FILM REVIEW ANNUAL

1999

Films of 1998

Film Review Publications
JEROME S. OZER, PUBLISHER

Editor: Jerome S. Ozer
Associate Editor: Richard Zlotowitz

ISBN 0-89198-153-5
ISSN 0737-9080

Manufactured in the United States of America

Jerome S. Ozer, Publisher
340 Tenafly Road
Englewood, NJ 07631

TABLE OF CONTENTS

FILM REVIEWS **1**

Affliction 1
Air Bud: Golden Retriever 10
Alan Smithee Film, An: Burn Hollywood Burn 11
Alarmist, The 15
All the Rage 18
Almost Heroes 19
Amy Foster (see Swept from the Sea)
American History X 21
Antz 27
Apt Pupil 33
Arguing the World 36
Armageddon 40
Artemisia 48
Avengers, The 52
Ayn Rand: A Sense of Life 57
Babe: Pig in the City 60
Bad Manners 67
Barney's Great Adventure: The Movie 69
BASEketball 72
Battle of Chile, The: Part 2: The Coup d'Etat 75
Belly 75
Beloved 77
Best Man, The 87
Beyond Silence 89
Big Hit, The 93
Big Lebowski, The 96
Big One, The 105
Billy's Hollywood Screen Kiss 109
Black Dog 112
Blade 114
Blues Brothers 2000 119
Borrowers, The 123
Boys in Love 126
Brandon Teena Story, The 127
Break, The 129
Bride of Chucky 133
Brigands: Chapter VII 135
Broadway Damage 136
Brother 137
Buffalo '66 139
Bug's Life, A 145
Bullet on a Wire 153
Bulworth 155
Burn Hollywood Burn (see Alan Smithee Film, An: Burn Hollywood Burn)
Butcher Boy, The 164

Cannibal!: The Musical 171
Can't Hardly Wait 173
Carla's Song 176
Caught Up 182
Celebration, The 184
Celebrity 187
Central Station 195
Chairman of the Board 199
Chambermaid on the Titanic, The 201
Character 210
Charlie Hoboken 215
Chicago Cab 216
Chile, Obstinate Memory 218
Chinese Box 219
City of Angels 225
Civil Action, A 232
Clay Pigeons 237
Clockwatchers 240
Comrades, Almost a Love Story 243
Concert of Wills: Making the Getty Center 245
Cousin Bette 246
Crossing Fields 252
Cruise, The 253
Cube 255
Dance With Me 259
Dancer, Texas Pop. 81 261
Dancing at Lughnasa 264
Dangerous Beauty 269
Dark City 271
David Searching 275
Day at the Beach 277
Dead Man on Campus 278
Dear Jesse 280
Deceiver 282
Dee Snider's Strangeland 284
Deep Impact 285
Deep Rising 291
Deja Vu 294
Desperate Measures 298
Destiny 302
Didn't Do It for Love 304
Digging to China 306
Dirty Laundry 308
Dirty Work 309
Disturbing Behavior 312
Divorce Iranian Style 316
Dr. Dolittle 317
Down in the Delta 322
Dream for an Insomniac 325
Dress, The 327
East Palace, West Palace 330
Eden 332
Eel, The 333
Elizabeth 338
Emperor's Shadow, The 346
Enemy of the State 348

Ever After: A Cinderella Story 356
Everest 362
Faculty, The 364
Fallen 369
Fallen Angels 373
Farm, The: Angola,U.S.A. 376
Fear and Loathing in Las Vegas 379
54 385
Firelight 390
Firestorm 394
Fireworks 395
First Love, Last Rites 400
Four Days in September 403
Free Tibet 406
Friend of the Deceased, A 407
Frozen 410
Full Speed 411
Full Tilt Boogie 414
Funny Games 416
Further Gesture, A (see The Break)
Gadjo Dilo 420
Genealogies of a Crime 425
General, The 427
General Chaos: Uncensored Animation 432
Gingerbread Man, The 433
Go Now 440
Gods and Monsters 441
Godzilla 447
Gonin 455
Governess, The 457
Great Expectations 461
Half Baked 468
Hallelujah! Ron Athey: A Story of Deliverance .469
Halloween: H2O 471
Hana-Bi (see Fireworks)
Hanging Garden, The 476
Happiness 480
Hard Core Logo 492
Hard Rain 493
Hav Plenty 497
He Got Game 500
Healing by Killing 509
Henry: Portrait of a Serial Killer 2 511
Henry Fool 512
Hi-Life 519
Hi-Lo Country, The 521
High Art 527
Hilary and Jackie 531
Hit Me 538
Holy Man 539
Hombres Armados (see Men with Guns)
Home Before Dark 544
Home Fries 546
Homegrown 548
Hope Floats 550
Horse Whisperer, The 554

How Stella Got Her Groove Back 563
Hurlyburly 569
Hurricane Streets 572
Hush 575
I Got the Hook-Up 578
I Love You, Don't Touch Me! 580
I Married a Strange Person! 582
I Still Know What You Did Last Summer 584
I Think I Do 587
I Went Down 589
I'll Be Home for Christmas 593
Illtown 595
Impostors, The 597
In God's Hands 601
Inheritors, The 603
Insomnia 607
Jack Frost 610
James Ellroy: Demon Dog of American Crime Fiction .613
John Carpenter's Vampires 615
Journey to the Beginning of the World (see Voyage to the Beginning of the World
Junk Food 618
Junk Mail 619
Keep the Aspidistra Flying (see A Merry War)
Killer Condom 622
Killing Time 624
Kingdom, The: Part 2 625
Kissing a Fool 631
Knock Off 634
Krippendorf's Tribe 636
Krzysztof Kieslowsi: I'm So-So 639
Kurt and Courtney 640
La Sentinelle 646
La Séparation 649
La Vie de Jesus (see Life of Jesus)
La Vita e Bella (see Life Is Beautiful)
Land Girls, The 652
Land Is White, The Seed Is Black, The 656
Last Big Thing, The 657
Last Days of Disco, The 658
Lawn Dogs 664
Leading Man, The 667
Leather Jacket Love Story 669
Lena's Dreams 671
Lenny Bruce: Swear to Tell the Truth 672
Les Miserables 674
Lethal Weapon 4 679
Let's Talk About Sex 684
Life Is Beautiful 685
Life of Jesus (La Vie de Jesus) 693
Like It Is 697
Little Boy Blue 699
Little Dieter Needs to Fly 701
Little Men (see Louisa May Alcott's "Little Men"
Little Voice 703
Live Flesh 709
Living out Loud 715

Lolita 722
Lost in Space 733
Louisa May Alcott's "Little Men" 738
Love and Death on Long Island 739
Love Is the Devil 746
Love Walked In 749
Madeline 751
Mafia! 755
Magic Sword, Quest for Camelot (see Quest for Camelot)
Major League: Back to the Minors 757
Man in the Iron Mask, The 759
Marie Baie des Anges 764
Marius and Jeannette 768
Mark Twain's America 772
Mask of Zorro, The 773
Meet the Deedles 779
Meet Joe Black 781
Men With Guns (Hombres Armados) .788
Mendel 795
Mercury Rising 797
Merry War, A (Keep the Aspidistra Flying) 801
Midaq Alley 805
Mighty, The 806
Mighty Joe Young 810
Mirror, The 815
Mr. Jealousy 816
Mr. Nice Guy 819
Mrs. Dalloway 822
Modulations 830
Monument Ave. 831
Moon Over Broadway 834
Mother and Son 837
Mulan 841
My Giant 847
My Knees Were Jumping: Remembering the Kindertransports 850
Negotiator, The 851
Neil Simon's 'The Odd Couple II' 857
Newton Boys, The 860
Next Step, The 864
Next Stop Wonderland 865
Niagara, Niagara 869
Night Flier, The (see Stephen King's 'The Night Flier')
Night at the Roxbury, A 871
Nightwatch 874
Nil by Mouth 875
No Looking Back 882
No Ordinary Love 885
Notes From Underground 886
Object of My Affection, The 887
Odd Couple II, The (see Neil Simon's 'The Odd Couple II')
Off the Menu: The Last Days of Chasen's 896
Ogre, The 898
One Tough Cop 902
One True Thing 903
Opposite of Sex, The 909
Orgazmo 914

Out of the Past 918
Out of Sight 920
Outside Ozona 927
Oyster and the Wind, The 929
Palmetto 930
Parallel Sons 933
Paralyzing Fear, A: The Story of Polio in America 935
Parent Trap, The 936
Passion in the Desert 941
Patch Adams 943
Paul Monette: The Brink of Summer's End 949
Paulie 951
Pecker 954
Pereira Declares ("Sostiene Pereira") 957
Perfect Murder, A 958
Permanent Midnight 965
Phantoms 967
Phoenix 969
Pi 970
Place Called Chiapas, A 974
Players Club, The 975
Pleasantville 978
Polish Wedding 987
Post Coitum, Animal Triste 989
Practical Magic 992
Price Above Rubies, A 996
Primary Colors 1000
Prince of Egypt, The 1014
Proposition, The 1020
Psycho 1023
Quest for Camelot 1031
R.I.P. (Rest in Pieces: A Portrait of Joe Coleman) 1034
Ratchet 1035
Rats Tale, A 1037
Reach the Rock 1038
Real Blonde, The 1040
Regeneration 1044
Replacement Killers, The 1048
Return to Paradise 1052
Ride 1057
Ringmaster 1058
River Red 1061
Ronin 1062
Rounders 1069
Rudolph the Red-Nosed Reindeer: The Movie 1075
Rugrats Movie, The 1077
Rush Hour 1081
Rushmore 1085
Safe Men 1093
Saltmen of Tibet, The 1096
Saving Private Ryan 1099
Savior 1123
See the Sea 1127
Senseless 1129
Seventh Heaven 1131
Shadrach 1134

Shakespeare in Love 1137
Shampoo Horns 1145
Shattered Image 1146
Shooting Fish 1149
Shopping for Fangs 1152
Siege, The 1154
Silver Screen, The: Color Me Lavender 1162
Simon Birch 1163
Simple Plan, A 1166
Six Days, Seven Nights 1174
Skin and Bone 1180
Slam 1181
Slamnation 1186
Slappy and the Stinkers 1187
Sliding Doors 1189
Slums of Beverly Hills 1193
Small Soldiers 1197
Smoke Signals 1202
Snake Eyes 1205
Soldier 1213
Soldier's Daughter Never Cries, A 1216
Somewhere in the City 1221
Sonatine 1223
Souler Opposite, The 1227
Sour Grapes 1228
Spanish Prisoner, The 1232
Species II 1239
Sphere 1242
Spice World 1249
Star Kid 1253
Star Trek: Insurrection 1254
Steam: The Turkish Bath 1260
Stephen King's 'The Night Flier' 1262
Stepmom 1263
Still Breathing 1269
Stolen Moments 1272
Storefront Hitchcock 1272
Sue 1275
Suicide Kings 1277
Swept From the Sea 1280
Swindle, The 1284
T-Rex: Back to the Cretaceous 1285
Talk of Angels 1288
Talk to Me 1290
Tarzan and the Lost City 1291
Taste of Cherry 1293
Ten Benny 1302
Theory of Flight, The 1304
There's Something About Mary 1308
Thief, The 1315
Thin Red Line, The 1319
Three Ninjas: High Noon at Mega Mountain 1334
Tokyo Fist 1336
Touch of Evil 1339
Tranceformer: A Portrait of Lars von Trier 1342
Trouble on the Corner 1343

Truce, The 1344
Truman Show, The 1348
Twilight 1361
Two Girls and a Guy 1366
U.S. Marshals 1371
Ugly, The 1374
Un Aire de Famille 1377
Under the Skin 1380
Unmade Beds 1384
Urban Legend 1387
Velvet Goldmine 1389
Very Bad Things 1398
Village of Dreams 1404
Voyage to the Beginning of the World 1405
Waking Ned Devine 1409
War Zone 1414
Waterboy, The 1416
Wedding Singer, The 1419
Welcome to Woop Woop 1424
West New York 1425
Western 1426
What Dreams May Come 1429
Whatever 1436
When I Close My Eyes 1439
Who the Hell Is Juliette? 1440
Why Do Fools Fall in Love 1442
Wide Awake 1447
Wild Man Blues 1449
Wild Things 1456
Wilde 1460
Without Limits 1466
Woo 1471
Wrongfully Accused 1474
X-Files, The 1475
Your Friends & Neighbors 1483
You've Got Mail 1489
Zero Effect 1495

ADDENDUM 1500

Deep Crimson (Film Review Annual 1998) 1500

AWARDS 1504

INDEX 1515

Cast 1515
Producers 1548
Directors 1552
Screenwriters 1554
Cinematographers 1556
Editors 1558
Music 1560
Production Crew 1562

AFFLICTION

A Lions Gate Films release of a Reisman/Kingsgate production. *Executive Producer:* Nick Nolte and Barr Potter. *Producer:* Linda Reisman. *Director:* Paul Schrader. *Screenplay:* Paul Schrader. *Based on the novel by:* Russell Banks. *Director of Photography:* Paul Sarossy. *Editor:* Jay Rabinowitz. *Music:* Michael Brook. *Music Editor:* Shari Johanson. *Sound:* Patrick Rousseau and (music) Bill Jackson. *Sound Editor:* Tony Martinez. *Casting:* Ellen Chenoweth and Kathleen Chopin. *Production Designer:* Anne Pritchard. *Art Director:* Michel Beaudet. *Set Decorator:* Ginette Robitaille. *Special Effects:* Louis Craig. *Costumes:* François LaPlante. *Make-up:* Diane Simard. *Stunt Coordinator:* Dave McKeown. *Running time:* 114 minutes. *MPAA Rating:* R.

CAST: Nick Nolte (Wade Whitehouse); Sissy Spacek (Margie Fogg); James Coburn (Glen Whitehouse); Willem Dafoe (Rolfe Whitehouse); Mary Beth Hurt (Lillian); Jim True (Jack Hewitt); Marian Seldes (Alma Pittman); Holmes Osborne (Gordon LaRiviere); Brigid Tierney (Jill); Sean McCann (Evan Twombley); Wayne Robson (Nick Wickham); Eugene Lipinski (J. Battle Hand); Tim Post (Chick Ward); Chris Heyerdahl (Frankie Lacoy); Janine Theriault (Hettie Rogers); Paul Stewart (Horner); Sheena Larkin (Lugene Brooks); Penny Mancuso (Woman Driver); Danielle Desormeaux (Elaine, LaRiviere's Secretary); Charles Powell (Jimmy Dane); Donovan Reiter (Short-haired Local); Brawley Nolte (Young Wade Whitehouse); Michael Caloz (Young Rolfe Whitehouse); Joanna Noyes (Sally Whitehouse); Marcel Jeannin (State Trooper); Susie Almgren (Mrs. Gordon); Steve Adams (Mel Gordon); Martha-Marie Kleinhans (Lena); Mark Camacho (Clyde); Ralph Allison (Reverend Doughty).

CINEASTE, Vol. XXIV, no. 1, 1998, p. 72, Leonard Quart

Paul Schrader has always worked on the margins of the movie mainstream, writing brilliant scripts for Martin Scorsese *(Taxi Driver* and *Raging Bull)* and directing his own singular films *(Blue Collar, Mishima)*. His films have been much darker, more austere, and less conventional and commercial than the Hollywood norm. Schrader's protagonists are often men besieged by demons—cosmic and personal ones—they can't control. They seek redemption in the midst of their oppression and confusion, but rarely find a road that will lead them there. *Affliction,* adapted from a lyrical, multi-layered novel by Russell Banks *(The Sweet Hereafter)*, is in that tradition.

Schrader's films tend to be violent, even apocalyptic, but usually remote emotionally. *Affliction,* however, is an emotionally immediate and charged work. It's set in Lawford, an economically depressed New Hampshire village, during what seems like a winter of eternal snow and cold. It centers on Wade Whitehouse (Nick Nolte), a native son who survives by doing a variety of odd jobs—village policeman, snowplow driver, and well digger.

Wade is a blue-collar loner, though also an integral part of the town. Nolte seamlessly and meticulously fits the role with his hulking maleness and attractive, unthreatening demeanor. He makes us believe he's just a decent, ordinary, working-class man with unrealizable dreams, who feels defeated by life. Wade has strong feelings of class resentment about being stuck in dead-end jobs and a trailer home; has an embattled relationship with his tough, more successful ex-wife, Lillian (Mary Beth Hurt); and is rejected by his nine-year-old daughter Jill (Brigid Tierney), who sullenly desires to return to her mother as soon as she goes off for a weekend with him. Most importantly, he lives with the traumatic memories of drunken abuse from his father (strikingly performed by macho Fifties and Sixties star, James Coburn).

At first, Wade, who is alcoholic, chain-smoking, and depressed, seems to be holding his demons relatively in check. *Affliction* follows this pained man's (he also has a gnawing toothache) descent from anger and frustration into uncontrolled paranoid and murderous rage. What sets him off is a hunting accident that he begins to think is a murder conspiracy. The genre trapping—the solving of a murder or a crime—is a red herring that Schrader has used in past works. The murders are never the real subject of his films. They are just used as a plot device that is a metaphor for something emotionally deeper.

About two/thirds through *Affliction,* we begin to see that Wade's obsession with the murder serves both as an attempt to evade dealing with the emotional chaos of his life and, conversely, as something he feels would help right that overwhelming sense of disorder. On another, more oblique level, his conviction that a younger, ex-minor-league pitcher friend, Jack (Jim True)—whose erratic life is almost a mirror of his own—has committed the murder, is unconsciously a way of punishing himself for the life he's led. If his life is a total muddle, the murder is something Wade sees as open to a solution. Wade, however, never calibrates what he's going to do. He goes off self-destructively, like a mad, avenging angel, violently confronting and attacking friends and employers about the murder until he has lost all his jobs and is totally out of control.

Schrader has made a film that is in a minor key about class and money in America. In an America divided between those who have power and live well, and the Wades, who are close to the bottom of the class system and have few economic options, Schrader's sympathies are clear. Wade's boss, small-town mogul and selectman Gordon LaRiviere (Holmes Osborne) and Evan Twombley (Sean McCann), putative murder victim and porcine Boston union official, are crass, complacent, and money-hungry, while Wade, for all his profound failings, has a strong moral sense and a soul that suffers. He lives, in Banks's words, "on the edge of his emotions."

Affliction's central focus, however, is not on American class divisions or entrepreneurial greed. Schrader may provide a detailed depiction of the grinding down and alienation of auto workers on the assembly line in his most socially conscious film, *Blue Collar,* but the prime interest in his films is usually in the fate of the individual, not the nature of political or social institutions. *Affliction*'s primary subject is the painful legacy of violence and machismo—of male swaggering, bluster, and misogyny—that some fathers perniciously pass on to their sons, and how two sons, Wade and his younger brother Rolfe (Willem Dafoe), try to deal with that destructive bequest. Wade's father Glen, seen in overexposed, black-and-white flashbacks looking like a boozed-up, macho monster, torments and beats his sons and wife. The flashbacks are telling, but a bit too broad and overdetermined. It's also not only Wade, but also Rolfe who Glen has emotionally crippled (he feels like a whipped dog").

Rolfe—the film's narrator and Banks's stand-in—has fled Lawford for a career as a professor of history in Boston. He's Wade's one confidante—the recipient of late-night calls in which Wade spills out the agony of his life. Rolfe is unmarried and an ex-alcoholic, who has chosen detachment as a survival technique rather than Wade's blundering impulsiveness. Wade sloppily storms about, while Rolfe is cautious and reticent, but just as alienated.

Rolfe makes only a brief appearance in the film, although from the beginning he states that Wade's story is his as well. He's the catalyst for Wade's downward spiral. It's Rolfe who suggests to Wade that there has been a murder conspiracy. He does it, perhaps, to move Wade, who always has been his protective buffer, to act out Rolfe's repressed rage against the world. It also can be interpreted as Rolfe's unconscious desire to punish Wade out of some envy of his being the stronger and more loved/hated by his father.

Affliction barely provides a glimpse of Wade's mother, but we learn that she is a sweet, suffering woman, who has "lived her life with the sound turned off." Glen's abusive relationship with a passive wife sets an indelible pattern for Wade and Rolfe's relationship with women. Rolfe self-protectively seems to have none, while Wade's women are all problematic. There is the ex-wife who has only contempt for him, and his daughter, Jill, who tries to mollify Wade by saying she loves him, but behaves in the same derisive manner as her mother. Wade's carelessness, rage, and his blue-collar style and status (his penchant for fast food, the kind of car he drives) only repel the ballet student Jill. The film handles the scenes between Wade and his daughter with such unusual subtlety that we sympathize both with the anguished Wade, who does nothing right in her eyes, and the harshly dismissive Jill. At the same time, we understand there is justification for Jill's feelings of irritation and wariness with his awkward, often irresponsible attempts at being a father.

There is also Margie (Sissy Spacek)—the warm, supportive waitress—his longtime girlfriend and a stand-in for his mother. Wade finds some consolation in the compassionate Marge, but although Wade is under the illusion that he desires a real relationship with her, he's clearly not capable of more than a sexual connection. She's just a receptive, warm body to him. Wade's model for marriage is built on his father Glen's domination of his mother, and he lacks the ability to respond to a woman's needs.

After his mother's death, Wade brings Margie to live in his father's house, and that act sets into motion the film's final horror. An aged, venomous Glen, who pathetically clings to his machismo—drinking himself senseless, inveighing against women who don't know their place, and calling his sons "wimps"—and Wade, possessed by his unlived life and the murder—stalk about the house swigging whiskey out of the bottle, acting as doubles of each other. They even share the habit of putting salt on their hands and licking it. Even the acquiescent Margie perceives that sustaining a relationship with Wade is hopeless and leaves—seeing him as an heir (despite his denials) to his father's destructiveness.

Affliction then moves to a stylized operatic climax, which avoids feeling incongruous despite the film's essential commitment to verisimilitude. It's true that Schrader conceives Wade as a wayward man who lives in a town of realistically portrayed bars, coffee shops, and town halls, but there are moments when he seems to view him as a larger-than-life, almost tragic and crucified figure (Schrader inserts a shot of Wade lying in the snow in that position.) Schrader's generally realistic film also heightens the desolately beautiful snowscapes, and blue-winter darkness to evoke a fabulistic vision of an utterly barren and solitary world. The film moves into the territory of fable when Wade instinctively reacts to his father's drunken physical attack by smashing and inadvertently killing him with a rifle butt. Driven by hatred, Wade then burns the barn down with his father's body in it—and watches, in a lingering long take, the flames from a distance. The imagery transcends the particular act of Wade killing Glen, and moves into another realm—an archetypal act of parricide. We learn then, in Rolfe's final eloquent voice-over, that Wade kills Jack and disappears. There is no salvation here for Wade—he's just fated to drift anonymously until he dies.

Rolfe's final narration provides the audience with an explanatory hook—something to sum up what has transpired—but in a grand, somewhat abstract style that reinforces the film's fable-like conclusion.

Rolfe intones that "our stories, Wade's and mine, describe the lives of boys and men for thousands of years, boys who were beaten by their fathers, whose capacity for love and trust was crippled almost at birth and whose best hope for connection to other human beings lay in elaborating for themselves an elegiac mode of relatedness, as if everyone's life were already over."

Affliction is an uncompromising, emotionally expansive film, very different stylistically from Schrader's more formally rigorous, emotionally detached films like *Mishima* and *American Gigolo*. It's also a bleak work that offers few sops to its audience—like humor or a lilting score—to mute its profound pessimism. Nevertheless, Schrader, Banks, and Nolte have created a deeply flawed, raging character in Wade whose basic innocence and agonizing bewilderment still evoke audience sympathy. *Affliction* is Paul Schrader's most emotionally accessible and expressive film.

LOS ANGELES TIMES, 12/30/98, Calendar/p. 1, Jack Mathews

[The following review by Jack Mathews appeared in a slightly different form in
NEWSDAY, 12/23/98, Part II/p. B15.]

Novelist Russell Banks, filmmaker Paul Schrader and small-town New England cop Wade Whitehouse are soul mates in a tortured hell on Earth. Each of these middle-aged men is haunted—in ways either real or imagined, physical or psychological—by violence, and each has devoted much of his life to trying to fathom his relationship with his father.

With the intense, almost overwhelming "Affliction," a movie adapted by Schrader from a novel by Banks about a character named Whitehouse (Nick Nolte), all the anger and resentment built up in the first two men are transferred to the third, leading to an emotional meltdown and an explosion of homicidal rage.

Rarely have a novelist and filmmaker been better matched. In their separate mediums, the 57-year-old Banks (author of "The Sweet Hereafter") and the 52-year-old Schrader (screenwriter for "Taxi Driver") are true auteurs, using their art to confront their own demons, and, in doing so, finding career-fulfilling outlets for their pain.

Wade Whitehouse, alas, doesn't have that option. In fact, he doesn't have many options to anything. He's the broken-down product of a broken-down childhood, a man whose ability to trust and form strong attachments to others was crushed while growing up in the small New Hampshire town of Lawton by his abusive, alcoholic father (played in flashbacks and present tense by James Coburn).

Wade's brother Rolfe (Willem Dafoe), who is the narrator of "Affliction," escaped his father's wrath, as younger sons often do, and moved away in early adulthood to become a college teacher and reasonably normal person.

No such luck for Wade, who is anchored to Lawton, to his past and to his father. As we join him decades later, he is barely functional: as a ridiculed part-time cop and school crossing guard; as a divorced father whose 9-year-old daughter (Brigid Tierney) is wary of him; as the noncommittal lover of sympathetic waitress Margie Fogg (Sissy Spacek). He can't even take care of himself, allowing an abscessed tooth to go untreated for so long, the pain eventually compels him to yank the offending molar with his own pliers.

That toothache is a metaphor for Wade's life ache, and as madness gradually overtakes him—and as he investigates a hunting accident as a murder and conspiracy that only he can solve—it's only a question of which will erupt first, his abscess or his fury.

This is a great performance by Nolte, the best of his post-Hollywood, post-movie star career. It's not easy to watch. Wade is one of the most pathetic figures to reach the screen in years. Yet he is a heroic figure, out of a Greek tragedy. He does confront his monsters, particularly his monster of a father, and though the film supplies no definitive answers, he seems to find a certain peace for himself.

Nolte seems a sure bet for an Oscar nomination, and there's a strong push for Coburn for best supporting actor, as well. Coburn is convincingly menacing, but totally unconvincing as the younger man in the black-and-white flashback scenes. Coburn is 70 and looks 70, both with dark hair in the flashbacks, and with stringy gray hair in the contemporary settings, and we'd need some of that Canadian whiskey he swallows between breaths to accept the illusion.

Still, "Affliction" is one of the year's strongest dramas. Schrader, a lapsed Calvinist who's written some of the boldest scripts of his generation, knows something about the dark side of the human soul, and directs Nolte as if he were looking into a mirror.

NEW YORK, 1/11/99, p. 50, Peter Rainer

In writer-director Paul Schrader's *Affliction*, small-town New Hampshire looks like hell frozen over. It's a vast meat locker of a locale, except the dead meat is walking around instead of hung up on hooks. The affliction here is metaphoric, but it's literal too. That's the Schrader specialty, and it's also the stock-in-trade of Russell Banks, upon whose 1989 novel the film is scrupulously based. The confluence of Schrader and Banks is almost too perfect—their dual oppressiveness wipes you out before the movie is ten minutes old.

Wade Whitehouse (Nick Nolte) is the chief afflictee of the piece. Divorced twice from the same woman (Mary Beth Hurt), he attempts to be a part-time father to his 9-year-old daughter, Jill (Brigid Tierney), who regards him in the same way her mother does—as a brawling, dangerous nuisance. His response, typically self-humiliating, is to sue for custody. As the town's sole police officer, Wade mostly acts as a crossing guard. To make ends meet, he does menial work for a local developer (Holmes Osborne), whose response to him isn't much more admiring than Jill's. Wade's father, Glen (James Coburn), is a roaring, vicious drunk, and just in case we thought this a recent incarnation, Schrader periodically intercuts flashbacks showing the brute pummeling his young son.

Barreling his way through his frostbitten inferno, Wade is the prototypical walking wounded, Schrader-Banks-style. He may try to wriggle out of his fate, but it's bigger than he is. In the film's take-no-prisoners view, this is the fate of all men, who must either self-destruct or visit their ills upon a new generation. What makes Wade such a heroic presence is that he's self-aware enough to know he's in torment. He's a good man gnarled by primal circumstance. He reaches out to his daughter because she represents for him the bliss of the normal; his sessions with her are botched and rancorous because he wants much more from her than she could ever give. Jill resents being used as an angel for her father's salvation. In his dotingness she spots the note of inauthenticity—Wade responds not to her but, rather, to his idealization of her.

Wade's waitress girlfriend, Margie (Sissy Spacek), is another of his angels-in-waiting. Her mercifulness toward him is the tenderest thing in the movie. If Wade is the archetypal male screwup, Margie is the archetypal silent sufferer. In their scenes together, he has a ravaged calm and she looks ethereal from longing. She wants her bliss, too. Everybody in this movie—not just Wade and Margie—has a long-ago look in his eyes. They're pulled in by the past, by its damages. Wade's brother, Rolfe (Willem Dafoe), who also narrates the film, has a death's-head countenance. He's a Boston University history professor with no sense of his own history. Speaking to Wade about their father, he says, "At least I was never afflicted by that man's violence," and Wade responds, "That's what you think."

The last film to have this kind of marrow-deep glumness was Atom Egoyan's *The Sweet Hereafter,* also based on a Banks novel, in which a school-bus accident wipes out virtually all of a village's children. I wasn't such a big fan of that movie. Its horrors were displayed as an emanation of small-town anomie—as if its villagers deserved their tragedies because of the littleness of their lives. Schrader's film also suffers from a heavy-going approach to rural malaise; he's offering up a sophisticated intellectual's take on the material, and there's something distanced and diminishing about his methods. (At one point Wade holds up traffic by posturing as if crucified.) His people are all so fixed in their fates that there's no possibility for joy. There never is in his movies. He turns winter-bound New Hampshire into a Hieronymous Bosch canvas: blasted souls topped by Wade's father's leering-gargoyle grin.

And yet this film is far more roiling and powerful than *The Sweet Hereafter.* It has the indrawn obsessiveness of male mythology, and even if you reject most of what it's saying, it's tough to shake off. It transcends your better judgment. Movies like *Straw Dogs* and *Deliverance* also operated in this realm of hallucinatory machismo; the survivalist tactics on display were framed as crucibles of masculinity. *Affliction* shares with them a sense of the world as a battlefield of male privilege, but it has a much drearier and more tragic overview. *Affliction* is the long hangover to those films. Schrader and Banks are saying that it's impossible to break the long chain of brutality at the core of maleness. Rolfe's narration near the end of the novel, in which he speaks on behalf of himself and Wade, and which Schrader largely incorporates, talks of boys and men who for thousands of years "were beaten by their fathers, whose capacity for love and trust was crippled almost at birth and whose best hope for a connection to other human beings lay in elaborating for themselves an elegiac mode of relatedness, as if everyone's life was already over. It is how we keep from destroying in our turn our own children and terrorizing the women who have the misfortune to love us."

This is highfalutin pop-psych palaver, and it carries a cock-of-the-walk gloat—especially that business about the "women who have the misfortune to love us." But this sort of weepy-brawly riff has its deep-down appeal to men, and perhaps to women too. It explains, and it explains away. Schrader lays the blame for Wade's sorry state on his father, but then he also casts the father as stand-in for a patriarchal line going back to the beginnings. Wade is both a special case and an unwitting player in a primordial procession. It's Freudian and it's biblical—quite a heavy load to lug.

But the film is blessed with a performance by Nolte that has real grace and sinew. Wade is the kind of character who is usually presented as a "type" in the movies—he's the Joe Six Pack we take for granted. It's Nolte's genius as an actor to bring out the delicacy and hurt in hunky parts. He's perfectly cast as Wade because he shows us how the man is miscast in his own life. Wade may be his father's Frankenstein monster, but his innards are his alone. He's too sensitive for the role he's been assigned. Wade wants to do the right thing in his world, but he's trapped not only by his own demons but by the unchangeable perception he has created in the town. When he sees a divorce lawyer about retaining custody of Jill, Wade halfheartedly tells him, "I'm not as dumb as I look." Wade knows it, but does anybody else? When, in torment, he looks in the mirror, a stranger stares back at him. The whipped boy is ever present in the adult, and Wade seems to be playing out some elaborate, furious penance for having been that boy. He's almost blithely unaware of his own need for protection: In a snowfall he's often hatless, and he has a raging toothache that he finally takes a pair of pliers to. The grimace on his face when he pulls the tooth is scarily identical to his broadest smiles. His smiles are like scars. He's afflicted, all right—beyond reckoning. The movie is his rightful dirge.

NEW YORK POST, 12/30/98, p. 37, Rod Dreher

As a filmmaker, Paul Schrader has long been interested in men tormented to the edge of madness by their proud masculinity. There was Travis Bickle in "Taxi Driver," then Jake LaMofta in "Raging Bull"—two great antiheroes brought to life by screenwriter Schrader for director Martin Scorsese. And now there is Wade Whitehouse, the protagonist of "Affliction."

"Affliction," which Schrader adapted from Russell Banks' novel and directed, isn't nearly as good as "Taxi Driver"and "Raging Bull"—there's the difference between a great screenwriter and a great director, perhaps—but it's still a compelling, at times bone-chilling study of the male character in crisis.

In one of his choicest roles and best performances, Nick Nolte creates an indelible tragic hero, a confused Everyman whose chaotic good intentions can't hold back the force of destiny.

We know from the opening lines that Wade is headed for trouble. In voice-over, Wade's younger brother (Willem Dafoe) tells us, "This is the story of my older brother's strange criminal behavior." Odd, this, because when we first meet Wade, we can tell by his uniform that he's a cop. Turns out he's a glorified crossing guard, but still he's the closest thing to the law in his one-stoplight New England village.

Wade is a middle-aged mess. He's desperate to claim custody of his young daughter (Brigid Tierney) from his ex-wife, Lillian (Mary Beth Hurt), though it's obvious that the child fears him. To make ends meet, Wade supplements his income by working as an all-purpose flunky for the town's wealthy businessmen (Holmes Osborne). Wade feels cheated by life and demeaned by having to labor for a man he doesn't respect.

When a wealthy big-city hunter dies in an accident while in the company of Wade's friend Jack (Jim True), Wade sees a chance to redeem his failed existence. He senses that this may have been a mob hit; the hunter had been involved in a controversial bit of business back in Boston, and Jack, who is just barely scraping by, would have had reason to commit murder. Fancying himself a backwoods Joe Friday, Wade makes a nuisance of himself trying to solve the shooting.

Either Wade will be a hero or he's making the most colossal blunder of his hapless, crumb-bum life. Schrader offers the audience only Wade's perspective, shrewdly keeping us in the dark as to whether he is a reliable interpreter of events.

In a series of flashbacks to Wade's childhood, we're given reason to doubt his judgment. His father (James Coburn, rivetingly malicious), a foul-mouthed alcoholic, beats and humiliates the boy frequently. Yet adult Wade still takes care of the old bastard, who continues to abuse his son and Wade's patient girlfriend, Margie (Sissy Spacek).

The film's title refers to the curse of violence, which has been visited on Wade through his father. Wade is a violent man, but he is neither crude nor simple. Nolte's great accomplishment here is to draw out the chiaroscuro shadings of Wade's anger. Here is a man who instinctively wants to do the decent thing, yet Nolte shows us the steam rising in hot jets from deep within Wade, and his moment by moment struggle to see clearly with clouded vision.

Nolte's depiction of Wade's tumultuous inner agony is breathtaking to watch—and he pierces us with empathy, for it's clear that Wade hasn't any conscious idea why his life seems so ungovernable. Circumstances inexorably drag him into awareness, with mounting tension for the audience and increasing danger for all those who get in Wade's way.

The supporting cast, Coburn in particular, is exemplary. So what's wrong with "Affliction"? I'm not exactly sure, but my sense is that Schrader's limitations as a visual stylist cramp the film. His straightforward realism serves this story ably, but a more stylized, less workmanlike way of storytelling—particularly a more painterly eye for the stark winter landscape, which mirrors the harsh moral environment in which Wade's fate is worked out—might have launched this solid, bleak film toward greatness.

NEWSWEEK, 1/11/99, p. 65, David Ansen

Novelist Russell Banks, the author of "Continental Drift" and "The Sweet Hereafter," is a specialist in the bruised, violent male psyche, and he couldn't have found a more ideal interpreter to bring "Affliction" to the screen than writer-director Paul Schrader, the screenwriter who dreamed up "Taxi Driver's" Travis Bickle. Wade Whitehouse (Nick Nolte), the protagonist of this ferociously bleak film, is a part-time cop and divorced dad in a working-class New Hampshire town.

Angry, hard-drinking, resentful of his daughter's preference for his ex-wife, Wade tries to be a good man but his rage keeps getting in the way. The violence inside him is bred in the bone, beaten into him by an alcoholic father (James Coburn) who still taunts him as if he were a child.

"Affliction"—which is narrated by Wade's brother, Rolfe (Willem Dafoe)—unfolds, deceptively, as a murder mystery. A wealthy man is shot and killed while deer hunting in the snowy woods. Wade doesn't think it was an accident. He becomes obsessed with the crime, finding evidence of a conspiracy that involves his own boss. As long as he can stay focused on the crime, he doesn't have to look at the wreckage of his own life, which is spiraling out of control.

Nolte presides over this movie like a raging, wounded animal. He's at once dangerous and doomed, threatening and pitiable. You can see why his daughter is afraid of him, why his new girlfriend (Sissy Spacek) must tread carefully around him. But Nolte and Schrader allow us to see the terrified little boy inside Wade, the inheritor of a tradition of violence that has been passed on from father to son for generations. Nolte gives this blighted man an almost tragic stature. The unexpected casting of Coburn is inspired: fathers don't get much scarier or meaner than this.

This may be the finest work Schrader has done. There's nothing flashy about his style here. Quietly, relentlessly, he burrows deep inside this place, these people. But the grittily realistic, seemingly objective style slowly takes on the intensity of a cold fever. By the end of this paranoid American nightmare, "Affliction" has achieved an almost hallucinatory power. Schrader has never been one to coddle an audience, and this is as uncompromising a vision as he has given us. That's both warning and strong recommendation.

SIGHT AND SOUND, 3/99, p. 36, Kevin Jackson

Lawford, New Hampshire; a snowbound, economically precarious town, at the start of a typically harsh winter. Wade Whitehouse, Lawford's only policeman, is in a bad way: he's divorced, living alone in a shabby trailer, agonised by a bad tooth, drinking heavily and forced to eke out his scanty earnings with menial jobs. All his attempts to be a good father to his young daughter Jill backfire miserably, and he is clearly still in thrall to his elderly father Glen, an alcoholic bully who used to beat and berate Wade mercilessly.

Wade's only sources of comfort and sanity are the few hours he manages to spend with his girlfriend Margie and his nightly phone call to his younger brother Rolfe, who has escaped Lawford to become a history professor in Boston. Despite their support, Wade grows ever more troubled.

When a wealthy weekend visitor dies in a deer-hunting accident, Wade suspects first murder, then a conspiracy. But he is distracted from his ham-fisted attempts at investigation by the death of his mother (which brings Rolfe back to town for the first time in years), by his anguished steps to regain custody of Jill from his ex-wife Lillian, and by his excruciating toothache, which he finally cures by tearing out the rotten molar with pliers.

Desperate to regain his daughter's love, he abducts the little girl, but is so infuriated by her frightened resistance that he finally lashes out at her.

Immediately horrified by himself, he lets Margie, who is leaving him for good, take Jill back to her mother. Glen taunts him, and father and son launch into a brawl which ends with Wade killing the old man and burning his corpse. Rolfe, who has been the film's narrator, explains that the supposed conspiracy was all in Wade's imagination, and that Wade's circumstances are now unknown.

Though *Affliction* is a high-fidelity adaptation by Paul Schrader of Russell Banks' semi-autobiographical novel of 1989, it also tends to put you in mind of earlier literary works—Zola, perhaps, or the less mirthful flowerings of Scandinavian drama. Pinched by poverty, in constant pain, humiliated by the local burghers (in one scene, even the local burger chef, Wade Whitehouse is afflicted in more ways than an assiduous social worker could catalogue) and most grievously by his emotional make-up. As the film's final voiceover underlines, he's been predestined to uncontrollable rage by his father's bullying.

The themes of a toxic childhood and the cycle of masculine violence are hardly uncommon these days, but here they have been made into the stuff of tragedy rather than soap, and Schrader has added a hint of sociology: one of his reference points when shooting was *Demonic Males,* a recent study of primate aggression. Almost everything about the film is scrupulously sombre, from its pallid skies and deathly winter landscape—an eastern cousin (it was actually shot near Montreal) of the Midwestern snows of *Fargo,* and of Schrader's youth in Michigan—to the fuzzy, desaturated memory-images which replay the horrors of Wade's childhood as fragments from a broken home movie.

Like its hero, however, the film is more often agitated than sullen, with scene after scene suddenly taking off in unexpected directions or hitting unsettling tones. A small instance: when Wade goes to see a lawyer about renegotiating custody of his child, the set-up looks like a routine confrontation between poor working stiff and greedy professional, until a reverse shot reveals that the lawyer is confined to a wheelchair. Yet another damaged male? *Affliction* casts many such doubts, large as well as small, and sometimes where you'd least expect them. Even its own narrator is unreliable, for example, since it's Wade's younger brother Rolfe (at first sight an escapee from their father's evil, and voice of sweetly pained reason among the drunken, brawling rednecks) who eggs Wade on to believe in a non-existent murder conspiracy.

Rolfe, the articulate brother, helps give voice to *Affliction*'s more abstract concerns—with the temptations and betrayals of storytelling, among other matters—and his final, weary account of Wade's doomed attempt to find plots where none exists sounds suspiciously like a film director's unhappiness with the glib patterns demanded by genre fiction. Wade, the inarticulate brother, embodies the film's horror. Nolte's acting of the part is almost dismayingly accomplished. His portrait of a wrecked man with futile aspirations towards common decency may be the best work he's done, and the scenes in which he tries to show tenderness for his daughter are so remorselessly exact that they're hard to watch without flinching.

After Schrader's last two unsuccessful digressions into mongrel forms of comedy with *Witch Hunt* and *Touch, Affliction* amounts to an overwhelmingly forceful return to earlier form and earlier themes. One can imagine Wade as Travis Bickle who stayed home instead of going to the wicked city, married, had a child, got a good job, knocked himself out to be sane and normal and still ended up in middle age as a solitary brooder, inwardly howling for a savage act of redemption.

Barring some freak response to Nolte's outstanding acting, *Affliction* is plainly far too austere a piece of film-making to hold its own in the multiplexes, but it invites at least three superlatives: it's Schrader's bleakest film, and his most mature, and it boasts a central performance of unmatched rawness and conviction.

TIME, 12/28/98-1/4/99, p. 174, Richard Corliss

Critics love films about simple folks dying in the snow *(Fargo, The Sweet Hereafter, A Simple Plan).* And they revere Nick Nolte, who has a lock on the role of the tough man—out of sorts, time and control—in a world with no use for his strengths. No surprise, then, that *Affliction,* Paul Schrader's film from a Russell Banks novel about family violence in New Hampshire, has placed strongly in the year-end critics' polls, and that Nolte won some Christmas laurels as best actor.

Wade Whitehouse (Nolte) is a part-time cop and a full-time burnout. His wife has left him; his daughter squirms as he tries charming her; his sadistic father (James Coburn) poisons Wade's prospects. His educated brother (Willem Dafoe) is too far away. His girlfriend (Sissy Spacek) can't soothe his dark side. His best pal may have killed a rich man for hire. And Wade has this awful toothache!

As screenwriter *(Taxi Driver)* and director *(Patty Hearst),* Schrader specializes in people spiraling into madness; for him it is their purest, most photogenic state. *Affliction* dawdles over small-town life: lots of boozy bonhomie and dazed snarling. The raging losers here often seem like sullen stereotypes. We could also have done without Nolte's self-crucifixion scene. But the actor finds truth in Wade's emotional clumsiness, in the despair of a man who hasn't the tools or the cool to survive. There are too many of these men in life, and not enough films that tell their sad tales. That gives *Affliction* a therapeutic worth.

VILLAGE VOICE, 1/5/99, p. 58, J. Hoberman

So the day before New Year's Eve, my candidate for the best-directed Hollywood movie and least enticing title of 1998 sneaks into town as volatile and vulnerable as its befuddled antihero. *Affliction,* cagily adapted by writer-director Paul Schrader from Russell Banks's 1989 novel, is as chilly a spectacle as you're likely to see. It's like watching a comeback in an empty stadium.

Raging rider, easy bull: Peter Biskind's "new Hollywood" tell-all introduces the young Schrader as a "bomb waiting to go off [who] massaged his reputation as a wild man when he realized he could make it work for him." Edging out *Bulworth* in the what-coulda-been sweepstakes, *Affliction* is the sort of American movie nostalgically associated with the first half of the 1970s. Low-key and downbeat, character-driven and well-written, Schrader's orchestration of a male self-destruct act could be a belated follow-up to *Five Easy Pieces* and *The King of Marvin Gardens.* "His story is my ghost life and I want to exorcise it," the hero's younger brother (Willem Dafoe) explains in an introductory voice-over that, although taken from the novel, sounds like it could have come straight from the director's own mouth.

Affliction opens on a suitably discomfiting note, the last night of October, in an unpretty New Hampshire town with divorced dad and part-time cop Wade Whitehouse (Nick Nolte) trying and failing to prod his unhappy nine-year-old daughter Jill into the Halloween spirit. The next morning, deer season starts on this forlorn planet and, before the morning is out, Wade's cocky young pal Jack (Jim True) will become involved in a fatal hunting accident that might or might not have wider implications.

Nolte's Wade is a big, tormented guy with a convoluted sense of injustice and a sympathetic waitress girlfriend played, in a richer performance than written, by Sissy Spacek. (There's a poignant postcoital image of this life-battered, flannel-wrapped couple in a cold room on a too-small bed.) In 1973, Nolte's would have been the Jack Nicholson role, but Wade is not exactly a beautiful loser. That he's apparently the town's last smoker only underscores his anachronism. Our antihero wanders around town nursing a monstrous toothache, muttering to himself that he's a whipped dog who just might bite back, but his real affliction is the legacy of male violence inherited from his drunken, abusive father Glen.

James Coburn (once the most jovially ironic of '60s action heros) plays Glen as a primeval terror in a few memorable flashbacks and in the present, even more vividly, as an evil old coot, cursing his children as "Jesus freaks and candy-asses," slugging Seagrams from the bottle, and ranting about the disappearance of "real men" like his father. Wade drinks a lot, too, and *Affliction* catches him on his downward spiral—planning a crazy child-custody suit, making late-night phone calls to his kid brother (a repressed college history professor living somewhere near Boston), stumbling onto some sort of real estate scam orchestrated by his oily boss (Holmes Osborne).

Wade absorbs a lot of punishment but, in attempting to justify himself by avenging a crime, he's a lot closer to Travis Bickle than he is to Jake LaMotta (or Jesus) in the Schrader gallery of masculine archetypes. Ignoring the reality principle, whether it's embodied by a freezing farmhouse or a divorce lawyer in a wheelchair, Wade can't prevent himself from turning into his father-as much as he hates him. If anything, each attempt to forestall the transformation brings him that much closer.

Did I mention how well-constructed *Affliction* is? Disaster has been lurking all movie long but things fall apart with a frightening suddenness. At the very moment when Schrader orchestrates a tracking shot to underscore Wade's bereftness, Glen comes chuckling out of the family farmhouse like a bad dream: "I love you, you mean sonofabitch." *Affliction's* ending reminds some people of the small apocalypse with which Andrei Tarkovsky closed out *The Sacrifice* but, like everything else in this nuanced film, it's rueful and distanced, understated rather than grandiose.

As personal as *Affliction* seems, it's neither solipsistic nor overweening. Indeed, Schrader's self-effacing direction allows ample room for his performers to stretch (and they repay him with a half-dozen superb ensemble scenes). This raw, troubling movie isn't anyone's idea of a Christmas tree but it illuminates the darkness anyway—*Affliction* radiates with humility.

Also Reviewed in:
CHICAGO TRIBUNE, 2/5/99, Friday/p. D. Mark Caro
NATION, 1/4/99, p. 36, Stuart Klawans
NEW REPUBLIC, 2/1/99, p. 24, Stuart Kauffmann
NEW YORK TIMES, 12/30/98, p. E1, Janet Maslin
NEW YORKER, 1/11/99, p. 94, David Denby
VARIETY, 9/1-7/97, p. 76, Todd McCarthy
WASHINGTON POST, 2/12/99, p. C1, Stephen Hunter
WASHINGTON POST, 2/12/99, Weekend/p. 46, Desson Howe

AIR BUD: GOLDEN RETRIEVER

A Keystone Pictures release in association with Dimension Films of a Robert Vince production. *Executive Producer:* Michael Strange, Anne Vince, and William Vince. *Producer:* Robert Vince. *Director:* Richard Martin. *Screenplay:* Paul Tamasy and Aaron Mendelsohn. *Based on the character "Air Bud" created by:* Kevin DiCicco. *Director of Photography:* Mike Southon. *Editor:* Bruce Lange and Melinda Seabrook. *Music:* Brahm Wenger. *Music Editor:* Bob Stewart. *Sound:* Kevin Sands and (music) Armin Steiner. *Casting:* Abra Edelman and Elisa Goodman. *Production Designer:* Rex Raglan. *Art Director:* Eric Norlin. *Set Decorator:* Grant Pearse. *Set Dresser:* Raul Casillas, Dave Parke, Johanna Mazur, and Tamara Susik. *Visual Effects:* Christopher Chen. *Digital Effects:* Geoff Richardson. *Costumes:* Patricia Hargreaves. *Make-up:* Jo Ann Fowler. *Stunt Coordinator:* Scott Ateah. *Running time:* 91 minutes. *MPAA Rating:* G.

CAST: Tim Conway (Fred Davis); Dick Martin (Phil Phil); Kevin Zegers (Josh Framm); Cynthia Stevenson (Jackie Framm); Gregory Harrison (Patrick Sullivan); Nora Dunn (Natalya); Perry Anzilotti (Popov); Robert Costanzo (Coach Fanelli); Shayn Solberg (Tom); Suzanne Ristic (Principal Salter); Alyson MacLaren (Andrea Framm); Tyler Thompson (Oliver); Rhys Williams (Goose); Shahri Khaderni (Juan); Jason Anderson (Weeble); Myles Ferguson (J.D.); Cory Fry (Cole Powers); Jeff Gulka (Pudge); Marcus Turner (Giants Quarterback); Jay Brazeau, Frank C. Turner, and Scott Ateah (Officials); Mark Brandon (Richard); Jaida Hay (Tammy); Richard Martin (Guy in Stands); Doreen Esary (Receptionist); Julio Caravetta (Giants Coach); David Lewis (Herb); Monica Marko (Lady with Broom); Ritch Renaud (Photographer); Barry MacDonald (Sportscaster); Simon Isherwood (Rams Coach); John Keelan (Ice Cream Boy).

LOS ANGELES TIMES, 8/14/98, Calendar/p. 10, Kevin Thomas

[The following review by Kevin Thomas appeared in a slightly different form in NEWSDAY, 8/14/98, Part II/p. B6.]

Last summer's screen fare was considerably brightened by a delightful family comedy called "Air Bud," in which a boy, who has just lost his father, befriends a golden retriever that turns out to be a terrific basketball star. Not surprisingly, the charm and success of this modest film has led to a sequel, "Air Bud: Golden Receiver," which unfortunately disappoints keenly.

The problem is that it is much more retread than sequel. Instead of the basketball court, Air Bud now demonstrates his prowess on the football field, but with much less conviction. Instead of Michael Jeter's memorably nasty clown, Air Bud's cruel original owner, we've got a tiresome Nora Dunn playing a Russian animal circus impresario who wants to steal Air Bud and take him home to turn him into a star performer. Instead of Bill Cobb's wise basketball coach, we've got Robert Costanzo's equally wise football coach.

Kevin Zegers returns as young Josh Framm, still grieving over the loss of his father. He actively tries to sabotage a budding romance between his mother (Cynthia Stevenson, replacing Wendy Makkena) and the new veterinarian in town (Gregory Harrison, very good). Even more disturbing than writers Paul Tamasy and Aaron Mendelsohn recycling old ideas from the first film is the way Josh's reaction to the vet is handled.

The coach does try to help Josh move beyond grief but doesn't really discuss his mother's right to try to find happiness with another man. His mother is totally ineffectual and never considers seeking help for her son. She actually gives up her romance to please her son, with the vet reinstated in her life only after he proves to be a hero in crisis. This is scarcely a healthy message to send to young audiences, and, frankly, Josh comes across as more in the grip of an intense Oedipal phase rather than suffering lingering grief.

Richard Martin directs energetically, but overall "Air Bud: Golden Receiver" is a washout.

NEW YORK POST, 8/14/98, p. 46, Thelma Adams

Close your eyes and say, "Air Bud: Golden Receiver." I hear groaning?

Only the most die-hard Lassie fans—or grown-ups who consider anything with a "G" rating to be kid-friendly—will welcome the arrival of this sequel to "Air Bud."

In director Richard Martin's movie, from a script by Paul Tamasy and Aaron Mendelsohn, the hoop-shooting golden retriever gets a second season, this time playing football.

Martin's extended stupid pet trick finds Bud (played with pep by Rush, Zak, Chasse and Chance) catching a football in his teeth. At least it's more believable than those three-pointers off the nose.

Buddy not only saves the Fernfield Junior High Timberwolves from certain budgetary death, he also solves the domestic traumas of 13-year-old Josh (Kevin Zegers). While the teen mourns his late father, mom (Cynthia Harrison) brushes off her little black dress and throws herself back into the dating pool.

The blue-eyed, deep-dimpled Zegers must have studied Method acting since he originated his role in "Air Bud." He's sulkier than Monica Lewinsky when the president didn't return her calls. Only Bud senses that the veterinarian, Dr. Patrick (Gregory Harrison), is stepdad material.

In a post-Soviet subplot, Russian circus fiends (Perry Anzilotti and Nora Dunn) dognap Buddy. Popov and Natalya are pure Boris and Natasha. They end up covered in fish guts, a fate that should also befall director Martin.

The movie heads for the Gipper speech like a trained dog making for the supper tent. The obese coach pauses, hogie in hand, to tell his athletes that it's not about winning, it's how they play the game.

Excuse me, but if these movies must end in the big game montage where the good guys win in the last seconds, let's be straight with kids and admit that it is about winning, after all.

Martin does throw us a bone: He cast his dad, "Laugh-In" co-host Dick Martin, and pal Tim Conway. The pair ad-lib the play-by-play at the big game. If only the director had had money in the budget to score a decent gag writer.

Also reviewed in:
CHICAGO TRIBUNE, 8/14/98, Friday/p. I, Monica Eng
NEW YORK TIMES, 8/14/98, p. E14, Anita Gates
VARIETY, 8/10-16/98, p. 43, Leonard Klady
WASHINGTON POST, 8/14/98, Weekend/p. 40, Michael O'Sullivan

ALAN SMITHEE FILM, AN: BURN HOLLYWOOD BURN

A Hollywood Pictures and Andrew Vajna release in association with Joe Eszterhas of a Cinergi production. *Executive Producer:* Andrew G. Vajna. *Producer:* Ben Myron. *Director:* Alan Smithee. *Screenplay:* Joe Eszterhas. *Director of Photography:* Reynaldo Villalobos. *Editor:* Marcus Manton and Jim Langlois. *Music:* Chuck D. and Gary G-Wiz. *Music Editor:* Mark Green. *Sound:* Felipe Borrero. *Sound Editor:* Richard E. Yawn. *Casting:* Nancy Foy. *Production Designer:* David L. Snyder. *Art Director:* Melanie J. Baker. *Set Designer:* John Goldsmith. *Set Decorator:* Claudette Didul. *Set Dresser:* Richard Wright, Kevin Chamber, Richard Chirco, Greg Lynch. *Special Effects:* Joshua Hakian. *Costumes:* Laura

Cunningham-Bauer. *Make-up:* Ashlee Peterson. *Stunt Coordinator:* Mark De Alessandro. *Running time:* 86 minutes. *MPAA Rating:* R.

CAST: Ryan O'Neal (James Edmunds); Coolio (Dion Brothers); Chuck D (Leon Brothers); Eric Idle (Alan Smithee); Richard Jeni (Jerry Glover); Leslie Stefanson (Michelle Rafferty); Sandra Bernhard (Ann Glover); Cheri Lunghi (Myrna Smithee); Harvey Weinstein (Sam Rizzo); Gavin Palone (Gary Samuels); MC Lite (Sister II Lumumba); Marcello Thedford (Stagger Lee); Nicole Nagel (Aloe Vera); Stephen Tobolowsky (Bill Bardo); Erik King (Wayne Jackson); Jim Piddock and Naomi Campbell (Attendants); Marianne Muellerleile (Sheila Caslin); Suli McCullough (S.L.A.); Dina Spybey (Allessandra); Robert Littman (Cousin Andrew); Doug Walker (Photographer); Robin Chivers and Robin Dugger (Bonnie 'N Clyde); Leslie Segar (Big Lez); Duane Davis (Black Policeman); Hideo Kimura and Earl Kim Shiroma (Japanese Businessmen); Jesse Rambis (Lakers Fan); Christopher Kelley (British Bartender); Sylvester Stallone, Whoopi Goldberg, Jackie Chan, Dominick Dunne, Robert Evans, Larry King, Robert Shapiro (Special Appearances).

LOS ANGELES TIMES, 2/27/98, Calendar/p. 1, Kenneth Turan

"An Alan Smithee Film Burn Hollywood Burn" tells of a director who incinerates his own work because he didn't want to inflict another terrible movie on the world. Too bad he didn't get his hands on this one.

Actually, burning is too good for such a wretched fiasco; only a surgical nuclear strike could suitably destroy what has to be one of the most enervating comedies ever made. More sluggish and not nearly as entertaining as the world of Hollywood moviemaking it nominally satirizes, "Smithee" is more painful and dispiriting to watch than anyone could possibly imagine. If this truly is, as the film's tag line claims, "The Movie Hollywood Doesn't Want You to See," Hollywood has rarely done the world a bigger favor.

The inspiration, if that is the right word, for "Smithee's" Joe Eszterhas script, is a Directors Guild of America rule that states if a dissatisfied filmmaker wants to remove his or her name from a project, Alan Smithee is the pseudonym that has to be used. What would happen, Eszterhas wondered, if a director whose name really was Alan Smithee wanted to take his name off a picture?

From such acorns do stunted dwarf oaks grow. Though the egotism, doublespeak and duplicity of modern Hollywood have been ably spoofed in films like "The Player" and 1989's underappreciated "The Big Picture," this venture so miscalculates everything it can't even elicit a chuckle.

Overlong at 86 minutes, "Smithee" is so misbegotten that its director, the much-traveled Arthur Hiller (who also appears in a cameo), took his name off the picture. That's right, "An Alan Smithee Film" is officially an Alan Smithee film, and that piece of metaphysical humor is funnier than anything that appears on screen.

In form, "Smithee" is a mock documentary postmortem on "Trio," an imaginary big-budget action film starring Sylvester Stallone, Whoopi Goldberg and Jackie Chan (all briefly playing themselves) that never reached theaters despite having a budget of more than $200 million and play dates confirmed on 7,000 screens.

Talking about the film's genesis and sad fate are the usual smattering of industry players. There's a thuggish producer (Ryan O'Neal) who gets offended when he's called a pimp, a social-climbing studio head (comic Richard Jeni), an agent from Talentless Artists Agency and a party girl by the name of Aloe Vera. Anyone laughing yet?

Then there's director Smithee (played without much enthusiasm by Monty Python-veteran Eric Idle, who has funnier lines in his press kit bio than he does on screen). Interviewed as a patient in the Keith Moon Psychiatric Facility (that's right, it's a joke), Smithee clutches his Tibetan holy rocks and his Tanzanian walking stick and explains, to no noticeable comic effect, how things went so terribly wrong on his film.

The only thing "Smithee" really succeeds in doing is illustrating the axiom that nothing is as painful to experience as a film that's not as hip and clever as it thinks. Typical of "Smithee's" approach are its documentary-style identification lines. Stallone's reads "superstar, rocket scientist, brain surgeon," Eszterhas' says "screenwriter and penile implant," and Dominick

Dunne's says "author and big mouth." This stuff isn't more amusing observed on the screen, it's less.

Aside from Eszterhas and Dunne, "Smithee" is overloaded with real celebrities (ranging from Robert Evans to Robert Shapiro) looking unhappy playing themselves. Then there are celebrities trying to act, like rap artists Coolio and Chuck D, who play the Brothers brothers, independent filmmakers who (don't ask) become Smithee's passionate defenders. Only Miramax's Harvey Weinstein, of all people, comes off well in his deadpan portrayal of deadpan private investigator Sam Rizzo.

A working screenwriter since 1977, Eszterhas knows his Hollywood territory, but making the business funny is completely beyond him. Neither self-referential jokes about how bad "Showgirls" was nor a cameo appearance by venerable little person Billy Barty can make a dent in the overall gloom. Barty, whose feature career goes all the way back to 1930s Busby Berkeley musicals, spends his brief time on screen looking confused. Who can blame him?

NEW YORK POST, 2/27/98, p. 45, Thelma Adams

Did you hear that? It's the screech of Joe ("Showgirls") Eszterhas in "An Alan Smithee Film Burn Hollywood Burn."

It isn't pretty. Neither is Eszterhas, the embittered big-bucks scribe who turned in an earnest bit of semi-autobiographical, self-important self-justification in last year's "Telling Lies in America" and now gives vent to a boundless rage, an attack of biting the hand that feeds.

"Burn Hollywood Burn" is a sap's "Sunset Boulevard," a quick and cheap assault on Hollywood's easiest targets. Told in the form of a mockumentary, it's a joyless parade of talking heads. Their lament? The conflict between art and commerce, the studio system and its discontent.

The movie opens with Brit Alan Smithee (Monty Python alum Eric Idle) directing a film within a film called "Trio," a mondo auctioneer starring Sylvester Stallone, Whoopi Goldberg and Jackie Chan (all smugly appearing as themselves).

In Holly-chat, Smithee is the pseudonym used by a director who removes his name from a film's credits, typically out of embarrassment or disgust. In fact, "Burn Hollywood Burn" goes out under the Smithee name.

It's an open secret that ex-Academy honcho Arthur ("Love Story") Hiller helmed the conceited comedy. Whether the director, who appears briefly at the end, removed his name as a publicity stunt or out of Eszterhas-fluenza is unclear.

Hiller's screen alter-ego, Smithee, broadly played by Idle, has a nervous breakdown when venal producer James Edmunds (Ryan O'Neal) and studio honcho Jerry Glover (Richard Jeni) refuse to give the director the final cut on "Trio."

In an effort to wrest control of his baby, Smithee steals the master negative, goes into hiding with the black filmmaking underground (Coolio and Chuck D), watches Orson Welles in "The Third Man," and burns the neg on the banks of the LaBrea tar pits.

Along the way, we meet a heartless, cussing, cunning assortment of self-described bitches and bastards. Probably wishing they could remove their names as easily as the director are tanned producer-director Robert Evans, CNN host-for-hire Larry King, O.J. apologist Robert Shapiro and Miramax chieftain Harvey Weinstein.

Replete with racial slurs and fellatio gags, crude attacks on critics and feeble gestures about artistic integrity, "Burn Hollywood Burn" will send audiences fleeing up the aisles before the final credits, as if the theater itself was on fire.

Idle's Smithee might feel "a responsibility to protect the world from bad film," but Eszterhas has no such scruples. The writer puts his name on a project that is, in fact, worse than "Showgirls,"

NEWSDAY, 2/27/98, Part II/p. B3, Jack Mathews

In the last 30 years, writer-director-producer Alan Smithee has been associated with some of the most embarrassing film and TV movies ever to slither out of Hollywood. But his latest, "An Alan Smithee Film Burn Hollywood Burn," may be his greatest embarrassment yet. If he had any sense, he'd withdraw his name from the title *and* the picture.

Of course, Alan Smithee has no sense, or pride. He doesn't even exist. He is nothing more than a pseudonym, a mask behind which real filmmakers with real names and at least some pride hide from work that has gone terribly, terribly wrong. And no movie bearing his name has gone more wrong than "Burn Hollywood Burn."

Written by Joe Eszterhas, a name associated with no few embarrassments itself, "Burn" is a stunningly bad, sophomorically vulgar parody of modern Hollywood. It's a feature-length series of in-jokes that should be of no interest to people outside the industry, and an object of scorn within.

Done as a faux documentary, "Burn" chronicles through talking head interviews and flashbacks the plight of "Trio," a $200-million action film starring Sylvester Stallone, Whoopi Goldberg and Jackie Chan. The movie's director (Eric Idle), an unstable Brit who is browbeaten to the point of madness by his insufferably intrusive producer James Edmunds (Ryan O'Neal), had stolen the negative and threatened to feed its ashes to the La Brea Tar Pits.

The one-joke idea that spawned the entire movie is that because the director's real name is Alan Smithee, it would do him no good to take his name off the picture. It would still be an Alan Smithee film. That Eszterhas was able to sell this idea to the folks at Disney says more about the level of delusion out there than any film could.

How bad is it? Well, irony of ironies. Arthur Hiller, the Oscar-winning veteran hired to direct "Bum," had his name taken off the film in protest of the final editing, making it a parody of Alan Smithee, "directed by Alan Smithee," That's as funny as this thing gets.

"Burn" is a butt-squiggler to sit through. Eszterhas ("Showgirls") is a mediocre writer even in his specialty areas—bondage, sexual violence, exhibitionism, voyeurism, obsession, humiliation—and he has no touch at all with satire or farce. The writing here is junior high school level stuff, in which the magazines Time and Newsweek become "Slime" and "Newsleak," and TV personalities like Larry King are labeled "hyenas." Much of the dialogue is so bad, particularly that of the stars playing themselves, you may suspect it was ad-libbed—and, who knows, maybe even improved—on the spot.

The first image in "Burn" is a close-up profile of Stallone, who barks out "Yo, AdriaNNNNNNNN!," then turns to the camera and volunteers that he and Adrian never got it on in "Rocky," meaning that their parenthood in the sequels was a miracle of biblical proportions. Throughout the movie, Stallone returns, in this same setting, with equally riveting speeches, all of which both mock his image as a musclebound, dimbulb narcissist, and confirm it.

It's safe to say that Stallone is above being embarrassed, as is the notoriously icky producer Robert Evans, who plays himself as a sort of patriarch of Hollywood smarm. But "Burn" also appealed to the vanity of such non-pros as O. J. Simpson lawyer Robert Shapiro and novelist/journalist Dominick Dunne, and their resumes will be forever stained.

Mainly, "Burn" is built around interviews with "Trio's" principals—Smithee, Edmunds, studio boss/Michael Ovitz-prototype Jerry Glover (Richard Jeni), and the Brothers brothers (rappers Coolio and Chuck D.), the ghetto filmmakers who befriend the fugitive Smithee and negotiate on his behalf at the studio. Only Jeni, a stand-up comic, manages something like a measured performance.

In evaluating the quality of "Trio," one of the characters says "it's worse than 'Showgirls,'" a playful reference to Eszterhas' most notable past embarrassment. We'll have to take his word for it. In the meantime, "Showgirls" has definitely been replaced at the bottom of the Eszterhas heap by "Burn Hollywood Burn." Alan Smithee should sue.

VILLAGE VOICE, 3/10/98, p. 118, Michael Atkinson

If a movie attains astonishing badness by clubfootedly parodying itself, is it still bad? If you're an infamously unfunny script-belcher like Joe Eszterhas and you write a scurvy dog called *An Alan Smithee Film*, does the film's subsequently lousy direction, by aged hack Arthur Hiller, become an act of destiny itself? If Hiller opts for the Smithee pseudonym himself, which he has, is it publicity or shame or both?

However pleasant it may be to ponder the humor holocaust that is *An Alan Smithee Film: Burn Hollywood Burn* as a Borgesian equivoque—*Merton of the Movies* by Pierre Menard—and however fiercely it may cut us off at the pass in loudly declaring its own ineptitude, the horsemeat hash that has resulted from this fit of self-amused Industry navel-gazing is Amnesty International-grade torture. Eszterhas tried for an in-your-face "Duck Amuck"ness—to be a nonfilm, the fragments of a film-in-the-unmaking—but since the Writer's Guild has no Smithee-like bylaw, one can only wonder why he chose to so proudly splatter his name, as well as his gruesome puss, across such a leaden disaster. Unlike the Smithees of lore, Eszterhas knows no shame, and has about as much right to satirical high ground in regards to Hollywood excess as Michael Cimino.

Still, all would be forgiven if the film hit a single funny note on its way down the crapper, but all we get is whiffs. Structured as a laborious faux-documentary and crammed with stellar guest stars (Sylvester Stallone, Whoopi Goldberg, Billy Barty, Shane Black, et al.), *AASFBHB* centers on a debut director infortuitously named Alan Smithee (a sadly doughy Eric Idle) who becomes unhinged when he loses control over his first film (a $200 mil cop movie called *Trio* that, though we see only a single scene, looks a lot worse even than *AASFBHB)*, realizes opting for the DGA pseudonym is useless, steals the negative, and burns it.

The screwed-over director is an old Hollywood story; if he had any chutzpah, Eszterhas would've lampooned screenwriters getting $5 million for hokey scripts about strippers. But what really wounds is the relentless direct-to-the-camera address, the sub-sitcom timing, the self-aggrandizing gags about sex and drugs, the I-know-it-sucks-but-we're-having-such-fun cameos, the amateurish dubbing, the bio titles that introduce the characters (wittily labeling them "scumbag," "bitch," "Oreo" etc.), the aural punctuation (scenes of Idle in a padded room are scored with a lullaby, that sort of thing), the cheap camerawork, the poundingly awful song score, and the jokes, not one of which is worthy of *Crack'd* magazine. Hiller's cop-out may have been intended as just another yock, but his directorial résumé is free of this buzz bomb forever.

Also reviewed in:
CHICAGO TRIBUNE, 2/27/98, Friday/p. B, Michael Wilmington
NEW YORK TIMES, 2/27/98, p. E10, Janet Maslin
VARIETY, 10/6-12/97, p. 54, Todd McCarthy

ALARMIST, THE

A Lions Gate Films and Key Entertainment release in association with a Bandeira Entertainment presentation of a Dan Stone Flynn/Simchowitz production. *Producer:* Dan Stone and Lisa Zimble. *Director:* Evan Dunsky. *Screenplay:* Evan Dunsky. *Based on the play "Life During Wartime"* by: Keith Reddin. *Director of Photography:* Alex Nepomniaschy. *Editor:* Norman Buckley. *Music:* Christophe Beck. *Music Editor:* Zoran Borisavljevic. *Sound:* Felipe Borrero and (music) Casey Stone. *Sound Editor:* Dean Hovey. *Casting:* Carolyn Long and Concetta Di Matteo. *Production Designer:* Amy B. Ancona. *Art Director:* Rachel Kamerman. *Set Decorator:* Melissa Levander. *Special Effects:* Andre Ellingson. *Costumes:* Denise Wingate. *Make-up:* Carol Strong. *Stunt Coordinator:* Rick Avery. *Running time:* 93 minutes. *MPAA Rating:* Not Rated.

CAST: David Arquette (Tommy Hudler); Stanley Tucci (Heinrich Grigoris); Mary McCormack (Sally Brown); Kate Capshaw (Gale Ancona); Tricia Vessey (April,Howad's Girlfriend); Ryan Reynolds (Howard Ancona); Hoke Howell (Henry Fielding); Ruth Miller (Mrs. Fielding); Michael Learned (Beth Hudler); Lewis Arquette (Bruce Hudler); Richmond Arquette (Andrew Hudler); Gabriel Dell, Jr. (Skippy Hudler); Valerie Long (Doris, Andrew's Girlfriend); Kim Tobin (Bambi, Skippy's Girlfriend); Colin Campbell (Waiter); Eric Zivot (Shelly, the Director); Vincent J. Bilancio (Assistant Director); Clea Duvall (Suzy); Dave Brisbin (Detective Gary Flinkman); Bradley J. Gorman (Grigoris Employee); Dennis Cockrum (Vendor); Matt Malloy (Morgue Technician); Alex Nepomniaschy (Installer).

LOS ANGELES TIMES, 10/23/98, Calendar/p. 16, John Anderson

[*The following review by John Anderson appeared in a slightly different form in* NEWSDAY, 10/16/98, Part II/p. B7.]

If "The Alarmist" were a houseguest, it would amble in, sit down, prop its golf-shoed feet up on the Duncan Phyfe, chug-a-lug the Chateauneuf du Pape and charm the shirt off you. You'd ask it to stay while praying for an evacuation order. And despite the stress, the visit wouldn't be entirely without its minor epiphanies.

Among them? That enough good acting can salvage a movie even when burdened with the structural missteps of writer-director Evan Dunsky's debut feature; that charm is as valuable as sense; and that Stanley Tucci is easily one of the finer actors in the country.

Admittedly, Tucci's Heinrich Grigoris—home-security charlatan, seducer-mentor-betrayer of babe-in-the-woods Tommy Hudler (David Arquette)—may not be the best showcase for any actor's talents. But then again, maybe that's the point. Tucci takes a morally bankrupt con man like Heinrich, makes him totally human without sacrificing any of his latent malevolence and does it all within the framework of what might be called a comedy-thriller with a debt to David Mamet.

The injustice is that Oscars and their ilk are so often determined by size—of the movies' budgets, of the characters' handicaps—rather than the small turn, the internal combustion, that really proves an actor's artistry.

And speaking of naivete, Arquette's Hudler is Exhibit A in the wide, wide world of cluelessness, although he can sure sell home-security systems—which, naturally, steals Heinrich's heart.

That Tommy can do it with such boyish clumsiness knocks Gale Ancona (Kate Capshaw), the beautiful widow with the giant son (Ryan Reynolds), off her feet as well. Tommy, of course, is caught on the horns of an ethical-comic dilemma of sorts, since he is having sex with a client, who clearly has no problem with any of it.

Besides, ethical dilemmas are the movie's meat and potatoes, although it's best when it stays in Tommy-Heinrich world, where Heinrich and his cohort, Sally ("Murder One's" Mary McCormack), teach Tommy the finer points of salesmanship—Heinrich's staging break-ins at clients' homes to justify their faith in him, for instance—after which Tommy begins the long, lonely road to disillusion.

It gets even weirder when the movie makes a big left turn into horror and something happens to make Tommy think that perhaps Heinrich isn't just a schemer but a monster. At which point, "The Alarmist" is getting a bit out there, as they say, and you have to wonder how the tight scripting, editing and overall flow of the movie's earlier episodes got so snarled up.

It's hard to imagine anyone better than Arquette as Tommy. He communicates a kind of dreamy, semi-self-awareness and takes it, seemingly effortlessly, into determined irrationality. Capshaw, whose recent efforts have been a bit lackluster, is as winning here as she's been in years. And Tucci conducts a virtual seminar on acting whenever he gets on screen, which, we're happy to say, seems to be more and more often.

NEW YORK POST, 10/16/98, p. 44, Larry Worth

David Arquette has become an overnight celebrity—not so much for his consistently fine film work, but for being Courteney Cox's intended.

But if Arquette's current status gives his latest film—an off-the-wall, initially rewarding indie, "The Alarmist"—a bit more attention, so much the better.

The bad news: Writer-director Evan Dunsky's debut film divides into two halves, the first of which is deliciously dark and perverse. Sadly, the darkness goes one step too far, after which the effort merely founders.

The story line focuses on a home-security company's timid salesman (Arquette) who travels door to door to sing his product's merits. That's all well and fine until he meets a '90s Mrs. Robinson (Kate Capshaw) whose idea of security has more to do with the salesman than the sale.

Complicating matters further, the guy's boss (Stanley Tucci) reveals his unique method for burgeoning sign-ups: breaking into an individual's home so that he or she will be panicked into grabbing an alarm.

That setup comprises an edgily amusing mix of hucksterism gone amok, awkward pauses and situations that hilariously push the envelope. Unfortunately, Dunsky segues to a grim development that cripples the production and sends it spiraling downhill.

But that's no fault of Arquette, whose blend of vulnerability and dawning cynicism provides pure pleasure for viewers. And he's nicely complemented by the chameleon-like, wonderfully unctuous Stanley Tucci.

Granted, supporting roles aren't as well defined. Still, Capshaw holds her own as the all-consuming matron, while Mary McCormack is a first-rate Lady Macbeth to Tucci's avarice incarnate.

Ironically, the film's highlights are why most viewers will feel betrayed by subsequent failings. Like its salesmen protagonists, "The Alarmist" promises far more than it ultimately delivers.

SIGHT AND SOUND, 11/99, p. 38, Kieron Corless

LA, the present. Heinrich Grigoris, the owner of Grigoris Home Security systems, demonstrates his sales pitch to tyro Tommy. On his first home visit, Tommy is seduced by older widow Gale. Tommy's new career proceeds swimmingly until he encounters a fractious man with an extensive domestic arsenal. Heinrich selects Tommy to star in the company's commercial in which he shines. Heinrich reveals to a horrified Tommy how he increases sales in a neighbourhood by driving at night to clients' houses and surreptitiously setting off their alarms. Tommy invites Gale to the country to stay with his parents. Having shocked them with her drunken behaviour she returns home during the night where she and her son Howard are murdered by an unseen intruder.

Gale's ghost visits a grief-stricken Tommy in a dream, and hints that Heinrich murdered her. Bent on revenge, Tommy tricks Heinrich into breaking into the house with the arsenal. Escaping in a hail of bullets, Heinrich confronts Tommy and denies he's the murderer. Tommy quits his job in disgust and elicits Howard's girlfriend's help in kidnapping Heinrich. He drives Heinrich to a deserted quarry and threatens to kill him unless he confesses. As Heinrich bargains for his life, Tommy receives a call from a talent agency wanting to represent him. Heinrich begs him to call the police to check if they've caught anyone. It transpires a suspect has confessed to the murders. On the drive home, Heinrich offers Tommy freelance work until his acting career takes off.

With *The Alarmist* debut director Evan Dunsky serves up a cinematic experience not unlike being savaged by a sheep. The central idea is not without promise: a slick, stop-at-nothing home-alarm salesman, Heinrich, keeps his business buoyant by moonlighting as a burglar, while schooling his wide-eyed protégé, Tommy, in the cynical ways of the world. *Repo Man* and *Glengarry Glen Ross* are clear points of reference here, but the vivid, freewheeling mania of the first and the incisive analysis of the second are well beyond the grasp of this limping satire. Bland torpor permeates the film's every nook, sapping the momentum of its scattershots at sundry easy targets.

Early on Tommy attempts to sell a security system to a paranoid client, who in turn fishes out every conceivable weapon, extolling its virtues. No doubt this exaggerated role reversal is meant to be funny, but it misses the mark considerably, not least because the scene plods on interminably. Virtually every attempt at black comedy bottoms out thanks to a similar combination of vacuous ideas, flat dialogue and laboured execution. Despite the thin gruel of ironic knowingness, it soon feels like a film running on empty.

As well as comedy and social critique, we get romance, murder mystery and a tacked-on ghost. None of these disparate, collaged elements works in its own right or melds with the others into anything vaguely coherent, although the film manages a productive tonal collision in one scene. Widow Gale and her son Howard's murders occur silently off screen in the kitchen while we see Heinrich's cheap, scaremongering commercial on their television set. It's a nicely judged if not particularly original moment, summoning a queasy, humorous chill.

It's when the script tries to weave Tommy's new relationship in with Heinrich's schemes—sacrificing consistent characterisation along the way—that things begin to feel forced. David Arquette as Tommy clings to innocent, doltish charm and refuses to budge. Stanley Tucci can make no sense of his character Heinrich and retreats into subdued perfunctoriness. Kate Capshaw's Gale conveys warmth and earthy sensuality in her early scenes until she's required to skip into noisy, unmotivated caricature, followed by her swift execution. If only someone had seen fit to visit the same fate on this ill-starred project at an early stage.

VILLAGE VOICE, 10/20/98, p. 160, Justine Elias

Heinrich Grigoris, the owner of a sleazy L.A. home-security firm, has a plan that guarantees profits: he burglarizes clients' houses until they purchase his expensive "armed response" upgrade. But when Grigoris (portrayed with insinuating charm by Stanley Tucci) reveals the scam to Tommy, his newest sales rep (an endearingly meek David Arquette), he finds that his protégé is far too honest for corporate criminality. Based on Keith Reddin's Off-Broadway play *Life During Wartime, The Alarmist* shifts uneasily between Mamet-esque satire and awkward erotic comedy. It's as though first-time writer-director Evan Dunsky didn't want to assert himself over rich source material, even as he shows that he's more than capable of doing so.

Also reviewed in:
NEW YORK TIMES, 10/16/98, p. E12, Stephen Holden

ALL THE RAGE

A Pink Plot Productions release in association with Jour de Fete Films. *Producer:* Roland Tec. *Director:* Roland Tec. *Screenplay:* Roland Tec. *Director of Photography:* Gretchen Widmer. *Editor:* Jon Altschuler. *Music:* Roland Tec. *Sound:* Doug Snyder. *Production Designer:* Louis Ashman. *Costumes:* Sarah Pfeiffer. *Running time:* 90 minutes. *MPAA Rating:* Not Rated.

CAST: Jay Corcoran (Larry); John-Michael Lander (Christopher Bedford); David Vincent (Stewart); Peter Bubriski (Tom); Paul Outlaw (Dave); Merle Perkins (Susan); Jeff Miller (John); Alan Natale (Kenny).

LOS ANGELES TIMES, 10/30/98, Calendar/p. 4, Kevin Thomas

Roland Tec's "All the Rage" offers one of the sharpest satires of gay life and values ever filmed. It's sexy, amusing and has an ending so inspired, so totally revealing, that the effect is all the more stinging for coming out of left field. It is also so cinematic you would never have guessed that Tec, in an especially adroit feature debut, had adapted it from his 1994 play "A Better Boy."

"All the Rage," a standout at the 1997 Outfest, takes us into a world of perfection. John-Michael Lander's Christopher Bedford has it all, including chiseled good looks and a good job as a lawyer in a Boston firm. His office is perfectly appointed as is his apartment in a fine old building. Outside the office his life is a regular routine of visits to the gym, trendy restaurants and bars, where he has no trouble picking up any man who catches his eye. Love 'em and leave him could be his motto, for he goes through men faster than you go through a box of Kleenex when you have a really rotten cold.

Still, since he's gotten everything he ever wanted, he wonders whether he shouldn't go for love as well. When his neighbors, longtime lovers Tom (Peter Bubriski) and Dave (Paul Outlaw), have him over for dinner they surprise him by inviting yet another neighbor, Stewart (David Vincent), an editor at a book publishing company recently arrived from the Midwest. Stewart is a nice-looking young man with large soulful eyes, and he meets one of Christopher's key qualifications: He loves both baseball and ballet.

Christopher regularly goes to the gym with one of his friends at the office, Larry (Jay Corcoran), who exclaims, "Are you telling me that you're going out with a man who doesn't work out!?" (As attractive as Stewart is, he is just a bit thick at the waist.) However, Stewart has a roommate, Kenny (Alan Natale), who not only works out but goes to the same gym Christopher goes to—needless to say, Kenny is a hunk.

Christopher is living in a house of cards and doesn't know it. It's not just that having been a glib, callous chaser he's not prepared for the warm and embracing love Stewart offers; he's also not prepared for the fate that awaits him once he makes a misstep. Setting himself up in his own eyes as the model of perfection, he's faced uniformly with unforgiveness—it's as if people are gratified to see him mess up.

VILLAGE VOICE, 10/20/98, p. 164, Elliott Stein

Writer-director-composer Roland Tec tackles the touchy subject of gay narcissism in this adaptation of his stage play, *A Better Boy*. The film's antihero Chris (John-Michael Lander), a gym-bodied Boston lawyer, flits from pickup to pickup until he settles down temporarily with Stewart (David Vincent), a sweetie-pie country mouse. When Chris starts playing the field again, he loses Stewart—and feels the loss deeply—and gets his comeuppance from an embittered old flame. This cautionary tale is curiously schizoid. The climactic scene is memorably intense, as are the brief sequences in which Chris delivers wrenching monologues directly to camera. But the rest of the film—repetitious visits to Boston's queer haunts with concomitant bitchery, endless shots of Chris grooming himself, dull subplots leading nowhere— is riddled with clichés and boneheaded dialogue.

Also reviewed in:
NEW YORK TIMES, 10/16/98, p. E20, Anita Gates

ALMOST HEROES

A Warner Bros. release of a Turner Pictures presentation of a Di Novi Pictures production. *Producer:* Denise Di Novi. *Director:* Christopher Guest. *Screenplay:* Mark Nutter, Tom Wolfe, and Boyd Hale. *Director of Photography:* Adam Kimmel and Kenneth MacMillan. *Editor:* Ronald Roose. *Music:* Jeffrey CJ Vanston. *Music Editor:* Christopher Kennedy. *Choreographer:* Adam Shankman. *Sound:* Mark Weingarten and (music) David Cole and Robert Fernandez. *Sound Editor:* Hamilton Sterling. *Casting:* Mary Gail Artz and Barbara Cohen. *Production Designer:* Joseph T. Garrity. *Art Director:* Pat Tagliaferro. *Set Decorator:* Linda Allen. *Special Effects:* Thomas "Brooklyn" Bellissimo and Charles "O.G." Belardinelli. *Visual Effects:* Brad Kuehn. *Costumes:* Durinda Wood. *Make-up:* Kate Shorter. *Stunt Coordinator:* Max Kleven. *Running time:* 87 minutes. *MPAA Rating:* PG-13.

CAST: Chris Farley (Bartholomew Hunt); Matthew Perry (Leslie Edwards); Bokeem Woodbine (Jonah); Barry Del Sherman (Sergeant); Robert Tittor (Priest at Fort Adams); Franklin Cover (Nicholas Burr); Patrick Cranshaw (Jackson); Eugene Levy (Guy Fontenot); Lisa Barbuscia (Shaquinna); Christian Clemenson (Father Girard); Steven M. Porter (Higgins); David Packer (Bidwell); Hamilton Camp (Pratt); Jonathan Joss (Bent Twig); George Aguilar (Chief Two Roads); Gregory Norman Cruz (Iowa Indian); Lewis Arquette (Merchant); Don Lake (Elias); Brent Hinkley (Trapper); John Farley (Bartender); Kevin Dunn (Hidalgo); Tim DeKay (New Bartender); Keith Sellon-Wright (Meriweather Lewis); Scott Williamson (William Clark); David Barrera (Ferdinand); Jay Lacopo (Hector); Frank Sotonoma Salsedo (Old Indian); Billy Daydodge (Strong Like Mountain); T. Dan Hopkins (Running Puma); Axel Lindgren (Salmon Brave); Harry Shearer (Narration).

LOS ANGLES TIMES, 6/1/98, Calendar/p. 4, David Kronke

Christopher Guest demonstrated last year, with "Waiting for Guffman," that he couldn't direct traffic. But that was OK, because he surrounded himself with some smart comedians well-versed in the art of improvisation—Eugene Levy, Catherine O'Hara, Fred Willard and Guest himself. With that troupe in front of the camera, behind-the-camera technique hardly mattered.

With "Almost Heroes," Guest has only Matthew Perry of "Friends," who's more adept when working off an urbane script, and the late Chris Farley, whose improvisational skills were limited to yelling and wildly shaking. The screenplay—credited to sitcom writers whose previous credits unpromisingly include "Nurses," "Full House" and "The Jeff Foxworthy Show"—is indifferently crafted, and since Guest himself doesn't appear and Levy is relegated to a tiny role that merely requires mad eye-rolling and sputtering with a bad accent, there's no one around to punch things up with some noodling in the movie's margins.

All we're left with is a lame script and dithering direction, a lethal combination.

"Almost Heroes" concerns a pair of deservedly obscure explorers who race Lewis & Clark across the Northwest Territory to the Pacific Ocean, the boorish Bartholomew Hunt (Farley, inevitably) and the foppish Leslie Edwards (Perry). With a motley band of crass, largely interchangeable crew members in tow, they pratfall their way through the wilderness, stumbling through an inconsequential series of formless sketches before they reach their final destination: the requisite 90-minute running time to qualify this as a feature film.

Hunt and Edwards actually manage to cover some ground, but the jokes go nowhere. The crew members cavort with straw mannequins passed off as hookers. They endure bagpipe music. They panic at the sight of a squirrel. They confront a vain conquistador who brags about his luxuriant mane of hair. Hunt battles an eagle for its eggs; the joke is that the same cheesy stock footage of a soaring eagle is used repeatedly.

It also appears that a running gag was set up concerning a crewman who leaves body parts strewn across the Pacific Northwest, but it's abandoned after only two missing appendages. Indeed, Ronald Roose's editing suggests a mercy killing: He cuts abruptly away from many scenes before they reach any payoff, suggesting he was trying to put them out of their misery.

In his last movie, Farley wasn't attempting to stretch himself; his fans will get what they expect. Perry mugs rather too broadly and delivers his lines as if he's playing the easily scandalized genteel guy in some low-rent burlesque show.

"Almost Heroes" is as misguided as its protagonists; the only difference is that while Hunt and Edwards nominally reach their destination, Guest and his cast remain lost throughout, fumbling around in the wilderness in search of even one inspired comic moment.

NEWSDAY, 6/1/98, Part II/p. B9, Gene Seymour

By the third or fourth time in "Almost Heroes" that Chris Farley hoists a tankard of ale and lets much of its dark amber contents engulf his chin, you wonder whether you should laugh at what he's doing or laugh at the kind of mind-set that finds what he's doing funny.

Farley, especially at the start of this slapstick pastiche of early 19th-Century America, does a lot of things that make you wonder; growling, snarling, stuffing his face with fatty meats, smelling buffalo droppings in sheer rapture and, in general, letting his outsized body ramble all over the scenery like a rogue elephant.

If you loved such implausibly lucrative movies as "Beverly Hills Ninja" and "Tommy Boy," you won't be too disappointed. As far as the rest of us are concerned, there are precious few signs of the growth in range and resources that many believed were within reach of Farley before his shocking death last December.

There is, for instance, one gag in the film in which Farley doesn't say a word. Yet it's the only time in the movie that I actually laughed out loud. It involves a nest at the top of a very tall tree, three eggs and a very protective mother eagle. Evidently, the filmmakers are with me on this since Momma Eagle makes a crucial return appearance toward the end. More than this I dare not say.

I can tell you, for what it's worth, the storyline. Farley plays Hunt, a rough-hewn tracker, recruited by a foppish explorer named Edwards (Matthew Perry) to blaze a trail through uncharted American territory in 1804 toward the Pacific Northwest. Undaunted by Lewis and Clark's huge head start, Perry, Farley and a motley, misbegotten crew are determined to be the first to get to the continent's left side.

Another "Saturday Night Live" alum, Christopher Guest ("Waiting for Guffman"), is the director, and while he applies a crisp polish to the proceedings, it's hard to believe that *he* believes there's much humorous capital in the odd-couple antics of Perry's Edwards and Farley's Hunt. Perry's quite fine, by the way. And so is Eugene Levy as a seedy French trapper and Kevin Dunn as a malevolent Spanish conquistador. But their efforts just don't seem to add up to much except a diverting afternoon watching people frolic by a river.

By the way, there's no easy way to bring into this discussion Thursday's equally shocking death of Farley's fellow SNL-er Phil Hartman except to say that, if nothing else, "Almost Heroes" offers tentative confirmation that Farley, like Hartman, may have been closer to better things that anyone realizes.

Also reviewed in:
CHICAGO TRIBUNE, 6/1/98, Tempo/p. 1, Mark Caro
NEW YORK TIMES, 5/30/98, p. B15, Anita Gates
VARIETY, 6/1-7/98, p. 34, Joe Leydon

AMERICAN HISTORY X

A New Line Cinema release of Turman-Morrisey Company production. *Executive Producer:* Lawrence Turman, Steve Tisch, Kearie Peak, and Bill Carraro. *Producer:* John Morrissey. *Director:* Tony Kaye. *Screenplay:* David McKenna. *Directory of Photography:* Tony Kaye. *Editor:* Jerry Greenberg and Alan Heim. *Music:* Anne Dudley. *Music Editor:* Richard Ford. *Sound:* Steve Nelson and (music) Paul Hulme. *Sound Editor:* Frederick Howard. *Casting:* Valerie McCaffrey. *Production Designer:* Jon Gary Steele. *Art Director:* Dan Olexiewicz and James Kyler Black. *Set Decorator:* Tessa Posnansky. *Set Dresser:* Craig Lafferty, Lisa Roman, Le'Von Webb, and Chris Griffiths. *Special Effects:* Thomas "Brooklyn" Bellissimo. *Costumes:* Doug Hall. *Make-up:* Christina Smith and John E. Jackson. *Special Effects Make-up:* Matthew W. Mungle. *Stunt Coordinator:* Ernie Orsatti, Noon Orsatti, Denney Pierce, and Paul Short. *Running time:* 118 minutes. *MPAA Rating:* R.

CAST: Edward Norton (Derek Vinyard); Edward Furlong (Danny Vinyard); Beverly D'Angelo (Doris Vinyard); Fairuza Balk (Stacey, Derek's Girlfriend); Jennifer Lien (Davina Vinyard); Ethan Suplee (Seth); Avery Brooks (Dr. Robert Sweeney, Principal); Elliott Gould (Murray); Stacy Keach (Cameron Alexander); William Russ (Dennis); Guy Torry (Lamont); Joe Cortese (Rasmussen); Jason Bose-Smith (Little Henry); Antonio David Lyons (Lawrence); Alex Sol (Mitch McCormick); Keram Malicki-Sanchez (Chris); Giuseppe Andrews (Jason); Michelle Christine White (Lizzy); Jonathan Fowler, Jr. (Jerome); Chris Masterson (Daryl Dawson); Nicholas R. Oleson (Huge Aryan); Jordan Marder (Curtis); Paul Le Mat (McMahon); Cherish Lee (Kammi); Sam Vlahos (Dr. Aguilar); Tara Blanchard (Ally); Anne Lambton (Cassandra); Steve Wolford (Reporter); Richard Noyce (Desk Sergeant); Danso Gordon (Buddy); Jim Norton (Randy); David Basulto (Guard); Alexis Rose Coen (Young Ally); Kiant Elam (Lawrence's Partner); Paul Hopkins (Student); Keith Odett (Random Skinhead); Paul Short (Stocky Buddy); Nigel Miguel (Basketball Player).

CHRISTIAN SCIENCE MONITOR, 11/6/98, p. B3, David Sterritt

[*American History X* was reviewed jointly with *The Siege*; see Sterritt's review of that film.]

LOS ANGELES TIMES, 10/28/98, Calendar/p. 1, Kenneth Turan

The mischievous shenanigans of director Tony Kaye have created a considerable show-biz fuss over "American History X," his debut film that depicts neo-Nazi racism infecting one man's family. As often happens in Hollywood, however, the fuss turns out to be more original than the movie.

Kaye, whose name remains on the film as both director and cinematographer despite his efforts to remove it, has run a well-publicized conceptual art campaign designed to protest what he considers the damage New Line Cinema has done to his film. He even showed up for a meeting with executives accompanied by a rabbi, a priest and a Tibetan monk to add some "spirituality" to the proceedings.

Though on the silly side, all this is more intriguing than the film itself, which, though well-intentioned, turns out to be a simplistic and unconvincing look at a serious problem. There's a kernel of a good idea here, plus a forceful, mesmerizing performance by the always impressive Edward Norton, but, all those protests notwithstanding, it's hard to see that this film could have been noticeably different no matter who had final cut.

That kernel, screenwriter David McKenna has said, is the notion of presenting a racist who is articulate and intelligent. As played by a bulked-up Norton, Derek Vinyard is that young man, a former high school honors English student whose head was turned by a combination of personal tragedy and the oily words of neo-Nazi guru Cameron Alexander (Stacy Keach).

His almost glistening body covered with inflammatory tattoos, most noticeably a huge swastika on his chest, Derek cuts a compelling figure courtesy of Norton's bravura performance. He's got the devil's own convincing tongue, using propaganda, statistics and half-truths to convince "insecure, frustrated, impressionable kids" that racism is the way.

"American History X" opens in black and white at a turning point in Derek's life. We see him, in brutal and graphic detail, murdering two black teenagers who are trying to steal his truck, an act that leads to three years in prison.

The present, filmed in color, has younger brother Danny (Edward Furlong) getting into trouble in high school on the same day Derek is getting out of prison. Danny is also a budding neo-Nazi who so idolizes his brother he's written a book report celebrating "Mein Kampf." The school's black principal (Avery Brooks) decides to teach Danny in a one-person tutorial (which he calls American History X) and assigns him a paper about his brother's influence on the family.

Much to that family's surprise, however, the newly freed Derek turns out to be a changed person. He's let his hair grow back to normal length, encourages long-suffering mother Doris (Beverly D'Angelo) to watch her health, and astonishes Danny by urging him to give up smoking and the skinhead ideology that once motivated them both.

"American History X" goes back and forth between the past and the present, between color and black and white, with Danny's and Derek's voice-overs guiding us through the central events of their family's life.

Given that we're supposed to think Derek's change of heart is great news, it's unfortunate that, despite Norton's best efforts, he was a considerably more magnetic and involving individual as a Nazi, which in turn takes some of the interest out of his character once converted.

Troubling in the same vein is the way director-cinematographer Kaye was jazzed by the opportunity to place on screen a wide range of disturbing events, including a nightmarish attack on a local Korean grocery, graphic sexual violence and waves of venomous and inflammatory hate speech. We're told this is all bad, of course, but Kaye's facility for razzle-dazzle cinematography (he's one of the world's top commercial makers) merely underlines the excitement he feels at capturing it on film.

A bigger, finally insurmountable problem is the bombastic, clumsy nature of much of "American History X's" script, which seems to feel that because racists aren't subtle a film about them needn't be either. Many of the supporting characters are either embarrassingly conceived or clumsily acted, and the explanations for radical changes in behavior tend to be relentlessly one-dimensional.

For all its surface verisimilitude and for all its focus on a problem that couldn't be more current, this film can't manage to feel more than sporadically real.

NEW YORK, 11/9/98, p. 59, Peter Rainer

Edward Norton specializes in using his ordinariness to spook us. In *Primal Fear,* playing a defendant accused of a horrible crime, his kid-next-door looks disguised a cunning depravity. In *Rounders,* he played a compulsive gambler whose anonymous mug was the perfect foil for his card-sharp hustle. As the neo-Nazi skinhead Derek in *American History X*, Norton has found the perfect role to bring out the scary undertone to his (seeming) blandness. Buff and goateed, tattooed with swastikas and white-power insignias, Derek is the face of the faceless mob, an ordinary-guy monster.

The film's point is that this monster wasn't born that way: When Derek was a boy, his firefighter father served up racist lectures at the breakfast table. Finally he was shot dead trying to put out a blaze in a crack house controlled by black dealers. In a rage of vengeance, Derek has become the youth leader of a Venice Beach white- power movement, and his younger brother Danny (Edward Furlong) has also been brought into the fold. Derek ends up jailed for three years for killing two black kids trying to steal his car, but his prison experiences transform him. Realizing that his Aryan brothers in the clink aren't exactly soul mates—they gang-rape him in the shower for being friendly around a black inmate (Guy Torry, in a superb cameo)—he emerges clear-eyed and with a full head of hair, yet. He returns home to salvage Danny, who has just written a high-school term paper praising *Mein Kampf,* before it's too late.

By making Derek highly intelligent and middle-class, the filmmakers cut against stereotype. They're trying to make a case for how his hate is a learned response to social misery; the implication, of course, is that what is learned can also be unlearned. But with its razzmatazz mayhem and its deadweight social conscience, *American History X* ultimately resembles nothing so much as an Oliver Stone special: It's *Unnatural Born Killers*. Tony Kaye, the award-winning British TV-commercial director making his feature-film debut, is so juiced by the badness of these people that his attempts to delineate their rehabilitation fall flat. Working from a script by David McKenna, he barely fills in Derek's redemption. The message seems to be: If you gang-rape a skinhead, he'll come to his senses. (Kaye, it should be noted, disowns the present cut of the film, which was assembled by its distributor, New Line.)

There's something highly suspect about *American History X*. Kaye gets so carried away by depictions of hate that the horror we see loses its context; it becomes pulped. (This is an even greater problem in the recent *Apt Pupil,* where a suburban high-school student—Brad Renfro—blackmails an old Nazi-in-hiding—Ian McKellan—to do his bidding. What, finally, is sickening about *Apt Pupil* is that it commodifies the terrors of the Holocaust: It's a Holocaust genre thriller.) *American History X* isn't terrible, but it still doesn't sit well with me. The pummelings and racist exhortations are showcased as if they were musical numbers. *Springtime for Hitler* was funnier—and more incisive, too.

NEW YORK POST, 10/28/98, p. 40, Rod Dreher

Meet Derek. See Derek hate. Hate, Derek, hate. Bad Derek! Hey, kids, don't be a Derek. (Cue angelic choir, cut to wrinkly Native American weeping a solitary tear.)

OK, so there's no crying Indian. Otherwise, that's "American History X", an intense film boosted by director Tony Kaye's bombastically beautiful black-and-white imagery, and yet another astonishing performance by Edward Norton. But the picture is smothered by solemn right-mindedness, and hobbled by scripter David McKenna's simplistic, knee-jerk liberal take on suburban white racism.

The story begins in the dead of a suburban California night, with junior skinhead Danny Vinyard (Edward Furlong) alerting his brother Derek (Norton) to the presence of black vandals breaking into his vehicle. Seconds later, pistol-wielding Derek blows a couple of the thieves away before cops arrive to cart him off to the pokey.

Kaye shot that in-your-face opener in shimmering black-and-white, which he uses to indicate flashback scenes. He introduces color in the next scene, which takes place in the present. School principal Dr. Sweeney (Avery Brooks) comes down hard on Danny for having turned in a paper on Hitler's Mein Kampf as a history report on a civil-rights hero. He tells Danny to write a report on the experiences of his older brother, just released from jail.

Jumping from present to past and back again, the movie shows us how Derek went from being a good kid to a satanically charismatic, powerfully muscled skinhead leader. The last half of "X" focuses on Derek's jailhouse conversion away from white-power nuttery, and his mission to save his hero-worshipping little brother from the hatemongers.

What's right with this movie? Start with Edward Norton. With his magnetic screen presence and astonishingly nuanced acting, Norton proves again that he is the best actor of his generation. And director Kaye's gift for creating extraordinarily potent images is remarkable—even if his use of Nazi skinhead iconography and lurid violence falls just short of pornographic.

McKenna's screenplay is another matter. Though at times psychologically astute, a couple of skinhead conversions late in the film are too tidy to ring true. And the story is downright schoolmarmish in its predictable left-wing lecturing on the causes of white racism.

Hate starts at home, the film says, especially if your home is headed by a white male conservative. "X" links racist rhetoric inseparably to mainstream conservative opinion about the injustice of affirmative action, diversity curricula, black crime, immigration and similar issues. There are no principled conservatives, only neo-Nazis and fatherly fascists; meanwhile, all the good, reasonable people are by-the-book liberal Democrats.

This is condescension and bigotry of a very high-minded sort, a lazy smear job that absolves liberals from having to confront honestly the complex social realities and issues that contribute to white working-class alienation. Write all their concerns off as racist, says "American History X", which will have zippo credibility with anyone but the choir to which it preaches.

Confoundingly, the movie at times makes the skinheads' case. Black gang violence against whites is a problem here, and white-power gangs seem a natural, if tragic, response. In one scene, the mere threat of skinhead attack stops three black goons from beating up an innocent white kid. What sort of message does this send to kids at risk of falling prey to neo-Nazi lies?

NEWSDAY, 10/28/98, Part II/p. B3, Jack Mathews

For those who follow the brutal infighting that occasionally precedes the arrival of a film, today's debut of "American History X," Tony Kaye's mangled morality play about the poison of racism, is something of a milestone. Not since Terry Gilliam fought his successful public war against Universal Pictures over the release of "Brazil" in 1985 has a director made such a spectacular pest of himself in Hollywood.

But the issues stand in stark contrast. Where Gilliam was fighting for his completed version of "Brazil," which the studio did not like, Kaye rejected his first version of "American History X," which New Line Pictures claimed to love, and insisted on being given additional funds and time to continue working on it.

"I'm fully aware that I'm a first-time director," said the 45-year-old Kaye, an award-winning director of TV commercials, "but I need the same autonomy and respect that Stanley Kubrick gets."

Right, and Shane Spencer deserves the same respect Mark McGwire gets. It's hard to imagine how "American History X" might have been made into something special with extra resources. The story is such a painfully obvious and preachy screed against racism, it totally undermines its only genuine ambition, which is to humanize a hate-mongering neo-Nazi.

When demographic statistics are read as lines of race-baiting dialogue, you know you're in for some painstaking sociology, and "American History X" doesn't get much more complicated than that.

From a first script by David McKenna, "American History X" focuses on one family in California's multi-racial Venice Beach. Derek (Edward Norton) is the older brother, the reigning prince of the skinhead crowd, and Danny (Edward Furlong) is the younger brother following in his goose steps. There's a heartsick mother (Beverly D'Angelo) struggling to hold the family together and preserve Danny's innocence. A sister, Davina (Jennifer Lien), is a college student and conveniently contrasting liberal, and another sister is barely out of diapers.

Narrated by Danny, in the form of a school paper he's been ordered to write about his brother, "American History X" intercuts three time periods. The present, shot in color, joins the family on the day of Derek's release from prison. The recent past, in black and white, gives us Derek's transformation from A student to neo-Nazi, and shows us—in the film's first and best sequence—what he did to earn that three-year prison term. And there is a deeper flashback, also in black and white, revealing in a scene of jaw-dropping simplicity how the seeds of racism were sown in Derek by his fireman father.

Norton, whose contributions to the film's final editing put him in the middle of the controversy, gives a performance that is alternately brilliant and banal. As the festering, goateed Nazi in the flashbacks, he creates a genuine menace, wearing a look of concentrated hatred. In Derek's reformed state, the reasoned parolee converted by his prison experiences and determined to rescue his brother from the grip of the neo-Nazis, Norton seems lost.

Part of the problem is that the character's turnaround in prison is so deliberately contrived. Some of the prison scenes have a raw, repelling power, but at the same time, they lead to insultingly predictable results. Not everything is black (evil) and white (purity), Derek is astonished to learn.

Minus the script's obviousness, in speeches and standoffs, Kaye has succeeded in giving life to a figure of grotesque inhumanity. Derek seems real enough, and his relationship with Danny is genuinely affectionate. D'Angelo is convincing, as their widowed, ineffectual mother.

Elsewhere, the movie is mired in stereotypes and caricatures. Stacy Keach is a joke as the neo-Nazi movement leader, directing the actions of his Hitler Youth from his office, like some Kurtzian ghost in the cave, while Fairuza Balk, as Derek's mindless girlfriend, does nothing more than bellow and snarl, as if she'd been told to portray a snake in an acting class.

In the end, "American History X" is no more than a remedial course in elementary humanity. Hatred is baggage, life's too short to be angry all the time, never judge a book by its cover and be kind to strangers. Class dismissed.

NEWSWEEK, 10/26/98, p. 78, David Ansen

In "Primal Fear," the movie that made his reputation as one of the most multicolored chameleons of his generation, Edward Norton played a guy with two distinct faces. His character in "American History X," Derek, a racist L.A. skinhead who comes to see the error of his ways, is almost as divided. The violent neo-Nazi Derek (seen in black-and-white flashbacks) is a mad-dog killer whose eyes glow with satisfied blood lust after he viciously murders a young black thief. The reformed, post-prison-term Derek, determined to save his impressionable kid brother (Edward Furlong) from following his hate-filled footsteps, is a brave, thoughtful fellow who's worked through his rage. Norton is convincing as both sides of Derek's personality, but his virtuosity cannot entirely disguise the fact that Derek's conversions—we also see him flip-flop from thoughtful student to racist—seem more dramatically convenient than psychologically coherent.

There's no doubt that this sometimes powerful, frequently overheated, cautionary tale is deeply felt. "American History X" is at its best showing us how Derek's rage (triggered by the murder of his racist father) tears his ideologically divided family apart. As Derek's sullen, worshipful younger brother, Furlong is touching. Director Tony Kaye (who disavows this cut of the film) and screenwriter David McKenna show some daring by making their antihero smart and articulate: the villains get more than equal time stating their xenophobic case. But the filmmakers are so appalled by the hysterical racial venom of the skinheads, so eager for us to be equally appalled (We are! We are!) that they work themselves into a cinematic hysteria of their own. This material is charged enough without piling on the melodrama and the lip-smacking violence—not to mention the slow motion and heavenly choirs. If only the filmmakers trusted themselves—and us—a little more. But the movie too often sacrifices reportage for razzle-dazzle: when somebody gets killed in a public place, no one comes to help because it would clutter up a cool shot. Is that filmmaking or showing off?

SIGHT AND SOUND, 5/99, p. 36, Andrew O'Hehir

Derek Vinyard, the former leader of a white, racist, skinhead gang in Venice Beach, Los Angeles, is being released from prison after serving three years for manslaughter While Derek has been away, his younger brother Danny, also a skinhead, has been torn between two men: Dr Sweeney, a black high-school principal; and Cameron, a local neo-Nazi leader. The Vinyards' father, a firefighter with racist views, was shot and killed years earlier in a black neighbourhood. At Cameron's urging, Derek organised the disgruntled white youths of Venice Beach into a violent gang who committed hate crimes. Before the killings, Derek alienated his mother and sister. Only Danny still sees him as a hero.

On Derek's release, Cameron, Danny and the other skinheads assume Derek will retake control of the gang. But Derek was betrayed and raped by neo-Nazis in prison, and was then befriended by a black prisoner. He has abandoned his racist views. He agrees to work with Dr Sweeney and the police to save Danny from the gang. Derek attends a skinhead gathering, beats up Cameron and escapes. He convinces Danny to leave the gang, but the next day, on his way to school, Danny is shot and killed by a black student he had confronted the day before.

This is an easy movie to make fun of—in virtually the first scene, skinhead Danny protests when a teacher threatens to fail Danny's essay, "Oh, come on, Sweeney! it took me a week to read *Mein Kampf*! It's not fair!" Elsewhere, characters tend to speak as if they were members of a college debating society or, in the case of Avery Brooks' high-school principal Sweeney, as if they were narrating a melodramatic novel. ("Cameron Alexander found in Derek his shining prince," he tells the cops.) Almost as much time is spent exploring Danny's older brother Derek's hate-filled past in arty, portentous black-and-white flashbacks as in the flat Pacific light of the film's more naturalistic present tense. And are we really expected to believe that a pack of skinheads could come up with a creed as colourful as: "I believe in death, destruction, chaos, filth and greed"?

Despite all that, and despite the wrangle over director Tony Kaye's efforts to remove his name from the finished product, *American History X* is a work of impressive scale and craft and not a movie that's easy to dismiss in the end. Its structure, storytelling method and emotional goals resemble those of grand opera. It seeks to link a simplistic, almost mythic tragedy of brotherhood and sacrifice to a set of powerful, non-verbal tableaux. The comic-book story of *American History X* comes to seem less important than the extraordinary image-making as Kaye's scenes gather cumulative force. The cinematographer as well as the director here, former director of advertisements Kaye has a gift for arresting compositions. What we remember is the sudden, kinetic explosion of Derek and his masked goons into a supermarket where they terrorise the Latino staff, the eerie clarity of the horrifying scene in which Derek kills a would-be car thief, and the documentary realism of the enormous outdoor skinhead gathering at which Derek confronts neo-Nazi leader Cameron.

If Edward Norton's Oscar-nominated performance is the film's magnetic centre—Derek often seems to glow with an insane inner luminescence, like a new Charles Manson—we could do without the clumsy efforts of David McKenna's script to provide the character with specific psychological anchors. To suggest Derek becomes a racist because his father delivers a bigoted dinner-table speech before dashing off to be killed, and then reforms because one black prisoner does him a favour, is reductive to the point of inanity. At its best, *American History X* reaches for a richer, more ambiguous notion of evil as an insidious force that's almost impossible to keep at bay. But whatever Kaye and McKenna's intentions may have been, Derek seems to be essentially the same arrogant jerk after his release from prison as he was before. Only his ideology has changed, and that's not enough to keep his family from tumbling over the tragic precipice.

For my money, the finest performance here comes from Edward Furlong as the sweet, bright and easily manipulated Danny, a boy both eager to please his morally upright black teacher and the moronic Venice Beach neo-Nazi leader (an enjoyable cameo role for Stacy Keach). The excellent supporting cast also includes Fairuza Balk as Derek's sycophantic girlfriend; Ethan Suplee as a beefy small-minded skinhead lieutenant; and Guy Torry as Derek's black workmate in prison. Beverly D'Angelo merits a special mention for her restraint as Derek and Danny's coughing mother, possibly suffering from emphysema (an operatic character if ever there was one). In a film whose memorable atmospherics are probably its primary virtue, the clutter and claustrophobia of white-trash Californian poverty are captured with startling accuracy.

TIME, 11/2/98, p. 100, Richard Corliss

With a swastika tattooed on his left pec and a gaudy line of rage against minorities, Derek Vinyard (Edward Norton) is the very model of a modern neo-Nazi—the model, at least, to his doting younger brother Danny (Edward Furlong). While Derek simmers in jail for killing two black malefactors, Danny gets the evil message. He writes a paper on *Mein Kampf*, shaves his head and becomes a good little Hitler youth. Monkey see ...

American History X, a confused, randomly compelling family melodrama, is at the center of a Hollywood controversy—not, so far, over its grim subject matter but over the firing of director Tony Kaye during editing. Thus it's hard to know whom to blame for the film's choppiness, its mixture of rage and sentimentality, the stridency of some of the acting.

Kaye, a Brit who shoots the film with familiar pizazz (low-angle shots, portentous slo-mo, some black-and-white scenes), made his name directing TV commercials in Europe. What's not clear is the product on sale here. It seems to be brotherhood among the races. But David McKenna's script is either cunningly ambiguous or desperately muddled. In racially torn Venice Beach, Calif., the neo-Nazis are pathetic lowlifes, crying out for our contempt. And of course Nazism is a thug ideology. Yet much of the film's violence is committed by blacks; most of the victims are white. So what's the moral?

The moral is as old as South Pacific: you've got to be taught to hate. Derek's father makes racist remarks, so the liberal-minded lad turns into a neo-Nazi; then Derek sees his beliefs are wrong, so skinhead Danny does too. It's nice that today's kids are so easily swayed by their elders. Or is it? Monkey see ...

VILLAGE VOICE, 11/3/98, p. 140, Gary Dauphin

American History X apparently had some paternity issues long before it headed to theaters. A leaden, presumptively shocking exposé about skinheads and surrogate fathers, *X* was reportedly marred by budgetary squabbles, a temporarily AWOL director, and an editing-room battle for control of the final cut. Neat industry chatter, to be sure, but on the screen, *X* is a mess of a film no matter who its daddy is.

X's title is taken from a school assignment skin-in-training Danny (Edward Furlong, chain-smoking where he could be acting) is forced to write after handing in an appreciative five-pager on *Mein Kampf.* Danny's been told to detail the trials and tribulations of his older brother, Derek (Edward Norton, slogging admirably through *X*'s overall muddle), a local neo-Nazi bigwig. Derek's been doing time for the gleeful murder of some Crips, but he's remembered by little bro as a good student, an emotionally wounded fatherless child, a semi-courageous guy willing to stand up to Venice, California's black and Latino toughs.

Having reduced racism to a kind of adolescent coping mechanism, *X* takes a mildly curious path to its foregone conclusion, writer-director Tony Kaye putting his leads through the somehow comforting 'hood-film paces. A proud, been-there black principal (relentlessly noble Avery Brooks) acts on the assumption that your average teenage skinhead needs love and guidance as much as your average movie Crip, making the big question not why or how our boys will abandon hate but whether they can do it before various first-act chickens come home to roost. *X* strikes such ghettocentric chords as wasted potential, haggard single moms, gang-banger camaraderie, old friends who can't accept newfound positivity, and, of course, prison-house set pieces aplenty, from the ever poignant moment when a convicted murderer takes up reading to the always life-altering shower-room rape. The 'hood movies certainly don't own these clichés, but *X* turns its meager insight about the stupid things marginal boys of all races do into a victimization pissing contest. There is something perversely pleasing in watching white guys strain to play urban-myth catch-up, but new and daring it ain't.

Also reviewed in:
CHICAGO TRIBUNE, 10/30/98, Friday/p. D, John Petrakis
NATION, 11/30/98, p. 32, Stuart Klawans
NEW YORK TIMES, 10/28/98, p. E1, Janet Maslin
VARIETY, 10/26-11/1/98, p. 41, Todd McCarthy
WASHINGTON POST, 10/30/98, p. D1, Stephen Hunter
WASHINGTON POST, 10/30/98, Weekend/p. 64, Michael O'Sullivan

ANTZ

A DreamWorks Pictures and PDI release. *Executive Producer:* Penney Finkelman Cox, Sandra Rabins, and Carl Rosendahl. *Producer:* Brad Lewis, Aron Warner, and Patty Wooton. *Director:* Eric Darnell and Tim Johnson. *Screenplay:* Todd Alcott, Chris Weitz, and Paul Weitz. *Story:* Zak Penn. *Editor:* Stan Webb. *Music:* Harry Gregson-Williams and John Powell. *Music Editor:* Brian Richards and Adam Smalley. *Choreographer:* Adam Shankman. *Sound:* Steve Maslow, Gregg Landaker and (music) Alan Meyerson. *Sound Editor:* Richard L. Anderson and Elliott L. Koretz. *Casting:* Leslee Feldman. *Production Designer:* John Bell. *Art Director:* Kendal Cronkhite. *Set Designer:* Don Weinger. *Special Sound Effects:* John Pospisil. *Supervising Animator:* Rex Grignon and Raman Hui. *Running time:* 83 minutes. *MPAA Rating:* PG.

VOICES: Woody Allen (Z); Dan Aykroyd (Chip); Anne Bancroft (Queen); Jane Curtin (Muffy); Danny Glover (Barbatus); Gene Hackman (Mandible); Jennifer Lopez (Azteca); John Mahoney (Drunk Scout); Paul Mazursky (Psychologist); Grant Shaud (Foreman); Sylvester Stallone (Weaver); Sharon Stone (Bala); Christopher Walken (Cutter).

CHRISTIAN SCIENCE MONITOR, 10/2/98, p. B3, David Sterritt

"I've always loved ants," says Dan Aykroyd, with just the hint of a smile. "They crawl across my desk and they're really like dogs, you know? They'll stop, they'll stand on your finger, they'll look at you, and if you put a paper clip on them they'll carry it away. I've always loved ants!"

If the DreamWorks movie studio has its way, everyone else will soon be loving ants as much Aykroyd claims to. Or at least one particular ant: Z-4195, the unlikely hero of "Antz," opening today after one of the season's most energetic promotional campaigns.

Z is played by Woody Allen, supported by Sharon Stone as the princess he falls in love with, Gene Hackman as a military ant with evil plans for their colony, and Sylvester Stallone as a soldier ant who trades places with Z in a poorly planned romantic scheme. Aykroyd and Jane Curtin, who play a pair of friendly wasps, were among several "Antz" talents visiting the recent Toronto International Film Festival to beat the drum for their movie.

Danny Glover, also on hand to publicize the picture, waxed more philosophical than Aykroyd when asked why he agreed to a voice-only part in an insect-based movie—not an obvious choice for the star of the "Lethal Weapon" series and the dramatic "Beloved," a far more serious film coming later this month.

"Human beings always try to displace their own emotions—and understand themselves better—through animals," he says. The idea that we can take such an insignificant little being and [use it] to understand something about loving, ideas, dreams is very intriguing to me."

Eric Darnell and Tim Johnson, who directed the movie, were drawn to ants for similar reasons. "They're hard-working," Darnell notes. "They have a social structure; they build things that are greater than themselves. In those and many other ways, they mirror ourselves." Honeybees have comparable habits, he adds, "but I don't think [a honeybee movie] would have been as interesting. They don't battle termites!"

How do Darnell and Johnson know so much about the insect world? Before embarking on the 18-month filming process for "Antz," which follows "Toy Story" as the second all-computer-animated film in Hollywood history, they spent a full year researching and preparing the project.

"We read books and studied [ants] any way we could," Darnell reports. "And we learned that [their] world is far more frightening, horrifying, and bizarre than you'd ever want to bring to the screen! But we were able to [use] a few nuggets."

While most of "Antz" is pure fun, centering on a neurotic hero amazingly close to the characters Allen has played in his own live-action movies, the directors acknowledge a political undertone in its depiction of a society filled with job-obsessed conformists at the mercy of self-centered rulers and a military tyrant who could destroy them all.

"Something animated filmmaking allows you to do—and it's particularly exciting—is to be far more mythological than in a live-action film," Johnson says. "You can have a stronger theme and moral to the story, without feeling you're beating people over the head or being overly cute.... We wanted a layer of the story [to be] about the politics of this ... sprawling and rather fascist world."

Still, messages and subtexts were hardly the point of the film, which ultimately cares less about ideas than comedy, action, and romance. "There was about a year of preparation," Johnson says, "when we worked it all out traditionally, pencil on paper, then filmed that and watched it. If you're entertained by stick figures, you know you've got a movie that's telling a good story."

Viewers here generally agreed that "Antz" succeeds well at its lively tasks, although few considered it superior to "Toy Story," still the high-water mark for computer-animated entertainment. "Antz" may meet its biggest test in two months when Disney releases "A Bug's Life," pitting a flea circus against a wicked grasshopper. Whichever film wins at the box office, moviegoers are in for a more insect-friendly year—and some lucky creepy-crawler might even emerge with an Oscar in its mandible.

LOS ANGELES TIMES, 10/2/98, Calendar/p. 1, Kenneth Turan

Of the numerous apocryphal stories clustering around legendary producer Samuel Goldwyn, one concerns "The Life of the Bee," a book by Nobel Prize-winning author Maurice Maeterlinck. Goldwyn, or so the story goes, purchased the rights to this popular volume, not realizing it was a work of natural history until he read a treatment. "My God," he said, storming out of his office, "the hero is a bee!"

Sam Goldwyn, meet "Antz."

Not only is the hero of this computer-animated feature an ant, so is (except for some stray wasps and a horde of nasty termites) just about everyone else who matters. Basing an entire movie on the lifestyle of these industrious insects, even if some of Hollywood's most recognizable voices do the talking, is something of a lunatic idea. It halfway works, but unlike the computer-generated "Toy Story," there is no magic in the air, and "Antz" ends up more impressive than embraceable.

The visual side of "Antz" (put together by computer animation firm PDI) is its most convincing aspect. Directors Eric Darnell and Tim Johnson are strongest when scenes require a sense of scale, and, given technology that can handle crowds of up to 60,000 ants, shots that illustrate the enormous business of the colony are something to see.

The gimmick of "Antz" is that, guess what, these tiny insects act exactly like people. The film employs distinctive, well-known and probably pricey voice talent to beef up this illusion, bringing together performers like Woody Allen and Sylvester Stallone for probably the first and last time.

Allen plays Z, an ant who wants to be all he can be in a colony that, not surprisingly, values team effort over individualism every time. But that doesn't stop Z from amusingly whining to his therapist about the problems of being "the middle child in a family of 5 million" and complaining that "handling dirt is not my idea of a fulfilling career."

Even Z's pals, fellow worker ant Azteca (Jennifer Lopez) and brawny soldier ant Weaver (Stallone), feel this is an odd attitude in a place where everyone definitely has his place. But Z keeps wanting to strike a blow for himself as an individual, and when Princess Bala (Sharon Stone) goes slumming in a workers' tavern, he sees his chance.

The daughter of the wise and prolific Queen (Anne Bancroft), Bala has problems of her own, the most pressing being her impending marriage to the darkly efficient General Mandible (Gene Hackman), an ant so tough he is thinking of overthrowing the queen and going into business for himself.

Smitten by Bala, Z will do anything to see her again, including switching places with Weaver during a parade of soldier ants. This casual changing of roles has far-reaching effects for all concerned, as does a tall tale Z hears in a bar about a "better place," a veritable Insectopia, where, wonder of wonders, "you can be your own ant."

One of the drawbacks of this scenario is that, to be frank, all ants look pretty much alike, which puts a crimp in the film's style. And having ants stand upright so they look more like people places an awkward emphasis on the insects' protruding tail-like appendages.

All those celebrity voices are intended to get us over the movie's rough spots, but while some actors, notably Stallone and Danny Glover as a soldier ant named Barbatus, do terrific jobs, Allen's trademark whining gets tiresome here in a way it doesn't in his own films.

When everything is added up, "Antz" is more weird than funny, a film that has the potential to make both parents and young children uncomfortable. A portion of its nominal humor involves jokes about drinking beverages out of "an aphid's anus" and its menacing termites are animated versions of creatures who'd be more at home in Paul Verhoeven's "Starship Troopers."

"Antz" is brief enough, clocking in at 83 minutes, but its story is too predictable to make an impact even in such a short space. Unlike "Toy Story," the dialogue here, written by Todd Alcott and Chris & Paul Weitz, is pro forma all the way. While it's amusing to hear ants mouthing Marxist dogma like "It's the workers who control the means of production," lines like "What kind of a chance do you have with a princess?" do not sound any better just because an insect is doing the talking. Sam Goldwyn, I feel your pain.

NEW YORK, 10/12/98, p. 82, David Denby

At the climax of *Antz*—the first animated feature from DreamWorks—Z (Woody Allen), an ordinary worker ant, and the Princess Bala (Sharon Stone), a very great ant indeed, burst out of their home beneath the ground and discover the fabled land of Insectopia. In front of the two ants lies an imposing mass of towers and bulky layered structures, glowing like the Emerald City in *The Wizard of Oz*—the remaining Pepsi cans and wrapped tuna sandwiches of a Central Park picnic. Oh, joy! But then, suddenly, an enormous corrugated rubber surface with pink ectoplasm stuck to it—a boy's sneaker with bubblegum in the cleats—comes down on Z and Bala like some indifferent, conquering God. *Antz* is a terrific joke about scale. Beneath the ground, the ant colony looks huge, with enormous tunnels, battlefields, and meeting halls. Z, who calls himself "the middle child in a family of 5 million," natters on to his shrink about depersonalization, and winds up the unwitting leader of a rebellion against a fascist society. Above the sod, however, the ants are too insignificant to be worth killing.

Antz, with its deadpan witticisms, its heart-stopping shifts of perspective, is completely entertaining, a kids' movie that will leave grown-ups quoting the best lines to one another. The script has been fashioned for Woody Allen's personality, and Woody delivers the lines with his own peculiarly incisive petulance. He's a drone who whines: As a voice coming out of an ant, he's even more like Woody than he is speaking in his own body. The team at the animation company PDI, devising the entire film with computers, renders the ants as caramel-colored stand-up creatures; they have wide skulls and big eyes, and some of them are spookily beautiful, like Egyptian sculpted heads. They are easy to look at, and flexible enough, even in massed groups, to enjoy without animation fatigue. The faces suggest ever so slightly the actors who are taking the various characters—Gene Hackman as a megalomaniacal general; Sylvester Stallone as a bluff soldier; and Dan Aykroyd and Jane Curtin, very proper indeed, playing not ants but a pair of buzzing, preening, distantly solicitous Wasps.

NEW YORK POST, 10/2/98, p. 39, Thelma Adams

Woody Allen needs "Antz." The world hasn't gotten smaller; Allen has. It's fitting, and even a step forward, to see the Woodman abandon his body and give voice to Z-4195, the worker ant struggling for self-esteem amid a colony of conformists in DreamWorks SKG's first computer-animated comedy.

Yes, Z sees a shrink. He spits out one-liners like a spider spews his web. He's appealing because he's powerless. He needs protection and we understand that he uses his humor like an exoskeleton.

Z is the under-ant, a quality that long ago added to Allen's charm; we could take the bitterness because we knew he wasn't sitting on top of the hill. He was under it, shoveling dirt like the rest of us.

"Antz" rehabilitates Allen. The small-scale world of ants—humming, conflicted, hierarchical, sexually charged, prolific—isn't that different from the two-block strip on the Upper East Side he takes for the world.

While Allen clearly shaped his dialogue, Todd Alcoft, Chris Weitz and Paul Weitz penned the script. Eric Darnell and Tim Johnson directed, creating a believable idiosyncratic world from an army of desktops and a stable of vocal talent.

"Antz" is a standard fairy tale with Marxist overtones. The worker schnook falls for Princess Bala (Sharon Stone, who manages to squeeze a wiggle in her walk into her tone of voice). To get closer to the girl, Z trades spots with warrior buddy Weaver (Sylvester Stallone, also benefiting from leaving his body at home).

By stepping out of line, Z gets embroiled in a palace coup led by ruthless Gen. Mandible (Gene Hackman). Mandible's scheme threatens the position of the queen (Anne Bancroft) and sacrifices the lion's share of the ant army to acid-spitting termites.

The senseless death of the good soldier Barbatus (Danny Glover) serves Z a straight shot of reality. He eventually sees beyond his own self-interest—and Bala's pretty thorax.

The insect hero harnesses his individual strength—his creativity—to save the collective and institute an Insectopia on Earth.

It's all very '70s. There's no use telling that bold little bug that communal life will always have its discontents. Still, "Antz" stands as a clever and accomplished 'toon about a misfit who creates a better world, gets the girl and finally grows up.

NEWSDAY, 10/2/98, Part II/p. B3, Jack Mathews

The major character in the computer-animated "Antz" is a pint-sized, wisecracking, neurotic worker ant who sees a shrink, frets about being the middle child in a family of five million, and is somehow attractive to the leggiest ant-babe in the colony. If this little fellow sounds like Woody

Allen—and it is his stammering voice we hear—then "Antz" may be best thought of as the latest Allen movie rather than the first animated feature from DreamWorks.

It took guts, or perhaps it's foolhardiness, for the fledgling studio formed by David Geffen, Steven Spielberg and former Disney honcho Jeffrey Katzenberg to build an animated film around a personality who has few admirers outside the urban centers, particularly among parents, and whose humor, in any event, is out of the range of children.

But "Antz," as Katzenberg has been anxious to say, isn't directed at small kids. It carries a PG rating, and earns it with sexual innuendo, oblique cultural references, and a wealth of in-jokes and hip movie allusions. Some of the biggest laughs, at least at my industry screening, came from the customized nature and delivery of lines from Allen, as the hero Z-4195; Gene Hackman, as the megalomaniac colony commander General Mandible; Christopher Walken, as his appalled second-in-command Colonel Cutter, and Sharon Stone, as the slinky Princess Bala.

While most of the film's voices are easily recognized, it's Allen's that dominates the foreground. "Antz" is a computer's idea of what Allen might have done during his "early, funny period," when he transported himself—over-analyzed, over-read, overwrought Manhattan Jew—into adventures in the future ("Sleepers"), the past ("Love and Death"), and the erogenous zones ("Everything You Always Wanted to Know About Sex"). It is vintage Allen, and for those who appreciate it, his performance breathes needed life into an otherwise glib film exercise.

There's nothing glib about the animation. "Antz" is a visual sensation, a great leap forward in computer animation over Disney's "Toy Story." The computer creates more realistic character movements and three-dimensional depth than classic animation, and there's seemingly much greater detail, in scenes ranging from panoramas of busy ant-hill interiors and trash dump nirvanas to character close-ups. You don't have to look hard to see the features of Allen, Stone, Hackman, and, as soldier ant Barbatus, Danny Glover. And you'll recognize muscle-bound Weaver even before you hear the voice of Sylvester Stallone.

But the storytelling largely belies Katzenberg's professed aim at an older, more sophisticated audience. The plot, about a reluctant hero's efforts to save his colony from a military coup, takes a slight, episodic cartoon route to a predictable ending, creating what I suspect will be little genuine wonder for children along the way.

Its script, by three credited writers with obvious input from Allen, depends mostly on its "Allen moments," in Z's nervous banter with Bala, his interaction with the evil Mandible, in his pithy, non-stop observations about life and revolt in an urban anthole.   Certainly, the word anthropomorphic has never been more appropriately applied.

SIGHT AND SOUND, 12/98, p. 41, Jonathan Romney

Worker ant Z-4195 is a neurotic loner in a rigorously stratified ant colony under New York's Central Park. Princess Bala, daughter of the colony's Queen, visits the workers' bar incognito and shares a dance with Z. Smitten, he persuades his soldier friend Weaver to swap places with him and joins the troops' review, hoping to spot Bala. But army commander General Mandible—Bala's fiancé—plans a coup. He sends the Queen's troops on a suicide mission to battle termites. Z is the only survivor of the ensuing massacre.

Returning home, Z is welcomed as a hero. Accidentally ejected into the perilous outside world, he and Bala make their way to Insectopia, the fabled land of plenty (actually a picnic area). But Cutter, Mandible's second-in-command, captures Bala, and Z returns home to look for her. Mandible plans to drown the colony and establish a military republic, but Z, Bala and Weaver unite the ants to build a ladder to safety. Mandible is killed, and the ants build a new colony.

Two years ago, promoting the release of Toy Story, the first entirely computer-animated feature film, director John Lasseter announced that his follow-up would be about insects. That film, A Bug's Life, is forthcoming, but in a coup that has caused red faces at Disney and jubilation at DreamWorks SKG—and much discussion in the trade press—DreamWorks has preempted Lasseter with Antz. Made with digital production house PDI, Antz already looks enough of a technical advance on Toy Story to cause Lasseter's Pixar company considerable concern. But then, CGI is Hollywood's boom sector—it's awfully competitive out there.

It has become commonplace to say that the new blockbuster cinema takes us back to film's silent origins as purveyor of spectacle, wonder and, above all, unimaginable novelty. But entirely digital animation is rather different—it takes us back further, to the history of painting. What arrests us in a film like *Antz* are very specific visual effects that strike us because we've never seen them achieved before: for example, the textures of stone in the workers' tunnels; a beam of sunlight captured underground; a wisp of dust in the air; and—one of CGI's several holy grails—a whole range of convincingly fluid and luminous water effects. These are all small miracles, but miracles none the less. The film's range of light effects is considerably more complex than the relatively flat, candy-colour palette of *Toy Story*. Ironically, though, the often cloying lighting of *Antz*, mainly in the outside-world sequences, seems very much informed by traditional Disney colour schemes (for instance, *The Lion King*'s), as well as the kitsch excesses of new-age and sci-fi illustration.

Ultimately, the two most impressive achievements of *Antz* are its rendering of character and multiplicity. While an insect can be easily reduced to a set of geometrical, machine-like parts, there are enough of those parts—legs, antennae, separate body sections—to provide a real challenge in coordinating the entire body, and even more of a challenge when masses of insects move together. Several set-pieces achieve both effects with astonishingly intricate dynamism. In the bar sequence, for example, hordes of ants move together as the workers dance in robotic unison to a twitchy Devo-like rendition of 'Guantanamera'—all except protagonists Z and Bala, who launch into their own routine, with nods to *Pulp Fiction* and Michael Jackson.

In sharp contrast are the two remarkable scenes that bookend the film, in which thousands of ants interlock to produce the solid shapes of a wrecking ball and a swaying tower, each a mass of chaotically squirming body parts. This, of course, is the narrative's central metaphor—the single unit that takes its place (or refuses to) in the mass—but it also reflects the overall nature of CGI, in which a multiplicity of individual pixels take their place in a vast, ever-shifting overall picture.

The film's other distinctive achievement is its character depiction. Where *Toy Story* focused on a small group of sharply differentiated characters, *Antz* derives an astonishing range of variations on the insect model, using basic distinctions (male/female, worker/soldier, and so on) to yield up precisely limned individuals. They still have a plastic, cartoon look, but that works to their benefit, especially in the creased scowls of General Mandible and the chunky Weaver, the latter modelled on Sylvester Stallone, who provides his voice. PDI claims to have developed a facial animation system considerably more complex than anything seen previously, corresponding to the anatomical make-up of the human face, but it's often the smallest details that make the faces marvellous, such as the delicate crow's feet around the Queens' eyes.

Antz's most immediate commercial appeal is its use of instantly recognisable character voices, and Woody Allen's self-parody as Z makes the film a sort of Allen film by default—perhaps a belated sequel to his sci-fi spoof *Sleeper* (1973). Allen extends various commonplaces of his comedy-kvetch persona. Z begins the film in therapy and ends up getting back in touch with "his inner maggot". All the actors' distinctive vocal inflections work much as Robin Williams' improvisations did in Disney's *Aladdin*, providing a template of unusually idiosyncratic human rhythms on to which the visual material has to be grafted. This seems to underline the film's theme—that it's ultimately the individual, the human factor, that controls the machinery, rather than the other way round.

Antz doesn't entirely work to plan in that thematic respect: there's still an odd tension between the human character traits and the visuals, with their geometric abstraction and plasticity. Somehow, rather than the voices humanising the visuals, the visuals defuse the immediacy of the humour. This may simply be a formality: PDI may yet come up with a neat new programme that automatically meshes the human and inhuman registers. But the problem may prove inherent to CGI itself (although it wasn't quite so apparent in the more emotionally engaging *Toy Story*). Perhaps, after all, computer animation's future may lie not in winning us over with anthropomorphic charm, but in opting even more brazenly for the machine made, for the radically inhuman. Genuine insect cinema is yet to come.

Also reviewed in:
CHICAGO TRIBUNE, 10/2/98, Friday/p. E, Mark Caro
NEW YORK TIMES, 10/2/98, p. E12, Janet Maslin
NEW YORKER, 10/19/98, p. 93, Anthony Lane

VARIETY, 9/21-27/98, p. 104, Todd McCarthy
WASHINGTON POST, 10/2/98, p. D1, Rita Kempley

APT PUPIL

A TriStar Pictures release of a Phoenix Pictures presentation of a Bad Hat Harry production. *Executive Producer:* Tim Harbert. *Producer:* Jane Hamsher, Don Murphy, and Bryan Singer. *Director:* Bryan Singer. *Screenplay:* Brandon Boyce. *Based on the novella "Apt Pupil" by:* Stephen King. *Director of Photography:* Newton Thomas Sigel. *Editor:* John Ottman. *Music:* John Otttman. *Music Editor:* Amanda Goodpaster and Lia Vollack. *Sound:* Geoffrey Lucius Patterson and (music) Tim Boyle. *Sound Editor:* Chuck Michael. *Casting:* Francine Maisler. *Production Designer:* Richard Hoover. *Art Director:* Kathleen M. McKernin. *Set Designer:* Amy Shock and David Eckert. *Set Decorator:* Jennifer Herwitt. *Set Dresser:* Jenny Baum. *Special Effects:* Philip Beck, Jr. *Costumes:* Louise Mingenbach. *Make-up:* Joni Meers Powell. *Stunt Coordinator:* Gary Jensen. *Running time:* 100 minutes. *MPAA Rating:* R.

CAST: Brad Renfro (Todd Bowden); Ian McKellen (Kurt Dussander); Joshua Jackson (Joey); Mickey Cottrell (Sociology Teacher); Michael Reid MacKay (Nightmare Victim); Ann Dowd (Monica Bowden); Bruce Davison (Richard Bowden); James Karen (Victor Bowden); Marjorie Lovett (Agnes Bowden); David Cooley (Gym Teacher); Blake Anthony Tibbetts (Teammate); Heather McComb (Becky Trask); Katherine Malone (Student); Grace Sinden (Secretary); David Schwimmer (Edward French); Anthony Moore (Umpire); Elias Koteas (Archie); Kevin Spirtas (Paramedic); Michael Byrne (Ben Kramer); Jan Triska (Isaac Weiskopf); Joe Morton (Dan Richler); Michael Artura (Detective Getty); Donna Marie Brown (Mother); Mark Flythe (Darren); Warren Wilson (Newscaster); Jill Harris (Reporter); Norbert D. Singer and Mildred Singer (Hospital Administrators); Mary Ottman (Doctor).

CHRISTIAN SCIENCE MONITOR, 11/6/98, p. B3, David Sterrit

[*Apt Pupil* was reviewed jointly with *The Siege*; see Sterritt's review of that film.]

LOS ANGELES TIMES, 10/23/98, Calendar/p. 8, Jack Mathews

[*The following review by Jack Mathews appeared in a slightly different form in* NEWSDAY, 10/23/98, Part II/p. B2.]

Adapted from a Stephen King novella, and staged like a two-character David Mamet play, Bryan Singer's "Apt Pupil" is a curious big-screen project, to be sure. Add in the subject matter, a teenage boy's obsession with an ex-Nazi's concentration camp reveries, and the experience is like staring at molecular evil through an electron microscope.

Ultimately, the view is too close for either comfort or scrutiny. The film leaves you no room to breathe, to step back and clear your mind with a quick whiff of humanity, and appreciate the point of the exercise. Nor is there enough psychological development of the boy's character to make his evolving relationship with the old man entirely convincing.

Nevertheless, the subject and the outstanding performances of Brad Renfro ("The Client") and Sir Ian McKellen give "Apt Pupil" a magnetic grip on the audience. Just as Renfro's Todd Bowden and McKellen's Kurt Dussander are attracted to and repulsed by each other, so are we.

The story is launched on a spectacular coincidence: the sighting of the ex-Nazi by 16-year-old Todd, who has just finished a week of Holocaust study in high school and become obsessed with the subject.

On a public bus, he recognizes Dussander, a scruffy loner in the neighborhood, from 40-year-old photos in the library. Todd then creates an airtight dossier on his concentration camp crimes and shows up at his door with an offer he can't refuse. If Dussander will tell Todd the detailed truth of his experiences, exactly what he did, to how many, and how it felt, Todd will not report him to Nazi hunters. And in case the old man gets any ideas, the evidence is stored in a safe deposit box.

And so, a lethal game of cat-and-mouse begins, with Dussander—at first cautious and reluctant, then with greater and greater, alcohol-fueled enthusiasm—recalling his role in the Final Solution. Though we are mercifully spared dramatizations of his deeds, Dussander reveals himself to have been a true patriot of the Third Reich, a dehumanized killing machine, and his foul soul is revived by the boy's encouragement.

The deeper the pair delve into Dussander's memories, the stronger their attraction and repulsion, and the more dangerous the game becomes—not only for them, but for anyone who tests their venom, including Todd's supportive, disbelieving principal (David Schwimmer), and the homeless man (Elias Koteas) who stalks Dussander, hoping for handouts.

Singer, who made a splash three years ago with the serpentine thriller "The Usual Suspects," directs with less certainty here. Working with a first script by Brandon Boyce, Singer attempts to blend the novella's more conventional thriller elements with the Holocaust issues, and the results are at best awkward, and at worst trivializing.

A scene showing Dussander relapsing into active duty while goose-stepping in a store-bought Nazi uniform sends chills directly up the spine, but one immediately following has him clumsily stuffing a live and vigorously uncooperative cat into his oven. It's played as black comedy, as if Dussander were a reformed vampire falling off the wagon. But considering that the cat represents the lives of 6 million slaughtered Jews, it's comedy of a truly odious sort.

Ultimately, "Apt Pupil" doesn't have the courage of its convictions. If it were truly concerned with the seductive power of evil, it would spend more time helping us understand what it is about Todd, and what it was about Dussander, that predisposed them to becoming monsters. As it is, and despite the riveting performances of Renfro and McKellen, we're left with classic horror-movie sociopaths, evil-doers without conscience, or much to say about the nature of evil.

NEW YORK POST, 10/23/98, p. 45, Thelma Adams

Stephen King and the Holocaust? Will horrors never cease? In "Apt Pupil," one of four novellas in the 1982 collection that also inspired the movies "The Shawshank Redemption" and "Stand By Me," King brought the war—WWII—home to suburban America.

The wretched title refers to red-blooded American high school honor student Todd Bowden (Brad Renfro). He's the squeaky-clean kid who has everything: two caring parents, a beautiful home, a promising college future and a girl.

But Todd isn't really alive to the world around him until his history class undertakes a one-week Holocaust course. He tears into the material—and then thinks he spots an infamous Nazi war criminal on the local bus.

Kurt Dussander (Ian McKellen) is the picture of Old World charm. He passes the time in self-imposed solitary in a big, rundown house. Todd tracks Dussander down and blackmails the fugitive SS guard into playing Scheherazade about his war crimes.

As coolly directed by Bryan Singer in a daring break from his first hit, "The Usual Suspects," "Apt Pupil" becomes a psychological confrontation between innocence and corruption.

At the movie's dark center is McKellen, a charming, old villain with the devil's wisdom and more moves than Bobby Fischer. Whether he's puttering around his kitchen or goose-stepping, carting groceries from the store or tossing a live cat in the oven for old time's sake, McKellen makes Dussander a hypnotic old snake.

Renfro has the tougher part. He's a keen actor, a listener, but "Apt Pupil" never quite clarifies his character's leap from teen-age curiosity to full-blown obsession.

"Apt Pupil," adapted from King's novella by Brandon Boyce, offers a harsh vision of Middle America, where clean sidewalks, basketball games and two-car garages are no protection from the evil that lurks within.

SIGHT AND SOUND, 6/99, p. 35, Kim Newman

Santo Donato, California, 1984.

Sixteen-year old Todd Bowden becomes fascinated by Nazi war crimes while writing an essay on the subject. He recognises that local resident Arthur Denker is really Kurt Dussander, once the commander of Patin concentration camp. Todd takes fingerprints to confirm the identification, then approaches Dussander and threatens him with exposure unless he tells Todd stories about the Holocaust. Todd buys a Nazi uniform and makes Dussander wear it.

Months pass. Haunted by nightmares, Todd starts to fall behind with his schoolwork. Dussander poses as Todd's grandfather for an interview with school counsellor Edward French, then forces Todd to work until he gets straight "A's". Dussander points out that their relationship has gone on for so long his exposure would prove disastrous for Todd too. Archie, a tramp who glimpsed Dussander wearing his Nazi costume, inveigles his way into the house. Dussander has a heart attack while trying to murder him. He calls Todd, then locks him in the basement with the wounded Archie. Todd kills Archie, and an ambulance is called for Dussander.

In hospital, Dussander is recognised by a fellow patient who was an inmate at Patin. The authorities interrogate Todd, who is not suspected of any wrongdoing. As Todd gives the valedictorian speech at his high-school graduation, Dussander commits suicide to avoid trial in Israel. Realising Dussander was not Todd's grandfather, French threatens a further investigation of their relationship. But Todd threatens to accuse French of making homosexual advances to student, and cows him into silence. Todd plans to go to college.

Bryan Singer's first feature *Public Access* was an almost non-supernatural adaptation of Stephen King's novel *Needful Things*. In it, a stranger in town uses a cable-television slot to bring out all the suppressed nastiness of the apparently archetypal good citizens. *Apt Pupil,* Singer's follow-up to his breakthrough *The Usual Suspects,* returns to King territory. It's adapted—as were Rob Reiner's *Stand by Me* and Frank Darabont's *The Shawshank Redemption*—from a novella in the 1982 collection *Different Seasons*. King's first attempt to emerge from his self-created modern horror genre and essay more ambitious literary efforts, this assembly has the feeling of raw America, stripping naked the everyday horrors King usually dresses up with vampires and ghosts. Though one of the best things King has ever written, 'Apt Pupil' has proved problematic for would-be adapters—an earlier filming, starring Ricky Shroeder and Nicol Williamson, was abandoned after financing fell through.

The story could have been reduced to two people spinning yarns that feed each other's fantasies (which are sometimes most persuasive when least truthful). It would have been natural for Singer to mount it exactly in the style of *The Usual Suspects,* with dramatisations of Dussander's stories and Todd's tales of detective work. However, he refuses to dramatise even the most truthful anecdotes (Todd's explanation that he has identified Dussander through fingerprints sounds unlikely, but is later confirmed by a throwaway shot). Instead, Singer relies on getting close to two remarkable performances to convey the shifting fascination between a Nazi war criminal and an all-American boy. We get surprisingly few scenes of Todd's life away from Dussander, though we sense the slipping of his normal relationships through an argument with his best buddy and a failed tryst with a girl. In fact, Singer prunes away much extraneous material from the novella, which ends with an exposed Todd becoming a freeway sniper.

What is most admirable about the film is how genuinely complicated its central relationship is. It is heavily hinted, not only by the casting of gay activist Ian McKellen, that there is a homoerotic undertone to the attraction between his character and often shirtless teenage boy. But the significance of the scene in which the girl can't arouse him and wonders if he's interested in girls at all is that his awareness of horror has blotted out all kinds of sexuality. A gay undertone is also present when, during a shower scene, Todd imagines he sees not healthy football players but shrunken camp inmates. Even more explicitly, Dussander lets a tramp think he's about to take sexual advantage of him when he's actually reaching for a knife. This scene, which features a weird cameo from Elias Koteas in an extraordinary jumper as the tramp, climaxes with a classic dialogue exchange as Archie offers his body with, "don't worry, I've done this before," and Dussander slips in the blade with a sad, self-amused, "So have I."

The exchanges of power between the two central characters are beyond the sexual. The film is deeply disturbing not only in the effective but obvious scene as Todd makes the old man put on a theatrical Nazi uniform like a little girl playing with a Klaus Barbie Doll, but also in the creepy interview scene where Dussander's Grandpa Walton act persuades the school counsellor to give Todd another chance. Though anchored in the Holocaust, Dussander represents a larger, possibly Satanic, European evil that finds its younger successor in Todd's high-school valedictorian. There is never any discussion of why Dussander became a Nazi or indeed of his politics and beliefs. He is just a plausible monster, recognising that Todd has the potential to be just like him. It is a credit to McKellen's sly, sad, sinister playing that the role never becomes melodramatic.

Apt Pupil lacks the flamboyance that made *The Usual Suspects* an audience favourite, but it is a highly assured piece of storytelling, confident enough to elide its worst horrors with a few brief speeches. It may well not find the favour which greeted *Stand by Me* and *The Shawshank Redemption,* both hymns to human endurance and courage, but it is the purest cinematic adaptation of a strain of true dread that even Stephen King is usually afraid to confront. Singer borrows a tiny trick from *The Shining* that reduces King's stream of pop-culture references to snippets from junk television, somehow disturbing in this context: *Mr Magoo, I Dream of Jeannie, The Jeffersons.* The film is set in 1984 simply because it is impossible to conceive of a Nazi senior enough to command a concentration camp as anything but a senile invalid in the present day. However, the finale—as Todd stitches up the school counsellor using a mix of cajoling and threat he has not learned from Dussander but found in himself—does pose the truly terrifying question of what that kid is up to these days.

VILLAGE VOICE, 10/27/98, p. 135, J. Hoberman

Apt Pupil is an altogether less uplifting story [the reference is to *Life is Beautiful*; see Hoberman's review of that film]. Because Bryan Singer's follow-up to *The Usual Suspects* is a sort of naturalized *Nightmare on Elm Street,* it is free to acknowledge—or at least hint—that its frissons, such as they may be, are the cold breeze off an Everest of corpses.

Singer's source is a Stephen King novella from the same collection that yielded *The Shawshank Redemption.* Published in 1982, it's pre-Schindler. Nevertheless, its cautionary account of an enterprising high school lad named Todd, who discovers a real Nazi war criminal living incognito in his idyllic American suburb and is consequently corrupted through his fascination with this absolute evil, is a Faust story with a neat-o Spielbergian resonance. (If *Life Is Beautiful* is the anti-*Sophie's Choice,* this is the anti-*E T.*)

In the original, the somewhat younger hero is disappointed when his SS man fails to sound like Colonel Klink on *Hogan's Heroes.* So it is with the movie. Singer tries in vain to find equivalents to wartime atrocities—as when the reawakened Nazi (Ian McKellen) stuffs a pussycat in his oven or young Todd (Brad Renfro) slams his basketball on a wounded bird. This exotic Euro horror is as alien as Count Dracula. One might have made *Apt Pupil* an allegory of postwar realpolitik—or at least the rehabilitation of rocket scientist Werner von Braun—but Singer has something more Hitchcockian in mind and, after the Nazi becomes Todd's superego, the guilt starts flowing freely. To complicate things, Singer imbues their relationship with an undercurrent of homosexual attraction while Renfro's cloddish character, who seems to be reinventing the s/m dress-up of *The Night Porter,* slyly encourages audience sympathy for McKellen's foxy grampa.

Disagreeable and exploitative as it is, *Apt Pupil* insists on something that *Life Is Beautiful* tries to hide in plain sight: the individual acts of courage found in the testimony of Holocaust survivors can never compensate for the knowledge gleaned of human depravity. There is no light at the end of that tunnel or even an end. It leads to a place with neither redemption nor closure.

Also reviewed in:
CHICAGO TRIBUNE, 10/23/98, Friday/p. I, Michael Wilmington
NATION, 11/2/98, p. 34, Stuart Klawans
NEW YORK TIMES, 10/23/98, p. E14, Janet Maslin
VARIETY, 9/14-20/98, p. 35, Todd McCarthy
WASHINGTON POST, 10/23/98, p. B1, Stephen Hunter
WASHINGTON POST, 10/23/98, Weekend/p. 55, Michael O'Sullivan

ARGUING THE WORLD

A First Run Features release of a Riverside Film Productions/WNET production. *Producer:* Joseph Dorman. *Director:* Joseph Dorman. *Screenplay:* Joseph Dorman. *Director of*

Photography: Peter Brownscombe, Barrin Bonet, Wayne de la Roche, and Boyd Estus. *Editor:* Jonathan Oppenheim. *Music:* Adam Guettel. *Sound:* John Cameron, Nick Clark, Jeff Hansell, Peter Karl, John McCormick, Haven McKenney, Rick Mills, Caleb Mose, Jeff Pullman, Mark Roy, Saul Rouda, and Dale Whitman. *Running time:* 107 minutes. *MPAA Rating:* Not Rated.

WITH: Alan Rosenberg (Narrator); Daniel Bell; Irving Howe: Nathan Glazer; Irving Kristol.

LOS ANGELES TIMES, 5/29/98, Calendar/p. 6, Kevin Thomas

At the beginning of "Arguing the World," a lively, incisive account of four of America's leading thinkers of the 20th century, documentarian Joseph Dorman tells us that when the quartet began arguing radical politics at the City College of New York, "they discovered the world, and through the power of their ideas they hoped to change it."

They are eminent sociologist Nathan Glazer; political essayist Irving Kristol, a key intellectual architect of the Reagan and Gingrich "revolutions"; Irving Howe, literary critic and leading voice of the left, a loyalist to the socialist ideal all four once embraced; and social theorist Daniel Bell, a man of the liberal center. Dorman has framed his group portrait with crisp commentary from colleagues and a treasure trove of largely unfamiliar archival footage, which brings alive an ever-changing New York over a period of some 65 years.

"May you live in interesting times," the famous Chinese saying, applies with full force to these men, all of them New York Jews from poor immigrant families who were coming of age in the late '30s. The combination of the impact of the Great Depression, the rise of fascism in Europe and what Kristol calls "the historical consciousness" they learned at their families' kitchen tables attracted them to the socialist movement of Eugene V. Debs and Norman Thomas.

At City College, the institution for higher learning for the city's "brightest poor," these four and many others gathered in the school cafeteria at Alcove 1, a haven for anti-Stalinists. (Alcove 2 was reserved for Stalinists—those who "read palookas like Howard Fast," huffs Howe. There's another alcove for jocks and so forth—an instance, perhaps, of interior design as destiny?)

With admirable clarity and comprehensiveness, Dorman traces how these four grappled with the great issues and events of their lives. Like most Americans of their generation, three of the four served in the war effort—Kristol and Bell were sent to Europe, and Howe to Alaska (which gave him much crucial time for reading and thinking). Glazer, several years younger than the others, was still a student.

The postwar years found them condemning both Soviet-style communism and the deplorable excesses of the anti-communist congressional hearings while attempting to defend leftist views and liberal causes. Through the Partisan Review and many other journals that the men became involved in, they began to deal with the arts as well as politics, while writing their landmark books and becoming university professors. In a 1968 essay, Howe came up with the phrase "New York intellectuals" to describe his group, which constituted some 60 people spanning several generations.

By then, however, these four titans, who had gradually moved to the center, except for Howe, had come to a bitter clash with the anti-Vietnam War protest generation. Glazer arrived at Berkeley just in time to confront the Right to Free Speech movement that tore apart the campus, and Bell was at Columbia in 1968 when the students shut down the university.

These men felt the students were too ignorant of history not to repeat its mistakes, too intent on wrecking the universities, whereas the student leaders felt, in the words of L.A. Councilwoman Jackie Goldberg, then at Berkeley, that Glazer, whom she had idolized, and his fellow professors were "control freaks" who wouldn't take the students seriously.

Even though initially sympathetic to the Students for a Democratic Society movement, Howe says Tom Hayden "had a strong manipulative streak. We could see the commissar in him." Bell dismisses Hayden, long a California state senator, as "the Richard Nixon of the left." Hayden in turn accuses them of a "paternalism beyond Abraham."

The advent of the '90s saw Howe holding steadfast to democratic socialism as a vision and goal while Kristol had long since traveled to the right, decrying the failure of liberalism. His old friends regard him with dismay, none more so than Howe, who regarded him as a "political enemy.... I wish him a long life—and many political failures."

But Howe himself was not to have a much longer life, dying suddenly in 1993 at the age of 72, which gives "Arguing the World" its unexpected and poignant coda. "Arguing the World" is yet another example of a documentarian getting to his key people just in the nick of time. Indeed, since the film's completion, Diana Trilling, who provides occasional acerbic, patrician commentary throughout, has died. Trilling was one of the few women among the New York intellectuals, and she deserves the last word on them: "Unless a man in the intellectual community was bent on sexual conquest he was never interested in women."

NEW YORK, 1/19/98, p. 51, David Denby

There are still plenty of intellectuals in New York, but "the New York intellectuals" as a compact group with common passions and a great magazine at their disposal—*The Partisan Review*—have all but vanished, leaving behind a disputatious roomful of books, memoirs, fallings-out, and reconciliations, as well as many studies of the group, not the least of which is the superb documentary *Arguing the World*. This film, written and directed by Jonathan Dorman, a public-TV veteran, is firm yet nuanced, accurate yet never pedantic. Using interviews and newsreel footage, Dorman has woven together the life and work of four representative members of the species—Irving Kristol, Daniel Bell, Nathan Glazer, and the late Irving Howe—all of whom came from poor Jewish-immigrant backgrounds in New York and attended, in the thirties and early forties, City College, where they partook in endless debates over socialism, capitalism, democracy, and tyranny. All four were members of the anti-Stalinist left, but except for Howe they moved rightward after the war—all the way right in the case of Kristol, who wound up tutoring the Reagan administration on the failures of liberalism. Dorman follows the complex pilgrimage of each with proper regard for detail and variation, and he lets us hear the men speak at some length. For the record: I am devoted to Irving Howe, whose writings have greatly affected my views of a hundred things; the movie brings his severe but humane consciousness back into focus with startling force.

NEW YORK POST, 1/7/98, p. 44, Michael Medved

"Arguing the World" is an epic adventure, not in the realm of car chases or special effects but in the far more complex—and dangerous—world of ideas.

Focusing on four hugely influential Jewish intellectuals (Irving Kristol, Daniel Bell, Nathan Glazer and the late Irving Howe), this ambitious documentary follows their differing trajectories over the course of 60 years.

Using candid, wry first-person interviews and the comments of colleagues and acquaintances (ranging from Tom Hayden to William F. Buckley Jr.), together with haunting archival footage of old New York neighborhoods and radical rallies, producer Joseph Dorman struggles to make sense of four complicated, often contradictory careers.

He first shows his heroes as idealistic Trotskyists in the 1930s, rubbing shoulders at lunch hour in City College's "Alcove 1," engaged in intellectual combat with the Stalinists of "Alcove 2."

Following their involvement with magazines such as Partisan Review, Commentary and Dissent, their academic careers at Columbia, Harvard and Berkeley, and their varied destinations as Reagan Republicans or democratic socialists, the film necessarily simplifies key ideas and transitions but still crackles with the excitement of passionate personalities.

Its chief flaw involves its exclusively careerist focus, with no description of personal or familial relationships—an especially puzzling gap in the case of Kristol, whose wife (Gertrude Himmelfarb) and son (William Kristol) are both significant political figures in their own right.

Nonetheless, even those with little interest in political movements will feel captivated by the charm and intensity of four unforgettable, world-class talkers.

VILLAGE VOICE, 1/13/98, p. 57, J. Hoberman

The documentary *Arguing the World*, which had its premiere in a slightly longer version at last year's New York Jewish Film Festival, provides a particular kind of local history. Although the geography with which it is concerned is largely mental, the movie might have been made for the riders of the Broadway local—it's an epic tale of the Upper West Side.

As written and directed by Joseph Dorman, the story is that of four brilliant boys of working-class origins and cosmopolitan aspiration, born in the city's immigrant Jewish neighborhoods and raised amid the poverty of the Great Depression. This quartet of New York intellectuals—the sociologists Daniel Bell and Nathan Glazer, public policy maven Irving Kristol, and literary critic Irving Howe—were all educated at City College, then something like the world's largest *kheder*. For them, speech was synonymous with self-assertion; "ideas," in the words of one, "meant arguing."

Their youth was a time when New York City was known as the most interesting part of the Soviet Union and a contentious wiseguy named Howe might recruit another named Kristol to the Young Trotskyites, to the ridicule of CCNY's far more numerous student Stalinists. Their colleague Clement Greenberg once noted, "Some day it will have to be told how 'anti-Stalinism,' which started out more or less as 'Trotskyism,' turned into art for art's sake, and thereby cleared the way, heroically, for what followed." *Arguing the World* is not exactly that story, but punctuated with old photos and flavorsome archival footage, it does a good job in tracking the path from CCNY Trotskyism through Cold War liberalism to post-'60s neoconservatism and beyond—which is, not coincidentally, the same trajectory that took the film's four subjects from their childhood ghettos to the (relatively) bourgeois splendor of the Upper West Side and, in some cases, from political marginality to the center of state power.

Like a good family drama, *Arguing the World*'s story is multigenerational. Independent intellectuals without advanced degrees, our heroes were absorbed into the university—Glazer at Berkeley, Bell at Columbia—just in time to confront the radical students of the '60s. In this, they were dealing not so much with their younger selves as with the children of the despised Popular Front, whose seemingly uncritical support for Third World revolutionaries Castro and Mao seemed to echo the Stalinism of the 1930s and '40s.

Of course, then as now, foreign policy was not identical with domestic politics. SDS took its cues more from the civil rights movement than the pages of *Partisan Review*. Ex-SDSnik Tom Hayden suggests that the New York intellectuals were more talk than action, but what's most compelling about these guys is their conviction that ideas matter. Rather than found a political movement, they start a magazine. Howe, declining to join the Cold War consensus, founded *Dissent*. Breaking with that consensus a dozen years later, albeit moving to the right, Kristol and Bell started *The Public Interest*—a journal more successfully Leninist (in form if not content). As William Buckley explains, the conservatives learned sociology from these old Marxists.

Not everyone was so attentive. Hayden, who butted heads with Howe in the mid '60s, skirts the edge of anti-Semitism when he explains that "I was not raised—thankfully—in a household of people shouting about the current line, and so I couldn't comprehend the decibel level these people would reach." His second point, evoking a "paternalism beyond Abraham" is even more inadvertently revealing, illuminating the sexual politics of the New York intellectuals more clearly than the film itself. *Arguing the World* manages to be as sexist as its subjects. A formidable intellectual in her own right, Kristol's wife Gertrude Himmelfarb has no past and barely appears.

Basically a Tale of Two Irvings, *Arguing the World* ends with Irving H.'s death and might be titled, after his most famous book, *The World of Our Fathers*. For New Yorkers of a certain age, the movie is a potent generational experience—not least in the light of Ruth Messinger's abject defeat, satirized in *The Weekly Standard* as the last gasp of an Upper West Side cult. History is written by the winners. Having placed his son inside the Bush White House, Kristol these days bestrides Riverside Drive like a colossus. Who would have ever imagined that the crowning triumph of American Trotskyism would be the capture of Dan Quayle's brain?

Also reviewed in:
NATION, 3/2/98, p. 36, Stuart Klawans
NEW YORK TIMES, 1/7/98, p. E5, Stephen Holden
VARIETY, 12/15-21/97, p. 61, Daniel M. Kimmel

ARMAGEDDON

A Touchstone Pictures release of a Jerry Bruckheimer production in association with Valhalla Motion Pictures. *Executive Producer:* Jonathan Hensleigh, Jim Van Wyck, and Chad Oman. *Producer:* Jerry Bruckheimer, Gale Anne Hurd, and Michael Bay. *Director:* Michael Bay. *Screenplay:* Jonathan Hensleigh and J.J. Abrams. *Adaptation*: Tony Gilroy and Shane Salerno. *Story:* Robert Roy Pool and Jonathan Hensleigh. *Director of Photography:* John Schwartzman. *Editor:* Mark Goldblatt, Chris Lebenzon, and Glen Scantlebury. *Music:* Trevor Rabin. *Sound:* Keith A. Wester and (music) Steve Kempster and Alan Meyerson. *Casting:* Bonnie Timmermann. *Production Designer:* Michael White. *Art Director:* Geoff Hubbard. *Set Designer:* John P. Bruce, Daniel Jennings, Kevin Ishioka, George R. Lee, R. Gilbert Clayton, William Taliaferro, Mindi Toback, Patricia Klawonn, Steven M. Saylor, Gary R. Speckman, and Domenic Silvestri. *Set Decorator:* Rick Simpson. *Set Dresser:* John Ceniceros. *Special Effects:* John Frazier. *Costumes:* Michael Kaplan and Magali Guidasci. *Make-up:* Rick Stratton and Fred Blau. *Make-up (Billy Bob Thornton):* Lynne Eagan. *Make-up (Liv Tyler):* Kathy Jeung. *Stunt Coordinator:* Kenny Bates. *Running time:* 144 minutes. *MPAA Rating:* PG-13.

CAST: Bruce Willis (Harry S. Stamper); Billy Bob Thornton (Dan Truman); Ben Affleck (A.J. Frost); Liv Tyler (Grace Stamper); Keith David (General Kimsey); Chris Ellis (Walter Clark); Jason Isaacs (Ronald Quincy); Will Patton (Charles "Chick" Chapple); Steve Buscemi (Rockhound); Ken Campbell (Max Lennert); William Fichtner (Colonel William Sharp); Jessica Steen (Co-Pilot Jennifer Watts); Grayson McCouch (Gruber); Owen Wilson (Oscar Choi); Clark Brolly (Freddy Noonan); Michael Clarke Duncan (Jayotis "Bear" Kurleenbear); Peter Stormare (Lev Andropov); Marshall Teague (Colonel Davis); Anthony Guidera (Co-Pilot Tucker); Greg Collins (Lt. Halsey); J. Patrick McCormack (General Boffer); Michael Kaplan (NASA Tech #5); Ian Quinn (Astronaut Pete Shelby); Christopher Worret and Adam C. Smith (Operators); John Mahon (Karl); Grace Zabriskie (Dottie); K.C. Leomiti (Samoan); Eddie Griffin (Little Guy); Mark Boone, Junior (New York Guy); Deborah Nishimura, Albert Wong, and Jim Ishida (Clients); Stanley Anderson (President); James Harper (Admiral Kelso); Ellen Cleghorne (Helga the Nurse); Udo Kier (Psychologist); John Aylward (Dr. Banks); Mark Curry (Stu the Cabbie); Seiko Matsuda (Asian Tourist-Female); Harry Humphries (Chuck Jr.); Dyllan Christopher (Tommy); Judith Hoag (Denise); Sage Allen (Max's Mom); Lawrence Tierney (Hollis Vernon"Grap" Stamper); Judith Drake (Grap's Nurse); Steven Ford (Nuke Tech); Christian Clemenson (Droning Guy); Duke Valenti, Michael "Bear" Taliferro, and Billy Devlin (Roughnecks); Frank Van Keeken (NASA Planner #1); Kathleen Matthews, J.C. Hayward, Andrew Glassman, and Alexander Johnson (Newscasters); Shawnee Smith (Redhead); Dwight Hicks (FBI Agent #1); Odile Broulard (Geo Tech #1); Vic Manni (Loanshard); Jim Maniaci (Biker Customer); Layla Roberts (Molly Mounds); Joe Allen (Kennedy Launch); Bodhi Elfman (Math Guy); Kathy Neff (Reporter); Victor Vinson (Sector Director); Joseph Patrick Kelly (Marine); Peter White (Secretary of Defense); Rudy Mettia (G-Man); Patrick Richwood and Brian Mulligan (Dr. Nerd); Greg Warmoth (KSC News Reporter); John H. Johnson (Pad Director); Charles Stewart (Vacuum Chamber Tech); Scarlet Forge (Young Grace); John Frazier (Priest); Andy Ryan (Greenpeace Guy); Michael Tuck (American Newscaster); Patrick Lander (British Newscaster); Anne Vareze (French Newscaster); Fritz Mashimo (Japanese Newscaster); Dina Morrone (Italian Newscaster); Ruben O'Lague (Spanish Newscaster); James Fitzpatrick (NORAD Technician); Wolfgang Muser (German Newscaster); Charlton Heston (Narrator).

CHRISTIAN SCIENCE MONITOR, 7/3/98, p. B3, David Sterritt

Science fiction has taken a paranoid turn lately. The friendly aliens of "E.T.: The Extra-Terrestrial" and "Close Encounters of the Third Kind" are being zapped off the screen by nasty-looking monsters with Washington accomplices, and outer space has become our enemy as heavenly bodies zoom toward catastrophic collisions with Earth.

Another such cataclysm looms in "Armageddon," the latest in what might be called the Count-down Category of Hollywood adventure movies. An asteroid as big as Texas is heading our way, and the clock is ticking. No matter what part of the globe gets the direct hit, life as we know it will be wiped out forever.

No one can save us except Bruce Willis, as a rough-and-ready oil engineer with a knack for drilling far beneath the earth's surface. Government agent Billy Bob Thornton recruits him and his scruffy assistants to become instant astronauts, rocket to the asteroid, and blow it to bits.

Everything about the first half-hour of "Armageddon," devoted to early signs of the impending calamity, is so coarse and crude that if you are watching this Disney movie, you might hope the asteroid will land on the very theater where you're watching it.

True, this vulgarity may not damage the picture's popularity. But people looking for glimmers of sensitivity may find themselves less dismayed by the on-screen action than by what it reveals about a world that would spend its treasure making such trash.

Things improve once Willis and company land on the asteroid, allowing director Michael Bay to concoct some of the season's more imaginative special effects. Yet while the movie's emotions grow a bit gentler, they remain as forced and artificial as ever, pushing market-tested buttons—heroics, patriotism, family values—with a monotony that denies us any chance to think or even feel for ourselves.

"Armageddon" may sell tickets, thanks largely to a high-powered marketing machine that's been conducting its own countdown for the past several months. But it's not a pretty picture.

LOS ANGELES TIMES, 7/1/98, Calendar/p. 1, Kenneth Turan

You know you're not in the intended demographic group for "Armageddon," the loud new film about how a Bruce Willis-led team of roughnecks tries to save the world from a deadly asteroid, if:

* you even notice it's loud;
* you don't consider two hours and 30 minutes an ideal length for this kind of thing;
* you find yourself missing the barely there sensitivity of "Deep Impact";
* you think of roughneck Steve Buscemi as a mainstay of American independent films, not one of the co-stars of "Con Air";
* you have your doubts about lines like "Let's chew this iron bitch up";
* you notice a shot lifted from a Robert Frank photograph and wonder what it's doing there and if he's going to get residuals;
* you recognize plot elements so venerable that they can be categorized by name, like "the blue wire or red wire dilemma" and "the damn kid knocked me out and flew the plane himself";
* you actually care that director Michael Bay's filmmaking style is so frantic and frenetic that it's often impossible to figure out exactly what is happening;
* you decide that rooting for the asteroid is a viable option.

Big and clumsy the way only $140-million projects manage to be, "Armageddon" is finally undone by its grandiosity as much as by anything else. Sporadically watchable, it's at its best at those infrequent moments when it doesn't take itself too seriously. But the film's general tendency to overplay its strengths and emphasize its weaknesses is a tough obstacle to overcome.

One of those squandered strengths is Bay. He is a celebrated commercial director whose previous features ("Bad Boys," "The Rock") demonstrate, as this film does, a sharp, slick look (here achieved by cinematographer John Schwartzman) linked to an ability to move things along.

"Armageddon's" story is set up by a prologue (read by Charlton Heston) that relates the widely believed theory that the last time a large object from outer space hit the Earth, it eliminated the dinosaurs. "It happened before," Heston intones as only Heston can; "it will happen again. It's just a question of when."

The first warning that that time is now comes when high-speed debris destroys a space shuttle and plows into Manhattan, creating a wave of flying taxis and exploding buses and causing the top of the Chrysler Building to flip point-first onto the street like an oversized dart.

It's only going to get worse, warns Dan Truman, the executive director of NASA (Billy Bob Thornton, expertly handling the take-charge Texan role usually reserved for Tommy Lee Jones). An asteroid the size of that great state will hit Earth in 18 days and function as "a global killer.

Half the world will be incinerated by the heat blast; the rest will freeze to death in a nuclear winter. Basically, it's the worst parts of the Bible."

The only way to stop this cataclysm, the government somehow decides, is to rocket a team of drillers onto the asteroid, have them dig an 800-foot hole, plant an atomic bomb and then get the hell out of Dodge before the thing goes off. If you think a lot can go wrong within that scenario, you've been peeking at the script.

The world's best deep-core driller just happens to be oil wildcatter Harry S. Stamper (Willis). No touchy-feely tree-hugger, Stamper divides his time between hitting golf balls at anti-drilling Greenpeace activists and trying to kill A.J. Frost (Ben Affleck), the top man on his crew, who happens to have fallen in love with Stamper's daughter Grace (Liv Tyler).

Naturally, Stamper won't take on the job without his Dirty Dozen-like seven-man gang, a group of well-cast wacky eccentrics that includes Will Patton, Buscemi and "Bottle Rocket's" Owen Wilson. Military types aren't happy "leaving the fate of the planet in the hands of a bunch of retards you wouldn't trust with a potato gun," but that's Hollywood for you.

Speaking of Hollywood, what is hard to figure out is why "Armageddon" needed so many writers. Five of them got screen credit, arrayed in a configuration so complex (story by Jonathan Hensleigh and Robert Pool, adaptation by Tony Gilroy and Shane Salerno, screenplay by Jonathan Hensleigh and J.J. Abrams) you practically need a directive from the Writers Guild to understand exactly who did what.

Also, and this may be a first, the film's press kit boasts about and even lists by name some of the high-profile uncredited writers (Paul Attanasio, Ann Biderman, Scott Rosenberg, Robert Towne) who worked on the script. All this talent has led to some amusing moments, but overall their use only underlines the manufactured nature of filmmaking on this scale.

Despite this horde of writers, the emotional side of "Armageddon" remains stubbornly and conspicuously weak, and it's an area the filmmakers have regrettably fallen in love with. Considerable screen time is devoted to the sensitive romance between A.J. and Grace, but their moments together can most charitably be called unconvincing.

Just as lacking are the film's pseudo-meaningful scenes of the people of the world, arranged in photogenic groupings from Mont-Saint-Michel in France to the Taj Mahal in India, worrying about the future of mankind. Anyone who remembers the Reach Out and Touch Someone commercials will get the picture.

"Armageddon's" action sequences should be its great strength, but these are also flawed. Using three editors, Bay has so sliced and diced the jittery camera work he favors that anyone who didn't work on the film will be hard pressed to explain exactly what is happening during several of its crisis sequences. This is not pushing the envelope, it's tearing it to shreds, and though Bay's skills may make us want to go along for the ride, we end up too motion sick to actually enjoy it.

NEW STATESMAN, 8/7/98, p. 42, Gerald Kaufman

What I love about movies like "Armageddon" is that they are beyond derision. With a proper film, comments about the plot may be appropriate. But "Armageddon," like other entertainments of its type, has no plot, simply a premise. An asteroid (the size of Texas, actually) is heading for the earth and, unless deflected, will on impact become a "total killer", inflicting "global damage".

To give an indication of what the planet is in for, showers of meteorites burst down from the heavens, destroying New York's Chrysler Building (this summer's target of choice, since it receives its quietus in "Godzilla" as well) and putting paid to much of Paris. London, however, is left intact—a disappointment for those who would have relished seeing the British Library zapped.

On-screen catastrophe has already threatened the earth this summer: in "Deep Impact" the potential agent of our oblivion was a comet. Here, just 18 days remain before "Armageddon's" asteroid is due to make lethal contact. All that stands between it and "the end of mankind" is Bruce Willis. It is perfectly obvious from the outset that Willis's rough diamond of a character, who is named Harry S Stamper and happens to be "the world's best deep-core driller", will go up in a spaceship and drill that asteroid into good behaviour.

Among those chosen to accompany him is his daughter's boyfriend, AJ Frost, played by Ben Affleck with a jut-jawed determination that renders him rather less lifelike than a Disney cartoon character. As soon as we are introduced to Stamper's six other roughneck chums, including "two guys who have done serious time", we know that what is in store is an outer-space version of "The Dirty Dozen." Stamper informs his team: "The United States government just asked us to save the world." One fastidious observer comments: "The fate of the planet is in the hands of a bunch of retards I wouldn't trust with a potato gun." Another bystander snorts: "Talk about the Wrong Stuff."

Those with experience of this genre of movie will know better than to expect anything in the way of what might be regarded as drama school acting. "Sense and Sensibility" this is not. The cast go competently through their paces but—apart from one manly tear shed by Willis (the nineties equivalent, surely, of Garbo laughing) there is not much—or, to be brutally frank, anything—to be seen in this film that would make Merchant Ivory look to their laurels.

So the Dirty Eight and an astronaut crew blast off on their assignment to drill a shaft into the asteroid, pop a nuclear weapon down it, detonate the bomb, and then get the hell out. At this point, it is my duty to report a difference of method adopted by the experts in, respectively, "Deep Impact" and "Armageddon". Both deploy a nuclear bomb, but in "Deep Impact" the idea was to destroy the comet, and disaster threatened when the bomb only split it. In "Armageddon", however, splitting the asteroid is Stamper's main objective. Ah, well—with luck we shall never find out which film is right.

Stamper's mission is not without incident; after all, there is still 75 minutes' running time. Touching down, the Dirty Eight encounter a rock storm. Yet drill they do and, thanks to meddling among squabbling functionaries down at Mission Control, the nuclear weapon's remote-control detonator is snafu'd. Someone will have to remain on the asteroid to carry out the detonation manually. Straws turning out, providentially, to be among the space ship's supplies, a draw takes place.

Should there be a single person among the entire movie-going public who cannot guess who is left behind, I will not dream of spoiling the surprise. Let me content myself by saying that this film about a global holocaust has the chutzpah to end with a lovers' clinch, followed by a white wedding. Planet Earth has been made safe for Middle America.

The director responsible for this magnificently enjoyable tosh is Michael (The Rock) Bay, assisted, of course, by zillions of digital-effects nerds. Between them, they have manufactured numerous sequences which, while at the cutting edge of movie technology, are almost totally incomprehensible. But, since no one who pays money to see this picture will do so with the intention of exercising their critical faculties for so much as an instant, why should the Disney Organisation ("Armageddon's" proud progenitors) worry? After all, the only line in the film which is certain to raise eyebrows in disbelief is the exclamation: "This is as real as it gets."

NEW YORK, 7/13/98, p. 41, David Denby

Charlton Heston, speaking in the voice of God (at the very least), is heard at the beginning of *Armageddon* warning of death and destruction from an asteroid. But after that solemn initiation into the higher terrors, the movie turns into a clangorous, hyped-up entertainment. *Armageddon* is not a good movie, but it's probably the best movie that ever gave you a ringing headache—exciting, fast, often funny. Producer Jerry Bruckheimer has turned the total destruction of the world into a sentimental, frivolous action film. But what else can he do with it? Action is what Bruckheimer (The *Rock, Con Air,* etc.) specializes in, and Bruckheimer appears to have his wits about him—he was smart enough not to commit the errors of the other asteroid movie, *Deep Impact, in* which we were actually instructed in how to behave when the world ends (make up with Dad, stand on a mountain). Ivan Bekey, the scientific adviser to *Armageddon,* has admitted that if an actual giant asteroid is heading this way, and we have anything less than four or five years of advance warning, we can do nothing to stop it but pray. So both movies offer improbable fantasies of heroic rescue. A few jokes would seem to be in order.

Armageddon is squarely plotted, but it isn't squarely cast or written. Bruckheimer and director Michael Bay have shrewdly gathered together a group of idiosyncratic actors from independent movies. I've never been much of a fan of Billy Bob Thornton, but his hairy-faced scowl and slightly flattened malevolence work very well in the central role of the executive head of NASA—the guy who has to run the crisis center, issue orders, and save the world. Thornton's withering bluntness has a certain authority. Here's what he says: The thing is coming our way at 22,000 miles an hour; we have eighteen days in which to try to blow it up or deflect it; we need to land on the asteroid, drill a hole 800 feet deep, plant a nuke, take off, and detonate the nuke. The only person who can do this is "the world's best deep-core driller," who sounds like the hero of a porno movie and turns out to be Bruce Willis.

Willis, of course, is not an actor from independent films (though he has appeared in a few), but when his oil driller, Harry Stamper, demands his own raffish crew for this adventure in the skies, a whole bunch of actors from left field get to play at being astronauts. Suddenly, Bruckheimer and Bay are making "The Dirty Dozen in Space." Ben Affleck, of *Chasing Amy* and *Good Will Hunting*, is the young oil-rigging hotshot who happens to be in love with Willis's daughter (a mopey, dopey Liv Tyler, who looks eager to put a thumb in her mouth and crawl into a large crib). Also along for the ride are a fatty (Ken Campbell), a basso-voiced meatball (Michael Clarke Duncan), a naïve mystic (Owen Wilson), and a sardonic genius who loves whores (the invaluable sourman Steve Buscemi). In mocking imitation of *The Right Stuff,* Bay gives us heroic shots of these flakes walking straight toward the camera in their orange astronaut suits. In training, and aloft, the crew wisecrack their way through saving the world, as if they were teens trying to put up a pup tent on the first day of camp.

Michael Bay has a feeling for pace and bustle: The movie never lets up, and such things as the Houston control-room scenes, with everyone milling about purposefully, are done with much greater conviction and energy than usual. But Bay, who shoots action in fragments, continues to send asteroids into the collapsing body of film aesthetics. When *The Rock* came out, I complained that you rarely saw where one person firing a gun was in relation to another, and Bay does the same kind of thing again, creating excitement by cutting very rapidly from one close-up to another, filling the soundtrack with thuds, and shaking the camera as if it were in the grip of an electric paint mixer. Bay is a bit of a faker, but he gets away with it, because the movie is too much fun to argue with. The jolts and thrills, plotted against the ticking clock, just keep coming. *Armageddon* is both up-to-date and very old-fashioned. Some of the clichés (like Bruce Willis's not wanting Ben Affleck to marry his daughter because Affleck's daredevil reminds Willis of himself at the same age) are so ancient that the filmmakers seem to be counting on the audience's having forgotten them—or being so young as to have never experienced them. Still, *Armageddon* is a better joke than most of the other disaster and spectacle movies. Early in the picture, a group of flaming meteors tears into New York, completing the rehabilitation of Grand Central Terminal and bringing the needle-nose top of the Chrysler Building right down on our heads. When Paris gets it from another meteor later on, the conflagration is seen from the point of view of a grinning gargoyle atop Notre Dame. The New York and Paris scenes were stuck into the movie at the last moment at the suggestion of studio chief Joe Roth, but that gargoyle bears more than a passing resemblance to Jerry Bruckheimer.

NEW YORK POST, 6/30/98, p. 57, Rod Dreher

"The United States government just asked us to save the world," cocky roughneck Bruce Willis tells his men. "Anybody want to say no?"

No! Which is to say, "Yes, yes, yes!" to "Armageddon," a barreling, badass testosto-fest that's like being strapped onto a screaming Fourth of July bottle rocket for 2 breathless, head-banging hours. Houston, we have liftoff, and it's a lollapalooza.

Michael Bay, the dogged terminator of action filmmakers, directs in a jackhammery, ba-da-boom style that leaves you feeling pummeled. And, true, "Armageddon" is a juiced-up compendium of action-movie cliches: macho grandstanding, buddy bonding, techno-fetishry, rah-rah patriotism, Bruuuuuuuuce—the whole megillah. But when a movie gives you a speedball ride this stupendously exhilarating, it's hard to complain.

"Armageddon" is light years better than the comparatively drowsy "Deep Impact," this summers other killer space-spitball flick. The plot is similar. Astronomers discover a massive asteroid—this one as big as Texas—hurtling toward You Know Where. NASA has mere weeks to figure out how to deliver us all from damnation.

The doomsday asteroid hurtles through space surrounded by a swarm of meteors, some of which streak through the atmosphere like warning shots and land with devastating effect. Boom! goes New York, boom! Paree. It's decided that the only way to stop the thing is to send a crew of astronauts to the rock, drill a hole to its core and drop a nuke in—which will crack it in two "like a firecracker in a fist."

Gruff NASA chief Dan Truman (Billy Bob Thornton) dispatches a helicopter to an oil rig in the South China Sea to fetch Harry Stamper (Willis), the world's greatest oilfield driller. When we meet him, Harry's taking time away from knocking golf balls at a Greenpeace ship to chase hired hand A.J. (Ben Affleck) around the rig with a shotgun. Reason? Stamper's caught A.J. in bed with his grown daughter, Grace (Liv Tyler).

Before long, Stamper and his crew of misfits—including Affleck, Will Patton and the mighty Steve Buscemi—are being blasted off into space aboard two whiz-bang versions of the space shuttle. ("Talk about the wrong stuff," an astronaut cracks.) They rendezvous with the Russian space station, a jalopy kept running, barely, by a pleasantly scuzzy Soviet (Peter Stormare).

Disaster after disaster follows the mission. People die, guts clench, nails are bitten and circulation is lost in one's legs from sitting on the edge of one's seat. With his constantly moving cameras and strobe-light editing, director Bay is not kind to his audience. As in "The Rock," he never gives the picture time to breathe.

But his movie careers ahead like a well-oiled machine—or, rather, a well-oiled athlete, because perfect casting helps "Armageddon" transcend the genre. It has heart, and characters you really care about—which, I think, will make women care about the movie as much as men will. The script strikes a good balance between hard action and companionable humor without resorting to the kind of cold "Hasta la vista, baby" wisecrackery that usually mars this kind of movie.

Thornton, looking a little underfed, nevertheless masterfully conveys authority as the NASA bigwig. Affleck's and Tyler's puppy love is sweet and tender, and the supporting cast members are lively and likable. And say what you will about the smug, superior, Farrakhan-praising, Demi-divorcing Bruce Willis, the guy rocks action movies like nobody else on the planet.

The movie is beautiful to look at. The techno-thriller segments are sleek, clean and metallic, while the other parts feature creamy, saturated colors bathed in warm, clean light. It looks like an ad for Tommy Hilfiger's America, but it's shamelessly effective. Three cheers for a big fat lump in the throat and cheap melodramatic thrills!

How absorbing is "Armageddon"? At one point mid-movie, Billy Bob turns to the NASA engineers and gravely tells them that if they feel like praying, now would be a good time to start. I bowed my head for a second to intercede for the imperiled astronauts, then laughed out loud at how caught up in the movie I was. I leaned over to my wife and whispered, "I actually was praying for those guys."

"Me, too!" she confessed. Now that's a movie.

NEWSDAY, 7/1/98, Part II/p. B2, Jack Mathews

Early in Michael Bay's "Armageddon, a bulldog charges into a New York street vendor's supply of green Godzilla dolls and begins snapping at the helpless creatures. It's a clever joke, a nose tweak for the film that was expected to battle with "Armageddon" for the summer's box office championship.

That dogfight's over. With less than $140 million in grosses through seven weeks, "Godzilla" has been a flop—by blockbuster standards—and Bay's thundering, rapid-fire, alternately farcical and straight-faced sci-fi thriller is not going to be. For its targeted young audience, this is summer entertainment at its superficial, excessive best, a combination roller coaster ride and fireworks show, with doomsday as its funhouse theme.

In its other head-to-head match, "Armageddon" should easily out perform, "Deep Impact," the first of the season's celestial-body-on-a-collision-course-with Earth movies. Where "Deep Impact" put the emphasis on some tedious character relationships, "Armageddon" dives head-first into a meteor storm, slowing. only occasionally to pop its own corn.

After a spectacular opening, in which Manhattan is pelted by Volkswagen-sized meteors that take out such landmarks as Grand Central Terminal and the Chrysler Building, world leaders are alerted by astronomers to an incoming asteroid the size of Texas (its puny counterpart in "Deep Impact" is barely the size of Mt. Everest). Earth has just 18 days to alter the asteroid's course and save mankind from the fate of the dinosaurs, and the only plan they can come up with on short notice is to send an oil-drilling crew into space to plant a nuclear bomb in the rock's core and run for it.

This is a job for Harry Stamper (Bruce Willis), deep oil driller par excellence, and his merry band of roughnecks, a motley crew that forms a modern equivalent of a band of Old West outlaws. Call them The Hole in the Rock Gang.

Signing on for such perks as lifetime tax immunity and summers in the Lincoln Bedroom are: Rockhound (Steve Buscemi), a slumming genius with a sharp wit and a weakness for busty strippers; Oscar Choi (Owen Wilson), an existentialist who finds joy on the edge; Bear (Michael Clarke Duncan), whose name denotes his girth, and A.J. (Ben Affleck), the cocky maverick whose romancing of Harry's daughter (Liv Tyler creates some absurdly strained tension between the two during the mission.

Can these undisciplined rogues get space-trained in two weeks? Will the real astronauts the politicians, military leaders and scientists ever accept them? Will they overcome a thousand obstacles to blow up the asteroid a split-second before it's too late? Will A.J. prove his mettle and earn Harry's blessings as a future son-in-law? And will they all be worthy of a movie, partially narrated by Charlton Heston?

Bay ("The Rock") uses every ploy of the action trade to overload the senses and deflect attention from the plot holes and incongruities (why do the heroes go through antigravity training when the asteroid has plenty of its own gravity?). There are slashing camera movements, smash cuts, extreme close-ups, strobe editing, a soaring musical score, and sound effects that send waves of thunder rumbling right up from the floor.

The script, which has more authors than amazon.com, goes from one cliffhanger to another without making the slightest transitional sense. An encounter with the Russian space station Mir exists for no apparent reason other than to stage a hairbreadth escape and to pick up comic relief in the form of a vain, half-drunk cosmonaut (Peter Stormare).

Technically, "Armageddon" is a far better thing than "Deep Impact," and generally has a better sense of humor. There are great lines fed to each of the asteroid wranglers, but Buscemi's wisecracking Rockhound gets the best of them. Even when he comes down with a case of space dementia out there, Buscemi keeps the apocalypse rocking.

There's also plenty of unintended humor, most of it supplied by the awkward father-daughter relationship between Willis and Tyler. Here's a roughneck dad who wants to protect his little girl from the kind of man he is even while he alone has been chosen to save the world? How bad a model can he be?

"Armageddon's" 2½-hour running time is way too long for the material. This is a live-action cartoon, and the action gets quickly repetitive. For the audience, there's not much difference between explosions in Manhattan, on an oil derrick, on Mir, or on the asteroid. And not much doubt about the outcome, either.

SIGHT AND SOUND, 9/98, p. 36, Andy Richards

A shower of meteors destroys parts of New York City. NASA chief Dan Truman and his team identify a huge asteroid on a collision course with the earth. Renowned oil driller Harry Stamper is approached to head a team that will intercept the asteroid and break it up with a nuclear charge, saving the planet. Stamper agrees, on condition that his own crew of "roughnecks" accompany him. They undergo an intensive training programme before departing in two separate shuttles, one headed by Harry and one by A. J. Frost—a young rigger involved with Stamper's daughter Grace against her father's wishes.

After a refuelling stop at a Russian space station nearly ends in disaster, A. J.'s shuttle crashes on to the asteroid's surface. Stamper's crew land elsewhere on the rock and begin drilling through the iron crust, but encounter difficulties. When Stamper argues with the NASA officer accompanying the mission, General Kimsey at Mission Control attempts to remote-detonate the nuclear device. Stamper and the officer thwart Kimsey and recommence drilling, but the drill is accidentally destroyed, and the mission seems doomed. A.J., presumed dead, rejoins Stamper, having manoeuvred his own drilling machine across the asteroid's treacherous surface. They successfully drill the hole. A. J. draws the short straw to stay behind to detonate the bomb manually. Stamper, however, forcibly takes his place and sacrifices himself to save the world. The mission survivors return safely to earth.

Jerry Bruckheimer's latest opus kicks off with a meteor shower hurtling down into the heart of Manhattan, a scene of fiery destruction and breathtaking special effects that not so long ago would have provided a fitting climax for a film of this type. But the stakes have upped since *Independence Day*, and *Armageddon* slyly sets out its commercial ambitions early on when a dog attacks a street vendor's *Godzilla* toys moments before a stray meteor decimates his wares. Indeed, just as the Bruckheimer-produced *Con Air* raised the ante of the action film by lifting it into realms of parodic, gratuitous excess, so *Armageddon* achieves much the same for the disaster epic.

Produced with full NASA co-operation, *Armageddon* plays like an extended promo for American manhood and expertise. In Ronald Neame's *Meteor* (1979), the US relies on Soviet support; here, a dilapidated Russian space station almost compromises the mission. The rest of the watching world stands by in impotent awe, rendered in stylised, clichéd *tableaux vivants* that parody the original function of such scenes in earlier global-threat movies. The politicians persevere in their unscrupulous machinations, but American heroism, allied with state-of-the-art technology, prevails. It is this crude triumphalism that most obviously separates this film from the similarly premised but less optimistic *Deep Impact*.

Armageddon reassembles generic tropes with predictable calculation, extending the testosterone trajectory of *Con Air* and Bay's *The Rock* by combining the former's *Dirty Dozen*-style characterisations with the latter's do or-die mission scenario. *Titanic*'s influence makes itself felt in the contrived romantic subplot. (Liv Tyler's Grace loves Ben Affleck's A. J. in defiance of her father's hopes for a better match for her.) *Armageddon*'s neo-Hawksian perspective on male group dynamics, mentorship and 'disruptive' female sexuality sits atop the mock-Fordian aspirations of the larger pioneering adventure against the "global killer". ("Talk about the wrong stuff," an onlooker wryly comments over a panoramic shot of the roughnecks in their astronaut gear.)

The irony, however, seems almost lost on Bruce Willis' Stamper, who serves up some risibly straightfaced heroics that become beguilingly difficult to separate from the script's intentional humour (centred, unsurprisingly, on Steve Buscemi's demented, bug-eyed Rockhound). "I've been drilling holes in the earth for 30 years," Stamper defiantly intones. "I will make 800 feet, I swear to God I will." Stamper's final self-sacrifice—for the sake of Grace's earthly happiness with A. J.—is the ultimate kitsch apotheosis, one that will have many more cynical viewers in fits of giggles. His tearful face fills the screens in Mission Control, almost sublime in its stoicism. "I love you," scream both A. J. and Grace at him. "I'll look in on you from time to time," he cherishably consoles, before pressing the trigger.

In a film which, in title alone, stands as the culmination of the pre-millennial disaster cycle, this arch refinement of a Hollywood formula generates its own curious pleasures, parading a slam-bang aesthetic of emotional and material excess glimpsed elsewhere but never so blatant to behold, *Armageddon* spews its money across the screen, dispenses with any pretence at subtlety or intelligence, and successfully batters senses and sensibilities into delirious submission.

VILLAGE VOICE, 7/7/98, p. 117, Dennis Lim

You can't fault a Jerry Bruckholmer-Michael Bay movie for being loud, boorish, illogical, choppy, and chaotic, but *Armageddon* decisively crosses the line from mindless, relatively painless garbage into a whole new dimension of summer-movie hell. Like being yelled at by idiots for 144 minutes, the *Armageddon* experience is pointlessly traumatizing, but, with audiences as benumbed as they are, the film should have no trouble passing off its abusive hysteria as manly bravado.

If nothing else, *Armageddon* gets right down to business; in about 15 minutes, it annihilates midtown Manhattan, gets in a *Godzilla* dig, and establishes the premise in its entirety: big asteroid coming. (While a similar death sentence in *Deep Impact* brought on fits of hand-wringing and soul-searching, here it triggers an epidemic of terrible one-liners.) In an attempt to nuke the offending space rock, the U.S. government turns to Bruce Willis, inventor of a Very Powerful Drill so fiendishly intricate that even NASA can't figure out how to assemble it (its phallic quality does not go unremarked). Smugly impassive, Willis at least knows how to negotiate the stinking Michael Bay quagmire, which is more than can be said for his cast mates: Ben Affleck (charmless and horribly serious), Liv Tyler (pouty and confused), Steve Buscemi (nervously wisecracking).

Cocksure yet somehow insecure, Bay leaves nothing to chance; all situations are incoherently life-or-death. Real thrills are beyond him, so the director simulates their presence through quick cuts, snazzy low angles, sudden camera swivels, deafening explosions, big sharp objects coming right at you! You have no idea what's going on, but It would seem rude not to at least fake excitement. Designed to strong-arm viewers into a bogus frenzy, *Armageddon* makes less sense as entertainment than as an experiment in social control.

Also reviewed in:
CHICAGO TRIBUNE, 7/1/98, Tempo/p. 1, Michael Wilmington
NEW YORK TIMES, 7/1/98, p. E1, Janet Maslin
NEW YORKER, 7/13/98, p. 78, Daphne Merkin
VARIETY, 6/29-7/12/98, p. 37, Todd McCarthy
WASHINGTON POST, 7/1/98, p. D1, Stephen Hunter
WASHINGTON POST, 7/3/98, Weekend/p. 46, Michael O'Sullivan

ARTEMISIA

A Miramax Zoë release of a Premiere Heure Long Metrage presentation of a Premier Heure/ France 3 Cinema/Schlemmer Film/3 Emme Cinematografica co-production.   *Executive Producer:* Lilian Saly, Patricia Allard, and Daniel Wuhrmann.   *Producer:* Patrice Haddad. *Director:* Agnès Merlet.   *Screenplay (French with English subtitles):* Agnès Merlet.   *Director of Photography:* Benoît Delhomme.   *Editor:* Guy Lecorne.   *Music:* Krishna Levy.   *Sound:* François Waledisch and (music) Didier Lizé.   *Sound Editor:* Pierre Choukroun.   *Casting:* Bruno Levy.   *Production Designer:* Antonello Geleng.   *Art Director:* Emita Frigato.   *Set Decorator:* Emita Frigato.   *Special Effects:* Zed.   *Costumes:* Dominique Born.   *Make-up:* Maurizio Silvi. *Running time:* 96 minutes.   *MPAA Rating:* R.

CAST: Michel Serrault (Orazio Gentileschi); Valentina Cervi (Artemisia Gentileschi); Miki Manojlovic (Agostino Tassi); Luca Zingaretti (Cosimo Quorli); Brigitte Catillon (Tuzia); Frédéric Pierrot (Roberto); Maurice Garrel (The Judge); Emmanuelle Devos (Costanza); Yann Trégouet (Fulvio); Jacques Nolot (The Lawyer); Silvia De Santis (Marisa); Renato Carpentieri (Nicolo); Sami Bouajila (Tassi's Assistant); Dominique Raymond (Tassi's Sister); Alain Ollivier (The Duke); Liliane Rovère (Rich Merchant's Wife); Patrick Lancelot (Academy Director); Rinaldo Rocco and Enrico Salimbeni (Students at the Academy); Catherine Zago (Mother Superior);   Anna Lelio and Claudia Giannotti (Wise Women);   Lorenzo Lavia (Orazio's Assistant); Edoardo Ruiz and Aaron De Luca (Tassi's Assistants); Guido Roncalli (Duke's Servant); Pierre Bechir (Rich Merchant's Son); Massimo Pittarello (The Executioner).

LOS ANGELES TIMES, 5/8/98, Calendar/p. 10, Kevin Thomas

No Renaissance maiden ever got sprung from a convent faster than Artemisia Gentileschi, widely regarded as Western civilization's first major female painter. The way French filmmaker Agnes Merlet tells it in her overheated "Artemisia," the 17-year-old girl somehow manages to find a mirror big enough in which to pose for a nude self-portrait.

Bam! The scandalized mother superior summons the girl's elderly father, Orazio (Michel Serrault), a renowned Roman painter who immediately realizes his talent has passed on to his daughter. Slam! He's yanked Artemisia (Valentina Cervi) out of there, whereupon she's soon exclaiming, "I'll never get anywhere if I can't paint naked men!" Pow! A hunky young fisherman is dropping his drawers so that they won't, as Artemisia explains, "break the flow of your body."

Oh, for a soupcon of Bressonian gravity. With her pow-in-the-kisser style, Merlet starts in such frenzied high gear that when she gets to her story's well-orchestrated payoff, you feel that its considerable impact would have been so much greater had she built rather than streaked toward it. Actually, Merlet has a fine sense of structure and skill with her actors, but she leaves you feeling that starting out in such a needlessly fevered pitch has a lot to do with feminist fervor, working us up instead of trusting us to comprehend the quite stark implications of the fact that, in 1610 Rome, women weren't supposed to be painting any kind of pictures, let alone anatomically correct renderings of naked male torsos.

Orazio gets a choice papal commission, painting the frescoes in a quite large church, but he must share it with the up-and-coming Florentine, Agostino Tassi (Miki Manojlovic). Deciding that she's learned all she can from her father, Artemisia persuades him to let her go off to the beach to learn perspective from the virile Agostino. His Casanova reputation seems to be completely unknown to the trusting Gentileschi, who has always dutifully painted exactly what his patrons requested and has apparently lived a more sheltered and genteel life than we might have imagined.

Actually, both father and daughter are innocents: When Agostino inevitably seduces Artemisia, he is genuinely shocked to discover she's a virgin.

Up until then Merlet's tone has been so hysterical that she invites you to snigger at the lovers (and a whole lot of other hot 'n' heavy orgying as well). In his enraged naivete, Orazio sues Tassi, accusing him of raping his daughter in hopes of forcing him to marry her to save her honor. (Never mind that Tassi is already married, although separated.)

The ensuing trial brings out all the hypocrisy, cruelty and severe puritanism you would expect of the times. Amazingly, at its fade-out this lush period piece strikes a note of maturity, realism and wisdom—leaving you to wish you could say the same for all that has gone before it. Perhaps Merlet, as a filmmaker, was growing up with her heroine.

NEW YORK, 5/25/98, p. 79, David Denby

What's most interesting in "Artemisia," an account of the art and semi-scandalous life of the Baroque-era female painter Artemisia Gentileschi, is the details of how the paintings were done—the arrangements of studios, the management of light, the deployment of helpers and naked models in a period when heroic painting was as natural to Italians as movies are to us. The feminist issues are more obvious and more familiar, and Valentina Cervi, who has small features and a slender body, is not singular enough to bring them to life. If you are going to portray your heroine as a revolutionary, you had better not cast a young actress who purses her lips and holds herself in.

NEW YORK POST, 5/8/98, p. 50, Larry Worth

There's a great epic to be told in the life and times of 17th century artist Artemisia Gentileschi. But the big-screen portrait—aptly titled "Artemisia"—mistakenly tells its tale in very broad strokes.

Rather than re-creating what's known about the young woman who earned a place in art history books by painting "Judith Beheading Holofernes," director Agnes Merlet treats the material like fodder for a dime-store romance. The central character's complexities are reduced to the stuff of a high schooler in heat.

When the narrative opens, teen-ager Artemisia is seen as the loyal apprentice to her painter father. But she's frustrated by society's restrictions on ladies taking up the brush or sketching anatomical shapes.

So it's no surprise when Artemisia is reduced to spying on lovers on the beach, then resting her body in the sandy cavity where the earth moved. Soon, the 17-year-old is willing to trade her virtue for the chance to sketch a male model's private parts.

Things change when the studly protege of Artemisia's dad begins tutoring her on the fine points of "perspective." A few steamy encounters later, he's charged with rape—and the screenplay moves onto an even less satisfying course.

Though the script, which Merlet co-wrote, is identified as a true story, it seems specious from the get-go. Not helping is florid language that sounds more like Jackie Collins than history brought to life.

In addition, one plot point after another is hinted at, then abandoned—as in the professional and personal jealousy that dear old pop channels toward his student after hearing of Artemisia's seduction. And is that all-important seduction a case of youthful lust or forced brutality? It's anyone's guess.

Valentina ("The Portrait of a Lady") Cervi's pouty turn as the titular heroine is another nail in the coffin. She's superficial, at best, failing to convey the character's artistic or sexual passions.

On the other hand, ever-reliable Michel ("Nelly et Monsieur Arnaud") Serrault delivers yeomanlike work as the confused father. He's nicely complemented by Miki ("Underground") Manojlovic's turn as the heavy-breathing landscape artist who captures Artemisia's heart.

The requisite period costumes and sets— along with an epilogue that's more interesting than anything in the main narrative—also distract. But, assets aside, "Artemisia" is as interesting as watching paint dry.

NEWSDAY, 5/8/98, Part II/p. B7, John Anderson

Although she seems to be in the throes of one long, continuous fit of pique from the moment the movie opens, Artemisia Gentileschi (Valentina Cervi), the sultry, tempestuous, willful, brazen, defiant subject of Agnes Merlet's "Artemisia," was really repressed. Although she seems perfectly capable of seducing and/or arm-wrestling the entire College of Cardinals, her life was one long struggle to throw off the yoke of femininity.

A gifted painter, Artemisia was real—her wonderful paintings continue to be exhibited around the world—and she really was denied, under Vatican stricture, the tutelage available to male artists in the early 17th Century. She fought the power and was raped and abused along the way. Such are the skeletal facts of her life, which has been adapted—or perhaps contorted—into Merlet's movie.

Films that tell a historical story with a strictly modern sensibility—endowing their heroine with an unrealistically progressive attitude about gender, for instance—are usually bores and frauds. They tell neither an accurate story nor an honest one, because the conclusions are foregone and the facts become conveniences. They remove their subjects from their own time, and make them tools of agitprop.

No one ever accused film, or art in general, of being historically accurate, or said it had to be—Shakespeare's histories were more than politically expedient; Dürer's Christ was a bit fair for an Aramaean—and history in service of art has had a much better record than art in service of history. But when the factual controversy is the *raison d'etre* of the movie, then contorting that history for crass commercial reasons is, well, crass.

As readers may know already from such anti-"Artemisians" as Gloria Steinem, the film takes what seems to have been a perfectly serviceable plot line and twists it into a far more conventional (and, presumably, marketable) story.

The skeletal facts are these: Artemisia, the convent-educated daughter of the painter Orazio Gentileschi (Michel Serrault), was sent by her liberal-minded father to study with acclaimed painter Agostino Tassi (Miki Manojlovic). In the movie, she and Tassi fall in love, have sex, and when Orazio finds out—motivated by envy for Tassi's talent—he accuses Tassi publicly of rape.

At the trial—which is prolonged by Merlet to an extraordinary, tension-extinguishing degree—Artemisia undergoes torture to prove her love for Tassi and his innocence. In order to stop the torture, Tassi declares that he did indeed rape Artemisia and accepts his punishment.

Merlet follows the record up to a point, replete with dramatic adornment: Artemisia spots a couple having sex on a beach, and studies them—not out of lust, but for the opportunity to study the forbidden male figure. She tries desperately—a bit too desperately—to find male models to draw, her efforts becoming both comic and controversial. She exhibits enormous talent and Tassi helps develop it.

What actually happened: Artemisia was raped by Tassi over a long period of time; he promised to marry her (the standard way of avoiding prosecution) but already had a wife and children, and children by his sister-in law as well.

At the trial, Artemisia underwent torture, but only to prove to the court that she was telling the truth about Tassi—who was busy using any means possible to smear her reputation and demolish her story.

So why change the plot? To get a love story into the movie. Do we live in weird times? Hypocritical times?

A film such as "Artemisia" uses a nearly 400-year-old feminist archetype as a de facto coverup of male villainy. They say there are no unhappy endings in the movies anymore, but if "Artemisia's" any example, that's all we get.

SIGHT AND SOUND, 5/99, p. 37, Adrian Searle

Rome, 1610, Artemisia, the precocious teenage daughter of successful painter Orazio Gentileschi, is forbidden by the strictures of the church from becoming a painter. But her father recognises her talent and sets her to work in his studio. Unable to study anatomy, Artemisia uses her own body as a model and spies on a couple having sex on the beach. She flirts with a young fisherman, and draws his naked body in exchange for a kiss.

Agostino Tassi, a Florentine painter and master of new perspective techniques, arrives in Rome. Artemisia is fascinated by the newcomer. Tassi, who has a reputation for debauchery, moves nearby and begins to work with Orazio on a church-fresco commission. Artemisia, watching through a window, witnesses an orgy in Tassi's house. Artemisia becomes Tassi's pupil. Between lessons she has Tassi model for her. He seduces her, confessing his love.

They continue to meet as lovers, under the guise of his tutelage. Orazio discovers the truth and has Tassi arrested for rape in order to force a marriage, while Tassi's friends try to blacken Artemisia's name, using her life-drawings of men as evidence. At the trial Artemisia insists she is still a virgin but the truth is found out. It is revealed that Tassi has an estranged wife and son in Florence. Artemisia visits Tassi in prison and works furiously in her studio. The judge orders her torture and Tassi confesses to rape to save her suffering. Tassi goes to jail for two years. Artemisia never sees him again, but her reputation is established as the first great female painter.

Agnès Merlet's film is no exception to the rule that bio-pics and fictionalisations invariably get art and artists wrong. This film has already attracted the wrath of art historians, especially in the US, for its distortion of the life of Artemisia Gentileschi (1593-1652). The film has the headstrong Artemisia as a willing lover to Agostino Tassi and ignores evidence that, as well as raping his 17-year-old pupil, Tassi also murdered his wife and child and committed incest with his sister.

Gentileschi's artistic career is also foreshortened, having her completing in her teens a self-portrait she wasn't to paint for another 20 years. But what the hell—this is a movie, and the fact that Artemisia has been the subject of intense study by feminist art historians for the past 20 years or so (see art-historian Griselda Pollock's article in *S&S* November 1998) hasn't put Merlet off. Instead, she wants us to see Artemisia and Tassi as Cathy and Heathcliff.

It is surprising that Merlet has made a movie about awakening sexuality and forbidden knowledge, rather than a post-feminist Jacobean tragedy And while she may not care for art history, she is fascinated by all those art-theoretical discourses about creativity, desire and the gaze. Artemisia spies on a couple having sex on the beach and others through a window. She bribes a boy with a kiss for a look at his cock, and is in turn spied on by her father. The prison bars are equated with the grid frame used for perspective drawing, and Artemisia's erstwhile lover talks meaningfully about "a spurt of white" on a canvas. When alone, Artemisia spouts the kind of stuff usually found in the writings of theorist Julia Kristeva, as she acts out an artistic-Oedipal conflict with her dad and contemplates the sun.

Valentina Cervi holds our attention as a believably ambitious and sexually curious late-adolescent, but she's hardly credible as the girl-genius artist, painting the suicidal Lucretia and Holofernes-slaying Judith by candlelight in her Wendy House studio in dad's back garden. The way Merlet has it, the theoretical crisis in representation was alive and well 400 years ago.

The movie is grounded by a fascination with the paraphernalia of the baroque painter: winged Caravaggiste cherub-boys suspended from wires in the father's studio; the *camera obscura,* perspective frames and lenses—the high-tech stock in-trade of seventeenth century painting. We meet a gossipy old pigment-grinder, vain patrons, and an assistant with a nice line in illicit porno-drawings. There's even a wicked stepmother. With camerawork and lighting out of Caravaggio, Le Nain and the Pre-Raphaelites, and *Don't Look Now*-style flashes of blood and paint, the film is sophisticated to look at. This is a genre film, in just the same way that Gentileschi's paintings are largely genre, mythological or religious subjects. Art history has created a modern myth out of Artemisia too, and the film is no more or less than a variation on the theme of the suffering female artist. If it wasn't supposedly based on such an iconic figure as Artemisia Gentileschi, it would make for a decent enough post-watershed costume drama on television, which is where *Artemisia* will probably end up.

VILLAGE VOICE, 5/12/98, p. 123, Amy Taubin

With so many great French films begging for distribution in the U.S. (along with Akerman's oeuvre almost in its entirety, there are, for starters, the recent films of Pascale Ferran and Naomi Lvovsky), it's obscene that Miramax is giving a push to Agnès Merlet's clumsy and banal *Artemisia*. A biopic about the 17th-century Italian painter Artemisia Gentileschi (the first female member of the Academy of Florence, famed for her depiction of *Judith Slaying Holofernes*), it's deficient in its understanding of history, economics, and painting. Artemisia is a terrific subject, but here she seems like a starry-eyed schoolgirl who had some mysterious immunity to one of patriarchy's basic strictures—that women were made not to look, but to be looked at. Merlet reduces painting to voyeurism. Just like the male painters around her, Artemisia is turned on by looking. And when she's turned on, she not only wants to paint, she wants to fuck her brains out.

Maybe Merlet thought she was being as bold as Artemisia when she let her camera linger not only on t&a, but on male full frontals as well. Miramax may have lost their eye for art films, but they know soft-core when they see it.

Also reviewed in:
CHICAGO TRIBUNE, 8/17/98, Tempo/p. 1, Michael Wilmington
NEW YORK TIMES, 5/8/98, p. E12, Stephen Holden
VARIETY, 9/29-10/5/97, p. 64, Derek Elley
WASHINGTON POST, 5/15/98, p. D1, Stephen Hunter

AVENGERS, THE

A Warner Bros. release of a Jerry Weintraub production. *Executive Producer:* Susan Ekins. *Producer:* Jerry Weintraub. *Director:* Jeremiah Chechik. *Screenplay (inspired by the television series "The Avengers"):* Don MacPherson. *Director of Photography:* Roger Pratt. *Editor:* Mick Audsley. *Music:* Joel McNeely. *Music Editor:* Michael Connell. *Sound:* Clive Winter and (music) Shawn Murphy. *Sound Editor:* Peter Joly. *Casting:* Susie Figgis. *Production Designer:* Stuart Craig. *Art Director:* Neil Lamont. *Set Decorator:* Stephenie McMillan. *Special Effects:* Josh Williams. *Visual Effects:* Nick Davis. *Costumes:* Anthony Powell. *Make-up:* Daniel Parker. *Make-up (Uma Thurman):* Peter King. *Stunt Coordinator:* Marc Boyle. *Running time:* 100 minutes. *MPAA Rating:* PG.

CAST: Ralph Fiennes (John Steed);   Uma Thurman (Dr. Emma Peel);   Sean Connery (Sir August De Wynter);   Patrick Macnee (Invisible Jones);   Jim Broadbent (Mother);   Fiona Shaw (Father);   Eddie Izzard (Bailey);   Eileen Atkins (Alice);   John Wood (Trubshaw);   Carmen Ejogo (Brenda);   Keeley Hawes (Tamara);   Shaun Ryder (Donavan);   Nicholas Woodeson (Dr. Darling);   Michael Godley (Butler);   Richard Lumsden (Boodle's Porter);   Daniel Crowder (Messenger);   Nadim Sawalha, Christopher Godwin, David Webber (World Council of Ministers).

LOS ANGELES TIMES, 8/17/98, Calendar/p. 5, Gene Seymour

[The following review by Gene Seymour appeared in a slightly different form in **NEWSDAY, 8/15/98, Part II/p. B3.]**

Movies spawned from old television series have less to do with a particular show than with whatever it is we think we remember—or love—best about it. Otherwise, what's the point, right?

So what then is the point of making "The Avengers" as a feature film? And what is it, exactly, that's worth reviving?

One remembers from the British adventure series' mid-1960s heyday a weekly parade of wildly improbable plots in which several people died in elaborate, exotic ways; solutions to which crimes could only be brought about by a pair of impeccably dressed secret agents: debonair "top professional" John Steed and versatile "talented amateur" Emma Peel.

Most of those episodes were warm souffles; empty inside for the most part, but served with flair and decorated with just the right amount of spice. Still, it's not the stories we remember so much as the chemistry between Patrick Macnee's Steed and Diana Rigg's Peel. Within the confines of the small screen, both actors were graceful, magnetic presences. Rigg, especially, spurred a cult of fevered devotion among the original show's younger fans that hasn't grown old even if those same fans have.

So how then do you duplicate a magic aura from 30 years ago? You don't. But that apparently hasn't stopped those who made this new incarnation of "The Avengers" from trying. Needless to say, they fall short—though not by as much as one might have expected. Or feared.

For one thing, they've got the tone right, beginning with a suitably preposterous plot: Mad meteorologist (Sean Connery) plans to pulverize London with bad weather unless he gets (Do I have this right?) "10% of Britain's gross national product." Several dotty touches are scattered about, including mechanical killer bees, henchmen dressed as giant teddy bears and a sweet old lady spy who knows her weaponry.

The rapport between Ralph Fiennes' Steed and Uma Thurman's Peel is agreeably droll and briskly seasoned with double-entendres. They're almost, but not quite, as charismatic as the originals. Yet Fiennes, though lacking Macnee's physical stature, adds a layer of gimlet-eyed implacability to Steed's elegance, reminding you that, as well-mannered as he is, the man will kill you in a blink if he has to.

Thurman has a far tougher task of competing not only with a previous actress' portrayal, but with a generational icon. She has the right physique and she seems to be enjoying herself through all the leaping, kicking and running. But still... well, what's fair? Put it another way: Ray Knight had to follow Pete Rose's act in Cincinnati and proved himself a great ballplayer in his own right. Let's leave things at that.

In any case, the movie lets them both down with a patchwork climax that feels rushed and perfunctory. And while it's always nice to see Connery do anything on screen, he somehow never convinces you that he really and truly wants to destroy the world.

Which, as is the case with Thurman, may not be his fault. After all, the same kids who grew up watching Steed and Mrs. Peel dispatch evil-doers also remember Connery as another British agent of note, battling villains far more scary than the one he plays here.

NEW YORK POST, 8/15/98, p. 21, Rod Dreher

"The Avengers" features Sean Connery dressed as—are you ready for this?—a malicious Hibernian Care Bear. More on which anon.

But first: If "The Avengers" were a silent movie—and you didn't have to hear the excruciating dialogue, or feel obligated to follow the absurd plot—it would still be quite dreadful, but minimally tolerable.

Stuart Craig's futuristic sets, which undoubtedly cost a fortune, are sleek and sophisticated, if a huge waste of talent. Uma Thurman (as Emma Peel) and Ralph Fiennes (as John Steed) cut dashing figures in their costumes, by Anthony Powell.

GQ cover boy Fiennes looks smashing in bowler and bespoke Savile Row tailoring, and La Dolce Uma sports sizzling minis and hubba-hubba catsuits that hug dangerous curves like a Testarossa going lickety-split on a test track.

So much for the good news. There's an excellent reason Warner Bros. refused to show "The Avengers" to critics, and why none of the stars could bear to show their faces at any of the advance parties to promote the film: It's a big fat gob of maximum crapulosity, the kind of shallow, stupid, big-budget cowpile that smells of Joel Schumacher (director of "Batman & Robin").

The Schumacher manque in charge here is a Mr. Jeremiah Chechik, who directs as badly as he can, from a fizz-free Don MacPherson screenplay that bears comparison to the crudulent works of Akiva ("Batman & Robin," "Batman Forever") Goldsman.

What I wouldn't have given to have been on set the day poor Chechik told Sean Connery, who plays the villainous Sir August De Wynter, that he and his evil co-conspirators would have to dress up in candy-colored teddy bear costumes.

The film is based on the smarmy but fun English TV program of the 1960s, which enjoyed a stateside run through the early 1970s. Patrick Macnee played the unflappable British secret agent

Steed, who partnered with sexy sidekick Peel (Diana Rigg) to fight baddies in Swinging London style.

There's nothing the least bit fun about the deadly dull film version, which had potential for timely, Cool Britannia appeal. Neither Fiennes nor Thurman has the slightest idea what to do with their characters, and they have zippo chemistry.

The usually brilliant Fiennes plays Steed as an international master of butt-clench. Thurman is actively awful. She delivers her lines in that same clunky, tap-dancing-in-clogs way she did as Poison Ivy in "Robin & Batman."

The menace-free plot has to do with an attempt by Sir August to blackmail the world by gaining control of its weather. Steed and Peel, of course, have to stop him. The screenplay has little coherence, either narratively or character-wise, and yanks us senselessly from one moronic scene to the next.

Only Austin Powers could save this hopelessly un-groovy movie, baby.

NEWSWEEK, 8/24/98, p. 59, David Ansen

It seemed like a good idea, but the more you think about it, the clearer it becomes that "The Avengers" should never have been turned into a movie. Not in 1998. It's not that it's the worst movie of the summer—it's merely the most irrelevant. It sits up there on the screen, as stiff and out of place as John Steed's black bowler. Who needs it?

A little explanation is in order for those who weren't around in 1966, when this cult British import took America by storm. Secret agent John Steed, played by Patrick Macnee, with his umbrella, bowler, antique car and veddy-upper-crust manner, was a parody of an Englishman. The character was matched with Diana Rigg's mod, mischievously unflappable Emma Peel, sexily decked out in midriff-revealing, chain-linked Carnaby Street fashions. "The Avengers"—located on the Zeitgeist halfway between James Bond and the Beatles—was something new on TV, with its tongue-in-cheek black comedy, its emotional cool, its champagne-popping hipness. No matter how many grisly deaths each episode recorded, the strongest reaction from Rigg and Macnee was an arched eyebrow.

But what could it mean today? Few things have dated so thoroughly as the absurdist whimsy of the late '60s. Looking at episodes of the show now, its hipness seems terribly quaint; the strongest emotion it evokes is nostalgia. The director of the movie, Jeremiah Chechik, and screenwriter Don MacPherson seem to think that all it takes to bring "The Avengers" into the '90s is computer-generated special effects. This is an elaborate production, but all the jazzy sets and explosions in the world can't disguise the story's complete lack of urgency. Do we care if Steed and Peel can stop the evil mastermind Sean Connery from his maniacal plan to control the world's weather? Even with the estimable Connery in the role, the character seems like a nefarious reject from one of Joel Schumacher's grim "Batman" sequels.

The overriding tone of "The Avengers" is archness gone flat. As Steed and Peel, Ralph Fiennes and Uma Thurman, cool customers both, can't transcend the wan material. How many times can you get a laugh out of the idea of a tea break? Thurman (playing with a Brit accent) seems locked in one heavily ironic gear, while Fiennes underplays to the point of near invisibility. They make an attractive but juiceless couple.

Chechik does manage to pull off a few striking visual effects: a conference room full of men disguised in colorful teddy-bear suits; a creepily surreal sequence in which Thurman can't escape from a marble room and the almost Magritte-like vision of an invisible bureaucrat, identifiable only by his glasses and his pipe (his voice is supplied by Patrick Macnee). More indicative of the film's general wrongheadedness is its misuse of the gifted stand-up comic Eddie Izzard, who plays a sinister heavy and is given a grand total of two words to say. It's now clear why Warner Bros. refused to screen the movie for the press, and didn't bother to throw a premiére. Quite simply, the champagne has lost its fizz.

SIGHT AND SOUND, 10/98, p. 38, Kim Newman

England. The Prospero Shield, a weather-control system, fails and the climate gets colder. Secret agent John Steed is summoned by Mother, his male commander, and required to investigate Doctor Emma Peel, a scientist who developed Prospero. A security camera filmed her sabotaging the device. Mrs Peel claims she is not the saboteur, and Steed's suspicions turn to Sir August De Wynter, a weather-control and cloning boffin. He now runs Wonderland, a private firm which tailors the weather locally for a fee. De Wynter has suborned the Prospero team and created an evil clone of Mrs Peel. He plans to blackmail the world into buying their weather from him.

Together Steed and Mrs Peel come up against the clone and De Wynter's henchman Bailey, who tries to kill them with robot insects. It transpires that Father, Mother's female second-in-command, is also working with Sir August. While Steed researches the madman's background with invisible archivist Jones, Mrs Peel is kidnapped by Father and the clone and spirited off in a balloon. An arctic winter descends upon London as De Wynter makes his demands to the world and turns up the cold as a demonstration. Mrs Peel escapes from the balloon, which crashes, killing Father and the clone. Steed and Mrs Peel penetrate De Wynter's stronghold and defeat De Wynter and Bailey, and then destroy the weather-control device. Mother gives them the thanks of a grateful nation.

The business of retooling cult television series as movie franchises seems simpler than it actually is. Hollywood seems to think that so long as original stars are present in cameos while currently hot box office names take over the roles the originals created, nothing much can go wrong. The fact that the field is littered with such corpses as *Car 54, Where Are You?*, *Sgt Bilko*, *The Beverly Hillbillies* and *The Saint* doesn't stop the industry from still wanting to emulate the financial success of *Mission Impossible* or *The Brady Bunch Movie*.

The Avengers poses a unique problem for its adapters. The original show evolved over 15 years. The gritty 1996 crime drama which partnered Ian Hendry's vigilante doctor with Patrick Macnee's elegant secret agent Steed turned into a chic fantasy as Steed became the central figure and Honor Blackman, Diana Rigg and Linda Thorson in turn took over the sidekick role. (The fact that only Hendry had anything to avenge was never mentioned.) Even the 70s coda of *The New Avengers* proved that the format was still evolving. This film, however, wants to be *The Avengers* circa 1966, with Steed partnered by Emma Peel in bizarre pulp plots pitting the unflappable agents against monomaniacal masterminds amid minimalist sets and dotty English surrealism. To that end, Jeremiah Chechik—who made a hash of the remake of *Les Diaboliques* but still hinted at a fondness for extreme chic with Sharon Stone's outfits—creates a world "in which the 60s never ended". The cars and clothes of the classic series are still in style and Steed swans about with a bowler and umbrella as if his *New Avengers* partner Gareth Hunt had never existed.

Visual style is about all the film gets right. The script has a witty central nugget, revolving (as did the television episode 'A Surfeit of H20') about that most English of concerns, the weather. This at least excuses Steed's umbrella and gives Uma Thurman as the evil clone a splendid entrance out of *The Lion, the Witch and the Wardrobe*, astride a sleigh in a catsuit with a giant fur wrap. However, screenwriter Don MacPherson is otherwise content to lift business from old shows (such as the disorienting labyrinth of 'The House that Jack Built'; the tropical enclave in the home counties from 'Small Game for Big Hunters'; and an invisible spy from 'The See-Through Man'). He also accommodates Sean Connery with some Bond villany (one scene replays a sequence from *Goldfinger*, but this time dresses all the characters as giant candy-coloured teddy bears). There is a little equivocation in the use of Mother (originally Patrick Newell), who belongs to the slightly later, Linda Thorson period, when the formula was settling somewhat. There is also an almost pointless degree of devotion in the resurrection of the one-off character of Father (Iris Russell in 'Stay Tuned') for the traitor, a reversal far less transgressive than revealing good old Jim Phelps as a villain in the *Mission Impossible* movie.

There are vulgarities, such as talk about tight-fitting boots. The kiss between the leads drew a deserved boo at the screening I saw, because it breaks the titillating tension carefully established throughout the series (a lesson learned by *The X Files*)—the only way the old heroes could ever kiss was if they had been possessed by villains ('Who's Who'). The business with the clone is so bungled (a major Uma-on-Uma fight has been cut) that we never get the obligatory moment where Steed is fooled by the doppelgänger (her, he could kiss). Action set-pieces (an attack by robot bees, a high-wire between Thurman and a chubbily unthreatening Eddie Izzard) hang unthreaded into the plot, evidence some desperate cutting made in an effort to salvage something from a project that went awry perhaps because *The Avengers* series is so ineffably itself it doesn't offer the cracks for a revisionary re-reading along the lines of *The Brady Bunch Movie* or *Mission Impossible*.

But the real failure of the film is in the performances. Ralph Fiennes is misleadingly suited by aristocratic looks and charm for Steed, but his weaselly hesitancy suggests deeply subdued neurosis rather than Macnee's unflappable confidence and sly hedonism. He would be excellent as Ian Fleming's basketcase Bond, but he searches for depth when he needs to deliver style. Uma Thurman, as she was as Poison Ivy in *Batman & Robin* is disastrous: striking as a clothes horse, she unwisely tries for a Diana Rigg imitation that is beyond her. The show was smart in replacing its leads, realising Steed was the eternal clubman but sidekicks needed to change with the times. A cleverer movie would have partnered him with a woman as 90s-specific as Blackman, Rigg or Joanna Lumley were for their seasons. And Sean Connery simply adds to the extraordinary number of bad performances he has given in bad films, confident that the next project or the one after that will be worth the effort of reminding the world he's a real star.

TIME, 8/24/98, p. 74, Richard Corliss

Critics long ago stopped even pretending they had any effect on the moviegoing habits of the mass audience. So to be forbidden an early peek at a film, as we were last week with *The Avengers*, is to be momentarily flattered that we matter. Hiding a film—especially a big-budget action-adventure with a certain pedigree—is a studio's open signal that the picture smells. It is a mystery how moguls think they can tell an epochally awful movie from a routinely bad one; last year, for example, there were plenty of press previews for *The Saint*, to name just one other dyspeptic update of a '60s British TV spy series. And one wonders why a studio would advertise its low opinion of a film, in effect encouraging journalists' pans. Well, we critics are an agreeable lot. So here goes.

The TV show, which was created by Sydney Newman (*Doctor Who*), ran in Britain from 1961 to 1969, and in the U.S. from 1966 to 1969. It starred Patrick Macnee, an actor of dumplingy face and no fixed appeal, as John Steed, infallible British agent with a Pierre Cardin wardrobe and a lethal umbrella. His most notable partner (of three) was Diana Rigg as Emma Peel, a jump-suited vision of protofeminist swank; she could handle a quip, a karate kick and power tools with equal authority. Each week they saved the world from suave nasties and gave viewers a cozy thrill or two.

Now Steed is played by Ralph Fiennes, an actor of such autocratic reticence that director Jeremiah Chechik and writer Don MacPherson must have thought it'd be fun to embarrass him at every turn. So there he is, naked, reading a newspaper and muttering feeble double entendres, as he first meets Mrs. Peel.

She is now Uma Thurman, who has a figure for high boots and miniskirts, but who affects an imperious mid-Atlantic accent that strives to recall the early Bette Davis. The thin smiles of the leads are meant to lend insouciance to the sub-Bondian dialogue. Or perhaps they are simply suppressing an impotent scream. We need only watch *The Avengers* for its endless 90 minutes. They had to be there daily, inuring themselves to dismay.

The plot could have been pertinent; it is about a powerful madman, Sir August De Wynter (Sean Connery) seizing control of the weather. But MacPherson botches even this. Instead of global warming, we get global cooling: London in a wedding-cake snow storm. (Exasperated note to filmmakers: London always has lousy weather. You may as well threaten Angelenos with smog.) Connery never connects with his role, but part of the problem is that *The Avengers* has the sloppiest dubbing since *The Jazz Singer*, Connery's lips move a macrosecond before we hear the words. The cast also includes a host of theater royals: Jim Broadbent, Eileen Atkins, John Wood, Fiona Shaw. May they have earned enough from their ordeal to buy estates in Majorca.

Some bad movies are bold outrages; many others become hits. This one hasn't the juice to be either. It is an inert gas. Chechik doesn't attain even the workmanlike facility of the old show's directors; if he were to take the pseudonym Alan Smithee, the name directors affix to movies they're ashamed of, he'd be boasting. And *The Avengers* is that most depressing and disposable of movie failures: the anonymous atrocity.

Also reviewed in:
NEW YORK TIMES, 8/15/98, p. B7, Janet Maslin
VARIETY, 8/17-23/98, p. 35, Godfrey Cheshire
WASHINGTON POST, 8/15/98, p. B1, Stephen Hunter

AYN RAND: A SENSE OF LIFE

A Strand Releasing and A G Media Corporation Limited release in association with Copasetic, Inc.   *Producer:* Michael Paxton. *Director:* Michael Paxton.   *Screenplay:* Michael Paxton. *Director of Photography:* Alik Sakharov.   *Editor:* Lauren Schaffer and Christopher Earl. *Music:* Jeff Britting.   *Music Editor:* Jeff Briting.   *Sound:* Michael M. Moore.   *Sound Editor:* Greg La Plante and Leslie Wolf.   *Production Designer:* Cathy Carr.   *Animation Director:* Cynthia Wells. *Make-up:* David Alan-Dittmar.   *Running time:* 145 minutes.   *MPAA Rating:* Not Rated.

WITH: Sharon Gless (Narrator).

CHRISTIAN SCIENCE MONITOR, 2/27/98, p. B3, David Sterritt

"Ayn Rand: A Sense of Life" turns its lens on a novelist, philosopher, and public intellectual who became a small-scale celebrity during the 1950s and '60s. Unfortunately, the movie doesn't live up to its subject and is likely to remain a long shot for the best-documentary Academy Award.

Born in Russia not long before the Communist revolution, Rand developed a deep hatred for the Soviet system's emphasis on self-sacrifice and collectivity. Passionate about movies and individualism, she emigrated to the United States and made her way to Hollywood, where no less a mogul than Cecil B. DeMille took her under his wing and helped her find work in a studio script department.

It apparently didn't dawn on Rand that moviemaking, a team enterprise from start to finish, was hardly an ideal profession for her fiercely independent spirit. Hollywood treated her reasonably well, though, and introduced her to actor Frank O'Connor, who became her husband of more than 50 years. Turning to novels and nonfiction, she wrote several books and made her mark on bestseller lists and TV talk shows before her death in the early '80s.

Rand is best known for two massive novels, "The Fountainhead" and "Atlas Shrugged," which dramatize her philosophy (Objectivism) through flamboyant stories about larger-than-life characters who triumph over altruism, religion, and other petty proclivities of modern society. "The Fountainhead" also became a 1949 movie, with a clearly bewildered Gary Cooper muddling through her wordy screenplay.

Unabashedly romantic in style, story, and subject, Rand's books sold increasingly well even as critics questioned their far-fetched plots and dubious views. Liberals derided her love of laissez faire capitalism, conservatives applauded her obsession with individualism, and she attacked both groups with gusto, regarding liberals as self-loathing weaklings and conservatives as mushy-minded frauds.

All of which makes Rand an excellent subject for a serious nonfiction film. "Ayn Rand: A Sense of Life" assembles the necessary materials, from childhood snapshots to her TV conversations with Mike Wallace.

Instead of analyzing her ideas and exploring her impact, however, director Michael Paxton turns his movie into a syrupy commercial for her philosophy. Not one opponent of Rand's ideology gets to counter the earnest anecdotes of her friends and colleagues—unless Phil Donahue's politely skeptical questions are meant to cover this ground. From the film's account of American history, you'd never guess that unregulated capitalism might breed monopolies, child labor, and other well-documented concerns.

It's as if Oliver Stone told the story of "Wall Street" financier Gordon Gekko without mentioning the downside of his "greed is good" credo. Rand thought greed was one of humanity's greatest inventions, and that notion deserves more scrutiny than Paxton and company choose to give it.

LOS ANGELES TIMES, 2/13/98, Calendar/p. 14, Kenneth Turan

If logic were any guide, Ayn Rand would be little more than a footnote to history. Objectivism, the philosophy she created and espoused, has not taken hold in any substantive way, and her linked betes noires, the Soviet Union and the collectivism it insisted on, have just about disappeared off the face of the Earth.

Yet Ayn Rand is still with us. Her novels, 1943's "The Fountainhead" and 1957's "Atlas Shrugged," continue to sell hundreds of thousands of copies every year. And a new Oscar-nominated documentary called "Ayn Rand—A Sense of Life" aims to illuminate her life for the uninitiated.

It is quite a life, involving a strong-willed heroine, a flight from the USSR, a chance meeting with a famous director, success first as a screenwriter, then as a novelist, and finally the worshipful attention of acolytes forever grateful for the way her thoughts revolutionized their life.

It's a mark of how much the world has changed that Rand's philosophy of "rational self-interest," its disapproval of altruism and staunch defense of individualism and self-centered behavior, seems much less controversial now that it did half a century ago. With voters turning down school bonds and aid to immigrants, with everyone from Ronald Reagan to "Wall Street's" Gordon Gecko promoting the notion of looking out for No. 1, the idea that selfishness was once out of favor seems a relic of a simpler, quainter time.

Given the potential a dispassionate examination of Rand's life and thought has, its unfortunate that Michael Paxton, "A Sense of Life's" writer and director, is unashamedly in the acolyte camp. While Rand's story is strong enough to create interest no matter what, having the filmmaker be someone whose eighth-grade discovery of "The Fountainhead" "changed my life forever" is not ideal for the sense of perspective that would benefit this kind of film.

Young Ayn (the name, appropriately enough, rhymes with "mine") determined to be a writer as a 9-year-old in St. Petersburg after reading a boy's adventure novel called "The Mysterious Valley" and deciding that its self-reliant hero was the ideal example of masculine courage and resolve.

Her youthful passion for individualism conflicting with the group-think of the young Soviet state, Ayn left home for America, "her heart," the narration breathlessly informs us, "skipping beats in anticipation." Determined to break into the movies, she took a train to Hollywood and used a chance meeting with Cecil B. DeMille as a steppingstone to both extra work in his "King of Kings" and employment as a screenwriter.

With the Jennifer Jones-starring "Love Letters" as her biggest credit, Rand embarked on her magnum opus, the writing of "The Fountainhead." Its story of an architect (loosely inspired by Frank Lloyd Wright) who blows up his own masterpiece rather than sully his hands with compromise, was rejected 12 times before Rand, who characteristically refused to change a single word, placed it with a publisher.

One of "Sense of Life's" best sections involves the making of the King Vidor-directed film version of the novel. Joan Crawford and Barbara Stanwyck apparently coveted the role that went to Patricia Neal, and after Frank Lloyd Wright's demand for $250,000 to design the film's buildings was rejected, the studio did the plans and hoped no one would notice they were structurally unsound.

"Sense of Life" does briefly spotlight some of the more controversial areas of Rand's life, including her friendly testimony to the House Un-American Activities Committee and her romantic infatuation with disciple Nathaniel Branden, but it handles them very gingerly, as if embarrassed at what genuine scrutiny might uncover.

Rand herself was apparently quite the media celebrity in her day, and the film offers clips from interviews with Mike Wallace, Phil Donahue and even Tom Snyder, all of whom seem unsure what to make of this determined woman who was completely convinced of her own eternal importance.

Unfortunately, "Sense of Life" is more convinced of that importance than it should be. To properly examine a figure like Rand, a natural polarizer whom people either loved or hated, a film needs to offer at least a sample of dissenting voices, not just proponents like Leonard Peikoff, grandly identified as "Ayn Rand's intellectual heir." Rand herself would have been delighted with this film, which takes her place in history for granted and shows her every action in the best possible light, but nonbelievers will be harder to convince.

NEW YORK POST, 2/13/98, p. 52, Michael Medved

Novelist, philosopher and a self-described "fanatic for individualism," Ayn Rand receives admiring treatment in the engaging, sober—and now Oscar-nominated—documentary "Ayn Rand: A Sense of Life."

Producer/director Michael Paxton, long associated with Rand's work, follows her eventful life from childhood in Russia (where she was born Alyssa Rosenbaum), to early years as an extra and screenwriter in Hollywood, to her triumphant best sellers "The Fountainhead" and "Atlas Shrugged," and to her role in developing the "Objectivist" movement, ending with her death in 1982 at age 78.

In telling this story, he uses an extraordinarily rich collection of intimate still photographs and some remarkable TV interviews featuring the heavily accented tiger lady with the burning black eyes parrying ideas with the likes of Mike Wallace and Phil Donahue.

Unfortunately, this 2½-hour film relies too heavily on recollections from just two of her friends and followers, while ignoring potentially important issues in her life.

How did she feel about the lack of children in her 50-year marriage to Frank O'Connor? With her Jewish background, how did she react to the Holocaust or the rebirth of Israel? The film also glosses over feuds and fissures in her movement (some complicated by her affair with Nathaniel Branden), and would have benefited from some commentators critical of Rand—providing perspective on the life-long controversy surrounding her.

One of the intellectual heroines of this century also deserves more heroic background music, but on balance this biography still succeeds in bringing her to life; it should please Randroids and intrigue all others.

NEWSDAY, 2/13/98, Part II/p. B6, John Anderson

It's tough to say what's more depressing: That the hagiographic "Ayn Rand: A Sense of Life" should be Oscar-nominated as Best Documentary while something like "Fast, Cheap and Out of Control" is not. Or, as the film's TV clips remind us, afternoon television once consisted of Phil Donahue and a writer/philosopher like Rand, instead of Jerry Springer and the two-headed children of Satan-worshipping troglodytes.

While the "Donahue" clips included in Michael Paxton's docu-biography are pretty discouraging, so is the movie. The life of Rand—author of "We the Living," "The Fountainhead" and "Atlas Shrugged" and the founder of the philosophy she called "objectivism"—is recounted with, all the awe and reverence accorded the Lives of the Saints. Which is strange considering that Rand rejected all religious, social or political movements as "collectivism" in favor of enlightened self-interest and rational thought.

Nowhere in this tale—which begins with Rand's birth in czarist St. Petersburg (as Alice Rosenbaum), traverses the Hollywood of Cecil B. DeMille (who gave her her first screenwriting job) and follows her successes as one of the world's best-selling novelists and the conscience-salving guru of big business—does it ever entertain the notion that she might have been a crank.

And given the controversy that surrounded Rand and her philosophy—simply, that every person has the inalienable right to their pursuit of happiness—it seems incumbent to at least explore what her critics had to say. As narrated by TV actress Sharon Gless, however, Rand's life was one long striving toward genius, with those who might have interrupted her dismissed as not just misguided but possibly evil.

During the staging of her first produced play, "The Night of January 16th" (a courtroom drama in which audience members were chosen for the jury), we're told Rand had to withstand "the tortuous process of trying to protect her script from changes." We are told about neither the nature of the changes nor the torture. When Rand, while married to actor Frank O'Connor, gets swept off her feet by the correspondence of her lover-to-be Nathaniel Branden it was because "his letter was so intelligent, his questions so astute." We're given no evidence. After "Atlas Shrugged," the book's critics "viciously attempted to discredit her and her work." Why? Why not?

For a film about a woman so opposed to religion, this one depends a lot on faith. And Rand probably deserves better—even though her work, like a lot of pop-philosophic phenomena, has the popularity it has because it appeals to people's worst interests. The gifted deserve to realize their dreams, she says. All well and good. But it's like Nietzsche's view of the *ubermensch*. Rare is the person who thinks of himself as merely a mensch.

VILLAGE VOICE, 2/17/98, p. 111, J. Hoberman

Ayn Rand—subject of Michael Paxton's two-hour-and-20-minute documentary—was a unique combination of Adam Smith, Nietzsche, and Jacqueline Susann. Rand's bestselling novels, *The Fountainhead* and *Atlas Shrugged*, were blatantly tendentious, written to illustrate her engagingly solipsistic mix of libertarian politics, free-market fundamentalism, and heavy-breathing hero worship.

Like the Marxist regime she fled (and whose term "objective" she appropriated), the Russian-born Rand was an outspoken atheist. She did, however, loathe collectivism, considering self-sacrifice an evil and big business the nation's most persecuted minority. "This odd little woman is attempting to give a moral sanction to greed and self-interest," is how Gore Vidal put it in 1961, summing up Rand's subsequent popularity among middle-level Reaganauts, despite her juicy contempt for Reagan himself. Nothing if not rational, she despised his opposition to abortion.

Ayn Rand—A Sense of Life opens with its subject on TV explaining her credo to newsman Mike Wallace. with her '20s-style bobbed hair, heavy accent, and iconic dollar-sign brooch, the founder of Objectivism was perversely mediagenic—so positive in her giddy pronouncements she seems an avatar of Camille Paglia. Too bad Sam Fuller never told her story for, never less than worshipful, Paxton's doc is a sluggish hagiography—its cultish quality accentuated by the flowery narration and reliance on the same few talking heads.

Perhaps to emphasize Rand's rugged individualism, Paxton makes no mention of her Jewish background (a factor in her blunt disregard for Christian pieties). Nor does he acknowledge her most influential disciple, Alan Greenspan. Indeed, a bit of HUAC testimony aside, there's no indication of any role Rand played in American politics—no references to the Young Americans for Freedom, the Goldwater candidacy, or the *National Review*. (Her assertion that "if anyone destroys the country, it will be the conservatives" is left tantalizingly unelaborated.) TV talk shows rule, although Paxton's greatest scoop is the footage of Rand as an extra in Cecil B. DeMille's silent *King of Kings*.

If Rand's greatest show-biz triumph was compelling Warners to shoot her exact script for *The Fountainhead*, her most endearing fantasy was that Marilyn Monroe's onscreen beauty proved that she was "born and reared in some radiant utopia." What could be more rational than that?

Also reviewed in:
NEW YORK TIMES, 2/13/98, p. E16, Janet Maslin
VARIETY, 2/16-22/98, p. 57, Todd McCarthy

BABE: PIG IN THE CITY

A Universal Pictures release of a Kennedy Miller film.   *Executive Producer:* Barbara Gibbs. *Producer:* George Miller, Doug Mitchell, and Bill Miller. *Director:* George Miller. *Screenplay:* George Miller, Judy Morris, and Mark Lamprell. *Based on characters created by:* Dick King-Smith.   *Director of Photography:* Andrew Lesnie. *Editor:* Jay Friedkin and Margaret Sixel. *Music:* Nigel Westlake. *Music Editor:* Christo Curtis. *Sound:* Ben Osmo and (music) Christo Curtis. *Sound Editor:* Julius Chan, Gareth Vanderhope, and Wayne Pashley. *Casting:* Alison Barrett, Nicki Barrett, Barbara Harris. *Production Designer:* Roger Ford. *Art Director:* Colin Gibson. *Set Designer:* Tony Raes. *Set Decorator:* Kerrie Brown. *Set Dresser:* Glen W. Johnson.   *Special Effects:* Tad Pride. *Costumes:* Norma Moriceau. *Make-up:* Lesley Vanderwalt. *Stunt Coordinator:* Guy Norris. *Running time:* 90 minutes. *MPAA Rating:* G.

CAST: Magda Szubanski (Mrs. Esme Hoggett); James Cromwell (Farmer Hogget); Mary Stein (Landlady); Mickey Rooney (Fugly Floom).

VOICES: E. G. Daily (Babe);   Danny Mann (Ferdinand); Glenne Headly (Zootie);   Steven Wright (Bob);   James Cosmo (Thelonius);   Nathan Kress and Myles Jeffrey (Easy);   Stanley Ralph Ross (Pitbull and Doberman);   Russi Taylor (Pink Poodle); Adam Goldberg (Nigel and Alan);   Bill Capizzi (Sniffer Dog);   Miriam Margolyes (Fly);   Hugh Weaving (Rex); Roscoe Lee Browne (Narrator).

OTHER CAST AND VOICES: Paul Livingston (Hot Headed Chef);   Babs McMillan (Matriarch);   Matthew Parkinson (Nervous Waiter);   Julie Godfrey (Suspicious Neighbor); Kim Story (Judge);   Richard Carter and Simon Westaway (Detectives);   Margaret Christensen (Haughty Woman);   Katie Leigh (Kitten);   Janet Foye and Pamela Hawken (Mrs. Hoggett Friends);   Basil Clarke (Doctor);   Cecilia Yates (Flight Attendant);   Damian Monk and Terrell Dixon (Customs Guards);   Gabby Millgate (Female Officer);   Anthony Phelan (Security Guard); Van Epperson (Night Cleaner);   Mark Gerber and Ken Radley (Motorcycle Cops);   John Samaha (Van Cop); Paul Moxley and Gareth Clydesdale (Tough Guys); Ken Johnson (Court Stenographer);   Jennifer Kent (Lab Lady);   Richard Huggett (Cop);   John Walton (Padded Raider);   Gandhi MacIntyre and Christian Manon (Lab Technicians);   Sacha Horler (Night Nurse);   John Upton (Sick Boy);   Peter Callan (Hospital Doctor);   Dean Nottle (Doctor in Tails);   Paul Maybury (Hospital Orderly);   Saskia Campbell (Woman in Billowing Gown); Kristoffer Greaves (Chef);   Dominic Condon (Kitchen Hand); Elizabeth Allen (Lady Zammitt); Evelyn Krape (Old Ewe and Alley Cats);   Charles Barlett (Cow);   Michael Edward-Stevens (Horse);   Al Mancini and Larry Moss (Feisty Fish);   Jim Cummings (Pelican);   Dann Mann (Tug);   Russi Taylor (Choir Cat);   Nathan Kress (Tough Pup).

LOS ANGELES TIMES, 11/25/98, Calendar/p. 1, Kenneth Turan

Anyone who earns more than $100 million worldwide is going to lose some of their innocence. Even if it's a pig. Especially if it's a pig.

Undeniably clever and inventive, "Babe: Pig in the City" has nevertheless sacrificed part of the freshness and buoyancy that made the original "Babe" so luminous. This sequel is more elaborate, more calculated and more self-consciously dark than its deservedly beloved predecessor.

Part of this comes from the inevitable Hollywood reflex to throw money at the follow-up to a success. This "Babe" reportedly cost nearly three times the original and is said to have four times the animatronic and computer-generated special effects of its predecessor.

Unable to resist the dictum that bigger means better, "Pig in the City," impressive technological wonders notwithstanding, has a tendency to flounder in its overproduced elements.

The first "Babe's" success also influenced Australian director George Miller, who produced and co-wrote (with director Chris Noonan) the original, to step in and direct as well this time around. This may not have been such a good idea.

Miller is a much-admired director, with films like the "Mad Max" trilogy, "The Witches of Eastwick" and "Lorenzo's Oil" to his credit. But as those titles show, he naturally gravitates toward darker material and that tendency inevitably colors "Pig in the City."

Unsettling, though not quite nightmarish, this new "Babe" includes among its incidents a chase by a terrifying bull terrier, a human character carried out in a very realistic coma, animals that barely escape being shot to death, drowning, suffocating and hanging themselves, as well as assorted scenes of animal humiliation and unhappiness. This may not be what parents have in mind for their smallest children.

It's true that bad things happened in the original "Babe," but the picture's overall tone was nowhere near as somber as the new version's is, despite numerous moments of humor. Though it doesn't go that far, "Pig in the City" does put one in mind of the penchant for the grotesque that marked Tim Burton's ill-fated "Batman Returns."

"Pig in the City" nominally picks up where the original "Babe" left off, with the beloved porker basking in the adulation of "Welcome Home Pig" parades after proving himself to be a sheepherder without peer. Almost immediately something bad happens: Fanner Hoggett (James Cromwell) nearly gets crushed to death by an errant piece of farm machinery (and in fact is barely a presence in the rest of the film).

With sullen bankers threatening to foreclose on the farm, wife Esme (Magda Szubanski) has no choice but to accept an offer for a personal appearance by Babe in a distant locale.

Tagging along are some of the funniest elements from the first film, animals who have lost none of their charm in the transition. Ferdinand the self-important duck still says what the others will not ("You'll be in the company of a serial killer," he quacks to Babe about his trip with Esme) and the trio of singing mice amusingly enlarge their repertory to include Edith Piaf s "Non, Je ne Regrette Rien" and the Elvis Presley hit "Are You Lonesome Tonight."

Changing planes in a mythical city, Esme and Babe run into more problems. An officious drug-sniffing dog maliciously fingers the pair, leading to an unhappy strip-search for Esme and causing Babe and his human to miss their connection and get stuck in the metropolis.

They end up in the Flealands Hotel run by an animal lover (Mary Stein) who is as tall and angular as Esme is short and round. Dogs live on one floor, cats on another, but the most troublesome animals are a family of hipster show-biz chimpanzees named Zootie, Bob and Easy who board with a melancholy orangutan named Thelonius and work for aging vaudevillian Fugly Floom (Mickey Rooney).

Things don't work out well for Esme in the city; she even manages to get herself arrested. In the interim, Babe interacts with the hotel animals and runs into a whole gang of abandoned strays on the city streets.

"Pig in the City" definitely has its amusing moments, and these new animals provide their share. There's a tiny kitten who wails, "I'm hungry," (and makes an amusing reappearance at the tail end of the film's very long credits) as well as a pink poodle who has the regrets of "A Streetcar Named Desire's" Blanche DuBois.

Fortunately, despite a change in vocal talent from Christine Cavanaugh to E.G. Daily, Babe is still Babe. Though told it's "a dog-eat-dog world and there's not enough dogs to go around," this pig on a mission continues to be upbeat and positive.

As for the rest of the production, its smarts notwithstanding, audience members will find it harder than it should be not to empathize with the animal who asks, "When is something good going to happen to me?" Not soon enough.

NEW YORK, 12/14/98, p. 58, Peter Rainer

The advance word on *Babe: Pig in the City* was that it was "problematic"—studiospeak for uncommercial. Its benefit premiere in Los Angeles had been canceled amid dire rumors that the picture was too scary, too loud, too violent, too everything. This piqued my interest. *Babe II. Dark Meat*—what a concept! The first *Babe* was such a transcendently charming experience that redoing it wouldn't have worked anyway; it would be like trying to be a virgin again. Better to shake things up.

As it turns out, the new *Babe* isn't the horror show that was rumored. But it's certainly more raucous and rough-edged than the original. Arguably, it's even better. George Miller, the co-producer and co-writer of *Babe*, has directed and co-scripted the sequel, and his *Mad Max* dark roots are showing. The set pieces have a hearty grotesqueness, and the action is full-throttle. The film's showcase sequence is an extended chase in which the wee pig is pursued by a pit bull, and it has as much vroom as anything in *The Road Warrior*. I can understand why the executives at Universal were concerned: This sort of thing doesn't bode well for the franchise. So what? *Babe: Pig in the City* is every bit as funny as its predecessor, but it's funny in a screwler, twistier way.

By bringing the pig into the urban hell of strays and pet impounders, Miller—with his co-writers, Judy Morris and Mark Lamprell, and his animal trainers and animatronic experts—opens up a brave new world. Babe is the country rube in the big city, but he's also the rube as holy fool. By the film's end, his goodness triumphs over the Gotham grunge. ("I'm just a pig on a mission," he says.) In *Babe*, he was a leader of sheep. Now he's a leader of men—and ducks, chimps, poodles, even pit bulls. His innocence proves cast-iron.

Babe is first brought to the city by Farmer Hoggett's ovoid wife, Esme (Magda Szubanski), in a botched plan to feature him in a fair and use the fee to stave off the farm's foreclosure. They end up residents in a four-story rooming house—the Flealands Hotel—catering to pets. From its attic lookout, Babe surveys the skyline—it's the shot used in ads for the film—and sees a scrunched melange of Manhattan, Hong Kong, Hollywood, Paris. It's an intimidating vista. By contrast, the rooming house is a romper-room oasis. The rickety, dark-toned majesty of the place suits its denizens, including the courtly orangutan Thelonius; Bob the hepcat chimp and his wife,

Zootie, and brother, Easy; and, among other squallers and squawkers, a Neapolitan mastiff, an English bulldog, and a fleet-fingered capuchin monkey. If Charles Dickens had created a bestiary, it might have resembled this one: It's positively jovial with oddity.

Miller doesn't ask us to recognize the humanness of these critters. He doesn't go in for a lot of goopy anthropomorphism. Instead, he exults in his menagerie's animalness. In *Babe: Pig in the City,* being an animal is the highest station in life. The people we see—not just the porcine Esme but also her flamingo-thin husband, Farmer Hoggett (James Cromwell), and the rooming-house landlady (Mary Stein), with her whippet profile, and the chipmunk-cheeked clown Fugly Floom (Mickey Rooney)—haven't quite achieved the full-fledged look of their bestial counterparts. They're honorary members of the club, animals-in-transition.

The film is full of exemplary gestures, like the way Thelonius attempts to save his goldfish friend from marauding animal impounders without thinking to save himself, or the pelican who transports the wisequacking Ferdinand the duck in his bill before releasing him high above the city with the words "Farewell, noble duck." Flealick the arthritic terrier spins out in a chase and has an enchanted, end-of-life reverie in which he leaps loose-limbed at butterflies. And then there's Babe's finest moment, when he suddenly wheels around in that pit-bull chase and calmly asks his pursuer: "One simple question. Why?"

Babe doesn't comprehend why animals—or people— self-destructively play out their natures. The pit bull clues him in: "I have a professional obligation to be malicious." And yet, when Babe's generosity redeems his attacker, it's as if all of evolution had suddenly been overruled. Babe brings together dogs and cats, pink poodles and pit bulls. Kids barred from this movie by wary parents are missing out on a helluva role model.

Still, I don't want to overstate the film's goody-goodyness. *Babe: Pig in the City* is no *Gandhi.* It's also not an archetypal quest. In interviews, Miller has attempted to frame Babe as a mythic hero a la Joseph Campbell and all that jazz. But this is not at all how we experience the porker. (Miller blabbed the same line when he made the *Mad Max* movies, and *Lorenzo's Oil,* too. He's got myth-on-the-mind.) If the new *Babe* should be compared to anything, it's to those epic questers the Marx Brothers. Whether he admits it or not, Miller is a gonzo first and an educator second—a distant second. His new film is too *spirited* to be instructional. It's all over the place. At times it seems to summon up the whole history of show business, from fleabag vaudeville animal-novelty acts to the latest in animatronic whoop-de-doo. The animals are like the apotheosis of all the performing pets we've ever seen in the movies; each one is a stunner, and because they can talk, they're more vivid—and, for that reason, a bit more nightmarish too. They assume personalities that remind us of everybody from mafiosi to the Beats, and the shock is in how easily we buy the transformation. After a while, there's no dissonance at all: The alternate universe has become the real universe.

Miller loves the clangor of butting high culture with low. It's no accident that the Hollywood sign sits across from the Eiffel Tower in his skyline. Once again, as in the original *Babe,* he mixes in music from Saint-Saëns's Third Symphony—and it has never sounded better than when it's being trilled by singing mice. Elvis and Edith Piaf are similarly mouseketeered. He has the film's narrator say: "You can't always put things back together, but sometimes you can look at things afresh," and that's what he's done here. He's bid a frenzied farewell to the old *Babe* and given us a delirious new joyride.

NEW YORK POST, 11/25/98, p. 47, Rod Dreher

[*Babe: Pig in the City* was reviewed jointly with *A Bug's Life*; see Dreher's review of that film.]

NEWSDAY, 11/25/98, Part II/p.B3, Jack Mathews

Whatever was lost in the frantic, eleventh-hour editing of George Miller's sequel to his 1995 sleeper hit "Babe" is not apparent in the final product. "Babe: Pig in the City" is a terrific sequel, building on the magical qualities of the first film, while telling a completely new story in a new and even more inventive landscape.

Framed by scenes at the Hoggetts' farm, where orphaned Babe went from ham-on-the-hoof to national sheepdog champion, "Babe 2" takes the porcine hero to the Big City to end all Big

Cities, a metropolis that looks like a combination of Manhattan, Paris, Hollywood, Sydney, San Francisco, Rio, Seattle and... well, just see how many landmarks you recognize.

Our view of the city is Babe's view, from an attic portal of the ramshackle hotel where he and Mrs. Hoggett settle. It's the only hotel in town that allows animals, and the hotel's other pet guests are breeds apart from those at the farm—a family of chimps, a solemn orangutan, a Capuchin monkey, a Tabernacle Choir of cats and every conceivable breed of dog except those who would herd sheep.

Miller, and his co-writers Judy Morris and Mark Lamprell, have conceived a simple adventure, and placed the emphasis on characters, dialogue and effects. An accident has left farmer Hoggett (James Cromwell) bed and debt-ridden, and in order to save the farm, Mrs. Hoggett decides to take Babe to a fair where he's to receive a handsome fee for a sheep-pig demo.

En route, Mrs. Hoggett and Babe miss a connecting flight. No sooner do they settle in the hotel than Mrs. Hoggett is thrown in jail, leaving Babe alone, having to prove himself all over again with a new clique of strange animals.

in one of the film's two main set pieces, Babe is sent into a dark alley by the mischievous chimps, thinking he is there to herd sheep, but finding instead a ferocious pit bull, which chases him all over the neighborhood. From a technical standpoint, this is one of the most amazing film chases in years, though small children are also likely to find it frightening. But the payoff is enormous. Babe not only survives but rescues his pursuer from a drowning, making a friend who, when the animal catchers raid the hotel, will change the course of the animals' immediate destiny.

"Babe 2" is a big movie, with sets nearly as elaborate as those in the Batman series, and its costs reportedly soared $30 million over budget. But the money is all there—in the detail of the architecture and settings, in the canals and shadowy walkways of the Venice-like neighborhood where the action takes place. And, most important, it's there in the special effects, in the anthropomorphing of the animals' dialogue.

You've seen talking animals before, but you've never seen their lips move like this. For a while, you're doing doubletakes, wondering if the mouths really go with the faces. But you soon give up and simply accept that they do.

Originally rated PG for language (The most shocking line that remains has a cat calling a dog a "butt-sniffer."), "Babe" was also said to be in trouble for its darkness. It's still dark, in some of its themes, and parents should still use discretion, but it seems to me the farther we get from the Brothers Grimm, the sillier we get about the dark side of the fairy tale.

NEWSWEEK, 12/7/98, p. 74, David Ansen

"Babe: Pig In the City" has already taken a certain amount of abuse for what it isn't. It isn't "Babe." And why should it be? The original was complete unto itself. Not content to repeat himself, George ("Mad Max") Miller, who produced the first and now directs the sequel, comes up with an equally but differently wondrous fantasy. Darker, deeper, more Dickensian, it's one of the most visually dazzling films of the year; if it weren't considered a kids' movie, it might better be recognized as a stunning example of surrealist filmmaking. And it's fun, too: where else could you hope to encounter that trio of singing mice crooning "Non, Je Ne Regrette Rien?

Leaving the bucolic Hoggett Farm behind, Babe is taken via jet to the big city by Esme Hoggett (Magda Szubanski) on a desperate money-raising mission to save the farm from its creditors. The trip is a calamity. Stranded in a chaotic and threatening metropolis—brilliantly imagined as a timeless distillation of New York, Tokyo, London, Paris, L.A. and Venice—the open-hearted Babe gets a fast education in the school of urban hard knocks.

The movie really comes into its own inside the dusty, Gothic rooms of the Flealands Hotel, a haven for homeless animals run by a towering landlady (Mary Stein). Here we meet an astonishing menagerie: a chorus of full-throated cats, an arthritic Jack Russell terrier and, most remarkable of all, a family of hipster showbiz monkeys who perform for a decrepit clown played by Mickey Rooney. The family includes the dapper, magisterially melancholy Thelonius (an orangutan) and the bubble-gum-popping chimp Zootie (voice of Glenne Headly), a soulful, pregnant floozy in tattered bathrobe. Miller has evoked more humanity in his animal ensemble than many recent human casts have been able to generate. Refusing to take the broad, crude "Dr. Dolittle" route, he aims for emotional realism, daringly mixing slapstick, melancholy, wit and horror, often in a single scene. The new "Babe" hits chords you don't expect in "family entertainment." The results may, at moments, be too disturbing for the very young (strangled dogs; dark alleyways), but anyone over 10 should be delighted.

Over and over, the virtuoso Miller and his team of designers, FX experts and animal trainers come up with jaw-dropping "how'd they do that?" moments. What "Pig in the City" lacks is the kind of rousing emotional climax the original achieved at the sheep-herding contest. Well, you can't have everything. But what this wildly inventive sequel delivers is more than enough. Don't look a gift hog in the mouth.

SIGHT AND SOUND, 2/99, p. 38, Nick Roddick

Having won the local sheep trials, Babe the pig returns to Hoggett Farm in triumph as his fame spreads around the world. Farmer Hoggett and his wife Esme turn down all invitations for Babe to make personal appearances, until an accident leaves Hoggett laid up in plaster. Esme is unable to cope and the bank threatens foreclosure. The Hoggetts then accept an invitation for Babe to open a state fair for a large appearance fee, and Esme and Babe set off for the city by air.

Babe strikes up a conversation with a drug-sniffing dog at the airport, resulting in Esme being detained and them missing their connecting flight. Stranded in the city, they end up in the Flealands Hotel—the only one which will take pigs. The Flealands is home to a wide selection of animals, many of whom work in Fugly Floom's circus. Excepting Babe's difficulty with a group of light-fingered monkeys, things go well enough until the little pig disrupts one of Fugly's shows, setting off a series of disasters which culminate in a raid on the Flealands by the city authorities, who impound all the animals.

Babe and several others escape and mount a successful rescue plan, after which Esme returns to the farm with rather more animals than she left with.

Although there can be no denying its extraordinary (and well deserved) success, the original Babe was never quite the out-of-nowhere film hailed by commentators at the time. Like Crocodile Dundee, it carefully calculated its appeal for the North American market; and, as with the Paul Hogan hit, international distribution was handled by a US major, ensuring the worldwide release would follow if it scored in the US. But, for all the calculations that went into its making, it did preserve a sweetness and a limited focus—with the exception of the prologue and the climactic sheep trials, it never left Hoggett Farm—which, in retrospect, account for much of its success. Babe Pig in the City, by contrast, goes for the big effect wherever possible and adds so many new talking animals that Babe himself (or herself, as one injudicious close-up reveals) begins to function rather like Spanky in The Little Rascals: as the leader of the gang but no longer the subject of the film.

It starts promisingly, with Babe's triumphant return from the sheepdog trials, even if the crowds do look a little thin. And the farcical series of events that leads to Farmer Hoggett's injury, perfectly timed and counterpointed by the deadpan narration, has all the élan of the earlier film, culminating in the sequel's best single moment, when the Singing Mice burst into a passionate rendition of 'Je ne regrette rien'. After that, however, it's all downhill.

True, production designer Roger Ford's 'global city' is a triumph: a surreal juxtaposition of a Gaudíesque neighbourhood vaguely modelled on Venice, California, a megalopolis that seems to be Sydney Harbour out of Fritz Lang, and the Manhattan skyline (with Rio's Sugar Loaf, the Eiffel Tower, Big Ben and the Hollywood sign thrown in for good measure). But, for all the pre-release talk of a "dark, Felliniesque vision" which was supposed to have scared Universal into cancelling preview screenings, what we get is not so much Fellini as John Landis, as each potentially comic set-up is laboriously worked through and gussied up with stunts.

Comedy, it seems, is not writer/director George Miller's forte. Some ideas, like the enormous cats' chorus lined up in one room of the Flealands, are simply wasted. Others, like the climax, in which Esme, Babe and assorted animal aides disrupt a charity dinner, seem not to know when to stop—particularly so with an extremely difficult stunt which has Esme bouncing across the room on some kind of elasticated harness. Frankly, the whole thing was done much better in Dunston Checks In, which had several of the same jokes, but the added bonus of seeing Faye Dunaway buried in a giant cream-cake.

TIME, 12/7/98, p. 226, Richard Schickel

Like so much in this harsh world, Babe the sweet-souled, stouthearted pig worked better as a surprise than he does as a sequel. You can't blame the little porker; fame has not gone to his head. But his handlers, led by director George Miller, have succumbed to a desire to test the powers of his innocence against creatures more ferocious than those that inhabited Farmer Hoggett's essentially benign barnyard. Or maybe it was the powers of their special-effects wizardry that they wanted to strut, for the cast members of "Babe: Pig in the City" are larger, busier and—shall we say?—more emotionally complex than their predecessors. They are mostly residents of the Flealands Hotel, a flophouse in a hellish—well, anyway, heckish—imaginary metropolis where Babe and Mrs. Hoggett (Magda Szubanski) are obliged to take refuge when a personal appearance Babe was supposed to make goes awry.

Babe's new pals are a testy, teasing, but not entirely lovable lot, among them a poodle that owes a lot to Tennessee Williams' damaged females, a pit bull whose lineage might be traced back to The Godfather's family, and a game, crippled mutt that seems to have been inspired by old Lon Chaney roles. In short, they are knowing yet desperate inventions. So is the farcical but flat rescue that Babe and Mrs. Hoggett lead when their friends are impounded by motivelessly malign city authorities. Studio executives ordered last-minute fixes on the film because they found it too dark in tone, but its inherent, insoluble problem is that in its frenzy to top the original, it has lost touch with the first film's gently whimsical spirit.

VILLAGE VOICE, 12/8/98, p. 134, Amy Taubin

Babe: Pig in the City is both rougher and more sophisticated than the original Babe. Its story line is more fragmented, its politics less profoundly progressive. There are no scenes in the sequel as elaborately choreographed as Babe's foray into the house to confiscate the alarm clock, no relationships as complex and moving as the one that bound two genuine eccentrics—the pig and Farmer Hoggett (James Cromwell).

There is, however, a great set—as Dickensian as it is postmodern—that collages bits of New York, Hollywood, Sydney, Hong Kong, Venice, and a half dozen other cities. And there are some winning new characters: a taciturn, elderly orangutan; a well-matched chimpanzee couple who become the parents of darling twins; a pink-dyed stray poodle who sounds like Blanche Dubois; and an arthritic Jack Russell terrier who speeds along with the help of wheels attached to his back legs.

Babe himself is little changed from when we last saw him. If anything, he seems slightly smaller than before, about the same size as the pit bull who becomes his guardian during his adventures in the big city. He still has that snuffly wet nose, those mournful blue eyes, and, even though there's a new actress speaking for him (E.G. Daily), that beguilingly soft, eager, yearning voice.

This Babe opens with the pig and Farmer Hoggett's triumphant return from the sheep-herding competition where, if you remember, Babe took first prize. But Babe has little time to enjoy his newfound fame as a sheep-pig. A horrible accident caused by Babe's clumsiness leaves Farmer Hoggett in head-to-toe casts and braces. Attempting to save the farm from bankruptcy, Babe and Mrs. Hoggett (Magda Szubanski) wind up in a foreign city where no one seems to like animals or country folk, and where law enforcement is more predatory than the human and animal populations it's meant to control.

Introduced by the sly title "Chaos Theory," the teeming bohemian quarter of the city—packed with skinheads, leather freaks, bikini-clad women, blank-faced cops in Ray-Bans—looks like something out of director George Miller's other signature film, Mad Max. Babe goes through most of the film wearing a spiked collar given to him by the pit bull whose life he heroically saves. Accessories, however cool, do not make over the pig. Babe doesn't accept the eat-or-be-eaten ethos of the city, and it's well that he doesn't. Instead, the new kid (and only pig) on the block proves that "a kind and steady heart can mend a sorry world" by rescuing several dozen pets and stray animals and shepherding them to a better life. As a theme or moral, this one is more conventional than the celebration of difference and the critique of hierarchies and stereotypes that enlivened the original Babe.

Hollywood scuttlebutt has it that the film was considerably toned down after the alarmed reactions of children at a preview screening. The hasty reedit (there were too many product tie-ins in place to delay the Thanksgiving release) may account for the patchy story line and a tone that's more frantic but less emotionally varied than in the first *Babe*. The chase scenes are as inventive as in the best *Road Runner* cartoons, but there's probably one too many of them, and the final one (despite the shower of blue balloons as ecstatic as the falling feathers in *Zero de Conduit* and the enthusiastic acrobatics of Mrs. Hoggett, who is the butt of some nasty fat jokes) goes on much too long.

Still, *Babe: Pig in the City* is enormously appealing and, like the original, appropriate for both children and adults, although not perhaps for tiny tots. The combination of live animals and animatronics is as wondrous as ever. What the narrator (Roscoe Lee Browne) says of the Hoggett farm, "It's in a place slightly to the left of the 20th century," also could be said of *Babe: Pig in the City*. Or, in the words of the pit bull, "What the pig says, goes!"

The secret of Babe's success is not only what he says but how he says it. The pig has one of the most seductive voices in the history of cinema—right up there with those of Delphine Seyrig, Jean-Luc Godard, and Marlon Brando. Most discussions of actors and of that mysterious quality called "presence" revolve around their faces and bodies—around distinctive features and parts, and how they work and move in concert. What's seldom mentioned is the voice, although, even more than the eyes, it's the mirror of the psyche, the index of intelligence, emotion, and physiology.

Also reviewed in:
CHICAGO TRIBUNE, 11/25/98, Tempo/p. 1, Mark Caro
NATION, 12/21/98, p. 35, Stuart Klawans
NEW YORK TIMES, 11/25/98, p. E1, Janet Maslin
VARIETY, 11/30-12/6/98, p. 64, Leonard Klady
WASHINGTON POST, 11/25/98, p. D1, Rita Kempley
WASHINGTON POST, 11/27/98, Weekend/p. 56, Michael O'Sullivan

BAD MANNERS

A Phaedra Cinema release of a Davis Entertainment Classics presentation in association with Skyline Entertainment Partners and Wavecrest Pictures of a J. Todd Harris/Stephen Nemeth production: *Executive Producer:* John Davis. *Producer:* J. Todd Harris, Stephen Nemeth, and Alan Kaplan. *Director:* Jonathan Kaufer. *Screenplay (based on his play "Ghost in the Machine):* David Gilman. *Director of Photography:* Denis Maloney. *Editor:* Robin Katz. *Music:* Ira Newborn. *Sound:* Ben Patrick and (music) Les Brockmann. *Casting:* Georgianne Walken and Sheila Jaffe. *Production Designer:* Sharon Lomofsky. *Set Decorator:* Susan Ogu. *Set Dresser:* Michelle Barker. *Costumes:* Katherine Jane Bryant. *Make-up:* Kelly Macneal and Rebecca Turner. *Running time:* 88 minutes. *MPAA Rating:* R.

CAST: David Strathairn (Wes Westlund); Bonnie Bedelia (Nancy Westlund); Saul Rubinek (Matt Carroll); Caroleen Feeney (Kim Matthews); Julie Harris (Professor Harper); Robin Pooley (First Musiciologist); Daniel Koch (Second Musicologist); Steve Forbert (Coffeehouse Troubadour).

LOS ANGELES TIMES, 10/9/98, Calendar/p. 4, Jack Mathews

[The following review by Jack Mathews appeared in a slightly different form in NEWSDAY, 10/9/98, Part II/p. B7.]

In the early moments of "Bad Manners," the filmed adaptation of David Gilman's "Ghost in the Machine," middle-aged academics Wes and Nancy Westlund (David Strathairn, Bonnie Bedelia) return to their New England home to find the wife's old college boyfriend Matt (Saul Rubinek) and his latest girlfriend Kim (Caroleen Feeney) standing at the door.

Though Matt is expected, it takes a moment for Nancy to recognize him. He's gained so much weight, she says.

The line would be innocuous enough if it weren't such a matter of the pot calling the kettle black. Bedelia has become so large that our immediate impression, given her shock at seeing Matt's girth, is that Nancy's pregnant. On the contrary, we soon learn, the couple haven't had sex since Methuselah was a freshman.

I'm not trying to show my own bad manners. This double-take is just an example of the odd mistakes made in this otherwise energized version of Gilman's play, a kind of knockoff of "Who's Afraid of Virginia Woolf?" The ages and relative conditions of the characters are important to the elements in the story, and movie audiences aren't accustomed to supplying quantum leaps of imagination.

"Bad Manners" throws these sexually contrasting couples, the barren academics and their nocturnally active guests, under one roof for two or three days of airy contention, sexual misconduct, jealousy, envy, accusations and remorse. Here are the dynamics of the foursome:

* Wes resents Matt, a renowned musicologist who's staying over while doing a series of lectures at nearby Harvard. At the same time, he's having trouble resisting his apparent seduction by Kim.
* Nancy is a tenured university professor, bewildered by her husband's faded passion and his dimming ambition.
* Matt's a condescending, self-adoring bore who regards Kim as a glorified assistant, even though it was her computer wizardry that isolated a musical mystery he's about to propose as evidence of the existence of God.

* Kim is a mystery in herself, a temptress who, when she's not thrashing the sheets with Matt, is coming on to Wes or trying to convince Nancy to recapture her sexual youth with the available studs at nearby college bars.

Compounding all this is a disappearing $50 bill. Wes believes Kim has stolen one from him, she believes he's stolen one from her, and their mates are caught in the cross-fire. Unlike his play, Gilman's script answers the mystery of the $50 bill as well as the question of whether Wes and Kim consummate their flirtation, as Matt charges. The information is more than we want, or need, to know.

The real fuel of the tory is in the nature and tensile strength of the relationships, and until they give into their urges to tie up the loose ends, Gilman and director Jonathan Kaufer ("Soup for One") keep us off balance and interested.

The four actors give solid performances, despite some odd casting. Feeney ("Denise Calls Up" is gorgeous, but too old and too obviously wise to be playing someone the others would regard, even for a minute, as a college bimbo. Still, her performance, and the lion's share of the script's best lines, maker her "Bad Manners'" best asset.

NEW YORK POST, 10/16/98, p. 44, Larry Worth

From first to last, the four protagonists of "Bad Manners" exchange a lot of grimaces and uneasy glances. In all likelihood, viewers will do the same.

The story concerns two couples—one a pair of fortysomething academics, the other a younger, hipper couple—who spend a weekend engaging in word games and power plays in a rambling old house.

Clearly, any parallels to the classic "Who's Afraid of Virginia Woolf?" are intentional. But the similarities end there.

This adaptation of playwright David Gilman's "Ghost in the Machine" not only feels stagey but utterly artificial. And the subjects for a few days' worth of arguments—ranging from a missing $50 bill to infidelities—are addressed with matching credibility.

Neophyte director Jonathan Kaufer deserves most of the blame, having choreographed the proceedings with the elan of Gomer Pyle. The ensuing mishmash actually takes about a dozen detours before its conclusive dead end.

Photography of the film's Cambridge, Mass., locale isn't a redeeming feature. Aside from a throwaway foray into Harvard Square, repeated shots of the focal residence make one assume Kaufer's resume includes a stretch at Architectural Digest.

But the saddest component is seeing an actor of David Strathairn's quality marooned by Gilman's stilted dialogue. Granted, Strathairn tries hard to rise to the occasion, but his role as a has-been scholar is a lost cause.

Making out slightly better is Bonnie ("Heart Like a Wheel") Bedelia—a pleasure to have back on-screen after a four-year absence—whose turn as a feisty college prof married to Strathairn allows for a few highlights.

Saul Rubinek and sexy newcomer Caroleen Feeney, cast as the central duo's sparring partners, are also light-years smarter than the screenplay. For that matter, how did Julie Harris, who barely registers in a virtual walk-on, get talked into this?

Star power aside, the film has little reason for being. In short, "Bad Manners" lacks style, grace and charm.

Also reviewed in:
CHICAGO TRIBUNE, 12/18/98, Friday/p. F, John Petrakis
NEW REPUBLIC, 11/2/98, p. 26, Stanley Kauffmann
NEW YORK TIMES, 10/9/98, p. E26, Stephen Holden
VARIETY, 6/9-15/97, p. 69, Todd McCarthy

BARNEY'S GREAT ADVENTURE: THE MOVIE

A PolyGram Filmed Entertainment release in association with Lyrick Studios. *Executive Producer:* Ben Myron. *Producer:* Sheryl Leach and Dennis DeShazer. *Director:* Steve Gomer. *Screenplay:* Stephen White.   *Story:* Stephen White, Sheryl Leach, and Dennis DeShazer. *Director of Photography:* Sandi Sissel. *Editor:* Richard Halsey. *Music:* Jan Rhees. *Music Editor:* Chris McGeary. *Choreographer:* Debra Brown. *Sound:* James LeBrecht. *Casting:* Ronna Kress.   *Production Designer:* Vincent Jefferds. *Art Director:* Collin Niemi. *Set Decorator:* Diane Lamothe.   *Special Effects:* Antonio Vidosa. *Costumes:* Francesca Chamberland. *Make-up:* Marie-Angèle Protat. *Stunt Coordinator:* Stéphane Lefebvre. *Running time:* 75 minutes. *MPAA Rating:* G.

CAST: George Hearn (Grandpa Greenfield); Shirley Douglas (Grandma Greenfield); Trevor Morgan (Cody Newton); Kyla Pratt (Marcella); Diana Rice (Abby Newton); Jeff Ayers (Baby Bop, Body); Jeff Brooks (BJ, Body); Julie Johnson (Baby Bop, Voice); David Joyner (Barney, Body); Bob West (Barney, Voice); Patty Wirtz (BJ, Voice); Alan Fawcett (Dad Newton); Jane Wheeler (Mom Newton); David Larouche and Edouard Larouche (Baby Fig); Renée Madeleine Le Guerrier (Mildren Goldfinch); Roch Jutras (Mr. Millet); John Dunn-Hill (Policeman); André St. Jean and Paul Vachon (Parade Stilt Walkers); Barry Taras (Sousaphone Player); Sheena Larkin (Woman With Hat); Matt Holland (Waiter); Alain Gendreau (Maître d'); Normand Carrière (Chez Snobble Delivery Man); Jean Filion and François Hébert (Circus Clowns); Ruby Rowat (Trapeze); Luc Tremblay (Acrobatic Bicycle); Mathieu Roy (Chinese Pole);   Jinny Jacinto (Contortionist); David Lebel (Trampolinist/Teeter Board Pusher); Alain Gauthier (Teeter Board Flyer); André St. Jean (Teeter Board Pusher); Roch Jutras (Teeter Board Spotter); Molly Saudek (Female Wire Walker); Michael Davis and David Lebel (Jugglers); Steffen Foster (Collector); James LeBrecht (Twinken's Voice).

LOS ANGELES TIMES, 4/3/98, Calendar/p. 20, David Kronke

The creators of the great purple scourge, Barney the Dinosaur, have an unspoken contract with parents palatable for all involved: We buy their videos and an occasional plush toy for our 3- and 4-year-olds and make Barney's brain trust obscenely wealthy; they in turn create benignly lobotomized entertainment that holds our non-demanding kids in thrall; our kids watch TV and allow us a few precious minutes of peace.

The most important element is parental trust in Barney to be blandly wholesome, so that we have to endure only a few seconds of it while we cue up the VCR for our tykes.

Family movies, on the other hand, imply a rather different contract: Parents buy tickets and popcorn for the whole family; filmmakers deliver light entertainment that kowtows to kids yet is not so brain-dead as to alienate sentient adults. "Barney's Great Adventure: The Movie," the first theatrical film featuring the green-bellied beast, takes that big old fat foot of Barney's and stomps that contract beyond recognition.

For a long stretch, "Barney's Great Adventure" is essentially plotless, as some kids and a token African American pal are left with farmer grandparents.

Two girls, about 7 or 8 (and therefore too old to like Barney in the real world, but I guess the filmmakers couldn't find 4-year-olds capable of competent line readings), love Barney, while the obnoxious, too-cool-for-the-room 10-year-old boy dismisses him—"Imagination? That's kid's stuff!" he snorts derisively, before Barney comes to life and upbraids him.

In a way, "Barney's Great Adventure" serves as a rare sort of revenge fantasy for younger siblings who have been constantly abused by older, "cooler" brothers and sisters; here, the bratty older kid is taught a lesson.

It also—finally!—shows that Barney indeed does have a mean streak, as he secretly, disingenuously delights in humiliating those who disparage him.

Initially, the film is taken up with singing public-domain songs and tuneless original ditties. The second half gets a little more surreal, as Barney and the kids chase a magical egg around town, encountering along the way a parade, a circus, a balloon show, a few drab eccentrics and Barney stalwarts B.J. and Baby Bop.

This section of the movie recalls, in turns, "8 1/2," "The Adventures of Baron Munchausen," "2001: A Space Odyssey" and "Close Encounters of the Third Kind," if only Mssrs. Fellini, Gilliam, Kubrick and Spielberg had been functional morons.

NEW YORK POST, 3/27/98, p. 44, Thelma Adams

For a big, purple dinosaur with a green belly and an insipid giggle, Barney inspires intense emotions. His parents despise his sticky-sweet "I'm OK, you're OK" television embrace, but they're not above plopping their entranced toddlers in front of the tube for some unfailing electronic baby-sitting.

Pre-schoolers adore Barney. What? Is it in the milk?

The only unbelievable thing about this fuzzy reptile from the PBS vaults is that public TV still has fund drives. The overstuffed star is a gold mine.

Now Barney is ready for his close-up in the feature-length "Barney's Great Adventure: The Movie." It opens today at Radio City Music Hall with a live pre-show, and next Friday in theaters everywhere.

Directed by Steve Gomer from Stephen White's script, the movie takes Barney from the schoolyard to the farm, the circus and into the heavens. He accompanies Cody and Abby Newton (Trevor Morgan and Diana Rice) and their multiculti friend (Marcella) Kyla Pratt to the country.

Cody, a crabby kid in shades, stands in for Barney haters everywhere. The girls are true believers. After a parade of pigs, sing-alongs and production values that would pass muster by the tough standards of Tony and Ridley Scott, even city slicker Cody finds himself adoring Barney.

Cody comes to believe in the imaginative powers Barney represents. We can't pretend to understand the cult of the nelly purple dino, but we recognize star power when we see it.

NEWSDAY, 3/27/98, Part II/p. B7, Bob Heisler

You won't die if you have to take your preschooler to see "Barney's Great Adventure: The Movie." For 73 of its 75 minutes, you might even find a charming, warm and surprisingly treacle-free story, unlike Barney's ubiquitous and occasionally preachy TV series.

For recent arrivals to planet Earth, Barney is a stuffed animal who, through the imagination of young children, turns into a 6-foot-tall, purple parent substitute. He's a soft authority figure who always wants to play make-believe, always has a new song to sing and is never bored. This makes him a public broadcasting and marketing franchise. It also makes usually rational people despise him with an anger reserved for uncurbed dogs and Martha Stewart.

But the very uncoolness of Barney to kids older than 7 is spun with winning effect into a plot device as the parents dump big brother Cody (Trevor Morgan), Barney owner Abby Newton (Rockville Centre's Diana Rice) and Abby's friend Marcella (Kyla Pratt) at the farm of Grandma and Grandpa (George Hearn and Shirley Douglas). The kids are older than the typical Barney rugrats. They aren't so sweet, either. They do sing and dance.

The cynical Cody's transformation into a kid with full powers of imagination is played out against a brightly colored quest to retrieve the egg of something called a Dreammaker. Yes, it will wind up as a plus-toy product extension. Just bear with it ... and sing. You know the words.

Barney and the kids do a lot of singing. They search for the egg while Barney distracts a fancy French restaurant full of adults with a snappy version of "If All the Raindrops Were Lemon Drops and Gum Drops." They chase it through a parade and into a circus (Cirque du Soleil), and finally back to the farm.

About those final two minutes. They sing The Song. The Song sets grown-up teeth on edge, like the words "Niagara Falls" in the old vaudeville skit. Just when you're starting to think you've gotten through a Barney movie without hearing it, everyone on screen starts: "I love you. You love me ..." If you know, the next line, you'll wish you were zipping up little jackets and talking about how wonderful it was to see Barney on the big screen.

And you can survive two minutes of The Song. You're a grown-up.

SIGHT AND SOUND, 7/98, p. 36, Amanda Lipman

Cody and Abby, with her friend Marcella and a baby go to stay at their grandparents' farm where Barney transforms from a kids' cuddly toy into a lifesize, talking purple dinosaur. When a mysterious rainbow-coloured egg lands in the barn, the children visit a local bird expert to find out what sort of egg it is.

They discover that it will reveal something important as long as it hatches where it was found. It disappears, and they embark on a chase to retrieve it through the local town, into a high-class restaurant, a circus and a ballooning expedition. They manage to return the egg to the barn just as it hatches Twinken, a little furry creature who shows them their dreams before flying off into the night sky in an explosion of fireworks. When all is quiet again, Barney and Twinken turn back into cuddly toys.

We may sigh that our kids have been encroached upon by yet another tacky merchandising gimmick, but children seem undisturbed by the aesthetics of the garish purple and green dinosaur who adorns more and more of their clothes and toys. Essentially, Barney has one characteristic: his goofy cheerfulness. Although he instructs kids in the power of the imagination, he only confirms what the children in *Barney's Great Adventure* (directed by Steve Gomer who made the kids' basketball film *Sunset Park*) already seem to know. It makes explicit an idea about imaginative power that has run through children's books and films since time began. This is all well and good as the children find themselves able to turn logs into aeroplanes and rusty old wheels into chariots, but it takes a disappointing turn at the end when the rainbow egg cracks and the great moment of truth they have been waiting for turns out to be a furry, gonk-like creature whose contribution is bathetic, to say the least.

More cheering is the film's notion that kids can and should be kids, that the sophistication to which big brother Cody aspires closes him off to other possibilities. Perhaps as a consequence, the film is quaintly reminiscent of a bygone era of children's musicals. There are nursery rhyme-like songs and a number of rather stagey dance routines. At the same time, the surreal appearances of Barney's dinosaur friends doing their comic turns throw in a touch of *Sesame Street*. All this is served up with the visual variety provided by the different locations to which the children's search takes them. One such, the absurdly posh restaurant, where waiters dance and strike dramatic poses until Barney shakes them out of it with a jazz number, takes us to the heart of the dinosaur's philosophy—that anything dislikable can be made likable by cheering it up.

So it becomes clear that childhood is intrinsically linked with a bonhomie that allows for no other feelings. And as a result, once they have learned the lesson, these kids are strangely well behaved. Even the baby does nothing but suck contentedly on his dummy. Children will probably take this as it comes, but accompanying adults may be left feeling just a little cheated.

Also reviewed in:
CHICAGO TRIBUNE; 4/3/98, Friday/p. D, John Petrakis
NEW YORK TIMES, 3/27/98, p. E28, Anita Gates
VARIETY, 3/30-4/5/98, p. 41, Todd McCarthy
WASHINGTON POST, 4/3/98, Weekend/p. 53, John F. Kelly

BASEKETBALL

A Universal Pictures release of a David Zucker production.   *Executive Producer:* Cleve
Landsberg. *Producer:* David Zucker, Robert LoCash, and Gil Netter. *Director:* David Zucker.
Screenplay: David Zucker, Robert LoCash, Lewis Friedman, and Jeff Wright.   *Director of
Photography:* Steve Mason. *Editor:* Jeffrey Reiner. *Music:* James Ira Newborn. *Music Editor:*
Terry Wilson. *Choreographyer:* Miranda Garrison. *Sound:* Hank Garfield and (music) Joseph
Magee. *Sound Editor:* Richard LeGrand, Jr. *Casting:* Junie Lowry-Johnson and Libby
Goldstein. *Production Designer:* Steven Jordan. *Art Director:* Bill Hiney. *Set Designer:* John
D. Jefferies Sr. *Set Decorator:* Anne D. McCulley. *Set Dresser:* John H. Maxwell. *Special
Effects:* Dave Kelsey. *Costumes:* Catherine Adair. *Make-up:* Nena Smarz. *Special Make-up
Effects:* Gil Mosko. *Stunt Coordinator:* Monty Cox. *Running time:* 105 minutes.   *MPAA
Rating:* R.

CAST: Trey Parker (Joe Cooper); Matt Stone (Doug Remer); Dian Bachar (Squeak Scolari);
Yasmine Bleeth (Jenna Reed); Jenny McCarthy (Yvette Denslow);   Ernest Borgnine (Ted
Denslow); Robert Vaughn (Baxter Cain); Trevor Einhorn (Joey); Bob Costas, Al Michaels,
Robert Stack, Reggie Jackson, Dan Patrick, Kenny Wayne, Tim McCarver, Jim Lampley,
Dale Earnhardt, Kareem Abdul-Jabbar, Victoria Silvstedt, and Reel Big Fish (Themselves);
Curt Gowdy (World Series Announcer);   Justin Chapman (Little Coop);   Matthew Murray
(Little Remer); Mark Goodson (Dirk Jansen); Matt Sloan (Darcy); Peter Navy Tuiasosopo
(Tuttle);   Robert E. Lee and Greg Grunberg (New Jersey Informants); Michael Garvey (San
Antonio Defender); Paul Michael Robinson (Psyche-Out Victim); Kevin Michael Richardson
(Peripatetic Player); Micah McCain (Heather); Cory Oliver (Brittany); Keith Gibbs (Davis);
Jayme Gallante (Redmond);   Francis X. McCarthy (Dr. Kaiser);   Blair Besten (Stephanie);
Stanley G. Sawicki (Skidmark Steve); Bret Lewis (News Anchor);   Richard Johnson, Joey
"Coco" Diaz, and Michael Matthys (Referees); Jill Gascoine (Hospital Nurse);   Charlotte
Zucker (Surgery Nurse); John Fink (Surgeon); Kato Kaelin (Driveway Announcer); David
Alan Osokow (Driveway Player); Iqbal Theba (Factory Manager); Susan Breslau (Denslow's
Niece Susan); Danielle Zucker and Maureen Ardolino (Inheritors); Andrew Herman (Cabbie);
Jeff Wright (Fireman);   Ray Xifo (Riverdance Referee); Titius Napoleon (Sumo Wrestler);
Julie Dolan (Beer Barrel).

LOS ANGELES TIMES, 7/31/98, Calendar/p. 10, Jack Mathews

[The following review by Jack Mathews appeared in a slightly different form in
NEWSDAY, 7/31/98, Part II/p. B2.]

   Matt Stone and Trey Parker, the... uh, talent behind Comedy Central's IQ-challenged "South
Park" cartoon show, take their act in front of the cameras in David Zucker's "BASEketball,"
where they prove to be dumber than "Dumb & Dumber," more adolescent than Beavis and Butt-
head, and about as funny as Bud Abbott and Lou Costello, now that they're dead.
   And the stars are the least of the film's problems!
   "BASEketball" is by far the most inane and badly written of the comedies made by any of the
creators of the classic 1980 sendup "Airplane!" There are about as many jokes attempted here,
but most of them travel like Stealth bombers, flying so low they can't even be detected by radar.
If this movie's a hit, the dumbing-down of America is complete.
   What's wasted here, besides time, money and the effort of innocent below-the-line wage
earners, is the ripely plump satirical target of contemporary professional sports. Basketball,

baseball, football, hockey, take your pick, they're all played by disloyal, largely thug morons who are overpaid by profiteering, antitrust-avoiding, jock-wannabe owners who would sell their souls, if they had 'em.

The film opens with a clever recap of the self-destruction of commercial American sports, bringing us to the doorstep of the new millennium, when a jaded country pines for a rebirth of cornfed innocence, a time when games were played by men who felt lucky to be playing like boys and when a Yankee or a Dodger was forever.

Enter Coop (Parker) and Remer (Stone), the almost literal live-action incarnations of Beavis and Butt-head (can cartoon characters sue?). Ten years out of high school, they're still knocking back brews and mumbling "Dude," fantasizing about women who'd rather undergo marrow transplants than have sex with them, and sharing a childhood dream—begun the day Coop caught Reggie Jackson's third home run during the 1977 World Series—that they'll someday be sports stars.

Their opportunity comes when they're challenged to a game of two-on-two half-court basketball at a party they've crashed. Rather than be shown up, Coop improvises a game that combines the rules of baseball and basketball with a defensive move called the "psych-out." The psych-out rule allows defensive players to do essentially anything they want to distract opponents from making shots.

Anyway, they win, and soon, the game is skyrocketing from a neighborhood craze to the new national pastime, with Coop, Remer and their runt pal, Squeak (Dian Bachar), the stars of the awesome Milwaukee Beers (to provide a micro-hint of the film's sophomoric flavor). The Beers have their own version of the Dallas Cowboy Cheerleaders, taken from the Merry Widow pages of the Victoria's Secret catalog, they have a stadium filled with rabid fans, and they are the new heroes of America's youth.

The plot itself is similar to "Major League." When the Milwaukee Beers owner (Ernest Borgnine) dies and leave the team to Coop, with the proviso that the team win the national championship or else, his idiot widow (Jenny McCarthy) takes up with a conniving rival owner (Robert Vaughn) in an attempt to ruin the Beers' chances.

Along the way, Coop will fall in love with a goody-two-shoes volunteer ("Baywatch's" Yasmine Bleeth, and the casting is meant to be a joke) at a Make a Wish-type foundation, and Remer will be seduced by the trappings of stardom, all leading to the big game and a buzzer shot.

The material is worse than banal. It's redundant.

"You smell like Christian Slater," one character comments to a drunk in one scene.

"You smell like Robert Downey Jr.," another character tells another drunk in another scene seconds later.

At least, Stone and Parker don't have reputations to uphold. No one expects much more than anatomical humor from these guys. The big losers of "BASEketball" are the sportscasters lending their names, presence and dignity to the proceedings. Namely, Bob Costas and Al Michaels, who appear as recurring characters—themselves—trying to breath life into the BASEketball games, while vulgarly mocking their own images.

At one point, Michaels expresses his excitement at the outcome of a game.

"You're excited?" Costas yells. "Feel these nipples!"

If you're old enough to see this movie without a parent or guardian and all that sounds encouraging, this review has failed, and failed badly.

NEW YORK POST, 7/31/98, p. 45, Thelma Adams

"No flipping," is Garry Shandling's anthem on HBO's "The Larry Sanders Show."

I watched the Comedy Central hit "South Park" once. It was OK. A commercial arrived. I flipped the remote control. I never looked back.

Watching David Zucker's "BASEketball," starring the Boyz N the Park, Trey Parker and Matt Stone, my trigger thumb ached to change the channel. I won't censor their sophomoric comedy; I just want my constitutional right to channel-surf.

Parker and Stone star as two losers, Coop and Remer. Unfit for anything but drinking "Cock" beer and throwing hoops, the perpetual adolescents stumble on a new sport, a driveway combo of baseball and basketball.

In a plot that makes "Major League III" look labyrinthine, the game becomes wildly popular. After team owner Ernest Borgnine chokes on a hot dog, Coop and Remer fight for the sport 's integrity against the venal Robert Vaughn.

Yasmine Bleeth and Jenny McCarthy limp along in the good-girl, bad-girl subplot. Like it or lump it, this is not a world where women count for much more than a way to psych out an opponent (e.g., your mother sucks socks in hell).

"South Park" visitors will recognize the easy comic targets: road kill, homosexuality, masturbation, boobs and bodily fluids, Zucker ("Naked Gun") co-wrote this junk before casting Parker and Stone; he helms with all the suspense of a Royals-Twins doubleheader.

At the climactic moment, Coop mockingly asks Remer: "Are you such a big star you're going to act in a Hollywood movie? F--kin' sellout." I've seen "South Park." What's to sell out?

NEWSWEEK, 8/10/98, p. 66, Jeff Giles

You'd think the success of "There's Something About Mary" would be a boon to other adolescent comedies this summer—that it would get audiences in touch with their inner 13-year-old and send them rushing back into theaters in search of laughs. But "Mary" is so genuinely demented that David Zucker's "BASEketball," for one, seems tepid by comparison. Trey Parker and Matt Stone, the creators and vocal talents behind "South Park," star as Coop and Remer, two slacker buddies who've never outgrown high school. One night, they invent a combination of baseball and basketball that storms the neighborhood—and then the nation. They hope BASEketball will return pro sports to a more innocent era. Before long, though, they're superstars, fighting over money and the love of a woman (Yasmine Bleeth). Zucker directed "Airplane!" and "The Naked Gun," and he relies on the same formula here: violent slap-stick, breast jokes, penis jokes and goofy casting. Jenny McCarthy and Ernest Borgnine—together at last.

"BASEketball" feels stale and inert. Still, Parker and Stone have a nice, giddy rapport, and it's a kick to hear traces of Cartman and Kenny in their dude-speak. The actors didn't write "BASEketball," but it might as well be their life story. They were college buddies who created a subversive cartoon out of paper and scissors, then found themselves—well, on the cover of this magazine, for one thing. The parallel is not lost on Parker and Stone, now 28 and 27. At one point, Remer (Stone) sits in the dugout, bedecked in gold chains and reading a script. Coop (Parker) scowls at him: "Now you're such a big shot you're gonna act in a Hollywood movie? F---ing *sellout*." For his sake, let's hope Remer picks a movie better than this.

VILLAGE VOICE, 8/11/98, p. 150, Dennis Lim

To get an idea of how unpalatable *BASEketball* could have been, you simply have to imagine the movie with Chris Farley and David Spade, or Cheech and Chong, or Matt LeBlanc and David Schwimmer. Which isn't to say that *South Park* creators Trey Parker and Matt Stone are charismatic in any conventional sense. More to the point, there's an affable, almost childlike enthusiasm that defines their work—as both trash auteurs and unlikely movie stars.

In David Zucker's latest bit of nonsense, Parker and Stone play two good-for-nothings who come up with a baseball-basketball conflation, the centerpiece of which is the "psyche-out—distracting the opposition by any means necessary. Couched as a satire of professional-sports venality, *BASEketball* unfolds against a busy backdrop of sight gags. Its transgressions don't measure up to *There's Something About Mary*'s more carefully calibrated gross-outs; Zucker and the boys—who improvised (it shows)—set the frat-house tone early on with a bout of underwear sniffing and vibrator licking. But the film works because of its borderline-surreal absurdity, and not its rudeness. *BASEketball*'s hit-and-run comic style is strictly hit-and-miss, but in the frenetic, manically indiscriminate Zucker universe, one hit for every 20 misses still works out to something like a chuckle a minute.

Also reviewed in:
CHICAGO TRIBUNE, 7/31/98, Friday/p. A, Michael Wilmington
NEW YORK TIMES, 7/31/98, p. E10, Stephen Holden
VARIETY, 8/3-9/98, p. 35, Leonard Klady

BATTLE OF CHILE, THE: PART 2: THE COUP D'ETAT

A First Run/Icarus Films release of an Equipo Tercer Año production with the collaboration of the Cuban Film Institute and Chris Marker. *Director (English and Spanish with English subtitles):* Patricio Guzmán. *Director of Photography:* Jorge Müller. *Editor:* Pedro Chaskel. *Music:* Robert M. Lepage. *Running time:* 91 minutes. *MPAA Rating:* Not Rated.

CAST: Patricio Guzmán (Narrator).

Also reviewed in:
NATION, 9/28/98, p. 34, Stuart Klawans
NEW YORK TIMES, 9/9/98, p. E5, Lawrence Van Gelder

BELLY

An Artisan Entertainment release of a Big Dog Films production. *Executive Producer:* James Bigwood. *Producer:* Ron Rotholz, Hype Williams, Robert Salerno, and Larry Meistrich. *Director:* Hype Williams. *Screenplay:* Hype Williams. *Story:* Anthony Bodden, Nasir Jones, and Hype Williams. *Director of Photography:* Malik Sayeed. *Editor:* David Leonard. *Music:* Stephen Cullo. *Music Editor:* Stuart Levy. *Sound:* Tod Maitland and (music) Gary Chester and Lawrence Manchester. *Sound Editor:* Steve Borne. *Casting:* Winsome Sinclair. *Production Designer:* Regan Jackson. *Art Director:* Nicholas Lundy. *Set Decorator:* Carol Silverman. *Costumes:* June Ambrose. *Make-up:* Sharyn Cordice. *Stunt Coordinator:* Julius LeFlore. *Running time:* 110 minutes. *MPAA Rating:* R.

CAST: DMX/Earl Simmons (Tommy); Nas/Nasir Jones (Sincere); Taral Hicks (Kisha); Tionne "T-Boz" Watkins (Tionne); Lavita Raynor (Kionna); Method Man/Clifford Smith (Shameek); Power/Oliver Grant (Knowledge); Louie Rankin (Lenox); Benjamin F. Muhammed (Reverend Saviour); Hassan Iniko Johnson (Mark); Tyrin Turner (Big); Stanley Drayton (Wise); James Parris (Lakid); Kurk Loder (Himself); Jay Black (Black); Shaun Morrison (Housekeeper); Frank Vincent (Roger); Eric Keith McNeil (Shorty); Xavier Simmons (Young Tommy); Monica Michaels (Club Manager); Jennifer "Nen" Gatien (Girl in Office); Anthony "Az" Cruz (Born); Micaal Stevens (Killer); Michael Woodhouse (Older Barber); Tyrone Lewis (Younger Barber); Carmen Yannuzzi, Jr. (Guard); Crystal N. Johnson (Knowledge's Cop Girlfriend); James Gresham (Speaker); Michael Manning (Teacher).

LOS ANGELES TIMES, 11/4/98, Calendar/p. 2, Kevin Thomas

Hype Williams' "Belly" starts its story of lifelong pals turned drug dealers at a provocative point—the pinnacle of their success. Tommy Brown (DMX) and Sincere (Nas) grew up in the projects in Queens, but now live in Long Island splendor.

First Sincere and finally Tommy begin to examine their lives, which is requiring them to take greater risks by peddling increasingly dangerous drugs. (Tommy only acts when he's blackmailed by government agents into attempting to assassinate a charismatic preacher, portrayed by actual minister Benjamin F. Muhammed.)

The entire thrust of "Belly" involves taking the duo on a series of adventures, from Omaha, Neb., to Kingston, Jamaica, which serve to bring about confrontations with themselves.

"Belly" has all the sex and violence of the urban black action genre, but it builds refreshingly and unexpectedly to a spirit of redemption and responsibility. Unfortunately, "Belly" is highly uneven. Williams comes from music videos and knows all about flashy techniques. His sure sense of the visual reveals potential, but he needs to learn to tell a story far more coherently.

His script, from a story he wrote with Nas and Anthony Bodden, rambles and is often heavy-handed in delivering its message. Rap stars DMX and Nas have lots of presence, especially

DMX, but both have more to learn about acting. Neither is particularly convincing as a major drug lord. The best performances are by Tionne (T-Boz) Watkins as Sincere's concerned, down-to-earth wife; Taral Hicks as Tommy's gorgeous but bored and neglected girlfriend; and, most notably, by Louie Rankin as a totally believable Jamaican drug overlord who lives in exactly the kind of baronial estate that F. Scott Fitzgerald's Jay Gatsby called home.

"Belly" looks great, thanks to Malik Sayeed's stunning, noirish camerawork, and moves well. Hype Williams now needs to concentrate on wedding style and substance more persuasively.

NEW YORK POST, 11/4/98, p. 53, Rod Dreher

Old buddies end up on opposite sides of the law. Hmmm, there's an original storyline, huh?

Actually, "Belly" would be lucky to get confused with the likes of "Angels With Dirty Faces." But since it has none of the star power, directorial talents or crackling dialogue of the 1938 classic, that isn't a real possibility.

Stepping into Pat O'Brien and Jimmy Cagney's now-dusty shoes, the protagonists are both drug dealers who learned their trade in the rougher sections of Queens. But while Tommy is flourishing in the fast lane, the aptly named Sincere wants to move to Africa with his wife and baby.

But nothing's that simple. The opening credits haven't ended before gang warfare has a shower of bullets ripping through umpteen bodies. So much for peaceful resolutions.

That's not the worst of it. Enter music-video director Hype Williams, whose inky photography makes it seem as if he'd filmed in a cave. Add to that a rainbow of filters that tint the murkiness in blue, yellow and red. Clearly, he's a real artiste.

The actors, meanwhile, are mostly rap stars with one-word names like DMX (a.k.a. Earl Simmons), Nas (a.k.a. Nasir Jones), Power (a.k.a. Oli Grant) and Method-Man (a.k.a. Clifford Smith). While all may be very talented singers, their range as thespians goes from A to B.

But the production's most laughable aspect is saved for the big finale—taking place on Dec. 31, 1999 in Times Square, no less—as one character delivers an interminable speech about putting an end to mindless violence and saving mankind, all as a hallelujah chorus plays in the background.

That's why, with nothing but a few camera tricks to divert attention, "Belly" sticks squarely in one's craw.

SIGHT AND SOUND, 8/99, p. 40, Kay Dickinson

New York, February 1999. Tommy and Sincere make money from robbery and drug-dealing. Tommy, who relishes the hustler lifestyle, is two-timing his loyal girlfriend Kisha. Sincere, on the other hand, encouraged by his partner Tionne and the writings of the Reverend Saviour, is more disillusioned. Tommy acquires large quantities of a new, more addictive type of heroin through his big-shot contact Lennox, and he and Sincere start selling it in Omaha, Nebraska. Tommy and Lennox travel to Jamaica to annihilate their competitor, a dealer who supplies New York. They return to find the Omaha operation has been busted. Several associates have been arrested, including Kisha.

The increasingly paranoid Tommy goes on the run. Sincere longs more and more for a law-abiding existence and even contemplates moving his family to Africa. The police eventually catch up with Tommy, offering him a deal in return for his freedom: he must assassinate Saviour before an important speech on New Year's Eve. As Tommy approaches his target, Saviour reasons with him and they eventually embrace. A voiceover tells us that Sincere's family are now happily living in Africa.

Over the past few years, music-video director Hype Williams has warped and morphed the fortunate likes of Busta Rhymes and Missy Elliot with his effects-heavy promos to the betterment of their careers. His first feature *Belly*—a tale of two gangsters running out of time and chances—offers an opportunity to see whether his talent can burn brightly enough to fill a big screen. The traces of Williams' past can be spotted in the film's glib if striking visuals and its muddied narrative in which figures waft in and out, their actions often unexplained and unmotivated. While frequently witty in its critique of masculine swagger and mindless *arriviste* consumption, the film unfortunately falls back on the moral-parable tradition which swamps the work of many African-American film-makers assaying conscientious representation (see *Boyz N the Hood).* Revolving around a pattern-book good friend/bad friend scenario (the dissatisfied Sincere and wide-boy Tommy, respectively), *Belly* is painted in slapdash, though striking, abstract brushstrokes.

True to music-video convention, what we encounter is aesthetically shallow but handsome nonetheless. Gorgeous hues, surreal fish-eyed perspectives and pulsating varispeed camerawork offer an alternative to the drab realism that so often cloaks films about the underclasses and denies their characters the suave confidence that makes their criminality interesting. After a daring armed robbery, the protagonists return to their lair to watch *Gummo*, but the disorienting sheen of *Belly* owes little to the avant-garde tradition to which *Gummo* aspires.

But should we read these characteristics as shortcomings? Maybe the film is simply an advert luring us to its soundtrack and is itself happily resigned to cinema's growing financial reliance on the music industry. Clues to this are easily spotted: MTV plays in the background of Kisha and Tommy's apartment and the cast form an extensive 'Who's Who' list of contemporary hip hop. While admittedly charismatic, these performers (Nas, DMX, T-Boz, Method Man) seem a little bewildered, unable to immerse themselves fully in characterisation.

Also reviewed in:
CHICAGO TRIBUNE, 11/4/98, Tempo/p. 2, Monica Eng
NEW YORK TIMES, 11/4/98, p. E5, Lawrence Van Gelder
VARIETY, 11/9-15/98, p. 32, Leonard Klady
WASHINGTON POST, 11/4/98, p. D1, Rita Kempley

BELOVED

A Touchstone Pictures release of a Harpo Films/Clinica Estetico production. *Executive Producer:* Ron Bozman. *Producer:* Edward Saxon, Jonathan Demme, Gary Goetzman, Oprah Winfrey, and Kate Forte. *Director:* Jonathan Demme. *Screenplay:* Akosua Busia, Richard LaGravenese, and Adam Brooks. *Based on the novel by:* Toni Morrison. *Director of Photography:* Tak Fujimoto. *Editor:* Carol Littleton and Andy Keir. *Music:* Rachel Portman and Deva Anderson. *Music Editor:* Suzana Peric. *Choreographer:* Dianne McIntyre. *Sound:* Willie D. Burton. *Sound Editor:* Skip Lievsay. *Casting:* Howard Feuer. *Production Designer:* Kristi Zea. *Art Director:* Tim Galvin. *Set Decorator:* Karen O'Hara. *Set Dressers:* Robert Holtzman, Kristina Kilpe, Victor Littlejohn, William Hennessy, Allen Mamet, Tom Scruggs, Tom West, and Patrick Trowbridge and John Ottesen. *Special Effects:* Tom Ward. *Visual Effects:* Steve Rundell. *Costumes:* Colleen Atwood. *Special Effects Make-up:* Carl Fullerton and Neal Martz. *Make-up (Oprah Winfrey):* Ellie Winslow. *Make-up (Danny Glover):* Diane Hammond. *Stunt Coordinator:* Tony Brubaker. *Running time:* 172 minutes. *MPAA Rating:* R.

CAST: Oprah Winfrey (Sethe); Danny Glover (Paul D.); Thandie Newton (Beloved); Kimberly Elise (Denver); Beah Richards (Baby Suggs); Lisa Gay Hamilton (Younger Sethe); Albert Hall (Stamp Paid); Irma P. Hall (Ella); Carol Jean Lewis (Janey Wagon); Kessia Kordelle (Amy Denver); Jude Ciccolella (Schoolteacher); Anthongy Chisholm (Langhorne); Dorothy Love Coates (M. Lucille Williams); Jane White (Lady Jones); Yada Beener (Denver aged 9); Emil Pinnock (Howard aged 14); Calen Johnson (Buglar aged 13); George E. Ray (Reverend Pike); Ramona Castle, Brooklyn James, and Nora Marlowe (Carnival Kids); Frederick Strother (African Savage); Lillian Smith (Lemonade Server); Aliya Robinson (Denver's Carnival Friend); Joe Toutebon (Frenchie); Brittany Hawkins (Young Girl Sethe); Alerte Belance (Nan); Ayoka Dorsey (Sethe's Mother); Ashleigh Watson (Baby Denver); Dajon Matthews (Howard aged 5); Norris Wiggins, Jr. (Buglar aged 4); Harry Northup (Sheriff); Tracey Walter (Slave Catcher); Terel Gibson (Buglar aged 21); Damani Baker (Howard aged 22); Robert Castle (Mr. Sawyer); Paul Lazar (General Store Proprietor); Leigh Smiley (General Store Helper); Dan Olmstead (Policeman); Charles Glenn (Helpful Gentleman); Jason Robards (Mr. Bodwin); Anthony S. Calypso (Denver's Boyfriend); Wes Bentley and Dashiell Eaves (Schoolteacher's Nephews); Tyler Hinson (Baby Beloved); Brian Hooks (Young Paul D); Angie Utt (Mrs. Garner); Hill

Harper (Halle);   Jim Roche (String Show Barker);   Vertamae Grosvenor (Grace);   Jiggs Walker (Good Samaritan).

CHRISTIAN SCIENCE MONITOR, 10/16/98, p. B3, David Sterritt

"Beloved" arrives with some of the season's most impressive movie credentials: based on the novel by Nobel Prize-winner Toni Morrison, directed by Oscar winner Jonathan A Demme, featuring stars Oprah Winfrey and Danny Glover. And it tells one of the season's most harrowing stories. Set in the Midwest shortly after the Civil War, it focuses on a house hold that's literally haunted by the aftereffects of slavery and the awful secret of a woman who loved her children too much to let them suffer its torments.

As powerful as its subject is, Morrison's novel gains most of its intensity not from plot or psychology but from the language with which it's told. Instead of shaping her tale for maximum drama, Morrison twists it into fractured, tortured convolutions that reflect the traumas its characters have endured and the oppressiveness of the memories inflicted by slavery on all who have borne its traces.

Demme's version serves the worthy purpose of summoning up those memories, holding them under Hollywood's bright lights, and reminding us of the racist heritage that Americans have yet to transcend.

But what his movie lacks is the sense of earthiness and urgency that surges through Morrison's pages. Aside from some searingly violent moments, the film is bathed in glossy colors and ear-soothing music, as if the filmmakers didn't trust their material to move us on its own.

Much of the acting is solid, but earnest performances can't give the picture all the bite and excitement it sorely needs. Hollywood is watching "Beloved" to see if white audiences will respond to a black-centered story. If it languishes at the box office, though, the reason may simply be that it's more picturesque than involving.

LOS ANGELES TIMES, 10/16/98, Calendar/p. 1, Kenneth Turan

To see "Beloved," all two hours and 52 minutes of it, is to understand at once all its confounding contradictions. Visible is both why it took 10 years to reach the screen and why star and driving force Oprah Winfrey would not, could not rest until it happened. Visible as well are the difficulties of translating a spectacular work of fiction into film and the bounty that can be gained by those determined to persevere.

Directed by Jonathan Demme, "Beloved" is ungainly and hard to follow at times, like the proverbial giant not quite sure how to best use its strength. But that power exists, present and undeniable, and once this film gets its bearings, the unsentimental fierceness of its vision brushes obstacles and quibbles from its path.

Already a modern classic, "Beloved" the novel was awarded the Pulitzer Prize and was critical to author Toni Morrison's receiving the Nobel Prize in literature. Set just before and just after the Civil War and telling the story of Sethe (Winfrey), the survivor of an unspeakable hell for whom "the future was a matter of keeping the past at bay," it deals as potently as only fiction can with the nightmare legacy of slavery and the deadly, terrifying weight of the past.

Yet as devastating as the book is, its use of a multilayered narrative, its complete acceptance of the supernatural plus its exceptional way with language add up to a story that seems to be too large and too poetic to fit comfortably into a film of any length.

"Beloved" is director Demme's first feature since 1993's "Philadelphia" and only his second since 1991's Oscar-winning "The Silence of the Lambs," and in some ways this film combines the social consciousness of the former with the facility for horror (and by extension the supernatural) of the latter. The work that has resulted, strange, troubling and powerfully imagined, is rough going at first, but the more time you spend with it the more the strength of the underlying material exerts its will.

"Beloved's" screenplay (credited to Akosua Busia and Richard LaGravenese and Adam Brooks) takes the sane way out, paring the book down to its essential events, most of which take place in 1873 in and around a small house on the outskirts of Cincinnati. What's been sacrificed is the book's extended look at life at Sweet Home, the ironically named Kentucky plantation where the horrors begin, though the flashbacks that are shown (shot by longtime Demme cinematographer Tak Fujimoto on special, deliberately grainy film stock) are critical to the film's impact.

All this, however, takes awhile to unfold. Initially, almost from its opening "Poltergeist, the Early Years" sequence—a chaotic, demonic night when a tormented dog called Here Boy gets tossed around, mirrors break and two young brothers flee for their lives—"Beloved" comes across as a film that knows its source so well it underestimates how confusing its events are to nonreaders.

The next scene reintroduces Sethe and her daughter Denver (Kimberly Elise) on a sunny day in 1873, eight years later. Coming up the road is a man Sethe hasn't seen in 18 years, Paul D (Danny Glover), a friend from the prewar days at Sweet Home and an intimate of Halle, Sethe's husband and Denver's father, whom Sethe also hasn't seen since the day in 1855 she precipitously fled the plantation.

Invited into their house, Paul D is unnerved to find a room filled with undulating, vibrating red light. It is, Sethe tells him matter-of-factly, the sad but not evil ghost of her baby daughter who died at the age of 2. It's the same ghost that drove her two sons away eight years ago, the ghost that keeps neighbors from coming over and relieving the bleak isolation these women live in.

Paul D's presence does two things. It precipitates a physical struggle with Baby Ghost, as Denver calls it, who apparently leaves, though Denver does say, "I think the baby ain't gone, I think the baby got plans." And having Paul D around leads Sethe to relive, and us to see in flashback, the agonies of her final night at Sweet Home.

What happens at Sweet Home, the multiple tortures inflicted on Sethe by the white men who run things, are painful, deeply difficult to watch even in the brief shards of flashback we're given, and aesthetically problematical. What we see on screen, perhaps to protect our sensibilities, is shown in short, often frenzied bursts. When that frantic tone combines with the film's determination to give its actors accurate accents, past events end up rushing by in a not completely comprehensible blur. In fact, to read Morrison's novel after seeing the film is to frequently say, "So that's what that was all about."

Determined to bring some normalcy into Sethe and Denver's lives, Paul D takes them to a local carnival. When they return home, however, they find in their front yard a beautiful, almost catatonic young woman whom we've seen emerge fully clothed and soaking wet out of a nearby stream. Asked her name, the woman croaks a single word in the deepest of voices: Beloved.

Partly young woman, mostly child, Beloved can't or won't say where she came from and has to learn from scratch what it is to act her age. She slobbers, drools, snores, eats sweets with a vengeance, and, though Denver is eager for her companionship, it is Sethe that Beloved is hungry for. As Morrison's limpid prose notes, "Rainwater held on to pine needles for dear life and Beloved could not take her eyes off Sethe," who in turn felt that "the company of this sweet, if peculiar guest pleased her the way a zealot pleases his teacher."

With the appearance of Beloved, the film that's her namesake comes fully alive, and Thandie Newton's performance in the role is the largest part of the reason. Previously seen in "Flirting" and "Jefferson in Paris" among others, Newton hits the right unnerving notes with her work here. Pleading, screaming, importuning, her Beloved is a truly disconcerting, unfathomable presence that deeply troubles Paul D. It gives the film the critical sense of unease the book has, in effect freeing it to be itself.

Because her eerie, insinuating "Tell me" can't be resisted, Beloved's persistent questions lead Sethe to slowly recount even more of her past. We see how she escaped from Sweet Home, the circumstances of Denver's birth, and how she got to Ohio and the comforting presence of her mother-in-law, the unchurched preacher Baby Suggs (Beah Richards). Sethe also gets closer and closer to her own terrible secrets as well as the hard truths that are in the possession of Beloved and Paul D.

It was Winfrey's persistence as a producer that got "Beloved" made, and though her relative inexperience as an actress is visible, it turns out not to be a problem. Winfrey is convincing enough to make an impact with lines like Sethe's "I will never run from another thing on this Earth, you hear!" declaration to Paul D; at other times, her untutored quality makes a good fit with the stoicism that is Sethe's touchstone.

Winfrey is also helped by the excellent actors she's surrounded with, starting with Glover as the soul of humanity Paul D and Elise as the troubled but striving Denver. Lisa Gay Hamilton is so convincing as the young Sethe you forget at times she's not Winfrey, and Albert Hall effectively plays the pivotal role of Stamp Paid. Most satisfying of all, perhaps, is Richards, Oscar-nominated 30 years ago for "Guess Who's Coming to Dinner," who poignantly conveys the mystical, healing presence of Baby Suggs.

What finally pulls "Beloved" over the shoals of its initial awkwardness and uncertainty is the strength contained in its exceptional source material. By the time Paul D tells Sethe, "We got more yesterday than anybody, we need some kind of tomorrow," we have gone through enough with them to calculate the cost of survival down to the last drop of blood.

NEW YORK, 10/20/98, p. 80, Stanley Crouch

It has always been possible to make a good movie from a bad book, which is not what happened with *Beloved* but *could* have. Since Oprah Winfrey is never less than a sequoia of humanity, since Danny Glover is capable of whatever might be asked of him, and since Thandie Newton gives an astonishingly original performance, a good script and the right director might have triumphed over Toni Morrison's willfully gothic merging of tanning-salon Holocaust tale, self-help homilies, and *The Exorcist*. The film is both too faithful to all of the book's shortcomings and utterly lacking in the spiritual depth that it, like Morrison's story, really only pretends to have. Spiritual grandeur in the face of heartbreak and injustice makes the Negro, as Richard Wright pointed out, America's metaphor. What we get in this film, by contrast, is less a humbling recognition of the complexities of slavery and its aftermath than a sticky New Age mess of uncleaned chitlins.

In telling the story of *Beloved,* the film attempts to layer on elements from its heroine's past in imitation of Morrison's overwrought imitation of Garcia Marquez and William Faulkner, neither of whom translates very well to the screen. Their densely lyrical rhetoric cannot be replicated visually; it lives too much in the mind of the reader, where all the filling-in is done by the person moving from sentence to sentence, expanding the images out into the realm of myth. A film director has to have a comparably mythic vision, one that is cinematic and not dependent on a literal reading of the text. That is where Jonathan Demme swings the wrecking ball into his own edifice. He makes the same mistakes Morrison did.

The director uses differently developed film for high MTV contrasts, as well as extremely quick intercutting flashbacks like those popularized by Sidney Lumet's *The Pawnbroker,* which is about bitter Holocaust guilt and, like *Beloved,* the psychological havoc wrought by memories of helplessness. We are shown snippets of what is ailing Sethe, the matriarch who escaped from plantation bondage and killed one of her female babies rather than allow the infant to be taken back into slavery. We are also given brief horrific images of chattel life that bear an interesting relationship to Lumet's film, where we see the day the Nazis came and took the family, the loss of a child in a boxcar on the way to the concentration camp, the beatings, and the father having to witness a Nazi rape his wife.

Similar horrors are also the staples of Negro victimization fiction. Such outsize periods of darkness, over there or over here, demand extraordinary artistry to avoid the melodramatic or the shrill, to avoid trivializing such heightened suffering. So the opportunity provided by making a film of *Beloved* was monumental: Here was a chance to bring the humanity and the pain of the slave experience and the post-slave experience into the world of art. And indeed, there are more than a few moments when just such a transformation takes place, just as there are in the novel. But as in the fiction itself, these moments never last long enough to overcome the lightweight core not of the tale, but of the teller.

Everything that takes place in *Beloved* exists so that by the end Sethe can be saved from the domineering ghost by a vision of Negro female solidarity—all blown up into a three-hour, New Age revelation message. Sethe, portrayed by Winfrey with a face that is classically masklike in its constancy of sorrow, is told that the best thing she ever produced was *not* the child she murdered, whose vengeful shade has finally been exorcised, leaving her catatonically broken and alone. No, her most splendid creation, she is told, is, of course, herself, to which she responds, "Me... me... me..." Thus slavery and the human suffering that attended it, and continued once it was over, are made no more than a vehicle for a simple-minded, self-help conception of human transcendence.I murdered my baby child but I got *me.*

Along the way to this epiphany, every point is made over and over, yet Demme never allows the past to have an actual presence in the film. We are never really shown the father of Beloved, which is the catchy name of the ghost girl; he zips by so quickly that his significance to this story doesn't add up or transfer the power of Sethe's memory and feeling to the viewer. As if to underscore what has been sacrificed, there is one extraordinary moment when Albert Hall, playing Stamp Paid, silently moves close into the camera as he helps Sethe cross the river into Ohio, his visage the entire story of southern Negro men. He alone achieves a mythic presence so lacking in almost all of the film. After we have looked at the same facial expressions, and the same landscapes, and the same cloud formations again and again, and after we have heard for the umpteenth time the same insipid bookstore music, the power of the past has been lost and the tale arrives as something merely episodic; requiring no emotional investment, it has no emotional payoff.

And yet there are moments when *Beloved* is unquestionably beautiful and full of feeling. Winfrey, never afraid to express feeling, makes Sethe an actual person—shy, witty, frightened, bitter, repressed, erotic, lonely, stoic, devastated. Winfrey's gift, which is the source of her success, is her inability to sell out emotionally. Even if she really believes every word of "me... me... me..." She remains as purely empathetic of tragedy as she is of human horror on her TV show. While we know we are looking at a woman of enormous fame and power, she makes us forget that. Winfrey almost always avoids anything close to glamour; when she does dress up, the fairy-tale magic of her own story intersects with the character as we notice how the charming piggly-wiggly remade herself into quite a swell-looking babe.

Danny Glover is good, but he could have been so much better had more been asked of him. Here, he is used to reiterate the noble field hand he played in *Places in the Heart*. *To Sleep With Anger,* his finest movie, proved that Glover can move from light to dark with ease and authority, which he does only intermittently in *Beloved*. To be sure, there is plenty of magnetism between his Paul D. and Winfrey's Sethe. Developing in tenderness, the romance expands upon what *Sounder* brought to the world of black images—the cinematic recognition of the blues, sweet and slow. Glover's best moments come when Paul D. is either hot for his lady or a murky suspicion begins to rise in him when the ghost who came to dinner reveals aspects of her sour identity. Yet in the end, Paul D. is expendable, because the moral of this movie is that when push comes to cold-blooded shove, the men run off and the women either face the brittle world alone or become a band of angels singing unsoulfully and waving Bibles that paddle bad spirits into total disappearance.

That is also why Sethe's two boys haul ass as soon as the movie opens, terrified of the ghost that shakes, rattles, and rolls things around. This makes a perfect frame for a certain kind of leaden feminism. It leaves the mother with her daughter and a number of tales in which she had to pull her heavy, heavy load alone. *No-account colored mens. They didn't do what they should have when everybody was supposed to run off from the plantation—cowards.* Sethe's man even stayed in the loft and watched the white folks suck her mother's milk from her brown breasts and rape her and whip her, too! *Double* coward. Sethe still ran off, pregnant and near bursting; a crazy white girl in the woods helped her birth her baby: Push and pull together, girls.

We can be mightily grateful that none of this obscures what Thandie Newton brings to the screen. She labors through a froggy *Exorcist* voice at the beginning, but when she moves fully into the ghost character, her infantile body rhythms and her nuanced facial expressions expand upon Boris Karloff's most touching and horrifying moments as the Frankenstein monster. Kimberly Elise, as Sethe's daughter Denver, also has greater-than-average talent, but she is locked in a narrow range of reaction shots until the film is almost over.

No matter its fundamental failures: *Beloved* still represents an act of courage. In structure and length, it has nothing commercial going for it other than Winfrey's admittedly formidable name. Perhaps, if the New Age Lord is willing, we shall someday see the marvelous Winfrey play a woman more like herself, or Leontyne Price or Hazel O'Leary, all of whom—like Toni Morrison, as it happens—are far more interesting and challenging than any of the characters created by the author of *Beloved*.

NEW YORK POST, 10/16/98, p. 37, Rod Dreher

The advance hype on Saint Oprah Winfrey's "Beloved" has been so relentless and awe-filling, one might wonder if it's permissible to enter the theater without having first been to confession.

It may be sacrilegious to say, but "Beloved" is not so hot.

While there are beautiful moments in the picture, it's a movie more to admire for its worthy intentions and undeniable dignity than to love for what's actually on screen.

Winfrey says nothing brought home the horrific legacy of slavery to her like Toni Morrison's novel, but that searing sense of pain and immediacy are conspicuously absent from director Jonathan Demme's overlong, laborious rendering.

Set in rural Ohio in 1873, "Beloved" concerns a runaway slave named Sethe (Winfrey) who lives in a wood-frame house with her teen-age daughter Denver (Kimberly Elise) and a rowdy, malicious ghost. When Paul D. (Danny Glover), who had known Sethe back on the plantation, turns up at her door, the poltergeist goes berserk. Creepy? And how.

Sethe is half-mad and literally haunted by her past. The ghost is the restless spirit of Sethe's dead child, who lost her life violently because of slavery. (The gruesome particulars are explained late in the film.) Paul D. moves in and the ghost departs, but soon after, another visitor arrives: A strange young woman with bugs crawling on her turns up at Sethe's door.

Her name is Beloved, and she seems not quite human. In fact, she's almost a cartoon freak. As the jarringly lovely Thandie Newton plays her, Beloved gawks and drools and yammers and carries on like a "Cosby" show version of Linda Blair in "The Exorcist"—which, alas, is funny. This is not supposed to be a funny movie.

Newton's stunt performance aside, the acting here is exemplary, particularly Elise's as the teen-ager trapped by her mother's suffocating devotion to the past.

If Oprah doesn't match her devastating turn in "The Color Purple," she nevertheless makes us forget that she's, well, Oprah. Her Sethe is a woman who has not so much made peace with her soul as reached a truce; what the narrative needs, and gets so little of, is a sense of the horrific past, which intrudes so rudely on the present.

Demme revisits Sethe's devastating back story in brief flashbacks to Sweet Home plantation, depicting the sexual assaults, lynchings and whatnot in abrupt episodes. It's not enough. Though we mercifully see little of the monstrous cruelties inflicted upon Sethe and the other slaves, we have to see more to feel Sethe's pain, to establish an emotional context in which to place the events of the film's present.

Slack and meandering, the occasionally brilliant "Beloved" pulls its punches, failing to deliver the healing catharsis the material calls for. It's a noble disappointment.

NEWSDAY, 10/6/98, Part II/p. B3, Jack Mathews

"They took my milk... They held me down and took my milk... They took my milk!"

It happened 18 years ago, at the Kentucky plantation from which the slave Sethe was trying to escape, and the white men did a lot more than that to her. They had raped and beaten her many times, and that very night whipped her so viciously, the scars would form an embossed silhouette of a densely branched tree on her back. But for Sethe, there could be no greater horror than the thought of not being able to feed her baby.

As horrific as these memories are, related by Sethe (Oprah Winfrey) to her old friend and new lover Paul D (Danny Glover) in the film version of Toni Morrison's Pulitzer Prize-winning novel "Beloved," they pale next to an unspeakable related secret that haunts her all these years later. Literally haunts her, by way of the angry spirit of her dead child, the one for whom that stolen milk was intended.

It's now 1873, in rural Ohio, where Sethe and her other daughter, Denver (Kimberly Elise), have just been joined by the roguishly charming Paul D and a strange, almost feral woman-child who seems to attract both insects and butterflies and calls herself Beloved (Thandie Newton). Who is this drooling, babbling woman and why does she have such power over Sethe? Where did she come from, why does she ask so many questions, and what does she want?

"Beloved" is a tough, painful, provocative story about the damaged souls of freed slaves, and, frankly, it works better as a novel than as a movie. You can step back from the book, and, in the case of "Beloved," you must. Morrison weaves such a tight tapestry of history, romance, adventure, and metaphysical mystery that readers have to pause now and then to absorb and reflect.

You can't do that with a movie, and even under the clear-headed direction of Jonathan Demme ("Silence of the Lambs," "Philadelphia"), working with a sharply adapted script by Richard LaGravenese, Akosua Busia, and Adam Brooks, the movie invites some confusion. There are a lot of characters and issues intercut from different time periods, and unless you know the story in advance, it's hard to keep them straight.

In large part, the story is split between a pre-Civil War period when Sethe (Lisa Gay Hamilton) is running from slavery, and the contemporary post-Civil War period when she's dealing with her tortured history, keeping it alive even as she wishes it away. Something terrible happened 18 years ago, something that tested a mother's love beyond reason, and it won't leave her alone. It shakes her house, breaks dishes, moves furniture, and appears in morbid apparitions.

Morrison used this ghost story as a metaphor for the weight of slavery bearing down on a single soul, making the point that it was a system of such profound inhumanity that there could be no genuine escape, no real freedom. Sethe remains a slave to her past.

Though the fantasy elements are done sparingly in the movie, they give it the feel of a good horror-mystery. Still, the film moves slowly, and with a running time of 2 hours and 52 minutes, few will complain that it's too short.

It's impossible not to at least partially review "Beloved" as an Oprah Winfrey movie. She shepherded the novel from the page to the screen, optioning it shortly after its publication in 1987, and getting the script developed and adopted as a major studio project. No mean task, any of this. And Disney deserves credit for taking on a project whose weighty subject matter would seem to make it a commercial longshot.

I'm not so sure. "The Color Purple," a critically far lesser movie, was a major hit for Steven Spielberg, and Winfrey, who's promoting "Beloved" like nothing she's promoted before, has no less influence on mainstream America. It takes some getting used to accept her as an illiterate slave (in fact, I never fully made the leap), but she gives a solid, assured performance.

Better yet is the work of Glover, as a goodhearted man set adrift by his freedom, wanting a life he's not sure how to live, and Newton, as the not-so-loveable Beloved. Brain-damaged, disabled, off-balance physically and mentally, Beloved is the catalyst who brings Sethe's past and present together and forces her to try to reconcile them. Newton, twisting her body and facial muscles in ways that are genuinely uncomfortable to watch, makes her simultaneously beautiful and grotesque, angelic and demonic, fragile and dangerous.

Other strong performances are given by Beah Richards, as Baby Suggs, the wise, gentle ex-slave preacher, and Hamilton, who plays Sethe in the most difficult scenes, including the one where she's milked like a cow. Its an image that won't be easily shaken.

NEWSWEEK, 10/19/98, p. 76, David Ansen

Nearly three hours long, filled with marvels and *longueurs*, the poetic and the pedestrian, Jonathan Demme's adaptation of Toni Morrison's Pulitzer Prize-winning "Beloved" is a bold and frustratingly uneven movie. In the novel, Morrison's dense, lyrical prose swoops and soars around her story, conjuring ghosts and visions, darting between present and past as it contemplates the harrowing legacy of slavery. The tale is inseparable from the teller—but how do you translate Morrison's voice into images? That's the challenge faced by Demme and writers Richard LaGravenese, Adam Brooks and Akosua Busia. To their credit, they haven't gone for easy, sanitized Hollywood solutions. Set in Ohio in 1873, and flashing back to the 1850s and '60s, "Beloved" creates a truly lived-in past: bleached-out, rough-edged and filled with strong, primal images that attempt to match the primal issues of blood and sacrifice that "Beloved" is about.

On one level, this is a ghost story. Sethe (Oprah Winfrey) and her daughter Denver (Kimberly Elise) are sharing a house with the spiteful spirit of Sethe's other daughter, dead for 18 years. Sethe's two sons have abandoned her, and the sullen, terrified Denver is a virtual prisoner in her own home. Sethe, who gave birth to Denver as she was escaping from the slave plantation Sweet Home, is a prisoner of the past, her mind as scarred with a secret guilt as her back is scarred with lashes. Into their lives come two figures promising hope. Paul D (Danny Glover) is a former Sweet Home slave who moves in with Sethe, offering her his love. The other is a mysterious feral creature who calls herself Beloved (Thandie Newton), speaks in a ghastly croak and is the age Sethe's baby would have been had she lived. Is this wild child the ghost made flesh? Is she an agent of destruction or salvation?

A chamber drama stretched into epic form, this sprawling movie is an odd mixture of the intimate and the grandiose, historical gravity and Gothic claptrap. One of the difficulties of translating the book to screen is that most of the story's crucial events take place in the past: it's Sweet Home that forged Sethe's character. Demme is understandably reluctant to linger on the horrors of slavery, but it's a dramaturgical mistake. The quick, shocking flashbacks of Sethe's brutalization by her white masters don't do the job—they're horrific, but with a B-movie luridness. The present-tense story of Sethe, Paul D and Beloved doesn't work properly unless we feel in our guts the burden of those years. That's what the story's about—slavery's spiritual fall-out—yet that's what's excised from the movie. Jumping about in time, the film often feels as if it were searching for its center. It takes a long time to get pulled in; it's not until its final hour that it's able to sustain any emotional momentum.

Yet along the way there are scenes that transfix you. The film bursts into life whenever Beah Richards is on screen. As Sethe's mother-in-law, Baby Suggs, a freed slave turned preacher woman, she delivers a sermon from atop a rock as men dance joyously around her; the moment is magical. Elise is astonishing as Denver: her transformation from outcast to independent woman gives the movie its defining arc. As for Winfrey, any fear that her TV persona would distract us is instantly erased: she effortlessly slips inside Sethe's stoic, haunted skin. Playing the young Sethe, Lisa Gay Hamilton uncannily matches up with Winfrey. You almost forget you're watching another actress in the role. Glover captures Paul D's charm, and the long miles as man has traveled in his life. As for the unearthly, grotesque Beloved, it's a part that may be as unplayable as the novel is ultimately unfilmable. There are moments when Newton's grimacing, sepulchral-voiced performance unfortunately invokes "The Exorcist." Like the movie itself, Newton takes big risks and doesn't always succeed. But you have to salute the attempt. However flawed, "Beloved" never plays it safe.

SIGHT AND SOUND, 3/99, p. 34, Charlotte O'Sullivan

Ohio, 1873. Sethe lives in a house passed on to her by her late mother-in-law Baby Suggs. Also sharing the house are her daughter Denver and an angry baby ghost. One evening Paul D arrives. He knows Sethe from their time together at Sweet Home farm, where they were both slaves. Sethe invites Paul D to stay the night and he frightens off the ghost.

A beautiful young girl arrives at the house, calling herself Beloved. Denver and Sethe take an instant liking to her. Paul D is suspicious but, against his will, has sex with her. He decides to confront Sethe with his fears but instead asks her to have his baby. Local man Stamp Paid informs Paul D that Sethe was prepared to kill her children rather than hand them over to her former owner, Schoolteacher. One baby girl died. When Paul D confronts Sethe she tries to explain her actions, but he fails to understand and leaves.

Sethe finally realises who Beloved is—an embodiment of the baby girl who died. She leaves her job and dotes on Beloved, but the latter, now pregnant, proves insatiable. Money runs out and Denver, prompted by the ghost of Baby Suggs, turns to the community for help. One evening, Denver is waiting for her white boss Mr. Bodwin to pick her up for work. Meanwhile, a group of the town's women gather outside the house. When Sethe see Mr Bodwin she runs to attack him. The women stop her and Beloved disappears. Paul D returns. He and Sethe are reunited.

Toni Morrison's novel *Beloved* is an extraordinary feat, a version of the judgement of Solomon. In the Bible story we learn that a natural mother would do anything rather than see her child cut in two. Morrison's project is to show how Sethe, a former slave, when pushed to nightmarish extremes could fight for the right to commit the bloody act herself.

Unfortunately, the film of the book seems to have aroused similar passions. Its parentage is also contested: is this an Oprah Winfrey project (Winfrey, one of the film's co-producers, has been nursing this baby for over a decade), or a Jonathan Demme movie? As a result it doesn't quite fit together. It's impossible, of course, to know who exactly did what, but it feels as if Winfrey claimed as her own the parts concerning her character Sethe and Sethe's mother Baby Suggs (Beah Richards), while Demme adopted Beloved (Thandie Newton), the title character who may or may not be a reincarnation of the daughter Sethe slaughtered rather than let her become a slave. Either way, both Winfrey and Demme get a lot wrong. Winfrey, for instance, should never have cast herself in the lead. She is very good in some scenes, but she is never startling or overwhelming, her pleasant, sturdy face capable of projecting only one feeling at a time.

More importantly, she has altered the contexts surrounding Sethe and Baby Suggs. We never learn, for instance, how Beloved's gravestone gets her name carved on it (in the book, Sethe has to have sex with the stonecutter). It's as if such a detail might sully our notion of the noble Sethe. Nor do we see, or even hear about, the magnificent party which in the book alienates the community from the two women. Essentially Sethe and Baby Suggs' beneficence makes the people fizzle with jealous rage. As a result, they don't want the two women of sadistic slave owner Schoolteacher's imminent arrival. A crucial passage in the book, the party demonstrates the limits of both the group and the individual. By having this out, a myth is kept alive: if you need it, the group will be there for you, while the big-hearted female can never give too much of herself. This is the logic of *The Oprah Winfrey Show*—too quick and easy by half.

This emphasis on the 'empowering', supportively spiritual female (Baby Suggs' sermons also feature heavily) unbalances the film. Lost are the male stories in the book, an irony given that when *Beloved* as first published, a number of critics accused Morrison of undermining black men. Denzel Washington allegedly turned down the role of Paul D on the grounds that there was too much bowing and scraping in the role. Such a view bristles with machismo, but in the film, somewhere along the line, black men have been pushed to the sidelines.

Danny Glover plays the part beautifully, but Paul D's individual story (about how he escapes from a chain gang in Georgia, just as he's decided to risk death rather than fellate a white guard) has disappeared. So too has Stamp Paid's explanation for how he got his name. On the written page, the words 'Stamp Paid' can almost explain themselves—heard, their significance can easily be missed. *Beloved* the film doesn't have room for the autonomous black male, and ironically this makes the triumphs of its black women less impressive. When Glover tells Winfrey, "you your best thing", the uncharitable thought surfaces: she doesn't need convincing of *that*.

Director Demme is just as guilty of recreating the film in his own image. For Beloved's birth scene, for example, we're plunged into the beautiful, surreal rankness of *The Silence of the Lambs* (not surprisingly, the two films share the same cinematographer, Tak Fujimoto). *Silence*'s killer's basement hideout crawls with insects; Beloved, similarly, is surrounded by fluttering wings and her body covered inch-thick with ladybirds (not in the book). Later, she drapes herself against a tree and her serpentine awkwardness—a mixture of shamelessness and self-disgust—remind one of Demme's psychopath.

Much work has gone into Newton's Beloved, perhaps too much. Her voice—like something out of *The Exorcist*—at first works well (combined as it is with bouts of enchanting, wide-eyed sweetness) but soon becomes distracting. In the book, the hope that Beloved can be made happy keeps flaring into life; here, thanks to that monster-voice, it's impossible not to realise she's trouble. Furthermore, it makes her seem culturally rootless. In the book she gradually begins to talk like the rest of the family and develops a poetic, sophisticated point of view. In the film her charisma is entirely other-worldly and we never identify with her. She's just wonderful and scary to watch. This one-note performance, though, is all of a piece with Demme's gothic-horror vision. The wigs get more demented and determinedly unreal by the minute. He even gives her pearly, vampiric teeth. It's as if whenever Beloved is before the camera Demme is back producing colourful exploitation for Roger Corman. Luckily, there are a number of scenes which seem to belong neither to Demme nor to Winfrey, but to embody the best of both. The family's trip to the carnival, for example, transforms a fairly insignificant part of the book into a bold, haunting set-piece. It looks just right, not a soft thing in sight (even the sky looks like a rough piece of metal). Best of all, potentially big points—such as the irony of ex-slaves being entertained by the sight of white "freaks"—are not rammed home. Chains and rusty prison bars are allowed to sink in slowly or not at all (for once, even the music is low key). It's the bright, grimly carnal colours that stay with you, colours which contrast with the shots of wildlife that crop up throughout the film, of animals roaming free and not a human in sight. Often such visions are beautiful, often they're ugly (such as two tortoises mating, wrinkled necks stretched to breaking point). In either case, the screen feels too full. We pull back, overwhelmed as if by an obscenity. What Fujimoto does so well is to produce a natural landscape that appears unnatural, or *too* natural. *Beloved* captures what Morrison has to put into words: that once we become accustomed to slavery, freedom becomes frightening and strange.

Implicating the audience in such thinking is the film's real achievement. *Beloved* may be as discombobulated as the flesh-and-blood ghost herself, but its various bits and pieces prove fascinating (contrary to advance warning, its three hours do go quickly).

VILLAGE VOICE, 10/20/98, p. 155, J. Hoberman

Dutiful as it is, Jonathan Demme's *Beloved* doesn't succeed so much as it abides. Nearly three hours in length, this largely faithful adaptation of Toni Morrison's 1988 Pulitzer Prize winner moves in leisurely fits and—unencumbered by style or narrative complexity—never loses its forward momentum.

Morrison's novel was inspired by the true tale of a runaway slave who chose to murder her infant rather than allow the baby's capture. For the writer, that gesture was a means to evoke an experience so extreme it confounded expression—circling around the life of the escaped Sethe (and hence the condition of slavery), Morrison created a terrifying vortex. Eight years after the end of the Civil War, Sethe is living in a haunted house (like everyone else in America) with her surviving daughter, Denver, when her ghosts take the form of the mysterious young woman who gives the book its title. Named for the heart's desire, *Beloved* is everything to everybody: daughter, sister, lover, the return of the repressed, slavery in a new and awful form.

Deprived of Morrison's dense style and oblique narrative, *Beloved*'s plot is as luridly melodramatic as anything by Faulkner or Hawthorne were they so baldly synopsized. In his infamous critique of the novel as an exercise in martyrology, Stanley Crouch imagined the trailer for the inevitable TV adaptation: "Meet Sethe, an ex-slave woman who harbors a deep and terrible secret..." Demme's movie is scarcely so crass but, as Morrison's *Beloved* was a sort of gothic, so his overwrought adaptation is, in part, a horror film.

Demme's dilemma isn't so much straightening out Morrison's artfully convoluted storyline as making her essentially literary fiction something literal. The supernatural must be established. When, after years of wandering, the ex-slave Paul D (Danny Glover) finds Sethe (coproducer Oprah Winfrey) living on the outskirts of Cincinnati, her house welcomes him with mad creaks, a red Kryptonite glow, and visions out of *The Shining* as a prelude to the full-scale table-throwing attack which Morrison describes in a single offhand paragraph. Similarly, the inexplicable Beloved (Thandie Newton) drags herself out of the swamp, covered with bugs and croaking like the possessed child in *The Exorcist*.

The implicit meaning of every scene is here made explicit—not just the shock centerpiece but also runaway Sethe's dreamlike meeting with the half-crazed white indentured servant who helps her give birth.(Paradoxically, these scenes make the film stranger by confounding its narrative fluidity. *Beloved* doesn't feel like other Hollywood movies—least of all the inept *Color Purple*, which its casting unavoidably references.) *Beloved* is best when Demme embeds the drama in a raw sense of place—the seasons changing around Sethe's cold frame house, the revivalist meetings her mother, Baby Suggs, leads out back. As the sensory assault of Cincinnati's hog pens is stronger than a poltergeist attack, so the ribbon-festooned party Sethe throws for Beloved and Denver is the most hallucinated sequence.

Hyperaware of his responsibilities, Demme admits no distance from the material. (In a fascinating slip, the director told *Time* that his fidelity to the book was "slavish.") It is fruitless to imagine what Charles Burnett might have brought to the table—having not only guided Glover's strongest performance in the subtly magic-realist *To Sleep With Anger*, but also delivered an extremely credible picture about slavery in *'nightjohn*. Another useful corollary would be Jim Jarmusch's laconic (and doggedly uncommercial) western, *Dead Man*, but that would have involved recasting the material—in both sense of the word.

Slack-jawed and wide-eyed, Thandie Newton throws herself into the title role—executing a sepulchral buck and wing with a variety of rag-doll moves—but the most uncanny presence in the movie is, of course, Winfrey's. A project she struggled to make for a decade, *Beloved* is the celebration of her you-go-girl tenacity. The subject is a family crisis—and who knows more about that than her? Ditto the healing message (reiterated in repeated shots of two slavery-scarred survivors making love). Glover helps ground the action, as does Kimberly Elise's grave and self-contained Denver, but the spectacle of a de-(or rather, differently) glamorized Winfrey living out her roots is a psychodrama stronger than acting.

Beloved is less Oprah's vehicle than her time machine. Even more than Morrison, Winfrey—who sees herself as a medium for the spirits of specific Negro slaves—has assumed the role of a tribune. *Beloved*'s oscillating tone and close-up-driven absence of perspective become more coherent once the movie is understood as an epic version of *Oprah*—a show in which the star naturally shifts between autobiographical confession and maternal advice, reliving personal adversity and offering the model of her own empowerment as New Age therapy.

In the logic of *Beloved*, Winfrey is not just Sethe but Baby Suggs and the eventually actualized Denver as well. (Her audience is represented by the redoubtable church ladies who mobilize to exorcise the past.) Marilyn Monroe returned from the grave invested with Meryl Streep's chops and Barbra Streisand's will in a movie bigger than *Titanic* wouldn't stand a chance of wresting away Oprah's Oscar. It's the performance of her life. She has made herself her own best guest.

Also reviewed in:
CHICAGO TRIBUNE, 10/16/98, Friday/p. A, Michael Wilmington
NEW REPUBLIC, 11/16/98, p. 26, Stanley Kauffmann
NEW YORK TIMES, 10/16/98, p. E1, Janet Maslin
NEW YORKER, 10/26 & 11/2/98, p. 248, David Denby
VARIETY, 10/5-11/98, p. 67, Todd McCarthy
WASHINGTON POST, 10/16/98, p. D1, Stephen Hunter
WASHINGTON POST, 10/16/98, Weekend/p. 48, Michael O'Sullivan

BEST MAN, THE

An October Films release of a Luigi and Aurelio De Laurentiis/Antonio Avati presentation of a Filmauro-Duea Film production. *Producer:* Aurelio De Laurentiis and Antonio Avati. *Director:* Pupi Avati. *Story and Screenplay (Italian with English subtitles):* Pupi Avati. *Director of Photography:* Pasquale Rachini. *Editor:* Amadeo Salfa. *Music:* Riz Ortolani. *Sound:* Raffael De Luca. *Production Designer:* Alberto Cottignoli and Steno Tonelli. *Costumes:* Vittoria Guaita. *Running time:* 100 minutes. *MPAA Rating:* PG.

CAST: Diego Abatantuono (Angelo Beliossi); Ines Sastre (Francesca Babini); Dario Cantarelli (Edgardo Osti); Cinia Mascoli (Pepina Campeggi); Valeria D'Obici (Olimpia Campeggi Babini); Toni Santagata (Malio Lobianco); Nini Salerno (Sauro Ghinassi); Mario Erpichini (Sisto Babini); Ugo Conti (Marziano Beliossi).

LOS ANGELES TIMES, 8/21/98, Calendar/p. 6, Kevin Thomas

If Pupi Avati's "The Best Man" had as much vitality as it has charm, humor and perception, it could have been an unalloyed delight. It has so much going for it—an attractive cast, an amusing story, gorgeous period locales, a sweepingly romantic Riz Ortolani score—it's hard to understand why Avati allowed it to become so listless. As a result, it's a decidedly minor film.

As untold millions of women before her—and since—the ravishingly beautiful Francesca (Ines Sastre) is all set to marry a man (Dario Cantarelli) she does not love for financial security. If she does not go through with the ceremony, to take place on the last day of the 19th century, it will mean, just for starters, that her parents will lose their magnificent palazzo in the storybook northern Italian town of Sasso. Francesca balks and balks again. Then, while reciting her marriage vows, her gaze falls on a handsome stranger (Diego Abatantuono). It's love at first sight.

Refreshingly, Avati does not have Abatantuono's swarthy, bearded Angelo fall instantly in love with Francesca in return, and when Cantarelli's bald, sharp-featured Edgardo realizes that his bride has instantly fallen in love with another man, Avati comes up with a clever master stroke for the bridegroom to deal with it. Avati is also an amused observer of the behavior of the wedding's many guests, who are soon to be scandalized by Francesca's refusal to play the demure bride.

There's a lovely scene in which a man announces what every guest has brought as a wedding gift, and there's a funny sequence involving a ritualistic preparation of the nuptial chamber, which culminates with a maid, grilled on her chastity by the bride's aunt, exclaiming in exasperation, "I don't need a note from my doctor to make a bed!"

"The Best Man" is a movie of many exquisitely staged, amusing moments, but there's just not much substance to string them together. There's not much that's distinctive about Francesca outside her willfulness or looks that would serve to captivate us, and Angelo, who has just returned after 16 years in America, where his brothers have made a fortune, is a bit stolid.

In any event, when Avati is not making his astute social observations, his energy decidedly flags. He does, however, get across his larger point that the turning of the century points to a time when, hopefully, a woman no longer, in Avati's words, "confuses love with respect, resignation, duty and routine."

NEW YORK POST, 8/14/98, p. 46, Larry Worth

Song lyrics aside, love and marriage don't always go together like a horse and carriage. It's a point that's nicely driven home—in golden-hued storybook fashion, no less—in Pupi Avati's "The Best Man."

The storyline is pretty basic. A gorgeous young woman (Lancome model Ines Sastre) is walking up the aisle to tie the knot with a man she doesn't love (Dario Cantarelli). The good news is that her family will be kept from financial ruin. The bad? She'll never get to know the handsome stranger—hubby-to-be's best man (Diego Abantantuono)—who's clearly got her eye.

Writer/director Avati uses that premise to explore social etiquette at the turn of the century (the tale takes place in the final hours of Dec. 31, 1899), but also to gorgeously detail the minutiae of wedding preparations, the ceremony and its aftermath in a small Italian town.

Though some might consider it feather light, that's part of the charm. Much like a wedding cake's sugary confections, "The Best Man" is easy to digest, beautiful to look at and sweet as can be.

NEWSDAY, 8/14/98, Part II/p. B7, Bob Heisler

At Midnight, the small Italian town that stands for the Old World in "The Best Man" will enter the 20th Century. Its most beautiful daughter, Francesca Babini, is about 100 years ahead of it.

In an engaging story richly told and lushly photographed, director Pupi Avati never quite explains what a thoroughly modern woman—even her striking face looks out of place among the townspeople seemingly drawn from old, sepia-toned pictures—is doing there, so out of step with her family and her times.

Yet the story and its execution in golden hues and almost operatic staging, with a chorus of relatives and friends filling the Babini home for a combination wedding party and New Year's celebration, is thoughtful and entertaining. The expectation that everything is about to change seems to forgive even the sharpest break from tradition. And if you're thinking "Fiddler on the Roof," you're not far off.

Francesca (Spanish actress Ines Sastre) chooses her wedding day—and the last day of the old century—to inform her parents that their arranged marriage to the bloodless business prince Edgardo (Dario Cantarelli) won't work, though it will ruin her family's reputation and prospects. She has determined without reason or cause that, contrary to her mother's careful instruction, love does exist, cannot be conjured to suit public opinion, and must exist before marriage.

Purposeful and emotionally unstable, she kneels at the marriage altar, looks at Edgardo's best man, loses her heart and—is Neil Simon Italian?—flees to a vestibule only to return with her heart resolved: Her "I do" will be for the man standing next to Edgardo, the stranger Angelo, just returned from America with a fortune (not that his wealth matters), a deep tan and the face of a young, thin Pavarotti.

Angelo (Diego Abantantuono) speaks with the uncertainty of a man who sees the old order changing—socially and economically—and doesn't know whether he wants all that responsibility.

He is the maybe between the bedrock of the past and the golden haze of the future. And his hesitancy is charming.

While the roles seem cut from a common bolt of movie cloth, Avati's detail work gives "The Best Man" its attractive fit. The wedding preparations, supervised with spiritual exactness by spinster Aunt Pepina (Cinia Mascoli) and a gaggle of servants, and the formal recitation of gifts make entertaining side business. Valeria D'Obici as Francesca's mother-in-denial, is a gracious though grieving hostess.

VILLAGE VOICE, 8/18/98, p. 116, Leslie Camhi

Set in a small Italian town on the final day of the 19th century, Pupi Avati's *The Best Man* focuses on Francesca (Ines Sastre), a young woman who is marrying an aristocratic cad (Dario Cantarelli) to save her family from ruin. Luckily, while walking down the aisle, she falls for Angelo (Diego Abantantuono), the groom's best man, a former laborer who's just returned from America, where he made his fortune.

This nouveau riche victory over the old social order falls strangely flat. Sastre's chilly, model-like demeanor is oddly paired with Abantantuono's inarticulate bumbling, and their presumptive attraction pales beside Avati's evident passion for the accoutrements and protocols of an upper-middle-class, 19th-century Italian wedding. The camera lingers lovingly over gifts, toasts, and drawers full of linens; the films most vivid character is eccentric Aunt Pepina (Cinia Mascoli), a devotee of matrimonial rites involving holy water and virgins. If this is a story about the pull of modernity, it's entirely turned toward the past and its rituals.

Also reviewed in:
CHICAGO TRIBUNE, 8/28/98, Friday/p. M, Monica Eng
NEW YORK TIMES, 8/14/98, p. E12, Stephen Holden
VARIETY, 2/9-15/98, p. 71, Leonard Klady

BEYOND SILENCE

A Miramax Films and Buena Vista International release of a Claussen+Wöbke Filmproduktion and Roxy Film-Luggi Waldleitner production in association with Bavarian Broadcasting company (BR)/South German Broadcasting Company (SDR)/Arte/Swiss Television (DRS). *Executive Producer:* Uli Putz. *Producer:* Thomas Wöbke, Jacob Claussen, and Luggi Waldleitner. *Director:* Caroline Link. *Screenplay (German and German sign language with English subtitles):* Caroline Link and Beth Serlin. *Director of Photography:* Gernot Roll. *Editor:* Patricia Rommel. *Music:* Niki Reiser. *Sound:* Andreas Wölki and (music) Thomas Strebel. *Casting:* Risa Kes. *Production Designer:* Susann Bieling. *Costumes:* Katharina von Martius. *Make-up:* Heidi Moser. Running time: 97 minutes. *MPAA Rating:* PG-13.

CAST: Sylvie Testud (Lara); Tatjana Trieb (Lara as a Child); Howie Seago (Martin); Emmanuelle Laborit (Kai); Sibylle Canonica (Clarissa); Matthias Habich (Gregor); Alexandra Bolz (Marie); Hansa Czypionka (Tom); Doris Schade (Lilli); Horst Sachtleben (Robert); Hubert Mulzer (Mr. Gärtner); Birge Schade (Ms. Mertens); Stephan Kampwirth (Bank Teller); Léa Mekhnéche (Johanna); Laurel Severin (Martin as a Child); Selestina Stanisavijevic (Clarissa as a Child); Julia Lorbeer (Bettina); Alexis Segovia (Uli); Anna Bickhofer (Bea); Stefan Spreer (Walter); Susann Bieling (Sales Clerk in Toy Store); Karin Lehmann (Secretary of Music School); Stefan von Moers (Associate of Conservatory); Marta Rodriquez (Lady at Concert); Jutta Schaad (Employee of Conservatory); Ute Cremer and Franz-Hermann Hanfstingl (Professors at Conservatory). Pfarrer Groll (Priest); Axel Hauguth (Colleague at Print Shop); Carmen Härdle and Stephan Lewetz (Pair of Lovers in Movie).

LOS ANGELES TIMES, 6/5/98, Calendar/p. 18, Kevin Thomas

Caroline Link's highly accomplished and engrossing Oscar-nominated German film "Beyond Silence" has the look of an idyll. An attractive couple, Martin and Kai Bischoff (Howie Seago, Emmanuelle Laborit), live with their beautiful 8-year-old daughter (Tatjana Trieb) in a lovely 19th century farmhouse in the Bavarian countryside. When it snows the place is as inviting as an old-fashioned Christmas card.

The Bischoffs are in fact a happy, deeply loving family but one with special challenges: The parents are deaf-mutes who communicate with each other and their daughter through sign language.

"What would we do without you?" asks Martin rhetorically, after Lara has interpreted for her parents at the local bank. That question becomes the film's point, for as Lara matures she will face a very real struggle to assert her independence from parents who have relied upon her so strongly. Already Lara is falling behind in her reading and writing skills because of their often unwitting demands.

Such responsibilities have matured Lara well beyond her 8 years, and as an interpreter she has learned to become an amusingly clever diplomat, tailoring her parents' questions and the replies to them in what she considers the family's best interests.

Lara's heroine is her father's elegant older sister Clarissa (Sibylle Canonica), a clarinetist who encourages her to follow in her footsteps. This is an immediate source of tension because Martin has an understandably deep-seated resentment toward his parents, who have never learned to sign, and a certain jealousy of Clarissa. Martin's enduring sense of isolation reveals Germany's reluctance to endorse sign language, insisting that it inhibits the deaf from learning to speak and that they are better off reading lips, an attitude that is by and large considered outdated in the U.S.

As the film moves forward 10 years we discover that Lara (now played by Sylvie Testud), whose special responsibilities to her parents have continued to foster her self-assertiveness, is flowering into a first-rate clarinetist. She now has a younger sister to help interpret for their parents, and she has become determined to take up her aunt's offer to come to Berlin to prepare for the exams that will gain her entry into the conservatory there. Fate then pulls a cruel trick, making Lara's difficulties in leaving home infinitely tougher.

Link and her co-writer, Beth Serlin, illuminate Lara's entire world beautifully, making clear very realistically that her parents' deafness is hardly the only challenge Lara will have to face, starting with the fact that her aunt, as loving as she is, would like her to be the daughter she never had and would like her to excel musically but not to better her. (If Martin's austere, autocratic father has in effect rejected him, he has also made it clear to his daughter that she has not lived up to his expectations as a musician.)

However, Lara is lucky in meeting a warm, caring young man, Tom (Hansa Czypionka), who is making a career in teaching deaf children, as his own father is deaf. Unlike most young lovers, Lara and Tom have recourse to another language should ever words fail them. Also supportive is her uncle (Matthias Habich), increasingly estranged from the unhappy Clarissa.

With its deft interplay of sound and silence, "Beyond Silence" is a rich, handsome film of passion, energy and joy as well as pain, and as any of us who have had a parent with a serious hearing loss can tell you, it rings all too true in its depiction of the ways in which deafness can exacerbate the often already difficult communication between parent and child. Link assembled a most affecting cast.

NEW YORK POST, 6/5/98, p. 46, Thelma Adams

"Beyond Silence" is this years "Shine."'

German director Caroline Link, who co-wrote "Beyond" with Beth Serlin, uses deafness as an emotional metaphor for the strains within a combative musical family.

Link's moving, warmly acted movie lost the 1997 Oscar for foreign-language film to the Netherlands' more self-conscious father-son drama "Character." In "Beyond," the central character is Lara (child actress Tatjana Trieb, followed by Sylvie Testude). The strong-willed girl acts as her hearing-impaired parents' ears.

Lara often interprets language to suit her own interest—imagine a parent-teacher conference translated by the child in question.

The world of Lara and her parents, Martin and Kai (Howie Seago and Emmanuelle Laborit, both deaf), is cozy and cut off, like a chalet in a snowstorm.

As Lara develops independent interests, conflicts arise. Lara's childless Aunt Clarissa (Sibylle Canonica) introduces her niece to the clarinet and the world of music.

The bond between Lara and Clarissa threatens Martin: as a child, Clarissa's musical ability was a threat to her brother's place in their bourgeois family. She was always a rival for his father's love, a reminder of his handicap.

What's beautiful about "Beyond Silence" is the way this discord between hearing and deaf, brother and sister, father and daughter is amplified by the tension between music and silence. The central conflict is universal: a daughter's struggle to separate herself from her parents while maintaining their love and respect.

NEWSDAY, 6/5/98, Part II/p. B7, John Anderson

Certain movies are considered critique-proof. Maybe they have Sylvester Stallone, Leonardo DiCaprio or some other expensive special effect. Or, maybe their subject simply puts them beyond reproof.

So it is with "Beyond Silence," German director Caroline Link's venture into the world of the meaning, very honest soap opera that seems to know it can coast on its own benevolence. In short, you won't find Sly or Leo, but you will find a movie whose sum is far more important than its parts.

But while it may falter dramatically, "Beyond Silence" goes where so few films have gone before that much of it, for the hearing world at least, will be pure revelation'

The engine of the film is the relationship between Lara (Sylvie Testud as an adult, Tatjana Trieb as a young girl) and her deaf parents, Martin (Howie Seago) and Kai (Emmanuelle Laborit); more precisely, the way Lara's musical talents create a rift between them. But it's the day-to-day stuff that really opens a window on the world of deaf parents, especially those trying to raise a hearing child.

Although her sensibility can be a bit cloying, director Link wisely finds both pathos and humor in the family's domestic life: Lara sitting below their TV screen, providing signed "subtitles" for her mother as she watches a weepy movie; young Lara conscientiously talking to her baby sister so the child will learn language; Lara interpreting for her parents and her teacher during a school conference, and twisting everyone's words to her benefit.

The music, however, on which so much of the plot revolves, is badly faked; the actresses playing Lara should at least have watched a clarinetist breathe so their playing wouldn't seem so stagey. From the moment Lara's aunt, the beautiful Clarissa (Sibylle Canonica), gives Lara her old instrument as a Christmas gift, the girl is tooting away squeaklessly. Given how much music means to the movie, its execution seems to have been treated offhandedly.

Clarissa is a really intriguing character, an artist/libertine whose cultivation of Lara and her talents seem at least equally as self-serving as generous. She knows, for instance, that deafness and music have always divided her from her brother, Martin; at her first recital, he got hysterical at the soundless sight of his sister playing. Excluded from the music and raised by a family that refused to learn sign language—a common situation, especially in Germany, the theory being that the deaf should learn regular speech—Martin is an angry guy. And he channels that anger toward music, something he won't even try to understand.

Seago is particularly good (deaf since birth, he's been seen in "Star Trek: The Next Generation," as well as in stage productions by David Byrne and Peter Sellars). He's a slow-burning but incendiary Martin, from whom music is stealing his daughter.

Lara, caught between her dependent parents and a career in music, progressses from childhood to young artistry without once combing her hair (someone please explain that hair to me) and finding along the way love, sex and independence—oh yes, and an Oscar nomination. "Beyond Silence" was in the running for Best Foreign Film this year, making it, ostensibly, one of the five best films in the non-English-speaking world. Which says more about the priorities of the Academy Awards than it does about the film: Good intentions, and hence political correctness, carry far more weight than craft, it seems, and in the case of "Beyond Silence," doesn't that really just equal pity and a patronizing attitude? The film is being released with special subtitles for deaf audiences (such as "Singing and Laughing," for whenever sound is fulfilling a plot function). It's a nice idea. In fact, it wouldn't be a bad idea in films that aren't about deaf people.

SIGHT AND SOUND, 5/99, p. 40, Nick Kimberley

Germany, the present. Martin and Kai are deaf-mutes who depend on their eight-year-old daughter Lara to interpret for them, through sign language, the world beyond the family. Lara sometimes uses her power to her own ends, but her relationship with her parents, particularly with her father, is close. The three spend Christmas with Martin's parents and his sister Clarissa, a gifted clarinettist whose music entrances Lara. Clarissa gives Lara a clarinet which becomes her obsession. Martin worries Lara devotes too much time to music and is wary of her relationship with Clarissa. Meanwhile, Kai gives birth to another girl. Lara confirms her baby sister can hear by playing clarinet to her. She continues to translate for her parents and persuades her mother she should learn to ride a bicycle, something she's avoided because of her deafness.

Ten years later, Clarissa suggests Lara come to Berlin to develop her musical talent. When Martin discovers their plan, a row ensues and he throws wine over Clarissa. Nevertheless Lara comes to Berlin, where she meets Tom, a teacher at a school for the deaf. A romance develops. When Lara learns her mother has died while cycling, she returns home. Martin suggests that Kai would still be alive had Lara not encouraged the riding. He discovers Lara's relationship with Tom which angers him. Rejecting her father, Lara returns to Berlin and auditions for music college. Martin attends the audition, which puts Lara off until he tells her in sign language that he wants to understand. Rapprochement is at hand.

In a movie with sound, can deafness ever be presented as anything other than a lack? If music is a healing force, where does that leave those for whom there is no music? Caroline Link has made a decent and honourable film, which might fit in the genre of disability-centred 'problem movies'. But it's hard not to feel that here deafness is a device that enriches our understanding not of deaf-mutes Martin and Kai, but of their daughter Lara. She is the fulcrum of the movie, her centrality emphasised by the fact that just as she uses sign language to mediate between her parents and the outside world, so she must also translate for us, the spectators. Why else does she speak while signing if not to let us know what is being communicated? Deafness (not her own) is a problem that she must solve in order to grow, while Martin's failure to accept the limitations imposed by deafness is the problem he must solve.

At only one point during the movie does Link attempt a point of view that might be read as representing deafness: the opening sequence has Lara skating on a frozen lake, our view of her sometimes interrupted by the view from beneath the ice, where the sound of her skates reaches us as if across a great distance and through immense muffling barriers. It is a beautiful, almost hallucinatory passage, yet even here we are aware that what's being communicated is frozen experience. Real life goes on out of sight, out of reach.

Carefully made and sensitively acted (particularly by the two actors playing Lara: Sylvie Testud and the remarkable Tatjana Trieb as the child Lara), *Beyond Silence* is a touching, at times even a tear-jerking film. Indeed, in one interview, Caroline Link has remarked wistfully, not to say enviously, "People like to cry in American movies." Why, then, the implication goes, shouldn't they cry while watching a European movie? An emotional response does not preempt understanding. Nor, on the other hand, does it guarantee it, but by and large *Beyond Silence* earns our snuffles.

And Link is clearly aware of the problem she has set herself. As in so many movies, music here is healing, enriching, Lara's means to escape. Yet when she visits the school where Tom teaches deaf children, she finds him in a music class. He gets the children to lie on the floor while music is playing and Lara joins them. When the children feel the sound through the floor, one by one they get up and begin to dance. Lara, however, remains on the floor. She can't feel the music. "Poor Lara," says Tom.

It's a sweetly ironic moment, and reminds me of what it feels like to attend signed opera performances. These are routine performances in every respect save one: there's a signer at the side of the stage. Yet by some strange alchemy, the signer's gestures intensify the dramatic, perhaps even the musical experience, although I can't read sign language and certainly cannot understand the experience of those for whom the signer is translating. *Beyond Silence* has no duty to educate us about deafness, nor to make us empathise. It does, however, make us think and feel. 'Problem movie' or not, it deserves credit for that.

VILLAGE VOICE, 6/9/98, p. 148, Kaelen Wilson-Goldie

How does a little girl explain to her deaf father her fear of thunder? Or her love of music? The German film *Beyond Silence* tells the story of a hearing child born to deaf parents and her efforts to unearth feeling beneath sound.

Acting as a bridge between her parents and the hearing world, young Lara (Tatjana Trieb) translates bank negotiations, telephone calls, and teacher conferences. When she's given a clarinet, Lara discovers a passion in music her parents seem incapable of understanding. Here the film jumps ahead 10 years to 18-year-old Lara (Sylvie Testud), who is anxious to break free from family obligation. Her music has ripped through her family, dividing sound from silence and father from daughter.

Director Caroline Link, who cowrote the script with Beth Serlin, fills *Beyond Silence* with witty exchanges the characters express both verbally and physically through sign language. The deaf actor Howie Seago, for example, registers a father's alienation from his daughter in a single wince. Though *Beyond Silence* has all the trappings of a typical affirmation-through-music tale, the subtle complexities both Trieb and Testud explore onscreen give Lara's character, as well as the film, unexpected depth.

Also reviewed in:
CHICAGO TRIBUNE, 6/12/98, Friday/p. D, Michael Wilmington
NEW REPUBLIC, 6/22/98, p. 26, Stanley Kauffmann
NEW YORK TIMES, 6/5/98, p. E12, Stephen Holden
WASHINGTON POST, 6/12/98, p. B5, Rita Kempley
WASHINGTON POST, 6/12/98, Weekend/p. 44, Michael O'Sullivan

BIG HIT, THE

A TriStar Pictures release of an Amen Ra Films/Zide-Perry/Lion Rock production. *Executive Producer:* John Woo, Terence Chang, and John M. Eckert. *Producer:* Warren Zide and Wesley Snipes. *Director:* Che-Kirk Wong. *Screenplay:* Ben Ramsey. *Director of Photography:* Danny Nowak. *Editor:* Robin Russell and Pietro Scalia. *Music:* Graeme Revell. *Music Editor:* Joshua Winget. *Sound:* Douglas Ganton and (music) Mark Currie. *Sound Editor:* Wayne Griffin and Michael O'Farrell. *Casting:* Roger Mussenden. *Production Designer:* Taavo Soodor. *Art Director:* Andrew Stearn and Craig Lathrop. *Set Decorator:* Enrico Campana. *Set Dresser:* Jacques A. Veilleux. *Special Effects:* Kaz Kobielski. *Costumes:* Margaret Mohr. *Make-up:* Donald J. Mowat. *Stunt Coordinator:* John Stoneham, Jr. and Lau Chi-Ho. *Running time:* 93 minutes. *MPAA Rating:* R.

CAST: Mark Wahlberg (Melvin Smiley); Lou Diamond Phillips (Cisco); Christina Applegate (Pam Shulman); Avery Brooks (Paris); Bokeem Woodbine (Crunch); Antonio Sabato, Jr. (Vince); Lainie Kazan (Jeanne Shulman); Elliott Gould (Morton Shulman); Sab Shimono (Jiro Nishi); Robin Dunne (Gump, The Stutterer); Lela Rochon (Chantel); Danny Smith (Video Store Kid); Joshua Peace (Lance); David Usher (Sergio); Hardee T. Lineham (Accountant); Gerry Mendocino (Slave Trader); Robert Vernon Eaton and John Stoneham, Sr (Pimps); Nicola Jones (Blond); Alexa Gilmour (Aly, Keiko's Friend); John Stoker (Sid Mussbergr, The Neighbor); Cotton Mather (Moe); Derek Peels (Windbush); Tig Fong (Kaya); Danny Lima (Aaron The Limo Driver); Morgan Freeman (Boy in Hotel Lobby); Giovahann White (Paris' Son); Bobby Hannah (Paris' Driver); China Chow (Keiko Nishi, Jiro's Daughter).

LOS ANGELES TIMES, 4/24/98, Calendar/p. 6, Jack Mathews

[The following review by Jack Mathews appeared in a slightly different form in
NEWSDAY, 4/24/98, Part II/p. B7.]

Hong Kong director Che-Kirk Wong's first American feature, "The Big Hit," is that rarest of all genre hybrids, the screwball-romantic-action-situation-blackcomedy. Rare for good reason. Who'd want to see a thing like that?

The gamble here is that kids will. The elements of Hong Kong action—the cartoon spectacles of high-flying, heel-kicking, pyrotechnic, Jackie Chan death-defying stunt violence—have become a hot commodity in Hollywood, where recruited Hong Kong directors have added their flourishes to such otherwise conventional studio fare as "Face/Off ' and "Broken Arrow."

"The Big Hit," which was brought to Wesley Snipes' production company by Hong Kong legend John Woo, attempts to take the East-West merger even further, and the result is an only fitfully funny comic mongrel.

Here's the situation comedy: Melvin Smiley (Mark Wahlberg) is a soft-spoken, Maalox-gulping professional hit man with a home in the 'burbs and the demeanor of a grown-up Beaver Cleaver.

He's a walked-on romantic, engaged to Pam (Christina Applegate), a "Jewish American princess" who doesn't love him, and fooling around with Chantel (Lela Rochon), an abusive black mistress who wants only his money. (This sitcom skews toward a wide ethnic audience.)

Here's the action comedy: Mel is a member of a hit squad, a foursome of hard-bodied killers who show off their abs and buns in an early group nude scene (size does matter: They all have small brains), then dress up like the Village People and go on a killing spree in the penthouse of a white slave trader.

Here's the screwball comedy: After a kidnapping caper goes wrong, Mel's angry mistress dumps the hostage, a bankrupt Hong Kong producer's daughter named Keiko (China Chow), at his house, where he's entertaining his potential in-laws, Pam's sad-sack drunk father (Elliott Gould) and her overbearing mother (Lainie Kazan).

Mel keeps shuffling Keiko from the garage to the bathroom, only to have his fiancee and her parents head for temple with the hostage in their trunk.

Here's the black comedy: Along with Keiko, Chantel drops off a couple of garbage bags full of body parts that Mel had collected on an earlier job. Now, he's having to keep his uncooperative hostage hidden while running outside to play tug-of-war with a dog trying to get to the goodies in the garbage bags.

Here's the romance: Mel and Keiko, who actually meet cute (he puts a bullet in the head of a kid who's assaulting her), are falling in love. She's a bored rich girl, he's a lonely killer, they're almost a computer match.

If any of this sounds good, go. Some of it does work. Wahlberg, the star of "Boogie Nights," is an amiable antihero, the kind of guy who would risk his life to return an overdue video of "King Kong Lives." Lou Diamond Phillips has a high time overacting as Cisco, the hit squad double-crosser who blames Mel when he discovers their hostage is the goddaughter of an underworld menace (Avery Brooks). And newcomer Chow, the daughter of the guy who owns the tony Mr. Chow's restaurant chain, is a dish.

Even by Hong Kong standards, the action sequences here are dizzy cartoons, with people jumping higher than they could, surviving events that they couldn't, and daring us to believe things that we can't.

"The Big Hit" is nothing more, or less, than a big goof.

NEW YORK POST, 4/24/98, p. 41, Rod Dreher

"The Big Hit"—add a well-placed "s" and the title of this breathtakingly bad flick becomes a succinct and spot-on review.

If you doubt that the hit-man comedy genre that has spawned such great pictures as "Reservoir Dogs"and "Pulp Fiction" is now as dead and reeking as Pol Pot rotting on his jungle bier, buy a ticket to this wretched thing and see for yourself.

And yet we can be grateful to its makers for one thing: introducing the marvelous China Chow to the movies.

Chow, the daughter of Manhattan restaurateur Michael Chow and his late wife, Tina, is hardly in the movie long enough to demonstrate her acting ability. But Chow is such a strong and sexy screen presence that she'll emerge from this steaming pile smelling like a rose, and poised to become Hollywood's next Young Big Thing.

Mark Wahlberg, who had a big thing in "Boogie Nights," goes slumming here as Melvin Smiley, a contract killer whose attempts to please his boss (Avery Brooks), his fiancee (Christina Applegate) and his mistress (Lela Rochon) are driving him to the bottle—the Maalox bottle, that is.

I know just how he feels. After listening to the torrent of sewage coming out of these characters' mouths, and watching the gut-wrenching savagery of "The Big Hit"'s first half hour, in which Melvin and his muscleboy buds (Lou Diamond Phillips, Antonio Sabato Jr., and Bokeem Woodbine) mow down their enemies, I was ready to heave. And leave.

The filthy dialogue is straight out of gangsta pictures, and the crudely balletic killing is typical of Hong Kong action films. Director Che-Kirk Wong, making his U.S. debut here, certainly fills the screen with enough graphic homicidal mania to thrill people who like this kind of vicious garbage.

But when these guys off a room full of men, then come on to three shaking and terrified women standing in a hot tub full of bloody water with the line: "I wanna pour milk on you and become part of your complete breakfast." you don't know whether to be more appalled by the vulgar witlessness of scripter Ben Ramsey's dialogue, or at the exploitation of extreme viciousness to entertain drooling morons.

The plot centers around a Japanese millionaire (Sab Shimono) and the kidnapping of his daughter (Chow). Though the killers work as part of a corporate team, Mel's cohort Cisco (Phillips, doing an incredibly irritating and profane wigger routine) decides to moonlight one weekend with a kidnap job to earn extra cash. Only after they've nabbed Keiko do they discover that she's the goddaughter of their ruthless boss, Paris (Brooks).

Paris puts Cisco in charge of tracking down the kidnappers and liquidating them. To save his own hide, Cisco tries to put the blame on Mel. In addition to dealing with his Jewish-American princess fiancee and her stereotypically shrill parents (Lainie Kazan and Elliott Gould), Mel has to outsmart Cisco while he's holding Keiko hostage—and falling in love with her.

Chow's entrance into this thoroughly repulsive and incompetent film brightens it considerably, but she has to struggle against a comic sensibility so puerile it makes "South Park" seem like a lost play of Oscar Wilde. Keiko and Mel's romance begins to bud when, no kidding, he pulls down the handcuffed girl's panties so she can pee. Beautiful.

About the only other thing to be said about "The Big Hit" is that they blow stuff up real good.

SIGHT AND SOUND, 7/99, p. 36, Danny Leigh

California. Neurotic assassin Melvin Smiley and three fellow hitmen break into the home of a wealthy pimp on behalf of crimelord Paris. Melvin shoots the pimp dead. His cohort Cisco asks him to take part in a kidnapping the following day. Melvin refuses. He returns to the suburban condo he shares with his fiancée Pam. She has lent Melvin's savings to her parents to square her father's gambling debts. Panicked, Melvin accepts Cisco's invitation.

Cisco's quarry turns out to be Keiko, the teenage daughter of film producer Jiro Nishi. After her abduction, a reluctant Melvin agrees to hold Keiko at his house, despite the presence of both Pam and her visiting parents. Melvin and Keiko find themselves attracted to one another. On learning Nishi is a close friend of Paris, Cisco blames the kidnapping on Melvin; Paris orders him to kill Melvin. When Cisco arrives at Melvin's house, Melvin and Keiko flee. Cisco pursues Melvin to a video shop. In the subsequent mêlée, both men are apparently killed when the building explodes. Weeks later, Keiko's chauffeur picks up Melvin—he was shielded from the blast by a promotional display for one of her father's films. The pair decide to elope.

For its first ten minutes the *raison d'être* of Che-Kirk Wong's US debut seems obvious. As bullets fly in fetishistic slow motion, turning a pimp's jacuzzi red with his own blood, *The Big Hit* resembles little more than a compendium of brutal stylised action sequences, assembled to introduce the Hong Kong-born director of *Crime Story* and *Rock 'n' Roll Cop* to western audiences—which, according to Wong himself, is exactly what was intended. Initially, this purpose-built précis of past glories for international consumption proves grimly effective: camera angles are vertiginous, dialogue minimal, the violence reliably stylised.

But after the frenetic opening the film reveals ambitions beyond amassing a prodigious body count. There is, for example, something slightly odd about a graphic gun battle in which attention is repeatedly drawn not to the on-screen carnage but to the costumes and set dressing. Wong was once a fashion designer. While the abundant ballistic hardware on display is, of course, subject to innumerable ardent close-ups, no less reverence is invested in the detailing of a Gaultier shirt or a gangster's pristine office space. Similarly, Ben Ramsey's labyrinthine narrative has grander aspirations than simply providing dialogue to punctuate the gunplay. Littering his script with the kind of priapic badinage young, male screenwriters now routinely ascribe to the criminal fraternity, Ramsey often appears eager to get the bloodshed over as quickly as possible in order to accommodate the next wisecrack.

A jarring uncertainty of tone is the outcome. Juxtaposing comedy and extreme violence is precarious, requiring masterly timing. But even the darkest humour looks glib when the punchline is a gunshot wound. The ceaseless flippancy and farcical motifs at the heart of *The Big Hit* make queasy companions for the storyline's slew of corpses. Yet although Wong's attempts at black comedy are badly misjudged, he has made the effort to learn from some of his more successful antecedents. *Grosse Pointe Blank,* in particular, seems to be a touchstone here Unfortunately Mark Wahlberg brings none of John Cusack's range or subtlety to his role. Instead he reprises his performance as *Boogie Nights'* Dirk Diggler with unnerving precision. With few of the supporting cast able to rouse themselves from a stupor, it is left to Lou Diamond Phillips to inject zest into the proceedings. Mugging his way through every scene with incipient mania, he shows all the signs of an actor relishing his work; in which case, some good has come of this otherwise vacant and ill-conceived film.

VILLAGE VOICE, 5/5/98, p. 124, Dennis Lim

Cloaking its obnoxiousness in an aggressively cartoonish mantle, *The Big Hit* marks the latest dubious U.S. debut of a Hong Kong director—in this case, *Crime Story*'s Che-Kirk Wong. As Mel, a hit man described as "charming in a *Rain Man* sort of way," Mark Wahlberg (or is it Dirk Diggler?) doesn't exactly test himself. With his pretty-boy cronies—Bokeem Woodbine, Antonio Sabato Jr., and Lou Diamond Phillips (who pops a blood vessel every other minute or so)—Mel abducts a Japanese tycoon's feisty daughter (China Chow) and, before you can say Stockholm syndrome... well, I won't spoil it for you.

Incidentally, our dumb, virile hero is also juggling a scheming fiancée (Christina Applegate doing Fran Drescher) and a scheming girlfriend (Lela Rochon). The multi-ethnic cast has been assembled at the behest of Ben Ramsey's self-consciously boorish screenplay, an equal-opportunity offender that's never smart enough to pull it off. Wong understands the mechanics of farce, but he's most comfortable turning pyrotechnical cartwheels. Mere minutes in, he's staging a gargantuan fireball and reflecting it in a swimming pool—just what you'd expect, really, from a film whose philosophy can be expressed in three words: Hell, why not?

Also reviewed in:
NEW YORK TIMES, 4/24/98, p. E12, Lawrence Van Gelder
VARIETY, 4/27-5/3/98, p. 59, Leonard Klady

BIG LEBOWSKI, THE

A Gramercy Pictures release of a PolyGram Filmed Entertainment presentation of a Working Title production.   *Executive Producer:* Tim Bevan and Eric Fellner.   *Producer:* Ethan Coen. *Director:* Joel Coen.   *Screenplay:* Joel Coen and Ethan Coen.   *Director of Photography:* Roger Deakins.   *Editor:* Roderick Jaynes and Tricia Cooke.   *Music:* Carter Burwell.   *Music Editor:* Todd Kasow.   *Choreographer:* Bill Landrum and Jacqui Landrum.   *Sound:* Allan Byer and (music) Michael Farrow.   *Sound Editor:* Skip Lievsay.   *Casting:* John Lyons.   *Production Designer:* Rick Heinrichs.   *Art Director:* John Dexter.   *Set Designer:* Mariko Braswell.   *Set*

Decorator: Chris Spellman. *Set Dresser:* Lisa S. Corbin, Beth Emerson, and Tim Park. *Visual Effects:* Janek Sirrs. *Mechanical Effects:* Peter Chesney. *Costumes:* Mary Zophres. *Make-up:* Jean Black. *Make-up (Jeff Bridges):* Edouard Henriques. *Running time:* 117 minutes. *MPAA Rating:* R.

CAST: Jeff Bridges (The Dude); John Goodman (Walter Sobchak); Julianne Moore (Maude Lebowski); Steve Buscemi (Donny); David Huddleston (The Big Lebowski); Philip Seymour Hoffman (Brandt); Tara Reid (Bunny Lebowski); Philip Moon and Mark Pellegrino (Treehorn Thugs); Peter Stormare, Flea, and Torsten Voges (Nihilists); Jimmie Dale Gilmore (Smokey); Jack Kehler (Dude's Landlord); John Turturro (Jesus Quintana); James G. Hoosier (Quintana's Partner); Carlos Leon and Terrance Burton (Maude's Thugs); Richard Gant (Older Cop); Christian Clemenson (Younger Cop); Dom Irrera (Tony the Chauffeur); Gérard L'Heureux (Lebowski's Chauffeur); David Thewlis (Knox Harrington); Lu Elrod (Coffee Shop Waitress); Michael Gomez (Auto Circus Cop); Peter Siragusa (Gary the Bartender); Sam Elliott (The Stranger); Marshall Manesh (Doctor); Harry Bugin (Arthur Digby Sellers); Jesse Flanagan (Little Larry Sellers); Irene Olga Lopez (Pilar); Luis Colina (Corvette Owner); Ben Gazzara (Jackie Treehorn); Leon Russom (Malibu Police Chief); Ajgie Kirkland (Cab Driver); Jon Polito (Private Snoop); Aimee Mann (Nihilist Woman); Jerry Haleva (Saddam); Jennifer Lamb (Pancake Waitress); Warren David Keith (Funeral Director).

LOS ANGELES TIMES, 3/6/98, Calendar/p. 1, Kenneth Turan

The Coen brothers are not twins but they might as well be. Like many close siblings, writer-director Joel and writer-producer Ethan share a private cinematic language. The films they make together are self-contained, almost hermetic alternative universes, worlds that amuse the brothers no end but are not guaranteed to connect with anyone else.

The Coens' career has alternated between pictures where the connection to audiences was made with exhilarating success (the recent "Fargo") and others (the completely baffling "The Hudsucker Proxy") where all circuits were down. Their latest, "The Big Lebowski," turns out to be a little of both.

Though the film has so much plot that the Coens consider "Lebowski" a '90s version of a Raymond Chandler detective novel, the story line is in truth disjointed, incoherent and even irritating. What you remember and enjoy about this film (if you remember and enjoy it at all) is not the forest but individual trees, engaging rifts as only the Coens can concoct them that amuse and entertain though they connect to nothing else in the film, not even one another.

Set during the Gulf War and framed by the words of a narrator/guardian angel with a thick cowboy accent (Sam Elliott), the Coens' film involves two different Jeffrey Lebowskis. Only one of them, however, is "the laziest man in Los Angeles County," a genial deadbeat who insists on being known simply as "the Dude" (Jeff Bridges).

Introduced in a supermarket sampling milk from the carton, the Dude is a proto-slacker, terminally befuddled by the constant smoking of weed and the drinking of White Russians. "Huh?" is his most common expression, "Take it easy" his advice on every subject, and bowling with buddies Walter (John Goodman) and Donny (Steve Buscemi) his sole reason for making it out of bed in the morning.

Though the Dude is not in the business of seeking out excitement, it comes unbidden one night to his Venice shack in the form of a pair of sadistic thugs, one of whom urinates on the Dude's cherished rug to make the point that he better make good on his wife's mounting debts.

As even the thugs soon realize, they've got the wrong Lebowski. The other, bigger Lebowski (David Huddleston) is a millionaire who lives across town in Pasadena with his sex-obsessed trophy wife Bunny (Tara Reid) and plaques commemorating earnest philanthropies like the Little Lebowski Urban Achievers.

Though this Lebowski throws the Dude out when he shows up asking for compensation for his rug, the millionaire soon calls back. It seems Bunny has been kidnapped and the services of the Dude are requested to act as intermediary. A well-compensated intermediary.

From this (relatively) straightforward beginning, "The Big Lebowski" soon spins rapidly and completely out of control. Though the Coens, working as usual with master cinematographer

Roger Deakins, are impressive visual stylists and clever writers, this film feels completely haphazard, thrown together without much concern for organizing intelligence.

That's because, despite concocting an incomprehensible plot that comes to include pornographers, anarchists and an avant-garde painter (Julianne Moore), the Coens don't seem to be very interested in it. What they care about are the private jokes and odd bits happening at the extremes of their picture, things like a peripatetic tumbleweed, a Busby Berkeley-inspired dream sequence and a marmot used to terrorize the unwary. Without coherence, there is anarchy, and when the wealthy Lebowski barks to the Dude, "What in God's holy name are you blathering about?," he's speaking for the audience as well as himself.

Yet as tempting as it is to completely dismiss "The Big Lebowski," it's hard to do because the Coens are able to create wickedly funny eccentrics and possess the ability to energize certain actors to inhabit them completely. The adept Philip Seymour Hoffman is properly unctuous as an executive assistant, and John Turturro has the time of his life as Jesus Quintana, a flamboyant bowler who's also a registered sex offender. These are tiny roles but they're more than memorable.

Strongest of the major players is Goodman as Walter Sobchak, a classic self-absorbed Coen brothers lunatic, as oblivious to the rest of the world as it is to him. A short-tempered, overwrought Vietnam vet forever warning everyone, "You're entering a world of pain," Goodman's Walter always surprises us with the extent of his manias, and his insistence that he is "shomre Shabbes," a Sabbath-observing Jew, turns into a classic sequence.

Unfortunately it's the nature of this film that all of "Lebowski's" good things exist in a vacuum. Unconcerned about creating a coherent center, the Coens haven't cared that the Dude is not only too laid-back to pay his rent, he's also too laid-back to function as a protagonist. Comparing Bridges' narcoleptic character to the more focused and humane heroine Frances McDormand played in "Fargo" goes a long way toward accounting for the relative success levels of the two films.

Whatever else you say about the Coens, they do have a knack for anticipating criticism. "It was a pretty good story, don't you think?" Elliott's folksy narrator says at the close. "It made me laugh. Pause Parts of it anyway." Partner, you got that one right.

NEW STATESMAN, 4/24/98, p. 45, Chris Peachment

Films from the Coen brothers divide into types: those that aspire to nothing more than comedy, and rather more serious ventures. Not that the Coens are ever entirely serious. The grim plot of their last film *Fargo,* which featured their first ever "ordinary" heroine in the sweet-natured cop played by Joel Coen's wife, Frances McDormand, was supposedly based on a true crime story. The movie was a mature inquiry into the nature of wickedness and its comeuppance. Though it still contained moments of wayward humour, it was their least tricksy, least wacky work.

The Big Lebowski is a step backwards; in fact, more like four steps backwards, to their second film, *Raising Arizona,* where the plot, such as it is, soon goes AWOL and the humour is like a surrealists' mass outing.

There are actually two Lebowskis living in LA, although Jeff Bridges does not know this when a couple of thugs burst into his room, shove his head down the toilet and demand that he tell them just where their money is. He suggests that they push his head in the toilet again, since it's probably lurking down there somewhere. Once the thugs look around Bridges' decrepit apartment they realise they've probably got the wrong Lebowski. They depart, although not before urinating on the rug.

Bridges was fond of his rug and so he goes in search of the other Lebowski to demand a nice new rug in compensation. This Lebowski is a millionaire recluse, who lives in a small palace in Pasadena. He is averse to giving Bridges a new rug but hires him instead to deliver the ransom for his kidnapped wife. It is at this point that any attempt to synopsise the plot gives out. Matters get so hopelessly twisted up that you feel there are two or three other films all scrabbling to make themselves heard.

It is on the incidental details of a film that the brothers put their stamp. The opening shot shows a piece of tumbleweed in the desert making its way into the streets of LA. A drawling voice-over talks in frontier style about what a cool dude Lebowski is. It looks like the first film ever to be narrated by a piece of tumbleweed and it also looks as if we're in for a western. But it soon mutates into a sub-Chandleresque thriller, first signalled by the millionaire Lebowski sitting in a wheelchair like General Sternwood in *The Big Sleep*. The bag given to Bridges for the pay-off contains no money, the errant wife seems only too happy to be kidnapped, double-cross follows deception, and everyone seems to be working to their own hidden agenda.

But Bridges is no Philip Marlowe. That tarnished knight died out years ago with Bogart. His Lebowski follows in the footsteps of Elliott Gould in Robert Altman's version of *The Long Goodbye:* a shambling, rueful no-hoper who hasn't a clue what is going on and is too dumb to care. This Lebowski prefers to be known as "the Dude" and his brain stopped somewhere in 1973, stalled on whatever illicit substance was fashionable at that time. He wanders around in baggy shorts, scratching his goatee beard and muttering hippy platitudes. It's the least stretching role Bridges has ever had, though he is as good as ever, which is to say one of the best actors in Hollywood.

Bridges is partnered by John Goodman, a good-natured weapons freak with an alarmingly short fuse. They spend much of the movie ten-pin bowling, with the mousy Steve Buscemi making up their team. This is an excuse for the Coens to indulge their taste for the myriad byways of American subculture. One of their rival bowlers, for example, is John Turturro at his freakiest, springing a purple jumpsuit painted fingernails, a hairnet and a name tag that says "Jesus". There is a Busby Berkeley dream sequence in which Saddam Hussein dispenses bowling shoes, and a point-of-view shot from inside the ball as it rolls down the bowling lane.

It's all very diverting, and there's even a catchphrase to take away if you're one of those people who likes to do so: "The Dude abides."

But reflecting on it all doesn't yield anything more than that the Coens are just messing around. And they are much funnier when they are being serious.

NEW YORK, 3/16/98, p. 55, David Denby

The funniest thing in the Coen brothers' comedy *The Big Lebowski* is a cameo appearance by John Turturro as a gay Latino bowler, a dandy of the lanes who urges on his ball with insolent thrusts of the pelvis. This egotistical madman—Jesus, his name is—wears a satanic goatee and directs ferocious carnal threats at the other players. What is he doing in the movie? Well, like other Coen brothers works-*Barton Fink* and *The Hudsucker Proxy*—this new comedy could be called an epic shaggy-dog story. Just about everything winds up in it. There are abrupt, nutty jokes, surreal episodes, people flying through the air. The Coen brothers lyricize bowling, turning it into a slow-motion fantasia of heavily rolling balls and sultry pins. It's fun, for a while, watching the Coens blow off the enormous discipline required to make *Fargo*, fun to watch them do any damn thing they please. The trouble is, the bowling-as-eros motif doesn't really fit the rest of the movie's portrait of the alleys as a refuge—a place where losers, dreamers, and blowhards form a little community and find peace.

The Big Lebowski is an off-kilter thriller with a sad-sack hero—Jeff Lebowski, known as the Dude (Jeff Bridges). The Dude shuffles through life in a fumy, pothead haze; he's so stack-brained he can't finish a sentence. He gets involved in a bizarre intrigue involving another man named Lebowski, a millionaire with a promiscuous young wife who may or may not have been kidnapped. Hired to deliver the ransom money, the Dude suffers a series of disasters, the result of his own ineptitude and the arrogant interventions of his friend Walter (John Goodman), a Jewish paranoid so hostile and aggressive that he misinterprets literally everything he sees. Goodman has his monstrous melancholy; he's funny—a huffy elephant—but Bridges and Goodman stumble through far too many superfluous adventures together. It's only amusing the first time the Dude gets lost in his own story—a story so incoherent that he can't explain it to anyone. What's the point of scoring off morons who think they are cool? Jeff Bridges has so much dedication as an actor that he sacrifices himself to the Coen brothers' self-defeating conception. Even Bridges can't open up a character who remains unconscious.

NEW YORK POST, 3/6/98, p. 47, Thelma Adams

If Paul Bunyan lived in L.A., drove a junker, smoked weed, drank white Russians, wore Bermuda shorts and lived for bowling, he'd be a lot like Jeff Lebowski, a.k.a. the Dude.

Joel and Ethan Coen have left "Fargo" behind for "The Big Lebowski." This tall tale will tickle audiences willing to drift through its pot-driven story like the tumbleweed that breaks away from the Mulholland chaparral and crosses the Hollywood freeway during the opening credits.

The Sons of the Pioneers sing "Tumbling Tumbleweeds" in the background while the cowpoke narrator (Sam Elliott, in his most resonant Louis Lamour voice) introduces us to the hero: "He's the man for his time and place."

Jeff Bridges is Lebowski, a large man without ambition who initially seems capable of only a minor role in his own destiny. We meet Lebowski in bathrobe and slippers. He's shambling down the aisles of Ralph's grocery store, stopping only to chug stolen milk, which dribbles in his beard.

In the next scene, milk sprays all over Lebowski's bathroom as shakedown artists flush the Dude's shaggy head down his filthy toilet. "Where's the money, Lebowski?" they ask. Welcome to L.A., Coen brothers style.

Where *is* the money? Lebowski doesn't have it. The thugs have confused the Dude with a wheelchair-bound industrialist (David Huddleston) of the same name. A few mistaken identities and many bowling frames later, Lebowski finds himself entangled in the kidnapping of the rich man's porn-star wife, Bunny (Tara Reid)—who may or may not be missing after all.

The ridiculous kidnapping caper brings the Dude and his bowling buddies (John Goodman and Steve Buscemi) into contact with an heiress *artiste* with a Peter Pan fetish (the zesty Julianne Moore), the bowling sex offender Jesus (the hilariously macho John Turturro) and a pack of incompetent nihilists (Flea, Peter Stormare and Torsten Voges).

"The Big Lebowski" reaches its hallucinogenic zenith with a gushy Berkeley-style extravaganza. It's complete with a chorus of dancing beauties flaunting bowling pin headdresses. The dazzled Bridges dances with Moore's bowling Brunhilde, then exits flying, face up, between the chorus girls' gams. More than a flight of fancy, the sequence is a strike, a preposterous, perfect 10.

But it's Bridges, working with a great cast, who carries "The Big Lebowski" when the plot skips town. Not since "Cutter's Way" has Bridges captured the laidback Californian with such aimless charm and feckless honesty. The Dude's too true to be Oscar-worthy, but we'd bowl with him anywhere.

NEWSDAY, 3/6/98, Part II/p. B6, Jack Mathews

The winsome melodic tune of the Sons of the Pioneers' "Tumbling Tumbleweeds," Joel and Ethan Coen's "The Big Lebowski" gets under way, following a tumbleweed on a westbound wind out of the southern California desert through the Los Angeles basin and all the way to the surf at Malibu. Rarely has the gist of a movie been announced with more apt symbolism.

"The Big Lebowski" is a big lark, as hollow, harmless, silly, random and memorable as that tumbleweed. The Coens have taken a break after "Fargo," their brilliant 1996 black comedy, to riff on bowling, blue-collar camaraderie, '30s pulp fiction, '70s stoners, post-traumatic stress syndrome, marmot terrorism, performance art, philanthropy, Busby Berkeley musicals and the stain resistance of Persian rugs.

There are hilarious bits strewn throughout, and a deft set of performances from people who clearly are having as good a time as the Coens. But there also are more comic misfires, more uninspired gags and meaningless camera tricks than the Coens have accounted for in all their previous films combined.

Like "Fargo," and their earlier "Raising Arizona," "The Big Lebowski" develops around a kidnaping theme. The teenage daughter (Tara Reid) of a philanthropist named Jeffrey Lebowski (David Huddleston) has disappeared from their Pasadena estate, a ransom note has been received, and another fellow named Jeff Lebowski, who prefers to be called the Dude (Jeff Bridges), is asked to make the money drop.

The Dude, a bearded, long-haired welfare case who's been stoned since the '70s, is a bad choice for any assignment more complicated than making a seven-pin spare at the local bowling alley, where he hangs out with pals Walter (John Goodman), a Vietnam vet in a terminal rage, and Donny (Steve Buscemi), a clueless Milquetoast with a bad heart. But the Dude seizes the opportunity to make a few bucks and maybe get back at the hoodlums who, earlier having mistaken him for the big Lebowski, broke into his apartment, dunked his head in the toilet and relieved themselves on his living room rug.

As things unfold, the Dude will have close encounters with a porn publisher turned gangster (Ben Gazzara), a group of nihilists and the big Lebowski's wife, Maude (Julianne Moore), a flaky artist who seduces him in the midst of her ovulation cycle, then, while he's enjoying a post-coital smoke, does yoga exercises to increase the chances of insemination.

Among these "real" events are a series of drug-induced fantasies. In one, the Dude flies over Los Angeles like Superman, a trip tragically shortened with the realization that he's still holding on to his bowling ball. Another takes place in the bowling alley, with a Busby Berkeley number, a chorus of gutter girls and the first-ever bowling ball's eye view of a strike.

In a way, the whole movie has the impact of a kaleidoscopic Berkeley production. It's an assault of images and gags that keeps you awake, if not necessarily alert. Ten minutes after "The Big Lebowski" ends, you will have trouble remembering that, oh, yeah, this is sort of a send-up of Raymond Chandler, with the Dude as a pothead-pacifist version of Philip Marlowe, and a second homage (following "The Hudsucker Proxy") to the rapid-patter comedies of the Coens' favorite director, Howard Hawks.

Bridges, inhabiting his character with a hazy insouciance, slows things occasionally, but Goodman, as the pal prodding him into deeper and deeper trouble, is in full shout throughout, and much of the action is borderline hysteria.

You can't blame the Coens for having fun. Their sense of humor, their affection for movies and their technical cleverness are the reasons they've become cult heroes of critics and cineastes. And with "Fargo," their best-written and most disciplined film, they threatened to take their act into the mainstream.

On that score, "The Big Lebowski" is either a setback, for those who'd like to see them raise their game to a new level, or a relief, for those diehard fans who want to keep them for themselves. The Coens have had few greater fans, but I think they should take their cue from that tumbleweed and move on.

NEWSWEEK, 3/16/98, p. 72, Jack Kroll

The Coen brothers have always walked a fine line between cleverness and catastrophe. Joel studied film at NYU, Ethan philosophy at Princeton: they're the two-headed monster of postmortem film. "Blood Simple" teetered toward the cleverness side; "The Hudsucker Proxy" pratfalled into catastrophe; "Fargo" was their best balancing act. As for their new one, move over, "Hudsucker," here comes "The Big Lebowski."

In this film, the Coens are afflicted by a new syndrome: Multiple Parodosis. Frothing from two mouths, they parody film noir, 1940s musicals, flower-child flicks, megaviolent thrillers, sports allegories, ravaged-war-veteran movies, existentialist Westerns... but this is a short review. The Doublemint Coens give us double Lebowskis: Jeff, a.k.a. the Dude (Jeff Bridges), a zonked-out Californian with beach sand in his gears, and Jeff, a.k.a. the Big (David Huddleston), a mysterious wheelchair-bound millionaire. When a trio of "nihilist" thugs mistakes the penniless Dude for the loaded Big, breaking in and urinating nihilistically on his rug, a hornet's nest of old movie themes explodes.

The ingredients in this overboiled cinematic stew include the Dude's Vietnam-vet bowling buddy John Goodman), the Big's performance-artist wife (Julianne Moore) and a cowboy-philosopher (Sam Elliott), whose tumbleweed tones provide the insufferably unfunny voice-over narration. The takeoff-mad Coens even lay their parodic mitts on Busby Berkeley musicals. The genius of Berkeley included its own parody. Didn't they teach that at Princeton?

SIGHT AND SOUND, 5/98, p. 42, Jonathan Romney

Los Angeles, 1991. Jeff 'the Dude' Lebowski, an aging hippie bowling buff, is atacked by thugs mistaking him for another Jeffrey Lebowski, whose wife is in debt to a Mr Treehorn; they beat him up and urinate on his rug. Seeking reparation, the Dud visits his namesake, a paraplegic millionaire, who gives him a hostile welcome. But later Lebowski hires the Dude as courier to hand over the ransom for his kidnapped young wife Bunny. The handover is ruined by the Dude's meddling buddy Walter, and the Dude is left with Lebowski's money, until it disappears when the Dude's car in which he's keeping it is stolen.

Lebowski's artist daughter Maude shows the Dude a porn video starring Bunny and German nihilist Uli, produced by Jackie Treehorn. She believes Bunny has faked her kidnap to extort money from Lebowski, and wants the Dude to retrieve the ransom. Lebowski shows the Dude a severed toe, apparently Bunny's. The Dude is attacked by Uli and his cronies. At the bowling alley, he encounters the Stranger, a mysterious cowboy.

The Dude is take to see Treehorn, who is still after Bunny and her debt. Back at his apartment, the Dude sleeps with Maude, who tells him she has had him vetted as a potential father for her child. Realising Lebowski has used him as a pawn to embezzle money from the Lebowski family foundation, the Dude confronts him at his mansion, where Bunny has returned, toe intact. At the bowling alley, the Dude and Walter have a run-in with the nihilists, during which their friend Donny dies of a heart attack. The Stranger wraps up the story and announces that a little Lebowski—Maude's child—is on the way.

The success of *Fargo* put to rest a long-held myth about the Coen Brothers: that their films were strictly esoteric or enigmatic. This belief seems to be based partly on the way their earlier films are rich in strands that can't easily be assimilated into a conventional narrative pattern—the stray hats in *Miller's Crossing*, the blatantly formal play of circles in *The Hudsucker Proxy*—and partly on the frustrating impression that there is always less to the Coens' work than meets the eye. Every film up until then seemed flawed by the sense that the brothers were being wilfully cavalier, refusing to play their genre games by the rules or, conceivably, just not trying hard enough. Their new film gives some credence to that interpretation: it could almost be subtitled 'In Praise of Goofing Off'.

The Big Lebowski serves as a reminder that the Coens are nothing more enigmatic than this: the most purely ludic of contemporary American film-makers. Played entirely for laughs—at the expense of the audience and of the detective genre—the film warns us from the start not to expect any of its narrative threads to lead anywhere. With a title echoing *The Big Sleep*, we're in for a Raymond Chandler-style entertainment, a labyrinthine route followed solely for the diversions encountered along the way. The story enables us to enjoy a whole catalogue of narrative dead ends, cruel gags and bravura character routines.

The Coens get the jump on us from the opening sequence: the drawling voice-over by the Stranger, a Will Rogers-like philosopher cowboy, makes us expect a Western; but the tumbleweed we see rolls straight into early 90s LA, an urban wild frontier even more untamed than in Chandler's day, and consequently demanding a rougher and readier Marlowe. We're told Jeff Bridges' superannuated slacker is "the man for his time and place", and is consequently several degrees of weathered somnolence beyond even Elliott Gould in Robert Altman's 1973 *The Long Goodbye*.

The Dude is on a doomed, albeit humble, quest from the start—to be paid back for his rug, ruined by debt collectors. But he's also out to answer the question posed by his millionaire namesake: "What makes a man, Mr Lebowski?' It's a pointed question in a universe which classifies the Dude as effectively a non-person—out of step with a culture of cool, malicious surface, in which he's effectively castrated by the loss of his car.

The Big Lebowski echoes such 70s neo-Chandlerian thrillers as *Cutter's Way* and Arthur Penn's *Night Moves*, which also recycles *The Big Sleep*'s wayward-nymphet opening premise. Like Penn's detective hero, the Dude will learn that the deeper you work your way into a labyrinth, the less likely you are to get anywhere. But the Coens actually defuse the paranoid implications of the plot complexities, making sinister machinations look like nothing more than obstacles devised to waste the Dude's leisure time. Sent in search of the other Lebowski's missing pom-star wife, the Dude will work his way into a world not so much of evil as of bizarre, misguided pretension. En route he encounters Lebowski's daughter Maude (Julianne Moore), an artist who does her work suspended in mid-air, and the sinister German nihilist Uli (Peter Stormare), whose prime weapon is a live marmot and whose most menacing threat is to "sqvishh" the Dude's "Johnnsonn".

The Coens seem also to have extended their crime reading to novels by and about 70s survivors. The hip jokiness suggests Kinky Friedman *(The Love Song of J. Edgar Hoover, God Bless John Wayne)*, or the cultivated weariness of the novels of James Crumley *(Mexican Tree Duck)*, in which action is measured not in plot points but in the amount of time spent recovering from benders. The convoluted plot seems designed purely to accommodate its various cameos and acid-inflected nightmare routines, such as a flashy but leaden Busby Berkeley spoof with Julianne Moore as avenging Valkyrie. The range of acting turns is rich, if wayward, with such Coen regulars as Steve Buscemi and John Turturro pointedly reappearing—if to remind us whose film we're watching. Best of all, in a memorably unctuous cameo, is Philip Seymour Hoffman from *Boogie Nights*, the best character-actor find in years. Less plausible are the ludicrous modems': Moore's clipped-voiced practitioner of "vaginal art" (perhaps jibing at her own loopy Dora Maar in *Surviving Picasso)*, a hyper-arch David Thewlis, and Peter Stormare's hissing heavy. But these characters help to flesh out the Coens' vigorously unglamorous portrait of LA. The Dude shuttles between the dreary nether regions—a bowling milieu all the drabber for such touches of tawdry flash as Turturro's purple-lurex lane shark—and the privileged enclaves where everything is phony, where even the dark secrets that once surrounded Chandler's Sternwood mansion no longer frighten.

Within this world, the Dude—a 70s activist with The Seattle Seven and signatory of the "Port Huron Statement"—functions as a resilient lapsed idealist, the old counter-culture dreams now regarded as period jokes. He is laudable not for his moral integrity as such, but because deep-ingrained inertia makes him impervious to corruption. He's an aesthetic dissident—honourably out of step with LA -*zeitgeist* he listens to Captain Beefheart and, in a neat reversal of stereotype, recoils when a black cab driver plays the Eagles.

The casting of Jeff Bridges slyly capitalises on his image as Hollywood's last good guy, an actor who can convincingly and affably embody nonconformist righteousness. He makes a wonderfully calibrated double act with John Goodman's irascible Vietnam veteran converted to Judaism ("I don't roll on Shabbas")—a perfect character for what looks like prime sitcom material. That might be finally what this is—a Seinfeld-style 'film about nothing', or about nothing more than the in-jokes that make the Coens giggle (the Dude, by all accounts, is based on a real-life acquaintance of theirs, one Jeff "the Dude" Dowd, who really was a member of the activist group The Seattle Seven). But then, to make a film this thick with non-sequiturs, this defiantly slight, looks like a heroic act in contemporary US cinema. *The Big Lebowski* is at once utterly inconsequential and a blow for a cinematic slacker aesthetic. Its moral payoff is that, like Marlowe, the Dude finally stays the same—he doesn't need to be redeemed, brought into line with the world he inhabits. Likewise, the Coens, flouting the genre rules and gleefully pursuing their own amusement reserve the right to stay their ineffable, not remotely enigmatic selves.

TIME, 3/2/98, p. 85, Richard Schickel

There are, difficult as it may be to believe, two Jeff Lebowskis living in the Greater Los Angeles area. There's the rich, shady one (David Huddleston) ensconced in a Pasadena mansion, who gives *The Big Lebowski* its title. His opposite number is better known as "Dude." Played by Jeff Bridges, he's a burned-out beach bum whose mental clock stopped sometime in the '70s. But when some thugs, mistaking him for his namesake, invade his pad, beat him up and, worse, ruin the rug that ties the whole living room together, he seeks redress. Or at least some replacement carpetry.

Since the mental calendar of filmmakers Joel and Ethan Coen is often turned back to the 1940s, Dude is a shambling version of Philip Marlowe, the incomprehensible plot and the all-too-comprehensible visual references homages to the film-noir tradition—as if we needed more. Happily, however, the Coens have established a tradition of their own: deeply weird characters (let John Goodman's great portrait of one of those paranoid know-it-alls who actually know nothing stand for the mad multitude this movie contains) embedded in profoundly banal settings (much of the film is set in a bowling alley). So even when they don't achieve the glorious farce of a *Fargo*, there is always something fascinating about following the Coens' rapt gaze as they peer into the American nut bowl.

VILLAGE VOICE, 3/10/98, p. 61, J. Hoberman

The most cold-blooded of American filmmakers, Joel and Ethan Coen recalibrated their formula in *Fargo* with what must have been heartwarming results. Although scarcely less nasty than previous Coen snarkfests, *Fargo* seduced critics, audiences, and even Oscar voters by centering its comedy on the likably dumb-smart persona expertly created by Frances McDormand.

Have the Coens gone feel-good? *The Big Lebowski*, their latest perfectly stylized (and pleasing discombobulated) jape, similarly draws on Jeff Bridge's loser charm as one Jeff Lebowski, a Kahlua-swilling, unemployed old hippie who prefers to be called "The Dude" and spends most of his time bowling with his equally dead-beat friends Walter (John Goodman) and Donny (Steve Buscemi). The Dude—who takes as his theme a half-forgotten, faux modest Dylan anthem, "The Man in Me"—is a paradigm of '60s go-with-the-flow. The movie's vaguely 1950s ambience is actually "'50s" retro, the action being presciently—if pointlessly—set during the late 1990 buildup to Operation Desert Storm.

Introduced shopping for munchies in a flannel bathrobe, the Dude generally favors a wardrobe of shapeless sweatshirts and baggy shorts. Such looseness can be a liability in one bit of business, he cricks up his car by inadvertently flicking a roach down his pants. Countercultural balance is provided by Goodman's crazed Viet vet, a trove of pseudo-militarist idiocy. Still, as deceptively amiable and easygoing as its star (the most versatile and underrated movie actor of his generation), *The Big Lebowski* is far mellower than any previous Coen movie. The brothers' fondness for grotesque stereotypes is evident mainly in the redoubtable John Turturro's turn as a fetishistic hissy-macho flamenco bowler.

Indeed, *The Big Lebowski* is so relaxed as to be all but free-associative. The cliché cowboy narrator (Sam Elliott)—who adds a further degree of surrealism to the proceedings with his tumbleweed homilies—calls the story "stupefying" and then promptly loses his train of thought. The movie, which intermittently references Howard Hawk's adaptation of *The Big Sleep*, is a wacky series of L.A. adventures featuring a stoned slacker as a surrogate Philip Marlowe. Improbably mistaken for another Jeffrey Lebowski, the Dude is menaced by a pair of thugs who invade his pad and piss on his rug. After attempting to get the rug replaced by the real Big Lebowski, the Dude is hired by his rich namesake (David Huddleston) to act as a bagman—the young Mrs. "Bunny" Lebowski (Tara Reid) having been kidnapped and held for ransom.

Lit like a Christmas tree and rich with set pieces *The Big Lebowski* is hardly a noir. But no less than Marlowe, the Dude is regularly roughed up and drugged by an assortment of Nazis and pornographers, hassled by the LAPD, shadowed by mysterious operatives, and vamped (after a fashion) by shady ladies—or at least by Julianne Moore as the Big Lebowski's estranged daughter, her hair bobbed like Louise Brooks, in a hilarious impersonation of a pretentious performance artist waited upon by the even funnier David Thewlis.

When it was shown in competition at the recent Berlin Film Festival, *The Big Lebowski* was reportedly attacked for being about itself—which is to say, dialogue, acting, and mise-en-scène. The *Times* reported that, when asked if his movie had any point beyond laughing at Nazis and "Hispanic pederasts," Joe Coen pondered and replied, "I guess you hit the nail on the head." Spoken like the Dude. David Thomson's BFI monograph celebrates *The Big Sleep* as the original pulp fiction, the first Hollywood movie to ditch narrative logic and celebrates its own movie-ness—"a picture about its own process, the fun of making fun." It's in this sense that *The Big Lebowski* is closest to its model. The Coens lack anything approaching the erotic chemistry between Bogart and Bacall, but on a lesser libidinal note, their score—which mixes Creedence with Esquivel and Mussorgsky—is the most playfully inventive since *Austin Powers*.

In its way, *The Big Lebowski* is pure pop rumination. Narrative, such as it is, is periodically ruptured by the Dude's dreams and visions. The most elaborate manifestation of his trip, set to "Just Dropped In (To See What Condition My Condition Was In)," has the Dude hallucinating himself into a Busby Berkeley extravaganza where Saddam Hussein presents him with the bowling shoes he wears to teach Moore—here dressed as a Wagnerian Valkyrie—how to bowl. One would like to imagine that this image inspired the movie.

Also reviewed in:
CHICAGO TRIBUNE, 3/6/98, Friday/p. A, Michael Wilmington
NATION, 3/30/98, p. 35, Stuart Klawans
NEW REPUBLIC, 4/6/98, p. 26, Stanley Kauffmann
NEW YORK TIMES, 3/6/98, p. E31, Janet Maslin
NEW YORKER, 3/23/98, p. 98, Daphne Merkin

VARIETY, 1/26-2/1/98, p. 68, Todd McCarthy
WASHINGTON POST, 3/6/98, p. D1, Rita Kempley
WASHINGTON POST, 3/6/98, Weekend/p. 50, Desson Howe

BIG ONE, THE

A Miramax Films release in association with   Mayfair Entertainment International, BBC Production and Dog Eat Dog Films. *Executive Producer:* David Mortimer and Jeremy Gibson. *Producer:* Kathleen Glynn. *Director:* Michael Moore. *Screenplay:* Michael Moore. *Director of Photography:* Brian Danitz and Chris Smith. *Editor:* Meg Reticker. *Music:* World Famous Blue Jays. *Sound:* Sarah Price. *Sound Editor:* Andy Kris. *Production Designer:* Devorah Devries. *Running time:* 96 minutes. *MPAA Rating:* PG-13.

WITH: Michael Moore, Garrison Kellor, Studs Terkel, Rick Nielson, Phil Knight.

LOS ANGELES TIMES, 4/10/98, Calendar/p. 12, Kenneth Turan

Michael Moore is definitely a prankster, but calling him merry is stretching the point. Writer, director and protagonist of his own documentaries, a practiced performer who knows how to be amusing on camera, Moore is deadly serious behind the fun and games. He's determined to make audiences ponder reality as well as laugh, and "The Big One," his latest film, overcomes some odds to succeed in both areas.

Social concerns have always spurred Moore's films, starting with his 1989 debut, "Roger & Me," which showed the filmmaker doggedly attempting to confront General Motors Chairman Roger Smith about the closing of GM factories in Moore's hometown of Flint, Mich. Moore never got quite the satisfaction from Smith he wanted, but his film won numerous awards and claims to be the highest-grossing, nonconcert documentary of all time.

That success gave Moore the visibility and credibility to turn himself into a biting agent provocateur, someone who may look jolly and harmless but who mainlines indignation about what he considers the injustices of America's political and economic system.

Much of the humor in "The Big One" comes from Moore's tart comic observations, honed during numerous live appearances: HMOs are said to stand for "hand the money over," and the last presidential election is called "the evil of two lessers."

But Moore doesn't just make jokes, he acts. When he discovers that Republican candidate Steve Forbes almost never blinks, he finds a doctor who's shocked by that, and then asks Forbes campaign workers if their man is a space alien. And wanting to see if candidates would accept money from anywhere, he sent out checks in the name of organizations like Satan Worshippers for Dole, Abortionists for Buchanan and Pedophiles for Free Trade. More of them were cashed than you'd like to believe.

"The Big One" (the title comes from Moore's tongue-in-cheek proposal for a new, more descriptive name for the United States) started in a decidedly haphazard fashion. Sent on a tour to promote his latest book, "Downsize This!," Moore apparently decided pretty much on the spur of the moment to film his experiences on the road.

This seat-of-the-pants approach is reflected in the final film, whose ramshackle structure seems to include anything of interest Moore ran into, from an airport chat with Garrison Keillor to an improbable evening singing Bob Dylan with Cheap Trick's Rick Nielsen in Rockford, Ill., Money magazine's choice as the worst place to live in America.

Given that Moore's subject is corporate downsizing, it's a given that much of his energy in the film goes into investigating and criticizing a dichotomy he finds troubling: Despite making millions in profits, many corporations seem intent on throwing their employees out of work so they can contract for cheaper labor elsewhere.

That may sound like the dry stuff of newspaper think pieces, but nothing is dry when Moore gets hold of it. He leaves a tiny Post-it note for the CEO of massive Pillsbury asking why the Doughboy needs millions in corporate welfare, and then tries to present a company called Johnson Controls with a giant check made out for 80 cents, enough to magnanimously pay for the "first hour of work for the first Mexican worker" after the company completes a projected factory move south of the border.

Moore's secret, aside from his refusal to ever turn the camera off even when he says he has, is that he is so determined and dangerously funny that if you're in the frame with him when film is rolling, you're in trouble. The only person who comes close to matching him in self-confidence and nerve is the one CEO who does agree to appear on camera, Nike's Phil Knight, whose one-on-one with Moore provides a boggling climax to the filmmaker's quixotic journey.

Sensitive and genuinely passionate as he is about injustice and the economic problems of America's working class, Moore does not necessarily come off as a swell person in this film. An adroit self-promoter capable of playing an unpleasant practical joke on one of the escorts hired by his publisher, he doesn't protest overly much when Cheap Trick's Nielsen pegs him as potentially mean-spirited. But with an old-fashioned populist zeal that's a throwback to the likes of Mother Jones and Big Bill Hayward, Moore's gift is making us think about things we'd rather not think about, and making us chuckle while he's doing it.

NEW YORK POST, 4/10/98, p. 42, Thelma Adams

Michael Moore's follow-up to his 1989 corporate ambush "Roger & Me" would make a great HBO comedy half hour. Unfortunately, "The Big One" stretches for 96 minutes.

The sloppy, episodic documentary has many comic moments, layered like the thin patties in a Big Mac hamburger. The film's premise is a trip into Middle America, courtesy of Random House, the monolithic publisher of Moore's 1996 working-class lament, "Downsize This!"

While promoting his book, the mouth from Flint, Mich., nettles local corporations from Centralia, Ill., to Seattle, Wash. Meanwhile, on TV, Clinton battles for reelection, preaching to Middle Americans who regard the president, in the words of one citizen, as "the evil of two lessers."

Before a college audience, Moore, in merry prankster mode, gets under the skin of campaign financing. He describes sending checks from bogus organizations to presidential hopefuls—for example, "Abortionists for Pat Buchanan" or "Pedophiles for Free Trade for Ross Perot." The punchline is that the candidates cashed the checks.

Maverick Moore also hits pay dirt in Centralia, home of the Pay Day candy bar factory. Moore discovers that every day is Pay Day—until the company closes the plant and lays off its workers. The kicker is that the factory and its parent, Leaf Inc., are profitable.

Moore's biggest coup is luring Nike chairman Phil Knight into a queasy, on-camera dialogue. Knight, a pale, blinking redhead, tries to smile his way through Moore's revelations that no Nike shoes are made in the U.S.A. Instead, according to Moore, the company farms 36 percent of its shoes to Indonesia, where they're cheaply made, free from domestic labor laws.

Moore produces two tickets to Indonesia and invites Knight on a free trip to visit his underage workers. Knight declines. Unsettling as it is, the segment never gets beyond demonizing Nike's CEO. Moore doesn't address the more complex issue: Why do working Americans pay the extravagant prices Nike commands and that have made Knight a corporate titan?

Likewise, "The Big One" (Moore's alternative name for the United States) invites an ambitious film student willing to ambush Moore. Why does he sit in business class while his crew flies coach? Why isn't he hammering away at Random House, that corporate giant that feeds him on his 47-city book tour? Wait, isn't this whole operation a canny way to market "Downsize This!" in paperback?

In the end, "The Big One" cheapens Moore's image. If the chunky filmmaker enters one more company foyer, pointed question on his tongue and camera at his back, he'll begin to look like the Dr. Ruth Westheimer of corporate avengers, an excursion into, self-parody.

NEWSDAY, 4/10/98, Part II/p. B6, John Anderson

Michael Moore is a populist with a mean streak—most of the great comedians have mean streaks—sort of a hybrid of Will Rogers and W.C. Fields. He's never met a man he didn't like, particularly if that man was out of work. He thinks there are a lot of people who've never gotten an even break, and that a lot of them are suckers.

But rather than take the Fieldsian position that comedy is tragedy happening to someone else, Moore presents the tragedy of a downsized America as just that, tragedy—absurdist tragedy, but awful just the same. The comedy comes in when we realize what size suckers we are and how, so often, we get what we deserve.

"The Big One" (Moore's suggested new name for the United States) follows his breakthrough 1989 feature "Roger & Me," the short "Pets or Meat" and his travels into "TV Nation," and is structured around the promotional tour for his book "Downsize This: Random Threats From an Unarmed American." The film's themes are those of the book—and of what has become Moore's life's work—pointing out the increasingly shameful disparity between rich and poor in this country, the untenable greed of corporate America and the way most of the country (the poor part) allows itself to be steam-rolled by a small minority (the rich part). As he makes his way through the various armpits of America—signing books, sympathizing with the laid-off and torturing Nike chairman Phil Knight about his use of child labor and sweatshops—Moore certainly raises a lot of ugly issues that need to be raised.

That he presents himself as the avuncular avenger of the downtrodden—while doing fairly well for himself, thank you very much—doesn't make what he says any less funny, or less true.

"How many millions has Congress spent on investigating what happened to just seven people in the White House travel office, and not a dime has been spent investigating what happened to millions of Americans and their jobs?," he asks, as we watch him do a ear-phone interview. As Moore well knows—and so do we, really—it's because the electoral process has become nothing but a race for Big Money.

Suspecting that the 1996 presidential candidates would take money from any despicable group, Moore tells a college audience, "I formed four despicable groups myself" and sent off $100 contributions from each.

"So Bob Dole got $100 from the Satan Worshippers for Dole Club, Clinton got a $100 contribution from the Hemp Growers of America, Pat Buchanan got $100 from Abortionists for Buchanan, and Ross Perot got $100 from Pedophiles for Free Trade." Buchanan was the first to cash his check; Perot sent a letter thanking "all you pedophiles."

This is smug, but very funny and it points up where a movie like "Primary Colors" went so very wrong. Cynicism isn't shocking, amoral politicians aren't the exception, they're the rule, and it's depressing to watch a movie cluck its tongue at a system that movies have done as much to corrupt as anything else. Moore doesn't necessarily think anything's going to change about all this—he's a critic, after all, not a social reformer—but he does know that satire is a lot more effective than diatribes in changing minds. Think James Carville meets Gore Vidal.

As he wends his way through some pretty low-rent metropoli—Rockford, Ill.; St. Louis—it's banality he finds, rather than evil. Sure, at the top there's unbridled avarice, but in the long, long ladder down to the laid-off people whom Moore champions, there are a lot of people who are just following orders, pushing him and his cameras out of their lobbies so they can keep their own jobs. You kind of hope Moore would say something to recognize this fact—that in our day-to-day lives, as well as in election years, we're all a little guilty. But he doesn't, because at heart he's a pragmatist, and comedy needs a fall guy.

VILLAGE VOICE, 4/7/98, p. 63, J. Hoberman

Once upon a time, documentary filmmakers were thought to be modest types—objective in their reportage and dispassionate in their judgements, representing the world rather than interpreting it, lest they be accused of making propaganda. It wasn't ever true, of course, but personality is the coin of our realm and during the 1980s, films of fact really went subjective: Ross McElwee documented his quest for love, Dennis O'Rourke his fascination with a Bangkok prostitute, Emile de Antonio his search for his FBI file.

Such auto-docs were as close to Maya Deren's psychodramas (or Madonna's music videos) as they were to *Nanook of the North*. None of their makers, however, achieved greater onscreen success than Michael Moore. No previous documentarian had ever cast himself as quite the same type of comic-strip avenger. Moore's 1989 docu-blockbuster *Roger & Me* projected the filmmaker as a cartoon icon who, baseball cap on head and camera crew in tow, bestrode like a colossus the economically ravaged landscape of Flint, Michigan, looking for the corporate villains to blame. Did the act play in Peoria? (Is Bruce Willis a multimillionaire?)

The Big One, Moore's latest, is somewhere between a sequel to and a remake of *Roger & Me*. The movie was shot during the 1996 presidential campaign, which, as bogus as it was, provides Moore with one of his best gags: showing the canceled checks he'd sent the various candidates on behalf of invented organizations like Satan Worshippers for Dole and Abortionists for Buchanan. Still, its evident that —with his emphasis on layoffs, plant closings, and feeling the heartlands economic pain—Moore himself is running a replay of Clinton's winning 1992 strategy. (Those with short memories are directed to John Travolta's address to the workers of New Hampshire in *Primary Colors.)*

Compounding the political post-modernism is Moore's other agenda. His personal campaign is a book tour. Solidarity merges with self-promotion. The marketing of Moore's bestseller is not only a photo-op for the author but—his well-publicized support for unionizing Borders Books notwithstanding—also the sole form of collective action available to his benighted fans. Not long ago, Moore's onetime advocate Alexander Cockburn took him to task for creating what was, in effect, a virtual working class—"a mythical body of folks who more and serve as extras in Michael Moore's movies and columns." Here, the job description is expanded to include laugh track.

What manner of entertainment is this? Michael Moore is a funny guy, he has a gift for symbol making, his performance-art stunts can be extremely effective. Self-mockery is even part of the act. The man pranks his handlers and has himself filmed boarding a plane and settling into first class as his crew shuffles back toward the cabin. (That *The Big One* was produced with union labor seems even less likely than Moore's distributor, Miramax, running a union shop. But then Jean-Luc Godard's idea of making political films in a "political fashion" would doubtless strike him as the ultimate in infantile leftism.)

Moore's biggest wink is his Dylan imitation, bellowing "The Times They Are A-Changin'" with a member of Cheap Trick discovered living back home in Rockford, Illinois. Changed beyond recognition, I'd say. Cynic that he is, Moore has approximately the same post-Reagan relationship to a self-proclaimed people's tribune like Woody Guthrie as Bill Clinton does to Franklin Roosevelt, or Hillary (hailed by Moore in his book as "ONE HOT SHIT-KICKIN' FEMINIST BABE") to Eleanor. Initially entertaining, ultimately sour, *The Big One* is an exercise in sound bite, image, and merchandising. The anti-NAFTA message isn't invalid although the juggled chronology that marred *Roger & Me* hardly inspires faith in Moore's use of statistics as he rolls through the Midwest dispensing hugs to the unemployed, mocking marketplace pieties ("If it's just about profit, why doesn't GM sell crack?'), and paying his trademark corporate house calls.

It's during one of the latter that Moore meets his match in Nike CEO Phil Knight. A relaxed and jovial middle-aged hippie type, Knight provides the world's largest shoe company with a human face while deflecting the filmmaker's various ploys (a free airplane ticket to visit Nike's Indonesian sweatshops, an appeal to his conscience regarding East Timor, a challenge to arm wrestle). Unsuccessful in his bid to persuade the sympathetic Knight to open a shoe factory in Flint, Moore finally gets him to match Moore's own $10,000 donation to the Flint school system—a dirt-cheap product placement for Nike and an inexpensive special-effect for Moore, with good vibes and tax deductions all around.

Heartbreaking in its capacity to inspire a longing for something beyond the cult of personality, this is the only movie I know which *opens* with applause for the director. It's as if Moore is providing his own sycophantic rockumentary. *The Big One* takes its title from Moore's proposed new name for America, but long before it ends it's describing his ego. There's not even room for "Roger" this time around. Why not call it *Me?*

Also reviewed in:
CHICAGO TRIBUNE, 4/10/98, Friday/p. B, Michael Wilmington
NEW YORK TIMES, 4/10/98, p. E1, Janet Maslin
VARIETY , 9/15-21/97, p. 75, Joe Leydon
WASHINGTON POST, 4/10/98, p. B7, Stephen Hunter
WASHINGTON POST, 4/10/98, Weekend/p. 46, Michael O'Sullivan

BILLY'S HOLLYWOOD SCREEN KISS

A Trimark Pictures release of a Revolutionary Eye production.   *Producer:* David Moseley. *Director:* Tommy O'Haver.   *Screenplay:* Tommy O'Haver.   *Director of Photography:* Mark Mervis.   *Editor:* Jeff Betancourt.   *Music:* Alan Ari Lazar.   *Music Editor:* Alan Ari Lazar. *Choreographer:* Michelle Spears and Joseph McKee.   *Sound:* John H. Gilman.   *Sound Editor:* Scott Schirle.   *Casting:* Robert McGee.   *Production Designer:* Franco-Giacomo Carbone.   *Art Director:* Ioannis Papadopoulis.   *Costumes:* Julia Bartholomew.   *Make-up:* Francie Paull. *Running time:* 92 minutes.   *MPAA Rating:* R.

CAST: Sean P. Hayes (Billy Collier);   Brad Rowe (Gabriel);   Richard Ganoung (Perry); Meredith Scott Lynn (Georgiana);   Matthew Ashford (Whitey);   Christopher Bradley (Andrew); Armando Valdes-Kennedy (Fernando);   Carmine D. Giovinazzo (Gundy);   Kimiko Gelman (Donna);   Niles Jenson (Deidre);   Les Borsay (Les);   Annabelle Gurwitch (Gallery Owner); Holly Woodlawn (Holly);   Paul Bartel (Rex Webster);   Mr. Dan (Drag Queen);   Chad Boardman, Rodney Chester, and Eric Davenport (Drag Chorus); Mark Anderson (Peter); Shanti Reinhardt (Ju-Ju, Performance Artist);   Kiff Scholl (Rio, Performance Artist);   Shawn Nicholson (Young Billy);   Jaime Spencer (Kent Bartlett);   Michelle Karén (Billy's Mom); Aaron Wilde (Chris Jungblut);   Bonnie Biehl (Connie Rogers);   Jason-Shane Scott (Brad);   Kim Campbell (Natalie);   Mark Conley (Raymond);   Robbie Cain. (Joshua).

LOS ANGELES TIMES, 7/24/98, Calendar/p. 6, Kevin Thomas

Tommy O'Haver's "Billy's Hollywood Screen Kiss" is a giddy yet wise romantic comedy about a self-absorbed young gay photographer from Indiana who has come to L.A. in search of love and success. Sean P. Hayes' boyish Billy loves old Hollywood movies, particularly women's melodramas, and O'Haver makes his film a witty homage to vintage screen romance while keeping its perspective on the here and now.

The film's title comes from Billy's dream project, which is to re-create famous film love scenes with drag queens playing the female roles—why he wants to do this is none too clear.

Billy is feeling mighty sorry for himself, unhappy at having to share his hunky lover (Armando Valdes-Kennedy) with another man and frustrated in his career, when Gabriel (Brad Rowe), a handsome coffee shop waiter, comes into view. Billy is transfixed and hesitantly begins his pursuit. It's a very old story: Gabriel has charm to go with his looks, he seems a nice guy, and he's tantalizingly uncertain as to his sexual orientation. "Billy" has a fantasy look, but its payoff is refreshingly anchored to reality.

Hayes and especially Rowe, in the more opaque and therefore more intriguing role, reveal that they are actors of considerable range and ability, but O'Haver's chief accomplishment is how he has managed to make the most of what is surely a decidedly modest budget. His camera moves only slightly more frequently than that of Japanese master Yasujiro Ozu, yet his visual resources seem endless. A drag trio lip-syncing and dancing to old pop songs bridge sequences as well as express themes and moods; collages of Polaroid Instamatic photos work as flashbacks; and a bold sense of color and a flair for pastiche create a distinctive style for the picture, which celebrates an exuberant gay sensibility.

O'Haver's stylized approach yields some static moments, but "Billy" always regains its momentum swiftly. The 29-year-old director, in his feature debut, has had a strong assist from his creative team: cinematographer Mark Mervis, composer Alan Ari Lazar, production designer Franco-Giacomo Carbone and costume designer Julia Bartholomew.

By no means are Billy and Gabriel the whole story, and O'Haver surrounds them with a large number of effective characters. Meredith Scott Lynn is Billy's shrewd, caring best buddy but she's not a stereotypical gal pal of a gay man.   Richard Ganoung plays an established photographer, a good-looking man a decade or so older than Billy who kindly insists on being Billy's mentor yet does not exploit the fact that he's secretly fallen for the younger man. Paul Bartel, in one of his funniest roles ever, plays a famous, flamboyant photographer, and Carmine D. Giovinazzo is hilarious as a serious doper who attracts Lynn at a moment when she's at odds with her steady (Christopher Bradley).

"Billy" makes some satirical points and tells the truth about the ruthless power of physical beauty in gay life yet wisely does not take itself so seriously that it is unable to live up its maker's own description: "A Tommy O'Haver Trifle."

NEW YORK POST, 7/24/98, p. 42, Thelma Adams

"I am a homosexual" is the first line of "Billy's Hollywood Screen Kiss." Movies have come a long way out of the closet, baby. Writer-director Tommy O'Haver's debut is a big, wet kiss to the old-fashioned Hollywood romance. There's no lewd "money shot," no attempts to shock, no violence, just the story of an average American gay guy trying to make a better love life for himself.

Goateed Indiana photographer Billy (Sean Hayes) flees the Midwest for L.A. Unemployed, single, unhappy, he channels his energy into a project as romantic as he is: taking Polaroid snaps of classic Hollywood screen kisses, using drag queens and dream boats as models.

Billy falls for dreamboat Gabriel (Brad Rowe). This blond angel claims to be straight, but is his hand on the closet door? Is he Burt Lancaster to Billy's Deborah Kerr? Will they go from here to eternity together?

Not exactly. As good as they are, Hayes and Rowe have more in common with Matthew Broderick and Rob Lowe than Lancaster and Kerr. The main problem in O'Haver's Sundance-kissed debut is that there's not enough spark to the boy-meets-boy plot to last from here to Encino.

While "Billy" fades like an old snapshot, the low-budget comedy's funny start and intensely poignant moments show O'Haver's promise. (Next stop: He's writing and directing the "Archie" comics movie.) Like his endearing screen alter ego, we welcome O'Haver as "a misfit of a different kind: a romantic."

NEWSDAY, 7/24/98, Part II/p. B11, John Anderson

If the definition of fluff is feel-good, audience-intoxicating fantasy, then "Billy's Hollywood Screen Kiss" is fluff on the level of a Sealy Posturepedic: It may do for Petula Clark what "Muriel's Wedding" did for ABBA, but that doesn't mean it's insubstantial.

It may, in fact, be something of a breakthrough. The debut feature of director-writer Tommy O'Haver—and several of his leading actors as well—it moves gay comedy, or just gay filmmaking, a step toward further liberation. If explaining it this way is actually ghettoizing the movie, we'll apologize in advance. But like this summer's "Hav Plenty" and "I Went Down"—one black, the other Irish—"Billy's" is a mainstream-directed, minority-oriented film that doesn't dwell on the Other, or how its characters are filtered through some at-large world view. The problems and history of being homosexual aren't ignored, but they're not the purpose of the movie either. The characters—just like in straight films!—are busy enough with their other obsessions.

In the case of Billy (Sean P. Hayes), our Polaroid-wielding photographer hero, this means reality-be-damned romance with a fatal edge, the type engendered by a lifetime of watching Douglas Sirk and Erica Kane. Already involved with Fernando (Armando Valdes-Kennedy), who's involved with someone else, Billy takes one look at divine "coffee boy" Gabriel (Brad Rowe) and throws empiricism to the wind.

Gabriel is handsome and hetero—too handsome to be hetero, as the subtext goes—but Billy harbors hope that something besides his camera is going to click. He's not much of a strategist, though. After asking Gabriel to pose for a series of Cindy Shermanesque photos, he introduces him to the lascivious art photographer Rex Webster (Paul Bartel) and sets himself up for the coup de heartbreak—aggravated by tantalizing invitations to violate Gabriel's straight facade.

"Billy's" is a comedy, though, so there's more wryness than misery. Billy's pals—the Streisand-esque Meredith Scott Lynn as George (she's straight) and Richard Ganoung as Perry (he's not) provide much of the humanity and humor. The drag-queen trio lip-synching Petula Clark (including "'This Is My Song," written by noted songsmith Charles Chaplin!) provides well-timed musical comedy relief. And with a "Dick Tracy"-evoking set design, melodramatic irising and the heart-on-the-sleeve direction, O'Haver is putting the squeeze on the soft udder of our movie-weaned sentimentality, milking soft, moist responses out of celluloid memories. Which may sound a bit much, but isn't inappropriate.

Although smartly punctuated by Billy's ever-present Polaroids, some self-deprecating narration and a solidly gay sense of humor, "Billy's" lags at times, no doubt about it. But when it's being good, it's being very funny. And Hayes, notably, whose Billy is easily as charming as Gabriel—more so, since he doesn't know it—has gotten his movie career off to a more than auspicious beginning.

SIGHT AND SOUND, 7/99, p. 36, Peter Matthews

Los Angeles, the present. Billy Collier, a 26-year-old gay photographer, is broke and tired of being the 'other woman' in his relationship with the already partnered Fernando. His best friend Georgiana proposes he realise a long-cherished dream of shooting a photo series recreating great screen kisses from Hollywood's golden era using drag queens. Perry, a more successful photographer, will be his financial backer. Needing a romantic male lead, Billy spots waiter Gabriel and soon becomes infatuated, but Gabriel claims to be straight. At an exhibition, the celebrated artist Rex Webster invites Gabriel to test for a modelling job in Catalina. Gabriel asks Billy back to his apartment for beers, but their cosy evening is interrupted by a phone argument between Gabriel and his girlfriend Natalie.

Billy and Gabriel's first photo shoot goes well. Later, the two begin to have sex, but Gabriel can't go through with it. He curtly informs Billy that he's accepted the modelling gig. Billy follows him to Catalina while Perry follows Billy to stop him making a fool of himself. Billy finds Gabriel at a party thrown by Rex, but another model, Brad, shows up, and he and Gabriel walk off arm in arm. Billy throws his camera into the ocean. Perry confesses he once longed for Billy in the same way Billy desires Gabriel and then kisses him. Some time later, Billy holds an exhibition called "Hollywood Screen Kiss" featuring Polaroids of his friends where he meets a young admirer named Joshua.

The gay romantic comedy *Billy's Hollywood Screen Kiss* gets listed in the credits as a "Tommy O'Haver Trifle", and that's certainly the word for it. The movie is so slender and ephemeral you emerge from the theatre thinking, can this dinky tale of the average fag-in-the-street and his crush on an unobtainable blue-eyed hunk really be all there is? Perhaps the film doesn't resemble a layered trifle so much as a spongy meringue. It's difficult to explain why gay audiences remain so eager to gobble up these light-headed confections, as if the slightest hint of *gravitas* automatically stigmatises a picture as boring and straight. Billy belongs in the same pipsqueak class as *Jeffrey* and *Beautiful Thing*, both of which proved how gay subjects can be marketed for the multiplex crowd. That's progress as long as you don't mind movies whose flat obviousness emulates the style of television soaps and sitcoms. What raises this debut feature a notch or two above the competition is that O'Haver shows signs of being a film-maker.

Here one-dimensionality is arguably part of the concept, with a few scenes attaining the perky modernist look of such 50s sex farces as *Pillow Talk* or *The Girl Can't Help It*. O'Haver, cinematographer Mark Mervis and production designer Franco-Giacomo Carbone swathe interiors such as Billy's apartment in vibrant pop colours that lend the film the graphic simplicity of a comic book (an effect heightened by the use of shallow space, which seems to turn the actors into bluntly scissored cut-outs). But what is all this witty stylisation in aid of? On the one hand, it comes across as a pastiche of the clean-scrubbed Hollywood fantasies with which our hero (who has Doris Day dreams of monogamy and white-picket fences) is meant to be sated. But on the other, squaresville is affirmed as what every normal gay guy supposedly inwardly craves.

While that may be true, the film barely registers the bottomless irony of it—and indeed, there are any number of promising ideas that die for lack of oxygen. Having Billy cast himself and his inamorata Gabriel as the lovers in a variety of screen genres is a pretty mouldy gimmick to begin with. But given the slack way the director stages these set pieces, you can't even tell for sure which movies are being spoofed. O'Haver's obscurantist rendering of a Fred-and-Ginger number boils down to a few apathetic twirls while a drag-queen chorus frisks randomly in the background. A more philosophical theme that gets mooted is the artist's growth from innocence to experience, represented by neophyte photographer Billy, his spiritual mentor Perry and an oily Warholian/Hockneyesque character named Rex Webster.

But there's one brilliantly astute sequence that lifts the film clear above itself. A boozy evening of mutual confession at Billy's leads to Gabriel's ostensibly idle request to stay the night. From that moment, the atmosphere is charged with an erotic tension that mounts until it becomes claustrophobic and terrible. Perched directly over the bed where the chaste couple lie apart, the camera simply watches and waits as they creep together by agonising millimetres. First, a hand brushes accidentally against a back; then, a shoulder arches outwards to meet it—finally, an arm pinions a chest to seal the deal. The scene is a small classic because, whether homo or hetero, we've all been in that bed. For a minute or so, this flyspeck movie gets transformed into triumphant *cinéma vérité*.

VILLAGE VOICE, 7/28/98, p. 124, Andrew Huang

As time goes by, a kiss becomes more than a kiss. Tommy O'Haver's debut, *Billy's Hollywood Screen Kiss,* is a dream-drenched romantic comedy that explores one man's search for love. Billy, played by Sean Hayes, is a regular-joe gay photographer whose ideal man comes in the traffic-stopping form of Gabriel (Brad Rowe), a struggling musician with a girlfriend.

To keep things lively, O'Haver mixes old-style Hollywood movie footage and campy musical interludes, weaving fantasy and reminiscence into a delirious rhapsody that mirrors the mind's desires. He directs Hayes into too much broad comedy, but the actor redeems himself in the heartfelt climactic moments. Handsome and painfully expressionless, Rowe gives a rigid performance—appropriate since his character is best understood as an icon seen through Billy's eyes. O'Haver never quite integrates his larger themes of Hollywood idealism, but his paean to the possibilities of infatuation has an undeniable appeal.

Also reviewed in:
CHICAGO TRIBUNE, 8/7/98, Friday/p. D, Monica Eng
NEW YORK TIMES, 7/24/98, p. E14, Stephen Holden
NEW YORKER, 7/27/98, p. 78, Daphne Merkin
VARIETY, 2/2-8/98, p. 32, Dennis Harvey

BLACK DOG

A Universal Pictures and Mutual Film Company release of a Prelude Pictures production in association with Rafaella De Laurentiis. *Executive Producer:* Mace Neufeld, Robert Rehme, Gary Levinsohn, and Mark Gordon. *Producer:* Raffaella De Laurentiis, Peter Saphier, and Mark W. Koch. *Director:* Kevin Hooks. *Screenplay:* William Mickelberry and Dan Vining. *Director of Photography:* Buzz Feitshans IV. *Editor:* Debra Neil-Fisher and Sabrina Plisco-Morris. *Music:* George S. Clinton. *Music Editor:* Mike Flicker and Joanie Diener. *Sound:* Mary Ellis and (music): John Whynot. *Sound Editor:* Dean Beville. *Casting:* Elisabeth Rudolph. *Production Designer:* Victoria Paul. *Art Director:* Ken Hardy and Randall Richards. *Set Designer:* Jonathan Short, Julia S. Sanford, and Bill Davis. *Set Decorator:* Diana L. Stoughton. *Set Dresser:* Eric Luling, Clifton T. Cooper, Kip Bartlett, Michael Hicks, John T. Bromell, Drew Meyers, Hal Gardner, Michael Pisani, Larry Sauls, and Polar Bear Shaw. *Special Effects:* Trevor Neighbour. *Costumes:* Peggy Stamper. *Make-up:* Lynn Barber. *Make-up (Patrick Swayze):* Scott Eddo. *Stunt Coordinator:* Vic Armstrong and Gary Hymes. *Running time:* 105 minutes. *MPAA Rating:* PG-13.

CAST: Patrick Swayze (Jack Crews); Meat Loaf (Red); Randy Travis (Earl); Gabriel Casseus (Sonny); Brian Vincent (Wes); Graham Beckel (Cutler); Brenda Strong (Melanie); Rusty De Wees (Junior); Cyril O'Reilly (Vince); Erin Broderick (Tracy); Charles Dutton (Ford); Stephen Tobolowsky (McClaren); Lorraine Toussaint (Avery); Hester Hargett (FBI Tech); Stuart Greer and Whitt Brantley (Troopers); Mark Steven Robison (Chicken Truck Driver); Elizabeth Jaye Moore (Linda).

LOS ANGELES TIMES, 5/4/98, Calendar/p. 7, Bob Heisler

Patrick Swayze is caught between the pedal and the metal in "Black Dog," a movie lacking the charm and style to raise it above a demolition derby with a country music soundtrack.

Deliver a truckload of illegal guns to Newark with the FBI and double-crossing transporters on his tail or lose his wife and daughter to the really bad guys and his house to the bank. And all this without a driver's license.

"Black Dog" asks the pressing philosophical question: Is it still a special effect to have a truck ram into a gasoline tanker and blow up?

Oh yes, people die, too. Many people, all bad in some way. And most deserve to die for turning their trucks into weapons of mass destruction. Is there no American Society for the Preservation of Trucks and Other Internal Combustion Vehicles to object to the cruel and inhumane treatment various 18-wheelers, car-carriers, pickups, motorcycles and cars receive?

Remember all those convoy movies back in the days of CB radios, when the road promised romance and escape? Not here. There's grit in the oil, bitter water in the gas tank. It's not "The Dukes of Hazzard," more like "Really Mad Max" meets "Smokey and the Gun Runners."

The plot runs along well-lighted roads with plenty of chases, crashes, escapes and corn-fed dialogue. As Swayze tells the man who set him up: "I'll do what I have to."

But there's hope for Randy Travis fans: He acts rings around Swayze, who has swagger and the sneer but stays too cool throughout. There's a camera in front of your windshield, Patrick. Do something for it. His only emotional moments are spoken; he is a trucker who doesn't even listen to country music.

Travis sings a little, sometimes in the truck cab, sometimes on the score. See, it's his hobby. He turns the boredom of the highway (not to mention those life-threatening moments that come his way as moving contraband from state to state) into country songs. Maybe one day his truck will crash into a radio station.

The ever-icky Meat Loaf makes an appearance in a role that fits him like a spiked glove: He's a Bible-quoting, cigar-chomping, lunchmeat-coupon-clipping bad guy who lets loose most of the truck-crunching action.

There may be an interesting movie somewhere in "Black Dog" and in the character of Jack Crews. But it prefers to rub metal together, rather than people or ideas.

NEW YORK POST, 5/1/98, p. 51, Larry Worth

Truck movies come in only two styles: rare classics like "Duel" and "The Wages of Fear," and scrap-heap specials of the "Convoy," "Maximum Overdrive" and "Breaker! Breaker!" variety.

With that in mind, "Black Dog"—which essentially exists to show a half-dozen 18-wheelers crashing and burning in slo-mo—should bypass theaters and head straight to the junk yard.

Ostensibly, it's a story about Jack Crews, a sweet-natured ex-con who's mighty tempted to haul a suspicious load of who-knows-what from Atlanta to New York. Though he lost his license for falling asleep at the wheel (and plowing into an innocent family), that $10,000 check would pay off the $9,000 foreclosure notice on his house.

Natch, this salt-of-the-earth guy doesn't want to pull up stakes and move back to evil Newark, where his precious little daughter would attend a school with—gasp!—metal detectors. So he drowns out ever-loyal wifey's protests and climbs back into the driver's seat.

Even then, he can't conceive of the roadblocks ahead: his two-timing pistol-wielding boss, a suspicious trio of passengers, FBI and ATF agents tracking his every move and a Bible-thumping redneck determined to steal his cargo.

Yes, there's a surplus of villains, not the least of which is director Kevin Hooks and his two sad-sack screenwriters.

Though Hooks keeps the action rolling, the endless chases soon look like "Smokey and the Bandit" leftovers. Further, Hooks' idea of suspense is having the wife and kid spend most of the movie at gunpoint, a device that's not only tired but cheap.

On the other hand, viewers who always wanted the inside scoop on highway weigh stations will certainly get their fill. But that's a dramatic high point, aside from probing queries about a possible informer in the rig, the unmasking of yet another traitor and a finale that's straight out of fairytale land.

The production also stalls as a comeback vehicle for Patrick ("Dirty Dancing") Swayze. He's less strong and silent than alarmingly stiff. Trying to let his ever-darting eyes do the talking, he comes off like a man in need of an ophthalmologist.

The supporting players fare better. Country-western crooner Randy Travis is nicely at ease with his good ol' boy charms, though one can't blame him for cautiously hiding behind a scruffy beard.

Another singer—a cleaned-up Meat Loaf—also outacts Swayze. As an ultra-religious Wile E. Coyote-like hijacker, Meat Loaf goes the camp route, spouting the Good Book one minute and raising hell the next.

A fine score—featuring one of Travis' latest tunes—occasionally diverts, too. But by the time Steve Earle belts out "Nowhere Road," it pretty much sums up where "Black Dog" has been—and where it's going.

Also reviewed in:
CHICAGO TRIBUNE, 5/7/98, Tempo/p. 13, John Petrakis
NEW YORK TIMES, 5/2/98, p. B16, Lawrence Van Gelder
VARIETY, 5/4-10/98, p. 84, Joe Leydon

BLADE

A New Line Cinema release of an Amen Ra Films production in association with Imaginary Forces. *Executive Producer:* Lynn Harris, Stan Lee, Avi Arad, and Joseph Calamari. *Producer:* Peter Frankfurt, Wesley Snipes, and Robert Engelman. *Director:* Stephen Norrington. *Screenplay:* David S. Goyer. *Based on "Blade and Deacon Frost" characters created for Marvel Comics by:* Marv Wolfman and Gene Colan. *Director of Photography:* Theo Van de Sande. *Editor:* Paul Rubell. *Music:* Dana Sano and Mark Isham. *Music Editor:* Tom Carlson, Carlton Kaller, and Paul Rabjohns. *Sound:* Lee Orloff and (music) Stephen Krause. *Sound Editor:* Jonathan Miller. *Casting:* Rachel Abroms and Jory Weitz. *Production Designer:* Kirk M. Petruccelli. *Art Director:* Barry Chusid. *Set Designer:* Thomas C. Reta, Chad S. Frey and A. Todd Holland. *Set Decorator:* Greg Grande. *Special Effects:* Lou Carlucci. *Visual Effects:* Matthew Justice. *Costumes:* Sanja Milkovic Hays. *Make-up:* Perry M. Germain. *Make-up Effects:* Greg Cannom. *Make-up (Wesley Snipes):* Cyndi Reece-Thorne. *Body Make-up:* Jane English. *Stunt Coordinator:* Jeffy Ward, Jr. and Henry Kingi, Jr. *Running time:* 120 minutes. *MPAA Rating:* R.

CAST: Wesley Snipes (Blade); Stephen Dorff (Deacon Frost); Kris Kristofferson (Whistler); N'Bushe Wright (Karen); Donal Logue (Quinn); Udo Kier (Dragonetti); Arly Jover (Mercury); Traci Lords (Racquel); Kevin Patrick Walls (Krieger); Tim Guinee (Curtis Webb); Sanaa Lathan (Vanessa); Eric Edwards (Pearl); Donna Wong (Nurse); Carmen Thomas (Senior Resident); Shannon Lee (Resident); Kenneth Johnson (Heatseeking Dennis); Clint Curtis (Creepy Morgue Guy); Judson Scott (Pallantine); Sidney Liufau (Japanese Doorman); Keith Leon Williams (Kam); Andray Johnson and Stephen R. Peluso (Paramedics); Marcus Aurelius (Pragmatic Policeman); John Enos III (Blood Club Bouncer); Eboni Adams (Martial Arts Kid); Lyle Conway (Reichardt); Freeman White III (Menacing Stud); DV De Vincentis (Vampire Underling); Marcus Salgado and Esau McKnight, Jr. (Frost's Goons); Erl (Von Esper); Matt Schulze (Crease); Lennnox Brown (Pleading Goon); Yvette Ocampo (Party Girl); Irene A. Stepic (Slavic Vampire Lord); Jenya Lano (Russian Woman); Levani (Russian Vampire).

CHRISTIAN SCIENCE MONITOR, 8/21/98, p. B3, David Sterritt

Blame it on the approaching millennium, or on Hollywood's desperation to please moviegoers starved for excitement in the late-summer doldrums. Whatever the reason, the new thriller "Blade" begins with such a burst of apocalyptic violence that you'd think the sequels to

"Armageddon" and "Godzilla" had already arrived, wrapped in a single package to double the box-office body count.

Things quiet down after the first 10 minutes or so, but with characters like these, tranquillity never lasts for more than a few seconds at a time.

Blade, our hero, is a sort-of vampire who stifles his evil impulses with an exotic serum so he can devote his life to exterminating full-fledged vampires. Frost, a former human who's become one of the latter, has devoted his life to studying vampire lore so he can summon up a demonic god who'll wipe out humanity. Dragonetti, an undead aristocrat, heads a vampire board of directors trying to uphold tradition against troublemakers like Frost.

Like many pop-culture artifacts in these postmodern times, "Blade" has a knowing sense of irony about the genre it belongs to. By their nature, as many observers have noted, vampire tales generally have a racist undercurrent, with the monsters standing in for whatever racial group the mainstream society considers strong, scary, and inferior. And in recent years, the vampire myth has been used as a ready-made metaphor for the AIDS crisis. "Blade" alludes to such notions in its imagery and makes them explicit with references to racism ("half-breed," "Uncle Tom") and illness ("sexually transmitted disease") in the dialogue.

This doesn't mean the movie is thoughtful about such matters, just that its savvy enough to cast a knowing wink in the direction of contemporary anxieties. For most of its two-hour running time it simply flings a barrage of horrors at the audience, enhanced with the most imaginative science-fiction atmospherics this side of "Dark City," which incidentally was a far more original picture.

Wesley Snipes makes Blade as commanding as any comic-book hero around, although one can't help wondering why he's chosen to appear in so many throwaway entertainments since his early promise in some of Spike Lee's movies. Stephen Dorff, whose roles range from John Lennon's best friend in "Backbeat" to a transvestite in "I Shot Andy Warhol," gives Frost a queasy blend of menace, machismo, and charm.

Kris Kristofferson's stolid performance as Blade's sidekick is the dead opposite of his sensitive acting in "A Soldier's Daughter Never Cries," a superb film coming in autumn, but the role demonstrates his versatility, if little else. N'Bushe Wright is her usual irresistible self as a scientist who helps the good guys, and as the head vampire Udo Keir is perfectly cast, given his experience in Warhol's campy "Dracula" and "Frankenstein" knockoffs. Traci Lords and Arly Jover are also on hand.

"Blade" was directed by Stephen Norrington from David S. Goyer's screenplay, but the movers and shakers of the production were clearly designer Kirk M. Petruccelli, cinematographer Theo Van de Sande, editor Paul Rubell, makeup artist Greg Cannom, and music supervisor Dana Sano, who stitched together the technopopping score.

LOS ANGELES TIMES, 8/21/98, Calendar/p. 4, Gene Seymour

[The following review by Gene Seymour appeared in a slightly different form in **NEWSDAY, 8/21/98, Part II/p. B3.]**

If memory serves, the last Marvel Comics hero to headline a major motion picture was "Howard the Duck." The dimensions of that 1986 fiasco were such that poor Howard never recovered his once respectable popularity. Whatever the fate of James Cameron's on-again, off-again plans to bring Spider Man to the big screen, recent pop culture history suggests that Marvel's stable of superheroes should go no further than the TV screen.

"Blade," the feature film debut of Marvel's half-human, half-vampire mercenary, gives faint hope that this precedent could be broken. The movie is nowhere near the disaster that "Howard" was. But it's going to take stories more interesting than the one told here to turn "Blade" into the kind of franchise that producer-star Wesley Snipes hopes it'll become.

Snipes himself is the movie's biggest asset. He may snarl, hiss and twitch in ways that are often disorienting, but you can't take your eyes off him, even when he's standing still. Which isn't often.

Blade, after all, is a very busy man with a time-consuming mission: to rid humanity of vampires—which, if you buy into this movie's garish vision, are as plentiful as cockroaches. Their growing population has been helped along by a ruthless little bloodsucker named Deacon

Frost (Stephen Dorff, who comes on like a sticky, satanic version of a record company executive—or does that sound redundant?).

It isn't enough for Frost and his fellow renegade vampires to stay several steps ahead of Blade and his mentor-sidekick Whistler (Kris Kristofferson). Frost wants to rule humanity, and he thinks he's found the means to do so with a long-suppressed curse that, if revived, will literally create hell on Earth. To make it work, he needs to, once again literally, bleed Blade dry.

After all, the very thing that makes Blade a social outcast (his mix of vampire and human blood) also makes him a valuable resource for scummy yuppies like Frost to exploit. "You have all our strengths," Frost tells Blade, "and none of our weaknesses." Complicating both Frost's malevolent plans and Blade's work schedule is a beautiful doctor (N'Bushe Wright), who's fighting infection by one of Frost's goons.

The dark ooze that even tinges "Blade's" daylight sequences is so omnipresent that, if this thing were a comic book, the black ink would come off on your fingertips. Director Stephen Norrington and his production team deserve credit for giving this story the jarring, angular design found in some of the more ambitious mainstream comic books.

The noir atmosphere doesn't quite smother the dialogue's cheesy smell, though David S. Goyer's script is efficient enough in its pacing. All the actors, even Traci Lords as a vampire vixen, play their roles with as much conviction as the story's pulp conventions allow without looking too ridiculous.

"Blade's" real attraction, however, is the swordplay and hand-to-hand combat. The movie only takes off when Snipes and his antagonists leap, kick, slash and gouge one another with heavy-metal flamboyance.

Such techno-action may give "Blade" enough power for a sequel, but one is left wondering whether there's any room for its central character to sustain interest beyond this flashy debut.

NEW YORK POST, 8/21/98, p. 57, Rod Dreher

"Blade" has a sharper edge than you might expect from a late-summer action flick based on a comic book. While this sci-fi horror tale about a martial-arts vampire vigilante never draws serious blood, it's a surprisingly satisfying rock'em, sock'em escapist romp through a techno-styled urban nightscape. The ephemeral pleasures of "Blade" are all on the sleek surface, but what's wrong with that?

The film's opening set piece goes for the jugular with imaginatively gory glee. A black-clad sexpot (Traci Lords) takes a horny guy for a ride to a nightclub. They pass through a gruesome abattoir and enter a secret door leading to an underground disco, where cool clubsters are dancing up an electronics frenzy. Then, the room's sprinklers come to life, spewing blood onto the ecstatic revelers—vampires, natch, who have worked up quite a thirst.

Enter Blade (Wesley Snipes), a musclebound avenger who has no truck with this slaughterhouse jive. Firing silver bullets and opening up a can of martial-arts whup-ass, Blade slices, dices and juliennes the bloodsucking baddies, saving his brutal best for Quinn (Donal Logue), a hairy, beer-bellied henchman whose appearance suggests what you might see if members of Lynyrd Skynyrd went off on a Dracula jag. Blade nails him to the wall with silver spikes and sets him on fire.

Yee-ha. It's gory as hell, but in an affectless, video game way, and executed by director Stephen Norrington with real flash and panache. "Blade" never again reaches this fever pitch of ghoulish glitz, but Norrington and screenwriter David S. Goyer, who penned "Dark City" earlier this year, sustain more interest than a story this silly has a right to.

Snipes is visually impressive as Blade, the vampire exterminator who, with a serum devised by grizzled scientist Whistler (Kris Kristofferson), keeps the vampire taint in his own body at bay while using its preternatural strength to destroy the disciples of Dracula.

But the role doesn't give him much opportunity to be more than a buff killing machine. That, in a movie that depends almost entirely on visual stimulation to jazz its audience, is no small thing.

The real payoff in "Blade" is Stephen Dorff, who plays Deacon Frost, an up-and-coming vampire determined to oust his mild-mannered assimilationist elders and declare jihad on pathetic humanity. With his greasy locks, snarly mouth and Prada-ish lounge wear, Dorff dazzles as a *louche* Lestat whose kinky cunning bedevils Blade at every turn.

The story has high-tech Deacon trying to translate an ancient vampire text, intending to learn the secrets of a ceremony to conjure the ancient Blood God, who will help him rule the world, yada yada. (Trust me: This isn't nearly as dopey when you're watching the movie.) Blade and Deacon play a cat-and-mouse game, with our leather-clad hero protecting a doctor (N'Bushe Wright) who was bitten by Quinn on the autopsy table, and who may or may not turn undead at any moment.

The producers clearly would love for "Blade" to become a "Batman"-like franchise, but the character isn't interesting enough to call for more of the same. Yet it's hard to complain about the movie's nifty fight scenes, the Anne Rice-ish combination of rock'n'roll and vampirism and, above all, the terrific production design. "Blade" is not as cutting-edge as it wants to be, but it'll do.

SIGHT AND SOUND, 11/98, p. 42, Andrew O'Hehir

The US. In 1967, a pregnant woman dying of blood loss after a mysterious attack gives birth. The present. The infant has grown up to become Blade, a human-vampire hybrid who has been trained by Whistler, a human hunter of vampires, to kill the creatures of the night, whose activities are becoming increasingly brazen and organised. Blade's nemesis, a vampire named Frost, hopes to defeat the established vampire aristocracy and set off a series of apocalyptic events—foretold in vampire prophecy—that will lead to vampires ruling over humanity. When one of Frost's minions attacks Karen, a hospital haematologist, Blade rescues her and takes her to Whistler to save her from becoming a vampire. A lengthy series of battles between Blade and the vampires ensues. The vampires kill Whistler and capture Blade and Karen, but not before she has devised a new drug that destroys vampire blood cells.

Frost kills and captures members of the vampire leadership but needs the blood of a "daywalker"—a hybrid such as Blade—to bring the demonic Blood God to life. Karen escapes and frees Blade, but not before Frost has drained a lot of his blood. The serum that keeps Blade's bloodlust at bay has worn off, so Karen permits him to drink her blood to give him strength. Frost transforms himself into the seemingly indestructible Blood God, but Blade uses Karen's new drug to kill him.

People often say that movies have become like comic books, but how often is it true? In the case of *Blade*—actually based on a popular Marvel Comic—I am happy to report that all the lurid colours, phantasmagoric imagery, relentless action, Byzantine plotting and sublimated homoeroticism that typify the comics genre at its best are here in loving detail. Especially in this year of big-budget Hollywood disappointments, *Blade* is smashingly successful entertainment. Pre-adolescent boys will find it serious and satisfying and surely not be happy with fewer than a half-dozen viewings. The rest of us can pronounce it delightful camp fluff, without admitting how thrilled our inner little boys (and tomboys) are.

On this occasion, at least, Wesley Snipes abandons his career-long struggle for dramatic credibility to embrace a role that is part Terminator, part RuPaul. When he isn't riding his motorcycle through walls or slashing vampires into sizzling fragments with a silver samurai sword (holy water and crucifixes are useless against the night creatures, but garlic and silver work as advertised), Blade displays his impressive physique in a series of stoney-faced but outrageous poses, clad in a pectoral-enhancing leather costume and wraparound sunglasses.

The arrival of a woman in his life, of course, is meant to show that the monosyllabic half-breed has a softer side. The lovely N'Bushe Wright does about as well as anyone could with the chaste helper role of Karen—her only erotic union with Blade comes when she allows him to drink her blood. However, it remains clear that Blade's real affections lie with his murdered mother and Whistler, the grizzled, Creedence Clearwater-blasting hippie vampire-slayer played by Kris Kristofferson (always better as an actor than as a singer).

Drawing analogies between the decadent, urban nightlife scene and the world of vampires is nothing new, but Stephen Dorff's portrayal of Frost as a trendy club entrepreneur with a Mick Jagger smirk and a Leonardo DiCaprio haircut, surrounded by bitchy supermodels and sycophantic hooligans, is no less enjoyable for its familiarity Frost is every inch the 90s vampire, using a PowerMac to decode ancient texts, eschewing the vampire oligarchy's power suits for hip synthetic casual wear, even venturing out by daylight coated with high-powered sunblock.

While the elaborately choreographed action sequences in *Blade* feature many of the temporal and spatial improbabilities you'd expect, the film's extensive scenes of violence are more grotesque than realistic. Director Stephen Norrington *(Death Machine)*, screenwriter David S. Goyer and *Blade*'s design team have constructed a consistent universe and taken it seriously From its nightmarish opening scene in a blood-drenched vampire dance club to the special-effects extravaganza of its hero's final battle with the Blood God (which winks at *Raiders of the Lost Ark*), *Blade* moves propulsively, and even sometimes lyrically, from episode to episode, lubricated by Mark Isham's haunting electronic score. Unlike so many action adventure films aimed at younger viewers (such as *Spawn* or the *Mortal Kombat* movies), it never lapses into incoherence or derides its audience for wanting an outlandish yarn told respectfully and well.

VILLAGE VOICE, 9/1/98, p. 114, Justine Elias

Let no one say that *Blade*, a blindingly overwrought hybrid of horror, action, and Oedipal drama, fails to mark some kind of great leap forward for vampire cinema. Not only does the film feature one of the genre's first African American slayer-heroes (he was introduced in a 1973 Marvel comic), but its version of Dracu-lore makes explicit connections between vampirism and sickle-cell anemia. But *Blade* is less interested in representing a watershed than in delivering the usual bloodshed, and director Stephen Norrington, a special-effects wizard on films like *Alien 3*, wastes no time in getting down to his real business: chic carnage for the wish-they-were-smart set.

A brief prologue depicts the hero's tragic origins: his pregnant mother was gruesomely attacked by an undead fiend, so baby Blade grows up to be Wesley the Vampire Slayer, torn between his altruistic and bloodsucking natures. Then we leap forward to the present day, to a nameless city of technoir gloom, where a young man is lured into a vampire-sponsored nightclub, featuring the very latest in recherché Downtown entertainment: carcasses of indeterminate species hanging from meat hooks, an overhead sprinkler system that drenches the crowd with blood, and clubgoers having sex right in front of everybody. Like, they're so undead they don't even care about conventional morality. Our hapless victim is too besotted with his hostess (Traci Lords, looking very fit) to notice his predators, but Blade comes to the rescue, armed to the pointy teeth with weapons custom-made by his human helper (undead actor Kris Kristofferson, in a luxuriant gray wig).

Thus, in this sequence alone, *Blade* manages to include at least 50 identically revolting shots of staked and machine-gunned bloodsuckers, who rot, burn, or disintegrate before our eyes. And there's more to come: dissections, beheadings, reanimated corpses, giant syringes stuck into human necks, and a smelly Jabba the Hut-sized vampire librarian. Children of the night, what disgusting movies they make.

Blade may not be for the faint of heart, but it's sure to please those who adore lots of complicated, contradictory back story (vampire overlords, a mysterious "Blood God," and an ancient, supposedly undecipherable sacred text that can be swiftly translated via Windows 95). Though Snipes makes a fine martial artist, he spends much of the movie hidden behind dark glasses and layers of body armor, and he turns in a rather muted, humorless performance. As the villain, a snotty little upstart vampire, Stephen Dorff—astoundingly unlikable even under the best of circumstances—brings his most odious qualities to bear in what might be described as a very committed performance. When he menaces the kidnapped heroine, an impossible-to-gross-out hematologist played by N'Bushe Wright, his sexually charged threats sound like they were written in a junior high school study hall: "What's the matter? You seem kind of... pent up. Blade not ... giving it to you?" You can't blame her when she responds with a blasé "Bite me."

Also reviewed in:
CHICAGO TRIBUNE, 8/21/98, Friday/p. A, Michael Wilmington
NEW YORK TIMES, 8/21/98, p. E27, Stephen Holden
VARIETY, 8/24-30/98, p. 27, Dennis Harvey

BLUES BROTHERS 2000

A Universal Pictures release of a Landis/Belzberg production. *Producer:* John Landis, Dan Aykroyd, and Leslie Belzberg. *Director:* John Landis. *Screenplay (based on "The Blues Brothers"):* Dan Aykroyd and John Landis. *Director of Photography:* David Herrington. *Editor:* Dale Beldin. *Music:* Paul Shaffer. *Music Editor:* George A. Martin. *Choreographer:* Barry Lather. *Sound:* Glen Gauthier and (music) Harvey Goldberg and Jeff Wolpert. *Sound Editor:* Scott A. Hecker. *Casting:* Ross Clydesdale and Joanna Colbert. *Production Designer:* Bill Brodie. *Art Director:* Dan Yarhi. *Set Designer:* Gord White. *Set Decorator:* Steve Shewchuk and Clive Thomasson. *Set Dresser:* Tracy Budd and Bill Johnson. *Special Effects:* Martin Malivoire. *Costumes:* Deborah Nadoolman. *Make-up:* Patricia Green. *Stunt Coordinator:* Rick Avery. *Running time:* 105 minutes. *MPAA Rating:* PG-13.

CAST: Walter Levine (Same Guard);   Dan Aykroyd (Elwood Blues);   Tom Davis (Prison Clerk);   Frank Oz (Warden);   Shann Johnson (Matara);   B.B. King (Malvern Gasperon); Kathleen Freeman (Mother Mary Stigmata);   J. Evan Bonifant (Buster);   Gloria Slade (Police Receptionist);   Joe Morton (Cabel Chamberlain);   Jennifer Irwin and Liz Gordon (Nuns); Junior Wells (Himself); Lonnie Brooks (Himself);   John Goodman (Mighty Mack McTeer); Willie Hall (Himself);   Nia Peeples (Lt. Elizondo);   Michael Bodnar, Slavko Hochevar, Wally High, Richard Kruk, and John Lyons (Russian Thugs); Igor Syyouk (Tstetsevkaya);   Victor Pedtrchenko (Ivan);   Matt Murphy (Matt "Guitar" Murphy);   Lou Marini ("Blue Lou" Marini); Aretha Franklin (Mrs. Murphy); Esther Ridgeway, Gloria Ridgeway, and Gracie Ridgeway (Mrs. Murphy's Friends);   Donald Dunn (Donald "Duck" Dunn);   Steve Cropper (Steve "The Colonel" Cropper);   Tom Malone ("Bones" Malone);   George Sperdakos (Priest);   Alan Rubin ("Mr. Fabulous"); Johnny Lang (Custodian);   Murphy Dunne (Murph);   Eddie Floyd (Ed); Wilson Pickett (Mr. Pickett);   Jillian Hart (Phone Operator); Steve Lawrence (Maury Sline); Susan Davy and Soo Garay (Indiana State Troopers);   Jeff Morris (Bob);   Howard Hoover (F.B.I.); Darrell Hammond (Mr. Robertson);   Chris Marshall (Skinhead);   Nicholas Rice (County Fair Announcer); Max Landis (Ghostrider); Sandi Ross (Church Woman);   Danny Ray (Deacon);   Sharon Riley and the Faith Chorale (Choir);   Sam Moore (Reverend Morris); James Brown (Cleophus James);   Candide Franklin (Ton Tons Macoutes);   Erykah Badu (Queen Moussette);   Patrick Patterson (Sheriff);   Paul Shaffer (Marco).

LOS ANGELES TIMES, 2/6/98, Calendar/p. 2, Jack Mathews

[*The following review by Jack Mathews appeared in a slightly different form in* NEWSDAY, 2/6/98, Part II/p. B3.]

"18 Years Later."

With that pre-credit title nudge, the sequel to John Landis' supercharged 1980 car chase and R&B comedy "The Blues Brothers" begins, and you are warned: If you don't have a detailed and reverent memory for the first film, rent it and love it, or save your money for the soundtrack. "Blues Brothers 2000" is the best noise you're going to hear all year.

"BB 2000" actually plays more like a self-celebrating 20-year reunion of aging hipsters than a sequel. John Belushi, Cab Calloway, who played the brothers' orphanage mentor, and John Candy, the Chicago cop who chased the brothers all over Illinois, are gone, and remembered with a dedication. But every member of the Blues Brothers Band is back, as are blues legends Aretha Franklin and James Brown, and almost every scene is a tribute to its predecessor.

The absence of Belushi, who is replaced by not one but three new Blues Brothers, is fatal in itself. The Blues Brothers weren't a concept, they were Jake and Elwood, the Abbott and Costello of cool, and the act was so much a collaboration of Belushi and Dan Aykroyd, so dependent on the moves and attitude and talents that each brought to his character, that it's frozen in time.

Belushi's trio of replacements—John Goodman, as the bartender-turned-Blues Brother Mighty Mack McTeer; Joe Morton, state trooper-turned-brother Cab Chamberlain; and J. Evan Bonifant, orphan brother Buster—gives "BB 2000" some of its best moments.

Goodman and Morton can really sing the blues, and 12-year-old Bonifant, decked out in black suit, black hat and black sunglasses, does a perfect imitation of Aykroyd's seemingly inimitable dance style.

But no one will mistake the act for the original. Aykroyd can't do those moves anymore. Nor can Brown, as a swollen Rev. Cleophus James, still start a fire under his feet. And Franklin can't begin to get her substantial body in sync with her voice when she launches into Otis Redding's jumping "Respect."

The script, co-written by Landis and Aykroyd, is a near replica of the first, without the purpose. In the first film, Jake is picked up from an Illinois prison by Elwood, and they set out to reunite their band and earn a quick $5,000 to save their old orphanage for Sister Mary Stigmata (Kathleen Freeman). Jake undergoes a quick religious conversion, at a rockin' gospel service led by Brown, and from then on, the brothers are on "a mission from God."

In "BB 2000," Elwood is released from prison, visits now Mother Mary Stigmata (Freeman again), then sets out to reunite his band, not with a mission but with the redundant shrug, "The Lord works in mysterious ways." That mystery gives Landis free rein to go from one set piece, either a destruction derby of a car chase or a music production number, to another.

There are funny sight gags strewn throughout, but because so many scenes and confrontations are repeated from the original, there's a staleness and sense of melancholy to the whole affair. It is so dependent on the audience's familiarity and affection, you get the feeling of sitting around with old college chums, trying desperately to relive the past and stay awake at the same time.

In the most self-indulgent moment, Elwood gives his band a pep talk, closing with a litany of the greatest names in blues history, including Robert K. Weiss.

"Who's Robert K. Weiss?" someone asks. Elwood doesn't answer, but Weiss is an old friend of Landis', and the producer of both "The Blues Brothers" and the earlier "Kentucky Fried Movie."

All that said, the soundtrack album has to be a best buy. Besides Franklin and Brown, and the Blues Brothers Band, the film's all-star cast of musicians includes B.B. King, Junior Wells, Lonnie Brooks, Jonny Lang, Wilson Pickett and the Louisiana Gator Boys, a pickup bank that includes Eric Clapton, Jon Faddis, Lou Rawls, Bo Diddley, Isaac Hayes, Josh Redman and Steven Winwood.

It's only when the Louisiana Gator Boys and the Blues Brothers jam in the film's final moments that "BB 2000" approaches the energy of the original film.

NEW STATESMAN, 5/22/98, p. 47, Nick Hasted

How to blow your budget the Blues Brother Way.

It's instructive, sometimes, to see just how far talent can fall. The first half an hour of "Blues Brothers 2000" (certificate PG) provides charts, graphs and the point of thudding impact. When Dan Aykroyd and director John Landis made the original "Blues Brothers" in 1980, they seemed to have comic talent to burn. In this belated sequel, co-written by the two of them, the fire has fizzled out.

The plot once again has a band of blues-loving reprobates being chased across America. But in the intervening 18 years, the sense of proportion that jokes need has been lost, the sense of development that sequels demand has been ignored. Worst of all is the loss of John Belushi. It was he who gave the original Brothers their faint tinge of anarchy.

No fewer than three new Brothers—a young boy, an upright half-brother, and John Goodman—are employed to fill Belushi's shoes. They just make the essentially straight Aykroyd look all the more out of place, all the less capable of the rebellious spirit the film requires. It's curious, then, how likeable and even enjoyable it becomes.

The first secret is the music. The Blues Brothers cult may have been based on car crashes, Belushi and the iconic cool of its leading men's black suits, shades and hats. But, to Belushi and Aykroyd, the music they played was always the point. The original film's most significant impact was in its rehabilitation of the careers of forgotten black music giants, from Aretha Franklin to Cab Calloway.

The sequel repeats the close. Landis calls it a musical and, after its flat opening, the singing and dancing never stops. Inspiration sometimes flags, though, as when Aretha sings "Respect" yet again. But there are many more moments when the energy and conviction of the score could make a corpse dance.

In the only speech written with purpose, Aykroyd spells out the movie's message: that traditional American music must be preserved in the face of inferior, modern forms. These are reactionary words. Times have changed, and the Brothers' revivalism can't be repeated. But that doesn't prevent a performance of "Ghost Riders in the Sky"—to a Kentucky crowd, as a real storm howls and real riders coast through the clouds—being any less thrilling, or less movingly American.

It's a scene that also contains two more points in this shoddy film's favour. First the sense, as we cruise down America's backroads, that as well as being a musical this is a road movie. There's something restful about watching this enormous country pass by, shot as it is with tender care. It's an effect spoilt only briefly on learning that the film was made in Toronto. Then, too, there's the crazed excess which the appearance of real ghost riders suggests. The Brothers' car can fly; a revival meeting makes a convert levitate through the roof; the first film's famously record-breaking rate of police-car demolition is beaten in a single two-minute scene. There's a sense, frankly, that Landis and Aykroyd knew this was their last shot at success. And that, rather than make them careful, the knowledge made them blow their budget in as many indulgent ways as they could before someone called "Cut!"

NEW YORK POST, 2/6/98, p. 39, Michael Medved

"Blues Brothers 2000" pursues two primary purposes: generating enough musical numbers for a socko soundtrack album, and smashing even more police cars than the original film.

On both counts, director John Landis can say his mission has been accomplished, but when it comes to more traditional elements of movie-making—like humor, plot, characterization, originality or pacing—"Blues Brothers 2000" doesn't even try, crashing fond memories from the original film in a sad pileup of its own.

The non-fun begins with Elwood Blues (the always appealing Dan Aykroyd) released from prison, discovering that his old Chicago orphanage has been torn down, and learning that both brother Jake and beloved janitor Curtis (their surrogate father) have passed on to the big blues club in the sky.

The old man, however, left a previously unacknowledged, illegitimate son, who's now an uptight, authoritarian state trooper (Joe Morton, whose substance and smarts as an actor somehow shine through the shabby material).

With Elwood trying to mentor a know-it-all 10-year-old orphan (J. Evan Bonifant) and reassemble his old band, the nasty cop seeks to capture him, while Russian mafia and right-wing militia unpersuasively pursue the hero's head.

The story line is much too predictable to win laughs, as in Elwood's recruitment of a new partner. Clearly requiring another salt-of-the-earth fat guy, he merely grabs John Goodman from his job as bartender of a strip club.

Every sequence mechanically echoes the first film. Cameo performers from last time (James Brown, Aretha Franklin, Steve Lawrence) conveniently reappear, along with other legendary names (Lou Rawls, Eric Clapton), but all the big numbers feel over-produced and puffed out of proportion.

Eighteen years ago, the original project displayed plenty of flaws, but struck sparks of lunacy that could only be described as joyful and youthful; this cautious and constipated sequel, on the other hand, feels decidedly (and fatally) middle-aged.

SIGHT AND SOUND, 7/98, p. 36, Geoffrey Macnab

Fresh out of prison and still mourning the death of his brother Jake, Elwood Blues heads to the big city. He tracks down his half-brother Cabel, a strait-laced cop who wants nothing to do with him. He also reassembles his old band, The Blues Brothers. New recruits include Mack, a singer, and Buster, a 10-year-old orphan.

Elwood wants The Blues Brothers to play in Queen Mousette's Battle of the Bands, a prestigious event held deep in Louisiana's bayou country. With the cops and some vengeful Russian mobsters hot on their trail, Elwood and his cronies drive across America, stopping for a warm-up gig at a bluegrass festival in Kentucky. Cabel has vowed to arrest Elwood but after a life-changing experience at a religious revivalist meeting, ends up joining the band himself. The Blues Brothers audition for Queen Mousette and are accepted to compete in the Battle of the Bands. They come up against The Louisiana Gator Boys, a huge R&B outfit comprising some of the best-known names in blues history. As both bands perform rousing sets, Queen Mousette uses her magical powers to prevent the Russian mobsters from stopping the concert.

Eighteen years after the original *Blues Brothers* movie, director John Landis and his co-writer Dan Aykroyd have decided to revive the franchise. Although without the late John Belushi, the set-up is exactly the same as before: show-stopping musical interludes from an array of stars (from James Brown and Aretha Franklin to Junior Wells, Bo Diddley and B. B. King) interspersed with noisy, Keystone Kop-style slapstick. Unfortunately, as B. B. King might put it, the thrill has gone. While the music is as brash and energetic as ever and Elwood's stunt driving continues to astound, the absence of anything approaching a coherent plot is a major drawback.

Blues Brothers 2000 lurches from set-piece to set-piece in random fashion. Most of Hollywood's stunt drivers seem to have taken part in the extraordinarily crass demolition derby of a pile-up (reportedly one of the biggest in movie history) which Landis tosses gratuitously into the action. The huge, ghostly skeletons of cowboys which gallop across the night during The Blues Brothers' spirited rendition of 'Riders in the Sky (A Cowboy Legend)' look impressive in themselves, but likewise have no bearing on the story.

At times, there is something almost invigorating about the way that characters we've never seen before suddenly burst into song (in fine musical tradition) but too often, an impression is created that the film-makers are stuffing as much music, noise and as many star cameos as possible into the mix in the hope that we won't notice the holes in the narrative. Blues fans will doubtless relish the wealth of musical talent on display (it's a far richer array than the first film's). Perhaps over time *Blues Brothers 2000* will attain the same cult status as its predecessor, but only the most indulgent of audiences is likely to be happy with such a slapdash sequel.

VILLAGE VOICE, 2/17/98, p. 120, Gary Susman

John Landis's 1980 film *The Blues Brothers*—a musical-*Saturday Night Live* sketch-demolition derby-r&b tribute—was a monument to the directorial bloat of the *Apocalypse Now-Heaven's Gate* era, albeit one whose enthusiastic overkill made it very entertaining. Compared to his belated and superfluous sequel, *Blues Brothers 2000,* the original is a masterpiece of tight plotting, rich characterizations, and singularity of purpose. The Brothers were "on a mission from God" then, using their talent to spread the soul music gospel and help children; here, Landis and cowriter-star Dan Aykroyd are out to fleece them. To replace John Belushi, Aykroyd's Elwood Blues needs three sidekicks, chosen for broad demographic appeal: a 10-year-old pickpocket (too-cute J. Evan Bonifant), whom Elwood is supposed to be keeping out of trouble; a white Boomer bartender (John Goodman, who sings with more zeal than talent) Elwood meets in an oddly wholesome strip club; and a black police commander (a humorless but musically talented Joe Morton) who belatedly realizes that it's his calling to help these white boys preserve black roots music. The plot is a pale xerox of the original, with Elwood shaming the band into reassembling while pursued by cops, Russian mobsters, and redneck militiamen (instead of neo-Nazis). Automotive mayhem, unwitting gigs at country music venues, and other familiar high jinks ensue. The film displays heart only in the joyous musical sequences spotlighting blues and soul greats young and old, notably a climactic jam with B.B. King, Bo Diddley, Eric Clapton, and a couple dozen others that is almost worth the price of admission. The overstuffed roster of musical all-stars is the only part of *Blues Brothers 2000* that proves the virtues of excess.

Also reviewed in:
CHICAGO TRIBUNE, 2/6/98, Friday/p. A, Mark Caro
NATION, 3/16/98, p. 36, Sturt Klawans
NEW YORK TIMES, 2/6/98, p. E14, Lawrence Van Gelder
VARIETY, 2/9-15/98, p. 70, Joe Leydon
WASHINGTON POST, 2/6/98, p. B1, Stephen Hunter
WASHINGTON POST, 2/6/98, Weekend/p. 41, Desson Howe

BORROWERS, THE

A PolyGram Filmed Entertainment release of a Working Title production. *Executive Producer:* Walt De Faria. *Producer:* Tim Bevan, Eric Fellner, and Rachel Talalay. *Director:* Peter Hewitt. *Screenplay:* Gavin Scott and John Kamps. *Based on the novels by:* Mary Norton. *Director of Photography:* John Fenner and Trevor Brooker. *Editor:* David Freeman. *Music:* Harry Gregson-Williams. *Music Editor:* Brian Richards, Graham Sutton, and Dina Eaton. *Sound:* David Stephenson and (music) Alan Meyerson. *Sound Editor:* Peter Joly. *Casting:* Nina Gold. *Production Designer:* Gemma Jackson. *Art Director:* Jim Morahan. *Set Decorator:* Careen Hertzog. *Special Effects:* Digby Milner. *Visual Effects:* Peter Chiang. *Costumes:* Marie France. *Make-up:* Joan Hills. *Stunt Coordinator:* Jim Dowdall. *Running time:* 83 minutes. *MPAA Rating:* PG.

CAST: John Goodman (Ocious Potter); Jim Broadbent (Pod Clock); Mark Williams (Exterminator Jeff); Celia Imrie (Homily Clock); Hugh Laurie (Officer Steady); Ruby Wax (Town Hall Clerk); Bradley Pierce (Pete Lender); Flora Newbigin (Arrietty Clock); Tom Felton (Peagreen Clock); Raymond Pickard (Spiller); Aden Gillett (Joe Lender); Doon Mackichan (Victoria Lender); Andrew Dunford (Dustbunny); Bob Goody (Minty); Patrick Monkton (Swag); George Yiassoumi (Wrigley); Dick Ward (Milkman).

LOS ANGELES TIMES, 2/13/98, Calendar/p. 8, Jack Mathews

[The following review by Jack Mathews appeared in a slightly different form in NEWSDAY, 2/13/98, Part II/p. B11.]

Things are missing in the Lender residence. Small things, like hat pins, tape measures, double-A batteries, spools of thread, refrigerator leftovers. Just enough to be an annoyance to the family, especially Pete, an innovative 10-year-old who has begun setting nasty little traps for the thieves.

But the missing items aren't stolen, they're merely borrowed. They're the raw materials of life for the house's other residents, a 4-inch-tall family of four, who live just beneath the floorboards of the upstairs landing.

The premise of director Peter Hewitt's "The Borrowers" is full of promise that the film, unfortunately, doesn't fulfill. Adapted from Mary Norton's children's book series, "The Borrowers" does a superb job of creating a scaled environment for its Lilliputian characters, but neither the characters nor the story matches the innovation of the design.

Hewitt and the screenwriters, Gavin Scott and John Kamps, seem to be caught in a familiar creative gap, trying to tell a story that will hold the attention of small children while amusing their parents, and not quite accomplishing either. "The Borrowers" is so anxious to get into its adventure—which has Pete (Bradley Pierce) and the Clocks trying to save the Lender/Clock home from a malicious lawyer (John Goodman)—that you can only tell members of one family from the other's by their size.

Like the recent "Mouse Hunt," "The Borrowers" borrows most from the "Home Alone" movies. The essence of its comedic action has the Clock children, Arrietty (Flora Newbigin) and Peagreen (Tom Felton) and a friendly scamp Borrower named Spiller (Raymond Pickard), tormenting their giant adversaries, Ocious Potter (Goodman) and the pest exterminator (Mark Williams) he hires to delouse the Lender house.

Potter is the primary aggressor-victim, having each attempt to kill the Clocks double-backfire on him in the form of hair-raising electrocutions, facial acid baths, submersions in dairy cheese and head-to-toe binding—a la "Gulliver's Travels"—by armies of Borrowers rallying to the Clocks' defense.

The surprise is not that the cast is over the top but that it's also flat. Goodman is a by-the-numbers villain, neither terribly funny nor particularly scary. British actor Jim Broadbent seems more lost than in command of Pa Clock's oversized world. And the kids simply aren't defined well enough for even the most superficial bonding with children in the audience.

NEW YORK POST, 2/13/98, p. 52, Larry Worth

If James ("Titanic") Cameron is right—that "size does count"—it'll be news to "The Borrowers." The Lilliputian-sized family living beneath the floorboards of a cozy house can outsmart their Gulliver-like counterparts any day of the week. And that's a necessity when their cubby—complete with thimble furniture, button plates and retractable tape-measure elevators—is about to be demolished.

Actually, the borrowers (as they call themselves) don't dislike all "human beans." Specifically, the 5-foot plus mother, father, and boy who reside above the floorboards are deemed relatively tolerable.

But an evil lawyer who's intent on gutting the dwelling is another matter. Ultimately, the borrowers team with the tenants' son to save the day. And that's when the tall tale kicks into overdrive.

Based on Mary Norton's popular series of children's books, the level of fun jumps from zero to 60 in the opening credits, then keeps on going. And though director Peter Hewitt is obviously indebted to Swift, he's equally inspired by "The Incredible Shrinking Man," "Tom Thumb' and "Home Alone."

The result is a magical world that's easy to buy into. One reason: Hewitt never skimps on details, providing the borrowers with their own manner of dress, habits and credos. And while echoes of '50s London surface, the purposely ambiguous time and place add to the whimsical charm.

Shot in warm sepia tones, the action is further enhanced by delightful special effects, garishly amusing closeups and a subtle anti-prejudice message.

Among the uniformly colorful actors, John Goodman is a total hoot as the unctuous, land-hungry attorney Mr. Potter (a tribute to Lionel Barrymore's evil Mr. Potter from "It's a Wonderful Life," perhaps?). He's deliciously cartoon-like without ever going over the top.

Other characters, however, suffer personality changes with no warning. One can't help wondering if the finished print got chopped down to a more kid-friendly 83-minute running time.

Thankfully, the production's wit and imagination nicely compensate, making "The Borrowers" into a fantasy fit for parents and kids alike.

SIGHT AND SOUND, 12/97, p. 39, Charlotte O'Sullivan

Ten-year-old Pete Lender has noticed that objects in his home keep disappearing. The culprits are the diminutive Clock family, Pod, Homily and their two children, Arrietty and Peagreen. The Clocks live under the skirting boards and "borrow" whatever they need from "human beans".

Pete's family are about to lose their home. An evil lawyer, Ocious Potter, intends to evict them on the pretext that the house's deceased owner, Great Aunt Mary, left no will. In the meantime, Peter has captured Arrietty and made friends with her.

For the move to the Lenders' new home, Pete helps pack the Clocks into the delivery van, but along the way Arrietty and Peagreen tumble out. They make their way back to the old house, where they come across Potter, extracting from a safe the will which actually leaves the house to the Lenders. Arrietty and Peagreen borrow the will, but Potter calls in Exterminator Jeff. The children evade capture and take a short cut to the Lenders' new home, but Peagreen gets stuck in a milk bottle along the way and is taken off to the dairy. Arrietty meets Spiller, an 'outie' (a borrower who lives outdoors) and they form an alliance.

Everyone heads for the dairy. Peagreen is eventually rescued but Potter snatches back the will. He goes to City Hall to order the demolition of the house, but gets locked in a store cupboard there. He is besieged by the Clocks, along with hundreds of their 'outie' friends and is tied up and lectured to. Potter is arrested and both families return to their original home.

At last, a kids' film about New Age travellers and the perils of homeownership. Swampy (the recently famous eco-warrior) will be pleased. But how did Mary Norton's classic 50s children's books get involved? After all, the original emphasis of the *Borrowers* books—a series of adventures concerning the Clock family—was on the little cockney clan's upward mobility. Home (and self) improvement was what they liked (with the mother Homily, in particular, a sucker for books and aristocratic left-overs).

Peter Hewitt's movie, however, problematises such aspirations. Creating a schizoid world—part modern-day America, part 50s Britain—*The Borrowers* testifies to a crisis in Western values. These Clocks are timid squatters, but instead of indulging their desire for legitimacy, Hewitt quickly turfs them out into the wide world. He's not interested in seducing us with furniture. Instead, he wants us to realise that the property boom (the lawyer Potter intends to turn the Clocks' house into a block of luxury flats) makes all indoor living dangerous.

With their colourful, scruffy wool garb and recycled tools and clothes, the Clocks even look like New Age travellers. And, indeed, they are a persecuted, panicky lot—constantly compared to vermin, these 'little people' (in both senses of the word) rightly fear attack. The full-sized little boy Pete, a sort of charitable liberal, has no power to help them. The Clocks only gain control of their lives when they meet up with the 'outies', the borrowers who live outside. The outies, in the form of handsome, natty-haired Spiller, are not afraid to "be seen". Father Pod and Homily's watchword for their behaviour is "inconspicuous". "Yeah, invisible more like," spits the politicised Spiller. To him, the Clocks are "dependent" on humans. Just like Swampy, Spiller's solution involves going underground, roaming the passageways where such scoundrels as Potter can't reach him.

But this is not, thankfully, a dogmatic film. All the characters are affectionately drawn (even Potter and Exterminator Jeff), and the ending is a triumph of pluralism. Jim Broadbent (Pod Clock) gets the big speech, where he reiterates the idea that his tribe are civil, not disobedient. The raggle-taggle mob swarm behind him, not sinister, but simply alert. Pod tells Potter "you are seen", marking a shift from the borrowers as hiding creatures to watching ones. But it's even more significant that at the end, the two families get their secure housing but without having been shown to have 'earned' it. The Lenders have merely inherited the property from Great Aunt Mary; the Clocks live off Pete. So if the film has a message, it's that ownership is a false dream—we're all parasites. And there are no strings attached: these Clocks (unlike those in the Norton books) do not ape the lifestyle of their benefactors—theirs may be a culture of dependency, but it remains their own. Meanwhile, the children go one step further: at the conclusion, Arrietty and Spiller take off into the tunnels in a tiny car—rootless and outward bound.

The Borrowers is a superbly bold piece of film-making, full of lovely performances (especially John Goodman as Ocious Potter) and gripping set pieces. The only odd thing about it is that Bradford & Bingley ("Britain's second-biggest building society") are promoting it. Have they seen this film?

VILLAGE VOICE, 2/17/98, p. 116, Leslie Camhi

Pins, keys, floss, and fabric disappear from our lives each day. Based upon the classic children's series by Mary Beth Norton, *The Borrowers* tells the story of tiny people who live beneath the floorboards of old houses. Making away with household scraps, they ingeniously transform them: Christmas lights illuminate their dwelling, a match provides a man's walking stick, a retractable tape measure does the job of an elevator. One day, a boy, Peter Lender, discovers Borrowers—Pod and Homily Clock and their children, Arrietty and Peapod—hidden in his family's house. And just in time huge, odious lawyer (John Goodman) wants to evict the Lenders and put up luxury apartments. Together, boy and Borrowers become embroiled in a plan to save their home from destruction. With shades of *The incredible Shrinking Man*, Peter Hewitt has fashioned an appealing fable about little people's enduring power. It's so much fun figuring out what their tiny world is made of that you forgive the broad performances, which anyway should appeal to children. Most important, Hewitt manages to convey "the Borrower way"—a complex morality of living by your wits, and an allegory about the remnants of magic, politeness, and community in a world that's often just too big.

Also reviewed in:
NEW YORK TIMES, 2/13/98, p. E28, Janet Maslin
VARIETY, 12/8-24/97, p. 112, Derek Elley
WASHINGTON POST, 2/13/98, p. D1, Stephen Hunter
WASHINGTON POST, 2/13/98, Weekend/p. 47, Desson Howe

BOYS IN LOVE 2

A First Run Features release of seven short films. *Running Time*: 97 minutes. *MPAA Rating*: Not Rated.

TWILIGHT OF THE GODS: A Zee Films production mad in association with The New Zealand Film Commission. *Producer:* Michele Fantl. *Director:* Stewart Main. *Screenplay:* Stewart Main. *Running time*: 15 minutes. *MPAA Rating*: Not Rated.

CAST: Greg Mayor (Toa);   Marton Csokas (Soldier).

ACHILLES: *Director:* Barry Purves.   *Animation:* Barry Purves.   *Narrator:* Derek Jacobi. *Running Time:* 11 minutes.   *MPAA Rating:* Not Rated.

BOOT CAMP: A Body and Soul Productions film.   *Producer:* Melinda Hsu.   *Director:* John Matthews.   *Screenplay:* John Matthews. *Director of Photography:* Kate Phelan.   *Music:* Jeffrey Hoffman.   *Choreographer:* Bill Fabris.   *Costumes:* Goran Sparrman.   *Running Time*: 6 minutes. *MPAA Rating*: Not Rated.

CAST: Mathew Solari (Novice);   John Cantwell (Master);   Alex Benjamin (Bartender);   Doug Bradford (Master with Whip);   Tyne Firmin (Slave on Leash);   David Kibbe (Slave in Shackles);   Sam Lipton (Master with Leash).

SPF 2000: A First Run Features release in association with Ambrosia Entertainment of a Willing Suspension production.   *Producer:* Patrick McGuinn.   *Director:* Patrick McGuinn.   *Screenplay and Story:* Patrick McGuinn.   *Director of Photography:* Amy Gissen.   *Editor:* Patrick McGuinn. *Music:* William Loose, R.D. Granados, and The Ventures.   *Running Time:* 10 minutes.   *MPAA Rating:* Not Rated.

CAST: Joseph Paolini (Kip);   Kelvin Walker (Pucci);   Peter Gingerich (JJ);   Colleen O'Neill (Gretchen).

DIRTY BABY DOES FIRE ISLAND: *Director:* Tod Downing.   *Screenplay:* Todd Downing. *Director of Photography:* Todd Downing.   *Editor:* Todd Downing.   *Sound:* Chris Larsen. *Running time:* 8½ minutes.   *MPAA Rating:* Not Rated.

CAST: Dirty Baby (Dirty Baby);   Rosy Ngo (Voice of Deer).

KAREN BLACK LIKE ME: *Producer:* David Briggs.   *Director:* David Briggs.   *Screenplay:* David Briggs.   *Editor:* David Briggs.   *Running time:* 6 minutes.   *MPAA Rating:* Not Rated.

CAST: Ira Rosenberg (Emil);   Anita Gillette (Mother).

MY BODY: *Producer:* Matthias Visser.   *Director:* Joel Moffett.   *Screenplay:* Joel Moffett. *Director of Photography:* Andrew Thomas.   *Editor:* Mark Catalena.   *Production Designer:* Kelly Perry.   *Running time:* 30 minutes.   *MPAA Rating:* Not Rated.

CAST: Joel Moffett (Charlie);   Mitchell Sternard (The Body);   Kim Strauss (Dr. Lockerman); Donna Peroni (Mrs. Sparky);   Sheila A. Grenham (Tina);   Jeremy D. Lawrence (Heart Patient); Michael Nissman (Mr. Sparky);   Mark Eric Howell (The Butcher);   Lee Everett (911 Operator); Tia Texada (Hospital Receptionist);   Kalena Coleman and Robyn Rice (Nurses);   Brianna Shebby and Danielle Shebby (Little Indians).

VILLAGE VOICE, 7/21/98, p. 124, Elliott Stein

There's long and fairly noble tradition of "portmanteau" or "omnibus" films (*Dead of Night, Love at Twenty*)" composed of several different stories, often, but not always, directed by different hands, usually linked by a narrative thread or common theme. *Boys In Love 2* is a looser latter-day compilation, a roundup of seven shorts, all concerned with the affairs of gay males. There are three standouts in the program: the American *Boot Camp*, directed by John Scott Matthews, Barry Purves's *Achilles* from Great Britain, and Stewart Main's *Twilight of the Gods* from New Zealand. *Boot Camp*, set in New York's s/m scene, concerns the song-and-dance courtship of a timid novice and a leather master. It's charming and droll, deftly done without a wasted frame. Purve's extraordinary animated film, narrated by Jacobi, recounts the passionate and ill-fated amours of Achilles and Patroclus against the background of the Trojan War, all in 11 minutes flat. This genuine oddity's eroticism is a bit unsettling—Purves animated puppets are markedly more sexy than nearly all the guys in the live-action flicks. *Twilight,*an exquisite period piece, is a poetic idyll about the love affair of a Maori warrior and an English soldier. Its Edenesque forest setting is depicted with rhapsodic black-and-white impressionism àla *Rashomon*.

Also reviewed in:
NEW YORK TIMES, 7/17/98, p. E12, Stephen Holden

BRANDON TEENA STORY, THE

A Zeitgeist Films release of a Bless Bless Productions film. *Executive Producer:* Jane Dekrone. *Producer:* Susan Muska and Greta Olafsdottir. *Director:* Susan Muska and Greta Olafsdottir. *Screenplay:* Susan Muska and Greta Olafsdottir. *Director of Photography:* Susan Muska and Greta Olafsdottir. *Editor:* Susan Muska and Greta Olafsdottir. *Music:* Lorri Morgan, Dinah Washington, April Stevens, and The Brown Brothers. *Sound:* Lora Hirschberg. *Running time:* 90 minutes. *MPAA Rating:* Not Rated.

LOS ANGELES TIMES, 3/12/99, Calendar/p. 16, Kevin Thomas

When 21-year-old Teena Brandon, who called herself Brandon Teena, left Lincoln, Neb., in mid-November 1993 because too many people had discovered she was a woman and not a man, moving to nearby Falls City (pop. 1,769), she could scarcely have made a worse choice of a place to try to live as a male.

It is a community of high unemployment and incidence of spousal abuse, a drab little burg where, according to one resident, any known gay person arriving there would be immediately escorted out of town. How could it be expected to be hospitable to a young woman in a self-described "sexual identity crisis" who was said to have wanted a sex-change operation?

In "The Brandon Teena Story," a devastatingly calm, revealing, step-by-step tracing of the last several weeks of Brandon's life, documentarians Susan Muska and Greta Olafsdottir don't tell us who or what it was that drew Brandon to Falls City; she could expect to be relatively safe only in the country's largest and most cosmopolitan cities. We don't know if she longed to go to San Francisco, for example, but as an individual known to forge checks in desperation, she clearly couldn't afford to go very far away.

Those who spoke of Brandon to the filmmakers say two things. First, the women Brandon dated as a male all praise her for being considerate, for treating them "like a lady." And second, when Brandon's physical gender was inevitably revealed in Falls City, everyone, men and women alike, expressed outrage that Brandon was "living a lie," but it's clear that none of them would have accepted Brandon as a transsexual—a term, let alone a concept, surely little-known in the community.

Sophocles could not have come up with a greater sense of inevitability in Brandon's tragic fate. Craving love and acceptance, Brandon quickly started dating lovely Lisa Tisdel of Falls City. When Brandon's chronic forging exposed her gender, two young men, John Lotter and Tom Nissen, with whom she had been hanging out, were especially enraged, and they attempted to rape her on Christmas Eve as a culmination of trying to confront Lisa with the truth about her "boyfriend." Instead of fleeing town, Brandon naively sealed her fate by reporting them to the local sheriff, whose recorded interrogation of Brandon reveals him to be a man of crudeness and insensitivity, to put it mildly. The sheriff was slow to press charges.

When Brandon's accusations swiftly became public knowledge, the heterosexuality of the young men was ridiculed: Why did they want to have sex with a woman who had been successfully passing as a man? As ex-felons knowing what kind of prison terms they were facing if convicted of rape, Lotter and Nissen tracked Brandon down at the home of her friend Lisa Lambert, who lived 30 miles away outside the even tinier town of Humboldt. On New Year's Eve they shot Brandon fatally, also subjecting her to further abuse to make sure she really was dead. They also shot to death Lisa and her visitor, Philip LeVine. Only Lisa's 9-month-old son survived.

A social worker interviewed in the wake of Lotter's conviction (which followed Nissen's) sums it up best when she states that she does not feel that Falls City, with its climate of hatred and ignorance, is aware of its responsibility in Brandon's fate. What "The Brandon Teena Story," reinforced by the fate of Mathew Shepard in neighboring Wyoming, makes clear is that the rural heartland of America can be a frightening place for those who don't fit into an extremely narrow view of human sexuality.

NEW YORK POST, 9/23/98, p. 51, Larry Worth

It's a story that's tailor-made for a head-turning National Enquirer cover, or at least a "Ripley's Believe It or Not" exhibit.

Indeed, "The Brandon Teena Story"—a documentary about a Nebraska girl who disguised herself as a teen-age boy in the early '90s—sounds like a deliciously lurid walk on the wild side. But within 30 minutes, any hint of sensationalism is replaced with a collection of facts that are as disturbing as they are fascinating.

Reminiscent of a real-life take on, alternately, "The Crying Game," "Glen or Glenda," "M. Butterfly" and "The Accused," it's the most sobering, downright shocking look at homophobia since 1984's "The Times of Harvey Milk."

But that's no thanks to co-directors Susan Muska and Greta Olafsdottir. The stranger-than-fiction scenario makes the film succeed in spite of their missteps.

For starters, the duo initially give the production an inappropriately campy tone. Interviews with Brandon's former girlfriends and associates seem meant to make viewers smirk.

Granted, there's a twisted logic to be found in ex-lovers describing Brandon as a great kisser and "knowing how to please a woman." But things go well beyond that level of amusement, complete with a condescendingly folksy soundtrack of Christmas carols played on an accordion or xylophone.

Then, out of nowhere, comes a jaw-droppingly dramatic turn. A series of sick and sicker revelations—the less they're described in advance, the better—will leave audiences reeling.

Suffice to say that a sheriff best described as a bigoted ignoramus won't attract many tourists to the Cornhusker State. He makes billboards reading "Nebraska... the good life" take on a special irony.

But as the directors haphazardly cross-cut between news reports and yet more interviews, it's easy to fantasize how a skilled auteur would mold such material into a masterpiece. Muska and Olafsdottir, on the other hand, operate solely with good intentions.

Thankfully, the very facts of what happened to Brandon and those in his/her sphere amply compensate. Drawbacks or not, it's a tale that demands to be seen and heard.

VILLAGE VOICE, 9/29/98, p. 128, Amy Taubin

Freud's proposition that "anatomy is destiny" is most clearly proven by those who attempt to live as if that were not the case. Brandon Teena (née Teena Brandon) spent her late adolescence in several Nebraska towns trying to pass as a boy. She was extremely popular with young women, some of whom were so charmed by her gentleness, skill at kissing, and by the respect she showed them that they were more than willing to accept her various stories—that her strap-on was the real thing, or that she was undergoing a sex-change treatment. Once involved, it was hard for them to admit that Brandon was female—because of what that would mean about them.

Eventually Brandon was exposed by local law enforcement when she was arrested for theft. Exposure made her vulnerable. Bailed out of jail by one of her girlfriends, she was raped on Christmas Eve and murdered a week later. The men responsible were ex-cons, whose incarceration had only heightened their homophobia. They raped her because they were enraged and threatened by her sexuality ("Brandon's gender was a real problem," one of them opines) and they murdered her to keep her from fingering them as rapists. Brandon Teena was 21 when she died.

While Susan Muska and Greta Olafsdottir's documentary, *The Brandon Teena Story,* doesn't do justice to its fascinating and heartbreaking subject, it's not without interest.

The filmmakers interview all the crucial characters: Brandon's mother and sister, many of her girlfriends and their relatives, and the two convicted killers.

The interviews are somewhat revealing, but they might have been more so had they been allowed to run longer. The filmmakers are at such pains to keep the film moving that they end up with little more than sound bites. Yanked out of context, the talking heads are edited together to tell the story the filmmakers want to tell. And because the filmmakers' understanding of gender and sexuality is implicitly so much more sophisticated than that of any of the people we see on-screen, it feels as if the film is both manipulative and condescending.

The film replicates, albeit to a lesser extent, the very us-against-them mentality that was the cause of Brandon Teena's tragic death. The pathology of homophobia, misogyny, and sexual self-hatred is hardly limited to Midwestern farm country, but the film makes it seem as if it is. Attempting to make connections between violence and poverty, homophobia and lack of education, Muska and Olafsdottir accessorize the film with tacky country-western music, and cliché shots of frozen empty highways, isolated houses, and folksy road signs ("Falls City, A Nice Place To Live").

What makes this disappointing is that the filmmakers clearly had the raw material with which to make a great film. In one extraordinary sequence, they play an audiotape of Brandon being grilled by the sheriff after she has reported being raped. The sheriff treats her as if she's the criminal, implying that she was asking for it, that if she lied about being a boy, she'd lie about anything. As we listen to Brandon's choked-up, scared voice, we see photos of her. In one she's in a hospital bed, her arms half covering her bruised, swollen face. In the other she's sitting on the edge of a pool table, looking both confused and thrilled by the success of her masquerade.

Also reviewed in:
CHICAGO TRIBUNE, 3/5/99, Friday/p. Q, Michael Wilmington
NEW YORK TIMES, 9/23/98, p. E5, Stephen Holden
VARIETY, 3/2-8/98, p. 88, David Stratton

BREAK, THE

A Castle Hill Productions release in association with Channel 4/Road Movies/Bord Scannan/NFD International. *Executive Producer:* David Aukin, Ulrich Felsberg, Rod Stoneman, and Michiyo Yoshizaki. *Producer:* Chris Curling. *Director:* Robert Dornhelm. *Screenplay:* Ronan Bennett. *Based on an idea by:* Stephen Rea. *Director of Photography:* Andrzej Sekula. *Editor:* Masahiro Hirakubo. *Music:* John Keane. *Sound:* Simon Willis and Brian Miksis. *Sound Editor:* Simon Gershon, André Schmidt, and Catherine Hodgson. *Casting:* Ros Hubbard and John Hubbard. *Production Designer:* Kalina Ivanov and Tom McCullagh. *Art Director:* Anna Rackard. *Set Decorator:* Diane Lederman. *Costumes:* Stephanie Maslansky and Maggie Donnelly. *Make-up:* Morag Ross. *Stunt Coordinator:* Patrick Condren and Manny Siverio. *Running time:* 96 minutes. *MPAA Rating:* R.

CAST: Stephen Rea (Dowd); Alfred Molina (Tulio); Rosana Pastor (Monica); Brendan Gleeson (Richard); Pruitt Taylor Vince (Scott); Maria Doyle Kennedy (Roisin); Jorge Sanz (Paco); Robert Taylor (Visiting Room Prison Officer); Catriona Hinds (Richard's Wife); Sean McGinley (Tommy Breen); Deirdre O'Kane (Breen's Girlfriend); Toby Bradford (Charlie);

Frankie McCafferty (Danny);   Richard Dormer (Joe);   B.J. Hogg (Albert);   Roy Haybeard (Food Lorry Driver);   James Duran (Gate Prison Officer);   Seamus Ball (Tallylodge Prison Officer);   Paul Ronan (Liam);   Brian Vincent (Lorenzo Bausch);   Caroline Seymour (Junkie); Myra Carter (Neighbor);   Paul Giamatti (Hotel Clerk);   Claran O'Reilly (Passer-by);   Jerry Grayson (Restaurant Manager);   Ken Solarino (Subway Man);   Sheik Mahmud-Bey (Knifeman); Richard Council and John Rothman (FBI Agents);   Coati Mundi (Pepe);   Alba Oms (Stall Owner);   Marlo Mendoza (Mustachioed Man);   Teresa Yenque (Indian Woman);   Graeme Malcolm (Lattimer);   Barry Snider (Eamonn);   Ndehru Roberts (Kid Gun Dealer);   George Bass (Ramon's Driver);   Luis Argueta (Ramon's Bodyguard);   Esteban Fernandez (Ramon).

LOS ANGELES TIMES, 5/1/98, Calendar/p. 16, Kevin Thomas

Robert Dornhelm's compelling "The Break," an offbeat romantic political thriller, opens with an exciting, faultlessly staged, 20-minute escape from a Belfast prison. A weary long-term IRA convict, Dowd (Stephen Rea) is in the visitor's room telling his lover that she should give up on him when all of a sudden a fellow prisoner whispers to him that a mass breakout is about to be set in motion. "Take your time to think it over," says his friend. "You've got a minute-and-a-half"

Deciding to join in, Dowd plunges into a new life—or is it so new, after all? Instead of life underground in Northern Ireland, he decides to try his luck in New York.

A loner by nature and appreciative of his newfound freedom, Dowd is grateful to live in a seedy hotel and work as a restaurant dishwasher. But when an older woman, also a hotel resident, begs him to come to the rescue of a woman, attacked by her lover (or pimp), screaming for help, Dowd reluctantly steps in and handles the attacker with dispatch. Outraged that he should bloody her attacker's "beautiful face," the woman knifes Dowd in the ribs.

As an escaped convict, Dowd dare not try to get help but is ultimately discovered by a restaurant co-worker Tulio (Alfred Molina), a kindly Guatemalan refugee who saves his life, sending a hospital orderly (Pruitt Taylor Vince) to tend to the wound. Dowd regains his strength in the comfort and security of the apartment Tulio shares with his sister Monica (Rosana Pastor), who works as a hotel charwoman.

Dowd is smitten with Monica and also becomes caught up in the brother and sister's plan to execute a particularly brutal Guatemalan colonel, now living in exile in suburban New York.

Having worked all over the world in a notably wide variety of films, Dornhelm is the ideal director to express the dislocation of the foreigner, and his film, so stunningly shot by Andrzej Sekula, and equally well-designed by Kalina Ivanov and Tom McCullagh, is especially good at suggesting how a cozy apartment or a hearty Irish bar can seem a refuge, if only temporarily, in a cold and dangerous universe.

"The Break" also benefits from Harald Kloser and Shaun Davey's gentle, keening score.

Born in Romania, then moving to Vienna with his parents at age 13, Dornhelm first came to attention with his Oscar-nominated "The Children of Theater Street," about the young students of the Kirov Ballet. More recently, he returned to Romania to make "Requiem for Dominic," a masterful, elegiac expose of the brutal Ceausescu regime.

With his worn, sensitive expression, Rea is perfectly cast as an essentially passive man whose life keeps being turned upside down when he tries to do what he thinks is the right thing. "The Break" is an intensely fatalistic film, and Rea, who supplied the idea for Ronan Bennett's script, is just the actor to portray a man stalked by danger and doom.

He is well-matched by the endlessly versatile Molina and the impassioned Pastor, so memorable in Ken Loach's recent "Land and Freedom." The plot description of "The Break" makes the film sound contrived.

In actuality, it is a beautifully expressed story of a man caught up in the remorseless workings of destiny.

NEW YORK POST, 2/20/98, p. 46, Larry Worth

Opening credits announce that "The Break" is based on an idea by Stephen Rea. Sadly, it comes off more like a thought, and a half-hearted one at that.

The concept is familiar: the inability to escape one's past. So when an IRA prisoner breaks out of a Belfast jail and sneaks into Manhattan on a bogus passport, one never assumes his troubles remain on the Old Sod.

Sure enough, the ex-con has no sooner found work washing dishes at a greasy spoon than he stumbles into an assassination plot hatched by Guatemalan coworkers.

It's all a bit too convenient to accept at face value. But under Robert Dorhelm's direction, the scenario gets even dicier.

Granted, major chunks of the story prove undeniably involving. But melodramatic twists, clumsy scenes and sloppy editing pull viewers out of the vortex.

And though the production could use more suspense, it's certainly not lacking in violence. Whenever a knife or gun is spied, a bloodied body part is about 30 seconds away.

On the plus side—and it's a big plus—evidenced in "The Crying Game," "Princess Caraboo," "Interview With the Vampire" and "Michael Collins," Rea's hang-dog face and soulful eyes bring a stunning dimension and authenticity to the most mediocre of productions.

When forced to communicate a rebel's passions—for either a pretty face or a not-so-pretty fight—Rea can say it all with an arched eyebrow. That's no easy feat.

Fine backup comes from the very reliable Alfred Molina playing Rea's sole friend among the mean streets of Manhattan. Also impressive are Rosana Pastor and Jorge Sanz, well cast as Molina's murder-inclined cohorts.

Finally, Dorhelm gets surprising mileage out of his Times Square and Queens locales, capturing gritty ambience while setting the stage for urban romance.

The bottom line? Good acting makes "The Break" worth seeing. But for future reference, Rea should give a little more thought to any bright ideas.

SIGHT AND SOUND, 1/98, p. 42, Geoffrey Macnab

A high-security prison in Belfast. Long-term IRA prisoner Dowd joins several of his fellow inmates in a daring escape plan. The escape goes wrong, but Dowd and his fellow IRA officer Richard make it to freedom. Dowd says his farewells to his lover Roisin and then sets out on his own for a new life in the US. He gets a job as a dishwasher in a New York restaurant and dosses down in a cheap hotel. One day, there is a fight in the hotel. Dowd intervenes and ends up being stabbed. Although he is bleeding badly, he refuses to call a doctor. Tulio, a Guatemalan from the same restaurant, finds him bleeding on his hotel bed and offers him treatment and accommodation in his own home, where he lives with his friend Paco and sister Monica. Meanwhile, the hotel clerk reports Dowd to the authorities.

Dowd recuperates, nursed by Monica. He begins to fall in love with her. He learns that Monica and Tulio's father was killed in Guatemala by a brutal dictator, Ramon, who now lives in the US. Monica, Tulio and Paco are planning to assassinate Ramon. Dowd, dismayed by their amateurism and worried about Monica, agrees to help. They procure guns, getaway cars and successfully carry out the hit.

Dowd has arranged for Irish contacts to spirit him and Monica out of New York. He goes into the Irish bar to meet their contact (his old friend Richard) while Monica waits in the car. But the FBI are tailing Dowd, so when he and Richard walk out onto the street, FBI officers stop them at gunpoint. Dowd runs. He sees he is hopelessly outnumbered, but rather than give himself up for arrest, he pulls out his gun. The FBI officers shoot him dead.

As Neil Jordan's *Angel* proved way back in 1982, there are few other actors whose faces can register melancholy and yearning as effectively as Stephen Rea's. His character here, a burned-out IRA prisoner by the name of Dowd who has somehow lost his ideals along the way, makes an intriguing counterpart to his saxophonist in Jordan's film. Both are men whose humanity dries up in the face of the violence which blights their life.

Almost inevitably, the opening shot of *A Further Gesture* is a big close-up of Rea. The camera pulls back to reveal him talking to his lover Roisin inside the prison where he is a long-term inmate. Their elliptical, painful exchange ("As long as I'm around, you have no life," says Dowd mournfully, later), beautifully written by Ronan Bennett, suggests that this is going to be a closely focused character study. But no sooner are they separated than the film shifts gear. There follows an exhilarating escape sequence, shot by Andrzej Sekula *(Pulp Fiction)* and edited by Masahiro

Hirakubo *(Trainspotting)* with real virtuosity. Like the convicts-on-the-marsh overture to David Lean's *Great Expectations* (1946), it stands as a film-within-a-film.

In a way, the sequence is a distraction. Nothing which follows matches it in tempo or excitement, or makes such effective use of Sekula and Hirakubo's skills. It is also the one occasion in which we do not see matters exclusively from Dowd's point-of-view. True, it tells us certain facts about his character (he's resourceful, handy with a gun and capable of extreme violence), but the escape might almost belong in a different movie. As if acknowledging the fact, the film-makers cut abruptly from an image of Dowd clinging onto a bridge for dear life, to him preparing to embark for New York, presumably many months later.

The idea of the outsider adrift in the big American city has been explored countless times before. As Dowd checks into a cheap hotel and gets a job as a dishwasher, we could almost be in the world of Jim Jarmusch's *Stranger than Paradise* or Paul Auster's fiction. The sequences showing him marvelling at the size, the buildings, subways and ethnic diversity of New York are effecti but the deeper reason *why* this exile is running remains a mystery. Apparently, he wants to break all his old ties, to cut himself off completely. Given his nihilism, it is perplexing why he sought to escape in the first place.

Bennett's script confronts Dowd with a situation which mirrors the one he faced back home in Ireland. Taken in by three Guatemalans, one of whom, Monica, he falls in love with, he sees that they are committed to a cause with a passion he no longer feels for his own. (They want to kill the fascist dictator Ramon, now living outside New York, who persecuted them and their families in their homeland.) Bennett's novel *Overthrown by Strangers* is set in civil-war torn Guatemala. But here, he is much more interested in Dowd's personal quest and in his interaction with his new friends than in explaining what happened to the Guatemalans or why Dowd has grown disillusioned with the IRA. The film laudably avoids preaching, but more of a historical context, more engagement with Irish and Central American politics, would have helped to give the film more grit.

The tourist-eye scenes of Dowd and Monica strolling the New York streets, testing out the Mexican food and clothes shops, and the bickering between Dowd and young hothead Paco inevitably lessen the intensity of the storytelling. With a starker, more focused approach, director Robert Dornhelm *(Requiem für Dominik)* could surely have elicited a major performance from Rea in a film that was designed as a vehicle for him. He is still effective enough as the forlorn, fatalistic hero, but throughout there remains a frustrating sense that he is not being pushed to his limits.

VILLAGE VOICE, 2/24/98, p. 128, Michael Atkinson

A radically less distinguished and honest portrait of international displacement [the reference is to *Comrades, Almost a Love Story*: see Atkinson's review of that film], Robert Dornhelm's *The Break*, based upon "an idea" by lead Stephen Rea, starts with an Irish prison break and then tracks its central hangdog tough guy to New York. There he reluctantly falls in with a cadre of Guatemalan dishwashers-amateur terrorists (Alfred Molina, *Land and Freedom*'s Rosana Pastor) intent on assassinating a national traitor. What Rea's "idea" was, besides aping *The Crying Game*'s structure, is hard to guess at, and Dornhelm's film is a graceless, clichéd sleepwalk. (Rea's cheap hotel room even has a neon light outside the window, but at least it doesn't blink.) Easily the moment's unlikeliest movie star, even for dourly sentimental Irish indies, Rea delivers little but slow-motion mannerisms. You can't help thinking that being an Irish escaped con hiding out in New York with gun-crazy Guatemalans has got to be more interesting than this.

Also reviewed in:
NEW REPUBLIC, 3/15/98, p. 26, Stanley Kauffmann
NEW YORK TIMES, 2/20/98, p. E12, Stephen Holden
VARIETY, 5/26-6/1/97, p. 71, Derek Elley

BRIDE OF CHUCKY

A Universal Pictures release of a David Kirschner production. *Executive Producer:* Don Mancini and Corey Sienega. *Producer:* David Kirschner and Grace Gilroy. *Director:* Ronny Yu. *Screenplay (based on characters created by):* Don Mancini. *Director of Photography:* Peter Pau. *Editor:* David Wu and Randolph K. Bricker. *Music:* Graeme Revell. *Music Editor:* Ashley Revell. *Sound:* Owen Langevin and (music) John Kurlander. *Sound Editor:* Stephen Barden. *Casting:* Joanna Colbert and Ross Clydesdale. *Production Designer:* Alicia Keywan. *Art Director:* James McAteer. *Set Designer:* Gordon White. *Set Decorator:* Carol Lavoie and Mike Harris. *Set Dresser:* Richard Ferbrache and John Rankin. *Puppet Effects:* Kevin Yagher. *Special Effects:* John Chilvers. *Visual Effects:* Michael Muscal. *Costumes:* Lynne MacKay. *Make-up:* Patricia Green. *Stunt Coordinator:* John Stoneham, Jr. *Running time:* 97 minutes. *MPAA Rating:* R.

CAST: Jennifer Tilly (Tiffany/Voice of Tiffany Doll); Brad Dourif (Voice of Chucky); Katherine Heigl (Jade); Nick Stabile (Jesse); Alexis Arquette (Damien); Gordon Michael Woolvett (David); John Ritter (Chief Warren Kincaid); Lawrence Dane (Lt. Preston); Michael Johnson (Norton); James Gallanders (Russ); Janet Kidder (Diane); Vincent Corazza (Bailey); Kathy Najimy (Motel Maid); Park Bench (Stoner); Emily Weedon (Girl at One-Stop); Ben Bass (Lt. Ellis); Roger McKeen (Justice of the Peace); Sandi Stahlbrand (Reporter).

LOS ANGELES TIMES, 10/19/98, Calendar/p. 4, John Anderson

[The following review by John Anderson appeared in a slightly different form in
NEWSDAY, 10/19/98, Part II/p. B7.]

As we're oft being told, there's simply not enough respect for our national institutions and after 10 years of cutting, ripping and tearing his way to the top, Chucky—the Doll of Death, the Toy of Terror, the Plaything of Pure Evil—deserves some respect. It's not easy keeping a franchise like this alive for 10 years.

"Bride of Chucky" stars Jennifer Tilly as Tiffany, the doll who's the ex-girlfriend—and, subsequently, the fellow FAO Schwarz refugee—of slain serial killer Charles Lee Ray, whose soul has inhabited the Chucky doll since 1988's "Child's Play" (followed by "CP 2" and "3"). If, like me, your favorite scene in Woody Allen's "Bullets Over Broadway" was when Jennifer Tilly finally got blown away by Chazz Palminteri, then the mayhem in "Bride of Chucky" will probably make you feel warm all over.

Chucky (voice of the not-so-oft-seen Brad Dourif, who's also playing in "Urban Legend"), has become a camp classic and, fortunately, the makers of "Bride of Chucky" know it.

Onetime Hong Kong action director Ronny Yu milks the utter inanity of Chucky's existence for all it's worth and knows the conventions of the genre well enough that horror fans should feel total gratification—in the levels of both mayhem and grotesque humor. Any real terror, outside of the standard false-alarm quick cuts, is minimal. But even if Yu hasn't quite done a "Scream"-style deconstruction of the form, you know that he knows that this stuff is a hoot.

The Chucky-Tiffany romance has a rocky start, although Tiff's heart has always been with Chucky. A goth named Damien (Alexis Arquette) is hanging around and getting nowhere, except of course dead. "You know me," Tiffany tells Damien. "I'll kill anybody, but I'll only sleep with someone I love."

Enter the Chuckster, who wants to go to Hackensack, N.J., and retrieve the magic amulet that will allow him to possess another human body. Jersey, as usual, is treated as a joke and it's interesting that while Todd Solondz has incurred the wrath of the Garden State for setting "Happiness" there, no one's said a word about Chucky. Which says something.

NEW YORK POST, 10/19/98, p. 40, Larry Worth

The ads read Chucky gets lucky. Sadly, the same can't be said for "Bride of Chucky" audience members.

As the title implies, the killer doll from "Child's Play," "Child's Play 2" and "Child's Play 3" has spawned a new knockoff—with still another clearly threatened at No. 4's finale.

In the meantime, this installment is even sillier—if that's possible—than its predecessors.

The good news is that "Bride of Chucky" actually features a few clips from its classic inspiration, "Bride of Frankenstein." Suffice it to say that those are this effort's highlights.

It opens with Jennifer Tilly's Tiffany—a bleached-blonde, buxom, stiletto-heeled and tattooed incarnation of trailer trash—stitching and stapling Chucky's mangled little body together. It seems he's her long-lost love, thus explaining why she performs a black-magic incarnation to bring him back to murderous life.

Probably because Tilly had the good sense to disappear after the first 35 minutes, Tiffany and Chucky both end up as humans trapped in a doll's body, soon becoming the Bonnie and Clyde of the Ken-and-Barbie set.

Of course, Ken and Barbie never had a sex scene like these two. And that's definitely a blessing. On the other hand, it at least distracts from the woefully awful acting of John Ritter, Alexis Arquette, Katherine Heigl, Kathy Najimy and pectoral-perfect soap veteran Nick Stabile.

True, director Ronny Yu supplies the requisite violence, but he's noticeably shy of anything akin to suspense or even fun. Indeed, "Bride of Chucky" is a toy story in which everything is purely mechanical.

SIGHT AND SOUND, 7/99, p. 37, Linda Ruth Williams

The US, the present. Tiffany steals Chucky the doll from a police-evidence depository. She takes him back to her trailer where she rebuilds and reanimates him using a book called *Voodoo for Dummies*. She brings back to life the personality of Charles 'Chucky' Lee Ray, Tiffany's dead lover, who inhabited the doll before (as recounted in the three previous *Child's Play* films). Tiffany gives him a bride doll to keep him company. However when she is electrocuted to death by the television falling into her bath, her personality transmigrates into the body of the bride doll.

Tiffany's neighbour Jesse agrees to take both dolls to Charles Lee Ray's grave in New Jersey where a buried amulet provides the couple's only hope of being made human again. Jesse brings his girlfriend Jade along on the journey. Tiffany and Chucky plan to possess their bodies once the voodoo ritual with the amulet has released them from the dolls. However, at the grave the dolls fight; Chucky is killed and Tiffany gives birth to his child.

As any jobbing film theorist will tell you, the pleasures of horror must always be framed by sadomasochism. You might think these dubious desires would be the main forces animating this latest outing of Chucky, the infernal doll star of the *Child's Play* film franchise which in the UK was accused of influencing perpetrators of at least two appalling crimes. But the thrills of *Bride of Chucky*, the possessed doll's fourth cinematic outing, are laudably cerebral. Like Wes Craven's *Scream* its sequel and its imitators, *Bride of Chucky* plays to the connoisseur, inviting viewers to tick off the cinematic references, so deeply embedded is this film in its genre's history.

From the opening shots, *Bride of Chucky* establishes its quite complex sense of place in the line-up of usual suspects: alongside Chucky in the evidence depository lie Jason's hockey mask (from the *Friday the 13th* series), Freddy's glove *(Nightmare on Elm Street)*, Michael Myers' mask *(Halloween)* and Leatherface's chainsaw *(The Texas Chain Saw Massacre)*. Two feet tall and less than human he may be, but this sequence suggests the slasher film's pantheon of serial killers have embraced Chucky as one of their own. The only crimes Ronny Yu's witty and knowing film will be associated with are those of other movies. So embedded are these references in a context of fiction, it's absurd to try to relate them to fact. *It's Alive, The Exorcist, Hellraiser, Natural Born Killers* even David Cronenberg at his most gynaecological, are all points in the film's reality co-ordinates, along with its own fictive past referred to in Tiffany's newspaper cuttings. Of this history, Chucky himself quips, "It's a long story. In fact, if it was a movie it would take three or four sequels." Unlike *Scream*, where the participants redirect their world so it looks like a movie, *Bride of Chucky* refuses to countenance that there is a world beyond the movie.

For something so schlocky and—quite frankly—bizarre, *Bride of Chucky* also generates the curious sense that if its makers have done their homework, then so should you. Relentlessly erudite, as *Bride of Chucky* piles on the references you get the strange sensation you're watching a parody of a parody, a film which gleefully grabs this very 90s form of filmic self reflexivity, chews it up and spits it out: been there, done that, bought the T shirt. "Chucky? He's so 80s," says Tiffany's lowlife boyfriend Damien before being dispatched, clearly a thought which also occurred to writer Don Mancini and Yu (a veteran Hong Kong director who made the recent *Warriors of Virtue*). So Chucky's Bride makes herself over by out-parodying horror as parody.

If all this sounds too clever by half, it's also very funny. Dolls and toys are the most conventional props of the uncanny: scary and sinister alter egos in *Dead of Night* (1945) and *Magic* (1978); grotesquely murderous in *Dolls* (1987, which also features a giant killer teddy bear) and in the long-running 80s-90s *Puppetmaster* series made in Hong Kong. But in Ronny Yu's hands they also become the building blocks of fun: essential elements of child's play as well as *Child's Play*. Tiffany plays at dressing up, transforming her new bride-doll body into an approximation of the foxy lady she was in human form to the tune of Blondie's 'Call Me', invoking the opening of *American Gigolo*. The film's weirdest moment, in which Tiffany and Chucky have sex, reminded me of Todd Haynes' all-doll avant garde short *Superstar*. The scene's sheer unabashed strangeness crystallises horror's much vaunted relationship with surrealism. As Chucky and Tiffany get it on in front of an open fire, bobbing up and down in a bizarre frenzy of plastic passion, they pause for a safer sex moment—a failure, as the ending proves.

Bride of Chucky is an impeccable construction, well wrought and efficiently paced. Like its hero, it is small but perfectly formed. It also has aspirations: if Freddy *et al* are left in the lock-up in that opening sequence, this is only so the film can make its bid to occupy a more substantial place in film history. *Bride of Frankenstein* (1935) is clearly the most obvious benchmark—Elsa Lanchester is seen on the television which kills Tiffany. *Bride of Chucky* also knows it's a monster made of many parts: *The Godfather* (1972), *Bonnie and Clyde* (1967), even a fleeting flirtation with *I Walked with a Zombie* (1943) when Tiffany sombrely marches through the long moonlit grass at the film's climax. Whether this parody is plagiarism, pastiche or punk postmodernism is perhaps irrelevant given the fun *Bride of Chucky* has with its sources. Mixed together in this unholy way, what emerges is a loving homage to a movie history gleefully raided by body snatchers.

Also reviewed in:
CHICAGO TRIBUNE, 10/22/98, Tempo/p. 2, John Petrakis
NEW YORK TIMES, 10/17/98, p. B16, Lawrence Van Gelder
VARIETY, 10/19-25/98, p. 77, Leonard Klady

BRIGANDS: CHAPTER VII

An Anthology Film Archives release of a Pierre Grise Productions/Soyuzkinoservice/Bim Distribuzione/Carac Film AG coproduction in association with Canal Plus, National Committee for Cinematography, Gosudarstevenny Komitet Rossiskoi, Federachii Po Kimematografii, Kartuli Filmi, Petropol.   *Producer:* Martine Marignac.   *Director:* Otar Iosseliani.   *Screenplay (Georgian and French with English subtitles):* Otar Iosseliani. *Director of Photography:* William Lubtchansky. *Editor:* Otar Iosseliani. *Music:* Nicolas Zourabichvili. *Sound:* Florian Eidenbenz. *Production Designer:* Emmanuel De Chauvigny, Jean-Michael Simonet, and Lena Zukova *Costumes:* Ludmila Gainceva and Cori D'Ambrogio. *Running time:* 129 minutes. *MPAA Rating:* Not Rated.

CAST: Amiran Amiranchvili (Vano);   Guio Tzintzadze (Spiridon);   Dato Gogibeidasvili (Sandro);   Nino Odzonikidze (Eka);   Keti Kapanadze (Lia);   Aleksi Dzakeli (Viktor);   Niko Kartsivadze (Kola).

NEW YORK POST, 3/13/98, p. 44, Larry Worth

Everyone knows that history repeats itself. So why watch a two-hour-plus movie that reaches such a familiar conclusion?

For starters, it's the only part of "Brigands: Chapter VII" that doesn't seem strikingly original, what with its time-jumping plot that lurches between Middle Ages Georgia, early 20th-century Russia and present-day Paris.

And as the settings keep varying, viewers may legitimately ask: Where is writer-director Otar Iosseliani going? Though requiring some patience, the rhythm becomes increasingly clear. Each story bears the same actor, the wonderful, craggy-faced Amiran Amiranachvili. And whether playing a king, communist carpetbagger or pickpocket, his adventures point out—in increasingly alarming fashion—man's inhumanity to man.

The tone is a mix of humor and horror, as when a young boy bonds with his fascist dad when getting a look-see at the torture devices used to extract confessions. When rejoining his mom, she casually asks, "Was it interesting?" The child then demonstrates through his giggles how fingers are cut off.

Throughout, the arbitrariness of violence is conveyed ,with minimal dialogue, making for some pretty powerful images. And as Alfred Hitchcock so often demonstrated, the screams are more effective when brutality takes place off-screen.

But be forewarned: Director Iosseliani never makes things easy for audiences. Is it part-dream, part-nightmare? Has the anti-hero been reincarnated? And what's up with the cryptic title?

There are no definitive answers, though viewers will have plenty of theories. They'll also have suggestions for the finale, which is about 15 minutes late in coming.

Granted, "Brigands: Chapter VII," doesn't always score a bull's-eye. But the anti-violence message consistently hits home.

Also reviewed in:
CHICAGO TRIBUNE, 7/3/98, Friday/p. D, Michael Wilmington
NEW YORK TIMES, 3/11/98, p. E5, Lawrence Van Gelder
VARIETY, 9/23-29/96, p. 130, David Stratton

BROADWAY DAMAGE

A Jour de Fête Films release. *Producer:* David Topel. *Director:* Victor Mignatti. *Screenplay:* Victor Mignatti. *Director of Photography:* Michael Mayers. *Editor:* Victor Mignatti. *Music:* Elliot Sokolov. *Production Designer:* Dina Goldman. *Running time:* 110 minutes. *MPAA Rating:* Not Rated.

CAST: Mara Hobel (Cynthia). Michael Shawn Lucas (Marc). Hugh Panaro (David). Aaron Williams (Robert).

NEW YORK POST, 5/29/98, p. 44, Larry Worth

Does anyone—besides Shari Lewis—consistently call someone Lamb Chop?

It just doesn't ring true, like so much of "Broadway Damage." On the other hand, one understands the puppet allusion since zaftig leading lady Mara Hobel indulges in a two-hour Miss Piggy imitation. Unfortunately, she's nowhere near as much fun as Kermit's better half.

Hobel plays an over-weight, fashion-conscious poor-little-rich-girl who moves into a Greenwich Village apartment with a handsome, struggling actor (a.k.a. Lamb Chop). But romance isn't about to bloom; he's as gay a blade as they come, established early on when he "secures" the lease with a hunky landlord.

Ultimately, it's all about unrequited amour: the golden-boy thespian falls for the caddish musician across the courtyard. Of course, he should be romancing his awkward, hopelessly lovesick best bud, but that would make things too quick and easy.

To his credit, writer/director Victor Mignatti rarely travels the expeditious route, which proves a mixed blessing. On the plus side, Mignatti studiously establishes each character and their various scenarios. But along the way, he provides a textbook example of why writer/directors shouldn't edit their own movies.

In addition, too many setups are achingly cute, predictable or in-joke dependent. Even more distracting: The nerdy best friend is only borderline nerdy. If he'd simply lose the Gilligan hat and Coke-bottle glasses, he'd be a popular little boy toy.

That's why one can't blame Aaron Williams for failing to bring the geek to life. Or the fact that his exchanges with over-the-top Hobel—best known for playing young Christina Crawford in 1981's "Mommie Dearest"—are too annoying for words.

Far more convincing is newcomer Michael Shawn Lucas. He provides a hero who'll never be mistaken for Schwarzenegger, but steers clear of all gay stereotypes—even while making convincing goo-goo eyes at Hugh Panaro's bad boy. The latter holds his own, too, emanating more than enough charm to convey a gigolo's appeal.

Sad to say, Lucas and Panaro's efforts—along with the production's admittedly sweet nature—can only do so much "Damage" control.

Also reviewed in:
CHICAGO TRIBUNE, 10/30/98, Friday/p. L, Michael Wilmington
NEW YORK TIMES, 5/29/98, p. E18, Lawrence Van Gelder

BROTHER

A Kino International Films release of an STW Film Company/Roskomkino production. *Producer:* Sergei Selianov. *Director:* Aleksei Balabanov. *Screenplay (Russian with English subtitles):* Aleksei Balabanov. *Director of Photography:* Sergei Astakhov. *Editor:* Marina Lipartija. *Music:* Slava Butusov. *Production Designer:* Vladimir Kartashov. *Running time:* 96 minutes. *MPAA Rating:* NR.

CAST: Sergei Bodrov, Jr. (Danila); Viktor Suhorukov (The Brother); Svetlana Pismichenko (Sveta); Mariya Zhukova (Kat); Yuri Kuznetsov (Guerman); Slava Butusov (Butusov).

NEW YORK POST, 7/8/98, p. 41, Thelma Adams

A young man crawls up an embankment in the Russian countryside, drawn by blaring pop music. He crosses a commercial film set, past a half-naked blonde and right through the shot. The director explodes. He sends in security. Cut to the local police station. The young man looks bad. What was that music?" the young man asks.

That young man is Danila (Sergei Bodrov Jr.), the unlikely hero of Alexei Balabanov's dry gangster comic drama, set on the Wild East frontier of post-Soviet Russia.

Danila wears his quiet like the trusty Sony Walkman that hangs from his belt, gunslinger style. He's just out of the army and seeking his place beside the golden arches of the McDonald's that are springing up all over his country.

The police chief offers Danila a job; he declines. His mother nags him and lionizes his older brother Viktor (Viktor Suhorukov) When Danila goes to visit this successful mover-and-shaker in St. Petersburg, he learns Viktor is a hit man.

He fills his brother's current contract by modifying a pistol with a plastic soda bottle and coolly liquidating a rival Chechen crime boss.

What did Danila really do for the army? While his past remains mysterious, his present alternates between murder-for-hire, various flings, the search for the perfect CD and the shifting power relationship between Danila, the apprentice, and Viktor.

From wife-beating to anti-Semitism, the black market to the music scene, writer/director Balabanov touches on contemporary society without ever dropping a stitch in his complicated plot.

At the center of "Brother" is Bodrov's disarming performance as a stealthy vet making his way on the frontier between socialism and capitalism, a place where it doesn't hurt to know how to saw off a shotgun.

NEWSDAY, 8/21/98, Part II/p. B7, John Anderson

Danila, played with nihilistic aplomb by young Russian star Sergei Bodrov Jr., is a typical footloose post-teen, his army service behind him, little future before him, metal music pounding his eardrums, women and parties preoccupying his mind. But everyone has a talent, it is said. And Danila's happens to be a ruthless efficiency in knocking people off.

In Alexei Balabanov's rather ironically titled "Brother," we get the New Russia unadorned, a St. Petersburg who's czarist glories are obscured by the degree of mob violence, homelessness and dissipation on its streets. It is at once frightening, grossly funny and self-deflating. Upon arriving home from the army, Danila wanders onto a film shoot and is attacked and beaten by the stooges of the New Russian Cinema.

Danila holds his own, though, and from then on shows a talent for mayhem, mugging a sidewalk extortionist, chasing fare beaters off a city bus at gunpoint. His mother, bemoaning Danila's lack of promise, tells him that Viktor, his elder brother (Viktor Suhorukov) is her "only hope"—not knowing that Viktor is a killer for the mob, a double-dealer who introduces Danila to his new line of work.

"Brother" is a fascinating movie, perhaps in spite of its subject matter. The hired-killer movie at this point has become a flourishing. self-contained subgenre, and while the hired killer-as-prodigy hasn't been done quite to death (pardon the pun), it *has* been done—as out-and-out black comedy ("Cold Blooded" with Jason Priestley), or as tragedy ("Little Odessa" with Tim Roth). And there's always an element of absurdist humor in the portrait of the hitman as young hopeful.

But for all the buoyancy of Balabanov's movie—not music-video buoyancy, just youth-movie bounce—Danila is never struggling, or questioning, or aspiring to anything particularly. He is a well-meaning, oft-times gallant sociopath who falls for a trolley driver (Svetlana Pismichenko) with an abusive husband, and devotes as much real thought to parties and music as he does to street killings.

Which is not to say that his preparations for murder aren't meticulous, and fascinating. The mixing of materials, the filling of shell casings,

The taping of matchbook bombs to be used as diversionary tactics during a hit on a mob rival, all are detailed lovingly by Balabanov, the way he might show an artist mixing paint.

And this is part of what makes "Brother" such a thrilling, off-kilter thing; this essential amorality that infects even the camera angles and attitude. The ruthlessness of the New Russia may be a given, but Balabanov's on-screen philosophy suggests the Hughes' Brothers' 1993 "gangsta" classic, "Menace II Society" in the Caucasus—a mix of irony and viciousness and no apologies.

VILLAGE VOICE, 7/14/98, p. 141, J. Hoberman

A young man arrives in the big city from the provinces and, with surprisingly little difficulty, becomes a professional killer. Less case history than cautionary folk tale, Alexei Balabanov's tough, mordantly comic *Brother* is a two-fisted travelogue through the vast thieves' market of the former Soviet Union.

The most popular Russian movie of 1997, *Brother* is also of the few post-Communist East European films to find an appropriate contemporary mode of address. Balabanov's direction is neither arty nor crass; his tone is sardonic without being cute; his intent is serious but hardly overweening. In its knowing deployment of genre conventions, *Brother* manages to be both a commercial movie and a comment on commercialism.

A brief prologue has the just-demobilized soldier Danila (Sergei Bodrov Jr.) wander onto a movie set and through a camera setup. The shoot, in a local park, appears to be some sort of semi-pretentious softcore porn, but the siren song that attracts Danila to the set is "Wings" by the pop group Nautilus. Danila's ongoing pursuit of this elusive melody becomes one of *Brother*'s running gags. So does Danila's elided brawl with the production's bodyguards, an unseen confrontation that establishes the unprepossessing soldier as a formidable character.

A veteran of the war in Chechnya, the twentyish Danila is played by one of the stars of Sergei Bodrov Sr.'s *Prisoner of the Mountains*. As *Prisoner* updated a Tolstoy story to deal with the contemporary Russian-Chechen conflict, *Brother* might almost be its sequel. Having received an education, the warrior returns home to apply his lessons. With his open face and crooked half-smile, Bodrov projects a sly innocence. Most of the time he seems like a sweet, not terribly bright, kid. He's polite but lethal-calm, single-minded, industrious, clever, and, as it turns out, a brilliant dirty fighter.

After turning down a job with the local police, Danila arrives in St. Petersburg, looking for his older brother Viktor, who, we know even if he doesn't, is a somewhat cowardly hit man. Danila, more of a natural, makes his own bones en route to Viktor's flat. He watches a street vendor getting shaken down, then punches out the extortionist and confiscates his revolver, continuing his career as a petty vigilante by using the weapon to make a deadbeat pay his bus fare. Once the brothers meet, the never less than opportunistic Viktor subcontracts Danila to whack the Chechen gangster who has apparently muscled in on one of the city's outdoor markets.

Although *Brother* turns out to be a movie with a fairly high body count, it's amazingly discreet by American standards. Much of the violence is offscreen, and the most gruesome visible carnage is specifically linked to pornography. The 39-year-old writer-director's modus operandi is as modestly understated as that of his frighteningly self-possessed protagonist. *Brother* is never more low-keyed than when showing Danila's total concentration in producing a sawed-off shotgun and, always efficient in his mayhem, loading it with homemade shrapnel.

Permanently plugged into his Discman, our hero makes his own soundtrack and constructs his own scene, in part by latching onto the various characters the metropolitan maelstrom tosses his way. *Brother*'s ballad structure—and the blackouts that punctuate its chance meetings—gives it the quality of an illustrated proverb. Danila makes his way through a world of hustling club kids, dumb tourists, and grandiose mafiosi, at one point taking up with a battered wife who drives a transport tram. At times he seems the only urban denizen who can keep the entire equation in his head. Bored with a stakeout, he goes upstairs to investigate a party in the flat above-the self-absorbed intellectuals oblivious to the killer enjoying himself in their midst.

Shot in a semidocumentary style, Balabanov's neorealist action film employs typecasting throughout. The story unfolds in a succession of cramped apartments where you can practically smell the spilled vodka and boiled cabbage. *Brother* is laconic but rich—not least in its autumnally brown-and-ochre milieu. With its decadent bars, public drunks, timorous victims, and ruling thugs, St. Petersburg is a regular Dodge City. If Danila were an American hero, we'd call him Cowboy or worse. This displaced veteran and one-man gang of destruction is the Russian Rambo. (Indeed, the writer-director is already planning a *Brother 2* to be partially shot in Chicago.)

Brother is set in a brutal, survivalist world where—animal self-interest aside—the only value would seem to be a free-floating nationalism, flavored with casual xenophobia. "The city is a force and everyone here is weak," Danila concludes with evident satisfaction. The lad from the provinces has learned something of how life is, and so have we. *Brother* is not only a highly entertaining genre film but a political statement as well—it imagines, even as it warns against, the strong man's return.

Also reviewed in:
NEW YORK POST, 7/8/98, p. E5, Stephen Holden
VARIETY, 5/26-6/1/97, p. 69, David Stratton

BUFFALO '66

A Lions Gate Films release of a Lions Gate Films/Muse Productions film. *Executive Producer:* Michael Paseornek, Jeff Sackman, John Dunning and André Link. *Producer:* Chris Hanley. *Director:* Vincent Gallo. *Screenplay:* Vincent Gallo and Alison Bagnall. *Story:* Vincent Gallo. *Director of Photography:* Lance Acord. *Editor:* Curtiss Clayton. *Music:* Vincent Gallo. *Sound:* Brian Miksis. *Production Designer:* Gideon Ponte. *Art Director:* James Chinlund.   *Set Decorator:* Jeanne Develle. *Special Effects:* Paul Murphy. *Costumes:* Alexis Scott. *Make-up:* Gucci Westman. *Running time:* 110 minutes. *MPAA Rating:* Not Rated.

CAST: Vincent Gallo (Billy Brown); Christina Ricci (Layla); Ben Gazzara (Jimmy Brown); Mickey Rourke (Bookie); Rosanna Arquette (Wendy Balsam); Jan-Michael Vincent (Sonny);

Anjelica Huston (Janet 'Jan' Brown);   Kevin Pollak and Alex Karras (Sportscasters);   John Sansone (Little Billy Brown); Manny Fried (Donut Clerk); John Rummel (Don Shanks); Bob Wahl (Scott Woods); Penny Wolfgang (Judge Penny M. Wolfgang); Anthony Mydcarz (Motel Clerk); Michael Maciejewski (Guy in the Bathroom); Jack Claxton (Denny's Host); Dominic Telesco (Prison Guard);   Carl Marchi (Cafe Owner); Kim Krah (Denny's Waitress); Julius DiGennaro (Information Booth Clerk);   Terry Braunstein (Tap Teacher);   Jack Hunter (Gas Station Clerk);   Norma Gelose (Bus Station Woman);   Jame King and Janel King (Tap Dance Kids); Kevin Corrigan (Goon).

LOS ANGELES TIMES, 7/10/98, Calendar/p. 12, Kevin Thomas

Many movies start out with a man being discharged from prison, but "Buffalo '66," Vincent Gallo's compelling debut film as a writer-director, has come up with a way for us to identify immediately with his ex-con: The guy has to urinate and there's no place to do it, a universal predicament.

The guard thinks he's crazy to be asked to let back in the prison to go to the restroom, so there's nothing to do but take the bus and wait till it pulls into the Buffalo, N.Y., terminal—where the men's room is closed for cleaning, natch. Right from the start, too, Gallo has introduced a note of humor that will prove to be absolutely crucial in the telling of a volatile, solitary young man's otherwise bleak struggle to come to terms with himself.

There's nothing like an urgent bladder to fuel an already frustrated, rage-filled man. Gallo's Billy tries to use a bathroom at a dancing school facility only to end up kidnapping one of its pupils.

Billy had been in prison on a foolish fluke and had kept his incarceration secret from the parents who've ignored him all their lives, but from whom he still craves love and approval. He's told them he is some sort of government agent whose work takes him out of the country for long periods of time. He figures he will impress them all the more if he returns with a beautiful wife.

Fate, for perhaps the first time in his life, has dealt kindly with Billy in the choice of the young woman he has grabbed, and Gallo and his co-writer Alison Bagnall keep us guessing until the final frame as to whether he's going to realize it or not. For Christina Ricci's Layla is not only beautiful, blond and bosomy, but intelligent and needy. She could get away from Billy almost immediately but stays along for the ride out of her own craving for love and attention.

Arriving at his parents' nondescript tract house, Billy is greeted by his father, Jimmy (Ben Gazzara), yelling, "It's your son!" to his wife, Jan (Anjelica Huston), who has spent most of her life glued to the TV rooting for the local football team. Billy has been on bad terms with his father since Jimmy got rid of his 7-year-old son's pet dog for not becoming housebroken quickly enough.

Jan, who can be pleasant enough in her maddeningly obtuse way, has never forgiven her son for being born on the very day in 1966 that her beloved team was last a winner. Gazzara and Huston, as you would expect of actors of their caliber, know how to use humor to keep Jimmy and Jan from becoming all-out monsters. Meanwhile, Layla gets into her role-playing so intensely she charms Billy's parents to the extent that they ignore their son all the more, inflaming his jealousy.

As it turns out, Billy's visit home is but a prologue to his setting in motion a vendetta, which in its sheer childishness reveals Gallo's key point: The child denied parental love and approval is the individual who, in forever trying to win it, will never grow up without a herculean struggle.

Intense, pale, gaunt with haunting light blue eyes, Gallo has been a vivid presence in a number of films, including Abel Ferrera's "The Funeral," a period gangster picture in which he played Mafioso Christopher Walken's fiery, idealistic younger brother. With "Buffalo '66" Gallo does himself credit not only as an actor but also as an equally distinctive filmmaker. He has a terrific instinct as to how much reality and how much fantasy to draw upon in telling his story. Similarly, Gallo and his cinematographer Lance Acord, using color in a shadowy film noir way, express the film's blend of grit and romanticism in striking images found in impersonal, everyday urban settings.

Actors more often than not instinctively know how to present not only themselves but also others to advantage, and Gallo, who also composed his film's spare score, is no exception. Fresh off raves for "The Opposite of Sex," Ricci further establishes her versatility playing a young woman of whom we are told nothing, but who captivates us with her compassion and insight, her determined composure and wisdom beyond her years. (It's Gallo's risky but effective strategy to tell us all about Billy and then let us infer that Layla's experiences must be lots like his.) Kevin Corrigan is appealing as Billy's dim but dogged loyal pal, and Gallo has come up with sharp cameos for Mickey Rourke, Jan-Michael Vincent and Rosanna Arquette, all of whom are right on the money. Alternately satirical and romantic, full of pain and humor, "Buffalo '66" is a winner.

NEW STATESMAN,10/9/98, p. 36, Gerald Kaufman

Truly enchanting (and visibly ingenious), despite being set in the urban wastes of an ugly American City, is *Buffalo '66*. Billy, returning to Buffalo after five years in jail, has deceived his parents into believing he has established a solid family life in another town. Desperate for a gents' lavatory, he blunders into an encounter with a plump tap dancer, Layla, whom he kidnaps and forces to pretend to be his wife, Wendy, promising her: "If you do a good job you can be my best friend." Layla takes so ardently to the deception that Billy has to explain to her: "We're a couple that doesn't touch each other."

Anjelica Huston turns up here, too, as the mother from hell who would rather watch the Buffalo Bills on TV than listen to the pseudo-Wendy's enthusiastically fictional account of her perfect marriage to Billy. Christina Ricci is adorable as the unexpectedly guileful Layla. And there are simply not enough Oscars to go round to do justice to Vincent Gallo, who wrote, directed, composed and performed the music and, in the role of the scrawny, resentful, magnificently inarticulate Billy, is the year's most unlikely but most irresistible lover.

NEW YORK, 7/20/98, p. 63, David Denby

In *Buffalo '66*, Vincent Gallo, acting in a movie that he wrote (with Alison Bagnall) and directed himself, has a face like an unsheathed knife. Pointed beard, pointed nose, pressed-together lips, filthy hair, a screw-you stare—Gallo, a former Calvin Klein heroin-chic model, takes his own neurotic singularity very seriously. He believes in it, he enacts it, and he appears to have very little distance from it. Watching *Buffalo '66* is a little bit like landing in the hands of a ratty hustler who lives in a bus station ("Hey, can I talk to you for a second? Just for a second..."). Which is not to say that Gallo doesn't have talent and a scraggly kind of wit. He plays Billy Brown, a jumpy young loser who leaves prison and spends a long time looking for a place to pee. Billy kidnaps a girl (Christina Ricci) with heavily tinted eyes and fluttering lashes—an erotic doll with a pliant disposition. The early scenes have a scary, paranoid realism, bordering on farce. Billy is terrified of sex with the girl; he kidnaps her so she will accompany him on a visit to his parents, who hate him and wish he did not exist. Angelica Huston and Ben Gazzara produce successful vicious caricatures, but in the family scenes, Gallo begins to play with trick staging and trick editing, and the movie comes grinding to a halt. Baffled, we feel like he's working through some sort of private obsession. From there on, it's strictly touch-and-go—some good scenes, some things that don't work at all, and a rushed, unsatisfactory ending. If Gallo is going to have a teenage girl fall for scary Billy, the movie needs more psychological realism than it has. Who, and what, is *she?* Gallo may be too self-obsessed to care. *Buffalo '66* has an authentic rotgut flavor, but here's the question for the future: Will Gallo learn to criticize his own ideas or continue to pride himself on screwing up?

NEW YORK POST, 6/26/98, p. 52, Thelma Adams

The upstate grunge drama "Buffalo '66" marks skanky Calvin Klein model Vincent Gallo's directorial debut.

Like Gallo, who made his reputation wearing undershorts, "Buffalo '66" would have looked better in a shorter version, although the feature was a hot ticket at the Sundance Film Festival and MoMA's New Directors/New Films series.

Gallo plays jailbird Billy Brown, an antihero as unlovable and flat as an Eternity ad. Paroled, Brown heads for his parents' Buffalo home. On the way, he kidnaps Layla (Christina Ricci). He forces the chunky tap dancer to impersonate his fantasy wife, Wendy.

The best scenes are those with Brown's folks, Janet and Jimmy (Anjelica Huston and Ben Gazzara). As in a John Cassavetes movie envisioned by Isaac Mizrahi, the characters are tossed into a small, tatty, overdecorated room, and then Gallo puts the Buffalo Bills on the tube and improvises family dysfunction.

Gazzara and Huston are game, showing promise for a better movie written and directed by a less-pretentious son. Former child star Ricci has been in the zone ever since "The Ice Storm"—see "The Opposite of Sex"—and "Buffalo '66" is no exception. She's a bruised angel in pale blue, the sky to Gallo's earth.

Perhaps Ricci's delicious Layla made it too tempting for Gallo to turn sentimental, but the moment he goes soft, the movie dries up and turns to dust.

NEWSDAY, 6/26/98, Part II/p. B6, Jack Mathews

Watching Vincent Gallo's "Buffalo 66" is what I imagine it would be like reading papers for a freshman creative writing course. Okay, you told the class, let it go, be inventive, look inward, focus on details, be honest and don't worry, because no one will see it but me.

Then, this thing lands on your desk. The story of a wrongfully convicted social reject who, upon graduating from prison, runs all over Buffalo looking for a place to pee, kidnaps a woman whom he compels to portray his wife in a charade for his mentally incompetent parents, goes bowling, whines constantly, plots the murder of a failed Buffalo Bills placekicker, falls in love and generally has an eventful day.

Now, imagine that the student took his paper, which you gave a C—with the advice that he get counseling, and turned it into a full-length feature film, starring himself as his own anti-hero. And you want tenure?

"Buffalo 66" is the price of the popularity of the independent film movement, and of the seemingly bottomless pit of small change available to filmmakers on a vanity binge. Gallo, a former artist and rock musician, is a character actor with some 17 credits to his name, but we know of nothing that would explain why he thinks his alter ego here is a worthy subject for a movie.

From the moment Gallo's Billy Brown emerges from the prison gate at the film's opening, you want to get away from him and his surroundings. The movie wallows in bleak, gray, decrepitude, the image that stopped people from shuffling off to Buffalo decades ago. And Billy, with his greasy, long, black hair and scruffy, unshaven face, looks like the "before" picture in an ad for a delousing ointment.(By the way, Mickey Rourke is in this movie, playing the bookie who sets up Billy for a prison term.)

In some ways, "Buffalo 66" is a routine badboy/good-girl-on-the-road-movie. You know that when a pretty kidnap victim doesn't run from her abductor when opportunity presents itself that she's going to fall for him, seeing the vulnerable, sweet boy behind the gruff exterior. And Christina Ricci's Layla is more impetuously love-struck than just about any kidnap victim in film history.

It could be because she has no apparent life beyond those aerobics classes. In one of the film's two clumsy fantasy sequences, she does a lazy tap dance in a bowling alley, suggesting that she's been to one—no more than two—tap classes, as well. But otherwise, her background is a blank.

We know just a little more about Billy's cartoon parents. Dad (Ben Gazzara) is a brute who, in front of young Billy, killed the family dog for doing its business in the house (thus, Billy's painful commitment to finding a rest room). And Mom (a tramped-up Anjelica Huston) is a Buffalo Bills fanatic who rues the day Billy was born (it caused her to miss a Bills game).

The film's long centerpiece at Billy's home, where Layla wins over his parents with outlandish tales of her and Billy's romance, is nothing short of agony, for him and us. Gallo's awkwardly experimental direction seems to suck the talent right out of Gazzara and Huston, who appear restless beneath the thin surface of their characters.

Ricci, who's probably the most compelling young actress around, does fill out her undefined character with suggestions of depth and empathy, and manages to be sympathetic even while nothing Layla does makes any sense.

Not that she or anybody else matters. "Buffalo 66" is a story of personal revelation; it's the story of an insecure, rejected, misfit whose attempts to cover his weaknesses with thorns fools everyone but the sweet young thing whose kidnaping—Billy's only felony—proves to be the smartest thing he's ever done. Class dismissed.

SIGHT AND SOUND, 10/98, p. 39, Geoffrey Macnab

Billy Brown is released from prison after serving time for a crime he didn't commit. He picks up Layla, a young woman whose dance class he barges through while looking for the men's room, and talks her into pretending to be his wife. Together they visit Billy's parents. Janet and Jimmy Brown don't realise their son has been in jail all these years. Layla spins them a far-fetched story about how she met Billy while he was working for the secret service.

The Browns are ardent supporters of the Buffalo Bills, the local football team. Billy ended up in prison because he made a huge bet on Buffalo winning the Super Bowl and lost when Buffalo's kicker missed a vital conversion. Unable to pay the bookie the money he owed, Billy wrote off his debt by confessing to a crime committed by one of the bookie's associates. Billy plans to revenge himself by killing the football player who missed the kick. He learns that the player now runs a successful strip club. Billy and Layla kill time roaming around town, moving from a bowling alley to a diner to a motel room. After leaving the motel, Billy fantasises about shooting the football player as planned and then pulling the gun on himself. In the end, he goes into a diner to buy Layla a hot chocolate instead.

Vincent Gallo is one of the most idiosyncratic actors of his generation. With his lank hair and cadaverous features, his face would not be out of place in a German expressionist horror film or a Bruegel painting. He brings an extraordinary degree of nervous energy to his roles. In *Arizona Dream*, he recreated the crop-dusting sequence from *North by Northwest* as a piece of wild performance art. In *The Funeral*, he invested his role as a young mobster with an almost demonic intensity.

Buffalo '66, his directorial debut which he also co-scripted, foregrounds performance in the same way as actor-turned-director John Cassavetes' films did. Gallo offers less a conventional story than a series of set-pieces loosely strung together. The opening, which follows ex-con Billy (played by Gallo himself as he roams through Buffalo trying to find somewhere to piss, could stand as a short comic movie in its own right. Likewise many of the subsequent sequences, whether set around the dinner table in Billy's parents' house or in the diner where he runs into a woman he was at school with and fancied from afar, have a self-contained, theatrical quality. Although Gallo doesn't shirk from shooting dialogue in an unusual way (the camera sometimes lingers on a character who isn't speaking) or from occasional formal flourishes (for example, the high-angle, Chinatown-style shot of Billy and Layla lying on the motel bed), he always allows his actors to perform their party pieces. We have Ben Gazzara (as Billy's father) miming away to old Sinatra songs; a jowly, weather-beaten Mickey Rourke (the bookie Billy owes money to) giving a monologue straight to camera; and Anjelica Huston (Billy's mother) reminiscing about 30 years as a die-hard Buffalo Bills fan and cheerleader.

At times, however, *Buffalo '66* is heavy-going. Unfolding in Buffalo in the dead of winter, its tone sometimes seems as dull and grey as its settings. Scenes are drawn out, and rather than involving us in the story, they occasionally look more like acting-school exercises. Billy's self obsession, like that of the actor-director playing him, can become wearisome. (Do we really need to see him showing off his expertise at the bowling alley?) Presumably, Billy pays so much attention to himself because nobody else does; abused as a child, even now his bickering parents ignore him. Only Layla (played with ingenuous charm by Christina Ricci) sees anything in him.

Yet Gallo has an eye for the telling detail. He is able to sum up Billy's slovenly friend Goon simply by training the camera on the character's huge belly. He uses music (which he also wrote) sparingly but effectively. The flashbacks to Billy's tormented childhood are ingeniously edited—they start as tiny shots-within-shots and grow to fill the screen. The slow-motion violence in the nightclub is so stylised it's almost surreal. Gallo treats the relationship between Layla and the scowling oddball who abducted her with humour and tenderness. Way off the mark, she calls Billy "the sweetest guy in the world", whereas he's actually rather truculent and boorish. Nevertheless, as this strangely likable malcontent struggles to cope with a rough, cynical world, she can't help but root for him.

TIME, 7/13/98, p. 78, Richard Schickel

Billy Brown (Vincent Gallo) emerges from the prison where he's just done a five-year stretch with three missions. The first, and most hilariously pressing, is to find a place to take a pee. The next is to find a girl willing to pose as his fiancé and help him convince his sublimely indifferent parents (Anjelica Huston and Ben Gazzara) that he's been doing topsecret CIA work all the years he was in jail. The last is to assassinate the Buffalo Bills placekicker whose missed field goal caused him to lose the bet that led him into a life of crime.

That's a lot for a young man, pretty much incapacitated by rage, and not too bright to begin with, to handle. But Gallo, who also wrote, directed and scored *Buffalo '66*, is a smart young filmmaker, not least in his casting. Gazzara, angrily mourning his lost career as a local lounge singer, and Huston, obsessing on the Bills' football frustrations, are glorious eccentrics. And Christina Ricci as the tap
dancer Billy forces to play his faux fiancé, is just lovely. She falls into instant love with her abductor, and with a kind of patient ferocity redeems his sanity.

And this says nothing about Gallos own demonic charm as Billy or his directorial boldness in juxtaposing the emotional surreality of his story with the bleak reality of his hometown in winter, creating a sort of but strangely haunting weirdness.

VILLAGE VOICE, 6/30/98, p. 133, J. Hoberman

Vincent Gallo's interviews are predicated on a self-regard so excessive and manic as to seem a cartoon shriek. There's a similar principle at work in *Buffalo '66*, the independent feature that everyone within earshot knows that Gallo cowrote, directed, scored, and set in his hometown—while appearing in every scene but one. The Vincent show's single-minded focus makes Truman's seem diffuse by comparison.

Would that every vanity production were this funny, soulful, and genuinely experimental. Having served five years in prison, Gallo's Billy Brown is cast out shivering into the Buffalo winter—dungaree jacket absurdly thin, pants all but falling down, his feet squeezed into a pair of ridiculous red Beatle boots. This derelict dandy has one of the most indelible faces in current American movies. Depending on the angle, Gallo's flattened nose, ascetic lips, and pale eyes give him the ethereal presence of a Medici princeling or the haunted look of a Kansas dirt farmer traumatized by the blizzard of 1889. Not that he treats himself to a glamorous makeover—appearing unshaven beneath his lank helmet of greasy hair and bent double in physical agony.

Gallo is a master of irritation whose unique strategy in enlisting audience sympathy is to have his character spend the movie's first 10 minutes desperately searching downtown Buffalo for a pot to piss in. (Call it Gallo's humor.) It's during this quest for a usable public toilet that Billy, at once tightly wound and totally unwrapped, kidnaps an innocent dumpling named Layla (Christina Ricci), dolled up as a cross between a big-eyed Walter Keane waif and a drag queen's impersonation of Elizabeth Taylor on Oscar night, from the seedy dance studio where she's been learning to tap.

Layla appears to be living out some indescribable Halloween fantasy; Billy's mad scheme is to visit his parents, unaware of his jailed time, and present Layla as his adoring wife. "This is acting," he impatiently explains (not for the last time). "You've been in love with me all your life." Layla is instructed to make Billy "look good" but, once in operation, the plan grows increasingly bizarre. Suddenly silent, the son sits glowering while his mother (Anjelica Huston, managing an impressive upstate New York accent) dithers around in agitated denial and his father (Ben Gazzara) twitches in the pre-coronary stages of spite-choked aggravation.

The family reunion is superb theater of embarrassment and one of the movie's best jokes is that Billy's own mixture of self-absorption and paranoid hostility is obviously derived from these parental models. This lengthy scene, which Gallo has suggested is loosely autobiographical, makes Billy "look good" mainly by illuminating his misery. Father and son can neither look at nor talk to each other, until, imagining that Billy's table knife is pointed at him, his dad goes ballistic. Layla, meanwhile, gets enthusiastically into her role, explaining at some length how she and her glamorous husband met through their jobs with the CIA.

Gallo compensates for his on-screen silence by orchestrating dinner as a series of long takes, the camera setup rotating around the table to showcase the actors in various combinations. Indeed, as character driven as it is (Rosanna Arquette and Kevin Corrigan have stellar cameos), *Buffalo '66* is not deficient in visual pleasure. Gallo contrives to film the dreary precincts of his old neighborhood as if touring the Garden of Allah. The contrast is high, the colors are either supersaturated or washed out. The shallow space dissolves much of the background in a diaphanous haze. This power-pop verité look is epitomized by Ricci's outfit—baby blue nightgown with matching tights, sparkly silver pumps, blindingly blond hair, iridescent lip gloss, and glitter mascara. As Gallo's scene-stealing foil, she's a far more enigmatic and compelling presence than was her bratty bad girl in *The Opposite of Sex*.

Largely reactive, Ricci is both docile and dynamic—grave mien wildly at odds with sugarplum fairy getup. (Like the movie itself, her performance is sweet but not cloying.) As much as it concerns anything, *Buffalo '66* is a movie about self-presentation. Gallo twice stops the action and drags in the spotlight to allow his costars to perform. Gazzara's lip-synched rendition of "Fools Rush In" (sung, according to the credits, by Vincent Gallo Sr.) is topped only by Ricci's sub-Ruby Keeler tap dance. But is it Billy who is ordering sulky Layla about—or is it Gallo (taking a leaf from the Jack Smith method of existential performance) directing his leading lady while they're both on camera? "Look like you like me," he tells her as they pose for a series of photo-booth portraits. Layla obligingly mugs for the camera; Billy, of course, remains hilariously frozen.

Buffalo '66 is some kind of psychodrama—but what sort? Rejection is built into the narrative along with revenge. Billy's braggadocio is repeatedly interrupted by spasms of vulnerability: "Would you hold me...Don't touch me." Family, self and place are subject to the same active ambivalence. billy is the spirit of suffering Buffalo, born on the day that the Bills won the AFL championship. His fanatical mother has never forgiven him for making her miss the game; a more recent Bills-based disaster precipitated his five years in stir, having taken the rap for a bookie (played by Mickey Rourke as if sculpted from congealed lard).

Long before *Buffalo '66* reaches its emotional climax in a strip joint owned by a former Bills placekicker—an incongruously golden heaven of grinding houris—the viewer may wonder if Layla is playing a fantasy Iris to Billy's half-cracked Travis Bickle. (There is a sense in which *Buffalo '66* rewrites *Taxi Driver*, or rather overwrites it—imagining the antidote to its loner protagonist's rage and alienation.) Why, one might ask, does Layla find her abduction an adventure? Is it because the situation compels her to become an actress? By the movie's end, it's clear that, no less than Billy, she's been inventing her own romantic fantasy all along.

Buffalo '66 itself is so self-contained, sincerely needy, and sui generis a directorial performance that it's difficult to imagine Gallo's encore—whatever he does, it could scarcely be more surprising than this. The movie is a tale of redemption; the real miracle is that Gallo's narcissism would prove so generous.

Also reviewed in:
CHICAGO TRIBUNE, 8/7/98, Friday/p. A, Mark Caro
NEW YORK TIMES, 6/26/98, p. E16, Janet Maslin
VARIETY, 2/2-8/98, p. 32, Todd McCarthy
WASHINGTON POST, 7/10/98, p. D1, Stephen Hunter

BUG'S LIFE, A

A Walt Disney Pictures release of a Pixar film.   *Producer:* Darla K. Anderson and Kevin Reher. *Director:* John Lasseter. *Screenplay:* Andrew Stanton, Donald McEnery, and Bob Shaw. *Story:* John Lasseter, Andrew Stanton, and Joe Ranft.   *Director of Photography:* Sharon Calahan. *Editor:* Lee Unkrich. *Music:* Randy Newman. *Music Editor:* Lori Eschler Frystak. *Sound:* Gary Rydstrom and (music) Frank Wolf. *Sound Editor:* Tim Holland.   *Casting:* Ruth Lambert.   *Production Designer:* William Cone. *Art Director:* Tia W. Kratter and Bob Pauley.

Set Dresser: Sophie Vincelette, David Eisenmann, and Derek Williams. *Supervising Animator:*
Glenn McQueen and Rich Quade. *Running time:* 94 minutes. *MPAA Rating:* G.

VOICES: Dave Foley (Flik);   Kevin Spacey (Hopper);   Julia Louis-Dreyfus (Princess Atta);
Hayden Panettiere (Dot);   Phyllis Diller (Queen);   Richard Kind (Molt);   David Hyde Pierce
(Slim);   Joe Ranft (Heimlich);   Denis Leary (Francis);   Jonathan Harris (Manny);   Madeline
Kahn (Gypsy);   Bonnie Hunt (Rosie);   Michael McShane (Tuck & Roll);   John Ratzenberger
(P.T. Flea);   Brad Garrett (Dim);   Roddy McDowall (Mr. Soil);   Edie McClurg (Dr. Flora);
Alex Rocco (Thorny);   David Ossman (Cornelius).

LOS ANGELES TIMES, 11/20/98, Calendar/p. 1, Kenneth Turan

Computer-animated movies, like computers themselves, are only as clever and funny as the
people who program them. What "A Bug's Life" demonstrates is that when it comes to bugs, the
most fun ones to hang out with hang exclusively with the gang at Pixar.

Though "Antz" has a sharper title and came first to theaters, the eccentric, off-the-wall "A
Bug's Life" is the insect-themed computer-animated film to see if you can only manage one. And
the wacky sensibility of the Pixar Animation Studio is very much the reason why.

It was Pixar that created the sensational "Toy Story," the film that made computer animation
a commercial and artistic force. While "A Bug's Life" is not that good, it has enough visual
surprises and gee-whiz moments to sustain its brisk 94-minute length.

It's probably just coincidence, but "A Bug's Life" and "Antz" have several plot points in
common. Both are grounded in ant colonies facing ruinous attack from outside insects, both
feature queens training their daughters in the finer points of monarchy, and both focus on a rift
between conservatives who want to do things the time-honored way and a rebel with ideas of his
own.

What "Bug's Life" has that the other film lacks is an unfettered imagination, a willingness to
tolerate the kind of harum-scarum, anything-goes sensibility that would come up with ideas like
a delightful series of outtakes of bugs blowing their lines and calling for retakes that plays
alongside the final credits.

This footloose humor comes both from the writing and the direction. Co-writer Andrew Stanton
was one of the team that received an Oscar nomination for the "Toy Story" script, and his
collaborators, Donald McEnery & Bob Shaw, contributed to the underappreciated "Hercules."
Directing (with Stanton getting co-direction credit) is Pixar stalwart John Lasseter, who also did
the honors for "Toy Story."

Another key to "Bug's Life's" success is that it's cast a much wider net, so to speak, in terms
of how many different kinds of insects make it onto the screen. And though its voices are not
always big stars (the film's story supervisor Joe Ranft did such a good job with the gemutlich
caterpillar Heimlich in the first reading he got the part), they are always at one with the material.

"A Bug's Life" starts with a typical example of its humor. As a line of ants carrying foodstuffs
snakes its way through the grass, a leaf falls, obscuring the trail and causing consternation. "'Do
not panic, we are trained professionals," cries a group of leaf removers, who clear things up
while commenting, "This is nothing compared to the Twig of '93."

The ants are gathering food as tribute for the annual visit of a gang of marauding grasshoppers,
led by the mendacious Hopper (Kevin Spacey). Don't worry, the Queen (Phyllis Diller) tells her
daughter Princess Atta (Julia Louis-Dreyfus), "it's the same year after year: They come, they eat,
they leave."

No ant colony is apparently complete without its resident iconoclast, in this case a well-meaning
but chronically inept young man named Flik (Dave Foley of TV's "NewsRadio"). When Flik
unintentionally causes a problem with Hopper's gang over the tribute, he decides the only way
to redeem himself and save the colony is to venture off of Ant Island and seek help from other
insects.

While "A Bug's Life" was apparently inspired by the Aesop's fable about the grasshoppers and
the ants, at this point the picture cleverly turns into an entomological version of Akira Kurosawa's
classic "Seven Samurai," where warriors are recruited from the big city to help embattled farmers
fight off brigands.

It's not exactly warriors this time around though. While Flik is on the road, the film allows us a peek inside the bedraggled circus of P.T. Flea (John Ratzenberger) and introduces a particularly zany and irresistible group of performing insects: cheerful Heimlich, feisty male ladybug Francis (Denis Leary), the stick-thin Slim (David Hyde Pierce), friendly black widow Rosie (Bonnie Hunt), the team of Manny the Mantis and Gypsy Moth (Jonathan Harris and Madeline Kahn), rhino beetle Dim (Brad Garrett) and the irrepressible twin Hungarian pill bugs Tuck & Roll (Michael McShane).

Visually satisfying is the film's "Blade Runner" vision of the Big (or is it Bug?) City, where a beggar wears a sign saying "A Kid Pulled My Wings Off." Ditto for the local bar (probably inspired by the cantina in "Star Wars"), where mosquitoes quaff genuine Bloody Marys and hardier insects quench their thirsts with Black Flags.

It's at the bar that Flik meets up with newly unemployed insects from P.T. Flea's. He mistakes them for "tough bugs" and they think he's a patron of the arts when he begs them to go back to Ant Island. "These guys," one of them says, "are sure hard up for entertainment." This confusion eventually clears up, and the circus bugs have to try to use what skills they have against Hopper and his pesky clan.

If the film's press notes are to be believed, "A Bug's Life" was hell on Earth to make, with some sequences demanding more than 100 hours per frame to render. It was worth all the effort. Just like Aesop's tale of the tortoise and the hare, this summer's insect derby is one race that did not go to the swift.

NEW YORK, 12/7/98, p. 75, Peter Rainer

The bugs'-eye view in disney's *A Bug's Life* is an iridescent marvel. This is only the third fully computer-animated feature—after the 1995 *Toy Story* and DreamWorks' recent *Antz*—but the palette is richer than anything we've ever seen before. The opalescence of the visuals has a poured-plastic quality that's highly pleasing; there's a voluminous smoothness to the imagery that's reminiscent of Salvador Dali's dreamscapes, but with an entirely different spirit. *A Bug's Life* is a storybook fantasia with the kick of a good carny act.

It's also buggy with tie-ins. According to *Business Week,* everyone from Mattel to McDonald's is churning out *Bug's Life* paraphernalia. All this should not get in the way of our enjoyment. In the corporate-conglomerate era—when films routinely resemble entire Sears catalogues of product placement—it's crucial to our sanity as pop-cult consumers to maintain some kind of distinction between a movie and its merchandising. Not an easy task. The commodification of movies has fuzzied our aesthetic sense: Are we responding to something new or just succumbing to another species of sell? A good rule of thumb here is that a movie shouldn't be blamed for its marketing unless the movie *is* the marketing. *E. T* was no less a classic for all the gewgaws it spawned. And *A Bug's Life* is delightful even though we know its rhino bugs will be staring back at us from the toy-store shelves until the Apocalypse.

For all its visual enticements, *A Bug's Life* is powered primarily by its story and characters. The visual superfluidity that is possible with computer animation finds its counterpart in a lickety-split yarn—a wiseacre Aesop's fable. The ants on Ant Island have been terrorized by grasshoppers into harvesting food each fall as ritual offerings. When one of the ants, the perky, eccentric Flik, accidentally spills the grasshoppers' bounty, the colony is endangered. Exiled, he seeks help from the raggle-taggle bugs in a traveling flea circus. The troupe is more like a menagerie of knockabout vaudevillians. The bashful rhino bug takes his place beside Helmlich, the chubby green caterpillar who sounds like a cranky Katzenjammer Kid. Slim, the walking stick, is effetely studious; Francis, the ladybug, is no lady—he's a guy with a macho complex. A pair of Hungarian pill bugs natter away in a speeded-up smattering of incomprehensible dialects. (They're like pipsqueak Sid Caesars.)

Co-directors John Lasseter and Andrew Stanton position these bugs in ways that make witty use of the wide-screen frame. This is, after all, a bug *epic*. The flea-circus performers plaster their mugs across the Cinemascope expanse, and they have every right to show off. A few of them, especially Francis and Heimlich, are as cantankerously memorable as the best of Disney's pre-computer animated characters.

One reason the bugs come across so well here is that the sheen of the wings and exoskeletons, and the segmented way in which these critters move, are tailor-made for the technical requirements of computer animation. But there's another explanation for why bugs are naturals in this family-entertainment universe: They bring out the kid in everybody. *A Bug's Life* gets inside the way you used to feel when you hunkered down in the tall grass and got up close and personal with beetles and katydids. (Their creepy-crawly world seemed to exist for your delectation.) But the movie's bugs aren't "realistic." They're more like a smart kid's reimagining of what the ideal bug would be.

Regrettably, in order to soften the ick factor in this material, the filmmakers have gone in for some sanitizing: The ants, for example, have two sets of arms and legs instead of six, and there's no hair, or cilia, or whatever you call it, on any of the bugs. On the other hand, the filmmakers gave the grasshoppers an extra set of appendages in order to make them scarier. They'd be pretty scary anyway. Their honcho, Hopper, is voiced by Kevin Spacey; issuing from a jut-jawed mandible, his feral unctuousness has never sounded more appropriate. Madeline Kahn, Phyllis Diller, Denis Leary, and others also sound off memorably. Some actors are positively liberated by this kind of exercise. Spacey doesn't need to be a grasshopper to be good, but you may have noticed that Woody Allen and Sylvester Stallone, voicing ants in *Antz,* were better than they've been for years in their live-action movies—where they've turned themselves into far less funny cartoons.

Everywhere you direct your eye in *A Bug's Life* there's something to look at. In the subterranean-ant-colony scenes, the mushrooms have a cool phosphorescence that soothes the screen like a night light. Aboveground, the Pixar Animation Studios wizards—the same crew, under Lasseter's direction, who made *Toy Story*—achieve a hyperrealistic clarity. This world of twigs and dewdrops is more than just our fantasy of what a bug's realm would be. It looks like a *bug's* fantasy, too. There's an enraptured nuttiness about the landscape: The oddments of civilization become props, totems. In the flea-circus scenes, a discarded ice-cube tray becomes the bleachers; a poodle collar is the circus ring.

There's also a refreshing lack of cant. Although I enjoyed *Antz* for most of the way, it wound itself into a paean to individuality—which is not what we go to see a movie called *Antz* for. *A Bug's Life* never makes that kind of high-minded mistake. The heartfelt epithets spouted by its characters are all along the lines of: *It's a bug-eat-bug world.* Say it isn't so. After seeing this film, you want only the best for the bugs. And from now on, watch what you're stepping on.

NEW YORK POST, 11/25/98, p. 47, Rod Dreher

Garrulous mammals or blabbermouth insects? Take your pick: You can't go wrong with either "A Bug's Life" or "Babe: Pig in the City" this holiday weekend.

Both are sweet, gleefully imaginative family films whose artistry, great good cheer and after lack of cynicism provide ample reason for giving thanks.

See them both, but if you have to choose one, by all means make it "A Bug's Life," the Disney-Pixar combustively colorful follow-up to 1995's brilliant "Toy Story."

The tale of a hapless but resourceful ant and his heroic measures to save his colony from bully-boy grasshoppers lacks the emotional depth of Buzz Lightyear's saga, but it's still an irresistible charmer. What's more, "A Bug's Life" marks a bounding leap forward in the wholly computerized animation process Pixar pioneered to such wondrous effect in its rookie effort. Thanks to technological advances of the past three years, the creatures are noticeably more lifelike and expressive—and rendered in eye-popping detail (the filmmakers studied the fantastic bugumentary "Microcosmos," and, boy, does it show). And the riot-in-a-candy-store palette that the filmmakers use makes "Toy Story" seem downright somber. In fact, the luscious marzipan shadings as well as a much more kid-friendly story line make "A Bug's Life" a lot more buoyant fun than "Antz."

To wit: The ants in "Antz" were plain brown; in "A Bug's Life," they look like fruit-punch Jelly Bellies lit from within, like Japanese lanterns. That says a lot about the difference between the look and feel of the two movies.

"A Bug's Life" begins with a colony of oppressed ants collecting winter food for their fearsome grasshopper overlords, led by the fierce Hopper (voice of Kevin Spacey). A clumsy buglet named Flik accidentally causes the mound of grasshopper groceries to tumble into the water, enraging Hopper and his crew. Hopper thunders that if the ants don't spend their summer replacing the food, he and his boys will squish them flatter than, well, bugs.

"It's a bug-eat-bug world out there," Hopper snarls. "It's a circle of life thing." Though entirely geared at a kid's level, the script is clever without being smart-alecky—something of a rarity in movies for children these days. The grossest it gets is a waitress in a bar dismissing dung-munching flies as "poo-poo heads." Hey, 8-year-olds will be rolling in the aisles.

Flik's queen (voice of Phyllis Diller) and the curiously Elaine Benes-like Princess Atta (voice of Julia Louis-Dreyfus—OK, so it's not so curious) are completely outdone by Flik, who swears he can make it up to them by going out into the world to find insect mercenaries who can fight off the grasshoppers.

Flik makes his way to a garbage dump behind a house trailer, which strikes him as mandible-dropping: "Wow, the city!" In a terrific scene recalling the cantina episode in "Star Wars," Flik meets and recruits a motley band of insect soldiers. Trouble is, they're not troopers but troupers: naive country ant Flik has mistaken runaway members of a flea circus for fighters.

For their part, the troupe members think they've been hired away from P.T. Flea, their slave-driving ringmaster (voice of John Ratzenberger), and offered a gig entertaining the grasshoppers.

And what a large and entertaining cast they are! Among them: Francis (voice of Denis Leary), a gruff ladybug; jittery doodlebug duo Tuck & Roll (voice of Michael McShane); snooty walking stick Slim (David Hyde Pierce); Dim, a lovable lug of a rhino beetle (voice of Brad Garrett); and, best of all, Heimlich (Joe Ranft), a jolly, blubbery German caterpillar whose voice and demeanor suggest Sgt. Schultz slurping beer and sausage at a perpetual Oktoberfest.

Flik and his goofy friends face down foes—including a marauding, T. rex-like robin—with wit, ingenuity and humor. The creepy-crawly cretins get what's coming to them, and the audience gets not only scene after scene of buggy delight, but a hilarious outtakes sequence during the closing credits—a cute, cherry-on-top of a big, boisterous banana split of a movie.

After the Pixar-induced delirium of talking bugs, talking animals don't seem quite so special. Though "Babe: Pig in the City" suffers by comparison not only with "A Bug's Life" but also with its wonderful 1995 predecessor, it is nevertheless much better than recent news had led us to expect. Universal canceled the "Pig in the City" premiere, reportedly because of last-minute edits to remove dark story elements that turned off young test audiences.

Whatever the truth, it's a relief to report that brave little Babe brings home the bacon once again. The story picks up where the first "Babe" left off, with Babe returning home with Farmer Hoggett (James Cromwell, in a cameo here) in triumph after winning the national sheepdog trials. Unfortunately, Babe's childlike curiosity soon causes an accident that leaves Farmer Hoggett bedridden, and brings creditors to foreclose on the farm.

The farmer's wife, Esme (Magda Szubanski), sets off for the State Fair with Babe in tow, hoping the celebrated porker's personal appearance will raise the money needed to save Hoggett Farm. But they miss their flight connection and get stranded in the big city, which, in Roger Ford's design, is an amalgam of New York, Los Angeles, Paris, Sydney and Venice Beach. They find lodging in a weird hotel that secretly shelters animals.

When poor Mrs. Hoggett is detained by the police, and the hotel's owner (Mary Stein) takes leave of the storied menagerie, the animals are left to fend for themselves. Good old Babe (voiced, this time, by E.G. Daily) takes command, and wins the confidence and affection of all—and their freedom once the jackbooted thugs of the Animal Control agency round them up.

This movie is noticeably edgier, and certainly more action-oriented, than the first "Babe" (we're not in Kansas anymore, Toto) and this version prepared for release bears signs of hasty editing to remove potentially depressing material. Yet there's still plenty of whimsy afoot, with adorable new characters joining old faves (including Ferdinand the Duck, and the Singing Mice Trio) for more endearing, Dr. Dolittle-like enchantment.

Though "Pig in the City" is not quite the warm, joyous fable we fell in love with three years ago, rest easy, "Babe" fans: This little piggy remains one happy, huggable ham. We've still got you, Babe.

NEWSDAY, 11/25/98, Part II/p. B2, Jack Mathews

Most hot-footed races between studios trying to be first in the market with same-subject movies end in disappointment for audiences. There were two bad Jean Harlow movies, two bad Robin Hoods, two terrible Christopher Columbus pictures, and—just this summer—two wretched action thrillers about outer space masses on a collision course with Earth.

But the great animation ant war between DreamWorks' "Antz" and Disney's "A Bug's Life" has proved to be a win-win for everyone. Despite virtually identical plot lines—unlikely hero ant sets out to save his colony from invasion and win the heart of a princess—and shared computer technology, the two movies will make a dream double-bill at home entertainment centers for generations to come.

And there are some clear distinctions between the films. Where "Antz" derives most of its humor from the hip by-play written for the famous voices (Woody Allen, Gene Hackman, Sharon Stone) behind its characters, "A Bug's Life" follows Disney tradition, creating a host of wonderful anthropomorphic figures, and allowing the energy and humor to flow from their actions.

The only downside of "A Bug's Life" losing the release race to "Antz" is that its reviews inevitably must be shared with the first film, which is still in theaters. Personally, I find it hard to declare a winner. Both films announce the true coming-of-age of computer animation, software artistry that creates nearly three-dimensional fictional worlds, landscapes of virtual unreality, if you will, where the camera roams freely in, out and around its imagined universe and characters.

The main difference between the movies, and the one that makes "A Bug's Life" the better bet for small children, is the emphasis on adventure. "Antz" has its great physical inventions—foremost, a harrowing ride by two characters trapped in a wad of gum on the bottom of a human's tennis shoe—but there are fewer primary characters and fewer moments of sheer visual exhilaration.

"A Bug's Life" gets off to an oddly slow start, introducing its hero Flik (voice of Dave Foley), a genial, industrious worker ant, and the Royal House of Ant Island, which includes the retiring queen (Phyllis Diller) and heir apparent Princess Atta (Julia Louis-Dreyfus). We also meet Hopper (Kevin Spacey), and his gang of pillaging grasshoppers who drop by Ant Island annually to consume the ants' store of winter food.

Said to be inspired by an Aesop's fable about a beggar grasshopper, "A Bug's Life" plays more like a toy-box version of "Seven Samurai," with a ragtag band of flea circus dropouts coming to the rescue, against their better judgment and avowed cowardice, of an oppressed town. And what a band it is!

Included among the troupe recruited by Flik is the timid rhinoceros beetle Dim (Brad Garrett); proud walking stick Slim (David Hyde Pierce); pompous praying mantis Manny (Jonathan Harris) and his moth girlfriend Gypsy (Madeline Kahn); warmhearted black widow Rosie (Bonnie Hunt); and Francis (Denis Leary), a male ladybug who's definitely not in touch with his feminine side.

There's also an overeating caterpillar, a flea P.T. Barnum, a pair of sow bugs who have more ham in them than bug, and, on the treacherous trip from the circus to Ant Island, a carnivorous red bird who, from a bug's-eye view, is the size of Godzilla. That bird will return later, both in person and in a cleverly detailed model created by the ants, to scare the grasshoppers.

"A Bug's Life" is a product of Pixar, the computer house that, in conjunction with Disney, created the 1995 animation hit "Toy Story," and like the earlier film, is directed (overseen?) by John Lasseter. Nothing but cost will ever threaten the place of classical cell animation, but the two ant movies demonstrate that the new technology is here to stay, as a related, but still unique, film medium.

Computer animators have far greater flexibility than their drawing-board-bound colleagues, and can clearly come as close, in their detail and movement, to three-dimensional photo-realism as they wish. And, as they show with some cleverly whimsical out-takes during the final credits of "A Bug's Life," they can even afford to make their characters work overtime.

SIGHT AND SOUND, 2/99, p. 39, Leslie Felperin

On a tiny island dominated by one large tree, a colony of ants gather their yearly midsummer grain offering to appease a marauding grasshopper gang led by the ferocious Hopper. Worker-ant

Flik, while demonstrating his new grain-harvesting contraption, accidentally dumps the offering into deep water. An incensed Hopper demands the ants provide twice their usual offering by the time the last leaf falls from the tree. Flik offers to get help from bigger bugs in the mainland city (a rubbish pile). Princess Atta, training to take over from her mother the Queen, agrees to let him go.

In the city, a troupe of circus bugs are fired by their ringmaster P. T Flea after a disastrous performance. Flik sees them fighting with some flies and mistakes them for warriors, while they mistake him for a talent scout. Flik leads them back to the island. When the misunderstanding is clarified, the circus bugs try to leave, but stop to help save Atta's sister Dot from a hungry bird. Flik is inspired: he persuades the colony and the bugs to build a fake bird to scare off the grasshoppers. But when Flik realises that no one expected him to succeed, he leaves with the circus bugs whom Flea has rehired.

The grasshoppers arrive, intending to squish the Queen. Dot finds Flik and persuades him to return. Flik's fake-bird plan partly succeeds until the bird catches fire. Flik stands up to Hopper and makes the ants realise that they vastly outnumber the grasshoppers. The ants attack *en masse*, Hopper battles Flik, but is tricked into falling into the clutches of a real bird and is eaten by its chicks. The circus bugs set off, leaving behind Flik, now considered a hero by the colony.

Insects have an impressive employment record in animation. In 1909, Ladislaw Starewicz experimented with animating dead stag beetles, eventually featuring them in *Cameraman's Revenge* (1911) a variation on the *Bride Retires* cycle of voyeuristic films, one so convincing critics were amazed that Starewicz had managed to train his tiny cast so well. Animation pioneers the Fleischer Brothers made *Mr Bug Goes to Town* (1941), a great *film maudit* which features a colony of urban insects whose home is threatened by the inexorable forces of property development. This was their second unsuccessful attempt (after *Gulliver's Travels in Lilliput*, (1939) to mount a viable alternative to Disney's monopoly on animated features.

It's tempting to make parallels with the current battle between DreamWorks SKG and Disney circa 1998. DreamWorks, who released their own wisecracking, New York-set ant movie *Antz* a few months ago, might seem plucky inheritors of the Fleischers' upstart-underdog title if they were not themselves so efficient, canny and corporate. Still, history is repeating itself in the sense that Disney has the upper hand with this co-production (with Pixar) of *A Bug's Life*—traditionally bucolic, better executed, more tightly constructed and more commercially successful. This latest insect movie uses the same basic plot structure as *Antz*, a colony threatened by other more powerful insects is saved by ostracised members' ingenuity. *A Bug's Life* burrows a little less deeply into the muddy individual-versus-conformity soil ploughed by *Antz*. It's a far lighter film—literally so, with much more of its action taking place above ground rather than inside the anthill (which in *Antz* made a wonderfully murky, *Metropolis*-like setting).

It's no accident, though, that an anglepoise (star of award-winning short *Luxo Jr.*) is Pixar's mascot. Subtle use of light and colour has emerged as director John Lasseter and Co's trademark and their deployment of these elements in *A Bug's Life* is quite astounding. Where the last film, *Toy Story*, was set mainly indoors and afforded opportunities to mimic incandescent lighting and sunlight filtered through windows, *A Bug's Life* goes for an even more complex palette of effects. As the summer wanes and autumn kicks in, the shades darken and the angles of illumination change almost imperceptibly. In this arena, computers really can achieve things cel animation would struggle to get right: it's a matter of mathematical programming to calculate shadows from preset sources. A kind of lapidary realism is generated that would have equally impressed those fooled by Starewicz's stag beetles.

Nonetheless, the film's makers are canny enough to realise the value of stylisation. *A Bug's Life* really has the edge over *Antz* in the graphic simplicity of its characterisation. Where *Antz* made things harder for itself with anatomically correct six-legged ants given almost human-proportioned faces, Pixar's film takes an opposite strategy, reducing faces to huge, white-filled eyes and giving the ant bodies only four limbs. Meanwhile, the grasshoppers (their relentless leader Hopper wittily voiced by Kevin Spacey) have a lobster-shell texture, their joints constantly clicking menacingly, forming a sharp contrast with the soft, incandescent burnish on the pastel-coloured ants. Little of it will wash with entomologists, but *A Bug's Life* achieves the aim of reducing the squirm factor inherent in having insect protagonists. Nevertheless, the script has fun playing with our common knowledge of insects. The film's best line is a bored fly at the circus dismissing the bugs' performance with, "I only have 24 hours to live and I'm not wasting it on this." This fly would be less likely to say this of the film in which he appears. The rest of the film has similar fun mixing bug-world givens with anthropomorphism.

TIME, 11/30/98, p. 110, Richard Corliss

A colony of peaceful, industrious little creatures is ripped off by marauders from afar. Ants and grasshoppers. That too. But in conspiratorial hindsight one might see "A Bug's Life," the first feature from John Lasseter and his Pixar whizzes since their 1995 computer-generated hit "Toy Story," as the company's rearview metaphor for its battle with DreamWorks' "Antz." That similar computer-animated cartoon was conceived after the Pixar pic but released before it. It's bug-eat-bug in Hollywood's animation wars.

Is there room for two? Yes, when the "second" movie is as rich and rewarding as "A Bug's Life". Its design work is so stellar—a wide-screen Eden of leaves and labyrinths populated by dozens of ugly, buggy, cuddly cutups—that it makes the DreamWorks film seem, by comparison, like radio. If that movie was Ant-Z, this one is Ant-A.

The story has the ants in servitude to Hopper (voiced by Kevin Spacey) and his band of gangster grasshoppers, who fly in each year to receive their tribute of vittles. Hopper is a thug among bugs, and no ant dares stand up to him. But one little fellow, Flik (Dave Foley), a misfit with big ideas, decides to venture outside the colony and hire some tough guys to fight the grasshoppers. All right, the new hired guns are actually a troupe of circus performers with prima-donna dispositions and tender carapaces. But what Hopper doesn't know can't hurt the ants. Can it?

The fable of the grinds vs. the goons, played out daily in suburban schoolyards, gets sophisticated tweaks from Lasseter, co-director Andrew Stanton and their colleagues. The movie teems with political infighting, with carnage and compromise, at the grass-roots level—"Michael Collins" meets "Microcosmos". Indeed, for the first half hour or so, "A Bug's Life" is so dense with characters and illustrative detail that it nearly chokes on its own banquet. The filmmakers encourage you to wander through the glamorous terrain of their imaginations as if the picture were a product reel for 21st century cinema.

But as Walt Disney knew, animation is more than sublime trickery; the word means giving life. With a different kind of mouse, Lasseter does just that as his film finds its heat and heart. The plot matures handsomely; the characters neatly converge and combust; the gags pay off with emotional resonance. And at the end, the movie tops itself with comic outtakes, undoubtedly the funniest finale of any cartoon feature. "Antz" may have amused viewers with its sidewise wit, but as a comprehensive vision of computerized moviemaking, Pixar's dream works. And when "A Bug's Life" hits its stride, it's antastic.

VILLAGE VOICE, 12/1/98, p.122, Amy Taubin

A Bug's Life is the little kids' version of *Antz*: sweeter, funnier, simpler to follow. I like that the ants in *A Bug's Life* are lavender and that they have the blissed-out eyes of Teletubbies, even when they're running for their lives. The brown ants in *Antz* are just a shade too realistic for anyone who has experienced a water-bug invasion. I also like that most of *A Bug's Life* takes place aboveground (the *Metropolis*-like anthill in *Antz* is very depressing) and that the Cinemascope landscape and Randy Newman's buoyant Americana score remind me of John Ford westerns. The casting in *A Bug's Life* is better, too. *Antz's* Woody Allen and Sharon Stone are simply too old to speak for young insects in love.

That said, it's staggering just how similar the premises and plots of both movies are. As Disney's *Armageddon* was to DreamWorks/Paramount's *Deep Impact*, so Disney's *A Bug's Life* is to DreamWorks's *Antz*.

Like *Antz*, *A Bug's Life* has as its hero an individualistic young male who's struggling to come of age in a rigidly conformist society. The hero, who's named Flik and given a friendly voice by Dave Foley, falls in love with the princess (and future queen) of the ant colony to which he belongs. He eventually wins her hand (these bugs have humanlike arms and legs) by saving her and the entire anthill from annihilation.

To this end, he must journey afar and win strangers to his side. Flik recruits P.T. Flea's Insect Circus (its star performers include a caterpillar, a moth, a couple of chiggers, an even-tempered black widow spider, and a macho ladybug) to help save the ants from mean, marauding grasshoppers who've been eating them out of house and home. (In the more sophisticated *Antz*, the danger comes from within: a warrior ant is plotting a military takeover.) The grasshoppers hang out in a dilapidated desert saloon that's more Sam Peckinpah than John Ford. Kevin Spacey provides the voice of their leader, Hopper, and he sounds as if he's been lubricating his vocal cords with that icky stuff that oozes out of bugs when they get crushed.

What's so peculiar about both *A Bug's Life* and *Antz* is that this basic patriarchal myth (young man marries princess after saving society as we know it) is imposed on a matriarchy. You know, the ants, the bees, they're ruled by queens, not kings. And the queens don't have consorts, just workers, drones, and warriors to feed them, fertilize them, and defend them. So what both these films are basically saying is that if a bug society could produce one freethinking individual, that individual would inevitably be male, and he'd turn that society into a patriarchy overnight. Or to put it slightly differently: the way to anthropomorphize a colony of ants is to make its most fully conscious and active member a young male.

The Pixar animation in *A Bug's Life* is much more fluent than it was in *Toy Story*, where the only expressive characters were Buzz and Woody. Here, there are about two dozen featured insects with distinct personalities. There are big crowd scenes, intimate close-ups, and lots of bug's-eye point-of-view shots. Call me gullible: I believed every second of it.

Also reviewed in:
CHICAGO TRIBUNE, 11/25/98, Tempo/p. 1, Michael Wilmington
NATION, 12/21/98, p. 34, Stuart Klawans
NEW YORK TIMES, 11/25/98, p. E1, Janet Maslin
VARIETY, 11/16-22/98, p. 33, Todd McCarthy
WASHINGTON POST, 11/25/98, p. D1, Stephen Hunter
WASHINGTON POST, 11/27/98, Weekend/p. 56, Michael O'Sullivan

BULLET ON A WIRE

A Provisional Production Company release. *Producer:* Jim Sikora. *Director:* Jim Sikora. *Screenplay:* Joe Carducci and Jim Sikora. *Director of Photography:* John Terendy. *Editor:* Chris Taylor. *Music:* Denison-Kimball Trio and Handsome Family. *Sound:* Gary Day. *Running time:* 84 minutes. *MPAA Rating:* Not Rated.

CAST: Jeff Strong (Raymond Brody); Lara Phillips (Tanya Strickland); David Yow (Ed); Paula Killen (Norma Brody); Richard Kern (Jake); Rex Benson (Dave); Robert Maffia (Wayne); Turk Muller (Mr. Strickland); Molly Reynolds (Mrs. Strickland).

LOS ANGELES TIMES, 11/6/98, Calendar/p. 6, Kevin Thomas

Jim Sikora's taut neo-noir "Bullet on a Wire" is one of those minimalist, deadpan tales of the collision of character and fate that is always so satisfying, particularly amid a clutter of mindless big-budget pictures. It's a small gem, with nothing wasted, everything sharply observed and expressed cinematically with cool aplomb.

Talk about cause and effect. A stocky, bespectacled man (Jeff Strong) wearing a suit, tie and topcoat enters a Chicago neighborhood cafe, notices a woman sitting at the bar but heads directly to the men's room to put drops in his eyes. (We later learn that the unflattering glasses, which give him an older, nerdy look, are only for effect; wearing them, despite his contact lenses, gives him an image of himself that boosts his confidence for making his phone pitches as an insurance salesman.)

Once back in the barroom, he's so disappointed that the woman has left that he heads for a county hospital where his attractive sister (Paula Killen), a busy, conscientious nurse, has little time to console him but assures him that she loves him and that she'll make dinner for him the following night. Strong's Raymond Brody, an ex-con with a short fuse, is not so easily assuaged.

While his sister has momentarily left her office, in a moment of extreme pique, he grabs a memo pertaining to tests taken by one of her patients, a young woman (Lara Phillips), and dials the number on it. When the woman's mother answers, Brody tells her that her daughter not only is pregnant but has also tested HIV-positive. (The first is most likely to turn out to be true but not the second.) The consequences for Phillips' Tanya are drastic.

Raymond and Tanya, so flawlessly portrayed by Strong and Phillips, are nondescript in the utmost, but there's lots more to them than meets the eye. Initially, we get the impression that Raymond is merely a nut, but he's actually a man who was once religious but furious about his fate in life.

Tanya is in love with a shiftless guy (David Yow) who's only too quick to exploit the predicament in which she now finds herself. Tanya is a woman, however, not only of unexpected intelligence and depth of character but also of a compassionate nature. While darkly humorous, "Bullet on a Wire" surprises us with its concern for redemption rather than revenge.

You find it sadly ironic that the lives of Raymond and Tanya intersected in such a calamitous way, because they are actually right for each other—but they probably would never have crossed paths otherwise. Sikora, who co-wrote the script with Joe Carducci, tells their story beautifully in black-and-white, perfect for expressing the drabness of Raymond's and Tanya's lives.

Expressing most effectively the shifting moods of "Bullet on a Wire" is the spare, evocative music of the Denison-Kimball Trio and the Handsome Family. "Bullet on a Wire" delivers just the kind of experience you hope for from a low-budget independent feature.

NEW YORK POST, 4/23/98, p. 59, Larry Worth

Based on his direction of the ultra low-budget film "Bullet on a Wire," it's obvious that Jim Sikora hits potential as an indie auteur. But it's equally obvious that he's still got a way to go.

The story, which Sikora co-wrote, is undeniably quirky, kicking off when a nerdy, middle-aged loser impulsively makes a prank phone call that results in murder. (Hence, the title.) What follows isn't as intriguing though the reactions of the anti-hero and his victims are never predictable.

That's the good news. The bad: Sikora introduces too many sub-plots, each of which seems less interesting than its predecessor. Worse, the grainy black-and-white photography, awkward segues, attempts at symmetry and scenes that beg for editing prove increasingly tiresome.

Among the cast of unknowns, Jeff Strong's disturbed protagonist is pretty memorable, with supporting turns from Paula Killen and Lara Phillips confirming that actors can hold up when dialogue doesn't.

Sure enough, the titular bullet hits the intended target, but it's light years from a bull's-eye.

VILLAGE VOICE, 4/28/98, p. 75, Amy Taubin

Jim Sikora's malign little psycho-drama *Bullet on a Wire* has *Detour* written all over it. And its not merely that both films make the telephone a lethal weapon. Like Ulmer, Sikora turns extreme poverty into a virtue. The lo-con black-and-white look evokes the affectless fog of paranoia. The bleak, generic locations (they seem as much like the '50s as the '90s) are correlatives for a dead-end existence. Sikora is also very good with the actors. Jeff Strong, as the sociopathic protagonist, and Lara Phillips, as his hapless victim, who has murderous impulses of her own, give understated but intense performances. With his cannonball head, clumsy body, and pale, fishy eyes, Strong cuts a particularly repellent figure. In these days of frisky, audience-friendly indies, the controlled creepiness of *Bullet on a Wire* makes Sikora an anomaly as a director, and one who's worth watching.

Also reviewed in:
NEW YORK TIMES, 4/24/98, p. E12, Lawrence Van Gelder
VARIETY, 11/9-15/98, p. 34, Lael Loewenstein

BULWORTH

A Twentieth Century release of a Warren Beatty film.   *Executive Producer:* Lauren Shuler Donner.   *Producer:* Warren Beatty and Pieter Jan Brugge.   *Director:* Warren Beatty. *Screenplay:* Warren Beatty and Jeremy Pikser.   *Story:* Warren Beatty.   *Director of Photography:* Vittorio Storaro.   *Editor:* Robert C. Jones and Billy Weber.   *Music:* Ennio Morricone.   *Music Editor:* Bob Badami.   *Sound:* Thomas Causey and (music) Fabio Venturi.   *Sound Editor:* Mark P. Stoeckinger and Paul Timothy Carden.   *Casting:* Victoria Thomas and Jeanne McCarthy. *Production Designer:* Dean Tavoularis.   *Art Director:* William F. O'Brien.   *Set Designer:* Dianne Wager.   *Set Decorator:* Rick Simpson.   *Set Dresser:* J.D. Smith and Greg Nestor. *Costumes:* Milena Canonero. *Make-up:* Valli O'Reilly.   *Make-up (Halle Berry):* Mary Burton. *Stunt Coordinator:* Garry Hymes, Daniel W. Barringer, and A. J. Nay.   Running time: 130 minutes.   MPAA Rating: R.

CAST: Warren Beatty (Jay Bulworth); Oliver Platt (Dennis Murphy);   Paul Sorvino (Graham Crockett);   Kimberly Deauna Adams (Denisha);   Vinny Argiro (Debate Director);   Sean Astin (Gary);   Kirk Baltz (Debate Producer); Ernie Banks (Leroy);   Amiri Baraka (Rastaman); Christine Baranski (Constance Bulworth); Adilah Barnes (Mrs. Brown); Graham Beckel (Man with Dark Glasses); Halle Berry (Nina); Brandon N. Bowlin, Michael "Big Mike" Duncan, Larry Mark, and Gary H. Walton (Bouncers).   Mongo Brownlee, Terry Cooley, and Kenn Whitaker (Henchmen);   Thomas Jefferson Byrd (Uncle Rafeeq);   J. Kenneth Campbell (Anthony);   Scott Michael Campbell (Head Valet); Jann Carl (Herself);   Kerry Catanese, Xiomara Cuevas Galindo, Ava Rivera, and Andrew Warne (Video Reporters);   Don Cheadle (L.D.); Dave Allen Clark (Himself);   Kevin Cooney (Rev. Wilberforce);   Christopher Curry (Journalist);   Stanley De Santis (Manny Liebowitz); Nora Dunn (Missy Berliner);   Jerry Dunphy (Himself); Dartanyan Edmonds (Man with Blunt); Edward J. Etherson (Mr. Sasser); V. J. Foster (Photographer);   Leon Curtis Frierson (Osgood);   George Furth (Older Man); Robin Gammell (Geoffrey);   Life Garland (Darnell's Bud);   Jackie Gayle (Macavoy);   Jim Haynie (Bill Stone);   Randee Heller (Mrs. Tannenbaum);   Barry Shabaka Henley (Man at Frankie's); James Hill (Journalist); Kene Holliday and Lee Weaver (Men in Church); Myra J. and Jedda Jones (Women in Church);   Mario Jackson (Snag); Ariyan Johnson (Tanya); Michael Kaufman, Deborah Lacey, Deborah Moore, and Brooke Skulski (Reporters); Larry King (Himself); Mimi Lieber (Mrs. Liebowitz); Elizabeth Lindsey (American Politics Host); Joshua Malina (Bill Feldman);   Helen Martin (Momma Doll); Armelia McQueen (Ruthie);   Laurie Metcalf (Mimi);   Michael Milhoan and Chris Mulkey (Cops);   Debra Monk (Helen);   Michele Morgan (Cheryl);   Patrick Morgan (Studio Employee); Juli Mortz (Larry King's Assistant); Scott Mosenson (Video Cameraman);   Paul Motley (Janitor in Senate Office);   Lou Myers (Uncle Tyrone);   Shawna Nagler (Technical Director);   Jonathan Roger Neal, Tony Tomas Randle, Arthur Reggie III, Kenneth Randle, Jamal Mixon, and Jerod Mixon (Little Gangstas). Ron Ostrow (Staff Member); Norman Parker (Irwin Tannenbaum); James Pickens, Jr. (Uncle David);   Wendell Pierce (Fred);   Oliver Platt (Dennis Murphy);   Adrian Ricard (Aunt Alice); Richard Sarafian (Vinnie);   Robert Scheer (Journalist);   Sam Shamshak (Fundraiser Guest); Sarah Silverman (2nd American Politics Assistant);   Bee-Be Smith (Aunt Harriet);   Robin Thomas (Reporter in Hallway); Roberto Soto (Reporter); Florence Stanley (Dobish); Quinn Sullivan (Fundraiser Server);   JoAnn D. Thomas (Rapper);   Sheryl Underwood (Woman in Frankie's); Jack Warden (Eddie Davers); Isaiah Washington (Darnell); Jermaine Williams (Paul Robeson); John Witherspoon (Revernd Morris);   Sumiko Telljohn (Lady at Banquet).

LOS ANGELES TIMES, 5/15/98, Calendar/p. 1, Kenneth Turan

Like Newt Gingrich singing "My Yiddishe Mama" or Hulk Hogan doing needlepoint, the sight of Warren Beatty rapping is not on the top of most people's must-see list. Will "Bulworth" change their minds? That's an easier question to ask than to answer.

A chaotic but somehow endearing mishmash, "Bulworth" is an amusing, self-consciously outrageous attempt at a shotgun marriage between knockabout comedy and serious political commentary. Produced, directed, co-written and starring Beatty, it's a lively, undisciplined one-of-a-kind vanity project from a smart and politically savvy movie star used to getting his own way.

Those looking for confirmation of how close Hollywood and Washington have become will notice how at home Beatty is as the incumbent California Sen. Jay Billington Bulworth seen in the campaign spots that start the film. Handsome, charismatic, with his jacket slung over his shoulder and slogans like "I believe in a hand up, not a hand out" on his lips, Beatty's Bulworth could probably parachute into the current California gubernatorial race and end up on top.

The Bulworth we actually meet, however, is not this paragon of confidence. Rather it's an exhausted-looking man in the middle of a nervous breakdown, someone whose personal life has degenerated into a charade and whose professional work has become a series of cave-ins to wealthy special interests.

So disgusted is Bulworth with himself that he acquires large amounts of life insurance from a corrupt lobbyist (Paul Sorvino) and contacts a man known only as Vinnie (Richard Sarafian) for what is euphemistically called "a weekend research project." Sick of it all, Bulworth has gone and hired someone to take his life.

Marking time back in Los Angeles, making his usual "we stand at the doorstep of a new millennium" campaign speech to a black audience at the First A.M.E. church, Bulworth is suddenly stricken, like Jim Carrey in "Liar, Liar" with the compulsion to tell the truth.

After outraging his African American supporters by blandly announcing that their community will never be treated seriously by politicians unless they either vote or contribute more money, Bulworth next appears at a fund-raiser composed mainly of wealthy Jews in show business, where he asks how such smart people can turn out so many stupid motion pictures.

Being Peck's naughty but honest boy turns out to be a balm to Bulworth's soul, and he starts to reconsider whether life is worth living after all. The fact that the stunning Nina (Halle Berry) has unaccountably attached herself to Bulworth after his A.M.E. speech doesn't hurt the senator's will to live either.

The reason "Bulworth" is more engaging than expected is Beatty's good-humored willingness to look completely silly. Whether it's engaging in classic pratfalls like walking into poles and slipping into pools or wandering through scenes in faux-rapper outfits complete with wool cap and baggy shorts, the actor reveals a gift for slapstick and self-parody that has not always been apparent.

The heart of this willingness to play the fool is the new Bulworth's determination to speak as much as possible in amusing rap-type rhymes, something that seriously disconcerts the senator's all-business staff, played by Oliver Platt, Jack Warden and Joshua Malina.

What gives "Bulworth" its unique character is that all this silliness is periodically punctuated by cogent, carefully thought-out mini-manifestos about such serious issues as the state of African American leadership, why health care costs so much and how those in power have always tried to drive a wedge between the poor of all races.

It is surprising to hear commentary like this in any kind of Hollywood picture, let alone a comedy. But even though Beatty makes sure these sound bites are delivered in a glib, antic manner engineered to be audience-friendly, their presence is too awkward to mix well with the slapstick. The audacity of the concept carries things along for a while, but, as "Bulworth's" peculiar ending points up, it is far from a seamless weld.

What is most fascinating about "Bulworth" (co-written by Jeremy Pikser) is how personal a film this is, how many Beatty-specific agendas it covers, from reinventing himself (via use of a rap soundtrack and a co-star like Berry) for a younger audience to expressing sincerely held political frustrations. Imagine Barbra Streisand interrupting "Yentl" for some pithy remarks about the N.R.A. and you'll get some idea of what's going on here.

It is also fascinating to see how cannily Beatty covers all his bases. Do you think Berry is too young to be a romantic interest? Bulworth makes sure to say the same thing himself. And anyone troubled that a film that says more than most about the plight of the black underclass still has to resort to urban stereotypes to get laughs will be brought up short by the presence of veteran writer-activist Amiri Baraka as a shaman-type figure.

Frequently awkward, peppered with moments that make you shake your head, "Bulworth's" singular nature makes it a film that can't be shrugged off. If Beatty, Robert Redford, Jack

Nicholson, Julia Roberts and others of their stature got together and set up a Big Star Sundance, this could be the opening night film.

NEW YORK, 5/18/98, p. 51, David Denby

At the beginning of *Bulworth*, Warren Beatty's thrillingly dangerous political comedy, the campaign smile of Senator Jay Billington Bulworth has collapsed into a grimace. Running for re-election in California, the senator (Beatty) has fallen into a hapless funk. In his dreary Washington office, as rain falls on the windows and uneaten pizza pies lie moldering all around him, he looks at his campaign ads in horror. "We stand at the doorstep of a new millennium...the ads begin, resounding with a Clintonian efflorescence of nothingness. The senator is a former sixties liberal with pictures of Bobby Kennedy on his wall. He even has pictures of the young Warren Beatty on his wall. Yes, years ago, he hung out with Warren. But in recent days, Bulworth has been attacking "welfare cheaters" and taking up other modishly conservative positions, and now, guilty and convictionless, he stands for nothing at all. In his office he makes a corrupt deal with an insurance-industry lobbyist: Bulworth will thwart a certain piece of legislation injurious to insurance interests in return for a $10 million policy payable to his daughter. When the lobbyist leaves, the senator, in utter misery, hires a professional hit man. Alas, poor Bulworth! He hasn't eaten, slept, or shaved in days; he can't stand the sight of himself on TV; and he's going to commit suicide.

The rest of *Bulworth*, I suppose, can be seen as a morally ambitious variant of *Liar Liar*, in which Jim Carrey, a career lawyer, is forced by a magic spell to tell the truth. Exhausted and nearly hallucinatory, Bulworth goes so far into his suicidal depression that he bums right through it and is delivered into a skittish, giddy exhilaration—a state of joy balanced on a rapier-point of terror. He's going to die—what has he got to lose? In the final days of his campaign, he races around California telling off his constituents. *Bulworth*, which Beatty directed and also wrote (with Jeremy Pikser and—uncredited—Aaron Sorkin) turns into wild, disorderly farce, mean and reckless, with an element of lethal uneasiness churning beneath the comedy. In a Los Angeles church, Bulworth tells a black audience that the Democratic Party won't take them seriously until they "put down that malt liquor and chicken wings"; no, not until they stop supporting a running back who murdered his wife and start contributing money to the party. His candor is not only annihilating, it's self-annihilating. Bulworth attacks the Jews who run the movie business ("It's funny how lousy your stuff is. I guess the money turns everything to crap") before an audience of Jews who run the movie business. He becomes an insult comic without malice; the words burst out of him, not with anger but in a friendly, almost happy way, as if he were only saying what everyone knows to be true. He has become a holy fool—in political terms, an idiot; a man without guile.

The movie is a comedy, but Warren Beatty has set off an explosion beneath the thick, insulated floorboards of American politics. *Bulworth* goes well beyond the usual late-night-TV attack on political correctness: It says that our politics are now so completely devoted to propitiatory lies that anyone who speaks candidly would have to be—by definition—half-crazy. Here is a populist left-wing movie, the first in years, and it offers its protest over the abandonment of liberalism not in the pained, earnest tones of, say, an editorial in *The Nation*, but as a blast of craziness and scorn. The movie is a scandal, an outrage—and irresistibly entertaining.

At the black church, Bulworth catches the eye of a beautiful young woman, Nina (Halle Berry). She crowds into his limo with two raucous girl rappers, and they all wind up, with Bulworth's flustered campaign aide (Oliver Platt) in tow, at a druggy black club somewhere in Los Angeles. Beatty turns to the comedy of white discomfort. He gets stoned, dances (clumsily) with Halle Berry; Bulworth doesn't quite have the beat, but he's too far gone to know how much he's missing it. "Is you a real nigger?" one of the club's less friendly inhabitants inquires. "Is you?" says Bulworth, dancing into the guy's face. Enjoying himself now, he no longer wants to die and tries to call off the hit. But he sees thugs shadowing him everywhere, and he's constantly throwing himself to the floor to avoid imagined gunshots. With a skittering little run, he flees the scene, and the entire media and political world runs after him. In form (and in form only), the movie becomes a goofy chase comedy—not all that different from something starring Dean Martin and Jerry Lewis or Bob Hope from decades ago. But the emotional tonalities are dark and threatening. As Beatty runs, we're pitched right into his excitement and his fear. We know that Bulworth is going too far, that the movie is also going too far, and that there's no turning back.

Nothing Beatty has directed in the past *(Heaven Can Wait, Reds, Dick Tracy)* has prepared us for this kind of dizzying momentum—though, of course, Beatty as producer and star was the guiding force behind the most famous farce of the seventies, *Shampoo.* That movie was an attack on political and sexual hypocrisy; this one attacks Clintonian mush-mouth rhetoric and big money's influence on politics. But, as ever, Beatty's rebellion is joyously eccentric and hedonistic—he's an entertainer with political ideas, not a slumming moralist. Senator Bulworth may turn on and drop out, but the spirit of the movie owes less to the sanctimonious sixties counterculture than to the sixties literary rebel Norman Mailer, who wrote two books in that decade, *The American Dream* (fiction) and *The Armies of the Night* (nonfiction), in which a man at the end of his tether bursts through the usual bourgeois restraints, commits crimes, falls in with low company, and seeks redemption. Beatty and Mailer celebrate the perilous spree of self-destruction and self-renewal; *Bulworth* offers Mailer's dread and liberating shenanigans without the metaphysical pretensions.

Despite his off-screen legend as a supremely confident seducer, Beatty has usually played sheepish, fumbling, and confused men in the movies—the impotent Clyde Barrow, the dreamer McCabe, the woman-bedeviled Bugsy Siegel. As Bulworth, he registers ten varieties of puzzlement; his quizzical, off-center delivery takes the righteousness out of the lines. He's a man amazed by his own transformation—his manner says, "What's next? Show me." Led by Halle Berry (who has never been more beautiful), he falls into the malign wonderland of the black underclass; he takes up with gangsters and even baby gangsters (homies) in South Central Los Angeles, the very people (in this telling) who have been both abandoned by liberalism and blamed for shifts in the economy not of their own making. The movie mixes white guilt with the old admiration of blacks for their alleged greater sexual confidence, their ease with their own bodies, with language, with violence. The combination of guilt and admiration would be sickly and dumb if it weren't pulled off with such rueful comic candor. Beatty is not a liberal of the high-minded variety who would like to believe that blacks are the same as everyone else, only more deserving. The movie doesn't turn its poor black characters into innocents. They may be soulful, but they have been hurt, even corrupted, by their social defeat—that's the bitter point.

Dressed like a homie in knit cap and shorts, Bulworth, as pixilated as a character out of *A Midsummer Night's Dream,* wanders into a TV station and recites his diatribe against big money in rhyming rap stanzas ("As long as you can pay, I'll do it all your way," etc.). Halle Berry lectures him on the collapse of manufacturing in the inner cities—it has to be the strangest romantic banter ever heard in a movie—and he turns that into rap, too. Beatty obviously means us to believe that rap is the language of protest, of social truth; I think he underestimates the amount of posing and commercial calculation in rap, but this is not a movie one should take too literally. Beatty's excitement in speaking his mind is all but incendiary: That a white politician could say what he thinks only in rap lyrics has to be the weirdest, funniest experiment in downward mobility since Preston Sturges deposited a rich director among hoboes in *Sullivan's Travels.* It's white-guy rap—pronounced slowly enough so that even the editorial writers of the *Wall Street Journal* can hear it. *Bulworth* is already a media sensation. It would be nice to think that its tormented but gleeful jokes will attract a large audience. Now that would be a *real* sensation.

NEW YORK POST, 5/15/98, p. 45, Rod Dreher

According to "Bulworth" and its auteur Warren Beatty, there's nothing wrong with America that socialized medicine, income redistribution, free airtime for political candidates and an interracial orgy can't fix. Got that? What's more, Beatty, a 61-year-old white guy, raps, and has a gorgeous young inner-city fly girl fall in love with his wrinkled cracker self.

It's a science-fiction movie, I think.

A mind is a terrible thing to lose, but in this movie, Beatty has just about done it. His "Bulworth" is an audacious, highly original attempt to critique contemporary American politics, but one ultimately wasted by its preachiness, dramatic incoherence and infantile limousine leftism.

Written (with Jeremy Pikser) by, directed by and starring Beatty, "Bulworth" is a satire about a veteran U. S. senator, J. Billington Bulworth, a Clinton-style Democrat who, in a fit of self-loathing over how he's sold out his liberal principles to stay in office, suffers a breakdown.

He takes out a mob contract on his own life, and heads home to Los Angeles for a final campaign swing. Babbling and foaming (think of The Great Cornholio as a "Crossfire" guest) Bulworth loses all discretion. Having nothing to lose, he begins telling his constituents what he really thinks.

Freed from the doublespeak required of American politicians, Bulworth feels reinvigorated, and decides he doesn't want to die after all. He spends the movie dashing around making outrageous speeches and avoiding his killer. Along for the rambunctious ride are his nervous chief of staff (a hilarious Oliver Platt) and Nina (Halle Berry), a sexy homegirl who Viagras the senator's exhausted libido with a sizzling nightclub dance number.

After a terrific half hour, the movie disintegrates when the uptight senator begins morphing into a gangsta rapper. Beatty can't rap, but that's the comic point, and its refreshing to see the notoriously vain playboy make fun of himself.

But from the moment when the senator gets misty-eyed and nostalgic for the visionary leadership of Black Panther thug Huey Newton, "Bulworth" sharply divides its audience. It's either a brave *cri de coeur* of the '60s Left, heartbroken over what's happened to liberalism, or it's the last pitiful gasp of radical chic.

Though Beatty slams some richly deserving targets—the insurance industry, big media, cynical politicians, lousy movies—the alternative he offers is romanticized silliness. Beatty advances, for example the Great Society idea that chronic social problems would disappear if more taxpayer money were thrown at them. What's new, pussycat? Not much.

In a telling scene, the film has two straw-men white L.A. cops harass a gang of crack-selling, gun-toting black children. Bulworth sticks up for the kids, naturally, but the moment turns cheap and ugly. Nobody's going to argue that racist cops are anything but a disgrace. But come on, are bigoted patrolmen a greater threat to inner-city than drug-dealing children packing heat?

"F---your mama, you f---ing pig crackers," are the words screenwriter Beatty puts into the mouth of a child, insulting a policeman. Beautiful. The next time Warren Beatty needs police assistance in his fancy-pants neighborhood, it'll serve him right if the cops remember this.

"Bulworth" does have its moments, and despite its politics, would be worth recommending if it were only cleverer and more consistently amusing. See Michael Moore's "Roger & Me" for an example of how to sell a radical populist message by making it a rib-tickling kick to watch.

Granted, the movie will utterly delight people who share the movie star's unreconstructed '60s radicalism (Greenwich Village, this one's for you). It recalls Abraham Lincoln's line about spiritualism: "For those who like that sort of thing, I should think it is just the sort of thing they would like."

NEWSDAY, 5/15/98, Part II/p. B2, Jack Mathews

The Hollywood political movie is such a rarity in the play-it-safe '90s that the release of three of them within five months of each other would seem to transcend mere coincidence and qualify as a plague of economic self-destruction.

What fools Barry Levinson and New Line ("Wag the Dog"), Mike Nichols and Universal ("Primary Colors"), and Warren Beatty and 20th Century Fox ("Bulworth") be to think there's a viable audience for political soul-searching in America. Even with spoonfuls of parody, satire and, in the case of "Bulworth," outright farce, moviegoers may find this unpleasantly serious medicine.

We'll see if Beatty has more luck. Despite great reviews, "Wag the Dog" and "Primary Colors" have done only modest business, and Beatty's film is going head-to-head with "Godzilla."

However it does at the box office, Beatty deserves credit for having the audacity it takes to shove a personal political agenda down the throats of an audience, and for one of the most eccentrically funny and charming performances of his career.

Beatty, who conceived the story, co-wrote the script, and produced and directed, also stars as Jay Bulworth, a corrupt U.S. senator from California who, in the waning days of his re-election campaign, suffers a nervous breakdown, hires an assassin to kill him, and then takes a chaotic plunge into political straight talk, done mostly in rhyming rap, and, while trying to stay a step ahead of his unknown assassin, reinvents himself as pure American populist. He also falls in love with an angry, young, black woman (Halle Berry) with her own agenda.

"Bulworth" is a hilariously crazy movie on the surface, with the senator ascending mountains while seemingly digging himself into a hole. When we meet him, he hasn't eaten or slept in days, and is plotting his own death, leveraging a $10-million life insurance policy from a lobbyist (Paul Sorvino) and negotiating with a mobster (Paul Sarafian) for his own execution.

Once that contract is made, Bulworth is liberated. Suddenly, he's throwing away his prepared speech of campaign platitudes and venting on his audiences the corrupting realities of politics and the suckerism of the public. Why hasn't he kept his promises to the black community, he's asked at a church meeting in South Central Los Angeles. Because blacks didn't contribute much money to his campaign, he tells them, and because they frankly have no choice but to vote for a Democrat.

Bulworth goes on to insult Hollywood Jews at a sessions with contributors in Beverly Hills, and, to their faces, indicts lobbyists for corrupting the political system by buying votes that raise the profit margins in industry at the expense of the health and well-being of the public. Presumably, it's Bulworth's complicity in the process that has driven him to the brink, and it's his compulsive disavowal of it that brings him back.

Beatty, cashing in an IOU that Fox gave him when it rejected "Dick Tracy," reportedly pitched "Bulworth" to the studio as a film about a senator who buys a contract on himself, then changes his mind. And that is the chassis upon which the story is built. The euphoria of confession has made the senator's life worth living, and in the broad stroke, "Bulworth" is a conventional comedy chase movie.

But that's the only convention observed. "Bulworth" takes sharp aim at everything that Fox godhead Rupert Murdoch represents, the power of the rich to maintain the disproportionate spread of wealth, and of the profit-driven media empires to define the issues of public debate.

Occasionally, the dialogue in "Bulworth" sounds just like that. But more often, it's done in a white man's version of hip-hop rap. Beatty's wildest conceit here is taking Bulworth into the ghetto, as an irrepressibly clownish emissary of Bobby Kennedy liberalism. With his flustered aides and a C-Span film crew in tow, he spends a night of drunken, drugged revelry in an after-hours bar in South Central, and later ends tip on the streets outside, in full rap regalia—baggy pants, tennies and sunglasses—jiving the locals with extemporaneous policy rhymes, and rescuing black kids from racist white cops.

The odds of a middle-class white man's dressing and talking like that in the inner city and coming away a hero, as Bulworth does, are about the same as the odds of winning the lottery. And this is where Beatty's ambitions get the best of him. The scenes are very funny, in a kind of "I can't believe he's doing this" sort of way, but their over-the-top silliness undermines the film's serious concerns.

Still, "Bulworth" is a terrifically entertaining piece of counterprograming for this politically correct decade, and the fun that Beatty, looking younger than he should for a man of 60, clearly had in making it is enough to win my vote.

NEWSWEEK, 5/18/98, p. 70, David Ansen

Warren Beatty has been famous for almost 40 years. Stardom, which has allowed him access to the major corridors of American power, is not just the atmosphere he floats in: it's his subject. What links almost all the roles he's played in the movies he's produced or directed is celebrity. His characters always have one eye on the public, and the public returns the gaze. Some may be real people—the bank robber Clyde Barrow in "Bonnie and Clyde," for whom fame was as arousing as Viagra; the revolutionary John Reed in "Reds," or mobster Bugsy Siegel in "Bugsy." Some have been fictional, such as the legendary crime-stopper "Dick Tracy," the pro quarterback in "Heaven Can Wait," the ex-quarterback turned TV host in "Love Affair" or even George the hairdresser in "Shampoo," a star in the bedrooms of Beverly Hills. But all these Beatty heroes are in pursuit of, or retreat from, the limelight.

Perhaps having been a star so long, Beatty can't imagine telling a story that unfolds in a purely private universe. But if his heroes are celebrities, they are not necessarily heroic, larger than life—or even outgoing. What other movie star has such a reticent, skittish presence on screen? Beatty the actor projects inwardness, hesitation, a self-consciousness that flirts with narcissism.

But Beatty the filmmaker is, to borrow a phrase from his childhood, "outer-directed," an observer and student of history and politics. His curiosity about the workings of power has made him the rare American director with an overt political agenda. Which brings us to his nervy farce "Bulworth," in which the public and private Beatty team up for a startlingly personal cry from the liberal heart.

Once again he plays a public figure—the Democratic senator from California, Jay Bulworth. In the midst of an election campaign, this lapsed idealist, now in the pocket of corporate lobbyists, mentally unravels. Taking a contract out on his own life, the unhinged candidate proceeds to make his appointed campaign rounds—but instead of emitting the usual high-minded gas, out of his mouth issue rude, uncensored truths about politics, race, the media and money. In an anarchic TV debate, he insults not just his rival politicians but the TV journalists who feed from the same corporate trough. "It's a club," he announces. "Let's have a drink!"

"Bulworth" is a comedy, of course, but not one that can be easily laughed off. Like Bulworth, Beatty the director and co-writer (with Jeremy Pikser) is throwing caution to the wind, producing a genuinely political movie in an era deeply suspicious of political passion. Savaging Hollywood, as well as Washington, Beatty then compounds the risk by sending his discombobulated hero into the inner city for a crash course in socioeconomic consciousness-raising. Acquiring soul from the brothers and sisters, the runaway politician, swear to God, begins to rap. "Bulworth" is a singular summer movie in many ways; it's certainly the only one in which the hero speaks in verse for half the movie.

The audience at "Bulworth" may find itself startled—not just by the senator's hilarious lapses into the politically incorrect, but at the chutzpah of Beatty's fusion of knock-about farce and unrepentant political didacticism. The movie might have been overbearing if Beatty weren't smart enough to make fun of himself at every opportunity. "How old do you think I am?" the vain candidate asks his love interest, the much younger Nina (Halle Berry), prepared for a flattering low-ball reply. "Sixty," comes the mincingly accurate reply. Bulworth's meltdown, and the panicky attempt of his chief handler (a terrific Oliver Platt) to find political method in his boss's madness, is wonderfully demented satire. "Bulworth" gets off to a fast, funny, sure-footed start. The plot device of a guy's hiring his own assassin—and then changing his mind when he falls in love—may be an old standby (there's even a just-released *Ukrainian* movie, "A Friend of the Deceased," with that premise), but it hardly matters because Beatty tosses it off so lightly. But when the movie takes us on its seriocomic tour of South-Central L.A., Beatty's touch grows more earnest—and clumsy. How are we supposed to take Jay Bulworth? One minute he's used as a vehicle to express the ugly, money-grubbing, racist id of political life; then he's a Chauncey Gardner-like blank screen who parrots the political lessons he learns from Nina or from a smart but evil drug dealer (Don Cheadle). Then he seems to be a genuine political hero, whose soul-stirring speeches have the power to transform that same drug dealer (in the movie's most embarrassing Capra-cornish moment) into a community activist. Beatty invests Bulworth with considerable frazzled charm; nonetheless, he's such a crazy quilt of traits and ideas that one is baffled when Nina falls for him: even by farce standards, it seems a stretch.

A dizzying mixture of the sophisticated and the naive, the deft and the clumsy, "Bulworth" is overstuffed, excessive, erratic—and essential. No other Hollywood movie raising these issues, or puncturing so gleefully the conservative pieties of our day (like, for example, the truism that business is more efficient than government). There should be something in it to provoke and annoy just about everybody, right and left, black and white. Just as surely as there is something in it to make just about everybody laugh.

SIGHT AND SOUND, 2/99, p. 40, Richard Kelly

1996, the eve of US primary elections. Jay Bulworth, Democratic senator for California, promises lobbyist Graham Crockett he will obstruct a healthcare bill in return for $10 million of life insurance. Intending to provide for his family, Bulworth contracts his own assassination with mobster Vinnie. At a South Central Los Angeles church, Bulworth abandons his campaign speech to tell the black congregation that the Democratic Party disdains them. Outside, he is intrigued by a young woman, Nina. At a Hollywood party, he denounces the film industry. Bulworth feels revitalised. He accompanies Nina to a rap club, but fears his assassin is pursuing him.

At a fundraiser the next day, Bulworth 'raps' a tirade against big business to an appalled audience. Bulworth decides to cancel his assassination, but is thwarted by Vinnie's death. Bulworth is unaware that Nina is his contracted killer. During a television debate, Bulworth lambasts the networks and alienates Crockett. His aide Murphy sabotages proceedings but realises Bulworth's outspoken approach is impressing people. Bulworth hides out with Nina's family. Wearing hip-hop clothes, Bulworth gives a controversial television interview. Afterwards, he and Nina are cornered by the 'assassin'—actually a paparazzo. Back at Nina's, she confesses her secret, but lets him live. Bulworth wins the election, and the media descend on Nina's home. She and Bulworth kiss before the cameras; but he is shot dead, the bullet coming from a vantage where Crockett was lurking moments earlier.

Just how much of a Marxist is Warren Beatty? Perhaps this question has never detained younger film fans, who might know Beatty only as a semi-legendary seducer and the perpetrator of *Dick Tracy* (1990). But consider the red thread political thread which runs through his acting credits alone: *Bonnie and Clyde* (1967) and *McCabe & Mrs. Miller* (1971), *The Parallax View* (1974) and *Shampoo* (1975), *Bugsy* (1991) and (yes) *Ishtar* (1987), Beatty has always professed a certain idea of the Left, and he has the cuttings to prove it. Prominent amid Bulworth's set-dressing are authentic snapshots of Beatty with Robert Kennedy and Huey P. Newton: incompatible ghosts of a radical past. Beatty was a vigorous cheerleader for George McGovern in 1972, and throughout the 80s he counselled Gary Hart, albeit to little obvious avail. Between these engagements, he was a charismatic incarnation of John Reed in *Reds* (1981), extolling Bolshevism to the American proletariat.

Now, here's *Bulworth,* a polemical assault on present US political torpor. As with *Reds,* Beatty wears the Wellesian mantle of star-writer-producer-director. "What animated Hollywood in the 70s," Beatty recently opined, "was politics. You can mark the end of that with the election of Carter. There's nothing that can destroy the Democratic Party like a Democrat." American leftists have swallowed this poisonous lesson for several decades now, so it comes as quite a thrill when, midway through *Bulworth,* Beatty's campaigning senator throws down an unfashionable gauntlet: "Lemme hear that dirty word—socialism!"

Bulworth's fundamental plank—that the Republican and Democratic Parties are bankrolled by the same venal corporate elite—is a numbing truism. Bulworth, mortally ashamed of his part in this puppet-show, abandons the 'bipartisan' drivel of his stump speeches (Clintonoid-Blairesque staples such as "I believe in a hand-up, not a hand-out") and becomes a holy fool. Initially, he can muster only a stream of 'incautious' remarks—impoverished blacks should lay off the malt liquor, Hollywood's "Big Jews" should quit churning out garbage—seemingly tailored by Beatty to generate nervous laughter in the cinemas. But gradually, the road of 'politically incorrect' excess leads Bulworth to radical wisdom, and he bites the hand of the corporate oligarchy which has sustained him.

Naturally, being a Beatty hero, Bulworth is doomed—much like *The Parallax View*'s patsy journalist Joe Frady. But *Bulworth* has bigger fish to indict than the conspiratory phantom that was the Parallax Organisation. Here, real menace is revealed, in the precise form of those profiteers from the US medical-insurance racket. Lurking behind these scoundrels, *Bulworth* implies, is the present Democratic incumbent of the oval office. Clinton slouched to power in 1992 pledging to deliver universal healthcare, and so abolish the strict fee-for-service fiddle which does such violence to the United States' poor. But he capitulated, shamefully, before the bullish lobbying of the insurance industry.

So where stands the *Bulworth* ticket on healthcare? In the film's linchpin scene, Bulworth publicly rebukes his insurance paymasters, calling for a single-payer, socialised national health system. Facing down the tissue-thin consensus that governments are best run like private corporations *Bulworth* makes a stirring case statism: "You think these pigs are gonna regulate themselves?" asks the senator.

Bulworth's wrangles with race are a bit trickier. Admirably, Beatty has argued that class is a more formidable social partition than skin colour. Nevertheless, his movie is possessed by a very Los Angelean notion that the US suffers from a specific Black Problem, compounded of drugs, guns and inveterate gangsterism. But *Bulworth* is also suggestive of the Democratic Party's very own Problem With Blacks. In the 70s, its hierarchs abandoned the legacy of the civil-rights movement. Twice in the 80s, Jesse Jackson offered the Party a populist "Rainbow Coalition", with himself as its chieftain. But Jackson was deemed (politely speaking) "unelectable"—as opposed to Walter Mondale and Michael Dukakis, of whom history, already, remembers nothing. Small wonder, then, that Bulworth informs a South Central congregation that his Party "pretty much forgot" about blacks.

Yet Beatty shows Bulworth to be redeemed by a dose of black urban culture, embodied in Halle Berry's exquisite Nina. He becomes a connoisseur of chicken wings, Philly blunts, and "the nappy dug-out", and delivers his polemics in tortuous rap. All of this might be risible, were it not for a flabbergasting scene where Bulworth, alone at last with Nina, muses over the spirit of Huey Newton, and the absence of "black leaders". Just as we fear Warren is about to offer a personal reminiscence, Nina cuts in to inform him that her mother was a Panther, that the 'leaders' Bulworth frets about were mostly rubbed out by Nixon's damnable Cointelpro operation; and that the malaise of Black America stems from the decline of post-war manufacturing, which provided such vigorous foot-soldiers for civil rights. Dispute that last thesis if you wish, but only John Sayles has served up such brazen dialectical materialism in recent American cinema.

If one wished to cavil: Beatty's highly accomplished visual triumvirate (cinematographer Vittorio Storaro, designer Dean Tavoularis, costumer Milena Canonero) may have given the film too polished a veneer. Throughout, there's a fairly central-casting conception of 'coloured folk'. At one point, Bulworth humiliates a racist LAPD cop, which resembles nothing so much as Beatty collecting a debt on behalf of Rodney King. And Bulworth's heroics are accompanied by too many shots of 'I-like-what-the-man-says' expressions on beaming black faces. Nevertheless, Beatty has once again taken handsome advantage of his Hollywood clout to make a film of dissenting intelligence. He leaves us with a turn from playwright Amiri Baraka, as a panhandler with a gift for muttering ominous oaths. This type of character is already shop-worn from liberal Hollywood pictures such as *Grand Canyon*. But Baraka's words have resonance: "You gotta be a spirit, Bulworth. You can't be no ghost." This clarion call to political engagement splendidly caps one of the best films to emerge from a Hollywood studio in the 90s.

VILLAGE VOICE, 5/19/98, Film Special/p. 131, Amy Taubin

Do you think Warren Beatty's womanizing compulsion was aggravated by a secret fear that he looked like Nixon? You may remember the shot in *Shampoo* where Beatty stands for a long time in front of Nixon's bejowled puss. Was he daring us to notice a resemblance that nearly 25 years later is as obvious as the ski-jump nose on his face?

Because film speaks in a language of faces, what *Shampoo* suggests about fleeting beauty and the ineffable difference between an attractive man and a repellent one is not insignificant. But it's only one of many prophecies embedded in a movie that passed itself off as a bubbly bedroom farce but that today looks like one of Hollywood's most subtle social and political satires. Made in 1975 but set in 1968, *Shampoo* looks back on Nixon's election as the crucial nail in the coffin of the '60s.

Like *Shampoo, Bulworth* takes place on the eve of an election, but as befits the times, its view of the body politic is even bleaker. Directed, cowritten, and coproduced by Beatty, who also starts, it's a less elegant film than *Shampoo*, but it's also a lot more risky. This may have something to do with the fact that Hal Ashby, who directed *Shampoo*, wasn't around to keep Beatty's unconscious from leaking all over every scene, and even more to do with the fact that, today, South Central makes the denizens of Beverly Hills more nervous and guilt ridden than Watts did 30 years ago when it went up in flames.

A once progressive politician now totally owned by fat-cat campaign contributors, Senator Jay Billington Bulworth (Beatty) is a slimy mess of a man. Consumed by self-loathing, he takes out a hit on his own life. But the imminence of death has a liberating effect on Bulworth. Soon he finds himself irrepressibly laying it on the line for a black church congregation. do they wonder why the Democratic Party doesn't care about the African American community? "It doesn't care because you don't contribute," he says, relishing the shocked expressions on the faces gazing up at him. Once the tongue loosens, the dick is sure to follow. "Let's call a spade a spade," Bulworth quips blithely, his eye drifting to a beautiful black woman (Halle Berry) who's enigmatically sucking on a lollipop.

Overnight, Bulworth becomes black-identified, turning his campaign rhetoric into rap songs, exchanging his boring dark suits for a gangbanger's baggy shorts and knit cap, and waxing nostalgic for Huey Newton with the mysterious black woman whom he has major hots for and whose political line about the necessity of building the economic base of the inner city he embraces as his own. But having thus rediscovered his zest for life (and with his poll numbers skyrocketing), he's at a loss for how to shake the assassin on his tail.

Raucous, unpredictably paced, self-conscious, and superarticulate, *Bulworth* is the most overtly liberal political movie to come out of Hollywood in many a long year. It basically says that without campaign finance reform, socialized medicine, freedom of the airwaves, and a more suitable distribution of money and power, we are doomed. Beatty manages to lay that out quite rationally within the framework of a movie that's anything but rational" *Bulworth* is couched as the desperate redemption fantasy of a '60s sellout on the verge of suicide.

Opening on a semicomatose Beatty twisting in his office chair, his face scrunched into a hideous hybrid of Nixon and Nicholson, the movie plunges us into Bulworth's psyche and never let us out. It's a '60s psyche, which finds in Wilhelm Reich the cure for racism. "Everyone's got to keep fucking everyone until they're all the same color," says Bulworth, talking with his dick while looking for approval from the taboo object of his affection.

What makes Bulworth's embarrassing, not to mention inescapably racist, embrace of African American 'tude so hilarious is Beatty's performance, a comic tour de force that should make Jim Carrey writhe with envy. There's nothing so absurd as the spectacle of a control freak who's overcome with the impulse to let it all hang out, or a member of the ruling class identifying with the disenfranchised while squirming around to hold on to his power.

Let's put it this way: even if the last thing you want to see is a movie driven by some stupid white guy's guilt and confusion about race and sex, you can't hate *Bulworth* as much as Rupert Murdoch undoubtedly does. Murdoch's company, 20th Century Fox, seems committed to burying the movie through benign neglect (much as Disney did with *Kundun*). So buy a ticket and savor the capitalist contradiction. You can't slap Murdoch in the face without putting money in his pocket.

Also reviewed in:
CHICAGO TRIBUNE, 5/22/98, Friday/p. A, Mark Caro
NATION, 6/15 & 22/98, p. 32, Stuart Klawans
NEW REPUBLIC, 6/8/98, p. 24, Stanley Kauffmann
NEW YORK TIMES, 5/15/98, p. E19, Janet Maslin
VARIETY, 5/11-17/98, p. 57, Todd McCarthy
WASHINGTON POST, 5/22/98, p. F1, Stephen Hunter
WASHINGTON POST, 5/22/98, Weekend/p. 20, Michael O'Sullivan

BUTCHER BOY, THE

A Warner Bros, release of a Geffen Pictures production with support and investment incentives for the Irish film industry. *Executive Producer:* Neil Jordan. *Producer:* Redmond Morris and Stepehn Woolley. *Director:* Neil Jordan. *Screenplay:* Neil Jordan and Patrick McCabe. *Based on the novel by:* Patrick McCabe. *Director of Photography:* Adrian Biddle. *Editor:* Tony Lawson. *Music:* Elliot Goldenthal. *Music Editor:* Michael Connell. *Sound:* Kieran Horgan, Brendan Deasy and (music) Steve McLaughlin. *Sound Editor:* Eddy Joseph. *Casting:* Susie Figgis. *Production Designer:* Anthony Pratt. *Art Director:* Anna Rackard. *Set Decorator:* Josie MacAvin. *Costumes:* Sandy Powell. *Make-up:* Morag Ross. *Stunt Coordinator:* Patrick Condren. *Running time:* 106 minutes. *MPAA Rating:* R.

CAST: Stephen Rea (Da Brady);   Fiona Shaw (Mrs. Nugent);   Eamonn Owens (Francie Brady);   Alan Boyle (Joe Purcell);   Niall Buggy (Father Dom);   Brendan Gleeson (Father Bubbles);   Peter Gowen (Leddy); Stuart Graham (Priest at College);   Ian Hart (Uncle Alo); Tom Hickey (Gardener);   Sean Hughes and Gerard McSorley (Psychiatrists);   John Kavanagh

(Dr. Boyd);   Rosaleen Linehan (Mrs. Canning);   Pat McGrath (Farmer on Tractor);   Sean McGinley (Sergeant);   Gina Moxley (Mary); Sinéad O'Connor (Our Lady/Colleen);   Ardal O'Hanlon (Mr. Purcell);   Milo O'Shea (Father Sullivan);   Aisling O'Sullivan (Ma Brady); Anita Reeves (Mrs. Coyle);   Andrew Fullerton (Phillip Nugent);   Anne O'Neill (Mrs. McGlone); Joe Pilkington (Charlie McGlone); Jer O'Leary (Dublin Man); Pat Leavy (Dublin Café Woman); Janet Moran (Dublin Shopkeeper); Páraic Breathnach (Man on Lorry); John Olohan (Mr. Nugent);   Mikel Murfi (Buttsy);   Brendan Conroy (Devlin);   Gregg Fitzgerald, John Finnegan, Gavin Kelty, and Eoin Chaney (Bogmen).   Ciarán Owens and Shane O'Connor (Boys at Fountain);   Paolo Tullio (Mr. Caffolla);   Siobhan McElvaney and Aine McEneaney (Girls in Shooting Gallery);   Pat McCabe (Jimmy the Skite);   Tony Rohr (Bogman in Mental Hospital);   Birdy Sweeney (Man in Well);   Marie Mullen (Mrs. Thompson);   Macdara O'Fatharta (Alien Priest);   Ronan Wilmot (Policeman);   Vinnie McCabe (Detective);   Dermot Healy (Bogman in Hospital).

LOS ANGELES TIMES, 4/3/98, Calendar/p. 1, Kevin Thomas

Ireland's Neil Jordan has made some unforgettable movies, "Mona Lisa" and "The Crying Game," among them, but "The Butcher Boy" may just be his best.

Jordan is remarkable in his ability to reveal people's inner lives and the interaction between everyday life and an individual's imagination and driving passions. Never has this been more evident than in his unique and uniquely challenging film of Patrick McCabe's celebrated coming-of-age novel, which has been compared to "Catcher in the Rye" and "Huckleberry Finn."

To state that "The Butcher Boy" is about a 12-year-old small-town Irish boy with a demented mother and an alcoholic father inevitably suggests gloom and doom. The most amazing aspect of a consistently amazing film is that as dark as it gets, it is so exuberant, as irrepressible as its young hero, jaunty even to its deadliest moment. The combination of Jordan and McCabe results in humor emanating from even the direst of circumstances and deeds.

Maybe it's because the parents (Stephen Rea, Aisling O'Sullivan) would be free spirits by nature were they not tethered by their demons, for their son Francie (Eamonn Owens) is possessed by an indomitable, fearless spirit and a strong sense of humor. He's by nature quick-witted, outspoken, hearty, prankish and a fighter, and he has a characteristically Irish, poetic way with speech. He forever comes on too strong, as people lacking in a loving stability in their lives so often do.

The time is the early '60s, which is crucial in shaping Francie's sensibility and destiny. He and his best friend, Joe (Allan Boyle, a strong foil to the formidable Owens), are enraptured by comic book and TV heroes and '50s alien movies at a time when the U.S. is heading toward the Cuban missile crisis. Joe's a nice, ordinary kid who has no trouble distinguishing between fantasy and reality.

But all these influences, coupled with a serenely accepted Roman Catholicism, and a sad, isolating chain of events that overtakes Francie, fuel in him an apocalyptic vision that is expressed by Jordan and his gifted cameraman Adrian Biddle with a witty, poignant conviction. Fate, implacable and unjust, as usually it is, however, threatens to overwhelm a boy left alone in the world, faced with enemies that are at once real and imagined. The experience of aloneness that everyone knows at one time or another gives the film a sense of universality. Indeed, McCabe has reported that Francie's story has been said to show "the mask of unbearable sadness through the ages."

Francie's nemesis, who takes on cosmic significance in his imagination, is a neighbor (Fiona Shaw) who represents a killjoy sense of bourgeoise propriety so relentless and controlling that it reminds us anew of how destructive, how contagious, such individuals can be. Always the most resourceful and compelling of actresses, Shaw is at once funny and scary in her implacability.

Rea and O'Sullivan convey beautifully the ultimate sense of doom of the truly defeated, and Milo O'Shea plays a priest with bizarre demons of his own. Sinead O'Connor is the exquisite, loving but down-to-earth Virgin Mary of Francie's visions. Elliot Goldenthal's jazzy score is attuned perfectly to the film's quicksilver changes in mood and tone and incorporates pop standards in a startlingly apt way.

"The Butcher Boy" seems in every way a film destined to be a classic, faultlessly shaped, buoyant and idiosyncratic. It's a work of awesome power and passion with an often hilarious sense of absurdity in regard to the human condition. And in Eamonn Owens it has a youthful actor whose talent is clearly protean. Redheaded and freckled, he recalls Butch Jenkins, the most adorably real and natural of Hollywood's boy actors of the Golden Era, but Owens is capable of expressing a manic drive and outrage way beyond the ken of any vintage family epic.

NEW YORK, 4/13/98, p. 49, David Denby

At his best, Neil Jordan, the Irish writer-director who earlier made such wonderful films as *Mona Lisa* and *The Crying Game*, pushes realism into dreams—sometimes bad dreams—without quite losing the bedrock of actuality from which dreams are sprung. In *The Butcher Boy*, Jordan stays close to the most extreme fancies of his lead characters little boy fighting off misery. When the action of *The Butcher Boy* turns out to be all too literally true, we are shocked in a way that we rarely are at the movies.

Jordan's hero, the 12-year-old Francie Brady (Eamonn Owens), grows up in a small Irish town with a drunkard and liar for a father and a beautiful madwoman for a mother. The boy receives no guidance at all—just the fervent guilty nonsense of his dad (Stephen Rea), a forlorn trumpet player who never finishes a tune. Yet there's wild gaiety in *Butcher Boy*. The movie is based on a novel by Patrick McCabe and records a moment, in the early sixties, when Ireland was irradiated with the nuclear energy of American popular culture—TV and old movies, and the glittering American Irish, the Kennedys, conquering the New World. Francie and his close friend Joe put together a mental life that is part fantasy, part role-playing. They live by their games and oaths, yet Francie is not recessive; on the contrary, he's an irrepressible entertainer, a put-on artist surging in and out of rooms like a whirlwind. Little Eamonn Owens has a face like a big piece of pie—luscious red hair, avid eyes—and a mouth that won't stop, and the movie built around him goes like a fever. Jordan's direction is incisive and at times electrifying, with sudden outbreaks of violence—farce yielding to terror—that should warn us something bad is coming. Part of the ominousness is produced by sheer incomprehension. Much of the dialogue is delivered in the deep accents of County Monaghan, near the border with Northern Ireland, where Patrick McCabe grew up and Jordan shot the exteriors. I understood no more than half of what Eamonn Owens says, so I find myself in an embarrassing position: I *think* this is a great movie, but I'm not sure.

NEW YORK POST, 4/3/98, p. 50, Thelma Adams

"The Butcher Boy" is deeply shocking.

Director Neil Jordan's killer-coming-of-age story, co-written with Patrick McCabe, the author of the novel on which it's based, isn't shocking for the obvious reasons.

Yes, Pope-taunting rocker Sinead O'Connor plays the Virgin Mary—and says the "F' word. But her comforting portrayal of the Blessed Virgin is warm and welcome, fuzzy even, despite the profanity. She's a dream apparition at the center of a nightmare.

"The Butcher Boy" is no more shocking because it arrives in the wake of the Jonesboro, Ark., schoolyard massacre. Yes, it shows 12-year-old Francie Brady (convincing newcomer Eamonn Owens) armed with a pistol. But if that alone were mortifying, we'd have to recoil at "Lost in Space," which shows young Will Robinson with a futuristic Uzi programmed to respond to his command alone.

No, "The Butcher Boy" shocks because, like the classic "A Clockwork Orange," it's eye candy and heart poison. Jordan, the director of "The Crying Game" and "Interview With the Vampire," creates a velvet nightmare, a '60s small-town Ireland that is hallucinogenic in both its quaintness and claustrophobia.

At the story's center is freckle-faced bully Francie. At first he seems like a regular rake, playing wild Indians against a gorgeous green landscape with his best pal, Joe (Alan Boyle). We laugh at Francie's antics, his aggression, the blackly comic disparity between the redhead's narration of events and what's happening on screen.

But, soon, Francie is truly running amok (in the Malayan, murderous frenzy sense at the word's root). His father (Stephen Rea) is a drunk; his mother (Aisling O'Sullivan) is a suicidal manic depressive. Francie, after a turn in a Catholic reformatory, shock treatments and a part-time job in a slaughterhouse, vents his rage on nosy neighbor Mrs. Nugent (Fiona Shaw).

Where did this pug-nosed monster come from? Was it nurture or nature? The rise of TV and the threat of the atom bomb that cracked the isolation of his small hometown? Was it comic books and pop culture? Was it the absence of a stable mom and pop to guide him through adversity? Was he manic like his mother, brutal like his father?

Ultimately, we don't know. One minute we're laughing, and the next we're nauseated. We've spent two hours with a killer and we still don't recognize the face of evil. Next stop, Jonesboro.

NEWSDAY, 4/3/98, Part II/p. B11, Jack Mathews

It's a little eerie watching Irish director Neil Jordan's "The Butcher Boy" just days after the middle-school massacre in Arkansas.

What could drive a child to cold-blooded murder? a nation now asks itself, and while there are no direct parallels between the real and fictional events, the movie does shed light on the question.

Adapted by Jordan and Pat McCabe from McCabe's 1992 novel, "The Butcher Boy" is a troubling, highly original study of a child slipping into insanity. The story is told almost entirely through the boy's perspective, in a series of flashbacks accompanied by his own voice, speaking decades later and with no small nostalgia from a mental institution.

It's madness filtered through madness, and very little of the movie fits the events we're watching. The music doesn't underscore the danger brewing, it underscores the often sanguine delusions of 12-year-old Francie Brady (Eamonn Owens). The narrator's voice has a tone of lightness at odds with the boy's grotesque behavior. And moments of magical realism—among them, appearances by the Virgin Mary (Sinead O'Connor, if you can beat that)—that defy you to enjoy them.

The movie opens in a small Irish village in the early 1960s, the weird Cold War period where children were caught in a kind of cultural schizophrenia, being simultaneously enthralled by American television series and unsettled by warnings of nuclear holocaust. One moment, images of cowboys and Indians, the next, mushroom clouds. Playtime, feartime. Fantasy, reality. For Francie, the messages are further mixed by his circumstances. His father (Stephen Rea) is a depressed alcoholic, and his mother (Aisling O'Sullivan) is mentally ill and suicidal. Francie's response is to delve deeper and deeper into his fantasy life, through elaborate games with his one and only friend Joe (Alan Boyle), and by adopting as a surrogate father his Uncle Alo (Ian Hart).

When he begins to lose these people, to death and disillusionment, Francie acts out against the person he irrationally blames for all of his troubles, his busy-body neighbor Mrs. Nugent (Fiona Shaw), and becomes either the town hero (his view) or the town monster (everyone else's view).

Jordan, working on a smaller canvas after "Interview With the Vampire" and "Michael Collins," has taken a very daring approach with the material, and it's not always effective. The book may have gotten away with moments of black comedy, but the events are too gruesome and disturbing on film, and Francie is too toxic a figure, for the audience to feel a sense of comic relief. And fair warning: the dialect of the characters takes a keen ear.

But it's all worthwhile. "The Butcher Boy" is a haunting Greek tragedy, featuring a remarkably energetic and assured performance from novice actor Owens. The freckled, pudgy-faced redhead creates the immediate impression of Francie as the classic grade-school bully, and then takes him far beyond that. There's nothing really evil about Francie other than his deeds. He's a kid floundering in a moral vacuum, taking his behavioral cues from comic books and television, and protecting himself from pain by deferring it.

The role calls for a lot of heavy lifting. Francie is in and out of institutions, undergoes shock therapy, deals with parents who are beyond hope, and encounters betrayals in the most unlikely places. But Owens, who had never acted before, is up to the task, and has helped Jordan craft his best film since "The Crying Game."

NEWSWEEK, 4/13/98, p. 72, David Ansen

There's a racket going on inside the head of 12-year-old Francie Brady (Eamonn Owens), the exuberant, apple-cheeked and terrifying hero of Neil Jordan's "The Butcher Boy." Francie, who has at best a hit-or-miss relationship with reality, has retreated into a personal fantasy world fed by comic books, the TV show "The Fugitive" and the apocalyptic anxieties spawned by the Cuban missile crisis. In his daydreams, priests appear with the insectlike heads of space aliens, and the Virgin Mary (Sinead O'Connor) floats down from the sky to give him advice.

Francie has good reasons to prefer the carnival going on inside his head to the real world of his small Irish town in the early 1960s. His father, Benny (Stephen Rea), is a hopeless alcoholic; his ma (Aisling O'Sullivan), subject to nervous breakdowns, is in and out of the mental hospital. As his losses mount, he clings with fanatical devotion to his best friend, Joe (Alan Boyle), with whom he can act out his cowboy-and-Indian fantasies, and he turns all his rage onto the demonized figure of Mrs. Nugent (Fiona Shaw), his stuffy and meddlesome neighbor.

"The Butcher Boy," based on Patrick McCabe's novel, is a raucously sardonic black comedy about a boy's descent into madness and murderous rage.(That it opened the week after the schoolyard massacre in Jonesboro, Ark., is a chilling coincidence.) Young Owens, who had not acted professionally before, gives an alarmingly brilliant performance, pitched at a level of feverish adolescent energy that seems inspired by the nuclear explosions on Francie's black-and-white telly. Owens beguiles us with his manic Dennis the Menace charm, then sends a shiver of horror down our spines as he evolves, after a grotesquely hilarious stint in a Roman Catholic reform school, into a pint-size Jack the Ripper.

This is another high-wire act from the director of "The Crying Game," and Jordan pulls it off with savage virtuosity. Narrated by Francie as a grown man (the voice is Stephen Rea's), the movie traps us inside the antic and demented world view of its protagonist, a hysterical (in both senses) place to be. Like the novel, Jordan and McCabe's screenplay refuses to abandon its gallows humor even after its bloody descent into tragedy. Francie's manic energy can become exhausting, but Jordan's too good a filmmaker to lose his grip on the audience. Beautifully designed and shot, with a superb soundtrack that ranges from "Mack the Knife" to Sinatra's heartbreaking "Where Are You?" to Elliot Goldenthal's hauntingly jaunty score (shades of "The Third man" theme), "The Butcher Boy" takes us on a whirling trip inside an imagination running amok. It's an uncomfortable yet strangely giddy place to be.

SIGHT AND SOUND, 3/98, p. 44, Leslie Dick

Carn, Ireland, the early 60s. Francie Brady, a boy of about 12 years, lives with his alcoholic Da and his mentally disturbed Ma. He spends most of his time with his friend Joe. When Francie and Joe taunt schoolmate Phillip Nugent, Francie incurs the wrath of Phillip's mother Mrs Nugent, who calls the family "pigs".

Ma Brady has a breakdown and is sent to a sanatorium. She returns, but Da Brady beats her, prompting Francie to run away to Dublin. When he gets back, he finds that his mother has committed suicide and everyone blames him for it, saying he broke her heart. Francie vandalises the Nugents' home, defecating on the floor. Caught bare arsed, he is sent to a harsh reform school where the priests who run the school force the children to work cutting turf. Francie starts to have visions of the Virgin Mary. After being sexually abused by a priest, he is released.

Back home, Da Brady is dying of tuberculosis and Joe has become friends with Phillip Nugent. Francie gets a job in the local slaughterhouse; his visions/hallucinations of the Virgin are mixed with ones of nuclear bombs going off, prompted by the Cuban missile crisis, and of aliens from outer space. Da dies. Ostracised and increasingly obsessed with his hatred of Mrs Nugent, Francie kills her with an abattoir bolt-gun, smears her house with blood and chops up her body. After a spell on the lam, Francie is tracked down and incarcerated in a mental institution. On the day of his release, many years later, he has a final vision of the Virgin.

The Butcher Boy walks a borderline, no, it dances a borderline, the film's stunning momentum and reckless wit careering between comedy and tragedy, laughter and horror. The film depicts the insanity implicit in a boy's view of his small town in Ireland, circa 1962. It moves with the urgency, intensity and sheer hilarity of this boy whose fantasies know no limits, who apparently enjoys the havoc he wreaks, in reaction to an unremitting series of disasters which befall him. The boy is an ordinary boy, and he's also a psychopath—like all little boys? The film lets us in on the emotional logic of his situation, until his borderline psychosis seems built into the very stuff of childhood.

We become complicit with Francie Brady: we see how his world makes sense to him, though his understanding of it drives him to bloody murder. We're on his side, even when he picks up a meat cleaver to hack up the body: it's outrageous, it's funny, and the violence is both horrifying and unreal, as it would be to him. Yet to emphasise the violence distorts the feel of this film: it is endlessly surprising, as what looks at first to be an Irish art movie (the detail in the locations and the interiors almost too perfect) jerkily transmutes into something else entirely, something not nearly so easy to categorise: a great film.

Francie's Ma is bonkers, a manic depressive. He finds her in the kitchen, chair on the table, on the verge of hanging herself. All she can say is, "Francie, you'd never let me down, would you?" His Da drinks all day, every day, and beats her up when he's had enough. But Francie is off to the river with his best friend Joe, to shout at the fish: "Fuck off, fish!" Their games are made up out of the remnants of movies and television cowboys and Indians, sci-fi monster movies, gangsters—all muddled up with the power of the nuclear bomb and the real threat of the Cuban missile crisis. Francie meets every setback with a joke: when his Ma's had a "breakdown" and is taken away, he and Joe say she's gone to the garage, and propose the treatments as car repair: "unscrew her head", and so on. Kids, they are propelled towards laughter, towards action, despite everything, and the passionate attachment between Francie and Joe almost saves him, almost makes up for the misery of his parents' lives.

The two boys torment a posh, studious kid and Francie's tragedy is set in motion when they steal his comic-book collection. The other kid's irate mother Mrs Nugent storms down to Francie's house, to shout in the street that the whole family live like pigs. This sets off a weird and wonderful concatenation of fantasies in Francie's head: pigs, mushroom clouds and the Holy Virgin appear and reappear, functioning as imaginary tools for him to negotiate the increasingly impossible situation of his family. The humour is unrelenting, as each real crisis is matched by a further paranoid construct, making Mrs Nugent into the prime cause of all his troubles. Francie's love for Joe, his nostalgia for their days together before it all began to deteriorate, is at the centre of the film. It is poignant and precise: we watch the abyss between them opening, as Joe seeks safe ground, repudiating Francie's craziness. It's heartbreaking, and ridiculous, and hopeless, like Francie himself.

The Butcher Boy is based in Patrick McCabe's prize winning novel, and in what is possibly a unique situation, Neil Jordan, also a writer of fiction, co-wrote the screenplay with him. (McCabe himself appears in the film as the local town drunk.) This movie works because the script is careful, detailed and rock solid. It is structured entirely around a voice-over, so we both watch Francie and listen to his self-dramatisation, transforming each event, pushing it over the border into play. The momentum, the beautiful sudden rhythm of the film, is partly a function of the cinematography, so sure of itself, the relentless music, the simple magic realism of Francie's hallucinations. But it's also an effect of the torrent of words that make up Francie's inner world.

Neil Jordan isn't scared of too many words, here, but then he isn't scared of anything. Within this whirlwind of language, he has made possible a set of great performances, from Stephen Rea as Da Brady, Fiona Shaw as Mrs Nugent, and most especially from Eamonn Owens as Francie, who moves from being a very funny, wild kid to being something other: someone so hurt by events that he's more than capable of murder, capable of enjoying it, and even, amazingly, capable of surviving. The music, a combination of popular songs, Da's trumpet-playing and the orchestral score, is stupendous: integrated into the deep structure of the film, its dynamism picks us up by the scruff of the neck, sets us dancing too. The Butcher Boy sustains its breakneck pace, hurtling along like Francie's own unstoppable fabulations, yet nothing is sacrificed. It's razor sharp—Neil Jordan's best film yet.

TIME, 4/6/98, p. 70, Richard Schickel

Mum is going mad, Da is a drunk, and what's worse, 12-year-old Francie Brady (played by the remarkable Eamonn Owens) lives in a provincial town in Ireland in the early '60s. That means neighbors who are either dim or actively disapproving as the Bradys fall further and further into disarray. It also means that Francie's racing imagination is being fed with cultural junk food—cheap religious icons and TV purveying low-end sci-fi and images of the atomic Armageddon that everyone brooded on in those days.

"It'll be a bitter day for this town if the world comes to an end," a lady in the grocery shop sighs during the Cuban missile crisis, and that about sums up the locals' world view. But it does not begin to suggest the complexity of the movie Neil Jordan has fashioned from Patrick McCabe's novel The Butcher Boy.

It is narrated by the grownup Francie (Stephen Rea, who also plays the boy's father and Francie himself in the film's last scene) in the wryly humorous tone of a man looking back self-indulgently on a mischievous boyhood that came out all right in the end. But the personal history he recounts includes hugely destructive vandalism, arson, murder and a descent into decades of madness. The latter encompasses visions of the Virgin Mary (Sinead O'Connor, no less) appearing to him looking like a gaudy lithograph and behaving like a seductress; of priests looming up as giant science-fiction insects; and of his town's being destroyed by The Bomb, which incidentally turns all the corpses into pigs.

The contrast between the chuckly narration and the horrific scenes it plays over is brilliantly dislocating. So is the way the film slowly, gently reveals its true colors, as a tale not of amusing, forgivable youthful high jinks but of the making of a psychopath.

In the beginning, Francie is just a bright, apple-stealing, school-skipping lad, someone you can easily see as "going through a phase." But as he loses mother, father and finally his best friend (Alan Boyle), those pop cultural pictures—hard to say whether the carelessly violent or irrelevantly instructional are more damaging—fill up the empty spaces in his mind. Fill them to a kind of ghastly overflowing, which—the film recounts with perverse but curiously appropriate good cheer.

Appropriate because Francie never fully realizes how this imagery has eased him across the line separating delinquency from criminality. The scariest thing about this difficult duplicitous movie is the invincibility of Francie's ignorance on this point and the vivid gloss this offers on our unending concern about the power of crud culture to bend vulnerable minds to its heedless will.

VILLAGE VOICE, 4/7/98, p. 68, Amy Taubin

Somewhere in the middle of Neil Jordan's *The Butcher Boy*, the picture-perfect image of the Irish countryside is suffused by the sound of Frank Sinatra singing "Where Are You?" The first bars are disconcerting. What does the 1957 love song, the bittersweet timbre of Sinatra's voice, the sophisticated nuance of his phrasing, or Gordon Jenkins's silky pop orchestration have to do with this story of a 12-year-old, small-town Irish boy driven into a homicidal rage by a lifetime of loss and betrayal?

But as the song continues, it begins to seem like the perfect choice, and all the more for being so blatantly out of keeping with every other element. Jordan must think so too, because he repeats the song in the closing credits, sending you onto the street with that aching sound and those bald heartbreak lyrics ("Where are you?/ Where have you gone without me?/I thought you cared about me/Where are you?") mixed up with the memory of Francie Brady (Eamonn Owens): his clownish face, his manic energy, the frantic way he tears through his constricted, lonely life, the desperate pleasure he takes in revving the engines of his imagination and his pre-adolescent body, and the bloody, grotesque, homicide he commits.

The thing about madness is that it doesn't make sense, neither from inside nor outside. The wildly associative styles in *The Butcher Boy* are Jordan's way of suggesting Francie Brady's experience, which is that of a lunatic. It also evokes the experience of living during the height of the Cold War in rural Ireland, where world politics and culture came at one from a great and alienating distance. What makes *The Butcher Boy* more complicated than the average case study of a crazy kid is its historic specificity. Francie internalizes comic books, the Atom Bomb, and the narrative of *The Lone Ranger,* which he watches on TV while his drunken jazz musician father plays the William Tell theme on his trumpet. It's no accident that Francie, who works in an abattoir, goes on his rampage during the Bay of Pigs crisis. In *The Butcher Boy,* piggery is massively overdetermined.

In Francie's imagination, he and his best friend Joe (Alan Boyle) are the Lone Ranger and Tonto rolled into one. As long as they stick together, they can survive the Bomb and the fury of Francie's nemesis, the prying, stuck-up Mrs. Nugent. Francie's obsession with Mrs. Nugent is his undoing. When Joe rejects him, scared off by his rage and his increasing violence, Francie feels that Joe has betrayed not only him personally but also the myth on which his fantasy of power is based. Add in that his mother commits suicide, that his father dies of cancer, that he's abused by every social institution meant to protect him, and you have a kid headed for certain disaster.

In co-adapting Patrick McCabe's novel, Jordan kept the first-person narrative structure intact. *The Butcher Boy* is couched as a memory piece with the voice of the middle-aged Francie (Stephen Rea, who also plays Francie's father) commenting on the actions of the young Francie. The rush of words is as expressive as the child's rubber face. The words put you inside Francie's head, a fearsome place where the distinctions between childhood make believe and psychosis arc blurred.

This split between Francie as a kid and as an adult intensifies the sense of a fractured psyche. So does the disjunction between the generically picturesque mise-en-scéne and Francie's manic behavior, not to mention the apocalyptic imagery, that erupts from his imagination onto the screen.

At the heart of the film is Owens's relentless, fierce performance, a mix of intelligence, intuition, and adrenaline. Owens elevates an extremely interesting film to near greatness.

Though *The Butcher Boy* eschews sentimentality, it's a tad too romantic about madness. Painting Francie as a combination of victim and unknowable monster, it places most of the blame on the social order. In doing that, it suggests that it's more courageous to express one's rage by hacking someone up than to succumb to petit bourgeois hypocrisy. Maybe the problem is that we never see Mrs. Nugent except though Francie's eyes. And since, for Francis, she's inhuman, it doesn't matter all that much that she die. That's my only quibble with the film and it's not a big one. With cliché about underaged murderers newly eclipsing the president's errant dick on the talk shows, *The Butcher Boy* is a timely corrective.

Also reviewed in:
CHICAGO TRIBUNE, 4/17/98, Friday/p. A, Michael Wilmington
NEW YORK TIMES, 4/3/98, p. E16, Janet Maslin
NEW YORKER, 4/6/98, p. 107, Daphne Merkin
VARIETY, 7/21-27/97, p. 37, Emanuel Levy
WASHINGTON POST, 4/17/98, Weekend/p. 56, Michael O'Sullivan

CANNIBAL!: THE MUSICAL

A Troma Entertainment release of an Avenging Conscience/Cannibal Films Ltd. production. *Executive Producer:* Jason McHugh, Alexandra Kelly, and Andrew Kemler. *Producer:* Alexandra Kelly and Matt Stone. *Director:* Trey Parker. *Screenplay:* Trey Parker. *Director of Photography:* Robert Muratore and Chris Graves. *Editor:* Ian Hardin. *Music:* Trey Parker and Rich Sanders. *Production Designer:* Dave Hedge. *Running time:* 95 minutes. *MPAA Rating:* Not Rated.

CAST: Trey Parker (Alferd Packer); Toddy Walters (Polly Prye); Jason McHugh (Frank Miller); Matt Stone (Humphrey); Jon Hegel (Israel Swan); Dian Bachar (George Noon).

LOS ANGELES TIMES, 10/16/98, Calendar/p. 14, Kevin Thomas

"Sweeney Todd" it's not, cinema art it's not, but "Cannibal! The Musical" has its hilarious moments for sure. Produced five years ago by a group of enterprising University of Colorado film students for $125,000, rejected by Sundance and picked up by Troma for direct-to-video release, "Cannibal!" has acquired a sufficiently large cult following for the Nuart, which screened it once at midnight last June, to book it for one week starting today.

That its prime mover, Trey Parker, went on to become a co-creator of TV's "South Park" has surely helped to give it a shot on the big screen. (In collaboration with some of his "Cannibal!" pals, Parker has completed the NC-17-rated comedy "Orgazmo," about a pious Mormon porn star who must rescue his kidnapped girlfriend.)

A spoof of inane musicals and B-western movie plots in which the hero loves his horse more than the girl—and with a nod to Donner Party mythology and a tip of the hat to Chaplin's "The Gold Rush"—has been crossed with the gore-and-entrails genre.

No doubt Troma would like to hit the midnight movie circuit jackpot, and the film just might, but you should know that between the hysterical musical numbers, things can seem mighty amateurish and a bit tedious up there in all the grandeur of the Rockies. Those looking for rambling, laid-back nonsense will be better served than those expecting the slick professionalism of "The Rocky Horror Picture Show."

The most amazing aspect of the movie is that its story is basically true: In the winter of 1874, a fur-trapper named Alferd Packer became the first man in American history to be convicted of cannibalism.

He led a party of five gold-seekers, and when he emerged from the wilderness alone months later in Saguache, Colo., he did not look sufficiently starved, arousing suspicions. When the mutilated bodies of his companions were eventually found near Lake Fork Gunnison, he denied that he killed them, saying that they were murdered by one of the party members, Wilson Shannon Bell, whom he in turn killed in self-defense. He further said that cannibalism was the only way he could survive the harsh winter.

The way the movie tells it, Packer, played by Parker, was so intent on finding his beloved horse, which had wandered away, that he led his party south in search of the animal instead of north, to Breckenridge, its destination.

The loss of the horse leads to one of the movie's funniest songs, the fulsome Barry Manilow-esque anthem "She'll Never Know What She Meant to Me." Other gems include "Let's Build a Snowman," sung by the group's optimist, who also does a soft shoe in snow nearly up to his knees, and "Hang the Bastard!," the chant of lynch-minded locals upon Packer's arrest.

Besides Parker and his pals, playing gold-seekers, fur-trappers and the like, is pretty Toddy Walters as intrepid reporter Polly Prye, surely a reference to newspaper legend Nelly Blye. Everyone involved with "Cannibalism! The Musical" seems to be having a ball. You may too.

NEW YORK POST, 7/25/98, p. 27, Larry Worth

Lots of bloodied limbs. Segues to song-and-dance numbers. More fleshy snacks. That about sums up "Cannibal! The Musical."

Those familiar with the crude humor of TV's "South Park" won't be surprised that the hit show's creators—Trey Parker and Matt Stone—cut their teeth on 1993's "Cannibal!" which is only now getting a big-screen release.

As evident from "South Park," the boys' manner of getting laughs isn't for everyone. But even diehard fans may find things a bit too redundant—and repulsive—this time around.

In the opening five minutes, viewers get to see an arm torn from its socket, a larynx yanked out and an elongated tongue-ectomy. And that's just for starters.

The story, set in Colorado in 1870, then shifts to the culprit's courtroom trial. The mad miner is accused of chowing down on his companions after getting lost on a gold-seeking expedition. Yet a noose is of less concern to the defendant than his fickle horse's affections.

Such twisted sentiments lead him to break into wink-wink, nudge-nudge songs like "When I Was on Top of You." Meanwhile, the townsfolk swing their partners around the gallows while harmonizing on "Hang the Bastard."

Not surprisingly, those musical numbers—all lip-synced to purposeful non-perfection—provide the film's sole highlights. They're sadly overshadowed by a string of gross-out yuks and predictably over-the-top acting from Parker, Stone and the rest of the would-be cutups.

The bottom line: "Cannibal! the Musical" is —at best—an acquired taste. At worst, it's plain unsavory.

VILLAGE VOICE, 7/28/98 p. 118, Gary Dauphin

Trey Parker's 1993 undergrad film *Cannibal! The Musical* already had a cult following before he and Matt Stone, created the potty-mouthed *South Park*, but a little fame and fortune obviously never hurts. Not so much rejected by '94's Sundance festival as politely ignored (Parker's musical didn't even rate a form rejection letter), *Cannibal!* was screened in Park City guerrilla-style anyway, drawing the attention of trash movie-heads dreaming of the next *Rocky Horror*-type live show. Now that the worm's turned for Parker and Stone, from cable to the upcoming *BASEketball* and *Orgazmo, Cannibal!* has gotten a new lease on life, singing and occasionally munching its cheesy low-budget way into theaters.

Although the poster promises a cross between *Oklahoma* and *Bloodsucking Freaks, Cannibal!* tells the true life story of Alferd Packer (director Parker playing under the name "Juan Schwartz"), an idiot 1870s mountain guide. Packer left Utah one winter with a group of miners and schlepped into Colorado a year late alone, claiming to have somehow "lost" his party. Townsfolk decided he seemed a little too plump for a wilderness survivor, and Packer became the first man ever to be tried for cannibalism in a U.S. court.

As portrayed in *Cannibal!*, Packer was a good-hearted loser whose only crime was an overenthusiastic desire to be reunited with his stolen horse Liane, hence the winking but chaster number "When I Was on Top of You." Instead of leading his group to Colorado, Packer takes them deeper into the Rockies in search of Liane, the party (which includes Matt Stone) starving, singing, and dancing before going completely Donner behind his unwitting back. In the way of most movies aiming for cult chuckles, *Cannibal!* is a mix of deadpan sight gags, in-your-face laziness, and randomly sharp interjections. Stan Brakhage makes a cameo (he was teaching at UC Denver that year), the Packer party visits an "Indian" tribe composed of Japanese martial-arts enthusiasts, and the requisite pus-spattering wounds make an appearance, but the worst and best parts are those song-and-dance bits. Despite being wholly ridiculous and interminable, the musical sequences are weirdly sincere, capturing the single-minded visionary awfulness of good junk. It's hard to imagine *Cannibal! The Musical* becoming the next *Rocky Horror*, but it does have the distinction of mixing in a thin local history with its thick groans, making it the first sick-puppy flick you could write about for extra credit in a hip Denver high school.

Also reviewed in:
NEW YORK TIMES, 7/24/98, p. E22, Anita Gates

CAN'T HARDLY WAIT

A Columbia Pictures release of a Tall Trees production. *Producer:* Jenno Topping and Betty Thomas. *Director:* Harry Elfont and Deborah Kaplan. *Screenplay:* Harry Elfont and Deborah Kaplan. *Director of Photography:* Lloyd Ahern. *Editor:* Michael Jablow. *Music:* David Kitay and Matthew Sweet. *Music Editor:* Carlton Kaller and Stuart Grusin. *Sound:* David Kirschner. *Sound Editor:* Roxanne Jones. *Casting:* Mary Vernieu and Anne McCarthy. *Production Designer:* Marcia Hinds-Johnson. *Art Director:* Bo Johnson. *Set Designer:* Donald B. Woodruff, Joseph P. Lucky, and Eric Sundahl. *Set Decorator:* Jan Bergstrom. *Special Effects:* Lou Carlucci. *Costumes:* Mark Bridges. *Make-up:* John Damiani. *Stunt Coordinator:* Clay Boss. *Running time:* 95 minutes. *MPAA Rating:* PG-13.

CAST: Jennifer Love Hewitt (Amanda); Ethan Embry (Preston); Charlie Korsmo (William); Lauren Ambrose (Denise); Peter Facinelli (Mike); Seth Green (Kenny); Michelle Brookhurst (Girl Whose Party It Is); Alexander Martin (Exchange Student); Erik Palladino (Cousin Ron); Channon Roe, Sean Patrick Thomas, and Freddy Rodriguez (Jocks); Joel Michaely and Jay Paulson (X-Philes); Brian Hall (Real Homeboy); Branden Williams and Bobby Jacoby (Homeboys); Johnny Zander (Guitar Player); Donald Faison (Drummer); Alaa Khaled (Bass Player); Jamie Pressly, Tamala Jones, and Jennifer Lyons (Girlfriends); Seth Peterson (Keg Guy); Angelo Vacco and Nick Paulos (Beer Drinkers); Chris Owen (Klepto Kid); Vicellous Shannon (Reddi Whip Kid); Victor Togunde (Reminiscing Guy); Monica McSwain and Marisol Nichols (Groupies); Liz Stauber (Gossipy Girl); Nicole Bilderback (Ready to Have Sex Girl); Jason Segel (Watermelon Guy); Paige Moss (Ashley); Clea Duvall (Jana); Leslie Grossman (Ready to Have Sex's Friend); Ali MacLean (Language Lab Girl); Brian Klugman (Stoner Guy); Meadow Sisto (Hippie Girl); Eric Balfour (Hippie Guy); Selma Blair and Jennifer Paz (Girls Mike Hits On); Sara Rue (Earth Girl); Nils Larsen (Skinny Guy); Steve Monroe (Headbanger); Eric Brice Scott (Hockey Guy); Chris Wiehl (Horny Guy); John

Patrick White (Tassel Guy);   Jamie Donnelly (Teacher);   Reni Santoni, Rob Roy Fitzgerald, and Corinne Reilly (Cops);   Jerry O'Connell (Trip McNeely);   Jenna Elfman (Angel).

LOS ANGELES TIMES, 6/12/98, Calendar/p. 6, Kevin Thomas

[*The following review by Kevin Thomas appeared in a slightly different form in* **NEWSDAY, 6/12/99, Part II/p. B11.**]

Before the credits are over for the fast and funny "Can't Hardly Wait" the word ripples through the ranks of capped-and-gowned seniors of Huntington Hills High that the unthinkable has happened: The class of '98's top jock (Peter Facinelli) and its perennial prom queen (Jennifer Love Hewitt) have broken up.

This is news of seismic implications—especially for nice-looking but timid Preston (Ethan Embry), who has had a crush on Hewitt's gorgeous Amanda since they were freshmen. As it happens, one of their classmates is throwing a graduation party at her lavish, elegant home while her parents are conveniently away. Will Preston take advantage of what may well be his last chance to make his feelings known to Amanda?

Writer-directors Harry Elfont and Deborah Kaplan, in their directorial debuts, know where they're going and how to get there. They cram their background with no end of incident, comic gags, sharp asides and raucous, increasingly out-of-control "Animal House" boorishness.

But they're also able to bring to life not only Facinelli's bewildered Mike and Hewitt's newly perceptive Amanda but also Seth Green's Kenny, who mistakenly thinks it's cool to talk and dress like a black rapper, and Lauren Ambrose's Denise, a redhead who's never resorted to hiding her superior intelligence. And don't forget William (Charlie Korsmo), the class valedictorian, a constant object of peer contempt, who proves to be a closet rock'n'roller—and is bent upon vengeance against his principal tormentor, Mike.

For all its nonstop energy and high spirits, "Can't Hardly Wait" allows its characters to emerge as fully dimensional individuals; they've been written with care and perception and played with equal aplomb by a roster of talented young actors.

For Amanda, graduation proves to be a wake-up call: She can no longer deny that Mike, who has given her a sense of security throughout high school, is an immature jerk who hasn't grown at all over the past four years.

Mike, in turn, is faced with the instant eroding of his heretofore unchallenged authority, as he has a hard time persuading his best pals to break up with their girlfriends simply because he's no longer with Amanda. It clearly never occurred to Mike that being a high school hero would come to an abrupt end with graduation—or that once apart from the gracious Amanda that so many, especially the girls, consider him an oaf.

Trapped together in an upstairs bathroom, Denise and Kenny discover that layers of bad attitudes toward each other have been gradually building up since second grade. You could wish that would-be writer Preston weren't such a tiresomely dreamy nerd, but he learns a lot of life in a brief encounter with a stripper ("Dharma & Greg's" Jenna Elfman, a standout in a cameo role) as they vie for the same pay phone at 2 in the morning; she ends up advising him that "fate can take you only so far." Her serious point is presented in an amusing context typical of the film: Her big regret is that when Scott Baio once made an appearance at the local mall she didn't try to make direct contact.

"Can't Hardly Wait" bounces along without ever missing a beat. With summer vacation imminent, its arrival is an instance of perfect timing.

NEW YORK POST, 6/12/98, p. 46, Larry Worth

Once a decade, a coming-of-age movie surfaces in which a group of high school teens—played by unknowns who later graduate to major-star status—defines a generation.

In the '70s, it was George Lucas' "American Graffiti" with Ron Howard, Richard Dreyfuss and Harrison Ford. In the '80s, it was Amy Heckerling's "Fast Times at Ridgemont High" with Sean Penn, Jennifer Jason Leigh and Nicolas Cage. And in the '90s, well, that slot' still up for grabs.

Harry Elfont and Deborah Kaplan's "Can't Hardly Wait" doesn't doesn't even come close, try though it does to ape its famous predecessors.

For starters Elfont and Kaplan's script never hints of anything akin to originality or talent. Nor do its stars give any indication of future potential.

The moronic story takes place—a la "Graffiti"—over one night as its half-dozen protagonists attend a high school graduation bash before leaving town to pursue their dreams.

The usual suspects include a brainiac who wants revenge on some mean-spirited jocks, the tart-tongued girl who can't get a date, the white boy and his Caucasian posse who think they're rappers, bimbo cheerleaders and bespectacled nerds.

And at the tale's center is an average joe who's secretly in love with the reigning prom queen. Though she doesn't know he's alive, hope survives since the girl just broke up with her obnoxious football hero boyfriend.

Directors Elfont and Kaplan frantically cross-cut between the deja-vu storylines, demonstrating that one comic subplot is as deadly as the next. By the time they reach for a serious message near finale time, the joke's on them.

As for the lack of acting talent, it starts with Jennifer ("Party of Five") Love Hewitt's miscasting as the local beauty. Though decked out in a revealing tank top with a wind machine blowing her perfect 'do, Hewitt never convinces—physically or emotionally—as the hottest babe since Marilyn.

Equally forgettable: Ethan ("That Thing You Do") Embry as the dopey protagonist, Seth ("Buffy the Vampire Slayer") Green's would-be homey and Lauren Ambrose's smart-mouthed homage to Janeane Garofalo. Even cameos from Jenna Elman, Jerry O'Connell and Melissa Joan Hart barely register.

That leaves the perfunctory soundtrack to carry the day, which is asking a lot. Accordingly, "Can't Hardly Wait" is more than bad grammar. It's bad moviemaking.

VILLAGE VOICE, 6/23/98, p. 146, Dennis Lim

A looking-for-love, coming-of-age, last-night-of-high-school ensemble piece, *Can't Hardly Wait* has so many obvious antecedents you'd think the filmmakers could at least get some of it right. But the movie, written and directed by first-timers Deborah Kaplan and Larry Elfont, is at once supremely cynical and totally clueless.

As anyone who lived through the Brat Pack will attest, stereotypes in teen movies are not a problem; it's when they're uniformly witless and charmless that trouble arises. *Can't Hardly Wait* is a supposed showcase for Hollywood's new wave of young talent. On this evidence (corroborated by various ongoing Kevin Williamson franchises), there is no wave, just a wading pool of barely distinguishable, passably photogenic, extremely white nonpersonalities.

The usual suspects gather for a post-graduation blowout. Vapid homecoming queen Amanda (Jennifer Love Hewitt) has just been dumped by her Neanderthal jock boyfriend Mike (Peter Facinelli), and her googly-eyed longtime admirer (Ethan Embry) is working up the nerve to finally make his move. The outcome is never in doubt, and essentially irrelevant, since *Can't Hardly Wait* is devoid of the basic good-natured empathy that is the genre's lifeblood (and that directors like Richard Linklater, Amy Heckerling and Cameron Crowe have evoked with relative ease in the past).

The script makes half-hearted stabs at pop-cult knowingness, but it's most notable for its tedium and for a wretched homophobic streak. Don't be fooled. This film is not the new *Say Anything*; it's not even the new *Porky's Revenge*.

Also reviewed in:
CHICAGO TRIBUNE, 6/12/98, Friday/p. J, Mark Caro
NEW YORK TIMES, 6/12/98, p. E14, Janet Maslin
VARIETY, 6/8-14/98, p. 67, Emanuel Levy
WASHINGTON POST, 6/12/98, Weekend/p. 45, Michael O'Sullivan

CARLA'S SONG

A Shadow Distribution release of a Channel Four Television Corporation and The Glasgow Film Fund presentation of a Parallax Picture in co-production with Road Movies Dritte Produktionen and Tornasol Films S.A. with the support of The Institute of Culture, Nicaragua and ARD/DEGETO Film/Filmstiftung Nordrhein-Westfalen/Television Española and Alta Films/the European Script Fund/Scottish Film Production Fund. *Producer:* Sally Hibbin. *Director:* Ken Loach. *Screenplay:* Paul Laverty. *Director of Photography:* Barry Ackroyd. *Editor:* Jonathan Morris. *Music:* George Fenton. *Sound:* Ray Beckett and (music) Paul Hulme. *Casting:* Jean Bacharach and Wendy Ettinger. *Production Designer:* Martin Johnson. *Art Director:* Llorenç Miquel and Fergus Clegg. *Special Effects:* Reyes Abades. *Costumes:* Daphne Dare and Lena Mossum. *Make-up:* Christine Blundell. *Running time:* 127 minutes. *MPAA Rating:* Not Rated.

CAST: Robert Carlyle (George); Oyanka Cabezas (Carla); Scott Glenn (Bradley); Salvador Espinoza (Rafael); Louise Goodall (Maureen); Richard Loza (Antonio); Gary Lewis (Sammy); Subash Singh Pall (Victor); Stewart Preston (McGurk); Margaret McAdam (George's Mother); Pamela Turner (Eileen); Greg Friel (Keyboard Player); Ann-Marie Timoney (Warden); Andy Townsley (Taxi Driver); Alicia Devine (Hospital Sister); John Paul Leach (Doctor); Norma Rivera (Norma); José Meneses (Harry); Rosa Amelia López (Carla's Mother).

CHRISTIAN SCIENCE MONITOR, 7/17/98, p. B3, David Sterritt

No filmmaker is more sensitive than Ken Loach when it comes to charting the connections between personal and political experiences. He's been exploring large-scale issues through human-scale movies for more than 30 years, and his new picture, "Carla's Song," continues this commendable practice.

Robert Carlyle, ("The Full Monty" and "Trainspotting") plays a likable Scottish bus driver who makes a new friend when he lends a helping hand to a young Nicaraguan immigrant. Their relationship blossoms into romance, but its clear the woman has unhappy secrets stemming from her recent past.

Eventually they travel to Nicaragua in search of her brother, who has undergone great torment for his political actions and beliefs. There the couple gets involved with a former American agent who has turned against US policies that he now considers wrong. The story reaches its climax with an attack by Contra rebels, which crystallizes the movie's themes in pungent and polemical terms.

Throughout his career, Loach's filmmaking has been most effective when he's conveyed his messages through direct, everyday stories that anyone in the audience might feel close to, as in "Ladybird, Ladybird" and "Raining Stones," which deal with family life. He's less adept at tales of intrigue ("Hidden Agenda") and action-based melodramas ("Land and Freedom") that stretch his modest budgets and his cinematic capabilities.

Not surprisingly, "Carla's Song" works best in its most intimate moments, as the working-class hero and memory-haunted heroine fall in love and try to build a caring relationship despite the obstacles in their paths.

It's less convincing when it breaks into Hollywood-style action, and it nearly falls apart when the American operative (played by Scott Glenn, of "The Right Stuff") goes into a political rant that's overwritten, overacted, and overwrought.

In the end, "Carla's Song" is a flawed but worthy effort that carries on Loach's fine tradition without deepening or broadening it as much as his admirers might hope.

CINEASTE, Vol. XXIII, no. 4, 1998, p. 52, Jonathan Buchsbaum

While Ken Loach's *Land and Freedom* featured the internecine battles of the Spanish Civil War of the Thirties, the travails of Sandinista Nicaragua in 1987, chronicled in Loach's recent *Carla's Song,* are even more remote for most North Americans. The electoral defeat of 1990 ended the rule of the Sandinista Front for National Liberation (FSLN), which has unraveled as a dominant political force ever since, following internal strife, including the recent lurid charges of sexual abuse against former President Ortega. Once the contra war ended and the Sandinistas relinquished power, Nicaragua disappeared from the front pages of newspapers, buried in the rubble of the Berlin Wall and the end of the Cold War. *Carla's Song* resurrects that forgotten time when the contra war was still raging.

Loach collaborated on the script with a Glasgow lawyer, Paul Laverty, who worked in Nicaragua during the Eighties as a human-rights monitor. Well aware of the human suffering caused by the contra war, he became frustrated by the difficulty of combating the American media's promotion of the contra cause. Laverty suggested to Loach that the project could "give shape to just one of those thousands of statistics, and tell his or her story set against the real backdrop of Nicaragua."

This dual focus on the personal and the political explains the film's oscillation between a love story and incidents detailing the real backdrop of Nicaragua." The film's opening lays the groundwork for the eventual convergence of these two strands. A young bus driver named George (Robert Carlyle) offers to pay the fare of a young woman named Carla (Oyanka Cabezas), who appears unable to speak English. George's sense of justice leads to a week's suspension, and eventually his dismissal after he commandeers the bus for a picnic outing with Carla in the hills outside the city. After a suicide attempt by Carla, George learns that this Nicaraguan dancer remains haunted by the atrocities of the war in Nicaragua, in particular the memories of Antonio, the boyfriend she left behind. As the love story of George and Carla develops, George recognizes that Carla cannot recover until she confronts her feelings for Antonio. Hence, he buys tickets for Nicaragua, where the rest of the film takes place.

As in *Land and Freedom,* Loach foregrounds a naive male protagonist who encounters a committed, experienced, and attractive female character to guide him through the confusion and violence. Furthermore, the couple comes together romantically, not ideologically, for the man knows virtually nothing of the complexity of the real situation. Interestingly, the man leaves a girlfriend behind in both cases, suggesting the erotic pull of war. Both films, then, try to use a conventional narrative form in order to draw a wide audience to an examination of ideological struggles.

No doubt Loach believes that the film's linkage of love and war is more than a mere rickety plot device. Loach and Laverty are obviously more concerned with informing audiences of Nicaragua's troubled past and the rewriting of history which demonizes the Sandinistas and neglects the criminal war sponsored by the United States. The film endeavors to set the historical record straight by cataloguing—and at times celebrating—the good works of the Sandinistas. On the plane to Nicaragua, for example, Carla's return to her homeland triggers a flashback to her happy days with Antonio in a literacy brigade. Once in Nicaragua, *campesinos* insist on showing George their new title to land. Carla's friends are active in the local Sandinista women's organization and teach literacy to *campesinos*. Throughout this journey, George, who speaks no Spanish, trails after Carla as an onlooker.

While championing the ideological virtues of the Sandinista project—agrarian reform, literacy, and women's newfound militancy—the film succumbs to a certain schematic didacticism. Each encounter instructs George—as well as the audience—about the Revolution, but does not change the relationship with Carla. The search for Antonio, moreover, takes them from the city into the countryside, the terrain of the most horrific violence of the war. Carefully instructed by the CIA to wage a campaign of terror against civilians, the contras specifically targeted health-care workers, farmers on cooperatives, and other Sandinista centers of progressive social change. The protagonists' descent into hell is explicitly designed to immerse us in the reality of a war which was obscured during the Reagan Administration with a massive disinformation campaign that eventually imploded in the Iran-Contra affair.

By ludicrously maintaining that Nicaragua had become a Soviet puppet threatening its neighbors with Marxist revolution, the United States transformed this country of three million people into the Cold War's last battleground. Understandably enough, in an attempt to correct these distortions, Loach and Laverty endorse the policies of the revolutionary government. Unfortunately, the didicaticism of *Carla's Song* precludes a more nuanced examination of the Sandinista experiment. Loach and Laverty overlook Nicaragua's real internal political tensions, since the Sandinistas faced opposition within the country, and not only from former Somocistas and the United States. In fact, the FSLN, self-professed vanguard of the revolution, progressively lost popular support not exclusively because of the war and the attendant convulsions in Nicaraguan society. Particularly in the countryside, the Sandinistas pursued economic policies which alienated sectors of the rural population. Some peasants even joined the contras in response to such measures as the imposition of collectivized forms of farming. While such strategies were intended to improve the lives of Nicaraguans and were not coercive (no one was forced to join cooperatives, many *campesinos* resisted these intrusions into their traditional way of life. Furthermore, the application of these policies often led to real economic hardship for *campesinos*, such as lower compulsory prices for their products offered by the state purchasers, failure to provide transport of their produce, and even forced relocation of communities from their familiar surroundings. The *campesinos* in *Carla's Song* who proudly display their land title obviously support the Revolution's policies; many others did not.

The film refers briefly to one such problem, but fails to pursue it in detail. When Carla asks her friend Rafael about the fate of Antonio's family, she learns that one of Antonio's brothers has been killed while fighting with the contras. Loach and Laverty's Manichaean representation of the war cannot account for such an unlikely character. How could any Nicaraguan, let alone a brother of the saintly Antonio, support the evil contras? A more nuanced narrative, which acknowledged the well-known fact that families throughout the country were split by the war, could have taken us closer to the real politics of the revolution and the war.

Although the film's version of history is overly simplified, it manages to successfully capture the texture of daily Nicaraguan life, a feat that eluded earlier films shot in Nicaragua such as *Alsino and the Condor, Latino, Walker,* and even the Nicaraguan *Specter of War.* Arriving in Nicaragua, George is disoriented by the chaos of the Huembes bus station in Managua, and the sequence's tight shots of tortilla makers and beverage vendors emphasizes his confusion. The buses are bulging with passengers, often carrying the overload on the roofs. Bars and restaurants operate out of nondescript houses with few amenities beyond some chairs and tables set up haphazardly on dusty porches, as Nicaraguan beer magically appears out of hidden interiors. Vehicles are constantly breaking down, repaired in makeshift ways until the next malfunction. Houses are extremely bare inside, with little furniture and often without electricity. Loach neither sanitizes nor dramatizes this poverty.

In an admirable reversal of standard conversion scenarios *(Under Fire, Missing, Salvador),* George does not decide to become an *internacionalista* recruit to the Sandinista Revolution. Instead, he realizes that he cannot commit himself to this foreign cause. Loach and Laverty refuse to imbue this doomed love affair with any sense of redemption; Carla must stay behind, since she cannot abandon either her country or her beloved Antonio.

The enigma of Antonio's fate lies at the center of the narrative. Bradley (Scott Glenn), a former CIA adviser who works as a Witness For Peace, ultimately informs George that Antonio was brutally tortured by the contras. Since Carla witnessed her lover's agony, she fled her trauma by remaining in Europe after her dance troupe's European tour. Antonio, appearing only at the end, functions as an allegorical condensation of what was done to the Sandinista project—suffering, paralysis, disfigurement, and silencing. By turning Antonio into an allegorical figure, the film further weakens the love story of George and Carla—George is not competing with a real person, but with a damaged country that he can never hope to repair.

Even though *Carla's Song* awkwardly grafts a love story onto an exposé of the contra war, the film succeeds in evoking the popular optimism of the Sandinista Revolution and conveying the brutality of its defeat. Ken Loach deserves credit for upholding the hopes of the anti-Stalinist left during the post-Cold War period. Films which examine the internal tensions of the Sandinista regime remain to be made, but Loach's film at least bears witness to the most recent Good Fight.

LOS ANGELES TIMES, 8/28/98, Calendar/p. 6, Kevin Thomas

Ken Loach's "Carla's Song" is a lesser "Land and Freedom in that both films focus on a young man from Britain who goes abroad and experiences love and revolution. Alas, "Land and Freedom" was such an excellent film in its illumination of the complexities of the Spanish Civil

War—and of an intimate relationship—that "Carla's Song," which takes its hero from Glasgow to Nicaragua in 1987, suffers all the more in comparison.

The primary problem for "Carla's Song," which was made in 1996, is one of structure. First-time screenwriter Paul Laverty, a former Glasgow lawyer who spent 2½ years in the mid-'80s working in Central America with human rights organizations, has written a script that requires spending 54 minutes of its 125-minute running time to get George (Robert Carlyle), a free-spirited Glasgow bus driver, on a plane for Nicaragua, just as the contras are overwhelming the Sandinistas.

While in Glasgow, George crosses paths with Carla (Oyanka Cabezas), a beautiful but traumatized Nicaraguan street performer, and you know that they will fall in love. The film deftly establishes George as a rebel—and then keeps reiterating that point, while a number of cliches of romantic comedy are awkwardly played against the unfolding of Carla's fragile emotional state. In short, the Glasgow sequence, essentially a prologue, takes on a protracted, contrived quality from which the film, for all the passion and commitment Loach consistently brings to it, never recovers.

On the plus side are the wiry Carlyle, who went on to star in "The Full Monty," and the lovely Cabezas; both have endless charm and magnetism. Indeed, Carlyle is an actor of formidable concentration and expressiveness. But even the pleasure we can take in the stars' performances is marred by the fact that both have such thick accents that we lose about half of what they're saying (this is so even when considering the film's sound has been carefully set at optimal level).

In any event, Carla had come to the U.K. to promote the Sandinista cause in the wake of the terrible fate that had befallen her lover and so many of her people, only to find herself adrift and increasingly suicidal. Once she and George fall in love, they agree that Carla must return to discover whether her lover is, in fact, still alive, and where she stands with George, who decides to accompany her.

"Carla's Song" picks up considerably when the couple finally arrive in war-torn Nicaragua, where they contact Bradley (Scott Glenn, very good), an American who has thrown his lot with the Sandinistas but who is tormented by a dark past. There could be more clarity in regard to the complexities of Nicaragua's tragic predicament, but one of the film's real pluses is that it is not preachy: The CIA's role in the suffering and oppression of the Nicaraguan people is expressed by Bradley in one angry, damning outburst.

In its last 20 minutes or so, "Carla's Song," so beautifully photographed by Barry Ackroyd, catches fire and blazes with suspense and emotion, but its powerful conclusion leaves you regretting that getting there was so labored.

NEW YORK POST, 6/26/98, p. 52, Larry Worth

British director Ken Loach never tackles easy subjects or particularly commercial ones.

In "Ladybird, Ladybird" it was domestic abuse and the travails of a single mom. In "Hidden Agenda" it was human rights activists in Northern Ireland. And in "Land and Freedom", he reinterpreted the Spanish Civil War through an anti-fascist's eyes. Great movies, one and all—though ignored by the general movie-going public.

Thematically and quality-wise, "Carla's Song" follows the Loach tradition, telling of a bus driver who, through an odd set of circumstances, ends up in Nicaragua battling contras alongside his Sandinista-oriented lady love.

OK, it'll never generate lines outside the box office. But one can't help admiring Loach's persistence in addressing worthwhile, thought-provoking subjects—and refusing to play it safe.

For instance, he makes "Carla's Song" more than a study of star-crossed lovers. Instead, it's a leisurely told drama with lots to say about culture clashes, societal alienation and political machinations.

The somewhat episodic story breaks down into two chapters. The first takes place in Scotland, where the tale's working-class hero comes across a lovely Nicaraguan native who dances on Glasgow's streets to pay rent. He pursues her, but with unexpected results.

The tale's remainder, set in the mid-1980s, places viewers in the hell of Nicaragua's war zone, with personal secrets and contra-inflicted horrors unfolding at a dizzying rate.

Like "Men With Guns," John Sayles' excursion earlier this year into Central America's jungles, "Carla's" is an intelligent, eye-opening and suspenseful riff on "Heart of Darkness," told with enough soul to make it accessible.

Fine location photography and uniquely expressed anti-war sentiments are other pluses, helping to compensate for Loach's tendency to let scenes run too long or inclusion of a dopey love montage.

The actors also deliver the goods, starting with omnipresent Robert Carlyle. After attention-getting turns in "Priest," "Trainspotting" and "The Full Monty" (never mind bits in less-popular movies such as this year's "Go Now" and Loach's "Riff-Raff"), Carlyle keeps finding new ways to reinvent himself. He's a consistent revelation.

As the titular Carla, newcomer Oyanka Cabezas is equally electric. She has the beauty of a young Bianca Jagger and the fiery passion of Anna Magnani. Scott Glenn ("The Right Stuff") also lends a strong presence as the man who holds the key to Carla's heart.

NEWSDAY, 6/26/98, Part II/p. B11, John Anderson

It may be more potent politically than dramatically, but "Carla's Song," a star-crossed romance about a Scots bus driver and Nicaraguan refugee, certainly serves a useful purpose. We should remember occasionally about Ollie North and potted palms, CIA "advisers," the sanctity of the Constitution and presidents with memory problems.

Too bad we need a Brit to help us do it. Or, in this case, two: Ken Loach, the director of such naturalistic, English working-class dramas as "Raining Stones," "Riff Raff" and "Ladybird, Ladybird," as well as the recent Spanish Civil War epic, "Land and Freedom;" and Paul Laverty, former Glasgow lawyer who developed the screenplay out of his work with human-rights organizations during the U.S.-backed contra war. It's angry stuff and, as usual when anger is a factor, intemperate. At the same time, sincerity isn't all that common a commodity.

Returning to work with Loach is Robert Carlyle, of "The Full Monty," "Trainspotting" and "Go Now," who starred in "Riff Raff" back in 1991. At his most profane and pugnacious, he plays George, a maverick, garbage-mouthed Glasgow bus driver who seems eager to be dismissed—and who, after helping a beautiful fare beater named Carla (Oyanka Cabezas) is. At loose ends in Glasgow, and deathly afraid of deportation, she resists his attentions at first. But before you know it they're in love. And before he can say "_____" they're heading for Central America.

Carla's history—and her political/romantic history with a missing contra victim—make up a large part of the story. So do the dramatic recreations of U.S.-supported ambushes, torture and disfigurements. Shot in small Nicaraguan villages (with the almost total support of that country's coalition government), "Carla's Song" has convincing atmosphere and pretty convincing plotline, although Loach may find himself preaching to the converted.

George, for whom Nicaragua is a cultural/political traumatic awakening, is a two-legged extended metaphor: The private citizen with nothing much motivating his life, who finds love and along with it a conscience about the state of the world. His world. As George, Carlyle outclasses the rest of the cast, from relative newcomer Cabezas to Scott Glenn, whose jungle-wise Bradley—a human-rights activist with a shady past—is well over the top. But Carlyle is thoroughly enjoyable to watch, even at his most indignant. And Loach, whose movies get more marginalized as the corporate movie monster eats its young, continues to be a valiant voice in the wilderness.

SIGHT AND SOUND, 2/97, p. 38, Paul Julian Smith

Glasgow, 1987. George, an independent-minded bus driver, sticks up for a young, female fare dodger threatened by an officious bus inspector. The woman escapes, but goes to the council estate where George lives with his mother and sister to offer him a gift. Attracted to this elusive and enigmatic figure, George tracks her down to a hostel and inadvertently causes her eviction. After George finds her a spare room in his friend's house, Carla gradually opens up to him: she is a traumatised exile from war-torn Nicaragua where her boyfriend Antonio is left behind in mysterious but perilous circumstances. George makes an unscheduled trip in his bus to show Carla the beauties of Loch Lomond. Having lost his job as a result and fallen in love with Carla, he produces plane tickets to Managua and persuades her to return with him.

On their arrival, the couple visit a number of Carla's friends, beginning with Bradley, a US human rights activist, with whom George has a violent argument. Travelling north they meet Norma, active in the women's movement, and Rafael, a literacy worker. All of them deny knowledge of Antonio's whereabouts. Finally Bradley admits that he himself was once a CIA agent; and that Antonio, horribly mutilated by the Contras, is sharing his house. After witnessing a Contra attack on Carla's home village (in which he displays great courage under fire), George tells Carla that he is leaving for Scotland, sickened by the violence he has seen. Carla steels herself to meet Antonio. As George departs, she sings a song called 'Guerrilla of Love' accompanied by the mute Antonio on guitar.

Carla's Song marks Ken Loach's third recent foray into things Hispanic, following the domestic drama *Ladybird Ladybird* (which features a Latin American exile in Britain) and the historical epic *Land and Freedom* (which focuses on a British volunteer in the Spanish Civil War). And there is much to enjoy here: Robert Carlyle's sensitive interaction with non-professionals; Oyanka Cabezas' endearing attempts to translate for her countrymen; a 'look, no hands!' love scene in which the central couple remove each other's clothes with their teeth; and even a Nicaraguan *campesino* arguing about the relative merits of Yul Brynner and Paul Newman. These incidental pleasures are, however, marred by structural problems which begin with the plot. With 30 minutes elapsed before the word "Nicaragua" is spoken and an hour before the cross-cultural couple reach Managua, the pace is leisurely.

Flat, semi-improvised dialogue ("We'll see this through together") is matched by hackneyed plot devices curiously out of sync with the seriousness of the film's moral and political intent. Thus the audience is strung along with quest motifs ("Where is Antonio?"), enigmas ("What is Bradley's secret?"), and ironic parallelisms (George drives a bus in war torn Nicaragua just as he did in, workaday Glasgow).

For all these familiar devices (the bus trip in the country is oddly reminiscent of *Summer Holiday*), the basic structure is inert. Loach has said that he and scriptwriter Paul Laverty were looking for a story in which an English-speaker was central to the action. The problem is that this seems not so much Carla's song as George's: certainly George is as voluble as Carla is tongue-tied by linguistic inadequacy. Moreover, after we arrive in Nicaragua, the story is told from the perspective of English-speaking characters: the camera keeps cutting back from FSNL (Sand-inista) *compañeros* to the bemused but well-meaning George; Bradley's US activists are shown in a protracted and wordy meeting. Loach is surprisingly close here to one Hollywood version of the Sandinistas: Roger Spottiswoode's *Under Fire*, which uses photojournalist Nick Nolte as the identification character for Anglo audiences bemused by or indifferent to Central American politics. But where Nolte's change of consciousness over the course of the film (he goes from dispassionate observer to active supporter of the Revolutionaries) carries the audience with it, George's well-intentioned puzzlement ("All this stuff—it's hard to believe, man.") carries no conviction. It is tempting to relate the hesitancy and diffidence of the actors, professional and non-professional alike, to Loach's refusal to give them advance knowledge of the script beyond the scene they are shooting. Both plot and characters lack a satisfying 'arc' to lead the audience through complex political issues.

The love story thus undermines the war story, rather than reinforcing it. It is clearly no stretch for George to love Nicaragua when that country is represented to him by the tousle-haired Carla, a role identical to that equally beautiful Rosana Pastor in *Land and Freedom*. George's quest would appear more disinterested had he encountered a less photogenic war victim. And the photography and music respectively by Loach veterans Barry Ackroyd and George Fenton also conspire to effect an exotic aestheticisation: the swelling strings added to Carla's song in the final sequence are incongruous. Moreover the war story is as schematic as the love story, with the Nicaraguan characters simply ciphers called upon to illustrate aspects of FSNL policy. Seeing as we do through the eyes of Loach's sympathetic but ignorant hero, we are left as much in the dark as the linguistically challenged George. Even in the Scottish scenes there is a curious sketchiness to the social context. Thus George is wholly indifferent to the loss of his job or, again, Carla's eviction is magically solved by a free room in a friend's house. Rarely can unemployment and homelessness have been treated so cavalierly. On the other hand, the denunciation of the horrors of US policy in Central America is so insistent and hectoring that it leaves no opportunity for the audience to exercise its imagination and no space for the fiction to take hold.

In spite of the concessions to commercial criteria (an English-speaking hero, an attractive love interest, a recognisable plot line), *Carla's Song* is not compelling enough as drama to hold the attention of a general audience, nor is it detailed enough as a document to serve as a serious analysis of Nicaraguan history. It is perhaps significant that not one member of the FSLN is mentioned by name; and issues such as land reform, which continue to divide Nicaraguans, are presented as wholly unproblematic. *Carla's Song* thus asserts simple Leftist pieties in a Central American context for European audiences who would no longer accept them if they were voiced in their own countries.

Loach's producer Sally Hibbin has said that the Centre-Right government of Nicaragua, in power at the time the film was shot, welcomed the film-makers even though they knew the latter's political sympathies were wholly opposed to their own. Pathetically, perhaps, the government hoped *Carla's Song* would "help put Nicaragua back on the international map." Such an attitude reveals the complexity of politics on the ground, a complexity which *Carla's Song* dares not acknowledge: few could guess from the film that Nicaragua was shortly to elect a Coalition Party opposed to the FSLN; or that even after six years of economically disastrous Coalition rule, half of the population would still vote against Sandinista Daniel Ortega in the 1996 elections. A small measure of this complexity is suggested by Loach's commendable refusal of a happy ending. The song Carla sings in the final sequence may be called 'Guerrilla of Love' (*'Guerrillero de amor'*), but when George returns alone to Scotland leaving Carla behind, the film appears at last to concede that the love story and the war story cannot be reconciled and that good intentions are not enough to heal the wounds of history.

VILLAGE VOICE, 6/30/98, p. 138, Amy Taubin

In Ken Loach's *Carla's Song,* Robert Carlyle plays a Glasgow, bus driver whose resistance to authority and identification with the underdog leads him to befriend and then fall in love with an exiled Sandinista played by Oyanka Cabezas (a talented first-time actress who's also an amazing dancer). Eventually he follows her back to Nicaragua, where the poverty and violence are too much for him to cope with. The same could be said of Ken Loach, who loses control of the film once it leaves Scotland. Happily, *Carla's Song* is only a minor slip for Loach, who's back in form with *My Name Is Joe*, a favorite at Cannes (Peter Mullan, its unknown star, won the best male performance award); it will probably show up in New York in the fall.

Also reviewed in:
CHICAGO TRIBUNE, 1/1/99, Friday/p. F, Michael Wilmington
NEW YORK TIMES, 6/26/98, p. E14, Stephen Holden
VARIETY, 9/9-15/96, p. 118, Deborah Young

CAUGHT UP

A Live Entertainment release.   *Producer:* Peter Heller.   *Director:* Darin Scott.   *Screenplay:* Darin Scott.   *Director of Photography:* Tom Callaway.   *Editor:* Charles Bornstein.   *Music:* Marc Bonilla.   *Sound:* Ben Patrick.   *Casting:* Tony Lee.   *Production Designer:* Terrence Foster.   *Costumes:* Tracey White.   *Running time:* 95 minutes.   *MPAA Rating:* R.

CAST: Bokeem Woodbine (Daryl); Cynda Williams (Trish/Vanessa); Joseph Lindsey (Billy Grimm);   Clifton Powell (Herbert/Frank Lowden);   Basil Wallace (Ahmad); Tony Todd (Jake);   LL Cool J (Roger); Snoop Doggy Dogg (Kool Kitty Kat);   Damon Saleem (Trip);   Shedric Hunter, Jr. (Jerome); Jeffrey Combs (Security Guard).

LOS ANGELES TIMES, 2/27/98, Calendar/p. 6, John Anderson

[*The following review by John Anderson appeared in a slightly different form in* NEWSDAY, 2/27/98, Part II/p. B7.]

As if to concede that there's no escape from stereotyped portrayals of African Americans in mainstream movies, Darin Scott lards his debut feature, "Caught Up," with chronic criminals, cartoon Rastafrians, bad cops, tosses in a gay villain from Central Casting and concludes with a character so transparently racist that it's all got to be tongue in cheek.

Doesn't it? Let's assume too that the bad acting is a goof. Bokeem Woodbine, as Daryl, the ex-con who's trying to go straight, keeps getting led down blind alleyways by the seductive but none too trustworthy Vanessa (Cynda Williams) who looks a lot like his old girlfriend Trish (Cynda Williams).

This causes Woodbine to lapse into what seems to be an impression of Frank Gorshin doing an impression of an exasperated Kirk Douglas. Vanessa, who's gotten involved with some diamonds that belong to the not-to-be-fooled-with Ahmad (Basil Wallace), reads fortunes. If she were any good at it, she would have known not to get involved with this movie.

Scott uses a lot of expressionistic touches that occasionally lift the film out of its exasperating morass of criminality and cliche. But they're not enough to keep Daryl out of a whole pack of trouble, or us very interested in Daryl.

NEW YORK POST, 2/27/98, p. 44, Larry Worth

Toward the climax of "Caught Up," a man is tied to a chair and sulfuric acid is poured on his head, burning clear through to his brain.

Not pretty. But his pain can't compare to that suffered by "Caught Up" audiences.

It's an insulting mix of film noir and blaxploitation, complete with a plot in which the holes could accommodate a convoy of pile drivers.

That's in addition to one deja vu moment after another, as when the sad-sack hero leaves prison at the film's outset and comments: "Nobody was waiting for me but a dude named Destiny, so I walked off to meet him."

Actually, it's a her. Fate comes in the form of a gorgeous fortune teller dressed in more scarves than Salome. And one needn't be among Dionne Warwick's psychic friends to know she's trouble with a capital T.

One quick Kama Sutra lesson later, the twosome are a hot item, having displayed more tongue action than anteaters in heat. But the lovers haven't unlocked limbs before a masked gunman tries to unite them for eternity.

So begins a ridiculously complicated pattern of double- and triple-crosses that would confuse Raymond Chandler. Worse, it's filled with one stereotype after another—the African-American principals are either drug dealers or killers—and dialogue that works the N-word or motherf---er into every sentence.

Neophyte filmmaker Darin Scott might have been aiming for a 'hood-based actioner, but hilariously awful direction and screenwriting create a parody to rival Keenen Ivory Wayans' "I'm Gonna Git You Sucka." But, this time, viewers will laugh at the film rather than with it.

One can't blame the cast for zombie-like performances. As the slinky femme fatale, Cynda Williams displays none of the potential that jumped off the screen in 1992's "One False Move." Instead, she deals Tarot cards, screams on cue and bares her breasts with the same bored expression.

And despite male-model good looks and presence to spare, leading man Bokeem ("Gridlock'd") Woodbine barely registers. Cameos from Snoop Doggy Dogg and LL Cool J are equally unmotivated.

Even the ad campaign is lame. "Caught Up" posters scream: "This game has only two rules: Do or die." Ticket buyers should opt for a third alternative: Disappear.

Also reviewed in:
CHICAGO TRIBUNE, 2/17/98, Friday/p. H, Michael Wilmington
NEW YORK TIMES, 2/28/98, p. B14, Lawrence Van Gelder
VARIETY, 3/2-8/98, p. 84, Leonard Klady
WASHINGTON POST, 2/27/98, Weekend/p. 43, Desson Howe

CELEBRATION, THE

An October Films release of a Nimbus Film production in collaboration with DR TV and SVT Drama. *Producer:* Birgitte Hald. *Director:* Thomas Vinterberg. *Screenplay (Danish with English subtitles):* Thomas Vinterberg and Mogens Rukov. *Based on an idea by:* Thomas Vinterberg. *Director of Photography:* Anthony Dod Mantle. *Editor:* Valdis Oskarsdottir. *Sound:* Morten Holm. *Casting:* Rie Hedegaard. *Stunt Coordinator:* Thomas B. Larsen. *Running time:* 106 minutes. *MPAA Rating:* Not Rated.

CAST: Ulrich Thomsen (Christian);   Henning Moritzen (Helge);   Thomas Bo Larsen (Michael);   Paprika Steen (Helene);   Birthe Neumann (Elsa);   Trine Dyrholm (Pia);   Helle Dolleris (Mette);   Therese Glahn (Michelle);   Klaus Bondam (Master of Ceremonies); Bjarne Henriksen (Kim);   Gbatokai Dakinah (Gbatokai);   Lasse Lunderskov (Uncle);   Lars Brygmann (Receptionist);   Lene Laub Oksen (Sister);   Linda Laursen (Birthe);   John Boas (Granddad); Erna Boas (Grandma).

CHRISTIAN SCIENCE MONITOR, 10/16/98, p. B3, David Sterritt

[*The Celebration* was reviewed jointly with *The Inheritors:* see Sterritt's review of that film.]

LOS ANGELES TIMES, 10/16/98, Calendar/p. 10, Kenneth Turan

A family comes together to celebrate its patriarch's 60th birthday, but everyone is not in a festive mood. Adult children gather to nominally salute their father, but darker thoughts prey on their minds. It may sound familiar, but "The Celebration" ("Festen" in the original Danish) overturns expectations.

Winner of this year's special jury prize at Cannes, "Celebration" is a remarkably mature work to be only the second feature from 29-year-old director Thomas Vinterberg. A beautifully calibrated and carefully thought out film about a completely out-of-control situation, it is raw without being off-putting and wrenching without losing its sense of humor.

Best of all, "Celebration" allows the audience to share the same sense of emotional danger and uncertainty its characters feel. We're in there with them, watching the chaos happen all around, wondering where it can possibly end.

"Celebration" is so successful because it's that rare film that's as compelling for the way it tells its story as for the tale itself The techniques used by the director and cinematographer Anthony Dod Mantle are as potent and effective as the excellent actors in conveying what Vinterberg and co-writer Mogens Rukov intended; any attempt to separate the film's elements, even in the mind, is bound to be futile.

"Celebration's" look stems from Vinterberg's commitment to the tenets of a collective of Danish directors (including "Breaking the Waves"' Lars von Trier) who call themselves Dogma 95. Dogma's rules include shooting on location without added props, using natural sound and available light at all times and doing all filming with nothing but a hand-held camera.

While some of Dogma's rules, like "the director must not be credited," have not been carefully attended to, the overall impact of this emphasis on naturalism is exceptional.

Hand-held camerawork, which can seem like an affectation, is used here to remarkable effect. It adds intimacy, immediacy and vitality to the piece, giving "Celebration" a connection to throbbing life it would not otherwise have. Moving around like one of the family, the camera brazenly eavesdrops on delicate situations, shrinking from nothing, showing and telling all.

Everything starts quietly enough as the camera picks up Christian (Ulrich Thomsen) walking with a suitcase through the Danish countryside. The family's serious, sober prodigal son, he's just flown in for the celebration from Paris where he runs two restaurants.

Headed down the same road in a sports car is younger brother Michael (Thomas Bo Larsen), a bullying, unpleasant hothead who immediately reveals his character by forcing his wife, Mette (Helle Dolleris), and their children to walk the rest of the way to the celebration so he can offer brother Christian a chance to ride in comfort.

Arriving by speeding taxi is sister Helene (Paprika Steen), a scattered, emotional woman who appears alternately strong-willed and on the verge of a collapse.

Waiting for everyone at what appears to be a family-owned hotel are mother Elsa (Birthe Neumann) and father Helge (veteran Danish actor Henning Moritzen). He's a bit stern but caring and in general happy to see his children, especially Christian, who has not been in close touch.

Once upon a time, it's revealed, Helge and Elsa had four children. But Christian's twin Linda has committed suicide so recently that when Helene is given her room she almost can't bear to stay there. Could you say a few words about Linda at the celebratory dinner, Helge asks his son, and Christian says yes, he was planning to say something.

Extended family members and guests arrive by the dozen and everyone proceeds to get fearfully drunk. Michael has what feels like one of innumerable intense brawls with his wife, Helene explores her room to startling effect, and Christian has a reunion with childhood friends Kim (Bjarne Henriksen), now the evening's chef, and Pia (Trine Dyrholm), who's always had a crush on him.

Then, in the midst of considerable inebriated merriment, Christian rises to speak. Barely able to stand, he makes a horrifying accusation against his father. The words have an air of finality, but in fact a Pandora's box of jealousies, rivalries, countercharges and recriminations is just beginning to open.

Wonderfully acted by a well-cast ensemble, "Celebration" never quite goes where you expect it to, even managing to throw in comic moments amid its terrifying family dynamics. While most films about dysfunctional relationships fit neatly into a problem picture box, this wrenching but uplifting film finds its own way with energy and aplomb.

NEW YORK POST, 10/7/98, p. 44, Thelma Adams

From the moment "The Celebration" begins we are in motion, tossed in with a bourgeois Danish family united by the patriarch's 60th birthday and rent by a daughter's recent death.

Like a fifth sibling, we quickly form our alliances, made intimate by Thomas Vinterberg's hand-held camera and urgent exposition. We trust the prodigal eldest son, Christian (Ulrich Thomsen). We warm to Helene (Paprika Steen), the effervescent daughter.

After Michael (Thomas Bo Larsen) tosses his wife and three kids out of his car to give Christian a lift, we know he's not our favorite kin—and that's well before the youngest son leads the guests at his father's country estate in a rousing racist song.

As for mom and dad, stuffy codger Helge (Henning Moritzen), a wealthy burgher known for his steely disposition, alternates bad jokes with threats. His elegant wife (Birthe Neumann) smiles graciously no matter the family bombshells shattering the china.

At the black-tie dinner that is the movie's centerpiece, Christian unmasks his father in a scathing toast. The family's immediate reaction is to deny Christian, to claim that his mortifying accusation is the product of an overheated imagination.

After this night, the family will never be the same. The taut dramatic structure is a perennial favorite. Like some Chekhov or Bergman ("Fanny and Alexander" is visually quoted) or the recent Academy Award winner "Burnt by the Sun," the comedic drama brings into burning focus all the ties and trials of a family in a single day, at a single moment in time.

While the structure is familiar, Vinterberg's technique comes from the Danish Film Collective known as Dogma. Lars Von Trier ("Breaking the Waves") is also a member. The group created a set of rules to shoot by that rejects genre movies and demands location shooting, natural lighting and the use of hand-held cameras, among others.

Instead of being restrictive, this so-called Vow of Chastity set Vinterberg free to create a vivid portrait of a family in crisis and catharsis.

Watching "The Celebration" (screening today and tomorrow at the New York Film Festival and opening Friday in theaters), we feel as if we are experiencing actions in progress at the very moment they melt into memory.

NEWSWEEK, 10/19/98, p. 81, David Ansen

Few events are as emotionally loaded as a family reunion—even the happiest families must traverse a minefield of ambivalence. Even so, the fireworks generated by the family gathering in

"The Celebration" are unusually explosive. At a lavish country estate turned hotel in Denmark, the well-heeled family and friends of Helge Klingenfeldt gather to celebrate this powerful patriarch's 60th birthday. At the heart of the tale are his three children. Michael, the volatile black sheep, arrives uninvited with his bickering wife and two children. The rebellious, emotionally disheveled Helene awaits the arrival of her black American boyfriend, knowing full well that the proper bourgeois guests will be secretly outraged by his presence. Christian comes from Paris, where he is a successful restaurateur. It is not just his blandness or his nationality that puts one in mind of Hamlet. The introspective Christian is also haunted by a ghost—that of his twin sister, whose recent suicide is still fresh on his mind. And he, too, wants to catch the conscience of a king—in this case his father. When the revenge-seeking Christian rises to toast the guest of honor, out of his mouth comes a family secret so dark and disturbing that the assembled guests have no choice but to ... completely ignore it. But this is just round one: Christian is determined to puncture the party's surreal gentility.

Thomas Vinterberg's gripping and savagely funny movie—winner of a special jury prize at the Cannes Film Festival this year—is shot with a handheld camera in a raw, urgent style that gives the story an almost *cinéma vérité* immediacy. Allowing himself no musical score, no makeup, no special effects, and shooting on video (which was then transferred to film), this gifted young director and his veteran co-writer, Mogens Rukov, dispense with cinematic slickness to home in on the characters. It's remarkable how swiftly and sharply each of them is brought to life—tribute to both the artfully concise script and the superb cast. It's not just the immediate family who claim our attention: aiding and abetting Christian's subversive plans are the banquet's chef and the hotel staff. To ensure that the guests remain throughout the increasingly scandalous evening, they hide everyone's car keys. "The Celebration" may have been intended as a specific assault on the complacency and hypocrisy of class-conscious Danish society, but the family emotions this supercharged movie taps into are sure to push universal buttons.

VILLAGE VOICE, 10/13/98, p. 119, J. Hoberman

The suburban domesticity of *Happiness* encompasses murder, rape, pedophilia, compulsive phone sex, free-floating humiliation, and syndromes which psychobabble has not yet named. *The Celebration,* in which Thomas Vinterberg presents one of the most disturbed Danish families this side of Elsinore, is a demented *Rules of the Game* with intimations of madness, incest, and suicide.

Solondz provides a democracy of despair, Vinterberg reminds us that the family is essentially a feudal institution. Gathering at their manor on the occasion of dad's 60th birthday, three grown sibs—all haunted by one sister's death and each wildly acting out—stage an extended domestic quarrel that escalates through insult, tantrum, and fistfights to the brink of patricide. Nothing is particularly subtle, although there's a particularly chilling equation of the family and the nation when the clan closes ranks to serenade one daughter's African American date with a rowdy racist drinking song.

Vinterberg, an associate of Lars Von Trier, orchestrates his ensemble with a gusto worthy of Robert Altman. *The Celebration* was impressively shot on Hi-8 video and successfully transferred to film; Vinterberg's brain-jarring camera swoops, outrageous tilts, and eccentric angle, as well as his frantic crosscutting, help compensate for the somewhat hackneyed characterizations. Like Gaspar Noë's more harrowing (and still distributor-less) *I Stand Alone, The Celebration* is basically a stunt—in this case, one that's too self-congratulatory in its craziness to achieve much more than momentary impact.

Also reviewed in:
CHICAGO TRIBUNE, 11/13/98, Friday/p. D, Michael Wilmington
NEW REPUBLIC, 11/2/98, p. 26, Stanley Kauffmann
NEW YORK TIMES, 10/7/98, p. E1, Janet Maslin
VARIETY, 5/25-31/98, p. 57, Godfrey Cheshire
WASHINGTON POST, 11/6/98, Weekend/p. 46, Michael O'Sullivan

CELEBRITY

A Miramax Films release of a Sweetland Films presentation of a Jean Doumanian production. *Executive Producer:* J.E. Beaucaire. *Producer:* Jean Doumanian. *Director:* Woody Allen. *Screenplay:* Woody Allen. *Director of Photography:* Sven Nykvist. *Editor:* Susan E. Morse. *Sound:* Les Lazarowitz. *Sound Editor:* Robert Hein. *Casting:* Juliet Taylor and Laura Rosenthal. *Production Designer:* Santo Loquasto. *Art Director:* Tom Warren. *Set Decorator:* Susan Kaufman. *Special Effects:* Russell Berg. *Costumes:* Suzy Benzinger. *Make-up:* Rosemarie Zurlo and Helen M. Gallagher. *Running time:* 114 minutes. *MPAA Rating:* R.

CAST: Hank Azaria (David); Kenneth Branagh (Lee Simon); Judy Davis (Robin Simon); Leonardo DiCaprio (Brandon Darrow); Melanie Griffith (Nicole Oliver); Famke Janssen (Bonnie); Michael Lerner (Dr. Lupus); Joe Mantegna (Tony Gardella); Bebe Neuwirth (Hooker); Winona Ryder (Nola); Charlize Theron (Supermodel); Greg Mottola (Director); Jeff Mazzola (Assistant Director); Dick Mingalone (Camera Operator); Vladimir Bibic (Director of Photography); Franciso Quijada (Erno Delucca); Aleksa Palladino (Production Assistant); Dan Moran (Jackhammer Operator); Pete Castellotti (Sound Recordist); A. Lee Morris (Second Assistant Cameraperson); Douglas McGrath (Bill Gaines); Maurice Sonnenberg (Dalton Freed); Craig Ulmschneider (Daniel, Production Assistant); Mina Bern (Elderly Homeowner); Janet Marlow (Singing Nun); Tommie Baxter (Second Nun); Kathleen Doyle, Arthur Berwick, and Jodi Long (Father Gladden's Fans); John Carter (Father Gladden); Monique Fowler (Jan, Robin's Friend); Mary Catherine Wright (Pious Diner); J.K. Simmons (Souvenir Hawker); Dylan Baker (Priest at Catholic Retreat); Melinda Eng (Fashion Designer); Isaac Mizrahi (Bruce Bishop); Alma Cuervo and Eve Salvail (Bruce Bishop's Admirers); Polly Adams and Brian McConnachie (Exercise Tape Fans); Irina Pantaeva, Mark Vanderloo, and Frederique Van Der Wal (Supermodel's Friends); Michael Moon Band (El Flamingo Band); Anthony Mason (Himself); Daisy Prince (Waiting Room Nurse); Tina Sloan, Dayle Haddon, and Bill Gerber (Waiting Room Patients); Julie Halston (Patient with Jowls); Renee Lippin (Second Examining Room Patient); Kate Burton (Cheryl, Robin's Friend); Reuben Jackson (Cameraman at Lupus Office); Debra Messing (TV Reporter at Lupus Office); Carmen Dell Orefice (Pinky Virdon); André Gregory (John Papadakis); Skip Rosa and Alicia Meer (Couple on Beach); Becky Ann Baker (Doris); Michael Kell (Nat); Steve Mellor (Eddie); Gerry Becker (Jay Tepper); Ileen Getz (Reunion Announcer); Robert Cuccioli (Monroe Gordon); Larry Pine (Philip Datloff); Surinder Khosla (V.J. Rajnipal); Marian Seldes (Datloff Party Guest); Frederick Rolf (Book Reviewer); David Margulies (Counselor Adelman); Ramsey Faragallah (TV Program Director); William Addy and Patrick McCarthy (Klansmen); Bernard Addison (Minister Polynice); Mary Schmidtberger and Sarah Buff (TV Production Assistants); Heather Marni (Teenage Obese Acrobat); Bruno Gioiello, Sean Daloise, and Matthew Sweeney (Skinheads); Kyle Kulish (Overweight Achiever); Tony Sirico (Lou DeMarco); Kenneth Edelson (Rabbi Kaufman); Sam Gray (Tony's Father); Marilyn Raphael (Tony's Mother); Antonette Schwartzberg (Tony's Grandma); Patti D'Arbanville (Iris); Frank Pellegrino (Frankie); Gabriel Millman (Ricky); Adam Sietz (Vince); Gretchen Mol (Vicky); Jim Moody and Robert Torres (Security Guards); Steven Randazzo and John Costelloe (Cops at Hotel); Mary Jo Buttafuoco (Herself); Joey Buttafuoco (Himself); Adrian Grenier, Sam Rockwell, and John Doumanian (Darrow Entourage); Lorri Bagley (Chekhov-style Writer); Ralph Pope (Comic's Agent); Rick Mowat (Comic); Tony Darrow, Victor Colicchio, Robert Cividanes (Moving Men in Loft); Donegal Fitzgerald (Moving Man on Street); Leslie Shenkel ("Manhattan Moods" Assistant Director); Donna Hanover ("Manhattan Moods" Anchor Woman); Allison Janney (Evelyn Isaacs); Howard Erskine (Senator Paley); Celia Weston (Dee Bartholomew); Donald Trump (Himself); Wood Harris (Al Swayze); Ray Cohen (Pianist at Wedding); Angel Caban (Limo Driver); Aida Turturro (Psychic); Ingrid Rogers (Off-Off Broadway Actress); Jeffrey Wright (Off-Off Broadway Director); Karen Duffy (TV Reporter at Premiere); Brian McCormack (Phil); Gigi Williams (Fan of Robin Simon).

LOS ANGELES TIMES, 11/20/98, Calendar/p. 10, Kenneth Turan

"Celebrity" sounds like something Woody Allen knows a thing or two about. Lionized as a writer, filmmaker and stand-up comic, with a personal life that's been as talked about as President Clinton's, who better than Allen to examine what it is to be famous? Or so you'd think.

Scattered, phlegmatic and an all-around weak effort, "Celebrity" turns out instead to be one of Allen's periodic misfires. And, ironically enough, one of the reasons for its off-putting nature is a miscalculation on someone's part about the nature of Allen's own celebrity.

Allen structures this episodic film around the messy misadventures of a pair of unsympathetic neurotics who are married at first but split up almost at once. Robin Simon (Judy Davis) is a teacher and her ex-husband Lee (Kenneth Branagh) is a journalist, blocked novelist and would-be screenwriter who is trying to get a script he describes as "an armored car robbery with a strong personal crisis" into production.

For reasons unknown, Branagh has been allowed to play this part as a close imitation of how Allen himself would have done it. Hearing the mannerisms and verbal patterns that characterize this most distinctive of American comic voices come awkwardly out of the mouth of someone else is disconcerting and irritating, the equivalent of having Daniel Day-Lewis spending an entire movie talking like Sylvester Stallone. It's a personality transplant miscalculation "Celebrity" never recovers from.

It doesn't help matters that Lee Simon is a thoroughly despicable person, a callow and ambitious phony always on the make—and one who is whiny and mean-spirited in the bargain. Allen has written parts like this for himself, most recently in the scathing but memorable "Deconstructing Harry," but absent his own leavening presence this character is simply too miserable to care about.

Lee's work as a journalist leads him to a motley collection of celebrity encounters with the likes of movie star Nicole Oliver (Melanie Griffith) and a top model played by Charlize Theron, whom he typically greets by saying, "If the universe has any meaning, I'm looking at it."

These vignettes, plus scenes at literary hangout Elaine's and the offices of a plastic surgeon to the stars, play like a random collection of pro forma celebrity-related items. There is no insight and surprisingly little humor, and even the presence of Supernova-of-the-Moment Leonardo DiCaprio doesn't manage to liven things up.

Lee's ex-wife Robin has the good fortune to meet a swell guy named Tony Gardella (Joe Mantegna), who works as a TV news producer, but all she can do about it is neurotically dither about her options. And Lee's romantic entanglements with book editor Bonnie (Famke Janssen) and waitress-actress Nola (Winona Ryder) are equally tedious.

Shot in black and white by the veteran Sven Nykvist, "Celebrity" revisits many of Allen's by now familiar situations, themes and preoccupations, from attractive women in skimpy clothing to jokes about oral sex. It's capable of surprising a laugh out of you from time to time, but mostly it has the feeling, as Allen's lesser efforts often do, of an early draft that should have been reworked before it went before the camera.

"Celebrity" makes periodic stabs at being about something, with one character saying, "You can tell a lot about a society by who it chooses to celebrate," but once it's over it doesn't seem to have gone anywhere. The last image on screen is the word "HELP" being spelled out by a skywriter. It's what this film desperately needs.

NEW STATESMAN, 6/21/99, p. 38, Jonathan Romney

Everything you really need to know about Woody Allen and celebrity you can get from Barbara Kopple's recent documentary *Wild Man Blues*, which followed Allen as he reluctantly toured the world with his jazz band. Allen *kvetched* about the showers and the sandwiches, grimaced behind the backs of adoring Venetian matrons and then returned to New York, where his nonagenarian parents put him firmly in his place. He'd have done better, they carp, if he'd become a pharmacist. Allen himself couldn't have devised a more deflating portrait of a star cushioned by fame, sneering defensively at his admirers, but finally humbled by a different kind of infantilisation. *Wild Man Blues* was all the more telling in that it coincided with *Deconstructing Harry*, Allen's own scathing picture of the kind of person we imagine him to be—a writer in the

Philip Roth mould, recruiting people from his own life as characters for his novels but signally lacking insight into his own nature.

These two films offer such a comprehensive impression of Allen's attitudes to public life and the media that his latest, entitled *Celebrity*, looked certain to be anti-climactic. It's worse than that. For a start, you could always count on an Allen film clocking in neatly around the 100-minute mark, This one runs to 113; that may seem a niggling complaint, but it's a sign that he's not pulling his strokes with quality control. This is the first Woody Allen film that's made me check my watch throughout.

Celebrity reeks of world-loathing as much as—but not nearly as compellingly as—the bilious *Stardust Memories* (1980). It's a journey through a bright, noisy funfair of worldliness, undertaken in parallel by a divorced couple, Lee (Kenneth Branagh), a writer, and the lapsed academic Robin (Judy Davis). Lee wants to be a serious writer but spends his time writing intimate personality profiles of the *Vanity Fair* ilk. He gets closer to the stars than most European profile-writers, allotted their 60 minutes, might find credible. He falls into bed with the actress Nicole (Melanie Griffith), has a wretched night out with a supermodel (Charlize Theron), then crashes his implausibly flashy car into a shop window and resists being inveigled into several-way sex by the star brat Brandon (the film's scoop—Leonardo di Caprio parodying his spoilt-puppy image). Meanwhile, Robin (Davis mangling herself into her inimitable angst-knots) passes through several shades of torment before re-inventing herself as a glib daytime TV personality reporting on Donald Trump's dining habits.

What are *Celebrity*'s great revelations? Only that Allen can still be unpleasantly dyspeptic, is still seriously hung up on Fellini's *La Dolce Vita* and is pretty much a write-off as a social satirist. Branagh's Lee, blabbering and twitching in a grotesque and distracting impersonation of Allen himself, gets sucked into the whirlpool of glitz in too many repetitive sequences. Allen has nothing to say about the shallow and famous, other than: "So beautiful, so rich—yet look how they waste their time!" He doesn't present their world as anything genuinely novel or seductive—it's all shorthand to justify the morally instructive spectacle of smart people such as Lee and Robin frittering away their talent.

Allen is no more optimistic or insightful about contemporary appetites for culture and spirit—religion, therapy and the literary world all get carved up in mechanical fashion. Lee is made to look as dopey in his airier aspirations as he is when drawn to the carnival. He falls for a bohemian princess—Winona Ryder, who must get sick of being cast as wafty and vaguely cerebral. She's another version of Allen's precocious, brainy dreamgirls who are best left alone, like Rain in *Husbands and Wives*. Then there's the novel that Lee finally writes, which his angry girlfriend (an incisive Famke Janssen) throws off the back of a boat. The old paper-fluttering-in-the-wind routine—can this wash any more? Is it pedantic to object that no sane writer today has only one draft of a novel? Lee can surely afford a laptop, or did he file all those profile pieces by carrier pigeon? The scene is a romantic cliché exposed by sloppy elderly thinking.

This impression of half-baked thought comes across in a formless succession of ugly routines that are less trenchant about fashionable emptiness than Brett Easton Ellis's *Glamorama* (which at least tackles the abyss from the inside) and less energetically silly than Robert Altman's much-maligned *Prêt à Porter*. Some sequences—at a cosmetician's, at various media beanfeasts—strain for a busy simultaneity of impressions in the manner of Fellini and Altman, but they're just blustery, as if Allen can't really stand the noise. Little is really said about the media other than that things get jumbled up in frivolous promiscuity. The single good gag is a TV chat show that programmes rabbis, Nazis and gangsters together—"Where are the bagels? The skinheads ate all the bagels already?"

Most of this is just deadening but the film becomes objectionable in its peevish handling of ordinary people. Lee attends a class reunion—that stalest chestnut of American social insight—and is shocked to see how staid and middle-aged everyone seems. Look, there's even a pony-tailed goon singing "The Impossible Dream"! It's meant to be Lee's moment of self-knowledge, as he realises that he's no spring chicken to be running around with club kids. But the scene reeks of distaste for the everyday.

If all you find is bourgeois stagnation on the one hand and tinselly neurosis on the other, what's there to do but retreat into contemplation of your own inner depths (which is more or less what the writer ends up doing in *Deconstructing Harry*)? You can only hope that the older and wiser

Lee succeeds in this better than his creator, because Allen's creative depths seem to have dried up for the moment.

NEW YORK, 11/20/98, p. 121, Peter Rainer

Woody Allen doesn't physically appear in *Celebrity*, but he seems to be inhabiting the corporeal substance of at least two of his stars. It's *Invasion of the Woodman*. In the past, Allen has restricted this sort of thing to just one player; usually his leading ladies are the ones who assume his vocal inflections and body language. (Think of Diane Keaton in *Annie Hall* or Mia Farrow in just about anything of his.) In *Celebrity*, Kenneth Branagh is doing Allen at least as well as Allen's been doing himself lately (especially as an ant in *Antz*). It's a dead-on impersonation rather than a performance, and the effect is weirdly comic—as if Allen were dubbing Branagh. Judy Davis plays Branagh's bitter ex-wife, and she seems dubbed, too. When these two go at each other, we might as well be seeing double. How much of this is intentional self-parody on Allen's part? Maybe he just thinks we miss not having him around. But turning actors of the caliber of Branagh and Davis into animated pod people isn't the brightest idea he's ever had.

Shot in austere black-and-white, *Celebrity* has its sly amusements, but it's a minor entry in the canon. Allen really doesn't have much to say about the nature of fame, because his whole persona disdains it. He can't stand the idea that it's the stars—simpering boobs and tantrum-throwers, in his view—who call the showbiz shots. They are the ones you need to have in your movies in order to be bankable. Branagh's Lee Simon is a hack magazine writer, and he has three celebrity-subject encounters that are meant to be illustrative. In the first, he accompanies a movie queen (Melanie Griffith) back to her childhood home, where he puts the make on her and she responds—at least from the neck up. Later, a supermodel (Charlize Theron) at a fashion show he's covering comes on to him and plays him for a gaga fool. Then he walks in on a hot movie star (Leonardo DiCaprio) as the brat tears up his hotel suite and lunges at his cowering girlfriend (Gretchen Mol). It all comes across as so much slapstick sleaze. The only aspect that rings true in all this is that Lee wants to buy into the sleaze. The author of two failed novels, he's constantly trying to palm his screenplays off on his subjects. He's both fawning and acrid—the perfect hack combo.

Judy Davis's Robin is a schoolteacher involved with a guy (Joe Mantegna) who produces star-powered drivel for television and loves her unconditionally. Her story is instructive, too. Instead of being frazzled by the celebrity circus, she settles into its lunacy. She's found an outer world that matches her inner one, and it calms her down. She ends up an on-air host for a top-rated schlock TV interview show and can finally say of herself, "I've become the kind of woman I've always hated, but I'm happier." Which may be the most uplifting words anybody has spoken in a Woody Allen movie in a very long time. For him, coming to terms with the cult of celebrity is a bit like resigning yourself to the apocalypse. He could have subtitled his film *How I Learned to Stop Worrying and Love the Biz*.

NEW YORK POST, 9/25/98, p. 37, Rod Dreher

In "Celebrity," the opening-night extravaganza of the New York Film Festival, Woody Allen tells us that celebrities are shallow, vain, flighty and bad examples of how to live. All together now: Duh.

It's probably time for Woody to settle down and be less prolific. While not at all a bad film, "Celebrity" is as tossed-off and inconsequential as anything he's ever done. Aside from a few lively star cameos, this very modest entertainment—Allen's first black-and-white film since the dreadful "Shadows and Fog"—is a ho-hum slog through exceedingly well-trod territory.

For this slight comedy about the manic chase of a false idol, Allen must have finally taken to heart critics' complaints that, at age 62, he's too old to credibly play older men looking for love with significantly younger women. He cast poor Kenneth Branagh in the Woody role, with bizarre and wildly unsuccessful results.

Branagh is an excellent actor, of course. But as the confused magazine writer Lee Simon, he does nothing more than a terribly unconvincing impersonation of Woody Allen. Lee is a celebrity journalist who has a midlife crisis and dumps his wife, Robin. He falls victim to the siren song of celebrity, and, like Fellini's Roman scribe Marcello, fancies the dolce vita of hanging out with stars.

But Branagh's neurotic lines and his stammering delivery are utterly Woody, to the point of complete distraction. Never mind us—what about the women in the picture? Lee dallies with several babes, including Famke Janssen as a book editor, Winona Ryder as an aspiring stage actress and, in a brief but show-stopping performance, Charlize Theron as a supermodel. What on earth any of these women would see in a yammering yutz like Lee is anybody's guess.

The usually dependable Judy Davis doesn't fare much better in her underwritten role as the wife who suddenly finds herself abandoned by her selfish husband. She attracts the sincere romantic attentions of a TV talk-show producer (Joe Mantegna), but insecure and untrusting, she resists his advances. In one embarrassingly unfunny scene, she visits a courtesan (Bebe Neuwirth) for oral-sex lessons involving a banana. This kind of cheap tee-hee-hee humor is beneath Allen's comic sensibilities—and it's done better by the Farrelly brothers, anyway.

What keeps "Celebrity" interesting and mildly fun is the fast-moving plot, which whisks us from scene to scene at a revolving-door pace, and, paradoxically, lets us gawk at celebrities making cameo appearances. The one destined to be the most talked-about is Leonardo DiCaprio's 10 minutes as Brandon, a bratty young film superstar who travels with a posse and carouses wildly with drugs and groupies. Sounds like type-casting.

Does Woody have any new ideas? "Celebrity" is crammed with either shopworn Woodyisms or exceedingly banal observations. Woody Allen is a smart man, but any fresh-out-of-Harvard junior writer on "The Simpsons" could make hash of Woody's startlingly unsavvy take on celebrity culture.

Though "Celebrity" tries—Lord, how it tries—it can't find anything amusing or insightful to say about famed plastic surgeons, trendy religious gurus, exploitative TV talk shows and bubble-headed TV entertainment reporters. Allen has made an entire movie commenting on the crassness of celebrity and hasn't even touched the sharpness and acerbity of the Alan Alda character in "Crimes and Misdemeanors."

The one half-good idea in "Celebrity" is Allen's likening of the pursuit of celebrity to the pursuit of true love. Both are capricious and involve personal and psychological risks, but only one has the potential for fulfillment. Woody seems to suggest that a society in which people take their cues on how to behave and what to esteem from self-absorbed celebrities is one that will have a tough time knowing what is good and lasting in life.

That's the movie lost somewhere in "Celebrity," which, like what it purports to criticize, is diverting but feather-light and pseudo-profound.

NEWSDAY, 11/20/98, Part II/p. B7, Jack Mathews

It's hard to think of someone better qualified to noodle on the cult of celebrity in America than Woody Allen. Allen has been a marksman at assaulting cultural phonies, usually played by Alan Alda, and he's certainly fostered his own cult.

But satire, which Allen attempts here, is not his specialty. His social commentaries have tended toward broad anthropological parody, and his sharpest observations about real behavior have led him to such humorless, deadweight dramas as "Interiors" and "September."

"Celebrity," a lazily episodic film following the parallel lives of a recently divorced New York couple, is a rare Allen comedy. It's not very funny. And it isn't funny because it has no focus, no particular insight, and no Woody Allen, though Kenneth Branagh does an annoyingly specific impression of him. Nervous stutter, hand-waving gestures, rolled eyes... the works. Branagh is Allen, except he's not. The imitation not only undermines every scene he's in, but belies any point Allen might be trying to make about his subject.

Branagh's character, Lee Simon, is a writer testing the romantic waters after his separation from insecure schoolteacher Robin (Judy Davis, doing the same neurotic flush she has done in past Allen films). The movie, shot in black and white, intercuts the Simons' life-altering adventures, scraping against celebrities—real and imagined—along the way.

The film's starry cast includes Leonardo DiCaprio, as a spoiled film idol (tough stretch), Melanie Griffith, as a married actress who shares Bill Clinton's narrow view of infidelity (oral sex doesn't count), and Bebe Neuwirth, as a hooker who, in a vulgar comic bit unworthy of Allen, instructs Robin in the performance of that "so-called" non-sexual act.

Inadvertently, Allen made a much stronger statement about the cult of celebrity with "Stardust Memories," his 1980 film about a dyspeptic director icon who rues his life, his loves, and his success. That is the Allen we know, and, with a nice try to Kenneth Branagh, he's the only one who can play it.

SIGHT AND SOUND, 7/99, p. 38, Leslie Felperin

Manhattan. Lee is an unsuccessful novelist and travel journalist who's now doing well as a celebrity-profile writer; his ex-wife Robin is an English teacher, adrift in life now that her marriage has ended. Lee gets a blow-job from Nicole Oliver, a famous movie star, chats up a waitress/actress named Nola, and later picks up a supermodel, even though he is in a serious relationship with Bonnie, a book editor. While visiting a plastic surgeon for a consultation, Robin meets handsome television producer Tony. On their first date at a film premiere they run into Lee and Bonnie. Robin gets drunk and hurls abuse at Lee. Nonetheless, Tony is smitten with her, and offers her a job at his production company where she eventually flourishes despite her initial lack of experience.

Encouraged by Bonnie, Lee works on a novel for a year. But he meets Nola again at a restaurant and becomes infatuated with her. On the day Bonnie is to move in with him, Lee splits up with her, so she chucks the only copy of his novel in the Hudson river.

Time passes. Lee is in a fractious relationship that seems poised to fail with the flighty Nola. Robin has become the presenter of a society-focused news report produced by Tony's company. Jittery and apprehensive, she leaves Tony standing at the altar on their wedding day, but they eventually marry. At the premiere of Nicole's film, a happy Robin and Tony arrive together and warmly greet Lee, now lonely and adrift.

The first 'Woodyless' Woody Allen film since *Bullets over Broadway, Celebrity* tempts you to think that Allen may suddenly have wised up to the fact that audiences find it increasingly hard to swallow the notion of him as a lady-killer alluring enough to pull the comely likes of Elisabeth Shue *(Deconstructing Harry)*, Julia Roberts *(Everyone Says I Love You)* or Juliette Lewis *(Husbands and Wives)*. So for *Celebrity* Allen has brought in sexier, younger Kenneth Branagh as his representative on screen. Always a better actor than he is a director, especially at comedy, Branagh clearly enjoys his jaunt in Woody-drag, hugging his corduroy jacket around him like a protective girdle and mimicking the nasal stutter, but it's more a top-grade impersonation than a performance.

Giving the persona a facelift by casting someone a generation younger still leaves a few ugly scars that mar this comedy of manners. The fit is just not quite right. For a start Branagh looks too *goyische*, so the New York-Jewish locutions of the dialogue make him seem even more the ventriloquist's dummy. He's completely out of place in a flashback to a high-school reunion populated by the kind of middle-aged, lower-to-middle-class grotesques Allen so often contextualises himself against, and among whom the director himself looks exactly of a piece. And sure, guys Lee's age can be just as sexist and groin-fixated as their fathers, but they're usually a bit smoother about disguising the fact and generally more cautious, crabbed and calculating. So it makes practically no sense that an ambitious lad like Branagh's Lee would throw over successful, well-connected and frankly stunning Bonnie for dippy Nola *unless* he was afflicted by a certain 50s-to-60s-vintage romanticism that prizes selfish spontaneity, the love-at-first-sight myth and Twiggy-shaped, quasi-pubescent girls. It's a mind-set straight out of Doris Day movies, but with a hard-on.

The analysis of celebrity itself, ostensibly the meat of the movie, is similarly that of a much older man. A whiny despair that the talentless usually rise to the top and that people become famous for the flimsiest of reasons seems to be the main thesis of the film. It's a worn complaint, and *EdTV* and *The Truman Show* have had fresher thoughts to contribute on the matter recently. At one point, Judy Davis' Robin (a magnificent performance of spite, wounded pride and touching resilience), having become a reporter-courtier to the rich and famous, casually mentions that everyone's a celebrity now—she just profiled Sunny von Bulow "and she just lies there." (Sunny is the now-comatose high-society wife whom Claus von Bulow allegedly tried to kill.)

Allen's darts at fatuous publishers and film critics fly with more accuracy than his barbs at fashion folk, modern Catholicism or the hedonism of Hollywood types (incarnated by a hilarious, self-immolating cameo by Leonardo DiCaprio). *Celebrity* lacks the misanthropic gusto of *Deconstructing Harry* as well as that film's flashy formal control and feels like Allen on autopilot.

TIME, 11/16/98, p. 104, Richard Schickel

Lee Simon (Kenneth Branagh) is a man in a rumpled corduroy jacket with his nose pressed eagerly against the double-glazed windows of fame. A failed novelist, he writes celebrity profiles for magazines and subsists emotionally on such crusts—a bit of gossip, a moment of false intimacy—as the famous discard as they pass by.

Robin Simon (Judy Davis) is Lee's estranged wife, a former teacher of Chaucer and a quivering mass of neuroses, willing to try anything—religious retreats, plastic surgery—to get her postdivorce life back together.

Woody Allen's "Celebrity" tracks the former's possibly predictable fall and the latter's entirely unexpected rise within the tensely striving world of Manhattan's media and cultural demimonde. Since Branagh's performance (rather daringly) imitates Allen's anxiously stammering screen persona, and Davis is doing something she has done—expertly—for the writer-director before, playing a jilted, tilted woman, it may sound as if this is yet another of Allen's comically discordant chamber pieces about the impossibility of permanent connection between postmodern urbanites who think too much about themselves and feel too little for each other.

But as Allen traces Lee's and Robin's parallel courses toward opposite fates, "Celebrity," even though it is shot in austere black and white on palpably real locations, turns into something new for him: an epic. It contains 242 speaking parts and 5,128 extras—forces sufficient, if deployed in a different context, to make a biblical spectacle. Or—better comparison—a screen version of Thackeray's "Vanity Fair" or some other satirical, multilayered saga of halfway decent, halfway desperate people trying to make their way in a corrupt society.

The pilgrim's path is made easier, Allen says, if he or she is armored by innocence rather than made vulnerable by naked need. It also helps if there is someone utterly indifferent to fame who can lend a guiding hand. It's Robin's good luck that such a figure interrupts her consultation with the cosmetic surgeon. He's a television producer named Tony Gardella (Joe Mantegna) doing a story on the currently hot doctor, and he thinks Robin looks fine just the way she is. And he thinks she might shake her funk if she comes to work for him.

Good idea. Like Allen himself, Tony brings clear vision but no reformist zeal to the business of chronicling celebrity life. It's just something he, like a dwindling few of his fellow citizens, is trying to live with (and in his case, make a living from) as rationally as possible. He guesses that Robin's self-consciousness, her sense that she doesn't belong in the same room with the rich and famous, will play well on TV. She's as addled as anyone in her audience would be in fast company, so of course viewers identify with her. And grant her stardom.

The secret of her success naturally eludes her former mate. Close, yearning observation has led him to believe that the celebrated are mostly not more gifted or harder working than he is. He thinks if he can just worm his way closer to the center of their world, he will be allowed to partake of their magic.

Bad idea. They can smell his desperation. It invites their casual contempt. When a movie star (Melanie Griffith) grants him a sexual favor, it's one of those once-in-a-lifetime benisons queens sometimes bestow on a lucky serf, not the beginning of a relationship. When a supermodel (Charlize Theron) catches a glimpse of his only glamorous asset, a classic Aston Martin sports car, she thinks its owner may do as an escort for a night on the town, but her attention keeps wandering.

The feckless journalist has a dreadful movie script he's trying to push on his interviewees, and that leads to the film's central, most harrowing passage. For when he arrives to discuss it with Brandon Darrow (Leonardo DiCaprio, in a chilling performance), the star is exercising his power by beating up a girlfriend and trashing a hotel room. Undaunted, Lee starts pitching. And pitching—through a night of high-stakes gambling (he loses, of course), drugs and group sex. Slyly, sadistically, Brandon alternately encourages and discourages him. Degradation is power's prerogative. And besides, it amuses him.

The experience briefly sobers Lee. He has, but fails to appreciate, an equivalent to Robin's Tony. She's a pretty, sensible book editor (Famke Janssen) who supports his return to fiction. But even with her patient encouragement, he can't stay straight for long. He betrays her for a promising, utterly self-absorbed young actress (Winona Ryder). Maybe he can get in on the ground floor of her celebrity.

VILLAGE VOICE, 11/24/98, p. 117, J. Hoberman

As entertainment grows ever more self-reflexive, the burden of celebritude is presented as an acute social problem—at least from the supply side. The past few months have brought several meditations on the subject—*The Truman Show, Pecker, Why Do Fools Fall in Love, Velvet Goldmine.* Woody Allen's *Celebrity* is another, even opening with the image of a cosmic cry for help—as well it might.

Predicated on a paradoxical mix of secrecy and exhibitionism, the Allen persona has always blurred the distinction between his art and his life. Still, one would scarcely expect Allen's attempt to satirize daily life in the National Entertainment State to be this tired, sour, and depressed. Whether or not the filmmaker regards the condition of celebrity as a curse, his meditation on the subject is extraordinarily punishing. *Celebrity* is as nasty as *Mighty Aphrodite* or *Deconstructing Harry*, and without the jokes.

Perhaps responding to those (myself included) who have wondered how much longer this incipient codger would continue to cast Hollywood's hottest young babes as his adoring sex toys, Allen has anointed a younger surrogate in Kenneth Branagh. It is a chastening experience—mainly for us. The spectacle of earnest Branagh imitating the body language and cadences of the obsequiously dithering Woody, without showing the slightest facility for the master's comic timing, is enough to make one wish for Allen's return, even if it requires a face-lift, dental surgery, and a triple bypass. To compound the misery, the Branagh character is married—at least initially—to Judy Davis, who is playing another whining, neurotic Woody clone.

Ostensibly, Branagh thrashes through the role of a craven, horny celebrity journalist, visiting movie sets and hanging out at literary parties, as he attempts to write his own novel on ... the curse of celebrity. (The movie is a generational mishmash. Branagh plays the only 40-year-old writer in America who davens at Elaine's and names as his inspiration William Saroyan.) The movie's premise, an opportunistic journalist exploring decadent high society, is loosely modeled on the 1959 Fellini warhorse *La Dolce Vita*—something *Celebrity* acknowledges with such Fellini-esque gargoyles as a TV priest, a star plastic surgeon, and most spectacularly, the gorgeous supermodel (wittily embodied by Charlize Theron) who leads Branagh on a merry chase to the end of the night.

To add to the carnival atmosphere, the large cast is augmented with such real-life media thugs as Anthony Mason, Donald Trump, and Joey Buttafuoco. If their celebrity weren't scary enough, Allen adds a bad-boy á clef. In the film's equivalent of a money scene, Branagh joins the entourage of a drug-crazed young star (Leonardo DiCaprio) and tags along to Atlantic City, haplessly trying to peddle a film script while the star beats up his girlfriend (Gretchen Mol), trashes their hotel suite, and engineers an orgy. All is possible when celebrity is the coin of the realm. But what exactly is Woody's complaint? If anything, the world of *Celebrity* is what his movies have always been. Allen is no stranger to self-absorption. Nor, beginning with the Marshall McLuhan gag in *Annie Hall,* has any filmmaker made more of the celeb cameo. The horror, I suppose, comes from his imagining himself being on the outside looking in.

Several have already noted the bizarre reversal in which a big star (Melanie Griffith) fellates Branagh's celebrity journalist. But this apparent misunderstanding of media dynamics is rectified with the even more embarrassing scene in which Davis—who has now made one Woody Allen film too many—pays a hooker (Bebe Neuwirth) for oral-sex tips. Supposedly this lesson is preparation for her upcoming second marriage to an adoring TV producer (Joe Mantegna); in reality, it's her symbolic initiation into a new role as a TV interviewer. If the Griffith character goes down on Branagh's Woody surrogate, it may be because Allen suspects that the only BJs he's going to get for this movie are from himself.

Also reviewed in:
CHICAGO TRIBUNE, 11/20/98, Friday/p. A, Michael Wilmington
NATION, 10/16/98, p. 34, Stuart Klawans
NEW REPUBLIC, 12/21/98, p. 26, Stanley Kauffmann

NEW YORK TIMES, 11/20/98, p. E22, Janet Maslin
NEW YORKER, 11/23/98, p. 113, Anthony Lane
VARIETY, 9/14-20/98, p. 35, Todd McCarthy
WASHINGTON POST, 11/20/98, p. F5, Stephen Hunter
WASHINGTON POST, 11/20/98, Weekend/p. 49, Michael O'Sullivan

CENTRAL STATION

A Sony Pictures Classics release of an Arthur Cohn production. *Executive Producer:* Elisa Tolomelli, Lillian Birnbaum, Don Ranvaud, and Thomas Garvin. *Producer:* Martine de Clermont Tonnerre and Arthur Cohn. *Director:* Walter Salles. *Screenplay (Portuguese with English subtitles):* Joao Emanuel Carneiro and Marcos Bernstein. *Based on an original idea by:* Walter Salles. *Director of Photography:* Walter Carvalho. *Editor:* Isabelle Rathéry and Felipe Lacerda. *Music:* Antonio Pinto and Jaques Morelenbaum. *Sound:* Jean-Claude Brisson, François Groult, Bruno Tarrière, and Waldir Xavier. *Sound Editor:* Waldir Xavier. *Casting:* Sérgio Machado. *Production Designer:* Cássio Amarante and Carla Caffé. *Running time:* 115 minutes. *MPAA Rating:* R.

CAST: Fernanda Montenegro (Dora); Marilia Péra (Irene); Vinícius de Oliveira (Josué); Soia Lira (Ana); Othon Bastos (César); Otávio Augusto (Pedrao); Stela Freitas (Yolanda); Matheus Nachtergaele (Isaias); Caio Junqueira (Moisés); Socorro Nobre (1st letter, Rio); Manoel Gomes (2nd Letter, Rio); Roberto Andrade (3rd Letter, Rio); Sheyla Kenia (4th Letter, Rio); Malcolm Soares (5th Letter, Rio); Maria Fernandes (6th Letter, Rio); Maria Marlene (7th Letter, Rio); Chrisanto Camargo (8th letter, Rio); Jorsebá-Sebastiao Oliveira (9th Letter, Rio); Sidney Antunes (Religious Man, Station); José Pedro da Costa Filho (Stall Owner); Esperança Motta (Young Prostitute, Letter Rio); Marcelo Carneiro (Thief); Manula-Manuel José Neves (Walkman Owner); Preto de Linha (Shoeshine Man); Mário Mendes (Joao, Yolanda's Husband); Gildásio Leite (Man on Bus); Sonia Leite and Estelina Moreira da Silva (Women on Bus); Zezao Pereira (Bus Driver); Felícia de Castro (Cashier); Harildo Deda (Bené); Marcos de Lima (Bené's Son); Maria Menezes (Waitress); Telma Cunha (Lipstick Woman); José Ramos (Pilgrims' Driver); Dona Luzia (Pilgrim Singing in Truck); Bertho Filho (Pilgrim 1); Edivaldo Lima (Jessé's Son); Antonieta Noronha (Violeta); Rita Assemany (Maria, Jessé's Wife); Edivaldo Lima (Jesse's Son); Antoinieta Noronha (Violeta); Rita Assemany (Maria, Jessé's Wife); Gideon Rosa (Jessé); Dona Severina and Joao Rodrigues (Pilgrims Praying); Nanego Lira (Preacher, Northeast); Antonio Marcos (Singer); Iami Rebouças (Woman in Photograph); Joao Braz (Photo Stall Owner); Antonio dos Santos (1st Letter, Northeast); Patricia Brás (2nd Letter, Northeast); Ingrid Trigueiro (3rd Letter, Northeast); Inaldo Santana (4th Letter, Northeast); José Pereira da Silva (5th Letter, Northeast); Eliane Silva (6th Letter, Northeast); Cicero Santos (7th Letter, Northeast); Andra Albuquerque (8th Letter, Northeast); Everaldo Pontes (9th Letter, Northeast); Diogo Lopes Filho (Cashier); Fernando Fulco (F-Street Man).

LOS ANGELES TIMES, 11/25/98, Calendar/p. 8, Kevin Thomas

In Walter Salles' "Central Station," a film that is as beautiful as it is wrenching, the camera picks out a worn, unhappy-looking older woman who sets up a table and chair every day in Rio's vast railroad terminus. She earns a pittance writing letters for the illiterate, whom she regards with a cold matter-of-fact disdain.

She is a retired schoolteacher who must augment her minuscule pension in this manner and takes scant pains to disguise her bitterness. Indeed, if she regards what is being dictated to her as rubbish she refuses to mail the completed letter entrusted to her by the customer. A drawer stuffed with such letters in a bureau in her tiny apartment attests to the magnitude of her disdain for her fellow human beings.

In short, Fernanda Montenegro's Dora is a mean-spirited, dishonest, highly judgmental individual—the very last person with whom you would trust a child. Yet when a woman, one of Dora's customers, is struck fatally by a car, Dora is the only person in all of Rio with whom the woman's 10-year-old son Josue (Vinicius de Oliveira) has had any contact, even though fleeting.

You may want to resist this movie as much as Dora resists Josue. You may say to yourself, "Not yet another movie about an aging curmudgeon melted by an irresistible kid." But that is to discount the profound scope and vision that Salles brings to his story. "Central Station" belongs to the grand humanist tradition of Italian neo-realism and has been made with the care and concern for values and emotions that have always characterized the films of its producer, five-time Oscar-winner Arthur Cohn. It is also to underestimate the power of Montenegro, widely regarded as Brazil's greatest actress, and the remarkable natural acting ability of de Oliveira, who in fact was spotted by Salles at Rio's airport, where he had been spending several hours a day shining shoes to help out his poor family.

The world of "Central Station" is all too universal—a place where older people, even those who've led responsible, respectable lives, are in effect discarded, left to fend for themselves, and a place where children are even more vulnerable at a time when families seem increasingly far-flung and fragmented. Indeed, a few deft plot developments propel Dora and Josue on a long railroad journey in search of the father he doesn't even know. (It has been suggested that their journey represents on another level a kind of quest for a sense of Brazilian identity.)

Dora is actually capable of an evil and indifference that won't be revealed here except to observe that the woman's hatefulness gives Montenegro all the greater a range in which to depict with the utmost understatement her ever-so-gradual regeneration—not so much an awakening of maternal instincts but a warming to the simple contact with another human being. In her relationship with the resilient yet inescapably vulnerable Josue, Dora is moved to confront the painful losses that have left her so emotionally calcified.

(The only other role of substance goes to none other than Marilia Pera, unforgettable as the prostitute in "Pixote." She plays Dora's good-humored neighbor, whose sense of decency proves to be pivotal.)

"Central Station" becomes transcendent in its stunning, unexpected climactic sequence that attests to the formidability of Montenegro's gifts as an actress. Her portrayal of Dora, one of the year's finest performances, attests to a career spent bringing to life a large portion of the stage's most challenging heroines. It also attests to Montenegro's unfailing grasp of the fact that acting for the cinema—in which she has appeared only a handful of times—requires no less than revealing your soul. For Fernanda Montenegro, who bears more than a passing resemblance to Italy's late Giulietta Masina (Federico Fellini's wife and frequent star) in appearance and talent, "Central Station" is a personal triumph and a rich cinematic experience.

NEW YORK, 12/14/98, p. 67, Peter Rainer

I can't join in with the prevailing opinion that Walter Salles's *Central Station* is on par with early De Sica—I love early De Sica too much. But in this otherwise rather schematic swatch of social catharsis, Brazil's Fernanda Montenegro gives the best performance by an actress I've seen all year. De Sica might not have made this movie, but he would have recognized in her bitter, beseeching portrayal a kindred character.

NEW YORK POST, 11/20/98, p. 64, Thelma Adams

There's an unlikely race heating up in this year's lackluster Oscar derby: best foreign language film. Italy's offering, Roberto Benigni's "Life Is Beautiful," is already an art-house hit. Enter the Brazilian contender: "Central Station."

Walter Salles Jr.'s touching road pic recalls John Cassavetes' 1980 melodrama, "Gloria" (currently being remade with Sharon Stone in the title role). It's about the unlikely kinship between a mature woman and a young boy forced on the lam.

Dora (Fernanda Montenegro) writes letters for Rio de Janeiro's illiterate amid the city's chaotic Central Station. One day, she meets Ana (Soia Lira) and her son Josue (Vinicius de Oliveira).

Ana dictates a melancholy letter to the boy's distant dad seeking reconciliation. The embittered Dora assumes the father is a drunk and doesn't mail the letter.

When Ana dies in a bus crash, Dora takes Josue in. No softy, she sells the boy to an adoption agency and buys a new TV. When she discovers the "agency" is harvesting kids' organs for foreign recipients, Dora kidnaps Josue.

Fleeing from the fake adoption ring, Dora escorts Josue to his father's last known address. Like Salles' previous film, "Foreign Land," which played the Anthology Film Archives last year, "Central Station" becomes a road movie tracing the landscape of the human heart.

Dora's flight across Brazil's harsh interior forces the frustrated middle-aged woman to confront her family legacy. Like Josue, she is an emotional orphan. She comes to face her drunken father's abandonment of the family; her mother's early death; and her own inability to fill the void with romantic love, alcohol or the fervent Catholicism the duo encounters on the road.

Montenegro, a Brazilian star who appeared briefly as a busybody in "Four Days in September," delivers an unsentimental, complex and moving performance. Her Dora is guardian and orphan, Madonna and child. She restores Josue to his family; he restores her hope.

"Central Station," in turn, restores our faith in the power of human relationships—and authentic movies—to help us look at the world anew, as if after a sudden, cleansing downpour.

NEWSDAY, 11/20/98, Part II/p. B11, Jack Mathews

In the teeming central train station in Rio de Janeiro, a young teenager is running for his life. He's just been spotted lifting something from one of the commercial vendors and security is right behind him. The chase comes to a quick end in the railroad yard, where the boy is tackled by one cop, then casually shot to death by another.

With that succinctly graphic sequence, Brazilian director Walter Salles establishes the stakes for his main characters in "Central Station": a 9-year-old boy left alone by his mother's death, and a 67-year-old former schoolteacher who makes her living writing letters for Rio's large class of illiterates.

Dora (Fernanda Montenegro) had just written a letter to the father of young Josue (Vinicius de Oliveira) when his mother stepped in front of a car, and though she thinks she has long since quit caring about the plight of Brazil's vast population of abandoned children, there's something about this one she can't shake.

Seeing Josue alone and forlorn at the train station the next day, Dora invites him to her apartment, then tries to do each of them a good deed by turning him over to a couple who supposedly arrange private adoptions. She'll get enough money to buy that new TV; he'll get a new home, though all he really wants is to find his father.

When Dora's neighbor suggests that Josue will more likely be killed for his organs than adopted, Dora pulls off a daring rescue, and takes to the road with Josue in tow.

Much of what follows is superficially formulaic. The kid hates the old lady, she resents him, they fight, they bond, they separate, reunite, each somehow enriching the other's life. But there's so much more going on in this tight, two-character play. Salles, a veteran documentary filmmaker, is reaching out through this relationship to call for a more determined effort by the Brazilian government to care for its lost children.

In a way, "Central Station" is a continuation of Hector Babenco's despairing 1981 "Pixote," a movie that follows in verite style the lives of a pack of homeless in Sao Paolo, as they cheat, steal, maim and otherwise play the urban-feral survival game. The boy shot in the opening of "Central Station" is kin to them.

You do not have to have seen "Pixote" to understand that Josue's future, without the intervention of Dora, or some other Samaritan, is no brighter. Dora knows that, and the audience knows, but Josue, on the brink, does not. As Dora goes farther down this road, literally and figuratively searching for miracles, she rediscovers her humanity, her emotions, even her sexuality (though she picks the wrong evangelical truck driver to hit on).

Montenegro, who looks like Imogene Coca's long-lost twin, gives a heart-wrenching performance, taking her character through a spectacular range of emotions and change. Some of this is slam-dunk territory; an old person comforting a child, and vice versa, is irresistible sentimentality. And yet, her most powerful scenes are those when Dora is alone, assessing her situation, reading her conscience and coming to like the person she finds inside.

De Oliveira, a shoeshine boy discovered during the proverbial national talent search, shows what would be called, in describing a veteran's performance, great restraint against so much opportunity for excess. With Salles' apparently gentle coaching, de Oliveira makes an effectively quiet hero, an innocent wending his way down a confusing path with cool determination.

The end of his and Dora's search is an anticlimax; after all, they will have found each other and much more. Still, you might wish Salles, who's credited with the story but not the script, had come up with a less convenient conclusion. Sometimes the journey is better than the getting there.

SIGHT AND SOUND, 3/99, p. 38, Nina Caplan

Dora is a letter writer in Brazil's Central Station. She transcribes the loves and longings for Rio de Janeiro's illiterates and sends the results—or not—as she and her neighbour Irene see fit. When one of her clients is run over and killed, nine-year-old Josué is left motherless. Dora takes him in and sells him, but later steals him back. Dora and Josué go in search of his father Jisus, using the address of the letter Dora had written but failed to send for Josué's mother.

Dora tries to leave Josué on the bus but he follows her, forgetting his rucksack which contains Dora's money. Penniless, they are picked up by a kindly, religious truck driver who abandons them when Dora grows too friendly. By hitching they reach Jisus' house but he has sold it to buy alcohol. In the town, Josué saves them from destitution by suggesting Dora write letters for pilgrims. This time, she posts the letters.

By chance, they find Josué's two half-brothers. Their father has disappeared, but Dora reads the letter he had sent six months ago: he had gone to Rio in search of Josué's mother and the son he has never seen. The brothers realise he too must be dead. The next morning, while Josué sleeps, Dora takes the bus for Rio. Josué wakes up too late to prevent her departure. Both are left with a photo by which to remember one another.

The trouble with road movies is they often go nowhere. Walter Salles' *Central Station* makes a virtue out of a common failing. It's a time-honoured scenario: haphazard travelling companions take a trip down Self-Discovery Highway, destination Understanding. For nine-year-old Josué, the search for his father marks his coming of age. His companion Dora, a retired teacher, rediscovers her humanity when she leaves her post writing letters for Rio's illiterates in Central Station to help him.

Salles *(Foreign Land)* takes recent upheavals in Brazil as his starting point and tackles individual quests within the context of the pain, loss and redemption of the whole community. Josué spends most of the film trying to join a community which is a metonym for the Brazilian society Dora abandoned along with her teaching career. As a letter writer, she interprets rather than instructs: if knowledge is her currency, she has exchanged generosity for avarice. She and Josué approach one another from opposite ends of the social spectrum: he seeks a place, she has abandoned hers. These two disparate but coinciding quests for rehabilitation are the film's heartbeat.

With his brothers, Josué will find a trade and a place in society. It is at his instigation that his mother Ana writes—via Dora—to her abusive drunken husband Jisus, tentatively pleading for reconciliation while the boy plays with a wooden top, symbol of his soon-to-be-lost childhood realm. He will lose top and mother simultaneously. His search for male role models will place him behind the wheel on a paternal truck driver's lap when he and Dora hitch a lift. Later, he will strike a similar pose with his older brother Moisés in front of the latter's lathe: the man behind, guiding the boy's hands. Under Moisés' guidance, Josué makes a top, no longer just a toy but a symbolic token of initiation into the community. This process begun, Dora leaves, having rediscovered the selflessness of the teacher/guide.

Like the trains, *Central Station* starts from the eponymous station and radiates outwards. People and trains move past with equal smoothness, making their random trajectories through the umber light that permeates the film. Characters collide with one another with seeming incoherence, like the letters which Dora posts, keeps or destroys according to her whim. Life is not linear. Dora tells Josué that one should always take buses because they have regular routes and preordained stops. She associates taxis with instability; her father's unfaithfulness; her mother's death. Dora's world contains its own insecurity: a perpetual liar whose lies are never believed she imputes her own untruthfulness to others. "How do they measure a kilometre?" asks Josué during their journey. "They make it up," replies Dora.

Vinícius de Oliveira is extraordinary as the proud, vulnerable Josué, chin raised as the tears fall, dictating Dora's clothes and make-up and initiating macho sex talk as he tries to seem grown up.

Like a teacher brushing up on a rusty foreign language, Dora relearns her moral grammar for his benefit and posts the letters she used to jettison. The film takes religion as its point of stability, replicating the developing country's conflict between industrialisation and tradition. The two travellers bounce from evangelist truck drivers to places of pilgrimage. In a stunning visual depiction of faith, the screen fills with points of light from pilgrims' candles. The family unit, seen as irrevocably lost, is idolised: Dora becomes a virgin mother to Josué, while his brothers create a shrine commemorating Ana and Jisus. When Dora leaves, the image which remains to comfort her and Josué for their mutual loss is a photo of them taken with a picture of a saint, a parody of the nuclear family, suggesting the duplication which replaces intimacy in a fragmented society. Salles takes this one step further: the result, a random microcosm of Brazilian life both intimate and eloquent, is *Central Station*.

VILLAGE VOICE, 11/24/98, p. 128, Gary Dauphin

Set in the backwoods and cinder-block slums of Brazil, *Central Station* is a mildly saccharine but kind-hearted movie. Part gorgeously photographed road trip, part socially aware South American docudrama, it tells the gently rewarding tale of how people can learn to care for one another under unlikely circumstances, standing fast for friend and adopted family when the easiest thing to do would be to run.

Dora (Fernanda Montenegro) is an aging ex-schoolteacher turned scam artist who takes the money of the illiterate in exchange for writing letters she never mails. Her life is a series of petty misdemeanors until she meets Josué (Vinicius de Oliveira), a motherless boy who lives in the train station where she plies her trade. Sensing the potential for profit, the old woman sells the outspoken child to an "adoption agency" that might be a back-alley organ bank, but after a predictable but credibly rendered attack of conscience she steals him back, the two going on the lam in Brazil's dusty, outback-like interior. Although their ultimate destination is the rural home of Josué's long-missing father, the pair take quite different emotional journeys. Josué, like any lost kid, is looking for an adult he can finally trust, while Dora is taking a trip back in time, discovering not only motherhood but the possibility of other kinds of love and affection.

Winner of the best picture prize at this year's Berlin film fest, *Central Station* works a subtle kind of sentimental magic despite occasional cloying lapses. Director Walter Salles sets his story against sweeping and lonely backdrops, the human figures either crowded into the frame or tiny specks against man-made and natural expanses. *Central Station* may be prototypically "life-affirming," but sometimes there's nothing wrong with an old-fashioned tearjerker that gets the formula right.

Also reviewed in:
NATION, 12/7/98, p. 35, Stuart Klawans
NEW YORK TIMES, 11/20/98, p. E10, Janet Maslin
NEW YORKER, 11/30/98, p. 129, David Denby
VARIETY, 2/9-15/98, p. 70, Todd McCarthy
WASHINGTON POST, 1/15/99, p. C5, Rita Kempley

CHAIRMAN OF THE BOARD

A Trimark Pictures release of a 101st Street Films/Trimark Pictures production. *Executive Producer:* Mark Amin. *Producer:* Peter M. Lenkov and Rupert Harvey. *Director:* Alex Zamm. *Screenplay:* Al Septien, Turi Meyer, and Alex Zamm. *Story:* Al Septien and Turi Meyer. *Director of Photography:* David Lewis. *Editor:* Jim Hill. *Music:* Chris Hajian. *Sound:* Christopher M. Taylor and Peter V. Meiselmann. *Casting:* Ed Mitchell and Robyn Ray. *Production Designer:* Aaron Osborne. *Set Decorator:* Danielle Berman. *Special Visual Effects:* John Lindauer. *Costumes:* Seok H. Yoon. *Running time:* 95 minutes. *MPAA Rating:* PG-13.

CAST: Carrot Top (Edison); Courtney Thorne-Smith (Natalie); Larry Miller (Bradford); Raquel Welch (Grace Kosik); Mystro Clark (Ty); Jack Plotnick (Zak); Jack Warden

(Armand);   Estelle Harris (Ms. Krubavitch);   Bill Erwin (Landers);   M. Emmet Walsh (Freemont);   Jack McGee (Harlan);   Glenn Shadix (Larry);   Fred Stoller (McMillan Gate Guard).

LOS ANGELES TIMES, 3/16/98, Calendar/p. 5, Kevin Thomas

Carrot Top, whose frazzled, fright-wiggy red locks remain his most finely developed gag, inspires marvel among many in the comedy world, mainly because he still manages to find work despite an almost utter lack of talent. The payoff of one episode of "The Larry Sanders Show," in fact, hinged on the fact that he's such an execrable comedian—why the guy agreed to be on a show in which his own ineptitude was a punch line is bewildering. Maybe he hoped he'd seem hip being such a good sport, or perhaps he just doesn't get sophisticated humor.

Carrot Top, who makes his film debut with "Chairman of the Board," is a manic prop comic whose objects tend to focus on mammillae and the scatological, making Gallagher look like a model of restraint. On the other hand, Carrot Top is reticent to bring the sheer level of crazed commitment to his persona that Paul Reubens did with Peewee Herman, so basically he's an irritant who can't stay in character and can only barely deliver his lines. (Fans must love him, though—I was the only person in the theater at one screening during the weekend.)

"Chairman of the Board" presents a standard-issue rags-to-riches plot, enlivened by only by a tchotchke-heavy production design that might engage those entranced by bright, shiny objects. Alas, the filmmakers can't hold back the urge for smutty or potty gags, so the thing's not even appropriate for the few kids who might find Carrot Top palatable (think of "Good Burger," another movie with kid-pleasingly idiotic protagonists, only with French tickler jokes).

Mr. Top portrays Edison, a wacky layabout who'd like to be an inventor if only it would fit into his surfing-and-loafing regimen. Edison meets an elderly eccentric and inherits the old coot's business when the guy croaks soon thereafter. To the dismay of apoplectic conniver Bradford (Larry Miller, a funny comic who turns up in too many movies like this), who wants the company for himself, Edison's unorthodox behavior makes the corporation wildly successful. Mayhem doesn't really ensue, but you can piece it together from there.

Two questions are posed: Does it never occur to anyone at this abject level of filmmaking to at least try to sell their stupid premise to audiences? And are finances so tight and meaty roles so few that respected character actors like M. Emmet Walsh, Estelle Harris and Jack Warden and beloved bombshells like Raquel Welch and Courtney Thorne-Smith must accept assignments in junk like this?

Technically, the thing is a shambles. Director Alex Zamm can't set up a gag to save his life, routinely putting the camera in the exact wrong place for a joke to work, and editing is so clunky it takes several beats for characters to react to incidents. In one scene, Carrot Top refers to Thorne-Smith's character, Natalie, as "Courtney," a mistake no one apparently cared about enough to correct. For what it's worth, the film gives Thorne-Smith a centerpiece scene in which she belches loud enough to be measured on the Richter scale. And the explosive finale turns on a shirt that makes flatulent sounds.

If Carrot Top is indeed destined for celluloid stardom, look for a lot of film critics' and movie projectionists' jobs to open up in the coming years.

NEW YORK POST, 3/14/98, p. 23, Larry Worth

When it comes to red-haired comics, it's safe to say Carrot Top will never best Lucille Ball. Heck, he'll never best Bozo.

Making his screen debut in "Chairman of the Board," the russet-headed imbecile brings irritation to an all-new high. He's enough to have one longing for the relative subtlety of Pauly Shore.

But in fairness, "Chairman" leaves viewers with lots to think and talk about after the end credits. For instance:

1) How does such a moron-geared formula movie—in which an idiotic hero battles, is victimized and finally triumphs over a smarmy corporate villain—get financed?

2) With foul-mouthed golden-agers, surfer dudes, bathroom humor and countless kicked-in-the-groin scenes, did first-time writer-director Alex Zamm miss any cliches?

3) Why would Raquel Welch, Jack Warden, Courtney ("Melrose Place") Thorne-Smith, M. Emmet Walsh and Larry Miller besmirch their reputations with this cinematic swill?

4) And, most important, why does Carrot Top have a career in entertainment? An industrial-strength microscope would find no trace of talent, charisma or humor beneath his freckled flesh.

Neither will filmgoers. It's not that the human Carrot—a pathetic mix of Pee-wee Herman and Gallagher—would ever be confused with high art. But watching his antics is a level of torture that Torquemada couldn't dream up.

That's why Carrot Top, and "Chairman," merit early retirement.

Also reviewed in:
CHICAGO TRIBUNE, 3/19/98, Tempo/p. 11C, John Petrakis
NEW YORK TIMES, 3/14/98, p. B17, Anita Gates
VARIETY, 3/23-29/98, p. 89, Glenn Lovell

CHAMBERMAID ON THE TITANIC, THE

A Samuel Goldwyn Company release of a UGC YM/La Sept Cinema/France 2 Cinema/Rodeo Drive Mate Production/Tornasol Films/Westdeutscher Rundfunk coproduction with the support of the Eurimages fund of the Council of Europe and the participation of the Centre National de la Cinematographie, Canal+ and Soficas. *Producer.:* Yves Marmion and Daniel Toscan du Plantier. *Director:* Bigas Luna. *Screenplay (French with English subtitles):* Bigas Luna, Cuca Canals, Jean-Louis Benoît. *Adapted from the novel by:* Didier Decoin. *Director of Photography:* Patrick Blossier. *Editor:* Kenout Peltier. *Music:* Alberto Iglesias. *Sound:* Jean-Paul Mugel, Laurent Quaglio, and Christain Fontaine. *Production Designer:* Walter Caprara and Bruno Cesari. *Costumes:* France Squarciapino. *Running time:* 96 minutes. *MPAA Rating:* Not Rated.

CAST: Romane Bohringer (Zoe); Olivier Martinez (Horty); Aitana Sánchez Gijón (Marie); Didier Bezace (Simeon); Aldo Maccione (Zeppe); Jean-Marie Juan (Pascal); Arno Chevrier (Al); Marianne Groves (Bathilde); Didier Benureau (Simeon's Secretary); Alberto Cassadie (Giovanni); Giorgio Gobbi (Mano); Yves Verhoeven (Gaspard); Vincenzo De Caro (Lacroix); Salvador Madrid (Leon); Barbara Lerici (Blanche); Stefania Orsola Garello (Mimi); Maurizio Solda (Lou); Jim Adhi Limas (Chinese Photographer).

FILM QUARTERLY, Winter 1998-99, p. 35, Marsha Kinder

Bigas Luna's *The Chambermaid on the Titanic (La Camarera del Titanic,* 1997) is a fascinating film dealing with the erotic power of narrative. Given its close to synchronous release with James Cameron's record-breaking blockbuster, *Titanic* (which it actually preceded), this witty French-Italian-Spanish co-production (based on a French novel by Didier Decoin and released in French with English subtitles) provides a telling comparison with Hollywood's high-tech megahit.[1] Rather than Cameron's dazzling special effects, here it is Bigas Luna's imaginative metanarrative intricacies that drive a contrived romance to new heights of emotional giddiness and financial success (in this case, the success of the character rather than of the film). Both films use the sinking of the Titanic as the historical anchor for a fictional love story involving class conflict, a sad tale told in retrospect by the surviving lover. Both feature a young, handsome working-class hero who gains access to the luxurious liner by winning a ticket—a stroke of luck that forever changes his life. The similarities end there.

Chambermaid begins in 1912 in a foundry in Northern France where, after competing in an arduous contest of physical endurance, a young worker named Horty (Olivier Martinez) wins a ticket to witness the launching of the Titanic in Southhampton. Hoping to seduce Horty's wife Zoe (Romane Bohringer) while he is away, the owner of the ironworks factory gives him only one ticket (instead of two). During his one night at a luxurious English hotel, a beautiful young Frenchwoman named Marie (Aitana Sánchez-Gijón), who claims to be a chambermaid on the

Titanic with no place to spend the night, comes to his door and asks him to give her his room. In response to this improbable request, he offers to share his suite, and she, in turn, offers to share the bed which he has gallantly relinquished to her. Although it is at first ambiguous as to whether they actually make love, in the morning he awakens alone and then rushes to the dock, arriving just in time to witness not only the launching of the luxurious ship but also the photographing of Marie on-board. When he later sees a copy of that same photograph for sale in the street, he purchases it as a souvenir. As soon as he returns home, he hears gossip about his wife having slept with the boss and then learns he has been promoted, which further arouses his suspicions. When one of his co-workers sees the photo of Marie, he urges Horty to describe his adventure. At first denying he made love to her, Horty soon begins to embellish his story with graphic sexual details that draw growing crowds of listeners at the local bar. These crowds include not only his fellow male workers but eventually also their wives whose erotic lives are increasingly affected by his sensual tales. Once news of the sinking of the Titanic reaches his town, his stories become even more compelling. Although his wife is jealous and urges him to stop, she allows him to continue because his storytelling brings more money than his hard labor had at the foundry. One night a circus showman named Zeppe (Aldo Maccione) hears his performance and persuades him to do a theatrical version with props, a melodramatic adaptation which proves even more successful than his original accounts. Then one night, a surprising event occurs (which I will not reveal here) but which changes his and our understanding of what happened that original night—an event that drives Horty to burn Marie's image and that unleashes the image of another watery death. When Horty resumes his tale, this new revision proves to be even more compelling and draws even more tears from his audience than had his earlier versions.

Like most films by Bigas Luna, *Chambermaid* focuses on an erotic obsession that narrativizes desire in a way that is transformative and potentially murderous. Yet, when compared with other works by this outrageous Catalan filmmaker, *Chambermaid*'s representations and excessiveness seem remarkably restrained. According to Bigas Luna, "The film is about imagination and too much explicitness would not have suited the tone."[2] Still, it is one of Bigas Luna's most compelling works. Peter Brooks' *Reading for the Plot* is useful here in understanding the film's power, partly because of his insistence that a story's ending and its "expansive middle" are always essential to narrative desire.

Many of the most suggestive analysts of narrative have shared this conviction that the end writes the beginning and shapes the middle... We can, then, conceive of the reading of plot as a form of desire that carries us forward, onward, through the text. Narratives both tell of desire—typically present some story of desire—and arouse and make use of desire as dynamic of signification... In the motors and engines I have glanced at, including Eros as motor and motor as erotic, we find representations of the dynamics of the narrative text, connecting beginning and end across the middle and making of that middle—what we read *through*—field of force.[3]

Simply from the allusion to the Titanic in the title, we expect that *Chambermaid*'s ending will involve death by water—which helps prepare us for its antithetical opening, an extravagant montage of molten fire from the foundry that almost literally erupts on screen. Like the fiery opening of Visconti's *The Damned*, another melodrama combining historical facts with outrageous fictions, this introductory montage functions as a visual overture that establishes the symbolic register against which the narrative is to be read—a register that is at least partially anchored by the respective titles of the two movies. Whereas Visconti's infernal fires evoke the fusion of evil and lust (as well as the historical crematoriums of the Holocaust and the complicity of big industrial firms like Krupp, which survived the war with their fortunes and corruption intact), Bigas Luna's images link the volcanic eruptions of industry with a smoldering vaginal desire. The sexual associations of this extravagant imagery are as apparent as those of the gigantic testicles of the black bull billboard at the opening of Bigas Luna's internationally successful crossover film *Jamón, jamón* (1992), only here the tone is sublime rather than satiric.[4] Yet *Chambermaid*'s extravagant hyperbole and surprising narrative twists do subsequently arouse humor but without ever undermining the film's erotic fire, which is ignited in the opening and burns full-blaze till the end. Apparently several Spanish filmmakers are skillful at achieving this difficult fusion of humor and eroticism, as we have learned from the films of Almodóvar, who was influenced by Bigas Luna.

From the opening moments of *The Chambermaid on the Titanic* we know that this narrative will forge an elemental fusion of fire and water, sex and death. The smoldering red-hot images of the opening are immediately followed by a cut to a cool grey-blue exterior, as the exhausted workers, including our impassive, tight-lipped hero, pour out of the factory into the night. This juxtaposition suggests the contrast between inner heat and exterior calm, which recurs in the opposition between the subdued hotel encounter and the wild flashbacks it spawns. The ironworks also evokes the historic context of the industrial revolution, out of which the Titanic and its generative fantasies of class privilege and invincible capital were forged. Against this muted landscape we hear the film's first narrative murmurs: fragments of proletarian gossip about alleged acts of cuckoldry, which reveal how the workers' longing for power is displaced onto the sexual realm and how it genders the foundry's smoldering fires female. As Linda Williams pointed out in her seminal essay on "Body Genres,"

> Even when the pleasure of viewing has traditionally been constructed for masculine spectators, as is the case in most traditional heterosexual pornography, it is the female body in the grips of an out-of-control ecstasy that has offered the most sensational sight... It is thus through what Foucault has called the sexual saturation of the female body that audiences of all sorts have received some of their most powerful sensations.[5]

This dynamic helps explain the hunger felt by these disempowered men for Horty's erotic tales of the ecstatic chambermaid's insatiable appetite and of his own sexual prowess ("Twelve times in one night!" his admiring listeners exclaim)—a prowess they had already witnessed in his winning performance during the grueling contest of physical endurance. The desire and capacity for endurance are easily transposed to the narrative, which generates new prolific variations that keep expanding the middle—a "field of force" that is also gendered female like the fire.

The "expansive middle" of the narrative extends desire by presenting a series of erotic representations of Marie's body and thereby forestalling her premature death. According to Brooks, "The complication of the detour is related to the danger of short-circuit: the danger of reaching the end too quickly, of achieving the improper death." (103-104) This expansive middle also underscores the pun in the English possessive form of Horty's name (whore-tease). For, not only does he withhold himself sexually from Marie in London, but like Shahrazad he uses his fictional heroine to tease his narratees with small doses of pleasure and thereby ensures the survival of his honor if not his life. Brooks' description of the "metaseductive" *Thousand and One Nights* (what he calls "the story of stories") could also apply to *Chambermaid* (only with Horty doubling as both clever narrator and troubled narratee):

Shahrazad's storytelling takes a desire that has gone off the rails—the Sultan's desire, derailed by his wife's infidelity... and cures it by prolonging it, precisely by narrativizing it..Narration, in this allegory, is seen to be life-giving in that it arouses and sustains desire, ensuring that the terminus it both delays and beckons toward will offer what we might call a lucid repose, desire both come to rest and set in perspective (60-61).

As Horty reawakens desire in his downtrodden fellow-workers, he simultaneously heals the wounds suffered by his own male honor over the scandals concerning his wife (yet it is equally possible that his jealousy is merely staged to alleviate his own guilt over his adulterous fantasies about Marie). At a pivotal point in the film he stands perched on the factory tower, as if contemplating a melodramatic suicide, but then throws a wrench down at his boss. It conveniently falls short and merely breaks the windshield of his boss's luxurious car, resulting in Horty's being fired. Yet this abortive performance of Promethean revolt succeeds in freeing him to commit himself to his "true" calling as storyteller. Thus, in many ways the compelling power of his stories is based on lack—his audience's lack of power, his own lack of a job, his lack of sexual fulfillment with Marie, his lack of effective follow-through as an action hero, and (by extension) the film's lack of sexual explicitness in what is represented on screen. Speaking as a Catalan filmmaker who grew up under Francoist repression, Bigas Luna describes the film as:

the story of the birth of a great storyteller ... Telling lies is the very essence of the creative process, Horty himself lives out his inventions and transforms those around him to survive and escape a reality he can no longer bear ... Creation [is] often born from a constraint. Total liberty is not very good for creativity.[6]

The expansive middle of the narrative also serves *our* pleasure. Given that we already know the Titanic will sink and most of its passengers and staff will die, the narrative must seek alternative hermeneutic questions to arouse and sustain our curiosity and desire. To solve this problem, Bigas Luna turns our attention to ellipses—those gaping holes in the narrative into which a profuse number of imaginative elaborations, hyperbolic variations, and lurching reversals can be inserted.

The first blatant ellipsis occurs in the hotel room. As the two beautiful young strangers lie quietly side by side in bed, there is a brief dissolve to a fleeting image of their making love. We are left wondering: is it a dream or did it really happen? Before we can answer, we see Horty awakening alone in bed, then hurriedly dressing and rushing to the dock. We do not know what happened in that gap between the dream-like dissolve and his abrupt awakening, which is precisely where Horty positions his first elaborate stories.

The most blatant ellipsis occurs during the break in one of Horty's theatrical performances, a rupture which draws hisses and boos from the bourgeois audience and a young juggler on stage to fill the interlude. This interruption imposes seriality onto the theater, turning his story into a "cliff-hanger"—a narrative strategy that is more commonly found in other forms of melodrama (in literature, movies, and television). During that interlude, surprising events occur off stage (but not off-screen) which are adapted to the dramatic narrative once his performance resumes. But it is obvious that other elaborations could just as easily have been inserted into this gap. Once Horty returns to the stage, the story of Marie is reborn like a phoenix out of the flames of her burning photo, which is an enlargement of the "original" reproduction. During this performance we realize that it is not the woman, man, or their actions that are inherently erotic, but rather their narrativization. The film shows us that desire is driven by narrative and, conversely, narrative is driven by desire—whether it is an erotic scenario performed for (or with) others, or a private fantasy used to mobilize bodily sensations and perceptions for one's own sexual climax. As Brooks puts it, "Desire as narrative thematic, desire as narrative motor, and desire as the very intention of narrative language and the act of telling all seem to stand in close interrelation."(54)

These two blatant ellipses in *Chambermaid* lead us to rethink all of the seams of the narrative, and as soon as we do this, the whole narrative fabric begins to unravel as a total fabrication. It is no longer merely a question of whether Horty actually made love to Marie, for a whole series of questions come to mind concerning the improbabilities of this narrative, each moving us further backward toward the beginning: Did he really become rich and famous as an actor and storyteller by telling this one story? Did she really come to his hotel room and ask him, a total stranger, to give it up to her? Did he really stay at that elegant hotel, supposedly the best in London? Did he ever go to England or win the ticket, or were these ideas sparked by his wife's fantasy of a special prize that might enable them to get away together for a brief holiday? Did he ever win that contest of physical endurance not just once but three years in a row, the proverbial number that triggers the magical event in fairy tales? Did he fantasize the whole narrative as he lay in the warm bath while his wife Zoe diligently scrubbed his body, speculating that those red marks on his flesh must have come from his having gotten too close to the fire? Or did the fantasy begin with the opening montage, a fantasy trained by fire and water—the molten iron begetting the burning image of Marie, just as the warm bath begets the icy sea in which the Titanic disappeared and the later scenes of sex and death at the water's edge?

The verisimilitude of the story seem to hinge only on two things: the sinking of the Titanic, which is an historical fact, and the photo of the chambermaid, a souvenir which is the only tangible evidence of their encounter. Yet both are treated in the story primarily as commodified visual spectacle—desirable objects to be seen rather than ridden. On the docks, the luxury liner is merely a pretty image looked at from afar; like the chambermaid, this narrative vehicle is entered and intimately explored only within the erotic flashbacks. For, Horty's winning ticket grants him not passage on the Titanic but merely an opportunity to witness its launching, and his night with Marie enables him to conquer not her body but her image.

Marie's photo is the germinal image for Horty's fantasies and those of his narratees, for it first arouses their interest and expectations. Not only is this haunting image reproduced and enlarged in the theater, but his wife Zoe begins to simulate and embody it. Marie's image becomes fetishized like the various erotic mementos in Bigas Luna's earlier film *Bilbao* (1978).[7] But ironically here, this photo also raises doubts about the story's authenticity. Was Marie ever really a chambermaid on the Titanic or were her costume and story merely part of a masquerade? And if so, then how could her photograph have been taken on the ship? And even if it were, how would it's reproduction appear so quickly on the streets? And how coincidental that he would immediately be able to find it. So ironically the photo becomes a contradictory sign of both the story's authenticity and its contrivance.

Similarly, it may be our prior knowledge of the Titanic's sinking that makes this story and the character of Marie sound more like an erotic fantasy. The mere coupling of the chambermaid and the Titanic in the film's title already begins to eroticize class conflict, for it evokes fantasies of dangerous servitude in the lap of luxury. Moreover, a sexual adventure with a chambermaid is a well-known sub-genre of porn, and pornography doggedly recurs throughout the work of Bigas Luna, usually driven by fantasies of sex and death.

This structure of an unraveling narrative can also be found in Buñuel's *Belle de jour* and in Bigas Luna's own earlier masterpiece, *Bilbao*.[8] Both of these films share with *Chambermaid* a similar slippage across genres—from pornography, to melodrama, to meta-narrative—and an implicit concern with class issues that gives these texts some grounding in everyday social reality. The close relationship between pornography and melodrama has been noted by Linda Williams in her essay on "body genres." After citing Laplanche and Pontalis's claim that "fantasy is not so much a narrative that enacts the quest for an object of desire as it is a setting for desire," she argues:

> Because these genres display fewer fantastic special effects and because they
> rely on certain conventions of realism—the activation of social problems in
> melodrama, the representation of real sexual acts in pornography—they seem
> less obviously fantastic. Yet the usual criticisms that these forms are
> improbable, that they lack psychological complexity and narrative closure,
> and that they are repetitive, become moot as evaluation if such features
> are intrinsic to their engagement with fantasy.[9]

Like *Bilbao* and *Belle de jour; Chambermaid* implies that this fusion of pornography and melodrama and their common root in erotic fantasy lie at the heart of *all* narrative. In the film's most passionate sequence, Horty pushes one of his fingers into Marie's mouth, and she rubs his sensual lips in response. Both acts are represented in huge eroticized close-ups, fetishizing the mouth as the most important erogenous zone in this film about storytelling. In another sex scene, where the couple makes passionate love on the Titanic under an elegant banquet table on which a lavish meal is being prepared for the elite first-class passengers, the class conflict is clearly part of the turn-on. In another erotic scene particularly beloved by his audience, Horty describes how he sprayed Marie's body with expensive champagne, and the image momentarily simulates both a "golden shower" and ejaculation (what Williams calls the classic "money shot" in movie and video porn).[10] The mere fact that some listeners (including his wife) are eager to reenact the scene testifies to its success. For, "The success of these genres is often measured by the degree to which the audience sensation mimics what is seen."[11] Yet, here this vicarious sensation acquires a class dimensions for the luxury liner and posh hotel prove ideal "settings for desire" for both the proletarian listeners savoring the pornographic tales at the local bar and the middle-class spectators watching their adaptation to melodrama in the theater.

In *Chambermaid* this movement across narrative genres (from gossip, lies, and dirty jokes, to bawdy fabliaux, to pornography, to serial melodrama, to intellectual meta-narrative) is accompanied by a similar movement across media: from private fantasy, to ordinary conversation, to oral recitation, to theatrical performance, to the novel and its adaptation to the screen. Partly as a result of this chain of adaptations across media, we are able to see Cameron's Hollywood blockbuster—like the Titanic itself, with all of their conspicuous consumption—as obscene. Bigas Luna claims the Titanic "is the symbol of a century going under... our sombre epoch sinking. Maybe culture itself is soon going to disappear swallowed up by the enormous media monster. And to survive the only thing we'll have left is our imagination. That's the message of the film."[12]

From this perspective, Cameron's dazzling special effects appear to be merely an elaboration of the theatrical gimmickry that was tacked on to Horty's tales and the heart of the movie's success seems similarly to lie in the melodramatic loss of the lover. For, this is the emotional anchor that survives across divisions of genre, media, class, and culture and that drives those passionate Leonardo DiCaprio fans (like Horty's avid listeners) to keep returning to the theater for more. This is hardly big news. Yet perhaps more surprising, *Chambermaid* enables us to see that Cameron's lavish technological extravagance (like Horty's expensive champagne and luxurious settings) as well as his trappings of class conflict are used merely to eroticize a simple tale of romantic conquests point that gives more ironic resonance to DiCaprio's celebrated line which Cameron echoed at the Oscars: "I'm King of the World!" I do not mean to suggest that Bigas Luna's film is more "sincere" in its sentiments, for the narrative's emotional hook and its earnest class-based context are deconstructed along with the gimmickry through the playful contrivance of *Chambermaid*'s flashback structure, which is driven not by romantic nostalgia (as in *Titanic*), but by a frank desire to salvage one's losses for profit and pleasure. The final irony is that, following in the wake of Hollywood's record-breaking *Titanic*, Bigas Luna's robust narrative vehicle might well prove unsinkable in the global market, despite all its ingenious unravellings.

Notes

1. For a perceptive discussion of Bigas Luna's approach to transnational filmmaking, see Marvin D'Lugo's essay, "*La teta i la lluna*: The Form of Transnational Cinema in Spain," *Refiguring Spain: Cinema/Media/Representation,* ed. Marsha Kinder (Durham and London: Duke University Press, 1997), 196-214. D'Lugo argues that the trilogy of Bigas Luna films that preceded *Chambermaid* all "are pointedly cast within the reordered commercial space of transnational European cinema."(200)
2. Quoted in an interview contained within the films's press kit, 5.
3. Peter Brooks, *Reading for the Plot: Design and Intention in Narrative* (New York: Vintage, 1984), 22, 37, 47.
4. For a discussion of this film, see my review, "Jamón, Jamón" in *Film Quarterly* 47, no. 1 (1993), 30-35.
5. Linda Williams, "Film Bodies: Gender, Genre, and Excess," *Film Quarterly* 44, no. 4 (1991), 4.
6. Press kit, 2, 4.
7. According to Bigas Luna, "At the beginning, she [Aitana Sánchez-Gijón] couldn't do the film. But I kept a photo of her on me. I'm slightly fetishistic with photos, a bit like Horty with Marie's." Press kit, 5.
8. For an extended discussion of this film, see my book *Blood Cinema: The Reconstruction of National Identity in Spain* (Berkeley, Los Angeles, London: University of California Press, 1993), 262-275.
9. Linda Williams, "Film Bodies," 10.
10. See Linda Williams, *Hardcore: Power, Pleasure, and the "Frenzy of the Visible,"* (Berkeley, Los Angeles, London: University of California Press, 1989).
11. Williams, "Film Bodies," 4-5.
12. Press kit, 4.

LOS ANGELES TIMES, 9/11/98, Calendar/p. 16, Kevin Thomas

"The Chambermaid" is a deliciously amusing celebration of the power of romantic imagination from Bigas Luna, a Spanish master of sly wit and psychological insight. This light, consistently original and delightful period fable is the kind of film in which sophisticated European filmmakers excel, but they don't come along as frequently as they once did.

A French production, it marks the largest-scale film yet from Luna, best known for "Jamon, Jamon," which helped establish Javier Bardem as an international star.

The film's opening sequence could be straight out of "Germinal," only the setting is a bleak steel mill community instead of a company mining town. For three years the winner of an absurdly grueling triathlon held by the Simeon Foundry in northern France is the handsome young Horty (Olivier Martinez, star of the equally romantic "The Horseman on the Roof'). Since the year is 1912 the prize is a week's stay in Southampton to witness the launching of the Titanic.

Cad that he is, foundry President Simeon (Didier Bezace) tells Horty that so costly is the prize that it is for him only—which means Simeon will have no interference in his intended play for Horty's pretty wife, Zoe (Romane Bohringer).

No sooner is Horty ensconced in unaccustomed splendor in a Southampton hotel than he receives a knock on his door from a beautiful young woman, Marie (Aitana Sanchez-Gijon), who tells him she is a chambermaid on the Titanic and has no place to stay. When Horty returns home, telling his foundry pals of the beautiful chambermaid, Zoe and his friends believe that he has been unfaithful; he, in turn, believes an unexpected promotion out of furnaces and into the foundry office is due to his wife letting Simeon have his way with her.

At once "The Chambermaid" becomes the story of the tough-minded and determined Zoe's struggle to rescue her marriage and of Horty's discovery of his storytelling gifts. Soon it matters not whether he and the chambermaid actually had an affair or not; his barroom cronies and soon their wives as well crave escape from their grim, hard existences by demanding to hear him weave tales of his fleeting romance with the beauty, now presumed drowned in the wake of the Titanic sinking.

This thoroughly engaging film takes yet another turn when a veteran traveling player (Aldo Maccione) comes to town to watch Horty tell his story and turns his routine into a professional act that can be taken on the road to wow audiences everywhere. (This new, improved version turns Horty into a Titanic survivor, telling in heart-rending fashion of his inability to save his love—a reverse of the Leonardo DiCaprio-Kate Winslet predicament in "Titanic.")

What actually did—or did not—happen between Horty and Marie becomes less and less important, even if Horty risks exposure as a fake, because it's plainly apparent that Horty, faithful or otherwise, has fallen in love with Marie and the naked honesty of his emotion is what rivets audiences. Indeed, Zoe, in her striving to win back her husband's heart, insists on becoming part of the act, playing the drowning Marie. The way Luna works out Horty and Zoe's fate is inspired, clever and wise.

It's hard to see how Luna's cast could be better, with special honors to Bohringer's loving wife, who finds herself competing for her husband with a woman who lives on only in his imagination. In every aspect and detail the film pleases, with a special nod to Alberto Iglesias' beguiling score.

When the distributors discovered that the film's original title, "The Chambermaid on the Titanic" was misleading to American audiences, they shortened it to merely "The Chambermaid. By any name this Samuel Goldwyn release is a pure pleasure.

NEW YORK, 9/7/98, p. 49, David Denby

In *The Chambermaid on the Titanic*, Horty (Olivier Martinez), a good-looking but rather depressed French foundry worker, wins a contest and receives a peculiar prize—a ticket to England to witness the departure of the *Titanic* on its maiden voyage. At Horty's hotel in Southampton, a French-speaking woman, claiming to be a servant aboard the ship, rather improbably presents herself at his door—she needs a place to spend the night, she says, before leaving in the morning. Her silk underwear just barely restraining rich expanses of bosom and rear, Marie (Aitana Sánchez Gijón) stretches herself out on Horty's bed, and Horty freezes. Aitana Gijón's clothes are so easily removable that I almost reached out to the screen myself, but Horty, in love with his wife, does nothing, and in the morning the woman is gone.

An honorable evening or a missed opportunity? When Horty returns to France with the chambermaid's picture, his factory buddies demand to hear about his exploits, and his wife (Romane Bohringer), who may or may not have slept with Horty's boss when he was away, turns on him in fury. Horty becomes a storyteller, a semi-articulate man who nevertheless holds a roomful of men in rapt silence with his tales of fabulous erotic goings-on in the empty ship and the dark hotel room. The sinking of the *Titanic* and presumed drowning of the chambermaid only enhances the tales, which now take on the glamour of doomed romance and shattering catastrophe. Horty and his chambermaid become enshrined as a myth of eros.

The Spanish-born director Bigas Luna is an imagist: He arranges sensuous palettes of color and texture—gray rain and slag for the mucky industrial scenes; white, gold, and red for the luxe hotel and shipboard episodes that Horty concocts for his avid listeners and that we get to see. Most of the scenes are short and rather too simply conceived in terms of Luna's color-coordinated moods. Luna, who has worked extensively as a painter, doesn't seem to know how to dramatize his material. But Luna has a talent for romantic-erotic fantasy, and the movie is seductively beautiful. Onboard the docked *Titanic,* the lovers frolic under a banquet table like dirty-minded children, and Aitana Sánchez Gijón receives a prolonged dousing in foamy white champagne that must set some sort of record for giddy obscenity. The actors keep their clothes on, but this movie, dreamy and rhapsodic in tone, knowingly teases our interest in pornography. Horty the erotic fabulist casts his spell with repetition, exaggeration, and the myth of inexhaustibility, and his audience—grimy married factory workers eventually joined by their fluttering wives—are all too willing to be fooled. It's 1912, and the movies are in their infancy. What else have the foundry workers got? Horty is their moviemaker.

Bigas Luna feasts on the two women— not just the luscious Gijón but sad-eyed Romane Bohringer, who looks at her husband with real adoration. Unfortunately, Olivier Martinez seems to share her opinion. We know what Eurotrash is, and now we know what Euro-narcissism is: Horty, sleek and slender with a sensual mouth and beautiful dark eyes, whispers passionately to his audience, but Martinez is completely unfocused: He never seems to make contact with anyone else; he never seems to *see* anyone else. His performance is shapeless; we never understand what he feels for his wife.

If Luna had had a great leading man, he might have made a classic fable of the late-industrial age. What the factory workers and their wives want is not so much sex but narratives about sex—they hold on to erotic fantasy as an escape from the dreary every day. After a while, Horty falls into the clutches of a bombastic Italian theatrical impresario, and Horty and his wife (who tries to live up to the fantasy figure in her husband's head) take to the road and entertain both bumpkins in the fields and well-dressed bourgeois audiences. The movie turns Felliniesque—there are charming scenes of primitive theatrical effects, with Bohringer, dressed in the chambermaid's uniform, swimming among painted wooden waves. Horty, we gather, is so much in love with an image that he grows fairly indifferent to the beautiful woman in front of him. The movie has a neat ironic ending, in which the story's mysteries are explained, but Horty is not judged harshly—he's a dreamer, as much a member of the audience, hoping to be enchanted, as he is an enchanter himself.

NEW YORK POST, 8/14/98, p. 47, Thelma Adams

Rumblings from Lake Winnipesaukee. In a press release dated Aug. 12, 1998, an elderly woman at the Sleepy Hollow Home for Shipwreck Victims has confessed to polishing Leonardo DiCaprio's silver in steerage while the starving artist tried to land a rich wife on the upper deck.

Calling herself "The Chambermaid on the Titanic," Madam Doe claims to have a semen-stained French maid's uniform, a cherished memento of their night of love.

News flash. Across the Atlantic, another chambermaid has stepped forward. This is her story, as told by Spanish director Bigas Luna ("Jamon, Jamon") from Didier Decoin's novel.

On the eve of the launch, Titanic chambermaid Marie (Aitana Sanchez Gijon from "A Walk in the Clouds") has no lodging. The porcelain-faced French servant knocks at a stranger's hotel room.

The door opens. It's Horty (darkly sexy Olivier Martinez). The French foundry worker won a trip to bid the Titanic good-bye. The solo ticket was a ploy by his boss to get Horty's wife, Zoe (Romane Bohringer), to himself.

Back at the hotel, Horty gives Marie his bed and takes the chair. When the beauty invites him to share, he slides between the linen but never dips into Marie's lingerie. Like Jimmy Carter, his hands remain faithful; his mind's another story.

The next day, Marie embarks. Horty returns home, the maid's photo wrapped in his hankie. His fellow laborers are abuzz: Zoe has been playing upstairs/downstairs with the foundry chief.

Enraged, Horty hits the tavern. Drunk, he confesses to sleeping with Marie without consummating their love. But soon, high on free brandy, he embellishes a thousand and one erotic tales of his English one-night stand.

Horty describes lifting the maid's uniform and making love while standing on the pier next to the virgin Titanic. He describes stealing kisses beneath a table in the ship's opulent dining room.

Night after night, like Sheherezade, Horty tells stories. Crowds gather and Horty achieves celebrity, inspiring romantic passion while describing dousing Marie with champagne and drinking her dry. When Zoe overhears her husband, she becomes jealous of a domestic who presumably drowned alongside Leonardo.

With minimal special effects and gorgeous stars, Luna guides audiences on a fantastic sensual voyage through love on the rocks, no ice. "The Chambermaid on the Titanic" is a delicious and inventive counterpoint to James Cameron's high seriousness.

NEWSDAY, 8/14/98, Part II/p. B6, Jack Mathews

You are excused if recent political obsessions have convinced you that all sex-lies told by married men are denials. The same guys who swear "I never had sexual relations with that woman" to their wives and constituents may be telling a completely different kind of lie to their pals at the pub, and it's no crime if they do.

Spanish director Bigas Luna's delightful, magical "The Chambermaid on the Titanic" is about the second kind of lie, the embroidered tale of conquest, the time-honored tradition among insecure men of inventing sexual adventures that only their imaginations can arrange.

In the larger,sense, "Chambermaid" is also an earnest endorsement of the lie as the lifeblood of theater. Without lies' there'd be only history. There'd be no morals, only lectures. There'd be no scandals, only legal pundits. Not a pretty picture.

"Chambermaid," on the other hand, is a very,pretty picture. Set in 1912 northern France and Southampton England, it's a parable about a married foundry worker named Horty (Olivier Martinez), whose victory at an annual company race wins him a weeklong trip to England where he is to observe the launching of the Titanic.

On his first night in his Southampton hotel, Horty is visited by the stunning Marie (Aitana Sanchez Gijon, Keanu Reeves' co-star in "A Walk in the Clouds"), who tells him she is to report the next day to her job as a chambermaid on the Titanic. In the meantime, she has no place to stay. Perhaps, a stranger would kindly share his room with another stranger?

What happens next is not precisely clear. What we see is Horty fighting off temptation, then dreaming of a torrid affair with Marie. In the morning, she's gone, and he goes to the ship, catching a glimpse of her being photographed on a deck of the Titanic, just before it sails.

Horty follows the photographer and buys his picture of Marie, which he carefully wraps in a handkerchief and brings home. Depressed by a promotion that rumors attribute to his wife's affair with his boss, a drunk Horty shows Marie's picture to his friends and attempts to tell them of his platonic night alone with her.

His friends reject the notion that there was no sex, and their persistence, along with the news of Titanic's sinking, and with it any chance of his story reaching Marie, he begins giving them what they want. First, sketchy tales of lust fulfilled, then waves of prurient detail. Soon, he's holding the entire town in thrall with stories of an endless night of passion, the details becoming so elaborate and engrossing that the truth is no longer an issue with anyone but his wife, Zoe.

The once shy and uncommunicative Horty becomes such a potent storyteller that he's recruited by a traveling acting troupe and, with Zoe insisting on assuming the role of Marie, they go on the road, eventually coming face to face with the truth—or, is it an even more elaborate lie?

Luna, best known to U.S. arthouse patrons for his deliriously raunchy "Jamon Jamon," shares the romantic sensibilities of "Like Water for Chocolate's" Alfonso Arau, allowing emotions and fantasy to blend as magical realism. The intercut scenes with Horty and Marie cavorting in bed, on the dock, and under tables in Titanic's dining room, grow proportionately outrageous as his story picks up steam, but they're never so outrageous that we can totally write them off to invention.

Martinez plays his role very close to the vest. Horty, at first annoyingly withdrawn, grows more confident and demonstrative, but Martinez is always holding back a little, leaving it unclear whether Horty views himself as an impostor or genuine lothario. Romane Bohringer is perfect as a wife competing against a ghost, and Gijon is coy, sexy and mysterious as Marie.

By the film's marvelously clever ending, Luna has expanded Horty's incredible tale into such pure theater that the truth has no relevance to the experience at all. The film offers an apparent clarification, for those who simply won't go home without it, but the rest of us are free to use our own imaginations.

VILLAGE VOICE, 8/18/98, p. 116, Leslie Camhi

A question lingers as we approach the millennium—will the European art film survive into the next century? Hellbent on nostalgia, directors have been lavishing attention on the last fin de siècle as a way of coping with this anxiety, using love (a leap of faith) and disaster (a deus ex machina) to bridge the gap between eons.

James Cameron's *Titanic* celebrated the demise of Old World hierarchy in the face of America and its glorious stepchild, cinema, the pseudo-democratizing institution that united rich and poor in fantasy. Bigas Luna's *The Chambermaid on the Titanic,* a post-modern tugboat beside that behemoth of ambition and vanity, emphasizes the powers of eroticism and the imagination over the charms of spectacle.

Horty (Olivier Martinez) and his wife, Zoe (Romane Bohringer), work at a foundry in muddy, gray, small-town Normandy. When Horty comes in first among workers in his company's annual contest of strength, he's rewarded with a trip to England to witness the *Titanic*'s launching. Settling into his hotel room, he's interrupted by a fetching chambermaid (Aitana Sánchez Gijón), due to start work on board the next morning, who asks to share his quarters. A chaste Horty returns home to find his wife and his world have changed; the woman, the boat, and the disaster capture his imagination, and he begins to tell stories of a night of love aboard the fabulous ship.

Adapted from the novel by Didier Decoin, *The Chambermaid on the Titanic* captures the peculiar poignancy of missed experience. Horty's near brush with both disaster and another human being—his tragedy and his love manqué—transform him from a simple worker into a producer of imaginary lives and sensations. Bigas Luna's direction is rarely subtle, but its overheated tone seems apt for the panting visions with which Horty beguiles his companions. He gives them the gift of perversion. They could hardly ask for more.

Also reviewed in:
CHICAGO TRIBUNE, 5/21/99, Friday/p. C, John Petrakis
NATION, 9/7-14/98, p. 44, Stuart Klawans
NEW YORK TIMES, 8/14/98, p. E6, Stephen Holden
VARIETY, 10/27-11/2/97, p. 43, Jonathan Holland

CHARACTER

A Sony Pictures Classics release of an Almerica Film B.B. production in co-production with NPS made with the support of Nederlandse Programma Stichting/Stichting Nederlands Fonds voor de Film/Stichting Nederlands Fonds voor de Film/Stichting Co-productiefonds Binnenlandse Omroep/Stimuleringsfonds voor Nederlandse Culturele Omroeproducties/Fonds Film in Vlaanderen/Stichting Film Fonds Rotterdam/Gemeente Rotterdam/Filmnet Benelux B.V./ABN-AMBRO BANK N.V. *Producer:* Laurens Geels. *Director:* Mike van Diem. *Screenplay (Dutch with English subtitles):* Mike van Diem, Lauren Geels, and Ruud van Mega. *Based on the novel "Karakter" by:* F. Bordewijk. *Director of Photography:* Rogier Stoffers. *Editor:* Jessica de Koning. *Music:* Het Paleis van Boem. *Sound:* Marcel de Hoogd and (music) Michel Schöpping. *Casting:* Jeanette Snik. *Production Designer:* Jelier & Schaaf. *Art Director:* Roland Mylanus and Andrzej Rafal Waltenberg. *Set Decorator:* Robert de Brujin. *Costumes:* Jany Temime. *Make-up:* Kathy Kühne. *Stunt Coordinator:* Henk Wams. *Running time:* 114 minutes. *MPAA Rating:* Not Rated.

CAST: Jan Decleir (Dreverhaven); Fedja van Huet (Jacob Katadreuffe); Betty Schuurman (Joba Katadreuffe); Tamar van den Dop (Lorna Te George); Victor Löw (De Gankelaar); Hans Kesting (Jan Maan); Pavlik Jansen op de Haar (Jacob, age 12); Jasper Gottlieb and Marius Gottlieb (Jacob, age 6); Bernhard Droog (Stroomkoning); Lou Landré (Rentenstein); Frans Vorstman (Inspector de Bree); Fred Goessens (Schuwagt); Marisa van Eyle (Miss

Sibculo);   Wim van der Grijn (Second Inspector);   Jos Berbist (Brigadier);   Jaap Spijkers
(Upstairs Neighbor);   Mark Rietman (Van Rijn);   Jack Hedley (Mr. Forester).

LOS ANGELES TIMES, 3/27/98, Calendar/p. 12, Kenneth Turan

Both here and in its home country of the Netherlands, "Character" has created considerable interest, taking film festival honors and even winning this year's Oscar for best foreign language film. Determining what the fuss is about is not difficult, but wholeheartedly sharing in it is another matter.

"Character" is made with an assurance and visual flair that belies the first-time status of director Mike van Diem, who also adapted the popular 1938 Dutch novel of the same name. Set in a convincingly re-created Rotterdam of the 1920s, "Character" is more than anything intent on telling its tale at breakneck speed, determined to operatically heighten every situation for maximum effect and exhibiting the same force Van Diem showed at the Oscar ceremony Monday night. While that makes the film instantaneously melodramatic and involving, it doesn't serve its long-term interests equally well.

The film opens with a furious young man named Jacob Willem Katadreuffe hurtling down the streets of Rotterdam. He storms into the office of an aged troll and screams that despite the troll's best efforts he's succeeded in becoming a lawyer. How do you know I wasn't working for, not against you?, the troll asks. Katadreuffe leaves in a huff, changes his mind, storms back into the office even more furious and literally hurls himself at the older man as the scene fades out.

Soon enough there is a large group of police at Katadreuffe's door. Dreverhaven, for that is the old man's name, has been found dead in his office, and this morose young man is the main suspect. Interrogated in a prison cell by a sympathetic official, Katadreuffe reveals the story behind the confrontation we've witnessed.

Dreverhaven (played with great presence by Jan Decleir) is no ordinary man. Called "the law without compassion" by understandably terrified citizens, he's a court bailiff who specializes in evicting the poor.   Wearing an impressive medallion and a large black hat like the one the Shadow favors, Dreverhaven is heartless and implacable, capable of tossing dying people into the street and even, if need be, "evicting the devil from hell."

Dreverhaven is allowed one quasi-human moment, a night of dalliance with his silent, grim-faced servant Joba (Betty Schuurman). Naturally the child Jacob Willem is born of that episode, but though Dreverhaven offers marriage, the independent Joba is determined to turn him down.

The refusal leads to a miserable childhood for our protagonist, who's taunted for being a bastard. Only two things even momentarily lighten his torment: a love of books and the friendship of an earnest young radical named Jan Maan (Hans Kesting), whom Joba takes in as a boarder.

Jacob Willem grows into a young man (played by Fedja van Huet, an actor who looks uncannily like Robert Downey Jr.) and takes his mother's name because Dreverhaven absolutely refuses to acknowledge his paternity. Katadreuffe attempts to make his way in the world but finds that every step he takes, even his flirtation with the pretty Lorna Te George (Tamar van den Dop) locks him deeper and deeper into a battle of wills with a father who appears to be a monster pure and simple.

Director Van Diem, aided by cinematographer Rogier Stoffers and an ominous symphonic score from Het Paleis van Boem, brings considerable verve and style to this story, but the film is not without problems. The most obvious is that being the son of two such grim automatons has not done much for Katadreuffe's personality. He's deadly serious and something of a pill, and we don't particularly care for him any more than we do his father.

More of a problem is Van Diem's attempt to tell this bleak story in a highly stylized way. The film does have energy, but it's so much the energy of a soap opera that none of the terrible things that happen to Katadreuffe seems real enough to involve us to any measurable extent.

That, finally, is probably the reason for "Character's" success. It provides all the trappings of a tragic story without any of the pain that real tragedy involves. What we get instead is a fun-house version of a serious film, made in a style that lets us ooh and aah at the characters' troubles without having to take them too seriously. There's some genuine filmmaking involved in "Character," but the darkness it so proudly evokes is strictly bogus.

NEW YORK POST, 3/27/98, p. 45, Thelma Adams

A week before "Character" won the foreign-language-film Oscar, Dutch director Mike van Diem told a crowd of New Yorkers in a private screening room: This is my first born, "treat her gently."

It's easy to treat van Diem's first feature more gently than his battered hero, Katadreuffe (Fedja van Huet). The ambitious young lawyer is the bastard son of a chilly mother (Betty Schuurman) and a wicked, absent father, Bailiff Dreverhaven (Jan Decleir).

The bailiff is the kind of bureaucratic Nosferatu who gets his kicks by evicting a woman on her deathbed. Had a tough day? Feeling rejected? Evict some more people and then justify the actions by claiming to be "the law without compassion."

The handsome, Kafkaesque drama opens when Katadreuffe attacks the bailiff. The police discover Dreverhaven's corpse and arrest the blood-soaked lawyer. Their formal investigation becomes the bitter story of Katadreuffe's life and moral development.

Is Katadreuffe the murderer? Is it a patricide? The movie flashes back to reveal the lawyer's life, from cradle to knife. Was the killing a justifiable homicide?

Based on a classic Dutch novel set in Rotterdam in the 1920s, "Character" shows promise but is bleak and heavy-handed. That it won the Oscar is not a poor reflection on the state of foreign films but on the Academy's selection process.

NEWSDAY, 3/27/98, Part II/p. B7, John Anderson

Those who watched Mike van Diem's quasi-delirious acceptance speech during the Academy Awards might well expect his Best Foreign Film, "Character," to reflect a similar kind of goofy exhilaration. Savvy Oscar watchers, on the other hand, knowing the tastes of the Academy, might be expecting a predictable, maybe even juvenile movie, thoroughly accessible to all but the oyster.

They'd all be wrong. "Character," based on the classic Dutch works by author/lawyer Ferdinand Bordewijk (a 1928 novella, a 1938 novel), has its predictable aspects, and a certain tongue-in-cheek quality that owes something to retrospection (an awareness that the past is prologue). But it's an epic in its' way, a period piece and character drama that operates as an adventure film, even while its subject matter consists mostly of bankruptcy and paternity.

Shot on locations in Belgium and Germany in order to replicate 1920s Rotterdam (the appropriate settings having been bombed into rubble during World War II), "Character" is Dickensian in its story line, Marcusian in its politics. Framed within the investigation of a murder—the feared and ruthless court bailiff Dreverhaven (Jan Decleir of "Antonia's Line") 'has been found dead—the story is told in flashback about Katadreuffe (Fedja van Huet), literature's quintessential self-made man. The son of the unmarried Joba (Betty Shuurman) and maligned as illegitimate, he is self-taught, ambitious, a borrower and poor—and at every turn he meets the visage of Dreverhaven, who not only hounds him with threats of bankruptcy and ruin but happens to be his father.

In an earlier era, Dreverhaven might have been played by Lionel Barrymore, a la Capra's Mr. Potter, but Decleir brings a physical presence to the role that both embellishes Dreverhaven's menace and shrivels Katadreuffe's manhood virtually before our eyes. With an uncanny resemblance to Robert Downey Jr., van Huet manages to be the picture of poignancy, but not without a certain voluptuous corruption around the edges. Dreverhaven, whose already winning personality has been soured by Joba's rejection of his marriage proposals, is a dark, cape-wearing angel of unrequited love.

Van Diem is an excitingly visual filmmaker (this is his first feature after a successful career in Dutch television) and "Character" is no less affecting in its story than in its look, which finds in the brickwork and alleys of faux Rotterdam a neo-gothic dread. It's an unusual film, granted—how often are a hero's personal finances the fulcrum of a plot? But at the same time, and for all its novelistic flourishes, "Character" possesses an appreciation of archetype that makes it worthy of the literature that spawned it.

SIGHT AND SOUND, 9/98, p. 40, Philip Horne

Rotterdam, Holland, the 20s. Jacob Katadreuffe quarrels with the city's most feared bailiff, Dreverhaven. Katadreuffe is later arrested for Dreverhaven's stabbing. Claiming innocence, he gives the police his account of the events leading up to the death.

Years before. Jacob is Dreverhaven's illegitimate son by housekeeper Joba Katadreuffe, who refuses to marry Dreverhaven or accept money. Jacob grows up in poverty, socially ambitious and obsessed with his father. Jacob obtains a loan and buys a tobacconist's shop, but goes bankrupt. At Stroomkoning's, the loan company's lawyers, he wins a post as a clerk. Jacob discovers Dreverhaven was the bailiff on his bankruptcy; the loan company also belongs to his father, who insists on taking Jacob to court. When Jacob confronts Dreverhaven, he tries to provoke Jacob to violence. Jacob falls in love with Lorna Te George, a secretary at work. He pays off the debt, but borrows a further large sum on hard conditions. Two years later, he becomes an office manager. He snubs Miss Te George and Dreverhaven demands the money back at once; in court Jacob wins only on a technicality.

Two years on, Dreverhaven yet again proposes to Joba, unsuccessfully, and vents his frustration by evicting poor people from his tenements. Jacob meets Lorna, now married and a mother, and realises his mistake. Joba dies. Jacob goes to Dreverhaven's and quarrels with him; they struggle. Dreverhaven, badly beaten, pleads with Jacob to kill him, but he refuses and leaves. Dreverhaven stabs himself and jumps to his death. Released, Jacob finds Dreverhaven has left him all his property in a letter signed "Father".

Winner of an Academy Award for Best Foreign Language Film, debut director Mike van Diem's *Character,* inspired by the Dutch novel *Karakter* (1938) by F. Bordewijk, is set in the grey, rain-soaked streets and canals of Rotterdam in the 20s, and recreates a harsh world of economic pressure, class conflict, emotional repression and grotesque obsession.

The book's subtitle is *A Novel of Son and Father,* and the film vividly realises the Oedipal struggle between young Jacob Katadreuffe and his remote, terrifying progenitor and persecutor, the austere but troubled Dreverhaven. Fedja van Huêt as the nervous, driven young lawyer has a touch of Robert Downey Jr about him, but his earnest striving and bafflement also recall Buster Keaton and Harry Langdon. Meanwhile, Jan Decleir as the universally hated and feared Dreverhaven resembles Max Schreck, the vampire in Murnau's 1922 *Nosferatu.* The joint appropriation of period styles of comedy and horror (consciously intended: Jacob goes to the cinema in 1924 and watches some classic Hollywood silent comedy) nicely furthers the grotesque, Kafkaesque aspects of the story.

Character is a tale of doubles (with father and son instead of twins), recalling Poe's 'William Wilson' (1839) in the hauntingly inescapable persecutor who seems to provoke acts of violence towards himself. But the world portrayed here is not just a sketchy background for a psychological case study: Jacob's desperation and Dreverhaven's brutal evictions of defaulting tenants are linked not only to their bizarrely embattled relationship but also to the social and political conditions of the time. Jacob's mother's lodger Jan Maan is a communist agitator. And we see Communist Party rallies and armed police suppressing a strike, as well as Dreverhaven boldly facing down crowds of distressed tenants "in the name of the law".

Van Diem is suggesting clearly here the unpleasant underpinnings of the comfortable bourgeois status quo to which Jacob aspires. And though we sympathise with Jacob, as he gains in power he does not seem to escape from the tyrannical Dreverhaven, and may be coming to resemble him, despite his protestations at one point that he "no longer exists for me".

The central mystery in the film is Dreverhaven's motive for repeatedly proposing to Jacob's silent, stubborn mother, and for shadowing his son like a malign guardian angel. "I want to know why you're doing this," Jacob fruitlessly asks him. There are intriguing hints. It may be that Dreverhaven deliberately denies Jacob his love, as Joba Katadreuffe refuses him hers, in order to force her to accept him. But it also seems a form of perverted parental care. He declares to Jacob's mother at a late stage, in a quasi-Nietzschean register, that "I'll strangle him for nine tenths and the last tenth will make him stronger"; but when she refuses marriage again, says "Maybe I'll strangle him for the last tenth too."

Repeatedly, his self-destructive urges lead him to offer Jacob a knife, and to confront angry mobs of evicted tenants. In one of the film's most hyperbolic scenes, he breaks through police lines and confronts a besieged striker with a gun, allowing him several shots before the police shoot him down. Dreverhaven seems to see the young man as Jacob for a moment: the intimacy of violence substitutes for the other kinds he refuses or is refused. The film's strength throughout is the intensity with which it conveys the central characters' predicaments, trapped in family romances which they cannot fully comprehend.

TIME, 4/13/98, p. 208, Richard Schickel

It is set in the early years of this century. It features an unreasonably implacable villain, a talented and idealistic young man determined to rise out of poverty, and a tender love story that ends on a poignant, not to say tragic note. And it was unaccountably named last year's Best Picture by the Academy of Motion Picture Arts and Sentiment a couple of weeks ago.

Best Foreign Picture, that is. Whereupon, to extend the analogy between Character and *Titanic*, as the director accepted his Oscar, his ego succumbed to an attack of St. Vitus' dance, causing some among us to avert embarrassed eyes. But it's worthwhile, in the case of Dutch director Mike van Diem, to refocus them on his work, which is a true epic-long, dark, complex, enigmatic and curiously riveting.

Character's protagonist, a young man named Katadreuffe (Fedja van Huet), lives in emotional country bordered on one side by Kafka, on the other by Dickens, or, if you insist on being literal, in dank, gloomy Rotterdam in the 1920s. He is the product of a one-night liaison between a chilly, brutal man named Dreverhaven (Jan Decleir) and his stony housekeeper (Betty Schuurman), sex that one suspects was a once-in-a-lifetime experience for both of them. He keeps asking her to marry him, she keeps refusing him, and he takes his frustration out on his son.

That's easy for him to do, for Dreverhaven is an all-powerful figure. He is a bailiff enriching himself by collecting everyone's bad debts, and his tentacles reach everywhere. He is never too busy, though, to keep a baleful eye on his son, eventually ensnaring the lad in debt and squeezing him mercilessly for the money.

The obsessiveness with which the old man pursues this perverse relationship, recounted in flashbacks after the son is arrested on suspicion of murdering him, is horrific. This is especially so since the lad is apparently everything his father is not—clean-cut, eager to please, lovable. But therein lies the story's cunning. For the father recognizes in his son qualities that they share. The son is wily, a demon for work, and not comfortable or clever with women, as he proves by sadly fumbling an office romance as he rises from clerk to partner in a law firm.

As the movie proceeds, taking time to linger with complex subsidiary characters, letting us absorb the detailed richness of its imagery, contextualizing its story in a broader social history (unlike most movies, it is aware of working-class unrest and Marxist attempts to organize it early in this century), two withering ironies are drawn. The first is that the father is one of those sad souls who can express love only by tormenting the object of his affection. The other is that his rationale for bad behavior—that he's building the boy's "character"—is not entirely wrong. In the end, Katadreuffe is strong, though at what cost in future psychiatric bills the movie wisely does not say. It is content to offer us only this bleak, useful thought: life's problems are not all small stuff, and we do need to sweat them. It helps us get rid of our baby fat.

VILLAGE VOICE, 3/31/98, p. 64, Dennis Lim

Like *Genealogies of a Crime* [see Lim's review], the Dutch period drama *Character* in a sequence of flashbacks triggered by the interrogation of a murder suspect. The similarities end there, for *Character* is as matter-of-factly transparent as *Genealogies* is willfully opaque. Set in 1920s Rotterdam, Mike van Diem's good-looking adaptation of a classic Dutch novel charts the lifelong antagonism between the evil town bailiff (Jan Decleir) and his idealistic bastard son (Fedja van Huet) Themes and twists are so instantly recognizable that any remotely alert viewer will have reached the finish line long before the film (which takes two bustling hours). The kind of billowy epic in which momentous events are scheduled for rainy nights and punctuated by thunderclaps, *Character* may, in any case, have won the Best Foreign Film Oscar by the time you read this.

Also reviewed in:
NEW YORK TIMES, 3/27/98, p. E14, Janet Maslin

NEW YORKER, 5/11/98, p. 107, Daphne Merkin
VARIETY, 5/26-6/1/97, p. 68, Godfrey Cheshire
WASHINGTON POST, 4/17/98, p. B1, Stephen Hunter
WASHINGTON POST, 4/17/98, Weekend/p. 56, Michael O'Sullivan

CHARLIE HOBOKEN

A Northern Arts Entertainment release of an Only Child production. *Producer:* Linda Crean.
Director: Thomas F. Mazziotti. *Screenplay:* Thomas F. Mazziotti. *Director of Photography:*
Mike Slovis. *Editor:* Thomas R. Rondinella. *Music:* Peter C. Lopez. *Production Designer:*
Dina Goldman. *Running time:* 85 minutes. *MPAA Rating:* Not Rated.

CAST: Austin Pendleton (Harry Cedars);   Ken Garito (Charlie Hoboken);   Tovah Feldshuh
(Angie Cedars);   Anita Gillette (Stepmother);   George Morfogen (Father).

NEW YORK POST, 6/5/98, p. 46, Larry Worth

The concept of funny hit men started in 1994 with Quentin Tarantino's "Pulp Fiction." Four
years and countless imitators later, it's time to move on.

Unfortunately, writer/director Thomas F. Mazziotti thinks otherwise. The result?   "Charlie
Hoboken" a film that brings new meaning to the phrase D.O.A.

Austin ("What's Up Doc?") Pendleton does his best to enliven the ho-hum proceedings, playing
a senior contract killer who's in constant conflict with his ever-amorous wife (Tovah Feldshuh)
and a young, super ambitious partner (Ken Garito).

What follows is a lot of would-be comic dialogue and an occasional detour into drama, all of
which seems incredibly labored. With Pendleton's talents as the sole diversion, viewers are left
to ponder what possessed the usually reliable Feldshuh to deliver such an unconvincing New
Yawk accent, why the lackluster Garito isn't a full-time waiter and what turn of events persuaded
Broadway vet Anita Gillette to play a cliched shrew.

An even better question: Why should anyone—with the exception of diehard Pendleton
fans—waste two seconds of time or the price of admission on "Charlie Hoboken"?

NEWSDAY, 6/5/98, Part II/p. B7, John Anderson

You know how it goes. Just when things are flowing along smoothly, no troubles, no hitches,
no bumps in the road, somebody gets ideas. They get restless. They start talking about their
dreams. Increasing their vocabulary. Using astringents.

Harry Cedars (Austin Pendleton) is a small-businessman who's happy with the old precepts and
policies; contentment is his middle name. Sure, there have been some sacrifices: He and his wife
Angie (Tovah Feldshuh) have never had children, for one thing. But they don't have a lot of
complaints. Business is good.

And his younger partner, Charlie (Ken Garito)? Who wants more upscale clients, a chance for
advancement, a career rather than just a solid job? No, he's a yuppie in a workaday world, and
there's going to be trouble.

That Harry and Charlie are hit men puts Tom Mazziotti's "Charlie Hoboken" in a very
congested field—one that will soon become even more crowded, with films like Anders
Dalgaard's Beckettian "Nether World" and Saul Rubinek's Mamet-esque "Jerry and Tom." Has
the vortex of cinematic satire spun so far around that just making a hit man film now qualifies
as postmortem? Or is it still just a cliche? We get the hired-killer metaphor, I think, and it ought
to take early retirement. What distinguishes "Charlie Hoboken," though, is its snowballing
dialogue, recited by a band of very capable actors—especially Pendleton and Feldshuh as the
cuddly Harry and Angie—and Mazziotti's penchant for taking every pedestrian conversation to
absurdist degrees. There isn't much story, but the script and cast are so voluble it's impossible
to be bored.

You don't usually get Pendleton in a leading role, and we haven't seen much of Feldshuh either lately, and both are fun to watch as a couple very devoted to their work (even if it does involve homicide) and whose love has survived all the vagaries of murder-as-vocation (one particularly romantic moment, Harry says, "reminds me of our first conjugal visit"). As Charlie, who lives in a church, overdresses for work and wants to upscale the industry (which is what gets him into trouble), Garito resembles a young John Travolta and is suitably shallow for the role of the scheming Charlie. But as the film itself instructs, older is often wiser, sometimes even better.

VILLAGE VOICE, 6/16/98, p. 154, Salma Abdelnour

Imagine *My Dinner With Andre* as a gangster buddy movie—we interrupt this murder for a lengthy philosophical discussion—and you'll understand *Charlie Hoboken*'s problem. For intellectual young Charlie (Ken Garito), a job as hired assassin seems promising enough—more challenging and lucrative than his insurance day-job. *Grosse Pointe Blank* already did the portrait of a hit man as cynical careerist and had fun with the premise, whereas *Hoboken* insists on gravitas.

En route to each hit, Charlie and partner Harry (Austin Pendleton) struggle to decode love, work, and destiny, knowing they shouldn't trust each other but trying to anyway. Unfortunately, director Tom Mazziotti's script buries their chemistry under precious repartee, and stage veteran Pendleton's studied enunciation chokes the spontaneity even more. Minor characters are wordsmiths, as well. When the partners ambush their first hit—a shrink—and pretend they're lost, the victim asks, "in what sense?" Don't get them started. Charlie's stepmother eventually screams, "Let's drop the metaphors!" But the metaphors win; even sex brakes for wordplay. Soon it's clear every character deserves a mercy killing: they know too much, and so do we.

Also reviewed in:
NEW YORK TIMES, 6/5/98, p. E20, Lawrence Van Gelder

CHICAGO CAB

A GFT Entertainment release of a Child's Will production in association with New Crime Productions. *Executive Producer:* Gary Howsam, Kathy Morgan, Charles Weber, John Cusack, D.V. Divincentis, and Steve Pink. *Producer:* Paul Dillon and Suzanne De Walt. *Director:* Mary Cybulski and John Tintori. *Screenplay (based on his play "Hellcab"):* Will Kern. *Director of Photography:* Hubert Taczanowski. *Music:* Page Hamilton. *Sound:* Joe Yarid. *Casting:* John Parsidera. *Production Designer:* Maria Nay. *Costumes:* Carolyn Greco. *Running time:* 96 minutes. *MPAA Rating:* Not Rated.

CAST: Paul Dillon (Cab Driver); Michael Ironside (Al); Laurie Metcalf (Female Ad Executive); John C. Reilly (Steve); Gillian Anderson (Southside Girl); John Cusack (Scary Man); Julianne Moore (Distraught Woman); Laura Kellogg Sandburg (Bug-Eyed Woman); Michael Shannon (Crackhead); Shulie Cowen (Stoner Girl); Philip Van Lear (Father-to-Be).

LOS ANGELES TIMES, 10/2/98, Calendar/p. 18, Bob Heisler

[*The following review by Bob Heisler appeared in a slightly different form in* NEWSDAY, 9/18/98, Part II/p. B10.]

There's no bulletproof divider between the cab driver and his passengers in the episodic and uneven "Chicago Cab." The barrier is between the driver, whose name we never learn, and the audience.

The double-shift worth of fares feel compelled to reach across the space between front seat and back, to use the driver as a sounding board, a counselor, an accomplice, a minister, a bank, a mirror and a pal.

He is none of those things. That's the point. He's a kind of hooker, taking money to get folks from where they are to where they think they want to be. And when he lets his fares get to him, he exposes his own hopeless soul. By the time he chooses to get involved in the serial tragedy of cab riders in Chicago—telling people what he thinks, what he'd do, what he knows—the driver (Paul Dillon) has already established a character who does not want to be touched or spoken to or bothered by life.

Looking like Lee Marvin's little brother, Dillon's driver spends a very long winter day driving around Chicago, picking up fares, listening for a few moments to the back-seat view of the universe, then moving on.

Buried in what is a bumpy sketch movie, there's an interesting treatise on how people talk to one another when they are strangers and not likely to meet again. But without irony or humor, with high-decibel street language taking the place of dramatic action, "Chicago Cab" is likely to leave you a little carsick. It goes nowhere because the driver has nowhere to go.

After a while, you begin to feel sympathy for Travis Bickle, Robert De Niro's overpowering character in Martin Scorsese's "Taxi Driver" (1976), who felt compelled to take action against an imagined sea of outrageous fortune.

There's enough outrageous fortune to go around in "Chicago Cab." You never know who'll get into Dillon's bomb of a cab. The drugged, pregnant, unemployed, bruised, used, abused, cheated and cheating fill the back seat. A woman announces her rape, another opens her garage door and invites both cab and driver inside. A man offers to save his soul, another offers advice on the proper way to bite a cuticle.

In the end, like an out-of-control radio talk show, the voices blur, the faces—even the TV-familiar faces of Gillian Anderson and Laurie Metcalf in R-rated cameos—disappear and your focus is on the host behind the wheel. And even though you feel empathy, you begin to blame him for his plight and for your slightly soiled feeling as the lights go up.

NEW YORK POST, 9/18/98, p. 58, Larry Worth

Where's Travis Bickle when you need him? Robert De Niro, with a little help from Martin Scorsese, knew how to make a ride in a taxi into the stuff of art. "Chicago Cab" will never be accused of the same, and not just because the locale has changed from NYC to the Windy City.

The problem is a collection of pointless anecdotes, with one crazed customer after another climbing into the vehicle of a lackluster driver. Indeed, the hack's most interesting feature is his appearance: Sideburns and one continuous eyebrow are the only hairs on his head.

The less-than-hirsute hero consequently tries to cope as one woman wants to deliver her baby in a hurry, a pimp disses his lady, couples emulate Bill and Monica's tricks or engage in the ugliest of fights.

The law of averages would dictate that at least one fare would be normal, or perhaps seeking a little quiet time. But as day turns into night, it's just one garrulous, utterly redundant lunatic after another.

The irony is that, almost two-thirds of the way through, things get better. John Cusack's turn as a mystery man who barks instructions to a godforsaken alley is menace incarnate. And that's followed by Julianne Moore's heartbreaking bit as a woman who's just been raped.

Both sequences hint at the endless potential that directors Mary Cybuiski and John Tintori ignored. Aside from focusing on cliches, the pair play too many moments for cheap laughs. Worse, they fail to knock the storyline out of its stagebound origins.

Paul (TV's Pretender) Dillon re-creates his Hellcab stage role as the everyman behind the wheel. But despite an obvious familiarity with the part, he fails to give it much credibility or nuance.

Featured bits from Gillian Anderson, Laurie Metcalf, Kevin J. O'Connor and Michael Ironside contribute little, adding only to the level of yelling in the back seat.

Also reviewed in:
CHICAGO TRIBUNE, 10/2/98, Friday/p. M, John Petrakis
NEW YORK TIMES, 9/18/98, p. E16, Stephen Holden
VARIETY, 2/20-4/5/98, p. 44, Emanuel Levy

CHILE, OBSTINATE MEMORY

A First Run/Icarus Films release of a National Film Board of Canada and Les Films d'Ici production. *Producer:* Yves Jeanneau and Eric Michel. *Director:* Patricio Guzmán. *Director of Photography:* Jorge Müller. *Editor:* Pedro Chaskel. *Music:* Robert M. Lepage. *Sound:* Boris Herrera. *Running time:* 58 minutes. *MPAA Rating:* Not Rated.

WITH: Patricio Guzmán (narrator).

CINEASTE, Vol. XXIV, no. 4, 1999, p. 44, Dennis West

In Chile in late 1972, documentary director Patricio Guzmán and his filmmaking collective foresaw the upcoming collapse of the popular Unity coalition government headed by President Salvador Allende. In spite of the dangers, the collective was determined to document the unprecedented economic, political, and ideological struggles that were ripping apart the nation during the months preceding the brutal right-wing military coup which toppled the popular-front government on September 11, 1973. The politically committed collective successfully used semiclandestine measures to document key events and sociopolitical movements across the political spectrum—from extreme left to extreme right.

After the coup d'etat, this treasure trove of actuality footage was smuggled out of Chile; and the production crew, except for cameraman Jorge Müller Silva, left the country and reunited ill Cuba, where the footage was edited with the support of the revolutionary film institute ICAIC. The result was the three-part *The Battle Of Chile,* a wide-ranging chronicle of history-in-the-making as well as a clearly conceived Marxist-socialist president. *The Battle of Chile* starred on the festival circuit when it was released in the mid-1970s, and it was voted by *Cineaste* one of the top political films of all time. Not Surprisingly, however, the documentary never screened publicly in Chile because of the deadly repression imposed by General Augusto Pinochet and his cohorts after the coup.

Twenty-three years later Guzmán returned to Chile with a videotape copy of his magnum opus. His new documentary, *Chile, Obstinate Memory,* records the emotion-charged discussions amongst audience members after screenings of *The Battle of Chile.* Many young spectators, largely ignorant of their nation's recent history, are clearly devastated after viewing actuality footage showing the brutality of the military coup. But other viewers argue in support of General Pinochet and the historical necessity of the coup. Guzmán's discussions with viewers lead him to understand that he has returned to a Chile very different from the one he had fled two decades earlier. Indeed, his principal finding in *Chile, Obstinate Memory* refers to the very changed socioeconomic and political situation in his country at this time: much of the citizenry is apolitical; neoliberal economic policies have triumphed; and most young people know little about the Popular Unity period because memory has been repressed.

In *Chile, Obstinate Memory,* Guzmán aims to explore the labyrinths of memory in contemporary Chile—and recuperate it. With this goal in mind, he interviews those least likely to have forgotten the past—the friends and relatives of the desaparecidos, and the Allende supporters who were his spokespersons, bodyguards, servants, and those who marched in the massive demonstrations in support of Popular Unity. Allende's widow tells how the military, in their frantic efforts to erase any trace of the President and his political vision, confiscated or destroyed all his photographs and other personal effects—thus leaving the widow nothing tangible to pass on to the couple's heirs.

As interviewees examine film footage and photos of the Popular Unity period in order to identify and reminisce about former comrades, one nefarious term keeps recurring: "*desaparecer,*" to disappear. During the Pinochet period, the Spanish intransitive verb "*desaparecer*" came to be used transitively as the military "disappeared" suspects following this macabre protocol: summary detention, interrogation and torture, extrajudicial execution, and clandestine burial. The bodies of these victims are still being found; thus far, however, the remains of Jorge Müller Silva, the only disappeared member of Guzmán's original collective, have not surfaced.

The most unforgettable interviewee is the spectral Carmen Vivanco, who is not certain whether a face that confronts her from the past—of a marcher in a pro-Allende demonstration—is really hers. Whether this woman is truly uncertain about the identity of the younger face, or is in fact fearful of publicly admitting her participation in a pro-Popular Unity event, remains unclear. What is clear is Vivanco's stone-faced, unflinching enumeration of her family members disappeared during the post-coup terror—husband, son, brother, sister-in-law, nephew.

Chile, Obstinate Memory is not only a sensitive meditation on memory and the weight of the past. It is also a powerful 'educational film' in the loftiest sense of that term. Since memory remains so repressed in contemporary Chile, Guzmán will inform and educate us—for instance, about the coup itself and its bloody aftermath. The documentary sketches a geography of repression as we tour historical sites with survivors at our side: The infamous Villa Grimaldi torture center; The National Stadium, where prisoners were tortured and executed, and Guzmán himself was detained; and the Moneda Palace, where Allende and his bodyguards resisted heroically in the face of aerial bombardment. Visionaries who dreamt a more just society for their nation—the *"Via Chilena"* path towards a democratic socialism offer us glimpses of their dreams and motivation. Guzmán even educates us in an auditory sense when he films a youthful marching band winding through downtown Santiago playing the Popular Unity anthem to the Surprise of passersby, who have not heard those strains in many years. And, finally, *Chile, Obstinate Memory* reveals how *The Battle of Chile*'s irreplaceable footage was saved: stored clandestinely by Guzmán's uncle and then smuggled out of the country in a diplomatic pouch on board a ship bound for Stockholm.

Guzmán achieves a high level of artistry in *Chile, Obstinate Memory* in spite of relying on conventional documentary techniques. Much of the emotional power of the film is owing to the use of a first-person narrator, Guzmán himself, who deftly guides us through the labyrinths of memory, while also capturing our interest in his own remarkable personal journey both as filmmmaker and as Popular Unity supporter during the movement's heyday—and as a fortunate survivor of all that. Guzmán completed *Chile, Obstinate Memory* before the detention of "Senator for Life" Aususto Pinochet in London on charges relating to crimes against humanity. That unprecedented international incident, of course, has ignited debates in Chile concerning the nation's recent past. If widely screened in his country, Guzmán's exceptionally moving documentary can contribute greatly to an understanding of how contemporary Chile was born and where it is heading.

Also reviewed in:
NATION, 9/28/98, p. 34, Stuart Klawans
NEW YORK TIMES, 9/9/98, p. E5, Lawrence van Gelder
VARIETY, 11/10-16/97, p. 45, Leonard Klady

CHINESE BOX

A Trimark Pictures release of an NDF International, Ltd. & Pony Canyon, Inc. and Le Studio Canal+ co-production.   *Executive Producer:* Michiyo Yoshizaki, Reinhard Brundig, Akinori Inaba, and Jean Labadie.   *Producer:* Lydia Dean Pilcher, Jean-Louis Piel, and Wayne Wang.   *Director:* Wayne Wang.   *Screenplay:* Jean-Claude Carriere and Larry Gross.   *Story:* Jean-Claude Carriere, Paul Theroux, Wayne Wang.   *Director of Photography:* Vilko Filac.   *Music:* Christopher Tellefsen.   *Sound:* Drew Kunin.   *Production Designer:* Chris Wong.   *Costumes:* Shirley Chan.   *Running time:* 100 minutes.   *MPAA Rating:* R.

CAST: Jeremy Irons (John); Gong Li (Vivian); Maggie Cheung (Jean); Michael Hui (Chang); Ruben Blades (Jim).

LOS ANGELES TIMES, 4/17/98, Calendar/p. 8, Kevin Thomas

Drenchingly romantic, world-weary and perhaps not just a little foolish, "Chinese Box," Wayne Wang's love letter to his native Hong Kong, is the kind of film that can be rewarding if you embrace it for its bold attempt rather than its easy success.

There are certainly plenty of inducements: Jeremy Irons and Gong Li's glamorous star-crossed lovers, Maggie Cheung's movie-stealing portrayal of a young woman living by her wits and, above all, a staggeringly rich visual evocation of Hong Kong on quite literally the eve of return to China after 156 years of British rule. To be open to this film is to be moved by it.

It's understandable that Wang, having achieved considerable success in the U.S. in the last 15 years, starting with the beguiling "Chan Is Missing" and including the large-scale "The Joy Luck Club," would want to tell a story that climaxes just as the turnover occurs. The challenge, of course, was to come up with a tale worthy of the complicated and contradictory historic event that serves as its background.

The obvious choice would be a love story, and to tell it he lined up the distinguished screenwriter and Buñuel collaborator Jean-Claude Carriere, novelist Paul Theroux, an old Asia hand, and a Hollywood veteran writer, Larry Gross.

Inevitably, Irons' English journalist, Li's mainland refugee bar hostess with a past and Cheung's native street vendor symbolize Britain, China and Hong Kong. But, golly, did they have to go and lay on Irons' John "a rare form of leukemia" that gives him only six months to live—exactly the film's time span, New Year's Eve 1996 to June 30, 1997? Talk about a literally dying empire!

Nonetheless, "Chinese Box" captures so much of Hong Kong's raw essence: the naked, rampant materialism, the sense that life is cruel and cheap, the uncertainty of the future under Chinese rule with its inevitable curtailing of democracy and free expression, and the terrific energy of the city's daily life that gives it hope.

John is the dashing, reflective but impassioned Anglo-Saxon and Li's Vivian the dazzling Asian beauty from countless movies and plays past. Anyone hear strains of "Love Is a Many-Splendored Thing"? Echoes of "Suzie Wong"?

Luckily, John is exceptionally well-drawn and played beautifully by Irons, and the reticent Vivian fits Li's limited English comfortably. But love for them is such a many-tormented thing, involving so much anguish of the hand-wringing, seesawing variety, that it's Cheung's Jean who grabs attention.

This is not surprising because Cheung could be said to embody the vital spirit of Hong Kong as much as the character she portrays and is a resourceful actress of widely varied experience, shining in everything from kung foolery to an admirable portrayal of the great Shanghai screen star of the '30s, Ruan Ling-yu. In creating the character of Jean, Wang drew on a short story by Rachel Ingalls, "Last Act: The Madhouse," and has said that for him she is the most important character in the film. The plot unfolds as John, on receiving his grim prognosis, begins to realize that for 15 years he's been covering the economics and politics of the British crown colony so single-mindedly that much of its essence has eluded him.

One side of her face badly scarred and partly hidden by a scarf, Jean peddles any kind of trinket on the street she can to survive. Persuaded by John to let him interview her and be photographed by his friend and colleague (Ruben Blades), Jean spins a lurid tale of a sexually abusive father because she thinks that's what John wants to hear, but her actual story involves classic British racism toward its colonial subjects.

John and especially Vivian are believable characters, but John's terminal illness gives their relationship an inevitable aura of contrivance while Jean and her story have the stinging punch of reality.

In all this interaction, Wang and his colleagues, who include his awesomely talented cinematographer Vilko Filac, who incorporates great documentary-like shots of actual events, charge "Chinese Box" with ambiguity and emotion about Hong Kong's past, present and future.

With its beguiling Graeme Revell score, the film pays tremendous—and redeeming—attention to nuance and detail. Among the touches: Gross' inspired idea of having Vivian become fascinated by watching Marlene Dietrich singing Frederick Hollander's memorably cynical "Black Market" from Billy Wilder's postwar Berlin classic "A Foreign Affair."

Sophisticated, ironic and highly complex, "Chinese Box" is to Wang's traditional narratives what the exotic and worldly "The Bitter Tea of General Yen" was to Frank Capra's cherished Americana.

FILM QUARTERLY, Fall 1998, p. 31, Wena Poon

Recent English-language filmmaking about doe-eyed Asian female superstars has developed to such a degree that the genre has already taken on a life of its own. A canon is in the making; soon one will be able to order boxed sets from Time Life Videos of these prolific outpourings of giddying fin-de-siècle Orientalism. It is thus quite impossible to watch *Chinese Box* without noting its place as the latest among an (inadvertent) trilogy of international films specializing in parading Chinese-speaking actresses before English audiences.

Wayne Wang's most recent film succeeds where its "sister" films, Peter Greenaway's *The Pillow Book* and Olivier Assayas's *Irma Vep*, fail... by satisfactorily accounting for the need to "orientalize." *The Pillow Book* and *Irma Vep* are films about filmmaking; one suspects that substituting for their Asian components those of any other major world culture would hardly disturb what Greenaway and Assayas have to say about their art. The directors are more enchanted by the *look* of Asia than by its life. By contrast, Wang does not allow Orientalism to play second fiddle to his ruminations about himself and his métier; he prefers to deploy his art to uncover and define what it must be like to exist in that world. *Chinese Box*, possessing both the aesthetic fancies of Greenaway and the music-video chic of *Irma Vep*, attains its own luminescence simply by realizing and sharpening the focus of an incredibly unsatiated nostalgia: the loss of Hong Kong in July 1997, seen through the eyes of John, a dying British expatriate.

Nostos, the pain Odysseus felt sitting on the rock looking across the sea toward an unseen Ithaca, has always been the flip side of voyages toward the exotic. Nostalgia and strangeness reverberate within these three films. In Greenaway, Nakiko's memories of her father and her childhood, encased in the lonely cheer of "Rose, Rose, I Love You" from a cracked radio in the background, and her subsequent self-exile in the giddying modernism of Hong Kong, are all elements of an incredibly rich and nostalgic Orientalist extravaganza, as bold and thick and luxuriant as the calligraphic swathes that litter the film. In Assayas, the nostalgia of silent movies of the 20s and the ludicrous strangeness of flying in real-life Maggie Cheuing to substitute for a long-dead French actress play against each other to terminate in a crazed, mutilating video montage in the last few tattered moments of the film as its thought (and originality) finally spins itself out.

These two films embody the tireless craving of auteurs whose imaginations have somehow expired. We understand their longing, but—at least those of us who find it impossible to empathize with their fetishes—remain unimpressed. Ethereal, beautiful, and substanceless, *Irma Vep* and *The Pillow Book* enchant and leave behind a vaporous trail in the movie-goer's imagination. One rummages in the refrigerator after this spread, unsatisfied.

Chinese Box, however, scalds with its own thought-out intelligence; the steely undertone of the political agenda puts the brains back into these Orientalist cinematic excursions. The *nostos* exists as a cry not simply from a Western director's aesthetic heart but from the hearts of two nations who have been strange bedfellows on a tiny island nation for a hundred years. Here, Wang says, we really have something to shed nostalgic tears about: the lowering of a rain-drenched Union Jack after one hundred years of misrule, the exodus of the last British expatriates on a vast ocean liner, like the final flush of the toilet; the traditional Scottish bagpipes of farewell played by a band with Chinese faces; the last salutes of Her Majesty's services; the student demonstrations and suicides in fear of a new world without democracy; finally, the evidently insurmountable cultural barrier between mainland Chinese and the Cantonese-speaking, Westernized people of Hong Kong—the return of a fostered child to its strange-smelling mother. Here is the nostalgia and strangeness all mixed up in a heady brew and given the gravelly undertone of politics.

Chinese Box is a thinking picture; in contrast to Greenaway's riotous calligraphy and Assayas's fuzzy video-image scribbles, there is calculation, depth, and sagacity before the ink hits paper in Wayne Wang's piece. Filmed both in the snapshot-quick tempo of video montage and the languorous pace of drama, *Chinese Box*'s handheld camera style envelopes the viewer in media res the moment the film opens. A haunting vocal score, as well as punchy contemporary pop, accompanies the camera as it plunges into crowd scenes, records noises of traffic and construction work, spies into houses, and eavesdrops on cocktail conversations, as if daring the viewer to absorb the eloquent array of details, faces, gestures, sound bites.

Wang seems to be speaking when the lead character, a journalist, declares his interest in camcording the last days of "Pompeii" before the handover. What Wang does with his own camera amounts to a type of time-capsuling, an archaeological preservation of poignant fragments that will perhaps vanish in the near future. It is an aesthetic mission first recognizable in Wang's early *Chan is Missing,* where he follows his lead men around Chinatown in search of the inscrutable Chan, careful to document errant strains of Chinatown life along the way; no senior citizen, looking out of a dark doorway, is too humble for his camera. Unpretty yet evocative, threadbare yet lush, this rigorously inclusive vision bursts into full blossom with *Chinese Box.*

Wang and his cinematographer Vilko Filac surprise us with their photo-journalistic dedication to show, never to judge, myriad images of Hong Kong's pulsating mass of dense-packed humanity. Thus, even while pursuing the lead story, Wang's camera alights on the cigarette drooping from the mouth of an aged trash collector, a periwinkle bush growing out of concrete. it records cell phones ringing, horns blaring, and prostitutes cussing over a mahjong game. Whether it is the lightning-fast motion of a woman slurping her instant noodles, or the slow put-put of a solitary barge in the harbor; whether it is the fizzle-zoom of the furious subway, or the entirely wordless minutes of Maggie Cheung regarding herself in the camcorder, the film surprises the jaded moviegoer with a seemingly effortless dramatic rhythm that is at once lustrous for the eye and nourishing for the brain.

However elusive the emotions of an adulterated people in their celebrated return to an estranged parent, Wayne Wang has managed to convey some of their bittersweetness without corresponding pedantry or editorializing. Like the metatheatricality of *Irma Vep*, a film about a filming, *Chinese Box* opens out into a series of many little boxes, mini-films, about Hong Kong. Jeremy Irons plays John, a consumptive scarecrow of a British financial reporter, a man who feels deeply about the subterranean Hong Kong that most expatriates don't get to see, and who tries to capture the last days of British rule with a roving videocam, his mechanical substitute for declining sensory opportunities. Like many of his compadres, he has a British wife and kids back in England but never returns their messages, choosing instead to fall in love with the ever-idolized Chinese überdoll, Gong Li.

That Wang's film fittingly comes after *The Pillow Book* and *Irma Vep*, like a main course accented by familiar ingredients, can be illustrated by their overarching spiritual similarity. "Rose, Rose, I Love You," which permeated Greenaway's film, repeatedly plays through *Chinese Box,* and thus can be considered the most "Chinese" of all Chinese traditional songs, a sort of statutory anthem common to all filmmakers who want stock Oriental-ness in the background. Greenaway's voyeuristic fascination with juxtaposing raw-looking, pallid European men with peachy bathrobed Asian women in a series of lovemaking montages lives on in *Chinese Box,* a gesture which, if one wanted to be generous, could be interpreted as illustrating the strangeness and pain of experiencing "the unknown," "the Other," etcetera; and which, if one wasn't feeling particularly generous, would simply be adduced as evidence of the fact that sex sells foreign art-house films. Indeed, the clichéd sexual interplay between Jeremy Irons and Gong Li—however important it was for the film's marketers—is perhaps the only disappointing pit in a film of glorious heights.

Nevertheless, John's relationship with the two Chinese female leads belong to a succinct and provocative allegory which crowns the film in a way that leaves *The Pillow Book* and *Irma Vep* behind. Maggie Cheung, reprising her jazzy, English-speaking personality in *Irma Vep*, plays a furtive gamin, Jean, the ultimate product of Hong Kong's gritty streets and narrow alleyways. Years ago, she attempted a biracial romance with a British classmate à la Cho Cho San, and tried to commit suicide when his father broke them up. Gong Li, with her usual incredible repertoire of facial expressions, is Vivian, a prostitute from mainland China who waits in vain for her Hong Kong businessman boyfriend to marry her.

If the characters are allegorical stand-ins for their respective countries, what the film shows us is that, by dying, "Britain" forces "Hong Kong" to wake up from its long reliance on imaginary British support—John reunites Jean with her English boyfriend, who doesn't remember her at all. Yet all is not lost: what was good of the old Empire, despite having drawn its last breath (i.e., John), is enough to send the reborn Hong Kong off in a brave new direction free of its ancestral moorings and illusory obligations—Vivian breaks up with her traditional boyfriend, knowing that he will never marry her, and takes courage from John's death to strike out on her own.

An interesting departure in Wang's film from that of Greenaway or Assayas is that Wang is as interested in the Asian characters' relation to other Asian characters as he is in their rapport with the European lead. The relationship between Vivian and her boyfriend Chang (veteran Hong Kong actor Michael Hui) exhibits a multi-dimensional cultural subtlety that does not seem to interest the Greenaways and Assayases of the film world. Chang proves that even in a side plot, *Chinese Box* offers round rather than flat characters. Not a typical rat-fink boyfriend who, once successful, dumps the woman who supported him, Chang is devoted to Vivian; his love for her is obvious, as are the cultural constraints that limit it. Michael Hui's perpetual mask of genteel, self-defeating resignation aptly summarizes the plight of the Chinese entrepreneurial class who fear risking the passion along with the prose.

As John's blood and life ebbs out of him, the tide drains out of Hong Kong harbor and the Great Empire's sun sinks in the East. With this last scene in mind, it is easy to see how a motion picture about the Hong Kong handover, with an international cast and sponsored by international budgets, could have been maudlin and didactic. But the reflective, timely, encyclopedic, and focused *Chinese Box* surprises with its eloquence about a complex subject. Although it will be some time before Chinese-born actresses can enjoy great roles in English films, Wang at least gave his female leads a fair chance to play Chinese characters the way a Chinese audience would expect to see them, and not as dislocated, glittering sexual ornaments in a Western director's art-house pastiche.

NEW YORK POST, 4/17/98, p. 52, Thelma Adams

The puzzle of Wayne Wang's "Chinese Box" is how a movie this fascinating on paper can be so lifeless in reality.

The cast includes three great actors: Jeremy Irons (the unseen "Lolita") and Chinese superstars Gong Li ("Farewell My Concubine") and Maggie Cheung ("Irma Vep").

Novelist and travel writer Paul Theroux contributed to the story that inspired screenwriters Jean-Claude Carriere and Larry Gross.

The plot couldn't have more natural drama: The central event is the British handover of Hong Kong to the Chinese in 1997. It's the end of an era, a topic that most Hong Kong filmmakers have addressed indirectly.

Wang, the Hong Kong-born, American-educated director ("Chan Is Missing"), attacks the split romantically. The end of the colonial reign—and the love-hate relationship between East and West—is mirrored in the relationships of three interracial couples.

"Box" is Wang's most ambitious, poetic film. It's also his most pretentious. Irons, a terminally ill journalist, roams Hong Kong with a videocam and a mournful expression.

The journalist interviews Cheung's waif, a scarred beauty. He seduces Li, a successful bartender who resists his marriage proposals. He bounces ideas off photographer Ruben Blades, who in turn serenades Irons with bitter-sweet love songs.

There's an immediacy to Wang's approach, but the movie fails to come together, to gain in emotional power. Hong Kong's seductive complexity eludes the self-involved journalist like quicksilver.

Who else caught the irony of the Asian-born Wang handing over the central narrative voice to Irons, the one-time star of "Brideshead Revisited," Evelyn Waugh's brilliant saga of the fall of the British Empire and the end of an era?

NEWSDAY, 4/17/98, Part II/p. B6, John Anderson

That the Hong Kong-born filmmaker Wayne Wang would want to make a film about the '97 Chinese takeover is understandable, and his "Chinese Box" will surely not be the last to contend with that particular upheaval. A riper moment for pre-millennial allegory comes along only about once every thousand years.

But even considering his personal resume of East-West influences, why make one that echoes so loudly and sympathetically with the fall of the British Empire? Jeremy Irons, the poster boy of Brit-flavored dissipation, decadence and weathered ennui? As a dying English journalist with leukemia in love with a Chinese former prostitute? Forget the fact that he's already done "M. Butterfly." You'd need Puccini to get this creaky motif up and moving.

As John the journalist (and his name is no accident), Irons is a business correspondent braced for the deluge, one for whom Hong Kong is "a great big department store," and who watches a student activist shoot himself on New Year's Eve with the same essential resignation with which he greets businessmen scurrying about Asia. As the resident symbol of a weary western world, Irons couldn't be more superciliously bored stiff.

You sympathize with him, however, when you watch his scenes with Chinese star Gong Li, who plays Vivian, the beautiful bar hostess and girlfriend of dubious businessman John Chang (Michael Hui). As unconvincing as Wang makes every other relationship and character in his film—with the exception of Ruben Blades' news photographer, Jim, who blows through the movie like a breath of fresh air—theirs is the most painfully rigid. Gong, it's pretty clear, speaks no English and is reciting her lines by rote. Irons, in turn, speaks to her as if he's talking to himself, which in effect he is.

This could, one supposes, be symbolic of the fabled Occidental-Oriental gap, especially given the other 800-pound ancillary metaphors that gradually sink Wang's foundering ship. Chief among them is Jean, a street hustler with whom Irons' character becomes intrigued, who has a face that's horribly scarred but all the instincts to survive the new Hong Kong. That Jean is played by the wonderful Hong Kong actress Maggie Cheung almost makes her palatable. There are, however, recurring scenes of a pit bull, tethered to a treadmill, that will do anything for its master, and the image of a severed fish, lying on a vendor's cart, whose heart continues to beat even though it's split in two. And with subtleties like these, you might as well march in Chinese troops and blow the place to bits.

The script is co-written by Jean-Claude Carriere, whose work with Luis Bunuel suggests that something more mischievous is afoot here. But essentially, "Chinese Box," which is a lot less complex than its title implies, is a romance—a fractured, hopeless romance about two disparate people from irreconcilable cultures who find themselves in a tragic place, at a tragic point in history. If the timing weren't completely off, you'd think maybe Wang had been seen "Titanic" too many times.

VILLAGE VOICE, 4/21/98, p. 72, Michael Atkinson

Wayne Wang's *Chinese Box* evokes Hong Kong and its delivery to Chines rule as a soul-searching millennial metaphor, and as soul-searching millennial metaphors go, HK ain't bad—less garishly horrifying than Bosnia, more fashionably edge-of-the-West than Kuwait, and more emblematic of capitalistic apocalypse than New York or L.A. Recombing aspects of *Sans Soleil, Tokyo-Ga,* and *The World of Suzie Wong,* Wang's movie is more rueful meditation than drama, though it has enough tragic corn to float a Ross Hunter movie. (Wang steered clear of Paul Auster this time, recruiting instead of postcolonialist exoticists Paul Theroux and Jean-Claude Carriere to come up with the story.)

Superficially sophisticated though it might be, *Chinese Box* is also superbly textured filmmaking, thrumming with gritty visual intelligence; if at times the narrative dawdles with contrived literary ideas rather than having a coherent story line, at least it dawdles beautifully.

Wang is an HK native, but that didn't encourage him to center his saga around an Asian. Instead, we have terminal (with cancer) and terminally jaded journalist Jeremy Irons wandering through the crisis-fraught city's alleyways wondering What It All Means, salving his broken-by-Gong Li heart by videotaping a portrait of the town, eventually choosing Maggie Cheung's scarfaced street urchin as a walking symbol of HK's orphaned commerce culture. Portraits fly thick as hailstones (gotta love that butchered fish with the still-beating heart), and Irons's marvelous dissipation is so thick-necked a metaphor for the sorry State of Things I wondered why he just didn't wear a placard ("Honk If You Symbolize the Spiritual Death of Civilization").

At the same time, Wang and company are grandly nebulous about their fears and doubts, just as the title promises thematic intricacy the film never delivers. Likewise, the romance is discussed rather than manifested. While Gong and Cheung are merely iconic, Rubén Blades (as Irons's comic-relief photog pal) steals every scene he's in, and Irons, despite his metaphoric burden, is regally convincing, like a sick lion trying to find a corner of veldt to die in. Still, all the star power in the open market can't disguise the fact that *Chinese Box* is masterfully executed laziness, an Asian guided tour for the epochally depressed.

Also reviewed in:
CHICAGO TRIBUNE, 5/1/98, Friday/p. B, Michael Wilmington
NEW REPUBLIC, 5/4/98, p. 27, Stanley Kauffmann
NEW YORK TIMES, 4/17/98, p. E18, Stephen Holden
VARIETY, 9/8-14/97, p. 79, David Rooney
WASHINGTON POST, 5/15/98, p. D5, Stepehn Hunter
WASHINGTON POST, 5/15/98, Weeken/p. 55, Michael O'Sullivan

CITY OF ANGELS

A Warner Bros. release in association with Regency Pictures of an Atlas Entertainment production.   *Executive Producer:* Arnon Milchan, Charles Newirth, and Robert Cavallo. *Producer:* Dawn Steel and Charles Roben.   *Director:* Brad Silberling.   *Screenplay:* Dana Stevens. *Based on the film "Wings of Desire" by:* Wim Wenders, Richard Reitinger, and Peter Handke. *Director of Photography:* John Seale.   *Editor:* Lynzee Klingman.   *Music:* Gabriel Yared.   *Music Editor:* Robert Randles, Katherine Quittner, and Carl Kaller.   *Sound:* David MacMillan, and (music) Paul Hulme and Ben Georgiades.   *Sound Editor:* Mark Mangini. *Casting:* David Rubin.   *Production Designer:* Lilly Kilvert.   *Art Director:* John O. Warnke. *SetDesigner:* Martha Johnston, John Goldsmith, and Anthony D. Parrillo.   *Set Decorator:* Gretchen Rau. *Special Effects:* David Blitstein. *Costumes:* Shay Cunliffe. *Make-up:* Hallie D'Amore.   *Stunt Coordinator:* Doug Coleman and Daniel W. Barringer.   *Running time:* 112 minutes.   *MPAA Rating:* PG-13.

CAST: Nicholas Cage (Seth);   Meg Ryan (Dr. Maggie Rice);   Dennis Franz (Nathaniel Messinger);   André Braugher (Cassiel); Colm Feore (Jordan);   Robin Bartlett (Anne);   Joanna Merlin (Teresa);   Sarah Dampf (Susan);   Rhonda Dotson (Susan's Mother); Nigel Gibbs (Doctor);   John Putch (Man in Car);   Lauri Johnson (Woman in Car);   Christian Aubert (Foreign Visitor in Car);   Jay Patterson (Air Trafic Controller);   Shishir Kurup (Anaesthesiologist);   Brian Markinson (Surgical Fellow);   Hector Velasquez (Scrub Nurse); Marlene Kanter and Bernard White (Circulating Nurses); Dan Desmond (Mr. Balford);   Deirdre O'Connell (Mrs. Balford); Kim Murphy (Balfords' Daughter); Chad Lindberg (Balfords' Son); Alexander Folk (Convenience Store Clerk);   Rainbow Borden (Hold-up-Man);   Harper Roisman (Old Man in Library);   Sid Hillman (Librarian);   Wanda-Lee Evans (Nurse in Messinger's Room); Wanda Christine (Station Nurse);   E. J. Callahan (Waiter at Johnnie's);   Tudi Roche (Messinger's daughter); David Moreland (Husband Frank); Kristina Malota (Hannah);   Stan Davis (Construction Foreman);   Mik Scriba and Nick Offerman (Construction Workers); Kieu-Chinh (Asian Woman);   Geoffrey A. Thorne (Big Orderly);   Peter Spellos (Mac Truck Driver);   Jim Kline (Store Clerk);   Cherene Snow (Woman Sewing).

LOS ANGELES TIMES, 4/10/98, Calendar/p. 1, Kenneth Turan

Like most cinematic love stories, "City of Angels" starts with a misunderstanding. A major misunderstanding.

When plucky L.A. heart surgeon Dr. Maggie Rice (Meg Ryan) first runs into the dishy Seth (Nicolas Cage) in a hospital corridor, she thinks she's meeting a great-looking guy with deep, soulful eyes. But while Seth is undeniably attractive, he is not the man of her or anyone else's dreams. He's not a man at all; in fact, he's... an angel.

While having an angel for a suitor may sound dreamy (think of the high-powered backrubs you could get), messengers, as they call themselves, turn out to be problematic in the romance department. They're not human, never were, so they exist without feelings of any kind. They spend their time just out of our sight, providing comfort, guiding the dead and acting like, yes, angels.

The idea of an angel who was tempted to give it all up for love did not originate with screenwriter Dana Stevens but rather German writer-director Wim Wenders. His 1987 "Wings of Desire," winner of the best director award at Cannes and beautifully shot by then 78-year-old master cinematographer Henri Alekan, is one of those foreign language films with a small but devoted following, though most Americans have not even heard of it.

"City of Angels" does not attempt to directly remake "Wings of Desire," a wise choice given how poetic, ethereal and determinedly nonnarrative that film was. Wenders himself says he considers his original to be no more than "a point of departure" for the new film (which he has publicly sanctioned) and that is probably the best way to look at it.

Still, with commercial echoes of the Demi Moore/Patrick Swayze-starring "Ghost" colliding with the spirit of rarefied European art cinema, "City of Angels" is in fact a fascinating hybrid. A Hollywood fantasy at its most fantastic, the film is equal parts true innocence and shameless calculation. Deciding whether the glass is half empty or half full depends on which part you are willing to embrace.

Certainly much has been done to make "City of Angels" as artistic as possible. While the material is by nature sentimental and romantic, Stevens' script is as literate and understated as the situation allows, Cage and Ryan do excellent work with it, and cinematographer John Seale (last year's Oscar winner for "The English Patient") succeeds in making Los Angeles look positively otherworldly.

Brad Silberling, whose only previous directing credit was "Casper," as in the Friendly Ghost, was an unexpected choice for this assignment. But he turns out to have been a shrewd selection, as only someone who believed absolutely in the norms of Hollywood could have any hope of turning this kind of rarefied material into a commercial undertaking.

Yet, despite all this good work, "City of Angels" remains a film that succeeds largely to the extent that audiences, eager to suspend disbelief, want it to going in. As slick as it is sincere, and burdened by a second half that is more schematic than it needs to be, this film is calculated to do many things, but softening the hearts of cynics and scoffers is not one of them.

Building on the visual imagery of Wenders' film, "City of Angels" does a haunting job of creating a lifestyle and a look for its heavenly creatures. Prone to perching above L.A. on things like freeway signs and Sunset Strip billboards, angels like Seth's buddy Cassiel (Andre Braugher) meet at the ocean's edge twice a day, at sunrise and sunset, to hear the music of the spheres. They spend a lot of time at the main library (San Francisco's dazzling new one was the location used), an ideal spot to hone in on people's thoughts.

For angels, who meet people only after they've died and are themselves invisible to mortals unless they choose to be otherwise, occasionally tire of their spiritual existence and display curiosity about what it's like to be human, about what touch feels like and what taste is all about. Not to mention romantic love.

When Seth, at work in an operating room calling a heart surgery patient to the next world, accidentally locks eyes with Dr. Maggie Rice, those vague longings take on a more concrete focus. And when Dr. Rice, an excellent surgeon, has a loss of confidence because of losing that patient, Seth is moved to allow her to see him so he can help her through her malaise.

So begins a highly unorthodox courtship. Seth can hear Maggie's most intimate thoughts, but because he's not human he feels next to nothing about them. He also can materialize at will wherever Maggie is. This turns him into something like a sensitive, solicitous stalker, boyish, eager and with a peculiar curiosity about the facts of human life.

Because of the nature of the material, both leads have to rely more than usual on their core personas. Cage has the presence needed to play this part, and he has the gravity to keep his constant questions from turning silly. And Ryan, once again, as she did in "Courage Under Fire," takes her innate likability to the challenging area of a driven doctor who has to question everything she thought she believed. Less successful is Dennis Franz, whose role (based on Peter Falk's in the Wenders film) as a patient of Maggie's who knows a few things about Seth's dilemma and the possible ways out of it, is on the overdone side.

Once Seth makes his decision, "City of Angels" takes turns that work against the originality it strives for. But if the film is not quite all there, it is closer than we might expect. Attractive as well as off-putting, it manages to leave a pleasant afterglow for those in the mood for its kind of loving.

NEW STATESMAN, 6/19/98, p. 43, Gerald Kaufman

They do make them like that any more. Although "City of Angels" is adapted from Wim Wenders' 1987 German film set in Berlin, "Wings of Desire," it is the ultimate Hollywood product (right down to a huge close-up shot of the celebrated Hollywood sign). And while Wenders' movie was variously regarded as either a masterpiece or else the epitome of pretentiousness, director Brad Silberling has here come up with one of those lush weepies, complete with ethereal heavenly music, that used up forests of Kleenex in the 1940s and 1950s.

Both films, though, are about angels. Silberling's lead angel, Seth, is played by Nicolas Cage with much soulful rolling of the eyes, which gives the impression that he is suffering from chronic constipation. Like all his fellow angels, Seth dresses in a long, black overcoat that must be rather uncomfortable in southern California. For the City of Angels of the movie's title is none other than Los Angeles (get it?).

Seth is a rather restless angel, roaming round the city and performing miracles when the fancy takes him. His policy for interfering in human predicaments seems inconsistent and arbitrary, a readiness to prevent robberies being counterbalanced by callousness in allowing the deaths of heart patients, ranging from infants to the elderly at the hospital where Maggie (played by Meg Ryan) operates as a cardiac surgeon. Maggie tends to get moody if her nifty scalpel fails to achieve 100 per cent success (though, given that she listens to blues music while carving up her patients, the casualty rate is rather lower than might be anticipated).

In any case, being operated on (a process that, I must warn the squeamish, involves lots of blood and handling of internal organs) is here a good deal more traumatic than dying, which simply involves changing into a clean nightie and being led off to heaven by a solicitous, if black-coated, angel. This, it should be pointed out, is an equal opportunities heaven, populated by seraphim of varied ethnicity. Relatives of the deceased, meanwhile, get the chance to practise their acting skills by emoting in a noisy bereavement scene.

Seth, who is generally invisible, appears to Maggie, asking her (much eye-rolling here): "Are you in despair?" From the tears in her eyes and her propensity to vomit—scarcely surprising in the context of this yucky picture—the answer has to be "Yes". Yet, after Seth has regaled her with a few of the totally meaningless aphorisms beloved of Hollywood scriptwriters (example: "Some things are true whether you believe them or not"), Maggie is soon smiling away as she carves her way to success in the operating theatre.

One of the survivors of her ministrations, a Jewish ex-angel named Nathan Messinger (get it?), played with intolerably twinkling bonhomie by Dennis Franz (of TV's "NYPD Blue"), is soon acting as mentor both to Maggie and to Seth. Will Seth, who has fallen in love with Maggie and—helped by trick photography—keeps popping up as a sort of celestial stalker, follow Nathan's example and abandon angelhood? Will he become mortal and die happily ever after? Though I shall obey Warner Brothers' request and keep the ending a secret, I can confidently predict that the final fade-out will leave many spectators in tears—whether of sadness or laughter I had better not say.

NEW YORK, 4/20/98, p. 62, David Denby

The great Australian-born cinematographer John Seale, who gave *The English Patient* such a luminous, sexy glow—Seale's images managed to be crystal-clear and erotically textured at the same time—is back in action in the beautifully photographed *City of Angels*. The movie is set in Los Angeles, a very horizontal city, but Seale, working with the director Brad Silberling, gets his camera up in the air—on rooftops, at the top of skyscraper construction sites, on the hills looking down into the city. The images are very crisp but slightly spooked. This is a movie about angels—real angels. The seraphic presences, who dress in long dark coats, like somber gangsters, stand silently on the successive balconies of a rotunda-like library. One of them pitches himself down from way up high, his arms outstretched, like a giant bird making a slow sweep to the ground. The movie is occasionally on the verge of breaking into surreal fantasy. Though I wish I could say that it amounts to more than a few startling images, it doesn't. *City of Angels* is the brainchild of the late producer Dawn Steel, who fell in love with Wim Wenders's 1987 classic *Wings of Desire* and decided to make an American version of it. The movie has its affecting moments, but the drearily inevitable has come true—an original and rather haunting poetic conception has been turned into a literal-minded love story. Take a chance on love: Fall for an angel.

Wenders's movie, elegantly written in collaboration with Peter Handke, was set in Berlin when the Wall was still up—a divided city, somber and scarred, with its war memories, its distinctive melancholy and bitter-sweet humor. Two very serious angels (Bruno Ganz and Otto Sander) wander about, listening in on the thoughts of ordinary people, offering a slight touch of reassurances breath, a tiny pressure—in moments of anxiety. For better or worse, the movie had a super-earthly delicacy—it breathed the spirit of German poetry and chamber music. Shot in silvery black-and-white, it shifted to color only at the end, when the angel played by Bruno Ganz falls in love with a female trapeze artist and decides to give up immortality for eros.

City of Angels, which was written by Dana Stevens, is a love story right from the beginning. Nicolas Cage plays an angel named Seth, invisible except when he wants to be seen, who hangs around the operating rooms of an L.A. hospital, waiting to take away the patients who die. He doesn't kill anyone; he executes orders, presumably from above, and he sits there looking on with tender sympathy, his eyes wide open. No one can be more beseeching than Nicolas Cage—he's like a dog who hasn't eaten for a week. Yet there's now something creepy about the story. It's no longer a poetic conceit: This angel is a sweet-tempered death junkie.

When a wired-up surgeon, Maggie Rice (Meg Ryan), loses a patient on the operating table, Seth falls in love with her, comforting her with an invisible hand as she weeps (it's a lovely moment, equal to anything in the original). Meg Ryan gives one of her best performances; her Maggie feels the strange, consoling presence, and when Seth makes himself visible and stares right into her soul—he's an angel, *boy* is he an angel; no "boorish" advances here—Ryan, stunned, disbelieving, struggles to understand what's happening to her.

But the movie quickly takes a tumble—it becomes an argument for life, for sensuous experience, for not living in the vacuum of immortality. Ah, to feel that water on your back when you jump into the Pacific! To taste some real food! But this is a movie set in Los Angeles, not in shattered, soulful, guilty Berlin. It is set in the narcissists' capital of the world. Could anyone possibly argue against pleasure in the sunlit paradise? There might have been an element of dramatic tension if someone had, but nothing so witty as that happens. The movie becomes a compellingly photographed advertisement for the good life, and nothing, in this setting, could be more redundant or banal. Will Nick accept love—and death? Will Meg take a chance on this strange guy? In other words, Hollywood has made the idea more realistic, more emotional, more communicative, more plausible. But how can it be plausible? The material is entirely fanciful. Silberling, whose only previous feature credit was the kids' fantasy *Casper,* has some talent, but he directs with too confident a belief in his own banalities. The movie is physically beautiful, but the ideas are kitsch—it's a New Age love story, the latest version of the doomed romances of 50 years ago.

NEW YORK POST, 4/10/98, p. 35, Rod Dreher

"City of Angels" provides a Hollywood gloss on profound themes of love, sacrifice and immortality. Our angel-obsessed culture is bound to make this a heaven-sent hit for Warner Bros., but the picture's pop spirituality and superficial romance left me wanting more.

"City of Angels" borrows its basic ideas from "Wings of Desire," Wim Wenders' dense, German, art-house film about an angel in Berlin who loves a woman and longs to be mortal.

Yet it avoids the poetic pensiveness that made "Wings of Desire" such tough, but rewarding, going. Instead, it substitutes a sunny, laid-back L.A. sensibility and a preoccupation with melodramatic matchmaking. *Auf Wiedersehen, Weltschmerz;* hi ya *Welt*-schmaltz.

Nicolas Cage is Seth, one of a stylish coterie of angels who spend their days lingering unseen around Los Angeles, eavesdropping sympathetically on the thoughts of its people, comforting the troubled, and observing the city from its rooftops.

One day, he falls for Dr. Maggie Rice (a radiant Meg Ryan), a surgeon and strict materialist. Yet after losing a patient, she becomes haunted by despair. Reeling from a sense of futility, Maggie begins groping for a spiritual life.

Lucky Maggie. After one look at her, Seth, who's pure spirit (and one handsome devil), begins craving a sensual life. He suddenly wants to know what a pear tastes like, and how the wind feels on one's face, how well Maggie fits into his embrace.

One of Maggie's patients, played with bemused gusto by Dennis Franz, lets Seth in on a secret: He has free will and can choose to renounce his abstract state; to fall from the heavenly heights and become human.

But there's a price. Seth discovers that the physical world can be a place of great tenderness and beauty, but also of violence, filth and degradation. The lesson here is that joy and suffering, pleasure and pain, are inextricable; you can't have one without the other.

The celestial conceit aside, "City of Angels' is really about the risks and rewards of falling in love. Cage and Ryan (the thinking man's Melanie Griffith) aren't bad together, but they don't exactly burn up the screen.

Screenwriter Dana Stevens should have given the would-be lovers longer scenes of conversational intimacy.

Director Brad Silberling knows how to keep things moving, but I kept wishing he had a more acute pictorial sense, and feeling for light and texture. We know Seth wants to be sensual because the achingly sincere Cage keeps telling us so, and his eyes do a constant slow yearn. You don't feel it, though.

For all its shortcomings, this pleasant but slight film will resonate deeply with audiences, who, I suspect, will ignore its artistic shortcomings and connect with it in much the same way that they did with the flawed "Titanic." The questions raised by "City of Angels," though, are a lot more interesting than the movie itself.

NEWSDAY, 4/10/98, Part II/p. B3, Jack Mathews

Star-crossed lovers are no strangers to Hollywood, but the conditions facing Nicolas Cage's Seth and Meg Ryan's Maggie in Brad Silberling's romantic curiosity "City of Angels" are special.

She's a heart surgeon, he's an angel.

She lives in Los Angeles, he's in the fourth dimension.

She's visible, he isn't.

He has complete faith in her, she isn't even religious.

What Seth and Maggie share—the thing that separates him from the scores of other black-clad angels hanging out in L.A. and that threatens to end her career—is the vulnerability they bring to their jobs.

Maggie takes each of her failures in the operating room personally, while Seth constantly anguishes over human despair. But he's there for her, and once she understands him, only God can separate them.

"City of Angels" is loosely adapted from German director Wim Wenders' 1988 "Wings of Desire," the story of an angel so envious of human life, he turns in his wings and, for the love of a woman, joins, the mortal coil. Wenders' film was a visualized philosophical poem, in which the angel Damiel's empathy was used as an allegory to study the range of human experience.

But that was Germany, this is Hollywood.

"Wings of Desire" was a cerebral art film. "City of Angels" is a "Sleepless in Seattle"-style romance. And given the TV-tested appeal of such spiritual drama as "Touched by an Angel," it's less an exploration of human experience than an appeal for faith.

When we meet Seth, he's on routine assignment, picking up the soul of a young girl whose body just gave out, and escorting her to the next world. "What was your favorite thing?," Seth asks the girl's spirit. "Madonna," she answers. Or, maybe she said "Doughnuts," I'm not sure.

His next assignment brings him to Maggie's operating room, where a patient she thought she had saved has suddenly died.

The depth of Maggie's despair hits Seth hard, and he decides to hang around and see if he can buoy her spirits. He falls in love instead, and when he makes himself visible to her, as a mysterious, gentle drifter, it's mutual. She's ready to dump her surgeon boyfriend (Colm Feore) for Seth, but it's not such an easy decision for him. He has to give up his career, his immortality, his ability to read minds, the whole nine yards.

Silberling, who earned his wings on "Casper," serves all this up as straight-faced romantic melodrama.

Seth has much more in common with Cary Grant's Dudley, an angel who falls in love and ponders mortality with Loretta Young in the 1947 film "The Bishop's Wife," than he does with

Wenders' Damiel. Silberling, and screenwriter Dana Stevens ("Blink"), have shifted the emphasis from envy to longing.

Damiel is curious about the things in life that make humans so reluctant to give it up. Seth is obsessed with knowing how those things feel to Maggie.

You don't know what a pear tastes like?," Maggie asks of the still heavenly Seth. "I don't know what a pear tastes like to you," he answers.

Much of the attraction between Seth and Maggie must be taken on faith. When she first meets him, in an empty hospital hallway, he's looking at her as if into the face of God and speaking in a kind of whispered fortune cookie dialogue. The normal reaction would be to cut and run. Instead, she's mesmerized.

The film's best moments are those when Seth finally crosses over and gets to experience the sensations of life, particularly those he has in the rack with Maggie. But as engaged in his role as Cage is, Seth comes off as a pathetic angel. Ryan has been here before, playing a woman searching for an idealized romance, and this one's a pip. Providing welcomed comic relief is "NYPD's" Dennis Franz, as an angel-turned-robust-family-man named Messinger.

NEWSWEEK, 4/20/98, p. 63, David Ansen

Meg Ryan might not be the first person you'd cast as a heart surgeon, and Nicolas Cage is far from the wispy, ethereal types usually drafted to play angels, yet here they are as the surprisingly convincing lovers—one mortal, the other celestial—in *City of Angels*. He is the seraphim Seth, grown restless with the incorporeal calm of his life, and she is the rational Maggie, who thinks life and death are under human control. Watching her fight to save a patient, the invisible Seth falls in love with her, and must face a choice: should he give up eternal life to become a mortal and experience pain and pleasure, love and death in Maggie's arms?

The premise and the images of grave, black-clad angels who congregate in the public library and eavesdrop on the thoughts of mankind are all taken from "Wings of Desire," Wim Wenders's haunting 1988 German film. Think of this lyrical, unabashedly romantic remake, transposed from Berlin to Los Angeles, as "Wings Lite." Instead of Wenders's brooding meditation on history, director Brad Silberling and writer Dana Stevens go straight to the love story. Ryan, curtailing her cute act, has rarely been so appealing. Cage, gliding through the film like an enchanted sleepwalker, once again pulls off a high-risk role. Dennis Franz, as a heart patient with a surprising past, and Andre Braugher, as Seth's celestial partner, lend strong support. The mood is hushed, the swooping, angel-eyed views of L.A. ravishing, the quirky eruptions of comedy well timed. Only near the end does Silberling fall to earth, when the mix of melodrama, mush and message gets out of hand. Till then, however, "City of Angels" earns its wings.

SIGHT AND SOUND, 7/98, p. 37, Nick Roddick

Dr Maggie Rice, a Los Angeles heart surgeon, is deeply shaken by the death of a patient on the operating table even though she did nothing wrong. Her distress is observed by Seth, an angel who is there to comfort the dying man. Seth is one of a host of invisible beings who watch over the city's inhabitants, but who are not allowed to intervene in their affairs. However, he finds himself experiencing an entirely new emotion towards Maggie, and begins to break the rules by following her around and, eventually, making himself visible to her.

Maggie, who has an ongoing but unsatisfactory relationship with another doctor, also experiences a strange attraction for Seth, despite being unable to understand who he is or where he comes from. After discussing the matter with fellow angel Cassiel and with Messinger, a patient of Maggie's who is himself a former angel, Seth decides to 'fall'—an irreversible step which will rob him of immortality and make him subject to such human experiences as pain and death, but will also let him experience physical sensation. However, an emotionally confused Maggie has fled to Tahoe. Seth follows her, and they finally consummate their relationship.

The next day, Maggie is accidentally killed in a road accident while bicycling back from the grocery store. Seth mourns her, but is comforted by Cassiel and Messinger and learns to accept his and Maggie's fate.

Although it is not wholly successful, *City of Angels* stands out from the dreary succession of recent Hollywood remakes of European movies. This is partly due to Dana Stevens' screenplay and Brad Silberling's direction, which grab hold of the theme of Wim Wenders' 1987 *Wings of Desire* and head off very much in their own direction with it.

Initially the brainchild of the late Dawn Steel, the former studio production chief (at Paramount and Columbia) turned independent producer who died while the film was in post-production, *City of Angels* changes the entire balance of Wenders' story by having Nicolas Cage's angel and Meg Ryan's doctor come face to face in the first act. The film thus becomes a more straightforward, less metaphysical story of love against the odds, with everyone but the two principals reduced to a kind of chorus. Among the latter, Dennis Franz is magnificently rumpled as a very fallen angel. Robin Bartlett also scores strongly as one of Maggie's co-workers with a disastrous line in relationships, including one with a gynaecologist that prompts the line: "Never date a man who knows more about your vagina than you do."

Most of all, however, *City of Angels* pleases because it is quite simply so surprising for a mainstream Hollywood movie. Almost entirely thematically driven, it has a plot which could quite adequately be summed up as "angel meets girl; angel loses girl." Much of the appeal comes from John Seale's glowing cinematography which, with all due allowance for the very different light in Southern California, is an almost exact equivalent of Henri Alekan's black-and-white lensing of Berlin (which is to say that it is totally different). And director Brad Silberling plays along cleverly, situating his angels in a number of iconographic locations (on top of an Arby's restaurant sign, on a freeway sign, and—of course—atop the Hollywood sign) as they look down on the mortal Angelenos. Costume designer Shay Cunliffe likewise hits the tone precisely, clothing the angels in post-Armani baggy suits and long black duster coats, which are especially effective when they gather in some of their preferred meeting places—the beach at dawn and dusk; in the city library during the day—invisible to all but each other (and us).

There is nothing in Silberling's previous career—which comprises directing episodes of *LA Law* and *NYPD Blue*, followed by the kids' film *Casper*—to prepare one for the confidence with which he handles a film in which tone is all. It starts with a quite astonishing scene in which a little girl dies in the emergency room after doctors have failed to calm her fever and with her mother looking on. The scene introduces both Seth and the idea of guardian angels, and at the same time makes it clear that this is a film about something that Hollywood hardly ever tackles: transcendence. The success is not total, and some may feel either that Wenders' film has been sentimentalised, or that the whole thing is just too airy-fairy.

In particular, Cage's performance, at once intense and ethereal, often suggests a kind of narcoleptic trance. What is more, some of the lines, as Maggie tries to figure out just what this mysterious stranger does, abruptly make one realise just how badly the film could have gone wrong. Seth is, he tells her, a sort of courier. So what does he deliver? "Messages from God," says Seth dreamily. Any normal person would run a mile. Paradoxically, though, it is its ability to survive such moments that demonstrates the film's strength and the fact that, in an era of narrative cloning and general dumbing down, *City of Angels* is the kind of one-off we should surely welcome.

TIME, 4/20/98, p. 81, Richard Schickel

[*City of Angels* was reviewed jointly with *The Object of My Affection*; see Schickel's review of that film.]

VILLAGE VOICE, 4/21/98, p. 72, Dennis Lim

Wim Wender's *Wings of Desire* continues to resonate in many ways—as a hand-on-heart love story, a wide-eyed urban fantasy, a sweet and wistful meditation on the trials of modern life and the vagaries of history. *City of Angels* is none of the above, less a remake than a despairingly imbecilic perversion of Wender's 1987 film. Director Brad Silberling and writer Dana Stevens have drained all the poetry, grace, and humanity from Wenders's talc of invisible seraphim among contemporary mortals, whittled it down to a precious gimmick, and—the final insult—imposed on it the exigencies of Hollywood romance, or what passes for it in the age of *Titanic*.

The results are horrific—from the forced jokiness of Stevens's script to the torturous VH1-targeted soundtrack to the embarrassingly dopey performances. Nicolas Cage plays Seth, a rebel angel who develops a libido when he lays eyes on Meg Ryan, a morose Los Angeles heart surgeon (does symbolism get more concussive?). If anyone could have saved this film, it's Cage, a consistently unpredictable actor who's often best when seemingly miscast. But here, he utters his uniformly awful lines in a slow, whispery monotone, seeming less like he's fallen from the heavens than fallen behind in special ed. Once Seth sheds his celestial skin, all the attempts at humor and pathos are of the oh-look-the-angels-become-human variety—there's Seth bloodied and bruised, there he is getting soaked in the rain, there he is being mugged, there he is even enjoying a handjob.

The filmmakers are apparently opting for the don't-call-it-a-remake defense. It won't wash: in the greater scheme of things, this is a cheapening experience; on its own terms, it's still a rotten movie.

Also reviewed in:
CHICAGO TRIBUNE, 4/10/98, Friday/p. A, Michael Wilmington
NEW YORK TIMES, 4/10/98, p. E12, Stephen Holden
VARIETY, 4/6-12/98, p. 46, Emanuel Levy
WASHINGTON POST, 4/10/98, p. B1, Rita Kempley
WASHINGTON POST, 4/10/98, Weekend/p. 45, Michael O'Sullivan

CIVIL ACTION, A

A Touchstone Pictures and Paramount Pictures release of a Wildwood Enterprises/Scott Rudin production. *Executive Producer:* Steven Zaillian and David Wisnievitz. *Producer:* Scott Rudin, Robert Redford, and Rachel Pfeffer. *Director:* Steven Zaillian. *Screenplay:* Steven Zaillian. *Based on the book by:* Jonathan Harr. *Director of Photography:* Conrad L. Hall. *Editor:* Wayne Wahrman. *Music:* Danny Elfman. *Music Editor:* Ellen Segal. *Sound:* David MacMillan and (music) Shawn Murphy. *Sound Editor:* Larry Kemp. *Casting:* Avy Kaufman. *Production Designer:* David Gropman. *Art Director:* David J. Bomba. *Set Decorator:* Tracey A. Doyle. *Set Dresser:* Loren Lyons, Dean Lakoff, Christopher Pascuzzo, and Alan L. Porter. *Special Effects:* Guy Clayton. *Costumes:* Shay Cunliffe. *Make-up:* Whitney L. James. *Make-up (John Travolta):* Michelle Bühler. *Make-up (Kathleen Quinlan):* Hallie D'Amore. *Stunt Coordinator:* Mark Riccardi. *Running time:* 113 minutes. *MPAA Rating:* PG-13.

CAST: John Travolta (Jan Schlichtmann); Robert Duvall (Jerome Facher); Tony Shalhoub (Kevin Conway); William H. Macy (James Gordon); Zeljko Ivanek (Bill Crowley); Bruce Norris (William Cheeseman); John Lithgow (Judge Skinner); Kathleen Quinlan (Anne Anderson); Peter Jacobson (Neil Jacobs); Mary Mara (Kathy Boyer); James Gandolfini (Al Love); Stephen Fry (Pinder); Dan Hedaya (John Riley); David Thornton (Richard Aufiero); Sydney Pollack (Al Eustis); Ned Eisenberg (Uncle Pete); Margot Rose (Donna Robbins); Daniel Von Bargen (Mr. Granger); Caroline Carrigan (Evelyn Love); Paul Desmond (Shaline); Michael P. Byrne (Barbas); Tracy Miller, Paul Hewitt, and Clayton Landey (Grace Workers); Paul Ben-Victor (Pasqueriella); Elizabeth Burnette (Lauren Aufiero); Alan Wilder (Insurance Lawyer); Gregg Joseph Monk (Insurance Lawyer); Harout Beshlian (Insurance Lawyer); Josh Pais (Law Clerk); Haskell Vaughn Anderson, III (Courtroom #7 Clerk); Kaiulani Lee (Mrs. Granger); Howie Carr (Radio Talk Show Host); Denise Dowse (Judge); Pearline Fergerson (Court Clerk); Scott Weintraub and Robert Cicchini (Personal Insurance Lawyers); Christopher Stevenson (Insurance Plaintiff); Kevin Fry (Waiter); Brian Turk (Mover); Rikki Klieman (TV Reporter); David Barrett, Ryan Janis, and Rob McElhenney (Teenagers on Property); Mike Biase (Market Clerk); Richard Calnan (Woburn Traffic Cop); Gene Wolande (Hotel Clerk); Sam Travolta (Grace Attorney); Gregg Shawzin, Juli Donald, Sayda Alan, and Cathrine Leahan (Reporters); Bruce Holman (Federal Marshall); John LaFayette, Charles Levin, Byron Jennings, and Jay Patterson (Geologists); Charlie Stavola (Detective); Taylor Bernard (Trustee's Assistant); Molly Allen (Saleswoman).

LOS ANGELES TIMES, 12/25/98, Calendar/p. 2, Kenneth Turan

"A Civil Action" comes close, achingly close, to greatness. Finely cast, classically shot, written and directed with sureness and skill and based on a book compelling enough to stay on bestseller lists for two years, it's a story told so confidently and well that it seems fated to succeed.

But as proficient a job as writer-director Steve Zaillian and his team do, "A Civil Action" has unmistakably unraveled by its close. It gets into difficulties all those combined skills can't overcome, upended both by the situation it wants to accurately portray and by a crucial casting decision. "A Civil Action" is good enough to perhaps have surmounted one of those difficulties, but both of them prove to be too much.

The book in question, written by Jonathan Harr, details a real-life legal battle in the 1980s that took eight years to play out and 500 pages to describe. It follows a liability lawsuit filed by eight blue-collar families from Woburn, Mass., just outside of Boston. Two large corporations, Beatrice Foods and W.R. Grace, were charged with dumping chemicals that eventually poisoned the town's water supply, leading to the leukemia deaths of several children.

Taking on the case is the unlikeliest of white knights, Jan Schlichtmann, played by John Travolta. He's a personal injury lawyer, a breed, he himself admits via voice-over, that even other attorneys deride as "ambulance chasers, vultures, bottom feeders."

Successful and opportunistic, favoring red power ties and a fast black sports car, Schlichtmann prides himself on being pragmatic above all else. "A dead plaintiff is rarely worth as much as one who's alive," he dispassionately informs us, "and in the calculus of personal injury law, a dead child's worth least of all."

All we need to know about Schlichtmann's modus operandi is shown in the film's exactly calibrated opening sequence, where a retreating camera reveals the lawyer carefully wheeling a disabled young man in a wheelchair—his client—down a long corridor and into court. Just the sight of this pair sends the opposing attorney into a sweat, which is just what Schlichtmann intended.

"The whole idea of lawsuits is to settle," his voice-over informs later in the film. "Trials are for fools."

Because of his calculation about the futility of litigating over dead children, Schlichtmann is wary of taking on the Woburn parents' case, even though his partner Kevin Conway (Tony Shalhoub) favors the idea. Two things win him over: the persistence of parent Anne Anderson (Kathleen Quinlan) and his chance discovery that the suspected local polluters are owned by large corporations with very deep pockets.

Though Travolta, who hasn't made his reputation playing professional men, was something of an unconventional choice for the role, the actor is solid in these introductory sections. He plays Schlichtmann as slick and street smart with just a veneer of sophistication, an opportunist and an operator with his eye always on the main chance, a characterization that is well within his range.

His main legal opponent Jerome Facher, the attorney representing Beatrice, is ideally cast, with superb actor Robert Duvall playing a wily master of legal manipulation. Beautifully introduced in a lunchtime scene that underlines his lethal combination of folksiness and a killer instinct, Duvall's Facher is the smiler with the knife, a purposeful eccentric who believes "if you're going to knock a guy down, do it so he can't get up again."

Duvall's well-cast co-stars are equally effective. John Lithgow as the case's touchy, acerbic judge, Dan Hedaya as the obstreperous operator of a suspect tannery, James Gandolfini as an employee torn about what he knows, Quinlan as the determined mother, David Thornton as a father whose child has died, all do work that could not be improved on.

Zaillian, who wrote the Oscar-winning script for "Schindler's List" and previously directed the exemplary "Searching for Bobby Fischer," handles both tasks expertly. As a writer, he never puts so much as a word wrong; as a director, he has a sureness surprising in someone who's only done two films, and, helped by the great cinematographer Conrad L. Hall (seven Oscar nominations, one victory), he displays a strong visual sense. More than that, he's able to give emotion its due and understands how to ground his characters in reality. So what possibly could have gone wrong?

Given that fitting all of a 500-page story into a two-hour-plus film isn't possible, "Civil Action" sensibly focuses on what the case does to Schlichtmann. It becomes, to put it mildly, an obsession for this previously uninvolved man, threatening to ruin his law firm financially and to take all his partners with him. (In the film's shrewd moments of comic relief, William H. Macy amusingly portrays the team's increasingly frantic financial advisor, James Gordon).

The problem with this focus is that it doesn't play to Travolta's strengths. His performance is acceptable as far as it goes, but the intangibles are off for him, he is simply not the right actor for the role. So much of the film comes to pivot around Schlichtmann's crisis of conscience, on the nature of his moral dilemmas, that what's needed is an actor better suited to conveying those kinds of predicaments. Ralph Fiennes in "Quiz Show" comes to mind, as does Ian Holm in "The Sweet Hereafter." But Travolta's screen success has never depended on the projection of a complex and troubling interior life, and this film probably isn't the best place to start.

Making this casting lapse more unfortunate is the complex way the plot of "A Civil Action" resolves, a conclusion that places even more emphasis on Schlichtmann's psychological journey. Reversal of expectations can be a wonderful thing in a book, but, as much as we don't like to admit it, it's not always satisfying in a film.

There's nothing to be done about the way "A Civil Action" ends, the facts presented are difficult to change with impunity, and those looking for a reason this often excellent film leaves an unsatisfied feeling in its wake might consider "defeated by reality" as an apt summing up.

NEW YORK, 1/11/99, p. 54, Peter Rainer

Reportedly, Jonathan Harr's nonfiction best-seller *A Civil Action* is being used as a textbook in law schools. The movie that has been made from it is unlikely to be used as a model in film schools. Written and directed by Steve Zaillian, *A Civil Action* has more negative virtues than positive. It's commendable for not doing many of the things we expect from legal thrillers in this Grisham era, but we're left with a long trudge through the ambiguities of civic virtue.

The case in question is an eight-year wrongful-death suit spearheaded by personal-injury attorney Jan Schlichtmann (John Travolta, not in top form) against W.R. Grace & Company and Beatrice Foods for dumping toxic chemicals in the Woburn, Massachusetts, water supply and allegedly causing the deaths of five children and one adult. What makes the story a movie natural is that Schlictmann, who starts out as a high-gloss ambulance chaser and "one of Boston's most eligible bachelors," ends up obsessed with the moral rightness of his case even as it drags down to the last penny the resources of his firm. What makes the story a movie bummer is that it doesn't end on a high.

I'm all for films that don't flow from the usual Hollywood test tubes, but *A Civil Action* is basically the standard formula with a dash of downbeat. Schlictmann is the sharpie crusader who gives himself up for righteousness; his legal adversary, played maliciously well by Robert Duvall, is fond of saying stuff like "The courtroom is not the place to look for truth." It may not be enough anymore for filmmakers to frame legal thrillers in the same old self-righteous ways: Having passed from O.J. through Zippergate, we've perhaps become too wised-up for that approach. Zaillian may think he's playing up to us, but he's playing down. He's made a movie where the chicanery of the legal profession is treated as breaking news.

NEW YORK POST, 12/23/98, p. 43, Rod Dreher

The children of Woburn, Mass., are dying from poisoned water, and eight mourning families want hotshot personal injury lawyer Jan Schlichtmann (John Travolta) to help. All the slick Boston attorney can say is, "Show me the money." By the time "A Civil Action" ends, they will have introduced him to something priceless: a sense of honor.

Steve Zaillian has written and directed a solid, unconventional legal drama based on Jonathan Harr's nonfiction account of the town's battle with two large corporations, W.R. Grace and Beatrice Foods, whom they accused of dumping toxic waste into their groundwater. Like the book, the film centers not on the townspeople, but on their lawyer, who waged a fierce and tortuous war against the deep-pocketed corporate Goliaths.

For the first 45 minutes, "A Civil Action" moves quickly and efficiently, with savvy Schlichtmann working the legal system like a pinball wizard, setting the stage for his clients' triumph, and building our expectations for a predictable payoff. Charismatic lawyers representing the families of dead kids against big corporations always win, right?

Not in real life, and certainly—admirably, atypically—not in this Hollywood movie. Schlichtmann hasn't counted on the understated brilliance of Beatrice's lawyer Jerome Facher, played magnificently by Robert Duvall. Facher's old-school eccentricity belies his wily genius; he lawyers circles around the overconfident Schlichtmann. Duvall shades his performance so perfectly that, while we don't want him to prevail in court, we can't help liking and admiring him.

Having entered the case expecting another high-profile victory, and a rich payday when his clients collected, Schlichtmann runs into serious trouble. He becomes obsessed with the case, and steadily leads his small firm, which is working on contingency, into bankruptcy. Why does he do it? Is it hubris? Or does he really want to do right by the suffering families?

A flashier, more brittle actor than the well-cushioned John Travolta, who is slightly miscast here, would have brought the conflicting passions and instincts within the man closer to the surface. The melancholic, downbeat ending will put off audiences who don't like rules of the courtroom genre broken, but it makes "A Civil Action" a more poignant film.

NEWSWEEK, 12/21/98, p. 67, David Ansen

Even if you weren't told that "A Civil Action" was based on a true story, you'd feel it. Steven Zaillian's engrossing legal thriller has the density, complexity—and somewhat misshapen quality of real life. It's based on a well-known case of toxic pollution that occurred in Woburn, Mass., in the 1970s. An unusual number of children were dying of leukemia, the cause unknown. When personal-injury lawyer Jan Schlichtmann (John Travolta) agrees to take the case, the finger of blame points at two giant corporations—W.R. Grace and Beatrice Foods. He wants to prove that their factories were illegally dumping poisonous chemicals, and he smells big money for both his firm and the victims' families. Following Jonathan Harr's best-selling book, Zaillian concentrates not on the families or the environmental issues, but on the lawyers who duked it out in civil court for almost a decade—a byzantine ordeal that had less to do with justice and human suffering than with pride, legalistic maneuvering and, above all, money.

Schlichtmann is a fascinating protagonist, an ambiguous mixture of greed and idealism, vanity and altruism. He's an ambulance chaser who is so obsessed with the case that his small firm, working on contingency and spending millions, is driven into bankruptcy. Unlike in more conventional courtroom dramas, Schlichtmann's passionate pursuit of the truth actually clouds his judgment as a lawyer. He keeps refusing to settle, even though he knows that "only fools with something to prove end up in court."

Zaillian, best known for writing "Schindler's List" and directing "Searching for Bobby Fischer," can turn dry depositions into riveting drama, And he has assembled a rock-solid cast. Travolta has just the right mixture of flash, tenacity and narcissism to bring this paradoxical hero to life. As his wiliest foe, attorney Jerome Facher, Robert Duvall is as good as it gets. Lethal as a snake behind his frumpy exterior, Facher is a brilliant legal mind in the service of a malign corporate master; you can't help but admire his Machiavellian expertise. These are the juiciest parts, but mention must be made of many others: James Gandolfini, David Thornton, Wilham H. Macy, John Lithgow, Dan Hedaya, Sydney Pollack.

"A Civil Action" is one movie that could have been longer. The other members of Schlichtmann's Boston firm are too sketchily developed: why do they let him drag them into penury with so little protest? And too many vital events are crammed into the last half hour. But far better a movie with too much story to tell than the usual lean cinematic cuisine. Zaillian's meaty movie, at once bleak and hopeful, speaks volumes about the maddening distance between justice and the justice system.

SIGHT AND SOUND, 4/99, p. 39, Stella Bruzzi

Boston, Massachusetts. Jan Schlichtmann is a successful lawyer specialising in personal-injury claims. He is contacted by Anne Anderson, a mother seeking legal representation in her fight to win an apology from whomsoever caused the deaths of several children—including her own—from leukaemia by contaminating the well water in Woburn, Massachusetts, with chemical waste. Since the case is difficult to prove, Schlichtmann turns it down, but changes his mind after witnessing the dumping of waste from factories owned by Beatrice Foods and Grace & Co. The motion to dismiss brought by Beatrice and Grace's defence lawyers (Cheeseman and Facher, respectively) is denied, and the case comes to trial.

Schlichtmann and his colleagues are bankrupting themselves to pursue the case, but only two employees from either company will affirm the plaintiffs' story. The defence team is ready to strike a deal, but Jan deliberately demands an unrealistic compensation fee that is refused. The trial falters as Grace is acquitted by the jury. A paltry settlement of $375,000 per family is agreed with Beatrice Foods. Schlichtmann and his firm part company. He goes back on the case, finding another witness willing to testify. The case is brought to the court of appeal (not by Schlichtmann), and this time both plants are closed down. $69.4 million is paid out in compensation and clean-up costs by the companies. Jan switches to environmental law.

Based on a real case concluded in 1990, *A Civil Action is*—like many courtroom dramas—a conscience film, which constructs a complex narrative from gritty moral material. Its realism is manifested in two distinct ways: through a functional but slick visual style (using montage to show the witnesses' testimonies, but refraining from other flourishes); and a tortuous attention to legal details. It's believable in a way that other courtroom dramas from *12 Angry Men* (1956) to *Philadelphia* are not. Disillusionment-fuelled legal dramas, such as Sidney Lumet's *The Verdict* (which focuses on an ambulance-chaser jolted out of moral limbo by getting involved in an emotive negligence case) are, of course, common. But given the bad rap lawyers have in the US these days, *A Civil Action* is not heavy with cynicism. Comments about the system shortcomings are almost ironic asides: "Trials are a corruption of the whole process," Jan's voiceover observes, while his rival, the defence lawyer Facher, says, "Here you're lucky if you find anything that resembles the truth." Overall, *A Civil Action* has a lightness of touch uncharacteristic of the genre.

Director Steven Zaillian (who made *Searching for Bobby Fischer* and is the screenwriter of *The Falcon and the Snowman*, *Schindler's List* and *Patriot Games*) cannily notes that in Jonathan Harr's original book, "All the important events happen outside the courtroom." Liberated from the constrictions (physical and otherwise) of making the trial its foundation, *A Civil Action* the movie puts its heart into the environmental-disaster case and Schlichtmann's hubristic rise and fall. Most moving is the depiction of the David-and-Goliath struggle between the parents (all lumberjack shirts, big jackets and shapeless cardigans), who simply seek an apology for their children's deaths, and the polluting factories and their haughty lawyers. Cinematic convention in the liberal trial film dictates (see *The Accused)* that a natural correlation exists between the emotional and the legal: whomsoever the audience identifies with almost always wins the case, with back-slappings, embraces and sanctimony all round. *A Civil Action* permits this fantasy for a while, only to let us down as the law outsmarts the grieving parents.

The form mimics the inherent cynicism of the script. When the trial is well under way, the judge retires the jury to consider whether or not there is a clear contamination case to be answered. Before they return, there is a protracted exchange between Schlichtmann and Facher. Schlichtmann stands restlessly and ponders the significance of the jury's lengthy deliberations, while Facher calmly eats his packed lunch and casts gentle aspersions on his profession. A legal drama in the celebratory mode would ensure that Facher—too clever, too recognisably the 'homespun' archetype epitomised by James Stewart in *Anatomy of a Murder* (1959)—wouldn't win. Instead, Schlichtmann is the one who fails and is professionally ruined.

This twist sets up the remainder of the film, encapsulating the realistic premise that worthy cases are rarely capable of withstanding the well-oiled legal machine, an equivocation represented in Schlichtmann himself, a figure vacillating between swaggering superficiality and moral integrity. The only way Schlichtmann can win his final victory at appeal is to lose everything—job, money and possessions—until all he has left is a moral victory, its hollowness echoed by the almost cursory announcement of the settlement in a rapid, intertitled montage at the end. And so concludes a subtle indictment of both the law and its cinematic romanticisation.

TIME, 12/28/98-1/4/99, p. 174, Richard Schickel

It's always nice, at the holiday season, to see a man get religion. It's especially rewarding to see him do so in a smart, tough, yet curiously moving film like *A Civil Action*, which is based on Jonathan Harr's true, best-selling account of how an insanely complicated Massachusetts case involving deadly environmental pollution was endlessly litigated.

The perps are subsidiaries of two giant corporations, carelessly dumping poisonous chemicals into a small town's water supply. The victims are kids, dying of leukemia as a result. The plaintiffs are their distraught, financially hard-pressed parents. Their unlikely champion is a lawyer named Jan Schlichtmann (John Travolta), who risks all and finally loses all that he and his partners have gained through the hot, slick pursuit of ambulances, as this case turns into an obsession.

Not, thank heaven, a particularly magnificent one. Travolta and writer-director Steve Zaillian, compressing complex issues and characters with admirable craft, make it clear that greed and ego, more than compassion, drive Schlichtmann. Only when he reaches straits as dire as his clients does he (non-melodramatically) achieve something like full humanity. Meantime, we've enjoyed a richly acted—see especially Robert Duvall's dreamy-fox opposition lawyer—subtly suspenseful, blessedly unmoralizing morality play.

VILLAGE VOICE, 12/29/98, p. 120, J. Hoberman

John Travolta conveys more authority in a single scene as a meat-faced general in *The Thin Red Line* [see Hoberman's review] than he does as a bionic, Porsche-driving personal-injury attorney in the whole overblown legal drama that is Steven Zaillian's *A Civil Action*. Adapted from Jonathan Harr's page-turner, a true story of industrial pollution and corporate chicanery, *A Civil Action* is a slick, shameless job that takes way too long to make its point (namely, we need the EPA).

There's a vaguely Clintonian feel to the war between Travolta's cocksure, crypto-Democrat ambulance chaser and Robert Duvall's eccentric, if Republican-respectable, Harvard law prof. The chuckling Duvall is an even more opportunistic con man than Travolta—as the better actor, he deserves to win the case. Like *Schindler's List,* which Zaillian scripted, *A Civil Action* concerns a cynic's redemption. But it's a transformation that the movie can't dramatize. Travolta's part might just have well been given to Sylvester Stallone.

Also reviewed in:
CHICAGO TRIBUNE, 1/8/99, Friday/p. A, Michael Wilmington
NEW YORK TIMES, 12/25/98, p. E1, Janet Maslin
NEW YORKER, 1/11/99, p. 95, David Denby
VARIETY, 12/21/98-1/3/99, p. 73, Emanuel Levy
WASHINGTON POST, 1/8/99, p. B1, Rita Kempley
WASHINGTON POST, 1/8/99, Weekend/p. 38, Michael O'Sullivan

CLAY PIGEONS

A Gramercy Pictures release of a PolyGram Filmed Entertainment presentation in association with Intermedia Films of a Scott Free production. *Executive Producer:* Tony Scott, Guy East, and Nigel Sinclair. *Producer:* Ridley Scott and Chris Zarpas. *Director:* David Dobkin. *Screenplay:* Matt Healy. *Director of Photography:* Eric Edwards. *Editor:* Stan Salfas. *Music:* John Lurie. *Music Editor:* Amanda Goodpaster. *Sound:* Robert Eber and (music) Pat Dillett. *Sound Editor:* Marc Fishman. *Casting:* Risa Bramon Garcia and Randi Hiller. *Production Designer:* Clark Hunter. *Art Director:* Max Biscoe. *Set Decorator:* Tracy Kirshbaum. *Set Dresser:* Joseph B. Arnold. *Special Effects:* David Wayne. *Costumes:* Laura Goldsmith. *Make-up:* Gina Monaci. *Stunt Coordinator:* Edward Conna. *Running time:* 104 minutes. *MPAA Rating:* R.

CAST: Joaquin Phoenix (Clay); Gregory Sporleder (Earl); Georgina Cates (Amanda); Scott Wilson (Sheriff Mooney); Vince Vieluf (Deputy Barney); Wayne Brennan (Minister); Joseph D. Reitman (Glen); Vince Vaughn (Lester Long); Nikki Arlyn (Gloria); Jeff Olson (Mark); Monica Moench (Kimberly); Kevin Rahm (Bystander at Amanda's); Jesse Bennett (Dr. Jaffe); Phil Morris (Agent Reynard); Janeane Garofalo (Agent Shelby); Zane Parker (Dr. Buckley);

Ryan Mouritsen (Pizza Delivery Kid);   Kari Peterson (Dolores);   Duane Stephens (Bartender); Steve Anderson (Old Man Waiter).

LOS ANGELES TIMES, 9/25/98, Calendar/p. 2, Kenneth Turan

Blame it on Quentin and the Coens if you have to pin it somewhere, but murder comedies that mix black humor and bloody doings are lately thick on the land. It's a subgenre that's so new it's already old, and "Clay Pigeons," the latest example, shows why it's both promising and played out.

Set in the mythical town of Mercer, Mont. (though filmed, not for any obvious reason, in Utah), "Clay Pigeons" echoes more than Coen brothers classics like "Fargo." There are several bits of Hitchcock lurking in its off-kilter tale of how love and friendship can make dupes of us all.

"Pigeons" is smartly written (by Matt Healy) and stylishly directed (by David Dobkin), both making their feature debuts. It follows the fortunes (misfortunes is more like it) of an earnest if not particularly bright young man named Clay (the engaging Joaquin Phoenix) whose last name isn't pigeon but might as well be for all the times he plays the dupe.

Garage mechanic Clay and buddy Earl are out drinking beer and using the bottles for target practice when the talk gets serious: "I hear you've been sleeping with my wife," Earl says. "Who told you?" "She did."

Before Clay can talk his way out of that one, Earl has taken his own life, but not without terrifying Clay by telling him he's making that death look like his erstwhile pal murdered him. (The reality, of course, is that gunshot suicides are much harder to fake than the film would have you believe, but if plausibility is a problem for you, you might as well leave now.)

Clay hopes for some sympathy from Amanda (Georgina Cates), the object of both men's affections, but she refuses to help him explain things to amiable local Sheriff Mooney (Scott Wilson) and his sleepy deputy Barney (Vince Vieluf). Still, she continues to be so voracious in her sexual demands that Clay ends up slapping her in the local pool hall. Big mistake.

That slap gets the attention of Lester Long (Vince Vaughn), new in town and dressed to be noticed in flashy cowboy hat and shirt. As fake as Lester's clothes are his friendliness, his sincerity and his sense of humor, but Clay, too hapless to notice, is so happy to have someone to talk to they end up going fishing together.

What happens at the lake ups the ante in this relationship, and Clay gradually realizes he's in over his head more than usual. Gradually, without really thinking about it, he's gotten himself involved in someone else's plot and the scenario is way too complex for him to easily extricate himself.

Adding to Clay's troubles is the arrival in town of laconic, ironic FBI Agent Dale Shelby, on the lookout for a serial killer responsible for the deaths of numerous women. Agent Shelby is played by the always-welcome Janeane Garofalo, whose deliciously blank style ("a murder scene is not crowd appropriate") is perfectly tailored to the film's attitude. Garofalo adds interest to all her scenes and she elevates Vaughn's otherwise iffy work in the key moments she has with him.

"Clay Pigeons'" trademark is how quickly and without warning it moves from comedy to horror. Both director Dobkin and writer Healy have a nice feeling for this transition, and Dobkin, a protege of Ridley Scott who's worked largely in videos and commercials, has a gift for counterpointing the action with unexpected music from an excellent soundtrack. Using Elvis Presley's "It's Now or Never" behind someone considering murder, for instance, is probably not what the King intended.

But as its excessively convoluted and implausible plot unfolds, "Clay Pigeons" keeps asking if style and attitude make up for excessive improbability and a baffling denouement. Not here it can't, at least not for as long as it tries to. "You've got a sense of humor, I like that," Lester Long proclaims at one point. Well, we all like that, but would it be asking too much to have a little coherence to go along with it?

NEW YORK POST, 9/25/98, p. 44, Thelma Adams

I was skeptical about "Swingers" cover boy Vince Vaughn playing Norman Bates in Gus Van Sant's "Psycho" remake—until I saw "Clay Pigeons."

Vaughn plays Lester Long—or, as he introduces himself in a Montana bar, Lester the Mo-lester, with rockin' pelvic thrusts to match.

Lester is Ted Bundy with a white hat, an amiable, ingratiating sociopath without a shred of psychology to explain his bloody habits. Way up in Big Sky Country, he bonds with gas jockey Clay (Joaquin Phoenix, at his most likable) over long-neck bottles of beer, fishing and dishing women.

Clay was neck-deep in trouble even before a serial killer became his new best friend. You see, there was a vacancy: Clay's old best friend, Earl (Gregory Sporleder), just shot himself.

And that's not the worst of it. Clay was sleeping with Earl's wife, Amanda (Georgina Cates, doing a wicked Sheryl Lee). Now the new widow is a little too merry—and she refuses to clear Clay's name with Sheriff Mooney (Scott Wilson). She has issues.

Suddenly, corpses start littering the breathtaking landscape. Promise you'll stop finding dead people, Mooney tells Clay. Before you can say "Toss me another longneck," Clay is the prime suspect.

Just as the story begins to go south of Red Rock West, FBI agent Shelby (Janeane Garofalo) arrives with comic reinforcements. The no-nonsense city lawgal has a brassy attitude that says: Don't mess with me, because I might break—but not before I take a piece of you with me.

Shelby unwittingly flirts with her prey at the local watering hole, where she tries to resist his charms. You're very colorful, she tells Lester. She doesn't yet know his favorite color is blood red.

"Clay Pigeons," directed by newcomer David Dobkin from Matt Healy's script, proves the rule that a thriller is only as irresistible as its villain is. "Lounge Lizard's" rocker John Lurie's score heightens the black comedy, and Lester climaxes a night of lovemaking with a little knife play to Elvis crooning It's "Now or Never."

NEWSDAY, 9/25/98, Part II/p. B7, Jack Mathews

In the shock-intended pre-credit opening of David Dobkin's black comedy, "Clay Pigeons," best friends Clay (Joaquin Phoenix) and Earl (Gregory Sporleder) are knocking back Buds and shooting the empty bottles in the great Montana outdoors when, suddenly, Earl turns his gun on Clay, accuses him of sleeping with his wife, then turns the gun on himself, announcing his plan to frame Clay for his murder.

After Earl's widow, Amanda (Georgina Cates), refuses to confirm the affair to the police—thus leaving him on the hook—Clay blows up his friend's body in a faked accident, then switches his romantic attentions to a pretty waitress (Nikki Arlyn) at a local diner. But no sooner is he in bed with her than jealous Amanda shows up, shoots her dead (ruins his water bed, too), and then compels him to dump that body in a nearby lake.

All this and we still haven't got to the meat or real meanness of "Clay Pigeons." This first-time film, for both Dobkin and screenwriter Matt Healy (who once toiled in Newsday's sedate art department), is about another killer, a stray woman-hater who has been trapping his prey in Big Sky Country for two years. His only connection to Clay is a certain sympathy, engendered by the sight of Clay whacking Amanda across the mouth in a neighborhood bar.

What good is a serial killer if he can't give a stranger a helping hand? "Clay Pigeons" is on one of the little sub-waves following the crashing of "Pulp Fiction" on our cultural shores. It is a riot of violence, where the laughs are squeezed out of wounds and bad karma, and where the most attractive characters are those with the least humanity. It is pure film exercise, not intended for scrupulous story analysis, not to mention weak stomachs.

Is it any good, you wonder? Well, Dobkin is clearly a promising filmmaker. "Clay Pigeons" is beautifully shot and paced, and he benefits from the spectacularly contrasting performances of Phoenix, who's somber enough to turn light to dark, and Vince Vaughn, making serial killer Lester the life of the party. Vaughn, who's getting the next-Paul-Newman treatment in Hollywood, is a still-unrefined actor, but his presence, as well as his future, are undeniable.

The film's scene-stealer is actually Janeane Garofalo, as a savvy FBI agent biting her tongue while working with the rubes in the local police department, one of whom (Vince Vieluf) is overtly fashioned after Don Knotts' Barney Fife. Garofalo says she took the role to counter the story's violence against women. Talk about a full-time job. Anyway, the film and the audience are lucky to have her.

VILLAGE VOICE, 10/6/98, p. 123, Dennis Lim

An allegedly comedic thriller about serial killing, David Dobkin's *Clay Pigeons* strives for the kind of edgy humor that, when misjudged, can make the relevant parties look extremely foolish, not to mention morally bankrupt. Joaquin Phoenix plays a hapless Montana mechanic who, covering up the suicide of a friend (whose wife he was screwing), finds himself in a predictable mess, swiftly complicated by the mysterious arrival of a swaggering cowboy-hatted psychopath (Vince Vaughn, having fun, though I couldn't begin to tell you why). Midway through the film, an FBI agent (Janeane Garofalo) shows up on cue. A last-minute twist seems in the cards—but is it really? It's never clear, by the way, why any of this is supposed to be even remotely funny.

If Vaughn's flashy, mannered performance is any indication of the actor's grasp of character, his forthcoming Norman Bates will be a major embarrassment. Garofalo is reduced once again to being gruff and snide and deadpan, directing her barbs at the obvious-target yokels (there's a deputy sheriff named Barney). Phoenix is a solid enough presence, but his role, as written, is restrictive and unflattering.

This is the kind of movie asinine enough to believe that the mere juxtaposition of sadistic violence and a jaunty tune on the soundtrack is, in itself, clever. That said, the main problem with *Clay Pigeons* isn't even questionable taste. First-time director Dobkin (a Ridley Scott protégé who doesn't show much of the stylistic surefootedness that that implies) and writer Mark Healy are intent on being provocative, but they lack a strategy; the film has trouble establishing a tone, and gets progressively more flaccid.

Also reviewed in:
CHICAGO TRIBUNE, 9/25/98, Friday/p. D, Mark Caro
NEW YORK TIMES, 9/25/98, p. E22, Stephen Holden
VARIETY, 9/21-27/98, p. 108, Dennis Harvey
WASHINGTON POST, 9/25/98, Weekend/p. 63, Michael O'Sullivan

CLOCKWATCHERS

A BMG Independents release of a Goldcrest Films International presentation of a Gina Resnick production.   *Executive Producer:* John Flock.   *Producer:* Gina Resnick.   *Director:* Jill Sprecher.   *Screenplay:* Jill Sprecher and Karen Sprecher.   *Director of Photography:* Jim Denault.   *Editor:* Stephen Mirrione.   *Music:* Mader.   *Sound:* Christopher M. Taylor.   *Casting:* Jeanne McCarthy.   *Production Designer:* Pamela Marcotte.   *Set Decorator:* Greta Grigorian.   *Costumes:* Edi Giguere.   *Running time:* 96 minutes.   *MPAA Rating:* PG-13.

CAST: Toni Collette (Iris); Parker Posey (Margaret); Lisa Kudrow (Paula); Alanna Ubach (Jane); Helen Fitzgerald (Cleo); Stanley DeSantis (Art); Jamie Kennedy (Eddie); David James Elliott (MacNamee); Debra Jo Rupp (Barbara); Kevin Cooney (Mr. Kilmer); Bob Balaban (Milton Lasky); Paul Dooley (Bud Chapman).

LOS ANGELES TIMES, 5/15/98, Calendar/p. 8, David Kronke

"Clockwatchers," which premiered at the 1997 Sundance Film Festival, is the estrogen version of a celebrated alumnus of that year's festival, "In the Company of Men." It explores how the soulless machinery of the workplace can destroy the spirit and reduce worker drones to, if not exactly the amoral monsters of Neil LaBute's scabrous work, then at least unpleasantly petty bickerers.

The film centers on a close-knit group of temp workers: Iris (Toni Collette of "Muriel's Wedding"), mousy and observant; Margaret (Parker Posey), mouthy and brash; Paula (Lisa Kudrow), flirty and delusional; and Jane (Alanna Ubach), unambitious and engaged to a scoundrel. They're all trapped at a monumentally mediocre credit company straight out of "Dilbert," where actually doing work can get you into trouble.

Like any good mega-corporation, the company exploits the young women's abilities without offering them any allegiance, blindingly dismissing them as poorly paid contract players of limited talent. Despite their contributions—they know their way around the company and keep things running—they're easily ignored or diminished.

Which is enough, of course, to make anyone bitter, but at least they have one another's camaraderie and the free grub of nearby pubs' happy hours to make life worthwhile. Things get even worse, however, when a nearly mute, bug-eyed young woman is hired over them into a permanent position. Frustration and jealousy mount, and a most peculiarly small-minded crime spree erupts, which adds paranoia to the mix.

"Clockwatchers" is written by the sister act of Jill and Karen Sprecher and directed by Jill. For a while, it's acceptable deadpan fun as it examines the deadening nature of a workplace committed to mediocrity, and Sprecher's mannered shot compositions accentuate the budget-minded production design's clever eye toward god-awful corporate blandness.

But, really, not much happens. Were it not for Iris' voice-over narration, we wouldn't have a clue that any of this matters a whit to anyone. And once the jokiness of the Sprechers' screenplay starts petering out, things get as dreary as a 9-to-5 shift chained to a desk.

What keeps things watchable are the principals' performances—these four really look and feel like the minions who populate offices looking borderline sharp but utterly frivolous, whose career options are dwindling and whose biggest thrill is sticking it to the Man by getting away with some tiny office taboo. "Clockwatchers" opens with fresh, quirky panache, but by film's end, those most closely consulting their watches may be those in the audience.

NEW YORK POST, 5/15/98, p. 53, Larry Worth

Having an eye for detail is a crucial trait for a director—but not as important as seeing the overall picture.

Jill Sprecher has the first down to a science, but she remains fuzzy on the latter, as demonstrated in her feature film debut, "Clockwatchers."

Set in a particularly sterile office building, the tale of four temps begins on Day One for timid newcomer Iris (Toni Collette). She's quickly befriended by Margaret (Parker Posey), a seasoned pro who knows where all the paper clips are buried; Paula (Lisa Kudrow), whose chief concern is maintaining her Veronica Lake 'do; and Jane (Alanna Ubach), a young woman biding time until her wedding.

Ultimately, the quintessential quartet fights the good fight against arrogant full-time secretaries, no-nonsense bosses and office Muzak, at least until supplies start disappearing and paranoia turns worker against worker.

That's also where Sprecher loses her way, letting the comedy's surreal elements get out of hand and shifting moods into an unsatisfying dramatic mode. It's as if she's run out of ideas.

That's a shame, because the level of humor Sprecher taps is all too rare, a nervous kind of wit that Martin Scorsese used in "After Hours." Here, it encapsulates the pure hell of temp work, the after-work pickup scene, office politics, cafeteria horrors, co-workers' pettiness, and the art of mastering busy work.

A prime example comes when Iris is told by a nasty superior, "Don't make too many typing errors." Sprecher cuts to a shot of Iris in the ladies' room, throwing away wads of paper stuffed into her purse.

Like the schizoid screenplay, the actors fall into two camps. Parker Posey and Lisa Kudrow thrive as the more flamboyant pencil sharpeners; but Toni ("Muriel's Wedding") Collette recycles her mouse-who-finally-roars routine and Alanna Ubach just goes through the motions.

Maybe their antics would have made a better short than a feature. Indeed, only the first half of "Clockwatchers" refers to the fearsome foursome. The remainder refers to viewers.

NEWSDAY , 5/15/98 , Part II/p. B8, John Anderson

The '90s will be remembered as an exalted, glorious age in the history of western civ, at least by shareholders and CEOs. And among its more cancerous symptoms—which include recreational vehicles and cell phones—temp workers will be remembered as the invisibles, the untouchables, the slaves who built the pyramids. Necessary, but anonymous. And, in the greater corporate sense, nonexistent.

So there's a good movie idea in "Clockwatchers," a stark and deceptively honest film about four temps who meet, bond and eventually get the company shaft. It seems to present itself as a comedy, but is so frank in its depiction of modern office life—and the way people sabotage each other as well as themselves—that it's far too real, and depressing, for laughs.

Written by the sisters Sprecher, Jill and Karen, "Clockwatchers" is set amongst the cubicles of Global Credit, one of those seemingly useless companies that move money from one place to another and whose employees have so little to do that the rules become rites. The music is someone's Muzak nightmare, the atmosphere is antiseptic, the office-supply manager is a mutant (Stanley DeSantis) and the temps become allies out of what is basically caste unity.

They might be immigrants, they might be welfare recipients, they might be anything that sets them apart, but in Global Credit they're the ones without the real jobs. Iris (Toni Collette) seems to be sleepwalking and is afraid of her own shadow; Margaret (Parker Posey) is an operator who knows just how far to push the system; Paula (Lisa Kudrow) is a man-crazy would-be actress without any noticeable talent and Jane (Alanna Ubach) is the engaged one with the negligent but rich fiance and some obsessive compulsions. Theirs is a gallows humor informed by the fact that they can work for years and never get hired, never get benefits, never get a recommendation. When someone starts stealing around the office, they immediately fall under suspicion.

"Clockwatchers" might have been more stinging had its chief characters not had such obvious flaws. Iris—who provides the narration, which gives the film an occasionally otherworldly aspect—perpetrates a fraud on her father (Paul Dooley), who thinks she has actually arranged her big interview with an associate of his. Margaret, so cocky, so flippant, lies about her career to her parents. Paula is kidding herself about acting, Jane about her groom-to-be. That they're so averse to success makes their plight their own fault. And this is self-destructive for an otherwise insightful film about the modern corporate condition and its metaphoric content.

The insights include the way the company divides and conquers, once the four start talking about striking. Fed up with the paranoia, their second-class status and the music (it's ungodly) they decide to walk out. And then things change. And they start fighting among themselves. Did someone overhear them? Or is Big Brother on the job? With "Clockwatchers," the paranoia is contagious.

VILLAGE VOICE, 5/12/98, p. 130, Rowan Morris

In *Clockwatchers*, Toni Collette of *Muriel's Wedding* appears once again as a shy heroine who watches everything but says nothing. As Iris, the new girl in a large credit bureau, she is relegated to the temp clique, with Lisa Kudrow as the big blond and Parker Posey's Margaret as the inevitable ringleader showing the ropes of coffee making and bathroom smoking. But just when the temps are beginning to establish themselves, random objects start to go missing, with Iris and company the obvious suspects. Soon the women begin to lose their trust in one another; an oddly frightening sequence of events imbues even pencils and letter openers with unexpected significance. To the point that, in one heavy-handed moment, the buzzing of the fluorescent lights screams at us. Writers Jill and Karen Sprecher show promise in the occasional clever lines, but it is Posey's knack for them that carries the film. Not quite the Coens yet, the Sprechers reveal only small flashes of genius—like casting Kudrow as a tragic figure.

Also reviewed in:
CHICAGO TRIBUNE, 5/22/98, Friday/p. A, Monica Eng
NEW YORK TIMES, 5/15/98, p. E23, Stephen Holden
NEW YORKER 5/25/98, p. 122, Daphne Merkin
VARIETY, 1/27-2/2/97, p. 77, Todd McCarthy

COMRADES, ALMOST A LOVE STORY

A Rim Film release of a Golden Harvest Entertainment presentation of a United Filmmakers Organization production. *Executive Producer:* Peter Chan. *Producer:* Raymond Chow and Eric Tsang. *Director:* Peter Chan. *Screenplay (Cantonese and Mandarin with English subtitles):* Ivy Ho. *Director of Photography:* Jingle Ma. *Editor:* Chan Ki-hop and Kwong Chi-leung. *Music:* Chiu Tsang-hei. *Art Director:* Yee Chung-man. *Costumes:* Dora Ng. *Running time:* 116 minutes. *MPAA Rating:* Not Rated.

CAST: Leon Lai (Li Xiaojun); Maggie Cheung (Li Qiao); Kristy Yeung (Fan Xiaoting); Eric Tsang (Pao); Irene Tsu (Rosie); Christopher Doyle (Jeremy); Ting Yu (George); Michelle Gabriel (Prostitute); Joseph Cheung (Restaurant Owner).

LOS ANGELES TIMES, 3/6/98, Calendar/p. 22, Kevin Thomas

Peter Chan's captivating "Comrades, Almost a Love Story" is an epic romance with just enough echoes of the original "Love Affair" to remind us yet again that nowadays a number of foreign filmmakers are more adept at making the classic Hollywood heart-tugger than most contemporary American writers and directors.

Best known for the sparkling gender-bending comedy "He's a Woman, She's a Man," Chan knows how to draw you into Ivy Ho's exceedingly shrewd script and how to present star actors at their charismatic best.

Indeed, "Comrades, Almost a Love Story," which launches the "New Chinese Cinema" series at the Grande 4-Plex, represents a career peak for Maggie Cheung, a young actress of such talent and versatility that she's equally at ease in action and martial arts fantasy or portraying the ill-fated '30s Shanghai movie star Ruan Ling-yu, one of the greatest actresses ever to face a camera. "Comrades" offers Cheung the kind of role actresses rightly adore, calling for a wide range of emotions yet allowing for plenty of glamour.

Cheung is a formidably expressive actress, and Chan misses no opportunity for her to glow. She's well-matched by tall, clean-cut pop singer-turned-actor Leon Lai, who matures from naivete to self-knowledge without losing a fundamental innocence. ("Comrades" won nine prizes in last year's Hong Kong Film Awards, including best picture, best director, best screenplay, best actress and best supporting actor.)

Spanning the decade between 1986 and 1996, "Comrades" finds Cheung's Qiao and Lai's Xiaojun meeting at a Hong Kong McDonald's where Qiao works. Xiaojun has arrived from Tientsin with the promise of shelter from an aunt—and speaking only Mandarin. By contrast, Qiao is from the south, Guangzhou, "where we get Hong Kong TV," but luckily for him she's as fluent in Mandarin as she is in her native Cantonese.

Xiaojun just wants any job and dreams of marrying his girl back home, but Qiao seethes with ambition and determination to achieve financial success. Her stamina and her resourcefulness are awesome, but underneath a toughened veneer she's able to take pity on Xiaojun and try to help him get started.

Xiaojun and Qiao work such incredibly long hours at a variety of menial jobs they really have no friends other than each other. Young and attractive, they end up in bed together. But Qiao is the kind of woman who reacts to moments of vulnerability by hardening herself She rebuffs the sweet-natured Xiaojun, convinced that they are such fundamentally different people that he could only hold her back.

At this point "Comrades" starts leapfrogging over the decade, picking up Qiao and Xiaojun's chance encounters. Xiaojun actually does well enough in the business world to bring his fiancee to Hong Kong and to marry her while Qiao opens a florist shop and then a bridal gown shop as well. She's hooked up with a wise, kindly gangster (Eric Tsang), an older, caring man without illusions. Gradually, however, Qiao and then Xiaojun himself realize how deeply they are in love with each other—and how they've messed up their lives by disregarding their true feelings.

Moving on to Taiwan and then to New York "Comrades" follows the ups and downs of their lives and starts building with great skill—and necessary shamelessness—incredible suspense over whether the two will ever cross paths again, whether they will ever have their chance at happiness. "Comrades" has you rooting for them the way fans root for home teams.

Of course, "Comrades" is drenchingly romantic, but Chan has also mastered the old trick of spinning an emotionally extravagant tale with a well-defined hero and heroine and turned them loose in a sharply observed, rapidly changing real world. Spectacularly photographed by Jingle Ma and accompanied by an unapologetically potent hearts-and-flowers score by Chiu Tsang-hei, "Comrades" has scope, depth and most important, the wisdom and courage to wear its heart on its sleeve.

NEW YORK POST, 2/20/98, p. 48, Thelma Adams

"Comrades, Almost a Love Story" is a Hong Kong award-winner that begins with such charm and energy, it almost surprises us when it sours like a relationship that runs aground without any warning arguments.

Maggie Cheung ("Irma Vep") and Leon Lai ("Fallen Angels") are two charismatic hicks from mainland China. It's 1986. They meet cute at a Hong Kong McDonald's while searching for a better life in the bosom of capitalism.

Both actors are appealing, and it's easy to root for them as Li Xiaojun (Lai) gets his first taste of freedom while delivering chickens throughout the city, and Li Qiao (Cheung) tries to pass herself off as a sophisticated local, even while wearing the red cap and striped shirt of a fry-girl at Mickey D's.

As directed by Peter Chan ("He's a Man, She's a Woman") from Ivy Ho's screenplay, the romantic comedy has a screwball energy. Anyone can see that the two are made for each other, except for the couple themselves.

There are many offbeat touches: a homage to William Holden; a cameo by cinematographer Chris ("Chungking Express") Doyle; and a funny scene in which duped mainlanders learn English from a western: "Jump, you son of the b----, jump"' they repeat, watching the video.

As 10 years pass, the plot strains. Xiaojun and Qiao's romance might survive two marriages (to secondary characters) and a trans-Pacific trek, but director Chan loses his grip in a sharply stereotyped Manhattan. By the end, I fell out of love with the pair, with the same pangs of regret I once felt for a failed love affair.

NEWSDAY, 2/20/98, Part II/p. B7, John Anderson

As Asian markets reel and Wall Street remains in what just might be perpetual hysteria, the arrival of "Comrades, Almost a Love Story" seems particularly serendipitous—to the point that the film's own cosmic coincidences seem almost less than outlandish.

The story of two lovers who can't make the connection—mainlanders Xaiojun (Leon Lai) and Qiao (Maggie Cheung), going for the gold in '80s Hong Kong—is a pageant of opportunities met and missed. As a love story, it isn't a particularly new idea: Two people whose passion is caught on the proverbial horns of circumstance, other loves, other dreams, etc. As plight, it's pretty pedestrian.

But Peter Chan's film, all westernized style and quasi-ancient story also wants to confirm at least half of Francis Fukuyama's "End of History" thesis that struggle has ended because the American way has triumphed. There's struggle left to be had, Chan says. But the sole plot device is money.

As such, "Comrades" is a universal movie, in which fortunes rise and fall and fall again. On the rise, ever so slowly, is Xaiojun; a painfully naive peasant who arrives in Hong Kong looking for his Aunt Rosie (Irene Tsu)—an aging, half-crazed prostitute fixated on William Holden (with whom she may or may not have had a thing during the filming of "The World of Suzie Wong"). Friendless, speaking only Mandarin, Xiaojun moves into the bordello and sets out to taste the finer things of colonial life—including McDonald's, where he meets the avaricious Qiao.

Qiao is a creature born to commerce. Hiding her mainland origins, she nevertheless steers the trusting Xiaojun to an English-language school for her usual commission (where the Australian-born cinematographer Christopher Doyle, whose work is so ubiquitous in current Asian movies, does an amusing cameo as the school's drunkard teacher). Somehow, they become inseparable, sleep together even as Xiaojun maintains his long-distance relationship with Xaioting (Yang Kung-yu) and weather the crash of '87, which in a somersaulting of exchange rates virtually wipes out Qiao.

What they did for love is subordinate to what they did for money—Qiao, at any rate. She and Xaiojun, in a Chinese rendition of the grasshopper and the ant, take divergent paths to success—she with a mobster named Pao (Eric Tsang), he by apprenticing as a chef. Like all adventurers and economic tidal waves, they eventually arrive in New York, where director Chan teaches more timeless truths and confounds us with kismet.

Chan's fluid filmmaking is pure Hollywood—right down to the music, which will rival John Williams' "Amistad" score for any Oppressive Music of the Year awards. This isn't necessarily bad, especially when you have the first-rate Cheung ("Irma Vep") in a first-rate role. At the same time, "Comrades" is a near-parable about lost opportunities and the preeminence of love. And combined with its rather frank recognition of the state of the world, "Comrades" is almost nonfiction.

VILLAGE VOICE, 2/24/98, p. 128, Michael Atkinson

Maggie Cheung is an international treasure—for my money, not another actress alive has such a masterfully pensive face, such an ice-melting smile, such a fluid romantic presence. Without her, Peter Chan's *Comrades, Almost a Love Story* might be merely the French-est Hong Kong movie ever made, down to the boulevard-minstrel score. With Cheung, it's a landslide, a culture-shock fable of capitalistic tribulation, rueful intimacy, and sweet, Demy-like melancholy. *Comrades* measures out a full decade in the lives of its woebegone characters, and there's no underestimating how Cheung's empathic glow allows Chan to take leaps through the narrative—we're jacked in before we know it. Just as *Fallen Angels* suggests the wry sadness of verging millennialism without actually expressing it, *Comrades* wins drenching melodramatic payoffs while quietly steering clear of melodrama.

The film's title sounds ironic going in, but nouvelle vague he movie's marrow—with time, that "almost" purples like a bruise. Cheung and *Fallen Angel*'s Leon Lai are two mainlanders in 1986 making their way through the profiteering chaos that is Hong Kong; he is a starry-eyed innocent intent on earning enough to import his childhood sweetheart, she is a fervent capitalist with her fingers in a dozen small-time pies. They partner up and, as the years roll on, glance romantically off each other like moths, their separate paths eventually crossing in New York. The tragic romance-in-suspension is foregrounded by the progressive love-hate tension between China and HK, one the embarrassing hillbilly cousin of the other, and both struggling to attain Western-ness. Filthy with intimate textures and disquieting pauses, Chan's film is true at heart even as it straddles the line, as HK movies so happily do, between rapture and absurdist treacle. (You gotta love Cheung identifying the body of her gangster boyfriend by the small Mickey Mouse tattoo on his heavily tattooed back.) A ripe-off-the-vine pop ballad, *Comrades* is a late masterpiece from the fading HK zeitgeist that may fade further still—like his more famous compatriots, Chan has struck a Hollywood deal.

Also reviewed in:
NEW YORK TIMES, 2/20/98, p. E26, Lawrence Van Gelder
VARIETY, 3/3-9/97, p. 68, Derek Elley

CONCERT OF WILLS: MAKING THE GETTY CENTER

A Maysles Films Inc. release.   *Producer:* Susan Froemke.   *Director:* Susan Froemke, Bob Eisenhardt, and Albert Maysles.   *Screenplay:* Susan Froemke, Bob Eisenhardt, and Albert Maysles.   *Editor:* Bob Eisenhardt.   *Music:* Joel Goodman.   *Running time:* 100 minutes.   *MPAA Rating:* Not Rated.

WITH: Richard Meier; Harold M. Williams; Stephen Rountree; Ada Louise Huxtable; John Walsh; Michael Palladino; Kurt Forster; Robert Irwin; Thierry W. Despont.

NEW YORK POST, 8/26/98, p. 49, Larry Worth

It would be Los Angeles' Acropolis. Such was the prediction of one art critic after seeing plans for the Getty Center, a six-building art complex to sit atop Tinseltown's hills.

But designing the Parthenon must have been a piece of cake compared to architect Richard Meier's Sisyphean struggle to construct the Getty Center while pacifying Getty trust members, Brentwood residents and fellow planners alike.

Thankfully, Meier's incredible 12-year battle was painstakingly documented by Susan Froemke, Bob Eisenhardt and Albert Maysles in the remarkable "Concert of Wills: Making the Getty Center."

Told in linear fashion, the tale begins with initial meetings about making the late John Paul Getty's dream for an art center into reality. But it assumes a near-epic feel as Meier's vision is scrutinized, debated, argued and vilified by his countless masters.

Maysles and Froemke (who earlier collaborated on "Grey Gardens"), capture the laid-back and not-so-laid-back bantering, filtered so amusingly through the niceties of California-speak. In the process, they provide crystal-clear insight into an artist's dreams, frustrations and genius.

Upon viewing the breathtaking results of all the blood, sweat and tears (the Getty Center opened to the public last December), audiences will know that Don Quixote wasn't the only one to dream an impossible dream. But Meier's miracle aside, the documentarians are a close second: They've made "Concert of Wills" into a compelling, utterly entrancing exploration of the creative process.

VILLAGE VOICE, 9/1/98, p. 109, Leslie Camhi

Architecture may be the handmaiden of power. Yet rarely has power's shaping hand been so clearly manifest as in *Concert of Wills*, which traces the creation of the Getty Center, the sprawling acropolis that overlooks the San Diego Freeway.

"We were like two rival armies coming together." So museum director John Walsh describes his meetings with Richard Meier, the High Modernist architect chosen to build a home for the Getty Trust's collections of medieval to 19th-century European art and antiquities. Early on, the Getty engaged filmmakers Froemke, Eisenhardt, and Maysles to record this 14-year process. In *Concert*'s opening scenes, predictable turf lines are drawn between Meier, Walsh, and the local Brentwood (read: Philistine) community. In his white office, sporting a white shirt, a mane of white hair, and bushy white eyebrows, Meier explains that he was hired with the proviso that he abstain from the use of his signature color.

Part consummate diplomat, part manic control-freak, and a total visionary, Meier takes repeated hits from artist Robert Irwin, who redesigned the central gardens, and architect Thierry Despont, who warmed up the interiors with Old World frills and color. He exults with Getty VPs as the first slabs of his travertine fall in an Italian quarry; on opening day, he carps over crookedly arranged chairs in the Getty cafeteria.

Commissioned by its subject, this fascinating film falls short of objectivity. Playing fast and loose with superlatives, it skirts any real engagement with the issues at stake in creating a new museum based upon a 19th-century model. Meier's building certainly looks like exciting architecture. But the age of monuments is long past, and we're left to wonder, what is the relation of this temple of connoisseurship to the grimy, chaos-laden city beyond it?

Also reviewed in:
NEW REPUBLIC, 9/14 & 21/98, p. 35, Stanley Kauffmann
NEW YORK TIMES, 8/26/98, p. E5, Lawrence Van Gelder

COUSIN BETTE

A Fox Searchlight Pictures release. *Executive Producer:* Susan Tarr, Lynn Siefert, and Rob Scheidlinger. *Producer:* Sarah Radclyffe. *Director:* Des McAnuff. *Screenplay:* Lynn Siefert and Susan Tarr. *Based on the novel by:* Honoré de Balzac. *Director of Photography:* Andrzej Sekula. *Editor:* Tariq Anwar and Barry Alexander Brown. *Music:* Simon Boswell. *Music Editor:*

Kevin Lane. *Choreographer:* Jane Gibson.   *Sound:* Drew Kunin and (music) Geoff Foster. *Sound Editor:* Derek Trigg.   *Casting:* Mary Margiotta, Karen Margiotta and Liora Reich *Production Designer:* Hugo Luczyc-Wyhowski.   *Art Director:* Didier Naert.   *Set Decorator:* Robert Le Corre.   *Costumes:* Gabriella Pescucci.   *Make-up:* Jenny Shircore.   *Running time:* 112 minutes.   *MPAA Rating:* R.

CAST: Geraldine Chaplin (Adeline Hulot);   John Benfield (Dr. Bianchon);   Hugh Laurie (Hector Hulot); Jessica Lange (Bette Fisher);   Paul Bandey (Priest);   Laura Fraser (Mariette); Toby Stephens (Victorin Hulot);   Kelly Macdonald (Hortense Hulot);   Janie Hargreaves (Célestine);   Gillian Martell (Portress);   Elisabeth Shue (Jenny Cadine); John Sessions (Musical Director);   Henrik Wagner (Baritone);   Aden Young (Wenceslas Steinbach);   John Quentin (Elderly Aristocrat);   Bob Hoskins (Cesar Crevel);   Jefferson Mays (Stidmann);   Tim Barlow (De Forzheim);   Heathcote Williams (Nucingen);   Philip Jackson (De Wissembourg);   Toby Jones and Kenneth Jay (Gentlemen in Café des Artistes);   Simon McBurney (Vauvinet); Geoffrey Carey (Duelmaster);   Dermot Keaney (Chief Gendarme).

LOS ANGELES TIMES, 6/12/98, Calendar/p. 2, Kevin Thomas

In her long and varied career, Bette Davis played many a memorable heroine, but she never got to play her namesake, Balzac's Cousin Bette. Davis would have been perfect as the plain, impoverished spinster who engineers revenge against her rich, selfish relatives.

Had she had the chance, her film probably would have been more serious and melodramatic than the delightfully tart yet blithe-spirited "Cousin Bette" that director Des McAnuff and his adapters have fashioned so artfully for Jessica Lange, a talented star who never stops trying to extend her range as an actress.

That no one seems to notice what a beautiful, sensual woman Lange's Bette is—even given the severe attire and hairdo appropriate to her station in life—serves to underline the cruel yet often comical obtuseness of all who surround her. The exception is Elisabeth Shue's lively Jenny Cadine, an artiste at a music hall where Bette is employed as a costumer. (The two women become fast friends when Bette exposes Jenny's admirable derriere in one outfit.)

It's Paris, 1846, and France is heading toward revolution, and you can be sure that Bette is one person who'll be able to take that in stride when it arrives. Life for the 40ish Bette has been one long affront. As a child, she was treated like Cinderella without the fairy godmother while her cousin Adeline (Geraldine Chaplin) was pampered and groomed to marry well. ("A family like ours could only push forward one girl," says a tight-lipped Bette.)

When Adeline dies, her widower Hector (Hugh Laurie), a rake who's running through the family fortune, leads Bette to believe he's proposing marriage—only to ask her to stay on as housekeeper for his Parisian palace, vast enough for a Bourbon. Such indignities dog Bette until she at last feels driven to turn the tables.

The charm of this "Cousin Bette," which plays emotion against the artifice of a grand theatrical style of speech and gesture, lies in the fact that while Bette sets those who have wronged her on a course of disaster, they really are responsible for their fates in all their self-absorbed, featherbrained foolishness. If they possessed an ounce of self-knowledge or perception, they might pick up the tinge of bitter irony in so many of Bette's remarks.

And if Bette is no monster—we sympathize fully with her every move—neither are her victims. They're in fact rather likably shallow: Hector wouldn't intentionally hurt a fly, and the starving yet lazy sculptor, Wenceslas (Aden Young), captures not only Bette's heart but also that of Hector's silly daughter Hortense (Kelly Macdonald) and even apparently that of the hard-headed Jenny Cadine, Hector's mistress. The worthiest of the men in Bette's world is the plain-spoken Crevel (Bob Hoskins), who says he values money above all else yet proves a loyal friend to Hector.

Although the elegant, highly formal world of "Cousin Bette" seems remote from ours, its truths are timeless: the price of self-involvement can spell disaster not only for the individual but also society at large; the only person on which you can ever truly rely is yourself in a world where ultimately you are alone. All this is familiar wisdom, and McAnuff was wise to approach Balzac with tongue slightly in cheek. The point of his "Cousin Bette" is that its dissection of human frailties be fun.

At first you have the feeling that Shue might not get to shine as brightly as Lange, but she gradually comes to the fore as the film unfolds. Through the friendship of Bette and Jenny, so unlikely on the surface, we're able to see the precariousness of the position of women at the time.

This graceful, effervescent and amusingly arch "Cousin Bette" is, amid its catalog of human follies, more about endurance than revenge.

NEW STATESMAN, 9/18/98, p. 39, Gerald Kaufman

This movie is of greater value [the reference is to *Men With Guns*] than pictures costing 20 times as much—films, for example, like, *Cousin Bette*, an adaptation from Balzac ("the Jackie Collins of the French Revolution" is the learned literary comparison emanating from joint-producer and scriptwriter Susan Tarr) which comes under the category of Hollywood-tasteful.

Set in 1840s Paris, this tale deals with the complex and comprehensive revenge inflicted by spinster Bette (Jessica Lange, all smirks and grimaces, in a role Bette Davis would have killed for) on her young cousin Hortense (Kelly Macdonald, pouting prettily but a long way from her success in *Trainspotting*) for stealing the love of Bette's life, an artist named Count Wenceslas (Aden Young, pouting prettily but a long way from his native Australia). Young speaks in a generic Eastern European accent. Kelly Macdonald speaks in BBC standard English. Our beloved Bob Hoskins, as "the richest man in Paris", is an Englishman who plays a Frenchman speaking, for some incomprehensible reason, in an American accent. The rolling credits at the end of the film (which concludes with a final, triumphant smirk from Jessica Lange) pay proper tribute to a "Cordon Bleu Consultant".

NEW YORK POST, 6/12/98, p. 46, Thelma Adams

If Honore de Balzac's "Cousin Bette" had met Jane Austen's sunlit "Emma" on a transcontinental voyage, the old spinster would have plucked the young girl's feathers, spun her around for a lark and sent her off to marry the most wretched suitor.

Balzac (1799-1850) tore into novels like day-old bread tossed at a starving man. The Frenchman escaped poverty with "The Human Comedy," a darkly funny postmortem on post-Napoleonic France that included novels and short stories.

At its simplest, the 1845 novel "Cousin Bette" is about vengeance. Bette (Jessica Lange) approaches premature old age, bitter, angry and unloved. She has sacrificed her life to her beautiful cousin, Baroness Adeline (Geraldine Chaplin).

With no independent means, the homely spinster must rely on Adeline's charity. Meanwhile, Adeline's womanizing husband, Baron Hulot (Hugh Laurie), squanders the family fortune on mistresses. The latest is burlesque singer Jenny Cadine (Elisabeth Shue), the spoiled Madonna of her day.

When the baroness dies Bette pounces. With a poor relation's pent-up pain, she schemes to destroy the baron and his unmarried daughter (Kelly Macdonald) and wrest control of the family's fate.

Bette draws Jenny into her plot and does the same with a suicidal sculptor (Aden Young) with an angel's lips and a fruit fly's libido. Crevel (Bob Hoskins), representing new money, also jockeys for position.

It's so wicked I could see Paul ("Showgirls") Verhoven directing with an S & M subtext. Noted stage director Des McAnuff, making his film debut with a script by Lynn Siefert and Susan Tarr, is too nice for this poisonous period piece.

Lange rustles and bustles in black and shakes her arms like a beaten spider, but she's no Amanda Plummer. She can't do ugly. The overrated actress is out of place.

When Cadine exposes her arse on the Paris stage, we're hardly scandalized. Been there. Seen that.

The star is British comedian Laurie ("Sense and Sensibility"). Like a perfect martini, he concocts the right mixture of humor vanity and vanity, and self-pity.

This weak-willed gent ruins his family for the love of a skirt without a single moment of insight or regret—and remains likable. That's the brilliance and folly of Balzac's human comedy!

NEWSDAY, 6/12/98, Part II/p. B11, Jack Mathews

In her most fevered ego-dreams, it's unlikely that Jackie Collins ever saw herself in the company of the 19th-Century French novelist Honoré de Balzac. But there they are, weirdly linked in a quote in the production notes for "Cousin Bette," the very loose, lively and uneven Des McAnuff adaptation of Balzac's last great novel.

In a way, Balzac was the Jackie Collins of the French Revolution, says the film's co-screenwriter Susan Tarr, going on to Tarr Balzac's reputation further by saying: He was scandalous and there is a racy, potboiler quality to his work. He wrote about getting ahead, greed, success, money and revenge.

Well, yes, all those things existed in French society before, during and after the French Revolution, and Balzac wrote about that society with a realist's eye. But his mammoth output, under the collective title "The Human Comedy," was hardly titillation for the masses. His vast array of characters was used to demonstrate how social pressure defines human behavior; he wrote about class conflict and the evil within.

What former film executive Tarr might more accurately have said of the script she co-wrote with Lynn Siefert ("Cool Runnings") is that it was inspired by the modern pop novel. It's a superficial, bawdy, audience-friendly movie without credible social context. It's "Balzac for Dummies."

As scandal, however, it works pretty well. Jessica Lange may be hard to accept as any family's ugly duckling, but as the vindictive Bette Fisher, a poor relation to the aristocratic Hulots, she's a marvelous soap-opera vixen. And Elisabeth Shue, as the actress-singer-courtesan Jenny Cadine, reveals—among other things—a fine touch for sexual farce.

This telling of "Cousin Bette" (it was previously done as a BBC Miniseries) has a convenient two-act structure. The first act establishes Bette as a sacrificing, unfulfilled seamstress whose final hopes for a better life are dashed by one major rejection and one spectacular betrayal.

First, her dead cousin's husband, the philandering Hector (Hugh Laurie), asks her to become his housekeeper rather than his wife. Then, Hector's teenage daughter Hortense (Kelly Macdonald) steals from her the handsome artist Wenceslas (Aden Young), whose career and affections Bette had been attempting, with her meager resources, to nurture.

Now, Bette's mad as a hornet and out to destroy both the Hulots and Wenceslas, setting one after another of her enemies against each other, often with the help of the opportunistic Jenny Cadine, whose friendship Bette had earned while designing costumes to show off the vain star's finest asset (Jenny's derriere is constantly exposed on stage).

McAnuff obviously knows his way around a theater, and he's imbued the stage and backstage scenes with great energy, humor and affection. The last shot in the movie, from a stage production that features several endings at once, is priceless.

But McAnuff is equally adept at composing the landscape of Paris, circa 1840s, contrasting the narrow cobblestone streets of Bette's smothering neighborhood with the fading elegance of the Hulot's mansion. And there are able performances at every position.

Laurie creates an earnestly befuddled Hector, whose love for Jenny, his longtime mistress, puts his entire estate at risk. And Bob Hoskins, borrowing George C. Scott's voice, is terrific as the wealthy vulgarian Crevel, who believes—as the rich often do, even outside Balzac's world—that money can buy anything.

SIGHT AND SOUND, 9/98, p. 41, Douglas MacCabe

Paris 1846. Adeline Hulot, the wife of philandering Baron Hector Hulot, dies. Adeline's cousin Bette, a seamstress for singing star Jenny Cadine, rejects Hector's offer to become his housekeeper (she'd hoped to become his wife). Bette saves the life of Wenceslas, a starving sculptor who lives upstairs from her, and tries to take control of his life. Intrigued by Bette's stories of Wenceslas, Hector's teenage daughter Hortense meets him in secret. Wenceslas visits Hector to ask for permission to court Hortense and Hector arranges for Wenceslas to be commissioned to make a bronze statue of the baron's uncle. When Bette discovers that Wenceslas and Hortense are having an affair, she plans her revenge.

Seven months later, Wenceslas and Hortense are married and have a baby, but Wenceslas flirts with other women. The statue is considered a disaster when it is finally unveiled and Hector demands that Wenceslas pay back the commission he's already spent. Hortense approaches a former suitor, Mayor Crevel, to borrow the money from him. He agrees, but Bette intercepts the cash.

In the meantime Bette persuades Wenceslas that he should approach Jenny for support. Wenceslas and Jenny become lovers, just as Bette had planned. Bette lures Hortense and Hector to a Paris hotel with a fake letter and they find Jenny and Wenceslas in bed together. Hortense steals Hector's gun to shoot Jenny but accidentally shoots Wenceslas. Six months later, Bette is seen taking care of Wenceslas and Hortense's son.

Written in 1846, *La Cousine Bette* was the first part of the culmination of Honoré de Balzac's ambitious cycle of almost 100 novels, *La Comédie Humaine*. Profoundly cynical but extremely funny, it draws on dozens of characters to tell an enthralling revenge story set against an intricate portrait of what Balzac saw as the debauched society of contemporary Paris. The plot centres on two generations of the aristocratic Hulot family, the decline of which eerily shadows the nation's social and political upheavals. The tone and general outline of *Cousin Bette*, a solid adaptation by theatre director and playwright Des McAnuff, won't offend literary purists. Though his screenwriters Lynn Siefert and Susan Tarr have stripped the story back to the bare bones—impecunious seamstress Bette vengefully schemes against her cousins, the patronising Hulot family—McAnuff competently fleshes out the novel's ironies, such as the shifting fates of the characters and the backfiring effects of snobbery.

Balzac's style is theatrical and melodramatic, and McAnuff sticks to the conventions of such costume dramas about sordid French aristocracies as *Dangerous Liaisons* and *Ridicule*. Although *Cousin Bette* is not as well executed as these two, it has a feel for the subtleties of its genre. Indeed, the film paints a hilarious picture of a wretched society from the opening shots. At the deathbed of his wife, Hector apologises to her for having had so many affairs, her doctor demands his payment, and Bette unconvincingly denies that she had tried to drown the baroness many years before. ("It was an accident.") At the funeral, Hector lusts after a friend of the family and Mayor Crevel is later found drooling over the baroness' teenage daughter Hortense. In seemingly every early scene, a young woman cries uncontrollably at the edge of the shot.

McAnuff and his photographer Andrzej Sekula (*Reservoir Dogs, Pulp Fiction*) exploit every opportunity to apply exaggerated lighting: bright for the dim but sly Hortense; darker than dark for her spiteful cousin Bette. However, it is Jessica Lange's incongruously deadpan performance as Bette which brings these self-conscious dramatic devices to life. Dressed in black and with dark marble eyes you have to struggle to see in her dingy room, she is a baleful human presence in an inhuman world. The irony is that the other characters are blissfully unaware of her spiteful intentions, especially since she never cries or expresses her emotions apart from two or three occasions. Lange is unlikely to play a role that will attract less attention than this one, yet her physical embodiment of Balzac's description is uncanny and without her the film would be too hysterical and emotionally vapid.

Unfortunately, *Cousin Bette*'s repetitiveness weakens it in its second half as Bette attempts to manipulate and control ever more complex situations. Almost all of the book's background characters (and therefore the professional, political and social worlds they inhabit) have been removed, so there is nothing to relieve the relentless family conflict. Neither is there any attempt to make sense of the Hulot family's financial and social downfall. One of the most important and moving scenes shows Jenny and Bette bonding over the fact that they both come from the country rather than the city. Bette's origins are what separates her from her cousins and causes them to "sacrifice" her, yet the same origins are what makes Jenny alluring to cosmopolitan society.

Regrettably, this theme (which should also involve the Pole Wenceslas) is never adequately explored and so both of these relationships become a bald expression of Bette's malevolent personality. Given more time, say in a television adaptation over several episodes, Bette could have been shown to be a complex monster surviving in a complex world.

TIME, 6/22/98, p. 69, Richard Schickel

Bette is the country cousin those aristocratic ninnies the Hulots patronize, exploit and fatally underestimate. They think she's plain (the one aspect of this character that Jessica Lange can't quite convince us of), they know she's repressed, and they seem to feel she's not quite bright.

What savage fun it is to see her wreak revenge on this superbly cast chateau of sublimely overconfident fools.

For by the end of this marvelously complex, wickedly comic adaptation of Honoré de Balzac's schoolroom classic, she has brought them all to ruin—the philandering father (Hugh Laurie), the spoiled daughter (Kelly MacDonald), the clueless son (Toby Stephens) and, for good measure, a self-absorbed young sculptor (Aden Young) who takes her generosity for granted, not realizing that she loves him. She spares only Elisabeth Shue's actress-courtesan, partly because she too is socially unacceptable, partly because she is so useful as the seductress Bette needs to bring off her schemes.

It's not clear how deeply she has preplanned them and how much they are inspired responses to the shifting circumstances of her shiftless victims. But in a day when intricate plotting has become a lost art, one of Cousin Bette's great pleasures is its capacity to plausibly surprise. It's not its only pleasure. Lange's work is wonderfully controlled, her hidden passions expressed with glancing delicacy. And stage director Des McAnuff, making a smashing film debut, subtly poises the endless, deadly ironies of this tale against the efficiently suggested feverishness of Paris just prior to the revolution of 1848. Rarely has a period film spoken with such energy and immediacy to our impatient modernism.

VILLAGE VOICE, 6/16/98, p. 160, Leslie Camhi

Bette Davis rather than Balzac seems to have been the inspiration for this adaptation of Cousin Bette, the gripping novel that's but a chip in his multivolume social mosaic, La Comédie humaine. Director Des McAnuff and screenwriters Lynn Siefert and Susan Tarr have played fast and loose with plot, streamlining a complex tale of aristocratic decrepitude, middle-class hypocrisy, and demimonde ambition into a latter-day feminist fable of jealousy and vengeance.

A serpentine Jessica Lange plays Bette, a poor, unmarried woman of 40 who's always lived in the shadow of her beautiful cousin Adeline. Twenty years earlier, Adeline married a Baron (Hugh Laurie); when the film opens she's dying and makes Bette promise to look after Hortense (Kelly Macdonald), her spoiled, pretty daughter. Bette instead returns to her job as costumier at a musical theater,where she befriends Jenny Cadine (Elizabeth Shue), an actress and the Baron's mistress. Love (the unreciprocated variety) finally arrives in the form of her neighbor Wenceslas (Aden Young), a starving young Polish sculptor. But spurned and betrayed, Bette makes Jenny the agent of her revenge. Bette is the motor of Balzac's brilliant novel; the pleasure she takes in destruction is the flip side of both an artist's creative energy and women's procreative function. Lange makes this marvelous character's power almost Medean. Macdonald is perfect as the insuperable Hortense, as is Bob Hoskins in the role of a ridiculous and wealthy ex-perfumer. The problem lies with Jenny, whose character has been cobbled together from several of the Baron's mistresses, including the splendidly sinister and sophisticated Madame Marneffe. Shue seems unconvincing as the embodiment of Old World perversion; so does the filmmakers' approach to whoredom as good, clean, profitable fun.

So see Cousin Bette for its fine dialogue, hilarious vulgarity, galloping plot, and the guilty pleasure of watching a powerful female character get away with murder. Just don't mistake it for literature or history.

Also reviewed in:
CHICAGO TRIBUNE, 6/12/98, Friday/p. A, John Petrakis
NEW REPUBLIC, 7/6/98, p. 28, Stanley Kauffmann
NEW YORK TIMES, 6/12/98, p. E14, Stephen Holden
VARIETY , 6/8-14/98, p. 68, Leonard Klady
WASHINGTON POST, 6/26/98, p. B5, Rita Kempley
WASHINGTON POST, 6/26/98, Weekend/p. 47, Michael O'Sullivan

CROSSING FIELDS

A Thalia Theater presentation. *Producer:* James Rosenow and David Hannah. *Director:* James Rosenow. *Screenplay:* James Rosenow. *Director of Photography:* Dejan Georgevich. *Editor:* Angelo Corrao. *Music:* Walter Thompson. *Production Designer:* Kathleen Harding. *Running time:* 101 minutes. *MPAA Rating:* Not Rated.

CAST: Reedy Gibbs (Carol); Gwynyth Walsh (Jessica); William James Jones (James); J.K. Simmons (Guy); Meadow Sisto (Denise).

NEW YORK POST, 11/6/98, p. 70, Bill Hoffmann

Dyed-in-the-wool New Yorkers looking for a fast, breezy trip to a very foreign planet should head straight for the Thalia, where "Crossing Fields" opens today.

No, this quirky independent isn't a high-tech, sci-fi flick, although entering the cloistered world of the Bradley family is like landing on Mars.

Carol Bradley (Reedy Gibbs) is a plumpish, 40-something Midwestern housewife who lives life by the book—the good book.

Life is lily white until Carol takes the bold step of inviting a young, unthreatening African-American man named James (William James Jones) to board so he can save money for college.

The family's most liberal act ever quickly spells doom for their Waltons-like lives.

Mom's all-but-dead libido is slowly reawakened as she watches him doing outdoor chores—his shirtless, pumped-up bod melting away layers of oppressed sex drive.

Of course, she can't do anything about it and has to watch in painful silence as her rebellious teen daughter (Meadow Sisto) and her best friend (Gywnyth Walsh) end up seducing him.

Carol's fury over the affairs soon turns into curiosity, and she and James become close friends. But as her sexual angst grows, she's faced with the inevitable question of will-I-or-won't-I.

Writer/director James Rosenow could've taken the easy way out by using the film to make fun of this little world of silent majority oddballs.

But after a half-hour of letting us laugh at them, Rosenow grinds into high gear, letting the characters explain their quirks. At the end, we're all family. Few films these days have that kind of insight.

A lot of the magic is thanks to Rosenow's highly spirited cast, anchored by Gibbs and Sisto, who are also mother and daughter in real life. Gibbs' feisty yet fragile turn as a tortured matriarch ranks as one of the best female performances of the year.

VILLAGE VOICE, 11/10/98, p. 120, Laurie Stone

Why is fortysomething Jessica (Gwynyth Walsh) screwing all the men in church-going, white-bread Ashton? Everyone knows about the affair her husband's been having but by the lights of this rural, Midwestern enclave, if Jessica were the right kind of wife her spouse wouldn't be straying. While Jess is acting up, James (William James Jones), a young, studly black man comes to board with her best friend, Carol (Reedy Gibbs). James spreads his joy.

Nailing the double standard and sex panic are the missions of writer-director James Rosenow's first feature. The film moves at the snail's pace of life in Ashton, and its promotion of sex, drugs, and rock'n' roll as antidotes to conservative pieties is served like a sex-ed bromide. Nonetheless, interest builds in the central women characters, with Walsh and Gibbs delivering finely tuned performances. Though disappointed by each other, the women are real to one another in ways neither is to anyone else. Rosenow exposes the deprivations of domesticity and shows how, in this world, female friendship is the ongoing, subversive alternative.

Also reviewed in:
NEW YORK TIMES, 11/6/98, p. E15, Lawrence Van Gelder

CRUISE, THE

An Artisan Entertainment release of a Charter Films presentation of a Bennett Miller production. *Executive Producer:* J.B. Miller, Theodore Miller, David Yamner, and David Cohen. *Producer:* Bennet Miller. *Director:* Bennet Miller. *Director of Photography:* Bennett Miller. *Editor:* Michael Levine. *Music:* Marty Beller. *Sound:* David Novack. *Running time:* 76 minutes. *MPAA Rating:* Not Rated.

CAST: Timothy "Speed" Levitch.

LOS ANGELES TIMES, 11/6/98, Calendar/p. 10, Kevin Thomas

If you are lucky, you might land Timothy (Speed) Levitch as your Gray Line tour guide of New York City. Lots of guides can summon the statistics that Levitch can ("The Empire State Building has seven miles of elevators"), but the brilliant and wildly imaginative Levitch—a thin, tousle-haired man of 28 with the utmost passion and intensity—brings a poet and philosopher's vision to his job. He sees the tour as no less than a metaphor for the journey through life and views his relationship to Manhattan and the universe itself in exuberant, cosmic terms.

He frequently uses the term "the Cruise," which he has said that, as a philosophy, means "the pursuit of the fullest amplification of self and the art of crafting moments out of time, while moving in a positive, forward direction." He has defined what he means by "the Anti-Cruise" as "agony and fear trying to justify themselves in our lives, attempting to control what is beautifully out of control."

With his film "The Cruise," documentarian Bennett Miller not only takes us along on Levitch's bus tours and his strolls through the city but also celebrates Levitch's brave spirit, his determined assertion of individuality and self-worth in the face of poverty, loneliness and his family's disappointment in him. At the same time, "The Cruise" is a paean to the glories of the city that Levitch views as a living organism, to which his relationship is in constant flux.

With his poet's metaphysical sensibility, he envisions buildings as being capable of feeling intimidated by more impressive structures and the entire city as collectively capable of making him feel gloomy or upbeat. To him, the city can seem alternately a Cyclops or a mermaid "who sings to me alone."

Levitch's words can soar and his spirit takes flight, but he is well-grounded in the everyday reality of survival below the poverty line. It is wonderful to watch him communicate easily and warmly with co-workers and tourists in plain language, leaving his poetic expressions for his tour spiels and for pouring out his confessions for Miller's camera. There is nothing precious in the sentiments of Levitch, a man who has looked inward deeply in order to look outward more acutely; he is not less aware of people than of buildings, which can transport him to ecstasies. He is an original thinker, constantly speculating on the relationship between the individual and society, between mankind and nature.

His tours, as a result, are gloriously idiosyncratic. A journey on a double-decker bus through Greenwich Village unleashes in him a torrent of names of the great writers and thinkers who lived there, when and where, and in what proximity to one another. A stop at Central Park prompts the observation that since its planners were transcendentalists, they did not intend its use for sports.

He knows full well that only a few tourists can connect with him, yet when two women from Argentina thank him affectionately, despite their shaky grasp of English, he looks back at them as they walk away with the simple pronouncement, "Style"—a quality Levitch and this film have in abundance.

Levitch represents a stand against a consumer-driven, materialistic society that promotes ruthless competition and total self-absorption. No fool, Levitch does not want to end up badly, as his grandparents fear he will. He concludes with a haunting fable about the Baal Shem Tov, the founding figure of Hasidism, and the Lamed-Vavniks, the 36 righteous people on whose shoulders rest the problems of the world. His essential goal, Levitch tells us, is "to be able to extol that I'm thrilled to be alive and still be respected." "The Cruise" validates beautifully a life that is its own validation.

NEW YORK, 11/2/98, p. 119, Peter Rainer

Timothy "SPEED" Levitch is a shambling, homeless, scraggly-haired motormouth who conducts his own free-form New York City Gray Line bus tours. In the documentary "The Cruise," directed by Bennett Miller, we get a full dose of Levitch's nutty spritzes. He can be amusing—as when telling tourists that "the Fulton Fish Market is more an odor than a landmark." He can be helpful: He points out the neighborhood where Dylan Thomas expired. (The bard's last words: "I just had my sixteenth martini.") Miller certainly found a "character" to build a movie around, but there's something Diane Arbus-y in the whole enterprise. Levitch, about whom we learn very little, is a whirling dervish in pain, and the camera's steady, unblinking gaze does him no favors. We don't feel closer to him at the end; we feel farther away. He describes New York as "a scintillating, streamlined mermaid who sings to me at night." We don't hear the song.

NEW YORK POST, 10/23/98, p. 45, Thelma Adams

"The sun, another great New York City landmark, above you on the left," mobile tour guide Timothy (Speed) Levitch tells a double-decker busload of unresponsive Gray Line tourists in Bennett Miller's entertaining black-and-white documentary.

Levitch is a yiddische Spalding Gray, a whiny-voiced monologist who tells his exuberant tales of the city to passing strangers and lives a marginal existence just inches away from the glamorous streets he celebrates.

This self-described "fifth wheel at an orgy" is a philosopher of a kind. His five years of "going in circles" for Gray Line is consistent with his vision of life as a cruise, an ecstatic unfolding of New York's mysteries—sensual, dangerous, ironic.

Miller follows the charismatic Levitch like an acolyte, recording every pithy phrase, every borderline psychotic rant, pausing only to catch a seagull in flight or ogle the Brooklyn Bridge's curves.

While the first-time filmmaker has picked a ripe subject, "The Cruise" would have benefitted from more investigation and less adoration. A segment during which Levitch discusses his prior arrest (complete with mug shot) has a glaring omission: What was the crime?

And would it have hurt to have dropped Levitch's shabby coattails for a moment to talk to his co-workers, friends or, God forbid, his disappointed mama up in Westchester?

NEWSDAY, 10/23/98, Part II/p. B11, John Anderson

Boswell had his Johnson, Richard Ellmann had his Joyce, Woody Allen had Mariel Hemingway, and director Bennett Miller has Timothy (Speed) Levitch, whose expectations for the people he meets along his daily journey are as modest as anyone's. "I expect the total transformation of their life," he says. "The rewriting of their lives..."

Doctor? Therapist? White House intern? No, Levitch's mission, at least within the confines of Miller's invigorating "The Cruise," is guiding tourists through the streets of Manhattan and along his own personal, transcendentalist trek—his "cruise," which traverses the "lascivious eroticism of the tour bus," the "different gradations of cruising manifestations," the wide, wide world of massacred malapropisms and a jazz-improvisational approach to language and perception.

If not quite as original as Levitch himself, "The Cruise" is that oft-unseen thing, a film completely unsellable. How would one pitch a movie about a homeless, adenoidal, often unkempt and occasionally forlorn figure, whose main asset is his stream-of-consciousness, one-sided dialogue with New York City? It can't be done. You simply have to see the movie, after which you will be glad you did.

Levitch is a shrug-shouldered philosopher, but he's also very funny and he knows it, despite the mock-grandiose posturing. One reason Miller's film is so engaging is the intimate way in which it shows all this. Cruising by the World Trade Center, Levitch offers his riders "a good view of commuters running to their destinations... and from themselves," the last bit delivered with theatrical click of the mike and quick spin in place, so the riders can't see him smile.

You learn things from Levitch, sort of: how early maps of the city don't even show Madison Avenue, because it was a service road for Fifth. Or that the population of Manhattan is 2.4 million. ("I heard it was 1.7 million," he confides to his driver, "but I don't care.") His cataloging of Greenwich Village writers and their homes—Poe, Twain, Wharton, O'Henry, Henry Miller, Arthur Miller, John Reed, Max Eastman—is such a rapid-fire spiel it can't possibly be correct, given that he's in a moving vehicle and the directions are so precise. But the performance—and Levitch's life is a performance—is completely seductive.

In one rambling walk around the Flatiron District, Levitch rails against the Manhattan grid plan—the arrangement of streets in numerical, right-angled fashion—which is about as Sisyphean an argument imaginable. But Levitch's passion isn't just for randomness and happenstance, it's against people who accept life's rules and regulations unchallenged. "She said, 'Everybody loves the grid plan,'" he recalls one female customer chirping, inferring that such a statement further isolates him from the mainstream of society. Or society at all. And he's right.

And when he's right he's right. "I think one of the great tragedies of this experience called civilization is the fact that people have to work for a living." It's all part of what Levitch calls the "anti-cruise" and his resistance is inspiring. As is the film.

NEWSWEEK, 11/2/98, p. 78, Jack Kroll

"The Cruise" is a long days journey into urban weirdness. The cruiser is Timothy (Speed) Levitch, a 28-year-old New York tour guide and home-grown existentialist prophet who spritzes mad odes about the city and his own psychic demons to busloads of tourists. Bennett Miller's documentary is a sharp portrait of a true original. Microphone in hand, Levitch spews forth evocations of New York's splendors and miseries. He points out the house where Tom Paine died, another where Garbo loved to be alone, the place where Dylan Thomas spoke his last words: "I just had my 16th martini." With his Jewish afro, his whiny but eloquent voice, Levitch is a nutty mix of Harpo Marx and Allen Ginsberg. Against Miller's vivid obligato of towers and bridges, he rants about his bad acne, his family, his treacherous friends. Creepy but unforgettable, there's clearly only one future for him—mayor of New York.

VILLAGE VOICE, 10/17/98, p. 140, Amy Taubin

Perhaps I wouldn't have despised Bennett Miller's *The Cruise* so much had I not seen it two days after *Lenny Bruce*. Its subject, Timothy "Speed" Levitch—monologuist and guide to New York City, who makes double-decker buses his performance-art venues and their tourist-passengers his captive audience—seems to fancy himself a mix of Abbie Hoffman and Bruce, but he lacks their intelligence and courage, not to mention their brilliant manipulation of language. Levitch—whose principal targets are his mother (when his rant turned gynecological, I nearly left the theater) and fans of Manhattan's "grid pattern"—is one of those irritating people who believe that words can man anything they want them to mean at the moment they spring to their lips.

Shot in digital-8 video and transferred to 35mm, *The Cruise* looks like black-and-white newsprint photos in motion. Miller seems to have worked hard to make the image look clean and professional, which, given his subject, seems exactly the wrong choice. *The Cruise* is being hailed as a harbinger of a future in which indie film will be liberated by low-cost technology. If this is where we're going, I want off the bus.

Also reviewed in:
CHICAGO TRIBUNE, 11/20/98, Friday/p. F, John Petrakis
NEW YORK TIMES, 10/23/98, p. E22, Stephen Holden
VARIETY, 4/20-26/98, p. 46, Todd McCarthy

CUBE

A Trimark Pictures and The Feature Fim Project release of a Cuba Libre production with the participation of Telefilm Canada/Ontario Film Development Corporation/The Harold Greenberg Fund/Viacom Canada. *Executive Producer:* Colin Brunton. *Producer:* Mehra Meh and Betty Orr. *Director:* Vincenzo Natali. *Screenplay:* Andre Bijelic, Vincenzo Natali, and Graeme Manson. *Director of Photography:* Derek Rogers. *Editor:* John Sanders. *Music:* Mark Korven.

Sound: Steve McNamee.   *Sound Editor:* Steve Barden, Craig Henighan, and Jill Purdy.
Casting: Deidre Bowen.   *Production Designer:* Jasna Stefanovic.   *Art Director:* Diana Magnus.
Special Effects: Louise Mackintosh, Ray Mackintosh, and Russell Cate.   *Costumes:* Wendy May
Moore. *Make-up:* Louise Mackintosh. *Stunt Coordinator:* John Stoneham, Jr.   *Running time:*
91 minutes. *MPAA Rating:* R.

CAST: Nicole de Boer (Leaven);   Nicky Guadagni (Holloway);   David Hewlett (Worth);
Andrew Miller (Kazan); Julian Richings (Alderson); Wayne Robson (Rennes); Maurice Dean
Wint (Quentin).

LOS ANGELES TIMES, 9/11/98, Calendar/p. 17, Kevin Thomas

Imagine a square cage, 14 by 14 feet, covered on all sides by what looks to be translucent
panels with geometric Art Deco designs. This is the space in which Canadian filmmaker Vincenzo
Natali has trapped six people in his highly ambitious and cerebral sci-fi thriller "Cube," a
veritable nightmare of a movie.

Even though there are tedious stretches with less-than-riveting characters, the film gradually
pulls you into its claustrophobic spell and becomes acutely suspenseful in its final half-hour.
"Cube" was named best Canadian debut feature at Toronto last year, and there's no questioning
Natali, clearly a visionary, is an important new talent.

The six people are Leaven (Nicole de Boer), a young math whiz; Holloway (Nicky Guadagni),
a middle-aged female physician; Worth (David Hewlett), a technologist with a dark secret; Rennes
(Wayne Robson), an escaped convict; Kazan (Andrew Miller), a young autistic savant; and
Quentin (Maurice Dean Wint), a policeman. None of them knows how they got into the cube,
but each may possess a skill, if everyone is willing to cooperate—a big "if," given human
nature—that may enable them to escape.

The cube possesses massive steel doors in the center of all its sides, which slide open with
the turn of a large handle. Soon it becomes apparent that the six are trapped in a veritable maze of
similar cubes, each of which seems to be equipped with sensors that can trip all manner of lethal
devices. The understandable terror that engulfs the six leads to personality clashes, which while
completely credible, are nonetheless predictable and tiresome.

"Cube" really kicks in when Leaven starts trying to figure out the meaning of the serial numbers
engraved on the lower sill of each of the doorways. Even if your grasp of mathematics is tentative
at best you can understand that she may be on to something.

A storyboard artist with "Johnny Mnemonic" among his credits, Natali has made several short
films, including "Elevated" (1996), in which three people, trapped in an elevator, are menaced
by an unseen force. Natali wisely avoids explaining who constructed the cube maze or why these
six people were selected to be placed in it, playing on our fears of claustrophobia and powerful
unknown forces.

Natali has had a major assist from his production designer Jasna Stefanovic, a master at creating
an elegant but menacingly high-tech environment; his resourceful cinematographer Derek Rogers;
and his composer Mark Korven, whose score adds just the right subtly unsettling note. Among
the characters only Leaven becomes fully engaging, and the cast, short on charisma and
personality, is merely competent. (Think of how distinctive and involving the people, caught in
a somewhat similar predicament, were in Robert Wise's "The Andromeda Strain" without being
"movie stars.")

Sci-fi fans, however, are not likely to be disappointed by "Cube." It is worth noting that "Cube"
is the fifth production of the Feature Film Project, which was launched four years ago by the
Canadian Film Center, a training institution founded in 1986 by Canada-born director Norman
Jewison.

NEW YORK POST, 9/11/98, p. 68, Larry Worth

At one point in "Cube," a character assumes he's in hell. If so, he's no worse off than audience
members.

This pointless sci-fi-cum-horror knockoff is not only derivative of TV's "Twilight Zone" and "The Prisoner," but provides an embarrassing Pirandello parody, kind of like "Six Characters in Search of a Movie Plot."

What passes for a script concerns six strangers who wake up inside a giant cube, equipped with many escape hatches into identical cubes. But the problem, the sextet quickly discovers, is that some doors lead to booby-traps.

Within minutes, one hapless adventurer passes through the portal into a nigh-invisible razor-sharp net, only to collapse into a pile of perfectly square-shaped body parts. Clearly, colleagues should proceed at their own risk.

Ditto for filmgoers. Writer-director Vincent Natali not only makes his protagonists into contrasting stereotypes (Joe Fascist vs. Joanne Liberal, math wiz vs. idiot savant, etc.) but lets things get redundant within 15 minutes.

The performers—all unknowns, and likely to remain so—do nothing to up the interest ante. In fact, the only real credit goes to intriguing set designs and some momentarily amusing gobbledygook about algebraic formulas.

But that's hardly a recommendation. The bottom line: "Cube" equals boredom squared.

NEWSDAY, 9/11/98, Part II/p. B6, John Anderson

As a strictly technical exercise, "Cube" is a square deal. Reportedly shot in less than a month, inside a single, 14 x 14 set, it's an impressive looking sci-fi thriller that was voted Best Canadian Feature Debut at last year's Toronto Film Festival and constitutes a nice resume line for both director Vincenzo Natali and Canada's Feature Film Project.

However: The set-up is essentially that of Sartre's "No Exit" that jocular, existential romp in the park in which three not entirely pleasant characters find themselves locked up together in an inescapable place. In "Cube," the characters number six and the captor is some vague political oppressor. But with no hope offered in either work, the setting is essentially Hell—be it man-made or theological.

And, frankly, I don't want to go to Hell, not really, not in virtual reality, not even for an hour and a half. It takes the audience for Natali's melodramatically acted movie a lot less time than it takes his characters to figure out what's going on, and by the time they do, the word EXIT starts to read like THIS WAY TO THE FREE BUFFET.

Like the considerably more engaging indie "Pi," "Cube" is a math-based thriller; clues, all of them bogus, lie in the sequence and numbering of the various cubes traversed by our characters in their search for a way out. All the travelers have particular talents and backgrounds, but their makeup seems a bit too heavy handed and ought-to-be-conscience-stricken.

The overbearing Quentin (Maurice Dean Wint) is/was a police officer and appoints himself to leadership of the group. His natural antagonist, Holloway (Nicky Guadagni), worked as a doctor at a free clinic and carries a fat liberal chip on her shoulder ("Only the government could build something this ugly," she mutters about the cube system). Leaven (Toronto-based actress Nicole de Boer, who's quite good) is an upper-crusty kid with a very useful gift for mathematics. Worth (David Hewlett), a techie, was somehow involved in the building of the cubes; Kazan (Andrew Miller) is an autistic youth who's presence seems diabolically calculated to thwart whatever progress the group manages to make.

Frankly, you're not rooting for them all that much. Which is a good thing. Let's just say that, for a six-character, four-sided enterprise, "Cube's" journey into artificial anguish is much too one-dimensional.

SIGHT AND SOUND, 11/98, p. 44, Philip Strick

Two women (Leaven and Holloway) and three men (Quentin, Worth and Rennes) find themselves trapped in a maze of adjoining cubical rooms, many containing deadly traps. Needing to escape before they starve, Quentin, a cop, and Rennes, a jailbreak expert, lead them from room to room, testing each one before they enter it. Despite their caution, Rennes is killed. Leaven, a maths student, works out that the numbers on each threshold indicate which rooms contain traps. Soon they are joined by the autistic Kazan, whose gift for mental arithmetic is later helpful.

When Quentin is wounded in a supposedly 'safe' room, the reliability of the numbers becomes questionable. Worth reveals he's one of the maze's designers; he has no idea who commissioned the structure or why, but he helps Leaven reinterpret the numbers. They find a room with an outside wall, looking out on vertiginous blackness. Making a clothes rope, they lower Holloway on an exploratory descent. When everything shakes violently, Quentin allows Holloway to fall into the pit below.

Quentin becomes violent, so Leaven and Worth knock him out and abandon him. They find Rennes' body where they left it and assume they have been going in circles. Then they realise that the rooms themselves have been shifting and will eventually return them to the exit point. When they reach the escape room, Quentin attacks them but is crushed between the sliding cubes. Worth and Leaven are fatally injured, but Kazan steps out into the light.

Much of the fascination of *Cube* derives from its opening, an unforeseeable dice-with-death encounter: an instant fragmentation by a network of razor-wire. Enough to unsettle the audience for a good hour or so, it is an effective warning of what awaits the rest of the cast if they put a foot wrong. It also prompts admiration for a special-effects masterstroke. And what, we may wonder, happens to the residual bits and pieces? Does some kind of room service clean up each cubicle or are the remains left to rot?

If, as we are later led to believe, the giant cube contains hundreds of such slaughter sites shunting and sliding in perpetual rearrangement, they would surely—thanks to their noxious contents—soon become easy to avoid by future explorers. Conversely, since the prisoners we meet in the cube doesn't find any other corpses, we may theorise that the cruel maze has only recently been put in motion. Clues as to the origin and purpose of the structure are so sparse that *Cube* makes considerable headway as a mystery yarn before it becomes plain that no answer is forthcoming, or even relevant.

Even so, the idea that the cube might be an alien construction, although sensibly dismissed by the prisoners for lack of evidence, does have its attractions, linking the film to a whole range of recent man versus-puzzle contests in such films as *Contact, Sphere* and *Event Horizon*. There are echoes here, too, of *Alien* and its crew, whittled away by the unknown into the endless anterooms of space, and of the *Star Trek* crew's struggle with the Borg who seek to contain the universe within a malevolent geometry. Adding to the fun, the plot is teasingly tricked out with allusions to three-dimensional Cartesian co-ordinates, with handy theosophical connections. From this perspective, the only other main 'meaning' for *Cube* lies somewhere between metaphysics, symbolism and sheer bravado.

Vincenzo Natali's first feature extends the theme of an earlier short, *Elevated,* about three people under threat in a jammed lift. Co-written with Andre Bijelic, *Cube* became, Natali states in the press notes, "a nightmare version of the circumstances of our own lives: we were room mates entombed in our little apartment." He likens the characters' experience to that of ants "in a world of giants," never understanding "the forces that push and pull you through life." Interpreted on this basis as existential melodrama, *Lord of the Flies* in the manner of David Lynch, *Cube* heads for its final blaze of white—which could be birth, death or freedom according to taste—with only its players and its visual skills for protection.

Bearing vaguely prison-related labels Leaven/worth, Holloway, (San) Quentin the characters need all the script they can get and earnestly make what they can of the mostly irritable exchanges provided. Although some weight can be expected from the seasoned Wayne Robson (whose screen career began in *McCabe & Mrs. Miller,* 1971), and some promise is shown by Nicole de Boer, they hardly achieve more depth than cyphers in a video game. The cop who begins as a confident organiser but who becomes increasingly violent and irrational is a particularly unhelpful illustration of the film's mood of anti-authoritarian complaint.

But if the cast resorts to little better than owlish expressions of disapproval and a great deal of shouting, the assurance with which Natali and his team have turned a single 14 foot-square enclosure into a near infinite vista of calculated menace deserves plenty of praise. That *Cube* was shot in less than a month is equally remarkable. It feels, appropriately, closer to a lifetime.

Also reviewed in:
NEW YORK TIMES, 9/11/98, p. E24, Anita Gates
VARIETY, 10/20-26/97, p. 73, Ken Eisner

DANCE WITH ME

A Columbia Pictures release of a Mandalay Entertainment presentation of a Weissman/Egawa production. *Executive Producer:* Ted Zachary. *Producer:* Lauren C. Weissman, Shinya Egawa, and Randa Haines. *Director:* Randa Haines. *Screenplay:* Daryl Matthews. *Director of Photography:* Fred Murphy. *Editor:* Lisa Fruchtman. *Music:* Michael Convertino. *Music Editor:* Daryl Kell. *Choreographer:* Liz Curtis and Daryl Matthews. *Sound:* David Ronne and (music) Dave Marquette and Shawn Murphy. *Sound Editor:* John Nutt. *Casting:* Lora Kennedy. *Production Designer:* Waldemar Kalinowski. *Art Director:* Barry M. Kingston. *Set Decorator:* Florence Fellman. *Set Dresser:* Lauren Lustig, Tom Gebr, Hunter Cain, Jeff Hay, Jim Jackson, and Alan Burg. *Special Effects:* Stan Parks. *Costumes:* Joe I. Tompkins. *Make-up:* Rick Sharp. *Make-up (Vanessa Williams):* Kate Best. *Running time:* 126 minutes. *MPAA Rating:* PG.

CAST: Vanessa L. Williams (Ruby Sinclair); Chayanne (Rafael); Kris Kristofferson (John); Joan Plowright (Bea); Jane Krakowski (Patricia); Beth Grant (Lovejoy); Harry Groener (Michael); William Marquez (Stefano); Scott Paetty (Steve); Rick Valenzuela (Julian); Chaz Oswill (Peter); Liz Curtis (Kim); Bill Applebaum (Don Harrington); Angelo Pagan (Cuban Mailman); Victor Marcel (Fernando); Ana Sofia Pomales (Fernando's Daughter); Nelson Marquez (Fiance); Mike Gomez (Bartender); Charles Venturi (Waiter); Maurice Schwartzman (Man in Dance Club); Janette Valenzuela (Woman in Dance Club); Jim Mapp (Fisherman on Pier); Robert Pike Daniel (Emcee).

LOS ANGELES TIMES, 8/21/98, Calendar/p. 10, Jack Mathews

[The following review by Jack Mathews appeared in a slightly different form in **NEWSDAY, 8/21/98, Part II/p. B7.]**

At one of the many moments of precious insight in Randa Haines' "Dance With Me," Rafael, a handsome young Cuban cleaning mirrors in a Houston studio asks Ruby, the professional dancer he admires, how she can practice her steps without music. It's a routine, honed through repetition, she explains.

"But dance comes from the music; it tells you what to do," Rafael protests, adding impertinently, "That's probably why you look so stiff."

Besides setting up the film's romantic conflict, that exchange cues the film's raison d'etre, the notion that true dance is inspired, not learned, and that music is the door to the soul, or something like that. It also provides the film's greatest irony: It's not Ruby who's stiff—far from it, she's played by the graceful, stunning Vanessa L. Williams—it's the movie.

Haines, reportedly a salsa club aficionado, with a script written by the film's head choreographer, Daryl Matthews, is working on a film that its investors must have envisioned as a serious major studio version of Baz Luhrmann's "Strictly Ballroom." But the spontaneity of that imported Australian hit—the same self-esteem-through-musical-abandon theme that made subsequent hits of "The Full Monty" and "Shall We Dance?"—is missing here, smothered by the script's incessant cliches and Haines' deliberate direction. "Dance" can't dance.

There's plenty of dancing in it, along with a zesty Latin soundtrack. The musical backdrop for the story is an international ballroom dance championship in Las Vegas, for which the amateurs and professionals at Excelsior's, a small studio run by former dance champ John Burnett (Kris Kristofferson), have just 30 days to prepare.

Ruby, whose specialty is Latin dance, is numero uno at Excelsior's, hoping for a return to the glory that was—six years ago—when she and her former partner and lover Julian (Rick Valenzuela) won the world title. Julian's still a winner, still an egomaniac, while Ruby's raising their son alone and struggling with a new partner (Broadway star Harry Groener).

Enter Rafael (Puerto Rican recording star Chayanne), the son of John Burnett's onetime Cuban partner, who's come to live with Burnett and work at Excelsior's. Rafael's got the native beat and Latin heat; you can tell by the tongues hanging out of the mouths of the older women at Excelsior's, whose most rambunctious spice girl is played by a clowning Joan Plowright.

From Rafael and Ruby's testy exchange on the dance floor, the sparks continue flying between them. But the pain of her last romance boosts her resistance to his advances, even after he shows her the time of her life at a salsa club and, in the spray of a sprinkler system on the way home, does a clunky but spirited impression of Gene Kelly singing in the rain.

All of Haines' previous films have focused on people overcoming obstacles to connect with each other. In "Children of a Lesser God," it was a teacher falling in love with a deaf student. In "The Doctor," it was two cancer patients. In "Wrestling Ernest Hemingway," it was an elderly pair whose only reason for becoming friends was their shared loneliness.

"Dance With Me" follows suit, in a fashion. Before they can connect, Rafael and Ruby have to get over some terrible cliches placed in their path by Matthews' dreadfully predictable script. Talk about dancing without music: Ruby's got the my-man-done-me-wrong-single-mama-blues, and Rafael and John Burnett have to work out a problem whose obviousness would embarrass a soap opera writer.

Throughout the film, Haines treats these banal moments as epiphanies, telegraphing every feeling and thought with annoying coyness. There's so much brooding going on with Ruby, Rafael and Kristofferson's character, a sulking loner who prefers midnight pier fishing to the music that once set him free, you begin to listen for a Latin dirge.

Inevitably, the entourage will get to Las Vegas, and they'll hear the music. But the movie itself never finds a rhythm.

NEW YORK POST, 8/21/98, p. 65, Thelma Adams

When defrocked Miss America Vanessa Williams says "Dance with Me," Puerto Rican singing sensation Chayanne listens. Who wouldn't? Ever since "Soul Food," the multi-talented Williams has become the sister most likely to crack a whip.

Williams and Chayanne do the older woman, younger man tango in Randa Haines' nostalgic dance movie. Call it "How Vanessa Got Her Groove Back."

Williams plays Ruby, a name straight from the Ann Miller era. Dumped by pro dance partner Julian (Rick Valenzuela), the sulky single mom teaches the two-step at a rundown Texas studio. The even crankier John (Kris Kristofferson) owns the dive where Bea (evergreen Joan Plowright) rhumbas away her Social Security checks.

Along comes Cuban emigre Rafael (Chayanne) like a breath of fresh cigar smoke. He kisses Castro goodbye to seek father John (who doesn't know he has a son) and "werk een Amerika."

The Latin superstar does his best Ricky Ricardo. Rarely has a grown man so sexy been expected to be so passive. With his thick black hair and restless spit curls, his grease monkey pecs and shoulders, he's a Latin Kowalkski crying babaloo. No matter what Ruby and John toss his way, he smiles constantly, like a nervous headwaiter.

We don't need to know how to samba (like head choreographer and screenwriter Daryl Matthews) to realize that Rafael will awaken Ruby's inner rhythms and touch the heart of his jaded pop. In the spirit of "Strictly Ballroom," the movie is about losers becoming winners by dancing to the beat of their own hearts.

After 90 minutes of soap opera, "Dance" finally finds its footing in the big Vegas dance finale with showstoppers by Plowright, Chayanne, Williams and the villainous Valenzuela. But, by the time Vanessa gets her groove back, any dancer worth her cha-cha-cha would have already left the floor with Chayanne. Babaloo!

SIGHT AND SOUND, 5/99, p. 44, Kay Dickinson

Santiago, Cuba, the present. After his mother's death Rafael takes up a job offer from John, one of his mother's old friends, as a handy-man in John's friendly, ramshackle dance studio in Texas. Here he meets Ruby, a professional dancer who has a son by her arrogant former dance partner Julian. Ruby and Rafael gradually build a relationship, Rafael slowly coaxing from Ruby a warmth and naturalness lacking in her emotional life and her choreography. Rafael's temperament also benefits the studio's other dancers, one of whom he agrees to partner in a Las Vegas dance competition they have all been working towards.

In a last-ditch attempt to provide her son with a father and to further her dance career, Ruby teams up with Julian again for the contest. While the dance school's competitors enjoy performing in Las Vegas and even carry off a few trophies, Ruby finds her and Julian's eventual victory hollow. She declines a job offer in Chicago to return to John's studio, which is transformed under her and Rafael's influence. John finally admits that he is Rafael's mysterious absentee father.

By now the word 'salsa' is as likely to conjure images of a night on the town with a gaggle of British librarians as it is to make us think of ballroom dancing's glitzy pizazz. *Dance with Me* hawks the 'see the movie, buy the soundtrack, learn the steps' experience of this burgeoning middle-class craze. The spangled campness of its most obvious precedent, *Strictly Ballroom* is replaced by a sweet earnestness that caters particularly for Latin-dance neophytes.

The film's coy romantic protagonists—US-born Ruby and Cuban Rafael—with their reticent approach to sex, make for a tale of dancing far from dirty, though surface salaciousness is not altogether banished. The camera lingers on Ruby's legs and, in an egalitarian spirit, delectably frames Rafael's naked torso in a mirror, but these characters are too self-evidently nice to provoke any truly naughty thoughts. This is where the movie's charm lies: it recognises that the pleasures of dance are communal rather than sexual. Regardless of a faint attempt to construct a nuclear-family-centred happy-ever-after, the supportive surrogate community which the dance studio provides for its clients is *Dance with Me*'s real joy. The other community Rafael leaves behind in Cuba is embodied by the colourful dancing extras in his scruffy local courtyard bar which the studio begins to resemble faintly once Rafael tarts it up for a party with an abundance of fairy lights and holiday decorations. The political reasons for emigration from Cuba are casually softpedalled. There is no acknowledgement of how salsa's growth in popularity is linked to the US blockade that bans both Cuban music and cigars. The blockade stimulated the formation of US-based salsa bands to meet local Hispanic demand, and from there salsa caught on with non-Hispanic consumers.

The narrative pivot of a relationship between a Cuban and an American brings to mind director Randa Haines' earlier feature *Wrestling Ernest Hemingway*, though *Dance with Me*'s own Cuban iconography—all dominoes and burritos—is markedly more clichéd. As with *Strictly Ballroom* the championing of the maverick over the conventional is played out through a plea for 'instinctive' style, an elusive characteristic which both films firmly root in Hispanic culture. Rafael's supposedly intuitive approach—"the music tells me how to dance," he says, and later: "I'm Cuban, of course I know how to dance"—weaves itself into a 'natural-rhythm' stereotype, which is, thankfully, more risible than blatantly offensive.

However, these weak narrative themes—in the best Busby Berkeley tradition—are merely the humble supports holding the spotlight on the film's true star: its choreography. Exquisitely rendered, this is of such high quality you forgive and forget *Dance with Me*'s obvious conservatism. Neither leering, nor queasily vertiginous, the lengthy dance sequences strive for a clarity rare in recent dance films. Unlike the disruptive approach of, say, *Flashdance*, giddy thrills are induced not through editing, but through longer takes which capture the dancers' gyrations. *Dance with Me* may insensitively step on a few toes, but its footwork is otherwise exhilarating.

Also reviewed in:
CHICAGO TRIBUNE, 8/21/98, Friday/p. C, Michael Wilmington
NEW YORK TIMES, 8/21/98, p. E12, Stephen Holden
VARIETY, 6/8-14/98, p. 67, Leonard Klady

DANCER, TEXAS POP. 81

A TriStar Pictures release of an HSX Films production in association with Chase Productions and Caribou Pictures. *Executive Producer:* Michael Burns and Leanna Creel. *Producer:* Chase Foster, Peter White, and Dana Shaffer. *Director:* Tim McCanlies. *Screenplay:* Tim McCanlies. *Director of Photography:* Andrew Dintenfass. *Editor:* Rob Kobrin. *Music:* Steve Dorff. *Music Editor:* Chris Ledesma. *Sound:* Wayne Bell. *Sound Editor:* Darren Paskal. *Casting:* Laurel Smith and Michael Testa. *Production Designer:* Dawn Snyder. *Art Director:* Jeff Adams. *Set

Decorator: Beau Petersen. *Set Dresser:* Jeni Ryan. *Costumes:* Susan Matheson. *Make-up:* Dara Jaramillo. *Running time:* 95 minutes. *MPAA Rating:* PG.

CAST: Breckin Meyer (Keller);   Peter Facinelli (Terrell Lee);   Eddie Mills (John);   Ethan Embry (Squirrel); Ashley Johnson (Josie); Patricia Wettig (Mrs. Lusk); Michael O'Neill (Mr. Lusk);   Eddie Jones (Earl);   Wayne Tippit (Keller's Grandfather); Alexandra Holden (Vivian); Keith Szarabajka (Squirrel's Father);   Shawn Weatherly (Sue Ann);   Michael Crabtree (Mr. Hemphill); LaShawn McIvor (Mrs. Hemphill);   Joe Stevens (Leon);   Tommy G. Kendrick (Rusty);   Steven Bland (Wayne);   Craig Carter (Guy); Mary Ann Luedecke (Betty Sue);   Bill Brooks (Reverend); Felipe De Ortego y Gasca (Principal); Kessia Kordelle (Jean); Kendra Payne (Loretta);   Jack Vaden (Harvey);   Lynn Carter (Rancher);   Jon Bergholz (Bus Driver); Lucy Jacobson (Flora);   Lisa Billing (Sandra);   Emilie B. Severin (Mrs. Caldwell);   Leigh Eaton (Mrs. Hufheinz);   Billie Craddock (Mrs. Garcia).

LOS ANGELES TIMES, 5/1/98, Calendar/p. 6, Kenneth Turan

"Dancer, Texas Pop. 81" opens with four young men lounging in plastic beach chairs parked right across the middle of what has to be the least busy highway in America. It's an unnerving sight for those who have had enough of sullen slackers and disaffected youth, but worry isn't necessary. "Dancer, Texas" isn't that kind of film at all.

Likable, affectionate and unashamedly warm-hearted, "Dancer, Texas" is a sentimental little picture that goes gently against the grain. Its young people all have ambitions, though they haven't necessarily thought them through, and what the film sacrifices in terms of hipness it more than makes up for by allowing the audience to actually care about the choices these people end up making.

Waiting around for their high school graduation later that Friday afternoon, the quartet is engaged in writing a letter to Rand McNally politely insisting that their tiny town, a classic wide spot in the road, is worth being put on the map. "Dancer's isolated location," writes Keller (Breckin Meyer), the group's motivator, "makes it a perfect spot for the weary traveler."

Actually these four 18-year-olds, best friends who make up almost all of Dancer's graduating class, are ideally situated to boast about the town's virtues. On Monday morning, they're scheduled to fulfill a "solemn vow" they all took when they were 11 and board a bus taking them to Los Angeles and what the commencement speaker grandly characterizes as "that adventure called life."

No sooner does graduation end, however, than the town's laconic West Texas population starts to kibitz that decision. The last guy from Dancer who went to L.A., someone remembers, ended up murdered in prison. The four insist they're leaving, but the town's adults, who know "a lot can happen between now and Monday," begin taking bets on how many if any of the boys will be on the bus.

What that final weekend offers us is the opportunity to get to know the quartet as individuals, to see the forces driving them to leave as we]] as the ones pushing them to stay and to observe these young men as they try to decide if their upbringing made them miss out on chances or gave them things other kids didn't have.

Keller, who's been doing research and making charts on the trip for years, is clearly the ringleader. With a crusty fly-hating grandfather as his only living relative, he's the most intent on leaving. But his three friends turn out to be increasingly ambivalent as the weekend wears on, worrying about life in "a city of 13 million strangers" as well as their own personal dilemmas.

Terrell Lee (Peter Facinelli), the only son of the town's only oilman, has to contend with his relentless, steamroller mother ("thirtysomething's" Patricia Wettig), who yammers at him about his responsibility to tradition and doesn't hesitate to insist that he join his father in the family business.

If Terrell Lee is the town Valentino, going steady with two girls, Squirrel (Ethan Embry) is its lost soul, unable to connect with women and living with his reprobate father in a trailer that appears to be permanently tilted.

Finally, there is quiet, responsible John (Eddie Mills), whose taciturn rancher father says as much in a year as many men say in an evening. Still, John has an enviable bond with his younger sister (Ashley Johnson of "Growing Pains") and has come to enjoy ranch life almost in spite of himself.

One of the accomplishments of "Dancer, Texas" is to be even-handed about the virtues of going and staying, making a case for the pleasures of a population 81 town without being dishonest or excessive. It makes you believe the truth of the character who says, "Some folks don't belong in a small town, some folks don't belong anywhere else."

"Dancer, Texas" wouldn't be as pleasant as it is without the authenticity of its feeling for its specific time and place, much of which can be traced to writer-director Tim McCanlies. A fifth-generation Texan who has written in Hollywood for more than a decade without creating a sensation, McCanlies wrote the "Dancer" script in 1984 but was reluctant to let anyone else direct.

Helped by talented young actors who have completely embraced their roles, "Dancer, Texas" brings us back to a time in life when one yearns to do something big without really knowing what that might be. By the time that bus pulls into town Monday morning, we're as eager as those cagey local bettors to know who will go and who will stay.

NEW YORK POST, 5/1/98, p. 50, Thelma Adams

Somewhere out in west Texas, off Highway 91, there's a tiny town that Rand McNally doesn't recognize, where every man looks like Tommy Lee Jones and the high school class of '98 graduated four boys—and only four boys—who've known each other since they were knee-high to a longneck bottle of Lone Star.

Welcome to "Dancer, Texas Pop. 81."

Writer-director and fifth-generation Texan Tim McCanlies has blown in off the High Lonesome with the sweetest coming-of-age story in ages. There's no incest, no dirty little secrets, no fatal game of chicken on Highway 91.

In "Dancer, Texas" there are just gorgeous sunsets and wild mustangs and four teens with a sacred vow to move to Los Angeles.

Will the rich man's son (Peter Facinelli), the drunk's son (Ethan Embry), the rancher's son (Eddie Mills) and the dreamer (Breckin Meyer) get on that bus west come the Monday morning after graduation?

Sigh. "Dancer" is sweet as moon pies, and I'm jaded. When those pretty Texas boys (guess which ones) catch that bus out of paradise, I imagined this fantasy on a double bill with "johns," Scott Silver's scrungy 1997 drama about male street hustlers living on Hollywood's fringe. California, here I come!

NEWSDAY, 5/1/98, Part II/p. B6, Jack Mathews

With "Dancer, Texas Pop. 81," writer-director Tim McCanlies takes us to a West Texas town so small, its characters lament, that it doesn't even appear on the Rand McNally state map. If it did you would also not find it in any Frommer's travel guide, though you could easily do it on $5 a day, and anybody who happened by wouldn't remember it. In fact, you might say that anybody with a brain and a good thumb would be out of there as soon as possible, which is exactly what McCanlies' four heroes—Keller (Breckin Meyer), Terrell Lee (Peter Facinelli), John (Eddie Mills), and Squirrel (Ethan Embry)—plan to do. The buddies made a solemn vow years earlier to head for Los Angeles as soon as they graduate high school and their day of liberation has come.

The problem is, once the reality of heading west is upon them, they begin to discover that the desire to leave is no stronger than the fear of being somewhere else. Even the townsfolk, some of whom are dumb as stumps, know that the boys have been dreaming, and the good money is betting that none of them leaves.

McCanlies intends "Dancer" as a warm homage to Small Town, America, to the stoic characters and simple life which—at least to those with experienced perspective—in enviable contrast to life in the big city. It's likely that McCanlies is basing his characters on people he knew, and liked, and he does his best to cast them in a good light.

But "Dancer" the movie is pretty much what Dancer the town is: A dull, boring, dusty wretch of a place, with people who are lot more interesting to each other and to McCanlies, than they are as fictional characters. That there are probably kids just like these all across the not-ready-for-Rand McNally map doesn't make the time spent with them any more exciting.

Keller, the dreamer, has a crotchety gramp who spends day and night swatting flies and fending off the town's bounty of widows. Terrell Lee, the sociable hunk, has a ramrod mother ordering him to work in the family's dying oil business. John, the quiet one, is attracted to his father's offer to help him run their ranch. And Squirrel, who's sort of a desert version of Jerry Lewis, has a dad who's as perpetually tipsy as their squalid trailer.

There's not much narrative force behind any of this, so the resolutions don't have much impact. Keller, because he is the most determined and most likely to leave (and maybe some day make a movie about his life there), is the most sympathetic. There are, in the minds of his friends, good reasons to stay, but the reasons don't make compelling drama and they won't put Dancer on the map.

Rand McNally knows what it's doing.

VILLAGE VOICE, 5/5/98, p. 119, Amy Taubin

As titles go, this one is nicely associative. Could it be a western barroom musical set in the days of disco? But no, it's yet another insipid boys' coming-of-age story that plays like a beer commercial of the currently hip shaggy-dog variety extended to a soporific 90 minutes. And Dancer, Texas turns out to be a teeny-weeny town whose population of 81 will take a slide if four out of the five teenagers that constitute its high school graduating class fulfill their boyhood pact to escape to LA. (The fifth graduate is a girl, so it's only natural for her to lack a spirit of adventure.)

But, as the moment of departure nears, even the chirpiest of these fledglings gets nervous about leaving the nest. There are many scenes of the four friends watching the sun set, watching the sun rise, driving around in a broken-down convertible and talking, talking, talking.

Written and directed by Tim McCanlies, a first-time film maker who grew up in a Texas small town and who has been working in Hollywood rewriting Disney movies since the 80s, Dancer, Texas Pop. 81 is so mediated by TV cliché that even when it's autobiographical it's still unlifelike. It isn't helped by the naked fib at its center: The actors playing the four friends look and behave like they took their SATs 10 years ago. Furthermore, except for the one whose supposed to be a nerd (Ethan Embry), they're almost indistinguishable from one another. There's the one who looks a little like John Travolta crossed with Brad Pitt (Eddie Mills), and then there are the two dark-haired ones whose noses turn down (Breckin Meyer and Peter Facinelli). One of them looks more like John Cusack than the other but I'll be damned if I remember which one it is. Even as a calling card for the actors, Dancer, Texas Pop. 81 doesn't work.

Also reviewed in:
CHICAGO TRIBUNE, 5/1/98, Friday/p. M, Monica Eng
NEW YORK TIMES, 5/1/98, p. E14, Stephen Holden
VARIETY, 3/23-29/98, p. 87, Emanuel Levy

DANCING AT LUGHNASA

A Sony Pictures Classics release of a Capitol Films/Channel Four Films/Ferndale Films presentation in association with Bord Scannan na Éireann/The Irish Film Board/Radio Telefis Éireann of a Noel Pearson production. *Executive Producer:* Jane Barclay and Sharon Harel. *Producer:* Noel Pearson. *Director:* Pat O'Connor. *Screenplay:* Frank McGuinness. *Based on the stage play by:* Brian Friel. *Director of Photography:* Kenneth MacMillan. *Editor:* Humphrey Dixon. *Music:* Bill Whelan. *Music Editor:* Thomas Drescher. *Choreographer:* David Bolger. *Sound:* Kieran Horgan and (music) Philip Begley and Willie Mannion. *Sound Editor:* Jonathan Bates. *Casting:* Mary Selway. *Production Designer:* Mark Geraghty. *Art Director:* Conor Devlin and Terry Pritchard. *Costumes:* Joan Bergin. *Make-up:* Jennifer Hegarty. *Stunt Coordinator:* Martin Grace. *Running time:* 94 minutes. *MPAA Rating:* PG.

CAST: Meryl Streep (Kate Mundy);   Michael Gambon (Father Jack Mundy);   Catherine McCormack (Christina Mundy);   Kathy Burke (Maggie Mundy);   Brid Brennan (Agnes Mundy); Sophie Thompson (Rose Mundy);   Rhys Ifans (Gerry Evans);   Lorcan Cranitch (Danny Bradley);   Darrell Johnston (Michael Mundy);   John Kavanagh (Father Carlin);   Marie Mullen (Vera McLoughlin);   Peter Gowen (Austin Morgan); Dawn Bradfield (Sophia McLoughlin); Kate O'Toole (Chemist).

LOS ANGELES TIMES, 11/20/98, Calendar/p. 14, Jack Mathews

[The following review by Jack Mathews appeared in a slightly different form in **NEWSDAY, 11/13/98, Part II/p. B7.]**

Adapted from a play and given the heart of a novel, Pat O'Connor's "Dancing at Lughnasa" is one of the more quietly thoughtful experiences you may have at the movies this season. If that doesn't exactly sound like a ringing endorsement, let's break it down.

Thoughtful? Absolutely. Irish screenwriter Frank McGuinness' adaptation of Brian Friel's Tony Award-winning play and O'Connor's measured direction of it put the story of five unmarried sisters in male—and spiritually starved 1930s Ireland on a different course from most screen-destined stage productions.

The movie does open up the play, in the physical sense, allowing the characters to roam from the Mundy sisters' Donegal farmhouse. We follow schoolteacher and humorless, bossy older sister Kate (Meryl Streep) into her classroom. We go with slow, sanguine Rose (Sophie Thompson) when she sneaks off to meet her married boyfriend Danny (Lorcan Granitch). And we ride along with impetuous Christina (Catherine McCormack) and her sometime lover Gerry Evans (Rhys Ifans) when he comes to visit her and their 8-year-old son on his motorbike.

But those are brief digressions from the real purpose of the film. How and whether the Mundys—suffering great economic hardship and profound loneliness—survive additional pressures placed on them is the thrust of the play, and O'Connor uses the intimacy of the camera to expand on and heighten those elements. The film explores the dreams, emotions and interrelationships of the sisters—and, by extension, of the depressed rural Irish—without being totally dependent on dialogue. (Not that anyone will think there are too few words.)

If thoughtful suggests plodding, unfortunately that's also true of "Dancing at Lughnasa." The deliberately paced movie follows the form of a reflective novel, narrated by Christina's son, looking back as an adult at a time when things were changing too fast.

The catalysts for that change are the arrivals of Gerry, who stops by to quench his sexual thirst and tell Christina of his plans to join the anti-Franco forces in Spain, and the sisters' older brother Jack (Michael Gambon). An ailing, delusional priest returning from decades of missionary work with lepers in Africa, he is more enthralled with pagan beliefs than Catholic ones.

There is the further economic bad news of Kate's losing her job, and of the opening of a new textile mill that is cutting into her sisters' homespun knitting business. And, finally, there is the addition to the household of a working radio, which brings news and music from the outside, creating a strange mix of melancholy and elation.

The most powerful moment in Friel's play comes when the sisters, at about their lowest point, break into a spontaneous dance to a tune from the radio. That moment of release is also a showcase event in the film, but the exultation of it is diluted somehow.

With the play, we are literally under the same roof as the sisters, and having that free-spirited dance acted out in the confined space virtually draws the audience onto the stage. The additional choreography and editing that go into the film's dance sequence flattens it out, and O'Connor's decision to let the dance spill outdoors makes it tone-deaf as well.

The film's greatest strength is its superb ensemble cast. Streep, manufacturing her eighth or ninth immaculate screen accent, is convincingly unsympathetic as the sisters' self-appointed guardian; Kathy Burke provides needed jolts of energy as Maggie, the sister most resistant to Kate's rule; and Gambon is truly wonderful as the unbalanced figure symbolically perched on the line separating hope from despair.

NEW YORK POST, 11/13/98, p. 61, Thelma Adams

If you've caught the preview for "Dancing at Lughnasa," you've seen the ecstatic moment when five Irish sisters, including a dowdy Meryl Streep, cut a rug in honor of the titular pagan harvest feast.

That's it for joy in Pat O'Connor's Irish drama adapted from Brian Friel's play by Frank McGuinness. One's enjoyment is directly proportional to how much this scene makes you want to pull up your scratchy woolen knickers and dance away the soles of your much-patched shoes.

Set on the eve of WWII in a rustic Donegal hamlet so small it could be called a piglet, "Lughnasa" is more elegy than celebration. It's one of those nostalgic dramas about that last relatively happy summer before heartbreak struck.

Told from the perspective of 8-year-old Michael Mundy (Darrell Johnston), the "love child" recalls how green was his valley, how insular his world. "Lughnasa" opens with Michael flying—and losing—a kite. Unlike the toy, neither the boy, his mother, nor his aunts can pull free of their hardscrabble roots.

The Mundys include Streep's sharp-tongued schoolmarm, Kathy Burke's homely homemaker, Brid Brennan's silent but steady mother figure, Sophie Thompson's simpleton and Catherine McCormack's willowy unwed mom. The heady ensemble—led by Streep, anchored by Brennan and warmed by McCormack—is the reason to go "Dancing at Lughnasa."

The five unmarried Mundy sisters are united in their frustration. In the heavy symbolism held over from the stage, the women earn cash knitting; their world, however full of discord and internal knots, is about to unravel.

The arrival of two men in Donegal that summer of '36 marks the beginning of the end. Older brother Jack (crusty but wasted Michael Gambon) returns from African missionary duty after 25 years with a feathered hat and a broken body full of jangled nerves. Michael's wandering Da Gerry (Rhys Ifans) returns for a slap and tickle before joining the Spanish Civil War.

Like that damn kite, both Jack and Gerry must escape Ireland to experience life. Men become men when they leave home. Alas, women must keep the home fires burning and raise the sons; it's a tough job, but somebody's got to do it—and it eases the pain if you whistle while you work.

If we don't understand the symbolism, our narrator is there to come of age and hammer it in. Michael recalls his mother and aunts "dancing as if language no longer existed because words were no longer necessary."

Except, of course, in voiceover narration.

NEWSWEEK, 11/16/98, p. 81, Jack Kroll

In "Dancing at Lughnasa," Meryl Streep adds an Irish brogue to her world-class collection of accents. Streep is splendid in this adaptation of Brian Friel's prize-winning play, but here she's one of five superb actresses who should win the first Oscar for ensemble acting. They play the unmarried Mundy sisters, scraping a hard living in Friel's imaginary town of Ballybeg during the Depression '30s. These women—stalwart Agnes (Brid Brennan), feisty Maggie (Kathy Burke), simple-minded Rose (Sophie Thompson), lovely Christina (Catherine McCormack), severe Kate (Streep)—are a group portrait of the deprivation, spiritual, economic, sexual, of Ireland during a dark time. When two men show up—their priest brother, Jack (Michael Gambon), returning from 25 years ministering to a leper colony in Africa, and Gerry (Rhys Ifans), the vagabond father of Christina's illegitimate son, Michael—the story shifts into a high gear of tragic elation. This sounds like a paradox, but it's Friel's specialty as a writer: destiny may be dark, but the darkness is broken by lightning flashes of the human spirit.

Some of this darkness comes from the economic breakdown that deprives the sisters of their work—Agnes and Rose knitting gloves, Kate teaching at the local school. And some of the darkness comes from the church, painted as a grim and repressive force. During his years in Africa, Father Jack (in Gambon's moving performance) has become more pagan than Christian. He has forgotten some of his English in favor of Swahili, and he nostalgically recalls the ecstatic dancing of the Africans, even the lepers. This ecstasy is reflected in the pre-Christian festival of Lughnasa, which still goes on in the back hills of Ballybeg, with its Dionysiac dancing celebrating the harvest god Lugh. The tension between an emotionally negative Christianity and a positive pagan exultation drives the screenplay by Frank McGuinness and the direction by Pat O'Connor.

In a climactic scene, the five sisters, who will soon split up, break out into a wild spontaneous dance. This scene, both heartbreaking and jubilant, has more power than any showstopper in a $75 million musical.

SIGHT AND SOUND, 12/98, p. 42, Claire Monk

Rural Donegal, Ireland, 1936. The five unmarried Mundy sisters live with eight-year-old Michael, the son of youngest sister Christina and Gerry, a travelling salesman. Kate is a teacher and strict Catholic; Maggie keeps house; Agnes and the mentally slow Rose make money by knitting gloves. Their brother Jack returns sick and senile after years as a missionary priest in Africa. Gerry reappears, but only to announce his departure for Spain to fight against Franco. The sisters consider attending the summer dance held for Lughnasa, the Celtic festival of light. But Kate overrides their plan, infuriating Agnes especially. One night, Agnes vows to Rose that the two of them will leave.

On Lughnasa, Rose vanishes and Kate admits she's lost her job. Late at night, Jack finds Rose drunk with Danny, a married man who has been covertly seeing her. Back home, all five sisters throw themselves into a wild dance. Gerry leaves for Spain the next day. A new knitwear factory puts Agnes and Rose out of work; they depart and are never seen again, leaving Kate permanently grieving. In voice-over, the adult Michael muses on the power of music, dance and the women who raised him.

The press notes for *Dancing at Lughnasa* casually mention that the playwright Brian Friel—on whose 1989 stage hit this film is based—has "no interest in film-making". Perhaps the film's producers should have heeded Friel's writerly snubbing of movies, for it suggests an alertness to the difficulties of translating Lughnasa from one medium into the other. The outcome isn't wholly disastrous: screenwriter Frank McGuinness (also a playwright) does his best to produce a respectful adaptation with neat storytelling, and the performances are never merely routine. Unfortunately, the same can't be said for the film as a whole. It's the sort of middlebrow, bland film, lacking in emotional or intellectual bite, that vindicates Friel's caution.

The film's downfall is its insistence on translating Friel's imagery and metaphors into the literalisms of conventional period cinema. The direction by Pat O'Connor *(Circle of Friends, Inventing the Abbotts)* must shoulder much of the blame. Indeed, the mismatch between O'Connor's recent work (none of which has equalled the promise of his debut, the political thriller *Cal*) and Friel's concerns makes O'Connor seem a careless choice. A central aim of Friel's plays, including *Lughnasa,* has been to explore and interrogate the past in order to understand the roots of the present, and thus to rethink Irish national cultural origins, histories and identities. By contrast, O'Connor's major recent success, *Circle of Friends,* was in the business of ruthlessly commodifying Emerald Isle clichés for the international market.

In theory, *Lughnasa*'s content alone promises substance and edge. In its portrayal of the Mundys, it not only sets out an unconventional family structure (with its illegitimate child and patriarchless household), but deliberately locates it within a time and place (rural Ireland, 1936) commonly thought of as traditional and repressive—suggesting that such 'alternative' families have a history within the nation, and hence a valid claim to legitimacy in the national present. This was a time and place of change, in which values were in flux in both the public and private spheres. As the title's reference to Lugh, the Celtic god of light, implies, Lughnasa also seeks to celebrate Celtic pagan roots. Most importantly, McGuinness' script succeeds in hinting at parallels between the breakup of the Mundy family and the larger, darker forces of 30s history—and, disturbingly, between Kate's zealotry and fascism. A derisive reference to Mussolini by Agnes is tellingly slapped down by Kate, and we're reminded in one exchange that the Vatican was a supporter of Franco's dictatorship in Spain.

With material this heady, you'd expect the film to stimulate and provoke. Instead, it's no sooner seen than forgotten. The generic Oirish visual lyricism O'Connor imposes muffles the impact and interest of the larger themes. The landscape is treated as one big photo-opportunity. A gratuitously prolonged mood sequence in which Gerry and Christina deliriously ride on a motorbike cannot, of course, be accomplished without the camera overtaking them and flying across the rolling green fields. The scenes contrived as trailer highlights are lamentably easy to spot.

This is fatal, since given its very evident commercial aspirations, O'Connor's film fails to exploit its story's potential for melodrama and emotion. On paper, its events are moving and even harrowing: poverty, transgressive romance, a boy's longing for an absent father, and the break-up of a family. Yet *Lughnasa* impresses only as a showcase for fine acting, though even here there are disappointments. At least Michael Gambon persuades that his reputation for greatness is deserved, but Kathy Burke, untypically subdued, is wasted. As sexy free spirit Gerry, Rhys Ifans looks the part, but fails to erase memories of his car-thieving past in *Twin Town,* raising futile hopes that he will breathe life and irony into *Lughnasa* by wreaking similar havoc here. As for Streep, if your motive for seeing the film is to marvel at her virtuosity in impersonating a fierce Donegal matriarch, she's remarkable. An alternative view is that 'the Streep effect'—with its demand that the viewer should consciously admire the invisibility of the star's technique—is yet another factor that explains *Lughnasa*'s failure to engage.

VILLAGE VOICE, 11/17/98, p. 138, Amy Taubin

Dancing at Lughnasa might have been titled *The Five Sisters,* so closely is it modeled on Chekhov's play about women with great potential and almost no possibilities. Adapted from Brian Friel's much lauded and awarded stage-play, Pat O'Connor's film is set in rural Ireland during the Depression. The Mundy sisters, their expectations dwindling day by day, struggle to keep the roof of their family farmhouse over their heads.

Kate (Meryl Streep) is an unmarried schoolteacher, like Chekhov's Olga. As the sole wage-earner, she's become a bit of a patriarch, ordering her sisters about, trying to regulate their erotic lives, down to the last fantasy. Middle sister Rose (Sophie Thompson) is enamored, like Masha, of a married man. Where Chekhov's middle sister was a world-class neurotic, Rose is just a bit "simple," which makes her sisters fiercely protective of her. Christina (Catherine McCormack), the youngest, has borne a son out of wedlock. (She's a kind of fallen version of Irina.) There are two other sisters, Agnes (Brid Brennan) and Maggie (Kathy Burke), whose characters are less well defined. (Having no prototypes in Chekhov perhaps puts them at a disadvantage.)

The film is couched as a memory piece, told from the point of view of Christina's son Michael. It takes place during the summer of his eighth birthday, the summer that the sisters' world collapses every which way. I don't know how this framework functioned in the stage version, but in the film it's so meretricious as to be offensive. Having laid claim in the opening scene to a young boy's perspective, the director sloughs it off whenever it proves inconvenient—which is most of the time. (The film is filled with scenes that the child could not have witnessed.) O'Connor makes no expressive or narrative use of a child's way of seeing; rather, he takes it as a rationale for the clichéd prettiness of the mise-en-scéne and for not getting under the skin of his characters. It's not the fault of the actresses that, for the most part, the five sisters seem like noble, long-suffering abstractions rather than flesh-and-blood women.

There's as much misogyny involved in putting women on pedestals as in crushing them underfoot. Imagining the sisters as superhuman in their strength and resourcefulness lets the men off easy. When the grown-up Michael describes the sad fate of the sisters (including his mother), all I could think was, "What a bastard." He profited from their story. The least he could have done was send some money home.

Still, it's the actresses that everyone will be talking about. Burke, Thompson, and Brennan all have moments when they break free of the *Masterpiece Theatre* ambience. McCormack gives the only sustained performance as the quietly rebellious and most modern sister. As for Streep, it's not her fault that the camera knows her too well to allow her to blend into the ensemble. But O'Connor's direction doesn't help. Do we really need to see three close-ups of Streep's foot tapping before she joins the others in a climactic, overly choreographed eruption of primal female energy? Looked like your average jig to me.

Also reviewed in:
CHICAGO TRIBUNE, 12/23/98, Tempo/p. 1, Michael Wilmington
NEW REPUBLIC, 11/30/98, p. 32, Stanley Kauffmann
NEW YORK TIMES, 11/13/98, p. E1, Janet Maslin
VARIETY, 9/14-20/98, p. 38, Todd McCarthy

DANGEROUS BEAUTY

A Warner Bros. release of a Regency Enterprises presentation of an Arnon Milchan/Bedford Falls production. *Executive Producer:* Michael Nathanson and Stephen Randall. *Producer:* Marshall Herskovitz, Edward Zwick, Arnon Milchan, and Sarah Caplan. *Director:* Marshall Herskovitz. *Screenplay:* Jeannine Dominy. *Based on the biography "The Honest Courtesan" by:* Margaret Rosenthal. *Director of Photography:* Bojan Bazelli. *Editor:* Steven Rosenblum and Arthur Coburn. *Music:* George Fenton. *Music Editor:* Stuart Goetz and Tommy Lockett. *Choreographer:* Flavia Sparapani. *Fight Choreographer:* William Hobbs. *Sound:* David Stephenson and (music) John Richards. *Sound Editor:* Per Hallberg. *Casting:* Mindy Marin, Wendy Kurtzman, and Mary Selway. *Production Designer:* Norman Garwood. *Art Director:* Keith Pain. *Set Decorator:* Ian Whittaker. *Special Visual Effects:* Robert Stromberg. *Costumes:* Gabriella Pescucci. *Make-up:* Fabrizio Sforza. *Make-up (Jacqueline Bisset):* Edward Ternes. *Stunt Coordinator:* Neno Zamperla. *Running time:* 114 minutes. *MPAA Rating:* R.

CAST: Catherine McCormack (Veronica Franco); Rufus Sewell (Marco Venier); Oliver Platt (Maffio Venier); Moira Kelly (Beatrice Venier); Naomi Watts (Giulia De Lezze); Fred Ward (Domenico Venier); Jacqueline Bisset (Paola Franco); Jeroen Krabbé (Pietro Venier); Joanna Cassidy (Laura Venier); Melina Kanakaredes (Livia); Daniel La Paine (Serafino Franco); Justine Miceli (Elena Franco); Jake Weber (King Henry); Simon Dutton (Minister Ramberti); Grant Russell (Francesco Martenengo); Peter Eyre (The Doge); Carla Cassola (Caterina); Gianny Musy (Joseph); Michael Culkin (Bishop De La Torre); Ralph Riach (Lorenzo Gritti); Charlotte Randle (Francesca); Alberto Rossatti (Andrea Tron); Anna Sozzani (Marina); Luis Moltena (Giacomo Baballi); Tim McMullan and Richard O'Callaghan (Zealots); Lenore Lohman, Maud Bonanni, and Gaia Zoppi (Venetian Wives); Roberto Corbiletto (Tailor); Annelie Harryson (Fanatic Woman); David Gant (Bolognetti); Daniele Ciampi (Naked Workman); Elena Mita and Federico Mita (Elena's Children).

LOS ANGELES TIMES, 2/20/98, Calendar/p. 10, Jack Mathews

[The following review by Jack Mathews appeared in a slightly different form in **NEWSDAY, 2/20/98, Part II/p. B6.]**

The movie that arrives in theaters today under the title "Dangerous Beauty" has been on and off Warner Bros.' release schedule for nearly a year, having tested and rejected such names as "Courtesan," "The Honest Courtesan," "Indiscretion" and "Venice." None of the titles smacks of brilliance, but the studio's confusion is at least understandable. The movie, both blessed and cursed with inspiration, defies simple description.

Based on the biography of a]6th century Venice courtesan named Veronica Franco, "Dangerous Beauty" is all of the following: a "Tom Jones"-styled period sex romp; a bordello version of "Romeo and Juliet" set against war, plague, political collapse and the Inquisition; a costume drama; a peep show; a heretical argument for guiltless passion over church doctrine; and a rousing call for women's lib from the Joan of Arc of post-medieval call girls.

No small trick that last one. Director Marshall Herskovitz, co-creator of TV's "thirtysomething," and screenwriter Jeannine Dominy have found a modem feminist role model in the world's oldest profession. Veronica Franco (Catherine McCormack) is a commoner who, having had her heart broken by a man whose social station prevents their marriage, adopts her mother's former profession of courtesan—prostitute to the court—and punishes him by denying him the sexual favors enjoyed by his peers.

This is sweet revenge indeed for Veronica, who discovers she has both an aptitude and an appetite for the calling. After going through rigorous training in manners and the art of passive seduction, and losing her virginity on her first night on the job, Veronica awakes with a look of radiant satisfaction, and coos to her proud mom (Jacqueline Bisset), "Who's next?"

The answer is, just about everyone in a position of power in Venice, from military leaders to the Catholic bishop—everyone, that is, except heartsick Senator Marco Venier (Rufus Sewell), with whom she's still in love. Will she follow her mother's advice and keep her distance from Marco, for to love a man is to be under his power, or will her heart carry the day? And tell us again, what makes her a proto-feminist?

According to the movie, and the film's production notes, courtesans of the period were the only sophisticated, educated and liberated women in Venice. All others were skullery maids and aristocratic breed mares. Courtesans were allowed to read, to wear makeup, quote verse, ridicule men and ride in the annual gondola race (albeit with their breasts out). All things being relative, what a life! Oddly, it's the bawdy silliness of "Dangerous Beauty," and its jaw-dropping presumptions of Veronica's liberated lifestyle, that makes the film occasionally entertaining. But it's a movie without a consistent tone or creative vision. A scene of delirious slapstick, a sword fight between Veronica and her rival court poet Maffio (Oliver Platt), leads directly to the plot's two most dramatic turning points: Marco's rescue of Veronica retires their romance, and Maffio's public humiliation causes him to make up with the church and to look for revenge as an Inquisition prosecutor trying Veronica for witchcraft.

Some of "Dangerous Beauty" is funny because it's meant to be. Veronica's indoctrination as a courtesan by her mother, particularly a scene where Mom uses a nude Adonis to demonstrate man's involuntary sexual reflex, is a hoot. Some of it is funny because it is so earnestly preposterous, a condition that prevails throughout the long Inquisition sequence, which features a show-stopping pro-passion, anti-guilt speech that would have had the real Veronica's head rolling before she got the first sentence out.

McCormack, who could be Robin Wright Penn's twin sister, does an able job in a role that combines Madonna, whore, tomboy, poet, intellectual, concubine, militant and martyr. But Herskovitz and Dominy are so determined to make her, more than anything else, the spokesperson for the modern woman—Gloria Steinem, in a previous life—that her performance implodes from the pressure.

Sewell, as the sad-eyed Latin lover, is an amiably heroic figure, and Bisset, mocking herself as an aging beauty, creates the most steadily honest character in the film. Platt, a fine comedy actor, is badly miscast as the self-loathing Maffio, and Fred Ward looks out of time, out of place, as Domenico, the syphilitic patriarch of the Venier clan.

NEW YORK POST, 2/20/98, p. 42, Michael Medved

"Dangerous Beauty" is superficially beautiful and tries hard to be dangerous—strutting out and tarting up the tired (and discredited) old idea that prostitution represents the ultimate empowerment of women.

Over the years, Hollywood has perpetrated plenty of fantasies about whores with hearts of gold, but this 16th-century strumpet (played by the luminous Catherine McCormack of "Braveheart") proves not only kindly but downright saintly, a paragon of intellectual integrity, raw courage and self-sacrificing nobility.

The lovely, lively Veronica (McCormack) can't marry the rich young twit she adores (the effectively smoldering Rufus Sewell) because of her questionable family background, so her mother (Jacqueline Bisset), a former courtesan herself, trains the blushing beauty on how to sell her charms to the city's power elite.

Director Marshall Herskovitz (still best known as co-producer of TVs "thirtysomething") endlessly emphasizes the contrast between respectable wives, treated like ignorant property by their husbands, and the worldly courtesans whose carefully cultivated sophistication enables them to captivate their clients.

With its lavish, seductive costumes and elegant sets, "Dangerous Beauty" shamelessly glamorizes these late-Renaissance happy hookers, who live in a sensual utopia utterly untroubled by messy distractions like diseases or pregnancies or abusive customers.

They face their biggest problem in the person of one brooding, drunken poet (Oliver Platt), who sneers at the prestigious prostitutes he can't afford.

Not even the magnetic McCormack can avoid embarrassment when gasping out lines like "You, who hunger so for what I give, cannot bear to see such power in a woman!"

By the time tearful spectators begin rising in their seats and calling out from the courtroom galleries, "If *she* is a witch, then so is every woman in Venice!" the movie audience will feel ready to burn them all at the stake.

VILLAGE VOICE, 2/24/98, p. 61, Leslie Camhi

Feminist heroines can come in many guises—witness the life of legendary courtesan Veronica Franco. *Dangerous Beauty* tells the oddly inspirational story of this Renaissance sex worker who used her multiple talents to attain literary renown and political clout.

Sixteenth-century Venice was a mercantile metropolis filled with foreigners and art, and famous for its highly cultivated ladies of pleasure. Veronica (Catherine McCormack), a brilliant young woman from an established but impoverished family, loves Marco (Rufus Sewell), who claims to return her love but must marry within the ruling elite. Veronica's canny mother, Paola (Jacqueline Bisset), sensing a business opportunity, introduces her reluctant daughter to the world's oldest profession. As a courtesan (and unlike an aristocratic wife) Veronica is free to educate herself, publish poetry, talk politics, and mingle openly with powerful men. All goes well until the Turkish sultan, the plague, and the Holy Inquisition decide to pay her city a visit.

Leaving aside its innumerable anachronisms and tacky title, *Dangerous Beauty* is a terrifically glitzy movie, conveying Venice's heady, fetid exoticism. Director Marshall Herskovitz has fun with Franco's verse performances ("I save the goodly wives of Venice/from their husbands' lustful menace") and with the accoutrements of courtly eroticism: jewels, pet peacocks, and ermine massage mitts. McCormack makes a feisty, intelligent Veronica; Sewell plays her tender, aristocratic heartthrob with dignity and dreaminess. Concessions are made to latter-day probity: Paola dies repentant and in pain, and there's little doubt that Veronica would have preferred to have married Marco. Still, this affirmation of women's independent erotic lives resounds profoundly in these days of pseudomorality.

Also reviewed in:
CHICAGO TRIBUNE, 2/27/98, Friday/p. Q, Michael Wilmington
NEW YORK TIMES, 2/20/98, p. E26, Stephen Holden
VARIETY, 2/2-8/98, p. 28, Leonard Klady
WASHINGTON POST, 2/27/98, Weekend/p. 44, Rita Kempley

DARK CITY

A New Line Cinema release of a Mystery Clock production. *Executive Producer:* Michael De Luca and Brian Witten. *Producer:* Andrew Mason and Alex Proyas. *Director:* Alex Proyas. *Screenplay:* Alex Proyas, Lem Dobbs, and David S. Goyer. *Story:* Alex Proyas. *Director of Photography:* Dariusz Wolski. *Editor:* Dov Hoenig. *Music:* Trevor Jones. *Music Editor:* Simon Leadley. *Sound:* Ben Osmo. *Casting:* Valerie McCaffrey, Shauna Wolifson, and Vanessa Pereira. *Production Designer:* George Liddle. *Art Director:* Michelle McGahey and Richard Hobbs. *Set Designer:* Axel Bartz, Jenny Carseldine, Judith Harvey, and Sarah Light. *Special Effects:* Tad Pride. *Costumes:* Liz Keogh. *Make-up:* Lynn Wheeler and Bev Taylor. *Stunt Coordinator:* Glenn Boswell. *Running time:* 103 minutes. *MPAA Rating:* R.

CAST: Rufus Sewell (John Murdoch); Kiefer Sutherland (Dr. Daniel Schreber); Jennifer Connelly (Emma Murdoch); Richard O'Brien (Mr. Hand); Ian Richardson (Mr. Book); Colin Friels (Walenski); Mitchell Butel (Husselbeck); Frank Gallacher (Stromboli); Bruce Spence (Mr. Wall); Melissa George (May); John Bluthal (Karl Harris); William Hurt (Inspector Frank Bumstead); Ritchie Singer (Hotel Manager/Vendor); Justin Monjo (Taxi Driver); Nicholas Bell (Mr. Rain); Satya Gumbert (Mr. Sleep); Noah Gumbert (Mr. Sleep Filming Double); Frederick Miragliotta (Mr. Quick); Peter Sommerfield, Timothy Jones, and Jeanette Cronin (Strangers); Paul Livingston and Michael Lake (Assistant Strangers); David Wenham (Schreber's Assistant); Alan Cinis and Bill Highfield (Automat Cops); Terry Bader (Mr. Goodwin); Rosemary Traynor (Mrs. Goodwin); Edward Grant II (Hotel Manager); Maureen O'Shaughnessy (Kate Walenski); Debbie Oparei (Train Passenger); Marcus Johnson (Station Master); Doug Scroope (Desk Sergeant); Cinzia Coassin (Waitress); Tyson McCarthy

(Murdoch, aged 10);   Luke Styles (Murdoch, teenager);   Anthony Kierann (Murdoch's Father); Laura Keaneally (Murdoch's Mother);   Natalie Bollard (Naked Woman);   Eliot Paton (Matthew Goodwin);   Naomi Van Der Velden (Jane Goodwin);   Peter Callan (Taxi Driver);   Mark Hedges (Emma's Lover);   Darren Gilshenan (Fingerprint Cop);   Ray Rizzo (Policeman);   Bill Rutherford (Police Officer);   Marin Mimica (Hotel Lobby Cop);   William Upjohn (Forensics Cop);   Glenn Boswell (Tackling Cop);   Avril Wynne (Telephone Booth Woman).

LOS ANGELES TIMES, 2/27/98, Calendar/p. 10, John Anderson

[The following review by John Anderson appeared in a slightly different form in NEWSDAY, 2/27/98, Part II/p. B7.]

Like Hong Kong action directors reinventing the western, Australia's current crop of filmmakers are happily absorbing the received wisdom of Hollywood and boomeranging it back at us. Recalibrated film noir. The costume epic as psycho drama. Road movies with no maps. There's no end to the modifications and mutations.

Sometimes, of course, the boomerang catches you in the neck. In "Dark City," Down Under director Alex Proyas revisits some of the territory he created for "The Crow," a tale of murder and revenge based on James O'Barr's comic-art novel, which gothicized the city and made the set design as much a character in the film as the late Brandon Lee's unhappy character. With "Dark City," we're in a similar landscape, but this time the set design is paramount.

The hero, John Murdoch (Rufus Sewell), awakens in a bathtub and doesn't know where he is. Neither do we. Murdoch seems to be registered at the Hotel Raymond Chandler, the city itself seems to lie somewhere between Fritz Lang's Metropolis and Tim Burton's Gotham City.

There's a scene at an automat. Is it the '40s? No, there's a '61 Falcon idling beside a '90s Citroen. Jessica Rabbit look-alike Jennifer Connelly, playing Murdoch's estranged wife, Emma, is a torch singer in a bygone boîte. Kiefer Sutherland, as Dr. Daniel Schreber, looks like the kid from "A Christmas Story" all grown up and gone bad. He speaks in an asthmatic staccato and walks with a limp borrowed from Everett Sloane in "Lady From Shanghai." William Hurt, as bemused as ever, is Detective Bumstead, a refugee from pulp fiction.

So what have we? It all gets explained—and excused—but not until we finally find out just what the Strangers, a race of ghouls who've decided to squat on Earth, are up to (it doesn't make much sense, but we won't tell you anyway). Made up like Murnau vampires and able to "tune"—or "alter reality by will alone"—they nevertheless carry nasty knives with which they perform various atrocities on unsuspecting humans: Each midnight, the city's population passes out and its collective memory is erased. The Strangers clearly have the ability to cloud men's minds—except John, who wakes up unscheduled and finds he, too, can "tune."

If you had to guess, you might say that Proyas came out of the world of comic art himself, rather than music videos and advertising. "Dark City" is constructed like panels in a Batman book, each picture striving for maximum dread. But Proyas' roots are clear enough: A shot of the city suspended in space seems to be almost a direct lift from a British Airways ad of a few years back; the scenes of the Strangers assembled in their grotto recalls another commercial I seem to have seen, perhaps during some relatively recent Olympic coverage, which had a Big Brother theme and might have been made for Nike. Proyas made Nike commercials, according to his bio. Maybe he's paying homage to himself.

At a time when the news plays out like a movie, making a movie about manufactured people in a manufactured city doesn't amount to the subtlest of commentaries on the state of the world. But Proyas is trying simultaneously to create a pure thriller and sci-fi nightmare along with his tongue-in-cheek critique of artifice. And this doesn't work out quite so well.

British heartthrob Sewell (best bedroom eyes since Giancarlo Giannini) affects the flattest American accent possible with a performance to match, while trying to embody every Kafka-inspired movie hero from Edmond O'Brien in "D.O.A." to the unborn George Bailey in "It's a Wonderful Life." What he can't do is erase the distracting illogic of "Dark City" or create tension when all those around him are camping it up.

NEW YORK POST, 2/27/98, p. 45, Thelma Adams

In "Dark City," the pasty-faced, pointy-teethed, funereal aliens cross the night sky with the simple, effortless grace of Mary Poppins.

Instead of carrying umbrellas, the Strangers wield daggers. Instead of trying to imbed positive memories in their young charges ("Just a spoonful of sugar..."), these malevolent Marys pluck the memories from the heads of childlike adults.

If Alex Proyas' sci-fi stunner recalls movies as diverse as "Mary Poppins," "Manhattan," "Brazil" and "Blade Runner," it also does what no other movie has done so far this year: gripped audiences with its sheer visual intensity and delivered a clear, concise, humanist message. Study our minds all you want, demon Marys. Mankind's truth is in our hearts.

The director of "The Crow" devised the spiraling story (scripted with Lem Dobbs and David S. Goyer) of an ordinary man on an extraordinary quest.

John Murdoch (Rufus Sewell) awakens in a strange hotel with a blood spot on his forehead, a slaughtered hooker in the bedroom, a shred of childhood memory and the ability to will objects into motion.

Who is Murdoch? How did he get there? Did he kill the woman? Once he leaves the hotel and enters a Hopperesque landscape of automats and dirty diners, Murdoch's circle of questions widens.

Why does the city shut down at midnight! Why can't anyone remember how to reach the seashore? When was the last time anyone saw daylight?

Murdoch's search for answers leads him to a green-eyed chanteuse (the curvy Jennifer Connelly) and a gimpy doctor (Kiefer Sutherland).

But the hero-killer is also the quarry. An accordion-playing homicide detective (a dryly arresting William Hurt) and aliens Mr. Hand (Richard O'Brien) and Mr. Book (Ian Richardson) are in hot pursuit.

What's the line between healthy paranoia and unhealthy paranoia? We tread on this razor's edge with Sewell, the British heart-throb ("Cold Comfort Farm") whose dark, exaggerated beauty anchors the brooding skyline of "Dark City" like the Chrysler Building

Watching "Dark City" recalls the pleasures of old-fashioned serials. We're desperate to know what happens next. What lies beyond the cliffhanger? Will Flash Gordon save the world? But what makes the tension exquisite is that we never want the serial to end.

We don't want to leave "Dark City," even when a new dawn finally arrives and the theater lights come up.

SIGHT AND SOUND, 6/98, p. 43, Kim Newman

In a nameless city, mysteriously frozen at midnight, John Murdoch wakes in a hotel room with a corpse and is phoned by Dr Schreber, who claims to be his psychiatrist. Suffering from amnesia and gifted with telekinetic abilities, he eludes both the arriving police and the Strangers, a race of aliens hiding among humanity by animating corpses. Inspector Bumstead takes over the case from a colleague who has gone mad. John pieces together his former life. He encounters Emma, who may be his estranged wife, and learns that he grew up in a place called Shell Beach, to which no one can direct him.

At midnight, the city stops again. Only John sees the buildings change and the Strangers rearrange the lives and personalities of the inhabitants. Schreber tells John it is all an experiment on humanity; John has been given the past of a murderer to see if he will become one. In a cavern under the city, Mr Hand, charged by the Strangers' leader Mr Book with apprehending John, is injected with a phial that contains John's memories. Hand becomes homicidal. John questions the nature of the world, asking Bumstead why there is never any daytime. He blasts a hole in the wall that reveals the city is floating in deep space. Bumstead and Hand are sucked into the void and John defeats Book in a psychic battle. Advised by Schreber, John reshapes the city, building a sea around it and making the sun rise. Anna, who is Emma with a new identity, meets him at the shore.

During a lengthy production, Alex Proyas' second feature film metaphorically drew in its horizons: announced as *Dark Universe* and shot under the working title *Dark World,* it has finally arrived as *Dark City.* This last title is as apt as the others, and perhaps less of a give-away of the film's final revelation, while it also evokes numerous *films noirs* (*The Dark Past, The Dark Corner, Night and the City*), particularly William Dieterle's *Dark City* (1950). The strangest thing about the *noir*-science fiction setting which this latest *Dark City* adopts is that it has become such a familiar backdrop for recent movies. There's *Blade Runner* of course, but also *The Crow*, Proyas' debut, which was set in just such a city of dreadful night, a small-scale imitation of *Batman*'s Gotham City.

With its fedoras and trenchcoats, Edward Hopper-cum-Cornell Woolrich hotel rooms and diners, droning snatches of remixed period tunes (Jennifer Connelly wittily gets to sing a verse of 'The Night Has 1000 Eyes') and morphing buildings, *Dark City* shifts its allegiances slightly, taking much of its visual style from Terry Gilliam's *Brazil*. The underside of the city, where vast clanking machines work huge changes in the upperworld and bald-headed aliens float around in black leather robes, is equally indebted to Fritz Lang's *Metropolis* (1926, with Kiefer Sutherland's psychiatrist Schreber standing in for Rotwang) as well as to Clive Barker's *Hellraiser* and its first sequel. It is hard for *Dark City* to make its own space among its borrowings (there's even a touch of Dennis Potter). But *Dark City* at least has a narrative excuse for the elements deployed purely as stylistic devices by its predecessors. Schreber reveals that the city has been composed out of bits and pieces of humanity's remembered past, and the neverending night is an actual plot point rather than an atmospheric quirk.

Proyas dreamed up the original story but brought in several other writers, including David S. Goyer (*The Crow, City of Angels*) and Lem Dobbs (*Kafka*), to sort it out. The trouble is that the film has a strong premise (reminiscent of the 'conceptual breakthrough" gambits often deployed in 50s written science fiction), but keeps stumbling over the need to explain itself. Sutherland is too often required to deliver expository speeches, fudging the bits that haven't been thought out. The police investigation seems prominent at first, but later the film concentrates more on suspect-on-the-run John. The parallel business with Richard O'Brien as an alien who learns about humanity when injected with John's memories is hurried through before it can make the quite complex and emotional points the script suggests ought to be covered. Even Jennifer Connelly's role is rather neglected when the film stops for another session of effects. (For example, the city is reconfigured with morphing so that a slumbering slum couple can wake up in a mansion and resume their dinner chat in their new rich personalities.)

If *Dark City* is more interesting than satisfying, it may be that its ambitions to add a little more depth and despair to the comic-book plotting are frustrated by the need to throw in bits of spectacle. Sewell's amnesiac-telekinetic John is an interesting creation, but the revelation that almost nobody in the city has any real identity undercuts the intriguing impossibility of rewriting a decent man as a murderer. A surprising thread of solipsism runs through the film, which climaxes not with the hero finding out who he really is (*à la RoboCop*) but with his readjustment of the entire world to conform with memories that have only been implanted in him. He creates the hometown he falsely remembers growing up in and wins the woman he has been made to imagine was his wife. So although *Dark City* is a definite improvement on the paper-thin posing of *The Crow*, this is nevertheless not quite as achieved a film as it might have been.

TIME, 3/2/98, p. 85, Richard Corliss

With feel-good comedies and soapy ship operas dominating commercial cinema, the visionaries are in retreat. Ridley Scott (*Blade Runner*) and Paul Verhoeven (*Total Recall*)have renounced the form. That leaves the creation of dank, luscious worlds within worlds to Alex Proyas. And he'll do fine. The Egyptian-born, Australian-raised director of *The Crow* has a chilling new fever dream called *Dark City*—a reminder of how sensuous a visual trip movie watching can be.

John Murdoch (Rufus Sewell) wakes up in a strange room with a dead woman. Who is she? he wonders. For that matter, who is *he*? In this dark city, dour bald aliens, known as the Strangers, have refitted humans with fake memories. Perhaps John is married to pretty Emma (Jennifer Connelly), perhaps not. Perhaps his world will end before he finds out.

Sewell, a Pre-Raphaelite hunk who also shines in the sumptuous new *Dangerous Beauty*, flashes a sullen magnetism here. But the playing is not the thing; the play of images is. In this city—part Moderne, part Magritte, part Manhattan collapsed onto itself—houses sprout like tropical flowers; office buildings magically morph in a technique that might be called Virtual Realty. You have to watch carefully, for this is not an ingratiating film. It drops you into a foreign landscape without guidebook or translator. It is as cool and distant as the planet the Strangers come from. But, Lord, is *Dark City* a wonder to see.

VILLAGE VOICE, 3/3/98, p. 108, Dennis Lim

An eye-popping convolution of neogothic fantasy and old-school sci-fi paranoia, *Dark City* whizzes by so quickly and so eventfully you don't stop to consider its extreme silliness until it's over—by which time you'll most likely have been razzle-dazzled into submission anyway. The plot cuts corners and the logic routinely short-circuits, giving the film a madcap momentum. Add to that an unaccountably busy score and plenty of surface tension, and you have what seems suspiciously like a 100-minute trailer—albeit an extremely, cool-looking one.

Fragmentation and stylishness come naturally to director Alex Proyas, best known for the morbid-by-default revenge thriller *The Crow* and dozens of music videos; *Dark City* is, ostensibly, his stab at a somewhat more cerebral genre movie. (Cowriter Lem Dobbs scripted Steven Soderbergh's awkward but fascinating *Kafka*.) Twenty minutes in, and *Dark City*'s premise is recognizable as a crackpot pastiche of *Blade Runner, Total Recall, 12 Monkeys*, and *Invasion of the Body Snatchers*.

Not that it finally matters. Proyas's achievement here is chiefly aesthetic, and like the plot, the look of the film is less strictly original than it is boldly referential, suggesting Tim Burton in Fritz Lang mode, with a soupcon of Jeunet and Caro and a dash of the Coens at their most baroque. Working in rigorous color schemes, Proyas and production designer George Liddle have constructed a series of anxiety-inducing interiors (narrow corridors, low ceilings, steep stairways, objects that glow in the dark) and, more striking still, a time-warped, quaintly futuristic cityscape.

It's always night on this version of Earth, and the population lives in a state of perpetual disorientation. Pale, bald, bony aliens in cloaks and top hats ("the Strangers") rise periodically from the netherworld to mess with the architecture (buildings spectacularly morph and mushroom) and carry out their memory-transplant research (oddly low-tech in their methods, these intergalactic anthropologists extract and implant memories with what appears to be an oversize hypodermic). The one glitch in their plans: Rufus Sewell, the film's tabula rasa hero, an amnesiac who, in time-honored tradition, may or may not be a killer. Thanks to an "evolutionary anomaly," he's blessed with the Strangers' shape-shifting powers and is the only one who can stop them. Which he eventually does with help from Kiefer Sutherland's Peter Lorre-like doctor, William Hurt's hard-boiled detective, and Jennifer Connelly's wholesome vamp.

Dark City pauses occasionally to ruminate on what makes humans human (to wit, are we merely the sum of our memories?), but Proyas knows better than to dwell on the Big Themes. He serves up one final telepathic face-off and throws in a blinding, ecstatic burst of daylight.

Also reviewed in:
CHICAGO TRIBUNE, 2/27/98, Friday/p. A, Michael Wilmington
NEW YORK TIMES, 2/27/98, p. E8, Stephen Holden
VARIETY, 2/23-3/1/98, p. 73, Todd McCarthy
WASHINGTON POST, 2/27/98, p. D1, Stephen Hunter
WASHINGTON POST, 2/27/98, Weekend/p. 43, Rita Kempley

DAVID SEARCHING

An L4Ltd./Backpain Productions release. *Producer:* Leslie L. Smith and John P. Scholz. *Director:* Leslie L. Smith. *Screenplay:* Leslie L. Smith. *Director of Photography:* John P. Scholz. *Editor:* Toni Blye. *Sound:* Michael Jordan. *Art Director:* Tina Parise. *Running time:* 103 minutes. *MPAA Rating:* Not Rated.

CAST: Anthony Rapp (David); Camryn Manheim (Gwen); Julie Halston (Julie); Joseph Fuqua (Walter); David Courier (Michael); Michael Rupert (Beau); Kathleen Chalfant (Grandmother);

David Drake (Mark); John Cameron Mitchell (Man with Fruit); Stephen Spinella (Hummus Guy); La Chanze (God Truth); and with Susan Bruce and Craig Chester.

LOS ANGELES TIMES, 7/3/98, Calendar/p. 18, Kevin Thomas

Fledgling filmmaker Leslie Smith brings much care, commitment and considerable technical skill to his debut feature, "David Searching," but the result is a picture of parts rather than a cohesive whole. For every moment that rings true there are more that seem false.

The film, which cost only $22,500 to shoot but which never looks cheap, has a certain wistful charm, humor and wisdom, but it's finally not distinctive or fully enough realized to stand out in the crowd of low-budget independent pictures.

The film opens with an ample woman frolicking in Central Park, a thin, pale youth with a shock of reddish hair cradled in her arms. He kisses her passionately. This joyous moment occurs in a dream of the woman, Gwen (Camryn Manheim), who wakes up to the reality of an East Village apartment she is sharing with that young man, David (Anthony Rapp), who happens to be gay.

Although the wise Gwen and the wet-behind-the-ears David become soul mates of sorts, the film never really makes it clear as to whether she has really fallen hard for him or whether the dream merely symbolizes an easy solution to her longings.

Gwen, a coffee-shop waitress who's left her husband, and David, an aspiring documentarian—he's forever shoving a video camera in someone's face—share the problem of finding the right man. With Gwen the right man may in fact be her husband after all, but David hasn't a clue in regard to himself. In the course of this overly long film he does learn a great deal about life, love and himself but none of it is all that riveting, perhaps because he isn't all that riveting. David isn't notably attractive, intelligent or in any way distinctive, which places a heavy burden on a film in which he's the central character.

When men do come along, frankly, it's hard to see what they see in him: He's self-absorbed, rather colorless and even something of a prig. What is it that people perceive in David that makes him so appealing on any level?

You wish that Gwen and also Julie (cabaret performer Julie Halston), David's friend, got more screen time because they are far more involving than David. Also key is Walter (Joseph Fuqua), who manages to make the most of an improbable role: a former tenant of the apartment who shows up because he has no place to go.

Good-looking, perceptive and caring, he offers himself first to David, who reflexively rejects him, and then to Gwen, with whom he has sex but who ultimately rejects him, too.

Come to think of it, "Walter Searching" might well have been a more interesting film than "David Searching."

NEW YORK POST, 9/12/98, p. 48, Larry Worth

What could pass for a deodorant commercial—two people running toward each other across a park—opens "David Searching." True, the moment is meant to be a parody, but all that follows feels equally familiar.

It's yet another would-be comedy about a Chelsea boy seeking the man of his dreams, meanwhile commiserating with his zaftig, equally sex-starved female roommate. Need more be said?

But while writer-director Leslie L. Smith keeps dipping into cliche central, actors Anthony ("Rent") Rapp and Camryn (TV's "The Practice") Manheim try hard to make the roles credible and fully nuanced.

To Rapp and Manheim's collective credit, their efforts lessen viewers' suffering. Even so, "David Searching" never finds much reason for being.

Also reviewed in:
NEW YORK TIMES, 9/11/98, p. E16, Anita Gates
VARIETY, 4/7 -13/97, p. 46, Mark Woods

DAY AT THE BEACH

An Arrow Releasing release in association with Bushwhacked Productions and Miravista Films. *Producer:* Nick Veronis. *Director:* Nick Veronis. *Screenplay:* Nick Veronis. *Director of Photography:* Nils Kenaston. *Editor:* Mark Juergens. *Music:* Tony Saracene. *Production Designer:* Petra Barchi and Charlotte Bourke. *Running time:* 93 minutes. *MPAA Rating:* Not Rated.

CAST: Jane Adams (Marie);   Patrick Fitzgerald (John);   Neal Jones (Chuck);   Catherine Kellner (Amy);   Robert Maisonett (Herman);   Joe Ragno (Antonio Gintolini);   Ed Setrakian (Augie);   Nick Veronis (Jimmy).

NEW YORK POST, 5/29/98, p. 44, Thelma Adams

Nick Veronis' first film is no "Day at the Beach," despite its title.

The good-natured Nick is vaguely handsome but no actor. The former Newark Star-Ledger reporter ran up his credit cards to write, direct and produce a spaghetti indie about a would-be filmmaker who works at a ravioli factory.

Jimmy (Nick again) dreams of making what appears to be a truly terrible movie. Sometimes dreams really do come true.

"Day at the Beach" is notable for its cartload of cliches: a briefcase full of cash, a mob hit, a road trip in a convertible, a blonde love interest, family secrets seen in flashback and a soulful guitar score.

Veronis, the star-auteur, accidentally sliced four tendons in his hand on the first day of shooting, so Jimmy wanders through his scenes with a gleaming white cast explained by an amateurish prologue.

At one point, Jimmy returns to his crash pad. The sole reason appears to be to smoke weed and perch beneath posters for Jim Jarmusch's "Down by Law" and Roman Polanski's "Chinatown."

Veronis has boundless ambition and limited talent. "Day at the Beach" makes Jarmusch's self-indulgent "Dead Man" seem as lively as a Fred Astaire solo. It makes Polanski's "Pirates" look like a masterpiece of directorial control.

Hey, Veronis makes Ed ("She's the One") Burns look like Orson Welles. I hope Veronis didn't quit his day job. He might consider visiting a debt-consolidation consultant—soon.

VILLAGE VOICE, 6/2/98, p. 166, Dennis Lim

Nick Veronis's *Day at the Beach* occupies an agreeable middle ground that's too unassuming for most American indies. First screened at last year's Gen Art festival, the film doesn't work overly hard for audience approval, nor does it ever resort to rote slackerisms. Veronis himself plays Jimmy, a pasta-factory worker who, on the weekends, makes ultralow-budget movies with his buddies, glum family man John (Patrick Fitzgerald) and terminal blowhard Chuck (Neal Jones). Self-referential as it initially appears, this isn't really an independent film about independent filmmaking. Granted, you never forget that Jimmy's a movie buff (at the beach, he name-drops the battle scene from *The Big Red One),* but, as the plot progresses, it's clear that Veronis—as an actor, writer, and director—is anything but self-involved.

A quieter, more contemplative version of last year's equally likable *Daytrippers, Day at the Beach* spends its first half setting up knotty but surmountable problems—an accidental death, a romantic complication, vaguely defined mob entanglements—then, on a whim, sends the characters off to the Hamptons. There are the usual revelatory detours and neat resolutions, but Veronis doesn't make too much of any of them. Amusing and very well acted (the hangdog Fitzgerald is especially irresistible), this may not represent the freshest or most hype-friendly breed of Amerindie, but it still strikes me as $90,000 well spent.

Also reviewed in:
NEW YORK TIMES, 5/29/98, p. E22, Lawrence Van Gelder

DEAD MAN ON CAMPUS

A Paramount Pictures release in association with MTV Films of a Pacific Western production. *Executive Producer:* David Gale and Van Toffler. *Producer:* Gale Ann Hurd. *Director:* Alan Cohn. *Screenplay:* Michael Traeger and Mike White. *Based on a story by:* Anthony Abrams and Adam Larson Broder. *Director of Photography:* John Thomas. *Editor:* Debra Chiate. *Music:* Mark Mothersbaugh. *Sound:* Walt Martin and Willie Burton. *Casting:* Deborah Aquila and Jane Shannon-Smith. *Production Designer:* Carol Winstead Wood.   *Set Designer:* Antoinette Judith Gordon.   *Set Decorator:* Jan K. Bergstrom.   *Costumes:* Kathleen Detoro. *Running time:* 90 minutes.   *MPAA Rating:* R.

CAST: Tom Everett Scott (Josh Miller); Mark-Paul Gosselaar (Cooper); Poppy Montgomery (Rachel); Lochlyn Munro (Cliff); Randy Pearlstein (Buckley); Corey Page (Matt); Alyson Hannigan (Lucy); Mari Morrow (Kristin); Dave Ruby (Zeke); and with Mark Carapezza, Jeff T, Jason Segel, Linda Cardellini, and Aeryk Egan.

LOS ANGELES TIMES, 8/21/98, Calendar/p. 8, Kevin Thomas

How's this for a dubious comic premise?: Two college roommates, certain to flunk out their first semester, discover an obscure school regulation stating that if one roommate commits suicide, the other roommate automatically gets straight A's.

In the dreadful "Dead Man on Campus," which is about as funny as a funeral, the roommates (Tom Everett Scott, Mark-Paul Gosselaar) aren't even trying to drive each other to suicide—that might have had bleakly comic possibilities. No, they're simply trying to line up a fellow student whose files, obtained via a little breaking and entering, reveal suicidal tendencies. Then they persuade their various candidates (Lochlyn Munro's manic, self-destructive Cliff, Randy Pearlstein's paranoid computer whiz; and Corey Page's dour punk rocker) to move into their three-man dormitory suite and determine which of them could most likely be pushed over the edge before the semester's over. Maybe if "Dead Man on Campus" had been played as a pitch-dark comedy instead of routine boisterous collegiate gross-out fare with a trite coming-of-age theme....

Under Alan Cohn's straight-on direction, the film, written by various hands, huffs and puffs mightily just to keep a strenuously labored plot going. Everett Scott's Josh arrives a confident if innocent kid with a full scholarship for a six-year medical program. By contrast, Gosselaar's Cooper is a brash playboy who lives for the moment and has no intention of attending classes, certain that he's going to end up working for his father, a toilet cleaning tycoon—but, as his soon-to-be irate parent promises, "not in the office."

Cooper, who has no respect whatsoever for Josh's scholarship and need to study hard to hold on to it, diverts Josh from his books so swiftly with the tried-and-true combination of sex, drugs and rock enroll that you lose all respect for the spineless kid. Everett Scott, who starred in Tom Hanks' "That Thing You Do," and Gosselaar, who's in the TV series "Saved by the Bell," are likely to survive to move on to better things, as will other youthful members of the cast.

Of course, the filmmakers, who turn in a technically polished product, would argue that their film is a comedy, not to be taken so seriously. The trouble is that it's not remotely funny enough not to seem merely strained, silly and even disgusting in its ultimate endorsement of conning your way into academic survival.

NEW YORK POST, 8/21/98, p. 64, Larry Worth

Since when did teen suicide become comic fodder? Or how about driving drunk and shooting out the window at cops? And is plain, old, unprotected sex good for a giggle?

Granted, "Dead Man on Campus" is meant to be a very dark comedy. But that genre requires real talent to pull off. And director Alan Cohn's about as talentless as they come.

As the latest big-screen effort from MTV Films, "Dead Man" is geared to young hipsters. But even young hipsters have standards.

The sophomoric tone is downright insulting, assuming that recycled coed cliches, gross-out yuks and the constant drone of cutting-edge music will keep adolescent moviegoers entertained.

The idiotic script has hard-working scholar Tom Everett Scott entering Daleman College with the best intentions. Enter bong-bearing, sex-crazed, study-phobic roommate Mark-Paul Gosselaar. Of course, Scott's grades nosedive and his cool quotient soars.

That's where the movie's far-fetched premise kicks in. Upon finding an obscure university rule that gives 4.0 averages to students whose roomie succeeds at suicide, the party boys try to bunk with a frosh who's ready to slit his wrists.

Make no mistake, viewers who shelled out the price of admission will be the ones pulling out razors—and wondering what Hollywood buffoon green-lighted this garbage.

It's hard not to be appalled, regardless of age. Adults won't excuse the horribly inappropriate treatment of serious subjects, while kids will note the lack of creativity and characters with the depth of Archie and Jughead.

Heck, there's not even a flicker of star power to divert one's attention. As demonstrated in "That Thing You Do" and "An American Werewolf in Paris," Tom Everett Scott evidences zero charisma and even less acting potential.

Then there's Mark-Paul Gosselaar, a six-year veteran of TV's "Saved by the Bell." He comes off as the cheap-rate version of Matthew Broderick's Ferris Bueller, minus the seductive charm.

The only silver lining will be the quick demise of "Dead Man" at the box office. That's something Tinseltown suits won't consider a laughing matter.

NEWSDAY, 8/21/98, Part II/p. B6, John Anderson

While it makes convincing arguments against coed colleges—or any colleges, for that matter—"Dead Man on Campus" is really the creative equivalent of ketchup and hot water: You can call it tomato soup, but you really need the saltines.

"Dead Man"? No saltines. A feature-length comedy fashioned out of a single urban myth—the "dead man's clause" that is said to compensate college students for a roommate's demise—it has a nice cast, but the humor has all the snap of yesterday's crouton and the script is too weak to shore up what is essentially a nonexistent story. Far more interesting, however, is what happens when a movie's lack of substance gets processed through a creative marketing department.

Anyone who's seen and/or been persuaded by the ubiquitous TV commercials for "Dead Man on Campus" probably came away thinking this is a frenetic, out-of-control comedy about two roommates plotting only against a third—namely, the psychotic Cliff, played by "Dead Man" MVP Lochlyn Munro—and that the rest of the movie is an avalanche of frat jokes, sex jokes, beer jokes, drug jokes and enough grossout humor to make "There's Something About Mary" seem like a daily affirmation. And he/she would be wrong.

For about half of the film, what we get is a surprisingly conventional rite-of-passage story about Josh (Tom Everett Scott), an unassuming scholarship student from Indiana who comes east to study and gets his career track trashed by his roommate, Cooper (Mark-Paul Gosselaar), and the rest of the party crowd at Daleman College. It goes nowhere specific during that first half, but the cast is engaging, particularly Josh's love interest, Rachel, played by Poppy Montgomery.

Then, when the failing grades start piling up, Josh is faced with losing his scholarship, Cooper is faced with having to work in his father's toilet-cleaning business (one of the movie's characteristically limp jokes) and they discover The Rule: If a Daleman student dies, his surviving roommates get straight A's. And Josh and Cooper have available space.

And here, amid the ivy, Frisbees, juicers and potheads, director Alan Cohn (of MTV's "The Real World") puts Josh and Cooper in camouflage gear, has them break into the school records room to find the file on the student deemed Most Likely to Be Calling Dr. Kevorkian Before Finals, and takes the film in new and seemingly desperate directions. They come up with several candidates for death, the most memorable being Cliff, and the movie's obliviousness toward its own sociopathy takes all the sympathetic gas out of the balloon.

The accompanying press materials for "Dead Man on Campus" claim that research has found no school anywhere in the country that rewards college students in any way for the death of a roommate. Of course, these are the same press materials that refer to "Dead Man" as a "comedy with depth," so draw your own conclusions.

Also reviewed in:
CHICAGO TRIBUNE, 8/21/98, Friday/p. F, Monica Eng
NEW YORK TIMES, 8/21/98, p. E30, Anita Gates
VARIETY, 8/24-30/98, p. 27, Joe Leydon

DEAR JESSE

A Cowboy Booking International release of a BANG Inc. presentation in association with the N.C. Film Foundation. *Executive Producer:* Gill Holland.   *Producer:* Mary Beth Mann. *Director:* Tim Kirkman. *Screenplay:* Tim Kirkman. *Director of Photography:* Norwood Cheeck and Ashley McKinney. *Editor:* Joe Klotz. *Music:* John Crooke. *Running time:* 82 minutes. *MPAA Rating:* Not Rated.

WITH: Tim Kirkman; Jessse Helms.

LOS ANGELES TIMES, 11/6/98, Calendar/p. 16, Kevin Thomas

At the beginning of "Dear Jesse," documentarian Tim Kirkman lists all that he and the senator from North Carolina have in common as if he were writing Helms a letter: They were both born in Monroe, N.C., raised as Southern Baptists, attended Wingate University for one year and were interested in journalism.

Then he concludes, "But I believe we have a more significant similarity—for most of your 24 years in the U.S. Senate you've been obsessed with homosexual men; for most of my adult life, so have I."

Kirkman left North Carolina in 1990 for New York. Six years later, fleeing an exceptionally bitter winter and a breakup with his lover, Kirkman decided to pack his camera and discover whether or not another North Carolinian, Thomas Wolfe, was right about whether you can go home again. Kirkman found that he could, at least for a visit, and that his timing was good, as Sen. Helms was running for office again.

During that campaign Kirkman and his cinematographers pointed cameras and mikes at a wide range of people, and we're reminded of why Helms has earned the nickname "Senator No." He's anti-gay, anti-AIDS funding, anti-abortion, anti-funding of the arts, and at the beginning of his career, anti-integration. What he's for, everyone reiterates, is tobacco and big business.

Time and again Kirkman discovers that what keeps Helms in office is that people, even those who admit they do not agree with all his reactionary views, believe they know where he stands; he strikes them, rightly or wrongly, as that rarity in modem times, an honest politician. Novelist Allan Gurganus, who returned from his own New York sojourn to resume living in his native state, says, before expressing how much he deplores the man, that he credits Helms for being "hard-working, proud of his state, and he does what he says he'll do."

Kirkman reveals that his beautiful native state is also home to lots of admirable, creative people who are trying to make North Carolina a better place to live for all people, young and old, white and black, gay and straight. Several of the people Kirkman talked to are especially moving—a white woman, for example, who adopted a baby of mixed parentage, whose parents were HIV-positive drug addicts but whose child proved miraculously free of disease. She tells of taking the boy, now a toddler, to church and encountering racism from a child who looked to be no more than 4 years of age.

Also heart-rending are two elegant middle-aged women, both of whom lost their sons to AIDS and who have founded MAJIC (Mothers Against Jesse in Congress). By chance Kirkman encounters his junior high school principal, a black man who, with a sense of bemused resignation, predicts Helms will die in office.

Note: After Matthew Shepard was killed recently in a gay-bashing incident, Kirkman realized he had interviewed the University of Wyoming student for his documentary while Shepard was enrolled at North Carolina's Catawba College. Culling his outtakes, Kirkman found the footage, in which Shepard stated he did not believe that Helms represents the feelings of North Carolinians toward gays. Kirkman has appended this two-minute sequence as an epilogue to "Dear Jesse" in memory of Shepard.

NEW YORK POST, 6/26/98, p. 60, Thelma Adams

"Dear Jesse" is one constituent letter that North Carolina Sen. Jesse Helms won't answer.

Director Tim Kirkman's deeply personal docu-diary addressed to the politician is a surprisingly balanced look at the similarities and differences between the filmmaker, who fled the Tar Heel State in 1990 for the Big Apple, and the Republican senator, who has led the radical right in Congress for two decades.

As Kirkman coyly observes, both men have spent their adult lives obsessed with homosexuals. They also hail from tiny Monroe, N.C., are Southern Baptists and each spent a year at nearby Wingate College. Kirkman contends that he placed his first vote, at age 18, for Helms. Why? "Because he believes in God."

Part travelogue, part confession, part political film, Kirkman interviews everyone from a lesbian mother of an adopted HIV-infected toddler to his own father, a staunch Helmsian who is trying his damnedest to reach through the closet door and stay in touch with his son.

Kirkman doesn't have the confrontational bluster that made Michael Moore's "Roger and Me" such a hoot. He nearly makes up for the loss with earnestness and country boy charm. His Tar Heel diary is refreshingly uncynical and heartfelt, as much a love letter to his home state as a critique of its famous son.

NEWSDAY, 6/26/98 Part II/p. B7, Jack Mathews

Tim Kirkman's documentary, "Dear Jesse," is a plea from the heart from an openly gay North Carolina man to his state's openly homophobic senior senator, Jesse Helms, and even if Helms is twice the man Kirkman thinks he is, it will fall on deaf ears.

The mother of a gay son who died of AIDS recalls in the film how she wrote to the senator telling him of her son's death and asking him to rethink his public comments that homosexuals who die from the disease deserve their fate. Helms wrote back, unapologetic, expressing sadness only for her son's decision "to play Russian roulette with his sexuality."

"Dear Jesse" is a rambling, not particularly graceful but undeniably warranted diatribe, done in the form of an open letter, with Kirkman's emotionally charged narration interspersed with interviews of fellow North Carolinians, most of whom despair of Helms' politics-of-hate and his still-wide popularity.

"I believe Jesse Helms is an evil man," says young Mike Nelson, who is gay and the mayor of a small North Carolina town.

"Jesse is aggressively ignorant," says a church pastor. "If Jesus was here, he'd say, 'Pray for him, he's a very troubled man.'"

None of this is breaking news outside the state, and it's hard to imagine anyone going to see the film who doesn't already agree with it. But it does have merit beyond the obvious therapeutic value for Kirkman.

Jesse Helms isn't likely to change before he meets his maker at the Big Barbecue, but from the film's depiction of liberated gays and lesbians, North Carolina has already begun.

VILLAGE VOICE, 6/30/98, p. 141, Mark J. Huisman

Jesse Helms and Tim Kirkman have a lot in common—the same hometown, upbringing, religious background, education and vocational paths. And both, as Kirkman wryly observes, are obsessed with gay men. *Dear Jesse*—part road trip, part diary—is Kirkman's attempt to understand the homophobic ways of his home-state senator. The usual Helms is here, blasting gay rights, AIDS research, and arts funding, but Kirkman spends more film time talking about the senator with fellow North Carolinians—mechanics, mothers, poets, and pastors. Kirkman's approach is surprisingly balanced, eliciting some sympathy for a younger version of Helms who was labeled "obnoxious" in his high school newspaper. While *Dear Jesse* may be a little too self-referential Kirkman draws some forced comparisons in order to discuss how he came to terms with being a gay and the effect it had on friends, lovers, and family—one does get the sense

Kirkman put a few personal demons to bed. Helms, however, proves to be an even greater mystery, for filmmaker and viewer alike.

Also reviewed in:
NEW YORK TIMES, 6/26/98, p. E22, Lawrence Van Gelder
VARIETY, 10/13-19/97, p. 86, Daniel M. Kimmel

DECEIVER

An MGM Distribution and MDP Worldwide release of a Peter Glatzer production. *Executive Producer:* Mark Damon. *Producer:* Peter Glatzer. *Director:* Jonas Pate and Joshua Pate. *Screenplay:* Jonas Pate and Joshua Pate. *Director of Photography:* Bill Butler. *Editor:* Dan Lebental. *Music:* Harry Gregson-Williams. *Music Editor:* Adam Smalley. *Sound:* Peter Bentley and (music) Slamm Andrews. *Sound Editor:* Trevor Jolly. *Casting:* Laurel Smith. *Production Designer:* John Kretschmer. *Art Director:* Sonya Duvall. *Set Decorator:* Chuck Potter. *Set Dresser:* Peter "Beatle" Alvanos, Jamie Arbuckle, Michael Lane, and Steven J. Yetman. *Special Effects:* Ray Bivins. *Costumes:* Dana Allyson Greenberg. *Make-up:* Sara Seidman. *Stunt Coordinator:* Cal Johnson. *Running time:* 102 minutes. *MPAA Rating:* R.

CAST: Don Winston (Warren); Michael Parks (Dr. Banyard); Tim Roth (Wayland); Chris Penn (Braxton); Michael Rooker (Kennesaw); Renee Zellweger (Elizabeth); Ellen Burstyn (Mook); Rosanna Arquette (Mrs. Kennesaw); Mark Damon (Wayland's Father); J.C. Quinn (Priest); Jody Wilhelm (Mrs. Wayland); Ocie Pouncie (Boogie); Bob Hungerford (Jebby); Genevieve Butler (Mary Kennesaw); Chelsea Butler (Chelsea Kennesaw); David Alan Pickelsimer II (Billy Kennesaw); Paul Smith (Wayland's Girlfriend's Father); George Nannerello (Laughing Officer); Mike Flippo (Police Officer); James Middleton (Police Officer #2); Karina Logue (Sorority Girl); Ashley Rogers (Woman in Park).

LOS ANGELES TIMES, 1/30/98, Calendar/p. 22, David Kronke

[*The following review by David Kronke appeared in a slightly different form in* **NEWSDAY, 1/30/98, Part II/p. B13.**]

A murder has been committed, and, since this is a movie, it goes without saying that it is a sensational, grisly murder—a prostitute has been sawed in half, her body parts dumped miles from one another. A couple of detectives who specialize in polygraph tests are interrogating what amounts to the only, flimsily connected suspect, a guy otherwise not lacking for problems—he's an alcoholic epileptic estranged from his wealthy parents because he has no interest in putting his genius IQ to good use.

For a while, the unrelenting mind games of "Deceiver" are intriguing. But twin brothers Jonas and Joshua Pate, the filmmaking tyros who made a small splash at Sundance a couple of years back with "The Grave," have fashioned genre exercise that aspires to so much more, piling on the plot twists, tossing off eccentric asides, even reaching for some faux philosophizing.

By the end, there's a sort of anything-goes quality to the narrative and the film's distinctive look that defeats the coiled tension, and the Pate brothers' house of cards collapses. If just any old contrivance can be thrown out at any second, they fail to realize, then nothing has much weight or resonance.

Braxton (Chris Penn), and Kennesaw (Michael Rooker) are a couple of competent if unremarkable cops who are clearly in over their heads when they strap Wayland (Tim Roth) to the lie-detector machine. The gaunt, wiry Roth is a counterpoint in every respect to the soft, flaccid Rooker and Penn—as the film progresses, he proves to know more about the partnered cops than they know about each other.

The interrogation scenes are, until the over-the-top conclusion, effectively moody and claustrophobic. Too bad there are so many non-interrogation scenes littered throughout the movie.

Performances are strong, though each of the male stars are merely aping roles they've essayed several times before—Roth, the mercurial, potentially dangerous and definitely unhinged guy; Rooker, the bulky, hard-headed grunt; and Penn, the dumb but good-natured schmo.

The brothers Pate are trying to come across as the Coen brothers ("Fargo," etc.), Brian Singer ("The Usual Suspects") and, yes, "Pulp Fiction's" Quentin Tarantino, all at the same time. They work into the proceedings jokey title cards, split-screens, retro-timeless production design (everyone seems to have rotary-dial phones) and a willfully murky structure chockablock with flashbacks and/or fantasy sequences. But as the film's visuals become increasingly monochromatic, the already generous camera movements and expressionistic editing lurch into overdrive.

Alas, eventually such pyrotechnical stylishness, by calling attention to itself, undermines the suspense the Pates are attempting to create. Moreover, they make their story so willfully fuzzy that they seem to abandon logic. For example, the cops could have cleared up a whole lot of what they're trying to get out of Wayland simply by interviewing his parents.

And while the brothers are quite accomplished in scripting the confrontations between the cops and Wayland, their scenes between these men and the female characters are borderline embarrassing. The brothers wrote the role of the hooker especially for Renee Zellweger of "Jerry Maguire," which doesn't seem to be much of a gift—it's certainly not much of a role. Actresses, one would think, should raise an eyebrow or two if a role written specifically for them is that of a sleazy prostitute whose fate is to be cleaved in two.

Still, it's more than apparent from the film's evocative look and dialogue that these twins have talent enough for at least quintuplets. The Pates truly get jazzed cooking up oddball stuff and pulling things from their bountiful bag of cinematic tricks. Once they learn the pleasures inherent in a little restraint, both narratively and stylistically, perhaps they'll uncork a real gem.

NEW YORK POST, 1/30/98, p. 45, Thelma Adams

You gotta love a psycho thriller that prints the IQs of the principals right on the screen. Southern smart boys and identical twins, Jonas and Joshua Pate, the genealogical oddities behind "Deceiver," have an interest in letting the best IQ win.

Mirror, mirror on the wall, who's the smartest of them all? Prime murder suspect Wayland (Tim Roth), the son of a South Carolina textile fortune, rates a 151, the power of a strong rum, and the current requisite smarts for a serial killer (See *Desperate Measures*).

Batting for the police is the reasonably sharp Kennesaw (Michael Rooker). He comes in at an impressive, if not Stuyvesant-worthy, 122. Bruiser Braxton (Chris Penn) hits 102, ranking 125th out of 157 in his high-school graduating class.

Both blue-collar crime-fighters are trying to solve the grisly murder of a prostitute (Renee Zellweger, twitching and pouting her way to emotional vulnerability in a push-up bra and stilettos). The detectives' only lead is a scrap in her frock pocket with Wayland's number on it.

Like "Fallen," which opens with the apparatus of a gas chamber, "Deceiver" begins with the minutiae of a lie-detector test. We see Wayland hooked up and jerked around, we see the ink, the pens, the taut black bands crumpling his expensive shirt. Will the Ivy Leaguer be smart enough to outfox the box? Or does he have other tricks up his sleeves?

It doesn't take a more complicated symbol than a copy of a red book called "Truth Deception" lying on Braxton's desk to know where this exercise in "No Exit" will lead. The Oscar-nominated Roth ("Rob Roy") makes the medicine go down easily, despite an accent that never crosses the Mason-Dixon line.

The writer/director twins ("The Grave:) have a freaky sense of humor. The black comedy fuels the first half of the movie, but the Pates outsmart themselves with an overresearched and awkward subplot involving absinthe and a disease called Temporal Lobe Epilepsy. Apparently, absinthe does not make the heart grow fonder. A high point in "Deceiver" is Ellen Burstyn's crusty cameo as a bookie. Mook is a threatening and alien presence, her sparkling, reptilian eye shadow the only thing alive in her pale face. The weakest: a scene where Kennesaw's upper-class wife begs for rough sex, and we beg for better for the actress Rosanna Arquette, trapped in a sleazy "Cat on a Hot Tin Roof" slip.

Written and directed by the Pate brothers, the identical-twin discoveries of two Sundances past, *Deceiver* features a brilliant madman, the dissolute Southerner that's best done these days by Kevin Spacey. Tim Roth gets the call here, playing an absinthe-drinking textile heir accused of cutting a prostitute in two and dumping her halves in a Charleston park. He's interrogated by a lie-detector-wielding pair of cops (Michael Rooker playing the loud flatfoot, Chris Penn the dumb one), whom Roth variously befuddles, enrages, and lies to, all the while leading the audience down a *Unusual Suspects*-like path of fabrication.

If you can get over the fact that everything in *Deceiver* is, like a lie, it's halfway diverting. Josh and Jonas Pate lock their characters into stagy but effective three-way confrontations that open out onto an increasingly lurid series of interlocked flashbacks. But unlike Bryan Singer's ballsy fuck-you to audiences everywhere, *Deceiver* lacks what you'd call "originality," repeating the look and feel of a neat gambit that, having already been done once, has lost all its powers to astound.

Also reviewed in:
CHICAGO TRIBUNE, 1/30/98, Friday/p. J. Michael Wilmington
NEW YORK TIMES, 1/30/98, p. E12, Janet Maslin

DEE SNIDER'S STRANGELAND

A Raucous Releasing release.   *Producer:* David L. Bushell and Dee Snider.   *Director:* John Pieplow.   *Screenplay:* Dee Snider. *Director of Photography:* Goran Pavicevic.   *Editor:* Jeff Kushner.   *Music:* Anton Sanko.   *Casting:* Lee Ann Groff.   *Production Designer:* Debbie DeVilla.   *Costumes:* Jillian Ann Kreiner.   *Make-up Special effects:* Michael Burnett.   *Running time:* 90 minutes. *MPAA Rating:* Not Rated.

CAST: Dee Snider (Captain Howdy);   Kevin Gage (Mike Gage);   Brett Harrelson (Steve Christian);   Elizabeth Pena (Toni Gage); Robert Englund (Jackson Roth);   Linda Cardellini (Genevieve Gage);   Amy Smart (Angela).

LOS ANGELES TIMES, 10/5/98, Calendar/p. 8, Bob Heisler

Capt. Howdy is the kind of guy who likes to hear himself talk. So he sews together the lips of visitors to his surgical dungeon in otherwise lovely Helverton, Colo.

Unless the name Dee Snider means something to you from the heavy-metal group Twisted Sister, there's no reason to read on. "Dee Snider's Strangeland" is the kind of movie your parents warned you about. And they were right.

It's a disturbing, hopeless, irredeemable series of images that will scar you if you wander into it unprepared. The images are strong and violent, and ultimately shocking. But the effect is not horrific, just numbing. And there's no reward for sitting through "Strangeland," a standard crime-against-a-cop's-family plot larded with the tools and incantations of body-piercing and torture.

Far from being a new horror-genre icon, Snider's Howdy is a serial sadist who draws his victims from Internet chat/try-on rooms for a little sew and tell, until he traps the teenage daughter of Det. Mike Gage.

Then it's www.war.com.

In short order, he is arrested, found insane, learns to wear cardigans and take his medicine, returns to his home, is visited by the Helverton vigilante society, stops taking his medicine and sprouts his old studs and spikes in a revenge spree that sweeps up the town's moralizers. Robert Englund makes an appearance, which makes it an official horror movie. Even the technology ratchets up to full frontal video.

That the petard on which Howdy is hoisted is of his own making, not society's, is the best indication that "Strangeland" is strange for its own sake. Capt. Howdy—the name of the unseen hand that invited evil into "The Exorcist"—claims a spiritual foundation, but it's entirely one way. Howdy has no acolytes, only victims.

The only rite of passage his rituals offer is passage into death. And his own willingness to cross over removes him from the roster of characters to care about.

NEW YORK POST, 10/4/98, p. 41, Larry Worth

Dee Snider was never much of a singer, as demonstrated when he led Twisted Sister to its one-hit wonder status in the 1980s. But compared with his acting and writing, his vocal talents now seem legendary.

The proof lies in "Dee Snider's Strangeland," a supposedly suspenseful tale devoid of anything akin to chills or thrills. More damningly, it goes out of its way to disgust viewers with consistently stomach-churning imagery.

Here's the setup: Capt. Howdy (Snider)—whose multiply pierced face passes for a contorted pin cushion—cruises Internet chat rooms and lures teens to his home. Once they cross his threshold, each gets a one-way ticket to the torture dungeon.

After sewing shut the victims' mouth and eyes with surgical needles, Capt. Howdy strips and cages them. Egged on by their screams, he then inserts various hooks and monster-sized studs into their genitals. When a policeman's daughter joins the imprisoned, the cops engage in a cat-and-mouse hunt to nab the latter-day Torquemada.

Still, the only real mystery is how Snider attracted even B-movie actors such as Kevin Gage, Elizabeth Pena and Robert (Freddy Krueger) Englund. Saddest of all: the participation of Brett Harrelson, who shined opposite brother Woody in "The People vs. Larry Flynt."

Yet blame really belongs with director John Pieplow. He quickly proves himself a hack of the first order, particularly when trying to incorporate a vigilante-justice subplot.

But in the end, Pieplow's misdeeds diminish beside the histrionic horror of Snider, a screenwriter from hell and all-around sick pup. If "Strangeland" is indicative of the way his mind works, a lobotomy should be mandatory.

Also reviewed in:
NEW YORK TIMES, 10/5/98, p. E3, Anita Gates
VARIETY, 10/5-11/98, p. 68, Oliver Jones

DEEP IMPACT

A Paramount Pictures and Dreamworks Pictures release of a Zanuck/Brown production. *Executive Producer:* Steven Spielberg, Walter Parkes, and Joan Bradshaw. *Producer:* Richard D. Zanuck and David Brown. *Director:* Mimi Leder. *Screenplay:* Michael Tolkin and Bruce Joel Rubin. *Director of Photography:* Dietrich Lohmann. *Editor:* David Rosenbloom. *Music:* James Horner. *Music Editor:* Jim Henrikson. *Sound:* Mark Hopkins McNabb and (music) Simon Rhodes. *Sound Editor:* J. Paul Huntsman and Walter Newman. *Casting:* Allison Jones. *Production Designer:* Leslie Dilley. *Art Director:* Gary Kosko, Thomas Valentine, Dennis Bradford, and Andrew Neskoromny. *Set Designer:* Joshua P. Lusby, Richard F. Mays, Suzan Torres, and Dean Wolcott. *Set Decorator:* Peg Cummings. *Special Effects:* Michael Lantieri. *Costumes:* Ruth Myers. *Make-up:* John M. Elliott, Jr. *Stunt Coordinator:* M. James Arnett and Charles Croughwell. *Running time:* 120 minutes. *MPAA Rating:* PG-13.

CAST: Robert Duvall (Spurgeon Tanner); Téa Leoni (Jenny Lerner); Elijah Wood (Leo Biederman); Vanessa Redgrave (Robin Lerner); Maximillan Schell (Jason Lerner); Morgan Freeman (President Tom Beck); James Cromwell (Alan Rittenhouse); Ron Eldard (Oren Monash); Jon Favreau (Gus Partenza); Laura Innes (Beth Stanley); Mary McCormack (Andrea Baker); Richard Schiff (Don Biederman); Leelee Sobieski (Sarah Hotchner); Blair Underwood (Mark Simon); Dougray Scott (Eric Vennekor); Gary Werntz (Chuck Hotchner); Bruce Weitz (Stuart Caley); Betsy Brantley (Ellen Biederman); O'Neal Compton (Morton

Entrekin);   Rya Kihlstedt (Chloe);   Alexander Baluev (Mikhail Tulchinsky);   Caitlin Fein and
Amanda Fein (Caitlin Stanley);   Joseph Uria (Ira Moskatel);   Una Damon (Marianne Duclos);
Mark Moses (Tim Urbanska);   Derek de Lint (Theo Van Sertema);   Charles Dumas (Jeff
Worth);   Suzy Nakamura (Jenny's Assistant);   Alimi Ballard (Bobby Rhue);   Charles Martin
Smith (Marcus Wolf); Katie Hagan (Jane Biederman);   Denise Crosby (Vicky Hotchner);   Frank
Whiteman (Priest);   Jason Dohring (Harold);   Jasmine Harrison (Kid);   Rahi Azizi(Student);
Tucker Smallwood (Ivan Bronsky);   Hannah Werntz (Holly Rittenhouse);   Merrin Dungey
(Sheila Bradley);   Kimberly Huie (Wendy Mogel);   William Fair (Grey Man);   Francis X.
McCarthy (General Scott);   Ellen Bry (Stofsky);   Lisa Ann Grant (Reporter);   Leslie Dilley
(Waiter);   Concetta Tomei (Patricia Ruiz);   Mike O'Malley (Mike Perry);   Kurtwood Smith
(Otis Hefter);   Gerry Griffin (NASA Official);   Charlie Hartsock (David Baker);   Jennifer
Jostyn (Mariette Monash);   Don Handfield (Dwight Tanner);   Jason Frasca (Steve Tanner);
Cynthia Ettinger (Pretty Woman);   Benjamin Stralka (Little Boy);   Stephanie Patton (Brittany
Baker);   Michael Winters (NASA Guy);   John Ducey (Young Lieutenant);   Christopher Darga
(Section Leader);   Joshua Colwell (CAPCOM); Cornelius Lewis (Bus Sergeant);   Kevin La
Rosa (Pilot).

LOS ANGELES TIMES, 5/8/98, Calendar/p. 2, Kenneth Turan

Wolf-Biederman is a comet 7 miles long, roughly the size of Manhattan. Weighing in at 500
billion tons, it's got the heft of Mt. Everest. But instead of minding its own business in deep
space, this big bully is headed for direct contact with Earth, where a collision will cause the end
of life as we know it.

Sounds like a summer movie to me.

The latest in Hollywood's almost biblical procession of disaster films, "Deep Impact" tries with
moderate success to be more than just the sum of its special effects. The first of two pictures this
year ("Armageddon" is set for July release) about intrusive objects from outer space, "Deep
Impact" is standard fare crisply and professionally done. Though director Mimi Leder is expecting
a bit much when she hopes audiences "will walk out of this movie reevaluating their lives and the
choices they've made," at least they won't be embarrassed to have gone in the first place.

Disaster films, especially ones that flirt with the extinction of the entire human race, have a
delicate line to walk. Given that the best special-effects shots are more likely to close the picture
than open it, how do you keep viewers involved for the duration?

"Deep Impact" has opted for a somewhat upscale approach. The film employs actors such as
Robert Duvall, Vanessa Redgrave and Morgan Freeman, and asks a pair of reputable
screenwriters, Michael Tolkin ("The Player," "The Rapture") and Bruce Joel Rubin ("Ghost"),
to construct a story line that interweaves the reactions of different people to the impending
catastrophe.

Youngest of the group is Leo Biederman (Elijah Wood), a 14-year-old high school student who
discovers the comet on an astronomy field trip. He also discovers that he has a crush on classmate
Sara Hotchner (Leelee Sobieski), a situation that gets noticeably trickier as the possible end of the
world approaches.

Barely older than Leo is Jenny Lerner (Tea Leoni), a spunky, ambitious young TV newsperson
who stumbles on what the government has tried to keep secret, that that darn comet will hit in
less than a year and cause more trouble than Dennis the Menace. In addition to her career, Jenny
has to deal with the troublesome emotional situation between her divorced parents (Redgrave and
Maximilian Schell).

The government, led by President Tom Beck (Freeman), is not without a plan: A newly built
spaceship called Messiah will be sent to intercept the comet, plant nuclear devices below its
surface, and, with any kind of luck, blow it to tiny bits.

Mostly young and telegenic, the Messiah crew resents the presence of old-timer Spurgeon
"Fish" Tanner (Duvall), the last man to walk on the moon, who they feel was brought on the
spaceship strictly for P.R. reasons.

It is typical of the film's pleasant way of telegraphing its events that though the other crew
members think Tanner is expendable, the fact that he's played by a big star and they're not means
that he's going to turn out to be plenty important before the close.

Besides working out all these human equations, "Deep Impact" has a what-if strain that is perhaps its most interesting feature. The contingency plans the government has made, if all else fails, are rather fascinating, and director Leder shows, as she did in her previous "The Peacemaker," that she has a facility for putting large-scale logistics on screen. These sequences also allow Freeman to be so effectively presidential that you can't imagine voting for anyone else. No, not even Harrison Ford.

It would be nice to say that all this effort has turned "Deep Impact" into a model for getting top-drawer scripts for special-effects movies, but that's not the case. Though you rarely wince at what people say, and there are even occasional bright lines, (a Messiah crewperson on possible failure: "Look on the bright side. We'll all have high schools named after us"), these people's problems are more pro forma than involving.

Also, key emotional sequences are only sporadically convincing, and "Deep Impact" has trouble resisting the obvious. The film's closing moments, for instance, include scene after scene of women having emotional crises with infants or toddlers: Either they're being given away, or saved at terrible cost, or held up to be admired via video by tearful fathers in space. Even the impressive closing special-effects shots of walls of water crushing flimsy-looking models of New York and Washington, D.C., can't shake the feeling that we've somehow wandered into the outtakes of a Gerber baby food commercial.

Does this mean the end of the world will come not with a bang but with a Pamper? Stay tuned.

NEW YORK, 5/25/98, p. 79, David Denby

A huge comet is heading this way, and the world is about to end: Tidal waves will sweep over the sushi bars, ashes will blot out the sky over Six Flags Adventure, Maureen Dowd will write no more, there is nothing but death by burning and drowning to look forward to. And what do the unlucky earthlings do? In *Deep Impact*, it's mainly what they don't do that astonishes me. They don't splurge, they don't drink champagne, they don't experiment with interesting sexual possibilities between one creature and another. Nor do they convert to the doctrine of Lao-tzu or Jim Jones. Robert Duvall, as the level-headed boss of a spaceship trying to intercept the comet, reads *Moby Dick* to one of the less literate younger crew members, but the filmmakers let us hear no more than "Call me Ishmael." (Presumably, Duvall made it to the end of the first chapter.) The president of the United States, Morgan Freeman, talks turkey to the public: He tells us we will die. Nothing much is made of the fact that the first African-American president has the unfortunate luck to get hit with a problem almost equal in importance to Monica Lewinsky's sexual adventures. The president stays calm and tries to get other people to act calmly. *Deep Impact,* which was written by Bruce Joel Rubin and Michael Tolkin and directed by Mimi Leder, is very solemn and responsible—a sobering experience. I have been known to complain about the hollowly ironic manner of the recent big spectacles, but I don't know that I was longing for a literal-minded, "sensitive" movie about the end of the world. The filmmakers treat us as if we were badly in need of instruction as to how to behave on that mighty day. So we learn: Head for the high ground.

Once the comet splashes down in the Atlantic, there is a beautiful, enormous wave that cleans up Jones Beach once and for all. But that's about it, as far as special effects go—the rest are cheesy and obvious. The drowning of New York passes without an instant's terror—or emotion. There's a fine-looking traffic jam, but an attempt to set up a Noah's Ark situation, with two of every species transported to an underground limestone cave, falls flat for lack of humor and fantasy. The best parts of the movie come right at the beginning, when young Elijah Wood, a teen astronomer, discovers the comet by accident. For a moment, the movie has a Spielbergian sense of wonder, but despite Spielberg's presence on the project as executive producer, the rest of *Deep Impact* fizzles out.

NEW YORK POST, 5/8/98, p. 43, Rod Dreher

"Deep Impact"? Not much of one from this disappointing disaster flick, yet another puzzling dud from the would-be wonderboys at DreamWorks SKG. It's the Kohoutek of summer comet-crash movies: great advance hype, lousy payoff.

Hopped up on the tantalizing ad campaign, everybody wants to see the gargantuan tidal wave hose Manhattan. Lo, it is a most impressive moment. The monstrous wall of water rises high over the World Trade Center towers and flumes through the skyscraper canyons with the force of firehoses. Cool.

But you have to sit through *beaucoup* blather and lame exposition to get to the "money shot." The movie is a lot like amateur sex: initial excitement followed by buzz-killing chitchat, then the quickie Big Bang, concluding with a hasty over-and-out. Is that all there is? Yep.

The movie starts promisingly, with an intrepid MSNBC reporter (Tea Leoni) stumbling onto a story even bigger than the O.J. trial, if such a thing were possible: The government is covering up knowledge that a massive comet—larger than Mount Everest; as big as Manhattan—is heading straight for You Know Where.

President Beck (Morgan Freeman) swears her to secrecy in exchange for allowing her the first question at the White House press conference to announce the bad news. Beck says the comet will arrive in one year, and a joint U.S.-Russian space mission will shortly depart to attempt to destroy it with nukes.

Much of "Deep Impact" is about what happens while waiting for the comet to hit. How would people behave if they knew the world was likely to end on a specific date? It's a fascinating thought experiment, but one carried out without much style or substance in the bland, mushy screenplay, by Bruce Joel Rubin and Michael Tolkin.

Leoni's character dithers about whether to forgive her father (Maximilian Schell) for having abandoned her mother (Vanessa Redgrave). Leo, the boy discoverer of the comet (Elijah Wood), ponders his future, or lack thereof, with his teen sweetie (Leelee Sobieski). Et cetera.

Meanwhile, Robert Duvall labors mightily to work up some interest in his space crew's do-or-die mission. They land on the comet's surface and try to dose that bad boy with nuclear weapons. It's the only time this movie comes close to being riveting.

They fail, of course; otherwise, where would we get that tidal wave? The comet strike is pretty nifty, but it comes very late in the film. In a way, "Deep Impact" should be lauded for trying to provide real characters instead of the usual disaster-movie cutouts.

But the existential drama they find themselves in is flat and weirdly uninvolving: I've seen better TV miniseries. Director Mimi Leder kept things popping at breakneck speed in "The Peacemaker," her last film, but her pacing plods, bringing the movie to a standstill so quiet you can barely hear the ticking of the Doomsday Clock.

Those who go expecting to see an "Independence Day"-style destructo fest will be deeply impacted by the wussy conflagration on display here. We're told that the wave rolled over Europe and Africa, too, but apparently there wasn't enough change in the special effects budget to show the wall of water looming over the Eiffel Tower or the Sphinx. Some apocalypse.

One of the most egregious conceits of "Deep Impact" is the notion that people would watch the world end on MSNBC. As if! Then again, if humanity were facing utter annihilation, I'd probably be in the mood for that snarky Keith Olbermann to put a little ironic distance between me and oblivion.

NEWSDAY, 5/8/98, Part II/p. B3, Jack Mathews

"Ladies and gentlemen, the president of the United States."

A door opens and into a room filled with White House correspondents and TV crews strides Morgan Freeman's Tom Beck, apparently America's first black president. But in Mimi Leder's woefully misfired "Deep Impact," that's neither here nor there. The gravity of this press conference far overshadows any social milestones the country may have reached.

It seems that a comet the size of Mt. Everest is on a collision course with North America, and that the U.S. government, in cooperation with other major governments around the world, has been discretely preparing for an *Extinction Level Event*. The last one of those left Earth covered with dinosaur bones.

For the last eight months, the president soberly intones, caves in Missouri have been refurbished as a modern Ark, ready to house a million people and two of everything else. But that's only a precaution, Beck assures the nation, in the event that a crack team of astronauts aboard the encouragingly named Messiah spacecraft fails in its mission to interrupt the comet and nuke it. In the meantime, it's business as usual, fellow Americans. We'll keep you posted.

"Deep Impact" is the first of the year's two Earth annihilation movies—Michael Bey's "Armageddon" arrives July 1—and we can only hope "Impact" proves worse. The last time Hollywood held a special effects/disaster movie race, the subject was volcanoes, and both movies were disasters.

Given the cataclysmic premise of Leder's film, it is shockingly dull. This is a story about a world counting down to its execution, yet there is hardly any tension or compelling human drama. And the computer-generated effects themselves, once contact is made and the Eastern Seaboard is slammed by a tidal wave, are downright cheesy.

The script, by Bruce Jay Rubin ("Ghost") and Michael Tolkin ("The Player"), intercuts three spongy subplots. One is about the high school student (Elijah Wood) who first discovers the comet during an astronomy club outing in Virginia, and later attempts to rescue his girlfriend (Leelee Sobieski) from the big wave. The second is about a fledgling MSNBC reporter (Téa Leoni) who stumbles into the government's Ark program and passively compels the president to go public. And the third is aboard the Messiah with its four youthful astronauts and the NASA veteran they call Fish (Robert Duvall).

The TV reporter sequences are a hoot. Leoni's character is following a sex scandal about a Cabinet member she's been told is having an affair with a woman named Ellie. When she confronts him with the name, he babbles something about her having in her hands the biggest story in history, and soon after, she's being rushed to a meeting with the president in the White House galley.

It turns out that Ellie is ELE, the code name for the looming disaster, and its mere mention by an outsider is enough to unravel a secret involving thousands of workers and dozens of government officials that has been kept from the media for eight months! Where's a leaker when you need one?

Leder, who made her directing debut with DreamWorks inaugural film "The Peacemaker," tells these crocks with deadpan sincerity. She's clearly only interested in the action, and given the leaden script, you can't blame her. But without some viable human drama to set up and sustain the action sequences, they have no emotional urgency. You're likely to worry less about the characters' lives than the actors' careers.

Leoni gives us a sad-sack heroine, a melancholy Lois Lane for whom it's hard to have any rooting interest. Duvall seems lost in the role of an aging astronaut with the right stuff. And Wood's character exists for no apparent reason other than to show teenagers a familiar face.

Sadder still are the appearances of Vanessa Redgrave and Maximillian Schell. As Leoni's estranged parents, they have little to do but react to images on a television screen.

DreamWorks and Paramount, the studios that co-produced "Deep Impact," have beaten Disney's "Armageddon" to the market, but so far, all they've proved is the old adage that haste makes waste.

SIGHT AND SOUND, 7/98, p. 39, Philip Strick

Leo Biederman, a 14-year-old amateur astronomer, photographs an unknown object among the stars. His photo is checked by astronomer Marcus Wolf who is killed in a car crash just after he realises the object is a comet headed for earth. A year later, television reporter Jenny Lerner scents a government scandal but discovers that an Extinction Level Event (ELE) is pending: President Tom Beck announces that the Wolf-Biederman comet is heading towards earth. An experimental spaceship, the *Messiah,* is sent with veteran astronaut Spurgeon Tanner aboard to land on the comet and shatter it with nuclear bombs. While Jenny, having become a leading newscaster, covers the mission on television, Tanner succeeds only in splitting the comet. With two comets now threatening the planet, the president announces that underground 'arks' will shelter a limited number of selected people. Leo marries his sweetheart Sarah to ensure she survives with him in an ark, but she won't abandon her parents.

Leo hunts for his young wife amid the crowds desperately fleeing the expected tidal wave, and Jenny gives up her own place in the ark to a colleague to await the end with her father. The smaller comet hits the Atlantic and the wave destroys New York. Reunited, Leo and Sarah manage to stay just ahead of the devastation by fleeing inland on a motorbike. In space, Tanner steers the *Messiah* into the remaining comet and blows it into harmless fragments.

Where previous disaster movies have almost unfailingly implied that we deserve every piece of retribution we get, *Deep Impact* is peopled with decent types who fall over themselves to move aside when the panic starts. Perversely dragging a feelgood message from an apocalyptic tale, the DreamWorks team effort pays little heed to the juicier aspects of social chaos and firmly snubs the gospel according to Philip Wylie (who warned of divine displeasure in the novel *When Worlds Collide*) by reassuring us of God's vote for the US president.

The most predictable feature of this screen president is not so much that he ignores the rest of the world, nor even that he bounces back safely from the ark in the wake of the crisis, but that he is played by Morgan Freeman. Mellow of voice, assuaging of gaze, even conciliatory of surname, Freeman has all the advantages when it comes to suggesting balance, reason and acceptance. His presence sets such a tone of propriety that heroes seem to leap from the woodwork when he calls, wonderfully personified by noble Robert Duvall, astronaut extraordinaire, cleverly capable of halting a comet with a single blast of his weird been-there-done-that cackle. And with the tone set, couch-potatoes, who after all have seen far more of Mimi Leder's work than cinemagoers in the past decade, have a grand game ahead of spotting reliable television faces like Laura Innes and Ron Eldard from *ER*, Mary McCormack from *Murder One* and *ER*, Tucker Smallwood from *Space: Above and Beyond*, Derek de Lint from *Poltergeist: The Legacy*, and the saintly Denise Crosby from *Star Trek: The Next Generation*. These are not acquaintances to be washed away by a mere mile-high tidal wave. They'll be back next week in some other episode, old or new. Even in the meteoric rush of television, survival is written upon them.

That Téa Leoni *(The Naked Truth)* also fails to persuade us of collective vulnerability is the fault partly of her uneasy expression (in which, curiously, she resembles Nicole Kidman in Leder's *The Peacemaker*, rattling around in a role several sizes too large) and partly of her peculiarly masochistic function as identifier, interpreter, and finally passive victim of the bolt from the heavens. Clutching her father in forgiveness for having married a girl about her own age, she at last confronts the monstrous wall of water in a magnificent vision of suicide that could have wrung us dry if only we had managed to dredge up some enthusiasm for either parent or offspring. The objective of many disaster yarns is the destruction of New York, and *Deep Impact* pays its dues with splendid if all-too brief scenes of toppling skyscrapers. These evoke all the helplessness that audiences have come to expect when faced with special effects running riot, but they avoid generating much sense of tragedy. A far better director than given the credit for on *The Peacemaker*, Leder maintains admirable pace and fluency of editing and camerawork with her regular team. (The film is deservedly dedicated to her late director of photography, Dietrich Lehmann.) It is hard to imagine a better space-trip, all skills at full blast, than the journey to the comet. But it's in one way fitting to find the director's husband and daughter (Gary and Hannah Werntz) in small roles: somehow an awesome topic has become an almost cosy family picture.

VILLAGE VOICE, 5/19/98, Film Special/p. 134, Gary Dauphin

You get the gist of the Steven Spielberg-guided *Deep Impact* from its opening moments: two brainy teenage lovebirds playfully arguing about a speck in the night sky. Astronomy club member Leo Biederman (Elijah Wood) will get the dubious honor of codiscovering the hammer of god that's hanging over humanity's collective head, but initially the comet's import is of the small-scale variety: the innocent ribbing about fame from Leo's buddies, the happy glow from his family and girlfriend about the whole world knowing just how smart their boy really is. *Deep Impact* will evolve into a Hollywood summer disaster movie, but first there's the little Spielbergian bits of business to take care of, before the tidal waves and background music can start swelling. It can be slow going, but it's certainly one way of ending the world.

An event of this scale makes for great prime-time fodder, so, appropriately, another protagonist is up-and-coming MSNBC researcher Jenny Lerner (an emotionally credible Tea Leoni). On the trail of a White House scandal involving President Beck (Morgan Freeman, apparently unconcerned by the ironies of having the world end on a black commander in chief's watch) and a mistress named Ellie, Lerner soon discovers the bimbo is really an "Extinction Level Event" that's been kept secret while American and Russian scientists cobble together a response, the potential apocalypse her personal rocket to the big time.

Deep Impact doesn't offer many outsized sci-fi or disaster-related kicks until its final minutes, director Mimi Leder and screenwriters Bruce Joel Rubin and Michael Tolkin busying themselves with a Hollywood instruction in good citizenship. A fair-minded (but chilling) lottery for bunker space is established, families board up homes, and crowds mill about dejectedly but relatively peaceably as the army takes the lucky 1 million winners underground. President Beck calls press conferences, alternately explaining the nation's response to the last days like a smiling schoolteacher and leading global prayer sessions, Freeman successfully conveys a mix of competence and helplessness.

There is a running subplot about NASA's attempts to nuke the comet into oblivion (with these scenes weighted toward human drama by the presence of aging Apollo astronaut Robert Duvall). Still, *Deep Impact* is a curiously understated outing. Like *Titanic,* the film is laden with F/X but they're mostly below the dramatic skin, non-science-fiction forms of unreality like a Washington, D.C, skyline dotted with fleeing helicopters—the ultimate Saigon. Leder and the technicians at Industrial Light and Magic deliver the goods, but after insisting for 90 minutes that human beings are worth saving, they just can't bring themselves to linger on the horror implicit in *Deep Impact*'s own premise. The comet impact and climactic, reel three, 1000-foot tidal wave are treated as a kind of necessary evil. *Deep Impact* seems less interested in contemplating the end than it is in finding an acceptable highwater "Whew!" mark, where, despite the deaths of millions and the shattering of whole cities, what President Beck sonorously calls "our way of life!" can logically be expected to continue.

Unlike *Independence Day,* which gleefully smashed everything in its first act in order to put it all back together, *Deep Impact* is all teary, loving togetherness, its last moments just the thud of F/X realism hitting solid Hollywood reassurance. There's probably a middle ground between out-of-control digital hysteria and soft-focused hokum, but don't expect to find it in a summertime multiplex.

Also reviewed in:
CHICAGO TRIBUNE, 5/8/98, Friday/p. A, Michael Wilmington
NEW YORK TIMES, 5/8/98, p. E12, Janet Maslin
NEW YORKER, 5/18/98, p. 89, Anthony Lane
VARIETY, 5/11-17/98, dp. 57, Todd McCarthy
WASHINGTON POST, 5/8/98, p. F1, Rita Kempley
WASHINGTON POST, 5/8/98, Weekend/p. 61, Michael O'Sullivan

DEEP RISING

A Hollywood Pictures release of a Laurence Mark production. *Executive Producer:* Barry Bernardi. *Producer:* Laurence Mark and John Baldecchi. *Director:* Stephen Sommers. *Screenplay:* Stephen Sommers. *Director of Photography:* Howard Atherton. *Editor:* Bob Ducsay and John Wright. *Music:* Jerry Goldsmith. *Music Editor:* Kenny Hall. *Sound:* Rob Young, Frank Griffiths, and (music) Bruce Botnick. *Sound Editor:* Douglas Murray and Patrick Dodd. *Casting:* Mary Goldberg. *Production Designer:* Holger Gross. *Art Director:* Kevin Ishioka and Sandy Cochrane. *Set Designer:* Luis G. Hoyos, Masako Masuda, and William J. Newmon II. *Set Decorator:* Rose Marie McSherry and Ann Marie Corbett. *Set Dresser:* Kevin "Noogie" Park. *Special Effects:* Darrell D. Pritchett, Stewart Bradley, Tim Storvick, and Lars Lenander. *Visual Effects:* Mike Shea. *Costumes:* Joseph Porro. *Make-up:* Rosalina Da Silva. *Special Effects Make-up:* Stephan Dupuis. *Stunt Coordinator:* Gary Combs. *Running time:* 106 minutes. *MPAA Rating:* R.

CAST: Treat Williams (John Finnegan); Famke Janssen (Trillian); Anthony Heald (Simon Canton); Kevin J. O'Connor (Joey Pantucci); Wes Studi (Hanover); Derrick O'Connor (Captain); Jason Flemyng (Mulligan); Cliff Curtis (Mamooli); Clifton Powell (Mason); Trevor Goddard (T. Ray); Djimon Hounsou (Vivo); Una Damon (Leila); Clint Curtis (Billy); Warren T. Takeuchi (Radar Man); Linden Banks (Communications Officer); Jack Anker

(Corpse);   Anne-Simone (Video Vault Woman);   Leanne Adachi (Toilet Lady);   Melanie Carr (Dealer);   Colin McCarlie (Sonar Man);   Jim May (Mystery Man);   Jana Sommers and Marti Baldecchi (Party Girls).

LOS ANGELES TIMES, 1/30/98, Calendar/p. 16, Kevin Thomas

[The following review by Kevin Thomas appeared in a slightly different form in NEWSDAY, 1/30/98, Part II/p. B7.]

With the Titanic, it was a plain old iceberg that did it in. But with "Deep Rising's" brand-new $487.6-million pleasure ship the Argonautica, it's immense sea serpents lurking in the depths of the South China Sea, surfacing to feast on its guests and wrecking the vessel in the process.

Imagine a giant octopus, at least as big as a mansion with many more tentacles than eight. Each tentacle is like the hose of a vacuum cleaner, its opening like a Venus' flytrap surrounded by pincers. These man-eaters are designed to crush you to death and drink your blood—while you're still alive!

"Deep Rising" is shrewdly designed to churn up thrills and chills via first-rate special effects and inventive suspense, yet it invites deliberate laughter. You could call it a monster-from-the-deep action-adventure comedy. It aims to divert audiences, and writer-director Stephen Sommers, who combines a light touch with a breakneck pace, hits the mark.

Treat Williams stars as a devil-may-care mercenary with a boat. He's hired by bad-guy Wes Studi, who is involved in a shady scheme with the Argonautica's owner (Anthony Heald), but the serpent attack aborts it.

Sommers piles on the cliffhanging action but never loses sight of his sense of humor. Williams and everyone else play tongue-in-cheek without overdoing it, for Sommers wisely resists camp. There's no condescension to action fans, who may just make "Deep Rising" a hit around the world. It's a technically impressive production, although the destruction of the Argonautica is not in "Titanic's" league—but then what is? And it boasts an appropriately roaring, thundering all-stops-out score by none other than Jerry Goldsmith.

Sommers and his producers have lined up a distinctive international cast that includes Famke Janssen as a poised, elegant jewel thief aboard the Argonautica, and a scene-stealing, Kevin J. O'Connor as Williams' wide-eyed, naive mechanic, who has a Jimmy Stewart crack in his voice. The rest of Williams' crew are tough types, played by such versatile actors as England's Jason Flemyng and New Zealand's Cliff Curtis.

The only thing deep about "Deep Rising" is the water, but it's not all wet.

NEW YORK POST, 1/30/98, p. 43, Michael Medved

"We've got creepy crawlies all over the place, eating us up one by one! I'd say that's a tight jam!"

This desperate declaration by one of the endlessly imperiled characters in "Deep Rising" serves as an eloquent summary of the motion picture's story line. Think "Aliens" meets "Under Siege" and you'll get the basic idea behind this silly, slick and surprisingly scary screamer.

Treat Williams plays a soldier of fortune in the South China Sea who rents out his speedy boat to a gang of thugs led by Wes Studi ("The Last of the Mohicans") and including Djimon Hounsou (whose hammy performance hardly computes with his noble work in "Amistad").

The bad guys plan to cash in big time by interrupting the maiden voyage of a huge, gaudy pleasure ship that combines the most obnoxious elements of the Love Boat and the Titanic.

By the time the heavily armed and heavy-breathing intruders hit their target, however, nearly all of the passengers and crew have been mysteriously slaughtered, leaving behind bloody decks and huge piles of horribly mutilated carcasses.

"Are we talking some kind of mutated sea monsters here?" asks one of the doomed craft's newcomers.

Indeed, we are—the sort of creatures that not only chew their victims but definitely inhale. Among the few survivors on the glamorous ship are a gorgeous jewel thief (Famke Janssen) and the craft's conspiratorial owner (Anthony Heald), who join the adventurers in fighting for their lives against the wicked worms.

If you can't guess who will escape the hideous carnage, try putting your money on the best-looking bods in the bunch.

Writer-director Stephen Sommers, whose previous work includes Disney's dismal recent remakes of "Huck Finn" and "The Jungle Book," is much more in his slimy element here.

At its best, the film recalls "Tremors," a 1990 worm-in-cheek horror flick about gigantic, snake-like desert creatures with big-time eating disorders.

"Deep Rising" isn't as smart or savvy as its predecessor, but it delivers splashy, genuinely creepy effects, well-staged chase scenes, plenty of stomach-churning gore, innumerable explosions, macho firearms, bodacious babes, visceral chills, breathless pacing and even a few flashes of outrageous humor.

Kevin J. O'Connor, as Treat Williams' loyal partner and resourceful grease monkey, nearly steals the picture from the monsters with his especially endearing comic relief. No one would describe "Deep Rising" as deep, but it should get a rise out of its intended audience.

SIGHT AND SOUND, 11/98, p. 44, Leslie Felperin.

American-born John Finnegan and the crew of his boat-for-hire are transporting a band of mercenaries, led by Hanover, to a secret rendezvous in the South China Sea. The mercenaries are planning to raid and then destroy a cruise liner, the *Argonautica* with Russian missiles so that its owner Simon Canton can collect the insurance money. But before Canton and the crew can evacuate the *Argonautica* a giant sea-creature attacks the ship, killing almost everyone on board apart from Canton, the ship's captain, and Trillian, a woman jewel thief, who had been locked in a refrigerator.

Looking for machine parts to fix their own boat, Finnegan and the mercenaries board the *Argonautica* and find the survivors. But one by one, the monster kills them all until only Finnegan, Trillian and Canton are left. Canton tries to kill the other two in order to use the only means of escape, a waterbike, and ensure their silence, but Finnegan defeats him.

He and Trillian make it to an island just before the missiles destroy the *Argonautica* and the monster. Finnegan's engineer Joey miraculously washes up on the island alive as well, but something enormous is moving through the trees.

With its spooky ship and monster-meat crew who are picked off one by one, this aquatic rehash of the *Alien* movies breaks no new ground, providing a strictly by-numbers exercise in stalk-and-squelch. The cheaply animated creature of the deep (looking like it was rendered on an old Amstrad computer) is purportedly some kind of mutant octopus (though there's no biologist on board to identify it) each of its tentacles topped by a mouth dripping with corrosive digestive juice.

This makes for a few requisite gross-out moments, as victims seem to decay before other characters' (and our) eyes before collapsing in a heap of slime. More stomach-churning is the thought of how many dishes of *pulpo tapas* such an animal could provide for an ambitious Spanish restaurant.

One gets the feeling that this sort of fare was originally conceived for a lead like Bruce Willis or even Steven Seagal. Instead, and luckily, the coarsely featured but charismatic Treat Williams embodies the film's one redeeming feature, managing to make even the clunkiest of lines convincing—even that old standby: "I have a really bad feeling about this" (spoken as the soundtrack lurches into a tinny minor key). When one character expresses fears that the *Argonautica*'s crew might attack them if they board the ship, he responds, "With what? Margaritas and tanning oil?"—one of the film's few intended laughs.

Other meagre highlights include: a fun, monster-eye-view opening sequence as it attacks the *Argonautica*; a passably tense underwater escape through a flooded part of the ship (reminiscent of *Alien Resurrection)* which snatches the life from another character; and a tongue-in-cheek *Jurassic Park* joke in the very last scene. With little else to redeem it, one wonders how this film escaped going straight to video.

VILLAGE VOICE, 2/10/98, p. 102, Steven Boone

In a somewhat novel turn, *Deep Rising* has its featured mutant sea beast come aboard a luxury ocean liner and drink its passengers to death. Writer-director Stephen Sommers peoples this comical death-show well, with Djimon Hounsou and Wes Studi lending their chiseled ethnic scowls to the background, while Treat Williams and Famke Janssen soak up the good light and join forces against the monster. The story moves from a shipboard jewel heist to an *Alien*-like chase through dark, rusty corridors. Though Sommers keeps the tone light, the jokes are mostly dull and familiar. The F/X—by Rob Bottin, Industrial Light and Magic, and Dream Quest—are stunning retreads of creatures, explosions, and chest-bursts they've all done before. Still, when the movie's floating death trap strikes something early on, the shake-up is more convincing than *Titanic*'s pricey iceberg crash. The unsung star here is composer Jerry Goldsmith, whose rousing orchestral score, tinged with ghostly electronics, helps *Deep Rising* stir up the adolescent glee Sommers is after.

Also reviewed in:
CHICAGO TRIBUNE, 1/30/98, Friday/p. H, Elaine Richardson
NEW YORK TIMES, 1/30/98, p. E24, Lawrence Van Gelder
VARIETY, 2/2-8/98, p. 27, Leonard Klady

DEJA VU

A Rainbow Film Company/Revere Entertainment release of a Jagtoria film.   *Producer:* John Goldstone.   *Director:* Henry Jaglom.   *Screenplay:* Victoria Foyt and Jenry Jaglom.   *Director of Photography:* Hanania Baer.   *Editor:* Henry Jaglom.   *Music:* Gaili Schoen.   *Sound:* Tim Fraser.   *Casting:* Irene Lamb.   *Production Designer:* Georgina Lowe.   *Art Director:* Helen Scott.   *Costumes:* Rhona Russell.   *Make-up:* Kirstin Chalmers.   *Running time:* 116 minutes.   *MPAA Rating:* Not Rated.

CAST: Stephen Dillane (Sean Elias);   Victoria Foyt (Dana Howard);   Vanessa Redgrave (Skelly);   Glynis Barber (Claire); Michael Brandon (Alex);   Vernon Dobtcheff (Konstantine); Graydon Gould (Dana's Father);   Noel Harrison (John Stoner);   Rachel Kempson (Skelly's Mother);   Aviva Marks (Woman in Café);   Anna Massey (Fern Stoner); Wael Jolani (Jerusalem Shopkeeper); Karen Loevy and David Rubin (Young Couple in Café); Amnon Meskin (Tel Aviv Cab Driver);   Sabrina Jaglom and Simon Orson Jaglom (Children on Beach);   Vladimir Bershevitz (Street Musician/Violin);   Simon Goshmir (Street Musician/Cello); Alexander Shtempel (Street Musician/Trumpet);   Carl Duering (Jewelry Shop Owner);   Lily Martin (Lady Jeweler);   Thomas Poncelet (Eurostar Conductor);   Maureen Rimmer (Eurostar Humming Lady);   Barbara Hicks (Housekeeper);   Cathryn Harrison (Fern's Masseuse);   David Gant (Antique Shop Owner);   Jeremy Stoner (Street Musician);   Earl Cameron (Doctor).

LOS ANGELES TIMES, 4/22/98, Calendar/p. 2, Kevin Thomas

While on a visit to Jerusalem, a beautiful American woman (Victoria Foyt) joins a lovely older woman (Aviva Marks) she has never before met for lunch on a cafe terrace overlooking the ancient city. By the time the older woman has told her a story of love lost, Henry Jaglom has caught us up in the sophisticated world of his romantic fable "Deja Vu," in which he plays genuine sentiment against the artifices of traditional romantic comedy.

"Deja Vu," which he wrote with Foyt, his wife, represents a new level of accomplishment for Jaglom. "Deja Vu" has the easy elegance and verve of an Astaire-Rogers musical, yet its people speak as spontaneously as in his earlier, more obviously improvised films. There's indeed a palpable tension between spontaneity and formality in "Deja Vu" that breathes fresh life into the classic Hollywood romance. Such intimate yet large-cast pictures as "Eating" have attracted a loyal Jaglom following for years, but "Deja Vu" has a polish and a universal appeal that could make "Deja Vu" the independent filmmaker's most popular venture yet.

Jaglom aptly calls "Deja Vu" a film about love and destiny and leave us thinking that true love is destiny—provided you have the courage to follow your heart. That's no small issue as Foyt's character, Dana, swiftly learns. In a mesmerizing manner, the older woman tells Dana of a romance in which she fell for an American military man she met in Paris, apparently in the '50s or '60s, and who promised to send for her once he was back home. He marries another, as does she eventually, but she still pines for her great lost love.

She presses on Dana an exquisite butterfly clip, set with rubies and diamonds, one of a pair, that was a gift from her lost love, who was to give her the clip's mate on her arrival in America. When Dana excuses herself from the table momentarily she returns only to discover that the woman has vanished.

Due in London after a Paris stopover with Alex (Michael Brandon), her fiance, Dana is thrown as much by what her mystery lady has had to say as by her abrupt departure. Pausing to visit the famous White Cliffs of Dover after her channel crossing, she notices a good-looking young man, Sean (Stephen Dillane), painting a seascape. They lock eyes and boom!, it's love at first sight. What they experience is way beyond mere sexual attraction; it's nothing less than a cosmic convergence of two spirits.

What to do about it takes up the rest of the picture. Sean is happily married to Claire (Glynis Barber), and Dana doesn't want to hurt Alex, even though she now sees him as rather ordinary.

Jaglom gets away with piling on coincidence upon coincidence because he expresses so fully what's at stake for Dana and Sean and those they care about. These potential lovers are intelligent, mature, considerate people who feel they must think of others and strive to do the right thing. The more they struggle against their emotions, the more fate throws them together, principally as guests in a spacious old townhouse around London that is the home of a witty, longtime married couple, Fern (Anna Massey) and John (Noel Harrison), who, wouldn't you know it, turn out to be friends of both Sean and Dana.

Massey and Harrison are skilled scene-stealers, and they give security, stability and family life a very good name indeed. On the other hand, John's sister Skelly (Vanessa Redgrave) believes in following your heart no matter what the price. An inveterate wanderer, Skelly has a lively mother (Rachel Kempson, Redgrave's real-life mother) and a dashing suitor (Vernon Dobtcheff who wish she would come to London more often and stay longer.

Jaglom's cast glows under his clearly affectionate yet always controlled guidance, and Foyt is more radiant than ever. Her Dana may be on an emotional seesaw, but she always has the dignity and poise of classic leading ladies—she brings to mind Kay Francis, not only in appearance but in presence as well.

"Deja Vu's" photogenic locales gives Jaglom's longtime cameraman Hanania Baer a terrific opportunity to give the film both beauty and scope. But what gives this picture its special kick is the suspense it generates; you really are kept guessing what Dana and Sean are going to do with their lives right up to its final moments.

NEW YORK POST, 4/24/98, p. 48, Thelma Adams

Henry Jaglom is the court jester of therafilm, the nebbish John Cassavetes. His recent films—"Babyfever" and "Eating"—are contemporary chatfests. They are overrun by the semi-talented, self-involved creative folks who circle Hollywood. These are the people the B-list invite to their parties to make the hosts feel superior.

His latest film, the unabashed romance "Deja Vu," brings to mind late-night bull sessions in expensive houses inspired by equally expensive pot.

Jaglom clings as desperately to a plot as Kate Winslet held on to that driftwood in "Titanic." Two couples, one married, one engaged, are thrown into disarray when true love appears like an unwanted relative at a house party.

For a maverick, Jaglom relies heavily on nepotism. He puts his wife and co-screenwriter, Victoria Foyt, on a pedestal. She's an actress with a face for film and a voice for taking orders at a diner. She fills the screen and there becomes as trying as last year's wife.

Foyt's Dana is fleeing from a six-year engagement to Alex (Michael Brandon) when she meets a mysterious stranger (Aviva Marks) in Jerusalem. With all the foresight of someone who has already read the script, the silver-haired woman tells Dana to hold out for true love.

A string of coincidences—and references to the 1944 Irene Dunne romance "The White Cliffs of Dover"—lands Dana at those same bleached cliffs. She peeks over the shoulder of painter Sean (Stephen Dillane). The die is cast. There's a lot of talk about kismet and sex—and more nepotism—as the characters converge on a London house. A rakish Vanessa Redgrave arrives with her mother, Rachel Kempson. Rex Harrison's son Noel and Raymond Massey's daughter Anna (hilarious with her clipped, comic delivery) play hosts.

All the hustle and bustle is only a distraction from the lack of chemistry between Foyt and Dillane ("Welcome to Sarajevo"). After all, hubby Henry is always in the room.

With Jaglom pulling the strings, the international production must have been one mad tea party. The film is just the dirty dishes.

NEWSDAY, 4/24/98, Part II/p. B7, John Anderson

In the Jeremy Workman-Alex Rubin documentary "Who Is Henry Jaglom?" a bio that's simply too kind to be anything but propaganda—Jaglom explains his philosophy of film to an unfriendly questioner. "Filmmaking for me is not about imposing, it's about extracting," he says. "You have a very male aggressive view of... the process, which is that you should *determine*, control, make it *happen*. For me, what I'm trying to do is *allow, evoke,* let things *emerge...*"

Later, we see Jaglom browbeating an actress into delivering a line *just so* and for no other apparent reason than whim. So the question remains: Who—or rather what—is Henry Jaglom?

At this point in his surprisingly lengthy career—12 films as writer-director—Jaglom is a combination filmmaker/curiosity. He's a kind of phenomenon simply because he has gone on for so long and for so little gain—and despite negative audience reaction, critical disregard and an amorphous sense of what he's after or why. Jaglom earns a grudging respect, but only for sheer tenacity.

His genre, if it can be called that, consists largely of a kind of fiction-documentary hybrid, with seemingly improvised scripts and improvised acting (although the scene above sort of discounts that). Probably the best known and best received work was "Eating." His self-proclaimed feminist perspective is more about patriarchy than empathy (as evidenced in films such as "Baby Fever"). His quest for the insightful, candid moment on film seems more about capturing embarrassment and pain. His sense of visual logic is almost completely nonexistent.

So to say that Jaglom's latest, "Deja Vu," may be his best film is not to say much. Only that it's less agonizing to watch than a lot of the rest. It's also a fiction, albeit with ad-libbed moments and a rather amazing appearance by Vanessa Redgrave—amazing only because she agreed to be in it.

The star of the film—as she has been in his last several—is Jaglom's wife, Victoria Foyt, an awkward actress whom Jaglom clearly loves to photograph, because he does so incessantly and adoringly. You can't help but giggle when the camera spins around her more times than is possibly necessary, or when she adopts one of those meaningful gazes on which Jaglom loves to dwell. But this is a movie about love, so why not, start with the cast and crew.

"Deja Vu's" love story is about destiny and weird coincidence. Foyt's character, Dana, an affianced businesswoman traveling in Europe, meets a mysterious woman in Israel (Aviva Marks) who tells a story of love and betrayal that has strange connections with Dana's life. The woman then disappears, and Dana begins a journey that takes her not only from Jerusalem to Paris to London to New York—Jaglom clearly had a Spielbergian travel budget—but from her fiance Alex (Michael Brandon) to her man of destiny Sean (Stephen Dillane) and back and forth and back and forth.

All the Kieslowskian metaphysics are a bit much for a film that has so little sense of organic unity, or visual poetry or direction. There are moments of mirth—Noel Harrison and Anna Massey as an eccentric English couple have some funny scenes, even if they're completely digressive. Similarly Redgrave, who would be fascinating reading the phone book, which would be a step up from this script.

And what about the director? Henry Jaglom looking for the meaning of it all is like Ray Charles looking for the Empire State Building. But he's well on his way to getting it right and, at this rate, should do so somewhere around the year 2030.

SIGHT AND SOUND, 10/98, p. 41, Melanie McGrath

Dana, a young American, meets an older Frenchwoman in a café in Jerusalem. Dana compliments her on her ruby pin and is told an American serviceman gave it to her during the war. The serviceman took an identical pin back to the US with him. When the woman departs suddenly, leaving the pin behind, Dana travels to Paris in an abortive attempt to return it. En route to London to meet her fiancé Alex, she meets and finds herself drawn to Sean, an artist and architect who seems familiar. In London, Dana admires an unfinished painting of a woman in Sean's studio. They kiss. Dana arrives at the home of John and Fern Stoner where Alex is staying. She and Alex discuss their future, but Sean and his wife Claire turn up unexpectedly. At a dinner party, Dana and Sean can barely disguise their mutual attraction. Sean confesses his feelings to fellow guest Skelly who advises him to live life to the full.

Dana and Alex return to the US and prepare for their wedding. On the wedding day, Dana's father confesses that the love of his life was a French woman he met during the war and gives Dana a ruby pin which matches the French woman's. Dana calls off the marriage and flies back to England to be with Sean. In his studio, Dana notices that the now completed portrait is of the same woman she met in Jerusalem, wearing the pin. Sean tells her that the woman is his mother, who has been dead for a number of years.

It is a rare film that succeeds in being both modern and nostalgic, expressing both an investment in contemporary life and a sense of yearning for the (often fantasised) simplicities of the past. *Blade Runner* is such a film. So, too, is *Citizen Kane*. Undoubtedly *Déjà Vu* would like to be. What unites all three is their fascination with the textures of human vanity, the quotidian inevitability of compromise in life and love, the limitations of choice and the vanity of dreams. But unlike *Déjà Vu, Kane* et al are not in themselves vain productions. The questions they raise are embedded in narrative and they do more than merely reiterate their concerns.

It is precisely this reiterative quality which makes Jaglom's films so narcissistic. And while narcissism is, perhaps, the defining quality of our times, it is nonetheless a closed system. To qualify as art, film must rise above both its own form and the questions it sets itself. But *Déjà Vu* fails to do either: formally tired, even old fashioned, *Déjà Vu*'s direction at times recalls the episodic, jerky quality of pretentious home movies. If there were a prize for zooming, *Déjà Vu* would win it. And in one scene, the camera twirls round Victoria Foyt so many times the result is almost unwatchable.

Jaglom's version of passion as fractious, consuming and above all involuntary is a by-product of banality, sentimentality and adolescence. Like all narcissistic texts, *Déjà Vu* creates and celebrates the victim. Victoria Foyt's performance as the main protagonist Dana here is archetypal of this strategy. When Norman Mailer wrote that "sentimentality is the emotional promiscuity of those who have no sentiment," he might have had her in mind. Hers is a performance of such hysterical self-importance, such emotional incontinence, that it is impossible not to feel the numbness, the neurasthenia, the sheer unloveliness that occupies the shallowness under the skin.

Rarely does a film say so little by burdening itself with so much. "To cheat oneself out of love is an eternal loss," aphorises Sean, Dana's would-be lover, while the mystery woman rhapsodises over her great love—"We lived out our destiny... All my life since has been like a dream"—like a tumbleweed preacher. What charm and wit *Déjà Vu* allows is all in the improvised performances of Anna Massey and Noel Harrison, absolutely masterful as the old couple who have managed to sustain a coltish kind of banter through all the weary decades of mutual affection.

There is a moment in every filmmaker's career when they think they're about to pull another rabbit from the hat only to discover that what has taken up residence there is, in fact, a turkey Usually the experience is a useful one. It shakes the film-maker up a bit, invites them to return to tested formulae or to try something new. Henry Jaglom should be an old hand at this. He has been pulling out turkeys for years *(Babyfever, Last Summer in the Hamptons)* but still seems unable or unwilling to learn his lessons from them. *Déjà Vu* is yet another. Jaglom makes his point. We *have* seen all this before.

VILLAGE VOICE, 4/28/98, p. 124, Elizabeth Weitzman

Dana (Victoria Foyt) believes she's happy with her dull fiancé and predictable life, until an enigmatic old lady shows up to share a story of true love and urgent advice against settling for anything less. Soon after, her whole world is thrown out of whack when she meets Sean (Stephen Dillane), an artist to whom she feels mysteriously, soulfully connected. In fact, mysteriousness abounds: magical encounters with the dead truckloads of remarkable coincidences, and the sort of sappy love talk I'd assumed was legally banned to those out of high school. As we've seen before, Henry Jaglom films tend to be a stubbornly twisted package of pleasure and pain. *Déjà Vu* is super corny, full of pseudodeep talk, and features a whiny, neurotic woman desperate for love. But on the other hand, there's a certain sweet charm to its breathtaking sentimentality, and the first-rate support (Anna Massey, Noel Harrison, Vanessa Redgrave, and her mama, Rachel Kempson) takes over when proceedings threaten to induce eye-roll spasms.

Also reviewed in:
CHICAGO TRIBUNE, 5/1/98, Friday/p. K, Michael Wilmington
NEW YORK TIMES, 4/24/98, p. E12, Stephen Holden
VARIETY, 11/3-9/97, p. 100, Steven Gaydos

DESPERATE MEASURES

A TriStar Pictures release of a Mandalay Entertainment presentation of an Eagle-point/Schroeder/Hoffman production. *Executive Producer:* Jeffrey Chernov. *Producer:* Barbet Schroeder, Susan Hoffman, Gary Foster, and Lee Rich. *Director:* Barbet Schroeder. *Screenplay:* David Klass. *Director of Photography:* Luciano Tovoli. *Editor:* Lee Percy. *Music:* Trevor Jones. *Music Editor:* Suzanna Peric. *Sound:* Steve Nelson and (music) Simon Rhodes. *Sound Editor:* Ron Bochar. *Casting:* Howard Feuer. *Production Designer:* Geoffrey Kirkland. *Art Director:* Sandy Getzler. *Set Designer:* Bo Johnson, Randy Schmook, and Kelly Hannafin. *Set Decorator:* Jennifer Williams. *Special Effects:* Paul Lombardi. *Costumes:* Gary Jones. *Make-up:* Rick Sharp. *Make-up (Michael Keaton):* Robert Mills. *Running time:* 105 minutes. *MPAA Rating:* R.

CAST: Michael Keaton (Peter McCabe); Andy Garcia (Frank Conner); Brian Cox (Jeremiah Cassidy); Marcia Gay Harden (Samantha Hawkins); Erik King (Nate Oliver); Efrain Figueroa (Vargus); Joseph Cross (Matthew Conner); Janet Maloney (Sarah Davis); Richard Riehle (Ed Fayne); Tracey Walter (Medical Inmate); Peter Weireter (SWAT Team Commander); Keith Diamond (Wilson); Steve Park (Dr. Gosha); Steven Schub (SWAT in Airduct); Neal Matarazzo (Cell Guard); Dennis Cockrum (Pelican Bay Head Guard); Charles Noland (Cigarette Guard); Randy Thompson (Library Guard); Michael Shamus Wiles (Tough Inmate); Darren Pearce and Eric Tignini (Convoy Guards); Billy Kane (Laser Technician); Christine Ashe (Young ER Nurse); Donna M. Duffy (ER Nurse); Troy Robinson (Cop Escorting Frank); Robert Baier (Security Booth Guard); David Flick (SWAT Sharpshooter in Street); Joe Drago (Doctor at Walkway); Josh Kemble (SWAT Sniper on Roof); Scott Colomby (Patrol Cop); Howard Meehan (Policeman on Street); Tim Kelleher (Helicopter Shooter); Cliff Fleming and Dirk Vahle, and Craig Hoskings (SWAT Helicopter Pilots); Jack Gill, Scott Waugh, and Danny Rogers (Motorcyclists); John Meier (Cop Shot in ER); Norm Howell and John Rottger (Burnt Cops); Donna Keegan (Burning Nurse).

CHRISTIAN SCIENCE MONITOR, 2/6/98, p. 11, David Sterritt

Michael Keaton's acting has taken a zigzag course, from the comedy of "Night Shift" and "Beetlejuice" to the drama of "Clean and Sober" and the thrills of two "Batman" adventures. He started the current season as the eager-beaver cop in "Jackie Brown," and now he's going for contrast with "Desperate Measures," playing one of his meanest characters yet.

Unfortunately for him—and moviegoers—the new picture is too facile and forgettable to mark a crest in his up-and-down career. Ditto for Andy Garcia, who's overdue for a hit but has stumbled into just the opposite this time.

Garcia plays a San Francisco policeman with a difficult problem: His young son has been diagnosed with a grave illness, and transplant surgery appears to be the only solution. Plunging into cyberspace for information on possible organ donors, he finds that the nearest choice is a notorious psychopath locked up in the local prison.

The criminal agrees to help, asking a few favors—library privileges, release from solitary confinement—in return. But he's not as altruistic as he appears, and no sooner does he enter the hospital than nasty surprises start springing from his bag of tricks. The rest of the movie is a series of chase sequences, pitting the fatherly hero against a crazed killer who'll stop at nothing to escape.

For a while, "Desperate Measures" shows signs of becoming a thoughtful thriller with timely overtones. The premise raises interesting questions related to contemporary medical procedures, embodied by a loving parent who seeks help from both high-tech treatments and the kindness of a hostile stranger whose biological makeup just happens to fit certain formulas. Like last year's "Gattaca" and "Critical Care," this movie spotlights the hopes and anxieties sparked by health technologies that can lose contact with the human needs they're meant to serve.

David Klass's screenplay shows only short-lived concern with these matters, though, soon leaving them behind for a nonstop barrage of cat-and-mouse suspense scenes. More problems arise from the acting. Keaton's character is an all-too-obvious rip-off of Hannibal Lecter in "The Silence of the Lambs," while Garcia never quite blends the policeman's conflicting traits—doting dad on one hand, fearless hero on the other—into a convincing whole.

The picture was directed by Barbet Schroeder, whose career has zigzagged even more than Keaton's, embracing unique documentaries ("Idi Amin Dada") and articulate dramas ("Reversal of Fortune") as well as overwrought messes like "Single White Female." It's no pleasure to report that "Desperate Measures" falls into the latter category—a squandered opportunity to explore important issues through popular moviemaking.

LOS ANGELES TIMES, 1/30/98, Calendar/p. 8, Jack Mathews

[The following review by Jack Mathewsn appeared in a slightly different form in **NEWSDAY, 1/30/98, Part II/p. B11.]**

Put yourself in the place of Frank Conner (Andy Garcia), San Francisco P.D. You've cornered the escaped killer Peter McCabe (Michael Keaton) in a hospital hallway. You're armed, he isn't, and he's not about to surrender. You can't kill him because he's the only person on Earth whose bone marrow can save your dying son, who's waiting for his transplant just down the hall.

What do you do?

Of course, it's easy to be calm and rational from a theater seat, but rather than let this guy and his bone marrow get away, wouldn't you at least try to shoot him in the leg, maybe blow out a knee cap, knock a couple of toes off, or otherwise disable him? After all, you're target-trained, and he's standing just 10 feet away. Bam! Game over.

A good thriller doesn't give you the opportunity to second-guess the hero and deem him a fool for his actions. And though Barbet Schroeder's "Desperate Measures" looks terrific and moves like a runaway train, it's nothing like a good thriller. It's standard-issue Hollywood chase bunk, chockablock with moments where the audience will be thinking faster and better than the characters.

The assumption made by Schroeder ("Single White Female") and screenwriter David Klass ("Kiss the Girls") is that we'll forgive Conner his confusion, and occasional reckless abandon because he's distraught over his son's illness. What could be more human?

But it doesn't work that way. The genre calls for heroes who rise to the occasion, whose senses are sharpened rather than dulled by crises. Otherwise, you begin to look around for someone else to identify with, and McCabe, recruited from solitary confinement for the bone marrow transplant, is not an option.

McCabe, who volunteers to be a donor so he can attempt an escape, is a marked departure for Keaton. When we first see him, working out in his cell in San Quentin with a De Niro-size snarl on his face, our impulse is to laugh. Buffed as Keaton has made his body, it's adorned by that same cherubic face, only it's now twisted in mimicry of a hundred prison psychos who've crossed the screen before him.

Behind the steel-tempered glare, the model for McCabe is actually the deceptively genial Hannibal Lecter, a true sociopath with a genius IQ, and the detail that goes into McCabe's escape plan gets the film off to a reasonably solid start. You may question his ability to research the blueprints of the hospital from the prison library, but bureaucracy being no sanctuary of common sense, we'll give it that much. However, once he's freed and the chase is on, the clichés mount like fallen bricks.

"Desperate Measures" goes for the extremes, pitting a man who will do anything to save his son against one who will do anything to save his own butt, with 10-year-old Matthew (Joseph Cross), a tabula rasa of innocence, between them. The answer, the filmmakers would like us to believe, cuts to the marrow of human nature: Is man basically good or evil? Will McCabe, as he casually slaughters his way through pursuing police, come to care about the boy dependent on him?

That issue might be compelling, if we could take anything else about the, movie seriously. But it's no go. Though the chase eventually gets outside for traditional San Francisco road thrills, most of the action takes place in the halls, rooms and bowels of the hospital and of the adjacent prison wing.

As scores of nameless cops look for McCabe in all the wrong places, he has only two worthy rivals, Conner and oncologist Samantha Hawkins (Marcia Gay Harden), who will walk ledges and scale barbed-wire fences to get enough of McCabe's rare bone marrow to save Matthew's life.

From what we gather in all this, McCabe could have made his precious donation from his cell, which would have ended the story even before it began. No such luck.

NEW YORK POST, 1/30/98, p. 45, Thelma Adams

I can just hear Michael Keaton's grandmother after watching a preview of "Desperate Measures": "For this you left 'Batman'?"

"Desperate Measures" is a step backward for Keaton and for his co-star, Andy Garcia. The painfully improbable thriller places Keaton's brilliant serial killer, Peter McCabe, in a penitentiary.

Garcia warms up his righteous anger and gets those Latin brown eyes simmering, as widowed San Francisco cop Frank Connor. His only son (Joseph Cross) has cancer. Matt needs a bone marrow transplant—and McCabe is the only guy with a DNA match.

Painful in a way that no i.v. can fix, "Desperate Measures" is a cynical attempt by a top-drawer director to cash in. French-born Barbet Schroeder ("Barfly," "Reversal of Fortune") cuts between nail-biter set pieces and cheap sentiment hurled his way by the preposterous script of David Klass ("Kiss the Girls").

What can we say to good talent, bad choices?

Mr. Klass: It would only make sense that even if poor Matty has cancer, his survival shouldn't come at the cost of half of the San Francisco Police Department and numerous critical patients who happened to be in the path of killer McCabe.

And Messrs. Keaton, Garcia and Schroeder: Sometimes when you're offered a cheesy movie that exploits children in peril and revives yet another genius killer as if every Westinghouse scholar had a bad gene, just say no. Your career survival is at stake.

SIGHT AND SOUND, 4/98, p. 36, Edward Lawrenson

Trying to locate a bone-marrow donor for his leukaemia stricken son Matt, police detective Frank Connor breaks into the FBI's offices. He finds a perfect match in violent convict Peter McCabe. At first McCabe refuses to go through with the operation, but consents after meeting with Matt.

Once in hospital, despite being closely supervised by Connor's superior Cassidy, McCabe manages to escape. In the ensuing chaos, the hospital is evacuated. Cassidy's repeated attempts to shoot McCabe are thwarted by Connor trying to keep McCabe alive. After pursuing McCabe through the hospital, Connor confronts him in his son's isolation ward. McCabe manages to escape yet again, taking Matt hostage. McCabe finally breaks out of the hospital and hijacks a car. Connor follows closely. The car chase comes to a halt on a mechanical bridge, and the injured McCabe jumps into the river far below. Connor dives in after him, and takes McCabe to hospital where his bone-marrow is transplanted in Matt. Some time later, McCabe, recovering in hospital, pulls a gun on his guard.

In John Woo's *Hard Boiled,* two gun-wielding adversaries confront each other at either end of a busy hospital ward. In a moment of rare chivalry, both men call a truce to allow the innocent patients time to escape. But this respite from violence is short-lived, abruptly shattered by the arrival of another party who guns down the fleeing invalids for the hell of it.

Set almost entirely in a hospital, *Desperate Measures* is far kinder to the patients who fill its wards: director Barbet Schroeder has his hospital evacuated before he indulges in some decidedly Woo-like action sequences. Schroeder is astute to erase any sign of these patients so early on in the game. In the body-fetishistic world of contemporary action movies—where characters somersault through empty space to avoid slow-motion bullets and flesh wounds are swiftly forgotten about—hospitals and their inhabitants are unwanted reminders of physical fallibility.

Ordinarily, to raise such objections against so knowingly stylised a genre as this seems churlish. But when the action takes place almost exclusively in a hospital—as it does in *Desperate Measures*—it's difficult not to think about medical credibility, if only because Schroeder's anonymously efficient handling of spectacle is so unengaging. The villain McCabe's efforts to escape from hospital (at one point jumping several storeys down a conveniently placed laundry chute) are precisely the kind of activities that would land most of us in hospital rather than out of it. Indeed, set against such relentlessly paced hospital dramas as *ER*—where the relative calm of an emergency ward can suddenly descend into mayhem—Schroeder's decision to use the hospital building in *Desperate Measures* as a patient-free backdrop for a tiresome pursuit seems particularly unadventurous.

His efforts to explore the shared psychological ground that exists between Connor's cop-hunter and McCabe's psychotic-hunted feels strained also, a far cry from the complexities of Schroeder's *Single White Female*. Aside from the shared genetic attributes that enable McCabe to be the bone-marrow donor to Connor's son, the only thing that these two characters have in common is that they are both clichéd creations. Andy Garcia's Connor is faultless, both as a lawman and as a father, but irredeemably bland; while Michael Keaton as McCabe is menacing only by association, invoking more memorable performances by Robert De Niro in *Cape Fear* and Anthony Hopkins in *The Silence of the Lambs*.

Ultimately, Keaton's feeble attempts to show just how cold-hearted and brutal a killer McCabe is (in one unintentionally hilarious scene he even outgrowls some Alsatians) are undermined by the sudden redemption he achieves in donating his bone-marrow to Connor's son. Were such a saccharine conclusion tacked onto the end of a 30s Warner Bros crime movie (which Schroeder cites as the inspiration here) one could write it off as a necessary concession to the strictures of the Hays Code. As it is, it's an appropriately ridiculous finale to an inconsistent and at times ludicrous film from an otherwise talented director.

VILLAGE VOICE, 2/3/98, p. 54, Gary Dauphin

One of the oldest tricks in the action-movie handbook involves giving your bad guy some accent, thereby catapulting him from just "bad" to "evil genius." Although *Desperate Measure*-Peter McCabe (Michael Keaton) has a Southern instead of a Euro accent, he's a prime exemplar of the type: looking like a bespectacled, steroidal Perdue chicken, McCabe can nonetheless use 100-year-old blueprints to plot an underground escape route, self-prescribe antinarcotics to counteract the effects of anesthesia, and even properly dislocate his own thumb, the better to slip out of a wrist restraint, grab the nearest oxygen canister, and turn it into a makeshift blowtorch. It's all totally preposterous, but like Michael Jordan's Nike shoes, McCabe's prison-issue hornrims somehow make the impossible plausible.

McCabe has something else special-yet-invisible about him, namely his bone marrow. He's not only the smartest violent convict in America but also the only living human who can give a bone-marrow transplant to a certain cancer-stricken tyke. The boy's cop father, Frank Conner (Andy Garcia), has the canny killer transferred from solitary confinement to a poorly secured hospital for a marrow harvest, thereby starting a cat-and-mouse game where the convict skulks around the SWAT-ridden hospital while the cop tries to keep him alive (a corpse's marrow being useless to his son).

The setup's rife with possibilities for mano-a-mano hijinks, but despite keeping things on a fairly tight, three-act timetable, director Barber Schroeder prefers to let Keaton and Garcia ham in isolation, Keaton losing the glasses and transmogrifying into a fun-loving trickster, while Garcia's lower lip quivers for the entire movie, his "love for the boy" so strong he constantly seems about to pull his own hair out and collapse into tears. *Desperate Measures* wants to suggest these men are actually two sides of the same, driven coin, but you don't need an eye chart to see their real connection as the most half-baked of Hollywood clichés.

Also reviewed in:
CHICAGO TRIBUNE, 1/30/98, Friday/p. C, John Petrakis
NEW YORK TIMES, 1/30/98, p. E22, Janet Maslin
VARIETY, 1/26-2/1/98, p. 66, Godfrey Cheshire
WASHINGTON POST, 1/30/98, p. D6, Stephen Hunter

DESTINY

An Ognon Pictures/France 2 Cinema/Canal +/Fonds Sud/Misr International Films coproduction. *Producer:* Humbert Balsan and Gabriel Khoury.   *Director:* Youssef Chahine.   *Screenplay (Arabic with English subtitles):* Youssef Chahine and Khaled Youssef.   *Director of Photography:* Mohsen Nasr.   *Editor:* Rachida Abdel Salam.   *Music:* Kamal el-Tawil and Yohia el-Mougy. *Choreographer:* Walid Aouni.   *Sound:* Annette Dutertre.   *Production Designer:* Hamed Hemdane.   *Art Director:* Hamed Hemdane.   *Costumes:* Nahed Nasrallah.   *Running time:* 135 minutes.   *MPAA Rating:* Not Rated.

CAST: Nour el-Cherif (Averroës);   Laila Eloui (Gypsy Woman);   Mahmoud Hemeida (The Caliph);   Safia el-Emary (Zeinab, Averroës's Wife);   Khaled el-Nabaoui (Nasser);   Hani Salama (Abdallah);   Mohamed Mounir (Marwan);   Seif Abdel Rahman (Caliph's Brother);   Abdallah Mahmoud (Borhan).

NEW STATESMAN, 11/13/98, p. 36, Jonathan Romney

It comes as a shock to a British critic's habitual complacency, but every now and then you realise there are whole chunks missing from our map of the film world. Practically every year on the festival circuit, you learn about another major director whose existence you barely knew of and whose work seems to be common currency just about everywhere else (or at least, wherever they read *Cahiers du cinema*). These film-makers' work has rarely, or never, been seen in Britain because they come from one of those parts of the world that happen not to be fashionable among distributors.

Egyptian director Youssef Chahine is one—he's not just a missing country on the map, but a whole continent in himself, having made over 30 films since his career began in 1950. Apart from being credited with discovering Omar Sharif, he became most widely known in the late 1970s when he embarked on a series of stylised autobiographical films, beginning with "Alexandria... Why?", which have variously been compared to Fellini and Bob Fosse's "All That Jazz." Despite his cosmopolitan tastes and background (he was trained in Los Angeles), Chahine is known for his determination to make cinema that is, as he puts it, "nothing but Egyptian".

Chahine has been much criticised in the Arab world for his emphasis on liberalism, and his 1994 film "The Emigrant" was banned in Egypt, supposedly under fundamentalist pressure. His new film "Al Massir" ("Destiny") has been seen as his direct response. It's an impassioned polemical statement in favour of religious tolerance—which also happens to be an all-action medieval costume musical.

Destiny is costume drama of a kind we've rarely seen—a curious stylistic mish-mash that at first sight looks heavy-handed, antiquated and naive. But its bold, expansive energies quickly reveal it as a very sophisticated, forceful use of populist film traditions to carry a message. Set in the 12th century in Andalucia under the reign of the Caliph Al-Mansur, it's the story of the philosopher Averroes, judge, scholar, commentator on Aristotle and the first man to describe the workings of the human retina (something that, crammed as the film is, Chahine somehow just didn't manage to work in).

The story begins in Languedoc, with the translator of Averroes' works burnt at the stake as a heretic. Immediately, on sight of the gawping peasants and spear-wielding soldiery, our reflex reactions set in and we reach for the handy term "hokum", suspecting we're in the territory of Monty Python and the Holy Grail. Then the heretic's son heads for Cordoba, where Averroes is holding convivial court at his dinner table with his extended family. Among them are the two sons of the Caliph himself, one a dashing dilettante, the other—why, he's just a dancin' fool. By the time the film bursts unexpectedly into an all-singing, all-hoofing gypsy routine—tossing chairs in the air to the lyrics, "We defy life with song"—"Destiny" somehow doesn't seem like your average studious historical trawl.

The complex intrigues unfurl at a dizzying pace—it's like "Dynasty", or "Alexandre Dumas". Malevolent forces ally themselves with the Spanish against the Caliph; the sinister Emir masses his fanatical troops, who abduct and indoctrinate the Caliph's son Abdallah; intrigue drives a wedge between the feckless Caliph and the pensive, tolerant Averroes, who becomes the target of a fatwa. Even if the plot ramifications are sometimes hard to follow, there's always plenty to keep our attention: star-crossed love, masked skulduggery in moonlit alleys, the perils of white-water rafting in the Pyrenees.

It can sometimes be unsettling, this strange carnival diversity, with its mix of modern and apparently archaic styles. Chahine seems to draw on the Bombay musical, the Hong Kong historical action genre, and the Hollywood biblical epic—some of the night scenes are washed with Technicolor greens and reds straight out of 1950s Cecil B de Mille. Even the working-out of the fundamentalist theme has an odd cosmopolitan spin: Abdallah's induction into the Emir's green-clad cult has echoes of Californian cult indoctrination, with curious homoerotic overtones, and there's a bizarre sequence in which a big musical knees-up is used as an anti-cult deprogramming technique.

The engagingly gravitas-laden Nour el-Cherif as Averroes is no Charlton Heston—more like a jovial, careworn middle-aged academic torn between commitment to his work and the desire for a quiet family life. For all the film's scope and bravado, Chahine never lets go of the intimate human touch. A week's limited exposure at the ICA is better than nothing, but this is rattling entertainment, one of the rare films of the year that have a burning raison d'etre, and one of the even fewer ones that could conceivably change your picture of world cinema.

NEW YORK POST, 10/16/98, p. 44, Thelma Adams

An all-singing, all-dancing medieval epic about the power of ideas over tyranny?

"West Side Story" meets "Fahrenheit 451" in "Destiny," Egyptian Youssef Chahine's rousing musical morality tale about the 12th century Andalusian philosopher Averroes   The Muslim thinker penned "The Incoherence of Incoherence" and analyzed Aristotle.

"Destiny," a highlight of the 1997 New York Film Festival, closes the Film Society of Lincoln Center's Chahine retrospective at the Walter Reade and then moves to the Quad Cinema.

It's silly, sexy, entertaining—and more. The movie offers a trenchant critique of religious fundamentalism that makes it relevant to contemporary audiences worldwide.

Two years ago, the Cannes Film Festival honored Chahine ("Alexandria, Why?") with a well-deserved lifetime achievement award. It would be a shame to miss this rare opportunity to see the work of an international master—and savor his rich humanism and exuberant style.

VILLAGE VOICE, 10/20/98, p. 155, J. Hoberman

Egyptian filmmaker Youssef Chahine's *Destiny*—shown in the 1997 NYFF—is a big, lush, boldly kitsch piece of political pop. The script is scarcely more elevated than a comic book, but its intellectual pedigree rivals *Beloved*'s, concerning as it does the 12th-century Arab Andalusian philosopher Averröes.

Shot largely in Syria and Lebanon, *Destiny* suggests a form of Oriental orientalism. The scenes are lit like the portico of a Miami Beach hotel and it will sprain no brain to imagine Maria Montez as a player in this swashbuckling tale of rival princelings, gypsy dancers, religious assassins, and court conspiracies. There is, however, another agenda. Beginning with an auto-da-fé in which French clerics burn a fellow Christian for the heresy of translating Averröes, *Destiny* evokes a multicultural Europe and defends a particular mode of secular humanism—an exuberant alliance of intellectuals, entertainers, and free spirits devoted to tolerance and sexual equality. (The political is certainly personal: the 72-year-old Chahine grew up a Maronite in cosmopolitan Alexandria and studied film at UCLA.)

Although *Destiny* is filled with spirited production numbers and even the zealots perform a mass prayer dance on the battlements, the movie's most ecstatic scene has Averröes's Christian disciple return north to his chilly homeland, piloting a skiff filled with books. As a philosopher, Averröes did ultimately have a greater impact on Christian than Islamic thought. (Dante generously includes him along with Abraham and Socrates among the virtuous heathens in hell's first circle.) But that is not Chahine's point either.

Destiny ends as it begins, with a huge bonfire. The difference is that the barbaric Europeans burn people while the more civilized Arabs only incinerate ideas. Even more than *Beloved*, *Destiny* is a movie that directly addresses its audience. Would the *fatwa* the fundamentalists declare against Averröes and his friends apply to this film as well? As the distraught philosopher watches his life's work thrown on the pyre, a friend whispers consolation: "I know your books are safe in Egypt." Let's hope so.

Also reviewed in:
NEW YORK TIMES, 10/16/98, p. E20, Stephen Holden
VARIETY, 5/26-6/1/97, p. 65, Deborah Young

DIDN'T DO IT FOR LOVE

A First Run Features release of a Filmgalerie 451 production. *Producer:* Irene von Alberti. *Director:* Monika Treut. *Screenplay:* Monika Treut. *Director of Photography:* Ekkehardt Pollack and Christopher Landerer. *Editor:* Eric Marciano and Jeff Lunger. *Music:* Georg Kajanus and Tom Judson. *Sound:* Andreas Pietsch-Lindenberg. *Running time:* 80 minutes. *MPAA Rating:* Not Rated.

WITH: Jan Baracz; Rene Cardona, Jr.; Nicholas Echevarria; Juan-Jose Gurrola; Juan Ferrara; Franz Harland; Jose Flores; Jose-Luis Cuevas; Georg Kajanus; Johanne Kajanus; Micheline Kinery; Nadine Markova; Ronald Moglia; Eva Norvind; Gerard O'Neal; Luz Maria Rojas; Veronica Vera; Liisa Simola; Alice Vernstad; Paul Vernstad; Esther Maria Wiig.

LOS ANGELES TIMES, 12/11/98, Calendar/p. 19, Kevin Thomas

Ever the feminist explorer of sexual frontiers, Germany's Monika Treut has found a subject ideal in Eva Norvind, who has led—and continues to lead—a most unconventional existence. The documentary "Didn't Do It for Love" charts Norvind's life through several identities and countries.

Born 54 years ago in Norway to a Russian prince, who long ago renounced his aristocratic identity, and a Finnish sculptress, Norvind was a blond and bosomy 20-year-old living in New York when she took off for a vacation in Mexico. There her looks and figure soon made her a movie star in the Jayne Mansfield mold and led her to becoming a high-class call girl.

While on a return trip to Mexico, the matronly, gray-haired Norvind of today looks back with disdain on a fleeting fame based on image rather than knowledge. She may have had little or no training as an actress, but Norvind clearly has a fierce intelligence and assertive personality that led her to speak out on behalf of birth control and women's rights in Mexico. This triggered a deportation order that she evaded for years. She also had a daughter, from whom she is estranged, and became a photojournalist.

By 1980, Norvind was back in Manhattan as a film student and embarking on a career as a professional dominatrix known as Ava Taurel, who appeared on TV espousing the therapeutic benefits of sadomasochism with the slogan, "Out of the dungeon and into the classroom." (Norvind, who has described herself as a "pansexual sadomasochist," has said that "being a dominatrix was very important to me because it was like working out the woman warrior within myself.")

Norvind apparently continues in the dominatrix business, but also has moved on to earn master's degrees at NYU in human sexuality and psychology. She has treated both sex offenders and sexual abuse survivors, and performed a wide array of human services, including volunteer work with Mother Teresa's mission in India.

The problem with "Didn't Do It for Love" is that Norvind is simply too complex a personality with too wide-ranging a history to be contained in an 80-minute documentary. Norvind has lots to say about human sexuality and behavior from an unusual perspective, but really hasn't a chance to put it all together in an overview for us. Nonetheless, she emerges as a strong—make that very strong—woman who is determined to keep growing and learning.

Throughout the film, there are revealing encounters between Norvind and her friends and relatives, especially her now-frail mother. Like her own daughter, who dismisses her as a whore, Norvind's mother lives in Mexico. Her mother was a beauty, who blithely paraded her 15-year-old daughter nude before a bevy of French film producers. When Norvind angrily asks her mother today how she could have done that, she nonchalantly counters that since she was so fully developed by that age, why not? Similarly, her mother approved of her becoming a prostitute because her clients were high-class Mexican gentlemen. (Norvind observes that "from macho men I learned how to become macho myself.")

Norvind emerges as a woman formidable in personality, intellect and experience. Yet she can be an unattractive bully in an unsettling scene with her lover, a young black man, whom she can swiftly reduce to terrified stammering, simply because he does not know or recall where she put some everyday item. We need to know more about this relationship, just as we need to know more about Eva Norvind.

NEW YORK POST, 5/1/98, p. 62, Larry Worth

Scandinavian B-movie actress. South of the Border prostitute. Successful Manhattan dominatrix. Student at NYU.

Yes, Eva Norvind has played each part and led a pretty eclectic life. It should have made for a great documentary. It didn't.

In placing blame, one need look no further than director Monika Treut, who turns "Didn't Do It for Love" into a production that only flirts with success.

Basically, viewers gain little understanding into what makes Norvind tick. Treut goes for sensationalism over insight, whether showing grainy, overbleached interviews with Norvind's family members, clips from Norvind's Mexican movies (ranging from the seamy "Juan Pistoles" to "Santa Claus Conquers the Martians") or lurid footage of the S&M queen cracking a mean whip.

Stuck in a tabloid rut, the director continually misses the point. Sure, the material itself remains intriguing. But to be truly stimulating, "Didn't Do It for Love" needed more talk and less action.

VILLAGE VOICE, 5/5/98, p. 130, Elizabeth Weitzman

"What the heck am I doing?" professional chameleon Eva Norvind muses at one point during this low-budget look at her life, and there's no denying it's a fascinating question. Norvind—celebrity, activist, teachers dominatrix—was born in Norway in 1944 but landed in Mexico in the mid '60s, her "cascade at blond hair and big tits" quickly turning her into the exotic, adored star of such classics as *Juan Pistoles*. After high-living through the dangers of image-based fame," she moved or to journalism, sadomasochism and volunteering at Mother Theresa's mission. There's plenty to work with here, but in trusty documentary style the most compelling scenes are built around visits with family. Her estranged daughter, who considers Mom a whore, wouldn't talk: her father, whom she introduces as "a collector," indeed spends his days foraging blithely through garbage cans; and her prim-seeming mother remembers starting Norvind's career by parading her nude in front of film producers at 16.

Also reviewed in:
NEW YORK TIMES, 5/1/98, p. E28, Stephen Holden
VARIETY, 3/9-15/98, p. 45, Derek Elley

DIGGING TO CHINA

A Moonstone Entertainment release in association with Davis Entertainment Classics & The Ministry of Film of an Alan Mruvka/Marilyn Vance/John Davis/J. Todd Harris production. *Executive Producer:* Etchie Stroh, David Friendly, and Stephen Nemeth.   *Producer:* Marilyn Vance, Alan Mruvka, John Davis, and J. Todd Harris.   *Director:* Timothy Hutton.   *Screenplay:* Karen Janszen.   *Director of Photography:* Jorgen Persson.   *Editor:* Dana Congdon and Alain Jakubowics.   *Music:* Cynthia Millar.   *Casting:* Wendy Kurtzman. *Production Designer:* Robert De Vico.   *Costumes:* Mary Zophres.   *Running time:* 98 minutes.   *MPAA Rating:* PG.

CAST: Kevin Bacon (Ricky);   Marian Seldes (Leah);   Mary Stuart Masterson (Gwen);   Evan Rachel Wood (Harriet Frankovitz); Cathy Moriarty (Mrs. Frankovitz).

LOS ANGELES TIMES, 9/11/98, Calendar/p. 8, David Kronke

"Digging to China," actor Timothy Hutton's directorial debut, has managed modest theatrical distribution, but it's a decidedly small-screen endeavor. The film benefits from a strong performance from newcomer Evan Rachel Wood in the role of a precocious little girl who has far more energy and imagination than sense. Unfortunately, there's not much else to recommend this earnest and prosaic coming-of-age drama, which fairly screams "Lifetime Channel."

Wood plays Harriet, a tart-tongued pre-adolescent loner enduring the '60s with a boozing, eccentric mother (Cathy Moriarty) who is never far from a vodka bottle or her next ominous cough and a slatternly "sister" Gwen (Mary Stuart Masterson), never far from the next in a hopeless string of low-rent suitors. They live in an amorphously defined stretch of lush Pennsylvania backwoods, struggling to maintain a dilapidated roadside motel.

One day, a broken-down car sputters up to their doorstep, containing crotchety Leah (Marian Seldes) and her mentally disabled adult son Ricky (Kevin Bacon). Leah's taking her son to a hospital where he will be cared for after she dies of cancer (why they trekked from California to Pennsylvania to institutionalize Ricky is unexplained). Apparently, one dying mom isn't enough for this push-button weeper, so it thoughtfully serves up two.

While Leah's car awaits repairs (which, in the film's context if not quite in real time, seems to take weeks), Harriet befriends Ricky; though their antics are innocent enough, Gwen finds their age difference troubling. (Obviously she had never seen "As Good as It Gets" or "Six Days, Seven Nights" or "Horse Whisperer," etc.).

"Digging to China" seems to be intended as an actor's holiday for the usually versatile Bacon. Nonetheless, with wrists and elbows at angles usually reserved for bebop music and his head rolling about his shoulders like a ball weighted left of center, Bacon never manages to suggest anything besides a drama student tackling an acting exercise.

The film wants to remind you of "Rain Man" so badly that it even co-opts the song "Iko Iko," also used in the earlier movie for its requisite pop-ditty soundtrack. Hutton's directing is sensitive but patchwork. He leaves viewers too much downtime to ponder such questions: How do cheap helium balloons manage to remain aloft for days and days? And if Gwen is so concerned when Harriet turns up missing, wouldn't she do something besides lounge around the house? More vexing is the lack of psychological underpinning explaining why Harriet gets so close to Ricky so quickly. If "Digging to China" (the title refers to a toss-off scene run under the credits) really cared to explore the vicissitudes of a loveless childhood, it should have dug a little deeper.

NEW YORK POST, 9/11/98, p. 69, Bill Hoffmann

As brilliant as Jackie Gleason was, he did have his albatross in the form of a 1962 movie called "Gigot," in which he played an oafish French deaf mute.

Gleason believed it to be his finest work, but not for a minute did anybody believe that Gigot was a real character. Rather, it was the Great One doing two hours of undisciplined, misguided schtick in one embarrassing mess of a movie.

The same can be said for "Digging to China," a new drama starring Kevin Bacon.

Bacon has racked up a lot of impressive screen time in his 20-year movie career—but that track record screeches to a halt in his role as Ricky, a retarded 30-year-old.

With a pair of ill-fitting pants, a mane of uncombed hair and enough facial and body tics to make a statue nervous, Bacon certainly has the stereotypical look of somebody with severe mental disabilities.

But never do you believe this character is anybody other than Kevin Bacon pouring on the pathos.

The plot doesn't help. It's third-rate soap opera that belongs on Lifetime, not in theaters.

The setting is a ramshackle motel run by a booze hound (Cathy Moriarty) and her two daughters, Gwen the slut (Mary Stuart Masterson) and 10-year-old Harriet (Evan Rachel Wood), a precocious loner who believes in flying saucers.

Ricky enters the picture when, en route with his mom to a home for retarded adults, their car breaks down by the motel.

Ricky and Harriet are soon sticking together like glue—especially after her mom suddenly dies and sis reveals herself as Harriet's real mom, who got pregnant during one of her sleazy flings.

In the wink of an eye, the shaggy-dog pair run off into the woods and set up camp where they "marry" as prince and princess.

When they eventually return, Ricky's accused of touching his little friend and the drama goes on...and on...and on.

NEWSDAY, 9/11/98, Part II/p. B6, John Anderson

Into each life, it seems, a little "Rain Man" must fall. For actors looking to stretch their chops and/or portfolio, playing the Gump du jour can mean anything from OscarGlobes to recognition as a "serious" performer. For audiences, it means another unwinnable wrestling match between their senses and their social conscience, between what they're *supposed* to feel about the performance on screen, and what's actually taking place.

Add the unavoidable element of calculation and the best thing you can say about Timothy Hutton's "Digging to China" is: No dog. It has children, most notably Harriet Frankovitz (Evan Rachel Wood), a whimsical 10-year-old living in a Pennsylvania auto camp in the late '60s, with her alcoholic mother (Cathy Moriarty) and promiscuous sister (Mary Stuart Masterson). It also has a mentally handicapped adult in Ricky (Kevin Bacon), whom Harriet befriends against everyone's advice. It even has a dying mother in the cancer-stricken Leah Schroth (the movie's best and smallest performance, by Marian Seldes), who's taking Ricky to a home when their car breaks down at Harriet's motel. But no pets. Someone showed some restraint.

Which is more than you can say for Bacon's tic-ridden turn as Ricky, a character with predictable elements of Dustin Hoffman's Raymond Babbitt but who's also been prepared with a light dusting of Pee-Wee Herman. As a display of pure technique, Bacon's work has some merit, but any emotional content or connection seems smothered by the twitches and contortions of his very physical acting.

"Digging to China" is Harriet's story—and screenwriter Karen Janszen's predictable tale of a misfit childhood—in which the innocent bond between Harriet and Ricky appeals to everyone else's worst instincts. It's odd that the young Harriet herself would also narrate the story—the voiceovers are infrequent, but clearly told from an older perspective—and odder still that Hutton seems so intent on making a story about quirky individuality palatable to everyone. The result, of course, is that it will move almost no one.

The surfaces are too clean, the people too attractive. Harriet's allegedly miserable childhood seems quite tolerable; her mother drinks, but she never seems drunk, her house is clean and her family well fed. Her tendency to drive on the wrong side of the highway is a problem, yes, but she seems quite cogent when she does it. Perhaps she has other medical problems that are going unattended? That would be a real tragedy.

As it is, Hutton gives us no convincing motivation for Harriet's odd behavior—trying to dig a hole to China, or flagging UFOs, or trying to run off and volunteer for medical experiments—and this colors her odd-couple friendship with Ricky. There's an arms-length feel to the whole affair, a fear of squalor and a too-desperate striving for wonderment, all of which is aggravated by the medium-length shots Hutton uses so regularly. Famed Swedish cinematographer Jorgen Persson does achieve a kind of '60s postcard aesthetic, which may have been the intention. But even the best intentions sometimes go awry.

As befits an actor-turning-director, Hutton gets good performances out of a good cast, although the contrivances of the script frequently distract from the acting. It's always nice to see Mary Stuart Masterson, especially in an uncharacteristicafly slutty role like Gwen; Moriarty is the best blousy slattern in the business, and newcomer Wood has a fine presence on screen, even if you don't believe every other sentence she's required to read. As for Bacon, he's got too much celebrity for Ricky not to seem like a bit of stunt casting, but let's give him the benefit of the doubt. Maybe his appearance helped get the movie made. Or maybe it was just something he had to get out of his system.

Also reviewed in:
NEW YORK TIMES, 9/11/98, p. E18, Stephen Holden
VARIETY, 2/2-8/98, p. 33, Dennis Harvey

DIRTY LAUNDRY

An Artistic License Films release of a Hollywood Productions/Rogue Features production. *Producer:* Robert E. DiMilia and Robert Sherwin.   *Director:* Robert Sherwin and Michael Normand.   *Screenwriter:* Michael Normand.   *Director of Photography:* John Newby. *Editor:* Andrew Morreale.   *Music:* James Legg.   *Running time:* 97 minutes.   *MPAA Rating:* R.

CAST: Jay Thomas (Joey Greene);   Tess Harper (Beth Greene);   Tresa Hughes (Betty Greene); Michael Marcus (Max Greene); Stanley Earl Harrison (Lowel Bower);   Erin Underwood (Chloe Greene);   John Driver (Dr. Stoller);   Michael Mulheren (Nick); Antoinette La Vecchia (Cathy); Stuart Burney (Dale Gordon);   Dana Chaifetz (Amy);   Ray Xifo (Jerry);   Luba Mason (Ingrid).

LOS ANGELES TIMES, 9/25/98, Calendar/p. 16, Kevin Thomas

"Dirty Laundry" is a washout.

There is absolutely no good reason to bother seeing this trite, underdeveloped comedy of marital infidelity that offers nothing to differentiate it from zillions of others. Writer Michael Normand and co-director-producer Robert Sherwin display plenty of feeling for their people but virtually no imagination in giving them or their predicament any individuality or dimension.

Jay Thomas stars as a New Jersey drycleaning entrepreneur who's hit a midlife crisis, the withering of his love life with his wife of 15 years (Tess Harper) coinciding with the imminent collapse of his business. He finally agrees to his wife's suggestion that he seek counseling only to end up with one of those nitwit psychiatrists who have been spoofed to death on the screen since the sound era began. He advise Thomas to try a prostitute (Dana Chaifetz). He does, only to be caught with her in his own home by Harper.

Although an advice columnist for a women's magazine, Harper not only will not hear out her husband—who in fact has been unable to betray her out of his deep love for her—but also hypocritically has already had a secret one-time-only fling with her handsome young chiropractor (Stanley Earl Harrison), which she now intends to turn into a full-fledged affair. For added measure she's pregnant but unsure whether her husband or her lover is the father—a mystery that unaccountably seems of little concern to her.

"Dirty Laundry" resolves itself in thoroughly predictable fashion. Thomas and Harper are proven actors but cannot, no matter how hard they try, bring this couple to life or even suggest that there may in fact once have been a spark between them. That there are far worse pictures out there doesn't make "Dirty Laundry" any brighter.

NEW YORK POST, 9/25/98, p. 51, Bill Hoffmann

Two likable stars, Jay Thomas and Tess Harper, can't save "Dirty Laundry," a half-baked romantic comedy that seems more like an R-rated sketch from the old "Love American Style"TV series than a full-fledged feature.

Thomas plays Joey Green, whose dry cleaning empire and libido are both on the slide, much to the chagrin of his advice-columnist wife, Beth (Harper).

Joey turns to a hooker and Beth to her chiropractor for sexual solace, and their marriage teeters on the brink. But you know from the first 10 minutes that everything will eventually work out—and it does, of course.

None of the characters has an ounce of depth, and while "Dirty Laundry" is marginally watchable, you'll kick yourself for shelling out $8.75 for something that should have gone straight to cable.

NEWSDAY, 9/25/98, Part II/p. B9, Jack Mathews

The offbeat romantic comedy "Dirty Laundry" is among the horde of independent features that arrive, if and when they do, with long histories of financial struggle, of impassioned filmmakers keeping their hopes alive with credit cards and shoe leather, and with their noses thumbed at the know-nothing Hollywood executives who let the gem get away.

"Dirty Laundry"is no gem. On the contrary, it's a clumsily written, flatly directed affair that produces fewer laughs than you'll get watching the spin cycle of your own washing machine. But Hollywood may indeed have let one get away.

Writer, co-director, and former stand-up comedian Michael Normand (also a writer on "Leon the Pig Farmer") came up with some pretty nifty ideas about mid-life crises and the stale marriage blues, and with some polished writing and directing, it might have been a solid studio movie. Instead, it plays like a rough draft of a script treatment that would go something like this:

To bolster their self-esteem in the listless 15th year of their marriage, Joey and Beth Greene (Jay Thomas and Tess Harper) find lovers.

Joey, the owner of a struggling New Jersey dry cleaner, has taken up with a prostitute whom guilt prevents him from enjoying, while Beth, a magazine sex-advice columnist, has had an impetuous one-afternoon-stand with her handsome chiropractor Lowell (Stanley Earl Harrison), who is black. Now Beth is pregnant, and won't know who the father is until the baby's born and shows its color.

After the revelations and recriminations, Lowell moves in with the Greenes, over Joey's objections, and the three fight it out while they wait out Beth's pregnancy. The suspense could kill ya.

Thomas, a busy character actor and one-time regular on "Cheers," has some good moments as the insecure Joey, but Harper ("Crimes of the Heart") is out of her realm in a story inspired by French sexual farce, and Harrison makes no particular impression beyond his resonant baritone voice.

Meanwhile, the whole thing is so talky it could be a radio program. A little film expertise would have gone a long way.

Also reviewed in:
NEW YORK TIMES, 9/25/98, p. E27, Lawrence Van Gelder
VARIETY, 11/18-24/96, p. 61, Derek Elley

DIRTY WORK

A Metro-Goldwyn-Mayer Pictures release of a Robert Simonds/Brad Grey production. *Executive Producer:* Brad Grey and Ray Reo. *Producer:* Robert Simonds.   *Director:* Bob Saget. *Screenplay:* Frank Sebastiano, Norm Macdonald, and Fred Wolf. *Director of Photography:* Arthur Albert. *Editor:* George Folsey, Jr.   *Music:* Richard Gibbs.   *Music Editor:* Stephen Lotwis.   *Sound:* Bruce Carwardine and (music) Jeff Vaughn.   *Sound Editor:* Stephen Grubbs.

Casting: Roger Mussenden.   *Production Designer:* Gregory Keen.   *Art Director:* Gordon Lebredt.   *Set Decorator:* Jaro Dick.   *Special Effects:* Martin Malivoire.   *Costumes:* Beth Pasternak.   *Make-up:* Leslie Sebert.   *Stunt Coordinator:* Branko Racki.   *Running time:* 81 minutes.   *MPAA Rating:* PG-13.

CAST: Norm Macdonald (Mitch); Jack Warden (Pops); Artie Lange (Sam); Traylor Howard (Kathy); Don Rickles (Hamilton); Christopher McDonald (Travis Cole); Chevy Chase (Dr. Farthing); Bradley Reid (Mitch, 8 years old); Matthew Steinberg (Mitch, 6 years old); Joseph Sicilia (Sam, 8 years old); Austin John Pool (Sam, 16 years old); Gerry Mendicino (Manetti); A. Frank Ruffo (Aldo); Hrant Alianak (Kirkpatrick); Michael Vollans (Derek, 10 years old); Grant Nickalls (Jason); Deborah Hinderstein (Charlene); Scott Gibson (Frat Guy); Laura Stone (Veronica); Polly Shannon (Toni-Ann); Rummy Bishop (Homeless Guy at Apartment); James Carroll (Middle-Aged Guy); Henry Chan (Doctor at Fat Clinic); David Koechner (Anton Phillips); Paul O'Sullivan (A.D.); Uni Park (Saigon Whore); Boyd Banks (Creepy Harry); B.J. McQueen (Big Wet Man); Tony Meyler (Lobby Henchman); Shane Daly (Door Henchman); James Binkley (Unaffected Henchman); Jim Downey (Martin/Homeless Guy); Fred Wolf and Wilfrid Bray (Homeless Guys); Jessica Booker (Mrs. Murphy); Johnie Chase and Conrad Bergschneider (Policemen); Kay Hawtrey (Gladys); Lloyd White (Ron); Dini Petty and Mike Anscombe (Themselves); Howard Jerome (Foreman); Arturo Gil (Midget Paul); Rebecca Romijn (Bearded Lady); Joslyn Wenn (Jenkin's Fantasy Girl); Robbie Rox (Huge Prisoner); Chris Gillett (Suit Guy); Kevin Farley and Sanjay Talwar (Theater Workers); Trevor Bain (Henchman Jenkins); Gord Martineau (Himself); George Sperdakos (Opera Critic); Eleanor Davies (Opera Critic's Date); Laura Pudwell (Opera Lady); Emilio Roman (Baratone Errante); George Chuvalo (Ring Announcer); Gary Coleman and Ken Norton (Themselves); Christine Oddy (Aunt Jenny); Robert Shipman (Crossing Guard); Richard Sali (Ed); Silvio Olivero and MIF (Lowlifes); Cliff Saunders (Thief); Bess Motta and Arlaine Wright (Aerobics Instructors).

LOS ANGELES TIMES, 6/15/98, Calendar/p. 4, David Kronke

There's something vaguely subversive about comedian Norm Macdonald's insistence on depersonalizing everything and everyone. In his new movie "Dirty Work," he impersonally greets other characters with flat, under-descriptive monikers ("Hey, homeless guys"; "OK, building tenants"; "hey, fat lady").

He even regards himself in this reductive fashion, both in his sheer refusal to "act" and in the blithe way his character is routinely brutalized (he's the victim of an off-screen prison gang rape that's played—with shocking improbability and even more shocking success—for laughs). It's as if he's telling the audience that even trying with material like this would just be unhip.

"Dirty Work" centers on a revenge-for-hire business in which everyone, even the kindly grandmother of the pert love interest, is fair game for retribution or humiliation. It's a comedy driven not by character but rather by the utter lack of it.

"Dirty Work" clocks in at a flyweight 81 minutes, leaving the audience to consider the mountains of worse stuff left in the editing bay's trash can, and is a tone-deaf, scattershot and dispiritingly cheesy affair with more groans than laughs. Certainly Macdonald, a former "Saturday Night Live" regular, does uncork a few solid one-liners, so there are more real laughs here than in, say, the glossier and even more predictable "Six Days, Seven Nights." What thoroughly, irrevocably kills "Dirty Work" is its production-value-free, direct-to-video-quality tinniness.

Bob Saget, he of the soft stand-up routines, the lame sitcom and the wacky home videos, directs like he acts, with an eye decidedly on the obvious. More dismayingly, his performers act like Saget acts as well.

With the exception of Jack Warden and the late Chris Farley, who put way too much oomph into their small, thankless roles of old and young leches, respectively, no one in the cast ratchets his or her performance above the level of a listless shrug. Perhaps this is to divert attention from Macdonald's inability to put an ounce of conviction into his performance (which, in a roundabout way, is amusing in and of itself), but it doesn't help the movie much.

The plot is negligible. Macdonald is Mitch and Artie Lange plays Sam, two losers who couldn't hold a job if it were stuck to their fingers with Krazy Glue. Their only talent is indulging in schoolboy-style pranks, so when Sam's dad (Warden) falls ill, they decide to raise money for a heart transplant by opening a business in which they play pranks for bucks.

Their gags are largely uninspired, of the cherry-bomb-in-the-toilet variety. They encounter the usual pitfalls and pratfalls before the perfunctory happy ending, at which point Macdonald dismisses the audience with a desultory, "That's it."

"Dirty Work" got a little free publicity recently when NBC West Coast President Don Ohlmeyer got into a petty feud with Macdonald and initially refused to run spots for the film on his network (the edict was later partially rescinded). Now, we realize that Ohlmeyer was just doing his part in protecting America from a crummy movie. In the end, the best way to get revenge on someone who irks you is to force them to sit through this movie.

NEW YORK POST, 6/13/98, p. 23, Larry Worth

If "Dirty Work" is any indication, NBC honcho Don Ohlmeyer was right. Norm Macdonald *isn't* funny.

Supposedly, that was the reason Ohlmeyer kicked the "Saturday Night Live" comic from the show's anchor desk last January. Smart move.

Since then the pair's feud escalated as Ohlmeyer tried to get commercials for "Dirty Work" banned from NBC. Regardless of motivations, the act seems downright heroic—at least after seeing the finished product. The story, which Macdonald co-wrote, portrays a sad sack (Macdonald) who's been fired from 14 jobs in three months. On the day of his latest dismissal, he's thrown out of his girlfriend's apartment, then insulted beyond belief by a moviehouse manager.

Taking revenge on all his tormentors proves pretty easy, which makes the guy realize his real talent. He'll offer his services to helpless Davids seeking to humiliate Goliaths.

That much would be fine, at least if some semblance of humor manifested itself along the way. Those holding their breath for punch lines had better look good in blue.

But Macdonald isn't the only one to blame. It's fair to say that the director Bob Saget brings the same level of wit and sophistication to the film that he brought to hosting duties on "America's Funniest Videos."

Here, Saget can't even find a consistent tone, varying between all-out slapstick and attempts at dark comedy. Then again, it's hard to milk yuks out of murder, prison rape, bestiality, incest, homelessness and guns in school.

Nor can Saget alter Macdonald's line readings, which carry a range of A to B. The alleged comic's delivery is the equivalent of Sominex.

The supporting cast offers no relief, underlining the downward spiral of Chevy Chase, Christopher McDonald and Don Rickles. Their sad antics are interspersed with pointless cameos from Adam Sandler, John Goodman and Gary ("Different Strokes") Coleman. And that's not even mentioning the late Chris Farley's final demonstration of his comic lackings. Most pathetic of all, though, is witnessing the great Jack Warden's decline. Just when thinking that it couldn't get any worse for him than playing Carrot Top's foil in "Chairman of the Board," he has to walk around as Macdonald's sex-crazed mentor, talking about "hooter heaven." If this is the best he's being offered, retirement seems a viable option.

Actually, retirement seems a fit fate for Macdonald and Saget, too. Maybe Ohlmeyer can give that concept some thought.

NEWSDAY, 6/15/98, Part II/p. B11, Jack Mathews

Whatever else can be said for his talent as a film director, and it will be difficult to think of anything else, Bob Saget's got nerve. During the incredibly unfunny outtakes that come at the end of his incredibly unfunny "Dirty Work," Saget ("Full House") includes Don Rickles ad-libbing to star Norm Macdonald, "How you got this movie, I'll never know."

Macdonald laughs, but it's a serious question.

Whatever else can be said for Macdonald's gifts for film comedy (and it will be hard to think of anything else), the former "Saturday Night Live" "Weekend Update" star certainly pulled a good one on MGM. The studio was so embarrassed by "Dirty Work," it didn't bother to show it to critics in advance. (I caught it at the first matinee at my local theater, and can report that its total gross for that screening was $5.)

"Dirty Work" is appallingly inept. The script, co-written by Macdonald, Frank Sebastiano and Fred Wolf, is less a story than a series of enacted comedy ideas, hatched around a flip premise that someone might have come up with at an "SNL" brainstorming session.

Macdonald and Artie Lange are Mitch and Sam, lifelong buddies, step-brothers as it turns out, who hire themselves out as revenge artists in order to earn enough money for their father's heart transplant. The perennially unemployed goofs can't hold a job until the noon lunch whistle, but they have a knack for screwing things up, which they decide to sell as a service, called Revenge For Hire.

Soon, they're putting popcorn in the engine of a bulldozer to save an old lady's home, shaving the whiskers off a bearded lady for the dwarf she's been hassling, and destroying an apartment building to clear its tenants out for an evil landlord. When the film's not absorbed in these moronic antics, it's stealing jokes from "Airplane!," and demonstrating how that movie might have gone if nothing had worked.

"Saturday Night Live" alums going bad in movies is nothing new, but Macdonald's work here, showcased by a director who has no clue how to pace or when to cut a comedy scene, is exceptional for its lack of inspiration and polish. Comedy is supposed to be hard to do, not to watch.

No one comes away untarnished. Besides Rickles, who plays a boisterous theater owner, the supporting cast features Chevy Chase as a heart surgeon with a gambling addiction, Jack Warden as the lecherous heart patient, Christopher McDonald as the sinister landlord, Traylor Howard as Mitch's inexplicably amused girlfriend, the late Chris Farley as a skunk-wrangler and John Goodman doing a brief cameo as an announcer at an opera.

What they did to deserve this movie, we'll never know.

Also reviewed in:
CHICAGO TRIBUNE, 6/15/98, Tempo/p. 2, John Petrakis
NEW YORK TIMES, 6/13/98, p. B15, Lawrence Van Gelder
VARIETY, 6/15-21/98, p. 99, Joe Leydon

DISTURBING BEHAVIOR

A Metro-Goldwyn-Mayer Pictures release in association with Village Roadshow-Hoyts Film Partnership of a Beacon Communications production. *Executive Producer:* C.O. Erickson and Phillip B. Goldfine. *Producer:* Armyan Bernstein and Jon Shestack. *Director:* David Nutter. *Screenplay:* Scott Rosenberg. *Director of Photography:* John S. Bartley. *Editor:* Randy Jon Morgan. *Music:* Mark Snow. *Music Editor:* Jeff Charbonneau. *Sound:* Rob Young and (music) Larold Rebhun. *Sound Editor:* Fred Judkins. *Casting:* Lisa Beach. *Production Designer:* Nelson Coates. *Art Director:* Eric Fraser. *Set Designer:* Gary Myers and Patrick Banister. *Set Decorator:* Louise Roper. *Set Dresser:* Tony Beck, Patrick Kearns, and Laurie Marsh. *Special Effects:* Joel Whist. *Costumes:* Trish Keating. *Make-up:* Lisa Love. *Special Effects Make-up:* Toy Lindala. *Stunt Coordinator:* J.J. Makaro and Dave Hospes. *Running time:* 83 minutes. *MPAA Rating:* R.

CAST: Natassia Malthe (Mary Jo Copeland);   Tobias Mehler (Andy Effkin);   Nick Stahl (Gavin Strick);   Steve Railsback (Officer Cox);   Chris Owens (Officer Kramer);   Katharine Isabelle (Lindsay Clark);   James Marsden (Steve Clark);   Terry David Mulligan (Nathan Clark); Susan Hogan (Cynthia Clark);   Robert Moloney (Ferry Guy);   Ethan Embry (Allen Clark); Derek Hamilton (Trent Whalen);   Dan Zukovic (Mr. Rooney);   Tygh Runyan (Dickie Atkinson);   P. J. Prinsloo (Robby Stewart);   Michelle Skalnik (Randi Sklar);   Lalainia Lindbjerg (Kathy);   Brendan Fehr (Brendan-Blue Ribbon);   Chad E. Donella (U.V.);   Garry Chalk (Coach);   Crystal Cass (Lorna Longley);   Fiona Scott (Fiona-Blue Ribbon);   David

Paetkau (Tom Cox);   Erin Tougas (Shannon);   Ryan Taylor (Ryan-Blue Ribbon);   Jay Brazeau (Principal Weathers);   Sarah-Jane Redmond (Miss Perkins);   Bruce Greenwood (Dr. Caldicott); Carly Pope (Abbey);   Katie Holmes (Rachel Wagner);   John Destry (Middle-Aged Man);   A.J. Buckley (Chug Roman);   Glynis Davies (Coupon Lady);   Cynde Harmon (Mrs. Atkinson); Larry Musser (Coroner);   William Sadler (Dorian Newberry);   Andre Danyliu (Roscoe); Gillian Barber (Judy Effkin);   Stephen James Lang (John);   Peter LaCroix (Mr. Strick);   Lynda Boyd (Mrs. Lucille Strick);   Daniella Evangelista (Daniella-Blue Ribbon);   Sean Smith (School Bus Boy);   Zuzana Marlow (Shannon's Mom); Tamsin Kelsey (Detrice Wagner); Suzy Joachim (Female Doctor);   Fulvio Cecere (Anesthesiologist);   Bob Wilde (Shadow Man); Judith Maxie (Shadow Woman);   Doug Abrahams (Security Guard);   Christopher R. Sumpton (Screaming Man);   Jarred Blancard (Flossing Man);   Kate Braidwood (Make-up Girl);   Stephen Holmes (Toothbrush Boy);   Mark Aviss (Bald Man);   Julie Patzwald (Betty Caldicott);   Stephen E. Miller (Frankie);   MarciaRose Shestack (Reporter);   Robert Lewis (Moderator);   Dee Jay Jackson (Assistant Principal);   Kendall Saunders (Disrespectful Student);   Sean Amsing (Damon).

LOS ANGELES TIMES, 7/24/98, Calendar/p. 13, Jack Mathews

[The following review by Jack Mathews appeared in a slightly different form in **NEWSDAY, 7/24/98, Part II/p. B7.]**

Movies like David Nutter's "Disturbing Behavior," written by Scott Rosenberg, the author of last summer's worst movie, "Con Air," are the reason valet parking attendants in Beverly Hills leave scripts on the seats. They give hope.

Conceived as an upside-down "Clockwork Orange," this howler of a horror movie is set in the picture-book Northwest town of Cradle Bay, where the high school is infested with a growing crowd of Stepford jocks and pom-pom girls with severe superiority complexes. Sounds like Any School, U.S.A., if you ask me.

But these kids are different. They're former thugs and sluts and otherwise problem teens who have emerged transformed from the motivational Blue Ribbon workshop of Dr. Caldicott (Bruce Greenwood), a neuro-pharmacist who's devised a behavioral modification program combining simple brainwashing techniques with cybernetics. He plants microprocessors in the kids' brains that makes them dress well, study hard, hold bake sales and avoid heavy petting.

For parents looking for results, this is even better than getting their children hooked on phonics.

Of course, with any new scientific breakthrough, there's resistance, mostly from rebellious students hooked on free will, and there is one nagging side effect. If the Blue Ribbon kids are sexually aroused, their pineal glands are overstimulated, and their dopamine skyrockets, short-circuiting their implants and causing psychotic outbursts. Tempting one of them is like feeding a gremlin after midnight.

We see this phenomenon demonstrated in the opening scene, on lover's lane, where a reluctant Caldicott jock ("I have to save my body fluids for the game") is being overwhelmed by his concupiscent girlfriend. When his dopamine kicks in, a yellow beam appears in his suddenly dead eyes, his nostrils flare, his brow is furled, and he completely loses his manners, cracking the girl's head like a walnut.

Moments later, he kills a cop who happens by, and is then calmed and sent on his way by the dead cop's curiously unruffled partner (Steve Railsback). Enter Steve (James Marsden), Gavin (Nick Stahl) and Rachel ("Dawson Creek's" Katie Holmes), Cradle Bay's version of the heroes of "Rebel Without a Cause." Steve is the James Dean character, a handsome newcomer from a dysfunctional family, Rachel has the sweet bad girl role played by Natalie Wood, and Gavin, an eyewitness at the opening murder scene, is a smarter, more confident rendition of Sal Mineo's ill-fated Plato.

Together, the rebels will take on the Blue Ribbon menace, Dr. Caldicott, parental complicity and, with the help of their own Boo Radley, a high school Janitor (William Sadler) with simultaneous rat and Kurt Vonnegut fixations, attempt to make Cradle Bay safe once again for making out.

Nutter, an "X-Files" TV show veteran making his feature directing debut, demonstrates a talent only for mimicry. Stylistically, "Disturbing Behavior" is indistinguishable from the hordes of past B-horror movies. And Rosenberg's script is a veritable anthology of genre cliches.

"This might not be such a good idea," Rachel says, as she and Steve break into an asylum populated by the mutant human debris of past Caldicott experiments. You can laugh—or cry.

NEW YORK POST, 7/24/98, p. 43, Larry Worth

Halfway through "Disturbing Behavior," a frustrated teen bangs her head over and over against a wall. Long before then, ticket-buyers will want to do the same.

The story is a clear rip-off of "The Stepford Wives," with a few touches from "Children of the Corn" and "A Clockwork Orange" inserted along the way. But unlike its predecessors, the results are utterly lacking in suspense and imagination.

The action takes place in a sleepy little community where the kids are divided into two types: nose ring-wearing punks who rebel at the system and goodie two-shoes who sport letter sweaters and plan bake sales. Oddly enough, the former keep turning into the latter.

Precious little time elapses before a hunky new kid in town learns that the wayward teens are getting a drastic attitude adjustment. Namely they're lobotomized into civility. And the hero's parents are ready to sign him up for the program.

That much would be fine, if first-time director David Nutter had any sense of style or story-telling abilities. Instead, Nutter's adept only at recycling horror cliches, as when a hand on someone's shoulder or a face at the window is meant to make audience members jump.

Worse still are the alleged special effects, best exemplified when one of the Stepford urchins gets a murderous purple glow in the eye before an act of violence. If possible, the attempts at techno-wizardry are even sillier than Scott Rosenberg's moron-geared dialogue.

The cast is little consolation, headed by model-handsome newcomer James Marsden. Granted, his cheekbones are sharp enough to cut glass, but he could be out-acted by a store mannequin. Then there's Katie "Dawson's Creek" Holmes, who's got petulance—and histrionics—down to a science.

And how to explain the participation of Bruce Greenwood, who helped make last year's "The Sweet Hereafter" such a memorable cinematic achievement?) Here, his work as the mad scientist makes Boris Karloff look understated.

But while sadly shy of assets, the film does have great potential for a sequel. How about a movie on brain-altered directors whose cerebral implants prevent swill like "Disturbing Behavior"?

SIGHT AND SOUND, 10/99, p. 41, Danny Leigh

The small town of Cradle Bay, the US. Grieving over the suicide of their eldest son, the Clark family arrive from Chicago. On his first day at the local high school, remaining son Steve is introduced to its various cliques by alienated Gavin Strick and his albino friend U.V.: among them are the Blue Ribbons, an exclusive gaggle of overachievers. Later, Steve meets school guidance counsellor and Blue Ribbon-Svengali Doctor Caldicott, and Rachel, another of Gavin's friends. Gavin tells Steve he believes the Blue Ribbons are a murderous cult.

Meanwhile, a Blue Ribbon attacks Rachel in the school boiler room, only to be foiled by janitor Newberry. That evening, Gavin discovers his parents are planning to have him recruited into the Blue Ribbons. Terrified, he flees. However, the next day at school he appears among the Blue Ribbons. Steve and Rachel steal the school's staff files and learn Caldicott came to teaching from a career in neuropharmacology. They realise the Blue Ribbons are victims of his experiments in mind control. Steve and Rachel are captured by Caldicott, but Newberry intervenes once more, saving the pair in a kamikaze rescue bid which simultaneously wipes out the Blue Ribbons. Caldicott is also killed. Steve, Rachel and U.V. depart the now deserted Cradle Bay. Weeks later, in an inner-city high school, a new student teacher is introduced to the class: Gavin Strick.

Although mostly a recasting of Bryan Forbes' overwrought thriller *The Stepford Wives* (1974) as a morality tale for Marilyn Manson fans, *Disturbing Behaviour* nonetheless wastes little time in pillaging stylistic touches from a slew of other sources. Barely a frame goes by without a touch of *Twin Peaks,* a scintilla of *The Lost Boys,* or even—in its hysterical finale—a quick rummage through *A Clockwork Orange* (1971).

However, director David Nutter's primary influence is *The X Files* for which he directed several episodes, and *Disturbing Behavior* exudes—notably in the jarring fades to black which pepper the film—an essentially small-screen sensibility. Of course, this approach has its compensations (the pacing, for example, is agreeably brisk). On the whole, however, Nutter seems ill at ease with the physical expansion, and his narrow range of atmospheric panning shots and extreme close-ups of eyeballs only goes so far.

Nutter also hovers nervously around the semi-parodic without ever embracing the downright frothy tropes of, say, *The Faculty.* The dialogue in particular oscillates between one liners so studied they could almost pass for Gregg Araki ("Self-mutilate this, fluid girl," remarks one anonymous Blue Ribbon baddie) and impossibly banal, apparently straight-faced moments of exposition ("Neuropharmacology?" quivers Steve, "You mean *mind control?"*). Ultimately, the same schizophrenic impulse pervades the entire film: it's too pompous to be camp, but too silly to be genuinely engaging.

None of which is helped by the script's reliance on leaden clichés. The characterisation consists mostly of lazily written archetypes the chisel-jawed hero, mourning the dead brother, the feisty chick sidekick with her barbed-wire tattoos, and, with Gavin before his transformation, the Holy Fool. Yet even dealing with such ciphers, Nutter cannot maintain any narrative coherence: amid the series of virtual non-sequiturs which precede the resolution, for instance, we're left wholly in the dark over why the nefarious Caldicott would actually want to brainwash a bunch of pimply ingrates into improving their grades and side parting their hair. As a consequence, all that remains is a confused paean to a generic notion of individuality, tailor-made for the noble outsider fantasies of perpetual adolescence.

VILLAGE VOICE, 8/4/98, p. 53, Justine Elias

In gloomy, isolated Cradle Bay, something weirder than usual is going on at the local high schoo—in addition to the familiar assortment of suburban geeks, jacks, and burnouts, there are the Blue Ribbons, a scarily upbeat student group dedicated to enforcing school spirit, organizing bake sales, and pleasing their parents. These peppy teens are invariably described as "good kids" no matter the crimes they commit. Even for those too young to remember *The Stepford Wives* (or its campy made-for-TV sequel, *The Stepford Children),* it will come as no surprise that the über-youth of *Disturbing Behavior* are the monstrous creations of an evil scientist—who, abetted by an SAT-worshiping cult known as the local PTA, is bent on wiping out adolescent rebellion. That's bad news for the angry, withdrawn new kid in town (James Marsden, a Brad Pitt clone).

Although there are a few inspired moments, like a visit to a hellish psychiatric ward filled with the villain's catatonic victims, and a chilling scene in which the Blue Ribbons help a new member destroy his customized muscle car—the last vestige of his former life—the movie is grim rather than frightening. And with the exception of Nick Stahl, who plays the hero's stoned, cynical pal, the main characters—like Katie Holmes's pouty rock chick—remain sketchy and inarticulate, like the unfortunate kids who get killed during the first two minutes of every *Buffy the Vampire Slayer* episode. Despite the stylish efforts of three *X-Files* veterans (director David Nutter, cinematographer John S. Bartley, and composer Mark Snow), *Disturbing Behavior* is dragged down by its own overwhelming moodiness. And what a shame! Everybody knows how talented these filmmakers are. I wonder if they're really applying themselves. Any more of this sullen sarcasm and it's going on their permanent record.

Also reviewed in:
CHICAGO TRIBUNE, 7/24/98, Friday/p. F, John Petrakis
NEW YORK TIMES, 7/24/98, p. E22, Stephen Holden
NEW YORKER, 5/31/99, p. 94, David Denby
VARIETY, 7/27-8/2/98, p. 53, Dennis Harvey
WASHINGTON POST, 7/24/98, p. B5, Stephen Hunter
WASHINGTON POST, 7/24/98, Weekend/p. 38, Michael O'Sullivan

DIVORCE IRANIAN STYLE

A Women Make Movies release.   *Producer:* Kim Longinotto.   *Director:* Kim Longinotto and Ziba Mir-Hosseini.   *Director of Photography:* Zahra Saiedzadeh.   *Editor:* Barrie Vince. *Sound:* Christine Felce.   *Running time:* 80 minutes.   *MPAA Rating:* Not Rated.

CAST: Joann Rosethall (Narrator/Farsi with English subtitles).

NEW YORK POST, 12/9/98, p. 65, Jonathan Foreman

"Divorce Iranian Style" is a crude, amateurish film, but its subject matter is fascinating.

The movie reveals a society with much more complicated and ambiguous sexual politics than one might expect. It seems that 20 years of religious totalitarianism and legal misogyny have not succeeded in fundamentally changing Iranian family life.

The chador-wrapped women and girls you see presenting their divorce petitions in an oddly informal little Teheran courtroom are astonishingly feisty, often shouting at the mild-mannered judge and badgering the courthouse bureaucrats.

Sometimes the arguments are so riveting—at times it beats TV's "Cops" or "Jerry Springer" for voyeuristic interest—that you wonder if the whole colorful cast isn't laying it on for the camera.

But on a technical level the film wastes time with meaningless shots of Teheran storefronts, or people walking up and down courthouse stairs, while leaving vital questions unanswered. Like, what is an Iranian "marriage gift," and what happened to the principal character's when their trials ended?

Ultimately, this is a case, if ever there was, of structure spoiling substance.

NEWSDAY, 12/9/98, Part II/p. B11, John Anderson

Roiling across the screen like a medieval "Jerry Springer Show," the nonfiction "Divorce Iranian Style" is easy to digest, once you grasp its most fundamental concept: Women under the kind of Islamic law practiced in Iran have no rights. After that, everything makes perfect sense.

For instance: A woman who already has given up almost everything to get her divorce from an abusive husband—including her elder daughter—is ordered to relinquish her younger child, too, because she's remarried. A 16-year-old petitioner, married off by her parents at 14, who shocks everyone when she insists on actually collecting the marriage "gift" her 37-year-old husband promised her. A better-than-middle-aged woman, whose husband has taken a second wife, being told by the judge that she must make herself "more attractive" in order to coax him back to the marriage. And the school-aged daughter of a court employee, who can do such a frighteningly accurate impersonation of the Islamic divorce judge that it makes your skin crawl even while you're howling.

Filmmakers Kim Longinotto and her London-based Iranian ally, Ziba Mir-Hosseini, working predominantly within the one judge's claustrophobic Islamic courtroom, practice a kind of guerrilla-advocacy cinema (at one point, they actually have to testify themselves about a particularly nasty scene outside the courtroom). It's no question where their sentiments lie, but they needn't do much to make their case against the barbaric legal legacy of the Khomeini era (the late Ayatollah is glimpsed in several not-so-incongruous cameos).

As rigged as the court system may be against Iranian divorcees, the emotional punch of its stories are equally biased toward them: The women have to be so tenacious and resolute about even daring to bring their cases up within a system so oblivious to the concept of westernized justice that they assume heroic stature just by being there. The men? Almost everyone that Longinotto and Mir-Hosseini portray complains about his "prestige" or "honor" being damaged by divorce, while trying to weasel out of some kind of support payment. Of course, this is a westernized interpretation. The presumption of "Divorce Iranian Style" (whose title is a coyly satiric pun on the '60s films starring either Marcello Mastroianni or Dick Van Dyke is that there is an objective reality to matrimonial legal justice, an idea Iran would seem to view with some degree of skepticism.

VILLAGE VOICE, 12/15/98, p. 146, Amy Taubin

A small, direct, tantalizing documentary, *Divorce Iranian Style* challenges preconceptions about what life is like for women in Iran. The most startling thing about the film is simply that it was made. The filmmakers—Kim Longinotto, who codirected the fabulous *Dream Girls,* and Ziba Mir-Hosseini, an Iranian anthropologist who is divorced herself—set up their camera in family court and follow the cases of three women who are attempting to divorce their husbands. Although Iranian religious law frowns on divorce, a man is allowed to claim the privilege without needing to show cause, provided he pays his ex-wife compensation. A woman, however, can only sue for divorce if she can prove that her husband is sterile or mad, or if he agrees to let her out of their marriage contract. In the last case, the compensation becomes the bargaining chip: the man will sometimes give his wife her freedom if he doesn't have to pay.

The women are assertive, demanding, and persistent to a degree that confounds stereotypes of oppression. They challenge the judge, badger the uncooperative clerk for misplaced files, chew out their husbands and their husbands' families. At one point, the judge tells a little girl (the daughter of the court stenographer who has been a fixture in the court from the age of two months) that he has a man picked out for her who's "not like the riffraff that come in here." The girl has a more radical plan: "I won't marry ever, now that I know what husbands are like."

Also reviewed in:
CHICAGO TRIBUNE, 1/1/99, Friday/p. A, Michael Wilmington
NEW YORK TIMES, 11/9/98, p. E5, Stephen Holden
VARIETY, 12/14-20/98, p. 133, Derek Elley

DR. DOLITTLE

A Twentieth Century Fox release of a Davis Entertainment Company/Joseph M. Singer Entertainment production.   *Executive Producer:* Sue Baden-Powell, and Jenno Topping. *Producer:* John Davis, Joseph M. Singer, and David T. Friendly.   *Director:* Betty Thomas. *Screenplay:* Nat Mauldin and Larry Levin.   *Based on the Doctor Dolittle stories by:* Hugh Lofting.   *Director of Photography:* Russell Boyd.   *Editor:* Peter Teschner.   *Music:* Richard Gibbs.   *Music Editor:* Will Kaplan.   *Sound:* David Kirschner and (music) Robert Fernandez. *Sound Editor:* Michael J. Benavente and John A. Larsen.   *Casting:* Nancy Foy.   *Production Designer:* William Elliott. *Art Director:* Greg Papalia.   *Set Designer:* James F. Claytor, Gina B. Cranham, and Easton Michael Smith.   *Set Decorator:* K.C. Fox.   *Set Dresser:* Glenn Roberts, Jason Bedig, Robert Camron, Eric Ramirez, and Michael J. Vojvoda.   *Special Effects:* Burt Dalton.   *Visual Effects:* Jon Farhat.   *Costumes:* Sharen Davis.   *Make-up:* Ann Pala.   *Make-up (Eddie Murphy):* Toy R. Van Lierop.   *Special Effects Make-up:* Matthew W. Mungle.   *Stunt Coordinator:* Ernie Orsatti.   *Running time:* 85 minutes.   *MPAA Rating:* PG-13.

CAST: Eddie Murphy (Dr. John Dolittle);   Ossie Davis (Archer Dolittle);   Oliver Platt (Dr. Mark Weller);   Peter Boyle (Calloway); Richard Schiff (Dr. Gene Reiss);   Kristen Wilson (Lisa);   Jeffrey Tambor (Dr. Fish);   Kyla Pratt (Maya);   Raven-Symoné (Charisse);   Steven Gilborn (Dr. Litvack);   Erik Todd Dellums (Jeremy);   June Christopher (Diane);   Cherie Franklin (Mrs. Parkus);   Mark Adair-Rios (Intern);   Don Calfa (Patient at Hammersmith); Arnold F. Turner (Animal Control Officer);   Kay Yamamoto (Receptionist);   Kellye Nakahara-Wallett (Beagle Woman);   Beth Grant (Woman);   Yule Caise (Vet's Assistant);   Brian Kwan (Busboy);   L. Peter Callender (Policeman). Charles A. Branklyn (Security Guard);   Cliff McLaughlin (Mounted Policeman);   Richard Penn (Principal);   John LaFayette (Reverend); Raymond Matthew Mason (3 Year-old Dolittle);   Dari Gerard Smith (5 Year-old Dolittle);   Karl T. Wright (Reporter);   Stan Sellers and Ming Lo (Cops).

VOICES: Norm Macdonald (Voice of Lucky);   Albert Brooks (Voice of Tiger);   Chris Rock (Voice of Rodney);   Reni Santoni (Voice of Rat #1);   John Leguizamo (Voice of Rat #2);   Julie

Kavner (Voice of Female Pigeon);   Garry Shandling (Voice of Male Pigeon);   Ellen DeGeneres (Voice of Prologue Dog);   Brian Doyle-Murray (Voice of Old Beagle);   Phil Proctor (Voice of Drunk Monkey);   Jenna Elfman (Voice of Owl);   Gilbert Gottfried (Voice of Compulsive Dog); Phyllis Katz (Voice of Goat); Douglas Shamburger (Voice of Pound Dog);   Jeff Doucette (Voice of Possum);   Archie Hahn (Voice of Heavy Woman's Dog);   Tom Towles (Voice of German Shepherd);   Eddie Frierson (Voice of Skunk);   Paul Reubens (Voice of Racoon);   Royce D. Applegate (Voice of "I Love You" Dog);   James F. Dean (Voice of Orangutan);   Chad Einbinder (Voice of Bettleheim the Cat);   Jonathan Lipnicki (Voice of Baby Tiger);   Hamilton Camp (Voice of Pig);   Kerrigan Mahan (Voice of Penguin).

LOS ANGELES TIMES, 6/26/98, Calendar/p. 1, Kenneth Turan

[The following review by Kenneth Turan appeared in a slightly different form in **NEWSDAY, 6/26/98, Part II/p. B7.]**

Animals move their lips a lot in "Dr. Dolittle," but they have nothing of interest to say. And neither does anyone else.

Based on the Hugh Lofting stories about a man able to talk to all of God's creatures, "Dr. Dolittle" is a complete waste of time and potential. It so squanders the technology that makes owls, dogs and raccoons look as if they're conversing that it might as well be labeled the "Anti-Babe."

Given that "Dolittle" was already filmed as a musical in 1967 (with Rex Harrison in the starring role), what the current producers had in mind, said one, was "bringing a contemporary and hip '90s spin to the material." In practice this apparently meant the wholesale insertion of a witless barrage of off-color bathroom humor.

"Dolittle" begins with a burst of butt jokes, amplified later by unflattering shots of a woman's huge and blotchy posterior. Then there's the extended sequence of a thermometer getting stuck you know where, not to mention giving CPR to a dying rat and having pigeons defecate on unsuspecting bad guys. If this is supposed to be family entertainment, it's frightening to wonder exactly what kind of family it's intended for.

Presiding over this menagerie is Eddie Murphy's Dr. John Dolittle, as warm and cuddly a husband and father as any TV sitcom could wish for. It's frankly depressing to see Murphy, who had moments of pure hilarity in "The Nutty Professor," recede into a role so bland that some of his co-stars—animal and human—get more laughs than he does.

As a youngster, Dolittle had the power of talking to animals, but as he grew older he lost the gift. Now a successful San Francisco doctor with a beautiful wife (Kristen Wilson) and two fine daughters, he's even forgotten he had it.

Dolittle and his two partners (Oliver Platt, Richard Schiff) are in the process of selling their practice to the all-purpose evil of the moment, an HMO fronted by a greedy type named Calloway (Peter Boyle).

In the midst of these delicate negotiations, Dolittle grazes a dog named Lucky with his car and rediscovers his power. The animals, in turn, find out there's a doctor in the house who speaks their language, and suddenly every corner he turns is occupied by an ailing four-footed friend.

It is one of the more misguided cornerstones of this feeble screenplay (by Nat Mauldin and Larry Levin) that each of these animals is a miniature Borscht Belt comic, cracking wise and making more questionable jokes about their individual sexual proclivities than most people will want to hear.

Director Betty Thomas has gathered an impressive collection of voices, including Albert Brooks as an ailing tiger, Chris Rock as a manic guinea pig, John Leguizamo as a troublesome rat and Julie Kavner and Garry Shandling as an unhappily married pair of pigeons. It's theoretically amusing, but only up to a point, and that point arrives well before the movie comes to an end.

The moral of "Dr. Dolittle," that being true to yourself is the only way to go, is unobjectionable, but it hardly makes up for the nonsense that surrounds it. "No animal was harmed in the making of this film," reads the usual American Humane Assn. disclaimer at the close, but nothing is said about the debilitating effect this film will have on anyone with the bad luck to wander into it unawares.

NEW STATESMAN, 7/31/98, p. 42, Gerald Kaufman

"Dr Dolittle" is doing big business at American box-offices this summer. The reason for this success explains a great deal about Hollywood economics. A mass film audience no longer exists. Half a century ago 80 per cent of Americans went to the cinema every week. Now, only a fraction of the US (or British) population sees even a huge hit like "Titanic." Yet enormous sums of money can be made—in merchandising, in TV rights, in sales of videos—from a movie that wins a reputation based on purchase of tickets during theatrical release. So the appeal of a picture such as "Dr Dolittle" is planned with care.

Filmgoers these days consist of niche audiences. No big-budget picture can be made without targeting at least one niche: children, teenagers, the affluent middle-aged, gays, blacks. "Dr Dolittle" has in its sights two audiences which overlap—children and blacks. based, however remotely, on Hugh Lofting's stories about a doctor who can talk to animals, it has to be a sure-fire winner if it can get animals to talk. These days, with the availability of dazzlingly accomplished computerised special effects, any animal can be turned into an actor at least as accomplished as Eddie Murphy (who plays Dolittle).

Some of this film's most impressive effects are achieved with animatronic replicas of animals, which appear to have learned the script (not too hard, considering its banality) and to be acting it out. If you want to watch anthropomorphic rats cavorting in a garbage bin, then "Dr Dolittle" is the movie you have been waiting for. The problem for me was that not only the rats seem to be animatronic artefacts; so does Eddie Murphy.

It is far from surprising that Murphy, who seems these days to be concentrating on remakes of past successes (or, in the case of "Dr Dolittle," a past failure, one of Rex Harrison's direst flops), was recently seen in a new version of Jerry Lewis' "The Nutty Professor." He is turning into this generation's Lewis: frantic, voluble, mugging and gesticulating, a daunting sight to behold. Nevertheless, Murphy is that rare phenomenon, a black actor who does not seek to be a surrogate Caucasian, but has nevertheless crossed the ethnic boundary into superstar status. Here he is supported by a team of other black actors, several of whom are children.

Innocuous films for kids, however banal, have always accounted for a segment of Hollywood's output. This movie, though banal to the nth degree, is far from innocuous. It is, to my mind, repulsive, not just because Betty Thomas directs it crudely and noisily, but because much of its content is squalid and grubby. It does not simply appeal to its child audience; it soils that audience. The screenplay, by Nat Mauldin and Larry Levin, seems utterly preoccupied with scatology, concentrating almost obsessively on arses and excrement.

Right at the beginning a character poses the question: "Why do dogs sniff each other's butts?", and Dolittle as a child starts sniffing the behind of the local clergyman. A woman patient of the adult Dolittle has her naked behind exposed. For laughs, a pet dog has a thermometer stuffed up its anus. A guinea pig is flushed down a lavatory. An important plot-point—in so far as any point in this rubbish can be regarded as important hinges on Dolittle's daughter going to the lavatory. His triumph is sealed by a pigeon defecating on his enemy. This is, literally, a shitty film.

It is a relief to find that "Paulie", though its eponymous hero is a parrot which not only talks but converses almost incessantly, contains not a single bird dropping. Paulie, because of his garrulousness, is taken away from his loving owner and spends the rest of the movie on a mission to make his way back to little Marie.

Emanating as it does from Steven Spielberg's production company DreamWorks, "Paulie" is crammed with references to other movies. Paulie himself is an avian ET. His adventures with a group of human ne'er-do-wells owe more than a little to Disney's Pinocchio. The middle-aged fairy godmother (a lovely performance by Gena Rowlands), who takes him into her home for a while, seems to be modelled on the comforting role played by Lillian Gish in "Night of the Hunter". There is also a sly little episode in which the parrot cheers on the marauding birds while watching a televised extract from Hitchcock's "The Birds."

"Paulie", whose special effects are as skilled as those in "Dr Dolittle" but less ostentatious, stretches its exiguous material almost to breaking point. At only 91 minutes, it has its longueurs. Yet it is suffused with touching charm, containing evocative images of huge Spielbergian night skies, magical silhouettes and an exuberant moment (low-flying helicopter shots) when the timid parrot spreads his wings and soars into flight. Paulie may not be a big-budget blockbuster, but it has the far more precious quality of being the rare kind of movie that a little girl could love.

NEW YORK POST, 6/26/98, p. 45, Rod Dreher

As amusing talking critters go, 30 *gordita*-shilling seconds of that cute Taco Bell Chihuahua beats all of the distemperate new Eddie Murphy kiddie comedy."*Yo no quiero*,"Dr. Dolittle."'

In another waste of his talent, Eddie Murphy plays a San Francisco physician who rediscovers a repressed childhood talent for yakking with all creatures great and small. This wreaks havoc in Dolittle's buttoned-down professional and private life until the jumpy doc finally learns to relax and enjoy being a squirrel.

This "Dr. Dolittle," an update of the 1967 children's musical "Doctor Dolittle" that stars Rex Harrison in the title role of an eccentric who converses with animals, Push-Me-Pull-Yous the fondly remembered fable into the '90s. Progress, it's not.

It's enough to make you pine for the good old days of children's movies, when filmmakers appealed to children's innate sense of wonder. (Even "Babe," from two years ago, was wonderfully old-fashioned in this way.)

Here, screenwriters Nat Mauldin and Larry Levin take the low road, writing trashy, "South Park"-ish dialogue for Dolittle's beloved menagerie. If I could talk to the animals, I'd tell them to wash out their nasty little mouths.

For example, the likable wisenheimer Norm Macdonald is generally a hoot voicing Lucky, a scrappy street hound Dolittle takes in for his family. But when Dolittle, desperate for some private bedroom time with his wife (Kristen Wilson), shoos Lucky away, the dog sniffs, "Hey, you want a tip on a good position?"

We have here a children's movie whose idea of "edgy" is the family pet offering to advise his owner on how to have sex doggy-style. Think about that.

Some of the jokes will zip right over kids' heads. Comedian Chris Rock provides the voice of Rodney, a lively guinea pig who's the funniest thing about this movie. "Hey, why they call me a guinea pig, anyway?" he says. "I'm not Italian, and I ain't pork!" What a knee-slapper.

Irrepressible Rodney does a little rodent jig to LaBelle's "Lady Marmalade," which is actually pretty funny. Gilbert Gottfried cameos as the voice of a spastic terrier, who calls someone a "pussy," which isn't.

The animatronic animals, courtesy of Jim Henson's Creature Shop, and the special effects add welcome zoological zip to the flaccid story, which studiously avoids wit and madcap magic-making in favor of penny-ante sleaze and, in the sappy, be-true-to-yourself conclusion, canned sentimentality.

Betty Thomas directs with more than her usual professionalism. The animals really do look like they're communicating with people, which couldn't have been easy to pull off. Too bad the material is cruddy and the performances, in turn, are routine.

NEWSWEEK, 7/6/98, p. 67, Veronica Chambers

You know "Dr. Dolittle" has gone '90s when the good doctor lives in a spacious San Francisco condo, transports tigers in a jazzy sport utility vehicle and is stressed over whether to sell his HMO for millions of dollars. Eddie Murphy, as John Dolittle, is as hip and sardonic as ever, but the real revelation is how well he plays a straight man to a cast of talking animals. The creatures (wonderfully voiced by Garry Shandling, Julie Kavner, Norm Macdonald, Chris Rock and John Leguizamo) steal the show with wise-guy attitude. The remake also smartly broadens Dolittle's role. He isn't just a friendly vet, he's an all-around animal counselor. He doesn't just hear the animals, he *understands* them, tending to an alcoholic monkey, a suicidal tiger, rats in cardiac arrest and pigeons in couples therapy. "Dr. Dolittle" is a zoo—and a blast.

SIGHT AND SOUND, 8/98, p. 37, Charlotte O'Sullivan

Young John Dolittle can talk to animals, but his father disapproves. As a result John loses his gift. He grows into a successful doctor, poised to sign a deal merging his practice with a huge conglomerate. John then runs over a dog and suddenly his gift returns. Several days later John catches sight of the dog, rescues him from the pound and takes him home. His new facility dismays himself, his family and his colleagues.

Word gets around and Dr Dolittle soon finds a queue of sick animals at his door. Particularly desperate is a circus tiger. John's behaviour has by now so alarmed his colleagues that they have him placed in an asylum. He manages to escape but is determined to be 'normal'. One day remains for the business contract to be signed. Prompted by his 'weird' youngest daughter Maya, John decides to accept his calling and treats the tiger in hospital. The money men are impressed but John refuses to be bought and, with the support of his family, begins his new career.

Dr. Dolittle is a sneaky film. At first glance it looks perfectly formulaic, presenting us with a hero who learns to be himself via a string of jokes about ugly fat women, ugly bossy women and unpleasant anal penetration. In other words, a film horrified by everything conventional society deems horrible. But in fact *Dr. Dolittle* is a genuinely pro-freak movie.

Sense is most easily made of *Dr. Dolittle* if one compares it not to the Rex Harrison original of 1967, but to Murphy's most recent vehicle, *The Nutty Professor*. Like *The Nutty Professor, Dr. Dolittle* is a film concerned with the waywardness of the human body. Where the first film's hero, Sherman, is perverse by dint of his size, John disgusts those around him through his ability to understand animals. What's at stake here is the hermetic quality of we humans. Sherman's oral needs—his inability to control his appetite—make him animal-like. Similarly, John's mouth blurs the animal-human boundary. He is prepared to give mouth-to-mouth resuscitation to a rat, putting a vermin's orifice where his wife's should be (as soon as his gift returns, appropriately enough, John has trouble consummating his relationship with his wife). The doctor's animal-loving flesh, you might say, is too open to suggestion.

And if we are in any doubt about the link between weight gain and speaking in animal tongues, it's made crystal clear in the asylum Dr. Dolittle is sent to. There, the head doctor writes three words on the blackboard: "Aspects of Obesity". In this way John's madness/gift is placed in direct opposition to America's body fascism, it's love of the 'norm.

The head of the mental institution is an interesting case in point. John is able to blackmail him because a cat tips him off to his perversion—a love of pink tutus, which he keeps in the 'closet'. Evidently, it's not freaks this film condemns, but those who try to cover up their weirdness. Which brings us to the circus, the movie's ideal space. Filmed with more care than any other location (it looks enchanting at night), this is a place where bearded ladies and midgets walk around brazenly; where animals and humans are cosied up together as equals. They are constricted, yes, and profit making (this is a pragmatic movie, after all) but they are *free*.

Despite the fat-lady jokes, then, *Dr. Dolittle* constitutes a radical development of Murphy's macho persona. It whittles down the star's shtick and relocates it in the form of Rodney the guinea pig, as voiced by comedian Chris Rock. Rock has self-confessedly based his act on Murphy's—in other words, the shtick not only gets very few lines but is exposed as something entirely imitable.

It's no surprise to learn that one of the film's scriptwriters, Larry Levin, worked on television's *It's Garry Shandling's Show*, for this is as self-conscious and iconoclastic as story-telling gets. What kids will make of it, though, is anyone's guess.

VILLAGE VOICE, 7/7/98, p. 120, Michael Atkinson

In every way a harmless, airy, personalityless committee movie (albeit one that, according to one mystery blurbster, will make us "roar, howl and hoot with laughter," presumably at rifle point if necessary), the new *Dr. Dolittle* aspires to please damn near everyone and therefore achieves a kind of familiar, pablum-like goopiness most happily spooned up by preadolescents. It's not as if we didn't know it was a gelded bull right out of the gate—it's a talking-animal movie, with the now requisite big-butt jokes for teens. (Not to mention lavish dialogue quotes from *Sling Blade, The Usual Suspects, Austin Powers,* etc.—do stray dogs get pay-per-view?) Eddie Murphy, comfortably maturing into a Cary Grant-ish grownup leading-man goofball, plays harried straight man to every beast that crosses his path, most of them voiced by sitcom actors and provided with obvious digital mouths. (Effects, schmeffects, we haven't really progressed very far past the talking camel in *Road to Morocco.*) Ellen DeGeneres and Norm MacDonald are dogs, Chris Rock is a guinea pig, Julie Kavner and Garry Shandling are pigeons, Albert Brooks is a lame tiger, and you understand already that much of the film's fun is in guessing the voice behind the whiskers, and that I just kinda pissed on it for you.

What'd you expect, *Animal Farm*? God knows Betty Thomas's movie is less wearisome than the 1967 original, which is useful only as proof that any old shit can get a Best Picture Oscar nomination, but somewhat less engaging than its own trailer, which benefits from those hypercondensed karate-chop comedy edits. Lots of the throwaway lines are mint, and Macdonald's dry terrier mutt is a rip, but you can't escape the sense of *Dr. Dolittle* simply as a great business move.

The film might be amusing, but I bet the deal meeting was electric.

Also reviewed in:
CHICAGO TRIBUNE, 6/26/98, Friday/p. A, Michael Wilington
NATION, 7/27-8/3/98, p. 35, Stuart Klawans
NEW YORK TIMES, 6/26/98, p. E16, Janet Maslin
VARIETY, 6/29-7/12/98, p. 38, Leonard Klady
WASHINGTON POST, 6/26/98, p. B1, Rita Kempley
WASHINGTON POST, 6/26/98, Weekend/p. 46, Michael O'Sullivan

DOWN IN THE DELTA

A Miramax Films and Showtime release of an Amen Ra Films and Chris/Rose production. *Producer:* Rick Rosenberg, Bob Christiansen, Victor McGauley, Wesley Snipes, and Reuben Cannon. *Director:* Maya Angelou. *Screenplay:* Myron Goble. *Director of Photography:* William Wages. *Editor:* Nancy Richardson. *Music:* Stanley Clarke. *Music Editor:* Dean Richard Marino. *Sound:* Tom Hidderley. *Sound Editor:* Dean Hovey. *Casting:* Reuben Cannon. *Production Designer:* Lindsey Hermer-Bell. *Art Director:* Robert Sher. *Set Decorator:* Megan Less. *Set Dresser:* David "Rocky" Rockburn and Andy Joyce. *Special Effects:* Tim Good. *Costumes:* Maxyne Baker. *Make-up:* Lynda McCormack. *Make-up (Alfre Woodward):* Wynona Price. *Stunt Coordinator:* Wayne Downer. *Running time:* 113 minutes. *MPAA Rating:* PG-13.

CAST: Alfre Woodard (Loretta); Al Freeman, Jr. (Earl); Mary Alice (Rosa Lynn); Esther Rolle (Annie); Loretta Devine (Zenia); Wesley Snipes (Will); Mpho Koaho (Thomas); Kulani Hassen (Tracy); Anne Marie Johnson (Monica); Justin Lord (Dr. Rainey); Richard Yearwood (Marco); Sandra Caldwell (Volunteer); Colleen Williams (Tourist Woman); Richard Blackburn (Tourist Man); Philip Akin (Manager); Mary Fallick (Drug Addict); Sandi Ross (Pawn Broker); Barbara Barnes Hopkins (Prim Woman); Marium Carvell (Prim Sister); Quancetia Hamilton (Gina); Kim Roberts (Isabelle); DeFoy Glenn (Reverand Floyd); Jeff Jones (Man in Congregation); Michelyn Emelle (Dozing Woman); Johnie Chase (Grinning Man); Andrea Lewis (Cassandra); Nigel Shawn-Williams (Carl); Bernard Browne and Alison Sealy-Smith (Diners); Eugene Clarke anc Chris Benson (Citizens); Carol Anderson (Jesse's Wife); Neville Edwards (Slave Man); Yanna McIntosh (Slave Woman); Troy Seivwright-Adams (Collin); Kevin Duhaney (Justin); Joel Gordon (Jesse 1865, 17 Years old); Phil Jarrett (Jesse 1890, 42 Years old); Clinton Green (Soloist in Church).

LOS ANGELES TIMES, 12/25/98, Calendar/p. 16, Kevin Thomas

Unflinchingly, "Down in the Delta" goes straight to the heart with its powerful story of a young Chicago woman who finds redemption by returning to her ancestral roots in rural Mississippi.

In adding feature-film directing to her formidable list of accomplishments, poet and author Maya Angelou tells first-time screenwriter Myron Goble's absorbing and far-ranging story with simplicity and directness while guiding a splendid ensemble cast to an array of impressive portrayals.

Alfre Woodard's Loretta is a woman without a trace of self-confidence or self-respect. Her life has been on a downward spiral since her husband deserted her when their daughter Tracy (Kulani

Hassen) was diagnosed as autistic. She's been hitting the bottle pretty hard, and there's a strong suggestion that she has been involved in prostitution.

Meanwhile, her widowed mother, Rosa Lynn Sinclair (Mary Alice), a God-fearing retired nurse, has come to the decision that she must take drastic action to save her daughter and grandchildren. She pawns a cherished family heirloom—a magnificent solid silver candelabra that we discover has extraordinary symbolic significance in the family—and sends Loretta, Loretta's bright, responsible adolescent son, Thomas (Mpho Koaho), and Tracy "down to the Delta" to stay the summer with her brother-in-law Earl Sinclair (Al Freeman Jr.).

Loretta and her kids are transported (by bus) to a world in jolting, sometimes amusing, contrast to Chicago's dangerous South Side housing projects. Earl has as much strength, resolve and religious faith as his sister-in-law but has enjoyed far greater worldly success. A Korean War veteran, he is the owner of a sizable and attractive roadside restaurant and has acquired and restored the fine old frame farmhouse that once belonged to "the white Sinclairs"—the family that had owned Earl's ancestors as slaves.

Earl is a man of principle and discipline tempered by kindness and wisdom. Loretta is expected to go to work (for which she will be paid) at the restaurant, and Thomas is charged with keeping his sister as quiet as possible, so as not to upset Earl's wife, Annie (Esther Rolle), who has suffered from Alzheimer's disease for about five years. Running the house is the warm and capable Zenia (Loretta Devine).

Inarticulate, barely literate, wasted-looking Loretta registers this radically different way of life with expressions of amazement, disdain and increasing gratitude. The unstinting tenderness and devotion Earl shows the gentle but confused Annie causes Loretta to see men in a new way. When Annie visits Zenia, she is bowled over by the fact that, although also a single mother with children, she has been able to own her own home.

Despite its verdant setting, "Down in the Delta" is not paradise on Earth. The Sinclairs experience the inevitable tensions of every family. Earl's son Will (Wesley Snipes), a successful corporate attorney in Atlanta, hates to visit because his mother no longer recognizes him and because such family gatherings tend to exacerbate his already strained relations with his glamorous wife (Anne Marie Johnson). A traditionalist to the core, Earl has long resented that his late brother and Rosa Lynn went off to Chicago in the first place. (He'd like his son nearby, too.) Yet "Down in the Delta" trusts in the power of love to transcend such differences.

"Down in the Delta" evokes the cruel and outrageous heritage of slavery that is part of most every African American family and finds that a triumph over a tragic past can become a source of a fierce, sustaining pride. It also reveals how a sense of extended family—something that evaporated in countless families of every race a couple of generations ago—could be spread to embrace an entire community faced with crisis.

In short, "Down in the Delta" is a most heartening experience, and its cast is capable of moving you greatly. Woodard holds back resolutely in order to bring Loretta to new life in the smallest of increments. Al Freeman Jr. and Mary Alice give us a patriarch and a matriarch of dimension, not just of an abstract strength of character. Straight down the line every actor strikes just the right note, and Rolle, to whose memory the film is dedicated, remains a remarkable actress to the end, expressing Annie's fleeting moments of clarity amid increasing perplexity with the dignity and presence that characterized her long and distinguished career.

Of course, "Down in the Delta" is meant to be uplifting, and unapologetically so, harking back to a tradition established by black pioneer filmmaker Oscar Micheaux 80 years ago. Yet the film, appropriately traditional in style itself, comes full circle in a rich, substantial way that is all the more gratifying. It's not afraid to leave us with some loose ends, knowing that it has opened up so many possibilities for so many people.

NEW YORK POST, 12/23/98, p. 44, Rod Dreher

As movies about the black experience go, Maya Angelou's "Down in the Delta" is so old-fashioned it's almost radical.

Forget the rank, despairing thug-culture filth championed by so many young black filmmakers championed as cutting-edge.

Ignore movies portraying black folks as victims doomed by white racism to perpetual misery and helplessness. Banish the groaning, defeatist liberal pieties that typically inform films of this sort.

This plainspoken melodrama celebrates the triumph of the African-American family in the face of oppression. It has the nerve to argue that poverty, violence, drug abuse, fatherlessness and other crises besieging black America can be overcome through abiding strength of character. And it does so not with the rarefied aestheticism of a "Beloved," but with a modest, straightforward storytelling style accessible to a broad audience.

I'm making the picture sound like a sermon; it's not. The worthy message doesn't smother the sleepily paced but warm, engaging story, which was written by Georgia native Myron Goble. Writer turned director Angelou gives us a journey of redemption that takes her characters in (literally) a surprising direction: to the Mississippi Delta, South toward home.

Alfre Woodard is Loretta, a single mother ekeing out a miserable existence in a Chicago housing project. She is lazy, she is dissolute, she smokes crack and ignores her young children, dumping them on her hard-working mother, Rosa Lynn (Mary Alice).

Sick of her daughter's freeloading, and fearing for the future of her grandchildren, Rosa Lynn puts "Nathan," a silver candelabra that is a priceless family heirloom, into hock. The reason? To pay for bus tickets for Loretta and her kids South, to spend the summer with their Uncle Earl (the terrific Al Freeman Jr.) and away from the drugs and savagery of the inner city.

The candelabra (which has a heart-rending symbolic meaning we don't learn until much later in the film) has been in the family for ages, but as Rosa Lynn puts it, "What's the point of saving Nathan for the next generation if the next generation isn't going to be there?"

In the Delta, Loretta finds a new purposefulness to her life. Elderly Uncle Earl employs her in the small cafe he owns, and expects her to wake up early for work. He takes Loretta and her kids to church and abrades her insolence by showing her kindness and courtesy, and expecting the same. Dignity, he teaches, is her birthright, but it can be lost through moral slovenliness.

Every boy should be lucky enough to have an Uncle Earl. He shows Loretta's young son Thomas (Mpho Koaho) that manly virtue—as distinct from the macho posturing of big-city playaz—calls for heroic chivalry and sacrifice for women and children. The scenes where Earl cares tenderly for his Alzheimer's-stricken wife Annie (the late Esther Rolle, in her final part) are piercingly beautiful.

Wesley Snipes has a brief but key role as Earl's son, a successful Atlanta buppie who learns not to forget the country people and the country place that made him who he is.

"Down in the Delta" could be dismissed by some critics as a glorified TV movie, which is true to a point. It's also a bit hokey. But the film's strong, grace-filled conclusion, which explains how the virtues Uncle Earl lives by have enabled the family not only to endure extreme hardship, but to triumph over it, disarms cynicism. "Down in the Delta" is not a great movie, but it is an extraordinary one, a timely crowd-pleaser that jerks honest tears.

NEWSWEEK, 12/21/989 p. 68, Veronica Chambers

We'll say it first. "Delta" is this year's "Soul Food," a heartfelt drama by a first-time director about an African-American family struggling to keep it together. Of course, the first-time director on "Delta" is Maya Angelou. For those who know and love her work, the question is, what will the writer do with a movie camera? The answer is: shoot poetry.

Loretta (Alfre Woodard) is a single mother in Chicago with a 10th-grade education. She has a problem with drugs and alcohol and can't get a job. Her own mother, Rosa Lynn (Mary Alice), gives her an ultimatum: either she takes her children back to the family home in Mississippi or Mom will call Child Welfare Services and have the children taken away. Loretta boards a bus down to the Delta, to save her kids and to save herself.

It is this illuminating journey of reverse migration that distinguishes "Delta" from any number of urban dramas. Angelou manages to make the South a character with the ability to heal and nurture. In a role reminiscent of his turn as the last good black man in "Waiting to Exhale," Wesley Snipes shines as Loretta's cousin, Will, who helps her gain self-confidence. A prosperous Atlanta businessman, Will returns to the Delta seeking to make peace with family. Snipes plays him with a disarming tenderness and grace that you never see in films like "Blade." In one scene, Will's father, Earl (wonderfully played by Al Freeman Jr.), implores him to return to Mississippi.

"Your roots are here, son," Earl says. "You always taught me that my roots are here," Will says, pointing to his heart. It is a sort of sappy truth, but one that by the end of the film, Angelou persuades you to embrace.

VILLAGE VOICE, 12/29/98, p. 122, Amy Taubin

In the family-holiday spirit is *Down in the Delta,* a TV-style social drama unassumingly directed by poet Maya Angelou. The rift between city and country has been the subject of a number of African American films, most notably Charles Burnett's To *Sleep With Anger,* and, more indirectly, Julie Dash's *Daughters of the Dust. Down in the* Delta isn't in their league—its narrative is too contrived and formulaic—but gets more involving as it goes along, thanks largely to a jittery star turn by Alfre Woodard and generous support from Al Freeman Jr. (as understated a fox as the middle-aged Paul Newman), Wesley Snipes, Mpho Koaho, and Loretta Devine.

Woodard plays Loretta, an undereducated mother-of-two who's falling apart under the pressure of inner-city life. Loretta, a near alcoholic, can't get a job and can't cope with her kids, 12-year-old Thomas (Koaho) and three-year-old Tracy, who's autistic. To keep her from succumbing to the lure of the local crackhouse, Loretta's mother (Mary Alice) packs Loretta and the children off to live with Uncle Earl (Freeman Jr.), who lives in the Mississippi Delta. For Earl, family is everything. Not only does he welcome Loretta and her kids; he's also trying to lure his son (Snipes), the son's snobby wife, and their spoiled brats back from Atlanta.

Loretta, at first, is horrified to find herself making chicken sausages in Earl's restaurant and helping to care for Earl's wife, Annie (Esther Rolle), who has Alzheimer's. But the Mississippi air and the atmosphere of unconditional love in Earl's house have healing effects on the wounded city mice. Life is still tough—the local economy is collapsing—but the family that stays together and looks to its own history for courage and inspiration will survive.

I'm not so sure what a viewer who lives in the inner city and doesn't have an Uncle Earl in Mississippi will make of this film. The blanket indictment of city life—as either crackhouse degradation or buppie consumerism—is the weakest aspect of *Down in the Delta.* And the perfunctory picture of the small Delta town coming together to save its last factory isn't much more convincing.

But *Down in the Delta* is worth seeing for Woodard's performance. Woodard lets us feel the constant panic and the agonizing sense of inadequacy beneath Loretta's bravado. You can see it in her eyes every moment. Without sentimentalizing the character, she also gives us flashes, right from the beginning, of what's potentially valuable in Loretta—her desire to stand on her own feet, to do right by her children, to be generous with other people. Woodard gives voice not just to Loretta's desires, but to the desires of millions of women much like her—women who flaunt their bodies and say stupid things in loud voices, who'll do anything to keep from being invisible.

Also reviewed in:
CHICAGO TRIBUNE, 12/25/98, Friday/p. S, John Petrakis
NEW YORK TIMES, 12/25/98, p. E19, Stephen Holden
VARIETY, 9/21-27/98, p. 110, Joe Leydon
WASHINGTON POST, 12/25/98, p. C1, Rita Kempley
WASHINGTON POST, 12/25/98, Weekend/p. 8, Michael O'Sullivan

DREAM FOR AN INSOMNIAC

An Avalanche Films release of a Tritone Productions presentation.   *Producer:* Christopher Lloyd, Rita J. Rokisky, and John Hackett. *Director:* Tiffanie DeBartolo.   *Screenplay:* Tiffanie DeBartolo.   *Director of Photography:* Guillermo Navarro.   *Editor:* Tom Fries. *Music:* John Laraio.   *Production Designer:* Gary New. *Costumes:* Charles E. Winston.   *Running time:* 88 minutes.   *MPAA Rating:* R.

CAST: Ione Skye (Frankie);   Jennifer Aniston (Allison);   Mackenzie Astin (David Shrader);
Michael Landes (Rob);   Leslie Stevens (Molly);   Seymour Cassel (Uncle Leo);   Sean San Jose
Blackman (Juice);   Michael Sterk (B.J.) .

LOS ANGELES TIMES, 6/19/98, Calendar/p. 8, Kevin Thomas

Tiffanie DeBartolo's "Dream for an Insomniac" proves to be a snooze that seems more play
than movie but would probably be only marginally better on stage than screen. It's an overly talky
yet under-characterized romantic comedy of unstinting artificiality and triteness and no style
whatsoever.

Ione Skye stars as a San Francisco romantic, an aspiring actress who's looking for love and
who's determined not to compromise her dream. (She's so intense about romance and career she
can barely sleep.) So when her knight in shining armor (Mackenzie Astin) appears—and the
movie switches from black-and-white to color—she's not to be deterred, even though he has a
girlfriend and Skye's set to move to L.A. with her pal (Jennifer Aniston), also an aspiring actress,
within about 48 hours.

The film's stagy-looking setting is a coffee shop owned by an Italian immigrant (Seymour
Cassel), who lives above the store with his son (Michael Landes), who's gay but afraid to come
out to his father, and Skye, who is Cassel's niece. Since the place draws few customers—they'd
probably only get in the way of the histrionics—it's hard to see why anyone would see any need
to replace Skye, once she takes off. In any event, in walks Astin, who's looking for work, and
it's love at first sight for Skye.

There's not a whiff of real life or any distinction to "Dream for an Insomniac." It's likely to
be no more than a blip on the screen for its appealing actors, who've done fine work before and
since this wan effort was finished years ago.

NEW YORK POST, 6/19/98, p. 50, Thelma Adams

"I have lost the will to spell," laments Jennifer Aniston over a friendly Scrabble game.

In "Dream for an Insomniac," Aniston plays best pal Allison to Ione Skye's Francesca, who is
sleepless in San Francisco in Tiffanie DeBartolo's "Friends" for the Phi Beta Kappa set.

The beautiful Francesca, alternately sulky and sunny like summer by the Bay, is as fluent at
quoting Eddie Vedder as she is Aristotle. An aspiring actress, she works in her Uncle Leo's cafe,
a shrine to Frank Sinatra.

Seymour Cassel plays Leo with a phony Chef Boyardee Italian accent and the wisdom that
comes from a script that adores each character as a unique individual.

Francesca, nicknamed Frankie after the Sinatra-inspired Cafe Old Blue Eyes, can't sleep. She's
dreamin' of love at night and whining to her gay cousin Rob (Michael Landes) during the day
while they work the coffee bar.

Enter aspiring writer David Shrader (Mackenzie Astin). When David walks into the Blue Eyes
with those cute little gold earrings and a quote for every occasion, it must be true love because
the juke box goes on a "Night and Day" jag and the world shifts from black-and-white to color.

Writer/director DeBartolo makes a first-class debut with a second-rate girl-meets-boy plot. The
casting is nearly as smart as the dialogue, the onscreen chemistry is contagious and
cinematographer Guillermo Navarro ("Jackie Brown" gives "Dream for an Insomniac" a luster
few first films have.

NEWSDAY, 6/19/989 Part II/p. B6, John Anderson

Like little Nemo, Bobby Ewing or, yes, Dorothy Gale, life might just be a dream for Frankie
(Ione Skye), the well-read heroine of "Dream for an Insomniac."

Having had nary a full night's sleep since surviving the crash that killed her parents, she's *got*
to be suffering sleep deprivation, which may explain the Munchkin Syndrome-by-proxy that we
experience when Frankie sets her eyes on Mr. Right: The whole world turns from black and
white to color.

Does that mean the aforementioned Right—a k a soulful-looking would-be writer David Shrader
(Mackenzie Astin)—is a member of the Lullaby League? She should be so lucky. Or that Frankie

suffered a bump on the head during the freak tornado that must have lofted her uncle's Cafe Blue Eyes out of Frisco and into the Emerald City? Or am I reading too much into all this?

There is something remotely extraterrestrial about "Dream for an Insomniac," beginning with the Italian accent of Uncle Leo (played by the otherwise lovable Seymour Cassel) and the fact that none of those Frank Sinatra records we hear are *actually Frank Sinatra*. Not Ol' Blue Eyes *but an incredible simulation!* And you have to wonder about a movie that would center itself around a coffee bar full of Sinatra memorabilia, with a central character named after you-know-who, without having secured the rights to the music. Maybe it's the *pods*...

Synergy is a beautiful, life-giving, sometimes death-exploiting thing, and just like all UFO-related products that will be carried in the wake of the "X-Files" movie, "Dream"—made in 1996— may be a beneficiary of either the death of Sinatra or the rise of both Mackenzie Astin ("The Last Days of Disco") and Jennifer Aniston, the "Friends"-fatale who plays Frankie's fellow would-be actress Allison (and affects a different accent for every occasion). Ione Skye, whose Frankie is very sweet and lovely and swaps famous quotes (Aristotle to Eddie Vedder) with David, has never gotten off of indie Elba, and while it would take a would take a squadron of flying monkeys to get her out of this, she is quite lovely and deserving of some other dream.

VILLAGE VOICE, 6/23/98, p. 146, Dennis Lim

Ione Skye—still best known for inspiring John Cusack's boombox serenade—shows up in *Dream for an Insomniac, a* sickening little romantic comedy that's as pompous as it is trite. Full of absurdly arbitrary show-off references, the screenplay, by neophyte director Tiffanie DeBartolo, screams: "Cultured! Savy! Hip!" Characters don't so much speak as recite inanities. "If Bono was God, then Eddie Vedder would be Jesus," someone argues earnestly—at which point, any sensible audience member should start running for cover.

Skye plays Frankie, an insomniac caffeine addict who may have found her dream man in aspiring novelist David (Mackenzie Astin). He's attached, but she's determined tb seduce him—or, as she puts it, "to circumnavigate his soul until he's anchored on all sides by my love." Who could resist such lush verbiage?

Frankie and David's relationship takes the form of a deranged parlor game that involves smugly identifying song lyrics, movie dialogue, and literary and philosophical quotations. Excruciating as all this is, there is the odd payoff—it's uniquely unsettling for example, to see the utterance "Kierkegaard!" accompanied by a gooey expression of adoration. There's precious little chemistry between the two, but it's clear that they thoroughly deserve each other.

Also reviewed in:
NEW YORK TIMES, 6/19/98, p. E24, Stephen Holden
VARIETY, 4/29-5/5/96, p. 134, Dennis Harvey

DRESS, THE

An Attitude Films release of a Graniet Film production.   *Executive Producer:* Patricia McMahon.   *Producer:* Marc van Warmerdam, Tom Schippers, and Alex van Warmerdam.   *Director:* Alex van Warmerdam.   *Screenplay (Dutch with English subtitles):* Alex van Warmerdam.   *Director of Photography:* Marc Felperlaan.   *Editor:* Rene Wiegmans.   *Music:* Vincent van Warmerdam.   *Sound:* Ben Zijlstra.   *Casting:* Annet Malherbe.   *Costume Designer:* Leonie Polak.   *Running time:* 103 minutes.   *MPPAA Rating:* Not Rated.

CAST: Henri Garcin (Van Tilt);   Ariane Schluter (Johanna);   Alex van Warmerdam (De Smet);   Ricky Koole (Chantalle);   Rijk de Gooyer (Martin);   Elisabeth Hoijtink (Stella);   Olga Zuiderhoek (Marie);   Eric van der Donk (Herman).

LOS ANGELES TIMES, 1/23/98, Calendar/p. 10, Kevin Thomas

With "The Dress," Alex van Warmerdam follows a garment as it passes from one person to another as a way for plugging into the free-floating frustration and anger that permeate contemporary multicultural society.

Adding paranoia, racism, sex and the perverse workings of coincidence and pure chance to the mix, the Dutch director comes up with a sophisticated, darkly hilarious satire on the enduring absurdity of the human condition. "The Dress" would be welcome any time of the year, but it's just the ticket to chase away any lingering post-holiday doldrums.

Even the distinctive design of the dress' fabric emerges from an ugly and violent racial incident. A hapless fabric designer, dumped on by his girlfriend and told by a garment manufacturer that his designs, representing four months' work, are lousy, has only a week to save his commission. Peering out his window to observe a heated clash between blue-collar workers and his Indian neighbors over their native music, he notices the wife's sari, which features bold red-orange leaves on a bright blue background.

He copies it immediately. The garment manufacturer is pleased, forgetting that he had wanted pastels for spring, declaring it "optimistic" in feeling. (There's an entire subplot involving the dire fate of the employee, played by Henri Garcin, who gets in a fight with the garment manufacturer over his dislike of the striking design.)

The next thing we know, an older couple is stopping at a shop window to look at a dress made of the fabric. The husband (Rijk de Gooyer) thinks it's too youthful for his wife (Elisabeth Hoijtink), who buys it anyway. It lifts her spirits.

We realize how devoted the two are when tragedy strikes—and the dress floats away, landing in the countryside, where it comes into the possession of a pretty housekeeper (Ariane Schluter) at an elegant mansion. Wouldn't you know that while wearing it, both she and its next owner, a beautiful teenager (Ricky Koole), arouse the passions of a train ticket-taker (Warmerdam himself) whose loneliness, stronger than even his sexual longings, takes on increasingly scary implications?

Warmerdam effortlessly sustains the antic madness he generates, although he might have wound up his fable a tad more swiftly. His observations of human behavior—not confined to always-vulnerable bourgeois propriety—are consistently sharp and funny, and his cast is a marvel. "The Dress" is sure to wear well.

NEW YORK, 1/26/98, p. 93, David Denby

In the award-winning Dutch movie *The Dress*, a thin summer frock, enlivened with a pattern of golden leaves against a blue background, passes from one person to another and destroys, or nearly destroys, the women who wear it and the men in love with these women. *The Dress*, which was written and directed by Alex van Warmerdam, is based on a mysteriously whimsical idea: We never know why the garment has been cursed, or what the curse means. *The Dress* is a fairy tale without a witch. And the movie, though fascinating, is marked less by magic than by perversity. Two of the young women who possess the dress are very appealing, but van Warmerdam treats them rather badly. The housekeeper Johanna (Ariane Schluter), mistress of a brusque old painter, attracts the interest of a railway ticket collector (played by the director), who follows her home and climbs into bed with her when the painter isn't there.

Johanna, an easygoing woman with a quick smile and a beautiful figure, is shocked but not altogether indifferent, and at first the collector seems possible as a lover. When he is revealed as a creep, the moviegoer, as well as Johanna, feels cheated. And when this creep then pursues the next owner of the dress, young Chantalle (Ricky Koole), who is alone in the country and vulnerable (her parents are away), we are appalled. The sexual scenes are staged as comedy, but the comedy is devoted to a potential rape. I won't reveal what happens, but van Warmerdam seems little concerned with the pleasure of his audience. And why shouldn't he be? Why shouldn't he charm us? It's not as if he had anything profound to say. The curse hanging over the dress is removed from ritual or rage or guilt or anything else that might give it meaning. *The Dress* takes some unusual twists and turns, and the way the story just passes from one vignette to the next is deft, but I can't help feeling that the movie's conceits are at the service of a remorseless—a meaninglessly remorseless—view of life.

NEW YORK POST, 1/16/98, p. 44, Larry Worth

Black comedy is one thing Bad taste is quite another. And, clearly, writer-director Alex van Warmerdam can't tell the difference.

That's obvious from a look at the Dutch auteur's latest opus, "The Dress." It not only celebrates misogyny and offers prurience for no reason but uses attempted rape as a running joke.

Giving the benefit of the doubt, maybe van Warmerdam wanted to give an edgy feel to a well-worn premise: the old hand-me-down tale in which an article passes from one owner to the next to the next.

The gimmick has been used successfully in French classics, as with "The Earrings of Madame de..." and "La Ronde" as well as knockoffs such as "Twenty Bucks" and "The Yellow Rolls-Royce."

This time around, it's a dress. So viewers see the garment conceived, manufactured, put in stores and bought off the rack. And no matter who comes into contact with it, bad luck follows them.

The dress—a bright blue shift with an orange leaf pattern—is acquired by women of various ages and social status, first at a boutique, then a thrift shop, then a rag pile. And even though the ladies experience everything from robbery to bondage to death while sporting it, van Warmerdam insists on a whimsical feel. Granted, some of the early moments—as when a symphony of violence inspires the pattern's creation—provide fleeting amusement and work well visually. But the jokes get increasingly labored, forced and illogical, particularly as the subject matter focuses more on obsession and fetishes.

With one exception, problems can't be blamed on the engaging performers, with Henri Garcin, Olga Zuiderhoek, Ricky Koole and Ariane Schluter standing out as the dress' more unfortunate victims. And then there's van Warmerdam, whose appearance as the oh-so-jolly, would-be rapist is enough to turn one's stomach.

Accordingly, American audiences may find that the film's original Dutch title—"De Jerk" nicely sums up the creator.

NEWSDAY, 1/16/98, Part II/p. B11, Bob Heisler

New in the stores today; "The Dress," a bright blue Indian print summer frock. It buttons down the front, ties in the back. Purchaser should be aware that she will either die unloved or be stalked by obsessive creeps.

If "The Dress" is festival-award-winning social commentary on the state of love and creativity in The Netherlands, the movie, the festival and the country need a few alterations.

Finding a Manhattan theatrical run after two years on the festival trail, director-writer Alex van Warmerdam offers a series of angry, hopeless vignettes around the life and death of a little blue dress. He saves the least human role, a nondescript train conductor sexually obsessed by the dress, for himself.

Charmless, unfeeling, impolite and downright awful people begin to appear and disappear as the dress finds its way from creation to mass production to its first wearer, who apparently dies when her clot of a husband fails to recognize the signs of a broken heart. The dress then blows off a clothesline only to fall from the sky into someone else's life, a maid who toys with, then escapes one sexual encounter, only to be attacked by the bus driver who rescues her.

Thank goodness only one dress seems to have been sold in all of The Netherlands.

All this amounts to nothing, of course. Is it an absurdist farce? A black comedy? Not really. Is there a lesson for the society that allows a bag lady to freeze to death in a hole in the ground just yards from a busy outdoor skating rink? Perhaps "The Dress" is simply an inside joke designed to keep tourists from visiting The Netherlands this winter.

VILLAGE VOICE, 1/20/98, p. 94, Gary Susman

The Dress is a gleefully nasty piece of work. Dutch writer-director Alex van Warmerdam knows how to wring laughs from queasy situations. The structure of the film recalls *La Ronde* or *The Earrings of Madame De* .... but the movie owes more to the bleak, absurdist farce of *After Hours* (if that film had starred a garment instead of Griffin Dunne).

The Dress spins the tale of a frock from its creation to its ragged end. Its designer, Cremer, is inspired by a squabble he witnesses outside his window on the morning that his girlfriend dumps him and his boss chews him out. The pattern he submits, a bright, leafy print, precipitates a vicious argument between Van Tilt (Henri Carcin), a fashion executive, and a couture bigwig, leading to Van Tilt's firing. Conceived in supremely bad karma, the dress will proceed to make miserable the lives of everyone who wears or owns it.

Van Tilt's life spirals ever downward, while young women who wear the dress find themselves subjected to unwanted sexual attention. Doing most of the pursuing is De Smet, a man who becomes obsessed with the dress as a fetish object. When he first tracks down a woman wearing the dress, he seems merely a lonely nebbish, but as he continues to chase her (and later a teenage girl who wears the dress), he begins to come off as deranged. De Smet's attempts at seduction, as pitiful as they are threatening, are played for uncomfortable laughs, like similar scenes involving cuddly stalkers in Almodóvar movies, but there's an extra creepy edge if you know that De Smet is played by the filmmaker.

The movie's point, that horror and misery may be clothed in upbeat trappings, is obvious, but the film derives some complexity from Carcin's Van Tilt, who maintains a haughty dignity at even his lowest ebb, and from van Warmerdam's mastery of tonal shifts. Audiences may wince at the film's predatory view of sexuality even as they're chuckling at its shaggy-dog storytelling.

Also reviewed in:
NEW YORK TIMES, 1/16/98, p. E10, Stephen Holden
VARIETY, 10/7-13/96, p. 91, David Rooney

EAST PALACE, WEST PALACE

A Strand Releasing release of a co-production of an Amazon Entertainment Limited and Quelqu'un d'Autre Productions. *Executive Producer:* Willy Tsao. *Producer:* Zhang Yuan, Christophe Jung, and Christophe Menager. *Director:* Zhang Yuan. *Screenplay (Mandarin with English subtitles):* Zhang Yuan and Wang Xiabo. *Director of Photography:* Zhang Jian. *Editor:* Vincent Levy. *Music:* Xiang Min. *Sound:* Wu Gang and Shen Jianquin. *Art Director:* An Bing. *Running time:* 94 minutes. *MPAA Rating:* Not Rated.

CAST: Si Han (A-lan); Hu Jun (Policeman).

LOS ANGELES TIMES, 9/11/98, Calendar/p. 14, Kevin Thomas

The setting is familiar the world over—a section of a big-city park where gay men cruise, but in Zhang Yuan's stunning "East Palace, West Palace" the park happens to be the grounds of the Forbidden Palace in Beijing. The locale is crucial, for this means that this picture—even more so than "Farewell, My Concubine"—is one of the first modern Chinese films to deal so directly and outspokenly with gay themes.

Not surprisingly, it is an independent production and has been banned in China. Zhang, whose previous underground feature was the impressive "Beijing Bastard" (1992), a raw look at alienated youth set with a rock music background, has even been forbidden to go abroad to attend "Palace's" various stage adaptations that have been produced in cities around the world. The film's title refers to gay slang used to designate the two public restrooms on either side of the Forbidden Palace.

The film is every bit as bold and daring as its making. Naturally, park police harass, humiliate and sometimes arrest any gays they encounter, as they do most everywhere else. But A-Lan (Si Han), a good-looking young gay man, is different from the others. When a cop rounds them up, he refuses to run away or express shame for his sexual orientation; he looks the cop (Hu Jun) straight in the eye. A-Lan then steps up and gives the ruggedly handsome policeman a kiss, leaving him as startled as we are. A-Lan calmly strolls off.

The next time around, on night patrol, the policeman—we never learns his name—detains A-Lan, taking him to the park police station, a quaint Chinese-Victorian structure that might once have been a tea pavilion. The policeman's questions give A-Lan a pretext to tell his life story, which we see glimpsed in flashbacks. The black leather-jacketed cop is a classic macho male yet increasingly intrigued by what A-Lan has to say; such a cop is also a classic gay fantasy figure. In a drama that has only two major characters, both Si and Hu, who has the more complex role, shine in superb, selfless portrayals.

Not surprisingly, A-Lan has had a hard life as a gay man in a profoundly homophobic society, but it has made him resilient and developed in him self-respect. What's more, he's a writer possessed of poetic sensibility, even though he can't express it in the trashy romances he writes for a living. Brutal experience has shaped A-Lan's submissive, even masochistic nature, and as such he has made a profound discovery: the paradoxical power of the seemingly powerless, a major motif in Chinese culture. The policeman doesn't realize that in the course of a long night A-Lan will try to seduce him or at least bring him to some kind of self-knowledge. What A-Lan is attempting with such steady resolve is of course decidedly dangerous and a source of the film's increasing tension and suspense.

What makes "East Palace, West Palace" such a threatening film goes beyond the seesawing of sexual dominance. The shifting power between prisoner and cop easily becomes a metaphor for an authoritarian regime and its seemingly most helpless citizens. You can see how the film could easily be adapted to the stage, yet "East Palace, West Palace" is a richly cinematic experience that comes alive in the imagination of a man who's inspired rather than crushed by being questioned in an isolated little police station in a darkened park in the dead of night.

NEW YORK POST, 7/24/98, p. 42, Larry Worth

Gay dramas don't seem particularly ground-breaking in 1998. But what separates "East Palace, West Palace" is its land of origin: China, where censors don't take kindly to films about homosexuality.

Marketed as China's "first gay feature," "East Palace" opens by depicting men making discreet contact in and around the East and West palaces (the nicknames for public toilets that bookend the Forbidden Palace). But the screenplay quickly segues into an intense two-man drama.

The central duo is comprised of A-Lan, a good-looking young man tortured by his past, and a hunky policeman who takes him to the station for a night of intensive questioning. Obvious from the get-go is that the cop is both repulsed and fascinated by A-Lan's tales.

Before long, handcuffs, dresses and long-held secrets come out of the closet, letting the two protagonists engage in a chillingly erotic *danse macabre*. That's intercut with scenes from a seductive fable—which the two men will ultimately act out.

Accordingly, director Zhang Yuan slyly resurrects the clever framing device that Hector Babenco used to perfection in "Kiss of the Spider Woman." Better still, Zhang's razor-sharp editing and his ability to lend tension to dialogue have a mesmerizing effect.

Helping the film resonate are Si Han's gay outcast and Hu Jun's lawman, both of whom prove masters of subtlety. They help compensate for some occasionally stagy moments and a finale that's less than a revelation.

Lackluster conclusion aside, "East Palace, West Palace" is more than one small step for gay tolerance. It's a giant leap for China.

VILLAGE VOICE, 7/28/98, p. 124, Dennis Lim

Billed as "China's first gay feature," Zhang Yuan's stylized, deliberately paced, *East Palace, West Palace* plays too much like a Genetesque reverie to qualify as social realism. But what the film seems to lack in documentary value it makes up for with an intense yet delicate examination of power, desire, and the aphrodisiacal properties of repression.

Named for Beijing's prime cruising areas, the two public toilets that lie on opposite ends of the Forbidden Palace, Zhang's movie provides brief glimpses of what passes for the city's gay nightlife before morphing into a taut, two-handed psychological thriller. A young gay writer (Si Han) is detained for questioning by a brutish, ostensibly straight policeman (Hu Jun). Under interrogation, the former talks about his past and meanders off into elaborate fantasies, all the while taunting, provoking, and expressing desire for his captor; the cop simply glowers, but his repulsion/attraction grows more obvious by the minute.

East Palace, West Palace is an independent, and hence illegal, production—footage was smuggled out of China and edited in France. Still, the film is less radical than its notoriety implies. It's tempting to interpret the tortured central relationship as a microcosmic reflection of a totalitarian society, but *East Palace, West Palace* resonates most as a chamber piece, distinguished by thoughtful acting and elegant camerawork. In the end, the film is notable not for its insights into a secret subculture but for its vivid and moving articulation of personal desire.

Also reviewed in:
NEW YORK TIMES, 7/24/98, p. E24, Lawrence Van Gelder
VARIETY, 5/12-18/97, p. 65, Derek Elley

EDEN

A Legacy Releasing release. *Executive Producer:* Robert William Landaas. *Producer:* Harvey Kahn and Chip Duncan. *Director:* Howard Goldberg. *Screenplay:* Howard Goldberg. *Director of Photography:* Hubert Taczanowski. *Editor:* Steve Nevius. *Music:* Brad Fiedel. *Art Director:* Philip J. Meyer. *Special Effects:* Gene Warren. *Costumes:* Elizabeth Kaye. *Running time:* 106 minutes. *MPAA Rating:* Not Rated.

CAST: Joanna Going (Helen Kunen); Dylan Walsh (Bill Kunen); Sean Patrick Flanery (Dave Edgerton); Sean Christensen (Rick); Edward O'Blenis, Jr. (Sonny); Stephen Lennstrom (Johnny).

LOS ANGELES TIMES, 3/27/98, Calendar/p. 10, Bob Heisler

[The following review by Bob Heisler appeared in a slightly different form in
NEWSDAY, 4/3/98, Part II/p. B6.]

Nostalgia waves tend to skip the '60s, preferring the rockin '50s or the boom box '70s to the few guitar-strumming years when everything came undone.

The earthbound universe Howard Goldberg loosens in "Eden," may explain it: The shorthand of 1965—when rebellion at the coat-and-tie Mt. Eden Academy meant singing "Silent Night" while everyone else recites the daily hymn—provides none of the usual comfort of cliche, though it is full of familiar types, circa mid-'60s, who never quite rise above their symbolic burdens.

The result is a disturbing movie with a final exam's worth of unanswered question.

Goldberg's decision to root his very '90s story about spiritual awakening in the frayed, but still rockbound Mt. Eden—beautifully rendered, in an episodic, low-budget way—is distracting. Helen Kunen's descent into out-of-body escape from physical challenges (she has multiple sclerosis) and emotional ones (the draining expectations of a traditional, mom-at-home) would carry "Eden" without the insertion of an academic love triangle.

The other sides: Bill Kunen (Dylan Walsh), busy teaching economics at his alma mater and turning lazy boys into tomorrow's leaders, doesn't realize the times are a-changing and his sons and his daughters—to say nothing of his wife—are beyond his command.

And Dave Edgerton (Sean Patrick Flanery), who wants to be a writer like Richard Farina. While he's feeding his soul, he's also flunking out.

Meanwhile, Helen (Joanna Going) keeps finding excuses to fall asleep, liberating her soul from her worn out body and empowering it to find—what? That we are but small pulses of energy in a large, fuzzy-focus/light-show world out there? And if our world is but one of billions, how significant is our shell of skin and bone and braces?

Bill is a selfish, whining lock-jawed idiot; Dave is a selfish, whining, smartass. Neither changes. Helen's struggle is so internal that her epiphany comes while she's in a coma.

Most destructive to "Eden's" promise of new age transformation is Goldberg's failure to have his characters pay any price for their experience.

It's as if, suddenly, the hard choices demanded by a spiritual odyssey is replaced with simple acceptance—an unfortunate invasion of 1950s values.

NEW YORK POST, 4/3/98, p. 54, Larry Worth

As anyone familiar with Genesis knows, the Garden of Eden looked swell at the outset. But trouble quickly surfaced in paradise.

It's small consolation, but at least writer-director Howard Goldberg follows a tried-and-true pattern. "Eden" gradually evolves from intriguing original to out-of-control nonsense.

Granted, the story line deserves credit for going in new directions, but Goldberg's vision is terminally unfocused. It's as brave and unique as it is disjointed and frustrating.

Set within a posh boys school m 1965, the plot initially looks at the frustrations of a set-in-his-ways professor and his smart, pretty wife. The heroine is afflicted with multiple sclerosis, but that doesn't prevent her out-of-body experiences and fantasies of flying. Suddenly, "Goodbye, Mr. Chips" goes existential.

As it turns out, the only soul who truly understands her is a troubled student who can't keep his mind on his studies. He's too busy switching from preppy loafers to hippie sandals.

So, is Goldberg setting viewers up for a lover's triangle? A look at '60s activism? A critique of repressed feminism? It's anybody's guess. But by the time one character asks, "Can't anybody figure out what's wrong?" it's become a rhetorical question.

At the same time, Goldberg does a fine job of establishing his time and place: a storybook world on the verge of collapse and change. And despite increasing silliness, there are moments of surprising poignancy.

That's largely due to the fine cast. The ever-luminous Joanna Going is wonderfully compelling as the physically and emotionally troubled protagonist. Dylan Walsh is almost as good as her confused spouse, while Sean Patrick Flanery's angry young man is both earnest and spirited.

Accordingly, "Eden" isn't without merits. But like the Bible's Adam, Goldberg bit off more than he could chew.

VILLAGE VOICE, 3/31/98, p. 68, Angela Starita

Eden as in the Garden of, is a mean trick of title for a movie that is so painfully claustrophobic we can't wait to be expelled. Joanna Going plays Helen Kunen, a 27-year-old woman with multiple sclerosis who has returned to her childhood boarding school, Mount Eden with her husband Bill (Dylan Walsh)—he to teach, she "to raise our family." The campus rebel, Dave (a believably agitated Sean Patrick Flanery), boards with the Kunens; he moons after Helen while clashing with Bill. Helen prevents Dave from flunking school by sharing her treacly self-help philosophy, which Going delivers with a vapid saintliness. As Helen grows sicker, she decides that in all crucial ways, she's useless: not only can't she pick up the vacuum cleaner, but that leg brace is screwing up Bill's timing in bed. She finds a handy solution in astral projection—finally something that gets her out of the house. Yet the movie won't allow her to "project" very far; Helen's supernatural treks are reduced to a few blurry shots of clouds with airy space music as accompaniment, while Bill and Dave remain earthbound to work out their prep school oedipal woes.

Also reviewed in:
NEW YORK TIMES, 4/3/98, p. E24, Stephen Holden
VARIETY, 2/12-18/96, p. 83, Godfrey Cheshire

EEL, THE

A New Yorker Films release of a KSS/Eisei Gekijo Company/Groove Corporation production in association with Imamura Productions. *Executive Producer:* Kazuyoshi Okuyama. *Producer:* Hisa Iino. *Director:* Shohei Imamura. *Screenplay (Japanese with English subtitles):* Motofumi Tomikawa, Daisuke Tengan and Shohei Imamura. *Based on the story "Yami ni Hirameku"*

334   FILM REVIEW ANNUAL

["Sparkles in the Dark"] by: Akira Yoshimura. *Director of Photography:* Shigeru Komatsubara. *Editor:* Hajime Okayasu. *Music:* Shinichiro Ikebe. *Choreographer:* Hirofumi Nakase. *Sound:* Kenichi Benitanai. *Production Designer:* Hisao Inagaki. *Set Decorator:* Toshiharu Aida and Yoshio Yamada. *Costumes:* Kazuo Matsuda. *Make-up:* Shigeko Igawa. *Running time:* 117 minutes. *MPAA Rating:* Not Rated.

CAST: Koji Yakusho (Takuro Yamashita); Misa Shimizu (Keiki Hattori); Fujio Tsuneta (Jiro Nakajima); Mitsuko Baisho (Misako Nakajima); Akira Emoto (Tamotsu Takasaki); Makoto Sato (Jukichi Takada; Sho Aikawa (Yuji Nozawa); Ken Kobayashi (Masaki Saito); Sabu Kawara (Seitaro Misato); Etsuko Ichihara (Fumie Hattori); Tomoro Taguchi (Eiji Dojima); Sansho Shinsui (Citizen's Hospital Doctor); Shoichi Ozawa (Maternity Hospital Doctor); Chiho Terada (Emiko Yamashita); Koichi Ueda (Keiji); Hiroyuki Konishi (Prison Guard).

LOS ANGELES TIMES, 9/18/98, Calendar/p. 16, Kevin Thomas

In the pre-credit sequence of Shohei Imamura's unpredictable and captivating "The Eel" ("Unagi") a perfectly ordinary-looking Japanese office worker ("Shall We Dance?"'s" Koji Yakusho, ideally cast) receives anonymous letters outlining his wife's infidelity while he's off on nighttime fishing expeditions. Deliberately coming home early, he catches her with her lover, and, seized with rage, knifes her to death and immediately heads for the nearest police station to turn himself in.

Once past the credits, we learn that eight years have passed. Yakusho's Yamashita emerges from prison with a few personal possessions, plus an eel that became his pet. He's fortunate in his parole officer (Fujio Tsuneta), a kindly priest whose hometown, a sleepy port village, is where Yamashita will start a new life as a barber. Tormented by nightmares yet not really regretting his crime of passion, Yamashita asks only to live in obscurity with his eel, with whom he can carry on a one-sided conversation, thus avoiding anything he doesn't want to hear. Yamashita fits in the small community quite well, and his life proceeds just as uneventfully as he wishes.

Of course, this idyll, as emotionally desolate as it is for Yamashita, cannot last—there would be no movie otherwise. Two things happen: A beautiful but troubled young woman, Keiko (Misa Shimizu), who resembles his late wife, arrives in town, and a garbage collector (Akira Emoto), crude and drunken, turns out to be an ex-con poised to let the community know the truth about its new barber.

Imamura now has in place all the elements for a conventional melodrama, but it's what he does with them that won "The Eel" Cannes' Palme d'Or last year. For 40 years Imamura has been, as a critic once observed, expressing sympathy for "the primitive in the blue serge suit." In films such as "The Insect Woman" (1963), "The Profound Desire of the Gods" (1968), "Vengeance Is Mine" (1979) and many others, Imamura has explored an individual's deep-seated emotional conflicts with his traditional culture.

Yamashita is horrified at himself to the point of numbness for having murdered his wife and desiring nothing more than emotional isolation. Then along comes Keiko, a woman at once desirable and beset with problems. Typical of the film's unexpectedness is that the ex-con, while a potential source of big trouble, is the individual who tells Yamashita that it's folly for him to deny his capacity for jealousy.

Photographed expressively by Shigeru Komatsubara, "The Eel" is a quieter, more episodic and less driving film than many of Imamura's finest, including his devastating anti-nuclear film, "Black Rain" (1989), a highly personal account of America's atomic bombings and their aftermath. Keyed by Shinichiro Ikebe's beguiling score, as varied in mood as "The Eel" is itself, the film also embraces rowdy, even comical sequences, again unexpected yet typical of the idiosyncratic Imamura. They work beautifully, as Imamura's mastery of tone has always matched his capacity for compassion and acuteness of observation.

Now that Akira Kurosawa is gone, there is no question that Imamura, along with Masahiro Shinoda and Nagisa Oshima, are heirs to Kurosawa's position as Japan's leading veteran director.

NEW YORK POST, 8/21/98, p. 64, Thelma Adams

Never come between a man and his eel. Japanese director Shohei Imamura's shimmering drama, "The Eel," follows a white-collar worker who kills his unfaithful wife in flagrante delicto, does time and emerges with a pet eel.

The prison warden warns parolee Takuro: "Even if you see trouble around you, don't let yourself be drawn into it."

Of course, the near-silent Takuro, economically played by Koji Yakusho ("Shall We Dance?"), can't keep himself or his eel out of the riptides of daily life.

Obvious symbolism aside, Takuro is attached to his pet because, in his words, "he listens to what I say... he doesn't say what I don't want to hear."

When Takuro takes over a backwater barbershop, he attracts a circle of offbeat characters: a folksy reverend, an eel fisherman, a young man in search of UFOs and an embittered ex-con.

One day, the barber trips over a woman about to commit suicide. He saves her but sacrifices his isolation. The young woman becomes his assistant. As they fall into domestic rhythms, it doesn't help that Keiko resembles Takuro's late wife (and is also played by Misa Shimizu).

Erotic, elegant, comic, "The Eel" earned the Palme D'Or at the 1997 Cannes Film Festival. Writer-director Imamura's film seems as deceptively simple as the eel, and yet generates deep emotion ripples.

NEWSDAY, 8/21/98, Part II/p. B12, John Anderson

Shohei Imamura is one of only three directors to ever win the Cannes Film Festival's Palme d'Or twice—for "The Ballad of Narayama" in 1983, and for "The Eel" in 1997. Less well known here than such contemporaries as Akira Kurosawa or Nagisa Oshima, he is often seen as the portraitist of "unofficial" Japan—or, as he's put it, "I am interested in the relationship of the lower part of the human body and the lower part of the social structure."

He gets there directly in "The Eel," which may be more sedate than many of Imamura's movies but is a film of great delicacy and humanity, which expands structurally like a flower (if that isn't too conventionally Asian an image).

The heart of the film is Takuro Yamashita (Koji Yakusho, star of such crowd-pleasers as "Shall We Dance?" and such pure art films as "The Sleeping Man"), who receives an anonymous letter about his wife's infidelity. Coming home early, he surprises her in bed with her lover, murders her brutally and spends the next eight years in prison.

Takuro's only companion, which is allowed to leave prison with him, is an eel, which he's caught and kept in the prison pond. Takuro talks to the eel, and listens, too. But Imamura presents this as less a symptom of madness than of the rigid structure imposed on Takuro by both his keepers and his conscience. Besides, as Takuro says of the eel, "He listens to what I say ... He doesn't say what I don't want to hear."

It is characteristic of Imamura to make Takuro, through the character's utter humiliation, a totally sympathetic man. It's likewise characteristic of him to tamper with the conventions of Japanese cinema. One of Imamura's mentors was the great, formalist director Yasujiro Ozu, who celebrated Japanese reserve, and to whom Imamura pays homage in his shots of the home where bloody murder is about to break out. Similarly, but less facetiously, he punctuates his action with the kind of fourth-wall-violating flourishes (blood on the lens, men falling into fish tanks) that would have made Ozu choke on his tea.

He also surrounds Takuro, who opens a barbershop but is almost too reticent to operate it, with a cast of wacky locals, including a crusty boat builder, a UFO enthusiast, a mirror-shaded hipster and Keiko (Misa Shimizu), whom Takuro saves from suicide, hires as his aide and with whom he falls in love. Her life takes the movie in new and chaotic directions, but ultimately to a unity of elements that brings Imamura's concern about humanity into concentrated bloom.

SIGHT AND SOUND, 12/98, p. 38, Tony Rayns

Summer, 1988. Tipped off by anonymous letters, Tokyo salaryman Takuro Yamashita returns home early from a fishing trip and catches his wife having wild sex with another man. He stabs her to death and surrenders to the police. Eight years later he is paroled under the supervision of

Buddhist priest Jiro Nakajima, who gives him a temporary home in his temple in Sawara and helps him to acquire a derelict barber shop on the nearby lake. Shunning most human contacts but cherishing the eel which he kept as a pet in prison, Yamashita renovates the shop and opens it for business. His regular customers soon include carpenter Jukichi Takada, small-time yakuza Yuji Nozawa and young UFO freak Masaki Saito.

Keiko Hattori, afraid she may inherit her mother's mental illness and tired of being swindled by her lover Eiji Dojima, a crooked 'financial consultant', attempts suicide in Sawara. Yamashita finds her unconscious and summons medical help. Keiko recuperates at the temple, and Nakajima's wife Misako suggests that she could work as Yamashita's assistant. Keiko's presence brightens the shop and attracts more customers, but Yamashita rebuffs her attempts to penetrate his shell.

Ex-con Tamotsu Takasaki, who recognises Yamashita from prison, turns up in Sawara as a garbage collector. Jealous of Yamashita's apparent success, Takasaki drunkenly tries to rape Keiko and taunts Yamashita, provoking a fight. The shop is further disrupted by the arrival of Dojima, who wants Keiko back.

Yamashita tells Keiko the truth about his past. Keiko discovers that she is pregnant (by Dojima) and sets off to retrieve her mother's savings from Dojima's company. By the time she returns to Sawara, Dojima and his men are intimidating Yamashita, demanding the return of the money. During the increasingly violent argument, Yamashita claims that he is to be the father of Keiko's child.

Yamashita releases his eel and prepares to return to jail for violating the terms of his parole. Keiko asks if she may wait for him.

On the face of it, *The Eel* tells one of the simplest stories Imamura has ever told. A middle-aged man catches his much younger wife with a lover and stabs her to death. He is paroled after eight years in jail and tries to rebuild his life by opening a barber's shop in a rural backwater. Taciturn and inward-looking, he confides his thoughts and fears only to the eel he adopted as a pet while in prison. But a chance involvement with a young woman struggling to overcome difficulties of her own gradually draws him out of his shell. It's not hard to imagine a Hollywood remake of the story: a feel-good melodrama about the thawing of an emotionally frozen man.

The film Imamura has actually made does have a crypto-Hollywood dimension, which in some ways distances it from his earlier films—and very possibly explains why it won the Palme d'or at Cannes (Imamura's second) and has had a easier passage into international distribution than most of his other films. The narrative thrust is unusually direct and clear-cut, the dialogue sometimes makes underlying ideas nakedly explicit (as if acknowledging the shorter attention spans of 90s audiences), and there's even implied happy ending, albeit projected into the future, with the long shot under the closing credits of a woman in bridal costume boating along the River Tone to her wedding. What makes *The Eel* so interesting, though, is its refusal to play by the rules of conventional storytelling: its odd emphases, its unpredictable ellipses, its awareness of comic absurdity even in moments of high drama. In a word, its messiness. It's a film with all the rough edges that Hollywood routinely smoothes away.

The key to the film's idiosyncrasy is Imamura's characteristic assumption that fantasy is an integral part of reality. *The Eel* presents itself as a more or less realistic account of one man's psychological and emotional rehabilitation, but the startling glimpses of the man's subjective fantasies which erupt every so often suggest that very little in the film can be taken at face value. It gradually becomes clear that this is a kind of psychodrama: most of the characters and incidents are there as much to externalise the strange goings-on in the protagonist's mind as to construct an entertaining account of everyday life in a quiet corner of Chiba Prefecture.

Takuro Yamashita is more squarely middle class than most of Imamura's previous protagonists, but that doesn't make him any easier to figure out. (Casting Koji Yakusho, who played another Japanese commuter-everyman with rather sweeter dreams in Masayuki Suo's *Shall We Dance*, stresses the character's consummate ordinariness.) The opening scenes sketch the parameters of his life, from his middle-management desk in a Tokyo office to his leafy suburban home to the small community of all-night anglers he joins once a week. One succinct vignette sketches his relationship with his young wife; they can't have been married for very long, but their life together has already settled into a routine of passionless moments.

The insecurities seething beneath this placid surface are signalled by the anonymous letter accusing his wife of infidelity which Yamashita reads on the train home from work—a letter from an unknown woman which he later rationalises as a figment of his imagination. And when he cuts short his fishing expedition and comes home early to catch his wife *in flagrante delicto*, his intentions of murder are signalled by his vision of the street light outside the house turning blood-red as he pauses by the lover's parked car. The murder itself is brutal, but also oddly lyrical: an act of hatred and revenge which shades into something more sensual—in fact, something sexual—and ends with Yamashita tenderly covering his wife's corpse with a bedsheet. The unsettling shift in tone is underlined by Ikebe's brilliant score, which switches from excited, Herrmannesque strings to the quirky theme (probably played on a synthesiser but designed to sound like an aboriginal instrument) later associated with Yamashita's phallic pet eel.

Most of what happens in and around the barber's shop in Sawara in the main body of the film clearly dramatises Yamashita's attempt to understand himself and his crime. The three oddball locals who form the core of his clientele, all of them men living without women, reflect such aspects of his own twisted psyche as his new compulsion to be a loner and his castration nightmares. The coffin-maker Takada is a widower with no intention of remarrying who tries to persuade Yamashita to spear eels and teaches him about their singular life-cycle. The would-be yakuza Nozawa is a leftover from simpler times, a 'man's man' in a small but flashy retro car. And the UFO freak Saito (as one untypically clunky exchange of dialogue makes plain) is interested in extraterrestrials for the same reasons that Yamashita is interested in his eel: because they're easier to deal with than other humans are.

Imamura introduces two other characters who serve to precipitate the crisis which drags Yamashita back into the real world. One of them is largely imaginary: the ex-con Takasaki (very well played by Akira Emoto, who has since taken the title role in Imamura's *Dr.Akagi)*, who first taunts then literally haunts Yamashita with recriminations about his lack of guilt for the murder of his wife. Takasaki is first presented as a realistic character, a guy who met Yamashita in jail and happens to come across him again while collecting garbage from his shop, but his subsequent appearances in Yamashita's waking dreams pitch him as the return of the repressed incarnate. It's Takasaki who voices the 'forbidden' thoughts that the anonymous letters never really existed and that Yamashita's wife took a lover because Yamashita himself was a sexual let-down. And it's Takasaki—or his phantom—who forces Yamashita to defend his eel and to confront the possibility of fathering a child.

Yamashita's salvation arrives in the indubitably real form of Keiko Hattori (the excellent Misa Shimizu), the only main character to have an existence entirely independent of Yamashita's fantasies—and she has flashbacks to fraught episodes in her past to prove it.   She enters Yamashita's life when he nervously saves her from an attempted suicide and winds up working as the assistant in his shop. Keiko's life is considerably messier than Yamashita's. Her wealthy mother is mentally ill, and her married lover is a loan shark/venture capitalist posing as a financial consultant, whose chief interest in her seems to be the access she provides to her mother's money. The character resembles Imamura's usual working-class 'heroines' only in possessing the resilience to overcome these and other tribulations, but the way her drive to sort out her life is interwoven with her attempts to penetrate Yamashita's shell occasions some of the film's most skilful plotting.

It's too early to be sure whether *The Eel* is a great Imamura film or merely a good one, but after an episode of ill health and a gap of eight years since *Black Rain* it's certainly a sign that the director is determined to keep pace with changing audiences and a changing Japanese film industry. It's different from his earlier films because Japanese cinema as a whole is different. But it fits cleanly into Imamura's filmography because, like everything else he has done, it respects the intelligence and integrity of its characters and viewers alike.

VILLAGE VOICE, 8/25/98, p. 123, J. Hoberman

A less negative but even more extreme vision of the human sexual response may be gleaned from *The Eel*, Japanese master Shohei Imamura's first film in eight years [the reference is to *Your Friends and Neighbors*; see Hoberman's review of that film.] (and the movie that shared the Palme d'Or with Abbas Kiarostami's *Taste of Cherry* at the 1997 Cannes Film Festival).

Violence is not verbal nor sex consensual in Inamura's films—his wildly sensationalist oeuvre is populated by a raunchy assortment of killers, prostitutes, and pornographers. ("I am interested in the lower part of the human body and the lower part of the social structure" is the one-sentence manifesto that emblazons the Cinematheque Ontario's recent monograph on his work.) *The Eel's* pre-title prologue is a movie in itself. Tipped off by an anonymous letter, the innocuous salaryman Takuro—played by Koji Yakusho of *Shall We Dance?*—returns home early from an all-night fishing trip and, catching his wife in flagrante, stabs her to death. The credits come up as Takuro bicycles to the police station to turn himself in.

Eight years later, the wife-killer is paroled from prison, along with his pet eel—a symbol so blatant, and so quintessentially Imamura, that it soon becomes thoroughly defamiliarized. ("He listens to what I say—he doesn't say what I don't want to hear," is how Takuro explains his attachment to the creature.) Having trained as a barber while in jail, Takuro sets up shop in some obscure corner of Japan with his eel installed in a prominent fish tank. Takuro doesn't care much for human contact but, this being an Imamura film, his eccentricities scarcely set him apart from the rest of the species. His parole officer is a ridiculously understanding Buddhist priest; his nearest neighbor is engaged in constructing a six-pointed star with jerry-built flashing lights in the hopes of attracting a visitor from outer space.

Despite occasional shots from inside the fish tank, *The Eel* is more staid—and even more tentative—than the 70-year-old director's vintage film's. Still, the mood-shifting narrative line is adroitly handled. As slippery as its namesake, the movie starts like a thriller, settles into what might be an elaborate purification ritual, then—once Takuro has almost grudgingly saved the life of Keiki, a would-be suicide who resembles his murdered wife (and is played by the same actress)—blossoms into a sort of wistful romance. As obvious a symbol as the eel, Keiki's embodiment of Takuro's second chance appoints herself, against his wishes, as helpmeet—and thus, under the influence of their respective pasts, pushes the plot toward melodrama.

Ferocious yet gentle, its tone shifting once more to gangster drama and then black comedy, *The Eel* concludes with a lunatic yet symmetrical turn of events that culminates in an unexpectedly hallucinatory and touching ending. Ultimately, *The Eel* is the unconscious made tangible. Takuro becomes the eel and, in becoming the eel, he sets it free. This simple, sinuous fable may not be among Imamura's greatest films—it lacks the crazy libidinal energy of *The Pornographers* or *Eijanaika*—but it could hardly have been made by anyone else.

Also reviewed in:
CHICAGO TRIBUNE, 9/11/98, Friday/p. F, Michael Wilmington
NATION, 9/7-14/98, p. 43, Stuart Klawans
NEW YORK TIMES, 8/21/98, p. E24, Lawrence Van Gelder
VARIETY, 5/26-6/1/97, p. 65, David Stratton
WASHINGTON POST, 11/20/98, p. F5, Stephen Hunter

ELIZABETH

A Gramercy Pictures release of a PolyGram Filmed Entertainment presentation in association with Channel Four Films of a Working Title production. *Producer:* Alison Owen, Eric Fellner, and Tim Bevan. *Director:* Shekhar Kapur. *Screenplay:* Michael Hirst. *Director of Photography:* Remi Adefarasin. *Editor:* Jill Bilcock. *Music:* David Hirschfelder. *Music Editor:* Michael Higham. *Choreographer:* Sue Lefton. *Sound:* David Stephenson. *Sound Editor:* Mark Auguste. *Casting:* Vanessa Pereira and Simone Ireland. *Production Designer:* John Myhre. *Art Director:* Jonathan Lee and Lucy Richardson. *Set Decorator:* Peter Howitt. *Special Effects:* George Gibbs. *Costumes:* Alexandra Byrne. *Make-up:* Jenny Shircore. *Stunt Coordinator:* Terry Forrestal. *Running time:* 124 minutes. *MPAA Rating:* R.

CAST: Terence Rigby (Bishop Gardiner); Christopher Eccleston (Duke of Norfolk); Amanda Ryan (Lettice Howard); Kathy Burke (Queen Mary Tudor); James Frain (Alvaro de la Quadra); Jamie Foreman (Earl of Sussex); Edward Hardwicke (Earl of Arundel); Joseph

Fiennes (Robert Dudley, Earl of Leicester);   Kelly Macdonald (Isabel Knollys);   Wayne Sleep (Dance Tutor);   Cate Blanchett (Elizabeth I);   Emily Mortimer (Kat Ashley);   Geoffrey Rush (Sir Francis Walsingham);   Richard Attenborough (Sir William Cecil);   Angus Deayton (Waad, Chancellor of the Exchequer);   Eric Cantona (Monsieur de Foix);   Kenny Doughty (Sir Thomas Elyot);   Fanny Ardant (Mary of Guise);   Vincent Cassel (Duc d'Anjou);   John Gielgud (The Pope);   Daniel Craig (John Ballard);   Liz Giles (Female Martyr);   Rod Culbertson (Master Ridley);   Paul Fox (Male Martyr);   Peter Stockbridge (Palace Chamberlain);   George Yiasoumi (King Philip II of Spain);   Valerie Gale (Mary's Dwarf);   Sally Grey, Kate Loustau, Elika Gibbs, Sarah Owen, and Lily Allen (Ladies in Waiting);   Joe White (Master of the Tower); Matt Andrews and Liam Foley (Norfolk's Men);   Ben Frain (Young French Man);   Lewis Jones (Priest);   Michael Beint (Bishop Carlisle);   Hayley Burroughs (Elizabeth's Dwarf);   Joseph O'Connor (Earl of Derby);   Brendan O'Hea (Lord William Howard);   Edward Highmore (Lord Harewood);   Daniel Moynihan, Jeremy Hawk, and Donald Pelmear (Bishops);   James Rowe (Bishop in Cellar);   Tim Bevan (Handsome Man);   Charles Cartmell and Edward Purver (Dudley's Men);   Vladimir Vega (Vatican Cardinal);   Alfie Allen (Arundel's Son);   Daisy Bevan (Arundel's Daughter);   Jennifer Lewicki (Arundel's Nursemaid);   Viviane Horne (Arundel's Wife);   Nick Smallman (Walsingham's Man).

CINEASTE, Vol. XXIV, no. 2-3, 1999, p. 78, Kenneth S. Rothwell

Appearing almost simultaneously in theaters everywhere, two costume dramas, *Elizabeth* and *Shakespeare in Love*, mesmerize audiences with a Life and Times of William Shakespeare far gaudier than the introductory essay variety in undergraduate textbooks. Indian director Shekhar Kapur's "historical thriller," *Elizabeth,* is not a J.E. Neale scholarly biography, but it constructs myths to shadow forth higher truths. Actually, good Queen Bess mythologized herself into a kind of Elizabethan Princess Di. Her Elton Johns were the poets like Edmund Spenser who idealized her as Eliza, Diana, Cynthia, Laura, or Gloriana. A feminist subtext, however, explores the gritty political struggles of the daughter of antipapist King Henry VIII and Anne Boleyn. Gradually the young monarch rejects her know-it-all male protectors, though even more threatening were her Catholic female relatives, stepsister Mary Tudor and cousin Mary Queen of Scots. Kapur's film exploits cinematic synecdoche to make a collage out of Elizabeth's reign (1558-1603) when France and Spain, the allies of the Pope (portrayed by John Gielgud), conspired to destroy Protestant England. A golden-reddish haired Cate Blanchett, a Cinderella figure, evolves from a mere mortal into God's anointed deputy on earth.

Few will care that the eventful period from 1558 to 1573 has been squeezed like an orange to fit the scenario rather than the scenario fitting the events. For just two examples, Jesuit priest John Ballard (Daniel Craig) was implicated in the 1586 Babington cabal, not in the Ridolfi plot of some dozen years previously. Elizabeth spoke her famous line, "I know I have the body of a weak and feeble woman, but I have the heart and stomach of a king," in 1588 to her assembled troops, not privately years before to her counselor Sir William Cecil (Richard Attenborough). Half-accurate, the grisly establishing shot reenacts the barbaric execution of Master Ridley and two other Protestant "heretics" at the hands of Catholic Mary Tudor's pompous Bishop Gardiner (Terence Rigby). The source is the Reverend John Foxe's wildly popular *Book of Martyrs* (1563), an illustrated encyclopedia of atrocities, featuring rackings, whippings, disembowelings, gougings, flayings, amputations, beheadings, boilings-in-oil, crucifixions, and burnings-at-the-stake. In fact, Master Ridley was martyred at Oxford at another time along with good Bishop Latimer, who when tethered to the stake uttered the great exit line, "Be of good comfort, Mr. Ridley, and play the man; we shall this day light such a candle by God's grace in England, as I trust never shall be put out." The hideously scalped male and female burned with Ridley in the movie appear to be improvised, though the scalping of the female, as we shall see, later bolsters the film's pervasive hair fetish.

Striking camera angles, dramatic lighting, lavish costuming, a stirring soundtrack and skillful manipulation of images and events shape the artistic design, even when the director almost perversely shrouds the action in shadows to keep the spectator guessing about the actors' identities. Apparently Sir Robert Dudley, Earl of Leicester (Joseph Fiennes), the queen's lover, is fornicating with the unfortunate lady-in-waiting whose squeals of delight turn into shrieks of agony when the borrowed poisoned dress, a gift of Mary of Guise to Elizabeth, exacts its lethal price. Kapur also likes to have the camera peer down on people from lofty heights. A crane shot of the flames licking around Bishop Gardiner's shrieking, writhing victims foreshadows a similar tactic in the interrogation of Elizabeth at the Tower of London. Her tormentors, Norfolk (Christopher Eccleston), Sussex (Jamie Foreman), and Arundel (Edward Hardwicke), circle her like predatory animals, hurling incriminating charges, snapping at her, seeking to wring an admission of treason for conspiring in the Wyatt rebellion against her sister. The camera then pulls up, and looks down on a noble princess who has been shrunken into a bundle of rags. Again, after the failure of her Scottish expedition, she is shown from far above as a tiny figure in anguish before a portrait of her father, Henry VIII, who would not ever have made the mistake of taking bad advice, as she tells herself.

The movie might be thought of as a Masque of Night and Day, though the *filmnoir* side often eclipses the shafts of light. The nagging males surrounding Elizabeth mostly seem to be very dark. Norfolk (Thomas Howard, 4th Duke of Norfolk and suitor to Mary of Scots), her overbearing advisor, never walks. A control freak, he stomps, blusters, and crashes his way through castle corridors, or even into the queen's bedroom, always the man in charge. Sir William Cecil, not dark but white-haired, could be Polonius; Alvaro de la Quadra (James Frain) is the spooky Spanish emissary; and the Duc d'Anjou (Vincent Cassel), the cross-dressing French suitor. The scowling Earl of Sussex wears the obligatory black beard, while Monsieur de Froix (Eric Cantona) is equally gloomy but large, being off screen a professional soccer player. Not least of the retinue is Sir Francis Walsingham (Geoffrey Rush), the man with fifty-three agents and eleven personal spies, the originator of international espionage, who at his first appearance inexplicably cuts the throat of a young boy in a Paris brothel. To swell the scene, black-hooded, unidentified assassins roam the stony corridors of the drafty palaces.

Like Senecan tragedy, *Elizabeth* goes from dark to darker, with a gothic creepiness reminiscent of a Roger Corman B-movie like *The Fall of the House of Usher*. There is, for example, the Princess Elizabeth's entry into the dreaded Tower through Traitor's Gate, which features a bloody head on a spike. She is hustled by her captors through Stygian corridors with much banging of doors, clanking of chains, squeaking and groaning of hinges, clattering of boots. An S&M paradise. Another interrogation at Lambeth by her stepsister, Mary Tudor, played wonderfully by Kathy Burke, who has the face of a cruel pig, takes place in a shadowy crypt that could easily be renovated into a pit with a pendulum. As John Foxe wrote of Mary, she "united bigotry, superstition, and cruelty." Suffering from an immense tumor in the stomach, and attended by her grotesque dwarf, the wretched creature thinks she is pregnant, though a lady-in-waiting, who lasciviously licks Norfolk's hand, has previously whispered to him that the king (Philip of Spain) has not slept with the queen for months.

Occasionally the Masque of Light intervenes, as when Elizabeth is first glimpsed dancing on a green and wearing a bright red sash, a paragon of youthful freshness and innocence. This quintessentially Elizabethan vogue for dancing at court is celebrated in John Davies's long poem, "Orchestra Or a Poeme of Dauncing" (1596), which makes the terpsichorean art a central metaphor for the universe: "The turning vault of heaven/doe a musick frame, [and] still daunce unto the same" (Verse 19). Robert Dudley as Elizabeth's graceful partner brings light into the queen's life for a time but then unhappily proves as dark as all the rest, and Joseph Fiennes is stuck with this unsympathetic role that allows too little room for his talents. Elizabeth's inspired dancing correlates with her new decisiveness after the Scottish invasion fiasco. No longer inclined to be misled by wily counselors, in a series of jump cuts resembling out-takes, she rehearses like a schoolgirl, modulating her voice, changing her expressions, revising her argument, for the successful speech advocating the Act of Uniformity.

Walsingham's warning of an ultimate megaplot, the mother of all conspiracies, implicating even Norfolk and Leicester, generates a violent counterattack signified with a flurry of cross-cutting, analytical close-ups, and sonic punctuation. In montage, hands grasp sword hilts; Bishop Gardiner is surprised while self-flagellating; Sussex, ingloriously seated on the jordan; Norfolk, in bed with his lascivious mistress. A swelling chorale of sacred music on the soundtrack counterpoints the bloody deeds on the screen, after the style of the christening scene in Coppola's *The Godfather* when the camera cross-cuts between the baptismal font and the Corleone family's savage reprisals against its enemies. Even as the choir's "Te Deum," or "Requiem," reaches vocal heights, the axe held high over Norfolk's head thuds into the block.

At moments of high epiphany, backlighting or overexposure blinds the audience to Elizabeth's majestic image. With her Catholic foes defeated, Elizabeth, inspired by Walsingham's advice that the people need Protestant symbols to replace Catholic icons like the Virgin Mary, reinvents herself as The Virgin Queen. As Elizabeth's own beautiful hair is sheared off by her weeping ladies-in-waiting, she unites in sisterhood with the scalped female martyr at the beginning of the movie who perished with Ridley. A montage reprises key episodes from the film and the great choir again fills the sound track. At last beatified, and now truly God's deputy on earth—bepearled, berouged, bewigged, becorseted, all in white—she steps out of a backlit brilliance into a room full of kneeling courtiers. "I am married to England," she says. Then, she is freeze-framed in a familiar National Gallery portrait as the wooden icon of the history books, not as the kinetic creature that Shekhar Kapur has so plausibly reconstructed with his gifted cinematic and historical imagination.

The transition from the melancholy of *Elizabeth* to the farce of *Shakespeare in Love* may induce culture shock. Director John Madden and coscenarists Marc Norman and Tom Stoppard's wit and humor bring to mind the inspired nonsense of the *Blackadder* and *Monty Python* television series, the British *Carry on Cleo* (1964), or the old Hollywood farce, *The Boys from Syracuse* (1940). It's a genre the British excel at but that sometimes leaves North Americans baffled. With its multiple covert allusions to Shakespeare and his contemporaries, *Shakespeare in Love* resembles a Sunday supplement children's cartoon puzzle crammed with camouflaged objects awaiting discovery. Probably not by mere coincidence, the period covered in the movie roughly corresponds to the so-called "lost years" (1585 to 1592), when Shakespeare's biography fell off the radar and which remain a gnawing mystery even to the greatest scholars. The iteration by Henslowe and others of the phrase, "It's a mystery," may refer not only to the "lost years" but also quibble on "mystery," in the sense of the "craft" of the players, who can make shadows speak.

Moreover, as with all farce, *Shakespeare in Love* hides in its subtext a morass of repressed anxieties. Behind all the badinage, the movie almost nostalgically yearns for the transcendent power of words to represent human emotion. Meanwhile what a great jest it is to show Will Shakespeare (Joseph Fiennes) as a starving young hack with a bad case of writer's block, struggling to write a ridiculous play called "Romeo and Ethel, the Pirate's Daughter." in slothful despair, he doodles his famous six signatures, and becomes disillusioned by the fickleness of his Rosaline (Sandra Reinston), who as a lusty wench is something less than the idealized creature of Shakespeare's *Romeo and Juliet*. Really impressive replicas of streets, inns, and theaters constructed on a Shepperton Studios back lot recapture the grubby bustle of Elizabethan London. We overhear Makepeace (Steven Beard), the Puritan preacher who resembles Zeal-of-the-Land Busy in Ben Jonson's *Bartholomew Fair,* saying, "A rose by any name," and, railing against the rival Rose and Curtain theaters, "A plague on your houses." An apothecary shop that doubles as a psychiatrist's office invites associations with Romeo's vial of poison, and Will Shakespeare, an inveterate plagiarist, picks up helpful hints from Kit Marlowe (Rupert Everett) for doctoring the script of his unfinished play by having the Italian hero fall in love with his enemy's daughter. Ned Alleyn (Ben Affleck), who is duped into being cast as Mercutio when Will assures him the play will be called "Mercutio," simplifies the title to *Romeo and Juliet*. The Jacobean playwright, John Webster (Joe Roberts), author of the sinister *Duchess of Malfi* (1614), surfaces as a vicious adolescent with a taste for feeding live mice to cats.

No longer Walsingham—the thoroughly unfunny secret agent of *Elizabeth*—Geoffrey Rush as Henslowe emerges as a bumbling, debt-ridden wretch being hassled by the collection agents of "money man" Hugh Fennyman (Thomas Wilkinson). Ironically, Henslowe's own diaries reveal that he was himself the true "money man," dealing meanly with impecunious playwrights. He dismisses Will Shakespeare as a "nobody," only "a writer."

He wanders down the center of the narrow pre-Hogarthian lanes oblivious to the bucket loads of slops being dumped just behind him. The waste disposal system actually glosses the Capulet servant Sampson's line when he insists that "women, being the weaker vessels, are ever thrust to the wall" *(Rom.,* 1.1.15). Myriad other spoofs include a tavern waiter's trendy recitation of the daily special of marinated pig's foot, which is served on a "buckwheat pancake," and Will's Woody-Allen-type consultation about verbal impotence with his apothecary/shrink, Dr. Moth (Antony Sher), whose name comes from shrewd little page in *Love's Labor's Lost.* It's even possible that these absurd "presentist" episodes send up the "new historicist" Shakespeare Critics, who like to impose the present on the past.

At the core, though, is the star-crossed romance that mirrors *Romeo and Juliet* between impoverished William Shakespeare and heiress Viola De Lesseps (Gwyneth Paltrow). Coscenarist Tom Stoppard's trademark gift for epistemological games and metadramatic forays, as in *Rosencrantz and Guildenstern Are Dead* and *The Real Inspector Hound*, provides the templates for the clever intertwining of play and movie. The bitter stage rivalry between the Admiral's and Lord Chamberlain's men parallels the Montague/Capulet feud. Viola becomes Shakespeare's inspiration for Juliet, a kind of un-Dark Lady, and her stunning audition for *The Two Gentlemen of Verona* and later role in the Curtain theater *Romeo and Juliet* allows the opportunity for Shakespeare's beautiful language to upstage everything else. To make the puzzle a happy hunting ground for film as well as literary scholars, the movie also quotes from other Shakespeare films, like the Capulet ball sequence in Zeffirelli's *Romeo and Juliet* (1968), the realistic Globe playhouse in Olivier's *Henry V* (1944), and the near drowning of Violi and Sebastian in the opening sequence of Trevor Nunn's *Twelfth Night* (1996).

Still, the farcical plot only thinly papers over the film's deeper obsession with literary art as the preserver of truth and beauty. Kit Marlowe's sudden death in the Deptford tavern brawl strikes a somber note, and even though Fiennes's Shakespeare is not literally responsible for his rival's death, in a figurative sense he did kill him by eclipsing his rival's reputation. In contrast with Cate Blanchett's mercurial queen, a dour Queen Elizabeth (Judi Dench)—whose plain speaking is in inverse ratio to her extravagant costumes—brokers a wager of £50, between Will Shakespeare and Lord Wessex (Colin Firth), a mean-spirited surrogate for Paris, that a play can actually represent human love. The cad Wessex loses when the *Romeo and Juliet* at the Curtain succeeds so well that the queen herself, quite implausibly, arises in all her majesty from the audience to rescue Viola from Tilney's (Simon Callow) enforcement of the stern law against female players. Yet if Will and Viola, like Romeo and Juliet, must be separated, they remain forever inseparable through the wonder of the Sonnet (#18) that Will has composed just for her: "So long as men can breathe or eyes can see, / so long lives this, and this gives life to thee."

"It's a mystery," says Viola. And so it is.

LOS ANGELES TIMES, 11/6/98, Calendar/p. 4, Jack Mathews

[The following review by Jack Mathews appeared in a slightly different form in **NEWSDAY, 11/6/98, Part II/p. B7.]**

Period movies inevitably reflect more about the period in which they're made than the period of their subject, and rarely has that been more evident—or more distracting—than it is with Indian director Shekhar Kapur's "Elizabeth."

This Elizabeth is the Virgin Queen, the illegitimate daughter of Henry VIII and Anne Boleyn, a strong-willed woman who survived early conspiracies, male condescension and foreign invasion to begin a popular 44-year reign that saw 16th century England rise from the brink of collapse to a glory remembered in history as a golden age.

Virginity, illegitimacy, politics, conspiracy. How could those elements go through the filters of a storyteller working at the end of the millennium and not emerge as an allegorical blend of sex, dysfunction, feminism and melodrama?

Stubborn historians may insist that Elizabeth went to her grave a virgin, or that she at least deserves the benefit of the doubt. But this is not a golden age, or even a period of polite discretion. If we can unzip a sitting president, we can deflower a dead queen.

That's essentially what Kapur, who showed his Hollywood ambitions with the provocative 1994 "Bandit Queen," and screenwriter Michael Hirst ("Meeting Venus") have done. "Elizabeth" is the story of a woman with a healthy sexual appetite who gives it up, out of pride and responsibility, and becomes the virgin mother of a new England.

When we meet her, Elizabeth (Cate Blanchett) is living relatively carefree, kept under house arrest by her gravely ill Catholic half-sister, Queen Mary (Kathy Burke). Virginity is already history for Elizabeth, who is openly entertaining her lover, Lord Robert Dudley (Joseph Fiennes), while quietly wondering what she might someday do to restore the outcast Church of England.

Elizabeth and Robert continue their open affair after she's installed on the throne, and after her councils have made it clear she must marry into the royal house of either Spain or France in order to save weakened England from being absorbed by one or the other.

Her potential husbands include Mary's widower, King Philip II (George Yiasoumi) of Spain, and Duc d'Anjou (Vincent Cassel), the fey young son of Mary of Guise (Fanny Ardant), the conniving queen of France. Philip is quickly ruled out, since he refuses to even visit England, and a blind date with the French duke proves comically disastrous when, in the film's most overdone scene, Elizabeth catches him wearing a dress, entertaining a day's catch of young boys.

That fiasco, plus the discovery that Robert has been married all this time, turns Elizabeth's interests to affairs of state, for which she reveals tremendous aptitude. The young queen grows into the job with strength and resolve, knowing herself to be the target of assassins, the throne to be the object of conspiracies and England itself to be prey to its enemies.

Whom does she trust, the sincere worrywart Sir William Cecil (Richard Attenborough), the devious Duke of Norfolk (Christopher Eccleston) or the darkly enigmatic Sir Francis Walsingham (Geoffrey Rush)? She sure can't trust Lord Robert, who, after her rejection of him, starts taking meetings in dark corners with beady-eyed men.

Blanchett, who bears an eerie resemblance to the portraiture images of Elizabeth, is the film's saving grace. She, alone among the principals, has a commanding grip on her character and gives her a seamless transition from naive idealist to steely monarch. Fiennes has matinee-idol looks but zero magnetism as Robert, and Rush, so sensational as David Helfgott in "Shine," seems more lost than menacing as the Machiavellian Walsingham.

Kapur will have his Hollywood career. He's a bit of a pack rat, ordering camera moves that would please Brian De Palma and staging a purge of conspirators as an almost direct homage to Francis Ford Coppola. But the film looks fabulous, and in the costume dramas he prefers, that's often enough.

NEW YORK, 11/16/98, p. 63, Peter Rainer

"Elizabeth," about the daughter of King Henry VIII and Anne Boleyn, has real verve. It's not all that great even so, but in the historical-bio genre, liveliness counts for a lot. Cate Blanchett plays the young Elizabeth from the time she is nearly rendered headless by her half-sister Queen Mary (Kathy Burke) to her final ascension as the Virgin Queen. We are not to take that moniker literally. Ben Jonson doubted Elizabeth was marriageable: "She hath a membrane which rendereth her incapable of man" was how he put it. But the Elizabeth on view here is a frolicker who knows how to dangle her spinsterhood before her panting suitors. She's a sexy queen, especially when she realizes she needs to ensure her power by lopping off a few heads of her own. The Indian director Shekhar Kapur and his screenwriter, Michael Hirst, would like us to see her as a feminist icon: She could do it all—dance the volta with her lover Robert Dudley (Joseph Fiennes) in full scandalous view of her court *and* lord it over the old fuds in Parliament. "I am no man's Elizabeth," she cries out while still in her marriageable mode. Later, she amends that: "I am married to England." Lucky England.

NEW YORK POST, 11/6/98, p. 55, Rod Dreher

Few historical figures of her stature have as fascinating a biography as England's Elizabeth I, the so-called Virgin Queen whose judicious reign ushered in a period of prosperity and might for her nation—an era that now bears her name.

Treachery, religious hatred, wars, bastardy, deadly intrigue—all this and more surrounded the young Protestant Elizabeth Tudor's accession to the throne following the death of her barren Catholic half-sister, Mary.

The stuff of heady melodrama, to be sure, and director Shekhar Kapur "The Bandit Queen" dramatizes it with lurid sensationalism. This is Masterpiece Theater for the MTV generation, a Virgin Queen for people raised on Like a Virgin.

The visual potency of "Elizabeth" is never less than compelling, thanks to Kapur's swashbuckling camera, John Myhre's meticulous production design and the eye-popping splendor of Alexandra Byrne's costumes.

But Michael Hirst's scattershot, often disorienting script, coupled with the breakneck pace of Kapur's narrative, drives you crazy. You wish the movie would stop long enough to catch its breath and give us at least a farthing's worth of historical context.

And with a couple of small exceptions, Hirst's characters are played as they are written: with bland competence. "Elizabeth" has flash, dash and panache on the surface, but little more. While no one wants a corseted, airless recitation of historical occurrences, turning the passions of dynastic politics into a got-up "Dynasty" is tremendously off-putting.

At least they get the history more or less right—no small virtue these days. The film begins with the roasting at the stake of three Protestant heretics in London. England is divided between Catholic and Protestant, with the present sovereign, the ailing Mary (Kathy Burke, in a brief but powerful turn), frantic to return her realm to the Roman fold from the exile earned it by her much-married father, Henry VIII.

When Mary dies with no heir, the crown passes to Elizabeth (Cate Blanchett), Henry's daughter by Anne Boleyn.

A red-haired beauty of 25 who has lived a relatively untroubled life, Elizabeth inherits a hideous mess. The country is threatened abroad by the papacy, and its minions, England's Catholic natives—represented at court by the nasty Duke of Norfolk (Christopher Eccleston)—are restless, the treasury is empty and nobody respects the poor dear.

She recalls from overseas exile Sir Francis Walsingham (Geoffrey Rush), a Protestant nobleman who comes to serve as both a paterfamilias, consigliere and 007, sussing out palace plots against the Queen and engineering a few of his own on her behalf.

Her clueless retinue of advisers includes the bumbling Sir William Cecil (Richard Attenborough), who doesn't think her capable of much, and Robert Dudley (Joseph, brother of Ralph Fiennes), her secret lover, whose petulant temper and control of the Queen's heart puts her reign at risk.

Though a Protestant, Elizabeth was for her time no religious nut. She was eager to make peace between Catholics and Anglicans, but knew that was impossible without a settlement of the religious question.

We see Walsingham sneakily guaranteeing that Parliament would affirm England's Protestant status, and the Pope (John Gielgud) absolving English Catholics from loyalty to Elizabeth, as well as issuing a contract on her life.

Good Queen Bess finally gets it into her pretty little head that if she is to carry on the family business, she's got to deal with the Holy Father and his goons on their own terms. So, in an obvious reference to "The Godfather," she becomes Michael Corleone, sacrificing her humanity for the sake of what her 20th-century successor and namesake would call "The Firm."

But whereas Coppola ennobled pulp melodrama with his artistry, Kapur vulgarizes dramatic history with his garish sensibilities.

But maybe I'm just sore because I'm a loyal papist and consider the conversion of England to Protestantism an incalculable loss.

The final scene has a triumphant Elizabeth kneeling before a statue of the Virgin Mary, telling Walsingham she herself will have to replace the madonna as an object of veneration in her formerly Catholic people's hearts. This is a tremendous tragedy, but not the one Elizabeth has in mind.

SIGHT AND SOUND, 11/98, p. 47, Stella Bruzzi

England 1554. Catholic Queen Mary reigns and Protestants are burned at the stake. Mary is dying of cancer. She has her Protestant half-sister Elizabeth arrested for treason, but finds she cannot sign her death warrant. After Mary dies, Elizabeth is crowned queen. However, England is in a precarious state, threatened by the Scots, French and Spanish. The new queen is urged to marry and secure the succession, although she is having an affair with Robert Dudley, the Earl of Leicester. The French, led by Mary of Guise, build up their army in Scotland; Elizabeth is advised to go to war, but her army suffers heavy losses. In England, the Catholic bishops plot her downfall, but Elizabeth ensures her Act of Uniformity is passed, establishing a single Church of England.

The Duc d'Anjou arrives to pay Elizabeth suit. Dudley proposes to Elizabeth, but she learns later he's already married. She refuses Anjou's offer of marriage. The Pope declares Elizabeth is not a legitimate queen and sanctions any assassination of her. One of Elizabeth's ladies-in-waiting dies after putting on a dress doused in poison that was a gift meant for Elizabeth. Dudley warns Elizabeth she is in danger and should marry the King of Spain. Elizabeth's adviser Walsingham murders Mary of Guise and warns Elizabeth against the Duke of Norfolk and a priest, newly arrived from Rome. Under torture the priest reveals the names of traitors plotting against Elizabeth, including Dudley and Norfolk. They are all beheaded, except for Dudley. Elizabeth declares herself the Virgin Queen, married only to her country.

In charting the early years of Queen Elizabeth I's reign (she ruled 1558-1603), director Shekhar Kapur's film ignores the golden years of triumph, peace and empire-building and focuses instead on the unrest and violence that preceded them. *Elizabeth* is not a celebration of Englishness. Instead, it is marked by its distance from rather than veneration for its subject, a standpoint no doubt informed by its director's origins (born on the Indian sub-continent, he is the director of *Bandit Queen* and several other Indian films). Occasionally Kapur seems to fall back on research in order to reassert the historical basis of the story, simplistically using famous portraits and miniatures as the basis for the costumes and compositions. (For example, Hillyard's allegorical portrait *Man in Flames* seems to be the inspiration for one framing of Elizabeth's lover Dudley.) But much of the time he approaches his subject with fresh eyes, and gives the film a dynamism rooted in difference.

Elizabeth is excessively stylised, particularly in its camerawork. In the opening sequence, depicting the burning of Protestants as heretics (filled with vertiginous swooping shots, bold editing and soaring flames), it is the barbarism and not the historical facts of the religious wars that is foregrounded. The film gazes with disbelief at the primitivism of this supposedly sophisticated civilisation. Kapur's sensuous visual style is fascinated with and fetishises the extremes of this sixteenth-century court life. This society is propelled by conflict and instability, exemplified by Elizabeth and Dudley's *amour fou;* Mary's painful inner conflict between her religion and her affection for her sister; the dangerous and corrupt papal court, with its minions and their sinister satellites in England; Norfolk's seething obsession with power; and ultimately Elizabeth's sacrificial offering of herself to her country.

Even Elizabeth's dancing with Dudley is transfused with emotion. The first time they perform the volta, their favourite energetic Elizabethan dance, is after the Coronation, when the two are in love and synchronised, and the camera cavorts in time with them. Their second dance comes after Elizabeth has learned Dudley is married, and the two are literally out of step, while the camera remains detached.

The film's sumptuous freneticism can be draining and some of the intrigues and plottings are too sketchily dealt with, but *Elizabeth* is bold and moving. A far cry from the sterility of British heritage movies, its acting and characters are refreshingly unlike the cardboard stereotypes of *The Private Lives of Elizabeth and Essex* (1939) or the BBC's 70s series *Elizabeth R*. Rather than being a place of hierarchy, privilege and clipped tones, Elizabeth's court is a dark hive of imminent danger, where even her loyal adviser Walsingham is a slippery machinator. The ending is disappointing—Elizabeth's renunciation of youth and sexuality (scything her hair and painting her face white) and her declaration, "I am married to England," are rather perfunctorily dealt with and are immediately followed by a bizarre and patronising list of trivial facts. But what Kapur does capture is the age's intensity and oddity. In short, its otherness from us as well as him.

VILLAGE VOICE, 11/10/98, p. 115, J. Hoberman

Another outsider's view of British history, Shekhar Kapur's dark, gusty account of the young Elizabeth Tudor's ascension to the throne is steeped in precisely the sort of enjoyable hokum that *Velvet Goldmine* eschews. [See Hoberman's review of *Velvet Goldmine*.]

An exercise in court intrigue and controlled tumult, the *Elizabeth* show begins with three Protestants burnt at the stake, but that's about as much public spectacle as the film supplies. In order to survive, the 25-year-old queen (superbly embodied by Cate Blanchett) must elude a host of foreign conspiracies, Vatican fatwas, and trick marriage proposals. Such protection as she has is the province of the cold-blooded spymaster Sir Francis Walsingham (an impressively sinister Geoffrey Rush, who never quite gets the big scene his lurking warrants). This relatively economical period melodrama is mainly a succession of candle-lit interiors—although England has never seemed more English than in the exterior scenes of rude merrymaking. A parallel is established in the contrast between the intrigue-ridden court and Elizabeth's unassumingly fresh and frolicsome nature. The dance the young queen does with her boyfriend—*lover* seems too heavy a term—is at once courtly and pagan.

Any evocation of 16th-century England can bask in reflected Shakespearean glory, but Kapur pushes this even further. More disciplined than his 1994 cause célèbre, *Bandit Queen, Elizabeth* displays a Wellesian brio in its dramatic overheads, deep-focus compositions, and baroque bustling through cold castles, all serving to emphasize the heroine's search for a center in this unbalanced world. Verily, *Elizabeth's* most triumphant aspect is Blanchett's transformation from saucy, spirited toe-tapper to iconic Virgin Queen—preempting the cult of Mary with her own personification of the English Renaissance. As common-sensical as her Elizabeth proves to be, Blanchett anticipates the foppish pop savants of *Velvet Goldmine,* who advise, "The secret of becoming a star is knowing how to behave like one."

Also reviewed in:
CHICAGO TRIBUNE, 11/20/98, Friday/p. D, Michael Wilmington
NEW YORK TIMES, 11/6/98, p. E16, Janet Maslin
NEW YORKER, 11/16/98, p. 115, David Denby
VARIETY, 9/14-20/98, p. 33, David Rooney
WASHINGTON POST, 11/20/98, p. F5, Stephen Hunter
WASHINGTON POST, 11/20/98, Weekend/p. 50, Michael O'Sullivan

EMPEROR'S SHADOW, THE

A Fox Lorber release of an Ocean Film/Xi'an Film Studio production. *Producer:* Jimmy Tan and Chen Kunming. *Director:* Zhou Xiaowen. *Screenplay (Mandarin with English subtitles):* Lu Wei. *Director of Photography:* Lu Gengxin. *Music:* Zhao Jiping. *Art Director:* Cao Jiuping, Duo Guoxiang, and Zhang Daqian. *Running time:* 123 minutes. *MPAA Rating:* Not Rated.

CAST: Jiang Wen (Ying Zheng); Ge You (Gao Jianli); Xu Qing (Ying Yueyang).

NEW YORK POST, 12/18/98, p. 64, Jonathan Foreman

"The Emperor's Shadow" is the most expensive movie ever made in China, and it shows. Set 2,000 years ago, it is a breathtakingly beautiful film, its spectacular scenes of pageantry exceeded only by stunning interior shots. Unlike the acclaimed films of Zhang Yimou ("Judou" and "Raise the Red Lantern") and Chen Kaige ("Farewell My Concubine"), this epic harks back to the traditional, symmetrical, glossy, well-lit look of post-war Chinese movies.

Imagine a DeMille heavily influenced by MTV videos and you have a pretty good idea of director Zhou Xiaowen's style: Lots of slow motion, sledgehammer symbolism, saturated colors and dramatic lighting effects. But its energetic visual virtuosity is set off by crudeness in the storytelling, and by dialogue so corny that it sometimes distracts from the action.

Ying Zheng (Jiang Wen), the most powerful warlord in China, is on the verge of unifying the six warring kingdoms of what will be the first Chinese Empire. On conquering the last but one, he captures Gao Jianli (Ge You), a brilliant musician and composer who was his best friend as a boy. He asks him to compose an anthem for the united China, one that will bring the masses around to the new regime. But Gao, bitter at the slaughter of his countrymen, would rather die.

Ying is so convinced that only Gao can compose a national anthem worthy of the empire, that he keeps him alive. But he cannot make him write music. Then Ying's beautiful, crippled daughter, Princess Yueyang (Xu Qing), steps in. She's betrothed to a vicious Klingon-like general, but she wants to learn the Qin, the traditional Chinese instrument, and is fascinated by the old man who was her father's best friend.

Her seductive attentions break the composer's will to die. And in proper Freudian-operatic fashion, the moment she is deflowered by the imprisoned composer, she regains the ability to walk.

Emperor Ying is furious. But he still wants his anthem, despite the conviction of the court that the composer should be tortured and killed. In the end he will have it, but at a terrible cost.

In many ways, Emperor Ying Zheng's character is the most sympathetic. Unlike his generals and his equally nasty eunuch courtiers, he has a tremendous, genuine love of the arts. And his line that the bloody cost of unifying China is worth the peaceful benefits that unity will bring, seems persuasive. Composer Gao, on the other hand, is an artistic prima donna who gets a girl he doesn't really deserve.

All three main performances are strong and convincing, but that of Jiang Weng—at 35, one of China's biggest stars—as a ruthless yet sentimental warlord is superb. Xu Qinq, while not quite as breathtaking as the fabulous Gong Li, is gorgeous as the doomed love-driven princess.

The long-awaited anthem itself sounds peculiarly Western and is obviously played on Western instruments. In fact, with its (unseen) massed choirs it has a sort of Soviet ring, and you wonder if Zhou Xiaowen is not emphasizing the parallels between the First Emperor and Chairman Mao ZeDong. If he is, then the film maker himself is clearly torn between the causes of artistic independence and political unity.

NEWSDAY, 12/18/98, Part II/p. B6, John Anderson

Having graduated from the Beijing Film Academy a bit earlier than his better-known contemporaries Chen Kaige and Zhang Yimou, director Zhou Xiaowen doesn't get pigeonholed as "fifth generation" (the first class after the Cultural Revolution).

It's an elusive category, whatever it is. In Zhou's 1994 social satire, "Ermo," a wily peasant woman's pursuit of a big-screen television became one of the more mordant comments about consumerism and media. He describes his next film as a dual-narrative, modern urban drama about handicapped people in China. In the meantime, we get a period piece about feudal warlords, pageantry and ritual death. Clearly, Zhou's world is an oeuvre without borders.

Eight or so years in the making, "The Emperor's Shadow" is part of a dubious genre, the Chinese costume epic. While "The Emperor's Shadow" makes the most of its casual barbarism and cruel landscapes, it also revolves around several contemporary, and provocative, ideas.

Ostensibly, "Shadow" is a tale of tempestuous relationships—between China's first emperor (played by Jiang Wen) and his boyhood friend (Ge You), a brilliant musician and composer who the emperor wants to become his court composer; between the musician and the emperor's daughter (Xu Qing), who was crippled in a riding accident but can suddenly walk after sex with the musician holistically liberates her spinal cord; and, less prominently but no less potently, between the emperor and his daughter, for whom he will clearly do anything, except abandon his pursuit of conquest.

The tensions between the artist and the martial artist—one seeing art as ultimate, the other seeing it as a gentle weapon of oppression—is "Shadow's" engine, a look back at Soviet social realism and Mao's attempts to ape it. The musician, Gao Jianli, is branded, tortured, beaten, but resists having his music used as propaganda. (Actor Ge apparently mastered, in only two months, the gu'qin, or zither, that his character plays.) The emperor, Ying Zheng, is a visionary, in that he realizes the value of anthems and pageantry, the unifying sentiments that glorious music could instill is his fractured, multitribal kingdom. The freedom of the artist, as always, clashes with the wishes of the despot, although one has to admit that Ying Zheng is one of your more enlightened dictators.

Violent, overheated and large in scope, "The Emperor's Shadow" has many bodice-ripper qualities. It also, however, taps into some topical arguments about art and malice. This may be why Beijing couldn't decide to release it or ban it, and ended up releasing it and then banning it. And then releasing it.

Among contemporary filmmakers, Zhou isn't just elusive. He's downright slippery.

VILLAGE VOICE, 12/22/98, p. 127, J. Hoberman

Another imperial epic, set a thousand or so years after *Prince of Egypt,* in the third century B.C., *The Emperor's Shadow* also concerns the conflict between a pair of foster brothers—one of whom grows up to be the famous musician Gao Jianli and the other the first emperor of China.

Wills collide, long after the lads are separated, when the baby-faced potentate demands a national anthem and conquers his brother's native land to get one. Although subject to torture, Gao refuses to comply until he has been seduced by the emperor's partially paralyzed daughter. Their cosmic sex is crosscut with images of fluttering flags, a royal sword, and a battering ram. The revival-tent atmosphere is clinched afterward, when the princess stands up and walks, and smitten Gao composes a piece to the effect that "10,000 men must stoop so that one can reach heaven." Somehow this sentiment fails to satisfy the emperor, who orders the mass execution of his slaves, until Gao agrees to a rewrite. One thing leads to another, but suffice to say that all the principals are dead by the time the emperor ritually ascends to the top of the giant pyramid he's built himself.

Directed by Zhou Xiaowen (best known for the contemporary comedy *Ermo),* and the most expensive Chinese movie to date, *The Emperor's Shadow* traveled the international festival circuit in 1996 and has recently emerged as a cult success in San Francisco. It's not entirely kitsch. Ascetic as well as sensuous, the movie is predicated on symmetrical compositions, spectacular landscapes, and humans organized into an ornamental mass. *The Emperor's Shadow* has the feel of an elaborate ritual and the sense of a civilization refined even in its cruelties. The sequence in which the emperor has Gao blinded with horse piss should strike a responsive chord with movie reviewers everywhere.

Also reviewed in:
NEW YORK TIMES, 12/18/98, p. E17, Stephen Holden
VARIETY, 6/3-9/96, p. 55, Derek Elley
WASHINGTON POST, 10/16/98, p. D5, Stephen Hunter

ENEMY OF THE STATE

A Touchstone Pictures release of a Don Simpson/Jerry Bruckheimer production in association with Scott Free Productions. *Executive Producer:* Chad Oman, Jamees W. Skotchdopole, and Andrew Z. Davis. *Producer:* Jerry Bruckheimer. *Director:* Tony Scott. *Screenplay:* David Marconi. *Directory of Photography:* Dan Mindel. *Editor:* Chris Lebenzon. *Music:* Trevor Rabin and Harry Gregson-Williams. *Music Editor:* Bob Badami. *Sound:* Bill Kaplan and (music) Steve Kempster. *Sound Editor:* George Watters II. *Casting:* Victoria Thomas. *Production Designer:* Benjamin Fernandez. *Art Director:* James J. Murakami, Jennifer A. Davis, and Donald B. Woodruff. *Set Designer:* Peter J. Kelly. *Set Decorator:* Garrett Lewis. *Set Dresser:* Charles Nicholson and Joshua Persoff. *Visual Effects:* James E. Price. *Mechanical Effects:* Mike Meinardus. *Costumes:* Marlene Stewart. *Make-up:* Ellen Wong. *Make-up (Will Smith):* Laini Thompson. *Stunt Coordinator:* Charles Picerni, Jr. *Running time:* 128 minutes. *MPAA Rating:* R.

CAST: Will Smith (Robert Clayton Dean); Gene Hackman (Brill); Jon Voight (Thomas Brian Reynolds); Lisa Bonet (Rachel Banks); Regina King (Carla Dean); Stuart Wilson (Congressman Albert); Laura Cayouette (Christa Hawkins); Loren Dean (Hicks); Barry Pepper (Pratt); Ian Hart (Bingham); Jake Busey (Krug); Scott Caan (Jones); Jason Lee (Zavitz); Gabriel Byrne ("Brill"); James Le Gros (Jerry Miller); Dan Butler (Shaffer); Jack Black (Fiedler); Jamie Kennedy (Jamie); Bodhi Pine Elfman (Van); Jacob Chambers (Davis); Alexandra Balahoutis (Martha); Anna Gunn (Emily Reynolds); Jascha Washington (Eric Dean); Rebecca Silva (Marie the Nanny); Bobby Borriello (Dylan); Carl Mergenthaler (Mike, Law Firm); Mattias Kraemer (Gas Station Cashier); Lillo Brancato (Young Worker); John Capodice (Older Worker); Vic Manni (Vic, Old Mobster); T.R. Richards (Cook); Ivana

Milavich (Ruby's Sales Clerk);   Patsy Grady Abrams (Accident Bystander);   Beatriz Mayoral (Reynold's Nanny);   Elizabeth Berman (Ruthie);   Donna Scott (Jenny);   Allison Sie (Hotel Desk Clerk);   Mike Andolini (Sal);   Arthur Nascarella (Frankie);   Grant Heslov (Lenny);   John Cenatiempo (Young Mobster);   Joyce Flick Wendl (Waitress);   Frank Medrano (Bartender); Dennis S. Fahey (Cop with Ambulance);   Albert Wong (Mr. Wu);   Christopher B. Lawrence (Paramedic);   John Haynes Walker and Joe Patrick Kelly (Firemen);   Lennox Brown (Tunnel Maintenance Worker);   Martin Bosworth (Bike Messenger);   Nancy Yee (Mrs. Wu);   Troy Anthony Cephers (ANA Hotel Secutiry);   Carlos Gomez (FBI Agent);   Arnie Alpert (Robert Gersicoff);   Greg Collins (FBI Supervisor);   Doug Roberts (Hijacked Car Driver);   Larry King (Himself);   Warren Olney and Penny Griego (TV Anchors);   Rhona Overby, Lillie Shaw Hamer, and Brenna McDonough (Field Reporters);   Eric Keung and David Han (Mambo Kitchen Workers);   Mandy Kriss, Noel Werking and Sam De Crispino (Reporters);   Wayne A. Larrivey (Doorman);   Callison Slater and Colin Brodie (Children);   Daniel Cano (Hallway Lawyer);   Joy Ehrlich (Mom in Diner);   Eric Olson, Thomas Troy, and Adam Karkowsky (Aides);   Steve Uhrig (Electronic Store Employee);   Robyn Killian, Laura Eizenia, Angelica Pamintuan, Vené Arcoraci, and Charlie Curtis (Models);   Raichle Watt (Becky);   Michael J. Walker (Union Official);   Jackilynn Ward (Pintero's Sister);   Jason Welch and Joshua Ward (Pintero Kids);   Pete Sutton (Dean House Cop);   Thomas M. Quinn (Tunnel Technician);   Robert O'Rourke, John Allendorfer, and Henry Sandler (FBI Observers);   Chris Holt (Himself);   Jason Robards (Rep. Philip Hamersly);   Seth Green (Seth);   Phillip Baker Hall (Brian Silverberg);   Brian Markinson (Mark Blake);   Tom Sizemore (Pintero);   Betsy Brantley (FBI Agent 1);   Paul Herman (Paulie, Young Mobster 2).

CHRISTIAN SCIENCE MONITOR, 11/20/98, p. 15, David Sterritt

"Enemy of the State" is about violence and video, among other fashionable topics.

A rogue security agent (Jon Voight) kills a congressman who's showing too much concern for civil liberties, and it's all caught on videotape by an unwitting wildlife expert.

Dumped into the hands of an easygoing attorney (Will Smith) who doesn't even know he has it, this deadly piece of evidence becomes what Alfred Hitchcock would call the "McGuffin" of the movie—an object that's uninteresting in itself, but gives the characters something to chase and fight over until it's time for the grand finale.

Two qualities separate "Enemy of the State" from the current Hollywood crop. One is its success in spinning out action so explosively energetic that you scarcely have time to notice how preposterous the story is, how thin the characters are, or how the picture pounds at your senses until it's hard to say whether they belong to you or the Disney technicians who cooked up the spectacle.

The other is its paranoid view of the United States government and, more sweepingly, the awesome technologies the Feds allegedly use or misuse. If you're targeted like our hero, sinister gizmos will make your private life public and your public life an on-the-run nightmare.

The movie has a lot of power, in a roller coaster sort of way, thanks to director Tony Scott, who gives it a sense of half-crazed commitment that many of his thrillers sadly lack.

The cast also works wonders with material that often borders on the idiotic, especially Smith and the marvelous Gene Hackman, who deserves an Oscar nomination even though he's only in a fraction of the story.

LOS ANGELES TIMES, 11/20/98, Calendar/p. 1, Kenneth Turan

Forget about Santa Claus coming to town. The National Security Agency is already here, and it not only knows whether you've been bad or good, it can deliver some pretty nasty surprises if you get caught on its downside.

That, at least, is the message of "Enemy of the State," the Tony Scott-directed, Jerry Bruckheimer-produced thriller about a man on the run from a super-powerful government agency. It's a paranoid's nightmare brought energetically to life, a solid and satisfying commercial venture with more than enough pizazz to overcome occasional lapses in moment-to-moment plausibility.

To do that a film has to have convincing performers, and this one demonstrates why Will Smith is pretty much the hottest actor in Hollywood. As Robert Clayton Dean, the man unjustly placed at the top of the NSA's bad list, Smith adds dramatic skills to his comic gifts and his immense relaxed likability and ends up as everyone's favorite Everyman, in a jam but determined to get out alive.

Just as good are the two actors who control Dean's fate. A convincing Jon Voight plays NSA zealot Thomas Brian Reynolds, the devil in a Brooks Brothers suit, and Gene Hackman helps make this film "The Conversation" on steroids with a tough turn as a rogue surveillance wizard.

More than that, casting director Victoria Thomas has dotted "Enemy of the State" with excellent performers in smaller supporting roles, people like James Le Gros, Ian Hart, Gabriel Byrne, Tom Sizemore, Jason Robards and Lisa Bonet who make this probably the best-cast of Bruckheimer's efforts.

A man who didn't become the king of popcorn movies by worrying too much about real world credibility, Bruckheimer has broken with form by commissioning a straight-ahead, non-tongue-in-cheek script that has a disturbing core. As written by David Marconi, "Enemy of the State" is if anything more convincing in its broad outlines than its thriller specifics as it posits the existence of a surveillance-dominated society, where the collaboration of the government and the telecommunications industry makes the most complete invasions of privacy possible.

Director Scott has done some of his best work ("Crimson Tide," "Beverly Hills Cop II") for Bruckheimer, and, collaborating with cinematographer Dan Mindel, he does a compelling job of visualizing how satellites and computers could make this Truman-Show-for-real scenario actually happen. Practically an elder statesman compared to the technobrats Bruckheimer usually employs, Scott also pays attention to the acting and it pays off.

Smith's Dean is introduced as one of Washington's top labor lawyers, a suspenders-wearing Georgetown resident with the requisite strong-minded wife (Regina King who has a great way with suspicious looks) and an adorable son.

Dean's current case involves a mobster (Sizemore) who's trying to muscle in on a labor union. As always when things get tough, Dean uses his old law school girlfriend Rachel Banks (Bonet) to make contact with a secretive private investigator named Brill, who is capable of gathering the most hard-to-find information.

Simultaneous with this plot strand, bad guy Reynolds is getting a bead on a scientist named Daniel Zavitz (Jason Lee), who has possession of a tape the NSA official will do anything to keep from becoming public.

Though he's not aware of it happening, that tape ends up in Dean's possession. What the lawyer does become aware of is his life turning into a nightmare overnight, as Reynolds, the man who invented ruthless, conspires for his own nefarious reasons to ruin every aspect of Dean's life from his marriage to his credit cards to his career.

It's a measure of how audience-friendly an actor Smith is that he manages to keep viewers interested through the toughest part of movies like this—the long section when the audience knows exactly what's happening but the protagonist is without so much as a clue.

Helping to clue Dean in is Hackman's character, a convincingly angry and suspicious security expert who seems uncannily like what the actor's Harry Caul persona in "The Conversation" would be like more than 20 hard years down the road. (As a pleasant nod to that earlier film, a shot of Hackman as Caul is flashed briefly on screen as part of Brill's out-of-date identity badge.)

People in "Enemy of the State" do a great deal of running around, with Dean for one getting briskly chased along hotel corridors, out windows and even down long tunnels wearing nothing but his underwear and a stolen bathrobe. All this activity serves to divert us from the film's periodic departures from plausibility. But with the whole world stacked against Smith's likable character, it seems only sporting to give his film that kind of a break.

NEW YORK, 11/30/98, p. 120, Peter Rainer

"It's not paranoia if they're really after you," announces the ad line for the new Will Smith-Gene Hackman thriller, *Enemy of the State*. That disclaimer notwithstanding, the film still tries to rev our paranoia. It's set against the buggy backdrop of top-secret government surveillance, and I suppose it's all meant to be Kafkaesque. But since this is a Jerry Bruckheimer production, it's more like Kafka on steroids. Bruckheimer is the ringmaster of such recent cranium-splitters as *The Rock*, *Con Air*, and *Armageddon*, and for fourteen years he worked with the late Don Simpson on everything from *Flashdance* to *Top Gun* to *Crimson Tide*. The truth is, there's not much difference between the Simpson-Bruckheimer stuff and the Bruckheimer stuff. The decibels are still pitched at the heavy-metal level and the action is the same old pumped-up pap. Partnered or solo, Bruckheimer specializes in movies that come on like trailers for themselves; when they're over, you're still waiting for the movie to start. He often casts first-rate actors, but the famous faces—Sean Connery, Nicolas Cage, Bruce Willis, Gene Hackman—are like mounted heads on a big-game hunter's trophy wall.

In *Enemy of the State,* Hackman (ostensibly Will Smith's co-star) doesn't even make it onto the wall until an hour into the show. He plays a kind of defrocked former CIA agent named Brill who knows all sorts of clever secret-agent-type things—like the bit about crushing potato chips in a crinkly bag to foul up audio surveillance. (If the people who seem to regularly sit behind me in movie theaters are any indication, the CIA has infiltrated audiences big-time.) A true Underground Man, Brill reluctantly surfaces to offer his aid when a Washington lawyer, Robert Clayton Dean (Smith), is targeted by rogue National Security Agency operatives under the command of Thomas Brian Reynolds (Jon Voight), whose wire-rims and thick upswept hairline give him a preternatural (and no doubt intended) resemblance to Robert McNamara. Reynolds has already engineered the garroting of a senator (an unbilled Jason Robards) opposed to an over-the-top domestic snoop-and-spy bill. By accident, Dean finds himself in possession of a videotape of the murder, and runs for his life. Worse: Spymasters douse his wife's white poodle with pink dye.

Smith, who co-starred with Martin Lawrence in Simpson-Bruckheimer's execrable *Bad Boys,* has been giving a lot of interviews lately about what a challenge *Enemy of the State* was for him. The notion that any gifted actor would regard a role in a Bruckheimer movie as a dramatic stretch is pretty funny. Smith actually had his biggest challenge in his first major movie, the extraordinary *Six Degrees of Separation.* As the con man who insinuates himself into the lives of white Upper East Side snobberati, he had an unreachability that was all the more chilling for being camouflaged by his trademark cool. But because that film tanked, it doesn't rate high in the Hollywood scheme of things. Nobody talks about it much. The stretch for Smith in *Enemy of the State* consists of punctuating his personable light comic rifts with occasional outbursts of high dudgeon. (Sample: "I want my life back.") He also runs around a lot and gets shot at, but he's done that before. The role doesn't enhance his dramatic range; it just shows off his enhanced portfolio. Now he can fit into a greater variety of junk than before. In Hollywood, this often is what is meant by versatility.

Enemy of the State, scripted by David Marconi, is the kind of movie where every change in locale is signaled by an onscreen digital-time readout. Just in case we mislaid our glow-in-the-dark stopwatch. The director, Tony Scott, an old Simpson-Bruckheimer maestro *(Top Gun, Beverly Hills Cop II, Days of Thunder, Crimson Tide),* doesn't allow the audience to discover anything for itself. He's a highly proficient thrill-ride operator, but there's a techno-hollowness in his method. If, say, Hitchcock had done this scenario, he might have really brought out the wrong-Everyman-in-the-wrong-place element; he might have made us *care.* But the Hitchcock era has long since given way to the Grisham era, and much of *Enemy of the State*—the family-man lawyer cornered into an apparently no-win situation; the deus ex machina resolution—seems Grisham-ized.

If you're going to make a movie about how easy it is for our identities to be electronically stolen by the government, shouldn't you at least create people with identities worth stealing? The only character in the movie with any resonance is Brill, and that's largely because Hackman is playing him like a follow-up to his Harry Caul, the professional surveillance expert in *The Conversation.* (A photo of Harry—supposedly Brill as a younger man—actually turns up.) Brill is what Harry might have turned into if he stayed in the game but out of sight. He has the somewhat rabid, distracted look of a man for whom privacy is no longer an option; he seems to be forever picking up vibrations in the air. Brill is made the hero of the piece because, on the fly, utilizing low-rent equipment, he aces out the high-techie bad guys. His laptop jujitsu with the NSA is easily the most entertaining thing in the movie. Hackman may not be onscreen for very long, but he's amazing when he is. How much more amazing he might have been if the film had delved into the psychology of a spook who is spooked by the invasive world he helped create. The frustration in watching Hackman is that he has it in him to develop a character of almost Dostoyevskian richness—the Underground Man as Nowhere Man—and the filmmakers keep sabotaging his performance with digital-time readouts and satellite sky cams and exploding warehouses and skidding U-turns. In a movie riddled with nefarious conspiracies, this one is the most heinous of all.

NEW YORK POST, 11/20/98, p. 59, Rod Dreher

The apparently unstoppable Will Smith delivers the goods yet again in director Tony Scott's firing-on-all-pistons "Enemy of the State," a perfectly cast, first-rate paranoid thriller that falters only in shorting the "paranoid" in favor of the "thriller."

That is, this superslick Jerry Bruckheimer production of David Marconi's script is so hard-driving that it brushes only lightly against the psychological terror and political implication of its premise. It never gets under your skin like the best films of its kind from the 1970s, and this superficiality keeps a good movie from achieving greatness. But when a picture is as entertaining as this one, the complaint is relatively minor.

"Enemy" opens at a clandestine lakeside rendezvous, where an influential U.S. congressman (Jason Robards) has gone to meet Reynolds (icy Jon Voight), an official of the National Security Agency. Reynolds wants the lawmaker to give up opposition to a bill that would make it easier for the government to spy domestically. When the congressman refuses, Reynolds' goons kill him.

Someone has photographed the assassination, though, and after a convoluted chase, the film secretly falls into the shopping bag of yuppie lawyer Robert Clayton Dean (Smith).

Reynolds and his techno posse figure this out almost instantly, owing to their wowie-zowie surveillance capabilities. Mistakenly believing the clueless Dean is holding out on them, the NSA puts the hurt on the guy. In the blink of an eye, his life is a shambles: His house is ransacked, his wife throws him out, his firm fires him, his credit rating is shot and his entire identity is under siege.

The adrenaline rush doesn't really kick in until Dean goes underground and makes contact with an ultraparanoid security expert named Brill. Casting the terrific Gene Hackman in this role is an obvious homage to his Harry Caul in Francis Coppola's "The Conversation." Brill, a former NSA operative who knows the agency's capabilities, is so suspicious and fearful that he lives in a kind of technological hermitage, seen by no one and seeing all.

Once Hackman hooks up with Smith, the chase is on, and it doesn't let up for a solid hour of brilliant zigging and zagging and ducking into sewers. Scott brilliantly stages and edits these sequences, which, aside from the car chases in John Frankenheimer's "Ronin," are unmatched in movies this year for sustained white-knuckle excitement.

"Enemy" is intended as an Information Age cautionary tale about how vulnerable modern people are to those who have gained omniscience through technology, and who have the will to exploit that knowledge.

The most interesting idea the film offers is a villainous conspiracy in which the key baddies aren't brush-cut thugs but nerd geniuses, slobby slackers in the NSA's employ so jazzed by the cool things they can do with computers and satellites that they never reflect on the morality of their actions.

Yet unlike even throwaway episodes of "The X-Files," Scott's movie doesn't succeed at making the paranoia personal for us. Part of this, no doubt, is because Scott's a broad-stroke action filmmaker, not an expert at creating shadings of mood.

It's also true, though, that the audience is infinitely more jaded today than in the 1970s, when the idea of a conspiratorial abuse of power at the highest levels could still shock and appall. Nowadays, we just take this kind of thing in stride, because—haven't you heard?—It's Time to Get On With the Business of the Country.

NEWSDAY, 11/20/98, Part II/p. B3, Jack Mathews

While it is always a pleasure to see Gene Hackman in a movie, you have to question the judgment of casting him as a reclusive surveillance wizard in Tony Scott's political thriller "Enemy of the State." Since he played a younger, sterner version of this character in Francis Coppola's "The Conversation," one of the best domestic spy movies ever made, his presence serves as a sad reminder of just how weak Hollywood storytelling has gotten in the last 24 years.

It's gotten so bad, in fact, that Hackman doesn't even appear until the film is half over, and we're past wondering whether the movie exists for any reason other than to showcase Scott's talent for creating slick surfaces and to exploit the winsome appeal of Will Smith.

When Hackman does arrive, looking like "The Conversation's" Harry Caul gone severely to seed, the tension level is indeed raised a peg or two on this otherwise rote thriller. But, again, comparisons to "The Conversation," or any other of the fine 1970s paranoia thrillers it attempts to mimic, fail.

"Enemy of the State," written by TV veteran David Marconi, is another in the lengthening line of absurdist post-Cold War thrillers in which enemies are drawn from unlikely places in our own government. The villain du jour of this Pogo action cartoon is a careerist politician (Jon Voight) who, while on loan from the White House to the National Security Agency, orders the assassination of a political enemy, then mobilizes the NSA field force to recover and destroy a video recording of the crime.

Lifting the wrong-man theme from Alfred Hitchcock, "Enemy of the State" has the telltale tape pass from the hands of a nature photographer into the shopping bag of a former friend the photographer encounters while running for his life through downtown Baltimore. That friend is Will Smith's Robert Dean, an unsuspecting labor lawyer who, from that moment on, is the new target of the NSA manhunt.

For the first half of the film, we follow Dean as he runs for his life, having no idea why he's being pursued and framed for murder. For the second half, the better half, we follow him and his reluctant ally, Brill (Hackman), a former security agency operative, as they attempt to turn the tables on the G-men.

After a promising opening sequence, in which a congressman is coolly murdered by a lake outside Washington, Scott throws "Enemy" into high gear and sets a blistering pace throughout. The movie could be the Gadget Guru's fever dream, a running demo of state-of-the-art surveillance equipment. There are hidden mikes, satellite tracking, telephone tracers and enough shady agents to start a pyramid scam.

The baloney alarm goes off early and often, and rings loudest at the end, when antagonists come together for what may be the most preposterous staging of a Mexican standoff on film. I count members of two federal agencies, the Mafia, the American Bar Association and the International Kitchen Workers Local No. 201.

In fairness, Scott seems more interested in wringing laughs from his material than in building any genuine tension. His forte is showcasing major stars in glistening, high-speed, high-tech settings, whether it's in the air ("Top Gun"), on the race track ("Days of Thunder") or in a nuclear submarine ("Crimson Tide").

Since most of the action in "Enemy" occurs in invisible air, where images and sounds are being absorbed by dweeb-operated electronics, he's more dependent than ever on his star, and Will Smith is a funny guy.

The result is a fitfully entertaining mix of heightened paranoia (Big Brother is watching!) and electronic slapstick. On one extreme, you have Smith, who in his character's most stressful moments seems to be inviting smiles. On the other, you have Voight, who wears the look of a man passing a kidney stone the size of Brooklyn.

And in the middle there's Hackman, gamely reprising a role that needed the deliberate, intimate pacing of Coppola's 1974 gem. Paranoia just isn't what it used to be.

NEWSWEEK, 11/23/98, p. 83, Jack Kroll

Big Brother is mutating into a vast family of Big Siblings. With every satellite that's Frisbeed into space, the surveillance state moves closer. The most Orwellian take yet on this theme is Tony Scott's new thriller, "Enemy of the State." Ba-ba-boom action specialist Scott ("Crimson Tide," "Top Gun") tells the story of a successful labor lawyer (Will Smith) whose comfy life is jackhammered to bits when he stumbles into a conspiracy masterminded by a sinister executive (Jon Voight) at the National Security Administration. This guy stops at nothing, including assassinating a congressman, to ram through a bill that will give the government expanded powers to spy on everything under the sun. Shorn of career, family and upscale wardrobe, Smith hooks up with an underground high-tech counterspy (Gene Hackman) to battle an army of murderous eavesdroppers who boast: "The only privacy left is inside your head."

The scary fun of the movie is embodied in a brilliantly filmed and edited chase sequence in which Smith tries to escape the ubiquitous cyber-eyes that see every inch of his flight. In such passages Scott transcends his usual MTV style and creates new cinematic landscape out of hurtling satellite images and flashing computer screens, turning the whole earth into a claustrophobic space that affords no escape. The NSA techies are all cool Gen-X kids for whom the whole lethal operation is just the world's biggest computer game. But screenwriter David Marconi spoils the fun with a dumb, bloody denouement involving the Mafia. This ending is an offer that Tony Scott should have refused.

SIGHT AND SOUND, 1/99, p. 45, Kim Newman

Washington, DC. National Security Agency man Reynolds has his right-hand man murder a congressman who was threatening to veto a bill that would grant the NSA increased powers. By chance, the murder is recorded on a video set up by environmentalist Daniel Zavitz. Reynolds has his team kill Zavitz, although Zavitz manages to plant the tape on Robert Dean, a lawyer whom he meets accidentally. (Dean is unaware he has the tape). Dean is involved in a case against mobster Pintero, whom he plans to incriminate with another tape supplied by Brill, a shadowy surveillance expert who deals with him through Dean's ex-girlfriend Rachel Banks. Reynolds puts Dean under extreme surveillance, has him fired, puts pressure on his marriage and incriminates him on several charges, including Rachel's murder. While fleeing, Dean makes contact with someone he thinks is Brill but who's really an NSA imposter. He's approached by the real Brill, an ex-NSA agent named Edward Lyle. Brill agrees to help Dean.

Dean discovers the video, which is then ruined in an explosion when Reynolds' men home in on Lyle's hideout. After the pair are seized, Dean dupes Reynolds by saying that Pintero has the video. He takes the NSA crew to the mobster's headquarters which he knows is being watched by the FBI. When Reynolds demands the video from Pintero, the gangster assumes he is after the evidence against him. In a shoot-out, Reynolds, Pintero and most of both gangs are wiped out. Dean's life is restored, and Lyle vanishes again.

Surveillance has been the watchword of the paranoia thriller ever since Fritz Lang's *The Thousand Eyes of Dr Mabuse* (1960) introduced the much-imitated figure of the shadowy mastermind who sits before a bank of monitor, eavesdropping on everyone. The assumptions of the genre—that security agencies are entitled to violate everyone's freedoms in the name of democracy—were first seriously questioned in *The Prisoner* television series. This brand of conspiracy movie became a commonplace in the Watergate era, from *The Anderson Tapes* (1971) to *Three Days of the Condor* (1975), in which it was established that the evil government was spying on everyone. *Enemy of the State* is a definitive late-90s updating of this style of thriller, its plot serving as a demonstration for all manner of high-tech snooping equipment, from bugs sewn into trouser seams to geostationary satellites 150 miles up.

Crimson Tide (1995), the last Tony Scott-Jerry Bruckheimer-Gene Hackman epic before this, was a retooling of *The Bedford Incident* (1965) with an unimpeachably ethnic but apolitical hero pitted against an establishment psychopath whose personal misdemeanours did not reflect government policy. In this light, it's no surprise that *Enemy of the State* balances its scares with the get-out clause that its villain is an NSA rogue, explicitly condemned by his superiors. One of the things the crowded script has no time to establish is the extent to which Reynolds' crew know or care that their quarry is actually an innocent man.

As in *Crimson Tide* (and unlike, say, *The Parallax View*, (1974) any implied criticism of the system is mitigated by star power. In other words, the film doesn't say it's terrible that unaccountable men have been given power over ordinary people. Instead, it's only wrong to use all these gimmicks when the victim is someone as all-round decent as Will Smith, whose slightly self-satisfied screen persona is ideally suited to the role of a man slowly stripped of his life and identity. Given Smith's dressiness (he sneers when Hackman tries to get him into a Hawaiian shirt), a *frisson* is generated by divesting him of his classy threads and forcing him to continue his flight in underwear, later pulling on a decidedly proletarian hooded sweatshirt. The fact that all is put right so cleverly marks it out as a 90s movie. The 70s version would end with Smith's Dean shot dead by an anonymous sniper or reduced to living unnoticed on the streets, with Reynolds smiling smugly as the congressional bill granting him unlimited powers is passed.

Aside from Tony Scott's technically brilliant marshalling of the chase scenes, incorporating surveillance images and the comments of the voyeurs into the breathless action, the chief delight of the film is its clever casting. When Gabriel Byrne appears briefly as the fake Brill, the movie seems as if it will turn into a sequel to *The End of Violence,* where Byrne played a paranoid observer. But Gene Hackman's appearance as the real Brill/Lyle makes it a continuation of *The Conversation* (it even uses a still from *The Conversation* for Lyle's NSA file photo). His appearance feels like the cameo Kevin McCarthy made in the remake of *Invasion of the Body Snatchers* (1978) or the guest spots found for original cast members in big-budget remakes of cult television shows. He provides a welcome physical link to what went before but is also shuttled off to one side so Smith can carry the whole thing in an uncomplex 90s way.

Hackman's presence resonates with that of Jon Voight and Jason Robards (also early 70s faces), but the cleverest stroke comes in the casting of Reynolds' team, who are played by Generation X faces, mostly familiar from indie films (Ian Hart, Loren Dean, Barry Pepper and so on) with second-generation hard men (Jake Busey, Scott Caan) as the thick-headed muscle. The gossipy callousness of the crew—they steal Dean's prized blender and use it to whip up fruit drinks while watching Dean run from pillar to post—makes them more amusingly hateful than the assassins who populated 70s movies. It also adds an interesting level of generational conflict between those, like Hackman and Smith, who have earned their expertise and those who have simply been raised on computer games and turned loose on the real world.

TIME, 11/30/98, p. 111, Richard Schickel

With a thong in his heart, an otherwise respectable lawyer named Robert Clayton Dean (Will Smith) drops into a store to buy his wife some sexy lingerie for Christmas. There he bumps into—or rather is bumped into by—an old, if mysteriously agitated, acquaintance. Next thing he knows, he's an Enemy of the State—his house, his marriage, his job, all trashed by powerful, shadowy forces. There being no limit to their depravity, they even invalidate his credit cards.

There's a plausible explanation—well, all right, a plot line that made some kind of sense to producer Jerry Bruckheimer—for the troubles visited on this perfectly nice chap. What he doesn't know, but we do, is that his pal has dropped a computer disc into one of his shopping bags. On it is irrefutable photographic evidence that a Congressman has been murdered by agents of a faceless government security agency for opposing its plan to destroy privacy as we know it in the U.S.

You can doubtless imagine just how strenuous an effort—much of it shot in raked angles and presented in quick cuts by director Tony Scott—is required of Dean to get his life back and his tormentors chastened. You can probably imagine, as well, the gleam, sheen and extensiveness of the high-tech machinery that a well-endowed bureaucracy can deploy to torment a citizen on which its baleful eye has fallen. You may even be able to predict the chipper amorality of the techies manning the keyboards and terminals. What do they care about ends when the means to it are so much fun to play with?

All this—not to mention the film's paranoid take on big, secretive government—is familiar stuff. Nor are the principal characters unknown quantities. Under pressure, Smith's attorney demonstrates the kind of stamina and physical agility that people confined to desk jobs find within themselves only in the movies. His sole ally, Brill, a former government operative who has turned into a rogue counterintelligence specialist, is played by Gene Hackman as a funny, cranky imitation—right down to the horn-rimmed glasses—of the snoop he played so memorably in "The Conversation" almost 25 years ago. And, as their chief nemesis, Jon Voight does another variation on his late-life specialty: the midnight conspirator whose puffy face stands in such curiously menacing contrast to his steely soul.

There are really only two surprising things about the movie. The first is that it works rather nicely. Strong technique, intensely applied to a project by a director like Scott or by actors like the ones working for him here, offers us simple and not entirely common rewards. The bigger surprise is the ending supplied by screenwriter David Marconi. All one can say about it, without spoiling the fun, is that no justice meted out at the conclusion of any action movie in recent memory is more poetically just, more brashly astonishing or better worth the rigors of the trip to it.

VILLAGE VOICE, 11/24/98, p. 122, Dennis Lim

Enemy of the State isn't really a smart film, but it makes a concerted stab at pretending to be one, which counts as a massive step forward in the vacuum of thought known as Bruckheimer Films. Directed by Tony Scott from David Marconi's patchy but engagingly busy script (reportedly much doctored), the movie certainly covers its bases: it shrewdly zeroes in on au courant *Truman Show* surveillance fantasies, foams responsibly at the mouth about Fourth Amendment issues, respectfully references the definitive wiretap-paranoia pic *The Conversation* by casting Gene Hackman as a reclusive gizmo wiz, and competently goes through the foolproof *Fugitive* motions with the help of the new Harrison Ford, Will Smith.

Smith plays a hotshot D.C. lawyer whose life promptly falls apart when an old college buddy slips him a disk while being pursued to his death by mysterious men in suits. The film gathers momentum slowly, and is a little shapeless, but that somehow works to its advantage: it feels twistier and more unpredictable than it actually is.

Scott may be a hack, but he's no Michael Bay. He gets some mileage from sped-up, spliced-in surveillance footage, and the aerial satellite shots (the film's cautionary message is, don't look up) lend an extra charge to the rooftop action, though someone should really tell him that shooting at a 45-degree angle does nothing besides give the audience a stiff neck.

Its subject matter is creepy and eminently exploitable, but *Enemy of the State* is too concerned with showing you a good time to tap into primal anxieties. It eventually ditches you-are-being-watched dread for safe escapist stuff like buildings blowing up (you have to wonder what someone like David Fincher might have brought to the film). Also, the bad guys are curiously nonthreatening. A waxy-looking Jon Voight plays a megalomaniacal but not especially sinister N.S.A. head, and the other government ops are even less villainous—a couple, in fact, are decidedly hipsterish (Scream's Jamie Kennedy and *Buffy the Vampire Slayer*'s Seth Green, two appealingly quirky young actors who aren't given much to do but are nonetheless fun to watch). The net result is fairly low-tension yet satisfyingly off-kilter. Put it down to some fluke combination of half-baked hackwork and conscious convention-bucking, and pray that Mr. Bruckheimer doesn't try to mangle it into a formula.

Also reviewed in:
CHICAGO TRIBUNE, 11/20/98, Friday/p. A, Michael Wilmington
NATION, 12/14/98, p. 42, Stuart Klawans
NEW YORK TIMES, 11/20/98, p. E1, Janet Maslin
VARIETY, 11/16-22/98, p. 33, Emanuel Levy
WASHINGTON POST, 11/20/98, p. F1, Rita Kempley
WASHINGTON POST, 11/20/98, Weekend/p. 49, Michael O'Sullivan

EVER AFTER

A Twentieth Century Fox release of a Mireille Soria production. *Producer:* Mireille Soria and Tracey Trench. *Director:* Andy Tennant. *Screenplay:* Susannah Grant, Andy Tennant, and Rick Parks. *Director of Photography:* Andrew Dunn. *Editor:* Roger Bondelli. *Music:* George Fenton. *Music Editor:* Graham Sutton. *Sound:* Simon Kaye and (music) John Richards. *Sound Editor:* Campbell Askew. *Casting:* Priscilla John and Lucinda Syson. *Production Designer:* Michael Howells. *Art Director:* David Allday. *Set Decorator:* Judy Farr. *Special Effects:* Alan Senior and John Clark. *Costumes:* Jenny Beavan. *Make-up:* Tina Earnshaw. *Make-up (Anjelica Huston):* Tina Earnshaw. *Make-up (Drew Barrymore):* Kimberly Greene. *Stunt Coordinator:* Graeme Crowther. *Running time:* 120 minutes. *MPAA Rating:* PG-13.

CAST: Drew Barrymore (Danielle); Anjelica Huston (Rodmilla); Dougray Scott (Prince Henry); Patrick Godfrey (Leonardo da Vinci); Megan Dodds (Marguerite); Melanie Lynskey (Jacqueline); Timothy West (King Francis); Judy Parfitt (Queen Marie); Jeroen Krabbé (Auguste); Lee Ingleby (Gustave); Kate Lansbury (Paulette); Matyelok Gibbs (Louise);

Walter Sparrow (Maurice);   Jeanne Moreau (Grande Dame);   Anna Maguire (Young Danielle); Richard O'Brien (Pierre Le Pieu);   Peter Gunn (Capt. Laurent);   Joerg Stadler (Wilhelm Grimm);   Andrew Henderson (Jacob Grimm);   Toby Jones (Royal Page);   Virginia Garcia (Princess Gertrude);   Al Hunter Ashton (Cargomaster);   Mark Lewis (Gypsy Leader);   Howard Attfield (Jeweller);   Ricki Cuttell (Young Gustave);   Ricardo Cruz (Cracked Skull);   John Walters (Butler);   Elizabeth Earl (Young Marguerite);   Alex Pooley (Young Jacqueline);   Janet Henfrey (Celeste);   Ursula Jones (Isabella);   Amanda Walker (Old Noblewoman);   Rupam Maxwell (Marquis de Limoges);   Tony Doyle (Driver Royal Carriage);   Christian Marc (King of Spain);   Elvira Stevenson (Queen of Spain);   Erick Awanzino (Short Bald Man);   Susan Field (Laundry Supervisor);   François Velter and Dominic Rols (Choirmen);   Jean-Pierre Mazieres (Cardinal).

LOS ANGELES TIMES, 7/31/98, Calendar/p. 1, Kenneth Turan

The urge to update the classics, to modernize all around, can be an overpowering one. After all, aren't we the smartest, most sophisticated people who ever lived? Why shouldn't we remake everything in our own image?

The well-meaning, erratic "Ever After," starring Drew Barrymore as an empowered, post-feminist Cinderella, demonstrates that successful modernization is harder to pull off than it seems. While it's difficult to dislike what this film tries to do, the way it does it is more problematic.

Why, the thinking went, should Cinderella be so dam passive, nodding off like Sleeping Beauty until a likely prince hits the neighborhood? Why not make her a fearless and liberated 16th century avatar of girl power who makes her own breaks and is smarter than everyone except, well, Leonardo da Vinci?

The idea is an excellent one, and Barrymore, an actress who radiates spunky good cheer, was the natural and appropriate choice to play "I gotta be me" heroine Danielle and many of the film's effective moments can be credited to her spirited performance.

Though director Andy Tennant was enthusiastic about putting this kind of spin on Cinderella, his touch turns out to be counterproductive. Tennant's sensibility, witness previous films "It Takes Two" and "Fools Rush In," is on the sweetly sentimental side, and "Ever After" tends as well toward being too insistently endearing and pleased with itself.

After a brief mid-19th century prelude, in which an unnamed Grande Dame (a magisterial Jeanne Moreau) tells the brothers Grimm that they've got the Cinderella story all wrong, the film heads back in history to old France.

There we meet Danielle, a frisky and happy 8-year-old tomboy. But a twist of fate turns the girl into a sad-eyed orphan who spends the next decade doing chores for wicked stepmother Rodmilla (Anjelica Huston) and her two daughters, the conniving Marguerite (Megan Dodds) and the more amiable Jacqueline (Melanie Lynskey of "Heavenly Creatures").

Meanwhile, handsome Prince Henry (Welsh actor Dougray Scott) is having difficulties of his own. Not interested in being defined by his position or marrying the Spanish princess his father the king has in mind, Henry wants "nothing more than to be free of my gilded cage." Delighted when Da Vinci shows up as a kind of artist-in-residence at court, he pleads with the great man to drag his father into the 16th century.

Henry and Danielle meet cute not once but twice. The first time, she knocks him off a horse with a well-aimed apple; the second she masquerades as a noblewoman to gain the freedom of a loyal servant.

Though he doesn't recognize that it's the same woman he's dealing with, Henry is consistently charmed by this feisty young person who is always quoting from Sir Thomas More ("Utopia" is her favorite book) and lecturing him on his arrogant insensitivity whenever she has the opportunity.

"Ever After" tries to be amusing about this relationship, but the script (written by Susannah Grant and Tennant and Rick Parks) has trouble mastering a consistently funny tone. What it produces instead is glib, aren't-we-cute dialogue that gives anachronistic lines, such as "Have you lost your marbles?" and "Sit down before you have a stroke," a place of pride.

An allied difficulty is the film's unaccountable idea that sentiments that would be ho-hum if said in modern dress—Henry's gee-whiz "How do you do it, live each day with this kind of passion?" are somehow effective if delivered by people in costume. It ain't necessarily so.

Counteracting all of this as much as any one actress can is Huston, who gives a thoroughly delightful performance as the troublesome stepmother. Arch, haughty and imperious, she adds the perfect spin to her dialogue and provides the kind of energy the film is fortunate to have.

This Cinderella does without a pumpkin, thank you very much, but it does have a glass slipper (designed by Salvatore Ferragamo) and it follows the familiar line of a prince falling in love with a phantom all the way through to what has to be called a fairy-tale ending.

While a modernization like this will clearly find favor with the self-esteem builders of the world, it's hard not to notice that what's on screen is lacking in the spark and brio (not to mention the language of Shakespeare) that made Baz Luhnnann's snazzy updating of "Romeo & Juliet" so strong. Though it has its moments, "Ever After" never completely finds its footing, either in its century or our own.

NEW STATESMAN, 10/9/98, p. 36, Gerald Kaufman

This formula movie fails to understand who invented its formula. "Ever After" opens with a grande dame (Jeanne Moreau, whom I hope got extremely well paid for demeaning herself in this way) launching the film's flashback structure by summoning the Brothers Grimm to hear her story. Yet that story quite possibly the most irritating variant yet of Cinderella, was invented by Perrault.

Twentieth-Century Fox has done everything it can think of to tart up the legend. Although Drew Barrymore's slab-faced portrayal fails to bring Cinderella to life, the supporting cast is pretty classy. The excellent Timothy West, as the king of France, does the kind of turn which was Frank Morgan's routine in old MGM movies.

Also on hand, sending this movie into the outer regions of zaniness, is none other than Leonardo da Vinci (Patrick Godfrey), who is given the triplicate function of comic relief, eccentric inventor and matchmaker ("A life without love is no life at all"). Strayed in from another film entirely ("The Addams Family," actually) is Anjelica Huston as the wicked stepmother. Huston, made up to look like the evil queen in Disney's "Snow White" but speaking with the posh accent of a Sloane Ranger, is provided with the only dialogue in the film that approaches originality or wit ("No matter how bad things get, they can always get worse"). Yet, even with location shooting in six French chateaux and magic slippers supplied by Ferragamo, "Ever After" cannot be salvaged.

NEW YORK POST, 7/31/98, p. 37, Rod Dreher

"This is not your grandmother's Cinderella," say the press notes for "Ever After," as if that were a virtue.

This sweet, but very slight, revisionist version of the familiar fairy tale tries to infuse 16th-century France with a modern "girl power' sensibility. Here we have spunky Drew Barrymore, she of the tattooed heinie, as a cute-but-tough commoner chick who, far from being rescued by a man, liberates a lovelorn prince from the shackling conventions of royalty.

"Ever After" doesn't mean to be more than a creamy little bonbon, so it would be silly to hold it to high standards of historical accuracy. Still, shining the light of *liberte, egalite* and *fraternite* into the grand chateaux and upon these lavish costumes has a flattening effect, particularly when dragged down by such pedestrian dialogue ("Have you lost your marbles?").

Relevant, shmelevant—this kind of ill-executed modernization shoos out the magic that provides fairy tales with their enduring appeal. "Ever After" isn't a bad movie, by any stretch, and no doubt teen girls will have a fine time with it.

But, for me, watching "Ever After" was like sitting through one of those lame contemporary church services, where mystery and ceremony and sparkling artifice have been cast off, and the heights of ho-hummery duly scaled.

The movie opens with an aged queen (the wonderful Jeanne Moreau, croaking softly like a filter-tipped Harvey Fierstein) summoning the Brothers Grimm to let them know they got the Cinderella story all wrong. She flashes back to tell the story of her ancestor, Danielle (Barrymore), a perky tomboy and the pomme de her papa's peepers.

Pop (Jeroen Krabbe) introduces her to the intellectual pleasures of Sir Thomas More, and if you had no trouble buying Elisabeth Shue as a nuclear scientist in "The Saint," you should be able to swallow the idea Of "Utopia" as Drew Barrymore's favorite book. Alas, alas, her father dies shortly after marrying the evil Baroness Rodmilla (Anjelica Huston), and Danielle becomes a servant girl in her own father's home.

All grown up, Danielle meets Prince Henry (Dougray Scott) by beaning him with apples before realizing who he is. Later, she runs into him on palace grounds, disguised as a courtier in a scheme to free an unjustly imprisoned servant. Henry falls hard for Danielle, not knowing that she's really a commoner.

They carry on a secret romance while Danielle's wicked stepmother Rodmilla, the Sir Edmund Hillary of social climbers, plots to have Henry marry her beautiful but catty daughter Marguerite (Megan Dodds). Henry's folks, the king and queen of France, are pressuring him to marry a Spanish princess for reasons of state and social convention.

Naturally, true love will win out, but not before we see plucky Danielle save the prince's fanny from marauding Gypsies; deal harshly with a mossy-toothed creep (Richard O'Brien, who played Riff-Raff in "The Rocky Horror Picture Show") that Rodmilla sells her to; team up with Leonardo da Vinci (Patrick Godfrey); and confront the kind of social prejudice that leads to unhappy marriages and the marginalization of ethnic minorities and the economically disadvantaged.

Anjelica Huston's perfectly wretched stepmother is a welcome splash of vinegar that cuts a lot of the bland earnestness here.

If "Ever After" had half of Huston's panache, it would be a stylish charmer instead of nothing special. It's a treat to look at, though, having been filmed in the velvet-lined jewelry box of France's castle-studded Dordogne region. It's a fairy-tale setting without much of a fairy tale in it.

NEWSDAY, 7/31/98, Part II/p. B3, John Anderson

The idea of Drew Barrymore in a Cinderella movie sounded delicious: singing mice, fairy godmothers, enchanted pumpkins and a bouncy, blond Barrymore, whose smile alone has lifted movies like "The Wedding Singer" out of the drainage ditch of banality. Add Anjelica Huston as the wicked stepmother and the forecast called for tart archness and arch tartness.

But "Ever After," highly enjoyable and surprisingly intelligent, turns out to be something else entirely. No mice. No songs. No pumpkins. There is a glass slipper (it's the size of a small gunboat), but the closest thing to a fairy godmother is Leonardo da Vinci (Patrick Godfrey)—and given the sexual orientation of the historical Leonardo, that's a rather broad joke for a children's story. But then, it isn't strictly a "children's" story, either.

It is, instead, "a" Cinderella story, with a fabricated framing device involving the Brothers Grimm and a French royal played by Jeanne Moreau (talk about typecasting!) who flash back to feudal France and the alleged inspiration for history's hundreds of Cinderella tales: a poor peasant girl named Danielle (Barrymore) whose father has died, leaving her with a social-climbing stepmother (Anjelica Huston), two stepsisters and a copy of Thomas More's "Utopia."

"Ever After" sort of brushes up against the conventions of the traditional "cinder girl" fable. Barrymore, sturdy and dark, plays a young woman whose decisions have basically been her own: Rough and rustic, she's chosen to stay with her stepmother, Rodmilla, in order to keep her father's household together, even as Rodmilla sells off the candlesticks and the servants to pay her debts. Rodmilla—a character custom-made for Huston, who's terrific—is a complex character whose motivations may be base, but not baseless. Only one stepsister—the more conventionally beautiful Marguerite (Megan Dodds)—is inherently nasty; Jacqueline (Melanie Lynskey of "Heavenly Creatures") is sympathetic to Danielle's plight and does what she can to keep Marguerite from marrying the prince.

Oh, yes, the prince. There is a prince, and he's charming. Henry (Dougray Scott) isn't quite as smart as Danielle; it takes him all of the movie to discover that's she's a peasant, not the comtesse she's pretended to be (in a ruse to free a sold-off servant). He's goodhearted, though, and trainable: He listens to Danielle's democratic ideas; he doesn't even mind when she saves him from being killed by initially evil but ultimately festive gypsies. He has a bit of a problem with mixed marriages (class, not religion), but good sense and Leonardo have a way of setting these things straight.

Directed and co-written by Andy Tennant ("Fools Rush In"), "Ever After" takes a decidedly 20th-Century feminist stance, revels in the mud and squalor of 16th-Century France (they actually shot it in France) while at the same time giving it all a golden glow. It's a tad too long, but the film contains very little that isn't almost believable, or at least not totally unbelievable—all except the rating, which, as far as I can determine, is based on one bovine-scatalogical expletive that's more funny than offensive. Take the kids. Take your mother. "Ever After" is—like Danielle herself—solid and charming.

NEWSWEEK, 8/3/98, p. 66, Laura Shapiro and Corie Brown

[*Ever After* was reviewed jointly with *Parent Trap*; see Shapiro and Brown's review of that film.]

SIGHT AND SOUND, 10/98, p. 43, Charlotte O'Sullivan

Eight-year old Danielle's life changes when her beloved father marries the Baroness Rodmilla. Only days after the wedding, he collapses and dies. Years pass. Now 16-years-old and practically a servant, Danielle accidentally meets and argues with Prince Henry, doomed to marry the Princess of Spain, according to the wishes of his father. That same day, Henry rescues Leonardo da Vinci from a band of gypsies. Later, Danielle dresses like a noblewoman and goes to court, where she impresses the Prince. He begs to know her name and she identifies herself as a countess.

Rodmilla is determined Henry shall marry her eldest daughter, Marguerite. However, through a series of chance meetings, "the Countess" and the Prince fall in love. The King plans a ball, at which his son must announce his wife of choice; otherwise he must marry the Princess. He plans to announce Danielle is his choice but she, fearing her identity will be exposed, tells the Prince she can never see him again.

The day of the ball: Rodmilla discovers Danielle's secret meetings with the Prince and locks her in the cellar. Danielle eventually appears at the ball—rescued by da Vinci. But when Rodmilla reveals Danielle's true identity, the Prince rejects her. The Prince realises his mistake, but by this time Danielle has been sold to landowner Pierre Le Pieu. She manages to free herself. The pair marry.

Socialism and fairy tales tend not to mix, but for a moment in *Ever After,* they play footsie. In this ambitious version of 'Cinderella', the heroine is given to quoting Thomas More's *Utopia,* a tract generally thought to have influenced Marx, which (among other things) decries the need for private property and hereditary privilege, calling instead for a society where all are "partners equally". Set in sixteenth century France, *Ever After* is the world according to More: the Prince's father appears a typical tyrant—war-mongering, greedy and inflexible while the wicked stepmother, Rodmilla, is a typical noblewoman, selling servants so she can pay off her debts.

However, *Ever After* soon grows coy. *Utopia* is an extraordinary book, not least for its lack of faith in the rich and noble. The traveller who has 'discovered' the distant land Utopia, Raphael Hythloday, is constantly entreated to share his wisdom with princes, but over and over again asserts the uselessness of such a project: "If I should propose to any king wholesome decrees think you not that I should forthwith either be driven away or else made a laughing stock?" This is where he differs from the makers of *Ever After.* In the latter, both Danielle and Leonardo da Vinci act as advisers to Prince Henry, critiquing and correcting his arrogant ways. They have a more secondhand, but similarly significant, effect upon the King— causing him to become a benevolent father to the realm, an enlightened despot. In other words, where *Utopia* seems doubtful about the feudal system of government altogether (and given More's later beheading, presciently so), *Ever After* merely wants to improve it.

Of course, since this is a mainstream movie we shouldn't be too surprised. It does, though, place *Ever After* firmly in the blood-will-out camp, along with *The Lion King* and *Anastasia*—children's films which promote the idea that the only alternative to a 'bad' king is a 'good' one. This is reinforced visually, the camera interested in the big picture—grand, implacable nature or beautiful chateaux set in dewy countryside—not little details. The script is equally romantically conservative. It makes sense, for example, that the naughty Gypsies prove friendly. They steal from the rich a little (though Prince Henry saves the *Mona Lisa* from falling into their grubby hands), but since they belong to the forest and hence nature they are repeatedly identified as benign. In the same way, Rodmilla's crime is that she does not respect 'tradition' or property (she sells off Danielle's land and all the objects within it to pay for Marguerite's trifles). On top of this, she flirts (most ferociously) with a dwarf, in order to get her way. In other words, she is a deviant, a woman whose tastes and instincts unravel the logic of privilege.

Having said that, Anjelica Huston's skills as an actress make the kinks in Rodmilla's Iron Lady armour rather interesting. Indeed, when she stares at Drew Barrymore's Danielle, uttering the line, "there's so much of your father in you... [comic pause] your features are so masculine", it's mesmerising. But this is not just good acting. Like Barrymore, Huston is a celebrity by birth—someone whose face bears traces of "the father" both literally and metaphorically. In this interaction, for once, the psychosexual rivalry between Danielle and Rodmilla comes to life.

The rest of the film is a hodge-podge, impossible to take seriously, hard to enjoy thoroughly. Barrymore is cutesie to the bone, undermining the obligatory shows of 'girl power'. The earnest, highbrow tone also sits uneasily with chaotic attempts at irreverence (encapsulated in Leonardo da Vinci's ridiculous lines). It's certainly an improvement, though, on director Andy Tennant's last project *Fools Rush In*. Where that tale of love-across-the class-barrier got lost in the shuffle, *Ever After* stands out as genuinely bizarre. As for More's head, it must be turning in its grave.

VILLAGE VOICE, 8/11/98, p. 143, Justine Elias

When any instance of sudden Hollywood fame or improbable athletic victory is described as "a real Cinderella story," it's hard to see why anyone would want to be compared to such an unremarkable character. She is nice. She has special feet. She has, like most fairy-tale heroines, not a single girlfriend her own age. She is, in short, suspicious. There have been some 500 versions of Cinderella over the past 1000 years, but the best-known go like this: the heroine's trials begin when her mother dies and her father remarries. Next, you get an unmarried prince, party-crashing, a lost shoe, and the stepsisters mutilating their feet in a vain attempt to claim it. From the most familiar variations, here are the highlights:

Charles Perrault, 1697: Cinderella is aided by a fairy godmother and mice-turned-coachmen. Her stepsisters get forgiveness, husbands and real estate.

Brothers Grimm, 1826: Cinderella is aided by birds and a magic tree that grows on her mother's grave. Her stepsisters are blinded when birds peck out their eyes.

Disney, 1950: G-rated cartoon. A lot of singing. The stepmother's face moves, but Cinderella's doesn't.

The Ice Princess (made for German TV and shown here on cable in 1996): A demented ice-stravaganza staring Olympic gold medalist Katarina Witt, who impresses the prince by skating and performing rap music.

Cinderella (ABC TV movie, 1997): Pop stars Witney Houston and Brandy, color-blind casting, more singing.

Now there's *Ever After: A Cinderella Story*, a version that attempts to define its heroine not by what she is (a mild, put-upon, rescuable girl) but by what she does. And in the person of the cheerful and plucky Drew Barrymore, Cinderella does it all: she runs the family farm, saves fellow servants from slavery, hangs out with Leonardo da Vinci, ambles through the forest with her truffle-sniffing pig, until one day her schedule is interrupted by an eligible prince (Dougray Scott, suitably dreamy). Director Andy Tennant presents an activist Cinderella, and the movie is so crammed with public-spirited spectacle that it becomes absurdly entertaining, like watching Alec Baldwin pretend he's not campaigning for government office.

After all intriguing prologue—Jeanne Moreau as a grand 19th-century lady, telling the Brothers Grimm that they've gotten the tale all wrong—it's right back to the old femme-on-femme rivalry with the step-family (Anjelica Huston, doing a very funny Lady Bracknell act, and Megan Dodds and Melanie Lynskey as the spoiled daughters). Late in the story, Cinderella is sold into marriage to the villainous Monsieur Le Pieu (Richard O'Brien, Riff Raff from *The Rocky Horror Picture Show*), and things seem about to turn all gothic and Angela Carter-esque, as in the recent, lurid cable TV version of *Snow White* (subtitle *A Tale of Terror*). By this time, however, it's clear that this modern, well-read girl could just deconstruct the bad guy into submission. And, though she won't get a very thoughtful answer, this Cinderella dares to ask the most troubling question: Why must she and her stepmother be pitted against each other in the first place?

Also reviewed in:
CHICAGO TRIBUNE, 7/31/98, Friday/p. A, Michael Wilmington
NEW YORK TIMES, 7/31/98, p. E12, Stephen Holden
VARIETY, 7/27-8/2/98, p. 52, Leonard Klady
WASHINGTON POST, 7/31/98, p. B1, Rita Kempley
WASHINGTON POST, 7/31/98, Weekend/p. 47, Michael O'Sullivan

EVEREST

A Polartec presentation of a MacGillivray Freeman Films prouction.   *Producer:* Greg
MacGillivray, Alec Lorimore, and Stephen Judson.   *Director:* Greg MacGillivray, David
Breashears, and Stephen Judson. *Screenplay:* Tim Cahill and Stephen Judson.   *Director of
Photography:* David Breashears. *Editor:* Stephen Judson.   *Sound:* Ken Teaney and Marshal
Garlington. *Sound Editor:* Harry Cohen and Anne Sciabelli. *Music:* Steve Wood, Daniel May,
and George Harrison. *Running time:* 45 minutes. *MPAA Rating:* Not Rated.

CAST: Liam Neeson (Narrator).

LOS ANGELES TIMES, 10/16/98, Calendar/p. 8, Kenneth Turan

If you haven't quite gotten around to climbing the world's highest mountain, "Everest," the new
Imax look at the top of the world, will both show you what you've been missing and thoroughly
discourage you from attempting it yourself.

Just now reaching metropolitan Los Angeles seven months after its premiere, "Everest" is on
its way to becoming the most successful Imax film ever, and that's not only because its super-
large screen format is ideal for showing the astonishing heights of this 29,028-foot peak.

Also a factor is that circumstances put the Imax filmmakers on the mountain in May 1996 as
a real-life nightmare was unfolding. This was the moment when, as detailed in the best-selling
"Into Thin Air," eight members of other expeditions died in attempts on the summit.

Though none of that tragedy was filmed, a part of "Everest's" 48-minute length is devoted to
rescue efforts that led to the miraculous survival of climber Beck Weathers in wind-chill
conditions of 100 below zero and to the understandably emotional reaction the Imax climbers had
to the deaths of people who were friends and colleagues.

The idea that the bulky Imax camera could ever be transported up through the dread "death
zone" to the very top of Everest sounds preposterous. But in fact a slimmed-down model,
weighing 48 pounds when fully loaded and capable of operating at 40 degrees below zero, was
blessed by the Buddhist monks of Thyangboche Monastery and carried by hardy Sherpas all the
way to the summit.

Up there with the camera was David Breashears, the film's cinematographer and (along with
Greg MacGillivray and Stephen Judson) one of its three directors. Because the Imax camera's
magazine holds only 90 seconds of film before it needs to be replaced, Breashears and company
tried not to shoot anything that wasn't going to be in the final film. The result is a dizzying
collection of heroic vistas that words are not equal to describing.

"Everest" not only shows us the beauty of the mountain, it also details how painfully arduous
getting up and down on it is. Everest's most celebrated obstacles, with names like the Lhotse Face
and the Khumbu Icefall, are shown in discouraging detail, as are ice crevices that seem to extend
downward to eternity.

Expected to surmount all these difficulties was a four-person climbing team, the most prominent
being American Ed Viesturs, who had scaled Everest three times previously and who was enough
of a zealot to convince his wife, Paula, to take their honeymoon on the mountain. Joining them
were two female climbers, Araceli Segarra of Spain and Sumiyuo Tsuzuki of Japan, and Jamling
Norgay, the son of the great Sherpa Tenzing Norgay who had accompanied Sir Edmund Hillary
on Everest's first successful climb in 1953.

Watching these people train in preparation for the climb led to some of the film's most compelling footage, including shots of Segarra doing perilous rock-climbing in Cabo San Lucas and Viesturs taking a biking vacation in Utah's scenic badlands.

"Everest's" visuals are all they should be, but the film's script leaves a considerable amount to be desired despite being co-written by veteran outdoor journalist Tim Cahill. With narrator Liam Neeson getting all wound up about "a place where only the strong and lucky survive," a lot of "Everest's" narrative exhibits the gee-whiz sentimentality of true-life adventure and exploration films of the 1930s.

The climbers deserve all the acclaim they get; it would be nicer if it wasn't so portentously done.

NEW YORK POST, 3/6/98, p. 46, Larry Worth

Plain and simple, "Everest" takes moviemaking to new heights—in every sense of the phrase.

it's not only the best IMAX film to date, it features some of the most spectacular, breathtaking photography on record. And within the 45-minute running time, it also captures the heart-stopping excitement and unmitigated foolhardiness of attempting to climb the world's highest peak.

There's also a newsworthy factor to "Everest" since IMAX producers were scaling the mountain when tragedy struck fellow hikers in 1996. Climbers from two other expeditions were caught near the summit by the fiercest of blizzards, resulting in eight deaths.

The coverage of those horrifying hours—including a lost hiker's phone call to his wife in New Zealand, naming their unborn child before freezing to death—is positively bone-chilling. So are the teary reactions of the IMAX crew.

The fact that viewers get to know each member of the IMAX team (which included honeymooners!) also helps set the film apart, giving ample reason to care about their fate. Whether spinning prayer wheels in Katmandu prior to the ascent, walking on shaky ladders over bottomless chasms or finding a foothold on a wall of ice, the team emerges as bigger-than-life adventurers.

But the real star here is the mountain—a 29,028-foot, fear-inducing entity where the snow blows straight up, avalanches are a daily occurrence (shown at one point coming straight for the camera lens), temperatures dip to 100 degrees below zero and thin air leaves coughers with a broken rib.

Enhanced by Liam Neeson's soulful narration and hiker David Breashears' tight direction, the result is one fascinating, eye-popping moment after another—all while documenting the IMAX cameras' true *raison d'etre*. What other technology could provide such a dizzying, harrowing, exhilarating journey to a frozen hell on earth?

Indeed, the thrill-a-minute scenario makes "Everest" a must-see for all—even heavy-duty coughers.

NEWSDAY, 3/6/98, Part II/p. B7, Bob Heisler

"Everest," a too-brief visit to the 29,028-foot summit of Mt. Everest with an expedition that is part science, part death wish, part celebration of the human spirit, asks much from its audience.

For the most part, you have to supply your own emotion. It can be a moving experience if you forget the storyline, sit back and let the overwhelming IMAX screen propel you to the top of the world. All that's missing is the cold.

Sit in the last rows of the middle of the theater; these provide the best perspective for this two-dimensional collection of soaring images from the 1996 Everest climbing season. After acclimating to the vista, though, you're left with beautiful pictures filmed by David Breashears and his crew. Emotion is left to the narration to describe.

And there is human emotion, if only in the text. Members of other teams are caught in a hurricane of snow at 30 degrees below zero. Eight people die. In the best Hollywood storyline, one of the climbers ties a Buddhist prayer flag to a stake at the summit to honor the spirit of his father, who guided Sir Edmund Hillary on the first successful trip to the top.

But—and maybe because your senses are only teased by the IMAX format—you never quite share in one of humankind's great challenges. These are real people, not characters in a movie, but you still expect them to reach their goal. In the end, you do not ask, "Why did they do that?" but only "How did they get that shot?" And of course the answer is only: "Very carefully."

When the ride is over, walk down the five flights of stairs. After Everest, using the escalator seems a little silly.

VILLAGE VOICE, 3/17/98, p. 68, Gary Susman

Perhaps not even the world's largest film format can do justice to the world's tallest mountain. *Everest,* an IMAX 2D film, is an incredible technical achievement—codirector David Breashears shot much of the movie in double-digit subzero temperatures with a 25-pound IMAX camera he lugged to the top of the mountain himself—yet it manages to trivialize the mountain's awesome power to thwart even the most experienced climbers.

Shot during the notorious 1996 storm that killed eight climbers from various expeditions, Everest features a team whose stated reasons for climbing vary from the highly personal (Jamling Tenzing Norgay wants to duplicate the feat of his father) to the almost callously trivial (newlywed Ed Viesturs jokes repeatedly that "I figured Everest would be a cheap place to honeymoon"). The IMAX camera captures Everest's eerie vistas and vertiginous cliffs, but it has difficulty conveying the horror and grief of the lost moments of Rob Hall, an expert Everest guide who freezes to death while Viesturs listens helplessly on the radio. When the film's climbers finally reach the summit, an orchestral "Here Comes the Sun" swells on the soundtrack. Surely both Everest and those who surmount its challenges deserve more reverent treatment.

Also reviewed in:
NEW YORK TIMES, 3/6/98, p. E22, Lawrence Van Gelder
VARIETY, 3/16-22/98, p. 64, Godfrey Cheshire

FACULTY, THE

A Dimension Films release of a Los Hooligans production. *Executive Producer:* Bob Weinstein and Harvey Weinstein.   *Producer:* Elizabeth Avellan.   *Director:* Robert Rodriquez. *Screenplay:* Kevin Williamson.   *Based on a story by:* David Wechter and Bruce Kimmel. *Director of Photography:* Enrique Chediak. *Editor:* Robert Rodriguez. *Music:* Marco Beltrami. *Music Editor:* Billb Abbott and Jay Richardson. *Sound:* Steve Nelson and (music) John Kurlander. *Sound Editor:* Phil Benson. *Casting:* Mary Vernieu and Anne McCarthy. *Production Designer:* Cary White. *Art Director:* Ed Vega. *Set Decorator:* Jeanette Scott. *Special Effects:* John McLeod. *Costumes:* Michael T. Boyd. *Make-up:* Ermahn Ospina. *Stunt Coordinator:* Bobby Brown. *Running time:* 111 minutes. *MPAA Rating:* R.

CAST: Jordana Brewster (Delilah); Clea DuVall (Stokely); Laura Harris (Marybeth); Josh Hartnett (Zeke); Shawn Hatosy (Stan); Salma Hayek (Nurse Harper); Famke Janssen (Miss Burke); Piper Laurie (Mrs. Olson); Chris McDonald (Casey's Dad); Bebe Neuwirth (Principal Drake); Robert Patrick (Coach Dick Willis); Usher Raymond (Gabe); Jon Stewart (Mr. Furlong); Daniel von Bargen (Mr. Tate); Elijah Wood (Casey); Summer Phoenix (F*%# You Girl); Jon Abrahams (F*%# You Boy); Susan Willis (Mrs. Brummel); Pete Janssen (Meat); Christina Rodriguez (Tattoo Girl); Danny Masterson (F*%# Up 1); Wiley Wiggins (F*%# Up 2); Harry Knowles (Mr. Knowles); Donna Casey (Tina); Louis Black (Mr. Lewis); Eric Jungmann and Chris Viteychuk (Freshmen); Jim Johnston (P.E. Teacher); Libby Villari (Casey's Mom); Duane Martin and Katherine Willis (Officers); Mike Lutz (Hornet Mascot); Doug Aarniokoski (Brun Coach); Gary Hecker (Creature Vocals); Gus Araiza, Ray Melendez, and Danny Sasser (Students); Mark Edward Walters (Front Row Fan).

LOS ANGELES TIMES, 12/25/98, Calendar/p. 22, Kevin Thomas

Before you can say "Invasion of the Body Snatchers," a group of students at a small-city Ohio high school begin suspecting that their teachers are turning into aliens. Can the student body be far behind?

Amid the traditional year-end deluge of prestige pictures, a smart, lively and unpretentious exploitation picture is always a welcome treat.

And that's exactly the pleasure of seeing "The Faculty," a rip-roaring collaboration between director Robert Rodriguez and writer Kevin Williamson. It's a consistently funny and clever teen horror flick that in the Williamson "Scream" tradition of hip references to old films also offers nods to "The Thing," "Forbidden Planet" and "The Puppet Masters." Be assured that the filmmakers fill the screen with organisms a bit more active and grotesque than "The Body Snatchers'" famously ominous pods.

This well-crafted film plugs into universal teenage fears and emotions: Whoever made it through high school without either feeling one's self or everybody else to be an alien? "The Faculty" even sends an implicit message about the value of disparate kids needing to pull together and really using their heads if, in this instance, humanity is to survive.

After all, the aliens are out there trying to lure the young people with the promise of a fearless, eternally successful and glamorous life—but at the price of a total loss of emotion.

In adapting a story by David Wechter and Bruce Kimmel, Williamson draws six sharply defined roles for young people and an equal number for their elders, and Rodriguez elicits from one and all succinct, on-the-money performances. Jordana Brewster's Delilah is the school's top girl, and don't you forget it. When her likable football star boyfriend Stan (Shawn Hatosy) reveals he wants to quit the team and buckle down to his books, she threatens to dump him as bad for her image. Delilah also hurls homophobic epithets to Clea DuVall's Stokely, a sullen but very smart outsider, simply because she's a nonconformist. (Teen sexual insecurities typically breed homophobia, but you wish the filmmakers could have suggested that it's not a cool thing to feel or express.)

Laura Harris' blond Marybeth is the new girl in school, desperate to make friends and feel as if she belongs, and Josh Hartnett is another bright kid who wastes his time and brains selling drugs out of his car trunk. The film's true star and hero is Elijah Wood as Casey, a brilliant, nice-looking youth who's picked on simply because he's smaller than the school's bullies. Casey and Stokely are the first students to join forces and to dare to use their knowledge and imagination to figure out what's going on.

Christopher McDonald plays Casey's thuggish father and is among a solid lineup of prominent actors cast in the film's adult roles. "The Faculty's" faculty boasts no less than Piper Laurie as the drama teacher; Bebe Neuwirth as the principal; Salma Hayek as the school nurse; Famke Jannsen as a drab, insecure English teacher; Jon Stewart as the biology teacher; and Robert Patrick as the school's notably ferocious football coach. Filmed in and around Austin, Texas, and boasting solid special effects, "The Faculty" easily makes the grade.

NEW YORK POST, 12/25/98, p. 33, Hannah Brown

Kevin Williamson, who wrote the screenplay for "The Faculty," hasn't forgotten how scary—and icky—high school can be.

Williamson, best known for his "Scream" films, has created a teen sci-fi gross-out fest that can best be described as "Invasion of the Body Snatchers" meets "The Breakfast Club."

There are also more than passing nods to "Carrie," "Dazed and Confused," "Species" and the "Alien" franchise.

Director Robert Rodriguez ("El Mariachi," "From Dusk Till Dawn") directs this creepshow with manic energy and a real appreciation of the menace that can lurk in deserted high school corridors, gyms and bathrooms.

But what saves this from being joyless, formulaic schlock is Williamson's patented shtick (see his TV series, "Dawson's Creek") of making the characters talk like real, cynical, movie-obsessed kids.

His kids-vs.-adults message becomes a running joke in "The Faculty," as we see how the teachers of the title are only a shade creepier than usual after their bodies are possessed by worms from outer space.

The tense, winning-is-everything football coach, Mr. Willis (Robert Patrick, who was so effective as Arnold Schwarzenegger's nemesis in "Terminator 2"), actually mellows out when his body is snatched.

Frustrated, burned-out Principal Drake (Bebe Neuwirth) actually forgets about budgetary concerns and lets the staff use the air conditioner.

The druggie school nurse (Salma Hayek) becomes chillingly efficient. And the timid Mrs. Olson (Piper Laurie) begins to have a homicidal glint in her eye. No wonder, since the actress played the mom from hell in "Carrie."

The teen actors, who, for the most part, look as young as they're supposed to, turn in decent, if slightly blander performances.

Elijah Wood ("The Ice Storm") is winning as the hapless geek Casey, a kid who gets beaten up so much on a typical day that he has little to fear from the alien onslaught.

Jordana Brewster brings a knowing touch to the stock character of Delilah, a gorgeous cheerleader, evoking memories of Demi Moore and Phoebe Cates.

Clea DuVall makes her mark in the cleverly conceived role of Stokely, a brainy sci-fi buff who poses as a radical lesbian but secretly has a crush on the football hero.

And Josh Hartnett may make inroads on Leonardo DiCaprio's heartthrob territory as the drug-peddling Zeke.

He takes a major role in crushing the alien baddies by dousing them with a substance he sells as a cocaine derivative (but which is actually crushed caffeine pills).

There are a lot of references to science fiction flicks, as the characters try to figure out how to stop the alien menace by remembering what happened in "Invasion of the Body Snatchers." At one point, Delilah snaps at Casey, "When did you become Sigourney Weaver?" and Casey muses, "Maybe 'The X-Files' are right."

The story climaxes at a football game in which the alien teachers and students cheer, "Kill, kill!"

The aliens try to lure our teen heroes with promises of a pain-free "world where the class wuss doesn't have to live in terror." The message that conformity is bad and teen angst is good comes over loud and clear.

Toward the end, Rodriguez uses up his bag of special effects and the shocks become more predictable. There's only a certain amount of morphing you can use in one film and still scare audiences when tentacles sprout out of someone's mouth or a decapitated head starts walking on its own.

How much you like this movie may depend on how much you hated high school. The squeamish should avoid it, and anyone who's never heard of "Scream" will probably miss the point.

NEWSDAY, 12/28/98, Part II/p. B9, John Anderson

Before getting back to our regularly scheduled review, a word to Dimension Films, the Miramax offshoot that is releasing "The Faculty": Yes, we understand that you want to keep all of the movie's "shocking twists and turns" a secret so "the audience can enjoy them for the first time." And yes, it would be cruel and unusual to give anything away. It would deprive actual paying customers of delighting in the splendidness of your sci-fi/teen angst/comedy/gross-out film. We just don't think you have a problem.

Think about it: Anyone going to see an "Invasion of the Body Snatchers" knockoff with script by Kevin ("Scream") Williamson walks in with the presumption that no one will be what he seems to be, that everyone is a suspect—which was the message of original Red Scare sci-fi like "Body Snatchers" in the first place—and that the ante on horror movies has been upped (thanks in large part to Williamson) to the point that the outlandish has become routine. You can't be shocked, particularly, when you expect to be.

So expect to be. Directed by Robert Rodriguez—who has confined the promise of Sundance by making such auteurist cinema as "From Dusk Till Dawn"—"The Faculty" is poised to become huge, because its ploy is so obvious: The teachers are possessed. What teenagers always have suspected was true has come to pass. The instructors' bods have been inhabited by space creatures.

A group of student eccentrics—pretty attractive eccentrics, but that's what they tell us—is the last line of defense between total world domination by hideous multidentate slithering beasts. You know, the usual. They include the school newspaper person Delilah (Jordana Brewster of "As the World Turns"), the school's faux lesbian, Stokely (Clea DuVall of "How to Make the Cruelest Month"), the school genius-delinquent, Zeke (Josh Hartnett, "Halloween H2O"), Casey the nerd (Elijah Wood), quarterback Stan (Shawn Hatosy, "In and Out"), and the new kid, Marybeth (Laura Harris). Keep your eye on her. Oops, sorry.

The staff at Herrington High is played by a rather distinguished group that includes Bebe Neuwirth, Piper Laurie, Salma Hayek, Famke Janssen, Daniel von Bargen, Jon Stewart and Robert Patrick, who hasn't gotten to be this evil (ooops!!) since he played the protean hitman in "Terminator 2."

The production is pretty tongue-in-cheek, with the older actors overacting like crazy and the younger ones taking things pretty seriously. But it's understandable. They're not really getting the education that their parents' tax dollars are paying for. The school is crumbling, their hormones are raging. And now this. I mean, whatever.

SIGHT AND SOUND, 4/99, p. 41, Peter Matthews

Herrington High School, Ohio. After a faculty meeting Principal Drake is attacked by Coach Willis and slashed to death by another faculty member, Mrs Olson. The next morning new student Marybeth tries to befriend Stokely, a moody loner. Class nerd Casey finds a strange organism on the football field, and shows it to the science teacher, Mr Furlong. School-newspaper editor Delilah explores the faculty room with Casey. While hiding in a closet they espy Willis and Mrs Olson implanting an organism in the school nurse, Miss Harper, and find the corpse of another teacher. Casey and Delilah flee, but are stopped in their tracks by a resurrected Drake, to whom they describe what they saw. The police are called, but Miss Harper appears fine while the corpse is gone.

By now, the entire student body is acting strangely only Casey, Delilah, Stokely, Marybeth, jock Stan and school dope-peddlar Zeke seem themselves. Furlong attacks them but Zeke dispatches him by sticking an ampoule filled with drug powder in his eye. Examining the creature Furlong disgorged in his death throes, Zeke identifies it as an alien parasite that can be killed using his dehydrating caffeine-based compound. Stokely speculates that if the mother alien is killed, everyone will return to normal. Zeke tests the drug on himself and forces the five other kids to take it too: Delilah is exposed as an alien. Soon the other teenagers become aliens, until only Casey and Zeke remain. Marybeth reveals herself to be the mother alien, mutates into a huge gorgon and is finally slain by Casey. Life reverts to normal.

"You're that geeky Stephen King kid. There's one in every school," sneers class bitch Delilah to bullied misfit Casey in director Robert Rodriguez's sci fi horror-comedy *The Faculty*. At once you recognise the strange country you're in: it's 90s pastiche-land, where the citizens are all trash archetypes and the most prominent local custom is tireless self-referentiality. The film marks the historic union of Rodriguez *(El Mariachi, From Dusk till Dawn)* and screenwriter Kevin Williamson *(Scream* and *Scream 2)*. Perhaps because of the doubling up of such commensurate talents, *The Faculty* effectively cancels itself out. It isn't the least bit scary or particularly involving, but that seems to be the point.

Back in 1976, when Brian De Palma kicked off the whole metatrash industry with *Carrie*, the joke was that something synthesised from scraps of old teen exploitation pictures could still be so affecting. *The Faculty* salutes its great schlock ancestor by casting Carrie's mom Piper Laurie as one of the teacher-aliens (though it's pure synchronicity that the production designer is named Cary White). But the De Palma flick appears the soul of authenticity by comparison. For a radical evolutionary leap has taken place, and the new joke of *The Faculty* is how easily it can do without the traditional suspension of disbelief.

Inevitably, the script offers ample latitude for Williamson's signature conceit: the characters frequently break off their adventures to engage in learned colloquia on the very genre they inhabit. As in the *Scream* films, specialist knowledge of movie clichés becomes a survival tactic:

here sci-fi nerd Stokely deduces the existence of a queen-bee alien by remembering *Alien*. Unsurprisingly, the Ur-text is *Invasion of the Body Snatchers* (1956), and Williamson even pilfers one of its key lines of dialogue: "It is so much better. There is no fear or pain." However, *Body Snatchers* belonged to a world where cultural anxieties found metaphorical expression in pulp. Rodriguez and Williamson have gone beyond all that. Their version of pop cinema cheerfully dispenses with subtext. There's not the faintest pretence that *The Faculty* is about anything but its own sly nudging and winking at the viewer. You aren't seriously meant to care whether these kids succeed in resolving their varieties of teen angst; you're mainly supposed to twig their parodic resemblance to the gang in *The Breakfast Club*. And though the climactic monster puts on quite a bravura show, it doesn't generate a soupçon of primal horror. Instead, you sit there chuckling over the effects and when the camera ducks underwater for a brief swimming-pool contretemps—the stylistic cribs—from *jaws*.

Rodriguez's entire technique feels similarly hand-me-down. His gratuitous point-of-view tracking provides an ironic gloss on just about every thriller made in the past 20 years. But if *The Faculty* has all the poetic resonance of a round of Trivial Pursuit, at least it manages to be genuinely sportive. One advantage of the movie's elaborate gamesmanship is it demands interactive participation; audience and film-makers enter into a gleeful, knowing complicity. Rodriguez and Williamson assume young viewers these days have racked up considerable expertise in the rules of genre, and *The Faculty* is among other things a nifty meditation on genre mixing. Loosely yoking together creepy crawlies and teen anomie, the film takes as its emblem the cut-and-paste hero Zeke: part nihilist hipster and part brilliant boy-scientist. The script specifies him as a "contradiction", and indeed the character makes no sense until one realises that his whole purpose is to be a witty bricolage.

The Faculty consistently draws attention to its own ill-joined cracks and seams. There's no telling why alien possession acts as an aphrodisiac on the teachers, yet converts the students into stock zombies (though the latter leads to the film's funniest image: a classroom where every hand is raised). And it's equally useless to fret over the hazy rationale by which some characters get a second chance, while others seem polished off for good. For in a vertiginous postmortem enterprise like *The Faculty*, cleverness and clunkiness turn out to be the same thing.

VILLAGE VOICE, 1/5/99, p. 94, Gary Dauphin

In the latest Kevin Williamson script to hit theaters (this time directed by Robert Rodriguez), the old small-town alien-invasion gambit gets the *Scream* treatment, with a little teen alienation (alien nation, get it?) thrown in for good measure. Reassuringly derivative of everything from *Invasion of the Body Snatchers* to *The Puppetmasters* to *The Stepford Wives* (even *Men in Black* gets both a dialogue name check and a plot-point nod), *The Faculty* riffs on the "parents and teachers just don't understand" thing as a question of species, introducing us to a demographic cross section of Anywhere High School, America, infecting their authority figures with extra terrestrial earwigs and asking the kids to, like, save the world.

On the side of individualized humanity and good, there's the Cheerleader (Jordana Brewster), the Jock (Shawn Hatosy), the Nerd (Elijah Wood), and the cig-smoking Cool Guy (Josh Hartnett). Arrayed against them is the efficiently evil gang from the teacher's lounge, led by the diabolical alien infected Bitch Principal (Bebe Neuwirth) and Football Coach (Robert Patrick). Since the codes of science fiction are different from horror's cant, the patented Williamson method doesn't make a perfect fit with the material; *Faculty's* fun, but less fun than it could be. Williamson and Rodriguez don't ruminate on impaled, violent death (i.e., sex) with much gusto, choosing instead to go a half-baked ideological route: the alien's perfectly regimented communal order squares off against what one kid identifies most succinctly as the freedom to "be a D student." Although *The Faculty* provides effective action set pieces, quite a few scary sneak-up scenes, and some good sneak-up scenes, and some good wiser-than-their-years repartee, it's only subversive touch is its hep-cat attitude toward drugs: the test to determine if someone's been taken over by aliens involving snorting home-brewed (albeit caffeine-based) speed. In the end, *Faculty* offers none of the unsettling half-closures or frame-shattering outburst of FX and violence that mark the best of its chosen genre, but there is something cool about a mainstream, teen multiplex outing that identifies chemically altering consciousness as a fundamental part of being human.

Also reviewed in:
CHICAGO TRIBUNE, 12/25/98, Tempo/p. 2, Monica Eng
NATION, 2/15/99, p. 34, Stuart Klawans
NEW YORK TIMES, 12/25/98, p. E5, Lawrence Van Gelder
VARIETY, 1/4-10/99, p. 97, Dennis Harvey

FALLEN

A Warner Bros. release of a Turner Pictures presentation of an Atlas Entertainment production. *Executive Producer:* Robert Cavallo, Ted Kurdyla, Nicholas Kazan, and Elon Dershowitz. *Producer:* Charles Roven and Dawn Steel. *Director:* Gregory Hoblit. *Screenplay:* Nicholas Kazan. *Director of Photography:* Newton Thomas Sigel. *Editor:* Lawrence Jordan. *Music:* Tan Dun. *Music Editor:* Tom Kramer. *Choreographer:* Russell Clark. *Sound:* Jay Meagher and (music) Gray Chester. *Sound Editor:* Bruce Fortune. *Casting:* David Rubin. *Production Designer:* Terence Marsh. *Art Director:* William Cruse. *Set Designer:* Ron Yates. *Set Decorator:* Michael Seirton. *Special Effects:* Jim Fredburg. *Visual Effects:* Ken Houston. *Costumes:* Colleen Atwood. *Make-up:* Edna M. Sheen. *Stunt Coordinator:* Phil Neilson and Ernie Orsatti. *Running time:* 120 minutes. *MPAA Rating:* R.

CAST: Denzel Washington (John Hobbes); John Goodman (Jonesy); Donald Sutherland (Lieutenant Stanton); Embeth Davidtz (Gretta Milano); James Gandolfini (Lou); Elias Koteas (Edgar Reese); Gabriel Casseus (Art); Michael J. Pagan (Sam); Robert Joy (Charles); Frank Medrano (Charles' Killer); Ronn Munro (Mini Golf Owner); Cynthia Hayden (Society Woman); Ray Xifo (Society Man); Tony Michael Donnelly (Toby); Tara Carnes (Teenage Girl); Reno Wilson (Mike); Wendy Cutler (Denise); Aida Turturro (Tiffany); Jeff Tanner (Lawrence); Jerry Walsh (Fat Man); Bob Rumnock (Schoolteacher); Ellen Sheppard (Nun on Bus); Christian Aubert (Professor Louders); Bill Clark (Detective Bill Clark); Allelon Ruggiero (Executioner); Jill Holden (Gracie); Drucie McDaniel (Vendor); John Raphael Russell (Distinguished Gentleman); Lynn Wanlass (Complaining Woman); John Descano (Cab Driver); Cress Williams (Detective Joe); Rick Warner (Governor); Jim Grimshaw (Warden); Brandon Zitin (Muscle Builder); Rozwill Young, Michael Shamus Wiles, and Frank Davis (Prison Guards); Barry "Sha Baka" Henley (Uniformed Cop); Ben Siegler (Priest); Jason Winston George (College Kid); Anika Hawkins (Girlfriend); Stan Kang (Japanese Businessman); Thomas J. McCarthy and Sheila Bader (Witnesses); Elleanor Jean Hendley, Michael Aron, and Bryon Scott (Reporters); Pat Ciarrocchi, Steve Highsmith, and Kent Manahan (Anchors); Mike Cicchetti (Moustache Man); William C. Jeffreys III (Transit Cop).

CHRISTIAN SCIENCE MONITOR, 1/30/98, p. 16, David Sterritt

"Fallen" begins with the execution of a ranting serial killer in the California gas chamber. This is another sign that capital punishment, once considered a serious moral issue, has become just another spectacle for audiences to gasp at. It's not an edifying sight.

From there, the thriller gets better for a while.

Denzel Washington plays John Hobbes, the detective who put that murderer behind bars. What he didn't know was that the killer's soul had been stolen long ago by Azazel, a fallen angel who must inhabit human bodies to exist. It was this demon who caused the serial killings, and the execution of his condemned "host" has now freed him to dwell in other bodies—and to avenge himself on Hobbes as wickedly as possible.

Hobbes spends the first part of the story figuring out the nature of his enemy, helped by a grizzled partner (John Goodman) and an attractive theology professor (Embeth Davidtz) who teaches him about angels, fallen and otherwise. Then he enters a high-stakes duel with Azazel, in which his nearest and dearest become unwitting pawns.

The first casualty is the screenplay, which becomes increasingly contrived as it winds its way to a surprise ending that would have more oomph if it flowed more gracefully from earlier scenes.

At heart, "Fallen" is an updated remake of popular possession pix like "The Exorcist" and the '50s classic "Invasion of the Body Snatchers," which had a similar paranoia about normal-looking folks controlled by unseen forces. The garish "Angel Heart" also comes to mind when the plot takes some particularly lurid twists.

While the new movie isn't likely to attract as much attention as its more original predecessors, it's stylishly directed by Gregory Hoblit, who learned the police-drama trade with Emmy-winning efforts on "NYPD Blue" and "L.A. Law," among other shows. Washington and Goodman turn in solid performances, helped by Donald Sutherland as a moody lieutenant and Robert Joy as a hapless victim.

Newton Thomas Sigel's cinematography gives the tale an appropriately spooky look, and Tan Dun contributes a mildly interesting score—although the best music comes from the Rolling Stones, whose "Time Is on My Side" and "Sympathy for the Devil" are used as Azazel's theme songs.

On the downside, some of the dialogue in Nicholas Kazan's screenplay is awfully stilted. (Hobbes: "Can I ask you a personal question?" Friend: "Everythings personal if you're a person.") It's also questionable whether today's popular interest in angels will extend to such a morbid view of the subject, at a time when movies like "Michael" and TV programs like "Touched by an Angel" encourage a very different approach.

"Fallen" will sell tickets on the strength of its appealing cast and high-impact camera work, but will probably fade from the scene more quickly than its demonic villain does in the story.

LOS ANGELES TIMES, 1/16/98, Calendar/p. 1, Jack Mathews

[*The following review by Jack Mathews appeared in a slightly different form in* **NEWSDAY, 1/16/98, Part II/p. B3.**]

Somewhere in the dark woods of the cold Northeast, a man is crawling in a panic across the ground. He looks about done in, ready to chum for earthworms, when we hear the calm voice of a narrator saying he wants to tell us "about the time I almost died."

The velvet voice belongs to Denzel Washington, and as the camera moves in, we recognize him as the man in his death throes. But the voice and the face are a weird mismatch. This guy is talking to us from a point long enough after the event for him to have perspective and an ironic sense of humor about it.

The framing device for Gregory Hoblit's "Fallen" is a familiar one to fans of postwar film noir. Think of narrator, William Holden floating face down in a swimming pool at the start of Billy Wilder's "Sunset Blvd.," or of a poisoned Edmond O'Brien stumbling into a police department to report his own murder in Rudolph Mate's "D.O.A.," or a gut-shot Fred MacMurray dictating a confession in "Double Indemnity," another Wilder film.

"This better be good," we think, as the narrator launches into his story, and though "Fallen" is no "Sunset Blvd.," the payoff at the end of the road is a gem.

Written by the able Nicholas Kazan ("Reversal of Fortune"), "Fallen" is a hybrid of crime drama and supernatural thriller, which is no easy trick. This is a story about a conventional cop hero, Washington's noble homicide detective John Hobbes, being terrorized by a fallen angel who takes over the bodies of people and animals, and passes from one to another with a mere touch. This demon terrorizes for sport, and for the greater collapse of human faith, and from the clues intentionally scattered about, Hobbes knows his adversary is left-handed, anal retentive, keen on Corn Flakes, obsessive about the Rolling Stones song "Time Is on My Side," and determined to enter Hobbes' body and destroy his soul from within. You see the problem.

Hoblit, a producer on "L.A. Law," "Hill Street Blues" and "NYPD Blue" before making his directing debut with the clever 1996 courtroom drama "Primal Fear," knows the difficulty audiences will have suspending their disbelief when the genres collide, and attempts to make it easier for us by showing how tough the whole thing is for Hobbes to swallow. And there is a touch of whimsy to the voice of the narrator, an audible tongue-in-cheek, that distracts us from logical reasoning.

The film veers into dicey biblical theory a couple of times, as Embeth Davidtz's theology teacher gives Hobbes the lowdown on fallen angels, but Hoblit pulls it back quickly each time, before the baloney alarm goes off in the theater. In fact, he turns the film's most preposterous moments to his advantage, creating fascinating chase sequences with a villain who never actually materializes.

The demon spirit is invisible. It's merely manifested in whatever body it's currently occupying. To relocate, all it has to do is touch another person. Occasionally, fallen angels meet resistance when trying to enter particularly pure souls. That's the case with the demon, called Reese after the killer (a scary Elias Koteas) he's taken over, when we first meet him. He has to work through the bodies surrounding his prey.

So he can be anyone: Hobbes' timid brother Art (Gabriel Casseus); his nephew Sam (Michael J. Pagan); his partner Jonesy (John Goodman); his boss Lt. Stanton (Donald Sutherland); Davidtz's Gretta Milano, the daughter of a previous victim; or anyone else in the busy, unnamed city (actually, Philadelphia). The demon is not shy about letting Hobbes know where he is, and often toys with him by switching bodies as if playing tag.

Kazan's screenplay bears no scrutiny. The demon could kill Hobbes in the opening scene and make "Fallen" a short, or any time thereafter, the obviousness of which makes the final confrontation all the more fanciful. But for those who go along with it, it's a crafty piece of work nonetheless, ending with a pair of marvelous twists.

NEW YORK POST, 1/16/98, p. 39, Thelma Adams

In Gregory Hoblit's "Fallen," Denzel Washington gets touched by a demon.

Buff and broad-shouldered, Washington's John Hobbes is a clean cop in a dark, dirty, rain-soaked world that looks as if it came secondhand from the production company of "Seven."

Hobbes thinks he knows right from wrong, domestic beer from imported, the public good from self-interest. Then the homicide detective shakes hands with killer Edgar Reese (Elias Koteas). In some mystical way, the squeaky cop has been slimed by the supernatural.

Before long, Hobbes is flipping through arcane texts (like the Old Testament, apparently). He uncovers forbidden names with a lot of Zs and words like cubit. Who can explain the copycat killers springing up, eating corn flakes on the crime scene with an unnerving similarity?

Meanwhile, outside, a desperate rain falls. All that water would unnerve Noah, much less drown the eensie weensie spider.

Director Hoblit, upstaged by cinematographer Newton Thomas Sigel, turns every police station into a dark church, every crime scene into a desecrated altar. The cop-angels are lit from below, their chins and nostril-hair glowing while their foreheads disappear into deep thought.

The convoluted plot is awkwardly ironed out by scribe Nicholas Kazan as if he was leafing through the Bible with one hand and waiting for a call from his agent on his cell phone.

There's this wild wood spirit, a fallen angel, named Azazel. He gets his kicks hopping from body to body in an ectoplasmic game of button, button, who's got the button?

Once inside, Azazel does nothing more imaginative with his other-worldly powers than killing and killing again. Oh, yeah—occasionally he spouts Aramaic.

Hoblit and Sigel's greatest innovation is the demon cam. This devil's-eye-view of the action looks astonishingly as if the camera were peering through Andres Serrano's demonized, National Endowment for the Arts-funded artwork "Piss Christ."

But what we see is the same old slice 'n' dice. While Donald Sutherland provides foxy distraction, John Goodman obese conviviality, and Embeth Davidtz a victim-in-waiting, Washington squanders enormous star power and the Platonic form of pearly white teeth.

What "Fallen" descends to is a dry Sunday-school lesson by way of the "X-Files."

SIGHT AND SOUND, 3/98, p. 46, Andrew O'Hehir

John Hobbes, a homicide detective, witnesses the execution of Edgar Reese, a serial killer he arrested. Reese behaves oddly before the execution, and as he dies, his spirit leaves his body and enters that of a guard. Reese-style murders begin recurring, and Hobbes starts receiving anonymous late-night phone calls—another Reese trademark. Clues lead Hobbes to the case of another police detective, Milano, who committed suicide 30 years earlier after a similar series of copycat killings. In the remote cabin where Milano shot himself, Hobbes discovers several texts on demonology and a name scrawled on the cellar wall: "Azazel", an Aramaic name which translates as "demon of the wilderness".

Gretta Milano, a theology professor who is the dead detective's daughter, confirms what Hobbes is beginning to understand: Reese, like Gretta's father, was possessed by Azazel, a demon who travels from person to person by touch, but can live only briefly outside the human body. Azazel begins to appear to Hobbes in strangers he passes in the street—his co-workers, a neighbour's child, even his nephew who lives with him. Hobbes' supervisor, Lt Stanton, begins to view Hobbes as a possible suspect in the unsolved murder cases.

After Azazel kills Hobbes' beloved brother, Hobbes flees to Milano's cabin, knowing the demon will follow. Stanton and Jonesy, Hobbes' trusted partner, arrive to arrest Hobbes. But Azazel, inhabiting Jonesy, forces him to kill Stanton. Hoping to deny the demon a host, Hobbes ingests poison and then kills Jonesy.

After Hobbes dies, Azazel enters the body of a stray cat, thus surviving to continue his campaign of destruction and murder.

Although *Fallen* boasts a plot that is preposterous even by the standards of supernatural thrillers, and features more than its share of risible moments—notably when Denzel Washington is called upon to utter cut-rate exorcist incantations in Aramaic—it's also probably the best of the neo-gothic *Se7en* copycats, a stylish and expertly paced blend of autumnal atmosphere and compelling characterisation. Much of its success can be credited to Washington, whose sly, relaxed charm, leonine physicality, and aura of unimpeachable moral rectitude transform the sketchily scripted role of Hobbes into the film's ethical and emotional centre.

An apparently sexless bachelor who cares for his slightly slow brother and young nephew, Hobbes provides the audience with such a steady anchorage that at first he seems unaffected by the paranoid dream state—familiar to all connoisseurs of the genre—that director Gregory Hoblit (*Primal Fear*) painstakingly constructs around him. Using an ingenious mixture of shifting point-of-view shots, a subtly dissonant score by Chinese-born composer Tan Dun, and a production design that becomes progressively damper and gloomier, Hoblit paints Philadelphia as more a collapsing psychological state of mind than a geographical city. As in David Fincher's *Se7en* the lights in indoor spaces never seem to be on all the way, and even in the rare daylight scenes, the sun's rays are barely able to penetrate the gathering murk.

Virtually the only bright colours in the film are delivered through a device one might call DemonVision—flat, grainy, over-saturated video footage used to convey the demon Azazel's point of view as he stalks his prey. Like so much of *Fallen* this isn't exactly original. It at least suggests the 'ShakyCam' technique used by Sam Raimi in his *Evil Dead* films (which also feature a rural cabin where arcane texts are used to summon evil spirits). But it is eerily effective. Hoblit's finest moments here come in an electrifying sequence when the demon passes through some 20 individuals in rapid succession, into Hobbes' precinct house to goad him, and then back out on to the street. Hobbes pursues in half-disbelief, staring around him at the pedestrians rushing past with the awful realisation that any one of them—or all of them consecutively—could be the incarnation of pure evil.

This epiphany plays off every urban dweller's sense of unease and general menace, the feeling that the demons trying to bring down the fortress of civilisation—sober-sided theology professor Gretta (Embeth Davidtz) informs Hobbes that such is their goal—are indeed winning in increments. Like Azazel's taste for the mid-60s Rolling Stones catalogue (hilariously executed by John Goodman while the demon is inside Jonesy, Hobbes' partner), this sensibility seems to date *Fallen* slightly, as though it were conceived before the stock-market boom and the New York-led anti-crime offensive had swung the prevailing ethos of America's cities back towards a perhaps misguided sense of prosperity and security.

In fact, the very cold-heartedness of the script by Nicholas Kazan (son of the legendary director Elia Kazan, the younger Kazan has written several other interesting films, including *Frances* and *Reversal of Fortune*) itself recalls the anarchic popular cinema of the 70s, when thrillers and horror films celebrated the triumph of disorder and frequently let the bad guys win. All Hobbes' 90s righteousness and likability is not enough to save his family, his friends, or himself from total annihilation at the hands of a baby-boomer-savvy demon. In *Fallen* we see Hollywood's most agreeable romantic leading man performing one of his finest roles—in a film that offers absolutely no sex (Hobbes' relationship with Gretta remains frustratingly chaste; are producers still terrified of black-white romance?) and precious little hope of redemption.

VILLAGE VOICE, 1/27/98, p. 68, Gary Dauphin

The pitch meeting probably went no further than "a supernatural *Seven*"—that, or maybe, "Denzel—we can do for you what Fincher did for Morgan." Working like a dark-hued genre-flick blender, *Fallen* announces from the opening credits that it fully intends to crib the look and feel of the aforementioned David Fincher creepfest and from there borrows from about six other movies, including all three *Exorcists*, the low-rent sci-fi classic *The Hidden*, and even *Ricochet*, another Washington vehicle. *Fallen* doesn't nearly add up to the sum of its parts, but you appreciate the effort the way you'd appreciate a precocious little kid, taking notice of their use and pronunciation of big words even if you know they don't fully understand them.

Fallen actually displays a touch of perversity when it comes to the anxiety-of-influence thing, its central theme something to do with a compulsive evil that can take hold of folks as suddenly as a bad head cold. The film opens with Washington's painfully proper big-city cop crowing at the impending execution of a serial killer, but it isn't long before he and his cheerfully dense partner (John Goodman) are finding corpses fashioned in the playful style of their old, technically dead nemesis. At first, Goodman and Washington are thinking copy-cat or maybe multimember murder cult, but the answer is more biblical, the killings (and an awful lot of threatening staring) being committed by random folks under the control of—you guessed it—the fallen angel Azazel. Never seen, its basic mission seems to be jumping from person to person, wisecracking, and humming the Stones' "Time Is On My Side" between stops to stab people in the heart with a syring. Azazel hates Washington, though, for just being so damned good and handsome, and frames him for the new set of stiffs, forcing him underground to confront the demon and the vague but imperative question of what he'll do when his "moment' comes.

Director Gregory Hoblit (*Fear*) isn't a very impressive craftsman but he does know the lay of the thriller landscape, stoking the endlessly scary, malevolence-filled encounters between Washington (who gives a credible performance here, as always) and Azazel's host du jour. (The flick's other core image is also surprisingly effective, the angel moving like an invisible baton or ripple through city streets choked with rivers of humanity.) Overall, though, *Fallen* is like an old story you've heard plenty of times before. Although this time it's being mumbled sinisterly in ancient Aramaic, that's no reason to sit through it from beginning to end.

Also reviewed in:
CHICAGO TRIBUNE, 1/16/98, Friday/p. A, Michael Wilmington
NEW YORK TIMES, 1/16/98, p. E10, Janet Maslin
VARIETY, 1/12-18/98, p. 74, Emanuel Levy

FALLEN ANGELS

A Kino International release of a Jet Tone Productions film. *Executive Producer:* Wong Kar-Wai. *Producer:* Chin Yi-cheng. *Director:* Wong Kar-Wai. *Screenplay (Mandarin with English subtitles):* Wong Kar-Wai. *Director of Photography:* Christopher Doyle. *Editor:* William Chang and Wong Ming Lam. *Music:* Frankie Chan and Roel A. Garcia. Production Design: William Chang. *Stunt Coordinator:* Poon Kin-kwun. *Running time:* 96 minutes. *MPAA Rating:* Not Rated.

CAST: Leon Lai (Wong Chi-Ming, the Killer); Takeshi Kaneshiro (He Zhiwo); Charlie Young (Cherry); Michele Reis (Agent); Karen Mok (Blondie); Chen Wan-Lei (Father).

LOS ANGELES TIMES, 5/22/98, Calendar/p. 9, Kevin Thomas

With "Fallen Angels" Wong Kar-Wai returns to the vignette form and the razzle-dazzle style of "Chungking Express," the film that made him internationally famous. Once again Wong takes us into Hong Kong at night, a claustrophobic neon-streaked city that is a veritable rabbit's warren, a maze of dark alleys, tiny apartments, bustling shops, restaurants and clubs—to spin a pair of tales of fatalistic, passionate love.

"Fallen Angels" is an exhilarating rush of a movie, with all manner of go-for-broke visual bravura that expresses perfectly the free spirits of his bold young people. (Chris Doyle is again Wong's cinematographer in what is evolving into a remarkable collaboration.) Indeed, "Fallen Angels" celebrates youth, individuality and daring in a ruthless environment that is wholly manmade, a literal underworld similar to the workers' realm of "Metropolis"—only considerably less spacious. Life proceeds at a corrosive rock music beat.

The Agent (Michele Reis), a beautiful young woman, has a problem. For some time she's had an ideal partnership with Ming (Leon Lai). She lines up hit jobs and Ming carries them out. As he tells us on the soundtrack, he loves his job because he's lazy.

The Agent taxes Ming with instructions and he opens fire at the designated targets. Although they have little contact--and perhaps for that very reason—the Agent has fallen in love with Ming—just at the moment he's decided he's had to dig out one too many bullets from his body.

In the meantime, we meet Zhiwo (Takeshi Kaneshiro, who brings to mind the young Toshiro Mifune in looks and acting range), a handsome ex-con who tells us (also via soundtrack narration) that he's been mute since he lost his voice from eating bad canned pineapple at the age of 5. Zhiwo lives with his widower father (Chen Wan-Lei), a chef, with whom he has a loving bond.

Zhiwo makes a living of sorts breaking into people's businesses after they're closed, then opens them up and sells to customers after hours. He breaks into a slaughterhouse, a barber shop and an ice cream van with equal glee—and exuberantly presses products and services onto a not always eager public.

Wong builds "Fallen Angels" to a graceful, beautifully orchestrated finale that at last melds his two stories romantically into one, as character collide with fate.

"Fallen Angels" grew out of "Chungking Express" only to surpass it in complexity of style, perception and emotional impact.

Made in 1995 right after "Chungking Express," "Fallen Angels" leaves you wondering whether in today's receded Hong Kong if Wong could get away with making so irreverent a film.

NEW YORK POST, 1/21/98, p. 43, Thelma Adams

"Fallen Angels," the 1995 companion piece to Wong Kar-Wai's "Chungking Express," makes its New York theatrical debut at the Film Forum today after a brief appearance last fall at the New York Film Festival. Shot with the visual adrenaline associated with Wong's longtime collaborator Chris Doyle ("Happy Together," Chungking," "Ashes of Time"), this kinetic outlaw romance makes MTV look like "Sesame Street".

Together, Hong Kong's Wong and Australian-born Doyle, are a bleeding-edge Fred and Ginger, the foremost director-and-cinematographer team working in movies today.

Wong and Doyle return to Chungking's mean streets to link two slim tales of love and betrayal. A killer (Leon Lai), his female agent (Michele Reis), her landlord (Chen Wan-Lei), the landlord's mute son (Takeshi Kaneshiro), and two lovers, one named Cherry (Charlie Young), the other Baby (Karen Mok), have encounters both chance and profound.

While "Fallen Angels" doesn't reach the emotional and narrative heights of "Happy Together," the movie has moments of piercing romanticism, ribald humor, and undeniable poignancy as well as the extreme violence long associated with more mainstream Hong Kong actioners.

Wong's movie shocks the mind like repressed memories returning under hypnosis. Images linger: An assassin encountering an old school chum on the bus after a violent hit and being offered life insurance, the speeded-up sense of modern life broken up by the elongated tension of the kill.

But the most memorable sequence of "Fallen Angels" has nothing to do with murder or romantic love. As a kind of therapy, a rejection of crime, the landlord's son videotapes his father in daily routines. After his dad's death, the young mute replays a single loop: his father in the kitchen, cooking food and kibbitzing.

In this one straightforward, ordinary deeply moving bit, the boy and Wong capture slippery life as it's lived and represented. It's exquisitely tender, universal and, like the work of Wong himself, completely unexpected.

NEWSDAY, 1/26/98, Part II/p. B11, John Anderson

In his fifth feature film—an offshoot of his fourth, last year's acclaimed "Chungking Express"—director Wong Kar-Wai both satirizes and ennobles the conventions of Hong Kong cinema, including existential hit men, slo-mo executions, nihilist heroes and an arms-length approach to love.

The story is a romance, or two (or three, if you count Wong's infatuation with Hong Kong nightlife): A disillusioned contract killer (Leon Lai) is working for "the Agent" (Michele Reis), who also happens to be in love with him. At the same time, an ex-convict (Takeshi Kaneshiro), who hasn't spoken since eating a past-dated can of pineapple at age 5, is making a living opening other people's stores after hours and strong-arming customers into buying. That is, when he's not helping Cherry (Charlie Young) find her ex-boyfriend, and when Blondie (Karen Mok) isn't throwing the entire picture into an uproar.

Preposterous? Sure, and funny, and frenetic, hallucinatory and punkishly hip. But even while Wong works his palette of garish neon, wet asphalt and urban waste (brought to electric life by his longtime cinematographer, Chris Doyle), he's also after beauty and truth, the kind found in Degas barmaids and Hopper nighthawks and washed up on a Fellini beach.

And because he creates his own context, his own conventions and his own universe, Wong is among the most exciting directors working today.

VILLAGE VOICE, 1/27/98, p. 63, J. Hoberman

The acme of neo-new wavism, the ultimate in MTV alienation, the most visually voluptuous flick of the fin de siécle, *Fallen Angels* is Hong Kong auteur Wong Kar-Wai's quintessential movie—an intermittently violent, wildly stylized, garishly soulful gangster film with almost no narrative and a surplus of shaggy-dog digression.

Say what? Perhaps some of the critical warmth extended to *Fallen Angels*'s New York Film Festival teammate, Wong's somewhat quieter *Happy Together,* will rub off on this jazzy nocturne. But even if it doesn't, all romantic cinephiliacs owe it to themselves to take in the last installment of Wong's long goodbye to the now-lost paradise of colonial Hong Kong and the sensationally florid film culture that it incubated.

Wong's cinematic universe has its own narrative laws. Most simply described, *Fallen Angels*—which evolved out of the 1994 *Chungking Express*—circles around the unconsummated love affair between a baby-faced hitman (pop star Leon Lai) and his ravishing female agent (the former Miss Hong Kong, Michele Reis). Her eyes hidden by long bangs, his masked behind impenetrable shades, these youthful fashion plates are more icons than actors—Wong underscores their glamorous star entrances with wailing Canto rap or mega-closeups lavished on the neon lights reflected off Reis's vinyl minidress.

Existing mainly in each other's imaginations, the business associates meet only twice (and then very briefly). For, as insistent as its soundtrack is, *Fallen Angels* is a movie with almost no dialogue. The speech is mainly voiceover soliloquizing, which, too subjective to ever exert much authority over the plot, has the effect of casting events into the realm of dreamy regret even as they happen. Like Wong's extravagantly moody martial arts pageant *Ashes of Time, Fallen Angels* is a reverie—albeit one erupting periodically into slo-mo gunfights of pure, light-smearing energy.

Hong Kong is itself a character through which the principles search for something not there. Wong's favorite shot places a pair of dreamily disconnected actors in the foreground, oblivious to the mad tumult behind them. When not booking Lai's professional bloodbaths or setting up his hideouts, the insolently slouching Reis spends her time in a sort of simulated heroin trance, lost in fantasy, occasionally making love to a glowing Wurlitzer.

Lai himself is scarcely less solipsistic. In between jobs (which are blatantly staged as outrageous, John Woo-style shoot-outs), he's recognized by an old classmate (all of *Grosse Point Blank* in a far funnier three-minute bit) or picked up by an orange-coiffed hysteric (Karen Mok), who claims to be a figure from his now-forgotten past. Tangential to their lives, but central to the movie, is the mute slacker (Takeshi Kaneshiro) who tries on and abandons commercial identities, prowling the local market like an edgy Harpo Marx.

Half of *Fallen Angels* takes place in a monsoon; the rest is set in a pungent series of lovingly selected locations (deserted subway stations, an empty McDonald's, 24-hour noodle joints, impossibly narrow apartments, entropic dives where the jukebox plays Laurie Anderson). The director's throwaway style has its equivalent in the movie's world of fast-food parlors and one-night stands. The more disposable the experience, the more crucial the memory. Shot entirely at night and mainly in wide-angle—Christopher Doyle's camera racing down rain-slicked Nathan Road or positioning itself an inch from a performer's face—*Fallen Angels* is suffused with nostalgia for the present. As the director told one interviewer, his evocation of the 1960s, *Days of Being Wild*, was the "reinvention of the disappeared world while *Fallen Angels* attempts to seal some of the existing images onto the negative, while they are still there."

As absolutely original and confidently mannerist as *Fallen Angels* is, I don't doubt that sonic people will find it highly irritating. Using a strategy invented by Orson Welles, Wong has connected cinema to its contemporary media rivals—radio, video, cyberspace. What's more, the worshipful response to the recent revival of Godard's *Contempt* notwithstanding, the break-throughs of the early '60s-movies like Antonioni's *L'Eclisse* or Resnais's *Muriel* —were not exactly hits. And this director doesn't even come from France. (I was told that the editor of one fashionable monthly found the very idea of East Asian art movies to be a source of annoyance.)

Wong, who runs the risk of becoming the world's most imitated filmmaker, here pushes his style to the brink of self-parody. But I believe the audience is there. Just as the star-struck *Irma Vep* was last year's *Jackie Brown* and the romantic disaster of *Crash* (all right, a double bill of *Crash* and *The Sweet Hereafter)* the true *Titanic*, so *Fallen Angels* is an infinitely sweeter and sexier *Lost Highway*—a pyrotechnical wonder about mystery, solitude, and the irrational love of movies.

Also reviewed in:
CHICAGO TRIBUNE, 6/19/98, Friday/p. L, Michael Wilmington
NEW YORK TIMES, 1/21/98, p. E5, Stephen Holden
VARIETY, 10/2-8/95, p. 43, Leonard Klady

FARM, THE: ANGOLA, U.S.A.

A Gabriel Films release. *Executive Producer:* Gayle Gilman. *Producer:* Jonathan Stack and Liz Garbus. *Director:* Jonathan Stack, Liz Garbus, and Wilbert Rideau. *Director of Photography:* Samuel Henriques and Bob Perrin. *Editor:* Mona Davis and Mary Manhardt. *Music:* Curtis Lundy. *Running time:* 93 minutes. *MPAA Rating:* Not Rated.

WITH: Bernard Addison (Narrator) and with George Crawford; Vincent Simmons; Eugene "Bishop" Tannehill; Logan "Bones" Theriot; John Brown; Ashanti Witherspoon; Burl Cain; Wilbert Rideau.

NEW YORK POST, 6/10/98, p. 42, Thelma Adams

"Winning the lottery" means having the governor sign a pardon at the Louisiana maximum security prison profiled in "The Farm: Angola, USA."

At the former slave plantation on the muddy banks of the Mississippi, inmates check in but few check out.

According to startling stats from directors Jonathan Stack and Liz Garbus, 85 percent of the murderers, rapists and armed robbers who enter the Angola prison die there.

Stack and Garbus round up a felony dirty dozen: a 22-year-old lifer; a death-row slasher; an ordained minister sent up for murder in 1959; a cancer-stricken wife-killer; a double rapist arguing his innocence 20 years into a 100-year sentence; and a prison activist who dropped acid and blasted a pair of cops during an armed robbery in the '70s.

We also get a long look at the man responsible for the care and feeding of more than 5,000 hardened criminals. Warden Burl Cain emerges as a good-old-boy and sharp business man who takes as much pride in knowing how much he spends a year for toilet paper ($51,000) as in the spiritual progress of his 5,000 cons.

The tightly focused, moving account of prison life was the co-winner of the Sundance Film Festival documentary grand jury prize. There are blazing emotional moments: A prison visitor breaks down, reading the fear in her son's eyes; a review board denies parole to a convicted black rapist despite new exculpatory evidence and 20 years served.

The larger battles between hope and despair, recidivism and redemption played out within Angola prison are thrown into relief on "The Farm." The result is both inspirational and disturbing—does it take hell-on-earth for many men to find God?

As tough as the documentary is, with its images of execution by lethal injection and unflinching confessions, there's a lingering sense that it's not the whole story. What's really going on behind closed and padlocked doors? I'd kill to know.

NEWSDAY, 6/10/98, Part II/p. B9, John Anderson

Welcome to hell, where some statistics seem in order.

The Louisiana State Penitentiary is the largest maximum security prison in the United States. Once a slave plantation (some would say it still is), it encompasses 18,000 acres, is bordered on three sides by the Mississippi River, and houses 5,000 inmates, 85 percent of whom will die there. Once known as the bloodiest prison in the nation, it is a place where regimentation and routine are the highest ideals; hope is third: An inmate who's spent 20 years behind bars can have his parole petition rejected in less than a minute.

One could continue—last year, for instance, 900 prisoners checked in, more than half with life sentences, and about 77 percent of whom were African-American—but it would scarcely do justice to "The Farm: Angola, USA." A stoical but exhilarating documentary, it presents, without unnecessary pathos or particular bias, what life is like for men in a place designed to crush the spirit.

Filmmakers Jonathan Stack and Liz Garbus spent a year filming inside what is commonly known as Angola (its original inhabitants were from that country), and both their access and their level of intimacy with prison life are extraordinary. Credited as codirector is Wilbert Rideau, the much-honored editor of the prison's Angolite magazine, who helped them get the remarkable cooperation they got.

"The Farm" focuses on a handful of inmates, ranging from the 22-year-old, freshly incarcerated George Crawford to Eugene (Bishop) Tannehill, who arrived at Angola on Oct. 4, 1959—"It was a Wednesday"—and whose pardon papers wait on the governor's desk. Others: George Ashanti Witherspoon, a model prisoner who's served 25 of his 75-year sentence for armed robbery; Vincent Simmons, whose guilt the parole board affirms out of hand, despite the many questions surrounding his rape conviction (he was, for instance, the only one handcuffed during his police lineup), and John Brown, who's spent 12 years on death row and whose fate will be decided before the end of the film.

A top prize winner at Sundance this year, "The Farm" is a movie for everyone: If you suspect that this country might find better ways of administering justice, you'll be grateful that the film exposes what it does. If you feel that the only response to antisocial behavior is to construct an environment in which redemption is possible only in the afterlife, you'll be gratified to see your tax dollars hard at work.

VILLAGE VOICE, 6/16/98, p. 149, J. Hoberman

Crime maybe on the decline but punishment has never been more popular. *The Farm: Angola, USA*, winner of the documentary prize at the last Sundance Film Festival, is a compact, sober, and thoroughly engrossing look at the American growth industry of incarceration—in this case the warehousing of convicts in the vast state prison known as Angola.

Located in a remote corner of Louisiana, Angola is (as it's more than once observed) "a world into itself." This former slave plantation was known for much of the 20th century as the nation's "most dangerous and bloody prison." It has since been "civilized" into a huge punishment facility with 1800 workers and six complexes, plus an entire, on-site employee town—the safest town in America, one inhabitant proudly notes. Guiding filmmakers Jonathan Stack and Liz Garbus through his domain, warden Burl Cain articulates the conventional wisdom of the 1990s: "You have to be a pretty good businessman to run this place."

Cain's philosophy is simple: work the inmates, most of whom seem to be serving lifetime sentences, into submission. Most of the prisoners toil in the fields at four cents per hour. (It's ultimate workfare: When asked how he likes what he's doing, one young inmate admits that this is the first job he's had in his life.) Angola's regimentation seems total, even by prison standards, and totally successful in controlling its antisocial population. Warden Cain presides over the perfect suffering society—a hymn-singing, tough-love monastery of pain. Is the existence of the institution a deterrent to crime? Who knows? If the prisoners seem successfully rehabilitated by their epic sentences, those same sentences insure that 85 per cent will end their lives in Angola.

This catch-22 is embodied by Wilbert Rideau, the inmate credited as the movie's codirector and the editor of the prison's much-praised newspaper, *The Angolite*. Although *The Angolite* is typically described as "uncensored," it's difficult to know what that means in this context. (These imprisoned journalists must be nearly as beholden to their corporate sponsors as those who work for network TV.) What is evident, however, is that as obviously reformed as a man like Rideau might be, it is precisely this useful (and perhaps dangerous) rehabilitation that would seem to insure he will never be released.

Thus, *The Farm*—which [played] at Film Forum in conjunction with the Human Rights Watch Film Festival at the Walter Reade—begins with one inmate's funeral and ends with the aftermath of another's. The latter's relatives are amazed that he requested a plot on the prison grounds but, as family visits to prisoners typically end after three years, the inmates are all but buried alive. *The Farm* focuses on six of these entombed, both black and white, ranging in age from 22 to 70-something. Most are murderers although one, the distinguished-looking Ashanti Witherspoon, is doing 75 years for an armed robbery committed in 1971. (Although a prison trustee, he is not yet eligible for parole.)

A location for both *JFK* and *Dead Man Walking*, Angola has a showbiz past going back at least to the 1934 governor's pardon with which folk entrepreneur John Lomax secured the release of the influential blues singer Huddie "Leadbelly" Ledbetter. The prison has recently been the subject of programs on ABC, PBS, A&E, and the Discovery channel; the amazing, much-ballyhoo'd inmate rodeo, which is neither shown nor mentioned in *The Farm*, was the subject of a lengthy article, taken from Daniel Bergner's forthcoming book on Angola, in the February issue of *Harper's* magazine.

Where filmmakers Stack and Garbus claimed to have enjoyed "unprecedented access" to the Angola facilities, Bergner's more detailed account takes note of Cain's attempt to cut himself a piece of the author's advance. The warden too is a star. (Cain's observations in *The Farm* are mainly self-serving; in Bergner's piece, they're megalomaniacal. The warden calls himself a prophet and says of the prisoners, "I am their daddy.") A believer in forgiveness *and* capital punishment, Cain is clearly a man for all seasons. His job, he tells the filmmakers, is to keep hope alive. It's unclear whether this is embodied by the clown shown wandering through the cellblock on Christmas eve.

The Farm is clearly not the complete Angola story. But where it excels is in its existential appreciation of the prisoners' state. A rapist serving a century-long sentence has his case reviewed for the first time in 20 years. The convict has new evidence to present. But despite a strong suggestion that the guy might possibly have been sloppily tried and railroaded into prison, the parole board is totally unconvinced (and shockingly flippant as well). Angola creates its own sense of time. Prisoners spend years preparing for hearings that are offhandedly dismissed in a matter of minutes.

Time seems to expand toward eternity even in the face of impending termination. A death row inmate faces his final ruling. His victims speak out strongly for his execution but, listening to them, he remains weirdly calm and cheerful. "He don't think it will happen—right until the end" the warden explains. The condemned man is still smiling and hopeful, sorting through his meager belongings, at 16 hours to lethal injection. We're spared the sight, although the prisoner's demise is represented with a memorable shock image—a table laden with the detritus of his last meal, heaps of crayfish shell and empty Coke bottles. (His final word, we're told, was "wow.")

The bottom line: No one gets out of here alive. There isn't any Shawshank redemption. Perhaps that's why just about everybody to whom the filmmakers speak, from the Angola's prisoners to the guards to the warden, repeatedly affirms their belief in heaven.

Also reviewed in:
CHICAGO TRIBUNE, 9/4/98, Friday/ p. F, John Petrakis
NATION, 6/29/98, p. 36, Stuart Klawans
NEW YORK TIMES, 6/10/98, p. E3, Janet Maslin
VARIETY, 2/2-8/98, p. 30, Glenn Lovell

FEAR AND LOATHING IN LAS VEGAS

A Universal Pictures release of a Rhino Films/Laila Nabulsi production. *Executive Producer:* Harold Bronson, Richard Goos, and Patrick Wachsberger. *Producer:* Laila Nabulsi, Patrick Cassavetti, and Stephen Nemeth. *Director:* Terry Gilliam. *Screenplay:* Terry Gilliam, Tony Grisoni, Tod Davies, and Alex Cox. *Based on the book by:* Hunter S. Thompson. *Director of Photography:* Nicola Pecorini. *Editor:* Lesley Walker. *Music:* Ray Cooper. *Music Editor:* Kevin Lane. *Choreographer:* Joann Fregaletto Jansen. *Sound:* Jay Meagher. *Sound Editor:* Peter Pennell. *Casting:* Margery Simkin. *Production Designer:* Alex McDowell. *Art Director:* Chris Gorak. *Set Designer:* Lynn Christopher. *Set Decorator:* Nancy Haigh. *Set Dresser:* Paige Augustine and James Meehan. *Special Effects:* Steve Galich. *Visual Effects:* Kent Houston. *Costumes:* Julie Weiss. *Make-up:* Patty York. *Stunt Coordinator:* Noon Orsatti. *Running time:* 120 minutes. *MPAA Rating:* R.

CAST: Johnny Depp (Raoul Duke);   Benicio Del Toro (Dr. Gonzo);   Tobey Maguire (Hitchhiker);   Michael Lee Gogin (Uniformed Dwarf);   Larry Cedar (Car Rental Agent, Los Angeles);   Brian LeBaron (Parking Attendant);   Katherine Helmond (Reservations Clerk);   Michael Warwick (Bell Boy);   Craig Bierko (Lacerda);   Mark Harmon (Magazine Reporter);   Tyde Kierney (Reporter);   Tim Thomerson (Hoodlum);   Richard Riehle (Dune Buggy Driver);   Ransom Gates and Frank Romano (Dune Buggy Passengers);   Gil Boccaccio and Gary Bruno (Desert Room Doormen);   Richard Portnow (Wine Colored Tuxedo);   Debbie Reynolds (Voice of Debbie Reynolds);   Steve Schirripa (Goon);   Verne J. Troya (Wee Waiter);   Will Blount (The Black Guy);   Ben Yeager (Clown Barker);   Penn Jillette (Carnie Talker);   Christopher Callen (Bazooka Circus Waitress);   Cameron Diaz (Blonde TV Reporter);   Ben Van der Veen (TV Crew Man);   Lyle Lovett (Road Person);   Flea (Musician);   Alex Craig Mann (Stockbroker);   Gregory Itzin (Clerk at Mint Hotel);   Gary Busey (Highway Patrolman);   Troy Evans (Police Chief);   Gale Baker (Police Chief's Wife);   Chris Meloni (Clerk at Flamingo Hotel);   Christina Ricci (Lucy);   Chris Hendrie (Executive Director);   Larry Brandenburg (Cop in Black);   Michael Jeter (L. Ron Bumquist);   Donald Morrow (Voice of Film Narrator);   Harry Dean Stanton (Judge);   Jenette Goldstein (Maid);   Stephen Bridgewater (Human Cannonball);   Buck Holland, Mary Gillis, and Jennifer Elise Cox (The Shoppers);   Robert Allen (Las Vegas Car Rental Agent);   David Brisbin (Man in Car);   Ellen Barkin (North Star Waitress);   James O'Sullivan and Milt Tarver (TV Newsmen).

LOS ANGELES TIMES, 5/22/98, Calendar/p. 14, David Kronke

In his seminal '70s book "Fear and Loathing in Las Vegas," acclaimed burnout Hunter S. Thompson wrote the epitaph for the drug generation and it serves as a pretty good review for Terry Gilliam's film adaptation of the book: "Buy the ticket, take the ride, and if it occasionally gets a little heavier than what you had in mind, well, maybe chalk it up to forced consciousness expansion. Tune in, freak out, get beaten."

Feel free to take that "beaten" part literally. Gilliam's film (which he inherited from "Sid and Nancy's" Alex Cox, who was tossed off the project just before production was to begin) is a spectacular wipeout, a visionary mess that is so unrelentingly dissolute that it may prove to be impenetrable viewing for most tastes.

The rainbow coalition of drugs on display notwithstanding, this movie is simply a downer.

Perhaps that's as it should be, given the subject matter, but while Gilliam has always leavened his misanthropy with eccentric storytelling prowess in the past, here, he makes no effort to connect with an audience. (The Writers Guild ruled that Gilliam and collaborator Tony Grisoni should share the scripting credit with Cox and his partner Tod Davies.)

There's no story, but there never was. Raoul Duke (Johnny Depp), a "doctor of journalism," and Dr. Gonzo (Benicio Del Toro), his "attorney," high-tail it to Vegas, ingesting freely from their generous trunkful of drugs along the way, to cover an off-road race in the desert, most of which they manage to miss. They partake to excess, trash one hotel room, head across town to pick up the bad vibes of a conference on law enforcement and drug abuse, then trash another hotel room.

Along the way, tripping—and pratfalling—madly, they recoil from the sight of ubiquitous Vegas denizens, ghastly people made all the more ghastly by their chemical overloads. Duke babbles about searching for "The American Dream," but of course he has no idea what he's talking about and neither do we.

Twisting Vegas into a variety show from the bottom ring of hell is where Gilliam's at his most inventive, and if there hadn't been a glut of films lately, which had already reveled in Sin City's garish side ("Honeymoon in Vegas," "Casino," "Cool World," etc.), this part of the film at least might have been nominally more interesting.

There are so many scenes where colors blur madly, the camera swirls woozily and the characters scream incoherently at one another that you're likely to think you've wandered in on one of Andy Warhol's slapdash films from the '60s.

Gilliam vaguely attempts to put the dementia in context—with Vietnam and Nixon the signposts of the era, Thompson suggested that the only recourse to a free-thinker was to batter one's brain—but that slender bit of philosophizing gets pile-driven beneath the film's sludge of excess.

This odyssey "was to be an affirmation of everything that is right and true of the American character," Duke declares with an irony that is obvious in the book, but unfortunately is only understood much later in the film.

Something like this was attempted once before—"Where the Buffalo Roam," a 1980 catastrophe starring Bill Murray as Thompson. That one, at least, seemed to get closer to Thompson's outrageous sense of humor; this movie scarcely seems to remember that the writer's ravings were, at least, supposed to be funny (a dramatized audio version of the book featuring Jim Jarmusch and Maury Chaykin, released on CD last year, is much more entertaining than this film).

For all that, Depp gives a creditable performance as Thompson's fictional stand-in. He's mimicking Thompson more than creating a full-bodied character, but someone that plastered probably doesn't have much of an emotional interior life to begin with, and Depp, whose baldness here would be the main shock of any other movie, manages some inspired physical humor.

Del Toro, as the infinitely grating source of bad legal advice ("As your attorney, I advise you to take a hit out of my little brown bottle in my shaving kit") and wretched bodily functions, throws himself into his character with reckless abandon, and the discipline-free turn is quite a spectacle, if for all the wrong reasons.

Turning in cameo appearances to no real effect except to add to their own hipness quotients are Cameron Diaz, Lyle Lovett, Flea (of the Red Hot Chili Peppers), Gary Busey, Christina Ricci, Penn Jillette, Harry Dean Stanton, Mark Harmon, Ellen Barkin and Tobey Maguire.

There's one redeeming factor, maybe. Had "Fear and Loathing in Las Vegas" had more of Thompson's tone, it might have made pharmaceutical experimentation seem like a wiggy kick.

As is, anyone who sees this as a movie glorifying chemical abuse must be, well, on drugs.

NEW YORK POST, 5/22/98, p. 49, Rod Dreher

It's hard to think of a director better suited to bring Hunter S. Thompson's freakadelic memoir "Fear and Loathing in Las Vegas" to the screen than the spectacularly imaginative Terry Gilliam, the genius behind the 1985 masterpiece "Brazil."

It had been widely thought that Thompson's brilliantly observed diary of a lost weekend in the brackish backwash of a decade that had passed its high-water mark simply could not he filmed. Gilliam's lurid movie is a fascinating disappointment. Conventional wisdom wins again.

If "Fear and Loathing" will prove toxic to mainstream audiences, who may be viscerally repulsed by the assaultive intensity of certain scenes (e.g., the ultra-realistic chunks one character blows into the toilet during a binge), Thompson devotees and admirers of Gilliam's arresting, more-is-better visual style will find the movie a fairly potent stimulant.

This manic movie is about two men, circa 1970, slouching toward Vegas to be reborn as rough beasts. Thompson alter ego Raoul Duke (Johnny Depp) and: his attorney/drug supplier, Dr. Gonzo (Benicio Del Toro), barrel across the desert toward Vegas with a pharmacological cornucopia stashed in the trunk.

Journalist Duke has an assignment to cover a motorcycle race for a sports magazine, but as you watch the pair gobble LSD tabs like Fritos, you know the bike race will have to wait.

Gilliam's skilled hand (or, rather, eye) is evident early on, when Duke, an acid-fueled Buddy Rich solo battering his cerebral cortex, tries to check into a Vegas hotel. The carpet patterns creep and crawl (a more realistic depiction of a psychedelic experience you will not find in the movies), and he perceives that the Sansabelt savages in the bar around him have literally turned into lounge lizards.

Depp and Del Toro are magnificent, almost balletic in their blasted physical comedy. Depp, who has a gift for making interesting choices in roles, if not always commercially smart ones, had Thompson's peculiar, jittery mannerisms down cold.

Incredibly enough, he's the straight man to Del Toro's hazily sinister Dr. Gonzo, the lively Cheech to Del Toro's poleaxed Rabelaisian Chong. Del Toro's belly is distended, like a grotesque pustule, and it could function as a symbol of their corrupting appetites.

This faithful recap of the Thompson book is little more than an episodic collection of debauched moments in which we see how many drugs and how much booze two men can consume in one weekend without losing their minds.

It's great fun, but finally becomes too much; even excess eventually becomes boring. Gilliam converts Duke and Gonzo's wrecked hotel rooms into hideous, compulsively watchable landscapes (think a pop-art Bruegel) but it doesn't appear to be going anywhere, or, unlike the book, have much more than surface resonance.

It exhausts us long before it's over.

Yes, Virginia, there is a moral to this aggressively unbourgeois story. In one of the film's few quiet moments, Duke reflects on how naively romantic the counterculture had been to assume that we'd all be living better through mind-expanding chemistry. The sense of loss of the revolutionary promise of the '60s, dissipated in an orgy of druggy self-indulgence, is palpable.

"Fear and Loathing" is, in the end, a surrealist explication of that line from "Easy Rider": "We blew it."

NEWSDAY, 5/22/98, Part II/p. B3, John Anderson

If you got it then, you'll get it now. If you would have gotten it then, you'll get it now.

If you never got it, you're never gonna get it. And as your attorney, I advise you to drink heavily.

To wit: They said it couldn't be done, and maybe they were right, because Terry Gilliam's "Fear and Loathing in Las Vegas" is Terry Gilliam's "Fear and Loathing, etc.," not Hunter S. Thompson's novel, first run as articles in Rolling Stone way back when in 1971 A.N. (Anno Nixon), and as unhinged a bit of first-person insanity as had ever been seen in a major magazine.

It was never a piece meant to embrace the masses, any more than Gilliam's work is meant to soothe the savage breast of the impassioned insurance actuary, but what he has done here is exactly what he meant to do and if that isn't art what is?

Teeing off with archival footage (Vietnam protesters), insulin-shock-inducing music (the Lennon Sisters singing "My Favorite Things") and blood-splatter graphics (a nod to Ralph Steadman, whose warped illustration accompanied Thompson's R.S. pieces), Gilliam gets down to business.

"We were somewhere around Barstow on the edge of the desert," a voice intones, "when the drugs began to take hold." Inside the car are Hunter Thompson, aka Raoul Duke (Johnny Depp), his faithful albeit demented attorney Dr. Gonzo (an appallingly corpulent Benicio Del Toro) plus "two bags of grass, 75 pellets of mescaline, five sheets of high-powered blotter acid, a saltshaker half full of cocaine, a whole galaxy of multicolored uppers, downers, screamers, laughers... also, a quart of tequila, a quart of rum, a case of beer, a pint of raw ether and two dozen amyls." As well as whatever the passengers had already ingested.

While the preemptively censoring minions at Disney-owned ABC-TV may not want to run ads for "Fear and Loathing" (they're shocked—shocked!—to find that drugs are involved), drugs aren't what the movie's about, or the book either, for that matter. Gilliam safety preserves—amid the Nouveau Linoleum aesthetic of his movie—the sense of time and place and politics that infected Duke and Gonzo. The vanished hope of political change. The extinguished sense of generational unity. A war that kept pointlessly raging. Nixon. Kent State. Manson. Etc. The characters, more eloquently than most, articulate the moorless amorality of a crushed soul by swan-diving into the only remaining vestiges of an evaporated dream. In other words, pharmaceuticals.

"Fear and Loathing" may in fact serve as the great cinematic bridge between the oft-dismissed '60s "sensibility" and the cultural stagnation (if not hypocrisy) experienced by the so-called Youth of Today. What the film illuminates better than anything else is that it's a sense of loss that makes people nostalgic. "F&L" is all about loss, be it of hope, sanity, control or your sense of self-respect. Or about what you tell yourself is true.

Take, as exhibit A, today's family-friendly Las Vegas and a country where traditional values mean guilt-free gambling. The city now, as an idea, is probably more of an affront than the '70s version but, in either age, where better to find the concentrated effluvia of the American Dream? Duke and Gonzo, riding the Red Shark (their blood-red Cadillac convertible, rented), having already terrorized a stupefied hitchhiker (Tobey Maguire), hit the Strip, ostensibly so Duke can cover the Mint 400 desert bike race for Sports Illustrated and Gonzo can keep him out of trouble. Surrounded as he is by the "absolute cream of the national sporting press," Duke follows his standard business practice and misses the race almost entirely, wandering in a drug-fueled hallucination that turns Vegas into a combination Great Adventure and Circus Maximus.

Johnny Depp, proving himself again the most adventurous movie star around (Del Toro is no slouch either), is fully possessed by the Thompson persona, from polished skull to faux jungle wear to the staccato elocution and a stentorian flair for gibberish ("How long could we maintain, I wondered"). What often lifts "Fear and Loathing" above the strictly comic is the love of language Thompson exhibits, and which Gilliam clearly appreciates.

Visually, Gilliam is always a magician, although "Fear and Loathing" departs from his usual dreamscaping and occasionally breathtaking perspectives and mines the mother lode of Vegas kitsch, bad hotel rooms, lizard bars ("Somebody was giving booze to the--- things"), dirty bathwater, unkempt underage women (Christina Ricci) and excruciating neon. All the while, he loads the background with televised Vietnam carnage and '50s B-movie sci-fi. What we get is greasy dread and contagious hysteria.

Watching the characters navigate the minefield that is their Las Vegas (a district attorneys' convention, bill-waving hotel clerks, Debbie Reynolds), backed by a sound track that might have been recorded off '90s Classic Rock radio, there's bound to be a little drag time; you've seen one post-apocalyptic ether and adrenal-gland hallucination you've seen 'em all, I suppose, but "Fear and Loathing" is so funny and so honest it's almost unheard of. Then or now.

SIGHT AND SOUND, 11/98, p. 48, Linda Ruth Williams

1971. Journalist Raoul Duke and his attorney Dr Gonzo drive from Los Angeles to Las Vegas in a red convertible, beginning a huge drugs binge. They check into the Mint Hotel so Duke can cover the Mint 400 off-track race the following day, take more drugs and run up a huge room-service bill. They visit Bazooka Circus casino on ether.

The next day Gonzo departs and Duke drives to Baker, California. On the way he is stopped by a highway cop. He returns to the Flamingo Hotel in Vegas to cover a district attorneys' conference on drug abuse. Gonzo shows up with Lucy, an under-age girl, whom they send to a motel. They attend some of the conference, take the powerful drug adrenochrome, then terrorise a waitress in a north Vegas café. Duke and Gonzo leave Vegas separately, by road and plane respectively.

It may seem perverse to read a film so obsessed with the immediacy of excess as a period drama. But *Fear and Loathing in Las Vegas* comes from a director who has specialised in tales of time-travel, one of cinema's most brilliant and bizarre animator-narrators of the past. And here the film's setting in an excessively vulgar United States of 1971 is as crucial to its narrative as the immoderate amount of drugs its central characters obsessively ingest.

Director Terry Gilliam brings to this long-awaited project which he inherited from Alex Cox some of the virtues of a distanced perspective. As an American who settled Britain in the 60s, his vision is imbued with a peculiarly European sensibility and the eye he casts across the crass

Americana of *Fear and Loathing* is radically transnational. Hunter S. Thompson's novel, on which the film is based, is still a countercultural icon, revered for its verbal audacity. So handing the project to a director known best for his bravura visual style is a canny move: from bold word to excessive image this is a flamboyant adaptation. But most of all, Gilliam's ongoing fascination with how the past is viewed through the lens of the present receives one more twist. Unlike the pastiche medievalism of his Monty Python collaborations *(Jabberwocky, Monty Python and the Holy Grail)* or the heroic, child's-dream past of *Time Bandits* and *The Adventures of Baron Munchhausen* this is a past many of us remember and which therefore implicates us in its telling.

Yet many viewers will be resistant since the spectacle of psychedelic excess is no longer fashionable. Gilliam doesn't care. Dispensing with foreplay, *Fear and Loathing in Las Vegas* throws you straight into a demented cinematic 'acid test' by refusing to explain or justify the desires that drive Duke and Gonzo's anti-heroic double act. Even Gilliam's dystopian *Brazil* glimmers with moments of unabashed human warmth, but *Fear and Loathing* gets bleaker as it proceeds, so that towards its conclusion such scenes as the terrorising of Ellen Barkin's downtrodden waitress can only be shocking. This is a film that unsettles through its ruthless drive to implicate everyone in the twisted or the sordid—if you don't find it funny, you may well be appalled.

We are made to share our heroes' altered states via the nauseatingly accurate *mise en scène*. The set-piece when Duke and Gonzo check into the Mint and are besieged by swirling carpets, rubber faces and guests morphing into lascivious reptiles is a masterpiece of addled point of view, making LSD look like the imaginative precursor of CGI. Gilliam crams each frame with hideous, witty details, knowing references and cameo performances. (Harry Dean Stanton, Katherine Helmond and Lyle Lovett make blink-or-you'll-miss-them appearances; Cameron Diaz, Christina Ricci and Gary Busey linger for longer.) An exercise in excess on many levels, *Fear and Loathing* can seem a cinema of overkill, appropriate to its subject matter but difficult to watch. When paired with the surging images it accompanies, even the gloriously ironic pop soundtrack is stripped of nostalgic comforts.

This is not like Oliver Stone's yearning for a moment when psychedelia was seen as gloriously cutting edge. Rather, as the title suggests, psychedelia here is the handmaiden of misanthropy. In this Dantesque rendition of the American Dream, which recalls Hieronymus Bosch and Lewis Carroll by turns, the doors of perception open to reveal not a magical Oz peopled by the beautiful but a spiky underworld of corruption, embracing both the cabaret-crowd glitterati and the lumpen hoards of slot-addicts. The relationship between the establishment and its counterculture mutates into one of mutual dependence as the film progresses. "Ether is the perfect drug for Las Vegas," Duke intones as they enter Bazooka Circus. "In this town they love a drunk—fresh meat." Sinatra croons about sexual addiction ("You're getting to be a habit with me," he sings as Duke signs on to the district attorneys' drugs-abuse conference) and the film seems to ask how we define addiction and where and why we draw our lines of politically correct tolerance.

That this all takes place as a footnote to the stabbing at the Altamont concert, Tate-LaBianca murders and the Kent State shootings is heavy-handedly underlined by the regular intrusion of actuality footage flickering on hotel television screens. Technicolor excess in Vegas is underpinned by black-and-white televisual death in Vietnam, confusing the line between fact and fiction. (This is in the spirit of Thompson's 'Gonzo' journalism, which fictionalises its writer by placing him, confused and biased at the centre of the action.) My most recently purchased copy of the novel *Fear and Loathing* was bought in a bookshop that stocked it under nonfiction. Gilliam would be hard-pressed to pull off that categorisation, but the past of *Fear and Loathing* is nevertheless uncomfortably close, a foreign country Gilliam was all-too familiar with.

VILLAGE VOICE, 5/26/98, p. 132, J. Hoberman

Fear and Loathing in Las Vegas, Hunter S. Thompson's drug-crazed journalistic prose-poem, used a weekend in Las Vegas as a metaphor for America's season in hell. Sent to cover a cross-country motorcycle race, Thompson filed a postmortem on the '60s while reporting on his brain as though it were the dark side of the moon.

As extravagantly subjective, linguistically rich, and outrageously bad-behaved as it is, this lysergic tall tale (first published in *Rolling Stone* in late 1971) would seem to be problematic

Hollywood material. But, taking over the project from Alex Cox (himself something of a gonzo filmmaker), Terry Gilliam has returned from the desert bringing multiplex nation a fever dream that's as funny as it is poignant and as unencumbered in its performances as it is uncompromised in its worldview. How did this movie get made?

Like a belated sequel to *Easy Rider*, *Fear and Loathing* opens with two guys in Hawaiian shirts and a red convertible bombing, born to be wild, towards Nevada's neon Sodom: "We were somewhere around Barstow when the drugs began to take hold." Their search for America will be three days in Vegas and their twilight arrival in Glitter Gulch occasions the definitive LSD sequence in American movies—a farrago of glacially delayed responses, free-floating incomprehension, inadvertent word repetitions, and minor distortions blossoming into full-fledged hallucinations. To add to the comedy, Gilliam flips in and out of his hero's drastically expanded consciousness.

Bill Murray made an embarrassing stab at playing Hunter Thompson back in 1980 but Johnny Depp, here given the Thompson alias Raoul Duke, has the attitude as well as the look—receding hairline, orange aviator shades, jaunty cigarette holder—and the bonded-bourbon voice. His is the detached cool of a 19th-century explorer or a 1920s bon vivant. Depp, no less than Thompson, is a southern gentleman—and his coke-snort double takes notwithstanding, he's also an exemplary straight man. As his sidekick Dr. Gonzo, Benicio Del Toro—no less ambitiously unpredictable in his career than Depp—is given ample room to pulverize the screen.

Depp proves himself a master of moving as though someone had just pulled the plug on his power source, but the movie's edge is provided by Del Toro, who has gained 40 pounds and honed a paranoid glare that's sharper than the hunting knife he brandishes. From the moment he begins baying "One Toke Over the Line" to the scene he plays opposite hard-boiled waitress Ellen Barkin in an exaggeratedly realistic North Las Vegas diner, Del Toro is a force of nature. Depp thinks, Del Toro acts: its he who gets to woo catatonic Christina Ricci, woof Cameron Diaz in a scene of claustrophobic elevator terror, puke out a car window at a parallel vehicle filled with uptight squares.

Gilliam is an inspired conductor of manic behavior. *The Fisher King* showed him the only director in history to handle Robin William's personality at full throttle; Brad Pitt gave a career performance as a borderline lunatic in *12 Monkeys*. But nothing equals the jabbering gesticulations of Depp and Del Toro's stoned minuet. The scene in which they dose themselves with ether and surrender all motor skills to enter Circus Circus is a grunt-and-lurch ballet choreographed for Jovian gravity. This small classic of physical comedy is so deftly played and excruciatingly funny, you might reasonably fear that the movie has peaked too soon. Indeed, the trip turns a lot scarier once the action retreats to the pair's dark and increasingly trashed hotel suite. Thrashing around half-dressed in the bathtub, menacing Depp with his knife, the full-clothed, acid-ripped Del Toro is the weekend's real Godzilla—particularly if you recall that the monster's Japanese name was an amalgam of whale and gorilla.

Fear and Loathing has its longeurs. It's more obvious than need be—Gillian leans too heavily on interpolated TV news shows and old Be-in footage—but its also lighter than one might expect. The mise-en-scène is busy but not hysterical. (The true nightmare would have been to sit through a version directed by Oliver Stone.) Generous in its use of voiceover, the movie gets maximum mileage from Thompson's prose. It not only has the guts to dramatize Thompson's two-page flashback to San Francisco 1965 but also includes his rumination on the moment's drug-induced sense of generational manifest destiny. Scored to a Buffalo Springfield dirge, this evolutionary failure is even visualized: Depp wrapped in his microphone cord and, sporting a Halloween lizard tail, immersed in the primeval ooze of what once was a hotel suite.

Despite its world-famous title and for all its judiciously applied special effects, *Fear and Loathing* is deeply unfashionable. Oblivious to the Rat Pack revival, Gilliam is unrelentingly hostile to the swinging, grown-up entertainment of the era. "This was Bob Hope's turf. Frank Sinatra's. Spiro Agnew's," Depp is heard to mutter as he and Del Toro attempt to crash Debbie Reynolds's floor show and get bounced as she breaks into "Sergeant Pepper's Lonely Hearts Club Band." Given that the '60s remains the most maligned and oversold decade of the American century, *Fear and Loathing* may well be caught between the Scylla of squeamish tsk-tsking and the Charybdis of anti-Boomerism. (Don't expect the White House to call Universal for a weekend screening.)

Indeed, you could lose your mind trying to position this movie. The trailer, which has evidently been banned by ABC, is hopeless. At once prestigious literary adaptation and slapstick buddy flick, *Fear and Loathing in Las Vegas* is *Fellini Cheech and Chong*, a low-brow art film, an egghead monster movie, a gross-out trip to the lost continent of Mu. Flung in *Godzilla*'s path, this may be the most widely released midnight movie ever made, a hilarious paean to reckless indulgence that's as mournful as the sunset on an abandoned movie lot.

Also reviewed in:
CHICAGO TRIBUNE, 5/22/98, Friday/p. A, Mark, Caro
NEW REPUBLIC, 6/22/98, p. 26, Stanley Kauffmann
NEW YORK TIMES, 5/22/98, p. E14, Stephen Holden
VARIETY, 5/18-24/98, p. 72, Todd McCarthy
WASHINGTON POST, 5/22/98, p. F5, Stephen Hunter
WASHINGTON POST, 5/22/98, Weekend/p. 21, Michael O'Sullivan

54

A Miramax Films release of a Redeemable Features/Dollface/Filmcolonyproduction. *Executive Producer:* Bob Weinstein, Harvey Weinstein, Bobby Cohen, and Don Carmody. *Producer:* Richard N. Gladstein, Dolly Hall, and Ira Deutchman. *Director:* Mark Christopher. *Screenplay:* Mark Christopher. *Director of Photography:* Alexander Gruszynski. *Editor:* Lee Percy. *Music:* Marco Beltrami. *Music Editor:* Shari Schwartz Johanson, John Finklea, and Chris McGeary. *Choreographer:* Lori Eastside. *Sound:* David Lee. *Sound Editor:* Tom Bellfort and Robert Shoup. *Casting:* Billy Hopkins, Suzanne Smith, and Kenny Barden. *Production Designer:* Kevin Thompson. *Art Director:* Tamara Deverell. *Set Decorator:* Karin Wiesel. *Special Effects:* Michael Kavanagh. *Costumes:* Ellen Rutter. *Make-up:* Patricia Green. *Stunt Coordinator:* Shane Cardwell. *Running time:* 89 minutes. *MPAA Rating:* R.

CAST: Ryan Phillippe (Shane O'Shea); Salma Hayek (Anita); Neve Campbell (Julie Black); Mike Myers (Steve Rubell); Sela Ward (Billie Auster); Breckin Meyer (Greg Randazzo); Sherry Stringfield (Viv); Ellen Albertini Dow (Disco Dottie); Cameron Mathison (Atlanta); Noam Jenkins (Romeo); Jay Goede (Buck); Patrick Taylor (Tarzan); Heather Matarazzo (Grace O'Shea); Skipp Sudduth (Harlan O'Shea); Aemilia Robinson (Kelly O'Shea); Daniel Lapaine (Marc the Doorman); Erika Alexander (Ciel); Thelma Houston (Herself); Mary Griffin (Disco Star); Don Carrier (Julian); Domenick Lombardozzi (Kev); Mark Ruffalo (Ricko); Bruno Miguel (Boyd); Jason Andrews (Anthony); Laura Catalano (Rochelle); Kohl Sudduth (Rhett); Lorri Bagley (Patti); Lauren Hutton (Liz Vangelder); James Binkley (Rubell's Bodyguard); Arthur Nascarella and John Himes (IRS Agents); Louis Negin (Truman Capote); Lena Vajakas (Conrows); Barbara Radecki (TV Host); Ron Jeremy (Ron); Sean Sullivan (Andy Warhol); Vieslav Krystyan (Photographer); Nick Holt (Alpine Inn Waitress); David Blacker (Bouncer); Bruce MacVittie (Muisc Producer); Emmanuel Mark (Talent Manager); Kabriel Lilly (Little Girl); Michael York (Ambassador); Morgan Freeman (Angelic Boy); Lina Felice (Nicaraguan Woman); Elio Fiorucci (Himself); Drake Alonso Thorens (Man on Horseback); Justin Tensun (Blond Busboy); Jason Fruitman (Busboy); Andy Grote (54 Waiter); Jordan Paige (Young Shane); Georgina Kess (Shane's Mom); Mario Bosco (Mario); Coati Mundi Hernandez and Victor Sutherland (DJs); Janine Longley, Michael Henderson, and Chris Ingram (Kissing Trio).

LOS ANGELES TIMES, 8/28/98, Calendar/p. 2, Kenneth Turan

If you've never understood why people begged, wheedled and pleaded to get past the velvet rope and into the celebrated discos of the 1970s, don't look to "54" to enlighten you.

Decadence has rarely looked so pathetic, lethargic and dispiriting as it does in this listless film, based very loosely on the story of Manhattan's celebrated Studio 54 and its reigning spirit, Steve

Rubell. If the real 54 was this lacking in excitement and pizazz, it's a wonder all its patrons didn't fall asleep once they'd gotten inside the door.

Unlike writer-director Whit Stillman, who managed to infuse his own wry sensibility onto the nightclub scene in "The Last Days of Disco," first-time filmmaker Mark Christopher is as phobic about originality as a club doorman would be about a tourist in a polyester plaid leisure suit.

Not only is Christopher's "54" an unconvincing portrait of a particular moment in time, it's also completely uninspired dramatically. Imagine a lame "Love Boat" episode garnished with strictly pro forma drugs and sex and you'll get the picture.

Helping to make the film's treatment of that celebrated club even less accurate than it might have been was the decision to portray Studio 54 as completely Steve Rubell's enterprise. In fact, Rubell, who died a decade ago, had an involved partner named Ian Schrager, currently a successful hotelier, whose name and influence are never so much as mentioned.

Rubell himself is played, in a departure from the norm, by comic Mike Myers, best known in recent years as Austin Powers, International Man of Mystery. Granted that there's not a whole lot of competition, Myers' wistful performance remains the best thing about the film.

Myers plays Rubell as a kind of dissolute Andy Hardy; bad, maybe, but not evil—someone who kept the rabble out because the nephew of the king of Saudi Arabia was counting on him to uphold standards. Sure, Rubell skimmed money off the top, handed out drugs by the handful and baldly propositioned the male help, but, hey, this was a guy with a dream, a dream of "the best damn party in the world, a party that would last forever."

Those words come not from Rubell himself but the film's protagonist, Shane O'Shea (Ryan Phillippe). The year is 1979 and while 19-year-old Shane may be pumping gas in a dead-end New Jersey town, that doesn't stop him from—you guessed it—yearning for the glamorous night life of glistening Manhattan, just the way Brooklyn boy John Travolta did in "Saturday Night Fever."

Though he has no particular ability except his sullen, pouty good looks and a hot body, Shane catches Rubell's eye at the door of Studio 54. When he crosses the velvet rope, Shane experiences a quasi-religious epiphany. "I was chosen," he gushes. "I'd never been chosen for anything before."

Hired as a busboy, Shane is soon befriended by co-worker Greg (Breckin Meyer) and his wife, Anita (Salma Hayek), a coat-check girl and aspiring singer who is fixated on becoming "the next Donna Summer." As for Shane himself, his dream is meeting glamorous soap opera ingenue Julie Black (Neve Campbell), a fellow Jersey native who crossed the river and made good.

Quicker than you can say "clueless arriviste," Shane is promoted to bartender at 54, a position he considers "the best job in the world." Soon he is tooling around Manhattan with a "Shane 54" vanity license plate, "raising his profile" by appearing in beefcake magazine shoots and falling in terrible funks when there is no article to accompany the photos.

Yes, it's true, Shane is so dense it never occurs to him that he has no profile to raise and that there couldn't possibly be an article about him because there would be nothing to write. "54" turns out to be as dense as he is: When the film wants to indicate how badly Shane fits into upper-crust Manhattan dinner parties, it has him profess ignorance about, of all people, Errol Flynn. Forget writers, artists and musicians, it's a lack of knowledge about movie stars that spells doom on the East Side.

Given that "54" is told in voice-over flashback by an older and presumably wiser Shane, it's a given that at a certain point the young man will be disabused about his disco dreams, but it's hard to have the patience to wait around until it happens. As one of the lyrics on the film's soundtrack aptly puts it, "the feeling's gone and we just can't get it back."

NEW YORK POST, 8/28/98, p. 54, Rod Dreher

Mark Christopher, the writer-director of "54," was a boy growing up in the Midwest during Studio 54's late-'70s heyday, though he has become a student of the time and place. For all its diverting eye candy, his disappointing "54" calls to mind Brendan Behan's line comparing critics to eunuchs guarding a harem: They see it done every night, but don't know how to do it themselves.

That is, Christopher captures many of the glitzy textural details of the era, but his perfunctory screenplay fails to capture its Dionysian spirit. Like an archaeologist of popular culture, Christopher displays familiar Studio artifacts: the cocaine-snorting crescent moon (check), the velvet rope (check), the shirtless bartenders (check), outrageous fashions (check), Andy Warhol (check), the basement, the balcony and a dose of the clap (check, check and—ouch!—(check).

The gang's all here, but the movie has no compelling idea what to do with them. It's one thing to observe that bingeing on sex, drugs, money and fame leads to ruin—as it certainly did for many of Studio's habitues—but you have to show, as Paul Thomas Anderson did so well in "Boogie Nights," why ultra-decadence seemed so irresistible in the '70s.

With a rather too-obvious nod to "Saturday Night Fever," "54" is a generically written tale of Shane O'Shea (Ryan Phillippe), a working-class kid who escapes the dingy drudgery of Jersey life by using his androgynous beauty to cross the Rubicon of the velvet rope. Before long, the lecherous Steve Rubell, one of the owners of Studio 54, hires Shane to be a bartender, and he makes friends with other desperate strivers using their employment at the club to forward their ambitions.

Salma Hayek portrays a coat-check girl who wants to be a disco diva. Her husband, played by Breckin Meyer, is a barback who deals drugs to supplement his income as he waits to be anointed a bartender. Neve Campbell plays a soap-opera actress who prostitutes herself to the rich and famous, hoping to become one of them. The consuming hunger of these "little people" to escape their quotidian misery no matter the cost is understandable, and even poignant, but the screenplay's characterization suffers from two left feet.

Except in the case of Steve Rubell, the pitiful dweeb and former steakhouse owner who, for one dazzling moment, became the international arbiter of jet-set style. Working under a thinning wig and a prosthetic nose, Mike Myers does an exceptional job of humanizing the loathsome but miserably needy Rubell, who staggers around in a barbiturate haze.

By what sinister alchemy did this cruel, unstylish gremlin become so famous and important? Now there's a movie. In one sad but funny exchange, Rubell berates his staff for letting some "yids" into his swank club. Says the doorman: "But they were your family, Steve." There's more pathos in that than in anything that takes place among Rubell's employees, with whom, unfortunately, we have to spend most of our time.

"54" is far from a disaster, though, and it's more fun (if less smart) than Whit Stillman's similarly themed "The Last Days of Disco." Christopher moves things along at a steady clip, and savoring the hairdos and the occasional humor provides modest entertainment.

There's a toot of a moment when Rubell stops the music to have a boy angel descend from the ceiling to give Truman Capote (Louis Negin) a present to celebrate his face lift. "Thank you, sugah!" Tru chirps. That's the sort of vanity and frivolity "54" ought to be rolling in. But maybe you had to have been there.

NEWSDAY, 8/28/98, Part II/p. B3, Jack Mathews

The best thing that may be said for first-time writer-director Mark Christopher's "54," an empty portrait of the infamous '70s Manhattan disco mecca Studio 54, is that you won't have to beg, wheedle, bribe, strip, know or service somebody to get in. In fact, give it a week and you may be the only person in line.

"54" is as flat as the drops in a bottle of champagne left for the cleanup crew after a night of partying at the Midtown drug and disco den where the rich, famous, beautiful and simply foolish convened to strut, gawk, grope, drink, smoke, and otherwise celebrate having got in. What is success but privilege, and what better way—at least at the peak of pre-AIDS, post-reason laxity—to exercise the privilege than in Steven Rubell's glitzy joint down on 54th Street?

How could this movie go so wrong? It has it all: sex, drugs and rock and roll. Couples make love, undisturbed in the midst of the throng, nasal passages are filled with the finest mood-altering powders, beautiful people—invited or hand-chosen by Rubell from the crowd outside—rub together in a hormone rage, to a disco beat.

The answer is not simply that "54" is badly written and directed but that the artifact itself, the studio disinterred, is as dated as a tabloid headline, and the people in it, from the usual pop icons Truman Capote and Andy Warhol to our hero, wide-eyed Jersey adonis Shane O'Shea (Ryan Phillippe), seem less privileged than idiotic.

Christopher, a native Iowan who, like Shane, fulfilled a dream by passing through the portals of Studio 54, has fashioned an homage out of equal parts contempt and admiration. The contempt may not have been conscious, but it's there, in his alter ego.

Shane, a working class stiff who's all looks and no brain (his pop-culture IQ is so low, he doesn't know whether he's been flattered or insulted by being compared to Erroll Flynn), is driven by nothing more than an urge to leave home and a fan's infatuation with a soap opera star who's a 54 regular. After being hand-chosen by a lusting Rubell (Mike Myers), Shane gets a job as a busboy in the club, and quickly works his way up to topless bartender!

"54" begs comparisons to "Saturday Night Fever," but the disco connection is weak. Shane is no Tony Manero (and Phillippe is no John Travolta). He's closer kin to Dirk Diggler in "Boogie Nights," a well-endowed nobody who bathes in false esteem when he becomes a porn star. Shane and Dirk are flashes in a shallow pan, but where "Boogie Nights" creator Paul Thomas Anderson plumbed the depths of Dirk's vulnerable psyche, and through him, a weakness in the American character during the same period, Christopher is satisfied skimming along the surface of atmosphere and legend.

What little story there is involves Shane's relationships with fellow busboy Greg (Breckin Meyer), his singer wannabe wife Anita (Salma Hayek), soap star Julie Black (Neve Campbell), and the pill-popping Rubell, whose real-life problems with the IRS provide a convenient place for the film to stop, if not quite end.

Christopher might have done better to make Rubell the focus of the story. How a hustling entrepreneur could launch, as Shane says, the best party the world had ever seen, then bring himself down by cooking the books, is full of promise. But despite Myers' game efforts in his first dramatic role, Rubell comes off as nothing more than a creepy, perpetually stoned dilettante.

No other character in the film is vaguely compelling, and there's something repulsively ill-conceived about Disco Dotty (Ellen Albertini Dow), a foul-mouthed, coke-sniffing eightysomething vamp who Rubell keeps around the club—and Christopher keeps in the movie—as dark comic relief.

SIGHT AND SOUND, 2/99, p. 42, Liese Spencer

New York, 1979. Nineteen-year-old Shane O'Shea lives with his father and younger sisters in New Jersey One night he cajoles his friends to go to Manhattan's most exclusive disco, Studio 54. Only Shane is let in by owner Steve Rubell. Shane returns and is given a job. He moves in with fellow busboy Greg and his wife Anita, an aspiring singer-songwriter who works in the cloakroom.

Sexually promiscuous, Shane takes drugs and meets celebrity guests such as soap star Julie Black and geriatric regular Disco Dottie. Every night money is cleared from the tills to cheat the IRS. Greg is propositioned by Rubell, but refuses. Shane begins an affair with socialite Billie Auster. Greg begins to deal drugs. Shane contracts a sexually transmitted disease. After arguing with Greg on Christmas Eve, Shane goes home but is turned away by his father.

Steve spends a romantic afternoon with Julie Black. On New Year's Eve, Shane sees Julie with another man who suggests a threesome. Dottie dies on the dance floor during Anita's singing debut. Shane argues with Rubell and storms out. The IRS raid Studio 54 and arrest Rubell. Eighteen months later Rubell is released from prison and Shane, Anita and Greg meet again at a party at Studio 54.

Bowdlerised by parent company Disney, Miramax's 54 is a disappointingly conventional account of the 70s most notorious nightclub. Retracing the steps of *Saturday Night Fever* with heavy feet, writer-director Mark Christopher's urban picaresque opens with teenager Shane O'Shea fleeing his New Jersey home in search of excitement in Manhattan's most exclusive nightclub. With a grinding predictability, the next 90 minutes show us Studio's glittering bacchanalia turning into a strobe-lit nightmare of corruption and ugliness. As he progresses from gauche innocent to bare-chested hustler, Shane befriends fellow busboy Greg and his wife Anita, blue-collar grafters who understand that in the United States, "there is no such thing as royalty, only celebrity", and who ply their aspirations in the mosh-pit of social mobility that is Studio 54.

The script's decision to focus on these dim-witted dreamers is a mistake. Pretty enough, Ryan Phillippe as Shane lacks Travolta's charisma and dancing skills, while Breckin Meyer and Salma Hayek's truncated roles as Greg and Anita leave them little room to prove their abilities. So brutal is the editing that their ensemble relationship is reduced to a series of tenuous allegiances and confrontations which dissolve between scenes with little meaning or resonance.

Such flimsy characters are matched by the film's half-hearted portrayal of pre-Aids hedonism. Bianca Jagger's ride into Studio 54 on a white horse was a moment of iconic decadence. It seems representative of the film's fearful approach that what we get instead is a white goat, a poor Andy Warhol impersonator and a slightly lascivious cameo by Michael York.

More perniciously, the club's legendary pansexuality has been replaced by the acceptable face of debauchery. In *54* homosexuality can be heard about but not seen (a prudishness that stems, one suspects, from the studio rather than from Christopher, whose previous work includes a couple of gay shorts). Shane, Greg and Anita's love triangle is entirely proper (a much vaunted screen kiss between Shane and Greg was cut) while Greg shows an uncharacteristic squeamishness by refusing to have a career-enhancing exchange of bodily fluids with club-owner Steve Rubell.

Sporting a prosthetic nose and bald patch, Mike Myers' Rubell is the best thing about the movie. Whether writhing ecstatically on a bed covered in dollar bills or addressing the crowds from the DJ's box like some disco dictator, Myers' tragi-comic performance captures Rubell's sleazy charm to perfection. It helps of course that Myers has all the best lines. In one scene he tells the doorman not to let, "whores and yids in like last night," only for the bouncer to protest, "But those were your cousins, Steve." Later, as the IRS raid his club, Rubell can't help sneering, "even from here their suits look cheap."

A moral bankrupt from the sticks who buried his own sense of self-loathing in snobbery and substituted intimacy for a family of dancing drug-users, Rubell's impresario is the one character of any substance, the one we want to watch. Instead, we follow his brainless employees towards a trite ending about a dead granny who partied until the end.

Released at the fag-end of the recent 70s retrospective, Christopher's film already feels past its sell-by date, its banal characters and uninspired script inviting unfavourable comparisons with *Boogie Nights* and *The Last Days of Disco*. Studio's decor famously included the Man in the Moon, spooning cocaine into his nose. Despite a great soundtrack, watching *54* is more like swallowing a bottle of quaaludes: let's hope it's the last stop on the current nostalgia trip.

TIME, 9/7/98, p. 75, Richard Corliss

From here, it seems that the most recent decade when folks looked really sharp was the '50s. Nice haircuts, good posture, a coolly casual clothes sense. Every decade since, as shown in the current glut of reflective movies, looks tacky, toadish, its own parody.

That's certainly the case with the late-70s metropolitan New York division, in Mark Christopher's *54*. We are yanked back to Studio 54, the trash-glam Manhattan disco where, for a few years, simply everyone who did anyone was desperate to be seen. They had a blast at this all-night carnival of drugs, booze, sex, and a lot of pretty people who tawked funny. And the funniest was 54s co-owner and host Steve Rubell, the Elsa Maxwell of sleaze.

In Mike Myers droll, brave impersonation, Rubell is a starstruck lout a user-abuser, seductively snaky, cheerily malevolent; he could be *Lolita*'s Clare Quilty without the gaudy wordplay. It'd be fun to see a movie about this Rubell. Alas, *54* focuses on the kids who worked for him: Shane the blond busboy (Ryan Phillippe), Anita the coat checker (Salma Hayek) and other cutie losers. The film tries to toss *Saturday Night Fever*'s bridge-and-tunnel dreamers into the '70s' hottest disco. But for that to work, you need verve, edge and Travolta. All those are absent here.

There's some fun seeing Canadians like Myers and Neve Campbell (as a soap-opera star) try out their lumpen tristate accents. And the music still has its innocent juice. But the film is just one more sound-track CD in search of a plot. Or maybe we're already sick of the polyester '70s. Why couldn't *54* have been the year instead of the club?

VILLAGE VOICE, 9/8/98, p. 121, J. Hoberman

The actual flash-photos of totally hammered celebs that grace the end-credits of Mark Christopher's *54* are by far the liveliest thing this choppy, depressingly pointless celebration of Manhattan's greatest disco.

Studio 54 is introduced, in a dopey voiceover given to busboy Shane O'Shea (Ryan Phillippe), as owner Steve Rubell's dream of democratic decadence—nonstop party with no rules, once you were allowed past the velvet rope. Christopher's *54* is a vision of showbiz beatitude with hardly any beat and very little to show. Too bad Christopher didn't put Rubell himself at the center—particularly since, in an underwritten or severely scissored role, the Brooklyn mogul is played, in an inspired bit of casting, by Mike Meyers as the snickering, 'luded Nero of New York City nightlife.

As released, however, *54* seems a pale imitation of *Boogie Nights,* focusing on the education of the dumb but winsome Shane, who flees Jersey City become a bare-chested bartender serving (and servicing) the gods at their revels—"one big bender with business cards," in the conventional wisdom of the pretty soap star (Neve Campbell), also from Jersey, whom Shane covets. Rumor has it that the movie has achieved its relatively svelte 89-minute running time by eliminating Shane's opportunistic homosexual trysts. And that's not the only thing missing.

Anyone who sat through *The Last Days of Disco* might find themselves searching the balcony for the well-bred Stillmanettes who populated last spring's vision of the Great Good Place. *Last Days* wasn't much of a movie but it did create the occasion for a splendid CD. *54* can't even say that.

Also reviewed in:
CHICAGO TRIBUNE, 8/28/98, Friday/p. A, Michael Wilmington
NEW YORK TIMES, 8/28/98, p. E10, Stephen Holden
VARIETY, 8/31-9/6/98, p. 94, Emanuel Levy
WASHINGTON POST, 8/28/98, p. B1, Stephen Hunter
WASHINGTON POST, 8/28/98, Weekend/p. 41, Michael O'Sullivan

FIRELIGHT

A Hollywood Pictures release of a Wind Dancer/Carnival Films production. *Executive Producer:* Susan Cartsonis, Rick Leed, Matt Williams, David McFadzean, and Carmen Finestra. *Producer:* Brian Eastman. *Director:* William Nicholson. *Screenplay:* William Nicholson. *Director of Photography:* Nic Morris. *Editor:* Chris Wimble. *Music:* Christopher Gunning. *Choreographer:* Jane Gibson. *Sound:* Sandy MacRae and (music) Chris Dibble. *Sound Editor:* Ian Fuller. *Casting:* John Hubbard, Ros Hubbard, and Nancy Klopper. *Production Designer:* Rob Harris. *Art Director:* Peter Wenham. *Set Decorator:* Caroline Smith. *Costumes:* Andrea Galer. *Make-up:* Suzan Broad, Lisa Pickering and Françoise Cresson. *Running time:* 103 minutes. *MPAA Rating:* R.

CAST: Sophie Marceau (Elisabeth Laurier); Stephen Dillane (Charles Godwin); Kevin Anderson (John Taylor); Lia Williams (Constance, "Connie"); Dominique Belcourt (Louisa Godwin); Joss Ackland (Lord Clare, "Jimmy"); Sally Dexter (Molly Holland); Emma Amos (Ellen); Maggie McCarthy (Mrs. Jago); Wolf Kahler (Sussman); Annabel Giles (Amelia "Amy" Godwin); John Flanagan (Robert Ames); Harry Jones (William); Ian Crowe (Thomas); Valerie Minifie (Hannah); Diana Payan (Mrs. Maidment); John Hodgkinson (Carlo); Anthony Dutton (Dodds); Hugh Walters (Dr. Geddes); Peter Needham (Rector); Melissa Knatchbull (Mrs. Hurst); Frank Rozelaar-Green (Dancemaster); Trevor St. John Hacker (Fashionable Guest); Katharine Levy (French Maid); Valerie Sarruf (French Patronne); Thomas Fischer (Davey).

CHRISTIAN SCIENCE MONITOR 9/4/98, p. B4, David Sterritt

Movie screens aren't exactly swarming with governesses this season, but they do seem more numerous than usual, First we had "The Governess," with Minnie Driver as the title character, who falls in love with her wealthy 19th-century employer and helps him invent photography. Now we have "Firelight," a slightly darker but no less romantic tale that's arriving in American theaters straight from the World Film Festival here in Montreal.

The heroine is a young Swiss woman who needs to settle her late father's debts. To obtain the necessary funds, she agrees to bear a child for a wealthy man whose wife is a helpless invalid, but finds herself unable to pass this off as what would now be called a "surrogate mother" arrangement. Years later she tracks her daughter down, accepting a job as the little girl's governess. She also sets about renewing her relationship with the aristocrat who originally set these events in motion.

What gives this story an appealing feminist overtone is the governess's determination not just to regain her daughter's affection but to give the little girl a genuine education, thus helping her avoid the sort of second-class status that she herself, like most women of the 19th century and many of our own, has been trapped in all her life.

Other assets of the movie include the firelit camera work by cinematographer Nic Morris, and earnest performances by Sophie Marceau as the heroine, Stephen Dillane as the aristocrat, and Dominique Belcourt as their daughter.

Although these ingredients weigh in the picture's favor, they're ultimately outbalanced by serious flaws in the screenplay. Many scenes are trite, stilted, or simply hard to believe. And Christopher Gunning's music drenches much of the action in melodies so corny that they detract from the emotions they're supposed to enhance.

The movie was written and directed by William Nicholson, who scripted Jodie Foster's drama "Nell" and earned a well-deserved Oscar nomination for his "Shadowlands" screenplay five years ago. He shows promise as a director, but he needs to show more trust in his own material and leave those weepy violins on the recording room floor.

LOS ANGELES TIMES, 9/4/98, Calendar/p. 10, Kevin Thomas

"Firelight" isn't likely to give off much of a glow except to devourers of Harlequin-type period romances. For them, however, it delivers the goods in much tidier fashion than the potentially much better but seriously flawed "The Governess," which also opened this summer. For the rest of us, though, it's pretty heavy going. (When it comes to recent governess/poor relation movies, Jessica Lange's "Cousin Bette" is the best of the lot.)

A governess, explains Sophie Marceau's Elisabeth, is the only respectable position open to women without means in the early 19th century. Times have obviously changed drastically for most women in Europe and America but no doubt there are still plenty of women who can identify with a governess whose only hope for escape from a grim existence is for some dashing knight to rescue her from poverty and loneliness and sweep her up into a life of romance, luxury and high social position.

British writer-director William Nicholson, who has spoken of his admiration for '40s screen romances, tries to recall them yet brings to the genre a contemporary candor that is sometimes jarring—too real for what is essentially contrived hokum. His Elisabeth, who is Swiss, is a damsel in such distress that she agrees to sire a child for Stephen Dillane's Charles, an English aristocrat whose beloved wife has for two years remain paralyzed and comatose (but with her eyes wide open) from a riding accident. (It seems that Elisabeth means to spring her father from prison, presumably for debt, with Charles' payment of 5,000 pounds.)

Elisabeth and Charles agree to meet in Normandy and spend three nights together to try to make sure that Elisabeth becomes pregnant. By the third night, Charles, who has remained celibate, and Elisabeth, who most probably is a virgin, are enjoying themselves but stick to the agreement, which means that their child is to be deposited on the steps of an inn near Charles' vast Sussex estate. Alas, mother love sweeps over Elisabeth, who spends the next seven years tracking down Charles, whose name she never knew. The next thing he knows Elisabeth has been hired by his sister-in-law Constance (Lia Williams) as the newest governess for their spoiled-rotten daughter Louisa (Dominique Belcourt).

Of course, he's outraged; of course, she's a miracle worker with the incorrigible child; of course, they can't keep their hands off each other.

Now all this wealth of incident—there's much more, to be sure—is treated by Nicholson with the utmost solemnity, so much so that when Charles' pleasure-loving father (Joss Ackland) visits, we're made to notice how stiff and glum "Firelight" really is. (Not helping is that Marceau is herself not exactly an animated actress; Dillane, however, is as good as circumstances permit.)

For someone who takes his material so very seriously, Nicholson is careless with details. How did Elisabeth and Charles come into contact with each other in the first place? Personal ads seem unlikely. How did Charles make sure that he'd be the one to pick up the seemingly abandoned baby? Since we're decades away from intravenous feeding, how has Charles' absolutely rigid wife managed to survive 10 long years? If Constance, who not surprisingly is secretly in love with Charles herself, yields gracefully to Elisabeth and departs, where and how will she live? The more "Firelight" sputters the less you care about the answers.

NEW YORK POST, 9/4/98, p. 68, Larry Worth

If it's a talent to push overwrought melodrama to the point of parody, writer-director William Nicholson is a master.

Freely ripping off romantic classics—think "Jane Eyre", "Madame X" and "Stella Dallas"—and then throwing in a bit of "The Miracle Worker", he has produced the embarrassingly awful "Firelight" It's the kind of bodice-ripping soap opera where the tortured hero reluctantly falls for the ever-heaving heroine and admits: "I didn't expect it would be like this."

Clearly, he's the only one who didn't see it coming. This is about as paint-by-numbers as the genre gets. Even that's OK if it's fun. But this is bad moviemaking, plain and simple.

Set in Europe in the 1830s, the tale opens as Elisabeth, a feisty young beauty, is propositioned by Charles, a crusty but handsome English land owner, to father his child. It seems wifey's in a hopeless coma and there's no heir in sight.

Elisabeth agrees—to save her daddy dearest from debtors prison, mind you—and falls for her hunky British employer in the process. One daughter later, they part ways.

Seven years pass (though nobody ages a day) and Liz tracks down her ex-lover and the child she's never forgotten. Getting herself hired as governess to the now-spoiled brat, she has to keep her true identity from the girl and suppress l'amour with ol' Chuck.

There's enough emotional baggage here to keep the principals in therapy for decades, but Nicholson treats those issues like a joke. He's too intent on putting orange filters on firelight scenes and letting the music swell to syrupy crescendos.

Meanwhile, the script seems about as true to the period as its 1990s spin on feminism. Too bad Nicholson didn't pay more attention to rectifying gaping plot holes and lame symbolism. Thankfully, the photography momentarily distracts.

That's more than can be said of the cast. While Sophie Marceau's Elisabeth is undeniably gorgeous, she fails to convey much more than pouty lips. Stephen Dillane, who made such a fine impression in "Welcome to Sarajevo," is no better as the ever-confused Mr. Rochester clone.

In supporting roles, usually reliable Kevin Anderson comes off like a walking anachronism while Tony Award nominee Lia (Skylight) Williams, veteran trooper Joss Ackland and petite newcomer Dominique Belcourt deliver varying stages of histrionics.

As for the title, it refers to the myth of being able to say and do anything in front of a blazing hearth, only to have it completely erased from all memory afterward.

"Firelight" should be so lucky.

NEWSDAY, 9/4/98, Part II/p. B3, John Anderson

One of the remarkable things about "Firelight," and there aren't many, is how blithely it goes about presenting characters of such dubious virtue. The putative hero pays an impoverished woman to bear him a child, shuts her out of the child's life and, when it suits his purposes, euthanizes his invalid wife because "she would have wanted it that way.." Excuse me, but are we supposed to be rooting for somebody here?

It doesn't help that this rather benighted movie, written and directed by William Nicholson (the decent "Shadowlands," the wacky "Nell"), is populated by actors of such numbing qualities. Or that to think that because people lived in the 1830s, they comported themselves with painful theatricality.

Sophie Marceau may be one of the more beautiful women on the screen, but she's so stiff she makes Bob Dole seem like Robin Williams. She had little to do in "Braveheart" besides brighten the decor, but in "Anna Karenina" she had you rooting for the train. Perhaps she's better in French.

Stephen Dillane ("Welcome to Sarajevo") doesn't help matters with his tepid performance, but his problems have more to do with the script than his style.

His character, Charles, is the conscientious son of a dissipated lord (Joss Ackland) who is so concerned that his family line be continued—and whose wife was left in a vegetative state by a riding accident—that he hires a debt-ridden Swiss woman, Elisabeth (Marceau), to have his baby.

During their several, uh, business negotiations in a French hotel, she falls in love with him—why? We can't tell. Able to forget neither the father nor the baby she gives up, she manages, seven years later, to get the job as her unsuspecting daughter's governess.

Forget the unlikelihood that any of this would happen, or that the movie is so solemn you'll think you're in church. Or that Charles' attractiveness to every woman in the movie is such an utter mystery. Or that the kid (Dominique Belcourt) is such an unlikable brat. Or that Elisabeth gave up her child to begin with.

When the love between Charles and Elisabeth becomes too much to hide, and Louisa learns the truth, there's nothing to do but knock off the wife. And they all live happily ever after.

Maybe I'm old-fashioned, but this seems to be taking poetic license, to say nothing of convenient morality, to something of an extreme.

SIGHT AND SOUND, 8/98, p. 39, Charlotte O'Sullivan

In 1837 Elisabeth, a Swiss governess, agrees to bear a child for mysterious English aristocrat Charles Godwin. During the three days they spend together in order to conceive, an attraction develops. Nine months later, however, the baby girl is taken away from her mother. Seven years later Elisabeth tracks down her daughter, Louisa. Identified as Godwin's "adopted" child, the girl lives in Sussex, where Godwin has moved with his invalid wife to rear sheep. At first relations between Louisa and her new governess are fraught, but gradually both she and her father are won over. The reckless behaviour of Godwin's father means Godwin loses his home. He deliberately leaves a window open so his wife will die. Father, mother and child leave for America.

This melodramatic tale of upstairs-downstairs love is scriptwriter William Nicholson's first feature as a director. It doesn't work, but one can forgive a novice an inability to cope with big stars (Sophie Marceau spends far too much time biting her bottom lip) and bad luck with the soupy and insipid score.

What one can't forgive, given Nicholson's reputation (he wrote the play *Shadowlands* which he adapted for Richard Attenborough's film), is the crude, superficial script. The film's metaphors and themes, for instance, couldn't be more obvious (firelight versus lamplight; genetic engineering versus natural selection), while the dialogue fails to register any class tension and is ludicrously anachronistic. (Elisabeth and Godwin's father engage in playful banter using the word "fucked".) It isn't even original. As in Campion's *The Piano*, a mercenary 'contract' sows the seeds of independence and therefore love. As in *Jane Eyre,* we have a rebellious, witchy governess obsessed with the beneficial effects of education (for the oppressed) and plagued by the presence of an incarcerated first wife. But in choosing a heroine so buxom, vivid and irrepressible, Nicholson drains the tension from his romance. Jane Eyre's appeal lay in her fierce human weakness, but Elisabeth truly is a magician—her problems, one by one, disappear into thin air.

Louisa is the only figure with a spark of life. Educating Louisa, winning her over, weaning her off her father: this is what animates Elisabeth and the script itself. "I will do to her what I do to myself," is the mother's bizarre promise; later she croons, "I loved my father but what I wanted most was a mother." We discover that Louisa has been communicating with her mother's ghost—travelling across water in a rowing boat to sit in an apparently empty room (shades of Henry James' *The Turn of the Screw),* Elisabeth's job is to destroy the power of this deadly ideal. The pleasing irony is that she's competing with herself.

The scenes concerning Elisabeth's "repossession" of Louisa are the only ones strange enough to justify the existence of *Firelight.* Breathtakingly shot in greys and blues, the space this child has created for herself is rendered utterly seductive and the loss involved in her baptism into life (Elisabeth must literally raise her from the water) is palpable. Having had a mother all to herself, she must now share her with the world (and papa), and young Dominique Belcourt's stricken, spritish face registers this perfectly. The shame is that Nicholson didn't make this grief-filled, tender battle between mother and daughter the true romance of his film.

Also reviewed in:
CHICAGO TRIBUNE, 9/4/98, Friday/p. A, Michael Wilmington
NEW YORK TIMES, 9/3/98, E17, Stephen Holden
VARIETY, 9/29-10/5/97, p. 61, Lisa Nesselson
WASHINGTON POST, 9/4/98, p. D5, Rita Kempley
WASHINGTON POST, 9/4/98, Weekend/p. 37, Michael O'Sullivan

FIRESTORM

A Twentieth Century Fox release of a Loeb/Weisman production. *Executive Producer:* Louise Rosner. *Producer:* Joseph Loeb III, Matthew Weisman, and Thomas M. Hammel. *Director:* Dean Semler. *Screenplay:* Chris Soth. *Director of Photography:* Stephen F. Windon. *Editor:* Jack Hofstra. *Music:* J. Peter Robinson. *Music Editor:* Lisé Richardson. *Sound:* David Husby and (music) Robert Fernandez. *Sound Editor:* Frank Gaeta. *Casting:* Allison Gordon Kohler. *Production Designer:* Richard Paris and Linda Del Rosario. *Set Decorator:* Dominique Fauquet-Lemaitre. *Set Dresser:* Jonathan Lancaster. *Special Effects:* Chris Corbould. *Costumes:* Bruce Finlayson and Carla Hetland. *Make-up:* Lisa Love. *Stunt Coordinator:* Glenn Wilder and Ken Kirzinger. *Running time:* 100 minutes. *MPAA Rating:* R.

CAST: Howie Long (Jesse); Scott Glenn (Wynt); William Forsythe (Shaye); Suzy Amis (Jennifer); Christianne Hirt (Monica); Garwin Sanford (Pete); Sebastian Spence (Cowboy); Michael Greyeyes (Andy); Barry Pepper (Packer); Vladimir Kulich (Karge); Tom McBeath (Loomis); Benjamin Ratner (Wilkins); Jonathon Young (Sherman); Chilton Crane (Tina's Mom); Robyn Driscoll (Tina's Dad); Alexandria Mitchell (Tina); Terry Kelly (Lawyer); David Fredericks (Guard); Gavin Buhr (Childs); Danny Wattley (Moody); Derek Hamilton (Dwyer); Adrian Dorval (Belcher); Jon Cuthbert (Davis); Sean Campbell (Deputy); Deryl Hayes (Sheriff Garrett).

LOS ANGELES TIMES, 1/9/98, Calendar/p. 16, Kevin Thomas

"Firestorm" is as elementary as action pictures get, but it moves as fast as the raging forest fire it captures so spectacularly well. There's not much time to dwell on plot developments that don't bear close scrutiny in the first place.

"Firestorm" works well as a mindless diversion under cinematographer-turned-director Dean Semler's punchy, efficient helming and has engaging stars in Howie Long, the former football great and current, Fox NFL commentator, Scott Glenn, Suzy Amis and William Forsythe as a villain so evil you wish he had a mustache to twirl. Indeed, "Firestorm" has the primitive appeal of early silents with their melodrama, derring-do and last-second rescues.

A rugged giant of a man with an open countenance and a sly sense of humor, Long is perfect casting as a Wyoming wilderness hero. He's a smoke-jumper, along with his mentor Glenn, and they're faced with a doozy of a fire—two of them, in fact, all set to converge on the bad guys as well as the good guys. Forsythe, a state prison inmate, has devised a way to escape, pass himself off as a firefighter and then head for wherever it is he has hidden $37 million stolen off a train at the cost of 17 lives.

Neither he nor his fellow escapees has much of a sense of direction, but they do know enough to take ornithologist Amis hostage. By the time the picture is over, debuting writer Chris Soth has come up with more perils than Pauline ever faced and has even fashioned some decent repartee for Long and Amis.

Although "Firestorm" plays like a TV adventure, it has big-screen panache in its stunts, camerawork and special effects. J. Peter Robinson's score underlines the action strongly. And that forest fire really looks to be out of control.

NEW YORK POST, 1/9/98, p. 37, Michael Medved

Raging forest fires. Raging windstorms. A raging mass murderer who's escaped from prison. Raging helicopters and raging motorcycles. A raging ornithologist/wilderness survivalist who just happens to look like a supermodel.

"Firestorm" throws together all these disparate elements of raging bull in a desperate attempt to distract attention from a puerile performance by Howie Long in his first starring big-screen role.

The former Raiders All-Pro football star and current co-host of "Fox NFL Sunday" got an attention-getting supporting role in "Broken Arrow," but here he attracts penalty flags every time he tries for a big play.

With less acting range than Jean-Claude Van Damme, less screen presence than Steven Seagal, less graceful athleticism (oddly) than Chuck Norris, and less spontaneous charm than Al Gore, Long muddies and muddles even those rare sequences that have begun to generate some cinematic momentum.

He plays the leader of a team of fearless smoke jumpers who use their parachuting skills to battle wilderness blazes in the Northwest.

One such conflagration arises out of a conspiracy to free an imprisoned murderer and master thief (the capably menacing William Forsythe), who hopes to recover the $37 million he's stashed away after his last train robbery.

With three other convicts posing as firefighters, the evil genius takes hostage a gorgeous birdwatcher (Suzy Amis), who's been conveniently trained in various survival and combat skills by her Marine hero father.

To rescue the girl, capture the bad guys and escape from the towering flames before they're all as burned as Bambi's buddies, Howie Long deploys peerless courage, flying chainsaws, martial arts expertise, leaping motorcycles and a single gritted-teeth knitted-brow facial expression.

Debuting director Dean Semler, who previously served as cinematographer on "Dances With Wolves," "Waterworld" and other ambitious projects, has no sense of pacing or structure, but he does stage some fearsome fires.

There's also one nifty chase scene through burning woods that ends with an impressive, death-defying jump off a cliff. The scariest part of this project, however, is its genesis: Young screenwriter Chris Soth wrote the silly, overloaded script as his acclaimed master's thesis at USC, America's most prestigious film school.

If this is the way we're training Hollywood's creative talent of tomorrow, it will take more than muscular superheroes to save this imperiled industry.

Also reviewed in:
CHICAGO TRIBUNE, 1/9/98, Tempo/p. 2, Monica Eng
NEW YORK TIMES, 1/9/98, p. E20, Stephen Holden
VARIETY, 1/12-18/98, Joe Leydon

FIREWORKS (HANA-BI)

A Milestone Films release of an Office Kitano/Bandai Visual Company/Television Tokyo Channel/Tokyo FM Broadcasting Company production. *Producer:* Masayuki Mori, Yasushi Tsuge, and Takio Yoshida. *Director:* Takeshi Kitano. *Screenplay (Japanese with English subtitles):* Takeshi Kitano. *Director of Photography:* Hideo Yamamoto. *Editor:* Takeshi Kitano and Yoshinori Ota. *Music:* Joe Hisaishi. *Sound:* Senji Horiuchi and (music) Shinichi Takaka. *Casting:* Takefumi Yoshikawa. *Art Director:* Norihiro Isoda. *Set Decorator:* Tatsuo Ozeki. *Costumes:* Masami Saito. *Make-up:* Michiyo Miyauchi. *Special Make-up:* Tomoo Haraguchi. *Running time:* 101 minutes. *MPAA Rating:* Not Rated.

CAST: Beat Takeshi (Yoshitaka Nishi); Kayoko Kishimoto (Miyuki, Nishi's Wife); Ren Osugi (Horibe); Susumu Terajima (Detective Nakamura); Tetsu Watanabe (Tezuka, Junkyard

Owner);   Hakuryu (Yakuza Hitman);   Yasuei Yakushiji (Killer on the Loose);   Taro Itsumi (Detective Kudo, Young Cop);   Kenichi Yajima (Doctor);   Makoto Ashikawa (Detective Tanaka);   Yuko Daike (Detective Tanaka's Widow);   Edamame Tsunami (Stone Throwing Officer Worker);   Yurei Yanagi (Chef of the Japanese Restaurant A);   Sujitaro Tamabukuro (Hit and Run Victim Hooligan);   Tokio Seki (Driver of the Smaller Truck);   Motoharu Tamura (Chief Detective);   Hitoshi Nishizawa (Boss of Yakuza Loan Shark);   Hiromi Kikai (Yakuza Henchman A);   Shoko Matsuda (Girl Who Flies Kites);   Banshou Shinra (Yakuza Henchman Who is Shot in the Head);   Satowa Matsumi (Maid at the Inn);   Miki Fujitani (Florist Clerk); Keiko Yamamoto and Kiyoko Kitazawa (Nurses);   Ai Kishina (Daughter of Scrapyard Owner); Mari Nakamura (Kiosk Salesclerk);   Takao Toji (Old Man Visiting Temple with Grandson); Shindai Naya and Muneyuki Konishi (Detectives at Stakeout);   Yuzo Yada (Temple Priest); Kanji Tsuda (The Man Under Investigation);   Yoichi Nagai (The Cop Driving an Unmarked Car);   Kohsuke Ota (Bartender);   Muhoumatsu (Construction Worker); Omiyanomatsu (Chef of the Japanese Restaurant B);   Shaw Kosugi and Banbino Kobayashi (Brats).

LOS ANGELES TIMES, 3/20/98, Calendar/p. 4, Kenneth Turan

"Fireworks" is bracing and original, an indefinable film made from familiar elements. "Hana-Bi," its title in Japanese, is a combination of the words for "flower" and "fire," and filmmaker Takeshi Kitano has, in the same way, adroitly fused genres, creating a film in which almost every moment pops out in unexpected ways.

Nominally a crime story, and the first Japanese work to win the Grand Prize at Venice since "Rashomon" in 1950, "Fireworks" is much more than a hard-boiled film with a sense of humor. Elements of violence, comedy and sentiment so disparate it doesn't seem possible they belong to the same film are unified and made irresistible by an eccentric and unconventional structure that is Kitano's creation alone.

Kitano is a major media celebrity in Japan, where, among other things, he has published more than 50 books and hosts several TV shows. Besides writing, directing and editing "Fireworks," he created a series of paintings that are a key plot element and, utilizing his acting name of Beat Takeshi, portrays the unusual character who carries the film.

With a classic been-around face—handsome yet sad and accented by the inevitable sunglasses and an involuntary twitch—Yoshitaka Nishi is a formidable police detective in the humanitarian hard guy mold. He dislikes conversation, won't so much as grunt when silence will do—but, just to make things interesting, he's got a weakness for sudden and brutal violence that is terrifying when it's unleashed.

Nishi is supposed to be part of a gangster stakeout with his partner, Horibe (Ren Osugi), and two younger detectives. But Horibe tells Nishi to visit his hospitalized leukemia-stricken wife, Miyuki (Kayoko Kishimoto), and dismisses the other two policemen as well. This, of course, turns out not to have been a smart thing to do.

When Horibe's colleagues return to the hunt, things get even more out of hand, and Nishi, as an honorable Japanese, naturally feels responsible for each tragic event. The bulk of "Fireworks" deals with his attempts to make amends for the things that have gone wrong, confront the violent yakuza who've lent him money and spend meaningful time with his dying wife.

Summarized this way, "Fireworks" sounds rather straightforward, but the film's narrative is intentionally obscured. Kitano favors a structure that is intricately fragmented. He tells his story in jigsaw puzzle-like bits and pieces, which we have to piece together ourselves and which only gradually form a coherent whole.

This technique is especially effective when it comes to the way "Fireworks" uses violence. Intense it may be, but it's never shown for more than a few surreal seconds, and it never comes when you expect it. As for the bloody police action that is "Fireworks' " centerpiece, we see it gradually, over the course of the film, in startling shards of flashback memory that are revealed to us as they randomly cross Nishi's mind.

Involving as all this is, it doesn't exhaust this film's attractions. Kitano began his acting career as a comic, and "Fireworks" has a strong and consistent element of deadpan, almost wacky humor. When you are ready for it least, Nishi will pop in something so slyly funny you half-think you've started watching another film by mistake.

Similarly unexpected is "Fireworks'" use of sentiment, which comes out in Nishi's heartfelt relationship with the survivors of the police action as well as with his dying wife. Given the man's proclivities, it seems like a joke when Miyuki's doctor tells him what his wife needs most now is conversation, but the couple do end up forging a memorable bond.

Though "Fireworks" is nothing if not its own film, its concern with the permanence of sadness and the intractability of regret bring to mind Jean-Pierre Melville's Alain Delon-starring noir perennial, "Le Samourai," which begins with a manufactured quote from a Japanese sage. Like Melville, Kitano knows the power of genre norms. By simultaneously honoring gangster conventions and making his own idiosyncratic use of them, he's made a personal film that speaks to everyone, but always in its own way.

NEWSDAY, 3/20/98, Part II/p. B11, John Anderson

Takeshi Kitano, better known in his homeland as Beat Takeshi (or Takeshi Beat), is a movie star, magazine columnist, commercial spokesman, the star of seven prime-time television shows and the best-known media personality in Japan. He's also a poet, essayist, novelist and, since his near-fatal motorcycle accident in 1995, a painter of some delicacy. To say he's a renaissance man doesn't quite do him justice, given how he manages to straddle *two* such divergent worlds with such seeming ease.

Likewise his latest film as both actor and director, "Hana-Bi (Fireworks)," winner of the grand prize at the '97 Venice Film Festival (an earlier film, "Sonatine," is opening here soon as well). The very title, as hyphenated by Kitano—"hana" (flower) and "bi" (fire)—suggest the dichotomy to come. Set in a milieu of violence, yakuza and tormented detectives, it is modern in its subject matter, classical in effect, a Dashiell Hammett done in silk and watercolor.

Kitano is Nishi, the most controlled but potentially violent of detectives, whose wife Miyuki (Kayoko Kishimoto) is dying of leukemia. His fellow cops have been caught in two ambushes, both of which Nishi is blaming on himself. Coiled in silent anguish, Nishi is the all-but-mute action hero personified: Harassed by two yakuza about his outstanding loan, Nishi plunges a chopstick into the eye of one, kicks the other senseless and the whole thing is over before we know it's begun.

Kitano the actor carries himself with a kind of bowlegged confidence, like Charles Bronson at his most lethal, but with introspection and evident pain. Kitano the director makes maximum use of the smallest gestures, and moves with a rhythm that seems rooted in a heartbeat. Rather than unfurling his austere tapestry in one motion, he allows it to unfold in multiple flashbacks and bursts of action, the fire and flowers of his title.

Nishi's story—which includes some very funny scenes at a local junkyard—is juxtaposed to that of Horibe (Ren Osugi), Nishi's partner, now confined to a wheelchair. Having been abandoned by his wife and daughter, he suggests to Nishi that he might take up painting, if the materials weren't so expensive. He soon receives a gift box of art supplies and, in front of a florist, has an artistic epiphany, begins turning out startling work (the paintings we see are by Kitano himself). Nishi, meanwhile, completes the paint job on an old cab, transforming it into a counterfeit police car and setting off to rob a bank.

Kitano's humor is ever-present and ever-melancholy, his destination no surprise, perhaps, but his travel methods fascinating. "Hana-Bi " is a rare film—a hybrid. But so is Takeshi Kitano.

SIGHT AND SOUND, 8/98, p. 32, Tony Rayns

Ultra-taciturn detective Nishi leaves his colleague Horibe to stake out a killer's apartment while he visits his terminally ill wife Miyuki in hospital. The doctor is telling him that Miyuki will die soon when Nishi is called away by news that Horibe has been shot and wounded by the killer. (In subsequent flashbacks, we learn that Nishi joins detective Nakamura and Tanaka in tailing the killer to a shopping mall, where Nishi jumps him. But the killer wounds Nakamura and kills Tanaka before Nishi is able to shoot him. Nishi unloads all the chambers of his revolver into the corpse.)

Some time later, Horibe is permanently confined to a wheelchair; his wife and child have left him, and he attempts suicide. Nishi has left the police to look after Miyuki, now back at home, and has borrowed money from some yakuza loan-sharks to support Tanaka's widow; he also buys art materials and a beret to encourage Horibe to take up painting. When the loan-sharks refuse him more money, Nishi robs a bank. He uses some of the proceeds to pay off his debt.

While Horibe paints, Nishi takes Miyuki on a trip around Honshu and Hokkaido which recreates their honeymoon. He is hounded by the loan-sharks, who have smelled his ill-gotten gains, and he kills them. Nakamura (who guesses that Nishi was the bank robber) follows his trail, finds the yakuza corpses and eventually catches up with Nishi and Miyuki on a remote beach. Nishi asks him to wait a while before arresting him. He shares his last moments with the grateful Miyuki. Two shots ring out across the beach.

Opening slightly portentously with a caption identifying it as "Takeshi Kitano Volume 7", *Hana-Bi* turns out to be a highly sophisticated synthesis of everything Kitano has learned from his earlier films. This story about an ultra-taciturn cop with violent tendencies who blames himself for the crippling of a colleague has recognisable roots in *Violent Cop, A Scene at the Sea* and *Sonatine*, but every familiar idea or motif is transformed by the new context; as *Kids Return* suggested, Kitano is now thinking about things harder and more deeply. *Hana-Bi* (which is the Japanese word for fireworks, *hanabi* separated into its constituent parts: *hana*-flowers; and *bi*-fire) feels like a genre film from an unknown genre. Its fractured time structure, its scattering of apparent digressions and incidentals and its intricate cross-cutting within and between scenes would all make it seem daringly experimental if the film weren't anchored in Joe Hisaishi's lush Max Steineresque score and in a powerful emotional intensity.

Nishi (Kitano himself) says almost nothing, but is never hard to understand: he is an 'old-fashioned' Japanese man who sees his useful life coming to an end and determines to honour what he believes to be his responsibilities before it's too late. His decision to steal money in order to give his dying wife a second honeymoon and support the widow of his junior Tanaka (Makoto Ashikawa), killed in action, is thrown into relief by the fate of his crippled colleague Horibe (Ren Osugi), who is abandoned by his wife and daughter as soon as he comes home in a wheelchair. Horibe eventually overcomes the impulse to suicide thanks in part to his effort to express his unvoiced feelings through paintings; Nishi's actions, conversely, are governed by what he sees as the inevitable necessity of his own imminent death.

At the heart of *Hana-Bi* are two damaged men, both trying to cope with intolerable circumstances. Horibe loses his wife, his child and the use of his legs; encouraged by his mother and nudged by Nishi, he takes up painting and produces not only images which reflect his suicidal state of mind but also strange visions of the nuclear family (husband, wife and child against backdrops of a fireworks display or the cosmos) and mysterious fusions of the plant and animal worlds.

Nishi either resigns or is fired from the Tokyo Metropolitan Police and looks for ways to discharge what he believes to be his moral duties, including steering Horibe away from suicide and providing for Tanaka's embarrassed widow. The main challenge he sets himself, however, is to give his wife a second honeymoon before she dies; Miyuki (Kayoko Kishimoto) is seriously ill, and the sudden death of the five-year-old daughter was a blow from which she will never recover. Nishi's drive to end his own life as a 'justified man' maybe fundamentally narcissistic, but (as Kitano himself has noted) he pursues it with the ruthlessness of a hero from one of Chikamatsu's Edo-period revenge tragedies.

Kitano never shows us Nishi and Horibe working as a team, but we hear how good they were together from Nakamura—in a speech to a greenhorn cop which is neatly bisected by a scene showing Nishi's clash with the *yakuza* loan-sharks: "Whenever Horibe got too rough, Nishi would stop him. But when Nishi hit the roof, he was the more frightening." Instead, Kitano spends the second half of the film cross-cutting between the two men, drawing symbiotic parallels between their predicaments and states of mind. Nishi spraypaints a stolen taxi to disguise it as a police car; Horibe pauses outside a florist and imagines how he will fill blank sheets of paper with images of animals with flowers for heads. Nishi tries to light a firework (it eventually goes off in his face) for his wife; Horibe paints a picture of a family watching a huge fireworks display. The effect of the cross-cutting, which has only the slimmest of narrative pretexts, is to push the film towards a symbolic level, on which Nishi and Horibe are less distinct individuals than embodiments of contrasted responses to personal catastrophes. This level undoubtedly has strong submerged meanings for Kitano, who took up painting after his own near-fatal accident in 1994 and who uses his own pictures not only to stand in for Horibe's but also to decorate all the main locations, from the bank to the yakuza headquarters.

Kitano follows through the symbolic implications by placing the other main male character into a kind of continuum with Nishi and Horibe. Nakamura (superbly played by Susumu Terajima, a familiar presence in Kitano's films) sheepishly tells Nishi that he plans to get married at last; he was touched by the loyalty of the woman who visited him every day during his convalescence after the shooting.   Accordingly, Nakamura is next in line for the Nishi/Horibe role—a progression he tacitly accepts by taking over Nishi's brusqueness and taciturnity as he tracks him through the winter. And the constant presence of greenhorns asking stupid questions implies that the continuum will not end with Nakamura, either.

Around this central nexus are all the film's minor characters (the yakuza gang members, the women) and the peripheral characters, from the two bolshie car-park attendants in the opening scene to the girl with the kite in the closing one. With the exception of the glue sniffing tomboy in the scrapyard, who gives as good as she gets, the women are considerate and well behaved, sure of their place in the film's (and Japan's) social structure. The men, on the other hand, are conspicuously rude, self-aggrandising and stupid, providing both a corrective to the prevailing fantasy of ritualised Japanese politesse and a counterpoint to the central characters' struggles with the fallout from marital relations.

The car-park attendants, seen twice, provide Kitano with opportunities to push his oblique narrative strategies and elliptical editing to new heights of precision. the clashes between Nishi and the younger man, whom he finds eating take-out food on the bonnet of his car, are either elided through jump-cuts or register through shadowplay and the reactions of the other man. But the most telling use of these peripheral figures is a final cutaway, a single shot showing them glumly pondering the outcome of their second brush with Nishi. This shot defines them, like the other peripheral characters, as on-lookers, spectators of everything that happens at the core of the film. They are not audience surrogates but losers defined by their inability to dent Nishi or to penetrate the central drama. As such (and this is a measure of Kitano's latent cruelty), they are also figures of fun.

Much of the brilliance of *Hana-Bi* is found in such seemingly marginal details, because their obliqueness and ellipses exactly mirror the larger complexities of the film's structure. Kitano's editing, idiosyncratic from the start, has become quite masterly. The interweaving of the main narrative with flashbacks and occasional flash-forwards delivers nothing pre-processed; the viewer is obliged to work to make connections and draw conclusions. The use of the many paintings and the general sparseness of the dialogue add to the film's demands on the viewer, turning it into something with the kind of visual expressiveness found in late silent cinema. The rewards, however, are great.

VILLAGE VOICE , 3/24/98, p. 65, J. Hoberman

Call this a global village? It's taken more years than Clinton's been president for Takeshi Kitano—currently the world's most original action auteur—to rate a New York commercial release.

Fireworks—which won the Golden Lion at Venice (and was shown, as *Hani-Bi* at last year's NYFF)—is artier and more contemplative than Kitano's 1989 *Violent Cop* or 1990 *Boiling Point*, the movies that established his tough-guy rep on the international festival circuit. But this self-reflexive *policier* is scarcely less eccentric in shaking down, roughing up, and otherwise reassembling a terminally tired genre.

Don Siegel meets Yasujiro Ozu with actor-director Kitano casting himself in death-haunted Dirty Harry mode as a retired Tokyo cop turned Zen vigilante. An unpredictable mix of bathos, slapstick, and visual invention, *Fireworks* is a meditation on violence and its screen representation that, referencing and recombining elements from Kitano's six previous features, seems close to his best filmmaking. The sudden eruption of mayhem is in continual counterpoint to the precise camera placement and rigorous use of off-screen space. *Fireworks* is founded on parallel action and filled with editing jokes; most of its "fireworks" are a function of montage. (Eisenstein would surely appreciate the Japanese title—an ideogram combining the characters for fire and flower.)

Kitano, as usual, orchestrates bits of business unseen in any previous action flick. With neither comedy nor cruelty ever far beneath the surface, his originality as a director seems based on his showbiz training—he has a stand-up comics timing, as well as a fondness for sight gags. Certainly, this eloquently brutal filmmaker's fastidiously deployed postdubbing suggests that what he really wants to make is an animated cartoon or a silent movie. (For all the *yakuza* butt he's kicking, Kitano's character has but one line of dialogue in *Fireworks* first half hour.)

Austerely cute, *Fireworks* has a unique somber-yet-saccharine flavor. With its blatantly fake blood and matter-of-fact ghosts, not to mention the author's own paintings scattered throughout, it might be a sort of nouveau, hard-boiled Kabuki. Human, as well as formalist, in its treatment of mayhem, it's an antidote—although not necessarily an answer—to the loathsome *Funny Games* also playing at Film Forum.

Also reviewed in:
NEW REPUBLIC, 4/6/98, p. 26, Stanley Kauffmann
NEW YORK TIMES, 9/27/97, p. B12, Janet Maslin
NEW YORKER, 3/30/98, p. 124, Anthony Lane
VARIETY, 9/8-14/97, p. 77, David Rooney
WASHINGTON POST, 4/17/98, p. B5, Stephen Hunter

FIRST LOVE, LAST RITES

A Strand Releasing release of a Forensic/Toast Films production. *Executive Producer:* Jeffrey Levy-Hinte and Amanda Temple. *Producer:* Scott Macaulay, Robin O'Hara, and Herbert Beigel. *Director:* Jesse Peretz. *Screenplay:* David Ryan. *Story adapted by:* David Ryan and Jesse Peretz. *Based on the story by:* Ian McEwan. *Director of Photography:* Tom Richmond. *Editor:* James Lyons. *Music:* Nathan Larson and Craig Wedron. *Sound:* Brian Miksis. *Production Designer:* Dan Estabrook. *Costumes:* Yasmine Abraham. *Make-up:* Ellen Veira. *Running time:* 93 minutes. *MPAA Rating:* Not Rated.

CAST: Natasha Gregson Wagner (Sissel); Giovanni Ribisi (Joey); Robert John Burke (Henry); Jeannetta Arnette (Sissel's Mom); Donal Logue (Red); Eli Marienthal (Adrian); Hugh Joseph Babin (Bob); Earl S. Binnings (Mitch); Howard Barker (Security Guard); Trang Thanh Le (Restaurant Cook); L. Christian Mixon (Tattoo Artist).

LOS ANGELES TIMES, 8/7/98, Calendar/p. 10, Kevin Thomas

Jesse Peretz's "First Love, Last Rites" takes us into the Louisiana bayou country southwest of New Orleans. The setting is ravishing visually, with watery vistas and swamps with trees dripping with Spanish moss. The small fishing community in which its story takes place, however, is remarkably nondescript; it's a place where ordinary people live ordinary lives.

Too ordinary. In his feature debut, Peretz, in adapting Ian McEwan's short story, charts the course of a first love with a bemused sensitivity and displays a sure instinct for the cinematic. But the plain truth is that his young lovers aren't very interesting, despite the adroit casting of Natasha Gregson Wagner and Giovanni Ribisi. Ribisi's Joey has ended up in the community for the summer and soon meets and becomes involved with Wagner's local girl Sissel.

Sissel is a desirable, fully mature young woman and knows it, whereas Joey is still pretty much a gangling kid, even though they both seem to be 20ish. He soon falls hard for Sissel, who is more detached, insisting on remaining her own woman. Their romance awakens Sissel to her power over men. You sense that she instinctively knows that Joey is only the beginning for her whereas he envisions spending the rest of his life with her.

Sissel and Joey are very real, as is the course of their relationship. But there's not a lot to them. They have little education, few interests, no apparent goals. Little is going on around them or, it would seem, inside their heads, although Joey goes through much emotional churning.

You have to admire Peretz for resisting making more of them than they are simply to make a more entertaining film. Yet he needed to discover and reveal more about them that would involve us more deeply than they do. The only other major character is Sissel's father, played by Robert John Burke as a manic, none-too-swift guy given to crazy schemes and irritating his estranged wife by driving his vintage convertible back and forth on her tract house driveway, accompanied by loud Chinese music.

For such a determinedly independent production, "First Love, Last Rites" shares in common with countless Hollywood pictures a vagueness about finances. You wonder what its people live on, yet nobody is working much or worrying that they don't. (It would seem that when Sissel takes a job in a sugar factory it's more out of boredom than anything else.)

The film, which is very well-shaped and controlled, benefits from Nathan Larson and Craig Wedron's vital score and from Tom Richmond's superb cinematography with its muted palette. Peretz displays a fine sense of tempo and structure and reveals a subtle, understated sensibility. "First Love, Last Rites" is of more interest for what it portends for Peretz's future as a filmmaker than for what it actually delivers.

NEW YORK POST, 8/7/98, p. 47, Thelma Adams

A man. A woman. A swamp. A rat. An eel. Now that's a love story. The opening scene of "First Love, Last Rites" finds us in bed with Sissel (Natasha Gregson Wagner) and Joey (Giovanni Ribisi). Maybe it's just me, but I'd like a little foreplay.

Wagner, daughter of Natalie Wood, is a game young actress. We can confirm she is well-toned. She can lead equally well with her pointed chin or nipple.

Ribisi, the splattered medic in "Saving Private Ryan," expresses his sexual inexperience with a nervous giggle. Still, he appears largely competent (and gives up a full profile of his member).

What folks do behind a closed shack door within yards of the Louisiana bayou is fine—and largely either the missionary position or woman-on-top. But first-time director Jesse Peretz, adapting an Ian McEwan short story with screenwriter David Ryan, makes the coupling of Sissel and Joey less interesting than a Tuesday on "The Young and the Restless."

I know why that mystery rodent is gnawing in the wall next to the bed: It just wants out!

As a counterpoint to the rise of young lust, there is the fall of Sissel's parents' marriage. Mama (Jeannetta Arnette) is a slim, bottle-blonde who never earns her own name; Daddy Henry (Robert John Burke) is one tough customer, a Vietnam vet who moonlights as a stalker and encourages Joey to take up eeling.

The best scene finds Hank (played by the blue-eyed Burke with the intensity of a "Die Hard" villain) tromping in hip-waders through the swamp. Hunting rifle in hand, Henry quizzes Joey about the Brooklynite's sex life with Sissel.

Alas, Hank doesn't shoot and the odd juxtaposition of menace, wildlife and sexual tension quickly fades into trite dialogue and swirly Freudian dream sequences. My favorite line? A confrontational Sissel tells Joey, apropos of nothing, "You want to stick a baby in me so you can dangle it in front of me like a carrot."

Now that's an image!

NEWSDAY, 8/7/98, Part II/p. B11, John Anderson

The girl looks druggy and sluttish, the boy looks ghastly and fluish, they're all but holed up in an increasingly squalid bayou rental with a rat gnawing through the wall and the boy is supposed to be on vacation. Could all this be anything but exhilarating? Yes. Another foray into independent anguish—and another sound track in search of a movie—"First Love, Last Rites" is the debut feature by Jesse Peretz and proves that, while a background in making music videos shouldn't preclude a career in feature films, it's no endorsement, either. Peretz presumably knows that motion pictures are supposed to include motion. "First Love," however, is essentially inert. Somewhere along the line, the antic video aesthetic went south.

Which, by the way, is where we find our loving couple—Sissel (Natasha Gregson Wagner) and Joey (Giovanni Ribisi), whom we first meet as they make love on a mattress on their kitchen table by an open window. (In Ribisi's other current feature, "Saving Private Ryan," we watch people getting massacred before we know who they are. In "First Love, Last Rites," we watch people having sex before we know who they are. Call me old-fashioned, but sex without commitment? Out of the question.)

Joey is from Brooklyn and, for reasons never ever explained—although the question is begged and begged—is vacationing in this stump-jumper's paradise in southern Louisiana. Unlike most people on vacation here, he is having a relentlessly lusty relationship with the oblique Sissel and is fishing for eels with her father, Henry (Robert John Burke). Draw your own symbolic conclusions.

Henry, who's been tossed out by Sissel's mom (Jeanetta Arnette), is becoming increasingly unhinged. Or maybe he already was and that's why Mom threw him out. You don't get a lot of background from Peretz, just yards and yards of atmosphere, plus a mashed rat and some sexual details that add little to the story and would probably have been better off unmentioned. But then, without the occasional squirm-producing moment, there wouldn't be a heckuva lot else to watch.

Its flies buzzing, its squalor mounting, "First Love, Last Rites" is based on a story by Ian McEwan, and like McEwan's "The Cement Garden" uses the house as a metaphor for soullessness and corruption—although the movie itself more than services any metaphoric needs we may have in that particular area. The sound track, by the way, includes music by Billy Corgan, Liz Phair, John Doe and Jeff Buckley, who drowned a little more than a year ago in the Mississippi River near Memphis. The movie is dedicated to Buckley.

VILLAGE VOICE , 8/11/98, p. 143, Amy Taubin

And now for something completely different from *There's Something About Mary*. Jess Peretz's *First Love, Last Rites* is an elegiac rendering of the kind of intense end-of-adolescence love affair from which no one fully recovers.

A Brooklyn boy named Joe (Giovanni Ribisi) is shacked up with a Louisiana girl named Sissel (Natasha Gregson Wagner) in a one-room house on stilts in a bayou fishing village. We don't exactly know how he got there, and it doesn't matter. The only thing that matters is this love affair, which is new and vibrant when the movie opens and tarnished when it closes.

"Do you ever think about it?" Joe asks hesitantly. "It's like we're creating something. It's like taking on a shape." "I wouldn't worry about it," Sissel replies. What's amazing about *First Love, Last Rites* is the way the love affair has an organic shape produced by the two people involved and also by the DNA of love affairs in general. Joe has never been through anything like this before, but he has a subterranean awareness of how the death of love is programmed into its promise. Joe is introspective, with a a penchant for metaphor. Sissel is literal-minded and more shut-down emotionally than Joe. Joe can't figure out what she's feeling, and that gives her an edge in the relationship. It may be that she's less in love, and that gives her an edge too. The imbalance creates anxiety, the anxiety grows, and pretty soon that's almost all there is—anxiety and exhaustion.

Remarkably faithful to the 12-page Ian McEwan story from which it's adapted, *First Love, Last Rites* has no plot to speak of. And for a film that lives from one fuck to the next, it's less about passion than obsession and intimacy. Joe is bowled over by Sissel's matter-of-fact attitude toward her body—toward her menstrual blood or her foot rot. At first, his knowledge of her body makes him feel liberated and powerful. But when the knowledge doesn't lead anywhere, he begins to despair.

Ribisi (who can be seen as the medic, Wade, in *Saving Private Ryan*) moves like a cat and is very good at revealing mixed emotions—how desire is fueled by repulsion or elation by fear. In and out of clothes, Wagner is notably unselfconscious about her body; she also has the courage to make Sissel as wan and tight as she needs to be. But good as the actors are, they're not the most expressive element in the film.

Rather, it's the light—reflected off skin and water, filtered through curtains and clouds—that makes the film os achingly sensuous, so flat-out erotic. Cinematographer Tom Richmond is a poet of sunrises and sunsets, of translucent mauves and blues, of a dozen different whites. It's the light that lets us understand how ravished Joe and Sissel are by each other, how they see each other as radiant beings. And thus, when Sissel sits hunched on the bed with the hideous fuchsia smock that she wears at work pulled around her body, we see it as the violation she means it to be, and we know that the end is near.

It's also a bad sign when she starts boiling her favorite records on the stove. Peretz, who played bass with the Lemonheads and directs music videos, has a sure sense of when and how to use music. The score by Shudder to Think is basically an eclectic group of singles that Sissel might own, each written in a different style from r&b to post-punk. In a year of notable soundtracks, this is one of the best.

Also reviewed in:
NEW REPUBLIC, 9/7/98, p. 24, Stanley Kauffmann
NEW YORK TIMES, 8/7/98, p. E22, Stephen Holden
VARIETY, 10/20-26/97, p. 72, Emanuel Levy

FOUR DAYS IN SEPTEMBER

A Miramax Films release in association with Pandora Cinema of an L.C. Barreto & Filmes do Equador production. *Producer:* Lucy Barreto. *Director:* Bruno Barreto. *Screenplay:* Leopoldo Serran. *Based on the book "O que é isso, companhiero?" ("What's Up Comrade?")* by: Fernado Gabeira. *Director of Photography:* Felix Monti. *Editor:* Isabelle Rathery. *Music:* Stewart Copeland. *Music Editor:* Michael Dittrick. *Sound:* Rick Ash and Marty Hutcherson. *Casting:* Oliva Guimaraes, Sheila Jaffe, and Georgianne Walken. *Production Designer:* Angelo Gastal. *Art Director:* Marcos Flaksman. *Costumes:* Emilia Duncan. *Stunt Coordinator:* Jorge So. *Running time:* 105 minutes. *MPAA Rating:* R.

CAST: Alan Arkin (Charles Burke Elbrick); Pedro Cardoso (Fernando Gabeira/Paulo); Fernanda Torres (Maria); Luiz Fernand Guimaraes (Marcao); Claudia Abareu (Renée); Nelson Dantas (Toledo); Matheus Nachtegaele (Jonas); Marco Ricca (Henrique); Mauricio Goncalves (Brandao); Caio Junqueria (Júlio); Selton Mello (César/Oswaldo); Eduardo Moskovis (Artur); Caroline Kava (Elvira Elbrick); Fisher Stevens (Mowinkel).

CHRISTIAN SCIENCE MONITOR, 1/16/98, p. 12, David Sterritt

International politics are in the news, and on movie screens as well.

"Welcome to Sarajevo," which opened recently, explores moral, ethical, and professional dilemmas raised by the Bosnian war as experienced by journalists from various countries. Now a somewhat less gritty film, "Four Days in September," tells the fact-based story of a politically driven Brazilian kidnapping.

It's no coincidence that both pictures are released by Miramax Films, which seems more willing than some other movie distributors to present stories about times, places, and situations too remote or troubling to be considered marketable by most Hollywood studios.

Alan Arkin plays Charles Burke Elbrick, who was American ambassador to Brazil in the late 1960s, when the country was ruled by a military regime widely deplored for its oppressive attitudes and brutal behaviors.

Desperate to attract public attention to their anti-government cause, a group of young militants—idealistic in their motivations, but frequently callow and even naive in their political views—decide to abduct Elbrick and hold him hostage. He will be released if their demands are met, executed if the regime won't cooperate.

What sets "Four Days in September" apart from many tales of political violence is its desire to portray the militants as fully rounded individuals rather than either stereotypical villains, stopping at nothing to achieve their goals, or one-dimensional heroes, sacrificing normal lives for the sake of their cause.

Another asset is Arkin's restrained yet affecting performance as the ambassador. Around the time when this '60s story takes place, Arkin was making his first major mark on Hollywood with a series of mannered portrayals that often promised more than they delivered. But in '90s pictures like "Havana," and "Mother Night," he has emerged as a mature and thoughtful actor who can raise even contrived or melodramatic moments to unexpectedly high emotional levels. He does this again in "Four Days in September," even though much of the story calls on him to do little more than sit, wait, and brood.

Other aspects of the picture are less successful. Its effort to humanize the militants is undermined by bits of shaky acting, and some twists of the plot and dialogue are familiar from too many earlier movies. More important, the film's attitude toward the Brazilian military regime is regrettably vague, making the militants' motives harder to grasp than they would be if the governments misdeeds were more fully aired.

The movie was directed by Bruno Barreto, a member of Brazil's historically important Cinema Novo group. He hasn't had a major intercontinental hit since "Dona Flor and Her Two Husbands" two decades ago, and while "Four Days in September" isn't likely to break box-office records, it's a good vehicle for reintroducing his name and renewing his reputation with American viewers.

The screenplay is based on an autobiographical book by Fernando Gaberia, who took part in the actual kidnapping and is today a journalist and Brazilian congressman. Pedro Cardoso and Caroline Kava head the supporting cast. In all, "Four Days in September" may be a little too unusual and ambiguous for mass-audience popularity, but its underlying seriousness makes it worth welcoming despite its flaws.

LOS ANGELES TIMES, 1/30/98, Calendar/p. 24, Jack Mathews

[The following review by Jack Mathews appeared in a slightly different form in **NEWSDAY, 1/30/98, Part II/p. B6.]**

Do you remember where you were on Sept. 4, 1969, when Charles Burke Elbrick, U.S. ambassador to Brazil, was kidnapped by Marxist revolutionaries in Rio de Janeiro?

Of course not. If you were old enough to be politically alert then, you were probably too focused on the upheaval at home to be jarred by an overseas event that wasn't even meant to be taken personally by Americans. Elbrick, like other foreign diplomats seized during a reign of terrorist kidnappings, was merely a tool used to gain the release of political prisoners and to bring outside attention to the loss of civil rights under Brazil's oppressive military regime.

Now, nearly 30 years after that event and a decade after democracy has been restored to Brazil, the Elbrick kidnapping is reenacted in Brazilian director Bruno Barreto's "Four Days in September." And though it is too sincerely nonjudgmental to evoke the passion of its participants, it's a fascinating slice of political history.

The movie, adapted from a book-length autobiographical essay by one of Elbrick's abductors, uses archival footage and still photos from the period as backdrop to a very tight, appropriately claustrophobic drama during which we learn a lot about the political circumstances in Brazil but very little about the people actually involved in the story.

As it plays out, "Four Days" may be best absorbed as a representation of the forming opposition to the military government, which formally outlawed free speech in 1968, imposing censorship on the press and criminalizing protest. Dissidents, largely professors and college students, were routinely arrested and tortured and, in many instances, murdered.

Elbrick (Alan Arkin, in a wrenchingly authentic performance) is depicted as an honest, compassionate career diplomat who, like his bosses in the State Department, is keeping a safe distance from Brazilian politics. The U.S. had more or less supported the 1964 military junta, choosing it as the lesser of two evils over the ousted left-wing regime.

Elbrick becomes the target of a small, newly formed group calling itself the October 8th Revolutionary Movement, or MR-8, which is led by a firebrand named Maria (Fernanda Torres). Among her band of frustrated, inexperienced, middle-class young adults is Fernando Gabeira (Pedro Cardoso), an intellectual and journalist whose subsequent book, "What's Up, Comrade?," provided the source material for Barreto and screenwriter Leopoldo Serran (Barreto's collaborator on "Doña Flor and Her Two Husbands").

The four days in the title is how long Elbrick is held at a rented house outside Rio while officials run out the clock on the kidnappers' deadline. There are two demands: the freeing and transport to Mexico of 15 political prisoners and open media coverage of the event.

Barreto avoids one of the clichés of hostage movies by ignoring the government's decision-making during the four days. It's made clear, after Elbrick is abducted from a residential street in midday, that the world is watching (even if we weren't) and that the pressure is on.

Instead, Barreto focuses on the tension inside the house, as a rightfully scared Elbrick gets to know his captors and on the efforts of a determined secret service officer (Marco Ricca) to foil the operation.

The cop subplot, though intended to explore the conflicts of ordinary people duty-bound to commit atrocities, is the weakest, most conventional element in the film. What makes "Four Days" riveting drama is the ambivalence of the young kidnappers about their actions. When it's time to kill, will the nonviolent Fernando's political outrage defeat his own humanity?

It's at that moment that the story transcends its political setting and becomes universal. What are we willing to give up for an ideal? Our lives? Our souls? Our identities? Stories about revolutionaries are difficult to make sympathetic because, in the end, it's hard to tell the righteous from their oppressors.

"Four Days" is a flawed film, but in its efforts to feel the pulse of human conscience, as well as the heart, it's dead-on.

NEW YORK POST, 1/30/98, p. 45, Thelma Adams

"Eating your cooking is a true test of military courage," Comrade Paulo tells Comrade Maria over the rebels' campfire in Bruno Barreto's "Four Days in September." It's a moment verging on Woody Allen's "Bananas."

The Brazilian director of "Dona Flor and Her Two Husbands" spins a political thriller about the real life 1969 kidnapping of the American ambassador to Brazil in Rio. The movie recalls Costa-Gavras' "Missing" as much as Allen, as it shifts between humor and heroism, the mundane and the horrific.

Based on kidnapper Fernando Gabeira's memoir, *O que e isso, campanhiero,"* Leopoldo Serran's script portrays everyone involved—from the Brazilian torturers, to the hard-line terrorists, to the ambassador's wife—as human beings worth knowing and saving. This is both the movie's strength and its weakness.

Wry set pieces turn our memories of common historical events on their heads. In one scene, after a hard day demonstrating against the military dictatorship and tossing rocks at the police, three Brazilian university students return to their pad to watch TV.

It's July 20, 1969. American astronauts plant the Stars and Stripes on the moon. The students, including future author Fernando Gabeira, critique the moon walk as yet another giant step for Yankee imperialism. Meanwhile, at the American embassy, foreign service flack Mowinkel (Fisher Stevens) calls the event the greatest TV ever seen—"[it] only cost $180 million.

Before long, the students close the distance between their tiny apartment and the palatial embassy. Two of the three buddies join a revolutionary cell. The ambassador's kidnapping—an attempt to gain recognition and force the government's hand—is the brainchild of Fernando (Pedro Cardoso).

Seasoned revolutionary Maria (Fernanda Torres) renames Fernando "Paulo," a radical baptism. While Paulo, Maria and their inexperienced gang of middle-class intellectuals—rebels in sneakers—raise money robbing a bank, Barreto gives us a peek at how the other half lives.

Two secret policemen torture a prisoner with the physical effort and boredom of assembly-line workers. The men chat about soccer and girlfriends. One says casually to his partner: "He'll talk soon. We'll get out early."

With Alan Arkin achingly sympathetic as soft-spoken Ambassador Charles Burke Elbrick, the supple Brazilian actress Torres ("Foreign Land") as the revolutionary earth mama, and Cardoso as the smart kid on campus who discovers he's not so sharp in the university of revolutionary politics, Barreto has assembled an extraordinary ensemble.

But the Brazilian director sacrifices suspense for balance. The kidnapping is never as tense as it should be, and the movie presents and then forsakes a powerful ending in the name of tying up loose threads. For all that, it's still "Four Days" well spent.

VILLAGE VOICE, 2/3/98, p. 49, J. Hoberman

The week's mellowest *policier*, Bruno Barreto's *Four Days in September* recounts a political abduction staged in Rio during the apocalyptic summer of 1969. The situation has the makings of a grimly taut mock documentary, but Barreto—making his first Brazilian movie in nearly a decade—manages to put an astonishingly amiable gloss on this tale of late-'60s mishigas.

Having pulled off the biggest "revolutionary expropriation" (bank heist) in Brazilian history, the self-styled urban guerrillas of the MR-8 cadre kidnap the American ambassador (Alan Arkin) to secure the freedom of 15 imprisoned comrades. The gang—a bunch of poignantly confused grad-school types—simultaneously impress and dismay the hard-bitten Marxists who are dispatched from Sao Paulo to supervise the caper.

The odd we-are-the-world affability is established with Barreto crosscutting to show both would-be revolutionaries and ambassador mesmerized by the telespectacle of Men on the Moon. The main regime here is that of nostalgia. The cadre is obviously tuned in to youth culture—a glossy Woodstock flyer appears as a sacred artifact in their safe house only days after the event—and Barreto makes only mild fun of the class irony that the kids screw up because they are too bourgeois to cook for themselves.

Only minimally suspenseful in its bosso nova terrorism, *Four Days* is notable mainly for its performances. The normally glamorous Fernanda Torres is successfully cast against type as the group's skinny, intense leader; Pedro Cardoso gives a subtly comic edge to the role of the bespectacled intellectual who talks better than he shoots (and grows up to be a leader of Brazil's Green Party). The film's kindest, gentlest aspect is the costing of Arkin as the ambassador—the movie Yossarian, he's the embodiment of principled opposition to the Vietnam War.

Also reviewed in:
CHICAGO TRIBUNE, 2/6/98, Friday/p. C, Michael Wilmington
NEW YORK TIMES, 1/30/98, p. E8, Stephen Holden
VARIETY, 3/6-9/97, p. 70, Joe Leydon
WASHINGTON POST, 2/13/98, p. D7, Stephen Hunter
WASHINGTON POST, 2/13/98, Weekend/p. 48, Rita Kempley

FREE TIBET

A Shooting Gallery release of a Milarapa Fund production in association with Mammoth Pictures. *Executive Producer:* Jay Faires and Adam Yauch.   *Producer:* Maria Ma.   *Director:* Sarah Pirozek.   *Director of Photography:* Evan Barnard, Roman Coppola, and Spike Jonze.   *Editor:* Paola Heredia.   *Music Editor:* Jacob Ribicoff.   *Running time:* 90 minutes.   *MPAA Rating:* Not Rated.

WITH: A Tribe Called Quest: Beastie Boys; Bjork; De La Soul; Foo Fighters;   Fugees; Richie Beck; John Lee Hooker; Biz Markie; Tim Meadows; Yoko Ono; Pavement; Rage Against the Machine;   Red Hot Chili Pepper;   Sonic Youth;   Smashing Pumpkins.

LOS ANGELES TIMES, 9/18/98, Calendar/p. 15, Kristine McKenna

China has forcefully occupied Tibet, its tiny neighbor, since invading it in 1949. Since then China has done its best to destroy Tibet's Buddhist culture. In recent years the plight of Tibet has become a cause celebre among the rich and famous, but their protest has done little for the Tibetans.

The protest nonetheless continues. Its latest manifestation is "Free Tibet," an alternately silly and sublime documentary that chronicles the San Francisco Tibetan Freedom Concert, a two-day event organized in 1996 by the Beastie Boys that was held in Golden Gate Park and drew 100,000 people.

Featuring 20 performances, "Free Tibet" is not, however, a concert film in the manner of "Woodstock" or "The Last Waltz." Rather, it focuses on educating the viewer about the history and state of affairs in Tibet.

Interspersed with concert footage are interviews, archival film, news footage and information about the Milarepa Fund, an organization dedicated to promoting nonviolence. Founded by Erin

Potts and Beastie Boy Adam Yauch and named after an 11th century saint who brought enlightenment through music, the Milarepa Fund is the recipient of all profits generated by "Free Tibet."

Yauch's commitment to Tibet seems genuine and moving, and he's smart enough to know that the mightiest tool he can bring to this cause is music. He's recruited an impressive lineup for the festival, which opens and closes with solo acoustic numbers by the redoubtable Beck. From there we segue to the Foo Fighters, who sound as if they belong in a suburban garage, a snippet of rap from De La Soul and blues courtesy of Buddy Guy. Along the way, Buddhist scholar Robert Thurman (Uma's dad) weighs in, and we spot Yoko Ono, the mother superior of the avant-garde, watching from the wings.

The Beasties turn in a typically high-voltage set, and Japanese rappers Cibo Matto screech. Pavement's batteries seem to run down over the course of their one song, Smashing Pumpkins acquit themselves admirably and the Red Hot Chili Peppers are fabulously over the top.

Then comes a dreary string of rap acts with the collective effect of a herd of elephants plodding slowly across the veldt; one recalls nothing but the thud. Turning in the strongest performance is Icelandic vocalist Bjork. Bouncing around the stage like a sunbeam as she delivers a strange tune called "Hyper-Ballad," Bjork has the range of Yma Sumac and the inscrutability of a Buddha. She is astonishing.

Much in the film is unintentionally hilarious. Observing the roiling bodies at the lip of the stage, a Tibetan monk chirps, "They're very happy!" Despite this seal of approval, there's something weird about celebrating Tibet with a mosh pit.

We see a Tibetan patiently explaining the theory of karma to an incoherent stoner, and a Tibetan nun who innocently exclaims, "The devotion to music here is amazing! In my country this kind of gathering only happens for spiritual occasions." A particular favorite is the head-banger who cheerfully declares: "I care about Tibet and everything, but I got a short attention span."

If the future of the free world is in the hands of kids like this, I'm, like, totally bummed.

NEW YORK POST, 9/12/98, p. 21, Larry Worth

As the very least of its accomplishments, "Free Tibet" confirms that monks and mosh pits make an odd mix.

Taking cameras into San Francisco's Golden Gate Park for a 1996 concert to benefit the beleagured Asian country, director Sarah Pirozek captures musicians like the Foo Fighters, Bjork, Smashing Pumpkins and Beastie Boys in top form.

She then intercuts staggering footage of Tibetans being brutalized, their temples' destruction by invading forces, and first-hand accounts of religious leaders suffering unspeakable tortures.

Going one step further, Pirozek takes her lens into the park's crowds, getting some candid—and sadly sobering—reflections from teens who barely know of Tibet, never mind its political problems.

Granted, "Free Tibet" is all over the map—literally (multiple graphics drive home Tibet's proximity to China) and figuratively. But awkward segues aside, memorable components make this a fine show-and-tell.

Also reviewed in:
NEW YORK TIMES, 9/11/98, p. E16, Lawrence Van Gelder
VARIETY, 9/14-20/98, p. 89, Daniel Lorber

FRIEND OF THE DECEASED, A

A Sony Pictures Classics release of a Compagnie des Films/Companie Est-Ouest/National Dovzhenko Film Studio/Studios du Kazakhstan Aimanov co-production, with the participation of the Ministere de la Culture Francaise and the Ukrainian Arts and Culture Ministry. *Executive Producer:* Jacky Ouaknine. *Producer:* Mykola Machenko and Pierre Rival. *Director:* Vyacheslav Krishtofovich. *Screenplay (Russian with English subtitles):* Andrei Kourkov.

Director of Photography: Vilen Kaluta.   *Editor:* Eleonora Sumovska.   *Music:* Vladimir Gronski.
Sound: Gueorgui Stremovski.   *Production Designer:* Roman Adamovich.   *Costumes:* Lyudmila
Serdinova.   *Running time:* 105 minutes.   *MPAA Rating:* R.

CAST: Alexandre Lazarev (Anatoli);   Tatiana Krivitska (Lena/Vika, the Prostitute);   Eugen
Pachin (Dima, Anatoli's Friend);   Constantin Kostychin (Kostia, the Contract Killer);   Elena
Korikova (Marina, Kostia's Wife);   Angelika Nevolina (Katia, Anatoli's Wife);   Sergiy
Romanyuk (Ivan, Anatoli's Contract Killer).

LOS ANGELES TIMES, 5/15/98, Calendar/p. 13, Kevin Thomas

With the elegant and tantalizing "A Friend of the Deceased," director Vyacheslav Krishtofovich
and writer Andrei Kourkov take an old plot—hiring someone to kill you, only to change your
mind—and use it to reveal the desperation and corruption that grips post-Soviet Ukraine, reducing
the value of human life itself.

Yet when a man remarks that friendship, now replaced with purely business relationships, is
part of "the glorious Soviet past," this reference to the former USSR is expressed with bitter
irony. "A Friend of the Deceased" is not nostalgic for Communist Party rule but rather for the
warmth between human beings that is in danger of evaporating in a Darwinian struggle to survive
in the new market economy.

You would think that Alexandre Lazarev's Anatoli, a former academic fluent in English and
French, would have plenty of opportunities to prosper in the new world of capitalist expansion.
That the reverse is the case leaves us to suspect that men and women like Anatoli must be a dime
a dozen in the former Soviet nations.

In any event, Anatoli slips into such drunken despair in trying to survive as a translator (mainly
for crass new entrepreneurs) that he succumbs to a friend's urging that he hire a hit man to rub
out the more prosperous man to whom Anatoli has lost his ambitious wife.

He's not serious about having his rival executed but instead decides to shift the hit man's target
to himself After a rendezvous with a contract killer aborts when their meeting place, a cafe, closes
early, Anatoli is surprised to realize that he's glad to have a new lease on life, only to discover
that his execution is set in motion and it that it's too late to reverse it.

"A Friend of the Deceased," which was selected for Cannes' prestigious Directors Fortnight last
year, is an anti-thriller in the sense that its makers transform its inherent suspense elements into
an evocation of the paranoia that permeates Ukrainian society. Anatoli emerges as an engaging
man, adrift in a world he may not be strong enough either to negotiate or to resist succumbing
to its corruptions. The film's other characters are similarly well-drawn.

Visually, "A Friend" is a jewel, with cinematographer Vilen Kaluta capturing three distinct
areas of Kiev—the charming cobblestoned old city where Anatoli lives in a flat of faded elegance,
the sleek night-life district and a suburban high-rise community under construction, at once
impersonal and luxurious—that are virtually interchangeable with such developments the world
over. Krishtofovitch fulfills his stated intention beautifully, which is to show "the inability of an
intelligent, refined, cultured but weak man to find his place in the new society.... We can't ask
people to behave like heroes."

NEW YORK POST, 5/1/98, p. 50, Larry Worth

O. Henry has been dead for 78 years. But his penchant for deliciously ironic endings lives on,
as perfectly showcased in "A Friend of the Deceased."

Actually, Ukrainian director Vyacheslav Krishtofovich threads O. Henry-like twists within an
even older chestnut—the one about a guy who mulls death (here, after losing his wife and job),
then hires a contract killer to be put out of his misery, and only later has second thoughts.

That's when Andrei Kourkov's script takes some wildly original turns. Specifically, the hero
is too embarrassed by his change of heart to cancel the hit. So he hires a second murderer to rub
out the first. But nothing's ever that easy.

Director Krishtofovich uses such intrigue as a launching pad for wonderfully subtle humor, as
when the protagonist must supply the assassin with a shot of himself for ID purposes. Rather than
submit an unflattering image, he goes all-out with a studio photographer. Nice touch.

Suspense also comes into play, intensified by the plot's Kiev setting. Depending on what's happening within its confines, the city alternately appears postcard pretty and downright gloomy, all while reflecting today's every-man-for-himself politics in the former U.S.S.R.

Granted, the pacing occasionally makes for slow going, and it's almost halfway into the production before the setup truly kicks in. But the highs more than compensate.

For starters, Alexandre Lazarev's charismatic hero lends a commanding presence to the proceedings, seamlessly seguing between happiness, despair and all the stages in between. Tatiana Krivitska is a lovely complement as a prostitute who straightens out Lazarev's thinking while Elena Korikova makes a heartbreaking damsel in distress.

Collectively, they help set the stage for both romance and mystery. In the process, "A Friend of the Deceased" resurrects old-fashioned drama in newfangled hues.

NEWSDAY, 5/1/98, Part II/p. B7, John Anderson

While the post-Communist Eastern Bloc has yet to inspire quite as many movies as the Old West, what they're about in either case is freedom: What it means, what it costs, and how very often it's just another word (cue Kris Kristofferson) for nothing left to lose.

To Anatoli (Alexandre Lazarev), the dark-eyed Ukrainian protagonist of Vyacheslav Krishtofovich's "A Friend of the Deceased" the absence of the Soviet yoke simply means no jobs, no money, no wife. But while he, a translator, has languished, his wife Katia (Angelika Nevolina), an advertising executive—a breed that would have survived nuclear annihilation anyway—has done very well and leaves him shortly for a guy in a red car (Soviet-ironic symbolism, anyone?). When an old friend, Dima (Eugen Pachin) offers to call a hit man he knows to knock off the boyfriend, Anatoli accepts—but arranges the hit to be on himself.

Krishtofovich (of 1991's "Adam's Rib") is making metaphors, not the least of which involves Anatoli's languorous grasp on life. The world's changed, Anatoli hasn't and what he sees as his moral surrender—which includes providing well-paid-for false testimony at a divorce trial—isn't much more than survival tactics, since he'd never been called upon to make any moral decisions before, anyway. At the same time, his is just a dipping of the toe into the great ocean of runaway Kiev corruption.

Lazarev is a rather magnetic leading man and Tatiana Krivitska, as the prostitute Lena a k a Vika is an impish presence in an otherwise dour movie—which is the problem. Krishtofovich maintains both the dry, sardonic tone of his film, and its believability, even after Anatoli decides he wants to live, hires a second hit man to kill the first and winds up romanced by the dead killer's wife. But "A Friend of the Deceased"—unlike, say, Aki Kaurismaki's "I Hired a Contract Killer" which deals with much the same material—takes its mission a little too seriously. In this, it's a little like Anatoli himself.

VILLAGE VOICE, 5/5/98, p. 124, Dennis Lim

Prone to outbreaks of ponderous gloom (a condition exacerbated by its gruesome mutant-Muzak soundtrack), *A Friend of the Deceased* is a mildly intriguing but eventually irksome reflection on life's stranger twists of fate. Sifting through the transitional disorder of present-day Kiev, Ukranian director Vyacheslav Krishtofovich means to evoke the profound disorientation of newfound "freedom" but his none too elegant parable is hamstrung by its insistent irony (or, à la Alanis, by what it stubbornly misdiagnoses as irony).

Drunk one night, an out-of-work translator (Alexandre Lazarev) takes out a contract on his wife's lover. In a fit of self-pity, he then sets himself up as the target. After spending the night with a perky hooker, he decides he wants to continue living. But, instead of calling off the hit man when he has the chance, he hires *another* heavy to put things right. Big mistake, needless to say, but it paves the way for much guilt-tripping and do-gooding, and for a series of epiphanies, most of them fake.

Also reviewed in:
CHICAGO TRIBUNE, 5/22/98, Friday/p. D, John Petrakis
NATION, 6/1/98, p. 36, Stuart Klawans
NEW YORK TIMES, 5/1/98, p. E28, Stephen Holden

NEW YORKER, 5/11/98, p. 108, Daphne Merkin
VARIETY, 5/26-6/1/97, p. 68, Brendan Kelly

FROZEN

An International Film Circuit release of an Another Film Company/Shu Kei's Creative Workshop production in association with the Hubert Bals Foundation. *Executive Producer:* Pang Ming. *Producer:* Shu Kei and Xu Wei. *Director:* Wu Ming. *Screenplay (Mandarin with English subtitles):* Pang Ming and Wu Ming. *Director of Photography:* Yang Shu. *Editor:* Qing Qing. *Music:* Roeland Dol. *Sound:* Zhai Lixin, Wu Jiang, and (music) Paul Mourus. *Art Director:* Li Yanxiu. *Make-up:* Guo Junxia. *Running time:* 95 minutes. *MPAA Rating:* Not Rated.

CAST: Jia Hongshen (Qi Lei);   Ma Xiaoqing (Shao Yun);   Bai Yu (Sister);   Li Geng (Sister's Husband);   Bai Yefu (Bald Guy);   Wei Ye (Long Haired Guy);   Zhang Yongning (Lau Ling);   Qu Lixin (Doctor);   Liu Jie (Dao Shi).

LOS ANGELES TIMES, 3/20/98, Calendar/p. 20, Kevin Thomas

On June 20, 1994, a 23-year-old Beijing performance artist committed suicide, and a young filmmaker, using the pseudonym "Wu Ming"—which translates as "No Name"—was inspired to make a film that probes the reasons why.

The result is "Frozen," a stunning, spare and demanding film that takes us into the world of Beijing's artistic avant-garde. Wu is too subtle, too evocative a filmmaker to come up with easy answers, but by the time 90 minutes have passed he has left us with an understanding of why a young artist would seek death.

Of course, the most obvious motivation is the despair that swept over young people in the wake of the Tiananmen Square massacre in 1989. Surely, that is what the performance artist's girlfriend (Ma Xiaoqing) is referring to when she remarks that her boyfriend (Jia Hongshen) killed himself "to show that he lived amidst murderers."

But Wu, who made his film independently—i.e., illegally—gives a larger picture, a panorama of a new Beijing that's drab, sterile and impersonal. It's a place where, despite economic growth, Jia's Qi Lei is too poor to live anywhere but in a tiny, stark apartment with his older sister (Bai Yu), a physician and surgeon, and her husband (Li Geng). Qi's sister, easily 10 years older, tries hard to understand her suicidal brother and remarks to a colleague that her brother's generation has had it "so easy." He counters that maybe young people have had it too easy, that they haven't experienced enough pressure and that this can lead to depression.

The colleague could be right, but Wu, in an interview last July in Beijing with film critic Berenice Reynaud observed that "historically, in China, economy and culture have advanced in opposite directions. When the country's economy gets better, the cultural sphere experiences problems. The government wants to concentrate on economic development, and it is really afraid to see people getting original or different ideas."

Qi, who is also a woodcut artist, decides to simulate death in his work with the advent of each season—an "earth burial" for autumn, a "water burial" for winter, a "fire burial" for spring and an "ice burial" for summer requiring large slabs of ice—but says for the last he intends to die for real of hypothermia. Tall and handsome, Qi would seem to have much to live for—he's young enough to hope for real change to happen in his country—but he has become intoxicated with the whole notion of death.

Wu takes us through Qi's daily life once he's announced his intention to die on the first day of summer and thereby introduces us to a series of people who either try to dissuade him or to get him to think through what he's planning to do. Wu lets us draw our own conclusions about Qi, his motivation and his decision.

Wu then packs a surprise twist in the final sequence and suggests that when people start setting drastic courses of action in motion they can start believing they just have to go through with it.

"Frozen"—a title open to various meanings—is bleak, to be sure, but it is not without humor. Mixing professional and nonprofessional actors expertly, Wu gives us that kind of here-and-now sense of reality about China that seems possible only through its independent cinema. With difficulty Wu managed to get his film, including the negative, to Holland for post-production. As is the case with virtually all Chinese films with any real edge, "Frozen" can not be seen in China.

VILLAGE VOICE, 3/24/98, p. 70, Amy Taubin

If there's a cultural bureaucracy less open to films about sympathetic, suicidal, social misfits than Iran, it would have to be China. (You don't find many such films being made in the U.S. today either, even in the so-called indie sector, but here, the censor is the marketplace rather than the state. As far as the effect on filmmakers, it's hard to say which is worse.)

Based on the true story of a young art student whose performance pieces prefigured his actual suicide, *Frozen* is most interesting for its documentary-like depiction of a Chinese youth scene enamored of American adolescent excess. The filmmaker, who goes by the pseudonym Wu Ming which translates as No Name is obviously talented, but the film stalls midway. Unable to illuminate the protagonist's desire for self-obliteration, and unwilling to leave it unexplained, the director does a 180-degree turn at the last minute, pointing the finger at an adult villain who plays head games with his young protégé.

Also reviewed in:
CHICAGO TRIBUNE, 9/4/98, Friday/p. F, John Petrakis
NEW YORK TIMES, 3/25/98, p. E5, Anita Gates
VARIETY, 2/24-3/2/97, David Rooney

FULL SPEED

A Strand Releasing release of a Magouric Productions/Telema/France 2 Cinema/Rhone-Alpes Cinema co-production with the participation of Cofimage 7 and Canal +. *Producer:* Laurent Benegui. *Director:* Gael Morel. *Screenplay (French with English subtitles):* Gael Morel. *Director of Photography:* Jeanne Lapoirie. *Editor:* Catherine Schwartz. *Choreographer:* Evaldo Souza Santo. *Sound:* Ludovic Henault and François Groult. *Sound Editor:* Corinne Rozenberg. *Casting:* Jacques Grant. *Set Decorator:* Frederique Hurpeau. *Costumes:* Brigitte Faur. *Make-up:* Catherine Bruchon. *Stunt Coordinator:* Philippe Guegan. *Running time:* 82 minutes. *MPAA Rating:* Not Rated.

CAST: Elodie Bouchez (Julie); Stephane Rideau (Jimmy); Pascal Cervo (Quentin); Meziane Bardadi (Samir); Romaine Auger (Rick); Salim Kechiouche (Jamel); Mohammed Dib (Karim); Paul Morel (Quentin's Father); Bernard Villeneuve (Journalist).

LOS ANGELES TIMES, 2/6/98, Calendar/p. 6, Kevin Thomas

Gael Morel's engaging "Full Speed" opens in a sylvan setting with two handsome youths—one blond, the other swarthy—looking lovingly into each other's eyes. Suddenly the blond youth is shot to death.

We move two years ahead, and again meet the surviving youth, the Algerian-born Samir (Meziane Bardadi) and through him a circle of friends living in a French provincial city surrounded by beautiful countryside.

They are Jimmy (Stephane Rideau), a lean, rugged young man whose emotions run close to the surface and whose loyalties run deep; Jimmy's best friend Quentin (Pascal Cervo), who, though not yet 20, has written a best-selling novel about disaffected youth; and Julie (Elodie Bouchez), a recent college dropout involved with Quentin and living in her absent family's large and charming country house, the film's key setting.

You can already tell that this is familiar territory for French films—and indeed those of many other countries—but Morel has a commanding way of revealing these young people to us and to one another through their constantly shifting allegiances and interactions.

The pivotal Quentin is a nasty piece of work: He has sex with Samir--who promptly falls in love with him—just so he can get Samir to talk about his murdered boyfriend, apparently figuring he might be able to put the story to future use. In the meantime, Julie finds herself drawn to Jimmy, better-looking and far more likable than Quentin.

These young people are deeply into living for the moment, pessimistic or unsure of their futures. All the while Morel is widening and deepening his perspective, connecting his young people to the larger community, which is infected with an ugly and dangerous racism nakedly directed to the Arabs living there. Morel implicitly suggests that France is speeding toward a self-destruction that may take its young people with it.

Morel is a master of stylish economy and swift pacing and extracts total and unself-conscious portrayals from his people. They all excel, but Rideau actually reminds you of James Dean in his passion and vulnerability. "Full Speed" is fully realized.

If it reminds you of Andre Techine's superb 1993 "Wild Reeds" (which starred Rideau, Bouchez and Morel himself), it should. Techine has been a mentor to Morel, who has created a remarkable contemporary companion film to Techine's study of coming of age at a time when France was torn by the Algerian War.

NEW YORK POST, 1/16/98, p. 46, Thelma Adams

Is it only a coincidence that Quentin is the name of the precocious young novelist in French filmmaker Gael Morel's precocious debut, "Full Speed? On the verge of 20, the provincial Quentin (Pascal Cervo) becomes the toast of Paris after penning a novel about his inner circle. He's written about Jules and Jim—his best friend Jimmy (Stephane Rideau) and girlfriend Julie (Elodie Bouchez).

Morel co-starred with Rideau and Bouchez in Andre Techine's "Wild Reeds." The beautifully shot, award-winning film was about youth, first love, homosexuality and Algerian-French tensions bursting into violence.

Morel patterns himself after Techine. The shots of leaves taken from below, the intoxication with the forest, the reckless feeling of speed on a motorcycle, as well as the brilliant casting, all hark back to "Wild Reeds" and "Ma Saisson Preferee."

Like Techine's films, Morel's drama is searching, matter-of-fact, multi-layered. The young writer-director revisits similar themes, but he twists them in a less nostalgic direction.

Young movie-makers are less sentimental about youth, however tragic the consequences of immaturity.

"Full Speed" follows Jimmy and Julie's difficult adjustment to the changes within Quentin, and is coolly merciless in its dissection of a young artistic opportunist. What will Quentin, with his boyish, blank face untempered by experience, do for an encore when he's already mined his short autobiography?

The Gen X writer befriends an Algerian emigre, Samir (Meziane Bardadi). While trying to siphon off the tragic love story of Samir's life for use in his second book, Quentin encounters a real-life complication: Samir falls in love with him, warts and all.

Unlike Techine at his best, Morel lacks the restraint of experience. A gun that appears late in the second act promises the intrusion of the melodrama that his mentor avoids. And yet, there is a bravery to match Morel's cockiness, a desire to whittle away at difficult, even embarrassing questions, that should assure that the young director's career continues at "Full Speed."

NEWSDAY, 1/16/98, Part II/p. B6, John Anderson

What was it Jean-Luc Godard said? "All you need for a movie is a gun and a girl." Good advice, although he never said the gun actually had to go off. Or the girl, either.

Nor did he specify that all youth-oriented French films had to have gay themes, fascists, allusions to the Algerian situation or romantic triangles. But they all seem epidemic. Even contagious.

Repetition doesn't make a film good or bad, of course, and neither does imitation. They do, however, distract. With his first film, "Full Speed," Gael Morel, one of the stars of Andre Techine's much-honored "Wild Reeds" of 1993, not only casts his costars Elodie Bouchez and Stephane Rideau (as Julie and Jimmy, in a nod to Godard) but in many ways has remade Techine's movie. There's a similar dynamic between the characters; homosexuality is exotic; Algeria festers like a bad conscience.

But while Morel is in many ways replaying or perhaps updating the conflicts of "Wild Reeds" he's also performing an autopsy—or maybe it's an exhumation—on the morality of the artist. His stand-in, Quentin (Pascal Cervo), is a teenage novelist whose first book has been published to acclaim (or, better yet, attention from talk shows) and although we don't ever believe Quentin is a writer, he's thoroughly convincing as an opportunist. Which is Morel's point.

Bouchez' Julie is dating the feckless Quentin, but she responds much more glandularly to Rideau's Jimmy, a street-tough boxer and rap fan who is the embodiment of the basic male animal. Conversely, Samir (Meziane Bardadi), a gay Algerian youth whose great love, Rick (Romaine Auger) has been killed in a racist attack, falls—or, more correctly, collapses—for Quentin. The young novelist, for his part, sees in Samir a great source for material, stringing him along for his stories and then rejecting him cruelly when something sexually overt occurs.

Quentin is also conspicuously absent when his friends Julie and Jimmy have their own crises, or when, despite their differences, they develop a genuine friendship with Samir. But like the scorpion of the fable—who stings his benefactor because "it's my nature"—Quentin is doing what an artist does. He really doesn't exist in anything like real life, leaving it up to others to do the living that provides the fodder for his work. At the end of the film, when he encounters an accordionist playing among a family of gypsies at a roadside encampment, the coalescence of art and reality sparks within him an epiphany of insignificance.

Would it be at all surprising to say that despite all these lofty thoughts, "Full Speed" is not all that likeable a movie? Interesting, but not likeable. Morel wants to capture the surface tension of selfish, combustible youth, but his megalomaniacal characters often sound as if they've stepped out of a bad romance novel. However, Morel also shows a rare intelligence. And when he decides to make something besides a sequel, it could be very intriguing indeed.

VILLAGE VOICE, 1/20/98, p. 90, Amy Taubin

Which makes it mysterious why any company (in this case Strand) would put its logo on *Full Speed,* a French film with nothing much to recommend it except a few dozen young boys without shirts. A first feature by Gael Morel, who appeared in André Téchiné's *Wild Reeds, Full Speed* is a paler, clumsier version of several of the films in the French series "All the Girls and Boys of their Time" (of which *Wild Reeds* was a part).

The film concerns a precocious 18-year-old novelist who abandons the working-class friends who served as raw material for his stories when Paris beckons. Set against a background of murderous relations between French right-wingers and Algerian immigrants, *Full Speed* is largely a film about lost love and deflected desire. The narcissistic novelist is adored by a middle-class girl, a gay Arab immigrant, and a hapless but appealingly macho kid. All three of them come to bad ends, which leaves the novelist guilty but with his ambition unimpeded.

I presume that the title *Full Speed* is meant to refer to the breakneck pace of adolescent passion, but it's also a description of the way the actors have been directed to speak their lines—as rapidly and flatly as possible.

Also reviewed in:
NEW YORK TIMES, 1/16/98, p. E20, Stephen Holden
VARIETY, 5/27-6/2/96, p. 73, Lisa Nesselson

FULL TILT BOOGIE

A Miramax Films release in association with L. Driver Productions Inc. *Executive Producer:* Quentin Tarantino. *Producer:* Rana Joh Glickman. *Director:* Sarah Kelly. *Screenplay:* Quentin Tarantino. *Director of Photography:* Christopher Gallo. *Editor:* Lauren Zuckerman. *Music:* Cary Berger and Dominic Kelly. *Music Editor:* Matt Beville and Cary Berger. *Sound:* Ken Ahern. *Sound Editor:* Charles Ewing Smith. *Running time:* 111 minutes. *MPAA Rating:* R.

CAST: Harvey Keitel (Jacob Fuller);   George Clooney (Set Gecko);   Quentin Tarantino (Richard Gecko);   Juliette Lewis (Kate Fuller);   Michael Parks (Earl McGraw);   Tim "Stuffy" Soronen (Best Boy Grip);   Rick Stribling (Key Grip);   Amy Cohen (Seth Gecko's Asstistant); Ken Bondy (Craft Service Man);   Victoria Lucai (Richard Gecko's Asstistant);   Cecilia Montiel (Production Designer).

LOS ANGELES TIMES, 7/31/98, Calendar/p. 20, Kevin Thomas

Sarah Kelly's "Full Tilt Boogie" amiably chronicles the 10-week shoot in 1995 of "From Dusk to Dawn," that lurid, amusing and entirely forgettable vampire picture directed by Robert Rodriguez from an early script by his executive producer Quentin Tarantino, who also co-starred in the film with George Clooney.

Unfortunately, whatever interest "Full Tilt Boogie" might have had has pretty much evaporated, coming so long after the release of "From Dusk to Dawn" in January 1996. That's because movie fans are pretty familiar by now with Tarantino's bright, manic personality, and with Clooney, then making his feature debut as Tarantino's partner in crime, who kidnap a minister and his family and wind up in an elaborate south-of-the-border topless biker bar where everybody is a vampire.

What's more, nothing really all that exciting occurs during the shoot. Yes, there is the threat of a union shutdown, an explosion that turns out to be bigger than planned, requiring the repairing of the nightclub facade set, erected on a dry lake bed in Barstow, where the temperature hits 122 degrees. But these are hardly earth-shaking occurrences, and the documentary may be of greatest interest to film students wanting to get an idea of what it's like to make a mainstream movie. Not helping matters is that in clocking in at 99 minutes "Full Tilt Boogie" overstays its welcome by 10 or 15 minutes.

What emerges is a portrait of cast and crew who are largely young people. They're entirely professional, likably candid and collectively possess an admirable sense of humor. These people work hard and party later in a perfectly normal fashion.

By far the most interesting aspect of a jaunty if none-to-gripping experience are the interviews with the film's stars. Juliette Lewis, who played the daughter of minister Harvey Keitel, comes across as a natural; she says of acting, "You're lying pure and simple. If you understand acting as lying you can lie a million different ways."

By contrast Keitel, who did not want to participate in the documentary but finally agreed, providing that Tarantino interviewed him (off camera) rather than Kelly, waxes philosophical, talking about acting's essential mystery, the excitement of not knowing what may happen moment to moment. Keitel, formidable actor that he is, is seemingly trying to be dead serious, which in the context of "Full Tilt Boogie's" hip, comedic tone, comes across as pretentious.

Fred Williamson, a veteran of so-called "blaxploitation" pictures, talks with pride of his experiences as an independent filmmaker—you're not entirely sure Kelly knows who he is, and Michael Parks, cast as a sheriff, epitomizes class and cool, mentioning his high regard for Jean Renoir and describing acting as "a way of finding out about other people." As for the now-famously wary Clooney, he avoids direct exchanges with Kelly, and as the documentary progresses, clearly regards Kelly as an intruder—though he also wants to come across as a good guy who gets along with everybody.

There's considerable good-natured humor along the way, and while "Full Tilt Boogie" is pleasantly diverting, it's about as negligible as "From Dusk to Dawn" was itself.

NEW YORK POST, 8/1/98, p. 24, Thelma Adams

Figure me this: Robert Rodriguez's "From Dusk Till Dawn," with George Clooney and Quentin Tarantino, lasted a fire-blasted 108 minutes. Sarah Kelly's documentary about the making of the 1996 vampire actioner lasts 100 minutes. We're not talking "Apocalypse Now" here!

Part apologia for producer Lawrence Bender's union problems, part hymn to the working stiffs that weather 129-degree days with only wilted chicken sandwiches to eat, part star-struck newsreel, "Full-Tilt Boogie" is another meandering feature film concealing a really sharp short.

Highlights include: Clooney's personal assistant kvetching about waiting at Taco Bell to get the "ER" actor's fix; seeing what happens behind-the-scenes when Rodriguez's trademark fireballs go very, very awry, and George Clooney getting a marriage proposal from a Barstow local while half-concealing his revulsion behind his patented smile.

But for every tidbit, we get subjected to another Tarantino self-important speed rant; Juliette Lewis clueing us in on her method ("acting is lying, and you can lie a million different ways") and Harvey Keitel having a messianic rhapsody about the Actor and living in the Moment. Still, these moments beat the musical montage of buses and trucks skimming along the movie's primary location, a dried-out lake bed.

And Kelly, largely relegated to the company of grips, truckers, extras and assistants, never asks the question I'm dying to know: Why does the talented Rodriguez always direct with a guitar strapped across his chest like a troubadour trigger-man?

NEWSDAY, 7/31/98, Part II/p. B10, John Anderson

When people wear advertising on their clothing, or watch the commercials-disguised-as-programming on the E! channel, at least there's a purpose to it all—something's being sold, a consumer is being snookered. There's also the sense of camaraderie among viewers, the opportunity to be part of the common degradation of the American consumer.

But "Full Tilt Boogie"—whose title is as misleading as it is nonsensical—is a new animal entirely, a milestone in the death-by-advertising being suffered on American culture: a commercial with nothing to sell! It's a breakthrough! It's brilliant! It's ... what is it, exactly?

It's a home movie; it's a vanity production; it's an exercise in self-indulgence; it's anti-union propaganda and it's a chance to revisit the set of "From Dusk Till Dawn," the Robert Rodriguez blood-and-vampires freak show that few wanted to see in 1996 but apparently have been clamoring for ever since.

Why else release a feature-length documentary made with the kind of objectivity that hasn't been seen since Leni Riefenstahl (whose "Triumph of the Will" was a documentary about her friend Adolf Hitler) and allows one to get up close and personal with people who, were they your neighbors, would prompt you to sell your house? Gosh, there must be some reason. Compromising photographs, perhaps.

Director Sarah Kelly, presumed owner of said photographs, takes her camera on set and proceeds to capture the uncandid and unspontaneous. Quentin Tarantino and George Clooney doing a rehearsed approach to the first day of shooting; Juliette Lewis karaoke-singing (you thought the vampires were frightening?) and crew members discussing who's having a romance with whom. There are no revelations, save for the big one, about the lack of depth in certain cultural icons and the ease with which people will abandon self-respect when they hear the buzz of a video camera.

Outside of the car-crash qualities of "Full Tilt Boogie," the only part of the film that gets vaguely interesting is Kelly's propagandizing efforts to defend Rodriguez' movie against charges of unfair labor practices; the interesting part is her total failure to do so.

VILLAGE VOICE, 8/4/98, p. 58, Amy Taubin

After moldering in the Miramax storeroom for two years, *Full-Tilt Boogie*, a documentary about the making of *From Dusk Till Dawn*, is finally getting a theatrical release. This untimely gesture is meant either to appease or to undermine the ego of the Weinstein brothers' aging wunderkind Quentin Tarantino, the writer and costar of *From Dusk Till Dawn,* who makes no impression whatsoever in this documentary directed by his intern, Sarah Kelly. Or perhaps, as the definitive counter-programming to *Air Bud Golden Receiver* (which Miramax is releasing on August 14), *Full-Tilt Boogie* is proof of the Weinsteins' unparalleled eclecticism—they adopt all kinds of dogs.

But who on earth would want to sit through a giddily worshipful doc about the making of a movie that was a blight on the career of everyone involved? Of the principal players—Tarantino, director Robert Rodriguez, and actors George Clooney and Juliette Lewis—everyone except Clooney, who blossomed under Steven Soderbergh's direction, is in a holding pattern. Kelly's focus, however, is not the talent but the crew who evince good cheer and team spirit in the face of unspeakable working conditions: 18-hour days in 100-degree heat, garbage food, a casual attitude about safety (even the art director is shocked when her set burns to a crisp).

An $18-million movie, *From Dusk Till Dawn* was infamous for its attempt to bypass IATSE (the production union) to save a buck. Kelly gives producer Lawrence Bender a forum to defend his antiunion stance and seems totally unaware that he undermines his own position with his argument. The unions, Bender claims, are dinosaurs. They don't understand how independent filmmakers like Rodriguez work. Rodriguez needs to be free to do everything on his films—operate the camera, take sound, set up the lights. Well, maybe that's how he handled the $7000 *El Mariachi,* but here, all we see him doing is chumming around with his stars, sitting on his butt, and yelling "action"—exactly what directors do on movies that play by the union rules. When the Miramax representative shows up to retroactively bestow a few months of health benefits on the unquiet masses, you wish someone had had the guts to tell him to shove it. Maybe someone did, but you can bet they wound up on the proverbial cutting-room floor.

Also reviewed in:
NEW YORK TIMES, 7/31/98, p. E22, Janet Maslin
VARIETY, 9/22-28/97, p. 50, David Stratton

FUNNY GAMES

An Attitude Films release of a Wega Film production.   *Executive Producer:* Veit Heiduschka. *Producer:* Veit Heiduschka.   *Director:* Michael Haneke.   *Screenplay (German with English subtitles):* Michael Haneke.   *Director of Photography:* Jürgen Jürges.   *Editor:* Andreas Prochaska. *Music:* Georg Friedrich Handel, Pietro Mascagni, W.A. Mozart, and John Zorn. *Sound:* Walter Amann and (music) Hannes Eder.   *Sound Editor:* Bernhard Bamberger. *Art Director:* Christoph Kanter.   *Special Effects:* Mac Steinmeier, Danny Bellens, and Willy Neuner. *Costumes:* Lisy Christl.   *Special Effects Make-up:* Waldemar Pokromski.   *Running time:* 103 minutes.   *MPAA Rating:* Not Rated.

CAST: Susanne Lothar (Anna Schober);   Ulrich Mühe (Georg Schober);   Arno Frisch (Paul); Frank Giering (Peter);   Stefan Clapczynski (Georg "Schorschi" Schober);   Doris Kunstmann (Gerda);   Christoph Bantzer (Fred Berlinger);   Wolfgang Glück (Robert);   Susanne Meneghel (Gerda's Sister);   Monika Zallinger (Eva Berlinger).

NEW YORK POST, 3/13/98, p. 44, Thelma Adams

The hills are alive with the sound of music but, in Austrian Michael Haneke's slick, sadistic thriller, there are deadly screams down by the lake. And no one hears them.

By turns torturous, mortifying, funny and consistently self-conscious, "Funny Games" has opened at the Film Forum after amazing and offending festival audiences from Cannes to Hong Kong.

The brutal film begins with an image of yuppie contentment: A father, mother and son travel in a shiny Range Rover amid sun-dappled trees on a perfect summer morning. They're bound for their secluded lake house.

With their frisky German shepherd, the Schobers are the Austrian Cleavers. On the road, Anna (Susanne Lothar) and Georg (Ulrich Muhe) delight Georgie (Stefan Clapczynski) by playing a car game: One parent picks a classical music CD and the other must guess, Handel or Mozart, which orchestra and which piece.

Within the Range Rover, the Schobers' life is as perfect and self-contained as an egg. It's also as fragile. It's no coincidence that two crisp young men in tennis whites invade the family's elegant lakeside compound under the pretense of borrowing eggs.

Peter (Frank Giering) and Paul (Arno Frisch) are baby-faced bullies. They could be college mates on the rowing team, guests at a nearby estate. They're not. They're sport killers on a spree—and we know before the Schobers that, when the chips are down, it's no use calling the neighbors.

It's part of Haneke's controlled agenda that the pair have no motives, no psychology. The writer/director refuses to offer his fiends that much justification. Even Norman Bates had cause.

What starts as a minor disagreement between the pudgy Peter and Anna over broken eggs escalates into a night of terror. After the preliminaries—Peter demonstrates his golf swing by knee-capping Georg—the quintet settles in for a night of "funny games." To be sporting, Peter bets the Schobers they won't live to eat eggs for breakfast.

Haneke ups the discomfort by breaking the film's fourth wall. Peter winks at the camera as he leads Anna to the family dog's corpse in a game of hide and seek, hot and cold.

The killers' gestures become more overt, and gimmicky, as the evening progresses. After an hour, Peter, stalling for gory entertainment value before the next round of agony, turns to the audience and says conspiratorially, "We're not up to feature film length yet."

Like Wes Craven in his recent thrillers, Haneke reminds audiences that his little murders are a clever cinematic prank. By purchasing tickets, the audience sanctions the violence. It's a ruthless argument about supply and demand. But, with its repulsive slaughter of children, "Funny Games" takes Craven's "joke" one step further, and it's very possibly one step too far.

SIGHT AND SOUND, 12/98, p. 44, Mark Kermode

An upper-middle-class family—Anna, Georg and son young Schorschi—drive to their lakeside holiday home. While neighbour Fred and his acquaintance Paul help to moor Georg's boat, Peter introduces himself to Anna as a friend of Fred's wife Eva, and asks to borrow some eggs. When Peter breaks the eggs and drops Anna's mobile phone in the sink, she demands that he leave. Instead, Paul uses a golf club to kill Rolfi the dog and breaks Georg's knee.

When neighbours from across the lake drop by, Anna introduces Paul as a friend while Peter holds her husband and son captive in the house. Peter and Paul bet the family that within 12 hours they will be dead. Paul covers the child's head with a pillow case and forces Anna to strip. A scuffle ensues during which young Schorschi escapes to Fred's house, where he finds the now-dead neighbours' gun and unsuccessfully attempts to shoot Paul. Back at the house, Paul makes a sandwich while Peter shoots young Schorschi dead. When Peter and Paul leave, Anna flees the house, but is recaptured and returned, bound and gagged. Peter tortures Georg with a knife. Paul forces Anna to recite prayers, and then shoots Georg. Peter and Paul take Anna bound out to the boat, and throw her overboard to drown.

Paul arrives at the neighbours across the lake, and says Anna has sent him for some eggs.

"Anyone who leaves the cinema doesn't need the film, and anybody who stays does," director Michael Haneke has said of his efficiently executed experiment in the theatre of screen cruelty. Indeed, rarely has a film-maker exercised such perverse precision in his desire to torment an audience who have paid to watch his work, but for whom he clearly harbours unbridled contempt. Building on an argument developed in such less accessible works as *The Seventh Continent* and *Benny's Video*, Haneke here attempts to engage with his withering attack on thrill-seeking screen consumers. Littering the screen with gaudy images of blood-splattered television screens and making numerous allusions to televisual trivia (the killers call each other Beavis and Butt-head or Tom and Jerry), Haneke takes his scalpel to the media-saturated masses, intending to torture them into awareness.

His motives are both simple and simplistic: believing that sanitised media violence has inured us to the realities of pain, he offers a gruelling depiction of suffering designed to appal, revolt and traumatise those who have come to watch a violent film. The fact that relatively few Hollywood action fans are likely to wander into an Austrian art film in the first place doesn't hinder Haneke.

This lesson takes the form of an elaborate game of show and-tell in which Haneke shows the audience nothing, but tells them everything. The only actual instance of on-screen violence in *Funny Games* occurs during an aberrational appendix which momentarily breaks the flow of the film before being rewound and unwritten, leaving the explicit sight unseen. Elsewhere, Haneke tells us about the appalling events unfolding either by focusing on the pain in his victims' faces, or by letting us hear their screams of anguish on an intentionally abrasive soundtrack which juxtaposes classical tranquillity and gibbering thrash metal with the angry wasp-like buzzing of an interminable, infernal television set.

Although powerful, such stylistic devices are not perhaps as radical or original as Haneke seems to believe. While the averted gaze of the camera and incongruous use of music are techniques recently explored by such populist actioneers as Quentin Tarantino, Haneke's reliance on anguished screams rather than visceral visuals merely builds on Tobe Hooper's more experimental *The Texas Chain Saw Massacre* (1974) which did far more to unravel the conventions of a violent genre. Even the straight-to camera asides have long been a staple of mainstream cinema and theatre, as have the various self-reflexive quirks ("Look, it's a film!") which permeate such mainstream fare as *Wayne's World* and *Gremlins 2*. And, of course, the open-ended narrative itself, which starts and ends with the killers continuing their path of destruction, owes an enormous debt to John McNaughton's superior film *Henry Portrait of a Serial Killer* which made all the same points nine years ago, but rather more successfully addressed the demands of its intended target audience.

In fact, *Funny Games* would be little more than an elaborate formalistic exercise were it not for the horribly believable central performance of Susanne Lothar, whose suffering contrasts starkly with the icy detachment of Arno Frisch's bloodless killer. At times, the two actually seem to be in different movies, with Frisch nipping merrily back and forth between the film's world and ours (a theme tangentially addressed in Peter's rambling anecdote about matter and anti-matter), while Lothar remains resolutely locked within the hellish sadism of Haneke's narrative.

While the hideous kinkiness of Peter and Paul's white tennis garb and surgical gloves places them within a well-worn tradition of weirdo screen villains, Anna's naturalistic wardrobe and make-up are intended to assure us that she is a real victim, enduring real pain. She is so convincing, in fact, it's hard not to imagine that her bloodshot eyes, puffed cheeks and ravaged features were not achieved by being roundly beaten up between takes. Here is an actor who genuinely gives the appearance of suffering for her art, and the pain of *Funny Games* resides in watching her suffer over and over and over again.

All of which suggests that the, only reasonable response to *Funny Games is* to walk out of the cinema itself. Indeed, Haneke offers more than one opportunity for the horrified viewer to use the exit signs, starting with Anna's early plaintive plea: "Please leave now." Later, Paul breaks off from terrorising Anna in a vicious round of hot-and-cold to turn and wink at the camera, suggesting that if we've stayed this long, then we are now implicated in his "funny game". When the bedraggled and wretched mother asks, "Why don't you kill us right away," her tormentors' reply of, "Don't forget the entertainment value: we'd all be deprived of our pleasure", is clearly intended to include any remaining members of the audience. And when Paul finally ungags Anna so that she can more vocally react to his partner's live dissection of her husband, he explains in passing that: "The dumb suffer in unspectacular fashion. We want to offer the audience something..."

Under such clear instruction from the film maker, who could reasonably stay and gawp rather than stand and walk? Short of achieving some twistedly misguided pleasure from the atrocities depicted, the only conceivable reason for staying to the end would be an academic interest in seeing just how long Haneke can sustain his thesis—either that, or a macho desire not to wimp out and show yourself beaten by the humourless Austrian and his cohorts. Why else would anyone wish to continue enduring an intentionally unendurable work of art? Why would anyone stay when the film so explicitly challenges them to leave? As the actor says in that probably apocryphal story about a disciple of Antonin Artaud who stood on stage gently tearing the wings of a butterfly: "Why didn't you stop me?"

VILLAGE VOICE, 3/17/98, p. 59, J. Hoberman

There are some filmmakers who are less the directors of movies than the directors of audiences.

Alfred Hitchcock and Steven Spielberg are two masters of the emotional cattle prod; Austrian filmmaker Michael Haneke is another. Haneke's *Funny Games* isn't much to look at; as its title suggests, it's designed to mess with your mind. "I want the spectator to think," the 57-year-old director told *Film Comment*.

A modernist whose scrupulously faithful adaptation of Kafka's *The Castle* was included in the last New York Jewish Film Festival, Haneke sets out to implicate the viewer in the spectacle of violent cruelty. His movies are founded on the denial of catharsis and, to compound the creepiness, Haneke (who claims Robert Bresson as his model filmmaker) insists that he is occupying the moral high ground.

The protagonist of Haneke's best-known film, the repellent *Benny's Video* (shown in the 1992 NYFF), is a TV-addicted adolescent who murders a playmate; then, having videotaped it, he enlists his middle-class parents, surrogates for the audience, to help him dispose of the body. In the even more sadistic *Funny Games*, Haneke arranges for a family to be held captive in their lakeside vacation house and tortured, presumably for our delectation, by a pair of seemingly innocuous lads—one simpering and baby-faced, the second (played by none other than the now grown "Benny") thin and insolent—both wearing white gloves like characters in an old Walt Disney comic strip. Indeed, they refer to each other as Beavis and Butt-head or Tom and Jerry.

Cartoon or not, *Funny Games* evokes the ultimate bourgeois nightmare. The invaded household is a situation that D. W Griffith, who more or less invented the practice of directing the viewer, used repeatedly in his Biograph two-reelers (as well as at crucial moments in *The Birth of a Nation*). But Haneke has a different agenda. *Funny Games's* early emphasis on innocent, time-killing competitions is preparation for the sport Haneke will have with the spectator. Now you see it; no, you don't. To the degree that one can distance oneself from the narrative action, one may note the filmmaker's precise use of offscreen space. The violence is almost all mental—a factor of clever editing and the power of suggestion. Moreover, its sickening escalation is rigorously based on the host family's lack of "manners." The wife loses her temper with the visitors well before anything bad really happens; the husband strikes the first blow. But then...

Discipline is mandatory in Herr Haneke's classroom. His *Funny Games* is a punitive movie; the villains return everything in spades. One of the movie's insistent ironies is that the family's own toys are inevitably turned against them as weapons. More than once, they are trapped by their fancy security system and unable to escape. The same goes for the audience. The invasive pair occasionally address the camera, reminding viewers at one point that the show must continue because "we're not yet up to feature-film length." As theoretical as *Funny Games* is, however, it is difficult not to have a visceral response. Once Haneke gets you to admit your own bloodlust, he's got you.

When *Funny Games* was premiered last year at Cannes, Haneke introduced it is an "anti-Tarantino film." He regards his ironies as not only more ponderous but also more edifying than those of the dread QT. Relentlessly clever, *Funny Games* offers more un-pleasure than suspense. Do we secretly crave the spectacle of a helpless naked woman? Watch where the schoolmaster positions his camera. Are we getting bored? Do we need to see something else happen? Haneke—who skips just ahead of his characters, planting props for them to use—will provide ample time for us to consider just what that atrocity might be.

Symptomatic of the fascist mindset is the self-righteous application of a strict code of civility from which the viewer himself is naturally exempt. Thus, Haneke despises the mass audience's vicarious pleasure in make-believe mayhem while demonstrating his own capacity to dish it out. The most honest aspect of Haneke's movie is the evident satisfaction the director derives from the authoritarian aspects of his position—demonstrated most spectacularly in *Funny Games* when the worm, as it were, finally turns.

The wheel is rigged so that only Haneke can win. *Funny Games* succeeds to the degree that the viewer hates it. To call the movie punishing would be to award it the epithet it craves.

Also reviewed in:
CHICAGO TRIBUNE, 7/10/98, Friday/p. K, Michael Wilmington

NEW REPUBLIC, 3/23/98, p. 25, Stanley Kauffmann
NEW YORK TIMES, 3/11/98, p. E5, Stephen Holden
VARIETY, 5/19-25/97, p. 52, David Rooney

GADJO DILO

A Lions Gate Films release of a Princess Films production with the participation of Canal+/Centre National de la Cinematographie/Ministere de la Culture/SACEM. *Executive Producer:* Guy Marignane. *Producer:* Doru Mitran. *Director:* Tony Gatlif. *Screenplay (French, Romanian & Romany with English subtitles):* Tony Gatlif. *Director of Photography:* Eric Guichard. *Editor:* Monique Dartonne. *Music:* Tony Gatlif. *Sound:* Nicolas Naegelen and (music) Dominique Gaborieu. *Sound Editor:* Nicolas Naegelen. *Casting:* Marie de Laubier. *Art Director:* Brigitte Brassart. *Costumes:* Mihaela Ularu. *Make-up:* Leana Mocanu. *Running time:* 97 minutes. *MPAA Rating:* Not Rated.

CAST: Romain Duris (Stéphane); Rona Hartner (Sabina); Isidor Serban (Izidor); Ovidiu Balan (Sami); Dan Astileanu (Dimitru); Florin Moldovan (Adrjani); Mandra Ramcu (Mandra); Aurica Serban (Aurica); Radu Ramcu (Radu); Angela Serban (Angela); Vasile Serban (Vasile); Ioan Serban (Ioan); Gheorghe Gherebenec (Gheorghe); Valentin Teodosiu (Mayor's Secretary); Petre Nicolea (Grocer); Calman Kantor (Radu); Adrian Simionescu (Child Prodigy); Luninita Paun (Bride); Jean Paun (Father of the Bride); Petre Costescu (Father of the Groom).

CHRISTIAN SCIENCE MONITOR, 8/7/98, p. B3, David Sterritt

At the movies, strains of music are in the air—folk music, to be exact, although that label takes on very different meanings in two pictures opening this week.

"Gadjo Dilo" comes from director Tony Gatlif, who thrilled music lovers and movie fans with his lively "Latcho Drom," a celebration of Gypsy music that earned prizes and applause in 1993. Gatlif's biography is a study in multiculturalism—he's a French filmmaker born in Algeria to Gypsy parents of Spanish origin—and in "Gadjo Dilo" he capitalizes on his international roots by spinning the story of a wandering hero.

His name is Stéphane, and he's fallen in love with the voice of a singer on a cassette that was treasured by his late father. Determined to find the mysterious musician, he travels from France to Romania and makes his way to a rural Gypsy community where he hopes to find the clues he needs. There he's befriended by an aging musician named Izidor who spends his nights carousing and his days worrying about his son, a young rascal currently in jail on charges Izidor swears are spurious. Stéphane also draws close to Sabina, a dancer who's as fiery as she is talented.

The plot of "Gadjo Dilo" is very slim, reflecting the rambling and uncertain nature of Stéphane's quest. There are some eye-opening surprises, as when we eventually see the truth about Izidor's wayward son, but some moviegoers may be disappointed by its general lack of a hard-driving story. Others won't like its moments of sex and vulgar language, and still others may question Gatlif's decision to pair a professional movie actor (Romain Duris) with a nonprofessional cast in the Gypsy roles, creating occasional mismatches of style and talent.

Happily, such problems pale alongside the picture's main attraction: scene after scene of Gypsy music and dance, performed with a skill, energy, and sheer exuberance that no other current film can equal. In its vivid portrait of a culture that few moviegoers have experienced firsthand, its only direct rival is Robert Duvall's "Angelo, My Love," a 1983 docudrama that also focused on real-life Gypsies playing characters drawn from their own community.

More adventurous and enticing than earlier Gatlif successes like "Latcho Drom" and the gentle "Mondo," the best scenes of "Gadjo Dilo" have an audiovisual power that's close to explosive. The picture is not for everyone, but moviegoers with a taste for folkloric culture will find it a rare treat.

LOS ANGELES TIMES, 8/14/98, Calendar/p. 6, Kevin Thomas

With the warm, joyous "Gadjo Dilo," Algerian-born French filmmaker-composer Tony Gatlif completes his beguiling Gypsy triptych. The series began with his superb "Little Princes" (1982), a tale of the rugged, marginal existence of Gypsies in France, and continued in 1993 with the rapturously beautiful "Latchmo Drom" (Safe Journey), in which he celebrates the sustaining power of music in Gypsy culture as he retraces the migration of the original Gypsies to Europe from India beginning a thousand years ago.

Gatlif fuses the elements of the two previous pictures to create the unique "Gadjo Dilo," which means "crazy outsider." That's what a rural Gypsy community, not far from Bucharest, calls the stranger in its midst, a young Frenchman named Stephane (Romain Duris). Stephane is trying to locate a Gypsy singer whose music was much-loved by his late father. He has encountered Izidor (Isidor Serban), a village chieftain, just as the older man's son Adrjani (Florin Moldovan) has been arrested and taken away by Romanian authorities for either violating a curfew or an alleged theft or both.

Izidor is one of those overwhelming life-force figures whose feelings are close to the surface and quick to erupt. His determination to treat Stephane as a surrogate son overrules his community's wariness over Stephane, to whom they apply the stereotyped negative judgments so often applied to themselves. Amusingly, were Gatlif not of Gypsy descent himself, he might well be criticized for depicting Gypsies as so unrelentingly passionate, fiery and earthy. The point is that he does so with unabashed affection and furthermore suggests that extravagant displays of emotion are ways in which Gypsies have long survived hardship and injustice.

A lot of that emotion is of course poured into their intoxicating music, with which the film overflows; Izidor and his people make their living as musicians, performing in clubs and at weddings and private parties. Their makeshift village is primitive in the extreme, but they seem happy and quickly cast their spell upon Stephane, who is eager to learn their language and record their music (much of it composed by Gatlif himself).

Stephane is also attracted to the beautiful, independent Sabina (Rona Hartner), a talented dancer who left her husband/dance partner in Belgium when he decided he did not want to return home. Initially, Sabina is hostile to Stephane, equating him with the world of Western Europe that lured her husband.

As Stephane wins over Sabina and the community, the film wins us over so captivatingly that it comes as a jolt when the entire community suddenly becomes threatened with savage bigotry.

Duris, who was featured in Cedric Klapisch's delightful "When the Cat's Away," is a sensitive charmer who persuades us that Stephane could embrace such a primitive way of life because he comes to care so deeply for his new friends. Duris' enthusiasm and humor lend balance to the bombastic yet likable Serban, and the lovely Hartner has no trouble at all casting a powerfully seductive spell.

NEW YORK POST, 8/7/98, p. 46, Larry Worth

It may be time for Tony Gatlif to move on. While one understands that the director wants to explore his Gypsy roots, he seems to be stuck in a rut.

Over the last 16 years, Gatlif has successfully plumbed various components of Gypsy life, from 1982's fiction-based "Les Princes" to the 1993 documentary "Latcho Drom" and 1996's fairy-tale-like "Mondo." But with the current "Gadjo Dilo," the director is clearly running out of steam, and genres.

What results is an odd hybrid of fact and fantasy. And in too many sequences, Gatlif doesn't even bother with a narrative.

Instead, the camera simply lingers on native dancers, singers and storytellers in their makeshift camps. And though initially intriguing, the results cry out for editing.

Framing such moments is the physical—and, of course, emotional—journey of a handsome Parisian traveling through Romania with his trusty tape-recording of a Gypsy woman's song. His mission: to identify the mystery voice that fascinated his late father.

An elderly Gypsy comes to the hero's aid, soon serving as guide, surrogate dad and all-around mentor as the pair subsequently attend local weddings, funerals and just about everything in between.

422   FILM REVIEW ANNUAL

Not surprisingly, the production's chief selling point is its attention to detail, whether showing the Gypsies' jury-rigged attempts to harness electricity or the colorful garb that reflects their wild existence. In addition, Romain Duris makes for a charismatic hero, ably assisted by Isidor Serban's wily aide.

Unfortunately, the assets aren't enough to carry the film.

Not helping is Gatlif s use of an all-too-predictable love story between Duris and fiery newcomer Rona Hartner, nor a coda that feels forced and tacked on.

Ultimately, "Gadjo Dilo"—which translates as "crazy outsider"—proves a mixed bag. Despite the makings of a first-rate travelogue, its dramatic heart is as elusive as the singer's origins.

NEWSDAY, 8/7/98, Part II/p. B7, John Anderson

The gypsies or Rom people depicted in the various films of Algerian-born, Paris-based filmmaker Tony Gatlif ("Les Princes," "Latcho Drom") seem to possess all the traditional values so cherished by more stationary cultures. Love of family. Love of tradition. A suspicion of strangers. A bias toward blood.

So who is the subject of Gatlif's new "Gadjo Dilo"—the "crazy outsider" described in the title? It might be the gypsies themselves. It might be their equally rustic Romanian antagonists. It could be the young Frenchman, Stephane (Romain Duris), who upon arriving in the village is subjected to a gauntlet of gypsy derision ("He's trying to steal our chickens!") that mimics the usual treatment of the gypsies themselves. It might be Sabina (Rona Hartner), who because she's left her husband in Belgium and come back to the village has been culturally excommunicated (and liberated).

Or, it may be that Gatlif is letting us peel the onion, and figure it out for ourselves.

A warts-and-all portrait of gypsy life—even the warts have warts—"Gadjo Dilo" is bracing in its honesty and embracing in its affection. The gypsies of Eastern Europe, whose roots are in India but whose torment is transcontinental, are depicted by Gatlif (himself of Spanish-gypsy origin) as a people with emotions on their sleeves, petty larceny in their hearts and a profound depth of tradition—something that seduces the young Stephane, who arrives as a kind of impromptu anthropologist and becomes part of the fabric of the village.

This only works, of course, because Stephane is honest and candid and Stephane only works because of the candid, honest performance of Romain Duris ("When the Cat's Away"), who makes Stephane so guilelessly charming the gypsies can't possibly reject him. Taken under the intoxicated wing of local reprobate Izidor (Isidor Serban)—whose son is under arrest by the Romanian authorities—Stephane gets to experience a world of daily passion and, often, pain that is as far from his life as Bucharest is from Paris, and which takes him in entirely.

Serban is a rascal as Izzie, but just as profanely affecting is Rona Hartner as Sabina, whose checkered past has placed her squarely outside the community. Being ostracized has its perks, however. Although she's generally disregarded, she enjoys a freedom unknown in a patriarchal society. And she and Stephane—crazy outsiders both—gravitate toward each other naturally.

There are crises and drama, but Gatlif seems more interested in getting the heart of gypsy life and painting it with the hot palette and frank dialogue it deserves ("May the worms eat you" is a one of the more casual insults). He succeeds, which is why when the word "cleanse" is used toward the finale of the film, it has such a freshly shocking echo.

SIGHT AND SOUND, 8/98, p. 40, Jonathan Romney

Stéphane, a young Parisian, is searching Romania for the gypsy singer who recorded his father's favourite song. On foot in the snow he arrives at a village where he meets Izidor, an old gypsy and master fiddler whose son Adrjani has been imprisoned. Izidor gives Stéphane shelter for the night although the other gypsies distrust the Frenchman, whom they consider a *gadjo dilo* ("crazy outsider").

However, with Izidor's encouragement they come to accept him; the old man treats him like a son and refuses to let him leave. Aided by Izidor and Sabina—a young gypsy woman formerly married to a Belgian—Stéphane continues to search for the elusive singer and begins to record and document other local musicians.

After a visit to Bucharest Stéphane and Sabina—who was initially hostile towards him—finally make love. Adrjani returns home but after a fight in the local bar Romanians attack the village, killing him. Back on the road, accompanied by Sabina, Stéphane destroys his tapes and performs a gypsy burial dance.

Gadjo dilo begins with its French hero stranded in an unwelcoming snowy landscape, trudging icy roads in decomposing boots and finding people shouting abuse at him in an unfamiliar language. A stranger in gypsy country, Stéphane undergoes a version of the traditional gypsy experience: this time it is an outsider, a *gadjo,* who is the nomad, distrusted, unwelcome, suspected of the most sinister motives.

Eventually accepted into the gypsy community, adopted as a surrogate son by a local elder, Stéphane becomes a tolerated outsider in a world of outsiders, a gypsy community in the region around Bucharest where the film was shot. Director Tony Gatlif—who was born in Algeria of gypsy origins and raised in France—is, as far as one knows, unique in European cinema as a specialist in the gypsy experience. Completing an informal trilogy with *Les Princes* and the epic *Latcho Drom,* his latest film concentrates on the experience of a non-gypsy and the possibilities of rapport, especially through language.

For once a stranger has both to live the Romany experience—in this case (precariously) rooted rather than nomadic—and to learn the Romany tongue. Much of the film concerns Stéphane's linguistic apprenticeship. The exchange, in fact, joyfully flows both ways: Stéphane teaches Izidor to say "Le Pen is a motherfucker" while the village children teach him such juicy phrases as "Eat my cock with polenta". *Gadjo dilo* has a fabulously salty linguistic palette, especially as Stéphane's relationship with Sabina hots up. The scene in which they prepare for love—making with a kind of verbal heavy petting gets up a remarkable head of erotic steam through words and looks alone.

At once fiction and ethnographic document, *Gadjo dilo* derives much of its power from the fact that Stéphane's experience seems to reproduce that of the film's star, the engagingly bedraggled Romain Duris, best known as the hipster drummer in Cédric Klapisch's *Chacun cherche son chat.* When Duris arrives in the gypsy community he is instructed not to look to Gatlif for guidance but to make his own way among his new acquaintances. The result is an astonishing sense of immediacy, of connections being made before our eyes in exchanged words and looks, misunderstandings and lightning realisations.

But *Gadjo dilo* is also a film *about* spontaneity, presenting a range of surprisingly coded ways in which spontaneous expression takes place. Izidor—played with galvanising animation by Isidor Serban—airs his rage and grief in what seem like ritual gestures, mourning his son's death with an incongruously celebratory-seeming graveside dance, which Stéphane finally repeats as he bemoans the village's violent fate. And the film is also adept at catching the smaller, unforeseen moments for which there are no prepared gestures—notably a poignant sequence in which Izidor begs Sabina for a sympathy fuck.

A film that seems largely unstructured until the violent denouement, *Gadjo dilo* comes across as a kind of documentary musical. By contrast with the dour, largely silent Romanians who surround them—a slur on the national character, perhaps—the gypsies have music as a constant in their lives, a notion evident from the moment Izidor picks up his violin and gives Stéphane a welcoming virtuoso recital. But this sense of a continual party rarely seems to romanticise the eternal gypsy spirit'; this is anything but a glamorising film, with Eric Guichard's often beautiful but always stark photography constantly evoking the harshness and poverty of the community's existence.

When the documentary flow is occasionally arrested by a single poetic image—a horse in the snow at midnight, a cluster of double basses stacked in a barn—the effect is invariably a sobering one. We may be visiting an archaic world, one straight out of painter Marc Chagall or writer Isaac Bashevis Singer, but the implicit parallel with the Jewish *shtetl* experience is not fortuitous.

The film ends with an eruption of the Eastern European pogrom nightmare, as the Romanians pursue Adrjani with arsonous intent to "cleanse the village"—a reminder, if the subtitles are accurate, of murderous drives still extant in the Balkans. It's remarkable, after this, that the film can still leave you on a high, with its single closing look from Sabina, incarnated with abrasive verve by Rona Harmer. In one sequence, Izidor fantasises about France as a gypsy paradise, with "gypsy colonels, majors, state prosecutors." It seems a terrible injustice to Tony Gatlif that he doesn't mention the film-makers too.

VILLAGE VOICE, 8/11/98, p. 139, J. Hoberman

It's a truism that folk music is born only once the folk themselves have begun to disappear and the notion of a preindustrial "folk" existence, with its suggestion of lost community, has been invented.

The folk premise is founded on a hunger for realness. Thus, the better part of documentarian Les Blank's oeuvre is a gumbo that combines equal parts down-home music, soul food, and unabashed wannabe. French filmmaker Tony Gatlif, whose 1993 *Latcho Drom* was one of the most rhapsodic music docs made anywhere in the past dozen years, is a kindred ethnostalgist; but unlike Blank (who samples cultures ranging from Cajun to Tex-Mex to Polish American), Gatlif is forever in search of his own roots among the gypsies, or Rom.

Somewhere between exotic fiction and guided documentary, Gatlif's *Gadjo Dilo* (Romany for "crazy outsider") opens in the snowy wastes of deepest Romania with its eponymous hero, the young Parisian musicologist Stéphane (Romain Duris), seeking a legendary gypsy singer who had fascinated his late father. Rather than her, fate provides him with a new father in the person of old Izidor (Isidor Serban), a squat, muscular, gnomish fiddler who—perpetually drunk and either ranting or lachrymose—can out-Zorba even the most manic of life-affirming folk patriarchs while providing Stéphane's entry into the world of the Rom.

For at least 200 years, gypsies have been represented as the last remnants of tribal Europe—a repository of free-floating folk consciousness, identified with the traditional music of countries as disparate as Hungary and Spain. In *Gadjo Dilo,* as in *Latcho Drom,* the Rom are natural, voracious performers. The various plate-smashing weddings staged in an assortment of unheated taverns are the movie's production numbers—musicians cavorting on tabletops, women break dancing on the floor, guests (resplendent in their red sports jackets, wide-brimmed hats, and garish American-flag neckties) showering the impassive bride with wads of money.

There's no particular narrative; nor should there be. A sympathetic explorer, Stéphane inevitably goes native—learning to carry on gypsy-style, flirting with the irrepressible Sabina (Rona Hartner), who, having lived awhile in Belgium, can speak to him in French. Sabina is something of a modern woman, as well as a stellar performer whose whirling, hip-twitching, shouting solo dances suggest the theatrical "savagery" of a gypsy Josephine Baker. (Although this highly trained actress isn't a real gypsy, she is authentically Balkan, born, according to the press notes, in Bucharest to Greek Armenian parents.)

No less than the volatile gypsy queen, who provides an unforgettable introduction to Rom foreplay (talking dirty as a prelude to lovemaking, or at least to running naked through the woods), *Gadjo Dilo* strikes a note of insane ethno exuberance and holds it for 90 minutes. Gatlif's gypsies are almost too picturesqe—loudmouthed founts of colorful curses, baroque threats, and continual histrionics. Every other shot in this clamorous pageant is a crowd scene. The mode is less humanist than humanoid; given their hysterical group mind, you might say that the Rom have not been objectified so much as hyper-anthropomorphized.

Like Gatlif's previous movies, *Gadjo Dilo* is exceptionally well shot—the careful compositions belie the movie's totally frantic pace—and disarmingly packaged. A colleague of mine pointed out the irony of the audience prize that *Gadjo Dilo* won at the last Rotterdam Film Festival. It's like the German craze for klezmer music. As the most maligned and persecuted minority in Europe, gypsies arc hardly a welcome sight in its cities—the Rom are never more romantic than on the screen.

Indeed, as in *Mondo*—Gatlif's earlier fable of a gypsy urchin—the Rom are almost too pure to exist on this earth. When the irate Romanians inevitably storm and torch the Rom village that has been Stéphane's Eden, the despairing Frenchman—with the ironic ballad "I Even Met Happy Gypsies" pounding in his brain—smashes and buries his precious field recordings. Gatlif, of course, does not.

Also reviewed in:
CHICAGO TRIBUNE, 9/25/98, Friday/p. J, Michael Wilmington
NEW YORK TIMES, 8/7/98, p. E12, Anita Gates

GENEALOGIES OF A CRIME

A Strand Releasing presentation of a Gemini Films production in association with Madragoa Films and Canal Plus France. *Producer:* Paulo Branco. *Director:* Raoul Ruiz. *Screenplay (French with English subtitles):* Pascal Bonitzer and Raoul Ruiz. *Director of Photography:* Stefan Ivanov. *Editor:* Valeria Sarmiento. *Music:* Jorge Arriagada. *Production Designer:* Luc Chalon and Solange Zeitoun. *Costumes:* Elisabeth Tavernier. Running time: 113 minutes. MPAA Rating: Not Rated.

CAST: Catherin Deneuve (Jeanne/Solange); Michel Piccoli (Georges); Melvil Poupaud (René); Andrzej Seweryn (Christian); Bernadette LaFont (Esther); Monique Melinand (Louise).
LOS ANGELES TIMES, 4/10/98, Calendar/p. 14, Kevin Thomas

Catherine Deneuve's career is as enduring as her beauty because she has always taken roles that rely as much on her talent as her looks.

With Portuguese fabulist Raoul Ruiz's brilliant, bravura "Genealogies of a Crime" she has taken on one of her most challenging, complex films ever with the intelligence and willingness to reveal vulnerability that are the hallmarks of her performances.

In its style and daring it's right up there with Deneuve's classic Buñuel collaborations, "Belle du Jour" and "Tristana," and is as demanding of her as an actress as such recent films as the Academy Award-winning "Indochine," which brought her an Oscar nomination, and "Ma Saison Preferee."

In this psychological mystery, a Chinese puzzle of a movie, Deneuve plays dual roles. As Solange, she is a poised, successful Paris lawyer, a widow who, just as she has lost her 20-year-old son in a car crash, agrees to defend a young man, Rene (Melvil Poupaud), accused of murdering his psychoanalyst aunt, Jeanne (played by Deneuve, in a red wig and gowned glamorously by Yves St. Laurent).

Associated with the Franco-Belgian Psychoanalytical Society run by the sinister, volatile Georges (Michel Piccoli), Jeanne has become convinced that Rene, whom she's seen from the time he was a young boy, would grow up to be a criminal and that nothing could be done about it. Solange will argue, however, that Jeanne's years of analysis with her nephew programmed him to kill.

It would seem that consciously or unconsciously Jeanne made herself the target through her incest-tinged relationship with her nephew. Or was Jeanne somehow a pawn of Piccoli and his followers, rumored to engage in orgies and to embezzle large sums of money? Or is Rene simply a "bad seed," a case of pure primeval evil?

As Solange becomes caught up in defending Rene, she probes the bizarre world of Jeanne, who lived in a 19th century Gothic mansion, a former luxury brothel whose suffocatingly chi-chi decor she left unchanged—except to have her likeness replace the portraits of the prostitutes who once worked there.

All the while "Genealogies" is unfolding, Ruiz is having fun with the proclamations of the warring schools of psychoanalysis—Andrzej Seweryn plays Georges' principal opponent, the unctuous Christian. Abounding with baffling cinematic sleight-of-hand, "Genealogies" is at once funny and serious, a tragicomedy that debates free will and predestination.

It also abounds in scintillating portrayals from a large cast and what Ruiz calls "melancholy, Chekhovian flavor," created by his production designers and cinematographer. A work of the utmost wit, intellectual sophistication and originality—Ruiz disposes, thankfully, of Rene's trial in a collage of courtroom sketches—"Genealogies of a Crime" is the kind of film likely to inspire no end of discussion and interpretation.

NEW YORK POST, 3/27/98, p. 47, Larry Worth

Catherine Deneuve gives truth to the old line about getting older and better. Indeed, she stuns—in the looks and acting departments—in a dual role in "Genealogies of a Crime."

On the other hand, she can't work miracles. Nor redeem the terminally muddled "Genealogies."

Chilean-born director Raoul Ruiz spins a lethargic, purposely confusing tale of a rich psychoanalyst (Deneuve) who treats her charming but homicidal nephew. At least before he offs her.

A well-meaning lawyer (also Deneuve) then defends the young man while getting sucked into the same sordid world that brought down her predecessor.

The premise had considerable potential, but Ruiz quickly squanders it with hackneyed sendups of therapy groups, role-playing and revenge-seeking ghosts.

NEWSDAY, 4/3/98, Part II/p. B14, John Anderson

There are those among us who are of the opinion that you can never have too much Catherine Deneuve. By casting her in two roles in his Chinese box-like "Genealogies of a Crime," therefore, director Raoul Ruiz is already ahead of the game.

Gamesmanship, however, is what it's all about—to too great a degree, perhaps; certainly to the degree that we're not sure how many roles Deneuve is in. Framed by an allegedly ancient Asian tale—about a killer snared by the ghost of his victim—"Genealogies" ventures into some of the Chilean-born, Paris-based director's favorite territory, including the nature of identity, accented with a perversely polymorphous cast of characters and motivations. At times, it's a bit overwhelming.

It remains, however, fascinating to watch Deneuve, who as Solange—a defense attorney renowned for taking on lost causes and losing them—buries her son and then enlists as attorney for René (Melvil Poupaud), a troubled young man known as The Monster. From the time of his childhood, it has been thought that René had a criminal nature and would someday act on it. With the bloody murder of his psychiatrist/aunt Jeanne (Deneuve), it appears he has.

In flashback—sparked by Solange's reading of Jeanne's voluminous notebooks—we see Jeanne and René engaged in a kind of role-reversal therapy, which gets out of hand. Who, in the end, kills whom? For that matter—and given the fluidity with which Ruiz passes between the past and the present—who is whom?

"Genealogies" is alternately dryly comic, blackly droll, punctuated by low comedy, and as tongue-in-cheek as possible—even the set design is facetious. Ruiz was particularly careful about the sound of the film: From shoes across a floor to the opening of a book, what we hear is integral to the creepiness inherent in Ruiz' opinion of cavalier psychiatry. Occasionally, he uses music to contradictory effect—a comic passage to accompany a horror scene, for instance. Similarly, Deneuve has to walk a fine, dissonant line, maintaining Solange's demeanor even while all those around her are losing theirs. These include Michel Piccoli, the veteran French film star whose dyspeptic analyst Georges Didier (or, alternately, Didier Georges), orchestrates the war of prognoses that rages between psychiatric societies. And around René.

All in all, "Genealogies of a Crime" is not first-rate Ruiz, but it's fun to watch the structure take shape. In a way, it's sort of like Notre Dame—in essence a mélange, one that finds its glory despite its parts.

VILLAGE VOICE, 3/31/98, p. 64, Dennis Lim

Raoul Ruiz's films are at their bewitching best when the director merges his two personae—intellectual prankster and shaggy-dog storyteller. The happy collision occurs often enough in *Genealogies of a Crime,* a deliriously scrambled film that assumes the same poker face whether considering the validity of determinism or the defenestration of felines. Fiercely recondite for much of his 30-odd-year, 50-plus-film career, Ruiz coasted on the Mastroianni charm to something approaching commercial appeal in *Three Lives and Only One Death* (1996); here, no less shrewdly, he calls upon the still-valorous, still-glamorous Catherine Deneuve to remain amusingly composed as surrealist goof-ups pile up around her.

Dense and recklessly allusive (yet penetrable by Ruiz standards), *Genealogies* is based on the true, turn-of-the-century story of a psychoanalyst who supposedly detected homicidal tendencies in her young nephew and was eventually murdered by him. Deneuve plays the shrink (in flashback) and also the lawyer who defends the teenage killer (Melvil Poupaud). A cursory investigation implicates the Franco-Belgian Psychoanalytic Society, a legion of kooks (led by a spirited Michel Piccoli) whose group therapy sessions constitute the ritual stagings of elaborate *tableaux vivant* (a tongue-in-cheek echo of Ruiz's pseudo-art-doc, *The Hypothesis of the Stolen Painting*).

Ruiz's parallel universe isn't the most accessible of movie realms. (What other director working today delights as much in frames and mirrors—actual and otherwise?) With typical offhandedness, *Genealogies* combines baroque Wellesian angles, reconstituted Lacanian theories, and gratuitous Borgesian gold dust, and adds a liberal sprinkling of non sequiturs and Freudian slips. The result is utterly Ruizian, which is to say, principally, a meta-narrative. The lattice-work of overlapping fictions gets progressively more complicated and locked in. For those who care (and trust me, it isn't a prerequisite), the theoretical hooey is most distinctly articulated by an "ethnopsychologist" who spouts nonsense literary analogies ("Paul Auster without New York," he muses, inspecting the interior decor of a law office) and explicates the perils of "narrative syndrome." He classifies stories as diseases—viruses that prey on, possess, and ultimately destroy us. If that's the case, Ruiz—ever the wily fabulist—must be among the deadliest of filmmakers.

Also reviewed in:
CHICAGO TRIBUNE, 7/24/98, Friday/p. H. Michael Wilmington
NEW YORK TIMES, 3/27/98, p. E14, Stephen Holden
VARIETY, 2/24-3/2/97, p. 80, Deborah Young

GENERAL, THE

A Sony Pictures Classics release of a Merlin Films production in association with J&M Entertainment. *Executive Producer:* Kieran Corrigan. *Producer:* John Boorman. *Director:* John Boorman. *Screenplay:* John Boorman. *Story based on the book by:* Paul Williams. *Director of Photography:* Seamus Deasy. *Editor:* Ron Davis. *Music:* Richie Buckley. *Sound:* Brendan Deasy and (music) Brian Masterson. *Casting:* Jina Jay. *Production Designer:* Derek Wallace. *Costumes:* Maeve Paterson. *Make-up:* Maire O'Sullivan. *Stunt Coordinator:* Dominic Hewitt. *Running time:* 125 minutes. *MPAA Rating:* Not Rated.

CAST: Brendan Gleeson (Martin Cahill); Adrian Dunbar (Noel Curley); Sean McGinley (Gary); Maria Doyle Kennedy (Frances); Angeline Ball (Tina); Jon Voight (Inspector Ned Kenny); Eanna McLiam (Jimmy); Tom Murphy (Willie Byrne); Paul Hickey (Anthony); Tommy O'Neill (Paddy); John O'Toole (Shea); Ciaran Fitzgerald (Tommy); Ned Dennehy (Gay); Vinnie Murphy (Harry); Roxanna Williams (Orla); Eamon Owens (Young Martin Cahill); Colleen O'Neill (Patricia); Maebh Gorby (Sylvie); Pat Laffan (Higgins); Frank Melia (Lawless); Ronan Wilmot (James Donovan); Lynn Cahill (Arcade Woman); David Wilmot (Assassin); Stephen Brennan (Arthur Ryan); Don Wicherley (Henry Mackie); Kevin Flood (Judge); Pat Kinevane (Desk Guard); Barry McGovern (IRA Leader); Pat Leavy (Mrs. Duggan); Neile Conroy (Maeve); Peter Hugo Daly (Beavis); Aoife Moriarity (Young Frances); Brendan Coyle (UVF Leader); Owen O'Neill and David Carey (Revenue Men); Niamh Lineham and Jason Byrne (Reporters); Ann Doyle (TV Newsreader); Daragh Kelly (Young Detective); Des O'Malley (Himself); Patrick Condron (IRA Man); Darren Miley (Young Anthony); Mark Quigley (Young Paddy); Frank Laverty, Kieran Harley, and Anthony Fox (Garda); Anne Kent (Mrs. Cahill); Donnacha Crowley (1962 Priest); Clive Geraghty (Commissioner); John Cronin (Aiden); Des Cave (ILC Chairman); Brendan Conroy (Corporation Official); Brian McGrath (Doctor); Alan Barry (Judge); Emma McIvor (Woman Worker); Andrew Bennett (Hollyfield Priest); Gavin Kelty, Darren Healy, Jeffrey O'Toole,

Mark Dunne, and Ger Kearny (Young Hoods); Tony Flynn (Security Guard); Jim Reid (Mr. Crenshaw); Ami Hedges (Baby);   Karl Deegan and Mick O'Brien (Gardai).

LOS ANGELES TIMES, 12/23/98, Calendar/p. 1, Jack Mathews

[The following review by Jack Mathews appeared in a slightly different form in **NEWSDAY, 12/18/98, Part II/p. B7.]**

Though he's been dead only four years, Dublin gangster Martin Cahill is taking his place alongside Jesse James, Billy the Kid and Clyde Barrow as movie heroes from the wrong side of the law. Cahill became known as the General, and through the eyes of writer-director-producer John Boorman he takes on almost mythic qualities.

Boorman, a native of England who has lived in Ireland for more than two decades, followed the much-publicized exploits of Cahill, as he and his gang pulled off everything from cheap arcade robberies to jewelry heists to the daring burglary of a private collection of art masterworks. Along the way, Cahill embarrassed the Irish police and, in refusing to share his loot with political factions in the north, made mortal enemies of both the IRA and the loyalists.

Cahill's murder in 1994, which opens and closes "The General," was claimed by the IRA.

Boorman has a personal interest in Cahill. He has said in interviews that his home was one of Cahill's targets and that among his burgled possessions was a gold album given to him for the "Dueling Banjos" song in "Deliverance" (which Boorman directed). Without mentioning the homeowner's name, "The General" reenacts that burglary and uses the gold album as a symbol of Cahill's comically distorted view of the collapse of social values in the republic. Talk about converting a loss to a win.

"The General" has been both a big hit and a big target in Ireland, where Cahill was seen more as a cleverly elusive, self-gratifying thug than as a lovable rogue. Cahill did make goats of the unarmed police, which made for good newspaper reading, but his gang also brutalized its victims, and, in one audacious act of violence, crippled a key witness in a Cahill trial with a car bomb.

The film includes that car bomb incident, and another horrific scene where Cahill nails one of his gang member's hands to a pool table, thinking the man had stolen from him. In both instances, the violence segues quickly into humor, with scenes that feel designed to immunize Cahill from audience enmity.

Boorman signals that he may not like what the real Cahill did, but as a storyteller with a proven affection for larger-than-life subjects, he can't resist him, either. Cahill is a screenwriter's dream, part Michael Corleone, part Archie Bunker, a blue-collar godfather who uses intimidation and paternalism in equal measure, and follows, with fevered devotion, a skewed moral framework of his own invention.

Cahill doesn't smoke, drink, use drugs or cheat on either of the women—wife Frances (Maria Doyle Kennedy) and her younger sister Tina (Angeline Ball)—who share his bed and his brood. He's a good husband, dad and provider, whose hobby is raising pigeons, whose only vice (besides crime, of course) is pastries and who never returns from a night shift without a Santa-sized sack of stolen toys for his kids.

If you can forgive his romanticized nature, Cahill is a great role, and Brendan Gleeson, a robust Irish actor best known in the U.S. as Mel Gibson's sidekick in the film "Braveheart," has a high time playing it. He's a big man with the facial expressions of an imp, portraying Cahill as a mischievous man-child, at play in the field of the gang lords.

Cahill's cat-and-mouse game with the cops, especially its chief investigator (Jon Voight, with a flawless accent), is depicted as an extension of the rambunctious urchin (Eamon Owens) shown in early flashbacks, a product of the oppressed Dublin projects and a would-be victim of a predatory reform school priest.

That run-in with the priest has the look of myth-making to it, and it certainly sets up all subsequent authority figures for the gangster's showcased pranks. Cahill's real victims may be unamused by his scamp-hero image, but it's classic storytelling. As a John Ford character famously said in "The Man Who Shot Liberty Valence": "When the legend becomes a fact, print the legend."

NEW YORK, 1/4/99, p. 67, Peter Rainer

Few movie characters are as rollickingly complex as Martin Cahill, the real-life Irish gangster in John Boorman's mesmerizing new movie *The General*. Boorman hasn't made a dramatic feature in three years, but at 65, he's come back with one of his very best. Cahill, who was assassinated in 1994 by an I.R.A. gunman outside his suburban Dublin home, was a sort of thick-waisted cross between Al Capone and a Celtic chieftain. Brendan Gleeson, the Irish actor who played Mel Gibson's bearded friend Hamish in *Braveheart*, doesn't try to soften Cahill for us or explain him away. What's amazing—great, in fact—about the performance is the way Gleeson right to the end keeps us perplexed about this fanatically anti-authoritarian crook. Cahill despised equally the church, the state, the IRA, the police. In his twenty-year career his capers and his cunning made fools of them all.

The General has the structure of an American gangster classic: The boy thief from the slums grows up to run his own goon squad before finally ringing in his doom. And yet the film, shot in lustrous black and white, doesn't remind you of anything else, not even anything else by Boorman. Cahill is supremely unsettling: His brutality and his tenderness are on the same continuum. In the film's ghastliest comic sequence, he nails the palms of a gang member to a pool table when he suspects the poor dopehead of stealing from him; realizing the guy is innocent, he then un-crucifies him and considerately shepherds him to the emergency ward. Cahill is a family man who loves his wife (Maria Doyle Kennedy) and also, with her permission, his wife's sister (Angeline Ball), and has children by both. (We see him steal a little girl's toy train for his own daughter.) Away from his trade Cahill is bulky, but on the job, moving in and out of the shadows he's entrancingly graceful.

Cahill's frenzy for thievery is almost an artist's passion. He's the artist as plunderer. When he steals a Vermeer, he takes a proprietary pride in his haul—in that moment he and Vermeer are kin. You can't really warm to Cahill as a folk hero—you keep thinking of that nailed doper, or the people Cahill puts out of work when he robs a jewelry store and the business is forced to shut down. He has no remorse for any of this; his only cause, in the end, is himself. This general is a commander of one.

NEW YORK POST, 12/18/98, p. 65, Rod Dreher

Shot in luminous black and white, John Boorman's "The General" is an off-puttingly adoring homage to a complete savage: Martin Cahill, a real-life Dublin gangster assassinated in 1994. The robust Brendan Gleeson stars as Cahill, a.k.a. the General, a fat, greasy-haired lout whose purpose in life is to screw the system by any means necessary.

The well-acted, stylishly directed film traces Cahill's rise and fall as he masterminds a variety of heists while rooking the IRA, loyalist thugs and the Dublin authorities (Jon Voight plays Cahill's police-inspector nemesis).

Cahill was a low-down criminal genius who was out for no one but himself. He lived in a menage a trois with his wife and sister-in-law (who seem oddly acquiescent to these household arrangements), and gets by on nothing but an audacity that would be heroic if he were serving any cause but his own gratification.

Boorman is obviously enchanted by the knavish Cahill, and audiences are by now accustomed to rooting for anti-heroes. But whatever interest Boorman found in this creep is elusive in the telling, and the director's point of view seems to waver at times, in the face of Cahill's unregenerate nastiness (he's no Robin Hood).

Gleeson's tour de force performance is first-rate, and makes the film far more interesting than it would have been in less capable hands.

But "The General" is ultimately dismaying and emotionally remote because Cahill's physical and emotional brutality is not redeemed by anything, save for the bullet that the IRA assassin puts in his skull in the opening scene (Boorman constructs the movie as a flashback).

Unlike, say, Michael Corleone, this actual two-bit crime boss seems to have had no tragic dimensions. Nor do we see that society has done him any particular wrong that would justify, or even explain, his criminality. He's no more than a clever pig and that gets old fast.

SIGHT AND SOUND, 6/98, p. 44, Xan Brooks

Dublin, 1994. Upon leaving his home, Martin Cahill (aka "The General") is shot dead by an IRA gunman. Flashbacks show Cahill's formative years on the Hollyfield estate, where he grew from a child thief into an expert adult cat burgler, always one step ahead of police inspector Ned Kenny. Cahill refuses to leave the estate, even when it is bulldozed around him, but eventually he moves out to Rathmines, another part of Dublin. Cahill marries and raises a family with his childhood sweetheart Frances, but he also carries on (with Frances' consent) a long-standing affair with her sister Tina.

With his gang in tow, Cahill stages a daring raid on a wholesale jewellers. The IRA learns of the robbery and demands a 50 per cent cut, which Cahill refuses to hand over. Emboldened by success, Cahill's team steals a priceless hoard of paintings from a private collection. But by now the police have him under constant surveillance and the only buyers for the haul are the Ulster Volunteer Force. When word leaks out that he's dealt with the UVF, Cahill is seen as a traitor by his neighbours and comes under increased police harassment.

His gang disintegrates and Cahill becomes isolated and paranoid. On the morning of his death, he finds the police cordon around his house removed and walks unguarded towards his car.

Movies are the repository of myth," wrote John Boorman in his 1985 book *Money into Light* 'Therein lies [their] power. An alternative history, that of the human psyche, is contained and unfolded in the old stories and tales. Film carries on this tradition."

The General's success—as storytelling, as cinema—is that it seems so deeply infused with a mythic sensibility. On the face of it a down and dirty roustabout, its true-life subject emerges here as a reborn, archetypal hero of Celtic folklore. Martin Cahill is Cuchulain or King Arthur in a puffa jacket; his Camelot a palace of double glazing and flock wallpaper. By shooting his tale in high-contrast black and white, Boorman conspires to give the proceedings a still more mystical distance. Inner-city Dublin—with its terraced streets, shabby pool halls and police stations—becomes a landscape both grittily familiar and dreamily off-beam, a place haunted by ghosts and memories.

But there are a host of other influences flitting throughout the *General*'s storyline. At times its lovable rogue ensemble of working-class criminals calls to mind the Ealing comedies of post-war Britain. On other occasions, their clear-cut code of honour and the importance of loyalty and camaraderie call to mind the American Mafia movie. And yet all the while Boorman remains alert to these reference points, playing with them at times, debunking them at others. When Cahill and his righthand man Noel Curley embrace, Cahill is quick to break the hug. "We're not fuckin' Italians," he says curtly. Cahill's role as a neighbourhood folk hero is similarly scrutinised. Charming, clever and flamboyant, the man clearly wants to be seen as a hero by his neighbours. Ned Kenny, the dogged, decent police inspector on his trail, recognises this aim and is offended by it: "Robin Hood is it?" he says. "You scumbag."

In truth, Boorman's protagonist both hero and villain, Robin Hood and scumbag. Cahill is a complex, murky, never altogether sympathetic figure. He treats his gang fairly, divides his hauls equally, stays off drugs, doesn't drink or smoke, and steals toys for his kiddies. But he is also paranoid, misguided and brutal. Suspecting one accomplice of stealing a gold bar, he nails the man's hands to the pool table and then realises he's got the wrong guy. Later, when his gang is fragmenting and the surveillance biting, he suspects his sister-in-law mistress of grassing to the police.

As such, much of *The General* depends on Brendan Gleeson's towering performance in the central role. With his lank hair and blunt features, Gleeson initially looks a most unglamorous movie hero. In fact his appearance provides the perfect smokescreen. For Cahill is a Janus-like creature, who turns two very different faces on the world. Behind closed doors, with his family or his gang the man is in his element: alert, authoritative, robustly charismatic. Pull him into the harsh daylight, however, and the General blinks like a badger. Up goes the hood of his jacket; his strut turns into a cringe. He covers his face with one hand; peeking at the world through splayed fingers. In researching the role to perfect the evasive manoeuvrings of a man on the run, Gleeson studied archive footage in which the real life Cahill is doorstepped by a television reporter, and the mimicry is uncanny.

As a result, Gleeson's performance boasts a compelling snap of authenticity. Cahill's brand of criminality is revealed as a reaction to legitimate society. It is one means by which the disenfranchised empower themselves. Yet its success depends on invisibility, on keeping below the parapet of public perception. Martin Cahill becomes a king among his own strata (the remnants of Dublin's bulldozed Hollyfield estate). But in the outside world he proves a fish out of water. The film's tragedy is that the General is ultimately unable to keep these boundaries secure. By selling his art haul to the Ulster Volunteer Force, Cahill becomes fatally emboiled in the wider landscape of Irish politics, and is regarded as a traitor by members of his own community. His cover is blown, and the real world comes crashing in to claim him in the end.

Despite its narrow confines, *The General* boasts a heady, epic sweep. This subtle and absorbing picture is part crime parable, part portrait of society's fringes, part study of the tensions at work within modern-day Ireland. Moreover, in tackling this fact-based, contemporary story, Boorman has somehow succeeded where his more bombastic and ostensibly 'mythical' films *Zardoz* and *Excalibur* never quite could. In the stolid figure of Martin Cahill, Boorman has found his mythic hero, and from the General's life-history he has fashioned a fragment of folklore that speaks of and to our times.

TIME, 12/28/98-1/4/99, p. 174, Richard Schickel

Writer-director John Boorman says he thinks of Martin Cahill, protagonist of *The General,* as a throwback to those Celtic chieftains who haunt Ireland's misty past—cunning brutes whom legend often turns into romantic rogues.

Cahill (Brendan Gleeson) was, in fact, Dublin's master thug in the 1980s, leader of a gang that pulled off a string of gaudy robberies, and also a great local celebrity. Constantly tailed by the police, he went boldly about the city but always with his face hidden, if only by his own hands. Mocking authority in this way, he enhanced his mystery, hence his power.

Until he was finally hit by the I.R.A. (to him, just more authority to affront), he was equally capable of cheekily parking on a police-station bench all night to give himself an alibi, or of crucifying a suspected informer on a pool table, Happily married, he kept his wife's sister as a mistress and sired children with both women. In this admittedly fictionalized retelling, his other reliable relationship is with an implacably pursuing detective (superbly underplayed by Jon Voight) who hates himself for succumbing to a psychopath's irresistible charm.

That's what's great about Boorman's stunningly realized black-and-white film and about Gleeson's performance, which, like Irish weather, goes from sunny to stormy without warning. Neither film nor actor tries to resolve Cahill's contradictions or anyone's feelings for him. He just—monstrously—is, a force of nature, beyond our rational reckoning, but not, perhaps, our irrational fascination.

VILLAGE VOICE, 12/22/98, p. 132, Amy Taubin

The General opens with an assassination. A pudgy, balding, middle-aged man (Brendan Gleeson) leaves his house, looks warily over his shoulder, gets in his car, starts the motor, checks out the view from the side window, and locks eyes with his killer, who is drawing his gun as he runs toward his intended victim. The killer fires once, twice, three times. The car rolls slowly, then stops. A motorcycle drives up, the killer leaps on the back. Through the shattered car window, we see the victim's face in close-up, blood streaming from the bullet hole in his temple. People—family, neighbors, cops—crowd around the car. There's a cutaway to police headquarters—cops celebrating that "Tango one is down." We see the dead man carried away on a stretcher. And then this odd thing happens. We again see the dead man, but it's as if he's come back to life, again looking out the car's side window and locking eyes with his killer. This time, however, the sequence is running backwards; the killer is pocketing, rather than pulling, his gun. For a moment, we see a close-up of the man in the car again, his face slowly dissolving into the face of an adolescent boy.

We've entered a flashback that will last until the film comes full circle in its final seconds. And while the flashback structure in itself isn't unusual, the way in which it's announced—with that little reverse-time clip—makes us aware that there's a sophisticated filmmaker at work here, someone with a mastery of the expressive possibilities of what is handily referred to as film language.

Based on the life of Martin Cahill, the Dublin master criminal whose lifetime loot was valued at around $60 million and included the only privately owned Vermeer in the world, *The General* is written and directed by John Boorman, and it's something of a comeback, his most sharply executed film since *Deliverance*. Shot in color but printed on black-and-white stock, it has an old-fashioned, fine-grained luminosity that's reminiscent of '30s studio pictures like *Scarface*.

An underworld anomaly, Cahill had contempt for the sanctioned authority of church and state and for the I.R.A. and the Loyalist undergrounds as well. He lived in a ménage à trois with his wife and her sister, and fathered children with both of them. When he was gunned down in the mid '80s, the I.R.A. claimed responsibility; Cahill had infuriated them by selling a stolen painting to the Loyalists. Having held himself above the Irish troubles, he is nevertheless destroyed by them in the end.

Although his crimes were flamboyant, Cahill made his identity a mystery. He was never seen in public without a hood shrouding his face. The most memorable images in the film are the close-ups of Gleeson with his hand over his face, eyes peering through spread fingers.

Gleeson, who's nearly a double for the real-life Cahill, finds innumerable shades for the anger that drives the man. At first, he's exuberant, cocky, and quick-witted, but he turns paranoid and depressive when his gang abandons him and the community turns against him. An explosive mix of rebel and reactionary, he tolerates no rule except his own. His audacity would be irresistible if he weren't so brutal. (I can't believe those two women were as pleased with their situation as the film makes them out to be.)

Cahill should be right up Boorman's alley, the larger-than-life, rogue male who sets up a breakaway patriarchy that mimics the very system it's out to trash. But despite the fascinating character, and some bravura scenes (among them a spectacular jewelry-factory heist), the film is flat. Boorman's stand vis-à-vis his protagonist is so ambivalent as to be nonexistent. And without a clear point of view, the artful filmmaking reads as decoration. *The General* is a refined, traditional movie about a character who is never more traditional than when he imagines himself outside the law. It's a great paradox, but it barely comes alive on the screen.

Also reviewed in:
CHICAGO TRIBUNE, 1/22/99, Friday/p. A. Michael Wilmington
NATION, 1/11 & 18/99, p. 36, Stuart Klawans
NEW REPUBLIC, 12/28/98, p. 32, Stanley Kauffmann
NEW YORK TIMES, 12/18/98, p. E20, Janet Maslin
NEW YORKER, 12/21/98, p. 114, David Denby
VARIETY. 5/25-31/98, p. 63, Derek Elley
WASHINGTON POST, 2/12/99, p. C5, Stephen Hunter
WASHINGTON POST, 2/12/99, Weekend/p. 47, Desson Howe

GENERAL CHAOS: UNCENSORED ANIMATION

A Manga Entertainment release of 20 animated shorts. *Executive Producer:* Marvin Gleicher. *Director/Project Collector:* Jan Cox. *Director "American Flatulators":* Jeff Sturgis. *Director "Attack of the Hungry, Hungry Nipples":* Walter Santucci. *Director "Beat the Meatles":* Keith Alcorn. *Director "Body Directions":* Karl Stave. *Director "Donor Party":* Laurence Arcadias. *Director "Espresso Depresso":* David Donar. *Director "Junky":* Tony Nittoli. *Director "Killing Heinz":* Stefan Eling. *Director "Looks Can Kill":* Mr. Lawrence. *Director "Malice in Wonderland:* Vince Collins. *Director "Misfit":* Amanda Enright. *Director "Mutilator":* Eric Fogel. *Director "No More Mr. Nice Guy":* Brad Schiff. *Director "Oh Julie!":* Frances Lea. *Director "The Perfect Man":* Emily Skinner. *Director "Performance Art: Starring Chainsaw Bob":* Brandon McKinney. *Director "The Saint Inspector":* Mike Booth. *Director "Sex and Violence":* Bill Plympton. *Director "Sunny Havens (a.k.a. Meat!!!)":* Kathryn Travers. *Director "Zerox and Mylar":* Joel Brinkerhoff. *Director "Quest":* Tyron Montgomery. *Running time:* 90 minutes. *MPAA Rating:* Not Rated.

NEW YORK POST, 2/6/98, p. 46, Larry Worth

Spike and Mike's yearly anthologies are proof that sick and twisted cartoons have an audience. But "General Chaos: Uncensored Animation" will put even diehards to the test.

The string of 20-odd shorts—told via Claymation, puppetry, stop-motion or cels—feature enough bare bods and lopped-off limbs to put a stupid grin on any 12-year-old.

Accordingly, the bits fall into two categories: juvenile and witless (exemplified by ever-mutating orifices in "Malice in Wonderland") and extra-strength juvenile and witless ("The Hungry, Hungry Nipples.")

Sure, a couple of segments are palatable. But the only real highlight is Germany's 1996 Oscar-winning short, "Quest." It not only precedes "General Chaos," but demonstrates the originality and quality in animation that "Chaos" lacks.

NEWSDAY, 2/6/98, Part II/p. B11, John Anderson

Intentionally rude, casually crude, "General Chaos: Uncensored Animation" purports to be cutting-edge animation and, without belaboring the pun, it is. It's also something like a processional of body-piercing fetishists: You know the parts, you know they're being mutilated and the entire event carries a subtext of serious self-loathing.

On the other hand, anything called "Uncensored Animation" is going to include sex and violence, although this is a lot heavier on the latter than the former, and the former usually is presented with heavy lashings of the latter. Even Bill Plympton's suavely demented visual gags—collectively titled "Sex and Violence" and appearing throughout the program—mix the erotic with the evisceral. Plympton's work, however, establishes standards not everyone can equal.

An international collection, "General Chaos" includes the British fabulist Mike Booth, whose "The Saint Inspector" is one of the movie's highlights. Likewise Tyron Montgomery's "Quest," the wordless, Oscar-winning tale of a Sisyphean sand creature caught in circular Hell. And "The Donor Party," a four-minute gothic nightmare after Terry Gilliam, concocted by female animator Laurence Arcadias.

One of the inadvertent points "General Chaos" makes is just how slender the line is between what animation can achieve and what Hollywood wants to do with computer-manipulated live-action film. Women's fantasies, however, (even when realized by men) are given much more air, and much more venom, than Hollywood would ever consider. In "Looks Can Kill," a topless dancer's breasts turn into machine guns and mow down the audience. In "The Perfect Man" a princess creates her own Prince Charming. Vince Collins' "Malice in Wonderland" creates imagery Georgia O'Keefe never dreamt about (well, maybe she did). And in "Oh Julie!" by the talented Frances Lea, a couple's sexual encounter bogs down in anatomical enhancement and appliances.

Some of the material here is crashingly sophomoric, like "American Flatulators" and the Beatles spoof "Beat the Meatles." On the other hand, you're not going to find this stuff on Nick at Nite.

Also reviewed in:
NEW YORK TIMES, 2/6/98, p. E20, Lawrence Van Gelder
VARIETY, 2/2-8/98, p. 29, Godfrey Cheshire

GINGERBREAD MAN, THE

A PolyGram Filmed Entertainment release of an Island Pictures and Enchanter Entertainment production. *Executive Producer:* Mark Burg, Glen A. Tobias, and Todd Baker. *Producer:* Jeremy Tannembaum. *Director:* Robert Altman. *Screenplay:* Al Hayes. *Based on a story by:* John Grisham. *Director of Photography:* Changwei Gu. *Editor:* Geraldine Peroni. *Music:* Mark Isham. *Music Editor:* Helena Lea. *Sound:* John Pritchett and (music) Stephen Krause. *Casting:* Mary Jo Slater. *Production Designer:* Stephen Altman. *Art Director:* Jack Ballance. *Set Designer:* Glenn Rivers. *Set Decorator:* Brian Kasch. *Special Effects:* Tom Kittle.

Costumes: Susan Kaufmann. *Make-up:* Deborah Larsen and Vonda Morris. *Stunt Coordinator:* Greg Walker. *Running time:* 115 minutes. *MPAA Rating:* R.

CAST: Kenneth Branagh (Rick Magruder); Embeth Davidtz (Mallory Doss); Robert Downey, Jr.(Clyde Pell); Daryl Hannah (Lois Harlan); Robert Duvall (Dixon Doss); Tom Berenger (Pete Randle); Famke Janssen (Leeanne); Clyde Hayes (Carl Alden); Mae Whitman (Libby); Jesse James (Jeff); Troy Beyer (Konnie Dugan); Julia R. Perce (Cassandra); Danny Darst (Sheriff Hope); Sonny Seiler (Phillip Dunson); Walter Hartridge (Edmund Hess); Vernon E. Jordan, Jr. (Larry Benjamin); Lori Beth Sikes (Betty); Rosemary Newcott (Dr. Bernice Sampson); Wilbur T. Fitzgerald (Judge Russo); David Hirsberg (Tom Cherry); Paul Carden (Judge Cooper); Michelle Benjamin-Cooper (Principal); Christine Seabrook (Secretary); Bob Minor (Mr. Pitney); Myrna White (Tax Clerk); Jim Grimshaw (Desk Cop); Stuart Greer (Detective Hal); Nita Hardy (Policewoman); Ferguson Reid (Detective Black); Benjamin T. Gay (Court Clerk); Mark Bednarz, Bill Cunningham, and Chip Tootle (Effingham County Sheriffs); Sonny Shroyer, Mike Pniewski, and Jay S. Pearsonstorm (Chatham Count Sheriffs); L. H. Smith (Evacuee); Wren Arthur (Barfly Robin); Angela Costrini (Barfly); Gregory H. Alpert (Barfly Clerk); Lydia Marlene (Tattooed Bartender); Bill Crabb (Huey); Jin Hi Soucy, Richie Dye, and Chad Darnell (Patrons); Natalie Hendrix, Gregg Jarrett and Doug Weathers (Television Anchorpeople); Alyson E. Beasley and Angela Beasley (Puppeteers); Scott Troughton (Dredge Worker); Grace Tootle (Gas Station Attendant); Shane James (Ricky Butch Banks); Herb Kelsey and William L. Thorp IV (Doss Gang Members).

CHRISTIAN SCIENCE MONITOR, 1/23/98, p. B3, David Sterritt

"The Gingerbread Man" comes from major talents: director Robert Altman, stars Kenneth Branagh and Embeth Davidtz, and bestselling author John Grisham, who dreamed up the story. Like other Grisham tales, including "The Rainmaker," it's about an attorney's adventures. While it offers no great revelations about the hero's profession, it has enough suspense and surprises—along with striking camera work and sound—to make it the most gripping entertainment of this very young year.

Branagh plays Rick Magruder, a Georgia lawyer who's successful in the courtroom but dogged by personal problems. An ill-advised love affair gets him involved with a woman whose father appears to be threatening her safety. Magruder helps put him behind bars, then finds himself—and his children—the target of a dangerous scheme.

Parts of "The Gingerbread Man" seem like a replay of "Midnight in the Garden of Good and Evil," which also involves a Savannah attorney. "The Gingerbread Man" is more excitingly filmed, though, taking its tone from a feature of Southern life: hurricane season, which douses the story in more water than any picture this side of "Titanic."

The acting is also solid, starting with Branagh's believable Georgia accent. Robert Duvall etches the role of the father with his customary skill.

"The Gingerbread Man" won't go down as an Altman masterpiece, and its faithfulness to Hollywood-thriller rules makes it a touch less artful than some of his other films. But it's a pleasure to see the quality he brings to this genre.

LOS ANGELES TIMES, 1/23/98, Calendar/p. 2, Jack Mathews

[The following review by Jack Mathews appeared in a slightly different form in NEWSDAY, 1/23/98, Part II/p. B3.]

If there were a movie god, to whom so many fledgling actors and screenwriters regularly pray, he would not have had Robert Altman direct a John Grisham thriller like "The Gingerbread Man," or had Clint Eastwood direct a sociological comedy like "Midnight in the Garden of Good and Evil." He would have switched them.

Eastwood is a master at crime melodrama, and Altman is a master of atmosphere, irony and social interplay. Switching assignments wouldn't have guaranteed that either film would turn out great, or even better than they are, but you've got to like the odds As it is, we have two high-profile movies that share a professional slickness, competent performances, even the setting of Savannah, Ga., but that finally leave us mostly unmoved.

Altman, of course, didn't have much to work with. Grisham's novels barely have enough bone and sinew to fill out a feature-length script, and Grisham wrote "The Gingerbread Man" for the screen!

Fewer words doesn't always mean fewer ideas, but with Grisham, it's a safe assumption. The script was reworked by Altman, and the screenplay credit now appears as the pseudonymous Al Hayes, from an original story by John Grisham.

"The Gingerbread Man" is at least a different Grisham story. There's no conscientious young or under-powered Southern attorney taking on corruption in the halls and boardrooms of justice, corporate America or the mob. The Southern attorney in this tale is self-absorbed, middle-aged and more than a little arrogant.

He's Rick Magruder (Kenneth Branagh), a fast-talking lawyer with an upscale client list, a peevish ex-wife (Famke Janssen), with whom he shares custody of two small children, an occasionally reliable sidekick (Robert Downey, Jr.) and a red Mercedes 450 SL to covet.

Leaving a victory party after winning a big case in Florida, Magruder meets a hysterical woman whose car has just been stolen. He gives her a ride home, where they find her car, she gives him a hard luck story about her crazy father, they spend the night together, and he leaves, without even getting her name.

But he needn't worry. That next day, she shows up in his office, with legal questions about having her father committed, and no sooner does he learn that her name is Mallory Doss than he is drawn into a situation that can lead to love, double-cross or a little of both.

The problem with having a good director working with mundane material is that you're inevitably promised more than you get. The first half of "The Gingerbread Man," as Altman takes us through a nasty tropical storm leading to a hurricane aptly named Geraldo, is compelling groundwork for a story that eventually turns on deadly clichés. He creates tension that's relieved only by disbelief.

Branagh affects a convincing Southern accent, but he's a classically trained actor whose stage forcefulness doesn't carry over to the screen. Magruder isn't a likable hero, even though his motivation changes dramatically from lust and professional vanity to paternal panic after his children are kidnapped. And Branagh doesn't have the star voltage to overcome that.

The underused Embeth Davidtz, Ralph Fiennes' Jewish sex slave in "Schindler's List," has the most complex role and makes the best of it. She keeps Mallory wrapped in mystery and sensuality from her opening scene. But as that mystery begins to solve itself, the life is drained out of her performance.

Besides Downey, who enlivens his few brief scenes, the able supporting cast includes Robert Duvall as Mallory's seriously unstable father, Tom Berenger as her roughhewn ex-husband and Daryl Hannah, almost unrecognizable as Magruder's redheaded associate.

"The Gingerbread Man" is beautifully photographed by China's Changwei Gu, who's worked with Chen Kaige (on "Farewell, My Concubine") and Zhang Yimou (on "Red Sorghum" and "Ju Dou"). Altman had a fine time composing difficult shots, through screens, bushes and sheets of rain, and Chungwei's images, sometimes delicate, sometimes harsh, stick with you long after you've forgotten their context.

NEW STATESMAN, 7/24/98, p. 43, Gerald Kaufman

Gene Kelly once explained to me why he rejected the concept of the cinematic auteur. Himself a director of movies with a highly distinctive style, he insisted that a picture does not stem from one individual's brain, but is a team effort. In Peter Bogdanovich's recently published collection of interviews with directors, "Who The Devil Made It?," the veteran Alan Dwan put forward the same vehement argument.

Nevertheless, this week offers two movies that seek to have auteur stamped all over them. "The Gingerbread Man" is the work of one of the most revered maitres of Hollywood, Robert Altman ("M*A*S*H", "Nashville","The Player", whom publicity material describes as "an iconoclastic auteur".

At first sight, the subject matter (of what the opening credit proclaims as "A Robert Altman film") could not be more conventional: a story by John Grisham. When last year another alleged auteur, Francis Ford Coppola, brought a Grisham bestseller to the screen, "The Rainmaker" resisted its director's efforts to make it stylistically distinctive and ended up as just another routine courtroom drama.

Altman, on the other hand, has certainly achieved a distinctive style for "The Gingerbread Man". This style, however, belongs not to Altman but to the 1940s school of Hollywood noir directors. The Coen brothers' "The Big Lebowski" earlier this year set out to be cod noir. Altman aims at the real thing. Even his plot, based on what we are told is "an original story" by Grisham, turns out to be a standard last-minute-surprise formula that has been used over and over again during the past half century.

Rick Magruder (Kenneth Branagh, with his Iago beard and a deep-fried Southern accent), a hot-shot lawyer in Savannah, Georgia, becomes involved with a mysterious waitress, Mallory Doss (Embeth Davidtz, most recently noted as the Nazi sadist's tragic trollop in "Schindler's List"). He gets her father, Dixon Doss (Robert Duvall, made up to resemble a plump version of Ben Gunn in "Treasure Island"), who is allegedly harassing Mallory, committed to a mental hospital.

All sorts of baneful consequences flow from this premise, including the kidnapping of Magruder's children (though it is hard to understand how any abductor could tolerate their winsome company for even five minutes), assault (Rick clocks a school janitor), and murder (Dixon is shot, a demise which, considering Duvall's manic cavortings, occurs not a moment too soon). All this, in true noir style, is accompanied by special ominous music (by Mark Isham, who should, and almost certainly does, know better), by lashings of rain which obscures much of the action and mercifully drowns a good deal of the banal dialogue, and by a certain amount of nude sex.

This being the 1990s, we get to see all of Davidtz (who goes right through this film with a single facial expression, possibly the only one she possesses) and a considerable quantity of Branagh (who, playing his role on an unremitting note of hysteria, raises the question of how such an over-excitable lawyer ever appeared in court without instantly being held in contempt). Gloria Grahame and Robert Mitchum this pair decidedly are not.

Let me make clear that this film provides a couple of hours of perfectly acceptable entertainment, especially for those whose blood is curdled by spooky goings-on in a cemetery and by the sadistic garroting of a cat (though the American Humane Society reassuringly promises that no animals were harmed). The climax—in so far as it can be seen through the rain—is handled with considerable bravado. It is difficult, however, to understand why, at the age of 73, Altman has decided that this is the proper moment in his career to expend his energies on hommage to Jacques Tourneur and Nicholas Ray.

Writer-director Gregg Mottola, at the age of 30 young enough to be Altman's grandson, demonstrates his auteur-isitic aspirations with "The Daytrippers." Filmed in 16 days on a minuscule budget, this calling-card movie may indicate that Mottola has seen too many of Woody Allen's melancholy Manhattan comedies. All the same, the story idea—an entire suburban family sets off to the big city to confront the elder daughter's apparently unfaithful husband—is neat. Its development always sustains a quirky impetus.

John Inwood's location shooting creates the flavour of a coldly hostile New York that intimidates the rubes from out of town. While the two daughters, the almost catatonic Eliza (Hope Davis) and the featherbrained Jo (Parker Posey), achieve two dimensions at most, Liev Schreiber creates a perversely appalling character out of Jo's nerdish boyfriend, Carl, who has written an allegorical novel about a man with a dog's head and wants to replace democracy by autocratic government led by, well, people such as himself. Anna Meara turns the initially self-effacing Mom into an increasingly power-mad Gorgon.

Some of the one-liners are as sharp as Mottola would like all of them to be. When the family invades a stranger's apartment and Mom offers to cook lunch, her totally fed-up husband, Jim (Pat McNamara), who rightly fears the worst during the whole expedition, pleads: "For the love of God, don't let her make soup." The following exchange is overheard at a party: Guest A: "She was sexy, in a Rubens-esque sort of way." Guest B: "She was fat."

NEW YORK, 2/23/98, p. 114, David Denby

I was moved as well as entertained by Robert Altman's work in *The Gingerbread Man*. Here is the crankiest, most iconoclastic American director of the past 30 years—the sore and proud survivor of many victories, many defeats—devoting himself quite selflessly and effectively to telling an old-fashioned story. *The Gingerbread Man*, based on a John Grisham yarn that was fleshed out by Al Hayes, is an example of neo-*noir* (southern, or moss-hung, division). In Savannah, a hotshot criminal lawyer, Rick Magruder (Kenneth Branagh), falls for a neurotic and very available young woman (Embeth Davidtz) and undertakes to protect her from the aggressions of her crazy old father (Robert Duvall). Magruder thinks he knows all the angles; part of the pleasure of the movie lies in watching this cocky but likable man get himself bogged down in an intrigue, thicker than mulligatawny soup. Altman, lays aside his usual strategy of mixing a variety of narrative strands; he forgoes his chattering, overlapping profusion; instead, he sticks to a single, complex narrative, driving it ahead furiously through many ambiguities and mysteries, pushing the actors in and out of the most relentless tropical storm in the history of the movies (the outtakes must be full of sneezes).

There is, I hasten to add, a great deal of Altman's characteristic observation and humor in the background: The law-office scenes are rich with innuendo and flirtation, and the crazy old man is surrounded by a gaggle of bearded loonies who cackle with glee over his various outrages. Still, despite these divertissements, the movie forges ahead on the conventional strengths of script, acting, and atmosphere. At the risk of impiety, I can't help wondering if Altman might not have made a greater number of good movies if he had determined to become not an artist but a commercial director; the man has a real gift for conventional storytelling, and the result of its full exercise is something like unmitigated pleasure.

Grisham's story is a legal-world variant of the kind of classic forties stuff in which a smart guy falls for a screwed-up broad and turns into a rueful sap (the late Robert Mitchum would have played the role with heavy-lidded authority 50 years ago). It is saved from cliche by the way virtue and vice have become, in the character of the lawyer, inseparable; Magruder is trapped by decency as well as by greed and lust, by his professional victories as well as by his personal recklessness. Kenneth Branagh slips into the accent and persona of the fast-talking Georgia shyster without the slightest strain. He's quick, amusing, a man whose attention flickers like a water bug across the surface of a hundred calculations. In the past, everything has always gone easily for Magruder, and his ease leads him into folly. As the character, losing his grip, reaches the rock bottom of despair, Branagh, shocked, becomes more and more interesting, and he's surrounded by strong actors in support, including Robert Downey Jr. and Robert Duvall, whom Altman has cast with malicious accuracy as, respectively, a dissipated private eye and a vicious old son of a bitch.

NEW YORK POST, 1/23/98, p. 47, Michael Medved

At first blush, the idea of asking Robert Altman (the king of quirky, independent art cinema) to direct a project based on a short story by John Grisham (the king of streamlined, legalistic, populist potboilers) sounds like a royal blunder—making as much sense as assigning Quentin Tarantino to adapt Andrew Lloyd Webber, or expecting Martin Scorsese to handle Edith Wharton (or did they try that?).

In any event, the biggest surprise about "The Gingerbread Man" is how well this bizarre combination works on screen. This spellbinding thriller provides Altman with one of his most watchable films of recent years and easily amounts to the strongest Grisham adaptation to date.

The secret is the intoxicating sense of texture, atmosphere and authenticity, and the juicy, multidimensional characterizations, which vastly enrich the pulpy plot.

Kenneth Branagh leads a superb ensemble cast as a hot-shot Savannah attorney going through a painful divorce and custody fight (with glamorous Famke Janssen).

At a victory celebration for a big case staged by his no-nonsense partner (the surprisingly strong Daryl Hannah), Branagh meets a white-trash waitress with a tummy tattoo (played with supercharged sex appeal and admirable subtlety by the unlikely Embeth Davidtz of "Schindler's List") and ends up falling into bed with her.

Soon he goes to court to protect her from potentially deadly stalking by her demented, religious fanatic papa (the unforgettably chilling Robert Duvall), compelling the unwilling testimony of her smoldering ex-husband Tom Berenger.

But when the dotty, dangerous old man escapes from the mental institution to which he's been committed, the lawyer's life begins to unravel. Neither his loyal associate (Robert Downey, admirably cast as an alcoholic private investigator) nor the local cops can protect the anti-hero—or, ultimately, his innocent kids—from the menace of a tricky plot where nothing is what it first appears to be.

The movie includes a cameo by President Clinton's pal Vernon Jordan. A consummate professional, he is highly persuasive in his brief appearance as a lawyer. Whether he will prove similarly convincing in the new starring role that has been assigned to him in the latest White House scandal remains to be seen.

Working together, Altman and Branagh capture the eerie, decadent charm of Savannah so effectively that one can't help longing to see what might have been had they been assigned (in place of Clint Eastwood and Kevin Spacey) to the misbegotten "Midnight in the Garden of Good and Evil." The grand climax, complete with a raging hurricane, is literally overblown, but Altman's funky visual sensibility and electrifying camera work make even the most melodramatic elements seem fascinating.

Anyone who even vaguely enjoyed such intermittently entertaining Grisham gothics as "The Firm" or "The Client" should run, run as fast as you can, to catch "The Gingerbread Man."

SIGHT AND SOUND, 8/98, p. 41, Geoffrey Macnab

Savannah, Georgia, the present. Successful attorney Rick Magruder gives a lift home to Mallory, a waitress. The two have a one-night stand. He learns that she is being stalked by her father, Dixon Doss, the leader of a cultish sect. Magruder has Dixon arrested. In court the judge institutionalises him for psychiatric evaluation, but Dixon's followers break him out of the asylum. Magruder hires detective Clyde Pell to protect Mallory. Worried that Dixon might target his two young children, Magruder whisks them out of school and goes on the run. He holes up with Mallory and the kids in a motel but the kids are kidnapped. Sure that Dixon has taken them, he persuades Mallory to lead him to Dixon's hideout. Trying to defend himself, Magruder shoots and kills Dixon. The kids are recovered, but Magruder is arrested for murder.

As Magruder prepares his defence case, he realises Mallory isn't telling the full truth. She falsely claims to be divorced from her husband Pete. Magruder lies about Dixon's will (he left property worth millions) to catch her out, and she takes the bait. Magruder tracks her down to the boat where her husband is hiding. He discovers that Clyde has been murdered. Magruder and Pete come to blows on the deck as the rain lashes down. Mallory shoots Pete with a flare gun. She tries to kill Magruder too, but he disarms her. Later, Magruder's career is wrecked, but Mallory is arrested.

The pairing of Robert Altman, one of the most maverick and improvisational of film-makers, with John Grisham, a rigidly formulaic writer, can't help but seem incongruous. Given the relish with which Altman's *The Player* attacks movie-making-by-numbers, Altman is just about the last person one would expect to direct a straightforward genre thriller like *The Gingerbread Man*. The plotting is indeed conventional—yet another Grisham yarn about a lawyer in peril. In traditional *noir* fashion, his problems begin when he sleeps with the *femme fatale*. Embeth Davidtz's Mallory is a throwback to the kind of blue-collar temptress that Barbara Stanwyck or Joan Crawford might have played in an earlier era, a fantasy figure who appears out of nowhere to beguile the hero. In one voyeuristic sequence, the lawyer peers through a half-open doorway as she strips off her wet clothes. The scene rekindles memories of the moment in *Short Cuts* where Julianne Moore argues with her husband, oblivious to the fact that she is half naked, but the difference here is that the striptease seems more intended to titillate than to cast new light on the characters.

Altman has often compared filmmaking to jazz. He composes films, treating characters like musical motifs. The challenge he sets himself with *The Gingerbread Man* is to stick to the score. He takes few of the liberties here that he took when he adapted Chandler's *The Long Goodbye*, where he transformed Philip Marlowe into a shambolic, Charles Bukowski-like bum. He hardly even uses his trademark cross-cutting between a chorus of characters. But at least he manages to harness the elements—not many other directors would have made the weather such an integral part of the story. *The Gingerbread Man* is largely played out in the rain. We hear constant references on radio and television to Hurricane Geraldo. Mark Isham's rumbling soundtrack accentuates the mood of foreboding that the noise of the rain and thunder help to create. Given the Southern settings and the background of cinematographer Changwei Gu (whose previous credits include *Farewell My Concubine* and *Ju Dou)* one might have expected an explosion of colour, but the emphasis here is on sombre greys and browns.

The casting is more adventurous than in most Grisham adaptations. Rather than Tom Cruise or Matt Damon, the hero is a middle-aged, soured and slightly overweight Kenneth Branagh. It takes a moment or two to become accustomed to his Deep Southern twang (perhaps acquired by watching episodes of *The Dukes of Hazzard*) but at least he is never bland. Jealous of his ex-wife's lover, bad-tempered, violent (he thumps a school janitor) and self-important, he blunders his way through the film with an angry furrow on his brow. As the womanising, doped-up detective—a role which comes close to self-parody—Robert Downey Jr often seems to be improvising. He is the closest to the laid-back, freewheeling kind of character encountered in Altman movies from *MASH* to *California Split*. Daryl Hannah and Tom Berenger are given less leeway with their stock characters and even Robert Duvall as the bare-footed, backwoods patriarch isn't allowed much of a chance at getting under the skin of his character.

There are hints that Altman is trying to remould the film in his own image. We see traces of his characteristic bite and humour in the barbed exchanges between the lawyer and his ex-wife or the scenes in which Downey plays the barfly. In the end, though, Altman is defeated by the constraints of the genre. *The Gingerbread Man* is an efficient, atmospheric thriller, but what it lacks is the spontaneity and sense of mischief that you invariably find in the director's most distinctive work.

VILLAGE VOICE, 1/27/98, p. 63, J. Hoberman

The decade-long "Asian Century" may have ended, but the Age of Grisham rolls on. Following Francis Coppola's impeccably empty *John   Grisham's The Rainmaker* comes the altogether shaggier *Gingerbread Man,* adapted by Coppola's fellow '70s film god Robert Altman, from a Grisham tale of sexual obsession and legal shenanigans in the New South.

Where Coppola's style is fastidiously retentive, Altman's is looser than his villain's morals. As folks who follow the trades know, PolyGram—unhappy with the way *The Gingerbread Man* tested—recut the movie. Altman threatened to remove his name but, as the studio version tested just as poorly; the studio reverted to the Altman version—a victory of sorts for '70s auteurism. Thus *The Gingerbread Man* is a stormy farrago of uneven ensemble acting, overlapping dialogue, and nervous camera maneuvers. Whatsits whiz through the foreground, scenes are shot through a foggy windshield. Narrative suspense is less important than character. When a defense lawyer as high-powered as he is horny (Kenneth Branagh) gets picked up and taken home by a lithesome waitress in distress (Embeth Davidtz), you don't need a Ph.D. in noir studies to spot the blatant setup.

Altman's best joke may be casting clueless Branagh as a guy led by his dick into a crazy and unethical involvement with a grim, spooky chick whose past includes a below-the-navel butterfly tattoo, a sullen ex-husband, and a demented daddy—guru for a klavern of sinister hillbillies. (The father is Robert Duvall, nearly as scary here as in *The Apostle;* the cult appears to have been cloned from ZZ Top.) Branagh drones on and on—his accent seemingly modeled on Bill Clinton's lilting drawl—moving from the affable to the crazed once his young children are drawn into the narrative morass (along with a stumbling Robert Downey Jr. and an unrecognizable Darryl Hannah).

The Gingerbread Man is set in Savannah but, less tourist-friendly than in Clint Eastwood's *Midnight in the Garden of Good and Evil*, its local color is strictly *Cape Fear*. Big weather comes and goes. The impending hurricane that functions as the wrath of God heads out to sea and then returns for the climax—which is more than I can say for the movie.

Also reviewed in:
CHICAGO TRIBUNE, 2/20/98, Friday/p. A, Michael Wilmington
NEW REPUBLIC, 2/23/98, p. 24, Stanley Kauffmann
NEW YORK TIMES, 1/23/98, p. E1, Janet Maslin
NEW YORKER, 2/2/98, p. 81, Daphne Merkin
VARIETY, 1/19-25/98, p. 88, Todd McCarthy

WASHINGTON POST, 2/20/98, p. B1, Rita Kempley
WASHINGTON POST, 2/20/98, Weekend/p. 37, Stephen Hunter

GO NOW

A Gramercy Pictures release of a PolyGram Filmed Entertainment presentation of a Revolution Films production for BBC Films.   *Producer:* Andrew Eaton.   *Director:* Michael Winterbottom. *Screenplay:* Paul Henry Powell and Jimmy McGovern.   *Director of Photography:* Daf Hobson. *Editor:* Trevor Waite.   *Music:* Alastair Gavin.   *Production Designer:* Hayden Pearce.   *Art Director:* Frazer Pearce.   *Costumes:* Rachael Fleming.   *Running time:* 88 minutes.   *MPAA Rating:* Not Rated.

CAST: Robert Carlyle (Nick Cameron);   Juliet Aubrey (Karen Walker);   James Nesbitt (Tony); Sophie Okonedo (Paula);   Berwick Kaler (Sammy);   Darren Tighe (Dell).

LOS ANGELES TIMES, 5/27/98, Calendar/p. 5, Jack Mathews

[The following review by Jack Mathews appeared in a slightly different form in
NEWSDAY, 5/1/98, Part II/p. B6.]

To make a movie about a couple whose love for each other is tested by the sudden onset of a crippling illness is to risk being lumped in with the most glib and manipulative of all dramatic genres, the "disease-of-the-week" TV movie. But Michael Winterbottom, who takes that plunge with "Go Now," is anything but a glib filmmaker.

The British director has made a splash stateside with his last two films, "Jude," a tough, unsentimental adaptation of Thomas Hardy's "Jude the Obscure," and "Welcome to Sarajevo," his superb docudrama about a television reporter's experiences covering the war in Bosnia.

"Go Now" was made in 1995, before those films, and is being released in the U.S. now because of them. Better late than never.

"Go Now" stars the terrific Robert Carlyle, the leader of the bump-and-grind boys in "The Full Monty," as Nick, a young Scottish plasterer whose rough-and-tumble bachelor life in Bristol, England, has just taken on the smooth edges of romance with Karen (Juliet Aubrey), a woman he'd met in a pub on a night out with his weekend soccer mates.

Nick and Karen are living together, in as much harmony as newly-lovers can expect, when Nick's body begins to undermine him. He's missing plays on the soccer field, earning the wrath of the coach. He's dropping tools on the job, nearly braining his best friend Tony (James Nesbitt). He's seeing double, losing bladder control, becoming temperamental. He has, doctors will soon tell him, multiple sclerosis.

We're a good way into the movie when we get to this revelation, which is where the "disease-of-the-week" formula usually kicks in, with data-heavy speeches from the doctor about the nature of the illness, its frequency in the population and the prognosis for the hero. But when it gets to that point here, Winterbottom stays put, and sticks with his love story.

With a sharply written script by Jimmy McGovern ("Priest") and Paul Henry Powell, who based his original story on his own experiences with MS, "Go Now" is far less interested in exploring the effects of the disease on Nick than on the bond between him and Karen. How strong is their relationship at this early stage? Do they know each other well enough to adjust?

"Go Now" is a slice of life, not death, and it has all the variables of living—humor and melancholy, joy and anger, pleasure and pain. Nick and Karen are real people, confused by this catastrophic development, uncertain about themselves, and put off balance with each other. Nick is pushing her away, and she's tempted, by her relationship with her boss and former lover, to leave. But the bond won't break easily.

Carlyle and Aubrey make Nick and Karen enormously sympathetic, even as their behavior takes some wrong turns. We follow their relationship as we would a threatened marriage among our own friends. We like them both, and want them to be together, but we're as stumped for answers as they are.

It's a remarkable thing for a filmmaker to make that emotional connection between his characters and his audience, and more evidence that Winterbottom is one of the bright new talents in international film.

NEW YORK POST, 5/1/98, p. 62, Thelma Adams

"Go Now" is a contemporary British "Love Story" with Robert Carlyle in the Ali MacGraw role.

Made for BBC-TV by Michael ("Jude") Winterbottom, it makes it clear quickly that something's rotten in the city of Bristol.

Nick (Carlyle) falls for Karen (Juliet Aubrey)—and the earthy beauty returns the fervor. They move in together. They cook pasta. All in the first half-hour. It's too perfect.

Before long, Carlyle's soccer-playing plasterer is flubbing goals, dropping hammers and seeing double—and he has a problem Viagra might fix.

Will love keep Nick and Karen together?

Did Tammy Wynette (and Hillary Clinton) sing "Stand By Your Man"?

Funny, touching, sappy, "Go Now" (a title taken from a Bessie Banks song) shows a new side of Carlyle for those who wanted to see more than "The Full Monty." Aubrey brings a dusky naturalness to Karen and is more interesting to watch than Ryan O'Neal was in "Love Story."

VILLAGE VOICE, 5/5/98, p. 128, Michael Atkinson

If little else, *The Full Monty*'s berserk success has created a shopper's run on Robert Carlyle's catalogue—next month, Ken Loach's *Carla's Song* finally arrives, and presently we have Michael Winterbottom's expanded BBC drama *Go Now*, in which Carlyle plays a good-natured plaster worker and pub hound who romances smart, willowy Juliet Aubrey and comes down with multiple sclerosis. Though strictly TV fodder in structure, *Go Now* is nevertheless passionate and convincing, thanks to Winterbottom's energetic naturalism and the leads: Carlyle's *Full Monty* buoyancy is traded in for white-hot rage and venom put to good use in *Riff Raff* and *Trainspotting*, and Aubrey is never less than completely authentic. If Loach made a movie for Lifetime, it might feel like this, and that doesn't suck.

Also reviewed in:
NEW YORK TIMES, 5/1/98, p. E22, Janet Maslin

GODS AND MONSTERS

A Lions Gate Films release of a Lions Gate Films production. *Executive Producer:* Clive Barker, Stephen P. Jarchow, David Forrest, and Beau Rogers. *Director:* Bill Condon. *Producer:* Paul Colichman, Gregg Fienberg, and Mark R. Harris. *Screenplay:* Bill Condon. *Based on the novel "Father of Frankenstein" by:* Christopher Bram. *Director of Photography:* Stephen M. Katz. *Editor:* Virginia Katz. *Music:* Carter Burwell. *Music Editor:* Adam Smalley and Brian Richards. *Sound:* Shawn Holden and (music) Michael Farrow. *Sound Editor:* David Bach. *Casting:* Valorie Massalas. *Production Designer:* Richard Sherman. *Set Decorator:* James Samson. *Special Effects:* David Waine. *Costumes:* Bruce Finlayson. *Make-up:* Tarra Day. *Running time:* 105 minutes. *MPAA Rating:* Not Rated.

CAST: Ian McKellen (James Whale); Brendan Fraser (Clayton Boone); Lynn Redgrave (Hanna); Lolita Davidovich (Betty); David Dukes (David Lewis); Kevin J. O'Connor (Harry); Mark Kiely (Dwight); Jack Plotnick (Edmund Kay); Rosalind Ayres (Elsa Lanchester); Jack Betts (Boris Karloff); Matt McKenzie (Colin Clive); Todd Babcock (Leonard Barnett); Cornelia Hayes O'Herlihy (Princess Margaret); Brandon Kleyla (Young James Whale); Pamela Salem (Sarah Whale, Mother); Michael O'Hagan (William Whale, Father); David Millbern (Doctor Payne); Amir Aboulela (The Monster); Marion Braccia

(Starlet);   Jess H. Long (Assistant Director);   Owen Masterson (Camera Assistant);   Lisa
Vastine (Librarian);   Kent George (James Whale at 25);   Martin Ferrero (George Cukor);
David Fabrizio (Photographer);   Jess James (Michael Boone, Son);   Lisa Darr (Dana Boone,
Wife);   Paul Michael Sandberg (Sound Man);   Judson Mills (Young Man at Pool).

LOS ANGELES TIMES, 11/4/98, Calendar/p. 3, Kenneth Turan

Great performances don't have to appear in great films; they don't raise everything else to their
level; they can't even be counted on to make co-stars look good. All they do is astonish, which
is what Ian McKellen does in "Gods and Monsters."

Though he's also currently appearing in "Apt Pupil," McKellen, one of England's finest
theatrical actors, shows up only sporadically on screen. Vividly remembered for re-creating his
stage role in the fascist-themed "Richard III," McKellen usually opts for smaller films, and his
work, always impeccable, reaches a remarkable new plateau here.

Possibly that's because James Whale, the real-life character he plays, shares some biographical
elements with the actor. Like McKellen, Whale was from the north of England, worked
successfully in the movie business and, by the standards of the time (half a century ago and
more), was frank and open about his homosexuality.

Whale was also the director who brought the world the Boris Karloff-starring "Frankenstein"
and, in fact, helped design the monster's unnerving look. This film's title is part of an optimistic
toast to "a new age of gods and monsters" that comes from that celebrated sequel, 1935's "The
Bride of Frankenstein," also directed by Whale.

"Gods and Monsters," written and directed by Bill Condon, picks up Whale's life in 1957. He
hasn't worked in film for some time, devoting himself instead to painting. Just home from the
hospital, he's recovering from a stroke that, to the concern of good friend David Lewis (David
Dukes), has created a kind of jumble in his mind, causing memories of the past to seem as real
as the here and now.

Not all of Whale's facilities are impaired, however. Much to the chagrin of fussy housekeeper
Hanna (an amusing Lynn Redgrave), who grumbles about his "chasing after boys," Whale has
his eye on the new gardener, macho ex-Marine Clayton Boone (Brendan Fraser), who certainly
knows how to fill out a T-shirt.

Impeccably dressed and as well-manicured as his meticulous yard, Whale approaches Boone
with some classic spider-and-fly maneuvers, hoping the young man will agree to pose for him.
"You have the most architectural skull, your nose is very expressive," Whale says with a
supremely insinuating voice that's capable of charming a stone. Which is a necessary thing,
because Boone is an archetypal big lug whose favorite expression turns out to be "I don't get it."

This is obviously a familiar character, and one of the things that makes McKellen's performance
so spectacular is the subtlety and delicacy he brings to a role we think we've seen. His Whale
meets the world as a practiced performer with a knowing air and a wonderful mischievous quality,
but he's other things as well: a man of enormous dignity, proud and imperious, but also tortured
with regrets and possessed of a most sympathetic and almost wistful yearning for life.

Writer-director Condon has given Whale some dead-on lines, having him tease the yardman
about his "schoolgirl shyness" and gilding the lily with an authoritative "I have no interest in your
body, Mr. Boone, I assure you of that." Yet every word, even the ordinary ones, are handled
with perfect grace and casual skill. There are so many colors to McKellen's performance, so
many diverse emotions fleetingly play on his face, that resisting his art is out of the question.
Better work by an actor will not be seen this year.

"Gods and Monsters" is concerned mainly with the awkward friendship that develops between
these two men at the opposite ends of the sexual spectrum, one just finding his way as an adult,
the other confronting the waning of his powers.

While his performance isn't a rival to McKellen's, Fraser, best known for comedy roles like
"Encino Man" and "George of the Jungle," does a respectable job as the naive, guileless Boone,
who tells his suspicious romantic interest Betty (Lolita Davidovich) that he's never ever met
anyone like Mr. Whale.

Like Whale's "Frankenstein" films, "Gods and Monsters" tries to mix humor with the
increasing pathos of the director's situation and flashbacks to his personal past and the filming of
his classics. But while a lot of "Gods and Monsters" is acceptable, none of it, frankly, rises to

the levels of subtlety that McKellen's performance does. Even Condon's writing and directing seem more alive and involving when this exceptional actor is the focus of them.

Was James Whale exactly as he appears in this film? That's open to question. "Gods and Monsters" is adapted not from a Whale biography but a novel (Christopher Bram's "Father of Frankenstein"), so its specifics are not necessarily historically accurate. But as a psychologically acute portrait of a singular man at a crossroads in his life, nothing whatsoever is wanting.

NEW YORK POST, 11/4/98, p. 53, Rod Dreher

Is there anything Ian McKellen can't do? In "Gods and Monsters," he gives an extraordinarily nuanced and dryly unsentimental performance as retired filmmaker James Whale, the director of "Frankenstein" (1931), "Bride of Frankenstein" (1935) and other horror films, who died a suicide in the pool of his Hollywood mansion in 1957.

Riffing on themes in the self-made Whale's peculiar life, writer-director Bill Condon's absorbing and highly original story (based on "Father of Frankenstein," Christopher Bram's 1995 novel) imagines Whale's final days as an elderly gay libertine whose flesh, his only comfort and pleasure in life, is failing him.

Once the toast of Tinseltown, the silken dandy spends his time alone in his tasteful digs, forgotten by his friends and colleagues, but too worldly and self-aware to ripen and rot gloriously, a la Norma Desmond. Arch, elegant and brittle, he looks like a dessicated dragonfly.

Whale alights upon his muscular new gardener, Clayton Boone, played with great subtlety by the underrated Brendan Fraser. He fascinates the younger man with his stories of Old Hollywood, but the gardener becomes tense as a Rottweiler when it finally—duh—occurs to him that Whale might have more in mind than trimming the hedges.

The gardeners simple mind and hulking body (to say nothing of his boxy head) are obviously meant to suggest the monster, and the movie clearly presents Whale as the mad doctor Frankenstein and Clayton as the lump of flesh he attempts to electrify to do his bidding.

The possibility that the randy coot is trying to manipulate cloddish Clayton into serving him sexually gives "Gods and Monsters" a spark of danger. But the movie has something more perverse and fascinating on its mind.

The ongoing collapse of Whale's increasingly frail mind causes long-buried memories to unearth themselves like zombies. There he is as a young sorcerer, conjuring movie magic on the "Bride of Frankenstein" set.

We later see him as a child, slogging through the dull brutality of the English working class. There he is again, serving in the British army in the Great War, and seeing a young man he passionately loved killed in the trenches.

Whale's flight to America, and subsequent career as a pseudo-posh sybarite and member of Hollywood royalty, appears driven by his desperation to evade the agonies of mortality. And what better laboratory for this ambitious immigrant to set up in than a town and an industry dedicated to the beautiful image and eternal youthfulness?

Whale becomes both a Frankenstein figure creating new life—his own—and a lonely monster of his own creation. "Gods and Monsters" is a strange, wonderful movie, a quintessentially American tale.

NEWSDAY, 11/6/998, Part II/p. B6, Jack Mathews

In 1957, seven years after the release of Billy Wilder's "Sunset Boulevard," with its provocative drowned-narrator opening, the body of Hollywood director James Whale was found in a similar pose at his estate just up the road from Sunset Boulevard. And in Hollywood, at least, it had a similar impact on the imagination.

Why did he drown? Whale, long-retired since his heyday as a horror-film director ("Frankenstein," "Bride of Frankenstein"), was no swimmer; in fact, he'd installed the pool only as a recreational hub for the boy toys who gamboled there at his invitation. His body was fully dressed, in his favorite suit. He had given no warning.

Did he fall in? Was he pushed? Did one of the gay hustlers in his circle do him in? There was no sign of a struggle, no apparent robbery, nothing to tax the resources of the LAPD.

More than 40 years later, nothing more is known about Whale's death. But there is some fascinating speculative fiction available, in Christopher Bram's 1995 novel, "Father of Frankenstein," and in the new film "Gods and Monsters," writer-director Bill Condon's superb adaptation of that book.

"Gods and Monsters" ruminates on the last weeks of the British-born director's life, using his succession of strokes as a plot device that allows the strokes to merge Whale's actual experiences with events in his films, to merge his personal monsters with those he created. The result is a richly imaginative and moving human drama that is worthy of the filmmaker's own work.

Ian McKellen, in the best performance of his fine career, plays Whale as a man clinging by narrow threads to his sanity, cogent and sardonic one moment, hallucinatory the next. Essentially alone, abandoned by the homophobic film industry, and with only his devoted Austrian housekeeper (Lynn Redgrave, offering some hammy comic relief) and his painting hobby to occupy him, Whale's mind begins to misbehave like a computer with a runaway virus. Synapses are firing in all directions, plunging him into fantasies both nostalgic and nightmarish.

The prime conceit of the story is the introduction of the powerfully built young gardener Clay (Brendan Fraser), who triggers Whale's sexual imagination while remaining clearly unattainable. Whale nevertheless hires Clay as a model, hoping for the best, and the two begin a curious relationship built largely around Clay's own loneliness and need for human connection.

Clay is, in ways both subtle and blunt, the embodiment of Frankenstein's monster, heavy on brawn, light in the balcony, and Whale is the well-intentioned doctor attempting to make him whole. In turn, Clay's curiosity about the filmmaker's life and work both props up Whale's self-esteem and hurtles him into the past—to his glory years in Hollywood, when his "Frankenstein" movies (along with "The Invisible Man" and "The Old Dark House") had made him the pride of Universal, and to the battlefield of World War I, where he had the great love of his life with a doomed soldier.

Ultimately, his memories, his movies and his confusing relationship with Clay are overlaid in Whale's mind, making his behavior more and more erratic, and driving him finally to concoct plans for escape.

If the story is schematic, it's also essential. Had Bram and Condon speculated, as people did 40 years ago, on Whale's relationships with his known gay lovers, the parallel allegory would have been lost. Like Frankenstein and his monster, Whale and Clay begin as creatures on different dimensions, searching for a common ground of humanity. And the analogy is alive in Whale's mind.

Who knows what it was in Condon's sketchy resume, which includes a handful of horror scripts and directing jobs on the mediocre "Sister, Sister" and the sequel to "Candyman," that persuaded the "Gods and Monsters" backers to turn him loose on this. But it's a brilliant piece of writing and directing. He not only got the best that McKellen had to give, and a solid, unself-conscious performance from the rising star Fraser, but showed a masterful hand at combining the story's fantasy elements.

"Gods and Monsters" may not solve a mystery, but it certainly sheds light on a man's life, and on an industry that treats its human assets as disposable.

NEWSWEEK, 11/30/98, p. 82, David Ansen

Ian McKellen has never given a screen performance as delicate, seductive and deeply felt as he does in "Gods and Monsters, a fictionalized account of the final days in '50s Hollywood of James Whale, the gay director of "Frankenstein." Losing his mental grip, the charming, death-haunted Whale is flooded with memories of his working-class English childhood, the horrors of trench warfare, the delights of filming "The Bride of Frankenstein." What keeps him in the present is the arrival of Clayton Boone (Brendan Fraser), a hunky, rootless and decidedly straight gardener whom he asks to pose for a painting. Their complex relationship forms the heart of Bill Condon's touching, multileveled movie. Still every inch the director, Whale is determined to stage-manage his own death. But life proves less malleable than art, as this witty gem demonstrates.

SIGHT AND SOUND, 4/99, p. 42, Kevin Jackson

Pacific Palisades in Los Angeles, 1957. The English film director James Whale has settled into a comfortable but dull retirement.

His monotonous life is gradually disrupted first by an importunate film student who agrees to strip for Whale in return for nuggets of studio gossip second; by a minor stroke, which leaves Whale more dependent on his housekeeper Hanna; and third by his attraction to his new gardener Clayton boone, an ex-marine. Whale asks Boone to pose for some portraits. Boone agrees, despite his misgivings about Whale's intentions (he is worried when he learns Whale is gay). Boone becomes fascinated by the older man, especially after watching a television screening of Whale's movie *Bride of Frankenstein*. As Boone and Whale grow closer, Whale's neurological condition grows worse, and he is afflicted by memories of his impoverished childhood in Dudley, England, and of a love affair with a fellow soldier during World War I.

Whale asks Boone to be his guest at a reception George Cukor is holding for Princess Margaret. At the party, where Whale is briefly united with stars of his *Frankenstein* films, Boris Karloff and Elsa Lanchester, he suffers another "brainstorm". Boone drives him home and finally strips naked for his friend so that Whale can draw him. But Whale insists Boone wear a gas mask and then fondles him until the younger man explodes in rage and disgust, almost killing him. The following morning Boone and Hanna discover Whale's body floating in the swimming pool and find a suicide note which they destroy. Several years later Boone is happily married and showing *Bride of Frankenstein* to his small son, as well as Whale's original sketch of the monster, inscribed "Clayton Boone—friend?, an allusion to a key line in *Frankenstein*.

Who created Frankenstein? "A mad scientist," says the tabloid journalist, and turns back to writing his scare piece about genetically modified 'Frankenstein foods'. "Wrong as usual," says the horror freak. "Frankenstein *was* the mad scientist, his poor creature went unchristened. The right answer is the man who played the brute, Boris Karloff." "A plague on both your houses," says the graduate student. "The true creator was Mary Shelley, whose book was really about womb envy." Finally, enter the unreconstructed auteurist, who regards his three forebears with an air of pitying exasperation and points out that the only correct response to the question has to be the English director James Whale.

The auteurist exaggerates but not absurdly. Although there had been nineteenth-century plays and two previous *Frankenstein* movies made in 1910 and 1915, it was Whale's Universal version of 1931 which finally made Mary Shelley's overdetermined yarn into a fable for twentieth-century mass culture, and it was Whale who re-invented the monster's frightful face. Where her novel spoke of a being whose "yellow skin scarcely covered the work of muscles and arteries beneath" (resembling Christopher Lee in the 1957 Hammer *"The Curse of Frankenstein* perhaps), Whale conceived a literal deadpan of sunken and hooded eyes, a brow like the cliffs of Dover and a prematurely fashionable flattop. "I made drawings of [Karloff's] head," Whale explained, "adding sharp bony edges where I imagined the skull might have been joined." Instead of looking silly, it looked like a trench hallucination (Whale had served in Flanders), or a *momento mori* retrieved from a nightmare.

This act of night vision ought to have been quite enough to confer deathless fame on Whale, even if he hadn't gone on to make film after distinguished film. *The Bride of Frankenstein* (1935) broke the iron Law of the Duff Sequel by being one of the most quirkily lyrical, gently funny movies ever made by a major studio; the musical *Show Boat* (1936) was greeted as a triumph; *Remember Last Night?* (1935) was a pioneering screwball comedy; and the Whale filmography of 20-odd completed films also includes such achievements as *Journey's End* (1930) *Waterloo Bridge* (1931), *The Old Dark House* (1932), *The Invisible Man* (1933) and *The Great Garrick* (1937).

In a just world, James Whale's name would be at least as well known as that of his fellow countryman Karloff, if not Hitchcock. In the real world, he has until recently been remembered mainly by the scholarly and by the sad, which is one reason for welcoming the film *Gods and Monsters*, a thoughtful and entertaining dramatic portrait of Whale which, despite its title, is based not on James Curtis' meticulous biography *James Whale. A New World of Gods and Monsters* (1998) but on Christopher Bram's more fanciful 1995 novel *Father of Frankenstein*, and is directed by horror film-and-television veteran Bill Condon (*FX2: The Deadly Art of Illusion, Candyman Farewell to the Flesh*).

Less a conventional biopic than a speculation about Whale's last few weeks, *Gods and Monsters* focuses on a tentative dance of courtship between the ailing homosexual director (Sir Ian McKellen, making a fireworks display of the role) and his handsome, ill-educated young gardener Clayton Boone (Brendan Fraser, at once quieter and more affecting, Karloff to McKellen's Colin Clive, as it were). At first Boone is puzzled by Whale's interest in him, failing to twig that Whale is "just some fruit", as his buddies warn him, but soon experiences fascination, pity and admiration for the older man. Much of this is conducted as a comedy of misapprehension, akin to *Love and Death on Long Island,* which also concerned a decent, comely, naive American lad flattered and baffled by the attentions of a patrician and significantly older British artist. Broader humour comes in the person of Hanna (Lynn Redgrave, all but unrecognisable), the film's fictional Hungarian housekeeper for Whale who adores her employer as a man but loathes him as a "bugger", and is wont to hiss such gothic clichés as, "Zer MAH-ster is VAY-ting fur you". One suspects a little parallel with "Fritz', the dwarfish servant played by Dwight Frye in *Frankenstein,* is intended.

As in Whale's horror movies, lightness gives way to the sombre and grotesque. *Gods and Monsters* nearly ends with a near fatal struggle between Whale and Boone. The film is also interlarded with flashbacks to World War I and Whale's traumatic love affair with a fellow soldier, shot dead and left to rot on the barbed wire. (An episode not mentioned in Curtis' biography, and presumably as fictitious as the main plot.) The true ending, however, is a years-later coda which hints that Boone's existence has been somehow revivified by his brief encounter with genius.

Throughout, *Gods and Monsters* plays teasing variations on metaphors derived from the Frankenstein story: Boone as the noble, inarticulate monster, Whale as the creator; *Frankenstein* the movie as the monster from which Whale's creative reputation can never escape; Whale as the lonely, ardent monster, Boone as the rejecting Bride. Of all these conceits, the most subtly pervasive seems to be the one current since Vito Russo's study *The Celluloid Closet* put forward a gay revisionist line on *Frankenstein*: Whale, the monstrous homosexual outcast, driven out from his Hollywood career by bigots waving flaming torches. Well, maybe, although (as Curtis contends with some force) this reading doesn't fit the known facts. For that time, Whale was not only unusually comfortable with his sexuality but was also generally respected for his openness. The decline of his career seems to have owed a lot more to his arrogant, high-handed manner than to his gayness. What obsessed Whale was not sex but class—he came from an extremely poor working-class family in Dudley—and by touching on this obsession only briefly, *Gods and Monsters* denies itself one really meaty conceit. In terms of the British class system, Whale was at once mad scientist and suffering creature—as the saying goes, a self-made man.

But while Condon may not quite have captured an accurate Whale, he and his cast have brought a memorable creation to life. Some of the film's most complex scenes show a variety of spectators watching *The Bride of Frankenstein* on television: the heartless, like Boone's drinking buddies, sneer at the censorious, like Hanna, see only necrophilia; but the pure in heart—like Boone and later his son—glimpse the magic. Which takes us back to ideas of creation: whether Mary Shelley's book is actually about womb envy or not, it is demonstrably about artistic fecundity. *Gods and Monsters* takes its title from a line in *The Bride of Frankenstein* and its single most memorable sequence is a flashback to that film's shooting. Elsa Lanchester and Ernest Thesiger leave aside their camp banter, Whale calls "Action!" and the bitchy silliness gives way to poetry. No wonder Whale is moved to reminisce to Boone that, "making movies is the most wonderful thing in the world."

VILLAGE VOICE, 11/10/98, p. 120, Amy Taubin

The James Whale biopic *Gods and Monsters* sputters and stalls, but it's roadworthy enough to serve as a vehicle for Ian McKellen's dazzling, old-school performance. McKellen plays the director of *Frankenstein* and *Bride of* as a man who's lived inside his invented persona for so long that it seems to have been encoded in his DNA. Artifice becomes McKellen as it became Whale, or at least McKellen's version of Whale.

Based on Christopher Bram's novel *Father of Frankenstein*, Bill Condon's *Gods and Monsters* is a fictionalized account of Whale's last few months. (I leave it to the Whale buffs to sort out the facts from the fantasy.) Long retired from filmmaking, Whale lives a life of consummate taste and loneliness, attended to by his faithful housekeeper (Lynn Redgrave) and occasionally visited by his former boyfriend (David Dukes). The housekeeper believes that her Mr. Jimmy will burn in hell for his homosexuality; the ex-boyfriend, a Hollywood insider, is embarrassed by Whale's refusal to keep his queerness a secret.

Whale has had a stroke that leaves him subject to memory storms; he's gripped involuntarily by visual images of the past. This loss of control over his own brain makes poor Whale suicidal, but it's of great convenience to the filmmaker, who uses it as an opportunity to cram in back story, most of it involving Whale's experience as a soldier in World War I. It was in the trenches that Whale, who grew up in the slums of England, found a fleeting experience of true love with an upper-class 18-year-old: "He didn't mind that I was a working-class boy imitating his betters."

Condon gets maximum mileage from these blasts from the past, collaging, for example, the gunfire lighting up the sky over no-man's-land with a clip of the lightning storm from *Frankenstein*, or cutting between a vision of Whale's first great love and the hunky gardener who becomes the object of his desire in the last weeks of his life. Most of *Gods and Monsters* is focused on the frustrating but strangely tender relationship that develops between Whale and the gardener, a well-muscled innocent named Clayton (Brendan Fraser). Clayton, who grew up poor and had father problems just like Whale, finds himself sympathetic to the old man and immensely gratified by the attention lavished on him. But the discovery that Whale is gay—and therefore lusts after his body—throws Clayton into a confusion of terror, anger, and disgust.

There's a hint of *Lolita* (the Kubrick version) in these scenes of forbidden desire in the '50s—the sophisticated, highly literate foreigner enamored of a healthy, minimally educated, but disarmingly direct American who has no sexual interest in him but is captivated by the way power turns round and about. The relationship is touching, painful, revealing, and often funny, which is true of the film as a whole as well. There's a darkly camp scene in which Whale takes Clayton to a garden party given by George Cukor to honor Princess Margaret. "He's never met a princess before, only old queens," says Whale of Clayton, while the closeted Cukor squirms in fury and embarrassment.

Whale called *Frankenstein* a comedy about death. The same could be said of *Gods and Monsters*. It just takes place on a slightly more earthbound level.

Also reviewed in:
CHICAGO TRIBUNE, 12/4/98, Friday/p. D. Mark Caro
NEW YORK TIMES, 11/4/98, p. E5, Janet Maslin
NEW YORKER, 11/9/98, p. 106, Anthong Lane
VARIETY, 1/26-2/1/98, p. 69, Dennis Harvey
WASHINGTON POST, 11/20/98, p. F4, Rita Kempley

GODZILLA

A TriStar Pictures release of a Centropolis Entertainment production and a Fried Films and Independent Pictures production. *Executive Producer:* Roland Emmerich, Ute Emmerich, and William Fay. *Producer:* Dean Devlin. *Director:* Roland Emmerich. *Screenplay:* Dean Devlin and Roland Emmerich. *Story (based on the character "Godzilla" owned and created by TohoCo., Ltd.):* Ted Elliott, Terry Rossio, Dean Devlin, and Roland Emmerich. *Director of Photography:* Ueli Steiger. *Editor:* Peter Amundson and David J. Siegel. *Music:* David Arnold. *Music Editor:* Dina Eaton. *Sound:* Jose Antonio Garcia and (music) Shawn Murphy. *Sound Editor:* Per Hallberg. *Casting:* April Webster and David Bloch. *Production Designer:* Oliver Scholl. *Art Director:* William Ladd Skinner. *Set Designer:* Mikc Cukurs, Jann Engel, Robert Fechtman, Luis G. Hoyos, and Richard Reynolds. *Set Decorator:* Victor Zolfo. *Set Dresser:* Matthew Altman and John D. Maskovich. *Visual Effects:* Volker Engel. *Godzilla Design:*

Patrick Tatopoulos. *Costumes:* Joseph Porro. *Make-up:* Katalin Elek. *Stunt Coordinator:* R.A. Rondell. *Running time:* 139 minutes. *MPAA Rating:* PG-13.

CAST: Matthew Broderick (Dr. Niko Tatopoulos); Jean Réno (Philippe Roaché); Maria Pitillo (Audrey Timmonds); Hank Azaria (Victor "Animal" Palotti); Kevin Dunn (Colonel Hicks); Michael Lerner (Mayor Ebert); Harry Shearer (Charles Caiman); Arabella Field (Lucy Palotti); Vicki Lewis (Dr. Elsie Chapman); Doug Savant (Sergeant O'Neal); Malcolm Danare (Dr. Mendel Craven); Lorry Goldman (Gene, Mayor's Aide); Christian Aubert (Jean-Luc); Philippe Bergeron (Jean-Claude); Frank Bruynbroek (Jean-Pierre); François Giroday (Jean-Philippe); Nicholas J. Giangiulio (Ed); Robert Lesser (Murray); Ralph Manza (Old Fisherman); Greg Callahan (Governor); Chris Ellis (General Anderson); Nancy Cartwright (Caiman's Secretary); Richard E. Gant (Admiral Phelps); Jack Moore (Leonard); Steve Giannelli (Jules); Brian Farabaugh (Arthur); Stephen Xavier Lee (Lt. Anderson); Bodhi Elfman (Freddie); Rich Battista (Jimmy); Lloyd Kino (Japanese Tanker Cook); Toshi Toda (Japanese Tanker Captain); Clyde Kusatsu (Japanese Tanker Skipper); Masaya Kato (Japanese Tanker Crew Member); Glenn Morshower (Kyle Terrington); Lola Pashalinski (Pharmacist); Rob Fukuzaki (WIDF Co-Anchor); Dale Harimoto (WKXI Anchor); Gary Cruz (WFKK Anchor); Derek Webster (Utah Captain); Stuart Fratkin (Utah Ensign); Frank Cilberg, Jason Edward Jones, and Roger McIntyre (Utah Sailors); David Pressman (Anchorage Captain); Robert Faltisco, Chris Maleki, and Scott Lusby (Anchorage Ensigns); Alex Dodd (Anchorage Sailor); Jamison Yang, Nathan Anderson, Mark Munafo, and Dwight Schmidt (F-18 Pilots); Dwayne Swingler (Raven Pilot); Lawton Paseka (Officer); Greg Collins (Soldier on Bridge); James Black, Thomas Giuseppe Giantonelli, and Paul Ware (Soldiers); Monte Russell (Soldier on Plane); Christopher Carruthers and Daniel Pearce (Radio Technicians); Mark Fite (Radio Operator); Craig A. Castaldo (Radio Man); Eric Paskel (Rodgers); Lee Weaver and Leonard Termo (Homeless Guys); Joshua Taylor (Spotter); Al Sapienza (Taxi Cab Driver); Stoney Westmoreland (Tunnel Guard); Gary Warner (Gun Technician); Ed Wheeler (New York Cop); Bill Hoag (New Jersey Cop); Joe Badalucco, Jr. (Forklift Driver); Jonathan Dienst (Field Reporter).

LOS ANGELES TIMES, 5/19/98, Calendar/p. 1, Kevin Thomas

Godzilla, that gigantic mutant amphibian reptile, is back, bigger and much better than ever, cutting a swath of destruction from Polynesia through Panama and on to Manhattan, where he threatens to trample the entire island with his 140-foot strides. The Brooklyn Bridge crumbles as if it were a toy and Manhattan landmarks get rearranged and lopped off in an effort to contain the monster, whose size defies comprehension.

"Independence Day's" Roland Emmerich is just the man to raise the dragon-like star of 22 Japanese features from beneath the sea one more time. Emmerich has an affectionate respect for '50s sci-fi horror that avoids camp and condescension. There's humor in his "Godzilla," but it is above all an expertly designed theme park ride of a movie that packs nonstop thrills. Emmerich and his co-writers, which include his producer, Dean Devlin, are never at a loss for inspiration, and their pace is unflagging as that of old serials; wisely, they don't underline Godzilla's inherent allegorical aspect.

They actually manage to keep up with Godzilla, who can move, we are told, at a 500 mph clip. Above all, they maintain clarity, a quality notably absent from two recent summers' blockbusters, "The Fifth Element" and "Mission: Impossible."

The film's thoroughly likable hero, Matthew Broderick as biologist Nick Tatopoulos, is abruptly whisked away by his employer, the U.S. Nuclear Regulatory Agency, from Chernobyl, where he has been studying the effects of radiation on earthworms (they're getting bigger!). Nick is dispatched to Polynesia, where Godzilla has mutated as a result of nuclear testing and has destroyed a Japanese fishing vessel.

In the meantime, Nick's old girlfriend, Audrey (Maria Pitillo), who ditched him eight years earlier to put career first, is getting nowhere at a New York-based network TV news department. As Godzilla approaches Manhattan, Audrey is refusing to have dinner with an arrogant news anchor (Harry Shearer, an amusing casting), clearly a big career mistake. Of course, the arrival of Nick, hot on the heels of Godzilla, will give her the professional—and maybe even personal—chance of a lifetime.

The spectacle that is "Godzilla" is simply stupendous—and there's no point in revealing one jaw-dropping sequence after another, yet the film never loses either momentum or its human scale. What counts is Nick's attempt to figure out why Godzilla has sought out New York while Audrey and her cameraman colleague, Animal (Hank Azaria), try to get the story, and the trigger-happy military try to stop the monster in his tracks. When the military and Nick part company, he teams up with Jean Reno's astute and courageous Philippe, a French secret agent.

No matter how good—or poor—other special effects may be, the ultimate effect in a monster movie must, of course, be the monster. Thanks to the magic of computer-generated imagery, Godzilla is most convincing, a figure of innocent rapaciousness and ultimately of poignance, and in this instance the film's myriad other effects are up to the level of the monster, who was designed by Patrick Tatopoulos—and who provided the hero's surname, an expression of gratitude on the part of Emmerich for his efforts. (The film is dedicated to the late Tomoyuki Tanaka, producer of the original film and Toho Studios chairman.)

The necessity of shooting primarily at night in Manhattan proved to be a blessing: It allowed cameraman Ueli Steiger the opportunity to give the film a great sooty, neo-noir look, and there's nothing like shadows to enhance even the finest special effects money can buy.

"Godzilla" has a tremendously rich and complex visual texture, and production designer Oliver Scholl, visual effects supervisor Volker Engel, editors Peter Amundson and David J. Siegel and Emmerich's immense cast and crew have all contributed positively toward making the film a fully realized movie experience. David Arnold's score is worth singling out for managing to be stirring, eliciting a sense of awe and excitement without being bombastic.

Emmerich projects his vision of Godzilla's path of destruction so forcefully that you buy into its credibility with ease, although you could use a greater sense of pandemonium and presence among the New York's citizenry—not everyone could have managed to flee town, although at times it seems that way. In big-deal disaster movies characters have to be defined sharply and swiftly, which means actors have to flesh out their parts with personality and presence. Broderick by far has the most substantial role, and the combination of his boyishness and intelligence makes him a most appealing, down-to-earth hero, not Superman.

Pitillo manages several abrupt shifts in Audrey's character nimbly, and Reno, Azaria and Shearer are likewise strong. Among those leading a very large supporting cast is Michael Lerner as New York's opportunistic mayor, up for reelection. (The mayor's last name is Ebert; his key aide, played by Lorry Goldman, is called Gene; Ebert and Gene look much like a pair of famous Chicago-based movie critics.)

It's hard to imagine "Godzilla"—or any movie, for now—topping "Titanic" in popularity, and it seems unlikely that as many adults will be drawn to a fantasy of Manhattan being trampled by a monster as they were to that film. But "Godzilla," which delivers unpretentious fun with a blithe spirit, will surely give that box-office behemoth a healthy run for its money.

NEW STATESMAN, 7/17/98, p. 39, Anne Billson

In his original Japanese incarnation, Godzilla was a city-stomping metaphor for atomic destruction. Now he's just an oversized reptile, all special effects and no brain. Bring back the man in the rubber suit

There's a wonderful moment in the otherwise   unexceptional post-Tarantino botched-caper movie "Things to Do in Denver When You're Dead", when knife-wielding lunatic Treat Williams launches himself at an opponent with the words: "I am Godzilla! You are Japan!" After which, he does to the guy what the 400ft dinosaur with radioactive breath used to do to Tokyo, which is trash him royally.

You will note the line is not: "I am Godzilla! You are New York!" Nonetheless, the makers of the new Godzilla movie have elected to have their monster swim half-way round the world from its place of origin so that the Big Apple, rather than Tokyo, can be the designated trash object, the pretext being that Manhattan is dark and wet and there are plenty of nesting opportunities in those grand canyons we call streets. But by pitching their monster squarely at American audiences who can't summon up interest in anything that takes place outside the US, they've cut the mighty behemoth off at his roots, leaving him splashing around in a film which is all shallows and no depth, all show and no subtext. For Godzilla and his original stomping ground, Japan, are wedded together like Punch and Judy, Cain and Abel, Sid and Nancy. Japan is the point about Godzilla, or Gojira, as they call him there.

Transforming our worst fears into monsters is the first step towards taming them. Gojira, unlike Occidental cousins such as King Kong, Dracula or H R Giger's Alien, had nothing to do with sexual symbolism; he had hotter fish to fry. After the second world war, the world was all too familiar with cities getting trashed, but Japan's cities had been unusually traumatised—not just Tokyo, rebuilt after the great earthquake of 1923 only to be flattened in 1945 by bombing raids, but Hiroshima and Nagasaki, obliterated by the most monstrous weapon known to man. If ever a nation needed to get something off its chest so it could sleep at night, it was Japan.

There had been big reptiles before: "The Beast From 20,000 Fathoms," which had stomped New York in 1953, was not an atomic mutation but an authentic dinosaur, awakened by an atomic blast in the Arctic.

But it wasn't until Toho Studios' "Gojira" in 1954 that the atomic monster movie came home. This established the blueprint for a classic three-part ritual that was to be re-enacted so many times: the awakening, rampage and, finally, taming or suppression of the beast. The man in the rubber monster suit, stomping on scale models of urban sprawl, became the earthly representative of demon, god and scapegoat, like the priest of some arcane religion.

The Americans, naturally, trimmed those plot elements hinting at an Armageddon they themselves had brought about, including cutting most of the footage about the embittered eye-patch-wearing Japanese scientist whose kamikaze heroism saves the world. In his place they inserted footage of Raymond Burr as an American reporter called Steve Martin, dubbed the Japanese actors and retitled the film "Godzilla, King of the Monsters". It was, of course, a monster hit, but a strangely emasculated one.

But repeat something often enough, and you control it. Disturbing memories lose the power to disturb if they're described out loud, whether to friends, therapists or the public. Over the years, Godzilla, and what it stood for, was indeed tamed. Like Frankenstein's monster, Dracula, even Freddy Krueger from "A Nightmare on Elm Street," he lost his power to frighten and was transformed, literally, into a cuddly toy for children. As sequel followed sequel, Godzilla's features were subtly remodelled so they became less reptilian, his eyes became rounder, until, with "Gojira No Musuko" (aka "Son of Godzilla") in 1968, the second generation was revealed as a cute, galumphing baby monster, a sort of mutant cross between a bouncing foetus and the Andrex puppy.

As Godzilla became more endearing, so he gradually turned into one of the good guys, the sort of monster who would trash cities only when under the malign influence of the alien thought-beams in "Kaiju Soshingeki" (aka "Destroy All Monsters") in 1968. And his kind went forth and multiplied. Daiei Studios, rival to Toho, came up with its own monster franchise in the form of Gamera, a giant tusked turtle which turned into a flying saucer. Godzilla himself was joined by a veritable menagerie of monsterdom, including Rodan the giant pterodactyl (whose modus operandi consisted of flapping its wings really hard to cause a massive shock-wave), Mothra the giant moth (another destructive wing-flapper), and Manda the giant serpent.

Later Godzilla films invariably ended up with its reptilian hero having a stonking great fist-fight with enemies of the people such as Gaigan (a giant metal bird with a buzz-saw in its stomach), Ghidorah (a supersonic three-headed dragon), Ebirah (a giant lobster) or Hedora (a giant lump of toxic sludge). From his early rampages as an uncontrollable weapon of mass destruction, Godzilla was recast in the military-friendly sixties as our ultimate secret weapon to keep evil aliens at bay and, incidentally, the main attraction on an island theme-park called Monsterland.

The trouble with the new Godzilla is that it (and it's impossible to think of it as a he) is neither hero nor villain, simply a big lizard with a charisma bypass. Instead of maliciously stomping on buildings, it blunders into them by mistake; more tourist landmarks are destroyed by friendly fire from the US military, which may be accurate but it sure ain't as much fun. The only sign of personality demonstrated by the new oik is shortness of temper after its hatchlings have been destroyed. There's a half-baked attempt to blame its existence on H-bomb testing in Polynesia, with Jean Reno playing a French agent dispatched with his crack team to the US to make good his government's mistakes. It might have worked better if the creature had gone walkabout down the Champs-Elysees.

The main problem, though, is that "Godzilla," like so many other films of the nineties, is ultimately about nothing. Peel away the layers of story and what do we find? That there aren't any layers, let alone a proper story. Co-writers Roland Emmerich (who also directed) and Dean Devlin were apparently peeved when the LA Times gave away the part of the plot in which Godzilla lays eggs in Madison Square Garden and a lot of Babyzillas hatch out. Big deal! It's been more than 30 years since Gorgo's mum stomped on Big Ben after her baby was kidnapped, and we've already brought up "Son of Godzilla" (as you do). And if you really want the deep dish on reptilian parenting, it was dealt with comprehensively in "The Lost World: Jurassic Park," in which a couple of T Rexes taught Jeff Goldblum how to be a better dad, and "Alien Resurrection," in which the relationship between monsters and mothers was thoroughly explored.

No, the best bits of the 1998 "Godzilla" are the trailers and the build-up before the monster appears. In other words, the hype. If only Emmerich and Devlin had incorporated this aspect into their screenplay and run the whole yard with it, they'd have unleashed a truly formidable beast. For none can escape the dreaded Hype-Monster, which chews up everything that stands in its path.

NEW YORK, 6/1/98, p. 93, David Denby

Did the filmmakers responsible for the sodden *Godzilla*—Dean Devlin and Roland Emmerich—lack confidence in their own animation techniques? Were they afraid to put their computerized beast out there in the open daylight, as Steven Spielberg did with his brontosaurus and his raptors in *Jurassic Park?* It certainly looks that way. Long stretches of *Godzilla* were shot in slate-gray light with buckets of water miserably coming down on everyone's head, or in dark underground tunnels, or in a dim mock-up of Madison Square Garden. *Godzilla* is not a fiasco like *Waterworld* or *The Postman*; it is not an insult to the audience like *The Last Action Hero, Starship Troopers,* or *Batman and Robin*. Within its dreary wastes, there are a few scares, a few thrills. But the movie is soggy, murky, and depressing—a joyless and redundant experience that leaves one in a ghastly mood. It turns out that spending two hours watching a movie shot in a wet, dreary New York is not all that different from spending two hours walking around in the actual wet, dreary New York. It's true that in *Godzilla,* a rather large creature shows up now and then, but you can't always see more than a part of him (an enormous foot, the tail), and when you do, he's half in darkness. The star of the movie isn't quite there. And no one else is there, either.

Most of the fun is gathered into the first few minutes. Somewhere in the Pacific, in the middle of a nighttime storm, a Japanese trawler is attacked, its side smashed in by a gigantic scaly something. Later, there's a good Spielbergian scene in which an old bum sits at the end of a rain-soaked pier in New York and hooks a very big fish indeed. As he runs back to land, the planks of the pier go flying up in the air as if propelled by an explosion. Something's definitely coming. But even by this time in the movie—still very early on—you may begin to feel dismayed by the gray-black coloring. What, after all, is the expressive meaning of the endless downpour? The darkness and wet do not convey a necessary mood, as they did in those drenched *noir* thrillers of the forties that featured characters locked into neurotic or will-driven states of mind. I believe you can fight a 200-foot lizard in almost any kind of weather.

The practical reason for the shrouded imagery, I assume, s that it covers the seams—the places where the computer-generated monster is joined to the real-world backgrounds. Some of us may feel, however, that we've been cheated more than a little. At first, Devlin and Emmerich tease us by showing the monster only in parts; there is a good moment when Hank Azaria, as a daredevil local-TV cameraman, is so paralyzed by a combination of bravado and fear that he forgets to get out of the way and almost gets squished outside Grand Central Terminal by a taxi-crushing foot. But there isn't one great stunning moment when we see Godzilla clearly in all his glory. As the Monster runs through streets, tossing automobiles, gouging skyscrapers with his swinging tail, the camera races after him, sometimes from the point of view of helicopters flying through the stone canyons in pursuit. Such imagery is thrilling at first, but when it's repeated again and again, we begin to notice that the shots have the glib, too-easy virtuosity of an advanced video game. In movies, computer-generated animation may be a double-edged sword: You can do anything with it, but if you leave plausible, photographed reality too far behind, the thrill evaporates instantly. As a pop experience—and I can't imagine any other way of experiencing it—the movie is turgid and only occasionally exciting.

The despressingness extends to the characters and actors. Matthew Broderick, as a serious young scientist summoned straight from Chernobyl, talks very deliberately and just seems sweet and out of it, as if he had no real sense of what was going on. Maria Pitillo, from the TV series *House Rules*, plays an ambitious young woman stuck in her low-status job as assistant to a pompous local-new's anchorman; Pitillo, it turns out, once had a fling with Broderick and has always longed for him. But Maria Pitillo his an empty space in her eyes and a tinge of unredeemed ordinariness in her manner. Who cares whether she gets back together with Broderick or goes on the air as a reporter? Framing the disaster with local-news reports is just obtuse and banal in the most movieish way. The script has a tired, halfhearted sound to it, as if it had been intentionally simplified for the meanest intelligence in Bangkok.

The festive *Independence Day* was not my kind of movie, but in that one, at least, Emmerich and Devlin seemed shrewd. Now I'm not so sure. They allow such talented actors as Michael Lerner and Kevin Dunn (playing, respectively, the mayor and a lizard-fighting Army colonel) to shout and carry on like second-raters in a sitcom. No one in the movie has any authority or stature. And there's no suffering, no terror—no blood, no bodies. The monster rampages without, apparently, hurting anyone. All of this can be justified (and doubtless will be justified) as intentionally schlocky and antiseptic, but mediocrity is finally just mediocrity. As a director, Emmerich doesn't have the kind of tactile and sensuous style that makes a monster movie an alarming experience of the dangerous and the deformed.

The original Japanese *Godzilla*, from 1954, was made in the wake of American H-bomb tests in the Pacific, and fed into queasy memories of America's nuclear attacks on Japan; the monster, which was produced by genetic mutation, could be seen as an emanation of nuclear paranoia. The Japanese masochistically turned Godzilla loose on Tokyo, not on New York (they may have been too afraid of Americans to create a revenge fantasy). In the new *Godzilla,* however, the mutations occur after *French* nuclear testing in the Pacific. When the beast attacks New York, we're told that he likes the city because there are plenty of places to hide there, which is nonsense. Why didn't Godzilla head for the Eiffel Tower? The political and "allegorical" sides of the pop epic have been trashed by commercial calculation. New York has been chosen for its box-office qualities, and so has the French action star Jean Reno, who turns up to protect France's honor (i.e., to nail down the European market).

This boring, meaningless corporate product is opening on 7,363 American screens and may push some good movies into the gutter. If we accept this situation as normal, then *Godzilla*—however trivial in itself—will have done our damaged movie culture some further harm.

NEWSDAY, 5/19/98, Part II/p. B3, John Anderson

Like skirt lengths and exchange rates, the historical "Godzilla" mirrors the state of the world. In 1954, when he first started tearing up Tokyo, he was the misbegotten spawn of the atomic bomb, a Japanese projection of an American nuclear threat and fear of Armageddon. Twenty-odd movies and 40 years later, when the makers of the latest "Godzilla" first decided to bring him to New York, the idea probably made sense, symbolically: An unstoppable force of Japanese origin devastating an economically hobbled America.

Production time being what it is, however, the latest "Godzilla" arrives in a world that doesn't quite jibe with its world-view. Japan's economy is reeling. The atomic threat is on the subcontinent.

And an ill-tempered creature rampaging through Manhattan and munching on taxi cabs might as well be a metaphor for Rudolph Giuliani.

No one, of course, is going to go see "Godzilla"—the hotly anticipated tear-'em-up-and-spit-'em-out summer monster movie—for socio-economic analysis. They want thrills, chills, scaly, green, building-size lizards and valiant humanity. They might also want a story that makes a modicum of sense and effects that don't insult the intelligence. Like they say, you can't have everything.

It's a shame, really, that "Godzilla," directed by "Independence Day's" Roland Emmerich and starring Matthew Broderick, is so lazy about what it does, or even what it wants to do. With every technological advantage at his disposal, Emmerich has made a movie that is so emotionally uninvolving you can't help but scrutinize every minor detail—most of which come up lacking.

It may be a strictly personal taste kind of thing, but I prefer my enormous, mutated Komodo dragons not to change their proportions to fit a director's particular scene. First, "Godzilla" is the size of the Woolworth Building; then, he's hiding inside the subway system. It doesn't make any sense. And it destroys the illusion.

Unlike what Emmerich did in his sci-fi extravaganza "Stargate"—pile on the effects, but make the characters vaguely human—in "Godzilla" he makes the humans into paper cutouts and plays fast and loose with the visual aids. Once Godzilla has made his presence felt—tearing up a Japanese freighter and sending cartoon Japanese scurrying about as they did in the original films—you get the very standard-issue cast of incompetents and their interrelationships: The blustering Army colonel (Kevin Dunn) and his worshipful subordinate (Doug Savant of "Melrose Place"); the mayor of New York (Michael Lerner)—whose name is Ebert and who looks like film critic Roger—and his beleagured aide (Lorry Goldman); the crazy-courageous TV cameraman (Hank Azaria), his ditsy wife Lucy (Arabella Field) and her ditsy friend Audrey (Maria Pitillo), who can't get her boss, sniveling TV anchor Charles Caiman (Harry Shearer), to give her a break.

As in the box-office-ruling "Deep Impact," the end of the world, or even just a city, is never given dramatic priority over a character's career advancement or love life. The whiny, conniving Audrey—who along with Lucy is a kind of evolutionary throwback in the advancement of female film characters—spots her old flame Nick Tatopoulos (Broderick) on a news report about the search for the mysterious, lethal creature who's believed headed toward New York. Audrey's first and second concerns are how to get back with the guy she dumped and how to use the monster to get herself on the air.

You might think that imminent destruction would be at least an afterthought, but there's a lot going on. The mayor's worried about re-election. The colonel's worried about public opinion—the military immediately destroys more of New York with its planes than Godzilla has with his tail. Lucy's worried about her husband, and Caiman's worried about keeping Audrey's career on hold. Only Nick Tatopoulos, the mild-mannered, single-minded scientist played by Broderick, realizes that the monster's motivations are nesting, feeding and laying... eggs.

Broderick gives the movie's single real performance, and he's rather charming as the gentle Nick, sort of a post-silent era Harold Lloyd. Jean Reno, amusing as usual, is Nick's confederate, a French secret service agent trying to cover up the results of his country's Polynesian nuclear tests (a k a Godzilla) and complaining about American coffee. The rest are caricatures—which would have been fine, had the entirety of "Godzilla" not been a catalog of tension-flattening illogic, preposterous theater and Abbott and Costello-style slapstick.

While the picture is very careful to leave you with the sense that a sequel is not just possible but inevitable, a more satisfying final shot would have been Roland Emmerich, fleeing down a side street with a great black shadow in hot pursuit.

SIGHT AND SOUND, 8/98, p. 42, Andy Medhurst

The sudden sinking of a Japanese supertanker in the Pacific Ocean is followed by the appearance of enormous footprints in Panama. To analyse the phenomena the United States military assembles a team of scientists including Niko Tatopoulos, an expert in the effects of nuclear radiation on animals who has been studying earthworms in Chernobyl. Meanwhile a group of Frenchmen, supposedly insurance investigators, also track the creature's progress. Niko concludes that the creature is a gigantic reptile, mutated by French nuclear tests in the South Pacific.

The creature arrives in New York, causing panic and destruction. Audrey Timmonds, a television researcher who was engaged to Niko in college, recognises him on a news broadcast. The military wound the creature. Niko tests the creature's blood and realises it is about to lay eggs. Audrey finds Niko and, desperate for a scoop, steals a classified videotape from him. When the footage is broadcast Niko is sacked by the military but is kidnapped by the Frenchmen. Their leader Roaché reveals that they are a unit from the French secret service, keen to destroy the monster. Roaché, his team and Niko (followed by Audrey and her cameraman friend Animal) find the creature's nest inside Madison Square Garden.

The military attack the creature again and believe they have killed it. The hatching eggs release young creatures who kill some of the Frenchmen. However, Niko, Roaché, Audrey and Animal take refuge in the stadium's television studio and manage to broadcast a warning message. The stadium and the creatures are destroyed. Niko and the others escape, but the original creature reappears. They lure it on to the Brooklyn Bridge, where it becomes ensnared in the suspension cables and is killed. In the Garden's wreckage, a final egg cracks open.

As huge and relentless as the creature it is centred on, *Godzilla* has no pretensions to being anything other than a big hunk of dumb fun. On that level it works exceedingly well, fully aware of its own preposterousness and shamelessly skilful in milking every available cliché. The effects deliver, the monster is a star, the plot's nonsenses are largely covered up by pace and noise, and the actors are ruefully aware that nobody has come to the cinema to see them. Given that last point, it would be unkind to complain about Maria Pitillo's profound vapidity or the cartoon mugging of Michael Lerner and Arabella Field, and more constructive to enjoy the performances of Jean Réno and Matthew Broderick. Réno turns in a delightful study of self-parodic Gallic mysteriousness, every shrug and twinkle the sign of a man relishing how much you can earn for doing so little, while Broderick's geeky hero is suitably self-effacing. It's not the first time Broderick has had to underplay in the shadow of a rampaging monster threatening to engulf New York—he was, after all, Harvey Fierstein's boyfriend in *Torch Song Trilogy*.

The most pleasing thing about Broderick's role is how it enables *Godzilla* to back away from the appalling militarism of the same production team's *Independence Day*. Broderick's Tatopoulos is an unashamed nerd—he wears glasses early in the film, taps on a laptop, and uses such words as "incipient" and "anomaly"—and yet he consistently outsmarts the gung-ho military. The kneejerk blow-it-up mentality so celebrated in *Independence Day* is here embodied by Sergeant O'Neal (a clever little performance by Doug Savant), who makes mistake after mistake in the pursuit of the creature. He comes good at the end, of course, but only after he has learned that the brawny jock must sometimes take orders from the brainy weed. In addition, marking a further retreat from *Independence Day*'s flagwaving agenda, the brainy weed teams up with a foreigner, though any critique this suggests of American nationalism is compromised by the way the storyline blames the French for creating the monster in the first place.

As for Godzilla himself, the film sends out mixed messages. The Japanese Godzilla was often an endearing beast, especially towards the end of his career, frequently defending humanity against some other threatening monster, and displaying a particular interest in ecological matters (see *Godzilla versus the Smog Monster*, for example). Traces of that idea remain here: Godzilla is the product of nuclear foolishness; he attacks only out of self-defence; and his final struggle strains, rather clumsily, after the tragic sensibility of *King Kong* (1933). Indeed, his first rampage through New York is motivated not by destructive malevolence but by sheer clumsiness—he scythes through skyscrapers only because when you're that big you inevitably have a huge turning circle. Any sympathy we might have for Godzilla, however, is undercut once the film switches focus to his offspring. They offer the sheer evil an audience needs in order to cheer on the destruction of the closing sequences, so much so that once Dad re-emerges he's fair game too. Although it steals blatantly from *King Kong, Jaws*, the first two *Alien* films and, most of all, *Jurassic Park* (if the big creature is T-rex, his brats are a nursery of velociraptors), *Godzilla* lacks the mythic underpinnings that made those films so resonant. Industrious subtext-hunters might want to dwell on the psychosexual implications of the creature's ability to be male but still reproduce or on his status as an unwelcome immigrant from the Pacific Rim, and good luck to them if they do, but the film is best enjoyed for what it fundamentally is: an absurdly expensive way of saying "boo!"

VILLAGE VOICE, 5/26/98, p. 132, J. Hoberman

I'm not enough a fan of the original *Godzilla* to consider its gigabudget update much of a desecration, but, a few stomp-and-chase scenes notwithstanding, it sure is a bore—even by the degraded standards of the transnational, pre-sold wannabe summer blockbuster.

Roland Emmerich's retooled, bandy-legged Godzilla is less herky-jerky than his precursors, as well as less personable. The movie is similarly generic—heavily indebted, not just to Japan's most famous movie and its zillion sequels, but to *Jurassic Park*, the *Alien* quartet, and even the prehistoric *King Kong*. Despite such borrowings, *Godzilla* gives back little—unless you count the sleight of hand by which France, rather than the U.S., gets credit for irradiating the South Pacific with its nuclear testing, or the hard rain which falls on New York for virtually the movie's entire length.

More flippant than the sanctimonious *Deep Impact, Godzilla* means to be pure spectacle. But given the obvious blue-screen matting throughout, its most impressive effect is its fidelity to Manhattan geography; the best sequence (many, many minutes into the movie) reduces Madison Square Garden to its state the night the Rangers won the Stanley Cup. So much for local color. New York's terrorized population is represented exclusively by smarmy media types, a few working-class shnooks, some stray derelicts, and an obnoxious, self-promoting mayor named Ebert (with a Siskel-like deputy). Where are Donald Trump, Al Sharpton, and Sylvia Miles when you need them? If this soggy thumpfest is the best Sony can do, let them move the sequel to New Jersey.

Also reviewed in:
NEW YORK TIMES, 5/19/98, p. E1, Stephen Holden
NEW YORKER, 6/1/98, p. 76, Anthony Lane
VARIETY, 5/25-31/98, p. 55, Joe Leydon
WASHINGTON POST, 5/20/98, p. D1, Rita Kempley
WASHINGTON POST, 5/20/98, Weekend/p. 20, Michael O'Sullivan

GONIN

A Phaedra Cinema release of a Shochiku presentation of a Bunkasha Publishing/Image Factory production in association with First Production and Kanox. *Executive Producer:* Kazuyoshi Okuyama. *Producer:* Kanji Miura, Taketo Niitsu, and Katsuhide Motoki. *Director:* Takeshi Ishii. *Screenplay (Japanese with English subtitles):* Takeshi Ishii. *Director of Photography:* Yasushi Sasakibara. *Editor:* Akimasa Kawashima. *Music:* Goro Yasukawa. *Art Director:* Teru Yamazaki. *Running time:* 109 minutes. *MPAA Rating:* Not Rated.

CAST: Koichi Sato (Bandai); Naoto Takenaka (Ogiwara); Takeshi "Beat" Kitano (Kyoya); Masahiro Motoki (Mitsuya); Jimpachi Nezu (Hizu); Kippei Shiina (Jimmy); Megumi Tokoyama (Nammy); Kazuya Kimura (Kazuma); Shingo Tsurmi; Toshiyuki Nagashima.

LOS ANGELES TIMES, 1/30/98, Calendar/p. 18, Kevin Thomas

Film-noir thrillers don't get much more subversive than Takeshi Ishii's sleek, convoluted and drenchingly violent "Gonin." Rich, shadowy images combine with a dynamic, headlong pace as we're swept into the lethal, brutal Tokyo underworld. Plot developments come hurtling by like a spray of bullets, so pay close attention.

For a while we're under the impression that "Gonin" is a classic genre film par excellence, but then a most provocative subtext emerges as a group of five desperate men cross paths and decide to relieve the fearsome Ogoshi gang of a great deal of money.

They are a handsome young disco owner, Bandai (Koichi Sato) and a laid-off corporate executive, Ogiwara (Naoto Takenaka)—both victims of recession; a hotheaded, fearless male hustler-blackmailer, Mitsuya (Masahiro Motoki); a peroxided pimp, Jimmy (Kippei Shiina), with a grudge against the Ogoshi, of which he is a former member; and Hizu (Jimpachi Nezu), a rugged ex-cop who lost his job when accused of taking bribes.

Ishii, who began as a *manga* (adult comic book) artist, introduces these five with maximum wit and impact. ("Gonin" in fact means "The Five.") Amid escalating mayhem, Ishii suggests that Mitsuya has succeeded in seducing Bandai. When the Ogoshi gang seeks revenge, it hires a pair of the scariest hit men in town, Kazuma (Kazuya Kimura) and Kyoya, played with an eye patch by none other than that icon of Japanese cinema machismo, Takeshi "Beat" Kitano. You guessed it: Kazuma and Kyoya are lovers.

At once Ishii manages to smash gay stereotypes and have fun with the homoerotic, though generally unacknowledged, aspects of those ultra-savage, ultra-masculine epics involving a lot of male bonding. (No wonder "Gonin" has been described by one critic as a gay "Reservoir Dogs.")

In any event, the film builds inexorably to a showdown right out of "The Wild Bunch." Violence, suggests Ishii, is ultimately as absurd as the notion that gays are automatically effeminate types. On the other hand, nobody who wears lipstick could be tougher or more dangerous than Mitsuya.

NEW YORK POST, 1/16/98, p. 44, Thelma Adams

"Gonin" is "Reservoir Dogs" meets "The Gang That Couldn't Shoot Straight"—with subtitles. Japanese writer/director Takashi Ishii touches on John Woo, Ringo Lam, Wong Kar-Wai and Quentin Tarantino with his 1995 gangster film.

"Gonin" crosses the overheated neo-action genre with a modish homosexual subtext. Perhaps it seemed fresher three years ago, but, like the many corpses that turn up, it lacks a long shelf-life.

If you can follow the plot, there's an ill-gotten gang of five (translated, that's what gonin means): The gay hustler (Masahiro Motoki), the suave disco owner (Koichi Sato), the fallen cop (Jimpachi Nezu), the down-sized businessman (Naoto Takenaka) and the wacko pimp (Kippei Shiina) in love with a hooker.

Why these dimwits think they can rip off the yakuza for more yen than the market can bear is a case of guts outweighing gray matter. Before we can say last man standing, we've seen more torture and atrocities and two-fisted gunplay than even the magnificent Woo could stomach.

When the movie's chief innovations are a scene in which a man bathes with his late wife's green corpse, and another in which a pimp wears the scalp and dress of his murdered lover, the only rational response is gag me.

Japanese superstar Takeshi Kitano ("Hana-Bi") gets top billing for a secondary role as a ruthless assassin who gets his kicks by beating his accomplice and then consummating their disunion while surround by their victims. Ugliness reigns.

NEWSDAY, 1/16/98, Part II/p. B11, John Anderson

You can define Takashi Ishii's Japanese gangster flick "Gonin" as much by what it's not as what it is. It's "The Seven Samurai," but without the honor code. It's John Woo-grade, Hong Kong-flavored mayhem, sans ballet. It's Wong Kar-Wai's viscous neon night-scape, free of introspection. It's even "The Full Monty" without the bump-and-grind.

"Full Monty"? Well, at least one of The Five (which is what "Gonin" means) has been downsized and the rest have other personal problems that they are going to solve not by taking their clothes off, but through a brazen rip-off of some ruthless hoods. Bandai (Koichi Sato), the organizer of this affair, is a disco owner on the ropes because of his debt to the yakuza, or Japanese mob. Hizu (Jimpachi Nezu) is a dishonored ex-cop; Mitsuya (Masahiro Motoki) is a flamboyantly androgynous killer; Jimmy (Kippei Shiina) is a platinum-blond pimp with a drug-addled brain and a grudge. Oh yes, and the seriously deranged Ogiwara (Naoto Takenaka, of "Shall We Dance") is a laid-off corporate exec who's too ashamed to go home.

A motlier crew has never tried stealing 100 million yen, which Bandai knows is hidden in a safe at the Ogoshi gang's headquarters. But they do. And then they pay.

Fusing low comedy to bigtime chaos—including some fabulous shootouts and the torture of Jimmy and his Thai girlfriend Nammy (Megumi Yokoyama)—director Ishii constructs a suspenseful, high-speed crime story and one that aspires to a highly visceral visual style. Having come out of the world of Japanese comic book art—highly violent, gothicly urban—Ishii shows a clear desire to take that *outré* sensibility from page to screen. And it works, quite often. Whether his attempts at moral posturing are quite as successful is another story.

Takeshi (Beat) Kitano, a celebrated filmmaker in his own right—his "Hana-Bi (Fireworks)" won last year's, Venice Film Festival—is one of two lethal hit men assigned to bring down the robbery team, and his psychosexual relationship with his partner is one of Ishii's better bits of mischief.

That the rest of the story doesn't always hang together may be, we suspect, partly due to language gaps. But the film is a riot of color, and Ishii has a way with violence—from the nightclub slugfest that starts things off to the series of gunfights and maimings that follow. "Gonin" almost begs to be called a genre film, with its dash of cheap sentiment and gallon of blood. But it's also rather frank and ruthless in its depiction of criminal revenge, and while this may not be your cup of popcorn, at least "Gonin" doesn't pull any punches.

VILLAGE VOICE, 1/20/98, p. 61, Dennis Lim

Moody and propulsive, *Gonin* sets itself up as a *yakuza* flick, but it's no mere flashy bloodbath (though you won't be disappointed if that's what you're looking for). Takashi Ishii's first U.S. release is a wayward package of unpredictable thrills, drenched in homoeroticism and buoyed by a surprisingly moving gay love story.

On the surface, *Gonin* is an old-fashioned heist movie, hence its three neatly circumscribed segments: haphazard scheming (five mismatched partners-in-crime assemble), clumsy execution (someone—oops—gets killed), and gory aftermath—with the emphasis strictly on the latter. There are times when the film seems little more than a *Things To Do in Osaka When You're Dead*, but Ishii, a former *manga* artist, is fully aware of which clichés he wants to indulge and which he wants to smash.

What *Gonin* lacks in narrative shapeliness it more than makes up for in style and atmosphere. Most of the set pieces are impeccably staged and edited, full of reflective, neon-saturated surfaces; the absurdist frills are presumably a homage to Takeshi Kitano, who shows up in the final reel to kill everyone. Kitano plays a deadpan executioner, a persona familiar from his own films; it's a shock when he pauses midmassacre to sexually devour his male sidekick. The film's milieu is essentially all-male; men deceive, bond with, and humiliate each other, and Ishii detects sexual ripples everywhere. Among the gang of five are a down-and-out nightclub owner (Koichi Sato) and a pretty, occasionally transvestite rent boy (Masahiro Motoki) whose cockteasing relationship builds to a fantastically romantic finale. Ishii has since made *Gonin 2* —more of the same, but with five women.

Also reviewed in:
NEW YORK TIMES, 1/16/98, p. E14, Stephen Holden
VARIETY, 8/14-20/95, p. 56, David Rooney

GOVERNESS, THE

A Sony Pictures Classics release of a Pandora Cinema presentation with the participation of British Screen and the Arts Council of England in association with BBC Films of a Parallax production. *Executive Producer:* Sally Hibbin.   *Producer:* Sarah Curtis.   *Director:* Sandra Goldbacher. *Screenplay:* Sandra Goldbacher. *Director of Photography:* Ashley Rowe. *Editor:* Isabel Lorente. *Music:* Edward Shearmur. *Choreographer:* Rosy Sanders. *Sound:* Danny Hambrook and (music) Stephen McLaughlin. *Sound Editor:* Jupiter Sen. *Casting:* Michelle Guish.   *Production Designer:* Sarah Greenwood.   *Art Director:* Philip Robinson.   *Set Decorator:* Katie Spencer.   *Special Effects:* Chris Reynolds.   *Costumes:* Caroline Harris. *Make-up:* Veronica Brebner. *Stunt Coordinator:* Nick Powell. *Running time:* 114 minutes. *MPAA Rating:* R.

CAST: Minnie Driver (Rosina Da Silva, "Mary Blackchurch");   Tom Wilkinson (Charles Cavendish);   Florence Hoath (Clementina);   Jonathan Rhys Meyers (Henry); Harriet Walter (Mrs. Cavendish);   Arlene Cockburn (Lily Milk);   Emma Bird (Rebecca);   Adam Levy (Benjamin);   Countess Koulinskyi (Aunt Sofka);   Bruce Myers (Rosina's Father);   Diana Brooks (Rosina's Mother);   Raymond Brody (Litnoff);   Olga (Leonora);   Cyril Shaps (Doctor); Kendal Cramer (Young Rosina); Ralph Riach (Mr. Hewlett); Joe Bromley (Prostitute);   Stephen Robbins (Rabbi).

LOS ANGELES TIMES, 7/31/98, Calendar/p. 16, Kevin Thomas

Sandra Goldbacher's tempestuous "The Governess" tries to tell a "Jane Eyre"-like tale with contemporary sexual candor, but it lacks crucial wit and irony. It affords a terrific role for Minnie Driver, who holds the film together with her talent, star presence and distinctive beauty, yet even she can't save it from its serious shortage of humor and detachment. As a first-time feature writer-director, Goldbacher has an ambitious story to tell but as a director lacks the experience to make it work as effectively as it might have.

Driver plays Rosina Da Silva, the eldest daughter of a Sephardic Jewish family in London in the 1840s. Too headstrong to submit to an arranged marriage after her father is murdered, leaving the family in dire financial straits (yet somehow still able to live in a lavishly appointed townhouse), Rosina is, however, not defiant enough to try for a life in the theater she so craves.

Understanding the bigotry of the times, she decides to call herself Mary Blackchurch and swiftly lands a job as a governess that takes her to the remote Scottish isle of Arran. Her employers, the Cavendishes, are not a happy family. Mrs. Cavendish (Harriet Walter), trapped in a lonely, narrow existence, has become a killjoy martyr, while her husband, Charles (Tom Wilkinson), spends most of his time in his laboratory experimenting on a photographic process.

Mary is to care for their petulant adolescent daughter (Florence Hoath) but, as a bright, ambitious young woman with a background in natural sciences unusual for the era, she is soon Cavendish's lab assistant as well. It's Mary who through chance and intuition hits upon a method for "fixing" Cavendish's photos so they won't fade away. And in turning his camera on Mary, Cavendish becomes turned on by her.

The heart of the film finds Mary and Charles falling in love as they start discovering the transforming potential of the camera. The camera changes Mary into a stunning temptress, a veritable Salome, and when she photographs Charles sleeping in the nude she captures a masculine beauty that he can only regard as profoundly threatening; he's a middle-aged family man already engaged in an adultery that inspires in him a deep self-loathing. Obviously, the situation is as volatile as any chemical in Cavendish's lab, and Goldbacher really lays it on when Cavendish's son (Jonathan Rhys Meyers) is sent down from university in disgrace, only to find himself overwhelmingly attracted to Mary.

A worldly, sophisticated director like Otto Preminger in his prime probably could have saved "The Governess" from escalating into soap opera, viewing human folly with a sort of knowing, bemused compassion. Driver, who steadfastly carries Rosina/Mary through every stormy stage of her self-discovery, is consistently better than the picture, as is Wilkinson, who ironically, here does "the full Monty" in a way he didn't do in the hit picture of the same name.

NEW YORK POST, 7/31/98, p. 44, Thelma Adams

College-educated Jewish women like me can be torn when reading "Emma" or "Jane Eyre." We identify with the heroine, but we can't see ourselves passing in gentile society. How many times can a gal read Sir Walter Scott's "Ivanhoe," one of the rare 19th century novels with a Jewish heroine?

In "The Governess," British writer-director Sandra Goldbacher tries to reconcile this problem—and her own split heritage. Her father was a Sephardic Jew; her mother hailed from the Isle of Skye.

The titular governess is Rosina, which rhymes with Rowena, Ivanhoe's beloved and a gentile. Rebecca is Scott's "Jewess," and Rosina's sister's name.

Rosina Da Silva (Minnie Driver) is an Edwardian Jewish princess. She lives in a tight-knit London Sephardic community. Her world unravels when gentiles murder her father and the heirs discover they are less liquid than their lifestyle demands.

Rosina won't marry a wealthy fishmonger to save the Da Silvas. Instead, she adopts the alias Mary Blackchurch and becomes a governess on the distant Isle of Skye.

Upon arriving at the foreboding Cavendish castle, Rosina finds an assortment of damp Brits: the brooding master (Tom Wilkinson), the perverse pupil (Florence Hoath) and the dissolute scion (cupid-lipped cutie Jonathan Rhys Meyers).

Cavendish, estranged from his kvetchy wife (Harriet Walter), hides out in the laboratory (cue Mary Shelley). When he's not mangling wildlife, he's pioneering a process that will fix photographic images on paper.

Rosina enthusiastically assists Cavendish's experiments. One night, while making a Passover Seder in her room, her ritual salt water splashes on a fading photo. Voila!

The movie then aggressively pursues its romantic roots, adding a '90s frankness that's anachronistic. One minute the two are photographing gulls' wings, the next they're taking nudie photos as foreplay. We see more than Driver's freckles, and the slimmed-down Wilkinson shows us "the full monty" again.

When the sex starts, Driver goes from hot to overheated. As Cavendish tells Mary/Rosina: "Stop this nonsense! This all must stop." We hate to agree with Rochester—er, Cavendish—but it's a reasonable upper-crusty response to a servant so obsessed, she invites her lover to "suck the marrow from my bones." Oy, vey!

NEWSDAY, 7/31/98, Part II/p. B7, John Anderson

"I think the word 'Jewess' must be emblazoned upon my forehead," muses Rosina Da Silva, who loses her father, her virginity and nearly her identity in Sandra Goldbacher's "The Governess." As played by Minnie Driver, Rosina—who heads off to Scotland to pass as a Christian—is armed with a formidable 19th-Century wardrobe, an incongruous set of 20th-Century attitudes and at least one misconception: The word on her forehead is "Actress" and you're not allowed to forget it for a moment.

Does "The Governess" sound like a horror movie? It's not that bad, but director-writer Goldbacher does perpetrate something of a by-the-numbers period improve on the Bronte-Austen genre. Her heroine is endowed with every virtue but money. She's the victim of small-minded thinking. She's meant for greater things than this (whatever this is). But in pronouncedly '90s film fashion, Rosina-cum-Mary-Blackchurch—faux shiksa governess to the Cavendish household—is never part of her time and place. She is, instead, a miraculous anachronism who embodies her creator's petit philosophies while existing thoroughly apart from anything resembling the 19th-Century woman she's supposed to be. As a viewer, you're always perfectly aware that, should things get really tough, she can always go back to her trailer and have a Diet Coke.

That Rosina-Mary is Jewish is rather immaterial; that she's a high-born woman thrust on hard times is more the point. Her religion does come into play via one crucial plot turn, however. As Mary among the Cavendishes—where Mother (Harriet Walter) is wan and frustrated, daughter Clementina (Florence Hoath of "Fairy Tale") is charmingly incorrigible and young Henry (Jonathan Rhys Meyers) seems to be the resident junkie-in-training—she becomes essential to the work of Charles Cavendish (Tom Wilkinson of "The Full Monty"), whose pioneering studies with the primitive camera obscura is tantalizingly close to modern photography.

It is Charles who does the scientific work, but Mary who sees its creative potential (never mind that Vermeer was using camera obscura nearly 200 years earlier). But how to make the images on paper permanent? When Mary holds a bedroom Passover seder for herself, and spills some saltwater on an image, it's eureka time in the Scottish highlands.

However ... there is seldom a moment that's sincere or convincing in "The Governess," thanks largely to Driver's thrust-jawed performance and slack-mouthed Vogue poses. The latter are put to particularly hilarious use when things start developing between her and Cavendish and they shoot a series of biblically inspired "art" shots. Things grow progressively lustier from there. It's difficult not to laugh. In fact, don't try.

SIGHT AND SOUND, 11/98, p. 51, Peter Matthews

London, the 1840s. After her father is murdered, Sephardic Jew Rosina Da Silva becomes the family breadwinner. Rejecting an arranged marriage, Rosina seeks employment as a governess, assuming the gentile sounding alias "Mary Blackchurch" and concocting a tale of half-Italian ancestry. She secures a position with the Cavendish family on a Scottish island. She gradually wins the friendship of her pupil Clementina whose father Charles is engrossed by his experiments in photography while Mrs Cavendish ignores her governess.

Curious about Charles' research, Rosina becomes his assistant. One day she accidentally splashes a photograph with salt water which enables him to fix permanently the images he captures briefly on paper. Charles jubilantly embraces Rosina, and the two embark on a passionate love affair. The Cavendishes' son Henry arrives home and is immediately attracted to "Mary", but he learns her real name and religion. While Charles sleeps, Rosina takes a nude photograph of him, but is shocked by his angry reaction when he sees it. Henry informs Charles of his own feelings for Rosina and reveals her true identity. Charles vengefully takes sole credit for the fixation process when a scientist visits from the Royal Academy. Furious, Rosina resigns, but not before she shows Mrs Cavendish the nude snap of her husband. In London, Rosina learns her mother has died in a cholera epidemic. The surviving Da Silvas set up a photographic studio, specialising in portraits. One day, a contrite Charles drops in. She takes his picture and sends him on his way.

It's far from a bad thing for a filmmaker to show a talent for imagery but it helps if that visual flair is tempered by a bit of common sense. There is a sequence in writer-director Sandra Goldbacher's debut feature *The Governess* that sums up its peculiar strengths and limitations. The scientifically curious Victorian heroine Rosina Da Silva has just stumbled on the chemical agent that will enable photographic images to be fixed permanently on paper: simple salt water. Taking advantage of the story's setting on a picturesque Scottish island, Rosina and her paramour Charles renew their faded prints in the sea. Half the sheets are scattered by the wind, and this mishap allows the director to frame a handsome composition of the lovers scampering across the rugged landscape in eager pursuit. One cannot suppress the profane thought that neither of these geniuses would appear to be acquainted with that useful household innovation, the bucket. However, it's plain that Goldbacher conceives of her shots primarily in graphic terms and isn't too fussed about the prosaic business of motivating them. Pictorially, the movie is never less than sophisticated; only on a dramatic level is it silly.

There are some films (von Sternberg's *The Scarlet Empress*, 1934, or Powell and Pressburger's *Black Narcissus*, 1947) that take stylistic extravagance so far it seems impertinent to complain of their logical lacunae. *The Governess,* however, lacks the authority of true folly. You can see Goldbacher trying out different things—a colour filter here or some speeded-up motion there—but these isolated effects never quite metabolise into a style. Throughout the film, one registers countless finely observed details of locale and atmosphere—the undulating shape formed by the amassed male bodies at a segregated Sabbath or the necrophilic stillness of an upper-class drawing room straight out of Dickens. As perhaps befits someone who's made documentaries, Goldbacher sometimes attains an incredible sensory precision. The chalky texture of a sacred scroll is all but felt on the fingertips, while a Victorian domestic piano grates on the ear with tinny authenticity.

Yet these small triumphs remain inert because nothing organises them into a significant pattern. Goldbacher reportedly began her screenplay in the form of a fictional diary kept on behalf of the title character, and that's how the movie frequently comes across: as a series of loose, dissociated jottings on character and theme. The story's protagonists resemble crib notes for the half dozen most common types encountered in the nineteenth-century English novel: a governess, her weird charge, the arid man of science and his languid, tittering wife and so forth.

What's missing is that iron-clad armature of plot which even the second-rate Victorians could rely on to bring their characters into resonant conflict. It's a double pity that the material feels so half-baked, as it was evidently inspired by Goldbacher's need to explore the warring forces in her own background. But this personal genesis may itself account in part for the movie's slightness. Goldbacher sets up a whole slew of thematic oppositions—Jew versus gentile, tradition versus modernity, art versus science—all neatly resolved in the single person of her heroine.

The miraculous Rosina effortlessly blends the best of every conceivable world, being at once learned and intuitive, practical and sensual, devout and licentious, conservative and liberal. Emerging from the warm cocoon of her Orthodox creed, she proves a phenomenal autodidact—a dab hand at photographic technique and an instant wanton in the bedroom. A vaguely bohemian father is used to explain Rosina's more forward looking side. However, it's clear that so seamless a reconciler of contraries can only exist in myth, or (which amounts to the same thing) in feminist coming of-age movies whose makers don't care to face unpalatable truths.

Goldbacher invites an easy, modern response by eschewing the share of narrowness that would be natural in someone of Rosina's period and circumstances. But it's also clear that the director herself wants to believe in her plausibility, as the character bears all the hallmarks of authorial wish fulfilment. Though it may sound disrespectful of Goldbacher's obvious personal commitment to this movie, *The Governess* really isn't so far removed from Yentl, which was at least brassy and up front in its sentimentalising of the past.

VILLAGE VOICE, 8/4/98, p. 102, Jessica Winter

As tales of sexual awakening go, Sandra Coldbacher's debut film, *The Governess,* is too dirty-minded to fit the Merchant Ivory mold but not salacious enough to quality as bodice-ripping laff riot. Rosina (Minnie Driver) swans her way through a charmed life as the daughter of a wealthy Sephardic Jewish family in 1840s London until her dotting father is murdered by gentile loan sharks. Christening herself Mary Blackchurch, she secures employment as a governess with a Scottish Protestant family. No sooner does Rosina arrive than budding photographer Charles Cavendish (Tom Wilkinson), the family's stuffed-shirt patriarch, finds his inner debauchee; with Rosina as his muse, he embarks on what one can presume is a pioneering career in softcore porn stills.

Driver's cool efficiency, maintained throughout the film's seizures of inexplicable violence and passion, only strands her. Whether she is fixing a glassy gaze upon Charles's leering camera or staring at the ceiling in her boudoir, Driver is self-contained and monumentally bored. Too bad she didn't follow Jonathan Rhys Meyers's lead and give her role the bosom-heaving gusto it deserved: as the horny Cavendish son who pops up Tinkerbell-like whenever Rosina goes on a crying jag, the pouty, saucer-eyed Meyers treats his part as half modeling assignment and half aerobics session. To his credit, he's the only player who can't quite keep a straight face.

Also reviewed in:
CHICAGO TRIBUNE, 8/21/98, Friday/p. D, Michael Wilmington
NEW REPUBLIC, 8/31/98, p. 28, Stanley Kauffmann
NEW YORK TIMES, 7/31/98, p. E2, Stephen Holden
VARIETY, 6/15-21/98, p. 99, Ken Eisner
WASHINGTON POST, 8/14/98, p. D5, Rita Kempley

GREAT EXPECTATIONS

A Twentieth Century Fox release of an Art Linson production.   *Executive Producer:* Deborah Lee.   *Producer:* Art Linson.   *Director:* Alfonso Cuarón.   *Screenplay:* Mitch Glazer.   *Based on the novel by:* Charles Dickens.   *Director of Photography:* Emmanuel Lubezki.   *Editor:* Steven Weisberg.   *Music:* Patrick Doyle.   *Music Editor:* Roy Prendergast and Nicolas Ratner.   *Choreographer:* Julie Arenal.   *Sound:* Tom Nelson and (music) Paul Hulme.   *Sound Editor:* Frank Eulner.   *Casting:* Jill Greenberg.   *Production Designer:* Tony Burrough.   *Art Director:* John Kasarda.   *Set Decorator:* Susan Bode.   *Set Dresser:* Damian J. Costa, Chris Vogt, Bob Vogt, and Dennis Freeborn.   *Special Effects:* Steve Kirshoff.   *Costumes:* Judianna Makovsky.   *Make-up:* Cecelia M. Verardi.   *Make-up (Ethan Hawke):* Manlio Rocchetti.   *Make-up (Gwyneth Paltrow):* Vivian Baker.   *Make-up (Robert De Niro):* Ilona Herman.   *Special Effects Make-up:* Manlio Rocchetti.   *Running time:* 115 minutes.   *MPAA Rating:* R.

CAST: Ethan Hawke (Finnegan "Finn" Bell);   Gwyneth Paltrow (Estella);   Hank Azaria (Walter Plane);   Chris Cooper (Uncle Joe Coleman);   Anne Bancroft (Nora Diggers Dinsmoor); Rober De Niro (Arthur Lustig);   Josh Mostel (Jerry Ragno);   Kim Dickens (Maggie);   Nell Campbell (Erica Thrall);   Gabriel Mick (Owen);   Jeremy James Kissner (Finn Bell, age 10); Raquel Beaudene (Estella, age 10);   Stephen Spinella (Carter Macleish);   Marla Sucharetza (Ruth Shepard);   Isabelle Anderson (Lois Pope);   Peter Jacobson (Man on Phone);   Drena De Niro (Marcy);   Lance Reddick (Anton Le Farge);   Craig Braun (Mr. Barrow);   Kim Snyder (Mrs. Barrow);   Nicholas Wolfert (Security Guard);   Gerry Bamman (Ted Rabinowitz);   Dorin Seymour (Senator Elwood);   Marc Macaulay (Cop on Boat);   Ana Susana Gerardino (Clemma);

Francis DuMaurier (Waiter);   Pedro Barquin (Lover);   Kendall Williamson (7-year-old-girl); Shobha Jain (Singing Indian Woman);   Aditi Jain (Singing Indian Girl);   Margo Peace (Anchor Woman);   Kimmy Suzuki (Waitress);   John P. Casey (Doorman);   Adusah Boakye (Taxi Driver);   Dyan Kane (Gallery Waitress);   Anne Ok (Gallery Receptionist).

CHRISTIAN SCIENCE MONITOR, 1/30/98, p. 16, David Sterritt

Most recent movies based on classic literature, from "Sense and Sensibility" to "Mary Shelley's Frankenstein," have stayed true to the time of the original story.

But there's another tradition that runs in the opposite direction: the Hollywood Update, moving a tale from bygone times to the present. Recent examples include "Clueless," based on "Emma" by Jane Austen, and "Romeo & Juliet," in which the star-crossed lovers are undone by a late Fedex delivery.

The first three versions of "Great Expectations," made between 1934 and 1974, fall into the first category, taking Charles Dickens's novel on its own terms. The new edition, starring Ethan Hawke and Gwyneth Paltrow, is an Update with a vengeance.

Once a poor English marsh-dweller, Pip is now Finn, a would-be artist who travels from Florida to Manhattan in search of fame and fortune. Estella is still a strong-minded young woman, but a modern American context makes her seem more willful and whimsical than ever. The mysterious Magwitch becomes a death-row convict with a knack for jailbreaking, and Miss Havisham develops a taste for music and campy outfits.

What's going on here? Nothing but Hollywood's perennial search for a sensational story to showcase its loveliest young talents. Hawke and Paltrow are as lovely as they come, and director Alfonso Cuarón loses no chance to fill the screen with their charms.

This gives stargazers ample opportunity to savor the images of two current Hollywood favorites. It also indulges the season's most rapidly aging cliché: the nude sketching scene, already overdone in "Titanic" and "As Good as It Gets."

Cuarón is a gifted director, as he showed in "A Little Princess," one of the most undervalued family films of the '90s. The visual style of "Great Expectations" doesn't have as much magical impact, but it has enough energy and inventiveness to give the picture a fair amount of cinematic flair.

What it doesn't have is a literate screenplay. Dickens's novel is a continual feast of imaginative storytelling, compassionate character-building, and hugely entertaining dialogue. Mitch Glazer's script is a pale shadow by comparison, with limply written scenes—an art-gallery confrontation between the Pip character and his uncle is almost embarrassing to watch—and little indication of why the filmmakers chose the Update treatment to begin with.

In the leading roles, Hawke and Paltrow look so nice that demands for excellent acting seem beside the point. In the supporting cast, Robert De Niro shows little involvement with the shadowy character he plays, and Chris Cooper is defeated by the weak dialogue he has to deliver. Anne Bancroft's over-the-top acting has nothing to do with any Miss Havisham you've ever seen, but she gives needed momentum to the picture.

The best technical credits are Emmanuel Lubezki's colorful camera work and the tuneful music by Patrick Doyle. Like others connected with this "Great Expectations," he'd do well to stay with period pieces for a while. It's safer and sounder all around.

LOS ANGELES TIMES, 1/30/98, Calendar/p. 1, Kenneth Turan

Despite the occasional wounded cry from critics, updating a classic piece of literature for the screen is not a crime against nature. Not even when, as is the case with "Great Expectations," a superb film version of the story already exists.

For every reader who's enjoyed the irresistible Charles Dickens novel, for every film buff who's seen the splendid 1946 David Lean-directed interpretation, there are much greater numbers who've never so much as heard of the story of the ever-striving Pip, the convict Magwitch, the reclusive Miss Havisham and the unattainable Estella. And as Baz Luhrmanh's unchained version of "William Shakespeare's Romeo & Juliet" proved a few years ago, adding a contemporary sensibility to venerable material can accomplish a great deal.

But to succeed, a modern version has to know what it's about and be able to carry its own weight. Change is not sacrilege, but losing the spark that animated the original is. Unable to decide how serious it should be or how close to the source it can safely remain, the latest "Great Expectations" suffers from being neither here nor there. In its rush to modernize its story and attract a young audience with stars like Ethan Hawke and Gwyneth Paltrow, the film ends up problematic both in relation to the original and on its own terms.

As written by Mitch Glazer and directed by Alfonso Cuaron, this "Great Expectations" does convincingly move its story from London and vicinity to the Gulf Coast of Florida and glamorous New York. With expert Mexican cinematographer Emmanuel Lubezki (who also shot Cuaron's "A Little Princess," "A Walk in the Clouds" and "Like Water for Chocolate") doing the honors, this film has a lush, pictorial quality that is always inviting.

Growing up on that bucolic coast is a dreamy boy named Finn, well-played by young Jeremy James Kissner. Finn nominally lives with his sister but is closer to her fisherman boyfriend, Joe ("Lone Star's" Chris Cooper), who affably encourages the boy's desire to be an artist.

The larger world startlingly intrudes on these quiet lives with two unrelated incidents. A terrifying escaped convict (Robert De Niro) comes upon the boy and demands help with his chains. And something about Finn catches the eye of the eccentric Nora Dinsmoor, the richest woman on the coast, whose mind was unhinged when her fiancé left her at the altar 30 years before.

Paradiso Perduto, Dinsmoor's wonderland of a house on a wildly overgrown estate, is given a fine brooding look by production designer Tony Burrough, who did the near-contemporary "Richard III" starring Ian McKellen. But though she is made up to be as dilapidated as her surroundings, Anne Bancroft's Ms. Dinsmoor is not a success.

Choosing Bancroft, who has made over-the-top portrayals something of a habit in recent years, to play a woman who is extravagantly mad is asking for trouble. Wildly dressed, gesturing grandly with a cigarette holder and muttering things like "chicka-boom, chicka-boom" to various recorded versions of "Besame Mucho," Bancroft makes Ms. Dinsmoor the one thing she really shouldn't be, which is silly. Even worse, her excessiveness has been allowed to set the film's tone in a fatally off-putting way.

True to the novel, Finn meets the woman's young but already beautiful niece Estella (Raquel Beuadene), whom the vengeful Dinsmoor is raising to be a cold and effective enemy to all men. Naturally, Finn falls in love with her, a feeling that doesn't lessen when he grows up into Ethan Hawke and she into Gwyneth Paltrow.

Given that Finn is a poor fisherman and the haughty Estella is soon packed off to one of those European finishing schools, the better to ensure, says her aunt, that "she'll cut through [men] like a hot knife through butter," any chance of Finn's romantic dreams coming true seems limited.

But then a lawyer named Jerry Ragno (Josh Mostel) appears, announcing a secret benefactor who wants to make some of Finn's dreams come true, wants to ensure his success as an artist in the heady world of New York. Not sure who "wants to turn this frog into a prince" but suspecting Dinsmoor, Finn goes to Manhattan, where he spends his time looking cute in jeans, painting up a storm and, yes, pursuing the gorgeous Estella, who just happens to be in town.

Despite its glamorous and photogenic cast, "Great Expectations" has difficulty using its people effectively. Hawke gives the adult Finn an appealing innocence, but there is something excessively hangdog about the way he moons over the object of his affections. And though the ice-cold beauty of Estella can account for Finn's open-mouthed quality, Paltrow's is also a performance lacking in dimension. The result is that the passion that supposedly exists between these two never shows up on screen.

This is especially problematic because the film's clunky exposition alters the balance that made both the book and the still-vibrant Lean-directed adaptation so successful. Yes, "Great Expectations" is about undying love, but it should also be just as much about loyalty, maturity and the lessons life teaches. Those qualities are touched on, but in its rush to exhibit Paltrow in the sexiest manner possible and focus on the more salable romance angle, the film gives these less glamorous factors too short shrift. As the Hollywood Reporter headlined in a story about the "Great Expectations" movie tie-in novel, the filmmakers were probably thinking "Who needs Charles Dickens when Gwyneth Paltrow's lying around naked?" The answer is right there on the screen: Everyone.

NEW STATESMAN, 4/17/98, p. 44, Chris Peachment

A good word for *Great Expectations*, a modern update of the Dickens classic which, like *Clueless*, Amy Heckerling's version of *Emma*, proves that you can better illuminate the classics through imaginative reworking than with respectful costume drama. Ethan Hawke is the Pip figure, a po' white southern boy with a talent for painting. De Niro is a good choice for the shady Magwitch, who provides the wherewithal for the boy's entrée into the corrupt New York art scene. Gwyneth Paltrow will break your heart just as she does Ethan's.

NEW YORK POST, 1/30/98, p. 37, Michael Medved

If you don't think about the Dickens classic that inspired it, and you know nothing about the magnificent David Lean adaptation of 1946, then you can come to the handsome but hokey star vehicle "Great Expectations" without great expectations. And chances are that you will enjoy it.

In this ingeniously updated version, the story centers on a sensitive lad on the Florida Gulf Coast growing up with his sister and her earthy, tender-hearted fisherman boyfriend (the splendid Chris Cooper, of "Lone Star").

One day, the boy is brutally surprised by a desperate convict (Robert De Niro, formidably fierce) who demands his aid in an escape from prison; but an even more painful assault comes from a rich, eccentric, old lady (Anne Bancroft) who commands that he visit every Saturday.

She introduces the little dickens to her haughty, beautiful niece, Estella, and expects the girl to break his heart—in retribution for the aged woman's having been jilted by her bridegroom some 30 years before.

Gwyneth Paltrow plays the grown-up Estella, and her languorous, smoldering, incomparably seductive performance quite simply makes the movie. No one can blame the adult hero (the likably befuddled Ethan Hawke) for his obsession with this mysterious, manipulative, maddeningly unattainable woman—especially after she insists on posing nude for the aspiring artist.

Mexican director Alfonso Cuaron brought a "magic realism," fairy-tale atmosphere to his justly acclaimed film "A Little Princess," and the same approach works wonders here: "Great Expectations" unfolds like a lush, lavishly romantic fable.

Haunting music by Patrick Doyle and flavorful, exotic, screen-filling camera work by Emmanuel Lubezki ("Like Water for Chocolate") also contribute to the feverish, fateful, ain't-love-strange atmosphere.

Unlike the previous Dickens update by screenwriter Mitch Glazer (Bill Murray's misbegotten "Scrooged"), "Great Expectations" lets you forget about the source, never hitting you over the head with its ingenious variations on the Victorian original.

Earlier in our own century, incandescent actresses such as Greta Garbo and Marlene Dietrich proved that sheer glamour could carry even the most unlikely material, and in this oddly endearing bit of cinematic excess, Gwyneth Paltrow exceeds expectations by making the same point.

NEWSDAY, 1/30/98, Part II/p. B7, Jack Mathews

The story sounds familiar. An impoverished orphan does an escaped convict a kind deed, and years later the convict becomes that man's anonymous benefactor. Overnight, he is a person of means, free to pursue the elusive woman with whom he's been in love since early childhood.

It is, of course, Charles Dickens' "Great Expectations," the story of the good-hearted orphan Pip, his comical, aristocratic heartthrob Estella, her eccentric aunt Miss Havisham and the shadowy thief Magwitch. Only here, the setting is South Florida and Manhattan, and it is a century later. The orphan is now Finn (Ethan Hawke), his tormentor is still Estella (Gwyneth Paltrow), her weird aunt is Miss Dinsmoor (Anne Bancroft), and the convict is Lustig (Robert De Niro, rising from the sea, like Max Cady in "Cape Fear").

Dickens' 1861 novel about British classism and romantic longing has been adapted several times for the screen, most notably by David Lean in 1946. But the new version, by the Mexican director Alfonso Cuaron ("The Little Princess"), has the audacity to stretch the story's wings in the contemporary United States, and it lands with a jarring thud.

Adapting Shakespeare's "Romeo and Juliet" as a fantasy in contemporary Florida, as Baz Luhrmann recently did, makes some sense. That story of unconditional, dying love translates to any culture, in any period. But "Great Expectations" is one of Dickens' most homebound novels; it is so intricately related to 19th-Century British society that it can only travel with full meaning to a culture equally class conscious.

Americans only think we're class conscious. It's one thing to put an "Eat the rich!" sticker on your refrigerator, it's another to consider the rich a delicacy. And so we have in Cuaron's "Great Expectations," a fantasy without foundation, a story that presumes class barriers where they don't exist.

Cuaron, with a script by Mitch Glazer whose previous foray into Dickens was the comedy "Scrooged," acknowledges the difficulty in adapting the material by having Finn's off-screen voice warn us in the beginning that the story we're about to get exists in his memory, not necessarily in fact.

With that caveat, Cuaron attempts to have it both ways, creating what seems to be a story firmly planted in reality, but whose follies may be taken as blurred reminiscence. As they say in the South, where his "Great Expectations" begins, that dog won't hunt.

The film's leisurely opening introduces us to the young Finn (Jeremy James Kissner), a budding artist, his restless sister Maggie (Kim Dickens, no relation), and her jovial live-in companion Joe (Chris Cooper), who share a run-down upstairs flat in a shrimp village on the coast. Shortly after his encounter with Lustig, Finn is recruited by the batty Nora Dinsmoor, who looks like a combination of Blanche DuBois and Baby Jane, to entertain her and her lonely niece Estella (Raquel Beaudene).

Miss Dinsmoor, we learn through Bancroft's hammy speeches, was left a virginal bride at the altar 30 years earlier, and her bitterness toward men has been deeply imprinted on Estella. The girl seems to live to taunt Finn, to tease him with her interest and then withdraw.

In a nice dissolve that you may have seen in the film's trailer, Finn and Estella go from children to young adults dancing at Miss Dinsmoor's pleasure across a leaf-strewn patio. But the game's the same, and the night before Estella leaves for Paris, she leads Finn to the heated brink of consummation, only to casually walk away, uttering something about having a nice life. There's a name for this, probably used even in Dickens' day, but Finn, who is thickheaded if nothing else, continues to pine for Estella.

Then comes the windfall. A stranger from New York visits Finn and tells him he has a patron willing to support him while he prepares for a major art exhibition in Manhattan. Knowing that Estella is living there, and figuring that Miss Dinsmoor is his secret benefactor, Finn heads north, to fulfill his destiny—or have his heart broken in the process.

Hawke and Paltrow make a nice couple, but not a very believable one. Paltrow is stuck with the worst stereotype, the Victorian femme fatale, but as Miss Dinsmoor, Bancroft sets a standard in overacting that's going to be hard to top through the rest of the year. Even De Niro has a shaky time with the material.

If you're a fan of "Great Expectations," the book or any of the previous screen adaptations, see this version with no expectations at all.

NEWSWEEK, 2/2/98, p. 61, David Ansen

Alphonso Cuarón's "Great Expectations" has two tough acts to follow: Dickens's great Victorian novel and David Lean's stunning 1947 movie. I'm sure no one will be shocked to hear that this American update, reset on Florida's Gulf Coast and in the 1980s SoHo art world, is unlikely to erase one's memories of either. But don't dismiss it out of hand. Cuarón, as he demonstrated in "The Little Princess," is an authentic movie lyricist; his wildly romantic "Great Expectations," while not a total success, produces its own share of memorably enchanted moments.

Most of the names have been changed, but the framework is pure Dickens. The orphan Pip has become the orphan Finn (Ethan Hawke), now endowed with a gift for drawing. The escaped convict Magwitch is now Arthur Lustig (Robert De Niro), wanted for a gangland killing. Miss Havisham has turned into Anne Bancroft's mad Ms. Dinsmoor, the richest woman in the gulf, who lost her mind when she was stood up at the altar at the age of 42 and has vowed to take revenge on the male species. The agency of her revenge is still named Estella (Gwyneth Paltrow), the pampered beauty raised to break men's hearts, whom Finn falls hopelessly in love with when he is 10 years old.

This love story is the new version's raison d'être. The novel may have been about its hero's moral education, but Mitch Glazer's screenplay narrows the focus considerably. Will Estella come to her senses and realize that Finn is her only hope of happiness? This may be a seriously reductionist reading of Dickens, but when you have two stars as sexy as Hawke and Paltrow, and a director with an eye as sensually charged as Cuarón's, why not succumb to the pleasure principle? This is one dreamy movie, lusciously designed by Tony Burrough (Ms. Dinsmoor's mansion is a tropical Gothic delight) and beautifully shot by Emmanuel Lubezld. Cuarón tells Finn's story as a fable, bypassing reality for the heightened style of selective memory: even the streets of Manhattan seem burnished with a fairy-tale glow.

Turning the hero into a rising star in the New York art scene (his striking paintings are by Francesco Clemente) has its problems. His naiveté made sense in the 19th century; in these hip environs he can seem a bit dim, awfully slow to catch on to Estella's twisted games. Nonetheless, the heat that Paltrow and Hawke generate—not to mention the fun of Bancroft's performance—is its own seductive reward. "Great Expectations" has great style; that's not everything we want from the movies, but sometimes it's almost enough.

SIGHT AND SOUND, 5/98, p. 44, John Wrathall

Florida. Young Finn Bell is surprised by a runaway convict, Lustig, who terrifies him into helping him escape. Later, when Finn accompanies his sister's handyman husband Joe to Paradiso Perduto, the mansion of elderly recluse Miss Dinsmoor, he meets her niece Estella. At Miss Dinsmoor's request, Finn starts to visit every week. She encourages him to draw and teaches him to dance with Estella. As the years go by, Finn falls n love with Estella who toys with him, then leaves for Paris without a word. Miss Dinsmoor tells him that, since she was jilted on her wedding day years earlier, she has brought up Estella as her revenge on men.

Seven years later, a lawyer turns up and offers Finn a chance to show his art in New York. Finn flies there, starts drawing again and meets Estella. She models for him, and his work improves. Estella gets engaged to another man, Walter Plane. At the opening of Finn's one-man show, all his paintings are sold, but Estella doesn't show up. He meets Miss Dinsmoor, whom he assumed was his benefactor. She tells him that Estella has now left on her honeymoon. Returning to his studio, Finn meets an old man who is being chased by gangsters and asks if he can come inside. He reveals that he, Lustig, has been Finn's benefactor all along, and has bought all his paintings. Finn helps him escape from his pursuers, but they catch up with Lustig on a subway train and stab him. He dies in Finn's arms.

Years later, Finn returns to the now derelict Paradiso Perduto, and meets Estella, a mother but now divorced from Walter. Finn and Estella hold hands and look out to sea.

In contrast with Peter Carey's recent novel *Jack Maggs,* which also took Charles Dickens' *Great Expectations* as its inspiration, Alfonso Cuarón's adaptation uses the bare bones of the plot but radically changes the setting. This might seem a perverse way to tackle Dickens, a writer whose vivid evocation of place and social milieu has generally lasted better than his coincidence-laden plots. However, Cuarón manages to do for *Great Expectations* what Baz Luhrmann did for *Romeo and Juliet,* invigorating a much-adapted classic with a captivating barrage of late-90s style. The result, if light on Dickens, is far more exciting than one can imagine a straight version being.

After starting his career in Mexico, Cuarón earned his Hollywood spurs with a hugely imaginative version of the American children's classic *A Little Princess,* relocated to New York during World War One. Working again with cinematographer Emmanuel Lubezki, his eye for mysterious, fairy-tale imagery is just as striking here. Miss Dinsmoor's mansion Paradiso Perduto, for instance, is a crumbling Moorish palace smothered by creepers, quite as magical a setting as the remembered, studio-generated India of *A Little Princess.* David Lean's immortal version of the opening scene where Magwitch (now Lustig) pounces on Pip (now Finn) might seem a hard act to follow, but Cuarón gives the convict an equally startling entrance. As Finn searches in a shallow lagoon for fish to draw, he suddenly glimpses the submerged figure of Lustig in his orange prison uniform, surging up out of the water to grab him.

Throughout, the director finds playful, surprising visual ways to tell the story. Finn's journey to New York is deftly evoked with the help of a toy plane and a Manhattan subway map. Later on, there's an extraordinary moment where Finn looks up into the night sky and we soar through the clouds with his gaze, until we reach the aeroplane which is taking Estella away.

Almost uniquely for a fictional artist in a Hollywood film, Finn actually produces genuinely good paintings, huge slightly distorted portraits with strong, clean lines. (Compare, for instance, the sub-pavement-artist efforts of the Leonardo DiCaprio character in *Titanic,* which surely wouldn't have cut much ice with a girl who'd just bought herself a Picasso.) The high point of the film is a tantalising scene—breathtakingly edited to the music of Pulp—where Estella toys with Finn, stripping for him as he frantically sketches her, then flouncing out and leaving him in a state of creative *coitus interruptus.* In passing, the film neatly satirises the New York art world, with Manhattan club guru Nell Campbell (last best known as an Antipodean punk in Derek Jarman's *Jubilee)* sending herself up as the gallery owner who takes Finn under her wing. On the theme of art as a potentially soul-destroying means of social climbing, the film is more interesting than *Basquiat,* and has only a fraction of the self-indulgence.

The downside of Cuarón's directorial flair and perfect taste, however, is a lack of emotional weight. True, as Estella, Gwyneth Paltrow shows, for the first time since her debut in *Flesh and Bone,* how much more interesting she can be when allowed to be saucy and faintly nasty. Ethan Hawke, meanwhile, makes a novel, very contemporary sort of Hollywood hero, sensitive to a fault and almost entirely passive. However, Anne Bancroft and Robert De Niro play to the gallery shamelessly. When De Niro reappears late in the day as Lustig, it's almost as if Fagin has wandered in from *Oliver Twist,* and his return prompts a lurch into melodrama that's unconvincing after the sophistication of what has gone before. But until then it's the film's very lightness which confirms Cuarón as probably the most graceful director to emerge in Hollywood this decade.

VILLAGE VOICE, 2/3/98, p. 122, Michael Atkinson

We're not escaping Penguin Classics cinema anytime soon, and you gotta wonder, is it millennial doubt about the future that's compelling this reactionary trudge through the canon, or are ex-English majors, like computer geeks, taking over? Either way the measure of the movie is hardly in its fidelity to the old book, but in its mind for locating convincing viscera in overfamiliar sagas.

Nothing if not unfaithful, Alfonso Cuarón's courageously lyrical *Great Expectations* hangs like a wet silk shirt on the novel's nearly incidental skeleton, dispensing with Dickens in favor of a childlike, moths-humping-lightbulbs Floridian magical realism that, at least for the first half, transcends literariness and embraces the individually mythic.

Like Cuarón's opalescent *A Little Princess*—my ardor for which, I know, is less than completely rational—*Great Expectations* has its head in the storybook clouds, fixing on images (a boy standing shin-deep in a tidal lagoon sketching the fish at this feet, a pre-pubescent kiss in the arcing waters of a mossy garden fountain, etc.) at the expense of Dickensian plotwork. Cuarón's version rewrites Pip (renamed Finn and filled in after puberty by Ethan Hawke) as Pensacola Bay white trash who helps escaped con Lustig (Robert De Niro), hangs out in the tropically overgrown mansion of old-money bat Ms. Dinsmoor (Anne Bancroft, playing it like Norma Desmond in *Grey Gardens*), and falls hard for the haughty blondness of Estella (an idealized Gwyneth Paltrow, again after puberty).

Like *Titanic,* Cuarón's film fuels the rediscovered fad of nude-portrait-posing-as-foreplay. coming after *William Shakespeare's Rome & Juliet.* the film's subplots are streamlined to make the young romance fly faster, which it unfortunately does: the film's magic dries up once Finn becomes a New York art scene success (albeit solely patronized by Lustig, which Finn doesn't seem to mind), and the stalled end of the story is narrated at us rather than visually manifested. Still, for much of *Great Expectations,* it's as if Maxfield Parrish were alive and making Hollywood films, and there's no undervaluing Cuarón's overwhelmingly rueful sense that the men and women we all love were little, hopeful boys and girls once. It's a pity *Great Expectations* gets lost in adulthood.

Also reviewed in:
CHICAGO TRIBUNE, 1/30/98, Friday/p. A, Michael Wilmington
NEW REPUBLIC, 3/2/98, p. 26, Stanley Kauffmann
NEW YORK TIMES, 1/30/98, p. E10, Janet Maslin
VARIETY, 1/19-25/98, p. 88, Todd McCarthy
WASHINGTON POST, 1/30/98, p. D1, Rita Kempley
WASHINGTON POST, 1/30/98, Weekend/p. 48, Desson Howe

HALF BAKED

A Universal Pictures release of a Robert Simonds production.   *Producer:* Robert Simonds.
Director: Tamra Davis.   *Screenplay:* Dave Chappelle and Neal Brennan.   *Director of Photography:* Steven Bernstein. *Editor:* Don Zimmerman. *Music:* Alf Clausen. *Music Editor:* J.J. George. *Sound:* Owen Langevin and (music) Rick Ricco. *Sound Editor:* Gary S. Gerlich and Richard LeGrand, Jr. *Casting:* Joanna Colbert. *Production Designer:* Perry Andelin Blake. *Art Director:* Paul Austerberry. *Set Decorator:* Mark Lane. *Set Dresser:* Brian Patrick and Brenton Brown. *Special Effects:* Martin Malivoire, Dean Stewart, and Bob Hall. *Visual Effects:* Richard Mazahn. *Costumes:* Vicki Graef. *Make-up:* Inge Klaudi. *Running time:* 90 minutes. *MPAA Rating:* R.

CAST: Dave Chappelle (Thurgood); Guillermo Diaz (Scarface); Jim Breuer (Brian); Harland Williams (Kenny); Rachel True (Mary Jane); Clarence Williams III (Samson Simpson); Dave Chappelle (Sir Smoka Lot); Laura Silverman (Jan); Tommy Chong (Squirrel Master); R. D. Reid (Scientist); Gregg Rogell and Kevin Brennan (Potheads); Alice Poon (Supply Clerk); Rick Demas (Nasty Nate); David Bluestein (Jerry Garcia); Kevin Duhaney (Young Thurgoood); Matthew Raposo (Young Scarface); James Cooper (Young Brian); Michael Colton (Young Kenny); Paul Brogren (Burger Customer); Neal Brennan (Employee); Karen Waddell (Record Store Employee); Vincent Marino (Bodega Man); Domencio "Macio" Parrilla and Marcus Burrowes (Rasta Men); Mark Henriques (Delivery Guy); Jenni Burke (Overweight Woman); Gwenne Hudson (Bong Genie); David Mucci (Horse Cop); Reg Dreger (Judge); Kevin Rushton (Inmate); Paul Saunders (Doorman); Ho Chow (Hot Dog Vendor); Rummy Bishop (Homeless Guy); Jon Stewart (Enhancement Smoker); Snoop Doggy Dogg (Scavenger Smoker); Stephen Baldwin (McGuyver Smoker); Marc Cohen (McGuyver Friend); Tracy Morgan (V.J.); David Edwards (Addict); Paulino Nunes (Swat Cop); Jason Blicker and Dave Nichols (Detectives); Sharon Brown (Talking Joint); Christopher Mugglebee and Raymond Hinton (Security Guards); David Sutcliffe (After School Dad); Daniel De Santo (After School Son); Gladys O'Connor (Grandma Smoker); Willie Nelson (Historian Smoker).

LOS ANGELES TIMES, 1/19/98, Calendar/p. 8, Bob Heisler

[The following review by Bob Heisler appeared in a slightly different form in
NEWSDAY, 1/19/98, Part II/p. B11.]

It's time to rethink the influence of television on American cinema. Specifically, the role "Saturday Night Live" has played in killing comedy movies.

Unfortunate Exhibit A: "Half Baked," a mirthless, stoned-buddy movie starring marijuana, vs Chappelle and "SNL" player Jim Breuer, based on the notion that a scattering of cultural references and over-the-top characters can sustain a one-joke plot.

Chappelle is the only spark of life here, perhaps because he co-wrote it, and plays the only weed-head with half a brain and an ounce of motivation. He gives evidence of having an interesting, nervous kind of movie energy. But yo, yo, yo, Dave. Weren't you hip, man? What are you doing involved in this limp, predictable less-than-sitcom of a movie. It's a bomb, man, not the bomb. If you think this is what you have to do to get major multiplex screen time, you're reading the wrong press clippings.

"Half Baked," which Universal Pictures did not screen for critics, is billed as a Cheech & Chong movie for the '90s, as if every decade demanded one. The film finds a grass-blowing trio engaged in selling drugs—yes, even to children—to raise bail money for a fourth roommate in prison for killing a police horse.

Who knew the horse was diabetic and couldn't handle a couple of shopping bags full of sweets intended as munchies? This allows us to meet a handful of cameo smokers including Snoop Doggy (dope-rapper Sir Smoka Lot) Dogg, Willie "In the Old Days, a Dime Bag Cost a Dime" Nelson and Janeane "I Can't Write Poetry Until I Get High" Garofalo. Steven Wright wakes up briefly as the Guy on the Couch.

To spare you the search for a moral to this smoky, tie-dyed tale, there are two ways to take "Half Baked." You can be outraged that a major studio still thinks pot is funny enough to sustain a movie—including a scene in which our friends try a particularly potent toke and seem to fly out the window to good vibrations. Or you can be certain that anyone who sees the sad losers involved in this enterprise will never smoke anything again.

At just under 90 minutes, "Half Baked" seemed to take a lot longer. Days and days, man.

NEW YORK POST, 1/17/98, p. 19, Larry Worth

More often than not, the name of a film means little or nothing. But "Half Baked" is more than a title; it's a pithy critique.

Specifically, a lot of good ideas and funny jokes surface in this potential throwaway about four guys who live to get stoned. Sadly, their highs aren't maintained.

The central quartet is undeniably talented: Up-and-coming comedian Dave Chappelle, "Saturday Night Live" regular Jim Breuer, "Party Girl" veteran Guillermo Diaz and Harland ("Wag the Dog") Williams.

By playing a group of twentysomethings whose existence centers on their beloved water pipe—nicknamed Billy Bong Thornton—the boys get unexpected mileage from updated takes on Cheech and Chong. (Tommy Chong acknowledges as much in a brief supporting role.)

The semi-plot kicks in when a toked-out Williams feeds his munchies to a diabetic police horse, subsequently going to the big house as a cop killer.

To raise bail, his pals home deliver some evil weed to a clientele ranging from Willie Nelson to Janeane Garofalo to Stephen Baldwin to Jon Stewart to Snoop Doggy Dogg (all of whom contribute amusing cameos).

Less amusing, by a long shot, is Chappelle's growing ardor for fierce anti-druggie Rachel ("The Craft") True. As the unfortunately named Mary Jane, the actress' contributions are labored at best.

A bigger problem is the generally lackluster direction from Tamra Davis (of "Billy Madison" notoriety). Aside from killing any sense of pacing, she's a sucker for recycling cliches.

Typical is a scene wherein Breuer imitates Tom Cruise being fired as "Jerry Maguire." All too obvious by that point is Davis' show-me-the-money attitude toward "Half Baked."

Also reviewed in:
CHICAGO TRIBUNE, 1/22/98, Tempo/p. 8, Lawrence Van Gelder
NEW YORK TIMES, 1/17/98, p. B16, Lawrence van Gelder
VARIETY, 1/26-2/1/98, p. 66, Brendan Kelly

HALLELUJAH! RON ATHEY: A STORY OF DELIVERANCE

An Artistic License Films release.   *Producer:* Catherine Gund Saalfield.   *Director:* Catherine Gund Saalfield.   *Screenplay:* Catherine Gund Saalfield.   *Director of Photography:* Catherine Gund Saalfield. *Editor:* Aljernon Tunsil.   *Sound Editor:* Margaret Crimmons and Paul Hsu. *Running time:* 90 minutes. *MPAA Rating:* Not Rated.

WITH: Ron Athey; Vaginal Davis; Julie Tolentino Wood; Darryl Carlton; Johanna Went; Cathy Opie; Lawrence Steger; Franko B.; James Stone; Alex Binnie; Julie Fowells; Brian Murphy; Katia Esperanza; Mario Kovac; Russell McEwan; Theresa Saso.

LOS ANGELES TIMES, 12/4/98, Calendar/p. 10, Kevin Thomas

It's hard to think of anyone who puts the redemptive power of art to the test more severely than performance artist Ron Athey, who works out his Pentecostal upbringing, his former heroin addiction, his homosexuality and his HIV status in increasingly elaborate—and increasingly meaningful—tableaux vivants in which sadomasochistic practices act as a force of liberation from society's oppressiveness and also from the fear of death.

Catherine Gund Saalfield's absorbing 90-minute "Hallelujah! Ron Athey: A Story of Deliverance" offers a strong insight into why Athey has become a vital cultural force. Saalfield interviews not only Athey but also members of his large troupe, who are as much outsiders as he is.

The film includes generous portions of the troupe in performance in such far-flung locales as Mexico City and Zagreb, where Athey's "Deliverance," a deeply moving coming to terms with death, was presented—and which may be too expensive ever to be staged again anywhere. (It is the concluding segment of Athey's trilogy, which includes "Martyrs and Saints" and "Four Scenes in a Harsh Life," portions of which are also shown.)

Athey is a chunky man of 36 who has covered much of his body with striking tattoos, as have many of his colleagues. Athey explains his urge to perform grew out of his love of dancing in clubs and it started to find expression once he discovered seminal performance artist Johanna Went.

What Athey does is to evoke some of the harsher Christian iconography and infuses it with ceremonial body piercing and modifications, sometimes involving sex and bodily functions and much of which is surely too strong for many audiences. He incorporates dramatic vignettes, dance and movement that results in spectacles as powerful, for example, as the Living Theater's famous "Frankenstein."

At this stage of his artistic development Athey creates tableaux vivants as rich in texture and detail as those in the films of Sergei Paradjanov. What Athey has become is an exorcist, taking on the demons of drugs, homophobia, fear of AIDS, racism and the degradation of women, and his vision has become strong enough to transcend the repulsion most of us surely feel in regard to sadomasochism. As one of his colleagues so aptly defines his work: "They're rituals of identity and freedom."

NEW YORK POST, 12/11/98, p. 66, Rod Dreher

Ron Athey is a pierced and tattooed weirdo whose only talent, aside from self-promotion, seems to be in shoving things into his body and calling it art.

Whether it's needles under the skin of his skull in a blasphemous representation of Christ's passion or various substances into his rectum (which appears to have contained more foreign objects than your neighborhood Pier 1), the extravagantly untalented Athey is impressive only in his ability to take himself with complete seriousness.

Actually, he's not the only one. The blocky, bald-headed creep is a big deal in the performance art world, which says a lot more about the standards of that lot than it does about Athey's dubious gifts.

To the cognoscenti, Athey, a homosexual, is a revolutionary artist brilliantly expressing the pain and alienation he feels from his religious upbringing. Most others would likely see him as merely a very silly man with a chronic and extremely bizarre case of adolescent rage.

Catherine Gund Saalfield, the filmmaker behind the performance documentary "Hallelujah! Ron Athey: A Story of Deliverance," is in the pro-Athey camp. Her crudely shot film features interviews with Athey and members of his torture-loving troupe, as well as extended excerpts from his revolting performances. Athey talks about having been raised in a Pentecostal sect but finding his true calling within the Los Angeles sadomasochistic community.

He came to national prominence several years ago when a brouhaha at a Minneapolis performance involving his HIV-tainted blood revealed just what manner of weirdness the National

Endowment for the Arts was paying for. It sparked an enormous controversy on Capitol Hill at a time when the arts agency was fighting for its life.

Inexplicably, Saalfield spends only a few minutes on that episode, which made Athey famous (or notorious, depending on your point of view), and never talks to anyone involved in the controversy other than Athey and his crowd—this in keeping with the worshipful tone of the film.

"Hallelujah!" reveals more about the depths of human depravity than most of us will be able to stand (though Athey's unspeakable acts of self-mutilation do put his comment about the God-sized hole in his soul in an interesting light). The sicko exhibitionist gets misty-eyed reminiscing about the ghastly thing a friend did to his own private parts. Athey re-creates the act in a touching stage tribute to his now-dead friend, inserting an IV needle into an assistant's scrotum and swelling it with fluid until it's as red and round as a pomegranate.

Later, this Michelangelo of the fin de siecle receives an enema on stage and evacuates his bowels into a clear bucket for the audience's entertainment and edification.

I confess that I left this repulsive movie during the oral-anal, um, climax involving a limber assistant and a giant, salami-sized leather phallus. Some people are more capable than others of suffering for art.

VILLAGE VOICE, 12/8/98, p. 129, Michael Atkinson

In terms of performance art's potential for flabbergasting bullshit in the name of "transgression," Ron Athey tries and in a sense succeeds at beating all comers—an apparently fearless, gay, massively tattooed, HIV-positive thunder god of sadistic ritual and preposterous self-absorption who puts himself through Christ-like torture sessions onstage. Talk about ego. By the evidence given in Catherine Gund Saalfield's crude video portrait, *Hallelujah!*, which chronicles Athey's career from Pentecostal cherub to s/m-loving club boy to bloodletting auteur, Athey's aesthetic consists mostly of self-inflicted flesh wounds.

Athey himself is quite articulate, though with respect to Sick, another self-abusive-artist biopic, he is not by any stretch Bob Flanagan, whose debilitating congenital illness and knifelike sense of humor lent his act a redemptive grace. For all his theorizing, Athey comes off most convincingly as a happy theater nerd, chatting up his stage design and lighting, and going giddy over European perf-art spaces. He may justify the lacerations (of himself and others) as quasi-liturgical tribulation, but the onstage double-ended-dildo ass fuck, and subsequent suck, is tough to swallow as resonant self-expression. Saalfield's talking heads (coworkers, cast members, et cetera) are all engaged in a hard sell for Athey, but there isn't an artistic idea in sight that looms a tenth as high as Athey's arrested desire to piss in his parents' shoes. The heritage of midcentury Middle American religious fanaticism that Athey cites as his source is much more interesting, and the vestiges of it on view more mysterious and terrifying. But who needs a subject, when you can stick needles into your skull?

Also reviewed in:
NEW YORK TIMES, 12/11/98, p. E27, Stephen Holden
VARIETY, 3/9-15/98, p. 48, David Rooney

HALLOWEEN: H2O

A Dimension Films release of a Moustapha Akkad presentation of a Nightfall production. *Executive Producer:* Moustapha Akkad. *Producer:* Paul Freeman. *Director:* Steve Miner. *Screenplay:* Robert Zappia and Matt Greenberg. *Story (Based on characters created by Debra Hill and John Carpenter):* Robert Zappia. *Director of Photography:* Daryn Okada. *Editor:* Patrick Lusser. *Music:* John Ottman. *Music Editor:* Amanda Goodpaster, George Martin, and David Slusser. *Sound:* Jim Tanenbaum and (music) Casey Stone. *Sound Editor:* Frank Eulner. *Casting:* Ross Brown, Mary West, and Christine Sheaks. *Production Designer:* John Willett. *Art Director:* Dawn Snyder. *Set Designer:* Thomas Reta and Dawn Swiderski. *Set Decorator:* Beau Petersen. *Special Effects:* John Hartigan. *Costumes:* Deborah Everton. *Make-up:* Tania

McComas. *Stunt Coordinator:* Donna Keegan. *Running time:* 92 minutes. *MPAA Rating:* R.

CAST: Jamie Lee Curtis (Laurie Stode/Keri Tate); Adam Arkin (Will); Josh Hartnett (John); Michelle Williams (Molly); Adam Hann-Byrd (Charlie); Jodi Lyn O'Keefe (Sarah); Janet Leigh (Norma); LL Cool J (Ronny); Joseph Gordon Levitt (Jimmy); Nancy Stephens (Marion); Branden Williams (Tony); Larisa Miller (Claudia); Emmalee Thompson (Casey); Matt Winston (Matt); Beau Billingslea (Fitz); David Blanchard (Waiter); John Cassini and Jody Wood (Cops); Lisa Gay Hamilton (Shirl); Chris Durand (Michael).

LOS ANGELES TIMES, 8/5/98, Calendar/p. 1, Kevin Thomas

"Halloween:H20" is as stylish and scary as it is ultra-violent. It brings back a stunning Jamie Lee Curtis in the role that made her a star and it's a work of superior craftsmanship in all aspects. But it is so gory you really do have to brace yourself.

For all the considerable artistry that went into the making of a picture that would have the impact of John Carpenter's 1978 original, "Halloween: H20" is first and foremost a very brutal slasher movie that leaves nothing to the imagination. At least it doesn't linger morbidly over all the blood and guts it spills and is laced with dark humor. Hard-core horror fans and teenagers are likely to make "Halloween: H20" a big hit, but it's just as likely to turn off other segments of the movie-going audience.

It was perhaps inevitable that the "Halloween" franchise would be revived now that the horror film cycle was so successfully regenerated with "Scream" and then "I Know What You Did Last Summer," both written by the genre-aware Kevin Williamson, who serves, not surprisingly, as a co-executive producer of "H20."

Twenty years have passed, but baby-sitter Laurie Strode (Curtis), now 37, is understandably haunted by the specter of her demented, knife-wielding brother Michael Myers murdering their sister and barely escaping death herself. Laurie has even gone to the extreme of faking her own death in a car accident—never mind that Michael supposedly died in a fire—and taking the new name of Keri Tate. Today, Tate, a single mother, is the assured headmistress (and teacher) at a posh, exceedingly secluded—wouldn't you know?—private school in Northern California. (It's actually silent star Antonio Moreno's elegant Spanish-style estate in Silver Lake.)

Behind the scenes she's a pill-popper and is described by her son John (Josh Hartnett) as a "functioning alcoholic." Despite how haunted Tate feels, she does have the prospect of some happiness, caught up in a romance with a sensitive, adoring school counselor (Adam Arkin) on her staff.

But now that the 20th anniversary of the masked, crazed Michael's attack approaches, Tate is getting pretty jittery. Even so, she decides to stay on at her home on the school grounds, deserted for the holiday. Having grounded her son, she at the last minute OKs his going on a school outing, which Arkin will help chaperon. Unknown to her, John has decided to stick with his plans to do some secret partying on school grounds with his girlfriend (Michelle Williams) and another couple (Adain Hann-Byrd and Jodi Lyn O'Keefe).

In short, Michael (Chris Durand, truly chilling), who of course is going to turn up, has five targets on hand, not to mention others along the way, including the school's good-natured watchman (LL Cool J, one of the film's warmest presences).

Writers Robert Zappia and Matt Greenberg and director Steve Miner have shrewdly anchored their take-no-prisoners blood bath with a strong, sympathetic character for Curtis to portray. On one level, the film is about a woman gathering courage to fight back at her own demons. Tate evolves from a trenchant but fragile woman to one who learns to assert herself with the bold determination of the cop Curtis played in "Blue Steel." It's hard to imagine Curtis participating in a "Halloween" sequel unless her part was exceptional, and it is.

Curtis' physicality is matched by her far-ranging, sharply nuanced acting. Smart, sexy and earthy, Curtis is overdue for a big role that takes her beyond genre into more personal dramas. She is surrounded by capable players, including her own mother, a radiant Janet Leigh, who is amusing as a well-meaning busybody school secretary. (Note the car Leigh is driving; it's the same 1957 Ford Fairlane she drove in "Psycho," one of the film's many tributes.)

Hartnett, who first came to attention in the short-lived but much-praised TV series "Crackers," makes his impressive screen debut in a role that calls for him to reveal sensitivity, stubbornness and intelligence. Tall, boyishly handsome, Hartnett has a commanding screen presence.

As violent as "Halloween: H20" is, it nevertheless represents well-controlled direction on the part of Miner, who directed two "Friday the 13th" installments and "Warlock." "Halloween: H20" is a handsome film, and as essential to its impact as Curtis herself is the fluid, shadowy, mood-setting camera work of Daryn Okada. Another major asset in setting mood is John Ottman's portentous score, which incorporates the "Halloween Theme," composed by the original film's director, Carpenter.

"Halloween: H20" may be hard to take, but when it comes to suspenceful thrills and chills, there's no denying it delivers the goods.

NEW YORK POST, 8/5/98, p. 45, Thelma Adams

"A boy's best friend is his mother," Norman Bates says in "Psycho."

Was Tony Perkins' Norman always an only child, or did he exercise psychotic sibling rivalry like Michael Myers, the fiend of "Halloween"?

"Halloween: H20," the seventh and final (?) installment in the Myers Cycle, pays tribute to the 1960 Hitchcock thriller that launched a thousand kitchen knives. Long before Steven Spielberg made us fear going into the water, Hitch made us terrified of our showers—and he didn't need buckets of blood to do so.

"Psycho" is the sick son, dominant mom, haunted motel, transvestite granddaddy of a genre that never quite died the grisly death of its supporting characters—and got a transfusion with the hip teen postmodernism of Wes Craven's "Scream."

Since it began in 1978, "Halloween" hallmarks have always been twisted family psychology, big knives and babes who go bump in the night. The villain is chalk-faced slasher Myers (that's a William Shatner mask painted white in the original).

Mikey began the mayhem by stabbing his big sister on Halloween. Fifteen years later, he escaped the mental ward on Pumpkin Day and tried to murder his other sister, Laurie Strode (Jamie Lee Curtis, in her film debut).

Laurie survived, but the past 20 years found her faking her own death, entering witness protection and diving into a bottle. "H20" picks up with Laurie Strode, using an alias, as the headmistress of a tony California boarding school.

A single mom, Laurie's overprotective of her son, John (Josh Hartnett), guarded with her shrink beau (Adam Arkin) and looking over her shoulder for freaks that go slash in the night. John and his pals supply standard issue "Scream" victims who drink and fondle and then find themselves face to face with an early death.

The movie, directed by Steve Miner from a script by Robert Zappia and Matt Greenberg, is slick and snappy and a bit unnecessary. Those who have always wanted to see Arkin's kvetchy "Chicago Hope" surgeon on the other end of the blade will be content.

Brittle and appealing, Curtis is Hollywood victim royalty. Her mother, Janet Leigh, fell to Norman's blade as the beautiful embezzler who rented a room in the Bates Motel.

"Halloween: H20" aches to exploit this noble lineage, but it pales in comparison to "Psycho." The beautifully crinkle-faced Leigh appears as Norma (Get it? "Norma Bates"), Laurie's secretary. It's a casting coup of lost potential, but we savor the moment when Norma exits the plot in the winged sedan she drove in "Psycho," after telling Laurie: "We've all had bad things happen to us."

NEWSDAY, 8/5/98, Part II/p. B2, John Anderson

Suspension of disbelief is the lifeblood of fiction, but "Halloween H20," for all its giddy, gory good humor, seems to be made for the permanently suspended. Anyone who can still shriek "OH MY GAAAWD!!!! Michael Myers is STILL ALIVE!!!" probably tends to start the day with "HOLY MACKEREL!!! The sun came up AGAIN! And in the EAST!"

That old cutup Michael Myers (that's Chris Durand behind the whitewashed William Shatner mask) has, as we all know, been out for blood since 1978. That's when John Carpenter's original "Halloween" broke new ground in the horror genre and made the slasher film the staple of

Saturday night, backrow snuggling. Carpenter (like Wes Craven and the later "Nightmare on Elm Street") got out early to let his creature run amok (five sequels, although No. III wasn't really related). The results have generally been as unsatisfying as they were unpretty.

"Halloween: H20" (no, not water, just marketing) virtually ignores anything that happened since the original even though its star Jamie Lee Curtis—as the besieged Laurie Strode, sister of psychokiller Myers—was in the first sequel. C'est la guerre. She's now a single mother and the headmistress of the exclusive private school attended by her shaggy-haired son John (Josh Hartnett), his girlfriend Molly (Michelle Williams of "Dawson's Creek") and their pals, Charlie and Sarah (Adam Hann-Byrd and Jodi Lyn O'Keefe).

The kids, virtual clones of every menaced claque of teenagers to ever populate a horror film, are trying to skip the field trip to Yosemite in favor of a little surreptitious on-campus romance. Laurie, while trying not to be an overprotective mother, is also a functioning alcoholic with a cabinet full of prescriptions who knocks back full-strength vodka and can speed-order Chardonnay in a restaurant while her love interest, Will (Adam Arkin), is off to the men's room.

All of her malfunctioning, understandably enough, stems from that Halloween massacre of 20 years before, when Michael made the walls run crimson and the skin turn cold. He's (supposed to be) dead. But when everyone you knew was cut to ribbons by a madman who also happened to be your brother, it tends to leave an impression. And whattya know: It's Halloween again.

It's also been longer now since the first "Halloween" than it was between "Halloween" and "Psycho," Carpenter's obvious influence and one director Steve Miner would like us to remember: Janet Leigh, who made that ill-fated motel stop for Hitchcock back in 1960—and is Curtis' real-life mother—makes a couple of cameos, cracks one shower joke and heads for her '60s Ford Fairlane to the tune of "Psycho" music. In "H20's" better moments, we sense the dread of a Norman Batesian cutlery demonstration. But there are a lot of false alarms, a lot of cheap come-ons using quick cuts and trumped-up music and by the time the action (and the body parts) start to roll, it's well beyond the time for the Ill-Will Games to begin.

Although the lighting isn't doing her any favors, Curtis is passable, if not particularly engaged, as Laurie, who keeps seeing Michael's face wherever she goes (when he really does show up, there's a funny moment where she closes her eyes to make him go away). But her exchanges with son John are beyond trite, and the whole domestic storyline is soggy.

LL Cool J appears in an amusing subplot as Ronny the security guy, who writes soft-core potboilers in his spare time and whose wife (heard over the phone) either edits his prose or tries to convince him to get a real job. He gets caught up in the bloodbath, as do Will, Sarah, Charlie, Molly and John, who's sent off by his mother at the end so she can go *mano a mano* with her longtime nemesis— even though, after 20 years of worrying, she seems to have learned nothing useful. Yes, he's still alive. And he will be until the lifeblood of movie madmen (money) stops flowing.

SIGHT AND SOUND, 11/98, p. 51, Kim Newman

The US. It is 20 years after Laurie Strode was terrorised on Halloween night by her homicidal brother Michael Myers. Since then, she has faked her death, changed her name to Keri Tate and become the principal of Hillcrest, a private school in California. Now a heavy drinker, overprotective of her son John and in a relationship with school counsellor Will Brennan, Laurie is still plagued by visions of Michael.

On Halloween 1998, most of the school goes away on a field trip but John stays behind to be with his girlfriend Molly and his friends Charlie and Sarah. Meanwhile in Illinois, Michael learns of Laurie's new identity and address after he murders Nurse Marion, the assistant of the late Dr Loomis who once treated Michael. At Hillcrest, he sneaks past gatekeeper Ronny, then stalks and murders Charlie and Sarah. Laurie tells Will about her past and produces a gun when she becomes aware of Michael's presence. However, Will mistakenly shoots Ronny before he is himself killed by Michael. Laurie gets John and Molly to safety but stays on the grounds to go after her brother with an axe. Michael is apparently killed in a fall. Ronny turns out to be only wounded and the police arrive to mop up. But, convinced her brother is still alive, Laurie hijacks the ambulance in which his body is stirring. She crashes the ambulance, pinning Michael under the wreckage. The siblings almost hold hands, but Laurie finally decapitates Michael.

In 1978, *Halloween* was the spookiest kid on the block. After a decade of such increasingly intense, ultra-violent, downbeat movies as *Night of the Living Dead* (1968) and *The Texas Chain Saw Massacre* (1974), John Carpenter's low-budget sleeper rediscovered the fun of horror films. While George Romero, David Cronenberg and others used the genre to dissect a disenchanted post-Vietnam, post-Watergate America, Carpenter was old-fashioned in his commitment to being scary rather than horrific, playful rather than challenging. Wittily written and performed, with an admirable refusal to explain or understand its monster, the film was also technically innovative. Using a then-new Panaglide camera and his own memorably simple score, Carpenter delivered 91 minutes of real suspense, made a new star of embattled babysitter Jamie Lee Curtis and demonstrated that sudden appearances could be more shocking than buckets of gore. Then there were the sequels.

Halloween H20 Twenty Years Later is equipped with an old-fashioned, windy title. But inspired by the recent revival of the slasher cycle in the *Scream* movies (a brief clip from *Scream 2* plays on television in *H20),* it attempts to revive and tie off the franchise for the 90s. Oddly, though there are *Halloween* snippets in flashback, the storyline is rooted in the revelation of *Halloween II* (made in 1981, the era of "Luke, I am your father") that Michael is Laurie's brother. (The use of the Chordettes' vocative song 'Mr. Sandman' dates back to that too.) Since that disappointing follow-up and the one-off aside of *Halloween III. Season of the Witch* there have been three more drab sequels which squandered the late Donald Pleasence (seen here in a photograph). The body counts went up as the intelligence quotient came down. On the whole, *H20* ignores those movies—though the last one was made only three years ago—and uses the return of Jamie Lee Curtis as an excuse to pick up where her character, last seen in *II*, left off.

Given how dreary the Michael Myers sequels are, it is hardly much of an achievement that *H20* is the best of them. Steve Miner, who directed parts 2 and 3 of the *Friday the 13th* series (there's a hockey-mask gag in the opening scene), is not up to the John Carpenter of 1978 but shows a tighter grip than the Carpenter of recent years. The mis-step that the sequels took, prompted ironically by the *Friday* series and dozens of other *Halloween* imitators, was in upping the gore effects, emphasising the slashing over the stalking. There are nasty moments here (Sarah's leg trapped in a dumbwaiter) but Miner remembers that the Michael of *Halloween* was more interested in making his victims jump than in killing them.

H20 manages to pull off a great many of those distinctive shocks where someone, either Michael or an innocent party, lurches unexpectedly into the frame, prompting a collective gasp. The fate of Charlie is exemplary. The build-up involves the unfortunate kid retrieving a bottle-opener dropped into a dangerous looking garbage disposal. The pay-off simply has Michael appear—Charlie's face is reflected in a close-up of the killer's eye—then cuts on Charlie's unexpected reaction ("Oh, hello") without showing us his actual death.

Given that she was the initiator of the project, it is unsurprising that the film is tailored to Curtis' strengths. The first half gives us a credible grown-up version of the girl we saw suffering in the first films, uptight every Halloween and so afflicted by hallucinatory Michael appearances that when he really shows up she blinks and hopes he'll go away. Though Curtis is good throughout, the script is a lot blunter than Carpenter and Debra Hill's original screenplay. Here, the story is hung up on the sibling relationship but no one ever asks why Michael feels a need to murder his family. Curtis shines in a couple of scenes with Adam Arkin which require her to convey exposition with menace. And in a neatly unstressed joke she discusses trauma with *Psycho* veteran (and Curtis' real mother) Janet Leigh ("we've all had bad experiences," Leigh counsels). Curtis is most on the money, however, in the sustained finale which finds her making an attempt to settle the family business once and for all, paying off with a reversal as Michael finally shows feeling for his sister and Laurie responds by demonstrating that she too has his capacity for ruthless violence.

H20 is brisk (87 minutes), mostly involving and plays expertly on its audience's expectations—delaying the action for a long time, then replaying moments from the original but with different outcomes—but it's still a *Halloween* sequel. Even Carpenter and Hill dropped the ball in *Halloween II,* and a great many of the earlier films' failings are also reproduced here: the comic-relief character of Ronny is annoying; Josh Hartnett carries most dramatic weight but is least interesting of the four fresh teenage faces introduced; the story dawdles for half the film before kicking in; and you can't escape the nagging question of what Michael has been doing all these years and why he is still wearing the outfit (a stolen boiler suit and mask) he improvised in the first film. The final scene seems to offer definitive closure, but a close reading of the last reel reveals a loophole that could allow further sequels.

VILLAGE VOICE, 8/11/98, p. 150, Dennis Lim

Hack tendencies plus smirky pomo self-consciousness equals disgustingly lucrative career. Just ask Kevin Williamson, a man who knows a thing or two about formulas. The Williamson-produced *Halloween: H20*—the title is Hollywood-speak for *Halloween 7 I Know What You Did 20 Years Ago*—updates John Carpenter's 1978 schlock classic into the slasher-friendly-post-*Scream* era. The resuscitation of the moribund franchise was a laughable idea as recently as 1995, when Dimension released the ill-fated *Halloween : The Curse of Michael Myers*. In fact, the series has been in such miserable shape for so long that, in order to sustain an even remotely coherent story line (and, no less, to work original star Jamie Lee Curtis back into the mix), the makers of *H20* have had to pretend that the last four *Halloweens* never happened—which, admittedly, isn't asking too much of the audience.

Curtis's last sanguinary encounter with her mute, masked tormentor was in 1981's *Halloween II*; when we first see her character Laurie Strode in *H20,* she's still screaming, flailing about in the throes of a nightmare. Living under the alias Kerri Tate, she's now the headmistress of a California boarding school. The events of October 31, 1978, have, however, left her alcoholic, emotionally overdependent on her 17-year-old son, and an all-round nervous wreck. And what's more, it's that time of year again.

A model of manipulative terror, the Carpenter original remains, for all the clichés and bad habits it initiated, surprisingly resonant. Directed by Steve Miner (who made two of the *Friday the 13th* movies), *H20* is more competent than previous sequels but almost as uninspired. After a feeble opening sequence that Carpenter's Steadicam prologue puts to shame, the movie settles into a paroxysmal routine of cheap thrills, coming alive in fits and (false) starts. The plot lurches toward Laurie's ultimate rejection of victimhood—clunkily foreshadowed in a classroom discussion on *Frankenstein*. While the Williamson logic can be detected in *H20's* on-the-verge teen cast and its conspicuous nods to *Psycho, Scream,* and the first *Halloween,* it's really Curtis's film, and she's more than up to the task. Twenty years on, she brings to her defining role a toughness and a capacity for self-mockery that the likes of Neve Campbell and Jennifer Love Hewitt just aren't programmed to understand.

Also reviewed in:
CHICAGO TRIBUNE, 8/5/98, Tempo/p. 1, Michael Wilmington
NEW YORK TIMES, 8/5/98, p. E5, Lawrence Van Gelder
VARIETY, 8/3-9/98, p. 35, Dennis Harvey
WASHINGTON POST, 8/5/98, p. C1, Stephen Hunter
WASHINGTON POST, 8/7/98, Weekend/p. 41, Michael O'Sullivan

HANGING GARDEN, THE

A Goldwyn Films release of a Triptych Media/Gala Film/Emotion Pictures production with the participation of Telefilm Canada/The Harold Greenberg Fund/Channel 4/Nova Scotia Film Development Corporation/Nova Scotia Film Industry Tax Credit/Gouvernement du Québec (Programme de crédits d'impot) and Canadian Film and Video Production Tax Credit/Nova Scotia Department of Education Canada/Nova Scotia Cooperation Agreement on Cultural Development. *Producer:* Louise Arfield, Arnie Gelbart, and Thom Fitzgerald. *Director:* Thom Fitzgerald. *Screenplay:* Thom Fitzgerald. *Director of Photography:* Daniel Jobin. *Editor:* Susan Shanks. *Music:* John Roby. *Music Editor:* Rick Betanzos. *Choreographer:* Mary Ellen Maclean. *Sound:* Georges Hannan and (music) Jeff McCulloch and Mike Jones. *Sound Editor:* Rick Betanzos and Glenn Tussman. *Casting:* Martha Chesley and John Dunsworth. *Production Designer:* Taavo

Soodor. *Art Director:* Charlotte Harper. *Set Decorator:* Darlene Shields. *Costumes:* James A. Worthen. *Make-up:* Rose Klatt. *Running time:* 91 minutes. *MPAA Rating:* R.

CAST: Ian Parsons (Little Sweet William);   Peter MacNeill (Whiskey Mac);   Troy Veinotte (Teenage Sweet William);   Kerry Fox (Rosemary);   Mark Austin (Preacher);   Joel S. Keller (Fletcher);   Heather Rankin (Black Eyed Susan);   Christine Dunsworth (Violet);   Seana McKenna (Iris);   Joan Orenstein (Grace);   Chris Leavins (Sweet William);   Shendi (Old Peat);   Ashley MacIsaac (Basil);   Jocelyn Cunningham (Laurel);   Lucy (Young Peat);   Jim Faraday (Mr. MacDougal);   Sarah Polley (Teenage Rosemary);   Renée Penney (Grace the Nun); Martha Irving (Dusty Miller);   Annabelle Raine Dexter (Bud);   Michael Weir (Police Officer); Tom Chambers (Police Officer).

CHRISTIAN SCIENCE MONITOR, 5/15/98, p. B5, David Sterritt

Hollywood's fondness for fantasy points to moviegoers' enjoyment of stories that blur the boundaries between reality and illusion. Many independent pictures share this interest, including two new dramas focusing on the lives of characters as they actually are, and as they might have been if events had taken different turns.

"The Hanging Garden" arrives today on American screens after winning four Genie awards—the Canadian equivalent of Oscars—as well as the Audience Award at last year's Toronto filmfest. It centers on a young gay man returning to his rural home after a decade of living in very different surroundings.

Once an overweight and unhappy child, he is now a successful and attractive adult. But he vividly remembers his discontented past, and additional memories are sparked by interactions with family members who haven't matured as much as he has during the past 10 years.

His recollections and fantasies contribute much of the movie's content—sometimes happily, as when he recalls his childhood's contented moments, and sometimes disturbingly, as when he's haunted by a vision of his own corpse hanging from a tree in his father's garden.

Thom Fitzgerald, who wrote and directed the picture, describes it as "both a slice-of-life drama and a surrealist fantasy," meant to show that "even the most ordinary lives also operate on a poetic level." His experiments with time-jumping and memory-sketching aren't always smooth, but few recent movies do a better job of blending the visible world around us with the invisible world we carry around in our imaginations. Chris Leavins, Kerry Fox, and Sarah Polley star.

"Sliding Doors" takes its cue from the longstanding idea that a tiny event can have huge consequences if it occurs at the right moment in a person's life.

The heroine is a young Londoner who heads for home after a terrible day at the office. As she hurries to pass through the sliding doors of a subway car, the movie splits in two, alternating for the next 90 minutes between alternate versions of her story. In one, she hops into the subway and returns home to find her boyfriend cheating on her. In the other, she's spared the sight of his infidelity, but hits a different series of problems that have their own strong impact.

"Sliding Doors" is amiably acted by Gwyneth Paltrow as the heroine, John Lynch as her sneaky boyfriend, and Jeanne Tripplehorn as her romantic rival. Their efforts are weakened, though, by Peter Howitt's uninspired filmmaking. The basic concept is fine—who hasn't wondered how life might have turned out under slightly different circumstances?—but this is worked out in sadly unoriginal terms.

"Sliding Doors" begins as a novel treatment of a thought-provoking idea. It winds up spinning two uninteresting tales for the price of one.

LOS ANGELES TIMES, 5/15/98, Calendar/p. 12, Kevin Thomas

"The Hanging Garden" hangs itself about two-thirds through its 91-minute running time. Until then it's a venturesome and absorbing attempt on the part of first-time director Thom Fitzgerald to vary the familiar story of the homecoming of a young man to what proves to be a supremely dysfunctional family.

After a 10-year absence, William (Chris Leavins), a gay man in his mid-20s, returns to his parents' home beside a lake in Nova Scotia for his sister's wedding. But in this Irish Catholic household, all that's idyllic is the setting. The sister, Rosemary (Kerry Fox), a caustic type, is having a tough time negotiating the rustic pathway of her parents' elaborately landscaped hillside with her long-trained wedding gown, and she seems less than thrilled about tying the knot with her longtime boyfriend (Joel S. Keller).

But at least she seems glad enough to see her brother; their carefully coiffed mother (Seana McKenna) and their father (Peter MacNeill), who more than lives up to his nickname, Whiskey Mac, are decidedly self-conscious about the return of their son, who left weighing 350 pounds and is now a slim, nice-looking man who is openly gay. William's grandmother (Joan Orenstein), a ferociously devout woman, embraces him, although she's suffered from Alzheimer's disease too long to recognize him for certain.

You really have to wonder why William returned. Nothing has changed, clearly, except that his abusive drunk of a father may be a tad less likely to strike out at his now-adult son.

Trying to avoid the predictable confrontational family drama, Fitzgerald goes for lots of stylistic devices and intricate structuring but finally goes over the top with a highly improbable family secret and other unlikely developments that allow the film to verge on parody or burlesque. Fitzgerald well may develop the talent to match his passion, but as for "The Hanging Garden," there have been countless and far better darkly comic dramas about extravagantly dysfunctional families.

NEW YORK POST, 5/15/98, p. 52, Thelma Adams

Is there such a thing as a functional family anymore? Thom Fitzgerald's debut feature is a wry, artful reminder that home is where the heartbreak is.

As in Peter Howitt's recent romantic debut, "Sliding Doors," with Gwyneth Paltrow, ex-art student Fitzgerald fractures the narrative. In "The Hanging Garden," past and present collide in a single back yard.

Sweet William (charismatic newcomer Chris Leavins) returns home in time for the wedding of his sister Rosemary (Kerry Fox). It's been 10 years since he left remote Nova Scotia.

William is slim and attractive, a homosexual living openly with his boyfriend back in the big city.

During Rosemary's nuptials, the groom (Joel S. Keller) flirts with William; papa Whiskey Mac (Peter MacNeill) drinks; mama Iris (Seana McKenna) contemplates uprooting herself, and little sister Violet (Christine Dunsworth) behaves like a little brother.

All of this is the stock in trade of the dysfunctional comedy or drama. What's the twist? There's a strangulated corpse that reappears like the body in Alfred Hitchcock's "The Trouble With Harry."

The movie isn't called "The Hanging Garden" just because the characters have flower names. The bloated body swinging in the family garden turns out to be the teen-age Sweet William (eloquently underplayed by Troy Veinotte) as a fat outcast.

William's life could have gone either way: teen suicide, or slimmed-down success story. In Fitzgerald's eccentric script, an individual, to move ahead, must come to terms with his family, his past and his inner fat boy.

Fitzgerald also dramatizes the optimistic idea that, as dark as things seemed for Sweet William at 15, 10 years later, there was a positive future for him—if he could just hang on without hanging himself.

NEWSDAY, 5/15/98, Part II/p. B8, John Anderson

James Cameron occupies a perch so lofty, so ultra, so uber, so mega, that to compare him with other directors would embarrass them (as Sparky Anderson once said about Johnny Bench and catchers). But consider the other Canadian-born directors. David Cronenberg. Atom Egoyan. Guy Maddin. And... who?

Well, Thom Fitzgerald for one, at least as of the opening of "The Hanging Garden," which isn't just a good movie, it's been touted in some quarters as the Great White (North) Hope of Canadian filmmaking. This is an awfully heavy burden, even if true. Let's just say that Fitzgerald's black comedy—which is fluent with bare-knuckle familial knockdowns and dementia as it is skewed humor and magical realism—delivers more than just promise.

Rosemary. Sweet William. Violet. Iris. Black-Eyed Susan. These are the family members of Whiskey Mac (Peter MacNeill), a professional gardener and alcoholic with a mean streak and a preoccupation with flowers. His cruelty drove his son away 10 years before, but now it's the wedding day of Rosemary (Kerry Fox) and Sweet William (Chris Leavins) is coming home.

He's late, though, and Rosemary—no wallflower—has launched into a torrent of profanity and ill temper, turning her beer-and rain-soaked wedding into something as funny as it is messy. Senile Grandma Grace (Joan Orenstein) is bellowing out upstairs window, Mac is falling-down drunk, new little sister Violet (Christine Dunsworth) is being a brat, the bridegroom's gay proclivities are becoming more and more evident. Meanwhile, William is sneaking in, circling the action, five sizes thinner than when any one last saw him and realizing that other than himself, little has really changed.

Fitzgerald's movie is about reinvention; flashing back to William's boyhood, we see a sweet kid whose abuse by his father drives him to binge eating. We see the obese teenager (Troy Veinotte) he becomes, still abused and more unhappy. His relationship with teenage Rosemary (Sarah Polley of "The Sweet Hereafter") is good but his homosexual encounter wit Fletcher (Joel S. Keller)—who'll grow up to marry Rosemary—compels his mother, Iris (Seana McKenna), to take him to a local prostitute. Which compels William to hang himself in the garden.

Huh? Yes, the hanged William is suspended by rope for much of the film, visible to all, which moves "The Hanging Garden" from the realm of realism into pure allegorical mischief. That it all works is a credit to Fitzgerald's visual style (terrific camera work) and combination of dry humor and melancholic memory which makes all the brashness so palatable.

He has a good cast, too. Both Polley and the chameleonic Kerry Fox are terrific as Rosemary, whose self satisfaction at marrying Fletcher overrides any concern about his commitment to heterosexuality. Violet, little Christine Dunsworth is a cocked pistol. And as Grace the Nun—a bit part in a scene involving the Virgin Mary—obsessed Grandma Grace—Renee Penney is a riot.

There's a cool, dry tone that informs "The Hanging Garden," like an ocean wind strafing the Nova Scotia landscapes. It's a movie about a lot of things; as the dangling William attests, it's largely about second chances. Thom Fitzgerald should get one very soon.

SIGHT AND SOUND, 5/98, p. 46, José Arroyo

Nova Scotia. After a ten-year absence, William returns to his parent' home for his sister's wedding to his teenage friend and ex-lover Fletcher. During the wedding, William reencounters his abusive alcoholic father Mac, his resigned mother Iris, his now-senile, religious grandmother Grace—and Violet, a sister he never knew about. Grace had caught William and Fletcher having sex when they were teenagers. To help her son, Iris paid a prostitute to have sex with him. The next day he tried, unsuccessfully, to hang himself.

Ten years later, after the wedding, his mother abandons the family, his brother-in-law makes a pass at him, and he discovers that Violet is his daughter.

For some reason, Canada seems to have bred recently an abundance of talented young film-makers who are now making a diverse range of queer films: John Greyson *(Zero Patience, Lillies)*, Bruce LaBruce *(No Skin off My Ass, Hustler White)*, Jeremy Podeswa *(Eclipse)* and many others. Each deploys different tones and techniques to explore the experiences of characters who love members of their own sex in different contexts. *The Hanging Garden* marks the introduction of an excellent new addition, Thom Fitzgerald, to this list of talent. The film, inevitably informed by queer culture, makes sex and sexuality duly important in the plot without making them central to the narrative.

The Hanging Garden is a powerful study of relationships within a working-class family living in rural Nova Scotia. A stop-motion study of a flowering daffodil early on acts as a dramatic metaphor for the film itself: the stem begins to grow, the plant takes shape, the colour intensifies and then, quickly, the flower arches back and opens its blossom like a threat.

The film begins at a raucous wedding, but the communication between the characters initially seems minimal. Yet each revelation layers and intensifies the meaning of previous words, gestures and actions. Minimal means—a word, a look—gain the power to hurt. But the film opts for forgiveness: Sweet William, the protagonist, buries the past (although a more tender memory of it continues to lurk) and chooses the responsibility of a new family.

The film could easily have been stultifying and pretentious; the title suffocates with significance. The narrative is classically (and potentially preciously) structured in three acts each named after a plant: 'The Lady in the Locket', 'Lad's Love' and 'Mums'. With the revealing exceptions of the father and the love interest, Whiskey Mac and Fletcher respectively, the major characters are symbolically named. Sweet William, Rosemary, Iris, Violet, Herb of Grace. They live in a place where past, present and future intermingle to such an extent that characters can see past events happening within the film frame. The film's rigid lines and its attribution of a particular colour scheme to a particular character make conspicuous its attention to form. Moreover, *The Hanging Garden* is one of those films that plant surrealist elements within a realist setting in order to arrive at the poetic. Each element in it risks ridicule, yet the end result is a moving and rich film.

The fully fleshed characters' relationships are particularly detailed. Rosemary, the sister, is vulgar and loud, as a young woman, we see her strength in the way she refuses to make her father feel better by accepting his money. As a bride, Kerry Fox imbues an older Rosemary with a lust for living that is not dulled by her acceptance of the fact that she knows her life is going nowhere. Beer in one hand and cigarette in the other, her rough manner does not blunt a delicacy of feeling which she lovingly extends to the rest of the family, fully aware of their faults. In fact, all the women in the film are flawed, yet also strong and admirable. Of the men, desperation leads Sweet William, the gay one, to learn a quiet stubbornness that becomes strength, but Fletcher will follow his lust the way Mac follows his bottle. This is a film that loves and forgives straight and bisexual men (or fathers and lovers) but has few illusions about them.

If the relationships between the characters are complex, so is the film's view of those relationships. For example, the mother is shown trying to care and protect her children as best she can. The father is shown as tyrannical, with a lack of control that borders on the monstrous. Yet the mother's desperate action to 'save' her son (taking him to a prostitute so he can be straightened out) is seen as a catalyst to his attempted suicide while the father's physical abuse is metaphorically buried.

It is this father-son relationship which is privileged, beginning with the father teaching and abusing his young son and ending with the same young boy lovingly playing with his father's hair. This emotional complexity, brought to life beautifully by the actors, acts as a powerful anchor to the film's formal flights of fancy. Love and violence are interleaved with the quotidian into a poetic form that is at once individualised and representative, earthier and somewhat more exalted. It's a film of sophisticated pleasures, ones that continue to increase long after the film is over.

Also reviewed in:
CHICAGO TRIBUNE, 5/29/98, Friday/p. F, Mark Caro
NEW YORK TIMES, 5/15/98, p. E19, Stephen Holden
VARIETY, 9/22-28/97, p. 39, Brendan Kelly

HAPPINESS

A Good Machine Releasing release of a Good Machine/Killer Films production. *Executive Producer:* David Linde and James Schamus. *Producer:* Ted Hope and Christine Vachon. *Director:* Todd Solondz. *Screenplay:* Todd Solondz. *Director of Photography:* Maryse Alberti. *Editor:* Alan Oxman. *Music:* Robbie Kondor. *Sound:* Neil Danziger and (music) Matthew "Boomer" La Monica. *Sound Editor:* Tom Efinger. *Casting:* Ann Goulder. *Production Designer:* Thérèse Deprez. *Special Effects:* Drew Jiritano. *Costumes:* Kathryn Nixon. *Make-up:* Nicki Ledermann. *Running time:* 135 minutes. *MPAA Rating:* Not Rated.

CAST: Jane Adams (Joy Jordan); Elizabeth Ashley (Diane Freed); Dylan Baker (Dr. Bill Maplewood); Lara Flynn Boyle (Helen Jordan); Ben Gazzara (Lenny Jordan); Jared Harris (Vlad); Philip Seymour Hoffman (Allen); Louise Lasser (Monda Jordan); Jon Lovitz (Andy Kornbluth); Camryn Manheim (Kristina); Marla Maples (Ann Chambeau); Rufus Read (Billy Maplewood); Cynthia Stevenson (Trish Maplewood); Justin Elvin (Timmy Maplewood); Lila

Glantzman-Leib (Chloe Maplewood);   Gerry Becker (Bill's Psychiatrist);   Arthur Nascarella
(Detective Berman);   Molly Shannon (Nancy);   Ann Harada (Kay);   Doug McGrath (Tom);
Eric Marcus (Courteous Waiter);   Eytan Mirsky (Angry Picketer);   Lisa Louise Langford
(Radical Picketer);   Anne Bobby (Rhonda);   Socorro Santiago (Crying Teacher);   Wai Ching
Ho, Bina Sharif, and Tsepo Mokone (Students);   Dan Moran (Joe Grasso);   Evan Silverberg
(Johnny Grasso);   Hope Pomerance (Hysterical Woman);   Matt Malloy (Doctor);   Dan Tedlie
(Don);   Marina Gaizidorskaia (Zhenia);   Johann Carlo (Betty Grasso);   Joe Lisi (Police
Detective);   José Rabelo (Pedro);   Diane Tyler (Janet);   Olga Stepanova (Zhenia's Mother).

CHRISTIAN SCIENCE MONITOR, 6/12/98, p. B3, David Sterritt

[*Happiness* was reviewed jointly with *Henry Fool*; see Sterritt's review of that film.]

CINEASTE, Vol. XXIV, Nos. 2-3, p. 80, Cynthia Lucia and Ed Kelleher

Whenever a movie such as *Happiness* encounters censorship and distribution difficulties, one
is tempted to presume that those difficulties—in the hands of seasoned publicists—will wind up
being assets. Such has been the case with Todd Solondz's latest film. Standing at the center of
this controversy is the male organ. If not actually depicted, the penis is nonetheless much talked
about in *Happiness*. That was enough to create problems once October Films was acquired by
Universal Pictures, which, as signatory to the MPAA, had agreed not to release unrated films.
After October dropped *Happiness*, the film came out via its own production company, Good
Machine. Perhaps predisposed to support the film as a result of these difficulties, some critics of
Happiness reported on this censorship/distribution controversy as though that, in itself, signified
a meaningful film.

A complex film, *Happiness* interweaves the stories of more than a dozen characters. Allen
(Phillip Seymour Hoffman), a world-class self abuser in New Jersey, boasts of his sexual prowess
via obscene phone calls to his neighbor Helen (Lara Flynn Boyle), who has no idea that this
perverse crank lives just down the hall. Meanwhile, in a more stylish part of Jersey, Young Billy
(Rufus Read) longs to learn about sex and manhood from his father Bill (Dylan Baker), who also
has a secret to conceal. Both Allen and Billy share an interest in masturbating—Allen in
something of a rage, and Billy in what will be something of a wry epiphany in the movie's closing
moments.

As a soft-spoken psychiatrist, suburban Little League dad and pederast, Bill propels a key
narrative out of which other narratives are spun. For instance, we are first introduced to Allen
in Bill's office as he drones on about his secret sadistic fantasies involving his next-door neighbor
("I want to tie her up and pump her—pump pump pump—till she screams bloody murder... Not
that I could ever actually do that. See, if she only knew how ... deep down I really cared for her,
respected her, she would love me back."). As Bill pretends to listen, we hear him, in voice-over,
running down his list of household errands ("Gallon of skim milk, a dozen eggs ... pick up the
dry cleaning ... get the dog cleaned"), unaware—as we too are unaware—that Allen's fantasy
revolves around Bill's sister-in-law Helen.

Bill's list of after-work activities includes a trip to his own psychiatrist and then to the local
convenience store where he picks up *Kool*, a magazine for preteen boys, that later appears in his
own son's bedroom. Bill uses the magazine as an aid to his own sex fantasy, which he satisfies
by masturbating in the back seat of his car, still parked in the busy late afternoon parking lot,
where he might easily be detected.

Bill is married to Trish (Cynthia Stevenson), a relentlessly vapid suburbanite who is the sister
of Helen and Joy (Jane Adams), the former a trendy poet whose pretensions far outweigh her
talent ("Rape at Eleven," "Rape at Twelve," what the hell do I know about rape? ... Oh, if only
I had been raped as a child! Their I would know authenticity."), and the latter a would-be folk
singer who proclaims herself as "so happy" when, in fact, she is miserable in her role as the
underachiever of the three sisters. Joy's underachiever role is further underscored by Trish whose
condescension, though perhaps not as deliberate as Helen's, is nonetheless hurtful ("Just because
you've hit thirty doesn't mean you can't be fresh anymore... the truth is, I always thought you
would never amount to much... but now I see that's not true. There's a glimmer of hope for you
after all."). While Trish imagines that she "has it all"—a perky upscale home, husband who's a

successful shrink, two healthy sons, and a dog—her determined superficiality will not allow her to question her sexless marriage nor to adopt anything other than a dismissive attitude toward the moods of her prepubescent son Billy. Even as a pedophile with secret longings for Billy's young friends, however, Bill is a surprisingly sympathetic father, listening with compassion and candidly answering Billy's questions about his own burgeoning sexuality.

Nowhere near suburban New Jersey but within striking distance by phone, are the three sisters' retired parents, Lenny and Mona (Ben Gazzara and Louise Lasser), a long-loveless couple who have fled to a Florida retirement community in search of their own dismal happiness. Lenny has just announced his desire to separate from Mona, though he stops short of using the word "divorce." When Mona accuses him of having fallen in love with someone younger, he says simply, with an air of bleak finality, "I'm in love with no one." Lenny and Mona represent the emotional end-point at which most other characters are likely to arrive. Most have set their sights on objects of desire far beyond their reach. Joy breaks up with the overweight, whiny, and vindictive Andy in the film's opening scene, only to long for happiness in the shape of some other more attractive man, whom she never does find. Trish loves Bill, who prefers prepubescent boys, with whom he certainly cannot find sustained happiness. The bloated Allen is cloistered in his bedroom masturbating to porn pinups and thoughts of the attractive Helen, who may live down the hall but who is far out of reach. Meanwhile, Allen's other neighbor Kristina longs for him, though he initially finds her repulsive. In sex, as in consumerism, characters in Solondz's film continually try 'trading up,' beyond realistic expectations, often unaware that the object of attraction is engaged in a similar quest.

Solondz's screenplay, nothing if not intricate, is structured like a spider web, with characters venturing into other parts of the web, providing the audience with a sense of playful coincidence and disquieting revelation. In Altmanesque fashion (as in *Short Cuts*), relationships are cleverly revealed, sometimes catching the viewer unawares, as when we gradually recognize that Joy, Trish, and Helen are, in fact, sisters or that Mona and Lenny are their parents. The surprise of discovering these relationships is sometimes heightened yet often hampered by Solondz's falling back on cheap jokes that traffic in stereotypes and clichés. For example, when Allen's overweight neighbor Kristina (Camryn Manheim) casually orders an elaborate ice cream sundae in the midst of confessing to murder and dismemberment, Solondz is playing the fat-lady-joke card in an all too obvious and cruel manner. Ice cream sundae notwithstanding, it is as if nothing sweet can exist in this film called *"Happiness."* On the other hand, one cannot help feeling a secret pleasure when Bill, fresh from the back seat of his car, strolls into his well-appointed suburban kitchen, where Trish is cooking dinner. We Suddenly learn that this woman who proclaims she "has it all" has more than she's bargained for. Thus, a subversive charge rattles this archetypal hub of middle-class domesticity.

Despite the fact that many of the characters in *Happiness* are exaggerated stereotypes—as in the case of Kristina—the character of Bill resists this pigeonholing tendency, consequently upping the stakes of the film's subversive potential. Early in the film, Bill shares a fantasy with his own psychiatrist in which he enters a peaceful sun-drenched park and opens fire with a machine gun on happy couples, both gay and straight. Simultaneously shocking and cartoonish, this moment seems designed to identify Bill as a sociopath, yet even as the story unfolds and we become aware of his disturbing sexual tendencies, Bill remains a character difficult to dismiss in all of his complexity. Strategically surrounded by characters the audience is invited to laugh at fairly comfortably, Bill enlists our serious consideration as the film's would-be architect of subversion.

What Alfred Hitchcock understood instinctively forty years ago, drawing audiences in through the delicious thrill of the forbidden, Solondz attempts to put into practice in the scene where Bill engineers his rape of Billy's young sleepover friend. As Bill methodically empties capsules of sedatives into the hot-fudge sundaes he prepares for his family and little Johnny Grasso (Evan Silverberg)—though viewers might prefer to resist—they, perhaps, cannot help sharing his disappointment when hearing that Johnny hates hot fudge. As members of the family drop off to sleep one by one, the audience impatiently waits as Bill encourages Johnny to take a bite of the sedative-laced tuna fish sandwich Bill has prepared instead.

As in *Psycho*, when viewers share Norman Bates's anxiety as Marion Crane's car momentarily stops sinking into the swamp, in *Happiness* they very likely share Bill's apprehension as Johnny's tuna sandwich remains untouched. Just as the audience draws a sigh of relief when Marion's car takes its final plunge, viewers may feel oddly elated as Johnny bites into his sandwich. Even though we, as viewers, don't necessarily want harm to come to Marion Crane, after she is murdered our fickle allegiance is entirely, if only for the moment, with Norman because, arguably, we desire the disorder he can bring to a society so secure in its sense of order. In the same fashion, viewers quite probably don't *want* little Johnny Grasso to be harmed. In part, however, they may want Bill Maplewood to succeed because of the disorder he will bring into the ordered lives of those who "have it all" and "want it all." Ironically, Bill himself is one of these people. Through point-of-view editing linking us to Bill's perspective throughout this scene, the film powerfully implicates the audience in Bill's desires—not only his desires for Johnny but his desire to "have it all."

While the distribution controversy centered, in large part, on the subject of pedophilia, it seems more likely that this controversy has arisen less from the subject itself than from the manner in which Solondz elicits audience complicity. To examine such complicity in Bill's actions, it is useful to look at the contradiction in his character through the lens of American culture—while he is a pederast he also is a good father, which would give him a passing grade on many daytime TV talk shows. Yet in his role as 'good father,' he also becomes a recognizable cultural stereotype, with an earnestness reminiscent of Ward Cleaver. While the TV talk show encourages the studio audience to adopt a superior distance, passing judgment on guests by booing or cheering their revelations—some of which deal with issues like incest and pedophilia—Solondz both connects and distances his audience. On some level we, as film audience, may 'desire' that Bill succeed in raping a young boy, while at the same time congratulating ourselves that *we* would never do such a thing. And it is on this contradiction that many film critics have reached an uncomfortable impasse. While many have praised the film for providing the narrative grounding necessary to connect us with certain characters—even in their most stereotypical or over-the-top form—a handful of reviewers congratulate themselves on their wholesale rejection of the film for its reliance on such stereotypes a response that may have more to do with backlash than with careful criticism of the film's artistic failings.

While Solondz may expect viewers to recognize themselves in many of his characters—to greater or lesser degrees—audience laughter, paradoxically, seems to arise both from an uneasy self-recognition and from a superiority upon encountering broad cultural stereotypes. The question remains as to whether these are merely 'sick' or 'ridiculous' characters or whether their behavior resonates in some meaningful, and perhaps even political, manner, forcing us to question seriously the culture which produces them. Just as in some of Woody Allen's films (particularly *Hannah and Her Sisters, Crimes and Misdemeanors*), *Happiness* attempts, with varying degrees of success, to link such contradictory behavior with contemporary American values.

In a culture that encourages self-involvement and consumerism, often conflating them with sexual gratification, the search for happiness, almost by definition, reflects these same cultural excesses. The character of Vlad (Jared Harris) is emblematic of these intersecting pursuits of happiness in America. A Russian immigrant cab driver who equates happiness with instant acquisition—preferably by theft—Vlad befriends Joy in New York City, where she has taken a low salaried job as an English-as second-language teacher, having resolved to "help people," even if it means crossing a picket line. Behind the wheel of his taxi one day, Vlad encounters a dejected Joy, whom he eagerly drives home to New Jersey—in Vlad's eyes, a vision of paradise. He comforts Joy by sleeping with her but exacts payment for his services by helping himself to her stereo and her guitar as he makes a quick getaway.

When Joy later asks him to return the stolen articles, he does so only after charging her five hundred dollars. Drawn to a culture that encourages rampant consumerism, Vlad is incapable of imagining the spiritual and emotional dead end that Mona and Lenny have arrived at, for instance, after buying into that system all their lives. Through this seemingly minor character, Solondz presents viewers with an unpleasant caricature of American cultural values. Neither 'sick' nor 'ridiculous' this petty thief from Russia—ironically the quintessential self-made man exposes the casual self interest at the core of consumerist values, which middle-class manners so artfully conceal. Whatever revelations Vlad is positioned by the filmmaker to expose, however, they remain, in the end, rather commonplace.

Having achieved the enviable middle-class trappings Vlad can only long for, Bill makes use of these both as a form of subterfuge and retreat. Less protected, for example, than the successful ophthalmologist in *Crimes and Misdemeanors,* who orchestrates the murder of his mistress, Bill nevertheless remains somewhat cloaked from the law by virtue of his middle class 'respectability.' He claims to love Trish, even though he will not make love to her, and in one moving moment while she sleeps, he confesses he is "sick," asking, "Do you really love me? No matter what?" Once his crimes against Johnny Grasso and Ronald Farber—another of Billy's classmates—have been discovered, his middle-class neighbors—like a Jerry Springer TV audience—turn instantly against him, spray-painting "pervert" and "serial rapist" across the red brick facade of his home. In spite of all this, however, Billy still needs and loves his father, approaching him in an effort to understand his actions. Emblematic of a relationship based on Bill's frank responses to his son's concerns and insecurities, in this pivotal scene he is remarkably candid with Billy—some might say brutally honest. After Billy asks what his father has done sexually to his friends, Bill replies, "I touched them... fondled them... I couldn't help myself.. I made love... I fucked them." When Billy asks, "Would you ever fuck me?," Bill responds, "No, I jerk off instead," as both break down in tears.

Are viewers to condemn or admire Bill for these responses? Does the father's comment about "jerking off" signal his recognition of a line he should not cross with his son or do his words signal an erasure of that line? The viewer expects Bill to respond with, "No, I would never fuck you," or failing that, "No, I *would* jerk off instead." Bill is admitting that he masturbates as an alternative to raping his son. Upon hearing this, a tearful Billy seems fraught with an ambivalence perhaps reflecting the viewer's attitude toward Bill. Does Billy read his father's response as a warning or as an emotional (sexual) rejection? In refusing to answer, *Happiness* resists the 'either/or' judgment of a TV talk show.

But *Happiness* also refuses the implications of its own construction of Bill as a subversive force. Like Bill, who is capable of subversion but draws a line, of sorts, around *his* family, *Happiness* draws a line around the notion of family, while appearing to do quite the opposite. Solondz shields the audience from witnessing Bill's actual rape of Johnny and Ronald, thus reducing an understanding of his subversion to abstract terms. While arguably positioning viewers to desire the disorder Bill can bring to the ordered world of those who "have it all," the film fails to uncover the implications of such desires. That Bill is a good, loving father and at the same time a serial rapist may be precisely the essence of his potential for disorder. He is both gentle and brutal, and, like Norman Bates, he cannot help himself.

Unlike Hitchcock's conception of Norman Bates, however, which forces audience discomfort through an awareness of their own complicity (as when Norman spies on Marion undressing), Solondz's conception of Bill perhaps falls short of its full potential for subversion, in that—while somewhat complicit—the audience is never fully made to face the implications of its own complicity. In failing to show more sustained interaction between Bill and Johnny Grasso—though it surely would have invited even more serious censorship problems—the film also fails to implicate the presumably middle-class art house audience by allowing refuge into the same recesses of respectability where Bill himself has hidden. On the other hand, unlike *Psycho,* which places its subversive violence in the transitory space of a motel room and a forbidding Victorian house, *Happiness* establishes its setting for violence and abuse in the midst of a comfortable American kitchen and family room. In this respect, *Happiness* arguably does follow through on its subversive charge.

After Bill has been presumably incarcerated, the three sisters sit at a Thanksgiving table in Florida with Mona and Lenny, drinking a toast to happiness. Meanwhile, on the condo balcony, Billy gazes at a buxom sunbather and finally attains his much desired goal of "coming." He rushes inside to an indifferent audience, proudly proclaiming, "I came," an eager admission really addressed to his absent father, but one which provokes only confusion among his other relatives. The wry epiphany of Billy's experience is heightened by the absence of Bill, whose empty chair is conspicuous at the dinner table. The absence opens possible readings of Billy's statement, which is charged with the irony of our knowing that this breakthrough into 'manhood' could lead him down the path of Allen, a lonely guy jerking off in Jersey—a character to whom his physical resemblance seems more than coincidental or more dangerously down the path of his father, for whom sexuality is both clinical and compulsive.

Solondz has chosen a cautiously ambiguous path, even though he has created a character with subversive potential—a sexual outlaw, who wreaks havoc from within the confines of the

American home. Unlike Vlad, Bill is not some outsider bringing disorder to an ordered middle-class enclave. Rather, as father, husband, and psychiatrist, he embodies the very order and comfort which he comes to overturn. But if *Happiness* truly had the courage of its convictions, would the film's closing shots be so cartoonish? Billy's emission, dripping from the Florida balcony rail, is greedily lapped up by Kooki, the family dog, who runs happily to the dinner table, licking Trish's face. These images provide an all-too-obvious and vulgar punchline in a film that initially presents so much promise for meaningful satire and genuine subversion.

LOS ANGELES TIMES, 10/16/98, Calendar/p. 1, Kenneth Turan

Don't be surprised when the laughter "Happiness" creates sticks in your throat: It's supposed to. Writer-director Todd Solondz has come up with a desperate comedy of longing, misery and misplaced need whose effects are exactly calibrated. But along with being a handful in ways it intends, "Happiness" is also troubling in ways it does not.

Solondz's previous film, the Sundance grand jury prize-winning "Welcome to the Dollhouse," shares with "Happiness" a willingness to cause discomfort and a desire to see how far the boundaries of what an audience will laugh at can be stretched. But in this work, Solondz has pushed the envelope to uncompromising lengths.

A loosely paced, episodic film that follows the personal lives of three sisters, their parents and acquaintances, "Happiness" is happy to feature jaw-dropping dialogue and situations not always found in modern comedies. On the menu to be talked about (though not necessarily seen) are murder, rape, suicide, possible dismemberment, masturbation, vomiting, visible ejaculation, obscene phone calls and, in a coup de grace that caused parent company Universal to insist that October Films drop distribution, the sexual assault of a drugged child. "I Love Lucy" this is not.

Yet it's a tribute to the acting as well as writing and directing that "Happiness" doesn't feel exploitative and can, against major odds, at times make you laugh. Solondz has an impeccable ear for current speech patterns, for our passion for fake cheerfulness and the way mean-spiritedness often masquerades as candor. He also has a gift for skewering the self-centeredness that makes the search for modern love both painful and futile and leads to the predominance, in this film at least, of hollow, disconnected and destructive lives. But even those strengths, as well as expert performances across the board, do not necessarily add up to enough.

The first of the three Jordan sisters to be met is the seriously misnamed Joy (Jane Adams). Vague, spacey and the despair of her sisters for being still single at 30, Joy has dreams of being a singer-songwriter, and she's responsible for the film's strongly ironic anthem. "Happiness, where are you, I've searched so long for you," Joy chirps mindlessly. "Happiness, what are you, I haven't got a clue."

Helen (Lara Flynn Boyle) is that fixture of contemporary life, the literary celebrity who barely has time to take a phone call from Salman Rushdie and complains, "Everybody wants me, you have no idea what it's like."

One person who wants her in the worst way is Allen (the always effective Philip Seymour Hoffman), a lonely guy who lives in Helen's building and bombards her with ferocious obscene phone calls. Allen, it turns out, has an admirer of his own, the seriously heavy Kristina (Camryn Manheim), who is forever knocking on his door with more information than he wants on the murder of one of the building's security guards.

Trish (Cynthia Stevenson), the third sister, likes to put her hands up like quotation marks and say, "I've got it all," but despite her three children and a successful therapist (Dylan Baker) for a spouse, Trish turns out to have the biggest problem of them all: Husband Bill is a child molester.

The molestation subplot has become "Happiness'" flash point, the place where people tend to draw the line. As interviews and the film itself makes clear, Solondz is interested in exploring Bill, not judging him, and, helped by Baker's empathetic performance, succeeds in playing against expectation. Bill, for example, turns out to be a thoughtful father to his own son Billy (Rufus Read), who is worried about his approaching sexual maturity.

But though these unhappy moments are as close as "Happiness" gets to emotion, the film is so coldly conceived that even this segment feels lacking. Solondz's filmmaking style tries to make a virtue out of flatness and distance, and is always more comfortable indicating where feelings would go than actually providing them. Combining this with "Happiness'" glacial pace and unnecessary two hour and 19 minute length, the result is an undeniably clever and provocative film that has sacrificed an essential element in bringing its vision to the screen. Not only can't these characters connect with one another, they have just as much trouble connecting with us.

NEW STATESMAN, 4/9/99, p. 37, Jonathan Romney

What British critics make of Todd Solondz's film "Happiness," we'll know soon enough; chances are it will rub a few sensibilities up the wrong way, especially at the conservative end of the scale. In the US, however, much of the adverse response has been in direct reaction to the extravagant praise that has generally greeted the film. In the magazine Film Comment, Andrew Lewis Conn attacked it as an example of the "tyranny of the critic-proof movie", surrounded by "such an aura of dark hipness that critics may have been afraid to puncture it". American critic Charles Taylor, writing in the British Sight and Sound, says: "The joke is on the audiences and critics who've fallen for it. They think they're embracing an alternative to Hollywood. They're really just applauding "Revenge of the Nerds."

What is it about "Happiness" that gets people's goat? Partly it's Solondz's stance, which in the US independent film sphere resembles the geek-outsider pose once adopted in pop by "Talking Heads." He walks and talks the part of the embittered nerd made good, the kid who got sand kicked in his face until he hit the beach at Cannes. That attitude is reflected in his films. "Welcome to the Dollhouse" told the story of a schoolgirl mocked and tormented by her peers and parents alike. The film seemed gratuitously sadistic towards her, until you realised that the hapless Dawn might be Solondz's self-portrait—at which point it began to look rather more masochistic.

"Happiness," at first glance, seems sadistic all around, with a wider range of targets. Its cast includes three New Jersey sisters, their parents, spouses and ill-chosen partners. The Dawn figure here is Joy, single and 30, equally inept socially, romantically and as a folk singer. Other characters include a lonely, overweight masturbator and the lady down the hall with a murderous secret.

One character arrests us most of all, so much so that "Happiness" is generally regarded as being specifically about his "case". Played by Dylan Baker with a chillingly bland mask of suburban placidity, Bill is a psychiatrist, a loving husband and father—and a paedophile who lusts after his son's 11-year-old pals. Bear in mind that the overall tone of the film is that of a flip, urbane comedy— a flavour of Woody Allen, with atmospherics closer to David Lynch—and you can see why "Happiness" is so risky. Surely, we begin to protest, it's quite inappropriate to treat paedophilia comically. Surely, if it's to be handled at all, it should be with the social-worker earnestness of a TV movie-of-the-week.

Solondz certainly tests our prejudices about comic decorum, hitting a note of black farce from the outset: at one point, Bill's attempts to drug a boy are diffused into an absurd routine with spiked tuna sandwiches. The film's strategy here is brilliantly devious. It nudges us away from speculation about the deep psychology of Bill's passion, and instead demonstrates what a perversion might entail in terms of banal daily admin. It's only later, in the film's most devastating sequence—at once understated and forensically direct—that Solondz finally takes us under Bill's skin, as his bewildered son asks him to explain himself.

This scene gives the lie to accusations that "Happiness" lacks compassion. But the film's outlook is tragic: its broadest comic stroke, the come-shot that provides its punchline, marks another poor sucker's entry into the realm of adult sexuality, of "happiness"—or rather, its opposite. Sex has never had such bad press in American cinema: desire here oppresses people just as brutally as Solondz's decor and lighting.

"Happiness" isn't the only recent American film to present masturbation as the defining human characteristic. "There's Something about Mary" used gobbets of spunk both as a set-up for a hair-gel gag and to define its hero as a chronic but lovable schmuck. Neil LaBute's altogether more sombre "Your Friends and Neighbors" featured men who were happier with their fists than with their partners. The LaBute and Solondz films have been erroneously lumped in with Mary and with the inanely brutal sex-and-death farce. "Very Bad Things" as representing a new cinema of shock, of gross-out tactics in which the stakes have to be constantly raised. These films may all pursue extremes of subject matter, but that's the only similarity. While Mary shoehorns even the most outrageous material into an innocent romantic comedy, LaBute and Solondz propose serious dissections of the modern human condition. LaBute, an acolyte of Edward Bond, takes a detached, theatrical approach, while Solondz seems more directly invested in his film, and wants us to be invested, too.

No one who's seen "Dollhouse" can help suspecting that "Happiness" also contains an element of self-portraiture, or that Solondz is presenting a distorting mirror to his audience. He wants us to understand and identify with his ordinary and extreme cases alike, even if that entails accepting the pans of human desire (and its absence) that we'd rather ignore. If its characters are all fucked up, "Happiness" implies, it's because we all are, in whatever closely guarded ways of our own. Whether you like or despise Solondz's film, everyone will surely be impelled to reject it on some level—hence the unusually combative flavour of the critical opposition. "Happiness" gets under our skins in ways that no one could conceivably find comfortable. It may be the most genuinely psychoanalytical fiction that American cinema has yet produced.

NEW YORK, 10/19/98, p. 71, David Denby

Philip Seymour Hoffman, who plays one of the sexually stymied neurotics in *Happiness*, threatens women over the phone with killer-stud rant ("I want to pump you so hard that..."), and then he freezes, hanging up in terror. Burly, with red hair and glasses, Hoffman, a wonderful actor, specializes in nerds, cut-off young men yearning for connection from inside a heavy shell of unhappiness. You'll recognize him from *Twister*, where he was one of the counterculture techies obviously in love with Helen Hunt's daredevil, and from *Boogie Nights*, where, again a techie, he declared his love to the porno star Mark Wahlberg. In *Happiness*, his phone-sex warrior calls women at random, but he also calls the svelte, beautiful writer (Lara Flynn Boyle) who lives down the hall from him in a New Jersey suburban high-rise. He enters her apartment at last—and then can't squeeze out a word. *Happiness, the* scandalous American independent film written and directed by Todd Solondz *(Welcome to the Dollhouse)*, is, of course, about misery. The characters try to make connections and wind up nowhere; they love the wrong person, the forbidden person; they degrade themselves, destroy other people. The movie has an eager intimacy with the atrocious that is sometimes funny in a deadpan way, sometimes depressing and barbarously cruel. *Happiness* seesaws between empathy and distaste, between sexual longing and sexual loathing. Solondz draws in close, not just to Hoffman but to everyone; he gives his characters long monologues and, amazingly, gets extraordinary performances and beautiful moments. Then he pulls the rug out, dumping the audience on its rear. Welcome to the dollhouse, indeed.

The movie is a series of malicious vignettes, in raptly quiet and concentrated style—no hysteria, no screaming, no swirling camera. Each scene offers one or another aspect of the alleged anxiety and terror lurking beneath the respectable surface of middle-class life. In Boca Raton, in Florida, a retired couple in their sixties (Ben Gazzara and Louise Lasser), married for 40 years, have nothing left to say to one another. Appalled that he's in perfect health and has to live on for decades more, Gazzara momentarily falls into the clutches of a predatory Boca widow played by Elizabeth Ashley. Poor Ashley! Solondz turns her croaking voice and hawk-like eyes into a mask of death. One might well ask what is so awful about lust in the elderly that it needs to be demonized in this way. But Solondz exposes everyone. He's like a vengeful adolescent, convinced that anyone who ever bored or angered him was being eaten away by dirty secrets.

Back in New Jersey, the elderly couple owns an apartment, and one of their daughters, Joy (Jane Adams), a scared, talentless girl, lives there by herself. Joy can't hold a job or a man, but she means no harm, and Jane Adams, who is pretty in a defenseless, Raggedy Anne way, with lank hair and hurt eyes, becomes the movie's nominal heroine—an infinitely vulnerable creature. Joy, it turns out, is the good sister in a fairy tale. Her older sibling Helen, the slinky writer, longs for emotional violence and "authenticity"—she's a parody of chic, attitudinizing success, a suburban Kathryn Harrison. The other wicked sister, Trish, played by the gurgling comic actress Cynthia Stevenson, lives happily as an apple-pie-fascist mom, married to what seems to be a solid husband and dad—Bill (Dylan Baker), of the square forehead, a somber householder in his dark psychiatrist's suit. Bill makes love to his wife but is haunted by demons—he lusts after little boys, perhaps even after his own little boy, Billy, who, at 11 is trying to have his first orgasm. "Have you tried playing with yourself?" his father asks with excruciating solicitude. "Do you want me to show you?"

Let me say quickly that the subject of pedophilia, creepy as it is, doesn't necessarily fall outside the realm of art. A few years ago, the Canadian film *The Boys of St. Vincent* made something grave and shocking out of it—a study in grown-up hypocrisy. Solondz goes back and forth: One minute Bill is a troubled, sympathetic man with an unspeakable problem, the next he's the preposterous and grotesque hero of a sick joke. In his malicious mode, Solondz manages to do what Adrian Lyne didn't have the courage to do in *Lolita:* As Bill plots desperately to isolate and drug a visiting little boy, we are placed inside the desire of the violator; the scene is hideously funny. But the result of Bill's manipulations—a sodomized 11-year-old—is not funny, and the movie comes to a dead stop in a hospital scene in which we are asked to be amused by a detective's persistent questions.

A bad boy, this Solondz. When the other shoe drops during those long, quiet conversations, the foot within the shoe drops, too. In a restaurant or a living room, one person relates something to another, and Solondz goes right over the top into the perverse. Yet his joking nihilism covers what may be something like sympathy or even solidarity—that's why one cannot dismiss the movie as nothing more than a nasty game. The actors, obviously with Solondz's help, find the character inside the vicious deadpan satire. Hoffman does wonders with his sagging belly, his fumbled glasses, his pained smile. Cynthia Stevenson turns housewifely smugness into a niftily rhythmed kitchen patter; Jared Harris, using a lighter Russian accent than John Malkovich's Stolichnaya special in *Rounders,* makes something pragmatic yet scuzzily sexual out of the émigré Russian taxi driver whom Joy has an affair with (asked what his profession in Russia was, Harris responds proudly, "I was teef.")

While appreciating Solondz's daring and sangfroid, we may also wonder what, finally, he is doing. What does it mean when a cruel movie mocks cruelty? And how can a movie that is clearly erotophobic celebrate an 11-year-old's first orgasm—and then immediately turn it into a sick joke? Solondz punishes everyone with his own disgust. He brings his frustrated characters together, but no one gets it on but the child-molester and his victims. Quite a joke. The movie offers personal confessions, but Todd Solondz creates drama by pushing dysfunction into pathos—a little boy weeping as he questions his pedophiliac dad.

Aren't the American suburbs a fairly easy target by now? And who but the fantasists of the Christian right has any remaining illusions about the inviolate nature of the American family? It's more than a little naïve, I think, to be shocked that people are out for themselves, that family relations can cover self-seeking and competitiveness. Solondz subverts what has already been subverted. The view that middle-class life is poisonous, a sham, is now so pervasive among the American independents *(Kids, Buffalo 66, Your Friends and Neighbors)* that I have begun to think that it is a substitute for politics. In the absence of any coherent critique of this society, the outsiders are burning themselves up with meaningless rage. Solondz himself is split, unable to decide whether his dysfunctional characters are really holy innocents or just contemptible losers. *Happiness* is a brilliant, disturbing, but unstable and half-crazy piece of work.

NEW YORK POST, 10/9/98, p. 47, Thelma Adams

Director Todd Solondz is a nasal-voiced nerd with black-framed eyeglasses, a field of cowlicks on his head and a fascination for the domestic lives of serial rapist-killers. He obviously knows what it's like to be attacked in the schoolyard. What's unclear is whether he enjoyed it.

"Happiness", which follows a controversial reign at Cannes and Toronto with an American premiere at the New York Film Festival and a theatrical run starting Sunday, is a perverted Mary Hartman, Mary Hartman.

Set in contemporary suburban New Jersey, with excursions to Manhattan and Boca, "Happiness" is a wicked comedy about a daisy chain of pathetic losers and one chunky 11-year-old who comes of age.

Ambrose Bierce wrote in The Devil's Dictionary that happiness is an agreeable sensation arising from contemplating the misery of another. By that definition, the characters in Solondz's black comedy should be downright jolly.

As successful writer Helen (Lara Flynn Boyle) tells her underachieving sister Joy (Jane Adams): "I'm not laughing at you, I'm laughing with you."

The ironically named Joy responds, "I'm not laughing."

We're torn between Helen and Joy, between laughing at the characters' misery and empathizing with their pain. Like the sisters' exchange, some of the toughest moments come from casual familial cruelty as stronger family members prey on the weak under the pretense of love and concern.

This theme was central to the writer-director's less-brutal "Welcome to the Dollhouse", an ode to the feverish dreams of suburban misfits. "Happiness" is more twisted. The extended family includes a sympathetic pederast, an obese murderess who preserves chunks of her victims in freezer bags, an obscene phone caller, a Russian wife beater and a senior philanderer.

The most controversial subplot is the mournful love story of soft-spoken therapist Bill Maplewood (Dylan Baker). Bill's wife, Trish (Cynthia Stevenson), believes she has it all. What she has is a husband who rapes little boys and, down the hall, a bunk bed filled with 11-year-old Billy (Rufus Read) and his brother, Timmy.

I'm sick, Bill confesses to Trish.

Take a Tylenol, she answers.

Solondz plays this domestic train wreck for its comic potential, an exercise in bad taste that pushes buttons a la early John Waters. But what makes "Happiness" poignant is that he creates a relationship between Bill and Billy that is authentic, complex, open.

Early on, Billy approaches Bill, seeking sexual advice. Dad patiently explains ejaculation, reassuring his son with a paternal punch on the arm. Later, when the two discuss Bill's sexual assaults on Billy's classmates, the familiar intimacy remains. That makes Billy's realization that his father is a pervert and yet still somehow dear old dad devastating. Their sharp moment of connection—and betrayal—is as fleeting as happiness.

NEWSWEEK, 10/12/98, p. 87, David Ansen

"Happiness" had me hooked with its first scene. A plain, 30-year-old woman named Joy (Jane Adams) is breaking up with her schlumpy boyfriend (Jon Lovitz) in a restaurant. "Is it someone else?" he asks pathetically. "No, it's just you," this nice young woman says, unaware how deeply she has twisted the knife in an already open wound. The sad-sack suitor is not about to retire quietly, however. He launches into an obscene attack on his now former girlfriend, his viciousness so direct the viewer isn't quite sure whether to shudder in pain and embarrassment or laugh out loud. The appropriate reaction is both.

As anyone who saw "Welcome to the Dollhouse" knows, filmmaker Todd Solondz catalogs humiliation with a connoisseur's expertise. In that 1996 film, his unsentimental eye was trained on the horrors of junior high. "We all know the cruelty we have in the seventh grade," the 38-year-old writer-director explains. "That cruelty didn't evaporate. That capacity resides within us to this day, just like kindness does." "Happiness" expands and deepens "Dollhouse's" dark perception into the adult world, following the blighted romantic fortunes of three suburban New Jersey sisters and the men who enter their orbit. Deeply disturbing and shockingly funny, it's a movie made for audiences willing to be challenged and discomfited.

Following many plot lines and more than a dozen characters, "Happiness" creates an intricate counterpoint on themes of alienation, loneliness, lust and love. Of the three sisters, the sweetly discombobulated Joy is the most romantically hapless. Helen (Lara Flynn Boyle) is the glamorous one, a successful author whose confidence is belied by her self-hatred, which leads her into a masochistic flirtation with an obscene phone caller (Philip Seymour Hoffman). The happiest sister—the relentlessly cheerful housewife Trish (Cynthia Stevenson)—proves the most deluded. Little does she know that her kind, soft-spoken psychoanalyst husband, Bill (Dylan Baker), is a pedophile who's molesting their young son's schoolmates. Add a murderer, a larcenous Russian emigre and Louise Lasser and Ben Gazzara as the sisters' loveless parents, and this suburban dystopia is complete.

This is risky stuff—so risky that October Films, bowing to pressure from its corporate parent, Universal Pictures, refused to release the movie. What particularly upset the top brass at Universal was the movie's portrait of the molester. "It turned my stomach," says one executive. "I don't need to see a movie about a pedophile." It's not that the character's crimes are shown (they aren't) but that Solondz refuses to demonize him. He finds it far more interesting to try to understand what makes him tick. This is what is truly shocking to some. Though Solondz is a ruthlessly unblinking observer, the bleakness of his vision is tempered by his compassion for almost every one of his characters. "Happiness" is no trendy wallow in nihilism (like the nasty but hollow "Your Friends and Neighbors"). Solondz is treading a mighty fine line here between comedy, tragedy and grossness (including close-ups of semen). "Happiness" is unnerving because it forces us into uncharted waters: Solondz doesn't tell us how to feel but makes us thrash out our responses for ourselves. In doing so, he has made one of the few indelible movies of the year.

SIGHT AND SOUND, 4/99, p. 44, Xan Brooks

The New Jersey suburbs. Thirty-year old Joy breaks up with her boyfriend Andy at a local restaurant. Overweight loner Allen tells his psychiatrist Bill of his lust for Helen, a successful poet who lives in Allen's apartment block. Unable to approach Helen directly, he plagues her with obscene phone calls. Helen has two sisters: the now single Joy, and Trish, who is happily married to Bill the psychiatrist. The sisters' parents, Mona and Lenny, have retired to Florida and are separating.

Andy commits suicide and Joy quits her job. She takes a post filling in for striking teachers at a language school. This leads to a one-night stand with Vlad, a Russian cab driver who steals her stereo. Bill becomes obsessed with Johnny Grasso, an 11-year old friend of his eldest son Billy. When Johnny stays the night, Bill drugs the child then molests him. Later Bill visits another schoolmate of Billy's (whom he knows is at home alone) and molests him too. Helen decides she needs to live more dangerously and invites her mystery caller to visit her home. Allen, in turn, is bothered by his neighbour Kristina who tells him she has killed the apartment block's porter and hidden his body parts in her freezer. Allen eventually calls at Helen's apartment but, disappointed, she sends him away. Bill is caught by the police and confesses his crimes to Billy. Kristina is also arrested. Joy, Trish and Helen visit their reunited parents in Florida. Billy masturbates and runs in to tell his family that he's had an orgasm for the first time.

The first scene in *Happiness* details a forlorn break up in a New Jersey restaurant; the second a turgid therapy session where the analyst's mind wanders off to checklist his plans for the afternoon. Suburban life, it is implied, is drab, uniform and quietly despairing. But its semi-formal etiquette and chintz masks real runaway psychosis. We subsequently learn that, having finished his dinner, the dumped boyfriend goes home and kills himself. The man on the psychiatrist's couch makes dirty phone calls. The shrink himself is a child molester. Writer director Todd Solondz (as with his earlier indie hit *Welcome to the Dollhouse)* presents suburbia as a type of peripheral hell, a moral darkness on the edge of town where, in the words of Wallace Stevens, "the pure products of America go crazy."

All of which is nothing new. Contemporary film-makers—from Hal Hartley in the US to Alain Berliner *(Ma vie en rose)* in France and Mike Leigh in the UK—have found suburbia such a fertile creative territory that there's a danger it's become a kind of comic shorthand, a knee-jerk symbol for a certain strain of middle class pretension and hypocrisy. *Happiness* certainly doesn't shirk from hitting these buttons, but it hits them with such bravery and abandon as to conjure up a landscape at once blandly familiar and almost surreal. A perpetual, at times unbearable tension between normalcy and deviance, between comedy and tragedy is the fuel driving *Happiness*. Sex (the getting of it, the mastering of it, the getting rid of it) is the currency for all its inhabitants. Its genial caricatures turn abruptly black as pitch.

At the heart of Solondz's intersecting train wreck of lifelines sits psychiatrist Bill (an astonishing, no safety net performance from Dylan Baker), an outwardly upstanding suburban dad who masturbates to pre-teen magazines and romps off in dogged pursuit of his son's classmates. The portrayal of Bill is central to the success or otherwise of *Happiness*.   On the one hand, Solondz has undeniable fun with the character. Bill's interactions with little Billy view like a paedophilic pastiche of the father son chats in *Leave It to Beaver*, his attempts to dope the "girlish" Johnny Grasso are played as farce. Moreover, Solondz forces us to identify with this man. The dramatic medium favours his character: for all his faults, Bill is at least an active protagonist, a take charge contrast to the insipid toy who is dumped on by others, or the impotent Allen who can only release his desires by phone. Most crucially and problematically of all, the grim consequences of Bill's crimes are either lightly glossed over or omitted entirely.

By rights, such hurdles should be insurmountable. But *Happiness* conspires to get over them, and ultimately there is more to Solondz's film than shock tactics. It's undeniable that *Happiness* relies extensively on queasy comedy and the zap of the audience gross out. Yet these extreme flights of fancy finally take on a quality that hoists it far above the level of the supermarket tabloid. *Happiness* stretches its taboo subject matter to the limits, using a freak show explicitness to attain a rarefied altitude that other, supposedly 'brave' pictures (Adrian Lyne's *Lolita,* Roberto Benigni's *Life Is Beautiful*) perhaps dream of but are finally too dramatically conservative, too compromised, too burdened by perceived audience reactions to reach. By the time Bill has his last painful conversation with Billy, *Happiness* has come to rest in a dreamscape where alienation dovetails into shocking recognition, where disgust and delighted laughter exist side by side. We wouldn't want to live in the place where Solondz takes us, but somehow, we suspect, we do.

VILLAGE VOICE, 10/13/98, p. 119, J. Hoberman

It's dysfunction at the junction. Having showcased twin girls whose home is their prison *(The Apple)* and presented another teenager whose father is her, uh, destiny *(I Stand Alone),* not to mention the latest Woody Allen screed, the New York Film Festival plumbs the depths of Springerville with the spectacularly miserable families of Todd Solondz's *Happiness* and Thomas Vinterberg's *The Celebration.* Both, as their titles suggest, are comedies.

Solondz's cinema of cruelty was introduced to the world with his 1996 indie hit *Welcome to the Dollhouse,* a portrait of the tormented 12-year-old Dawn "Weiner Dog" Weiner, which not only offered the antidote to 40 years of domestic sitcoms, but remains the funniest, bleakest movie on the subject of suburban adolescence ever produced in this country. This shopping-mall *Los Olvidados* was not to every taste *(The New Yorker* declared it "hateful"), and *Happiness,* which has already strewn its share of psychological debris at the Cannes and Toronto film festivals, is scarcely less splenetic.

His ambitions having grown, Solondz creates in *Happiness* a world of Weiner dogs. A portrait of an upper-middle-class, nominally Jewish extended family, this is the *Hannah and Her Sisters* that the Woodman might make today, with an expulsive assist from the Farrelly brothers. In descending order of success—and ascending order of likability—the three sisters are a self-hating, bitchy best-selling author (Lara Flynn Boyle), a smugly self-deluded suburban hausfrau (Cynthia Stevenson) married to a shrink on the verge of a nervous breakdown (Dylan Baker), and a pitifully optimistic loser whose name is Joy (Jane Adams).

Even more than in his previous film, Solondz's style is clinical—if not pathological—in its lack of inflection. Every character is simultaneously the prisoner of desire and the victim of rejection. The mode is less black comedy than a particularly brutal and impassive mode of psychological slapstick. Joy's restaurant breakup with a fellow passive-aggressive (Jon Lovitz) and her erotic misadventures with a rakish Russian cabdriver (a hilarious, stellar vaudeville turn by Jared Harris) provide the least painful yocks—it's that kind of a movie.

Happiness is a relentless two hours and 20 minutes. As the misery mounts and the various trysts grow increasingly grotesque, the tormented father-son relationship that is the film's heart of darkness coalesces into an agonizingly explicit confession and explication of sexual guilt. Parents are supposed to discuss this stuff with their children, aren't they? Shot mainly in close-up, this man-to-boy dialogue is a scene that demands to be compared with Bibi Andersson's once shocking orgy description in Ingmar Bergman's *Persona.* If Hollywood were truly devoted to telling it like it is, Baker would win a special Oscar. To add to the creepiness, Solondz is (as he made clear in *Dollhouse)* an extremely sensitive director of kids.

Where *Welcome to the Dollhouse* derived a certain charge from being borderline tasteless, Solondz desecrates Ozzie-and-Harriet suburbia in somewhat the same spirit in which Freud's child patient Little Hans dreamt of smearing his mother's pocketbook with mucus. (As *Voice* readers know, *Happiness* had to be dumped by its original distributor, October, when its parent [sic] company Universal objected to the movie's alleged pedophilia.) *Happiness* may push gross-out pathos and ferocious geekiness too far in deconstructing the p.c. sex appeal of TV star Camryn Manheim, paired in masochistic misery with fellow tubster Philip Seymour Hoffman, but Solondz's Swiftian sense of human sexual practice as absurd, messy, and ridiculous could not be more topical.

Awash as it is in bodily fluids, *Happiness* conspicuously lacks the milk of human kindness. But then, as Solondz demonstrated so forcefully in *Welcome to the Dollhouse*, persecution does not necessarily make for generosity.

Also reviewed in:
CHICAGO TRIBUNE, 10/23/98, Friday/p. A, Michael Wilmington
NATION, 11/9/98, p. 34, Stuart Klawans
NEW REPUBLIC, 11/9/98, p. 28, Stanley Kauffmann
NEW YORK TIMES, 10/9/98, p. E10, Janet Maslin
NEW YORKER, 10/19/98, p. 94, Anthony Lane
VARIETY, 5/18-24/98, p. 73, Todd McCarthy
WASHINGTON POST, 10/23/98, p. B5, Stephen Hunter
WASHINGTON POST, 10/23/98, Weekend/p. 54, Michael O'Sullivan

HARD CORE LOGO

A Rolling Thunder Pictures release in association with Cowboy Booking International of an Ed Festus production. *Producer:* Christine Haebler and Brian Dennis. *Director:* Bruce McDonald. *Screenplay:* Noel S. Baker. *Based on the book by:* Michael Turner. *Director of Photography:* Danny Nowak. *Editor:* Reginald Harkema. *Music:* Schaun Tozer. *Production Designer:* David Wilson. *Running time:* 92 minutes. *MPAA Rating:* R.

CAST: Hugh Dillon (Joe Dick); Callum Keith Rennie (Billy Tallent); Bernie Coulson (Pipefitter); John Pyper-Ferguson (John Oxenberger); Julian Richings (Bucky Haight); Megan Leitch (Mary).

LOS ANGELES TIMES, 11/13/98, Calendar/p. B16, John Anderson

[*The following review by John Anderson appeared in a slightly different form in* **NEWSDAY, 11/13/98, Part II/p. B10.**]

The garbled voices, the grand-mal-seizure camera work, the "art shot" of the flaccid French fry being dragged through the catsup at the all-night diner—Bruce McDonald knows the rock-documentary shtick like he knows Johnny's Rotten.

"Hard Core Logo," his mockumentary about an '80s punk band that reunites for an anarchic, low-rent tour of Canada, is not just the best rock movie of the last several years, it creates/substantiates its own Descartian theory of cinematic existence: I pose, therefore I am.

McDonald, director of such rock'n'roll-scented road movies as "Roadkill" and "Highway 61," is fluent with the conventional mechanics of nonfiction filmmaking, which gives "Hard Core Logo" its hilarious bite. But he also knows the up-yours attitude of punk, the nihilism-meets-genuine passion of rock-gone-by and the premeditated nature of anger as a career tool. His movie, as antic and propulsive as it can often be, is also a commentary on the artist as bore.

Reassembled by lead singer Joe Dick (Hugh Dillon) to do a benefit/anti-gun tour after the shooting of seminal punker Bucky Haight (Julian Richings), the Logos—Billy Tallent (Callum Keith Rennie), John Oxenberger (John Pyper-Ferguson) and Pipefitter (Bernie Coulson)—hit the revival road with the doomed optimism of "Spinal Tap" and with the undigested bile of the second Nixon administration.

Playing to small rooms and increasingly small audiences, they start out well and rapidly deteriorate, both musically and personally. Billy is biding his time before he gets the "big gig" with the headlining band Jenifur; Pipefitter might just as easily be robbing gas stations as playing drums; and bassist Oxenberger is a medicated schizophrenic who can't find his medication. Joe Dick, the baseball cap-wearing rock general with the Mohawk hair, throws around band and audience abuse.

McDonald plays it straight at first, with the backstage-style footage and gyrating concert scenes but the film becomes increasingly expressionistic and cinematic, perhaps in proportion to how increasingly unfilmable the band becomes. We get little bits of history—some distinctly disturbing—about the band's early history. You certainly know why they might hate one another; you sense why they might stay together. You don't know, necessarily, about the loss of brain cells. In the film's most poignant segment, subtitled "Mary the Fan," an old camp follower-groupie (Megan Leitch) shows up with her visibly uncomfortable husband and small daughter and tries to revisit the past. After a rambling discussion about crimes of the past, Oxenberger asks, "What's your name?" Mary is as shattered as we are.

Everyone in the film is convincing, sometimes moving and always funny—abetted, of course, by McDonald's construct, which is intentionally tongue-in-cheek and jaded and cognizant of the foibles of modem celebrity. Similarly, McDonald marries two sensibilities—utter cynicism and rock romance—with a resulting combo platter that's tartly delicious.

VILLAGE VOICE, 11/17/98, p. 138, Michael Zilberman

This Canadian import is a mockumentary peculiarly devoid of mockery; it's hard, in fact, to recall a film so seriously fawning before so featherweight a subject. An unseen chronicler dogs a reunion tour of the titular band, conveniently there for every tussle between singer Joe Dick and songwriter-guitarist Billy Tallent (the names presumably forming a dichotomous pair). There's fertile ground for punk fury, but Noel S. Baker's script would much rather ladle on wink-wink homoeroticism, and director Bruce McDonald soon all but abandons the format: Let this stand as the first docu-styled enterprise to attempt a garish acid sequence.

Schaun Tozer's original songs ("Rock'n'roll is fat and ugly!") passably approximate old-school punk. But dressed up as it is in St. Mark's bric-a-brac, *Hard Core Logo* is essentially an earnest male weepie about friendships, and its backstage minutiae aren't all that different from, say, *That Thing You Do*. By the time the film reaches its "tragic" ending—humorlessly swiped from *Man Bites Dog*—it has demonstrated neither dick nor talent.

Also reviewed in:
NEW YORK TIMES, 11/13/98, p. E18, Stephen Holden
VARIETY, 5/27-6/2/96, p. 70, Brendan Kelly

HARD RAIN

A Paramount Pictures release in association with Mutual Film Company of a Mark Gordon/ Gary Levinsohn production. *Executive Producer:* Allison Lyon Segan. *Producer:* Mark Gordon, Gary Levinsohn, and Ian Bryce. *Director:* Mikael Salomon. *Screenplay:* Graham Yost. *Director of Photography:* Peter Menzies, Jr. *Editor:* Paul Hirsch. *Music:* Christopher Young. *Music Editor:* Tom Milano. *Sound:* Lee Orloff and (music) Michael Farrow and Dick Lewzey. *Sound Editor:* Sandy Berman and Cameron Frankley. *Casting:* Risa Bramon-Garcia and Randi Hiller. *Production Designer:* J. Michael Riva. *Art Director:* David Klassen. *Set Designer:* Charisse Cardenas, Al Hobbs, and Hugo Santiago. *Set Decorator:* Ron Reiss. *Special Effects:* John Frazier and Jim Schwalm. *Costumes:* Kathleen Detoro. *Make-up:* Mike Hancock and Sharon Ilson. *Stunt Coordinator:* Jeff Habberstad. *Running time:* 98 minutes. *MPAA Rating:* R.

CAST: Morgan Freeman (Jim); Christian Slater (Tom); Randy Quaid (Sheriff); Minnie Driver (Karen); Edward Asner (Charlie); Richard Dysart (Henry); Betty White (Doreen); Michael Goorjian (Kenny); Dann Florek (Mr. Mehlor); Ricky Harris (Ray); Mark Rolston (Wayne); Peter Murnik (Phil); Wayne Duvall (Hank); Ray Baker (Mayor); Lisa Fuhrman (Mayor's Wife); Jay Patterson (Mr. Wellman); Michael Monks (Father on Local News); Mackenzie Bryce (Baby on Local News).

LOS ANGELES TIMES, 1/16/98, Calendar/p. 10, Kevin Thomas

As a depiction of a small Midwestern city undergoing a major flood during a furious rainstorm, "Hard Rain" is as convincing as James Cameron's sinking of the Titanic. This documentary—like realism, alas, only underlines the preposterousness of its plot with its torrent of contrived, credibility-defying cliffhangers.

A lighter touch, a sense of not taking itself too seriously, could have helped, but this Paramount release is basically a standard action-adventure. Directed with more vigor and efficiency than inspiration by Mikael Salomon, it relies heavily on the sheer presence of its first-rate cast, whose roles tend to be short on characterization.

The film opens spectacularly with a dramatic aerial shot swooping down on to a classic 19th century Main Street, where at its key intersection the local sheriff (Randy Quaid) is directing the final stages of the evacuation of the city.

Meanwhile, armored truck drivers Christian Slater and Edward Asner are emptying the vault at the local bank of its cash deposits as part of an assignment to clear out a series of banks adjacent to a river on the verge of overflowing. On the way out of town, Asner loses control of the truck amid rising water and makes a signal for help that's picked up by ex-con Morgan Freeman, who is only too eager to grab the truck's holdings, which add up to $3 million plus.

From this point on, writer Graham Yost piles on plot complications as fast as the water rises, and what emerges is the notion that almost everyone can be tempted by greed. We don't know whether this applies to Slater till the finish; only Minnie Driver's stained-glass restorer seems pretty immune to temptation.

It's no stretch for Freeman to play a likable good-bad guy, but he seems too intelligent to have credibly assembled such inept partners in crime. The same goes for Slater, as an average Joe, or Quaid a disgruntled law enforcement officer. Similarly, little is asked of Driver, such a standout in "Good Will Hunting," beyond being tart-tongued and spunky.

There's some comic relief from Betty White as an amusing obtuse nagging wife and Richard Dysart as her long-suffering husband. Asner, the film's strongest presence, exits early.

"Hard Rain's" logistics really are impressive—it's as if we're watching the inundation of Grand Forks, N.D., all over again. However, the underwater sequences are too similar to those in "Titanic" for this film as a whole not to suffer in comparison. The absolutely convincing staging of the flood may just be enough for the least demanding of action fans.

NEW YORK POST, 1/16/98, p. 45, Michael Medved

The traditional disaster film formula presents a large, colorful cast of sympathetic victims, thrown together with a villain or two to provide additional trouble and excitement.

"Hard Rain" audaciously reverses this standard format, populating its story with a teeming array of depressingly despicable creeps, while only two likable misfits deserve to survive the devastation.

It's an intriguing experiment (from the writer and producer who previously collaborated on "Speed" and "Broken Arrow"), but the result is that the audience ends up rooting for the flood—hoping the inexorably rising waters will soon sweep away this disgusting cross-section of humanity.

The story unfolds in a fictional Midwestern town, where the weary sheriff (Randy Quaid), recently thrown out of office by his ungrateful neighbors, mobilizes his alternately bungling and corrupt deputies to deal with the usual looting and petty theft as people abandon their homes to the raging waters.

Christian Slater and his bossy uncle (Ed Asner) work as conscientious armored car drivers, emptying $3 million dollars from a local bank. When their vehicle gets stuck on a flooded roadway they radio for help, but their message is intercepted by a gang of murderous thieves.

Led by old pro Morgan Freeman, determined to make one big score so he can retire, the crooks open fire but Slater flees with the money and spends the rest of the movie playing a soaked version of cat-and-mouse with the bad guys.

His only reliable help comes from an artist (Minnie Driver) determined to save a venerable church she has recently restored in town.

The script offers its share of surprises as one after another of the purportedly wholesome Bedford Falls types show their sickening true colors.

The filmmakers seem determined to echo "Blue Velvet by exposing moral rot behind a nostalgic Main Street facade. Incoherent religious references emanate from one of the thieves, who constantly mutters biblical citations, and Driver's beloved church windows are spectacularly destroyed by greed and betrayal.

Chase scenes with all manner of speedboats and Jet Skis careening through the flooded halls of a high-school have been reasonably well staged but eventually they grow tedious, while the bad guys suffer from the annoying habit of requiring many different gruesome deaths before they finally go down for good.

The elaborate miniatures and flashy special effects, like all other elements of the film, display calculating, show-offy excess rather than humanity or realism.

NEWSDAY, 1/16/98, Part II/p. B7, John Anderson

To quote Sam Spade, "So many guns, so few brains." And so much water! Enough so you can't imagine how "Hard Rain" ever got so overheated. Or why, with so much wooden acting, the whole thing doesn't just float away.

But no. Moored in your field of vision for what seems to be 40 days and 40 nights, "Hard Rain" is a consistently illogical cartoon that has the courtesy—as it ladles up the inane—to explain what it is you're watching. And why.

For instance, consider Tom the armored-car guard (Christian Slater) who, having been ambushed and his partner (Ed Asner) killed, drags away millions in cash from his unmovable truck rather than simply flee through the rising waters of Huntingsburg. Is it out of a sense of duty to his employer? Out of venegeance for his partner and uncle? Greed? No way. "As long as he knows where the money is and we don't, we won't kill him," says ringleader Jim (Morgan Freeman), explaining Tom's motivation. Which doesn't explain why, since he's slogging though the water anyway, Tom wouldn't just get away as fast as he could. But then there wouldn't be a movie.

And what a movie! Cinematographer-cum-director Mikael Salomon, Oscar-nominated for his visual effects ("Backdraft," "The Abyss") creates a sodden, ark-needy world that doesn't quite demonize the elements (a la the wind in "Twister") but suggests that in their disinterest, they're pretty scary just the same. The problem is, just as special-effects techniques have grown more sophisticated, so have our expectations. And the look of "Hard Rain"—particularly in the opening aerial sequence, showing the town largely under water—is more cartoonish than convincing.

It's uncanny. Once Tom hides the money and the chase begins, you start asking yourself: How are they going to work a beautiful woman into all this moistness and—splash!—there she is, Karen the church restorer (no one has a last name) played by Minnie Driver with a new accent and a mission to keep her stained glass and candles from imminent submersion. She will save Tom, Tom will save her, the sheriff (Randy Quaid) will try to get her to evacuate the town like everyone else, and she'll become a hostage, like any good starlet would under the same set of circumstances.

Freeman lends a certain noble gravity to whatever he's in, and he's not in "Hard Rain" enough. Slater, who has a certain charm—even while delivering those spongy zingers that follow each small battle with Jim and his crew—is playing a role that's too young for him, given Tom's combination of dead-end job and intelligence. But "Hard Rain" is really about action—jet-skiing through flooded school corridors, motorboating around the streets of Huntingsburg, electrocutions from exploding transformers. (Wouldn't a utility cut the town's power once the water level reached 16 feet or so? Just asking). And remarkable resiliency by bad guys who by all rights should be dead; there haven't been this many soggy resurrections since "Cape Fear."

Although "Hard Rain" does try to explain all the plot holes as it goes along, it's still unclear why the sheriff and his deputies left Tom locked in a jail cell when it was clear that the water was coming in and up. I'm just guessing, but maybe they saw "Pump Up the Volume."

SIGHT AND SOUND, 5/98, p. 49, Andy Richards

Tom and his uncle Charlie are the drivers of an armoured car delivering $3 million in cash. Their vehicle breaks down in almost evacuated Huntingburg, Indiana, a small town suffering from torrential rain and flooding from the Ohio River. They are ambushed by Jim and his crew of robbers, who accidentally kill Charlie. Tom takes off and hides the money in a submerged graveyard.

The crew steal a motor boat and a pair of jet-skis, and pursue Tom through a flooded school. Tom escapes, and takes refuge in a church where he is mistaken for a looter and knocked out by Karen, a church restorer. Waking up in jail, Tom explains his situation to the sheriff, who leaves to retrieve the money. The flood gates open, and a tidal wave hits the town. Karen saves Tom from drowning in his cell. They are pursued by Jim's men, and take refuge with elderly eccentrics Henry and Doreen, but Tom is captured by Jim's men. Jim reveals that he was in league with Charlie all along.

Jim and the crew are ambushed by the sheriff and his deputies, who have decided to keep the money. Wayne, one of the sheriff's deputies, handcuffs Karen to her house's banister, and tries to rape her, but she stabs him dead. Another tidal wave hits the town as Tom and Jim have a series of gun battles with the sheriff and his cronies. Tom frees Karen. The sheriff is eventually shot dead by Tom just before he can shoot Karen. With the National Guard approaching, Tom allows Jim to escape with the money.

Following in the wake of *Twister, Daylight, Dante's Peak, Volcano* and *Titanic, Hard Rain* (originally titled *Flood)* offers itself as the latest in the deluge of big-budget, effects-driven disaster movies, while still managing to serve up a few surprises amid its retro-generic trappings. Director Mikael Salomon (cinematographer on *The Abyss)* successfully extracts several engagingly tense set-pieces from his film's 'high concept' (rising water levels)—notably Christian Slater's Tom struggling to escape from his jail cell. Meanwhile, the digital effects are definitely some of the best of their kind, combined convincingly with genuine water-tank effects. *Hard Rain*'s narrative benefits from its leanness and fast pacing, knowing when to up its ante and usher in the next tidal wave or gun battle.

Unfortunately, Salomon makes unconvincing and redundant attempts to add moral depth to his tale by trying to make us wonder whether Tom, having concealed the money entrusted to him, will attempt to make off with it himself. This is not a film that allows itself the time for anything other than broad-stroke characterisations (although Morgan Freeman has fun as Jim, managing to suggest a certain corrupted dignity under his gold earring and flamboyant hat). It later transpires that Jim's potentially interesting cohorts have been introduced primarily as expendables, their 'softness' merely intended to offset the viciousness and sadism of the real villains of the piece—Randy Quaid's rapacious sheriff and his cronies.

As soon as the sheriff reveals his true intentions, *Hard Rain* further mutates from its disaster-heist scenario to add elements from the paranoid *Deliverance/Southern Comfort* sub-genre of films wherein visitors to conservative isolated US communities uncover an ugly, primal viciousness that is ultimately mirrored in their own souls. The film is at pains to emphasise the apocalyptic starkness of its battleground (characterised by unremitting darkness and the claustrophobia of the film's water-logged studio sets) by adding Christian symbols (stained glass, crosses, Jim's crucifix earring, the church itself) and having Ray, one of Jim's men, quote with mock-portentousness from Jeremiah and other Biblical prophets. Yet the characters remain so much soaked cardboard, and the film's strivings for greater resonance are left unfulfilled. If *Hard Rain* is thus inadequate as a meditation on human fallibility and greed, it remains efficient and exciting enough as a gimmicky action vehicle with some diverting plot twists.

VILLAGE VOICE, 1/27/98, p. 68, Dennis Lim

Waterlogged crap for those who found *Titanic* too intricate, *Hard Rain* is the typical result of a Hollywood off-season bowel movement. Monumentally stupid, predictably ludicrous, and consistently audience-insulting, this is what happens when script development stops at "heist during flood." As far as I can figure, the film has no characters: Christian Slater, Morgan Freeman, Randy Quaid, and Minnie Driver are all here (as, respectively, an armored-car courier, a master thief, a redneck sheriff, and a feisty something-or-other), but have little to do besides get wet and sound trite. Assorted cops and crooks are present, mainly to pad out the body count.

The script is by Graham Yost,whose previous throw-aways (Jan De Bont's *Speed* and John Woo's *Broken Arrow)* at least benefitted from smidgens of directorial gall. Mikael Salomon, James Cameron's cinematographer on The *Abyss,* is a director with no discernible ideas, and he's curiously reliant on Christopher Young's score, which deafeningly cues every already transparent plot twist.

Freeman has finally run into a role that even he can't flesh out (there's an attempt at Eastwood-like ambivalence, which the brain-dead context essentially drowns out). Slater's blank, bland hero lacks charisma and, as usual, the harder he tries, the worse it gets, though, at one point, Los Angeles prison authorities may be interested to know, he pulls off a Houdini-worthy escape from a flooded jail cell.

Also reviewed in:
CHICAGO TRIBUNE, 1/16/98, Friday/p. F, Mark Caro
NEW YORK TIMES, 1/16/98, p. E10, Lawrence Van Gelder
VARIETY, 1/12-18/98, p. 63, Todd McCarthy

HAV PLENTY

A Miramax Films release in association with Wanderlust Pictures, Inc. and e2 filmworks in a dream by C.S.C.   *Executive Producer:* Tracey E. Edmonds, Kenneth "Babyface" Edmonds, Bridget D. Davis, and S.J. Cherot.   *Producer:* Christopher Scott Cherot and Robyn M. Greene.   *Director:* Christopher Scott Cherot.   *Screenplay:* Christopher Scot Cherot.   *Director of Photography:* Kerwin Devonish. *Editor:* Christopher Scott Cherot.   *Music:* Wendy Melvoin and Lisa Coleman.   *Sound:* Damian Canelos.   *Sound Editor:* Kevin Lee and Harry Bolles.   *Costumes:* Christina G. Miller. *Make-up:* Christina G. Miller.   *Running time:* 105 minutes.   *MPAA Rating:* R.

CAST: Chenoa Maxwell (Havilland Savage);   Hill Harper (Michael Simmons);   Christopher Scott Cherot (Lee Plenty);   Tammi Katherine Jones (Caroline Gooden);   Robinne Lee (Leigh Darling);   Reginald James (Felix Darling);   Margie St. Juste (Alexandria Beaumont);   Chuck Baron (Mr. Savage);   Kim Harris (Bobby Montgomery);   Betty Vaughn (Grandma Moore);   Michele Turner (Sylvia Savage);   P. G. Reese (Evelyn);   Wanda Candelario (Girl in Gas Station);   Nia Long (Trudy);   Shemar Moore (Chris);   Lauryn Hill (Debra);   Chilli (Kris);   Mekhi Phifer (Harold);   Leslie "Big Lez" Segar (Jane);   Christopher Batyr (Emcee);   Shontonette Crawford, Reginald Bruce, and Alaina Irizarry (Spectators);   Keith Hudson (Festival Participant);   Tracey E. Edmonds (Amy Madison);   Kenneth "Babyface" Edmonds (Lloyd Banks);   Bridge D. Davis, Shara P. Fleming, and Patrik Ian Polk (Caprice Films Entourage).

LOS ANGELES TIMES, 6/19/98, Calendar/p. 8, Kevin Thomas

Christopher Scott Cherot has no lack of nerve, for he not only wrote, directed and edited his debut feature, the engaging "Hav Plenty," but also stars in it—as a young man women just love to throw themselves at. (Never mind that Cherot's Lee Plenty is a writer so broke he's living in his car.)

He's trying—but not too hard, it would seem—to get his life together when he gets a call from a former classmate (Chenoa Maxwell) to come down to Washington, D.C., from New York for a New Year's Eve celebration.

Maxwell's alternately appealing and imperious Havilland ("Hav") Savage is an ultimate Black American Princess. She has a great job, her parents are rich (though divorced), and her mother has a luxurious suburban D.C. home, where much of the film will unfold. In conversation, she drops names like Eddie (as in Murphy) and Quentin (as in you-know-who). Hav's also engaged to a rock star described as "the next Marvin Gaye"—but she's just discovered he has, not surprisingly, a rather casual view of fidelity. They won't be seeing the New Year in together.

The group of people Hav has invited over to her mother's home—her mother is off somewhere with her fiance—includes her half-sister Leigh (Robinne Lee) and Leigh's husband, Felix (Reginald James), and Hav's lacquered pal Caroline (Tammi Katherine Jones), who one moment wouldn't give a homeless man the time of day and the next is coming on to Lee Plenty like gangbusters. But Lee isn't receptive to Caroline or anyone else, for that matter.

The point is that the passive Lee is not interested in casual sex, even with Hav, whom he loves as much as she does him—but it takes a whole movie for them to figure this out. Of course, that the good-looking Lee, a man whose empathy knows no limits, is determinedly impossible to get makes him all the more attractive to the women who hit on him.

Cherot has an ear for dialogue and a way with actors. Maxwell, as talented as she is lovely, expertly rings in all the self-discovery she experiences in the course of an extended weekend. (Robinne Lee is also a special delight as the reflective Leigh.)

The pleasure in watching "Hav Plenty" comes from seeing Cherot discover the possibilities of the medium as he goes along. As it unfolds, repartee gives way to an increasing sense of the visual, and by the time the film is over, Cherot has discovered how potent Maxwell can be in repose, expressing herself without resorting to words.

NEW YORK POST, 6/19/98, p. 50, Thelma Adams

Mrs. Cherot, your son has talent. And it was noble of you to mortgage you house to bankroll Christopher Scott's first feature, "Hav Plenty."

But did your son have to write, direct, edit and star in his first movie?

Cherot plays Lee Plenty, the title's better half. The charming but unemployed Manhattan writer turns a failed New Year's Eve weekend in D.C. with buppy maneater Havilland "Hav" Savage (Chenoa Maxwell) into a successful movie.

Fairy tales can come true—and in Cherot's case, Miramax picked up the autobiographical comedy. Tracey E. and Kenneth "Babyface" Edmonds, the musical couple who catered "Soul Food," executive produced and packaged the movie's steaming soundtrack CD.

There are funny, flirtatious exchanges and there is social commentary. After Hav shows Plenty her photo album, stuffed with pictures of evenings with Eddie Murphy and picnics with David Dinkins, Lee says, sarcastically: "Excuse me, you dropped something... a name."

Cherot has an ear for dialog—but no eye for composition and casting. The over-starched Maxwell is attractive but no comic foil.

The supporting players—with the exception of Hill Harper, as Hav's rapping fiance—make Queen Latifah look like Joan Crawford.

Mrs. Cherot, no disrespect, but, between us mothers, you took quite a gamble with your house. Your son has turned a sitcom situation into a long day's journey into New Year's Eve. Thank God for Miramax!

NEWSDAY, 6/19/98, Part II/p. B7, John Anderson

There's a symptom manifested by film-festival-attending critics that we'll call "festival head": The overreaction to any decent movie, because what you've watched for a week is unwatchable. Tangentially, movies also are funnier when you watch them with a real audience (not that festival audiences aren't real). It's an arguable point, I suppose, but comedy usually loves company.

None of which, by the way, has anything necessarily to do with "Hav Plenty," Christopher Scott Cherot's sophisticated debut feature, a movie about young people you almost never see onscreen, two of whom are blind to the love that's staring them in the face. But after not having seen the film for five months—since its popular screenings at the Sundance Film Festival in January—it now seems like a different movie. Cherot's strongest suit is his timing, which is something you can't fuss with—and someone seems to have fussed. The sound track seems saturated with music that wasn't there before and wasn't needed. Scenes are missing. Like I say, it's hard to really be sure, but something's amiss.

What's certain is that Cherot has a knack for the clever line, the well-crafted character and the modulated mood. His apartmentless New York writer, Lee Plenty (whose preoccupation is

Havilland "Hav" Savage, played by Chenoa Maxwell), probably shouldn't talk to the camera as often as he does, because it tends to be jarring, but he's a master of the disarming observation and pointed remark. And while he's a bit stiff cinemagraphically, the movie has a lot of heart.

Lee, whose big zit in the middle of his forehead adds a bit of *verité* to the goings on, is on the horns of an unspoken romantic/economic dilemma. When Hav invites him to her mother's Washington home for New Year's, he hustles on down, but at the same time neither he nor Hav even entertains the idea of a getting together. Having lost his home and his book contract, his prospects are such that she's out of his league (she may be a lawyer; it isn't very clear). And here Cherot is making some astutely understated observations about skewed priorities.

On the other hand, why would they get together? Hav is "Hav Plenty's" basic flaw. Although Maxwell does well by her, and she's beautiful, she's also icy, rigid and insensitive to those she supposedly loves. She offers her unemployed sister Leigh (Robinne Lee), a job in New York, even though Leigh's husband, Felix (Reginald James), is doing quite well in D.C. And although her ex-fiancee, big-time singer Michael Simmons (Hill Harper) is a creep—and Cherot's funniest invention—her unyielding anger at his infidelities is not very attractive.

It all works out, of course. It has to: The ending, which we won't disclose, is a devastating editorial on the very thing this movie went through. Tammi Katherine Jones is very good as Hav's love-hungry buddy Caroline, and Harper is hilarious as the narcissistic Michael. But what's the story behind the picture Hav finds in his Bible, showing his face beaten to a pulp? And what happened to Havilland's mother? I seem to remember something about them, but that was in another movie altogether.

VILLAGE VOICE, 6/23/98, p. 140, Amy Taubin

Lee Plenty (Christopher Scott Cherot) is madly in love with Havilland Savage (Chenoa Maxwell), even though he despises her ambitious buppie lifestyle. Lee, whose mocking way with words and laid-back demeanor (he never sits when he can sprawl) make him irresistible to everyone except Havilland, describes himself as "a thread-bare, fake, book-writing sucker who lives in his car." Certainly not the right guy for a hotshot-editor like Havilland who was born with a silver spoon in her mouth. So why does she invite him to spend New Year's weekend in the bourgie bosom of her family?

A romantic comedy of manners, *Hav Plenty* is one of a handful of films set in the upper-middle-class African American society of New York and D.C. Better observed and more biting than the generic *love jones*, it's remarkable for its hilariously accurate portrait of a black intellectual slacker, a wannabe novelist paralyzed by self-doubt. A low-budget, no-frills film, *Hav Plenty* doesn't lack for visual humor to underscore its verbal wit. Lee is never so vulnerable (or attractive) as when he turns up in Havilland's bed wearing a cartoon-mouse T-shirt.

Cherot is right on the money about the anger and resentment that drive romantic love and the power games lovers play to protect themselves and stay involved. It's exactly because Lee is a dropout from the middle class that he wants to conquer Havilland, the ultimate material girl. (And of course, only a guy who knows he has a middle-class mom with an extra bedroom could risk being jobless and homeless at 30—for the sake of his art.)

Invited to a family brunch with Havilland's software-tycoon father, Lee gets testy when the subject of her rap-star boyfriend Michael (Hill Harper) comes up. While everyone gazes in awe at Michael's latest platinum CD, Lee undertakes to read aloud from the lyric sheet. "I'm a crack addict. Girl, I'm addicted to your crack." He might as well be addressing the next table. When money and success are involved, even a dad who loves his daughter hears only what he wants to hear.

A first-time writer-director, Cherot hadn't intended to play the lead role in his openly autobiographical film. (*Hav Plenty* opens with the words "This is a true story.") But when his leading actor got a more lucrative job just days before *Hav Plenty* was scheduled to go into production, Cherot was forced to step in.

As an actor, Cherot has an easy, seductive presence. He convinces us (as few actors could) that the character he's playing is a talented writer, because (unlike most actors) he actually is a talented writer. Cherot's Lee Plenty is at once protagonist, witness, and narrator. Turning to the camera, he invites us into a screwball romance where the only operative point of view is his own.

Did I turn against him because of unfair advantage (as, for example, I often turn against Woody Allen)? I didn't at first, although perhaps I should have. It's creepy that most of the female roles are so one-dimensional. The problem with Havilland is a little different. Cherot has written an interesting character, but Maxwell, not the most subtle of actors, plays her on a single, strained, farcical note.

In the first version of the film (shown at last year's Toronto Film Festival), Lee doesn't get his heart's desire, and his failure undercuts the fact that Cherot was playing with a stacked deck. But when Miramax bought the film, they insisted on a more upbeat ending. The epilogue Cherot came up with has the opposite effect. It's one thing when a guy who's in total control comes out a loser. It's another when his only problem is the anxiety of getting what he wished for. Cynical and sophomoric, the new ending lacks the wit and intelligence that make the rest of the film such a pleasure.

Also reviewed in:
CHICAGO TRIBUNE, 6/19/98, Friday/p. B, Mark Caro
NEW YORK TIMES, 6/19/98, p. E26, Stephen Holden
VARIETY, 10/20-26/97, p. 71, Emanuel Levy
WASHINGTON POST, 6/9/98, Weekend/p. 48, Michael O'Sullivan

HE GOT GAME

A Touchstone Pictures release of a 40 Acres and a Mule Filmworks production. *Producer:* Jon Kilik and Spike Lee. *Director:* Spike Lee. *Screenplay:* Spike Lee. *Director of Photography:* Malik Hassan Sayeed. *Editor:* Barry Alexander Brown. *Music:* Aaron Copland. *Music Editor:* Maisie Weissman. *Sound:* Allan Byer and Mathew Price. *Sound Editor:* Kevin Lee. *Casting:* Aisha Coley. *Production Designer:* Wynn Thomas. *Art Director:* David Stein. *Set Decorator:* Caroly Cartwright. *Set Dresser:* Mark Selemon, Peter Von Bartheld, Bill Kolpin, Mark Simon, and James Callahan. *Special Effects:* Wilfred Caban. *Costumes:* Sandra Hernandez. *Make-up:* Anita Gibson. *Stunt Coordinator:* Jeff Ward and Manny Siverio. *Running time:* 131 minutes. *MPAA Rating:* R.

CAST: Denzel Washington (Jake Shuttlesworth); Ray Allen (Jesus Shuttlesworth); Milla Jovovich (Dakota Burns); Rosario Dawson (Lala Bonilla); Hill Harper (Coleman "Booger" Sykes); Zelda Harris (Mary Shuttlesworth); Ned Beatty (Warden Wyatt); Jim Brown (Spivey); Joseph Lyle Taylor (Crudup); Bill Nunn (Uncle Bubba); Michele Shay (Aunt Sally); Thomas Jefferson Byrd (Sweetness); Roger Guenveur Smith (Big Time Willie); John Turturro (Coach Billy Sunday); Lonette McKee (Martha Shuttlesworth); Arthur J. Nascarella (Coach Cincotta); Travis Best (Sip); Walter McCarty (Mance); John Wallace (Lonnie); Rick Fox (Chick Deagan); Al Palagonia (Dom Pagnotti); Leonard Roberts (D'Andre Mackey); Saul Stein (Prison Guard Books); Ron Cephas Jones (Prison Guard Burwell); Jade Yorker (Jesus Shuttlesworth, age 12); Quinn Harris (Mary Shuttlesworth, age 6); Gus Johnson (PSAL Announcer); Stuart Scott (TV Announcer); Ray Clay (Tech U Announcer); J.C. Mackenzie (Doctor Cone); Coati Mundi (Clerk in Motel); Avery Glymph (Sneaker Clerk); Ciara A. Shiels (Mary's Friend); Mark Breland (Man With Gat); Heather Hunter (Female in Sex Montage); Christopher Wynkoop (The John); Alonzo Scales (Goose); Lori Rom (June); Kim Director (Lynn); Felicia Finley (Molly); Tiffany Jones (Buffy); Jill Kelly (Suzie); Jennifer Esposito (Ms. Janus); Tony Paige (Correction Officer); Dean Smith, John Chaney, Roy Williams, Denny Crum, Clem Haskins, Jim Boeheim, Robert "Bobby" Cremins, Bill Walton, Reggie Miller, Scottie Pippen, Lute Olson, John Thompson, Nolan Richardson, Tom Davis, George Karl, Rick Pitino, Dick Vitale, Shaquille O'Neal, Charles Barkley, Michael Jordan, and Robin Roberts (Themselves).

CHRISTIAN SCIENCE MONITOR, 5/8/98, p. 15, David Sterritt

By a wide margin, Spike Lee is the most gifted and influential black filmmaker in American movies. His new picture, "He Got Game," is his most ambitious production since the sweeping "Malcolm X" six years ago.

It's far from perfect, and some scenes may strike viewers as overcooked, overblown, or offensive. But its best moments are as exuberant and insightful as anything the screen has given us this season, and its passionate concern for believable characters in a recognizably real world offers a refreshing change from the current spate of feel-good fantasies.

Denzel Washington plays Jake Shuttlesworth, a fundamentally decent man who's locked away in prison after accidentally causing his wife's death. The warden approaches him with an unusual offer involving Jake's son, a superb basketball player about to finish high school. Jake will be set free, the warden says, if he can persuade the boy to join the local college team instead of signing with a major school or turning pro.

Jake is willing to try, but his son has never forgiven him for the tragedy he caused and will barely speak to him, much less follow his wishes. Given just a week to accomplish his task, Jake returns to the city and reestablishes contact with his shattered family. There he discovers that his son is being bombarded with offers from a bewildering number of sports promoters with highly questionable motives.

On one level, "He Got Game" is a realistic family drama centering on a complex father-son relationship. On another level, it has elements of a religious allegory. Jake's son is named Jesus, and the offers he's getting from greedy basketball teams—many laced with enticements of sex or money—are portrayed as devilish temptations in the urban wilderness. At the same time, the worship he receives from admirers (constantly chanting "Jesus saves") serves as a pointed criticism of some people's tendency to seek "salvation" from material activities and human personalities.

On still another level, "He Got Game" is an energetic attempt to create a new kind of American mythology. The key to this is Lee's remarkable choice of music—a blend of rap songs from the group Public Enemy and, more surprising, lively renditions of classic pieces by composer Aaron Copland.

To hear this music alongside scrappy basketball scenes and other urban episodes is to experience an exhilarating new approach to portraying the American experience in movie terms. It marks one of the most brilliantly original moves in Lee's always-unpredictable career.

Not all of "He Got Game" is so successful. Washington's feisty performance is marred by a couple of flat scenes; certain story twists are less than convincing; and eruptions of explicit sexuality and drug use will jar some moviegoers despite their cautionary intent. In all, though, this stands with the most exciting pictures Lee has made since "Do the Right Thing" established him as one of the screen's most inventive young artists.

LOS ANGELES TIMES, 5/1/98, Calendar/p. 1, Kenneth Turan

Two men are shooting baskets in the opening montage of Spike Lee's "He Got Game"—two men with similar fluid outside shots, not surprising for a father and a son. The younger man is a gifted high school senior from Coney Island, his father a convicted murderer imprisoned in Attica in upstate New York. The city game was a factor in their separation, and now it's going to join their worlds once again.

Given that writer-director Lee is one of the most visible of the New York Knicks' celebrity fans, what's surprising is not that he made a film about the sport he cares so much about but that he waited so long. As with much of Lee's work, the director's passion is a source of great strength but it also occasionally hamstrings matters by encouraging him to include more than comfortably fits on the screen.

For single-focus filmmaking is not Lee's style. He is, thankfully, an ambitious director, someone who is prone to sending his films off into several different areas simultaneously. "He Got Game" is always watchable and often compelling, but it is also erratic and unwieldy, the result, perhaps, of having too much to say, of trying to do too much with the ball too much of the time.

As has become traditional with Lee's films, "He Got Game" starts with an involving credits sequence, and this one, with its shots of determined young men and women playing basketball in all kinds of environments across the country, strikes a note of almost poetic love for the game that is a constant theme. Lee's unexpected use of big chunks of composer Aaron Copland's sweeping music throughout the film points to his belief in the quintessentially Americanness of both the game and the story he's telling.

Lee almost immediately links his graceful tributes to the sport with a pure pulp story line. Jake Shuttlesworth (Denzel Washington), with 15 years left on his sentence, is called into the office of Warden Wyatt (Ned Beatty). The subject of the conversation is Jake's son Jesus Shuttlesworth.

Jesus, who plays for the real-life Lincoln High School in Brooklyn, is the No. 1 high school prospect in the country, labeled "Jesus of Coney Island" by Sports Illustrated. And celebrated college coaches (many of them, like John Thompson and the recently retired Dean Smith, making cameo appearances in the film) are just about drooling to get him on their team.

The governor, however, happens to be a major fan of mythical Big State University. If Jake can convince Jesus to commit to the school, his sentence might be reduced. With a week left before Jesus has to make a decision, Jake is clandestinely let out of prison in the care of two parole officers (one played by the veteran actor-athlete Jim Brown) and charged with getting his son to sign on the dotted line for Big State.

Washington is so consistently effective an actor that it hardly needs be said that his excellent performance as the beleaguered Jake carries the film. What is of interest is the way Washington makes subtle changes in his usually polished persona to be convincing as a man who has enough menace and violence in him to have landed in prison and to have survived six-plus years inside.

Playing son Jesus is a bona fide basketball All-American, the youthful-looking 22-year-old Ray Allen of the Milwaukee Bucks. Serious enough about acting to have devoted eight weeks of his off-season to working with a coach, Allen brings a verisimilitude to his part that is essential to yet another one of Lee's aims, the detailing of the pressures brought on highly coveted young athletes.

Some of "He Got Game's" strongest sequences involve what hard guy Big Time Willie (Lee regular Roger Guenveur Smith) calls "the Pygmy vultures" that swarm around someone in line for a big payday. No one can be completely trusted, not the coach, not girlfriend Lala Bonilla (Rosario Dawson), not even Uncle Bubba (Bill Nunn), desperate for the chance to just "wet my beak a little bit" in the below-the-table wealth everyone is sure Jesus' college or professional signing is going to mean.

As if all this wasn't more than enough to construct a film out of, "He Got Game" pulls in two other strands, one of which is a miscalculation. Jake is placed in a hotel room next to Dakota ("The Fifth Element's" Milla Jovovich), who is, no kidding, the umpteenth movie hooker with an untarnished heart. Nothing that happens to these two isn't the weariest of cliches, and the film would have been much the stronger if this entire subplot were surgically removed.

The film's final element, its examination of the dynamics of family and the possibilities for reconciliation, is one of its strongest. For it turns out that the death Jake is in prison for causing is his own wife Martha's (Lonette McKee in flashbacks), a situation that has completely estranged Jesus and led to difficulties with Jake's young daughter Mary (a charming Zelda Harris).

Though "He Got Game" is periodically awkward and unruly, it benefits, as many of Lee's films do, from the director's determination to connect with the troublesome issues of the real world. Too few American directors work with Lee's kind of social immediacy, and that makes his films, flawed and didactic though they sometimes are, essential viewing.

NEW YORK, 5/11/98, p. 52, David Denby

Spike Lee's ambitious new movie *He Got Game*, begins with a montage of basketballs slowly flying through the air and landing in the sweet embrace of hoop and net. The shooters, solitary teenagers, practice on outdoor courts all over America—in city playgrounds, in the suburbs, and in the country, too, with lush farms and fields in the background. The sequence is accompanied by Aaron Copland's music—Copland, the most American of American classical composers, whose work, with its mixture of hymns, homely western tunes, and pounding rhythms, seems at once pastoral and urban. Okay, we get Spike Lee's point: Basketball is now the American national game, the unifying sport. It is also a game that at the professional level has come to be dominated almost entirely by blacks, a game that increasingly seems an emanation of African-American style. (That opening montage pauses every once in a while for a closeup of a black basketball player staring proudly at the camera.) In *He Got Game,* Spike Lee celebrates basketball as the apotheosis of black-American glory without lying about the game's effect on the black community. The movie is startlingly candid. In the real world, removed from the idealism of lonely shooters, basketball is drenched in money, envy, and betrayal. The movie is a volatile combination of ambitious mythmaking and nasty reality, and like most of Spike Lee's work, it is also an inextricable combination of good and bad.

Lee, who also wrote the screenplay, has a slightly, gimmicky story to tell. Jake Shuttlesworth (Denzel Washington), a man serving time in Attica for murder, receives a week-long leave. The warden gives him a task: Jake has to persuade his own son, the star of Abraham Lincoln High School in Coney Island and the hottest prospect in the country, to accept an athletic scholarship from the alma mater of the governor. If he is successful, his prison time may be shortened. But the son hates Jake, a good athlete who failed to make the pros; Jake drove the boy too hard, and after one of their combative court sessions, a fight spilled into the kitchen, and Jake accidentally killed his wife. The center of the movie is a tug of war between a guilty father and a vengeful son who has lost his mother. But around this drama, Lee, in his abrupt, throw-everything-in-the-mix style, arrays the spectacle of enormous success in a poor and depressed neighborhood. Jake's son, a presumptive basketball millionaire, is leaving home, and people want to grab a piece of him—or pull him down.

The kid's name is Jesus Shuttlesworth, and he's a peculiar kind of American savior: He's going to succeed in order to redeem his fallen neighbors; he's going to play for everyone's sins. Spike Lee trained Ray Allen, the 22-year-old Milwaukee Bucks guard, to take on the role, and Allen, graceful and fast in the basketball scenes, gives a somberly effective minimalist performance. Jesus is a serious young winner, with the inflexibility and humorlessness of youth; his head is screwed on so tight he can see nothing but what's right in front of him—his career and his role as guardian of the kid sister left with him after his father was sent away. He's fanatically insistent on doing the right thing, and he regards his father as a destroyer and a loser. As Jake, Denzel Washington gives a confident and wide-ranging performance. In the flashback scenes, we see Jake's anger and frustration as he dominates the boy he knows is going to surpass him. (The only thing worse than a stage mother is a sports dad.) But after years in prison, he's a man who has mortified his instincts, and Washington is quiet, even abashed, his steps tentative, his body held in. His Jake doesn't want trouble, but he's hungry for any kind of love he can get. The prison officials (including a frighteningly unsympathetic Jim Brown) drop Jake in a Coney Island fleabag hotel, where he meets and sleeps with a beaten-up whore (Milla Jovovich). The scenes between Washington and Jovovich—not airborne this time, as she was in *The Fifth Element*—are about the most tender Spike Lee has ever filmed.

Jake approaches his son, tries to master him and can't. The father-son relationship—the missing connection in black life—has shown up in a number of recent movies, and although it has a slightly cozy feeling here, as of a thrice-told tale, at least it's strongly acted and brilliantly staged. The inevitable climactic game of one-on-one, with Copland's music throbbing under it, reverses the earlier father-son games. This time, Jake knows his son has to beat him if they are ever to have any kind of reconciliation.

At times, *He Got Game* has the feeling of a black morality play. More and more, Spike Lee exercises his citizenly function of telling the truth to the African-American audience, but always, of course, in his own style of flashing collage. He wants to get people to face things; he hardly ever lets up on his tense, aggressive, hectoring manner. Jesus Shuttlesworth is surrounded by people who try to cash in on him—not only his uncle but his girlfriend, his coach, a sports agent, all want a piece of the action. And other people want to pull him down. These creeps jump into a scene or two and recede. There is, for instance, an ambiguous local gangster who taunts Jesus with the dangers of drugs and whores, and Lee throws onto the screen little scenes of degraded people in crack dens. In his own antic way, Lee reinforces the disastrous impression among some black teens that they have no serious alternatives between overwhelming success as athletes and overwhelming catastrophe as crackheads.

Spike Lee is a very literal-minded moralist, and he's not above luridness. The hero has to face more temptations than the biblical Jesus did when he was under siege from Satan. In the movie's worst scenes, a sports agent rants on and on about money (his house has more fancy red cars than a Park Avenue showroom); later, Jesus goes off to look at a prospective university, only to be thrown by another black basketball player into bed with two sluttish blonde coeds. All the white college girls at this particular U appear to be pathetic whorish suck-ups, oohing and aahing over Jesus. Lee is offering some easy laughs to the black audiences here—the scenes are unworthy of him.

But just when the movie seems overwrought and cheap, something great will turn up—a series of straight-into-camera appearances by actual NBA and NCAA coaches, for instances. The men are so square that they are far out—obsessive, insanely emphatic, their faces contorted by the relentless desire to impose themselves on others. The comedy of pro basketball is produced by the big-money pressures and competition. The movie looks at all that with wary amazement, but Spike Lee knows there's no way of going back to the ecstasy of the single shooter, alone on his court somewhere in the city or way out in the country at dusk.

NEW YORK POST, 5/1/98, p. 43, Rod Dreher

From the orchestral music accompanying the gorgeous montage that opens Spike Lee's basketball drama "He Got Game," it's clear the director is up to something far more ambitious than the straightforward hoops-in-the-'hood drama we might have expected.

The music is by Aaron Copland, and the images are of young people—black, white, male, female, urban and rural—playing basketball with mystical seriousness and grace. It recalls Woody Allen's unforgettable appropriation of Gershwin in "Manhattan.'

In hallowing the game with this visual symphony of poeticized athleticism, Lee sets us up to see what follows as an American myth with resonance beyond the particulars of his Coney Island-based drama.

It's a daring shot to attempt, and, for the most part, Lee scores. "He Got Game" soars on Lee's strengths as a visual stylist and provocateur, but his chronic weakness as a screenwriter, especially his heavy-handed didacticism, hamstrings the storytelling.

"He Got Game" is a religious allegory about a high school basketball star, Jesus Shuttlesworth (Milwaukee Bucks guard Ray Allen), who is much sought after by college coaches. Jesus—Lee slam-dunks the Christ metaphor in our faces as obnoxiously as any TV evangelist—has a week to sign a letter of intent.

He must run a gauntlet of temptations from those who would corrupt the soul he's managed to keep pure through self-discipline as well as devotion to the game and the memory of his dead mother (Lonette McKee).

Jesus' father, Jake (Denzel Washington), suffers in jail for having killed the boy's mother. Authorities let him out for a week to persuade his son to sign with the state university. If he succeeds, the warden (Ned Beatty) promises his sentence will be lessened.

Trouble is, the son wants nothing to do with his dad, however chastened and penitent. We learn that Jake was a hard-driving coach who taught his son everything he knows about basketball. Jesus owes a debt to his harsh father, but he despises him for his murderous rage.

Having the power to ransom a captive—his father—is only one of the impossible pressures bearing down on the kid. His extended family demands a portion of the financial bounty headed his way. The extended black community comes off as jealous hanger-on out to exploit what Jesus has won for himself through talent, work and self-control. Unscrupulous agents and coaches tempt him with flattery, cash, gifts and girls. Distressingly, several near-pornographic sex scenes play as a cheap thrill that diminishes the film's dignity.

"He Got Game" posits healing the severed link between father and son as crucial to overcoming the degradation of one's surroundings. I wish Lee had tightened his meandering, sluggish narrative and given Washington and Allen more scenes together to talk about their sins and their redemption.

Jesus is too often less a flesh-and-blood man than a symbol. I don't think Lee brings either Jesus or Jake into satisfactory focus, but the problem lies with the screenplay, not with winning performances by Washington and neophyte actor Allen.

There's so much to admire in "He Got Game"—not least among them some terrific new songs by Public Enemy, a nice contrast to the Copland—that its shortcomings pale. This movie tries to say something fresh and important about what it takes to keep faith in family and oneself in this vale of tears.

I was so moved by the father and the son's struggle to connect and transcend their circumstances that even the magic realist ending, which might fairly be called hokey as hell, made me weep.

NEWSDAY, 5/1/98, Part II/p. B2, Jack Mathews

Most of Spike Lee's movies have shown more ambition than talent, more passion than clarity, more audacity than good storytelling sense. He's the runt, in the parlance of his favorite pastime, who'd rather dunk than dribble, and when he misses—as he invariably does in each film—he misses big.

Never have those misses been more disappointing than they are in "He Got Game," an urban fable about a high school basketball prodigy and the people who would exploit him. It's disappointing because, in many ways, Lee's 12th feature is his best, and it's probably the one that most sucessfully matches him with his subject.

It's not Lee's courtside devotion to the New York Knicks nor his Nike basketball commercials that qualify hun to tell the story, though his knowledge of the game certainly informs the backdrop. The basketball scenes, captured by cinematographer Malik Hassan Sayeed have both athletic credibility and a fluid, poetic beauty. There's purity and perfection in this game, the images tell us. The rest is original sin.

"He Got Game" is about the "rest," the corruption that, like a colony of barnacles, attaches itself to a clean surface. Money-hungry agents, coaches, girlfriends, even family members. The bulk of Lee's films have played as counterattacks on white racism. Here, he grants us the right to assume, without having it shoved down our throats, that the racial divide in America is responsible for the exploitation of black innercity athletes, and he takes dead aim at an even more insidious enemy: universal, colorless greed.

Lee isolates the purity of the game in a beautifully edited opening credit sequence, showing men, boys and girls, in basketball uniforms and street clothes—in one case, prison garb—shooting, or driving toward the basket, to the accompaniment of Arron Copland's spirited "John Henry." With exquisite dramatic pacing, Lee quickly introduces us to the story's two main characters, Coney Island basketball prodigy Jesus Shuttlesworth (Milwaukee Bucks guard Ray Allen), and his imprisoned father Jake (Denzel Washington).

Jake is about to got an offer he can't refuse. Seems the governor would like to see Jesus, the most hotly pursued high school player in the country, accept a scholarship to his alma mater, Big State University. Jake will be given a week's supervised furlough, and if he can convince Jesus to go to Big State in that time, the governor will commute Jake's sentence. Nothing in writing, mind you, just a promise conveyed through Attica's Warden Wyatt (Ned Beatty).

The problem is that Jake is doing time for killing his wife, Jesus' mother, and there's no forgiveness in the kid. The last thing he wants to do is help Jake, and the last thing he needs is another person trying to hitch a ride on his future. He's got college coaches chasing him, an uncle demanding that he share his presumed riches, a high school coach trying to shove agent money at him, and a girlfriend being paid to get him to turn pro. They all want a taste of his success, or, as Uncle Bubba (Bill Nunn) so colorfully puts it, "to wet my beak a little."

Casting dramatic athlete roles is always a problem. Cast a real player and you get honest athleticism with stiff acting. Cast an actor and you get a credible performance from someone who plays ball like your cousin Lorch. Given his fidelity to, the game, Lee made the only choice he could, and Allen, a first-round NBA draft pick two years ago, is a sensation on the court.

But Jesus is one of Lee's most fully developed, and most dramatically demonstrative characters, and despite an often natural ease in front of the camera, Allen is badly outmatched by the pros around him—particularly by Washington, who gives one of the most riveting performances of his career.

Jake is a completely convincing character. In fact, the inspiration for him might have come from the real-life father of one of the two ghetto basketball stars followed from the playground to college in."Hoop Dreams." He was a great player himself, who missed or didn't have any opportunities of his own, and who lives vicariously through the talent encouraged in his son.

In this case, the encouragement is abusive. In the flashback sequences, we see the half-drunk Jake putting a prepubescent Jesus through a punishing drill on a street corner playground, then following him home to pound him for quitting.

It's almost axiomatic that behind every great athlete is an overbearing father—think of Tiger Woods and *père*—and Jake plays that part with righteous zeal. If it weren't for the drunken outburst that results in the death of his wife (Lonette McKee), Jake and Jesus might be making the big decision about his future together.

This is a switch for Washington, who seems destined by his own intelligence and bearing to play cool, savvy professionals and men of conscience. In "He Got Game," he plays a man who's street-tough and cocky, and only discovers his conscience while trying to help himself. Because Jake can't get through Jesus' defenses, Lee lets us glimpse Jake's revelation through his tentative romance with Dakota (Milla Jovovich), the hooker who lives next door in the fleabag Coney Island hotel where the prison guards install him.

Lee's attempt to resolve the father-son conflict is an absolute botch, and the note of magical realism with which he ends the film is dreadful. Lee is hardly an adept sentimentalist, and this final image undermines much of the good work that's gone before.

For me, an even greater problem is the use of the late Aaron Copland's music as a dramatic score. The rap music by Public Enemy that's mixed in is appropriate, and for the first few minutes, the jaunty, symphonic sound of Copland's "John Henry" and "Appalachian Spring" almost feels inspired. But Lee's attempt to match the music to the scenes, while playing it too LOUD! (as he always does), becomes a recurrent distraction.

The film's great strength is the insight Lee brings to the process of college recruiting. He gets carried away at times, as he does when Jesus visits a campus that seems to be crawling with women from a Russ Meyer movie (what are these girls majoring in, "Baywatch"?), and where its evangelical coach (John Turturro, in another flashy cameo) has prepared a promotional reel comparing him to his namesake.

But there's painful truth beneath even these comic bits. A ghetto kid with talent is gruel for the American exploitation industry, and with so much at stake, for both the colleges and the NBA, no tool or temptation is off-limits to the recruiters. That point is made, with incidental irony, by the cameo appearances of more than a dozen famous college coaches, who ape themselves trying to recruit franchise players.

Their tone is amiably self-mocking, and Lee clearly intends no insult. But they're there for one reason: They're part of a process that is finally guided by colorless, universal greed.

NEWSWEEK, 5/4/98, p. 80, David Ansen

The strutting title, "He Got Came", doesn't begin to convey the reach or the feel of Spike Lee's ambitious, absorbing new movie. At once a celebration of the game of basketball, an exposé of the game's corruption and an exploration of a fraught father-and-son relationship, "He Got Game" merges the epic aspirations of "Malcolm X," the domestic concerns of "Mo' Better Blues" and the social issues explored in "Get on the Bus." Then it wraps it all in an epic-scale package and sets the tale to the music of Public Enemy and Aaron Copland. Those improbable musical credits—inner-city hip-hop shoulder to shoulder with the plangent, wide-open spaces of "Appalachian Spring" and the hortatory strains of "Fanfare for the Common Man"—give a much better sense of the expansive, eclectic taste of this movie.

Milwaukee Bucks guard Ray Allen plays Jesus Shuttlesworth, the most coveted high-school basketball player in the country. Denzel Washington is his father, Jake, who's spent the last six years behind bars in Attica, convicted of murdering his wife, Jesus's mother. The week before his son must choose one of the colleges clawing for his talents, Jake (a once promising player himself) is temporarily released. The governor wants him to get Jesus to sign with the guv's alma mater; success could shorten his sentence. Thus Jake, whom Jesus has never forgiven, joins a long line of supplicants who want a piece of the future millionaire's action: girlfriends, agents, coaches, groupies and greedy relatives who see Jesus as their ticket out of Coney Island into the promised land of the Lexus and the Rolex.

Washington is terrific as this decent, haunted, angry father, but the domestic drama isn't as fully realized as the lively pageant of worldly temptations that Jesus must face on the road to his fateful decision. When Jake's crime is finally shown, neither his sentence nor his reaction to his fate makes much sense. Lee's script, which is so sharp on the specifics of the sports world, gets fuzzy around Jake: we're never even told how he made a living before his incarceration. Lee also throws in an abused, heart-of gold hooker (Milla Jovovich) as Jake's quasi-romantic interest. Jovovich can act, but her part's a cliché and the subplot goes nowhere.

Flaws and all, this may be Spike's most purely enjoyable movie, and his best looking. It flows and breathes as few of his earlier, crunched-up movies ever did, borne along by a juicy cast that includes Hill Harper, Rosario Dawson, Zelda Harris and Bill Nunn. Allen is inexperienced but winning, and there are amusing cameos from such hoop heavyweights as Dean Smith, John Thompson, Charles Barkley and Shaquille O'Neal. "He Got Game" may be all over the place, but it's held together by Lee's passion for the game.

SIGHT AND SOUND, 10/98, p. 44, Richard Falcon

Jake Shuttlesworth, serving time in Attica for the manslaughter of his wife, is paroled secretly so he can persuade his son Jesus, a brilliant basketball player, to sign up for the warden's old college. Jake seeks out his young daughter, who has been brought up by Jesus, but his son shuns him. Jesus must make a decision about his future in a week. Also courting Jesus are his high-school coach, who wants to be his coach in the big time, and colleges and agents who want him to turn professional.

Jesus is in love with Lala, but he realises, after she has persuaded him to see an agent with mob connections, that she is two timing him and is only after his potential wealth. Jesus is given a tour of a college that's courting him. Jake spends the night with Dakota, a prostitute. Jesus tries to steer clear of his exploitative neighbourhood associates. Finally, out of desperation, Jake offers Jesus a game of one-on-one to decide whether he will sign the letter of intent and free his father. Jesus wins and Jake is taken back to Attica. At the end of the week, it is announced that Jesus has decided to go to Big State, the warden's alma mater, but it is unclear whether this will benefit Jake since Jesus didn't sign the letter.

Spike Lee's twelfth feature, *He Got Game*, opens in typically bravura style, with a montage of young men shooting hoops all across the US. On the soundtrack, we hear Aaron Copland's song 'John Henry'(Copland accompanies the basketball action throughout, most impressively in a game choreographed to 'Hoe Down'). Such an arresting opening declares both Lee's passionate love of basketball (documented in his recent book *The Best Seat in the House)* and his continuing commitment to producing mythic cinema from a black American perspective.

The story concerns convict Jake's mission to get his son Jesus' signature on a letter of intent committing him to the Attica governor's alma mater, thereby securing Jake's parole. Even though this premise is neat and the timescale restricted to one week, *He Got Game* feels like a big expansive movie which sprawls at the edges, an impression fostered partly by Lee's trademark multiple point-of-view sequences. It is as though basketball were too sacrosanct a subject for Lee to use it just to explore familial preoccupations, or for a study of the sport as a focus for black American male aspiration, or merely to satirise the commodification of sport—all of which the film pursues. Instead, *He Got Game* is almost a textbook example of the way mythmaking cinema attempts to reconcile the irreconcilable.

The result tells us less about college basketball and the pressures on talented young black sportsmen than the celebrated documentary *Hoop Dreams*. In the character of Jake, played superbly by Denzel Washington, we have almost a strange riposte to the criticism that *Hoop Dreams* played to pernicious stereotypes about absent black fathers. Jake is absent because he accidentally killed Jesus' mother. Her death is presented in the lengthiest flashback in a film whose dominant style otherwise consists of virtuoso, rapidly edited flashbacks which break up the expository dialogue. The accident arises from Jake's determination to make the young Jesus a basketball star—a reversal of the mother who keeps *Mo' Better Blues'* Bleek from playing baseball in the street in order to practise scales on his trumpet. It is important for *He Got Game* that her death is a tragic accident (she cracks her head on the sink) rather than a result of domestic violence because we can't dislike Jake for a moment.

However, this narrative sleight reduces the mother to a Madonna who stands in sharp contrast to the other female roles in the film, all of them implicitly or explicitly whores, from Jesus' two-timing girlfriend Lala to the white co-eds and hookers offering themselves to Jesus at one of the colleges. This treatment of women extends to a curiously stilted subplot introducing Milla Jovovich as tart-with-a-heart Dakota which looks shorn of the material that would lend it a substantial thematic point.

Even more awkward and fraught is *He Got Game*'s treatment of sports' commerce. In a series of commercials for Nike Jordan Air shoes, Lee revives Mars, one of the central characters from his debut *She's Gotta Have It*. One wouldn't want to be impossibly purist about product placement, but Lee's work for Nike may partly explain the muted nature of the satire on sports promotion here. On the one hand, there is the broad spoof contained in John Turturro's pricelessly funny cameo as a college sports coach, who greets Jesus with a basketball multimedia show including clips from *Jésus of Montréal* of all films and tells him he will be the salvation of college basketball. (Despite the fact that Jesus owes his name, we learn, to Jake's reverence for ballplayer Earl "The Pearl" Monroe, who worked as technical consultant on the film and was known as "The Black Jesus.") on the other hand, we have Jake visiting a sports store while wearing the electronic tag placed on him by his two minders. (Jake pretends that the device is for arthritis—"My brother has the same complaint," says the sussed salesman.) The scene discreetly tells us that the new Air Jordans cost $130 ("$150 with City Tax") and draws our attention to the shoe's new concealed laces.

Cultural critic bell hooks suggested at the time of its release that *Hoop Dreams* engaged a universal fantasy of sporting success which endeared it to mainstream white audiences in the US. This is perhaps even more true of *He Got Game*, which beyond the central relationship is so infatuated with the game that it presses into service numerous real-life basketball coaches and stars for on-screen cameos, and stars the immensely likable real life pro-basketball star Ray Allen as Jesus. Basketball fans, and admirers of all American mythmaking cinema, will love *He Got Game* and relish the film's final image in which Jake defies an armed Attica guard to throw his basketball miraculously, via a match cut, out of the exercise yard to the hall where his son is training. Shot in slow-motion, the *2001*-like Planet Spalding, the passing of a patriarchal torch, is only a piece of monumental symbolism too far for those of us wearing the wrong footwear.

VILLAGE VOICE, 5/5/98, p. 119, Amy Taubin

Spike Lee has never made a secret of his ambition—to make films that count as modern American classics. Lee aspires to the ranks of Ellington and Pollock—artists who, as Greil Marcus wrote in *Mystery Train* about a different pantheon, "broke rules, took risks ... deliver[ed] a new version of America."

It's rare these days for a Hollywood financed film to do any one of those things. Most of Lee's do all three (the exhausted *Girl 6* and the lazy *Four Little Girls* are exceptions). Lee's method is to fuse personal and political passions with familiar film genres, news-hook stories, a style that's grown increasingly bravura during his 14-year career, and a theatrical mix of realism and allegory that, from the first, has been his trademark. It goes without saying that what's newest about Lee's version of America is its African American perspective, a perspective that vehemently resists ghettoization. Lee's films arc insider views of black America that include how black Americans perceive and relate to white Americans.

Nothing in that prickly relationship prepared me for the aesthetic interracial marriage at the heart of *He Got Game*, which, from its opening to its closing frame, is set to the music of Aaron Copland. True, there are a couple of Public Enemy numbers in the mix including the title song, which has a hook so insistent that every time I hear it I want to see the movie all over again. But it's the combo of Lee and Copland that makes *He Got Game* such a complicated depiction of race and culture and what it means to be an American.

I'm not sure, for example, that without the Copland factor I would have noticed that Denzel Washington (giving a career-defining performance as the bedraggled, guilt-ridden jailbird Jake Shuttlesworth) sounds like the young Marlon Brando. Which shouldn't be surprising, since Brando absorbed into his acting persona the rhythms and behavior of the black dancers and musicians he hung out with when he came to New York from the Midwest in the '40s. *He Got Game* is, among other things, a meditation on Americana and on how much of it was shaped by the culture and fantasies of outsiders (Copland himself was the son of Jewish shopkeepers from Brooklyn). And on the connection between the great dance theater of the '40s and the improvised choreography of playground basketball. *Rodeo* originated as a score for an Agnes de Mille ballet set in the Wild West but *He Got Game* makes you wonder whether Copland had hoops in his mind's eye when he wrote it.

Even more than *Do the Right Thing* or *Jungle Fever, He Got Game* is structured like a musical. The functional plot (some will say it's a little too forced) is heartfelt enough to be emotionally involving beginning to end, and clear enough to serve as an armature for elaborate set pieces and the most fluid nonlinear editing in a Hollywood film since *Apocalypse Now* or maybe *Kundun*. The film is basically a father-son story. Jake Shuttlesworth is doing time for the unintentional killing of his wife. In his absence, his son, Jesus (played honestly and unassumingly by NBA rising star Ray Allen) has become the most promising high school basketball player in the country. The colleges all want him; the agents want him to forget college and turn pro immediately. Everyone in his Coney Island neighborhood is trying to bribe him or manipulate him. His talent is their ticket out of the projects.

Even his father needs Jesus to rescue him. Jake has been promised early release if he can convince his son to go to Tech U, the governor's alma mater. To this end, Jake has been let out of jail for one week. His chances aren't good. Jesus blames him for his mother's death. He hates his father so much that he doesn't care that Jake's teaching made him the player he is today.

Lee (with cinematographer Malik Hassan Sayeed) has photographed famed Coney Island locations (Lincoln High School, the Garden court, the boardwalk the flophouses, the amusement park rides) so they seem simultaneously real and phantasmagorical. The color is even more intense here than in *Clockers*—all lurid reds and iridescent greens and browns. All the world's a stage and, on top of that, there are cartoons.

The cartoons get a bit out of control—the cable TV sports show, for example, where half the coaches in the world plus Charles Barkley and M.J. himself pay Jesus homage (when have NBA stars ever been so generous?). The worst is the college recruitment sequence, where the bevy of coeds throwing themselves at Jesus and the T&A on display in a lewd and crude bedroom three-way are an obvious sop for the teenage male audience that might not be thrilled with the film's serious elements. Lee's madonna/whore complex is still out in force. Jesus's mother and sister are saints; every other woman in the film does it for money.

That said, the love scene between Jake and the hooker-next-door (Milla Jovovich) is as subtle and sexy as anything Lee has ever done. But *He Got Game*'s high points are the two basketball one-on-ones between Jake and Jesus. Lee has a truly cinematic talent for physicalizing the connections between his characters. And while these scenes are exceptionally intricate in the way they project emotional dynamics onto film space, the entire narrative is put together with a sure sense of rhythm and pace. *He Got Game* is a real movie, and I bet you haven't seen many of those lately.

Also reviewed in:
CHICAGO TRIBUNE, 5/1/98, Friday/p. A, Michael Wilmington
NATION, 6/1/98, p. 35, Stuart Klawans
NEW REPUBLIC, 6/1/98, p. 24, Stanley Kauffmann
NEW YORK TIMES, 5/1/98, p. E16, Janet Maslin
VARIETY, 4//27-5/3/98, p. 57, Emanuel Levy
WASHINGTON POST, 5/1/98, p. D1, Stephen Hunter
WASHINGTON POST, 5/1/98, Weekend/p. 53, Michael O'Sullivan

HEALING BY KILLING

A New Yorker Films release. *Producer:* Nitzan Aviram. *Director:* Nitzan Aviram. *Screenplay (German and English with English subtitles):* Nitzan Aviram. *Based on the book "Nazi Doctors"* *by:* Robert Jay Lifton. *Director of Photography:* Yoram Millo. *Editor:* Naomi Press-Aviram. *Music:* Oded Zehavi. *Running time:* 90 minutes. *MPAA Rating:* Not Rated.

WITH: Robert Jay Lifton, Camp Survivors, and Doctors.

NEW YORK POST, 4/22/98, p. 47, Larry Worth

When one thinks of World War II villains, Hitler and his henchmen immediately spring to mind. But according to "Healing by Killing," German doctors not only paved the way for the Holocaust but fomented Nazi ideology.

It's a startling concept, and the launching pad for writer-director Nitzan Aviram's exhaustively researched documentary. Specifically, early experiments with euthanasia resulted in officially sanctioned gas chambers, initially used for the infirm and the deformed, then for elders, then healthy political prisoners.

Having interviewed those who were sterilized as children as well as medical practitioners who took part in such atrocities, Aviram cross-cuts between their recollections. Collectively, they put a surprising spin on all-too-familiar horror stories.

Hearing one person after another telling of cremated bodies or citing stats of the experiments' "success" is as bone-chilling as one might expect. But the most numbing commentaries come from doctors who bought into the theory that they were working for the common good.

Unfortunately, Aviram doesn't present the material in a particularly compelling fashion. Incorporating minimal archival footage, he generally cuts between talking heads and shots of long-deserted sites where the "mercy killings" led to genocide.

Yet, in between endless segues of gates opening or doors slamming shut, many of the terror tales are duly stomach-churning. And when the camera shows a hospital wall bearing the motto "Love is the doctor's foremost concern," the irony is akin to a slap in the face.

The film may also raise eyebrows since, with one exception, Israeli filmmaker Aviram doesn't have any Jews speaking on camera. It's yet another interesting twist on the scope of the Nazis' victims.

That's why "Healing by Killing" truly resonates. Still, its unsettling, disturbing look at those who betrayed the Hippocratic oath merited a far more, commanding presentation.

NEWSDAY, 4/22/98, Part II/p. B9, John Anderson

The cool, dry tone of Nitzan Aviram's "Healing by Killing"—which indicts the '30s German medical profession as the practical founders of the Final Solution—is tactically brilliant, because it recognizes the Holocaust Film Paradox: The more earnest and sincere you try to be, the more you trivialize your subject matter.

So Aviram simply allows his interview subjects to speak, and renders us speechless: A now-elderly woman, dispassionately recalling her experience as a child at the Brandenburg euthanasia center in the early years of World War II; a local woman blithely remarking that "everyone in Brandenburg knew" what was going on, largely because of the smell of the incinerators; a former center guard with a confiding smile telling how he once kept a "patient" from escaping through an open window—all the way down to Vilhelm Brasse, Dr. Josef Mengele's still photographer at Auschwitz, remembering how "unpleasant" it was to be in the room where all those twisted experiments took place. And an SS doctor, Hans Munch, conceding that it probably was wrong for him to have signed the papers allowing the harvesting of "meat" from the camp crematorium.

It's a direct line Aviram contends, between the early "mercy killings"—a way of "healing" German society by killing off its "flaws"—to the Holocaust itself. Gas-chamber technology was perfected by doctors exterminating the disabled, retarded and enfeebled. A "bureaucratic distancing" made it more palatable for physicians to carry out their duties, because it separated the judges from the executioners. Eventually, one crime condoned the next.

Why Aviram concentrates on two doctors in particular—Irmfried Eberl and Carl Clauberg—isn't entirely clear at first. But his motives become obvious. Eberl was a second-rate medical student and something of a social misfit who was able to further his career by becoming an enthusiastic cog in the Nazi death machine. He eventually became the first chief of the Treblinka death camp, where only his bloodlust undid him.

Clauberg, on the other hand, was a respected gynecologist and fertility specialist whose mission became finding the most effective ways of sterilizing the thousands of woman who passed through his hands at Auschwitz. The Holocaust, in other words, was an equal opportunity employer of any doctor, skilled or unskilled, who wanted to pervert his Hippocratic oath to the point that it sanctified murder and mutilation.

It's almost inspiring to learn that Clauberg was eventually driven mad, less so to learn that the German medical profession never revoked his license—not after the war, not after he was imprisoned by the Russians, not after he was indicted for war crimes. Aviram, an Israeli and graduate of NYU who draws on Dr. Robert Jay Lifton's book "Nazi Doctors" for much of his information (and on Lifton himself for some of his better commentary), clearly wants a more forthcoming attitude from the current medical establishment, an admission of guilt.

His questioning of current German medical students about the value of ethics education is a too-distracting digression and gets predictably blase responses. His beginning and end shots of a flock of lambs—yes, lambs—is almost painfully obvious. But what lies in between is a brutal reminder not just of what was, but what could be: It was only two years, we're told, between the first Nazi mercy killing, of a blind, retarded and malformed baby, to the state-sanctioned murders of those whose handicaps were religion, race, politics and sexual orientation. Somehow, that makes the likes of Jack Kevorkian seem so much less benign.

VILLAGE VOICE, 4/28/98, p. 80, Leslie Camhi

Healing by Killing is Israeli director Nitzan Aviram's horrifying and compelling exploration of Germany's official "euthanasia" program, the state's sinister dress rehearsal for Auschwitz. Between 1939 and 1941, from 70,000 to 100,000 mentally ill and disabled men, women, and children were murdered by doctors, and thousands more were forcibly sterilized.

Inspired by psychiatrist Robert Jay Lifton's book *The Nazi Doctors*, this straightforward but powerful documentary focuses on the way such "mercy killing" lay the groundwork for genocide. Only two years separated the official end of the euthanasia program (discontinued due to widespread public protest, though it persevered in secret) and the first mass killings of Jews at Treblinka. The two operations shared bureaucracies, technologies (including gas chambers and crematoria), and personnel. More broadly, medicine became the great alibi of the death camps, which were conceived as a vast experiment in social "hygiene" while doctors mined the human laboratory of Auschwitz for raw material to use in "pure" research.

Aviram interviews doctors, students, psychiatric patients, historians, survivors of euthanasia, and even one doctor who "studied" at Auschwitz (you wonder why he's still at liberty). Perhaps the most horrifying witness is the Polish man who was Mengele's medical photographer, and who ruefully describes photographing the wombs of Jewish women, extracted from their bodies. The most poignant testimony comes from an elderly man, severely retarded but still sharp enough to weep at the memory of evil. Among his companions in the asylum, he alone was spared. "Let us pray for those poor souls," he says, with simple eloquence.

Also reviewed in:
CHICAGO TRIBUNE, 1/29/99, Friday/p. D, John Petrakis
NEW REPUBLIC, 5/25/98, p. 27, Stanley Kauffmann
NEW YORK TIMES, 4/22/98, p. E5, Janet Maslin
VARIETY, 5/4-10/98, p. 86, Godfrey Cheshire

HENRY: PORTRAIT OF A SERIAL KILLER 2

A Margin Films release of a Maljack Films production in association with H-2 Productions. *Executive Producer:* Waleed B. Ali and Malik B. Ali. *Producer:* Thomas J. Busch. *Director:* Chuck Parello. *Screenplay:* Chuck Parello. *Director of Photography:* Michael Kohnhurst. *Editor:* Tom Keefe. *Music:* Robert F. McNaughton. *Sound:* Jake Collins. *Casting:* Suzanne Gardner. *Production Designer:* Rick Paul. *Art Director:* Angela Howard. *Costumes:* Patricia L. Hart. *Running time:* 85 minutes. MPAA Rating: R.

CAST: Neil Giuntoli (Henry); Rich Komenich (Kai); Kate Walsh (Cricket); Carrie Levinson (Louisa); Daniel Allar (Rooter); Penelope Milford (Woman in Woods).

NEW YORK POST, 8/15/98, p. 23, Bill Hoffmann

Diabolical movie maniacs never go away—they just resurface in bad sequels. Jason Vorhees, Freddy Krueger and Michael Myers return every few years—so it was just a matter of time before Henry made a comeback.

He's the creepy nut job from John McNaughton's 1990 thriller "Henry: Portrait of a Serial Killer"—a sober, unsensational account of a multiple murderer's life and times.

The original movie was graphic, but the grisliest violence was kept just out of camera range, making the horrors even more disturbing.

Don't expect the same from "Henry 2"—which features a second-rate director, star and script—and lots of nasty, in-your-face gore. It's exploitative junk that deserves a quick death at the box office.

Also reviewed in:
CHICAGO TRIBUNE, 8/21/98, Friday/p. F, John Petrakis
NEW YORK TIMES, 8/14/98, p. E24, Anita Gates
VARIETY, 4/21-27/97, p. 66, Joe Leydon

HENRY FOOL

A Sony Pictures Classics release of a True Fiction Pictures/The Shooting Gallery production. *Executive Producer:* Larry Meistrich, Daniel J. Victor, and Keith Abell. *Producer:* Hal Hartley. *Director:* Hal Hartley. *Screenplay:* Hal Hartley. *Director of Photography:* Mike Spiller. *Editor:* Steve Hamilton. *Music:* Hal Hartley. *Sound:* Daniel McIntosh. *Casting:* Chelsea Fuhrer. *Production Designer:* Steve Rosenzweig. *Set Decorator:* Melissa P. Lohman. *Costumes:* Jocelyn Joson. *Make-up:* Claus Lulla. *Running time:* 138 minutes. *MPAA Rating:* R.

CAST: Thomas Jay Ryan (Henry Fool); James Urbaniak (Simon Grim); Parker Posey (Fay); Maria Porter (Mary); James Saito (Mr. Deng); Kevin Corrigan (Warren); Liam Aiken (Ned); Miho Nikaido (Gnoc Deng); Gene Ruffini (Office Buñuel); Nicholas Hope (Father Hawkes); Diana Ruppe (Amy); Veanne Cox (Laura); Jan Leslie Harding (Vicky); Chaylee Worrall (Pearl, age 7); Christy Romano (Pearl, age 14); Chuck Montgomery (Angus James); Melanie Vesey and Denise Morgan (Go-Go Dancers); Jill Morley (Afternoon Table Dancer); Paul Boocock (Steve); David Latham (Barry); Marissa Chibas (Newspaper Reporter); Julie Anderson (Woman Outside Store); Reggie Harris (Anchorman); Don Creech (Owen Feer); Camille Paglia (Herself); Maraya Chase (TV Reporter); Shoshana Ami (Young Woman in Library); Karen DiConcetto, Tiffany Sampson, and Rachel Miner (Girls in Library); Paul Lazar (Doctor); Gretchen Krich (Nurse); Valorie Hubbard (Patty, the Bartender); Dave Simonds (Bill); Fay Ann Lee (Lawyer); Paul Greco (Concierge); Blake Willett and Raymond Cassar (Cops); Katreen Hardt (Airline Ticket Clerk); Rebecca Nelson (Flight Attendant Lucy); Paul Albe (Angry Customer).

CHRISTIAN SCIENCE MONITOR, 6/12/98, p. B3, David Sterritt

American independents get special attention at the Cannes filmfest, where audiences hope the next "English Patient" or "sex, lies & videotape" may surface. Hence the advance interest in "Henry Fool," a pitch-dark comedy by Hal Hartley.

Cannes encouraged the buzz by bending its own rules, screening the movie in the Official Competition even though it had unspooled earlier at the Toronto filmfest. On closing night it won the prestigious Best Screenplay award, puzzling some critics who found it one of Hartley's less-enticing works.

This touched off speculation that the jury's American members—actresses Sigourney Weaver and Winona Ryder, and director Martin Scorsese, who chaired the panel—may have persuaded the seven additional members to honor Hartley in return for top-level prizes to European productions.

Overlooked in this ruckus was the possibility that Hartley's picture actually deserved the kudos it received A vocal minority of Cannes critics saw it as a bold, sometimes breathtaking story that may prove too unsettling for multiplex appeal—especially in its treatment of child abuse and other disturbing issues—but could take its place as an indie classic once the initial fuss dies down.

The title character is a mysterious stranger who drifts into the life of Simon, a young garbage collector. Henry hints at an exotic past that he's memorializing in his "Confession," an autobiography that will stun the world if he ever gets around to finishing it.

Spurred by his example, Simon writes a book-length poem of his own, greeted by his neighbors with very different responses. A mute woman bursts into poignant song after reading a few lines, yet others find it sick and disgusting. Henry and Simon pursue their literary destinies to expected conclusions, also intertwining their personal lives as Henry marries Simon's sister.

Detractors of "Henry Fool" find it long, slow, intermittently offensive, and evasive in its refusal to let us know what the characters' writing is actually like. Defenders note that its stylized treatment of offbeat material shows the influence of master filmmaker Jean-Luc Godard, a longtime Hartley favorite who has also explored unsettling material in movies closer to moral allegories than conventional stories.

"Henry Fool" finds Hartley assimilating Godard's ideas with far more assurance than in previous pictures like "Amateur" and "Flirt," which marked a downturn in his career.

It also has more emotional depth than his other movies, particularly in its candid treatment of child abuse, an evil also probed in Todd Solondz's new "Happiness," the best-received American film at Cannes this year. Both films suggest that sublime and sickening impulses may exist side by side in our all-too-human natures, and "Henry Fool" indicates that making art is one of the few means we have for sorting these out.

The cast includes Thomas Jay Ryan as the title character, James Urbaniak as his odd companion, Parker Posey as his sister, and Maria Porter as their mother. Hartley himself wrote the prizewinning screenplay.

LOS ANGELES TIMES, 6/16/98, Calendar/p. 10, Kevin Thomas

Watching Hal Hartley's "Henry Fool" is like reading a fine novel in which we come to know its people so well that their fates take on a mythic dimension.

After 10 years, five features and numerous shorts, Hartley approaches his 40th birthday with a maturity that his previous features, filled with quirky, frustrated individuals, many of them living in blue-collar Long Island, only hinted at. The result is a career milestone and a film that could become a landmark in American independent cinema.

That his two principal figures are as eccentric as any Hartley ever imagined gives him the space and distance to invite us to ever so gradually experience a sense of recognition with people with whom most of us would be hard-pressed to identify. Yet we share their experiences in self-awareness, their discovery of the meaning and conflicts of friendship and an acknowledgment of the unpredictable workings of fate. At this point it should be hastily mentioned that "Henry Fool" is a comedy, albeit a very dark one, and sometimes hilarious.

Thomas Jay Ryan's Henry could have wandered into the lives of Simon Grim (James Urbaniak), his layabout sister Fay (Parker Posey) and their demented mother Mary (Maria Porter) straight from the saloon of Eugene O'Neill's "The Iceman Cometh." On parole for a particularly foolish and entirely deplorable crime, the seedy, unshaven Henry has a certain boozy, beefy charm and assumes a grand air of intellectual authority that some might find a bit much at Harvard or Oxford. He says he's working on his "Confessional," which is to electrify and confound the world, but in the meantime he ends up laboring alongside Simon as a garbage man.

Painfully thin, profoundly introverted, Simon, a kind of ultimate geek, looks like Woody Woodpecker with thick glasses. Yet Simon sets the plot in motion when he allows Henry to read his work-in-progress, a vast poem that Henry pronounces in his professorial manner as possessed of "profound instincts." Henry's announced determination to see Simon published and in turn to see his own work in print has long-ranging, cataclysmic consequences.

For a considerable time you worry that Henry, for whatever perverse reasons, is simply conning the hapless Simon, but Hartley has much more in mind. In fact, his film, at just the right moment, shifts into high gear, with "Henry Fool" suddenly expanding its scope and vision. The film's scale remains intimate while Henry and Simon become figures in an epic tale of interlocked, ever-shifting destinies, requiring of them both either to rise or to fall in the face of life's big moral choices.

Within this grand unraveling, Hartley, while probing the mysteries of the human heart and psyche, has considerable fun with the ambiguities and treacheries of artistic reputation and with the folly of the kind of criticism that merely passes judgment on a work—while allowing that some stuff is just plain bad. "Henry Fool" soars but it's grounded in the muck of life's realities. In this it recalls James Joyce's "Ulysses"; Hartley in fact has cited Joyce and Samuel Beckett in general, and the legends of Faust and Kasper Hauser in specific, as key inspirations.

A young actor with considerable stage experience, Ryan, in his film debut, and Urbaniak, also from the stage and in his first key film, just about wipe you out with their seemingly endless resources, not merely of technique but of emotion and perception. Parker strikes all the brittle attitudes that have made her such a vivid presence on the independent film scene, then moves way beyond them to show us a woman with an unexpected strength and capacity for love.

With "Henry Fool" Hartley has done something fairly unusual in American movies, Hollywood or otherwise: He fills the screen with unapologetically smart people and then shows us that intelligence alone is not much defense against the workings of outrageous fortune.

NEW YORK POST, 6/19/98, p. 51, Thelma Adams

I'm a fool for Hal Hartley, but not enough of one to fall head over heels for "Henry Fool."

As the abrasive Fool (Thomas Jay Ryan), a pedophiliac writer-turned-garbage man, tells his friend Simon Grim (James Urbaniak), a garbage man-turned-Nobel Prize-winning poet: "There's no accounting for taste."

"Fool" is the fable of their friendship, which ends up being anything but grim and foolish. The absurd, Queens-set comedy begins with Simple Simon protesting, "I'm not retarded." Fool dryly responds: "I'll take your word on that."

The dialogue frequently crackles and confounds our expectations. In that, Hartley rivals David Mamet. Like Mamet, sometimes the Long Island auteur gets consumed in his own games and forgets to involve the audience.

"Fool" is an extended meditation, alternately funny and preachy, on love, sex, ambition, garbage and art in a society awash in pop culture, corrupted by commerce and get-rich-quick schemes.

As Henry Fool, Ryan can't carry the movie. The actor makes his film debut in a role that needs the loser charm of Hartley alum Martin Donovan ("The Opposite of Sex"). Urbaniak, with his square face and heavy head awkwardly balanced on a thin stalk of neck, is the movie's revelation, the nerd Brando.

Parker Posey, who appeared in Hartley's "Flirt" and "Amateur," starts off in raving nympho mode. She chews up and spits out the writer-director's dialogue in a funny, brittle way that perfectly matches Hartley's suburban sensibility. Posey improves when she stops using the dialogue as a shield, settles down and sinks deeper into the role of Fay, Simon's sister, Henry's lover and nobody's fool.

In a cameo, the cartoonish pundit Camille Paglia praises Simon's poetry as "pungent and squalid." She could be describing "Henry Fool."

Hartley consciously conceals Grim's poetry, words so moving they merit a Nobel Prize; similarly, he distances us from his characters' emotional lives. They apparently are profound, but they don't touch us.

NEWSDAY, 6/12/98, Part II/p. B7, John Anderson

From "The Searchers" to "Mary Poppins," one of the more potent characters in the movies has been the mysterious stranger—the one who changes everybody's life and then moves on. A legacy of literature, it's an enchanting myth, appealing to our near-genetically patterned belief that the individual is ultimately supreme, and just as disposable.

"Enchanting" might not quite be the word to describe the title character in Hal Hartley's "Henry Fool," a hard-smoking, beer-snarfing, unshaven, self-loving, rent-jumping, bath-eluding ex-offender who storms head-on into Hartley's viewfinder and alters his immediate universe. But he's an original, a modern-day twist on Lear's agent-provocateur crossed with the hard charms of Charles Bukowski. And along with poetry, publishing, hard-right conservatism, the Internet, product placement and art-as-commerce, he's in for a major myth-adjustment within "Henry Fool's" orgy of archetype-smashing comedy.

Henry (screen newcomer Thomas Jay Ryan) is a tough sell as a hero; certain elements of his minimum-security past are a little unsavory. But he's certainly a catalyst. Marching into Queens with a butt in his mouth and a bag in his hand, he takes a room somewhere on the outskirts of Oprahville: Mom (Maria Porter) is chronically depressed; her daughter Fay (Parker Posey, in the best role of her indie queen career) is a nymphomaniac; brother Simon (James Urbaniak), a sanitation man with all the symptoms of acute catatonia, is silent, stunned and treated as an idiot by his immediate family.

Henry, whose sweaty eloquence impresses everyone, is working on his "confessions," which he humbly portrays as a genre-busting opus lying somewhere between St. Augustine and Marcel Proust. He encourages Simon to write. And Simon does, despite the sneering of his mother and sister and the repugnance of his initial readers. Some of them anyway.

When Henry posts a Simon poem at the corner grocery owned by Mr. Deng (James Saito), his mute assistant Gnoc (Miho Nikaido) begins to sing. Others react more violently. After some local students run it in the high school paper, school board meetings are convened, decent folk are outraged, words like "scatalogical" and "pornographic" are bandied about like small-weapons fire.

All of which, naturally, sets Simon on the road to enormous success, leaving Henry in his literary dust.

"Henry Fool," fresh out of Cannes with a screenwriting award, has been labeled the first "indie epic," but any independent film that clocked in at more than two hours would probably get that tag. No, "Henry Fool" is an epic because of what it embraces and the scope of its sway. Like a 19th-Century novel it is a portrait not just of characters but of a time.

The celebration of Simon (whose work we never see or hear) isn't about art but celebrity; the publisher who initially rejects his poetry (Chuck Montgomery) and who is under siege by the self-serving entrepreneurs of the Internet ("You have to reinvent the publishing industry for the electronic age!") hates Simon's writing but publishes it anyway.

In Kevin Corrigan's thuggish Warren, who takes up the cause of a local, hate-mongering politician (Don Creech), we get the politics of fear. ("He takes complicated issues and totally simplifies them. And I appreciate that.") In the ever-changing Mr. Deng's, which transmutes from doughnut shop to coffee bar to discotheque, we get the nuts and bolts of the American dream.

Despite the cool, collected and maybe even clinical approach that Hartley has used in the past to dissect his troubled characters (in movies such as "Flirt," "Trust" and "Amateur"), "Henry Fool" is a far more accessible movie in its emotionalism, its flagrant comedy, its affection and grace. Has Hartley acquiesced to popular taste? Or is that the very question that makes "Henry Fool" the provocative thing it is?

NEWSWEEK, 7/6/98, p. 67, Malcolm Jones Jr.

Hal Hartley makes funny, weirdly moving movies ("Trust," "Amateur"). They're filled with hip, deadpan dialogue spoken by impossibly handsome characters who are tormented by the squarest set of values: loyalty, fidelity, filial devotion. "Henry Fool" is the best yet. The title character (brilliantly acted by Thomas Jay Ryan) is a lazy scoundrel who calls himself a writer, but his real talent is for making other people believe his blarney. He encourages his landlord, a laconic Queens, N.Y., garbage man (James Urbaniak), to write poetry, while hitting on the landlord's horny sister (Parker Posey). The garbage man becomes a successful writer. Henry doesn't. And before long his lies start piling up. When he's implicated in a murder, what had looked like rascality now suddenly seems like villainy. But the only thing you can count on in this exhilarating movie is that nothing is what it seems. Even the borough of Queens looks beautiful.

SIGHT AND SOUND, 11/98, p. 53, Geoffrey Macnab

A mysterious stranger named Henry Fool turns up in a small US town. He takes up residence in the basement of the house where garbage collector Simon Grim lives with his sexually promiscuous sister Fay and his ailing mother.

Simon becomes friends with Henry, who turns out to be a convict on parole. Henry is devoting his life to writing his memoirs. He encourages Simon to write as well, and soon Simon's scatological poetry is the talk of the town. Henry claims to be friends with an eminent publisher who might be interested in it. Simon approaches the publisher; he rejects the book. Behind Simon's back, his sister publishes the book on the internet, and it attains cult status. The publisher now offers to publish it. At first, Simon insists that he also publish Henry's book, even though neither of them thinks highly of the *Memoirs*. Henry's book is rejected.

Years later, Simon has become a famous author while Henry has married Fay and become a garbage collector. They have a child. Henry intervenes in a case of wife beating and accidentally kills the abusive husband. His young son tracks Simon down and brings him back to the town to help Henry. Since Simon is on his way to Stockholm to receive the Nobel Prize, he gives Henry his passport and sends him in his stead. Henry is last seen running across the airport tarmac.

In making a film about a mysterious, charismatic stranger who pitches up out of nowhere in smalltown America, Hal Hartley isn't breaking new ground. His debut feature *The Unbelievable Truth* started from roughly the same premise. The outsider in that film was a garage mechanic, but his counterpart in *Henry Fool* is a would-be visionary— a poet, philosopher and vagabond. He treats his chaotic life as the raw material for his *Memoirs,* a work-in-progress which he promises will startle the literary world.

As a character, Fool makes a change from the cool, ironic types who inhabit most of Hartley's movies. A Rabelaisian (or Henry Milleresque) figure with an unquenchable appetite for sex, alcohol and knowledge, he speaks in soliloquies rather than in the gnomic dialogue favoured by the typical Hartley protagonist. By contrast, the young garbage collector he befriends, Simon Grim, is shy and reticent. As in most buddy movies, opposites attract. The loquacious mountebank and his taciturn companion complement each other perfectly.

In its own stylised way, *Henry Fool* flirts with blue-collar realism. Hartley sketches in the social problems faced by his protagonists, touching on such subjects as wife beating, sex with minors, alcoholism and even politics. The Grims (as their name might suggest) are a typical dysfunctional family. Simon is in a dead-end job. His sister Fay compensates for the monotony of her life by having flings with any man she meets. Their ailing mother sits indoors all day, drugged on the medication her children feed her. The look of the film is deliberately grey, as if to underline the banality of the world that traps them. But Hartley's vision of smalltown life isn't quite like anyone else's. The usual idiosyncrasies still abound: be it the store where Fool buys his beer or the basement where he hides out, the settings are stagy. Likewise, the characters are a little too eccentric to conform to naturalistic stereotypes.

Unlike the Grims, Fool is held down by no ties—he comes from nowhere in particular, goes where he wants and does what he will. Only slowly does Hartley reveal Fool's past. An ex-con who was sent to prison for having sex with a minor, his parole officer always seems to be lurking in the background. But Fool blithely ignores him. He can't help but disrupt a community which never seemed quite normal anyway. Like Terence Stamp's character in Pasolini's *Theorem* (1968) who seduces an entire family one by one, or the devil in Dennis Potter's *Brimstone & Treacle* (1976), he is an unsettling and mischievous presence. He beds both Simon's mother and sister. ("Simon, I made love to your mother about half an hour ago," he tells his hapless friend.) Through him, the film poses provocative questions about hype, creativity and charlatanism which could equally well be asked of Hartley's work. Fool may play the role of the *poète maudit* to perfection, but when he finally finishes his *Memoirs,* he is revealed, at least in Simon's eyes, as a fraud: his writing stinks.

Henry Fool ends in a ragged fashion. The idea that Fool could escape the police by passing himself off as a Nobel Prize-winning novelist doesn't make much sense. Likewise, some of the satire is pretty lame. Simon's book-length poem is snapped up for a huge advance by the same publisher who had previously dismissed it as inept, changing his mind simply because he sees an opportunity to make money. Simon becomes a media phenomenon, fêted by cultural commentators (Camille Paglia among them) but since we don't see or hear his work we have to take his metamorphosis from garbage collector to world-class author on trust.

On the most basic level, this is yet another story about an apprentice outstripping his mentor. Fool, though, remains infinitely the more compelling character. Failure is in keeping with his narcissistic idea of the suffering artist. Thomas Jay Ryan plays him with great charm and tenderness. Even at his most abject moments—for instance during an attack of diarrhoea which, through an unlikely chain of accidents, leads him to propose to Fay—Fool retains a sense of innocence and idealism.

Hartley is often accused of mannerism and repetition. All his characters, from the ex nun in *Amateur* to the brothers in *Simple Men* invariably engaged in the same search for meaningful relationships. Their self-obsession and introspection can become wearing. In Fool, though, alongside his usual gallery of neurotic narcissists, he has created probably his first full-blooded hero, a rambunctious dreamer who behaves like a latter-day Walt Whitman. The fact that Fool is not the great writer he proclaims himself to be doesn't matter in the slightest. At least he plays the part to perfection.

TIME, 7/13/98, p. 80, Richard Corliss

They make a strange menagerie, the Hal Hartley clan. Thee people in his odd, alert comedies (*Trust, Amateur, Flirt*) inhabit some Long Island of the mind, where Amy Fisher-style melodrama rubs up against working-class angst. They are part strong, silent types, part East Coast neurotics. They revel in their own contradictions; one Hartley heroine, a nymphomaniac virgin, explains the anomaly by saying, "I'm choosy." His creatures will sit mute and mopey, then turn endlessly articulate once they get going. Self-conscious but not self-aware, skeptical yet wildly romantic, they have a horror of the personal commitment to which they are also drawn. A girl asks her dyspeptic beau, "Will you trust me?" and he says, "If you'll trust me first." They are exasperating, endearing—perfect totems for the seen-it-all '90s.

So far, audiences haven't chosen to see much of Hartley. Each of his first six features (two of which are compilations of short films) has earned less than $1 million at the North American box office. His wonderfully intransigent pictures—neither chipper enough to appeal to the indie-film date crowd nor exotic enough to qualify as critical cult objects—survive on funding from Britain, Japan and Germany, where they are art-house staples. If not for this offshore financing, Hartley, 38, might be working as a radio repairman or a garbageman—jobs that keep his heroes occupied when they aren't playing chess with their gnarly demons.

That could change with *Henry Fool*, the intimate epic that made a splash at festivals last year and has now opened in U.S. movie houses. No less quirkish and studied than his earlier films, this one has an expansiveness, a rowdiness and emotional generosity, that flows directly from its ribald antihero.

Henry Fool—what a guy! He materializes, like the answer to a dark prayer, in a Queens neighborhood where a sanitation worker named Simon Grim (the glumly funny James Urbaniak) is literally lying in the street waiting for ... something. Henry (Thomas Jay Ryan, pinwheeling raffish charisma) has everything, and too much of it. He swaggers, smokes, guzzles beer, grabs life by the butt and gives it a fat smack. He makes abrupt love to Simon's morbid mother (Maria Porter) and bored sister (Parker Posey). He is, he tells Simon, an artist, the author of a huge, unpublished tome called *My Confession*; and he encourages Simon to lift himself from lethargy and create his own masterpiece.

Dwelling in the sulfurously lighted basement apartment of Simon's house, Henry is the Devil—a devil, anyway—with a gift for inspiring those he does not repel. An apt pupil, Simon composes a long poem that some people hate ("Drop dead" reads a publisher's rejection note; "keep your day job") but others champion. Simon becomes a literary celebrity, and in gratitude to his mentor says he will insist that his publisher also issue Henry's opus. Then, alas, he reads it.

We never hear a line of either Henry's or Simon's work. One or both may have great lyrical beauty and ethical depth; one or both may be junk. It matters not, for this is less a tale of literary gamesmanship than a parable of friendship. What would you do for a friend, a lover, the family you feel trapped by? Who deserves your most annihilating sacrifice? What are friends for, anyway?

That question is answered, with a potent ambiguity, in the final act. It is seven years later: Simon is a Nobel prize winner, Henry a garbageman in a sad marriage. Both are called on to perform a treacherous good deed in a climax that mixes brutality and death with the desperate, deadpan tenderness that marks Hartley at his ornery best.

Be warned: this is a long movie, with weird excremental explosions amid the philosophizing and philandering. But it is pristinely acted; and its range and heart dwarf other summer films, so cogent is it about our common aches and dreams.

Early in *Henry Fool* Simon returns from a fearful beating administered by the local bully. "It hurts to breathe," he pants, referring to his bruised ribs. "Of course it does!" Henry snorts, referring to the hard job of getting through the day. Yes, it hurts, but in Hal Hartley's world the pain blends with humor in a way that gives one a reason to believe in the complexity of life and the future of movies.

VILLAGE VOICE, 6/23/98, p. 135, J. Hoberman

The widely acclaimed independent Hal Hartley is the sort of filmmaker who might appreciate the notion that his is a dialectical cinema. Too bad that Hartley's structural-minimalist romantic comedies are the synthesis of an overwhelming whimsical lightness and an unbearable deadpan gravity.

Henry Fool is a seriously frivolous allegory on art, fame, fate, the power of the Internet, and the anxiety of influence. (There seems to be a religious component too, which I'll leave for other exegetes.) Suffice it to say, this antic melodrama is the glumly ambitious epitome of Hartley's paralyzed romanticism. A movie that tries to fandango in lead clodhoppers, it's too weighted down to even take a pratfall.

The film, which won the award for best screenplay at Cannes, has already been hailed in some quarters as Hartley's breakthrough, and some of his fans may find this schematic yet lopsided tale of an alienated Queens garbageman and the mysterious derelict who changes his life to be the director's most personal film. Perhaps. *Henry Fool*, which runs a leisurely and ultimately tiresome 138 minutes, is so self-conscious it feels uncomfortable in its own skin.

Simon Grim (James Urbaniak) is a dour, thin-lipped borderline geek who works as a sanitation man and dreams of ... what? Introduced watching a couple of teenagers bong and ball in the alley behind the garbage garage, Simon lives with his depressed mother (Mary Porter) and unemployed, if sexually active, sister Fay (Parker Posey) in a modest frame house in what could be Jackson Heights. Out of his quiet desperation, Simon—I keep fighting the urge to preface his name with "saint"—conjures up the extravagantly disreputable Henry Fool (Thomas Jay Ryan), an unshaven, lank-haired, chain-smoking boho with an incantatory delivery.

Henry's high-flown bombast conceals an unsavory and pitiful past. At once Simon's repressed double (he's similarly unsmiling) and his Mephistophelian tempter, Henry moves into the Grim family basement to work on the "confession" that he maintains will upend the literary world.

His real aesthetic project, of course, is the reinvention of the Grims. Henry pursues both the women in the household, takes Simon out carousing to a topless bar, and, more successfully, inspires him to begin filling notebooks with a raging torrent of verse. Simon's first poem, posted by the cash register in the neighborhood deli, inspires the hitherto mute daughter of the Vietnamese proprietor to sing (and this member of the audience to sigh). This epic, to which we're never made privy, is a model for the movie— it's supposed to be shockingly scatological and it galvanizes the community.

Hartley is not one to shy away from cartoon characterizations. (Too tightly wrapped in the spandex of the Posey personality, Fay is a one-note brat.) But, abstract as it is, *Henry Fool* manages a sense of place better than any of Hartley's films since the modest and affecting *Trust*. The feeling of lower-middle-class stagnation is palpable, and Hartley almost has fun with the notion of a Budweiser-fueled Queens bohemia. The deli mutates into a modish literary coffee bar. But while Henry holds forth for his high school admirers, Simon ventures out into the world. His foray into the city to find a publisher for his poem begins, somewhat unsurprisingly, with his being mistaken for a messenger and ends, no less predictably, when he is rejected by the overbearing chief editor to whom Henry has sent him.

Inspired by the irrational, Simon is saved by technology. Has the curse of the unknown genius been lifted in the age of the personal computer? Misappreciated by the professionals, Simon's poem generates vast excitement on the Net—even as it is denounced as pornographic by local politicians. After Camille Paglia (playing herself) rallies to its defense, the snotty publisher too comes around—thus enabling Simon to finally shed his sanitation-man uniform (which his alter ego Henry promptly takes on). This is hardly the last of Simon's successes, nor of the movie's, role reversals.

Hartley's films are carefully plotted. Indeed, with their studied camera placement and precise mise-en-scène, deliberately worked out narrative ideas and iconic acting, they are scarcely more spontaneous than a military briefing—his performers seem drilled to be droll. This obsessive, form-conscious director may have one great film in him. (Perhaps he should bring his meticulous methodology to someone else's material.) Here, however, he fights a futile battle against his constricted style. *Henry Fool* is not exactly down and dirty, but, working domestic violence and pedophilia into the mix, it's somewhat dutifully all over the place.

The movie is at once precious and sensational, bone-dry and awash in leaky fluids—spilled milk, upchucked vomit, shed blood, Henry's verbiage, Simon's endless poem. The explosive violence peaks after Henry ODs on cappuccino. It's a memorably tasteless bit of business that gives a whole new dimension to the conclusion reached by the two writers that "the world is full of shit"—or what high school English teachers used to call "adolescent Ex-Lax."

Also reviewed in:
CHICAGO TRIBUNE, 7/17/98, Friday/p. A, Michael Wilmington
NATION, 7/13/98, p. 35, Stuart Klawans
NEW REPUBLIC, 7/13/98, p. 26, Stanley Kauffmann
NEW YORK TIMES, 6/19/98, p. E13, Janet Maslin
VARIETY, 9/15-21/97, p. 75, Derek Elley
WASHINGTON POST, 7/24/98, p. B1, Michael Colton
WASHINGTON POST, 7/24/98, Weekend/p. 37, Michael O'Sullivan

HI-LIFE

A Lion Gate Films release in association with Gun For Hire Films of a Silverman production. *Executive Producer:* Michael Paseornek, Jeff Sackman, and Steven C. Beer. *Producer:* Erica Spellman-Silverman. *Director:* Roger Hedden. *Screenplay:* Roger Hedden. *Director of Photography:* John Thomas. *Editor:* Tom McArdle. *Music:* David Lawrence. *Casting:* Deborah Brown. *Production Designer:* Sharon Lomofsky. *Costumes:* Isis Mussenden. *Running time:* 85 minutes. *MPAA Rating:* Not Rated.

CAST: Katrin Cartlidge (April); Charles Durning (Fatty); Daryl Hannah (Maggie); Moira Kelly (Susan); Peter Riegert (Minor); Campbell Scott (Ray); Eric Stoltz (Jimmy); Anne DeSalvo (Sherry); Saundra Santiago (Elena); Kathleen Widdoes (Frankie); Bruce MacVittie (Cluck); Tegan West (Phil); Carlo Alban (Ricky); Dean Cameron (Santa); Tucker Smith (Adrien).

NEW YORK POST, 12/4/98, p. 57, Jonathan Foreman

"Hi Life" proves that independent filmmakers can be every bit as tone-deaf and wasteful of money and talent as the big studios.

The movie is endurable only as a bleak primer on how bad writing, combined with incompetent direction, can elicit truly awful performances from a wonderful young cast.

"Hi Life" is intended to be an atmospheric ensemble piece about people who hang out in or work in bars on the Upper West Side. But for all the neighborhood feel evoked by writer-director Roger Hedden (who also wrote the pretentious "Sleep With Me") it could have been shot in downtown Phoenix.

Unemployed Upper West Side actor (Eric Stoltz) owes an Irish bartender (Charles Durning) $900 on college football bets. To raise the money, he tells his girlfriend (Moira Kelly) that his sister (Daryl Hannah) needs an abortion.

He tells his sister that his girlfriend needs money for the same thing.

Girlfriend persuades her bartender brother (Campbell Scott) to start collecting debts owed him by other bar and restaurant folk—including the Daryl Hannah character, who is the bartender's ex-girlfriend.

So the bartender visits a number of oddly empty watering-holes together with a regular who has a crush on him (Katrin Cartlidge). Everyone else also goes from bar to bar—narrowly missing the others—and encounters people who are supposed to be amusing "characters," including two grotesquely stereotyped Puerto Rican women.

In the end, everyone ends up in the Hi Life bar on Amsterdam Avenue, and all problems are ludicrously resolved.

Scott is more lugubrious than ever as the generous-but-uptight bartender. Hannah does little else but shake a strangely misshapen blond mane.

Stoltz gives what may be his first dreadful performance. Even Peter Riegert, so good in "Crossing Delancy" and "Animal House," here reads his lines as if he were waiting for the nightmare to end.

With the exception of Kelly—still the lovely, big-eyed ingenue of "The Cutting Edge"—and two relatively unknown actors, Bruce McVittie and Tegan West, the performers are adrift, and it is a painful spectacle.

The fact that Hedden received a playwriting grant from the National Endowment for the Arts should make even a Karen Finley wonder if Sen. Jesse Helms didn't have the right idea when he tried to close the Endowment down.

"Hi Life" will certainly make other real-life bars think twice before lending their name and reputation to a movie.

NEWSDAY, 12/4/98, Part II/p. B11, John Anderson

Imagine "It's a Wonderful Life" crossed with "Seinfeld." Got it? Now forget it. The only connection between "Hi-Life" and the former are the pronouncedly James Stewart qualities of star Campbell Scott; with the latter, that they both take place on an imaginary Upper West Side where no one but the principals seem to live.

And yet... and yet... this cockeyed and thoroughly inconsequential movie does combine character-driven urban cynicism with a yearning for life-affirming resolutions that will keep our chestnuts roasting another 12 months. It recognizes/exploits the tension between natural self-absorption and the phenomenon of the holidays. It possesses an infectious esprit de corps, thanks to the stable of light-heavyweights (thank you, Sports Department) that writer-director Roger Hedden has put together for his film. You hope for the best, given the cast.

Things don't get off to much of a promising start as regards either good will or narrative clarity, however. The lying and deception, in fact, are epic. If you can follow.

Jimmy (Eric Stoltz), an unemployed actor, needs $900 to pay off Fatty the Bookie (Charles Durning), so he tells his girlfriend. Susan (Moira Kelly) that he needs the money so his sister, Maggie, (Daryl Hannah) can get an abortion. Susan thinks she can get the money from her soft-touch brother, Ray (Scott), a bartender at the Hi-Life Bar & Grill, but since he's just broken up with Maggie—stay with us now—Susan tells Ray she needs the abortion. Which troubles him, and makes him think even less fondly of Jimmy.

Join the club. Minor (Peter Riegert), sent by Fatty to watch Jimmy while he collects the money, enlists his girlfriend's son, Ricky (Carlo Alban), to rip Jimmy off, but it doesn't work out and there's a gun, so things get messy. Meanwhile, our hero, Ray, the one guy who's on the level in this film, makes the rounds of every bar in the neighborhood, collecting all the money he's loaned out and never asked for, accompanied by the devout drunkard April (the wonderful Katrin Cartlidge), who helps him get his money and of course falls in love with him, too.

Scott, as usual, is a joy. Cartlidge, too. Riegert's always great and Durning's no slouch. Anne DeSalvo, who specializes in piquant ethnic broads, is Fatty's powderkeg of a wife and Stoltz is only mildly hateable, just the sort of villain, if you needed a villain, that you might get from Santa—although not Dean Cameron's belligerent Santa, whom proves there's no sanity, or any other Claus.

VILLAGE VOICE, 12/8/98 p. 140, J. Hoberman

It's been a good year for shaggy dog stories. First *The Big Lebowski*, then *I Went Down*, and now *Hi-Life*. Tales of loyalty tested by money, these films have had nothing much loftier in mind than enticing the viewer into the pleasure of following a leisurely, roundabout, often hilarious narrative.

Such unpretentiousness is a welcome change for Roger Hedden, whose two previous screenplays, *Bodies, Rest and Motion* and *Sleep With Me*, were similarly meandering in plot but were populated with whining Gen-X characters angsting over portentous sexual and existential crises. In *Hi-Life*, Hedden's directing debut, he merely seems out to have a good time, and his high spirits have clearly spread to his fine ensemble.

The title, a mildly ironic comment on the booze-fueled adventures of the film's down-and-outers, is the name of the Amsterdam Avenue bar where this jolly Christmas story begins and ends. Bartender Ray (Campbell Scott), a notorious soft touch, spends an evening making the rounds of Upper West Side taverns, accompanied by genial barfly April (casting coup Katrin Cartlidge), trying to collect on old debts to raise $900 for an emergency request from his sister Susan (Moira Kelly). Pursuing Ray and his money are Susan's unemployed actor boyfriend Jimmy (Hedden sine qua non Eric Stoltz) and Minor (Peter Rieqert), who is making sure Jimmy pays off a gambling debt to bookie Fatty (Charles Durning). Also thrown into the chase are Maggie (Daryl Hannah), who's Jimmy's sister and Ray's ex; two goofy EMS workers; a couple of angry wives and girlfriends; a ubiquitous mugger; and a surly Santa Claus.

The money notwithstanding, the film is less about greed than deceit. The characters demand honesty from each other while spinning elaborate lies and self-deceptions. Sometimes they know they're being lied to, but they're enjoying the spiel nonetheless.

Most of the performances feel both spontaneous and lived-in, particularly Scott's exasperated romantic, who's charming even when he's nervously intense; Cartlidge's unapologetic, cheerfully pragmatic drunk; and Riegert's harried grifter, whose half-baked scam attempt leads to a priceless argument with Stoltz in a taxi.

For most of the film, Hedden juggles these characters and their subplots with humor and dexterity. In a spirit of yuletide generosity, he lets most of his characters wind up with better than they deserve. For viewers, he offers no Dickensian sweetness or lessons, just a frivolous, festive cup of spiked eggnog.

Also reviewed in:
NEW YORK TIMES, 12/4/98, p. E12, Lawrence Van Gelder
VARIETY, 10/19-25/98, p. 77, Dennis Harvey

HI-LO COUNTRY, THE

A Gramercy Pictures release of a PolyGram Filmed Entertainment presentation in association with Martin Scorsese of a Working Title production with Cappa/DeFina Productions.   *Executive Producer:* Rudd Simmons.   *Producer:* Barbara DeFina, Martin Scorsese, Eric Fellner, and Tim Bevan.   *Director:* Stephen Frears.   *Screenplay:* Walon Green.   *Based on the novel by:* Max Evans.   *Director of Photography:* Oliver Stapleton.   *Editor:* Masahiro Hirakubo.   *Music:* Carter Burwell.   *Music Editor:* Adam Smalley.   *Choreographer:* Leslie Cook.   *Sound:* Drew Kunin and (music) Michael Farrow.   *Sound Editor:* Stefan Henrix.   *Casting:* Victoria Thomas.   *Production Designer:* Patricia Norris.   *Art Director:* Russell J. Smith.   *Set Decorator:* Leslie Morales.   *Set Dresser:* Jason Davis, Charlie Montoya, Lelan Keffer, and S. Mark Rich.   *Special Effects:* Dieter Sturm.   *Costumes:* Patricia Norris.   *Make-up:* Isabel Harkins.   *Make-up (Patricia Arquette):* Debbie Zoller.   *Make-up (Woody Harrelson):* Isabel Harkins.   *Stunt Coordinator:* Shawn Howell and Tim Trella.   *Running time:* 114 minutes.   *MPAA Rating:* R.

CAST: Billy Crudup (Pete Calder);   Woody Harrelson (Big Boy Matson);   Cole Hauser (Little Boy);   Enrique Castillo (Levi Gomez);   Darren Burrows (Billy Harte);   Jacob Vargas (Delfino

Mondragon); Robert Knott (Jack Couffer); Sam Elliott (Jim Ed Love); Sandy Baron (Henchman); Patricia Arquette (Mona); John Diehl (Les Birk); Craig Carter (Art Logan); Penelope Cruz (Josepha); Walter C. Hall (Auctioneer); James Gammon (Hoover Young); Will Cascio (Chickie Cobain); Richard Purdy (Bartender); Keith Walters (Man on Horse); Lane Smith (Steve Shaw); Sarge McGraw (Nick the Bartender); Rosaleen Linehan (Mrs. Matson); Rose Maddox (Grandmother); Bob Tallman (Rodeo Announcer); Buff Douthitt and H.P. Evetts (Rodeo Wranglers); Kate Williamson (Mrs. Young); Katy Jurado (Meesa); Don Pope (Sheriff Fitts); Monica Sundown and Amanda Cordova (Singers at Sano Dance).

LOS ANGELES TIMES, 12/30/98, Calendar/p. 5, Kenneth Turan

It was a horse named Old Sorrel that brought Pete Calder and Big Boy Matson together in the bleak, northeastern corner of New Mexico that gives "The Hi-Lo Country" its name. So it's fitting that a shot of Pete sitting cross-legged on Old Sorrel signals early on how this much-anticipated modern western is going to go astray.

Written by Walon Green ("The Wild Bunch") and based on Max Evans' celebrated novel, "The Hi-Lo Country" was a project "Wild Bunch" director Sam Peckinpah and several other filmmakers tried for decades to get on the screen. It finally fell to British director Stephen Frears to do the work, with Woody Harrelson as Big Boy, Billy Crudup as Pete and Patricia Arquette as Mona, the seductive woman who threatens to come between them.

Frears is one of the best of Britain's directors, and he's worked successfully in American settings before with "The Grifters." But there must be something about doing a western, about stomping around in the region John Ford celebrated, that makes a man push the mythic further than it can safely go. "The Hi-Lo Country" is a film of high quality, beautifully shot (by longtime Frears collaborator Oliver Stapleton) and all of that, but it's too self-consciously western, too much the exquisite copy rather than the living and breathing original, to be counted a complete success.

What that early shot of Pete artistically perched on Old Sorrel gives away is the film's tendency to be mannered, to present characters and situations that aren't capable of being as natural as they pretend. There's too much of the static museum piece about this authentic-looking film; it's so assiduously peopled by archetypes that much of what goes on feels like play-acting, though granted it's play-acting on quite a high level.

When Old Sorrel acts up once too often, Pete decides to sell the beast, and that's when he meets Big Boy and his brother Little Boy, or L.B. (Cole Hauser). A man with a ready grin, a rascal's sense of humor and an inability to worry about the future, Big Boy is presented as the Last Real Cowboy, the living personification of all the virtues of the traditional West.

The two men meet just before the start of World War II, and when they return to the Hi-Lo Country after the conflict, the West they know has changed. Jim Ed Love (Sam Elliott) bought up big chunks of Hi-Lo while everyone else was off fighting and represents a new class of managerial capitalism that threatens the cowboy ways Big Boy holds dear.

A good deal of "The Hi-Lo Country" is taken up with Big Boy and Pete displaying a wide range of quintessentially masculine behavior, from brawling and drinking to letting hand-rolled cigarettes settle in the corners of their mouths and pulling up chairs for high-stakes poker games. Men are men in this movie, make no mistake about that.

The placidity of this Eden is disturbed not only by Jim Ed's rapacity but also—wouldn't you know it?—by the presence of women. Josepha O'Neil (Penelope Cruz), Pete's prewar girlfriend, still clearly cares about him, but both her old beau and Big Boy are completely transfixed by Mona Birk (Arquette), the sultry wife of Jim Ed's aging foreman.

Mona has more than a classic film noir name, she's a through-going femme fatale, a New Mexico riff on the unattainable character she played in David Lynch's "Lost Highway." A dark-haired beauty who fears only boredom and is no more than nominally married, Mona drives all men wild, but most particularly Pete and Big Boy.

With Pete, the film's narrator, brooding over his obligations to Josepha, his passion for Mona, Mona's relationship with Big Boy, not mention his own relationship with Big Boy, "The Hi-Lo Country" turns unrelievedly grim awfully fast. With cowboy noir dialogue like "You're in my blood, Mona" and "Shootin's been a curse on our family," the film gets increasingly somber and fatalistic without becoming particularly convincing.

Though Harrelson and Crudup get the job done, it says something that in this most macho of films the two female leads make the biggest on-screen impression. Arquette as Mona feels completely authentic in a familiar role, and it's Cruz's Josepha who sums up the thrust of this self-involved drama in three well-chosen words: "Stupid, horny cowboys." Thirty years of trying to get this story on screen notwithstanding, that pretty much says it all.

NEW YORK, 1/18/99, p. 60, Peter Rainer

Lots of ink has been expended on *The Hi-Lo Country* lately because for years it was one of the late Sam Peckinpah's most cherished unrealized projects. There appears to be more excitement about the movie we don't have than about the one we do—a mild, by-the-numbers quasi-Western directed by Stephen Frears and starring Woody Harrelson and Billy Crudup. Scripted from Max Evans's 1961 novel by Walon Green, who wrote *The Wild Bunch,* no less, the film takes on fresh subject matter—the passing of the Old West and the encroachment of agribusiness just after the Second World War—and hammers it flatter than the proverbial pancake. Frears, who is British, is a remarkable talent, but his response to the New Mexico countryside and its cowboy rituals seems secondhand. It's not simply a matter of his being unfamiliar with America. After all, he made perhaps the best postwar *noir* genre piece in *The Grifters,* and from *My Beautiful Laundrette* to *Dangerous Liaisons,* he's always had a far-ranging, uncategorizable curiosity. He's a quick-change artist, but the chaps and Stetsons here prove an ill fit. He probably wishes he could have seen the Peckinpah version, too.

The prairie town of Hi-Lo comes off like a movie location, and for the most part, the performers who strut and sidle and sashay across it are actorish. This is not altogether unpleasing, at least for a while: The comfort level of most Westerns lies in their ability to remind us not of real life but of other Westerns. But with filmmakers such as Frears and Green involved, we keep waiting, in vain, for the genre to split open. *The Hi-Lo Country* isn't an homage, really—it's more like a simple retelling of something we all know by heart anyway. A movie like this can make even the dumb-dumbs in the audience seem prescient.

Pete Calder (Crudup) and Big Boy Matson (Harreleson) are best friends who return from the war to raise cattle and work the land. You know they're soulmates because they're always getting stewed together and helping each other in and out of bar brawls. For that all-important triangle effect, they're also both in love with the same woman, Mona (Patricia Arquette), who happens to be married to the foreman of the town's agri-bad-guy, Jim Ed Love (Sam Elliott, overdoing it). With her crimson hair and clingy dresses, Mona drives just about every male in Hi-Lo into Hi-Hi—although Arquette is so unconvincing that she might have ordered up her sultry moves from a catalogue. Mona evokes from Pete a volley of voice-overs that sound like Mickey Spillane-on-the-prairie. (Sample: "She came up against me like silver foil.") Most of the time, though, Pete is more reliably pedestrian, as when he looks out across the countryside and whispers, "The land, yeah, this is what I was born to do." Silver foil, meet tin ear.

What bails out a lot of this hogwash is the enjoyableness of the two lead performances. Crudup has a soft-spoken reticence that seems authentic to the period, and his handsomeness seems in period, too. He's a postwar cowboy with the stark, daguerreotype look of his forebears, and this makes sense in terms of the passing-of-the-old-ways story Frears is trying to tell. Based on his work here and as the long-distance runner Steve Prefontaine in Robert Towne's affecting, neglected *Without Limits,* Crudup has something of the quality of the young Robert Redford—inside his glossiness there's a crackle.

Harrelson is a much more flamboyant presence, but his Big Boy never lapses into total caricature—even when the movie does. Harrelson can be goony and overwrought, but with his crooked satyr's grin he has a slyness, too. No other actor around, except perhaps James Woods, has wilder eyes—he always seems to be looking out at you from atop a plunging roller coaster. Harrelson is able to make Big Boy both a good old boy and a son of a bitch; he flaunts his affair with Mona in front of her husband in a way that's close to sadistic. (Peckinpah would have made it plain sadistic.) Big Boy is made to stand for too much in this film—he's the rabble-rousing Life Force of the Old West—but Harrelson at least has a lot of life in him. When somebody accuses Big Boy of living in the past, he shoots back, "I don't want no goddamn future," and it's more than a boast; it's a war whoop.

NEW YORK POST, 12/30/99, p. 37, Rod Dreher

Woody Harrelson's surprisingly credible, yippie-ki-yay performance as the last of the old-time cowboys is the only reason—but just reason enough—to see "The Hi-Lo Country," British director Stephen Frears' pokey soap opera set in post-WWII, rural New Mexico.

There's a fair amount of drinkin', fightin', chasin' women and drivin' cattle, but a rueful, party's-over atmosphere pervades the action, and a supporting cast that can't match Harrelson's vivid portrayal bogs down the story.

The film has been adapted by Walon Green from a 1961 novel by Max Evans. The book was an elegy to a rough-and-tumble way of life that was eclipsed by social changes wrought by the Second World War, and a memorial tribute to a murdered friend of the author's, who was the inspiration for hell raising Big Boy Matson (Harrelson).

In a sense, "The Hi-Lo Country" is a post-Western Western, in which the rugged individualism represented by the cowboy of myth came to be seen as a positive liability.

As "The Hi-Lo Country" sorrowfully tells it, when America grew up after the war and got "sivilized," the cowboy, who used to be viewed as a romantic hero, now appeared as a boy—a Big Boy—who wouldn't grow up.

The film begins with Pete (Billy Crudup), sitting in his truck with a shotgun across his lap, contemplating killing a man. The story then slips into flashback, recounting events that led Pete to the cusp of murder. Director Frears quickly establishes the brotherly friendship between solemn Pete and boisterous Big Boy, who are separated when they are called to active military service.

When he returns to the boys' desert prairie home town of Hi-Lo, Pete develops an obsessive crush on Mona (Patricia Arquette), the trollopy wife of spineless Les Birk (John Diehl). Mona is trapped in an unhappy marriage, and makes it clear at a dance that she would appreciate a distraction.

But when Big Boy gets back from the Pacific, Pete soon discovers that his best friend has put his brand on Mona. Where Pete is shy, reflective and deferential, Big Boy is a hotheaded extrovert.

He's a half-crazy, intensely physical man who lives by his own rules. Though he is seriously flawed—he is, after all, carrying on shamelessly with another man's wife—Big Boy is admirably brave in his refusal to kowtow to Jim Ed (Sam Elliott), the cold-blooded rancher with a fat wallet and a crocodile smile.

As good as Harrelson is, he can't carry the movie alone. The tepid acting from Arquette and most especially from Crudup in a crucial role, make the picture go slack whenever Harrelson is off screen. That, and the downbeat (if realistic) ending, make "Hi-Lo" only so-so. N.B. the brief appearance of the great Texas swing musician and singer Don Walser, who performs with his band in a rodeo dance scene. Without question, Walser is one of "Hi-Lo"'s high points.

NEWSDAY, 12/30/98, Part II/p. B5, John Anderson

Looking for a New Year's resolution? Try this: If you're going to see a movie based on a book, don't read the book.

(Note: This may sound like a paradox-in-the-making, since it's usually only best-sellers that are made into movies. But it's OK to buy them. Just don't read them.)

Even with a good film, what becomes most striking when you sit down in the theater are the differences between the book and the movie, not the similarities. The screen becomes a funhouse mirror, reflecting a distorted vision of what's in your memory. The movie may actually be good. But you can't see its virtues for the warps in its vision.

Which is too bad, because once in a while, a movie will rise to the level of its source material ("To Kill a Mockingbird," "The Thin Red Line") and occasionally even surpass it ("The Godfather," "The Bridges of Madison County"). On occasion, a filmmaker has had the sense to realize he can't do justice to an entire book and films only part of it ("East of Eden"); others have had a terrific book and perhaps too much lawyerly advice to do it justice ("A Civil Action"). Left over, of course, is a vast number about which one wonders why anyone bothered.

These would include "The Hi-Lo Country," written in the early '60s by Max Evans, a novel the late Sam Peckinpah had wanted to film but never did. Wry, dry and as flat as its postwar New Mexico-Texas setting, it's an anecdotal book about larger-than-Texas characters, a vanishing way of life and a peculiar set of love affairs that intertwine like rattlesnakes. But its casual attitude toward the eccentricities of its people is a slippery thing, especially for a director like Stephen Frears ("Dangerous Liaisons," "The Grifters"), who tends to go archly where others fear to tread.

Frears may have a lot of fallow ground under him in "The Hi-Lo Country," but his prize bull is Woody Harrelson, who makes Evans' somewhat laconic Big Boy Matson into an energized, screen-dominating presence. Playing opposite Harrelson is the understated Billy Crudup, as saddle pal Pete Calder, another would-be cattleman trying to keep tradition alive in a noble-futile gesture of defiance. While Frears mines the homoerotic attraction between Big Boy and Pete to an extent Evans probably never even thought about, the film's entire sociologic message could be summarized in one scene from this year's documentary "The Saltmen of Tibet": yak-driving salt gatherers being passed along a roadside by high-speed trucks full of salt.

Yak drivers certainly don't have the romantic entanglements of Big Boy and Pete, who've arrived back from World War II ready to get rich, drunk and, uh, sexually satisfied, not necessarily in that order. Nor do they have anything like Mona Birk (Patricia Arquette, seemingly as stoned as Harrelson is hyper), wife of Les Birk (John Diehl), the scurrilous minion of local mogul Jim Ed Love (Sam Elliott), the guy who always seems to have hay for sale when the blizzard arrives. Les is something of a spineless worm, so Mona takes one look at Big Boy and, you know, vice versa. Pete, unhappily, has already fallen for the rather licentious Mona, despite the undying affection of his old girl Josepha (Penelope Cruz). So what we have are a lot of pretty volatile people, tossed together like the proverbial matches, dynamite and pyromaniacal chimpanzees.

What's missing from Evans' novel are its tone and structure, which weren't ingenious but made a lot more tactile sense out of the Mona-Big Boy-Pete fiasco than does Frears' (and screenwriter Walon Green's) more directly romantic approach. The original "Hi-Lo Country" interspersed minibiographies of the local characters—the hunters, drunks and hustlers of Hi-Lo—with the chronicle of romance gone bad. The romance—both sordid and inconsequential—wasn't given the prominence it has in the film. And somehow it made more sense that way. Which just goes to indicate not just the problems of adapting novels into films, but why, sometimes, it shouldn't be done at all.

SIGHT AND SOUND, 8/99, p. 44, Edward Buscombe

The town of Hi-Lo, New Mexico, the late 30s. Pete Calder and Big Boy Matson first meet when Big Boy buys Pete's horse, Old Sorrel. The two cowboys become close friends. Both join up and see combat during World War Two. When they return to Hi-Lo things have changed. Local rancher Jim Ed Love has grown rich and bought up many small holders. But Big Boy and Pete decide they can make it alone, although they accept help from the sympathetic rancher Hoover Young.

A feud develops between Love and the two cowboys, intensified when Big Boy begins a romance with Mona, the wife of Love's foreman Les Birk. Before the war Pete had himself been in love with Mona. Now he tries to forget her by resuming his relationship with the loyal Josepha. Big Boy's younger brother Little Boy goes to work for Love, and Big Boy constantly goads him, much to the distress of their mother Mrs Matson, who reminds them that both their father and grandfather died violent deaths. Big Boy's behaviour grows provocative and Pete has to save him from being shot by the jealous Birk.

In a drunken stupor, Pete has sex with Mona; Josepha breaks off with him in disgust. Mona leaves her husband and she and Big Boy plan to marry when she finds herself pregnant. But Big Boy and Little Boy fight and Big Boy is shot dead. Pete plans to shoot Little Boy in revenge, but is dissuaded by Mrs Matson. After saying goodbye to a grieving Mona, Pete leaves for California to seek out Josepha.

In the introduction to the reissue of his novel *The Hi-Lo Country*, first published in 1961, Max Evans tells of meeting Sam Peckinpah to discuss filming it. It's not hard to see what might have attracted Peckinpah to the book: the bonds of male friendship; the tragedy of a strong, even heroic man overwhelmed by the forces of modernity he barely understands; the Hispanic milieu of the South West; even the binary division of women into virgins and whores, though in truth that has roots deep within the Western genre.

But Stephen Frears has no need to apologise for not being Sam. He has made a handsome-looking and sounding version of the novel. From its confident opening on a huge, flat landscape, followed by (as with all proper Westerns) a shot under the titles of a man riding towards the camera, to its closing on a big rosy sunset the film delivers a satisfyingly broad visual sweep. There's a loving attention to period detail and local colour, and Carter Burwell's music is especially good, with a fine 40s sound in the extended dancehall sequence including a skilled recreation of 'San Antonio Rose', the best known number of Bob Wills and His Texas Playboys—and an on screen appearance by Austin's own Don Walser.

Like a couple of Peckinpah's Westerns, the film turns on the clash between the old cattle culture of the South West and the forces of modern commerce and technology. Big Boy wants to preserve things the way they've always been, or at least the way he's always seen them: small, independent ranchers working their land on horseback, leading lives of manly self-sufficiency. "This is what I was born to do," he says, riding through open country on a cattle drive. But, as he's told more than once, he's living in the past. The war has changed everything. While he and Pete have been away, the smugly smiling Jim Ed Love has been consolidating his holdings, swallowing up the smaller ranches, introducing mechanisation. Though real enough, Big Boy's attraction to Mona is also a way of getting back at forces too powerful to be confronted head on.

Morally, if not economically, the cards are stacked in favour of the good ol' boys. Jim Ed Love and his allies are an unappealing bunch: Big Boy's weasely brother Little Boy, Mona's husband Les with his small, mean moustache, Steve the moneylender. Against them are ranged, alongside Big Boy himself, his friend Pete, their employer Hoover Young (a wonderful cameo by James Gammon, whose face is a landscape in itself), and a handful of stalwart Hispanics. But the film doesn't necessarily take Big Boy at his own value. As the story unfolds, his behaviour coarsens. He flaunts Mona in front of the loyal Pete, likening women to horses: a good one has "bottom", he declaims to anyone who will listen. In a poker game Big Boy goads Steve to the point where the overweight moneylender dies of a heart attack, and then heartlessly triumphs in what he has done.

Josepha, finally reacting against Pete's continuing infatuation with Mona, dismisses him and Big Boy as stupid, horny cowboys. It's a point of view. There's something brutish about their constant fighting; in almost every scene, one or the other carries a facial scar from the last encounter. In Peckinpah's films the heroes, though flawed, retain enough stature to touch tragedy. But, in a generally excellent cast, Woody Harrelson is the one actor who slightly misjudges his performance. We have to believe he would inspire the undying love of Pete and Mona, but there's not enough charm. Too often his high spirits spill over into a boorishness the film seems uneasy with, neither condemning nor celebrating, but merely observing, half embarrassed. It's the only uncertainty in what is other-wise a rich and satisfying evocation of a culture under pressure.

TIME, 12/28/98-1/4/99, p. 177, Richard Schickel

Mammas, don't let your babies grow up to be cowboys. And while you're at it, don't let them grow up to make movies about cowboys either. Especially ones that place them in a pretty Southwestern light and solemnly invite us to contemplate their tragic inability to cope with the modern world.

In *The Hi-Lo Country*, a young man named Pete (Billy Crudup) goes home to New Mexico after World War II, determined to make a go of it as an independent small-scale rancher. Mostly, however, he watches, awed and complaisant, while his like-minded neighbor Big Boy (Woody Harrelson) proceeds along a mulishly macho course to self-destruction. This includes a feckless involvement with a trashy woman (Patricia Arquette), lots of sullen standing around in bars itching for a fight, and much hoo-hawing contempt for a competitor (Sam Elliott) who lets nothing distract him from building the kind of big operation that changing times require.

When all is finally lost, it's the failure to honor tradition, not the dopiness of clinging to it, that's blamed. Sam Peckinpah, who loved to celebrate bad-boyishness, apparently tried for years to adapt Max Evans' 1961 novel to the screen. It says something about the reach and persistence of decaying myth that British director Stephen Frears, creator of such eccentric delights as *My Beautiful Laundrette* and *The Grifters*, has succumbed to it. There's no need to follow his example.

Tracy McKnight. *Sound:* Noah Timan and Matt Armstrong. *Sound Editor:* Tom Efinger.
Casting: Billy Hopkins, Suzanne Smith, and Kerry Barden. *Production Designer:* Bernhard
Blythe. *Art Director:* Caryn Marcus. *Set Decorator:* Mechelle Chojecki. *Costumes:* Victoria
Farrell. *Make-up:* Mia Thoen. *Running time:* 96 minutes. *MPAA Rating:* R.

CAST: Ally Sheedy (Lucy Berliner); Radha Mitchell (Syd); Patricia Clarkson (Greta);
Gabriel Mann (James, Syd's Boyfriend); Bill Sage (Arnie); Anh Duong (Dominique, "Frame"
Editor); Tammy Grimes (Vera, Lucy's Mother); David Thornton (Harry, Syd's Boss); Helen
Mendes (White Hawk); Cindra Feuer (Delia); Anthony Ruivivar (Xander); Elaine Tse (Zoe);
Rudolf Martin (Dieter); Laura Ekstrand (Waitress); Charis Michelson (Debby).

LOS ANGELES TIMES, 6/12/98, Calendar/p. 8, Jack Mathews

[The following review by Jack Mathews appeared in a slightly different form in
NEWSDAY, 6/12/98, Part II/p. B19.]

I don't know about art, but people are definitely high in Lisa Cholodenko's arrestingly ambitious "High Art," a movie populated by characters who keep themselves so stoned on heroin they seem to be in a perpetual state of slow-motion.

It's a world, as the heroine Syd (Radha Mitchell) will learn, that you enter at your own risk. One line sucked into the nasal passage can turn your brain into drying cement. It's like being in one of those dreams where you try to run but your legs won't move. Only, these people aren't trying to move. They've stopped the world and gotten off, they've chosen stupor over struggle, to be loaded and disconnected.

That's the scene discovered by Syd, a fledgling New York photo magazine editor, when she knocks on the door of her upstairs neighbor, hoping to find the source of water leaking through her and her boyfriend's bathroom ceiling. About the only coherent person in the room is Lucy (Ally Sheedy), a former rich girl and prodigy in New York's photo-art world, who had gone off to Europe in a fit of material rejection and returned with Greta (Patricia Clarkson), a strung-out German actress, as her dependent lover.

Syd doesn't recognize Lucy, but she knows good photography when she sees it, and the walls of this drug den are covered in brilliantly intimate candid photos. Or so Syd—and later, her editors—say. They look like doable snapshots to me.

In any event, Syd returns, to snort some dope herself and laze around on Lucy's bed, drunkenly considering the unfamiliar pangs of passion she's feeling for another woman.

Syd's emotions become a tangle of envy, admiration, infatuation and ambition. She wants to score with her bosses by bringing Lucy to the magazine, and Lucy wants to score with her by cooperating. The magazine's deadline for Lucy's assignment becomes the catalyst that will alter several people's lives.

The fact that "High Art," which earned Cholodenko the screenwriting award at this year's Sundance Film Festival, is the third lesbian-themed film from producer Dolly Hall (the others were "The Incredible True Adventures of Two Girls in Love" and "All Over Me") has already pigeonholed "High Art" for a niche art-house crowd.

But the genders of the lovers are almost incidental to the true beat of this story. It's not about an experienced lesbian recruiting a straight; if anything, Syd is the aggressor. And nothing is made of it, even by Syd's angry boyfriend, who looks on Lucy as he would any rival.

Cholodenko's main interest is the self-destructiveness of Lucy, a heroin addict trapped in a cycle of doom, and the impact that the secure and relatively square Syd has on her. The key moment of truth in the film comes when Syd announces to Lucy, as they head upstate for a weekend tryst—their first—that drugs can't be a part of that experience.

"High Art" is, unfortunately, full of itself and its artistic pretensions. The dialogue and personalities of the magazine editors, though intended as humorously hip, will produce more sounds of gagging than laughter. And the hazy drug scenes, especially those with Greta, whom Clarkson portrays as a zonked-out Marlene Dietrich, have the stale odor of cliche.

But there's nothing wrong with the lead performances. Sheedy plays Lucy with a strength that gradually falls away as a facade over her vulnerability, and Mitchell ("Love and Other Catastrophes") is a revelation as the innocently ambitious Syd. Together they provide some of the most honest and hotly passionate romance you'll find in theaters this year.

NEW YORK, 6/15/98, p. 50, David Denby

High Art is tinged by the gray light of downtown seriousness. A fresh young girl (Radha Mitchell), a sub-editor at a highbrow photo magazine in Manhattan, gets pulled into the life and bed of a star photographer (Ally Sheedy) who lives in the SoHo apartment above her. Having withdrawn from work, the photographer sits around doing dope with her lover, a wasted German actress (Patricia Clarkson), and a bunch of terminally wrecked cronies. The atmosphere is one of apocalyptic languor—everyone speaks in a whisper, and the coffee tables groan under the weight of heroin. This may sound like a very dreary funeral, but it isn't. The writer-director Lisa Cholodenko sustains her intimate moods with skill, and bit by bit the love story takes hold. In the end, despite much resistance, I was fascinated by the movie's commitment to passion and to art. In its solemn way, *High Art* is a victory for both.

NEW YORK POST, 6/12/98, p. 47, Thelma Adams

Ally Sheedy: You've come a long way from the Brat Pack, baby!

"High Art" is not "The Breakfast Club." In writer/director Lisa Cholodenko's assured debut, Sheedy plays Lucy Berliner, a seedy, sinewy, heroin-snorting Jewish lesbian.

Berliner could have been a contender as a photographer, another Nan Golden, if she didn't have a nasty habit of self destruction.

Lucy lives with her junkie gal pal Greta (Patricia Clarkson). The faded, honey-haired actress dreams of her heyday with the late German director Rainer Werner Fassbinder.

The pair hang in their Manhattan loft with a handsome crew of drug-addicted hipsters who can hardly hold a thought together to play dominoes.

Enter Syd, an unlikely knight in shining armor. The ambitious golden girl (Radha Mitchell) has clawed her way from intern to assistant editor at Frame, an art photography magazine.

One night, while taking a bath, Syd sees a drip from the ceiling. She heads upstairs to fix the problem (she's a great fixer, that one).

When Lucy opens the door, Syd falls through the looking glass into a seductive world of ambiguous sexuality, heroin and hipness.

In Lucy's loo, the plucky Syd repairs the leaky tub and admires the older woman's photos. Lucy admires Syd.

The editor seduces the artist by deconstruction. In turn, when Lucy stares longingly at Syd, its as if she were looking over her shoulder into a mirror at a younger, better self.

Syd's encounter with "High Art"—a pun on drug-fueled creativity—launches an intellectual and sexual journey. Mitchell ("Love and Other Catastrophes") conveys both the 24-year-old's naivete in office and sexual politics—and her ambition.

Sheedy's lined, world-weary face contrasts with Mitchell's peach complexion. Sheedy resembles the older Genevieve Bujold, the pert, pixieish features of youth bowing to soulful eyes that swallow light.

Newcomer Cholodenko makes the relationship between Syd and Lucy stimulating—both intellectually and sexually. Together, they burn like the Malibu hills in September.

Columbia alum Cholodenko earned well-deserved praise at Sundance and Cannes. Her languid, witty and frank love story achieves what she aspires to: "High Art."

SIGHT AND SOUND, 4/99, p. 45, Leslie Felperin

New York City, Syd works at *Frame*, a photography magazine. At home one night with her boyfriend James, a leak in the bathroom leads Syd up to the flat of their neighbour Lucy, who's been snorting heroin with her live-in girlfriend Greta and their friends. Syd is bowled over by Lucy's photographs and later borrows a book of her work to show the editors at *Frame*. They explain that Lucy was once the hottest photographer in New York, but she turned her back on it all. At a meeting, Lucy agrees to do a spread for *Frame* as long as Syd has full editorial control.

A mutual attraction grows between Syd and Lucy. Syd tries some heroin at a party with Lucy, alienating James and making Greta jealous. Lucy insists Syd accompany her on a trip upstate. The two make love and in the morning Lucy takes intimate snaps of Syd in bed. Back in New York, Lucy considers leaving Greta and giving up heroin. She gives Syd the photos of their weekend, insisting *Frame* use them. Greta and Lucy fight about their relationship and then snort some heroin together; Lucy dies. Syd's image adorns the latest issue of *Frame*.

It's been a long time since I've been deconstructed," says a flattered Lucy Berliner after magazine assistant editor Syd raves about how Lucy's photographs illustrate a notion of Roland Barthes'. And it's been a long time since we've seen on screen so cerebral a seduction as Lucy's. It's to *High Art*'s credit that it flirts so frankly and eschews using complicated visual accessories to lure us into the bedroom. Given the hip, quasi-intellectual demi-monde the film is set in, other filmmakers might have been tempted to trick out the movie with retro new wave-style jump cuts or Warholian graininess. But Lisa Cholodenko (maker of the shorts *Souvenir* and *Dinner Party*) and cinematographer Tami Reiker confine themselves to coolly composed long takes and slow tracks richly lit. This suits what is after all a simple love-triangle story, and finds a correlative in Lucy's photographs (actually taken by JoJo Whilden) of her friends in various postures of

loucheness, which Syd describes as striking a balance between formal composition and spontaneity
If *Artforum* had a tabloid-style agony-aunt column with a photostory, it would look something like
High Art.

Some of the other photographs used in the film are by Nan Goldin, and Lucy's snaps bear more
than a passing resemblance to Goldin's confessional, lapidary portraits of herself and her
bohemian friends. Inevitably, this has wrought accusations that the film has plagiarised Goldin's
life, which seems a little unfair to both the film and Goldin, whose work has moved on from self-
focus to more distinctly other subjects, including drag queens and hospices. Nonetheless, *High
Art* does deal, perhaps with oblique criticism, with the 'cult of the artist's personality culture' that
dominates a strain of 80s and 90s metropolitan chic. ("You guys are so glamorous," says Lucy
to her friends as she watches them inject heroin.) The vampiric editorial crew at Syd's magazine
Frame all but slobber when they find out Syd knows Lucy and push the latter to produce a spread
based on her life at that moment, itching for the proximity frisson brought by her drug-culture
lesbian cachet. Though sympathetically incarnated in Radha Mitchell's russet-and-honey figure,
Syd gets to live out something of a star-fucking fantasy, albeit one for high-toned Ivy League
girls.

Who can blame her when Ally Sheedy's Lucy is the fulcrum of that fantasy? Whip thin and
kitted out in a selection of crisp hipster slacks, Sheedy oozes both the confident sexuality and
brittle intelligence required for the role. Adding another spin to the film's thematic games with
fame and reputation, her casting is an extra irony since Sheedy, like Lucy, also seemed to have
slipped disappointingly from view since she became famous for *The Breakfast Club*. She holds
the reins at the film's heart with confidence, leaving a wonderfully deadpan Patricia Clarkson,
whose Greta once worked with "FAAASbinder", to embody the bitterness of the wash-out.

If Lucy and Syd's relationship blossoms with a little too much abrupt ease, the scalding portrait
of Lucy and Greta's co-dependence is worth the price of a ticket alone, beautifully measured out
in spoonfuls of smack. The only real disappointment in this otherwise excellent film is that the
conclusion goes for childish 'live fast, die young' melodramatics instead of evolving something
more provocative out of the subtle portrait that's gone before.

TIME, 8/24/98, p. 74, William Tynan

O'Haver, who evokes the retro spirit with such expert élan, has signed with Universal Pictures
to direct a movie of the Archie comic book. We can't wait to see if Archie gets to pining over
Jughead.

Not every gay film wants to be a Minnelli musical. Three of the new gay dramas, all about
artists in extremis, are traditional in another sense. They locate the not so divine decadence—all
that is theatrical, naughty, self-destructive—in gay sex. Bill Condon's *Gods and Monsters* stars
Ian McKellen in a parable about '30s Hollywood director James Whale (*Frankenstein, Show
Boat*). Like Billy, he is consumed with sexual longing, but here it is the ultimate form of
masochism: a desire to be killed. The erotic charge sizzles in Lisa Cholodenko's *High Art*, a
pensive throwback to the drug-and-sex angst of the '70s. It tosses Ally Sheedy into heavy, fraught
clinches with Patricia Clarkson and Radha Mitchell. (Mitchell: "It's hot in here." Sheedy: "No.
You're hot.")

John Maybury's *Love Is the Devil: Study for a Portrait of Francis Bacon* examines the English
painter's long affair with a petty thief and his need to be the submissive partner in
sadomasochistic sex. The film is broken into shards of images like shrapnel: coupled male bodies
mime the exertions of Greco-Roman wrestling; Francis bends over for a whipping, or to be
tattooed with a hot cigarette. Which makes the film both exquisitely observed and tough to watch.

The reach of either of these genres—happy-gay or sad-gay—is limited. They appeal to people
who are open to gays and to modestly experimental films. Jenni Olson, whose *PopcornQ* website
compiles data on gay and lesbian movies, warns against expecting one with *Titanic* or even *Full
Monty* box office. "They can cross over to a straight art-house audience," she says. "We're not
talking about an 'Oh, let's take the kids to a gay movie' crossover." The point isn't that everyone
needs to see these films. It is that "out" films are finally and fully out there.

VILLAGE VOICE, 6/16/98, p. 154, Amy Taubin

The actors in *The Land Girls* have the benefit of sensitive direction and an intelligent script. In *High Art*, Ally Sheedy, playing a downtown photographer grossly based on Nan Goldin, gives a memorably ironic, sad, and wise performance despite the banality of almost everything going on around her. It's very difficult to make a film about an artist when you have no discernible aesthetic of your own and when the supposedly great works of art that you show on the screen look as if they were executed by a mediocre college photography major. First-time director Lisa Cholodenko fails in good company: Vincente Minnelli, Robert Altman, and Jacques Rivette made similarly ludicrous films about the lives and loves of famous artists.

On the other hand, the junk-saturated downtown bohemia of the '80s has been exactingly depicted in two films—Jim Jarmusch's *Stranger Than Paradise* and Julian Schnabel's *Basquiat*. Cholodenko's desire to make a feminist intervention in the genre is admirable, but aside from Sheedy's performance and that of Radha Mitchell as an ambitious but starstruck young editor with a strong sense of self-preservation, the film is strictly by the numbers.

Also reviewed in:
CHICAGO TRIBUNE, 7/3/98, Friday/p. A, Michael Wilmington
NEW YORK TIMES, 6/12/98, p. E12, Janet Maslin
VARIETY, 2/2-8/98, p. 29, Emanuel Levy
WASHINGTON POST, 6/19/98, Weekend/p. 48, Michael O'Sullivan

HILARY AND JACKIE

An October Films release in association with Film Four and Intermedia Films of an Oxford Film Company production with the participation of British Screen and The Arts Council of England. *Executive Producer:* Guy East, Nigel Sinclair, and Ruth Jackson. *Producer:* Andy Paterson and Nicholas Kent. *Director:* Anand Tucker. *Screenplay:* Frank Cottrell Boyce. *Based on the book "A Genius in the Family" by:* Hilary du Pré and Piers du Pré. *Director of Photography:* David Johnson. *Editor:* Martin Walsh. *Music:* Barrington Pheloung. *Music Editor:* Bob Hathaway. *Sound:* David Crozier and (music) Joel Twataki and Mike Ross-Trevor. *Casting:* Simone Ireland and Vanessa Pereira. *Production Designer:* Alice Normington. *Art Director:* Charmian Adams. *Set Decorator:* Tricia Edwards. *Special Effects:* Evan Green-Hughes. *Costumes:* Sandy Powell. *Make-up:* Lois Burwell. *Running time:* 121 minutes. *MPAA Rating:* R.

CAST: Emily Watson (Jacqueline "Jackie" du Pré); Rachel Griffiths (Hilary du Pré); James Frain (Daniel "Danny" Barenboim); David Morrissey (Kiffer Finzi); Charles Dance (Derek du Pré); Celia Imrie (Iris du Pré); Rupert Penry Jones (Piers du Pré); Bill Paterson (Cello Teacher); Auriol Evans (Young Jackie); Keely Flanders (Young Hilary); Grace Chatto (Teresa); Nyree Dawn Porter (Dame Margot Fonteyn); Maggie McCarthy (Margaret); Vernon Dobtcheff (Professor Bentley); Anthony Smee (BBC Nabob); Delia Lindsay (Tweedy Woman); Linda Spurrier (Twinset); Nick Haverson (Photographer); Kika Mirylees (Patron); Pal Banda (Maestro); Robert Rietti (Italian Flunky); Tamsin Pike (Harpsicord Player); David Shimwell (Man in Suit); Peter Czajkowski (German Admirer); Stella Maris (Spanish Admirer); Carla Medonca (Spanish Maid); Anna Barkan (Acolyte); Steven Atholl (Bookish Man); Heather Weeks (Guest); Ralph De Souza (Violinist); Andrea Chaialton (Dressmaker); Jon Rumney (Rabbi); Kate Hetherington (Middle Jackie); Ariana Daykin (Middle Hilary); Oliver Lee (Baby Piers); Hayley James-Gannon and Melissa James-Gannon (Hilary's Children); George Kennaway (German Concert Conductor); John Gough (Wigmore Accompanist); Brian Perkins (Radio Announcer).

LOS ANGELES TIMES, 12/30/98, Kenneth Turan

It takes two to be sisters, two to have a rivalry, and two exceptional actresses to turn "Hilary and Jackie" into a compelling look at the most intimate and troubling of family dynamics. An assured take on the nature of sibling bonds, "Hilary and Jackie" also provides an unorthodox examination of the burden being gifted places on all concerned—the one with the talent as well as those in the emotional vicinity.

"Hilary and Jackie" is based on "A Genius in the Family," a book by Hilary and Piers du Pre about their celebrated sister, Jacqueline du Pre, the brilliant young English cellist who died in 1987 at age 42 after being stricken by multiple sclerosis 16 years earlier at the height of her career.

One of the great musicians of her generation, celebrated for her interpretation of the Elgar cello concerto and half of a golden couple with conductor and pianist-husband Daniel Barenboim (who once described her as having "the gift of making you feel she was actually composing the music she was playing"), Du Pre is next door to deified in Britain.

So her siblings' book and its revelations about what life with Jackie could be like caused a tremendous ruckus, with one critic huffily proclaiming he could do without Du Pre being turned into "Du Praved, the sexual predator."

The resulting film promises to create equal discord, and in fact ends its credits with the most detailed disclaimer in memory, admitting in part that "composite characters, representative incidents, adjusted chronology and context, constructed dialogue and other fictionalized elements have been used for dramatic purposes... No implication should be drawn that any of the persons depicted have authorized or approved this production."

While this fuss is intriguing it's largely beside the point. In fact, viewers in this country, where Du Pre is hardly a household word, are likely in a better position to appreciate what should be viewed as something inspired by reality instead of the exact real thing. Screenwriter Frank Cottrell Boyce ("Welcome to Sarajevo") and first-time feature director Anand Tucker have created an absorbing human story and told it with an unexpected structure and a determination to be evenhanded to all its conflicting parties.

Tucker, whose BBC background is in documentaries, shows off his strong storytelling sense and visual assurance with an opening dream sequence whose meaning doesn't become completely clear until later in the film. In a sequence that is both fun and somehow sad, he introduces two little girls playing by the shore, bright girls with vivid imaginations and sisters for sure.

These would be young Hilary (Keely Flanders) and younger Jackie (Auriol Evans). Their mother, Iris (Celia Imrie), is determined to give them a strong musical education, under which they both thrive. It is Hilary, two years older, who excels first on the flute, with Jackie's flowering as a prodigy on the cello shown to be inspired by their mother's edict, "If you want to be together, you have to play as well as Hilary."

This pair of child actresses do a remarkable job of underlining the poignancy of young girls working ever so hard on their adult music. Once Hilary and Jackie grow up, the parts are taken even further by two of the best actresses working today, Rachel Griffiths and Emily Watson.

The Australian Griffiths, best known for her role in "Muriel's Wedding," brings a keen mixture of melancholy and resilience to the part of Hilary, who feels the separation Jackie's sudden success brings with it and whose own life as a musician becomes reduced to answering the question, "And how is your marvelous sister?"

As Jackie du Pre, British actress Watson more than fulfills the promise of her celebrated Oscar-nominated work in "Breaking the Waves." She completely inhabits the role of the troubled young cellist, living it as much as acting it. As Jackie appears to gradually turn into a kind of beautiful monster, selfish and needy in a way that feels directly proportional to her amazing gift, Watson knows how to create involvement without special pleading on her part.

Once Hilary and Jackie become adults, the narrative splits in two. In a device reminiscent of Akira Kurosawa's celebrated "Rashomon," the story of their troubled but deep interaction is told first from Hilary's point of view and then, about 45 minutes later (and announced by a large "Jackie" on the screen) from her sister's.

It's a mark of how evenhanded "Hilary and Jackie" manages to be that this technique works as well as it does, forcing us to recognize the honest subjectivity and selective memory that makes up each woman's view of reality. As a general rule, Hilary tends to feel abandoned by her soul mate, while Jackie finds herself lonely and even desperate, trapped by her talent in a bizarre life. Even as simple an act as Jackie's sending her dirty laundry home to England during her first European tour is depicted from a pair of radically different perspectives.

Though loving, the two sisters are always competitive, even where men are concerned. Hilary gets involved first, marrying Christopher "Kiffer" Finzi (David Morrissey), the son of composer Gerald Finzi, whose brash persona is a breath of fresh air for her after her cloistered life at home. Not one to be overshadowed, Jackie snags the celebrated young musician Barenboim (James Frain). As Jackie gets more insecure and voracious, the personal lives of the sisters get even more intimately intertwined—an agony that worsens when Hilary's MS is diagnosed.

There is, inevitably, something of "Shine" about this story of music and emotional torment, but "Hilary and Jackie" feels completely its own picture. The powerful yet delicate ties of sisterhood it illuminates are so intricate and mysterious, and so superbly acted, that this exploration is difficult to resist.

NEW STATESMAN, 1/15/99, p. 39, Dermot Clinch

Jacqueline du Pre was a brilliant cellist who contracted multiple sclerosis and died young. This you know already. Did you also know she had sweaty armpits? That she slept with her sister's husband and crouched by the side of rivers muttering, "All I want is a fucking fuck, for fuck's sake"? No? Then you haven't seen the film.

Du Pre is our modern Chatterton: she has become a myth—a Channel Island genius, an English rose, cut down in full bloom. She was also—crucially for present purposes—famous, more famous than her sister or her brother. Indeed, neither Hilary nor Piers du Pre were famous at all, until last year when they published a book about their sister. Jackie wrote letters home on lavatory paper signed "PS Unused!", they revealed. She was selfish. The only way to make her happy had been "to give her what she wanted". Hilary gave, or lent, Jackie her husband.

The film of the book has now been made, and brother and sister have a petit success, at last, to match their sister's big one. The film is enraging Jacqueline du Pre's musical friends and colleagues; her former husband, Daniel Barenboim, has been threatening. But of course. It is not a film for them. It is a film for those whose deserts have not, or so they feel, been just.

The film offers little Jackie and Hilary in its opening scene. Trim, prim girls in fair isle knits and woolly hats, they dance on a beach, embarking on life's adventure with joint abandon. They are both musicians. But the story sours. At the Coulsdon and Purley annual competition they both win prizes, not just clever Hilary; soon Jackie starts winning them all. Metal cups with bug-eared handles will encumber their emotional lives for ever.

"Hilary and Jackie"—note that Jackie's name is not first—is Anand Tucker's motion picture debut. The camera twirls round the cellist as she plays ever dizzier cellistic feats, and we feel a little sick; Jackie leaves her cello—the priceless Davidov Strad—in the sun and the snow; the early zoom on Jackie's, ear—an organ of superfine musical sensitivity, you understand—leaves one hoping that Desmond Morris or Jonathan Miller will pop up and take us on an internal guided tour. But they are minor disappointments in a pleasingly constructed period drama.

Is it, musical types may ask, authentic? The exaggerated swing and swagger of Emily Watson's playing seems true to the du Pre we know from film. But is her Jackie meant to be mentally unstable, or just eccentric? Rachel Griffiths' Hilary is an acute study in embittered love. And in the small authenticities "Hilary and Jackie" is a joy: Jones the Milk delivering pints on sturdy London doorsteps; Mummy offering tea from tartan flasks (the action predating the time when thermoses got cold); a Morris Traveller proving just the size for some yeomanly rumpy-pumpy. And the scene in which Daniel Barenboim (James Frain) breaks into jazz during a recording of Beethoven Trios is memorably, convincingly deflating.

Is it truthful? That is a harder question. The closing credits provide a mundane answer: "composite characters, adjusted chronology... constructed dialogue and other fictionalised elements" have been used for dramatic purposes, they explain. But the more important question is left hanging in the air. By telling its story twice—from Hilary's point of view, then from Jackie's—the film feigns fairness. Given this modern recognition of truth's relativity, one wonders, why stop there? What about the milkman? What was his take on events? And what, say, of Daniel Barenboim's mum?

It is too late for fairness when the film's premise—the sister's book—is partisan already. "You should meet Hilary's husband," says Jackie to Dame Margot Fonteyn (who else?) in one scene. "He was the best fuck I ever had." We leave the cinema with a queasy feeling that this—recrimination, separation—is what the film is about. Jackie does it with sister's husband; sister does it with husband to patch things up. A Bactrian camel of a film, the story of two humps.

NEW YORK POST, 12/3/99, p. 36, Jonathan Foreman

Gutsy, moving, provocative, intelligent and thoroughly grown-up, "Hilary and Jackie" is one of the best movies of the year.

It has nothing to do with American First Ladies. It is the true story of the great English cellist Jacqueline du Pre, whose meteoric career and life were cut short by multiple sclerosis.

Based on the memoir by her sister, Hilary Finzi, "Hilary and Jackie" boasts a terrific script by Frank Cottrell Boyce, stylish direction by first-timer Anand Tucker and two sensational, Oscar-caliber performances, by Emily Watson and Rachel Griffiths.

Watching a person play a musical instrument on film can be even duller than watching people play cards. But Watson, who with her big, round eyes looks something like a young Susannah York, captures the sensual, almost spastically hyperactive way that the real du Pre played her cello. Combine that with the way Tucker whirls his camera to the rhythms of his film's swirling, beautiful score, and the result is gripping.

"Hilary and Jackie" is actually a love story spanning four decades. It's a tale of two sisters whose childhood closeness is destroyed by sibling rivalry when one achieves fame and glory and the other domestic happiness.

We see the du Pre sisters growing up in the sheltered, middle-class England of the 1950s in one of those musical families that put too much store on talent and success. Hilary (Griffiths) is the older daughter. The pushy Mrs. du Pre (the excellent Celia Imrie) believes her daughter is destined for greatness, thanks to her skill with the flute.

But Jackie (Watson) turns out to be the more talented daughter. And the fact that she plays the cello—the instrument closest in range to the human voice—helps to make her famous at a very young age.

When she marries Daniel Barenboim (James Frain), the handsome Argentine pianist and conductor, they become the first classical-music superstar couple.

But while Jackie's genius takes her around the world, it also makes her lonelier and more insecure than her sister. Always selfish, sexually voracious and occasionally spiteful, she becomes a needy monster who emotionally blackmails Hilary into organizing an affair between her and Hilary's husband, Kiffer (David Morrissey). And it's at this point that the illness that will cripple and eventually kill her begins to manifest itself physically.

Emily Watson (Oscar-nominated for "Breaking the Waves") gives another intense, all-out performance as the difficult, doomed cellist. And Rachel Griffiths, who resembles Juliette Binoche, is magnificent as Hilary, providing the film with a strong moral and dramatic center.

Movies have an irritating tendency to treat artistic genius in a fetishistic manner, to push the notion that if you are a great artist, it's somehow OK to behave badly. "Hilary and Jackie" is far too subtle and intelligent for that. And the ambitious if slightly unwieldy structure that Boyce and Tucker employ—they show us some key events first from one sister's point of view, then the other's—makes Jackie's awful behavior understandable without ever justifying it in terms of her talent or her illness.

While Jackie's decade of multiple sclerosis is compressed into a few minutes, "Hilary and Jackie" does offer an uncompromising, heart-rending portrayal of that cruel disease that is harsh enough to wring sniffles from even a hardened film reviewer.

NEWSDAY, 12/20/98, Part II/p. B7, Jack Mathews

If you've seen concert footage of the late cellist Jacqueline Du Pre, or—lucky you—actually saw her perform before she was disabled by multiple sclerosis in the early 1970s, you know what it looks like when a musician and her instrument become a singular force of nature.

Du Pre played the cello with a passion and abandon that were both awe-inspiring and a little bit frightening. With her bow flying, her left hand a blur against the bridge, and the rest of her body writhing to the music, she appeared to be a person possessed. But by what, devil or angel?

In "Hilary and Jackie," first-time director Anand Tucker's brilliantly conceived biographical drama about Du Pre and her older sister, the answer is, a little of both.

Played by Emily Watson, in her most demanding role since her Oscar-nominated performance in "Breaking the Waves," Jackie is a woman buffeted by contradictory impulses. On one hand, she wants to indulge her reputation as one of the world's greatest cellists, and the privileges of class that come with it; on the other, she wants to live her sister's simple life, in the English countryside, sharing her sister's virile husband (David Morrissey).

Based on a controversial family memoir, co-written by Du Pre's sister Hilary and brother Piers, "Hilary and Jackie" goes beyond the typical hagiography of a genius cut in her prime. It is, instead, a rather sensational tale of sibling rivalry, a case of the have envying the have-not, and abusing that sister's loyalty by demanding—and receiving—the physical love of her husband.

Nobody seems to be disputing that Hilary's husband, chicken farmer and sometime conductor Kiffer Finzi, slept with the sisters during a 16-month period after a depressed Jackie left her husband, Daniel Barenboim (James Frain), and came to the country to stay with them. But few accept that the relationship was quite the selfless sacrifice depicted in the memoir and movie.

Some also dispute the nature of the sibling rivalry. The movie shows Jackie becoming obsessively competitive after being chastised by her mother for not being a worthy accompanist to Hilary, a perennial award-winning flutist. Soon after, Jackie shoots past Hilary, leaving big sister in her dust as she moves into the international spotlight.

But Jackie does look back, continuing to envy whatever it is Hilary has that she doesn't—a husband, children, a home—and trying to claim a share for herself. No question, the story favors the character of Hilary, who suffers the abuse and snubs of Jackie, and remains loyal to her to the bitter end, when Jackie is a bedridden knot of flesh, half-mad and alone.

Whether Hilary's account is accurate or not, it makes a great story, and Tucker, with a sharply adapted script by Frank Cottrell Boyce ("Welcome to Sarajevo"), knows what to do with it. Opening with dreamlike images of the sisters as small children playing together on an empty beach, "Hilary and Jackie" takes the form of a musical piece itself, with movements and solos and crescendos, and returning to the beach.

As beautifully written and shot as it is, the power of the film is in the performances of Watson and Griffiths, both of whom might claim Oscar nominations in the coming weeks. Watson has the showiest and most physical role, miming Du Pre's kinetic cello style on stage before becoming imprisoned in a twisted body. But Griffiths' is the sympathetic role, and the actress gives her a quiet dignity throughout.

If it didn't happen this way, it should have.

NEWSWEEK, 1/11/99, p. 66, David Ansen

The Jackie of "Hilary and Jackie" is the great, passionate English cellist Jacqueline du Pré, whose career—and life—was cut short by multiple sclerosis. Knowing only this bare outline, you'd have reason to fear another hagiographic account of a great spirit nobly felled by a movie disease. But what director Anand Tucker has wrought is something far more spiky and complex. Informed by the memoirs of Jackie's sister, Hilary, and brother, Piers, this double portrait of sibling love and sibling rivalry treads a richly ambivalent line between tribute and exposé. Emily Watson's turbulent Jackie is both a brave, adventurous talent and a tormented solipsist, whose selfishness flowered in the self-indulgent Zeitgeist of the '60s.

Hilary (played with just the right mixture of adoration and masochism by Rachel Griffiths) was a gifted child musician herself until Jackie eclipsed her glory. Dropping out of the music world, Hilary settles into domestic life with her adoring husband (David Morrissey). But even then she is forced to share when Jackie, fleeing her marriage to the pianist-conductor Daniel Barenboim (James Frain), descends on her country home and begs to share Hilary's husband's bed. Told from both women's points of view, this fascinating, if sometimes overwrought, tale packs a wallop. Watson's bravura performance shows us the agony, the ecstasy and the ruthlessness of genius.

SIGHT AND SOUND, 2/99, p. 44, Nick Kimberley

Encouraged by their mother Iris, Hilary and Jacqueline du Pré develop precocious musical talents. Hilary is invited to play in a children's concert and insists Jackie join in. But when Jackie disrupts rehearsals, Iris angrily says she must learn to play as well as Hilary. Jackie is soon attracting more attention as a player than Hilary, and makes a prestigious concert debut.

Jackie's success undermines Hilary's confidence, but when Kiffer asks Hilary to play with his orchestra, she agrees. The two fall in love and marry. Jackie falls in love with pianist Daniel Barenboim, converts to Judaism and marries him, but is unhappy. While visiting Hilary, Jackie announces she wants to sleep with Kiffer. Daniel makes an unsuccessful attempt to rescue their marriage. After he leaves, Hilary encourages Kiffer to sleep with Jackie, although it does little for anyone's peace of mind.

Flashbacks now show events from Jackie's point of view. She meets Daniel, and they begin playing together. Signs of Jackie's multiple sclerosis emerge until finally, after a performance conducted by Daniel, she can't stand up to acknowledge the applause. She spends time in hospital, where the dancer Margot Fonteyn offers Jackie her flat to recuperate in. Daniel, now artistic director with the Orchestre de Paris, visits London less and less frequently. Confined to a wheelchair, Jackie plays tambourine at a children's concert. Hilary and Jackie are close again, but driving back from visiting Jackie with their brother Piers, Hilary hears the radio announcement of Jackie's death at the age of 42.

The cellist Jacqueline du Pré was one of the most talented musicians Britain has produced in the last 50 years. Talented enough that for some European and American writers she alone gave the lie to the myth that Britain was "a land without music". And it's certainly true that, in 60s Britain, she seemed to embody a passion and a *joie de vivre* not always apparent in the world of classical music. Her success was instant and meteoric; the illness that killed her brought her playing career to an end when she was only 27.

A Genius in the Family, on which Frank Cottrell Boyce *(Butterfly Kiss, Welcome to Sarajevo)* based his screenplay for *Hilary and Jackie,* is an often painfully underwritten book in which Hilary and her brother Piers take turns to tell the story of growing up in sister Jackie's shadow. The film acknowledges that Hilary's is the more gripping story by all but writing Piers out of the plot. In this, he is no more than an agreeably grinning buffoon, semi-detached from the emotions which seethe beneath the prim demeanours of the women around him. Similarly, the du Prés' father retreats into the background, although in the book his illness, barely mentioned in the movie, provides an anguished counterpoint to Jackie's multiple sclerosis. His stroke serves only to occasion Jackie's angry accusation that he's trying to upstage her.

These are all acceptable, even welcome changes. Any movie that attempted to replicate the emotionless monotone of the du Prés' prose would be dull indeed, and by narrowing the focus to the relationship between the two sisters, *Hilary and Jackie* undoubtedly locates the heart of the matter. In the process it gives us a kind of *Amadeus* for English suburbia, with Hilary playing Salieri to the extravagantly gifted but tortured Mozart of Jacqueline du Pré. Yet where the Salieri *Amadeus* (not the historical figure) was an embittered inferior trying to grasp the nature of Mozart's genius, Hilary is a decent soul repeatedly put upon by Jackie's spoiled behaviour. Music doesn't have much in the way of healing power here, and Jackie's genius only makes her and everyone else unhappy. Of course there's a long history of movies depicting the gifted who are brattish and unhappy—in fact these seem to be the very qualities by which cinema defines genius.

But if the film predictably fails to get a grip on what 'genius' might be, it first does a decent job of making sense of the hard work without which talent means little. It then illustrates the slow and disturbing progress of an illness that is particularly insidious in its attack on mind and body. Of course, it attacks genius and non-genius alike, but there is something inevitably poignant about the fact that Jacqueline du Pré was so young when she succumbed to the disease: had she not done so, she might now be at the height of her powers as a musician. It's these 'might-have-beens' that give *Hilary and Jackie* its dramatic power.

Sensibly, the movie chooses not to get involved in the controversy over whether or not Daniel Barenboim neglected du Pré during her illness—or rather, it suggests that he did, but without dwelling on the matter. If its decision to include only the briefest fragment of du Pré's playing seems an odd one (nearly all of the music was specially recorded), that at least steers it away from the fetishisation that has marked the cellist's posthumous career. Although music is at the heart of the film, it is not a film about music, but about an English middle-class family in suppressed emotional turmoil. If that limits its scope, its impact is increased by some finely measured performances. This is an actors' film, and the actors are actually rather good. That may not make it a fashionable movie, but it's not a negligible achievement.

VILLAGE VOICE, 1/5/99, p. 94, Michael Atkinson

As opportunistic and portentous as your average tragic-genius biopic—the genre is, after all, beholden only to history and hindsight—*Hilary and Jackie* eventually earns its scars in ways you can't anticipate from the way first-time director Anand Tucker clods up the story's groundwork. It's not unusual: moviemakers have long forgotten the art of introducing us into a film's environment without obvious exposition, sketchy dramatic highlights or punch-projected symbolism. In a hammy, *Shine*-like whorl, *Hilary and Jackie* tries far too hard to dictate emotional involvement right out of the gate, and you're left counting off the doom-laden cues for things that are sure to return full circle.

That Tucker's restless bolero does build into a relevant and eloquent thunder is largely due to Emily Watson, making her latest crucifixion count like all get out, and to the story of Jacqueline du Pré itself. At first you're convinced the movie will glibly extol the passionate bond of siblings; by the end, it has played out the ambivalent ballad of sisterhood like few movies have managed. The du Pré sisters were both '50s musical prodigies; though Hilary was first to be lauded for the flute, she was soon passed by Jackie, whose operatic affair with the cello made her, by her teen years, an international phenomenon. (In the film, they have a brother, Piers, who does little more than hold the family radio and TV antennae.)

As with another Pré oversubjected to biopicity, Jackie's fame cost her big-time. (Would there be a film if it didn't?) Intimate but cruelly competitive since they were kids, married country mouse Hilary (Rachel Griffiths) and lonely celebrity Jackie (Watson) spend their lives envying each other, until the balance shifts in Hilary's favor when Jackie begins to slip gears, sabotages her relationships, turns up at her sister's manse, and begs to screw her Liam Neeson-esque husband (David Morrissey).

That Jackie ends up being plagued with MS isn't the cliché it might be, not as it's seen here, fogging over her perceptions as her hands and cello seem to furiously play an Elgar concerto without her. Screenwriter Frank Cottrell Boyce divides the narrative up into two *Rashomon* halves, and though Griffiths shines in the quieter role, Watson shakes the rafters. Her Jackie isn't just a disjointed talent, she's thorny, girlish, anarchic, given to mocking foreign languages right to natives' faces, and prone to self destructively leaving her priceless cello behind at airports. Watson is a mercurial presence with huge, nervous baby eyes, and when she cuts loose, an otherwise conventional film shudders with anxiety. Still, the movie's money moment belongs to the two of them, huddled in bed together during the late stages of Jackie's affliction, and it's worth waiting for.

Also reviewed in:
CHICAGO TRIBUNE, 1/15/99, Friday/p. A, Mark Caro
NATION, 1/11 & 18/99, p. 36, Stuart Klawans
NEW REPUBLIC, 12/21/98, p. 26, Stanley Kauffmann
NEW YORK TIMES, 12/30/98, p. E1, Stephen Holden
NEW YORKER, 1/18/99, p. 89, Anthony Lane
VARIETY, 9/14-20/98, p. 37, David Stratton
WASHINGTON POST, 1/15/99, p. C1, Stephen Hunter
WASHINGTON POST, 1/15/99, Weekend/p. 32, Michael O'Sullivan

HIT ME

A Castle Hill Productions release of a Slough Pond Company presentation. *Producer:* Steven Shainberg and Gregory Goodman. *Director:* Steven Shainberg. *Screenplay:* Denis Johnson. *Based on the novel "A Swell Looking Babe" by:* Jim Thompson. *Director of Photography:* Mark J. Gordon. *Editor:* Donn Aron. *Music:* Peter Manning Robinson. *Production Designer:* Amy Danger. *Running time:* 123 minutes. *MPAA Rating:* R.

CAST: Elias Koteas (Sonny); Laure Marsac (Monique); Jay Leggett (Leroy); Bruce Ramsay (Del); Kevin J. O'Connor (Cougar); Philip Baker Hall (Lenny Ish); J. C. Quinn (Bascomb); Haing S. Ngor (Billy); Jack Conley (Bodyguard); William H. Macy (The Cop).

LOS ANGELES TIMES, 10/9/98, Calendar/p. 10, John Anderson

[The following review by John Anderson appeared in a slightly different form in NEWSDAY, 10/2/98, Part II/p. B6.]

Given that it's adapted from a Jim Thompson novel ("A Swell-Looking Babe"), "Hit Me" is a predictably plug-ugly, fatalistic thriller, a kind of Kafka after dark. And although director Steven Shainberg drifts a bit between dark absurdity and hard-boiled pulp, he does capture the desperation of small-time minds and the crazy logic of violence, as well as the sickly pallor of all-night employment and the desolation of an unwelcome dawn.

He also has—as the ill-fated hotel night man Sonny—Canadian actor Elias Koteas, who for years has done solid character turns in everything from Atom Egoyan's "Exotica" to "Teenage Mutant Ninja Turtles," but now he has center stage. He plays a cluelessly doomed, two-bit operator who succumbs to every temptation—including grand larceny—that comes his way. Even as he tells himself he shouldn't.

Sonny's is a take-out-the-trash, take-up-the-bags existence, exacerbated by his obese, mentally deficient brother Leroy (Jay Leggett), whom social services would like to take off his hands. Beleaguered at work, overburdened at home, Sonny is overwhelmed by the beautiful Monique (Laure Marsac), a troubled hotel guest who proves that Shainberg is best on the absurdist tack because she's strictly unbelievable.

But she's also the engine of Sonny's disaster, staging a theatrical suicide attempt, seducing him on the floor of her room and exhibiting such a lust for money that Sonny's involvement in a poker-game rip-off spirals out of control and directly into mayhem.

Shainberg, making his feature debut, is blessed with a first-rate cast that includes Philip Baker Hall (Seinfeld's library cop, as well as the star of "Hard Eight"), William H. Macy in a virtual cameo as Sonny's interrogator, and the late, Oscar-winning Haing S. Ngor, who could and probably should have been cut from the film; his fate is eerily and distastefully similar to the incident that took his life two years ago. It's a distracting moment in a movie that's otherwise handled with a great deal of style and a definite sense of where it's going.

NEW YORK POST, 10/2/98, p. 44, Thelma Adams

Sonny is anything but sunny. Which is exactly what you'd expect from the walking wounded who venture out after dark in Jim Thompson's jaundiced novels.

"Hit Me," directed by Steven Shainberg from grisly cult novelist Denis Johnson's adaptation of "A Swell-Looking Babe," has the misfortune to follow two better Thompson noirs, "After Dark, My Sweet" and "The Grifters."

Like its predecessors, "Hit Me" spirals downward in a dangerous world where no man is innocent and no woman trustworthy. Sonny (Elias Koteas), the central character, is a disturbed schlepper, an angry, aging bellhop.

Sonny works the night shift. He delivers room service and services the occasional patron at a seedy Tacoma two-star hotel with walls as jaundiced as its inhabitants.

When Sonny meets Monique (Laure Marsac), a suicidal femme fatale with a get-rich-quick scheme, the hop discovers he can actually fall lower than he already has. His first mistake is to assume she's "a four-star woman in a two-star hotel."

What "Hit Me" has that its predecessors lacked is the kind of dysfunctional loser-hero that Thompson cultivated and that actors Jason Patric and John Cusack ("Sweet" and "Grifters," respectively) were simply too pretty to deliver.

As Sonny, Koteas ("Exotica" and the upcoming "A Thin Red Line") has the savage intensity of Robert De Niro's taxi driver, without the cabby's easy charm and good manners.

Alternately ferally attractive and fiercely repugnant, tender and corrupt, Koteas' Sonny hurtles toward the inevitable noir bloodbath (overplayed by Shainberg and overwritten by Johnson), with an outsized rage and a "Hit Me" sign firmly planted on his backside.

VILLAGE VOICE, 9/29/98, p. 130, Justine Elias

Honor among thieves is the focus of *Hit Me*, an uneven adaptation of the Jim Thompson novel *A Swell-Looking Babe,* in which a bellhop (Elias Koteas) and a suicidal prostitute (Laure Marsac) become embroiled in a conspiracy to rob a high-stakes poker game. For a draggy hour or so, this first film by director Steven Shainberg is nearly overwhelmed by neo-noir gloom: the setting is the creepiest, kitschiest flophouse ever seen on celluloid, and the idea that the owner hopes to upgrade his establishment's rating—from two stars to three—is ludicrous. (He might as well hang a sign out front that says, "Management has steam-cleaned ALL bloodstained carpeting!") But as the scam gets more complicated, and more deadly, *Hit Me* develops an unexpected emotional force. The bellhop, you see, has fallen in love, and as played by Koteas (who looks and acts like a young Robert De Niro), passion becomes the most alluring, confusing gamble of all.

Also reviewed in:
NEW YORK TIMES, 10/2/98, p. E12, Lawrence Van Gelder
VARIETY, 12/16-22/96, p. 84, Emanuel Levy

HOLY MAN

A Touchstone Pictures release in association with Caravan Pictures of a Roger Birnbaum production. *Executive Producer:* Jeffrey Chernov and Jonathan Glickman. *Producer:* Roger Birnbaum and Stephen Herek. *Director:* Stephen Herek. *Screenplay:* Tom Schulman. *Director of Photography:* Adrian Biddle. *Editor:* Trudy Ship. *Music:* Alan Silvestri. *Music Editor:* Michael T. Ryan and Kenneth Karman. *Choreographer:* Lori Eastside. *Sound:* Peter J. Devlin and (music) Dennis Sands. *Sound Editor:* Tim Chau and Donal J. Malouf. *Casting:* Amanda Mackey Johnson and Cathy Sandrich. *Production Designer:* Andrew McAlpine. *Art Director:* James Tocci. *Set Designer:* Richard Fojo and Stephanie Girard. *Set Decorator:* Chris Spellman. *Set Dresser:* Stephen Durante and Chris Alicea. *Special Effects:* Kevin Harris. *Costumes:* Aggie Guerard Rodgers. *Make-up:* Joe Campayno. *Make-up (Eddie Murphy):* Toy Russell Van Lierop. *Stunt Coordinator:* Alan Oliney. *Running time:* 113 minutes. *MPAA Rating:* PG.

CAST: Eddie Murphy ("G"); Jeff Goldblum (Ricky Hayman); Kelly Preston (Kate Newell); Robert Loggia (John McBainbridge); Jon Cryer (Barry); Eric McCormack (Scott Hawkes); Sam Kitchin (Director); Robert Small (Assistant Director); Marc Macaulay (Cameraman, Brutus); Mary Stout and Edie McClurg (Laundry Ladies); Kim Staunton (Grace); Morgan Fairchild, Betty White, Florence Henderson, James Brown, Soupy Sales, Dan Marino, Willard Scott, and Nino Cerruti (Themselves); Barbara Hubbard Barron and Cristina Wilcox (Sunbathers); Clarence Reynolds (TV Host); Mal Jones and Jody Wilson (Elderly Couple); Pamela West (Fresca, the Foot Model); Tim Powell (Doctor Simon); Lori Viveros Herek and Angel Schmiedt (Nurses); Whitney Dupree (Laurie); Jennifer Bini Taylor (Hot Tub Girl); Robert Walker (Farmer); Elodia Riovega (Housekeeper); Avrohom Horovitz (Rabbi); Al Kamaar

(Moslem Theologian); Dan Fitzgerald (Priest);   Mark Brown (Grass Mat Salesman);   Mike Benitez (Bullet Proof Vest Man);   Deborah Magdalena (Control Booth Technician);   Adriana Catano and Andrea Lively (TV Hostesses); Kim Alexis (Keratin Girl, Amber);   Veronica Webb (Keratin Girl, Diandre);   Lee Bryant (Money "Meg");   Nick Santa Maria (Sword Salesman); Aaron Elbaz (Glue-Gun Boy);   Scotty Gallin and John Bosa (Jock Salesmen); Jeffrey Wetzel (Stage Manager);   Erin Morrissey, Daryl Meyer, and Ronda Pierson (Hosts); Brett Rice and John Archie (Detectives);   Armando Ramos (Grace's Little Boy);   Nancy Duerr, Tonya Oliver, Fred Workman, Jacqueline Chernov, and Roger Reid (Reporters);   Peter Paul DeLeo (Stagehand); Errol Smith (GBSN Staffer); Dave Corey (Announcer); Alan Olivey (Stunt Coordinator/ "G"'s Stunt Double);   Mike Christopher (Ricky's Stunt Double);   Alejandro Acosta Fox (Flamenco Guitarist);   Maria Alejandra Carpio (Flamenco Dancer);   Laurie Wallace (Facial Mist Girl); Willie Gault (Nordic Track Guy);   Amanda Lynn (Nordic Track Girl); Charlie Haugk (Party Animal);   Margaret Muldoon (Attractive Party Guest);   Mark Massar (Set Dresser);   Toy Van Lierop Van Lierop ("G" Makeup Artist);   Dana Hawkins and Denise Heinrich (Hair Chat Girls); Antoni Cornacchione (Chain Saw Host);   Marc C. Geschwind (GBSN Electrician);   A.J. Alexander O. Parhm (UPS Guy);   Alan Jordan and Mike Kirton (Marksmen).

LOS ANGELES TIMES, 10/9/98, Calendar/p. 1, Kenneth Turan

A series of high-concept notions in search of a film, "Holy Man" falls apart right in front of our eyes. It's not an inspiring sight.

This comic examination of America's parallel manias for shopping and gurus, starring Eddie Murphy, is an appealing notion, and "Holy Man" manages some amusing moments. But the satire never takes hold, the dramatic and romantic aspects are indifferently executed, and the whole thing has the authenticity of one of those celebrated zirconium diamonds.

The Good Buy Shopping Network, GBSN for short, has gone beyond selling those ersatz gems, but not by much. Easily the funniest parts of Tom Schulman's script are the network's mock infomercials for products like Hood Buddy, which cooks meals while your car drives; a glue gun useful for attaching children to the ceiling; and the James Brown Soul Survivors System, which in case of emergency has the hardest working man in show business scream out, "Help me, help me, good God!"

In nominal charge of GBSN is hard-charging Robert "Ricky" Hayman (Jeff Goldblum), a confident-seeming salesman whose daily mantra is "Good, better, best: Never let it rest until your good is better and your better is best." Ricky, however, is really running scared. He's in danger of losing both his convertible and his glamorous Miami Beach apartment to the bank, and an unknown quantity named McBainbridge (Robert Loggia) has just bought GBSN.

McBainbridge turns out to be a cranky sort who is incensed that sales at the network have been flat for 27 months. He tells Ricky he has two weeks to turn things around and assigns his driven No. 2, media analyst Kate Newell (Kelly Preston), to help figure out an identity for GBSN.

It's at this point, when a flat tire on the highway strands these two, that G (Murphy) appears, wearing white pants and a flowing shirt and blithely walking across several lanes of traffic to ask, "Are you in trouble and in need of my help?"

Hayman, who G amusingly calls Robert Ricky, is suspicious of this wandering savant who stops periodically to smell the grass and whose response when hooligans hit him with a plastic cup full of soda is a heartfelt and cheerful, "Thanks for not using a can." But Kate takes a liking to G, and since Ricky is smitten with her, G is soon living in Ricky's penthouse and mixing with celebrities like designer Nino Cerruti at fancy parties.

G has no last name ("A consonant is here to see you" is how they refer to him when he visits the station), no visible past and a sorrowful attitude toward a society where a "Baywatch" lifeguard is more of a role model than the Dalai Lama. So of course Ricky is going to hit on the idea of using G as a pitchman to sell the flotsam and jetsam of the universe to gullible consumers, and of course G is going to agree.

Murphy was originally thought of for the role of the fast-talking Ricky, and it's to his credit that he wanted to go past the obvious and play G. The guru is someone you can't quite figure out, a "Don't Worry, Be Happy" individual who is simultaneously warm and opaque, like a rock left outside in the sun, and Murphy has the strength of personality and ability to turn in a properly comic and enigmatic performance.

But though Murphy makes an acceptable wise child, someone whose seeming innocence makes people think there's something deep going on, one problem with "Holy Man" is that that kind of character has been done earlier, and better, in numerous films, including "Being There," "Michael" and even "Forrest Gump."

Also, though the setup here is passable, what happens once G gets on TV is so obvious and banal you could predict it in your sleep. G's philosophy turns out to be so mild ("You never feel more whole than when you love another person"), it's almost not there, and the crisis Ricky and Kate have about whether they're going to, horror of horrors, sell their souls is close to embarrassing.

Not helping the story problems is Stephen Herek, a director whose gift for branding things out has been rewarded with tedious box-office successes like the live-action "101 Dalmatians," the "Three Musketeers" remake and "Mr. Holland's Opus." With iffier material than usual here, that kind of touch is fatal, and a film that thinks it's saying a whole lot more than it actually is sinks quietly under the waves.

NEW YORK POST, 10/9/98, p. 41, Rod Dreher

Consumers, beware. The transcendentally awful "Holy Man" violates truth-in-packaging laws. Purportedly an Eddie Murphy comedy, this disastrously unfunny film trots out someone who has the body of the once-hilarious comic but the blissed-out, "Got milk?" soul of Carol Brady. (Here's a stay-awake tip: During Eddie's close-ups, look for the lobotomy scar.)

The idea of Eddie Murphy playing a televangelist dragooned into hawking trinkets on a home-shopping channel is pregnant with comedic possibilities. Can't you see Eddie cutting loose as a Pentecostal firebrand, marshaling all the gaudy rhetorical tactics of a stump preacher to work viewers into a Holy Roller froth over cubic zirconia? Say amen, somebody!

Great concept, wrong religion. Eddie plays G, a bland, quasi-Buddhist, New Age nice guy happened upon by Ricky (Jeff Goldblum), a venal programming exec told to boost ratings or lose his job. Ricky observes Zen master G's easy charm and uncanny ability to soothe all those he meets, and figures he'd be a great salesman.

He puts the holy man in front of cameras, and guileless G delivers a bland, beige-toned homily against materialism, with a light misting of eau deself-affirmation. It's not the least bit amusing or catchy, as Tom Schulman's woebegone screenplay conceives this character without the least sense of irony.

Why would people respond to a guy with a pleasant smile who serves up mild aphorisms like spoonfuls of Mylanta? How can you expect an apostle of renunciation to plausibly provoke acquisitiveness? Because this is Movie World, where nothing has to make sense.

G's yogurt-brained homilies move junky merch by the truckload, and even inspire a passionate nationwide following. This leads Ricky to a moment of crisis as he admits to himself that he has exploited this sweet-natured guru to save his job and romantically impress station executive Kate (Kelly Preston).

"Holy Man" wants to say something about the commodification of spirituality, but has no idea what. There are approximately 1 laughs in this deadly dull dramedy. Goldblum mutters his way through, looking concerned without saying anything smart, and Preston is at best attractive wallpaper. Though no actor could have taken a character as misconceived and tap-water bland as G and made him compelling, the fact that Eddie Murphy thought such a crap role worth attempting is bizarre.

Playing G apparently is part of Eddie's effort in recent years to smooth his image. In "Holy Man," he's had every edge sanded down and every quirk of his personality smoothed agreeably flat, as if by Prozac. The guy who was once America's hottest comic is rendered as huggably soft as that annoying fabric-softener bear.

Eddie "Snuggles" Murphy? Sheesh. What's next for Ed—pushing pudding pops on TV? A starring role in "Leonard Part 7"?

NEWSDAY, 10/9/98, Part II/p. B3, John Anderson

There's this technique they use in radio and TV advertising wherein a commercial gets played and played and played until you can't stand it anymore, but at the same time you can't get it out of your head. Then, after a certain period of what can only be called low-level brainwashing, a shorter version starts getting played, your freshly laundered mind filling in the blanks.

Ingenious? Evil? Perhaps, although that's not how one would describe "Holy Man," which is far too inert to be either. But the technique behind the film is a lot like those ads: Give people a familiar framework filled with cliched gestures and well-known faces and they'll fill in the blanks themselves.

Eddie Murphy. He's funny. Right? Right, right. So cast him as a shaved-headed spiritual wanderer named G., so guileless and charming that when he starts selling chain saws and soup bowls on a home-shopping cable channel, the entire nation falls in love with him. For wry counterpoint, cast Jeff Goldblum as the failing network manager for whom G. is an ongoing nightmare and add Kelly Preston—providing modest babe factor—as a go-get-'em media analyst who's supposed to be smart and savvy but for reasons never quite clear is immediately in thrall to G. She thinks he'll be the salvation of the station.

And then... don't do much of anything. Murphy, whose career arc has taken him from young, acerbic black comedian to a kind of suburban transparency, would seem ripe for a role like G., but he brings almost nothing to the movie (I kept hoping for a reprise of his Cameroonian loon from "Trading Places," but no dice). It is, perhaps, the sad price of success, or the second-class status of comedy, that some of our funniest performers—Murphy for one, Robin Williams for another—seem to think it's beneath them to make people laugh anymore.

As for Goldblum, his mannered delivery has become a parody of itself (for evidence, see "The Lost World") and Preston is too mature an actress to be putting on such perky airs. But the more pressing problem with "Holy Man" is that it operates totally on faith, providing no proof of anything it wants us to believe.

G.'s attraction, either to Ricky (Goldblum), Kate (Preston) or the rest of the nation, is never convincingly presented. When the new station owner, McBainbridge (Robert Loggia, sporting some of the more painful looking plastic surgery in recent film history), threatens to revamp the station and get rid of Ricky, there's no reason to think he shouldn't, since Ricky never gives us reason to think he's anything but a useless hack. G. becomes a success, but we don't see it happen, can't imagine why it might have happened. Kate complains to Ricky that she's worried about G.; we don't know why, except that the film needs to get from happy point to crisis point.

That Hollywood movies have largely become collections of demographically tailored conventions is nothing new (see "Deep Impact" as a recent appalling example). "Holy Man," however, seems to set new standards in the substitution of gesture for plot and suggestion for performance. Tom Shulman, who once wrote "What About Bob?" but also perpetrated "Eight Heads in a Duffel Bag," is credited with "writing" this movie, but "amassing" it might be a more apt description, given the collection of cliches that pass as a script.

Take G., the strange visitor who changes everyone's life: He's "The Bishop's Wife." He's "Down and Out in Beverly Hills." He's "Oh, God!" He's "Free Willy." Goldblum's Ricky Hayman? He's "The Bishop's Wife." He's "Down and Out in Beverly Hills." He's "Scrooged" (the climactic scene really is "Scrooged"). Preston's Kate Newell? Her type is too ubiquitous for any catalog, but let's just say she's isn't storming any barricades.

Morgan Fairchild and Betty White are among the people playing themselves and the people playing themselves are the gamest performers in the film—which not only blows the chance of satirizing TV shopping but pales in comparison as entertainment. The teaser for G.'s shopping show is "Higher Thinking, Lower Prices." Judging by "Holy Man," that's precisely the opposite of the state of the cinema.

NEWSWEEK, 10/19/98, p. 81, Jack Kroll

There are tear-jerkers, and there are laugh-jerkers. "Holy Man" gets its laughs and "The Mighty" pumps its tears from the same place, our bleeding hearts. Eddie Murphy is G., an L.A. guru who strides the roads in white PJs, pausing to kiss the ground—grass or asphalt, this Saint Francis of the freeways smooches all surfaces. He encounters Ricky (Jeff Goldblum), director of a TV shopping network, who realizes he can use the lovable G. to pump up his floundering sales. G. is an instant smash, lending a spiritual aura to the selling of items like cleaning balls (don't ask) and the Clam, a sex-enhancing device (really don't ask). The holy huckster's redemptive message touches everyone, including leaders of the Christian, Jewish and Muslim faiths.

Director Stephen Herek ("101 Dalmatians") has made a kind of laughed-up "Network," taking off on our consumerist, TV-templed society. It's harmless fun, but it underutilizes Murphy, who's largely reduced to doing virtuoso variations on his iconic smile: there's the vast, all-embracing Sacred Smile, the melting Compassionate Smile, the I-see-through-you Forgiving Smile. (We miss his Dirty Smile.)

The indomitability of the human spirit is nothing to laugh at in "The Mighty," with its story of two outsider kids, Max Kane (Elden Henson), an overgrown, seemingly underbrained perpetual seventh grader, and Kevin Dillon (Kieran Culkin), a genius type crippled by a fatal degenerative disease. Tormented by their punky peers, the unlikely pair bond in a brawn-brains combo that reaches a sad but uplifting destiny. Directed by Peter Chelsom ("Hear My Song") from a prize-winning young-adult novel by Rodman Philbrick, the film is sweet but soft. With a cast featuring deglamorized roles for Sharon Stone and Gillian Anderson, the movie is carried by the two young actors, the stolid Henson and the feisty Culkin, Macaulay's brother, who turns out to be the actor in the family.

SIGHT AND SOUND, 3/99, p. 40, Andy Richards

Miami, the present. McBainbridge, the new owner of the Good Buy Shopping Network which broadcasts live 'infomercials', threatens to sack executive Ricky Hayman unless he can increase his sales figures. After a blow-out on the freeway, Ricky and network media-analyst Kate Newell encounter G, an enigmatic, itinerant "holy man" on a personal spiritual pilgrimage. When Ricky accidentally reverses his car towards G, G appears to halt the vehicle with psychic powers before collapsing from the effort. Ricky and Kate take G to hospital, where Ricky agrees to pay his fees. While awaiting medical assessment, G stays in Ricky's apartment. At a party G hypnotises Nino Cerruti and helps him overcome his fear of flying. After G wanders on to some of the network's sets and inadvertently succeeds in increasing sales through an advocacy of spiritual values, Ricky proposes he work as a salesman for the network. G agrees, as a favour to Ricky.

Sales soon soar, and G becomes a media sensation. Ricky and Kate become lovers. A woman causes a brief scandal by claiming G is her husband and the father of her children, but then confesses she was bribed to lie by a jealous rival of Ricky's. McBainbridge, wanting to put G on prime time, offers Ricky a promotion if he gets G to sign a contract. Ricky lies to G about his medical tests. Kate is appalled, and breaks up with Ricky. G signs the contract. However, Ricky relents and tells G to continue his pilgrimage. Live to the network's audience, Ricky explains his own changed values. Kate sees his recantation and races to the studio, where they reconcile in front of the cameras. Together, they return G to where they found him.

Eddie Murphy's late-90s career resurgence is a prime instance of a star distancing himself from the style of material that once made him famous but subsequently proved too constraining. *The Nutty Professor* self-consciously deconstructed the Murphy persona, while last year's *Doctor Dolittle* softened the actor's macho reputation. Here, as G—a modern-day saint seeking an Inner rather than a Golden Child—Murphy again largely effaces his *48Hrs.* Axel Foley shtick, leaving Jeff Goldblum to dominate as flash womaniser Ricky whose grandstanding rants offset G's still small voice of calm. This balance—between Murphy's restrained placidity and Goldblum's manic spieling—proves crucial to the film's overall success.

Television shopping may not be the most elusive of satirical targets, but the film at least manages to do a thorough and entertaining job of putting the boot in. Director Stephen Herek (*Bill & Ted's Excellent Adventure, 101 Dalmatians*) has fun with a succession of witty vignettes: James Brown endorses the Soul Survivor's Alarm System which emits his trademark cry of "Help Me, Help Me, Good God!"; a sexagenarian plugs 'Clam' perfume by gently orgasming on camera.

The film displays a clear contempt for the masses glued to the shopping networks, so spiritually bereft they fall instantly in love with Murphy's G and his anti-materialistic sermonising, buying in greater quantities of goods than ever before and feeling better about themselves in the process. What G offers is literally a grass-roots philosophy. When he exhorts his audience to go outside and look at some grass, they do so, in wide eyed wonderment, before phoning in to buy some of Ricky's cheap grass mats. This scene is a clear variant on Peter Finch's famous "I'm mad as hell..." rant from *Network* (1976), to which Herek's film is clearly indebted. Like Finch's character, G is gleefully exploited and commodified by a ruthless network.

While Finch' s Messianic anchorman gave extemporaneous editorials on societal breakdown, G offers pantheistic panaceas, advice on how to rediscover life's essential purity. G's faith, of course, is non-specific and non-denominational, and as with almost any Hollywood film that confronts 'spirituality' in its nebulous, catch-all form, certain confusions arise. *Holy Man* would like to reconcile commerce and the soul, and the film while poking fun at the excesses of a specific sales culture never indicts selling per se. It is Ricky's betrayal of G's friendship that makes Kate leave him, and Ricky's subsequent 'conversion' seems principally motivated (like most of his actions) by his desire for Kate. Yet despite this thematic fuzziness, born of a desire to be both satirical and feel-good, *Holy Man* is well enough crafted to trick you into believing you've just bought a slice of both.

VILLAGE VOICE, 10/20/98, p. 160, Gary Dauphin

You almost feel sorry for Eddie Murphy while watching *Holy Man*. Murphy's done funny-funny, funny-violent, and funny-sweet, but he hasn't done funny-serious, hasn't had his *Truman Show*. Considered abstractly, *Holy Man's* traipse through the wilds of consumerism and higher purpose must have seemed like a chance for the proverbial stretch, but not even Eddie can save this ill-conceived mess of a movie.

First glimpsed walking down a Miami causeway in ashram/pajama-party wear, Murphy plays his itinerant spiritualist, G, as preternaturally good-natured, a fully actualized update of his *Coming to America* turn. G is on a vague pilgrimage when he's almost run down by two home shopping network execs. Ricky (Jeff Goldblum) thinks G is a fruitcake but Kate (Kelly Preston) thinks he's the nicest human she's ever met. They offer him aid and shelter and it's a short hop from there to the thoroughly clichéd main action, wherein G teaches his new buds the meaning of life, loyalty, love, et cetera. As written by Tom Schulman *(Dead Poets Society)*, *Holy Man's* stab at relevancy involves setting G loose in Ricky and Kate's office. G takes over the soundstage, railing against materialism, but those dopey viewers in TV land not only connect with G, they buy oodles of the crap on sale behind him. G's martyr-like disaffection with stardom grows in lockstep with Ricky's spiritual side. This is a low yuk outing (all the jokes fit in the trailer), with the focus on Goldblum and Preston's listless romance. The star does some work here, but like the station he invades, *Holy Man* is in the business of pitching cheap knockoffs of better wares.

Also reviewed in:
CHICAGO TRIBUNE, 10/9/98, Friday/p. A, Michael Wilmington
NEW YORK TIMES, 10/9/98, p. E14, Janet Maslin
VARIETY, 10/12-18/98, p. 39, Leonard Klady
WASHINGTON POST, 10/9/98, p. D5, Rita Kempley
WASHINGTON POST, 10/9/98, Weekend/p. 49, Michael O'Sullivan

HOME BEFORE DARK

A Scout Productions and Hazelwood Films release. *Executive Producer:* Robert Laubacher. *Producer:* Michael Williams, Dorothy Aufiero, David Collins, and Maureen Foley. *Director:* Maureen Foley. *Screenplay:* Maureen Foley. *Director of Photography:* Brian Heller and Mark Petersson. *Editor:* James Rutenbeck. *Music:* Jeanine Cowen. *Sound:* G. John Carrett. *Casting:* Susan Willett. *Production Designer:* Kathleen Rosen. *Art Director:* Sophie Carlhian. *Costumes:* Susan Anderson. *Running time:* 110 minutes. *MPAA Rating:* Not Rated.

CAST: Stephanie Castellarin (Nora); Brian Delate (Martin); Katharine Ross (Rose); Patricia Kalember (Dolores); Helen Lloyd Breed (Sister Concilia).

CHRISTIAN SCIENCE MONITOR, 7/10/98, p. B3, David Sterritt

Dysfunctional families have become such a movie-screen cliché that even sex comedies like "Talk to Me" and action fantasies like "Lost in Space" manage to work one in somehow. Less common are pictures that treat this serious subject with the seriousness it deserves, and that's what makes the understated drama "Home Before Dark" worth noting.

The heroine is 11-year-old Nora, an ordinary schoolgirl growing up in a Massachusetts town during the early 1960s. Her life would be commonplace and contented if not for the emotional instability of her mother, Dolores, who's bereft over the accidental death of her eldest children and—in a more recent development—obsessed with the notion that the late President Kennedy had a close connection with her and her family.

Dolores is eventually hospitalized, and when her husband decides that single parenting is beyond his capabilities, Nora goes to live with a well-meaning aunt. This proves unsatisfactory for all concerned, and Nora returns home to her dad, determined to find some way of making the household work. This leads to a series of dilemmas and confrontations that call on Nora to be far more resourceful and resilient than she dreamed she could be.

"Home Before Dark" marks the movie-making debut of Maureen Foley, a Massachusetts resident who clearly has firsthand familiarity with the sorts of places and personalities that populate her story. Although her directing style is rarely innovative or surprising, it has the virtues of sincerity and authenticity, and it's refreshing to find a filmmaker who cares so deeply about her characters.

Good acting also helps. Stephanie Castellarin is an excellent Nora, supported by a well-chosen roster of established talents: Patricia Kalember, of "Sisters" and "thirtysomething," as the mother; Katharine Ross, of "The Graduate" and "Butch Cassidy and the Sundance Kid," as the aunt; and Brian Delate, of various movies and TV shows, as the father. Their efforts help make "Home Before Dark" one of the season's more worthwhile independent entries.

NEW YORK POST, 7/10/98, p. 46, Larry Worth

If awards were given for good intentions, first-time writer-director Maureen Foley's efforts on the low-budget "Home Before Dark" would make her a winner.

But they don't, and she's not. Sadly, the meandering, unfocused plot of this film is reminiscent of watching wallpaper dry—an event viewers in fact get to observe not once but twice.

The story is set in western Massachusetts of 1963 a period when 11-year-old Nora is going through a particularly hard time. With her JFK-obsessed mother on the verge of mental collapse and Dad battling his own demons, Nora is officially in charge of her two young siblings.

At the same time, she's coming to terms with puppy love, her body's maturation, no-nonsense nuns in her Catholic school and some very catty schoolmates. But those troubles are soon dwarfed by her ice-queen aunt, with whom Nora's sent to live when Mom is institutionalized.

That leads to yet more subplots, none of which catch fire or coalesce into anything vaguely original or meaningful. Worse, the film has a naggingly amateurish feel, no doubt due to Foley's inexperience behind the camera.

But Foley lucked out in the casting department. In particular, newcomer Stephanie Castellarin does her best to make Nora into a fully developed individual, often compensating for lackluster dialogue. Her big scenes nicely convey confusion and an overwhelming sense of loss.

Patricia Kalember, best known from TV work in "thirtysomething" and "Sisters," also scores as an emotionally damaged mother who can't face up to a tragic past. She's best when playing off Brian Delate, who delivers a complex turn as the frustrated family leader.

Unfortunately, Katharine Ross—back on screen after a lengthy hiatus from her "Graduate" and "Butch Cassidy" heyday—falls flat as the overbearing aunt. In fairness, she was saddled with an ill-defined character: wannabe mother one minute and a venomous virago the next.

With varied themes making it similarly schizophrenic, "Home Before Dark" illuminates little but its young heroine's talents.

VILLAGE VOICE, 7/14/98, p. 146, Rown Morris

Set in 1963, Maureen Foley's debut feature *Home Before Dark* is the dramatic tale of an 11-year-old trying to save her family from itself while she struggles in the throes of early pubescence. With a severely depressed mother (Patricia Kalember) and a painfully befuddled dad (Brian Delate), Nora (Stephanie Castellarin) tries to cobble together a cohesive family existence between girl talk and writing stories in her journal. At a moment of crisis, Aunt Rose (Katharine Ross) arrives to whisk Nora off to suburban hell, where shopping trips replace country-road bike rides. After a few visits to her mother in a psychiatric ward, though, Nora brings her family back together in an ending too pat to be believable.

Something of a variation on *Are You There God? It's Me, Margaret, Home Before Dark* clumsily mixes preteen angst with Catholicism, budding sexuality, and self-awareness. Unfortunately, this young girl's awkwardness seems to stem more from the unsophisticated dialogue and the director's inexperience than anything inherent in Nora's circumstances. Foley's choice to narrow her focus to an 11-year-old girl means the film rides on one 11-year-old actress, who, for all her fresh-faced appeal, seems more naive than the character she plays. With the exception of Ross, who is marvelously cast as an uptight suburban queen, the adult actors seem equally confused about how to feel about their characters problems. Perhaps inspired by her own experiences as a young girl, Foley has tried to have a child tell a story about adult pain.

Also reviewed in:
NEW YORK TIMES, 7/10/98, p. E24, Lawrence Van Gelder
VARIETY, 5/5-11/97, p. 70, Daniel M. Kimmel

HOME FRIES

A Warner Bros. release of a Mark Johnson/Baltimore Pictures/Kasdan Pictures production. *Executive Producer:* Romi Lassally.   *Producer:* Mark Johnson, Barry Levinson, Lawrence Kasdan, and Charles Newirth.   *Director:* Dean Parisot.   *Screenplay:* Vince Gilligan.   *Director of Photography:* Jerzy Zielinski.   *Editor:* Nicholas C. Smith.   *Music:* Rachel Portman.   *Music Editor:* Jay Richardson and Will Kaplan.   *Sound:* Jennifer Murphy and (music) Mike Trevor Ross.   *Sound Editor:* Stephanie Flack.   *Casting:* Jill Greenberg Sands and Debra Zane.   *Production Designer:* Barry Robison.   *Art Director:* Phil Dagort.   *Set Designer:* Andrew Menzies.   *Set Decorator:* Suzette Sheets.   *Set Dresser:* Jack Colmenero, Melinda Pharr, Steve Sawhill, and Colleen Saro.   *Special Effects:* David Blitstein.   *Costumes:* Jill Ohanneson.   *Make-up:* Kimberly Greene.   *Stunt Coordinator:* Greg W. Elam.   *Running time:* 105 minutes.   *MPAA Rating:* PG-13.

CAST: Drew Barrymore (Sally);   Catherine O'Hara (Mrs. Lever);   Luke Wilson (Dorian); Jake Busey (Angus);   Shelley Duvall (Mrs. Jackson);   Kim Robillard (Billy);   Daryl Mitchell (Roy);   Lanny Flaherty (Red);   Chris Ellis (Henry Lever);   Blue Deckert (Sheriff);   Mark Walters (Deputy);   Tommy Shane Steiner (Soldier in Jeep);   Theresa Merritt (Mrs. Vaughn); Jill Parker-Jones (Lamaze Instructor);   Morgana Shaw (Lucy Garland);   Robert Graham (Reverend);   Zeke Mills (Tobacco Warehouse Supervisor);   John Hawkes (Randy);   Brady Coleman (Doctor);   Jean Donatto and Mona Lee Fultz (Nurses);   Marco Perella (Good Ol' Boy in Pickup);   Meason Wiley (Photo Lab Employee);   Zachary Moore (Benny).

LOS ANGELES TIMES, 11/25/98, Calendar/p. 1, John Anderson

[The following review by John Anderson appeared in a slightly different form in NEWSDAY, 11/25/98, Part II/p. B9.]

At one point, Drew Barrymore seemed destined to become the Louise Brooks of the second half of the 20th century, mixing liberal doses of healthy sex appeal with an irresistible complicity with her audience; a wink always seems to accompany her smile. Most recently, her career has been heading down a depressingly wholesome track ("The Wedding Singer," "Ever After"), but she still can exude a wry sweetness disarming enough to excuse just about anything.

This includes "Home Fries," a thoroughly unhinged comedy from Dean Parisot, best known for his Oscar-winning short, "The Appointments of Dennis Jennings." Visually fluid and understatedly droll, it's also narratively addled and needs all the distraction Barrymore can provide, lest one ask too many questions.

The film gets rolling when a heavyset, middle-aged man is chased by a state-of-the-art Air Force helicopter, which terrorizes him to the point of a fatal heart attack. Among the grieving are his wife (Catherine O'Hara), his sons Angus and Dorian (Jake Busey and Luke Wilson) and his very pregnant girlfriend Sally Jackson (Barrymore), the drive-thru girl at the local Burger-Matic.

In making its informal and none-too-kindly overview of their lives (Sally's house hasn't been painted since the Civil War and her father is a drunk), "Home Fries" asks us to swallow a lot. Angus and Dorian were the helicopter pilots; their jealousy-crazed mother has put them up to the harassment-turned-murder; and none of these people—in a town where the population's got to be in the high two-figures—knows one another (never mind the fact that the Air Force National Guard, to which the two lads belong, is located conveniently in their own hometown).

The search for Sally, with whom Dorian falls quickly in love, takes up most of the mileage in this story, which requires everyone to run pretty much in place.

Parisot makes deliciously ironic use of his music (like Dean Martin singing "Memories Are Made of This") and good use of Wilson, who really dominates the film. If he seems to be grimacing through a lot of it, it's understandable: Busey's Angus is a madman, as is Mom, and Dorian looks at Sally as his sanctuary and ticket to sanity.

Of course, the baby's going to be both his brother and his son ("my brother...my son...my brother...my son"), but what's one more distraction in a town, or a movie, like this?

NEW YORK POST, 11/25/98, p. 49, Thelma Adams

There has been an illustrious history of films named after potatoes. Who can forget "French Fries" ("Frites"), the coming of age of a young French Jew during World War II? And, of course, there was "Scalloped," the horrific tale of the radioactive cream sauce that threatened to overrun Boise.

Now there's "Home Fries," a ditzy romantic caper that casts Drew Barrymore as an unwed mother-to-be. Saucy Sally slings beef at the Burger-Matic, unaware that she's the target of a murder plot. The unborn infant's father's wife (Catherine O'Hara) and his stepsons (Luke Wilson and Jake Busey) are out to fry her.

With bouncy red curls and a basketball stuffed under her smock, Barrymore somehow brings a Shirley Temple spunk and innocence to the role of the pregnant hick. But love spud Luke Wilson ("Bottle Rocket"), who shuffles in to woo Sally when his stepdad wavers, is about as charming as yesterday's meat.

It's all small potatoes, energetically packaged by director Dean Parisot and screenwriter Vince Gilligan. If you prefer your "Home Fries" well-done rather than half-baked, send this one back to the kitchen.

NEWSWEEK, 11/30/98, p. 82, David Ansen

Fans of Drew Barrymore will find her sweet, Kewpie-doll charm in full blossom in "Home Fries," a modest, off-the-wall black comedy written by "The X-Files's" Vince Gilligan. Barrymore plays Sally, a pregnant drive-through cashier at a small-town Burger-Matic, whose older ex-lover turns up dead in a country field after being strafed by two attack helicopters. The pilots of those choppers were the dead man's stepsons (Luke Wilson and Jake Busey), acting on behalf of their jealous mother (Catherine O'Hara). Unfortunately for Sally, her Burger-Matic headset picked up the radio transmission between the pilots, which means they may have to kill her. Wilson, entrusted with the job, falls in love with her instead. First time director Dean Parisot serves up this convoluted tale with amiable, offhand, flair.

VILLAGE VOICE, 12/1/98, p. 128, Gary Dauphin

Just plain folks in *Home Fries*—down home, slightly slow, and desperate for happiness—would make great *Jerry Springer Show* guests if they weren't so damned pretty.

Starring Drew Barrymore as the nicest little unwed mother-to-be you ever did meet, *Home Fries* begins with an accidental murder by helicopter chase (don't ask), moves on to a "My Dead Stepfather Impregnated My Girlfriend" scenario (Luke Wilson plays the dim-witted stepson of the father of Barrymore's baby), and ends up with another helicopter chase, as Fries's faux Coen brothers-ish dumb-smart flourishes and attention to backwater detail explode inexplicably into action-movie high jinks. Veering uncontrollably between black comedy (murder attempts) and feel-good fuzziness (a Lamaze class), *Fries* is actually much less complicated and therefore less interesting than it sounds. Tooling through the same white-trash hood as *Ringmaster* but with a bigger Hollywood engine, this is an unexpectedly snide and mean little movie despite its gauze wrapping. *Home Fries* misses its intended target of rural quirk and hits just plain dumb instead.

Also reviewed in:
CHICAGO TRIBUNE, 11/25/98, Tempo/p. 2, Mark Caro
NEW YORK TIMES, 11/25/98, p. E6, Stephen Holden
VARIETY, 9/21-27/98, p. 109, Glenn Lovell
WASHINGTON POST, 11/27/98, Weekend/p. 57, Michael O'Sullivan

HOMEGROWN

A TriStar Pictures release. *Producer:* Jason Clark. *Director:* Stephen Gyllenhaal. *Screenplay:* Nicholas Kazan and Stephen Gyllenhaal. *Based on a story by:* John Raskin and Stephen Gyllenhaal. *Director of Photography:* Greg Gardiner. *Editor:* Michael Jablow. *Music:* Trevor Rabin. *Production Designer:* Richard Sherman. *Running time:* 95 minutes. *MPAA Rating:* R.

CAST: Billy Bob Thornton (Jack); Hank Azaria (Carter); Kelly Lynch (Lucy); Jon Bon Jovi (Danny); Ryan Phillippe (Harlan); Judge Reinhold (Policeman); Jon Tenney (Pilot); Matt Ross (Ben Hickson); Matt Clark (Sheriff); Ted Danson (Gianni); John Lithgow (Malcolm/Robert); Jamie Lee Curtis (Sierra Kahan).

LOS ANGELES TIMES, 5/8/98, Calendar/p. 8, David Kronke

Marijuana is notorious for inducing paranoia, but the huffing and puffing antiheroes of "Homegrown" take it to extremes. When they witness the brains behind their cash crop being gunned down, they go into hiding in a half-hearted, stoner sort of way: In their random lucid moments, they realize that anyone—even intimate pals—could be behind the hit.

Perhaps appropriately, "Homegrown" topples between the bar stools as a genre movie: It's a little too funky and shambling to provide much mystery or tension, it's not funny enough to qualify as a comedy and it doesn't add much of substance to the debate over legalizing marijuana.

Still, in the fashion of the sought-after product of the title, for good patches it's a diverting little hybrid.

"Homegrown" is the third in a mini-trend in contemporary cannabis cinema, following the stewed stoners of "Half-Baked" and "The Big Lebowski" (add to these the drug humor of the recent "Senseless" and the upcoming, higher-profile "Fear and Loathing in Las Vegas"). Since moviegoers have largely resisted the urge to inhale these releases, one must wonder what they're smoking at the pitch meetings that get these things green lights.

Jack (Billy Bob Thornton) and Carter (Hank Azaria) are the brains, such as they are, of a motley outfit protecting its primo on prime real estate beneath the shade of Northern California redwoods Assisting them is a dopey doper named Harlan (Ryan Phillippe), and Lucy (Kelly

Lynch, perhaps playing her "Drugstore Cowboy" character gone further to, well, seed), who provides them with occasional shelter and affection.

When their boss Malcolm (John Lithgow) is dispatched to that greenhouse in the sky, they bolt with a few pot plants, just enough to sell to pay for their troubles, with a little left over. Later, they discover that their hidden harvest, worth millions, has not been appropriated as aggressively as Malcolm's life was. Predictably, and ineptly, the guys get a little too greedy.

The film's most pointed joke is the local community's lax attitude toward, if not downright acceptance of, the pot peddlers. When they pay the local law enforcement to look the other way, the sheriff's deputy accepting the payola exults over the new high school auditorium: "We never had a place like that when lumber was the cash crop."

The truth behind Malcolm's murder is eventually revealed, amusingly enough; let it not be said that dopers don't have some ethics. Bit parts and cameos by Jamie Lee Curtis, Ted Danson, Judge Reinhold and Jon Bon Jovi add to the quixotic confusion.

Director Stephen Gyllenhaal, who made the terrific cable TV film "Paris Trout," has proved, with features "Losing Isaiah," "A Dangerous Woman" and "Waterland," that he has a distinct nose for sniffing out unique, difficult material; alas, he can be hampered by an inability to fully realize his ambitions. Gyllenhaal, who co-wrote the script with Nicolas Kazan ("Reversal of Fortune," "Fallen"), tells his story too fuzzily to be fully satisfying.

As Gyllenhaal's story buzzes around, it's easy to feel like one of his befogged characters, knowing there's a logic to what's going on but incapable of piecing everything together coherently. As far as entertainment goes, "Homegrown" provides more of a contact high than the real thing.

NEW YORK POST, 5/8/98, p. 50, Larry Worth

Was there something in the water out in Hollywood?

What else could account for a top-notch bunch of actors signing on for an unfocused film about Northern California pot growers?

Among the suckered: Billy Bob Thornton, Hank Azaria, Kelly Lynch, Jon Bon Jovi, Ryan Phillippe, Judge Reinhold, Jon Tenney, Ted Danson, John Lithgow and Jamie Lee Curtis. Heck, it's got everybody but Cheech and Chong.

Granted, heavy-duty star power can dress up dreck, but it can't disguise it. Proof comes via the thread-bare plot of four hemp-happy marijuana farmers—Thornton, Azaria, Phillippe and Lynch—who secretly take over the biz when their boss is killed.

In between sampling the wares, the quartet fight each other, the Mafia and police as paranoia takes its toll. But who cares?

The movie is only slightly more interesting as a start-to-finish look at the evil weed's journey from seedling foliage to reefer being stuffed into baggies by pregnant moms. The concept—pot farming as a cottage industry—was the film's best shot at success.

Too bad it evaporates as fast as director Stephen Gyllenhaal's half-hearted attempts at black comedy suspense and drama. By all appearances, cast and crew appear to be improvising, badly.

Of the troupers, Bon Jovi's turn as a wholesale drug dealer is the sole standout, with Azaria's soulful stares and Lynch's naturally sexy ways earning honorable mentions. The rest wasted their time and efforts, much like ticket buyers might.

Essentially, "Homegrown" is a bust.

VILLAGE VOICE, 5/19/98, Film Special/p. 131, Michael Atkinson

Something of a tempest in a bong tank, *Homegrown* hardly comes off as the crusading personal project director-cowriter Stephen Gyllenhaal has been hawking, or the picketable, weed-revering hooligan Sony at first seemed extremely reluctant to release. Now that the dust has begun to settle, it's apparent that the corporate bone to pick with Gyllenhaal's pot farce probably had as much to do with marketing confoundedness as with post-drug-war butterflies. It isn't, after all, the easiest movie to sell, a tasteful wacky tabbacky movie for tax-paying ex-dropouts who feel fouled by the low-down bon mots of movies like *Half-Baked*.

There is, in any event, little for reeferheads to giggle at in *Homegrown*, and for a satire the film generally suffers from a shortfall of laughs. The scenario sounds promisingly absurd: after their boss (John Lithgow) is mysteriously tossed out of a helicopter, a dopey crew of NoCal pot growers (overseer Billy Bob Thornton, dippy horticulturist Hank Azaria, grungy neophyte Ryan Phillipe) decides to bury the body, and harvest the latest crop for sale themselves. With the help of romantic interest-weed processor Kelly Lynch, the stooges slowly dip into the deep, dark world of cash-crop capitalism, maintaining the ruse that the boss man is merely in hiding. Paranoia, betrayal, the law, sabotaging competitors, and malevolent customers all contribute to the schmucks' inevitable comeuppance for dealing dope (if not possessing or consuming it), climaxing in an open-air tribute to *The Killing*.

Gyllenhaal can shoot, and his movie has an attractively sullen, shadowy feel, but it never cuts loose—you can't help but think it might've benefitted from a spliff or two behind the scenes. Even Azaria, who is initially fascinating as the clan's unreformed, hair-trigger stud, runs out of opportunities.

Also reviewed in:
NEW YORK TIMES, 5/8/98, p. E16, Lawrence Van Gelder
VARIETY, 4/20-26/98, p. 44, Leonard Klady

HOPE FLOATS

A Twentieth Century Fox release of a Lynda Obst production in association with Fortis Films. *Executive Producer:* Mary McLaglen and Sandra Bullock. *Producer:* Lynda Obst. *Director:* Forest Whitaker. *Screenplay:* Steven Rogers. *Director of Photography:* Caleb Deschanel. *Editor:* Richard Chew. *Music:* Dave Grusin. *Music Editor:* Curt Sobel. *Choreographer:* Patsy Swayze. *Sound:* Felipe Borrero and (music) Al Schmitt. *Sound Editor:* Jim Brookshire, David Kern, Nils C. Jensen, and Don Malouf. *Casting:* Ronnie Yeskel. *Production Designer:* Larry Fulton. *Art Director:* Christa Munro. *Set Decorator:* Douglas A. Mowat. *Set Dresser:* Evelyn Colleen Saro, John Parker, Jack Colmenero, Lawrence Heyman, Robert Tate Nichols, and Steve Sawhill. *Special Effects:* Randy E. Moore. *Costumes:* Susie DeSanto. *Make-up:* Christina Smith. *Make-up (Sandra Bullock):* Pamela Westmore. *Stunt Coordinator:* Kiante Elam and Danny Castle. *Running time:* 112 minutes. *MPAA Rating:* PG-13.

CAST: Sandra Bullock (Birdee Pruitt); Harry Connick, Jr. (Justin Matisse); Gena Rowlands (Ramona Calvert); Mae Whitman (Bernice Pruitt); Michael Paré (Bill Pruitt); Cameron Finley (Travis); Kathy Najimy (Toni Post); Bill Cobbs (Nurse); Connie Ray (Bobbi-Claire); Mona Lee Fultz (Teacher); Sydney Berry (Orange Julia); Rachel Lena Snow (Big Dolores); Christina Stojanovich (Kristen); Allisa Alban (Debbie Reissen); Dee Hennigan (Dot); Martha Long (Waitress); Norman Bennett (Mr. Davis); James N. Harrell (Harry Calvert); Chris Drewy (P.E. Teacher); Meason Wiley (Young Man at Dance); Tisa Hibbs (Suzy); Art Michael Tamez (Bartender); Jeanette Sieh (Volleyball Captain); Tara Price (Young Birdee); Richard Nance (Priest).

LOS ANGELES TIMES, 5/29/98, Calendar/p. 1, Kevin Thomas

"Hope Floats" has a terrific opening. Tempted by the offer of a free make-over, a Chicago housewife and mother (Sandra Bullock) goes on a Jerry Springer-type TV show (hosted by a deliciously unctuous Kathy Najimy) only to be confronted unexpectedly by her best friend (an unbilled Rosanna Arquette), who promptly announces that she's having an affair with Bullock's husband.

Completing the horrendously public devastation is the appearance of the unfaithful husband (Michael Pare) who has no idea he's going to be confronted with his wife and lover.

Totally devastated, Bullock's Birdee Pruitt does what many women with few options would do under the circumstances: run home to mother. In this instance mother happens to be Ramona Calvert (Gena Rowlands), a free spirit living in a fine old house in a beautiful small town in West Texas.

Yet as inviting as this Norman Rockwell community looks to be, it is not an unalloyed safe haven. Ramona is a beautiful woman with a dynamic personality and a lot of wit, much wisdom and self-knowledge but she does not realize she has failed to express the love she genuinely has for her daughter. It's always been her father (James N. Harrell) who gave Birdee the warm embraces and made clear his affection, but now he is in a rest home suffering from Alzheimer's; his ability to comprehend life is wavering at best.

"Hope Floats" itself wavers. At its core is a strong drama about the need for the mothers and daughters to communicate their love for each other and about how a woman with few resources copes with having to rebuild her life from scratch.

In his second feature (following "Waiting to Exhale") the formidable actor Forest Whitaker sensitively directs a sterling cast in Steven Rogers' in many ways admirable script. But "Hope Floats" is undercut by that soft, sentimental Hollywood glow, a lot of artificial cutesy-poo comic touches around the edges—does Ramona really have to have a thing for stuffed animals?—and too many golden oldies on its soundtrack edging out Dave Grusin's apt score.

The filmmakers might have benefited from a screening of the timeless "Picnic" as an example of how to portray small-town American life free of quaintness and caricature but not of humor. A sharper edge could have taken a pretty good, if uneven, picture to greater heights, considering its potent ingredients and actors.

Even so, "Hope Floats" gives good value, starting with Bullock's and Rowlands' knockout performances. Pare is likewise impressive as a man whose good looks have belied an essential weakness of character, and so is Cameron Finley as Birdee's imaginative, sweet-natured little nephew, left to Ramona by her sister who's gone off to pursue a career in Hollywood.

At its best "Hope Floats" delineates insightfully not only Birdee and Ramona's relationship and that of Birdee with her little daughter Bernice (Mae Whitman, easily as effective as Bullock and Rowlands) but also of Birdee and Bernice to adjusting to small-town life. Birdee left home as the gorgeous prom queen who married the handsome high school star quarterback and has now returned, humiliated on national TV, with no job skills, too many bad hair days and too many contemporaries with long-held jealousies unable—or unwilling—to hide their gloating at her return in defeat.

If Birdee is going to have any kind of life she's really going to have to dig in. Similarly, Bernice has to go through the familiar ordeal of being the new kid in school, adjusting to a radically different environment, and therefore longing only for her beloved father—she too is a father's girl—to come rescue her.

Not all is grim for Birdee, because who should be Ramona's handyman but Justin Matisse (Harry Connick Jr.), ruggedly handsome in tight jeans, who adored Birdee in high school but was too shy to say so. It seems Justin, an artisan-level carpenter, is back from California, where his painstaking qualities made him "too slow" on the job and is now building his own Neo-Craftsman cottage in a forest, happy to be back where he can be "doing things the right way."

There's no doubting Connick's impact as Justin, but speaking of "Picnic," this man could use at least a measure of character development afforded William Holden's unforgettable Hal, the archetypal sexy guy in a small town.

The patient Justin is your basic Sensitive Hunk, but Connick and the story warrant more than this. We know nothing of Justin's personal life. Is he divorced? Has he been seeing anyone else when Birdee returns? We need to know more about the man to make him seem more than a plot contrivance. (Justin's improbable surname does elicit a genuine laugh when Birdee's daughter says she never wants to be known as "Bernice Matisse.")

"Hope Floats," which fortunately does pull together for a strong finish, is nevertheless a real plus for Bullock, who served as the film's co-executive producer. She's had difficulty capitalizing on her career-making appearance four years ago in "Speed" after some dismal choices ("Speed 2" among others) and this is a step in the right direction.

Birdee requires Bullock to dig deep to portray a woman who above all else has to define for herself whatever responsibility she had for the failure of her marriage. To her credit Bullock gave herself the challenge of acting opposite the eternally radiant Rowlands, one of the movies' enduring vital presences—and, under Whitaker's caring direction, more than holds her own.

NEW YORK POST, 5/29/98, p. 39, Rod Dreher

"Hope Floats" is pleasant and marshmallowy enough to achieve a certain kind of buoyancy, but it wears its goopy, leaden screenplay and cutesy curlicues by director Forest Whitaker like a pair of cement penny loafers. The movie doesn't sleep with the fishes, but it struggles to keep its head above water.

It starts promisingly, with Birdee Pruitt (Sandra Bullock) finding out on a trashy "Jerry Springer"-ish chat show that her best friend, (Rosanna Arquette) is having an affair with her husband, Bill (Michael Pare).

Shattered, Birdee packs her things and their daughter, Bernice (Mae Whitman), into the car and heads home to Smithville, Texas, to lick her wounds. She moves in with Ramona (Gena Rowlands), her strong-willed, eccentric mother, whose idea of helping her daughter get over her caddish hubby is setting her up with ruddy local hunk Justin Matisse (Harry Connick Jr.). Birdee, wearing her bathrobe like sackcloth, resists.

I bet people will buy tickets to "Hope Floats" solely because of the enormously sexy idea of a romance between such world-class charmers as Bullock and Connick. Aside from being easy on the eyes both have disarming smiles and knockabout gracefulness.

Chemistry. Oh, you bet.

Why, then, does Steven Rogers' screenplay keep Connick at the margins? "Hope Floats" is not about Justin and Birdee falling in love—that would have been a movie worth seeing. It's about Birdee getting over her no-good husband so she can be ready to fall in love again. When Justin shows his frustration with Birdee's constant rebuffs, we feel his pain.

With "Waiting to Exhale," Whitaker established himself as a director who understood how to make a "woman's film." Most women I know would find his habit of clumsily highlighting poignant screen moments amateurish. It's as if he didn't trust the strength of his actors or the material, which is sugary enough without him having to add an extra layer of frosting. Cavity emptor, babe.

Despite all the formulaic sentimentality, there really is a good movie somewhere here, not trying hard enough to get out. As the high school beauty queen who returns home in disgrace, Bullock is quite good showing the pained dignity with which she has to face the people she had been mean to way back when. Her scenes with Rowlands, in which Ramona's past shortchanging of love and support for Birdee becomes an issue between them, have real resonance.

Connick, too, is a treat to watch flirting with Birdee, and is developing real leading-man potential. Which only makes the relative lack of lovey-dovey between the two all the more disappointing. And we're left wanting to know more about this mysterious carpenter's back story. Connick is misused as merely a prop for Bullock's character.

By far the most emotionally wrenching moment comes near the end, when little Bernice, who misses her father and can't understand why he can't be with them, is left sobbing in the driveway as her father speeds away in his car. This child actress does what Bullock cannot: make the hot pain of divorce raw and real.

SIGHT AND SOUND, 11/98, p. 54, Stella Bruzzi

The US. On a daytime talk show (*Toni*) Birdee's best friend reveals that she is having an affair with Birdee's husband Bill. Birdee goes with her daughter Bernice to Texas to live with her mother Ramona, who is already looking after another grandchild, Travis.

Birdee goes to an employment agency to find a job. Her one skill is photography and she lands a position in a local photographic store. Justin, who has been in love with Birdee since they were teenagers, comes courting. Ramona is keen to foster the relationship and invites Justin to the house. After Bernice tells Birdee that the separation with Bill is all her fault, Birdee goes to a bar and gets drunk. Ramona dies suddenly in bed. Bill attends the funeral and asks Birdee for a divorce. Bernice packs her bags and wants to go with her father, but he drives off alone. Birdee and Bernice are reconciled. Justin appears at the photo store. Later, Justin, Birdee, Bernice and Travis walk into the house together.

Like *Waiting to Exhale*, Forest Whitaker's last film as director, *Hope Floats* is a benign, romanticised movie which blunts its potentially hard edges with soft focus and even softer colour filters. Both films go partly against the grain of their material. In *Hope Floats*, there are a few sequences in which strong emotions are permitted to surface from the sentimental soup. One is the opening talk-show scene which enacts the nightmare that underlies all the *Ricki Lake, Oprah Winfrey* and *Jerry Springer* shows: that someone may be genuinely oblivious to the tragedy that is about to befall them. As Birdee (ex-prom queen in neat clothes, pearls and Alice band expecting to be given a make-over) sits rigidly on the homely sofa, her life falls apart, yet all she can do is look at her daughter sobbing in the audience.

The pain that is hinted at throughout *Hope Floats* is consistently more interesting than the schmaltz that swathes it. Justin was stung by his experience of LA and so moved back to the tranquillity of Smithville. Travis' mother abandoned him and he seeks solace in mimicking people or affecting disguises. Bernice idolises her philandering father. Yet little of this is developed. Whitaker seems to believe the pain will be all the more affecting if it's used sparingly In some cases, this strategy pays dividends, such as after Ramona's funeral when Bill is about to leave and Bernice pleads with him to her, wailing, holding on to the car, waiting for her father's capitulation. Evidently, Bill has no intention of fighting for custody of his "princess", and Bernice's despair as this realisation dawns is *Hope Floats'* most wrenching moment.

For the most part, however, *Hope Floats* deals in clichés. Ramona is a stereotyped southern eccentric whose main income has come from taxidermy and who can't express her emotions. Justin is the good, faithful local boy whose sensitive side comes out in his slow renovation of his house. This is film-making by numbers, not altogether unenjoyable, but just too easy, and the contrast between the text and subtext means that the film's tone becomes difficult to gauge. In the scene in which Birdee goes back to Justin's place, for instance, reference is made to Justin's copious use of "tongue and groove". By this stage in the film it is truly unclear whether this is an isolated piece of innuendo or merely an unfortunate moment to comment on interior decoration.

VILLAGE VOICE, 6/2/98, p. 155, Elizabeth Weitzman

Birdee Pruitt (Sandra Bullock) has always been golden: Texas beauty queen, head cheerleader, married to the captain of the football team. But when she finds out on TV that her husband's cheating, her world shatters, and all she can do is run back to the small-town site of her former glory. Mama (Gena Rowlands), who is already taking care of one sad grandchild (Cameron Finley), is waiting with open arms for Birdee and her heartbroken young daughter (Mae Whitman). She won't brook any nonsense, however: neither moping nor self-delusion is allowed, even in the face of Birdee's catty former classmates, who are thrilled to see the Queen fallen. Slowly, despite overwhelming obstacles, all three generations begin to lean on and learn from each other.

Sound impossibly saccharine? What did you expect? The adult protagonist is named *Birdee*. But Bullock is believable and sympathetic in a role that requires her to smile bravely and declare, "Once upon a time your mama knew what it meant to shine," while Rowlands, naturally, gets tough-but-loving just right. And even though a testosterone-free Harry Connick Jr. appears vaguely mentally deficient in his role as Birdee's stubbornly sweet suitor, his gentleness ultimately fits the context. However, the best work comes from the children, who, though adorable, don't possess a shred of cuteness. Whitman's character, in particular, is as fully created and understood as any of the adults'. Forest Whitaker reconfirms the empathy for women's stories he displayed as the director of *Waiting To Exhale,* and thanks to so many graceful performances, there's a rather charming film caught inside all the determinedly upbeat sentimentality.

Also reviewed in:
CHICAGO TRIBUNE, 5/29/98, Friday/p. A, Mark Caro
NEW YORK TIMES, 5/29/98, p. E12, Janet Maslin
VARIETY, 5/25-31/98, p. 57, Todd McCarthy
WASHINGTON POST, 5/29/98, Weekend/p. 49, Rita Kempley

HORSE WHISPERER, THE

A Touchstone Pictures release of a Wildwood Enterprises production.   *Executive Producer:* Rachel Pfeffer.   *Producer:* Robert Redford and Patrick Markey.   *Director:* Robert Redford. *Screenplay:* Eric Roth and Richard LaGravenese.   *Based on the novel by:* Nicholas Evans. *Director of Photography:* Robert Richardson.   *Editor:* Tom Rolf, Freeman Davies, Hank Corwin.   *Music:* Thomas Newman. *Music Editor:* Bill Bernstein.   *Choreographer:* Katherine Kramer.   *Sound:* Tod A. Maitland and (music) Dennis Sands.   *Sound Editor:* Richard Hymns and Frank Eulner.   *Casting:* Ellen Chenoweth and Gretchen Rennell Court.   *Production Designer:* John Hutman.   *Art Director:* W. Steven Graham.   *Set Designer:* Clare Scarpulla. *Set Decorator:* Hilton Rosemarin and Gretchen Rau.   *Set Dresser:* Grant Sawyer.   *Special Effects:* Neil Trifunovich.   *Costumes:* Judy L. Ruskin.   *Make-up:* Gary Liddiard.   *Make-up (Diane Wiest):* Lee C. Harman.   *Make-up (Sam Neill):* Noriko Watanabe.   *Stunt Coordinator:* Gary Combs.   *Running time:* 164 minutes.   *MPAA Rating:* PG-13.

CAST: Tom Booker (Robert Redford);   Kristin Scott Thomas (Annie MacLean);   Sam Neill (Robert MacLean);   Dianne Wiest (Diane Booker); Scarlett Johansson (Grace MacLean); Chris Cooper (Frank Booker); Cherry Jones (Liz Hammond);   Ty Hillman (Joe Booker);   Catherine Bosworth (Judith);   Austin Schwarz and Dustin Schwarz (Twins);   Jeanette Nolan (Ellen Booker);   Steve Frye (Hank);   Don Edwards (Smokey); Jessalyn Gilsig (Lucy);   William "Buddy" Byrd (Lester Petersen);   John Hogarty (Local Tracker);   Mike La Londe (Park Ranger);   C.J. Byrnes (Doctor);   Kathy Baldwin Keenan (Nurse);   Allison Moorer (Barn Dance Vocalist);   George Sack, Jr.   (Truck Driver);   Kelley Sweeney (Nurse);   Stephen Pearlman (Voice of David Gottschalk);   Joelle Carter, Sunny Chae, and Anne Joyce (Office Workers); Tara Sobeck and Kristy Ann Servidio (Schoolgirls);   Marie Engle (Neighbor);   Curt Pate (Handsome Cowboy);   Steven Brian Conard (Ranch Hand);   Tammy Pate (Roper);   Cliff Fleming and Dirk Vahle (Pilots).

CHRISTIAN SCIENCE MONITOR, 5/15/98, p. B3, David Sterritt

Robert Redford is one of those unquenchable movie stars who look ever more fascinating as they mature. His new drama, "The Horse Whisperer," shows him at his rugged best.

His countless fans will naturally be delighted with this, although his handsome face dominates so many scenes that skeptics may consider it too much of a good thing. It's hard to concentrate on other characters when Redford is smiling or frowning or looking pensive in an elegantly framed close-up, and as director of the film, he's made certain the camera points in his direction as often and intently as possible.

Based on Nicholas Evans's bestselling novel, the story focuses on a teenager named Grace who suffers a grievous injury in a riding accident with Pilgrim, her favorite horse. Her physical condition improves but emotional scars remain, growing deeper when she learns that her beloved Pilgrim is also in bad shape.

Determined to help, her mother drives Grace and Pilgrim to a Montana cattle ranch whose owner, Tom Booker, is renowned for a "horse sense" few cowboys can equal. Tom agrees to help the horse, only to find that the mother and daughter also need his tender, increasingly loving care. By the end of the movie everyone has changed from the experience: Grace feels better about life, her mom has learned that motherhood is more important than career, and yes, Pilgrim is almost his old self again.

The screenplay of "The Horse Whisperer" is as unsubtle as the cinematography, coaching us through a series of unsurprising emotions and predictable plot twists, including an apparent love affair between Tom and Grace's mother that throws a curve into the story's otherwise traditional morality. The picture's biggest problem is its constant wobbling among the three important characters—the girl, the mom, and the horse—who need Tom's attention. That's a lot of subplots, even for a film almost three hours long, and Redford's storytelling skills aren't strong enough to make the tale appear as seamless as it should.

Compensating for this is a nonstop stream of gorgeous Montana landscapes, and solid acting by Kristin Scott Thomas as the mother, Scarlett Johansson as the daughter, and Redford as the title character. Dianne Wiest and Sam Neill head the supporting cast, helped by six sturdy horses who take turns playing Pilgrim.

LOS ANGELES TIMES, 5/15/98, Calendar/p. 1, Kenneth Turan

Reverence is a wonderful quality, but, as the Bible says, for every thing there is a season, and "The Horse Whisperer" is not the kind of project you want to be getting too worshipful about.

It's true that the novel by Nicholas Evans has been translated into 36 languages and sold more than 10 million copies worldwide. But at its core "Horse Whisperer" is a piece of romantic pulp whose spirit is best captured by the breathless paperback blurb: "A child wounded in body and spirit, a horse driven mad by pain, a woman fighting to save them both and the man who is their only hope..." You get the idea.

Robert Redford, who for the first time stars in a movie he's also directed, has taken this soap opera material and treated it like something inscribed on yak vellum by the Dalai Lama. While it's almost unheard of for critics to complain that a movie has been made with too much sensitivity, too much care, that's the situation here.

One result of "The Horse Whisperer" being too fussed over is that its running time is an excessive two hours and 44 minutes. Redford and company were so entranced by their own work they didn't realize what a long slog they turned out. The film is set in Montana, and by the time it's over you feel like you've walked there.

Having said all this, it should be added that there is a considerable amount of impressive work here. Redford gives himself some appealing movie star moments; he's smartly selected his co-stars, including young Scarlett Johansson from the indie success "Manny and Lo" and New York stage icon Cherry Jones, and, as photographed by Robert Richardson (who works most often with Oliver Stone) Montana has never looked lovelier.

Moreover, if it hadn't been imprisoned by respect, "Horse Whisperer" is just the kind of heart-tugging story that could make an involving film. And, as its clean and direct opening sequences unfold, you think it just might.

Young Grace MacLean (Johansson) is first seen at her family's country home, a 14-year-old getting up so early to ride with her best friend on a snowy morning that lawyer father Robert (Sam Neill) is still asleep.

Scenes of the girl saddling her horse, Pilgrim, and heading off are intercut with shots of Grace's hard-driving mother, Annie (Kristin Scott Thomas), a Manhattan magazine editor whose job running a Vanity Fair knockoff called Cover is all-consuming.

High-strung, impatient, used to giving orders and getting her way, Annie just about snaps when she's told about something we are shown via a superbly executed piece of special-effects work. A terrible accident has killed Grace's friend, caused Grace to lose part of her leg and put Pilgrim in such horrid shape that vet Liz Hammond (Jones) says she's "never seen an animal with these injuries still breathing."

Seemingly shaky to begin with, the MacLeans' marriage is sorely stressed by having to contend with a daughter traumatized and a mad horse that Annie refuses to have put down despite being told that the animal is beyond help.

A bear for research, Annie discovers the existence of a class of horse trainers called "whisperers," savants who "could see into the creature's soul and soothe the wounds they found there." Against reason and without the slightest encouragement from anyone, Annie packs Grace into the car, shoehorns Pilgrim into a trailer and sets out for a Montana cattle ranch called the Double Divide, the home of Tom Booker (Redford), the whisperer's whisperer.

Reluctantly at first, and only after Grace gruffly agrees to be part of the process, Tom starts to work with Pilgrim. Unlike the novel, which provides detailed explanations of what the whisperer does and why he's doing it, the movie frustratingly chooses to show but not tell, leaving the audience to figure out the specifics. This provides Redford with strong moments of star charisma, but it also gives some of his scenes with Pilgrim the air of a staring battle with a surly studio executive.

Given that he believes what he does is "helping horses with people problems," Tom Booker naturally turns out to be a therapist in chaps and jeans. Though he is older than the 46-year-old

Booker of the novel, Utah-based Redford is comfortable and convincing around horses and looks awfully good wearing his custom-tailored western wear.

Still, Redford has too sophisticated a presence for his character's determinedly folksy persona to be convincing.

Scott Thomas, usually the most reliable of actresses, is similarly uninvolving. In part it's the schematic, nature of her role, the way she turns on a dime from obsessed career woman to mellow cowgirl. It's also because the charismatic attraction that is supposed to exist between Annie and Tom is rarely visible on screen.

Screenwriters Eric Roth and Richard LaGravenese have done what they could with Evans' novel, but they are often caught trying to invest emotions in scenes that aren't able to hold them. When Tom and Annie kiss, you wish they wouldn't; it's like watching the consummation of an arranged marriage. In that context, Redford's decision to eliminate the book's sexual component was perhaps a wise idea.

That lack of identifiable passion is "The Horse Whisperer's" most vexing problem. Redford directs everything smoothly but from a distance, with too few natural moments. This kind of story needs to be more vital, to capture audiences by force and make them believe. Redford's careful, respectful style can do a lot, but that is not within its powers.

NEW STATESMAN, 8/28/98, p. 42, Gerald Kaufman

With "The Horse Whisperer," "Lady in the Dark" meets "Shane." In the Kurt Weill-Ira Gershwin musical "Lady in the Dark," a woman "New York" magazine editor who is a control freak learns to soften up and let men make the decisions. In the western "Shane," a lone man enters a family's life, solves its problems, wins the wife's love and the child's hero-worship, and then bows out.

Annie MacLean strides into "The Horse Whisperer" by marching into her "New York" magazine office with all the dominant authority of Kay Thompson in "Funny Face" (but, unfortunately, without her dazzling musical number, "Think Pink"). She scatters and shatters male egos as she issues her orders for the day. Little does she know that her life is about to be transformed by a virtuoso sequence of movie editing (credits: Tom Roll, Freeman Davies and Hank Corwin), depicting an equestrian accident which results in her 14-year-old daughter, Grace (Scarlett Johansson), undergoing a leg amputation and Pilgrim the horse suffering serious injuries.

Annie (Kristin Scott Thomas, with the frown and a fringe) refuses to have the animal destroyed. Instead, after regaling herself—and the audience—with a potted history of horses on her computer screen, she tracks down on the Internet a man in Montana who might cure Pilgrim of his newly-acquired ultra-nervous disposition.

Enter Robert Redford as Tom Booker, the horse whisperer. Redford refuses to come to New York and abandon his picturesque western locations which are just waiting for Robert (Oscar-winner for "JFK") Richardson's camera. So Annie sweeps up Grace and Pilgrim and drives west, the screen obligingly widening to accommodate all those snow-covered mountains.

We all know what's going to happen, even if we haven't read Nicholas Evans's best-selling novel. Tom is going to cure Pilgrim. Grace is going to snap out of her moodiness (thereby imposing on Scarlett Johansson the necessity to replace the sulky expression she has worn during most of the movie with a very slightly less sulky expression, her entire acting range thus being displayed). Divorcee Tom and married Annie are going to fall in love.

The one unresolved question is: do Tom and Annie do it together? Audiences will have to wait almost all of the film's two hours and 48 minutes to find out, since Redford has tampered with the book's ending.

So how does director Redford fill in all that time? First, with lots and lots of very pretty pictures. Second, with a camp fire singsong and a hoedown (during which Tom and Annie risk setting every tongue in Montana buzzing with a smoochy dance the like of which cinemagoers haven't seen since "Picnic"). Third, with resentment at Annie's intrusion into her family by Tom's sister-in-law, Diane (Woody Allen regular Dianne Wiest venturing out of the Big Apple to play the role reserved for Mercedes McCambridge in "Giant"). Fourth, with a bit of cattle-branding (simulated, the squeamish will be relieved to learn). And fifth, with a little thrifty product placement (Sony and Calvin Klein brand names to the fore).

And then, in addition to Tom's love affair—consummated or not—with Annie, there is Redford's love affair with Redford. Seldom has any director set out so determinedly to mythologise his male star. Despite Redford's raddled right cheek, the man's features can still, if photographed appropriately, be made to look both pretty and rugged. So we are treated to lots of crinkly-eyed views of Redford, with the sun (or the lighting) haloing his golden locks.

Yet even he is outdone by a rival performer. If Redford seems to be recreating himself as the new millennium's Gary Cooper and Kristin Scott Thomas has a sporting chance of becoming Emma Thompson Mk II, then High Tower (chief of the six horses who play Pilgrim), with rolling eyes—photographed in extreme close-up—and quivering nostrils, clearly aspires to be the new Bette Davis.

Anyone seeking highly professional middle-brow entertainment could do a lot worse than "The Horse Whisperer." But a warning is in order: this is an extremely anti-feminist film. Annie only learns to be a true woman by stopping being bossy and accepting that men know best. She replaces her east-coast power dressing with comfy western outfits (provided, of course, by Calvin Klein). She is far from put out when she is fired from her swanky job, accepting that she can be kept quite comfortably by her lawyer-husband (Sam Neill, written out of most of the script until his income comes in handy). She even—the ultimate abasement—meekly accepts Tom's orders not to use her mobile phone while he is whispering to Pilgrim.

NEW YORK, 5/25/98, p. 78, David Denby

In some of her early roles (say, in *Four Weddings and a Funeral)*, Kristin Scott Thomas spoke with such crisp, elocutionary panache that she might have been an escapee from Noel Coward's plays—one of those rueful and bittersweet Englishwomen who enunciated their lines with unimaginable poise. Brittle and tense, she was attractive in an odd, distant way: One wondered if she was heading for a career in BBC period pieces, permanently wrapped in a cocktail dress. But in *The English Patient,* she unwrapped herself and gave an impassioned and elegant performance as an adulterous woman; she blossomed into a romantic heroine. Audiences love to see the ice queen melt (the same fascination worked to advance the career of Katharine Hepburn); Scott Thomas, with her lean, long figure and her directness and bite, may be the perfect actress to play contemporary women fighting for love and power at the same time. I cannot imagine that *The Horse Whisperer,* from the popular Nicholas Evans novel, would have been anything but a very soft pillow to lay one's head on without her. As it is, the movie, directed by Robert Redford, is most leisurely, a rich-toned mixture of romance and earnest therapy. One is soothed by it, bored by it, touched by it. One is grateful when it is over.

Nicholas Evans, who worked in TV and movies before writing fiction, knows what is meant by the term *high concept.* Despite the engaging equine lore in *The Horse Whisperer,* the basic idea of the story is no more than "What if Anna Wintour fell in love with a cowboy?" Kristin Scott Thomas plays Annie MacLean, a strong-willed Brit magazine editor in New York, a woman who defines things too explicitly in order to control them. Annie's horse-loving daughter, Grace (Scarlett Johansson), suffers a terrible accident and loses a leg; the horse, Pilgrim, bashed by a truck and badly scarred, rears and kicks when anyone comes near. But Annie takes action; she packs up her damaged daughter and horse, leaves her husband (Sam Neill) in Manhattan, and heads for Montana and the ministrations of the famous horse trainer Tom Booker (Redford). Grace will be restored to life, Annie reasons, only if Pilgrim is restored to life. Tom is the man to do it: He's a trainer of the whispering school; he doesn't break a horse but gentles it.

Since I know nothing about horses, I'm easily impressed by anyone who does, and I admit to being charmed by the scene in which Redford crouches in the tall Montana grass and just waits as the overwrought Pilgrim wanders about, stares, and finally makes his way back to the man waiting for him. But what brings the horse back? We never find out. It's not quite clear what Tom Booker's special gift consists of, apart from patience. He understands that every horse has its own soul, that a horse's individual temperament has to be respected. The same with mother and daughter. He lets the horse, the girl, the woman—all unhappy creatures—express their misery before he turns them, with a gentle hand, back to their true nature. It's a fantasy, of course, a fantasy directed at women, which Evans and now Redford have created, of a man who is sexually powerful but never aggressive. Tom Booker waits for Annie to come to him. Redford, who has always cultivated a modest demeanor to set off his burnished good looks, plays the role lightly and easily. At 61, he's in great shape, a little weathered, even worn around the eyes, but physically convincing when he works the horse in a ring, rope wrapped around his thighs.

The Horse Whisperer is the kind of pop mythmaking that makes hearts ache all over the world. In the past, you see, Tom Booker has been hurt; his woman has left him, and now he wants nothing for himself and lives in contentment on the Montana ranch with his brother (Chris Cooper), his brother's wife (Dianne Wiest), and their children, all kindly, impeccably polite people, thoroughly rooted in their land and house, and set up, of course, in reproving contrast to the Brit editor from New York, who is power-mad and materialistic, an unsatisfied wanderer. *The Horse Whisperer* is about the seduction of Annie—not just by the faultless Tom Booker but by the soothing open spaces and magnificent mountains and imperial air of southwestern Montana. In the New York scenes, the cutting is jagged, the colors monochromatic and stark. When the movie moves west, Redford slows down; the colors warm to gold, blue, purplish-black; and as Tom and Annie endlessly ride across the mountains, the camera takes to the air for long sweeping shots of man at peace with nature. All this soft, didactic cliché is harmless enough as long as one doesn't take it too seriously. It seems not to have occurred to Redford that rough-and-tumble journalistic and cultural life in New York may have spiritual satisfactions that Montana ranchers can't imagine. The movie is pitched toward people easily intimidated by the big city, people prepared to think that a tough, impatient woman who thinks she can run things has to be humbled and reformed. These assumptions are unlikely to hurt the movie's commercial prospects.

The structure of *The Horse Whisperer* is implicitly condescending to Annie, but Redford, both as a director and as an actor, doesn't condescend to Kristin Scott Thomas. He gives her all the time in the world to set the character and then slowly to change and develop it. In the beginning, her Annie uses charm as an instrument like any other—like rudeness, in fact—as a way of getting things from people. By degrees, she begins to talk to people, not batter them. Her eyes seem to widen; she listens more. Removed from England, Kristin Scott Thomas is no longer as pale as a teacup, and the Calvin Klein western outfits are perfect for that lean body. By the end of *The Horse Whisperer,* she makes the deep stillness of this movie seem like something genuinely earned.

NEW YORK POST, 5/15/98, p. 53, Thelma Adams

Dear Bob:

I can't hate you because you're beautiful.

I've tried. I've tried to forget you. You were my first love. I was the loud-mouth radical from across the tracks when I loved and lost you in "The Way We Were."

Ah, memories, like the corners of my mind (if my mind had corners).

In "Butch Cassidy and the Sundance Kid" I fantasized I was Katharine Ross. Raindrops kept fallin' on my head, but it wasn't water torture. You were easy on the eyes.

Bob, can I call you Bob? You were Brad Pitt before he was born.

But that was a long time ago, and "Three Days of the Condor" ago. When I heard you were directing the Nicholas Evans best seller "The Horse Whisperer," I groaned.

I knew you had this rivalry with Clint. He was always more macho. And, face it, he was an independent filmmaker long before you made Sundance your personal sandbox.

So, Clint looks better in a cowboy hat and his face got leathery first. Get over it, Bob.

I told you we'd cross "The Bridges of Madison County" when we get there. But you couldn't wait. There you were, optioning "The Horse Whisperer," taking Madison to Montana and two-stepping into the silent senior stud role.

You cast yourself as Tom Booker, the dream man who sold a million books, Dr. Dolittle in denim, the horse whisperer, the soulful cowboy who could tame the blackest stallion.

I can't fault you for casting Kristin Scott Thomas as your love interest. We all saw "The English Patient." She can act. But why make Annie a Tina Brown-style Manhattan editrix and bitch goddess? Why not make her a Manhattan film critic bitch goddess?

Bob, people will say it's far-fetched that this self-involved word jockey would shlep her desperately injured horsy daughter and the teen's spooked stallion all the way from Manhattan to Tweedledee, Mont., for some equine healing. So what? The trip brought Annie and me closer to you.

Oh, Bob, we didn't want to fall in love. We had deadlines. Hair appointments. Sample sales. Underlings to boss around. Black-tie dinners to blow off. But you roped us, lassoed us, whispered in our ears, and wore chaps with fringe.

We were yours, Annie and me.

But, before another gilded cloud rolls by in Big Sky country and the camera catches another perfect cattail waving in a dewy pasture, a stallion stamping in the distance, let me unburden myself: Sometimes, I want a director with a slow hand.

Bob, blow in my ear and I'll follow you anywhere. Will I respect you in the morning, you whisper? Who knows, but we'll always have tonight.

NEWSDAY, 5/15/98, Part II/p. B3, John Anderson

My favorite moment in Robert Redford's "The Horse Whisperer"? When guitarist John Fahey is picking "Desperate Man Blues" and the cowboys are on the range and Redford's hair is waving like $30,000-a-bundle wheat and his teeth are flashing like flight-path indicators for international aircraft and a palpable schism opens up between the travelogue aesthetics and saddlebag psychology of the film and a feeling of simple pleasure.

Let's face it: For all its new-age posturing about old-fashioned virtues and the inherent evils of urban life, pleasure is what "The Horse Whisperer" is all about. The aging-like-old-walnut pleasures of Redford; the pleasure of watching Kristen Scott Thomas act; the pleasurable catharsis of a young girl like Grace (Scarlett Johansson) recovering from the trauma of losing her leg and almost losing her horse. The pleasures of being transported to a place and time that never quite existed and watching a "horse whisperer" like Tom Booker (Redford) "gentle" a wounded animal back from the psychic dead (whether horses have souls is a theological question, but the movie seems to think they do).

And, of course, the deluded pleasure of thinking that if only we could all move out to Montana and get back to our roots—even if our roots are in concrete and exhaust fumes—we'd all be perfect people.

One of the more anticipated entries in what has become an earlier and earlier summer movie season, "The Horse Whisperer" isn't a bad film. It isn't even two films, which is where its internal conflicts want to send it. But it's certainly irritating in its simplicity, a fault that lies in the source material as much as in Robert Redford's vision of it.

A western, a romance and virtual science-fiction, too, "The Horse Whisperer" requires that one forget about gangrene, madness, bad dentistry and all the other hazards of primitive western life. Forget about the implicit hypocrisy of ga-ga Hollywood demonizing a hyperactive control freak/Tina Brown-impersonator like Annie MacLean (Scott Thomas). And please, forget about "The Bridges of Madison County," which has enough parallels with "Horse Whisperer" to fill a hay loft.

But neither should we forget that Redford really is a director to be reckoned with. He gets believable emotion out of his actors and makes their interrelationships seem just as genuine. And where he really shines is in those places where he can depart from the dictates of the Nicholas Evans novel (which has been adapted into a very intelligent screenplay by Richard LaGravenese and Eric Roth) and flex his visual muscles.

The opening scene, in which Grace and her doomed chum Judith (Catherine Bosworth) head out for their ill-fated early morning ride, is a jewel-cut winter dream, full of halftones and muted conversation. The accident, in which Judith is killed and Grace is maimed—and which her horse Pilgrim miraculously survives—is a horrific collision of horse and horsepower and expertly edited (in accordance, naturally, with the American Humane Association). And the sequences that lead up to Annie, Pilgrim and the reluctant Grace schlepping out West by car and trailer—so Booker can cure their ills and fall in love with Annie—possess a twitchy, nervous disposition that is perfect for its Annie-centric story.

From there it's mostly, gradually, downhill. Redford feels the animal's pain but is otherwise static. Chris Cooper and Dianne Wiest as Booker's brother and sister-in-law are more than capable (Ty Hillman, who plays their son, is a real charmer) but Scott Thomas is the star of the film, regardless of what the billing says, and she's a little too subtle for outdoor life. And her character is about everything the movie preaches against. Strong-willed women. Ambition. Sophistication. Urbanity. And something less than revulsion at the thought of infidelity: When she headed West, Annie wanted to flee her too-nice husband Robert (Sam Neill) as much she wants to help Grace. Booker is a sitting duck.

There are incongruities aplenty in "The Horse Whisperer," most glaringly this unlikely barnyard romance between Annie and Tom, whose own brief marriage was to a city gal, showing some consistency on his part, if not wisdom. And what has he got to offer besides wisdom? A firm hand with a horse and enough gentlemanly wit to tell a woman she's got a "nice seat"—but only when she's on horseback.

NEWSWEEK, 5/18/98, p. 74, Jeff Giles

Nicholas Evan's best selling novel "The Horse Whisperer" is about a traumatized girl, a spooked horse and the Marlboro Man who puts everything right. Robert Redford has donned three cowboy hats in bringing the book to the screen—he's the director, co-producer and star—and he stages the novel's initial tragedy, at least, masterfully. One winter morning a 14-year-old named Grace (Scarlett Johansson) rides through the woods of Connecticut with a friend. Suddenly the friend's horse rears, throwing her out of the saddle and dragging her into the road as a 16-wheeler bears down. Grace tries to help, and loses a leg while her horse, Pilgrim, is maimed.

These opening scenes are brutal and beautifully choreographed. Then Grace and the mother she hates go West, and the movie goes south—it's punishingly dull for fully half of its two hours and 45 minutes. Grace's mothers Annie (Kristin Scott Thomas), is a highly charged magazine editor clearly based on Tina Brown. She refuses to put Pilgrim down. Instead, she abandons her doting husband (Sam Neill) and hauls Grace and Pilgrim to Montana because she believes a horse trainer named Tom Booker (Redford) can rehabilitate the animal.

Scott Thomas recently said in an interview that she prefers understatement, but that Redford demanded a showy performance. Ironically, he himself is all but a no-show here. We're supposed to believe that Booker carries great pain from a failed marriage and that he fears falling for Annie, but Redford is a big bore beneath a big sky. He stares soulfully into Pilgrim's eyes, dispenses homey wisdom, squats in pastures. It's a vain performance. It's as if Redford figures he's such an icon he can break hearts just standing still. And for a man who has criticized the media's preoccupation with looks, there's an awful lot of sunlight—and moonlight and firelight—in his hair.

For her part, Scott Thomas's Annie is such a palpably real mix of urban arrogance and self-loathing that you never for a moment believe she'd fall for this condescending cowboy. Even if you do, you can hate her for excluding her husband from the most pivotal moments of their daughter's life and for even contemplating an affair that would destroy her already devastated girl. Redford has radically altered the novel's soap-operatic ending. As a director, he does a canny job of rendering Annie's imploding marriage—there's no doubt that this is the man who directed "Ordinary People"—but his heart isn't in the subsequent "Bridges of Madison County"-style melodrama. Neither is ours.

SIGHT AND SOUND, 9/98, p. 43, Peter Matthews

Upstate New York. Thirteen-year-old Grace MacLean loses part of her leg when she and her horse Pilgrim are both severely injured in an accident. When Grace falls into a deep depression, her mother Annie, a magazine editor, realises that her daughter's well-being is mystically bound up with the now crazed Pilgrim's. Annie consults Tom Booker, a 'horse whisperer' dedicated to soothing the spirits of troubled equines. When he proves unwilling to help, Annie drives to his cattle ranch in Montana with Grace and Pilgrim. Tom reluctantly agrees to work with the horse.

Tom slowly gains Pilgrim's confidence. Tom's brother Frank suggests that Annie and Grace stay at the ranch for the duration of the therapy. Mother and daughter pitch in with the chores, and Grace's sullenness gradually lifts. Tom and Annie become emotionally involved. Tom explains that his wife abandoned him for life in the city; Frank's wife Diane fears that history will repeat itself with Annie. Having neglected her duties at the magazine, Annie is fired. Annie's husband Robert makes a sudden appearance at the ranch, just in time to witness Grace's triumphant ride atop Pilgrim: the therapies of both horse and girl are complete. Robert invites his wife to take her time deciding which man she wants. Robert and Grace return to New York, where Annie promises to meet them. Tom watches Annie drive away with Pilgrim.

Whatever else may be wrong with Robert Redford's film adaptation of Nicholas Evans' international best-seller *The Horse Whisperer,* it's extremely well acted—especially by the horses. The story concerns a spirited young steed named Pilgrim who is traumatised by his involvement in a violent road accident; Redford plays the benevolent equine therapist who rallies him. It's a concept tailor-made to appeal to soppy anthropomorphisers the world over—but damned if it doesn't work. Through a combination of editing, psychological projection and histrionic ability on the horse's part, you really come to believe that Pilgrim has a turbulent inner life, even a soul. When the maddened animal is forcibly restrained in a gloomy old barn, you can read the helpless panic and bewilderment in its eye. (Redford provides some of the most eloquent non-human close-ups in film history.) Later, after the treatment has been terminated, you can tell from the fresh spring in his trot that Pilgrim is a changed beast. Cynical film scholars will no doubt put it all down to the Kuleshov effect, but I vote for the horse. The main trouble with the movie is the people.

For its first hour or so, *The Horse Whisperer* canters along smoothly enough to remind one that pretty good movies can sometimes be made from slushy, middle-brow books. As a director, Redford has evolved a stately and imposing style that few in Hollywood know how to do anymore. His previous film *Quiz Show* represented bourgeois film-making of a high order: the shots were finicky, literal-minded and over-composed, but the total effect was monumental and impressive. The new movie also favours orderly, academic imagery punctuated by ceremonious lap dissolves. The main innovation is that the equestrian scenes force Redford into bouts of quick cutting (in part to palm off half a dozen stunt horses as one). The smash-up that maims Pilgrim is a thrilling example of classical montage, the split-second alternation of viewpoints working almost subliminally to induce a sense of paralysed horror.

Even when Redford reverts to his more usual princely mode, it yields much traditional pleasure for the viewer. There's a long, grandiloquent passage recording the cross-country trek of the horse and its owners to the healer's ranch in Montana. The deluxe iconography of this sequence could be literally summed up as spacious skies and amber waves of grain. Yet the vistas are so stirring and Redford frames them with such formal pomp that you can't help capitulating to the whoosh of elevated emotion. For a while at least, the human performers hold their own with both beasts and scenery. Kristin Scott Thomas uses her clipped, high strung quality to bring out the tensions in Annie, the Tina Brown-ish magazine editor who (rather unaccountably) develops an interest in horse whispering. And in the role of despondent daughter Grace, Scarlett Johansson gazes at a colt with more brooding intensity than any screen tot since Elizabeth Taylor in *National Velvet.* Then actor Redford ambles into view and the movie rapidly collapses. "I kinda reckoned you didn't jest happen to be passing through," his horse shrink drawls to Annie on her arrival. It momentarily appears that the star (who was born in 1937) is following in the footsteps of such ageing matinée idols as Clark Gable and Gary Cooper, who, when the big romantic parts dried up, were obliged to turn cowpoke. *The Horse Whisperer* soon bears all the hallmarks of a vanity production. The setting western sun has never been so golden as in one shot where it glints off that celebrated hair, forming a hagiographic—if suspiciously soft-focus—aureola. In the novel, Tom is a lean, athletic 45-year-old; otherwise he's an absolute ringer for the actor. Whether or not Evans wrote the entire book anticipating the movie deal—far from impossible—he has certainly dreamed up a character calculated to stroke a decaying screen hunk's narcissism. Besides being gifted with a near-magical power over horses, Tom is centred, intuitive, empathetic, endlessly patient—not to mention the world's most spectacular lay. The only change that Redford and screenwriters Eric Roth and Richard LaGravenese have made in this paragon is to improve him still further.

In the novel, Tom's weakness is the torch he carries for Annie, which unbalances his instinctive yin and yang. Realising that "he had been whole and now he was not," our hero immolates himself beneath the hooves of a symbolic white stallion. Cooler heads have prevailed for the movie: Annie simply drives away as Tom watches, heart-sore but eternally resilient. That way, the character remains self-sufficient to the last—and that way the star comes out on top. Regrettably, so much screen time is wasted on this tedious love affair that Pilgrim and his neuroses get relegated to the side. You glimpse Tom lassoing the horse, immersing it, massaging it, but you rarely understand what he is doing or why. If Redford had dared to scrap the romance, honed in on the cagey duel of man and animal and shot the whole film in a style of limpid semidocumentary plainness, he might have had something. But then he would have needed to stop reflecting the sun off his hair.

TIME, 5/18/98, p. 86, Richard Schickel

In the movie's emblematic sequence, a horse named Pilgrim and an actor-director named Robert Redford stare at each other—the former nervously, the latter reassuringly. They're both handsome creatures, and the high Montana plain where this confrontation takes place is pretty too. But really, folks—endless minutes of screen time devoted to this silent, essentially motionless sequence? You get the feeling that someone is indulging himself and that his name isn't Pilgrim.

Not that one doubts the purity of purpose that led Redford to *The Horse Whisperer*, based on Nicholas Evan's best-selling, critically dissed novel about an uncannily simpatico wrangler. His patient ministrations are needed to restore psychological wholeness to Pilgrim and, more important, to Grace (Scarlett Johansson), the horse's adolescent rider, after a bloody confrontation with a truck on an icy road.

Redford the director has long been drawn to stories of young people whose innocence has been soiled by cruel circumstance, starting with *Ordinary People*, later in A *River Runs Through It* (and even, stretching a point, *Quiz Show*). In these films there's usually an adult whose failures of understanding are a big part of the problem. In *The Horse Whisperer*, that's the damaged girl's mother (Kristin Scott Thomas). She has her virtues, most notably a determination not to let either Grace, who has lost a leg in the accident, or her mount succumb to despair. But she's a driven, unforgiving sort of woman—chic, brittle, chilly, not at all ideal-mom material. To put the point bluntly, we know what she needs, which is a good, horse whisping.

Redford's Tom Booker is up for that as well. Not anything so vulgar as a raw sexual encounter, mind you—nothing that would interfere with our contemplation of the simple, natural life that this movie us determined to idealize. But some soulful slow dancing, some rides into the sunset—the saintly Tom all rueful smiles an gentle wisdom, can winsomely manage that. The question is can we manage nearly three hours in the company of so perfect a male animal, a figure from whom, in fact, everything animalistic—for that matter anything jaggedly human—has been blanched? There comes a time when you'd give anything if Tom would yell at the kid, swat the horse on the nose or maybe just tell some dumb, dirty joke by the campfire.

Doubtless Redford believes in the ideals that animate this movie—as who among us does not? But the very fact that he is so well known and widely applauded for his many good, politically and artistically correct works offscreen helps make the movie seem self-regarding, self-righteous, even smug. There was once something of the wicked kid in Redford's screen character, and one fondly imagined that he would someday grow up to be, if not a dirty old man, then a subversive and obstreperous one. Certainly we never guessed he'd end up a rustic bore like Tom Booker.

VILLAGE VOICE, 5/19/98, Film Special/p. 131, Amy Taubin

It's too weird, as we used to say, that two big-budget movies, each directed by and starring a romantic icon of the '60s and '70s, are opening on exactly the same day. Robert Redford's *The Horse Whisperer* is no less an auteurist project than *Bulworth*, but it's nowhere near as interesting.

I am, I confess, part of the target audience for this tale about a wounded 14-year-old girl, her traumatized horse, and the gentle rancher from the West who helps them become whole again. Growing up in the city, I named my bike Black Beauty and lived from one Walter Farley horse book to the next. Later, after seeing *Three Days of the Condor*, I nurtured a momentary fantasy of escaping my complicated life by running off to Utah with Robert Redford and raising horses. But even for me, *The Horse Whisperer,* running 165 minutes, outstayed its welcome. Maybe it's just too humiliating to see fantasies you haven't outgrown paraded before you on the big screen. In any case, once Tom (Redford), the "horse whisperer" from Montana, and Annie (Kristin Scott Thomas), the 14-year-old's magazine-editor mother, started galloping together over the prairie in slo-mo and caressing their horses' muzzles while averting their yearning eyes from each other, I wanted to flee the theater.

The Horse Whisperer begins promisingly enough. Teenage Grace (Scarlett Johanson) and her best friend are riding their horses in the snow. Chattering about boys, they decide to take a shortcut, oblivious to the ice under the horses' hooves. The horses lose their footing, and slide, sickeningly, down the hill, dragging their riders with them into the path of an oncoming truck. Grace's friend and her horse are killed instantly. Grace's leg is so badly injured that it has to be amputated. And Pilgrim, her horse, becomes so crazed that his trainer thinks it would be better to put him to sleep.

Redford directs this opening sequence so that you're right in the middle of it without quite knowing how you got there. All the scenes involving kids (with or without horses) arc exceptionally well observed, understated, and quite moving. The problem is the silly love story and the landscapes that look too much like Hallmark cards to be as awe inspiring as Redford wants them to be.

Also reviewed in:
NEW REPUBLIC, 6/15/98, p. 26, Stanley Kauffmann
NEW YORK TIMES, 5/15/98, p. E10, Janet Maslin
VARIETY, 5/4-10/98, p. 83, Todd McCarthy
WASHINGTON POST, 5/15/98 p. D1, Rita Kempley
WASHINGTON POST, 5/15/98, Weekend/p. 55, Michael O'Sullivan

HOW STELLA GOT HER GROOVE BACK

A Twentieth Century Fox release of a Deborah Schindler production. *Executive Producer:* Terry McMillan, Ron Bass, and Jennifer Ogden. *Producer:* Deborah Schindler. *Director:* Kevin Rodney Sullivan. *Screenplay (based on the novel by Terry McMillan):* Terry McMillan and Ron Bass. *Director of Photography:* Jeffrey Jur. *Editor:* George Bowers. *Music:* Michel Colombier. *Music Editor:* Chris McGeary and Tom Kramer. *Choreographer:* Russell Clark. *Sound:* Susumu Tokunow and (music) Mick Guzauski. *Sound Editor:* Steven D. Williams. *Casting:* Francine Maisler. *Production Designer:* Chester Kaczenski. *Art Director:* Marc Dabe. *Set Designer:* Christopher S. Nushawg and Eric Orbom. *Set Decorator:* Judi Giovanni. *Special Effects:* John Hartigan. *Costumes:* Ruth E. Carter. *Make-up:* Judy Murdock. *Running time:* 99 minutes. *MPAA Rating:* R.

CAST: Angela Bassett (Stella);   Whoopie Goldberg (Delilah);   Regina King (Vanessa); Suzzanne Douglas (Angela);   Taye Diggs (Winston Shakespeare);   Michael J. Pagan (Quincy); Sicily (Chantel);   Richard Lawson (Jack);   Barry "Shabaka" Henley (Buddy);   Lee Weaver (Nate);   Glynn Turman (Doctor Shakespeare);   Phyllis Yvonne Stickney (Mrs. Shakespeare); Lou Myers (Uncle Ollie);   James Pickens, Jr. (Walter);   Carl Lumbly (Judge Boyle);   Denise Hunt (Ms. Thang);   Lisa Hanna (Abby);   Phillip Casnoff (Kennedy);   D'Army Bailey (Minister);   Art Metrano (Doctor Steinberg);   Phina Oruche (Leslie);   Tenny Miller (Kitchen Worker);   Andrew Palmer (Buffet Server);   Harold Dawkins, Kenneth Buckford, and Simon Street (Upbeaters Band);   Craig Blake (Winston's Friend);   Elizabeth Granli (Girl in Jamaica Commercial);   Steve Danton (Man in Commercial);   Elly McGuire (Stella's Friend);   Selma McPherson and Fern Ward (Friends at Party).

CHRISTIAN SCIENCE MONITOR, 8/14/98, p. B3, David Sterritt

Jack Nicholson did it in "As Good as It Gets," and Harrison Ford did it in "Six Days, Seven Nights," and Warren Beatty did it in "Bulworth." So shouldn't Hollywood's women get to do it for a change?

It happens in "How Stella Got Her Groove Back," one of the rare movies where an older woman wins the heart of a younger man, instead of some weather-beaten male star strolling into the sunset with an actress who's a whippersnapper by comparison.

And who could blame the younger man in question? His name is Winston, he's 20 years old, and he's cooking at a Jamaican resort while deciding whether to become a doctor like his dad. That's where he meets Stella, a 40-year-old executive who's been downsized from her job and wants to forget her troubles with a few days of tropical sunshine. One conversation is all Winston needs to fall in love with this brainy California beauty, and if people worry about their ages, a look at their starry eyes will prove this is real romance, not a mere flirtation with novelty.

Based on a novel by Terry McMillan, whose "Waiting to Exhale" inspired a Hollywood hit not long ago, "Stella" appears to be aimed at the same audience of women in general and African-American women in particular. Additional box-office power may come from older women and, yes, men of all ages who find Angela Bassett, the gifted star of "Malcolm X" and "What's Love Got to Do With It," among many other films, as appealing as any star today.

Not that "Stella!' stands with the season's best movies. The story doesn't hold enough surprises to justify its running time of more than two hours, and the filmmakers fall back on R-rated sensationalism more often than a genuinely mature movie would need, as if they didn't trust the central relationship to sustain interest on its own.

There are lots of lively performances, though: The cast ranges from newcomer Taye Diggs as Winston to veteran Whoopi Goldberg as Stella's best friend—and the scenery is splendid in Jamaica and San Francisco alike. First-time filmmaker Kevin Rodney Sullivan directed.

In addition to their age difference, Stella and Winston also hail from different countries, giving a touch of multiculturalism to their tale.

Cultural differences play a darker role in "Return to Paradise,"a new drama that raises more difficult moral issue than it's prepared to handle convincingly.

The story begins by introducing three young Americans on vacation in Malaysia, where casual drug use is among their dubious recreations. When two of them head back to the United States, the third decides to stay and pursue a career in environmentalism.

A couple of years later, the returned New Yorkers are shocked to learn that their companion was arrested on drug charges soon after their departure and will be executed as a narcotics dealer unless they go back to Malaysia, confess that some of the drugs belonged to them, and agree to serve time in a very frightening prison. What will they do? And what would we do if we were in their position?

"Return to Paradise" asks hard ethical questions centering on trust, honesty, and self-sacrifice, and it makes them vividly real by linking them with everyday people who never planned to face them in such an urgent, unsettling way.

But what promises to be a challenging and engrossing movie is weakened by two serious flaws. One is the decision to dilute its primary issues with a trite romantic angle involving one of the New Yorkers and a lawyer (Anne Heche) representing the condemned prisoner. The other is a very weak performance by rising star Vince Vaughn as the man involved in this mistimed affair. He's supposed to be facing the most difficult crisis of his life, but through most of the story he barely manages to look nervous.

The picture takes a truly surprising turn near the end, and Joaquin Phoenix turns in such strong acting as the prisoner that he almost compensates for Vaughn's shortcomings. But ultimately "Return to Paradise" is more a squandered opportunity than an enlightening moral tale. Almost a dozen years have passed since director Joseph Ruben reached the top of his form in "The Stepfather," still one of Hollywood's most memorable thrillers. His new effort is more ambitious but a lot less impressive.

LOS ANGELES TIMES, 8/14/98, Calendar/p. 1, Kenneth Turan

You could call it "Femmageddon." Or "The Jailbait Trap." Under any name "How Stella Got Her Groove Back" is a glossy, good-humored romantic fantasy directed as purposefully toward women as "The Parent Trap" is toward youngsters and "Armageddon" toward males.

Taken from the best-selling novel by "Waiting to Exhale's" Terry McMillan, "Stella" may be frothy and paper-thin, but it's also another great success for star Angela Bassett, who transforms the film into an infomercial for her considerable abilities.

Looking gorgeous in more Ruth E. Carter-designed outfits than Imelda Marcos has shoes and displaying a smile that could light several cities, Bassett also has the skill and force of personality to make this frivolous concoction as close to real as it's going to get. During those frequent moments when "Stella" trembles on the brink of complete unbelievability, it's always Bassett who brings it back more or less alive.

Her Stella is a strictly business San Francisco stockbroker who has made all kinds of money by asking clients, "Do you want to be rich or do you want to wallow in regret?" Divorced from her husband, she is doing a hell of a job raising son Quincy (Michael J. Pagan) and coping with her sisters, bossy busybody Angela (Suzzanne Douglas) and sassy Vanessa (Regina King, Cuba Gooding Jr.'s wife in "Jerry Maguire").

Money she may have, but 40-year-old Stella is without a man, something her sisters delight in moaning and groaning about. Even Quincy, a candidate for the best-behaved young man in America, pleads with his mother as he heads off on a two-week vacation to "try and have some fun while I'm gone."

Strictly on a whim, Stella decides to spend that time in Jamaica. Her companion of choice is longtime best friend Delilah (Whoopi Goldberg), a Manhattan department store window dresser who is the film's designated comic relief, a reliable source of irreverent attitude and laugh lines.

A veteran of fending off more mature suitors, Stella is astonished by the attentions of a 20-year-old Jamaican named Winston (Taye Diggs in his feature debut). "There ought to be a law against being young and sexy" is her thought when she spies him, but against her better judgment she finds herself fatally attracted to someone she worries is not legally of age.

From this point on, "Stella" becomes one of those low-maintenance movies that can be left for 10 minutes without losing track of the plot. Since its surprises are minimal (the title, after all, is "How Stella" not "Did Stella"), the main source of astonishment is that screenwriters McMillan & Ron Bass have been able to coax as many minutes out of this situation as they have.

Some recent French films, including last year's "Post Coitum" and the forthcoming "School of Flesh," have realistically treated the difficulties of relationships between young men and older women, but "realism" is not a word in this picture's vocabulary. While everyone within the sound of Stella's voice is upset by her "trolling the kindergarten yards" for a romantic mate, all the obstacles she and Winston face are no more than eggshell thick.

Winston's mother, Stella's sisters and even a worried Stella herself take turns treating this love affair as if it were the outre pairing of Ruth Gordon and Bud Cort in "Harold and Maude," but the film goes out of its way to minimize any factors that would make the romance even borderline unsuitable and thus disturb the fantasy.

First of all, with the dynamic Bassett coming off as years younger than 40 and the handsome Diggs (a New Jersey-born actor who does a convincing Jamaican accent) having a receding hairline, the two look much more like brother and sister than mother and son.

Cutting the age difference even more is Winston's earnestness, solicitousness and a remarkable maturity that is way beyond the reach of your average 20-year-old. Add in a set of wealthy, cultured parents, plus his own potential interest in medical school, and Winston stands revealed as the same kind of paragon Sidney Poitier's character was in "Guess Who's Coming to Dinner."

Under the workmanlike direction of Kevin Rodney Sullivan, "Stella" offers a few sensual moments and some passable comedy. But it's mostly a smoothly artificial soap whose likable people do the most predictable things. Delilah calls Stella's situation "The Young, the Restless and the Colored," and we know better than to argue with her.

NEW YORK POST, 8/14/98, p. 39, Thelma Adams

Angela Bassett is as good as it gets. She's Hollywood's reigning diva.

Bassett is beyond Sharon Stone because this girl can act—the Academy robbed her of an Oscar for her tear-me-up, tear-me-down Tina Turner in "What's Love Got to Do With It." And when Bassett cries, she has that Julia Roberts look-gorgeous-through-the-tears act down.

In the title role of "How Stella Got Her Groove Back," Bassett is not just your average fabulous 40-year-old stockbroker. Sure, the super single mom has the best San Francisco pad a production designer can fantasize, and a wardrobe to match.

She also is one colossal piece of womanhood, completely confident within her skin yet vulnerable—but not so vulnerable that she feels compelled to peel off her shirt or sit with her crotch exposed. Bassett puts the groove in Stella, another go-girl movie from the pages of novelist Terry McMillan. Stella is another bourgeois black woman waiting to exhale; she's caught up in her job, her house, her anger, her son. In the back of her head there's a little voice saying, "It's over, babe. The peak is past. It's downhill and blind dates from here to the grave."

Then Stella sees an ad for Jamaica. She grabs her best gal, Delilah (Whoopi Goldberg), and away they go. Whoopi's sarcastic schtick makes her the perfect foil for Bassett. Not only does the dreadlocked comedian bring out the diva's humor and warmth, without Whoopi, Bassett would be too good to be true. Audience envy would cancel out empathy.

Why envy Stella just because she looks gorgeous in a bikini and sarong? On her first morning at the upscale Jamaican resort, she meets Winston Shakespeare (Taye Diggs). Young Winston is 20 going on 21, a premed student from an upper-crust island family whose mother is only a year older than Stella.

We want to believe the age difference is a complication, that there are doubts that Stella and Winston will overcome the older woman-younger man taboo. But with an episodic, poorly structured script by McMillan and Ron Bass, and uneven pacing from first-time director Kevin Sullivan, there are no surprises and too many spots where the movie shudders to a halt.

Bassett's charisma keeps the love alive. Flawed though it is, "Stella" is this summer's women's movie, the romance most likely to get female viewers calling out for a full-frontal-nude shot of newcomer Diggs. The May-September pair seduces us: Every shower scene, every sunlit swim, every candlelit supper cries out that this is vitamin "L," and no obstacle can come between Hollywood and a potent fantasy romance.

NEWSDAY, 8/14/98, Part II/p. B3, Jack Mathews

In the competition for America's tourist dollars, the tropical paradise of Jamaica gets a big jump over its rival Malaysia at U.S. theaters today.

Kevin Rodney Sullivan's "How Stella Got Her Groove Back," adapted from Terry McMillan's novel about an island romance between a 40-year-old woman and a 20-year-old hunk, is a joyful audience pleaser that plays like a two-hour product placement for the Caribbean island, while Joseph Ruben's "Return to Paradise," the story of three young Americans accused of drug trafficking in Penang, could do for Malaysia what "Midnight Express" did for Turkey.

First, the good news.

With aerial introductions to the pristine aquamarine surf and palm-studded beaches of Jamaica, followed by pastel-colored drinks, reggae music, hard bodies and pajama dances, "Stella" is enough to get everybody's groove back. McMillan's novel, inspired by her own midlife rescue by a stud muffin, follows Stella (Angela Bassett), a successful San Francisco investment broker and single mom, and her chatty friend Delilah (Whoopi Goldberg) on a week's vacation to Jamaica.

There, Stella finds it impossible to resist Winston (Taye Diggs), an age-blind colt with an electric smile and a body that had women in both the movie and the audience swooning. But when their aerobic passion gets serious, when he takes her home to meet the folks and she reciprocates, they're a scandal, Lolita and Humbert in reverse, and their puppy-yuppie love is put to the test.

That's a pretty thin story line for a feature, and it's made even thinner by the expansion of the role of Delilah, a minor figure in McMillan's novel and the driving comic force of the movie. It's the gamey, adventuresome Delilah who pulls Stella from the rat race to kick back in Jamaica. With Delilah touting some mindless sex with a pair of broken-down NFL players, Stella draws the unflinching stare of young Winston, and a bad case of *amour fou* soon follows.

Goldberg hasn't had a better opportunity to ham it up in a film, and she's howlingly funny in the movie's first half. But when the story narrows its focus to Stella and Winston, the tone shifts, too. Though there are more good laughs, particularly from Stella's envious sister Vanessa (Regina King), and a superb star turn from Bassett, the last section of the movie slogs through a swamp of sentimentality.

By making Delilah so strong, and casting the scene-stealing Goldberg, Sullivan and his co-writers McMillan and Ron Bass ("Rain Man") essentially created two different stories, a screwball comedy followed by a strained tale of star-crossed lovers. Though Winston acts older than 20, and Stella, with Bassett's face and body, looks younger than 40, apparently only the audience can be fooled. Everyone else in the movie looks at them as if they each had two heads.

Structural problems aside, "Stella" seems to me to be better-directed than Forrest Whitaker's adaptation of McMillan's "Waiting to Exhale," which also starred Bassett. Sullivan, a veteran TV director on his first feature assignment, has a terrific feel for light comedy, and knows how to showcase both his actors' talents and his surroundings. Jamaica, and San Francisco for that matter, have never looked better.

Now, I've been to Malaysia, and I recommend it. Great beaches, beautiful water, lush jungles, incredible exotic fruits and night music right out of a Tarzan movie. But I don't recommend you buy illegal substances while you're there. The Malaysian government has an ongoing war on drugs, and a death penalty for anyone caught with an amount that qualifies as trafficking.

In Joe Ruben's "Return to Paradise," loosely adapted from the 1990 French film "Force Majeure," the amount in question is a brick of hash weighing more than 100 grams. It was bought by Sheriff (Vince Vaughn), Lewis (Joaquin Phoenix) and Tony (David Conrad), three Americans who met and traveled together through Malaysia, and was left with Lewis when the other two returned to New York.

Two years later, Sheriff and Tony are contacted by Beth (Anne Heche), a woman claiming to be an attorney representing Lewis, who has been in a Penang prison all that time. Seems he was caught with the drugs shortly after the others left, and is now just eight days from being hanged. His life will be spared only if Sheriff or Tony, preferably both, return to Malaysia and share the responsibility. If one does, he and Lewis will serve six years in prison. If both do, the sentence is three years each.

The long middle section of "Return to Paradise," done as a countdown to hanging day, deals with the crisis of conscience facing Sheriff and Tony, whose friendship didn't extend beyond the trip, and Sheriff's relationship with Beth, whose commitment to the case seems to go far beyond normal professional ethics and compassion.

It is a fascinating moral dilemma for both of the free men. After all, they only knew Lewis casually. Tony, a construction worker, is now engaged to a woman determined to keep him home, and Sheriff is a Manhattan limo driver whose self-interest seems firm against any challenge. Nonetheless, one or both will return with Beth; otherwise, there's no movie. The suspense hangs on what awaits them there.

And this is where Malaysia gets trashed. Even the beautiful opening footage, with the boys cavorting innocently through the countryside, is shot in other countries, mostly in neighboring Thailand. When the entourage returns, it's to a Third World sewer, and a prison that resembles a medieval dungeon.

The good news for the Malaysian government is that the real villain of the piece, the institution upon which the fate of the three men really rests, is the American media. Throughout the movie, Beth is accosted by M.J. Major (Jada Pinkett Smith), a pitbull New York newspaper reporter who's threatening to blow the story before Beth can negotiate Lewis' reprieve.

"Return to Paradise," co-authored by Bruce Robinson ("The Killing Fields") and Wesley Strick ("Cape Fear"), ventures through some riveting psychological terrain before hurtling into a last-act thicket of cliches. There's no bigger cliche than M.J., a kill-for-a-story reporter who seems to operate independently of ethics or editors.

Newspapers are having a bad enough time, thank you.

NEWSWEEK, 8/17/98, p. 61, Allison Samuels

Nineteen ninety-five's "Waiting to Exhale" was a surprise hit at the box office, and here's another Terry McMillan adaptation that should make women giggle with vengeful glee. "How Stella Got Her Groove Back" concerns a 40-year-old professional woman (Angela Bassett) on vacation in Jamaica. She catches the eye of a brother (Taye Diggs) who's as fine as Michael Jordan, but half her age. Stella falls for him against the backdrop of the lush tropical island. Rarely have we seen black love be this sensual. But when Stella and her new beau return to the real world, troubles arise and both of their families object to their relationship. "Stella" is a much smoother ride than "Waiting to Exhale," partly because it's focused on one main character. It also has a big dose of sister-girl humor from Whoopi Goldberg, as Stella's best friend, and Regina King ("Jerry Maguire"), as Stella's younger sister. Anyone who's ever lost her groove will relate.

SIGHT AND SOUND, 2/99, p. 45, Nina Caplan

Stella is a stockbroker and single mother who jogs daily and looks far younger than her 40 years. The only thing she is bad at is having a good time. However, when she takes a holiday with her best friend Delilah in Jamaica she soon starts a romance with Winston Shakespeare, a Jamaican half her age. The romance ends badly but unknown to Stella, Delilah gives Winston her phone number. When she loses her job and Winston phones, she agrees to go back to see him, despite the disapproval of her sister Angela.

Winston wins over Stella's son Quincy, but Winston's own parents disapprove of his relationship with Stella. Meanwhile, in New York Delilah goes into hospital with cancer, an illness she had hidden from Stella. When it worsens, the doctor calls Stella who flies back to be with her friend when she dies. Winston appears at the funeral to offer support and moves in with Stella and Quincy. Most of Stella's friends and family overcome their disapproval, although Angela still disdains Winston. The age difference becomes a problem between them: their tastes are different and the fact that Winston is jobless, penniless and undecided about his future aggravates their difficulties. Nevertheless, he asks Stella to marry him; when she dithers, he decides to return to Jamaica and resume his interrupted medical studies. Stella lets him go, but follows him to the airport and agrees to the marriage.

A love story between a 40-year-old woman and a boy half her age, *How Stella Got Her Groove Back* makes a valiant effort to be contentious without actually annoying anyone. The film tries to examine the antiquated prejudices still lurking beneath the glossy new-age surface of the US in the 90s, but it backtracks immediately by casting youthful-looking Angela Bassett in the title role. Her paramour, the gloriously named Winston Shakespeare (Taye Diggs)—calm, mature, self-directed and monogamous—hardly behaves much like your average 20-year-old man either.

Other reasons make it hard to take the film's central premise seriously. First-time director Kevin Rodney Sullivan fumbles the key love scenes in Jamaica where the couple meet, making them stylistically reminiscent of the travel-advertisement type of 80s pop video (think of Duran Duran's 'Rio'). The copulating couple even groan in time to the soundtrack, while coy pans to the surrounding mountains provide more viewing interest than the couple on the bed. The film also has a bad case of tunnel vision, homing in on its older woman-younger man problem at the expense of other issues. Why, for example, does Stella assume that a holiday romance would make her a slut? The film could have used her assumptions to examine different attitudes to sex between the generations but it doesn't. Winston accepts that his penury is a problem because a 'real man' would take financial responsibility for 'his woman'.

The incipient rivalry between Stella's 11-year-old son Quincy and Winston is also brushed over. Quincy comments on Mom's and Winston's ages once to his cousin, is won over and then pipes down—apart from once in a man-to-man talk where he warns Winston not to hurt his mother. The scene leaves the spectator wondering why an age gap is worth making a film about when even an 11-year-old seems ready, in emotional terms, to apply for a pension.

That the film skips along is thanks largely to Stella's best friend Delilah. In this, her trademark role—spunky black woman with the heart of gold—Whoopi Goldberg provides a colourful contrast to Bassett's pastel sartorial and dramatic style. Unfortunately Goldberg's character is also used to ram home the message that if you look like a film star, the world is your five-star hotel suite. If not, you face either neglect or humiliation. Winston even upstages Delilah's funeral by arriving halfway through for an impassioned reconciliation with the grief-stricken Stella.

This is one of the film's few emotional outbursts. "Don't go there," various characters say when others bring up personal, hurtful or humiliating topics, as if emotions comprised an actual landscape with pockets of forbidden territory. All very well as topography for touchy-feely dialogue, but a somewhat timid approach given that the film revolves around an uneven relationship and a hard-edged family duality—Stella's sister Angela embodies the self-righteous disapproval of the outside world, while younger sister Vanessa is the money-conscious, prurient element. So, despite its glorious Jamaican setting, *How Stella Got Her Groove Back,* doesn't travel as far as it should in its exploration of putative taboos and relationship problems. Stella's groove, like the film itself, doesn't run deep.

VILLAGE VOICE, 8/25/98, p. 132, Gary Dauphin

Hollywood didn't really discover the black female audience with *Waiting to Exhale*, at least not the way Columbus discovered America. Terry McMillan's bestselling romance novel was already a recognized phenomenon before there was a movie version and so the dream industry was just along for the ride. *Exhale* was a very profitable ride of course, hence *How Stella Got Her Groove*

Back, an April-August romance starring Angela Bassett that's return trip, community service, and mercenary raid all rolled into one. It's not a very well-made movie, *Stella's* many limitations will probably be a side issue among its target audience, irrelevant next to those repeating images of Angela being so rich and beautiful and black.

The divorced, 40-year-old Stella is the typical girl who has everything...except, you know, love. Introduced like a video personal ad, she powers through million-dollar deals with unquestioned ease, lives in a generically scenic home, mothers her teenage son with firm, smiling wisdom and takes slow-motion morning runs through the hills. (Unlike the hug-centric *Exhale* Stella is built around gasp-producing money shots, Bassett's tri-athlete body, her home, and her young lover drawing equal amounts of oohs.) After enduring some ribbing from her sisters about being blackman-less, Stella decides what she really needs is restful trip to Jamaica with gal pal Whoopi Goldberg (who gets all the best lines). There she meets Winston (Taye Diggs), a 20-year-old hardbody. It's not a wholly unbelievable love connection. Besides having those muscles, Winston has no real competition, his main obstacles a pair of flabby ex-football players and the psychic scars Stella's developed where her groove used to be.

One of those "if you have to ask..." things, Stella's vaguely metaphysical groove doesn't really get an on-screen exploration beyond the tastefully sexy kind. (You know it's definitely back when a single postorgasmic tear erupts from Stella's eye midway through the movie.) Director Kevin Rodney Sullivan pares McMillan's turgid hand-wringing about love and living life to the fullest down to simple aesthetic determinism (Winston and Stella look too good not to be together). But where *Exhale* extended its beautiful ladies the courtesy of consistently glossy surroundings, *Stella* is kind of chintzy, its high-end black spaces as superficially textured as an episode of *Melrose Place. Stella* deserves a grudging nod for giving black women the kind of soapy images white women take for granted, but that doesn't mean it couldn't have tried harder to make them shine.

Also reviewed in:
CHICAGO TRIBUNE, 8/14/98, Friday/p. A, Michael Wilmington
NEW YORK TIMES, 8/14/98, p. E9, Stephen Holden
VARIETY, 8/10-16/98, p. 41, Todd McCarthy
WASHINGTON POST, 8/14/98, p. D1, Rita Kempley
WASHINGTON POST, 8/14/98, Weekend/p. 39, Michael O'Sullivan

HURLYBURLY

A Fine Line Features release.   *Executive Producer:* H. Michael Heuser, Frederick Zollo, Nicholas Paleologos, and Carl Coplaert. *Producer:* Anthony Drazan, Richard N. Gladstein, and David S. Hamburger. *Director:* Anthony Drazan. *Screenplay, (based on his play):* David Rabe. *Director of Photography:* Changwei Gu. *Editor:* Dylan Tichenor. *Music:* David Baerwald and Steve Lindsey. *Production Designer:* Michael Haller. *Costumes:* Mary Claire Hannan. *Running time:* 122 minutes. *MPAA Rating:* R.

CAST: Sean Penn (Eddie); Kevin Spacey (Mickey); Robin Wright Penn (Darlene); Chazz Palminteri (Phil); Garry Shandling (Artie); Anna Paquin (Donna); Meg Ryan (Bonnie).

LOS ANGELES TIMES, 12/25/98, Calendar, p. 2, Kevin Thomas

"Hurlyburly" takes us into the hills of Hollywood to acquaint us with a group of people we've met many times before, on the screen and in life—and would take pains to avoid whenever we could. Yet playwright-screenwriter David Rabe writes such juicy parts that he's attracted as glittering a lineup of stars for the new film version as he did for the original play 14 years ago.

We now get to see Sean Penn, Kevin Spacey, Robin Wright Penn, Chazz Palminteri, Garry Shandling, Anna Paquin and Meg Ryan in roles that were created by William Hurt, Christopher Walken, Sigourney Weaver, Harvey Keitel, Jerry Stiller, Cynthia Nixon and Judith Ivey. Under Anthony Drazan's assured direction the screen cast acts just as impressively as the stage cast did, but ultimately to no more avail. The problem remains: For all Rabe's sound and fury, he doesn't come up with any profound revelations about the human condition to match the intensity of his ranting and raving, or to make up for the fact that, to put it mildly, most of his people are off-putting in the extreme without being very interesting.

The passing of time has further undermined the impact of "Hurlyburly" because it suffers in comparison with the films, for example, of Todd Solondz and Neil LaBute, who have the knack of making the dark and destructive compelling and even amusing.

Even so, in adapting his play to the screen, Rabe had a chance to create something better of it had he not been so self-indulgent of his often tortuous dialogue and trusted in the power of images to express alternating desperation, superficiality and aimlessness.

"Hurlyburly," photographed with a bleak sleekness by "Farewell My Concubine's" formidable Changwei Gu, has been opened up with considerable ease and grace, but it just doesn't know when to shut up. (And if it has the pluses of Gu's mobile camera work and the late Michael Haller's spot-on production design, it also has the assist of David Baerwald and Steve Lindsey's supportive, varied score.)

The film's talkiness erodes the impact of an absolutely galvanic Penn as Eddie, a coked-up casting director who starts coming apart when he realizes that he has fallen in love with Wright Penn's Darlene, the kind of cool, poised blond that has always cut a swath in Hollywood. Eddie didn't think he'd mind Darlene having a casual fling with his business partner and apartment mate, Mickey (Spacey), a glib, polished type that has flourished in the motion picture industry since its beginnings. (Both Penn and Spacey had first played their roles on stage.)

But unexpected jealousy has plunged Eddie into an emotional tailspin, intensified immeasurably by steady lines of cocaine. The recognition of love has caused the scales to drop from his eyes. He's forced to realize that most of the people around him live skittish, dicey existences purely on the surface, that the world may be going to hell in a handcart—the time is just as the Gulf War is about to break out—and that he's in desperate need of being loved by a woman who, enraging him further, regards him as casually as she does Mickey.

Only Mickey, played by Spacey with a delicious oiliness, may have the edge because he has magnanimously maneuvered Darlene back into Eddie's arms, making Mickey all the more attractive to her. (How a suave wheeler-dealer like Mickey can remain partners and live under the same roof with Eddie is one of the movie's key mysteries.) You can identify with Eddie's pain, and could even more so were Penn not required to do so much grandstanding.

Mickey is probably right when he observes that Palminteri's Phil makes Eddie feel that there will always be somebody lower than he is no matter how far he may fall. Phil is an ex-con with delusions of being an actor and with a terrifying streak of violence, most often directed toward women. When Eddie arranges for him to take out a likably forthright exotic dancer, Donna (Ryan), he's soon shoving her out of her car.

Now Phil can gaze with pure love upon the baby he's kidnapped from his estranged young second wife, but that's scarcely enough to keep him from being an otherwise dangerous, self-deluding jerk. Shandling is Eddie's and Mickey's crass neighbor, another Hollywood wannabe, who passes on to them Bonnie (Paquin), a pretty 15-year-old drifter who proves to have a better grip on herself and the universe than everybody else.

"Hurlyburly" isn't a movie about Hollywood the way, for example, "The Big Knife" is. The Hollywood setting certainly intensifies the slipperiness of its people's existences and heightens their on-the-make natures. But since the drama does take place here, Rabe might have made more of Eddie's connection to Hollywood to reveal more of him to us. We never know if he came here with a dream of doing something creative in films or from the start was just out to make big bucks.

"Hurlyburly" means to be a scabrous screwball comedy, but it's too grueling, too heavy-handed and too obvious to be very funny. You find yourself agreeing with Donna's observation that she finds Eddie and his friends without socially redeeming value, and you're again left to wonder why, apart from casting coups, there's such a hullabaloo about "Hurlyburly."

NEW YORK, 1/18/99, p. 61, Peter Rainer

There's a whole lot of overacting going on in *Hurlyburly*, which stars—take a deep breath—Sean Penn, Kevin Spacey, Robin Wright Penn, Chazz Palminteri, Garry Shandling, Anna

Paquin, and Meg Ryan. It's like a Master Thespian convention. (To be fair, Spacey and Shandling don't overact, exactly; they over-under-act.) David Rabe's celebrated 1984 play, which he adapted for the screen and Anthony Drazan directed, doesn't satisfy in the transition. Being up-close and personal for two hours with a gaggle of Hollywood sleazeballs is repellent, all right, but on the big screen, it's clearer than ever that Rabe wants to enlarge the meaning of our repugnance—he wants to turn the coke-snorting, swinging-sex eighties L.A. scene into some kind of template for all our spiritual ills. But what's funny about this mixed-nuts assortment of casting directors, producers, strippers, unemployed actors, and Lolitas is precisely the *smallness* of their existence. They don't stand for anything—not even themselves. They should call *this* movie *A Bug's Life.*

NEW YORK POST, 12/23/98, p. 45, Rod Dreher

Is there a year-end award for Best Acting in Worst Movie? Give it to the exemplary cast of the appalling "Hurlyburly."

How bad can a movie be when the great Sean Penn leads a cast that includes Kevin Spacey, Chazz Palminteri, Garry Shandling, Robin Wright Penn and Meg Ryan?

You have no idea.

It's like this: Do you want to see the perky "You've Got Mail" girl playing a character joked about by a bunch of guys for having performed oral sex on one of them while her small child was in the back seat? Do you want to see Anna Paquin playing a runaway whore passed around by the same fellows like an inflatable doll?

Nothing says "Happy Holidays" like a two-hour coked-up, motormouthed wallow with some of the most hateful, degraded and altogether unbearable characters to sputter across the big screen all year. And they won't shut up!

It came from the '80s. David Rabe adapted the screenplay from his Broadway play about sleazy, self-absorbed Hollywood guys extending their adolescence with easy sex, piles of drugs and casual, corrosive cynicism. Penn plays Eddie, a squirrelly casting agent who shares a luxury house with Mickey (Spacey), his business partner. Mickey is "taking a break" from his wife and kids.

They drink, do drugs, screw around, and entertain themselves trading nasty barbs with their friends Artie (Shandling) and luggish Phil (Palminteri). Eddie can't seem to get any work done, so distracted is he by jealousy over Mickey's brief affair with Darlene (Wright Penn), his old flame.

Meanwhile, Lolita-on-the-lam Donna (Paquin) turns up to serve as recreation for the big boys, who later recruit and abuse exotic dancer Bonnie (Meg Ryan) for their sexual amusement. In "Hurlyburly," all the women and children are there solely for the amusement of these no-count dirtbags, who yammer incessantly—incessantly!—about their vulgar and pointless lives.

Eddie spends the movie skittering along from one nervous crisis of meaning to another. He senses something is deeply wrong with his life, yet has no idea how to get things in order. Fear, paranoia, confusion, and loathing come sputtering out in a geyser of profane, jackhammery gibberish.

As pointless, headachy and unrelenting as this picture is, there is unusually fine ensemble acting on display. Sean Penn is simply phenomenal, as usual, giving another of his electric performances in a film far beneath his talent ("U-Turn," and "She's So Lovely" being recent examples). Spacey modulates self-interest and hostility with cold, silvery malice. Indeed, all the performances are far better than the verbose dross of a script.

At the film's fevered height, Darlene spouts, "I cannot stand this semantic insanity anymore!" Truer words...

VILLAGE VOICE, 12/29/98, p. 120, J. Hoberman

More grueling than anything in *The Thin Red Line*, [See Hoberman's review], *Hurlyburly* is another spectacle of men together doing bad things—if not an argument for war. Indeed, the only reason not to ship the guys played by Sean Penn, Kevin Spacey, Chazz Palminteri, and Garry Shandling to Guadalcanal would be to keep them out of your foxhole.

Directed by Anthony Drazan from David Rabe's mid-'80s ensemble drama of Hollywood hacks coking up and getting down, *Hurlyburly* is a raging torrent of misogynist self-pity—mostly staged in the unaccountably beautiful pad shared by manic Penn and fastidiously suave Spacey. As the most conflicted of the group, Penn gives a flamboyant, lurching performance—rivaled for stridence by the Method conundrum of Palminteri's badly-acted impersonation of a bad actor. (Palminteri's scenes with the slightly more skillful Meg Ryan, playing an up-for-anything tart, have the behavioral fascination of a community college acting class.)

Given that these characters are even more delusional than the movies they make, Rabe's dialogue is not without its mordant zing. "I am my own biggest distraction," Penn complains to his love object (an eloquently inarticulate Robin Wright Penn). Not so. Drazan's heavy-handed direction and clumsy camera-placement cuts the performers too much slack, then competes with their antics for attention.

Also reviewed in:
CHICAGO TRIBUNE, 12/25/98, Friday/p. P, Michael Wilmington
NEW REPUBLIC, 1/18/99, p. 26, Stanley Kauffmann
NEW YORK TIMES, 12/24/98, p. E1, Stephen Holden
VARIETY, 9/14-20/98, p. 36, David Rooney
WASHINGTON POST, 12/25/98, p. C5, Stephen Hunter
WASHINGTON POST, 12/25/98, Weekend/p. 8, Michael O'Sullivan

HURRICANE STREETS

A United Artists release of a (giv'an) production.   *Executive Producer:* L.M. Kit Carson and Cynthia Hargrave.   *Producer:* Galt Niederhoffer, Gill Holland, and Morgan J. Freeman. *Director:* Morgan J. Freeman.   *Screenplay:* Morgan J. Freeman.   *Director of Photography:* Enrique Chediak.   *Editor:* Sabine Hoffman.   *Music:* Theodore Shapiro.   *Sound:* Robert Taz Larrea.   *Sound Editor:* Margaret Crimmins and Paul D. Hsu.   *Casting:* Susan Shopmaker. *Production Designer:* Petra Barchi.   *Art Director:* Iliana Sakas.   *Special Effects:* Ralis Khan and Robert Yoho.   *Costumes:* Nancy Brous.   *Make-up:* Callie French.   *Running time:* 88 minutes. *MPAA Rating:* R.

CAST: Brendan Sexton III (Marcus);   Antoine McLean (Harold);   Mtume Gant (Louis); Carlo Alban (Benny);   David Roland Frank (Chip);   Adrian Grenier (Punk);   Lynn Cohen (Lucy);   L.M.Kit Carson (Mack);   Edie Falco (Joanna);   Isidra Vega (Melena);   Andrew Ko (Little Kid);   José Zuniga (Kramer);   Terry Alexander (Duane);   Heather Matarazzo (Ashley); Shawn Elliott (Paco);   Socorro Santiago (Gloria);   Jin S. Kim (Lee);   Damian Corrente (Justin); David Moscow (Shane);   Preston B. Handy and Terry Sturiano (Detectives);   Anna Basoli (Social Worker);   Richard Petrocelli (Hank);   Leslie Body (Police Man).

LOS ANGELES TIMES, 2/13/98, Calendar/p. 24, John Anderson

[The following review by John Anderson appeared in a slightly different form in **NEWSDAY, 2/13/98, Part II/p. B11.]**

Brendan Sexton III, the self-styled "rapist" of "Welcome to the Dollhouse," has a still-forming, pimple-flocked face with the kind of downy deposit under the nose that an adolescent never shaves for fear it won't grow back. It's a face that, even after the several nasty beatings it takes in "Hurricane Streets," retains an engaging aspect, even when wrapped around an asthma inhaler, a most unorthodox sidearm for a budding teenage criminal.

"Budding" may not be the word; "destined" may be more apt. In "Hurricane Streets," a kind of East (Village) Side Story, Sexton's young Marcus is turning 15, growing up around his grandma's bar, racing his bike around Alphabet City, shoplifting in Chinatown and selling contraband CDs and sneakers to kids at local public schools; it's small-time stuff with a lot of growth potential. He has a good heart; Melena (Isidra Vega), his 13-year-old paramour, certainly thinks so.

But his mother (Edie Falco) is in prison, his father is dead. Melena's father is an obsessively protective nut ball. In the dubious moral universe of independent movies, what these ingredients add up to is Marcus, resist though he may, being sucked into a vortex of larceny and mayhem.

And whether that is really justifiable in the great scheme of things is one of the more dubious presumptions in what is otherwise a generally entertaining little street drama. The acting is particularly good—not just that of Sexton and Vega but also of Marcus' sidekicks (David Roland Frank, Antoine McLean, Carlo Alban and Mtume Gant) and Lynn Cohen as his grandmother and L.M. Kit Carson (who with wife Cynthia Hargrave executive-produced the film) as the barfly-felon Mack. Frequently, however, the cast's best efforts can't surmount the more sophomoric qualities of the script—it strains terribly hard, for instance, to use teenage slang without really incorporating it. Occasionally, you can see what might have been terrific performances undone by ungraceful dialogue and less than sure-handed direction.

But at the same time, "Hurricane Streets" (which, as "Hurricane," was a much-talked-about participant at the '97 Sundance festival) has a lot of heart. Debuting director Morgan J. Freeman can be credited with creating something that's more urban fantasia than verite street fare. Kids with beepers and guns and casually violent attitudes or problems at home aren't rare or new, but dreamers are. And whether it's the New Mexico of Marcus' mind or the moon of Melena's, what Freeman's characters are about is space and hopes. In this, "Hurricane Streets" is less about the way things are than the way we think they might be, or should be, or could be.

NEW YORK POST, 2/13/98, p. 53, Larry Worth

It sounds like a sequel to "Twister," which it's not. But the ill winds that define "Hurricane Streets" are no less daunting.

First-time writer-director Morgan J. Freeman has turned a formulaic coming-of-age story on its ear, opting for, a gritty, downbeat, utterly compelling look at street-wise kids from Manhattan's Lower East Side.

The focus is on 14-year-old Marcus, who cuts school, mourns his late dad, shoplifts with pals and dreams of a better future. On a typical day, Marcus cruises a music store's aisles, trying to decide the resale value for stolen Hanson CDs.

Marcus believes it's a temporary way of life, one that will change when Mom's released from prison and they can move to New Mexico. In the meantime, there's Melena, a likable teen who roller skates through the neighborhood and gives his hormones reason to rage.

But once accepting his Artful Dodger-like existence, peers push Marcus toward a higher criminal profile. And as family secrets threaten to explode, the stage is set for a new level of tragedy.

With the exception of a final twist too many, Freeman seamlessly weaves the melodrama within the tale's slice-of-life setting. That's what makes his vision of adolescent agony, first love, the death of hope and a world of violence seem fresh and vital.

It's further enhanced by a great score, best exemplified as Supple's version of "Stayin' Alive" brings dark new meaning to the Bee Gees' classic lyrics.

Best of all, Freeman avoids genre pitfalls, as in refusing to make parents and authority figures into easy foils for the young protagonists. Instead, he lends dignity and a three-dimensional quality to all in his sphere.

Leading the fine cast is Brendan Sexton III, a remarkable young actor who first made his mark in Todd Solondz's "Welcome to the Dollhouse." As Marcus, he exudes a likable quality while conveying inner turmoil, honesty and vulnerability with the subtlest gesture or inflection.

Newcomer Isidra Vega also stands out as the girl caught between Marcus and her over-protective dad. Brief turns from Edie Falco as Marcus' guilt-ridden mother and Heather "Welcome to the Dollhouse" Matarazzo's confused onlooker help fuel the emotional juggernaut.

Though it's been 13 months since "Hurricane Streets" stormed Sundance (and emerged with three top awards), the end result more than justifies the wait.

SIGHT AND SOUND, 6/98, p. 46, Charlotte O'Sullivan

New Yorker Marcus is 15 years old. With his mother in prison and his father dead, he lives with his grandmother, hangs out in   his 'den' near the river and goes shoplifting with his gang. He meet Melena, a Latino girl. She and Marcus begin seeing each other secretly because of her overprotective father. When Marcus is arrested for selling stolen goods, the police let slip that his mother is in jail for shooting his father. Meanwhile, one of Marcus' gang, Chip, is keen to commit a serious crime and Melena's father Paco discovers she's been seeing Marcus and confronts them. Marcus punches him; the couple spend the night in a tent.

Marcus and Melena plan to go to Alaska. Since Marcus now needs money, he agrees to Chip's plan to break into a house, where Harold, another member of the gang, finds a gun. While they are out, Melena's father breaks into the den and hearing the boys returning from their robbery, hides in a cupboard. Harold fire the gun and the bullet kills Melena's father. Harold turns himself in and the police start rounding up the gang. A penniless Marcus tries selling the gun. When this fails, he commits a hold-up. He meets Melena at Penn Station and they board their train.

Hurricane Streets comes laden with awards from the Sundance festival and there's certainly much to recommend it. Star Brendan Sexton III (the soulful bully from *Welcome to the Dollhouse*) gives a beautifully awkward performance as Marcus, a trouble-beset urchin, alternately cringing and swaggering beneath his pastrami-red spots. Meanwhile, fellow *Dollhouse* star Heather Matarazzo—hunched, myopic, prematurely middle-aged—packs more idiosyncratic charm into her split-second cameo than most grown-up actors manage in a whole movie.

Sadly, the film itself resembles a cross between the Hughes Brothers' cliché-ridden *Menace II Society* (even down to the opening shot of a hold-up, which functions here as a flashforward) and the rambling, sunny-sad soap *The Kids of Degrassi Street*. The trouble lies primarily with Freeman's old-fashioned script, which has limitless sympathy for its hero and heroine but little to spare for anybody else. These days, we expect youth films to be more sophisticated. For instance, Larry Clark's *kids* had its moralistic side, but at least it threw a dead, contemptuous eye over *everyone*.

Director Freeman goes to great lengths to show Marcus as an ideal leader, while suggesting it's only freedom and love that he craves. New York is the glamorous enemy (Marcus' asthma is an obvious metaphor for the contaminating dangers of city life), because good-American boy Marcus is a frontiersman at heart, dreaming of going to New Mexico. He often says he just wants "to have some space" and he is repeatedly referred to as a "cowboy".

Of course, rights and responsibilities go hand in hand. We get a whole subplot involving blasted ex-hippie Mack to prove that Marcus is mature enough to give up his dream if someone weak needs it more than he does (Marcus gives Mack his New Mexico plane ticket). Freeman's attempt to justify certain juvenile crimes is truly a worthy endeavour. But Marcus is so saintly, and the rights and wrongs so tidily organised, we feel no tension at all.

Full of short scenes which do nothing except push the plot along, *Hurricane Streets* is also flawed by overlong camera shots and wistful bouts of harmonica playing. And while Enrique Chediak's interior cinematography is polished (the scenes in Marcus' grandmother's bar have a pleasantly rootless, *Trees Lounge* feel), the outdoor takes lack originality. In particular, Freeman's desire to get the pulse moving with chase scenes (the movie seems to be itching to get back to its pumping, trendy soundtrack), reduces New York to a predictable series of busy streets.

However, the most complexly treated theme in the film concerns fatherhood. It turns out both Marcus and Melena come from homes in which the father physically abused his wife and child; both men die violently, with their last moments shrouded in secrecy. The film ends with the young lovers, Melena and Marcus, calmly slumped in a train. Has Melena discovered the truth about papa? On the one hand, we can assume her demeanour indicates that she is blissfully unaware, but it could just as well signal apathy. It's a nice ambiguity, leaving us to decide whether abusive fathers should be mourned, especially when their deaths bring freedom. The jolting, queasy mix of feelings we experience on realising that the couple may "get away" with their dream provides (at long last) something of a surprise.

VILLAGE VOICE, 2/17/98, p. 116, Amy Taubin

It sounds like the movie you've seen once too often: Loisaida 15-year-olds from broken homes ride bikes, shoplift, fall in love, fear for their lives, and dream of escaping the city's potholes for the wide open spaces of New Mexico and Alaska. But *Hurricane Streets* (which was titled *Hurricane* when it won three major awards at Sundance in 1997) is, moment by moment, more compelling and heartfelt than its plot summary suggests. First-time filmmaker Morgan J. Freeman and actor Brendan Sexton III (who impressed as the wannabe rapist in *Welcome to the Dollhouse*) have collaborated on a memorable character. Marcus is the leader of a small group of bike-riding adolescents who gleefully rip off the downtown Tower Records and neighboring Broadway boutiques and sell their loot to elementary school kids. As introspective as he is impulsive, Marcus has a sense of responsibility beyond his years. Maybe he gets it from his grandmother, a life-affirming Avenue A bartender who's been taking care of him most of his life. His father's dead; his mother's in jail. Powerless to win her release, Marcus displaces his rescue fantasy onto his peers, and in particular onto a sly 14-year-old Latina whose father brutalizes her. Marcus's fantasy is so strong that it transcends the limits of the screen. It makes us want to save him.

Sexton brings a startling honesty and sense of moral purpose to his characterization. One of the few young actors who is able to silently reveal inner thoughts and emotions, he carries the film from beginning to end. The rest of the cast is quite good, particularly Edie Falco as Marcus's mother and Isidra Vega as the girl he falls in love with. Freeman knows how to shape a scene dramatically. Because he gives the actors the time they need to get from here to there emotionally, *Hurricane* almost never feels hyped-up or exploitative. And his direction is abetted by Enrique Chediak's cinematography, which is fluid and expressive without being obtrusive.

That's not to say the film doesn't have awkward moments. Freeman's not as sophisticated a writer as he is a director. As Marcus's predicament becomes increasingly dire, Freeman's plotting becomes predictable. First there's one gun in the picture, then there are two, then the character who's the biggest obstacle to our hero's happiness just happens to get in the way of a bullet that's not meant for him. Imperfectly wrought and matter-of-factly unoriginal, *Hurricane* is, nevertheless, a winning filmmaking debut.

Also reviewed in:
NEW YORK TIMES, 2/13/98, p. E28, Stephen Holden
VARIETY, 2/3-9/97, p. 44, Todd McCarthy

HUSH

A TriStar Pictures release of a Douglas Wick production. *Producer:* Douglas Wick. *Director:* Jonathan Darby. *Screenplay:* Jonathan Darby and Jane Rusconi. *Story:* Jonathan Darby. *Director of Photography:* Andrew Dunn. *Editor:* Dan Rae, Lynzee Klingman, and Robert Leighton. *Music:* Christopher Young. *Music Editor:* Thomas Milano. *Sound:* Jay Meagher. *Sound Editor:* Sandy Berman. *Casting:* Heidi Levitt and Billy Hopkins. *Production Designer:* Thomas A. Walsh and Michael Johnston. *Art Director:* James Truesdale. *Set Designer:* Easton Michael Smith. *Set Decorator:* Michael Seirton. *Set Dresser:* Michael D. Harrell and Bob Renna. *Special Effects:* David P. Kelsey. *Costumes:* Ann Roth. *Make-up:* Vivian Baker. *Stunt Coordinator:* Glory Fioramonti. *Running time:* 110 minutes. *MPAA Rating:* R.

CAST: Jessica Lange (Martha); Gwyneth Paltrow (Helen); Johnathon Schaech (Jackson); Nina Foch (Alice Baring); Debi Mazar (Lisa); Kaiulani Lee (Sister O'Shaughnessy); David Thornton (Gavin); Hal Holbrook (Dr. Hill); Richard Lineback (Hal Bentall); Richard Kohn (Clayton Richards); Faith Potts (Georgina Richards); Tom Story (Priest); Jolene Carroll (Church Warden); Jacob Press (Usher); Joe Inscoe (Doctor); Catherine Shaffner (Nurse); Lenny Steinline (Paramedic); Rick Gray (Banker); Tom Holmes (Auctioneer); Owen Valentine (Official); Ricardo Miguel Young and Woody Robertson, Jr. (Policemen); Charles

Thomas Baxter (Racing Enthusiast);   Jayne Hess (Nursing Home Nun);   Sarah Elspas, Rebecda Elspas, and Jacob Elspas (Helen's Baby).

LOS ANGELES TIMES, 3/9/98, Calendar/p. 4, David Chute

It's probably not the filmmaker's fault that "Hush" is being peddled as a family-pathology slasher film, like "The Stepfather" or "The Hand That Rocks the Cradle." Still, the prospect of catching Jessica Lange in a late-period Bette Davis role, as a smother-mother gargoyle, is bound to attract some unwary thrill-seekers. And they are bound to be disappointed.

"Hush" is a would-be suspense film without a single major plot twist that isn't ham-handed. You can spot every portentous clue the second director Jonathan Darby shoves your nose in, usually in a giant close-up. Flashing neon arrows might make the plot signals easier to read, but only slightly.

The movie's legitimate ancestors are such Golden Age gothic romances as "Rebecca," in which an ingenuous willowy young thing is introduced into the claustrophobic atmosphere of a sinister family manse, and then menaced until all the household's dark secrets are revealed.

Long-stemmed Gwyneth Paltrow, as Helen, has the Joan Fontaine beleaguered-innocent part, an awkward Christmas guest at the palatial Virginia horse-breeding estate of her architect boyfriend, Jackson (Johnathon Schaech) and Martha, his filterless-Camel-puffing widowed mom.

Martha wants her beloved son to return home and take over the family business, which has been on the skids recently, and her interest in breeding seems to have shifted focus from thoroughbred foals to thoroughbred grandchildren.

Lange provides Momma Martha with an impressive array of quivery seductive mannerisms; she simpers and shrugs and toys with her frizzy curls, wired and watchful. We can practically hear the gears meshing. Lange seems to be having fun with this jittery, crafty character, but her weirdness is so overt that it strains credulity.

"Hush" deploys many classic visual indicators of suspense; maybe a few too many. There are strange murmuring interludes in front of bedroom mirrors, a shower of stiff rat corpses from an attic trap door and the looming shadow of a huge veterinary syringe, gliding across the floor toward a helpless woman in the throes of childbirth.

Nothing works, and almost nothing pays off. The transformation of victim into aggressor, just in time for the limp finale, is so abrupt and unmotivated that it doesn't deliver a satisfying table-turning charge. Jackson's character is a blank, and Schaech is from the Victor Mature-Peter Gallagher class of bland handsomeness. He's a trophy hunk.

The strangest aspect of "Hush" is its seeming squeamishness about the clingy central relationship. It introduces with leers, and then primly dances away from, the obvious possibility that Martha's feelings toward her strapping son are not altogether healthy. The pivotal issue seems to be class rather than family. Martha is typed as a social climber, a former stable girl who set her sights on the young lord of the manor and has been scheming ever since to scoop up all the marbles.

All the good people in the film are bluebloods, and all the proles are predatory. (Helen's social standing isn't specified, but nobody in movies looks more effortlessly aristocratic than Paltrow.)

So it isn't mother-love but a thirst for status that shoves poor Martha off the deep end. That's a less than enthralling premise, and Lange never does get a chance to cut loose.

NEW YORK POST, 3/6/98, p. 47, Larry Worth

If nothing else, "Hush"—a thriller that's virtually devoid of thrills—marks a turning point in Jessica Lange's career: Professionally speaking, she's got a bigger monkey on her back than 1976's "King Kong."

So the question remains: Why would a two-time Oscar winner—who long ago proved naysayers wrong after squirming in the big ape's grip—sign on for such unredeeming claptrap?

Well, maybe Lange thought it would be challenging to play a dragon lady. As for co-star and current golden girl Gwyneth Paltrow, she probably wanted to work with Lange.

The sorry script has Paltrow traveling with boyfriend Johnathon Schaech to his boyhood home in Kentucky's bluest hills, a Tara-like manse with its own version of Scarlett. But mommie dearest Lange makes Miss O'Hara's machinations into mere fiddle-dee-dee.

Lange—who's desperate for a grandson—has no sooner toyed with Paltrow's diaphragm than a pregnancy is announced. So Paltrow and Schaech tie the knot, move in with the skirted menace and live happily ever after, right?

Well, that *would* be a surprise in this utterly predictable, Oedipally-edged nonsense. Virtually every development is telegraphed light years ahead of its happening. For instance, when Paltrow says that she'll never forget an assailant's voice, you can bet the house on her hearing it again pre-finale.

It's no secret in Hollywood that "Hush" has been kicking around for a couple years, endured various title changes and revised endings. But the implausible, no-payoff conclusion which Darby settled on will have boo-birds in full chorus.

In his feature-film debut, Darby shows zero potential. A clear graduate of the Sledgehammer School of Directing, he doesn't even provide enough fun to make "Hush" a guilty pleasure.

He also wastes most of his stellar cast. Paltrow and Schaech make a very handsome couple, but have precious little opportunity to shine. Equally sad, supporting players Hal Holbrook, Debi Mazar and Nina Foch barely register.

To her infinite credit, Lange still delivers the goods. Rather than settling for a "Dynasty"-like matriarch, she drips honeyed Southern tones into a steel magnolia persona. And even when exposing those iron claws, she never goes over the top.

But one good performance can't justify this lunacy. Even Lange would doubtless agree that—when it comes to "Hush" (never mind "King Kong")—the less said, the better.

NEWSDAY, 3/9/98, Part II/p. B2, John Anderson

How many blondes does it take to make a thoroughly unconvincing, overheated-to-the-point-of-lukewarm psycho-drama-cum-"Medea"-goes-gaga about a son-fixated mother, a mother-fixated son and the daughter-in-law with suspicions about one, when she should be giving both the brush-off?

Two. In "Hush" (which wasn't made available to critics, which means no one had any confidence in it, anyway), Jessica Lange is Martha, queen of Kilronan, a failing horse farm in … well, horse country. Gwyneth Paltrow, looking as gilt as any lily, is Helen, who's living with Martha's son, Jackson (Johnathon Schaech), in New York, where both have lovely jobs. Martha wants Jackson to come home and save the farm, Helen to give her a grandchild (and we mean give her a grandchild) and then go away, because what she really wants is Jackson.

Lange, whose Martha is a reprise of her Broadway Blanche DuBois with a side order of Mrs. Danvers ("Rebecca"), is a pretty, hysterical, fading southern belle, one with a morgue's-worth of skeletons in her closet—and, as much as we hate to say it, a son who's none too swift. But, as directed by Jonathan Darby, one never gets the sense that the characters, played by Lange and Schaech (or Lange and Schaech themselves, for that matter) had ever met before the shooting started.

Paltrow, on the other hand, doesn't have a lot to do besides look golden and blow-dried, despite the fact that Helen was an orphan and had the toughest of rows to hoe. But hers is a big future. After returning from Kilronan to their ratty New York apartment (which would bring, let's say, $3,500 a month on the open market), she gets to impersonate George Bush, throwing up on her boss during a big meeting. There's only one conclusion to draw, of course, and once she's mugged in her own home, Helen is more than willing to split the city and raise the little yuppie-to-be on the stately grounds of stately Kilronan (directions: start putting two and two together here).

Let it be said that "Hush" is totally unconvincing—thrillers are always far more satisfying when the villain's motivation is more than just lunacy—but there are ways of amusing oneself while watching this thing. Helen's pregnancy, for example: At any given moment, the bulge beneath her maternity wear could be anything from a throw-pillow to a '47 Buick. The climactic childbirth—which Martha makes Helen go through with nary a bullet to bite on—has little long-lasting effects on Helen, who gets up in the morning and knocks Martha on her can. That old Jackson seems to spend the entire film in a state of suspended animation is something that's not worth the time to discuss, since this is, after all, a film about cosmic, metaphoric femaleness, however disturbed and unreal.

Also reviewed in:
CHICAGO TRIBUNE, 3/6/98, Friday/p. N, Michael Wilmington
NEW YORK TIMES, 3/7/98, p. B10, Stephen Holden
VARIETY, 3/9-15/98, p. 41, Todd McCarthy
WASHINGTON POST, 3/6/98, p. D7, Rita Kempley

I GOT THE HOOK-UP

A Dimension Films release in association with No Limit Films & Priority Films of a Shooting Star Pictures production. *Executive Producer:* Master P. *Producer:* Jonathan Heuer. *Director:* Michael Martin. *Screenplay:* Master P., Leroy Douglas, Carrie Mungo. *Director of Photography:* Antonio Calvache. *Editor:* T. David Binns. *Music:* Andrew Shack. *Music Editor:* Lionel Ball. *Sound:* Rich MacLane. *Sound Editor:* David Bach. *Casting:* Stevie "Black" Lockett. *Production Designer:* Michael Pearce. *Art Director:* Daina Kramer. *Set Decorator:* Jennifer Fraser. *Set Dresser:* Nancy Dahl. *Special Effects:* Wayne Beauchamp, Eric Beauchamp, and Kevin Beauchamp. *Costumes:* Jhane Isaacs. *Make-up:* Gloria Elias. *Make-up Effects:* Marc Linn. *Stunt Coordinator:* Julius Leflore. *Running time:* 93 minutes. *MPAA Rating:* R.

CAST: Master P (Black); A.J. Johnson (Blue); Gretchen Palmer (Lorraine); Frantz Turner (Dalton); Richard Keats (Jim Brady); Joe Estevez (Lamar Hunt); William Knight (Agent in Charge); Anthony Boswell (Little Brother); Mack Morris (Andrew); Mia X (Lola Mae); Tomm "Tiny" Lister, Jr. (T-Lay); Corey Miller, Edward Smith, and Michael L. Taylor (T-Lay Boys); Pablo Marz (Hispanic Man); Tangie Ambrose (Nasty Mouth Carla); Harrison White (Tootsie Pop); Howard Mungo (Mr. Tucker); Laura Hayes (Mrs. Tucker); Richard Balin (Communications Trucker); Ella Mae Evans and Judy Jean Berns (Customers); Kourtney Locke (Little Girl); John Witherspoon (Mr. Mims); John Wesley (Minister); Lawrence Williams (Family Member #1); Vercy Carter (Family Member #2); Izetta Karp (Ms. Rose); Paula Bellamy Franklin (Old Lady #1); Dollie Butler (Old Lady #2); Helen Martin (Grandmother); Tommy Chunn (Dooley); Leland Ellis (Man); Sacha Kemp (Woman); Duffy Rich (Policeman #1); Andrew Shack (Policeman #2); Cindy L. Sorensen (Martha); Dana Woods (Big Daddy); Will Gill, Jr. (Black Lamar); Jerry Dixon (Black Jim); Ice Cube (Gun Runner); Daniel Garcia (Lorraine's Lover); David Garcia and Eric Vidal (D.J.s); Michael D. Harris (Homeless Man); Sheryl Underwood (Bad Mouth Bessie).

LOS ANGELES TIMES, 5/27/98, Calendar/p. 4, David Chute

The movie subgenre once known (and denigrated) as "blaxploitation" is alive and well, although today's specimens (like the recent "Players Club"), unlike the older examples, are often actually made by African Americans, rather than by whites cashing in. The predatory nature of this kind of fare is a constant, though. Is it really a sign of progress that black audiences are now being ripped off by their own?

One thing can be said for the newest of these pictures, "I Got the Hook-Up," an alleged comedy celebrating the fun and excitement of inner-city crime (drive-bys as slapstick): It's at least consistent; the film itself is a crime in progress.

This is the first movie written and produced—as an acting vehicle for himself—by rapper and music industry entrepreneur Master P, whose No Limit label is (according to the press packet) "the most successful independent record company in the country." (Nineteen No Limit tunes and/or artists are showcased on the soundtrack.)

In fact, P himself is the film's strongest element, a sturdy, steadying presence in the midst of grating chaos. Most of the supporting characters are garish eccentrics who face off periodically to scream obscenities at one another.

Master P and the super-hyper stand-up comic A.J. Johnson ("Players Club") are known as Black and Blue, con artists who have set up a sprawling off-the-books department store in a vacant lot in South-Central L.A. Their scam du jour is peddling jury-rigged illegal cell phones that bug out as often as they ring true. The comic possibilities in the premise of a city full of crossed connections are barely explored. Within minutes, a scary thug (Tommy "Tiny" Lister Jr.) gets a bum phone, a money drop goes wrong, and the picture devolves into a chase comedy set to a sledgehammer beat.

The subject matter, as such, is not the problem. Similar material has been deployed by some of the strongest rappers and by the hard-boiled masters of street-level black crime writing: Chester Himes, Iceberg Slim and Donald Goines.

As a filmmaker spinning a tall tale of players, hustlers and thieves, Master P may believe he's carrying on that urban folklore, Staggerlee tradition. But his actual touchstones seem to be so-called"chitlin circuit" farces, faded reruns of "Sanford and Son:" (the junkyard setting) and even the all-in-fun stereotyping of "Amos 'n' Andy," to which the film refers in passing.

NEW YORK POST, 5/27/98, p. 42, Larry Worth

When a pair of urban hustlers run one scam too many, vengeful mobsters, ripped-off customers, disgruntled FBI agents and a buxom ex-accomplice want them to disappear—but no more so than "I Got the Hook-Up" audience members.

It's hard to feel anything but revulsion for the protagonists—rapper Master P (who co-wrote the hideous script) and would-be comic A.J. Johnson—never ming the disgusting production that spotlights them.

This is a world where every man is a crack-smoking idiot, every woman is a 'ho whose sass ranges from tart to Tourette's, and guns are the toy of choice. With flying bullets used as comic fodder, is it any wonder kids think they're playthings?

What passes for a plot has the two snake-oil salesmen fencing a cache of bootleg cellulars. When the gadgets' crossed wires leads to a blown drug deal for the local crime czar, the boys go on the lam.

Sure enough, chase scene after chase scene follows, along with such cliched standbys as the foul-talking granny, bare-breasted fly-girls, a 6-foot transvestite and nerdy white folks.

And, of course, the mastermind behind the boys' phone scheme (stunner Gretchen Palmer) is an African-American vamp, whose dirty dealings get her fired by her uptight honky boss. Exploiting the race card further still, whites and blacks masquerade as each other (via latex masks) to manipulate the boys in the 'hood. Nice.

Completing the scenario: requisite bathroom humor, an ear-blasting hip-hop soundtrack, pointless cameos from Ice Cube and Snoop Doggy Dog and more profanity—in the first 10 minutes alone!—than Martin Lawrence at his ugliest. There's something to offend everyone.

For that, one can thank first-time director Michael Martin, who proves beyond all doubt that he's got bad taste down to a science.

On the other hand, Martin dutifully remembers to thank Mom and Dad in the end credits. They must be so proud.

NEWSDAY, 5/27/98, Part II/p. B9, Bob Heisler

Meaning no disrespect to Master P, the rap entrepreneur who grew his Los Angeles record store into a major independent record company, but is the collection of ugly, humorless stereotypes who populate his "I Got the Hook-up" any less offensive because the creator is down with the homeys?

The sound track to "I Got the Hook-up" is already on the Billboard charts, so let's call the movie bad and move on. Master P will be back on the big screen. But someone should risk the master's wrath and suggest that he hook up with a writer to make a movie that reflects the strength and power of his music and the styling of his videos instead of stringing together a series of awkward, badly filmed, improvised scenes that consist primarily of words that rhyme with words that can't appear in this newspaper.

Not that there's anything worth quoting. The dialogue would have embarrassed Redd Foxx. All right, here is one line:

"Is that a cell phone in your pocket or are you just happy to see me?"

Master P stars as Black, the smart/serious half of a fenced-goods shopping center partnership in South Central L.A. That his partner is called Blue (A.J. Johnson) suggests the wit and wisdom of the script. The pair get a load of cellular phones (the delivery man mistakes Black for a Mr. Goldstein), Black connects with a friend who can activate them and an old girlfriend who can cover things at the phone company. Lorraine (Gretchen Palmer), the girlfriend eager to squeeze Black into her over-booked sex schedule, is the only character with a legit job.

But instead of a rip-off-the-oppressors attitude that would make Black and Blue the heroes, P's script makes them simply another set of chumps ripping off their friends and relatives. Apparently, the genre that is "urban caper comedy" absolves its makers from responsibility for any motivation except the pursuit of cash.

When that pursuit interferes with a neighborhood criminal's operation—and the phone company gets wise—the music kicks and the chases begin with only short breaks to put down family, religion, women, friendship and people who are different in all the ways that make a community.

That's a lot of folks to abuse, but director Michael Martin's pace takes care of business with time left over to give an on-screen shout to rappers, including Snoop Doggy Dog and Ice Cube, and to let things get out of hand completely when characters change their race at the drop of a mask.

VILLAGE VOICE, 6/9/98, p. 148, Gary Dauphin

Multimillionaire rapper Master P's second film, *I Got the Hook-Up*, Is a typical sophomore letdown that keeps it real only in traditional, bad-meaning-bad ways: real dumb, real stupid, really badly made. Unlike his single-minded debut, the straight-to-video revenge fantasy *I'm 'Bout It*, *I Got the Hook-Up* is a disjointed comedy about two street-corner hustlers (bigman P and A.J. Johnson as his gruff, Chihuahua-like sidekick) who luck into a batch of cell phones. Running afoul of the mob and the feds, the pair skitter from half-baked gangsterism to aimless rounds of the dozens to pointless mack set pieces. Having managed to will two feature films into existence, P apparently didn't have time to spare on things like character or story. Few shots are fired, and the fantasy ghetto P creates is full of wild Jerry Springer-meets-William Gibson flourishes (the transvestite prostitutes and hot-sex skeezers give head and hack data-bases with equal skill), but *I Got the Hook-Up* is really no more than another interesting footnote in the ongoing story of how people can get rich selling the same old shit.

Also reviewed in:
NEW YORK TIMES, 5/27/98, p. E5, Lawrence Van Gelder
VARIETY, 6/1-7/98, p. 34, Joe Leydon

I LOVE YOU, DON'T TOUCH ME!

A Goldwyn Entertainment Company and   Westie Films release in association with Big Hair Productions. *Executive Producer:* Jennifer Chaiken. *Producer:* Julie Davis and Scott Chosed. *Director:* Julie Davis.   *Screenplay:* Julie Davis.   *Director of Photography:* Mark Putnam. *Editor:* Julie Davis. *Music:* Sharal Churchill and Jane Ford. *Sound:* Lee Howell. *Casting:* Karen Church. *Production Designer:* Carol Strober.   *Set Designer:* Karen Numme.   *Set Decorator:* Caroline Halili.   *Set Dresser:* Dorothy Drysdale. *Costumes:* Wendy Greiner. *Make-up:* Brandi Robertson. *Stunt Coordinator:* Ignacio Alvarez. *Running time:* 90 minutes. *MPAA Rating:* R.

CAST: Marla Schaffel (Katie); Mitchell Whitfield (Ben); Michael Harris (Richard Webber); Meredith Scott Lynn (Janet); Darryl Theirse (Jones); Nancy Sorel (Elizabeth); Wally Kurth (David Barclay);   Jack McGee (Lou Candela); Julie Ariola (Mom);   Victor Raider-Wexler (Dad); Sara Van Horn (Analyst); Debbie Munro (Margo); Tim deZarn (Vagrant); Janine Venable (Deirdre); George P. Saunders (Ted); Michael Candela (Audition Man); Ramesh Pandey (Bob Yager);   Jackie Debatin (Jenny);   Nell Balaban (Nina);   Julie Davis (Lisa);

Michael Dell, Matthew R. Eyraud, Tom Hodges, and Mitchell Rose (Assholes); Geoffrey Infeld and Mark St. James (Club Sin Hunks);   Shannon McLeod (Ben's Dream Date);   Melanie Wachsman (Naked Blonde);   Julia Bruglio (Naked Woman in Shower);   Andrew Camp (Clark's Lover).

LOS ANGELES TIMES, 2/20/98, Calendar/p. 16, Kenneth Turan

"I Love You, Don't Touch Me!" is a comedy of eros, an amusing and mischievous look at the push-pull ambivalence and confusion that accompanies the quest for pure and perfect romance in a world that values physical thrills, not eternal commitment.

Written, directed, co-produced, edited and just about willed into existence by 27-year-old Julie Davis, "I Love You" is also the debut of a fresh new voice, one that's honest, sexy and consistently funny.

One of the hits of the American Spectrum section at last year's Sundance Film Festival, Davis' warm and playful examination of the complications of intimacy benefits from its heroine's high energy; it's also welcome for showing the comic side of searching for love in unlikely places from a young woman's point of view.

Twenty-five-year-old aspiring singer Katie (Marla Schaffel) no sooner appears on screen than her voice-over is insisting, "I can't help it, I'm a romantic. I'm in love with love." A charming theory, but hell to put into practice in the real world, where Katie's personal life is a self-described "romantic holocaust."

In the four years since she broke up with the man she thought she loved, it seems that every guy Katie's met (some of whom amusingly appear on screen) is either "a troll, a pervert or a liar." Complicating her love life is Katie's virginity and her determination that everything be perfect for the first time.

You'd think (or at least hope) that Katie's friends would be sympathetic to her situation, but they're not. Janet (Meredith Scott Lynn), a fellow office temp, thinks all this insistence on love before sex is a way of hiding from the joie de vivre that only the physical act can provide, and Katie's sexually active neighbor Jones (Darryl Theirse) definitely agrees.

And then there's the Ben question. A decent, calling guy who's more attractive spiritually than physically, Ben (Mitchell Whitfield) is Katie's best friend, someone she knows far too well to consider as romantic material. "Sexual attraction," she says with typical confidence, "is not negotiable."

Ben thinks otherwise, but when he insists he's in love with Katie, she insists right back that he's not and sets him up with her least attractive girlfriends to prove it, all of which leads to some wry ranting sessions between Ben and his understanding analyst (Sara Van Horn).

Then Ben surprises and shocks Katie by getting into a serious relationship, and she makes use of an accident at a traffic light to meet suave composer Richard Webber (Michael Harris), the kind of guy who manages to say, "There are no accidents, only cosmic coincidence," without making you hate him. That's when the romantic complications really begin.

Self-centered and vulnerable, assertive and touchy, confident and uncertain, Katie is the strong and vibrant center of "I Love You." A character written from the heart (Davis calls the film "autobiographical in spirit"), Katie is unmistakably Jewish in the Woody Allen mold, with all the comic neurosis and eagerness to over-anaylze to prove it. She never hesitates to use her know-it-all tongue to say precisely what's on her mind. Consequences? There's plenty of time to worry about them later on.

While some of "I Love You's" plot line is familiar, the premium the film puts on smart dialogue, its unexpected bursts of candid and even biting humor, sustains our interest. Katie's kind of conflict isn't often seen on screen these days, and the way it's played for poignancy as well as humor makes this romantic perils of Pauline a first-time film that's both promising for the future and awfully appealing right now.

NEW YORK POST, 2/20/98, p. 43, Michael Medved

Katie, the deeply endearing heroine of the Sundance Film Festival hit "I Love You, Don't Touch Me!," is a mass of puzzling contradictions: a hopeless romantic "in love with love," who's somehow remained a virgin at age 25.

She's an aspiring nightclub singer with guilty fantasies, but still a nice Jewish girl who gets along with her mother.

As played by earthy, unconventionally appealing newcomer Marla Schaffel, sh won't inspire wild passions from most men in the audience, but they can't help liking (and even respecting) her, while all women should feel a profound, powerful identification.

Her story makes for a smart, sweet, audacious, funny, original and hugely impressive debut project for Julie Davis, the 27-year-old writer-director-producer-and-editor who completed this project on a miraculous budget of $64,000. (That's about 1/3000th the cost of "Titanic.")

Katie, who feels that life is passing her by, considers various romantic alternatives. Mitchell Whitfield (of TVs "Head Over Heels") beautifully plays her devoted, dependable best friend, who writes poetry admiring her hair but hardly arouses her physically.

Her handsome, married boss (Wally Kurth) at her part-time secretarial job wants to introduce her to the joys of uncomplicated sex. And then there's the suave, wealthy British pop composer (Michael Harris), 22 years her senior, who claims he's ready to give up his wandering ways in order to build a relationship.

Meanwhile, she feuds with her female friends, including the sexually voracious Meredith Scott Lynn, who falls into a lusty but loveless relationship with the male best friend Katie has wounded.

The meandering (and generally predictable) plot isn't exactly edge-of-your-seat material, but all characterizations of these nice neurotics are strong, with splendid performances by the entire cast.

Even Darryl Theirse as Katie's wild, wise, worldly African-American neighbor and confidant, brings unexpected depth to this hackneyed role. Leading lady Schaffel, best friends with the director since they were both 13, has a striking, transparently expressive face and truly outstanding singing voice.

Writer-director Davis occasionally mars her crisp, perceptive dialogue with misplaced, show-offy "F" words—as if straining to show that her tender-hearted old-fashioned heroine is still somehow a "hip" woman of the '90s.

Despite a subtle shot of a wine glass accidentally breaking (suggesting the Jewish wedding to come?) at the movie's final clinch, the conclusion feels anti-climactic. But then, for a talent as formidable as that of Julie Davis, the big cinematic climaxes lie ahead.

VILLAGE VOICE, 2/24/98, p. 124, Elizabeth Weitzman

I Love You, Don't Touch Me! suffers from a terminal case of the postadolescent cutes. Twenty-five-year-old virgin Katie (Maria Shaffel) is a self-declared "hopeless romantic," and as she and her best friends search frantically for some action, we're unfairly led to believe she incredibly irritating simply because she needs to get laid. This is not so; her faux-analytical interior monologues ensure that Katie will remind you of any smug, whiny person you can't stand long after she's deflowered. A comic " exploration of sex and relationships in the '90s" (though despite the indiscriminate bed-hopping, there seem to be few safety concerns for these folks), the film is clearly a labor of love, born out of a million midnight bitch sessions. So there is some honest humor in all the clichés about Jewish mothers and the power of Ben and Jerry's to ease heartache, and there are certainly plenty of opportunities for you to elbow your companion and whisper, "That is so true!" But then again, you could just stay home and watch *Friends* together for free.

Also reviewed in:
NEW YORK TIMES, 2/20/98, p. E14, Janet Maslin
VARIETY, 2/10-16/97, p. 68, Joe Leydon

I MARRIED A STRANGE PERSON

A Lions Gate Films release of an Italtoons production. *Producer:* Bill Plympton. *Director:* Bill Plympton. *Animation:* Bill Plympton. *Director of Photography:* John Donnelly. *Editor:* Anthony Arcidi. *Music:* Maureen McElheron. *Sound:* David Rovin. *Backgrounds:* Greg Pais and Graham Blyth. *Running time:* 114 minutes. *MPAA Rating:* Not Rated.

VOICES: Charis Michelsen;   Tom Larson;   Richard Spore;   Toni Rossi;   J.B. Adams;   John Russo;   Max Brandt;   Ruth Ray;   Chris Cooke;   Etta Valeska.

LOS ANGELES TIMES, 8/28/98, Calendar/p. 10, Kevin Thomas

The moral of "I Married a Strange Person," Bill Plympton's adult feature-length cartoon, is perfectly clear: Know that if you have a satellite dish and happen to be watching TV when some lovemaking ducks crash into it, you're in for some bizarre, kinky adventures.

No wonder suburban newlywed Kerry Boyer feels she married a strange person. Her husband, Grant, a Clark Kent look-alike—he even has a flash of himself as Superman—having been watching TV at just the wrong time, has wound up with a lobe at the back of his neck, which causes him to develop supernatural powers that automatically turn anything he thinks or imagines into reality. When his sour mother-in-law expresses her distaste for bugs, for example, they start popping out of her various orifices. And when it comes to lovemaking, bewildered Kerry exclaims, "Damn it, Grant! When I have sex with you, I want to have it with you alone!"

While ingenious and clever, "I Married a Strange Person," which marks Plympton's feature debut, never really develops much of a rhythm or becomes all that involving or hilarious and is therefore best left to animation fans. Plympton's drawing style is simple and unpretentious, resulting in nicely textured graphics. His film is also graphic in the sexual sense but stays on the far side of porn in that its sex fantasies are too grotesque to be erotic.

NEW YORK POST, 8/28/98, p. 60, Larry Worth

It's no coincidence that a Pablo Picasso quote—"Taste is the enemy of creativity"—opens Bill Plympton's latest feature-length cartoon, "I Married a Strange Person."

The sentiment aptly sums up what follows: endless imagination and vulgarity galore. Actually, that would be fine, if the result was consistently entertaining. But it's not.

Instead, "Strange Person" suffers from heavy-duty redundancy, the same disease that crippled Plympton's first 70-minute animation, "The Tune." It's quickly apparent that a little of his mindset goes a very long way.

The story certainly had potential, dealing with a just-married groom's new-found ability to make fantasy into reality. That starts with a randy romp in the honeymoon suite, the least of which has hubby resculpting wifey's breasts into balloon animals.

The protagonist—empowered by a mysterious boil on his neck—proceeds to target everything from a recalcitrant lawn-mower to grumpy in-laws. And so it goes, until a power-mad army tries to channel the magical powers for its own aims.

But long before the protracted finale, Plympton recycles his own gimmickry. That becomes increasingly obvious, especially in attempting to gross out the audience.

Ultimately, Plympton never masters the medium, a trait he shares with fellow "adult cartoon" director Ralph Bakshi. As the latter demonstrated in everything after "Fritz the Cat," pushing the NC-17 envelope on a sketchpad rarely produces quality.

In all fairness, there are highlights. As apparent in his umpteen shorts, Plympton's style of drawing is always interesting and visually appealing. And one has to give credit for trying to break new ground.

Even so, "I Married a Strange Person" confirms what the cartoonist's biggest fans already know: Less of Plympton is definitely more.

VILLAGE VOICE, 9/1/98, p. 114, Michael Atkinson

A tabletop sensibility that lives and breathes in a very small world all his own, Bill Plympton has a way of making his animated sketch movies dumbly ponder their own collapse into flesh-rending chaos. When nothing is moving, his pencil lines still do, as if shifting uncomfortably with the helpless knowledge that something horrific is about to happen.

Plympton seems to have learned a lesson from his earlier, disappointingly hokey feature *The Tune,* and with *I Married a Strange Person* he pops the cork off every vision of distended human flesh he ever had. Plympton is famous for his runaway distortions of uncomprehending human physicality (often tying numb middle-aged men in knots through their nostrils, etc.), and his new feature spills more blood and guts than *Saving Private Ryan*. It's hardly a restrictive scenario Plympton's dreamed up for himself: thanks to a misdirected laser or something, a dim-witted newlywed hunk acquires a swollen neck lobe, which, for better or worse, materializes his every daydream.

What you get is in-laws overrun by beetles, lawn grass that stalks its owner, a copulating wife (this year's most outrageous sex scene) whose breasts grow until they invade the yard. There's no subtext here—it's all right there on a plate for you—but Plympton's strength is his visual timing; he's a master of the pregnant pause cut short by the abrupt punch-image of slow-motion calamities abbreviated by the sudden ka-thunk of gravity. However hampered by poor vocal acting and lousy songs, *Strange Person* is packed with Plymptonian thwacks, like the fantastically still moment before a giant corporate thug punches a flack's brain out his mouth. It's the pause that separates the men from the boys.

Also reviewed in:
CHICAGO TRIBUNE, 10/23/98, Friday/p. G, Michael Wilmington
NEW YORK TIMES, 8/28/98, p. E20, Anita Gates
VARIETY, 1/12-18/98, p. 64, Joe Leydon

I STILL KNOW WHAT YOU DID LAST SUMMER

A Columbia Pictures release in association with Mandalay Entertainment of a Neal H. Moritz production.   *Producer:* Neal H. Moritz, Erik Feig, Stokely Chaffin, and William S. Beasley. *Director:* Danny Cannon.   *Screenplay:* Trey Callaway.   *Based on characters created by:* Kevin Williamson.   *Based on the novel by:* Lois Duncan.   *Director of Photography:* Vernon Layton. *Editor:* Peck Prior.   *Music:* John Frizzell.   *Music Editor:* Abby Treloggen.   *Sound:* David Ronne.   *Sound Editor:* John Morris.   *Casting:* Jackie Burch.   *Production Designer:* Douglas Kraner.   *Art Director:* Charles Butcher and Scott Ritenour.   *Set Designer:* Louisa Bonnie, John D. Jefferies, Joseph Lucky, and Ann Harris.   *Set Decorator:* Jan Bergstrom.   *Special Effects:* John D. Milinac.   *Costumes:* Dan Lester.   *Make-up:* Bonita DeHaven.   *Stunt Coordinator:* Freddie Hice.   *Running time:* 96 minutes.   *MPAA Rating:* R.

CAST: Jennifer Love Hewitt (Julie James);   Freddie Prinze, Jr. (Ray Bronson);   Brandy (Karla Wilson);   Mekhi Phifer (Tyrell); Muse Watson (Ben Willis/Fisherman);   Bill Cobbs (Estes);   Matthew Settle (Will Benson);   Jeffrey Combs (Mr. Brooks);   Jennifer Esposito (Nancy);   John Hawkes (Dave);   Ellerine! (Olga);   Benjamin Brown (Darick the Dockhand); Red West (Paulsen);   Michael Bryan French (Doctor);   Dee Ann Helsel (Nurse);   John Harrington (Todd);   Mark Boone, Jr. (Pawn Shop Owner);   Dan Priest (Professor);   Sylvia Short (Old Woman).

LOS ANGELES TIMES, 11/13/98, Calendar/p. 8, Kevin Thomas

[*The following review by Kevin Thomas appeared in a slightly different form in* NEWSDAY, 11/13/98, Part II/p. B7.]

If you're up on your capitals of South American countries, you'll smell a rat when a Boston college student wins an all-expenses-paid Fourth of July weekend vacation at a posh Bahamian island resort for guessing Rio as the capital of Brazil.

But if you're Julie James (Jennifer Love Hewitt), survivor of "I Know What You Did Last Summer," you'll let your vivacious roommate Karla (Brandy), the contest winner, talk you into going along.

Anything would be better than returning home to South Port, a charming old North Carolina coastal community where two Independence Days earlier a drunken youth driving down a remote beach highway struck a man, presumably killing him. Of the four passengers only Julie, the most intelligent and mature of the four, insisted they contact the police, but she was forcefully outvoted.

One Fourth of July later, the supposedly dead man, Ben Willis (Muse Watson), garbed in his fisherman's slicker and face-concealing rain hat, surfaces with a hook in place of his right arm and ready for revenge for having been the victim of a hit-and-run accident. He succeeds in killing the car's driver and his girlfriend, and Julie and her boyfriend Ray (Freddie Prinze Jr.) think they in turn have succeeded in killing Willis.

Had that been the case, there wouldn't have been a sequel, right? "I Still Know What You Did Last Summer"—shouldn't that be "Summer Before Last"?—finds Julie, Karla, Karla's boyfriend Tyrell (Mekhi Phifer) and Will (Matthew Settle) off to the resort. Ray has told Julie he can't get away, and Karla thinks Will is just the guy to cheer up the fragile Julie, who is subject to nightmares and hallucinations that constantly confront her with images of past terrors. (She really needs professional help, not a vacation.) Of course, an island soon to be cut off by a storm is just the spot to be trapped with a crazed killer.

If "I Know What You Did Last Summer" wasn't the virtuoso work that "Scream," also written by Kevin Williamson, was, it was fun, energetic and fairly scary. But "I Still Know" is merely a fairly silly and ultra-gory schlocker/shocker. Danny Cannon directs Trey Callaway's serviceable script with tremendous drive and zest, but the film is so bloody without being all that persuasive that you start thinking how delightful it could be to be watching the poised and lovely Hewitt and Brandy, overflowing with talent and personality, in a movie other than an especially bloody slasher picture.

NEW YORK POST, 11/13/98, p. 61, Larry Worth

Ten minutes into "I Still Know What You Did Last Summer," Jennifer Love Hewitt is slinking through darkened corridors holding a carving knife in front of her heaving, brassiere-clad chest and calling out, Is anybody there?

Ah, some things never change. Chief among them: the out-and-out stupidity with which knockoff slasher flicks like this are mindlessly thrown together.

How else to explain when, after being menaced by a maniac on a deserted island, Love Hewitt's character slides into a coffin-like tanning bed while wearing a blaring Walkman. He'd never bother her there, right?

Believe it or not, this sequel to "I Know What You Did Last Summer" makes 1997's tepid tale of four teens stalked by a claw-handed ringer for the Gorton's fisherman seem the ultimate in sustained terror. Though Sarah Michelle Gellar and Ryan Phillippe lost the battle with Captain Hook, Love Hewitt and Freddie Prinze Jr. lived to scream another day, which brings audiences to this sad-sack epilogue.

Now in college, Love Hewitt is plagued by constant nightmares. So when corn-rowed roomie Brandy wins a free weekend for four in the Bahamas, Love Hewitt goes along for fun in the sun with their boyfriends.

But no sooner has the quartet made steam rise from the secluded resort's hot tub than hurricane season arrives. That means plenty of pounding rains, thunder claps and nonstop lightning bolts to illuminate the slicker-clad ripper and his curved stiletto.

The storm also brings on the genre's requisite dumb dialogue (I'm not going crazy. That guy was hanging in the closet.), predictable plot twists, cheap jolts, an intrusive rock score and a level of idiocy that killed this genre until "Scream" rejiggered it.

Hack director Danny Cannon probably figured that viewers wouldn't care if the body count kept climbing. Consequently, one never gets to know half the victims. Anybody who wanders in front of the camera is fair game for a hook through the head.

As for the principals, their acting does them in before any blood is spilled. Even Love Hewitt's smile, meant to see so natural and coltish, comes across as phony. Meanwhile the histrionics of pop chaunteuse Brandy would drive anyone to drink.

As for the washboard-stomached guys—Prinze, Mekhi Phifer and Matthew Settle—they'll certainly make girls' hearts skip a beat. But their inability to recite a declarative sentence with credibility assures them a room at the Troy Donahue Home for Pretty-Boy Has-Beens.

Even so, it comes as no surprise when the finale promises yet another chapter to the saga. They can call it: I Still Know What You Did Last Summer—and You're Never Gonna Hear the End of It.

SIGHT AND SOUND, 5/99, p. 51, Kim Newman

Although she survived an encounter with psycho-killer Ben Willis (now missing, believed dead) student Julie James is still haunted by dreams in which Willis pursues her. At college, she is drifting away from Ray, her boyfriend from back home who also survived Willis. Her room-mate Karla is trying to fix her up with genial Will Benson. When Karla wins a radio contest she invites Julie to come with her and her boyfriend Tyrell on a Fourth of July weekend break on a Caribbean island. Julie asks Ray to make a fourth but he turns her down so Karla invites Will instead.

Changing his mind, Ray drives to Boston but is attacked by a slicker-clad killer who looks like Willis. Ray escapes from hospital, and to buy a gun he pawns an engagement ring he bought for Julie. When they arrive in the Caribbean, the party discover that it's the last day of the season and a hurricane is expected soon. Julie is tormented by messages like the ones Willis used to send, and the hotel's few staff are murdered one by one. Estes, the voodoo-practising caretaker, explains that Willis used to work at the hotel, but left after he murdered his wife. Tyrell is also killed by the murderer, and Will helps Julie to escape only to reveal himself as Willis' son, working with his father to complete the family's revenge. Ray arrives with the gun, and he and Julie are able to overcome and kill the murderers. A year later, Ray and Julie are married, but Willis still seems to haunt them.

Picking up from *I Know What You Did Last Summer,* in which the heroine seemed to be killed by the mad Ben Willis, this sequel opens and closes with scenes of Julie meekly going about her business when Willis attacks her. Evidently, these shocks are all supposed to be dreams. But they are no more contrived or hokey than the supposedly real scenes they bookend, and have the effect of turning the whole film into little more than a feeble series of jolts. If Julie's death can be revoked at any moment by having her wake up screaming, then there's no point getting too concerned about her.

The original film, itself no masterpiece, at least had a strong premise, from Lois Duncan's novel, and complicated its characterisations by an unusual class awareness. This follow-up briefly evokes the pressures making Julie and Ray break up. The strain stems more from their earlier ordeal than from the fact that she's an A student destined to make it in the big city and he's a fisherman stuck in a small town. And in place of the first film's credible fishing-town setting, this one plays out in an unlikely Caribbean resort which shuts up over the Fourth of July weekend but still rents out suites during the storm season. Director Danny Cannon claimed he wanted to evoke the deserted Overlook mansion of *The Shining.* But this is a cramped hotel and all the settings are anonymous (except in a silly scene in which Julie is trapped on a sunbed as her friends struggle to free her without thinking to turn it off. The hurricane's meteorological threat, meanwhile, proves no more than a stiff downpour.

Having gone from being promising to washed-up without passing through a phase of success, Cannon—who turned down the original film and has pretended not to be humiliated in interviews—here does a job calibrated solely to score enough at the box office in order to make him bankable again after his *Judge Dredd* fiasco. However, this kind of picture is unlikely to impress anyone after the opening-weekend grosses are in. For a moment it seems some satiric point about the dumbness of slasher-movie characters is being made when three college students don't know what the capital of Brazil is. Yet that thread is never picked up and instead we get a sustained exercise in irritating black stereotyping from Brandy and Mekhi Phifer and thin-faced quivering from Jennifer Love Hewitt.

The self-awareness and 90s attitude Kevin Williamson brought to the *Scream* films and *I Know What You Did Last Summer* have by now completely washed away. Along with *Urban Legend,* this does its best to seem like an exact copy of such middling slasher films of the 80s as *He Knows You're Alone, The Burning, Madman,* and *Hell Night.* When Tyrell mocks the panicky Julie by asking her if she saw Jason or Freddy in the shadows, the film overreaches itself. With its father-and-son villain team, it is at once a whodunit and a franchise wannabe that hopes to elevate Willis, with his fisherman's slicker and Captain Hook hand, to the psycho pantheon. In 20 years time, characters in slasher movies won't be invoking Ben Willis the way this one invokes Jason and Freddy. Moreover, given that this sequel is set two years after the supposed crime of the original, and the finale of the first film revealed that Julie and her friends hadn't actually done anything they should feel bad about, even the title of *I Still Know What You Did Last Summer* doesn't bear thinking about.

Also reviewed in:
CHICAGO TRIBUNE, 11/13/98, Friday/p. A, Mark Caro
NEW YORK TIMES, 11/13/98, p. E14, Stephen Holden
VARIETY, 11/9-15/98, p. 31, Leonard Klady
WASHINGTON POST, 11/13/98, Weekend/p. 43, Richard Harrington
WASHINGTON POST, 11/14/98, p. G1, Stephen Hunter

I THINK I DO

A Strand Releasing release in association with Robert Miller/House of Pain Productions & Danger Filmworks/Sauce Entertainment/Daryl Roth Productions of a Lane Janger production. *Executive Producer:* Robert Miller, Marcus Hu, Jon Gerrans, and Daryl Roth. *Producer:* Lane Janger. *Director:* Brian Sloan. *Screenplay:* Brian Sloan. *Director of Photography:* Milton Kam. *Editor:* François Keraudren. *Music:* Gerry Gershman. *Sound:* Robert Taz Larrea. *Sound Editor:* Dan Kramer. *Casting:* Stephanie Corsalini. *Production Designer:* Debbie Devilla. *Art Director:* Matteo De Cosmo. *Costumes:* Kevin Donaldson and Victoria Farrell. *Make-up:* Kim Behrens. *Running time:* 91 minutes. *MPAA Rating:* Not Rated.

CAST: Alexis Arquette (Bob); Guillermo Diaz (Eric); Jamie Harrold (Matthew Edward Lynch); Christian Maelen (Brendan); Marni Nixon (Aunt Alice); Lauren Vélez (Carol Anita Gonzalez); Tuc Watkins (Sterling Scott); Patricia Mauceri (Ms.Rivera); Marianne Hagan (Sarah); Maddie Corman (Beth); Elizabeth Rodriguez (Celia Gonzalez); Dechen Thurman (Wedding Photographer); Jordan Roth (Caterer/Sterling Admirer); Mateo Gomez (Mr. Gonzalez); Arden Myrin (Wendy); Richard Salamanca (Father Paulson); Leonard Berdick (Mr. McPherson); Chris John (Tracks Bartender); Lane Janger (Wedding Bartender); Anthony Patellis (Band Leader); Carlos Rodriguez (Drummer); Nathaniel Bonini (Porter); Gabriella Bring (Sterling Admirer).

LOS ANGELES TIMES, 4/15/98, Calendar/p. 9, John Anderson

[The following review by John Anderson appeared in a slightly different form in **NEWSDAY, 4/10/98, Part II/p. B12.]**

Here's an idea you haven't heard more than four dozen times: Take a group of demographically diverse college friends, ones who never seemed to like one another that much to begin with, and toss them like a salad with croutons of unresolved sexual attraction, floriated radishes of career anxiety, the occasional legume of substance abuse, serve it all up at a wedding—it could be a funeral, but let's keep things light—and watch the comedic indigestion begin!

Just to remind us that we're all fin de siecle postmodernists and that life is an absurdist romance, pepper the soundtrack with the Partridge Family. And garnish the entire dish with the processed cheese of marketing savvy (read cynicism).

"I Think I Do," which for 91 minutes asks the all-but-obvious question of whether gay Bob (Alexis Arquette) and straight Brendan (Christian Maelen) will, in fact, make Bob's long-suppressed dream come true, attempts to put classic screwball comedy in a gay context—as if it weren't there already. Uh, by making homosexuality the hook in an otherwise cliche-ridden enterprise, aren't you really making something like an exploitation flick? Just a question.

"I Think I Do" is, among other things, about how things change Director-writer Brian Sloan's earlier short film, "Pool Days," was a subtle, sensitive snapshot of a young man's sexual awakening and it got him a lot of attention (especially as part of the "Boys Life" anthology released in 1994). Having been subtle and sensitive once was apparently enough, because "I Think I Do" is as heavy-handed and overacted as might be possible in ostensibly light comedy.

The main characters are a diverse collection, or a motley crew, depending on your POV. Bob, the group's resident gay male, was in love with Brendan all the while they were roommates at school, although Brendan never knew. By the time they're brought together at the Washington wedding of their close friends Carol and Matt (Lauren Velez and Jamie Harrold)—along with Eric (Guillermo Diaz), Beth (Maddie Corman) and Sarah (Marianne Hagan)—the playing pieces have moved: Bob, a soap writer, is in a long-term relationship with the show's hunky star, Sterling (Tuc Watkins); Brendan, of now-unspecified sexuality, remains a babe magnet for both sexes, especially Sarah, a slightly shrewish sexual adventuress now working for a Republican senator. Carol and Matt seem to be marrying at precisely the moment when the romance is over.

To get where it's going, "I Think I Do" has to leap cliched dialogue, a bloated sense of its own relevance and some serious misdirection. The biggest casualty of the latter is Maddie Corman, a seemingly talented comedian playing the Joan Blondell-inspired (but not otherwise inspired) role of Beth.

The characters are mostly cartoons, especially Carol's parents. At the same time, this is a cast of what are fairly charming, personable actors. One can only guess that ethnicity keeps the talented Diaz from breaking out of movies like this. Arquette has a great deal of screen presence. Watkins is very funny. However, they and their movie are a marriage not made in heaven—just to rework one more cliche.

SIGHT AND SOUND, 4/99, p. 45, Rob White

Bob, Brendan, Sarah, Matt, Carol and Eric all share an off-campus apartment at George Washington University in Washington DC. Bob is in love with his room-mate Brendan. At a Valentine's Day party, Bob makes a clumsy pass at Brendan and is punched, then sleeps with Sarah. Five years later, the former flatmates gather again for Matt and Carol's wedding. Bob is accompanied by his soap-star lover Sterling Scott. Sarah still carries a torch for Brendan but, unknown to anyone else, Brendan has realised he's gay. After the wedding, Brendan declares his love for Bob, while elsewhere a drunken Sterling announces he and Bob are going to 'marry'. Having been accidentally locked out of their room by Sterling, Bob ends up sleeping with Brendan. At brunch the next morning Bob's love-bite gives the game away. After some soul-searching and discussions, Bob and Brendan eventually leave happily together.

I Think I Do barely contains enough material for a 25-minute sitcom pilot. The central thread of the film concerns the tribulations of Bob, who having been rebuffed by his college roommate Brendan finds out five years later at a wedding that Brendan is now gay and wants to wind back the clock. But Bob is going out with soap-star Sterling Scott. How will this mélange resolve itself. Since this is a feel-good, gay affirmative film, and Sterling is too smug even for Bob's breathtakingly vapid group of friends, there's not much suspense.

Yet this lack isn't compensated for elsewhere. A key song comes from *The Partridge Family*, but it is never reinvented or allowed enough space to become perversely agreeable (as 'California Dreamin'' was in *Beautiful Thing* and *Chungking Express*). Rare stabs at visual invention (for instance, a descriptive intertitle) are half-hearted and seem hackneyed. There is some comic characterisation—the bride's stoned sister and fractious parents, the born-again Sarah who also pursues Brendan, and the Aunt Alice—but these fall very flat, never testing let alone threatening decorum. The lead actors, by the same token, are wearisomely benevolent.

A comparison with the sitcom *Friends* demands to be made, since *I Think I Do* revolves around six people in their 20s trying to cope with life and relationships. The dazzling writing and performances in *Friends* always veil an underlying desperation. Should the energy of the talk ever subside, all that will be left is people living in a depressurised bubble. This scary edge to all the talk is reminiscent of the best screwball comedy, which director Brian Sloan (who made the short *Pool Life)* claims unconvincingly to have tried to emulate here. *Friends* wouldn't work without its dangerous subtext, but *I Think I Do* forsakes this in favour of teenage fantasies. What made Brendan decide that all he ever wanted was Bob? He was worried that, unless it was Bob, he would never "find someone to stay up all night [with], bullshitting about bad TV."

Perhaps the makers of *I Think I Do* set out to score a political-generic point by letting gay characters take over a wedding movie. But to do this necessarily involves relinquishing the tension which conventionally pertains in the thematic conjunction of homosexuality and marriage. It's simply boring when there's no friction in this situation, when a gay love triangle is nothing more than a genial distraction for the wedding guests. Such a strategy reduces everything to an anodyne, 'we're all the same' view, and says nothing worthwhile about sexuality or personality. *I Think I Do* makes one grateful for the subversively genteel gay characters of *Four Weddings and a Funeral* and the estimable *My Best Friend's Wedding*. And as Rose Troche's forthcoming *Bedrooms and Hallways* shows, far more enjoyable entertainment is to be had when the poles of sexual behaviour are juggled around so that orientation becomes an unpredictable bond between people rather than a label. In that film gay characters are neither stereotyped nor, as in *I Think I Do*, just further examples of a banal norm.

VILLAGE VOICE, 4/14/98, p. 64, Michael Atkinson

A predictable and timid gay-slanted variation on *Friends*, Brian Sloan's *I Think I Do* tracks seven theme party-addicted college students from senior-year romantic blunders to "a few years later," when two of them (nerdy Jamie Harrold and hair-trigger nervous wreck Lauren Velez) are getting married. Way back when, Bob (Alexis Arquette) had a crush on his roommate, Brendan (Christian Maelen), and got slugged for it; today, Brendan shows up single, gay, and on the prowl. Unfortunately, Bob, now a soap opera writer, is semiengaged to studly soap star Sterling (Tuc Watkins). The blunders resume, and Sloan manages a fresh line of dialogue for every 10 in what is, in the end, yet another wedding indie. Arquette and Maelen are colorless, but the supporting perfs shine, by Velez, Maddie Corman as a sarcastic party girl, and especially Watkins, whose preposterous good looks make his comic timing and spot-on line readings all the wigglier. Marni Nixon shows up as a family battle-ax in flapper gear, and the soundtrack is festooned with *Partridge Family* songs, but *I Think I Do* has few surprises besides Watkins's expression as he gears up to catch the garter.

Also reviewed in:
CHICAGO TRIBUNE, 9/31/98, Friday/p. B, Michael Wilmington
NEW YORK TIMES, 4/10/98, p. E14, Anita Gates
VARIETY, 6/30-7/13/97, p. 66, Dennis Harvey

I WENT DOWN

A The Shooting Gallery release of a BBC Films and Bord Scannàn na hÉireann/Irish Film Board presentation in association with Radio Telefís Éireann and Euskal Media of a Treasure Films production. *Executive Producer:* Mark Shivas, David Collins, and Rod Stoneman. *Producer:* Robert Walpole. *Director:* Paddy Breathnach. *Screenplay:* Conor McPherson. *Director of Photography:* Cían De Buitléar. *Editor:* Emer Reynolds. *Music:* Dario Marianelli. *Sound:* Simon J. Willis and (music) Andrew Boland. *Sound Editor:* Michael Redbourn. *Casting:* Deirdre O'Kane. *Production Designer:* Zoë Macleod. *Art Director:* Tom McCullagh. *Special Effects:* Maurice Foley. *Costumes:* Kathy Strachan. *Make-up:* Debbie Boylan. *Stunt Coordinator:* Philippe Zone. *Running time:* 107 minutes. *MPAA Rating:* R.

CAST: Brendan Gleeson (Bunny Kelly); Peter McDonald (Git Hynes); Peter Caffrey (Frank Grogan); Tony Doyle (Tom French); Antoine Byrne (Sabrina Bradley); David Wilmot (Anto); Michael McElhatton (Johnner Doyle); Joe Gallagher (Steo Gannon); Liam Regan (Little Boy at Teresa's); Kevin Hely (Petrol Station Attendant); Eamonn Hunt (Cork Barman); Frank O'Sullivan, Jason Byrne, and Eamon A. Kelly (Cork Men); Carly Baker (Caroline); Carmel Callan (Teresa); Margaret Callan (Caroline's Mum); Denis Conway (Garda); Donal O'Kelly ("The Friendly Face"); Amelia Crowley (Receptionist); Conor McPherson (Loser in Nightclub); Rachel Brady (Git's Girlfriend); Anne Kent (Bunny's Girlfriend); Johnny Murphy (Sonny Mulligan); Don Wycherley (Young Frank Grogan); John Bergin (Young Tom French).

LOS ANGELES TIMES, 7/1/98, Calendar/p. 4, Kevin Thomas

"I Went Down" is one of those droll little Irish comedies that start out in such a low gear it risks tedium before finally kicking into high. When it does it becomes clearer as to what all the fuss has been about, for it became the highest-grossing independent Irish film ever.

It's hard to see how it could give another charmer, "The Full Monty," a run for its money, but there's no denying that this bit of blarney, concocted by writer Conor McPherson and directed by Paddy Breathnach, is ultimately beguiling.

As in "The Full Monty" we're treated to a screen full of fairly ordinary men who reveal various quirks and vulnerabilities. Whereas "The Full Monty" guys turned to stripping in the face of dire unemployment, "I Went Down's" are petty criminals. Actually, its young hero Git (Peter McDonald) is no criminal at all. Fate, however, propelled him wrongly into an eight-month prison term, and now Git's concern in doing the right thing by his trouble-prone best pal Anto—never mind that Anto (David Wilmot) has stolen Git's girl—has led him to make Dublin crime boss Tom French (Tony Doyle) seriously angry.

So outraged in fact that he orders Git to go down to Cork and pick up 25,000 pounds from French's onetime partner Frank Grogan (Peter Caffrey) and deliver Grogan to an associate known only as "a friendly face." Accompanying Git will be Bunny Kelly (Brendan Gleeson), a 40ish small-time crook whom French has under his thumb.

Git and Bunny are very different men, and a generation apart. Twentysomething Git is handsome, sober and highly principled. Bunny is a seasoned, beefy, red-headed middle-aged guy with scythe-like sideburns that make him look silly. What the two have in common—and what will make them so finally appealing—is that both are just intelligent enough to realize that they haven't been smart enough to stay out of various troubles yet capable of regretting the consequences of their foolishness.

Once Git and Bunny hit the road and all those Irish bogs, "I Went Down" threatens to bog down itself as they meander all over the countryside. At 108 minutes it's hard to see how the film couldn't have benefitted from some deft trimming, especially for American audiences, who are conditioned to expecting a livelier pace. But "I Went Down" gathers steam as its string of funny incidents start accumulating with greater frequency, and Grogan at last becomes a part of the action.

Grogan, bless him, is an easygoing nonstop talker and therefore a source of much humor, and Git and Bunny come to realize that the long history between Frank and Tom is so complex and treacherous that it could prove dangerous indeed for one and all. (In a way, "I Went Down" is a less complex "Miller's Crossing.")

In the meantime, we become acquainted with Git and especially Bunny, who proves to be the most likable of crooks. Bunny is miserable over a bad patch in his 12-year marriage, and he never wants to go back to prison. But you have to wonder if he is capable of surviving outside the world of crime, just as you have to wonder whether Git can extricate himself from that same world before it's too late.

The way "I Went Down," with its lovely score, plays out under Breathnach's gentle, compassionate touch becomes wryly amusing, ironic and entirely satisfying. Its cast is a glory, adept at setting off a sly humor with a touch of pathos, and it brings to the fore Brendan Gleeson, so good in so many supporting parts, as a seriocomic powerhouse in the central role.

NEW YORK POST, 6/24/98, p. 45, Thelma Adams

How's this for creative torture: Two kidnappers leave their hostage tied up in a motel watching a TV show on algebra's fundamental theorem. Did that explanation of a quadratic equation force the victim to break his bonds and, flee?

The two thugs, Git, Hynes (Peter McDonald) and Bunny Kelly (Brendan Gleeson), are the Art Carney and Jackie Gleason of larceny and payback in Paddy Breathnach's bawdy Irish caper "I Went Down.'

The movie opens with Git leaving prison. The boyish con immediately lands in debt to crime boss Tom French (Tony Doyle). French orders Git to Cork to fetch the mysterious Frank Grogan (Peter Caffrey). Of course there's a catch: Bunny, a hardened criminal with a deadly tendency to improvise, escorts Git.

Like Carney and Gleason, Jack Lemmon and Walter Matthau, Eddie Murphy and Nick Nolte, Git and Bunny (the hardass with a heart of gold and sideburns that haven't seen a razor since 1970) discover that mutual irritation is the sincerest form of male bonding. The odd couple band together when they realize they share two things in common: If one screws up, they both go down; and neither has any luck with the ladies. Thanks to writer Conor McPherson, the dialogue has more sense than the men do, if you can understand the wisecracks beneath the accents.

Breathnach's Guinness noir includes a number of hilarious episodes and, in what is considered in the press notes as a refreshing departure from contemporary Irish lips, no mention of "the Troubles."

"I Went Down"—a title which refers to Git's prison hitch, his trip to Cork and is a euphemism for oral sex—exposes, chatty Dubliners who have less to do with James Joyce than with "Pulp Fiction."

NEWSDAY, 6/24/98, Part II/p. B2, Gene Seymour

Git Hynes (Peter McDonald) has been sprung from prison and finds himself back on the streets of Dublin with little money and zero prospects. Worse, his girlfriend has dumped him for his best buddy, Anto (David Wilmot), a loser who owes the local crime boss, Tom French (Tony Doyle) lots of coin.

Just this much of "I Went Down's" set-up makes you brace for yet another dismal tour of a poor young boyo's struggle for survival in contemporary Ireland. Not so fast.

After saving Anto from having his fingers smashed by a couple of French's goons, Git is ordered by the scary French to take what seems a leisurely ride to Cork to pick up 25,000 pounds from the boss' former partner, Frank Grogan (Peter Caffrey) and deliver Grogan to what French will only describe as a "friendly face." If Git messes up, Anto will lose more than the use of his thumbs.

To ensure success, French arranges for Git to be chaperoned by one Bunny Kelly (Brendan Gleeson), a 40-ish thug who resembles a loaf of unbaked bread wrapped in polyester and garnished with muttonchop sideburns and corny jewelry. The match of Git's laconic, insecure personality with the brash, loutish Bunny would seem to announce that you're in for another odd-couple series of uproarious mishaps and chronic misunderstandings.

You get plenty of those, to be sure, beginning with an impromptu gas-station holdup right up to the peculiar twists the story takes when the pair finally nab Grogan and find him to be an untrustworthy, rheumy-eyed motormouth.

And, as the droll title cards scattered throughout the film announce, there's sporadic gunplay, a car chase, a little romance on the fly and nasty stretches of tension to offset the dry, ribald humor in Conor McPherson's ingenious script.

But if what you've read so far makes you think that "I Went Down" is just another comic crime movie, think again. In fact, you're compelled to challenge whatever preconceived notions you have about the movie even as you're watching it.

For all its quirky impudence, "I Went Down" is no Tarantino-esque pastiche of chic *noir* references, but a cooly ingratiating, beautifully paced amalgam of road movie, crime melodrama and character study. Imagine what would happen if Elmore Leonard wandered into Roddy Doyle's neighborhood by accident.

Even this comparison won't prepare you for the film's deftly assembled characterizations and brilliant performances, especially by the two leads. Newcomer McDonald shows surprising poise in evoking both Git's reserve and resolve while Gleeson's comparable magnetism and bearish bravado leaves just enough room for the audience to see Bunny's psychic wounds. (Though tough enough to have stuffed his own grandfather into a trash bin during an argument, Bunny also hurts deeply from being estranged from his wife and child.)

These are little guys who aren't even sure whether they want to be big. But by movie's end, they achieve the stature of "Rio Bravo's" motley, overmatched, but dauntless heroes. As the reference implies, such men are hardly unique in movies. But their presence in "I Went Down" feels so fresh compared with what passes for heroism in most Hollywood thrillers that it makes the movie seem almost revolutionary.

SIGHT AND SOUND, 2/98, p. 44, Philip Kemp

Dublin. Git Hynes is visited in prison by his girlfriend Sabrina, who tells him she's now going with his best friend Anto. After being released, Git visits Anto to find him being menaced by two hoods who work for crime boss Tom French. Git disables the hoods. Furious, Tom demands that, as compensation, Git brings in Frank Grogan, who once stole £25,000 of Tom's money. Git is paired with the unstable Bunny Kelly.

The pair miss their rendezvous with their contact, "The Friendly Face", who can tell them where to find Frank and to whom they must hand him over. Even so, they trace and kidnap Frank from the house he's sharing with a rival gang. Frank begs them not to hand him over to the Friendly Face. He relates a rambling tale about himself, Tom, a long-vanished associate called Sonny Mulligan and some counterfeiting plates for US bank notes. Git feels sorry for Frank, but Bunny is implacable.

Git delivers Frank to the Friendly Face, who is about to shoot both of them when Bunny kills him. Striking a deal with Tom, the pair take Frank to a hotel and tie him to the bed for the night, but he escapes. They track him down, abduct him and take him to meet with Tom in the woods. There they dig up the missing £25,000, plus the printing plates and Sonny Mulligan's skeleton. Tom explains that years ago he, Frank and Sonny were partners in crime; Tom and Frank conspired to cheat Sonny. Later, Frank shot him dead. Tom now kills Frank and wounds Bunny, but Git kills Tom. Back in Dublin, Bunny gives Sabrina money from Git before he and Git take off for the US.

The foot-soldiers of crime, those stumbling petty operatives taking most of the risks and reaping little of the glamour, in many ways offer a more fertile field for drama than the flashier *capos* and Mr Bigs at the top of the heap. Several recent films from different countries, from *Donnie Brasco* to *Trojan Eddie,* have explored this territory. If the tone of Paddy Breathnach's second feature (after *Ailsa)* is a lot closer to that of Gillies MacKinnon's *Eddie* than to Mike Newell's *Donnie,* that's hardly surprising: *I Went Down* takes place in the same grim Irish underworld of seedy pubs and fatalistic violence, leavened by straight-faced, Guinness-black humour. Peter McDonald's Git Hynes, the put-upon loser who finally strikes lucky, could easily be Trojan Eddie 20 years earlier. The two films also share the actor Brendan Gleeson, who is here offered a plum role as Git's mismatched partner Bunny Kelly.

I Went Down according to Breathnach, started out "very plot driven...but as we went on, the humour began to emerge". Hence, perhaps, some intermittent uncertainty of tone and a denouement that packs in far too much exposition for its own good. By the time we get to the grave in the woods for the final showdown, Tom's narrative flashback is more explanation than we need: who winds up shooting who is all that matters. If you're going to introduce a Macguffin, it's best to have it in and dealt with early on, while the narrative's still picking up speed. Otherwise, the film sustains its momentum, and its bad-taste scabrous humour, with likeable aplomb.

It's not hard to guess that the odd couple of Git and Bunny will eventually bond and end up with the loot, although Conor McPherson's script has enough minor twists to hold our interest. But essentially this is a character-driven piece, fuelled by dialogue, and the actors seize their chances with both hands. Peter Caffrey's Frank Grogan, spieling tirelessly, exudes all the dubious charm of a snake-oil salesman, and McDonald, in the least showy of the three main roles, holds the centre appealingly. But it's Gleeson who steals the film: his Bunny Kelly, with his teased orange quiff, addiction to cowboy novels and compulsion to commit pointless petty crime, is a glorious creation, borderline psychotic yet endearing in his emotional incapacity.

The film also allows us a refreshing view of rural Ireland: no wild, craggy Kerry or Connemara landscapes, but flat dull fields, characterless hotels and townships where the most unprepossessing venues make half-hearted gestures towards a dated notion of Stateside glamour. When Git and Bunny stop at a petrol station in the middle of nowhere, we note that adjacent to it stands a faded pink construction called "The Boom Boom Room." Bunny Kelly, with his USA-fixation, drawn from television shows and dime novels, would find his spiritual home there.

VILLAGE VOICE, 6/30/98, p. 138, Amy Taubin

A not dissimilar trip through the rituals of bonding and one-upmanship among the criminally inclined, the Irish film *I Went Down* lacks some of the pizzazz of *Out of Sight*, but it has something else that's just as alluring From beginning to end, the film feels like an open-ended collaboration among its talented director (Paddy Breathnach), dazzling writer (Conor McPherson), and actors (the flawless cast is headed by Peter McDonald, Brendan Gleeson, and Peter Caffrey). The plot keeps taking unpredictable turns, the characters are totally confused about where they are and what they're doing but in retrospect it's all perfectly logical.

I Went Down (yes, the title has a multitude of meanings) has a streak of antic humor that borders on the surreal—it's like an Irish *Down by Law*. Breathnach shares Jim Jarmusch's attachment to the western. There's a running gag with a six-shooter that's hilarious and an even funnier bit involving the handsome and droll McDonald disguising himself in what's supposed to be a ski mask but looks more like the kind of knitted cap his granny would wear to bed. You have to see it to believe it.

Also reviewed in:
CHICAGO TRIBUNE, 7/1/98, Tempo/p. 2, John Petrakis
NEW YORK TIMES, 6/24/98, p. E5, Janet Maslin
VARIETY, 10/13-19/97, p. 98, Derek Elley
WASHINGTON POST, 7/3/98, Weekend/p. 46, Michael O'Sullivan

I'LL BE HOME FOR CHRISTMAS

A Walt Disney Pictures release.   *Executive Producer:* Robin French.   *Producer:* David Hoberman and Tracey Trench.   *Director:* Arlene Sanford.   *Screenplay:* Harris Goldberg and Tom Nursall.   *Story by:* Michael Allin.   *Director of Photography:* Hiro Narita.   *Editor:* Anita Brandt-Burgoyne.   *Music:* John Debney.   *Music Editor:* Tom Carlson.   *Sound:* Rob Young and (music) John Richards.   *Sound Editor:* John Benson.   *Casting:* Roger Mussenden and Karen Church.   *Production Designer:* Cynthia Charette.   *Art Director:* Alexander Cochrane.   *Set Designer:* Peter Stratford.   *Set Decorator:* Lin MacDonald.   *Set Dresser:* Craig Reynolds.   *Special Effects:* William H. Orr.   *Visual Effects:* Dale Fay.   *Costumes:* Maya Mani.   *Make-up:* Sandy Cooper and Connie Parker.   *Stunt Coordinator:* Jacob Rupp and Tony Morelli.   *Running time:* 86 minutes.   *MPAA Rating:* PG.

CAST: Jonathan Taylor Thomas (Jake);   Jessica Biel (Allie);   Adam LaVorgna (Eddie);   Gary Cole (Jake's Dad);   Eve Gordon (Carolyn);   Lauren Maltby (Tracey);   Andrew Lauer (Nolan);   Sean O'Bryan (Max);   Lesley Boone (Marjorie);   Amzie Strickland ("Tom Tom Girl" Mary);   Natalie Barish ("Tom Tom Girl" Darlene);   Mark De La Cruz (Esteban);   Kathleen Freeman ("Tom Tom Girl" Gloria);   Jack Kenny (Gabby);   Celia Kushner ("Tom Tom Girl" Mama);   Blair Slater (Ian); P. J. Prinslow (The Brandt-Man);   James Sherry (The Murph-Man);   Kevin Hansen (The Ken-Man);   Alexandra Mitchell (Little Girl in Hospital);   Eric Pospisil (Little Boy at Bus Station);   Cathy Weseluck (Wendy Richards);   Peter Kelamis (Clyde);   Betty Linde (Older Lady on the Bus);   Awaovieyi Agie (Service Man);   Brenda Beiser (Bellhop);   Graeme Kingston (Pizza Eating Santa);   Ian Robison (Mayor Wilson);   Ernie Jackson (Kenyan Santa);   Kurt Max Runte (Taxi Driver);   Nicole Oliver (Ticket Agent);   Tasha Simms (Parade Manager);   Dimitry Chepovetsky (Angel);   Dolores Drake (Fraulein Maid);   Chris Willes (Race Official);   Nick Misura (Groundskeeper).

LOS ANGELES TIMES, 11/13/98, Calendar/p. F, Kevin Thomas

It's not even Thanksgiving yet, but here comes "I'll Be Home for Christmas," which Disney is releasing early in hopes of attracting audiences before the holiday deluge of films begins in earnest. It's a broad, shiny teen comedy that showcases Jonathan Taylor Thomas, the middle son in TV's long-running "Home Improvement." The film is formulaic but its energy never flags, and it fills the family entertainment bill.

Thomas' Jake is a Los Angeles-area college student, a fast-talking con man (right out of an old Warner Bros. picture) who tries to wrangle airplane tickets for a Christmas getaway in Mexico with his girlfriend Allie (Jessica Biel of TV's "Seventh Heaven"). But she wants to spend the holidays with her family, and Jake's father (Gary Cole), estranged from Jake for having remarried only 10 months after his wife's death, bribes his son by promising to give him his cherished '57 Porsche if he arrives home, in upscale Larchmont, N.Y., by 6 p.m. on Christmas Eve.

Writers Tom Nursall and Harris Goldberg have thus set the stage for one misadventure after another as Jake attempts to cross the country in time to win the car. When an elaborate scheme he's devised to help some classmates cheat on their finals backfires, Jake winds up in the desert wearing a Santa Claus suit, its hat glued on his head, the white beard glued on his face. He has neither money nor any identification, but you know that's not going to stop an irrepressible guy like Jake.

Some of Jake's mishaps inevitably are more effective than others—one of the best features the one and only Kathleen Freeman as an elderly Tom Jones fan—but director Arlene Sanford, a TV sitcom veteran, socks them all for maximum impact. She's a forceful director who'll zap you with cynicism one moment, then offset it with schmaltz the next, keeping everything moving along all the while. Thomas is nothing if not brash, Biel is a down-to-earth charmer, and Adam LaVorgna scores as Thomas' dense but determined rival for Biel's affections.

"I'll Be Home for Christmas" resembles lots of other pictures in the family genre, but it deserves credit for taking values seriously. Jake, the guy who concocts classroom cheating schemes at the beginning of the picture, has grown up and got his priorities straight by the time the picture is over.

NEW YORK POST, 11/13/98, p. 60, Thelma Adams

Call me a Grinch, but I don't want to see any Christmas gewgaws—or movies—until Thanksgiving at the earliest. "I'll Be Home for Christmas" with its peppy, poppy Xmas soundtrack and materialistic values, would be unwelcome at any time.

I confess: I'm not attracted to star Jonathan Taylor Thomas, the teen heartthrob from TV's "Home Improvement." I like a guy who shaves. That removes me from the only conceivable audience for Arlene Sanford's shameless comedy about the moral resuscitation of Jake, an obnoxious California college student.

Jake's dad (Gary Cole) wants his son in Larchmont for the holidays. To drag the kid's sorry butt east, Dad (he has no given name) offers the brat a 1957 Porsche if he arrives home by 6 p.m. Christmas Eve.

In the universe of screenwriter Harris Goldberg and Tom Nursall, that motivates Jake to cash in his Cancun tickets for a New York flight. But vengeful jocks foil Jake's plans. Left jilted at a history final by one of Jake's get-smart-quick scams, the cheaters retaliate. They dump our hero in the desert wearing only a Santa suit.

Jake awakens in Red Rock West, glued to a white beard. He bonds with a buzzard and then heads east on foot, penniless, to score that Porsche while Elvis sings "Here Comes Santa Claus."

Whatever inadvertent happiness Jake brings to sick children, lovesick waitresses and jogging Santas along the way, the central motivation remains crass. Despite the fact that we know the repulsive wheeler-dealer will somehow find his heart on Route 66, the plot's chief tension is, will Jake get the Porsche or won't he? That's a spirit of Christmas we don't need.

NEWSDAY, 11/13/98, Part II/p. B10, John Anderson

Ah, Christmas. A time for men and women to be of good cheer, to remember what unifies all people rather than divides them. A time to reject the pedestrian matters of this temporal world and consider the true meaning of life. A time for family. A time for movies about family. A time for a movie about a family that would offer a kid a Porsche if he would just come home for Christmas.

This is, in fact, the rather obnoxious premise of "I'll Be Home for Christmas," but one must remember that it is, after all, a fantasy. How else to explain the Porsche? How else to explain why anyone would want Jonathan Taylor Thomas home for Christmas? The diminutive actor has had his fans since growing up on TV's "Home Improvement," but he seems to be an acquired taste, like depilation or colonoscopy. The objective correlative, as T.S. Eliot might say, therefore seems a bit lacking in this Arlene Sanford comedy.

However: We watched it. You can at least listen to the plotline.

Attending college in a faraway land of nose jobs and trust funds, Jake Wilkinson (Thomas) is a hustler of fake IDs, concert tickets, etc. Crossing the wrong bunch of knuckleheads one night, he regains consciousness in the California desert, glued into a Santa suit. (How he became unconscious to begin with is never explained, but that's show biz.) His father (Gary Cole) has offered him the cherry red '57 Porsche that they restored together if he can get home to New York by 6 p.m. Christmas Eve. The race is on.

The hilarity presumptive is based on Jake's adventures crossing the country by thumb, dressed as Santa. He'd had a plane ticket—and had one as well for the lovely Allie (Jessica Biel of "Ulee's Gold"), whom he'd been trying to woo to Mexico until the Porsche appeared on his horizon—but his excursion into the desert leaves him afoot. And dateless, since Allie had to accept a ride from the obnoxious lothario Eddie (Adam LaVorgna), whose van keeps crossing Jake's path as they all make their way east. En route to his Porsche—and, oh yes, his family—Jake visits a children's hospital, runs in a 5K Santa Race (donating his winner's proceeds to charity, naturally) and, lacking any ID, eventually hitches a plane ride to Kennedy Airport with a smelly mastiff in a pet carrier.

Shall we continue? Or has the point been made that this is pure, unadulterated manipulative pablum, in keeping with the yearly tradition of like-minded movies, and that it's enough, to paraphrase a colleague, to make one join the Baha'i faith and forget about Christmas entirely? Holidays come and go, but bad Christmas movies are forever, and even the promise of a Porsche wouldn't be enough to watch this one again.

Also reviewed in:
CHICAGO TRIBUNE, 11/13/98, Friday/p. K, Monica Eng
NEW YORK TIMES, 11/13/98, p. E18, Lawrence Van Gelder
VARIETY, 11/16-22/98, p. 34, Lael Loewenstein
WASHINGTON POST, 11/13/98, Weekend/p. 44, Michael O'Sullivan

ILLTOWN

A Shooting Gallery and Donald C. Carter release of a Shooting Gallery production. *Executive Producer:* Larry Meistrich. *Producer:* David Bushell. *Director:* Nick Gomez. *Screenplay:* Nick Gomez. *Director of Photography:* Jim Denault. *Editor:* Tracy Granger. *Music:* Brian Keane. *Sound:* Jeff Kushner. *Production Designer:* Susan Bolles. *Set Decorator:* Paul Weathered. *Costumes:* Sara Slotnick. *Running time:* 97 minutes. *MPAA Rating:* R.

CAST: Michael Rapaport (Dante);   Lili Taylor (Micky);   Adam Trese (Gabriel);   Kevin Corrigan (Francis);   Angela Featherstone (Lilly);   Tony Danza (D'Avalon);   Isaac Hayes (George);   Paul Schulze (Lucas);   Saul Stein (Gunther).

LOS ANGELES TIMES, 1/23/98, Calendar/p. 6, Kevin Thomas

In 1991, writer-director Nick Gomez made a terrific debut with "Laws of Gravity," an ultra-realistic tale of three blue-collar Brooklyn thieves. He followed it up, in 1995 with the less effective but worthy "New Jersey Drive," about some Newark young people becoming caught up in crime. Gomez's impulse to try something different is understandable, but "illtown" misfires badly.

Gomez tries to tell the entire film as a memory, expressed as a drug-induced vision, related by his key character, who has just shot up. Unfortunately, "illtown" seems merely silly and preposterous, not to mention incoherent.

Perversely, Gomez's previously gritty style is again what is called for in depicting a devoted couple (Michael Rapaport and Lili Taylor), seasoned Miami drug dealers eager to start a family but whose operation is becoming disastrously unstuck. (Taylor allows she would like to bring a child into the world who wouldn't grow up to kill another child; Rapaport's idea of heaven is a golf course.)

Very swiftly you stop caring who's wasting whom, or why, as enemies start popping out of the woodwork and the bodies pile up beyond count. Soon packs of deadly adolescent males start swarming over the landscape.

Gomez's deliberately hallucinatory style works against generating any concern for the drug-dealing couple, as much as they seem to care for each other. That's too bad because Rapaport, so often the wacky guy, is very good in a serious portrayal, and Taylor has her usual strong presence.

Others include Kevin Corrigan as the couple's pal, Adam Trese as a key nemesis, Tony Danza as a veteran criminal kingpin and Isaac Hayes as a mysterious type who pops up from time to time. (Production notes helpfully tell us that he's Rapaport's "police contact-spiritual advisor.")

As resoundingly disappointing as "illtown" is, it is nonetheless clearly the work of a talented filmmaker who in this instance has miscalculated disastrously.

NEW YORK POST, 1/16/98, p. 46, Thelma Adams

There's a law of gravity: What goes up must come down. So, too, Nick Gomez's career. The independent film wonder got off to a powerful start with "Laws of Gravity." With "illtown," he's taken a turn for the worse.

The director of the more mainstream, underappreciated "New Jersey Drive" makes a huge misstep in a pretentious, portentous tale of Florida drug dealers. The movie had its New York premiere at the 1996 New York Film Festival but has had the distribution flu ever since.

This is the movie in which I learned that a little of Michael Rapaport and Lili Taylor goes a long way. Rapaport is one-note and Taylor, so good in "I Shot Andy Warhol" and "Household Saints," is limited by her vocal range. In "illtown," her mannered, somnolent whisper has us leaning away from the shallows, not into the depths, of her pregnant dope peddler.

You know you're in trouble when you welcome the arrival of Tony Danza as a mob kingpin/gardener/swami. Is there a sitcom there?

One interesting aspect to Gomez's script: Rather than glorifying drug use, he gives us back-story tragedies that are all by-products of substance abuse. We can give Gomez a pat on the back for experimenting, but do we have to consume the mistakes like a batch of burnt cookies? No.

VILLAGE VOICE, 1/20/98, p. 90, Amy Taubin

A hallucinatory tale of young Florida dope dealers who haunt one another's waking dreams like the ghosts they already are, Nick Gomez's *illtown* is as strange and original as any American film of the decade. Imagine Jean Cocteau crossed with Takeshi Kitano with traces of Jacques Tourneur thrown in for good measure and you might get a sense of its trance-like rhythms and sudden jolts of violence.

Gomez had intended to make a straightforward genre picture but ran out of money during production. He took what he had and reshaped the narrative on the editing table into something more elliptical and disassociated, where memory and prophecy merge in an extended anxiety-ridden present moment. If you've ever been behind the wheel of a car that's skidding out of control toward a concrete wall, well, that's what *illtown* feels like for most of its 97 minutes.

Which is not to say that its devoid of action or plot. Dante (Michael Rapaport), his girlfriend Micky (Lili Taylor), and their best friend Cisco (Kevin Corrigan) have a low-key, well-organized operation dealing heroin to Florida club kids. But their relative security is shattered when their former partner Gabriel (Adam Trese) gets out of jail. Gabriel believes that Dante and company sold him out to the cops—and he might be right. With a crew of teenage boys so feral they make the kids in *Kids* look like Hanson, he comes looking for revenge.

As plots go, this one isn't particularly inspired or revelatory. Nor does it help that Gomez has an adolescent weakness for religious symbolism. (Thus Gabriel is a fallen angel and Dante is trapped in a purgatory of guilt and addiction.)

But if Gomez isn't a first-class screenwriter, he has a great gift for creating images that go straight to your solar plexus. They change the rhythm of your breathing, they shake up your body chemistry, they transform the way you see the world. For all its narcoleptic languor, *illtown* is no less kinetic than Gomez's first feature, *Laws of Gravity*, where the jazzed-up hand-held camera danced so close to the actors it seemed a member of the cast.

illtown, on the other hand, is all about the distance between the psyche and the environment. Gomez and cinematographer Jim Denault create images that are as shimmering and translucent as a Fata Morgana. It's a rare psychodrama in which wide-angled sunlit landscapes seem as claustrophobic as dank underground passageways. This is a world where there is nothing to hold on to and where death is a constant presence—in the off-screen space behind the camera. That the characters, in scene after scene, see their death coming toward them from a place that's off limits to the viewer not only ritualizes the violence, but also raises it to a metaphysical level.

And indeed, *illtown* is so ritualistic that it might have seemed hokey were not the actors so fleshy, so vulnerable. With his chiseled features, pale skin, and habit of materializing out of thin air, Trese's Gabriel is the exception. Rapaport and Corrigan, in particular, have a gravity and weight that they've not shown before. (Taylor is fine but underused; Gomez just isn't interested in women.) Nearly as memorable are a baby-faced teen playing a low-level dealer who's shot down beside his much beloved car and a redheaded kid who plays Micky's deaf-mute younger brother (and who could be a stand-in for the director himself). Gomez coaxes performances from these nonprofessionals that are both subdued and electric—no easy combination.

Given its extraordinary beauty, its horrifying violence, its indelible performances, one wouldn't have thought *illtown* would have had to wait a year and a half after its New York Film Festival debut for a theatrical release. Not merely an independent, *illtown* is an art film without subtitles or British accents. And these days, that's the kiss of death.

Also reviewed in:
CHICAGO TRIBUNE, 1/30/98, Friday/p. I, John Petrakis
NEW YORK TIMES, 1/16/98, p. E14, Janet Maslin
VARIETY, 9/23-29/96, p. 125, Todd McCarthy

IMPOSTORS, THE

A Fox Searchlight Pictures release of a First Cold Press production.   *Executive Producer:* Jonathan Filley.   *Producer:* Beth Alexander and Stanley Tucci.   *Director:* Stanley Tucci. *Screenplay:* Stanley Tucci.   *Director of Photography:* Ken Kelsch.   *Editor:* Suzy Elmiger. *Music:* Gary DeMichele.   *Music Editor:* Steve Borne.   *Choreographer:* Jo Andres.   *Sound:* William Sarokin and (music) Craig Williams.   *Sound Editor:* Bob Hein.   *Casting:* Ellen Lewis. *Production Designer:* Andrew Jackness.   *Art Director:* Chris Shriver.   *Set Decorator:* Catherine Davis.   *Costumes:* Juliet Polcsa.   *Make-up:* Carla White.   *Stunt Coordinator:* George Aguilar. *Running time:* 102 minutes. *MPAA Rating:* R.

CAST: Oliver Platt (Maurice);   Stanley Tucci (Arthur);   Walker Jones (Maitre D');   Jessica Walling (Attractive Woman);   David Lipman (Baker);   E. Katherine Kerr (Gertrude);   George Guidall (Claudius);   William Hill (Bernardo);   Alfred Molina (Jeremy Burtom);   Michael Emerson (Burtom's Assistant);   Jack O'Connell (Stage Manager);   Matt Malloy (Mike/Laertes); Ted Blumberg (Francisco);   Lili Taylor (Lily);   Tony Shalhoub (First Mate);   Teagle F. Bougere (Sheik);   Elizabeth Bracco (Pancetta Leaky);   Steve Buscemi (Happy Franks);   Allison Janney (Maxine/Maxi);   Matt McGrath (Marco);   Richard Jenkins (Johnny/Frenchman); Isabella Rossellini (Queen/Veiled Woman);   Campbell Scott (Meistrich);   Billy Connolly (Sparks);   Dana Ivey (Mrs. Essendine);   Hope Davis (Emily);   Arden Myrin (Stewardess with Luggage);   Allan Corduner (Captain);   Christopher Pomeroy (Steward);   Sarah McCord (Stewardess with the Queen);   Lewis J. Stadlen (Bandleader);   Phyllis Somerville (Woman at Bar);   Amy Hohn (Woman with Captain);   Michael Higgins (Older Man);   Ken Costigan (Bartender);   Woody Allen (Theatre Director).

LOS ANGELES TIMES, 10/2/98, Calendar/p. 19, Jack Mathews

[*The following review by Jack Mathews appeared in a slightly different form in*
NEWSDAY, 10/2/98, Part II/p. B6.]

To fully enjoy "The Impostors," writer-director-star Stanley Tucci's homage to early slapstick movie farce, one has to be in a particularly open, perhaps even unhinged, mood. You can't simply appreciate its encomiums to the Marx Brothers, the Three Stooges and Laurel & Hardy; you have to accept those teams as if they had been collectively reincarnated in the persons of Tucci and his co-star, Oliver Platt.

As Maurice and Arthur, a pair of would-be Depression-era actors who end up as stowaways on a Europe-bound cruise ship (think: "Monkey Business"), Platt and Tucci bear an easy physical resemblance to Laurel & Hardy. And in each of them are traits of both Laurel & Hardy, as well as of Curly, Larry and Moe, and Chico, Groucho, Harpo and Zeppo, and a few others we may have missed. Tucci is nothing if not ambitious, and courageous.

It takes guts to open a comedy with scenes that remind you of "Ishtar," an earlier failed attempt at slapstick homage. Coming off his (and Campbell Scott's) critically celebrated "Big Night," a hefty first film about immigrant Italian restaurant brothers reaching for the elusive American dream in 1950s New Jersey, Tucci has not only spun off in another direction, but in one that would test the most seasoned comedy director.

Look what happened to Blake Edwards, the modern master of movie slapstick, when he made a run at doing Laurel & Hardy in a movie so aptly titled "A Fine Mess." "The Impostors," at least, isn't a total mess. Tucci and Platt both reveal strong deadpan comedy sensibilities, and on occasion the inventiveness of their bits rises above imitation. But too often, we watch them doing deliberate pratfalls, or telegraphing punch lines. They're working hard to fill the time, and there's no story, suspense, or so much as a romantic interest to give it ballast.

In its opening moments, we go through a series of sketches showing us that Maurice and Arthur are bona fide losers. Practicing their art by faking fights and death scenes in public places, they can't even remember who's dying on which day. When they do get a break, they can't get a break. During an audition for which they've been guaranteed roles, the wife of the director (an unbilled Woody Allen) calls to say she's leaving him for another man, and taking the play's funding with her.

After later being chased out of a bar by a drunken, mean-spirited stage actor (Alfred Molina), the boys spend the night in a dockside crate, only to awaken aboard a cruise liner whose passenger list happens to include that same ferocious actor.

It includes a further variety of thieves, murderers and mysterious royalty, and while Maurice and Arthur hide behind their own guises, they begin to peel away the veils of a shipload of impostors. Most of these secondary characters are even less interesting than our frightened heroes. There are exceptions in Campbell Scott's mime of a sadistic German ship's officer, and Steve Buscemi's hangdog portrayal of a jilted crooner.

Otherwise, this ship of fools doesn't sail.

NEW YORK POST, 10/2/98, p. 45, Thelma Adams

In a season when a cigar is no longer just a cigar, when even third-graders make jokes about the presidency and social studies, Stanley Tucci's "The Impostors" is refreshing. The shipboard comedy is an irony-free zone: fizzy, uncynical fun.

Following "Big Night"—a less slapstick, more tender comedy—Tucci wrote, directed, co-produced and crocheted the tea cozies for this Depression-era farce about two unemployed actors named Arthur and Maurice (Tucci and the uproarious Oliver Platt). After a run-in with pompous Hamlet portrayer Jeremy Burtom (Alfred Molina), Arthur and Maurice stow away on an ocean liner.

Molina delivers one of those fabulous set-pieces, like Richard Dreyfuss' Richard III in "The Goodbye Girl," where the actor skewers Shakespeare. Molina's British actor lards the Dane with a generous portion of ham. His wig askew, his lips vodka-smeared, Burtom lances Laertes/Mike (Matt Malloy) with his rapier, drawing blood from the actor and howls from the audience.

In the following scene, Maurice and Arthur commiserate with Mike. The greatest insult is that Burtom has cheated their friend of the serious actor's reward: a tragic death scene. In a fit of beer-induced bravery—part loyalty, part envy—Platt's Maurice stands up and roundly dismisses the absent Burtom: No, boozie boy, bye, bye.

Of course, Burtom has entered the bar and witnessed the insult. Burtom chases Maurice and Arthur into the night. When they hide in a shipping case and awaken on the sea, the pair enters a world of fakery and intrigue, all the more delightful because Tucci has cast every actor against type.

Twitchy Steve Buscemi plays a suicidal crooner named Happy Franks—and even sings a number before folding into heartbroken sobs. The incandescent Hope Davis hides beneath thick pancake and a book of the Psalms of Loss, the pale, bleary-eyed daughter of a fallen socialite.

Whispery, intense Lili Taylor takes a break from playing blind, telepathic killers to step into the happy shoes of inqenue Lily. She even dances! The sweet-cheeked Campbell Scott (Tucci's partner in "Night") plays a Teutonic steward with a dueling scar and a have-goosestep-will-travel attitude.

Tony Shalhoub, Billy Connolly, Isabella Rossellini and Dana Ivey join the fray as if they were out-of-stock characters in a road show of Agatha Christie's "Death on the Nile."

As a bomb threat and a double-murder scheme thickens the plot, it's the comedic gifts of Platt and Tucci, fat and skinny, one generous and dense, the other nervous and shrewd, that keep the pace hectic and hilarious. The pair revives the spirit of Hope and Crosby, Bob and Bing.

It's no surprise that Platt finishes the action in drag, or that neither comedian gets a girl as the weary travelers pair off in the exuberant finale. Maurice and Arthur are meant for each other and I'd happily follow them on the road to Bali or Morocco.

NEWSWEEK, 10/12/98, p. 88, Jeff Giles

"Big Night" was one of 1996's biggest winners—it was showered with praise, if not box-office receipts. The comedy was set in a struggling Italian restaurant. It was so rich and languorous—and its performers were given so much room to breathe—that it almost had to have been directed by actors: Stanley Tucci and Campbell Scott. Tucci's follow-up, "The Impostors," is an altogether different movie, a frantic shipboard farce that begins wonderfully but drifts farther and farther out to sea.

We open in Manhattan in the '30s. Arthur (Tucci) and Maurice (Oliver Platt) are starving actors. They perform hilarious, histrionic deaths in the park for spare change. They try to con a neighborhood baker out of some cream puffs. They attempt to wow a playwright (Woody Allen), who completely ignores them and spends their audition arguing with his wife on the phone. Maurice and Arthur are never deterred. They're an adorable pair, convinced of their own greatness for no clear reason.

Early on, Arthur and Maurice take in a production of "Hamlet," loudly ridiculing the star, a famous, fatuous drunk named Jeremy Burtom (Alfred Molina). That night, they mock Burtom in a bar. Arthur and Maurice wind up fleeing for their lives, hiding in a crate and accidentally stowing away on an ocean liner. Burtom, who's now in a murderous mood, is on the same cruise. So is a queen (Isabella Rossellini), a nut with a bomb (Tony Shalhoub), a depressed lounge singer (Steve Buscemi), a Nazi-ish ship steward (Campbell Scott), a kindhearted young woman (Lili Taylor), and on and on.

What follows is meant to be an electric farce, but someone forgot to plug this contraption into the wall. "The Impostors" devolves into an anthology of every screwball antic you've ever seen. Maurice and Arthur race through the inevitable disguises, pretending to be stewards, doctors, rich passengers. They hide in closets and under beds. They run endlessly through the ship's corridors. Platt and Tucci have a sweet rapport, and there are funny moments here.

When all hope seems lost, Maurice turns to a terrified Arthur and says, "Your dream has come true. You'll have your great tragic death." To which Arthur squeals, "I don't want a real one!" In general, though, "The Impostors" is overly familiar and distressingly flat. Tucci and Platt are hugely gifted actors—as are just about all the zillion cast members. It's too bad they got all dressed up for a cruise to nowhere.

SIGHT AND SOUND, 1/99, p. 47, Peter Matthews

New York City, the 30s. Arthur and Maurice are struggling actors who pull a series of scams to acquire food. A plot for cream puffs goes wrong, but Maurice gets two tickets to a performance of *Hamlet* starring Jeremy Burtom, a drunken ham. After the play, Burtom overhears Maurice complaining about his bad acting and a scuffle ensues. Dodging the police, Arthur and Maurice hide inside a packing crate and soon find themselves on board the *S.S. Intercontinental* headed for Paris. Burtom is also on board, so the two impersonate stewards with the help of the head stewardess Lily.

Glimpsing Arthur and Maurice, Burtom demands that they be apprehended. The friends conceal themselves in a succession of passengers' cabins and learn about their fellow voyagers, who include a queen deposed in a military coup, a sheik and a tennis pro named Sparks. In addition, the newly widowed Mrs Essendine is looking for a rich husband, while her daughter Emily moons over the ship's entertainer Happy Franks. Arthur uncovers a plot hatched by Maxi and Johnny—a couple posing as French sophisticates—to kill the sheik and Mrs Essendine and abscond with their wealth. Maurice learns that the first mate is a secret revolutionary planning to assassinate the queen.

At the captain's ball, Maurice tries unsuccessfully to warn the sheik and Mrs Essendine. The captain recognises the queen as his lost love and the pair embrace. The first mate tries to kidnap the queen and blow up the ship. Johnny snatches Mrs Essendine, while Maxie spirits away the sheik. However, the three abductress turn out to be Lily, Maurice and Arthur in disguise. When the first mate accidentally drops the detonator, Happy catches it and saves the day. All the deserving couples are united.

In theory, US independent filmmakers are free to tackle offbeat and daring themes that Hollywood won't touch. So it's always a little depressing when they choose to grind out the kind of genre pictures that studio hacks in former days were compelled to make. After the success of *Big Night*—a warm, wistful comedy about Italian food and the failure of the American dream—director Stanley Tucci could presumably write his own ticket. But of all the conceivable subjects for a follow-up, he has decided to recreate a Paramount art-deco farce circa 1932. Not to infuse it with a modern sensibility, but to bring back the antique conventions just as they were. It was clear from *Big Night* that Tucci likes to snuggle up in what he sees as a gentler, more innocent past. Yet at least the 50s of that picture had a genuine nostalgic glow. By contrast, *The Impostors* is as thoroughly ersatz as the title suggests. You are never allowed to forget that the actors are actors or that their one-dimensional parts (the *ingénue*, the money-hungry dowager, the foreign revolutionary and so on) have been lifted almost bodily from the repertoire of 30s crazy comedy.

As if to confer his blessing on the project, Woody Allen appears uncredited in the role of a theatre director whose marital angst gums up the audition of down-and-out actors Arthur and Maurice. Allen's guest shot is certainly apt since *The Impostors* belongs to the same frisky metatextual species as *Bullets over Broadway* and the film-within-a-film sequences of *The Purple Rose of Cairo*. Tucci even includes a final stunt analogous to the postmortem shenanigans in *Purple Rose*, the happily paired off couples step down from the ocean-liner set, dance past the smiling camera crew and shimmy out into the street. Far from disrupting the theatrical illusion à la Brecht, Tucci wants to affirm the magic of old Hollywood fakery and schmaltz. But the sad fact is the clock can't be turned back. The featherweight comedies which *The Impostors* tries to simulate were catalysed by the need of Depression-era audiences to escape into a universe of high style wit and romance. There's no way for Tucci to recover that historical frame of mind, and so all he ends up with is fossilised froth.

You can vaguely entertain yourself ticking off the allusions: a paraphrase of the state-room scene from *A Night at the Opera* (1935) here, a reprise of the "nobody's perfect" gag in *Some Like It Hot* (1959) there. Indeed, watching the movie is like enrolling in a course on screwball themes and leitmotifs (not anybody's idea of a party). Despite much rushing about in corridors and characters being knocked over like bowling pins, *The Impostors* is almost studiously unfunny.

The chief exception is the elegantly designed title sequence in which conmen Arthur and Maurice enact a slapstick argument that spirals into mock murder. This silent routine works because it depends on pantomime skills that haven't dated—unlike the specifically 30s forms of archness and naughtiness the film invokes elsewhere. Steve Buscemi's catatonic warbling of 'The Nearness of You' is also worth catching because it's the one time when something bizarrely, unpredictably contemporary breaks into the mothballed farce structure.

The large ensemble cast enters avidly into the spirit of the piece and seems to get a bang out of embodying the period clichés. It's a bit dismaying to observe indie stalwarts like Buscemi, Lili Taylor and Campbell Scott divesting themselves of their wacko originality and playing cute for the camera, even with irony. Still, these professionals supply the movie with some crisp edges. It's the centre that goes out of focus.

The nominal conceit is that Arthur and Maurice are compulsive hams who try to act their way out of scrapes, but this idea is only perfunctorily developed in practice. By a fundamental miscalculation, Tucci's script has our heroes mainly reacting from the sidelines to the various zany goings-on. What's worse, you sometimes see them positively recoiling from the craziness like the squarest of the square. When Arthur rolls his eyes at the music-loving sheik's invitation to the dance or when Maurice prudishly squirms out of the embrace of the besotted tennis champ, they forfeit a good deal of audience sympathy Tucci doesn't seem to recognise that true clowns don't resist the comic anarchy: they give in to it.

Also reviewed in:
CHICAGO TRIBUNE, 10/2/98, Friday/p. C, Mark Caro
NATION, 10/26/98, p. 34, Stuart Klawans
NEW YORK TIMES, 10/2/98, p. E12, Stephen Holden
VARIETY, 5/25-31/98, p. 58, Todd McCarthy
WASHINGTON POST, 10/2/98, p. D1, Stephen Hunter

IN GOD'S HANDS

A TriStar Pictures release of a Tom Stern production. *Executive Producer:* Zalman King, David Saunders, and Aladdin Pojhan. *Producer:* Tom Stern. *Director:* Zalman King. *Screenplay:* Zalman King and Matt George. *Director of Photography:* John Aronson. *Editor:* James Gavin Bedford and Joe Shugart. *Music:* Amanda Scheer-Demme. *Sound:* Adam Joseph. *Sound Editor:* Richard King. *Casting:* Cathy Henderson-Martin and Dori Zuckerman. *Production Designer:* Marc Greville-Masson and Paul Holt. *Art Director:* Jacqueline R. Masson. *Set Decorator:* P. J. Boston. *Set Dresser:* Russell Maki and Michael Kaahanui, Jr. *Costumes:* Jolie Anna Andreatta. *Make-up:* Deborah Huss. *Stunt Coordinator:* Chad Randall. *Running time:* 92 minutes. *MPAA Rating:* PG-13.

CAST: Patrick Shane Dorian (Shane); Matt George (Mickey); Matty Liu (Keoni); Shaun Tomson (Wyatt); Maylin Pultar (Serena); Bret Michaels (Phillips); Brion James (Captain); Brian L. Keaulana (Brian); Darrick Doerner (Darrick); Pete Cabrinha (Pete); Rush Randle (Rush); Mike Stewart (Stewart); Brock Little (Brock); Tom Stern (Shane's Father); Amy Hathaway (Girl On Train); Vince Klyn (Madagascar Prince); Leontina Santos Miranda (Madagascar Princess); Chad Randall (Boxer); Buffalo Keaulana (Chief of Police); Monica Kuhon (Lily); Joey Van Hekken, Jessie Ryan, and Marielle Landi (Wyatt's Children); James K. Kaina (Piano Player); Titus Kinimaka and Alekai Kinimaka (Kauai Boys Band); Darren D. Foy (Hugh); Tahitia Hicks (Sunshine); Judge (The Poet); Tim Skold (Rocker); Duke Decter (2nd Rocker); Camerina Arvizu (Maria); Ayesha Moreno (Lady of the Night); Jade Sun (Prostitute); Jimmy Helen (Chieftain); Maria Sviland (Soul Alley Follower); Philip Boston (Aggressive Australian); Mario Heras (Fisherman); Gwyne Redner (Nurse); Henric Nieminen (Orderly); Kimo Hugho and Michael Moore (Sheriffs); Carl A. McGee (Longshoreman George).

LOS ANGELES TIMES, 4/24/98, Calendar/p. 19, Kevin Thomas

"In God's Hands" takes us into the heart of the surfer mystique, suggesting powerfully that, for those for whom surfing becomes a way of life, riding an enormous wave becomes a form of communion with nature.

It's the moment when "everything makes sense"—in the words of the reflective, reserved Shane (Patrick Shane Dorian), one of three world-class surfers we follow from Madagascar to Bali to Hawaii in their pursuit of stupendous waves.

The lure of those waves has been explored in countless pictures over the three decades since Bruce Brown's classic "Endless Summer," yet "In God's Hands" has impressive depth and poignancy, thanks to the fortuitous teaming of filmmaker Zalman King and Matt George, who both co-stars and co-wrote the script with King. A former top professional surfer who has been involved in every aspect of surfing and in many aspects of filmmaking, George, in the role of the aging Mickey, gives the film its strength and resonance.

King, himself an experienced swimmer and diver, is equally well-cast behind the camera: as one of the movies' resolute sensualists dedicated to revealing the extremes of sexual passion—e.g. "9½ Weeks"—he has the right sensibility to delve into the extremes of sport.

"In God's Hands," photographed by John Aronson with plenty of jazzy panache, is a supremely gorgeous film—all those lush locales, thundering waves and perfect bodies—that unfolds accompanied by a rapturous, rousing score by Paradise.

King was lucky in that he was able to find three top surfers who can act. It would seem that King keyed the natural reticence of Dorian, currently the No. 2-ranked professional surfer in the world, to his portrayal of Shane, whereas third surfer, Matty Liu, a five-time Hawaiian champ, would seem to bring his own high spirits to his playing of the 17-year-old Keoni.

Trim, rugged, his head shaved bald, George's Mickey is a figure of good-natured virility whose sunny, reckless personality hides the self-knowledge that at 35 he's by his own admission burned out. He's deeply concerned that Shane will resist turning pro, as he did, until it's too late to cash in.

King takes the strands of travelogue and surfing documentary and gradually weaves them into a compelling drama that reaches its moment of truth on an outer reef in Hawaii, where turbulent 50-foot, 35 mph waves normally require that a surfer be towed into them by a watercraft traveling faster than 35 knots.

"In God's Hands" has some of the most spectacular surfing footage ever; more important, it has people we can care about.

NEW YORK POST, 5/16/98, p. 34, Larry Worth

Watching world-champion surfers guide their boards into, over and around a 40-foot wall of water is as fascinating as it is frightening.

Such thrill-inducing footage could have made the best documentary on riding the waves since "The Endless Summer." Instead, soft-core director Zalman ("Red Shoe Diaries") King made "In God's Hands" into the dopiest sand saga since "Beach Blanket Bingo."

The script is hilariously bad, starting with half-baked subplots about jail breaks, stolen pearls and Day of the Dead festivities, then arbitrarily dropping those for dopey romances, malaria outbreaks and fiery dream sequences. Worse, the acting skills of real-life surfer hunks Patrick Shane Dorian, Matt George and Matty Liu are as wooden as their boards.

But once in the water, Dorian, George and Liu are master craftsmen. Watching their death-defying stuntwork, exploring a wave's curl in the most jaw-dropping manners imaginable, is a bona fide treat. So are shots of exotic South Seas locales and a score that varies from native chants to pop that rocks.

The bottom line: Thanks to King, "In God's Hands" is cinema's equivalent of "Baywatch": a visual dream and a verbal nightmare.

Also reviewed in:
NEW YORK TIMES, 5/15/98, p. E24, Lawrence Van Gelder
VARIETY, 4/27-5/3/98, p. 59, Leonard Klady

INHERITORS, THE

A Stratosphere Entertainment release of a DOR Film productions with ORF and Bayerische Rundfunk. *Executive Producer:* Manfred Fritschoski. *Producer:* Danny Krausz and Kurt Stocker. *Director:* Stefan Ruzowitzky. *Screenplay (German with English subtitles):* Stefan Ruzowitzky. *Director of Photography:* Peter von Haller. *Editor:* Britta Nahler. *Music:* Erik Satie. *Sound:* Karoline T. Heflin. *Sound Editor:* Heinz Ebner. *Casting:* Barbara Vögel. *Art Director:* Isi Wimmer. *Special Effects:* Joe Joachim. *Costumes:* Nicole Fischnaller. *Make-up:* Helga Klein and Georgie Schillinger. *Running time:* 95 minutes. *MPAA Rating:* Not Rated.

CAST: Sophie Rois (Emmy); Simon Schwarz (Lukas); Lars Rudolph (Severin); Tilo Prückner (Foreman); Ulrich Wildgruber (Danninger); Julia Gschnitzer (Old Nane); Susanne Silverio (Lisbeth); Kirstin Schwab (Liesl); Christoph Gusenbauer (Stable Boy); Werner Prinz (Policeman); Dietmar Nigsch (Sepp); Elisabeth Orth (Rosaline); Gertraud Mayböck (Gertrud); Norbert Perchtold (Danninger's Nephew); Michael "Pogo" Kreiner (Elephant Keeper); Johann Naderer (Priest); Eddie Fischnaller (Florian).

CHRISTIAN SCIENCE MONITOR, 10/16/98, p. B3, David Sterritt

The far-flung network of international film festivals is a favorite launching pad for non-American movies hoping for success in US theaters.

"The Inheritors" and "The Celebration" have come to commercial screens after a busy tryout period on that circuit, including a last-minute stop at the eclectic filmfest in Mill Valley, a northern California town.

"The Inheritors," by Austrian filmmaker Stefan Ruzowitsky, tells a sardonic rural tale. The heroes are seven peasants who inherit a farm from the sour old man who owned it, then astonish their community by deciding to run the place themselves instead of selling it for an influx of easy money.

Although the movie roots for these unlikely landowners, it doesn't romanticize them by suggesting they have a natural talent for the activities they now have to manage.

Instead it weaves a complicated story of high ideals, hard realities, and escalating intrigues, some of them unexpectedly dark and violent. This isn't a particularly original or startling film, but it has enough twists to make it a strong candidate for box-office prosperity.

"The Celebration" comes from Thomas Vinterberg, a Danish film-maker who joined "Breaking the Waves" director Lars von Trier in signing the so-called "Dogma 95" statement, pledging to avoid artificiality and manipulation in a no-nonsense search for cinematic truth.

The results of this manifesto have been very mixed so far: Von Trier's most recent movie, "Idiots," is a disaster as both art and entertainment, but the most pungent moments of "The Celebration" indicate that it may pay some dividends in the long run.

The story centers on a party organized by a rich family man to celebrate his 60th birthday. The festivities get off to a shaky start when his grown son abruptly accuses him of child abuse in bygone years, and emotional tensions continue to grow as resentments and rivalries emerge in a scathing series of revelations.

As bitter as many of its characters are, the movie's ultimate message is not entirely cynical, suggesting that honesty may be the best policy even if it causes great discomfort when it first appears. The acting is crisp and lifelike, establishing Vinterberg as a major new player on the world movie scene.

LOS ANGELES TIMES, 10/30/98, Calendar/p. 18, Kevin Thomas

Stefan Ruzowitzky's "The Inheritors" is a tragedy of caste, rich in pathos as well as humor. It's an impassioned yet disciplined film in which the fullness of life is expressed with such subtlety and lyricism that you may not catch all its meanings and insights on just one viewing. By any measure, it's one of the most accomplished and rewarding films of the year.

The year is around 1930, but take away electricity and it could be centuries earlier. Time seems to have stood still in the ravishingly beautiful Austrian countryside where the film is set.

And that's just how the region's rich farmers want to keep it. One of their kind, named Hillinger, has been murdered and he has done the unthinkable—he has written an outrageously frank will, telling one and all what he thinks of them and leaving everything to his 10 peasants. To put it mildly, this news does not sit well with the rural community's ruling class; its dominant figure, Danninger (Ulrich Wildgruber), is absolutely apoplectic.

No less shocked are the peasants themselves. The peasants have defied their brutal foreman (Tilo Pruckner), who without their permission has told Danninger that the group would sell the farm to him at a price well below its actual value. The foreman leaves in a fury with two followers. The seven remaining new landowners will ultimately be required to buy these other three out.

Not surprisingly, shock gives way to euphoria. Old Nane (Julia Gschnitzer) dares to think she might indulge herself and buy her first-ever umbrella; Emmy (Sophie Rois) can now bring her young son, born out of wedlock, to live with her; and Lukas (Simon Schwarz), known in the community as the Foundling, brings Hillinger's Gramophone to the stable, flooding the place with Caruso's robust "La Donna e Mobile," which he confidently announces is being sung "in American."

Brought to the farm by Old Nane as a foundling some 20 years earlier, Lukas has been kept illiterate by Hillinger. The hard-working Lukas is not stupid, but he is naive. Blond and handsome, he is a happy-go-lucky playboy. By contrast, Emmy, his sometime lover, is a strong and smart woman, a proto-feminist who from the get-go tells herself that their little group can't afford to make mistakes.

The seven are scarcely a formidable group: They are Severin (Lars Rudolph), the film's narrator, an outsider, a slight, secretly gay man attracted to Lukas; two ineffectual young girls; and a stable boy. Against great odds, they do pull together making the farm more productive than ever. Success, even modest, only makes their position in the community more vulnerable, and it is not surprising that Danninger finds this turn of events increasingly intolerable.

As "The Inheritors" grows darker it grows more complex, with the unraveling of the circumstances of Hillinger's murder combining with the increasing fragility of the former peasants' situation to reveal the evils of the class system at its cruelest, most exploitative and most hypocritical.

Meanwhile, the local priest seems to keep himself above the fray. That this is a society ripe for the Nazism so soon to sweep over it seems utterly inescapable. Yet there is another layer, a history of tangled relationships that won't be revealed here, that gives "The Inheritors" a personal dimension so essential to yielding its ultimately tragic effect.

Evocative, ribald, painful, compassionate and perceptive, "The Inheritors" is a beautiful, stylish film and an uncommonly satisfying and stirring experience.

NEW YORK POST, 10/7/98, p. 44, Larry Worth

There's an old cliche about being careful for what one wishes. But there's nothing old or cliched about "The Inheritors," a cinematic exploration of that time-honored tenet.

Writer-director Stefan Ruzowitzky bases his tale in a sleepy little Austrian village in the 1930s. There, a hateful old farmer is found dead in the mud and everyone—workers, neighbors, officials—is a suspect. Thankfully, that's as close as this gets to Agatha Christie.

Instead, Ruzowitzky shifts gears with the reading of the will, during which seven peasants working the dear departed's land become beneficiaries. They form a collective known as the one-seventh farmers—and take on the wrath of class-conscious landowners in the process.

What follows is an almost mythic tale of seven rebels with a cause, employing a tone that never sugarcoats. Rather, Ruzowitzky lets things get downright ugly as the stakes heighten, meanwhile incorporating themes as lofty as dawning feminism, prejudice and socialism without getting pretentious.

That's all in addition to appropriately moody photography that captures verdant picture-postcard views of Tyrolean countryside one minute, then makes the same terrain into a terrifying maze of deadened trees and jutting rocks minutes later. Similarly, the mood can change in a flash from charming to brutal.

Equally electrifying is a troupe of actors—all unknowns—each of whom weighs in with strong impact. Led by Simon Schwarz and Sophie Rois' three-dimensional turns as doomed lovers, the cast makes for a grim, Marxist, utterly magnificent seven.

As a result, "The Inheritors" turns viewers into the real beneficiaries.

NEWSDAY, 10/23/98, Part II/p. B6, Jack Mathews

It's no wonder that Austrian director Stefan Ruzowitzky's next film will be made for Columbia/TriStar Pictures. His second one, "The Inheritors," has so many conventional Hollywood elements in it that it virtually cries out for an American remake. And that isn't a criticism.

"The Inheritors" is a warmly told story about a group of peasants who are bequeathed the farm where they have been on slave duty by its murdered owner. The prime suspect in the murder is an old lady who is found on the farm, mute and unknown.

The story returns to the mystery of the old lady, and her eventual story has a genuine last-act payoff. But "The Inheritors" is really about the struggle of the suddenly landed peasants to organize their lives and withstand attempts by their outraged neighbors to run them off.

There are 10 original inheritors of the farm, named in the dead man's will out of spite and in defiance of the church and fellow landowners—and with the malevolent hope that the ragtag peasant band will kill each other fighting over it. The number of inheritors is quickly reduced to seven, when the vicious foreman and two allies are sent packing by the others, led by the robust Lukas (Simon Schwarz), who was found abandoned as baby on the farm 20 years earlier, and Emmy (Sophie Rois), a bawdy dairy maid who sees her inheritance as a chance at respectability.

But for Emmy and Lukas and the others to succeed as farmers, they have to overcome the power of the local land baron Danninger (Ulrich Wildgruber), who will stop at nothing to humiliate, harass and destroy them.

If this sounds like something inspired by American Westerns, Ruzowitzky isn't likely to argue. In fact, he acknowledges it as an homage to the popular Austrian genre known as Heimatfilm, or heartland film, which is noble kin to the Western.

"The Inheritors" has the look and feel of an American movie set in the late 1800's even though its period is ostensibly the 1930s, and Ruzowitzky has given it both the scale and dramatic impulses of the Western. It is a drama of class, of have-nots ascendant, but it plays like classic Hollywood melodrama.

Young, impulsive and innocent, Lukas isn't quite the image of the rugged frontiersman Americans favor, but Schwarz, who bears more than passing resemblance to tennis star Boris Becker, has genuine appeal, while Rois' Emmy is Thelma and Louise rolled into one. And Wildgruber creates a cold-blooded villain that would do Lionel Barrymore proud.

SIGHT AND SOUND, 3/99, p. 42, Geoffrey Macnab

Rural Austria, the early 30s. A farmer is murdered. The killer, an elderly peasant woman, is imprisoned. The farmer's will leaves all the land to the peasants who work it. The foreman tries to bully the peasants into selling up to the neighbouring farmer, Danninger. Deciding to tend the land themselves instead, Severin and the rest of the peasants refuse. After working extremely hard to make enough money to pay their taxes, they succeed. The local landowners resent them. At a summer fête, angry words are exchanged between Lukas, one of the seven peasants turned farmers, and Danninger. Later, Danninger and the old foreman steal on to the land and set fire to the barn and crops. The foreman beats up Lukas. When the foreman's back is turned, Lukas thumps him on the head and kills him.

Lukas goes into hiding in the woods, hunted by vagabonds seeking the reward for his capture. Before departing for America, Lukas visits the prison where the murderess is under lock and key—he has learned she is his mother. Lukas was conceived when the farmer raped her years ago, but she isn't pleased to see him. Trying to escape, Lukas shoots the jail warder and several townsfolk and is wounded himself. Danninger leads a posse to the peasants' farm. Emmy, Lukas' old girlfriend, is raped. The others are tied up and tortured. Lukas tries to intervene, but is beaten to death. All the peasants in the area attend Lukas' funeral. Emmy leaves town with Severin but not before they have Danninger murdered.

Stock images of snow-capped mountains and happy little rural communities don't exactly tally with rugged cowboy stereotypes. Nevertheless, Austrian writer/director Stefan Ruzowitzky's description of his second feature (after *Fetzig*), *The Inheritors*, as an Alpine Western makes perfect sense. The iconography of this story about small-timers fighting for their land may be different from *Shane's* but the struggle is largely the same.

What starts off like a piece of bloody folklore, with the old farmer having his throat slit, gradually becomes a rich and strange allegory which touches on class oppression, rape, property relations, murder and theft. Despite the beauty of the surroundings, there is never any sense of a rural idyll. The storytelling is barbed and ironic. The voiceover narration and Ruzowitzky's eye for the absurd (an elephant passing by the farm, the peasants talking to the cows, the little boy who never speaks) rekindle memories of Volker Schlöndorff's adaptation *The Tin Drum*. Severin, the narrator, is one of seven peasants who inherit the land when the tyrannical farmer is killed. A dishevelled *idiot savant* his seeming naiveté masks considerable insight.

"And now I'm going to hell," reads the will of the murdered farmer. The document is intended as a provocation—he leaves the land to the peasants not out of any sympathy for their plight but because he wants to outrage his fellow farmers. Without his martinet foreman to order them around, it is assumed the farm must fail. This is a strictly hierarchical society, after all. Bosses are bosses, workers are workers. Characters are heard to mutter repeatedly, "a peasant can't be a farmer," as if it is an unshakeable axiom. Even the local priest frowns on the new experiment. In one magnificent shot, Lukas, an illiterate foundling, expresses his delight at his new status by embracing the earth. With the rain lashing down, he rolls around like a puppy in the mud, yelling out, "It's mine now!" He seems an impulsive, simple-minded figure, but he changes during the course of the film as he gains self-respect and learns to read.

Ruzowitzky switches easily between slapstick, comic caricature and a much darker vein. His villain, the obese, bearded bourgeois farmer Danninger, looks as if he has just stumbled from some George Grosz cartoon. In the film's most grotesque scene, we see him finish off an enormous dinner as Emmy, one of the peasant girls, strips in front of him in a bid to save Lukas' life. Venal, lazy, cruel and an inveterate snob, Danninger epitomises all that is worst about patriarchal feudalism. On one level, *The Inheritors* can be read as a morality fable about the attrition between bosses and workers—a tale of class warfare transplanted to the countryside. On another, it's a coming-of-age story. Emmy, Lukas and Severin are all youngsters perched on the edge of adulthood, idealists pitted against a society which wants to grind them down. The film also works as a murder mystery—only slowly do we learn the tragic details about who killed the farmer and why.

It is to be expected that a rural tale should be cyclical. Seasons roll on, one generation follows another. In *The Inheritors* Ruzowitzky's protagonists try to break the chain. Their relationship with the land is signalled symbolically: when they are in control, reaping the harvest or tending their cattle, nature itself seems benevolent. When their experiment begins to go awry, the weather changes and the mood darkens. At times, the film resembles an old-fashioned fairytale. The forest in which Lukas hides out from his pursuers is a magical and mysterious place, his foundling story might have come straight from the Brothers Grimm where there is always something dark and disturbing lurking within. *The Inheritors* ends on a violent but ambivalent note. The peasant-farmers' dream may be shattered, but at least they have planted the seeds of defiance.

VILLAGE VOICE, 10/13/98, p. 119, J. Hoberman

A more focused critique (The reference is to *Happiness* and *The Celebration*; see Hoberman's reviews of these films.) of the family (among other things), Stefan Ruzowitzky's *The Inheritors* is a satiric and deeply antiauthoritarian reworking of a long-lived sentimental German genre—the *Heimatfilm* or paean to the homeland. In this variant, set in rural Austria in the early 1930s, the seven newly masterless peasants of a murdered farmer have to learn to feed themselves.

Ruzowitzky's sardonic, economical movie—whose German title is a neologism translating as "The One-Seventh Farmers"—doesn't have much dialogue. Indeed, given the archaic feel, excellent sight gags, and spare Satie piano accompaniment, it could almost be a (very eccentric) silent film. The acting is skillfully broad, with the shrilly provocative Emmy (Sophie Rois) and goofy golden-boy Lukas (Simon Schwarz) particularly memorable as the peasants most active in their struggle against the intractably hostile "full" farmers who surround them.

To a far greater degree than the madcap families of *Happiness* and *The Celebration*, these unsentimentally simple-minded communards—ranging in age from child to crone—have a more complicated relationship to the surrounding society. Their haphazard organization harks back to the matriarchal, sexually promiscuous collective imagined by Friedrich Engels in *The Origin of Private Property, the Family, and the State*. Not only does each local custom (including "leisure") have to be reinvented, their very presence is understood as a threat, sexual as well as economic, to the neighboring farmers who, predictably, mobilize religion against them.

Ruzowitzky is telling a timeless tale but his folkish faux innocence has a distinctly modernist backbeat. (In one privileged moment, the one-seventh farmers discover that they have inherited a gramophone complete with disc of Caruso's "La donna è mobile.") This Marxist comedy has an inevitably brutal denouement. *The Inheritors* may be overshadowed by the week's other releases but there hasn't been a sharper, funnier, more socially astute German-language import since the halcyon days of Rainer Werner Fassbinder.

Also reviewed in:
NEW YORK TIMES, 10/7/98, p. E5, Janet Maslin
WASHINGTON POST, 12/4/98, Weekend/p. 56, Michael O'Sullivan

INSOMNIA

A First Run Features/Castle Hill Productions release of a Norsk Film/Nordic Screen production with the participation of the Norwegian Film Institute and Gunnar Svensrud. *Executive Producer:* Petter Borgli, Tomas Backström and Tom Remlov. *Producer:* Anne Frilseth. *Director:* Erik Skjoldbjaerg. *Screenplay (Norwegian with English subtitles):* Nikolaj Frobenius. *Director of Photography:* Erling Thurmann-Andersen. *Editor:* Hakon Overas. *Music:* Geir Jensen. *Sound:* Kari Nytro. *Set Designer:* Eli Bo. *Set Decorator:* Tom Gammelsrod. *Special Effects:* Pal Morten Hverven. *Costumes:* Runa Fonne. *Make-up:* Veslemoy Fosse Ree. *Running time:* 97 minutes. *MPAA Rating:* Not Rated.

CAST: Stellan Skarsgard (Jonas Engstrom); Sverre Anker Ousdal (Erik Vik); Gisken Armand (Hilde Hagen); Bjorn Floberg (Jon Holt); Maria Bonnevie (Ane, Hotel Receptionist); Kristian Figenschow (Arne Zakariassen); Thor Michael Aamodt (Tom Engen); Bjorn Moan (Eilert, Tanja's Boyfriend); Marianne O. Ulrichsen (Froya Selmer); Frode Rasmussen (Chief of Police); Guri Johnson (Mia Nikolaisen); Maria Mathiesen (Tanja Lorentzen).

LOS ANGELES TIMES, 6/5/98, Calendar/p. 10, Kevin Thomas

As the opening titles unreel for "Insomnia," an imaginative psychological thriller from Norway that demands total attention, we glimpse a pretty young woman meeting a grisly fate. Her death brings to a town in the north of Norway a pair of veteran Oslo police investigators, Jonas Engstrom (Stellan Skarsgard) and Erik Vik (Sverre Anker Ousdal).

Engstrom, celebrated in his field, takes charge of the investigation and swiftly devises a plan to snare the young woman's killer. But incomplete information on the part of the local police force causes the plan to backfire tragically, and "Insomnia" turns into a harrowing portrait of a man struggling against disintegration as he strives to conduct his investigation with his customary authority.

By now moviegoers know well the impact and range of Skarsgard; among his better known recent films are "Breaking the Waves," in which he played the warm, earthy oil rigger who meets a shocking fate, and "Good Will Hunting," in which he was an MIT mathematics professor jealous of Matt Damon's untutored genius. Skarsgard's Engstrom, who had left his native Sweden in the wake of a scandal, becomes a man who switches from investigating to covering up.

Plaguing his effort to keep a grip on himself is his insomnia, heightened by the fact that he's wound up in the land of the midnight sun during the summer—in a hotel without blackout blinds and drapes. Skarsgard persuades us to empathize with Engstrom while never flinching from the ruthlessness the man displays in protecting himself.

In formidable feature debuts director Erik Skjoldbjaerg and writer Nikolaj Frobenius do such a terrific job of realizing their story visually—Hitchcock would approve—that if your attention wanders at just the wrong moment you can miss something that will prove to be a major development. Hitchcock believed that true suspense derived from letting the audience in on key information that other characters cannot know—then make us grow more anxious about how everything will turn out.

Also like Hitchcock, the filmmakers concern themselves with themes of guilt and transference as Engstrom and the killer begin to echo each other. "Insomnia," which its director calls "a film noir with light, not darkness, as its dramatic force," is a work of style and irony with a strong sense of mood and atmosphere. It's virtually flawless as it builds inexorably to a finish that is as impossible to predict as it is satisfying.

NEW YORK POST, 5/29/98, p. 44, Thelma Adams

The crossover between movie and TV critics must be minimal. What else could explain all the advanced buzz for the Norwegian whodunit, "Insomnia"?

It must come from critics who've never watched "Prime Suspect" or "Cracker" or the many excellent PBS mysteries that consume my Thursday nights when I'm not hanging with "Seinfeld" and his kvetchy friends.

I confess I feel like I've visited Scandinavia's meanest streets by reading the crime novels of Maj Sjowall and her husband, Peter Wahloo.

In "The Laughing Policeman," the mystery of nine bus riders snuffed out by a sniper, I learned that Superintendent Martin Beck of Stockholm Homicide drinks more than he laughs.

Stellan Skarsgard, the intense star of "Insomnia" (and "Breaking the Waves"), never laughs either. His Detective Engstrom is the pro from Dover, the Swedish homicide detective imported to northern Norway to solve the murder of a 17-year-old party girl.

The oddest kink in Erik Skjoldbjaerg's film debut is not who murdered the girl, but the detail that the killer washed the corpse's hair. If "Insomnia" was NBC's "Homicide," we'd know the shampoo and whether the murderer did one rinse or two.

Since the mystery itself is tame, the heat (if there is any in this land of endless sun sketched in bleak blues and grays) is in the fact that Engstrom accidentally shoots his colleague Erik Vik (Sverre Anker Ousdal) while in pursuit of the murderer. (By the way, there won't be a spelling quiz.)

The fact that Engstrom doesn't confess to killing his partner, a justifiable homicide if ever there was one, gives the stone-faced but handsome detective a mean case of insomnia.

Early in the mystery, I leaned over to Post Plus's Su Avasthi and asked, "Why do I find Skarsgard so attractive?" Without missing a beat, Avasthi answered: "He looks like your husband."

For me, that exchange was the movie's high point. "Insomnia" isn't bad; it's just not the existential sleeper that advanced word promised.

SIGHT AND SOUND, 12/98, p. 46, Nick Roddick

Having moved to Oslo because of some unspecified past misdemeanour (possibly sexual), Swedish cop Jonas Engström is sent with his ageing partner Erik Vik to investigate the brutal killing of a teenage girl in a northern Norwegian town. Because it is midsummer, the sun never sets. A trap is set with a key piece of evidence to catch the killer. But the plan goes wrong when the police map fails to include an important element of the scene and, in the confused chase through thick mist, Engström mistakenly shoots and kills Vik.

Engström rearranges the evidence to suggest Vik was shot by the fleeing killer.

With the help of local cop Hilde Hagen, Engström uncovers evidence that links the murdered girl to crime writer Jon Holt, a local resident.

Unable to sleep because of the constant sunlight, Engström becomes increasingly obsessive in his behaviour, but succeeds in locating and finally trapping Holt. Hilde decides not to follow through on her suspicions about the death of Vik.

Psychological thrillers are one of the staples of Nordic film production, usually only getting international distribution when they have a handsome cast *(Nightwatch)* or are the work of established auteurs such as Bo Widerberg *(The Man From Majorca)*. *Insomnia* the debut feature of Norwegian director Erik Skjoldbjaerg, who has some prize-winning shorts to his credit, seems to have slipped through the net because it was in the Cannes Critics Week in 1997. And we should be glad it has: *Insomnia* is an ambitious combination of a fairly straightforward murder inquiry with an extended study of a tortured individual coming apart at the seams.

Nothing entirely new there, of course. The history of cinema is full of burnt-out cops. But what holds the attention here is that the cop in question, Engström, a Swede working in Norway (read a Yank in Canada or Englishman in Scotland), is as much plagued by existential angst as by the fact that he can't sleep during the midsummer nights because it never gets dark. The basic plot—murdered girl (killed in an edgy, strikingly lit pre-credit sequence); small community; dark secrets; sinister villain with Nietzschean undertones—resembles a feature-length episode of *Taggart,* combining the details of police work (an autopsy, a bungled stake-out) with a sardonic study of the detectives involved.

Whether the voyage to (almost literally) the end of the night that Skjoldbjaerg has grafted on top of this generic staple entirely works is a moot point. It certainly throws up some surprises and some very real pleasures, most of them from watching Stellan Skarsgård (as Engström) get twitchier and twitchier as the film goes on. The setting is also significant. Reassigned to Norway, Engström does not relish his latest posting to the frontiers of civilisation. Resolutely questioning everyone in Swedish—a detail likely to be lost on audiences who don't pay close attention to the subtitles—he spends his nights in increasingly desperate battles to tape up the defective blind in his sun-filled hotel room.

By the end of the film, he can scarcely keep his eyes open and is beginning to hallucinate. Since by then we are seeing things almost entirely through his eyes, what is real and what isn't becomes pretty blurred for us too, and the atmosphere of the film begins to resemble one of those pre-dawn half-dreams which come at the end of sleepless nights.

Skjoldbjaerg studied at Britain's National Film and Television School, which may partly account for the British television cop-thriller pacing of the film. He is extremely skilful at keeping us locked on Engström, even when his behaviour is at its most erratic. In one nasty little scene Engström uses an over-inquisitive guard dog to falsify ballistic evidence by shooting it, cutting out the spent bullet, and substituting it for the one that killed Vik.

In fact, a lot of what we feel about Engström is mediated by Vik in their early scenes together. But the amiably world-weary Sverre Anker Ousdal disappears before half an hour is up, reappearing briefly in one delightful dream (or hallucination) sequence in which he calmly finishes a story he'd started telling his partner before his death. By then, however, we have accepted that the film is as much about Engström as it is about who killed the girl.

Showing a nice eye for specific settings—Don Siegel himself would have been proud of the rotting pier on which the final confrontation takes place—Skjoldbjaerg balances thriller and psychological study for most of the film's brief running time. Only a disastrous sexual encounter with the desk clerk at the hotel where the Swede is staying and a rather over-the-top final shot appear miscalculated. The strand involving Engström's outsider status might have been further developed: the local cops seem genuinely impressed by Engström's powers of detection (which, on the evidence presented here, are only slightly above average), while the murdered girl's classmates are disdainful of his big-city Swedishness, claiming not to understand half of what he is saying. Perhaps this comes across more strongly for Norwegian audiences.

All in all, though, the very distinctive tone of *Insomnia*—and particularly the way in which it manipulates its bleak, end-of-the-line setting—leaves one wishing that Skjoldbjaerg had got the job (instead of Bille August) of directing *Smilla's Feeling for Snow* with its similar themes and settings and its almost identical sense of Nordic angst.

VILLAGE VOICE, 6/2/98, p. 160, Michael Atkinson

Scandinavian cinema has never been the ground zero for "waves" per se, preferring to nurture the obsessions of dour lone wolves (Bergman, Kaurismaki, Von Trier) and generally enrich the standard concept of the region as a desolate, lachrymose outland. There is the minor exception of the extremely depressed, breaking-as-we-speak Norwave, which with Pal Sletaune's *Junk Mail* and Erik Skjoldbjaerg's *Insomnia* seems more interested in smartening up and dressing down Hollywood conventions than locating its own aesthetic or voice. Not that there's anything wrong with that—*Insomnia* is a particularly eloquent, creepy, arresting piece of psychosexual police work, shot and cut with a knuckle pressed to your temple, and even if that's the best the wave can offer, American thriller makers should stand aside.

The movie's got a fabulously dyspeptic premise: Engstrom, a sullen Swedish detective (Stellan Skarsgard), finds himself sent to arctic Norway in the summertime, when there is simply no night, to investigate a murder, and finds it impossible to get any sleep. That Engstrom accidentally shoots his partner (Sverre Anker Ousdal) during a stakeout in the fog and then decides to blame it on the at-large perpetrator only clouds his vision even more intensely—he must unravel one murder while covering up another, and often evidence of the two collides. When Engstrom eventually corners the killer, things only get sweatier: the killer witnessed the cop killing, and so an uneasy bargain is struck.

As in an old Richard Matheson story, you're never sure the hero isn't simply imagining part or all of the story; Engstrom's battle with sleeplessness (and the inexorable sunlight stretching into his hotel room 24 hours a day) takes a vicious toll on the character and the filmmaking alike. As the paranoid wakefulness persists, Skjoldbjaerg begins to subtly fragment Engstrom's perspective, keeping the camera uncomfortably close to Skarsgard's giant, perspiring face, creating jolting gaps in traveling shots (Skarsgard will walk off-frame and then reappear elsewhere a moment later coming through a doorway, et cetera), and editing revelatory scenes with jaws-of-life abruptness. The bulk of *Insomnia*'s substance is detective-story routine, but *Insomnia*'s cool visual evocation of dissolving consciousness could give real insomniacs the shivers.

Also reviewed in:
CHICAGO TRIBUNE, 7/10/98, Friday/p. M, Mark Caro
NEW YORK TIMES, 5/29/98, p. E14, Janet Maslin
VARIETY, 5/19-25/97, p. 52, Steven Gaydos
WASHINGTON POST, 8/14/98, p. D5, Stephen Hunter

JACK FROST

A Warner Bros. release of an Azoff Entertainment/Canton Company production. *Executive Producer:* Matthew Baer, Jeff Barry, Richard Goldsmith, and Michael Tadross. *Producer:* Mark Canton and Irving Azoff. *Director:* Troy Miller. *Screenplay:* Mark Steven Johnson, Steve Bloom, Jonathan Roberts, and Jeff Cesario. *Story:* Mark Steven Johnson. *Director of Photography:* Laszlo Kovacs. *Editor:* Lawrence Jordan. *Music:* Trevor Rabin. *Music Editor:* Will Kaplan and Tom Kramer. *Sound:* Thomas Brandau and (music) Steve Kempster. *Sound Editor:* Gregory King and Robert Grieve. *Casting:* Marci Liroff. *Production Designer:* Mayne Berke. *Art Director:* Gary Diamond. *Set Designer:* John P. Bruce, Mindi Toback, and Stan Tropp. *Set Decorator:* Ronald R. Reiss. *Special Effects:* Steve Galich. *Costumes:* Sarah Edwards. *Make-up:* Sharon Ilson. *Stunt Coordinator:* Buddy Joe Hooker and Chad Randall. *Running time:* 100 minutes. *MPAA Rating:* PG.

CAST: Michael Keaton (Jack Frost); Kelly Preston (Gabby Frost); Mark Addy (Mac MacArthur); Joseph Cross (Charlie Frost); Andy Lawrence (Tuck Gronic); Eli Marienthal (Spencer); Will Rothhaar (Dennis); Mika Boorem (Natalie); Benjamin Brock (Alexander); Taylor Handley (Rory Buck); Joe Rokicki (Mitch); Cameron Ferre (Pudge); Ahmet Zappa (Snowplow Driver); Paul F. Tompkins (Audience Member); Henry Rollins (Sid Gronic);

Dweezil Zappa (John Kaplan); Steve Giannelli (Referee); Jay Johnston (TV Weatherman); Jeff Cesario (Radio Announcer);   Scott Thomson (Dennis's Dad);   Googy Gress (Spencer's Dad); Scot Kraft (Natalie's Dad); Jimmy Michaels (Devil's Goalie); Ajai Sanders (Interviewer); John Ennis (Truck Driver);   Wayne Federman (Dave the Policeman);   Golden Henning (Bank Customer); Pat Crawford Brown (Storekeeper).

LOS ANGELES TIMES, 12/11/98, Calendar/p. 14, Jack Mathews

[The following review by Jack Mathews appeared in a slightly different form in **NEWSDAY, 12/11/98, Part II/p. B6.]**

Warner Bros. got even with critics for a year's worth of negative reviews last week when it compelled them to see "Jack Frost" on a Saturday morning. "We're going to make you see it with children," a publicist said, with a detectable note of glee.

Fair enough. But if the movie is to be reviewed as a total experience, yours and an auditorium filled with kids, then we must report both reactions. Not much.

There was some enthusiastic laughter throughout the film, which is a fairy tale about a man who dies one Christmas and returns the next as a snowman. But it was the laughter mostly of adults, presumably those who find Michael Keaton endlessly amusing, even as a disembodied voice.

"Jack Frost" is the jackalope of this holiday season. Its overlong first half, which establishes Keaton's Jack Frost as a blues-rock musician torn between his love for his family and excitement over his suddenly promising career, seems aimed mostly at an older audience.

Aside from a marvelously inventive playground snow fight in the opening moments, this section deals seriously, and effectively, with a man's sincere struggle to balance his time between his supportive wife (Kelly Preston) and a son (Joseph Cross) who idolizes him, but finding the seduction of success almost irresistible.

The second half of the film is a grade-schooler's fantasy, the cartoon adventures of a boy and his talking, walking snowman, and a voice-over Keaton interior monologue, apparently written with the purpose of keeping parents' minds from wandering.

"Talk about separation anxiety," the snowman says to himself, after his head has rolled a few feet away from his body.

One could, in fact, get genuine separation anxiety at the point where Jack Frost dies, in a car accident while trying to join his family for Christmas in their cabin in the Rockies, and his return as Frosty the Snowman—blobs of snow with attitude. One moment, you have some serious grief issues for wife Gabby and son Charlie, the next, Dad is peering through his son's bedroom window, looking like a happy face on a pumpkin wrapped in white terry-cloth.

Coming to theaters on the heels of "A Bug's Life" and "Babe: Pig in the City," "Jack Frost" is something less than a miracle of illusion. The snowman moves like the proverbial man in a gorilla suit. He's an animatronic puppet, created by Jim Henson's Creature Shop and George Lucas' Industrial Light & Magic.

There are a couple of action scenes that will please kids. In one, Jack Frost turns his tree branch arms into rotary fans to help his son overwhelm some snow-fight opponents. And in the same sequence, Frosty mounts a snowboard and leads the neighborhood bullies on a merry downhill chase.

But the writers, and director Miller, an MTV veteran making his feature debut, are never able to mesh the film's contradictory tones. For kids, it doesn't even make sense on an identification level. The first half ends with a young boy losing his dad; the second half ends him with him losing his dad. And it's a pretty fine line between flesh and snow.

NEW YORK POST, 12/11/98, p. 66, Thelma Adams

"Jack Frost" doesn't have a snowball's chance in hell. Michael Keaton plays the title character, a Rocky Mountain rocker who neglects his hockey-playing son, dies disastrously, returns as a snowman—and is a better father for the experience. It's not exactly "It's a Wonderful Life."

"Frost" is a comedy of heartache slapped together by a posse of Hollywood writers (including stand-up comic Jeff Cesario) and forced onto the screen by TV hack Troy Miller.

It reeks with the kind of driven-daddy guilt that pervades Hollywood's workaholic serial-marriage set and saturates dysfunctional family comedies such as "My Giant," "Bye Bye, Love" and "One Fine Day," to name a very few.

Keaton's Frost is a warm, fuzzy, harmonica-playing dad. He's trying to make it as big as Bruce Springsteen so that he can support his wife (Kelly Preston, the poor man's busty Meg Ryan) and his pouty son (Joseph Cross) in a style that would make Hollywood set designers happy.

Frost's biggest crime is that he misses his son's hockey game while jamming in the studio. We're not talking physical abuse here, or hard drinking, or even being momentarily grumpy. He's just a hard-working bar band leader trying to make it—and his sulky, ungrateful kid (whose movie is this, anyway?) can't get over it.

Surely, the Frost man doesn't deserve to die young, but how else to fulfill some evil writer's over-caffeinated idea to animate a snowman and make him act like Beetlejuice in whiteface?

There is nothing more tasteless than a sneering snowgent delivering off-color jokes with twinkly coal eyes.

This is all very bad news for Keaton. The darkly charming actor— whose looks are gradually going the way of Jack Nicholson's—has been in career meltdown since he turned in his Batman wings. As Frost asks when he's reincarnated into a snowdrift, "Why me? Why a snowman?"

Some questions even an agent can't answer.

SIGHT AND SOUND, 3/99, p. 44, Amanda Lipman

Jack Frost is a singer in a rock band on the brink of success. When he's not on the road or in a studio somewhere, he lives with his wife Gabby and their 11-year-old son Charlie in Colorado. Jack breaks a promise to Charlie to watch him play in an ice-hockey match. To make up for it, he promises the three of them will spend Christmas together in a cabin in the mountains. At the last minute Jack is invited to a music mogul's party with the lure of a big record deal. Half way there, he decides to go back to his family for Christmas after all, but is killed on the way in a car accident.

A year later, Charlie is still grieving for his dad. After a new fall of snow he decides to build a snowman in the garden, something he and his father did each year. He dresses it in his father's old scarf and hat. That night, the snowman comes to life as Jack. Charlie is at first horrified, then drawn to the snowman who saves him from the school bullies and becomes the father he never was before. Jack drags himself across the rapidly melting snow to see Charlie play gloriously in the ice hockey team. Desperate not to lose his father again, Charlie takes Jack up to the cabin in the mountains to cool him down, but Jack realises he has to leave and says goodbye to Charlie and Gabby.

From its opening rock version of 'Frosty the Snowman' onwards, Jack Frost makes the point that it is a children's film with an adult theme about loss and bereavement. This old-fashioned rites-of-passage story is knowingly overlaid with contemporary psychological references. When Jack returns as the snowman he even talks his way through the various 'stages' of mourning—denial, anger, grief—as he works out how he's been reincarnated.

The story is played out almost entirely through the relationship between Jack and Charlie and moves fairly adeptly between the experience of each of them. When Jack is alive, his world revolves around his band and his love for his wife and son, endlessly anguished with guilt for never being there enough. Once he's dead, he becomes both a comic recreation, trying to come to terms with his new outer self and, now free of his life's other distractions, an utterly involved father. Keaton plays out the living Jack with manic enthusiasm, allowing himself to relax into comedy as the voice of the snowman. Meanwhile, Charlie zigzags sensitively and convincingly between hero worship and anger towards his living father and we see how that anger becomes part of his depression once Jack has died. When he finds Jack again, there is something touching both in his love, which overcomes any sense of the ridiculous, and his tenacious determination to keep Jack against all the odds.

The message—that children have to learn to deal with loss as part of growing up—may sometimes feel rather crudely put, but it is certainly a potent one. As Jack leaves for the last time, promising to be always in Charlie's heart, we can all weep with Charlie as he learns that, contrary to all our existential fears, 'dead' does not have to mean 'forgotten'. Even the film's bad boy, the orphaned school bully, seems to have learned this lesson when (via the kind of instant magic only found in films) he is touched by Charlie's determination to keep his father and, muttering "snowdad is better than no dad", helps him on his way.

The film is so tied up in its father/son dynamic that, inevitably, other characters remain less than satisfying. In particular, the sexy, understanding, perfect-mother Gabby is always just one step behind the real emotional dynamic, acting as a foil for the relationship between Jack and Charlie, and never quite coming to life herself. But it hardly needs saying that this is not, ultimately, a piece of social realism. It's a modern fairytale, complete with a magic harmonica that brings the snowman to life and a picture-postcard setting, featuring row upon row of twinkling Christmas lights and endless snowy vistas. And these also provide the backdrop for the impressive and exciting fight-and-chase scenes full of giant snowballs, sleighs, ice skates and snowboards, guaranteed to appeal to snow-hungry kids.

VILLAGE VOICE, 12/22/98, p. 132, Gary Dauphin

Despite having all the charm of a department store snow scene, *Jack Frost* is a serviceable kid pic, as counterfeit as Muzak but still able to strike a few seasonal chords. *Frost* is too insubstantial to evoke memorable Christmas movie chestnuts (or the 1996 horror flick of the same name), but its briskly paced tale of a dead dad (Michael Keaton) who comes back to the mortal plane one Christmas as a snowman does the heartwarming thing with workmanlike enthusiasm, never becoming so boring as to be offensive.

A very minor parable on paying attention to family while you can, *Frost* offers a wide range of passing diversions, from snowboarding derring-do to a minimally annoying computerized title character to lots of tender snowman-son bonding moments. Although you could cite *Jack Frost* as an example of all that is dire and generally lame about all things Christmassy, enough small children flocked to the inflatable *Jack Frost* lobby promo after an advance screening to suggest that, despite the cheap banalities flying from the screen, no one in the theater had lost an eye. Some parents may, Scrooge-like, lament the lost 90 minutes of life, but it sure beats standing in line at Toys "R" Us.

Also reviewed in:
CHICAGO TRIBUNE, 12/11/98, Friday/p. A, Mark Caro
NEW YORK TIMES, 12/11/98, p. E28, Janet Maslin
VARIETY, 12/14-20/98, p. 131, Joe Leydon
WASHINGTON POST, 12/11/98, Weekend/p. 51, Jane Horwitz

JAMES ELLROY: DEMON DOG OF AMERICAN CRIME FICTION

A First Run Features release of a Fischer Film production in association with ORF. *Producer:* Markus Fischer. *Director:* Reinhard Jud. *Screenplay:* Reinhard Jud and Wolfgang Lehner. *Director or Photography:* Wolfgang Lehner. *Editor:* Karina Ressler. *Music:* Sam Auinger and Deedee Neidhart. *Sound:* Sam Auinger. *Running time:* 90 minutes. *MPAA Rating:* Not Rated.

CAST: Phil Tintner (Narrator) and with James Elroy; Bill Moseley; Helen Knode; Barko (The Pit Bull).

NEW YORK POST, 3/25/98, p. 45, Thelma Adams

"As good as the movie is, the book is better," crime writer James Ellroy bragged to Conan O'Brien while stumping for "L.A. Confidential" on late-night TV last fall.

The so-called demon dog of American crime fiction is not one for false modesty—and the fact that the howling, obscene author creeped Conan out so much made for freaky, must-see TV.

The Film Forum, coming as close as that saintly shrine of cinema can to exploiting the Oscar gold, is opening "James Ellroy: Demon Dog of American Crime Fiction" today, following the win by L.A. Confidential" of the Oscars for adapted screenplay (by Brian Helgeland and the movie's director, Curtis Hanson) and for supporting actress (Kim Basinger).

"Demon Dog" is a fascinating exercise in truth being stranger than fiction. Austrian director Reinhard Jud's jazzy 1993 documentary cruises L.A. in a big-finned, crystal blue caddie convertible with Ellroy hunched over the wheel, spinning dark stories of L.A.'s past.

"Demon Dog" is a bio-pic, the story of what makes the writer tick, as well as an incestuous caress of the Los Angeleno's beloved, reviled, "smog-bound fatherland."

For all Ellroy's on-camera howling, the best-selling author is a lot tamer than the wild print shirts he wears. With his wire-rimmed glasses, long face and stringy comb-over, he resembles a high school chemistry teacher, Bill Nye the Science Guy as recovering alcoholic.

The obsessive, prolific author wrote 10 books in the 11 years following his 1979 debut, "Black Dahlia," including "White Jazz," and the autobiographical "My Dark Places."

On camera, Ellroy gets in touch with the "dim reptile part" of himself and gleefully shares it with the filmmakers. It's surprising how such a curmudgeon a confessed panty-sniffer, shoplifter, dog-kisser, sometime golf caddy and ex-drunk, can be this cuddly. It's part of Ellroy's shtick, his self-promotion, his circus act: pet the demon dog.

The doc, co-written by Jud and Wolfgang Lehner, trails Ellroy to 39th and Norton, the site where policemen found the tortured, bisected body of the Black Dahlia murder victim. It was 1947, the year before Ellroy's birth only a few miles away.

As chilling as this moment is, Ellroy tops it. He visits the spot in the East L.A. suburb of El Monte where three divorced, alcoholic mother was strangled. The killer dumped her naked corpse, wrapped in a coat, a single stocking around her neck, in the bushes near the local school.

Ellroy was 10 when he discovered the news. He had spent the weekend with his father. They'd caught a Randolph Scott double feature together.

Ellroy calmly tells the story of his mother's unsolved murder while standing in front of the tumble of bushes where her body was discovered. Nearby, the Arroyo Varsity Cheerleaders practice their kicks.

Not since the Oscar-winning "Crumb," has a documentary focused on an artist this articulate with a family history of equally ferocious dysfunctionality—and been so engrossing.

NEWSDAY, 3/25/98, Part II/p. B11, John Anderson

Los Angeles: Vice cops. Bail bondsmen. Bad girls. Dead girls. And writer James Ellroy, who calls his hometown "a city of nightmares," portrays it as the place the Dream came to die, and perches on its shoulder like, a particularly hyperactive bird of prey.

Or a dog. In "James Ellroy: Demon Dog of American Crime Fiction," the impressionistic 1993 documentary by Austrian director Reinhard Jud, we get an Ellroy's-eye view of a city he holds in sneering wonder and affectionate contempt, as well as a guided tour into the neo-gothic soul of the most admired figure in crime fiction since Hammett and Chandler, escorted by the soul himself.

"I wanted to be Tolstoy," he tells Jud. "I wanted to be Dostoyevsky, I wanted to be Balzac, I wanted to be all those guys that, quite frankly, I've never really read ..." But what he really wanted was to make crime fiction on an "epic, transcendent scale." If he hasn't—in novels such as "White Jazz" and "The Big Nowhere"—he's at least pumped fresh blood into what had been a very tired genre.

The film, completed long before the filming of Ellroy's 1990 "L.A. Confidential," finds the author completely cynical about making movies from his books. "Just give me the check," he snarls.

Cruising the streets in his sloop-sized Cadillac, he reflects on the investigation of one murder case—perhaps the most notorious in the city's history and an investigation he actually calls "a one-way ticket to Nowheresville."

That case, the Black Dahlia, was also the title of an Ellroy book. And, as he does in the book, Ellroy segues from the Dahlia story—the killing of a 22-year-old woman whose torso was severed, her blood drained and the two halves of her body almost ritualistically deposited beside each other in a vacant lot—to his mother, the victim in 1958 of a strangulation murder that was never solved.

When he isn't acting like an R. Crumb character or howling like a dog, Ellroy makes insightful comments about his own past, the technical aspects of his writing, and the city that spawned it. He can write about Los Angeles only in the past because "it's a place that's gotten so completely out of control it isn't even believable to me anymore."

Jud goes on long, scavenging excursions, picking up a police roust here, a prostitute negotiation there, trying to capture something to match the spiritual possession and verbal digressions of his subject. It's tough to match Ellroy, though, that rare breed of writer who is—almost—as entertaining as his fiction.

VILLAGE VOICE, 3/31/98, p. 59, Michael Atkinson

A self-styled Orpheus bellowing about his infernal journey in the patois of Eisenhower-era racetrack lowlife, James Ellroy may not deserve his fame so much as seize it with two meaty hands and dare us to wrench it away. With crime-fiction credentials Jim Thompson couldn't even approach (the still-unsolved murder of Ellroy's mother when he was 10, the odd interfacing with the Black Dahlia case, his subsequent bottom-feeding), Ellroy has made the most of his materials, and exactly how much of his story is destiny and how much is opportunism is a question he answers with every book: destiny, baby, fast, hard, and dirty. But too often, Ellroy merely sucks from the well of demimonde nostalgia. In the 1993 Austrian doc *James Ellroy: Demon Dog of American Crime Fiction* opening two short days after *L.A. Confidential* will have either won or lost its Oscars, Ellroy turns flamboyantly Ellroyesque—hard-charging, fucked up on old slang, and as self-important as a bull stud in a meadow of cows. Taking the mute camera crew on a brawny guided tour of L.A. as if it were Sarajevo Ellroy sketches out his *My Dark Places* tale, visits his various ground zeros, talks about his work as if he were plunging into the black truth of human nature, not just writing pulp. Launching into a kind of shibboleth-filled rant aimed at the camera, Ellroy calls us "hepcats," picks over his own "demonic" urges, and discourses on where exactly "Jack Kennedy played bury the brisket with Marilyn Monroe." In his memoir Ellroy prioritized the forensic reality of his life and its latent theme—the victimization of women; on film, Ellroy only tells us how tortured, savvy, leather-tough, and supercool he is. He makes an impression, but I doubt it's the one he wanted.

Also reviewed in:
NEW YORK TIMES, 3/25/98, p. E3, Janet Maslin
VARIETY, 7/26/93, p. 29, Leonard Klady

JOHN CARPENTER'S VAMPIRES

A Columbia Pictures and Largo Entertainment release of a Storm King production. *Executive Producer:* Barr Potter. *Producer:* Sandy King. *Director:* John Carpenter. *Screenplay:* Don Jakoby. *Based on the novel "Vampires" by:* John Steakley. *Director of Photography:* Gary B. Kibbe. *Editor:* Edward A. Warschilka. *Music:* John Carpenter. *Sound:* Hank Garfield. *Sound Editor:* John Dunn. *Casting:* Reuben Cannon and Eddie Dunlop. *Production Designer:* Thomas A. Walsh. *Art Director:* Kim Hix. *Set Decorator:* David Schlesinger. *Special Effects:* Darrell D. Prichett. *Costumes:* Robin Michel Bush. *Make-up:* Jill Cady and Janna B. Phillips. *Special Make-up Effects:* Robert Kurtzman, Gregory Nicotero, and Howard Berger. *Stunt Coordinator:* Jeff Imada. *Running time:* 107 minutes. *MPAA Rating:* R.

CAST: James Woods (Jack Crow); Daniel Baldwin (Montoya); Sheryl Lee (Katrina); Thomas Ian Griffith (Valek); Maximilian Schell (Cardinal Alba); Tim Guinee (Father Ada Guiteau); Mark Boon, Jr. (Catlin); Gregory Sierra (Father Giovanni); Cary-Hiroyuki Tagawa (David Deyo); Tommy Rosales (Ortega); Henry Kingi (Anthony); David Rowden (Bambi); Clarke Coleman (Davis); Mark Sivertsen (Highway Patrolman); John Furlong (Father Molina); Angelina Calderon Torres (Cleaning Lady); Jimmy Ortega and Gilbert Rosales (Male

Vampires);   Danielle Burgio (Woman Vampire);   Laura Cordova (Girl Vampire);   Troy Robinson, John Casino, Chad Stahelski, and Steve Blalock (Male Masters);   Marjean Holden, Anita Hart, and Cris Thomas Palomino (Female Masters);   Julia McFerrin and Lori Dillen (Hookers);   Jake Walker (County Sheriff);   Michael Huddleston (Motel Owner);   Todd Anderson (Deputy Sheriff);   Steven Hartley (Clerk);   Dennis E. Garber (Limousine Driver); Robert L. Bush (TV News Anchor);   Frank Darabont (Man with Buick).

LOS ANGELES TIMES, 10/30/98, Calendar/p. 22, Kevin Thomas

Twenty years ago John Carpenter came up with "Halloween," which became a classic, but for this Allhallows Eve his savage horror comedy "Vampires" is more trick than treat, and more trash than anything else. It's so ludicrous—every scene is a sendup, intentionally or otherwise—that it would seem that Carpenter is making an all-out attempt at what he surely knows to be impossible: to drive a stake through the entire vampire genre.

At least Carpenter, who also composed the film's hard-driving score, proceeds with exuberance and energy. That's also true of his star James Woods, who sets the film's tone for sheer outrageousness as a manic, foul-mouthed vampire slayer in the employ of the Vatican. The Vatican?

According to Don Jakoby's determinedly lurid script, back in 1340 a priest named Father Johann Valek led a revolt of a group of presumably oppressed Bohemian peasants, which resulted in the Church conducting an exorcism of Valek that somehow—don't ask precisely how—backfired. The effect of all this was to turn Valek into the world's first vampire.

Woods' Jack Crow, his burly sidekick Montoya (Daniel Baldwin) and his crew of Vatican mercenaries, who look to have been recruited from the Hell's Angels, have been summoned to New Mexico to exterminate a nest of vampires. Crow is a whiz with a crossbow, and the downed vampires are hauled out to the sunlight via a winch attached to Crow's truck.

Once the sun's rays hit them they incinerate. It's a dangerous, bloody business but somebody's gotta do it, and who better than Jack, whose introduction to the profession came when he was forced to slay his own father when the man turned into a vampire.

The local padre understands that these vampire slayers, having finished their grisly task, are going to want to have a little R&R, and he's arranged for booze and girls at a local motel. Just when the party starts to swing, with the priest himself getting a little tiddly, Valek (Thomas Ian Griffith), who has a specific reason for being in the Southwest, turns up to be the ultimate party pooper, leaving in his wake 19 dead, with Crow and Montoya barely escaping with their lives.

They have in tow a hooker (Sheryl Lee), whom Valek has put the bite on, but, because she now has a telepathic link to Valek, can theoretically lead Crow and Montoya to him for a final showdown. Along the way, Crow is determined to find out who set up him and his crew. Meanwhile, Crow has a meeting with his boss, no less a cardinal (Maximilian Schell), who assigns to him a scholarly young priest (Tim Guinee), a colossal good sport and a handy expository device for the filmmakers.

Woods has all the lines, but everybody's game, and we get a sizable slice of New Mexico scenery and historic locales thrown in. But in the end "John Carpenter's Vampires" is junk, and it leaves you with the feeling that its makers know it, too.

NEW YORK POST, 10/30/98, p. 40, Thelma Adams

James Woods strides across the main drag of a New Mexico backwater. Huddled in a leather jacket, his skinny legs weighed down by combat boots, his big head poking forward on the stalk of his neck, he looks like a really angry star ready to tear his agent a new contract.

Woods is vampire slayer Jack Crow, the hotshot impaler in "John Carpenter's Vampires." Crow has reason to be mad. Bloodsuckers bit his parents, forcing him to stake his own father.

Raised by the church, orphan Crow has become the Vatican's secret weapon, its champion in a secret war against the undead.

One bright and shiny New Mexico night, Crow comes face to face with the Pope's nemesis, Valek (Thomas Ian Griffith). The 600-year-old fallen priest doesn't look a day over 29.

Carpenter (Halloween) plays this confrontation as a duel under the moon. Valek and his fang gang walk cross the desert abreast in Wild Bunch formation. Meanwhile, Woods and his band of vampire crunchers get down with bra-less hookers in a raunchfest that Sam Peckinpah could have choreographed.

It's been ages since a mainstream movie has been this misogynist or anticlerical. Sheryl Lee got better treatment as the dead Laura Palmer in "Twin Peaks" than as the undead hooker beaten, then beloved, by chunky vampire killer Daniel Baldwin.

But when it comes to vampire flicks, good taste isn't the main criterion. We want bloodsuckers with good bite. Thanks to Maximilian Schell's foxy supporting performance and Don Jakoby's hard-bitten script, "Vampires" is a guilty pleasure, a Halloween horror howler.

NEWSDAY, 10/30/98, Part II/p. B6, John Anderson

Sucking the lifeblood out of the vampire genre, "John Carpenter's Vampires" opens with a pan across a southwestern desert tract. To a seemingly deserted house. Where a posse of vampire hunters arrives. Armed and ready. For an epic battle with the undead...

Pretty exciting, even if it is an almost verbatim quote from "Lord of Illusions"—which shows how desperate things have gotten for onetime fright master John ("Halloween") Carpenter. Ripping off Clive Barker? Can it get any more humiliating than this?

Only for his actors. James Woods, looking a bit like the undead himself, is Jack Crow, a kind of emissary of the Catholic Church, which raised him from childhood after his parents fell victim to vampirehood. Sounds like papal bull to me, but it might explain the joy Jack takes in physically abusing members of the priesthood, especially Adam Guiteau, a young priest who doesn't quite spill all he knows about the unholy and unbeatable Valek (Thomas Ian Griffith) while helping Jack and his partner Tony Montoya (Daniel Baldwin) hunt down the blood-thirsty agents of Satan.

"Vampires" should come with a warning label, something like "Movies named after their creators are liable to be harmful to your mind and / or stomach." Straining for gasps with his comic-horrific eviscerations / decapitations / amputations and for laughs with the abuse of priests and women—notably prostitute-turned-vampiress Katrina, played by Sheryl Lee, who has been through enough—Carpenter isn't just appealing to the lowest common denominator, he's groveling at its unhygienic feet. And then there's the script. "How do you like your stake?" Jack asks one vampiresicle-to-be. Bada-bing, bad-a-boom: How about in another theater?

Throw in a little homophobia, a dash of illogic, a total disregard for physics and what you're left with is Woods. You can't really picture him playing Hamlet, but he does seem to be an actor of some talent, who in "Vampires" makes every effort not to show it. Lee and Baldwin, who looks like any other Baldwin, if Baldwins retained water, are along for the ride. Which is too long, stupidly gory and, oddly enough, painfully anemic.

VILLAGE VOICE, 11/3/98, p. 135, Amy Taubin

John Carpenter crosses the vampire genre with the western-according-to-Peckinpah, adds some digital camera moves and hi-tech mutilation effects, and voilà!, a gorefest of epic proportions. More bodies are decapitated, crunched, pierced, gutted, and incinerated than in any movie in memory. Is it scary? Not at all. Is it funny? Occasionally, as when James Woods (playing a vampire slayer trained by the Church and assigned to clean up New Mexico) interrupts his labors to offer such cogent observations as "A master vampire able to walk in the sun! Unstoppable unless we stop him."

Vampires is so over-the-top that Woods's performance seems restrained—except when he's throwing Sheryl Lee across the room or bashing her head against the furniture. Lee plays a prostitute who's bitten by a master vampire. Since Carpenter is nothing if not literal-minded, the vampire attends to Lee's neck for only a second or two before sinking his fangs into her cunt. Poor Sheryl. Having begun her career as a corpse for David Lynch, she's now undead for John Carpenter. She's so mistreated in this film (when she's not being bitten or punched, she's naked and tied to the bedposts) that it's positively uplifting when she becomes a full-fledged vampire. Her first victim is Woods's partner, who's played by Daniel Baldwin. (No, she does not bite his dick.) Baldwin's character feels pretty conflicted about becoming a vampire. But not Lee's. When she struts down the highway, blood dripping from her fangs onto her cleavage, you know she's having the time of her life even though she's undead. And she's earned it. You go, girl!

Also reviewed in:
CHICAGO TRIBUNE, 10/30/98, Friday/p. A, Michael Wilmington
NEW YORK TIMES, 10/30/98, p. E21, Lawrence Van Gelder
VARIETY, 5/4-10/98, p. 83, Lisa Nesselson
WASHINGTON POST, 10/30/98, Weekend/p. 65, Michael O'Sullivan

JUNK FOOD

A Junk Food Connection release for Stance Company. *Producer:* Toshihiro Isomi. *Director:* Masashi Yamamoto. *Screenplay (Japanese with English subtitles):* Masashi Yamamoto. *Director of Photography:* Hiroshi Ito. *Editor:* Syuichi Kakesu. *Music:* DJ Krush and Ko Machida. *Running time:* 84 minutes. *MPAA Rating:* Not Rated.

CAST: Shizuko Yamamoto (Blind Woman); Miyuki Ijima (Miyuki); Akifumi Yamaguchi (Boss); Keigo Naruse (Murdered Man); Yoichi Okamura (Miyuki's Husband); Yoshiyuki (Hide); Onimaru (Ryo); Mia (Myan); Ali Ahmed (Cawl); Esther Moreno (Mariarna).

NEW YORK POST, 6/24/98, p. 45, Larry Worth

Despite its easy appeal, junk food has little nutritional value. So it's only fitting that the cinematic "Junk Food" has more style than substance.

It's more like celluloid eye candy, chock-full of attention-getting visuals and shock effects. But under Masashi Yamamoto's direction, that's not so bad.

Basically, the film spends 24 hours among Tokyo's down-and-outs. Yes; it's another day in the big city. But this time, it ain't pretty.

The tale segues from a fetching young office worker who's desperate for a fix to a murder-bent Pakistani, a homesick lady wrestler, a gang of no-nonsense thugs, a blind woman who wanders the streets, and countless others. As luck would have it, several of those paths cross that evening for a memorable rendezvous.

That's about it for plot, with the real focus on nuance, mood and atmosphere. Often, there's minimal dialogue as the metropolis' refugees go about their generally distasteful dealings.

Even the least interesting protagonist proves alluring, and nicely captured by Yamamoto's sweeping camerawork. Perhaps inspired by Hong Kong auteur Wong Kar-Wai and his hipster, style, Yamamoto's vision always seems fresh and unpredictable.

And since viewers will be clueless as to where the story's headed, they'll be jolted with regularity when graphic violence erupts from nowhere.

Though that mindset gets a little redundant before the film wraps up, "Junk Food" is hard to resist.

VILLAGE VOICE, 7/7/98, p. 117, J. Hoberman

Masashi Yamamoto's *Junk Food* is a walk on Tokyo's wild side framed by sequences in which an elderly woman (the 42-year-old filmmaker's mother) putters around her neighborhood. She's blind—and thus oblivious to the outrages her son is committing to film.

Junk Food's marginally more intriguing first half might be called, after Debussy, "The Morning of a Crackhead." Even as Mrs. Yamamoto does her daily shopping, a young woman wakes in a cold-water hovel, smokes the last of her coke, murders her trick, and then takes off on the commuter train for the high-rise office where she works. A certain amount of mordant comedy is derived from her drug-induced desperation amid decorous surroundings—she nods out midconference, intrudes on her boss's lunch to demand money, attempts to purchase dope in a posh boutique. Yamamoto punctuates these antics with subjective flash frames and slo-mo blurs until, like just about everything in *Junk Food,* the narrative dissolves into a degrading, bloody mess.

After the crackhead has made it home to hubby with a big bruise and five quarts of milk, *Junk Food* switches to a more documentary style—stitching together a patchwork of vignettes, mainly involving foreigners in nighttown. These include a Mexican woman wrestler, several Pakistanis, and a Chinese American hooker. The mode is lowlife, low-budget splatter, but the mood is cosmopolitan. If you tough it out, you'll be rewarded with the spectacle of the survivors dancing to salsa at dawn—just as Mrs. Yamamoto rises to face another day.

Also reviewed in:
CHICAGO TRIBUNE, 8/21/98, Friday/p. F, Michael Wilmington
NEW YORK TIMES, 6/24/98, p. E5, Stephen Holden
VARIETY, 3/30-4/5/98, p. 59, Ken Eisner

JUNK MAIL

A Lions Gate Films release of a Norsk Film AS and Atlas Film AS production.   *Producer:* Dag Nordahl and Peter Boe.   *Director:* Pal Sletaune.   *Screenplay (Norwegian with English subtitles):* Pal Sletaune and Jonny Halberg.   *Director of Photography:* Kjell Vassdal. *Editor:* Pal Gengenbach.   *Music:* Joachim Holbek.   *Sound:* Ragge Samuelson, Sturla Einarson, Berndt Frithiof, and (music) Peter Brander.   *Casting:* Liv Sandvik, Kjersti Paulsen, and Eva Isaksen. *Production Designer:* Gudny Hummelvoll and Carina Brattvik. *Art Director:* Karl Juliusson. *Set Decorator:* Vida Thune.   *Special Effects:* Pal Morten Hverven.   *Costumes:* Bente Winther-Larsen.   *Make-up:* Eva Rygh.   *Stunt Coordinator:* Wolfgang Wedde.   *Running time:* 83 minutes.   *MPAA Rating:* Not Rated.

CAST: Robert Skjaerstad (Roy Amundsen);   Andrine Saether (Line Groberg);   Per Egil Aske (Georg Rheinhardsen);   Eli Anne Linnestad (Betsy);   Trond Fausa Aurvag (Espen);   Adne Olav Sekkelsten (Per);   Bjorn Sundquist (Stein);   Karl Sundby (Rune);   Rold Arly Lund (Postmaster); Geir Morstad (Einar Karlsen);   Rolf Dolven (Security Guard);   Helge Sveen (Second-hand Bookseller);   Geir Johnsen, Henrik Hole, and Harald Kolaas (Junkies);   Marit Syversen (Woman at Dry Cleaners);   Henning Syverud, John Ivar Bye, and Runar Johannessen (Post Office Colleagues);   Bentine Holm (Nurse);   Jan Zaborowski (Pole);   Suzanne Paalgaard and Lars Frogner (Couple in Café).

LOS ANGELES TIMES, 4/24/98, Calendar/p. 8, Kenneth Turan

Roy is a postman, but he's not exactly in the heroic Kevin Costner mold. Downtrodden, woebegone and about the loneliest guy around, Roy is so listless he doesn't hesitate to throw mail away when his load weighs him down. "Junk Mail" is his story and what a wonderfully eccentric black comic fable it turns out to be.

Winner of the International Critics Week prize at Cannes last year and a top box-office attraction in its native Norway, "Junk Mail" is a Scandinavian delicacy possessed of the fine sense of bleak but amusing absurdity that invariably characterizes comedies from that part of the world.

Yet, as put together by co-writer (with Jonny Halberg) and first-time director Pal Sletaune, "Junk Mail" boasts appealing elements missing from similar films by Finnish director and art-house favorite Aki Kaurismaki. The pace is faster, the sense of narrative greater, and the humor, while still off-beat, is considerably more accessible.

The heart of "Junk Mail" is actor Robert Skjaerstad's performance as Roy, the all but lifeless romantic hero of the piece. The soul of ineptitude, with a gift for making everything he touches worse, Roy is such a lost soul even his misfit postal buddies in Oslo can't think of anything he's good at. "Walking," someone tentatively suggests, but even that appears to be suspect.

With Skjaerstad supplying the look of fearful desperation that is Roy's constant companion, "Junk Mail" imagines and observes his character in such careful detail that though the situations he's involved in get odder and odder we never have any doubt of their reality.

Initially Roy leads a life of almost monastic solitude. After a day spent delivering as much mail as he can handle, Roy retires to an evening in a chaotic apartment steaming open pilfered letters and eating unheated spaghetti out of an ancient can. The last time he washed a dish, or himself, could well have been decades ago.

One day, killing time in a bookstore when he should be working, Roy notices a young woman (Andrine Saether) shoplifting a book. The sense of complicity with her life that moment gives him provides an almost erotic charge that curiously galvanizes the slovenly postman.

Through a combination of amateur sleuthing and blind luck, Roy discovers that the woman, named Line, works at a cleaners and has hearing difficulties. Without even the shadow of a life of his own, the opportunity to eavesdrop on someone else is more than a natural snoop like Roy can resist. When fate puts the keys to Line's apartment in his hands, he can't help but let himself in and look things over when she's not around.

Crossing that most ordinary threshold and investigating a living space most notable for Line's impressive supply of Kellogg's Frosted Flakes turns out to be a through-the-looking-glass experience for the befuddled Roy. After that moment, nothing about his life has any chance of being the same again.

Though it's characterized by a dark and droll, pleasantly surreal sense of humor, "Junk Mail" balances its mordant sensibility with elements of a thriller plot. Armed robbery, physical violence, a suicide attempt, bad sex and drunken nights out with blotto postal workers doing karaoke versions of "Born to Be Wild" suddenly appear like apparitions in Roy's existence. It's hard to imagine a more bizarre romantic scenario than the one "Junk Mail" illustrates, and that is the heart of its charm.

NEW YORK POST, 4/10/98, p. 42, Thelma Adams

Who knew Oslo had a dark side? In "Junk Mail," being a mail carrier has its romantic side—if you consider steaming open the love letters of strangers a passionate act.

Norway's bid for the 1997 Academy Award is an unpretentious thriller-cum-love story by newcomer Pal Sletaune. In this Nordic "Il Postino," Roy (Robert Skjaerstad) is an Oslo postal worker; Line (Andrine Saether) works at a dry cleaner.

They're a match made in Oslo: He wears filthy clothes; she cleans them. No one listens to him; she's deaf. He reads strangers' mail; she read strangers lips. He tosses mail he's too apathetic to deliver in an abandoned tunnel; she tries to toss her life away by drowning in a bath.

Roy and Line meet very uncute: She forgets her keys in her mailbox, and he lets himself into her apartment. He squats in the flat while she's at work, and falls in love with a woman he's never formally met.

The postman quickly discovers that behind he girl's pretty, quiet facade lies a secret life of stolen cash and brutality. His voyeurism unlocks a door to the danger zone. Likewise, "Junk Mail" is anything but junk; it's an unexpected key into a dankly funny world of intrigue and unlikely affection.

NEWSDAY, 4/10/98, Part II/p. B7, John Anderson

Some Scandinavians have described the mise-en-scene of "Junk Mail" as the "other side of Oslo" because relative to the image we usually get out of Norway, it's an urban ruin and moral cavity. Well, it's certainly not tidy and white, but it could be the other side of anywhere. In fact it probably is.

Confirming the (unwarranted!) suspicions of postal customers everywhere, "Junk Mail" delivers Roy (Robert Skjaerstad)—unenthusiastic, unhygienic, unmotivated and possibly unstable. Roy is a mailman who opens people's letters, throws away mail he doesn't want to deliver and generates a general aura of unsavoriness. The miracle of Pal Sletaune's debut feature film is that you empathize with him anyway.

This, despite the fact that his co-workers find him repulsive, he eats cold spaghetti out of a can (occasionally smearing it on the mail and when he finds that one of the women on his route, Line (Andrine Saether), has left her apartment keys in her mail box, he has a set made for himself.

From this point in Roy's squalid life, things get dicey and it's Sletaune's gift that he's able to juggle so many disparate elements at once and still get where he wants to go. Even as Roy is rooting around in Line's apartment—discovering as he does that she and Georg (Per Egil Aske) were involved in a mugging that left a man hospitalized—we don't want him to get caught, because he has suddenly become the good guy. Goodness is, as Sletaune well knows, a relative value.

Roy's still a dope—bringing his vomit-strewn jacket to Line's dry cleaning shop and then asking her out. But as "Junk Mail" becomes a romance as well as a slouchy thriller, it also jousts with the ludicrous nature of bureaucracy: When some junkies try to steal Roy's post bag, the strap gets caught on his arm and he receives a commendation for protecting the mail. And the officials presenting the award have even fewer reasons to live than Roy.

Ah, but Line gives him one, and "Junk Mail" turns out to be sweet despite the squalor. There are many coolly executed narrative twists, unexpected shifts in mood (although the overall tone is slyly dispassionate) and deftly deadpan performances by Skjaerstad, Saether and Aske as the evil Georg. "Junk Mail" is, in fact, this year's delightful surprise. And it should be a big hit down at the post office.

SIGHT AND SOUND, 4/98, p. 40, Jonathan Romney

Oslo Postman Roy Amundsen becomes fascinated with Line, a deaf woman who works in a dry cleaners. One day Line forgets her keys in her mailbox in an apartment block on Roy's route. Roy steals into her flat where he picks up the card of a man called Georg. Mugged by derelicts, Roy ends up in hospital, where he discovers a man in a critical condition—a security guard who was violently robbed. Discharged, Roy is mistakenly hailed as a hero because he didn't lose his mail sack and is awarded a gold watch. Snooping around Line's flat one day, Roy saves her from a suicide attempt.

In a club, Roy meets Betsy, an ageing good-time girl and, posing as Georg, takes her back to Line's. She discovers a bag of money, and the night ends in a row. Roy finally talks to Line at the dry cleaners. Later, he overhears her talking to Georg about the attack on the guard. Wanting no more involvement in the crime, Line gives Georg the money. Roy corners Georg in a toilet and grabs the money, but Georg catches hold of the watch with Roy's name on it. Roy hides the money. He strikes up a friendship with Line. Georg ambushes him at his flat, but Roy gets away. Betsy turns up at Line's, and her heavies beat up Georg, mistakenly thinking that he is Roy. Roy arrives and rushes off with Line in a stolen van. Georg pursues them, but finally collapses. Line guesses that Roy has been in her flat and, even though he tells her he saved her life, angrily walks off. Roy follows her down the road.

For his lead role as *Junk Mail*'s anti-social, downbeaten postman, actor Robert Skjaerstad spent four months in worn-down shoes perfecting his walk. This painstakingly unspectacular variant on Method preparation is typical of the film's style: a lot of careful contrivance has gone into it, yet it comes across as a very uncontrived film. Pal Sletaune's debut feature—part thriller, part black comedy—operates at a delicate pitch of lugubriousness, which pushes it out of the realm of realism, yet not so far that it looks like stylised grotesqueness. It has been compared to the studied moroseness of Aki Kaurismaki, although the feel is closer to a French strain of the Cinema of Abjection, to certain Bertrand Blier films or to Alain Corneau's *Série Noire*.

Roy is about as abject as a protagonist can be while remaining essentially sympathetic—a shyly malicious slacker who thinks nothing of dumping his mailbag and taking petty revenge on a customer, and whose attentions to Line are little short of stalking. But at least he stands out as borderline redeemable compared with his colleagues—a Gogolian crew of pasty-faced martinets and no-hope nerd subordinates. Roy is brought to life by the subtle energies that Skjaerstad brings to the role, nervously peering over his shoulders, rarely cracking a smile, looking altogether like Tim Roth gone drastically to seed.

The film is memorable for the thoroughness of its look and feel, its soundtrack underscored with an ambient drizzle of urban noise. The dominant colour is washed out khaki green, with the characters' skin tones drably matching the uniforms and decor. Grim little touches of set dressing flesh out the characters' lives: Roy's lunch of tinned sausages and spaghetti is matched by the strangely eloquent sight of the Kellogg's Frosties in Line's larder (he tries to bond with her by claiming to be devoted to the stuff). Other touches are equally inspired but very nearly verge on cartoonishness, such as the boozy, hard faced Betsy belting out a karaoke version of 'I Love Rock'n Roll'.

Sletaune subtly handles the seedy nature of Roy's voyeurism, but the narrative is less successful when the crime intrigue gets under way, leading to incongruous comedy-thriller touches (a menacing Georg emerging from the darkness singing the *Postman Pat* song). The crime story is too involved to let the film remain only a character sketch, not quite complex enough to make for a full-blown Hitchcockian exercise. Sletaune and co-writer Jonny Halberg are better on ironies arising out of character traits. When Roy is attacked, he tries to give up his bag but his strap gets caught; he's therefore assumed to be a hero, defending his mail. His rare acts of decency invariably misfire: giving water to the ailing guard in hospital, he immediately causes a drastic relapse. Most eloquent of all is the business of Line's vomit stain on his coat, which he comes almost to cherish, and oddly, there *is* a suggestion of mutual tenderness when he takes his coat to her for cleaning.

In its less effective moments, *Junk Mail* could feel like a wallow in other people's misery. There's certainly no sign of the spiritual resources that we are able to infer in Kaurismaki's characters even at their most wretched. The film is also flawed by being so exclusively centred on Roy, with Line never emerging as much more than the hazy object of his yearnings. But if finally not quite satisfying, this is a striking debut, and at a time when European low-budget cinema is increasingly mired in spurious glamour, it's quite a thrill to see a film so committed to the pleasures of the glum and the grimy.

VILLAGE VOICE, 4/14/98, p. 64, Dennis Lim

Hailed as the forerunner of a supposedly imminent "Norwave" Pal Sletaune's first feature, *Junk Mail,* takes the stereotype of a supersterile Scandinavia and empties a slop bucket on it. A fanciful gross-out both clever and aimless, the film centers on—or, more accurately, runs circles around—Roy (Robert Skjaerstad), an Oslo postman for whom routine invasion of privacy constitutes the sole job perk. A jowly, sullen fellow, he opens anything in his mailbag that looks like it might be a fun read, delivers only what he feels like, and dumps the rest in a tunnel. Roy's also a slob—and in case his elaborately scuzzy pad isn't enough of a giveaway, he's shown wolfing down cold spaghetti straight from the can and applying dishwashing liquid to his armpits by way of ablutions.

Don't let the in-your-face slovenliness fool you, though; *Junk Mail*'s underlying exactitude is positively, well, Nordic. No detail is inconsequential—the film is as streamlined, incident-filled, and hermetically plotted as a superior *Seinfeld* episode (i.e., one from about five years back). Midroute one day, Roy wanders into the apartment of a hearing-impaired blond (Andrine Saether) and is soon trapped in a crime caper populated by grotesques. There's a violent thug, a man in a coma, and some missing loot involved, not to mention multiple cases of mistaken identity, and Sletaune keeps the reasonably familiar setup tightly wound and slightly off-balance.

Save for one priceless moment—an indescribable karaoke rendition of "Born To Be Wild"—the film sticks with low-key absurdism (the closest reference point, tonal and geographical, is deadpan Finn Aki Kaurismaki). There's less to *Junk Mail* than meets the eye. For all its very palpable grime, the film is ultimately content to evaporate into whimsy. Still, Sletaune's unquestionable way with vivid detail shouldn't be taken lightly.

Also reviewed in:
CHICAGO TRIBUNE, 5/8/98, Friday/p. D, Mark Caro
NEW YORK TIMES, 4/7/98, p. E5, Janet Maslin
VARIETY, 5/19-25/97, p. 52, Derek Elley

KILLER CONDOM

A Troma Entertainment release of an Ascot Filmproduktion/ECCO Film production. *Executive Producer:* Michael Stricker. *Producer:* Ralph S. Dietrich and Harald Reichebner. *Director:* Martin Walz. *Screenplay (German with English subtitles):* Ralf Koenig, Martin Walz, and Mario Kramp. *Based on the comics by:* Ralf Koenig. *Director of Photography:* Alexander Honisch. *Editor:* Simone Klier. *Music:* Emil Viklicky. *Sound:* Jochen Hergersberg. *Art Director:* Agi Ariumsaichan Dawaachu. *Set Designer:* H.R. Giger. *Special Effects:* Jorg Buttgereit. *Costumes:* Anja Niehaus. *Running time:* 90 minutes. *MPAA Rating:* Not Rated.

CAST: Udo Samel (Luigi Mackeroni);   Peter Lohmeyer (Sam O'Connery);   Iris Berben (Frau Dr. Riffelson);   Marc Richter (Billy);   Leonard Lansink (Babette);   Henning Schlüter (Robinson);   Gerd Wameling (Professor);   Ralf Wolter (Boris Smirnoff);   Merte Becker (Phyllis);   Otto Sander (Mr. Higgens);   Monika Hansen (Mrs. Higgens);   Hella von Sinnen (Polizistin); Adriana Altaras (Putzfrau); Ron Williams (Boss/Police Chief); Evelyn Künnecke (Wilma);   Inga Busch (Inga);   Georg-Martin Bode (Dick McGovern);   Lillemor Malau (Edelnutte).

NEW YORK POST, 7/31/98, p. 44, Larry Worth

Admittedly, no one will be looking for high art in "Killer Condom," a film whose advertising slogan is "the rubber that rubs you out." A few chuckles, on the other hand, isn't a lot to ask.

Instead, German director Martin Walz specializes in dumb, heavy-handed yuks, as in the name of the gay hero: Detective Mackeroni. It's assumed that all subsequent wet-noodle jokes will have viewers doubled over.

Even sillier—and more inappropriate—is a finale that preaches about the need to honor gay contributions to society. Good message, bad venue.

Basically, the schizo plot follows Mackeroni's search through Manhattan's sleaziest dives for a carnivorous condom that jumps across rooms at will and squeaks its disapproval at gay liaisons—kind of like Disney's purring green "Flubber" creature, but with razor-sharp teeth and an attitude.

And the clues to the condom's whereabouts? A bloody trail of castrated genitals. Funny stuff, huh?

Between battling the prophylactic "Jaws," the detective also tackles his ex-boyfriend-turned-drag-queen, never mind a handsome hustler whose tricks in the Hotel Quickie put him in ongoing danger.

But no matter what direction this stupidity takes, it triumphs only at time wasting and recycled gags. Rather than being drawn into the dark comedy, viewers will find themselves wondering why all Big Apple cops are speaking German. Not a good sign.

To his credit, Udo Samel, who looks like Berlin's Bob Hoskins, brings dignity to his character. Avoiding any limp-wristed routines he not only plays it straight but ignores the dialogue's endless double-entendres. Though Marc Richter's pretty-boy prostitute also strives for subtlety, histrionics from the supporting cast dominate.

Granted the title gets a laugh. But it's the only one "Killer Condom" generates.

VILLAGE VOICE, 8/4/98, p. 106, Laurie Stone

Dicks are biting the dust at the Hotel Quickie—an epidemic of dismemberment due to cheapo condoms the management distributes. In this German fantasy of mongrel, sexually emancipated New York—directed by Martin Walz and based on Ralf Konig's smut-friendly comic *Kondom des Grauens*—the government underwrites free rubbers to encourage safe sex. Designed by slime connoisseur H. R. Giger, who did the creatures for *Alien,* the killer condoms at first look like ordinary sheaths but, once unfurled, grow a ring of razor teeth and a funnel of pulsing, mucus-spewing tissue. They can wriggle out of packages, make taunting, giggly sounds, and leap from long distances onto unsuspecting extremities. It happens that Luigi Mackeroni (Udo Samel), a guy detective with a penchant for lonesome rent boys and a *shvantz* so long it gives new resonance to the term short-arm inspection, tricks at the Quickie. During a session with pouty, beguiling Billy (Marc Richter), Luigi loses his right ball to one of the wolves in latex clothing, and his resolve to uncover the plot becomes personal.

Though scenes repeat and the story meanders, the movie lofts over longueurs with a tone of deadpan farce, bravura sleaziness, and Samel's pleasingly dissonant world-weariness. In one amusing interlude, a coroner—played by an elderly blond with a cigarette dangling from her lower lip—declares the condoms part virus, part worm, and part piranha. It's fun, too, catching German touches, like trough-sized mugs of beer served in bars. *Killer Condom* trumpets a sex-positive moral: the culprit turns out to be a religious fanatic, punishing deviance and pleasure. But the movie's soupy undercurrents are more libidinal, chief among them a *vagina dentata* with a phallic mission to bust penises.

Also reviewed in:
NEW YORK TIMES, 7/31/98, p. E21, Lawrence Van Gelder
VARIETY, 3/17-23/97, p. 56, David Stratton

KILLING TIME

A Pilgrim Films release in association with Metrodome Films of a Richard Johns production. *Executive Producer:* Paul Brooks. *Producer:* Richard Johns. *Director:* Bharat Nalluri. *Screenplay:* Neil Marshall, Fleur Costello, and Caspar Berry. *Director of Photography:* Sam McCurdy. *Editor:* Neil Marshall. *Music:* Christopher Slaski. *Production Designer:* Ronald Gow. *Running time:* 88 minutes. *MPAA Rating:* Not Rated.

CAST: Craig Fairbrass (Bryant); Kendra Torgan (Assassin); Peter Harding (Madison); Neil Armstrong (John); Ian McLaughlin (George); Stephen D. Thirkeld (Charlie); Rick Warden (Smithy); Nigel Leach (Jacob Reilly); Phil Dixon (Frank).

LOS ANGELES TIMES, 1/30/98, Calendar/p. 16, John Anderson

[The following review by John Anderson appeared in a slightly different form in NEWSDAY, 1/30/98, Part II/p. B11.]

With Eastwoodian effectiveness, the Hit Woman With No Name struts into and over the bad guys in Bharat Nalluri's "Killing Time," mowing' em down, blowing' em up and making them share her pain, even if she doesn't remember it. She has no history, so we have the luxury of projecting. Picture a female grim reaper in group therapy with Austin Powers and Dr. Laura.

Or, consider how essential death is to the movies—like popcorn to the theaters, like hot dog to the roll—and consider Kendra Torgan's lethal seductress the *chef de cuisine* with no name. Why shouldn't she who prepares the main course be exalted to the level of artiste?

The number of hit men/women in the movies seems to be rivaling the number of smokers on screen as the least representative example of the American public, although this is a British movie. And besides, the Assassin is Italian (she listens to English-language tapes while trying to shoot a pomegranate off a victim's head). But why shouldn't we be made to look for provocative questions while being spoon-fed inanity? Isn't that what separates us from the beasts, finding meaning where there isn't any?

There's a recurring anecdote in this blood-soaked suspense yarn about how Burmese women had to walk behind their men until 1945, when they got to walk in front and check for land mines. If the intention is to cast the beautiful and quite lethal Assassin as a feminist ideal, it's not clear this is quite what Betty Friedan had in mind. But the Assassin certainly controls her own destiny and that of the rest of the characters, too.

The film starts promisingly. The evil Jacob Reilly (Nigel Leach), speaking to a soon-to-be-dead victim of his lust for bloodshed, catalogs the sexual peculiarities of his literary heroes—Andre Gide, Joyce, Dostoevsky, Byron, T.E. Lawrence—and compares them with his own erotic peculiarities (think of Professor Moriarty as imagined by the Marquis de Sade). His argument in defense of himself isn't quite on the order of Nietzschean *Übermensch* entitlement, but rather that the depravities he enjoys automatically rank him with his idols. Either way, he's the kind of guy you'd like to spend some (screen) time with.

Instead, we find ourselves among a hapless gang of working-class Cockney mobsters, whose as-yet-unexplained assignment is to get the Assassin as soon as she gets her target, which is Reilly. It's like watching RuPaul slug it out with the Seven Dwarfs. She walks through them the way she walks through Reilly's headquarters, like an avenging Amazon angel wielding a harp full of bullets.

So no real tension, just a lot of gauzy, arch poses by Torgan (the once and present model gets the coveted "and introducing" line in the opening credits), who is as photogenic a hired killer as has ever committed mass murder. Director Nalluri, unwisely, tries to operate on multiple levels of mood, shifting sensibility as he cuts from the two detectives (Craig Fairbrass and Peter

Harding) investigating the slaughter at Reilly's, to the rapidly diminishing gang of hoods, to the Assassin herself, all Bond girl-style light and vapors and accented by the suggestion that she responds to killing the same way Reilly does.

Tawdry? *Of course.* Also, hilarious, but Nalluri's embrace of camp is only halfhearted, so the film only half works. When the Assassin (the press notes for the film say her name is Maria, but we never hear it) wields two guns, she's John Woo's Chow Yun-Fat; when she dresses in black, she's Mrs. Peel. When she shoots another hood, she's your pal, because the cast is only so large and eventually, you pray, she's going to get to the end of the line.

NEW YORK POST, 1/30/98, p. 44, Michael Medved

Even the shabbiest films from Hollywood offer world-class technology in re-creating wounds and gunshots, so the amateurish pistol play and garish mutilation makeup of the British import "Killing Time"' come as something of a shock. This is no small defect in a film that offers absolutely nothing beyond 20 badly staged murders pointlessly stretched out over 90 minutes.

A glamorous Italian hit-woman (model Kendra Torgan) is hired by a British cop (Craig Fairbrass) to avenge the death of his partner. Between listening to her English-language tapes, and taking countless baths and showers, she's supposed to rub out a depraved pseudo-intellectual (Nigel Leach).

The cop who hired her, however, wants to destroy evidence of his crime, so he pays four goofballs to assassinate the assassin when she's done her job.

The film tries to evoke spaghetti Westerns with the lanky, buxom, black-clad, nameless contract killer in the Clint Eastwood role. Flashes of warped humor, like the bonehead dialogue of paid killers "killing time," play like junior-varsity Tarantino.

The project will never earn a fistful of dollars—even with camera work and acting that's occasionally good—because the script and shoot-em-up scenes are bad and ugly.

VILLAGE VOICE, 2/3/98, p. 54, Gary Dauphin

Brit indie *Killing Time* starts out with what's probably the most ridiculous opening monologue in movie history (the punchline goes something like: "I kill to climax, and that makes you, Inspector So-and-So, my first lay of the evening!") and quickly degrades from there. *Killing Time* centers on a police-ordered contract killing gone bad, with do-gooder bobby (Craig Fairbrass) hiring not only an Italian hit woman to assassinate an untouchable sex-and-violence fetishist but also a group of local lads to kill her in turn. The plan goes awry from the very beginning, but not so completely as director Bharat Nalluri's debut. A stumbling farrago of slick sleaze and hooligan humor, *Killing Time* doesn't live up to the ironic reading of its title, as its more likely to bore you to death than to distract you.

Also reviewed in:
NEW YORK TIMES, 1/30/98, p. E16, Lawrence Van Gelder

KINGDOM, THE: PART 2

An October Films release of a Zentropa Entertainments and the Danish Broadcasting Corporation with the cooperation of Liberator Productions. *Executive Producer:* Peter Aalbaek Jensen. *Producer:* Vibeke Windelov and Svend Abrahamsen.   *Director:* Lars von Trier and Morten Arnfred.   *Screenplay (Danish with English subtitles):* Lars von Trier and Niels Vorsel. *Director of Photography:* Erik Kress. *Editor:* Molly Malene Stensgaard and Pernille Bech Christensen. *Music:* Joachim Holbek. *Sound:* Peter Christian Hansen. *Production Designer:* Lene Nielsen. *Art Director:* Jette Lehmann and Lars Christian Lindholm. *Special Effects:* Annette Rolfshoj and Lars Kolding Andersen. *Costumes:* Annelise Bailey. *Make-up:* Birthe Lyngsoe and Jeanet Keil. *Special Make-up Effects:* Kim Olsson and Lis Olsson. *Stunt Coordinator:* Hans-Peter Ludvigsen. *Running time:* 300 minutes. *MPAA Rating:* Not Rated.

CAST: Ernst-Hugo Aregard (Stig G. Helmer);   Kirsten Rolffes (Mrs. Sigrid Drusse);   Holger Juul Hansen (Dr. Einar Moesgaard);   Soren Pilmark (Krogen);   Ghita Norby (Rigmer Mortenson);   Jens Okking (Bulder);   Birthe Neumann (Miss Svendsen);   Otto Brandenburg (Porter Hansen);   Erik Wedersoe (Ole);   Baard Owe (Palle Bondo);   Birgitte Raaberg (Judith Peterson);   John Hahn-Petersen (Bob, Director General);   Peter Mygind (Mogge);   Vita Jensen and Morten Rotne Leffers (Dishwashers);   Henning Jensen (Nivesen, Hospital Manager);   Udo Kier (Little Brother/Aage Krüger);   Soren Elung Jensen (Man in Top Hat);   Paul Hüttel (Doctor Steenbaek);   Holger Perfort (Professor Ulrich);   Klaus Wegener (Casualty Doctor);   Michelle Bjorn-Andersen (Pediatrician);   Timm Mehrens (Operating Theater Doctor);   Louise Fribo (Susanne "Sanne" Jeppesen);   Tine Miehe-Renard (Night Nurse);   Julie Wieth (Pediatric Nurse);   Annette Ketscher (Casualty Nurse);   Birthe Tove and Lise Schroder (Nurses);   Dorrit Stender-Petersen (Assisting Nurse);   Ole Boisen (Christian);   Thomas Stender (Student);   Cecilie Brask (Young Woman in Therapy);   Claus Nissen (Madsen);   Thomas Bo Larsen (Falcon);   Steen Svarre (Man in Overalls);   Laura Christensen (Mona);   Mette Munk Plum (Mona's Mother);   Michael Philip Simpson (Man from Haiti);   Fash Shodeinde (Philip Marco);   Kim Jansson (Detective Jensen);   Claus Flygare (Detective Nielsen);   Nils Bank-Mikkelsen (Hospital Pastor);   Britta Lillesee (Woman in Bed);   Henrik Flig (Car Crash Victim);   Birger Jensen (Janitor);   Peter Hartmann (Removal Man);   Lars Lunoe (Minister of Health);   Jens Jorn Spottag (Attorney Bisgaard);   Helle Virkner (Emma);   Annevig Shelde Ebbe (Mary);   Torben Zeller (Crematorium Functionary);   Jannie Faurschou (Orthopedist);   Stellan Skarsgard (Swedish Lawyer);   Klaus Pagh (Bailiff);   Vera Gebehr (Gerda);   Mette Hald (Cross Girl);   Bjarre G. Nielsen (New Hospital Pastor);   Anders Hove (Celebrant);   Ingolf David (Death);   Philip Zandén (Jönsson from Lund);   Ruth Junker (Voice of Dishwasher 1);   Peter Gilsfort (Voice of Dishwasher 2);   Evald Krog (Voice of "Little Brother");   Ulrik Cold (Narrator).

LOS ANGELES TIMES, 5/8/98, Calendar/p. 6, Kevin Thomas

Something is still rotten in the state of Denmark!

Having affirmed the possibility that faith can work miracles in his go-for-broke, internationally acclaimed "Breaking the Waves," Denmark's endlessly venturesome Lars von Trier returned to television to create "The Kingdom II," a sequel to his mind-blowing account of supernatural occurrences—and all-too-human shenanigans—at the National State Hospital in Copenhagen.

With co-director Morten Arnfred, Trier continues the miniseries with four more chapters, which add up to a whopping four-hour, 46-minute running time. A lot of people who submitted to the similarly lengthy "The Kingdom" at the Nuart last year will find it rewarding to return to the theater for more. (A concluding Part III is already planned.)

"The Kingdom II," which Trier wrote with Niels Vorsel, is at once a greater challenge both to its makers and its audiences. That's because it's basically a restatement of the first part's warning against the disdaining of the spiritual in the modern world.

Yet Trier and Vorsel are so imaginative, so hilariously comprehensive in their perceptions of the foibles of human nature, that a revisit to the Kingdom, as that immense hospital is referred to, is worth the effort.

Be warned, however: "Effort" is the operative word here, for this time there are a staggering 11 plot lines going on instead of the mere five of the first part. If you lose a thread momentarily you can't afford to worry because you're in imminent danger of losing another; besides, everything does tie together at the end of this soap opera of the supernatural.

As viewers of Part I will recall, this state hospital, rated Denmark's finest, was constructed over the site of an ancient marshland used as bleaching ponds, which gave off a seemingly permanent fog. With the construction of the hospital "ignorance and superstition were never to shake the bastions of science again." Yeah, sure.

The key figure among many is again Sigrid Drusse (Kirsten Rolffes), a 70-ish retired journalist with psychic powers. A determined malingerer, Drusse actually leaves the hospital at the beginning of Part 2 only to be struck by a car. Back in the Kingdom she senses, after a course of bizarre events, that the hospital itself is somehow "wounded" and that someone on staff for whatever reason has summoned the powers of Satan.

The most extraordinary occurrence is that an intern, Judith (Birgitte Raaberg), has given birth to a baby with a man's head. The baby rapidly develops a gigantic yet fragile body and speaks adult thoughts in a baby's voice. He has been sired by Aage Kruger, a demon who also fathered little Mary, the ghost of Part 1; ever-sinister Udo Kier is a natural for Kruger, but he also plays, in one of his most daunting roles, the baby—a noble, pathetic creature. Setting the incredibly complex story in motion is that Stig Helmer (Ernst-Hugo Jaregard), the hospital's Swedish consulting neurosurgeon, has botched an operation on a brain-damaged girl, Mona (Laura Christensen), and he now faces a summons.

The pompous, inept Helmer is the star in the film's large gallery of hypocritical, corrupt old fools. (Trier has lots of fun with the self-importance that accrues with age and power.) Other key medicos are head of neurosurgery Einar Moesgaard (Holger Juul Hansen), whose search for relief from an imminent nervous breakdown allows von Trier to skewer faddish therapies); Bondo (Baard Owe), a professor of pathology and a self-dramatizing martyr who has had a cancerous liver transplanted in himself in the dubious name of research; and Krogen (Soren Pilmark), a hospital administrator who has decided that sustaining the lives of hopelessly disabled patients is not cost-effective. There is much, much more.

As "Waves" was before it, "The Kingdom II" is shot entirely with hand-held cameras, which gives it an eavesdropping cinema verite quality. And once again the immense cast dazzles from start to finish, none more so than the assured, compelling Rolffes (and including a cameo by "Breaking the Waves" star Stellan Skarsgard). If you feel up to the demands of its running time, the Kingdom is well worth a new visit.

NEW YORK POST, 5/6/98, p. 47, Larry Worth

Not many movies can clock in at nearly five hours and leave audiences begging for more. but "The Kingdom, Part 2," the continuation of 1994's look at the haunted happenings in a Copenhagen hospital, is sheer joy.

The lunatic patients and even loonier doctors are all back for another ghost-filled go-round, though this one is both funnier and gorier than the original.

Director von Trier again proves a master weaver as he cuts between at least 10 subplots that range from apparitions and zombies to unrequited love and malpractice. The highlight is a twist on "Rosemary's Baby" that'll produce shudders, laughs and tears in equal measure.

Best of all, the same characters that distinguished the first chapter of "The Kingdom" are back on board. Seeing them again is like catching up with old friends, each with a unique history and eccentric quirks: the double-dealing, Dane-hating neurosurgeon, the meddling but oh-so-wise lady ghost-hunter, the pair of slow-witted dishwashers who hear "whisperings," and on and on and on.

Great writing has made the principals particularly memorable—along with one of the best ensemble casts in memory. Ernst-Hugo Jaregard, Kirsten Rolffes and Ghita Norby stand out as three of the saga's senior members while Fassbinder veteran Udo Kier goes above and beyond in a dual role that must be seen to be believed.

Of course, those who missed 1994's 4½-hour installment of von Trier's masterpiece will be in the dark, essentially having walked into a story in progress. Thankfully, the situation is easily rectified as "The Kingdom" is available on video.

But beware: the series is highly addictive. With the current production culminating in von Trier's trademark "to be continued," followers will be counting the days until "Kingdom III.

NEWSDAY, 5/6/98, Part II/p. B7, John Anderson

Gambling, drugs and sexual "research" preoccupy the staff at Copenhagen's Kingdom Hospital, where the files have been written in code ever since the patients gained legal access to them—and where a mob of restless spirits makes the rounds, keening and waiting for the personification of evil to rear his/her ugly head.

The loathsome Swedish neurosurgeon Stig Helmer (Ernst-Hugo Jaregard) faces prosecution for having left little Mona (Laura Christensen) in a vegetative state; he covers his tracks by putting Haitian voodoo poison in the coffee of Krogen the registrar (Soren Pilmark). Meanwhile, Little Brother (Udo Kier), the grotesque baby born to Judith (Birgitte Raaberg) and fathered by the evil Aage Kruger (Udo Kier), grows at an and somewhat disgusting rate of speed while Christian and Mogge (Ole Boisen and Peter Mygind), when not transfixed by the hospital-organized ambulance racing, circle Sanne (Louise Fribo), the intern obsessed with splatter films but who faints at the sight of real blood.

The malingering Mrs. Drusse (Kirsten Rolffes) communes with the undead souls stirred up by the hospital's disintegration. The fatuous Dr. Moesgaard (Holger Juul Hansen) evades bureaucrats while undergoing gestalt therapy from a drum-beating Danish shaman. And down below, in the belly of the beast, two young dishwashers with Down's syndrome (Vita Jensen and Morten Rotne Leffers) wax philosophical about the nature and the growing power of the evil that surrounds them.

Funnier and far less dark than "The Kingdom," his original made-for-Danish-TV gothic soap opera, Lars von Trier's "The Kingdom II" is a squalid, sprawling, subversive comic epic that's being shown in two parts at Manhattan's Film Forum and demolishes virtually all it surveys. Medicine, sex, health-care reform, spirituality, motherhood, Sweden—none are safe; all fall victim to von Trier & Co.'s sardonic world view, which possesses an almost giddy willingness to stick its figurative finger in the metaphoric sore.

Von Trier, whose "Breaking the Waves" established him here as a formidable if somewhat inscrutable talent, works in a system where television is both unavoidable and acceptable and where he's done some astounding work. His small-screen "Medea" was a masterpiece of the medium and used the constraints of the form to his and the play's advantage. The first "Kingdom" was a huge success in Denmark; here, the length is a problem for filmgoers, although the option of either one- or two-day viewings should make it more audience-friendly. And besides, "Kingdom II" should do nothing to allay the suspicion that in Denmark resides one of the truly original minds in current film.

Alongside its audacity and dark humor, "The Kingdom II" has a structural kinship with its forebears on daytime TV—not just the cliffhanger endings that conclude each installment, but in the regular, rhythmic rotation of storylines and signature shots. From Helmer's problems—which include his pursuit by the matrimony-minded Rigmer (Ghita Norby)—we head to the ambulance race, then to the ominous outside shot of the hospital itself, then to the basement where the dishwashers dwell. There's a deliberateness to von Trier's technique, which includes a gradually disintegrating picture—like in a bad old videotape, the surface of the film seems to be dissolving as we watch, and as the Kingdom's evil grows. Is this von Trier asserting that the genre as well as his characters exist in the realm of the dead? It would seem to be, especially if—as I suspect—that's the director himself appearing in the uncredited role of the morgue attendant.

SIGHT AND SOUND, 8/98, p. 46, Peter Matthews

Supernatural occurrences continue to plague the staff of the Kingdom Hospital in Copenhagen. Elderly spiritualist Sigrid Drusse is struck by a speeding ambulance and later dies on the operating table. She finds herself in an antechamber to the next world, where little Mary (whose ghost she had previously laid to rest) advises her that the kingdom still needs her, so Mrs Drusse comes back to life. Neurosurgeon Stig Helmer returns from Haiti with the voodoo potion he hopes to use to turn his blackmailer Krogen into a zombie. Helmer slips the poison into Krogen's coffee and the junior registrar collapses, apparently dead. Intern Judith has successfully given birth to the baby fathered by her ex-lover, evil spirit Aage Krüger. But the child—Mary's half brother—starts growing at an alarming rate. Director-general Bob announces a thorough investigation of the hospital.

Head of neurosurgery Einar Moesgaard samples a variety of alternative treatments from Ole, an ageing hippie psychiatrist. Proud to know that the world's biggest sarcoma has been transplanted into him, professor of pathology Bondo turns down yet another liver donor for the sake of medical research. Fearing a murder charge, Helmer consults with the hospital's voodoo expert, who informs him that Krogen is only "skin dead". Armed with the antidote, Helmer races to the crematorium but is gunned down by his disgruntled girlfriend, anaesthesiologist Rigmer, before he can rescue the coffin from the flames. The wound proves superificial. Moesgaard's son Mogge is too exhausted to study for his upcoming viva because of his endless rounds of sex with a sleep researcher. Fellow medical student Christian dotes on Sanne, but she has eyes only for Mogge. Christian volunteers to take over the daredevil ambulance run on which the students secretly wager after the regular driver Falcon accidentally kills an innocent motorist.

Mrs Drusse convenes the spirits in the lecture theatre, but when the hospital chaplain unexpectedly drops in, he meets a ghastly death. The perpetrator is Aage, who turns out to be an incarnation of Lucifer. Judith's monster baby is slowly being crushed under its own weight. When Aage proposes a satanic deal in order to save it, the child—nicknamed Little Brother—pleads with Judith to resist temptation. Krogen gets rescued in the nick of time by the porter Hansen, who hears him banging inside the coffin. Thereafter, he undergoes a personality change and becomes obsessed with eliminating the weak. Krogen attempts to kill little Mona—brain-damaged in a bungled operation by Helmer—but desists when he notices that she has spelled out an incriminating message with her building blocks. Hearing that Mona's case has been transferred to the state prosecutor, Helmer tries to avoid being served with a writ. Hoping to bribe Helmer—an examiner at his viva—Mogge wheedles out of Krogen the hiding place of the damning anaesthesia report. However, the document turns out to be blank: Rigmer has located the real report and blackmails Helmer into attending an impromptu marriage ceremony.

Taking delivery of a new Volvo, Helmer discovers that the bailiff has tricked him into signing the writ. Mrs Drusse, her son Bulder and Hansen go flying above the hospital. When the plane spins out of control, the spirits carry it to safety—but a sizeable chunk lands on Helmer's Volvo. Mrs Drusse uses a word-association game to lure the sleep researcher into admitting that she is a devil-worshipper. Bondo has his sarcoma removed, but needs bone marrow from a near relative to stem the spreading cancer. Mrs Drusse reveals that he and Bulder are half-brothers and the operation proceeds. Learning about Mona's building blocks, Helmer hurriedly gives Mogge a *cum laude* at his viva—then kidnaps the helpless girl and conceals her.

Christian smashes into a car containing Mogge and Sanne. At Little Brother's desperate urging, Judith puts him out of his misery—but instantly regrets her decision and calls Aage for help. Krogen shuts off the Kingdom's power supply, thereby dooming those patients on life support. Mrs Drusse is trapped in a plummeting lift. A stranger arrives from Sweden with greetings from Helmer's wife and seven children. The drama continues.

Lars von Trier's occult hospital soap opera *The Kingdom* ended with one of the great practical jokes in film history. After waiting more than four hours for the half a dozen intersecting storylines to sort themselves, and just when events had reached a furious apocalyptic boil, the viewer was pulled up short by a spiteful title card that read "To Be Continued". Since one had no way of knowing whether a sequel was being planned, this denial of narrative closure was as frustrating as *coitus interruptus*—though a whole lot funnier. While it rather spoils the joke, *The Kingdom II* provides blessed relief from years of accumulated suspense. But von Trier does it again—twitting the gullible audience with a cliffhanger of even more seismic proportions. This time, fortunately, *The Kingdom III* has already been announced.

As a kind of colossal leg-pull, the series (first shown in slightly different form on Danish television) is so enjoyable that it seems unsporting to point out its shallowness. Nor would it be necessary if the general incense-burning surrounding von Trier's *Breaking the Waves* hadn't inspired some people to read *The Kingdom* as a significant allegory of faith. In *Breaking the Waves*, the heroine's self-victimising actions border on the obscene, and the picture hedges its bets about whether she is a saint, a madwoman or both. Even when the purity of her belief results in a literal miracle, the director deliberately italicises it by laying on a saccharine peal of bells and a final image of the sickliest religious kitsch. Von Trier is a practising Catholic, but it may be equally relevant that he was brought up by atheists. What comes across in his movies is a certain defensiveness concerning the spiritual—a simultaneous desire to disavow it. Though the supernatural flimflam of the *Kingdom* films is only a few cuts above *The Omen*, it's clear that von Trier and co-director Morten Arnfred aim at more than a spook show. But if the creaky machinery of ghosts and demons is a way of encoding theological truths it also supplies the film-makers with an out: they can pre-empt the viewer's scepticism—and protect themselves from embarrassment—by taking refuge in the self-consciously ersatz.

Like its predecessor, *The Kingdom II* seems to hinge on one uncertainty over whether von Trier is kidding or not. The only scenes of any authentic feeling are those between solicitous mother Judith and her innocent spawn-of-the-devil Little Brother. Here von Trier manages to pluck something tender and human out of the most arrant gothic claptrap. But instead of trusting the emotion, he undercuts it with a knowingly slurpy string arrangement on the soundtrack. In common with other postmortem ironists, von Trier appears to labour under a paranoid fear of being caught out as naive. That's what separates him from incorruptible artists like Carl Dreyer and Robert Bresson (to whom he has been rashly compared). Those austere masters never courted popularity and never achieved it, but their works are permanent if any are. Granted that he may not have much choice in the matter, von Trier is possibly too embroiled in the Euro-blockbuster game for his entire good as a film-maker. He wants to be clever, stylish and spiritual all at once.

But this is written as a small corrective to the hype. There's still plenty to be glad of in *The Kingdom II*. Mainly, there are the characters, each one a skewed original. It's a little rich that von Trier should claim the series is about the revenge of the irrational on modern scientific hubris when the personified non sequiturs inhabiting the hospital so patently give the lie to his thesis. However, if one considers what more ham-fisted satirists would have made of this putatively soulless bureaucracy, one is grateful for the inconsistency. As in the previous part the woolly-minded consultants are too absorbed in selfish intrigues to pay much heed to the pandemonium breaking out. There's no illusion of getting to know these crabbed eccentrics any better the second time around. Von Trier, Arnfred and co-writer Niels Vorsel simply build on our familiarity with them and allow them to behave more like themselves than ever. Once again, the star monomaniac is that formidably dew-lapped Swedish bulldog, Dr Stig Helmer—a hypocrite of truly Pecksniffian dimensions. Ernst-Hugo Järegard is peerless in the part, whether soliloquising over a toilet bowl or enthusing about how a child whom the surgeon's negligence has made a drooling vegetable lights up the ward with her "energy and vivacity". Vice has rarely been so adorable. For all his metaphysical ambitions, von Trier is enough of a secular entertainer to realise when he's hit pay dirt—without resistance or protest, he permits this cuddly crook to walk off with the show.

VILLAGE VOICE, 5/12/98, p. 130, J. Hoberman

I have a mixed message for fans of *The Kingdom*, Lars von Trier's 1994 miniseries, the pinnacle of Danish TV—an unholy, alternately comic and yucky mix of *ER*, *The X-Files*, and *Twin Peaks* set in a haunted hospital of fools. The epic's latest five-hour installment—which had its local premiere at the last New York Film Festival and is currently screening in two parts, at Film Forum—is more of the same. Unfortunately, more, in this case, is also somewhat less.

The neophyte may be baffled, but the experienced *Kingdom* head will be plunged back into a familiar morass of conflicts and scandals. Here, once more, are the hospital's ridiculous fraternal lodge and idiotic director, the girl who has been brain-damaged through negligence, the unexplained voodoo trip to Haiti, the mutant birth, the Swedish Dr. Helmer's compulsive anti-Danish jibes, the secret satanists, the bizarre New Age therapy sessions down in the basement, the Down's syndrome dishwasher couple who never interact with the movie's dozen or more principals but offer mysterious commentary throughout: "It may start as stupidity but it will end as evil."

Von Trier is as aggressive as ever. The visuals are deliberately choppy—with flailing, brain-jarring camera moves that are further pulverized by the director's habitual use of jump cuts. The attitude is brash and the humor reliably scatological. If some of the jokes are wearing thin, von Trier nevertheless manages to up the film's nastiness level by having the medical interns, who seemingly spend most of their time watching splatter films on the hospital VCR, wager on blindfolded ambulance-races. Mrs. Drusse, the Kingdom's resident medium, is struck by one such ambulance, occasioning a tantalizingly brief trip to von Trier heaven.

Mostly, however, *The Kingdom, Part 2* threatens to turn into *Rosemary's Baby*. Even newcomers to the mini-series will be able to follow the trail of slime that leads through the hospital to the grotesque talking infant who made his ghastly appearance in the final shot of the first *Kingdom*. The creature (played by Fassbinder favorite Udo Kier, or at least by Kier's head) has grown beyond all reason, too big for his bed and effectively crucified on his grossly extended skinny limbs. This plight is played for maximum mocking bathos. The baby's high plaintive voice—heard in endless conversations with his doting mother, a young neurologist—suggests von Trier driving a stake through his Hans Christian Andersen's mawkish heart.

When the show aired on TV, von Trier appeared intermittently as his own master of ceremonies, ending the proceeding with a big grin and a sung synopsis of *The Kingdom*'s "slalom course" narrative. Myself, I felt like I was in the ski lift going up rather than on the mountain heading down. *The Kingdom, Part 2* seems mainly to be marking time. Given that nothing is resolved, it's reasonable to assume that von Trier is preparing an ultimate blow-out for the millennium.

Also reviewed in:
NEW YORK TIMES, 5/6/98, p. E10, Stephen Holden
VARIETY, 9/15-21/97, p. 80, David Rooney

KISSING A FOOL

A Universal Pictures release in association with R.L. Entertainment and Largo Entertainment of a Tag Mendillo/Andrew Form production. *Executive Producer:* David Schwimmer and Stephen Levinson. *Producer:* Tag Mendillo, Andrew Form, and Rick Lashbrook. *Director:* Doug Ellin. *Screenplay:* James Frey and Doug Ellin. *Story:* James Frey. *Director of Photography:* Thomas Del Ruth. *Editor:* David Finfer. *Music:* Joseph Vitarelli. *Music Editor:* Allan K. Rosen. *Sound:* David Obermeyer and (music) Dan Wallin and Nicholas Vitarelli. *Sound Editor:* Richard E. Yawn. *Casting:* Ferne Cassel. *Production Designer:* Charles Breen. *Set Decorator:* Tricia Schneider. *Costumes:* Sue Kaufmann. *Make-up:* Denise Wynbrandt. *Running time:* 94 minutes. *MPAA Rating:* R.

CAST: David Schwimmer (Max Abbitt); Jason Lee (Jay Murphy); Mili Avital (Samantha Andrews); Bonnie Hunt (Linda); Vanessa Angel (Natasha); Kari Wuhrer (Dara); Frank Medrano (Cliff Randal); Bitty Schram (Vicki Pelam); Judy Greer (Andrea); Ron Beattie (Priest); Doug Ellin (Bartender); Tag Mendillo (Wedding Guest at Bar); Justine Bentley (Beautiful Woman at Bar); Liza Cruzat and Jessica Mills (Dara's Friends); Sammy Sosa and Jerry Springer (Themselves); Doug Ellin and Tag Mendillo (Springer Guests); Mike Squire (Spanish Man in Bed); Marco Siviero (French Man in Bed); Steve Seagren (Heckler); Philip R. Smith (Fan on the Street); Jayson Fate (Rudolpho); Ross Bon (Blue Kings Lead Singer); Antimo Fiore (Tony).

LOS ANGELES TIMES, 2/27/98, Calendar/p. 12, Kevin Thomas

[The following review by Kevin Thomas appeared in a slightly different form in
NEWSDAY, 2/27/98, Part II/p. B13.]

You've got to hand it to David Schwimmer. Not only did he sign on as an executive producer of "Kissing a Fool," he also turned over the picture to his co-star, Jason Lee, who made a strong impression in last year's "Chasing Amy."

That's because Schwimmer's Chicago sportscaster, Max, is too often obnoxious rather than likable while Lee gets considerable opportunity to reveal charm as Max's best pal Jay, a budding novelist.

It's no great gift Lee is getting, for "Kissing a Fool" is romantic comedy at its slightest and most contrived, passable date-night fare for the easily diverted and as disposable as an empty popcorn bag.

As a local celebrity, Max is an unabashed playboy, but Jay thinks that his lovely and dedicated editor, Samantha (Mili Avital) might just be the woman Max could take seriously. It's an instance of opposites attracting, for Max, proud of his disdain for books, and Sam, who has no interest in sports events, swiftly become caught up in a passionate affair—so passionate that Max proposes marriage after only two weeks.

Schwimmer has his best moments when Max starts having second thoughts: Is he really prepared to accept the idea that there are to be no other women in his life? Such a notion is entirely in keeping with the kind of man Max is, but it inspires him to make a harebrained decision. He insists that Jay try to seduce Samantha, figuring that if she has the capacity to be faithful to him, maybe he can summon the resolution to be faithful to her.

Max has got to be pretty dense not to notice that Jay has more in common with Samantha than he does. In fact, Jay, getting over heartbreak from a breakup, finds Samantha most attractive but understandably thinks making any moves on her would complicate their working relationship.

But work takes Max out of town a lot, and Sam and Jay, who has rejected Max's proposal, do spend an awful lot of time on developing that novel... You don't have to be Sherlock Holmes to deduce what's going to happen next.

Director Doug Ellin and his co-writer, James Frey, haven't come up with anything to freshen up the plot.

Otherwise solidly crafted, "Kissing a Fool" works best as a showcase for Avital as well as Lee, both of whose roles have some dimension. Bonnie Hunt is fun as a tough, gossipy publisher. With luck, Schwimmer will survive this trifle.

NEW YORK POST, 2/27/98, p. 37, Michael Medved

By kissing a fool—or even a frog—a fairy-tale princess can transform even the lowest life form into a handsome prince. In "Kissing a Fool," the altogether adorable Hollywood newcomer Mili Avital proves herself the perfect princess for the job, transforming pleasant but hum-drum material into a handsome, irresistibly charging romantic comedy.

Avital, one of the most popular stars in the history of Israeli cinema, speaks perfect, unaccented English in playing the focus of the film's romantic triangle.

One of her suitors is a shy novelist (Jason Lee, of "Chasing Amy) whose first book describes his heartbreak over a lost love; Avital is the editor assigned to whip the project into shape.

The novelist's best pal is a glib TV sportscaster (good "Friend" David Schwimmer). When the brooding writer introduces his best bud to his glamorous editor, the shocking result is instant attraction. They announce their engagement and move in together.

Schwimmer, however, worries that he's not cut out for monogamy and suspects that the lady he loves may also be tempted to stray. As a test, he insists that his bookish, reluctant friend try his best to seduce her, and only if she successfully resists will the marriage go forward.

The story artfully unfolds in flashbacks, as narrated by Avital's chain-smoking boss (Bonnie Hunt) at a wedding reception; only in the movie's final minutes do we discover who actually got married.

Debuting director (and co-writer) Doug Ellin cherishes the summery Chicago locations that decorate his movie, but displays even greater affection for his cast.

Schwimmer, so downbeat and disappointing in "The Pallbearer," is perfect as a self-centered, obnoxious but endearing lug.

Jason Lee may seem a bit laid-back (off camera, he's a former skateboard pro) for the part of a tormented poet, but his understated, easygoing appeal covers any lack of substance.

As for Avital, who previously played little-noticed parts in "Stargate" and "Dead Man," this film should make her a significant star, allowing smitten moviegoers to forget all about the likes of Gwyneth and Julia.

SIGHT AND SOUND, 10/98, p. 45, Andy Medhurst

At a lavish Chicago wedding, publishing executive Linda tells two fellow guests how the bride and groom met. Flashback to before the wedding. Aspiring author Jay Murphy arranges a date between his new editor Samantha Andrews and his best friend, sports journalist Max. The match exceeds all expectations. Max, hitherto horrified by commitment, proposes marriage to Sam and moves in with her. Jay is delighted, though he is still broken-hearted over his break-up with girlfriend Natasha. Max and Sam continue being the ideal couple until Max starts to panic. Paranoid over Sam's trustworthiness, Max suggests to Jay that he test her loyalty by attempting to seduce her. Horrified, Jay refuses but, under pressure to finish his book, he spends more time with Sam and grows ever fonder of her.

While Max is away working in Detroit, Jay and Sam go to a club where they meet Natasha. Sam impresses Jay with how she handles the situation and on returning home they kiss. Confused over his feelings, Jay leaves and visits Natasha who tries to seduce him. Jay calls Max in Detroit and is furious when he realises Max has spent the night there with a female colleague. Back in Chicago, Jay and Max argue, Sam finds out about the loyalty test, and all three part acrimoniously. Some time later, Max engineers a meeting between Jay and Sam which rekindles their love and leads to their wedding.

The most useful way of approaching *Kissing a Fool* is to consider it as a curious little essay about the anxieties of stardom. David Schwimmer, clearly, is unhappy with forever being seen only as Ross Geller from *Friends,* and this film groans with the effort of trying to break him out of that ridiculously lucrative straitjacket. He not only stars, but is one of the film's executive producers, while the film's publicity material laboriously delineates his career outside sitcom, insisting that Schwimmer is a "serious writer and director" and has appeared at "the Edinburgh Festival in Scotland" (as opposed, one presumes, to the Edinburgh Festival in Paraguay).

Schwimmer himself asserts that this film allows him to "flex different acting muscles"—all too evidently, *Kissing a Fool* is a bid to extend his range and name. The irony here, of course, is that the film's chances of success hinge entirely on luring the *Friends* audience off its collective couch and into the cinema, so straying too far from Ross would be an alienating move. Hence *Kissing a Fool* wavers between asking genuinely new things of Schwimmer and letting him fall back on those puppyish pouts and affronted double takes which have made Ross America's favourite sentimental geek.

The non-Ross aspect of Schwimmer's role lies in the fact that Max Abbitt is a hugely dislikable character, a shallow, immature, exploitative womaniser, and there are some scenes where Schwimmer's portrayal of him is convincing enough to push all thoughts of Ross aside. This, however, creates a further problem for the film, since at those moments the intended atmosphere of light comedy sours into something dark and bitter, so Schwimmer and the film go scuttling back to Ross-world, reassuring the fan base but undermining Schwimmer's aspirations to show off his versatility. It's the nastier elements which hold the most interest in *Kissing a Fool:* Max's jealousy is horribly damaging to all concerned, once or twice veering towards *Othello* territory, and it threatens to break out of the sugary coating that the wedding-day flashback structure coats the film with. That this isn't allowed to happen is disappointing, since it's only in those uneasy, queasy glimpses that the film manages to be anything other than a piece of polished fluff.

Schwimmer aside, the rest of the cast inhabit their stereotypes enthusiastically enough. Jason Lee plays a tactful second fiddle behind Schwimmer's big solos, and Mili Avital manages to convey a sense that Sam is really too good for both her suitors. Although the film ducks out of taking her strength as far as it might, her punchiness is another clue that *Kissing a Fool* fancies itself as heir to the screwball comedies of classic Hollywood. Yet all it can do is lamely ape them, as evidenced by the use of Harry Connick Jr's pastiche Sinatra act as soundtrack to the opening titles, and by Bonnie Hunt's game attempts to inject some Eve Arden style waspishness into the underwritten role of Linda. It tries hard, but the overall effect is one of hand-me down pastiche.

VILLAGE VOICE, 3/10/98, p. 118, Elizabeth Weitzman

When Jay (Jason Lee) sets Sam (Mili Avital) up with Max (David Schwimmer), they fall in love immediately. But Max needs to know that Sam will stay faithful, and enlists Jay to test her. Jay, however, is as sensitive as Max is smarmy, and he's not interested. Except maybe, he is. Schwimmer's a pretty funny boor, while Lee, so oafish in *Chasing Amy,* is such a mensch you may find yourself pondering which of your girlfriends you'd fix him up with. (The words "chick flick" should have just flashed across your brain, by the way.) You'll mostly be doing this to pass some time, because the film, like Avital's Sam, is cute, spunky, and very thin. You'll chuckle a few times, maybe wander Into the lobby to refill your courtesy cup, and certainly contemplate why the marvelous Bonnie Hunt is never the bride. The movie is set up in flashback, with Hunt, as Sam's boss, explaining the story to guests at Sam's final-scene wedding. If you for a minute wonder who she marries, this one's for you.

Also reviewed in:
CHICAGO TRIBUNE, 2/27/98, Friday/p. A, Monica Eng
NEW YORK TIMES, 2/27/98, p. E23, Anita Gates
VARIETY, 2/23/-3/1/98, p. 73, Todd McCarthy

KNOCK OFF

A TriStar Pictures release of a Knock Films, A.V.V. and MDP Worldwide presentation of a Film Workshop Company Ltd./Val D'Oro Entertainment production. *Producer:* Nansun Chi. *Director:* Tsui Hark. *Screenplay:* Steven E. de Souza. *Director of Photography:* Arthur Wong. *Editor:* Mak Chi Sin. *Music:* Ron Mael and Russell Mael. *Music Editor:* David Trevis. *Sound:* Gary Wilkins and (music) Brian Reeves. *Sound Editor:* Nelson Ferreira. *Casting:* Illana Diamant and Lauris Freeman. *Production Designer:* James Leung and Bill Lui. *Visual Effects:* Joe Bauer. *Costumes:* Ben Luk, William Fung, and Mable Kwan. *Make-up:* Kwan Lee Na. *Make-up (Jean Claude Van Damme):* Prisana Traechai. *Make-up (Rob Schneider):* Rosa Librizzi. *Stunt Coordinator:* Yuen Bing. *Running time:* 110 minutes. *MPAA Rating:* R.

CAST: Jean Claude Van Damme (Marcus Ray); Rob Schneider (Tommy Hendricks); Lela Rochon (Karen); Paul Sorvino (Johansson); Carmen Lee (Ling Ho); Wyman Wong (Eddie); Glen Chin (Skinny); Michael Fitzgerald Wong (Han); Moses Chan (Officer Fong); Raymond Leslie Nicholas (Karl); Jeff Joseph Wolfe (Skaar); Michael Miller (Tickler); Steve Brettingham (Hawkeye); Mark Haughton (Bear); Peter Nelson (Biff); Kim Maree Penn (Chip); Thomas Hudak (Kyle); Steve Nation (Kip); Rosa Librizzi (Buddha CIA); Noel Rands (Racemaster); Dennis Chan (Choy); William Chow (Papa Wang); Stuart Kavanagh (Colonel Carrington); Noorie Razack (Fruit Market Old Man); Heung Hoi (Fruit Market Accountant); Dennis Chan (Eddie Kid); Cheung Simon (Supermarket Kid); Leslie Cheung (Young Worker "Skinny Freight"); Matt Grant (Tarzan); Nyree Hansen (Jane); Kent Osborne (Pachy); Lynne Francis (V-Six Secretary); Cordelia Choy (Mel); Leon C. Somera, Jr. (Eddie's Ringer).

LOS ANGELES TIMES, 9/7/98, Calendar/p. 3, Kevin Thomas

"Knock Off"—that's what TriStar would seem to be doing in opening this high-energy, high-spirited thriller Friday without press previews. The irony is that this is the kind of action adventure with real crossover appeal: It's fast, light and funny and not top-heavy with special effects and epic-scale destruction. It's a much tighter, far less outre film than Jean-Claude Van Damme and director Tsui Hark's last outing, "Double Team"—and no Dennis Rodman or Mickey Rourke on hand this time.

Indeed, "Knock Off" is one of Van Damme's best movies ever. What's more it has Sammo Hung, as much a Hong Kong legend as Tsui, on board as second unit director and Steven E. de Souza, who has "48 Hours" and "Die Hards" 1 and 2 among his credits, as writer of the film's lean, witty yet scary script.

Van Damme is well-cast as the free-spirited King of Hong Kong knockoffs. His partner (Rob Schneider) of four years has strived to get Van Damme to go legit in manufacturing jeans for a major U.S. company, whose no-nonsense rep (Lela Rochon) arrives to check out suspicions of counterfeiting. It seems that Van Damme's brother-by-adoption (Wyman Wong) not only has continued knocking off the jeans but also has been trading with the Russian Mafia in cheap transistor radios and toys, perfect items for concealing mini-bombs, as well as in jeans buttons. Nothing, and almost no one, is what or who he or she seems.

Opening 72 hours before Hong Kong is to be handed back to China by the British, "Knock Off," which was shot during the transfer, starts off with a zany rickshaw race held for charity and never really lets up. When it comes to action, Tsui, backed by Arthur Wong's breathtakingly mobile camera work, is the most kinetic of directors who never misses the comic potential in rough-and-tumble action.

Yet amid the nonstop mayhem there emerges the all-too-timely idea of how the world is becoming increasingly menaced by terrorist acts—and how Hong Kong's elaborate hand-over celebrations and ceremonies last year could well have been vulnerable to sabotage.

In Tsui's films actors have to be fast on their feet not only physically but also in establishing the characters and personalities of the people they are playing. Van Damme, Schneider and

Rochon are exceptionally adept under Tsui's direction, as is Paul Sorvino, as a veteran CIA section chief. From his classic "Peking Opera Blues" to "A Better Tomorrow" and countless other films, Tsui expresses a well-developed sense of life's dark absurdities that subtly shadows even his zaniest moments.

NEW YORK POST, 9/5/98, p. 24, Larry Worth

Making the rounds on the TV talk-show circuit this week, Jean-Claude Van Damme has talked of turning over a new leaf. Though maintaining his rep as the Muscles from Brussels, he says he's kicked drugs and stopped womanizing. Oh yes, he also wants to aid mankind.

Quitting acting would be a nice start. Short of that, how about swearing off incoherent action flicks like "Knock Off"?

The lamentable script is a collection of totally implausible setups as the Russian Mafia tries to wreak havoc on the world. Their M.O. is planting pea-shaped bombs in Hong Kong exports, set to go off as the Chinese take the island back from the Brits.

It's like a cheesy James Bond plot, minus anything akin to exciting tableaux or a suave 007. Instead, Van Damme shows up as a lady-killing fashion designer(!) who's partnered with manic, ever-frantic Rob Schneider. But their shenanigans come to a halt when tough-talking exec Lela Rochon accuses them of using counterfeit materials on their duds.

Believe it or not, there actually is a tie-in between the boys' rip-off rags and global destruction. That's because no one is quite who they seem to be. In fact, the principals take turns being a suspected terrorist.

But the real enemy here is director Tsui Hark, last heard of when he paired Van Damme opposite Dennis Rodman in "Double Team." This time, Hark achieves a bad John Woo imitation, trying to mix nonstop fight scenes and quirky photography.

Accordingly, his camera dives beneath an empty sneaker's tongue before Van Damme's foot slips into it for a chase scene. Or the lens burrows through a revolver's snout before a bullet explodes from a chamber. Rather than innovative, Hark comes off like a fetishist.

As if that's not silly enough, the dialogue is wedged between one slo-mo destruction scene after another. But it's virtually impossible to tell who's doing what to whom, or why. Tension simply doesn't exist, maybe because editing appears to have taken place in a blender.

For his part, Van Damme has evolved from a second-rate Stallone to a third-rate Jackie Chan. When he cries out, I'm doing my best, it's obvious that it'll never be enough.

And as Van Damme's high-kicking backups, sad sacks Schneider and Rochon seem more like Rockette rejects. Only veteran Paul Sorvino emerges with dignity intact, maybe because he has the smallest role.

On the other hand, the title is right on target. Like its subject matter, "Knock Off" is about as worthless as cheap imitations get.

SIGHT AND SOUND, 7/99, p. 43, Jamie Graham

Hong Kong, 1997. Marcus Ray and Tommy Hendricks deal in 'knock offs', inferior imitation goods. Their scam is exposed when sales executive Karen Leigh arrives from the US. But Karen is really after Eddie Wang, a Chinese gangster who is Marcus' adopted brother. She insists Marcus and Tommy raid Eddie's factory that night. Before the operation Marcus discovers Tommy is an undercover CIA agent working for a division headed by Johansson—the CIA plans to oversee the raid. But the factory is bombed before Marcus and Tommy can enter. Marcus finds a remote-controlled nanobomb hidden in a knock-off trainer. Dismayed at the treachery, Marcus agrees to get Eddie to testify to the CIA.

Wang pleads he only provided a group of Russians with the knock-off goods. Another bomb detonates, killing Wang. Marcus and Tommy discover Karen is also a CIA operative, looking for a mole in Johansson's team. Learning there will be a shipment of nanobombs that night, both CIA divisions, Marcus and Tommy sneak aboard. During a shoot-out Johansson is revealed as the mole. The ship blows up but the protagonists escape, Marcus and Tommy with Johansson's detonator which later accidentally sets off a nanobomb that kills Johansson.

Whatever you think of Jean-Claude Van Damme's acting skills, there is no denying his acumen when it comes to career-development choices. Graduating swiftly from his early, funnier films

(Black Eagle) to martial-arts contest movies *(Kickboxer),* there was even a brief moment following *Universal Soldier* when stardom beckoned. But then he chose to anchor his place in the mainstream by turning to Hong Kong action flicks, a sub-genre which largely supplanted the Schwarzenegger-Stallone heroics of the 80s. *Knock Off* is the fourth movie in six years in which Van Damme has teamed up with cult eastern directors, and his second outing for Tsui Hark after *Double Team.* It is of interest only in that this is far more the director's picture than his own.

Tsui's imprimatur is apparent in both the convoluted plot (involving nanobombs and Russian gangsters) and the staging of the fight sequences. It has long been accepted that Van Damme's fans don't come to his films wanting the labyrinthine complexities of *The Big Sleep,* but they do expect plenty of roundhouse kicks, splits and at least one 'butt shot'. *Knock Off* has none of these, Tsui seemingly preferring to show off his own techniques rather than his star's. The fight sequences are often filmed in disorienting close-ups, while slow and fast motion, freeze frames and *Evil Dead*-style crash zooms whip up plenty of sound and fury to camouflage the central emptiness.

Tsui's fondness for style over substance even extends to his use of the Hong Kong handover as a backdrop. Despite frequent bulletins counting down the hours and intermittent shots of Al Gore, Chris Patten and the lowering of the British flag, the historic event is irrelevant, only adding to the overall cacophony Even Wayne Wang's ill-advised *Chinese Box* made better use of the handover than this, which is particularly disappointing considering his track record of bolting politics on to pyrotechnics in the *Once Upon a Time in China* movies.

Also reviewed in:
NEW YORK TIMES, 9/5/98, p. B17, Lawrence Van Gelder
VARIETY, 9/7-13/98, p. 72, Joe Leydon

KRIPPENDORF'S TRIBE

A Touchstone Pictures release of a Morra-Brezner-Steinberg-Tenenbaum/Dreyfuss-James production. *Executive Producer:* Whitney Green and Ross Canter. *Producer:* Larry Brezner. *Director:* Todd Holland. *Screenplay:* Charlie Peters. *Based on the book by:* Frank Parkin. *Director of Photography:* Dean Cundey. *Editor:* Jon Poll. *Music:* Bruce Broughton. *Music Editor:* Patty Carlin. *Sound:* James E. Webb and (music) Armin Steiner. *Sound Editor:* George Anderson. *Casting:* Jackie Burch. *Production Designer:* Scott Chambliss. *Art Director:* Bill Rea. *Set Decorator:* Karen Manthey. *Set Dresser:* Merdyce McClaran. *Special Effects:* J.D. Streett and Archie K. Ahuna. *Costumes:* Isis Mussenden. *Make-up:* Ben Nye, Jr. *Running time:* 98 minutes. *MPAA Rating:* PG-13.

CAST: Richard Dreyfuss (Krippendorf); Jenna Elfman (Veronica); Natasha Lyonne (Shelly); Gregory Smith (Mickey); Carl Michael Lindner (Edmund); Jacob Handy and Zachary Handy (Young Edmund); Lily Tomlin (Ruth Allen); Stephen Root (Gerald Adams); Doris Belack (President Porter); Julio Oscar Mechoso (Simon Alonso); Siobhan Fallon (Lori Heyward); Amzie Strickland (Gladys Schmades); Phil Leeds (Dr. Harvey); Frances Bay (Edith Proxmire); Susan Ruttan (Mrs. O'Brian); Barbara Williams (Jennifer); Elaine Stritch (Irene Hargrove); Zakes Mokae (Sulukim); David Ogden Stiers (Henry Spivey); Sandy Martin (Nurse); Tom Poston (Gordon Hargrove); Lance Kinsey (Principal Reese); Mila Kunis (Abbey Tournquist); Robin Karfo (Mrs. Tournquist); Tim Halligan (Mr. Tournquist); Peter Tilden (Larry Swift); Shashawnee Hall (Mabu); Timothy Wells (Ruth's Guide); Kari Leigh Floyd (Party Guest); Michael Steve Jones (Alcove Man); Ian Busch (Flagpole Boy); Grace Lee and Todd Cattell (College Students); Chris Duque (Outpost Man); Valerie Reid (Divorced Woman); Rachel Winfree, Suanne Spoke, and Catherine Paolone (Lecture Women); Bill Rosier and Robb Derringer (TV Store Customers); Laura Cayouette (TV Studio Woman); China Brezner (Elevator Teen); Bruce Jarchow (Andrews); Wendy Worthington (Secretary).

LOS ANGELES TIMES, 2/27/98, Calendar/p. 4, Kevin Thomas

[The following review by Kevin Thomas appeared in a slightly different form in **NEWSDAY, 2/27/98, Part II/p. B11.]**

If you thought that blackface went out with Al Jolson, you're wrong. If you thought "jungle bunny" humor of tales set in "darkest Africa" or way up the Amazon went out with serials, B-pictures and Tarzan, you're wrong. "Krippendorf's Tribe" revives all those old demeaning racist stereotypes in the most horrible ways—and at the very moment when the world's few remaining isolated native populations face extinction.

Tastelessness can be hilarious if it is sufficiently affectionate and substantially funnier than it is offensive. The trouble is "Krippendorf's Tribe"—arguably the worst movie ever to come out of Disney—induces more chagrin than laughter. It's a jaw-dropper, not a thigh-slapper, and its sensibilities are so appallingly out of touch that they harken back to those innocent old Osa and Martin Johnson travelogues in which Pygmies danced to the Johnsons' Victrola.

The movie does raise some perplexing questions: What did director Todd Holland and writer Charlie Peters have in mind in bringing Frank Parkin's book to the screen? How did this project get the green light? What induced an actor of the caliber of Richard Dreyfuss to star? And why did Jenna Elfman, the red-hot young star of TV's "Dharma & Greg," have to make this her first featured role in a movie?

Dreyfuss plays Krippendorf, a recently widowed anthropologist with three children, a delinquent mortgage and a $100,000 research grant that's supposed to yield a major paper on a lost New Guinea tribe that Krippendorf's late anthropologist wife had become convinced existed. Devastated by his wife's death, Krippendorf has done zero work, and his fumbling presentation is patently fake, yet for unfathomable reasons his description of the tribe he has invented passes muster with everyone except a prissy colleague, played by Lily Tomlin, no less.

Meanwhile, an obnoxiously aggressive young anthropologist named Veronica (Elfman) has latched on to Krippendorf and winds up selling the prof's phony treatise as a TV series. This means Krippendorf has to blacken up himself and his kids to shoot fake jungle footage in his backyard and pad it out with material he and his wife shot in New Guinea with some real tribal people. (They're the ones who told the Krippendorfs about the alleged "lost" tribe.) When Krippendorf has a TV hit on his hands, he and Veronica fake "mating practices of the natives," tape, apparently a porn reel, for more bucks.

"Krippendorf's Tribe" isn't remotely intelligent or sophisticated enough to make it as a pitch-dark comedy or satire. It's just sheer crassness overlaid with single-parent sentimentality, not to mention the notion that it's OK to cheat as long as you don't get caught.

It's sad to report that, along with Tomlin, other notables appearing in the picture are Elaine Stritch and Tom Poston (as Krippendorf's starchy in-laws) and David Ogden Stiers (as the TV series producer). When it comes to lost tribes, it's "Krippendorf's Tribe" that needs to get lost.

NEW YORK, 3/9/98, p. 48, David Denby

Dr. James Krippendorf (Richard Dreyfuss), anthropologist and widower, layabout and fraud, a man possessed of three kids who don't respect him and a research grant that has long run out, is clearly at the end of his tether. Krippendorf has to deliver a report to his university. Where's his proof? That is, where's the documentary evidence of the previously undiscovered New Guinea tribe that he claims to have stumbled across with his late wife some years ago? The tribe, of course, doesn't exist. Professor Krippendorf bluffs his way through a lecture, concocting the tribal name—the Shelmikedmu (emphasis on the second syllable)—from the names of his three cranky children, Shelly, Mickey, and Edmund. Krippendorf then manufactures, in his suburban backyard, a film illustrating the curious habits of these remarkable people. Dressed in body paint and rings, with white wigs scrunched like sugar donuts about their ears, the Krippendorf children gambol among thatched huts with little pigs and other New Guinea creatures, and perform ritual circumcision—or so it seems—on the youngest boy. Krippendorf and his older son mix in some footage of an actual New Guinea tribe, and the academic audience is fooled. The director, Todd Holland, and the screenwriter, Charlie Peters (adapting a novel by Frank Parkin), don't bring this out, but it's implicit in the movie's entire scheme that the university types, despite their alleged high standards, take a voyeuristic, even pornographic, interest in aboriginal people. Excited by those shocking native customs, they can't see that the documentary is rubbish. A sycophantic female anthropologist (Jenna Elfman) gets drunk at Krippendorf's house, and the professor tricks her into wearing native garb; he then puts on tribal-chieftain rig himself and makes a film of the two of them exploring a great many more native customs.

Once it gets going, *Krippendorf's Tribe* is pretty damn funny—and at times uproarious—but there's no use pretending that the comedy is anything but disrespectful and crude. Thrown together without grace or beauty, *Krippendorf's Tribe* falls below the level of satire—it's burlesque, really, the kind of movie that might have been made in the thirties and forties, before Americans had been educated or bullied into respect for native people. As far as this movie is concerned, someone dressed with chicken bones sticking out of his nose is ridiculous, and that's that. The movie louses up native dress and ritual, body paint and phallus sheaths, and even anthropology in general, which is portrayed as a pretentious crock that could interest no one but phonies. Krippendorf's nemesis, the head of the department, Dr. Allen (Lily Tomlin), herself discovered a new tribe some twenty years ago and has been dining out on it ever since. She lives by vanity alone, and Tomlin, pale and enraged, makes her a creature of the most extreme paranoia.

Todd Holland has worked as both a producer and a director on *The Larry Sanders Show,* and he has a TV veteran's rough-and-ready attitude toward comedy. The camera setups and the line readings are obvious and overemphatic, and Holland allows (or encourages) Jenna Elfman to come on so hard that we have trouble accepting her as a love interest for Richard Dreyfuss—she seems like a creep. The movie might actually have been funnier if it were a little closer to realism; if Holland were able, now and then, to rise above caricature. The university people are all portrayed as jerks; everyone is a jerk except Krippendorf's three little kids, who are struggling to grow up in the wake of their mother's death. The title has two meanings—the kids are also Krippendorf's tribe—and the movie suggests that this self-pitying widower had better discover *them* before it is too late.

Richard Dreyfuss has always possessed a talent for squashed dignity. Now 50, he seems sadder than before, more resigned. When he shows up at the university disguised as the Shelmikedmu tribal chief, wearing enough feathers, teeth, and whatnot to decorate the entire Banana Republic chain in 1983, he doesn't do much but grunt and slam the table, but he's funny anyway. He pours all of Krippendorf's wounded self-love into the chiefs demand for respect. *Krippendorf's Tribe* is too casually made and too silly to take seriously, and yet too funny to ignore. When Dreyfuss and Elfman get interviewed together on TV—he as the chief, she as an anthropologist—the profanities emerge from beneath the pidgin New Guinea they speak to each other. The jokes are the kind of things we laughed at as children in old movies and in slapstick episodes of *I Love Lucy.* The picture represents a regression, I suppose, though there's something exhilarating about academic pieties falling to the floor like a tableful of old dishes.

NEW YORK POST, 2/27/98, p. 44, Michael Medved

"Krippendorf's Tribe" represents one of Hollywood's first ever adventures into the sexy, glamorous, ruthlessly competitive world of big league anthropology, but the disappointing results hardly suggest a speedy follow-up expedition.

Prodigiously gifted stars (Richard Dreyfuss, Jenna Elfman, Lily Tomlin) save this odd project from abject disaster, but this feeble farce feels fatally forced.

Dreyfuss plays James Krippendorf, a distinguished anthropology professor so distracted by the death of his wife that he's squandered a foundation grant intended to finance his study of an undiscovered tribe in the wilds of New Guinea.

Unprepared to present the lecture that's supposed to summarize his research, he improvises at the podium, making up details about an exotic jungle people who go by the name of the "Shelmikedmu"—a synthesis of the names of his three kids, Shelly, Mickey and Edmund.

Those children (Natasha Lyonne, Gregory Smith, Carl Michael Lindner), covered in full body paint and elaborate headdresses, soon become the stars of backyard home movies that Krippendorf splices together with old film of his actual trip to New Guinea in order to authenticate the existence of the bizarre tribe he has discovered.

The Shelmikedmu soon become a national sensation, featured on cable TVs "Primal Channel," celebrated for their unique social structure (with families headed by a single father) and uninhibited mating rituals.

Krippendorf's ambitious young colleague in the anthropology department (Jenna Elfman of TVs "Dharma and Greg" wants to cash in on this fad while harboring a longstanding crush on the professor himself. But another academic, the crusty, cynical Lily Tomlin, is determined to prove that the entire business is a hoax.

Based on a novel by Frank Parkin, the movie is at its best when emphasizing inventive, ingenious aspects of Krippendorf's fakery, but it quickly heads into groan-inducing "I Love Lucy" territory with the professor himself impersonating a heavily painted native chief who's inexplicably appeared on the scene.

Dreyfuss displays energetic, undeniable gifts for this frantic foolishness, but clumsy TV director Todd Holland maintains no sense of proportion—and simply can't seem to keep microphone booms out of crucial shots.

The romantic twist comes across as a lame afterthought, with Dreyfuss and Elfman demonstrating far more convincing chemistry when they're supposed to hate each other than in their limp lust scenes.

Countless unfunny gigs about 6-foot-long penis sheaths, prehistoric dildos and jungle circumcision help give phallocentrism a bad name, and may count as this picture's distinguishing characteristic.

The movie's underlying "serious" theme—that "going native" and playing at aboriginal authenticity can heal and liberate dysfunctional moderns—hardly registers with the audience because this particular "Tribe" remains entirely too primitive.

Also reviewed in:
CHICAGO TRIBUNE, 2/27/98, Friday/p F, Elaine Richardson
NEW YORK TIMES, 2/27/98, p. E12, Lawrence Van Gelder
VARIETY, 3/2-8/98, p. 84, Joe Leydon
WASHINGTON POST, 2/27/98, p. D7, Stephen Hunter

KRZYSZTOF KIESLOWSI: I'M SO-SO

A First Run Features release of a Kulturmode Film/Staens Filmcentral production. *Producer:* Karen Hjort. Director: Krzysztof Wierzbicki. *Screenplay (Polish with English subtitles):* Krzystof Wierzbicki. *Director of Photography:* Jacek Petrycki. *Editor:* Milenia Fiedler. *Music:* Zbigniew Preisner. *Sound:* Michael Zarnecki. *Running time:* 56 minutes. *MPAA Rating:* Not Rated.

WITH: Krzysztof Kieslowski

NEWSDAY, 8/5/98, Part II/p. B11, John Anderson

[*Krzysztof Kieslowski: I'm So-So* was reviewed jointly with *Tranceformer: A Portrait of Lars von Trier*; see Anderson's review of that film.]

VILLAGE VOICE, 8/11/98, p. 143, Michael Atkinson

In a virtual world of E! profiles and publicity "films," movies about moviemakers evoke about as much knee-jerk cachet as buying a bag of peanuts. But both Krzysztof Wierzbicki's film on Kieslowski and Stig Björkman's film on Von Trier are seriously respectful, not genuflective, toward their subjects, and the worshipful drool is kept to a trickle. Both are dead lucky, too, that their subjects are so engaging and eloquent, Kieslowski coming off like Philip Baker Hall playing a relaxed old-school metaphysician, and Von Trier like a modest, bratty anarchist who can't keep a straight face about the bomb that's about to go off under your chair.

Kieslowki's is the more affecting portrait of course, because he's dead, and this bio, as well as his entire oeuvre, chimes like a funeral bell. The surprise is how relaxed he is spilling his guts, showing the camera his dog-scratched cornea, musing on the question of an afterlife ("It's a beautiful secret"), and considering the reoccurrence of horse images in his films just as a horse walks over and licks his head. However gimmicky (a graphologist, a clairvoyant, and a priest are interviewed to define Kieslowski's persona), Wierzbicki's minimovie is the best trailer for the Kieslowski filmography the filmmaker could've hoped for. (He might've appreciated the subtitled mistranslation of "sine wave" into "sinus wave.") Still, *The Decalogue* is strangely scanted (one scene from No. 1), and *Blue White* and *The Double Live of Veronique* are elided altogether in favor of the earlier films, *Camera Buff* in particular.

Von Trier's portrait is a good deal more erratic, culled from years of interview snippets, even featuring "very arty" 8mm footage Von Trier shot when he was "10 or 12," including traveling shots and a handheldness that's a mere stumble from *Breaking the Waves*. From Von Trier's childhood acting an TV (from what we see, a kind of Danish Lance Kerwin) to *The Kingdom* and *Waves*, Björkman busies himself cataloguing the filmmaker's notoriously incapacitating phobias, even though Von Trier himself appears rarely ruffled. If nothing else, *Tranceformer* reminds us how formally remarkable *Epidemic, The Element of Crime* and *Zentropa* are, all made before Von Trier become the doyen of faux-doc turbulence.

Also reviewed in:
NEW YORK TIMES, 8/5/98, p. E5, Stephen Holden
VARIETY, 8/5-11/96, p. 50, Derek Elley

KURT AND COURTNEY

A Roxie Releasing presentation. *Executive Producer:* Nick Fraser. *Producer:* Nick Broomfield. *Director:* Nick Broomfield. *Director of Photography:* Joan Churchill and Alex Vendler. *Editor:* Mark Atkins and Harley Escudier. *Sound:* Sarah Jeans and (music) Mark Rozett. *Production Designer:* Daniel Harris. *Running time:* 95 minutes. *MPAA Rating:* Not Rated.

WITH: Nick Broomfield; Mari Earle; Tracy Marander; Alice Wheeler; Hank Harrison; Rozz Rezabek; Tom Grant; Dylan Carlson; Al Bowman; Jack Briggs; El Duce; Chelsea; Victoria Clarke; Larry Flynt; Vincent Schiavelli; Courtney Love.

LOS ANGELES TIMES, 4/17/98, Calendar/p. 4, Kenneth Turan

"Kurt & Courtney," the new hot potato documentary about rockers Kurt Cobain and Courtney Love that's being publicized as "the most talked-about film that didn't play at the Sundance Film Festival," has finally arrived, but in all honesty, "Kurt & Courtney & Nick" would be a more descriptive title.

Nick is Nick Broomfield, the British guerrilla documentarian whose shameless hussy style, developed over decades of work, invariably includes generous portions of himself. Here's Nick, camera always running, barging into the wrong apartment, sweet-talking antagonists on the car phone, striding unannounced into an office in fearless pursuit of the answer to "just a little question." Lack of self-confidence is not a problem area here.

As always, too, Broomfield's choice of subjects involves individuals on the fringes of morality and society. Given that his previous documentaries include "Chicken Ranch's" examination of a Nevada brothel, "Aileen Wuornos: The Selling of a Serial Killer" (his best work), "Heidi Fleiss: Hollywood Madam" and "Fetishes," which looks at a New York S&M establishment, it's not likely that the Disney Channel will be calling on his services any time soon.

Broomfield's films—and "Kurt & Courtney" is no exception—are structured around his dogged quest for information, in this case about the suicide death of Nirvana lead singer Cobain in 1994. Broomfield claims to have come to the subject with no preconceptions, but in the blink of an eye

3

he is wading hip deep in an open sewer of raucous accusations that the rocker was murdered and that Love was in some way involved in the death.

Not surprisingly, as Broomfield portentously intones, this was "a story some people have not wanted to tell." Love was understandably irked, and when two songs on the soundtrack turned out not to have the proper clearances, enough pressure was brought to have the film yanked from Sundance. The troublesome music has since been changed and it's now possible for general audiences to experience what the fuss was about.

Unreliable and categorically unfriendly to Love though it is, "Kurt & Courtney" is thoroughly watchable in a bad car accident, trash TV kind of way. All kinds of bizarre people get to hold the floor, a regular carnival sideshow of accusers, self-mythologizers, burnt-out cases and berserk tale-spinners, some of whom aren't even identified with full names.

One of the characteristics of Broomfield's work is that it's impossible to tell whether anyone is telling the truth or not: If you can hold the screen, you can appear in his film. So while it is arresting to hear the insalubrious El Duce, part of a rock group known for the song "You Are My Sex Slave," claim that Love "offered me 50 grand to whack Kurt Cobain," it's anyone's guess the reality level of that statement. Broomfield doesn't help matters by trying to have it both ways, giving screen time to unvetted gossip and then piously covering his tracks by saying things like "I was beginning to doubt everything" and "I wondered how much of anything anybody was telling me was true."

The most emotionally affecting part of "Kurt & Courtney" is its brief portrayal of Kurt Cobain. Starting with time spent with his Aunt Mary, the person who introduced Cobain to music, and including home movie footage and snippets from a very poignant (and uncredited) interview done near the Seattle waterfront, the movie quickly sketches the rock star as sincere, thoughtful and, at least at that moment, very much in love.

After spending time with grunge pals and Tracy Miranda, "Kurt's one and only true love" before he became famous, Broomfield moves on to bigger game. Using his fluid chameleon voice, which can be simultaneously ingratiating, insinuating and instigating, he first debriefs private investigator Tom Grant, a major conspiracy theorist. Then he turns to, of all people, Hank Harrison, Courtney's father, still locked into a fierce ego battle with his offspring, a tough love parent who does not feel his daughter's involvement in murder is beyond the realm of possibility.

Still, even if one is moved to dismiss the murder-conspiracy theories as incredible, it's not surprising that Courtney Love was not happy about this one-sided film. For "Kurt & Courtney" portrays her as a seriously unpleasant person, prone to violence, and in general not someone you would comfortably invite into your life.

It's more than the fury of ex-boyfriend Rozz Rezaback, who screams "a kinder, gentler Charlie Manson is still Charlie Manson," it's the chilling interactions Love has had with reporters. Vanity Fair writer Lynn Hirschberg, who Broomfield claims was too frightened to appear on camera, apparently told the director of a death threat and of being attacked by Love, no kidding, brandishing Quentin Tarantino's Oscar. Chilling phone threats both Love and Cobain are heard to make to a British writer are on the soundtrack, and the woman in question talks of being dragged across a club floor by the outraged Love.

In a classic Broomfield sequence, the director ambushes Love at a Los Angeles ACLU banquet and then brazenly strides onto the podium to briefly denounce her in front of an astonished black-tie audience before being hustled off stage. It's a typically surreal moment in a film that creates its own reality as it goes along. "You might not be a reliable witness your own self," the outrageous El Duce says to Broomfield, a statement that could serve as an epitaph for this singularly unnerving film.

NEW YORK POST, 6/5/98, p. 47, Thelma Adams

"Kurt and Courtney" is the documentary Courtney Love doesn't want you to see.

Filmmaker Nick Broomfield revisits the 1994 suicide of grunge messiah Kurt Cobain. With less journalistic integrity than "Inside Edition," the British director implicates Love, Cobain's widow, in the Nirvana front man's "murder."

Love's father, Hank Harrison, claims the junkie Cobain wasn't a suicide but was a victim of a killer with a shotgun. Harrison, who abandoned Love as a tot, suspects his daughter. Talk about tough Love!

Broomfield pumps Courtney's ex-boyfriend for bile on the Hole singer. The Portland rocker claims that Love's ambition ruined his career. He describes their first meeting ("She... threw a drink at me") and then says: "Courtney, you're not that good in bed."

No wonder Courtney would rather watch "The People Vs. Larry Flynt." Meanwhile, Cobain gets the tortured-artist treatment. His first girlfriend wanders her Seattle flat, which remains a shrine to her long-ago love. The chubby brunette does confess that "we had problems with him not cleaning the house."

Now that's dirt—but not the kind Broomfield wants. The egotistical documentarian with a taste for the sensational ("Heidi Fleiss: Hollywood Madam") has a field day prodding unreliable witnesses. He interviews disgruntled ex-employees, junkies, deviants and drug dealers.

Broomfield tracks down an S & M rocker known as Il Duce. The singer performs in an executioner's mask and claims that Love offered him $50,000 to kill Cobain. The director opens his interview by saying: "People might think you're not a reliable witness."

Il Duce has Broomfield's number. The ugly thug spits back "You may not be a reliable witness your own self" before promising to dish more if he gets paid in beer.

It's no wonder Love threatened legal action, a tack that kept "Kurt and Courtney" out of its official Sundance Film Festival slot. The move backfired: The film became a must-see unofficial event in a lackluster year.

Broomfield also pillories the widow Cobain for barring his use of Nirvana songs. Love may be unlovable, but she doesn't have to provide the soundtrack when she's burnt like a witch.

The outspoken, aggressive Love is an easy target, but there's a more interesting story than this tacky hate fest. Kurt and Courtney were two needy, talented, lonely children of divorce. He was a troubled troubadour with the face of an angel who shunned the spotlights; she was a hell-raiser who craved fame like a father's love.

Like Sid Vicious and Nancy Spungen, Kurt and Courtney waded through a cesspool of drugs and self-indulgence. One drowned; the other swam to safety. As Tina Turner would say, what's Love got to do with it?

NEWSDAY, 6/5/98, Part II/p. B6, Jack Mathews

Nick Broomfield, a British documentary filmmaker with the genes of a stalker, has a real racket going. He makes movies that reveal nothing so much as his incompetence at making movies.

They're quasi-exposes whose subjects—serial killers, hookers, dead rock stars, Margaret Thatcher—are incidental to the main theme, which is how hard it is to be Nick Broomfield trying to get a story.

People with real information won't talk to him, and some of those who have nothing to offer but rumor and speculation want money for it. His only friendly sources tend to be tangential figures with axes to grind or books to sell, and if he didn't ambush every subject and record every telephone conversation, he wouldn't have a movie at all.

How a lame sensationalist like Broomfield has found a critical fan club in the United States is as big a mystery as what he was doing on the documentary jury at this year's Sundance Film Festival, an event that was to host the world premiere of his latest picture, "Kurt & Courtney." That screening was canceled because of a threatened lawsuit over the use of music.

This is a really terrible movie, a cheesy tabloid clip job about the life and suicide of Seattle grunge rocker Kurt Cobain, with a pornographic array of interviews with spectacularly unreliable sources accusing Cobain's widow Courtney Love of plotting his death. One of Love's accusers is her own father, a breast-beating egocentric from whom she's been estranged since childhood, and who now writes books about his own bad seed.

Another "key" source, located for Broomfield by a man identified as the pimp of Hugh Grant consort Divine Brown, is some blubbery trailer trash called El Duce, who tells Broomfield that Love once offered him $50,000 to "whack" Cobain in a faked suicide. El Duce, who's more than a few bricks short of a full load, offers to reveal even more to the credulous filmmaker if he'll buy him a drink,

Later, with breathless gonzo urgency, Broomfield follows a note left on his windshield to a murky basement apartment in Seattle, where an apparently strung-out hooker introduces him to a woman claiming to have been the Cobains' nanny. Her vital testimony: Courtney was such a harpy that if she didn't kill her husband, she drove him to suicide.

By the time Broomfield acknowledges that he doesn't believe Love ordered Cobain's death, he has already elevated the conjecture to a dramatic theme, and it's apparent why. After charming his way into the lives of such past subjects as serial killer Aileen Wuornos and Beverly Hills madam Heidi Fleiss, Broomfield ran into a stone wall with Love, who went out of her way to undermine the financing for his film.

As a target for character assassination, Love is as nimble as a beached whale. She's damned by her own contemptible nature, as evidenced here by a ranting, audiotaped threat she made to the author of a tell-all book on the Cobains, and by an equally rancid letter she wrote to Lynn Hirschberg, the author of an unflattering article in Vanity Fair.

If there's a thread of documentary truth in "Kurt & Courtney," it's the influence that the steamrolling Love had over the passive, emotionally disabled Cobain. That's a good story for someone to tell, whether in a book or a film. But that's for another day, another reporter. All you'll learn from "Kurt & Courtney" is that Broomfield had no idea how to get it.

NEWSWEEK, 2/2/98, p. 60, David Ansen

The most talked-about film at the sundance Film festival is the one they were too afraid to show. "Kurt and Courtney", Nick Broomfield's documentary about the late rock star Kurt Cobain and his wife, Courtney Love, was removed from the festival under threat of a lawsuit. The legal issue was the use of two songs for which Broomfield had not secured the rights. But as Cassian Elwes, Broomfield's agent at William Morris, points out, "probably 80 percent of the films showing here don't have music clearance." The real issue was the film's scathing depiction of Love as a violent, manipulative, ruthlessly ambitious harpy—not to mention its inclusion of the dubious views of conspiracy theorists who claim Love was directly involved in Cobain's death despite its being ruled a suicide.

Broomfield, who happens to be on the jury of the documentary competition at Sundance this year, offered to cut the two songs from this film, but the Utah festival still believed there were unresolved legal issues. Enter Slamdunk, one of several underground mini-festivals that have sprung up in the wake of Sundance's success. It agreed to show the film at midnight at the old Elk's Lodge on Park City's Main Street (the original Sundance headquarters in its funkier days). An excited crowd of 150 handpicked filmmakers, distributors, celebrities, critics and reporters hunkered down on folding chairs, and though it was nearly 2 in the morning when the film ended, no one was in danger of dozing.

Disturbing and luridly entertaining, "Kurt and Courtney" is a freakish journey into the sleazier corners of the entertainment world and a devastating act of character assassination. "Stay away!" one of Love's former lovers, a Portland ex-rocker, says to the camera, addressing the absent Courtney."I don't care if you are Jesus and your lawyers are the 12 disciples." We hear of a death threat writer Lynn Hirschberg received from the star after her unflattering 1992 Vanity Fair article (Love, we are told, tried to attack the journalist at the Academy Awards, brandishing Quentin Tarantino's Oscar as a weapon). Hirschberg, the film says, was too scared to even appear in Broomfield's movie, but there are many other anti-Courtney testifiers, including a burly, tattooed rocker named El Duce, who claims courtney "offered me 50 grand to whack Kurt Cobain" (he later adds, "but I didn't think she was serious"), and private eye Tom Grant, who is obsessed with proving she was involved in killing Kurt. Oddest of all her enemies is her own father, the author of "Who Killed Kurt Cobain?," who seems to revel in waging public war against his daughter. (This is a guy who disciplined her as a little girl by scaring her with pit bulls.) These folks are not the most reliable witnesses, and Broomfield makes it clear he doesn't buy into the conspiracy theories. Nonetheless, we do hear from the nanny who was present in Kurt and Courtney's home shortly before his suicide; she says that Love was obsessed with his will. the film is relentlessly one-sided: Love receives no credit from anyone for her music or her amazing performance in Milos Forman's "The People Vs. Larry Flynt."

Broomfield says he didn't set out to attack Love. As in his previous films about Heidi Fleiss and serial killer aileen Wuornos, he expected he'd be sympathetic to her. The focus of his film shifted when it became clear Love and her powerful allies in Hollywood were trying to keep him from making his film. (Love's publicists, PMK, also represent Sundance founder Robert Redford, who said at a press conference he hoped Broomfield's film would eventually get released.) The pressure exerted on Sundance is a continuation of what we see in the film, which records a phone call from Showtime informing Broomfield it is withdrawing its funding from the film. In a scene that will prove deeply embarrassing to the ACLU, we see Broomfield take the stage at an ACLU dinner celebrating the First Amendment and Milos Forman, at which Love had been a speaker. He begins to denounce her hypocrisy, given her attempts to stifle journalists, but he is strong-armed off the stage before he can finish.

As soon as the screening ended, offers to distribute the film came in. Broomfield is certain his movie will get released, but it will now have a new ending. The Sundance brouhaha will make a perfect coda. If the film is a success, he'll owe a big debt to Courtney. Her campaign to suppress it has give the movie a publicity send-off no money can buy.

SIGHT AND SOUND, 7/98, p. 44, Mark Sinker

In the wake of rock star Kurt Cobain's 1994 shotgun suicide, Nick Broomfield plans to discover if there's any truth in the conspiracy theories claiming this was murder: that fellow rock star Courtney Love, wife and mother of Cobain's child Frances, ordered a hit on him—since if divorced, she'd lose out on his money. Broomfield talks to Cobain's aunt and a pre-fame ex-girlfriend, Tracy Marander, then meets people from Love's past: her long-estranged biological father Hank Harrison, who calls her "violent" and speculates on her role in Kurt's death; and former lover and rock failure Rozz Rezabek, who reads from journals she left behind.

Love hired private detective Tom Grant to find Cobain when he vanished from drug rehab: Grant is today convinced she had Cobain killed. However, Cobain's friend Dylan Carlson refuses to endorse the murder theory. Self-styled 'stalkerazzis' Al and Jack point Broomfield towards El Duce, a lowlife rock singer who claims Love offered him $50,000 to kill Kurt, and who dies days after being interviewed. Nevertheless, Broomfield loses confidence in the conspiracy theory. Was suicide the only way Kurt could escape a domineering Courtney? After detailing Love's extreme hostility to reveal-all articles and books written about her in the past, Broomfield confronts her at a Constitutional Free Speech junket in Hollywood, where she's speaking: he attempts to storm the stage and denounce her, but is hustled away.

A celebrity marriage with offspring, followed by the suicide of one partner: as Ted Hughes and Sylvia Plath proved long ago, whoever shares the departed's life will be accused of 'soul murder' by those besotted fans who alone understand (as they see it). At issue here is unaddressed envy. Certainly Nick Broomfield's latest clownish exercise in doorstepping documentary underscores the very similar price rock star-turned-actress Courtney Love is paying, for refusing to act the passive priestess at the shrine of St Kurt.

Yet this confused, self-regarding, misogynist tabloid character assassination suggests more that the would-be journalist at its centre is perhaps as naive as he pretends to be. Sure, this pretence is a device: playing the bumbling innocent, Broomfield can present his subjects as fools and grotesques without coming across as manipulative, or, a bully. He has in past documentaries (on South African fascist Eugene Terreblanche, on Mark and Margaret Thatcher, on Hollywood madam Heidi Fleiss) enjoyed showing himself failing to get key interviews—here he also fails to get key co-production backing or the rights to use Nirvana songs on the soundtrack. As always, we're to conclude that when so charming an inadequate is refused access, there's villainy afoot.

Not that it's the skull-and-crossbones evil he set out to uncover after an investigation at once interminable and cursory—it consists primarily of ringing on doorbells, a grey furry boom-like bobbing alongside Broomfield's ambulatory bald spot—our far-from guileless gumshoe concludes that the alleged rub-out ordered by Love on Cobain is so much conspiracy-nut nonsense.

No, the 'real story', as he belatedly affects to realise, is that the fragile future suicide simply couldn't cope with Love's monstrous ambitions for him. The 'proof' of this, beyond the hearsay of the disgruntled, is that her support of Free Speech is mere hypocrisy, as witness her various (apparent) attempts to shut journalists up.

Now this has the outline of a genuine issue, even a scoop. Unfortunately, it's precisely here that the film tumbles over into plain misrepresentation. Whether or not we believe him, part of the Broomfield shtick is that he does almost no pre-shoot research: because we're witness at such length to his improvised, ill-informed interviews, we perhaps don't recognise quite how effective he can be at omitting crucial facts. Concerning Rozz Rezabek, an earlier consort who couldn't cope with Love, we're never told that he is fully ten years older than her, or that she was just 17 years old when they lived together. Concerning her estranged father, today so unabashed an advocate of 'tough love', we never learn the extent of his delinquency as a parent back when she was an unhappy and unloved 12-year-old, especially with regard to drugs. Concerning her own career, we never learn that her band Hole's acclaim—for the LP *Pretty on the Inside*—predated and set the context for Nirvana's.

Whether by her choice or Broomfield's design, Love puts no case in her defence—but if the charge against her is suppression of the facts from her past (about stripping, about addiction), then consider her friend Poppy Z. Brite's authorised biography *Courtney Love: The Real Story*. We needn't accept a single page as gospel: the fact is, this official version of events dwells, at quite exhaustive length, on all that it's here implied she's hiding. We learn nothing of this. Instead, she's once more punished for a refusal: for denying parasitic media the automatic right to transform her honesty (and rage and mistakes and confusion) into just another showbiz turn. Paradoxically, music-industry unwillingness to back this project is an index less of its cowardice—or of payola—than of its grudging respect for this artist's creative integrity Ergo collapse of scoop.

Of course Broomfield's last-ditch excuse could be that his films are not independent investigative journalism, but rather deconstructions of its excesses and pretensions: and that, above all, he is himself the patsy here, a version of comedian Harry Enfield's Tim-Nice-But-Dim stumbling about trying to be reporter Roger Cook. Certainly out of the collision of so many self-serving, self-deluded agendas, some of these incoherent, damaged, no-hope chancers emerge with dignity surprisingly intact. Love herself, briefly ambushed, meets a potentially awkward moment with admirable grace and restraint. But this is a tip of the hat to them, not their interlocutor.

OK, so Love can be volatile, paranoid, controlling, irritating and ferociously ambitious; can exhibit the same extremes of selfishness, self-doubt, self-dramatisation and oversensitivity as any former or still-using junkie. But Broomfield himself is today an operator whose fading public-school charm can no longer disguise his deeply conventional opinions, a once-talented documentarist gone to waste. As Ruby Wax proved with O. J. Simpson, earnest objectivity is not the only way to deliver documentary revelation. But Wax sets standards Broomfield consistently falls below. Frankly, it's time a few more people thought twice before returning his phone calls.

VILLAGE VOICE, 6/9/98, p. 143, J. Hoberman

Elsewhere in celebrityland [The reference is to *The Truman Show*; see Hoberman's review of that film.] we have Nick Broomfield's *Kurt and Courtney*—a documentary notorious for not only wondering whether Courtney Love had a hand in the death of her husband, Kurt Cobain, but for being bounced at the last minute from the Sundance Film Festival.

As Michael Moore documents his quest for corporate CEOs, so Broomfield makes movies about his fascination with "difficult" women. The early films concerned female soldiers and Nevada prostitutes; he hit his stride with portraits of serial killer Aileen Wuornos, ex-PM Margaret Thatcher and Hollywood madam Heidi Fleiss. It's not surprising that Broomfield would have found Love a sympathetic subject but—unlike Aileen and Heidi—she declines to play along.

Thus, with Kurt dead and Courtney unavailable, what we have is Nick—bottom-feeder deluxe, orchestrating a grunge freak show, and explaining why he can't use Nirvana's music or complaining about Courtney's attempts to suppress his project. A presence at once cool and harried in taking his revenge, Broomfield assembles a crew of negative character witnesses—Love's pre-Kurt rocker swain, the private eye she apparently hired to investigate Cobain's "disappearance," the journalists she threatened and/or physically attacked, a woman claiming to have been the Cobain baby's nanny, and her father—a spectacular lowlife creep who has written two books on Cobain's "murder" and admits to using pit bulls to discipline Courtney. "It's still tough love and I'm still her father," he explains, availing himself of Broomfield's camera to address his daughter directly: "I'll kick your ass!"

Right. At one point, Broomfield is taken by Divine Brown's pimp to meet El Duce, and s/m metallista who brags Love offered him 20 grand to waste her husband. (El Duce's subsequent death further feeds the conspiracy.) While Courtney's alleged role in Kurt's alleged death is surely a question for *The X-Files*, Broomfield makes a strong case for Love as a violent, unstable, narcissitic control freak. No scoop that. The real surprise is that he is able to find something more exploitative than his own project—a black-tie American Civil Liberties Union dinner with Love presenting the Torch of Freedom award to Milos Forman.

After documenting the star's barely coherent natterings on the First Amendment, Broomfield manages to ask a public question about her attempts to intimidate journalists and then have his own media martyrdom filmed as he is dragged away from the microphone—thrown off the set of Love's *Truman Show*.

Also reviewed in:
CHICAGO TRIBUNE, 6/5/98, Friday/p. D, Greg Kot
NEW YORK TIMES, 6/5/98, p. E12, Janet Maslin
VARIETY, 1/26-2/1/98, p. 71, Dennis Harvey
WASHINGTON POST, 7/17/98, p. B5, Richard Harrington
WASHINGTON POST, 7/17/98, Weekend/p. 44, Michael O'Sullivan

LA SENTINELLE

A Strand Releasing release of a Why Not Productions/2001 Audiovisuel/La Sept Cinema/Films A2 production. *Producer:* Arnaud Desplechin. *Director:* Arnaud Desplechin. *Screenplay (French with English subtitles):* Arnaud Desplechin. *Director of Photography:* Caroline Champetier. *Editor:* François Gedigier. *Music:* Marc Sommer. *Sound:* Laurent Poirier. *Production Designer:* Antoine Platteau. *Running time:* 144 minutes. *MPAA Rating:* Not Rated.

WITH: Emmanuel Salinger;   Thibault de Montalembert;   Jean-Louis Richard;   Valerie Dreville;   Marianne Denicourt;   Jean-Luc Boutte;   Bruno Todeschini;   Philippe Duclos; Fabrice Desplechin;   Emmanuelle Devos;   Phillippe Laudenbach.

LOS ANGELES TIMES, 1/15/98, Calendar/p. 20, Kevin Thomas

A complex and truly original film, Arnaud Desplechin's 1991 "La Sentinelle" on the surface is the story of a young medical student (Emmanuel Salinger) adjusting to life in Paris after spending years in Germany as the son of a diplomat.

At the outset, however, two tremendously jarring incidents—Salinger's exceptionally harrowing interrogation by a semmingly deranged border patrolman and his discovery of a mummified head in his luggage—let us know that we're in for more. For all its Hitchcockian twists, "La Sentinelle" is a lot closer to Jacques Rivette's "Paris Belongs to Us"; the Cold War may be over, but its paranoia lingers on dangerously.

NEW YORK POST, 10/16/98, p. 44, Larry Worth

Any film treat starts with an analysis of the Yalta Conference obviously signals heavy going ahead. In that respect, "La Sentinelle" doesn't disappoint.

Ironically, the film is too ambitious for its own good. As written and directed by Arnaud Desplechin, the man who put his name on the cinematic map with "My Sex Life... Or How I Got Into an Argument," the film tackles a dizzying amount of subject matters. The problem: Too many of them lead down dead ends.

As the tale opens, a young pathologist en route from Germany to his native France is accosted on a train by a burly guard who not only ransacks his luggage but leaves an additional item: a mummified head.

After getting past his shock, the protagonist becomes increasingly obsessed with the severed noggin, conducting his own investigation into its identity. What he uncovers leads to an even bigger mystery, and enough intrigue for a half-dozen John le Carre novels.

But what of the subplots? Watching the guy endure endless squabbles with his roommate, sister, girlfriend and on and on wears thin, especially when it becomes obvious that they're mere filler for the script's more engaging political themes.

Desplechin, using camerawork that's nearly drained of color, certainly presents some fascinating scenes and complex exchanges. But as the film reaches its climax after two hours and 20 minutes, it's hard not to feel a sense of letdown and frustration.

For the most part, a young cast that includes "Sex Life" veterans Emmanuel Salinger and Emmanuelle Devos makes for achingly—and aptly—conflicted characters. That's particularly impressive since their fully nuanced efforts were lensed four years before cameras rolled for "Sex Life."

Regardless, "La Sentinelle" fails to satisfy. But as the observant title implies, Desplechin is a man who always bears watching.

NEWSDAY, 10/16/98, Part II/p. B11, John Anderson

Two of the more telling moments in Arnaud Desplechin's "La Sentinelle" come at opposite ends of the movie and, on first blush, seem precisely opposite.

The first takes place at the French Embassy in Bonn, September, 1991. A senior diplomat is relating an anecdote about an alleged post-war meeting between Churchill and Stalin, at which they divvied up Europe in about a minute and a half. Don't tell anyone about this, Churchill is said to have told Stalin, or they'll accuse us of having cynically decided the fate of millions.

The second involves a young Parisian named Nathalie (Valerie Dreville), a singer who walks into a room, tosses her bag on a piano, and it lands on the keys. It's a banal moment— a throwaway, if you will. At the same time, the resulting clash of notes says as much about callous indifference and carelessly led lives as Winnie, Joe and the apportioning of Bulgaria.

What they remind us about director Desplechin is his ability to marry big ideas to small, to get at the essence of individual lives through major philosophical or political concepts, and to illuminate large ideas through the minutiae of his characters. The same approach helped make last year's "My Sex Life ... (or How I Got Into an Argument)" last year's best French import and one of it's better films. And it does the same for "La Sentinelle."

Of course, "La Sentinelle," which is more than caustic about dilettante Europe and the aftermath of the Cold War, might have had a bit more impact had it been released here after screening at the New York Film Festival—in 1992. The delay has diluted some of its potency. Even so, it's a remarkable movie.

Appropriately Kafkaesque, the movie's ostensible, beleagured hero, Mathias (Emmanuel Salinger), a doctor and the son of a French diplomat, is stopped on a train en route from his former home in Germany to Paris. His papers are not in order and a sweaty official (Jean-Louis Richard) grills him, not just about his identity but about the shallowness of his existence.

Soon after arriving in Paris, Mathias finds something planted in his bag: a mummified, severed head. The metaphors are obvious; the reasons for it being there are a complete mystery.

Desplechin paints a rather clinical picture of a despicable crowd, the young musicians and diplomats Mathias meets through his estranged sister Marie (Marianne Denicourt), a group whose capacity for shallowness is matched by their capacity for viciousness. Mathias, considered something of a rube, becomes obsessed with the head, what it means to the interrogator who put it in his bag, and eventually how to give it a decent funeral, a process so fraught with Jesuitical nuance that you suspect Mathias may at any moment metamorphose into a dung beetle.

The details are fascinating, occasionally revolting (Mathias' pursuit of the head's identity involves a bit of scraping and tearing) and in the end add up to a world in which knowledge of the flesh is a good deal more advanced than our knowledge of the soul. And a so-called free world that may be a bit less than complete, and more like a headless body in glorious retreat.

VILLAGE VOICE, 10/20/98, p. 160, Amy Taubin

Few films are as successfully Kafkaesque as Arnaud Desplechin's *La Sentinelle,* the story of a young French forensic pathologist named Mathias (Emmanuel Salinger) who becomes obsessed with a well-preserved human head that has been stowed in his suitcase. "The dead are your patients," says Mathias's teacher. Acting on that instruction, Mathias attempts to discover the identity of the head so that it can have a proper burial.

Sound strange? Well, it is and it isn't, though the film does have its grisly moments (rather like *E.R.* crossed with the recent British vogue for taxidermic art). What's remarkable—and Kafkaesque—about *La Sentinelle* is how Desplechin grounds the phantasmagoric aspects of his tale in the details, routines, and conflicts of daily life. The film can be interpreted as a realist narrative about a young man whose family background (his father was a diplomat) and profession make him an unwitting tool of political intrigue between France and what was about to become "the former Soviet Union." *(La Sentinelle* is set in 1991.) Or, one might read everything that follows the opening scene as the anxiety dream of a young man who, leaving home for the first time, feels guilty toward his parents and alienated from his peers.

In either case, the film is a political allegory about the emergence of the new Europe, which in its rush toward prosperity has crassly and crudely repressed its own history. Alone among his friends, classmates, and family, Mathias feels burdened by the ghosts of the Holocaust, the Resistance, and the near-50 years of divided Europe that followed World War II. He cannot move from adolescence to adulthood unless he finds a way to honor the past and keep its memory alive.

Subtract the spy shenanigans and *La Sentinelle* is very much like *My Sex Life... or How I Got Into an Argument,* the film Desplechin made in 1996 and the first of his three films to get U.S. distribution. (His first, *The Life of the Dead,* has never been shown here.) Mathias's psychological dilemmas—the anger and competitiveness he feels toward his more careerist peers, his desire for women just out of reach—are the same as those of the hero of *My Sex Life. La Sentinelle* is less visually fluid and less emotionally naked than the later film, but it's just as intellectually compelling.

The continuity between the two films is the result of their open-ended, porous narratives and the fact that many of the same actors are cast in both of them. Emmanuel Salinger, who plays the overwrought Mathias, also plays Nathan, the self-possessed best friend of the hero of *My Sex Life.* Emmanuelle Devos, who appears as Mathias's object of desire, appears in *My Sex Life* as the long-term girlfriend the hero is desperately trying to dump. That hero is named Paul, but he's played by an actor named Mathieu-Mathieu Amalric. Amalric, who can be glimpsed in *La Sentinelle* as one of Mathias's medical school classmates, has rapidly become as much of an axiom of French filmmaking in the '90s as Jean-Pierre Leaud was of the '60s New Wave. He also plays the lead role in Olivier Assayas's recent NYFF entry *Late August, Early September,* which is strikingly similar in its themes to *My Sex Life.*

If Assayas is the stylist of this generation of French filmmakers (which also includes Pascale Ferran, Danielle Dubroux, and Noemie Lvovsky), then Desplechin is the intellectual. While his films pack an emotional punch, they're also a workout for the brain. He has a knack for revealing the life of the mind in characters so consumed with anxiety that they can only act spasmodically. Mathias, the fish out of water in yuppified Paris, is an unforgettable character—so unsophisticated that he inquires of a colleague he's just met, "Are you Jewish?" and so diligent in applying his forensic skills that he analyzes history even as it's being shredded and dumped.

The more I look at the films of Desplechin and the others in this group (and they are definitely a group, not only because they share actors and ideas, but also because they actively assist one another in the filmmaking process), the more I'm convinced that they are as expressive and complicated reflections on their time as were the films of the New Wave. Like those earlier films, these are actors' movies, though the performances are less flamboyant and more inner-directed.

The most commercial New Wave films seduced American audiences by flattery. We loved them for fetishizing Hollywood movies. This new generation of French filmmakers trains its sights on Europe—on its history and its future. Thus, their films are a more difficult sell. And yet, there are few contemporary American movies that treat a young man's struggle to define himself in relation to friends, enemies, and family, and to make his way (pay the rent) in a cosmopolitan city, as brilliantly as *La Sentinelle.* See it in New York, and recognize yourself.

Also reviewed in:
NEW REPUBLIC, 11/16/98, p. 26, Stanley Kauffmann
NEW YORK TIMES, 10/16/98, p. E14, Stephen Holden
VARIETY, 5/25/92, p. 54, David Stratton

LA SÉPARATION

A Phaedra Cinema release of a Renn Productions/France 2 Cinema/DA Films/CMV Productions production with the participation of Canal Plus. *Executive Producer:* Pierre Grunstein. *Producer:* Claude Berri. *Director:* Christian Vincent. *Screenplay (French with English subtitles):* Dan Franck and Christian Vincent. *Based on the novel by:* Dan Franck. *Director of Photography:* Denis Lenoir. *Editor:* François Ceppi. *Sound:* Claud Bertrand and Jean-Paul Loublier. *Casting:* Frederique Moidon. *Art Director:* Christian Vallerin. *Costumes:* Sylvie Gautrelet. *Running time:* 88 minutes. *MPAA Rating:* Not Rated.

CAST: Isabelle Huppert (Anne); Daniel Auteuil (Pierre); Jérôme Deschamps (Victor); Karin Viard (Claire); Laurence Lerel (Laurence); Louis Vincent (Loulou); Nina Morato (Marie).

CHRISTIAN SCIENCE MONITOR, 10/2/98, p. B3, David Sterritt

France has been showering American moviegoers with riches since the days of silent cinema. None of this year's French offerings is more captivating than "La Séparation," which tells a small but insinuating story with characters so tenderly written and vividly acted that they will be recognizable to audiences of any nationality.

As the title hints, "La Séparation" is about a marriage that's slowly and sadly coming apart. This subject has been handled in countless melodramas on both sides of the Atlantic, of course, but what makes this treatment different is its lack of sensationalism, exploitation, or overstatement. It's as if director Christian Vincent knew this couple personally and wanted to explore their problems without risking the slightest suggestion of tactlessness or indiscretion.

The result is a series of compassionately filmed scenes from a marriage, delicate and sensitive from beginning to end.

Key to the movie's success is the acting by two of France's most luminous stars: Isabelle Huppert, whose career ranges from "The Lacemaker" and "Madame Bovary" to "Amateur" and some of Jean-Luc Godard's movies, and Daniel Auteuil, who captivated US audiences in "Jean de Florette," "Manon of the Spring," and "Queen Margot." Both are at their expressive best in "La Séparation," as is director Vincent.

Statistics show that Americans attend subtitled movies far less often than they used to, which means they may sacrifice the subtle pleasures of "La Séparation" because it doesn't have English dialogue. At a time when many criticize Hollywood for its frequent violence and vulgarity, how heartening it would be if audiences decided to support the maturity of "La Séparation" and other intelligently made imports—including such thoughtful French dramas as "An Autumn Tale" and "The Dreamlife of Angels," both coming soon—as an alternative to the slam-bang heroics of business-as-usual studios.

LOS ANGELES TIMES, 10/23/98, Calendar/p. 10, Kevin Thomas

Isabelle Huppert and Daniel Auteuil, two of the French cinema's most accomplished actors, are teamed—surprisingly for the first time—in Christian Vincent's astute "La Separation." It is a film in which the full range of love and pain are expressed with an appreciation for nuance and subtlety and viewed with a sense of detachment and compassion.

French films have been relatively scarce in recent years, so much so that the arrival of this beautiful, harrowing and completely captivating film—four years after its completion, but never mind that—is cause to reflect on some of the classic elements of French movies: their quality of intimacy, sense of everyday life (more often than not lived in a tasteful if smallish Paris apartment), the presence and value of children, and, of course, the paramount importance they place on passionate love.

In a sense you could say that we've seen "La Separation" many times before, but the French have a special gift in making every relationship, every love story, seem unique and important.

When we learn well into the film that Huppert's patrician Anne and Auteuil's tousled, unshaven Pierre are not married it's not surprising, for that too is commonplace in French pictures.

However, they are in need of a marriage counselor for sure—but like lots of otherwise intelligent people in emotional crisis, it apparently never occurs to them to seek professional help.

What has happened to Anne and Pierre, who have a 15-month-old son, after several years together is familiar enough. They're not paying enough attention to each other, and as a result, they've started getting on the other's nerves. They're finding it impossible to let the least little disagreement pass. In such an atmosphere it does not shock us to hear Anne announce, "I've fallen in love with another man," although the news devastates Pierre, who has been feeling that he is no longer important to her. She explains, in time-honored words, "You wouldn't listen to me... I met a man who listens to me, who's interested in me and pays attention to me."

Where Anne is different from many other women in a similar situation is that she does not want to leave Pierre or want him to leave her. Anne sees her romance (with a man unknown to both us and Pierre, who does not want to know his identity) as transient, yet of course there's no way of knowing when or if it really will ebb. The question thus becomes whether or not Pierre will be strong enough to weather the storm—and whether or not he'll be able to forgive her.

Huppert and Auteuil work deeply from within, creating a foundation for the formidable command of expression, gesture and movement that allows them to act with the utmost naturalness and spontaneity. Based on writer-actor Dan Franck's acclaimed 1991 novel, "La Separation" has a masculine point of view yet is as fair-minded toward Anne as it is toward Pierre.

Neither Vincent, best known for "La Discrete," nor Huppert is afraid to show Anne as unsympathetically cool to Pierre's pain. No one is denying that she has placed Pierre in a difficult, excruciatingly painful position, for he clearly loves her deeply. Yet we can see in Pierre an unfortunate tendency to bungle those opportunities to reach through to Anne when they come along.

"La Separation" has been filmed with that rich yet clear, natural light that make so many French films glow. It has style, economy and understatement in dealing with the contradictions of the heart, traits that have always characterized the best of French cinema.

NEW YORK POST, 10/2/98, p. 44, Larry Worth

A story about a couple on the verge of breaking up is bound to seem familiar, no matter what permutations their relationship assumes.

That's where a dream cast can make all the difference. By featuring two of France's very best actors—namely Isabelle Huppert and Daniel Auteuil—as the troubled protagonists, "La Separation" guarantees that a viewer's attention will be riveted to the screen.

To a great degree, the production's look and feel go way beyond the script. Much more is said in the way Auteuil's posture evolves from cocky to crippled, the manner in which Huppert alternately meets and averts his gaze, and how their eyes convey a fire that's equal parts passion and rage.

When the film begins, the two seem content with each other, and totally smitten with their 2-year-old son, nicknamed Loulou (perhaps a nod to Maurice Pialat's 1980 film that cemented Huppert's reputation). But when Huppert's character announces that she's taken a lover, the central relationship begins its unavoidable spiral into hell.

To director and co-writer Christian Vincent's credit, a few surprises surface alonq the way. Neither principal reacts as one might expect. Better still, there's no real villain; each is at fault as the power plays pass from one to the other and back again.

Make no mistake: This isn't "Who's Afraid of Virginia Woolf?" where the badinage is as entertaining as it is painful. As staged by Vincent, these clashes are filled with a raw anger and honesty that will convince audiences they're peeking through a neighbor's keyhole.

Still, it's Huppert and Auteuil who define the boundaries between alienation, growing tension, full-fledged battle and acceptance of the inevitable. They're the '90s version of Gallic greats Simone Signoret and Yves Montand.

Auteuil, whose previous interpretations of amour gone amok include "Jean de Florette," "Manon of the Spring" and "Ma Saison Preferee," provides as penetrating a look into one man's soul as it's possible to imagine. And Huppert continues to prove why she's a performer of such international acclaim.

Together, they elevate "La Separation" into an experience that's as wrenching as it is insightful, as ultimately draining as it is thoroughly satisfying.

NEWSDAY, 10/2/98, Part II/p. B7, John Anderson

Although it's a form that gives most of the movie industry hives, tragedy is a useful, meaningful, exhilarating thing. It's ennobling. It conveys immediacy, poignancy, mortality. It may even cause us to count our blessings.

"La Separation," a crafty, deftly deflating film by French filmmaker Christian Vincent, is that rare thing, a tragedy—not of the grand variety, but the French. When the increasingly chilly Anne (Isabelle Huppert) announces to common-law husband Pierre (Daniel Auteuil) that she's fallen in love with another man, his reaction isn't anger or outrage or violence. He will confront this problem with civility and reason and affectionate rationality. And only slowly drive himself to the point of perspiration.

"La Separation," which is a small film only because of the commonality of its situation, uses adultery the way Hitchcock used murder. Once Anne declares her love for her never-seen paramour, we wait nervously for the other shoe to drop. Will she sleep with him? This seems obvious, but when? Will we know? Will Pierre? And will Pierre maintain his continental cool? Considering what's at stake—a home, a child, a life—the tension builds in luxurious domestic layers.

Vincent, whose 1992 "La Discrete" failed to engage because it lacked an empathetic character, has atoned for that here by giving us two. Anne, played with icy resolve by the austere Huppert, is possessed of an arrogant self-indulgence but is also a kind of victim; her condition is like a disease ("I'll get over it," she tells Pierre), one she views with a certain distance and resignation.

Pierre, for his part, is quietly shattered, his videotaping of infant son Loulou (Louis Vincent) taking on progressively poignant overtones, beginning as a playful history and gradually evolving into what may in the end be the last umbilical link to the boy he obviously loves. There's more than a bit of feminist antipathy here. As Pierre is told by an adviser at court, hiring a lawyer would be useless: Since he and Anne are not married, he has no real claims to their child and is effectively out in the cold.

Vincent uses the family's household routines to morph and change according to the domestic atmosphere within and mines the inherent perversity in their oh-so-civilized dissolution. As their relationship becomes increasingly poisoned, their occasional moments of tenderness seem almost illicit; the uncertainty of their relationship becomes more unsettling than Anne's philandering. The wild card in it all is babysitter Laurence (the lovely Laurence Lerel), who is clearly available to Pierre should he want her, although he hardly seems aware she's there. And while the Laurence factor is a red herring, it adds another element of risk to an already dicey situation.

Ultimately, what makes "La Separation" a significant film is its sophisticated handling of a very adult scenario and the emotional fallout it produces. No wailing, no gnashing of teeth, but a measured, cancerous collapse of two people who have the great misfortune to love each other.

VILLAGE VOICE, 10/6/98, p. 132, Leslie Camhi

It can start with a peculiarly quiet breakfast, an unshaven afternoon, a gesture of affection shrugged off or rejected. La Separation follows a trajectory many will find familiar—the downward spiral of eroding intimacy. Pitiful and disgusting, the ends of relationships are a staple of European arthouse cinema—Rossellini and Bergman weighed in with classics of the genre. French director Christian Vincent (La Discrete, 1992) takes a stab at greatness with this wrenching portrait of the senseless disintegration of a household, and comes up short, but delivers fine performances from two big stars—Isabelle Huppert and Daniel Auteuil—who give their all to the pettiness and ugliness of la vie a deux.

"I knew there was something wrong," Pierre (Auteuil), a children's book illustrator, says about Anne (Huppert), a businesswoman, "when for a fortnight she didn't nag me." La Separation is most disturbing in its vivid portrayal of the bickering and daily abuse that binds couples when it doesn't break them. No one looks particularly pretty—neither the perennially self-pitying Pierre nor the blindly narcissistic Anne, who thinks she can philander while maintaining a cozy home life with Pierre and Louis (a/k/a Loulou), their adorable toddler son.

Innocent bystanders are particularly unbearable—Pierre's friends, self-involved intellectuals, spout idiocies, in the guise of advice or consolation, about how "people once mated as they pleased" or "all couples have their crises." A real estate agent's spiel about the "communicating rooms" of a country house in Normandy underscores the larger theme here—this pair's inability to attend to each other and to make themselves understood. "I don't have anything specific against you," Anne says to Pierre. "I just met someone who listens." Perhaps that's why much of the dialogue falls flat, and why Huppert and Auteuil are most affecting when, with eyes averted or cast into a coffee cup, a moment of silence is among the few remaining things they share.

Subtly, the film is skewed toward Pierre's perspective. The intense focus on tiny slights, the sly glances at Loulou's winsome young baby-sitter, the sense of rage and helplessness are his. And so it also suffers from the cloying claustrophobia of his oddly passive personality; he never really fights the loss of his family, he just rails at Anne and privately mourns her. Anne's emotions (and her work) remain strangely opaque, and the world beyond their household barely exists. Is this a flaw in the narrative or a symptom of modern alienation? Either way, it's part of a horror story that's simply all too real.

Also reviewed in:
NEW YORK TIMES, 10/2/98, p. E27, Stephen Holden
VARIETY, 12/5-11/94, p. 75, Lisa Nesselson

LAND GIRLS, THE

A Gramercy Pictures release of a PolyGram Filmed Entertainment presentation from Intermedia Films with the participation of the Greenlight Fund and Channel Four Films of a Greenpoint Film in association with West Eleven Films. *Executive Producer:* Ruth Jackson. *Producer:* Simon Relph. *Director:* David Leland. *Screenplay:* Keith Dewhurst and David Leland. *Based on the novel "Land Girls" by:* Angela Huth. *Director of Photography:* Henry Braham. *Editor:* Nick Moore. *Music:* Brian Lock. *Sound:* Stuart Wilson and (music) Martin Astle. *Sound Editor:* Ian Fuller. *Casting:* Jeremy Zimmerman. *Production Designer:* Caroline Amies. *Art Director:* Frank Walsh. *Special Effects:* Ian Wingrove and Jeff Clifford. *Costumes:* Shuna Harwood. *Make-up:* Jenny Shircore. *Stunt Coordinator:* Nick Powell. *Running time:* 112 minutes. *MPAA Rating:* R.

CAST: Catherine McCormack (Stella); Rachel Weisz (Ag); Anna Friel (Prue); Steven Mackintosh (Joe Lawrence); Tom Georgeson (Mr. Lawrence); Maureen O'Brien (Mrs. Lawrence); Lucy Akhurst (Janet); Gerald Down (Ratty); Paul Bettany (Philip); Nick Mollo (Barry); Michael Mantas (Desmond); Nicholas Le Prevost (Agricultural Officer); Celia Bannerman (District Commissioner); Ann Bell (Philip's Mother); Nigel Planer (Gerald); Edmund Moriarty (Harry, the Airman); Shirley Newbery (WAAF at Dance); Russell Barr (Jamie, Scottish Airman); John Gill (Doctor); Crispin Layfield (German Pilot/Stunt Artist); Grace Leland (Baby Barry); Alan Bennett (Reverend Alan Bennett/himself); Martha Mackintosh, Felix Davis, and Jacob Leland (Children at Christening); Jack O'Hampton (Jack the Dog).

LOS ANGELES TIMES, 6/12/98, Calendar/p. 18, Kevin Thomas

When World War II broke out in 1939, Britain revved up its Women's Land Army, founded in 1917 during World War I to recruit young women to take over the plows when farmers went off to the battlefields. Over the years, 100,000 women became part of the WLA, which was not disbanded until 1950.

"The Land Girls," adapted from Angela Huth's well-received 1994 novel by writer-director David Leland and co-writer Keith Dewhurst, is a sure-fire heart-tugger that resonates with American audiences, especially those of us old enough to remember life on the home front, even if we were only children at the time. It was an era when people really pulled together, to a large extent laying aside "for the duration" differences in race, class and gender for the war effort.

"The Land Girls" is an old-fashioned women's picture but told with a candor not possible in the movies of its time. World War II marked the beginning of a social revolution in which women began to consider alternatives to their traditional roles as housewives and mothers.

The war, of course, was a time of terrific emotional upheaval and uncertainty; young people of conventional backgrounds were tempted to throw aside strictures against premarital sex and to question whether they really loved those whom they were supposed to many.

Against this backdrop, three beautiful young women—Stella (Catherine McCormack), Ag (Rachel Weisz) and Prue (Anna Friel) become Land Girls assigned to a farm belonging to the Lawrences (Tom Georgeson and Maureen O'Brien) in the gorgeous English countryside. Engaged to a naval officer, Stella is a banker's daughter. Ag is a virginal Cambridge graduate, superficially a bit of a snob, and Prue is a hairdresser, the earthiest and most realistic of the three. Since he is so badly needed at the farm, the Lawrences' hearty, handsome son Joe (Steven Mackintosh) has delayed enlisting in the Air Force.

Even with the arrival of our trio, "The Land Girls" keeps delaying Joe's enlistment to the extent that the film spends precious little time with the women plowing the fields and lots more in the hayloft, where in time all three are eager to end up with Joe. Prue means to seduce the guy from the get-go and also decides he's just the man to relieve Ag of her virginity. Stella, who has a personality clash with Joe, is naturally the one who falls for him the hardest—and vice versa.

"The Land Girls" plays out quite effectively with its potent blend of wartime romance, sacrifice and bravery in the face of inevitable tragic losses, and it benefits from its first-rate cast in largely well-drawn roles and its verdant natural locales.

But it's a picture that doesn't know when to quit while it's ahead. There's a moment when the camera pulls way, way back from Stella and Joe sitting in a field, at last confronting their feelings for each other fully, thereby arriving at a moment of truth that could have been the perfect signal for a fade-out of a modest but engaging film.

But no, "The Land Girls" goes on to pile on drastic developments and beyond that to a stiff-upper-lip epilogue in which the women gather again at a christening and all turn up in extreme versions of the New Look. By the time it's over, "The Land Girls" has lapsed into soap opera.

NEW STATESMAN, 9/4/98, p. 39, Gerald Kaufman

I really want to be nice about British pictures. I was as nice as I possibly could be about the pretentious "Jane Eyre" rip-off, "Firelight", by not writing about it at all. I did the squalid and amateurish Glasgow druggy epic, "The Life of Stuff"—and myself—a favour by leaving its last 40 minutes to my imagination. But I don't want to ignore or walk out of every product of our island's studios.

So, what can I say in favour of "The Land Girls"? Set in 1941, it deals with an aspect of the last war that is certainly worth recording. Young women from an urban environment volunteered to help out on farms whose labourers had been conscripted to the forces. Though their overcoats were designed by Worth, the conditions they had to endure were often straight out of Stella Gibbons. A film about land girls could say something interesting about culture clashes, about city-dwellers for the first time seeing life in the raw.

The movie's dark, gloomy look depicts how primitive life could be in the countryside nearly 60 years ago and how the wartime black-out oppressed everyone's spirits. A beautifully organised crane-shot of a hay-making scene demonstrates how back-breaking farm work was before mechanisation. Sadly, though, David Leland (the director and, with Keith Dewhurst, co-scriptwriter) has left no cliche under-utilised in this adaptation of Angela Huth's novel.

We are treated to the Saturday-night dance during which romance dawns, the hurried wedding followed by the stock announcement of the bridegroom's death in action, the love affair blighted by loyalty to a wounded boyfriend. The farmer, Mr Lawrence (Tom Georgeson), is that over-familiar figure, the ogre who turns out to have a heart of gold. The three land girls are all cut-outs: the snob who learns to muck in (Rachel Weisz), the vulgar lass from Lancashire with yet another heart of gold (Anna Friel), and the ingenue whose experience leaves her wiser but sadder (Catherine McCormack).

The film is so old-fashioned that it could actually have been made in 1941, apart from the explicit sex scenes. These three women really must have been desperate for male company to fall so easily—and, indeed, actively to seduce—such a thorough-going wimp as the farmer's son, Joe (Steven Mackintosh).

NEW YORK POST, 6/12/98, p. 53, Thelma Adams

David Leland's "The Land Girls" is a WWII romance about the women who took up hoes and milked cows in the English countryside while their lads went off to fight the jerrys.

Unfortunately, the earnest period saga about the Women's Land Army plays like an extended farmer's daughter joke. OK so its feminist: The farmer's son is the joke.

Three lasses—the virgin, the slut and the sophisticate—move to a Dorset farm. Sooner or later, the farmer's son services all three. Is that the hayseed's contribution to the war effort?

Audiences wishing for another "Wish You Were Here" from Leland will be disappointed. The director goes for a cliche-ridden, golden-tinged "Rosie the Riveter.'

Catherine McCormack, Rachel Weisz and Anna Friel are three of the prettiest actresses ever to don snoods and *shmutz*. Each woman has her cross to bear—and there are no surprises for anyone who's ever watched the most stilted of British war propaganda.

The chief nod to the '90s is that the girls' sisterly solidarity is in the foreground. They also talk openly about sex—way too openly for an era when "swing" meant Benny Goodman, not a key party.

As Stella, the banker's daughter engaged to a naval officer, McCormack ("Braveheart") makes a lovely centerpiece. She even drives a tractor with stunning posture. Her star turn gives the production more backbone than it deserves.

Both Weisz and Friel disappear as complex characters once their assigned sexual relationships with the young planter become moot. And, as the epicenter of this pig wallow of country love, the lanky Steven Mackintosh is hardly a D.H. Lawrence fantasy, much less a compelling romantic figure.

Director Leland telegraphs every plot point until all actions seem like a bad case of deja vu. The best that audiences can do is sit back and admire McCormack's complexion and the gorgeous Dorset countryside.

NEWSDAY, 6/12/98, Part II/p. B7, John Anderson

Now that there has been a motion picture made for every person who actually fought in World War II—cinematically, at least, the defining event of our century—why not a movie each for the people who didn't?

"Land Girls," adapted from the Angela Huth novel about young English women who subbed for the farm boys at war, isn't really treading new ground. "Mrs. Miniver," probably the most famous of folks-back-home melodramas, was made at precisely the same time "Land Girls" is set (1941) and was even a factor in generating U.S. public support for the English war effort. But "Mrs. Miniver" was a *war* movie. "Land Girls" seems to be something else entirely.

It's largely about sex, for one thing. And it's also about evoking an era through the conventions of its films (although no wartime movie would have ever been so sexually candid). The three young women in question, whose patriotic assignment brings them to a remote farm in rural Dorset, are, of course, a cross-section of the female world at large: the Cambridge-educated but charmingly naive Ag (Rachel Weisz); the working-class-and-that-means-sluttish Prue   (Anna Friel); and, of course, Stella, the most generous, the most noble, the most betrothed of a naval officer—whose escape from every sexually compromising situation is one of the movie's major accomplishments. That she's played by the beautiful Catherine McCormack, with her '40s starlet looks, only enhances the sense of deja vu.

Temptation comes via young Joe Lawrence, son of ill-tempered Farmer Lawrence (Tom Georgeson), whose ever-pending enlistment in the RAF precipitated the arrival of the girls in the first place. Joe is played by Steven Mackintosh, a fine actor (his transsexual in "Different for Girls" was a tour de force) but who comes across physically as a hybrid of Peter O'Toole and Stan Laurel. Granted, there's not an abundance of men running loose about England, but Joe still seems a dubious source for the kind of sexual combustion that erupting on the Lawrence Farm.

And while "The Land Girls" is a well-intentioned and generally well-acted film, there are some basic structural problems. As someone in another World War II movie once said, the problems of three little people don't amount to a hill of beans in this crazy world, and he was right. In "Land Girls," there's a war on—the war is, in fact, an essential element in the drama we're watching—and the romantic entanglements of what are basically bit players in that much wider drama can't be less than compelling. Add to this a shortage of romantic integrity—people say "I love you" as freely as Ken Starr serves subpoenas—and what you have is an emotional/logical free-for-all

At the same time, the cast is a heady lot, the landscapes are lovely and the time re-created is one of unity and valor. One does get the feeling that certain scenes were cut out of the film, scenes that might have improved things tremendously. Perhaps one in which the girls take the captured Messerschmidt on a joyride down the Champs d'Elysee...

SIGHT AND SOUND, 9/98, p. 44, Geoffrey Macnab

England 1941. Three young women arrive at a remote farm in rural Dorset to work for the Women's Land Army. Ag is a somewhat naïve Oxbridge graduate. Stella is quiet and serious, and engaged to a naval officer. Prue is a hairdresser with an irrepressible sense of mischief. The farmer, Mr Lawrence, sets them to work in the fields. Prue decides to seduce Lawrence's son Joe. Although he is already engaged, he has sex with her in the barn. Prue encourages Ag, who is a virgin, to sleep with him and eventually he does. Ag strikes up a friendship with a Canadian airman she meets at a dance. Prue ends up marrying a young British pilot. Despite already being engaged, Stella realises that she is falling in love with Joe, who is turned down as unfit for military service. Prue learns that her husband has been killed in combat. Stella leaves the farm to visit her fiancé, vowing to Joe that she will break off the engagement, but when she discovers that her fiancé has been badly wounded, she changes her mind.

After the war, the three women meet again at a function. Prue is now married to a wealthy but much older man. Ag is married to her Canadian airman. Joe is also married. Stella, in love with Joe all along, is divorced. The three women reminisce about their time as land girls.

At its peak during World War Two the Women's Land Army numbered more than 80,000. Recruits were drawn from all classes to fill in for the male farm workers who were away at the Front. As historian Angus Calder notes, they were not really an army as such. They worked wherever they were sent, and were as likely to be employed as rat catchers or gardeners as agricultural workers. Nevertheless, the image of the woman tractor driver or farm labourer carries a special resonance, apparently signalling a breakdown in old gender stereotypes. David Leland's *The Land Girls,* adapted from a novel by Angela Huth, evokes the war years with the same mix of scepticism and nostalgia that Leland brought to *Wish You Were Here,* his film about a young woman growing up in the 50s. In Prue, the working class hairdresser turned farm girl, he even has a character moulded along well-nigh identical lines to the rebellious but naïve adolescent heroine of the earlier film. When Prue gazes longingly at muscular farmer's son Joe and announces with a glint in her eye, "I'm going to have him—total fornication," it is hard not to be reminded of the equally lecherous Lloyd with her famous chorus, "Up your bum!"

Rural wartime Britain has been recreated before by filmmakers, for instance in Michael Radford's *Another Time, Another Place.* Like Radford, Leland pays close attention to landscape. The meadows, ploughed fields and country roads are all filmed in fetishistic detail. The lyrical mood is a long way from the anger and aggression Leland brought to the television films he wrote for Alan Clarke, most notably *Made in Britain.* Here, consensus rules and mild eccentricity is celebrated. When the women arrive in the countryside, there is obvious class-tension between Prue and Ag. At first the old farmer seems a curmudgeonly figure, vastly resentful of the three new employees who have been foisted on him, but inevitably he turns out to be a benevolent soul at heart.

In its treatment of sex, *The Land Girls* often steers close to sub-D. H. Lawrence cliché. Whether seen on his motorbike or out in the fields, Joe is the earthy, Mellors-type figure who stirs up troubling emotions in the three women. Stella clearly prefers him to her upper-class, Clifford Chatterley type fiancé. There is also a strong vein of sentimentality here. Although the weather is harsh and the work of milking cows and shovelling shit is hardly glamorous, the women soon become firm friends and seem to relish the lifestyle. When they meet up again after the war, all wearing floral dresses, they look back on their time together with an unlikely yearning.

The gentleness of *The Land Girls* certainly marks a radical departure from the bloody machismo of *The Big Man*, Leland's uncompromising film about a bare knuckle boxer. Arguably, though, his vision of 40s rural Britain is just a little bit too cosy. The period is recreated in such loving detail that the film risks looking like a museum piece, complete with old planes, Hovis ad-like farm workers in breeches and braces, and even fun-loving GIs. A more abrasive approach would surely have revealed the tensions, bitterness and loneliness behind the stock images of rural life.

VILLAGE VOICE, 6/16/98, p. 154, Amy Taubin

Set during World War II, David Leland's *The Land Girls* is a modern version of a "women's picture." Meaning that the women seem like real people rather than fantasies of good girls and bad girls, and sex is very much part of the picture—in word and deed. Don't be put off by the mawkish TV trailers. This is one of the rare films that, without being smug or judgmental, nails the difference between first true love and an exuberant, mutually satisfying roll in the hay.

The hay's not metaphoric here. Stella (Catherine McCormack), Ag (Rachel Weisz), and Prue (Anna Friel) are members of the Women's Land Army, the volunteer corps that filled in for the U.K. farmers who went off to war. The three young women wind up on a small farm near the coast, where German bombers light up the night sky. They milk cows, plow fields, win the respect of the crusty old farmer, Mr. Lawrence (Tom Georgeson), and his more openly affectionate wife (Maureen O'Brien), and bond with one another despite or, maybe, because of the fact that each of them in turn has sex with Joe (Steven Mackintosh), the Lawrences' accommodating son. A character who's every bit as complicated as the three heroines, Joe has a tendency to take the course of least resistance, and it works against him in the end.

Photographed in dark earthy tones, *The Land Girls* is pleasant enough to look,it, but the script and acting are unusually fine. Without being didactic or pushy, *The Land Girls* shows how the war disrupted the lives of three very different young women, and, at the very least, changed their perspective on doing what history and culture had programmed them to do. Leland lets the character details accumulate slowly. At first, it's not that easy to tell the land girls apart. Prue is working-class and a little bit boy crazy. Friel makes her a bit of a tart, but then takes full advantage of the Ophelia-like bathtub scene where she abandons herself to grief and loss. Weisz gives a sweetly comic edge to the privileged Ag, undercutting her lush pre-Raphaelite looks by stomping around like a prep-school hockey player. And McCormack and Mackintosh make us root for the romance between Stella and Joe—all the more inevitable for being so very ill timed.

Also reviewed in:
NEW REPUBLIC, 7/13/98, p. 26, Stanley Kauffmann
NEW YORK TIMES, 6/12/98, p. E12, Stephen Holden
VARIETY, 2/2-8/98, p. 30, Emanuel Levy

LAND IS WHITE, THE SEED IS BLACK, THE

A Balfour Films release.   *Producer:* Didier Creste and Catherine Mathis.   *Director:* Koto Bolofo.   *Story:* Koto Volodo and Claudia Mapula Bolofo.   *Editor:* Karina Mitrecey.   *Running time:* 48 minutes.   *MPAA Rating:* Not Rated.

NEW YORK POST, 12/2/98, p. 44, Rod Dreher

Koto Bolofo grew up in exile from his native South Africa after his schoolteacher father was forced to flee in 1963. The reason? Trumped-up charges of communist sympathies. Bolofo went to art school in Europe, and now works in Paris as a fashion photographer. He revisits his native land's racial past in two short films playing at Film Forum.

By far the better of the two is "The Land Is White, the Seed Is Black," a documentary-style account of his father's run-in with the South African authorities, and what it cost the Bolofo family. Shot in black and white, the film is an elegant montage of images exploring the beauty of the country's land and its (black) people. Bolofo is concerned with how the casual cruelty of the white-ruled government dispossessed his ancestors of their land.

Even when the film's images are discordant—contrasting the grandiosity of white dwellings and buildings with the ramshackle shanties many blacks have to live in, for example—they remain poetic and powerfully heartfelt, even if the film doesn't tell us anything new about the human cost of South African racism.

"African Violet" is a pretentious, amateurish mess, though. I was surprised to read in the production notes that the narrative, such as it is, goes inside the minds of five white women in 1960s South Africa. Oh? The film is such a confusing, surreal montage of sound and visual imagery that it's hard to know what's going on.

The point seems to be: Rich White People Are Uppity Bastards—which is uncontroversial enough, I suppose, in an apartheid context. But what's the deal with the talking teddy bears spouting lines from "1984"?

VILLAGE VOICE, 12/8/98, p. 134, Kathy Deacon

In *The Land Is White, the Seed Is Black*, filmmaker Koto Bolofo accompanies his father, a history teacher and 30-year refugee from apartheid, on a journey back to South Africa. He had been a critic of the racist Bantu education system and the brutal disciplinary methods of his school's Afrikaner principal. The film juxtaposes Professor Bolofo's flight to asylum with vibrant scenes from the daily life of his village. This is not a documentary of explanation—of politics, of sociology—but an outpouring of images of the people given life by an artist and photographer.

Also reviewed in:
NEW YORK TIMES, 12/2/98, p. E5, Stephen Holden

LAST BIG THING, THE

A Stratosphere Entertainment release of a Byronic Pose Productions film. *Producer:* Vladimir Perlovich and Anthony Rubenstein. *Director:* Dan Zukovic. *Screenplay:* Dan Zukovic. *Director of Photography:* M. David Mullen. *Editor:* Markus Lofstrom. *Music:* Cole Coonce. *Production Designer:* Martina Buckley. *Running time:* 98 minutes. *MPAA Rating:* R.

CAST: Dan Zukovic (Simon Geist); Susan Heimbinder (Darla); Sibel Ergener (Magda).

NEW YORK POST, 9/23/98, p. 51, Larry Worth

If there's anything more difficult than creating humor, it's sustaining it. And while writer-director-actor Dan Zukovic has mastered the former, the latter is another story.

That quickly becomes obvious in his debut feature film, "The Last Big Thing". It's a tale about bucking the mainstream that has no shortage of potential, at least in its first third.

Actually, the opening shot is downright hilarious, with manic Simon Geist (Zukovic) entering a Blockbuster-like video store and denouncing its new-releases section as garbage. He maintains that classic and foreign selections are cinephiles' only hope.

Simon follows up by harassing cultural icons to their face (You're called a hunk, but a hunk of what? he taunts a beefy star-de-jour) and bashes popular trends with unnatural glee. Meanwhile, acolyte-cum-girlfriend Darla dutifully records all antics in her diary.

And so it goes, until the increasingly unhinged Simon meets his match in a would-be victim—a curvy model who's not as vacuous as she appears. A couple of catwalk struts later, her actions are posing a threat to Simon's crusades.

Unfortunately, they also topple director Zukovic's inspired premise. It's as if his imagination only went so far, after which redundancy or stupidity is meant to carry the day. And what's with those exaggerated, headache-inducing sound effects?

Perhaps Zukovic was simply overburdened by duties behind and in front of the camera. Coincidentally or not, his direction and writing go south at the same time his acting loses focus.

Susan Heimbinder proves more consistent as Darla. The screen newcomer projects a mix of wonderment and hero worship while subtly hinting at dark secrets to come. It's nice work.

That's why, despite the ultimate failure of "The Last Big Thing," it's safe to assume that Zukovic and Heimbinder have bigger things ahead.

NEWSDAY, 9/25/98, Part II/p. B6, Gene Seymour

One version of the pre-millennial jitters promotes the possibility that something very big—and, most likely, awful—will take place at the turn of the century. "The Last Big Thing," however, may well be the first pre-millennially minded movie to speculate that nothing whatsoever will happen by Year 2K, except the awful stuff going on now.

Which is to say the kind of air-brained cultural drift viewed with deadpan acidity by Simon Geist (Dan Zukovic), a dark-eyed vigilante against a society that values celebrity over talent.

Geist's weapon is a nonexistent magazine called "The Next Big Thing," for which he interviews second-rate actors, rock bands, models and stand-up comics. He doesn't so much interview these "up-and-comers" as use the encounters to deflate their pretensions and insult their aspirations.

Simon wages this campaign from a dreary tract house on the outskirts of Los Angeles. He shares this bland space with Darla (Susan Heimbinder), a tightly-wound enigma who views her platonic boyfriend's guerrilla war against pop culture with awe and trembling. She admires, to the point of envy, his principled elitism, but fears, to the point of hysteria, that he'll stumble onto her secret stash of lunch boxes commemorating 1960s TV shows.

In her high-strung way, Darla is a stand-in for those, driven nuts by consensus superficiality, who yearn for something better without going to extremes. As for Simon... well, you'd be right in assuming he is not entirely what he seems, especially when he starts making moves on a clever model (Pamela Dickerson), who's on to his game from the moment they meet.

Zukovic wrote and directed this dry, ramshackle farce in a manner reminiscent of such edge-of-the-apocalypse L.A. satires as "Repo Man." The movie's as grimly funny as a celebrity lawsuit, only a lot more intelligent. Be wary, though, of its insolent tone. Beneath the movie's acerbic skin, after all, are its own hopes for cutting-edge fame and glory.

VILLAGE VOICE, 9/29/98, p. 130, Justine Elias

The world of Simon Geist, mastermind of a cutting-edge-but-bogus—publication called *The Next Big Thing*, is defined by a vicious clarity. His mission, bankrolled by a neurotic, rich admirer, is to set up interviews with up-and-coming actors, comics, and musicians, and then harangue them about their absurd, derivative artistic pretensions. In less capable hands, *The Last Big Thing* could have become as smug as its bizarre, forhorn-voiced hero, but star, director, and writer Dan Zukovic—who looks like a cross between Bruce Campbell of the *Evil Dead* movies and Beaker from *The Muppet Show* has more on his mind than roasting the celebrity industry. Simon would be appalled by the idea, but this furiously original movie could become the *Repo Man* of the '90s.

Also reviewed in:
CHICAGO TRIBUNE, 12/11/98, Friday/p. I, Michael Wilmington
NEW YORK TIMES, 9/23/98, p. E5, Stephen Holden
VARIETY 9/21-27/98, p. 83, Ken Eisner

LAST DAYS OF DISCO, THE

A Gramercy Pictures release of a Castle Rock Entertainment production. *Executive Producer:* John Sloss. *Producer:* Whit Stillman. *Director:* Whit Stillman. *Screenplay:* Whit Stillman. *Director of Photography:* John Thomas. *Editor:* Andrew Hafitz and Jay Pires. *Music:* Mark Suozzo. *Music Editor:* Joe Lisanti. *Choreographer:* John Carrafa. *Sound:* Scott Breindel and (music) Ted Spencer. *Sound Editor:* Paul P. Soucek. *Casting:* Billy Hopkins, Suzanne Smith, and Kerry Barden. *Production Designer:* Ginger Tougas.   *Art Director:* Artemis Willis. *Costumes:* Sarah Edwards.   *Stunt Coordinator:* Peter Bucossi.   *Running time:* 112 minutes. *MPAA Rating:* R.

CAST: Chloe Sevigny (Alice); Kate Beckinsale (Charlotte); Chris Eigeman (Des); Mackenzie Astin (Jimmy);   Matt Keeslar (Josh); Robert Sean Leonard (Tom);   Jennifer Beals (Nina); Matthew Ross (Dan);   Tara Subkoff (Holly); Burr Steers (Van);   David Thornton (Bernie); Jaid Barrymore (Tiger Lady);   Sonsee Ahray (Diana): Edoardo Ballerini (Victor);   Scott Beehner (Adam); Zachary Taylor (Backdoorman); Neil Butterfield (Rick); Michael Weatherly (Hap);   James Murtaugh (Marshall);   John C. Havens (Steve);   Amanda Harker and Brandi Seymour (Models); Leslie Lyles (Sally); Cate Smit (Helen); Kathleen Chalfant (Zenia); Jan Austell (Bob);   Robin Miles (Josephine);   Carolyn Farina (Audrey Rouget);   Taylor Nichols (Charlie); Bryan Leder (Fred); Dylan Hundley (Sally Fowler); Taylor Nichols (Ted Boynton); Debbon Ayer (Betty); Mark McKinney (Rex);   Linda Pierce (Real Estate Lady);   Carlos Jacott (Dog Walker); Sharon Scruggs (Justine Prashker); Ajay Mehta (Pharmacist); Norma Quarles (Anti-Disco Rally Reporter).

LOS ANGELES TIMES, 5/29/98, Calendar/p. 1, Kenneth Turan

Writer-director Whit Stillman makes wonderfully clever and confident films about insecure young people who are smarter than they are wise. Ferociously verbal types who chat knowledgeably about the propaganda value of language but worry that ordering the wrong drink will typecast them forever. "What if 'thine own self' is pretty bad?" someone wonders in reference to Shakespeare's famous line. "Wouldn't it be better not to be true to it?"

Those kinds of quintessentially youthful dilemmas from the heart of Stillman's latest film, the sharp-eyed and charming "The Last Days of Disco." Made with Stillman's trademark dry wit and whimsical sense of humor, it is a continuation of the filmmaker's equally stylish first venture, 1990's "Metropolitan."

While "Disco's" ensemble of recent college graduates is older than the characters of "Metropolitan," they inhabit the same unmistakable universe of Manhattan's youthful upper crust. It's a small yet quite specific world where the women have subsidized jobs in publishing and the men went to Harvard, but Stillman captures it with such fine-grained exactness that thoughts of Jane Austen's tiny romantic cosmos are not out of place.

Working together as editorial assistants in "the very early 1980s" are recent Hampshire graduates Alice Kinnon (Chloe Sevigny) and Charlotte Pingress (Kate Beckinsale). Drones during the day, they glamorize at night and head to Manhattan's hottest disco (unnamed but modeled after Studio 54), where they inevitably wonder whom they'll see, whom they'll meet, whom they'll pair up with, and, most important, whether any of it will lead to love.

Alice is blond, acerbic and borderline mousy, which is why she overcompensates for her fear of being mistaken for a kindergarten teacher by telling men, "I live dangerously, on the edge." A decent person under her anxieties, Alice deserves better than Charlotte for a best friend, but Charlotte is whom she's got.

Beautifully played without the hint of an accent by British actress Beckinsale (memorable in "Cold Comfort Farm"), Charlotte is bossy and self-promoting, the kind of person who makes cutting comments and then claims she's just trying to be honest and/or helpful. With Charlotte as a guide, it's no wonder that her friend's romantic waters are choppy.

Two men are on Alice's short list for possible romance. Tom Platt (Robert Sean Leonard) is a Kennedy-esque lawyer interested in environmental causes and a collector of original Carl Barks comic art. Jimmy Steinway (Mackenzie Astin) is a young advertising man whose main function is getting his clients into the same hot disco club Alice and Charlotte hang out in.

Helping Jimmy out in that department is Des (Stillman veteran Chris Eigeman), one of the club's managers, who has the unfortunate habit of telling women who get too close that he's just discovered (via watching "Wild Kingdom" of all things) that he's gay. Also in the club a lot is another college pal, the earnest Josh (Matthew Keeslar), a passionate believer in the disco ethos who happens to work for New York's district attorney.

"Disco's" exceptional acting ensemble is especially successful at capturing the brittle rituals of this specific group of genteel, well-spoken young people on the cusp of adulthood who say things like "What I was craving was a sentient individual" and "It's far more complicated and nuanced than that." Overflowing with that once-in-a-lifetime combination of naivete and sophistication, blindness and self-awareness, these yearlings are trying mightily to impress both one another and themselves.

Believing that "before disco this country was a dance wasteland," these folks are also united by their love of the disco lifestyle. And with a hopping soundtrack of 22 favorites, including Blondie's "The Tide Is High" and "Heart of Glass," "The Last Days of Disco" almost makes you believe that those sweaty, snobbish and overcrowded clubs might have been fun.

"Disco" is the third film ("Barcelona" followed "Metropolitan") in what writer-director Stillman calls his "Doomed-Bourgeois-in-Love series." He talks in the press notes (it's impossible to know how seriously) about doing next an 18th century historical adventure film. "Real movie-making—dialogue films no more!" he writes. "Maybe still some talking, but on horseback."

While that would be something to see, Stillman handles this world so adroitly it would be a shame if he didn't see his way clear to revisiting it, if only from time to time.

NEW YORK, 6/15/98, p. 50, David Denby

In *The Last Days of Disco*, Whit Stillman, the director of *Metropolitan* and *Barcelona*, drains the life out of a potentially terrific subject—the end of that period in which a thumping beat and easy access to drugs made nightlife in Manhattan an ecstatic release. Stillman's downtown clubgoers, by contrast, are prattling yuppies; they don't want to lose themselves, they want to seek status. This may have been intended as a satirical idea, but it doesn't play as funny. In the middle of the disco floor, with the music somehow suppressed, the young men and women hold peculiar discussions about manners and protocol. Should a certain person be kept out of the club? Should they all engage in "ferocious pairing off"? Or should they party together as a group? But is anyone in the audience interested in the answers? If you are 25 and eager to have sex with another human being, you are not likely to be deterred by a vote against it. As far as we can see, Stillman revels in the priggishness of these dialogues. His fussy, over-explicit men natter on like Henry James characters without intellect; they seem more eager to split hairs than to make love or even to dance. Indeed, it is most difficult to imagine a Whit Stillman character being "ferocious" about anything.

I was a fan of Whitman's first movie, *Metropolitan*, a comedy of manners set among the white-gloved teens of the Peter Duchin world. Stillman gently satirized the formal speech of his privileged kids—or so it seemed at the time. Now I'm not so sure: In Whitman's subsequent two movies, the same kind of twits have appeared, but this time as adults. Whit Stillman, it would seem, has found the world he wants to live in—a world spiritually bounded by the outer edges of Harvard Yard. His work has a fatal knowing insularity, the sound of college wits entertaining one another with trivial ironies. In *The Last Days of Disco*, the men (Chris Eigeman, Matt Keeslar, Mackenzie Astin, and Robert Sean Leonard) are quite hopeless—so boring, weak, and self-absorbed that one can hardly tell them apart. The women, at least, come off a little better. Chloë Sevigny, as a respectable girl who works in publishing, is charming, and Kate Beckinsale as her malicious colleague might have been charming, too, if only Stillman had not made her character into such a dummy. Yet I suppose there is hope: If Stillman preserves his female characters as carefully he does the male ones, these two may have further conversational adventures. In a Paris café, they could talk about the propriety of public smoking; in a Mexican whorehouse, about the wearing of mantillas at funerals; and so on.

NEW YORK POST, 5/29/98, p. 45, Thelma Adams

When was the last time you heard someone Yell "disco sucks"? The last time you passed the graffito "Die yuppie scum"?

With the "Last Days of Disco," Whit Stillman, the bard of the Upper East Side, takes us back to the disco daze in true bourgeois white-guy style: He dances, but he never moves his pelvis.

Stillman ("Metropolitan" and "Barcelona") is a filmmaker who's more interested in talk than action, a novelist writing adult picture books. He loves the nightlife, but he'd rather observe than let go.

Stillman's movies are brittle, sharp, witty and status-conscious. His elegy to disco makes even those who loathe the Bee Gees wax nostalgic over their lost youth as one character says about the dance craze of the early '80s: "Disco will never be over...Those who didn't understand will never understand."

The writer-director has the power to make us mourn something as silly and transient as disco. His plot is the stuff of '50s fluff. Two women straight out of crunchy Hampshire College head for Manhattan. Once there, they ponder the big questions while dancing the night away: careers, sex, babies, marry a millionaire?

Alice (Chloe Sevigny) and Charlotte (Kate Beckinsale) are the Betty and Veronica of the club scene (think Studio 54). The pair shimmy on the dance floor amid naked tiger ladies, drag queens and a weathered George Plimpton. With all this wildness going on, the women still end up with a gaggle of Harvard men.

Stillman regular Chris Eigeman, Matt Keeslar, Mackenzie Astin and Robert Sean Leonard dance around the women in an extended yuppie mating ritual. These Ivy League losers, loners and lovers confront manic depression, drug abuse, infidelity, venereal disease and the death of idealism—and still manage to have a good time and a vodka tonic.

The casting is original and brilliant. Sevigny ("Kids") and Beckinsale ("Cold Comfort Farm") should displace Neve Campbell as the "it" girls of the moment—and they have range.

Leonard, Keeslar and Astin are appealing and Eigeman once again reveals the vulnerability beneath the high-class jerk.

But the real flights of fancy are in Stillman's script, the moments when "Disco" spins off and dissects pop off culture. Who else could lay the roots of contemporary environmentalism at the death of Bambi's mom in Disney's animated classic, or analyze "The Lady and the Tramp" with the insight of a Harvard lit major and the precision of a marriage counselor?

There's a reason this director is named Whit.

NEWSWEEK, 6/8/98, p. 66, David Ansen

It's only fair to warn viewers that "The Last Days of Disco", Whit Stillman's romantic comedy, has little feel for the period, the clothes or the music of that lurid, druggy early '80s moment in New York City night life. This is not to slam the movie, but you should adjust your expectations. Like Stillman's previous films, "Metropolitan" and "Barcelona," the true subject is East Coast WASPs, the tone arch and fondly ironic, the mode chatty and the sensuality buttoned down. Stillman's comedy may be filled with songs by Blondie and Evelyn (Champagne) King, but it could just as well have been called "The Last Days of Peter Duchin."

Stillman's focus is two Hampshire College grads who share an apartment but have little else in common. Alice (Chloe Sevigny) is serious and shy and awkward with men, Charlotte (Kate Beckinsale) is vivacious, crafty and back-stabbing. By day they work in publishing jobs; at night they go out clubbing with a circle of guys who used to go to Harvard. What Stillman does capture is what it feels like to start your adult life in a big city; to find yourself roommates with people you don't really like; to rush into relationships without quite knowing why. As in "Metropolitan," he has a keen sense of group dynamics and a fine comic ear for the way his petulant, privileged but penurious WASPs talk. The cast, including Stillman regular Chris Eigeman and Matt Keeslar as an eager assistant D.A., is right on the money, though Sevigny's virtuous schlumpiness becomes one-note. Glitter is not what this movie is after—a wry glimmer of amusement is more like it.

SIGHT AND SOUND, 9/98, p. 44, Rob White

In the early 80s, Des works at a New York nightclub where his friends regularly meet: Alice and Charlotte work as publishing assistants; Jimmy is in advertising; Josh is a state attorney; and Tom is an environmental lawyer. Jimmy, who relies on being able to take clients into the club, is barred and forced to slip in by the back door. Under threat of dismissal from Bernie the boss, Des throws Jimmy out. Alice sleeps with Tom.

Alice, Charlotte and another friend Holly rent a flat together. In the club, Jimmy is spotted again and thrown out. Several months pass. Josh is angry with Des for taking drugs. Jimmy is sacked when he can't get clients into the club. Charlotte embarrasses Alice in front of others by surmising that she has gonorrhoea. Over dinner with Tom, Alice discovers that it was he who gave her both herpes and gonorrhoea. Josh is falling in love with Alice and is jealous when he sees Des kissing her. He asks to be taken off the case he's working on—a federal investigation of the club. Jimmy admits to Des that he now realises that the clients he was taking into the club were undercover agents. The club is raided by Josh and the police, though he warns Des in advance. Jimmy flies to Spain. Des and Josh are unemployed, as is Charlotte after a takeover of the publishing house. But Alice has been promoted and she dances on a subway train with Josh.

The Last Days of Disco is the third of a loose trilogy of films written and directed by Whit Stillman. Like Metropolitan and Barcelona, it's a comedy of East Coast morals and manners in which the scions of the "urban haute bourgeoisie" (or 'UHBs', to use the acronym bandied about in Metropolitan) fend off real life with a largely ineffectual combination of talk, arrogance and fading social codes. The film is set at the beginning of the 80s in and around a New York nightclub that Des (Chris Eigeman, who took lead roles in Stillman's other features) helps to run, and where his young professional friends congregate. These yuppies avant la lettre include Charlotte (a wonderfully waspish and bitchy Kate Beckinsale), the passive, put-upon Alice (Chloë Sevigny, from kids, Trees Lounge and Gummo) and a group of male Harvard graduates, among whom are ad man Jimmy and state attorney Josh. Structured around Alice's point of view and her and others' couplings, the film is character-based for the most part but held together by a plot involving the busting and closing down of the club.

The elegiac title is cleverly disingenuous. Last Days is not dealing with an earlier era's tarnished glamour (as in Boogie Nights) or spangly spectacle (Velvet Goldmine). Instead, disco serves here as part of an essentially classless popular culture against which Stillman's characters stand out awkwardly for all their attempts to be part of it, or rather to mould it to their own habits. This club is no Studio 54. To use a contemporary, British analogy, it's more Annabel's than Ministry of Sound—a space where pampered young professionals can be secure, a salon where they can dress smartly, sip cocktails and imagine their future careers.

The use of music exemplifies the way this group of friends are dislocated from disco culture. While the soundtrack offers plenty of crowd-pleasing favourites—Chic, Blondie, Evelyn 'Champagne' King—the most striking musical moment comes when Charlotte breaks into 'Amazing Grace' on a hospital bed. (This moment is echoed later when Josh tells Alice about how the hymn 'Dear Lord and Father of Mankind' comforted him during a period of depression.) The disco standards are historically relevant. But the snatch of 'Amazing Grace'—staid, nostalgic, childish—is Charlotte's deeper, inner music, perversely old-fashioned and claustrophobic, a melody which interferes with and retards the buoyant disco that surrounds it.

Accomplished film making helped by generally fine performances and polished wit, The Last Days of Disco also sports some terrific set-pieces, including a hilarious ensemble disputation about the morality of The Lady and the Tramp. Charlotte has many of the best lines, a whole repertoire of self-gratifying nonsense summed up in her declaration late in the film that "I have to start looking out for myself now." In another scene, Alice takes Charlotte's advice to drop the word "sexy" into conversation with marvellous ineptness ("there's something really sexy about Scrooge McDuck").

Beneath such pleasurable stuff, though, there's a sharper message which is crystallised in Alice. Like the central couple of Metropolitan, she seems to deplore the shallow, over intellectualised chat which surrounds her, but she makes no real effort to separate herself from it. So she can't help but be tainted, and this is made literal when after her first real sexual encounter she contracts two sexually transmitted diseases. The film could have led towards a tragic dénouement—and we're surely supposed to infer this—in which Alice, of all the group the least obnoxious, falls victim to Aids, only just emerging at that time. Instead she catches herpes and gonorrhoea—grubby, workaday afflictions which symbolise the social realities that she, though less so than her friends, clumsily resists.

VILLAGE VOICE, 6/2/98, p. 155, J. Hoberman

Just as FM radio locks in certain demographics—specific stations supplying, for example, dentist-office music for those who graduated high school in 1978—so movies seek to illuminate with laserlike precision the generational nostalgia for golden ages one hardly knew existed.

Whit Stillman's mock elegiac *The Last Days of Disco* is set, somewhat coyly, in "the very early 1980s"—the gap between *Boogie Nights* and *The Wedding Singer*. An indie at once anecdotal and convoluted, this is a movie of small—very small—pleasures. (Some might call them details.) The context is New York nightlife and clique formation. Where once there was the amphetamine-fueled Warhol Factory of extroverted exhibitionists, Stillman presents a well-bred group of young white clubgoers who—whatever their state of romantic excitement or the noise level in the crypto—Studio 54 they favor—never fail to communicate in complete sentences.

Too cool for screwball comedy but too attached to its clubbiness to be successfully sardonic, Stillman's wryly titled opus lacks the ethnographic edge that made his 1990 prep-and-deb fest *Metropolitan* so exotic. Nevertheless, Stillman remains the most caste-conscious of indie directors, even if class distinction merges somewhat schematically with gender. In his 1994 *Barcelona* an oblique lament for the end of the Cold War, the boys were American and the girls Spanish; in *The Last Days of Disco*, the barely individualated men hail from Harvard and the slightly younger women, Alice (Chloë Sevigny) and Charlotte (Kate Beckinsale), are recent graduates from hippie-tinged Hampshire.

A well-chosen, if somewhat anachronistic, score propels the action past the velvet rope into the movie's recreation of Studio 54. "God ... isn't this place great?" someone sighs upon gaining admission. The club is a source of identity for Alice and Charlotte as well as fascination for the fogies who work with them in a midtown publishing house. But, despite a chorus effect accentuated by Stillman's reflexive cutaways to the weirdly decorous, Darien prom-like dance floor where the song always seems to be "More, More, More" *The Last Days of Disco* lacks even the conceptual rigor of the Edgar G. Ulmer cheapster *Club Havana*—a B movie which never leaves its eponymous single set.

More evocative than the club's paradigm of controlled merrymaking amid byzantine intrigue are the scenes shot in the cramped railroad apartment that Alice and Charlotte share with a third roommate. The missed communications, cattiness, incestuous socializing, and blabbing out each others secrets suggest a sour episode of *Friends,* although, to the degree that it's about anything, the movie concerns Alice's search for herself in the funniest scene, she stage-manages her own seduction by applying Charlotte's lessons (telling a collector of Disney duck art that she finds Uncle Scrooge "sexy") and is thereafter misused, even by Stillman.

Chloë Sevigny projects a certain vulnerability, but, far too vague and dreamy, her Alice spends most of the movie reacting to Charlotte's compulsive bitchiness. "Women prefer bad over weak and indecisive," one guy tells another. So it is with audiences, too. Beckinsale makes the most of her screen time in the Parker Posey vixen role as the outrageously outspoken Charlotte. The other performers fare less well. Chris Eigeman, an axiom in Stillman World (who appears to greater advantage in Noah Baumbach's upcoming *Mr. Jealousy),* seems a bit tired, unnecessarily burdened with absurd bits of business in the role of the club's Ivy League assistant manager. And, call me racially insensitive, but it took two-thirds of the movie to confidently distinguish between his classmates, the young lawyer Josh (Matt Keeslar) and adman Jimmy (Mackenzie Astin).

Given that the scene's black, Latino, and gay aspects are scarcely more than window dressing, *The Last Days* theorizes the Disco Era as a preppie recuperation of the orgiastic '60s. The further suggestion is that the era was itself wiped out by an excess of sexual license (here epitomized by herpes). It's a thought that Stillman allows anple time to ponder. Initially entertaining, *The Last Days of Disco* grows increasingly sluggish—fatal for a film that celebrates propulsive rhythm.

Like Stillman's previous features, *The Last Days* is self-consciously literate (my guess is that his models are more likely to have been F. Scott Fitzgerald and J. D. Salinger than any particular film directors), and its major strategy is to let a bit of uncomfortable reality intrude on the preciosity. Thus, Alice's wonderland is variously contaminated by the IRS, venereal horror, and the recession of the early Reagan years. Gloria Gaynor is mercifully unplayed, but Alice is designed to survive everything—except perhaps the movie's soggy middle.

Also reviewed in:
CHICAGO TRIBUNE, 5/29/98, Friday/p. A, Mark Caro
NATION, 6/15 & 22/98, p. 34, Stuart Klawans
NEW YORK TIMES, 5/29/98, p. E12, Janet Maslin
VARIETY, 5/25-31/98, p. 55, Todd McCarthy

WASHINGTON POST, 5/29/98, p. B1, Stephen Hunter
WASHINGTON POST, 5/29/98, Weekend/p. 48, Michael O'Sullivan

LAWN DOGS

A Strand Releasing release of a Duncan Kenworthy production. *Executive Producer:* Ron Daniels. *Producer:* Duncan Kenworthy. *Director:* John Duigan. *Screenplay:* Naomi Wallace. *Director of Photography:* Elliot Davis. *Editor:* Humphrey Dixon. *Sound:* Michael Barosky and (music) Simon Rhodes. *Sound Editor:* Jonathan Bates. *Casting:* Ronna Kress. *Production Designer:* John Myhre. *Set Decorator:* James Edward Ferrell, Jr. *Set Dresser:* Joseph R. McGuire, Jr., Jimmy Smith, and Alice Baldwin. *Special Effects:* Peter Kunz. *Costumes:* John Dunn. *Make-up:* Patricia Schenkel Regan. *Stunt Coordinator:* Peter Bucossi and John Copeman. *Running time:* 101 minutes. *MPAA Rating:* Not Rated.

CAST: Mischa Barton (Devon);   Sam Rockwell (Trent);   Kathleen Quinlan (Clare); Christopher McDonald (Morton);   Bruce McGill (Nash);   Eric Mabius (Sean);   David Barry Gray (Brett);   Miles Meehan (Billy);   Beth Grant (Beth);   Tom Aldredge (Jake);   Angie Harmon (Pam).

LOS ANGELES TIMES, 5/15/98, Calendar/p. 10, Kevin Thomas

In the beguilingly offbeat "Lawn Dogs," Australian director John Duigan, who has always had an affinity for outcasts and the young, and Kentucky poet and playwright Naomi Wallace team up to create a memorable fable of friendship and betrayal involving a 10-year-old girl and a 21-year-old man.

Exceptionally intelligent and having survived heart surgery, little Devon (Mischa Barton) is notably precocious. She's captivated by a Russian folk tale centering on Baba Yaga, a creature who eats little girls, and disenchanted by her unctuous, determinedly upwardly mobile parents, Morton and Clare Stockard (Christopher McDonald and Kathleen Quinlan), a lethal pair of phonies.

The Stockards have just moved to a grandiose suburban development called Camelot Gardens—the actual locale is outside Louisville—featuring pretentious outsized houses of dubious architectural design. At least these homes are surrounded by substantial lawns, and that's where Sam Rockwell's Trent comes in.

A rugged free spirit, Trent lives in a forest not too far away in a ramshackle trailer, drives a '65 Ford truck and mows the Stockards' lawn. He's the sexy redneck of a thousand other movies, the kind of man who makes other men feel jealous and insecure and draws women to him like moths to the flame—only they wouldn't dream of acknowledging him in social situations. He also appeals to Devon as the only authentic human being in her artificial world.

Trent is smart enough to realize that Devon's instant attachment could spell big trouble for him in Camelot Gardens, where he's already looked down on as trailer trash. Morton has been condescending to Trent from the get-go, and Camelot's security guard (Bruce McGill), a burly ex-cop, likes to give him a hard time. He's further targeted by two obnoxious college boys, Brett (David Barry Gray), who's having an affair with Clare, and Sean (Eric Mabius), who's attracted to him.

These characters and Devon's parents are deliberately one-dimensional; they're meant to seem like ogres in a fairy tale. On one level a satire, "Lawn Dogs" comments on the widening gap between the self-isolating haves and increasingly vulnerable have-nots in American society.

In the midst of this extremely hostile atmosphere, Devon remains absolutely determined that Trent will be her friend, and she begins to wear down his resistance. You can see from virtually frame one that trouble lurks ahead; it's just a question of when and how it will erupt and what the consequences will be.

From this predicament Duigan and Wallace reveal how Devon may be exceedingly bright yet still be limited by her 10-year-old's perspective. That "Lawn Dogs," imaginatively photographed by Elliot Davis, itself is shaped like a folk tale, ever so slightly stylized, allows it to get away with a satisfyingly surreal finish.

Even though vital, risk-taking performances are a Duigan trademark—think of the nasty Nicole Kidman in "Flirting"—Barton is in a class by herself in making Devon come alive in all her passion, iron will and naivete. Rockwell emerges as a compelling actor and McDonald and Quinlan have the dreadful Stockards nailed from frame one. The supporting cast is also strong.

Longtime moviegoers will be surprised to see again, after a 16-year absence, the once-familiar Rank Film Distributors logo, a strong man beating a gong, that heralded the beginning of many classic British films. Alas, now that Rank has been bought by the Carlton conglomerate, the Rank logo may now be gone for good.

NEW YORK POST, 5/15/98, p. 52, Thelma Adams

In the recent hubbub about Adrian Lyne's "Lolita," JonBenet Ramsey and Internet pedophilia, a conflicting home truth is being overlooked. There can be healthy relationships between prepubescent girls and adult males. Call it the "favorite uncle syndrome."

John Duigan's surreal sex comedy, "Lawn Dogs," is a funny, moving portrait of two idiosyncratic friends, one of whom happens to be below the age of consent.

Indie star Sam Rockwell ("Box of Moonlight") plays Trent, the Kentucky lawn dog in question. The high school grad mows grass at Camelot Gardens, one of those idyllic suburban communities with mansions set on postage stamp lawns.

Devon (Mischa Barton) is a Camelot Gardens princess with the soul of a Tim Burton outcast; she presses dead flies into the cookies she bakes with her mother (Kathleen Quinlan.)

The girl befriends trailer trash Trent. Before you know it, they're having cookouts, raiding chicken coops and showing each other their scars. He took a shotgun hit; she had open-heart surgery.

In a memorable scene, the pair caper on the cab of Trent's rusty Ford pickup to a Bruce Springsteen tune. He's 21, she's 10; he knows the risks, she doesn't.

Trent and Devon bring out the truth in each other. "Sirens" director Duigan and screenwriter Naomi Wallace capture the rush of finding a soulmate in an otherwise lonely landscape.

Attraction is a part of the friendship, but orgasm isn't. That queasy distinction is what makes these relationships so dangerous and powerful.

Faster than Trent can say my trailer is your trailer, the paternal villains of Camelot (Devon's father, Christopher McDonald, and security guard Bruce McGill) swoop down on the lawn dog like the hounds of hell.

Maybe a contemporary look at a man and his girl can't go anywhere else. But, before "Lawn Dogs" reaches its florid and overwrought ending, it illuminates a taboo busting truth about the favorite uncle syndrome and little girls made of sugar and spice and squashed black flies.

NEWSDAY, 5/15/98, Part II/p. B9, John Anderson

It's hardly a fresh observation, but some of the more trenchant films about American life and culture over the last few years have been made by foreign or foreign-born directors. And what has distinguished the direction—by Ang Lee, Jane Campion, Gillian Armstrong and others—is an already keen eye magnified by distance.

The English-Australian filmmaker John Duigan has exhibited a gift for communicating telling gesture and elemental detail, whether in his early Australian youth movies or in the art farce "Sirens." And despite many audaciously implausible plot points, he does the same in "Lawn Dogs," which could never have been set anywhere else but here.

It's the South, to be precise, in a gated, wealthy and esthetically sterile "community" with the loaded name of Camelot and as much energy as a lawn jockey. The atmosphere is suffocating. The houses are overbuilt. The rooms are too large for the people, the furniture too large for the rooms; the land has been stripped for building, so there are no trees—only grass mowed by a platoon of self-employed landscapers eyed with contempt and suspicion by the happy-and-we-mean-it homeowners, all of whom grow more paranoid with every car alarm and deadbolt.

The most prominent of these scrappy entrepreneurs is Trent (Sam Rockwell), who goes about his business but can't help attracting the unwanted attention of Camelot's security chief (Bruce

McGill), or the admiring eyes of the local women, especially when, on a hot afternoon, he stops traffic on a bridge and dives *tout nude* into the river below. He's a born outsider, pitched by Duigan against an enclave whose ethos is conformity and escape and who finds his natural ally in a girl with a bad heart and head full of fantasy.

As Devon, daughter of the get-ahead Morton (Christopher McDonald) and the get-in-bed Clare (Kathleen Quinlan), Mischa Barton is fascinating—so fascinating, in fact, that it's tough to tell whether the young actress is giving a terrific performance or not. There are few paradigms for a fictional 10-year-old girl who has died twice on the operating table and, as a result, has the kind of weary worldview her vacuous parents can only wonder about; a child who sneers at other children (taking a toy gun from a local brat, she shoves the barrel in his mouth and says, "You'd be doing the community a favor."); who becomes enthralled with Trent and becomes his friend, basically because they're the only really mature people for miles around.

The conflicts in "Lawn Dogs" are born of a very modern brand of dread and a very old-fashioned strain of meanness. Not all of the story works; not all the things that Trent or Devon do are easy to swallow. "Lawn Dogs" is really a mixed bag (of clippings, perhaps) whose charm is in the friendship between the two damaged people and a psychological climate that's both very American and very disturbing. And in these things, Duigan gives us something worth watching.

SIGHT AND SOUND, 11/97, p. 46, Xan Brooks

Summertime in Kentucky. Lonely ten-year-old Devon lives with her parents Morton and Clare in Camelot Gardens, a sterile suburban complex patrolled by Nash, an aggressive security guard. Fascinated by a Russian fairytale about a witch in a forest, Devon roams the surrounding countryside. There she meets Trent, a young drop-out who lives in a remote hippie trailer and works as a "lawn dog" mowing lawns in Camelot Gardens. A friendship develops, which Trent insists must remain secret.

The residents regard Trent with contempt and suspicion: Nash thinks him a petty thief, and Morton and Clare are horrified when he gives Devon a tortoise to raise as a pet. College boys Brett and Sean suspect him of stealing their CDs, and destroy his lawnmower, ruining his livelihood.

Trent takes Devon to visit his own family. On the way back he accidentally runs over Sean's rottweiler. Distraught, Devon flees home, where her tearful explanation of the relationship is misconstrued as an allegation of child abuse. With Devon in tow, Morton, Sean and Nash storm Trent's trailer and beat him up. Devon shoots Sean with Morton's gun, and holds Nash and her father at bay while Trent escapes. As he drives away, the river and forest rise up magically in his wake, shielding the lawn dog from his pursuers.

Man-versus-nature has been the dominant theme in John Duigan's canon, and his first American-set film finds the Australian director in this mode again. In *Flirting*, he explored the liberating power of young love at a repressive boarding-school; in *Sirens*, two buttoned-down Brits visiting an idyllic Australian paradise came spectacularly unbuttoned; while in *The Leading Man*, a libidinous American got more stiff Brits to loosen up a bit. In *Lawn Dogs'* rural Kentucky, this dynamic has been transplanted wholesale. The continent may change, but the concerns stay solidly the same.

The opening two shots perfectly embody the conflict in *Lawn Dogs*. The first shot offers us a dreamy portrait of Devon, a child heroine in shaggy grass and a shimmering blue dress—and from her we cut to an establishing shot of the Camelot Gardens suburb, its identikit houses perched on manicured lawns. Wilderness and civilisation are put in stark opposition, with soulful Devon the bridge between the two worlds. Everything that follows is mere embellishment.

This said, the plot casts quite a spell, as mere embellishments go. The script (by first-time screenwriter Naomi Wallace) is a classic slice of magic-realist yarn-spinning: Devon's beloved Russian fairytale (about Baba Yaga the witch) echoes pleasingly throughout the narrative, as groundwork for the final vault into fantasy, when rivers and forests sprout from nowhere, an affecting end to an absorbing picture.

Elsewhere matters aren't quite so smooth-running. The child-abuse subtext sometimes feels too stock and convenient a plot device, while Devon's parents are cartoony, caricatured villains at best—and the visit to Trent's folks strikes a clunkingly melodramatic note (complete with Bob

Dylan wailing *Knockin' on Heaven's Door* on the soundtrack). Ordinarily such minor flutters wouldn't be particularly distressing, but the world of *Lawn Dogs* is so richly all-enveloping and strange that anything even slightly out of tune jars horribly.

The chief sources of the film's success are lead actors Sam Rockwell and Mischa Barton. The latter veers towards the cutesy at times, but generally manages to portray outcast Devon in heartfelt fashion, as she shuns other neighbourhood children, who "smell like TV." And Rockwell has had practice at this type of role before: earlier this year he was fine as the Kid, the mobile home-dwelling drop-out hero of Tom DiCillo's not dissimilar *Box of Moon Light*. Both roles are Christ-figures: where the Kid—who's hyper—is the liberator of repressed modern mankind, the introverted Trent is its victim, and this more intense, anguished part fits Rockwell's skills more snugly.

His performance—sympathetic, but unreadable in all the right places—is perfectly in keeping with the film's overall tone. For much of its course, *Lawn Dogs* is a twiddly variation on a familiar tune, a standard coming-of-age plotline twisted into eccentric new shapes, its rural South backdrop conjured into something almost mystical, a lush Eden of storybook forest clearings and crackling campfires.

What it ultimately calls to mind, in fact, is a warped modern overhaul of Mark Twain's *The Adventures of Huckleberry Finn*, with Devon as Huck and Trent as embattled outcast Jim. Although less interested than Twain's book is in racial friction, *Lawn Dogs* does explore the clash between old wilderness and new civilisation as opposing ideals. But where Twain's America was a land of limitless space, where Huck and Jim could dart off down the Mississippi, *Lawn Dogs'* inhabitants are hemmed in, captives with nowhere to run, their only escape the internal flight into the realms of fairytale and fantasy.

Also reviewed in:
CHICAGO TRIBUNE, 5/15/98, Friday/p. H, John Petrakis
NEW YORK TIMES, 5/15/98, p. E10, Janet Maslin
VARIETY, 9/1-7/97, p. 78, Todd McCarthy
WASHINGTON POST, 6/5/98, Weekend/p. 59, Michael O'Sullivan

LEADING MAN, THE

A BMG release in association with Northern Arts Entertainment. *Producer:* Bertil Ohlsson and Paul Raphael. *Director:* John Duigan. *Screenplay:* Virginia Duigan. *Director of Photography:* Jean-Francois Robin. *Editor:* Humphrey Dixon. *Music:* Edward Shearmur. *Production Designer:* Caroline Hanania. *Art Director:* Andrew Munro. *Costumes:* Rachel Fleming. *Running time:* 99 minutes. *MPAA Rating:* R.

CAST: Jon Bon Jovi (Robin Grange); Lambert Wilson (Felix Webb); Anna Galiena (Elena Webb); Thandie Newton (Hilary Rule); Barry Humphries (Director); Nicole Kidman (Unbilled Cameo); David Warner (Tod); Patricia Hodge (Delvene); Diana Quie (Susan).

LOS ANGELES TIMES, 3/6/98, Calendar/p. 27, Kevin Thomas

[The following review by Kevin Thomas appeared in a slightly different form in **NEWSDAY, 3/20/98, Part II/p. B7.]**

Rocker Jon Bon Jovi continues the careful building of his film career with "The Leading Man," a witty English romantic comedy not likely to attract a large swath of his fans. It is nonetheless a shrewd artistic choice, one that shows just how easily he can command the screen in unexpected material for him.

The film's modest booking suggests that the distributor and exhibitors are unsure how to play it; the best bet would probably be an art-house approach because its famous singing star sings nary a note.

Bon Jovi plays Robin Grange, a major Hollywood star who opts for a role in a serious London play and winds up showing how the West End is no match for West Coast smarts. Successful playwright Felix Webb (Lambert Wilson), heretofore ensconced for 14 years in one of the English theater's perfect marriages (to Anna Galiena's beautiful Elena), has become caught up in a passionate affair with Hilary (Thandie Newton), his play's gorgeous ingenue.

Felix is too love-struck to be discreet, and his wife's outrage and his lover's growing impatience with him for not making a choice between her and Elena jeopardize the entire production. Felix is in such a state of escalating emotional turmoil he actually accepts Robin's cool proposition that he create some space and diversion for him by seducing Elena.

"The whole thing is absurd," remarks Felix, in one of his saner moments, but veteran Australian director John Duigan and his writer-sister Virginia are too clever to allow that judgment to be applied to their film. They have the knack of turning potential contrivance into effective dramatic convention the old-fashioned way: through attractive, well-developed characters whose plights involve us. It helps that they are played flawlessly by well-cast actors under Duigan's customarily astute direction.

Sleek, leonine Robin just oozes confidence onstage and off. He knows just how dazzling a star's megawatt concentration and charisma can be for a lovely but miserable woman. Robin is so far ahead of everyone in knowing how to play games, romantically and professionally, there's just no telling where his romancing of Elena will go. And what are we to make of his attempt to seduce Hilary while he's at it? There's such charm and ambiguity of intention enveloping Robin you just can't help but be intrigued. The thorny situation allows two stunning and intelligent women to come to terms with themselves while Felix thrashes about in the throes of weakness and self-absorption. Wilson is such an accomplished actor that you come away with compassion for Felix if not exactly respect. The film's ending is notably tart and ironic.

Always a man with a gift for the succinct phrase, Robin remarks that he plays a "hit man in a play about politics and morality," and the glimpses we get of Felix's play, which stars an urbane David Warner, suggest that the Australian Duigans are getting in a few deft digs at West End high seriousness.

The play's director is a warm Barry Humphries, out of his famed Dame Edna Everage drag, and there's an un-billed cameo by Nicole Kidman, who appeared with Newton in "Flirting," one of Duigan's best films. A handsome, polished effort, "The Leading Man" is a sly, traditional-style delight.

NEW YORK POST, 3/20/98, p. 50, Thelma Adams

Is Jersey rocker Jon Bon Jovi ready to play "The Leading Man"? The answer's a resounding yes. With those pillowy, kiss me lips, that honey mane and charisma to spare, Bon Jovi could probably cross-dress and play a leading woman. But that's another movie.

In John ("Sirens") Duigan's backstage sex comedy, Bon Jovi's Robin Grange is an American pop star with acting aspirations. It's not much of a stretch.

Grange flees Hollywood for the London stage after a scandal with a producer's wife. Once there, he pads his role as a wily assassin by making a Faustian pact with playwright Felix Webb (Lambert Wilson).

The prolific writer resembles Sam Shepard with an Oxbridge accent. He has a beautiful wife, Elena (Anna Galiena), and a beautiful life: three kids, a host of awards and a script deal with Paramount.

Webb also has a beautiful mistress, Hilary (Thandie Newton). The ambitious young actress is cast as the leading lady opposite Grange in the drama-within-the-movie, described as "a moral fable for an amoral time."

Webb is, in fact, caught in a web—and Grange is just the spider to exploit him. The American opportunist offers to woo Elena to give the writer more time with Hilary. Grange also plays a few angles for himself, seducing Hilary when he isn't squiring Elena.

The plot unfolds in a witty, sexy roundelay. Galiena ("Jamon Jamon") and Newton (the love slave in "Jefferson in Paris") are ripe and appealing. British pros David Warner and Patricia Hodge add wry commentary as Grange's fellow thespians.

The urbane script gains texture in the scenes of domestic discord at the Webbs' posh home. The kids sense that their parents are drifting apart and desperately, touchingly try to fill the void.

But there's ultimately no place for children in Duigan's sex farce—and that's a shame. In the end, the emotions get broader and the plot strands knit up all too neatly. The juicy commentary on sex, marriage, family, fidelity and the theater has no third act. The playwright recedes from the action, leaving "The Leading Man" to become a cartoon, a rough drawing of its early promise.

VILLAGE VOICE, 3/10/98, p. 66, Dennis Lim

In John Duigan's *The Leading Man*, Jon Bon Jovi's acting technique depends on what might broadly be termed charm, though reflex smarminess is closer to the mark. The film itself is a moth-eaten, London-set drama (the likes of which the Brits only produce for gullible foreign markets), but, as the titular blank enigma Robin Grange, Bon Jovi has the kind of foolproof non-role that could keep him employed in movies for years to come.

Robin's a rising Hollywood star who's passed up some big-budget shoot-'em-up for a cred-boosting stint in a musty West End abomination called *The Hit Man*. Felix Webb (Lambert Wilson), the floppy-haired middle-class bore who wrote it, is casually identified as "Britain's greatest living playwright." Is this soft satire or gross stupidity? Same difference, as it turns out. The tone of the film is fuzzy and absurdly fluid: you're never sure if you're supposed to laugh, and if so, why. (In the opening scene, Robin gazes at the Houses of Parliament as "Burning Down the House" blares from his headphones— is he a Talking Heads fan or does this hint at the anarchist within?)

Bon Jovi's main function here is as sex-god-for-hire. Felix is in love with his leading lady (Thandie Newton) but can't leave his scissors-wielding Italian wife, Elena (Anna Galiena), for fear of reprisals. Robin offers to help—he bones up on Elena's bedside reading (Umberto Eco, no less), sniffs her underwear, and proceeds to woo her. The scheme backfires, degenerating swiftly into farce; the film unintentionally follows. As for Bon Jovi, he just about passes muster as a mystery man, but you can't help feeling that opacity suits him a little too well.

Also reviewed in:
CHICAGO TRIBUNE, 3/13/98, Friday/p. E, John Petrakis
NEW YORK TIMES, 3/20/98, p. E12, Lawrence Van Gelder
VARIETY, 9/16-22/96, p. 68, Derek Elley

LEATHER JACKET LOVE STORY

A Leather Jacket Productions release. *Executive Producer:* Bruce Baker. *Producer:* Jerry Goldberg. *Director:* David DeCoteau. *Screenplay:* Rondo Mieczkowski. *Director of Photography:* Howard Wexler. *Editor:* Jeffrey Schwarz. *Music:* Jeremy Jordan. *Sound:* Jack Lindauer. *Production Designer:* Jeannie Lomma. *Art Director:* Brian Virwani. *Set Decorator:* Jeffrey Morris. *Costumes:* Edward Hibbs. *Running time:* 85 minutes. *MPAA Rating:* Not Rated.

CAST: Christopher Bradley (Mike); Sean Tataryn (Kyle); Geoffrey Moody (Ian); Hector Mercado (Sam); Arlene Golonka; Nicholas Worth; William Butler; Madame Dish; Erin Krystle; Craig Olsen; Mink Stole; Momma; Ruby Tuesday; Moist Towelette.

LOS ANGELES TIMES, 5/22/98, Calendar/p. 9, Kevin Thomas

David DeCoteau's "Leather Jacket Love Story" could well be the sunniest gay movie ever made, yet it is also genuinely poignant. It's campy, raunchy and funny as well, glowing with an unabashed gay sensibility. It's no less perceptive for having been made with a light touch and an ear for broad humor and has an easy, graceful style heightened by Howard Wexler's beautifully modulated black-and-white cinematography.

An aspiring 18-year-old poet, a towheaded Valley boy named Kyle (Sean Tataryn), decides to take an apartment in Silver Lake for the summer before enrolling in UCLA in the fall. He's gotten tired of hanging out with his best friend Ian (Geoffrey Moody), a determined hedonist with a house in the hills with a pool populated by a revolving door of "Chads and Brads," well-built guys who swim in the nude. Ian thinks Kyle is crazy to forsake West Hollywood sex and glitz for Silver Lake bohemia, but Kyle is serious about his poetry.

Kyle is drawn to a local coffee shop, a magnet for drag divas and a site for poetry readings hosted by none other than "Pink Flamingos'" Mink Stole. One day Kyle is transfixed when in walks a good-looking man in a leather jacket, having arrived on a motorcycle, natch. The newcomer spots Kyle staring at him, and in turn likes what he sees.

He's Mike (Christopher Bradley), a 29-year-old carpenter and roofer in a seven-year partnership, now more professional than romantic, with Sam (Hector Mercado). Mike is a hunky, easygoing guy who effortlessly sweeps Kyle off his feet.

Writer Rondo Mieczkowski and DeCoteau know exactly what they're doing and where they're going with their blithe romantic fantasy. Their romance is as tender as it is hot, and the filmmakers could not be more deft in steering it in a credible direction. They know how to camp it up and take sex right to the edge of hard core, but they also know how to be subtle and sensitive in depicting Kyle and Mike's relationship.

Most important, perhaps, is that the filmmakers are inclusive. In their gay world there's room for young guys like Kyle, older guys like Sam (about to celebrate his 40th birthday) and leather types like Mike. At a poetry reading there's pioneer gay rights activist Morris Kight, amusing as a grumpy poet. And then there are the local divas—Madame Dish (Stephen J. McCarthy), Erin Krystle, Craig Olsen, Momma (Worthie Meacham), Daniel Escobar, Ruby Tuesday and Moist Towelette—on hand to dispatch gay bashers, dispense bitchy humor and not a little wisdom besides.

The best advice to Kyle comes from a middle-aged poet (Nicholas Worth, in a stylishly theatrical turn) who reminds the youth that he needs to write about what he knows—and what he needs to know most is love.

Amid much that's deliberately and delightfully outrageous, DeCoteau directs Tataryn and Bradley toward giving legitimate, winning portrayals. "Leather Jacket Love Story" may be a fantasy, a crowd-pleaser with lots of laughs, but Kyle and Mike are for real.

NEW YORK POST, 2/20/98, p. 47, Larry Worth

In the old days, love meant never having to say you're sorry. Now, it means wearing a nipple ring for your significant other.

As documented with nauseating detail in "Leather Jacket Love Story," piercing is just one sacrifice made by blond, doe-eyed Kyle to keep hunky biker Mike coming back for more.

Worse, director David DeCoteau puts the emphasis on bared bods and graphic sex scenes rather than on character. Is it a coincidence that nude men keep walking straight into the camera—with the lens focused just below their navels?

Even then, DeCoteau can't settle on a consistent tone; one minute it's a Greek chorus of drag queens and '50s sitcom music, the next it's handcuffs and heartbreak.

But the most unsettling business comes via casting. As 18-year-old Kyle, Sean Tataryn looks 12. And as 30-year-old Mike, Christopher Bradley looks 40. Together, they make "Leather Jacket Love Story" look like a cross between "Lolita" and "Chicken Hawk."

VILLAGE VOICE, 2/24/98, p. 128, Mark J. Huisman

After a long B-movie career, director David DeCoteau makes his first gay-themed film with the low-budget *Leather Jacket Love Story*. Budding, blond, dreaming-of love Kyle meets Mike, a 30-plus rough-trade wannabe. Mike doesn't want to commit but Kyle, poetry pad in hand, won't say die. The movie has the makings of a high-energy film funtasia: two studly protagonists, more crotch shots than Robin Byrd's TV show, a cameo by John Waters diva Mink Stole, and a bouncy Erasure soundtrack. But somehow—perhaps because the story is compressed into two days—the film misfires, turning clever lines and deft editing into rather cloying cuteness. The most potentially interesting character—Sam, a graying, 40-year-old black guy—is sidelined with only a birthday cake to console him. "It's not just about getting your rocks off," Kyle laments at one point. "It's about having a special experience." The movie, however, provides only the first.

Also reviewed in:
NEW YORK TIMES, 2/20/98, p. E26, Stephen Holden
VARIETY, 7/21-27/97, p. 40, Dennis Harvey

LENA'S DREAMS

An Olympia Pictures release. *Producer:* Chip Garner. *Director:* Heather Johnston and Gordon Eriksen. *Screenplay:* Heather Johnston and Gordon Eriksen. *Director of Photography:* Armando Basulto. *Editor:* Steve Silkensen. *Music:* Don Braden. *Sound:* Noah Vivekananad Timan. *Art Director:* Robert Nassau. *Costumes:* Jennifer L. Eriksen. *Running time:* 85 minutes. *MPAA Rating:* Not Rated.

CAST: Marlene Forte (Lena); Gary Perez (Mike); Susan Peirez (Suze); Jeremiah Birkett (Johnny); David Zayas (Jorge); Judy Reyes (Maritza); Kai Adwoa (Angela).

NEW YORK POST, 12/18/98, p. 64, Hannah Brown

The cast of this rambling film, directed by Gordon Eriksen and Heather Johnston, probably learned a lot while working on it, but that doesn't make for compelling drama.

Lena (Marlene Forte) is a Cuban-American aspiring actress who waits tables, lives in a Brooklyn walk-up and dreams of stardom.

She promised her actor-director boyfriend, Mike (Gary Perez), that she would quit show business by age 30 if she didn't make it. But now it's her 32nd birthday and she agonizes over whether she has wasted her life.

Mike, frustrated by living in poverty, wants them both to become "civilians" and get regular jobs.

After a painful audition in which she is told that she looks and sounds "too upper-class" to play a nanny and "not upper-class enough" to play the nanny's boss, she decides Mike's right.

But just then, her agent tells her that she has gotten her dream part—the female lead in a Broadway show about Fidel Castro—and she has to reassess her decision.

Her choice, after much Sturm und Drang, won't come as a surprise to many.

This shakily photographed, low-budget film looks as if it were made by people who maxed out their credit cards to finance it (and didn't have very high credit lines to begin with).

Still, the audition scenes have charm and give the versatile Forte a showcase to display her considerable talent. "Lena's Dreams" may not catapult Forte into stardom, but it's clear that she won't be waiting tables forever.

VILLAGE VOICE, 12/22/98, p. 132, Amy Taubin

Few films could be further from *The General* (see Taubin's review of that film) than Heather Johnston and Gordon Eriksen's *Lena's Dreams*. A no-budget, no-frills portrait of a Cuban American actress in crisis, it's a film John Cassavetes almost certainly would have loved, and not just because his *Opening Night* is such a clear influence. As filmmakers, Johnston and Eriksen wear their hearts and politics on their sleeves. There's an enthusiasm and sense of purpose in all their films that has to do with putting difference—sexual difference, racial difference, and to a lesser degree, class difference—out front.

Lena's Dreams is the third, and easily the most focused, film they've made. That's not to say that it doesn't have awkward moments (the first 15 minutes are remarkably unpromising) or that it's chock-full of aesthetic pleasure. But it's bold, resourceful, honest, and smart, and, more than any film besides *Opening Night,* it gets inside the process of acting and all the craziness that's part of a great acting talent.

Except for a few flashbacks, the film takes place within a single day, the day that Lena (Marlene Forte) turns 32. Lena's been pounding the pavement for years. She's confident of her talent but she also knows that great parts for Latinas who don't do what Jennifer Lopez does for a skirt are almost nonexistent. Years ago, she promised her boyfriend Mike (Gary Perez) that if she didn't make it by the time she reached 30, she'd quit. Now she's two years past her deadline, and she's still addicted to the hope that tomorrow everything will change. Every callback is a fix, and because Lena's an exciting actress, she gets lots of those. But she's never landed a role commensurate with her talent. "I'm too middle-class to play a maid and too ethnic to play middle-class?" she inquires scornfully of the casting agent who has just rejected her. It's the first of many bridges she burns on the day she decides to give up acting. She kisses off her manager, her answering service, her boyfriend. And she doesn't change course even when she finds out that she's been cast as the female lead in the big Broadway show (Castro starring Andy Garcia) she'd auditioned for weeks earlier. It's mad, it's nearly tragic, and it's just what an actor has to do when she creates a role—choose an action and follow it through no matter where it leads.

Working on a minimal budget, Johnston and Eriksen shot the film in very long takes with a hand-held camera (their cinematographer Armando Basulto is a wiz). It's a dangerous choice—and it doesn't always work—but it's also wildly appropriate because it lets the actors (rather than an editor) determine the pace and the momentum of each scene. Forte, a fiercely concentrated performer with a big emotional range and a deft sense of humor, rises to the occasion. She builds a character before our eyes, exposing the process whereby she makes Lena's dreams her own. The film is unimaginable without her.

Also reviewed in:
NEW YORK TIMES, 12/18/98, p. E17, Lawrence Van Gelder
VARIETY, 4/14-20/97, p. 95, Emanuel Levy

LENNY BRUCE: SWEAR TO TELL THE TRUTH

A Whyaduck Productions release in association with HBO Documentary Films. *Executive Producer:* Sheila Nevins. *Producer:* Robert B. Weide. *Director:* Robert B. Weide. *Screenplay:* Robert B. Weide. *Editor:* Geof Bartz and Robert B. Weide. *Running time:* 94 minutes. *MPAA Rating:* Not Rated.

CAST: Robert De Niro (Narrator) Sally Marr, Honey Bruce, Kitty Bruce, Martin Garbus, Paul Krassner, and Nat Hentoff.

NEW YORK POST, 10/21/98, p. 42, Larry Worth

Any production that focuses on Lenny Bruce has got a built-in advantage: The man is utterly fascinating to watch, hear and absorb. Better still, the eclectic characters in his sphere were right out of central casting.

Clearly, Bruce's life was like a movie waiting to happen—which director Bob Fosse discovered with 1974's justly celebrated "Lenny." (The film received a half-dozen Oscar nominations, including those of best actor and actress contenders Dustin Hoffman and Valerie Perrine.)

Now, 24 years later, Robert B. Weide improves on Fosse's drama by offering the real thing in the documentary "Lenny Bruce: Swear to Tell the Truth," opening today at Film Forum.

Writer/director Weide has compiled a stunning tribute to the legendary comic, as funny as it is poignant. Using Bruce's home movies, photos from the family album and early TV appearances with Steve Allen and Hugh Hefner, Weide charts Leonard Alfred Schneider's progress from rebellious Navy man to struggling comedian to headline-making satirist.

Complemented by Robert De Niro's eloquent narration, the film gradually recalls all the scandals for which Bruce is best-known: his attempts to push the envelope in stand-up routines via profanity and verbal taboos that rocked society in the '50s.

Whether exploring ramifications of the "N word," addressing never-mentioned body parts or commenting on the Catholic Church's "hypocrisy," Bruce was ready, willing and able to take on all targets. And for that, he paid a pretty high price.

But what could have been a standard bio-film ultimately becomes much more. That's largely due to interviews with those who were intimately aware of how Bruce thought and acted before his untimely passing at age 40.

First and foremost is Bruce's larger-than-life mom, Sally Marr. Offering deliciously off-the-wall comments while getting her hair styled at a beauty salon, Marr recalls taking her pre-teen son to watch strippers, perhaps setting the tone for his unconventional approach to life.

The comic's wife, ex-stripper Honey Bruce, is also filled with insights. She appears downright wistful in resurrecting details of their dawning romance, professional routines together and the pain of divorce.

Daughter Kitty and Lotus Weinstock (the woman with whom Bruce resided at the time of his death) provide yet more chapters in the ever-fascinating scenario.

So, was Bruce brought down by the system? Was he a victim who went down fighting for First Amendment rights? Were the feds' obscenity charges manufactured? Clearly, Weide thinks so, and makes a pretty credible case for his views.

Granted, detractors will take issue. But even they would agree that "Swear to Tell the Truth" is a mesmerizing look at a man who was light years ahead of his time.

VILLAGE VOICE, 10/27/98, p. 140, Amy Taubin

"If anyone in the audience believes that God made your body, and your body is dirty, the fault lies with the manufacturer." That's vintage Lenny Bruce, and while you can get an idea of how smart he was by reading his routines, you have to have seen him perform to appreciate his cosmic comic timing.

The timing was all the more extraordinary because he seemed to make up his routines on the spot (and often, that's exactly what he did). You could see these half-formed ideas and associations churning out of the dark recesses of his mind. He stumbled and mumbled, until, in a flash, the meaning of what he was saying became clear to him, and like the burlesque comic he was, he pivoted full-frontal and jammed the punchline home. The effect, like the material itself, was massively contradictory. Bruce was never so vulnerable as when he was most hostile, never so wary as when he was most reckless, never so heartbreaking as when he was most hilarious. His act was liberating because it found and exposed side-splitting humor in the ambivalences and disjunctions of mind, body, and emotions—and because he never hesitated to speak truth to power. Bruce's main targets were organized religion, racism, and sexual hypocrisy. It was probably his attack on the Catholic Church that made him a target of the Right.

Robert B. Weide's *Lenny Bruce: Swear To Tell the Truth* comes as close as a 94-minute biopic can to resurrecting its subject (at least, as a performer). Weide has got his hands on amazing footage: Bruce's 1964 appearance on the *Steve Allen Show* that was censored by the network and supposedly lost for 30 years; a TV gig with Nat Hentoff where Bruce, stoned on bennies, falls to the floor and bashes away at the piano with his feet; a fragment from an unfinished biker movie directed by Bruce in the '50s which looks like Kenneth Anger gone hetero; and news footage of Bruce's corpse, sprawled naked and face down in a doorway of his dilapidated Hollywood Hills home. (The LAPD allowed photographers an hour to shoot Bruce's body before they took it away to the morgue.) Weide also assembled a great cache of stills, and the film has Bruce's rhythms so right that when he plays tapes of Bruce's voice over the photos, it's almost as if you're seeing him in motion.

The story is pieced together chronologically by talking heads, among them Bruce's devoted mother, Sally Marr; his ex-wife Honey and their daughter; Hentoff, who compares the way Bruce transformed comedy to what Charlie Parker and Coltrane did to jazz; Martin Garbus, who assisted Ephraim London in defending Bruce when he was tried for obscenity in New York in 1964; and Richard H. Kuh, then lackey of New York D.A. Frank Hogan, who prosecuted the case. Kuh won. Although the conviction was reversed on appeal (18 months after Bruce's death), it destroyed Bruce as a performer (he never worked a big club again) and as a person (he spent the last two years of his life doing drugs and writing appeals, obsessed with the fact that he had never had a fair trial, and that not only he, but the Constitution of the United States, in which he profoundly believed, had been violated).

Weide gets the big stuff right, and he's also attuned to the echoes. Robert De Niro, who played "God's lonely man" in *Taxi Driver,* does the voice-over narration, and as you listen to him, you realize how much he owed his "Are you talking to me?" moves and timing to Bruce (whose signature song was "All Alone," a little ditty he wrote himself. Weide's choice of music is inspired: Rodgers and Hart's bereft "It Never Entered My Mind" becomes the theme of Bruce's final downward spiral, mixing at the end with "Three Satie Spoons," the early-'60s avant-garde art-world anthem, and then breaking out into The Clash's cover of "I Fought the Law" for the closing credits.

Twelve years in the making, *Lenny Bruce: Swear to Tell the Truth* could not be released at a more opportune moment. I can't begin to enumerate the parallels between the persecution of Bruce and right-wing hysteria around Clinton, but it's worth noting that Kuh, still nattering on about standards of decency and 12-letter words, is a minor-league Starr, and that the press, with few exceptions, cheered Bruce's persecutors on, as if their own constitutional rights were not at stake.

Also reviewed in:
NEW YORK TIMES, 10/21/98, p. E1, Janet Maslin
VARIETY, 11/9-15/98, p. 33, Oliver Jones

LES MISERABLES

A Columbia Pictures release of a Mandalay Entertainment presentation of a Sarah Radclyffe/James Gorman production. *Executive Producer:* Petr Moravec and Jean François Casamayou. *Producer:* Sarah Radclyffe and James Gorman. *Director:* Bille August. *Screenplay:* Rafael Yglesias. *Based on the novel by:* Victor Hugo. *Director of Photography:* Jörgen Persson. *Editor:* Janus Billeskov-Jansen. *Music:* Basil Poledouris. *Music Editor:* Curtis Roush. *Sound:* David John and (music) Tim Boyle. *Sound Editor:* Jonathan Bates. *Casting:* Leonora Davis and Petr Hartl. *Production Designer:* Anna Asp. *Art Director:* Peter Grant. *Special Effects:* Terry Glass. *Costumes:* Gabriella Pescucci. *Make-up:* Morag Ross. *Stunt Coordinator:* Gareth Milne and Ladislav Lahoda. *Running time:* 129 minutes. *MPAA Rating:* PG-13.

CAST: Liam Neeson (Jean Valjean); Geoffrey Rush (Javert); Uma Thurman (Fantine); Claire Danes (Cosette); Hans Matheson (Marius); Reine Brynolfsson (Captain Beauvais); Peter Vaughan (Bishop); Christopher Adamson (Bertin); Tim Barlow (Lafitte); Timothy Bateson (Banker); Veronika Bendová (Azelma); David Birkin (Courfeyrac); Patsy Byrne (Toussaint); Kathleen Byron (Mother Supervisor); Václav Chalupa (André); Ian Cregg (Feuilly); Ben Crompton (Grantier); Zdenek David (Peasant); Paola Dionisotti (Forewoman); Edna Doré (Old Woman); Louis Hammond (Letter Reader); Gillian Hanna (Mme. Thénardier); Janet Henfrey (Mme. Gilot); Shane Hervey (Gavroche); Zdenek Hess (Foreman); Gerard Horan (Digne Gendarme); Kelly Hunter (Mme. Victurien); Lennie James (Enjolras); Toby Jones (Doorkeeper); Jon Kenny (Thénardier); Pavel Koci (Coachdriver); Sylvie Koblizkova (Éponine); Jan Kuzelka (Furniture Dealer); Peter MacKriel (Doctor); Margery Mason (Nursing Nun); Shannon McCormick (Redheaded Gendarme); John McGlynn (Carnot); Philip McGough (Judge); David McKay (Informer); Mimi Newman (Cosette, age 8); Alex Norton (General); Ralph Nossek (Clerk); Frank O'Sullivan (Brevet); Zoja Oubramová (Old Woman); Jirí Patocka (Old Man); Petr Penkava (Beggar Child); Julian Rhind-Tutt (Bamatabois); Milan Riehs (Priest); James Saxon (Chabouillet); Petr Strnad (Young Homeless Boy); John Surman (Stonemason); Miroslav Táborsky (Gendarme); Terry Taplin (Prosecutor); Richard Toth (Gendarme); Edward Tudo Pole (Landlord); Zdenek Venci (Messenger); Tony Vogel (Lombard); Pavel Vokoun (Sergeant); Jan Unger (Officer); Joshua Wren (Old Homeless Boy); Libor Zidek (Wig Maker).

LOS ANGELES TIMES, 5/1/98, Calendar/p. 1, John Anderson

[The following review by John Anderson appeared in a slightly different form in
NEWSDAY, 5/1/98, Part II/p. B3.]

It's chichi in academia to reject the work of so-called dead white males, but despite what you might read, not all DWMs were defending the patriarchal status quo, or subjugating colonials, or writing in dialect.

Take Victor Hugo. Or, if you prefer a couple of hours to a couple of hundred pages, take Bille August's adaptation of Hugo's greatest work, "Les Miserables," an eager, earnest, broadly constructed pageant of ideas and characters whose greatest asset may be the service it pays to literature.

Mine may be a strictly CNN-saturated American point of view, but watching the Danish director take the French novel and an international cast through their weighty paces, the sly parallels and commentary seem obvious. Jean Valjean (Liam Neeson), who serves 20 years in prison for stealing a loaf of bread, embodies all the modern arguments about poverty, rehabilitation, reinvention and redemption. The doomed factory girl Fantine (Uma Thurman), fired for having an illegitimate daughter, represents everything about sexual double standards, public morality and welfare. And frankly, if the relentless, obsessive, self-righteous and sanctimonious Inspector Javert (Geoffrey Rush) doesn't have Kenneth Starr written all over him, I'll eat my tri-cornered hat.

So, what you have in "Les Miserables" is what you didn't have in the movie "Primary Colors," which might have been a mirror of contemporary events, but settled for a gelatinous sense of night and wrong—as well as a story that was more smirk than substance. And although it's an unwitting confirmation that original screenwriting is dead in Hollywood, "Les Miserables" certainly has a story. And, for the most part, a cast.

Thurman is good, but briefly seen (and seen in her briefs). As Valjean, the hardened convict who is forgiven by a priest he robs and is thereafter made a good man, Neeson is a monument—of penance, intelligence, charity. His physical presence, naturally, is a plus (although August underplays the cinematic potential of Valjean's famous rescue of the man under the horse cart). But so is the sense of warring instincts that Neeson modulates so beautifully.

It's Rush, however, who is the magnetic force here—darkness, as always, being so much more delicious—and his Javert, like Neeson's Valjean, is a simmering cocktail of emotions. Less sneering and unctuous than Charles Laughton was in the 1935 film ("Les Miserables" has been filmed at least 20 times, in various nations and incarnations), Rush is more reminiscent of Cedric Hardwicke in the 1939 "Hunchback of Notre Dame"—half angel of rectitude, half vampire.

When Javert discovers he's been right all along—that Valjean has become the owner of a prosperous factory and as mayor of Vigau defied him in the arrest and persecution of the hapless Fantine—he's also a picture of glee.

The first half of the film, which includes Valjean's flight, his rescue of Fantine's daughter Cosette and their sanctuary in a Paris convent, is more involving than the latter, and this is due both to the story line and the casting. As the grown Cosette, Claire Danes again proves herself an interesting actress, but one whose emotional repertoire is beginning to seem mannered, even at her ripe young age. A more mature romantic partner might have helped, but as Marius, the political firebrand trying to get the July Revolution of 1832 out of the blocks, Hans Matheson is a callow ingredient.

August ("Pelle the Conqueror," "Smilla's Sense of Snow") has less success orchestrating the large-scale scenes than he does the more intimate ones. This was evident in "Jerusalem," his as-yet-unreleased-hereversion of Selma Lagerlof's epic Swedish novel, and it's evident here. Neither is he immune to the cringe-producing moment of *Sturm und Drang* and schmaltz and gingerbread. But at the same time he "gets" what Hugo was about, what the story has to say a century and a half later and, most important, why literary adaptations don't always have to be exercises in sloth and convenience.

NEW YORK, 5/18/98, p. 52, David Denby

A moviegoing mother of my acquaiantance asked me what she could take her children to see, and my answer was "Les Misérables," Bille August's broad-backed version of the Hugo tale. August works soberly, without excitement or imagination, but decently, too, with a fine feeling for the heroic reach of a decades-spanning narration—misery and obsession stretching over years. Liam Neeson and Geoffrey Rush are both excellent as, respectively, the exemplar of Christian ethics Jean Valjean and the rule-bound, desiccated, implacable police inspector Javert.

NEW YORK POST, 5/1/98, p. 51, Thelma Adams

Misery loves company. That's the only reason I can come up with for Bille August's prissy adaptation of Victor Hugo's "Les Miserables." This 's a movie that makes "Masterpiece Theater" look risque.

Hugo had a few agendas in his 19th-century French novel besides letting rip on an epic romance. In the wake of the French Revolution, the question of whether man (and, by extension, society) could be reformed was a hot-button issue, the sexual harassment question of its day.

Director August, working from Raphael Yglesia's respectful script, removes the heat and leaves the righteous squalor. In keeping with the novel, the handful of previous movies and the Broadway musical, it is the story of a larger-than-life romantic hero: thief Jean Valjean (larger-than-life Liam Neeson).

Valjean is liberated after 20 years hard labor for stealing a loaf of bread. Will he return to a life of crime? Can he escape the cycle of poverty that drove him to desperation in the first place?

Aided at a crucial moment by a kindly bishop, Valjean rehabilitates himself. Years later, he turns up as the mayor of provincial Vigau.

Before you can say brie, gendarme Javert (Geoffrey ["Shine"] Rush) arrives in Vigau. He remembers Valjean from his prison days and tries to "out" him as an ex-con.

Meanwhile, on the romance front, Valjean falls for poverty-stricken prostitute Fantine (a sweaty-browed, busty Uma Thurman). Unable to save her from her fate, Valjean adopts Fantine's illegitimate waif, Cosette.

After a decade on the lam from Javert spent cloistered in a Parisian convent, Valjean is as kindly as ever and Cosette (Claire Danes) has blossomed.

On Cosette's first day out of the convent, she falls for Marius (Hans Matheson), a hot young revolutionary. The society convulses; Javert hunts Valjean; the noble giant makes a great sacrifice.

Oh, dear! Rarely has nobility seemed so dull as in the ample hands of Neeson. And if Danes' ball of a chin warbles on the verge of uncontained emotion once more, I'll scream.

As a snitch tells Javert about the young lovers: "They're in love. It's perfectly nauseating."

If only Rush weren't such a tedious villain (cue the organ, audience hiss), if only he were James Woods, we'd easily be rooting for the side of determinism over free will, death over liberty, monarchy over republicanism.

NEWSWEEK, 5/4/98, p. 81, David Ansen

Not even counting that musical that won't go away, there has been no shortage of "Les Misérables" to choose from. Four silent-movie versions were followed by six with sound (two French, one Italian, one TV movie). The most memorable was the 1935 Hollywood version with Fredric March as Jean Valjean and an unforgettable Charles Laughton as his implacable foe, Javert. Does the world really need another retelling?

Frankly, no.

But we've got one anyway, this time with Liam Neeson as the reformed convict trying to have a decent life and Geoffrey Rush, of "Shine" fame, as the obsessive, law-and-order police inspector who spends half a lifetime hunting him down. Rafael Yglesias has condensed Victor Hugo's immense novel into a tight, time-hopping script, and the Danish director, Bille August, who has made some excellent Scandinavian films ("Pelle the Conqueror" "Jerusalem"), finally shows that his encounters with the English language don't have to end in disaster ("The House of the Spirits"). This is a solid, handsomely mounted but seldom inspired "Les Misérables."

Perhaps it will prove enthralling to a viewer encountering Hugo's sweeping, romantic tale for the first time.

For Mizniks, however, the thrills seem diluted. It's a bit like listening to another recording of Beethoven's Fifth, hoping to find interesting variances between Kleiber's conducting and Abbado's. See how sternly and unsentimentally the abbe is played here, as he forgives Valjean his theft and sets him on the road to righteousness. Savor the heft and physicality the well-cast Neeson brings to the role, neatly mixing coarseness with delicacy. Marvel at Rush's reptilian, dead-eyed stillness and wonder: why doesn't he ever change his expression? Is it a reaction against playing the twitchy, hyperactive David Helfgott? It can also be diverting to watch Uma Thurman transform herself (a bit too strenuously) into the beat-up, sickly Fantine, whose daughter, Cosette, grows up to be Claire Danes, who in the movie's third act falls in love with the dashing young revolutionary Marius (Hans Matheson).

It's here, when the story jumps 10 years to 1832 Paris and we have to get to know a whole new set of characters, that "Les Misérables" begins to feel like "Les Interminables." The filmmakers can't surmount the stop-start structure. Hugo's themes may be timeless, but in this version the viewer is all too aware of the passing time.

SIGHT AND SOUND, 12/98, p. 49, Andrew O'Hehir

France, the early nineteenth century. The convict Jean Valjean is paroled after 19 years of hard labour. Years later, Valjean has assumed a new identity as a prosperous factory-owner and the mayor of a provincial town. Javert, a policeman who was once a guard at Valjean's prison, arrives in town. Once Javert recognises Valjean, he dedicates himself to exposing Valjean as a convict with forged identity papers. Meanwhile, Valjean has brought Fantine, a desperately ill prostitute who once worked in his factory, into his home. He tries to nurse her back to health and vows to reunite her with her daughter, Cosette, whom he sent to live with another family. Javert tricks Valjean into publicly revealing his identity. Fantine dies. Valjean poses as Cosette's father and flees with her to Paris. The two live in a convent for ten years.

After Cosette decides she wants to experience the outside world, she falls in love with Marius, a young Republican leader plotting a rebellion. Javert, now a Paris police official, sets off through the city on the day of the uprising in search of Valjean. Marius captures Javert and turns him over to Valjean for execution. Valjean refuses and releases him. The insurrection is crushed and Marius is wounded. Valjean carries him through the sewers of Paris, pursued by Javert. Valjean agrees to surrender if Marius is freed. Javert agrees, but when Valjean returns from reuniting Marius and Cosette, Javert kills himself, setting Valjean free.

Victor Hugo's classic novel of 1862 has been filmed more than 15 times. This is understandable, as *Les Misérables* remains a cracking good yarn, built around an archetypal confrontation between the letter of the law and the spirit of justice, its implausible coincidences and sentimental set-pieces played out against a vibrant social history of tumultuous post-revolutionary France. Bille August's addition to the list (adapted by Rafael Yglesias, screenwriter of *Death and the Maiden* and *Fearless*) is an impressive, brooding monolith of a film, dense with vivid, grimy detail and anchored by Liam Neeson's granite performance as Jean Valjean. Unfortunately, it really isn't much fun, a cardinal sin in this sort of epic spectacle.

As execrable as the Broadway/West End musical of *Les Mis* may be on many levels, it successfully carries its audience on an emotional roller coaster from laughter to tears, from mawkishness to celebration. August and cinematographer Jörgen Persson have certainly crafted a convincing vision of the last century as a realm of soot and dirt, perennially shrouded in haze and twilight. But the lack of sunlight is mirrored on a thematic level.

This film is a joyless, relentlessly sober exercise that takes no delight in its own outrageousness, with characters solemnly intoning such lines as, "With this silver I have bought your soul," or standing in a Parisian throng, calling out: "To the barricades!" It almost seems that in August's attempt to escape his reputation as the heir to Bergman's cinematic legacy, he has made a movie as grim as any of the Swede's most forbidding works, but without Bergman's concision or philosophical depth.

Neeson puts his imposing physicality to good use, stalking and smoldering his way through the film like a barrel-chested combination of Jesus Christ and Frankenstein's monster. If his saintliness finally becomes tiresome, that reflects more on the movie's lack of dynamics than on his abilities. Geoffrey Rush is better as Javert, his twitches and grimaces revealing that beneath this policeman's devotion to the rule of law lies a bottomless abyss of self-hatred. The first third of the film, in which the two are locked in a battle of wills as mayor and police chief of a provincial city, possesses a Bressonian intensity that makes it by far the most satisfying segment. Uma Thurman's luminous screen charisma is such that one wishes she had more to do as the tubercular Fantine than lie around in heavy make-up, beaming at Valjean and waiting to expire.

However, once Fantine dies and the scene shifts to Paris, everyone involved with the film (except the production design team and the battle choreographers) gradually seems to lose interest. As the teenage Cosette, Claire Danes is permitted to wander around vacantly like a visitor exploring the set, alternately screwing up her face at Neeson and opening her eyes wide at Hans Matheson, who brings nothing more than underwear-model good looks to the role of Marius. After Javert plunges into the Seine and before the credits roll, Valjean walks away with a peculiar expression, undoubtedly meant as a smile (his first of the entire picture). It also might be a wince of regret, an appropriate closure to a film that, despite its admirable craft, feels too ashamed of itself to stoop to entertaining its audience.

VILLAGE VOICE, 5/5/98, p. 128, Leslie Camhi

The product of an age of monuments, *Les Misérables* casts a considerable shadow. Victor Hugo packed his 1200-page novel with large chunks of the 19th century. His characters surface amid the flotsam of poverty as transcendent symbols of suffering and redemption. Can the epic be condensed into a standard-length film starring name-brand actors without sacrificing its two main heroes—history and the great unwashed masses?

Director Bille August has managed remarkably. His *Les Misérables* is both vast and intimate; most surprisingly, he's used a cast studded with celebrities to convey the anonymous power of the people and the soul of mercy that animates Hugo's oeuvre.

Liam Neeson stars as Jean Valjean, the peasant who steals a loaf of bread and pays for his crime with 19 years of hard labor. When we first see him, he's an ex-convict, fearfully strong and without a conscience. A local bishop's unexpected benevolence "ransoms his soul from evil"—nine years later he's buried his past and prospered as the charitable, solitary mayor of a provincial town.

Along comes the new police inspector, Javert (the meticulous Geoffrey Rush), a man morally emptied by his obsession with order. Javert smells the mayor's odor of sanctity and starts having suspicions. They clash over Fantine, a tubercular prostitute played by Uma Thurman with startling frailty and grace. Valjean's chaste love for the dying Fantine, at once fervent and beautifully understated, inspires his promise to care for Cosette (a slightly disappointing Claire Danes), her illegitimate daughter. His flight from Javert with Cosette will take him across the rooftops, through the sewers, into the convents and better homes of Paris, and, after another decade, onto the barricades of a revolution.

August manages to convey the novel's scope through sweeping camera movements and subtle changes in character. Prague, where most of *Les Misérables* was filmed, passes convincingly for Paris, and the period textures are all quietly accurate. This is no costume drama but a tale of the spirit, played out against the scale of history.

Also reviewed in:
CHICAGO TRIBUNE, 5/1/98, Friday/p. A, Michael Wilmington
NEW REPUBLIC, 5/25/98, p. 26, Stanley Kauffmann
NEW YORK TIMES, 5/1/98, p. E22, Janet Maslin
VARIETY, 4/27-5/3/98, p. 58, Emanuel Levy
WASHINGTON POST, 5/1/98, p. D1, Rita Kempley
WASHINGTON POST, 5/1/98, Weekend/p. 53, Michael O'Sullivan

LETHAL WEAPON 4

A Warner Bros. release of a Silver Pictures production in association with Doshudo Productions. *Executive Producer:* Steve Perry and Jim Van Wyck. *Producer:* Joel Silver and Richard Donner. *Director:* Richard Donner. *Screenplay:* Channing Gibson. *Story:* Jonathan Lemkin, Alfred Gough, and Miles Millar. *Director of Photography:* Andrzej Bartkowiak. *Editor:* Frank J. Urioste and Dallas Puett. *Music:* Michael Kamen, Eric Clapton, and David Sanborn. *Music Editor:* Zig Gron and Daryl Kell. *Sound:* Tim Cooney and (music): Bobby Fernandez and Lee Manning. *Sound Editor:* Mark Mangini and George Simpson. *Casting:* Marion Dougherty. *Production Designer:* J. Michael Riva. *Art Director:* David Klassen. *Set Decorator:* Lauri Gaffin. *Special Effects:* Matt Sweeney. *Costumes:* Kimberly Guenther. *Make-up:* Gary Liddiard and Robert Scribner. *Stunt Coordinator:* Conrad E. Palmisano and Mic Rodgers. *Running time:* 125 minutes. *MPAA Rating:* R.

CAST: Mel Gibson (Martin Riggs); Danny Glover (Roger Murtaugh); Joe Pesci (Leo Getz); Rene Russo (Lorna Cole); Chris Rock (Lee Butters); Jet Li (Wah Sing Ku); Steve Kahan (Captain Murphy); Kim Chan (Uncle Benny); Darlene Love (Trish Murtaugh); Traci Wolfe (Rianne); Eddy Ko (Hong); Jack Kehler (State Department Official); Calvin Jung (Detective Ng); Damon Hines (Nick Murtaugh); Ebonie Smmith (Carrie Murtaugh); Mary Ellen Trainor (Stephanie Woods); Steven Lam (Ping); Michael Chow (Benny's Assistant); Tony Keyes (Ng's Partner); Richard Riehle (INS Agent); Phil Chong (Yee); Roger Yuan (Chu); Jeff Imada and Simon Rhee (Thugs); Zu-Wu Qian (Uncle Chung); Danny Arroyo (Gomez); Ramond Ma (Doctor Cheng); Jennie Lew Tugend (Cheng's Receptionist); Elizabeth Sung (Hong's Wife); Jessica Jann (Little Girl); Dan Wynands (Human Tank); Paul Tuerpé (Helicopter Co-pilot); James Lew (Freighter Captain); Jeanne Chinn (Ping's Mother); Ray Chang (Ping's Father); Ryan C. Benson, Daniel Getzof, and Theodore Touré Johnson, Jr. (Construction Workers); Dana Lee (General); George Kee Cheung (Fan); Marian Collier and Cece Neber Labao (Maternity Workers); Glenn Tannous and Larkin Campbell (Patrolmen); Doug Weaver and Glenn Friedman (Police Officers); Brittany Gamble, James Oliver, and Rick Hoffman (Police Officers at Port); Sarah Sullivan (News Reporter); Tim Cooney (News Cameraman); Bill Henderson (Angry Patient); Philip Tan (Waiter); Judith Woodbury (Question Lady); Jey Wada (Master Printer); Wallace Gudgell (ATF Officer); Gary Hand (Coroner's Assistant); Nancy Rosenfield (Candy Striper); Kenneth Jackman (Hospital Employee); Nancy Hopewell (Patient with I.V.); Christina Orchid and Bruce Orchid (News Crew); Richard M. Sieker (Motorcycle Officer); Jen Wei Chang (Bicycle Guy); James W. Gavin and Craig Hosking (Helicopter Pilots).

LOS ANGELES TIMES, 7/10/98, Calendar/p. 1, Kenneth Turan

If we get the movies we deserve, what have we done to be worthy of "Lethal Weapon 4"?

A fourth-generation copy of a distant original, "Lethal 4" is less a movie than a habit. Like a too-long-running TV show, it makes a fetish of familiarity, featuring the usual faces doing one more time what they've done repeatedly in the past.

Because moviegoers can be counted upon to follow the naughty-boy police team of Mel Gibson and Danny Glover off the face of the Earth if necessary, "Lethal 4" apparently went into production without anything like a finished script.

It was also churned out, if news reports are to be believed, even though none of the principals particularly wanted to make it or cared about any aspect except the size of the payday. The result is a calculated, cynical piece of business that epitomizes the creative bankruptcy and contempt for the audience that infects so much of the blockbuster side of Hollywood.

Four people may have bravely put their names on the "Lethal 4" script (screenplay by Channing Gibson, story by Jonathan Lemkin and Alfred Gough & Miles Millar), but it's disturbing to see such an inert, haphazard piece of business reach the screen. There's no plot worth describing, no repartee wittier than "Oh shut up," no acting moments that rise above the level of posing.

What becomes obvious is that all things verbal are intended only to mark time until the next stunt. Anything capable of taking up space is given a chance, from an out-of-nowhere diatribe about cell phones to illogical and short-lived promotions to captain for our heroes, which lead to padded sequences of everyone congratulating them on their good luck.

Those action blocks, which range from oil tanker trucks exploding to houses going up in flames to a car hurtling in and out of an unfortunate high-rise, are done with the steady professionalism that marks the work of veteran action director Richard Donner.

But even destroying as many vehicles as a demolition derby and displaying beatings severe enough to disable a horse (including having a seriously pregnant woman brawling and breaking chairs with no ill effects) can't make up for the absence of the kind of surreal flair a virtuoso like John Woo brings to the table.

As has become the rule with the series, "Lethal 4" starts with a particularly showy sequence, during which detectives Martin Riggs (Gibson) and Roger Murtaugh (Glover) learn some intimate secrets. Riggs finds out that his live-in girlfriend, Lorna Cole (Rene Russo), is pregnant, and Murtaugh learns that his daughter Rianne is similarly expecting.

After this sequence, "Lethal 4" moves forward nine months, with Riggs lackadaisically trying to decide whether he and Cole should get married and Murtaugh attempting with equal lack of vigor to determine who his future son-in-law might be.

The action half of "Lethal's" plot revolves around the smuggling of Chinese refugees into Los Angeles, where they're forced into the equivalent of slavery to pay for their passage. All signs point to the sinister Uncle Benny, as in "if it's dirty and Chinese, Benny's doing it."

One of the least pleasant aspects of "Lethal 4" is the kind of things it finds funny. Lots of jokes are made at the expense of the Chinese, from mocking jibes about "flied lice" to threats to stick egg rolls into various parts of the human anatomy. Equally misguided are the contortions Murtaugh goes through when he thinks he is the object of a gay crush.

In an attempt to shake up this moribund franchise a la James Bond, "Lethal 4"—having wisely decided that the unhappy Leo Getz (a struggling Joe Pesci) is not exactly a sidekick for the ages—has brought in a pair of new faces.

Chris Rock, who plays the earnest Det. Lee Butters, is straitjacketed by his underwritten role. Chinese action star Jet Li, playing a villain for the first time, not surprisingly benefits from having almost no dialogue in English. His nifty Hong Kong martial arts moves add a welcome intensity to the picture, but even Bruce Lee couldn't bring this baby back from the dead.

NEW STATESMAN, 9/25/98, p. 66, Gerald Kaufman

Two cops—Riggs (Mel Gibson) and Murtaugh (Danny Glover)—are also featured in the noisy and raucous "Lethal Weapon 4", which is pervaded with the din of explosions, fire, thunder, shattering glass, shooting and shouting. Loma (Rene Russo), about to have Riggs's baby, even shouts her way into the maternity ward. Murtaugh accurately tells Riggs, "You're getting too old for this shit." Gibson looks gnarled, with valise-sized bags under his eyes.

When both heroes and their loved ones are left tied and gagged by the sinister oriental villain (Jet Li) in a house about to explode, this seemed to me a really neat way of winding up the Lethal Weapon series. But... they are rescued by—believe me—a child with a pair of scissors. Saccharine music swells the soundtrack when Murtaugh saves Riggs from drowning; for, despite a succession of tired jokes about homosexuality, the relationship between these two is this movie's true romance.

NEW YORK POST, 7/10/98, p. 46, Thelma Adams

"What happened?" "Gun fights, sharks, explosives—the usual," Mel Gibson tells live-in gal-pal Rene Russo after a night battling Chinese gangs in "Lethal Weapon 4."

And thus is summed up Richard Donner's merry movie of mass destruction.

Houses, cars, boats, warehouses, restaurants, piers, Chinese immigrants: They all disappear into that ravenous fireball that is the script of the fourth Gibson-Danny Glover buddy comedy.

Screenwriter Channing Gibson blends every action cliche, from Steven Spielberg's "Jaws" to John Woo's "Hard Boiled." The script—about Chinese mobsters in L.A. and the yellow slave trade—creaks under its own weight, with multiple starts and endings.

Fortunately, the best script polishers Hollywood can buy (including superscribe Shane Black) ride shotgun. The surface dialogue is fast and funny. Gibson and Glover, as the aging cops Riggs and Murtaugh, have the prickly rapport of Katharine Hepburn and Spencer Tracy circa "Desk Set."

In the earlier movies, Murtaugh's refrain was "I'm getting too old for this s---." He was the family man just this side of a pension who insisted that Gibson's reckless Riggs grow up and walk on the safe side. The fun was watching Glover go wild.

Now, four movies in, Riggs has mellowed. He's no longer aiming pistols at his own tonsils; he's no longer a cop so past caring he's a lethal weapon on two legs.

During a locker room tete-a-tete, Riggs and Murtaugh grouse about aging and then chant: "We're not getting too old for this s---." Sorry, boys, you are. "Lethal Weapon 4" is like watching Gibson and Glover on Viagra. They leap, they bicker, they shoot, but their passion's pill-induced.

Joe Pesci staggers in as Getz, a motor-mouthed former mob accountant turned private eye. Pesci's shrill act of self-parody climaxes in the bizarrely sentimental "Froggy speech" about his youthful befriending and accidental killing of an amphibian.

New addition Chris Rock is a misfire—a black Henny Youngman with a badge. As a Chinese enforcer, the magnificent Jet Li offers a calm moment in a manic sea. But, in the martial arts set-pieces, the filmmakers trot out the Hong Kong superstar like a trained monkey; he's less a character than fast legs in expensive pajamas.

The movie's most shameless twist is dual pregnancies. Riggs' Russo (his partner in crime-fighting in the last go-round) and Murtaugh's daughter are both preggers.

Before you can say "Parenthood," the Chinese fiends kidnap the expectant moms. It's no great moment for feminism when a third-trimester Russo kick-boxes her attacker after he puts a knife to her bulging belly. Did we burn bras to become macho mommies-to-be?

Murtaugh and Riggs are getting too old for this stuff—and, even though it's often lethally funny, so are we.

NEWSDAY, 7/10/98, Part II/p. B3, Jack Mathews

It has taken 11 years and four episodes, but the creators of the "Lethal Weapon" series finally have transformed their lucrative franchise into a pure situation action-comedy. Same characters, same explosions, same car chases, but new jokes and a pair of new guest stars. And, surprise, it's better—at least, funnier—than ever.

When "Lethal Weapon 4" was announced, I thought it should have been subtitled "Why?" No. 3, released six years ago, was a tired mess that struggled to get by on the chemistry between stars Mel Gibson and Danny Glover, and on Joe Pesci's reprise of Leo Getz, the bumbling private eye introduced in the second episode.

It didn't work. Ten points to anybody who can remember the plot. Five points to those who can remember if they even saw it. For the record, it's the one that introduced Lorna Cole (Rene Russo), the karate-kicking colleague who proved to be a match not only for Gibson's Martin Riggs but for the memory of Riggs' slain wife. You'll recall that her death is what made Riggs such a suicidal menace in the first film.

I mention these past events because "Lethal Weapon 4" brings them all together with Riggs, Glover's Roger Murtaugh, his wife and daughters, Lorna Cole, Leo Getz; plus a new character named Lee Butters, an L.A. detective who, unbeknownst to Murtaugh, is about to become the father of his granddaughter. Butters is a character obviously contrived to showcase the comic talent of Chris Rock, and it does. Rock, pretty much doing his own thing, is funny every time he appears, even in the midst of a gun fight, and there is one long, seemingly ad-libbed scene between him and Pesci that's worth the price of admission.

Bang for the buck is what you expect from popcorn movies, and "Lethal Weapon 4" delivers better than any other film so far this summer. The strength of the series has always been its willingness to pause between fireworks and fights for some lively, occasionally sentimental, banter between Riggs, the unstable cop, and Murtaugh, his rock-solid partner.

There's undeniable chemistry between the actors, but by the third film, even they seemed bored with the sameness of the series. But in the intervening six years, director-producer Richard

Donner, with a script by TV veteran Channing Gibson (no, relation), has revived it by seeming to kill it.

"Lethal Weapon 4" plays exactly like the last episode in a long-running TV sitcom. "Seinfeld" with a backdrop of death and destruction, a show about nothing... but fun.

There's a plot, not that it matters. Riggs and Murtaugh are investigating a Chinese slave-trade operation that leads them to a scheme by a local Chinese mobster to buy the freedom of four political prisoners in China with counterfeit money. The important thing that comes of all this is the Chinese hit man Wah Sing Ku, by far the best villain of the "Lethal Weapon" series.

Wah Sing Ku is Played by Asian action star Jet Li as a combination Bruce Lee-Jack Palance. Though he's used to playing heroes, Jet Li has a chillingly cold smile, and his athleticism in the fight scenes makes Riggs and Murtaugh look like the tired old guys they admit they have become.

The humor and the action overlap here. Before they give in to their instincts and go after Wah Sing Ku in the final scenes, Riggs and Murtaugh acknowledge being outmatched by one man, and briefly consider running away—to fight another day, or in a future episode.

But Donner doesn't dangle any promises of more to come. Riggs is now living with Lorna Cole and is about to become a father, which has him thinking about marriage and settling down. Murtaugh's relationship with his free-spirited daughter, Rianne (Traci Wolfe), is about to move to a new level when she gets around to telling him who his new son-in-law is. And Leo is going to finally feel the sense of acceptance that has eluded him throughout his life.

Whether "Lethal Weapon 4" is really the end of the series, it is buoyed by a sense of celebration. Everybody involved seems to be having a great time, and in this instance, it's contagious.

SIGHT AND SOUND, 9/98, p. 45, Andrew O'Hehir

Los Angeles police sergeants Murtaugh and Riggs—the first about to become a grandfather and the second a father—are fishing in the harbour aboard Murtaugh's boat when they encounter a freighter smuggling Chinese immigrants into the US. They overpower the crew. When they learn the immigrants are to be deported, Murtaugh agrees to shelter one family he finds huddled in a lifeboat. A few of the passengers have been murdered by the crew. Murtaugh, Riggs and their colleagues trace the crew to an ageing Chinatown crime boss named Uncle Benny and a mysterious newcomer from the Hong Kong underworld.

This gang leader, Wah Sing Ku, and his thugs abduct the immigrant family from Murtaugh's home, imprisoning Murtaugh and his family along with Riggs and his girlfriend and then burning the house down. The group barely escape alive. Murtaugh, Riggs and their subordinate Butters go in pursuit of the gang. Along the way Murtaugh learns that Butters is his grandchild's father. The gang, it turns out, are forcing the abducted family's uncle to counterfeit Chinese currency in an effort to buy freedom for imprisoned crime lords in China. After a lengthy battle on the LA piers, the police defeat the gang and Murtaugh and Riggs kill Wah Sing Ku. Days later, Riggs marries his girlfriend just before she and Murtaugh's daughter both give birth.

While the *Lethal Weapon* formula—dependent on running sophomoric gags, explosions and elaborate motor-vehicle chases, overlaid with a veneer of integrationist racial politics and leavened with a dash of sentimentality—has remained remarkably consistent since 1987, no one can say the franchise hasn't matured. Indeed in *Lethal Weapon 4,* the first new instalment in six years, the star duo of Mel Gibson and Danny Glover must face a villainous force even more indefatigable than the nefarious martial-arts master played by Jet Li—the ageing process. Both the screenwriters and the audience have apparently forgotten that Murtaugh, Glover's character, planned to retire at the end of *Lethal Weapon 3,* but much of the more winsome humour in this latest episode derives from the idea that the two wisecracking, property-destroying detectives are now greying, wrinkled baby-boomers grown "too old for this shit".

The portrait of *fin de siècle* masculinity drawn here is a somewhat chastened one. Riggs may be as insouciant as ever, but he absorbs a pounding in almost every scene (as he always does), first from a younger cop in the boxing ring and then from an assortment of Asian thugs, including the electrifying Li. Emotionally, reality is also closing in: his likable, long-suffering girlfriend Lorna, who must contend both with his chronic irresponsibility and his devotion to a long-dead first wife, manoeuvres him into proposing and marrying her while she's on the delivery table. Meanwhile, Murtaugh, always the stable and sensible one, seems ever more the harried househusband. Between shoot outs and freeway chases (and this film has some of the most ingenious in years), he passes out the money his wife earns to his college-age children, who are rapidly drifting away from him.

On hand to add a pinch of youth-culture appeal is Chris Rock, a major stand-up comedy star in the US, as Murtaugh's prospective son-in-law. Rock is hilarious whenever the script can be laboriously manipulated to create a monologue for him—and he and *Lethal Weapon* stalwart Joe Pesci perform a marvellously irrelevant routine about the uselessness of cellular phones—but he never really does any acting. You can't say the same about Li; although he hardly speaks in the film, his ample charisma is on display along with his balletic martial arts ability, and fans of his Hong Kong films won't be disappointed. For all the obvious appeal of Gibson and Glover's goofballing, audiences at a *Lethal Weapon* film expect elaborate action set-pieces. This movie's injection of eastern energy, while arguably leading to some unsavoury onscreen stereotyping, acts as a virtual dose of Viagra for Richard Donner's long-in-the-tooth franchise.

VILLAGE VOICE, 7/21/98, p. 120, Amy Taubin

Absence of ego is not the problem in *Lethal Weapon 4*. Director Richard Donner and stars Mel Gibson and Danny Glover are so determined to get their last licks and leave us feeling satisfied and well-disposed toward them and whatever they think they and the franchise represent that they deluge us with as much bonhomie as shattered glass and crushed steel. It's a veritable firestorm of good feeling.

While not as clumsy as *Lethal Weapon 3*, this finale (it better be) is almost as tired and empty. What in the first *Lethal Weapon* was a compelling tension (I wont go so far as to call it a dialectic) between Murtaugh (Glover), the family man, and Riggs (Gibson), the borderline psychopathic loner, has finally been resolved with Riggs becoming a family man himself. We always knew it would happen. Indeed, the recuperation of Riggs into the family is the narrative arc that bonds the four films into one. Its as if at the end of *The Searchers* John Wayne had started building a house instead of heading off alone into the prairie.

The total triumph of family values is particularly egregious given the abysmal treatment of all the women involved. Riggs's fellow cop and girlfriend (Rene Russo) is pregnant and the modern equivalent of barefoot. In her three measly scenes, she has only one thing on her mind—getting Riggs to marry her.

Murtaugh's wife accounts for a semi-important plot point, but she has, at most, five lines in the entire film. Murtaugh's daughter is sold out by the filmmakers—she has to marry Chris Rock.

One day the *Lethal Weapon* powers that be must have woken up panicked that their stars were both the far side of 50. Adding Rock was a no-brainer, demographically speaking, but the problem is he can't act a jot. He's a pretty funny fellow (and he'd be a lot funnier here if he didn't have to outscream Joe Pesci) but, as a cop, he just can't pass. Therefore it was necessary to supply a motivation for his perpetually self-conscious, weird behavior—like he's trying to impress Murtaugh because he's secretly married to his daughter.

Donner is still a whiz when it comes to fender benders (although there are too many vehicular explosions), and Gibson's *mano a manos* with Chinese action star Jet Li (playing a Chinese mafia assassin) rival those in the best Hong Kong movies. In his tunic, pigtail, and black silk tunic, Li looks like the son of Fu Manchu, and he's as hard to kill as any vampire. Murtaugh's parallel between Chinese boat people and runaway slaves notwithstanding, *Lethal Weapon 4*'s yellow-peril racism outstrips its misogyny and homophobia. Oh, did I forget the other rationale for Chris Rock's sorry-ass performance? Riggs gets to fool Murtaugh into thinking the flavor of the month is a fag.

Also reviewed in:
CHICAGO TRIBUNE, 7/10/98, Friday/p. A, Michael Wilmington
NEW YORK TIMES, 7/10/98, p. E13, Janet Maslin
VARIETY, 7/13-19/98, p. 53, Leonard Klady
WASHINGTON POST, 7/10/98, p. D1, Stephen Hunter

LET'S TALK ABOUT SEX

A Fine Line Features release of a Deborah Ridpath production.. *Executive Producer:* Susan Ainsworth. *Producer:* Deborah Ridpath. *Director:* Troy Beyer. *Screenplay:* Troy Beyer. *Director of Photography:* Kelly Evans. *Editor:* Bill Henry. *Music:* Michael Carpenter. *Casting:* Mary Jo Slater and Ellen Jacoby. *Production Designer:* Joe Warson. *Set Decorator:* Chandler Roneli. *Costumes:* Timothy Biel. *Running time:* 82 minutes. *MPAA Rating:* R.

CAST: Troy Beyer (Jazz); Paget Brewster (Michelle); Randi Ingerman (Lena); Joseph C. Phillips (Michael); Michaline Babich (Morgan); Tina Nguyen (Drew).

LOS ANGELES TIMES, 9/11/98, Calendar/p. 19, David Chute

"Hey, what's going on in that head of yours?" says director-writer-star Troy Beyer to her sulky best girlfriend in a key scene from "Let's Talk About Sex." And it's a fair question. The hapless moviegoer may be wondering the same thing. Seemingly, the movie is designed to satisfy our curiosity on that score. An aspiring TV talk-show host (Beyer) is filming a documentary audition tape in Miami with the help of her two gorgeous roommates.

Fictional scenes of the three friends bonding and wrestling with personal issues are interspersed with footage of actual ordinary real women discussing sex, men, romance and shopping—all the things women really care about. It's "women talking to women about women and women's problems," as Nora Dunn used to say on "Saturday Night Live." But authentic insights are few and far between. All the central conflicts are (to put it kindly) a tad shopworn. Michelle (Paget Brewster) is a cold-blooded "user" who dumps men because she's so afraid of being dumped herself ("I'm so angry!... When does the pain go away?") Her pal Lena (Randi Ingerman) is a sultry doormat who has to learn to respect herself and stop smoking so much pot. ("I'm only human. I hurt, I have feelings, I have needs.")

And Jazz, the aspiring interviewer, has split from her boyfriend, an understandably puzzled paragon (Joseph C. Phillips), because of an agonizing private disappointment. You know the one, the heartbreak that drives women to pursue careers as an outlet for their frustrated creative energies.

The odd thing is that the documentary snippets don't feel any more authentic than the fictional bits: You'd expect the mix of tones to be jarring, but for some reason it never is. It's as if the filmmakers and the "real" women had been all watching the same talk shows, so that they draw upon the same handy storehouse of cliches to express even their most private feelings. In that sense, perhaps, "Let's Talk About Sex" is revealing after all, if not quite in the way that Troy Beyer intended.

NEW YORK POST, 9/11/98, p. 68, Larry Worth

Jerry Springer may be the king of sleaze. But at least he's up-front about it.

Alleged writer-director-actress Troy Beyer, best remembered as Diahann Carroll's ditzy daughter on "Dynasty," pretends to champion the feminist cause in "Let's Talk About Sex." But her efforts speak more about hypocrisy.

Aside from an ad campaign featuring Beyer and co-stars Paget Brewster and Randi Ingerman in skin-tight jeans and snug crop-tops, the narrative shows women not only performing stupid cucumber tricks but plenty of supposedly hot lesbian action and catfights. That's in addition to enough soap opera developments to have the ladies going through a lifetime supply of Kleenex. "I'm human, I feel, I have needs," one sobs.

Ostensibly, the film puts Beyer's character—an aspiring talk show host in sunny Miami—and two fellow vixens on the street with their videocam to discover gals' biggest gripes about guys. That means lots and lots of graphic talk, though reading a public restroom stall would be more interesting, and illuminating.

The trio—whose acting ranges from hideous to horrific—ultimately showcase men as insensitive brutes and women their perpetual victims. So much for coming a long way, baby.

NEWSDAY, 9/11/98, Part II/p. B7, John Anderson

The come-on for "Let's Talk About Sex," a movie about sisterhood, empowerment, taking control and not taking any gas, features the three lead actresses in belly-baring half-Ts, sex-soaked expressions and the top of their jeans ajar. Contradiction? No, merely the pathology of the mall movie.

Connoisseurs of cultural cheese may find this film by Troy Beyer (she wrote the screenplay for the erratically amusing "B.A.P.S.") to be a best-case scenario: ersatz "Jerry Springer" shot on Supermodel World. Jazz (Beyer) and her roommates, Michelle (Paget Brewster) and Lena (Randi Ingerman), armed with camcorder, storm the Miami Beach-head in search of women willing to bare their sexual souls for a talk-show pilot—the operating ethos being that coarser is truer, blunter is better. And so, in mockumentary fashion, we watch dozens and dozens of young women—mostly very attractive young women—complain about the social/sexual inadequacy of men, the uselessness of men, the obsolescence of men and the sleep habits of men, never betraying anything but an obsession with men.

Which may be totally understandable, I can't really say, but the inadvertently fascinating thing about "Let's Talk About Sex" (which does not feature the hit song) is how it operates in a kind of parallel universe—the ever-expanding Movie Zone where the usual rules of human behavior or logic simply do not apply. Only the conventions of previous movies direct the action and the purpose, which becomes a kind of distillation process of stupidity.

This begins with the movie's premise—there really isn't one. The taping of interview subjects takes up the bulk of the film, particularly the first half, and the occasional interruption for a character crisis—Lena with a callous-lover, Michelle with a callous mother, Jazz with an ex-fiance—consist of hackneyed dialogue, tortured acting and laughable plot devices lifted from every TV Movie of the Week made since 1983.

Proving once again that the movies beget their own world view, we have three attractive women with little visible means of support living in an enormous beach-front house in Miami and suffering the tortures of the damned over matters easily resolved, abated or ignored. We also have a director-writer crowing about the liberation of women from conventional sexual warfare while larding her work with enough visual/verbal provocation to qualify as a soft-porn film. But then, there really isn't a film here, not in the sense of narrative, character or pictorial substance. "Let's Talk About Sex" is a film because its various conventions meet the necessary requirements of pop cinema, the way the East River is a tidal strait, or a tomato is a fruit.

Talmudic examinations aside, "Let's Talk About Sex" is coarse and unattractive, full of contempt for its audience, promises unfilled and contradictions abounding. Beyer's character, Jazz, even has the nerve to say at one point, "Everything happens for the best." It does? Then stop *whining* about everything. Either that or realize, as this movie will blithely attest, that in fact things can go terribly, terribly wrong.

Also reviewed in:
CHICAGO TRIBUNE, 9/11/98, Friday/p. F, Mark Caro
NEW YORK TIMES, 9/11/98, p. E29, Stephen Holden
VARIETY, 9/14-20/98, p. 89, Daniel Lorber
WASHINGTON POST, 9/11/98, p. D5, Stephen Hunter

LIFE IS BEAUTIFUL

A Miramax Films release of a Mario & Vittorio Cecchi Gori presentation of a Melampo Cinematografica production. *Executive Producer:* Mario Cotone. *Producer:* Elda Ferri and Gianluigi Braschi. *Director:* Roberto Benigni. *Screenplay (Italian with English subtitles):* Vincenzo Cerami and Roberto Benigni. *Story:* Vincenzo Cerami and Roberto Benigni. *Director of Photography:* Tonino Delli Colli. *Editor:* Simona Paggi. *Music:* Nicola Piovani. *Choreographer:* Leda Lojodice. *Sound:* Tullio Morganti and (music) Fabio Venturi. *Sound Editor:* Benni Atria and Silvia Moraes. *Casting:* Shaila Rubin. *Production Designer:* Danilo

Donati. *Set Decorator:* Danilo Donati. *Costumes:* Danilo Donati. *Make-up:* Walter Cossu and Enrico Iacoponi. *Running time:* 122 minutes. *MPAA Rating:* PG-13.

CAST: Roberto Benigni (Guido Orefice); Nicoletta Braschi (Dora Orefice); Giustino Durano (Uncle);   Sergio Bustric (Ferruccio); Lydia Alfonsi (Guicciardini);   Giuliana Lojodice (Headmistress); Amerigo Fontani (Rodolfo); Pietro De Silva (Bartolomeo); Francesco Guzzo (Vittorino); Raffaella Lebboroni (Elena); Giorgio Cantarini (Giosué Orefice); Marisa Paredes (Dora's Mother); Horst Buchholtz (Doctor Lessing); Claudio Alfonsi (Rodolfo's Friend); Gil Baroni (Prefect);   Massimo Bianchi (Man with Key);   Jürgen Bohn (German Orderly at Celebration);   Verena Buratti, Daniela Fedtke, Inger Lise Middleton, and Laura Rudeberg (German Auxiliary);   Robert Camero (Executed German Soldier);   Ennio Consalvi (General Graziosi); Giancarlo Cosentino (Ernesto, a Waiter); Aaron Craig (US Driver); Alfiero Falomi (King); Antonio Fommel (School Janitor); Stefano Frangipani (Player); Ernst Frowein Holger (German Sergeant); Alessandra Grassi (Schoolmistress); Hannes Helman (German Corporal); Wolfgang Hillinger (German General at Celebration);   Margareta Lucia Krauss (Soldier who Feeds Children);   Patrizia Lazzarini and Maria Letizia (Women at Grand Hotel);   Concetta Lombardo (Gigliola); Maria Rita Macellari (Queen); Carlotta Mangione (Eleonora); Franco Mescolini (School Inspector); Francesca Messinese (Lady at Opera); Andrea Nardi (Decorator); Günther Pfanzelter and Dirk Karsten Van Den Berg (German Soldiers);   Cristiana Porchiella (Unmarried Schoolmistress); Nino Prester (Bruno); Gina Rovere (Dora's Governess); Massimo Salvianti (Policeman at Map Shop);   Richard Sammel (Official);   James Shindler (Transfixed German);   Andrea Tidona (Grand Hotel Porter); Giovanna Villa (Registrar).

CHRISTIAN SCIENCE MONITOR, 10/30/98, p. B3, David Sterritt

For about an hour, the new comedy "Life Is Beautiful" lives cheerfully up to its title.

A young man named Guido moves to a small Italian town in the late 1930s and meets the woman of his dreams. True, she's already engaged to a fascist official, but Guido won't let details stand in his way. He pursues her with such sincerity that she can't help succumbing to his charm. So far, life is indeed beautiful.

But the second hour takes a different turn, A few years have passed, and while Guido's family is flourishing, the fascists have grown in power and brutality. An aspect of Guido that seemed innocuous before, his Jewish background, has assumed ominous new importance, putting his household in grave danger as the Holocaust gathers momentum.

Guido knows the future might be grim, there's one thing he's determined to do: protect his five-year-old son from all harm, both physical and psychological, even when the two of them are transported to a concentration camp.

This is a powerful story idea, and "Life Is Beautiful" has already received a slew of accolades, from the Cannes filmfest's Grand Jury Prize to eight awards in Italy's equivalent of the Oscar race. Miramax is now distributing it in the United States, promoting it as a comic fable about "love, family, and the power of imagination."

Enthusiasm for the movie has not been as unanimous as its ad campaign suggests, however, and audiences would do well to ponder its implicit attitudes. To be sure, few people would deny that love, family, and imagination are three of humanity's most precious resources. Yet it is folly to deny the overwhelming horror of the Holocaust, whose savage perpetrators wiped out uncountable numbers of families, including many as loving and as loyal as the heroes of this story. Oddly, the movie tends to minimize this.

Guido certainly deserves credit for his supple imagination; there's no situation he can't bluff, trick, or fast-talk his way out of. But does the film mean to suggest that quick-witted confidence was a match for the terrors of fascist death camps? The movie has a curious message about gender, too—paying tribute to Guido's sacrifices while almost ignoring the contributions of his wife, who treasures her loved ones so much that she enters the camp voluntarily just to be near them.

None of these criticisms means humor can't be a potent weapon against great evils. Charles Chaplin attacked fascism with comedy in "The Great Dictator," as did Ernst Lubitsch in "To Be or Not to Be" and Lina Wertmuller in "Seven Beauties." All used laughter to peel away hypocrisies, deflate pretensions, and inspire hope without understating obstacles.

"Life Is Beautiful" was written and directed by a less brilliant talent, Roberto Benigni, known to US audiences for his acting in some of Jim Jarmusch's pictures. His fable ultimately obscures the human and historical events it sets out to illuminate. Its intentions may be sound, but its achievements fall far short of the ambitious mark it sets for itself.

LOS ANGELES TIMES, 10/23/98, Calendar, p. 1, Kenneth Turan

When the narrator of the surprising "Life Is Beautiful" says, "This is a simple story but not an easy one to tell," he's speaking of the tale he's introducing. But the thought applies as well to the challenges facing co-writer, director and star Roberto Benigni, who set himself an impossible task with "Life Is Beautiful."

Best known in this country for brief appearances in Jim Jarmusch's "Down by Law" and "Night on Earth" as well as "Son of the Pink Panther," Benigni is one of Italy's cinematic heroes, an irresistible comic force whose films regularly set national box-office records. But when he and co-writer Vincenzo Cerami came up with the idea for "Life Is Beautiful," Benigni admitted he scared himself, and no wonder. A comic fable about the Holocaust set in part in a mythical concentration camp would give anyone pause.

A sizable hit in Italy, where it won eight David di Donatellos (the Italian Oscars), "Life Is Beautiful," despite its mild title and Benigni's comic genius, has not been without its vocal detractors. Even at Cannes, where it won the runner-up Grand Jury Prize and an ecstatic Benigni literally kissed jury president Martin Scorsese's feet, the film had some furious opposition.

That mixed reaction is understandable. For while it's futile to pretend that "Life Is Beautiful" completely triumphs—it's simply too tough a concept to sustain—what is surprising about this unlikely film is that it succeeds as well as it does. Its sentiment is inescapable, but genuine poignancy and pathos are also present, and an overarching sincerity is visible too.

That guilessness comes directly from Benigni, one of the world's most irresistibly funny people. A mischief-maker percolating with infectious energy and a machine-gun verbal style, he blends an Everyman aura with the ability to infuse his characters with believable innocence.

Innocence is especially hard to come by in the dark year of 1939, but Guido (Benigni) manages. As a completely assimilated Jew his feeling is "What could happen to me?" He and a pal come to the small Tuscan city of Arezzo to try their luck, but practically the first thing that happens to Guido is having the beautiful Dora (Nicoletta Braschi, Benigni's wife and perennial co-star) fall out of a hayloft and land right on top of him.

That style of chaotic comedy continues, as the first half of "Life" proceeds in an old-fashioned knockabout slapstick manner with jokes that could have come out of a silent film. Typical is the episode where Guido's out-of-control car stumbles into a motorcade for Italy's king, and his frantic gestures warning everyone out of the way are mistaken for crisp royal salutes.

When not courting Dora, Guido alternates between tormenting his romantic rival, a local fascist leader, and trying to learn from his tolerant uncle (Giustino Durano) how to be a waiter at the fancy local hotel. There he becomes friendly with a cultivated German named Dr. Lessing (a gray-haired Horst Buchholz), who shares his love of difficult riddles.

A characteristic of "Life Is Beautiful" that runs through both its comic and serious parts is how carefully planned everything is. If eggs are grabbed for whatever reason, you can be sure they'll eventually be squashed on someone's head, and many of the film's elaborate jokes take 10 or 15 minutes to completely play out.

Similarly, the hints of fascist repression that dot the film's first hour, including the tormenting of Guido's uncle by local hooligans, bear fruit about halfway into the film. Almost without warning, Guido, who is by now married to Dora with a wide-eyed child named Giosue (Giorgio Cantarini) for a son, finds himself and his family on a train headed for a concentration camp. What has been a genial romantic comedy suddenly takes a very different turn.

Determined to protect his boy from the knowledge of what's going on, Guido is desperate for a way to explain the inexplicable horrors of their new life to the child. He hits on the notion of telling Giosue that everything that's happening is part of a huge game in which everyone is competing for the chance to win that most outrageous boyhood fantasy, a genuine army tank. A classic scene where Guido pretends to speak German and translates the rules for camp safety into a speech about the game's rules ("no asking for your mother") is the manic centerpiece for this deception.

The concentration camp, like the film, is a strange hybrid, half faithful re-creation, half fabulistic dream. While the greatest suffering Guido experiences on-camera is having to carry heavy anvils, there is also a haunting, fog-shrouded shot of a huge mountain of corpses. Just dealing, even peripherally, with this kind of powerful material lends "Life Is Beautiful" its own kind of dignity. Guido's manic good cheer in the face of the end of his world, while something of a setup job, is moving even as we're tempted to resist it.

Given that good cheer, the film's considerable popularity at festivals worldwide is not surprising: the notion that the determined human spirit can find ways to triumph over this kind of hell on Earth can't help but be an appealing one. Balancing that is the question of whether this scenario trivializes the Holocaust, making it seem like a bad but not monstrous event just so audiences can feel reassured.

Clearly Benigni is an optimist and the willingness to buy into that point of view is the determining factor in reacting to his improbable experiment.

NEW YORK POST, 10/23/98, p. 45, Thelma Adams

Holocaust humor isn't a booming industry. One false joke can sink an entire production.

Mel Brooks' greatest movie, "The Producers" (1968), toyed with this idea. In his prescient "The Great Dictator" (1940), Charlie Chaplin attacked Fascism with his funny bone. Even Jerry Lewis entered the fray with his almost entirely unseen "Day the Clown Cried" (1972).

Now, along comes Italian comedian Roberto Benigni's "Life Is Beautiful" ("La Vita e Bella"). In a moving, controversial, heartbreaking, award-winning comedy, the director and co-writer plays his own version of the "Little Tramp" in big trouble.

Benigni opens his fable in 1939, as his character, Guido, barrels into the town of Arezzo after his car loses its brakes on the Tuscan hills.

With the same giddy downhill abandon, Guido, a secular Jew, falls for a gentile teacher, Dora (Nicoletta Braschi, a breath of Audrey Hepburn grace). Actually, she falls for him—tumbling from a hay loft into Guido's arms—and later jilts her fiance, the local Fascist chieftain, for the man who makes her laugh.

During the bright romantic half of the film, Benigni pokes easy fun at Fascism. When Guido asks a Tuscan upholsterer his political views, the answer comes when the man disciplines his children, Benito and Adolfo.

Guido and Dora share a short spring before he is sent to the death camps with their son, Giosue (Giorgio Cantarini). Dora, who refuses to be left behind, hitches a ride on the cattle cars as well. And here the movie switches tone, as Benigni tries to make the case for humor's power to overcome the most impossible of obstacles.

Guido shields Giosue by presenting their starkly changed circumstances as a game. In slapstick scenes, Giosue hides from the guards and a one-way ticket to the ovens. His life is at stake and he doesn't even know it.

While the humor occasionally strains and pulls, the humanity, the depth of the relationship between father and son, leads to a wrenching and life-affirming conclusion. "Life Is Beautiful" because humor survives even in the shadow of death.

NEWSDAY, 10/23/98, Part II/p. B13, Jack Mathews

When Italian comedian Roberto Benigni's "Life Is Beautiful," a tragicomedy about an Italian Jew's attempt to protect his son from the reality of the Holocaust, premiered at the Cannes Film Festival this year, critics immediately split into two camps. One accused Benigni of trivializing his subject, while the other found it a fable of profound humanism.

I'm in the second group (as were members of the Cannes jury, who gave it their Grand Prize). Though the film has a pacing problem—a repetitive prologue takes up nearly half the movie—it is, in the end, an extraordinary tale of parental love, and the affirmation of life.

Benigni's Guido Orefice is a nonpolitical bookseller with enough passion for life to suck the air out of Earth's atmosphere, a description that might equally apply to Benigni. The actor and role have the sort of perfect fit that makes it impossible to imagine a film working, or even being attempted, with any other actor.

"Life Is Beautiful" links two very differently styled movies. The first is a broad Italian romantic farce, in which Guido frantically courts and wins beautiful schoolteacher Dora (Nicoletta Braschi, Benigni's wife), literally sweeping her away from her fascist bureaucrat fiance.

The second part picks the couple up several years later, near the end of the war and on the eve of their son Giosue's fifth birthday, when father and son are herded into a truck with other Italian Jews, then placed aboard a cattle car bound for a German concentration camp. Dora, a gentile, demands that she be put on the train, too.

On their journey, Giosue asks his father where they're going. Guido, vamping an explanation as far from the scary reality as possible, says it's all part of a birthday surprise—a charade in which everybody pretends to be something they're not. At the camp, Guido expands the game to explain away the uniformed men shouting in German, the horrible barracks conditions, and the lack of palatable food. Giosue is made to believe he and his father are teammates in a game where you earn points for sacrifice, silence, and for all you do that keeps you out of trouble.

Is this trivializing the Holocaust? I don't think so. It's Guido's undauntable humanity, in the face of so much evidence of man's evil, that drives his story into your heart. Benigni intends the title "Life is Beautiful" to be literal, not ironic. It's Guido's genuine outlook, and his belief in it strengthens his determination to preserve it for his son, as well.

The wonder of Benigni's performance is in the outward continuity he creates for Guido's upbeat personality. In the first half, he's a playful, spirited man consuming life by the ton. In the second, he's drawing on every ounce of his reserve to keep up that facade, to keep the game—and Giosue's innocence—alive.

I wish the first half of the film were shorter. Benigni's instincts as a comedian got the better of him, and the result is an excess of bits that tend to make everyone else, Braschi in particular, look like wooden foils and straight men. Still, enough of the true nature of both Guido and Dora comes through to make her choice at the end of this segment convincing, and vital. Yes, she goes with her heart, but more than that, she goes with her conscience. Dora, like too few gentiles of her generation, chooses goodness over security, and that's exactly what Guido will have to do in the dark days ahead.

NEW STATESMAN, 2/12/99, p. 42, Francine Stock

Roberto Benigni's film "La Vita e Bella" jokes its way through the Holocaust. But Francine Stock isn't laughing. Laughter and fear linked: official. Or as official as research at the University of California can be. We laugh when we perceive a danger that subsequently turns out to be a false alarm, according to recent findings by one Professor V S Ramachandran. Or as James Thurber put it 40 years ago, with a nod to Wordsworth, humour is emotional chaos remembered in tranquillity.

But what if the alarm isn't false? Roberto Benigni's much lauded film "La Vita e Bella" ("Life is Beautiful") is set in Italy. It starts in 1939 in Tuscany—all gentle slopes and diffused sunlight. It ends in a concentration camp. Throughout, the Benigni character, Guido, clowns his way through romance and terror with equal animation.

A dreamer who wants to open a bookshop, Guido meets and wins, by a series of improbable sight-gags, a local beauty who is both rich and a teacher in the local school. She's played by Nicoletta Braschl, Benigni's wife and regular costar. Guido is Jewish (although Benigni is not). The bigotry that dogs their courtship soon turns to organised persecution. They marry and have a child—for a while all is well, in a fragile way, until the authorities come for him. And then the clowning really starts.

Guido refuses to play along with the regime. To ease his son through the horror of the camp, he pretends the whole thing is a game, played to absurd rules. If the child stays hidden, if he doesn't complain, if he doesn't miss his mama, then he might win a ride in a real tank. His father dies laughing.

Benigni has described the film as a fable. A cautionary subtitle has been inserted in the US by the distributors, indicating it should not be viewed as a representation of reality. Much is made of the fairy-tale romance of the first half, in contrast to the misery of the camp.

The tribute to Chaplin is clear. Benigni even resembles him, slight and rubber-limbed; he does not so much meet Braschi as she falls on him—a typical beginning for a Chaplin romance. She, in turn, with her wide eyes and grave expression, is a Paulette Goddard foil for the frantic little clown. In the early scenes in Arezzo there's a heavy whose hat he repeatedly steals. ("What are your politics?" Guido asks him. "Hey," says the big guy, distracted by his twin sons fighting on the sofa, "Benito, Adolfo, cut it out.")

Guido dares, he invents, he pushes his jokes to the border of danger—and beyond. But do we laugh? Only occasionally, in my case. For me, Chaplin is painful, beautifully observed and executed, wonderfully imaginative—but not funny. Guido isn't funny either, although he does have moments of impossible, implausible charm. In a foolhardy attempt to speak to the girl, he impersonates a local fascist official and (a direct echo of Chaplin's "The Great Dictator") makes a speech to children about Aryan superiority, stripping off his clothes to reveal a puny body, with the tricolore sash of office worn over his shoulder and between his legs like a happy.

There's a surreal moment when a huge cake in the shape of a camel ("Ethiopian style") is brought shoulder-high into an engagement party. In the camp, there's a perfectly timed irony where the prospect of reprieve appears briefly but turns out to be, in every sense, a very bad joke. But for the most part, "La Vita e Bella" is excruciating—a word Benigni himself uses—as we watch the father's increasingly frantic attempts to disguise the inevitable. In a recent interview Benigni talked of the fear that clowns can inspire, of their need to control. This is what Guido does. He sets up a parallel system in an attempt to save his five-year-old son. He uses humour as an act of dissent. It's an irrational and dangerous technique but, under the circumstances, who could condemn it?

That seems to have been the verdict in Israel, where the film won Best Jewish Film Experience at the Jerusalem Festival. It also picked up the Grand Jury prize at Cannes and eight Oscar equivalents in Italy. Amazingly, there has been broad support among Jews for this non-Jew's eccentric account of the Holocaust, with only occasional accusations of trivialisation or insensitivity.

Benigni has professed that his aim is to reach a peak of tragedy where laughter and weeping collide. Jerry Lewis tried something similar nearly 30 years ago with his film of a clown in a concentration camp. It remains unreleased, tangled in litigation. Reports of it suggest a grotesque mawkishness that might provoke nervous laughter. Benigni certainly doesn't avoid mawkishness in "La Vita e Bella," but he's inclined to knock it down again seconds later.

Whether or not you approve of the result, Roberto Benigni has transgressed the usual artistic convention in depiction of the Holocaust—a certain grieving restraint. Maybe this departure denotes a new compassion and sincerity; maybe it's a sentimental muddle. I don't want to see this film again. But, three days after the viewing, I wish it would leave me alone.

SIGHT AND SOUND, 2/99, p. 46, Colin MacCabe

Italy, 1939. Guido, a young Jew, accompanied by his friend Ferruccio, descends on Arezzo where Guido's uncle has promised to help him to set up a bookshop. Before they even arrive at the town, Guido has met and fallen in love with a local young schoolteacher, Dora, whom he calls his 'Princess'. Guido eventually woos his (non-Jewish) princess away from Rodolfo, the boorish fascist official with whom he has an unfortunate encounter when he tries to obtain permission to open his bookshop. While waiting for this permission, Guido works in his uncle's hotel where he meets, among others, a school inspector (whom he impersonates to see Dora at work) and Doctor Lessing, a German obsessed by riddles.

A few years later, Guido and his young son Giosué are deported to a concentration camp. Dora insists that she must suffer the same fate as well. Guido is determined to shield his child from the horrors that surround him and persuades Giosué they are actually engaged in a weird and wonderful game in which the prize is a life-size version of the toy tank which is the child's most treasured possession. As the camp is abandoned by the German guards, Guido hides his son and is killed trying to rescue Dora. Giosué finally comes out of his hiding place to encounter the tank of his dreams driven by a US soldier who reunites him with his mother.

Life Is Beautiful starts as an idyllic Italian comedy set in Mussolini's Italy, but from the opening sequence of the film, in which Guido and Ferruccio are mistaken for royal visitors and given the fascist salute, we are aware that this is a comedy firmly rooted in history. Nothing, however, prepares us for the shock that begins the second half of the film when Guido and his young son Giosué are escorted to a train destined for the death camps.

Comedy is the genre that celebrates the social. Traditionally, comedies end with a marriage, confirming the power of society to reproduce itself. Tragedy is the domain of the individual, traditionally ending with the death of the hero who can't conform to the demands of the community. *Life Is Beautiful* takes for its subject matter the Holocaust—the attempt to build a new social order on the systematic extermination of an entire race. The horror of the camps defies all genres. In a world where murder is an instrument of state policy, all notions of the individual or the social are negated.

Benigni's magnificent film attempts the impossible: to make a comedy out of the Holocaust, to find an affirmation of society in the death of all social relations.

This is not a work of realism. The central story—Guido hides his son Giosué in the camp as he persuades him that this is all a game—has no historical plausibility. But the film is not interested in this kind of realism. The marriage between Jewish Guido and gentile Dora is equally unlikely. Indeed the set, costumes and lighting in the second half of the film are all designed to produce a level of abstraction which does nothing to detract from the horror and brutality of the camps. However, this heightend *mise en scène* makes it seem otherworldly.

There is equally no attempt to understand the historical processes which produced Nazism and its millions of murders. The Germans are presented as an incomprehensible race whether they be brutal camp guards or the sophisticated Doctor Lessing. He reencounters Guido in the camp and arranges a private meeting, only to pose him yet more riddles, while the philosopher Schopenhauer is invoked by Ferruccio at the beginning of the film as the thinker who held that one could change reality simply by force of will.

This is what the concentration camps at one level are: the perverted and bureaucratic product of an idealism which would make the real and the 'rational' one. It is against this will that Guido opposes his own to produce a world where his child can be happy in this titanic mismatch of individual and system, Benigni, the supreme European clown of his generation, mobilises a comic heritage that reaches back through Chaplin to the *commedia dell'arte*. Never has Benigni's mobile face been put to more varied use; never has Nicoletta Braschi been so simply beautiful. The direction is as assured as the acting. The full resources of the cinema are harnessed to make the world of Arezzo live before us. The elegant farce of the hotel scenes are as good as anything produced in Europe this decade.

One could criticise the film for abandoning the terrain of the social, or rather for reducing it to the basic unit of the family. But the film's strength is its settled faith that the affective bonds of the family can overcome the worst that society can offer. If this is a fantasy, it is probably a compensation we need when facing the reality of history. It is not too fanciful to read in this fantasy of a father's protectiveness the real guilt of a generation of European children who grew up knowing they had been unable to save their own fathers.

But if much discussion of the film will turn around its narrative denouement, its real emotional strength comes from the simply acted and beautifully shot first hour in which Guido's love for Dora triumphs over all obstacles. "There is no greater sorrow," says Dante, "than to recall a time of happiness in misery." Throughout the second half of the film we are achingly aware of such happiness lost. It may be that the Holocaust will always defeat any attempt at representation or comprehension but Benigni's *Life Is Beautiful* is the first film that recognises the enormity of the task.

TIME, 11/9/98, p. 116, Richard Schickel

The place is clean, and though the work is hard and the rations are short, no one seems to sicken or die. There are references to mass extermination, but that brutal reality is never vividly presented. Indeed, the prisoners don't seem to see much of their jailers, who, when they do turn up, act as if they've drifted into this film from a Hogan's Heroes rerun—barking incomprehensible orders to cover their comic ineptitude.

This is life in a Nazi concentration camp as presented by Roberto Benigni, the star, director and co-writer (with Vincenzo Cerami) of *Life Is Beautiful*, which has been winning awards and high popularity in Europe. Benigni won't—can't—have it any other way, for even a hint of the truth about the Holocaust would crush his comedy and reduce to absurdity his "fable" about a man named Guido making a sort of hide-and-seek game out of camp life, diverting his four-year-old son (Giorgio Cantarini) from its harshness and encouraging him to lie low. The idea, of course, is to save the boy from the gas chamber, where the young, the old and the sickly—all those who can't work—are automatically sent.

It is perhaps fair to observe that Italian Jewry was spared the worst of genocide. Mussolini's Fascist government only belatedly and halfheartedly embraced the nightmare racial theories of its German ally. Not until after the Italians made a separate peace, late in the war, and the Germans occupied much of their country did deportations begin in earnest. This meant that many Italian Jews stayed only a relatively short time in the camps, which enhanced their chances of survival.

It is also fair to say that Benigni—whose self-love, if not his comic skills, could charitably be described as Chaplinesque, or perhaps more accurately as Robin Williamsish—devotes much of his film to peacetime passages overestablishing Guido's childlike yet shrewd, cheeky yet romantic character as a wise innocent, an idealized Everyman. His pursuit of his principessa, who is engaged to a local Fascist leader (and is sweetly played by Benigni's wife Nicoletta Braschi), and his casually farcical assaults on decorum and authority are, if you have a taste for simpleton comedy, inoffensive.

It would be a pretty thing to think that a gentle, genial spirit like Guido's could effectively resist totalitarianism at its most terrible. But it cannot—unless, of course, you rewrite the past and in the process travesty tragedy. The witnesses to the Holocaust—its living victims—inevitably grow fewer every year. The voices that would deny it ever took place remain strident. The newer generations hurry heedlessly into the future. In this climate, turning even a small corner of this century's central horror into feel-good popular entertainment is abhorrent. Sentimentality is a kind of fascism too, robbing us of judgment and moral acuity, and it needs to be resisted. *Life Is Beautiful* is a good place to start.

VILLAGE VOICE, 10/27/98, p. 135, J. Hoberman

It wasn't *Schindler's List* that made the Holocaust safe for show business. But it was Steven Spielberg's successful rethinking of mass extermination in terms of mass culture that created space for genre movies like Roberto Benigni's concentration-camp comedy *Life Is Beautiful* and Bryan Singer's Nazi monster flick *Apt Pupil*. What situation could be more extreme? What vampire scarier?

Life Is Beautiful, Benigni's most ambitious movie to date and an enormous popular success in Italy, announces itself as a "simple fable"—although if fable is defined as a tale told to convey a moral truth, it's neither. The film opens in Mussolini's Italy on the eve of World War II and for its first half is a cheerfully antifascist slapstick romp, heavily indebted to Chaplin's *The Great Dictator*.

Mildly scurrilous and monumentally speed-jabbering, the quick-witted Benigni arrives in a Tuscan village and mounts a campaign to win a pretty schoolteacher (Nicoletta Braschi). The assault is waged against the audience as well. In one calisthenic set piece, the voluble star passes himself off as a school inspector to impress Braschi and finds himself having to improvise an explanation of Italy's newly mandated race laws—using a mixture of double-talk, bombast, and exhibitionism.

Irrepressible, imaginative, and naturally anti-authoritarian, Benigni consequently rescues Braschi from a night at the opera and an unwilling engagement to a pompous fascist official. Only then is it revealed that his character is a Jew. Of course, Benigni is a purely abstract Jew except in so far as he resembles Chaplin (or, at times, Woody Allen). He is the lovably déclassé little guy, dexterous enough to tip his hat with his cane and manipulative enough to talk his way out of anything. It's a 20th-century trope: the Nazis sincerely hated Chaplin, who may not have been a Jew but was certainly a symbol of everything "Jewish."

In the movie's second half, Benigni leaps into the void. In a single shot, the action jumps ahead six years to become a version of *The Day the Clown Cried*, the legendary, never-released Jerry Lewis opus in which America's greatest comedian-philanthropist plays a clown in Auschwitz given the job of amusing children on their way to the gas chamber. Such gruesome psychodrama is (mercifully) beyond Benigni's grasp. Still, now married to Braschi, his character is snatched by the Gestapo on the afternoon of their son's fifth-birthday party and deported, along with the boy (Giorgio Cantarini), to a Nazi concentration camp.

Life Is Beautiful improves on reality in many small ways. It is never noted that Italian race laws forbade intermarriage between Jews and Gentiles or that, when Benigni is deported, Italy had been at war for five years and was under German occupation. Benigni's character seems unaware that most other Italian Jews were rounded up and sent to Auschwitz during the winter of 1943-44. Still, in some respects, the hero's experience parallels that of the best known of these deportees, Primo Levi, an assimilated Italian who survived a year in Auschwitz and later described the experience with devastating lucidity.

Levi is not exactly a feel good writer, although (as Lawrence Langer notes in his new collection, *Preempting the Holocaust)* American publishers have consistently tried to give his books an affirmative spin both by altering their titles (changing *If This Is a Man* into *Survival in Auschwitz* and *The Truce* to *The Reawakening)* and employing grotesquely upbeat jacket copy: "Primo Levi's luminous writings offer a wondrous celebration of life. His universally acclaimed books remain a testament to the indomitability of the human spirit." So too *Life Is Beautiful.*

Benigni may whine and complain while doing slave labor, but he helps his boy survive by explaining their incarceration as a sort of madcap outward-bound contest in which, so the child is led to believe, they engage in all manner of nutty behavior to rack up points for a grand prize. Responding to circumstance, Benigni's character invents this as he goes along and, for once, his hysteria almost feels genuine. Despite the jokes about showers and crematoria, the Toronto Film Festival audience with whom I saw the movie was clearly amused—except perhaps when the game's other "players" began to disappear.

It's stunningly inappropriate and yet, by turning the death camp into an improvised children's game, Benigni articulates a partial truth. Auschwitz was, in the deepest, most awful sense, an absurd place—a monstrous realm of institutionalized irrationality. Soon after his arrival, the parched Levi broke an icicle off a windowsill to quench his thirst only to have it snatched by a guard. Levi was shocked enough to asked why, to which the guard replied, "There is no 'why' here." Reason had no meaning in Auschwitz although there was a particular logic—which had to be grasped if one were to have any chance of staying alive—and it is this logic that Benigni takes as the basis for comedy.

But that can only be seen in retrospect. If the movie is a fable, its moral must be that lying makes life bearable. *Life Is Beautiful* shows not just an attempt to save a child but also an attempt to protect his innocence—and hence that of the spectator who may or may not know (or want to know) how the extremity of the death camps compelled parents and children to unbearable acts of sacrifice. Mel Brooks's bad-taste "Springtime for Hitler" implicated its audience but, like *Schindler's List*, Benigni's movie is above all reassuring—indeed, that is its greatest absurdity. Benigni, like Schindler, is the good father and little Giorgio Cantarini is his chosen son.

Life Is Beautiful is funny (kinda) and even tasteful (sorta). But in its fantasy of divine grace, it is also nonsense.

Also reviewed in:
CHICAGO TRIBUNE, 10/30/98, Friday/p. A, Michael Wilmington
NATION, 11/2/98, p. 34, Stuart Klawans
NEW REPUBLIC, 11/23/98, p. 26, Stanley Kauffmann
NEW YORK TIMES, 10/23/98, p. E14, Janet Maslin
NEW YORKER, 11/16/98, p. 116, David Denby
VARIETY, 12/22/97-1/4/98, p. 61, David Rooney
WASHINGTON POST, 10/30/98, p. D1, Rita Kempley
WASHINGTON POST, 10/30/98, Weekend/p. 64, Michael O'Sullivan

LIFE OF JESUS (LA VIE DE JESUS)

A Fox Lorber release of a 3B Productions/CRRAV/Norfilms co-production with the participation of Centre National de la Cinématographie, Ministère de la Culture/Canal+. *Producer:* Jean Bréhat and Rachid Bouchareb. *Director:* Bruno Dumont. *Screenplay (French with English subtitles):* Bruno Dumont. *Director of Photography:* Philippe Van Leeuw. *Editor:* Guy

Lecorne, Yves Deschamps, and Pierre Choukroun. *Music:* Richard Cuvillier.   *Sound:* Eric Rophé, Matthieu Imbert, and Olivier Denesles. Costumes: Nathalie Raoul and Isabelle Sanchez. *Make-up:* Férouz Zaafour.   *Running time:* 96 minutes.   *MPAA Rating:* Not Rated.

CAST: David Douche (Freddy);   Marjorie Cottreel (Marie);   Kader Chaatouf (Kader); Sébastien Delbaere (Gégé);   Samuel Boidin (Michou);   Steve Smagghe (Robert);   Sébastien Bailleul (Quinquin);   Geneviève Cottreel (Yvette, Freddy's Mother);   René Gilleron (René); Mme. Chaatouf (Kader's Mother);   M. Chaatouf (Kader's Father);   Daniel Tanchon (Gégé's Father);   Sophie Ruckebusch (Majorette);   Jean-Claude Lefèbvre (Inspector);   Gérard Wallyn (Majorette's Father);   Jean-Benoît Gros (Pierrot);   Suzanne Bertelot (Nurse);   Mélinda Deseure (Majorette's Leader);   Bernard Filebeen (Michou's Father);   Francis Desure and Alain Lenancker (Policemen with Freddy);   Hélène Blaevoet (Marie's Colleague);   Marie-Josée van Overbeke (Quinquin's Mother);   Nadir Ghilmoinou (Kader's Friend).

LOS ANGELES TIMES, 10/2/98, Calendar/p. 4, Kenneth Turan

Bruno Dumont's "Life of Jesus/La Vie de Jesus" is an exceptional French film that treats a familiar topic in ways we're not used to. Winner of the prestigious Prix Jean Vigo as well as a special mention for the Camera d'Or in Cannes, this somber, powerful and intimate film is as intense and deterministic as a novel by Zola though its subject is very much close to home.

Set in the town of Bailleul in Flanders (where first-time writer-director Dumont was raised), "Life" is a bleak, unblinking yet inescapably sympathetic look at the dead-end existence of marginal young people who feel, not without reason, that they're imprisoned in their own lives.

It's a subject that American independent films have an invariable tendency to foolishly romanticize, turning aimless teenagers with nowhere to go and nothing to do into the equivalent of knights of the round table. Dumont, working beautifully with a completely nonprofessional cast, manages instead to dispassionately convey the shape of these lives from the inside, increasing our concern as he avoids either lionizing or blaming his subjects.

The protagonist of "Life" is 20-year-old Freddy (David Douche), out of school, unemployed, living with his mother (Genevieve Cottreel) in the rooms above her neighborhood cafe and hanging out with a gang of motorbike-riding pals.

Largely inarticulate, Freddy is also subject to disabling epileptic fits. The condition infuriates him, adding to his overall feeling of being trapped and symbolizing how emotions have been blocked inside him. For though Freddy is prone to bursts of hot anger, even a casual look at his face reveals softer feelings trying to break through the mask.

That sensitivity comes out in the patience Freddy takes helping his pet finch Leo learn to sing, and in his passionate relationship with his girlfriend Marie (Majorie Cottreel), a cashier at the local supermarket.

Few films have better captured how the boredom and hopelessness of small-town surroundings can turn sexual activity into a completely involving obsession. Though the couplings between Freddy and Marie are brusque to the point of being mechanical (body doubles are used in the film's brief explicitly sexual moments), they do allow for tenderness and release in their quiet aftermath.

Because of the tedium of these lives, "Life" is played out against a heavy air of foreboding, a feeling that is justified when a young Arab named Kader (Kader Chaatouf) begins to take an interest in Marie. The clumsiness of Kader's bravado and the intensity of Marie's tie to Freddy puts Marie off at first, but whether she cares about Kader or not when the unthinking racism of the motorbike gang is added to the stifled, claustrophobic nature of village life, the result is sure to be disturbing.

Writer-director Dumont conveys all this in a wonderfully measured, dispassionate style, neither cloying nor preachy, that comes, he's said in an interview, from a background of shooting industrial films where "I learned how to create meaning and emotion out of nothing."

Whether it's using their motorbikes to challenge a hot sports car on narrow country roads or playing instruments in a barely alive local band, Dumont's characters touchingly illustrate how the grinding, stifling nature of their reality serves to deaden almost all emotions. While Dumont's style may sound pitiless, "Life of Jesus" (the title is never explicitly explained) arouses our concern. These may be limited, no-exit lives, but they are lives after all, and in this filmmaker's patient, sensitive hands, that is reason enough to care.

NEW YORK POST, 5/15/98, p. 58, Larry Worth

Those seeking the latest biblical epic about the New Testament miracle worker are in for a shock with "The Life of Jesus."

French wunderkind Bruno Dumont's study of one young man's stunted existence in present-day Northern France is pretty far removed from Christ's life and times. The teen-age protagonist undergoes more of a symbolic crucifixion and resurrection, with his emotional suffering leading to unsettling, duly evocative movie-making.

Essentially, the slow-moving plot documents the all-encompassing ennui of a sleepy Gallic town—where a marching band's performance is considered an event. That leaves locals with too much time on their hands—and too much time to mull their hatred for "outsiders."

Dialogue is kept to a minimum but facial expressions and darting eyes—all courtesy of a cast of non-professionals—say more than enough. In particular, David Douche provides a properly menacing presence as antihero Freddy, a young man whose embarrassment at epileptic spells is camouflaged with attacks on those who don't melt into his sphere.

Kader Chaatouf is equally memorable as a colt-eyed Arab boy who dares to befriend Freddy's girlfriend, providing the story with its much-needed heart and soul. Marjorie Cottreel also comes through as the romantic triangle's focal point.

But Dumont isn't interested in playing up any star-making performances. Rather, he uses his cast as part of the overall tapestry—with the exception of one extremely graphic sex scene. Even then, the coupling isn't for shock value, but to demonstrate a disturbingly blunted mindset.

Collectively, the neo-realist production's lack of action may be perceived as sluggish going. But the end result is stunningly provocative.

Granted, Dumont's handiwork will never be compared to headline-making small-town smut studies like "Peyton Place" and "Blue Velvet." But this look at rural malaise hits with an equal wallop.

NEWSDAY, 5/15/98, Part II/p. B8, John Anderson

On the surface, Bruno Dumont's anti-allegorical "La Vie de Jesus" has as much to do with Jesus of Nazareth as it does with "Lawrence of Arabia." Less, actually, because Dumont opens with a galloping sequence straight out of David Lean: the "hero," Freddy (David Douche), hurtling down a country road, his motorcycle whining, his face obscured by a helmet, his future a very uncertain thing.

The crash, when it comes, is figurative, but you know it's coming, because Freddy is a boy-man with doom written all over him. Sullen or dull, it doesn't much matter which, he leads an aimless existence in his northern French town, riding his bike with his equally unemployed friends, or having sex—sex as inarticulate as he is—with the beautiful Marie (Marjorie Cottreel), whose matchup with Freddy makes about as much aesthetic sense as the Venus de Milo and Groucho Marx.

Freddy is an epileptic, humiliated by his illness; the allusions to Dostoyevsky and his own Christian parallels in "The Idiot" seem pretty obvious and apt. But while "La Vie de Jesus" seems to exist in rough reality, nothing is real. The town where Freddy lives—with his indulgent mother, Yvette (Genevieve Cottreel), over a bar—is an eerily underpopulated place. Rather than pumping their heads with urban pop, the boys play drums in a marching band. Freddy competes with his pet finch in a strangely anachronistic bird contest. Occasionally, the bikers race a strange sports car that seems to challenge their supremacy, but otherwise, theirs is a place without specific time.

The intermittent intrusions of reality are like reports from the moon—a friend dying of AIDS, genocide in Rwanda—but these are the exceptions that prove the rule: Dumont may not be forthcoming about his religious allusions, but his movie is clearly a myth. And by calling his film a life of Jesus, he provokes the question: Where is Christ to be found? In Freddy? Why not? A former philosophy teacher, Dumont is promoting a kind of practical, rational Christianity (influenced, he says, by the French philologist Ernest Renan) and by imposing Jesus on such a rugged little story he creates an intriguing collision of contrasting (if not necessarily contradictory) perceptions.

Like so many recent youth-oriented films out of France, the crisis in "La Vie de Jesus" is rooted in racism: Kader (Kader Chaatouf)—whose family is baited as "wogs" by the locals in Freddy's mother's bar—pursues Marie with vigorous intention. And after Freddy and his pals are hung out to dry for the sexual abuse of a young girl, Marie gets intrigued.

"La Vie de Jesus" is cast entirely with non-actors, and the result is a frighteningly natural and disassociated portrayal of a tragic character. Whether it's Freddy's Calvary or Kader's that we watch is a good question. But there's no end of those in Dumont's movie.

SIGHT AND SOUND, 9/98, p. 95, Richard Falcon

Bailleul, northern France. Twenty-year-old Freddy is unemployed and lives with his mother Yvette in her café. An epileptic, Freddy spends his time racing around the countryside with his four friends on their mopeds, having frequent sex with his girlfriend Marie, and training his pet chaffinch.

Cloclo, the brother of gang-member Michou, dies of Aids. Freddy organises a trip to the beach at Dunkirk to help Michou with his grief. Following an Armistice Day parade in which the youths play in the marching band, Freddy, Michou and the others racially abuse Kader, a local Arab youth, and Kader's parents. Kader begins following Marie home on his moped and when Freddy espies them together, he refuses to see her. The youths sexually molest a cheerleader and the next day they are denounced by her father. Marie begins to show interest in Kader. Freddy and his friends waylay him on a country road and beat him up. Later, Freddy is informed that Kader died from his injuries; he crashes his moped and lies alone in a field.

Bruno Dumont's first feature, a study of small-town boredom and desperation, adopts the title of the most famous work by the unorthodox theologian Ernest Renan. This 1863 historicising of Christ's biography presents him as human, a great leader around whom supernatural narratives have been spun, Dumont reveals himself as an uncompromising new talent by sticking to the film title's invocation of Renan's spiritual humanism. In an early sequence, Freddy and his friends stand silently in a hospital room around the comatose Aids sufferer Cloclo until one of them seeks solace in a nearby biblical print of the raising of Lazarus. It is the film's one explicit reference to Renan, who considered the miracle a deliberate fraud. Cloclo does not rise from the dead.

This is a rare moment of commentary from Dumont in a film which primarily calls on our empathy by gearing its pacing to the daily rhythms of his unemployed protagonists' thwarted lives. The film's opening reels make almost tangible the time spent in aimless and stifling inactivity. A painful prolonged shot of Freddy and his friends sitting near the town's cemetery is reminiscent of Fassbinder's use of claustrophobic stasis to convey boredom in *Katzelmacher* (1969), which like this culminates in an outburst of racial violence. Dumont employs repeated slow fades to mark the incremental passage of time between late winter and summer, emphasising the lack of change in the characters' lives. Despite Dumont's justifiable aversion to speaking about influences, his slow-paced narrative technique is distantly related to Malle's *Lacombe Lucien*, in which wartime collaboration is set against a mundane context. Here, the tragic outburst of racial violence with which the film culminates is similarly placed within a precise context which demands, uncomfortably, that we suspend easy moral judgement.

Dumont also invokes our empathy through his characters' physiognomies, particularly the lachrymose, prematurely aged features of David Douche as Freddy. The opening shot has Freddy's helmeted face juddering with the motion of his moped as he races through the countryside. A later shot of Freddy and Marie having sex focuses on the rapid jerking of Freddy's buttocks between her legs. Another shows the youths banging their drums in a furious tempo, and Dumont's camera moves into one face jerking spasmodically as he drums. Finally, the kicking to death of Kader is played off Freddy's impassively convulsing face. It is almost as if the energy of youth, suppressed in these constrained lives, can only express itself in involuntary convulsions.

That the focus for violence should be the racial outsider Kader is a familiar liberal-film move. The social reality of racism among the young unemployed in this poor industrial region offers only a partial rationale. Despite his subaltern position in the narrative, Kader is presented in ambiguous terms which exceed but never fully escape the role of post-colonial Other. When he approaches Marie on his moped, he seems half-threatening, half-desperate, an echo of the racist protagonists. Superb restraint by Kader Chaatouf—like the rest of the cast a local first-time actor—keeps the character unreadable until Marie shocks him by thrusting his hand into her knickers.

La Vie de Jésus is centrally concerned with physical being and unrecognised spiritual needs. Dumont emphasises throughout the bodies of his protagonists amid their involuntary distresses and ecstacies. There are shots of Freddy's torso, scarred after repeated tumbles from his moped, and also of Freddy and Marie copulating. These include a close-up of Marie's hand guiding Freddy's erection into her body, a sacramental moment almost, and possibly the only, non-gratuitous, meaningful penetration shot in the history of cinema. Perhaps more startling in its emphasis on the physical aspects of spiritual suffering is the distressing sequence in which a cheerleader is molested by Freddy and the youths. As elsewhere, Dumont uses the *mise en scéne* effectively, juxtaposing the youths' later incredulity that this should be called rape with a heartrending shot of the overweight victim walking home alone through the impassive countryside.

Concentrating alternately on landscapes and close-ups of the inarticulate protagonists, Dumont has made a French film which is remarkably unreliant on dialogue. At one point Freddy and Marie take a sightseeing chairlift ride over the fields and Dumont's camera characteristically dwells on the vista as Marie comments to an impassive Freddy on its beauty. Which it undeniably is, but a sense of foreboding, of implacable gloom is distilled in these frequent shots of the Flanders countryside. These unpopulated images resist interpretation, their meaning to the characters unclear beyond a vague sense of oppression. It is only at the end that this landscape takes on an unambiguously expressive and metaphysical dimension. Freddy lies back, having deliberately crashed his moped again, and the image begins to darken, leading us to expect another fade. Instead a reverse point-of-view shot of the sky shows the sun disappearing momentarily behind a cloud, and a series of close-ups, of an insect transferring itself from the leaves to Freddy's body, of his cracked and grimy thumb, offers us Freddy's sufferings, a *Via Dolorosa*, representative of mankind's lot. It is—as the culmination of a film grieving for the cruelty of being in the world while holding out minimal hope for salvation—a transcendent moment of secular martyrdom and is almost unbearably and inexplicably moving.

Also reviewed in:
NATION, 6/15 & 22/98, p. 34, Stuart Klawans
NEW REPUBLIC, 6/1/98, p. 24, Stanley Kauffmann
NEW YORK TIMES,5/15/98, p. E10, Janet Maslin
VARIETY, 5/26-6/1/97, p. 68, Lisa Nesselson

LIKE IT IS

A First Run Features release of a Deep in You Ltd., Fulcrum Productions, and Channel Four production. *Executive Producer:* Christopher Hird. *Producer:* Tracey Gardiner. *Director:* Paul Oremland. *Screenplay (based on his story):* Robert Gray. *Story:* Paul Oremland and Kevin Sampson. *Director of Photography:* Alistair Cameron. *Editor:* Jan Langford. *Music:* Don McGlashan. *Sound:* John Avery and (music) Gary Wilkinson. *Production Designer:* Tim Sykes. *Art Director:* Louise Bedford. *Costumes:* Sarah Bowern. *Make-up:* Michele Baylis. *Running time:* 90 minutes. *MPAA Rating:* Not Rated.

CAST: Steve Bell (Craig); Ian Rose (Matt); Roger Daltrey (Kelvin); Dani Behr (Paula); Jude Alderson (Gloria); Emile Charles (Aylon); Christopher Hargreaves (Tony); Paul Broughton (Minto); PJ Nicholas (Jamie); Sean Simpson (Jack); Charlie Caine (Terry); Stephen Burke (Luke); Dicon Tolson (Dirty Dave); Chris Ross (Andy); Suzy King (Amy); Ursula Lea (Sonya); Suzanne Hall (Train Girl).

NEW YORK POST, 9/4/98, p. 68, Bill Hoffmann

The club scene has never looked more sleazy, more utterly disposable than in "Like It Is," a gritty, well-crafted little drama from Britain.

At first look, "Like It Is" is primarily about the sexual awakening of a twentysomething misfit.

Craig (Steve Bell) makes his living from illegal bare-knuckle fights in the back alleys of Blackpool, the garish beach resort/amusement park city in Northern England.

A bona fide loner, Craig one night finds himself coming out of the closet with a hip and handsome club kid Matt (Ian Rose), a free-spirited young gay who's visiting from London.

At first repulsed by their sex act, Craig soon finds himself obsessed by Matt and follows him to London and the club where Matt works for Kelvin, an aging pop impresario (played here with gusto by pop star Roger Daltrey).

It's here the film puts the magnifying glass on the flimsy, cynical, dishonest world of '90s pop culture.

Kelvin is an operator with a capital O. A gay, good ol' boy who enjoys the company of barely legal boys, he uses his power to make fleeting stars out of pop hopefuls who sleep with him.

Matt—who hopes to run one of Kelvin's new clubs—is one of the old lech's favorite kids, and things get tricky when Matt finds himself failing for Craig. With a jealous Kelvin in the wings, Matt must decide what's more important—15 minutes of fame or true love.

Bell, a real fighter who won Britain's Amateur Boxing Association featherweight title this year, has a likable, easygoing screen presence, as does Ian Rose, who's been in some of British TV's best soaps.

The revelation is Daltrey, the Who's legendary frontman, who again proves himself as talented in front of the camera as he is before thousands of screaming rock fans.

Daltrey, now in his 50s, is likable yet loathsome as the hardened showman who manipulates his underlings like stock commodities. Youth is everything in his oh-so-cool and calculated world—and when his proteges get too old, they're out.

Few films truly penetrate the glossy surface of pop culture—this summer's two Studio 54 movies are cases in point. "Like It Is" is a fine exception. With a razor-sharp knife, it cuts right into its subject and displays it from all angles.

NEWSDAY, 9/4/98, Part II/p. B11, John Anderson

The state of gay-themed cinema is better than it once was. But there are still few enough films in the category that something as torpid as "Like It Is" can get a U.S. release, while any number of international masterpieces (albeit subtitled masterpieces) go unseen and unloved. Ah well, such is commerce, which doesn't seem likely to grow any more enlightened anytime soon.

In the meantime, we have "Like It Is," starring Steve Bell as bare-knuckled club fighter Craig, a boy from the north who brings his fists and sexual dysfunction to London, falls for up-and-coming record producer Matt (Ian Rose) and gets mistreated by record execs like Kelvin, played by Roger Daltrey, once of The Who and the best actor in this movie.

As Joan Cusack once screamed, *"is everybody* gay!!?" They are here, with the exception of Paula (Dani Behr), a singer so popular that when her real age is disclosed it makes the front page of a London tabloid, but who still shares a modest flat with Matt and gets jealous of his romance with Craig. Which are just two of the many unlikelihoods that "Like It Is" tries to get us to swallow.

The others might include the casting of Steve Bell, who looks about 98 pounds, as a back-room boxer; Bell actually is the Amateur Boxing Association U.K. featherweight champ, but that doesn't mean you buy him as a fighter. He looks like he could walk on a pie without breaking the crust.

Rife with dictatorial music—which almost invariably overdoes its intended effects—and atrociously lit, "Like It Is" is sort of a Theodore Dreiser story as realized by John Waters, except that *that* might actually be interesting. Paul Oremland's film wanders around aimlessly, although at the same time both the acting and direction are incredibly stiff. Which is an accomplishment, of sorts.

The real offense, though, is the way Oremland treats sex and human bodies—like a voyeur. In a film that purports to be liberated and liberating, treating gay love and sex as if they're shocking seems like the cinematic equivalent of high treason.

Also reviewed in:
NEW YORK TIMES, 9/4/98, p. E19, Anita Gates
VARIETY, 5/18-24/98, p. 77, Derek Elley

LITTLE BOY BLUE

A Castle Hill Productions release of a Jazz Pictures presentation. *Executive Producer:* Virginia Giritlian. *Producer:* Amadeo Ursini. *Director:* Antonio Tibaldi. *Screenplay:* Michael Boston. *Director of Photography:* Ron Hagen. *Editor:* Antonio Tibaldi and Tobin Taylor. *Music:* Stewart Copeland. *Casting:* Michelle Guillermin. *Production Designer:* John Frick. *Set Decorator:* Gabriella Villarreal. *Costumes:* April Ferry. *Stunt Coordinator:* Walter Strait. *Running time:* 107 minutes. *MPAA Rating:* R.

CAST: Ryan Phillipe (Jimmy West); Nastassja Kinski (Kate West); John Savage (Ray West); Shirley Knight (Doris Knight); Jenny Lewis (Traci Connor); Devon Michael (Mark West); Adam Burke (Mikey West); Tyrin Turner (Nate Carr); Brent Jennings (Tom); John Doman (Andy Berg); Kaitlin Hopkins (Young Doris); Ryan Phillippe (Danny Knight); Dennis Letts (Sgt. Phillips); Jerry Cotton (Detective Fleaharty); Michael Boston (Leo Dalt); Gail Cronaur (Motel Clerk); Carine Chalfoun (Paramedic).

LOS ANGELES TIMES, 5/29/98, Calendar/p. 6, Kevin Thomas

[*The following review by Kevin Thomas appeared in a slightly different form in* **NEWSDAY, 6/19/98, Part II/p. B11.**]

"Little Boy Blue" is a penny-dreadful time-waster that turns upon a Vietnam veteran (John Savage) having had his genitals blown away during combat. He has ever since remained in a state of permanent anger, often inebriated.

Savage's Ray West lives with his worn-down but doggedly devoted wife, Kate (Nastassja Kinski), and three children, a 19-year-old (Ryan Phillippe) and two much younger boys in a ramshackle house in the Texas countryside. Kate runs a roadhouse in a nearby small town, where her husband lifts nary a finger to help her but hoists lots of drinks at the bar.

Ray holds his family in the thrall of constant fear of his rages. You may well be wondering who fathered the three boys, and that question allows writer Michael Boston to give his story a suspenseful framework. The problem with the film is not its material or even its mind-boggling twists and turns of plot but that Boston has failed to develop his characters sufficiently to allow us much sense of recognition in them; he's also left too many loose threads.

There are countless families as luridly dysfunctional as the Wests prove to be, people with not enough knowledge or confidence to know how to seek help in the direst of circumstances. "Little Boy Blue" simply doesn't give us enough reason to submit to witnessing such harrowing misery; it lacks illumination.

But not for the lack of effort on the part of clearly committed director Antonio Tibaldi or of Savage, who shows us Ray's torment and even capacity for love, and Kinski, both distinctive actors with a certain mystique created by erratic, offbeat careers. Savage, however, seems to be in too good shape for such a self-destructive layabout, and Kinski too young to have been involved with him before he was wounded in Vietnam.

The focal point of the film is Phillippe's Jimmy, who hesitates to take a way out when his rich girlfriend (Jenny Lewis) offers to pay for his college education—he also has the prospect of an athletic scholarship. He finds he just can't stand the thought of not being home to protect the younger boys from Ray's rages.

But if Jimmy is intelligent enough to go to college in the first place he would be intelligent enough to attempt at least to seek protection—especially when his best friend (Tyrin Turner) happens to be a cop. Jimmy can't entertain the possibility that he might be in a better position to help the boys once away from home. The strongest survivor of this downer of a movie is Shirley Knight, vivid as a woman obsessed with her mission of vengeance.

NEW YORK POST, 6/19/98, p. 54, Larry Worth

Most people know "Little Boy Blue as the horn-blowing hero of nursery rhyme fame. But on the big screen, he's not so innocent. This time around he's seen more action than the old woman who lived in a shoe.

Under Antonio Tibaldi's over-the-top direction, tales don't get much more lurid, or downright weird.

In its '90s telling, Boy Blue is the ever-masturbating son of Texas trailer trash. And it's fair to say he's the sanest member of the household.

Dad is a Vietnam War vet whose injuries mean he has to wear a catheter. So when impotent Pop flies into one of his all-too-frequent rages, he makes Boy Blue get intimate with barmaid Mom in the family station wagon, at gunpoint.

Not to worry Boy Blue and Mom truly love each other, but not like your average mother and son. And that's just for starters.

Things get increasingly melodramatic—and silly—as the film continues. But one gives Tibaldi grudging credit for at least treating this soap opera slop with such straight-faced gravity.

Without exception, the actors also make the best of bad situations. In the title role, baby-faced Ryan Phillippe—who's about to attain star status as the lead of the upcoming "54"—supplies a nicely textured look at lost youth and twentysomething angst.

Phillippe's at his best in scenes with the film's two youngest stars, Devon Michael and Adam Burke, providing a sense of sibling warmth that really rings true.

A bleached-blond John Savage also commands attention as the oh-so-warped head of the household, giving Gary Busey a run for his psycbo shtick. Meanwhile, Nastassja Kinski's waif-eyed mom is equally disturbing and wrenching.

Heck, even Shirley Knight's mystery woman provides allure, which says lot considering her utterly preposterous part in the plot. Ditto for Jenny Lewis' turn as Boy Blue's duly confused girlfriend.

So while "Little Boy Blue" is no longer fodder for children or discerning adults, it should still hold appeal for Savage and Kinski fans—and those who wallow in occasional guilty pleasures.

VILLAGE VOICE, 6/16/98, p. 154, Laurie Stone

Oh, the shrink bills! And the appearances on *Oprah* and *Sally!* Southern Gothic doesn't get much pulpier than the goings-on in *Little Boy Blue*, directed by Australian Antonio Tibaldi and written by first-time screenwriter Michael Boston. John Savage plays twisted-psycho Ray. His penis damaged in Vietnam, he gets kicks by forcing his 19-year-old son Jimmy (Ryan Phillippe) to have sex with his mother Kate (Nastassja Kinski). It turns out, however, that Jimmy's parentage is murky, as is that of the two little boys he's been raised to think are his brothers.

Further bizarre revelations, accumulating like flies on sticky tape, make the movie easy to lampoon. But the storytelling, unreeled from the perspective of the boys—in fragments and through peepholes, with as many mysteries churned up as solved—gathers hypnotic force. Tibaldi directs the fine cast with effects at once dreamy and terrifying. In the physical beauty of the wounded characters and in the thin-walled, cramped quarters of their isolated trailer house, he captures tensions more primal than words.

Also reviewed in:
NEW YORK TIMES, 6/19/98, p. E18, Stephen Holden
VARIETY, 6/2-8/97, p. 58, David Rooney

LITTLE DIETER NEEDS TO FLY

A Werner Herzog Filmproduktion release in association with Cafe Prods. for ZDF of a ZDF Enterprises/BBC coproduction. *Producer:* Werner Herzog. *Director:* Werner Herzog. *Screenplay (German and English):* Werner Herzog. *Director of Photography:* Peter Zeitlinger. *Editor:* Rainer Standke, Glen Scantlebury, and Joe Bini. *Sound:* Ekkehart Baumung. *Running time:* 80 minutes. *MPAA Rating:* Not Rated.

CAST: Werner Herzog (Narrator);   Dieter Dengler (Himself).

NEWSDAY, 4/8/98, Part II/p. B10, John Anderson

In his early features as well as in his more recent documentaries, there has been the sense that Werner Herzog believes an intelligence guides the universe, and that the Supreme Being is a nihilist. And having decided on a capricious God, Herzog is able to find beauty in His greatest works, namely chaos and enigma.

Thus he has given us fascinating madness (1972's "Aguirre, the Wrath of God," for instance), the profound aesthetic pleasures of an incinerating Kuwait (1992's "Lessons of Darkness"), and the martyrdom-without-purpose of Dieter Dengler, the subject of Herzog's latest film to make it here, "Little Dieter Needs to Fly."

Shot down over Laos in 1966, and subjected to barbaric torture and deprivation at the hands of his Viet Cong captors, Dengler, the German-born American pilot, saw friends beheaded, hope evaporate and death all but wrap its arms around him. And what has it all made him? Inspiring, charming, sad and all but tragic, in a Greek-literary sense—and a character who might have sprung from the brow of Herzog, if not Zeus.

Born in Germany during World War II, Dengler was the grandson of the only, man in town who voted against Hitler (and who was persecuted for it), the son of a German soldier who would die in the war (only to reappear to the hallucinating Dieter during his escape in '66), and a boy who wanted to fly from the time he watched an Allied pilot buzz his house. Reared amid the poverty of post-war Germany, apprenticed to a blacksmith who beat him, he immigrated to America, joined the Air Force, went to college while living in a VW microbus, joined the Navy and was shipped off to fly missions over Vietnam. From here, he becomes Herzog's Icarus.

As the director shows us, there is something aesthetically pleasing in the sight of a village being bombed, especially when combined with the precision/anonymity of long-range warfare; it's art, as practiced by governments. But there are prices to pay. Dengler, on his first mission, is shot down. Denying his heroism ("Only dead people are heroes," Dengler insists), he never denounces the war itself, talks little about what he lost (a fiancée, we presume, although we're never told) and is cast as a sacrificial lamb, albeit without the quid pro quo.

Now in his late 50s and living near San Francisco, Dengler tells his story in a torrent of words, as if he's been waiting 30 years for Herzog—or anyone—to show up and ask "What happened?" or "What was it like?" What he relates is an adventure story of the highest order, a tale of courage and a tenacity for living (which he credits to the lessons of his grandfather and the brutality of the blacksmith).

Herzog accents this reminiscence with stock footage, dramatic re-enactments (during which Dengler grows visibly nervous) and a score that ranges from Bartok to the throat singers of Tuva, and has made a truly engrossing film, about a man no one can really explain, whose experiences are beyond rationality. As such, Dengler serves the director not only as a muse but as a philosophic mirror as well.

VILLAGE VOICE, 4/14/98, p. 59, J. Hoberman

Werner Herzog is long past being the art-house star he became during the 1970s height of the old New German Cinema. But in working out his own solitary destiny, this obsessed and irascible figure now seems one of the greatest and most original of documentary filmmakers—a celluloid conquistador with an extreme and tragic sense of life.

All throughout February's now forgotten buildup to Desert Storm II, I kept wishing someone would revive Herzog's 1992 masterpiece, *Lessons Of Darkness*—an awe-inspiring vision of the Kuwaiti desert in the hellish aftermath of the Gulf War. Instead, we have another sort of war story: Herzog's *Little Dieter Needs to Fly*, the bizarre saga of a German-born American pilot improbably named Dieter Dengler.

Opening with a quote from the Book of Revelation (surely the only part of the Bible that Herzog might religiously read), *Little Dieter* begins as Dengler's at-home portrait. A fit, cheerful fellow with a slight accent and an exceedingly bright smile, Dengler has built himself a hilltop house somewhere north of San Francisco. His harmless idiosyncrasies include leaving the doors unlocked and stocking the basement with several years' worth of food. The reasons are soon evident. Prompted by Herzog, Dengler recounts the story of his Black Forest childhood, his father's World War II death, the American bombing mission that destroyed his town. Dengler maintains that the first time he saw airplanes they were strafing his home. Indeed, one flew so low that the boy actually made eye contact with the "almighty being" piloting the bomber: "From then on little Dieter needed to fly."

Dengler is the sort of figure a reactionary modernist like German novelist Ernst Jünger would have appreciated. The aviator, he wrote in the 1920s, was the new 20th-century man, "the living expression of a powerful life force," the fulfillment of Germany's national destiny. But that was before the Reich crashed and burned in 1945. Dengler is roughly Herzog's age and the filmmaker seems to appreciate him as a sort of fantastic alter ego. An urgent Carlos Gardel tango underscores newsreels showing Germany in ruins. As soon as he was 18, little Dieter left for victorious America to enlist in the air force. He spent years peeling potatoes before he was permitted to enter navy flight school, graduating in 1966. Dengler was sent to Vietnam, where 40 minutes into his first mission he was shot down and captured by the Pathet Lao.

Who could possibly invent this? Dengler went to war because he wanted to fly; he wanted to fly because his childhood had been traumatized by war. If Dengler is a war criminal—and a son of a Nazi one at that—he is also the fulfillment of a destiny distorted beyond Jünger's imagining. Hence Herzog's fascination. The filmmaker includes some stunning Vietnam footage of aerial napalm explosions. (There are, however, no images of napalm victims.) Herzog appreciates a bitter twist of fate—his imagination is nourished on the remnants of 19th-century romanticism: a love of nature and the heart of darkness, an affinity for Nietzschean supermen on one hand and outcast primitives on the other.

Still, Dengler's experience of "savage" captivity and escape through the wilderness is a story with a particular American resonance. The descriptions of hardship and torture surpass anything in *The Deer Hunter*, while the downed pilot's barefoot escape from a prison camp into the jungle defies synopsis. Dengler's accounts of his own visions notwithstanding, *Little Dieter* doesn't have the hallucinatory kick provided by Herzog's landscape films, *Fata Morgana* or *Lessons of Darkness*. It's less visual than it is incantatory. Throughout, Dengler's vivid yet matter-of-fact delivery compels the viewer to imagine the unrepresentable extremity of his adventure.

Dengler is battered by monsoons and devoured by leeches. He nearly drowns. His companion is abruptly decapitated. He is followed through the forest by a bear that is waiting to eat him, and he calls this embodiment of death his only friend. When he is finally (and miraculously) rescued, he weighs only 85 pounds. Mildly ironic, Dengler calls this saga the "fun part" of his life. What he means is, it is the part of his life when he was most alive. "Death didn't want me," he explains.

The haunting thing is, there is no explanation. Even in his waking hours, perhaps most in his waking hours, little Dieter is still living a dream.

Also reviewed in:
CHICAGO TRIBUNE, 10/2/98, Friday/p. M, Michael Wilmington
NEW YORK TIMES, 4/8/98, p. E5, Janet Maslin
VARIETY, 9/8-14/97, p. 80, Emanuel Levy

LITTLE VOICE

A Miramax Films and Scala Productions release of a Scala Production film. *Executive Producer:* Nik Powell and Stephen Wooley. *Producer:* Elizabeth Karlsen. *Director:* Mark Herman. *Screenplay:* Mark Herman. *Based on the stage play "The Rise and Fall of Little Voice" by:* Jim Cartwright. *Director of Photography:* Andy Collins. *Editor:* Mike Ellis. *Music:* John Altman. *Music Editor:* Andy Glen. *Choreographer:* Bruno Toniolli. *Sound:* Peter Lindsay. *Sound Editor:* Dennis McTaggart. *Casting:* Priscilla John; *Production Designer:* Don Taylor. *Art Director:* Jo Graysmark. *Set Decorator:* John Bush. *Special Effects:* Bob Hollow. *Costumes:* Lindy Hemming. *Make-up:* Peter King. *Stunt Coordinator:* Lee Sheward. *Running time:* 99 minutes. *MPAA Rating:* R.

CAST: Brenda Blethyn (Mari); Jane Horrocks (LV); Ewan McGregor (Billy); Philip Jackson (George); Annette Badland (Sadie); Michael Caine (Ray Say); Jim Broadbent (Mr. Boo); Adam Forgerty and James Welsh (Bouncers); Karen Gregory (Stripper); Fred Feast (Arthur); Graham Turner (LV's Dad); George Olivier (Pawnbroker); Virgil Tracy (Loan Advisor); Dick Van Winkle (Money Lender); Howard Grace (Talent Scout); Alex Norton (Bunnie Morris); Melodie Scales (George's Girlfriend); Kitty Roberts (Brenda Bailey); Fred Gaunt (Wild Trigger Smith); Alita Petrof (Elaine); Jonathan Clark (Fireman).

CHRISTIAN SCIENCE MONITOR, 12/4/98, p. 15, David Sterritt

England has a long-established film industry, and a large potential audience for movies made on its own territory. Still, many English directors dream of success in the United States, where the word "hit" conjures up extravagant visions of fame and fortune. So the makers of "Little Voice" and "Waking Ned Devine" are surely delighted to have their pictures playing on American screens.

Not every British filmmaker dances to this tune, of course. A serious-minded *cinéaste* like Ken Loach, who made the recent "Carla's Song" and the coming "My Name Is Joe," thinks of social value far more than commercial profit. Others will make almost any compromise to crack the American market, though, and the recent breakthrough of "The Full Monty" put enormous new energy into the trend.

This helps explain the recent trickle of British imports with strikingly similar traits:working-class characters, plain-and-simple settings, and stories combining quirky humor with intractable human problems. Some call this a new genre, The British Unemployment Comedy, but it's really an extension of a category dating to the early 1960s when hard-hitting pictures like "The Loneliness of the Long Distance Runner" and "Saturday Night and Sunday Morning" earned international acclaim.

Update the underlying atmosphere of those classics with the sardonic ironies that helped "The Full Monty" and "Secrets & Lies" grab Oscar nominations, and you have the basic pattern for "Little Voice" and "Waking Ned Devine."

Of the pair, "Little Voice" is the more original and entertaining. The title character is a shy young woman with a gift for imitating bygone movie stars, from Marilyn Monroe to Judy Garland. She could be a star herself, but she's painfully lacking in self-confidence and stage presence.

Fortunately, help is on hand from her wildly extroverted mother and a local talent scout who's eager to capitalize on her gifts. Unfortunately, these two are natural-born losers who are more likely to squelch her talent than to nurture it.

At its best, "Little Voice" is a gently told tale of human foibles, spicing its stage-struck elements with a romantic subplot (featuring Ewan McGregor as a pigeon-loving boyfriend) and poignant suggestions that Little Voice's shyness stems from her lack of a loving father. But the movie's most boisterous assets are its star performances by Jane Horrocks as the heroine, Brenda Blethyn as her mother, and Michael Caine as the sleazy entrepreneur—three of the most dependable acting talents on either side of the Atlantic.

"Waking Ned Devine" is less imaginative and a lot more sentimental. The story takes off when two rural Irishmen find that an elderly friend abruptly died upon learning that he won the lottery.

Hoping to keep the money in their community, they organize a friendly conspiracy designed to fool the lottery officials into thinking Ned is alive and well.

The scheme proceeds smoothly until a nasty old woman decides to demand more than her fair share of the ill-gotten loot.

Although it has an Irish veneer, "Waking Ned Devine" has a British writer-director (Kirk Jones) and star (Ian Bannen) and was reportedly filmed on British locations. While this won't matter to most US moviegoers, the picture's stereotypical acting and self-consciously cute characters may prove too cloying for comfort, and its love-story subplot seems perfunctory rather than heartfelt. For a funnier and more original tale of a town-wide conspiracy, you could see the hilarious "Local Hero" from 1983, and let Ned Devine slumber undisturbed.

LOS ANGELES TIMES, 12/4/98, Calendar/p. 1, Kenneth Turan

Everyone calls her L.V., short for Little Voice, because she's so quiet her vocal powers barely exist at all. Shy to the point of being reclusive, she lives with her mother in a depressed seaside town in England's North, sticking close to a crumbling apartment where she obsessively plays hits from her late father's record collection.

Yet it is the conceit of "Little Voice" that inside this dull and unpromising exterior lies an incredible jewel. For L.V. has somehow absorbed all those records and can, when so moved, turn out astonishingly accurate copies of the vocal stylings of legends like Judy Garland, Marlene Dietrich, Marilyn Monroe and Shirley Bassey, renditions that sound frighteningly identical to the real thing.

British actress Jane Horrocks plays Little Voice, and it is a transfixing, tour de force performance. Even given that the original 1992 London stage hit "The Rise and Fall of Little Voice" was written by playwright and friend Jim Cartwright specifically for Horrocks and her startling capacity to mimic, how much she does with the role is continually surprising.

An elfin, bird-like actress with an endearing, twitchy manner, Horrocks is known to American audiences primarily as the angry, bulimic daughter in Mike Leigh's "Life Is Sweet" and for a recurring role as PR woman Bubble in the Brit TV hit "Absolutely Fabulous." As much as her singing, it's her skillful acting that turns L.V. into a strange, unnervingly spooky presence.

Yet, just as the ethereal Little Voice is surrounded by the dross and rubbish of life on the skids, so Horrocks' delicate work finds itself in a willfully excessive film that wants nothing so much as to force its brashness down our throats. Written and directed by Mark Herman (who did the uneven "Brassed Off"), "Little Voice" gets solid work out of both Michael Caine and Ewan McGregor, but it's often as offputting as Horrocks' performance is heartbreaking.

The main victim of the film's determination to glory in crudeness is actress Brenda Blethyn. Coming off her nuanced, Oscar-nominated performance in Leigh's "Secrets & Lies," it's especially difficult to endure Blethyn's abrasive work as aging party girl Mari, L.V.'s mother.

Locked in a war of nerves and words with her silent daughter, and with the equally closemouthed Sadie (Annette Badland, also of the London stage production) as her only confidant, Mari is concerned only with her alcohol-fueled sexual escapades.

Her latest love interest is Ray Say (Caine), an on-the-skids agent, complete with a flashy convertible and personalized plates, who likes to think of himself as "agent to the stars, king of cabaret, maker of miracles." He's a man who grandly claims to have known Monroe, but confesses if pressed that Matt, the singing bus conductor, is the Monroe in question.

Though he's hampered, as everyone except Horrocks is, by "Little Voice's" crass, hectoring tone, Caine does a poignant job as the man who hopes to make a fortune out of L.V.'s skills. Memorable is his astonished look when he first hears her as Judy Garland doing "Over the, Rainbow," as is the pep talk he gives L.V. when he's trying to convince her to take her private world public.

Also doing strong work despite the odds are Jim Broadbent as Mr. Boo, the oddly named failed comic and local impresario, and the always impressive McGregor.

Usually seen in energetic, high octane roles like "Velvet Goldmine" and "Trainspotting," McGregor is convincingly well-modulated as the timid Billy. He's another nervous non-communicator, more at home up on the roof with his pigeons than downstairs with people. Billy becomes a prime candidate to share misfit love with L.V. when he shows up with his father to hook up telephone service for the garrulous Mari.

Given that it's built around Horrocks' role-playing abilities, "Little Voice" couldn't exist without giving her the chance to demonstrate what she can do on stage. The transformation, when it comes, transcends all thoughts of gimmickry and becomes a genuine astonishment. It can't completely redeem the movie, but it certainly is one heck of a show.

NEW YORK POST, 12/4/98, p. 49, Rod Dreher

Shout hallelujah, c'mon, get happy! There's big noise in "Little Voice," a pitch-perfect British tragicomedy that's as brassy and exuberant as a big-band blowout. A plucky pastiche of sentimentality, joy, sadness, vulgarity and rollicking good humor, "Little Voice" is like a torch song translated into a feature film.

Jane Horrocks makes what amounts to a show-stopping American screen debut in the title role of "Little Voice" (LV for short), a morbidly shy young woman who exists—"lives" seems excessively optimistic—shut up in the bedroom of the tumbledown flat shared with her widowed mother, Mari (a knockout Brenda Blethyn).

Mari—rhymes with "sorry"—is a foulmouthed, boozy slattern who spends her days working at a fish market in a dilapidated northern English town and her nights tramping around barrooms, trolling for a man.

LV escapes her motor-mouthed mum's torrent of verbal abuse by obsessively playing her sainted father's LPS. Judy Garland, Shirley Bassey, Billy Holiday, Marilyn Monroe—LV has learned to mimic them all perfectly (as has Horrocks, who does her own singing here, to astounding effect). Too withdrawn to speak in more than a tiny whisper, LV can express herself only in the voices and guises of these larger-than-life entertainers.

One fateful night, Mari staggers in with her idea of a great catch: Ray Say (Michael Caine), a sleazy, small-time talent agent who tries to book his awful acts into a tacky cabaret run by the washed-up Mr. Boo (Jim Broadbent).

While rolling on the couch with Mari, the gloriously gauche Ray overhears LV singing upstairs. Convinced that he can launch her career—and his own—from Mr. Boo's stage, Ray schemes to persuade the extremely reluctant waif to perform.

After some doing, Ray gets his wish, and the result—an electrifying set of show tunes and pop standards—is an unqualified triumph. But can the frail songbird carry off a repeat performance? And will this fantastic mimic ever find her own voice?

Horrocks, best known to American audiences as Bubble, Edina Monsoon's dink-brained secretary in "Absolutely Fabulous," originated the LV role in the acclaimed London stage production. Director Mark Herman has adapted Jim Cartwright's play for the screen, adding a minor subplot involving Ewan McGregor, playing a sweet-natured pigeon fancier who takes a shine to plain-faced LV.

He's also toned down some of Cartwright's eccentric dialogue, which is still pretty lively. Even so, American audiences may have to listen closely to catch the fast-talking Blethyn's hilariously tawdry expressions.

With characters this offbeat and vividly written, "Little Voice" provides a first-rate showcase for acting—and the cast is unbeatable.

Horrocks, Caine and Blethyn vault into the front ranks of Oscar contenders with their work here. What's remarkable is the humanity Caine and Blethyn bring to their horrid characters, the kind of Dickens-in-a-trailer-park wretches whose greed and desperation seem weirdly touching.

We aren't meant to sympathize with Mari and her would-be beau, but it's hard not to find some pity for folks on the verge of failure, grasping at anything they can, even despising the weak, to sustain the illusion that life will turn out grand for them after all.

"I love it when you talk swanky," Mari says to Ray, a hussified Josephine to her gold-chained Napoleon. Mari and Ray may be cheap, but their dreams are not. Bless their crabapple hearts, I loved them more than anybody else in the movies this year.

NEWSDAY, 12/4/98, Part II/p. B3, John Anderson

It seems fairly safe to say that "Little Voice," the half musical, half comedy, half horror story from director Mark Herman, is the wholly owned proprietary domain, realm and fiefdom of English actress Jane Horrocks; that it will propel her into heretofore unforeseen fame and fortune; that her performance will (or should) be celebrated with all appropriate plaques, scrolls, honoraria and statuettes, and that someone will miss the point entirely and offer her a contract to record cover versions of Judy Garland songs.

It seems inevitable, but we may hope that cooler 'eads prevail, as they did with the casting of this British play-turned-film. Miramax, reportedly, had wanted Gwyneth Paltrow for the title role of the near-catatonic musical savant Laura Hoff, aka "LV," who was created by playwright Jim Cartwright for Horrocks (best known as Bubbles on "AbFab" or as the daughter with the chocolate fetish in Mike Leigh's "Life Is Sweet"). Would this have turned the film from half horror to whole, or just half comedy to total farce? As it turns out, the film is disjunctive, but it's not the fault of the casting.

No, the casting's pretty much a dream, a dream in pursuit of nightmare. The gifted Brenda Blethyn ("Secrets and Lies") is LV's mother, Mari, a raucous, bawdy barfly whose nonstop pungency sucks the air out of the room; you might think she's compensating for LV's habitual silence, but her loyal friend Sadie (Annette Badland) never speaks either, so it must be the oxygen. Mari yearns for love and, eventually, Ray Say (Michael Caine) a low-rent local talent promoter with "a bit of Elvis about 'im" and an obvious example of midlife Alfie. In Ray, Mari sees love; in LV, Ray sees his passage to the big time. Neither is going to let a little emotional disturbance get in the way of destiny.

While Mari is painfully oblivious to the plight of her daughter—who, we learn, is in the grip of inconsolable grief over the long-ago death of her father—so is the movie. Although some of the fault may be in the play, Herman strives for the broadest possible comedy, the loudest laughs, the sloppiest pratfalls, all manner of cruelty passed off as humor. The fatties Mari and Sadie dancing to disco? Hilarity. The idea that someone Mari's age might be sexually attracted, and attractive, to Ray? Please, you're killing me.

There's a merger of class snobbery and slapstick here that tries to make you forget that the film is about a profoundly disturbed young woman whose freakish musical genius develops out of her love for her father's old records. And her father. It's crushingly sad, and Herman seems just the director to distract us from any unpleasantry.

Horrocks, however, will not be denied. Garland is just one of the people she mimics so effectively in the film, adapted by Herman from the Cartwright play ("The Rise and Fall of Little Voice"). Not precisely, just effectively. Her big moment performing for the dilapidated Mr. Boo (Jim Broadbent) carries with it an easy but nonetheless irresistible emotional catharsis. No one, however, could mistake for mere mimicry for what Horrocks does, capturing not just an echo of Garland—and Streisand and Marilyn Monroe and Dietrich ("Falling in luff again. . . but their spirit, mixing it all with the pathos of LV's loss. It's called acting, and as Gumpish as her role might be at times, Horrocks deserves a standing ovation.

SIGHT AND SOUND, 1/99, p. 38, Andy Medhurst

Scarborough, Yorkshire. Sexually voracious widow Mari Hoff lives with her daughter, whose shyness and reluctance to speak have led Mari to nickname her "LV" for "little voice". LV's prize possessions are the records left her by her father, and she has learned to do uncannily accurate impersonations of such singers as Judy Garland, Shirley Bassey and Billie Holiday, but only in the privacy of her own room.

When two telephone engineers visit the Hoff house one of them, Billy, sees and falls in love with LV. At the run-down nightclub Mr. Boo's, Mari meets showbiz agent Ray Say. She takes Ray home, where he hears LV singing in her room, realises her talent and persuades her to audition for Mr. Boo. LV's nerves make the audition a disaster. Billy continues his timid courtship of LV, despite Mari's attempts to scupper it. Mr. Boo overhears LV singing and offers to stage a show starring her. She agrees, but only for one night.

The show is a triumph, and a prestigious London agent travels to Scarborough to hear LV, but she refuses to go on stage a second time, despite Mari and Ray's aggressive attempts to persuade her. Ray viciously turns on Mari, who realises he has only been seeing her because of LV's potential.

Ray and LV argue, and a fire breaks out in the house. While Ray rants drunkenly at the club, LV is trapped in the burning house, but Billy rescues her with his truck's cherry picker. LV finally confronts her mother and goes to see Billy at his pigeon coop.

Nobody who buys a ticket for *Little Voice* is going to feel shortchanged. Crammed into its trim 96 minutes are a fairy tale, a psychodrama, a teen romance, a showstopper musical and a vulgar comedy so broad it threatens to burst from the screen just as Brenda Blethyn's backside constantly threatens to overflow her tights. Subtlety is not its trademark, and there's a full-bloodedness about the film which bludgeons you into admiration. It slaps you on the back, kicks you in the guts, dares you not to laugh and cry and leaves your subconscious reeling. In all honesty, I can't say that I particularly liked it, but liking is a fairly feeble criterion to apply to a film as aggressive and unrestrained as this. The sheer ferocity with which it operates is going to knock lots of audiences sideways. I can't imagine a film less likely to provoke indifference.

The story is deliberately schematic and fable like. From the moment you see frail, isolated, waif like LV (Jane Horrocks) and her boozy, foul-mouthed, cock-hungry mother Mari (Blethyn) it's clear that you're in Cinderella territory, with *über*-tart Mari as every imaginable Ugly Sister rolled into one. Prince Charming is Billy (Ewan McGregor), the cripplingly shy pigeon-fancier who sees in LV a kindred dysfunctional spirit, while the perverse Fairy Godmother is Ray (Michael Caine), the sleazy showbiz agent who realises that LV's astonishing ability to sing just like her favourite stars could be his last chance of netting a fortune. Will she perform or won't she? That's the crux of the plot, with Mari and Ray urging her in different ways to get on stage (Mari just nags, Ray finds more devious means), while Billy fears for the damage performing might do, and offers an escape route when the pressures become too much.

The trick *Little Voice* strives to achieve is the mixture of simplicity and profundity. While the actual narrative is so obvious it could have been painted on placards, the emotional and psychological resonances behind it delve in deep and distinctly murky waters. LV's devotion to the torch singers of past eras is a displacement of her devotion to her dead father, whose pantheon of *chanteuses* she has taken on wholesale. Her father recurs throughout the film, as the photograph pinned shrine like on her wall, as a reassuring ghostly presence to comfort her at night, and as a phantom in the audience on her big night on stage. Viewers inclined towards psychoanalysis can draw their own conclusions, but even as somebody whose favourite Freud is Clement I felt increasingly uneasy at the clammy implications of this relationship. The undertow of incest becomes even harder to ignore through various devices which equate LV's tongue-tied suitor Billy with the father she adores so disturbingly.

If *Little Voice* is a love letter to Dad ('My Heart Belongs to Daddy' is even one of the old songs we hear), it hates Mum with a vengeance. Mari is given no redeeming features at all, a state of affairs exacerbated by Blethyn's uncharacteristically one-dimensional performance. Just as we are told nothing about what made her late husband so wholly wonderful, there are no hints at why Mari has turned out to be such an irredeemable old slapper. Well, perhaps one, a blink and-you-miss it scene which shows Mari at her drainingly dead-end job at the fish docks, the kind of work that would incline anyone to prioritise having a good time in their brief leisure hours. That's the only glimpse, since *Little Voice* has no sociological leanings.

Unlike the writer-director Mark Herman's previous film, the incomparably rich, wise and moving *Brassed Off*, *Little Voice* has no interest in the cultural contexts of people's lives. It simply wants to zoom in on their individual traits. Hence Herman rather wastes the promising possibilities of setting the film in the faded Yorkshire resort of Scarborough, apart from a few loving shots which relish the heroically preposterous tat of British seaside culture, moments that briefly recall the way Peter Chelsom used Blackpool in his marvellous *Funny Bones*. Otherwise it's hard to suppress a worry that *Little Voice* risks serving up northern working-class lives for the condescending titillation of audiences elsewhere (Blethyn's foghorn stab at a Yorkshire accent doesn't help here), a possibility which, coming from the creator of *Brassed Off*, is as regrettable as it is perplexing.

Setting all these worries aside, *Little Voice* is best enjoyed for three of its performances. Jane Horrocks' impersonations of her heroines are truly amazing, though her non-singing LV rather overplays the semi-autistic card (even Lillian Gish was never this innocent and unworldly). Jim

Broadbent, one of the most reliably excellent actors alive, captures just the right blend of desperation and resignation as the tacky club-owner Mr Boo, and Michael Caine gorges like a starving man on the best script he's had since *Educating Rita*. There are unavoidable parallels between this film's Cinderella tendencies and *Little Voice*, but Ray here is a far darker proposition than the teddy-bear boozer Caine played in *Rita*. The one scene where *Little Voice* breaks out of its good-and-evil binary to stir up some real, complex emotions comes when Caine, drunk as a skunk and enraged that LV won't perform again, takes to the stage and bellows his way through Roy Orbison's 'It's Over', interjecting self-lacerating abuse to make the song's lyrics comment on his own screwed-up career. It's not just the best vertiginously perverse use of an Orbison song since the 'In Dreams' sequence in David Lynch's *Blue Velvet*. It might be the finest two minutes of Caine's screen life.

You should see *Little Voice* for that scene alone, indeed it deserves to be seen for its overall punchiness, vigour and verve, and while it's steaming along like a rhino on heat you won't have time to ponder its shortcomings. As for afterwards, well, I'm still troubled by its father-worship and its incitement to matricide, not to mention its class politics, its tediously laboured birds-in-flight equals freedom metaphor, and its recurring use of fat people to score easy laughs—this fat-phobia is so endemic that *Little Waist* might have been a better title.

It also avoids one glaring question: if LV's Dad's favourite singers were Judy Garland, Shirley Bassey, Marlene Dietrich, Gracie Fields and Marilyn Monroe, why has nobody twigged that he must have been gay as a goose? Feel free to discuss that in the pub after you've seen this shameless battering-ram of a film.

VILLAGE VOICE, 12/8/98, p. 134, Amy Taubin

Insofar as *Little Voice* is a film about a voice that defies expectation and how it came into being, it's quite interesting. It's also a creepy depiction of nuclear family dysfunctions and disassociations. At its center is Jane Horrocks, who, in the title role, gives the best female performance of the year.

Adapted by director Mark Herman from Jim Cartwright's stage play *The Rise and Fall of Little Voice*, the film is set in a working class backwater in the north of England. L.V. (Horrocks), a fragile, paralytically shy young woman, lives with Mari, her brassy, bawdy, drunken, frustrated mother (Brenda Blethyn, giving a performance that makes Shelley Winters's "noxious baba" in Kubrick's *Lolita* seem like a paragon of discretion and empathy). The two women loathe each other. L.V. blames her mother for her father's death. Mari hates her daughter for preferring her father, and also because the neurotic L.V. is a reminder of her misbegotten marriage.

L.V. spends all her time in her room listening to the records that her father loved—Judy Garland, Shirley Bassey, Marilyn Monroe. When L.V. thinks no one can hear her, she sings, channeling voices of the various divas through her own. Horrocks does all her own singing, and the sound is extraordinary, to put it mildly. L.V. never sounds more fully and nakedly like herself than when she's evoking someone else. (it's the paradox that underlies all great acting.)

Eventually, she's discovered by a desperate, sleazy talent scout (Michael Caine) who convinces her to perform at the local club. Although the mother-bashing, and the contempt for the working class in general (except for L.V. and Ewan McGregor, as her almost equally shy soul mate, everyone in the film is completely grotesque), nearly drove me out of the theater, the show that Horrocks puts on when she finally takes to the stage is more than worth the wait.

Also reviewed in:
CHICAGO TRIBUNE, 12/4/98, Friday/p. A, Michael Wilmington
NEW YORK TIMES, 12/4/98, p. E12, Janet Maslin
VARIETY, 9/28-10/4/98, p. 36, Derek Elley
WASHINGTON POST, 12/25/98, p. C1, Stephen Hunter
WASHINGTON POST, 12/25/98, Weekend/p. 7, Michael O'Sullivan

LIVE FLESH

An MGM release of an El Deseo presentation of a Ciby 2000, France 3 Cinema, El Deseo production. *Producer:* Agustín Almodóvar. *Director:* Pedro Almodóvar. *Screenplay (Spanish with English subtitles):* Pedro Almodóvar, Ray Loriga, and Jorge Guerriche Chevarria. *Based on the novel by:* Ruth Rendell. *Director of Photography:* Affonso Beato. *Editor:* José Salcedo. *Music:* Alberto Iglesias. *Sound:* Bernardo Menz and (music) José Luis Crespo. *Casting:* Katrina Bayonas. *Production Designer:* Alejandro Vazquez and Esther García. *Art Director:* Antxon Gómez. *Set Decorator:* Felipe de Paco. *Special Effects:* Molina. *Costumes:* José Maria de Cossio. *Running time:* 100 minutes. *MPAA Rating:* R.

CAST: Francesca Neri (Elena);   Javier Bardem (David);   José Sancho (Sancho);   Angela Molina (Clara);   Liberto Rabal (Victor Plaza);   Penelope Cruz (Isabelle);   Pilar Bardem (Doña Centro);   Alejandro Angulo (Bus Driver).

LOS ANGELES TIMES, 1/30/98, Calendar/p. 6, Kevin Thomas

Don't be put off by its lurid-sounding title; "Live Flesh" is an effortlessly articulated tragicomedy by Pedro Almodóvar, a world-renowned filmmaker at the height of his powers.

Almodóvar is as outrageous as ever when contemplating the folly and glory of the iron dictates of human passion as it collides with fate. But he brings to his vision ever greater breadth and depth of compassion and concern for the possibilities of redemption. The beautifully crafted "Live Flesh" continues the new mature cycle in Almodóvar's work that began two years ago with "The Flower of My Secret."

Simply setting the plot of "Live Flesh" in motion is a dazzling display of filmmaking assurance. After a prologue, in which one of the key figures, Victor, is born on a Madrid bus in 1970, we flash to 1990. The handsome Victor (Liberto Rabal—Antonio Banderas, move, over) is attempting to reconnect with the frizzy-haired blond Elena (Francesca Neri), who has just relieved him of his virginity. Unfortunately for Victor, he is the last person Elena, the tempestuous daughter of a rich Italian diplomat, wants to see at just this moment.

She in fact is strung out and waiting for a fix from her tardy drug dealer. But when Victor gains entry to her luxurious Madrid apartment and a tussle between him and the furious Elena is witnessed through a window, a pair of cops turn up.

They are the steady, intelligent David (Javier Bardem), a virile 30-ish man, and the drunken, middle-aged, hotheaded Sancho (José Sancho). Guns go off in a standoff so deftly staged that in this moment of mayhem even all four of the participants may not know what really happened.

Flash to 1996, and the lives of all four, plus Clara (Angela Molina), the elegant but abused wife of the insanely jealous Sancho, once again become entangled. A convoluted and volatile contemporary "La Ronde" has just been set in motion, accompanied by Alberto Iglesias' marvelously seductive and varied score.

The confidence Almodóvar gives his actors must be awesome, for the risks and emotional range he elicits from them is typically breathtaking. "Live Flesh" helps consolidate Bardem's position as Spain's leading male star of his generation. Molina, the last of Luis Buñuel's memorable discoveries, is harrowing as a woman who grasps at an unexpected chance for love, and Rabal, grandson of one of Buñuel's greatest stars, Francisco Rabal, is a newcomer of major promise. Neri and Sancho are equally fine, and Bardem's mother, the wonderful character actress Pilar Bardem, appears in the prologue as a tough, brassy but kindly madam.

Almodóvar has Buñuel's "The Criminal Life of Archibaldo de la Cruz" (1955) airing on Elena's TV set at the time of the gunplay. By now Almodóvar is more than worthy of making such a homage to the great Spanish iconoclast, not just for their similarly detached amusement at human behavior but also for Buñuel's determined stand for freedom of expression.

In its epilogue "Live Flesh" comes full circle as a narrative—and at the same time celebrates Spain's journey from the repression of Franco to the country's open society of today.

NEW YORK, 1/26/98, p. 43, David Denby

Victor Plaza (Liberto Rabal), a prostitute's son born in a Madrid bus—and on the very day in 1970 that Franco cracked down on personal liberties in Spain—gets in serious trouble as a young man, goes to prison, and emerges while still in his twenties, eager to claim his personal freedom in a newly energized country. Franco is dead, and the reborn Victor—the hero of Pedro Almodóvar's *Live Flesh*—has a galvanizing effect on everyone he meets. A lover with dark eyes and a small goatee, Victor is neither evil nor violent, but he's an inexperienced, hungry young man, and things go out of control when he's around (Rabal has rough edges that his predecessor in such roles, the handsomer, more skilled but more predictable Antonio Banderas, did not have). *Live Flesh*, the best movie from Almodóvar since that Iberian screwball classic *Women on the Verge of a Nervous Breakdown*, turns into a happy joke about passion as destiny, eros as the dominating force in life. Apart from eros, of course, there isn't much life in Almodóvar—the world of work and family hardly exists. But this Spanish bad-boy writer-director does the comedy of sexual passion better than anyone else. The entire history of Spanish repression and guilt seems to gather inside the heads of his men and women; they are naturally explosive in ways that Americans, with their lesser sense of sin, their hygienic attitude toward sex, could never be.

The story, which has been freely adapted from a Ruth Rendell novel, teases symmetry into an Almodóvarian pretzel. Eager to become the world's greatest lover, Victor sleeps with the wives of the two Madrid policemen who put him in jail—first Clara (the great Angela Molina, of the tragic mask), who is much adored by her murderously obsessive husband, Sancho (Pepe Sancho), who loves a woman by trying to dominate her and, if necessary, kill her. Clara cheats on her husband in order to survive him, in both body and soul. Taking Victor in hand, she teaches him some of the more essential points of lovemaking, and under Clara's tutelage, he becomes a saner and gentler fellow—a better man, in every sense. You might say he is healed by sex. *Live Flesh*, which begins and ends on Christmas, is about salvation; Almodóvar is eros's last true worshiper.

Bored with Clara, Victor pursues the exquisite Elena (Francesca Neri), the woman who lured him into trouble some years earlier. It was at Elena's house that the 20-year-old Victor accidentally shot Sancho's partner, a promising young police detective named David (Javier Bardem). After the shooting, Elena, the daughter of the Italian consul, a rich girl dabbling in drugs, was so guilty over her own role in the affair that she married David, who had taken a bullet in the spine and was confined to a wheelchair. He's a dynamite wheelchair basketball player and a thoroughly virile man in every sense but the literal one. So the adulterous joining of Victor and Elena is charged with the many varieties of desire, guilt, and ambivalence. It's a scene worth waiting for—certainly the most sensual of Almodóvar's heterosexual love scenes.

Almodóvar's electric, brightly colored hyperbolic style has always teetered on the edge of camp and pornography. When he's going well, he achieves a delirious freedom of tone; when not so well, he horses his way into silliness. In *Live Flesh*, Almodóvar has stabilized his manner somewhat. The movie is not as startling and fantastic as *Law of Desire*, or *Matador*, but it doesn't settle into commonplace realism either. For Almodóvar, sexual passion is part of the cruel joke of Spanish guilt and fatalism. Sex is a matter of life and death that drives people into absurd situations: Almodóvar's most tragic scenes slide into farce (and vice-versa). These men and women seem not to possess "psychology" but only desire; that's all the psychology Almodóvar needs. It's a view of character that dissolves social reality. Would an elegant woman like Elena, the daughter of a foreign diplomat, marry a young policeman? Would she leave him for a young nobody? In this movie, such questions are beside the point. Almodóvar embraces the Mediterranean, or celebratory, view of sex, familiar from Boccaccio's stories, in which eros is a democracy of matching bodies and temperaments. Society, money, status all shrink to nothing. Despite his erotic fixations, Pedro Almodóvar is the cinema's last true innocent.

NEW YORK POST, 1/16/98, p. 44, Thelma Adams

Pedro Almodovar's "Live Flesh" begins and ends with a birth. In a rush to be born, the main character arrives in Madrid one gloomy night during the Franco regime.

Unlike its hero, Victor (Liberto Rabal), "Live Flesh" is in no hurry.

Loosely based on a Ruth Rendell novel, the movie, which closed last year's New York Film Festival and opens in theaters today, is a densely plotted thriller about five sensual adults who keep crossing paths.

The scene shifts from the '70s to contemporary Madrid. David (Javier Bardem) and Sancho (Jose Sancho) are cops. Sancho drinks to forget the infidelities of his wife, Clara (Angela Molina); or is it that his drinking leads to the brutal beatings that have driven her into the arms of other men?

One night, the two cops bust into an apartment where an armed rape is in progress—or so it appears. (In a video footnote, Luis Bunuel's "Rehearsal for a Crime," a.k.a. "The Criminal Life of Archibaldo de la Cruz," plays on TV.)

While attempting to capture the hapless Victor and protect Elena (Francesca Neri), David takes a bullet in the back and is paralyzed.

Seven years later, Victor leaves prison, vowing revenge. What he gets is a sexual education. His liberation touches the lives of David, Pancho, Clara and Elena. Guilt, lust, blood and passion bind them together in a *menage-a-cinq*.

With "Flesh," Almodovar streamlines his narrative. Gone are the supporting actors bouncing off the leads and swinging the story in unexpected directions.

Even the interiors, energetic expressions of the characters they surround, aren't as garish as we've come to expect from the director of "Women on the Verge of a Nervous Breakdown." It almost looks as if real people could live in them—almost.

Bardem ("Mouth to Mouth") and Molina ("That Obscure Object of Desire") lead the strong cast. The faces and bodies of the actors are vine-ripened and hand-picked. How can we ever forget that Antonio Banderas was an Almodovar find?

Almodovar directs sex scenes like no other. The coupling between Elena and Victor ignites a passion that changes them both. The director presents images of the naked human that are as sensual as Georgia O'Keeffe canvases, as stirring as the flamenco ballads on the soundtrack.

"Live Flesh" is a sigh of relief—a lover's sigh—for how far Madrid has come since the fall of fascism; a reminder to cherish freedom, to relish life and to have faith in the power of rebirth.

NEWSDAY, 1/16/98, Part II/p. B7, Jack Mathews

If Spanish director Pedro Almodovar, the master of the cinema of excess, continues making movies like his 1996 "The Flower of My Secret" and his new "Live Flesh," some of his fans are going to start sounding like Woody Allen fans: "I like his early, garish films best."

Not me. I like the new, more restrained, more focused Almodovar best. "The Flower of My Secret," which takes us through the mid-life crisis of a female romance novelist, demonstrated Almodovar's depth of empathy when he is not distracting himself with gaudy stylistic flourishes. And "Live Flesh," a melodrama about the interlocking lives of five people in contemporary Madrid, is his most balanced, and most mature film yet.

"Live Flesh," which had its American premiere at last fall's New York Film Festival, is a superbly conceived story, adapted loosely from British crime writer Ruth Rendell's novel, that manages to be simultaneously clear and complex, and done with an economy of time (the film is 90 fast-moving minutes long) that Quentin Tarantino would do well to note.

Once again, Almodovar is focusing on people who've come of age in the post-Franco era, a generation that doesn't have or want a sense of the country's immediate history. But here, the 46-year-old filmmaker, whose artistic life is a reaction to the totalitarian Spain he grew up in, makes a direct link.

The movie opens in 1970, as the government is adopting policies that make civil liberties virtually nonexistent. A pregnant young prostitute is roused from bed by the eagerness of her baby to be born, and hustled by her landlady aboard an empty bus, where her son arrives before they get to the hospital.

This pre-credit sequence has a whimsical, existential quality; it's a singular moment of humanity, with the bus driver and the landlady pitching in to bring a very lively baby into a country as dead as the night.

Cut to 20 years later, when that boy, Victor (Liberto Rabal), is attempting to keep a date he'd made with a woman he'd had casual sex with in a nightclub bathroom. She's Elena (Francesca Neri), a diplomat's drug-addicted daughter, and she wants nothing more to do with Victor. An argument erupts, a gun drawn, police are called, a scuffle ensues, a shot is fired, and one of the cops is left paralyzed.

This sequence is brilliantly structured, with intercutting scenes bringing Victor, Elena and the two policemen, the ill-fated David (Javier Bardem) and his drunk partner, Sancho (Jose Sancho), together. By the time of the shooting, we know a great deal about them and Sancho's wife, Clara (Angela Molina), whom we've seen nursing a black eye given her by her suspicious husband.

A few more years go by, and we return to the five people. Victor is being released from prison, intent on getting revenge on Elena, whom he blames for his predicament. She has reformed and, out of guilt, married David. Soon, Victor has re-entered their lives, beginning an affair with Clara, and setting in motion events that will threaten the two marriages and bring violence back into play.

With the exception of Sancho, who remains little more than a peevish, righteously jealous wife-batterer, Almodovar has created wonderfully complex and sympathetic characters. Victor is a desperate figure, but behavior that makes him seem a dangerous stalker at first is fleshed out in ways that mirror the growth of post-Franco Spain itself. He enters a world of despair and emptiness and finds all that its reinvigorated state has to offer.

Almodovar takes each of the characters, or at least four of them, through great transformations, all of which feed the film's theme of liberation. It's as if Almodovar has said all he has to say in the way of pure rebellion, and is changing course toward the future.

The new direction may not have the trashy irreverence that made him the cult hero of Spanish film, but with "Live Flesh," he becomes a highly accessible international filmmaker, and the best work of his career is likely still ahead.

SIGHT AND SOUND, 5/98, p. 50 José Arroyo

Madrid, 1970. In the empty streets of the city during a curfew, a young prostitute gives birth on a bus to a son, Victor. Twenty years later, Victor shows up for a date with Elena, the drug-addicted daughter of an Italian diplomat, but she barely remembers him. She threatens him with a gun. Two policemen, David and Sancho, arrive. David is shot and Victor is sent to jail. Two years later, Victor sees David, now a paraplegic and married to a now-sober Elena, playing meets basketball in the Barcelona Paralympics. Victor vows revenge.

After being released from jail, Victor sees Elena at her father's funeral and s Clara, Sancho's wife, with whom begins an affair. Victor gets a job at the children's shelter Elena works at. When David tries to confront Victor, Victor reveals that it was really Sancho—wanting revenge because of David's affair with Clara—who shot him. Elena goes to bed with Victor. Meanwhile, Clara decides o leave Sancho for Victor and shoots him when he tries to prevent her from leaving. Elena confesses to her affair with Victor to David. He goes to tell Sancho of Clara's affair with Victor and a badly wounded Sancho goes to kill his rival. Instead, he finds Clara at Victor's and the two men kill themselves. Some time later, Elena gives birth to Victor's son in a taxi. Victor tells his child how lucky he is to be born in a new Spain.

Live Flesh/Carne Trémula is the latest instalment of *l'amour à* Almodóvar. Few directors have mined the terrain of love in so many forms and with such delirious insistence. There's the sexual explorations of *Labyrinth of Passions;* the unrequited lesbian desire of the Mother Superior in *Dark Habits;* the murderous passion in *Matador;* the homosexual desire and brotherly love in *The Law of Desire;* the despair of abandonment in *Women on the Verge of a Nervous Breakdown*; and the feelings between mother and daughters in *High Heels,* and so on. That *Live Flesh* is based on a Ruth Rendell novel seems almost incidental since Almodóvar reprises many of his previous concerns, such as passions that drive characters to murder, love which makes them suffer and occasionally seek revenge, and life in Madrid itself. Yet *Live Flesh* also represents a departure from his previous work. This film's view on love is now rueful if still generous. Madrid is no longer quite the utopian pleasure place of yore. Recent Spanish history is finally acknowledged. The usual repertory of players is mostly absent. And more significantly, the treatment of the material is his 'straightest' yet—camp figures less than in his other films and, interestingly, not to *Live Flesh's* disadvantage.

Live Flesh has an attempted murder at its heart and is loosely structured as a who- and whydunit. However, the discovery of the would-be murderer is incidental to the film. What's important is that Sancho loves Clara who has loved David and is now in love with Victor and that Victor and David are both in love with Elena who is married to David but is soon to love Victor. The film's focus is on lushly accented emotions. The Spanish title is more descriptive than the novel's original English title: 'carne' in Spanish means 'flesh' but it also means 'meat', while 'live' does not quite convey the connotations of trembling and pulsating that 'trémula' does. This is only worth indicating because the Spanish title so perfectly describes the film's emotional pitch: raw, fearful, passionate, possibly deadly, but possibly delicious.

As in previous Almodóvar films, the songs in *Live Flesh* mostly of loss and pain, at times adumbrate, at times directly express the rawness of the characters' feelings. The music is drawn from a wider range than one normally associates with Almodóvar; the usual *boleros* and *flamencos* are there, but here is also bluesy urban rock and mournful rural *coplas,* all of which underline, intensify and sometimes counterpoint the characters' emotions. The most emotionally repressed character, perhaps because she's an upper-class foreigner (albeit Italian), is Elena. The rest are not afraid to court ridicule in the expression of their emotions. Perhaps with less expert actors such lines as 'the greatest pleasure for a woman in love is to please her man' might seem ridiculous, but the actors in *Live Flesh* put them over with only slightly stylised naturalism. Even Victor's confession to Elena of his plan for revenge—to become the best lover in the world, make her fall in love with him and then dump her—comes across as charming.

It is worth singling out Angela Molina and Javier Bardem for praise. The power of their presence has as much to do with the way Almodóvar uses their established star personas as with their highly skilled performances. Molina is famous for playing talented low-class women with high-class looks. Almodóvar uses a vibrant and youthful painting of her in full flamenco regalia to remind us of the beauty she was in the films of Buñuel *(That Obscure Object Of Desire),* Gutierrez-Aragón *(La mitad del cielo/Half the Sky)* and especially Chavarri *(Las cosas del querer).* When she pleads with Victor not to leave her, her face—still beautiful in spite of the harsh photography—is deeply moving not only because we know that this is her character's last chance at love, but because we've been with her before on her journeys around the block, at least at the movies.

Likewise Bardem, especially in the films of Bigas Luna, has come to represent the dangers of traditional macho culture in the new Spain. Part of the effectiveness of his characterisation here is that it reminds us so much of how an excess of testosterone led the character he played in *Golden Ball/Huevos de oro* to end up as a crippled cuckold in Miami. Here he is also in a wheelchair, once again paying the price, as his T-shirt ironically reminds us, of having been "100 per cent animal".

Live Flesh succeeds on various levels, but the densely textured *mise en scène* is particularly worth savouring. The gorgeous scene where Victor and Elena finally have sex and the camera moves so closely that their bodies become an abstraction in motion, as if carnal pleasure had transmuted into a more metaphysical love, will be fully appreciated on first viewing. So might the blatant use of legs (often prominently foregrounded and sometimes used to frame whole shots) as a symbol. Other equally brilliant touches will probably be less consciously perceptible on a first viewing, including the brilliantly coloured carpet in Elena's apartment; the way Clara's face is framed through a wreath to look like a Madonna dressed in flowers; the way David is filmed behind out-of-focus bars and in front of clearly visible rainbows.

Live Flesh is arguably Almodóvar's best film since *Women on the Verge of a Nervous Breakdown.* The films in between have all had brilliant moments or sections, but *Live Flesh* is a fully realised work, a sustained examination of how betrayal, guilt, revenge, desire and loss relate to love. It is a complex and moving film that is beautiful to look at. You'll want to see it again.

TIME, 2/23/98, p. 88, Richard Corliss

Victor (Liberto Rabal) has a lofty ambition: to become "the best lover in the world." And Clara (Angela Molina) is eager to coach him. The first lesson, she sagely informs him, is that "making love involves two people." He smiles, then asks, "And the second...?" Victor is a quick learner.

People in Pedro Almodóvar films, though, never learn quite fast enough to cope with the wild, melodramatic twists the Spanish writer-director hurls their way like grenades. That's one of the lovely things about Almodóvar epics like *Women on the Verge of a Nervous Breakdown* and *Tie*

Me Up! Tie Me Down!: they give you three movies' worth of plot in a fast 100 minutes or so. His sensuous, delirious new film, *Live Flesh,* has plenty. Victor is involved with two women, Clara and Elena (the sorcerous Francesca Neri), both of whom are married to jealous policemen. The story (based on a Ruth Rendell novel) begins in 1970 with a prostitute giving birth to Victor on a Madrid bus and, within half an hour, doles out drugs, sex, a triangular gun battle and a paraplegic policeman (Javier Bardem) who plays basketball in the 1992 Paralympics in Barcelona.

Obsession has seldom looked as gaudy or thrilling as here. One of the cops José Sancho), who is as doting as he is abusive, tells his wife, "As long as I love you, you're not leaving me." After a quickie with her lover, a woman rapturously smells her body—it still has his musk all over it. Few films these days are about sex, let alone love. Almodóvar is that rare moviemaker who still thinks they are as important as a space invasion or a sinking ship.

VILLAGE VOICE, 1/20/98, p. 61, J. Hoberman

"Chance is the fool's name for fate," as some comic *secondario* says in an Astaire-Rogers musical that, if you substituted flamenco for Jerome Kern, gunfire for taps, and sex for dancing, might seem a distant precursor to Pedro Almodóvar's droll meditation on destiny, *Live Flesh.*

A soap opera as convoluted as it is overdetermined, *Live Flesh*—which closed the last New York Film Festival follows the fate of Victor Plaza, the son of a Madrid prostitute, born in the middle of the night on an empty bus during the January 1970 state of emergency. The birth scene is a discreet gross-out—a setup for the movie's title, as well as its symmetrical ending. Twenty years later, Victor has grown into a fresh-faced hunk (Liberto Rabal) who, in the course of pursuing the diplomat's daughter he met and coupled with in a nightclub toilet, becomes the fall guy in a shooting that leaves a police officer paralyzed.

The movie's key scene is a baroque tour de force. Smitten Victor is bringing a stolen pizza to the agitated Elena (Francesca Neri, looking like a freaked-out Michelle Pfeiffer), a crackhead ditz who has forgotten their earlier tryst and mistakes Victor for her dealer. They argue, Elena pulls a gun and squeezes off a shot that brings a pair of squabbling cops—handsome, smarmy David and drunken, jealous Sancho—to her rescue. Where earlier there was actual emergency, here the TV broadcasts *Hospital: State of Emergency*. The TV is also showing Luis Buñuel's *El*, setting up a system of allusions that the movie never satisfies. Another shot is fired and, when next we see them, David is a wheelchair-basketball star, married to Elena (now a social worker), while Victor languishes in prison.

The reference to *El* suggests that *Live Flesh* might be a dark comedy of male sexual jealousy. The material is there—like Buñuels, Almodóvar's characters are prone to impulse behavior. (In one grotesque altercation, a territorial fight between two machos is suspended by their fascination with a televised soccer goal.) Angela Molina, one of the title characters in Buñuel's *That Obscure Object of Desire*, is even on hand to complicate the proceedings. But, as *Live Flesh* runs its course with Victor's release from prison, any particular theme dissolves in a series of enjoyable non sequiturs founded on a posthippie hedonism of casual drugs and sex. Victor stalks Elena while carrying on with Sancho's wife Clara (Molina) as David spies on them, the fate that had earlier brought them all together in Elena's father's apartment continuing to play itself out.

Generous entertainer that he is, Almodóvar would seem to be looking for new sorts of material. (How I regret that he was not drafted to direct *Evita*). Here, the filmmaker has evidently taken a crime thriller and suavely twisted it to his own aggressively local devices—too bad they're so modest. The subtexts juxtapose Spain's increasing political liberalism with Madrid's changed landscape. The mise-en-scène of exotic profiles and designer apartments is confidently wide-screen, if more subdued than in previous Almódavar outings. Style is still substance: this is the sort of movie in which a woman puts on a red dress to go out and commit adultery (or, alternately shoot her husband).

"I've never lied to you," Elena tells David. "Yes, you've been offensively honest" is his considered reply. And so it is with *Live Flesh*. The movie is well constructed but weightless. Much of it is instantly forgettable and yet, there, are daring bits of business you will never see in a Hollywood movie—a prisoner reading a letter about his mother's cancer while his cellmate jerks off, or a woman in the shower, passionately sniffing her body after a night of sex.

Also reviewed in:
NEW YORK TIMES, 1/16/98, p. E18, Janet Maslin
VARIETY, 10/13-19/97, p. 84, Lisa Nesselson
WASHINGTON POST, 2/13/98, p. D1, Stephen Hunter
WASHINGTON POST, 2/13/98, Weekend/p. 47, Desson Howe

LIVING OUT LOUD

A New Line Cinema release of a Jersey Films production. *Producer:* Danny DeVito, Michael Shamberg, and Stacey Sher. *Director:* Richard LaGravenese. *Screenplay:* Richard LaGravenese. *Director of Photography:* John Bailey. *Editor:* Jon Gregory and Lynzee Klingman. *Music:* George Fenton. *Music Editor:* Nick Meyers. *Choreographer:* Frank Gatson, Jr. *Sound:* Petur Hliddal. *Sound Editor:* Stan Bochner and Stuart Levy. *Casting:* Margery Simkin. *Production Designer:* Nelson Coates. *Art Director:* Joseph Hodges. *Set Designer:* Bruce Hill and Jerry Sullivan. *Set Decorator:* Linda Lee Sutton. *Set Dresser:* Hawley Anderson, Mark Andersen, Rick Chinelli, Paul Penley, Joe Grafmuller, James Harper, and Randy Severino. *Special Effects:* John Ziegler. *Costumes:* Jeffrey Kurland. *Make-up:* Valli O'Reilly. *Make-up (Holly Hunter):* Kathrine James. *Stunt Coordinator:* Steve Davison. *Running time:* 102 minutes. *MPAA Rating:* R.

CAST: Holly Hunter (Judith Nelson); Danny DeVito (Pat Francato); Queen Latifah (Liz Bailey); Martin Donovan (Bob Nelson); Richard Schiff (Philly); Elias Koteas (The Kisser); Suzanne Shepherd (Mary); Mariangela Pino (Donna); Eddie Cibrian (Masseur); Clark Anderson (Gary); Ellen McElduff (Crying Woman); Ivan Kronenfeld (Angry Boyfriend); Fil Formicola and Nick Sandow (Santi's Men); Jenette Goldstein (Fanny, Pat's Wife); Lin Shaye (Lisa's Nurse); John F. Donohue (Sid); Fred Scialla (Johnny); Anthony Russell (Mo); Sy Sher (Lou); Sal Jenco (Len); Gina Philips (Lisa); Kate McGregor-Stewart (Female Diner); Mitch Greenberg (Anchorman Voice-over); Tamlyn Tomita (Bob's Wife); Henry Woronicz and Taylor Leigh (Fifth Avenue Parents); Matthew McKane (Andy); Robin McDonald (Heckled Singer); Yolanda Snowball (Jasper's Waitress); Deborah Geffner (Woman with Make-up); Rachael Leigh Cook (Teenage Judith); Christian Hill (Teenage Lover); Ed Fry (Formal Dress Man); Judith Regan (Formal Dress Woman); Sean Dooley (Late Teenager); Terry Rhoads (Across Hall Man); Susan Reno (Across Hall Woman); Claudia Shear (Drunken Fan); Mike G. Moyer (Jeweler); Roger Nehls and Mary Schmidtberger (Married Couple in Lawyer's Office); Lou Richards (Judith's Lawyer); Tom Howard (Bob's Lawyer); Michael Clair Miller (Couple's Lawyer); Willie Garson (Man in Elevator); Ellen Buckley (Pat & Judith's Waitress); Laura Salvato (Neo-Natal AIDS Volunteer); Hattie Winston (Hospital Nurse); Mario Piccirillo (Cousin Louie); Carole Ruggier (Italian Girlfriend).

CHRISTIAN SCIENCE MONITOR, 10/30/98, p. B3, David Sterritt

[*Living Out Loud* was reviewed jointly with *Pleasantville*; see Sterritt's review of that film.}

LOS ANGELES TIMES, 10/30/98, Calendar/p. 1, Kenneth Turan

"Don't treat me like I'm stupid, Bob," says Judith Nelson in the opening moments of "Living Out Loud," her husband lying to her and on the way to leaving after 16 years of marriage. But Bob's not the only one who treats Judith badly—she also does it to herself.

Written and directed by Richard LaGravenese, "Living Out Loud" is a film of eccentric charm, a warm and sympathetic character comedy about romance, vulnerability and the odd turns the search for one's self can take. Natural and playful, ragged but alive, "Living" is the kind of unexpected but welcome picture that doesn't have points it wants to make so much as lives it wants to explore.

What's not unexpected about "Living," given LaGravenese's presence, is the quality of the writing, with scenes filled with surprising, sophisticated dialogue and an empathetic touch where relationships are concerned.

With credits including the adaptations of "Beloved," "The Horse Whisperer," "The Bridges of Madison County, "A Little Princess" and "Unstrung Heroes" (which this film most closely resembles), LaGravenese has written more often than not about the dilemmas of women's lives, a knowledge that gets put to use here.

A writer before he is anything else, LaGravenese has made his direction serve the dialogue, not the other way around, and a welcome change of pace that is. As a first-time director, LaGravenese has also made sure to surround himself with excellent support, including such veteran behind-the-scenes personnel as cinematographer John Bailey, composer George Fenton and costume designer Jeffrey Kurland (who does fine things with Judith's clothes). Also impressive is a cast that includes stars Holly Hunter, Danny DeVito and Queen Latifah and supporting players Martin Donovan and Elias Koteas.

It's Hunter who plays visiting nurse Judith, and as she copes with being left for a younger woman by caddish neurosurgeon husband Bob (poker-faced Donovan, perfectly cast), it seems a familiar role.

Oppressed by the walls of her Fifth Avenue apartment, brittle, edgy and high-strung Judith shares her worries and fantasies, her fears of being invisible and the always-difficult New York question, "What if I wind up alone and wrinkled in Queens?"

What gets Judith through the early days is her love for the music of Liz Bailey, a Billie Holiday-type jazz singer who works out of a small club on the Upper West Side called Jaspers. Expertly played and sung by Queen Latifah in a series of exotic diva gowns, Liz Bailey's soulful way with standards like "Lush Life" and "Be Anything (But Be Mine)" acts as a kind of Greek chorus to Judith's uncertainties.

But one night at Jaspers, in an event that LaGravenese says was inspired by the Chekhov short story "The Kiss," Judith is passionately embraced by a man (Koteas in an against-type warm role) who has mistaken her for someone else but seems to want to know her better even after the misunderstanding is cleared up.

That kiss seems to open something up in Judith, so much so that she notices and begins to befriend the elevator operator in her building, someone we've already gotten to know as a kind-hearted, ill-starred man named Pat Francato (DeVito).

Though he doesn't share them with Judith at first, Pat has numerous troubles of his own. In serious debt to loan sharks, the father of a gravely ill daughter and living small after his wife of 25 years threw him out ("It kind of took the fun out of the marriage," he cracks), Pat still has dreams of being a success in business on his own terms.

If this sounds suspiciously like the start of an odd-couple cute-meet romance, it's a measure of the quality of "Living Out Loud" that what develops is a complex, fully human and unpredictable relationship. Roughly the same height but so physically dissimilar as to have come from separate universes, Hunter and her co-star turn out to work especially well with each other, and DeVito ends up giving one of the more low-key and appealing performances of his career.

But while "Living Out Loud" wouldn't be as successful as it is without those vivid performances from both DeVito and Latifah, it is Hunter's character the film is most interested in. As Judith interacts with a wide variety of New Yorkers, from her patients to a handsome specialist in erotic massage, her character starts to become more malleable, less brittle. It's a process rife with doubts, regrets and uncertainties, but in Hunter's accomplished hands, Judith begins to gradually, and believably, reclaim her sense of self and her own life.

None of this happens anywhere nearly that directly, for LaGravenese has elected to unfold his story in a quirky, completely unschematic way. "Living Out Loud" meanders through fantasy and reality, doing without rigorous plotting in favor of unexpected character moments. It's a film that knows its way around relationships, and it's difficult to ask for more than that.

NEW YORK, 11/9/98, p. 58, Peter Rainer

Set inside New York's carnival din, "Living Out Loud" has a sweet, almost numinous quality. It's a weepie that doesn't weep for itself, a sidelong glimpse at the comedy of woe. It's about two lonely people—Holly Hunter's Judith and Danny DeVito's Pat—who find each other and feel less alone. The writer-director Richard LaGravanese keeps things open and ambiguous and a little messy, just like life.

A starry-eyed realist, LaGravanese wants the world to be like the movies, but he's too levelheaded to sustain the illusion. He offers up the familiar trappings of movie romance but then subverts them, gently. Judith, for example, resembles a standard-issue wronged-woman waif, but she's much kickier than that. You can't get a fix on her. At the beginning of the film, she finds herself suddenly single after sixteen years as the well-appointed Upper East Side wife of a prominent cardiologist (Martin Donovan) who has dropped her for a younger woman. Alone in her chill, spacious co-op, she lip-synchs bluesy jazz vocals and keeps the lights down low. She might as well be living in a mausoleum. Pain has transformed her existence into a sort of wide-awake sleep walk; she's benumbed yet ardent. When she sits in the audience, alone, at her favorite neighborhood blues club, she wears a smile so tight it could pass for a wince. Liquor loosens her tongue. In the ladies room she accosts another woman, a total stranger, making up before the mirror: *What is the point? He's just going to dump you.* If your heart goes out to Judith, it's not because she sent an engraved invitation. She's a handful, and she doesn't try to make nice. But a delicacy comes through her anyway. She's so avid for human connection that at times she's as touching as Katharine Hepburn aching to be asked to dance in *Alice Adams*.

LaGravanese doesn't allow us to get a fix on Pat, either. The doorman in Judith's co-op, he's been turned out by his wife after 25 years. It's not so long since he was selling hot watches and driving a gypsy cab, and he seems ill-fitted and a little clownish in his doorman's duds. Wearing the uniform italicizes him; it showcases his failure. He's prideful, though: Out of uniform, he's quite a snappy dresser. He's surprisingly mulish too. He owes money to some local mobsters but can't stomach the thought of covering his debts by bartending for his brother Philly (Richard Schiff). Instead, he dreams of starting up an Italian-foods import business with an uncle in Sorrento.

Riding with Judith in the elevator late one evening, Pat lets slip that his terminally ill daughter has just died. It ought to be a terminally icky sequence, but LaGravanese has the elevator doors slam shut on them just as the moment sinks in. This slapstick heartbreak soon gives way to something sweeter: Judith sits with Pat in his cramped office and attempts to make him feel better. As down as he is, Pat is still aware enough to recognize her troubles. He tries to cheer her up, too. They get friendly, and because their emotions are so up-front, we never think of their involvement in class terms. Judith is still faintly enameled with an Upper East Side hauteur, but it's the part of her she's trying to chip away. Pat has so much spirit that we're never moved to condescend to him as a working-class Poor Soul. He's a lot closer to Chekhov than to Chayefsky (in fact, the film has vague links to two Chekhov stories, "The Kiss" and "Memory").

A true New York romance, *Living Out Loud* brings the city into the mix as an equal protagonist. In LaGravanese's view, Manhattan's raucous, close-packed unpredictability is all of a piece with the vagaries of love: You never know whose squall of a life you're suddenly going to be swept into. Pat's career running the elevators is a perfect metaphor for this: Every ride up and down is somebody's mini-drama. One of them becomes his own.

LaGravanese has a reputation for toning up sob-sister acts like *The Bridges of Madison Count* and *The Horse Whisperer*. But his scripts for the neglected *A Little Princess* and *Unstrung Heroes* and *The Fisher King* (at least the Mercedes Ruehl and Amanda Plummer parts) were dazzling. They showcased what also shines in *Living Out Loud*—a rapt intimacy. He's never directed a movie before, and he doesn't give us much to look at except the actors. But boy, does he love actors! He gives his fine supporting players—including the voluminously voluptuous Queen Latifah as a blues-club singer and, especially, Schiff—fully lived-in roles. And he draws out his leading actors in ways we haven't seen before. Judith's sudden singlehood is not, for the most part, framed as some sort of feminist growth experience. She's frankly miserable, and her pathos has a crazy, dangerous energy. LaGravanese has worked out a tricky structure in which Judith's daydreams and nightmares often seem visually inseparable from her actual life. The strategy is sometimes unnecessarily confusing, but psychologically it makes perfect sense: Judith is so vibrantly present that it seems only natural her fantasies should co-exist with her reality. Hunter, in her most daring performance, works both sides of the character equally well, whether sitting demurely by herself at a swank French restaurant, reading *House of Mirth,* or throwing elbow jabs at her ex-husband in an elevator. She has a powerhouse fortitude *and* a powerhouse winsomeness.

DeVito, too, is a revelation. I've often been turned off by his relentless pugnacity; he's not just a cartoon, he's a *bullying* cartoon. But when he cans the yammering and lets a real person come through, he can be effective. He was fine in the otherwise negligible *Renaissance Man,* playing a teacher on a military base, and he scored as an aluminum-siding salesman in *Tin Men.* In *Living Out Loud,* he has his best role yet, and he does it full justice. His bluster has converted itself into deep reserves of feeling. It's as if he finally figured out what acting can *do.*

Standard movie romances are fond of bringing mismatches together. LaGravanese shows us why they might be kept apart. Judith and Pat are made for each other, but they may not be right for each other, and therein lies the rub of this rueful duet.

NEW YORK POST, 10/30/98, p. 35, Rod Dreher

At last, a romantic comedy for grown-ups! The urbane, smartly written "Living Out Loud" is a lissome and light-footed October surprise, the kind of textured, mature picture that makes fall such a rewarding season at the movies.

This tale of a ritzy Manhattan divorcee struggling to get her groove back after her crumb-bum hubby dumps her for a pretty young thing has all the trappings of a high-gloss chick flick, a formulaic Lifetime channel movie on a Hollywood budget. Wrong.

The tip-off that "Living Out Loud" will be something special is the involvement of Richard LaGravenese, who wrote the film and also makes a remarkably self-assured directorial debut. In his previous film adaptations ("The Bridges of Madison County" and others), LaGravenese has demonstrated an uncommon facility for gracefully detailed dialogue that conveys emotional nuance, particularly with women characters.

In his first original screenplay since "The Fisher King," LaGravenese strikes gold, giving us larky, complex characters worth our time and our empathy. He takes them, dateless in Manhattan, on a bittersweet comic journey through the travails of midlife loneliness, vulnerability and uncertainty, making unexpected and often charming diversions along the way to an unpredictable ending.

Holly Hunter is spectacular as Judith Nelson, a fortysomething Fifth Avenue wife cast aside after 16 years by Bob, her unfaithful husband (Martin Donovan). She's alone and angry, antsy and miserable in her fancy East Side digs, terrified that she'll end up old and alone in Queens, and at a loss as to what her next move should be.

Desperate to get out of the house, Judith dresses up and makes solo journeys across Central Park to Jaspers, an Upper West Side jazz boite where she finds consolation in martinis and lush jazz standards crooned by the soulfully elegant Liz Bailey (Queen Latifah). One night at the club, Judith stumbles through the wrong door and into the arms of a stranger (Elias Koteas), who kisses her passionately.

It's a case of mistaken identity, and not the meet-cute it appears to be—LaGravenese's script keeps charmingly defying our expectations—but the kiss hits Judith like an epiphany. It awakens her to romantic possibility.

It also gets her to notice stubby little Pat (Danny DeVito), the elevator man in her building. He's stewing in his own midlife crisis: deeply in debt, estranged from his wife, worried about his sick child and hurting for a chance to redeem himself. Pat and Judith pour out their hearts to each other, and they do have a warm, appealing rapport. Their relationship plays out sweetly, but with a prickly, wide-awake sense of realism that years of sifting through by-the-numbers Hollywood romances hasn't prepared us for.

The marvelous Hunter has the high-strung act down to a science—imagine her "Broadcast News" character coming to life after years as a Lady Who Lunches—but it's DeVito and Latifah who give the film depth and resonance. If you only know her as a rapper, or from her gritty performance in "Set It Off," you will be amazed at how a gorgeous gown and a velvety jazz ballad brings out her softer side. And DeVito invests a character that could have been a shlumpy pity party with bright humor and sparkling dignity.

"Living Out Loud" is not perfect, but there's much easygoing pleasure to be found in watching these likable New Yorkers work out their destiny. There are no do-or-die scenes, just a playful grab bag of moments where these familiar folks relearn, in funny fits and starts, the art of living. It feels mighty real.

NEWSDAY, 10/30/98, Part II/p. B3, John Anderson

For all its understated charm and frankness, one gets the sense about "Living Out Loud" that screenwriter-turned-director Richard LaGravenese is purging himself of a lot of notions he's been collecting while watching his screenplays being executed by his various employers of the moment—usually an actor-turned-director.

Of course, when you've written movies for other people—better yet, when you've written movies that have frequently saved other people—you must store up a virtual catalog of directorial spare parts.

So: Is "Living Out Loud" a reaction movie? A contrarian but no less self-reflective survey of his work? You might read it that way. It's certainly an East Coast, urban romance—no "Horse Whisperer" holiness about the sanctifying wide open spaces.

Holly Hunter, who gives as naked and tic-less a performance as she's ever turned in, is shot by cinematographer John Bailey ("As Good As It Gets") with as little cosmetic enhancement as possible—no "Mirror Has Two Face Lifts"-style haloed backlighting, a la Streisand.

The characters are odd—not cartoon odd, as in LaGravenese's "Unstrung Heroes" or certifiably odd, as in his "The Fisher King"—merely Manhattan eccentric. Love? It's both elastic and elusive. And a long, long way from his "The Bridges of Madison County."

LaGravenese, who also adapted Tony Morrison's "Beloved," works from his own original screenplay, which is about Judith Nelson, an Upper East Side doctor's wife who loses her doctor. There's no warmup: LaGravenese drops us unceremoniously into a restaurant meltdown between husband and wife that tells us everything we need to know about her, him (the always terrific Martin Donovan) and why the marriage is kaput. There isn't a two-shot in the whole sequence. Each is shown as solitary as they are, will be and obviously have been.

LaGravenese will double back to this scene—just as he doubles back repeatedly, throwing us red-herring hallucinations and imagined encounters and makes us privy to Judith's internal monologues ("I hate these terrorists!" she sputters, in reaction to the news. "Why can't they just get over it!!!"). But first he has to give us Judith's counterweight in this minor tragedy.

Pat (Danny DeVito), a gambler with debts and a dying daughter, is a member of the occasionally unemployed working as Judith's doorman. We meet him en route to a meeting where he spies a woman crying bitterly on a park bench. He's not a bad guy. He wants to help. But first, he checks his watch. Which tells us a lot about Pat, and a lot about LaGravenese.

"Living Out Loud" is a dialogue-driven movie; there haven't been conversations this long, and visuals this static, since "My Dinner With Andre" (which he did not write). But it works, over all. Judith, snagged on the barb wire separating youth and age, is thoroughly believable—neurotic, generous, manic, self-pitying, looking for love but not quite desperate.

This is no fairy tale about unlikely lovers—unlikely friends, yes, but lovers no. Judith forms a sisterly bond with Liz, the torch singer played by rapper-actress Queen Latifah (who may not be Sarah Vaughan, but can do a sultry "Lush Life" nonetheless). She has an anonymous clinch with an anonymous man (Elias Koteas) that rocks her world. She has a few bad moments with her ex, but who hasn't? (In the movies, that is.)

And she reaches a certain level of contentment—not Hollywood resolution, not fantasy elation, just maturity and adulthood of a brand you can buy. You don't know what's in store for Judith when the movie ends, but you know she's given LaGravenese something he isn't getting anywhere else.

NEWSWEEK, 11/2/98, p. 78, David Ansen

Judith Nelson (Holly Hunter), The tightly wound, bottle-blond heroine of "Living Out Loud," may be the most fully imagined female character in an American movie this year. A lonely, angry divorcée who's full of surprises, she is—like the movie itself—as entertaining to watch as she is hard to pigeonhole. Judith is holed up in her big Fifth Avenue apartment after her 17-year marriage to a philandering doctor (Martin Donovan) has collapsed. She's locked inside her overactive mind, and writer-director Richard LaGravenese lets us eavesdrop on her internal conversations; he takes us inside her fantasies—some as drastic as suicide, others as banal as having someone to dine with. The film is about how this complicated, unfinished woman finds her way back into the world—back to living out loud, with a voice she can call her own.

No typical Upper East Side matron, Judith now works as a day nurse. At night, she takes her overdressed self to a jazz club to listen to her favorite torch singer, Liz Bailey (Queen Latifah). One night at the club, searching for a bathroom, she opens the wrong door, is yanked into a dark room and is passionately embraced by a total stranger. It's a mistake—the man was expecting another woman—but it lights her romantic fire. Flush with the prospect of a new love, she's reawakened to the world.

One of the first things she sees with her new eyes is her doorman, Pat (Danny DeVito), who confides in her about the recent death of his daughter. Estranged from his wife and deep in debt, Pat is touched by Judith's genuine concern—and eager to think her interest in him is romantic. It isn't, but he's determined to change her mind. You may think you know where this story is leading, but LaGravenese is too honest an observer to play by conventional Hollywood rules.

LaGravenese understands—and Hunter's daring, funny performance captures—just how fluid our identities can be. Judith doesn't always act "in character," because her personality is in constant motion. Hunter gradually unpeels the layers of pretense this Southern girl has acquired as she's traded up in the world, abandoning her old friends—and too much of her real self—along the way. Hunter has always had a great high-strung comic style, and the film gives her some hilarious opportunities to demonstrate her talent for rage and pent-up sensuality. "Living Out Loud" is full of moments we haven't seen before: there's a sexy and funny scene in which Judith summons an erotic masseur to her apartment, and the experience shoots her back in time to her first teenage experience of lust.

One of Hollywood's most-sought-after screenwriters ("The Fisher King," "The Bridges of Madison County," "The Horse Whisperer"), LaGravenese gets his first opportunity to direct here, and his assurance is impressive. He's gotten from DeVito the most subtle, touching performance of his career. Pat could have been milked for sad-sack pathos, but DeVito gives him spine: he fights for his right to be considered a romantic contender. Queen Latifah—big and sultry and wry—is an amazing screen presence, and her commanding way around a standard like "Lush Life" will startle those who know her only as a rapper. You want more of her story than the movie gives you. "Living Out Loud" is far from seamless—the last third of the movie has a choppy rhythm and an ending that doesn't quite work—but it's alive in all the ways that count. LaGravenese dramatizes nuances most filmmakers wouldn't even think to try. This un-hyped, delightfully grown-up comedy is the sleeper of the season.

SIGHT AND SOUND, 2/99, p. 47, Peter Matthews

New York City. After 16 years of marriage, home-nurse Judith Nelson's husband Bob dumps her for another woman. Meanwhile, Pat, the lift operator in Judith's building, desperately attempts to pay off his debt to some loan sharks. When his daughter Lisa dies, Pat's wife throws him out and he moves in with his brother Philly. At Jasper's Jazz Club, Judith listens to torch-singer Liz Bailey. Looking for the toilet, she finds herself in a clinch with a stranger expecting someone else. Later, a euphoric Judith invites Pat in for coffee. When their conversation is interrupted by the loan sharks, Pat borrows $200 from Judith.

Philly agrees to lend Pat $400 so that he can repay and woo Judith. Pat confesses to Judith his dream of importing Italian food. Philly consents to pay off Pat's debt and finance a trip to Italy if he will work part-time in his bar. At the club, Judith searches for her handsome stranger in vain. Returning home drunk, she rudely ignores Pat and seeks solace with a male masseur. Later, she apologises to Pat but hesitates to accept his offer of a romantic dinner. However, after Liz gives her some happy pills, Judith ravishes a baffled Pat in the lift. Accompanying Liz to a lesbian club, Judith slow-dances with a young woman. Pat invites Judith to Italy with him but she refuses. Some months later, a happier Judith spots Pat at the jazz club with an Italian woman.

Directed by Richard LaGravenese, screenwriter of *The Fisher King*, *The Horse Whisperer* and other films, the best that can be said for the feminist rites-of-passage comedy *Living Out Loud* is that it seems to suffer from a guilty conscience. The movie plays a complicated shell game with the viewer, raising a whole slew of issues and then juggling the story elements so that you won't notice what a phoney bill of goods you've been sold. Probably no one is fooled while

LaGravenese ties himself up in knots trying to explain why things can't work out between the madcap heroine Judith and her adoring suitor Pat. The film is ostensibly about two lyrical lost souls whose transient relationship gives them the courage to look life straight in the eye. But since he is the lowly lift operator in her exclusive Upper East Side building, their crypto-romance is flatly unequal—and the film would rather die than admit that.

There are, however, one or two strangely jarring scenes where the unstated irony of the picture almost spills out. In the first, Judith details the circumstances of her broken marriage and describes her long-term goal of becoming a paediatrician. Without a flicker of resentment, Pat replies that it must be nice if you're rich and can pick yourself up like that. While his subsequent request for a loan might be interpreted as class revenge, the disquieting ambiguity of this exchange is left hanging like a bad odour. Later on, Judith endeavours to dampen Pat's ardour by declaring her wish to be "authentic". Again, the film speedily backs away from its own nagging suspicion that her fumbling quest for personal meaning is strictly a middle-class enterprise. Judith's existential freedom and Pat's material determinism are silently registered in *a mise en scène* that contrasts the vast open spaces of her apartment with the claustrophobic confinement of the lift.

But though *Living Out Loud* gingerly concedes that class does matter, it also attempts to anaesthetise the viewer to this insight's nastier implications, just when you have Judith pegged as a moral leech who recharges her batteries at a working man's expense, the movie squelches this impious thought by a providential bolt from the blue: she is exposed as a former guttersnipe who has merely learned to 'do' the Upper East Side. By a similar sleight of hand, the misused Pat gets fobbed off with a buxom Italian beauty and a pasta import business, so we don't have to worry about him.

One hesitates to say it, but *Living Out Loud* seems very American in its social attitudes. The film would make up an instructive double bill with Ken Loach's *My Name Is Joe,* so emotionally devastating in its picture of the objective forces driving apart its two lovers. Admittedly, LaGravenese is making a comedy, but the facile melting-pot ideology he milks results in one of the more unintelligible and shape-shifting protagonists in screen history.

As if her class vampirism weren't enough, Judith has an incidental nibble at race in the form of a sisterly alliance with Liz, the sultry black chanteuse at a jazz dive. Does anybody really believe that this powerhouse would give a needy white woman like Judith the time of day? Yet LaGravenese seems determined to perform a clean sweep, since he also broaches the question of our heroine's inchoate sexuality. The film invents its own curious New York ritual of ladies who lunch and stare inquisitively at Judith over her copy of Edith Wharton. Finally, she's ready to take the plunge at an upscale lesbian club, which must have the strictest babe only door policy imaginable. After dancing in tight formation with a number of these foxes, Judith begins to nuzzle one experimentally—but the rest is silence. What's pathetic about the movie is that it tries to conjure away the unresolved class theme by replacing it with the lesbian theme, and then cops out on that too. You're meant to conclude that the newly empowered Judith has many choices to make and miles to go before she sleeps with anyone, a comfy platitude that's like a big red ribbon tying up this parcel of evasions and falsehoods.

VILLAGE VOICE, 11/10/98, p. 115, Gary Susman

Apparently, it's called *Living Out Loud* because its characters scream at each other and divulge their most intimate secrets to strangers. No, it's not a Jerry Springer episode, but a glossy comedy-drama about three New Yorkers of diverse backgrounds who make improbable emotional connections and help each other overcome their similar neuroses and live their dreams. In other words, it's *As Good As It Gets, Part Deux.*

Judith (a blond Holly Hunter) is a Fifth Avenue divorcee whose journey of self-discovery begins when she walks on the wild (Upper West) side and is kissed by a stranger in a jazz club. Suddenly, she is able to notice Pat (Danny DeVito), her elevator operator, who's also coping with financial and personal losses. In a more conventional romantic comedy, Judith and Pat would defy class barriers and become a couple, but her newfound self-realization does not extend to acknowledging her attraction to him. Judith does cross racial barriers to befriend a jazz singer, Liz (Queen Latifah), who avoids commitment by associating with gay men. While the film ridicules the use of African Americans as a pop-cultural symbol of raw emotional candor, that's nonetheless how it employs Liz.

Richard LaGravenese peppers his directorial debut with the narrative trickery (fantasy sequences, flashbacks) that often tangles his sceenplays *(The Fisher King, Beloved)*. He continues to display a rare sensitivity to women's emotional lives (he's also adapted such Lifetime-y novels as *The Horse Whisperer)*, and the scenes in which Judith enjoys a masseur's full-service visit and a grope session at a lesbian club are refreshingly nonjudgmental. They're also, like much of the movie, woozily absurd.

Also reviewed in:
CHICAGO TRIBUNE, 11/5/98, Friday/p. A, Mark Caro
NEW YORK TIMES, 10/30/98, p. E14, Janet Maslin
NEW YORKER, 11/30/98, p. 130, David Denby
VARIETY, 9/28-10/4/98, p. 44, Daniel M. Kimmel
WASHINGTON POST, 11/6/98, p. D5, Rita Kempley
WASHINGTON POST, 11/6/98, Weekend/p. 47, Michael O'Sullivan

LOLITA

A Samuel Goldwyn Films release of a Pathe production. *Producer:* Mario Kassar and Joel B. Michaels. *Director:* Adrian Lyne. *Screenplay:* Stephen Schiff. *Based on the novel by:* Vladimir Nabokov. *Director of Photography:* Howard Atherton. *Editor:* Julie Monroe and David Brenner. *Music:* Ennio Morricone. *Music Editor:* Bill Abbott. *Sound:* Charles Wilborn. *Sound Editor:* Michael O'Farrell. *Casting:* Ellen Chenoweth. *Production Designer:* Jon Hutman. *Art Director:* W. Steven Graham. *Set Decorator:* Debra Schutt and Steve Parenti. *Special Effects:* Joseph Mercurio. *Visual Effects:* Jeffrey A. Okun. *Costumes:* Judianna Makovsky. *Make-up:* Richard Dean. *Stunt Coordinator:* Danny Aiello III. *Running time:* 137 minutes. *MPAA Rating:* Not Rated.

CAST: Jeremy Irons (Humbert Humbert); Melanie Griffith (Charlotte Haze); Frank Langella (Clare Quilty); Dominique Swain (Lolita); Suzanne Shepherd (Miss Pratt); Keith Reddin (Reverend Rigger); Erin J. Dean (Mona); Joan Glover (Miss LeBone); Pat P. Perkins (Louise); Ed Grady (Dr. Melnick); Michael Goodwin (Mr. Beale); Angela Paton (Mrs. Holmes); Ben Silverstone (Young Humbert); Emma Griffiths-Malin (Annabel Leigh); Ronald Pickup (Young Humbert's Father); Michael Culkin (Mr. Leigh); Annabelle Apsion (Mrs. Leigh); Don Brady (Frank McCoo); Trip Hamilton (Dr. Blue); Michael Dolan (Dick); Hallee Hirsch (Little Girl in Bunny Suit); Scot Brian Higgs and Mert Hatfield (Accident Policemen); Chris Jarman and Jim Grimshaw (Policemen); Hudson Lee Long (Elderly Clerk); Lenore Banks (Nurse at Hospital); Dorothy Deavers (Receptionist); Donnie Boswell Sr. (Taxi Driver); Judy Duggan (Singer/Piano Player); Margaret Hammonds (Nurse); Paula Davis (Motel Clerk); Tim Gallin (Hospital Orderly).

CINEASTE, Vol. XXIV, No. 1, p. 71, Richard Porton

Despite the fact that Vladimir Nabokov condemned Humbert Humbert, the anti-hero of his most famous novel, *Lolita*, as a "vain and cruel wretch who manages to appear 'touching,'" moralists of all stripes continue to smear the Russian emigré's modernist classic as either nothing more than a dirty book or a full-blown example of sexist debauchery. Part of this misunderstanding may arise from the fact that many readers fail to recognize Humbert's unreliable first-person narration as profoundly ironic or the even more likely possibility that the Christian rightists and antiporn feminists who fume at the mere mention of Nabokov's name have not even cracked *Lolita's* spine.

The preemptive strike launched against Adrian Lyne's new adaptation of *Lolita*, a venomous campaign which surpasses the mildly hostile reception which greeted Stanley Kubrick's 1962 version, was undoubtedly engendered by the recent American preoccupation with child abuse and molestation. Although child abuse is certainly a heinous crime, the rage that was directed against Lyne's film long before it was released has little to do with actual sex crimes and is instead bound up with our ongoing confusion concerning the relationship between childhood and sexuality. As James Kincaid has recently pointed out, "Our culture has enthusiastically sexualized the child while denying just as enthusiastically that it was doing any such thing." Both Nabokov's book and Lyne's film are relatively chaste when compared with most modern depictions of sexuality, but they undeniably undermine the myth of childhood innocence (Lolita is unquestionably a victim, but not a virginal, asexual preteen) that our neo-Victorian guardians of morality cherish. The ad campaign for Stanley Kubrick's 1962 adaptation teased audiences by posing the question, "How did they ever make a movie of *Lolita*?" But despite James Mason's suave performance as Humbert and Peter Sellers's inimitably brilliant turn as Humbert's nemesis, Clare Quilty, the film remained an oblique—if extremely entertaining—black comedy that failed to confront the implications of Humbert's monstrous passion. As difficult as it may be for many critics to admit, Lyne, a director often regarded as a *schlockmeister,* produced a film that is more faithful to the spirit of Nabokov's tragicomic indictment of self-delusion and moral dementia.

Indeed, the sophisticated condescension that some of the tonier critics have directed towards Lyne's film is almost totally a product of their snobbery and fails to consider the significance of Nabokov's famous pronouncement that "there is nothing more exhilarating than philistine vulgarity." It is undeniable than no film version could possibly capture the idiosyncratic luster of Nabokov's prose, but to indict Lyne as a hack whose visual style mimics David's Hamilton's soft-core photographs of nubile adolescents (to paraphrase several critics) ignores the fact that an ironic deployment of soft-focus prurience may, in fact, be a totally appropriate visual accompaniment to Humbert's deranged, if manically lyrical, recollections.

It is common knowledge that Nabokov never had dalliances with little girls and remained a faithful husband with a largely uneventful personal life, but, as a European emigré, the circumspect novelist shared Humbert's bemused fascination with American coffee shops, motels, movies, and pop songs. The new *Lolita* is particularly satisfying for its meticulous evocation of American pop-culture detritus and a determination to faithfully render the late Forties ambiance of the original novel. Unlike many films which bombard the audience with period references, Lyne's film is a model of restrained production design. Kitschy details—a motel with cabins shaped like tepees, the Magic Fingers that delight Lolita during her cross-country jaunt, and a malevolent apparition of Dick Tracys that bedevil Humbert as his luck runs out—are subtly integrated into the film. The clash between an era in which the commercialization of childhood was only beginning (one of Lolita's most strenuously 'modern' teachers emphasizes the importance of "Dramatics, Dance, and Dating") and our own Jon Benet-obsessed consumer society provides much of the film's effectiveness—a resonance which would have been lost if Lyne and screenwriter Stephen Schiff had not resisted the temptation to update Nabokov's novel.

Given the American propensity to forgive almost any transgressor who expresses repentance, the most scandalous aspect of both Nabokov's novel and Lyne's film remains Humbert's rapturous hymn to the charms of his beloved Lolita, *neé* Dolores Haze. As Mark Lilly observed some years ago, Lolita shocks us because "the narrative has a casualness of tone, an improper lack of strong moral outrage... what the philistine/ prude really objected to was that Nabokov allows Humbert to have his say, to make a case." Lyne follows suit by casting the exquisitely vulnerable Jeremy Irons as Humbert; Irons's sensitive hangdog face and mellifluous voice enable us to, at least partially empathize with a calculating pedophile. Our troubling identification with Humbert is also facilitated through the stratagems Schiff borrows from Nabokov: Humbert, supposedly a stuffy, Old World litterateur, adeptly deflects the New World's pompous attempts to emulate European hauteur.

Of course, it is true that Charlotte Haze, Lolita's mother and the woman Humbert is obliged to marry in order to seduce his paramour, is treated with callousness, even cruelty, by Nabokov and both film versions. The pitiless scorn we feel towards her, however, is triggered by our contempt for her arriviste pose—her annoying habit of dropping French phrases and drooling over European high culture while hanging chintzy prints of famous paintings in her house. (It must be conceded, nevertheless, that Melanie Griffith's hesitant line readings cannot compare with the blowzy pathos that Shelley Winters brought to the role.)

Wittily reversing the premise of Henry James novels featuring naive young Americans bowled over by European sophistication, Humbert, whose mind is cluttered with quotations from Baudelaire and Chateaubriand, is as much in love with Lolita's ingenuous Americanness as he is with her nymphettish body. And despite the many differences between Nabokov's dense, allusive prose and the Kubrick and Lyne films, they all steadfastly refuse to offer psychological or sociological reasons for Humbert's illicit obsession. In a famous mock-foreword to *Lolita,* impishly attributed to the fictitious academic "John Ray, Jr., Ph.D.," Nabokov attacked the pretensions of so-called experts who offer facile analyses of complex, perhaps inexplicable, psychological phenomena. "Ray" concluded his foreword by proclaiming that *"Lolita* should make all of us—parents, social workers, educators—apply ourselves with still greater vigilance to the task of bringing up a better generation in a safer world." On the other hand, Schiff and Lyne, as well as Nabokov, are convinced that Humbert's perversity cannot be explained by hollow bromides.

Nabokov considered the character of Lolita one of his most finely honed creations, and Dominique Swain's (an irresistibly Nabokovian name!) performance as the central, although not particularly obscure, object of desire, is remarkably perceptive. Lolita is often mistaken for little more than a fetishized object, but Swain's impersonation of a flirtatious, highly intelligent brat convinces us that she is a young woman with a mind of her own who is not a mere projection of Humbert's madness and is profoundly aware of how she is being ensnared. She straightforwardly informs her stepfather that he is out of his "gourd," dispassionately assessing her fate and proving that she is far more than a passive victim.

Some of the gestures supposedly improvised by Swain are startlingly apt; the shot of Lolita removing her retainer before kissing Humbert drives home the casual violation of this ingenue's innocence with a pithiness that even Nabokov would have envied. Swain proves equally impressive in her transformation from a ravished preteen to a damaged young woman who rejects Humbert's final, plaintive advances.

Lyne's film proves weakest when it attempts to capture Nabokov's grim humor, particularly Quilty's near-Joycean word play. Quilty, a figure of maniacal intensity in the novel and Kubrick's film, is a shadowy figure in this relatively solemn film. Frank Langella's Quilty surfaces only occasionally, and his sardonic mutterings fail to bring to mind Nabokov's dastardly creation—a man who is both the embodiment of a Sadeian evil that goes far beyond Humbert's more pedestrian perversions and a magister ludi who spews forth puns, witticisms, and bogus clues with great alacrity. Since Lyne and Schiff pay scant attention to Quilty's diabolical brilliance, his death at the hands of Humbert emerges as strangely anticlimactic.

The current *Lolita,* inevitably more streamlined and linear than its labyrinthine source, is a far better film than almost anyone could have expected. What is missing from the film is the book's most disturbing—and admittedly one of its most uncinematic components: the chasm between Humbert, the self-described "murderer with a fancy prose style" and Humbert, the failed artist whose eloquence delights readers who abhor his deeds. The book never lets us forget the fact that a psychopath's macabre, and often hilarious, lyricism cannot help but estheticize the life of a young woman whose childhood he has robbed. While retaining fragments of Humbert's final monologue, the film, unable to completely bypass Hollywood conventions, leaves us with a more sentimental glimpse of a jilted, though regretful, lover.

FILM QUARTERLY, Spring 1999, p. 48, Devin McKinney

The *Lolita* remake has been allowed to muddy these chaste shores after two years in European quarantine, and in this case the remake really is a remake, as distinct from its precursor as leafy green is from forest black. Even we who have loved the 1962 Kubrick film knew it elided much that was unforgettable on the page; enough, certainly, to allow for a second take. The novel stands formal and integral and untouched as the two films regard it from their own oblique angles, catching certain textual truisms, glancing off others. Taken together, as complementary contradictions, they come close to capturing the novel's wonders.

The novel is as funny as sordid can be, and vice versa. Nabokov's humor is inseparable from his sense of the hidden, and he offers neither of these delicately; as piddling social satire, they combine to form the rot at the center of Humbert's soon-to-be-attacked heart as he writes his prison *pensées.* Comedy is deadly, death comic. Humor and ridicule have the power to kill, as when poor Charlotte is driven into the traffic by Humbert's diary of cackles and disdain. The illicit has the power to will murder—Humbert's execution of Quilty, carried out because he cannot fathom that illicit part of Lolita that would choose the indifferent pervert over his own tender, obsequious pedophilia. Nabokov's famously ecstatic prose, full of funny allusions and clever acrostic ploys and doublings-back, sprays his story with an exquisite perfume, but it never quite covers the stench of that rotting heart, which is not only Humbert's but the novel's. "It has bits of marrow sticking to it," says the character of his narrative, "and blood, and beautiful bright-green flies."

Kubrick went for the comedy, the macabre in the comedy, and found there the story of a squirming European pedant with a Pygmalion fixation on a sexy, mischievous, but finally fiercely conventional and rather dull American girl. As commercial (or merely narrative) film, this *Lolita* is an unwieldy object, lumpen in shape, dramatically diffuse, often banal; and despite this it has a near-greatness that issues from its actors and a pervading dank humor. Its anomaly is the latitude the director allows for subversive comedy and sideways-moving improvisation within the gilded, boxy frames of an otherwise four-square Hollywood literary adaptation. Scenes are dictated not by plot mechanics but by actorly rhythm and the natural life span of a comic interrelation between jarring personalities. It is Kubrick's only film in which, from first to last, he allows his actors to dominate space and spectacle rather than mug tightly in the constricted zones his monomaniac genius has allotted for them. To the extent one savors the visuals it is only because they have innocently, delightedly captured James Mason drunk in a bathtub; Sue Lyon's bacon-stuffed mouth sneering at Mother; or the Peter Sellers speed freak dropping the mask for a moment, chortling at his own absurdist riff on normality.

The rest of its achievement is how it breathes its singular atmosphere of suburban murk, as unwholesomely wholesome as a moldering loaf of Wonderbread—an accumulation of small twists, behavioral intangibles floating in a velvety black and white, encompassing the varieties of post-Kinsey American kink from Quilty's epicene fencing with Mr. Swine the night manager to a neighbor's coy suggestion of a wife-swap ("John and I, we're *both* broad-minded"). Kubrick catches the beautiful bright-green flies. Considering its time and place, his film is a remarkably eerie and unstable piece of mass-market absurdism, whispering of perverse delights and deaths under all the brushed and brocaded surfaces of a film that with the sound turned off could be mistaken for *The Parent Trap*.

The new film's presumption is that far more than its predecessor it will take Nabokov as writ, at least insofar as this can allow it to diverge from Kubrick. Firstly in physical detail: Lyne orchestrates a 40s period both audial (Lolita singing to novelty hits) and visual (closeups on archaic iceboxes, radios, automobile ashtrays) where Kubrick opted for the up-to-date. More generally, and impressively, there is a concentration on despair and derangement over comedy. Lyne flirts with satire but his heart is not in this by now benign aspect—he meat here is sex and death, the seduction of the aggressively youthful innocent, the ruin of the seducer. The Stephen Schiff screenplay, describing a narrative circle more sensible than the first film's, retains psychological detail Kubrick excised—hazy flashback to the original nymphet demon in the Humbert psyche, a quality of latent pathology in the titular girl's knowingness, and a voice-over patched from our narrator's most self-flagellating insights.

This seriousness, though wallowed in, isn't betrayed. Adrian Lyne, a third-rate stylist (textbook editing, post-Gothic trumpery) and fifth-rate thinker (flashy sex on the brain), has made a careful, second-rate *Lolita*-which as it turns out is more than nothing, for Kubrick's film also was second-rate.

Lyne (*9½ Weeks, Fatal Attraction, Indecent Proposal*) has been identified with a lack of aesthetic ethics—a technician's love of the effective effect, reliance on shock in cutting, insidious politics that rise like weeds from his favored fables of Womanly snakes loosed in the gardens of rational Man. So it isn't surprising that in its seriousness his *Lolita* should constitute a near-immersion in "Masterpiece Theatre" visuals: a soft-edged image and conventional framing, slow-rolling rhythm that subjugates lust with cool sophistication and situates as many scenes as possible in proximity to meadows, forests, shrubs. Scenes are as measured as medicine, fed the viewer through a formal construction of close-ups, vaguely subjective shots, reverse angles, cutaways to hands engaged in fussily detailed business. This sort of borrowed art, a congealing of good taste, is the talented hack's idea of serious. It's more elegant than Kubrick, but the price is a burden and studiousness the earlier film's irreverence easily threw off despite its cumbersome length.

And yet, split thus against itself, the movie haunts. It contains a hard center of melancholy. In its way it is tough and rigorous, because Lyne is mesmerized by the tale's downward spiral—ordinary human unpleasantness recovered and, to some extent, redeemed. Much of this strain exists in the screenplay, which selectively dices the novel for its lowest scenes of humiliation, arranges them artfully in a descension dwindling to the vanishing point and pitiful realization of the final scene. But even more it is in camerawork which gets harder and better as it goes. Lyne deserves credit for the precise staging of humiliation, the cultivation of actor's face and body into registers of non-diegetic feeling, camera placement which at one moment is sufficiently near the action to capture human volatility, at another remote enough to turn volatility into abstraction. He must do both, often in the same scene, for the art and tension of this story rest at the intersection of the abstract and the real, somewhere between Humbert's fantasy and Lolita's reality.

Example of how both interact is a three-way talk on a porch swing between Humbert, Lolita, and Charlotte, played well and straight by the actors as the dialogue makes fairly explicit points on mother-daughter sexual jealousy. Lyne's piquant undertext throughout, achieved with surprising, rude cuts that corrupt the measured surface of the scene, is of Lolita's physical intimidation of Humbert, her hands, feet, and arms in constant attack on his stoic manly limbs, his masochistic pleasure in the secret display. Fun, but sick fun. Another, even better example: a late scene of the two in bed, clawing violently over loose coins (she has raised her price mid-session), catches a curdled hysteria as it darts from tight to medium shot and back, a fierce thrusting of flying hair, gauze-obscured mouths—degradation played without self-consciousness, emotional impoverishment as a fragmented action piece. This isn't even fun. The quick scene hurts all the more for how it is thrown away, served as filler under a length of summary narration.

The film is impressively erotic. Impressive because it skirts the merely voyeuristic while doing all it can to characterize through precise physical action the dynamics of the sexual relationship, dynamics which change with each encounter. The first commingling between timid Hum and whispering Lo is realized delicately by a camera casting a wide eye, taking in white sheets and sunlight, soft cutting between the faces—lingering especially on Irons' priceless boyish giggle as Lolita slips out her retainer. We look down on him, up at her: Who has control here? Their final intimacy is rape, with Humbert beginning as attacker and ending as abject supplicant, a scene remarkable for its implication of the unseen penis as a siphon transferring power from man to girl. By this point we are looking down on her, up at him: again the presumption of control is complicated by viewpoint. Most frightening is a scene halfway between these two, with him apparently napping in his chair, her on his leg, enjoying the funnies. Spontaneously Lolita masturbates herself on Humbert's leg, and Lyne visibly must resist the impulse to porn up the sadness of a rocking-chair orgasm in a cheap motel on a dusty afternoon. But his slow zoom upon reaching the lovers melts into a premature fade, and sadness overpowers sex. Here we see both characters head on, neither looking at the other. It is their only moment of sexual equality.

The implication that power can be shared, transferred, ambiguous in such situations is neither politically correct nor morally exculpatory of child molesters, but it is emotionally valid and as real a perception as can be caught about these characters. It's the perception that lodges that melancholy at the heart of this *Lolita* and takes it to its necessary depths, which are perhaps more subtle than those of Kubrick. And in each case Lyne, summoning empathy from behind his mastery of sleaze and commerce, has made the perception alive with his eye.

This even though he elsewhere dawdles on tasteful frou-frou; disrupts visual and rhythmic integrity to no great purpose with tricks from an old bag (shock cuts to a bug-zapper as Quilty baits the nervous pedophile); and films a Humbert-Quilty showdown that is helplessly ugly, revolted at nakedness and glibness, not a transformation of the sordid but the plain, gross thing itself. The surprise seems to be that Lyne's good instincts increase in proportion to the sorrow of the material. It ends up not a simple, wet sorrow, but something more astringent, aggravated by a clash of ingredients, impulses, motives.

So, just as Kubrick's comic extrapolations defeated his own indifferent pacing, Lyne's fascination with the story's fatal momentum survives his first bout with a high, gelid seriousness.

His *Lolita* is a combination of prestige-picture quality and queasy despair whose ultimate effect is of a messy and harrowing woe. Movies exerting such a low, persistent pull to the dregs of a story are scarcely common. The last may have been Todd Solondz's *Welcome to the Dollhouse* (1996), a brisk, bitter masochism about an ugly schoolgirl's social damnation at the hands of among others, a girl named Lolita. And there was the clinical decay of Cronenberg's *Dead Ringers* (1988), which also gave a Jeremy Irons tour de force nowhere to go but down. The stronger sense, though, is of Eastern Europe. Early on in *Lolita* there is a preponderance of stars and stripes (a trope soon discarded), but more than anything American, the film in its echt European mood resembles those long-ago life-slices of the Prague Spring, *Loves of a Blonde* or *Closely Watched Trains*, that devolved from modest mirth to bleak apprehensions of abysmal lives and dead ends. This class of film seeks a refuge in glancing observations, found romance, and not coincidentally, the redemptive cachet of youth; but in it youth is always wasted, romance poisoned at the root, and possibility consigned to the middle distances of a barren landscape.

All of which was implicit in Nabokov's novel—as was the particular sort of comedy that Kubrick made of it. The two *Lolitas* are prime material for someone's college course on Film and Adaptation: in essence they divide the novel cleanly between them, each taking one cache of riches while leaving the greater treasure—and then, the accomplishment, succeeding even while being so limited. Is it in spite or because of this limit that they have succeeded? Certainly the latter, since neither film suggests it could replicate Nabokov's patho-comic integration even if it wanted to. Kubrick's comedy borrows drama and Lyne's drama borrows comedy, but both do badly by what is opposite to their natures: poignancy in Kubrick consists of Nelson Riddle music rising to meet an emotion that isn't there, while humor in Lyne is the smirk of recognition that one of Nabokov's wittier lines has been reproduced by the mouth of an actor. Each film is an instance of moviemakers consciously avoiding a level of complexity—in theme, performance, psychology—they cannot engage, and extrapolating from their single focus a world familiar from the novel but unique in itself. That Lyne has followed the pathetic implications of the story is, if not a greater imaginative act than Kubrick's, probably a tougher one: he ignores the bright-green flies but comes away with some of the marrow.

Depressive material more than any other kind requires its actors to be anchors for action we would otherwise emotionally resist, and each of the two stars is given his or her abiding specialty, an identity of body and carriage: for Jeremy Irons' Humbert it is a lithe physical misery suggesting incontinence more than tumescence, while Dominique Swain's Lolita, chicken dancing in the living room, comes across on goony charm, her face an unnerving glaze of self-centeredness. Interiorized in both performances is foreknowledge of the characters' fates, a spying of the downward spiral. There is a bitter logic to the way they interact, both with each other and with the camera: she seems constantly in motion, while he, a wilting licorice stick at the center of the screen, is whipped by the camera this way and that. Swain is particularly amazing in giving the impression of outward-pushing acting while remaining almost entirely opaque, insulated, an all but unreadable physiognomy: her face occasionally grins between long stretches of scary impassivity which suggest the inner life of a morose gangster.

This is not a great film, merely a nagging one, and disarming in its nag. The picture's grip on its true grim self is too tenuous for it to be anything like great, even the near-great of Kubrick. But Lyne has found a core of unmelodramatic doom and by observing a certain discipline he carries it through to a last scene in which the film's elements, elsewhere at war, are fused. It is unexpectedly perfect, this ending: as Humbert reaches his tether's end on a picturesque hillside, blood staining one cheek like an ambiguous cancer, the meadow-mongering of Lyne's seriousness is joined to his insistence on the characters' misery. At that moment, one feels loss. If false solemnity is this Lolita's folly, suppressed pain is its living, grumbling *bête noire*.

LOS ANGELES TIMES, 7/22/98, Calendar/p. 1, Kenneth Turan

When towering Abraham Lincoln met tiny Harriet Beecher Stowe, or so the story goes, he peered down at the woman whose "Uncle Tom's Cabin" had inflamed the North against slavery and said, "So this is the little lady who started the big war." And so it is on finally seeing "Lolita."

Shown to and refused by studio executives early in 1997, debuting in Europe in September and finally opening in Los Angeles 10 months later for a one-week Academy Award-qualifying run before going nationwide on Showtime, "Lolita" seems hardly likely to have caused so much trouble.

Was this reverential, overly long version of the Vladimir Nabokov novel going to start a conflagration in the hearts of the religious right? Was this careful, respectful but only sporadically involving vehicle the bombshell guaranteed to outrage moralists across America? Surely, there must be some mistake.

"Lolita's" subject matter of a grown man engaging in a sexual relationship with a pre-pubescent girl has been understandably controversial since Nabokov's brilliant novel was published in France in 1955 and went on to sell 14 million copies in this country. And the congressional passage in 1996 of the Child Pornography Prevention Act, precluding the use of body doubles by forbidding even what "appears to be a minor engaging in sexually explicit conduct," cast more of a chilling effect and made reediting on "Lolita" a necessity.

But on seeing the finished film, the pious spin the filmmakers have put on the chronicle of their lack of success in the American market—a tale of besieged genius confronting soulless philistines, of dark threats to creative expression and 1st Amendment rights—seems lamentably self-serving.

This is not the case of a brilliant film sandbagged by the nattering nabobs of negativity, but rather a rarefied, arty, distinctly noncommercial work whose refined air and considerable cost (a reported $58 million, double its original budget) clearly were as much factors as the threat of controversy in keeping distributors away.

Paradoxically, "Lolita" is also the least likely movie to have been made by director Adrian Lyne, whose previous works include such non-art-house fare as "Flashdance," "Fatal Attraction," "9½ Weeks" and "Indecent Proposal."

A passionate admirer of the Nabokov novel, Lyne, having rejected screenplays by Harold Pinter, David Mamet and James Dearden, elected to follow Stephen Schiff's careful script, retaining the novel's late-1940s setting and turning great stretches of Nabokov's hypnotic prose into voice-over material.

But though this "Lolita" is closer to the book than Stanley Kubrick's dazzling 1962 version (which starred James Mason, Sue Lyon and Peter Sellers), respect has not served it particularly well. Except for a memorably haunted performance by Jeremy Irons as the conflicted Humbert Humbert, what the new version lacks most of all is inspiration.

Humbert is the film's narrator as well as its protagonist, and it's his sad voice we hear crooning, "Light of my life, fire of my loins, my sin, my soul, Lolita," as, spattered with blood with a revolver next to him, he erratically drives his car along a country road.

Most of the film is a flashback from that moment, but before that can begin we go back even earlier, to Humbert's childhood, when he fell deeply in love with a girl of 12, only to have her die of typhus. "The shock of her death froze something in me," he remembers. "The child I loved was gone, but I kept looking for her—long after I had left my own childhood behind."

Humbert's tale proper begins in 1947 in the New England village of Ramsdale, where he has gone to spend a quiet summer before he begins teaching at nearby Beardsley College. Humbert inquires about a room rented by the affected Charlotte Haze (Melanie Griffith) and is about to turn it down when he catches sight of young daughter Lolita (Dominique Swain), lolling casually under a lawn sprinkler and smiling innocently through her dental retainer in a way he finds irresistible.

Humbert is, he tells us, a connoisseur of what he calls the nymphet, "the little deadly demon" with power enough to cloud his normally reasonable mind with thoughts of lust. From that moment on, Humbert's entire waking life is devoted to trying to seduce Lolita, to make her his own. It's a quest that takes strange turns, including the involvement of a mysterious author named Clare Quilty (Frank Langella), and has unlooked-for results.

It should be emphasized that though sex is very much on its mind, this "Lolita" is not prurient and not meant to be. What drama it has focuses on Irons' expert rendition of Humbert's various comic-tragic agonies, the contortions he has to go through to sustain a relationship with someone who, after all, is only 14.

Swain, who was a 15-year-old sophomore at Malibu High when filming began, does a respectable job as Lolita, but through no fault of her own this character is more problematic than

Humbert's. For one thing, in an age when a supermodel like Kate Moss can become an international sexual icon partly because she looks 15, Swain doesn't, as Sue Lyon didn't, really look as young as the novel has you imagine her.

Nabokov's book is a problem in another way: It is largely narrative, with very little dialogue. Though "Lolita" tries to remedy this with extensive voice-over, the movie has no choice but to replace the novel's incandescent language, its major source of excitement, with the kind of not particularly edifying dialogue that tends to come out of a 14-year-old's mouth.

When Kubrick's "Lolita" was released in 1962, the ad line teasingly asked, "How could they make a movie of Lolita?" A more appropriate question for this version is not how could they do it, but how could such a sincere, well-meaning effort end up so ineffectual on the screen?

NEW YORK, 10/12/98, p. 82, David Denby

The new version of *Lolita*, released at last, turns out to be a beautifully made, melancholy, and rather touching account of a doomed love affair between a full-grown man and a very young woman. But that, of course, is not what Vladimir Nabokov's masterpiece is about. As Louis Menand pointed out in *Slate*—in a necessary statement of the obvious—Nabokov's book is devoted to a love affair between a man and a child. The book *Lolita* is truly shocking and quite impossible to adapt "faithfully." (Stanley Kubrick didn't even try in his brilliant 1962 film version.) Nabokov's narrator, Humbert Humbert, is an educated but moldy European living in America, a pedophile who longs for downy, slender limbs and "delicate-boned, long-toed, monkeyish feet"—the gawky, undeveloped beauty of 12-year-olds. The book is a lyrical black comedy balanced between lust and humiliation, between perversion and rhapsody. It is a dizzying, morally dangerous work—and an extraordinary entertainment. Humbert the fetishist covers his criminal intentions with stuffy cultural superiority and a show of parental concern. He's a low, devious fellow, a worm, but a worm who, in the end, truly gives his love, and that's the other side of the joke. *Lolita* is both an undermining satire of obsessive love and a genuine love story.

Director Adrian Lyne *(Fatal Attraction, Indecent Proposal)* and screenwriter Stephen Schiff, who did the adaptation, have seized on the romantic side of this amazing fable and left out most of the satire and malevolent humor. What we see is not a *sui generis* erotic comedy about a very specialized kind of obsession but a recognizable descendant of European films in which a poor sap falls into all-encompassing love and is tormented by an unreachable bitch. Humbert is no longer an ironic hero—a haughty and hypocritical creep who is redeemed—but a very earnest man who loves too much. The joke has vanished.

When Humbert (Jeremy Irons) first sees Lolita (Dominique Swain), she is lying on her tummy in the sun, and water from sprinklers falls all around her. The image has the slightly banal prettiness of dozens of other romantic movies. Later on, Lolita and Humbert ride around the country (it is the late forties), and Lyne and cinematographer Howard Atherton give us deep, dark woods and the "naive" American beauty of lonely gas stations and rooming houses and empty golden-brown fields. The beauty has no particular thematic importance, but it soothes the audience—it makes the story seem more normal somehow. Except for one overwrought fantasia in the middle, and some grotesquely bloody violence at the end, this *Lolita* plays evenly and smoothly, with the gratifying emotional continuity of an old-fashioned narrative. The trouble is, there's no audacity in it, no surprise—no wicked fun.

Dominique Swain, who was 15 when the movie was made, has the long, powerful legs of an ice-skating champion, not the shy, clinging knees of, say, the child photographed on the cover of the Vintage edition of the novel. Swain, grinding jawbreakers one minute and pulling herself onto Irons the next, is the best thing in the movie—coltish and volatile, a young woman with girlish impulses. As for Irons, he gives a very decent performance, if only you can keep out of your head the sound of James Mason's inflections in the Kubrick version. Kubrick wasn't faithful to the book's erotic nature, either, but he knew that an adaptation of *Lolita* had to be a comedy. So James Mason conveyed some pleasure in the role; he didn't suffer so much; he made Humbert a cynical fake gentleman—whereas Jeremy Irons is a bit of a dullard who can't keep up with his energetic, ordinary, faithless American girl. And there are comparable diminutions in the other roles: In Kubrick's movie, Shelley Winters's Charlotte Haze (Lolita's overeager mom) was a brilliant parody of provincial vulgarity; Melanie Griffith, who plays Charlotte for Lyne, is just shrill. Clare Quilty—Peter Sellers's enormous, exuberant invention, the nasty consciousness needed to put Humbert in perspective—is here, in the person of Frank Langella, only a wearily caustic villain.

Yet this new *Lolita* is not negligible. I have seen it twice, and I can report that audiences are sitting raptly through it. What they are responding to, I believe, is not Nabokov's disturbing joke about romantic obsession but a more conventionally reassuring romantic drama. They are responding to pathos and heartbreak, to suffering and noble, unhappy love.

NEW YORK POST, 9/25/98, p. 44, Rod Dreher

Adrian Lyne's "Lolita" is not a great film, but it is an exceptional film, a believable film, an erotically potent and morally responsible film. In most ways, it exceeds Stanley Kubrick's 1962 version of the Nabokov novel, chiefly because Lyne and his brilliant leading players (Jeremy Irons as Humbert Humbert and Dominique Swain in the title role) are able to treat the material with far more frankness than Kubrick.

While not sexually graphic—the film is, after all, about an older man's relationship with a precocious adolescent—Lyne's "Lolita" eschews the mordant comedy of Kubrick's take, immersing us instead into the story's sinister, obsessive elements.

Swain is perfectly cast as a fatherless 14-year-old aware of her sexual power without having the slightest understanding of it. The petulant Swain is breathtakingly convincing as she whipsaws between gawky girlish innocence and perverse knowledge of an experienced older woman.

Irons always has about him an air of aristocratic Old World decadence—this is the man who played Claus von Bulow, remember—and it serves him well here. The intelligence he brings to the Humbert character keeps us from dismissing him as a mere pervert, but also shows why it is easy for Humbert to delude himself into thinking his vile behavior with the girl is acceptable.

There is real erotic spark between Irons and Swain, which makes Lyne's version much more affecting than its predecessor. But the shock that comes from it is one of recognition: that our culture eroticizes little girls and rationalizes it away. Lyne's deeply sensual eye conjures a persuasive atmosphere of stylish decadence, particularly when the story moves to sultry New Orleans.

Yet Frank Langella's Clare Quilty—an unambiguously satanic figure in this version, not Peter Sellers' comic freak—returns like a Greek chorus to remind us that below the aesthetic pleasure and intellectual contortions Humbert experiences to service his desire, lies a malignant rottenness that cannot be ameliorated, only dealt with harshly.

NEWSDAY, 9/25/98, Part II/p. B11, Jack Mathews

When last we checked in with Adrian Lyne's version of "Lolita," she was appearing on Showtime. This "Lolita," like the one Stanley Kubrick made in 1962, is a major motion picture, adapted from Vladimir Nabokov's extraordinary novel, but with its cost ($58 million), its subject (pedophilia), and things being what they are (timid), its producers were unable to find a major American distributor.

The movie was released in Europe last year about this time, and had its first Showtime airing on July 30, when we reviewed it in Newsday. It finally reaches its original destination, American theaters.

After providing some history, the review continued... "Lolita" wasn't turned down because of its quality. Lyne ("Fatal Attraction") got first-rate performances from Jeremy Irons, as Humbert, the British writer who migrates to America and falls in love with a 12-year-old girl—Melanie Griffith, as the girl's mother, the lonely, infatuated widow Charlotte, Frank Langella as Quilty, a debauched playwright with his own plans for the girl, and newcomer Dominique Swain, as Lolita.

Lyne's version of "Lolita," skillfully adapted by New Yorker writer Stephen Schiff, is a more faithful rendition than the one credited to Nabokov himself in Kubrick's film. For the earlier movie, the role of Quilty was enlarged and tailored to Peter Sellers' gift for disguise, and Lolita was aged to 15, to make her precocious sexuality more palatable for censors and audiences.

No question that Swain, who was 14 when the film was made, looks like a child, barely pubescent, rather than the saucy temptress portrayed by Sue Lyons. In Lyne's version, Lolita is a rebellious kid acting out her movie and fan magazine-enhanced fantasies. The genius of Nabokov's novel was the subtext of a rapidly changing culture, which Lolita's aggression, rebelliousness and confusion represent.

"Lolita" is largely a road movie, with Humbert and the girl aimlessly crisscrossing America, avoiding the reality and consequences of their actions. Humbert is a sick, sick puppy, savagely jealous and insecure, and incapable of resisting Lolita's increasingly sophisticated use of her sexual power.

Swain, in her first film performance, is remarkable, creating a Lolita whose sexuality is a pure reaction to Humbert's desire. It's behavior modification at its most twisted... "Lolita" ... has some uncomfortable, if not quite explicit, sex scenes. But the only graphic nudity involves a naked, 58-year-old Frank Langella running directly at the camera, with a gun-toting Humbert in hot pursuit. It's quite a sight, especially on the big screen.

SIGHT AND SOUND, 5/98, p. 51, Leslie Dick

The south of France, the 20s. Thirteen-year-old Humbert Humbert falls madly in love with Annabel Leigh, who dies shortly after they have sex. Humbert develops a fixation on pubescent girls. 1947. Humbert arrives in the US to teach at a Midwestern college. Taking a room at the house of Charlotte Haze, Humbert meets Charlotte's 12-year-old daughter Lolita. Humbert marries Charlotte to be near Lolita, but Charlotte is killed crossing the road after she reads his diary. Humbert collects Lolita from summer camp and the two of them sleep together. After Humbert reveals that Charlotte is dead, Lolita and he begin an aimless tour of the US.

Humbert and Lolita settle in the college town of Beardsley. While performing in a school play, Lolita meets the playwright Clare Quilty, an old acquaintance of her mother's. Humbert begins to suspect that she is seeing someone else. When they take to the road again, a car appears to be following him. Ultimately, his suspicions are confirmed when Lolita absconds.

Several years later, Lolita gets in touch. Humbert finds her pregnant and married, in need of money before she and her husband move to Alaska. Lolita reveals that the man she ran off with was Clare Quilty. Humbert tracks Quilty down and kills him. Intertitles reveal that soon after this, both Humbert and Lolita died.

Adrian Lyne's *Lolita* is a comic romp, an amusing escapade complete with motels—*It Happened One Night* for the 90s—that turns into a doomed romance, a full-on tragedy—interspersed with quasi-soft porn sequences so tacky they bring tears to your eyes. Nabokov would have liked the motels.

The first time Humbert Humbert lays eyes on Lolita, she is in the garden, lying on the grass under a sprinkler. Long sunbeams angle through the veil of falling water and, needless to say, Lolita is wearing a thin cotton dress, soaked to semi-transparency, which clings to her nubile body. Despite the plentiful droplets, she is reading a magazine, admiring a photo of Burt Lancaster. Lyne adds a childish detail in her retainer, which she reveals in a wildly improbable cover-girl smile directed at the stranger. (Later this retainer will perform a key semiotic function, as she gleefully pulls it out, in bed with Humbert Humbert, apparently in preparation for fellatio.)

The initial 'wet T-shirt on a pre-teen' scene gives the game away: no matter how hard the actors work (and they're good actors, doing their job against terrible odds) no matter how crisp the script (and there are only a few real gaffes, such as when Quilty says "Enjoy!" like a waiter in an LA restaurant), the erotic clichés spoil it all. For example, in the scene where Lolita drops her pajama bottoms, on her way downstairs to raid the icebox, the unnecessary undressing marks this out as soft-porn fantasy, rigorous in its conventionality—and suddenly it isn't sexy any more.

H. H.'s penchant for little girls goes way back: when he was 13, and she was 12, he loved Annabel by the sea (echoes of Edgar Allan Poe, who married a 12-year-old), a girl who died three months later. His life is an attempt to rediscover that first love: even the ribbon the youthful H. H. pulled from the ever-so-tasteful broderie anglaise camiknickers of the long-limbed Annabel reappears, fetishistically retained, folded into the leather-bound notebook where he records his secret thoughts. Nabokov does not hesitate to depict his protagonist's furtive masturbation on the bench at the playground, on the couch with Lolita. The movie inevitably romanticises: in place of abject wanking, Lyne gives us tasteful fetishism, a case of arrested development, golden sunlight, sheer romance.

Far more compelling is H. H. in his room, bathroom door ajar, listening transfixed to Lo brushing her teeth, listening to the loo roll spin, as Lolita's collusion—is she aware of him listening?—remains uncertain, ambient eroticism displaced into sound, a sense of bodily proximity, a familiar intimacy. Or when she drops her retainer into his glass of white wine—it's much more plausible, and much more complicated. The unseen presence of Lolita's mother Charlotte adds a special *frisson*, but she's the fall guy, the dupe. She's the fool who thinks Humbert's a disgusting pervert, a despicable criminal monster, when she finds out. She dies, of course, just as all the women in the story do, even Lo.

Lolita's point of view remains necessarily opaque: her isolation, after her mother's wonderfully *deus ex machina* death, is complete and as a result she turns to Humbert for comfort, even when he is the cause of her misery. She may be seductive, provocative, voracious even. But she is also a child, and as a child she has no power in the world. Ironically, Quilty offers her an escape route, yet what he asks of her is even less palatable than H. H.'s embraces: he wants her to take part in an orgy for the camera. But her tragedy is viewed entirely through H. H.'s eyes, and the film gives much more weight to *his* tragedy, his loss, his jealousy.

Given how glib the movie is stylistically, the fact that Jeremy Irons makes Humbert's love for Lolita credible is amazing. When the film tries for the tragic mode, when H. H. runs after her through the rain, the barking dog in the alley, the beautifully preserved 40s cars, the elaborate lighting, and the cinematography recall nothing so much as a very upmarket advert. Lyne's determination to include the whole audience in H. H.'s perverse passion is crucial: we must all partake of the forbidden fruit—a requirement that leads, with inexorable logic, to the wet, transparent dress, among other things—so that subsequently we can buy into Humbert's dubious expressions of guilt, his emotional intensity, so we can indulge him and ourselves. Lyne sets us up to identify with H. H.—maybe he cannot imagine a movie without that central structure of identification. The elaborate edifice of irony, distance, disgust and sympathy that Nabokov so magically sustained is thereby reduced to a story where ambiguity is almost absent, complexity discarded, and real transgression evaporates, like so many drops from a sprinkler.

VILLAGE VOICE, 10/6/98, p. 128, Michael Atkinson

Although the theatrical release of Adrian Lyne's beleaguered *Lolita* has by this time as much cultural significance as another post-Maris home run, it'd be wise to cast a cold eye on this baby, sans the cluttering context of its year in limbo, the apprehension of stateside distributors, the Child Pornography Prevention Act of 1996, the franc-fed budget ($58 million!), the imagined picket lines, the comparison to Kubrick's version, the NC-17 sex scenes left on the cutting-room floor. Circumstances are, after all, yesterday's entertainment-page filler; in a year, we'll have only the movie to be bored by. There's precious few yucks, for one thing, but you can't say you're surprised that the astonishingly humorless Lyne hadn't noticed or cared that the Nabokov original is a droll comedy of errors first and a self-pitying romantic tragedy second. (The funniest thing in Lyne's oeuvre is the fact that Michael Douglas needed Glenn Close to tell him he had a golf-ball-sized dollop of cream cheese on his nose in *Fatal Attraction*.)

Shot too gorgeously to be amusing in any event, *Lolita* attempts moments of light farce, encouraging the monstrously awkward Melanie Griffith and the up-for-anything Dominique Swain to deport themselves like actors in a car commercial, but these scenes have the grace of gunshot ducks. Lyne's idea of Nabokovian wit is having Swain snap her gum, and then cutting to Jeremy Irons's Humbert grinning in enraptured embarrassment.

Irons occasionally manages a funny bit of fumbling, and his handling of the Humbertian narration is adept. But it's Lyne's particular style of post-'80s-TV-ad filmmaking that fattens this movie for the chopping block. Outside of the lovely credit sequence, scored by Ennio Morricone with bars right out of *Once Upon a Time in America* and featuring the bloodied Humbert driving semiconsciously down a country road, *Lolita* is shot and cut with a gilt-edged sledge. When Quilty (Frank Langella) makes his ominous appearance on the hotel porch, Lyne cuts busily between him, Irons, and giant moths bursting preposterously into flame around an anachronistic bug zapper as if it were a shoot-out. When Humbert visits a pregnant Lo late in the tale, Lyne makes sure Swain blocks the doorway with her belly so Irons will have to squeeze shakily through, milking the silly and unrealistic moment by cutting to three or four angles. The assassination of Quilty is a veritable atrocity of overlighting, punctuation cuts, and grotesque theatrics. Every scene in the film is shaped with the same cement-heavy hand.

In the tradition of Spielberg-era hacks, Lyne doesn't strive to tell a story so much as lock a roped ring into your nose and pull. (Salacious as all get-out, Lyne makes the big mistake of bending over backward making Lo sensual and alluring—even though Humbert has detailed to us in the narration how "nymphets" are only discernible to those cursed with a yen for jailbait.) It's easy to miss Lyne's traffic-cop style when he's trucking in pulpy paranoia and romantic tosh, but taking on Nabokov makes him look like the TV-spot handyman he obviously remains.

Also reviewed in:
CHICAGO TRIBUNE, 11/13/98, Friday/p. K, Michael Wilmington
NEW REPUBLIC, 10/5/98, p. 26, Stanley Kauffmann
NEW YORK TIMES, 7/31/98, p. E1, Caryn James
NEW YORK TIMES, 9/25/98, p. E26, Janet Maslin
NEW YORKER, 2/23 & 3/2/98, p. 182, Anthony Lane
VARIETY, 9/29-10/5/97, p. 61, David Rooney

LOST IN SPACE

A New Line Cinema release of a Prelude Pictures production in association with Irwin Allen Productions. *Executive Producer:* Mace Neufeld, Bob Rehme, Richard Saperstein, and Michael De Luca. *Producer:* Mark W. Koch, Stephen Hopkins, Akiva Goldsman, and Carla Fry. *Director:* Stephen Hopkins. *Screenplay:* Akiva Goldsman. *Director of Photography:* Peter Levy. *Editor:* Ray Lovejoy. *Music:* Bruce Broughton. *Music Editor:* Patricia Carlin. *Sound:* Simon Kaye and (music) John Timperley. *Sound Editor:* Eddy Joseph. *Casting:* Mike Fenton, Allison Cowitt and Mary Selway. *Production Designer:* Norman Garwood. *Art Director:* Keith Pain. *Set Decorator:* Anna Pinnock. *Special Effects:* Nick Allder. *Visual Effects:* Angus Bickerton. *Space Costumes:* Vin Burnham. *Earth Costumes:* Robert Bell and Gilly Hebden. *Make-up:* Yvonne Coppard. *Stunt Coordinator:* Greg Powell. *Running time:* 121 minutes. *MPAA Rating:* PG-13.

CAST: William Hurt (John Robinson); Mimi Rogers (Maureen Robinson); Heather Graham (Judy Robinson); Lacey Chabert (Penny Robinson); Jack Johnson (Will Robinson); Gary Oldman (Dr. Zachary Smith/Spider Smith); Matt LeBlanc (Don West); Jared Harris (Older Will); Mark Goddard (General); Lennie James (Jeb Walker); Marta Kristen (Reporter #1); June Lockhart (Principal); Edward Fox (Business Man); Adam Sims (Lab Technician); Angela Cartwright (Reporter #2); John Sharian (Noah Freeman); Abigail Canton (Annie Tech); Richard Saperstein (Attack Pilot); William Todd Jones (Spider Smith/Shadow).

CHRISTIAN SCIENCE MONITOR, 4/10/98, p. B3, David Sterritt

The movie version of "Lost in Space" starts pretty much the same way as the 1960s television series its based on.

An adventurous family boards a spacecraft for a voyage to the stars; a nasty scientist sneaks in to sabotage their ship; his plan goes haywire, and he becomes an unwilling stowaway on the journey—but not before sending the vessel a jillion light-years in the wrong direction, which launches a great deal of intergalactic excitement for the Robinson clan and dashing Don West, the handsome pilot at the helm.

This said, there are inevitably a lot of changes in the '90s version, reflecting Hollywood's current ideas of high-profit material. Most obviously and predictably, the Robinsons are now a dysfunctional family, spending half their time airing the kinds of household problems—dad's too preoccupied, son feels neglected, younger daughter wants no part of this particular family outing—that stayed decorously beneath the surface of '60s television fare.

The new "Lost in Space" might have been interesting if it explored and resolved these personality clashes in a serious and creative way. But the filmmakers can't decide what sort of picture they're trying to cook up, so they keep oscillating among shallow psychological drama, high-tech action sequences, and comedy scenes that are themselves an uneasy mixture of sitcom-style dialogue and self-mocking campiness.

William Hurt and Mimi Rogers do their best with their shakily written roles—at least they seem a trifle more human than Guy Williams and June Lockhart, their TV predecessors—and Gary Oldman is his usual flamboyant self as the scientist. But in the end, "Lost in Space" is one expedition that should have been scrubbed long before the final countdown.

LOS ANGELES TIMES, 4/3/98, Calendar/p. 8, Kenneth Turan

"Lost in Space" is way more lost than it knows.

Yet another theatrical feature based on a decades-old TV show (what's next—"Modern Farmer: The Movie"?), this effects-loaded extravaganza has more trouble finding its dramatic bearings than the Space Family Robinson has in figuring out where the heck in the universe they are.

The original 1960s TV show—four of whose members make cameo appearances here—is remembered, by those who think about it at all, for its genially campy sensibility. The current model, by contrast, lacks a clear idea of what it wants to be.

Cute and off-putting by turns, "Lost in Space" is driven by the commercial imperative to dabble in anything an audience might be interested in. Sentimental family moments alternate with video game-inspired action and computer-generated monsters who seem to come out of another movie altogether and coexist with a saucer-eyed living toy called Blawp.

Made with an ensemble cast of seven (not counting an upscale robot that looks like it's on steroids), "Lost in Space" unmistakably has its eye on sequels extending well into the next century. But while "Star Trek," which set the franchise standard all aspire to, was bequeathed a distinctive and unmistakable sensibility by creator Gene Roddenberry, this film had to make do with the generically jokey vision of writer and co-producer Akiva Goldsman—a point of view that viewers of the last two "Batman" vehicles have come to dread.

Which is partially a shame, because "Lost in Space's" more than 750 effects shots create an arresting visual world and, taken individually, the cast members acquit themselves as honorably as the material allows.

William Hurt, for instance, adds a kind of gravity these films rarely aspire to as Professor John Robinson, a deep thinker who devotes less time to his family than to his upcoming space mission. The year is 2058 and planet Earth is headed for the last roundup. The professor and his family are being sent to a place called Alpha Prime to be space pioneers, paving the way for a mass evacuation.

While scientist daughter Judy (the always effective Heather Graham) is pleased to be going, other family members have mixed feelings. These include strong-willed scientist-mom Maureen (Mimi Rogers), boy genius Will (Jack Johnson, celebrated screenwriter Nunnally Johnson's appealing grandson) and sulky teenager Penny ("Party of Five's" Lacey Chabert), who gripes, "If there's no time for fun, what are we saving the planet for?"

Definitely not looking forward to the trip is Major Don West (Matt LeBlanc, the Joey of "Friends"), a hotshot fighter pilot of the "am I good or what" persuasion. "Taking the family camper on an interstellar picnic" is not high on his priority list, but then he meets the fetching Judy and utters one of Goldsmith's signature lines: "That's one cold fish I'd like to thaw."

Even more reluctant to be on board is the villain of the piece, Gary Oldman's traitorous Dr. Zachary Smith. Oldman is such an old hand at treachery that he's given top billing here, and the good news is that he's chosen to play Dr. Smith in a nonflamboyant manner. Scuttling around the ship, muttering, "Evil knows evil," and in general up to no good, Oldman's Dr. Smith makes us hang on his every word.

One of the odd things about "Lost in Space" is that it's not only based on a TV series, with a plot that's divided into four fairly self-contained half-hour segments, it feels like a series in and of itself.

First comes the prelaunch character introduction, followed by what goes wrong on board the Robinsons' ship to get everyone lost in space in the first place. Then comes an ominous interlude on yet another one of those spaceships that only seems deserted, followed by a final segment concerning time warps and alternate realities that will confuse anyone over the age of 12.

Director Stephen Hopkins, many of whose credits have numbers after them ("Nightmare on Elm Street 5," "Predator 2"), tries hard to make all this coherent but he has difficulty compensating for a script that alternates between sci-fi lingo about the dangers of entering hyperspace without a gate and family sitcom lines like, "We will discuss this at dinner."

The largest problem, however, remains the misguided nature of the project. By largely jettisoning the elements that made the TV series popular, the creative crew of "Lost in Space" embarked on a road not fated to meet with any kind of meaningful success.

NEW YORK POST, 4/3/98, p. 45, Rod Dreher

"Lost in Space" is about great production design and selling toys. Period. The movie looks terrific, but as with the last two "Batman" movies, also penned in part by scripter Akiva Goldsman, the sub-moronic screenplay quickly vaporizes interest and good will.

Nobody expects a big-budget sci-fi extravaganza based on a dopey 1960s TV series to be "Citizen Kane," but this is too much for anyone who isn't a pre-pubescent male mouth-breather to take.

This "Lost in Space" borrows the basic set-up from the TV series, but director Stephen Hopkins avoids the series' unintentional campiness. He fastforwards the story into the '90s with a turbocharged techie shine and a fast-and-furious sense of adventure.

The film's first hour is pretty swell, despite opening with a disorienting space battle sequence marred by the kind of coked-up Cuisinart editing that gives seizures to Japanese children.

Professor John Robinson (William Hurt) is preparing to take his family into space aboard the Jupiter 2, a sleek, swoopy, futuristic funhouse that's a wonder to behold.

Not so the blandoid Dysfunctional Family Robinson. The screenplay ill-advisedly panders to contemporary anxieties over absentee fathers by making Robinson a workaholic. Mother Maureen (Mimi Rogers) is trying to keep the family intact, while brainy son Will (Jack Johnson) suffers from neglect.

Bratty daughter Penny (the ultra-whiny Lacey Chabert) experiments with precocious club-kid styling and twerpy teen rebellion that just begs for a short sharp smack from Mom. You keep hoping they'll trade her to the Ferengi for a six-pack of malt liquor. No such luck.

Daughter Judy (Heather Graham) is a scientist like Pa, but her primary directive is to play hard-to-get around the ship's cocksure but dim pilot, Don West (Matthew LeBlanc). Also aboard: Dr. Zachary Smith (Gary Oldman), the prissy traitor who's part Guy Burgess and part Mr. Blackwell.

The Jupiter 2 loses its way when, thanks to Smith's evil programming, the rampaging Robot—a pumped-up insectoid version of the vacuum-cleaner-ish original—goes postal, forcing an emergency leap into hyperspace, and thus oblivion.

Aside from Oldman and that irritating Chabert, the rest of the cast is so colorless you don't much care what happens to them.

Squinty Hurt brings such genteel somnolence to his space professor role you expect to see elbow patches on his rubberized outfit. Rogers works her soccer-mom hairdo for all it's worth, but it's frankly disconcerting to look up in her big take-charge scene and think, "Shazbot! It's Marilyn Quayle!"

The movie veers irrecoverably off course right after the Jupiter crew has a run-in with vicious space spiders. This occasions the introduction of a simperingly cute, computer-generated monkey mascot, utterly irrelevant to the plot but key to moving "Lost in Space" merch in toy stores.

From then, the ship crashes hard on an unstable planet, which is not a bad metaphor for what happens to the picture, lost and flailing in a confusing denouement involving time travel, family values and a blatant rip-off of Darth Vader's shtick. Parents of Earth, you have been warned.

NEWSDAY, 4/3/98, Part II/p. B2, John Anderson

"Get lost" is the tag line on New Line Cinema's "Lost in Space"—which for those old enough to remember LBJ and young enough to be wandering awestruck through Nickelodeon's TVLAND, is a considerably more upscale version of the old CBS adventure program. For those who remember "Let's Get Lost," Bruce Weber's 1989 documentary on jazzman Chet Baker, "getting lost" meant taking heroin. But except for a certain narcotic quality in the newer film, I don't think there's any connection.

There is, instead, a decidedly forced nostalgia in this reheating of leftovers, which continues a trend that seems unlikely to stop until they cease making TV shows—or until the production of the films overtakes the production on TV, which at its present rate may be soon. Unless you were actually a fan of the old show—which looked like it was made for about $1.79—it probably doesn't matter how faithful the filmmakers were to the original. It seems necessary to mention, however, that June Lockhart, Angela Cartwright and several other members of the TV cast make cameo appearances; Dick Tufeld returns as the voice of the robot—then, as now, the funniest thing in it. There are a lot of catch phrases ("Danger, Will Robinson!") guaranteed to tickle the oldies. And it didn't cost $1.79.

Then, as now, gallantry is not necessarily a dramatic asset. Dr. Zachary Smith, the sniveling stowaway originated by Jonathan Harris, remains the centerpiece of the story, although as played by Gary Oldman—for whom typecasting as weird villains is no longer a danger but a reality—he's almost purely evil. In league with the New Global Sedition—there will be terrorists in space, we're reassured—Smith sets out with the soon-to-be-converted Robot to kill the already imperiled Robinsons, sending their 10-year, corporate-funded mission for ecology wildly awry. Please disregard the trainloads of scrap metal they leave hurtling through space.

Along with space cockroaches and time bubbles, Smith provides one of the obstacles to the Robinsons' finding their way home—or to their original destination, Alpha Prime, it's not clear which. But besides villainy, Oldman also serves as the audience's voice of emotional reason. Is every crisis going to be an occasion for sickening familial sentiment? he asks. Yes! And to an extraordinary degree!

A moment doesn't go by that the dysfunctional Robinsons—John (William Hurt), Maureen (Mimi Rogers), Dr. Judy (Heather Graham), Penny (Lacey Chabert of "Party of Five") and Will (Jack Johnson)—aren't whining, hugging or re-plighting their troths. Penny, particularly, who suggests Calvin Klein-meets-"Alphaville," is in need of therapy, or a pharmacy. And Graham fresh from "Boogie Nights," looks good in space sweats.

That's a factor certainly appreciated by Maj. Don West, the ace pilot and brash young hero played by Matt LeBlanc ("Friends"). Despite a crypto-Nazi sense of in-flight fashion, and nostrils that flare like a pair of black holes, LeBlanc's West is consistently fun and sympathetic, even as Judy keep disregarding his satellite transmissions.

But for all its occasional comedy, "Lost in Space" is more often dull and uninvolving, mostly for lack of story or visual rhythm. Screenwriter Akiva Goldsman—who, unsurprisingly, wrote Joel Schumacher's unwatchable "Batman and Robin"—is freshest when he's quoting the old TV show. Director Stephen Hopkins, the perpetrator of "Judgment Night" and "Blown Away," doesn't know if he wants to make "2001" or "Plan 9 from Outer Space."

To paraphrase an old management maxim, if you can't dazzle 'em, baffle 'em. The technological wizardry of "Lost in Space," as loud and flashy as it is, flies by too quickly to really be grasped, which is the strategy. Likewise: a lot of the action sequences, which are so frantic and chaotic it's impossible to know where you're supposed to be standing when your socks are knocked off. One needs, in other words, some kind of visual orientation for all the roller-coaster special effects to have the kind of visceral impact they're intended to have. If it's just sound and lights, well, it's just sound and lights.

SIGHT AND SOUND, 8/98, p. 48, Leslie Felperin

Earth, 2058. The planet is dying due to environmental breakdown. Plans have been made to colonise nearby planet Alpha Prime. Dr John Robinson has designed a pair of hypergates—one for earth, one for Alpha Prime—which will enable vehicles to travel between the two instantaneously. But first Robinson and his family—wife Maureen, daughters Judy and Penny, and son Will—must go via conventional space travel (a ten-year trip) aboard the *Jupiter 2* to Alpha. War hero Major Don West is conscripted to pilot the mission. However, Dr Zachary Smith, a terrorist spy, attempts sabotage, resulting in the ship being lost in space with Smith aboard.

The *Jupiter* crew find an earth spaceship from the future sent to look for them, but its crew have been wiped out by alien space spiders which attack West, the Robinsons and Smith (who is wounded by a spider). A temporal anomaly brings them to a planet where they eventually discover a grown Will Robinson, who has perfected the time machine he conceived as a child in 2058. The older Will is angry with his father, has grown close to Smith (now half space spider) and plans to go back to 2058 to stop the *Jupiter* mission. Spider Smith kills the other Smith, but is killed in his turn. The older Will helps his father travel back in time far enough to be reunited with his family in 2058. They escape the planet just as it breaks up due to earthquakes and, using the hyperdrive, they are lost once again in space.

Stranding the family Robinson on a desert planet with a hunky space pilot, an effete doctor and a robot resembling an industrial vacuum cleaner mated with a goldfish bowl, the original television series *Lost in Space* (1965-68) was somewhat misleadingly titled. Due to budget restrictions, for two series everyone stayed on one planet, lost in a cosmic sense but hardly in a local one.

Budgeted big, the new film *Lost in Space,* based on the series, can afford to explore what it means to be lost. The *Jupiter 2* floats against a dense bank of stars, while a flashy holographic map generated by the ship's computer, throwing up bigger-and bigger-scaled maps, looks set to keep on trying to locate the ship until told to stop. In one sweet scene Major West and Judy Robinson discuss how the earth's first explorers navigated by making charts of stars, and propose new constellations by drawing pictures of Daffy Duck and Bugs Bunny. The cliff-hanger ending (a signature in the television series) suggests that the film-makers were hoping that with so much space to be lost in, this could be the start of a healthy franchise.

Unfortunately, someone forgot to put a better screenplay in the hold on the maiden voyage, and the film has sunk at the box office in the US. Despite some cynical touches (Major West dismisses the whole venture of sending a family into space as a hollow PR exercise; much is made of the family's dysfunctionality)the script is wearisomely wholesome, punctuated by toe-curlingly pro-social messages. ("I guess sometimes friendship means listening to your heart, not your head. Put that in your memory," Will Robinson tells his pet robot.) When Will guides the robot with remote-holographic control, a touch clearly intended to tie in with a video or arcade game, the film feels all too much like a hollow merchandising exercise.

Yet despite the flat performances (even Gary Oldman with the fun character of Dr Smith looks bored), it's worth savouring *Lost in Space* for the visuals alone. Art directed to within an inch of its life, it offers a dazzling spread of curvy, matt-aluminium surfaces, rubberised fetish suits with intricate pleats and pockets, and discreet touch-sensitive computer interfaces with jewel-like buttons. Altogether, it's like something designed by Charles Eames in collaboration with Ron Arad, waiting for interiors-and-style bible wallpaper to arrive with the models for a fashion shoot. What a shame the fabulous space the film constructs is wasted on such an otherwise shabby enterprise.

VILLAGE VOICE, 4/14/98, p. 64, Gary Dauphin

Light years beyond the foamy, low-tech F/X of the mid-'60s series, the new *Lost in Space* is chock-full of vertiginous B+ eye candy that teeters between old-style, obsessively crafted miniatures and the vaporous digital immateriality of a video game. The 2058 of this updated Robinson family saga looks pretty plausible because it's so fake, cooked up on the fly in a technological pot heated by fast-cycling gadget-happiness. All that energetic randomness adds nothing to the people parts of the flick—little things like story, dialogue, and character—but it's hard to find fault considering the original source material; anyone who walks in expecting different is as crazy as that kooky Dr. Smith.

Now as then, *Lost in Space* tells the tale of the never ending wanderings of the egghead Robinsons: scientists Ma and Pop (William Hurt and Mimi Rogers); kids Judy, Penny, and Will (Heather Graham, Lacey Chabert, and Jack Johnson); pseudo-uncles Dr. Smith and pilot-hunk Major West (Gary Oldman and Matt LeBlanc), and, of course, the Robot. Looking for the ecological promised land of the planet Alpha Prime, the Robinsons blast off from Earth in their homey *Jupiter* starship and, you know, get lost, their main problem perpetual stowaway Smith, who's more malevolent than humbling this time around.

The comedic triumvirate of Dr. Smith, the Robot, and Will still provides *Lost in Space*'s low-gravity distractions, with Chabert's Penny updated into one of those waifish, oversexualized preteens you find in extremely naughty *anime*. Hurt and Rogers are paper-thin, and LeBlanc just can't pull off the suave space hero thing, but Oldman has a fine time making Smith an oily ideologic of evil who can't be killed or abandoned, just masochistically endured. Unless you've got an F/X fetish, *Lost in Space* will probably be an endurance test as well. The flick shoots its emotional wad with little more than the words "Danger! Danger!"

Also reviewed in:
CHICAGO TRIBUNE, 4/3/98, Friday/p. A, Michael Wilmington
NEW YORK TIMES, 4/3/98, p. E26, Janet Maslin
VARIETY, 4/6-12/98, p. 45, Dennis Harvey
WASHINGTON POST, 4/3/98, p. F1, Rita Kempley
WASHINGTON POST, 4/3/98, Weekend/p. 53, Desson Howe

LOUISA MAY ALCOTT'S "LITTLE MEN"

A Legacy release of a Brainstorm Media presentation in association with Image Organization of an Allegro Films production. *Executive Producer:* Meyer Shwarztein and Tom Berry. *Producer:* Pierre David and Franco Battista. *Director:* Rodney Gibbons. *Screenplay:* Mark Evan Schwartz. *Based on the novel by:* Louisa May Alcott. *Director of Photography:* Georges Archambault. *Editor:* Andre Corriveau. *Music:* Milan Kymicka. *Sound:* Tim Archer. *Casting:* Lynda Purdy and Francois Garcia. *Production Designer:* Donna Noonan. *Set Decorator:* Mario Hervieux, Michel Clement, Diane Gauthier, and Frances Calder. *Costumes:* Janet Campbell. *Running time:* 98 minutes. *MPAA Rating:* PG.

CAST: Michael Caloz (Nat Blake); Mariel Hemingway (Jo Bhaer); Ben Cook (Dan); Ricky Mabe (Tommy Bangs); Chris Sarandon (Fritz Bhaer); Gabrielle Boni (Nan Harding); Michael Yarmoush (Emil); Tyler Hynes (Dennis Brooke); Julia Garland (Daisy Brooke); B.J. McLellan (Jack Ford); Mathew Mackay (Franz); Kathleen Fee (Narrator).

LOS ANGELES TIMES, 5/8/98, Calendar/p. 14, John Anderson

[The following review by John Anderson appeared in a slightly different form in **NEWSDAY, 5/8/98, Part II/p. B7.]**

Here's the kind of movie they don't make anymore, because when they do, people don't go. At the same time, "Louisa May Alcott's Little Men" fills that frequently empty family-entertainment niche where movies for the whole brood are supposed to reside. For all its merits, the film won't attract any kids I know personally, but if yours are young enough it should be OK. The smaller they are, the less fight they put up.

"Louisa May Alcott's Little Men" shouldn't be considered in any way a cinematic sequel to Gillian Armstrong's 1994 "Little Women," a splendid film that did everything right. "Little Men," directed by Rodney Gibbons, is operating on a different level entirely, where the people are so nice they might have come from pods and where production values are so simple they might have come from television. Still, the lessons—honesty, friendship, family—are worthy ones, even if Alcott's book is the type that's romanticized both the institutionalizing of children and the institutions.

The one here is Plumfield, the house and grounds inherited by Jo (Mariel Hemingway), the key sister from the first book, who with her husband, Prof. Fritz Bhaer (the not-so-frequently-seen Chris Sarandon, who starred with Hemingway long ago in "Lipstick"), runs a boarding school for boys. The daily routine is disrupted by the arrival of Nat (Michael Caloz), a street urchin from Boston, whose street ethics clash with those of the school ("All we ask is honesty and a willingness to learn"). Nat adapts, but the arrival of his partner in crime, Artful Dodger impersonator Dan (Ben Cook) creates more discord of the moral and academic varieties.

No, Dan and Nat don't turn into Perry Smith and Dick Hickock and slaughter all the inhabitants. There are crises, but all are resolved with uplifting results. The kids learn much and Prof. Bhaer learns not to jump to conclusions. "Little Men" may lumber, but it does so with its head held high.

NEW YORK POST, 5/8/98, p. 50, Larry Worth

Louisa May Alcott should have left well enough alone after penning her masterpiece, "Little Women." Her sequel, "Little Men," couldn't compare.

So it's no real surprise that the same holds true for the stories' big-screen versions. Even so, director Rodney Gibbons goes above and beyond to make "Little Men" into cinematic treacle: It sems less Alcott knockoff than Hallmark card, complete with sugar-sweet sentiments and heart-warming imagery.

This Alcott saga concerns heroine Jo, now grown and running a school for boys with her husband in Concord, Mass. Sitting around the dinner table with ther Stepford-like charges, Jo, hubby and the boys make "The Waltons" seem deviant.

Paradise, however, is about to be invaded—courtesy of Oliver Twist and the Artful Dodger (here less imaginatively dubbed Nat and Dan). But under Jo's tender loving care, Nat can be brought over to the good side. That darn Dan is another matter.

Anyone left in suspense—Will Dan burn the house down when smoking cigars in the attic?—can find solace with a look at the nearby corral. Even the wildest metaphor—er, mustang—can be tamed with guidance.

Collectively, it's enough to put diabetics in a coma. That's obvious just from narrator Kathleen Fee's jolly tones in the opening sequence, delivering syrupy lines like: "Oh, what surprises were in store for the lads!"

The actors don't help. Mariel Hemingway's Jo tries hard to generate warmth and a spirit of fun. But whether exchanging oh-so-knowing glances with her spouse or troubled by the latest calamity, she's frightfully over the top.

Chris Sarandon is no better as her other half. But chld actors Michael Caloz and Ben Cook—the titular little men—play off each other well and deliver a few refreshingly cynical lines with relish.

Granted, the production means well and is chock-full of good intentions. But filmgoers would do well to remember what the road to hell is paved with.

Also reviewed in:
CHICAGO TRIBUNE, 5/8/98, Friday/p. F, John Petrakis
NEW YORK TIMES, 5/8/98, p. E12, Anita Gates
VARIETY, 5/11-17/98, p. 60, Lael Loewenstein

LOVE AND DEATH ON LONG ISLAND

A Lions Gate Films release of a Skyline/Imagex production with the participation of British Screen/Telefilm Canada/Arts Council of England/Nova Scotia Film Development Corporation in association with BBC Films/Mikado/The Sales Company. Developed in association with Alfalfa Entertainments and with the support of British Screen Finance Limited/BBC Films/The Nova Scotia Film Industry Tax Credit and the European Script Fund. Supported by the National Lottery through the Arts Council of England. *Producer:* Steve Clark-Hall and Christopher Zimmer. *Director:* Richard Kwietniowski. *Screenplay:* Richard Kwietniowski. *Based on the novel by:* Gilbert Adair. *Director of Photography:* Oliver Curtis. *Editor:* Susan Shipton. *Music:* The Insects and Richard Grassby-Lewis. *Sound:* Neil Kingsbury, Jim Rillie and (music) Steve Parr. *Sound Editor:* Kevin Brazier and Stephen Griffiths. *Casting:* Kate Day and Jon Comerford. *Production Designer:* David McHenry. *Art Director:* Fleur Whitlock and Emmanuel Jannasch. *Set Decorator:* Patricia Larman. *Costumes:* Andrea Galer and Martha Curry. *Make-up:* Tory Wright. *Stunt Coordinator:* Branko Racki. *Running time:* 93 minutes. *MPAA Rating:* PG-13.

CAST: John Hurt (Giles De'Ath); Jason Priestley (Ronnie Bostock); Fiona Loewi (Audrey); Sheila Hancock (Mrs. Barker); Harvey Atkin (Lou); Gawn Grainger (Henry, Giles's Agent); Elizabeth Quinn (Mrs. Reed); Maury Chaykin (Irving Buckmuller); Linda Busby (Mrs. Abbott); Bill Leadbitter (Eldridge); Ann Reid (Maureen); Danny Webb (Video Assistant); Andrew Barrow (Harry); Dean Gatiss (Rob); Robert McKewley (Video Salesman); Tusse Silberg (Abigail's Mother); Rebecca Michael (Abigail); Jean Ainslie and Nigel Makin (Ticket Sellers); Jonathan Stratt (Taxi Driver); Magnus Magnusson (Quiz Master); Shaughan Seymour (Quiz Show Contestant); Marguerite McNeil and Andrew Smith (Irv's Customers); Jeffrey Hirschfield (Policeman); Tommy Hurst (Mailman); Lex Gigeroff, Michael Pellerin, and Cecil Wright (Cab Drivers); Benita Ha (Weather Reporter); Jason Priestley (Mikey); Vincent Corazza (Corey); Geoffrey Herod (Brad); Ryan Rogerson (Tommy); Bruce Fillmore (Big Guy); Nancy Marshall (Corey's Mother); Elizabeth Murphy (The Stomper); Jennie Raymond (Molly); Charles Jannasch (Rusty); Shaun D. Richardson (Pete); Gabriel Hogan (Jake); Jeremy Akerman (Father Bryson); Christine Jeffers (Sitcom Mother); Morissey Dunn (Sitcom Father).

LOS ANGELES TIMES, 3/5/98, Calendar/p. 22, Kenneth Turan

As the determined enemy of all things modem, British cult novelist and "erstwhile fogy" Giles De'Ath (it's pronounced "day-ath," thank you very much) is not a person one expects to find in a movie theater. In fact, if he hadn't accidentally locked himself out of his London flat on a rainy afternoon, he wouldn't be there at all.

Expecting to see a refined E.M. Forster adaptation, Giles accidentally wanders into "Hotpants College II." Suitably horrified, he's about to leave when he catches a glimpse, just a glimpse, of a face on the screen. It's mega-dreamboat Ronnie Bostock, "one of Hollywood's most snoggable fellows," and against all logic, reason and expectation, Giles is overwhelmed and a magnificent obsession is born.

Starring John Hurt in one of the great performances of his career as the transfixed writer and "Beverly Hills, 90210's" Jason Priestley as teen idol Bostock, "Love and Death on Long Island" is sharp, sophisticated and completely delicious, a purposeful comedy that focuses on the power of screen images to uproot lives and the poignancy of amour fou, totally mad love.

"Love and Death" (taken from Gilbert Adair's novel of the same name) is also the impressive feature debut of British TV's writer-director Richard Kwietniowski. Wildly unlikely yet completely believable, droll enough to practically define the word, this film uses exactly calibrated bursts of dry wit and killing dialogue to uncover mania where others wouldn't even dare to look.

What gives "Love and Death" a special grace is the exquisite, nuanced performance of veteran actor Hurt, Oscar-nominated for his work in "Midnight Express" and "The Elephant Man." Hurt's grasp of the role couldn't be surer—who, after all, is in the actor's league when it comes to the quizzically raised eyebrow?—and his ability to squeeze all possible humor out of lines like "I've never really approved of the pre-Raphaelites" is unquestioned. There is an entire universe in Hurt's face, a world of bemusement, bafflement, comic hauteur and disdain that is intoxicating to observe.

At first Giles' fascination with Ronnie Bostock takes a conventional route. He scours fan magazines for color photos, pasting them in an album grandly titled "Bostockiana." And, not caring that Sight & Sound has called them "puerile romps without a single redeeming feature," he tries to catch up on "Skidmarks" and "Tex-Mex," earlier items from the Bostock oeuvre. It's a difficult proposition when a) you don't realize VCRs have to be connected to TV sets and b) you can't tell a TV from a microwave.

Then the madness goes up a notch. Giles imagines himself on a TV quiz show where the category is Bostock; he visualizes his new hero as the subject of the Tate Gallery's classic painting "The Death of Chatterton"; he even starts constructing a new novel around "the discovery of beauty where no one thought to look for it."

Inevitably, Giles decides to track this beauty to its source—and this from a man who hates to so much as leave his apartment. He makes a pilgrimage to the small Long Island town where Ronnie lives with a model named Audrey (Fiona Loewi) and puts his own considerable personal charm at the service of worming his way into the young man's life.

Under Kwietniowski's completely controlled direction, this film delights in exploring the clash of cultures that's inevitable when De'Ath hits Long Island and discovers places like a diner called Chez d'Irv. When the writer ignores a "Thank You for Not Smoking" sign and informs the astonished cabdriver, "As I am, I don't expect to be thanked," it's a moment of such heedless and hilarious urbanity you want to stand and cheer.

When the oblivious actor (nicely played by Priestley, tweaking his own teen idol image) and the conniving writer—two people who speak the same language only in theory—finally meet, it's an irresistible case of worlds colliding. Yet it's a mark of the skill with which "Love and Death" has been made that as his mania plays itself out, Giles never becomes ridiculous, never turns into a melancholy version of "Lolita's" Humbert Humbert.

The combination of Hurt's magnificent presence and Kwietniowski's uncompromising writing and direction give the lovelorn writer a dignity and an emotional heft he never loses. Not even when he's in the throes of the desperation born of what even De'Ath knows enough to call "the most irrational desire of all mankind, the desire to fall in love."

NEW YORK, 3/16/98, p. 54, David Denby

Here is the great enigma of pop, the great subversive mystery: Shallow prettiness, achieved without effort or style, may strike a susceptible soul as the most profound beauty in the world. So perhaps it's no surprise that a crusty English highbrow writer, Giles De'Ath (John Hurt), the hero of *Love and Death on Long Island,* falls in love with an image—the face of an American actor, a teen idol named Ronnie Bostock (Jason Priestley). But it certainly comes as a surprise to *Giles.* De'Ath (the second syllable is emphasized, but you may read the name as "death") is a London widower, the author of many distinguished and unreadable tomes (we get a whiff of classicism covered with mold). A creature of routine, De'Ath is entombed in a wood-paneled house; he regards the world outside with hauteur and fear. Going to the movies, he wanders into the wrong auditorium in a multiplex—the one playing the crass American comedy "Hotpants College 2"—and is about to leave in a rage when Ronnie Bostock appears as a waiter in a fast-food joint. De'Ath's astonished face, caught in the reflected light of the screen, suggests a man ravished from soul to bowels by an emotion he has never experienced before. The joke, of course, is that Jason Priestley—sideburns, full wavy hair, rotten-angel smile—looks like a second-rate teen fave from about 1954. He's not even that good-looking. But De'Ath becomes obsessed; he rants about a beauty of classical permanence. In a more practical vein, he starts a scrapbook and hides movie-fan magazines in his house as if they were the vilest pornography. He even rushes to eastern Long Island, where Ronnie lives with his girlfriend (Fiona Leowi), and turns himself into a seducer of considerable guile.

Writer-director Richard Kwietniowski has never made a feature before, but this debut effort is a triumph, a buoyant and elegant achievement—romantic and ruminative yet always precise, a comedy of longing propelled by a strong current of satirical observation. Kwietniowski plays the most beautiful effects off silence; he dwells on the baffled pause and strained hesitation. And yet the movie is never fussy or embarrassing; it finds the element of audacity in the love-struck aging artist and stays close to it. De'Ath may be a creep, but he's also a true hero. He's pulled by his obsession into the common life, and suffers the humiliation of getting things wrong. A video store is like a foreign planet to him; a TV set is an instrument of terror and wonder. The formality of English manners offers an extraordinary advantage to a nuanced actor like Hurt. With the slightest change of intonation—the verbal equivalent of a raised eyebrow—he suggests reserves of fear and rage. His sudden grin when he begins to get close to Ronnie is so flagrantly happy that one almost wants him to succeed. Everything Hurt does seems fresh, fully felt.

Love and Death on Long Island is based on a novel by an extremely witty British film critic named Gilbert Adair. I haven't been able to get hold of the book, but I would guess from the movie alone that Adair was playing with the themes of Thomas Mann's *Death in Venice* examining them through the lens of Nabokov's *Lolita,* in which an English writer is mesmerized by both a beautiful American nymphet and the siren song of American vulgarity. This connection alone is a perverse joke, since Nabokov's loathing of Mann's novella is famous. In the movie, the joke of American commonness works both ways. Ronnie Bostock's pizza-parlor and locker-room movies (which Kwietniowski re-creates with loving care) are appalling, but the ordinary folk whom De'Ath meets on Long Island are decent and friendly in a way that the sarcastic Londoners are not. Ronnie himself is an okay guy—no great brain or talent, but no stuck-up monster either. He's moved by what he takes to be De'Ath's interest in his mediocre movie career. Jason Priestley's performance is on the bland side, but he has one great moment. It is the look on his face—the shot is prolonged for what seems an eternity—when the Englishman proclaims, in the Long Island hash house Chez D'Irv, his undying love for the young actor. At that moment, Jason Priestley's Ronnie really does become someone worthy of eternal love.

NEW YORK POST, 3/6/98, p. 46, Thelma Adams

"This isn't E.M. Forster," veddy veddy proper British writer Giles De'Ath says with alarm at the beginning of "Love and Death on Long Island."

The conservative widower, played with aching sincerity by John Hurt, has wandered into the wrong theater at a London cineplex. De'Ath has stumbled onto the 20th century, which appears dressed in the short shorts of Ronnie Bostock (Jason Priestley), the star of the instantly forgettable teen exploitation flick "Hotpants College II."

As Dorothy so aptly put it: "We're not in Kansas anymore."

Those blue eyes, that all-American smile, that lack of any visible intellectual activity: De'Ath like millions of high school girls before him, is instantly smitten with Bostock/Priestley. Pushing aside his latest novel, De'Ath exercises his scholarly rigor in collecting scraps of pop culture related to the hunky heartthrob.

When De'Ath discovers that Bostock has a hideaway on Long Island, the author travels to the New World for "research." Once there, he charms Bostock's girlfriend, Audrey (Fiona Loewi), and gets close enough to the star to share sunglasses.

British writer/director Richard Kwietniowski's original debut is an odd-couple comedy that displays both male stars to their best advantage. Based on Gilbert Adair's offbeat novel, there's something so Long Island "Lolita" about this tale of late-blooming desire and the clash of high and low culture. Hurt is fabulous in the Humbert Humbert role and Priestley's easy on the eyes.

Like so many recent movies, this favorite from the Cannes and New York film festivals stumbles in the third act. But no one can fault "Love and Death on Long Island" for being predictable. As De'Ath might say, it's easily the finest work in the Priestley oeuvre.

NEWSDAY, 3/6/98, Part II/p. B6, Jack Mathews

During a painful dead spot in a radio interview with the reclusive and culturally insulated British novelist Giles De'Ath, in Richard Kwietniowski's wonderfully off-beat comedy "Love and Death on Long Island," the show's frustrated host asks the author, "Does the 20th Century play any part in your life?"

De'Ath (John Hurt) ponders the question with the look of someone who's just been handed an object that is both disgusting and unidentifiable. And he can't answer it because... well, someone's first going to have to define what is meant by 20th Century.

The reference is clear enough to us. It's the time we live in, with television, computers, supersonic travel, cybercommunications, pop art and the open, if often irrational, pursuit of love and happiness. De'Ath, a widower who's lived a cloistered literary existence, knows nothing of this world, but through a chance exposure to rising American teen heartthrob Ronnie Bostock (Jason Priestley), he's about to get a crash course.

Giles' introduction to Ronnie occurs in a movie theater that Giles ducks into during a rain storm. He's expecting to see an adaptation of E. M. Forster's "Eternal Moment." Instead, he finds himself watching some artless gruel called "Hotpants College II," and is about to leave when he is thunderstruck by Ronnie's appearance. It's as if everything unknown to Giles about the world outside his own, as well as a lifetime of missed emotions, were contained in that one bolt of electricity connecting him to the image on the screen.

From then on, Giles is overcome by adolescent passion. He begins a scrapbook of Ronnie Bostock magazine photos, pores through fan magazines for scraps of lifestyle details, buys a TV set and videocassette player and watches Ronnie's movies so many times he begins to believe the actor has real talent.

When Giles begins lacing his book-club lectures with spontaneous riffs about the power of images over words, his agent suggests a long vacation, and Giles already has a spot in mind. The woodsy hamlet of Chesterton, Long Island, where Ronnie Bostock lives. After days or weeks of hunting, Giles finds and befriends Ronnie's girlfriend, Audrey (Fiona Loewi), and is soon insinuating himself directly into the actor's life by proclaiming him a talent worthy of Shakespeare.

"Love and Death on Long Island," adapted by first-time director Kwietniowski from Gilbert Adair's novel, is a smart, bittersweet story of self-discovery and the power of infatuation, and Hurt makes De'Ath, who is alternately intellectual and clueless, confident and desperate, reasoned and mad, the performance of his career.

Death in the title refers both to the way people read Giles' last name, prompting each time the gruff correction, "Day-awth," and the shucking of his musty, buttoned-down former life. Giles' infatuation with Ronnie is cause for some nervous laughter in the audience. He envisions himself as the mentor/lover of old European "tradition," Cocteau to Ronnie's Radiquet, and even as the words leap out of his mouth, he knows how irrational they are.

This is dicey territory for comedy, but Kwietniowski handles it with a master's touch, collaborating with Hurt to create a character so rich, fascinating and sympathetic that the experience—for him, for Ronnie Bostock, and us—is ultimately liberating. And although Priestley is clearly mocking his own image as a "90210" phenom, he gives Ronnie enough dimension, character and compassion to convince us that, while he may not be ready for Hamlet, he has better ahead than "Hotpants College III."

By the way, don't look for familiar Long Island landmarks. The Chesterton scenes were shot in Nova Scotia, and the filmmakers are literally all over the place trying to locate it for us. In one scene, Giles scans the map for Chesterton and his finger settles somewhere in the Hamptons. But the train station marked Chesterton is actually the one in Huntington. Later, he takes a short cab ride from Chesterton to his motel in a cab marked "Oyster Bay."

But why quibble? This is one story about Long Island real estate where location isn't everything.

NEWSWEEK, 3/9/98, p. 59, David Ansen

John Hurt, whose talents are often wasted in big Hollywood movies, such as "Contact," has found a role he can sink his sharpest teeth into. In "Love and Death on Long Island," a comedy of unusual intelligence and poignancy, he plays a recently widowed highbrow British novelist named Giles De'Ath (pronounced Day-athe, not death), an old fogey so set in his ways he doesn't know one can't use a VCR without a television set to go along with it. One afternoon, locked out of his London house, he deigns to go to the cinema, thinking he'll catch one of the E. M. Forster adaptations he's been hearing about. Wandering into the wrong theater, he finds himself assaulted by a raunchy teen sex comedy called "College Hotpants 2." "This isn't E. M. Forster!" he protests, but before he can leave he is transfixed by the vision of teen idol Ronny Bostock (Jason Priestley).

So begins an obsession—fed by teen magazines and video rentals of such early Bostock works as "Skidmarks" and "Tex Mex"—that will drag this 19th-century man into the cheesy delights of 20th-century pop culture. As a man in the grips of a passion he knows is ridiculous and is helpless to abandon, Hurt gives one of his subtlest, funniest—and most touching—performances. "What exactly is a sitcom?" he inquires of his agent, disdain mingling with hidden excitement. Mastering the minutiae of "Bostockiana" (Ronnie's favorite author is Stephen King; his favorite athletic shoes, Reeboks), he flies to New York's Long Island on a mad quest to meet his idol and convince him that Giles should take charge of his career.

The first-time writer-director, Englishman Richard Kwietniowski, has adapted Gilbert Adair's novel with wit, economy and a delicate understanding that the funniest comedies are played with dead seriousness. Priestly gives a good-natured performance as the banal object of desire who's unaware of Giles's amorous motives, drolly tweaking his "90210" heartthrob image. "Love and Death on Long Island" owes an obvious debt to both "Death in Venice" and "Lolita," but the particulars of this collision between high and low cultures, age and youth, are pricelessly its own. Kwietniowski's re-creations of Ronnie's hopelessly tacky movies are dead on, but in De'Ath's transfixed eyes, the vision of Ronnie's playing a pizza-delivery boy prone on a counter and drenched in ketchup evokes hallowed comparison to the Pre-Raphaelite painting of the death of Chatterton. The hero of this wicked satire may be pathetically deluded, but the movie grants his quixotic, lovestruck quest a certain nobility. The movie is about, as De'Ath puts it, "the discovery of beauty where one wouldn't expect to find it." You could say the same about this small, clever beauty of a film.

SIGHT AND SOUND, 7/98, p. 45, Philip Kemp

British novelist Giles De'Ath, widowed and reclusive, spurns the modern world. One rainy day, accidentally locked out of his flat, he takes shelter in a cinema and finds himself watching a trashy American comedy, *Hotpants College II*. His attention is taken by a young supporting actor, Ronnie Bostock. Increasingly obsessed, Giles seeks out Ronnie's previous films and collects magazine cuttings about him. Learning that Ronnie lives with his girlfriend Audrey in Chesterton, Long Island, De'Ath travels there, checks into a motel and sets out to find his beloved.

Having engineered an encounter with Audrey in a supermarket, Giles is invited back to meet Ronnie. He becomes a frequent visitor, flattering the young man and filling his head with dreams of a distinguished acting career in Europe. Giles also helps Ronnie rehearse his forthcoming role in *Hotpants College III*. Audrey, at first delighted for Ronnie, grows suspicious and lets Giles know she understands his real feelings. Forced to act, Giles declares his love. Ronnie gently rebuffs him. Before leaving for the airport, Giles sends Ronnie a long fax recounting the story of his obsession. In it he includes a touching graveside speech for Ronnie to perform in the new film. When *Hotpants College III* is released, the scene is featured word for word.

In a perfect matching of sensibilities, Richard Kwietniowski has fashioned a slim, fastidious film from Gilbert Adair's slim, fastidious novel. All the ironies—the literary and cinematic allusions, the amused mockery of both high and popular culture—are deftly positioned. The whole exercise would be a touch too precious for its own good were it not for John Hurt, bringing a real sense of poignancy, late-flowering passion and assured comic timing to a role that cold easily have toppled into caricature. As he plunges, wincing but game, into the alien world of pre-teen fan mags ("Mega-dreamboat Ronnie Bostock!!") and stupid Hollywood college comedies, Hurt's Giles De'Ath presents the touching spectacle of a man prepared to risk not just ridicule, but (far worse in his own eyes) cultural contamination all for love.

Kwietniowski, here making his feature-film debut, shows a fine eye (and ear) for detail. He has fun creating pastiches of the daytime soaps and straight-to-video turkeys in which Ronnie's career has been mired, and even tosses in a supercilious *Sight and Sound* dismissal of one ("puerile romp without a single redeeming feature). At the other end of the cultural spectrum, he playfully sketches in Giles' literary standing as "an erstwhile fogey, now cult". The camera browses around his Edwardian, technology-free study and skims along a row of his novels published by Faber and Faber (translated into French by classy publisher Nouvelle Revue Française). Scornful of his public (it's easier to write one of his novels, he says, than to read one properly"), Giles disdains the suggestion he might swap his fountain pen for more modern methods, such as a word processor: "I don't process words", he sniffs. "I'm a writer. I write."

Not only is Hurt on top form, but Kwietniowski is well served by all his cast. As Audrey, far savvier than her hunky boyfriend, Fiona Loewi gives a likably unaffected performance, and there's a winning turn from Maury Chaykin as Irving Buckmuller, a diner-owner with intellectual pretensions. (His establishment is called Chez d'Irv.) Jason Priestley's Ronnie, dim intimations of thought swimming behind his furrowed gaze like fish in a murky pond, never overplays the crassness. (His casting is doubly apt, considering his career as a teen pin-up in the television series *Beverly Hills 90210*.) His response to Giles' declaration of love is appealingly simple: no outraged tirades or embarrassed mumbles, just a look of slow-dawning compassion. Standing up, he pats Giles' shoulder and walks off, leaving the novelist murmuring, "Dear God—what have I done?'

None of this bites too deep. It's Nabokov's *Lolita* without the anguish, *Death in Venice* without the mortality, touchstones of which Kwietniowski, like Adair, is clearly well aware, and with which he plays knowingly. Fantasy and reality may collide, but each gets off with nothing worse than a minor graze. Far from agonising, Giles will transmute the experience into an elegant, urbane novel—deriving far more satisfaction from it than from any brief spasm with Ronnie. Had Kwietniowski been prepared to confront real emotional damage, a hint of lasting waste and pain, then without doing violence to Adair's original he might have tapped a deeper, more disturbing vein. As it is, *Love and Death on Long Island* remains an accomplished soufflé of a film, witty and diverting—a thoroughly civilised pleasure that sometimes touches the heart.

TIME, 3/2/98, p. 85, Richard Corliss

We think ourselves ladies and gentlemen of taste, connoisseurs of finer books and deeper thoughts. Then we see some ravishing creature on the street or the screen, and we are starstruck kids, our brains shut off, hearts turned to mush.

Giles De'Ath (John Hurt), a reclusive English novelist, has had so little contact with the late 20th century that he can't tell a microwave from a VCR.

One day, by mistake, he watches a trashy teenpic called *Hotpants College 2* and finds, he thinks, a reason for loving. In an actor named Ronnie Bostock (Jason Priestley), Giles sees all the beauty of the ages in one glorious package. The donnish writer buys fan mags, rents B-minus films, immerses himself in the detritus of Bostockiana. To your eyes Ronnie might seem a bland dreamboat, but that is part of the fun in this delicious comedy. And part of the truth: for it is a mark of obsession that it fixes its gaze on an object whose appeal is inexplicable.

Director Richard Kwietniowski, adapting Gilbert Adair's novel, uses Priestley's fretful blankness to handsome comic effect. But Hurt is the big news here. Dignified and dithery, he makes Giles one of the most charming predators in ages. Like Von Aschenbach in *Death in Venice*, like *Lolita*'s Humbert Humbert, he is a man of culture finding beauty in youth, in coarseness—in "all that I myself have never been." To Giles, ecstasy comes in small packages. For viewers, this film is one of them.

VILLAGE VOICE, 3/10/98, p. 61, J. Hoberman

As *The Big Lebowski* recalls the movie-ness of *The Big Sleep*, so *Love and Death on Long Island*—the comic hit of the last New York Film Festival—riffs on Thomas Mann's *Death in Venice* in limning the hopeless passion of an elderly writer for a beautiful young boy.

Adapted by Richard Kwietniowski from sometime film critic Gilbert Adair's witty novella, *Love and Death* is an excellent joke—at once literary and lowbrow—that gives Mann's account of age yearning for youth an additional postmortem spin as high culture's unrequited longing for the vulgar mass market. Wandering out of the rain into his neighborhood 'plex, dourly mandarin British novelist Giles De'Ath (John Hurt) winds up in a softcore *Porky's* romp called *Hot Pants College 2*. As the writer rises to leave, he is smitten by the image of one Ronnie Bostock (Jason Priestley).

The transfixed De'Ath graduates from buying fan magazines and creating a scrapbook, carefully labeled Bostockania, to purchasing a VCR (which he first confuses with a microwave oven and initially believes needs no television to use) to delivering a lecture entitled "The Discovery of Beauty Where No One Ever Thought of Looking For It." The cineaste speaks from behind his character as the obsessive De'Ath explains to his uncomprehending audience that the effect of repeated VCR viewings is to incorporate fortuitous events into the movie text.

Innocently smug, fastidiously clueless, Hurt devours the role of the totally self-involved aesthete. The film's running gag is his character's confrontation with the contemporary world. Once De'Ath flies to the eastern Long Island town where Ronnie and his model girlfriend (Fiona Loewi) make their home, he can be amazed anew by the mirrored motel ceilings, talking automobile alarms, and no-smoking restaurants. Nevertheless, the apparently unworldly novelist proves himself increasingly devious and determined, his eloquently wrinkled face creased by a lizardy smile as he successfully insinuates himself into the Bostock household.

Perfectly cast as the obscure (and obtuse) object of desire, Jason Priestley maintains the entertaining illusion that he has failed to grasp the movie's premise. (In a sense, *Love and Death*'s second half is a reverse and unconsummated *Sunset Boulevard*, featuring a young never-will-be rather than an old has-been.) The big scene, across the table at a greasy spoon called Chez d'Irv, is a wonderful juxtaposition of disparate acting styles, the document of Priestley's guileless sincerity reacting to the artifice of Hurt's heartfelt guile.

Also reviewed in:
CHICAGO TRIBUNE, 3/13/98, Friday/p. A, Mark Caro

NATION, 3/16/98, p. 34, Stuart Klawans
NEW YORK TIMES, 3/6/98, p. E25, Janet Maslin
NEW YORKER, 3/9/98, p. 93, Daphne Merkin
WASHINGTON POST, 3/13/98, Weekend/p. 47, Desson Howe

LOVE IS THE DEVIL

A Strand Releasing release of a BBC Films/BFI/Premiere Heure/Uplink and the Arts Council of England presentation of a BFI production in asociaton with Partners in Crime. *Executive Producer:* Ben Gibson and Frances-Anne Solomon. *Producer:* Chiara Menage. *Director:* John Maybury. *Screenplay:* John Maybury. *Director of Photography:* John Mathieson. *Editor:* Daniel Goddard. *Music:* Ryuichi Sakamoto. *Music Editor:* Daniel Goddard. *Sound:* Ken Lee and (music) Goh Hotoda. *Casting:* Anne-Laure Combris, Mary Selway, and Emma Buckley. *Production Designer:* Alan MacDonald. *Art Director:* Christina Moore. *Set Dresser:* Philippa Hart. *Special Effects:* Bob Smoke. *Costumes:* Jemima Cotter. *Make-up:* Jacquetta Levon. *Stunt Coordinator:* Rod Woodruff and Glen Marks. *Running time:* 90 minutes. *MPAA Rating:* Not Rated.

CAST: Derek Jacobi (Francis Bacon);   Daniel Craig (George Dyer);   Tilda Swinton (Muriel Belcher);   Anne Lambton (Isabel Rawsthorne);   Adrian Scarborough (Daniel Farson);   Karl Johnson (John Deakin);   Annabel Brooks (Henrietta Moraes);   Richard Newbold (Blonde Billy);   Ariel De Ravenel (French Official);   Tallulah (Ian Board);   Andy Linden (Ken Bidwell);   David Kennedy (Joe Furneval);   Gary Hume (Volker Dix);   Damien Dibben and Antony Cotton (Brighton Rent Boys);   Anthony Riding (London Rent Boy);   Christian Martin (Bellhop);   Ray Olley (Boxing Referee);   Wesley Morgan and Nigel Travis (Boxers);   Eddie Kerr (Tailor);   George Clarke and David Windle (Wrestlers);   William Hoyland (Police Sergeant);   Mark Umbers (PC Denham);   Hamish Bowles (David Hockney).

LOS ANGELES TIMES, 10/9/98, Calendar/p. 12, Kevin Thomas

Sometimes it really is better to let a painter's work speak for itself.

That's the feeling that John Maybury's adventurous but off-putting "Love Is the Devil" leaves you with. Cautiously subtitled "Study for a Portrait of Francis Bacon," it concentrates on the painter's relationship with his lover and model George Dyer, the inspiration for a series of key works in the Bacon canon.

You can sympathize with Maybury's resistance to avoid the standard film biography approach to so unconventional a painter, widely heralded as one of the century's greatest for his often grotesque yet riveting depictions of human suffering and solitariness. But Maybury carries the elliptical to the extent that we never get to see the "George" paintings in question. Yet the film is so morbid you have the need to experience the redemption of misery by art.

For all of Maybury's barrage of arty-as-all-get-out flourishes, "Love Is the Devil" turns upon one of the movies' oldest devices, the flashback. It's 1971, and the 62-year-old Bacon (Derek Jacobi), at the Grand Palais in Paris, is being proclaimed the greatest living painter and the first British artist since Turner to be exhibited there. Meanwhile, back in Bacon's hotel suite, Dyer (Daniel Craig), is deliberately quaffing a fatal dose of pills washed down by alcohol. From what Maybury depicts of the men's relationship, which in fact lasted seven years, it is amazing he didn't do himself in years earlier.

In any event, as Dyer loses consciousness he relives his terrible time with Bacon, some of it depicted through distorted lens to suggest his woozy state. Dyer, a striking-looking young working-class burglar, breaks into Bacon's London residence, landing in a pile of photos, either of beautiful men such as himself or images of violence. Too bad he didn't get the picture, so to speak. Instead of jail, Dyer winds up in Bacon's bed.

Jacobi's Bacon is a spiffy dresser, a trim but aging gay man who dyes his hair and uses makeup to hold on to an appearance of youth. In sex he's a masochist who orders Dyer to beat him with a belt and even put out lighted cigarettes on his back. Since we repeatedly see the men sleeping, with Dyer clinging to Bacon, we're left to assume that some kind of tenderness follows the rituals.

But Dyer becomes plagued with nightmares—a recurring image is of himself, naked and covered in blood, rolling off a diving board, presumably into an abyss. Whether Dyer's dreams inspired Bacon's paintings or whether posing for the paintings triggers the nightmares is left to conjecture. Whatever the case, Dyer swiftly becomes totally dependent upon Bacon—who is generous with money and fancy clothes but nothing else—and commences a steady diet of booze and pills.

Throughout Dyer's disintegration Bacon remains ice-cold, a sarcastic wit indifferent to his lover's fate, so much so you start to wonder whether the younger man's coming apart is some sort of sexual turn-on and inspiration for the painter. After all, Bacon is an artist who rhapsodizes about the inherent beauty in car accidents, the bloodier the better, it would seem.

The heart of the matter seems familiar enough. Bacon, like many other self-absorbed creative geniuses, pours so much emotion into his work he has none left over for anything or anybody else. At the end of the day he heads to a bar where he spends his evenings with a group of regulars who are just as bitchy and boring as he is.

When Dyer, who unaccountably loves Bacon, comes along, he can be sure to be the subject of ridicule. (Maybury has said that the Bacon-Dyer relationship represents "a fatal attraction between the upper and working classes," but there's nothing very upper-classy about Bacon.)

Jacobi, formidable actor that he is, has re-created Bacon to a degree that's uncanny. His Bacon is so outrageously detached from Dyer's suffering that he would seem darkly funny had not Craig, in a portrayal that is harrowing in the fullest sense, made us so thoroughly believe in Dyer's pain and anguish. Perhaps Maybury, who worked with the late Derek Jarman as a costume and set designer, means to suggest that Bacon's hollowness as a man and the ferocity of his paintings represent an ultimate expression of gay self-loathing nurtured by a homophobic society.

Whatever the case, for all the brilliance of Jacobi and Craig, "Love Is the Devil," which has a bold, seductive Ryuichi Sakamoto score, doesn't yield enough fresh insight and meaning to make it worth putting up with its unrelieved degradation.

NEW YORK POST, 10/7/98, p. 44, Larry Worth

Films about artists have an admittedly sketchy history, ranging from old-style Hollywood's "Lust for Life" to 90s missteps like "Surviving Picasso." But "Love Is the Devil" takes form as a colorful exception.

One reason: Writer-director John Maybury plays by his own rules in bringing the life of 20th-century painter Francis Bacon to the screen. The emphasis here isn't on canvases; it's camera angles and compositions which evoke the artist's wonderfully unique style.

Not surprisingly, the plot isn't linear. Its two odes to conventional storytelling are symmetry (the tale begins and ends at the same spot—a 1971 tribute to Bacon at Paris' Grand Palais) and documenting the beginning, middle and end of Bacon's relationship with George Dyer, his lover of seven years.

Their tortured relationship hinges on Bacon's delight in ridiculing Dyer's blue-collar roots, particularly when surrounded by high-society pals. But Bacon's self-loathing also becomes apparent, manifested in games of dominance with burning cigarettes and leather straps as the oh-so-painful toys.

That tragedy will result is obvious from the start. But the way in which the director lets the story unravel is never predictable. Mixing MTV editing with recurring motifs, slo-mo photography and suffocating closeups, the production always feels as out-of-control as the focal relationship.

But all kudos for Maybury must be shared with Derek Jacobi's masterful interpretation of Bacon. The painter's talent and mindset are portrayed through Jacobi's every action, gesture and inflection. It's a brilliant turn.

Though far less flashy, Daniel Craig also shines as the ill-fated Dyer. His inability to fit in and desperation for love is evoked with properly heartbreaking results.

Further enhanced by the presence of ever-offbeat Tilda Swinton, "Love" proves that abstract art can be just as satisfying in cinematic form.

SIGHT AND SOUND, 9/98, p. 47, Michael O'Pray

1971. As Francis Bacon is being officially welcomed at a prestigious retrospective of his work at the Grand Palais in Paris, his lover George Dyer is dying of a drugs and drink overdose in their hotel room.

An unsuccessful minor criminal, Dyer becomes Bacon's lover when the latter discovers him burgling his house in 1964. Dyer is introduced to the *demi-monde* of the infamous Colony Room club in Soho. Their sado-masochistic love affair is at first a happy one a marriage of opposites until Bacon eventually begins to tire of Dyer's increasing misery with the coterie who surround the artist. Exiled from his own petty-criminal milieu and increasingly dependent on drugs and drink, Dyer drifts steadily into mental turmoil, expressed in a recurring nightmare. He feels sexual humiliation as Bacon encourages new lovers. Dyer's decline contrasts starkly with Bacon's rising fame, self-absorption and indulgent lifestyle. Although Bacon always remains loyal in the last instance, after a long period of mutual betrayals, stormy rows and separations, Dyer ends his life.

One can understand John Maybury's rather sniffy initial response to the idea of a film about Francis Bacon: it must have seemed miles away from his previous high-energy collage films, especially *Remembrance of Things Fast,* his hour-long experiment with high tech to explore sexual masquerade and cultural nihilism. A key figure in the influential early 80s New Romantic film 'movement' and one of his country's most successful music-video makers, with *Love Is the Devil* Maybury has shown he is also perfectly at home in the more conventional confines of narrative film-making.

Loosely based on Daniel Farson's biography of the painter Francis Bacon and stories culled from some of Bacon's friends, Maybury's effort forsakes the embarrassing self-consciousness endemic to films about artists (there are no grand "My Art..." statements here). Derek Jacobi's mesmerising portrayal of Bacon is tough-minded, suggesting behind a brilliant but often despicable facade a depth of feeling reserved for the paintings, not for humanity at large. In many ways, this facade is the film's core, thrown into relief by Dyer's vulnerability and uncontrollable mental collapse (another good performance in an exacting part by Daniel Craig). Without overstating the case, Maybury sets up the two as a fascinating pair of contraries: Bacon, the sexual masochist and social sadist, is the mirror image of Dyer. The inarticulate petty criminal's descent into a drugs-and-drink-inflamed excess gives shape to the film, while Bacon remains a steely, focused, detached constant.

The absence of any of the artist's paintings (many of Bacon's circle closed ranks against the film) helps to deflect it from being about 'Art' and instead makes it into a film about styles of life (something which has always fascinated Maybury). But he also includes fascinating material to illustrate Bacon's creative sources: photographs taken in a seedy studio by John Deakin for Bacon (who rarely used a model); films (notably Eisenstein's *Battleship Potemkin* 1925); a boxing match that leaves Bacon blood-spattered; and a strange scene of a nasty car accident which underlines Bacon's alienated sensibility as he fails to see anything there but a kind of beauty. (Artists often lead fairly boring lives; life in the studio by its very nature is intense, withdrawn and tedious for the onlooker.) The fact that Dyer modelled for Bacon is hardly shown, but Maybury does suggest that the unhappy working-class man's nightmares became the tortured figures of Bacon's canvases. The artist's cold stare penetrates his lover's inner turmoil, yet he still denies him the love he craves.

Maybury reins in his own sensibility for the social scenes with Bacon at their centre. This allows him to express Dyer's mental life—such as the dream sequences of a crouching, blood-drenched man—with a fully filmic imagination. It's a perfectly apt approach given Bacon's cruel objectivity and distance from life. He prized above all wit, quick sex and a no-nonsense view. But this does leave an emotional vacuum at the film's centre. Bacon's rigid aestheticism and emotional coldness never engage us (why should they?). Nor do Dyer's pathetic grasping for the unattainable and his self-destructive mania. Only in the brilliantly staged sex scenes between the two—the creaking leather belt tight around Dyer's fist as Bacon waits on his knees for the exquisite beating—are the two worlds brought together in what Maybury recognises as a gay cliché: the "fatal attraction between the upper and working classes".

Maybury creates a stifling, claustrophobic world in which post-World War Two society at large is rarely glimpsed. The fetid, squabbling, viscous atmosphere of the Colony Club is deftly conjured. Tilda Swinton, with a mouthful of bad teeth and bad language, turns in a fearsome Muriel Belcher. In one memorably sordid scene, Karl Johnson as the seedy *Vogue* photographer John Deakin takes nude shots of a young 60s 'liberated' woman in his studio. Bacon's own studio is photographed in muted colours to stress its cramped disorder. The only spatial relief to be found is in the kitchen/bathroom, where the lovers seem most content (Bacon cooks while Dyer lingers in a bath). These quiet moments are effectively worked with economy and tenderness, belying Maybury's reputation for excessive, sometimes overworked visual style.

The rather ponderous nightmare scene, laden with overbearing sound effects that never pay off in narrative terms, is where Maybury's ambitions seem least resolved. Perhaps if the identification of the nightmare with the paintings had been better established, these 'inner-life' sequences might have worked better. Of course, this leads back to the film's sex-class premise, which suggests that Bacon fed off Dyer's misery and pain, hinting that this is how it is with art. It's the classic view of the artist as vampire, social misfit and unfeeling bastard. Also lurking here is a sense of sexual self-disgust—of the upper-class gay toying callously, and sometimes to devastating effect, with working-class rough trade. Interestingly, Derek Jarman was also bewitched by this scenario, though at times he wanted to it as a sentimental education (which, in some cases, it no doubt was). Maybury seems much more ambivalent, which may explain the lack of resolution in this aspect of *Love Is the Devil*. There is no clear interpretation of Bacon and Dyer's relationship here, but that may be Maybury's point.

Also reviewed in:
CHICAGO TRIBUNE, 11/20/98, Friday/p. G, Mark Caro
NEW YORK TIMES, 10/7/98, p. E5, Stephen Holden
NEW YORKER, 10/12/98, p. 82, Anthony Lane
VARIETY, 5/25-31/98, p. 58, David Rooney
WASHINGTON POST, 11/13/98, p. D5, Stephen Hunter
WASHINGTON POST, 11/13/98, Weekend/p. 44, Michael O'Sullivan

LOVE WALKED IN

A TriStar Pictures release of a Jempsa Entertainment and Apostle Pictures production. *Executive Producer:* Jorge Estrada Mora. *Producer:* Ricardo Freixa. *Director:* Juan J. Campanella. *Screenplay:* Juan Campanella, Lynn Geller, and Larry Golin. *Based on a novel by:* Jose Pablo Feinmann. *Director of Photography:* Daniel Shulman. *Editor:* Darren Kloomok. *Music:* Wendy Blackstone. *Production Designer:* Michael Shaw. *Art Director:* Shawn Carroll. *Set Decorator:* Janine Ramsey. *Costumes:* David Robinson. *Running time:* 90 minutes. *MPAA Rating:* R.

CAST: Denis Leary (Jack Hanaway); Terrence Stamp (Fred Moore); Aitana Sanchez-Gijon (Vicki Rivas); Moira Kelly (Vera); Michael Badalucco (Eddie Bianco); Danny Nucci (Cousin Matt).

LOS ANGELES TIMES, 2/20/98, Calendar/p. 8, Kevin Thomas

In the final credits of "Love Walked In," a competent B-picture, special thanks are offered to Columbia Home Video. Well, the home screen is precisely where this picture belongs. It's intelligent and stylish but not nearly original enough to warrant a trip to your local multiplex.

It is best of all a solid showcase for Denis Leary, a comic actor with a real edge who's due for a big breakout role. Leary plays Jack Hanaway, a piano player and would-be writer with a drinking problem. Jack's booked at a small club in an Eastern seaside resort teamed with a torch singer, Vicki Rivas (Aitana Sanchez-Gijon), a smoldering beauty and his longtime lover.

Jack's patter is so sour that he and Vicki are fired—only to be promptly reinstated when a Mr. Moore (Terence Stamp) speaks up and states that he likes a "sardonic piano player." Fred Moore's opinion carries weight because he's an important local businessman married to a fabulously wealthy wife (Marj Dusay), who has a palatial estate nearby.

She also suspects he's being unfaithful and has hired a private eye named Eddie (Michael Badalucco) to investigate. It turns out that Eddie is an old pal of Jack's from Brooklyn. Although Jack and Vicki are happy and living rent-free in a charming beach cottage, they have no real security, and Jack so far isn't getting anywhere in his writing career. (We get glimpses of what's happening in his imagination as he tries to spin a prophetic tale of an especially savage and bitter lifelong rivalry between cousins, well-played by Neal Huff and Danny Nucci, with Moira Kelly as the girl they both want.)

A rich woman with whom Jack once had an affair tested him by throwing a diamond ring down toilet—and he unhesitatingly flushed it. But that was then; now Jack finds himself open to Eddie's proposal that Vicki come on to Fred Moore just enough to allow Eddie to snap some compromising photos to enable Mrs. Moore to nail her husband.

These three, however, have no idea of what they're getting into in dealing with Moore—and Stamp is such a compelling actor that he can show you more aspects of formidability and insight than you might ever have dreamed.

Adapted from a novel by Jose Pablo Feinmann by director Juan J. Campanella and writers Lynn Geller and Larry Golin, "Love Walked In" has some snappy repartes and an abundance of film noir mood and atmosphere but lacks that extra twist to make it distinctive and original. Like a lot of other neo-noirs, "Love Walked In," which could just as easily have been made in the '40s, draws more from other movies than real life. Even so, "Love Walked In" is a satisfactory diversion—especially if you wait to see it in the comfort of your own home.

NEW YORK POST, 2/20/98, p. 42, Larry Worth

Murder or blackmail usually sets film noir plots in motion. But the genre's latest—"Love Walked In"—features a different crime: killing an actor's career.

Terence Stamp zoomed to stardom in the '60s, then waned before his "rediscovery" in 1994's "The Adventures of Priscilla, Queen of the Desert." Since then, he's been in one bomb after another. But "Love Walked In" takes the cake, even though Stamp gamely gives his all.

He plays a wealthy millionaire whose wife wrongly thinks he's cheating. But the private investigator on the case sees a way to make a buck: He suggests that a buddy's wife seduce the fat cat while being photographed, and they all divide the payoff.

So, should the bud encourage his sultry lounge-singer spouse to sell her bedroom skills? That's the million-dollar question, much like Robert Redford's "Indecent Proposal" pondered by Woody Harrelson and Demi Moore a few years back.

But under the hopeless direction of Juan J. Campanella, who also co-wrote the script, the query leads to an incoherent snoozer.

As if the main storyline isn't mishandled enough, Campanella introduces a film within the film, meant to parallel the leads' shady lives with a parable about good and evil. It's double the stupidity.

Campanella may have recognized the error of his ways, which would explain some throwaway sex scenes that distract from the nonsense at hand. Worse, the climax is laugh-out-loud funny—never a good sign in an alleged thriller.

With the exception of Stamp's valiant attempt to swim above the dreck, the cast flounders. Denis Leary sleepwalks through his cuckold-to-be role, adrift without the edgy quality that's made him soar on screen in the past.

As the object of everyone's ardor, Aitina Sanchez-Gijon is stunning to behold. But she couldn't convince if her life depended on it. And in the secondary story, Moira Kelly and Danny Nucci are as one-note and annoying as ever.

Collectively, it's enough to make one long for "Indecent Proposal," which at least qualified as fun trash. "Love Walked In" is all trash and no fun.

VILLAGE VOICE, 2/24/98, p. 124, Elizabeth Weitzman

Jack Hanaway (in-his-element Denis Leary) is an embittered, alcoholic musician stuck in loser loungeville, haranguing the customers between songs with caustic asides. But things could certainly be worse: at least he has the love of his life with him both at work, where her sultry songs torch up his piano, and at home, where she edits the pulp fiction that emanates from his typewriter (and which the movie brings to heavy-handed life as a parallel of Jack's world). He knows he's pretty lucky: Vicky (Aitana Sanchez-Gijon) is beautiful, fun, and loyally content to be right by his side.

Therefore, when a long-lost detective buddy shows up with an indecent proposal (if Vicky will fool around with the husband of his moneyed client they'll all get rich off blackmail dough), you'd think Jack would firmly shake his head. But then, of course, we wouldn't have much of a movie. So Vicky does the Demi thing—agrees reluctantly and soon discovers the many advantages of sleeping with a rich older guy (Terence Stamp); Jack does the Woody thing—gets jealous, drunk, and crazy; and we watch and wonder why Campanella thought style was so important he could leave all character bonds and motivation completely underdeveloped.

There's not a lot of love here, just some smoke, a little liquor, a coupla guns, and a pretty girl, so as it turns out, we still don't have much of a movie. Aging as quickly as it should be, '90s noir is showing ever-stronger signs of going *gris*.

Also reviewed in:
CHICAGO TRIBUNE, 2/20/98, Friday/p. K, Michael Wilmington
NEW YORK TIMES, 2/20/98, p. E12, Stephen Holden

MADELINE

A TriStar Pictures release of a Jaffilms and Pancho Kohner/Saul Cooper production. *Executive Producer:* Stanley R. Jaffe.   *Producer:* Saul Cooper, Pancho Kohner, and Allyn Stewart. *Director:* Daisy von Sherler Mayer.   *Screenplay:* Mark Levin, Jennifer Flackett, and Malia Scotch Marmo.   *Based on the book "Madeline" by:* Ludwig Bemelmans.   *Director of Photography:* Pierre Aim.   *Editor:* Editor Jeffrey Wolf.   *Music:* Michel Legrand.   *Music Editor:* David Carbonara.   *Sound:* Michel Kharat.   *Sound Editor:* Stuart Levy.   *Casting:* Karen Lindsay-Stewart, Pat McCorkle, and Sylvie Brocheré.   *Production Designer:* Hugo Luczyc-Wyhowski.   *Set Decorator:* Aline Bonetto.   *Special Effects:* Graham Longhurst and Graham Hills.   *Costumes:* Michael Clancy.   *Make-up:* Nathalie Tissier.   *Stunt Coordinator:* Rémy Julienne, Daniel Vérité, and Michel Norman.   *Running time:* 105 minutes.   *MPAA Rating:* PG.

CAST: Frances McDormand (Miss Clavel); Nigel Hawthorne (Lord Covington); Hatty Jones (Madeline); Ben Daniels (Leopold the Tutor); Stéphane Audran (Lady Covington); Arturo Venegas (Mr. Spanish Ambassador); Katia Caballero (Mrs. Spanish Ambassador); Chantal Neuwirth (Helene the Cook); Kristian de la Osa (Pepito); Clare Thomas (Aggie); Bianca Ströhman (Victoria); Christina Mangani (Chantal); Rachel Dennis (Lucinda); Pilar Garrard (Beatrice); Jessica Mason (Serena); Emilie Jessula (Elizabeth); Eloïse Eonnet (Sylvette); Alice Lavaud (Veronica); Morgane Farçat (Marie-Odile); Alexis Desseaux (Louis the Painter); George Harris (Mr. Liberian Ambassador); Marie-Noëlle Eusebe (Mrs. Liberian Ambassador); Ash Varrez (Mr. Indian Ambassador); Vayu Naidu (Mrs. Indian Ambassador); Alexandre Arbatt (Mr. Uzbekhistani Ambassador); Katia Tchenko (Mrs. Uzbekhistani Ambassador). Julien Maurel, Raphaël Beauville, and Choukri Gabteni (Idiots Popopov); Luc Florian (Chief Gendarme); Luca Vellani (Chauffeur); Marianne Groves (Admitting Nurse); Christian Mulot (Hospital Doctor); Christophe Guybet (Paramedic); Nani (Genevieve); Emile Abossolo M'bo (Circus Barker); Alix Ponchon (Lolo);

CHRISTIAN SCIENCE MONITOR, 7/10/98, p. B3, David Sterritt

The early warm-weather season has offered plenty of wide-screen attractions for teenagers and young adults, at whom Hollywood has targeted the recent spate of special-effects fantasies. But there's been less on view for children, aside from the animated charms of Disney's colorful "Mulan" and Warner Bros.' short-lived "Quest for Camelot."

So it's a pleasure to welcome "Madeline," based on the series of children's books by Ludwig Bemelmans, which have sold more than 15 million copies in the six decades since the first volume appeared. At a time when "name recognition" is a key factor in mass-audience entertainment, it's hard to think of a more widely known and trusted commodity than the time-tested saga of "an old house in Paris all covered with vines" where "lived 12 little girls in two straight lines."

As innumerable kids could instantly tell you, those 12 little girls are the residents of a French school administered by Miss Clavel, their always orderly but frequently indulgent teacher. Madeline is the most venturesome of the pupils, known for her ability to shake up Miss Clavel with perilous stunts and unlady-like antics. The movie has two intertwined story lines: a suspense tale involving a naughty neighbor who's kidnapped by his tutor, and Madeline's effort to save Miss Clavel's school after its wealthy owner decides to close it down.

"Madeline" is not one of the rare children's movies that will delight parents as much as their youngsters. Adults will find the jokes familiar, the action predictable, and the filmmaking more efficient than imaginative.

This said, "Madeline" deserves credit for solid professionalism, starting with the audience-friendly acting of Frances McDormand as Miss Clavel and Nigel Hawthorne as the aristocratic Lord Covington, known as Lord Cucuface to Madeline and her irreverent friends. Also enjoyable are nine-year-old Hatty Jones as the title character and French star Stéphane Audrane as Lord Covington's ailing wife. Rounding out the cast are 11 first-time actresses from France, the United States, and Britain, bringing Miss Clavel's other students to energetic life.

Daisy von Scherler Mayer directed the picture from a screenplay by Mark Levin and Jennifer Flackett, based on four of Bemelmans's six beloved books.

LOS ANGELES TIMES,7/10/98, Calendar/p. 10, Jack Mathews

[The following review by Jack Mathews appeared in a slightly different form in
NEWSDAY, 7/10/98, Part II/p. B7.]

Who says blonds have more fun? When it comes to child heroines, there's nothing like red on the head. Just ask Annie, or Pippi Longstocking, or drop by a theater near you and meet the vivacious young star of "Madeline."

Adapted from several of Ludwig Bemelmans' enduring children's books about a fearless orphan at a French girls school, "Madeline" plays more like a pilot for a TV series than a stand-alone feature. It introduces Madeline (Hatty Jones), her schoolmates, their marvelously kind teacher Miss Clavel (Frances McDormand), and the school's curmudgeonly owner Lord Covington (Nigel Hawthorne), then cobbles together a semblance of an episode, hoping your kids will create the demand for more.

"Madeline" is for really small fry and for nostalgic adults—moms, mostly—with fond memories of the character conceived by Bemelmans in 1939. Given her rambunctious nature, her curiosity and her stubborn spirit, there has been no time like the present for her to matriculate to the big screen.

Jones, who sports one of the few dimpled noses I've seen, has the right balance of cuteness and spunk for the charismatic Madeline, whose challenges in this story are to (a) prevent recently widowed Lord Covington from selling the school, and (b) rescuing next-door neighbor Pepito (Kristian de la Osa), the spoiled son of a Spanish diplomat, from a gang of kidnapping circus clowns.

Director Daisy von Scherler Mayer ("Woo") generates real empathy for the children and opens the stage for supremely appealing performances by British newcomer Jones and veteran McDormand. But there is no visual magic to underscore the adventures.

Madeline and Miss Clavel, kindred spirits over the generation gap, are operating in a very stark, graceless environment, in a story that moves in fits and starts. But then, only a critic with no kid in tow is likely to notice.

NEW YORK POST, 7/10/98, p. 47, Thelma Adams

"Madeline" is the "Party Girl" of pre-pubescent Paris. No wonder, for "Madeline" director Daisy von Scherler Mayer was the force behind Parker Posey's 1995 indie hit. Here, she makes a smooth transition to Hollywood by adapting Ludwig Bemelmans' illustrated classic about the liveliest, littlest pupil in a strait-laced French private school.

Newcomer Hatty Jones plays the spunky, red-haired orphan. The breezy, 9-year-old Brit carries the comedy on her narrow shoulders. Brown-eyed, unpretentious and a staunch advocate for truth, justice and the French joie de vivre, Jones' Madeline has a charisma unrivaled since Shirley Temple was "The Little Princess."

Oscar-winner Frances McDormand ("Fargo") plays Miss Clavel, Madeline's headmistress and guardian angel. Clavel's tough love grounds both book and movie—and McDormand makes one hell of a nun.

The film shares the book's bright, whimsical view of Paris. Screenwriters Mark Levin and Jennifer Flackett hew closely to the original stories: Madeline has appendicitis, falls into the Seine and spars with neighborhood bully Pepito.

The school's owner, Lord Covington (the august Nigel Hawthorne), schemes to sell the school and evict the girls. Meanwhile, kidnappers target Pepito. In fact, overflowing with plot and plots, the movie periodically strains to gain momentum.

But this is a quibble in a charming and exuberant film. "Madeline" is enriched by its efforts to demystify villainy. We discover that both Pepito and Covington (a.k.a. "Cucuface") have sound reasons to ignore the needs of others. Once we understand them, they lose their power to frighten.

Director Mayer is respectful of the cult of "Madeline" without genuflecting. Moms who fondly remember the books will turn out in droves, their daughters in tow, dressed in what used to pass for Sunday finery. The shame would be if boys skipped the party.

SIGHT AND SOUND, 4/99, p. 46, Amanda Lipman

Madeline, an orphan, is the smallest of 12 small girls living in a school in Paris in the mid-50s with their teacher Miss Clavel, a nun. When Madeline is rushed to hospital with appendicitis, she meets Lady Covington, the school's benefactor. Lady Covington dies soon after and her husband decides to sell the school. Later, Madeline has a run in with Pepito, the spoilt, lonely son of the Spanish ambassador next door. Madeline falls into the river and is saved by a dog whom the girls take home and name Genevieve.

Madeline and the girls plot to sabotage Lord Covington's plans to sell the school. The girls visit the circus where Madeline sees Pepito being kidnapped by his tutor and some clowns. She's also taken prisoner. Distraught, Miss Clavel and Genevieve drive all night in search of her. Madeline and Pepito escape on a motorbike after a chase. The next day, Madeline tries unsuccessfully to talk Lord Covington out of selling the school. However, the new owner of the house, the Uzbekhistani ambassador, agrees to let the school and its residents stay.

The charm of Ludwig Bemelmans' *Madeline* stories resides in the stylised illustrations (well mimicked by UPA's 1952 cartoon) and the simplicity of the rhyming narrative. Capturing these qualities in live action is difficult, so this version, directed by Daisy von Scherler Mayer *(Party Girl, Woo)*, has taken the essence of the books—the obedient but naughty little girls, the doting, eccentric Miss Clavel, the colourful Parisian background—and imaginatively filled it out to create a jaunty, good-humoured film with a sumptuous retro look and a contemporary feel.

The repetition of the books' catchphrases is preserved: the girls' chorus of "Good night, good night, dear Miss Clavel" every bedtime, while Miss Clavel nightly intuits that "something is not right" with her girls. This remains charming rather than laboured, largely because of the film's fine performances. Hatty Jones, as the diminutive heroine, is as convincing when she is the rebellious straight talker (giving Lord Covington a piece of her mind, or launching herself at Pepito to save a mouse) as she is when hinting at the anxiety and essential loneliness of the orphaned child.

The other girls are defined by one-liner trademarks, but they spring to life as a group, demurely trotting about Paris by day and horsing around with the cook's enormous bra and cracking fart jokes by night. Nonetheless, crystallised in Madeline's rivalry with one particular girl is a sense of the ambivalence between loyalty and dissonance that occurs in a close community such as this.

Frances McDormand seems made for the role of the liberal, kooky nun, who allows her beloved girls to yell and cluck at each other in the name of "debate", then insists on them being "young ladies", while her own pious demeanour hides a love of fast cars and card playing. This is a Miss Clavel for the 90s; McDormand's Marge Gunderson (from Fargo) with a touch of Mary Poppins.

Nigel Hawthorne makes all the right noises as the uptight Lord Covington, sole representative of the books' ghoulish board of trustees, here given a specific reason for his bad behaviour. As

Madeline, with empathic perception, works out, he takes out his grief for his wife on the school. Pepito, too, compensates for his feelings of abandonment by acting like a bombastic little prince. And Madeline, it is hinted, is a little mixed up after her parents' death. But the bundle of explicatory psychology has just the right weight.

The film even pulls off the wickedly schematic touch that makes all the male characters bad, sad or hopeless, while the women are tough, funny and bright. Helene, the cook, is a gender reversal of the salty old French resistance member. A throwaway turn of the plot at the end reveals that the Uzbekhistani ambassador, who agrees to keep the school going, is not, as we expect, a man but a woman. And Genevieve, the brave dog who saves Madeline, is female yet not, as the book has it, so that she can produce enough puppies for each girl.

TIME, 7/13/98, p. 78, Richard Corliss

Give us the '40s Margaret O'Brien. Now there was a child actress who knew that childhood could be an orphanage, an abode of isolation, misery and misunderstanding. When Miss Margaret's lower lip got to quivering in *Meet Me in St. Louis,* why, it took a Judy Garland ballad to dredge the poor kid out of depressive hysterics.

Such geysers of emotion are out of fashion; today's movie children are action figures. Yes, girls too. Madeline (Hatty Jones), the heroine of Ludwig Bemelmans' children's books, is an orphan, but she spends little time pondering her fate. Instead, she does what contemporary movie kids have to do: get into cute trouble. She incites insurrection at the boarding-school dinner table, pontificates on a bridge railing and falls into the Seine, plots to set off firecrackers under the feet of innocent visitors—it is all meant to be super delicious fun.

Isn't, though. Director Daisy von Scherler Mayer and the screenwriters treat the original tale like a bottle of Perrier left too long uncapped; the effervescence evaporates. Fine actors (Frances McDormand, Nigel Hawthorne) get swallowed whole, and the child stars are, shall we say, not swathed in charm. Madeline does finally face up to her orphanhood (a touching little scene), but by then the film is a lost cause, and Bemelmans' Madeline a lost soul.

VILLAGE VOICE, 7/21/98, p. 115, Amy Taubin

Madeline is a great heroine—not because of her silky red-blond hair, her expressive brow, or even her adventurous spirit. It's because she fearlessly speaks truth to power, as if to do less would be unconscionable.

Adapted from Ludwig Bemelmans's books about the smallest girl in a French boarding school, the film is lovely to look at and quite lively once it gets going. Fans of the books will find all their favorite characters and situations strung together in a single story line. Madeline does indeed have her appendix removed; fall into the Seine, from which she is rescued by the hero-dog Genevieve; run away to the circus, where she foils an attempt to kidnap Pepito, the obnoxious son of the Spanish ambassador. Binding all this into a proper life-or-death plot is Madeline's determination to keep Lord Cucuface, er, Covington from closing the school that is her only home.

Daisy von Scherler Mayer gets wonderfully nuanced performances from both the child and adult actors. As head-mistress Miss Clavel, Frances McDormand is concerned but wry, maternal without being smothering. She's also very funny. Hatty Jones is a shining Madeline—as convincing in her thoughtful moments as when she throws caution to the wind. And in her big confrontation with Lord Cucuface, she's a veritable Joan of Arc.

Madeline is a class act in more ways than one. The film never talks down to its young audience or underestimates its intelligence. But it's hard to imagine what public school kids will make of these extremely privileged little girls who speak with upper-class English accents and crack jokes in French. Could Madeline, a natural-born lefty who always stands up for the underdog, also be inadvertently endorsing school uniforms and the veddy British film culture of Merchant Ivory?

Also reviewed in:
CHICAGO TRIBUNE, 7/10/98, Friday/p. B, Mark Caro
NEW YORK TIMES, 7/10/98, p. E18, Janet Maslin
VARIETY, 7/13-19/98, p. 54, Todd McCarthy

MAFIA!

A Touchstone Pictures release of a Tapestry Films production. *Executive Producer:* Peter Abrams and Robert L. Levy. *Producer:* Bill Badalato. *Director:* Jim Abrahams. *Screenplay:* Jim Abrahams, Greg Norberg, and Michael McManus. *Director of Photography:* Pierre Letarte. *Editor:* Terry Stokes. *Music:* Gianni Frizzelli. *Music Editor:* Abby Treloggen. *Choreographer:* Helene Phillips. *Sound:* David Ronne and (music) Bill Schnee. *Sound Editor:* Michael Hilkene. *Casting:* Jackie Burch. *Production Designer:* William Elliott. *Art Director:* Greg Papalia. *Set Designer:* Ann Harris, Colin de Rouin, and Jason Weil. *Set Decorator:* Jerie Kelter. *Set Dresser:* John H. Maxwell, Christopher Amy, Micael A. Belgrave, and Robert Lee Robinson. *Special Effects:* Bruno Van Zeebroeck. *Costumes:* Mary Malin. *Make-up:* Vera Yurtchuk. *Running time:* 86 minutes. *MPAA Rating:* PG-13.

CAST: Jay Mohr (Anthony Cortino);   Billy Burke (Joey Cortino);   Christina Applegate (Diane);   Pamela Gidley (Pepper Gianini); Olympia Dukakis (Sophia); Lloyd Bridges (Vincenzo Cortino);   Jason Fuchs (Young Vincenzo);   Joe Viterelli (Clamato);   Tony Lo Bianco (Marzoni);   Blake Hammond (Fatso Paulie Orsatti);   Phil Suriano (Frankie Totino);   Vincent Pastore (Gorgoni);   Marisol Nichols (Carla);   Carol Ann Susi (Clamato's Wife);   Gregory Sierra (Bonifacio);   Vera Lockwood (Rosa Cortino);   Martin Charles Warner (Jimmy Big Features);   Joseph Jumbo Rufo (Willy Denunzio);   Tyler Daniel Wenz (Toddler);   Jason Davis (Geno);   T.J. Cannata (The Boy Diane);   Louis Mandylor (Middle-Aged Vincenzo);   Georgia Simon (Middle-Aged Rosa);   Joey Dente (Middle-Aged Clamato);   Sebastian Aza (Young Joey); Seth Adkins (Tiny Anthony);   Andreas Katsulas (Narducci);   Joseph R. Sicari (Rizzo);   Allyson Call (Jenny);   Monica Mikala (Young Rosa);   Anthony Jesse Cruz (Young Clamato);   James Costa (Immigration Thug);   Mark Goldstein (Clerk);   Stefan Lysenko (Ruffo);   Sofia Milos (Young Sophia);   Anthony Crivello (Luigi Cortino);   Saverio Carubia (Villager);   Bill Livingston (Guess the Number Croupier);   Gerald Emerick (Guess the Number Player);   Franie Como (Waiter);   Brian Tahash (Bodyguard);   Richard Abraham (Evil Priest);   Frank Birney (Wedding Priest);   Don Bovingloh (Funeral Priest);   Henry Harris (Nonchalant Guy);   Karen Leigh Hopkins (Nurse);   Dan Klein (Judas);   Pat Harvey (Newscaster); Jerry Haleva (Saddam Hussein);   Mr. Oh (Korean Soldier);   Jack Bernstein (ATM Man with Double Chin).

CHRISTIAN SCIENCE MONITOR, 7/24/98, p. B3, David Sterritt

The easy way to review a comedy is to quote the movie's jokes. But in a gag-a-second case like "Jane Austen's MAFIA!" it would take thousands of words to fit them all in.

Not every one is worth repeating, of course. An enormous number are silly, stupid, vulgar, pointless, old, borrowed, or blue. But you can't help being impressed by their sheer quantity.

This picture does for dumb humor what "Armageddon" does for action shots and "The Mask of Zorro" does for swordfights, flinging them out so frantically that you feel you've gotten your money's worth long before the halfway mark.

What holds all this horseplay together is a satirical story poking fun at the classic "Godfather" pictures, with an over-the-top Marlon Brando impersonation at its core. "MAFIA!" gains a touch of class by entrusting that impersonation to the late Lloyd Bridges, a versatile actor whose comedy credits include "Airplane!"—the 1980 hit that launched today's wave of self-mocking Hollywood parodies.

Not coincidentally, "Airplane!" was co-directed by "MAFIA!" filmmaker Jim Abrahams, who has turned a flair for rapid-fire farce into a long-running career. One secret of his success is his talent for assembling gifted casts. "MAFIA!" would be far less bearable if not for Bridges as the klutzy mob patriarch, Jay Mohr as his basically decent son, Billy Burke as his basically indecent son, and Christina Applegate as a fiancée who inexplicably winds up as president of the United States.

What does any of this have to do with Jane Austen, you may be asking by now? Not a thing; it's just another joke. But since Abrahams has a great love for sequels, you can't help wondering whose unlikely name will grace the title of his next epic.

LOS ANGELES TIMES,7/24/98, Calendar/p. 8, Jack Mathews

[The following review by Jack Mathews appeared in a slightly different form in NEWSDAY, 7/24/98, Part II/p. B7.]

Here's a partial listing of the movies you'll need to be familiar with in order to appreciate the full idiotic flavor of Jim Abrahams' "Mafia!," the latest (but only the first of three this summer) descendant of "Airplane!":

"The Godfather," Parts 1, 2 and 3, "Casino," "Il Postino," "Child's Play," "GoodFellas," "Forrest Gump," "The English Patient," "E.T.," "Saturday Night Fever" and any version of Dickens"'A Christmas Story." And, of course, you also have to have seen all the other "Airplane!," "Hot Shots!" and "Naked Gun" derivatives, and laughed your fool head off.

If you have done all that, and lower your expectations, you may get a few laughs out of this one, too.

"Mafia!" takes its greatest inspiration from the first two "Godfather" movies; the third, after all, was a laugh riot in its own right. The late Lloyd Bridges plays Vincenzo Cortino, a Sicilian who swam from Sicily to America as a small boy to get away from the Mafia don he'd infuriated by splashing him with Miracle Grow.

Young Vincenzo brought with him the right thumb of a man who'd murdered his father, and in the decades since, while he was building an underworld empire with an olive oil front, he's carried the digit around with him, like a rabbit's foot, hoping to find its match.

Cutting back and forth between Vincenzo's youth and modern times (this is actually a parody of the special edition of "The Godfather: 1902-1958, the Complete Epic"), we get to know Vincenzo's sons, the hotheaded Joey (Billy Burke) and the college grad, war hero Anthony (Jay Mohr), Joey's girlfriend Diane (Christina Applegate) and the Cortino consigliare Clamato (Joe Viterelli).

The contemporary section of the story turns on a potential territorial mob war and an assassination attempt on Don Vincenzo. In revenge, young Anthony meets the rival don at a restaurant and shoots him between the eyes ("I hear the ocean," the victim says, before he falls). The new Anthony takes over the family business, treats his girlfriend badly, sends his brother to Las Vegas, and generally stumbles over the plot line of the first "Godfather."

There are amusing moments, but none of them involves Bridges, whose frailty dampers all his scenes. Bridges did some very funny work in Abrahams' earlier movies, but he clearly wasn't up for this assignment.

The funniest thing about "Mafia!" is in the film's press kit, where Abrahams seriously attempts to explain how he got the idea for it. Something about seeing reviews of a TV adaptation of a new gangster movie and having a lightbulb go on. Let's send up the mob! After parodying the combat, cop and disaster movie genres, we might have thought he'd simply got to the Ms.

In that same hilarious section, Abrahams says the key to the success of his movies is the time and effort that goes into the plots. No kidding! Francis Ford Coppola and Mario Puzo knocked themselves out writing their Oscar-winning "Godfather" scripts. In fairness, Abrahams and his "Mafia!" co-writers Michael McManus and Greg Norberg might have insisted on the credit line: Jokes written by....

I don't know about Coppola and Puzo, but the Mafia should sue.

NEW YORK POST, 7/24/98, p. 49, Thelma Adams

Here's another hoot from the bad-comedies-we-love file: "Mafia!"Jim Abrahams' mob parody (co-written by "Hot Shots!" writers Greg Norberg and Michael McManus) is as subtle as a day-old meatball. What do you expect from a director who routinely stamps exclamation marks at the end of his movie titles?

"Mafia!" (formerly "Jane Austen's Mafia!" for no reason other than a cheap goose) maintains the same hectic hilarity of Abrahams' high-flying, low-brow disaster satire, "Airplane!" "Mafia!" mixes "The Godfather" and "Casino," shuffling in every self-important movie from "Il Postino" to "The English Patient" to "Forrest Gump."

The main character is family scion and straight-man Anthony Cortino (Jay Mohr, the voice of parrot "Paulie"). Tony combines Al Pacino's war hero-turned-hit man Michael Corleone and Robert De Niro's compulsive Vegas narrator "Ace" Rothstein.

On the road from Korea to corruption, Tony battles his psycho sibling Joey (Billy Burke) for control of the family bus and the right to make a killing. The women in Tony's life are split between the good (Christina Applegate), the bad (Pamela Gidley) and the granny (Olympia Dukakis).

Shifting back in time, we revisit the making of Don Vincenzo "Clutzo" Cortino. The late Lloyd Bridges—Leslie Nielsen's comic stand-in—mumbles the oft-parodied Brando role. (Harry Belafonte is the best black Brando.)

The plot is as sturdy as Il Pacino, the name of the boat Vincenzo follows from Sicily to Ellis Island. "Mafia!" is a tale of love, honor, betrayal and murder in a family much like any other immigrant family—except that, from gassy granny to red-haired grandkid, they kill and kill again.

Abrahams' technique is akin to R. Crumb's '70s underground comics and the splatter humor of Mad magazine: He fills each frame with joke after joke, embroidering the slapstick action with sophomoric giggles.

Vincenzo's craggy Sicilian birthplace is called Salmonella ("the home of warm mayonnaise"). An ad pasted on a wall asks "Got Vino?" over a picture of Mussolini with a mustache. A sign in Vegas says: "Welcome, compulsive gamblers." The open-air market on the immigrant Lower East Side retails bupkis for a nickel alongside socks sold for soup.

"Any Sicilian in you?" Tony asks a stripper. "Not since last night," she replies. From the juggling nuns at Salmonella's black olive festival to the projectile vomiting at Don Clutzo's funeral, Abrahams makes us a tasteless offer we can't refuse: Let's just kick back and cackle and slaughter every sacred cow in sight.

Also reviewed in:
CHICAGO TRIBUNE, 7/24/98, Friday/p. D, Michael Wilmington
NEW YORK TIMES, 7/24/98, p. E14, Janet Maslin
VARIETY, 7/27-8/2/98, p. 52, Dennis Harvey

MAJOR LEAGUE: BACK TO THE MINORS

A Warner Bros. release of a James G. Robinson presentation of a Morgan Creek production. *Executive Producer:* Michael Rachmil, Gary Barber, and Bill Todman, Jr. *Producer:* James G. Robinson. *Director:* John Warren. *Screenplay:* John Warren. *Director of Photography:* Tim Suhrstedt. *Editor:* O. Nicholas Brown and Bryan H. Carroll. *Music:* Robert Folk. *Music Editor:* J. J. George. *Sound:* Carl S. Rudisill and (music) Tommy Vicari and Steve Sykes. *Sound Editor:* Victor Ray Ennis. *Casting:* Shay Bentley-Griffin. *Production Designer:* Ann A. Dunsford. *Set Designer:* Michael W. Devine and Colleen Ballance. *Set Decorator:* Frank Galline. *Set Dresser:* Otto Lindsey. *Special Effects:* Keith Williams. *Costumes:* James Grey Mathews. *Make-up:* Vivian Baker. *Stunt Coordinator:* Cal Johnson. *Running time:* 90 minutes. *MPAA Rating:* PG-13.

CAST: Scott Bakula (Gus Cantrell); Corbin Bernsen (Roger Dorn); Dennis Haysbert (Pedro Cerrano); Takaaki Ishibashi (Taka Tanaka); Jensen Daggett (Maggie Reynolds); Eric Bruskotter (Rube BAker); Walton Goggins (Downtown Anderson); Ted McGinley (Leonard Huff); Kenneth Johnson (Lance Pere); Judson Mills (Hog Ellis); Lobo Sebastian (Carlos Liston); Thom Barry (Pops Morgan); Peter MacKenzie (Doc Windgate); Tim DiFilippo and Tom DiFilippo (Juan #1); Ted DiFilippo (Juan #2); Bob Uecker (Harry Doyle); Steve Yeager (Coach Duke Temple); Larry Brandenburg (Chuck Swartski); Jack Baun (Chuck Ledbetter); Mike Schatz (Renegades Batter); Joe Kelly (Miracles Cather); J. Don Ferguson (Umpire); Brian Beegle (Young Player); Ted Manson (Miracles Manager); Ronald "Buzz" Bowman (Miracles Announcer); Alex Van (Billy); Tim Ware (Hot Dog Vendor); Robert M. Egan (Rockcats Announcer); Michael A. Lynch (Chief Umpire); Richard Bruce Dougthy (Boll

Weevils Announcer);   Al Hamacher (Diner Cook);   Natalie Hendrix, Stephen Hardig, Leroy Myers, and Gary P. Pozsik (Reporters); Andre Tardieu (Maitre D'); Brien Straw (Waiter); R.J. Kackley (1st Base Umpire); Bradley Crable (Twins Runner);   Ken Medlock (Twins Assistant Coach); Lucinda Whitaker and Kimberly Herndon (Bar Girls);   Elizabeth Diane Wells (Diner Waitress);   Gary Murphy (Home Umpire);   Scott Foxhall (2nd Base Umpire);   Warren Pepper (TV Reporter); Dee Thompson (Head Umpire);   Raymond Sterling (1st Base Umpire);   Ron Clinton Smith, Richie Dye, and Dolan Wilson (Tutu Men);   Laura-Shay Griffin (Stewardess); Mark Storm (Mr. Buzz).

LOS ANGELES TIMES, 4/20/98, Calendar/p. 7, David Kronke

The joke, such as it was, in the "Major League" movie mini-franchise—that the long-hapless Cleveland Indians actually become contenders—became decisively outdated when the real Indians stormed to the 1995 World Series. Now, in its third installment, the "Major League" series itself is the joke.

Even the blatantly contradictory title "Major League: Back to the Minors" admits that the series has run out of ideas. The film itself is simply a painful confirmation.

Long gone are Wesley Snipes and Rene Russo, as well as Tom Berenger and Charlie Sheen. Still on hand is Corbin Bernsen as Roger—though instead of a mockably vain third-baseman, he's now the sympathetic owner of the lowly Minnesota Twins—along with the just-collecting-paychecks thespians Dennis Haysbert (the wacky voodoo guy), Takaaki Ishibashi (the wacky Japanese guy) and Bob Eucker (the wacky play-by-play guy).

Brought in to shore up team morale this time around is Scott Bakula, who, despite spending half the movie hiding behind sunglasses, brings the movie the easy-going grace of a guy making the best of a bad situation.

No one's heart, apparently, is in going through these motions, except for maybe Ted McGinley, who does a pretty fair imitation of Mets manager Bobby Valentine; unfortunately, he aims for the cheap seats in the obnoxiousness department. Even the special effects are listlessly rendered—many of the baseballs hit and pitched are obvious fakes.

Hence, the movie isn't so much inept as merely tired and uninspired. The problem isn't that gags fizzle—though, certainly, they do—it's that writer-director John Warren, who replaces David S. Ward as the series' spit-balling auteur, doesn't even bother to create many comic setups in the first place.

Bakula stars as Gus, a career minor-league pitcher whose arm has lost whatever mustard it had. Along comes ostensible old pal Roger (they're so tight that Roger never mentioned Gus in the other movies) to offer him a gig managing a minor-league team.

Gus' team stinks; he teaches 'em some basics; their fortunes improve (based on these "Major League" movies, you and I aren't such abject klutzes that we couldn't become credible players with a little heart and the right coaching). The climactic game occurs too early in the movie, so a completely idiotic plot contrivance is tossed in to force a rematch and extend this to feature length.

Warren seems interested in "Bull Durham's" funky vibe more than "Major League's" manic antics, but if he can't ape the latter, he can't approximate the former. He doesn't even bother to build to the bottom-of-the-ninth climax. Time for this team to hit the showers.

NEW YORK POST, 4/18/98, p. 29, Larry Worth

Choosing instantly forgettable movies like "Terminal Velocity," "The Chase" and "Shadow Conspiracy"—never mind "Major League" and "Major League II"—over the last decade, Charlie Sheen isn't known for quality control. But even he had the good sense to duck "Major League: Back to the Minors," which opened yesterday without advance screenings for critics.

The latest installment in this torturous series about a sad-sack baseball team known for its wacky players is the worst yet. That's saying a lot.

Scott Bakula steps into the lunacy as a washed-up pitcher who's talked into managing the Buzz, one of South Carolina's sorriest collection of players. Naturally, the team's roster is the Three Stooges in triplicate, with the boys' natural inabilities making for an alleged comedy of errors.

After rounding up members of the old gang, Bakula opts to whip them all into shape, which brings a showdown challenge from the smarmy manager of the Minnesota Twins. Headlines scream that it's David vs. Goliath.

So, do the underdogs have a chance? Any audience members left wondering haven't suffered the earlier "Major Leagues," nor heard of "The Mighty Ducks," or "The Bad News Bears" or... you get the picture.

Meanwhile, idiotic writer-director John Warren's idea of humor is summed up as the Buzz's token Japanese member constantly asks, "Is it crear?" while a subtitle reads: "Is it clear?" So much for cutting-edge humor.

Thankfully, Bakula has a hefty reserve of natural appeal, which is more than can be said for rival coach Ted McGinley or "League" veterans Corbin Bernsen, Dennis Haysbert, Takaaki Ishibashi and Bob Uecker. Professionally speaking, they should be permanently benched.

Accordingly, one doesn't need an umpire to recognize this as strike three for the series. Hopefully, that means future "Major League" knockoffs are officially out.

Also reviewed in:
CHICAGO TRIBUNE, 4/23/98, Tempo/p. 4, John Petrakis
NEW YORK TIMES, 4/18/98, p. B16, Lawrence Van Gelder
VARIETY, 4/20-26/98, p. 43, Daniel M. Kimmel

MAN IN THE IRON MASK, THE

A United Artists release of a United Artists Corporation Ltd. production. *Executive Producer:* Alan Ladd, Jr. *Producer:* Randall Wallace and Russell Smith. *Director:* Randall Wallace. *Screenplay:* Randall Wallace. *Based on the novel by:* Alexandre Dumas. *Director of Photography:* Peter Suschitzky. *Editor:* William Hoy. *Music:* Nick Glennie-Smith. *Music Editor:* Laura Perlman. *Choreographer:* Christine Cullen Wallace. *Sound:* David A. Stephenson and (music) Malcolm Luker. *Sound Editor:* Kelly L. Oxford and Lon E. Bender. *Casting:* Amanda Mackey Johnson and Cathy Sandrich. *Production Designer:* Anthony Pratt. *Art Director:* François de Lamothe and Albert Rajau. *Set Decorator:* Philippe Turlure. *Set Dresser:* Perine Barre. *Special Effects:* George Gibbs. *Costumes:* James Acheson. *Make-up:* Giannetto de Rossi. *Stunt Coordinator:* Phillipe Guegan and Yannick Derrien. *Running time:* 131 minutes. *MPAA Rating:* PG-13.

CAST: Leonardo DiCaprio (King Lous/Philippe); Jeremy Irons (Aramis); John Malkovich (Athos); Gérard Depardieu (Porthos); Gabriel Byrne (D'Artagnan); Anne Parillaud (Queen Anne); Judith Godrèche (Christine); Edward Atterton (Lieutenant André); Peter Sarsgaard (Raoul); Hugh Laurie and David Lowe (King's Advisors); Brigitte Boucher (Madame Rotund); Matthew Jocelyn (Assassin); Karine Belly (Wench); Emmanuel Guttierez (King's Friend); Christian Erickson (Ballroom Guard); François Montagut (Blond Musketeer); Andrew Wallace (Peasant Boy); Cécile Auclert and Sonia Backers (Serving Women); Vincent Nemeth (Customer); Joe Sheridan (Fortress Keeper); Olivier Hemon (Fortress Head Guard); Michael Morris (Bastille Gate Guard); Emmanuel Patron (Fortress Guard); Leonor Varela (Ballroom Beauty); Michael Hofland (Ruffian); Laura Fraser (Bedroom Beauty); Brigitte Auber (Queen Anne's Attendant); Jean-Pol Brissart (Monk).

LOS ANGELES TIMES, 3/13/98, Calendar/p. 1, Kenneth Turan

"The Man in the Iron Mask" swashes until it buckles. Heavy on swordplay and spectacle, it's so intent on reviving the costume epics of the past it doesn't realize it's trying to be too many things to too many people until it collapses under its own weight.

Written and directed by Randall Wallace, Oscar-nominated for his "Braveheart" script, "Mask" has more energy than sense, but its tale of derring-do in 17th century France is watchable in a mock heroic sort of way for those who are forgiving and in the mood for a film that uses the classic "all for one and one for all" line no less than seven times.

Yes, this film features the Three Musketeers and is based on a celebrated novel by the prolific Alexandre Dumas. With Jeremy Irons, John Malkovich and Gerard Depardieu as the trio of swordsman, Gabriel Byrne as their pal D'Artagnan, and Leonardo DiCaprio as both King Louis XIV and the title character, no one can be accused of holding back in the casting department.

Production values are not lacking either. "Mask" is crammed with neighing horses, rowdy peasants, elegant French chateaus and servile courtiers bowing and scraping in more than a thousand authentic costumes. For those who want more, they've even worked in a pig chase.

But Wallace, in his first try at directing, has been unable to unify the film's disparate elements. There's swordplay and tragedy, slapstick and romance, lots of DiCaprio for all those teenage girls—there's everything but a consistent style. And events are handled so broadly it's not surprising to learn that the director's inspiration was the Classics Illustrated version of the Dumas novel he read as a youth.

The closest "Mask" comes to a unifying tone is, unfortunately, one of raunchy comedy, with numerous crude jokes about sex and bodily functions intended to appeal to who knows who. Creating the kind of sophisticated, tongue-in-cheek humor that Richard Lester brought to his beguiling 1974 version of "The Three Musketeers" was not on anyone's mind here.

"Some of this is legend, but at least this much is fact," the film's prologue proclaims, before noting that the dreaded Bastille really did have an inmate identified only as "Prisoner number 64389000—the Man in the Iron Mask." (Who knew the place had that kind of capacity?)

Initially we get only a peek at this gentleman, who is seen banging his metal headdress against prison bars in understandable frustration. He's been in a cell coping with a cast-iron covering for years, and no one has ever told him why.

Much more in control of his destiny is the young King Louis. A ruthless, long-haired dandy who cares more about the cut of his sash than his starving subjects, the king divides his time between military matters ("No, no, do not underestimate the Dutch" is his unfortunate first line) and his avocation as vile seducer and all-around bounder.

Having less fun are the grumpy old musketeers, retired from active service with lots of time to mull over their regrets and yearn for the good old days. Athos (Malkovich) lives only for his grown son, Porthos (Depardieu) is still eager to party though his bulky frame barely fits through brothel doors, and Aramis (Irons) has become a worshipful priest.

As for the steely D'Artagnan, he's still in the royal service, acting as the king's worrywart captain of the guards who believes "a fool's sword can be sharper than his brain." When he's not working, D'Artagnan's spare time is taken up exchanging passionate but discreet looks with Louis' mother, Queen Anne ("La Femme Nikita's" Anne Parillaud).

It's the king who unwittingly reunites this morose group. For one thing, he deputizes Aramis to stop those rascally Jesuits from criticizing the wars that are leading to general starvation. And his ruthless eye falls on a comely young woman ("Ridicule's" Judith Godreche) who just happens to be the beloved of Athos' prized son. The ramifications of both events lead directly to that unhappy masked man and all manner of swordplay.

While pains have been taken to assemble a stellar cast, no similar labors went into giving them anything memorable to do, and no one seeing "The Man in the Iron Mask" should expect lines more profound than the king's "I hope you know there is more of me to love than a crown." And "all for one and one for all" may be a heck of a motto, but repeating it seven times is not the way to any sane person's heart.

NEW YORK POST, 3/13/98, p. 39, Rod Dreher

A certain word comes to mind while watching long-tressed golden boy Leonardo DiCaprio in "The Man in the Iron Mask."

Is it "Valiant"? "Heroic"? "Passionate"?

Nope. Try "Mmmmbop."

As girlish, shallow and altogether Hanson-like as he is in this costume catastrophe, DiCaprio is at least keeping in step with the all-consuming lousiness of this phony-baloney picture, over two snoozy, talky hours of derring-don't.

When bloated Gerard Depardieu whines, "I expected action," he speaks for all of us.

The Alexandre Dumas novel on which this misbegotten adaptation is based is the story of an attempt by the Three Musketeers to save France from the tyranny of its evil king (DiCaprio) by replacing him with his good twin brother. The goody-two-shoes twin (guess who) has been imprisoned on a faraway island, his incriminating visage entombed in metal.

Aside from the prestige cast—Depardieu, Jeremy Irons and John Malkovich as the aging Three Musketeers, and Gabriel Byrne as their comrade-in-tights D'Artagnan, who remains loyal to the bad king—there's every reason to expect this version to be a rollicking smash too. That's because the writer-director is Randall Wallace, who penned the Oscar-nominated script for "Braveheart," a stirring mix of heroism, humor and terrifically well-staged battles royal.

Alas, alas. Wallace's "The Man in the Iron Mask" has to be the most notable gathering of top talent in service of a hopeless cause since "The Capeman" started rehearsals. The writing stinks like overripe Camembert ("To love you is a treason against France, but not to love you is a treason to my heart."), the direction is clueless and the acting is a squeamish joke.

And with apologies to fantasy-laden teenage girls, you might as well call this wheezy epic "Three Men and a Baby," such is DiCaprio's youthful inadequacy in his key role. The flavor du jour's prisspot Louis XIV is a skinny, petulant brat, and nothing more. His nascent hero, Philippe, is made of even weaker stuff—effete, neutered and harmless. DiCaprio may be Hollywood's ideal beau, but if he's the new beau ideal of a romantic action lead, Tinseltown's decreeing, "Let them eat milquetoast." Malkovich's turn is lazy and mannered, marked by the actor's by now tiresomely sour air of sophisticated decay. His Athos looks like he'd really rather be over at the Marquis de Sade's drinking absinthe and playing naked twister.

Bryne is a pill as D'Artagnan, and even Jeremy Irons, who generally acquits himself well as the soldier-priest Aramis, is humiliated by having to wear a Roseanne Roseannadanna wig when he tries to talk his way into Philippe's prison.

So why the lack of action? Perhaps Wallace, a first-time director, lacked confidence. He certainly lacked the wherewithal to give us even the most basic scenes. How do the Musketeers slip the king's brother into a royal masked ball, for example?

Who knows? A film that tries to pass off an ending as cockamamie as this one's—involving velvet Kevlar, dubious paternity and more kindness and gentleness than the 17th century had to offer—has bigger problems to worry about.

NEWSDAY, 3/13/98, Part II/p. B2, Jack Mathews

When you enter Hollywood's world of historical mythology, you are obliged to accept a few givens: (1) Heroes always know their place in legend and behave accordingly. (2) Heroes never die, except as martyrs in the act of either rescue or redemption. (3) No human events are random; they're all carefully interconnected. (4) The dialogue sounds like Shakespeare as translated by Errol Flynn.

If you're down for those pre-conditions, as well as a nostalgic reunion with middle-age versions of the Three Musketeers and D'Artagnan, you may have a good time with Randall Wallace's "The Man in the Iron Mask" or, as it is more commonly referred to these days, "Leonardo DiCaprio's "First Film Since 'Titanic'." If not, this is a two-hour-and-11-minute movie that will make "Titanic" look like a short.

DiCaprio who will likely end the weekend as the star of the top two films in America, is both the Man in the Iron Mask and his baby-face twin, the cruel French King Louis XIV. That much of Alexandre Dumas' last Musketeer novel, the three-volume "The Viscount of Bragelonne," has been preserved in Wallace's account of a legend that's been adapted on screen at least four times previously.

Wallace, a novelist, an Oscar-nominated screenwriter ("Braveheart") and a first-time director, has written an ambitious, dense script that combines the values of the old-fashioned swashbuckler with modern soap opera psychology, ending up with something that is, at times, a comically brooding epic.

Dumas set "The Man in the Iron Mask" three decades after the Three Musketeers were in their youthful glory, and in this telling, theirs is a fragile all-for-one, one-for-all bond. Gusty Porthos (Gerard Depardieu) is now portly Porthos, a flatulent carouser so depressed by his declining virility he's ready to hang himself from a barn beam. Aramis (Jeffrey Irons) has become a court priest and underground Jesuit activist, an inner-circle enemy of Louis XIV. Athos (John Malkovich) is enjoying a quiet retirement, about to see his son Raoul (Peter Sarsgaard) become a second-generation Musketeer.

Meanwhile, D'Artagnan (Gabriel Byrne) has become captain of the Musketeers, and is serving his new king with devotion, even though he hates the little punk. When the king sends Raul to his death on the battlefield, in order to call his fiancée (Judith Godreche) to the royal bed, D'Artagnan's continued loyalty to Louis breaks his bond with the Three Musketeers and sets him against them in a battle for the throne.

That's for starters. There are many other complications, involving past affairs, questions of paternity, mother-son and mother-lover reunions (separate events), guilt and redemption. It's "Days of Our Lives" in the 17th Century, with great furniture.

"The Man in the Iron Mask" is visually stunning, with authentic castles and palaces of the period serving as sets, and with detailed interiors—gold gilding, masters' paintings, marbled halls and all—duplicated on Paris sound stages. The climactic costume ball is enough eyewash alone to ensure the film consideration at next year's Oscars.

But the growingly outrageous storyline, the ripe prose and the self-conscious hype of the Musketeer myth—the phrase "one for all, all for one" is uttered like a mantra—undermines some interesting ideas.

Wallace, like Dumas, is fascinated with the maturation of the Musketeers, who, in middle age, are indeed legends in their own time. When D'Artagnan rides his horse into a throng of starving Parisians, quelling a riot with his mere presence, the reverence they have for him feels real. And the directions taken by the original Musketeers are believable enough, though Depardieu's sole function is comic relief.

But the movie lacks the resonance of Richard Lester's "Robin and Marian," which caught up with a middle-age Robin Hood and his old flame. With the exception of DiCaprio, whose youth and inexperience are magnified by the age of his co-stars, "The Man in the Iron Mask" plays more like a Who reunion than an extension of the earlier Musketeer stories.

NEWSWEEK, 3/23/98, p. 64, David Ansen

Thanks to "Titanic," which has made Leonardo DiCaprio at this moment the hottest actor in the universe, "The Man in the Iron Mask"—which offers up two DiCaprios for the price of one—will probably be the first movie to displace "Titanic's" 12-week run at the top of the box-office charts. With two books about DiCaprio on the best-seller list, we are in the midst of certified Leo-mania. The swoony symptoms resemble every other great teen-idol craze of the past, with one difference: this heartthrob actually has talent.

That talent isn't seen at its very best, however, in this loose retelling of the Alexandre Dumas classic. Not that he's bad. Just check out how easily he conveys through his eyes the difference between his two characters—the spoiled and treacherous boy-king Louis XIV, and his secret twin, the kind and courageous Philippe. But the more mainstream DiCaprio's choices in roles become, the less interesting he seems. Let's hope the brilliant character actor of "This Boy's Life" and "What's Eating Gilbert Grape" isn't sacrificed to stardom.

As it turns out, the royal twins are not this movie's true subject. Louis Hayward, who played the dual roles in the 1939 version, and Richard Chamberlain, who played them in 1977, were the swashbuckling centers of those films. DiCaprio's Philippe is more puppet than protagonist, for the heart of writer-director Randall Wallace belongs to his aging musketeers, d'Artagnan (Gabriel Byrne), Athos (John Malkovich), Porthos (Gérard Depardieu) and warrior turned priest Aramis (Jeremy Irons). A kind of 17th-century wild bunch, they are aroused from their middle-aged slumber by outrage at the King's injustice. Led by Aramis, who knows that the king's secret twin is locked up in the Bastille, three of the musketeers attempt to replace the ruler with his benign carbon copy. The fourth—d'Artagnan, captain of the royal guards—stands in their way, for he cannot break his vow of loyalty to the king.

Though this formidable quartet of actors share neither accents nor acting styles, they seem to be having a high old time together. Depardieu, as the lusty Porthos, wallows in the low humor like a pig in search of comic truffles. Irons, less neurasthenic than usual, seems happy to exhibit some extroverted energy. Malkovich, as the vengeful father whose son was killed to satisfy the king's lust for the boy's fiancée (Judiih Godrèche), has surprising panache, and Byrne cuts a fine, solemn figure as the conflicted d'Artagnan.

"The Man in the Iron Mask" is pleasant, old-fashioned fun, even if the filmmaking rarely rises above the pedestrian. First-time director Wallace, who wrote "Braveheart," has no real flair for action, and a sense of humor that's more "Animal House" than aristocratic. Still, he's a good storyteller and never condescends to his material But unlike Richard Lester's musketeer movies of the '70s, which put an absurdist spin on Dumas, Wallace's remake is more throwback than reinvention. Perhaps that's what makes it a distinctly late-'90s movie, an era in which we may increasingly find ourselves following "Titanic's" everything-old-is-new-again lead.

SIGHT AND SOUND, 4/98, p. 43, Rob White

Paris, France, 1662. The former musketeer Porthos is reunited with his one-time comrade-in-arms Aramis, now a priest. Their other colleague Athos has a heart-to-heart with his son Raoul about the latter's impending marriage. King Louis sends Aramis to find and kill the secret leader of the Jesuits. Louis tries to seduce Raoul's fiancée Christine, but is interrupted by an assassination attempt which is foiled by D'Artagnan, the king's bodyguard and the "fourth" musketeer. In a secret dungeon, Louis' identical twin brother Philippe is kept in an iron mask.

Louis has Raoul recalled to the front where he's killed. Furious, Athos arrives at the palace but is subdued by D'Artagnan. Louis seduces Christine. At a secret meeting, Aramis reveals that he is the Jesuit leader, and plans to depose the king. Athos and Porthos support him, but D'Artagnan refuses to help. Planning to put Philippe in Louis' place, Aramis smuggles him out of jail; Athos tutors him in courtly manners. At Louis' masquerade ball, the former musketeers effect the switch, but Philippe's kindness towards Christine alerts D'Artagnan. Philippe is captured, but the others escape.

Louis orders the others to be killed and Philippe to the Bastille. The musketeers, now reunited with D'Artagnan (who is shocked by Louis' actions), contrive to rescue Philippe again. Besieged by troops, D'Artagnan reveals he is the father of the twins. The royal troops refuse to shoot the musketeers. D'Artagnan throws himself in front of Louis' sword to protect Philippe. Louis is put into the mask, and Philippe takes his place as king.

Having written the script for *Braveheart,* Randall Wallace turns his hand to direction with this adaptation of Alexandre Dumas' novel *The Man in the Iron Mask,* the last in a sequence featuring the four musketeers. Unlike *Braveheart,* which is sometimes aggravatingly po-faced, this latest version of the book (there have been at least five other films of it and a television series) is a gleefully tongue-in-cheek romp reminiscent of Richard Lester's 70s musketeer films. It's stylishly photographed by Peter Suschitzky, who shows off the Fontainebleau locations and dazzling costumes to full effect.

But, like Lester's films which brought together Oliver Reed, Faye Dunaway and Raquel Welch, it's the stellar cast who grab all the attention here. Gérard Depardieu makes a wonderful Porthos, by turns maudlin and rambunctious. Gabriel Byrne is a preoccupied, severe D'Artagnan full of honour and secrets. John Malkovich, though his characteristically pedantic diction is occasionally frustrating, plays Athos subtly, hinting at a complexity beyond the film's remit. Leonardo DiCaprio is impressive in the dual roles of the near-psychotic Louis XIV and his virtuous, iron-masked twin brother Philippe. Only Jeremy Irons, as the pious Aramis, puts in less than his best, a bit too brooding to pull off the comic lines. All the principals keep their own accents, so we can enjoy both their star personas and their essays in stock characterisation.

Dumas' novel is inordinately long and wordy, and in his script Wallace rightly strips all of this out in order to maintain cinematic musketeer conventions. The novel concludes with D'Artagnan killed by a cannon ball in battle, and only Aramis is still alive by the end. Here, though, D'Artagnan alone is killed—throwing himself in front of Louis' sword as the king tries to murder his brother.

However, the script is still *The Man in the Iron Mask*'s weakest feature and, given to lesser actors, it could have been very ponderous. Even so, the film noticeably sags in the middle. Along the way, some interesting issues bubble under the surface. In a film so dependent on male characters, gender roles are disturbed and redistributed. A feminised Athos, grieving for his dead son, teaches Philippe courtly behaviour, and carries out the task gently. There are also hints of all sorts of trauma and dysfunction—in the royal family but also in the solitariness of the legendary musketeers' fading lives. Their precarious lonely masculinity is almost reminiscent of Sam Peckinpah!s *The Wild Bunch* (1969), which is recalled in the climactic slow-motion, seemingly suicidal charge of the musketeers against the besieging troops in the Bastille. But these issues never come into full view, and we are left with a film which, at all the right moments but especially in its last half hour, abandons seriousness in favour of swordfights, often to hilarious and completely satisfying effect.

Also reviewed in:
CHICAGO TRIBUNE, 3/13/98, Friday/p. A, Michael Wilmington
NEW YORK TIMES, 3/13/98, p. E14, Janet Maslin
VARIETY, 3/16-22/98, p. 63, Todd McCarthy
WASHINGTON POST, 3/13/98, p. C1, Rita Kempley

MARIE BAIE DES ANGES

A Sony Pictures Classics release of a Les Films de la Suane presentation of a Studio Image 2/La Sept Cinema/Lelia Films/Les Films des Tournelles co-production. *Executive Producer:* Pascal Judelewicz. *Producer:* Philippe Rousselet. *Director:* Manuel Pradal. *Screenplay (French with English subtitles):* Manuel Pradal. *Director of Photography:* Christophe Pollock. *Editor:* Valerie Deseine. *Music:* Carlo Crivelli. *Sound:* Gita Serveira. *Sound Editor:* Jean Goudier. *Casting:* Frank Saint Cast. *Production Designer:* Javier Po and Véronique Mellery. *Art Director:* Aziz Hamzaoui. *Costumes:* Claire Gérard-Hirne. *Make-up:* Valérie Tranier, Murielle Brot and Heidi Braumberger. *Running time:* 90 minutes. *MPAA Rating:* R.

CAST: Vahina Giocante (Marie); Frederic Malgras (Orso); Amira Casar (Young Woman); David Kilner (Larry); Jamie Harris (Jim); Frederic Westerman (Ardito); Nicolas Welbers (Goran); Swan Carpio (Jurec); Aladin Riebel (Hairdresser); Andrew Clover (Andy); John Dowling (John); David Gregg (American Marine); Roxane Mesquida (Mireille); Aurelle Moradet (Corinne); Patrick Serraf (Bob); Serge Merlin (The Watcher); Brigitte Roüan (Paule); Marc Brunet (Louis); Grégory Derangère (FI Pilot); Sauveur Campanella (Old Fisherman); Louisa Bouali (Louisa); Christophe Deslandes (Chris); Karim Saad (Claude); Laetitia Lefbèvre (Karine); Janvier Abelle (Fisherman).

LOS ANGELES TIMES, 7/3/98, Calendar/p. 6, Kevin Thomas

The bay around Nice in the south of France is called the Bay of Angels because it was once the habitat of a species of shark by that name. According to legend, the sharks, along with a pair of huge rocks that look like shark fins, guarded the bay from invaders. But once invasions waned, the sharks started feeding on the locals, requiring the rulers to make sacrifices of children to appease them and resulting in a new species, angel sharks.

Writer-director Manuel Pradal, in his dizzying, go-for-broke "Marie Baie des Anges," suggests that nothing really has changed. For the most part, his film is a headlong visual rush in which beautiful 15-year-old Marie (Vahina Giocante, a dancer with the Marseilles Opera) parades around the port and its craggy, pine-crested hills like a biblical—or DeMille—temptress, inflaming both a contingent of rowdy, crude young American sailors and a pack of youths, dangerous feral creatures, hired to harvest local wheat fields.

The film has the feel of an opera in its stylized emotional extravagance and of a ballet in its restless, graceful movement, as the two groups of males encircle and retreat, tension mounting and easing. "Marie" is distinctly disturbing: How could such a locale of awesome, inviting natural beauty also be a place of such lawless, constant danger?

Breaking out of that teen pack is the solemnly handsome 17-year-old Orso (Frederic Malgras, a 15-year-old of Russian Gypsy descent), who is as drawn to Marie as she is to him. She is the angel, he is the shark, and they enact the mythical fusion said to produce those long-vanished angel sharks. Marie is, however, an angel only symbolically, for she is a totally contemporary teen who moves in complete freedom from whatever family she may have or wherever they may be. She knows her wanton flirting can be dangerous and is turned on by the risks.

For his part, Orso is also not wholly a shark, deadly as he can be, but is yet another alienated kid looking for love. And sure enough, when Marie and Orso do manage to get away from corrupt, indifferent society to an abandoned island, they not only fall in love with each other but in their Eden regain some of the childlike delight in simple play that clearly had long since vanished from their lives.

Now all this is every bit as heady and exalted as it sounds. Yet because these teens have such beauty and vulnerability and because Pradal has such driving passion and visual panache—his cameraman Christophe Pollock is endlessly resourceful—this first-time writer-director gets away with a great deal of flashy technique and actually makes it serve in eliciting a genuine emotional response to his star-crossed lovers.

Unfortunately, Pradal also overreaches, punching up his narrative with a flood of strobe-like flashbacks that are too often more distracting, indeed confusing, than emotionally enriching. While this repeated indulgence makes "Marie Baie des Anges" too precious and arty for its own good, it does signal the arrival of a new, distinctive talent who leaves you curious to see what he'll try next.

NEW YORK POST, 6/19/98, p. 50, Thelma Adams

Just when I was thoroughly disenchanted with French movies about sexually overactive youths, newcomer Manuel Pradal seduced me with an ominous romance about two teens sexing and scamming their way along the Riviera.

"Marie Baie des Anges," recalls Rene Clement's 1960 sun-drenched noir "Purple Noon."

"Marie" opens with an idyllic vista that contrasts with the drama's dark driving forces. A passing tourist boat skimming Nice's Bay of Angels informs visitors and audience alike that the angels in question are angel sharks, usually docile, that turn on men when they become desperate or overcrowded.

Seventeen-year-old Orso (Frederic Malgras) could be called Orca. He's a predatory, dark-eyed thief whose clean-shaven face is set, but not yet hardened, by danger. Orso, who has the power to calm vicious guard dogs, kills a younger boy just as calmly.

Marie and Orso meet. They become dizzy in each other's company. They are angels swimming like sharks until Pradal's script delivers on its threatening promise. Both Giocante and Malgras are fiercely appealing in physically demanding roles.

Writer-director Pradal is a passionate, energetic talent shifting to dream states and fracturing the narrative, he occasionally severs the strings of logic. But the vivid image of Marie dancing, partnered by a platoon of sailors, or Orso initiating foreplay by moving his hand up Marie's tan thigh while they share a mini-bike with a third youth, express a native wildness as beautiful and dangerous as the Bay of Angels.

NEWSDAY, 6/19/98, Part II/p. B7, John Anderson

To paraphrase John Lennon: You say you want a resolution? If there's a sign of one-worldism in current cinema—besides the fact that we make films for the Chinese and the rest of the world makes films for us—it's the ability of so many youngish filmmakers everywhere to create intriguing set-ups that couldn't find their way out of their own conflict with a meat ax and a flashlight. Imagine there's no ending...

So many movies with the bold construction, the artful introductions, the seductive orchestration; so many with the cliched coda, the burst of obligatory gunfire, the portentously unsatisfying conclusion. If George Will were reviewing movies, he'd call all this a symptom of our lack of national resolve, or a systemic aversion to objective morality. Except that "Marie Baie des Anges" is French, so maybe it has something to do with NATO.

In this debut feature by Manuel Pradal, an obviously talented, thirtyish director who uses his native south of France to rather glorious effect, the infrastructure, as it were, is sound. Weaving flashback and flash forward around a corrupt present, he sucks us into a youth drama by creating real mystery: Who is this sociopathic delinquent Orso (Frederic Malgras), who kills another boy in the first few moments of the movie, robs a house, deals in guns and seems by every indication to be careening toward disaster? Who is this gorgeous creature Marie (Vahina Giocante), who glides so gracefully across the morally thin ice of the local American naval base, allowing herself to be wined, dined and escorted toward an equally disastrous end?

Who is the woman whose house Orso robs (Amira Casar), whose picture he carries on a purloined locket and who reappears with inscrutable timing? The fluidity with which Pradal executes his visual choreography, making abrupt and clashing cuts seem effortless and arresting, is all very masterful and seductive. He also has a stunningly beautiful leading lady in dancer-turned-actress Giocante—13½ at the time of filming who convincingly mixes imperious self-possession with adolescent uncertainty.

But three-quarters of the way through the film, when Marie and Orso are doing their "Blue Lagoon" routine, fleeing to paradise and finding it lacking, we're forced to recognize just how unsympathetic—you might even say boring—these tortured individuals are.

Orso is a thug, one of many who roam the tourist haunts of southern France and who scramble around its seaside cliffs like goats (the terrain is, like the characters, almost constantly off kilter). Perpetrating chaos around the Bay of Angels—whose signature is two cliffs shaped like angel shark fins—their crimes are stupid, venal, almost innocent; Pradal's scene in an amusement park, with kids in bumper cars handing off bottles of liquor to each other, may be the best thing he does here. But his use of Marie, the temporary toast of a group of boorish American sailors, seems a bit off. Giocante is visually captivating, but when Pradal uses her for decoration instead of illumination he pushes his movie over into an entirely different and wrongheaded realm.

Plus, when the sentiment shifts, the movie goes south. And we don't mean France. Despite the obvious comparisons, "Marie" is no "Lolita." For one thing, "Marie" is actually being shown in an American theater. For the Jeremy Irons film, which no one wanted to buy, we'll have to wait for Showtime to show it Aug. 2. Meanwhile watch "Marie" and figure out the difference.

SIGHT AND SOUND, 12/98, p. 40, Michael Temple

The Bay of Angels (not the Bay of Nice, known locally as the 'Bay of Angels', but an amalgam of various places in the South of France). According to a local legend, because of two fin-like rocks visible in the sea, the bay is said to be protected by two 'angel-sharks'.

The coastal area is populated by gangs of wild young adolescents, who regularly come into conflict with the authorities and with the American sailors stationed there. Among these outsiders, two individuals, Marie and Orso, stand out. Orso drifts between gangs and commits petty crimes. He gives some money to his friend Goran to buy him a gun, but Goran is mugged and loses the money. Meanwhile, Marie divides her time and affections between the rich foreign sailors and Jurec, one of the gang leaders. But she is finally rejected by both parties and this precipitates her coming together with Orso. Having fled to an island, they live happily until Marie is killed during an unsuccessful armed robbery. In revenge, Orso murders Goran whom he believes to have double-crossed him.

This is Manuel Pradal's second feature (after *Canti*), a tale of love and marginality set in an imaginary world peopled by teenagers supposedly located in the South of France. It is an astonishingly powerful debut, overflowing with colour, movement, beauty and emotion. Although the title may evoke memories of Jacques Demy's 1962 Nice-based gambling drama *La Baie des anges,* it would be wrong to suggest *Angel Sharks* is some kind of allusive cocktail or academic homage to classic European cinema.

On the contrary, Pradal's vision is so fresh and original even moments that in other films would seem like bookish references here seem like oneiric transformations of Demy's dancing American sailors or Pasolini's suburban thugs. Early films are inevitably haunted by certain major influences, but in this case those influences have informed rather than deformed a genuine cinematic talent.

Most impressive is the ease with which Pradal creates a tangible universe and an engaging set of characters while happily ignoring many conventions of dramatic and narrative coherence. As the summary given above may suggest, it is in fact very difficult to reconstruct the story of *Angel Sharks* without resorting to excessive detail. The film moves us swiftly through an intricate series of petty crimes, brief flirtations, tribal clashes, sudden embraces and acts of revenge, all of which somehow get us from start to finish, but we cannot then account for what has happened exactly.

In fact, the story is structured around a flashback, and it is only at the end of the film that we realise why in the opening scene we saw Orso shoot his friend Goran. Within this narrative loop, much of the action is edited in a fragmented, hallucinatory style. little or no psychological justification is given for the acts of the two main characters, Marie and Orso. He drifts between the various gangs of angel-sharks or lawless youths alluded to in the title, while she switches allegiance between the poor local kids and the rich American sailors stationed in the bay. In the end, Marie and Orso are brought together simply because they have been rejected by everyone else.

Despite this lack of conventional psychology and storytelling, the characters are strong and persuasive. The film achieves that rare feat of creating a narrative flow that is both incoherent and convincing, broken and harmonious. In a similar vein, Pradal's handling of time and space creates an impression of improvised, wilful disorder, as if a literary scenario had been carefully constructed for the purposes of acquiring finance and then was joyfully and rigorously destroyed in the chaos of the shoot and the magical transformations of the editing. For example, the Bay of Angels we see on the screen is not the Bay of Nice that geographers or Demy fans might expect. It is, in fact, a beguiling spatial artifice, assembled from scenes shot all over the South of France and Italy. At times even the most convincing shot/counter-shot is constructed from one image taken near Marseilles against another filmed six months earlier in the Roman countryside.

It is as if the exceptional depth and intensity of the images and rhythm of *Angel Sharks* had in part been derived from all that time and travel invested in the film's preparation. As for the casting process, this reportedly involved seeing thousands of young people, virtually all of them from impoverished backgrounds. Whatever questions this information may raise about the ethics of making a beautifully crafted film from such fragile human materials, the performances given by the principal actors are brilliant across the board, with Vahina Giocante as Marie and Frédéric Malgras as Orso putting to shame the drama-school dross that all too frequently finds its way on to French screens. This highly subjective projection of sounds and images, comprising the sort of highly personal investigation of places and faces that French cinema rarely explores, deserves attention and respect.

VILLAGE VOICE, 6/23/98, p. 135, J. Hoberman

For all its careful setups and lugubrious little epiphanies, *Henry Fool* is a movie with a dubious premise and one astonishing scene. Still, one good scene is one more than you'll find in Manuel Pradal's first feature, *Marie Baie des Anges*. A mild version of *Kids* transposed to the French Riviera, this Saint-Tropez day of the narcoleptics features a pair of blank young model types swanning through a primal landscape of sun-blasted stupefaction.

Oh, the restless boredom of teenage sensualists in a voluptuously wide-screen world without adults. Calling Henry Fool: the 15-year-old Marie (Vahina Giocante), who seems to have been sewn into a red, form-enhancing designer *shmatte,* spends her time vamping a base full of lustful American sailors, while 17-year-old Orso (Frederic Malgras) engages in petty larceny, picks fights, and gets sent to reform school before escaping into her life. Writer-director Pradal kills time waiting for the kids to connect by jazzing the action with all manner of jump cuts and ellipses. But, whether flashing forward or back (not to mention over, wider, sideways, down), *Marie Baie des Anges* is still swoony trash. Things only get worse once the lovers are free to explore their island—it's as if Pradal were trying to channel Bonnard's impression of *The Blue Lagoon.*

Its woods and crags constructed from a dozen different locations, *Marie Baie des Anges* is meant to be elemental and timeless. (A shot of a giant soccer stadium is designed to suggest the eternal Mediterranean of the Roman Empire.) Outweighing even his cynicism, Pradal's pretension crushes the life out of the movie, not to mention his sullen young leads; they barely have one expression between them. Marie does know how to strike a pose (Giocante was a dancer in the Opera de Marseilles when discovered by Pradal). Her Arabian number creates a distraction for Orso to steal a fisherman's boat, although she's mainly devoted to toe balancing in the woods.

Pradal's movie is named after Jacques Demy's 1962 evocation of Monte Carlo, as well as the bay where the action supposedly unfolds. If there were truth in advertising, this failed exploitation flick would be called *Marie Bain de Soleil.*

Also reviewed in:
CHICAGO TRIBUNE, 9/4/98, Friday/p. A, Michael Wilmington
NEW YORK TIMES, 5/19/98, p. E13, Stephen Holden

VARIETY, 10/6-12/97, p. 59, Deborah Young
WASHINGTON POST, 8/7/98, p. D5, Stephen Hunter

MARIUS AND JEANNETTE

A New Yorker Films release of an Agat Films production in association with La Sept Cinema and with the participation of Canal +. *Producer:* Giles Sandoz. *Director:* Robert Guédiguian. *Screenplay (French with English subtitles):* Robert Guédiguian and Jean-Louis Milesi. *Director of Photography:* Bernard Cavalié. *Editor:* Bernard Sasia. *Sound:* Laurent Lafran and (music) Jean-Yves Rousseaux and Jean-Pierre Laforce. *Casting:* Maya Sevleyan. *Production Designer:* Malek Hamzaoui. *Art Director:* Karim Hamzaoui. *Make-up:* Maïté Alonso. *Running time:* 102 minutes. *MPAA Rating:* Not Rated.

CAST: Ariane Ascaride (Jeannette); Gérard Meylan (Marius); Pascale Roberts (Caroline); Jacques Boudet (Justin); Frédérique Bonnal (Monique); Jean-Pierre Darroussin (Dédé); Laetitia Pesenti (Magali); Miloud Nacer (Malek); Pierre Banderet (Monsieur Ebrard).

LOS ANGELES TIMES, 6/19/98, Calendar/p. 13, Kevin Thomas

The warm embrace of Marcel Pagnol hovers over Robert Guediguian's irresistible "Marius and Jeannette." It can't be an accident that one of the films in Pagnol's classic Marseilles trilogy of the '30s is called "Marius."

In this contemporary *comedie humaine*, the setting is also Marseilles, in Estaque, the city's working-class district, where poverty can still look invitingly picturesque—and where Guediguian and his Marius, Gerard Meylan, grew up together. It's easy to see why "Marius and Jeannette" was last year's sleeper at the French box office and why it scored in the Cesars, France's Oscars, racking up seven nominations and a best actress nod for Ariane Ascaride.

Marius, a tall, handsome man in his 40s, is guarding an Estaque cement factory about to be demolished when he catches Jeannette (Ascaride), a vital woman about his age, stealing two drums of paint. The volatile Jeannette, who says of herself that if she shut up she'd get an ulcer—"and I can't afford rich people's diseases"—nonetheless heads home empty-handed. The next day she's dumbfounded when Marius shows up, the paint in hand, at her tiny apartment.

Jeannette, who has an inner glow that makes her seem beautiful, doesn't even invite the man in for tea, but Marius' gesture marks the beginning of an understandably tentative romance.

Jeannette's life has been hard: The father of her daughter Magali (Laetitia Pesenti), a teenager who wants to become a journalist, walked out on the family, and the father of her little son Malek (Miloud Nacer) was killed when some scaffolding collapsed. A strict but loving mother, voluble about injustices faced by the working classes, Jeannette hasn't been involved with a man for eight years. Marius, who is as reticent as Jeannette is garrulous, doesn't talk about his past, but you can see the pain of loss in his sensitive gaze.

Guediguian views the human comedy as affectionately as Pagnol and all the great French directors. It is a question of perspective, of seeing the middle-aged couple within their warm community and in the cycle of life with all its foibles and vicissitudes.

Jeannette's children and neighbors are just as interesting. They include Monique (Frederique Bonnal) and Dede (Jean-Pierre Darrousin), who have three children; Dede suffers plenty of derision from Monique and his neighbors for once having voted for the far right.

Also prominent are Caroline (Pascale Roberts), a life-affirming survivor who was sent to a German concentration camp at the age of 14 as a member of the Communist youth movement, and Justin (Jacques Boudet), a retired teacher and intellectual with a refreshingly ecumenical view of world religions. These are warm, wonderful people, and their sense of community and their larger, more compassionate view of people are enough to make you envious.

That Guediguian and Meylan were members of a Communist youth movement shows in the film's leftist but hardly doctrinaire sentiments. Disillusioned with communism, Guediguian discovered film as a way of expressing his idealism and concern for workers. He met Ascaride, his wife, at college, where she was a political activist. Her acting ambitions led to an opportunity for him to try his hand at screenwriting.

"Marius and Jeannette" is his seventh feature since his 1980 filmmaking debut and the first to be distributed in the U.S. This charmer surely won't be the last.

NEW YORK POST, 4/24/98, p. 48, Larry Worth

As the capital of chic, Paris is the perfect spot for beautiful people to fall in and out of love.

But there's nothing vaguely chic about Marseilles, and the titular "Marius and Jeannette" will never be confused with the beautiful people. Therein lies this Cesar-winning production's ever-refreshing charm.

Seeming right at home in the blue-collar seaport, Marius is a 40ish, limping, craggy-faced guard at a cement factory. And Jeannette, a middle-aged single mother of two, tries to make ends meet by cashiering at a supermarket.

The two first meet when Jeannette attempts to steal a couple of buckets of discarded paint from Marius' place of employment. He catches her red-handed and a nasty argument ensues. It's hardly the makings of a storybook romance.

Regardless, the twosome recognize a mutual spark and subsequently begin dating. Counterpointed against the budding union are the fates of two equally feisty, older couples, both of whom live in Jeannette's rundown section of Marseilles.

Writer-director Robert Guediguian uses the characters for a leisurely, bold look at daydreams, reveries and daily disappointments which should ring true for anyone past puberty. That's because the savvy script is filled with one moment after another of the small truths and bitter ironies that come to define everyday lives.

Traditional drama goes on hold as the protagonists vent their feelings while drying dishes, shelling peas or kissing their kids good night. What comes through is an authenticity that's lacking in more conventional love stories.

That's not to say Guediguian's script is flawless. Specifically, the screenplay has its share of forced humor and a resolution that comes about too neatly.

Thankfully, the fine ensemble cast distracts from any drawbacks. In particular, Ariane Ascaride is a positively luminous Jeannette, delivering a richly nuanced performance that's already won her France's equivalent of the Oscar.

And as Jeannette's better half, Gerard Meylan proves sentient and charismatic. To watch him expose long-hidden emotional baggage in an oh-so-slow manner is to observe a master at work.

Indeed, the principals help turn "Marius and Jeannette" into a cinematic valentine for those who know *l'amour* can bloom at any age.

NEWSDAY, 4/24/98, Part II/p. B6, John Anderson

It's a story as old as Karl Marx' prom picture: Woman with two kids meets slightly damaged single guy, they fall reluctantly but deeply in love, stumble over some personal history and 1) live happily ever after, or 2) split up entirely. And yet "Marius and Jeannette," the Cesar-winning French hit from Robert Guediguian is just as reluctant about love as its two title characters: The abrasive, politicized Jeannette (Ariane Ascaride), who has been both abandoned and widowed and has two children to show for it; the earthy, phlegmatic Marius (Gerard Meylan), a security guard at a derelict cement plant, who got his job by feigning a limp. Meeting angry when Marius stops Jeannette from appropriating some paint drums from the factory grounds, they are living hand-to-mouth and carrying a load of baggage. Neither is love material, both are symptoms of a capital-worshiping world. And they jump in with both feet.

But while Guediguian is making a romance—and has made a perfectly believable and touching one at that—his film arrives at love not by the usual careless, casual route, but over mounds of emotional obstacles, as a conscious, deliberate act: In a movie dedicated to the "thousands of unknown workers," amour is a political decision. If there were enough love, after all, there'd be no need for politics. Lovers of the world, unite!

They don't, as a rule, so the tiny cul-de-sac where most of the movie is set is an incubator of old leftist sentiment, a mini-utopia of worker solidarity. Fidel Castro is now wearing a suit?

Scandale! A husband who voted for the National Front? Don't expect peace from your wife anytime soon.

Of course, no one has a sou. There is no money, no jobs—which doesn't stop Jeannette from mouthing off and losing hers—and the ruins of the cement factory lie like the bleached white bones of a plundered economy. Kids dream of becoming footballers (think NBA) and they might just as well. Politics is less a subject of action than conversation: Dede (Jean-Pierre Darroussin) and his wife Monique (Frederique Bonnal) argue strikes and policy while their kids play.

The older, sexy Caroline (Pascale Roberts) now and then remembers being a Communist in the Nazi death camps; her occasional boyfriend, the professorial Justin (Jacques Boudet), teaches Jeannette's young son, Malek (Miloud Nacer), who's black, why his mother is Catholic and he's Islamic. Magali (Laetitia Pesenti), Jeannette's statuesque daughter, plans on leaving for journalism school so she can kick figurative government butt. Both kids like Marius, as does Jeannette. Theirs is a perfect terrarium of political stability.

Justin, naturally, has an unspoken history that at some point was destined to rear its ugly head and attempt a coup against the Jeannette-Marius alliance; even in a dream state such as this, conflict is a necessity. But this is a surmountable obstacle to happiness. There are so many that are insurmountable, Guediguian suggests, and so many people who cannot find what Marius and Jeannette find in this movie, which is a pure, sunny fantasy, intelligent fantasy all the same, of course, never any more than a movie.

SIGHT AND SOUND, 12/97, p. 46, Michael Temple

Jeannette is a single mother with two young children, Malek and Magali, by two different fathers who are dead or departed. She works as a checkout clerk in a supermarket in the impoverished l'Estaque area of Marseilles. Marius works as a security guard at an abandoned cement-works. They meet when he catches her stealing tins of paint from the factory site. When he ends up offering to help her redecorate her modest apartment, a romantic relationship gradually develops between them, and soon Marius is integrated into the routines of the close-knit family unit.

One day, however, he fails to turn up for dinner, and it becomes evident that something has profoundly disturbed him. Further evidence is provided by the fact that he starts drinking very heavily. Jeannette feels she has been let down once more by an unreliable man, and is reluctant even to find out what Marius' problem actually is. Eventually, two of her male neighbours, Justin and Dédé, join Marius in a massive drinking session. Marius reveals that he is troubled by the constant reminder, provided by Malek and Magali, of his own two children who died in a drink-driving accident for which he still feels responsible. Taking advantage of his drunken condition, Justin and Dédé carry him back to Jeannette's bed, and thus bring the couple back together again. Finally, a narrator reassures us that all will be well for each of the characters in the future.

This is an unashamedly sentimental story of love lost and found, of desire as an unexpected miracle bringing warmth and meaning to an otherwise harsh world. Robert Guédiguian's strengths as a director clearly lie in the dramatic aspects of film-making, notably his neat execution of a well-conceived scenario and his excellent direction of the actors, from whom he obtains a full range of fine performances. The narrative develops smoothly and is effectively paced, introducing us to the two main characters via the simple plot device of coincidence. When Marius catches Jeannette in the act of stealing paint from the disused factory, their first encounter is thus marked by confrontation and suspicion in a way which foreshadows their awkward, slightly embarrassed passage towards a sexual relationship. It also reflects the couple's markedly contrasting personalities: Marius is all masculine reserve and silence, while Jeannette is mercurial and voluble.

This progressive, classical unfolding of the narrative is extended throughout the whole film, and also brought into play gradually in the treatment of the secondary characters. Justin, the retired schoolteacher, has an on-off relationship with wartime deportee Caroline, providing both emotional and historical perspective. Similarly, the tempestuous couple formed by Dédé and Monique represents the rockier side of love's progress.

Guédiguian directs the children Malek and Magali with great economy and sensitivity (the latter, played by the beautiful Laetitia Pesenti, looks uncannily like the annunciative Angel in Pasolini's *The Gospel According to Matthew*). Not only does he encourage quietly persuasive performances from the two young actors, but he also uses their presence to counterpoint the tragic absence of Marius' own children, about whom we learn a dramatic secret which structures the film's plot, one revealed late in the game.

Guédiguian's handling of space and place is similarly intelligent. Although the cinematography is aptly simple and conventional, Bernard Cavalié's shot composition conveys the cramped living conditions, the narrow communal courtyard, and the winding backstreets of l'Estaque, as well as the constant promise of escape and eternity represented by the Mediterranean sky and welcoming sea. Equally effectively filmed is the former cement-works: dry, dusty, dilapidated, it says more about the social and economic context of the story than the rather heavy-handed attempts at political analysis which emanate from the characters themselves. The same could be said for the striking long tracking shot which follows Jeannette down a seemingly endless queue of unemployed women waiting for jobs outside a factory (reminiscent of certain effects achieved by Godard in the supermarket and factory scenes of *Tout va bien*).

It is no doubt the explicit political content of *Marius et Jeannette* which is its least convincing feature. The sentimentality of the romance feeds into the sentimental humanism of Guédiguian's world-view (expressed in such earlier films of Guédiguian's as *A la vie, a la mort!* and *L'argent fait le bonheur*). This is socialism of the heart, to put it mildly: poverty is good for you, the people are all kind and generous, and Communists don't build Gulags or persecute minorities. Even Dédé's brief flirtation with the Front National is presented more as an amorous indiscretion than a conscious political act. But as Bernard Tapie once famously commented, "people who vote Front National are bastards", not lambs who have innocently strayed from the democratic flock. Guédiguian's politics, however, are hardly crucial to the film's success, and if anything his ideological nostalgia and naïvety only add to the old-fashioned charm of this well-told story.

VILLAGE VOICE, 4/28/98, p. 75, Amy Taubin

Set in Estaque, the working-class district of Marseilles, Robert Guédiguian's *Marius and Jeanette* is a middle-aged fairy tale about love and labor. It has a generosity of spirit that recalls the '30s films of Jean Renoir (among them *Les Marseillaise*). And it also makes love and loss not only inseparable, but such an everyday part of what it is to be human that, by comparison, the formulaic disaster films that Hollywood deploys every summer seem all the more meretricious and manipulative.

Marius (Gérard Meylan) works as a watchman at a shuttered cement factory that's in the process of being torn down. He catches Jeannette (Ariane Ascaride)—a single mother of two whose outspokenness has just gotten her fired from her job as a supermarket cashier—helping herself to a few cans of paint from the trash heap. As much opposites as people from the same background can be, they are instantly attracted. She's buoyant and irrepressible; he's weighted down and taciturn. And they both have tragedies in their past that make them leery of attachment.

Marius and Jeannette, which won a bunch of big prizes in France, is something of an oddity these days in that it wears its leftist heart on its sleeve. Against a background of factory closings, record-high unemployment, and the rise of the Le Pen right, Marius, Jeannette, and their neighbors exhibit an old-fashioned working-class solidarity. It's the source of the film's ironic optimism and joie de vivre.

Made on a TV budget, *Marius and Jeanette* is nothing much to look at. But the actors are wonderful. Ascaride, who's married to the director and has appeared in all eight of his films, is impulsive, tenacious, and all the more seductive for her lack of glamour. Meylan, who's also a Guédiguian regular (and is a nurse by profession), is equally vivid—even when he's not saying a word. Among the supporting cast, Laetitia Pesenti and Miloud Nacer are nicely at ease as Jeannette's kids, and, as her neighbors, Jacques Boudet, Frederique Bonnal, Pascale Roberts, and Jean-Pierre Darroussin really seem like they've known each other for years. Though Ascaride won the César (the French Oscar) for her performance, *Marius and Jeanette* stays true to its subject by being a real ensemble piece. It makes you fantasize about the pleasure of living next door to everyone involved.

Also reviewed in:
NEW REPUBLIC, 5/4/98, p. 26, Stanley Kauffmann

NEW YORK TIMES, 4/24/98, p. E21, Janet Maslin
VARIETY, 5/26-6/1/97, p. 69, Derek Elley

MARK TWAIN'S AMERICA

A Sony Pictures Classics release of an Ogden Entertainment presentation.. *Executive Producer:* Mitchell Cannold, Isaac Palmer, and Jonathan Stern. *Producer:* James Lahti and Stephen Low. *Director:* Stephen Low.   *Screenplay:* Alex Low and Stephen Low.   *Director of Photography:* Andrew Kitzanuk.   *Editor:* James Lahti.   *Music:* Alan Williams.   *Sound:* Peter Thillye. *Production Designer:* Charles Braive.   *Running time:* 47 minutes.   *MPAA Rating:* G.

CAST: Anne Bancroft (Narrator).

NEW YORK POST, 7/17/98, p. 45, Larry Worth

The adventures of Tom Sawyer and Huckleberry Finn have entertained the general public for well over a century. But the story behind their legendary creator, Mark Twain, deserves its own telling.

Proof positive comes via "Mark Twain's America," a rambling picaresque about the early days of Samuel Clemens and how he grew up to take on the pseudonym "Mark Twain." Also revealed are the many tragedies that ultimately took their toll on the legendary author.

If writer-director Stephen Low makes Twain seem larger than life in the process, that's no accident. His tale unfolds in the wonder of the giant-screen IMAX format, with a wealth of vintage Twain photos taking on a glorious new look in 3-D.

Low, who previously lensed IMAX's "Titanica" and the 3-D IMAX treat "Across the Sea of Time," intercuts the sepia-toned shots of life on the Mississippi with present-day visits to Twain's hometown, Hannibal, Mo., and then to his later residence in Hartford, Conn. The mix of old and new is virtually seamless.

And, as expected, 3-D visions of riding the rails on a rickety locomotive, hovering alongside a steamboat's paddlewheel or seeing Civil War soldiers charging will have audiences ducking. Ditto for a sojourn to a local swimming hole, where the water seems to splash right into the viewers' collective lap.

Granted, the narrative, voiced by Anne Bancroft, sometimes seems all over the map. But it's easy to sit back and go along for the ride when the subject matter's as intoxicating as that of "Mark Twain's America."

NEWSDAY, 7/17/98, Part II/p. B11, Jan Herman

With his latest Imax 3-D film, "Mark Twain's America," director Stephen Low ("Across the Sea of Time") has brought a curiously old-fashioned and at the same time high-tech gloss to one of the longest-lived cottage industries in American social and literary history: Twainiana.

This 47-minute documentary is a must-see for Twain fans—but only because it has original stereo-optic archival photos of Twain in his familiar white linen suit, looking like a forebear of Col. Sanders.

Civil War buffs may also get a charge out of scenes from a stagy reenactment of the battle of Antietam.

Otherwise, the film generates no more excitement than you'd get from a nicely illustrated introductory lecture to a children's museum exhibit—even through the life and times of our wittiest, arguably greatest 19th-Century novelist is made of dazzling stuff.

One example of misplaced priorities: Tom Saywer gets more attention here than Huck Finn.

Twain's life is touched upon with 3-D stills interspersed with location filming (also in 3-D) of the annual July Fourth parade and fireworks in Hannibal, Mo., the facade of Twain's boyhood home, a latter-day Mississippi riverboat paddling loudly on the river, the interior of the Twain mansion in Hartford, Conn., and so on.

Though admirable for its good intentions, "Mark Twain's America" drifts along with no discernible climax and without the humor that would match the spirit of its subject.

Also reviewed in:
CHICAGO TRIBUNE, 7/2/98, Tempo/p. 1, Michael Wilmington
NEW YORK TIMES, 7/17/98, p. E18, Lawrence Van Gelder
VARIETY, 7/13-19/98, p. 55, Lael Loewenstein

MASK OF ZORRO, THE

A TriStar Pictures release of an Amblin Entertainment production. *Executive Producer:* Steven Spielberg, Walter F. Parkes, and Lauie MacDonald. *Producer:* Doug Claybourne and David Foster. *Director:* Martin Campbell. *Screenplay:* John Eskow, Ted Elliott, and Terry Rossio. *Story:* Ted Elliott, Terry Rossio, and Randall Jahnson. *Based on the character created by:* Johnston McCulley. *Director of Photography:* Phil Meheux. *Editor:* Thom Noble. *Music:* James Horner. *Music Editor:* Jim Henrikson. *Sound:* Pud Cusack and (music) Simon Rhodes. *Sound Editor:* Dave McMoyler. *Casting:* Pam Dixon Mickelson. *Production Designer:* Cecilia Montiel. *Art Director:* Michael Atwell. *Set Designer:* Noelle King. *Set Decorator:* Denise Camargo. *Set Dresser:* Bernardo Trujillo and Oscar Ramirez. *Special Effects:* Rocky Gehr and John Stears. *Costumes:* Graciela Mazon. *Make-up:* Ken Diaz. *Make-up (Anthony Hopkins):* Chrissie Beveridge. *Stunt Coordinator:* Glenn Randall and Glenn Randall, Jr. *Running time:* 130 minutes. *MPAA Rating:* PG-13.

CAST: Jose Maria de Tavira (Young Alejandro Murrieta); Diego Sieres (Young Joaquin Murrieta); Emiliano Guerra (Boy Crying); Yolandao Orizaga (Woman Crying); Paco Morayta (Undertaker); William Marquez (Fray Felipe); Stuart Wilson (Don Rafael Montero); Tony Amendola (Don Luiz); Anthony Hopkins (Zorro/Don Diego de la Vega); Pedro Altamirano (Squad Leader); Luisa Huertas (Nanny); Maria Fernandez Cruz and Monica Fernandez Cruz (Baby Elena de la Vega); Julieta Rosen (Esperanza de la Vega); Raul Martinez (Heavyset Lieutenant); Antonio Banderas (Alejandro Murrieta/Zorro); Victor Rivers (Joaquin Murrieta); L. Q. Jones (Three-Fingered Jack); Jose Perez (Corporal Armando Garcia); Tony Cabral (Soldier Holding "Wanted" Poster); Tony Genaro (Watering Station Owner); David Villalpando (Stupid Soldier); Matt Letscher (Captain Harrison Love); Maury Chaykin (Prison Warden); Paul Ganus (Prison Guard); Sergio Espinosa (Leper Zorro); Conrad Roberts (Black Zorro); Abel Woolrich (Ancient Zorro); Pedro Armendariz (Don Pedro); Moises Suzrez (Don Hector); Humberto Elizondo (Don Julio); Diego Sandoval (Padre at the Beach); Catherine Zeta-Jones (Elena); Enrike Palma (Bartender); Erika Carlson (Don Pedro's Wife); Manuel de Jesus and Vasquez Morales (Guitar Playing Soldiers); Oscar Zerafin Gonzalez (Giant Soldier); Vanessa Bauche (Indian Girl); Kelsie Kimberli Garcia and Kaylissa Keli Garcia (Baby Joaquin).

CHRISTIAN SCIENCE MONITOR, 7/17/98, p. B3, David Sterritt

Steven Spielberg is only an executive producer of "The Mask of Zorro," but the movie bears his mark as vividly as Zorro's enemies bear the fiery Z he carves as a sign of his power. The action is explosive, the romance is sentimental, and the message is a Spielbergian blend of "love conquers all" and "might makes right."

The story begins in 1821, as the people of California struggle for liberation from their Spanish oppressors. Their greatest champion is Zorro, a masked outlaw whose personal war against the Spaniards has become legendary. His foes are wily, though, and the movie is barely past its opening titles when the treacherous Don Rafael Montero manages to kill Zorro's wife, abduct his baby, and lock him in prison.

Nobody can keep a Hollywood hero behind bars forever, of course, and Zorro eventually leaves his cell. But two decades have passed, and he's a little old for the swordplay that used to be all in a day's work. What he needs is an apprentice, and if candidates aren't exactly lined up for the job, he'll have to make do with the material at hand: a dashing young bandit who needs a few lessons in technique, discipline, and charm. Soon teacher and pupil are an unbeatable team, determined to wreck Don Rafael's new scheme to build an independent California on the backs of its ruthlessly exploited population.

"The Mask of Zorro" is proudly old-fashioned in every way except the often excessive violence that director Martin Campbell splashes across the screen. Anthony Hopkins demonstrates his versatility as the older hero, Antonio Banderas keeps up nicely as his protégé, and Catherine Zeta-Jones couldn't be much better as his daughter. She's a bright new talent with a promising Hollywood future.

LOS ANGELES TIMES, 7/17/98, Calendar/p. 1, Kenneth Turan

"The Mask of Zorro" does not stint on its Zs: There's an Old Zorro (Anthony Hopkins), a Young Zorro (Antonio Banderas), even a Ms. Zorro (Catherine Zeta-Jones). No wonder the villains can be heard to gasp in fear, "It isn't just one man, damn it, it's Zorro!"

Spanish California's very own masked avenger and righter of wrongs is someone with a past: More than 50 features, serials and a TV series have been made about him worldwide, and everyone from Douglas Fairbanks and Tyrone Power to George Hamilton, Frank Langella and France's Alain Delon have carved that final initial on any and all available surfaces.

Reviving such a venerable franchise can be a tricky business, but "The Mask of Zorro" is not a corpse that came C.O.D. A lively, old-fashioned adventure yarn with just a twist of modern attitude, it's the kind of pleasant entertainment that allows the paying customers to have as much fun as the people on screen.

Much of the media attention for this new "Zorro" will understandably be on the beautiful but little known Zeta-Jones, a spirited and sensual British ingenue whose eyes flash as much as her sword. But she is matched by Hopkins, who brings his distinctive substance and dignity to the proceedings, as well as Banderas, whose casual charm is made for a movie like this.

"The Mask of Zorro's" unheralded mastermind would appear to be director Martin Campbell. Best known for reviving the James Bond franchise with his work on "Golden Eye," Campbell has an it's-so-old-it's-new knack for getting audiences excited about revered, not to say hoary with age, material.

So it matters not that the dazzling swordplay, the stunt leaps, the tricks with horses, were not new when Fairbanks and friends employed them in the 1920s. Campbell throws himself and his cast into the proceedings with so much energy and movement that he carries us along with him.

If "The Mask of Zorro" is not cutting edge, it's also not a film to look to for plausibility. How can Zorro stride through the center of a hot, dusty plaza without a spot of dust on him, appearing for all the world like he just stepped out of a dry cleaners? How can he still have the strength of 10 and the agility of Baryshnikov after spending 20 years heavily shackled in a pitiless Spanish prison? You're just not supposed to ask.

The first close encounter with the masked man is in Old California in 1821. A defender of the downtrodden with a rock star's popularity, Zorro, the secret identity of Don Diego de la Vega (Hopkins), is the idol of two young boys and the sworn enemy of the area's snuff-taking Spanish governor Don Rafael Montero (Stuart Wilson), who will stop at nothing, nothing do you hear, to put him away.

After a particularly dashing adventure that photogenically ends with his horse rearing up in front of an enormous setting sun, Don Diego tells his wife and infant daughter "today is Zorro's last ride." But instead of a quiet retirement, Don Diego endures a family tragedy and ends up imprisoned in all those chains.

Twenty years later, the villainous Don Rafael returns to California with an even more nefarious plan, accompanied by Elena (Zeta-Jones), a striking young woman who thinks (though we know better) that she's the evil one's daughter.

Escaped from prison and looking like Ben Franklin with the benefits of a personal trainer, Don Diego is searching for someone to pass his skill and ideals on to. Alejandro Murrieta (Banderas) was one of the worshipful young boys of 20 years past, but he lacks the patience for the Zen and the Art of Swordsmanship lessons the older man has in mind. All you have to know about the weapon, he insists, is that "the pointy end goes into the other man."

Alejandro, to be sure, needs instruction in this area, as he does about romance, horsemanship and fine manners. And though he's initially overmatched by the film's fine pair of believable villains, Wilson's shrewd Don Rafael and his icy American enabler Captain Harrison Love (Matt Letscher), this man is nothing if not a fast learner.

Written by John Eskow, Ted Elliott & Terry Rossio, "The Mask of Zorro" builds self-deprecating humor into all these situations in a way that amusingly undercuts the heroism. With good chemistry between Banderas and Zeta-Jones, especially in their numerous comic/passionate moments, this is one film that knows what to take seriously and what to leave alone.

NEW YORK, 8/3/98, p. 54, David Denby

In "The Mask of Zorro," Anthony Hopkins and Antonio Banderas work with professional skill in a ludicrous vehicle—a retro-style comedy-adventure with lots of explosions and fires and gold-toothed Mexicans falling down in a heap. In his black pants and cape, Hopkins, amazingly, has a rather mournful dignity; he uses his precise diction as if it were a weapon as potent as his whip and sword. He speaks with contempt to the messy Banderas—a thief who doesn't know how to fight—and then begins the arduous task of turning the young ruffian into a gentleman and a warrior. Banderas, with his flashing eyes, makes a good mock-Hidalgo, but the movie would be a lot more amusing if it weren't such kid stuff. The director, Martin Campbell, and a variety of screenwriters and producers have created a vaguely leftish tale of Zorro helping "the people" fight the Spanish grandees who want to take over old California. But no one on earth will be fooled by the movie's protestations of deep feeling. This Zorro is just another pop-culture jamboree. Zorro himself is less an aristocrat with a double life than an amalgam of Jackie Chan, Batman, and Obi-wan Kenobi. He lives in a huge black cave and employs martial-arts techniques to discipline his mind. The best thing in the movie is the swordplay. There's lots of it, in different places and styles, and even Catherine Zeta-Jones—a young and beautiful actress of the heaving-bosom school—gets into the act. She gives Banderas a good fight. When he prevails at last, he cuts the straps of her bodice with his rapier, but the camera, in the movie's only act of discretion, hides its eyes.

NEW YORK POST, 7/17/98, p. 37, Rod Dreher

"The Mask of Zorro" is a lot more fun than you might expect. What could be more dated and hokey than the dashing Mexican caped crusader, striking fear into the hearts of evildoers with his saber-slashing derring-do?

But this film's hero; played winningly by Antonio Banderas, has pulpy zing. Director Martin Campbell's playful, pleasurable film is old-fashioned without being stuffy, and jokey without descending into wink-wink irony. (It's what "The Man in the Iron Mask" could have been if it had taken itself a bit more seriously.)

Campbell is surprisingly successful at reinvigorating shopworn, Saturday-matinee conventions. Sure, the melodramatic and quite ridiculous "The Mask of Zorro" is silly con queso, but, like the tastiest junk food, it's hard to resist

The film opens in 1821, in Mexican-held California. Two small boys watch as the heroic Zorro (Anthony Hopkins) descends upon a crowded plaza, freeing political prisoners, thrilling the mob and thwarting the evil Spanish governor, Don Rafael (Stuart Wilson).

Zorro retires to his Bat-cave-like lair, ditches the get-up, and resumes his life as Don Diego, a mild-mannered Spanish aristocrat. But Don Rafael is on to his secret identity. They clash, and Don Diego's lovely wife is killed.

Don Rafael throws Don Diego/Zorro into prison, and takes his infant girl, Elena, to raise as his own daughter.

Twenty years later, an aged Don Diego escapes from prison and makes the acquaintance of Alejandro, a handsome, bushy-haired bandito (Banderas) who he selects to become the new Zorro. Lo, but Alejandro was one of the ninos on the plaza that day long ago! Diego does a Yoda on Alejandro, whipping him into shape, and the two set out to topple Don Rafael's tyranny.

Portraying a Spanish nobleman, el nuevo Zorro infiltrates Don Rafael's mansion and learns of his hidden goldmine, its slave-labor system and a nefarious plan to rule California like a Mafia kingdom. Our hot-blooded hero is also a Don Juan, forming a show-stopping, flamenco-style dance with grown-up Elena (Catherine Zeta-Jones), the hottest honey in the hacienda.

Banderas and Zeta-Jones are two peppers in a pot, and their three-alarm chemistry gives the flick real kick. In one scene, they face off as opponents in the horse barn. Zorro's sword goes snicker-snack, and Elena's dress is off in a trice. (Parents, don't, worry: You don't see anything untoward, as the scene is played for innocent comedy.)

Recalling this ravishing to Don Rafael, Elena breathlessly reports, "He was very *veegorous,* Father." That Zorro, what a swordsman.

"The Mask of Zorro" unspools with yee-ha, boyish brio as our hero performs feats of astonishing dexterity, faces down sneering baddies (including a corrupt American cavalry officer, played to ice-blond perfection by Matt Letscher) and defends truth, justice and honor with gee-whiz gallantry and spirited machismo.

Will Zorro save the toiling masses from their venal oppressor? Will he pierce the heart of the fair Elena? Will Zorro *pere* be happily reunited with the daughter he lost so long ago? "The Mask of Zorro" answers these questions with the kind of thrilling, cheddary-rich romanticism rarely seen at the movies these days. And look, Ma: No dirty words, trampy chicks, sick gun-violence or heartless cynicism. Cool.

NEWSDAY, 7/17/98, Part II/p. B3, Jack Mathews

In this era of the big bang and the big illusions, Martin Campbell's "The Mask of Zorro" seems almost quaint. It's the retro summer alternative, where the characters ride horses instead of asteroids, talk to each other in more than monosyllabic grunts and fight for such novel purposes as dignity and honor.

Oh, it's a spectacle, too. The production, with its Spanish missions and meticulously detailed haciendas, is huge. There are lavishly choreographed swordfights, with flying, leaping, somersaulting stunts, dramatic images of the masked hero and his black steed Tornado silhouetted against a burning orange sun, and—for those who just have to have them—a couple of teeth-rattling explosions.

But there's no mistaking the filmmakers' intentions. "The Mask of Zorro" is old-fashioned Hollywood adventure, meant to satisfy modern audiences' passion for romance in the same way their parents and grandparents were satisfied by the Zorro legend in the past.

Introduced by serialist Johnston McCulley in a 1919 issue of All-Story Weekly, "Zorro" was immediately embraced by a post-World War I America hungry for escapist adventure, and was forever imprinted on the public consciousness as a physical superman the following year by Douglas Fairbanks' portrayal of him in "The Mark of Zorro."

Fairbanks reprised the role in a 1925 sequel, and among the actors playing Zorro in ensuing installments were Tyrone Power, Clayton Moore (better known for his work as the Lone Ranger), Guy Williams and Frank Langella. For "The Mask of Zorro," the 15th American Zorro movie and the 52nd worldwide, Campbell has the benefit of two appealing stars. Anthony Hopkins plays the original Zorro, Don Diego de la Vega, and Antonio Banderas is Alejandro Murrieta, his personally trained replacement.

If you're new to Zorro, think of him as an Old West version of Batman, whom creator Bob Kane has acknowledged fashioning from McCulley's character (which, in turn, was inspired by Robin Hood and the Scarlet Pimpernel). Don Diego is a wealthy landowner who has adopted a masked and caped alter ego to fight the oppression of the local peasants by the Spanish governor of colonial Alta California.

In "The Mask of Zorro," Don Diego and Alejandro meet briefly in the opening scene, when Zorro rides into the town square to rescue four men chosen at random by the tyrannical Don Rafael Montero (Stuart Wilson) for public execution. Alejandro is the young boy who, along with his brother, helps Zorro escape.

Twenty years later, the two meet again, as fugitives. Alejandro is being hunted by the troops of the new ruler of free Mexico, Gen. Santa Anna, and Don Diego has just escaped from the underground prison where he has been since his wife was murdered and Montero returned to Spain with their baby daughter, Elena. Now, Montero is back, too, with the grown Elena (Catherine Zeta-Jones) and a scheme of establishing a California republic with gold taken from Mexican land.

MASK OF ZORRO, THE 777

Don Diego has to figure a way to settle an old score without destroying the innocent life of his daughter. Thus, the pact with Alejandro, a man with far more conviction than grace. Most of the first hour of the movie is devoted to Alejandro's often comic transformation, but when he emerges from Don Diego's secret cave to assume his own double identity as nobleman and masked avenger, he's Zorro reborn.

Much of what follows is comic book formula, with Alejandro fated for a showdown with the sadistic captain (Matt Letscher) who murdered his brother, and Don Diego moving toward a swordfighting reunion with Montero. Caught in the middle is the confused, feisty, beautiful Elena.

"The Mask of Zorro" is too long by at least 20 minutes, and I know where I'd cut. The swordfights go on and on and on. The movie is much better when the weapons being used are words. The script, which is credited to four different writers, features some of the sharpest and wittiest dialogue of the season, and is delivered by its stars with skilled aplomb.

Hopkins and Banderas make a smooth blend from their characters' contrasting personalities. Don Diego is serious, reflective, bearing the world on his shoulders, and Hopkins reads it with an emotional gravity that roots the story in genuinely human terms. Alejandro, on the other hand, is the pure romantic adventurer, picking fights to test his mettle, and courting Elena with boastful arrogance. If Banderas is fated to become a major star, it begins here.

Newcomer Zeta-Jones is stuck with the most conventionally modern role, the lady battler, but she has the glamour and presence of an old-fashioned Hollywood star, and we'll be seeing a lot more of her.

The question is, will we be seeing more of Zorro? Are audiences fed up enough with whiz-bang special effects and empty character posturing to relax with an old hero? Can Zorro, the wily fox of old California, rescue Hollywood? To be continued...

SIGHT AND SOUND, 12/98, p. 48, José Arroyo

Los Angeles, 1821. Outlaw "Zorro" saves some peasants from being killed by Don Rafael Montero. He is saved in turn by the young Murrieta brothers, Alejandro and Joaquin. After discovering Zorro is really Don Diego de la Vega, Montero accidentally kills Zorro's wife, steals his child and sends de la Vega to jail.

Twenty years later, Montero returns from Spain with his daughter Elena. De la Vega escapes from jail and Alejandro Murrieta watches Joaquin shoot himself rather than surrender to Captain Harrison Love, Montero's officer. De la Vega is set to kill Montero but balks when he realises Elena is really his own daughter. A drunken Alejandro fails to kill Captain Love. De la Vega promises to train Alejandro as the new Zorro. The two of them discover Montero plans to create an independent state of California by buying it from General Santa Ana with what is effectively Santa Ana's own money. After taking the gold from a secret mine being worked by enslaved peasants, Montero is planning to blow up both the mine and the peasants. Alejandro, the new Zorro, falls in love with Elena, who finally realises who her real father is. The two Zorros defeat their adversaries and, along with Elena, save the peasants. A year later, Elena and Alejandro are proud parents.

A dashingly old-fashioned adventure, *The Mask of Zorro* is an old and familiar story which has been turned into a foxy new movie. Ever since the publication of Johnston McCulley's short story in 1919, Zorro's story has been frequently adapted for the screen, ensuring the popularity of the character. Although arguably the part was most memorably played by Douglas Fairbanks (in *The Mark of Zorro*, 1920, and *Don Q Son of Zorro*, 1925) and Tyrone Power *(The Mark of Zorro*, 1940), there has been at least one screen Zorro per decade, including Robert Livingston, John Carroll, Guy Williams, Sean Flynn, Alain Delon and George Hamilton, to mention but a few. *The Mask of Zorro* boasts one of the very best incarnations of the character in Antonio Banderas. He's not the athlete Fairbanks was, but he's a passionately physical actor who moves gracefully. His romantic appeal is at least the equal of Power's, although Banderas, in spite of having played various gay characters, is less sexually ambiguous. It is perhaps significant that missing here is the previous versions' sub-plot in which de la Vega pretends to be a pansy so no one suspects he's Zorro, a device in one of Zorro's literary antecedents, *The Scarlet Pimpernel*. More importantly, Banderas' star persona highlights rather than obscures the ethnic identity of the hero.

Zorro has been done straight and spoofed up (see *Zorro The Gay Blade* for the latter). And the character forms the intertextual lynchpin, endlessly enduring and eminently adaptable like other myths, for a whole array of merchandising, from dolls to masks and whips (particularly during the television show's run in the 50s). This new version is so successful because the film-makers have wisely left the story's basic elements alone. *The Mask of Zorro* is still a kind of Western featuring an American Robin Hood, fighting the injustice of an old and despotic aristocracy in order to distribute justice, win the gutsy señorita and pave the way for the utopian civilisation of the new republic to come.

As the audience knows, the Spanish/Mexican *pueblo* in which the film is set will become Los Angeles. Also, the film doesn't forget that Zorro is a Hispanic-American hero. In fact, Antonio Banderas is the most Hispanic Zorro to date. Because of this, the casting is invariably implicated in complex ideas about ethnicity and national identity. These notions are given an explicit hierarchy in a way relatively rare in US cinema: at one end are the dark-skinned indigenous peasants, the saintly salt of the earth who absolutely *belong* here; at the other is the cruel and despotic Aryan Captain Harrison Love. In between, the old aristocratic order is split, one half represented by de la Vega (Anthony Hopkins with upper-class Brit accent) whose belongingness is assured by his support of the future American way of life; the other half by Montero and his cronies (darker skinned, accents tending more towards a Spanish inflection) whose un-American actions forfeit future citizenship. The film's resolution is to have the new swarthy Zorro, son of the people, defeat evil blondie and marry the raven-haired daughter of the old aristocracy. To a much greater degree than any of the previous versions, *The Mask of Zorro* succeeds in creating a hero who is explicitly Hispanic and unarguably American.

Part of the pleasure of the film lies in its joyous embrace of bombast. When Montero defeats de la Vega and is about to steal his baby and cart him off to prison, the house bursts into flames, the music swells, thunder erupts and we get close-ups of Anthony Hopkins emoting pain intensely through the bars of his prison in a vain attempt to reach his baby. It's the full cliché, with every flourish successfully realised. in fact one of the reasons the film is so enjoyable is the obvious craft with which the film-makers maintain the overall action/adventure structure while shifting fluidly between comedy, melodrama and romance, deploying clichés refreshed with irony.

There are some scenes that don't quite work. For example, the choreography of the dance between Banderas and Zeta Jones is awful. And the film does indulge in some of the worst excesses of contemporary film-making— can Zorro not steal a horse without the entire building blowing up? However, like the banter between Banderas and Zeta Jones, *The Mask of Zorro* might be nonsense but this doesn't make it any less delightful.

TIME, 7/20/98, p. 62, Richard Schickel

A swish, a swoosh, the snick-snack-snick of dueling blades—the nice thing about swordplay is that it doesn't make a lot of noise. When cold steel is their weapon of choice, men can actually exchange snappy dialogue while engaging in mortal combat. Better still, when heroism and villainy go at it *mano á mano*, a certain clearly identifiable humanity as well as a certain cinematic grace and fluidity is imparted to their conflicts.

This alone would be enough to recommend *The Mask of Zorro* and separate it from its competitors. Imagine a summer action spectacle that saves its only explosion until the end, where it has a genuine impact. Imagine one that leaves room for grace notes of humor and gallantry and does not bury them in showers of bad language and falling debris. Imagine one where you can actually hear yourself think. And better yet, hear the actors think.

Think? Well, all right maybe that's too strong a term. But the action in this movie, most of which takes the form of spectacular stunt work performed by real, as opposed to digitized, people (note especially the spectacular Roman riding gag), is motivated by simple, powerful emotions of an old-fashioned and rather melodramatic nature, which the characters are not shy about expressing. We're talking high romance, pure ideals, dashing heroism here—all the stuff that used to animate our big boyish movies.

Generous almost to a fault, this movie offers us not one but two Zorros. There's an aging one, Don Diego (played with impeccable elegance by Anthony Hopkins), making a comeback after suffering a long imprisonment, to fight a resurgence of tyranny in old, Spanish-controlled

California. In the process he recruits a young, nimbler apprentice, Alejandro (portrayed by Antonio Banderas), who's not afraid of acting a little dumb until his mentor smartens him up, cools his ardent blood and teaches him the skills that make him worthy of wearing the black mask of the gallant outlaw.

The pair need all their wit to thwart the relentlessly scheming Don Rafael. A blackguard worthy of the two Zorros' steel, he's richly realized by Stuart Wilson as a sort of Darth Vader of romance, helplessly embracing its dark side. Long ago he killed Diego's wife, with whom he was in love, and then abducted their daughter to raise as his own. Played in adulthood by the ravishingly beautiful and wonderfully spirited Catherine Zeta-Jones, she is, of course, destined to find both her true father and her true love behind one Zorro mask or another.

But not before our heroes have mercilessly tweaked, mocked, scorned and generally reduced Don Rafael to largely impotent rage. And just when he was on the brink of stealing all the gold in the state and setting himself up as ruler of an independent empire. Director Martin Campbell doesn't quite know when to stop. At some point the number of hair-breadth assaults and escapes approaches the tiresome. But they're all well choreographed, and since the good-natured conviction of all concerned with Zorro never flags, we are carried blithely along on their journey.

VILLAGE VOICE, 7/21/98, p. 124, Michael Atkinson

As part of the moviegoing public, I don't remember ever feeling a ripple across the cultural transom suggesting that we wanted or needed a new Zorro movie, and yet for our sins they gave us one, retrofitting the Old California chestnut into a kind of Spanish Batman (complete with cave lair and gym) and jacking the entire affair into a late-Spielbergian series of set-piece kabooms. We need no longer lament the recycling instinct that runs roughshod over any IQ genes in the Hollywood helix, but should instead acknowledge that through the marketeer's lens, we're no more sophisticated than our parents, or their parents, and that what was good for Douglas Fairbanks and Tyrone Power and Guy Williams fans is good enough for us. So, the Spanish imperialize, the Mexicans suffer. Old Zorro Anthony Hopkins (looking comically unspry) retires in time to be slammed in prison for 20 years, escapes, bumps into lavishly persecuted thief Antonio Banderas, and does an Obi Wan on him to turn him into the new Zorro, who confronts the smirking villains, woos a postfeminist maiden, and does so much somersaulting and vaulting around you can't help but think if they had the Olympics in 1840 he'd be an international star.

There's a fabulous moment midway through when love interest Señorita Catherine Zeta-Jones (who, by the by, is ravishing in such a strangely perfect way she may be computer generated) steps off a boat into a crowd of unhappy Mexicans and a little girl runs in from off-frame, hands her a huge flower, and scampers off—we're not supposed to wonder who she was, or why she had brought the flower to the dock, we're just supposed to register the cliché at the back of our skulls. (The bad guys do a lot of waiting-to-be-slugged and fumbling amongst themselves when a curtain falls on their heads.) Director Martin Campbell rises to his systems-management-man job adequately enough, but *Zorro* only attains the generally lifeless, contrived feel of a Thanksgiving Day parade, and that goes for the overproduced dubbing mix as well (horses laughing, throats gulping, etc.). At least Fairbanks did his own stunts.

Also reviewed in:
CHICAGO TRIBUNE, 7/17/98, Friday/p. A, Michael Wilmington
NEW YORK TIMES, 7/17/98, p. E12, Janet Maslin
VARIETY, 6/29-7/12/98, p. 37, Todd McCarthy
WASHINGTON POST, 7/17/98, p. B1, Stephen Hunter
WASHINGTON POST, 7/17/98, Weekend/p. 43, Michael O'Sullivan

MEET THE DEEDLES

A Walt Disney Pictures release of a DIC Entertainment production in association with Peak Productions. *Executive Producer:* Andy Heyward and Artie Ripp. *Producer:* Dale Pollock and

Aaron Meyerson. *Director:* Steve Boyum. *Screenplay:* Jim Herzfeld. *Director of Photography:* David Hennings. *Editor:* Alan Cody. *Music:* Steve Bartek. *Music Editor:* Angie Rubin. *Sound:* David M. Kelson and (music) Robert Fernandez. *Sound Editor:* Patrick Dodd. *Casting:* Amy Lippens. *Production Designer:* Stephen Storer. *Art Director:* Harry Darrow. *Set Decorator:* Robin Peyton. *Set Dresser:* Wayne Wulfenstein. *Special Effects:* Ray Bivins. *Costumes:* Alexandra Welker and Karyn Wagner. *Make-up:* Gina Homan. *Stunt Coordinator:* Lance Gilbert. *Running time:* 90 minutes. *MPAA Rating:* PG.

CAST: Steve Van Wormer (Stew Deedle); Paul Walker (Phil Deedle); A. J. Langer (Jesse Ryan); John Ashton (Capt. Douglas Pine); Dennis Hopper (Frank Slater); Eric Braeden (Elton Deedle); Richard Lineback (Crabbe); Robert Englund (Nemo); M. C. Gainey (Major Flower); Ana Gasteyer (Mel); Megan Cavanagh (Mo); Michael Ruud (Ludwig); Hattie Winston (Jo-Claire); Bob Eric Hart (Governor).

LOS ANGELES TIMES, 3/27/98, Calendar/p. 14, Bob Heisler

[The following review by Bob Heisler appeared in a slightly different form in **NEWSDAY, 3/27/98, Part II/p. B7.]**

Stew Deedle is the smart one. He wears glasses, can hack into Defense Department computers and knows without looking at a map that Yellowstone Park is in Wyoming.

His twin, Phil Deedle, is 4 inches taller, would need a map to find his way home, and even when he street-luges into Yellowstone wearing hijacked women's underwear, he thinks he's in Jellystone Park and Yogi Bear is waiting to teach him how to steal pick-i-nick baskets.

He also gets the girl.

Phil has the right cartoonland state of mind for "Meet the Deedles," a harmless dumbing-down of "Wayne's World" meets "Bill & Ted's Excellent Adventure" with all the intellectual content of "Scooby-Doo." If you can diagram the phrase "It's so diculous, it's re-diculous," welcome to the multiplex. Take any seat.

Before your popcorn can get cold, Stew and Phil (Steve Van Wormer and Paul Walker), budding but syntax-challenged surf-heirs, get expelled from school, are dispatched to this totally bogus Camp Broken Spirit, lose many of their worldly possessions, trash a campsite and nearly kill themselves at least three times—finally crashing into Yellowstone where they are mistaken for rookie park rangers.

Got it? Good. Now forget it. The real story is about how two well-meaning dudes save the day (and Old Faithful—played in an understated way by a hole in the ground, a helicopter engine, some tubing and a very large amount of water) by foiling the twisted plan of former head ranger Frank Slater (a miscast Dennis Hopper, abetted by special guest henchmen Robert "Freddy" Englund and Richard Lineback) to divert the geyser using an enslaved legion of prairie dogs and create his own theme park.

Things move quickly in an oddly sympathetic way until the outdoorsy sensibility is sacrificed for a cheap coda that should prevent the franchising of the Deedles.

NEW YORK POST, 3/27/98, p. 49, Larry Worth

The dialogue runs something like, "Hey, don't go getting neg on me, Brah." Nuff said?

Yes, "Meet the Deedles" brings new meaning to stupidity as it tells of the Deedle brothers, a bleached-blond, surfer-dude version of valley boys Bill and Ted.

When their no-nonsense dad catches them riding Waikiki's waves rather than attending Honolulu High, they're sent to a disciplinary camp in Yellowstone National ParK. Only newborns will be surprised when Deedle-dum and Deedle-dee cause calamities with the regularity of Old Faithful.

But will the boys become heroes before they ride their motorized skateboards into the end credits? Duh, do bears find relief in Yellowstone's woods?

Speaking of which, there's no end to the bathroom humor in the predictably awful script. And, of course, women are on hand only as fodder for sex yuks.

Less predictable is that newcomers Paul Walker and Steve Van Wormer actually put a funny spin on a few lines. Too bad the same opportunity wasn't afforded bad guys Dennis Hopper and Robert Englund, who barely get enough screen time to register.

But the biggest insult comes as director Steve Boyum assumes viewers can't tell the difference between a bona fide bruin and a man in a bear suit. Suffice it to say that "Meet the Deedles" will have viewers long for the relative intelligence of "Dumb and Dumber."

Also reviewed in:
CHICAGO TRIBUNE, 3/27/98, Friday/p. K, John Petrakis
NEW YORK TIMES, 3/27/98, p. E28, Anita Gates
VARIETY, 3/30-4/5/98, p. 42, Lael Loewenstein
WASHINGTON POST, 3/27/98, Weekend/p. 61, Jane Horwitz

MEET JOE BLACK

A Universal Pictures release of a City Lights Films production. *Executive Producer:* Ronald L. Schwary. *Producer:* Martin Brest. *Director:* Martin Brest. *Screenplay:* Ron Osborn, Jeff Reno, Kevin Wade, and Bo Goldman. *Director of Photography:* Emmanuel Lubezki. *Editor:* Joe Hutshing and Michael Tronick. *Music:* Thomas Newman. *Music Editor:* Bill Bernstein and Angie Rubin. *Sound:* Danny Michael and (music) Dennis Sands. *Sound Editor:* Scott A. Hecker. *Casting:* Juliet Taylor and Ellen Lewis. *Production Designer:* Dante Ferretti. *Art Director:* Robert Guerra. *Set Decorator:* Leslie Bloom. *Set Dresser:* Michael A. Saccio, Robert Currie, John Oates, Jr., Paul Gaily, Mitch Towse, John J. Flugel, Dennis Lee Causey, and Gary Levitsky. *Special Effects:* Connie Brink. *Costumes:* Aude Bronson-Howard and David C. Robinson. *Make-up:* Richard Dean and Randy Houston Mercer. *Make-up (Brad Pitt):* Jean A. Black. *Stunt Coordinator:* Buddy Joe Hooker. *Running time:* 179 minutes. *MPAA Rating:* PG-13.

CAST: Brad Pitt (Joe Black/Young Man in Coffee Shop); Anthony Hopkins (William Parrish); Claire Forlani (Susan Parrish); Jake Weber (Drew); Marcia Gay Harden (Allison); Jeffrey Tambor (Quince); David S. Howard (Eddie Sloane); Lois Kely-Miller (Jamaican Woman); Jahnni St. John (Jamaica Woman's Daughter); Richard Clarke (Butler); Marylouise Burke (Lillian); Diane Kagan (Jennifer); June Squibb (Helen); Gene Canfield (Construction Foreman); Suzanne Hevner (Florist); Steve Coats (Electrician); Madeline N. Balmaceda (Madeline); Julie Lund (Drew's Secretary); Stephen Adly-Guirgis (Hospital Receptionist); Leo Marks (Party Waiter); Michelle Youell and Gene Leverone (Party Guests).

LOS ANGELES TIMES, 11/13/98, Calendar/p. 1, Kenneth Turan

Death takes a holiday in "Meet Joe Black," but does that mean everyone else has to slow down?

The fanciful story of what happens when the original Big Chill takes human form and investigates life on Earth, "Meet Joe Black" is more convinced of its worth than we are. Clocking in at a self-important two hours and 59 minutes, this elongated romantic fable is impossible to sustain at a running time better suited to the fall of the Roman empire.

Once upon a time, in 1934 in fact, this same notion was filmed by Mitchell Leisen as "Death Takes a Holiday" and did a quite elegant job in a brisk 78 minutes. In this day and age, even as talented and meticulous a director as Martin Brest ("Beverly Hills Cop," "Midnight Run," "Scent of a Woman") has felt the need to inflate the tale until it floats around like one of those ungainly balloons in Macy's Thanksgiving Day Parade.

Not helping the time go faster is the way star Brad Pitt has ended up playing Death. Ordinarily the most charismatic of actors, with an eye-candy smile and a winning ease, Pitt approaches this role largely on a leash, hanging around more like the protagonist of "I Walked With a Zombie" than a flesh-and-blood leading man.

While this acting choice may be defensible in abstract terms, watching it on screen is nothing like fun. Perhaps Pitt, like Julia Roberts before him, is for the moment chafing at being considered no more than a pretty face and has determined to in effect hide his light under a basket. Love me, not my smile is the idea, but the absence of that singular likability is tough to swallow.

Making the loss worse is that the Pitt everyone has come to see—the grinning, tousle-haired knockout—makes an appearance in the film's first 15 minutes and then disappears. He plays a young man in a Manhattan coffee shop who hits it off with Susan Parrish (Claire Forlani), a beautiful but earnest doctor whose father has just sagely advised her that in terms of love she should be looking for "passion, obsession, someone you can't live without."

That father would be the patrician William Parrish, chairman of Parrish Communications and all-around wise tycoon. Played by Anthony Hopkins as a close relative of his role in "The Edge," Parrish has managed to remain a kindly captain of industry despite being one of the world's richest humans. He's so well-balanced, in fact, he tolerates the intrusive neuroses of his other daughter Allison (Marcia Gay Harden), who's planning to give him an over-the-top 65th birthday party.

Only one thing troubles Parrish, and that's an otherworldly voice he keeps hearing. Soon enough that voice takes over the body of Pitt (well, whose body would you take?) and shows up in Parrish's elegant apartment. He's Death, he says, come to take Parrish away, but before he goes he "wants to take a look around" at the world that so fears him.

Parrish, who hardly has a choice, agrees to have Joe Black, as he comes to be called, hang out with him around the clock. This confounds Drew (Jake Weber), Parrish's right-hand man and daughter Susan's boyfriend, and it completely dumbfounds Susan, who wonders, as much of the audience will, who stole the personality from that cute guy in the coffee shop.

"Joe Black's" crowd of screenwriters (Ron Osborn and Jeff Reno, and Kevin Wade and Bo Goldman) has followed the recent trend by having Death know very little of this earthly life. Like Nicolas Cage's character in "City of Angels," Death is no savvy traveler but kind of an idiot savant, someone who knows the big picture but has never tasted peanut butter and, cute as he is, never so much as been kissed. That, obviously, is going to change.

Personality-deficient though he may be, Joe Black is undeniably attractive, and it's no surprise that (a) Susan's going to be powerfully attracted to him and (b) that's going to present some problems. After all, Death has got to be a tougher guy to spend quality time with than Saddam Hussein.

Where "Meet Joe Black" runs into most of its trouble is that everything happens so terribly slowly it makes the suspension of disbelief this story has to have that much harder to sustain. And the addition of a completely predictable and time-wasting subplot about a potential corporate takeover of Parrish Communications is no help either.

"Meet Joe Black" does have some moments that shows what might have been. The romance scenes are pleasant once they finally arrive and the lively Jamaican woman (Lois Kelly-Miller) who recognizes Joe for his true self at a hospital almost steals the picture. "Joe Black's" grand finale creates a bit of emotion as well, but the film's been going on for so long, it's hard to separate those feelings from simple relief that the dam thing is finally over.

NEW YORK, 11/23/98, p. 85, Peter Rainer

Suppose you were death and you were visiting the mortal realm for the first time. What would you do for kicks? Maybe check out Graceland or take in the slopes at Aspen? Splurge at Barneys or cool out on the Côte d'Azur? Wouldn't you want to boogie? Wouldn't you want to feel *alive?*

The big cheese in *Meet Joe Black* doesn't think so. Joe (Brad Pitt) is Death personified, and he acts like death warmed over. He manifests himself in human form in order to mingle with mortals, but he doesn't look like he's having a lick of fun. Then again, *Meet Joe Black* isn't a comedy. Actually, it is, but the joke is on the filmmakers. Few movies in my lifetime have offered up so many inadvertent cues for audience wisecracks. The wisecracking is a form of self-preservation: If the film isn't going to entertain us, then we'd damn well better entertain ourselves.

This has been quite a month for ponderoso uplift at the movies: first *Beloved,* and now this. *Meet Joe Black* is like a Hallmark card with elephantiasis. Media tycoon William Parrish (Anthony Hopkins), to whom Death pays a visit, specializes in dispensing greeting-card-style wisdom. He counsels his marriageable physician daughter Susan (Claire Forlani) to hold out for the right guy: "I know it's a cornball thought, but love is passion, obsession. Forget yourself and listen to your heart." Forget the heart; is anybody listening to this dialogue (courtesy of four—count 'em—screenwriters: Ron Osborn, Jeff Reno, Kevin Wade, and Bo Goldman)? It *is*. cornball; just because the filmmakers admit as much doesn't make it any less so. The director, Martin Brest, wants to be both a schlockmeister and a serious artiste. But in the *Titanic* era, corn is best served up without all this coy self-consciousness. *Titanic* piled on the hearts and flowers, but at least its death cruise had a schmaltzy monumentality. It was an ersatz romance with enough ardor to resemble the real thing. *Meet Joe Black*, which lasts almost as long as *Titanic*, doesn't have that kind of oomph; it's dour and shrouded, a lifeless romance about the value of life.

At the outset, Parrish is visited by Joe Black as the tycoon nears his 65th birthday and his family prepares a big celebration. It seems Joe is curious to take a look around before he brings Bill into the Great Beyond. He sets out his nonnegotiable offer: As long as Bill keeps things interesting, he's spared. Joe may be a bit of a sadist but—here's the surprise—he's also a virgin. Death, where is thy stinger?

He warms to Susan, but it takes her a while to reciprocate. She's confused, you see, because she met an identical sweet-talker the day before in a coffee shop and went all ga-ga over him; he's the same gent Joe later dispatched in a car accident so he could inhabit his body. Talk about the perils of dating in the big city! Joe has no memory of having met Susan, who thinks he's a mope compared to the brash guy he replaced. And yet there is something about him—perhaps it's that he looks like Brad Pitt?—that pulls her in.

Pitt can't seem to get a fix on how to play Death. You can't blame him; after all, it's not exactly a role you can research firsthand. Still, his Joe doesn't add up: One minute he's coolly sinister with Bill, the next he's as innocent and dopey as Lenny tending the rabbits in *Of Mice and Men*. He develops an appetite for peanut butter, and it's barely different from his appetite for Susan. It's all the same to him—at first. When Joe finally gets carnal with her, their lovemaking is depicted in that lyrically slowed-down way that lets you know sex is truly a beautiful thing. No hot monkey love for these two. Getting down with Death turns out to be the ultimate in safe sex.

Joe claims he's lingering for the lessons: "I chose you for your excellence and your ability to instruct," he tells Bill early on. But what it really looks like to us is that Death digs the good life—not just Bill's peanut butter (chunky) and daughter (smooth) but his sumptuous New York penthouse and Versailles-style country estate. It's depressing but true: Death is a social climber. The filmmakers, too, seem inordinately impressed by Bill's riches even as they pretend that money can't buy happiness. The camera slavers over the parquet floors with inlaid borders and the carved moldings on the door frames. Bill is the kind of CEO Hollywood can feel sanctimonious about: He's a bit gruff in the boardroom, perhaps, but he's a philosopher-king who runs a good, clean empire and cherishes his wife's memory and has a really classy art collection. When it looks like Joe might take the unsuspecting Susan along with them into the hereafter, Bill even stands up to the guy. He scolds Death!

The filmmakers have described *Meet Joe Black* as a "meditation on happiness," but it's more like a *Twilight Zone* episode played at the wrong speed (an early *Zone* in fact featured a very young and blond Robert Redford as Death). The film didn't need to be three hours. I can only surmise that Pitt's clout kept it at that length. If so, he did himself no favors. The camera lingers for what seems like aeons on his face, but nothing new is revealed, no depths, no hollows, no sparkle; he's just a blank glamour-puss. Forlani also gets the walleyed treatment, and she offers up two expressions: a suggestion of a smile (to indicate thought) and a slight squint (to indicate passion). Hopkins does best with his opportunities, but this is not, to put it mildly, one of his most exacting performances. After a while, you just want to bring on the hereafter and get done with it.

Why does Death bother to show up at all? In the 1934 movie *Death Takes a Holiday*, starring Fredric March, Death crossed the human threshold because he wanted to discover why people feared him. In *Meet Joe Black*, which lifts a few plot elements from that film, Death just wants his close-ups. The film isn't about mortality; it's about star wattage. Audiences can take great comfort in knowing that Death looks like Brad Pitt. But hey, folks, its only a movie. Do not go gentle into that good night. And hang on to your peanut butter.

NEW YORK POST, 11/13/98, p. 53, Rod Dreher

In "Meet Joe Black," Brad Pitt becomes Death, but Death most certainly does not become him.

As the Grim Reaper walking among mortals in the guise of a spiritually aware studbot, pretty-boy Pitt is so vacant, mechanical and pretentious it occurs to you that this is what the Dalai Lama would be like reincarnated as an underwear model.

And his bizarre performance in a preposterous role is not even the worst thing about this visually exquisite corpse of a movie. The script has had more doctors than the Bride of Wildenstein, with similarly impressive results.

And Martin Brest's direction offers abundant lunacy—or, to be more precise, lunatic abundance. He drags nearly every scene out to unreasonable length, and the entire film out to three punishing hours. There may be a worse movie yet to come this year, but none so bad for so long.

"Meet Joe Black" is Brest's update of the slight 1934 fantasy "Death Takes a Holiday." The film begins with Pitt as a devastatingly sexy and likable guy in a coffee shop, charming a medical intern named Susan Parrish (Claire Forlani). After they part, the lovestruck guy dies in traffic, taking the film with him—with about 2 hours left to go.

We next see him in the posh country house of widowed, impossibly noble media mogul Bill Fiarrish (Anthony Hopkins). Except it's not Coffee Shop Guy, but the considerably less affable Death, inhabiting his body. He tells Bill he's come to take him away, ha-ha; but first, he'd like Bill to show him around for a few days.

Bill introduces him as "Joe Black" to his family, gathered at the dinner table, and they accept with suspiciously little protest the constant presence of this new weirdo in their father's life.

And he is a weirdo. Sometimes Joe has preternatural knowledge of people's dark histories, and other times he's as dumb as a stump. Pitt plays the character with a sort of glazed high-handedness, ordering Hopkins around in a mysterioso HAL 9000 monotone that keeps him aloof from our affections. Joe's "irie mon" jibber-jabber to a Jamaican granny provides unintentional hilarity.

Susan falls prey to Joe's androidal allure, even though he remains strangely remote, and kvells over peanut butter like a 3-year-old. There's no heat between Pitt and blank-slate Forlani, and the one money shot—Brad going shirtless to get jiggy with Claire—is not cuddly but creepy. Quasi-necrophilia is such a buzzkill.

Joe promises to let Bill stick around until after his swank birthday bash, and that's enough time for him to deal with a fiendish plot to take over his business, and advise all that a life lived without love is meaningless. Next time, Marty, send a Hallmark card.

By the time the credits roll, and the swelling violins have pushed the bile to the tip of your throat, and the scorched-earth schmaltz of the closing party sequence has you pining for the Bergmanesque austerity of "What Dreams May Come," the living may well and truly envy the dead.

On the other hand, Brad Pitt has great hair.

NEWSDAY, 11/13/98, Part II/p. B3, Jack Mathews

If you can imagine Sidney Sheldon retelling the story of "Little Red Riding Hood" as a dead-serious, epic-length philosophical meditation on life, love and mortality in which the Big Bad Wolf becomes a man, falls for Red, repents, then eats her grandmother anyway, you'll have a vague notion of Martin Brest's bloated, empty, self-important "Meet Joe Black."

Inspired by a 1920s play and the subsequent 1934 movie, "Death Takes a Holiday," "Meet Joe Black" is an allegory about the disruption of a wealthy New York family by the arrival of Death, in a commandeered body renamed Joe Black, and his romance with Susan Parrish (Claire Forlani), the moonstruck daughter of Bill Parrish (Anthony Hopkins), the man whose soul he has come to collect.

"Meet Joe Black" is the latest—and slowest—float to pass in Hollywood's current parade of star-driven paranormal love stories. First, doe-eyed angel Nicolas Cage fell in love with mortal surgeon Meg Ryan in "City of Angels," then Robin Williams searched heaven and hell for wife Annabella Sciorra in "What Dreams May Come." Now, we have a morally ambivalent Death getting a lesson in humanity from the super-rich.

Filmmakers are clearly reaching back to a time when "The Ghost and Mrs. Muir" met for old-fashioned romance. But they're failing to bring back the humor that made films like that levitate. This new stuff is dead serious, and deadly dull, and none more so than "Meet Joe Black."

The 1934 "Holiday" lasted a mere 79 minutes; "Joe" goes a full three hours. And the difference is mostly in repeated lines, pregnant pauses, longing stares and slow pans. Brest, who has made only six movies in 21 years and none since his 1992 "Scent of a Woman," treats this material as if it were leading up to a revelation about the meaning of life and is making sure you don't miss a single heartbeat along the way.

Slowly delivered lines are followed by silence, then repeated, with silence, then again. In the introductory scenes, Parrish is shown to be on the brink of a heart attack and hearing a voice saying, "Yes." What does it mean? he wonders. We know that it means he's going to die, and Brest must know we know. So why does he drag it out?

If he's making the point that Death is a tease, or a sadist, it's hardly worth the minutes spent. We'll stipulate that Death, also known as the Grim Reaper and the Dark Angel, is no joy. Get on with it.

In another Faustian deal, Death makes Parrish an offer he can't refuse. If he'll serve as Death's guide on an earthly holiday, Death will postpone the publishing magnate's heart attack—at least until his imminent 65th birthday party, being elaborately arranged at his 75-acre seaside mansion by his older daughter (Marcia Gay Harden).

Meanwhile, Joe is introduced to family, friends and associates as Parrish's personal consultant. He moves into the man's spectacular Manhattan penthouse, becomes proactive in his business, even helps him stave off an attempted boardroom coup. At the same time, he is falling deeply, desperately in love with peanut butter and Susan.

This romance will be of great interest to Pitt fans, who will envy Susan no end when she seduces, undresses, fondles and deflowers the virginal Joe Black. On the other hand, Pitt's mannered performance is a turnoff for anyone hoping to become involved in the story.

Pitt has his moments in an early coffee shop scene, as a young lawyer who charms Susan Parrish. But after that character is hit by a car (a heart-stopping stunt, by the way) and Death takes over his body, Pitt's performance shifts into low gear. His Joe Black is a stiff, deliberate, nearly inanimate creature who, at times, disappears into the wallpaper. At other times, such as a pair of embarrassing scenes in which Joe speaks in patois to comfort a dying Jamaican woman, you wish he would.

Given the sedated nature of most of the performances, Joe Black's sluggish personality was probably ordered by the director. Even Hopkins, while the most energetic and compelling presence in the picture, moves as if the bottom half of his body were under water. Forlani has little more to do than stare longingly into Pitt's generally vacant eyes.

In the end, "Meet Joe Black" is more memorable for questions unasked than those answered. Who is Death, an angel? Who's he working for, God or the Devil? What's it like on the other side? Bill Parrish may have made his fortune disseminating news, but when opportunity knocks, he's no reporter.

NEWSWEEK, 11/16/98, p. 82, Jack Kroll

Let's get one thing straight, sports fans. "Meet Joe Black" is not about the pitcher of that name who played for the Brooklyn Dodgers in the '50s. Maybe Joe should sue Universal Pictures for bringing his name into disrepute. The Joe Black of the movie is not even a guy. He's Death. How would you like to see your name, chosen carefully by your loving parents, given to the Grim Reaper? And in a movie as silly and boring and maniacally long as this one? Every once in a while a film comes along that's so inexplicably ghastly that there's just no point in making nice about it. Let's hate it and get on with our life.

Or what's left of our life after "Meet Joe Black" has taken nearly three hours out of it. Director Martin Brest ("Beverly Hills Cop," "Scent of a Woman") has been stricken with the dreaded syndrome *filmus elephantiasis*. He's taken the 1934 kitsch classic "Death Takes a Holiday," with Fredric March, and attempted to make an epic update of it. He's used a platoon of writers and spent $90 million (and that's not counting about $40 million in promotional costs). Universal studio chairman Casey Silver has said he's cool about the length and the cost, despite rumors to the contrary. He's got Brad Pitt playing Death, so what's to worry?

That's the gimmick, making Death cute and sort of innocent. He takes over a young guy's body and shows up at the baronial digs of tycoon William Parrish (Anthony Hopkins), delaying Parrish's scheduled demise so he can observe human life. Joe is so innocent that he doesn't even know about peanut butter, so we're treated to the sight of Death cutely licking spoons of the gooey treat. He falls for the tycoon's daughter Susan (Claire Forlani) and decides to take her with him when he sheds his cute body and goes back to being just plain Death. Parrish is outraged; he tells Death "You're violating the laws of the universe!"

Damn right. After all, Death's gig is to kill not only zillionaire tycoons, but starving wretches in Calcutta, infants, flowers and bacteria. So on his earthly vacation from his labors it's pretty Republican of him to ignore all living things except those in the highest tax bracket. In the 1934 film (which was 78 minutes long) there was the fun of seeing people surviving normally death-dealing situations; this interminable version has no time for that.

Pitt's (and Brest's) idea of Deathly innocence is to act like a zombie—a cute zombie. Hopkins, master of the throwaway style, seems more throwaway than ever, perhaps indicating that he knows this flick is a crock. Its one delight is the exquisite 26-year-old Forlani in her first major role. In the original "Death Takes a Holiday," the Reaper takes the girl. This Death, after three inane hours, gives back his cute body to its mortal owner and returns to sad cosmic celibacy.

SIGHT AND SOUND, 2/99, p. 48, Geoffrey Macnab

A few days before his sixty-fifth birthday, media tycoon William Parrish begins to hear voices but is too busy with his company's merger with a rival to pay attention. His daughter Susan is chatted up by a handsome stranger in a coffee shop. After they go their separate ways, the man is hit by a car and killed.

At dinner, Parrish is visited by Death who has taken the body of the stranger killed outside the coffee shop. Wanting to spend some time on earth, Death allows Parrish a few extra days of life. Parrish introduces the stranger to his family as Joe Black. Susan is astonished that Joe doesn't remember their earlier encounter.

When Parrish scraps his merger plans, his colleagues believe that Joe—who accompanies Parrish wherever he goes—is responsible. Parrish's deputy Drew, who is also Susan's fiancé, stages a boardroom coup and deposes Parrish. Meanwhile, Joe and Susan fall in love.

Joe warns Parrish that his time is almost up. Joe wants to take Susan with him to the other side, although it will mean her death. At his birthday party, Parrish discovers he was double crossed by Drew, whom he confronts. The other board members promise to safeguard the company. Joe tells Parrish he won't be taking Susan with him after all. The two men leave the party. As Susan is looking for them, Joe appears but can't explain how he got there. Susan realises that this is the original man she met in the coffee shop, whom Joe has allowed to come back to life in his stead.

Pitched in some grey purgatory between screwball comedy and metaphysical romance, *Meet Joe Black* suffers from a severe identity crisis. Director Martin Brest (inspired to make the film by Mitchell Lieson's 1934 *Death Takes a Holiday)* starts with the flimsiest of conceits and embellishes an epic three-hour tale around it. *Joe Black* may be a rarity—a big-budget studio picture that is character-led, not effects-driven but it's still weighed down by its own solemnity. The early scenes work best. Anthony Hopkins is well cast as Parrish, the benevolent patriarch troubled by an inner voice intimating his own death. He is a media mogul, but a good-natured and lyrical one with a flair for poetic language. When he dispenses fatherly advice to his daughter Susan, he sounds like Richard Burton declaiming Dylan Thomas poetry. As he suffers his heart attack—a genuinely frightening scene, shot in juddering close-ups—Susan's encounter with a dishevelled stranger in a coffee shop is handled with spontaneity and charm.

But just as the film looks set to develop into a likable romance along the lines of *Sliding Doors,* cracks begin to appear. By bringing Brad Pitt back as a not-so-grim reaper, the scriptwriters raise all sorts of questions which they never really answer. Why, for instance, does Death need Parrish's assistance to see around the world?

There is some neatly observed comedy when Parrish introduces Death to his family, but it is still hard to work out what Joe is supposed to represent. Pitt plays him in the same way that Nicolas Cage did the angel in *City of Angels*—that's to say deadpan and charming, almost like a silent film star. On those few occasions when Joe does speak, it's only to repeat a question that has just been asked or to thank his hosts.

When Sting played the Devil in Dennis Potter's *Brimstone & Treacle,* his beatific good looks made him seem all the more diabolic. Here, nice is as nice does—every so often, Joe might affect a deep voice and threaten to take Parrish away before his time, but we know he is an all-American boy at heart who likes peanut butter and cookies too much to do anything evil And he's certainly preferable to Susan's other suitor, the oleaginous businessman Drew (Jake Weber), whom Joe effortlessly antagonises.

Parrish himself, though played with gravity and pathos by Hopkins, is a surprisingly one-dimensional hero. There is no tension about his struggle with Death. He's not covetous, or desperate for a few extra days of life to atone for past misdeeds. Rich as Croesus, he is also wise, kind-hearted and despises making money for its own sake. Given that the film's poor performance in the US was partly responsible for Universal boss Casey Silver losing his job, there's more than a hint of irony about his business philosophy.

The longer Joe sticks around, the mushier the film becomes. His hesitancy and eccentric ways enrapture Susan: I love your smell, he tells her, as if invoking the memory of Al Pacino's courtship technique in Brest's earlier hit, *Scent Of a Woman* (1992). In the lovers' scenes together, Pitt gets the best close-ups: he is the object of desire, not Forlani. When Susan falls in love with Joe despite realising that he is not the man she met in the coffee shop, you're left with the impression that anybody in Brad Pitt's body would bowl her over, an impression the bizarre and unsatisfactory ending does nothing to change.

Watching *Meet Joe Black* one is reminded of A. J. P. Taylor's description of the British war machine at the beginning of World War Two as an expensive motor car, complete in every detail, but empty of petrol. The film too is lovingly crafted, well acted, impressive to behold, but lacks any narrative momentum. Back in 1988, Brest directed one of the tautest comedy thrillers in years, *Midnight Run* a movie which knew exactly where it was going. Perhaps he should have watched that film again before embarking on this extravagant, meandering piece of whimsy.

TIME, 11/16/98, p. 107, Richard Schickel

Pale and cadaverous, cowled and carrying a scythe? No, no, it's just so... medieval. You can't personify death that way anymore. Our age demands something hunkier, less menacing, sort of a surfer dude to help us catch the curl of our last wave gracefully.

To borrow a phrase (and a pseudonym), meet Joe Black, as played by Brad Pitt, who has a real gift for standing around looking cute and stupid. He appears, along with chest pains and some numbness in the left arm, at an inconvenient moment in the life of an even more unlikely figure—a media mogul with a conscience—named William Parrish (Anthony Hopkins). Parrish is fighting off a takeover bid from a less savory rival and grouchily submitting to having his 65th birthday celebrated at one of those parties of the century that seem to occur once a month in our better social circles.

Obligingly, Death agrees to take a short break from his grim reapings in order to let Bill wind up his affairs in an orderly fashion. In return, he asks only that his victim teach him something about life. It does not occur to director Martin Brest and the raft of screenwriters employed on this enterprise that this is an illogical request. Who would know more about life than the figure who confronts us in our final moments, when all pride, all pomp, all defenses are stripped away?

But then they've set him to knocking on the wrong door anyway. What do people as privileged as Parrish and his family, at least as they are presented in "Meet Joe Black," know about life? Mostly they are observed dressed to the nines, eating delicately prepared viands and enjoying life in either a Manhattan penthouse, where one prays the swimming pool does not spring a leak and ruin the library's first editions, or a riverside mansion, where the helicopter pad blends nicely into the landscape. There is no rage, pain or panic in any of these venues, and no wild laughter either. There are only the muttered discontents of the well favored.

In time their servants help Death discover the joys of peanut butter. In time Bill's serious daughter Susan (Claire Forlani)—you know she's serious because she works as a doctor instead of as an aromatherapist—helps him discover the joys of sex. In return he helps Bill fend off his corporate enemies and even allows him time to make a nice exit speech at his birthday bash before gently conducting him, through a shower of fireworks—anything for a big finish—to a world that, frankly, cannot possibly be better than the one he's leaving.

Brest thinks he needs three endless hours to turn Death into a glam and fully cuddlesome character. And as we watch his movie (a remake of 1934's blessedly brief "Death Takes a Holiday," in which Fredric March played the title role) slowly disappear into the blond hole of Pitt's affectlessness, we have plenty of time to observe just how profoundly he has misconceived Death. As anyone whose house he has visited can tell you, he's a vicious, merciless anarchist. Maybe Max von Sydow is now all wrong for the part. And we can certainly be glad Robin Williams didn't get it. But there is Jim Carrey, who is right for the role and can open bad pictures too.

VILLAGE VOICE, 11/24/98, p. 117, J. Hoberman

A mind-numbing three-hour update of the 1934 chestnut *Death Takes a Holiday, Meet Joe Black* suggests the sort of New Age drama that *Celebrity*'s Leonardo DiCaprio character might imagine for himself. Indeed, this ponderous, didactic weepie aspires to *Titanic* stature even if the only ship it sinks is itself.

As in *Celebrity*, social climbing is universal. Death decides to learn about life by appropriating the body of Brad Pitt and attaching himself to American media mogul Bill Parrish (Anthony Hopkins). A sort of domesticated Rupert Murdoch, Parrish has been scheduled to shuffle off this mortal coil but, in the interest of his own education, Death—now known as Joe Black—allows him to live on a bit, harrassed on the one hand by a fellow corporate shark and the other by the fussy, rejected daughter (Marcia Gay Harden) who is preparing his 65th birthday party.

More like a dazed puppy than the great devourer, Pitt's eye-batting Joe attends Bill's board meetings and family dinners while Bill, who never offers any explanation for the presence of his swanky young friend, keeps mulling about how crazy it all is. (Hopkins tries to act his way through this hogwash, although his part is really ready-made for wisecracks and Woody Allen, particularly given the climactic party's heavy dependence on the Astaire-Rogers songbook.) After a while, Joe falls for the mogul's beloved younger daughter Susan (Claire Forlani, forever blinking away or smiling back tears). That the feeling might be reciprocated is signalled by the modification of her oft-repeated line, "What are *you* doing here?" to "You're *here*!"

Although the media mogul lives surrounded by Rothkos and Kandinskys, the most immaculately lit objet d'art is, of course, Pitt. To watch this immaculately coiffed, boyishly smiling reaper provides less the chill of the grave than the sense of the blow-dryer lurking just off-camera to tousle his hair between takes. The movie's excessive length and ridiculous cost (reportedly $90 million) are nothing compared to this mystery: In all the snarky speculation about Joe's relation to Bill, why does no one ever wonder if this stud-muffin is the old guy's boyfriend? There really must be some things worse than death.

Also reviewed in:
CHICAGO TRIBUNE, 11/13/98, Friday/p. A, Michael Wilmington
NEW REPUBLIC, 12/7/98, p. 26, Stanley Kauffmann
NEW YORK TIMES, 11/13/98, p. E14, Janet Maslin
NEW YORKER, 11/23/98, p. 114, Anthony Lane
VARIETY, 11/9-15/98, p. 30, Todd McCarthy
WASHINGTON POST, 11/13/98, p. D1, Rita Kempley
WASHINGTON POST, 11/13/98, Weekend/p. 43, Michael O'Sullivan

MEN WITH GUNS (HOMBRES ARMADOS)

A Sony Pictures Classics release of a Lexington Road Productions and Clear Blue Sky Productions film in association with The Independent Film Channel and Anarchists' Convention. *Executive Producer:* Jody Patton, Lou Gonda, and John Sloss. *Producer:* R. Paul Miller and Maggie Renzi. *Director:* John Sayles. *Screenplay (Spanish, Nahuatl, Tzotzil, Maya and Kuna with English subtitles):* John Sayles.   *Editor:* John Sayles.   *Director of Photography:* Slawomir Idziak.   *Music:* Mason Daring.   *Music Editor:* Patrick Mullins.   *Sound:* Judy Karp and (music) Michael Golub.   *Sound Editor:* Philip Stockton.   *Casting:* Lizzie Curry Martinez.   *Production Designer:* Felipe Fernández del Paso.   *Art Director:* Salvador Parra.   *Set Decorator:* Miguel Angel Alvarez.   *Set Dresser:* Rigoberto Castañeda.   *Special Effects:* Alex Vázquez.   *Costumes:* Mayes C. Rubeo.   *Make-up:* Carlos Sánchez.   *Running time:* 128 minutes. *MPAA Rating:* R.

CAST: Federico Luppi (Dr. Fuentes);   Damián Delgado (Domingo, the Soldier);   Dan Rivera González (Conejo, the Boy);   Tania Cruz (Graciela, the Mute girl);   Damián Alcázar (Padre Portillo, the Priest);   Mandy Patinkin (Andrew);   Kathryn Grody (Harriet); Iguandili López (Mother);   Nandi Luna Ramírez (Daughter);   Rafael de Quevedo (General);   Carmen Madrid (Angela, Dr. Fuentes' Daughter);   Esteban Soberanes (Raúl, Angela's Fiance);   Alejandro Springall (Carlos, Dr. Fuentes' Son);   Maricruz Nanjera and Jacqueline Walters Voltaire (Rich Ladies);   Roberto Sosa (Bravo);   Iván Arango (Cienfuegos);   Lizzie Curry Martínez (Montoya); Luis Ramírez (Hidalgo);   Humberto Romero (De Soto);   Gabriel Cosme (Echevarría);   Horacio Trujillo (Arenas);   Efrine Elfaro and Pedro Hernández (Kokal drivers);   Dionisios (Salt Man); Loló Navarro (Blind Woman);   Maggie Renzi and Shari Gray (Tourists by Pool);   Paco Mauri (Captain);   Gilma Tuyub Castillo (Mother with Baby);   Armando Martínez Velásquez (Vendor); Luis Felipe Tovar (Barber);   Fernando Medel (Barber's Client);   David Villalpando and Raúl Sánchez (Gum People);   Diego Méndez Guzmán (Moisés);   Mariano Lápez de la Cruz (Gonzalo); Antonio de la Torré López (Isidro);   Ermenehildo Sáenz Guzmán (Sixto);   Cristóbal Guzmán Mesa (Artemio);   Domingo Pérez Sánchez (Junípero);   Oscar García Ortega (Sergeant);   Miguel Xocua (Modelo Boy); Guadalupe Xocua (Modelo Woman);   Celeste Cornelio Sánchez (Raped Girl);   Nazario Montiel, Francisco Váldez, and José Alberto Acosta (Guerrillas).

CHRISTIAN SCIENCE MONITOR, 3/13/98, p. B3, David Sterritt

American independent filmmaker John Sayles does something so bold in his new movie, "Men With Guns," that it deserves to be underscored as vividly as possible: He presents a story about Spanish-speaking people in which the characters actually speak Spanish!

This may sound like a minor point, but its implications are important. For many years now, United States audiences have been shying away from foreign-language films; theaters have been increasingly reluctant to show them; and journalists have been sluggish about covering them.

Ifs scandalous that such patterns should persist at a time when our world continues to shrink every day, making international interests more vital than ever. Where better than the movies to let our horizons grow?

In this atmosphere, it's an act of courage for Sayles to tackle a Latin American story and insist on its characters speaking the language of their own lives (with English subtitles) rather than translated "Moviespeak."

"Men With Guns," also known as "Hombres Armados," is praiseworthy in other respects, including the sensitive humanism of its story.

The hero is an aging Latin American physician who has never paid much attention to political events in his (unidentified) country but prides himself on his longtime career of training doctors to help poverty-stricken rural families.

Learning that many of his former students have abandoned their posts or disappeared, he begins an arduous voyage of discovery into the region's interior. There he encounters a series of new enigmas, accompanied by accounts of "men with guns" pursuing a frightful agenda of their own. This brings him to a new awareness of how political forces affect ordinary lives whether we want them to or not.

Sayles has never been a natural-born filmmaker, and "Men With Guns" often feels more like a photographed screenplay than a truly cinematic work. But its acting is admirable—standouts include Federico Luppi as the physician and Mandy Patinkin as a US tourist—and its mood only grows more engrossing as the story proceeds.

Most important, its integrity as a socially responsible drama is unimpeachable. Excelente!

CINEASTE, Vol. XXIII, no. 3, 1998, p. 43, Susan Ryan

John Sayles has such good intentions for his films that one always wants to like them. Whether taking on corruption in local government in *City of Hope*, siding with striking coal miners in *Matewan*, or exploring tensions on the U.S.-Mexican border in *Lone Star*, he is unique among independent filmmakers in expending considerable effort to bringing subjects of class and ethnicity to the screen in meaningful ways. In *Men with Guns (Hombres Armados)*, Sayles returns to a Hispanic theme with a beautifully crafted film about an upper-class doctor's political awakening in an unnamed Central American country. He gradually realizes that the brutal repression of the indigenous population can no longer be ignored. As in many of Sayles's films, however, *Men with Guns* does not always measure up to the importance of its subject, despite its good intentions.

The story revolves around a Dr. Fuentes (Federico Luppi), who, nearing the end of his career as a physician to the wealthy, decides to go on a journey to discover what has happened to the medical students he taught in an international health program (reminiscent of the Alliance for Progress program from the 1960s) which placed doctors in the countryside. In the process of searching for his former students, he also learns a great deal about himself and what it means to remain oblivious to the suffering of the poor, indigenous population. Fuentes meets with opposition from the outset, from his children who accuse him of naiveté, from an army general patient who warns him of guerrilla violence, and even from a former student, Bravo, who left medicine and now sells pharmaceuticals out of boxes in a squalid slum courtyard. Unable to explain why he left his medical post in the villages, Bravo dismissively informs Fuentes that he must find another student to learn what happened with the program. This final encounter begins the peripatetic wanderings of Fuentes, as he moves from village to village, deeper and deeper into the mountains, only to find that the doctors have "disappeared," victims of an unnamed dirty war against the indigenous population.

But why have the doctors disappeared or been openly murdered in front of their villages? Dr. Fuentes has always been isolated from the political turmoil happening in his own country, choosing to believe that accounts of atrocities are mere exaggerations, and that the papers print them because the "common people love drama." In each village he is confronted with the reality of innocent people being murdered, all at the hands of men with guns. Sayles chooses not to identify the country—although much of what happens in the film bears a strong resemblance to Guatemala in the 1980s—because he wants Dr. Fuentes's allegorical journey to stand for the many injustices experienced by indigenous peoples in Mexico, Brazil, Guatemala, and elsewhere. According to Sayles, the common denominator in all these countries can be simply explained by the fact that when men with guns take control, no matter what the culture, you do what they say. But this reductive observation begs the question of government complicity and legal systems which allow the military to operate with impunity. Placing the blame solely on ownership of guns avoids any systemic criticism of the powers that allow it to happen.

One of the most disturbing aspects of the film is Dr. Fuentes's purported innocence about the events occurring around him. It is hard to believe that he ever participated in a health program with the worthy ambition of helping the poor in the countryside when he rejects any knowledge of a conflict that is burning villages, uprooting entire communities and placing them in "model" camps, and slaughtering anyone thought to be associated with the guerrillas. According to Sayles, the character of Fuentes was based on stories told to him by friends, including one recounted by the novelist Francisco Goldman (*The Long Night of White Chickens*). Goldman told of an uncle in Guatemala whose students had been murdered by the same government that claimed to support their community health program.

Unlike Goldman's novel, however, which weaves elements of Guatemalan political history into the investigation of a mysterious death, Sayles's attempt to create an allegory results in rendering brutal acts which seem stylized beyond the point of credibility. As he remarked in an interview on his decision to create a mythical location for a setting, it is more important for the film to show that everyone has the responsibility to know "What your police force is doing, what your government is doing," making it impossible to plead ignorance in the face of widespread corruption and violence. *Men with Guns* manifests this liberal sentiment repeatedly, as Fuentes learns from the indigenous characters he picks up along the way, but, given the subject matter, one wishes that a more radical approach had been taken. Instead of merely discovering more oppression and discrimination, Fuentes could actually do something about it, or at least witness some pockets of resistance in the Indian communities he encounters.

At several points in his unusual road trip, Fuentes crosses paths with an American couple played by Mandy Patinkin and Kathryn Grody. While more informed about the political realities faced by the Indians than Fuentes himself, they come across as Ugly American tourists displaying as much interest in torture and death as they do in viewing ruins. One gets the feeling they would enjoy witnessing a massacre just so they would have an interesting story to report to the folks at home. In several scenes their fractured Spanish makes for some strained comic moments, yet their inclusion reveals a weakness that Sayles has exhibited in many of his films—introducing characters simply to make a point rather than integrating them into the narrative. If Sayles wants to comment on the American presence in this mythical country, why not make a more pointed reference to U.S. support for military governments which endorse the type of violence seen in the film?

Despite its political weaknesses, *Men with Guns* has a number of strengths which make it worth seeing. The framing story of an Indian woman, describing the movements of Fuentes and his entourage before they arrive at their final destination, injects a lyrical note of magical realism into the narrative. Beautifully photographed by Kieslowski's cinematographer, Slawomir Idziak, the film has an incredibly lush color scheme of intense greens and blues which makes the jungle environs palpable. The soundtrack, created by Sayles's longtime collaborator Mason Daring and music consultant Tom Schnabel, expertly weaves meringues, salsas, cumbers, and other types of Latin music to create an audio tapestry to complement the narrative action. Strong performances by Argentine actor Federico Luppi (also seen in *Time of Revenge)* as Dr. Fuentes, along with a number of regional actors bring a ring of truth to even some of the most naive formulations of the script.

While Sayles has created an affecting humanistic portrait of a man who realizes too late that ignorance is as much a part of the problem as the men with guns, the film will certainly disappoint viewers who want a stronger political statement. Allegorical treatments of sensitive subjects have a long history in socially conscious filming, particularly in Latin America (e.g., *Land in Anguish, The Promised Land*), but the lack of historical specificity in *Men with Guns* mystifies rather than illuminates the treatment of indigenous people. By presenting the Indians as only passive victims of the forces surrounding them, the film mistakenly ignores the power of the indigenous-rights movement in Latin America which grew out of conditions similar to the ones that Sayles shows in the film. The pressing issue is not only men with guns, but what needs to be done about them.

LOS ANGELES TIMES, 3/13/98, Calendar/p. 14, Jack Mathews

[The following review by Jack Mathews appeared in a slightly different form in
NEWSDAY, 3/6/98, Part II/p. B6.]

When John Sayles was out promoting his critically acclaimed and darn near commercial "Lone Star" a couple of years ago, he was inevitably asked what he intended to do next. He said he was writing a script with a political backdrop set in Latin America, and that it would be in Spanish and Indian dialects, with subtitles, with an all-Latino cast—if someone will pay for it.

Up stepped Sony Pictures Classics, which agreed to buy the rights to North America, England and Latin America. And now here's the movie, "Men With Guns," subtitles and all.

Looking at the films he's chosen to make in the past 10 years—from "Matewan," about a labor crisis in a 1920s coal town, to "City of Hope," about big-city corruption, to "The Secret of Roan Inish," a poetic ode to the myths of the Irish Sea—you can accuse Sayles of self-indulgence but never vanity or greed. He explores subjects that interest him, in novels that he writes with film.

And though he tends to focus on personal relationships within a political context, no two of his movies are alike. "Men With Guns," as Casey Stengel might have put it, is more unalike than any of them. It spirits us into the mountains and jungles of an unidentified Latin American country, where the recently widowed and ailing Dr. Fuentes (Federico Luppi) has set out on a working vacation to visit the medical students he had trained years before to work with impoverished natives.

It's a trip that will turn into a mystery, an adventure, a spiritual odyssey and a series of deep personal and political revelations. There's a war going on out there, between guerrillas and government troops, an endless battle that catches everyone else in the middle, including most of Fuentes' former students.

"Men With Guns" is a slow-paced trip, with a lot of translated conversation, and Sayles keeps it pure. The actors are said to be speaking in four dialects, and there's nothing about the film, other than the ill-conceived couple (Mandy Patinkin and Kathryn Grody) used as comic relief, to give away its American origin. Sayles has never been a visual stylist, and his latest film is as straightforward and plot-bound as any of the earlier ones.

The pleasures are in the nuances of the relationships that develop between Fuentes and the three companions he picks up along the way. The first is Conejo (Dan Rivera Gonzalez), a boy without parents, who takes Fuentes to the deserted school ground doubling as the military's killing field. Next is Domingo (Damian Delgado), an army deserter without a gun or a country. And the third is Padre Portillo (Damian Alcazar), a defrocked priest who's also lost his faith.

Sayles opens the film with a scene of a native woman telling her young daughter about a city doctor who can heal by touch. He's a sick man, fighting for his breath in the high mountain air, she says, and as Fuentes' small party trudges through the jungles, looking for a rumored paradise away from politics and war, the connection becomes clear.

But it's a weak connection, too facile for the kind of epiphany Sayles has in mind. "Men With Guns" is strong enough on its own. It doesn't need a higher power.

NEW STATESMAN, 9/18/98, p. 39, Gerald Kaufman

"Men with Guns" proves that money can't buy quality. Since starting as scriptwriter for Piranha in 1978, John Sayles has achieved a reputation as a director both for quality and for financial economy. "Lone Star" earned him an Oscar nomination for best original screenplay, and it made money as well.

Sayles shot "Men With Guns" in Mexico in six weeks on a budget of $ 2.5 million. Just one member of the cast has any kind of international reputation: Mandy Patinkin, who played opposite Barbra Streisand in "Yentl." Patinkin plays little more than a bit part, as a blundering American tourist. He and Kathryn Grody, as his wife, are the only characters who speak English. The rest of the dialogue, by Sayles (who directs and edits as well), is in Spanish (translator, Alejandro Springall).

Dr Fuentes (Federico Luppi), near to retirement, lives in the capital city of an unnamed Latin American country. He decides to travel into the interior in search of the students he trained for an international health programme. Warned not to go because of the dangers, he persists. The jungle and wasteland are pervaded by groups of guerrillas and by army units. Both are the men with guns. Both are equally lawless and trigger-happy. The inhabitants Fuentes meets along the way live in abject poverty, victims of the men with guns. Scraping a living off the soil, they are known by the products they harvest: Salt People, Sugar People, Coffee People, Banana People, Gum (for chewing gum) People, Corn People. "They're afraid of everything," Fuentes is told.

He soon finds there is much to fear. His camera is stolen. Then his car tyres go. There is nowhere safe to stay or to sleep. It makes every kind of sense for him to turn back. But, against all apparent rationality, he presses on.

Then, without Sayles making heavy weather of his allegorical theme, we cotton on to what is happening. Fuentes' risk-fraught progress is not simply a journey; it is a quest. It is a quest to acquire knowledge that becomes self-knowledge. It is the Pilgrim's Progress. Like Pilgrim, Fuentes acquires companions, comparable with John Bunyan's "Worldly Wiseman" and "Giant Despair."

First to attach himself to the doctor is a boy whose mother was raped. When Fuentes allows him to ride in his car, Conejo (Dan Rivera Gonzalez) exclaims: "I've never been on a plane before! "Next to join Fuentes are an army deserter (Damian Delgado) who had to prove himself to his mates by murdering a prisoner in cold blood; a priest (Damian Alcazar) who abandoned his faith after betraying villagers who consequently were massacred; and a mute girl who barely survived rape (Tania Cruz).

Along the way Fuentes learns that, though most of his students have been killed, one may still survive in a remote and inaccessible village, Cerca del Cielo—obviously a counterpart of

"Pilgrim's" Celestial City. Cerca del Cielo's inhabitants, Fuentes is told, are the Sky People: "They eat air and shit clouds." He shepherds his flock through to the slopes of the mountain at whose apparently impenetrable summit Cerca del Cielo may perhaps be found. Just as the narrative has been disturbing, even harrowing, so the finale is ineffably moving, even hopeful, though far from facile.

Fuentes is a noble character in a film of beauty, dignity and calm. Throughout all his travels, he stays true to his credo: "I'm a doctor. A scientist. I believe only in progress." "Men with Guns" is an old-fashioned movie. Sayles achieves his impact through the coordination of acting, no-frills filming (director of photography Slawomir Idziak worked in Poland with Andrzej Wajda) and plangent music (the composer is Sayles regular, Mason Daring).

NEW YORK POST, 3/6/98, p. 47, Thelma Adams

Sometimes John Sayles writes movies. Sometimes he writes novels. Sometimes he writes movies that would work better as novels. "Men With Guns" is a case in point.

That doesn't mean I don't appreciate "Men With Guns," but I'm a Sayles junkie who thought "Lone Star" was the smartest movie made in America in 1996.

"Guns," which is largely in Spanish and a collection of unspellable dialects from Nahuatl to Tzotzil, is a fable. Written, directed and edited by Sayles, the ultimate Yankee independent, it presents large themes as if they were embroidered on pillows. "Nobody is immune to" is one. "The people love drama" is another.

Set in an unidentified latin American country that resembles Mexico, "Men With Guns" is the story of a sophisticated urban M.D. (Federico Luppi). While Dr. Fuentes spends his days tending the rich and powerful, he prides himself on his humanist legacy: A few years earlier, he trained young doctors to treat the poor in the mountain jungles.

After his wife dies, Fuentes hears rumblings that his legacy might not be so enduring. A chance encounter with a former student (who bears a red zigzag scar on his cheek) reveals that something is horribly wrong with the program.

Fuentes borrows his son's four-wheel-drive and heads for the mountains, accompanied by composer Mason Daring's jaunty and compelling soundtrack. The doctors quest is a journey from ignorance to enlightenment, the unique story (in American films) of an honest, intelligent and apolitical man who has deluded himself into believing he is not responsible for his government's activities.

Along the way, Fuentes encounters a foreign land in his own nation. The verdant, wild landscape reveals the sugar people, the salt people, the coffee people and the skeletons of the victims of "men with guns"—both government soldiers and armed guerrillas.

While searching for his former students, Fuentes meets the bastard son of a soldier and a native woman, an AWOL soldier with a gun, a mute rape victim and a priest who lost his faith after betraying his village to the local gendarmes.

In Sayles' attempt to provide the people with their beloved drama, he creates a schematic plot that rings false—we didn't need a gun, a girl, a soldier, a priest and an innocent to get the point. And when all the plot strands are laboriously knotted on a remote hillside, we feel cheated rather than exhilarated.

Still, who else but Sayles would have attempted a Spanish-language journey into a contemporary heart of darkness—a world of torture, rape and murder—in the NAFTA era? Ironically, it's the figure of paternalism who rings truest. Luppi, a Latin American star who gained attention stateside in "Cronos," makes Dr. Fuentes a charismatic tragic hero.

SIGHT AND SOUND, 9/98, p. 49, Philip Kemp

Doctor Fuentes is an eminent elderly doctor in a Latin American capital city. Despite warnings, he decides to visit some of the students he trained to work as doctors in poor mountain villages for an international health programme.

In the first village, Fuentes is met with impenetrable suspicion. Finally he learns that his student, Cienfuegos, was burned alive by "men with guns". He treks onwards, guided by orphan boy Conejo, whom he finds in the second village. Fuentes hears similar stories everywhere. In some places everybody has been killed and the village burned to the ground; in others selected villagers, including the doctor, have been tortured to death. The tyres are stolen off Fuentes' car, and he is robbed at gunpoint by an army deserter, Domingo. But Domingo later returns wounded, with a stolen set of tyres, and joins the trek. They pick up a former priest, Padre Portillo, who tells them how his villagers were ordered by the army to shoot him as a subversive. When he fled, the villagers were all murdered in reprisal.

At a refugee camp Portillo surrenders to soldiers to save the others. Graciela, a mute young rape victim, attaches herself to Fuentes' group. There are rumours of a village high in the mountains where Montoya, Fuentes' last surviving student, may be working. They reach it after a long climb, but Montoya is not there. Exhausted, Fuentes dies. A young girl comes asking for medical help for her mother. Reluctantly, Domingo picks up the doctor's black bag.

In recent years, John Sayles has been moving steadily south. His early work stuck close to his New Jersey base, but *Passion Fish* found him in the Louisiana bayous, his novel *Los Gusanos* switched between Cuba and Florida, and his last film *Lone Star* straddled the TexMex border. *Men with Guns*, however, is set wholly in an unidentified Latin American country that could well be Guatemala or Mexico, and barring a few brief scenes is all in Spanish since Sayles wanted to let his actors concentrate on acting, rather than "struggling with their English". Even though Sayles speaks Spanish well, it was a bold decision. And it has paid off. The performances, as ever in his films, are focused and naturalistic. Several of the cast are making their film debuts, but you wouldn't guess it.

Compared with *Lone Star* with its intricate, multi-stranded narrative, *Men with Guns* is straightforwardly linear. It takes the classic form of an allegorical journey from urban to rural, from sophisticated to primitive, from ignorance to knowledge. Also from detachment to commitment: Doctor Fuentes, a widower whose children have long left home, goes in search of a surrogate family (his students, whom we see grouped around him in a treasured photograph). He doesn't find them, but instead, like the outlaw Josie Wales in Eastwood's classic 1976 Western, he picks up a far more ramshackle family of the injured and vulnerable. And again like Josie Wales, he is humanised by them: through them he comes to recognise that he's responsible to more than his family or his students, that his ignorance of political realities was a wilful abnegation of that responsibility

Fuentes' own words return to mock him. Instructing his students (in monochrome flashback) that proper equipment is crucial in medicine, he reminds them how Cortés could conquer an empire with a handful of men, "because he had guns and horses, and they didn't." Later, asking the villagers why they didn't resist their oppressors, he's told, "because they had guns and we didn't." People are defined by objects and artifacts: army and guerrillas alike are simply "men with guns" (though, when we meet some guerrillas, they're much more sympathetic than the soldiers); tribes don't have names but call themselves "Banana People" or "Gum People" according to the crop they harvest. Race is subordinate to political function. "When an Indian puts on uniform," we're told, "he becomes white." Fuentes, at last realising what his kind have done, sighs despairingly: "There should be somewhere where white people aren't allowed."

"Maybe innocence is a sin," says Padre Portillo, the fugitive priest who sacrificed his flock to save his own life, and who is given a second chance to redeem himself. *Men with Guns* tells a grim, bloody tale, but its underlying theme is redemption—of Fuentes, of Portillo, and above all of Domingo, the deserter haunted by the rapes and killings he perpetrated during his career in the army. First appearing as a hunched, brutal figure robbing the doctor at gunpoint, he finally becomes the doctor's successor, the sole fruit of his wish "to leave behind something practical".

Sayles is unusual, maybe even unique, among US film-makers in that his films are informed by a clear political agenda. It's their strength, but the downside is a weakness for the didactic, and this is what mars *Men with Guns*. Despite the excellence of the acting, the characters remain ciphers, placed to instruct Fuentes and us on what we owe each other. Fuentes himself (played by the fine Argentinian actor Federico José Luppi, the lead in Guillermo del Toro's *Cronos)* never comes convincingly to life: for the sake of the message, he's made far too naïve to be plausible. Would he really never have inquired how his prize students were making out in the programme he sees as his intellectual legacy? (And if he didn't ask, wouldn't the international body that funded it have done so?) In *Lone Star,* his best film so far, Sayles seemed able to loosen control and relax into his material—not so here. For all its powerful qualities, *Men with Guns* feels message-driven rather than character driven.

VILLAGE VOICE, 3/10/98, p. 66, Amy Taubin

there's not a lot I want to say about John Sayles's *Men With Guns*. It doesn't work and I'm not sure there was any way Sayles could have known that in advance. Especially since he doesn't have a filmmaker's instincts. Sayles is basically a writer who has extremely interesting things to say about the way people treat (mostly mistreat) one another in various social and political circumstances. He's also one of the few American filmmakers who refuses to allow commercial concerns to influence his choice of forms or subject matter. Sayles's last two films, *The Secret of Roan Inish* and *Lone Star*, were very fine and much more complicated and moving than anything he made before. *Men With Guns* (which is largely in Spanish with English subtitles) seems like an attempt to combine the fabulist narrative of the former with the social realism of the later, but it never comes together.

Set in some nameless Latin American country *Men with Guns* is about a wealthy physician (Federico Luppi) who has spent 60-odd years in denial about how people outside his privileged environment are forced to live. Of all his accomplishments, he's proudest of having trained seven young doctors who were sent to villages to care for the poor. Although his family and various sleazy army and police honchos caution him against going, he travels into the interior to find out how his students are faring. His journey takes him to one destroyed village after another, one mass grave after another, one encampment of starving people after another. He hears about "men with guns" (the army), who kill anyone who might support the guerrillas (who we never see). He meets a young boy who's learned to survive by not feeling anything about the horror in which he lives, a guilt-ridden army deserter, and a priest who's abandoned his parish to save his skin.

Didactic and politically confusing (what a combo), *Men With Guns* fails first and foremost because the doctor is not a believable character. Not only is he never able to admit what he sees with his own eyes, his mechanism for defending himself from the truth never changes. His denial doesn't intensify, his behavior doesn't become more contradictory. He's on auto-pilot first to last. And what could be more tedious than that.

Also reviewed in:
CHICAGO TRIBUNE, 3/27/98, Friday/p. C, Michael Wilmington
NEW REPUBLIC, 3/23/98, p. 24, Stanley Kauffmann
NEW YORK TIMES, 3/6/98, p. E29, Janet Maslin
VARIETY, 9/8-14/97, p. 79, Emanuel Levy
VARIETY, 3/9-15/98, p. 48, David Rooney
WASHINGTON POST, 3/27/98, p. C7, Stephen Hunter
WASHINGTON POST, 3/27/98, Weekend/p. 60, Desson Howe

MENDEL

A First Run Features release of a Northern Lights presentation in co-production with Zentropa Entertainments, Lichtblick Filmproduktion, Norsk Film and NRK with financial support from Audiovisuelt Produksjonsfond, The Danish Film Institute and Eurimages. *Producer:* Axel Helgeland. *Director:* Alexander Rosler. *Screenplay (Norwegian, German and Yiddish with English subtitles):* Alexander Rosler. *Director of Photography:* Helge Semb. *Editor:* Kirsten Bonnen Rask. *Music:* Geir Bohren and Bent Aserud. *Sound:* Fredrik Berg. *Casting:* Heta Mantscheff, Ellen Lande, and Nora Ibsen. Production Designer: Jack Van Domburg. *Running time:* 98 minutes. *MPAA Rating:* Not Rated.

CAST: Thomas Jungling Sorensen (Mendel); Teresa Harder (Bela); Hans Kremer (Aron); John Henning Gobring Hermstad (Markus); Martin Meingast (David); Bjorn Sundquist (Mitten Man); Charlotte Trier (Mrs. Freund); Wolfgang Pintzka (Mr. Freund); Lene Braglie (Mrs. Rosen); Geo Von Krogh (Mr. Rosen); Bjorn Jenseg (Ugland); Ketil Gudim (The Farmer).

LOS ANGELES TIMES, 5/1/98, Calendar/p. 14, Kevin Thomas

The enormity of the evil of the Third Reich revealed in the cinema of the Holocaust over the decades has reflected, by and large nobly, the vast geographical scope and equally vast diversity of experiences endured by its survivors. The latest addition to this immense, ongoing cinematic tapestry is Alexander Rosler's exquisitely expressed "Mendel," a coming-of-age tale with unusual circumstances.

The place and time is rural Bavaria in 1954, where a German Jewish family is leaving to begin a new life in Norway as part of a government program to relocate a small number of Jews Nine-year-old Mendel (Thomas Jungling Sorensen), whose family seems to have been living under the protection of kindly Herr Fischer, cannot understand why this is happening. "No Jew can stay in Germany after what they've done to us" is a constant refrain, but Mendel does not understand what this means. He is also constantly being told that there can be no explanations "until you're older."

You can certainly appreciate his loving, worn parents (Hans Kremer, Teresa Harder) wanting to protect their son from hearing about the horrors of the Holocaust until they feel he's old enough to handle them. Yet Mendel, who is very bright and high-spirited, is naturally curious, growing up in an atmosphere of uncompleted sentences and veiled allusions. He is, of course, aware of World War II but does not understand the way in which his parents and older brother David (Martin Meingast) are different from other war survivors.

Yet inevitably the boy will not be stopped from piecing bits of information together, and one of the film's key accomplishments is to evoke Mendel's occasional troubled dreams, composed of images of Nazi acts of oppression he's not supposed to have heard of, accounts of his parents' suffering, and a jumble of Jewish and Christian figures and symbols. As you might expect, the move to Norway is severely dislocating, with his nonreligious family initially crowded into an old apartment with an Orthodox family—these scenes are eerily reminiscent of life in Anne Frank's Secret Annex.

There are well-meaning Christians eager to convert Mendel's family, and a schoolteacher dumbfounded by having a little Jewish boy in her class.(There's clearly no separation of church and state here.) Amid so much contradiction and confusion, with his parents struggling to achieve their own equilibrium while inundated with horrifying memories, Mendel represents the eternal resiliency and adaptability of the young.

Rosler, a German Jew who emigrated to Norway as a child, misses no opportunity to find humor in Mendel's growing up. However, he's not entirely convincing when he depicts Mendel, once he learns the truth, as cursing Jews for having been, in his view, so passive in the face of the Nazis. You could wish, too, that Rosler could have let us know a little more about how Mendel's family lived between the time he was born and the emigration to Norway. On the whole, however, "Mendel" is a distinctive, acutely sensitive film that is capably sustained by Sorensen, yet another of those amazing child actors who've been emerging in large numbers in recent years.

NEW YORK POST, 3/20/98, p. 49, Bill Hoffmann

"Mendel," is a Holocaust film for people who can't stomach Holocaust films. The setting is Norway in 1954, where families of displaced Jewish survivors of Nazi Germany were allowed to resettle and begin a new life.

But as 9-year-old Mendel finds out, it's not that easy. While he's aware of the war, Mendel has been kept in the dark about the horrors of anti-Semitism and the atrocities that haunt his parents. And since nobody will talk to him about it, Mendel goes on a childhood quest to find the truth.

Director Alexander Rosler, a veteran documentary filmmaker, has made a warm, delicately textured film that's both funny and profoundly moving at the same time. Since "Mendel" is a little picture, it probably won't be around too long—so catch it now.

NEWSDAY, 3/20/98, Part II/p. B18, John Anderson

The Trotzig family, tattered refugees from Germany, pull into Norway in 1954, are greeted by a bigger-than-life-size roadside crucifix and run straight into the fjord of cultural nondiversity.

Christianity is doled out as firmly as the cod liver oil. Jews are as foreign as ketchup on herring. And the refugees themselves, operating as they do on various levels of devotion, play an ongoing game of "Who's the Jew?"

"Displaced persons" they are, none so much as young Mendel, played by the sweet-faced Thomas Jungling Sorensen, as a kid too young to remember the horrors of the war, and with too much sense to be blindly obedient.

Mirroring, at least to a certain extent, the personal history of director Alexander Rosler (who was born in Dachau in 1947 and emigrated to Norway in the '50s), "Mendel" gleans its humor from a rambling cast of characters—ex-resistance fighters, a mysterious horse driver, a man who lives in the attic, the families themselves—and its profundity from Mendel's plight. He is to accept without question the gravity of being a post-war Jew, the solemnity of tradition, the sacredness of others' secrets and the decorum expected of a non-Norwegian without any other information. Or any memory: He's told he must never forget, without knowing what. Mendel is representative of all peoples for whom ritual has lost any meaning other than habit, because the history is too painful to recall.

Rosler plays most of his story for laughs, even at its most dire. Mendel's typhus-ravaged father, Aron (the alternately tender and explosive Hans Kremer), had forgotten he was a Jew "until Hitler renewed his membership," as Mendel tells us in voice-over. His brother David (Martin Meingast), keeps a cherished photo he won't let Mendel see. And his mother, Bela (Teresa Harder), won't even entertain Mendel's pleas for more details. The secrets are driving the young man nuts.

Mendel spends his days adapting to Norway, his nights listening to his family scream in their sleep. It's a fine line Rosler walks in telling this story, which asks as many questions of the Trotzigs as it does of Norway. Despite a few anxious moments of unnerving sentiment, the director maintains an admirable balance.

VILLAGE VOICE, 3/24/98, p. 70, Leslie Camhi

It's 1954, and nine-year-old Mendel's world is full of mysteries. He can't understand why his family, along with other Jewish refugees, has left the familiar world of postwar Germany for Norway, a land of polar bears, cod-liver oil, and fish balls. Mendel's father and his teenage brother suffer from terrible nightmares; his mother, from memories she won't share with him. His questions about the number tattooed on their neighbor's arm are greeted with silence; his enthusiasm for Jesus and Santa gets a cold reception. "Like the Germans," he muses about these two, "You could never be sure what they might have done before."

Mendel, Alexander Rosler's first, loosely autobiographical feature, is an evocative exploration of the humor, melancholy, and strange growing pains of the average German-Jewish-Norwegian childhood. "What do you have to remember?" Mendel's brother asks him at one point, accusingly. This gentle film provides a most affecting answer.

Also reviewed in:
NEW YORK TIMES, 3/20/98, p. E18, Stephen Holden
VARIETY, 3/17-23/97, p. 56, Deborah Young

MERCURY RISING

A Universal Pictures and Imagine Entertainment release of a Brian Grazer production. *Executive Producer:* Joseph M. Singer and Ric Kidney. *Producer:* Brian Grazer and Karen Kehela. *Director:* Harold Becker. *Screenplay:* Lawrence Konner and Mark Rosenthal. *Based on the novel "Simple Simon" by:* Ryne Douglas Pearson. *Director of Photography:* Michael Seresin. *Editor:* Peter Honess. *Music:* John Barry. *Music Editor:* Cliff Kohlweck. *Sound:* Kim Ornitz and (music) John Richards. *Sound Editor:* Terry Rodman. *Casting:* Nancy Klopper. *Production Designer:* Patrizia von Brandenstein. *Art Director:* Jim Truesdale and Steve Saklad. *Set Decorator:* Maria Nay. *Costumes:* Betsy Heimann. *Make-up:* Leonard Engleman. *Make-up (Bruce Willis):* Jerry Quist. *Stunt Coordinator:* Joe Dunne. *Running time:* 131 minutes. *MPAA Rating:* R.

CAST: Bruce Willis (Art Jeffries);   Alec Baldwin (Nicholas Kudrow);   Miko Hughes (Simon);
Chi McBride (Tommy B. Jordan); Kim Dickens (Stacey);   Robert Stanton (Dean Crandell);
Bodhi Pine Elfman (Leo Pedranski);   Carrie Preston (Emily Lang);   L. L. Ginter (Burrell);
Peter Stormare (Shayes); Kevin Conway (Lomax); John Carroll Lynch (Martin Lynch); Kelley
Hazen (Jenny Lynch);   John Doman (Supervisor Hartley);   Richard Riehle (Edgar Halstrom);
Chad Lindberg (James);   Hank Harris (Isaac);   James MacDonald (SWAT Team Leader
Francis);   Camryn Manheim (Dr. London);   Jack Conley (Detective Nichols);   Maricela Ochoa
(Charlayne);   Peter Fontana (Pasquale);   Kirk B.R. Woller (Lieutenant);   Betsy Brantley
(Special Ed Teacher #2);   Ashley Knutson (Samantha);   Tom Gallop (Medic);   Margaret
Travolta (Autism Expert Nurse); Tiffany Fraser (Night Nurse); Koko Taylor (Koko Taylor);
Matt Levert (Tommy Jordan, Jr.);   Lisa Summerour (Dana Jordan);   Barbara Alexander
(Librarian);   Gwen McGee (Security Woman);   Ned Schmidtke (Senator);   Kristina Eliot
Johnson (Special Education Teacher #1);   James Krag (Rookie Agent Roger); Wadell Brown
(Bank Security Guard);   Tim Grimm (Ted);   John Scanlon (South Dakota Helicopter Pilot);
Annabel Armour (Ruth); Brent Freeman (Marine Guard);   Gary Hand (Kudrow's Assistant);
Michael Chieffo (Hostage);   Steve Key (Cop at Lynch House); Darryl Alan Reed (Ambulance
Driver);   Steve Rankin (WGEX Helicopter Pilot);   Maureen Gallagher (Flea Market Lady);
Mark Collins (Train Conductor);   Denise Woods (Nurse in Elevator);   Kim Robillard
(Motorman).

LOS ANGELES TIMES, 4/3/98, Calendar/p. 14, Jack Mathews

[The following review by Jack Mathews appeared in a slightly different form in
NEWSDAY, 4/3/98, Part II/p. B6.]

Here's something you don't see every day, a movie about a righteous, stubbornly independent
lawman who gets in trouble with his department and has to evade his own arrest while chasing
down the real bad guys. Not every day, more like every week.

And this week, it's Harold Becker's "Mercury Rising," the latest formula thriller out of
Hollywood, starring Bruce Willis as a dog-housed FBI agent; a slumming Alec Baldwin, as a
murderously zealous National Security Agency official; and young Miko Hughes, as the 9-year-
old autistic savant whose ability to decipher a top-secret Pentagon code makes him the target of
government assassins.

Actually, calling "Mercury Rising" a formula thriller suggests notes of complexity that aren't
here. The script, by Lawrence Konner and Mark Rosenthal ("Cop and a Half," "The Beverly
Hillbillies"), from the novel "Simple Simon" by Ryne Douglas Pearson, is more like a recipe for
simple syrup. Mix a boy, a hero and a villain in a bowl of overheated sentiment and lap it up.

The ingredients are laid out with a nonchalance bordering on parody. In the opening scene,
Willis' Art Jeffries is on an undercover job when overeager colleagues jump the gun and kill five
people, including a teenage boy to whom Jeffries has formed a paternal bond. Jeffries' subsequent
outburst gets him reassigned to stakeouts.

Meanwhile, the autistic Simon Lynch, while paging through a puzzle magazine, reads an
encrypted message and calls its 1-800 number, alerting the startled Pentagon computer geeks on
the other end to the fact that the sophisticated Mercury code, as unbreakable as the Titanic was
unsinkable, has been broken. They alert their boss, Baldwin's Lt. Col. Nicholas Kudrow, who
decides that in order to protect the lives of the spies for whom the code was created, the boy must
be "erased."

That's no easy task, once Jeffries divines the conspiracy at work and, against agency orders,
appoints himself the boy's guardian, determined not to let another child die on his watch. The rest
of the movie is a frantic chase through the streets and over the rails of Chicago, interrupted only
by Jeffries' attempts to make an emotional connection with Simon.

Simon's autism is the sole distinction between "Mercury Rising" and the great wad of brainless
contemporary action-thrillers rolling off the studio assembly lines, and seems a particularly
egregious one. Developmental disorder as plot device.

Though some effort is made to show autistic behavior in a clinically accurate way—the
repetition, the fascination with moving objects, the lack of eye contact—it's too much to ask of
a child actor to portray.

Dustin Hoffman had it down pretty well in "Rain Man," and won an Oscar for it. Hughes is working so hard to stay in character, all you see is the effort. He speaks in a robotic voice, walks as if battery-operated, and he doesn't just avoid eye contact, his eyes float in the sockets, as if there were no muscles attached. Autistics do have speech and coordination problems, but Simon's problems are related to a more commonly understood condition: bad direction.

Still, Simon is the most complicated character in the film, and Hughes is at least trying. Willis and Baldwin are operating under their own battery power. They add nothing to their good cop/bad cop caricatures, and they don't even share a scene until the movie lumbers into its last, numbingly cliched act.

If James Cameron wants to convince people what a fine writer he is, he should offer "Mercury Rising" as a comparison. Next to this, "Titanic" is Dostoevsky.

NEW YORK POST, 4/3/98, p. 51, Thelma Adams

Few images are more heart-rending than a scared kid in pajamas. It's the icon of the kid-in-peril movie, and director Harold Becker milks it for all its worth in the shameless thriller "Mercury Rising."

Let's take the star of "Rising," Simon (Miko Hughes).

The 9-year-old overhears his parents' assassination. In rapid succession,. he's the target of a bullet-head National Security Agency hitman, is shanghaied in an ambulance, is nearly flattened by not one, but two Chicago commuter trains, and is rescued by renegade G-man Art Jeffries (Bruce Willis)—all while still in his jammies.

If that isn't enough to tear our hearts in two, Simon is simple. At least according to the twisted script which Lawrence Konner and Mark Rosenthal culled from Ryne Douglas Pearson's novel "Simple Simon."

How simple? Simon is autistic. Get this: He's also a genius. Oh, no, let it "Rain Man"!

The poor poster child brings on the wrath of Lt. Col. Kudrow (Alec Baldwin) and his band of government nasties—and the dubious help of Willis' fed—when he cracks a billion-dollar government code (a.k.a. Mercury) embedded in a book of puzzles.

From the opening standoff to the final shower of glass, nothing is plausible in "Mercury Rising." Baldwin does his demon dimple act. Lone wolf Willis gets in some close scrapes, none closer than a buzzed hairstyle that rivals Demi's 'do in "G.I. Jane."

But did we really have to watch a young actor struggling to play a handicapped child for two hours to get off? Is this entertainment? Is this a body-strewn path to a broader awareness of autism? I think not.

Don't call the movie "Mercury Rising." Call it "Mercury Poisoning."

SIGHT AND SOUND, 10/98, p. 46, Andrew O'Hehir

South Dakota. FBI agent Art Jeffries is undercover with a group of anti-government militia men robbing a bank. The militia members, including two teenage boys, die in a botched FBI raid. Later in Chicago, a now psychologically unstable Jeffries is reassigned to routine duties. Investigating a missing-child case, he encounters Simon Lynch, an autistic boy whose parents have been murdered. Simon, a whiz at puzzles, solves a cryptogram used by government agents to test an expensive new secret code called Mercury. Fearing he may jeopardise Mercury's security, Kudrow, the head of the Mercury project, wants Simon killed. With the help of Tommy, a friendly FBI agent, and Stacey, a stranger he meets on the street, Jeffries and Simon stay one step ahead of Burrell, Kudrow's hired gun.

When the two cryptographers who designed Mercury learn what is happening and try to help Simon and Jeffries, Kudrow has them killed. But one of them has written a letter to Jeffries linking Kudrow to the murder of Simon's parents. He takes the letter to the Senate committee charged with overseeing Mercury. Kudrow learns of the plan and tries to kidnap the boy. Tommy uses the letter to convince his FBI superiors to fight Kudrow. In a shootout atop a skyscraper, Burrell and Kudrow are killed and Simon is rescued.

With its propulsive pacing and *noir*-inflected photography, *Mercury Rising* provides an agreeable, rapidly forgettable two hours in the dark. If its look and tone are rather too close to *The Fugitive,* at least it pays obeisance to a movie that people genuinely enjoyed. But the film's greatest strength actually exposes its greatest weakness. *Mercury Rising* features what may well be Bruce Willis' most compelling screen performance. Playing a haunted variation on his brooding man-of-action persona, Willis never winks or smirks at us behind the story's back. However, perhaps as a result, it comes off as a grim, dour, fundamentally trivial affair, neither good enough to be taken seriously nor relaxed enough to be any fun.

That's a shame, because as Willis demonstrates here, he is capable of doing a great deal with very little. Everything about agent Art Jeffries, from his slouch to his shabby clothing, his patchy, thinning hair and the pained gestures he makes while popping pills, bespeaks a lonely bachelor on a downward slope. It's entirely believable that this middle-aged failure drowning in his own hopelessness would seize on an uncommunicative boy as his lifeline to the world. Given the emotional context created by the powerful acting of Willis and young Miko Hughes (an undeniably eerie screen presence), the tedious flashbacks supplied by director Harold Becker *(Malice, City Hall* of the South Dakota massacre which screwed Jeffries up merely substitute banal clichés about trauma for genuine psychological complexity.

Adding to this banality, Alec Baldwin performs with a laziness that is all-too characteristic of the film. His hair styled in a Clintonian wave and reading his formula villain lines in flat, abstracted tones, Baldwin nonetheless gives a convincing impression of a Washington apparatchik. In one scene meant to be a key confrontation between Jeffries and Kudrow, Willis and Baldwin never appear in the same shot. Even if a viewer doesn't actually notice such trickery, it surely robs the drama of any intensity or verisimilitude it may have built up.

Mercury Rising employs the kind of mirroring device frequently encountered in thrillers: just as Jeffries' fragile emotional state is reflected in Simon's, the apparently irrational paranoia of the South Dakota militia men is echoed when Jeffries finds himself pursued by fellow agents of his own government. The film's attempt to resolve these doublings is cursory in the extreme—neither Simon nor his protector is miraculously restored to emotional health, and there's no indication that the US security apparatus will power down its nefarious operations—but this seems less like a dose of salutary realism than more of the garden-variety anomie of our age. This is, after all, the kind of movie where an intelligence agency employs just one man to execute a complicated kidnap murder assignment, where a senior spook explains the details of his plan in great detail to subordinates he doesn't trust, and where the committed effort of one actor only serves to highlight the fundamental shoddiness of the whole enterprise.

VILLAGE VOICE, 4/14/98, p. 64, Gary Dauphin

A by-the-numbers technothriller, the new Bruce Willis vehicle *Mercury Rising* pretends to aim for geopolitical complexity but mostly wants to wring cheap tears. The "Mercury" of the title is a cryptographic algorithm spawned in the bowels of the National Security Agency, a presumably unbreakable code designed to protect major American secrets. In the film's first five minutes, this code is miraculously broken by Simon (Miko Hughes), an autistic nine-year-old. The NSA, headed by a blithely evil Alec Baldwin, sends the spooks out to "neutralize" the problem, leaving Simon an orphan in the hands of FBI agent Willis, a downer-popping borderline psycho who has a thing for saving troubled kids.

Despite a few neat action sequences, *Mercury* is utterly unremarkable and consistently underdirected (the workings of Simon's ability are set up exactly like those of Steve Austin's bionic eye, right down to extreme close-ups of his iris and mechanical sound effects). Still, there is something mildly affecting in the relationship between Simon and his protector. Hughes does well as a terrified little boy with crossed wires, Simon's closed-in neuropsychological trauma concisely drawn. And you'd have to be an imitational rock not to fall momentarily for Willis, ever the big brutish lug trying desperately to be good.

Also reviewed in:
CHICAGO TRIBUNE, 4/3/98, Friday/p. A, Mark Caro
NEW YORK TIMES, 4/3/98, p. E14, Stephen Holden
VARIETY, 4/6-12/98, p. 47, Todd McCarthy
WASHINGTON POST, 4/3/98, p. F7, Stephen Hunter
WASHINGTON POST, 4/3/98, Weekend/p. 53, Michael O'Sullivan

MERRY WAR, A

A First Look Pictures release of an Overseas Filmgroup presentation in association with the Arts Council of England and Bonaparte Films of a UBA/Sentinel Films production. *Executive Producer:* Robert Bierman and John Wolstenholme. *Producer:* Peter Shaw. *Director:* Robert Bierman. *Screenplay:* Alan Plater. *Based on the novel "Keep the Aspidistra Flying:* by: George Orwell. *Director of Photography:* Giles Nuttgens. *Editor:* Bill Wright. *Music:* Mike Batt. *Sound:* Patrick Quirk and (music) Haydn Benall. *Casting:* Michelle Guish. *Production Designer:* Sarah Greenwood. *Art Director:* Philip Robinson. *Costumes:* James Keast. *Make-up:* Marilyn MacDonald. *Running time:* 101 minutes. *MPAA Rating:* Not Rated.

CAST: Richard E. Grant (Gordon Comstock); Helena Bonham Carter (Rosemary); Jim Carter (Erskine); Harriet Walter (Julia Comstock); Lill Roughly (Mrs. Trilling); Julian Wadham (Ravelston); Lesley Vickerage (Hermoine); John Clegg (McKechnie); Barbara Leigh Hunt (Mrs. Wisebeach); Grant Parsons (Beautiful Young Man); Dorothea Alexander (Old Woman); Peter Stockbridge (Old Man); Malcolm Sinclair (Paul Doring); Derek Smee (Lecturer); Ben Miles (Ravenscroft Waiter); Richard Dixon (Head Waiter); Roger Morlidge (Policeman); Roland Oliver (Magristrate Croom); Bill Wallis (Cheeseman); Liz Smith (Mrs. Meakin); Roger Frost (Orton the Undertaker); Harri Alexander (Dora); Lucy Speed (Factory Girl); Joan Blackman (Librarian); Roy Evans (Cabby); Maggie McCarthy (Customer).

CHRISTIAN SCIENCE MONITOR, 8/28/98, p. B3, David Sterritt

"And now abideth faith, hope, money, these three; but the greatest of these is money." That wry "adaptation" appears at the beginning of George Orwell's novel "Keep the Aspidistra Flying," a keen-witted satire of modern materialism. The movie version, "A Merry War," retains much of the novel's sharp skepticism about the power of money, although filmmaker Robert Bierman shares Orwell's reluctance to pursue his observations all the way to their logical conclusions.

The hero is a young poet who thinks about money all the time. This isn't because he wants it—poets are above that sort of thing, in his opinion—but because it permeates his professional and private lives. He believes it's a want of money that distracts him from writing, keeps him from marrying his girlfriend, and makes him uncomfortable around his wealthy best friend.

The only solution, he decides, is to declare war on the awful stuff. And if that lands him in the gutter, so much the better, because he'll be free of temptation and ambivalence in that relaxing place.

The filmmakers do a merry job of chronicling our hero's campaign, helped by rollicking performances from Richard E. Grant as the poet and Helena Bonham Carter as his sympathetic but aggravated sweetheart.

What ultimately reduces the movie's value is its too-faithful adherence to Orwell's book, which concludes with an abrupt happy ending unworthy of the author who galvanized world literature with "1984" and "Animal Farm," cautionary classics to this day.

NEW YORK, 9/7/98, p. 50, David Denby

In *A Merry War*, Richard E. Grant plays Gordon Comstock, a thirtyish moth-eaten failed poet who rails against the moneyed classes and ascribes all his failings to poverty. Gordon, the hero of this Robert Bierman adaptation of the early (1936) George Orwell novel *Keep the Aspidistra Flying*, could easily have become a bore or merely pitiful. The period is Depression-era London, and Gordon, of course, has a point: It is easier to become a man of letters if you have money. But it is also easier if you have talent, and Gordon obviously has neither. Grant *(Withnail & I)*, a lean, vivacious actor, delivers his lines with an exuberant theatricality—Grant has no interest in realism—and his anger and outraged vanity keep the movie aloft. Too much Orwellian masochism or withering bluntness would have been a mistake—an immersion in the grinding unhappiness of the Depression itself. Grant's baleful stare and ripe, ranting style turn the movie into comedy.

This is the same Robert Bierman who made the wonderfully goofy mock-horror film *Vampire's Kiss*, with Nicolas Cage, in 1988, and the only link I can find between the movies is intelligence. Bierman slightly exaggerates the period manners—he puts everything into quotation marks so we can morely relish the thirties as style. Gordon's upper-class socialist friend Ravelston (Julian Wadham), who publishes Gordon's poems and throws him a loan now and then, is so relaxed and debonair he seems to have been born in a dressing gown. And Ravelston's mistress, a self-consciously daring woman of the world, speaks of her orgasms with calculated naughtiness. The middle classes are stuffy and inquisitive, the working-class characters generous and honest. Orwell's socialist sentiment is all there, and also his honesty. Gordon is unspeakably lucky to have a girlfriend (Helena Bonham Carter) who, despite everything, loves him deeply. The movie's modest affirmation at the end, when a homely aspidistra plant becomes a symbol of life and continuity—the connection, for Gordon, with the vital existence that has eluded him—is surprisingly touching. *A Merry War* is a very small movie, but it gets everything right.

NEW YORK POST, 8/28/98, p. 61, Thelma Adams

George Orwell, the English author of "Animal Farm" and "1984," is better known for political allegory than satirical romance. There are no despotic pigs or Big Brothers in "A Merry War." There's not even much of a war as England muddles through the valley between the Great War and World War II.

Adapted by scenarist Alan Plater from "Keep the Aspidistra Flying," Orwell's semi-autobiographical 1936 novel, and directed by Robert Bierman, "A Merry War" is about class conflict and the battle between the sexes as seen through the eyes of a minor English poet. While the dialogue is merry, the compromises an artist makes to survive give the story satiric bite.

Poet Gordon Comstock (Richard E. Grant) is full of himself. Having published a grim volume entitled "Mice" to meager acclaim, Comstock ditches his successful London copywriting job. To pay the rent, he takes up bookselling and supplements his diminished wages by "sponging" off his sister, his girlfriend and his publisher.

Comstock proclaims himself an artiste with no class consciousness, but he can't escape the fact that he envies the rich, was born to the upper middle, and is rapidly failing into squalor.

A former co-worker, Rosemary, has the weighty task of being Comstock's loyal girlfriend and voice of reason. As she tells her beau, "You make the mess, I clean it up. That's the usual arrangement."

As the virginal Rosemary, Helena Bonham Carter ("The Wings of the Dove") tries desperately to seem plain. She delivers refreshingly adult dialogue with a stiff upper lip, enviable posture and dagger-thrust wit. Bonham Carter is wonderful without appearing so.

Grant, who has repeatedly played the fop and, most recently, the comic foil in the Spice Girls' screen mishap, is well cast as a poetic hero in the anti-Byronic mode.

That "A Merry War" ends happily is no cop-out, but another edge in the satire. Gordon gleefully abandons his art and toasts his return to respectability by buying an aspidistra, the lackluster houseplant that, for Orwell, symbolized the boorish middle classes.

Should we take Comstock's fall in poetry and rise in copywriting at face value? No. Big Brother Orwell is watching, after all, and he went on to write "Animal Farm" and "1984," not ads for Bovril.

NEWSDAY, 8/28/98, Part II/p. B8, John Anderson

George Orwell knew a few things about being down and out ("Down and Out in Paris and London," 1933), a few things about ruined ideals ("Animal Farm" and "Stalinists") and few presciently sardonic ideas about the future ("1984"). But he'd been a success for years before the publication of his early novel "Keep the Aspidistra Flying" and people realized how precociously and self-deprecatingly funny he could be, especially about writers.

"A Merry War" is no better a title than "Keep the Aspidistra Flying" (Orwell's third novel, published in 1936), but it's no worse, either, and at least it's pronounceable. The point is that Robert Bierman ("Vampire's Kiss") has fashioned a dryly witty and moving film out of Orwell's book, with Richard E. Grant as the poet Gordon Comstock, a fabulist and undiagnosed megalomaniac whose modest book of verse gets an encouraging review in the Times Literary Supplement, prompting him to quit his job at a London ad agency and become a bum.

In Gordon's view, he is now "a poet and a free man." Free, yes, from food, baths and decent lodging. A poet? William Carlos Williams was a doctor, T.S. Eliot was a banker and a publisher, and many of the rest of Gordon's contemporary wordsmiths were independently wealthy, or eccentric loons. Gordon is a middle-class dreamer who's chasing a myth, a romanticized image of poet as vagabond, which is not the same as writing poetry. He's an absurdity, frankly, a man who on one hand bemoans his lack of money—and his lack of sex because he has no money—while tossing away liquidity with the other.

And he might have been an extremely dislikable absurdity, if not for the warmly hysterical performance of Richard E. Grant. Grant is best known for Bruce Davidson's cult favorite "Withnail and I" but his particular gifts have subsequently been diverted toward such disasters as "Hudson Hawk" and, more recently, "Spice World." What Bierman's done for Richard E. Grant in "A Merry War" is what he did for Nicolas Cage in "Vampire's Kiss," which is put an unusual actor in the appropriate role (and may Grant have Cage's subsequent good fortune, but no "Snake Eyes" please).

Grant hardly does it singlehandedly, however. As Rosemary, the ad agency artist who supports almost all of Gordon's half-baked crusade, Helena Bonham Carter is a wonder of common sense and understated sex. And it is, of course, good to see her displaying what a splendid actress she can be, even when Merchant/Ivory aren't peering around the next Georgian pillar.

Grant and Bonham Carter are so wonderful together precisely because they are so different, both physically and temperamentally, and because Rosemary is so stalwart even though Gordon's Quixotic art quest is so antithetical to her worldview. They can't—and she won't—ignore the fact that they're middle class and British. Although the intramural class element is unspoken, Gordon begins to carry the air of contagion about him. Members of England's middle class don't chuck it all for art, after all; the system is too unforgiving and eager for casualties. When he gets a $50 check from a Californian review—thus making him a poet with an "international reputation"—he takes Rosemary and his wealthy publisher friend Erskine (the likable Jim Carter) to a wildly overpriced restaurant, gets stinking drunk and winds up in jail, thus cementing his status as nouveau boob. And destroying whatever shabby respectability he still maintained.

As Gordon grows gaunt and unwashed, and sinks to the lowest end of London life, he acquires an aura of saintliness about him. There's comfort in the fact that he can sink no further, and Grant dredges up in Gordon a giddy fatalism that's both troubling and endearing. This is the film's best section. Gordon's not writing anymore, but he does get sex. And sex, as it will, changes everything. His old job beckons. And the irony of it all makes for Gordon a situation that's not exactly surreal, but is certainly Orwellian.

SIGHT AND SOUND, 11/97, p. 44, Claire Monk

London, 1934. Gordon Comstock is a successful copywriter at a publicity company where he is teamed with his graphic-artist girlfriend Rosemary. Unhappy, he wants to be a full-time poet, so when promotion is offered he resigns. Comstock visits his upper-class socialist publisher Ravelston. To help, Ravelston finds Comstock a job in a Hampstead bookshop at half his old pay. Comstock blames Rosemary's refusal to have sex with him on his poverty and her middle-class prissiness. They fall out. He rents a room in a boarding-house and finds in it an aspidistra—a plant he loathes for its respectable connotations. Rosemary persuades him that a day in the country will help their relationship. After a drunken lunch, Rosemary agrees to sex in the woods, but refuses when Comstock has no condoms.

Comstock is paid $50 for a poem by a US magazine. Elated, he takes Rosemary and Ravelston to dinner at an expensive restaurant. Over dinner, Comstock gets offensively drunk, gropes Rosemary, drags Ravelston to a pub, uses up his $50, falls down and wakes in a police cell charged with "taking an aspidistra without the owner's consent". Ravelston pays his fine, but he loses the bookshop job and his room. Rosemary is promoted and, despairingly, dumps Comstock. Ravelston finds Comstock another, even worse-paid, bookshop job. There, with digs in a filthy attic where even prostitutes may visit, Comstock is happy. Rosemary, determined to learn the worst, visits and makes love with him. She vows never to return, but she discovers she's pregnant. Suddenly, Comstock is keen on middle-class life. He returns to his copywriting job, marries Rosemary and sets up home with her and an aspidistra in the suburbs.

From its crisp, period title graphics and pleasurably painstaking art direction to its equally crisp 30s dialogue, consistently well-judged performances and literary origins (George Orwell's novel was published in 1936), *Keep the Aspidistra Flying* is the kind of British film that oozes 'quality'. There is nothing really objectionable about the project—indeed, Alan Plater's meticulous script, which succeeds in capturing both the sourness of Orwell's prose and the (to 90s ears, weird) archaisms of 30s speech, is superb—but it leaves almost no lasting impression.

This forgettableness raises awkward questions about what we mean by, and how little we expect from, "quality British production at its best" (to quote the London Film Festival's 1997 programme). In this case the answer is clearly not intensity of cinematic, emotional, intellectual or even comic effect. (Though the film is intended as a comedy, its burnout is too often theoretical rather than laugh-aloud funny.)

Aspidistra's lack of impact has worrying implications given the tone and content of the original book. Based closely on his own experiences when working in a bookshop to support his writing, Orwell's novel is a bitter, vituperative rant. The film reshapes this black invective into romantic comedy, feminising the original story to allow a more active role to Comstock's girlfriend Rosemary. (She represents the pragmatism to which idealist Comstock is opposed, until her pregnancy makes him accede.) In the process, Orwell's themes (the stultifying effects of the class system on human creativity and libido; the literary world as an Old Etonian closed shop which a middle-class hopeful like Comstock cannot expect to penetrate) retain their centrality but are oddly neutralised. Nothing important seems to be at stake.

The failure is partly due to aesthetic and thematic *déjà vu* and partly to the casting. A key problem is that the liberal-bourgeois preoccupations which are supposed to provide *Aspidistra* with its central dramatic substance are now such well-worn themes of British literary drama, the film risks seeming like a pastiche. Robert Bierman has directed the *Dracula*-variant *Vampire's Kiss,* and such dramas as *Clarissa* and *The Moonstone* for the BBC. However, his direction lacks the self-awareness either to avoid this pitfall or to make an ironic virtue of it (as Ang Lee and Emma Thompson did in *Sense and Sensibility).*   An array of scene-stealing London locations does nothing to dispel the aura of unreality surrounding Comstock's poverty and despair.

This unreality is intensified by Richard E. Grant's performance as Comstock. In Jane Campion's recent *The Portrait of a Lady,* Grant proved himself capable of pathos and restraint. Here, his treatment of Comstock's escalating excesses veers close to his histrionics in *Withnail & I.* At times this is very funny—Comstock's abuse of the hated aspidistra plant in his room ("Look at this, you verdant bastard!") could have been written with Withnail in mind. But Grant's playing has a damaging side-effect: if Comstock's denouncements of the middle classes (rhymed in one of his poems with "horses' arses") are nothing but Withnail-like rants, then it follows that we can safely ignore them.

Perhaps this retreat into empty parody is an admission by Bierman that *Aspidistra*'s 30s preoccupations are increasingly hard to relate to in today's Britain where attitudes have radically changed. While the fashion world's current obsession with aristocratic models suggests that old hierarchies don't exactly die, the thought of, say, Damien Hirst or Will Self agonising over the conflict between filthy lucre and their art seems as quaint today as *Aspidistra*'s other core premise that middle-class girls don't like sex. As Comstock's down-to-earth ad agency boss puts it: "Poetry or advertising—they're the same words in a different order".

VILLAGE VOICE, 9/1/98, p. 109, Amy Taubin

Ambivalence about the comforts, constrictions, and compromises of bourgeois life is the subject of Robert Bierman's *A Merry War,* an adaptation of George Orwell's *Keep the Aspidistra Flying,* a satire about class and money in England between the two world wars. Richard E. Grant plays a successful advertising copywriter who quits his job to become a poet, descending from genteel poverty to bawdy, flea-infested poverty in the process. Helena Bonham Carter plays the coworker who loves him and tries to turn him into a proper husband and father. *A Merry War* is decently acted (Grant is amusingly curdled, Bonham Carter is sensible and efficient even when she's lying in a damp field in her underwear), but as filmmaking, it's too staid to make much of an impression.

Also reviewed in:
CHICAGO TRIBUNE, 8/28/98, Friday/p. H, Mark Caro
NEW REPUBLIC, 9/7/98, p. 24, Stanley Kauffmann
NEW YORK TIMES, 8/28/98, p. E10, Stephen Holden
WASHINGTON POST, 9/18/98, Weekend/p. 58, Stephen Hunter
VARIETY, 10/6-12/97, p. 57, Derek Elley

MIDAQ ALLEY

An Imcine presentation of an Alameda Films production in association with Fondo de Formento a la Calidad Cinematografica and Universidad de Guadalajara. *Producer:* Alfredo Ripstein, Jr. *Director:* Jorge Fons. *Screenplay (Spanish with English subtitles):* Vicente Lenero. *Based on the novel "Midaq Alley" by:* Naguib Mahfouz. *Director of Photography:* Carlos Marcovich. *Editor:* Carlos Savage. *Music:* Lucia Alvarez. *Sound:* David Baksht. *Running time:* 140 minutes. *MPAA Rating:* Not Rated.

CAST: Ernesto Gomez Cruz (Don Rutilio); Maria Rojo (Dona Cata); Salma Hayek (Alma); Bruno Bichir (Abel); Delia Casanova (Eusebia); Daniel Gimenez Cacho (Jose Luis); Claudio Obregon (Don Fidel); Luis Felipe Tovar (Guicho); Tiare Scanda (Maru); Margarita Sanz (Susanita); Juan Manuel Bernal (Chava).

NEW YORK POST, 4/24/98, p. 48, Larry Worth

Self-sacrificing moms. Good girls gone bad. Victimized spinsters.

It's the stuff of weepy soap operas from the '30s and '40s, when the likes of "Mildred Pierce," "Stella Dallas" and "Imitation of Life" had lines forming around the block. Well, those days may be long gone, but modern-day knockoffs like "Midaq Alley" still have a lurid appeal.

Based on Nobel laureate Naguib Mahfouz's novel of the same name, the screenplay concerns a dozen-odd principals of a poverty-stricken section of Mexico City, nicknamed Midaq Alley. There, unrequited love is in full bloom for those of all ages, sexes and orientations.

For example, a 50ish father chastises his grown son about spending too much time with a boyhood pal. But dad's the one who's having a gay old time. In the meantime, the son has the hots for a pretty neighbor, but she's got her eyes on bigger fish.

And the rich but homely landlady who owns this Latina Cannery Row dreams of passion with a thieving bartender. But he's only drawn to her cash drawer.

Sure, most of the couplings, breakups and makeups are predictable. Almost without exception, each major development is obvious to viewers long before it becomes reality.

But director Jorge Fons shakes things up by dividing the plot into separate episodes. All begin with the same cantina-set scene, then focus on different stories. So the main characters of Tale One serve as supporting players in Tale Two. Ditto for Tale Three, and on and on.

Is it all too much at nearly 2½ hours? That's a given. But within the ever-expanding framework, some fine acting gets showcased. A radiant Salma Hayek stands out as a confused vixen who discovers tragedy early on, then learns how to exploit it. Also effective are three-dimensional turns from Ernesto Gomez Cruz, Margarita Sanz and Maria Rojo.

Granted, the end result will never be confused with art. But in playing its cliches for all they're worth, "Midaq Alley" is an acceptable setting for some old-fashioned melodrama.

VILLAGE VOICE, 4/28/98, p. 80, Ed Morales

Based on the Cairo-set novel by Naguib Mahfouz, Jorge Fons's *Midaq Alley* adopts the setting of a poor Mexico City neighborhood so seamlessly you'd think the original book was part of the

Latin American fiction boom. One of the best Mexican films since *Like Water for Chocolate*, *Midaq Alley* is only now having an American theatrical run. But unlike its predecessor, *Midaq Alley* is a product of a more risk-taking strain of Mexico City's art scene—the film features a time-bending narrative, the cinematography of *Who the Hell is Juliette?* director Carlos Marcovich, and a quirky performance by *Danzon* star Maria Rojo.

Told from the perspective of three different characters in overlapping segments, and veering off into tangential plots in each one, the film flirts with being a latter-day *Rashomon* as it exploits an array of societal taboos. Fons likes to play with appearances, and gently scolds the viewer for making assumptions. Seemingly gay loners are just close friends who share a lust for the local women; the biggest patriarch of the bunch is a lecherous lover of young boys; a virginal teenager becomes a high-class coke whore. But as *Midaq Alley*'s ensemble cast expertly reveals how incestuously the characters are involved, a running theme emerges: the relentless victimization of the neighborhood women by rogues, lechers, and even well-meaning boyfriends.

Salma Hayek manages to dominate the film with a riveting, nuanced performance as Alma, a modern Mexicana who is torn between just wanting to get laid and the need to be a good girl. She is at once a miserable failure and a hero for deciding to make explicit her role as a prostitute and turn her back on the hypocrisy of morally acceptable marriage. Conversely, Abel (Bruno Bichir), her lowly haircutter suitor, tries to be the modern, sensitive male, but his chivalric earnestness does nothing to liberate Almita from her sexual prison. His ultimate act of self-sacrifice is little more than a macho ego trip.

Apart from its intricate story line, *Midaq Alley* is a vibrant portrait of millennial Mexico City, with its free-wheeling slang, circus-garbed, fire-swallowing street beggars, and Greek chorus of domino players. The feeling of economic uncertainty is palpable, intensifying the sex-for-money equation, but the bottom line is just how much it's still a man's world. While it may seem strange that an Egyptian novel could work so well in Mexico, perhaps the centuries-long Arabic conquest of Iberia had a defining role in developing what we understand to be macho.

Also reviewed in:
NEW YORK TIMES, 4/24/98, p. E12, Lawrence van Gelder
VARIETY, 3/20-26/95, p. 51, Joe Leydon

MIGHTY, THE

A Miramax Films release of a Scholastic Productions/Simon Fields production. *Executive Producer:* Bob Weinstein, Harvey Weinstein, and Julie Goldstein. *Producer:* Jane Startz and Simon Fields. *Director:* Peter Chelsom. *Screenplay:* Charles Leavitt. *Based on the novel "Freak the Mighty" by:* Rodman Philbrick. *Director of Photography:* John De Borman. *Editor:* Martin Walsh. *Music:* Trevor Jones. *Music Editor:* Jim Harrison. *Sound:* Bruce Carwardine and (music) Simon Rhodes. *Sound Editor:* Paul Clay. *Casting:* Barbara Cohen and Mary Gail Artz. *Production Designer:* Caroline Hanania. *Art Director:* Dennis Davenport. *Set Decorator:* Cal Loucks. *Special Effects:* Michael Kavanagh. *Costumes:* Marie Sylvie Deveau. *Make-up:* Christine Hart. *Make-up (Sharon Stone):* Tricia Sawyer. *Stunt Coordinator:* Rick Forsayath. *Running time:* 100 minutes. *MPAA Rating:* PG-13.

CAST: Harry Dean Stanton (Grim); Gena Rowlands (Gram); Elden Henson (Maxwell Kane); Douglas Bisset (Homeless Man); Joe Perino (Blade); Dov Tiefenbach (Doghouse Boy #1); Michael Colton (Doghouse Boy #2); Eve Crawford (Mrs. Donelli); Kieran Culkin (Kevin Dillon); Sharon Stone (Gwen Dillon); John Bourgeois (Mr. Sacker); Bruce Tubbe (Officer); Rudy Webb (Mr. Hampton); Ron Nigrini (Man in Diner); Nadia Litz (Girl in Diner); Gillian Anderson (Loretta Lee); Meatloaf (Iggy); Serena Pruyn (Girl in Hall); Telmo Miranda (Boy in Hall); Jordan Hughes (Denardo); Jennifer Lewis (Mrs. Addison); Bryon Bully (Fat Boy); Charlaine Porter (Girl with Limp); James Gandolfini (Kenny Kane); Lisa Marie Chen (Girl in Cafeteria); Lisa Mininni (Cashier); Ann Chiu (Nurse); Carl Marotte (Doctor); Nora Sheehan (Police Woman); Sophie Bennett (Little Girl); Willam Van Allen (Laundry Worker).

LOS ANGELES TIMES, 10/9/98, Calendar/p. 2, Kenneth Turan

"The Mighty" is based on a book called "Freak the Mighty," and that small but telling change is as good an indication as any of how the forces of conventionality have hamstrung what is in many ways a quirky and imaginative piece of work.

Directed by Peter Chelsom, whose previous credits are "Hear My Song" and the fiercely eccentric "Funny Bones," "The Mighty" seems at war with itself. Adapted from Rodman Philbrick's award-winning young adult novel about the unlikely alliance of two miserable 14-year-olds, the film is itself an unlikely alliance of earnest, well-meaning sentimentality and genuinely magical and moving filmmaking.

"The Mighty's" script (by Charles Leavitt, who wrote Michael Cimino's thankfully little-seen "Sunchaser") creates a literary overlay for the project, breaking the action into chapters and making extensive use of voice-over by Maxwell Kane, a very unhappy narrator.

Max (Elden Henson) has reasons to be woebegone. His mother is dead, his father, "Killer" Kane, is in prison, and he lives in Cincinnati in the basement room ("the down under") of the house belonging to the overmatched grandparents he puckishly calls Gram (Gena Rowlands) and Grim (Harry Dean Stanton).

Wait, there's more. Max is large for his age (though nowhere near as gargantuan as the voice-over insists) and his passive nature has made him an easy target for the group of local toughs called the Doghouse boys. Plus he's failed seventh grade two years running, with a third failure a distinct possibility. No wonder he says, "I never had a brain until Freak came along and lent me his."

Freak, known to his mother (Sharon Stone) as Kevin Dillon (Kieran Culkin), is the kid who moves in next door. Not your ordinary neighbor, but a brainy type who is hunched over and fitted with large leg braces and crutches because of a degenerative disease called Morquio's syndrome.

Kevin and Max do not take to each other at once, but when Kevin is assigned to be the large boy's remedial reading tutor, he naturally starts Max on his own favorite book, a collection of stories of King Arthur and the Knights of the Round Table that emphasizes the notion that "a knight proves his worthiness through his deeds."

A chance encounter with the Doghouse boys leads to the defining moment in the friendship, when Max suddenly hoists Kevin up on his shoulders. The team that results, which the pair name Freak the Mighty, is a natural fit. As glib Kevin puts it, "You need a brain and I need legs and the Wizard of Oz doesn't live in Cincinnati."

Joined this way, Freak the Mighty dedicates itself to fulfilling Kevin's fantasy of being a Knight of the Round Table. To his dreamer's eyes, "there are fair maidens to rescue and dragons to slay," even if the maidens turn out to be shopworn items like Loretta Lee ("The X-Files'" Gillian Anderson) with disturbing links to dark episodes in Max's past.

The appeal of this scenario to every picked-on kid who had visions of being powerful is as strong here as it presumably was in the book, and there are moments when it comes off beautifully. Actors Henson and Culkin (one of Macaulay's younger siblings) work extremely well together and help make what is essentially a literary conceit believable on film.

Also appealing is the deft way Chelsom repeatedly intercuts snippets of the knights of the boys' imaginations with their more mundane adventures in Cincinnati. This is a director who understands the sense of wonder, as well as one who genuinely cherishes each and every offbeat character moment he can manage to shoehorn into the production.

Everything about "The Mighty," however, is not pleasantly wacky. Though Stone (whose production company served as co-executive producer) does a solid job as Kevin's mother, her character would be richer if it had been allowed a quirk or two. And good as Culkin is, the film's determination to turn Kevin into a miniature wiseguy with a nonstop flow of snappy patter is as wearing here as a similar scenario was in "Simon Birch."

So, regrettably, this film tends to aim too patly at the heart and get too pleased with itself in the process. The best thing about "The Mighty," however, is that it is its own best antidote. If you stick with it long enough, you will gain sympathy for its quixotic attempt to do things differently and wonder exactly what director Chelsom might be up to next.

NEW YORK POST, 10/9/98, p. 47, Thelma Adams

"My father was a magician. He heard the words birth defect, and he disappeared," Kevin tells his new best friend, Max, in "The Mighty."

Thirteen-year-old Kevin (the elfin Kieran Culkin) has this year's fad illness, Morquio's Syndrome, a degenerative disease associated with premature aging. Like Simon Birch, he compensates for his twisted body and weak legs with a sharp tongue and wicked sense of humor.

Max (the hulking Elden Henson) has more body than he knows what to do with. He's a gentle giant, bully meat until Kevin comes along and inspires him to stand up—with the frail boy on his shoulders.

Inspired by Arthurian legend, the pair forms "The Mighty" or, like the title of Rodman Philbrick's teen novel, "Freak the Mighty", a modern-day knight in the land of Cleve.

The boys' exploits to combat injustice—and simply survive in a harsh blue-collar landscape—are sharply rendered by director Peter Chelsom ("Hear My Song" and, a personal favorite, the Jerry Lewis black comedy "Funny Bones").

The movie deftly weaves humor and pathos as the two navigate Cincinnati and their own individual demons. Max is also technically fatherless—his dad (James Gandolfini) is upstate for murder.

Chelsom, working from Charles Leavift's well-structured adaptation, doesn't lard the story with sentimentality. He does treat himself to flights of Monty Pythonesque fantasy as medieval knights in full regalia repeatedly pop up on the streets and bridges of Cincinnati.

The supporting cast is magnificent. Sharon Stone plays Kevin's mom with the unfussy beauty of well-worn denim, easily making the transition from femme fatale to motherhood that's been heralded in the press.

Gena Rowlands and Harry Dean Stanton play Max's parents; X-Files star Gillian Anderson shows off her wild side, perhaps too wild, as a local chippie.

The main stumbling block—besides a clunky voiceover narration and clumsy multiple endings—is who's the audience?

It's not young children. Max's paroled father leads "The Mighty" into dark territory. And, like Simon Birch, a Morquio diagnosis in Act One promises one young actor a noble death scene.

And it's not for Stone fans. Those waiting for the diva to remove layers of sweaters and stretch will be disappointed.

But the dark comedy's strong message of friendship's healing power and the importance of good deeds coupled with appealing performances make "The Mighty" uplifting entertainment.

NEWSDAY, 10/9/98, Part II/p. B7, Jack Mathews

While reviewing "Simon Birch" a few weeks ago, I resisted the urge to warn people away from that sappy tale of juvenile friendship and await "The Mighty," a movie I saw at the Cannes Film Festival in May but which wasn't due to be released here for a month. Though the films share several themes, it's not fair to compare one to the other until both can be seen. Now, they can. "The Mighty," adapted from Rodman Philbrick's award-winning Scholastic novella "Freak the Mighty," is opening in theaters in New York and Los Angeles today and expanding across the country in the next two weeks, by which time it may have already been accepted as a young adult classic.

Beautifully directed by England's gifted Peter Chelsom ("Hear My Song," "Funny Bones"), "The Mighty" is a fable about friendship, self-esteem and empowerment. It's the story of two adolescent outsiders, a timid, slow-witted giant named Maxwell (Elden Henson) and his new next-door neighbor Kevin (Kieran Culkin), a young genius and devotee of Arthurian legend whose growth is stunted by a degenerative, inevitably fatal bone disease.

To their cruel classmates, they are Frankenstein and Igor, but when Max impulsively lifts Kevin onto his shoulders one day, merging Max brawn and Kevin's brains, they proclaim themselves Freak the Mighty, the tallest, toughest, smartest kid in Cincinnati.

The parallels to "Simon Birch," which is based on a fragment of John Irving's "A Prayer for Owen Meany," are lifesize. Both stories are about the powerful bonds of friendship between outsiders struggling against personal and physical problems. Both feature a bright, diminutive, disabled character paired up with a boy carrying a serious grudge against his absent father. Both are told as flashbacks, by one of the friends recalling the other's life-changing impact on him.

Where Simon Birch made his friend believe in God, Kevin introduces Max to the noble glories of King Arthur. This is tricky material, in both instances. You can play it straight and leap into the sentimental quicksand, as the makers of "Simon Birch" did, hoping the audience follows you in. Or, you can elevate it to myth, heighten the reality, and ask the audience to suspend its disbelief and accept the sentiment as a literary gift. Such is the case with "The Mighty."

The latter is made easy by the quirky-comic writing of Philbrick and his adapter Charles Leavitt; by the high-wire direction of Chelsom, who keeps the film steadily balanced between reality and fantasy, and comedy and tragedy; and by the superb performances of a cast that includes Sharon Stone, as Kevin's nourishing mom, and Harry Dean Stanton and Gena Rowlands as Max' concerned but flummoxed grandparents.

But the greatest credit goes to the young costars. Henson, an alumnus of Disney's "Mighty Ducks" movies, has the tougher assignment, playing a kid whose confusion and conflicting emotions simmer beneath his frightened, nearly mute manner. As a child, Max watched his mother being murdered by his father (James Gandolfini), and the violence and scariness of their eventual reunion is what earned "The Mighty" its PG-13 rating.

To take nothing away from Culkin's engaging, sure-handed performance, Kevin is the film's can't miss role. He's a lovable, wisecracking dreamer who eases his hobbled existence with Arthurian fantasies, and deflects the grim reality of his future with the even greater delusion that he'll become the first human to have his brain grafted onto a bio-mechanical body.

The closest he will actually come to that is riding Max' shoulder, and it is in these exhilarating, galloping moments of triumph, when they're outsmarting or out-muscling a pack of school bullies, or rescuing a battered wife from her abusive husband in a local diner—and being accompanied on these adventures by horseback knights only they can see—that "The Mighty" soars into greatness.

Philbrick, and now the filmmakers, have envisioned these events through the exaggerated memories of the story's narrator, Max. From the opening image, of Max' grandparents posed in front of their duplex like the farm couple in American Gothic, "The Mighty" reflects Max's world, from his suddenly expanded vantage point. People who watch the film literally are going to be gravely disappointed; all others are in for something special.

NEWSWEEK, 10/19/98, p. 81, Jack Kroll

[*The Mighty* was reviewed jointly with *Holy Man*; see Kroll's review of that film.]

SIGHT AND SOUND, 1/99, p. 50, Charles Taylor

Cincinnati. Large and lumbering adolescent Maxwell Kane has lived with his grandparents ever since his father was imprisoned for murdering his mother. Maxwell, who has troubles reading and writing, is assigned a tutor, Kevin, a classmate his own age who is afflicted with a bone-marrow disease. Kevin and his mother Gwen have just moved in next door to Max and his grandparents. Under Kevin's tutelage, Max begins reading, delighting especially in stories of knights undertaking heroic quests and selfless deeds.

Kevin asks Max to accompany him to a local fair where, perched on Max's massive shoulders, he's able to see the fireworks display. The burgeoning friendship between the boys is cemented when Max saves Kevin from the wrath of the Doghouse Boys gang by wading into a muddy lake out of the gang's reach, holding Kevin aloft. The pair begin wandering around Cincinnati in the manner of the storybook heroes they revere, looking for worthy deeds to perform. A mission to return a woman's stolen wallet brings Max face-to-face with Loretta and Iggy, old friends of his father and reminders of a life he'd rather forget. Max's father Kenny is paroled and kidnaps his son. Kevin sets out on his own quest and succeeds in rescuing his friend. Having tried to prepare Max for his eventual death, Kevin succumbs to his illness. Max honors his dead friend by setting forth their adventures in a book he calls *Freak the Mighty*.

Neither as magical as it aspires to be nor as sentimental as it might be, Peter Chelsom's third film continues the director's approach of putting together odds and ends that, like the dismembered body parts floating through *Funny Bones,* don't quite make up a working whole.

So far, Chelsom's penchant for leapfrogging from genre to genre, for abrupt shifts in tone, remains more contradictory than cohesive. He resists the urge to sentimentalise the two damaged boys who are the film's heroes. But he's not above putting a melodramatic squeeze on you, for example when Kevin, entertaining some classmates at lunch in what appears to be a goofy, throwaway scene, begins choking and nearly dies, or when Max's murderer father (the scenery-chewing James Gandolfini) kidnaps the boy and holds him captive by tying him to a radiator. (Gillian Anderson does what she can to lighten this part of the movie by turning the role of Gandolfini's old barfly acquaintance into lively, trashy caricature.) And Chelsom's introduction of mythology, as in the sight of Arthurian knights journeying over a bridge in modern-day Cincinnati, lacks the obsessive burnish that a director like John Boorman or Terry Gilliam might bring it.

The Mighty is finally like an exceptionally good after-school special, but that doesn't mean it's without its pleasures. Chelsom is much better with the quotidian than he is with the extraordinary. Max and Kevin's working-class neighbourhood is rendered with scrupulous attention to lived-in detail; not a case study but a place where people are doing their honourable, unfussy best to live their lives. *The Mighty* works best in the scenes of simple and not-so-simple interaction between the characters, as in the moment when Gena Rowlands, as Max's grandma, gently persuades her husband (Harry Dean Stanton, whose character's name—Grim—perfectly describes his hangdog mug) to put away the rifle he's cleaning in anticipation of the arrival of Max's no-good father.

Similarly, there's the lovely moment when Sharon Stone takes out her fears and frustrations over her son's illness on a hospital vending machine. Stone's performance is one more piece of evidence that it's high time people stopped cattily commenting on her failed star vehicles and started paying attention to her as an actor. Playing a working-class mom, Stone is anything but a star trawling for credibility. The brainy flirtation that marks Gwen's relationship with her son allows Stone to indulge the quick-witted playfulness that's one of her best qualities.

The film's occasional lapses into melodrama hurt because of Chelsom's very genuine and unsentimental affection for outsiders and oddballs. He can't quite knock the well-oiled, show-biz-tyke reactions out of Kieran Culkin's Kevin. But he doesn't go soft with Elden Henson's bashful giant Max. Henson conveys the poignancy of a gentle soul housed inside a hulking body without ever asking for our sympathy. He shows a knack for maintaining a surface reticence while drawing us in with the promise of revealing Max's hidden sensitivity, bravery and smarts. It's a performance of disciplined stillness and quiet beneath which can be distinctly heard a large, beating heart.

Also reviewed in:
CHICAGO TRIBUNE, 10/16/98, Friday/p. M, Michael Wilmington
NEW YORK TIMES, 10/9/98, p. E14, Janet Maslin
VARIETY, 5/25-31/98, p. 60, Leonard Klady
WASHINGTON POST, 10/16/98, p. D5, Stephen Hunter
WASHINGTON POST, 10/16/98, Weekend/p. 49, Michael O'Sullivan

MIGHTY JOE YOUNG

A Walt Disney Pictures release of an RKO Pictures production. *Executive Producer:* Gail Katz. *Producer:* Ted Hartley and Tom Jacobson. *Director:* Ron Underwood. *Screenplay:* Mark Rosenthal and Lawrence Konner. *Based on a screenplay by:* Ruth Rose. *Based on a story from RKO pictures "Mighty Joe Young" by:* Merian C. Cooper. *Director of Photography:* Don Peterman and Oliver Wood. *Editor:* Paul Hirsch. *Music:* James Horner. *Music Editor:* Jim Henrikson. *Sound:* Richard Bryce Goodman and (music) Simon Rhodes. *Sound Editor:* Wylie Stateman and Kelly Cabral. *Casting:* Pam Dixon Mickelson. *Production Designer:* Michael Corenblith. *Art Director:* Dan Webster. *Set Designer:* Bill Hawkins, Patte Strong, and Al Hobbs. *"Might Joe Young" Creature Designer:* Rick Baker. *Set Decorator:* Merideth Boswell. *Set Dresser:* Alexander Kirst. *Visual Effects:* Hoyt Yeatman. *Costumes:* Molly Maginnis.

Make-up: Deborah K. Larsen. *Stunt Coordinator:* Terry Leonard.   *Running time:* 114 minutes. *MPAA Rating:* PG.

CAST: Charlize Theron (Jill Young);   Bill Paxton (Gregg O'Hara);   Rade Sherbedgia (Strasser); Peter Firth (Garth); David Paymer (Harry Ruben); Regina King (Cecily Banks); Robert Wisdom (Kweli);   Naveen Andrews (Pindi);   Lawrence Pressman (Dr. Baker); Linda Purl (Dr. Ruth Young);   Mika Boorem (Young Jill);   Geoffrey Blake (Vern);   Christian Clemenson (Jack);   Cory Buck (Jason); Liz Georges (Jason's Mother);   Richard Riehle (Commander Gorman); Cynthia Allison and Ken Taylor (News Reporters); Ray Harryhausen (Gentlman at Party); Terry Moore (Elegant Woman at Party); Judson Mills (Impatient Driver); Tony Genaro (Boxer Shorts Man); Flo Di Re (Bambi's Owner); Kaylan Romero, Hernan Ruiz, Jenilee Deal, and Matt Deal (Street Kids);   Bethany Bassler, Vicki Davis, Deborah Kellner, and Marguerite Moreau (Cabriolet Girls); Tracey Walter (Conservancy Guard); Larry Brandenburg (Animal Control Duty Officer);   Damien Leake and Neal Kopit (Cops);   Janet Eilber (Concerned Mother);   Wiley Pickett (Police Sharpshooter);   John T. Bower (Carjack Man); Hannah Swanson (Toddler); Laurie Kilpatrick (Toddler's Mom); Richard McGonagle (Panda Owner); Reno Wilson (Poacher); Theodore R. Hartley (Society Man); Dina Merrill (Society Woman); Lily Mariye (Ticket Clerk); John Alexander (Joe Young).

LOS ANGELES TIMES, 12/25/98, Calendar/p. 24, Jack Mathews

[The following review by Jack Mathews appeared in a slightly different form in **NEWSDAY, 12/25/98, Part II/p. B3.]**

If you were shut out of this season's toy-buying frenzy for Furbys and are dreading the disappointment you'll see on your kids' faces Christmas morning, take heart. The best new pet toy of Christmas '98 will be available at your local multiplex, for the price of a ticket to "Mighty Joe Young."

Joe's a darling, gentle, affectionate, obedient, warm and fuzzy with deep-set, expressive eyes and a playful-pup spirit. Furbys may have more to say, but Joe comes to play. Close your eyes and count to 10, and you're on for a game of hide-and-seek. Of course, you'll have to humor him—it's hard to hide when you're 15 feet tall and weigh 2,000 pounds, when you are, after all, the biggest gorilla this side of King Kong.

"Mighty Joe Young," directed by "City Slickers'" Ron Underwood for Walt Disney Studios, is a remake of a 1949 RKO film that was itself a knockoff of "King Kong." Like the first film, it's the story of a mutant giant gorilla, his surrogate human mother, Jill Young (Charlize Theron), and their adventures in Africa and the U.S.

We're dubious of remakes, especially remakes of knockoffs, but this one seems warranted. Five decades is a long time, and even though the '49 version earned Oscars for Ray Harryhausen and Willis O'Brien's stop-motion effects, creature illusions have come a long way.

Technically, this Joe is a sensation, perhaps the most lifelike giant of them all. Created by modern makeup and effects master Rick Baker, who's previously aped apes for "Gorillas in the Mist," "Greystoke" and the 1976 version of "King Kong," Joe runs, walks, roars and pounds his massive chest without showing any signs of his animatronic workings, or, in some sequences, of the man inside the gorilla suit.

He's so well executed, in fact, that you very quickly accept him as a real animal and begin to empathize with the feelings pouring from those soulful eyes. Joe's a big baby, orphaned on the same day and by the same bloody hands of poachers who killed both his and Jill's mothers. The killers did not get away scot-free; baby Joe bit off two fingers on one of the poachers' hands, sending him screaming into the night, promising revenge.

Twelve years later, Jill has grown into a statuesque beauty, and Joe into the most lovable companion a girl ever had. But their bucolic jungle playground is being threatened by encroaching civilization, not to mention poachers, and when the ingenuous zoologist Gregg O'Hara (Bill Paxton) offers Joe space and protection in a San Diego animal tourist attraction, Jill accepts.

In the first "Mighty Joe Young," the beauty (played by Terry Moore, who has a cameo here) and the beast come to America as a nightclub act, which leads to disaster because of Joe's disdain for the hedonist ways of club patrons. In the remake, written by Mark Rosenthal and Lawrence

Konner ("The Beverly Hillbillies"), Joe's problems are more people-specific. His mother's killers (Rade Sherbedgia, Peter Firth) are back, and there are scores for both sides to settle.

The feud will spill out of Joe's new home, and take him and his pursuers on a tour of some of the most famous landmarks in Los Angeles. King Kong had his Empire State Building, Mighty Joe Young has the Hollywood sign.

As silly as things get, parents of Furby-aged children are advised to pay heed to the film's PG rating. The early scenes with the poachers and the baby ape in the jungle are intense, and the violence in the climactic chase sequence is bluntly realistic.

Still, "Mighty Joe Young" may be the season's most appealing family bet. Certainly, it has an appealing cast. Paxton, who has the rutty look of a middle-age Huck Finn, is the perfect hunk—Everyman for this kind of adventure. And Theron (listen carefully, because I'm only going to say this a thousand times) is the most gorgeous woman working in film.

Merry Christmas. "Mighty Joe Young" is a Furby for the whole family.

NEW YORK POST, 12/23/98, p. 45, Jonathan Foreman

Don't get the wrong impression from the trailers: "Mighty Joe Young" may look like another lame, gutless remake of an old great by a Hollywood bereft of ideas, but it's actually the best family movie of the year, and a vibrant, delightful film in the classic, Disney mode.

It's a much better movie than "The Lost World—Jurassic Park II." It manages to be exciting in the old-fashioned way, with plenty of action, humor, real characters that you care about, as well as spectacular special effects. (There's also not a trace of political correctness, nor any of the anti-adult, anti-civilization messages that sometimes pop up in Spielberg's oevre.)

In addition, it also has a surfeit of wholesome sex appeal in the lissome sun-tanned form of Charlize Theron, who plays a sarong-clad nature girl with dazzling aplomb.

In fact, "Mighty Joe Young" establishes Theron as a genuine, 100 percent, atomic-powered movie star. She showed she could act in "Devil's Advocate." Here she displays the luminous beauty and overpowering screen presence of a golden-age movie goddess.

The film opens in Africa with the shooting of a Dian Fossey figure—one of those blonde babe scientists so numerous in the movies—by evil gorilla poachers. She is the mother of Jill Young, the little girl who will grow up to be Charlize Theron.

At the same time, the poachers also murder the mother of a preternaturally large and clever baby gorilla that young Jill has named Joe. Jill promises her dying mother that she will protect Joe.

Years later, when Joe has grown into a giant, feeding the local legend of a monstrous ape-deity protecting the valley, a hunky zoologist named Gregg (Bill Paxton) turns up in town. He hires some of the local poachers to help him find the real-life simian he's sure lies behind the legend.

They do sight Joe, but he's far too smart to be caught. Gregg is injured in the "Lost World"-style chase, and comes to in the hospital founded by Jill's mother.

He persuades Jill to bring Joe to a California animal conservancy, where he will be safe. Joe quickly becomes famous for his size, playfulness and intelligence. But the man who slaughtered his mother is now the world's leading poacher and he comes up with a fiendish plan to get hold of Joe so his parts can be sliced up and flogged off.

Unlike Paxton, solid as ever as a good-hearted but modest man of action, Theron is occasionally flat when playing opposite computer-generated effects or animatronic creatures. But she and Paxton generate plenty of chemistry.

The filmmakers have played it safe by making their wittily nasty chief villains a Lithuanian and a white South African. But there is some ethnic stereotyping that some may find offensive: Naveen Andrews, (the handsome Sikh in "The English Patient"), plays Pindi, a lying, cheating East African-South Asian. And David Paymer is Ruben, yet another ultra-nerdy Jewish scientist.

"Might Joe Young" is that rare thing, a movie that kids of all ages will enjoy.

NEWSWEEK, 12/21/98, p. 68, David Ansen

Talk about an odd couple. He's at least 15 feet tall, extremely hairy, and tends to beat his chest when speaking. She's an adorable blonde with penciled eyebrows and the kind of skimpy but trendy outfits that don't usually pop up in the remote African jungle. He, of course, is Mighty

Joe Young, the post-Kong gorilla first dreamed up by Hollywood in 1949. She is the orphan girl Jill (Charlize Theron) who dotes on his every roar and is doing her damnedest to save him from nasty poachers who would chop him up and sell off the rare pieces. To this end she moves him to a California animal preserve, having been assured by a remarkably foolish zoologist (Bill Paxton) that no harm can befall her big buddy there. Well, we all make mistakes.

This Disney remake, directed as broadly as Mighty Joe's chest by Ron Underwood, is not for grown-ups, at least not grown-ups bothered by clumsy dialogue, cartoonish performances and formulaic plots. Joe (a Rick Baker animatronic creation) is a gruff charmer, however, and if your kids can endure the terrors that jeopardize our hero, this might hit their spot. But be prepared for a grisly opener in which both Jill's and Joe's mothers are killed. In kids' films, moms are always the real endangered species.

SIGHT AND SOUND, 4/99, p. 48, Charles Taylor

Africa. Dr Ruth Young, an anthropologist studying gorillas with her ten-year-old daughter Jill, is killed during a night-time attack by poachers who also kill a mother gorilla. Jill and the gorilla's baby (whom she has named Joe) grow up together. Twelve years later, Jill is carrying on her mother's work, protecting the gorillas from poachers and trying to hide Joe, who now weighs over 2,000 pounds. Gregg O'Hara, an anthropologist, inadvertently leads poachers to Joe. Realising Joe is no longer safe, Jill accepts Gregg's offer to house Joe in the Los Angeles wildlife centre where Gregg works.

In LA, Joe has troubles settling into his new home. Strasser, the poacher who killed both Jill and Joe's mothers and swore revenge when the infant Joe bit off two of his fingers, poses as a protector of rare species. Seeing a CNN report on Joe, Strasser heads for LA and represents himself to Jill as the owner of a Bothswana preserve where Joe would be safe. At a fund-raising event, Joe goes on the rampage when he sees Strasser. About to spirit Joe to Strasser's "preserve", Jill stumbles upon Strasser's true identity and flees. Joe escapes Strasser and causes havoc in downtown LA. Jill, Gregg and Strasser track Joe to an amusement park where Joe kills Strasser and is then acclaimed a hero by saving a young boy from a ride that's aflame. Jill returns to Africa and opens a wildlife reserve where Joe is assured a safe home.

The idea behind the original *Mighty Joe Young* (1949) was to redo *King Kong* (1933) as a kid's movie, and the result was uncomfortably mawkish. (It doesn't take any talent to get an audience to react by showing an animal mistreated.) Ron Underwood, the director of the new remake, brought a loose-limbed, tongue-in-cheek approach to the horror-comedy *Tremors*, but any hopes he can do the same thing here are dispelled in the opening sequence. The guiding sensibility of *Mighty Joe* appears to be the Disney studio's. The approach is epitomised by the film's opening: we're treated to shots of baby Joe the gorilla screaming and crying while his mother is murdered. We also get a ten-year-old girl huddling with the distraught gorilla while *her* mother is murdered.

Things brighten considerably when Joe becomes a stunning full-grown behemoth and his protector becomes a stunning full-grown Charlize Theron (and brighten even a little more when the appealing sane Regina King turns up in a supporting role). But Underwood never hits on the funky satirical tone that made John Guillermin's sadly maligned 1976 remake of *King Kong* such a delight, though the way he shoots Joe, emphasising his huge liquid eyes, certainly hearkens back to the Guillermin film.

Designed by Rick Baker, Joe's an endearing enough presence, but because the script calls for him to spend too much time forlornly locked up in the zoo, he becomes more cuddly than he should. He shakes that off in the best-sustained sequence where Joe gets loose in Los Angeles, acting out our fantasies of flattening all the annoyances city life offers up, like the Porsche equipped with a shrieking alarm system. (At one point Joe passes a movie theatre with a poster for John Ford's 1950 *Wagon Master*, a sweet tip of the hat to the star of that film, Ben Johnson, who also starred in the original *Mighty Joe Young*.)

At nearly six athletic feet, Charlize Theron is well suited to stand up to her co-star. This isn't the role that lets out the hell-raising comedian her performances in *The Devil's Advocate* and Woody Allen's forthcoming *Celebrity* have suggested. But she manages to be a sunny presence without being a twinkie. Theron is a saucy punchline to the movie's riddle: what kind of girl plays hide and seek with a 2,000 pound gorilla?

TIME, 12/28/98-1/4/99 p. 177, Richard Schickel

When Willis O'Brien, the pioneering special-effects genius, went back to his drawing board in the 1940s, he gave Mighty Joe Young two things King Kong, his first and greatest ape, lacked: a user-friendly name and a lady friend who didn't burst into screams every time she caught sight of him. The result didn't quite match *King Kong,* arguably the movies' most intense portrayal of unrequited love but it remains a sweet memory, now happily recalled by director Ron Underwood's genial remake.

To put it simply, a big guy—even if he is just a gorilla with a pituitary problem—who has a playful sense of his own strength and deploys it only in good causes is an irresistible figure. Also, these days, an instructive one. Fifty years ago, there wasn't much you could do with Mighty Joe except display him exploitatively in a nightclub. Now he can be played as a lovable symbol for all our endangered species.

Underwood has a nice, humorous regard for the fact that Joe tends to make a scary first impression even on sympathetic souls, and the director is blessed with inviting performances by Charhze Theron as Jill Young, the light of Joe's life, and Bill Paxton as Joe's rival for her affection. Maybe the update on the old script strains a bit over the implacability and resources of Joe's enemies, but his daring, concluding rescue of an imperiled child—this time the setting is an exploding amusement park not a flaming orphanage—effectively stirs both suspense and sentiment. This Christmas you could do worse than introduce the kids to the big Furby, one who carries a certain moral weight very lightly.

VILLAGE VOICE, 12/29/98, p. 128, Gary Dauphin

Disney's African entertainment subdivision—recent offerings include the various incarnations of *The Lion King,* wilderness theme parks, and *George of the Jungle*—adds a new item to the product line with the big-screen technological trifle *Mighty Joe Young.* Remaking the strictly-for-kicks 1949 original as a holiday-appropriate feel-good outing *Young* is the perfect introduction to the Continent formerly known as Dark for the children of ecofriendly soccer moms and dads. Multiculti enough to depict an Africa whose local population includes South Asians, this picture is not so indifferent to tradition that its lithe, blond female lead can't effortlessly charm both man and savage beast.

Young opens neo-*Bambi*-style, with a baby ape and a little white girl bonded in blood when their mothers are murdered by poachers. The girl grows into gone-native protector of animals Jill (Chartize Theron, resplendent in Putu-mayo wrap skirts throughout), while the wide-eyed little monkey will become the biggest gorilla the world has ever seen. The impressively rendered Joe might be part-robot, part-digital figment, but he's all cutes at heart. Whether playing hide-and-seek with Jill or absently crunching a car to silence its alarm, Joe's just an "aw-shucks" problem child, too big for his own good.

Joe and Jill's African Eden has been steadily encroached upon by poachers and that dreaded social disease, civilization, so when they're "discovered" by American zoologist Gregg (Bill Paxton), they happily hightail it to a zoo in Los Angeles. Jill falls for Gregg despite Joe's disapproving, Homer Simpson-ish growl, while the caged-in ape becomes a media darling, drawing the attention of the same poacher who killed his mommy. After a rather Freudian freak-out during a fundraiser, Joe goes on the lam in LaLaland, *Young*'s main question becoming how to get him back to Africa in one piece. The movie's formulaic animal hi-jinks risk very little and therefore return less, the film unable to satisfy even the impulse toward ghoulish racial rubbernecking. (During some lengthy full-body rubbing and purring between Joe and Jill, I wanted to tell the person next to me that the film's sexual tension was becoming apparent, but he was six and still hiding his eyes from some earlier fright.) Joe himself is an admitted F/X marvel. Whether in huggy close-up or breezily bounding across cityscapes and savannas, he's seamlessly brought to life by the kids at Industrial Light + Magic, and director Ron Underwood *(City Slickers)* is surprisingly reserved in deploying him, Joe always subservient to the film's thin narrative line. *Mighty Joe Young* would scan just as legibly if it starred a normal-sized gorilla or an elephant, making, this great-ape movie disappointingly more akin to *Free Willy* than *King Kong.*

Also reviewed in:
CHICAGO TRIBUNE, 12/25/98, Friday/p. H, Michael Wilmington
NEW YORK TIMES, 12/25/98, p. E19, Stephen Holden
VARIETY, 12/21/98-1/3/99, p. 74, Lael Loewenstein
WASHINGTON POST, 12/25/98, Weekend/p. 6, Michael O'Sullivan

MIRROR, THE

A Cowboy Booking International release of a Rooz Film production. *Producer:* Jafar Panahi and V. Nikkah-Azad. *Director:* Jafar Panahi. *Screenplay (Farsi with English subtitles):* Jafar Panahi. *Director of Photography:* F. Jodat. *Editor:* Jafar Panahi. *Production Designer:* M. Motavalli. *Running time:* 95 minutes. *MPAA Rating:* Not Rated.

CAST: Mina Mohammad-Khani (Mina); R. Mojdehi, M. Shirzad, N. Omoumi, and T. Samadpour (People on The Street).

NEW YORK POST, 11/25/98, p. 57, Jonathan Foreman

"The Mirror" is everything you would expect from an Iranian art film written and directed by Oscar nominee Jafar Panahi.

It is beguiling, sometimes funny, deliberately rough in places and very slow. It is also shot through with what could be read as very subtle criticisms of Iran's Islamic fundamentalist regime.

"The Mirror" starts off documentary-style, as a girl whose mother fails to pick her up from school tries to find her way home. A camera kept low to simulate a 7-year-old's perspective accompanies actress Mina Mohammad-Khani through the traffic-clogged streets of Tehran and onto what she hopes is the right bus.

Then something bizarre happens. Mina tells director Panahi she's sick of acting and has had enough. Panahi lets her go, but the willful little actress is still miked, so he decides to follow her home with a camera crew.

Like the character she had been playing, Mina doesn't know her address, only that she lives near a big square and a fountain. So the journey becomes an odyssey through Tehran, where we hear Iranians talking about marriage, work, the role of women and the results of the Iran-South Korea soccer game.

For all the oppressiveness of a society that inflicts medieval garb on its women and forces even young girls to sit at the back of a bus, there is also a gentleness about the people Mina encounters on her journey.

There's no way of knowing whether the film is scripted and cut to look spontaneous, or if Mina really had no idea that Panahi's bus was following her.

To the extent that you can see her face under her head scarf, she's a plain, but oddly attractive little thing. And in a way her ordinariness gives you the opportunity to take in the fascinating slice of Tehrani life that is the filmmakers real subject.

VILLAGE VOICE, 12/1/98, p. 117, J. Hoberman

The featured film in the Walter Reade's current Iranian series, Jafar Panahi's *The Mirror* is a quintessential example of that national cinema—a spare slice of life, at once neorealist and self-reflexive.

Panahi, whose 1995 first feature, *The White Balloon*, proved to be the most commercially successful Iranian movie in the annals of American distribution, revisits the situation of a little girl coping with the vicissitudes of the big city—indeed, the child actress is the same (grave, chubby Mina Mohammad-Khani), although her predicament here is far more existential. Arm in a sling and oversize book bag slung across her back, first-grader Mina is waiting outside school for her mother—as it turns out, in vain.

The girl is as anxiously hypervigilant as the intersection is busy—the traffic accentuated by the amplified soundtrack and the squeezed space of the telephoto lens Panahi uses to keep Mina in situ. In some regards, the movie is a little primer—Mina crosses the street with adults and carries money to make an emergency phone call. Too bad she hasn't an emergency plan, can't seem to remember her bus number, and doesn't know her street address. (Nor is the school much help.) Mina nevertheless attempts to get herself home, taking buses and then jumping off, reversing field, forgetting to use the women's entrance on the bus, and finding herself left behind.

Panahi makes much of the child's solitude in the crowd, together with the relative disinterest evinced by the adult world babbling above her head. Midway through, at the point of maximum narrative involvement, *The Mirror* does what some might consider a very bad thing—abruptly switching from neo-neorealism to self-conscious cinema verité. "Don't look at the camera, Mina," someone tells the girl, and suddenly the crew is right there. At this point, the star rebels: "I'm not acting anymore," Mina cries, taking off her sling and chador and hopping off the bus. The crew is consternated, but, realizing that Mina is still on mike, they continue to document her progress through the streets of Tehran. But as the fiction appears to dissolve into life, the basic situation remains constant. Mina still must negotiate the adult world to find her way back home.

Shot largely from a child's perspective, punctuated by radio bulletins on a soccer match between South Korea and Iran, *The Mirror* is so concentrated in its elements and so single-minded in its narrative as to be practically a structural film. Nothing, however, is as insistent as Mina's high-pitched, piercing voice—at once admirable and grating in its constant interrogation of grown-up authority.

Also reviewed in:
NEW YORK TIMES, 11/25/98, p. E14, Stephen Holden
VARIETY, 8/25-31/97, p. 76, Derek Elley

MR. JEALOUSY

A Lions Gate release of a Joel Castleberg production. *Executive Producer:* Eric Stoltz. *Producer:* Joel Castleberg. *Director:* Noah Baumbach. *Screenplay:* Noah Baumbach. *Director of Photography:* Steven Bernstein. *Editor:* J.Kathleen Gibson. *Music:* Luna and Robert Een. *Costumes:* Katherine Jane Bryant. *Running time:* 105 minutes. *MPAA Rating:* R.

CAST: Eric Stoltz (Lester Grimm);   Annabella Sciorra (Ramona Ray);   Chris Eigeman (Dashiell Frank);   Carlos Jacott (Vince);   Marianne Jean-Baptiste (Lucretia);   Brian Kerwin (Stephen);   Peter Bogdanovich (Dr. Poke);   Bridget Fonda (Irene);   John Lehr (Lint).

LOS ANGELES TIMES, 6/5/98, Calendar/p. 16, Kenneth Turan

They don't call Lester Grimm "Mr. Jealousy" without just cause.

Back when he was 15, Lester lost his nerve when it came time for a good-night kiss, only to later spy his beloved in the arms of someone else. Fidelity, not surprisingly, became an issue with him, and in college he can be glimpsed trailing after his girlfriends' exes "like a detective shadowing a subject."

Set in neurotic Manhattan, "Mr. Jealousy" shows what happens when the thirtyish Lester (Eric Stoltz) meets Ramona Ray (Annabella Sciorra), a free spirit always on the alert for wounded birds to rescue. It's a film about both the improbability and inevitability of romance, a warm, playful and clever look at the precariousness of human relationships. Written and directed by Noah Baumbach, it's a success all the way around.

"Mr. Jealousy" is the 27-year-old Baumbach's second feature, following 1996's "Kicking and Screaming." Like its predecessor, this film has a way with the comic insecurities and obsessions of the modern age. And its easygoing and engaging quality masks how rare an accomplishment it is to create something achingly true as well as amusing, as wise about people as it is about the craft of film.

For a gambit like "Mr. Jealousy" to succeed, the writer-director has to be a matchmaker several times over. He has to first mediate between his characters and his actors, getting the performers to understand his off-center people as well as he does. Even harder is the mediation between the characters and the audience, the creation of a bond that makes viewers empathetic instead of dismissive when multiple quirks develop.

Baumbach and his cast manage to do all this and make it seem easy. This is more than a question of writing bright dialogue, though "Mr. Jealousy" does have numerous lines like "You can only find incompetence endearing for so long." Nor is it only the ability to relax actors and give them confidence, though Baumbach has managed to coax stars Stoltz and Sciorra into some of the most confident and natural performances of their careers (and given how potentially unsympathetic Stoltz's role might be, that is no small accomplishment).

Rather it's the writer-director's gift for truly seeing people, for imagining them whole, foibles and all, that is the critical element. And deciding to build the piece around a sophisticated, knowing voice-over that is bemused as well as caring is a structure that makes everything possible.

Lester and Ramona, the narrator tells us, are introduced by mutual friends Vince (Carlos Jacott) and Lucretia (Marianne Jean-Baptiste of "Secrets and Lies") who are themselves engaged and "feeling generous with love."

Ramona is a tour guide at the Brooklyn Museum who's working on a PhD in Abstract Expressionism, while Lester, the kind of substitute teacher who ends up teaching Spanish though he doesn't know a word, is a stalled writer who'd like to get down to it but doesn't quite know how.

A mass of insecurities at the best of times, a past master at torturing himself without reason, Lester goes into overdrive when he discovers that one of Ramona's (numerous) ex-boyfriends is the celebrated young novelist Dashiell Frank (smartly played by Whit Stillman regular Chris Eigeman), author of "Post Euphoria" and widely acclaimed as, yes, the voice of his generation.

Recognizing Dashiell Frank on a Manhattan street from his book jacket photo, Lester reverts to type and clandestinely follows his unsuspecting prey. When he discovers that the author is a member of a therapy group run by the avuncular Dr. Poke (director Peter Bogdanovich), Lester impulsively joins, giving himself the identity of his good friend Vince and not letting on that he and the writer have Ramona between them.

No good, clearly, can possibly come of this, but as Lester's deception gleefully spirals out of control, leading him and his friends into an increasingly desperate and comic series of dodges, half-truths and prevarications, we have to marvel at how easily Baumbach manages to juggle both emotional tones and plot twists. While predicting futures is a rube's game, it's hard to observe how well "Mr. Jealousy" manages it all without thinking this young man has quite a bright one.

NEW YORK POST, 6/5/98, p. 46, Larry Worth

It's a given, much as (a) that subject is a natural launching pad for laughs, (b) Noah Baumbach is a gifted writer-director and (c) Eric Stoltz, Annabella Sciorra and Chris Eigeman are utterly engaging, consistently bright performers.

So how did all the above add up to a movie as unsatisfying as "Mr. Jealously"?

The easiest explanation is that Baumbach suffered from sophomore slump, having debuted with 1995's New York Film Festival fave "Kicking and Screaming." Coincidentally or not, that also showcased Stoltz and Eigeman at their preppy, erudite best.

This time around, Stoltz (also the executive producer) plays a thirtysomething substitute teacher in Manhattan who was scarred for life—romantically speaking—at 15. It seems he caught his adolescent cutie with another guy.

Though he now finds himself attracted to a kooky Brooklyn Museum of Art guide (Sciorra), he's suspicious of her fidelity. After learning that she dated a successful author (Eigeman), paranoia kicks in: He assumes a false identity and joins the novelist's group-therapy sessions to get the real skinny.

Yeah, right. In a quest for madcap developments and deliciously oddball characters, Baumbach sacrifices credibility. People consistently react in silly rather than sensible ways, which only proves effective in farce.

The plot quickly becomes as obvious as the characters' names. Lester Grimm for the downbeat hero, Dashiell Frank as his literary rival, Ramona as the sexy object of their lust (who inexplicably becomes an eccentric clod at the halfway point) and Lucretia, her scheming girlfriend.

Baumbach's technical devices aren't a saving grace. He employs cartoon-like dissolves, jump-cuts, montages, flashbacks and unnecessary narration to segue from one thudding setup to the next.

Ironically, subplots about male bonding, psychobabble and half-developed supporting characters (gamely played by Marianne Jean-Baptiste, Bridget Fonda, Brian Kerwin, Carlos Jacott and Peter Bogdanovich) are welcome relief from the main storyline.

Maybe that's because Stoltz and Sciorra generate limited chemistry. One couldn't care less if they were to end up together or not. And as the third side of their triangle, Eigeman offers a funny though familiar variation on the pompous elitist he's clearly got down to a science.

At one point, a character comments: "I hate it when people don't live up to their stereotypes." Sadly, that's the chief area in which "Mr. Jealousy" won't disappoint.

NEWSDAY, 6/5/98, Part II/p. B6, John Anderson

The omnipotent narrator, the character named Grimm, the way the needs of the narrative supersede the logic of the situation and you don't even mind. Or notice. Yes, "Mr. Jealousy" is that oft-cited, rarely seen illusion, the urban fairy tale. Rarer still, it's a romantic comedy that's actually funny.

Funnier than it is romantic, perhaps, but certainly not the obsession-fired melodrama the title seems to suggest (sequel: "Mr. Jealousy II: The Armageddon"). No, a better one might have been "Mr. Can't-Quite-Resist-His-Own-Worst-Impulses." Our hero's not nuts. He's just insecure.

Which is something you certainly can't say about director-writer Noah Baumbach. It's quite a leap he's made from his debut film, "Kicking & Screaming," into "Mr. Jealousy's" atmosphere of finely measured mirth and casual hilarity—all of which merely buttress the very real emotional phenomena of the film. But he's also dancing along the edge of a snake pit. Young urbanites? Group therapy? Diner talk? The singed veterans of the dating game? Can we care, again? Yes. Where most Gen X-oriented comedy presents sophomoric fantasy as realism, Baumbach blithely uses the structure of fable, (and his own ironic/ paternal narration) to make something very real, something that acknowledges the artifice at the same time it mugs us, a technique as old as Hawks, Sturges and Lubitsch.

Baumbach gets terrific performances out of his actors. Eric Stoltz, who has suddenly aged out of callowness, is Lester Grimm, a teacher whose romantic history began in betrayal and has left him with a bit of a jealous streak. Annabella Sciorra, who always seems brittle when she plays hard, is delightfully sweet/smart as Ramona, a Brooklyn Museum tour guide and PhD candidate whose sexual history becomes Lester's obsession. The third plane in the triangle—although no one but Lester knows there is a triangle—is Dashiell Frank (Chris Eigeman), a best-selling writer but, much more importantly, Ramona's ex. ("Lester gritted his teeth," Baumbach intones. "Ramona had a life before him.")

Lester fixates on Dashiell, infiltrating his group-therapy sessions (a hilariously deadpan Peter Bogdanovich is the aptly named Dr. Poke). He derides Dashiell's accomplishments (that he's a writer who "writes about people our age" seems a self-deprecating dig by Baumbach). He makes paranoid phone calls, weird midnight trips.

One shouldn't say it, but "Mr. Jealousy" is kind of a Generation Ex comedy. In the love market, everybody is defined as somebody's ex; when he's about to blow it, Lester admits, "I was about to become the thing I hated most: Ramona's ex." The air of propriety even projects into the future: One person's ex always seems to marry someone else's ex. And Ramona, though delightful, isn't immune to temptation. In all of this, "Mr. Jealousy" rushes in where a lot of movies fear to tread, into territory about past lovers, lovers' past lovers, the idea that "when she thinks about him she has the affair all over again." It is on one level very dark stuff, mature stuff, and to Baumbach's credit that he keeps us laughing.

He's also got a good supporting cast, especially Carlos Jacott as Vince, whose personal history Lester appropriates when he infiltrates Dashiell's group. Bridget Fonda does virtually a cameo as Dashiell's girlfriend, whose stammer suggests a certain complexity in the haughtier-than-thou

Dashiells (Eigeman, also in "Last Days of Disco," is even better here). There are no easy endings or sugarcoated froth, just a comedy about a boy, his particular obsession and the girlfriend who likes to talk about her past. Hey, wait a minute, maybe this is a horror movie?

VILLAGE VOICE, 6/9/98, p. 152, Elizabeth Weitzman

Noah Baumbach's sophomore effort, about a crew similar to but 10 years older than his postcollegiate *Kicking and Screaming* navel gazers, offers us Lester Grimm (an amusing Eric Stoltz), a man permanently scarred by an unfaithful girlfriend at age 15. His lovers' old boyfriends are the stuff of Lester's nightmares. Soon after 31-year-old unpublished writer-apathetic substitute teacher starts dating Ramona (Annabella Sciorra)—whose 26 previous beaus include a famous, voice-of-his-generation author named Dashiell (Chris Eigeman)—he gets a little crazy. At first, it's enough to read Dashiell's book, searching for Ramona's presence in another man's life. But he needs something more tangible, and finds himself joining Dashiell's group therapy session. Though he's there to uncover dirt, the two slowly start merging their slightly unsatisfying lives.

Despite a surfeit of easy observational asides, *Mr. Jealousy* exhibits much of the sharp humor and accomplished direction that made Baumbach a critic's favorite his first time out (though he could have eased up on the iris shots and jump cuts). And he's got gold in Eigeman, who adds another shade to his multihued palette of assholes. Also wonderful is Carlos Jacott, a scene stealer as Lester's best friend Vince, who eventually also joins the group.

The film's women, however, don't fare as well. Baumbach, still a disciple of the why-show-if-you-can-tell school, sets up much of the story through a too intrusive narrator; despite what he repeatedly tells us, though, Ramona's quirkiness is less adorable than solipsistic. And both Marianne Jean-Baptiste, as Vince's fiancée, and Bridget Fonda, as Dashiell's girlfriend, are wasted in roles that suggest depths unprobed. But the biggest problem lies in the pair at this story's center, since their connection, all intellect and no emotion, is oddly tenuous. The strongest chemistry, in fact, occurs among the three men, either in therapy, where they exchange identities like participants in some misguided, psychiatric game of telephone, or at the low-key social events they turn into quests for the meaning of adulthood. Perhaps that's something we can look forward to—these Baumbach regulars agonizing over their own intriguing romance—when the director drop-kicks them into their ever-nearing next decade.

Also reviewed in:
CHICAGO TRIBUNE, 6/19/98, Friday/p. 1, Monica Eng
NEW YORK TIMES, 6/5/98, p. E15, Janet Maslin
VARIETY, 10/6-12/97, p. 57, Derek Elley

MR. NICE GUY

A New Line Cinema release of a Raymond Chow/Golden Harvest production. *Executive Producer:* Leonard Ho.   *Producer:* Chua Lam. *Director:* Samo Hung.   *Screenplay:* Edward Tang and Fibe Ma. *Director of Photography:* Raymond Lam.   *Editor:* Peter Cheung.   *Music:* J. Peter Robinson. *Music Editor:* Lisé Richardson.   *Sound:* Gretchen Thornburn and (music) Frank Fleming and Brian Pierret.   *Sound Editor:* Paul Clay.   *Casting:* Maura Fay.   *Production Designer:* Horace Ma.   *Art Director:* Chau Sai-Hung.   *Set Decorator:* Jill Eden.   *Costumes:* Lui Fung-Shan. *Make-up:* Poon Men-Wah, José Perez, and Paul Pattison. *Stunt Coordinator:* Jackie Chan and Cho Wing.   *Running time:* 100 minutes.   *MPAA Rating:* PG-13.

CAST: Jackie Chan (Jackie); Richard Norton (Giancarlo "The Saint" Lucchetti); Miki Lee (Miki); Karen McLymont (Lakeisha); Gabrielle Fitzpatrick (Diana); Vince Poletto (Romeo Baggio); Barry Otto (Baggio, Romeo's Father); Samo Hung (Cyclist); Emil Chau (Ice Cream Vendor); Mina Godenzi (First Woman Catcher in Cook Show Audience); Peter Houghton (Richard); Peter Lindsay (Gronk); David No (Victor); Rachel Blakely (Sandy); Judy Green

(Tina);   Sonny Notarfrancesco (Sonny, Romeo's Son);   Jake Notarfrancesco (Nancy, Romeo's Daughter);   Frederick Miragliotta (NEA Head Officer);   Keith Agius (Special Action Team Leader);   Greg Jamieson (Priest);   Matthew Dyktynski (Floor Manager);   Salik Silverstein (Cook Show Director);   Lynn Murphy (Babysitter);   Nicholas Bufalo (Passerby).

LOS ANGELES TIMES, 3/20/98, Calendar/p. 14, Kevin Thomas

[The following review by Kevin Thomas appeared in a slightly different form in **NEWSDAY, 3/20/98, Part II/p. B6.]**

"Mr. Nice Guy" could be the title of practically all the movies Jackie Chan has ever made, but it happens to be that of his latest, an entertaining, action-filled thriller that is pure pleasure for fans of the charismatic martial-arts superstar.

Not surprisingly, "Mr. Nice Guy" is a lot like a zillion other Chan films; what's amazing is how Chan's sunny personality, his graceful dexterity plus lots of inventive stunts and action sequences keep the formula fresh.

Directed by his longtime colleague, director-actor Samo Hung and featuring the work of Chan's own team of stunt coordinators, "Mr. Nice Guy" seems as much choreographed as it is filmed. It has the movement and structure of an exceptionally vigorous ballet, giving it a terrific sense of energy and unity. Hung's bravura sense of style and pace have been crucial in making "Mr. Nice Guy" one of Chan's best.

Edward Tang and Fibe Ma's lively, well-developed script finds Jackie a star in a popular Melbourne TV cooking show, whose cooking video gets mixed up with one belonging to a TV newscaster (Gabrielle Fitzpatrick). She has managed to record the city's premier drug kingpin (Richard Norton) engaged in dealings that would swiftly bring him down should the tape be played on the evening news.

The trouble is that Fitzpatrick's intrepid Diana has been discovered. She runs for her life, and luckily Jackie becomes her knight in shining armor. Alas, the subsequent tape mix-up now has the gangster Giancarlo and his no-less-than 42 henchman after Jackie as well.

There's just no end of awesome and amusing derring-do and kung-foolery in "Mr. Nice Guy": Jackie escorting a group of friends over an I-beam bridging two buildings high above the ground; Jackie crashing an outdoor group wedding of 50 Harley Davidson bikers and escaping via a balloon float; Jackie leaping onto a giant crane in pursuing the baddies. The action never lets up until a finale set-piece that's too good to give away and may well be the most elaborate ever staged for a Chan film. Hung himself shows up in a funny cameo as an irate cyclist.

Chan is as buoyant and appealing as ever, but the film gives him a sharp edge of rage because no sooner has his fiancee (Miki Lee) arrived from Hong Kong than she is kidnapped by Giancarlo's minions. As nonstop as the action seems, the film surrounds Jackie with lots of likable people in addition to Lee: veteran Australian actor Barry Otto (as Chan's senior cooking show partner and foster father), Vince Poletto (as Otto's policeman son) and Karen McLymont (as Jackie's loyal assistant). Tall, elegant Norton, who has Stewart Granger looks, is the wittiest of villains. He's a martial-arts master long associated with Chan.

"Mr. Nice Guy" is a quality effort that makes good use of a range of photogenic Melbourne locales, gleamingly photographed by Raymond Lam. Horace Ma's strongly contemporary production design includes a magnificent rural high-tech-style estate for Giancarlo that looks to be about size of the Getty Museum in Los Angeles. J. Peter Robinson's rich score expertly supports the action dramatically rather than merely frantically. Jackie Chan has done it again.

NEW YORK POST, 3/20/98, p. 50, Thelma Adams

In the final half-hour of the Jackie Chan throwaway "Mr. Nice Guy," there's an artfully choreographed fight sequence at a construction site. The lone Jackie battles a corps of gray-suited baddies in a maze of blue doors and unpainted cement walls. It's a satisfying bit of silent-movie schtick.

But it's too little too late in a movie that should have been called "No More Mr. Nice Guy."

On one level, it's heartwarming that the humorous Hong Kong action star is loyal to his longtime friend and director, Samo Hung ("Dragons Forever"). On another, if these guys have made so many movies together, how can they still be so amateurish?

Set in Melbourne, "Mr. Nice Guy" follows the travails of a chef named Jackie. When he's not kneading dough on Australian TV, the pleasant fellow finds himself in the middle of a pitched battle between Mafia kingpin Giancarlo (Richard Norton) and a ragtag gang of coke thieves known as the Demons.

It's a cliche of old Chinese chopsocky movies that the dubbed English voices and the actors' mouths don't match. But who can figure out why, when the majority of the actors, including Jackie, are speaking English, the dubbing here still looks phony.

Toward the end, when key characters have disappeared from the plot without a trace and all that remains is the chase, a mobster introduces a new character named Lucci. I was hoping it might be soap star Susan Lucci, on hand to give the actors some pointers on turning bad acting into high entertainment.

SIGHT AND SOUND, 9/98, p. 49, David Tse

Jackie is a popular television chef in Melbourne. He rescues reporter Diana when she is chased by thugs working for drug boss Giancarlo. Her videotape showing Giancarlo dealing drugs with the Demons, a biker gang, gets mixed up with Jackie's cookery tapes. The two gangs become aware of this and want the tape back. They disrupt Jackie's charity appearance in a shopping mall and attack him at his house, but Jackie holds them off and performs daring escapes on horse-drawn carriages and scaffolding.

Jackie's girlfriend Miki is held hostage by the Demons at a construction site, so Jackie rescues her. Jackie is captured and beaten by Giancarlo, but he turns the tables and demolishes Giancarlo's mansion with a giant mining truck. The tape falls into the cops' hands, Giancarlo is arrested, and Jackie returns to his cookery show.

Having taken a break from directing, Jackie Chan's recent work has consisted of hit-or-miss collaborations with big-name directors. This represents something of an identity crisis for the Hong Kong action-film star/auteur. The hits include the revival of his *Police Story* glory days with Kirk Wong Chi-Keung in *Crime Story,* and the reprisal of his star-making role in the period comedy *Drunken Master II*. However, *Mr. Nice Guy,* helmed by Chan's Chinese Opera School contemporary Samo Hung, is a miss.

Mr. Nice Guy is an attempt to find a middle ground between Chan's 80s blockbusters and the globe-trotting action comedies he has been starring in since the 90s. While a solid stunt coordinator, Hung's conception of what constitutes family entertainment is skewed. In lieu of a multi-layered narrative that an audience of all ages can connect with (as in the products of Disney and Castle Rock), the film tries to cater superficially to every target sector. This explains the presence of the greasy gangsters, warm family scenes, overabundant car crashes and unnecessarily scantily clad women. The insistence on location shooting often reduces the film to a travelogue, and the choppy re-editing by US distributor New Line doesn't help either.

When all else fails, Chan's kamikaze daredevilry is still magical. The best set-piece is a breathless chase inside a construction site, a studio-like environment with numerous props allowing Chan to do infinite variations on his vaudeville routines. Chan is now in his forties, and the constant pursuit of dangerous spectacle (to consolidate audience affection? to surpass himself? for masochistic atonement?) is punishing his body. Chan seems to be experiencing a hidden crisis, and as if to underscore his confusion, his latest return to blockbuster film-making is aptly entitled *Who Am I?* So, at the start of the third phrase of his career as a Hollywood player, one wishes that instead of rushed location shooting and costly hardware he would realise that there's no shame in staying at the studio to perfect his vision, as was the case with his 30s gangster comedy *Miracles,* still Chan's best film.

Also reviewed in:
NEW YORK TIMES, 3/20/98, p. E12, Lawrence Van Gelder
VARIETY, 8/25-31/97, p. 74, Leonard Klady

MRS. DALLOWAY

A First Look Pictures release of a Bayly/Parée production in association with with Film of Newmarket Capital Group and BBC Films presentation with the participation of The European Co-Production Fund UK/NPS Television/Dutch Co-producation Fund. *Executive Producer:* Chris J. Ball, William Tyrer, Simon Curtis, and Bill Shepherd.   Producer: Lisa Katselas Paré and Stephen Bayly. *Director:* Marleen Gorris. *Screenplay:* Eileen Atkins. *Based on the novel by:* Virginia Woolf. *Director of Photography:* Sue Gibson. *Editor:* Michiel Reichwein. *Music:* Ilona Sekacz. *Choreographer:* Sue Lefton. *Sound:* Peter Glossop, Brian Simmons and (music) Gert de Bruijn. *Sound Editor:* Marc Nolens. *Casting:* Celestia Fox. *Production Designer:* David Richens. *Art Director:* Alison Wratten and Nik Callan. *Set Decorator:* Carlotta Barrow and Jeanne Vertigan. *Special Effects:* John Horton. *Costumes:* Judy Pepperdine. *Make-up:* Joan Hills and Maggie Webb. *Stunt Coordinator:* Andreas Petrides. *Running time:* 97 minutes. *MPAA Rating:* PG-13.

CAST: Vanessa Redgrave (Mrs. Clarissa Dalloway);   Natascha McElhone (Young Clarissa Dalloway);   Michael Kitchen (Peter WAlsh); Alan Cox (Young Peter Walsh);   Sarah Badel (Lady Sally Rosseter); Lena Headey (Young Sally Seton);   John Standing (Richard Dalloway); Robert Portal (Young Richard Dalloway);   Oliver Ford Davies (Hugh Whitbread);   Hal Cruttenden (Young Hugh Whitbread);   Rupert Graves (Septimus Warren Smith);   Amelia Bullmore (Rezia Warren Smith);   Margaret Tyzack (Lady Bruton); Robert Hardy (Sir William Bradshaw); Richenda Carey (Lady Bradshaw);   Katie Carr (Elizabeth Dalloway);   Selina Cadell (Miss Kilman);   Amanda Drew (Lucy);   Phyllis Calvert (Aunt Helena);   John Franklyn-Robbins (Lionel, Clarissa's Father);   Alistair Petrie (Herbert);   Rupert Baker (Joseph Breitkopf);   Janet Henfrey (Miss Pym);   Polly Pritchett (Nursemaid);   Jane Whittenshaw and Sisoe Fairfax (Women by Lake);   Richard Bradshaw (Evans);   Hilda Braid and Derek Smee (Couple in Deck Chairs.);   Fanny Carby (Singer);   Denis Lill (Doctor Holmes);   Richard Stirling (Receptionist); Neville Phillips (Mr. Wilkins);   Peter Cellier (Lord Lexham); Kate Binchy (Ellie Henderson); Edward Jewesbury (Professor Brierly);   Jack Galloway (Sir Harry Audley);   Tony Steedman (Prime Minister);   Faith Brook (Lady Bexborough);   Nancy Nevinson (Mrs. Hilberry); Christopher Staines (Willie).

CHRISTIAN SCIENCE MONITOR, 2/27/98, p. B3, David Sterritt

Are filmmakers afraid of Virginia Woolf?

Novels by groundbreaking authors like Jane Austen and Henry James have filled movie screens in recent years, and stage productions have focused on Woolf's life and work. But film directors have steered away from her, perhaps because her writing is more experimental and therefore less easily adapted than most.

This makes Marleen Gorris's screen version of "Mrs. Dalloway" something of a news event as well as an impressive movie. In her first offering since "Antonia's Line," an Oscar winner two years ago, Gorris has met the challenge of Woolf's style, translating it into motion-picture terms with a surprising degree of success.

The story takes place on a June day in 1923, when England has recovered from the effects of World War I but is still coming to terms with the grim lessons it taught.

The heroine is a middle-aged London woman who appears to have built a comfortable life but is troubled by memories of the past—and by suspicions that the world might seem far less hospitable if she allowed herself to examine it more closely than her sheltered existence requires.

We watch her activities and listen to her thoughts as she prepares for a party she's giving, encounters a long-ago suitor, and hears about the death of a shell-shocked veteran whose image has haunted her.

Much of the film's interest comes from screenwriter Eileen Atkins's transformation of the novel's interior monologues—conveying Mrs. Dalloway's thoughts via streams of expressive prose—into an articulate voice-over narration. This preserves the story's introspective quality while making the heroine an engaging figure.

The other key element is Vanessa Redgrave's acting in the title role. This isn't one of her very greatest performances, since her radiance is so strong that it outstrips the personality of the somewhat unsteady character she's playing. Even at her second-best, though, Redgrave is one of the most compelling talents in movies today.

Gorris's filmmaking is also strong, avoiding the ideological overkill that made the feminist message of "Antonia's Line" less persuasive than it should have been. Rupert Graves and Michael Kitchen head a talented supporting cast, and Sue Gibson's cinematography makes the movie sparkle.

LOS ANGELES TIMES, 2/20/98, Calendar/p. 4, Kevin Thomas

There comes a moment with some women when you know they will be beautiful always. These are women whose inner glow and carriage are not dependent upon youth.

Even if you've had this feeling about Vanessa Redgrave long before seeing her in director Marleen Gorris and adapter Eileen Atkins' vaultingly ambitious though somewhat flawed film of Virginia Woolf s "Mrs. Dalloway," this experience will confirm it absolutely.

Elegantly gowned in a flowing pale green outfit and a hat with a flourish of yellow feathers, Redgrave's tall, stately Clarissa Dalloway is strolling through London's Bond Street on a sunny day in June 1923 when we meet her. Smiling a secret smile, she is pure enchantment, yet on this perfect day this perfect-looking woman is asking herself if her life is, for all intents and purposes, over.

She has been seriously rattled by the sight of a young World War I veteran (Rupert Graves) who finds himself coming mentally unhinged right there in the street. It is an encounter that propels her into memories of the summer of 1890, the turning point of her life.

In flashbacks we discover the young Clarissa (Natascha McElhone) immersed in the leisurely existence of an aristocrat living at her family's vast country estate. She's caught up in an innocent flirtation with her best friend Sally (Lena Headey) and is ardently pursued by the good-looking Peter Walsh (Alan Cox) who wants to whisk her off to a life of adventure. But Clarissa senses that Peter's kind of life is dangerous and that he asks too much of her. Poor Peter, desperately in love with her, realizes swiftly that for a husband she will choose the steadfast Richard Dalloway.

On this day more than 30 years later, which will unfold with a Aristotelian appreciation for dramatic unity, Clarissa is selecting flowers for the grand party she will be giving that evening in her splendid townhouse. In time we discover that Mr. Dalloway (John Standing) is a member of Parliament, that the prime minister himself will be in attendance, not to mention the duke and duchess of Marlborough. But no sooner has Clarissa arrived home than she receives an unexpected visitor—one she finds fitting, considering her state of mind. He is none other than Peter (Michael Kitchen), back from long years in India, enmeshed in a messy private life and still caring for her.

Along with moving back and forth in time within Clarissa's ruminations, "Mrs. Dalloway" also counterpoints her story with that of the unraveling young man, Graves' Septimus Warren Smith, who five years after the "Great War" is over, starts experiencing severe post-traumatic stress syndrome, reliving the witnessing of the death of his best friend. By the end of the day, his fate will impinge upon Mrs. Dalloway's conscience, even though they never meet, eliciting an epiphany in which she will make a crucial decision about life.

With her concern more for psychology than plot and penchant for interior monologues, Virginia Woolf represents a challenge for filmmakers, even though Woolf was intrigued and influenced by the new art form, the movies. Yet Gorris, whose "Antonia's Line" won a 1995 best foreign film Oscar, and actress-writer Atkins come to the task well-qualified.

Gorris is a venturesome storyteller in her own right with much skill in revealing the inner workings of the feminine psyche, and Atkins, co-creator of "Upstairs Downstairs," had already starred as Woolf in her own play, "Vita and Virginia," with Redgrave as Vita Sackville-West, the inspiration for Woolf's "Orlando."

They succeed in creating a reverie that will recall John Huston's film of James Joyce's "The Dead"—but then Joyce not only was Woolf's contemporary but also an exponent of stream-of-consciousness technique who took a similarly contemplative view of life as Woolf.

Gorris and Atkins carry off the difficult task of bringing Woolf alive on the screen, but they stumble on the prosaic business of matching actors playing the same character in youth and middle age. There's very little resemblance between Redgrave and McElhone—or for that matter, any of the actors playing the same character at different points in their lives—and this proves to be a serious distraction and even a source of initial confusion, requiring a real effort on the part of the viewer to suspend disbelief.

But for all its interior monologues and expressions of tormented imaginings, "Mrs. Dalloway" is otherwise a traditional screen narrative and not the kind of stylized venture in which close physical resemblance is not so crucial.

Even so, "Mrs. Dalloway" is a rich work, an insightful consideration of the nature of civilization in the wake of "the war to end all wars." And Redgrave is so transcendent—others are good but she soars—that you recommend the film anyway.

It's hard to watch "Mrs. Dalloway" without thinking of the impact of both world wars upon Virginia Woolf and how when the crucial moment arrived for Woolf herself she made a drastically different choice from that of her heroine.

Exquisitely crafted, "Mrs. Dalloway" leaves you with a sense of irony, intended or otherwise. The adventure Peter held forth in youth really boiled down to some posting in India. Would not Clarissa have found colonial society a mite stifling and just possibly more fatuous and myopic than the London high society she presides over with such skill and wry, even scathing, detachment?

NEW YORK, 2/23/98, p. 112, David Denby

In *Mrs. Dalloway*, the accomplished but slightly tedious adaptation of Virginia Woolf's great novel, Vanessa Redgrave displays again the devastating gentleness familiar from her performance in *Howards End*. In that movie, Redgrave appeared briefly as the dying Mrs. Wilcox, a beautiful, unselfish woman—and an emanation of the purest sympathy. With only a few lines of dialogue, Redgrave suggested fathomless spiritual depths. Her vagueness was dominating, almost imperial—a ruminative grandeur that would have made sentiment of any overt kind, expressed in her presence, impossibly vulgar. Vanessa Redgrave has always possessed a genius for doubleness. Tall and broad-shouldered, with long arms and enormous hands, she is, God knows, a very palpable physical object. Big as life (bigger, really), she stands, or lies, before us, and yet she often seems lodged somewhere else at the same time, far away and lost in communion with gods too intimate for public scrutiny.

The doubleness becomes explicit right at the beginning of *Mrs. Dalloway*. Walking down a London street on a beautiful June day in 1923, Clarissa Dalloway feels herself to be nothing, a mere nobody—and at the same time, she registers with delight every element of sunshine, the movement of traffic and the passersby, the glitter of shops. This prosperous woman—married to a member of Parliament—is preparing for her annual party. Obsessed with silverware and flowers, Mrs. Dalloway nevertheless lives in a spiritual realm. She is not without faults, but she is great in empathy and alertness, and Redgrave, capturing her formal gravity, speaks slowly but without pomp. The public words are entirely conventional, the internal monologues (which we also hear) vivid and rebellious. In the hours before the party, Mrs. Dalloway reviews her life, casting back 30 years to easy summer days at her family's country estate, where, as a young woman, she rejected a demanding, puppyish suitor, Peter Walsh, in favor of the more stable and successful Richard Dalloway. Did she marry the right man? Just home from India, Peter (Michael Kitchen) shows up on the day of the party, and we can see that he's still charming and boyish, still ardent, but also unfinished in some way, a failure.

Now, it has been much noted that Virginia Woolf's heroines are not bold and intellectually distinguished like herself but gracious mothers and housewives, women who preside over personal relationships and marshal the silverware. Years earlier, young Peter had taunted Clarissa with her fears, and he was right about her—and also wrong. She has become something more than a public man's hostess-wife, and the movie is devoted to the something more—the imaginative sympathy within the heroine that holds life together. Written by actress Eileen Atkins, who has adapted a number of Virginia Woolf's works for the theater, and directed by Marleen Gorris, the Dutch filmmaker who won an Oscar for *Antonia's Line,* this is a movie made with poise and distinction.

All day long, Clarissa Dalloway thinks of her disappointments, her fears, her jealousies, and she vibrates in unconscious sympathy with a man she never meets—a shell-shocked and increasingly suicidal war veteran (Rupert Graves) whose troubles she will first hear about that night, right in the middle of her party. The movie has no plot in the ordinary sense, but as Mrs. Dalloway, grief-stricken, takes a momentary break from the swirl of polite social chatter, the elements of past and present, mediocrity and success, death and life, all come together in her head. Has she led a good and worthwhile life or not? The movie offers its judgment.

In the early scenes in the streets and in St. Jame's Park, as the forlorn war hero and his wife try to get through the day, Gorris jumps freely but coherently from minute observation of street life to lyrical fancy. *Mrs. Dalloway* flatters the movie audience with its high, quivering delicacy, its clear-eyed sensitivity. I wish, however, that Gorris did not stage social meetings so stiffly. These people are all from the same class and share the same assumptions; they are knowing, perhaps witty, yet they never seem at ease with one another. The stiffness may be intentional, a way of highlighting the difference between conventional surface and seething interior, but Gorris bores us with punctilious ceremony. She seems to be observing this society from another planet. Anyway, an emphasis on social behavior misses part of the point.

Virginia Woolf's habit of running freely from past to present has been called cinematic, but that is a naïve description of a very complex method. Woolf may have been influenced by the cinema, but she creates perhaps the most densely woven web of allusion, memory, and observation in English prose. She doesn't simply mix two time frames; she melds everything together in long passages of ecstatically heightened consciousness. This rich mental atmosphere—thick, bounding, grave yet playful cannot be recaptured on film; anyone who tried it would simply get visual hash. The movie doesn't offer hash; it is well ordered, beautiful, and clear. But it does what movies do, not what Virginia Woolf does. The filmmakers' rather simple flashbacks to Clarissa's youth (and this stuff is staged much more affectionately than the grown-up social scenes) are not very different formally from such sequences in dozens of other movies. When the poor war hero falls into delusion, we see a very literal spectacle of blown-up bodies; Atkins and Gorris thereby lose one of the central points of the book—that the shell-shocked veteran responds to nature and the world as the alert Mrs. Dalloway does (that's what connects them), but whereas she sees joyous beauty, he receives a riot of sensuous impressions that overwhelms and defeats him. The book is endlessly subtle, the movie refined but rather obvious.

Mrs. Dalloway is at its most inventive, and most Woolfian, when Redgrave is front and center, behaving with elaborate social grace and thinking very different things to herself. Just hearing Redgrave pronounce the word "*dis-ahs*-ter" (her appraisal of her own party) is reason enough to see the movie. In any case, I can't imagine any other actress large enough (in every sense) to hold together this plotless story. Redgrave makes the heroine all of a piece—timid, conventional, but alive to every breeze of consciousness.

NEW YORK POST, 2/20/98, p. 42 Thelma Adams

Virginia Woolf's 1925 stream-of-consciousness" Mrs. Dalloway" is one tough novel to crack for the screen. On a glorious June day in 1923, a middle-aged socialite gives a party. A shell-shocked World War I veteran leaps out a window.

That's as much of a plot as you're going to get in a book that celebrates the moment, the quotidian, while straining to capture the past. As the top-hatted Hugh Whitbread (Oliver Ford Davies) tell Mrs. Dalloway (Vanessa Redgrave) on her stroll through a London garden bound for the florist, "The war may be over, but there's still the echo of it.

In one day, the full weight of past and present, of personal choices and external forces, falls on Mrs. Dalloway. She may seem to be a silly, petty woman, a born hostess without a lick of social conscience, a snob; but she gets it.

Mrs. Dalloway leans out her townhouse window in the middle of her enchanting party, her back turned to Mr. Dalloway, the prime minister and the rest of her guests, and asks the night: "Have I lost the thing that matters?"

Mrs. Dalloway's stirring wake-up call leaps off the screen thanks to a subtle adaptation by Eileen Atkins (who wrote and starred with Redgrave in the Woolf-inspired play, ("Vita and Virginia") and emotionally warm direction from Marleen Gorris ("Antonia's Line") of the Netherlands.

Redgrave is a willowy wonder as Dalloway, long-stemmed, petal-thin-skinned, burning bright just at the moment before she wilts into oblivion. At 50, Dalloway's heart ailment limits her actions but not her thoughts.

And her thoughts return to 1890, to the days when she was single and simply Clarissa (the luminous Natascha McElhone). with her life ahead of her. Clarissa flirts with the glib, passionate Peter Walsh (Michael Kitchen as a young man, Alan Cox, in 1923). She also flirts with the flamboyant Sally Seton (Lena Headey and Sarah Badel in middle age).

But Clarissa makes a pivotal choice. She opts for security in the figure of the dashingly dull Richard Dalloway (Robert Portal). She gilds her own cage, becoming a wealthy politician's wife. When, on the day of her party, she encounters Peter, and hears of the suicide of the war veteran (Rupert Graves), the door of the cage flies open for one brief hour and life's potential, both tragic and ecstatic, rushes in. Here's to you "Mrs. Dalloway."

NEWSDAY, 2/20/98, Part II/p. B7, Jack Mathews

Dutch director Marleen Gorris' ambitious and mostly successful attempt to adapt Virginia Woolf's highly interior 1925 novel "Mrs. Dalloway" opens with two contrasting, and, as we will soon learn, unrelated scenes.

The first shows the non-revealing face of a young British soldier named Septimus (Rupert Graves), who has just seen a friend killed on the battlefield of World War I. The other shows the story's heroine, a politician's wife named Clarissa Dalloway (Vanessa Redgrave), cheerfully welcoming a sunny June day that is to end like the book and the movie, with another of her famous parties.

Woolf, one of the innovators of the 20th-Century literary form known as stream-of-consciousness, used the parallel stories of Septimus and Clarissa as two sides of an emotional coin. Septimus has lost the ability to feel, and is driven mad by it; Clarissa feels so deeply that the simple act of opening her door, or looking at a bowl of flowers, fills her with joy.

But there is also a sense of emptiness plaguing Mrs. Dalloway, the nagging feeling—revealed through detailed flashbacks to a critical juncture 30 years earlier (when she is played by Natscha McElhone)—that she has missed something on the road presented but not taken. And in the most subtle and extraordinary ways, the choices made by Septimus on the day of Clarissa's party will affect her for the rest of her life.

Long books have been written about those dynamics in Woolf's short, dense, fitfully-bright and melancholy novel, the difficulty of which has left only the cockiest readers asking, "Who's afraid of Virginia Woolf?" The author moved freely through the minds of her characters, developing them from the inside out, and used their seemingly spontaneous thoughts to make the most profound observations about life and each other.

But let none of that scare you away from the movie. Gorris, whose 1995 "Antonia's Line" won the Oscar for best foreign language film, and screenwriter Eileen Atkins, a British actress who's made Woolf a major part of her career repertoire, have translated the novel with miraculous ease and with incredible fidelity. With few liberties, the movie is the book.

Just about everything that describes the novel—it leaps back and forth between characters, in and out of their thoughts, and back in time—is true of the film, yet it's never confusing, and never boring. It does get too precious at times, particularly during the climactic party scenes, and Redgrave wears a smile of open-mouthed wonder through so much of the film that you begin to suspect lockjaw. But the characters, whom we get to know in both their 20s and their 50s, are fascinating products of turn-of-the-century British high society.

The memories stirring in Clarissa's mind involve her early relationships with her would-be Bohemian friend Sally Seton (Lena Headey), her passionate, suffocating suitor Peter March (Alan Cox) and the earnest, boring Richard Dalloway (Robert Portal).

Clarissa's most sublime connection is with Sally, who stimulates her imagination and, in one chastely intimate scene, her sensuality. There's a wildness about Sally that is both appealing and dangerous to Clarissa, and the same is true of Peter's suffocating devotion. Ultimately, she chooses Richard, accepting a prescribed life over a gambler's, and is brought, all these years later, to wonder what she's missed.

As fate would have it, the older Peter (Michael Kitchen) shows up on the day of Clarissa's party, as boyishly irresponsible and lovestruck as ever. Sally (Sarah Badel) returns, too, tamed and matronly and a mother of five grown sons, as anxious as Peter to reclaim, if just for a nostalgic moment, what they all once shared.

What they shared is what gives "Mrs. Dalloway" its energy. Except for Graves' wrenching performance as Septimus, the day-of-the-party scenes are static next to Clarissa's memories. McElhone and Headey are especially engaging as the young women, and though nothing we learn about the futures of Peter and Sally questions Clarissa's choice, the unknown—like the roads not taken in all of our lives—is no less haunting.

NEWSWEEK, 3/2/98, p. 80, Jack Kroll

In a movie universe clanking with special effects, "Mrs. Dalloway" dares to luxuriate in art's greatest special effect: language. It's something of a miracle to succeed in adapting Virginia Woolf's landmark (and eternally popular) 1925 novel, written almost entirely in its characters' stream of consciousness. But it's been pulled off by a gifted and gutsy team headed by a noted writer-actor, Eileen Atkins; a supersensitive director, the Dutch-born Marleen Gorris (whose "Antonia's Line" won the 1995 Oscar for best foreign-language film), and a supreme actress, Vanessa Redgrave. They have made a million-faceted gem, flashing forth the world inside Clarissa Dalloway's head, and outside, with the sights and sounds of a teeming London on a fine June day in 1923.

Mrs. Dalloway's interior monologue, spoken on the soundtrack by Redgrave in her crushed-velvet voice, veers like a verbal dance between present and past. The Clarissa of 30 years before rejects the feverish idealism of one suitor, Peter Walsh, for the unexciting security of another, Richard Dalloway. Her best friend, Sally Seton, is a bohemian beauty who talks of "changing the world" and scoots naked through the halls of Clarissa's proper family house. Now, five years after the Great War, Mrs. Dalloway is a chiffoned pillar of society, her husband a minor M.P., her life measured out by her fashionable parties. Her odyssey through the great city is intercut with a more painful one by a shellshocked veteran, Septimus Smith. Mrs. Dalloway's day is climaxed by her party, Smith's by his suicide. But these contrasting events are two parts of a symbolic whole, Virginia Woolf herself. Mrs. Dalloway is a Woolf without the genius, while Smith's fate prefigures the troubled Woolf's own suicide in 1941. In her notebook Woolf wrote, "Mrs. D seeing the truth. SS seeing the insane truth."

This truth is that of spiritual death. At her party, attended by the decaying lions and lionesses of the English ruling class, Mrs. Dalloway ponders her loss of "the thing that matters" to a life of "corruption, lies and chatter." Her one moment of incandescent feeling occurred long ago when Sally kissed her, bringing a smile of ecstatic wonderment to her face. Natascha McElhone as the young Clarissa is part of a superb ensemble that seems to create a cityful of characters. Redgrave's haunting performance is a double incarnation. She is Mrs. Dalloway and she is Woolf, a gallant icon of a gracefully collapsing world.

SIGHT AND SOUND, 3/98, p. 53, Claire Monk

On 13 June 1923, Clarissa Dalloway, middle-aged wife of a politician, prepares for the society party she will host that night at her London home. The day's events send her thoughts back to her youth in 1890. Musing on her close friendship with the radical, mischievous Sally Seton (which might have been something more) and on Peter Walsh, the socialist suitor whom she rejected in favour of Richard, she reflects on the different course her life might have taken.

In the street, Clarissa glimpses a young man, Septimus Warren Smith, a war veteran tormented by delayed shell-shock, reacting in terror to a car backfiring. Peter Walsh unexpectedly reappears after years in India and confides that he is in love with a married woman. Septimus' wife Rezia takes him to see a shell-shock specialist, Sir William Bradshaw, because insensitive treatment by another doctor, Holmes, has failed. Bradshaw dismisses Septimus' suicidal urges, but later sends Holmes to institutionalise him, prompting Septimus to jump from a window to his death.

Clarissa greets her party guests. Present are Peter and Sally, now wife of a knighted mill-owner and mother of five—but hostess' duties and the arrival of the Prime Minister keep Clarissa from the two people she most wants to see. Bradshaw arrives late due to Septimus' suicide. Clarissa, repelled by his token concern, is traumatised by the news. Alone on a balcony, she anguishes over her fears of life and old age and admires the courage of choosing death, but returns to her party.

Virginia Woolf's formally revolutionary 1925 novel *Mrs Dalloway* offers multi-perspective inner monologues and leaps back and forth across space (1923 London) and time (between the 1923 'present', scarred by World War One, and a remembered 1890 'past'). It could be argued that any attempt to film this book demands a director committed to finding an equally radical cinematic equivalent.

Judged by such criteria, Marleen Gorris' *Mrs Dalloway*—the Dutch feminist director's first film since her matriarchal epic *Antonia's Line*—counts as a failure. Innocent of the critic-pleasing, audience-pulling devices of some recent literary adaptations (such as the tricksy cinematography and hyped-up raunch of *The Wings of the Dove*), its aesthetic recalls the European art cinema of an earlier, less commercially frenzied decade.

Designed as if the fiercely stylised spectacle of Sally Potter's *Orlando* had never happened, its realist, object-crammed *mise en scène* implies an unfashionable unconcern to be faithful to the period.

In fact, *Mrs. Dalloway*'s success is due to the nonchalance of Gorris (working from a script which actress and Woolf-buff Eileen Atkins had already written with Redgrave in mind) about such formal and narrative problems. As she indicated in her debut, the darkly comic radical-feminist classic *De Stilte rond Christine M./A Question of Silence*, Gorris is not a director who plays by the usual rules. *Mrs Dalloway*'s art-film appearances, like those of *Antonia's Line*, harbour a robustly female-centred sensibility; but a conventional period aesthetic also coexists with a ruthless unsentimentality and political bite which few recent British period films have fully achieved.

At the same time, *Mrs. Dalloway* marks a further mellowing of the black-and-white gender politics of Gorris' earlier films. In *Antonia's Line* men were either bad, benign or sperm-donors. Here, their peripherality to the lives women could lead in an ideal non-patriarchal Utopia remains a theme. (Although the unrealised implicitly lesbian partnership between the young Clarissa and the radical Sally Seton is treated with peculiar restraint.) However, the existence of women who use their power to poisonous ends is also admitted, most clearly via the figure of Lady Bruton. She exploits her status as a "mere" woman to persuade male politicians to sponsor a scheme to "encourage' unemployable casualties of war - such as shell-shocked Septimus Warren Smith—to emigrate.

A less commented-upon trait of both films is their atheistic humanism and it i! this which Gorris' *Mrs. Dalloway* develops into a broader exploration of freedom and power. Where in *Antonia's Line*, the aged Antonia's decision to die is presented as a positive step, *Mrs. Dalloway* embraces the idea that death—or, here, suicide—may be a positive gesture of autonomy for those made powerless. More ambiguously, the film juxtaposes the young Clarissa's 1890 decision to marry Richard with Septimus 1923 suicide, suggesting that her choice of a partner who will "leave me room" in preference to his more politically radical rival Peter is a similar gesture of necessity in the face of constraints.

Ultimately, though, *Mrs. Dalloway*'s real bite and significance derives less from its expected feminism than from its stance as one of only two recent period releases, along with Gillies MacKinnon's *Regeneration* to admit knowledge of the Great War and its traumas. In a pointed departure from Woolf's novel, its opening shot shows Warren Smith (whose final hours of anguish are juxtaposed with Mr. Dalloway's party preparations) in the trenches. As Mrs. Dalloway says at the outset: "The war may be over, but there's still the echo of it." The presence of this echo in the film, together with its chilling snapshots of the attitudes of the rich and powerful (given a grimly comic edge by flawless cast which includes Margaret Tyzack and Phyllis Calvert), make nostalgic viewing possible.

VILLAGE VOICE, 2/24/98, p. 61, Amy Taubin

What a surprise. *Mrs. Dalloway*, Virginia Woolf's novel of nonstop introspection, has been turned into an affecting and highly intelligent movie. The women responsible for this feat are Eileen Atkins, who wrote the adaptation; Marleen Gorris, who directed; and Vanessa Redgrave, who is so absolute an incarnation of Mrs. Dalloway (although she has neither a "narrow pea-stick figure" nor a "little face beaked like a bird") that it seems, impossible as it is, that she was Woolf's inspiration.

Set in London during the course of a single day in 1923, Woolf's novel is constructed basically as a set of interlocking interior monologues that collapse time present and time past in what used to be called stream of consciousness and now is more loosely dubbed subjectivity. With one exception, the main characters are all in their early fifties. Facing a limited future, they muse on their pasts, on the unfathomable separation between who they were at 20 and who they are now. They muse about themselves in the first person and the third person. And when their musing is interrupted by another person's words or activity, they incorporate the voice and the activity into the unbroken and unspoken commentary taking place inside their heads.

Here is Clarissa Dalloway lost in thought as she walks up Bond Street to buy flowers for a party she is giving that night. Clarissa is famous for her parties. "She had the odd sense of being herself invisible, unseen, unknown, there being no more marrying, no more having of children now, but only this astonishing and rather solemn progress with the rest of them, up Bond Street, this being Mrs. Dalloway; not even Clarissa anymore; this being Mrs. Richard Dalloway."

How, then, to translate into a movie a text that is so anticinematic even though it owes the fluidity with which it moves about in time and space to montage, the governing principle of a medium—film—that in 1923 was still in its most feverish period of development. Atkins and Gorris find relatively conservative formal solutions, while preserving the sense of Woolf's central character, her dilemma, and the historic forces that made her who she was. Pared down to core bits and pieces, Mrs. Dalloway's inner monologues come to us as a voiceover that's never obtrusive but does the trick of bridging the gap between emotions, thoughts, and actions, and also of cueing the frequent transitions between the here and now and the memory of the crucial summer when the young Clarissa chose to marry the reliable Richard Dalloway rather than the dependent and possessive Peter Walsh, though neither of them excited her as much as did her friend Sally Seton, who proclaimed that marriage was a prison and, of course, went on to become the wife of a wealthy tradesman and the mother of five sons.

What's best about the film—what differentiates it from Merchant Ivory costume claptrap—is its feminism, most of which comes from Woolf, but which is given an even sharper edge by Gorris. A Question of Silence, Gorris's first and most powerful film, was a homicidal assault on patriarchy in which laughter became the most lethal weapon of all. Her Oscar winner, Antonia's Line, was unbearably vulgar and silly, a mistake from beginning to end. What she brings to Mrs. Dalloway is a contemporary feminist sensibility and a kind of hindsight. She makes us understand that the choices Clarissa makes—the fact that she can't even contemplate running off with Sally Seton—have to do with the interaction of temperament and historical conditions.

The ensemble cast is adequate, though Natascha McElhone as the young Clarissa is a bit too well adjusted to metamorphose into Redgrave's neurasthenic Mrs. Dalloway. This is one of Redgrave's extraordinary performances. She deploys to the full her capacity for playing mixed emotions and psychological instability; she shows how Mrs. Dalloway's euphoria can exist simultaneously with despair, how she must fight to preserve her sanity, and how in that fight, repression is a double-edged sword.

Woolf gives Mrs. Dalloway an alter ego, a soldier who fought in the trenches in World War I and five years later is in the throes of a post-traumatic stress syndrome that London in the '20's is at pains not to acknowledge. Mrs. Dalloway sees him only once—through the window of the shop where she buys the flowers for her party—but his evident psychosis shadows her day. The soldier's story is what gives the narrative its psychological and political breadth. It's a measure of the filmmakers' intelligence and integrity that, however awkward it was to handle, they give the soldier's narrative its due. We could not know Mrs. Dalloway without him.

Also reviewed in:
CHICAGO TRIBUNE, 3/6/98, Friday/p. L, Michael Wilmington
NEW REPUBLIC, 3/9/98, p. 28, Stanley Kauffmann
NEW YORK TIMES, 2/20/98, p. E12, Janet Maslin
NEW YORKER, 2/16/98, p. 82, Daphne Merkin
VARIETY, 9/15-21/97, p. 75, Emanuel Levy
WASHINGTON POST, 3/6/98, Weekend/p. 50, Desson Howe

MODULATIONS

A Strand Releasing release of a Calpirinha production. *Producer:* George Gund. *Director:* Iara Lee. *Screenplay:* Peter Shapiro. *Director of Photography:* Marcus Burnett and Paul Yates. *Editor:* Paula Heredia. *Running time:* 73 minutes. *MPAA Rating:* Not Rated.

WITH: Afrika Bambaataa; Juan Atkins; Bundy Brown; DJ Spooky; Future Sound of London; Fumiya Tanaka; Hardfloor; Kodwo Eshun; Teo Macero; Christian Marclay; Giorgio Moroder; Robert Moog; Mixmaster Morris; Orbital; Prodigy; Simon Reynolds; Ed Rush; Karlheinz Stockhausen; Tetsu Inoue; Westbam.

LOS ANGELES TIMES, 9/4/98, Calendar/p. 14, Steve Hochman

Do you think of the techno-rave scene as cultural cotton candy: flavorful, but nutritionally empty? With "Modulations," director Iara Lee has managed to make a documentary on the phenomenon and fill it with fiber and vitamins—and put it in a very colorful wrapper.

The color was the easy, and obvious, part. After all, this is a world filled with pulsating beats, strobing lights and fashions that mix "The Jetsons" with Dr. Seuss. And the artists and fans in the scene affect a wide variety of philosophies—all touted with religious fervor—ranging from party masters to Zen-like self-tuning. Lee captures this in all its electric glory, using a mix of film and video textures and illustrative techniques in rave locales ranging from a New Jersey warehouse to the slopes of Mt. Fuji.

Where Lee offers something of more substance is with her explorations of the history of electronic music (fascinating interviews with such figures as Karlheinz Stockhausen and Pierre Henry and an examination of John Cage using vintage clips) and the way the classical, intellectual experiments took root in the visceral world of urban dance styles. Her interest in technology (her previous film, "Synthetic Pleasures," looked at new technology in pop culture) also adds meat to the material, with instructive and entertaining bits about how the nature of samplers and turntables have dictated the shape of the music.

Lee's technique is at times choppy and especially in the early going the distinctions between the numerous sub-genres of techno are not always clear. But she's managed to capture the essence of a very complex world for the uninitiated while at the same time engaging it in a way that offers something new for even the most devoted fans.

NEW YORK POST, 9/4/98, p. 68, Larry Worth

Those who don't know their breakbeats from their BPMS, mix up a sampler with a sequencer or—worse still—confuse a TR-808 drum machine with a TR-809 should steer clear of "Modulations."

Iara Lee's documentary about electronic music's genesis and growing influence will appeal to a very limited audience. For that matter, even techno-culture diehards may find it a trial.

That's surprising since Lee hit a bona fide home run with her debut film, "Synthetic Pleasure," an exploration of every man-made wonder imaginable. This time, the wonders never veer too far from a Moog synthesizer.

In the process, one gets to hear from composer Giorgio Moroder on how Donna Summer's "I Feel Love" launched a new age of sequenced, high-energy disco in the '70s. And this is an accomplishment?

The director also makes a giant leap in segueing from "pioneers" such as Neil Armstrong (showing his first steps on the moon) to those who've furthered the art of organized noise. Somehow, it's tough to make the connection.

In fairness, the narrative also covers electronic music's effects on Detroit, then jumps back to the '20s with inventor Leon Theremin's contribution to the cause. Without doubt, it's the most intriguing segment.

Lee fuses all that into a mix of MTV-style jump cuts and talking heads who discuss the "forever changing" sounds of electronics. And though a few recognizable names pop up, most speakers could be interchangeable.

For many, the soundtrack may justify the film's existence. At the very least, it's non-stop. But it's also headache-inducing. So's the grainy photography.

But the most damning factor is Lee's lack of attempts to cut through the verbiage and translate some of the jargon. That's a basic for any documentary, and what makes them accessible to dilettantes.

Yet, before "Modulations" reaches a protracted conclusion, it's almost a moot point. Electronica's fans—and certainly the non-fans—will have tuned out long ago.

NEWSDAY, 9/4/98, Part II/p. BII, John Anderson

A sort of sequel to Steven Martin's "Theremin" and an upscale sister to films such as Craig Baldwin's "Sonic Outlaws," Iara Lee's documentary, "Modulations," examines the birth and directions of electronic music, which the uninitiated might compare to the sound of someone banging on a garbage can (and we get to see several examples of people doing exactly that). What "Modulations" does is get one past one's trashy presumptions and into the heart of the music.

And it is music, even though the aesthetic—as a number of Lee's "witnesses" testify—is often about quasi-nihilism and the chemical effect of throbbing beats. You wish that Lee—who has an excellent editor in Paula Heredia—had spent a little more time on the artistic traditions inherent in electronic music (the technique of repetition, for one, which is as old as Gaelic poetry and as current as Top 40 radio) and had steered her subjects toward even more sociological ruminations about the attractions of electronic music. Still, where she goes is pretty fascinating.

Emulating the frenetic pace of a dance hall and applying a candy-shell finish to her pulsing imagery, Lee shows us that there are as many points of view and artistic philosophies behind the music as there are forms of the music itself (ambient, acid house, jungle techno, krautrock, hiphop and even disco). The true aficionado (unlike myself) might bring his or her own perspective to who and what Lee chooses to focus on; as like any form of music, of course, it all can sound alike to a disinterested audience. But by the end of Lee's primer, the squeak of packing tape and the whine of a dentist's drill start to take on tonal and rhythmic qualities.

"Modulations" pays homage to the pioneers—John Cage, Karlheinz Stockhausen, jazz producer Teo Macero, through to Kraftwerk ("Trans-Europe Express") and on to the DJs/sound mechanics of the '90s nightclub. There are moments that give one pause, of course. Take a crowd, cheering a record scratcher for his manipulations of an LP and a sound machine with the same lusty enthusiasm they might have afforded Horowitz. The difference, unacknowledged here, is that Horowitz was working within a familiar recognized framework, a tradition wherein subtleties and nuance meant something concrete. A cheering crowd at a nightclub, on the other hand, is exhibiting the same kind of crude response that a member of Future Sound of London, one of the groups Lee includes in her film, is railing against. "Most music is based on instant gratification for the artist," she says, "gratification through contact with an audience. With so many people basing their idea of entertainment on that concept, we think there has to be something interesting about the opposite." There is. But as in any other form of 20th-Century expression, the audience often has to play catch-up with the artist.

Also reviewed in:
NEW YORK TIMES, 9/4/98, p. E8, Stephen Holden
VARIETY, 2/2-8/98, p. 35, Dennis Harvey

MONUMENT AVE.

A Lions Gate Films release of a Spanky Pictures/Apostle Pictures production. *Executive Producer:* Joel Stillerman and Ted Demme. *Producer:* Jim Serpico. *Director:* Ted Demme. *Screenplay:* Mike Armstrong. *Director of Photography:* Adam Kimmel. *Editor:* Jeffrey Wolf. *Music:* Amanda Scheer-Demme. *Production Designer:* Ruth Ammon. *Stunt Coordinator:* Brian Ricci. *Running time:* 90 minutes. *MPAA Rating:* Not Rated.

CAST: Denis Leary (Bobby);   Ian Hart (Mouse);   Lenny Clarke (Skunk);   Jason Barry (Seamus);   Kevin Chapman (Mickey Pat); George MacDonald (Gallivan);   John Diehl (Digger); Lyndon Byers (Fitzie);   Herbie Ade (Herbie);   Noah Emmerich (Red);   Famke Janssen (Katy); Melissa Fitzgerald (Sheila);   Don Gavin (Brosnihan);   Billy Crudup (Teddy);   Colm Meaney (Jackie O'Hara);   Greg Dulli (Shang);   Brian Goodman (Gavin);   Martin Sheen (Hanlon); Victor Chan (Lee);   Marily Murphy Meardon (Mrs. O'Grady); Bill McDonald (Father Donahue); Gene Boles (John Kelsey);   Sandra Shippley (Mrs. Timmons);   Jeanne Tripplehorn (Annie); Karen White (Marcy);   François Joseph (Kid);   Sue McGinnis (Mrs. Turbody);   Jackie Sullivan (Bar Owner).

CHRISTIAN SCIENCE MONITOR, 9/25/98, p. B3, David Sterritt

Boston has become an active location for independent filmmakers, but the portrait they paint isn't always flattering. While the romantic "Next Stop Wonderland" uses bright colors and energizing music to lighten its sometimes doleful story, the downbeat "Southie" proved a somber and sometimes violent experience when director John Shea presented its premiere at the Montreal filmfest.

"Monument Ave." takes place in a different neighborhood but tells a similar tale of loyalty, rivalry, and betrayal in one of the city's staunchly Irish-American sections. Named after a street that divides long-entrenched residents from privileged yuppies moving into the area, it focuses on a small-time crime boss called Jackie 0. and a budding criminal.

"Monument Ave." follows in the footsteps of too many like-minded movies, dating back to "Mean Streets" and beyond, to be called original or surprising. It also has a weakness for self-conscious dialogue scenes that resemble acting exercises more than real life. But it has some chillingly suspenseful moments. The good cast includes Colm Meaney as the boss, Denis Leary as the edgy youngster, Billy Crudup as the ex-convict, and Martin Sheen as the cop.

LOS ANGELES TIMES, 9/25/98, Calendar/p. 4, Kevin Thomas

Ted Demme's bleak yet compelling "Monument Ave." takes its title from the street that has come to divide the old Boston neighborhood of Charlestown, whose working-class Irish settled there a century ago, and the surrounding area, which has become increasingly gentrified. Bobby O'Grady (Denis Leary) and his lifelong Charlestown pals may resent the intrusion of yuppies, but the newcomers also provide more goodies to steal.

At the beginning of "Monument Ave.," Bobby, at 33 and still living with his parents, pretty much accepts his lot in life, which means that he and his friends have chosen petty crime over factory work (which is probably dwindling anyway). While not so sophisticated as to resist wearing ridiculous outsized sideburns, Bobby is clearly more intelligent, more reflective, than the others he hangs with, and in a sense this will be his curse.

Mike Armstrong's relentlessly downbeat script allows Demme to develop an ensnaring camaraderie coupled with a dark destructiveness that recalls Eugene O'Neill. "Monument Ave." begins on a fairly light note, taking its time to acquaint us with Bobby and others, notably his best friend, Mouse (Ian Hart), and Seamus (Jason Barry), his cousin from Dublin, and to take us into their everyday lives, which are consumed with hanging out, mainly in neighborhood bars.

The cocaine they take on top of large quantities of liquor will prove to be the factor that unravels their lives. When yet another O'Grady cousin, Ted (Billy Crudup), fresh out of prison and high as a kite, starts talking loudly and loosely in a crowded pub, the local crime boss Jackie (Colm Meaney) has him gunned down on the spot.

(It doesn't help that Bobby is having an affair with Jackie's girl Katy Franke Janssen; the irony is that all these guys are so into seemingly full-time male bonding that neither Bobby nor Jackie has much time for her. Theirs is clearly a society in which women are good for one thing.)

In any event, the code of silence that gripped Charlestown, causing three out of four murders to go unsolved until recent years, kicks in immediately. But a local veteran cop (Martin Sheen), Irish for sure but from "across the bridge," is the kind of man who never gives up.

"Monument Ave." thus centers on Bobby, a man too smart not to see his entire way of life threatening to disintegrate but who may not be strong enough to resist the undertow. Demme and Armstrong depict with mounting tension—and looming dread—a group of criminals so closely tied to each other by either kinship or friendship or both, and so imprisoned by codes of behavior, that they can't handle the inevitability of change to the point of self-destruction. Careening around in a taxi belonging to a gang member, they spot a black man walking on "their" turf in the dead of night. Bobby goes berserk—or does he?—threatening a terrorist attack on the stranger. Is he driven to show up the cowardice of the worst bigot among his pals? Or is he in danger of displacing the rage of his own frustrations? Probably both.

You cannot watch "Monument Ave." without thinking of "Mean Streets." The filmmakers surely know this, and they respond to the challenge of inevitable comparisons with the Scorsese classic by generating a shattering raw power of their own through Demme's superb direction of a large ensemble cast, through cameraman Adam Kimmel's shadowy images shot in authentic locales, and through Armstrong's script, which steadily evokes an ever-mounting sense of inevitable tragedy.

In a screen crowded with impeccable portrayals, Leary's Bobby emerges as a dominating presence, haunting—and haunted by—an awareness the others lack. With "Monument Ave.," Leary fulfills the promise he's been revealing in bits and pieces all along in either smaller or less demanding roles.

NEW YORK POST, 9/25/98, p. 53, Thelma Adams

"Monument Ave. is Ted Demme's fierce, coke-driven, hard-drinking, mother-loving morality play set on the mean, green streets of Boston's predominantly Irish-Catholic Charlestown section.

If anything, it's a monument to Denis Leary.

The stand-up actor doesn't steal the picture as a car thief, but he strains to transcend his natural talent—ranting—to bring a blue-collar Irish sensibility to a stock character molded, then abandoned, by Scorsese.

We have seen him before, this Bobby, this charismatic man-boy who has one last chance to stand up in long pants, to uphold the immigrant code. Robert De Niro, Al Pacino and Ray Liotta have all played him.

Leary doesn't have the shadows and light of the Italians and is even less believable with a gun in his hand or liberating a Lamborghini.

But he shares with director Demme and screenwriter Mike Armstrong a passion for authenticity and a willingness to stare down the racism, sexism and pigheadedness that are as much a part of this insular Irish enclave as Guinness and great storytelling.

Demme surrounds Leary with a pack of buddies from birth played by Ian Hart, Noah Emmerich and John Diehl. Colm Meaney is the demi-godfather and Martin Sheen the cop bent on destroying him.

Leggy Famke Janssen strikes a false note as the neighborhood supermodel, an actress who could make the facial bruise left by a boyfriend's fist look chic.

Billy Crudup burns through the movie as Bobby's ex-con cousin, Teddy. Crudup's strung-out coke dealer just out of the joint is attractive and repulsive, boyish yet broken, a brazen liar whose blarney can't save him from street justice on Monument Ave.

NEWSDAY, 9/25/98, Part II/p. B7, Gene Seymour

With his serpentine features never too far from a smirk or a scowl, Denis Leary has been a paragon of the angry-white-guy school of stand-up comedy in the 1990s. His snarling, in-your-face delivery has been an effective tool for either selling motor oil or busting pop icons down to size. He's also given a charge to feature films such as "Wag the Dog" and "The Ref." Yet, despite such credentials, few have dared imagine Leary as having the potential for major, Bruce Willis-size film stardom.

"Monument Ave.," the moody crime thriller directed by "The Ref's" Ted Demme, should change that. As Bobby O'Grady, a small-time car thief and street thug living with his mother in Boston's Charlestown district, Leary is able to contain a swarm of moral ambiguities within the kind of magnetic swagger once associated with James Cagney. Even when he deploys some of the explosive elements of his stand-up persona, Leary puts them at the disposal of his character's melancholy and unfocused rage with a musician's sense of timing.

What makes Leary's work more impressive is that his fine performance is one of many that raise "Monument Ave." above other attempts to duplicate "Mean Streets." The story is set in an Irish working-class enclave of Charlestown at odds with the overall neighborhood's gentrification. Bobby and his buddies carry on a guerrilla war against the yuppies by burglarizing their homes and stealing their fancy cars.

Most of the spoils of victory, however, end up in the slimy hands of Jackie O'Hara (Colm Meaney), a gangster whose dominion over the neighborhood becomes more noticeably iron-fisted when Bobby's cousin Teddy (Billy Crudup in a bravura turn) is sprung from prison earlier than expected, arousing Jackie O's suspicions that Teddy turned rat. Bad stuff starts to happen all around Bobby and friends such as partner-in-theft Mouse Murphy (Ian Hunt), blowhard bigot Red Doherty (Noah Emmerich from "The Truman Show") and burned-out cabby Digger Bruce (John Diehl) maintain a tribal code of silence against the insistent queries of a veteran cop named Hanlon (Martin Sheen).

Under Demme's smooth, tight guidance, the story manages to flow and grip despite a somewhat improbable climax. And, as noted, every cast member delivers a strong performance. Special mention should also be given to Famke Janssen as Jackie's mistress and Bobby's sometime lover, who shares the latter's conflicted emotions and desperation.

VILLAGE VOICE, 9/29/98, p. 130, Justine Elias

Across the river from Boston's tony Beacon Hill—and a world away from the salt-of-the-earth Southie of *Good Will Hunting* lies the neighborhood of Charlestown, a mostly Irish, working-class enclave where, according to *Monument Ave.*, you definitely don't want to park your car. That's because a gangster called Jackie O (Colm Meaney, sounding more Irish than Irish-American) runs a crew of car thieves. Two of them, Bobby O'Grady (Denis Leary) and Mouse (the superb Ian Hart) are trusted members of this criminal underworld, but their boyhood pal (Billy Crudup, in a smashing cameo) is seen as a threat. Released early from prison, he's suspected of being a rat, and he soon pays the price for violating the local code of silence.

Though Bobby and his friends toy with the idea of vengeance, they strike out with predictable shortsightedness against easier targets: mothers, girlfriends, yuppie homesteaders, and a black college student who makes the mistake of walking home alone through Charlestown. Under Ted Demme's accomplished direction, the film unfolds with a kind of ruthless simplicity, observing, rather than stating, the neighborhood's intricate social connections. Leary is a quiet, mesmerizing dramatic actor, and another strong performance comes from Famke Janssen, a Dutch émigré who would be one of the most glamorous women in film if she were not so determined to forge a career as a gritty character actress. As Bobby's sometime lover, and Jackie O's mistress, she may seem a little too bright and beautiful to be marooned in this sorry world, but like Leary, she conveys the defeat and fear behind her tough facade, and like him, she is utterly believable.

Also reviewed in:
NEW YORK TIMES, 9/25/98, p. E15, Stephen Holden
WASHINGTON POST, 10/9/98, p. D5, Stephen Hunter
WASHINGTON POST, 10/9/98, Weekend/p. 49, Michael O'Sullivan

MOON OVER BROADWAY

An Artistic License Films release of a Pennebaker Hegedus Films and Mc*Ettinger Films presentation in association with Bravo Cable. *Producer:* Frazer Pennebaker and Wendy Ettinger. *Director:* D.A. Pennebaker and Chris Hegedus. *Director of Photography:* D.A. Pennebaker, Nick Doob, and James Desmond. *Editor:* D.A. Pennebaker and Chris Hegedus. *Running time:* 92 minutes. *MPAA Rating:* Not Rated.

WITH: Carol Burnett; Philip Bosco; Ken Ludwig; Tom Moore; Elizabeth Williams; Rocco Landesman.

LOS ANGELES TIMES, 3/6/98, Calendar/p. 24, Kevin Thomas

You have to wonder how the Carol Burnett-Philip Bosco 1995 Broadway hit "Moon Over Buffalo" could be more captivating than Chris Hegedus and D.A. Pennebaker's "Moon Over Broadway," which documents the course of the play's production from first rehearsal to opening night. Written by comparative newcomer Ken Ludwig and directed by boyish-looking Broadway veteran Tom Moore, "Moon Over Buffalo" is a traditional backstage farce in which Burnett and Bosco are cast as "the second-rate Lunts." They are performing "Private Lives" and "Cyrano de Bergerac" in repertory in Buffalo—the year is 1953—when they learn the electrifying news that Frank Capra is coming to see them for their possible casting in his upcoming film, "The Return of the Scarlet Pimpernel" (an unlikely Capra project, but no matter).

Of course, they're thrown into a tizzy, especially Burnett. The generous glimpses of "Moon Over Buffalo" in rehearsal and out of town in Boston's glorious Beaux Arts Colonial Theater suggest that it is a pretty funny show, a sturdy vehicle for its stars, and that audiences laugh a lot.

"Moon Over Broadway" takes us backstage in the assembling of a major stage production starring one of America's most beloved performers and one of the theater's—and film's—most distinguished character actors. Even allowing for the fact that Hegedus and Pennebaker's celebrated fly-on-the-wall technique could not possibly have caught every feeling and nuance experienced by cast and crew in bringing the show alive, "Moon Over Broadway" is in fact very comforting. It suggests that professionalism, civility and sophistication are alive and well in the top rungs of the American theater.

Burnett, who looks wonderful with or without makeup, is just as you would hope she would be: unpretentious, thoughtful and a good sport. (When the curtain wouldn't go up during the play's final dress rehearsal, Burnett came out and did 10 minutes of stand-up, to the delight of the audience.) There's less of Bosco, who early on makes a point of hoping Moore and Ludwig will want input from the actors and worries that he's being expected to play at the top throughout.

As it turns out, however, the star of the documentary is in fact Ludwig, a stocky, 40-ish man who has to come up with all those rewrites and, as one of the producers remarks, has the most at stake as the least-established of the production's principals. He's the one who needs the most reassurance, the most constructive of criticism; fortunately, Moore comes across as a man who knows both what he wants and how to be a master diplomat. There's also a lot of helpful input from the play's urbane producers, Rocco Landesman and Elizabeth Williams.

As is their style, Hegedus and Pennebaker, who made the Oscar-nominated 1993 documentary "The War Room," about the Clinton campaign for the presidency, don't ask questions—and they didn't let anybody involved see their film until it was finished. You're left to wonder how Ludwig reacted to learning that the producers seriously considered bringing in a joke-smith—a Long Island dentist—to get more laughs, and how Burnett felt when she heard Ludwig remark of star casting that "that's the pact you make with the devil in the modern theater."

The filmmakers' approach prevents them from asking Ludwig to explain who his ideal casting would be and how she would be different from Burnett. (You get the feeling that he might like a bit of underplaying, but Burnett gives the broad strokes her fans expect and she is swiftly validated.)

In any event, by and large Burnett and Bosco got the critical raves rather than Ludwig. There seems little doubt that Burnett, in her return to Broadway after a 30-year absence, was responsible for "Moon Over Buffalo's" nine-month run.

NEW YORK POST, 2/18/98, p. 38, Larry Worth

When it comes to documentarians who educate *and* entertain, D.A. Pennebaker is at the head of his class.

Pennebaker, who blossomed in 1967's "Don't Look Back" (capturing Bob Dylan's concert tour through England), got even better after teaming with Chris Hegedus for 1993's study of President Clinton's election campaign, "The War Room."

Now, Pennebaker and Hegedus triumph anew by switching gears for "Moon Over Broadway," a mesmerizing look at the daily anxieties, larger-than-life egos and constant compromises that dog a play en route to the Great White Way.

The subject of scrutiny is the 1995 farce "Moon Over Buffalo" (which ultimately opened at the Martin Beck Theater to mixed reviews and played for nine months). Despite the reassuring presence of comedienne Carol Burnett and co-star Philip Bosco, life backstage proves no laughing matter.

For starters, Burnett has trouble remembering her lines *exactly*. And with massive daily rewrites, who could blame her? Bosco, meanwhile, explodes when he doesn't feel his input is being taken seriously.

Then there's the whiny starlet who doesn't think her publicity picture is glamorous enough, writer Ken Ludwig—whose insecurities over script-doctoring seem warranted—and director Tom Moore's doubling as camp counselor and general punching bag.

The ever-unobtrusive Pennebaker and Hegedus record it all, from tenuous Boston tryouts to Burnett's superstitious ways and celebs' gushy dressing room visits. It's virtually impossible not to relish each fascinating tidbit.

One of the best moments occurs when a malfunctioning winch literally brings down the curtain during a preview performance. Reverting to her TV variety show persona, Burnett saves the day by taking audience members' questions—and producing funnier answers than anything in the show.

Ironically, if "Moon Over Buffalo" had been half as enjoyable as "Moon Over Broadway," it would still be playing.

NEWSDAY, 2/18/98, Part II/p. B10, John Anderson

In "The War Room," the wedded documentarians D.A. Pennebaker and Chris Hegedus braved the backstage of the 1992 Clinton campaign, a minefield of desperate ambition and raging egos. It was just a warmup.

While it probably could have used a bit of George Sanders playing Addison De Witt, their "Moon Over Broadway"—a less-than-venomous "making of" movie about "Moon Over Buffalo," in which Carol Burnett made her return to the New York stage after 30 years—is a fairly naked account of the mounting of one Broadway show and a CAT scan on much of the rest.

The show in question was not an Andrew Lloyd Webber musical, not a Bohemian rock opera, not even an Oscar Wilde revival. It was a rather moldy farce by Ken Ludwig, author of the successful though equally bacterial "Crazy for You," and one which the producers somehow thought would work with Burnett as the lead. Why they did is the biggest question raised by the film.

It's easy enough to sympathize with Ludwig, even though he comes off as the least likable of the bunch (comparing his work to the classic farceur Feydeau's, imposing himself on celebrities on opening night, etc). Having been instructed by the producers on the facts of Broadway life—you need a star, even a former TV star with a stalled career, to put fannies into seats—he concedes their points. But at the same time, he says, "It'll never be the play I wrote because you can't do it." Whether anyone would want to is another question, but the concerns of his vanity and the state of live theater in New York are not necessarily mutually exclusive.

Pennebaker ("Monterey Pop," "Don't Look Back," "Jane") and Hegedus are flies on the wall, giving us some rather appalling discussions about the play, the star and ways in which things are basically not working as the show makes its awkward way through first rehearsals, to Boston tryouts to the October opening at the Martin Beck. There are constant rewrites, arguments about changes ("Do you not want our input?" co-star Philip Bosco asks in his most stentorian tones when Ludwig resists.) Still, the play remains unfunny. Someone jokes that they should bring in Paul Rudnick to write some one-liners. Someone answers drily that, it's already been considered.

As she struggles with the play and with the unfamiliar task of actually learning lines (on TV, she admits, "we paraphrased a lot"), Burnett comes off as warm, professional and totally wrong for the play, even if she does save what there is to save. Pennebaker and Hegedus, in a gesture of enlightening cruelty, toss in a couple of clips from Burnett's old CBS show, in which the star pulls out all the schticky stops. Schtick is what everyone says they don't want in "Moon Over Buffalo." And it's what Burnett resorts to every time the going gets rough.

At the same time, the best moments in the film are hers, doing what she does best. When the main scenery-moving winch jams in the middle of a close-to-opening performance, Burnett and director Tom Moore virtually crawl under the curtain and the comedienne regales her elated audience for 20 minutes (not all of them are here) taking questions and doing spontaneous standup. It's a testament to Burnett's resilience as a performer, and to the Pennebaker-Hegedus knack for always being where the dramaturgy is hitting the rotary oscillator. And you can't help thinking that, during this uncharacteristically lighthearted chapter in the making of "Moon Over Buffalo" that the producers would have been delighted to keep that winch disabled for the play's entire nine-month run.

VILLAGE VOICE, 2/24/98, p. 61, Amy Taubin

It's hard to think of a female star who has less in common with Redgrave than Carol Burnett, who appears, not to great advantage, in Chris Hegedus and D. A. Pennebaker's *Moon Over Broadway*. The film documents the making of the Broadway play *Moon Over Buffalo* from its prerehearsal press conference through its New York opening some six months later. The film should appeal to the same audience of Burnett fans that kept the play running for nine months, despite the drubbing it received from the critics. Persons with a necrophiliac fascination for the current state of Broadway theater also might find the backstage back-biting slightly titillating.

Pennebaker first explored this turf in *Jane* (1962), which followed Jane Fonda through rehearsals and previews of the unfunny bedroom farce in which she made her Broadway debut. *Jane* is a lot more intriguing than *Moon Over Broadway*, partly because it's less painful to watch an emerging talent trying to survive in unfortunate circumstances than it is to watch a veteran haul out her shtick in the service of a project that never should have gotten off the ground. Burnett doesn't have a clue about acting but she's a pretty good stand-up comic. During one preview performance, there's a major technical glitch (the curtain refuses to rise). It's a lucky accident for the filmmakers and the star Burnett improvises 20 minutes of chatter to keep the customers in their seats. It's the only time during *Moon Over Broadway* when she deserves the laughs she gets.

Also reviewed in:
NEW YORK TIMES, 2/18/98, p. E5, Janet Maslin
VARIETY, 9/29-10/5/97, p. 65, Leonard Klady

MOTHER AND SON

An International Film Circuit release of a Zero Film, O Film, Severnyi Fond coproduction. *Executive Producer:* Katrin Schlösser, Martin Hagemann, and Aleksandr Golutva.   *Producer:* Thomas Kufus.   *Director:* Aleksandr Sokurov.   *Screenplay (Russian with English subtitles):* Iruii Arabov.   *Director of Photography:* Aleksei Fedorov.   *Editor:* Leda Semenova.   *Music:* Mikhail Ivanovich, Glinka, and Otmar Nussio.   *Art Director:* Vera Zelinskaia and Esther Rittersbusch. *Sound:* Vladimir Persov and Martin Steyer.   *Make-up:* Ekaterina Beschastnaia and Grit Kosse. *Running time:* 73 minutes.   *MPAA Rating:* Not Rated.

CAST: Gudrun Geyer (Mother); Aleksei Ananishnov (Son).

LOS ANGELES TIMES, 2/20/98, Calendar/p. 14, Kenneth Turan

It's a temptation to deal with Alexander Sokurov's magisterial and poetic new film "Mother and Son" by describing what it isn't. Absent from the screen are fast cutting, explosive action, glib dialogue and complex plotting. And in a sense this beautiful and serene film does stand as a welcome antidote to cinema's eternal obsession with what's new, what's hot, what's happening.

But more pertinent ultimately than what "Mother and Son" doesn't do is what it does by realizing potentialities in the medium that most films aren't aware even exist. Made with exquisite care by a director in formidable control of his skills, this Russian work makes demands on its viewers but then rewards them with an impressive largess.

Sokurov's delicate vision of a son caring for his dying mother couldn't be in less of a hurry though it lasts only 73 minutes. With its emphasis on long takes and the slowest of camera movements, "Mother and Son" creates a hypnotic mood that compels viewers to enter its simple, languorous world, forcing them to examine each frame and create their own focus of interest. Because it's in effect pulling us into a dream world, seeing this film requires an audience willing to submit to its pace, willing to participate in an experience that can in no way be rushed.

While he's been making features and documentaries since 1978, Sokurov is all but unknown in this country, partially because his tone poem style of filmmaking made him an artistic nonperson in the ideology-driven Soviet Union. "The fact that I was involved in the visual side of art made the government suspicious," Sokurov told director Paul Schrader in a recent Film Comment interview. "The nature of my films was different from others. They didn't actually know what to punish me for—and that confusion caused them huge irritation."

Yet unlike the work of some of the directors he's been compared to, including his Russian mentor Andrei Tarkovsky or Greek filmmaker Theo Angelopoulos, there is nothing obscure or ambiguous about this film. "Mother and Son" has a wonderful clearness and simplicity to its narrative with a story line as straightforward and direct as its title.

A nameless mother and son (Gudrun Geyer and Alexi Ananishnov, both nonprofessionals) are discovered together, their closeness underlined by the conceit that they apparently dream the same dreams. The setting is a rural cabin, the time could be any time in the last century, and the only fact that needs to be known is soon obvious: The mother is fatally ill.

What happens over the next hour are the small occurrences of a single day. The son combs his mother's hair, shares reminiscences as he reads to her from old, forgotten postcards, attempts to soothe her when she's in pain. Most dramatically he takes her for a walk in the surrounding woods and fields, carrying her gently in his arms. At times these two seem like lovers, which, the film is telling us, is in a sense what they are.

Critical to the impression "Mother and Son" makes is the powerful use of simple sounds like a crackling fire, a howling wind and a train whistle, and the impact of the carefully muted but indelible color scheme Sokurov created with cinematographer Alexi Fyodorov.

The film's emphasis on the importance of landscape and nature has a very Russian feel. Luminous shots of intense black clouds moving into the frame, of the wind rippling a field of grain like an ocean, and, most memorably, of the haunting vapor trail left by a distant locomotive, underline the strength simple yet poetic images can have.

It is the accomplishment of "Mother and Son" to use these straightforward ingredients to create a powerful piece of work. The dialogue by Yuri Arabov that passes between mother and son is sparse and almost exclusively small talk, but the film presents it in a way that makes the deep and abiding connection between these two, the sense of their inner life, inescapable.

An experience like "Mother and Son" is at odds with the way most Americans experience film, something the director himself recognized in a recent interview when he said, "In the West, people don't let themselves be as moved by art. Russian people allow it all the way into the depths of their soul." Anyone looking for that kind of sensation, anyone eager to reexperience the core power of cinema, could not do better than see "Mother and Son" for themselves.

NEW YORK POST, 2/4/98, p. 40, Thelma Adams

Michelangelo's Pieta is among art's most familiar images. Located at St. Peter's in Rome, the sculpture shows the Virgin Mary cradling Jesus after the crucifixion. It reflects both the Renaissance artist's tragic sense of human destiny as well as spiritual transcendence.

The Pieta is one of the most famous images of the mother-son bond. Aleksandr Sokurov's "Mother and Son," which opens today at the Film Forum after screening at the New York Film Festival, is also a portrait of a mom and her grown son.

Sokurov inverts the figures of Michelangelo's famed sculpture: He shows a strapping son (Alexei Ananishnov) cradling his dying mother (Gudrun Geyer), a pale, waxen figure draped in thin blankets. Above the pair, trees arch their limbs, artfully framing the characters in Mother Nature's embrace.

The much-lauded Russian film from the director of "Whispering Pages" rarely strays from the central pair and their undiluted emotion: the tenderness of maternal love and filial devotion, an oasis of profound affection in an empty landscape.

Very little happens. The son reads an old postcard to his mother; they reminisce; they stroll (he carries her) past an empty village; a train passes in the distance; they return to their barren cottage, where he strokes her brow on her deathbed; a chilly, heavenly light cracks the deep shadows.

Shot like a Russian folk tale—enchanted, mysterious and murky—Sokurov's rural inaction movie is both spare and impenetrable. The intimate look at son and mother may be a metaphor for the death of Mother Russia and a people adrift in grief. Maybe not.

The movie's press notes bear intellectual Susan Sontag's seal of approval: "It is one Of [Sokurov's] most beautiful, most important films. Sokurov is what cinema can be, at its greatest, at its most serious. No filmmaker active today matters as much to me as he does."

Watching Sokurov makes Sontag required reading, since what the Russian is trying to say is unclear simply by watching his film. When the son suggests that his mother take a nap, many in the audience will join her, calmed by the soundtrack's haunting lullaby of natures sounds and subtle piano.

SIGHT AND SOUND, 4/98, p. 46, Julian Graffy

A man tends his dying mother in a large dilapidated house in the country. They have dreamed the same dream. She wants to go for a walk, so he carries her out to a bench where he reads to her from old postcards. He takes her along a path and they recall his childhood. Eventually he carries her home and lays her down to sleep. The mother admits her fear of death and her pity that one day he will have to experience what she is going through.

The son leaves her sleeping and walks out into nature, running and pausing in the landscape into which he eventually merges. He seems to see a boat on a sea and sobs. He returns to his mother and lays his face on her hand; finding her dead, he cries out in pain. He reminds her to wait for him, and that they have agreed to meet in the hereafter.

Mother and Son is a film about fundamentals, about human love and human death, about man in nature. It combines an absolute paring down of the conventional ingredients of cinema—narrative, characterisation, even language (this is a film with almost no dialogue, and what there is is simple and crystalline)—with a hypertrophic richness of colour and light, sound and image, and the textures of wood and flesh.

In this sense, its compositional sources are less in the history of cinema than in that of painting. Director Aleksandr Sokurov has spoken frequently of his admiration for classical landscape painting and portraiture, and of his conviction of cinema's inability to match their achievement. Before embarking upon *Mother and Son,* he took cameraman, Aleksei Fedorov, on a tour of Russian and German galleries, and the visual stamp of the Russian nineteenth-century realists and of German Romanticism is evident in the film's evocation of nature. In particular, Sokurov acknowledges a debt here to the visionary landscapes of Caspar David Friedrich, while his capturing of the play of sunlight recalls Turner, another painter he greatly respects. To create the startling effects of lighting and composition, Sokurov and Fedorov used a complex, intricate optical system of filters, lenses and reflecting planes while shooting both nature and people. Just as important as its visual resolution to the creation of the film's atmosphere is its astounding use of sound. Natural sounds, especially wind and bird song, both precede the beginning and follow the ending of the visual film, and at times the rushing of the wind of the world achieves awesome power. Elsewhere, there is a sparing use of classical music or the noise of unseen insects or footsteps.

Sokurov is famously careful in his choice of actors, and demanding in his requirements of them. It is his practice to choose people who are not professionals, whose openness to experience equips them for the combination of plastic reticence and emotional intensity characteristic of his protagonists. Aleksei Ananishnov has previously played only the part of the hero of Sokurov's haunting fable of existential confusion *Days of Eclipse* (1988), and Gudrun Geyer heads the International Documentary Film Festival in Munich. Here they both display a capacity for intimacy and concentration, an alert, receptive stillness.

The relationship between mother and son (central to many cultures) is the subject of two masterpieces of Russian cinema of the last 30 years, Kira Muratova's *The Long Farewell* (1971) and Andrei Tarkovsky's *Mirror* (1974). (The latter is a film which shares Sokurov's concern with animated nature, for example with the power of wind in trees.) But it is not by chance that *Mother and Son* is the title of Sokurov's film and not theirs. For the earlier films, brilliantly alert and intuitive as they both are, inhabit the loquacious, busy world of human society, whereas Sokurov's dwells in the solitary expanse of last things.

Mother and Son is constructed out of archetypal imagery. Its characters are unnamed. The house they live in is isolated in nature, alone and ill cared for, reminiscent of the abandoned house of the émigré Tarkovsky in Sokurov's 1987 documentary *Moscow Elegy* or the deserted house-museum of Chekhov in his *Stone* (1992). The film is also full of symbolic images of journeys: the path they walk, the track of a passing train, a tiny figure passing unnoticed by their window, and the sailing boat that reduces the son to tears. And at the end of the film, a fragile butterfly flutters and dies on the mother's emaciated hand.

Central among Sokurov's concerns is death, a theme treated in *Stone* and, above all, in his stunning *The Second Circle* (1990), and these three films form a kind of trilogy. Comparisons with *The Second Circle* are especially instructive, for that film was seen to introduce the reality, the physicality of death into Soviet cinema, from which (as from most cinema) it had hitherto been hidden, elided from a process into an instantaneous, atemporal event. *The Second Circle* showed the consequences of the death of a father for an absent, estranged son. It was set in a city and in a recognisably Soviet world, and much of its attention was directed towards the practical exigencies of preparations for burial. *Mother and Son* by contrast, treats the hours before the death of a beloved mother in an unspecified place in the natural world. Both films make parsimonious use of language and music, but in *Mother and Son* Sokurov takes the process of distillation to a new and brilliant level. It makes even *The Second Circle* seem wordy and conventional. *Mother and Son* has a steady, concentrated gaze, never, perhaps, more powerful than in the close-up of the son's distended neck when he groans in anguish at the moment of his mother's death. Its majestic affective power makes most of cinema seem trivial, raucous, faked.

VILLAGE VOICE, 2/10/98, p. 61, J. Hoberman

Mother and Son is a movie as elemental as its title, as well as the most rarefied vision its famously uncompromising director, Alexander Sokurov, has yet produced. An artist whose fastidiously crafted movies concentrate on the most elusive, fugitive sensations, Sokurov here outdoes all previous efforts with this astonishing chamber piece—the equivalent of a visual whisper—about the last hours a child spends with his ailing parent.

The 47-year-old Russian's trademark twilight zone is here the shadowland between consciousness and oblivion. An enfeebled woman (Gudrun Geyer) is attended by her grown son (Alexei Ananishnov) in an isolated country cabin. Their speech is muffled, even as the noises around them are exaggerated. The light is fading, the perspective seems unfixed, the colors are barely present, and yet these flattened-out, smeared images have a startling precision. How does something so insubstantial project so much authority? The crackle of the logs in the fireplace might be the sound of burning film emulsion, even as the movie appears to float somewhere in space, casting its faint shadow on the screen.

Mother and Son (which was screened once at the last New York Film Festival) looks like no other film ever made. Sokurov has fused locations ranging from the Russian woods to the sandy cliffs of Germany's Baltic coast, synthesizing his own version of early-19th-century Romantic landscape canvases. (Caspar David Friedrich is the painter most frequently invoked, although Sokurov's images can also suggest William Turner's quieter compositions in mist and light.) Each shot is an individually worked-out composition. Indeed, *Mother and Son's* spectacular "creative geography" is doubly invented—the image modified by a system of mirrors and glass filters, some of them hand-painted, positioned both behind and before the lens.

Ethereal as it is, *Mother and Son* makes a stark contrast to Sokurov's most original movie, the 1990 *Second Circle*—a far more materialist view of death, where the protagonist spends most of his time in the miserable Siberian hovel where his father has just died, arranging for his parent's corpse. Shot nearly in real time, this sui generis borderline black comedy had as much to do with dreariness and discomfort as it did with grief. *Mother and Son* is different. "The relationship between a father and a son is more complicated" Sokurov told one interviewer. "Between a mother and son there is virtually only one relationship, that of love, irrespective of how it manifests itself." Be that as it may, the son here treats his enfeebled mother with a lovers tender solicitude. At times, the son seems the doting parent and his mother the child—refusing to sleep or eat, disdaining her medicine, drinking like a baby from a bottle, fretfully asking to be taken outside for a walk. The movie is triumphantly pre-Freudian, although not in its limiting the child's ambivalence, desiring—even as he fears—the release of his mothers death. The dying parent is a literal burden, who, for much of the movie, is carried through the world by her son in a sort of reverse pietà.

A movie of incredible stillness, *Mother and Son* evokes overwhelming solitude amid fulsome creation—the filmmaker's not the least. (Sokurov's subtlety and high seriousness was poorly served by the ludicrous trailer that Film Forum had the good sense to cease showing.) Sokurov is driven to strive for the sublime, working without the net of irony that served Lars von Trier in his similarly high-flown *Breaking the Waves*. In the films most stunning passages, the son leaves his mother alone and returns to the fields, wandering through the deep forest and windswept hills. A storm is gathering; black clouds cover the sky. He turns to watch the gradual progress of a distant railroad train traversing the valley—inexorable time, made tangible to crawl across the screen. (Seeing this, we understand that a life has passed.)

Interviewing Sokurov in a recent issue of *Film Comment*, Paul Schrader linked the director to the austerely spiritual Dreyer-Bresson-Ozu tradition he analyzed a quarter century ago in his book *The Transcendental Style in Film*. Sokurov's, however, is a bleak pantheism. Neither mother nor son makes mention of God. And, although the child speaks to her corpse as a Tibetan Buddhist might, the mother's last words are what hang in the air: "You will still have to go through all I have suffered. It's so unfair."

Also reviewed in:
CHICAGO TRIBUNE: 2/20/98, Friday/p. C, Michael Wilmington
NEW REPUBLIC, 2/9/98, p. 26, Stanley Kauffmann
NEW YORK TIMES, 2/4/98, p. E8, Lawrence Van Gelder
VARIETY, 3/10-16/97, p. 83, Deborah Young

MULAN

A Walt Disney Pictures release. *Producer:* Pam Coats. *Director:* Barry Cook and Tony Bancroft. *Screenplay:* Rita Hsiao, Christopher Sanders, Philip Lazebnik, Raymond Singer, and Eugenia Bostwick-Singer. *Based on a story by:* Robert D. San Souci. *Editor:* Michael Kelly. *Music:* Matthew Wilder and (Lyrics) David Zippel. *Music Editor:* Ken Hall. *Sound:* Lon E. Bender and (music) Frank Wolf and Bruce Botnick. *Sound Editor:* Kelly Oxford. *Production Designer:* Hans Bacher. *Art Director:* Ric Sluiter. *Visual Effects:* David Tidgwell. *Computer Animation:* Eric Guaglione. *Animator (Mulan & Fa Zhou):* Mark Henn. *Animator (Shang & Fa Li):* Ruben A. Aquino. *Animator (Mushu):* Tom Bancroft. *Animator (Yai & The Ancestors):* Aaron Blaise. *Animator (Chien-Po & Ling):* Broose Johnson. *Animator (Shan-Yu & Falcon & Elite Hunts):* Pres Antonio Romanillos. *Animator (Khan & General Li):* Alex Kupershmidt. *Animator (Chi Fu & Granmother Fa):* Jeffrey J. Varab. *Animator (Cri-Kee):* Barry Temple. *Animator (The Emperor):* T. Daniel Hofstedt. *Running time:* 86 minutes. *MPAA Rating:* G.

CHRISTIAN SCIENCE MONITOR, 6/26/98, p. B3, David Sterritt

Take a feisty heroine and a spunky sidekick; stir in songs, action scenes, and an exotic historical setting. Follow this recipe successfully, and you'll wind up with a stylish cartoon in the Walt Disney tradition—like "Mulan," the studio's first animated feature in years to look like a sure-fire hit.

The title character is a Chinese girl preparing for marriage when life changes: Huns invade the nation, and the emperor decrees every family must send a man to fight the coming battle.

Mulan feels her aging father couldn't survive the ordeal, so she hits on a novel solution—join the army under a false name and fool everyone into thinking she's a warrior. Helping her is Mushu, a diminutive dragon who makes up in sarcasm what he lacks in size.

"Mulan" could be a crucial picture for Disney, which scored lackluster results with recent animations like "Pocahontas" and "Hercules," and faces increasing pressure from competitors like Warner Bros., which released the colorful "Quest for Camelot" last month.

Auguring well for the future, "Mulan" combines strong pictorial appeal with amiable voice-acting by Ming-Na Wen as the heroine and Eddie Murphy as Mushu. While their efforts may not add up to a blockbuster in the "Aladdin" or "Little Mermaid" mold, it will be surprising if "Mulan" doesn't renew Disney's leadership in the animation field.

LOS ANGELES TIMES, 6/19/98, Calendar/p. 1, Kenneth Turan

It's a fine formula, and as displayed in Disney's "Mulan," the latest in the self-replenishing stream of animated features from the studio, it produces a number of sure-fire sentimental moments. But formula can be pushed too hard, serving as a crutch as well as a comfort. "Mulan" has its accomplishments, but unlike the best of Disney's output, it comes off as more manufactured than magical.

Disney has literally scoured the globe for different cultures to animate—only the wonderfully named Norse epic "The Prose Edda of Snorri Sturluson" has unaccountably been ignored. "Mulan," based on a popular Chinese legend, is set more than 2,000 years ago in a China that has built the Great Wall as security against Hun incursions.

No wall, however impressive, can keep out the fierce Shan-Yu (voiced by Miguel Ferrer), the Hun leader with gimlet eyes and a body like the Incredible Hulk. Reacting to the invasion, the kindly emperor (Pat Morita) thinks first of protecting his people. But he does send the officious Chi Fu (James Hong) to round up new recruits. "A single grain of rice can tip the scale. One man may be the difference between victory and defeat," the ruler says, which is why he's emperor and we're not.

Meanwhile, somewhere in the heart of China, a young woman named Mulan (Ming Na-Wen) is having her own kind of problems. The despair of her traditional parents, Mulan is a brainy tomboy who's unafraid of speaking her mind yet worries about not being appreciated. "When," she asks, "will my reflection show who I am inside?"

Mulan's real difficulty, of course, is that she is a completely modern young woman, a Valley girl who's been trapped with typical Disney shrewdness in a patriarchal civilization where marrying well is the only way for a woman to bring honor to her family.

It's at this point that the war comes to Mulan's village. The emperor has decreed that one man from each family will be drafted, and, anxious to prevent the sure death of her infirm father, Mulan cuts off her hair (a homage to "G.I. Jane"?) and joins up in his place.

The loutish men who are Mulan's comrades-in-arms are not so sure about this slender new youth at first. But under the command of a handsome young captain named Shang (B.D. Wong), Mulan becomes enough of a warrior to prove, to the surprise of no one in the audience, that the best man for even a military job can be a woman.

The simplicity of this story line (dressed up with impressive computer-animated Hun hordes) is not without its appeal. As a vivacious rebel who has to be true to herself no matter what, Mulan is an excellent heroine, perfect for the young female demographic the studio is most anxious to attract. And this resourceful, can-do young woman is a more likable and resourceful role model than Pocahontas was.

While an independent, not completely boy-crazy heroine is somewhat new for Disney, what finally undoes "Mulan," directed by Barry Cook and Tony Bancroft, are those standard elements that have not been re-energized. The by-now-standard hip patter (prepare for jokes about cross-dressing) is so tepid that not even five credited writers can revive it, and the songs by Matthew Wilder and David Zippel (with Lea Salonga and Donny Osmond singing for the leads) lack the spark that Zippel's lyrics brought to the underappreciated "Hercules."

On a visual level, there's too much familiar shtick as well, including excessive use of the oldest of animation cliches, like people's backsides catching on fire. Similarly, the sidekicks Mulan hangs out with in the army are always hitting the wrong person and falling to the ground in displays that are more familiar than funny.

Perhaps as a safety measure, Mulan is also given two cute, nonhuman sidekicks. One, a cricket named Cri-Kee, is not around much, but the other, a midget dragon guardian named Mushu, is voiced by Eddie Murphy and positioned as precisely the same kind of crowd-pleaser Robin Williams was in "Aladdin" and James Woods in "Hercules."

It's that reliance on schematic, fill-in-the-blanks dramatic structures that is "Mulan's" problem. Of course Murphy is amusing as a demoted family guardian who wants a chance to make good, but neither his patter nor his role is inspired.

Though "Beauty and the Beast," perhaps the best of the modern Disney animated features, was nominated for best picture, that's not going to happen here. For all the warmth and positive feelings its title character generates, "Mulan" is finally too much of a cartoon for its own good.

NEW YORK POST, 6/19/98, p. 51, Thelma Adams

As a girl, I had plenty of role models: Snow White, Sleeping Beauty and Cinderella. Close your eyes and Prince Charming might awake you to a life more rewarding than hanging around with a bunch of dwarfs.

If the shoe fits, wear it 'til death do you part.

Times have changed. Now, girls (and boys) have "Mulan." Voiced with spunk to spare by Ming-Na Wen ("One Night Stand"), Mulan is more brains than braids. This legendary Chinese heroine cuts her hair, dons her dad's armor and engages the Huns.

Going to war is as much opportunity as bravery: At least if Mulan jumps on her stallion she doesn't have to loiter under the cherry blossoms and wait for Prince C.

Mulan's aide de camp is Mushu, a pint-sized red dragon. Eddie Murphy, as the voice of Mushu, is spitfire funny on his longest tear without profanity since his career began.

Also on hand are a lucky blue cricket, a brave black stallion, a tart granny ("who spit in her bean curd?" she asks about the crabby matchmaker) and three stooge soldiers who end up in drag (no surprise when they include Harvey Fierstein).

B.D. Wong voices Captain Shang, one of those burly, barrel-chested heroes who finally figures out that that funny feeling in his heart isn't indigestion right before the final credits.

As directed by Barry Cook and Tony Bancroft from a script with five credited writers and David Zippel's lyrics set to Matthew Wilder's tunes, Disney's latest animated movie is light-hearted, not heavy-handed.

The tunes are forgettable, but the animation is memorable. Inspired by Chinese calligraphy and painting, the colors are rich, the lines simple and expressive, the horses noble, the blossoms delicate and, when the inevitable fireworks come, they command oohs and aahs.

Effects like candlelight, snowfall, steam curling above a teacup, lightning, rain and an avalanche are cunning. But what sets "Mulan" apart—besides cross-dressing—is the central character.

"Mulan" puts the fun back in feminism. She's Barbie by way of Bruce Lee, a charming young misfit who captures our affection while outfoxing the Huns. In the end, Mulan ends up with Prince Charming, but it's clear who will be wearing the sword in the family.

NEWSDAY, 6/19/98, Part II/p. B6, Jack Mathews

From pliant to defiant, from Snow White, Cinderella and Sleeping Beauty to Belle, Pocahontas and Esmeralda, the heroine of Disney fairy tales has undergone a dramatic personality change between the first and second of the studio's animation dynasties.

No longer a passive innocent, the new heroine is pro-active, a self-starter, a can-do kind of post-feminist cartoon figure who doesn't sit around humming "Some day, my prince will come." Even in "The Little Mermaid," the first and most traditional film of the second dynasty, which was begun a decade ago by Michael Eisner and Jeffrey Katzenberg, Ariel sets her story in motion by defying her father and following her curiosity about the lives of humans.

Ariel was followed by Belle, a bookish beauty who tamed a monster; Pocahontas, an aerobicized American Indian princess who mediated peace in the New World, and Esmeralda, the slinky Gypsy dancer who threatened to neuter her prince with a sword in "The Hunchback of Notre Dame."

And now, we have the star of "Mulan," the most determined Disney heroine of all, a child-woman combining a journey of self-discovery with the salvation of her family's honor and China's future. In the end, as with all fairy tales, she'll get her man, but it's through her own bravery, not his. This is the story of a princess who rescues a prince.

In fact, Mulan (voice of Ming-Na Wen), with the help of an ambitious, street-talking dwarf dragon (Eddie Murphy), comes to the rescue of three men in Disney's retelling of a popular Chinese folk story. She rescues her proud but lame father (Soon-Tek Oh) by disguising herself as a man and taking his place as a conscripted soldier in the war against the Huns. She rescues the emperor (Pat Morita), who is the object of the Hun invasion. And more than once, she rescues Shang (B.D. Wong), the handsome captain of her troop.

"Mulan" is one of Disney's most daring animated features and, at the same time, its most child-friendly since "The Lion King." It's daring not only in its depiction of the heroine as hero, but in its willingness—or is it commercial ruthlessness?—to Disneyfy a Chinese legend and, by extension, modern Chinese culture.

We'll see,whether "Mulan" softens China up for that long-planned Beijing Disneyworld, or is the final insult that scuttles it altogether. As the emperor in "Mulan" says, speaking perfect Hollywood fortune cookie, "A single grain of rice can tip the scale."

Having learned at least one lesson from "Pocahontas," where animators drew the American Indian heroine as a girl of a white man's dream, a buff, suntanned beauty with the neck of Audrey Hepburn and the legs of Cyd Charisse, Disney has given Mulan simple, ethnically authentic features. She does get the porcelain-doll treatment for an early sequence where she's made up for a bridal audition, but through the rest of the film, as either the timid soldier or her roused-to-heroism self, Mulan's look is a model of Chinese modesty.

The animators were less consistently correct with the other characters. The emperor, and Mulan's father, have strong Chinese features, but Shang looks like a Greek god. The Huns, led by Khan (Frank Weller), are dark, ethnically inscrutable figures. And with her baggy eyes, Mulan's hilariously meddlesome grandmother (June Foray) looks like Mr. Magoo's lost twin.

I'll leave it to other voices to assess the cultural damage or benefits of "Mulan." In an article in the Los Angeles Times, the Chinese-American author Gish Jen says Chinese will be appalled by underlying themes of female empowerment and the open display of emotions. But for her, "Mulan" is a perfect model for young girls in this culture.

Of course, the most urgent question is whether "Mulan" will keep kids entertained for an hour and a half, and the answer is, yes.

There are stunning action sequences, from cartoonish hijinks to an avalanche that bears down on the Huns and the heroes with a power that will have even adults in the audience ducking. The contrasting Chinese landscape, from mountains to villages to the Forbidden City, create a sensation of colors and images. And besides the red dragon, who is as unmistakably Eddie Murphy as Aladdin's geni was Robin Williams, "Mulan" is graced by the comic company of a loyal horse and a lucky cricket.

The songs, by Matthew Wilder and David Zippel, have the sound of Alan Menken knock-offs, and the big numbers aren't quite the show-stoppers we've come to expect in the second dynasty. But overall, "Mulan" is a treat, and, so far at least, the summer's best bet for families.

SIGHT AND SOUND, 10/98, p. 47, Jill McGreal

Ancient China. The barbarians, led by Shan-Yu, are preparing to invade. Meanwhile, the Fa family present their high-spirited daughter Mulan to the local matchmaker, but Mulan insists she'll only marry someone she loves. The Emperor issues a conscription order and Mulan's father, now elderly and infirm, prepares to go to war. That night, Mulan disguises herself as a young man in her father's armour and leaves in his place.

Answering her family's prayers to their ancestors, the tiny dragon Mushu embarks on the quest to protect Mulan with Cri-Kee, a lucky cricket.

At the army training camp, Mulan trains with the other raw recruits under the leadership of Captain Shang, helped by Mushu and Cri-Kee. Mulan distinguishes herself in training but must keep her growing love for Captain Shang a secret. With Shan Yu's barbarian hordes decimating the regular army, Captain Shang leads his recruits into battle. Mulan outwits the enemy but is injured in the process; her gender is discovered. She is thrown out of the troop, but soon learns that Shan-Yu is preparing another attack on the Emperor's palace. Shan-Yu and his men capture the Emperor but Mulan helps save him by disguising herself, Shang and several other warriors as dancing girls to sneak into the palace. She is rewarded for her bravery by the Emperor and returns home to her family with honour. Captain Shang realises that he loves her and asks Mulan's father for her hand in marriage.

The Disney strategy, in *Mulan* transposed to an Oriental setting and featuring a feisty heroine, is nevertheless formulaic and predictable. Once again, we are snared by a web of manipulative storytelling as the Disney machine steamrollers over local customs and cultures, imposing internationally translatable values (so effective at the box office) on this tale of disgrace and dishonour redeemed by bravery and love. *Mulan* tells the story of a legendary Joan of Arc figure who saves Imperial China from the barbarian hordes. Unlike the Maid of Orleans, who is sacrificed finally for her gender and non-conformity, this pre-Revolutionary Chinese counterpart singlehandedly takes on and overcomes not just the invading armies but also traditional attitudes towards gender and an array of other significant social and cultural norms.

Disney viewers fall into two camps. Fans refer to the quality of the animation, the burnout, the characterisation and the strong storytelling, none of which is denied by the detractors. But the detractors scorn the 'Disneyfication' process which reduces important cultural and historical texts such as Victor Hugo's *Notre Dame de Paris* or the Greek legend of Heracles to little more than cutesy sentimentality. There is some snobbery lurking in the detractors' camp, while those who defend these films have been accused of participating in the general dumbing down of culture. *Mulan* is certainly exemplary of the reductive, liberal Hollywood worldview. The opportunity for children to learn about cultural difference and history is rejected in favour of low-level, unchallenging entertainment.

But so what? Kids everywhere will love *Mulan* precisely for the entertainment that it does offer. The visual style, strong on calligraphic lines and often alluding to traditional Chinese painting techniques, also delivers typically uncomplicated Disney characters—dark, brooding baddies, brave, kind goodies and an assorted supporting cast with a Grumpey-to-Dopey personality range. The *Dirty Dozen*-style raw recruits training scene is fast and fun-packed and wittily offset by the song 'I'll Make a Man Out of You' as Mulan struggles, *G.I. Jane*-style, to keep up with the blokes. It's quickly followed by the *South Pacific*-style 'A Girl Worth Fighting For' sequence which also allows the audience to enjoy Mulan's secret. Later, in a Zulu-style battle scene when the invading army appears in huge numbers on a snowy ridge and descends on Captain Shang's small band of men, my young Disney-devotee friend gasped with pleasure at the virtuosity of the spectacle, an effect he later informed me was achieved by one of the most advanced uses of computer animation ever seen in an animated film.

As is common in Disney films, the hero and heroine are the blandest characters. Ever since *Snow White and the Seven Dwarfs* (1936) with its wobbly Prince, setting the male character has always been especially troublesome, and the tediously hunky Captain Shang is no exception. Mulan looks better as a young man than as a young woman, but without the thrill of a Garbo-style transformation. It's the supporting roles that provide more entertainment. The Grandmother is particularly enjoyable, her position as a widowed and decrepit, cackling old woman allowing her to be crude. But the star is Eddie Murphy's Mushu, a streetwise, heart-of gold semi-conman, and a performance worth catching. When the puffed-up, quarrelsome ancestors vie with each other for importance Murphy delivers a risky line about cross-dressing granddaughters which will raise a laugh from the adults and go straight over the heads of anyone under ten. The film is full of such moments.

TIME, 6/22/98, p. 69, Richard Corliss

The great wall of China snakes like a stem dragon through the opening shots of *Mulan*, a strange and beguiling new breed of Disney animated feature. This is, in part, a war movie that understands loss, desolation, death. Power and discipline are the motifs here: bending your will and others', bending the system while working within it. The villain, a crazed, WWF-style hulkster named Shan-Yu, has no comic irony softening his brute trapezoidal lines. He's just an evil machine with vampire teeth. The Wall, the vast plains and hills, the Forbidden City itself, all cringe at his shadow.

In other words, this is strong, supple entertainment, not a girlish cartoon in the style of *The Little Mermaid*, in which a girl becomes a woman. Here, a girl becomes a man. Mulan is the only child of a dutiful man tied to tradition. "I know my place," he tells his rebellious tomboy of a daughter. "It is time you learned yours." Her place, it turns out, is at the head of a ragtag platoon fighting Shan-Yu's Huns. This woman warrior will prove that the art of war is the smart of war, that one wins by cunning, not strength. And unlike most Disney heroines, she achieves her goal without much mentoring. As her sidekick, a spindly dragon named Mushu, proudly says, "You da man!"

Mulan is the first feature from Disney's Florida unit—those people who try to get work done as Walt Disney World tourists gawk at them through the huge windows of the animation pavilion. It doesn't seem to have distracted them a whit, for the team, led by directors Barry Cook and Tony Bancroft and producer Pam Coats, has created the boldest, most persuasive storytelling in a while, in a ravishing pastel palette (from production designer Hans Bacher) that recalls the color experiments of *Fantasia* as much as the delicacy of Chinese graphic art.

Yes, yes, it's a Disney cartoon, with comic relief—a little wheezy at first, in a matchmaker scene that seems to revel in inflicting pain—and yearning romance. It has some star voices, like Eddie Murphy, very funny as the Mushu shrimp, and a fine cast of East Asian and Asian-American actors (Ming-Na Wen, B.D. Wong, Soon-Tek Oh, James Shigeta) playing the main characters. But what's terrific about Mulan is its reaching for emotions that other movies run from: family love and duty, personal honor and group commitment, obedience and ingenuity. Nice notions for kids to think about.

The four songs, by Matthew Wilder and David Zippel, propel the plot with lyric efficiency. But then, at the end, the racy Eddie Murphy spirit that has been held in check during the film explodes with a Motownish rave-up, *True to Your Heart,* that cascades over the closing credits. The song doesn't have much to do with the girl-power theme of this briskly enchanting film, but it's a perky parting gift from the Disney folks. The R.-and-B. group 98°and Stevie Wonder trade harmonic and harmonica riffs with some sassy horns, and euphoria saturates the multiplex. Cap your soda cup before dancing out of the theater.

VILLAGE VOICE, 6/30/98, p. 142, Gary Dauphin

Perched at the exact opposite end of every category, *Mulan* is Disney's return to the earnest multiculti angle after taking a beating with the smarmily savvy *Hercules*. The story of a Chinese girl who cuts her hair off and joins the imperial army, Mulan pulls the yuks and heartstrings from its heroine's blossom-strewn household, which is headed by her poignantly long-faced and hobbled father. When a conscription order arrives for him, Mulan (played by Ming Na-Wen) impulsively takes his place, riding off not only to fight Mongol hordes and protect Daddy but find herself as well. Her only allies are natural-born wit and a slightly shady, but effortlessly jokey dragon (voiced by Eddie Murphy), who's more of a boon to the audience than Mulan, having been dispatched by the ancestors not to help her but to protect the family from dishonor.

Mulan's didactic songs are forgettable, and the action moves at a dipped, overfast pace, with only the middle scenes of Mulan's training and education in the ways of men providing any extended emotional rewards. The images throughout are beautiful in that Disney way, ranging from soft-toned domestic scenes to epic, wide views of huge, rolling countryside to imperial courts filled with a mobile sea of humanity. (A mountaintop battle is itself worth the price of admission.) On the intercultural tip, besides pseudo-Orientalist music, its sheer visual scope is probably the most "Chinese" thing about *Mulan*. The boys at Disney move heaven and earth to bring their girl into a kind of modern, livable adolescence, while China is still that familiarly crowded and exotic backdrop chock-full of faceless multitudes.

Also reviewed in:
CHICAGO TRIBUNE, 6/19/98, Friday/p. A, Michael Wilmington
NATION, 7/13/98, p. 36, Stuart Klawans
NEW YORK TIMES, 6/19/98, p. E13, Janet Maslin
VARIETY, 6/8-14/98, p. 66, Todd McCarthy
WASHINGTON POST, 6/19/98, p. B1, Rita Kempley
WASHINGTON POST, 6/19/98, Weekend/p. 47, Michael O'Sullivan

MY GIANT

A Castle Rock Entertainment release of a Face Production film.   *Executive Producer:* Peter Schindler.   *Producer:* Billy Crystal. *Director:* Michael Lehmann.   *Screenplay:* David Seltzer. *Story:* Billy Crystal and David Seltzer.   *Director of Photography:* Michael Coulter.   *Editor:* Stephen Semel.   *Music:* Marc Shaiman.   *Sound:* Jeff Wexler and Don Coufal.   *Sound Editor:* Robert Grieve and Gregory King.   *Casting:* Pam Dixon Mickelson.   *Production Designer:* Jackson DeGovia.   *Art Director:* Tom Reta.   *Set Designer:* Les Gobruegge and Christopher S. Nushawg.   *Set Decorator:* Kathe Klopp.   *Set Dresser:* Glenn H. Roberts, Daril Alder, Robert Bleckman, Carl Cassara, Frank Calvert, Fred M. Paulesen, and Keith McCormick.   *Special Effects:* Richard Ratliff.   *Costumes:* Rita Ryack.   *Make-up:* Peter Montagna.   *Make-up (Kathleen Quinlan):* Hallie D'Amore.   *Make-up (Steven Seagal):* Jef Simons.   *Stunt Coordinator:* John Branagan and Paul Weston.   *Running time:* 105 minutes.   *MPAA Rating:* PG.

CAST: Billy Crystal (Sammy); Kathleen Quinlan (Serena); Gheorghe Muresan (Max); Joanna Pacula (Lillianna); Zane Carney (Nick); Jere Burns (Weller); Harold Gould (Milt); Dan Castellaneta (Partlow); Raymond O'Connor (Eddie); Rider Strong (Justin); Doris Roberts (Rose); Carl Ballantine (Rabbi); Eric Lloyd (Young Sammy); Jay Black (Jay); Lorna Luft (Joanne); Tony Belton (Man on Street); Lindsay Crystal (Stephanie); Peter Schindler (Don); Martin Falty'n (Cinema Manager); Miroslav Dubsky (Camerman); Dale Wyatt (Dialogue Coach); David Steinberg (Himself); Ajay Naidu (Hot Dog Vendor); Estelle Harris (Aunt Pearl); Elain Kagan (Myrna); Philip Sterling (Uncle Nate); Max Goldblatt (Jerry); E.E. Bell (Ring Announcer); Michael Papajohn (Tough Guy # 1); Lincoln Simonds (Tough Guy #2); Steven Seagal (Himself); Heather Thomas (Showgirl); Rick Overton (Director); Richard Portno (Producer); Nikki Micheaux (P.A. Jeannie); Lawrence Pressman (Doctor); Yvonne de la Paix (Cleaning Woman); Miroslava Baburkova (Peasant Woman #1); Zoja Oubramova (Peasant Woman #2); Vaclav Kotva (Max's Father); Lena Birkova (Max's Mother).

LOS ANGELES TIMES, 4/10/98, Calendar/p. 4, David Kronke

[The following review by David Kronke appeared in a slightly different form in NEWSDAY, 4/10/98, Part II/p. B6.]

While shooting the 1987 delight "The Princess Bride," Billy Crystal met and befriended Andre the Giant, a European immigrant who had come to America and become a benignly fearsome TV wrestler. That friendship inspired "My Giant," a funny, good-natured tale about two men of vastly different statures, both physically and spiritually.

Crystal stars as Sammy, a Broadway Danny Rose-type talent agent whose fast sweet-talking as a child once convinced his rabbi to try ham. Alas, Sammy's powers of seduction have seriously waned of late—both his wife and his biggest client have dumped him—and he finds himself in Romania, out of work and luck and with a bad sense of direction in every sense of the phrase.

Until, that is, he meets Max (Washington Wizards center Gheorghe Muresan), a 7-foot-7 tower of unassuming power who rescues Sammy from an automobile accident. Since Sammy knows a nearby cheesy film production is seeking an imposing villainous sort, he begins wooing Max—who prefers his simple life as a monastery's caretaker, outside the gawking eye of the public—in an effort to get the big guy to agree to plant his sizable feet before the movie cameras.

This triggers a series of misadventures in which Sammy finds himself by turns exploiting and protecting his new charge. And Sammy is of course forced to reflect upon his own messed-up value system while coming to understand what simple if unattainable pleasures would make Max's life complete.

In order to get Max to deliver his one line in a gladiator movie, Sammy gets him hugely smashed (this is based loosely on some behind-the-scenes lore when Andre the Giant got good and loose to play a scene in "Princess Bride"). Later, to raise money, Sammy books Max for a wrestling gig against a passel of midgets—a surrealistically comic yet grave miscalculation, as he soon discovers.

Crystal, who also produced and developed the story with screenwriter David Seltzer, is a seasoned pro when it comes to this kind of material, and he serves it expertly, playing Sammy's wit and desperation for all its worth. Still, the film would not have worked if Muresan, who spoke limited English before this project got underway, hadn't been able to deliver a surprisingly soulful performance.

Muresan may not have the chops to deliver forcefully the lines of Shakespeare his character supposedly knows by heart, but he gets everything else blissfully right, from Max's gentle humor to his (literal, it turns out) heartache. Memo to Shaquille O'Neal: See this movie and you'll understand that there's more to being in movies than just having an appealing presence.

Max agrees to trek to America, but he's far less interested in auditioning for the Steven Seagal slugfest Sammy has in mind for him than reuniting with the woman he has loved from afar since sharing a fleeting kiss with her two decades back, before his pituitary gland began working overtime. (Seagal even proves a good sport here in a cameo, playing off his difficult behind-the-camera persona.)

At this point, the film loses a smidgen of steam as it ditches its comedic elements for a finale steeped in pathos. The subplot involving Max's unrequited love is a standard one with no conceivable resolution that could be both narratively satisfying and fresh.

Still, "My Giant" is both funnier and more sincerely heartfelt than some of the manipulative films Crystal has been in recently and it's his best movie since the first "City Slickers." Director Michael Lehmann ("Heathers," "The Truth About Cats and Dogs") devises a plethora of visual gags playing off Crystal and Muresan's pronounced height discrepancy, but shows admirable restraint in not running that joke into the ground.

NEW YORK POST, 4/10/98, p. 43, Thelma Adams

As funny as Billy Crystal was hosting the Oscars, there was a melancholy to his delivery. When the funnyman's "Father's Day" co-star, Robin Williams, received the best supporting actor nod, the emotion crested. Why? Crystal knew something that the audience didn't. He was following the desperately unfunny "Day," not with "Good Will Hunting," but with the abysmal "My Giant."

In Michael Lehmann's syrupy comedy, Crystal dispatches Catskills zingers as a talent agent named Sammy who's at the end of his rope. Child stars diss him. His relatives pity him. Sammy's estranged wife (Kathleen Quinlan) moves away and his kid (Zane Carney) scours Variety just to have things to talk about with his self-involved dad.

All this changes when Sammy meets Max (Gheorghe Muresan), a 7-foot-7 Romanian giant. Lehmann, the hip director of "Heathers," stoops to a comedy that relies largely on sight gags. Look at tiny Sammy in the shadow of Max, a melancholy outcast who's a giant in more ways than height. How funny is that?

A typical comic set piece finds us breaking brisket around the dinner table with Sammy's parents. Both his Yiddishe mama (Doris Roberts) and Aunt Pearl (Estelle Harris) are lifted from sitcoms ("Everybody Loves Raymond" and "Seinfeld"). It wouldn't be family embarrassment hour if Pearl didn't raise that most desperate of questions: Is *everything* giant?

As stale as this joke is, it's nothing compared to the sappy self-help message that follows. While Sammy learns how to be a giant of a man from Max, David Seltzer's script makes the sentimental comedy of Babaloo Mandel and Lowell Ganz ("City Slickers') seems as dark and alienated as Kafka.

The only figure who comes out of "My Giant" unscathed is Steven Seagal. The he-man actor has a cameo playing himself. At least he has a reason for not being funny. He never is.

SIGHT AND SOUND, 4/99, p. 49, Kevin Maher

On the Romanian location of a medieval film epic, talent agent Sammy Kanin is fired by his only client. Leaving, he crashes his car and is saved by Max, a local giant monk. With the promise of reuniting Max with his long-lost love Lillianna, who lives in New Mexico, Sammy persuades him to come to the US and star in movies. They arrive in New York. Sammy is broke, and so the only work he can get for Max is a job as a wrestler.

Sammy learns about a Steven Seagal movie filming in Las Vegas that would be perfect for Max. He asks his estranged wife Serena for the money to get to Vegas. Once there, Seagal likes Max and hires him. Through a medical check Max is found to have a terminal heart condition. Sammy contacts Lillianna but she refuses to see Max, and so he asks Serena to pretend to be Lillianna for one night. Moved by Sammy's altruism towards Max, Serena obliges. Their marriage is saved. Sammy takes Max home to Romania, reuniting him with the family he hadn't seen since he was a boy.

My Giant is a strange and slightly disconcerting movie. Actor-producer Billy Crystal is omnipresent, self-aware and carefully cloying from the first frame to the closing credits. Yet unlike his own directorial efforts—*Forget Paris* and *Mr. Saturday Night*—what this film mostly resembles is an uninterrupted stream of Crystal's now famous Oscar Night movie parodies pasted together. And so we have Crystal the talent agent and his new-found giant star Gheorghe Muresan 'doing' sales parlance from *Jerry Maguire,* road scenes from *Midnight Run,* and misfit drama from *King Kong* and *The Elephant Man*—all bound by an oppressive sentimentality yet sadly without benefit of a punchline.

From an idea born out of Crystal's friendship with his *Princess Bride's* co-star Andre Roussimoff (aka Andre The Giant), who died in 1993, writer David Seltzer (*The Omen*) and director Michael Lehmann (*Heathers*) have created a movie of unerring derivativeness where everything is telegraphed and literal-minded. Muresan's gentle giant Max is dying because his heart is enlarged—it's literally too big. Sammy is a bad father because he misses his son's birthday party. Through Max's benign influence, Sammy discovers that beauty is on the inside: "He wanted to be small, I wanted to be big, but what we were looking for had nothing to do with size."

Ironically this cod appearances-are-superficial philosophy turns out to be utterly disingenuous in a movie that hinges on the aberrant demeanour of its central character. *My Giant* is dragged along by a series of throwaway sight gags—Max in a tiny sports car, Max at a tiny table, Max sitting on a tiny horse—which all depend on first impressions. Muresan, with his indented forehead, huge angular jaw and gargled delivery, is blatantly objectified as the movie's 'freak'. Yet unlike its classical precursor, Tod Browning's *Freaks* (1932) where physical abnormality is also fetishised but used to accentuate a dramatic crisis (in this case a deceptive love triangle), here the movie tries both to ridicule Muresan's size and deny it at the same time. When Sammy's senile aunt asks Max how big his penis is, it's a nasty moment, which coupled with Muresan's limited acting ability strains against all the easy rhetoric about the power of personality. Crystal himself, bereft of stinging one-liners, is strangely muted as the Hollywood agent. Unlike the mischievous Broadway Danny Rose or the cynical suits in *The Player,* Crystal's softer post-*Jerry Maguire* agent wants only to be a good father and is prone to eulogising about movies in Academy Award MC-speak. "Movies are like life," he gushes, "only bigger, and better. On a movie screen everyone is 40 feet tall!"

My Giant certainly looks pretty, thanks to the efforts of Scottish cinematographer Michael Coulter *(The Neon Bible)*—the frequently filmed Czech countryside (standing in for Romania) has rarely looked more lush on screen. Yet next to the howling inadequacies of director, scriptwriter and performers alike, this is ultimately a small reward from a substandard film.

VILLAGE VOICE, 4/14/98, p. 68, Salma Abdelnour

We know Billy Crystal can do the neurotic-smartass-softie. He reminds us in semiannual permutations as supporting actor, cameo, or Oscar host. But even at his most somnambulant, he remains matchable, which says more about his workhorse shtick than about any of his movies.

In the latest tepid star vehicle by Michael Lehmann—who gave us the tart suburban cult classic *Heathers,* then promptly vanished into a world of *Hudson Hawk, Airhoods,* and *Meet the Applegates*—Crystal appears as a desperate C-list agent who fortuitously discovers a 7-7 Romanian named Maximus (real-life NBA player Gheorghe Muresan) and tries to cast him in a string of degrading roles as a hulk. Enter the gentle-giant sequences in which we discover Max is just a softie with a big ol' heart, and then the ending in which the clout-starved slickster learns that being big means more than having Bruce Willis on speed dial. *My Giant* is the kind of one-joke film that gives away its punch line on the poster (think *Twins,* which pinned its hopes on the same sight gag). Lehmann pulls a surprisingly moving performance out of Muresan but asks nothing of us and even less of Crystal.

Also reviewed in:
CHICAGO TRIBUNE, 4/10/98, Friday/p. D, Michael Wilmington
NEW YORK TIMES, 4/10/98, p. E20, Janet Maslin
VARIETY, 4/6-12/98, p. 47, Leonard Klady
WASHINGTON POST, 4/10/98, p. B7, Stephen Hunter
WASHINGTON POST, 4/10/98, Weekend/p. 45, Michael O'Sullivan

MY KNEES WERE JUMPING: REMEMBERING THE KINDERTRANSPORTS

An Anthology Film Archives and the National Center for Jewish Film release.   *Producer:* Melissa Hacker.   *Director:* Melissa Hacker. *Director of Photography:* John Foster, Kevin Keating, Jill Johnson, and Eric Schmidt.   *Editor:* Melissa Hacker.   *Music:* Joel Goodman. *Sound:* Alexandra Balthazuk, Susan Korda, Trisha Gouvanis, and Paul Koronkeiwicz.   *Running time:* 76 minutes. *MPAA Rating:* Not Rated.

CAST: Joanne Woodward (Narrator) and with Lore Segal;   Erika Estis;   Michael Roemer; Norbert Wollheim;   Kurt Fuchel;   Sonnie Better;   Eddie Better;   Kurt Goldberger.

NEW YORK POST, 12/2/98, p. 44, Hannah Brown

A simple and eloquent documentary, "My Knees Were Jumping: Remembering the Kindertransports," is a perfect antidote to the countless movies (such as "Apt Pupil") that use the Holocaust as little more than a lurid backdrop.

Director Melissa Hacker looks at the personal dimension of the tragedy by focusing on the story of her mother, Ruth Morley.

Morley was one of the nearly 10,000 Jewish children sent to England to escape Nazi-controlled Europe on the so-called "Kindertransports," a rescue effort undertaken just before the outbreak of World War II in 1938 and 1939. Most never saw their parents again.

Although Morley went on to become a movie costume designer ("Annie Hall" is among her credits), she was indelibly scarred by her wartime separation from her family.

With a gentle touch, Hacker weaves interviews with her mother with recollections from other Kindertransport survivors, footage from a 1990 Kindertransport reunion, newsreel footage and snapshots. Joanne Woodward provides the narration.

This film's opening today, at Anthology Film Archives, is timed to commemorate the 60th anniversary of the first Kindertransport. The title refers to Morley's feeling, when she learned her father was about to be arrested by the secret police, that "my knees were jumping out of my skin."

In a day and age when so many are eager to portray themselves as victims, the dignity and reticence of these survivors as they tell their stories is remarkable.

The one flaw is that, especially at the beginning, it's easy to become impatient as the survivors' testimony is interrupted by their American-born children, who describe their traumas growing up.

After all, Art Spiegelman mined this territory so brilliantly in his "Maus" books. What more is there to be said? But as portraits of several families emerge, it becomes clear how important each generation is in healing the other.

While many may feel that they know all they need to about the Holocaust from movies like "Schindler's List" and "Shoah," this quiet film makes the horror vivid all over again. And it does so not by the use of gory images, but by showing the faces behind the statistics.

VILLAGE VOICE, 12/8/98, p. 140, Elliott Stein

One of the little-known stories of the Holocaust is recounted in heartrending detail in Melissa Hacker's doc about the *Kindertransports,* a rescue mission organized by a group of British Jews and Quakers that saved nearly 10,000 children from the concentration camps. The movement was set up in 1938, after the British Parliament passed a bill allowing the threatened children to enter England. To its shame, the U.S. Congress turned down similar legislation.

Hacker intercuts talking-head interviews and passages of rare and moving archival footage. She centers the film on her mother, Ruth Morley—one of the lucky kids transported out of Austria—who eventually became a successful costume designer (*The Miracle Worker, Taxi Driver*). Like most of those interviewed, Morley admits that she had hardly ever spoken of her wartime experiences before—even to her own children. These grown-up *Kinder* all seem to have gone through adult lives haunted by lingering survivor's guilt.

Also reviewed in:
NEW YORK TIMES, 12/2/98, p. E1, Janet Maslin
VARIETY, 7/31-8/6/95, p. 38, Dennis Harvey

NEGOTIATOR, THE

A Warner Bros. release of a Regency Enterprises presentation of a Mandeville Films/New Regency production. *Executive Producer:* David Nicksay, Robert Stone, and Webster Stone. *Producer:* David Hoberman and Arnon Milchan. *Director:* F. Gary Gray. *Screenplay:* James DeMonaco and Kevin Fox. *Director of Photography:* Russell Carpenter. *Editor:* Christian Wagner. *Music:* Graeme Revell. *Music Editor:* Josh Winget. *Sound:* Russell Williams and (music) Dan Wallin and John Kurlander. *Sound Editor:* Mark Stoeckinger. *Casting:* David Rubin. *Production Designer:* Holger Gross. *Art Director:* Kevin Ishioka. *Set Designer:* Luis G. Hoyos. *Set Decorator:* Richard Goddard. *Special Effects:* Dan Sudick. *Costumes:* Francine Jamison-Tanchuck. *Make-up:* Marietta Carter-Narcisse and Tania McComas. *Stunt Coordinator:* Joel Kramer. *Running time:* 115 minutes. MPAA Rating: R.

CAST: Samuel L. Jackson (Danny Roman); Kevin Spacey (Chris Sabian); David Morse (Commander Adam Beck); Ron Rifkin (Commander Grant Frost); John Spencer (Chief Al Travis); J.T. Walsh (Terence Niebaum); Slobahn Fallon (Maggie); Paul Giamatti (Rudy); Regina Taylor (Karen Roman); Bruce Beatty (Markus); Michael Cudlitz (Palermo); Carlos Gomez (Eagle); Tim Kelleher (Argento); Dean Norris (Scott); Nestor Serrano (Hellman); Doug Spinuzza (Tonray); Leonard Thomas (Allen); Stephen Lee (Farley); Lily Nicksay (Omar's daughter); Lauri Johnson (Chief's Wife); Sabi Dorr (Bartender); Gene Wolande (Morewitz); Rhonda Dotson (Linda Roenick); Donald Korte and Anthony T. Petrusonis (Officers at Funeral); John McDonald (Pipes and Drums Leader); Jack Mclaughlin Gray (Priest); John Lordon (Linda's Attorney); Jack Shearer (D.A. Young); Donna Ponterotto (Secretary); Michael Shamus Wiles (Taylor); Mik Scriba (Bell); Joey Perillo (Tech I); Mary Page Keller (Lisa Sabian); Kelsey Mulrooney (Stacy Sabian); Brad Blaisdell (FBI Agent Grey); Bruce Wright (FBI Agent Moran); Robert David Hall (Cale Wangro); Guy Van Swearingen (Officer); Bernard Hocke (Sniper); Charles Valentino (FBI Agent); Robert Baier (Officer at HBT); Ted Montue (Officer at IAB); John Buckley and Darius Aubry (Detectives); Steven Mainz (TAC Officer).

CHRISTIAN SCIENCE MONITOR, 7/31/98, p. B3, David Sterritt

Samuel L. Jackson and Kevin Spacey are two of the most gifted, versatile, and downright matchable actors in American movies today. They also care about cultivating their skills in different kinds of projects, swinging from Hollywood haymakers to independent projects like "Eve's Bayou" for Jackson and "Glengarry Glen Ross" for Spacey.

They should have stuck with the indies this time around. "The Negotiator" is the sort of big-budget cliché festival that lets you imagine what the studio's story conference was like. Nobody but an isolated executive could think the world really needs another yarn about a cop thrown off the force ("I have no choice. Give me your badge and your gun.") because of trumped-up charges ("You just planted that evidence!") that only he can deny and disprove ("They've gotta listen to me! I'll do what I have to until they do!").

The twist is that our unjustly maligned hero (Jackson) is a hostage investigator himself, until the dark day when he's accused of killing an informant to cover up a financial scam.

He takes four hostages of his own to get the world's attention, then refuses to talk with anyone but a colleague (Spacey) who's an expert in the same field. With such dynamic actors portraying the dueling negotiators, this element of the tale has strong dramatic possibilities.

But the filmmakers are more interested in gimmicks and gunshots than in the psychological face-off between two brilliant criminologists, and this leaning toward the superficial is what determines the picture's overall direction. As an experienced maker of music videos and multiplex movies, director F. Gary Gray keeps the action popping at a frantic pace for most of its 139 minutes, with help from Christian Adam Wagner, the editor of "Face/Off" and other quick-moving entertainments.

But there's no disguising its lack of originality, conviction, and feeling. Jackson and Spacey should think long and hard before signing up for another potboiler like this.

LOS ANGELES TIMES, 7/29/98, Calendar/p. 1, Kenneth Turan

The less you think about "The Negotiator," the better off you are. It's a measure of how pulsating and energetic a visual style director F. Gary Gray has, and how vividly actors Samuel L. Jackson and Kevin Spacey come across on screen, that this film is intensely matchable from minute to minute, even though a lot of what's happening doesn't stand up to a moment's scrutiny.

The story of a police hostage negotiator forced by circumstances into taking hostages himself, this film is said to be based on an actual event. Its director and stars turn out to be so adept at pulling us rapidly through all kinds of situations that it's a shock when we encounter the periodic speed bumps that the clunky James DeMonaco and Kevin Fox script creates.

Jackson and Spacey, friends from early in their acting careers and co-stars in "A Time to Kill," apparently took this picture in part for the opportunity it presented to work together. Seeing these completely accomplished American actors light sparks off each other is a reminder of the way powerful performers elevate almost any kind of material.

Jackson has the more flamboyant role, playing Chicago police Lt. Danny Roman. He's a 12-year veteran whose specialty is talking deranged hostage-takers into giving up their prisoners unharmed, something we see him trying to do in the film's opening sequence.

Jackson is always a compelling actor, and in a film like this, which gives him wide latitude to be angry and unhappy, his intensity is as good as money in the bank. When Lt. Roman is holding the floor, nothing else, not even questions of plausibility, matter much at all.

Newly married and determined to leave his risky ways behind him, Roman nevertheless gets drawn into a scandal involving $ 2 million missing from a police disability fund. Suddenly (in fact, much too suddenly to be believed), Roman becomes a murder suspect, his badge gets taken away, and everyone he knows resolutely turns their back on him.

Especially onerous is Inspector Niebaum (the always reliable J.T. Walsh in his last role), the dour head of the Chicago police's Internal Affairs Division. When Roman charges into Niebaum's office, insisting he's being set up, all he gets in return is a practiced sneer. Not a wise choice.

Screaming "I'm not going to jail today" and the ever-popular "We're not leaving here," Roman takes Niebaum, his secretary, a weaselly criminal and a police commander named "Frosty" Frost (Ron Rifkin) hostage.

Naturally, Roman's experience as a negotiator means he knows more about the do's and don't's of taking hostages than anyone within earshot. Determined to clear his name, he insists that he'll only deal with Chris Sabian (Spacey), a negotiator from another precinct he knows by reputation as someone who will never stop trying to talk his way to a solution.

Cool and unflappable, a family man who reads history and biographies in his spare time, Sabian is presented as the cerebral opposite of the more visceral Roman. Despite the obviousness of the setup, Spacey gives the kind of involving performance he's known for, and both actors clearly relish the chance to match up and fence with each other as they try to get to the bottom of the crimes in question.

Because trigger-happy types like Commander Adam Beck (an excellent David Morse) are always trying to break in on Roman, "The Negotiator" is filled with moments of conflict as police helicopters continually hover and only the slightest encouragement is needed to get SWAT team members to rappel down skyscrapers.

None of this is particularly new and exciting, but director Gray, whose last film was "Set It Off," another gritty urban drama, acts like it is. Working with editor Christian Wagner, who also cut John Woo's "Face/Off," Gray sets a brisk, page-turner pace and refuses to let it flag. He won't be stopped, not even by cheesy plot points that no one will buy, and there is certainly something to be said for that.

NEW YORK POST, 7/29/98, p. 45, Rod Dreher

"The Negotiator" is about a wrongly accused police hostage negotiator (Samuel L. Jackson) who himself takes hostages in a desperate attempt to clear his name. Kevin Spacey plays a fellow negotiator, who tries to defuse the explosive situation.

It sounds like a routine action thriller, but the prospect of a wicked psychological duel between a pair of aces like Jackson and Spacey promises to make "The Negotiator" something worth talking about.

It's not. Even gifted actors are limited by what screenwriters give them to say, which in the case of James DeMonaco and Kevin Fox's paint-by-numbers screenplay, isn't much we haven't heard before.

An intellectual thrust-and-parry between two characters supposedly renown for their skill with wordplay might have been terrific, played by intense but nuanced thesps like these two. But the script plays it safe, hewing to standard action-movie hijinks and underusing the talents of its stars.

Danny Roman (Jackson) is a hostage negotiator with the Chicago police whose courage and rhetorical finesse have earned him the respect of his colleagues. When his partner is murdered under suspicious circumstances (he was looking into fraud involving the police pension fund), Roman suddenly finds himself accused of the crime.

It's a set-up, of course, but the noose tightens so rapidly (and so implausibly, from the audience's point of view) that Roman feels driven to execute an extreme strategy to save his neck: he takes hostages in the Internal Affairs office.

Maybe seizing captives isn't the best way to prove you're an innocent, law-abiding citizen, but it's best not to think too much in this movie. One of the hostages is an inspector, Niebaum (the late J.T Walsh), a sleazy IA guy whom Roman believes is in on the dirty scheme. The others include a secretary (Regina Taylor), Roman's captain (Ron Rifkin) and a hysterical small-time crook (Paul Giamatti).

Roman hopes to hold off his gung-ho colleagues long enough to force Niebaum to tell what he knows. He demands that Chris Sabian (Spacey), a police hostage negotiator from across town, serve as the go-between. Sabian is someone he trusts, and someone he can be sure isn't part of the hidden conspiracy, whose members would sooner kill Roman than have him out them.

"The Negotiator" shows promise when the deft Roman makes a hapless police talker do a clumsy verbal dance by peppering him with humiliating questions, as if he were just warming up for the formidable Sabian.

There are glimmers of intelligence in the eventual series of clashes between the red-hot Roman and the icy Sabian, but director F. Gary Gray has to rely on shoot-'em-ups, improbable escapes and a ludicrous conclusion to keep our attention.

Neither Spacey nor Jackson disgrace themselves in this overlong potboiler by any means, but we expect more out of them.

but, as the nervous con man whose computer skills later prove helpful to Roman, Paul Giamatti proves a welcome surprise, turning in another hilarious portrayal, a la his Pig Vomit in "Private Parts," of a shaky man on the verge of a nervous breakdown. But his bits are just about the only times this dull and disappointing "Negotiator" really sings.

NEWSDAY, 7/29/98, Part II/p. B2, Jack Mathews

At what would seem to be a pivotal moment in F. Gary Gray's "The Negotiator," hostage taker Samuel L. Jackson stands at an opening on the 20th floor of a Chicago high-rise daring marksmen to shoot him from a helicopter hovering a few yards away, while at the same time he's shouting to the hordes of news crews gathered on the street below.

Jackson's character, Danny Roman, is a cop himself, an expert in the art of negotiation and a hero to all but his most envious colleagues, but he's now on the other side of a hostage crisis.

Accused of murdering his partner and draining the police pension fund into a Swiss bank account, Lt. Roman has sealed himself and four others in a room, threatening to kill his hostages if his demands aren't met.

What he's demanding is help in unraveling the case of the disappearing pension fund and identifying the corrupt cops setting him up. Apparently, these are the same people now trying to kill him before he learns the truth, which is why he's standing at the window delivering a monologue that not even he could hear above the din of the helicopter.

It's a pivotal moment only for those collectors of Silly Scenes From Summer Movies.

"The Negotiator" may have the dumbest premise of any major studio movie this year, and there are still five months to go. But there is nothing dumb about the performances of its charismatic stars, Jackson and Kevin Spacey, who plays the wily cop with whom Roman has to negotiate.

The film is a creaky 40 minutes along before Spacey appears, as Chris Sabian, a negotiator for another Chicago division who's at home trying to broker a truce between his wife and his teenage daughter when he's called to the hostage scene uptown. Roman has demanded Sabian as his negotiator, because he doesn't trust anyone from his own department, and in the deal finds himself up against a man who is every bit his match.

"The Negotiator" seems to meet the minimum contemporary standard of summer excess, in size and number of explosions, fires, shootings, etc., but from Sabian's appearance on, his cat-and-mouse game with Roman, and the relationship that develops from it, ground the film in solidly sympathetic characters.

Gray, a music video veteran with two inner-city action features ("Set It Off," "Friday") to his credit, has a good sense of pace and an even better sense of comic timing. It's no mean task to get big laughs in the midst of the greatest tension, but they come in bushels here, mostly through a hilarious Paul Giamatti, as the frightened petty thief among Roman's hostages.

Elsewhere, veteran character actors Ron Rifkin, David Morse and John Spencer fill out conventional police genre roles, while the late J.T. Walsh, in a performance that seems clearly truncated, plays the internal affairs cop at the hub of the conspiracy.

NEWSWEEK, 8/3/98, p. 67, David Ansen

High inside a federal building in Chicago, Danny Roman (Samuel L. Jackson) is holding four hostages at gunpoint—two of them cops. He has a list of demands. One of them is that the police get Chris Sabian (Kevin Spacey) to act as the negotiator—the only man he's willing to deal with.

That may sound like a strange request, but Roman knows what he's after. He, like Sabian, is a skilled negotiator, a highly respected police lieutenant who regularly risks his neck talking maniacs out of taking lives. What's he doing on the other side of the law? In "The Negotiator," Roman has been framed for the murder of his partner. Just before he died, the partner told Roman that someone within the Chicago police force stole $2 million from the pension fund. Whoever is behind the crime has planted evidence pointing the finger at Roman. Cornered, he takes desperate measures to clear his name and find the culprit, knowing that the real crooks within the department now have a perfect excuse to kill him.

At first "The Negotiator" shows every sign of being just another slick, overwrought hot-weather action movie with a bombastic score. But I can pinpoint the exact moment when F. Gary Gray's movie won me over. Roman is on the phone with the first, inexperienced negotiator. Knowing far more about the job than this novice, Roman proceeds to lecture him on how badly he is handling the situation, hilariously reducing his hapless foe to jelly. It's amazing how a sense of humor can turn a formula film into a frolic. It also helps that one of Roman's hostages—played by the very funny Paul Giamatti—is a nervous wreck of a con man whose expertise will eventually come in handy in helping our hero get to the bottom of the plot against him.

Gripping and slightly off-the-wall, "The Negotiator" is guided by a particularly clever script by James DeMonaco and Kevin Fox: it manages to make us root for both Roman and Sabian when they are at odds with each other (we know, of course, that eventually they'll end up on the same side). Jackson and Spacey are two of the sliest actors around—there's always more than one thing at a time going on in their performances, ironies percolating under the surface. Jackson's irony is predominantly verbal—he draws out his words with a teasing sarcasm, toying with adversaries whose tricks he knows better than they do. Spacey's irony is visual: it's in his perfection of the tiny little smile, the droll twinkle of the eye, that turns the meaning of what he's saying upside down. They're the perfect stars for this double-edged battle of wits. They are backed up by an accomplished cast that includes David Morse, Ron Rifkin, Regina Taylor and the late J. T. Walsh, whose mastery of dead-eyed menace made him one of the most satisfyingly subtle villains of the past two decades.

Gray, directing his first big-budget feature, keeps the squeeze on the audience, escalating the suspense with an expertise that, most of the time, avoids the meaningless hysteria so many action directors now feel is *de rigueur*. This rousing and funny sleeper should catapult him onto the Hollywood A-list.

SIGHT AND SOUND, 12/98, p. 52, John Levac

Chicago. Danny Roman, a police hostage-negotiator, is told by his partner Nate that a group of their colleagues are embezzling the police pension fund. Roman later stumbles upon Nate's corpse. As the chief suspect, Roman has his house searched by his fellow officers: they find records there of off-shore bank accounts in his name.

Realising he is being framed, Roman takes hostage internal-affairs investigator Terence Niebaum, Niebaum's assistant Maggie, police commander Frost and police informant Rudy. Roman insists he will deal only with Chris Sabian, a negotiator from another precinct. Sabian begins his mediation, but the police ignore his advice and attack. Roman pretends to execute a captured cop in response. With the aid of Maggie and Rudy, Roman finds proof of Niebaum's involvement in both the pension fraud and his partner Nate's death. Niebaum reveals some of what he knows, but is killed when the FBI storm the building. Sabian helps Roman escape. The pair arrive at Niebaum's home, where they find evidence that Frost is behind the embezzlement. Frost pursues them, but inadvertently allows himself to be recorded admitting his culpability, and is arrested. Roman, his innocence proven, walks free.

Despite executing its remit as studio-generated spectacle with an efficiency bordering on the clinical, *The Negotiator* often appears notable less for what it is than for what it attempts to be, at least until the final act. Appropriating the role-reversal device of last year's *Face/Off* the script manages to inject a refreshing note of ambiguity into the strict binary logic of the good guy/bad guy paradigm. While Danny Roman's innocence is certain, he is never quite the moral centre. Equally, few conventional heroes display a streak of dispassionate professionalism as wide as that of Chris Sabian.

Similarly, a measure of subtlety informs the film's handling of race; the fact that the police department's most senior black officer is also being made its scapegoat is neither glossed over nor allowed to dominate. Instead, we're given the freedom to draw our own conclusions from the prosaic visual evidence of a sea of white faces taking aim at an African-American colleague. Here, Gary Gray's dexterity and almost journalistic eye for detail are redolent of both his last film, the female-gangster movie *Set It Off*, and his professional background as a cameraman for live news broadcasts.

Yet his ability to pace is much less certain. As the storyline grows increasingly hysterical in its later stages, the momentum of individual scenes oscillates manically, sagging under the weight of unnecessary plot explanation or becoming alarmingly frenetic. By the denouement the effect is one of an unusual delicacy being swallowed whole by generic fairground thrills. As a consequence, the film drifts from examining dualism and Otherness into becoming disappointingly routine cop melodrama. Not only is the resolution eminently predictable, its arrival is delayed by a series of explosions and gun battles which do not seem to be the director's real forte.

By this point, the mere presence of the two lead actors comes to resemble the project's entire *raison d'être* and, while both give the kind of astute performances on which their respective reputations are based, for much of their time together on screen they have little to do but showboat at each other. It is perhaps fitting that the posters for *The Negotiator* feature Jackson and Spacey posed as if preparing for some kind of heavyweight title fight. Though he hints at something altogether more cerebral, Gray ultimately contents himself with simple-minded if functional macho visceral thrills.

VILLAGE VOICE, 8/4/98, p. 58, Amy Taubin

Pity *The Negotiator*, a punchy, police-action flick that has the misfortune of opening a week after *Saving Private Ryan*. Since I was overwhelmed by only 50 minutes of Spielberg's 170-minute homage to the slaughtered soldiers of World War II (great scenes, not a great movie), I was a bit disconcerted when I discovered its high moral tone had rubbed off on me. *Saving Private Ryan* could accelerate the backlash against rollercoaster blockbusters, making viewers feel guilty about their acceptance, not to mention enjoyment, of movies that don't "earn" their explosions and torn flesh.

While the Spielbergian moral order allows for the kind of genre fantasy in which all hell breaks loose when science interferes with nature *(Jaws* and *Jurassic Park)*, it finds more virtue in the depiction of such real-life wholesale slaughters as the Holocaust, the Middle Passage, and the D-Day invasion—events that it would be obscene to view as entertainment. What's beyond the pale are the summer thrill drills from *Lethal Weapon* to *Armageddon*, where mayhem is an end in itself and the scattershot paeans to the nuclear family have all the authority of a psychologist's preface to an illustrated sex manual.

Like all Hollywood films *(Saving Private Ryan* included), F. Gary Gray's *The Negotiator* is a mess of contradictions. Basically a police corruption B picture with a subtext about racism that's all the more powerful for never being openly stated, it goes out of control when it turns into *Die Hard* midway through.

When we first see Danny Roman (Samuel L. Jackson), he's trying to talk an ex-marine psycho into giving up the little girl he's holding hostage, a rifle barrel pressed to her neck. Roman is reputed to be the best hostage negotiator in the Chicago P.D., willing to risk his neck when he can't turn some nutcase around with talk alone. But his skiff and courage may have given him a false sense of security. When he's framed for the murder of his partner and for embezzling big bucks from the pension fund, he's shocked by how easily his fellow officers are convinced of his guilt. Refusing to plea-bargain about crimes he didn't commit, and fearing that he'll never live to come to trial, Roman takes the head of internal affairs and his staff hostage, intending to trade them for information that will prove his innocence. He refuses to talk to anyone except Chris Sabian (Kevin Spacey), a negotiator whose reputation is based on his coolheaded approach. Sabian has been known to spend 50 hours talking a subject into surrendering. And time is what Roman needs to discover the identity of the bad guys.

It was inevitable, after the back-to-back successes of *Friday* and *Set It Off*, that director F. Gary Gray would be persuaded to harness his talent for nervy, outsider characters and adrenalized action into larger-scale, more mainstream fare. Unlike his previous boyz-or-girlz-in-the-hood films, however, *The Negotiator* takes the point of view of a black hero-cop who's nearly an anomaly in a white institution. I don't think there's a mention of race in the movie, and yet Jackson's performance and Gray's direction make us aware of how racism figures in Roman's predicament.

The Negotiator is also one of the rare Hollywood movies that's art-directed and photographed to the advantage of black skin. The saturated blue, green, and brown walls show Jackson to advantage. He may be out of place in the Chicago police department but, in a larger sense, he seems at home in the world while the white cops just look pasty-faced and bled out. If you don't consider such visual elements a crucial aspect of how movies make meaning, just think of *A Time To Kill*, where Jackson—supposedly playing a sympathetic character—was fit to look like a stereotypical crazed spook.

Jackson proves he can easily carry a big studio action picture. Gray makes the most of his star's physical authority and his ability to think and react with a camera tight on his face.

As a thinking actor, Spacey is Jackson's equal. Their one-on-ones are more exciting than the firepower and shattered glass, SWAT-team helicopter attacks, and ventilator-shaft escapes that blow a potentially intriguing *policier* out of proportion.

Also reviewed in:
CHICAGO TRIBUNE, 7/29/98, Tempo/p. 1, Michael Wilmington
NEW YORK TIMES, 7/29/98, p. E5, Janet Maslin
VARIETY, 7/27-8/2/98, p. 51, Emanuel Levy

WASHINGTON POST, 7/29/98, p. D1, Stephen Hunter
WASHINGTON POST, 7/31/98, Weekend/p. 47, Michael O'Sullivan

NEIL SIMON'S 'THE ODD COUPLE II'

A Paramount Pictures release of a Cort/Madden production. *Producer:* Neil Simon, Robert W. Cort, and David Madden. *Director:* Howard Deutch. *Screenplay:* Neil Simon. *Director of Photography:* Jamie Anderson. *Editor:* Seth Flaum. *Music:* Alan Silvestri. *Music Editor:* Kennet Karman and Andrew Silver. *Choreographer:* Michelle Johnston. *Sound:* Lee Orloff and (music) Dennis Sands. *Sound Editor:* Sandy Berman. *Casting:* Jane Shannon-Smith and Alex Rosenberg. *Production Designer:* Dan Bishop. *Art Director:* Jeff Knipp. *Set Designer:* Mary Finn and Julia K. Levine. *Set Decorator:* Kristen Toscano Messina. *Costumes:* Lisa Jensen. *Make-up:* Steve Artmont. *Stunt Coordinator:* Charlie Brewer. *Running time:* 90 minutes. *MPAA Rating:* PG-13.

CAST: Jack Lemmon (Felix Ungar); Walter Matthau (Oscar Madison); Christine Baranski (Thelma); Barnard Hughes (Beaumont); Jonathan Silverman (Brucey Madison); Jean Smart (Holly); Lisa Waltz (Hannah Unger); Mary Beth Peil (Felice); Doris Belack (Blanche Madison Povitch); Ellen Geer (Frances Ungar Melnick); Jay O. Sanders (Leroy); Rex Linn (Jay Jay); Richard Riehle (Detective); Lou Cutell (Abe); Mary Fogarty (Flossie); Alice Ghostley (Esther); Peggy Miley (Millie); Rebecca Schull (Wanda); Florence Stanley (Hattie); Estelle Harris (Flirting Woman); Joaquin Martinez (Truck Driver); Amy Yasbeck (Stewardess); Francesca P. Roberts (Woman Passenger); Amy Parrish (Computer Girl); Liz Torres (Maria); Myles Jeffrey (Little Boy); Carmen Mormino and Chuck Montgomery (California Troopers); Earl Boen (Fred); Ron Harper (Jack); Edmund Shaff (Ralph); Daisy Velez (Conchita); Beecey Carlson (Waitress); Terry L. Rose (Bartender); Alfred Dennis (Morton); Armando Ortega (Detective); Peter Renaday (Justice of the Peace); David Jean-Thomas (Bus Driver); Daniel Zacapa (Lead Cop); Cliff Bemis (Dance Partner); Frank Roman (Bellman); Lonnie McCullough (Roadblock Officer); Matt McKenzie (Pilot); Heath Hyche (Policeman); Irene Olga López (Cafe Waitress); Jerry Rector (Detective); Martin Grey (Immigration Officer); Michelle Johnston (Bridesmaid); Michelle Matthow (Wedding Guest); Mark McGee (Wedding Bartender); Barry Thompson (Male Passenger); Joanna Sanchez and Catherine Paolone (Passengers); Michelle Johnston (Airline Employee); Laura Russo (Stewardess).

LOS ANGELES TIMES, 4/10/98, Calendar/p. 16, Jack Mathews

[*The following review by Jack Mathews appeared in a slightly different form in* NEWSDAY, 4/10/98, Part II/p. B6.]

It's as funny as a banana peel. Or, a guy on laughing gas getting a root canal from a buxom blond. Or, take my wife... please!

It's vaudeville with a touch of burlesque, a reunion of Mutt and Jeff. It's "The Sunshine Boys" doing "The Out of Towners," starring those grumpy old men, directly from the Borscht Belt table at the Friars Club. Let's hear it for them, ladies and germs: Jack Lemmon and Walter Matthau.

Just what the group activities supervisor ordered, "The Odd Couple II," 30 years later. Yes, it's been that long since fussy Felix Unger moved in on slob sportswriter Oscar Madison and made Oscar so mad that he threw a bowl of spaghetti against the kitchen wall. Now, they're back, having survived three decades of fastidiousness and slovenliness on their own, thrown together on the road in California by Neil Simon and the popularity of the "Grumpy Old Men" movies.

Oscar and Felix reconnoiter 17 years after their last, apparently painful get-together, when news reaches each of them that Oscar's son Brucey (Jonathan Silverman) and Felix's daughter Hannah (Lisa Waltz) are getting married. By chance, both arrive at LAX at the same time, giving Felix the opportunity to sprain his ankle and Oscar to leave Felix's luggage—with a $6,000 wedding gift and $10,000 in cash—at the car rental office, and setting up a long road sequence that involves the worst writing Simon has ever done.

The story, such as it is, puts Oscar and Felix on the wrong road to a fictional town north of Los Angeles where their kids and their ex-wives are preparing for the wedding. But Oscar makes the wrong turn somewhere, sending them in a different direction and on a collision course with a pair of roadside bar tarts named Thelma (Christine Baranski) and Holly (Jean Smart), their pistol-packing redneck husbands, a road-straddling crop duster, a batch of undocumented immigrants and a short-tempered local sheriff to whose jail they keep returning.

"Odd Couple II," directed by "Grumpier Old Men's" Howard Deutch, is essentially a rehash of the feuding friendship dynamics of the first film, which are probably familiar to most of today's audiences through their incarnations in the TV series starring Jack Klugman and Tony Randall. Frankly, it's a little sad to see the 77-year-old Matthau and the 73-year-old Lemmon going back to the well, especially when the "Grumpy Old Men" movies have already supplied two de facto "Odd Couple" sequels.

There are, of course, some funny lines. Even in a knockoff mood, Simon can turn a phrase. And Matthau—getting the best of those lines—and Lemmon play off each other like an old married couple. But the laughs leave a melancholy aftertaste, a sense that we've encouraged an old song-and-dance team to cut a rug and are embarrassed by the spectacle.

NEW YORK POST, 4/10/98, p. 43, Thelma Adams

Walter Matthau and Jack Lemmon are as grumpy as it gets.

America's favorite codgers take their coot 'n' kvetch routine on the road to California in "Neil Simon's The Odd Couple II."

The comedians re-create their 1968 roles as mismatched roomies Oscar Madison and Felix Unger. The pair prove they have legs—even if they're criss-crossed with varicose veins.

Stealing a plot from the duo's "Grumpy Old Men" and cadging "Grumpier Old Men," director Howard Deutch reunites the guys when Felix's daughter weds Oscar's son in California.

Matthau has the best comic timing in movies—and funnyman Simon arms him with zingers to spare. Together with fussy Felix after 17 years, the sloppy sports-writer quips: "We mix like oil and frozen yogurt."

As he ages, Matthau's face is it's own sight gag. Caterpillars of black hair curl in his ears. His lizardy neck holds the face of a disgruntled basset hound.

Lemmon is Matthau's straight man, an all-purpose irritant allergic to life. He honks, he whines, he's a human blowfish.

Together, Lemmon and Matthau are as close to Hope and Crosby as we're going to get on the verge of the millenium.

Those lamenting the absence of Jack Klugman and Tony Randall, who played Oscar and Felix for five seasons on TV, will at least be at home with the sitcomy nature of Simon's script.

Getting Felix and Oscar on the road is the hilarious part: they roll rental cars, chase a corpse's toupee, wear glow-in-the-dark skivvies and are arrested for transporting illegal aliens in a borrowed truck.

Felix and Oscar also cavort with two tarts in a lowlife cantina in fictional California backwater Santa Menendez (like the brothers). Thelma (a cackling Christine Baranski) and Holly (Jean Smart) are a chip off feminist movie rebels T. and Louise.

The appearance of Baranski and Smart filling hot pants like helium allows a series of jokes that prove Simon and the boys are throwbacks to the golden age of sexism.

The climactic wedding is anticlimactic, but we no longer care. Our cheeks are sore from laughing. The door is left wide open for sequels, should the leads survive to play out their multi-picture deals.

If "The Odd Couple" has become so familiar it's no longer odd, take it in stride like the skirt-chasing Oscar: This is the biggest, goddamnedest deja vu anybody's ever had."

SIGHT AND SOUND, 12/98, p. 53, Robin Dougherty

After 17 years slovenly Oscar is reunited with his former housemate, the fastidious Felix, when Oscar's son announces his engagement to Felix's daughter. The two fathers meet in LA and rent a car together. They soon begin to annoy one another just as they had years earlier. Oscar accidentally burns their map, and the two find themselves lost in the desert. Their empty car rolls into a canyon and bursts into flames.

Distraught, the pair are picked up by a Mexican truck driver who leads them to a road block. Then, in the first of three occasions when they will be mistaken for criminals, the pair are arrested for violating immigration laws. Released, they continue to make their way to the wedding, by now five hours' journey from their destination. An elderly man volunteers to chauffeur them, but dies while driving. A bus they take is hijacked by the irate husbands of two biker women they had met earlier in a bar.

Finally, the duo arrive at their destination. By this time, Felix has become enamoured with Felice, Oscar's former sister-in-law, whom they met on the way. After the wedding Felix leaves LA with Felice, while Oscar goes home alone. Some time later, Felix arrives on Oscar's doorstep, suitcases in hand because it didn't work out with Felice, and suggests the two live together again.

"This is the biggest God damned *déjà vu* anyone has ever had," growls Oscar, one half of the mismatched pair of housemates reunited in *The Odd Couple II*, the sequel to *The Odd Couple* (1967). However, this affable comedy is less reminiscent of the original (which also starred Walter Matthau as Oscar and Jack Lemmon as Felix) or the 70s television series based on it than it is of the *Grumpy Old Men* series, which reunited Matthau and Lemmon in 1993 and again (with *Grumpier Old Men)* in 1995.

Author of the original stage play on which the first *Odd Couple* was based, Neil Simon both wrote the screenplay and produced this sequel. But there's none of the existential angst of the first movie, which mined the melancholy as well as the humour in the pairing of two divorced men, one of whom is mindbogglingly sloppy, the other obsessively clean. Instead, director Howard Deutch *(Pretty in Pink)* offers up low-intensity fun of the same variety that propelled the *Grumpy* movies (the second of which Deutch also directed). With its series of minor dramatic peaks and shallow valleys, the film feels like an extended television episode. Given the sun drenched shots of freeways, canyons and airports that dominate the visual landscape, the film makers didn't wander very far from Los Angeles in reality or imagination. No matter how synthetically constructed, however, *The Odd Couple II* is as lovable as any of the other minor works in the Matthau-Lemmon canon.

In fact, the plot—in which Oscar and Felix encounter a series of misadventures on the road while travelling to the wedding of Oscar's son and Felix's daughter is little more than an excuse for the two Hollywood veterans to play off each other's excellent comic timing. Curiously, despite the fact that neither Oscar nor Felix has been able to survive, much less maintain, a long-term relationship with a woman, the movie is very pro marriage. The joke, of course, is that Oscar and Felix are better suited to each other than the partners in many conventional marriages. Likewise, Matthau and Lemmon have the kind of chemistry (of three decades' standing) that can't be concocted by a studio marketing department. The two seem genuinely happy to be in one another's company and that alone rescues the movie from staleness.

Less fresh, perhaps, are the snatches of the original Neal Hefti composed theme song that crop up from time to time, gratuitously reminding us that we've seen these characters before. Also unnecessary is the foul language that dots the dialogue, possibly intended to forge a contemporary edge. Matthau conveys plenty of gruffness without needing to say "shit head". As for Felix, the words just sound ridiculous coming out of his mouth. More welcome is the appearance of Christine Baranski and Jean Smart, who play characters named Thelma and Holly, a pair of disgruntled biker chicks who pick up Oscar and Felix in a bar. Leave it to Matthau and Lemmon to find charmingly off-beat company everywhere they go.

Also reviewed in:
CHICAGO TRIBUNE, 4/10/98, Friday/p. A, Michael Wilmington
NEW YORK TIMES, 4/10/98, p. E25, Stephen Holden
VARIETY, 4/6-12/98, p. 48, Joe Leydon

NEWTON BOYS, THE

A Twentieth Century Fox release of a Detour filmproduction. *Executive Producer:* John Sloss. *Producer:* Anne Walker-McBay. *Director:* Richard Linklater. *Screenplay:* Richard Linklater, Claude Stanush, and Clark Lee Walker. *Based on the book by:* Claude Stanush. *Director of Photography:* Peter James. *Editor:* Sandra Adair. *Music:* Bad Livers. *Music Editor:* Alex Gibson. *Choreographer:* Eddie Baytos. *Sound:* John Pritchett. *Sound Editor:* Pat Jackson. *Casting:* Don Phillips. *Production Designer:* Catherine Hardwicke. *Art Director:* Andrea Dopaso and John Frick. *Set Designer:* Kevin Cross. *Set Decorator:* Jeanette Scott. *Set Dresser:* Darren Patnode, Bart Brown, Tom Christopher, Todd Morris, Shane Patrick, Jeff P. Schwan, and Terri L. Wright. *Special Effects:* John McLeod. *Costumes:* Shelley Komarov. *Make-up:* Patty York. *Stunt Coordinator:* Fred Lerner. *Running time:* 121 minutes. *MPAA Rating:* PG-13.

CAST: Matthew McConaughey (Willis Newton);   Skeet Ulrich (Joe Newton);   Ethan Hawke (Jess Newton);   Gail Cronauer (Ma Newton);   Jena Karam and Casey McAuliffe (Orphan Singers);   Regina Mae Matthews (Orphan Fiddler);   Lew Temple (Waiter);   Dwight Yoakam (Brentwood Glasscock);   Charles Gunning (Slim);   Glynn Williams (Farmer Williams);   Charles "Chip" Bray (Bank Teller);   Chloe Webb (Avis Glasscock);   Gary Moody (Crooked Banker); Julianna Margulies (Louise Brown);   Robert Iannaccone (Tailor);   Jennifer Miriam (Catherine); Anne Stedman (Madeline);   Marjorie Carroll (Old Woman);   Katie Gratson (Young Hotel Clerk);   Angie Chase (Kat);   Lynn Mathis (Arthur Adams);   Vincent D'Onofrio (Dock Newton);   Becket Gremmels (Lewis);   Ed Dollison (Night Guard);   Boots Southerland (Wagon Driver);   Bo Hopkins (K.P. Aldrich);   Tommy Townsend (Omaha Detective);   Mary Love (Hotel Maid);   A.G. Zeke Mills (Old Usher);   Abra Moore (Argosy Ballroom Singer);   Lori Heuring (Flapper);   Joe Stevens (Bank Association President);   Eddie Matthews, Scott Roland, and J.P. Schwan (Bank Messengers);   Rooster McConaughey (Tool Pusher);   Bo Franks (Barker);   Ali Nazary (Thug);   Ron De Roxtra (Murray);   David Jensen (William Fahy);   Brad Arrington (Hobo);   Richard A. Jones (Engineer);   Randy Stripling (Fireman);   Harold Suggs (Old Brakeman);   Chamblee Ferguson (Head Postal Clerk);   F.W. Post (Postal Turkey);   Grant James (Gangland Doctor);   Mark Fickert (Chicago Sergeant);   Kerry Tartack (Chicago Detective);   Luke Askew (Chief Schoemaker);   Blue McDonnell (Nurse);   Eduardo Cavazos Garza (Mexican Cab Driver);   Ken Farmer (Frank Hamer);   Daniel T. Kamin (District Attorney);   Ross Sears (Judge).

CHRISTIAN SCIENCE MONITOR, 4/3/98, p. B3, David Sterritt

Ever since the aptly named "Slacker," his 1991 debut picture, Richard Linklater has been the movie world's foremost expert on lackadaisical youths.

He continued his slacker-studying in "Dazed and Confused" and "subUrbia," and gave it a new spin in the talkative "Before Sunrise," his most sophisticated picture to date.

The trouble with being a slacker specialist is that you may run out of fresh approaches to the subject. Faced with that danger, Linklater tries a daring solution in "The Newton Boys," his latest enterprise. He draws his heroes from a real-life outlaw gang who pulled off an amazing string of bank robberies in a long list of states between 1919 and 1924.

In short, Linklater has made a slacker western—hardly the first in Hollywood history, but still a bold maneuver at a time when westerns are considered box-office risks.

What may give "The Newton Boys" some hope of prosperity is its winsome cast, populated by handsome young heartthrobs like Matthew McConaughey, Skeet Ulrich, and Ethan Hawke, a Linklater veteran who contributed much to "Before Sunrise" three years ago.

Also shooting up the screen are Vincent D'Onofrio as yet another Newton brother and Dwight Yoakam as the gang's explosives expert; and there are occasional glimpses of Julianna Margulies and Chloe Webb as two of the story's rare female characters.

These are fetching performers, but their built-in energy is about all "The Newton Boys" has going for it. The plot is familiar from decades of earlier bank-robbing sagas—the classic "Bonnie and Clyde" seems to have been a particular inspiration for its overall tone—and neither the action nor the dialogue rings meaningful changes on the genre.

The best part comes at the very end, when elderly members of the actual Newton gang reminisce briefly about their criminal careers. They don't arrive until the final credits are rolling, though, and that's a long time to wait for a movie's payoff.

LOS ANGELES TIMES, 3/27/98, Calendar/p. 6, Kenneth Turan

It's probably not fair to "The Newton Boys" to call it a slacker western. Or to lament that "Young Guns" would have been a sprightlier title if it hadn't already been taken. But absent much of anything that's distinctive in this film, comparisons to other movies are what come to mind.

Co-written and directed by "Slacker's" Richard Linklater, "The Newton Boys" is neither bothersome nor exciting. It has periodic bursts of action, as befits the story of "the most successful bank robbers in the history of the United States," but an edge-of-your-seat affair this is not. The film exists mainly on style and attitude, both of which wear thin as time marches on.

The four Newton brothers, robbers of more than 80 banks in Texas and the Midwest between 1919 and 1925, were real people, and the most fun this film provides is clips (run alongside the closing credits) of two of the siblings in their declining years. The sight of Willis Newton matching wits with Johnny Carson is more fun than everything that precedes it.

What Hollywood saw in the Newton saga is the chance to have four cute guys swagger around in period costumes. Matthew McConaughey, Ethan Hawke, Skeet Ulrich and Vincent D'Onofrio are the quartet of rascally individuals, good old boy bandits whom grateful victims invariably describe as "a bunch of please and thank you country boys."

Writer-director Linklater has made a career of detailing the peregrinations of the young and the restless in films like "Dazed and Confused," "Before Sunrise" and the unspeakable "subUrbia." He (and co-writers Claude Stanush & Clark Lee Walker) have conceived of the Newtons as kings of cool, and while this casual, relaxed feeling is pleasant for a while, it's not enough to build an entire picture around.

"The Newton Boys" starts in Uvalde County, Texas, in 1919, the kind of rural locale where squirrel dumplings is the plat du jour. Brother Jess (Hawke) is teaching baby brother Joe (Ulrich) the finer points of breaking horses when brother Willis (McConaughey) shows up after a stint behind bars.

Willis is irked, not just because he was put away for something he didn't do but because society is intent on holding that prison sentence against him. He's bothered enough to join career criminal and nitroglycerin expert Brentwood Glasscock (Dwight Yoakam) and a pal in a daring daylight robbery of a bank that doesn't quite turn out as planned.

Glasscock never wanted to do a daylight job to begin with; "that damn Jesse James routine," he complains, "went out at the turn of the century." He and Willis decide to be better prepared in the future, working out detailed escape routes and concentrating on old-fashioned square-doored safes that can be easily blown apart during late-night criminal forays.

Willis relocates in staid Omaha, where a question about what's fun brings a "you could chew gum" reply (the film's funniest line). Needing lookouts, Willis remembers his brothers, especially tough-guy Dock (D'Onofrio), but his younger siblings need convincing to depart from the straight and narrow.

Willis is up to the task, coming up with a speech about how taking insured money from banks is not the same as stealing from people. "We're just little thieves stealing from the big thieves" is how he puts it. "Banks have been dealing dirty to our people since before we were born."

The outlaw is equally glib with Louise Brown, a single mother he has his eye on, played by "ER's" Julianna Margulies. Unfortunately, none of the women in this picture, including the playful and eccentric Chloe Webb, who appears as Glasscock's wife, aren't given anything to do that isn't generic and predictable.

"The Newton Boys" presents several robberies for our amusement, but they are too lackadaisical to be more than moderately involving. The film tries to rouse itself for the traditional "one last big job and then we're outta here" finale, but doesn't quite manage to overcome its general level of genial torpor.

Though the actors, especially a well-used McConaughey, have charm to spare, nothing they do feels as if it matters, and the fraternal roughhousing that characterizes the boys' relationship has limited appeal. Nothing seems individual about "The Newton Boys," nothing compels you to watch it. Just because everyone wants to make a western doesn't mean everybody should.

NEW YORK POST, 3/27/98, p. 45, Thelma Adams

"The Newton Boys" will be boys. Hey, it could be called "Where the Newton Boys Are."

The chief pleasure of Texan Richard Linklater's all-pretty-boys, all-the-time period caper is watching Matthew McConaughey, Skeet Ulrich, Ethan Hawke and Vincent D'Onofrio in cute little tweed suits and felt hats, robbin' banks, breakin' ponies, chattin' up floozies and drinkin' bathtub gin.

Linklater, the drawling poet laureate of Gen X movies, switches from the contemporary aimlessness of "Slacker" to the fact-based story of four Lone Star brothers who aimed to rob banks without shedding blood. Willis, Jess, Dock and Joe Newton knocked over 80 banks from 1919 to 1924. Then they upped the ante, ambushed a mail train out of Chicago and got caught.

Texan McConaughey, a Linklater find in "Dazed and Confused," plays ex-con Willis, the brothers' ringleader. It's easier to believe M.M. as a thief than a lawyer, as proven in the strained disappointments of "Amistad" and "A Time to Kill." His Willis has the dimpled smoothie charm of Paul Newman in "The Sting."

Hawk is the bold, drunken, party brother, Ulrich is the sensitive, youngest son; the underused D'Onofrio is a big, loyal ox. Julianna Margulies shimmers as Willis' true love, Louise Brown.

Country singer Dwight Yoakam, the menacing stepdad in "Sling Blade," shows stretch for a part by sporting a bad combover. Yoakam is quietly satisfying as the brothers' frail explosives expert, Brentwood Glasscock. How's that for the name of a guy who blows safes?

The audience, when not simply sitting back and enjoying the pleasures of boy-watching, can also admire the "E.R." beauty Margulies' gorgeous costumes and bountiful hair. There's plenty of time since the film moves with the speed of a Texas summer, which is a surprise for anyone watching a film about bank robbers, but not to fans of Linklater.

Linklater gives "The Newton Boys" an easy charm and a sepia-toned patina of Hollywood period movies. The script is witty and romantic and entirely lacking in narrative tension.

NEWSDAY, 3/27/98, Part II/p. B3, John Anderson

Richard Linklater's prankster instincts—so evident in "Slacker" and "Dazed and Confused," so glaringly absent in "Before Sunrise" and "subUrbia"—are given their head in "The Newton Boys," a Jazz Age western about the most successful robbery team in American history and an adventure of hat-tipping, glad-handing archness.

The Newtons, who from 1919-24 robbed more than 80 banks between Texas and Canada—and lived to ripe old ages besides—are played by Matthew McConaughey, Ethan Hawke, Vincent D'Onofrio and Skeet Ulrich, four actors who represent the *idea* of being actors as often as they act. But, as the de facto posse pursuing Linklater's aim of the post-modern/modernized shoot-'em-up, they're also celebrating the *idea* of the western. And as canny Willis (McConaughey), bronc-busting, wisecracking Jess (Hawke), big old Dock (D'Onafrio) and sensitive Joe (Ulrich), they're beyond charming, not far from "Bonanza" and what they're always about is bringing types to life.

"The Newton Boys" takes the lads from their hard-scrabble Texas upbringing (erratic father, squirrel dumplings) to relatively high-tech safe-cracking (night jobs, nitroglycerine) to the biggest train robbery in U.S. history ($3 million, big mess). It's colorful and fast-paced, but you're always aware that amid the rollicking tempos and comedic swashbuckling, this is a movie that celebrates conventions and gestures—from the opening title cards (the "Butch Cassidy" echoes are distinct) to the hat-tipping cameos that introduce the players (including Julianna Margulies as Willis' love interest, Louise Brown, and Dwight Yoakam as the Newton's crafty, safe-blowing attache Brentwood Glasscock) to the full-blown, posturing illogic that announces we're somewhere near Farceville, Texas, population . . . who knows?

Linklater, given that he's working with a true-crime story, pushes the limits of disbelief in subtly mischievous ways. What's going on when the poverty stricken ex-convict/rube Willis gives a handful of dollars to a trio of hymn-singing street urchins? Or when, with relative sophistication, he sips a brandy during a meeting with confederates—Glasscock warms it with his palm; the thick-headed Slim, played by Charles Gunning, knocks his back like whiskey and then slips Glasscock a knowing look?

Willis reduces a romance derailed by the woman's father—"I'm not good enough for his daughter but I'm good enough to work his crop?"—to the kind of swell-chested non sequitur that may be permissible only in a western. And his epiphany about the Newtons' destiny as bank robbers—as Robin Hoods victimizing the victimizers—lies in an emotional territory somewhere between Emile Zola defending Dreyfus and Mickey Rooney saying, "Let's put on a show!" It is all show, Linklater is telling us, in a manner just short of erecting a billboard.

At the same time, the movie seems perfectly serviceable as straight adventure, or even as a family film (there's no vulgarity, nudity or compromising positions I can recall, and the violence, all non-lethal, is fairly tame too).

And while it's ostensibly McConaughey's picture, Yoakam ("Sling Blade") pretty much steals it out from under him, underplaying Glasscock perfectly, allowing the Newtons to orbit his gravitational field like antic moons. Hawke, who's always seemed irritatingly smug, uses his particular gifts to good advantage as the whiskey-drinking charmer Jess. Ulrich, as the doubting Joseph, is sweetly hunkish. Margulies ("E R") is solid enough (and lovely, although not the raving beauty the film pretends she is). But we wish there'd been more of Chloe Webb as Glasscock's salty wife, Avis, who is more than memorable and probably would have gotten more screen time if her performance wasn't so knowing, and therefore out of sync with a movie so intent on replicating it's own antique line of sepia-toned realities.

TIME, 4/6/98, p. 70, Richard Schickel

The Newton Boys were for real—a quartet of bank-robbing brothers out of Texas who pioneered the same territory that Bonnie and Clyde would bucket across to much larger celebrity a decade later. There were, however, important differences between the gangs. For one thing, the Newtons were far more successful, financially speaking, than their successors. More important, they did not come to a premature and legend-inspiring end. They all attained great age and modest respectability; one of them even turned up as a guest of Johnny Carson's in the '80s.

Their efficiency and longevity presented certain problems to director Richard Linklater (*Slacker*) and his co-screenwriters. He has cast some of Hollywood's hottest young guns—notably Matthew McConaughey, who plays smart very well, and Ethan Hawke, who has a nice slippery charm as the gang's smoothest talker. Best of all, Linklater chose ER's Julianna Margulies to play the woman McConaughey courts and marries. She is beguiling both in her initial skepticism and in her loyalty when things start to go bad for the boys.

When they move up to the big cities, they make a farce of a Toronto heist and a near tragedy out of an Illinois train robbery. Linklater isn't quite skilled enough to make a virtue of these mood shifts and settles for a tone of wry, slightly distant amiability. The result is an agreeable movie, but one that is lacking the edge and intensity that films more self-consciously aware of their moral ambiguities sometimes generate.

VILLAGE VOICE, 3/31/98, p. 68, Amy Taubin

Richard Linklater's first foray into a historical period more distant than his own '70s adolescence is a tastefully told, prettily executed western with a rollicking score that mixes Jelly Roll Morton with original music by The Bad Livers. Set in the decade between World War I and the Great Depression, when horses were outrun by Studebakers even in the heart of Texas, *The Newton Boys* is based on the true story of the most successful bank robbers in U.S. history.

Poor Texas farm boys, the four Newton brothers approached bank robbery as a legitimate profession, no different, they explained, from doctoring or lawyering. Their code of ethics involved absolute family loyalty, never harming women or children, eschewing violence as much as possible (though they claimed to have stolen more money than Jesse James, Butch and Sundance, the Dalton Brothers, and Bonnie and Clyde put together, they never killed anyone), and only stealing from the rich. Since banks were insured, the brothers figured it was the bankers and the insurers who felt the pinch, not the depositors.

For the Texas-raised Linklater, who is one of the least exploitative of '90s indie filmmakers, the Newton brothers' story offered an opportunity to make an anti-Western western and an anti-gangster gangster film rolled into one. And although the film is rife with genre references (so gracefully integrated you have to be as much of an aficionado as the director to spot them), Linklater seems more indebted to Truffaut's *Jules and Jim*.

Unlike the French new-wave favorite, however, the story of the Newton brothers isn't bittersweet or romantic. It's a flat-out comedy even in the classical sense of resolving in favor of the protagonists. Linklater is skillful at shooting and editing action for its comic potential, but his casting is way off the mark. In the title roles, Matthew McConaughey, Ethan Hawke, Vincent D'Onofrio, and even Skeet Ulrich, who's the best of them are model handsome and nothing much more. Freshly shaved and washed behind the ears, they're wiped clean of idiosyncrasy. It's the Bland Boys almost all the way, and who could give a fig about them? The only mildly arresting performances are obvious character types—Dwight Yoakam as the professional safecracker whose skills hold the Newton enterprise together and Chloe Webb as his faithful wife who gets a kick out of keeping nitroglycerin under the bed.

The Newton Boys doesn't pick up steam until the last 30 minutes, when the brothers, arrested in the aftermath of a botched train robbery, try to work their charms on the law. Linklater saves the best for the last possible moment, mixing the end credits with a hilarious videotape of one real Newton—a very senior citizen—appearing on the Johnny Carson Show and even funnier documentary footage of another real Newton in his comfortable ranch house. The film historian in Linklater must have found the footage irresistible, but for *The Newton Boys*, it's a mixed blessing. Sure it sends us out laughing but also wondering why Linklater's Newtons lack the pizzaz they radiated in real life.

Also reviewed in:
CHICAGO TRIBUNE, 3/27/98, Friday/p. A, Michael Wilmington
NEW YORK TIMES, 3/27/98, p. E14, Janet Maslin
VARIETY, 3/16-22/98, p. 67, Emanuel Levy
WASHINGTON POST, 3/27/98, p. C1, Stephen Hunter
WASHINGTON POST, 3/27/98, Weekend/p. 60, Desson Howe

NEXT STEP, THE

A Phaedra Cinema release. *Producer:* Aaron Reed and Hank Blumenthal. *Director:* Christian Faber. *Screenplay:* Aaron Reed. *Director of Photography:* Zack Winestine. *Editor:* Judd Maslansky and David Codron. *Music:* Roni Skies, Mio Morales, and Brian Otto. *Choreographer:* Donald Byrd. *Running time:* 87 minutes. *MPAA Rating:* Not Rated.

CAST: Rick Negron (Nick); Kristin Moreau (Amy); Denise Faye (Heidi); Taylor Nichols (Peter); Gerry McIntyre (Sean); Aubrey Lynch (Steven); Michell Pertier (Michelle); Donald Byrd (Austin); Fuchsia Walker (Receptionist).

NEW YORK POST, 2/6/98, p. 46, Larry Worth

You have to lose everything before you can find yourself. Yes, that's the moral of "The Next Step," which may be the most laughable collection of falling-star cliches since "Show Girls."

Specifically, it's "Chorus Line" meets "Midnight Cowboy" on "42nd Street" as an aging Lothario goes from Broadway hoofer to prostitute in the thud of a tap shoe.

With the exception of Taylor ("Barcelona") Nichols' all-too-brief supporting turn, acting ranges from poor (Rick Negron's footloose anti-hero) to pathetic (Denise Faber's monotoned heroine). And then there's choreography that would be laughed off the Great White Way, never mind Christian Faber's ultra-clumsy direction.

But the biggest problem? Dialogue such as "Maybe it's time for you to give something back," to which the leaden lead responds "I've got nothing left to give."

The same could be said for "The Next Step."

NEWSDAY, 2/6/98, Part II/p. B11, Gene Seymour

Theatergoers who sense the grimaces beneath the grins on a typical chorus line will have many of their worst suspicions confirmed by "The Next Step." There's plenty of up-to-the-minute grit in this backstage-Broadway melodrama—though, even (or especially) in its harrowing moments, it can't help acting like its glossier, soapier forebears.

Nick (Rick Negron), the protagonist, is a dancer in his mid-30s living from foot to mouth. His aching joints keep telling him he's also on borrowed time.

But he won't listen. "I want to dance. Forever!" he tells Heidi (Denise Faye), another gypsy dancer and one of a handful of women he loves and leaves; the exception being Amy (Kristen Moreu), his physical-therapist roommate.

Just when Nick thinks he may have to leave New York with Amy for suburban limbo, he gets a chance to perform in the revival of a show he'd done years before. The director (choreographer Donald Byrd) lets Nick go through the tryout gauntlet for old times' sake, but doubts whether his old pal can still come across as a teenage gangster.

There's so much shrewd observation on the dancing life in Aaron Reed's script that one wishes the story spent more time on such details and less on the philandering, self-absorbed Nick. Negron carries the story with skill and occasional daring. But one leaves the film wishing there were more of the magnetic Denise Faye, or Gerry McIntyre as Sean, a buoyant, witty colleague of Nick's, who rallies his crestfallen co-workers after a show's unexpected closing by holding their credit cards hostage.

VILLAGE VOICE, 2/17/98, p. 116, Elizabeth Zimmer

Making the transition out of a dancing career can be rough, especially if you're a total jerk. That's the situation of one Nick Mendez (played with slack-jawed sensuality by Rick Negron), a straight, unapologetically promiscuous Broadway hoofer performing in a show that closes. We (and a director played by choreographer Donald Byrd) can see that he's too old and achy to hack the eight-shows-a-week of a musical, but he sabotages his shot at a revival by beating up his competition, a talented younger guy, at the audition. He refuses the coaching gig offered by the director and proceeds to fuck up his love life, his restaurant job, his hustle as a male stripper—even his flirtation with suicide.

The dance class, auditions, and sex sequences are shot with the some lascivious, softcore attention; sure, dancing is sexy, but the real Broadway backstage scene concentrates more on precision and expression than on this insipid raunch. The script is stilted and clichéd. Though whites fill the big parts, the best acting is by a few African Americans: Fuchsia Walker's. receptionist, buddy Gerry McIntyre, and fairy godfather Byrd.

Also reviewed in:
NEW YORK TIMES, 2/6/98, p. E10, Stephen Holden
VARIETY, 4/1-7/96, p. 57, Emanuel Levy
WASHINGTON POST, 8/28/98, p. B1, Rita Kempley

NEXT STOP WONDERLAND

A Miramax Films release of a Robbins Entertainment production. *Executive Producer:* Mark Gill. *Producer:* Mitchell B. Robbins. *Director:* Brad Anderson. *Screenplay:* Brad Anderson and Lyn Vaus. *Director of Photography:* Uta Briesewitz. *Editor:* Brad Anderson and Deb Driscoll. *Music:* Claudio Ragazzi. *Sound:* Lenny Manzo. *Sound Editor:* Geof Thurbetr. *Casting:* Walken & Jaffe. *Production Designer:* Chad Detweiller. *Art Director:* Humberto Cordero. *Set Decorator:* Karen Weber. *Set Dresser:* Paul Richards, Gregory Richards, Mary Dicicco, Robert Schleinig, and Juliet Carter. *Special Effects:* Phil Cormier. *Costumes:* Dena Popienko. *Make-up:* Maria Scali. *Running time:* 111 minutes. *MPAA Rating:* R.

CAST: Hope Davis (Erin Castleton); Alan Gelfant (Alan Monteiro); Victor Argo (Frank); Jon Benjamin (Eric); Cara Buono (Julie); Larry Gilliard, Jr. (Brett); Phil Hoffman (Sean); Jason

Lewis (Rory);   Roger Rees (Ray Thornback);   Sam Seder (Kevin Monteiro); Robert Stanton (Robert);   Holland Taylor (Piper Castleton);   Callie Thorne (Cricket);   Jimmy Tingle (Lowrey the Bartender);   Lyn Vaus (Daryl);   Jose Zuniga (Andre DeSilva);   Robert Klein (Arty Lesser); Katherine Kerr (Candice);   Paul Wagner (Bob);   Ernest Thompson (Nathan);   Charlie Broderick (Desmond);   Bronwyn Sims (Traci);   Paul Plum (Denise Shebola);   Ken Cheeseman (Rick); Wayne Pretlow (Oliver);   Pamela Hart (Berit);   Diane Beckett (Seana);   Neil Gustafson (Yuri Spinov);   Luz Alexandra (Thalia);   Kemp Harris (Ben);   Dave Gilloran (Aquarium Volunteer); Emme Shaw (Bailey);   Greg Watson (Frank's Crony);   Robert Larkin (Arty Lesser's Crony); Elizabeth Lindsay (Lucy Bidwell);   Jack Sweet (Sal);   Jeremy Geidt (Bookseller);   Paula Lyons (TV News Anchor);   Arnie Reisman (Field Reporter);   Renita Whited (Arizona Reporter);   Alan Horwitz (Aquarium Guest);   Todd Robinson (Society Photographer).

LOS ANGELES TIMES, 8/21/98, Calendar/p. 1, Kenneth Turan

"Next Stop Wonderland" is a romance, but not just any romance. Smart and beguiling, it manages the impressive feat of believing wholeheartedly in the power of love without checking its mind at the door. Discriminating romantics will not believe their good fortune.

Though its plot echoes other films (including Claude Lelouch's "And Now My Love" and Krzysztof Kieslowski's "Red"), "Wonderland's" bemused, delicately ironic sensibility, supplied by co-writer, editor and director Brad Anderson, is strictly its own.

Helping to set that tone is the subtle yet sensual bossa nova music that dominates the soundtrack: classic Brazilian works by artists including Antonio Carlos Jobim and Astrud Gilberto. In fact, Anderson has said, it's the Brazilian concept of saudade, a kind of happiness and sadness at the same time, that helped inspire this film.

In Hope Davis, recently seen in "The Daytrippers" and "The Myth of Fingerprints," Anderson has found the classic personification of this notion. It's unusual for a young actress to have the opportunity to carry an entire picture, and rarer still does one succeed with the aplomb Davis displays here.

Set in Boston, where Wonderland is, in fact, a train station close to the airport, "Next Stop" introduces both its droll sensibility and Davis' Erin Castleton at a low point in her life.

Walking home from her night-shift job as a registered nurse, Erin is confronted by her live-in boyfriend, Sean (the dead-on amusing Philip Seymour Hoffman), frantically trying to move out before she returns. A gung-ho political activist, he's off to help a needy Native American tribe, leaving her with a cat named Fidel and a tape postulating "Six Reasons Why Our Relationship Is Doomed."

Understandably hurt and angry, Erin is, as it turns out, a self-sufficient woman perfectly content to be on her own and quite capable of turning a tart tongue on those who don't believe that, especially her social butterfly mother, Piper (Holland Taylor).

Though she can appear dismissive and judgmental, Erin, we come to realize partly as we experience her love of poetry, acts that way to protect a good and caring heart. She may proclaim to her friends that she doesn't believe in "the unseen hand leading to the garden path," but part of her would be delighted if the right man came her way down that very path.

Piper Castleton, however, is not one who waits for fate. Without her daughter's permission, she places a personal ad for Erin in a Boston alternative paper. Erin is furious at first, but when she checks in on her responses, she's astonished to discover there are 64.

Partly out of boredom, partly out of curiosity, Erin decides to meet some of her suitors, and the scenes that follow, with their deft skewering of male ego and vanity, are irresistible. The zealot who sells small rubber parts (played by Robert Stanton) is a standout, but look also for the putative divinity student who talks about God being "a big subject"—it's the film's co-screenwriter, Lyn Vaus.

Paralleling Erin's life is that of another Boston resident, Alan Monteiro (Alan Gelfant), who's beset by a different set of problems. A third-generation plumber who works part time at the Boston Aquarium while studying to become a marine biologist, Alan is a mature, hard-working young man who spends a lot of his life taking evasive action.

In school, Alan tries to avoid Julie (Cara Buono), an attractive fellow student with a crush on him, and at work he tries to avoid Frank (Victor Argo), the loan shark he owes money to, as well as Frank's boss Arty Lesser (Robert Klein), a mortuary kingpin locked in a battle with the aquarium.

Though Erin and Alan live lives that seem completely separate, "Next Stop Wonderland" adroitly insinuates that maybe, just maybe, they are meant for each other.

It starts with a simple shot that frames them together: he in a subway car and she seated on the platform seen through a window behind him. As the film progresses, we see, though neither one of them does, just how intertwined their lives have become without their actually meeting. Again and again, in the same room, even on the same telephone line, they just miss connecting.

This is a very delicate balance for a director to maintain, keeping audiences honestly on edge as to whether two people will finally mesh or not, and filmmaker Anderson, in only his second film (the first was the Sundance entry "Darien Gap"), keeps his footing beautifully.

"Wonderland" succeeds because it shares a sensibility with its heroine: Despite its clever dialogue, it's an empathetic vehicle at heart, a work whose well-developed characters, even the sillier ones, insist we care even as they're making us laugh.

Because we care most about Erin and Alan, and because there is just enough sadness in this film for us to know that things don't have to work out, we feel terribly protective of these two. And as their individual romantic lives get more complicated, and they do, we worry desperately about their vulnerability, and ours. Much as we'd like to, this is one outcome we can't predict with complete assurance, and few things are more delicious than that.

NEW YORK POST, 8/21/98, p. 64, Thelma Adams

"The real mystery is what keeps two people together after they meet," says a gay nurse in Brad Anderson's "Next Stop Wonderland," a quirky romantic comedy with Hope Davis in yet another star-making performance.

The quote, from a sharp, funny script by Anderson and writing partner Lyn Vaus, counters the potential sentimentality of a romance about two off-beat people who keep passing each other like Boston commuter trains in the daytime.

In "Wonderland," Erin (Davis) is a latter-day Alice with all the tart appeal of Lewis Carroll's heroine grown up into a beautiful contrary adult. The romance begins when Erin's activist beau dumps her, taking the futon and leaving behind a video break-up message.

The heartache sends the registered nurse through the looking glass, giving her a rare moment to contemplate her past and future. She's haunted by the death of her father, irritated by her mother's meddling, uncertain about her own destiny or if such a thing exists.

While Erin moons about her apartment chasing solitude and taking breaks to skewer suitors who answer the personal ads her mother has placed for her in the local paper, she gradually realizes her choice isn't between solitude and love, it's between embracing and rejecting life.

Meanwhile, Alan (Gelfant) is also at a turning point. The second-generation plumber is trying to reinvent himself as a marine biologist, but all the people at the Boston Aquarium want him to do is fix pipes. In an inventive subplot, the worlds collide when Gelfant abducts the aquarium's prize pufferfish to clear his father's gambling debts with an unsavory developer (Robert Klein).

Erin and Alan crisscross repeatedly. They brush by each other on Boston Metro's Wonderland line, they lock eyes, and they talk on the phone. Are they made for each other? Will they ever find out? It's a romantic mystery that loops back to the idea that the real mystery isn't getting together, but staying together.

The gruffly handsome Gelfant makes a low-key foil for Davis, the spurned wife in "The Daytrippers." The brown-eyed actress is the indie Meg Ryan. The slim blonde with the pale moon face doesn't have to smile if she doesn't want to—and she still glows irresistibly.

Davis captures the rhythms of Erin's life, rhythms reflected in Erin's favorite music, Brazilian songs like "Desifinado" and "Corcovado" that layer the soundtrack. The music's romantic melancholy underscores the mix of sweetness and sadness that makes "Wonderland" such an adventure.

NEWSDAY, 8/21/98, Part II/p. B12, John Anderson

The centerpiece of a much-publicized, multi-million-dollar deal at this year's Sundance Film Festival, "Next Stop, Wonderland" has been the victim of some post-post-production adjustments designed to make it more user-friendly. So does this marriage of big money and major miscalculation make it 1998's state-of-the-art indie?

Not quite, because despite a new and "improved" ending, the film is still too wry, too human and—most important—too adult for strict genre-fication. It may employ several of the thematic trendettes seen in other recent independent films (the Kieslowskian cosmic-coincidence theorem of "Sliding Doors," the venomous misogyny of "In the Company of Men"). But it's a *sui generis*, samba-percolating romance that bluntly acknowledges the complexity/perversity of a needy heart. Or two.

It also has the blue-chip asset of Hope Davis, the protean young actress of Greg Mottola's "The Daytrippers," who, if conventional stardom didn't seem such an obvious threat, would be poised to become a post-modern Rosemary Harris or Deborah Kerr. As Erin, the Boston nurse who's dumped by her activist boyfriend Sean (Philip Seymour Hoffman), she is emotionally harassed by her stridently well-meaning mother (Holland Taylor) and spends most of the movie never meeting the man she was meant for (Alan Gelfant). She's a marvel of understated irony and self-assertive sympathy.

She's also a chameleon, transmuting from bedraggled sad-sackiness to confident sexuality with all the unpredictability of a real person, which, is much of the movie's charm: You believe the people.

Erin, who left medical school for nursing when her beloved father died (all of which history is inferred from Anderson's artful dialogue), is leading a life without passion, but can't play the game. Alan (Gelfant), a would-be marine biologist, volunteer fish-feeder at the Boston Aquarium and reluctant heir to his father's plumbing business, is a late-blooming self-starter who's single-minded in his studies to the point that he doesn't seem to know just how alone he is.

They engage in a sometimes comic and sometimes overly calculated series of near-misses; he spotting her through the glass in the aquarium tank, she spying him through a restaurant window, both passing like trains in the night on the Boston el. Erin even becomes the target of a cruel bet between Alan's obnoxious brother Kevin (Sam Seder) and his oafish yuppie buddies, who answer the personal ad Erin's mother has placed for her in the romance columns; at one point, Erin and Alan even talk on the phone.

But while the movie's nut conceit is fated love and kismetic attraction, "Next Stop, Wonderland" is a romance that seems fixed on the notion that people can be happy alone—a point that may be moot if, like Erin and Alan, one can't abide the mating/culling process that involves such trite, tiresome and self-absorbed people. Erin's interviews of the men who answer her ad, for instance, is a terrific set piece that seems calculated to keep people single.

If Anderson's film has a major flaw, in fact, it may be its less-than-generous attitude toward all but its own main characters. Erin, who spends a lot of time looking a lot like the other weary souls on the subway or in bars, sees them and feels a fear of loneliness. What "Wonderland" never acknowledges is that they may look at her and feel exactly the same thing.

"Next Stop, Wonderland" (the ostensible reference is to Boston's Wonderland dog track/train stop) has a seductive Brazilian soundtrack, mostly of Antonio Carlos Jobim songs, which makes no sense until you remember that neither does love.

And, in fact. it does make sense. Melancholy—or better, the Brazilian-Portuguese *saudade*, as Erin's late-inning Brazilian suitor, Andre (Jose Zuniga), puts it—is what Erin's all about. Like the movie's opening tune, "Desafinado" which means "slightly out of tune" Erin is beautiful but slightly askew, waiting for—maybe—that missing link in her life. What the new ending does is remove the maybe, taking some of the sophistication out of the film. So ignore it. Whistle a samba. Think of Jobim. And remember how few movies get to take intelligence even this far.

VILLAGE VOICE, 8/25/98, p. 128, Amy Taubin

Among the myriad wrongs that Hollywood has committed, consider this: No studio has ever cast Hope Davis as the lead in a romantic comedy. Along with bossa nova and Boston, Davis is a key element in Brad Anderson's anti-formulaic *Next Stop, Wonderland*. If you find *Sleepless in Seattle* cloying and less than credible, if you suspect that the libidos of Meg and Gwyneth are cathected onto their mirrors, then *Next Stop, Wonderland* might be your kind of movie. And even if you go for those wide-screen, digitally enhanced Hollywood jobs, it's possible you'll find what you were missing in Anderson's affectionate and smartly understated rendering of a familiar genre.

Erin (Hope Davis) has just been abandoned by her lefty live-in boyfriend. The crisis in confidence that caused her to take up with such a self-serving jerk and also to drop out of Harvard Medical School and settle for a career in nursing has something to do with the death of her poet father and the insistent presence of her panicky mother. Erin is just beginning to enjoy being the sole occupant of her pretty Boston apartment when her mother takes it upon herself to place an ad for her daughter in the personals.

In a parallel Boston universe, Alan (Alan Gelfant) has left his father's plumbing business to study marine biology. Alan has parent problems too. His father's compulsive gambling leads to local mobster pressure on Alan. He's tapped to do a hit on a beloved resident of the Boston aquarium, Puffy the blowfish. Does that sound whimsical? It is, but Anderson grounds whimsy in the effluvia of daily life. The "Wonderland" of the title, for example, is, in fact, the last stop on one of Boston's subway lines. For the riders of that line, Erin and Alan included, the conductor's routine announcement, "Next stop, Wonderland" is devoid of magic or metaphor. The entire movie is about preparing Erin and Alan to hear those three words as an invitation to another way of living in this imperfect world.

Twisting a traditional romantic comedy structure, Anderson and his coscreenwriter Lyn Vaus invent one sight gag after another to prevent Erin and Alan from meeting head-on while letting us know that they're right for each other. Each of them is put through various trials, in order to find themselves before they find each other In Erin's case, some of those trials are dates with men who answered her mother's personal ad—a hilarious array of frauds and losers.

Here, as in his less polished but more complicated first feature, *The Darien Gap*, Anderson constructs characters that are filled with ambivalence and whose actions are always overdetermined. And in Davis, whose mobile face can express a dozen different categories of irony, he's found an ideal actress. Cheeky, wry, wistful, acerbic, Davis carries the picture. The actors are all quite good, but she takes the film to another level. Anderson can't bear to cut away from her for too long and he's right not to try, although the resulting imbalance between the Erin story and the Alan story causes the film to lose some of its impetus going into the final stretch.

The style of the filmmaking, the freewheeling handheld camera movement, the associative editing, and the buoyant Brazilian score convey Anderson's sense that chance play major role in our lives and that what's happening on the periphery is often more important than what's staring us in the face.

Having zeroed in on Anderson as a commercial talent, Miramax seems to have persuaded him (as they did Chris Cherot, director of the bleaker romantic comedy *Hav Plenty)* to change the ending of his movie. The new scenes—one is sappy, the other meanspirited—put a cork on *Next Stop, Wonderland*'s effervescence.

Also reviewed in:
CHICAGO TRIBUNE, 8/28/98, Friday/p. M, Michael Wilmington
NEW YORK TIMES, 8/21/98, p. E8, Stephen Holden
VARIETY, 1/26-2/1/98, p. 68, Todd McCarthy
WASHINGTON POST, 8/28/98, p. B1, Rita Kempley

NIAGARA, NIAGARA

A Shooting Gallery release of a Shooting Gallery production. *Executive Producer:* Larry Meistrich. *Producer:* David L. Bushell. *Director:* Bob Gosse. *Screenplay:* Matthew Weiss. *Director of Photography:* Michael Spiller. *Editor:* Rachel Warden. *Music:* Michael Timmins and Jeff Bird. *Sound:* Jeff Pullman. *Casting:* Sheila Jaffe and Georgianne Walken. *Production Designer:* Clark Hunter. *Art Director:* Max Biscoe. *Set Decoration:* Traci Kirshbaum. *Costumes:* Laura Jean Shannon. *Running time:* 96 minutes. *MPAA Rating:* R.

CAST: Robin Tunney (Marcy); Henry Thomas (Seth); Michael Parks (Walter); Stephen Lang (Pharmacist); John MacKay (Seth's Father).

LOS ANGELES TIMES, 3/20/98, Calendar/p. 2, John Anderson

[The following review by John Anderson appeared in a slightly different form in
NEWSDAY, 3/20/98, Part II/p. B7.]

That last year's Venice Film Festival turned down "Boogie Nights" in favor of "Niagara Niagara" should help American audiences get over any lingering inferiority complex they might have regarding European cinema, although it won't allay anyone's concerns about American independent pictures.

Robin Tunney ("The Craft") won a best actress award from the festival, playing a lovely loser with Tourette's syndrome (an honor that seems a classic example of "Rain Man" syndrome). But while Tunney is nice as Marcy, the bourbon-swigging loose cannon who hooks up with the introverted Seth (Henry Thomas, best known as the kid from "E.T."), the use of Tourette's as a plot device still feels like exploitation.

And for all the attempted romance and railing against intolerance—what's more obscene, we're asked, Marcy's mouth or the world at large?—the syndrome (which involves involuntary tics and uncontrollable vulgarity) dominates the movie, and makes Marcy a sideshow attraction.

Produced by the self-admitted geniuses at New York's Shooting Gallery, "Niagara Niagara" presumes a lot: unquestioned sympathy for Marcy and Seth, for one thing; a galloping contempt for the rest of the world for another. They're sensitive and sweet, and they're in love; and when Marcy wants her medication, the bourgeois pig pharmacist wants a prescription. The brute.

And when the two teenagers try to refill her ever-present silver flask at the local liquor store—alcohol and sex tend to keep Marcy from losing her grip—the system foils them again, What kind of world is it when a girl with a delirious look in her eye and a mouthful of expletives isn't immediately embraced by everyone she meets? Not a nice one, I can tell you that.

Director Bob Gosse's commitment to his characters is suspect, given how easily he swings away from them for the easy joke, visual or otherwise. But he has a good cast. Michael Parks (erstwhile star of the erstwhile "Then Came Bronson") is fun to watch as Walter, a reclusive eccentric who befriends the two and whom Marcy nearly beats to death; likewise, Stephen Lang, as a particularly short-tempered druggist with a shotgun.

Despite Tunney's Venice honor, it's really Thomas who anchors the movie, providing Seth with a convincing introspection and wariness, and the movie with the only proof of its assertion that in the lost soul lies truth.

NEW YORK POST, 3/21/98 p. 24, Thelma Adams

"Niagara, Niagara" is deadly, deadly.

First-time director Bob Gosse, working from Matthew Weiss' uneven screenplay, can't decide whether he's making a frank after-school special about Tourette's syndrome or a campy romantic remake of "The Getaway."

Slacker Seth (Henry Thomas) and sanitation worker Marcy (Robin Tunney) meet grunge cute while shoplifting in an upstate dime store. Soon the two are making for the U.S.-Canada border in Seth's Plymouth Grand Fury, pursuing Marcy's ridiculous quest for a black Barbie doll head. (Don't ask: Apparently they don't carry the dolls in Syracuse.)

The intermittently adorable Marcy twitches and stutters and unleashes profanities like Linda Blair possessed. On the road, she copes with Tourette's syndrome by drinking bourbon and skipping her medication.

When Marcy begins to come unglued, she tries to get medication. First, she forges a prescription. When that fails, the bumblers rob a pharmacy.

As "Drugstore Cowboy" lassos "Dirty Mary Crazy Larry," the teen lovers meet a sentimental, chicken-loving survivalist (Michael Parks) and a kinky pharmacist (Stephen Lang) who shares his bed with an inflatable girl.

As Seth, Thomas ("E.T." and TVs "Moby Dick") is a lanky blank page. The only reason to visit "Niagara, Niagara" is Tunney, who won the best-actress award at the 1997 Venice Film Festival.

Casting directors, take note: The young actress is ripe to play Kidder in a Lifetime cable-TV melodrama about the "Superman" star's lost days before police found her—filthy, paranoid and missing her two front teeth—hiding under a bush in a Glendale, Calif., back yard.

VILLAGE VOICE, 3/24/98, p. 70, Dennis Lim

Few film subgenres are more reliably objectionable than the disease-of-the-week road movie. *Niagara Niagara*, in which the featured condition is Tourette's, isn't as cloying or simplistic as, say, *Rain Man* or *The Eighth Day*, but it's as fundamentally wrongheaded. Directed by Bob Gosse (co-founder of the Shooting Gallery production company) from a script by Matthew Weiss, the film takes the much abused, increasingly sentimentalized doomed-lovers-on-the-lam scenario and adds little besides labored idiosyncrasy. The movie's afflicted heroine Marcy (Robin Tunney) twitches, grimaces, blurts out profanities, acts out obsessive-compulsive rituals, and seems to subsist on a steady diet of whiskey and pills. Out shoplifting, she meets the quietly befuddled Seth (Henry Thomas), who, in the interest of symmetry, has his own problems, thanks to a deranged, violent father. The pair sets off in search of a black Barbie hairdressing head (for no real reason), chancing upon the usual oddballs along the way, among them a trigger-happy pharmacist (Stephen Lang) and a hospitable codger (Michael Parks). Given their threadbare, superficially written roles, the leads do their best; unlike what most actors in her position have done, Tunney aspires to more than the sum of her spasms. It's to no avail, though, as the filmmakers shuttle her from one familiar, trivializing situation to another.

Also reviewed in:
CHICAGO TRIBUNE, 4/3/98, Friday/p. F, Michael Wilmington
NEW YORK TIMES, 3/20/98, p. E12, Stephen Holden
VARIETY, 9/22-28/97, p. 52, David Rooney
WASHINGTON POST, 4/3/98, Weekend/p. 54, Michael O'Sullivan

NIGHT AT THE ROXBURY, A

A Paramount Pictures release in association with SNL Studios of a Lorne Michaels and Amy Heckerling production. *Executive Producer:* Robert K. Weiss. *Producer:* Lorne Michaels and Amy Heckerling. *Director:* John Fortenberry. *Screenplay:* Steve Koren, Will Ferrell, and Chris Kattan. *Director of Photography:* Francis Kenny. *Editor:* Jay Kamen. *Music:* David Kitay. *Music Editor:* Terry Wilson. *Choreography:* Mary Anne Kellogg. *Sound:* Jim Tanenbaum. *Sound Editor:* Cameron Frankley. *Casting:* Jeff Greenberg. *Production Designer:* Steven Jordan. *Art Director:* Carl Stensel. *Set Decorator:* John Philpotts. *Costumes:* Mona May. *Make-up:* Alan "Doc" Friedman. *Stunt Coordinator:* Pat Romano. *Running time:* 83 minutes. *MPAA Rating:* PG-13.

CAST: Will Ferrell (Steve Butabi); Chris Kattan (Doug Butabi); Dan Hedaya (Kamehl Butabi); Molly Shannon (Emily Sanderson); Richard Grieco (Himself); Loni Anderson (Barbara Butabi); Elisa Donovan (Cambi); Gigi Rice (Vivica); Lochlyn Munro (Craig); Dwayne Hickman (Fred Sanderson); Meredith Scott Lynn (Credit Vixen); Colin Quinn (Dooey); Raquel Gardner (Hot Girl); Vivica Paulin and Paulette Francese (Porsche Girls); Jennifer Coolidge (Hottie Cop); Michael "Big Mike" Duncan (Roxbury Bouncer); Trish Ramish (Roxbury Club Girl); Gina Mari (Saturday Night Fever Girl); Roy Jenkins and Kip King (Flower Customers); Mary Anne Kellogg (Aerobics Instructor); Maree Cheatham (Mabel Sanderson); Kristin Dalton (Grieco's Lady); Deborah Krieger (Topless Woman); Betty Bridges-Nicasio (Zadir Receptionist); Yoshio Be and Victor Kobayashi (Japanese Men); Twink Caplan (Crying Flower Customer); Eva Mendez (Bridesmaid); Mark McKinney (Father

Williams);   Chad Bannon (New Club Bouncer);   Jim Wise, Patrick Ferrell, and Dorian Spencer (New Club Waiters);   Tina Weisinger (New Club Waitress).

LOS ANGELES TIMES, 10/2/98, Calendar/p. 16, Gene Seymour

[The following review by Gene Seymour appeared in a slightly different form in **NEWSDAY, 10/2/98, Part II/p. B7.]**

The "Saturday Night Live" skits featuring the head-bobbing, hip-shaking, we're-so-cool-it's-pathetic nightclub cruisers offered one of the few reasons to keep tuning in to the show, especially when Will Ferrell and Chris Kattan were joined at the bar by a similarly dressed guest star like Jim Carrey or Tom Hanks. There's a demented quality to the routine that keeps it fresh even when you know what's going to happen every time.

Which doesn't mean that it was necessarily a good idea for "Clueless" writer-director Amy Heckerling to co-produce a whole movie about these hopeless Butabi brothers. Nevertheless, she and "SNL" honcho Lorne Michaels went ahead and handed the directing chores to TV veteran John Fortenberry.

Together with Ferrell, Kattan and screenwriter-co-producer Steve Koren, they've given these guys... lives, for crying out loud! That is, if you call being past your mid-20s, living with your parents and working in your dad's fake-flower boutique with limited prospects a life.

Certainly Kattan's Doug Butabi doesn't think it's much of a life compared with the thrill of being thrown out of, or rejected by, every dance club in L.A. Doug, you see, has this dream, mildly unfocused, of owning his own version of the red-hot Roxbury club, with his own velvet rope, bouncers and gorgeous women. Ferrell's Steve—no less dim than his brother—is down with the plan, except he's also drawn to the idea of a normal life with Emily (Molly Shannon), the girl who works with her dad (Dwayne Hickman) in the lamp store next to the flower shop.

The most successful "SNL" spinoffs have been about people with dreams that are too big and visions that are too narrow. But unlike "Wayne's World" and "The Blues Brothers," it's hard to figure out which is lamer in "A Night at the Roxbury," the dream or the alternative. At times, one wants to join their dad (Dan Hedaya) and tell them to face reality and live within their limits. But their goofy quixotic quest goes on and on... and on.

Kattan and Ferrell do their best to fill out the shallow Butabis. But there are times when you wish they'd get out of the way and give more room to such supporting players as the inimitable Hedaya, playing an even more blustery version of his exasperated dad in "Clueless." Or Shannon, whose cheeky blend of nerdiness and eroticism needs a broader canvas.

Even Richard Grieco, cast in the role of a self-absorbed, club-hopping ex-TV star named Richard Grieco, is a revelation. If the Butabis deserve a movie of their own, so does this character.

NEW YORK POST, 10/2/98, p. 44, Thelma Adams

If there was ever any doubt about sending a platoon deep into occupied France to preserve the life of one lone soldier, consider this doomed quest: Two mentally incompetent brothers whose only goal is gaining access to the hottest nightspot in Hollywood.

Meet Steve and Douq Butabi (Will Ferrell and Chris Kattan). The Butabis are the clueless head-bopping unhipsters from the one-note Saturday Night Live skit that, thankfully, passes without dialogue. That should have been a clue that expanding to a feature-length movie was as doomed as "It's Pat" or "Stuart Saves His Family."

But producers Lorne Michaels and Amy Heckerling were unfazed. It didn't have to be "A Night to Remember;" it only had to part teens from their car fare.

The shameless producers gathered TV director John Fortenberry and tossed Ferrell and Kaftan in a room with co-writer Steve Koren. The only saving grace is a paycheck to supporting player Dwayne Hickman. The Dobie Gillis star looks on with a confused smile as if he's not getting the jokes. That's because there's nothing to get.

SIGHT AND SOUND, 2/99, p. 49, Danny Leigh

Beverly Hills. Ardent clubbers Steve and Doug Butabi are refused entry to exclusive LA nightclub, the Roxbury. Returning home, Steve is given a ticket by a policewoman with whom he immediately falls in love. Steve and Doug spend the following day working at their father's shop, where Doug sweet-talks a female credit-control telephonist and Steve is pursued by neighbour Emily. That night, the brothers unsuccesfully attempt to bribe their way into the Roxbury. En route home, television star Richard Grieco scrapes their car's bumper; worried about litigation, he gets the Butabis into the club.

Inside, they share a table with the owner Mr. Zadir, and are mistaken for businessmen by two women with whom they subsequently lose their virginity. In the morning, they visit Zadir's offices to tell him their idea for a new club, but are ejected by his chauffeur. Their conquests of the previous night abandon them. Distraught, the brothers argue; Doug moves out of the room he shares with Steve and into the family's guest house.

Emily and Steve become engaged. At the wedding, Doug appears brandishing a tape recorder playing his and Steve's favourite club anthem. Steve leaves Emily; the brothers track down Zadir, who becomes their business partner. At the opening of their own club, Steve and Doug spend the evening with their new girlfriends: the policewoman and the telephonist.

Despite the fitful nature of the results, a job on the venerable US sketch show *Saturday Night Live* has long been a golden ticket for comics seeking to transfer their talents to cinema. In the tradition of the first *SNL* spin off, *The Blues Brothers,* such vehicles are often little more than an extended riff based around characters already established on the small screen. *A Night at the Roxbury* is simply the latest variation on the theme. Despite some ferocious competition, it may also be the most profoundly unfunny.

When the formula works, as it did with Penelope Spheeris' *Wayne's World* (with its pair of dim-witted losers embroiled in an insular musical subculture), the secret lies in the instant recognisability of the protagonists. Even for a British audience denied the opportunity of seeing the characters in their original milieu, Wayne and Garth were given enough personality for the humour to resonate. Doug and Steve Butabi, on the other hand, have no believable existence outside this tired procession of set ups and punchlines.

Presumably we are supposed to empathise with their role as perennial outsiders, forever striving to make it beyond the Roxbury's velvet rope. Yet it is difficult to identify with the only defining traits of these pampered imbeciles: vanity and ignorance. Director John Fortenberry, whose unwillingness to venture beyond the most prosaic storytelling devices betrays his background in television comedy and exacerbates Roxbury's air of an over extended skit, simply casts us adrift in a sea of unfamiliar catchphrases and cultural references. The intertextuality of casting Richard Grieco, leading man of US series *21 Jump Street,* as himself will surely baffle anyone lacking a thorough knowledge of US television's lower depths.

Moreover, just as it fails to find an equilibrium between mocking the Butabis' naivety and deifying their innocence, *Roxbury* cannot decide whether to sneer at or fetishise its clubland locale. On the one hand, it is exclusively populated by shallow and mendacious airheads; on the other, the only visible alternative (marriage) is proposed to be more status-driven and soul-destroying.

Indeed, if there's one group of people Fortenberry appears to hate more than clubbers, it is women. Amid the countless scenes in which the Butabis harass innumerable mini skirted extras, every female character is a gold digger or a walking castration complex. The only exceptions, tellingly enough, are the boys' nameless dream dates referred to throughout as 'Hottie Cop' and 'Credit Vixen' and their own mother. In fact, with their admiring glances at the mother's surgically enhanced cleavage, their repressed hatred of their overbearing father and terror when confronted with aggressive female sexuality, the boys end up looking persistently Oedipal. Such inadvertent kinkiness may be intriguing, but it comes at the expense of any genuine comedy.

Also reviewed in:
CHICAGO TRIBUNE, 10/2/98, Friday/p. M, Monica Eng
NEW YORK TIMES, 10/2/98, p. E20, Anita Gates
VARIETY, 10/5-11/98, p. 68, Dennis Harvey

NIGHTWATCH

A Dimension Films release of a Thura Film/DR TV Fikton/Danske Filminstitut production. *Executive Producer:* Bob Weinstein, Harvey Weinstein, and Cary Granat. *Producer:* Michael Obel. *Director:* Ole Bornedal. *Screenplay (based on Bornedal's film "Nattevagten"):* Ole Bornedal and Steven Soderbergh. *Director of Photography:* Dan Laustsen. *Editor:* Sally Menke. *Music:* Joachim Holbek. *Music Editor:* Tom Kramer. *Sound:* Stephen Halbert. *Sound Editor:* Stephen Hunter Flick. *Production Designer:* Richard Hoover. *Art Director:* Kathleen McKernin and Adam Scher. *Set Decorator:* Brian Kasch. *Set Dresser:* Julie K. Smith. *Special Effects:* Dale Newkirk. *Costumes:* Louise Mingenbach. *Make-up:* Debra Denson. *Running time:* 105 minutes. *MPAA Rating:* R.

CAST: Ewan McGregor (Martin Bells); Nick Nolte (Inspector Cray); Josh Brolin (James); Lauren Graham (Marie); Patricia Arquette (Katherine); Erich Anderson (Newscaster); Lonny Chapman (Old Watchman); Scott Burkholder (College Professor); Brad Dourif (Duty Doctor); Michael Matthys (Guy in Pub); Alison Gale (Girl Friend of Guy in Pub); Robert Lasardo and Mongo (Pub Thugs); Candy Brown Houston (Female Paramedic); Michelle Csitos (Leanne Singer); Alix Koromzay (Joyce); Larry Cedar (Waiter); Lennie Loftin (Man in Theater); Bradley Gregg (Theater Actor); Nicholas Sadler (Theater Director); Jeff Davis (Stagehand); Nicholas Cascone (Male Paramedic); Ben Skortstad (Helicopter Pilot).

LOS ANGELES TIMES, 4/17/98, Calendar/p. 18, Jack Mathews

[The following review by Jack Mathews appeared in a slightly different form in **NEWSDAY, 4/17/98, Part II/p. B12.]**

If you didn't get enough swollen-corpse depravity out of David Fincher's 1995 serial-killer thriller "Seven," Dutch director Ole Bornedal's "Nightwatch" may fill your tank.

"Nightwatch," adapted by Bornedal and Steven Soderbergh from Bornedal's Dutch-language film "Nattevagten," is an empty exercise in the macabre. Like "Seven," it mixes the styles of suspense, horror and film noir, using murky lighting, odd angles and deliberately paced camera movements to create an atmosphere of constant dread.

What it lacks is purpose, psychological heft and a killer with his own sense of style.

I wasn't a fan of "Seven," but at least its villain was on a mission—to punish violators of the Seven Deadly Sins—that would be personally threatening to most members of the audience. The psycho in "Nightwatch" is a necrophiliac, the scourge of the county morgue, with the peculiar habit of killing and mutilating prostitutes before having sex with them.

Most of "Nightwatch" is set in that morgue, where law student Martin Bells ("Trainspotting's" Ewan McGregor) is the newly hired security guard. Graveyard shift. There are rooms where body parts are stored in jars or in vats of formaldehyde, and there's the refrigerated section where the newly dead await autopsies. And to warm him up for the job, the departing night watchman explains what to do in the event a corpse comes to life.

As if the job weren't stressful enough, Martin's kinky, thrill-seeking friend James (Josh Brolin) keeps sneaking into the morgue to scare him. He's under the supervision of a petulant, drug-addled duty doctor (the ever-creepy Brad Dourif) who's constantly threatening to have him fired. Bodies start getting moved around during his shift. And a smarmy detective (a slumming Nick Nolte) is asking him for a semen sample to test against evidence left at a murder scene.

Worst of all, the rotting breath Martin acquires from all that death-tainted air at work is a net loss in his love life with his live-in girlfriend, Katherine (Patricia Arquette).

A smart law student would consider quitting this job, but Martin presses on, doing his rounds with the look and nerves of a cornered rabbit, while evidence mounts that the serial killer is out to frame him for all the murders. One of the future victims has even been calling his home and telling Katherine what a pervert he is.

Bornedal keeps the real killer's identity secret through the first half of the film, by showing him only from the waist down, and by making everybody else so weird that they're all suspects.

"Nightwatch" is a seriously overcast B-movie with rote performances from everyone but Brolin, who gives James an edge of danger that says that if he isn't a killer, he will be.

VILLAGE VOICE, 4/17/98, p. 52, Larry Worth

In the first scene of "Nightwatch," an unseen killer hacks up a screaming prostitute, setting off a ruckus that makes an overhead fan fall from the ceiling and silences a chirping pet birdie. Not a pretty picture.

On the other hand, the gutted hooker and her feathered friend are released from their suffering early on. That's more than can be said for viewers.

That would-be thriller has been on Miramax's shelf for almost two years, despite a screenplay co-written by Steven ("sex, lies and videotape") Soderbergh and a cast led by Ewan McGregor, Nick Nolte, Patricia Arquette and Josh Brolin.

So what's the problem? Enter director Ole Bornedal, who has basically remade his earlier, Danish version of the same story, "Nattevagten." Sadly, he didn't maintain quality control the second time around.

The tale gets increasingly ludicrous as it proceeds, detailing the life of a young morgue attendant (McGregor) and the manner in which he's framed for a serial killer's increasingly bloody actions.

From the getgo, everything is connect-the-dots predictable, as when the hero is warned about the morgue's overnight alarm system—set off only if a body comes back to life, and pulls the chain above the autopsy table. So it's only a matter of time before the buzzer roars and the guard must take that endless walk to investigate.

Aside from predictability, nothing's vaguely plausible. That includes the culprit's identity—which is prematurely revealed anyway. Worse still, suspense-scene payoffs always disappoint.

On the plus side, Bornedal establishes a genuinely creepy setting for the morgue's midnight-shift flickering neon lights illuminating long, sterile corridors, black-plastic-wrapped shrubbery looming as tearsome sentinels at the building's glass-enclosed entrance and heavy metal music blasting from the watchman's earphones.

Speaking of the watchman, Scottish heartthrob Ewan McGregor tries hard to convince. But his American accent isn't all that falters. As the roguish best pat, Josh Brolin has more presence, exuding an edgy charisma and palpable appeal—despite his "Dumb and Dumber" dialogue.

Playing McGregor's love interest, Patricia Arquette is wasted as a victim-in-waiting. And though the actress' drone-like delivery has become a tiresome trademark, her monotoned scream seems appropriate.

One feels sorriest for Nick Nolte, miscast as a sentient detective. Seeing such a fine actor brought down by such hideously awful lines proves more horrifying than anything else "Nightwatch" has to offer.

Also reviewed in:
CHICAGO TRIBUNE, 4/17/98, Friday/p. C, Mark Caro
NEW YORK TIMES, 4/17/98, p. E16, Stephen Holden
VARIETY,4/13-19/98, p. 28, Leonard Klady
WASHINGTON POST, 4/17/98, p. B1, Stephen Hunter

NIL BY MOUTH

A Sony Pictures Classics release of a Luc Besson presentation of an SE 8 Group production. *Producer:* Luc Besson, Douglas Urbanski, and Gary Oldman.   *Director:* Gary Oldman. *Screenplay:* Gary Oldman.   *Director of Photography:* Ron Fortunato.   *Editor:* Brad Fuller. *Music:* Eric Clapton. *Music Editor:* Richard Bernstein. *Sound:* Jim Greenhorn. *Sound Editor:* Eliza Paley.   *Casting:* Sue Jones.   *Production Designer:* Hugo Luczyc-Wyhowski.   *Art*

Director: Luana Hanson.   *Costumes:* Barbara Kidd.   *Make-up:* Fae Hammond.   *Stunt Coordintor:* Rod Woodruff.   *Running time:* 128 minutes.   *MPAA Rating:* R.

CAST: Ray Winstone (Raymond); Kathy Burke (Valerie); Charlie Creed-Miles (Billy); Laila Morse (Janet); Edna Doré (Kath); Chrissie Cotterill (Paula); Jon Morrison (Angus); Jamie Forman (Mark); Steve Sweeney (Danny); Terry Rowley (M.C. in Club); Sam Miller (Club Comic); Leah Fitzgerald (Michelle); Gerry Bromfield (Drug Dealer); Neil Maskell (Schmuddie); Sid Golder (Old Guy in Window); John Blundell (Man with Knife); Kenan Hudaverdi (Laundrette Owner); Everton Nelson (Street Violinist); Ronny Fox (Peter/Pool Player); Frances Ashman (Club Singer).

CINEASTE, Vol. XXIII, no. 4, 1998, p. 49, Leonard Quart

Gary Oldman's first film, *Nil by Mouth* centers on the life of a destructive, and self-destructive, underclass English family. The family is part of a white, South London, dysfunctional world where almost everybody is permanently unemployed and lives on the dole, with the men having spent much of their lives in prison. The film gives no political or social explanations for the family's situation, but treats their unredeemable lives as a result solely of their own behavior. Oldman models the film after the work of John Cassavetes and Ken Loach films like *Cathy Come Home* and *Ladybird, Ladybird* (without their political and social agenda) rather than the formulaic Hollywood films that he has acted in ever since he came to Hollywood from England.

Oldman grew up in South London, so he intimately knows the milieu's look and vernacular (harsh, expletive-filled talk that is hard for an American audience to decipher), and avoids any hint of artifice or caricature in depicting it. *Nil by Mouth* plunges the audience into this desolate world without any establishing shots. It begins in a working-class pub with the film's garrulous, brutal central figure, Ray (Ray Winstone), sitting at a table with his loyal stooge, Mark (Jamie Forman), exchanging stories about orgies and planning a scam that includes his wife's ferretlike, junkie brother, Billy (Charlie Creed-Miles).

The film's extremely loose narrative does little with the scam, since Oldman focuses on the behavior of his characters, not on building tension or creating a strong, consistent plot. The camera observes a pathetic, filthy Billy begging on the subway, hanging around aimlessly on the street, ineffectually engaging in petty crime, and hungrily pursuing his next drug score. It then cuts to Ray, his sweating, bloated, raw face seen in tight-close-up. We watch him drink vodka straight from the bottle, snort a great deal of coke, and act in a sadistic and self-pitying manner. He casually beats somebody up outside a shop, bites off a piece of Billy's nose after he robs his drugs one night, and, in a fit of drunken jealousy, stomps on his wife Val (Kathy Burke) so badly that she miscarries their baby and looks, for a time, like a gargoyle. (Oldman never exploits the violence, however, shooting the beating off screen.)

Ray is an overweight, self-hating bully—an uncontrolled, raging force—without a single saving grace. In a drunken haze, miming boxing moves, he tearfully talks to his mirror image (a touch of Scorsese), speaking about his love for Val, and the need to punish himself for his behavior. Of course, his self-awareness is merely momentary, for he then totally demolishes the council flat he and Val live in. In another scene he indulges in an overlong monologue about his childhood pain, lachrymosely recalling a hated father who gave no kisses, cuddles, or love. Oldman inserts it as a partial explanation for Ray's behavior, but in no way absolves or explains away his abusiveness.

The women of the family—Ray's wife Val, her mother, Janet (Laila Morse), who is the only character who holds a job, and her grandmother, Kath (Edna Dore)—inhabit a separate, more stable, and caring world. They sit apart from the men in the pub, their relations with them dominated by a need either to fend off and repulse violence or pick up the broken pieces after the men commit one self-destructive and destructive act after another. A wrinkled, gray-haired Kath, who is in her late seventies, has to flee a drunken Ray (dressed in his underwear) when he grossly propositions her. Billy visits his mother, Janet, at her factory job, and, angrily shouting and cursing, demands cash to help feed his £60 a day habit. In that instance she refuses, but in another melancholy scene she drives him to his connection and sits in the front seat of the van as we see him, in great detail, shoot up in back.

A teary but volatile Ray tries to get back with Val, constantly harassing her with silent phone calls, violently trying to break into her mother's flat, and finally, with hard rain pouring down, bringing her a gift and telling her he still loves her. Val, who is thirty but looks a bruised, worn, suffering fifty, responds that, "He has a funny way of showing it," and, without high drama, searingly bemoans the life of alienation, pain, and oppression he has handed her. It's the one moment Val speaks back to Ray, since the women in Oldman's film masochistically accept their fate as victims of male rage and control.

Still, the women provide a network of emotional support for each other, and have a capacity for hope and kindness that the men lack. Kath and Val's daughter (who mutely watches all that goes on), let go of a red balloon and watch it float skyward—one faint metaphor of escape from their entrapment. In an ironically moving scene Kath and Val dance to "Last Chance to Paradise," and Janet rallies around Val after she's been beaten up by Ray.

The film focuses on claustrophobic interiors, but we do get a look at the scrub grounds of dismal council estates, playgrounds, and hallways scarred with graffiti, streets filled with debris, and a generally gray world where the rains never end. Oldman shoots the interiors in soft light, and avoids shooting the exteriors in sunlight so he can preserve the murky, dark, half-lit look of things. Shot mostly in close-up, there are a few striking long shots of Billy, utterly isolated within the frame, walking through the grounds of council estates. There is a *cinéma-vérité* look to the film, with Oldman's camera catching the faces of people in Soho strip clubs, South London pubs, and nighttime streets. He also sometimes obscures part of the image by having somebody pass in front of the camera—a directorial choice rather than an accident.

Nil by Mouth may have the feel of a documentary, but from Eric Clapton's vivid, bluesy score to the probing close-ups that get inside its characters, this is a carefully crafted and detailed realist film that is never visually dull. Oldman makes few wrong turns, except the too-theatrical set piece that Billy's tattooed friend Angus (Jon Morrison) indulges in when he repeats verbatim, gestures and all, Dennis Hopper's mad monologue from Coppola's *Apocalypse Now*. Oldman has chosen neither to sentimentalize, judge, nor patronize these members of the London underclass, whom he knows so intimately. Oldman feels no need to mention Thatcher or Tory economic policies to give this world a social context. For him, "People are politics, it's not the other way around." He simply observes them with a clear-eyed view that sticks to what is true, and serves no larger moral or social purpose.

Two scenes sum up his view of this milieu. Billy tries to hit up for cash a man who is sitting with his son in an estate playground. The man refuses, but, when he walks away, we get a peek at his son's face and it looks terrifyingly demonic. Oldman suggests that there is no innocence here, the virulent cycle of destruction beginning with childhood. Another scene sees Kath in a pub passionately singing, without a touch of irony, "I can't help loving that man of mine." A more conventional director would have underlined the absurdity of those words in this context, but Oldman remains faithful to his characters' perspective, knowing that the women learn to adjust to a male universe where misogyny is the norm. Men treat women like dogs, and the prime emotional links in a marriage are never between husband and wife, but between a man and his buddies.

What we learn from Oldman about this dead-end, South London world leads logically and jarringly to the film's final scene. Val is back with Ray, and the other members of the family, including the omnipresent Mark, are sitting around telling stories about Billy, whom they are going to visit in prison. They joke and laugh about the severe problems Billy has there (somebody wants to kill him), none of it daunting or disturbing them. Going to prison is an integral part of their ethos, something to make the best of (Val is totally at home with criminal argot). Just as they stoically accept that Val has reconciled with the frightening Ray, who will likely savage her again. Val may become enraged at Ray's abuse, but she's ultimately accepting and complicit with it. The scene suggests something even more ominous—that Ray's nuzzling closeness to his young daughter could turn into something sexually manipulative and abusive as she grows older.

For Oldman, *Nil by Mouth* is an auspicious debut. He elicits emotionally revealing performances from his actors that rarely strike a false note. Though less interested in the social world, he depicts enough of its texture to capture its barren grimness. This relentless, agonizing film is not *The Full Monty*—nobody leaves the theater feeling buoyant or sanguine about the human condition. It's also no Mike Leigh film, for there are few unpredictable shifts in emotional tone, or scenes that evoke absurd or comic behavior. (Oldman, of course, deals with an underclass, not the working class that populates most of Leigh's films.) What *Nil by Mouth* grants an audience is an unsparing look into a world so particularized and real that all sociological paradigms, political abstractions, or wish fantasies seem meaningless.

LOS ANGELES TIMES, 2/6/98, Calendar/p. 12, Kevin Thomas

Gary Oldman's raw and vital "Nil by Mouth" takes its curious title from a sign over a London hospital bed. "Nil" means "nothing" in Latin, so the sign simply indicates that the patient in the bed below it must not take any medicines by mouth.

Raymond (Ray Winstone), a burly alcoholic ex-con, mentions the sign while holding forth with his best pal Mark (Jamie Forman) on visiting his dying father, who never expressed any love for him—the abusive parent never said anything loving "by mouth" to the son craving for affection.

At the moment, Raymond is wallowing in self-pity, for he has just beaten his worn-looking wife Valerie (Kathy Burke) more savagely than usual and has wrecked their apartment in a Southeast London housing project. In a lesser film, this scene might have played as if Oldman is excusing Raymond's domestic violence because he felt his father didn't love him. (Hey, lots of us know what unloving fathers are like.)

But Oldman, drawing upon his memories of growing up in impoverished Southeast London in making his writing-directing debut, is projecting a much deeper vision, and the hateful Raymond comes off as a figure of pity.

Oldman loves these blue-collar people—yes, he has real compassion even for Raymond. He knows them through and through, and he is here celebrating their tremendous capacities for endurance, humor and loyalty.

At the same time, Oldman leaves you understanding why he had to get out of Southeast London himself, to move beyond the dead-end, suffocating routine of spending the better part of your life drinking ale—or stronger—and chain-smoking at the rowdy neighborhood pub. ("Nil by Mouth" is very strong stuff, in its violence and in its language, and is definitely not for everyone.)

The linchpin of Ray's family is his mother-in-law Jan (Laila Morse, Oldman's sister, who has never before acted), a plump, middle-aged, blond factory worker who may be the only one of her relatives who actually has a job. (You can't rightly call these people working-class anymore—the chronically unemployed is more like it.)

Jan lives in the projects with her feisty mother (Edna Dore) and worries about Valerie and her 20ish son Billy (Charlie Creed-Miles), who's taking heroin and who's just had his nose smashed by Raymond, a man of truly terrifying rages.

What Oldman does very well is to evoke a certain kind of mentality that allows his people to seek help only as the very last resort. When Billy shoots up right in front of Jan, she's upset but doesn't take action—not because she's in any way stupid but because she doesn't think it would do any good.

Similarly, neither Valerie nor any of her relatives reach out to any agency in regard to the insanely jealous Ray, with his hair-trigger raging. Among themselves, they circle the wagons to protect the battered Valerie, but none of them even thinks of calling the cops. These are people who have no faith in the system; they have only one another.

As an actor of intensity and versatility himself, Oldman not surprisingly molds his cast into a thoroughly convincing ensemble, with Burke, who won the best actress prize at Cannes for her performance, revealing Valerie to be a woman of more self-knowledge than you at first realize.

Beyond that, Oldman, working with ace cameraman Ron Fortunato, has a real feel for the cinematic, and "Nil by Mouth" has a driving, jagged style that is complemented by Eric Clapton's often melancholy score. Oldman's key achievement is to make you feel for people you wouldn't want to know in real life.

NEW YORK POST, 2/6/98, p. 46, Michael Medved

"Nil by Mouth" portrays a group of characters so cruel and so crude, so pathetic and primitive, that make the fun-loving junkies in "Trainspotting" look by comparison as refined and elegant as the figures in a Merchant-Ivory adaptation of E.M. Forster. The film invites you to spend more than two hours with these boozy losers in a foul alcohol-and-tobacco haze only occasionally interrupted by flashes of senseless violence or painful injections of cheap heroin.

Against all logic, however, Gary Oldman's debut as writer-director works a weird sort of alchemy on its audience, creating vivid grotesques who initially inspire abject disgust, then arouse outright horror, and finally earn grudging sympathy with the belated recognition that they're members of the human race after all.

Ray Winstone plays the films leading lout, a brooding brute with an explosive temper and an abundance of bad habits. Kathy Burke is his sad-sack, long-suffering wife who endures devastating abuse at his hands.

Her kid brother (the gangly, goofy Charlie Creed-Miles) is a childlike, slow-witted heroin addict who supports his habit by panhandling, theft and begging from their mother (Laila Morse), an aging, embittered bimbo with bleached hair.

The most sympathetic member of this disastrously dysfunctional clan is the silent grandmother (Edna Dore), who speaks no memorable lines except for her ironic, amateur-hour performance of Oscar Hammerstein II's "Can't Help Lovin' That Man."

As a matter of fact, you can help lovin' these people, but you can't stop caring about their self-destructive disasters.

Musical accompaniment for this earthy non-eloquence is provided in an edgy, gritty and effective score by Eric Clapton.

Director Oldman (known for the ferocity of his own acting in his various driven, downbeat and demonic roles) draws fierce, fiery performances from every member of his little-known cast.

His style as a director combines the improvisatory, *verite* approach of John Cassavetes's at the peak of his powers with the primal energy and emotional explosions of Scorsese's "Mean Streets."

It is an odd, audacious and deeply impressive debut as a filmmaker, in a film that is simultaneously riveting and revolting, succeeding in its efforts to discomfit and disturb even the most jaded audience.

NEWSDAY, 2/6/98, Part II/p. B7, John Anderson

Gary Oldman has inhabited a gallery's worth of twisted scum, from Sid Vicious to Lee Harvey Oswald to the homicidal space freak in Luc Besson's "Fifth Element." Oh, yes, and Dracula. But the inferences you draw watching "Nil by Mouth"—even as vaguely autobiographical as Oldman claims it is—are far more disturbing than as any mere character he's played.

A primal scream of a movie, "Nil by Mouth" is a purgation, a venting, a bitter screed—and a lot less about cause than it is about effect. The milieu depicted—lower-middle-class South London—and the portrait he paints—of a post-Thatcher family caught in a hamster wheel of drunkenness, drugs and self-perpetuating violence—are, frankly, brutal and sickening. And to say that is to grossly understate the case.

But like the films of Britain's Ken Loach or Mike Leigh, which share a world if not a style, this isn't "entertainment" in the feel-good sense; if you need a lift, go watch 1,500 people drown in the North Atlantic. No, Oldman's faux-documentary mannerisms, suffocatingly up-close shooting and often unintelligible dialogue are about re-creating the corrupted community of his childhood, a community that festers as you watch it rot.

The centers of the movie are Raymond (Ray Winstone) and his wife, Val (Kathy Burke), he a coke-snorting, pub-crawling bully, she an almost-vanquished victim of domestic violence and spousal contempt. Around these misshapen planets orbit moons—Val's mother Janet (Laila Morse), her heroin-addicted brother Billy (Charlie Creed-Miles), Janet's mother, Kath (Edna Dore), and Raymond's friends, a crew of sycophants and weaklings.

The violence is abrupt and its manifestations are vicious: In a cocaine delirium, Raymond nearly bites the nose off Billy. His beating of Val has few on-screen equals. While the film is simply too long—not because of its potency, but because it, or we, simply can't stand the pressure—Oldman certainly proves himself an astute observation of aberrant human behavior. And although *what* the characters say is often incomprehensible, at least to these American ears, the whys and wherefores are seldom in doubt, because the physical dynamics are so strong.

Burke won the best-actress prize when the film showed at Cannes last year, but Winstone gives an equally powerful and nuanced performance as Raymond, who's a two-headed spewer of belligerence and melancholy and really quite scary. The standard operating procedure in a movie like "Nil by Mouth"—not that there are many movies like "Nil by Mouth"—is to set things up so the perpetrators are as much victims as victimizers, lashing out at the weak because society has a boot-heel at their throats. But Oldman is neither sociologist nor sentimentalist and Raymond is a louse, whose soliloquy about his own unloving father toward the end of the film makes him, if anything, more contemptible—because he understands himself. It makes Oldman's dedication of his film—to his own father—the kind of thing you want to push away, and can't stop thinking about.

SIGHT AND SOUND, 10/97, p. 55, Geoffrey Macnab

South London, the present. Ray orders drinks for his mates. While they drink, Ray and his mate Mark enlist Billy, his wife Valerie's young heroin-addict brother, to help them in a scam planned for the following Sunday. Ray, Mark and Billy successfully carry out their plan. To celebrate, they go for a night on the town which takes in pubs, strip clubs and gambling. The next morning, Ray suspects that Billy has ripped off some of his drugs, and confronts the youngster, Billy refuses to admit his guilt so Ray beats him, leaving a gaping bite mark on his nose. Billy's mother Janet can't afford to keep on lending him money to support his drug habit. He breaks into Ray and Val's council flat, rummages through their possessions, and ends up stealing Ray's favourite painting.

Val, sickened by Ray's violence and constant drinking, is spending a quiet evening in the pub with Janet and a group of friends. She'd like to leave him, but with one child already and another on the way, she doesn't feel able to, Ray comes by, notices her playing pool with a strange man, and summons her home. She reluctantly goes. Later that evening, Ray accuses her of being unfaithful. She tells him not to be stupid, but he responds by beating her up. As a result of the brutal assault, she miscarries. In self-pity, Ray trashes the flat. He tries to get her back, but she tells him she is sick of being abused by him. Billy, meanwhile, is arrested and thrown into prison. At a family gathering, Janet reveals that he has been attacked by another prisoner. Ray has repaired the damage to the flat and seems to be off the booze. The family leaves to visit Billy in prison.

In the very first images of *Nil by Mouth*, we're confronted with a huge close-up of Ray at the bar, reeling off an order for drinks. Director Gary Oldman seems fascinated with Winstone's pustulous, sweaty face. It is a landscape in itself, registering a dulled brutality which seems entirely in keeping with the grey south-east council block where we later learn Ray and his family live.

The sheer fuzziness of the lighting, the dialogue a mumbled, overlapping vernacular, rich in expletives—and the fidgety camerawork mark out Oldman's debut feature as radically different from most British social realist dramas. There is none of the detachment of Terence Davies' *Distant Voices Still Lives* or *The Long Day Closes*. Nor does it tend towards the caricature of Mike Leigh's work, Rather, *Nil by Mouth* is an insider's film and its relentless, excoriating close-ups create a feeling of claustrophobia.

These characters are familiar as the butt of comedians' jokes. They're the types treated as Tommy Trinder-style cheery chappies, ridiculed by Peter Cook and Dudley Moore in their 'Derek and Clive' sketches, or made mock heroic in Steven Berkoff plays like *Greek,* and *Decadence.* In *Nil,* however, they are humanised. These South-London 'white trash' are as marginalised in their council flats as any poor share croppers. (Eric Clapton's bluesy soundtrack reinforces the comparison.) But Oldman neither condescends toward them nor sentimentalises their plight.

Whether sitting on his own in a pub at midday drinking whisky or remonstrating with his own mirror-image in a drunken haze after Val has left him, Ray is never a figure of pity. He's a violent alcoholic who beats up women, and even in his one moment of vulnerability, when he talks lovingly about his relationship with his father who never gave him a single kiss or cuddle, he fails to recognise that his own behaviour is equally remiss.

Oldman doesn't skimp on the gloom. The outdoor scenes are all lit in a pallid, grey half-light. The rain in South London seems never-ending. The streets are full of rubbish. The high-rise towers jut out like ugly eyesores. But just as in the Alan Clarke films *(Scum, Made in Britain)* which Oldman admires so much (he himself starred in Clarke's 1989 television movie, *The Firm*), the bleakness of the environment is always mitigated by the dynamism of the performances. Winstone, a former boxer with a face like a boot and an intimidating physical presence to match, dominates the screen. After his cameo as the husband who assaults Chrissy Rock in Ken Loach's *Ladybird Ladybird,* it would have been understandable if he had baulked at playing yet another wife-beater, but Oldman's shooting style, especially his Cassavetes-like use of long takes, enables the actor to get under the skin of the character. With his self-loathing always evident, Winstone plays Ray with an introspective intensity you expect from Robert De Niro in *Raging Bull,* but rarely find in a British character actor.

Men and women occupy mutually exclusive worlds in *Nil by Mouth.* They sit in different parts of the pub. When the men walk into a room, the women invariably leave it. In one typical scene, the grandmother runs upstairs shrieking after being propositioned by Ray in his underwear. (Given the brutality of the husbands and sons in the film, her final-reel rendition of 'Can't Help Lovin' Dat Man' seems cruelly ironic.) The attrition between sexes is only part of the story. It's also boredom which pushes the men into such extreme behaviour. The young Billy, it is implied, has nothing to do outside loitering on street corners, taking drugs or indulging in a little petty crime.

Oldman regards his characters with affection and avoids moralising at their expense. Even Ray at his most obnoxious is sometimes very witty, and there is plenty of incidental humour. Billy mixes up names and decides that an Alsatian is a dog called "all stations". His friend imitates Dennis Hopper's lunatic photographer in *Apocalypse Now.* Even in the scene in which they're both stuck inside a laundrette while the man they've just robbed bangs on the door threatening to kill them, the grimness is tinged with comedy.

From *This Happy Breed* to *Distant Voices Still Lives,* the heroic, long-enduring housewife has been a leitmotif in certain kinds of British film. Kathy Burke and Laila Morse shatter the stereotype even as they seem to reinforce it. As Ray's wife Val, and his mother-in-law Janet, respectively, they're resilient and level-headed, and yet their qualities of endurance are constantly undermined by the ever-more destructive antics of their men.

In one key scene, which could easily have slipped into bathos, Ray confronts Val not long after he has beaten her to a pulp. He tells her he still loves her. "You've got a funny way of showing it," is the inevitable reply. As the rain lashes down, she bemoans the dead-end life he has left her with. It's the one time that she speaks back to hurt after all that she has endured. The scene is all the more affecting for the understatement with which Burke plays it. Oldman places extraordinarily heavy demands on her, prying into the most intimate and vulnerable parts of a character who at first seems little more than a foil to Winstone's explosive drunken machismo. But all the other actors are similarly exposed to the unrelenting gaze of the camera. In the end, *Nil by Mouth* hinges on its performances, and neither Burke nor anyone else ever strikes a false note.

VILLAGE VOICE, 2/10/98, p. 61, J. Hoberman

Parents and children suffer together in Gary Oldman's *Nil by Mouth*—a brutally accomplished first feature that the actor turned director dedicates to his fathers memory.

Whatever this domestic horror story owes to Oldman's boyhood in the housing estates of southeast London, *Nil by Mouth* is an actor's movie—shapeless, empathetic (but unsentimental), and driven by a score of vivid performers with thick Cockney accents. Kathy Burke won the best-actress award at Cannes for her portrayal of the spud-like Valerie, beaten to a pulp by her husband Raymond, an oafish, besotted thief played with scary conviction by former boxer Ray Winstone, but the award might just as easily have gone to Laila Morse, the robust, profane, and leathery nonactress who plays Valerie's mother, Janet (the only character in the movie who seems to be gainfully employed).

In what might have been the Gary Oldman part of Valerie's younger brother Billy, Charlie Creed-Miles gets a star-making turn as a junkie with a hundred-dollar-a-day habit and a head as smooth and impenetrable as a billiard ball who, beaten (and bitten) by the terrifying Raymond, is compelled to push his bloody beak through the movie's mix of street brawls and prole pubs, its scenes of nonstop yapping and claustrophobic sense of a generational pile-up. "Get indoors, mother, you fucking cow—this has nothing to do with you," Janet screams at *her* mother (Mike

Leigh veteran Edna Dore, who later unnecessarily summarizes the film's grim representation of Stone Age sexual politics with a game rendition of "Can't Help Lovin' Dat Man o' Mine").

Not without its longueurs at 128 minutes, *Nil by Mouth* underscores its absence of moralizing with the director's fondness for an actor's set piece. Oldman allows one minor character, a tattooed lunatic who is Billy's partner in petty crime, to echo the entire Dennis Hopper scene from *Apocalypse Now;* somewhat more organically, he treats Ray Winstone to what feels like a 10-minute orgy of chronology-pulverized, furniture-smashing telephone soliloquies that owes more than a bit to Robert De Niro's most abject scene of self-loathing in *Raging Bull.*

As nervy a presence as any of the actors, Oldman's camera is in constant motion, considering and then reconsidering the action (appropriately abetted by Eric Clapton's eclectic, bloozy score). Blown up from Super 16mm, *Nil by Mouth* was shot largely in close-up. The long takes, shallow space, and near total absence of establishing shots submerge the viewer in a bustling naturalism that suggests John Cassavetes without the histrionics and Mike Leigh sans cuteness. It's a skillfully harrowing performance.

Also reviewed in:
CHICAGO TRIBUNE, 3/6/98, Friday/p. D, Achy Obejas
NATION, 3/2/98, p. 35, Stuart Klawans
NEW REPUBLIC, 2/23/98, p. 25, Stanley Kauffmann
NEW YORK TIMES, 2/6/98, p. E14, Janet Maslin
NEW YORKER, 2/9/98, p. 83, Anthony Lane
VARIETY, 5/12-18/97, p. 76, Derek Elley
WASHINGTON POST, 2/27/98, Weekend/p. 43, Desson Howe

NO LOOKING BACK

A Gramercy Pictures release of a PolyGram Filmed Entertainment presentation of a Marlboro Road Gang/Good Machine/South Fork Pictures production. *Executive Producer:* Robert Redford. *Producer:* Ted Hope, Michael Nozik, and Edward Burns. *Director:* Edward Burns. *Screenplay:* Edward Burns. *Director of Photography:* Frank Prinzi. *Editor:* Sue Graef. *Music:* Joe Delia. *Music Editor:* Patrick Mullins. *Sound:* Matthew Price and (music) Gary Solomon. *Sound Editor:* Bruce Kitzmeyer and Branka Mrkic. *Casting:* Laura Rosenthal. *Production Designer:* Therese Deprez. *Art Director:* John Bruce and Derrick Kardos. *Set Decorator:* Diane Lederman. *Set Dresser:* Kevin Mahon. *Costumes:* Sara Jane Slotnick. *Make-up:* Michael Bigger. *Stunt Coordinator:* Douglas Crosby. *Running time:* 96 minutes. *MPAA Rating:* R.

CAST: Shari Albert (Shari); Jon Bon Jovi (Michael); Connie Britton (Kelly); Edward Burns (Charlie); Blythe Danner (Claudia's Mom); Marcia Debonis (Marcia); Matty Delia (Bugsy); Kathleen Doyle (Mrs. Ryan); Jennifer Esposito (Teresa); Leah Gray (Leah); Kevin Heffernan (Sco); Lauren Holly (Claudia); Ellen McElduff (Waitress); Chris McGovern (Chris); Margaret O'Neill (Maggie); Susan Pratt (Annie); Stuart Rudin (The Foot); Nick Sandow (Goldie); Glenn D. Sanford (Glenn); Mark Schulte (Bno); John Ventimiglia (Tony); Kaili Vernoff (Alice); Welker White (Missy).

LOS ANGELES TIMES, 3/27/98, Calendar/p. 4, Kenneth Turan

When self-confident, charismatic Charlie gets off the bus in an unnamed burg and kick-starts the plot of "No Looking Back," it's momentarily reminiscent of the film version of William Inge's "Picnic," where a handsome stranger blows into town and causes all kinds of romantic complications. Except Charlie turns out to be no stranger and neither is Edward Burns, who plays him and wrote and directed this film, his third.

Burns' debut, the appealing "The Brothers McMullen," is a Sundance legend, winning the Grand Jury Prize and going on to be named the most profitable film of 1995 by Daily Variety.

Burns followed that with the similar but completely unsatisfying "She's the One," so with his latest outing he's tried to do something different.

One change is that "No Looking Back" is a serious drama that exists almost entirely without laughs. It's also the first of Burns' films to be told largely from a woman's point of view. But attempting that in a film in which Burns was so much the key creative force turns out to be tricky in ways that might not have been anticipated.

One thing Burns hasn't changed—and it's his greatest area of strength—is the sense he has of how working-class Americans, specifically those living in the Northeast, speak to one another. But while "No Looking Back" (set in an unnamed seaside town and shot in Far Rockaway, N.Y.) rings true in terms of ambience and dialogue, it has not completely managed to come up with a story that feels as right as the setting.

The woman in question is Claudia (Lauren Holly), a waitress in a diner who heads straight for a beer and the TV after hours, especially if her cute but hard-working boyfriend Michael (Jon Bon Jovi) is putting in his usual overtime.

Claudia and Michael live together like a married couple, but no wedding date has been set. Before we can examine why, Charlie, once Michael's best friend and Claudia's lover, saunters off that bus and back into everyone's lives.

Despite his roguish charm and king-of-the-hill attitude, hardly anyone is happy to see Charlie return, and that includes his mother who tells him "you act like an adult or you're out on your ass." Michael calls him "a mutt" and Claudia, still smarting from the circumstances of Charlie leaving town, is not crazy about reconnecting either.

It turns out, to no one's surprise either on or off screen, that Claudia is why Charlie came back after three years in (where else but?) California. No sooner does he take a job pumping gas at Bugsy's but he's trying to reenter her life, reminding her that he used to call her "Cloudia" because of her airy dreams, insinuating that she's sold herself short by living with Michael, and finally proposing that she go with him the next time he leaves town.

It's an interesting dilemma, or at least "No Looking Back" tries hard to make it interesting. Bon Jovi is completely creditable as a "where is it written you've got to be happy all the time?" kind of guy, and Holly, assisted by Blythe Danner's capable supporting work as her abandoned mother, works very hard to get this character right.

Despite all this, it's hard to watch "No Looking Back" without feeling that things are missing and out of kilter. Partly it's that while Claudia rings true around the edges, at her core this character comes off as more a generic "woman at a crossroads" than a specific individual, a situation that the script's tendency toward billboard-type speeches doesn't help.

As for Burns, starring in his own film is both a strength and a weakness. He easily holds the screen with an ingratiating screen presence, as witness his being cast to support Tom Hanks in Steven Spielberg's forthcoming "Saving Private Ryan," and he certainly understands all the aspects of the character.

But while Burns doesn't hesitate to show the duplicitous sides of Charlie, and though he's given himself a potent rival by employing Bon Jovi, casting himself in his own piece throws the film out of balance. Even without trying, "No Looking Back" gives his character an unfair advantage. Should he win Claudia's heart, it will seem too obvious a solution; should he not succeed, we will feel more misled than we should.

As to the more general question of whether audiences beguiled by "The Brothers McMullen" will have to resign themselves to being misled by a one-trick pony, that is still without a definitive answer.

NEWSDAY, 3/27/98, Part II/p. B6, John Anderson

Lacking any tangible history, in a town that might be constructed out of stilts and Styrofoam, the characters in Edward Burns' "No Looking Back" enjoy an emotional freedom unheard of in the raggedy genre of post-adolescent, blue-collar, can't-quite-hit-the-road romances. Virtually inseparable from the actors who play them—in their camouflage baseball caps and $200 haircuts—they exist in a cottony textured limbo constructed of other movies' devices and other people's anxieties.

This may be exactly what audiences want, of course: Movies that employ the machinery of angst without making us feel any, which use class as a prop instead of a problem. But who to root for? In his third feature (following the equally class-unconscious "The Brothers McMullen" and "She's the One"), Burns constructs a three-horned morality tale among characters with no sense of personal propriety.

There's Charlie (Burns, doing a passable impersonation of a young James Caan, sans irony), who has come back to the cars and bars of his shore town after three failed years in California. There's his old girlfriend, Claudia (Lauren Holly), a waitress with a runaway father and an unsteady mother (Blythe Danner), stratospheric cheekbones and a subliminal itch. And there's Michael (Jon Bon Jovi), Charlie's old pal, Claudia's live-in and a pretty decent sort, who is cast into the thankless role of cuckold-to-be, never to return.

Charlie, having gotten a warm greeting from Mom ("You stayin'?"), moves back into his bedroom (in a claustrophobic shot that suggests he's outgrown his old life, or is just a bad angle) and almost immediately starts dogging Claudia. There's no reason to think he's come back because of her. But there is reason to think he's the hero of the movie; if nothing else, the subtle-as-a-pneumatic-drill soundtrack tells us so. And as an irredeemable heel, he skews the dynamics of storyline that's otherwise happy to abide by all the rules of bad love.

Claudia is cool to Charlie, at first—he did, after all, virtually abandon her when she aborted their baby, a plot element that arrives on the doorstep like your grandmother's scratchy old sofa. And he is, as she knows, unreliable, despite his big talk of dreams and escaping the Town Where It Has Always Just Rained. But there's something between them—something missing with the too-reliable Michael—that makes the Charlie-Claudia intersection as inevitable as the Grand Central Parkway and the Van Wyck meeting at Kew Gardens.

Holly and Burns may or may not still be an off-screen item by the time this runs, and it wouldn't be relevant to a review of "No Looking Back" if Holly's responses weren't so contradictory and off-putting. Every time Charlie shows up, however inappropriately, she's so *delighted* it's like the actress has been rattled out of character. If nothing else, Claudia should be worried about getting caught or hurting Michael, but Burns the director, having made the Claudia-Michael relationship as chaste as possible, seems happy to make Claudia as debauched and unsympathetic as Charlie.

Which leaves Michael, the best realized character in the movie thanks to Bon Jovi's capable acting and, yes, charisma. It's tempting to credit this to the relief his presence offers from the Burns-Holly whine-a-thon, but the rocker-turned-actor seems to do fine on his own.

Burns loves those wistful beach scenes almost as much as the clichéd camera movement—when a schoolyard confrontation involves Claudia, you just know the camera is going to circle her and it does (she might as well be Kate on the stern on the Titanic). When the tentative couple finally have their low-rent rendezvous, they're shot in tentative silhouette—a bit that dates back to "Fatty and Mabel Adrift" in 1916.

Anheuser-Busch was clearly a proud sponsor of "No Looking Back," in which the director again proves his talent for putting together families of people who couldn't possibly be related. And for staying in one place—which, in its way, defies the film's own premise. Even though millions do it every day, being happy or content in a small town, with modest, decent aspirations, is never depicted in movies, because movies are dreams and the American Dream is one of perpetual motion. Getting out. Moving on. And looking back; if there's no looking back, then there has been no movement. And for all its concern about the need for change, that's precisely what's missing in "No Looking Back."

NEW YORK POST, 3/27/98, p. 44, Thelma Adams

If Jersey rocker Jon Bon Jovi is the star of Edward Burns' blue collar love triangle, "No Looking Back," why is the soundtrack wall-to-wall Bruce Springsteen and Patti Scialfa?

Because this serious turn in the writer-director's romantic trilogy, following "The Brothers McMullen" and "She's the One," plays like an extended Springsteen ballad. Bon Jovi may have a chance at being a serious actor, but his music may be too truly working class for a young man of Burns' pretension.

Bon Jovi, so charismatic in "The Leading Man," brings heart and the brushed softness of worn denim to his factory-working, Bud-drinking Michael. He's settled into a steady thing with live-in fiancee Claudia (Lauren Holly)—but there's still no ring on her finger.

Charlie (Burns) doesn't fail to notice the missing diamond. Years after dumping Claudia (and, yes, there's a hidden, soapy secret) and splitting for California, the mechanic returns home. He's come to reclaim his girl, or so he says.

Charlie's a no-account dreamer, a petty schemer (even I'm starting to catch that Springsteen rhyme thing.) Before long, Chuck is licking the back of Claudia's neck while Michael's at work.

Claudia, the most glam waitress ever to pour coffee at an off-season seaside diner, starts to wonder about her future while filing her already-perfect nails.

In what passes as the subplot, Claudia's father has left her mother (Blythe Danner) for a younger model in Vegas. Faced with a choice between steadfast Michael and charming Chuck, Claudia has to decide whether she's her mother's daughter—or her father's.

This three-minute pop tune of romantic loss and independence found plays out against the shabby-chic scenery of the Rockaways, nostalgically shot by Frank Prinzi. Burns expands his range by playing against his hero type, but it's not enough to carry a movie that's flying without a script over too-familiar territory.

VILLAGE VOICE, 3/31/98, p. 68, Amy Taubin

Heavy-handed and wooden, Ed Burn's third feature, *No Looking Back,* is at least an improvement on his second, the disingenuous *She's the One.* Burns deserves credit for not making what he's expected to make—a tie-the-knot comedy about love and marriage—and for letting the negative qualities of the romantic character he's played in all his films finally come to the fore.

Set in a blue-collar, Irish-American working class community in the Rockaways, *No Looking Back* is Burns's first film with a woman at the center. Claudia (Lauren Holly) has been living with Michael (Jon Bon Jovi) for 3 years. She got involved with him on the rebound after her high school sweetie Charlie (Burns) ran out on her in a circumstance so ludicrously clichéd it had the preview audience choking with laughter. Michael is good husband material, but Claudia can;t commit. She's confused about what she wants, and her uncertainty grows when Charlie unexpectedly skulks back into town.

Burns clearly wants to make a film about a culture so insular and repressed that nothing much ever happens and no one allows themselves a glimmer of the big picture. What he doesn't get is something that Cassavetes understood perfectly—that the more people feel trapped, the more they focus on minor inconveniences and trivial conflicts. Burns never gets the proportions right. *No Looking Back* is the kind of film where the peeling paint on the back stairs isn't just part of the texture of daily life. It peels in close-up, taking the weight of all the other details that are missing from the film.

Holly isn't much of an actress and she isn't helped by the fact that her role is massively underwritten. Bon Jovi is as solid and unexciting as he's meant to be. And Burns is still a scene stealer. Leaking guilt and hostility, his Charlie is the guy who never comes through in a crunch, who screws over his best friends, who, for chrissake, picks up an 18-year-old college freshman, and after talking her halfway into bed, asks if she'll pay for the motel room because he's a little short on cash. (It's the only compelling scene in the film.) What's appealing about Charlie is his evasiveness. He's a magnet for desire. *No Looking Back* might have been more interesting if Charlie had been its center. It's a bit late in the day to be making *Claudia doesn't live here anymore.*

Also reviewed in:
CHICAGO TRIBUNE, 4/10/98, Friday/p. I, Michael Wilmington
NEW YORK TIMES, 3/27/98, p. E24, Stephen Holden
VARIETY, 3/23-29/98, p. 88, Todd McCarthy

NO ORDINARY LOVE

Executive Producer: Adam Fast. *Producer:* Eli Kabillio. *Director:* Doug Watkins. *Screenplay:* Doug Watkins. *Editor:* John Orland. *Music:* Bob Christianson. *Sound:* Dan Slider. *Production*

Designer: Scott Carruth. *Art Director:* Anthony Bashford and Greg Ovard. *Set Decorator:* Bryce Holtshousen. *Costumes:* Sabina Huber. *Running time:* 104 minutes. *MPAA Rating:* Not Rated.

CAST: Smith Forte (Kevin); Erika Klein (Wendy); Dan Frank (Tom); Koing Kuoch (Vince); Antonio Rosas (Ramon); Marina Palmier (Gloria); Tymme Reitz (Ramon). Mark S. Larson (Ben); Robert Pecora (Andy).

NEW YORK POST, 1/30/98, P. 44, Larry Worth

Defining the difference between bad moviemaking and abysmal moviemaking probably means splitting hairs. But "No Ordinary Love" goes beyond bad. For that matter, abysmal may be an understatement.

Ostensibly, it's about a household of five twentysomethings—three gays, one male bisexual and one female man-hunter (all played by no-name actors likely to retain that status). Starting out as a goofy sex romp, the spotlight switches from one gay's overprotective mom to various one-night stands to yet more unmitigated stupidity.

But two thirds of the way along, writer-director Doug Watkins opts for a murder mystery, which plays out—at best—like a sad-sack Agatha Christie parody. The good news: most moviegoers will have walked out or fallen asleep long before.

NEWSDAY, 1/30/98, Part II/p. B13, John Anderson

The possibility does exist, however remote, that "No Ordinary Love" is supposed to be taken seriously—that all the sexual fence-jumping, operatic hysteria, the soap-meets-dope sensibility and the actress who looks like Jane Wyman aren't supposed to suggest "Falcon Crest" with nipple rings.

But if it is a spoof, and we're pretty sure it is (how else to explain the Douglas Sirk-meets-Danielle Steel title?), then "No Ordinary Love" is a prime candidate for a lengthy run of midnight screenings, where audiences can recite the overheated dialogue ad nauseam, throw things at the screen and (un)dress like the characters.

And to call them characters is to understate the case. Kevin (Smith Forte), is the overextended house mother-father trying to make ends meet by taking in roommates—punk-rocker Wendy (Erika Klein), who's pregnant by Kevin's dead boyfriend, Tom (Dan Frank); Vince (Koing Kuoch), a dare-to-be-in-drag college student with an ache for Ramon (Antonio Rosas), who's straight but possibly movable; Ben (Mark S. Larson), a cross between Richard Simmons and "Seinfeld's" Newman with a bank robbery in his background; and Andy (Robert Pecora), a studly narcissist who's seeing the woman next door and dances exotically.

In the great tradition of "Dynasty," "Dallas," "90210" and "Melrose Place," the characters in "No Ordinary Love" can produce mad passion over nothing and allow major tragedy to roll off their backs. Theirs is a universe complete unto itself, and as its inhabitants experience love and loss and gunshots and thefts and all manner of sexual experience, you can only nod and say, "Nice world."

Flouting and flaunting soap-opera conventions and filling his characters' mouths with all manner of histrionic palaver, writer-director Doug Watkins has created a minor classic of the genre, which is already minor. But at the right hour, at the right theater, "No Ordinary Love" could have 'em rolling in the aisles.

Also reviewed in:
NEW YORK TIMES, 1/30/98, p. E16, Stephen Holden
VARIETY, 6/12-18/95, p. 63, David Rooney

NOTES FROM UNDERGROUND

A Walkow-Gruber Pictures/RenegadeFilms production. *Executive Producer:* Gary Alan Walkow. *Producer:* Frank Gruber, Alicia Dollard, and Chris Beckman. *Director:* Gary Alan Walkow.

Screenplay: Gary Alan Walkow. *Based on the novella by:* Fyodor Dostoevsky. *Director of Photography:* Dan Gillham. *Editor:* Peter B. Ellis. *Music:* Mark Governor. *Sound:* Yehuda Maayan. *Casting:* Bonita Pietila. *Production Designer:* Michael Rizzo. *Art Director:* Mark Bensson and Cindy Vance. *Set Decorator:* Fred Cisterna. *Costumes:* Alina Panova. *Running time:* 87 minutes. *MPAA Rating:* Not Rated.

CAST: Henry Czerny (Underground Man); Sheryl Lee (Prostitute); Eammon Roche (Simon); Charlie Stratton (Jerry); Geoffrey Rivas (Tom); Jon Favreau (Zerkov).

NEW YORK POST, 3/6/98, p. 56, Larry Worth

After three big-screen versions of "Crime and Punishment," is there any need for a fourth?

Writer/director Gary Walkow makes the answer obvious. His acidly funny, dark and disturbing "Notes From Underground," at Anthology Film Archives, is a first-rate updating of Dostoevsky's classic.

It's also a stunning showcase for its actors. Henry Czerny brilliantly portrays the tale's anti-hero, an insecure buildings department clerk drowning in his own vitriol. And as the zaftig call girl who proves his ultimate victim, Sheryl Lee is heartbreaking and haunting.

But the real coup? With its consistently black-humored undertones, "Notes" is genuinely entertaining. Even Dostoevsky couldn't pull that off.

VILLAGE VOICE, 3/10/98, p. 118, Gary Dauphin

There isn't much the movies can add to Fyodor Dostoyevsky's concise but chatty ode to delusional interiority, so it's fortunate this celluloid version of *Notes From Underground* sticks close to the novella's relentlessly corrosive "I"; it insures that at the very least there are always those awfully beautiful words. Director Gary Walkow turns 19th-century bourgeois Russia into a vaguely La-La-land Present of sun-gathering sports cars and dingy basement apartments. The Underground Man (Henry Czerny) is unaffected by the change in scenery: a pathetic but prideful loser, he's brutally honest in a literal sense; his obvious intelligence is much more suited to various kinds of assault than insight. *Notes* manages to condense the novellas already short plot arc. The Underground Man's endless schlepp from work to below-ground level home is broken only by the nightmarish humiliations of dinner with smarmy college classmates and his viciously manipulative relationship with a needy, round-faced prostitute (Sheryl Lee). *Notes* indulges the unnamed protagonist's pinprick logorrhea with a mania that almost matches the original, Czerny giving a mannered but neatly unbalanced performance, while director Walkow chooses images so clinical they suggest the horror of an entire life lived in the head.

Also reviewed in:
NEW YORK TIMES, 3/6/98, p. E22, Anita Gates
VARIETY, 10/2-8/95, p. 43, Emanuel Levy

OBJECT OF MY AFFECTION, THE

A Twentieth Century Fox release of a Laurence Mark production. *Producer:* Laurence Mark. *Director:* Nicholas Hytner. *Screenplay:* Wendy Wasserstein. *Based on the novel by:* Stephen McCauley. *Director of Photography:* Oliver Stapleton. *Editor:* Tariq Anwar. *Music:* George Fenton. *Music Editor:* Nick Meyers. *Choreographer:* Paul Pellicoro and Eleny Fotinos. *Sound:* Michael Barosky and (music) John Richards. *Sound Editor:* Philip Stockton. *Casting:* Daniel Swee. *Production Designer:* Jane Musky. *Art Director:* Patricia Woodbridge. *Set Decorator:* Susan Bode. *Costumes:* John Dunn. *Make-up:* Naomi Donne. *Stunt Coordinator:* G.A. Aguilar. *Running time:* 11o minutes. *MPAA Rating:* R.

CAST: Paul Rudd (George Hanson); Kali Rocha (Melissa Marx); Jennifer Aniston (Nina Borowski); Lena Cardwell and Natalie B. Kikkenborg (Girls at Community Center); Lauren Varija Pratt (Sally Miller); Hayden Panettiere (Mermaid); Lauren Chen (Violin Player); Liam Aiken (Nathan); Alan Alda (Sidney Miller); Allison Janney (Constance Miller); Tim Daly (Dr. Robert Joley); Bradley White (Stephen Saint); Marilyn Dobrin (Mrs. Sarni); Midori Nakamura (Nina's Colleague); John Pankow (Vince McBride); Joan Copeland (Madame Reynolds); Steve Zahn (Frank Hanson); Kate Jennings Grant (Kennedy); Bruce Altman (Dr. Goldstein); Salem Ludwig (Mr. Shapiro); Antonia Rey (Mrs. Ochoa); Danny Darrow (Nina's Dance Partner); Sean Rademaker and Heather Thompson (School Children); Mary McIlvaine, Lisa-Erin Allen, and Fanni Green (Nurses); Samia Shoaib (Suni); Douglas Wert (Father); Michael Phelan (Son); Edward James Hyland (Doctor); Gabriel Macht (Steve Casillo); John Roland and Rosanna Scotto (TV Anchors); Miguel Maldonado (Colin Powell); Peter Maloney (Desk Clerk); Bette Henritze (Mrs. Skinner); Nigel Hawthorne (Rodney Fraser); Amo Gulinello (Paul James); Iraida Polanco (Carmelita); Kevin Carroll (Louis Crowley); Sarah Knowlton (Caroline Colucci); Steven Ochoa (Waiter); Kia Joy Goodwin (Juliet); Daniel Cosgrove (Trotter Bull); Damian Young (Romeo & Juliet Director); Rebecca Eichenberger and Jane Bodle (Wedding Guests); Audra McDonald (Wedding Singer); Sarah Hyland (Molly), Paz de la Huerta (13-year-old Sally); Jeffrey Marchett and Susan Bradford (Parents).

CHRISTIAN SCIENCE MONITOR, 4/17/98, p. B3, David Sterritt

The "Object of My Affection" is the latest in a recent line of movies featuring gay men tangled up with straight love affairs. Greg Kinnear earned an Oscar nomination for playing this role in "As Good as It Gets," and many felt Rupert Everett in "My Best Friend's Wedding" should have been similarly honored.

It's doubtful the new picture will make as strong an impression as its predecessors, since its story is more rambling and less amusing. But it boasts appealing performances, and it takes a reasonably tasteful approach to its subject, aside from a string of four-letter words that sound strangely out of place in this romantic comedy.

Jennifer Aniston, another veteran of the TV series "Friends" seeking a place on the wide screen, plays the likable heroine. Her name is Nina; she earns her living as a social worker, and she can't decide how committed she is to Vince, her well-meaning but overbearing lover.

Her life changes when a new roommate moves in: George, a gay teacher who expects to stay only a couple of weeks, becomes Nina's confidant. Their arrangement grows more challenging when Nina learns she's pregnant.

While the father is Vince, she decides to raise the baby without him, enlisting George as her partner. These two aren't really meant for each other, though, and various romantic complications arise.

Aniston is always enjoyable and sometimes touching as Nina, ably joined by Paul Rudd as George and John Pankow as Vince, plus a strong supporting cast including Nigel Hawthorne and Alan Alda.

Director Nicholas Hytner earns points for versatility since his previous pictures were "The Madness of King George" and "The Crucible."

He keeps "Object" rolling smoothly, helped by Oliver Stapleton's silky camera work, which makes New York look more like a folksy village than a city bursting at the seams.

Like other aspects of the movie, this portrait of urban life doesn't ring particularly true; but if Hollywood fantasy is what you're after, Hytner's romance is as matchable as most others this season.

LOS ANGELES TIMES, 4/17/98, Calendar/p. 6, Kenneth Turan

It's hard not to feel, well, affection for the characters in "The Object of My Affection." Are not George Hanson (Paul Rudd) and Nina Borowski (Jennifer Aniston) sweet and funny, and aren't the Wendy Wasserstein lines they deliver more amusing than not? Yes, but just as these two face trouble in their relationship, so this film has trouble delivering on its intriguing premise.

This is apparently the season for romantic obstacles. While last week's "City of Angels" tried pairing human and celestial lovers, "Object" presents us with two handsome young people on the way to becoming wild about each other. The difficulty this time is that George is gay and Nina is straight and neither is thinking of changing.

More than that, when these two meet, both are in serious relationships. George, who teaches first grade at a fancy Manhattan private school, is involved with Dr. Joley (Tim Daly), a college professor with literary aspirations. Nina, a social worker who counsels teenage girls, is dating Vince McBride (John Pankow), a penniless but obstreperous legal aid lawyer.

The two meet at the home of Nina's stepsister Constance (Allison Janney) and her husband Sidney (Alan Alda), who have a child in George's class. They get along well enough that when George needs a place to stay, Nina's spare room in Brooklyn seems the most obvious solution.

Under Nicholas Hytner's direction, "The Object of My Affection" is at its best showing the strong, caring and nonsexual love that develops between George and Nina. As played by the immensely likable Rudd and the perky Aniston, these two have believable fun together, whether they're ballroom-dancing or sharing a late-night ice cream snack. And having amusing characters around the story's periphery, like eagle-eyed landlady Mrs. Sarni (Marilyn Dobrin), helps a great deal.

The complications rise a notch when Nina gets pregnant and decides she wants to raise the child not with Vince, the father she doesn't get along with, but with George. Though George agrees after some hesitation, neither one of them gives much thought to what will happen if the serpent of sexual attraction, either toward each other or to someone else, ever rears its head in this idyllic platonic relationship. Which, of course, it does.

"The Object of My Affection" wants to be wise and adult in addition to amusing, but the nature of its plot development makes its characters more involving than the problems they encounter. Despite likable leads and a promising premise, the film's people make choices at variance with the honesty of their performances. The result: an inability to deliver on what's promised emotionally.

Wasserstein's script, which she worked on for 10 years is so major a departure from Stephen McCauley's charming novel that director Hytner has accurately called it "a free cinematic adaptation of the novel rather than a slavish retelling of it." There's nothing wrong with this in theory, of course. The problem in practice is that the changes, made in the name of greater audience accessibility, have made the story less emotionally compelling.

McCauley's novel was told first person from George's point of view. So when, as is inevitable, George gets seriously attracted to another man, the book gains much of its poignancy from how torn he is by two different and mutually exclusive kinds of love, the terrific bond he feels with Nina and the new sexual passion he feels for someone else.

The film, by contrast, is told from no specific point of view, and Nina's romantic and sexual needs are given full weight. A fine idea, perhaps, but giving everyone equal time means a wholesale jettisoning of the book's second half and the creation of numerous new characters to balance things out.

Some of these new people, particularly a drama critic played by Nigel Hawthorne (who starred in the Hytner-directed "The Madness of King George"), are engaging, but the changes have the effect of eliminating the focus on George's choice. What's substituted is a generic and uninspiring scenario about how sad unrequited love is when you're the one not getting loved back.

There isn't any reason why that sequence shouldn't have been as affecting as the original, but it simply is not. Perhaps that 10 years' worth of backing and filling and contrivance, which was needed to tidy up a different kind of story so it would fit into a conventional mold, took a greater toll than anyone anticipated. "The Object of My Affection" is an honorable and affecting attempt at something out of the ordinary, but it plays less like a breakthrough than an opportunity lost.

NEW STATESMAN, 6/26/98, p. 51, Gerald Kaufman

Affection? I object.

Here is George. George is gay. George is in love with Joley. But Joley is no longer in love with George.

Here is Nina. Nina is kooky. For reasons which are entirely impossible to explain but without which "The Object of My Affection" would have no plot, Nina invites George to live with her in Brooklyn after Joley dumps him. Nina then gets pregnant by the loutish Vinnie but falls in love with George.

The scene is set. The rest of this glossy film's action, such as it is, must now answer the following questions: will Nina (a pouting Jennifer Aniston) "cure" George (a totally expressionless Paul Rudd) of his homosexuality? Will Vinnie (John Pankow, who scowls) put some expression into George's face by punching him, as he constantly—and justifiably—seems about to do? What is the purpose of the black policeman who is abruptly and arbitrarily written into the script? Did Haagen-Dazs pay 20th Century Fox for the frequent on-screen appearances of tubs of its ice-cream, which George, Nina and yet another character, Paul (the sharp-chinned Amo Gulinello), are addicted to eating in potentially lethal quantities? How did a reputable British stage director, Nicholas Hytner, get mixed up in this glop?

Nigel Hawthorne, as an effete drama critic, and Alison Janney, as Nina's name-dropping stepsister ("I so wanted to see your show, but I got caught up in a lunch for King Hussein"), are allotted the best—actually the only—good lines, spatch-cocked into a script by Wendy Wasserstein that is otherwise dominated by such inspired exchanges as: "I adore you"; "I adore you, too."

The rest of the cast gets through the film without being called upon to indulge in so energetic an activity as acting. Although everyone is constantly going on to everyone else about how they feel (generally at the tops of their voices), two hours go leadenly by without anything resembling a genuine human emotion.

Hytner is quoted in this picture's publicity material as claiming to "probe the terrible ache" of insufficiently reciprocated affection. The only terrible ache is in the posterior muscles, shifting uncomfortably as this cynical, formulaic celluloid equivalent of junk food continues, apparently interminably. The huge mistake is made of having George and Nina dance to a soundtrack recording of Gene Kelly singing "You Were Meant for Me" from "Singin' in the Rain," and then showing a clip of Kelly dancing with Debbie Reynolds in that film. Those few grainy seconds from nearly 50 years ago supply more romance than the whole of Hytner's movie.

At first it seems that "Girls' Night 15"), too, will be nothing more than overblown soap opera, Coronation Street variety. Dawn (Brenda Blethyn) and Jackie (Julie Walters) are sisters-in-law who work in a multi-layer board factory in Rawtenstall, Lancs. Friday is their Bingo night and Dawn wins the [pounds] 100,000 jackpot.

Then real life takes over. Dawn finds out that she has a malignant brain tumour. Jackie uses the Bingo winnings to take her for a final splurge in Las Vegas.

That's all. Except that TV scriptwriter Kay Melior has written a screenplay that rings true practically every moment of its 93-minute running time; TV director Nick Hurran creates a genuine working-class Lancashire world in which there are no glib solutions and no happy endings; and director of photography David Odd's location filming is simultaneously gritty and lyrical. Oh, yes, and Brenda Blethyn and Julie Walters provide rich, honest, moving portrayals for which Oscars would be inadequate.

Dawn, who has seemed insipid, turns out to be tough, brave and ready to face brutal facts: "I've got cancer—and nobody on this earth can sort it." It is she who comforts the worldly wise Jackie, prone to make all the wrong choices, and who posthumously provides some sort of solution for the mess Jackie has got her life into. These two play like partners in a tennis match, neither upstaging the other, both contributing to their joint impact. Generally I flinch from any entertainment labelled "life-enhancing", but this duo and their supporting cast of factory workers rule that response out.

Ponette (PG), too, is about bereavement. Little Ponette is told that her mother has been killed in a car accident. Too young to understand what death means, she tries to bring her mother back by incantations and spells, and even attempts to dig her out of her grave. Victoire Thivisol was aged four when the film was made and her miraculous performance as Ponette, coaxed out of her by director Jacques Doillon, won her the best actress award at the Venice Film Festival. This gem of a film goes on rather too long and ends too glibly but, in exploring the inconsequential world of childhood, it is as good as anything Francois Truffaut ever directed.

"Girls' Night" and "Ponette" restore faith in the possibilities of the cinema. Yet, unlike "The Object of My Affection," which will saturate the multiplexes, neither will receive a circuit booking.

NEW YORK, 4/27/98, p. 57, David Denby

No subject, I suppose, can be categorically ruled out of bounds, but some subjects are a hell of a lot more difficult to pull off than others, and among the most difficult—the most embarrassing, the most awkward—is the love of a woman for a gay man. Such a relationship can be done gently and wistfully (Helen Hunt's fondness for Greg Kinnear in *As Good As It Gets*), and it can be done as farce. But if the woman's love is obsessive and needy, the story becomes stupid and painful, and that is what happens in *The Object of My Affection*, the Stephen McCauley novel that has been adapted for the movies with disastrous panache by playwright Wendy Wasserstein and director Nicholas Hytner. Jennifer Aniston plays Nina, a snippy-snappy young social worker in Brooklyn who takes as a roommate a lovable gay teacher, George (Paul Rudd). When Nina is made pregnant by her overbearing and unsuitable boy-friend (John Pankow), she asks George to raise the child with her. But Nina wants George's sexual love as well, and although George is willing to be daddy, he cannot be lover. Poor Nina is left with nothing to do but throw fits and turn her back in sorrow and furiously wash the dishes. *The Object of My Affection* is one of those cases, I think, in which the audience is so frustrated by an untenable situation onscreen that it shuts down on the movie: Paul Rudd is charming, and some of the scenes are intelligently written and played, but at a recent screening people on all sides of me were squirming in discomfort. Dramatically, *The Object of My Affection* has nowhere to go. Nigel Hawthorne shows up as a dapper old drama critic who loves a younger man, and he offers Nina rueful and worldly advice about her dilemma—the movie turns immensely sophisticated about the dumb situation it should never have allowed to develop in the first place.

Just when the country was beginning to like New York again, this picture comes along and ruins everything. Wasserstein has added to McCauley's rather modest novel all sorts of New York-style patter, and most of it is excruciating—the nervous, self-conscious chatter of a name-dropping literary agent (Alan Alda), the tense aggressions of his equally name-dropping, and unhappy wife (Allison Janney), and much more. Since the two characters are extraneous to the plot, who is dropping names but Wendy Wasserstein? There are scenes that are supposed to satirize the pretensions of powerful, knowing people, scenes that are themselves exactly an example of the display that is being satirized.

And the movie takes New York's ethnic and sex-preference variety to the point of boastful folly. *The Object of My Affection* is not just pro-gay (which is fine) and pro-diversity (ditto); it is programmatically and cheerfully committed to mixing everybody and everything together, as if life were just a problem that could be sorted out by creative casting at the Public Theater. This is the kind of fatuously self-approving movie that could bring Rush Limbaugh springing back to life.

NEW YORK POST, 4/17/98, p. 43, Rod Dreher

How can anything that sounds so wild be so, well, mild? True, "wild" is not an adjective that can describe anything involving cute-as-a-button "Friends" star Jennifer Aniston. But, still, the complications arising from the gay-straight romance at the heart of "The Object of My Affection" promise more daring than Wendy Wasserstein's sweetly bland screenplay delivers. Imagine "Chasing Amy" with a Gap-ad cast and scrubbed clean of its emotional prickliness and sex appeal. Aniston plays Nina, a Cobble Hill social worker whose job appears to be passing out condoms and bad sex advice like party favors to teenagers. She meets gorgeous George at a dinner party, and when his uppity boyfriend (Tim Daly) dumps him, Nina invites him to move into her spare room.

Nina and George quickly become best pals, taking dance lessons, walking hand-in-hand, lying in bed together watching old movies and sharing a pint of Haagen-Dazs. Nina finds George a lot more sympathetic and likable than her aggressively hetero boyfriend Vince (John Pankow), a lawyer who, like everybody else in her life, views life and love as competition to land the best deal.

When Nina becomes pregnant by Vince, she decides she wants her baby raised not by the jerky father but by the kind, loving George. Well, why not? "None of the old rules apply," she says.

That line's subtext screams "Danger, Will Robinson!" but George, feeling paternal, accepts. What he doesn't count on is Nina falling impossibly in love with him and the possibility that he will fall madly in love with a man.

It sounds like a great French farce, but it's actually played for tragedy, one we see coming like a train wreck. Not to worry, it's only toy trains. Despite their winsome appeal—and the whole cast, which includes Alan Alda and Allison Janney, is a treat to watch—neither Rudd nor Aniston conveys the terrible risk and destructiveness of giving oneself over to this kind of illusion.

You stick with "Object" because it keeps intimating more depth to come, but ultimately "Object" carries the emotional freight of a Very Special Episode of "Friends."

When the superb Nigel Hawthorne, playing a gay theater critic who also suffers from unrequited love, tenderly warns the confused Aniston that she's going to become a sad little "fag hag" if she doesn't wake up, both the grandly grave actor and his painful wisdom seem to have emerged from the heart-rending story nearly smothered by the movie's glib conventionality (epitomized by its dishonest, Hollywood happy ending)

What kept us involved with "Chasing Amy" was the understanding that sexuality is fluid and love is unpredictable. The gay-straight romance might, just this once, have worked. We're never given that hopeful illusion in "Object," which puts us in the awkward position of hoping, for their own good, that the romantic leads *don't* get together. Hmm.

What is different, and welcome, about "Object": The gay thing is treated as no big deal. Movie gays are as attractive but dull as movie straights. That's progress.

NEWSDAY, 4/17/98, Part II/p. B3, Jack Mathews

Playwright Wendy Wasserstein is said to have spent parts of the last 10 years writing and rewriting the script for Nicholas Hytner's "The Object of My Affection." Who knows how many worthwhile plays she might have written instead.

From what we see on the screen, the movie certainly didn't warrant that kind of commitment from that kind of talent. Wasserstein has a comic genius for exploring the psychological messiness of daily life. But "The Object of My Affection," the story of a pregnant New York social worker who falls in love with her gay roommate and invites him to be the father of her child, is so self-conscious and politically correct, it plays like a stiff "Guess Who's Coming to Dinner?" for the '90s.

Wasserstein's script is sort of doomed by the circumstances dictated in the Stephen McCauley novel she's adapting. The heroine, Jennifer Aniston's Nina Borowski, is a terrific person—intelligeint, warm, independent, caring. She has everything but the good sense to know (and it's been in all the papers) that homosexuals don't change their orientation just because someone they love wants them to.

Maybe in 1987, when the novel was published, enough people still believed in the possibility of a moonstruck conversion to have a rooting interest in the relationship between Nina, who becomes pregnant by her overbearing, narrow-minded lawyer boyfriend Vince (John Pankow), and George (Paul Rudd), the first-grade teacher who is her soulmate as well as her roommate. For the longest time, as George and Nina go dancing together, nuzzle in front of the TV, and otherwise play house, the movie expects us to believe in that possibility, too.

But to do that, we'd have to experience the movie solely from Nina's perspective, as she falls for George at first sight, invites him to live with her, and hopes against hope that they can make a life together. Since the book is written from George's point of view, from that of a gay man comfortable with his orientation, we begin to understand why it might take 10 years to redirect the narrative, and have it still come off unbalanced.

Despite a charming performance from Aniston, Nina's dogged pursuit of happiness with George is more frustrating than sympathetic. In the beginning, she's content to sleep with Vince, and communicate with George. However, when she discovers she's pregnant, she rejects Vince's proposal and asks George to assume the spousal role, rationalizing that since most marriages end up in sexless friendship, why not start at that point?

The moment George and Nina agree to this arrangement, a bonehead alert goes off and the questions pile up. What are the odds on their giving up their sexual lives? What will George do when friendship isn't enough for Nina? What will Nina do when George's old boyfriend (Tim

Daly) calls, or when he starts hanging out with that gay theater critic (Nigel Hawthorne) and his irresistible young lover Paul (Amo Gulinallo)?

Throughout Nina's pregnancy, these questions beget stress, and the reality gradually sets in. Yep, this is a bad movie. It's well-intentioned, and the occasional, Wasserstein zinger perks up the dialogue, but the dramatic arc makes it feel more like a tragic disease-of-the-week movie than a story of star-crossed lovers.

Part of its undoing is its surprising embrace of stereotypes. Vince is a lawyer, therefore, insensitive; George is a schoolteacher, therefore, a father figure. Vince is domineering, therefore, homophobic; George is gay, therefore, open. The movie would have been a lot more fun if George moved in with Vince.

The supporting characters are all used as contrast and comic relief, serving the former better than the latter. Steve Zahn is George's cartoonish hyper-hetero brother, a surgeon working his way through his hospital's nursing and female doctor corps. Alan Alda is, well, Alan Alda, playing an affected, name-dropping literary agent, and his wife (Allison Janney), Nina's stepsister, is a grating witch-snipe of superficiality.

Despite its multiple locations, "The Object of My Affection" has the rhythms and flow of a stage play, the understandable result of a collaboration between Wasserstein and Hytner, a British stage director whose previous films— "The Madness of King George," and "The Crucible"—were both adapted from plays. But in "closing" the novel, they've really highlighted the weakness of its premise.

NEWSWEEK, 4/20/98, p. 63, David Ansen

In most respects, the slick, lightweight "The Object of My Affection" is indistinguishable from dozens of other fluffy Hollywood romances. What's different about this romantic comedy—a loose adaptation of Stephen McCauley's 1987 novel—is the dilemma keeping our lovers apart: the heroine, a social worker named Nina (Jennifer Aniston), is a heterosexual woman and the schoolteacher George (Paul Rudd), the object of her affection, is a gay man. About the hero's sexual orientation the movie is blessedly nonchalant; it's neither cause for laughter, outrage or special pleading.

George, having just been dumped by his callow college-professor boyfriend (Tim Daly), takes up his new friend Nina's offer to move into her Brooklyn apartment. She already has a boyfriend of sorts—a civil-liberties lawyer (John Pankow) whom she keeps at arm's length. But Nina infinitely prefers the company of George; indeed, he feels so much like a soulmate that when she discovers she's pregnant, she asks George if he will raise the baby with her.

McCauley's novel was told from George's point of view; screenwriter Wendy Wasserstein and director Nicholas ("The Crucible") Hytner tell it from Nina's—the more conflicted and, in this version, more interesting character. Nina and George love each other, but it's harder for her to keep up her platonic end of the bargain. She's jealous of his affairs with men; he isn't jealous of hers. Aniston's Nina is always a little out of control;. she crashes through life hurting other people's feelings. Aniston comes into her own here, bringing all of Nina's contradictory emotions alive in a strong, likable performance. Rudd is also good as the sweet, sensitive schoolteacher, but he's blander than the novel's hero; removing George's edge makes the movie duller than it needs to be.

The straight woman/gay man dilemma is a fresh Hollywood subject. So why does the movie feel so conventional, so unexciting? It's as if, in trying to appeal to a wide audience, quirky material has been forced to fit a formula that can't really contain it. Since it's clear to us that Nina and George shouldn't become a romantic couple, we're in the odd position of watching a romantic comedy in which we know it's best the lovers stay apart. The scene where the two almost sleep together is one of the best: it has a complicated erotic tension that's missing in the rest of the story. More commendable than compelling, "The Object of My Affection" is a little too nice for its own good. Inside it there's a messier, funnier, more painful movie struggling to get out.

SIGHT AND SOUND, 7/98, p. 50, Stella Bruzzi

New York, the present. A school play directed by teacher George Hanson goes off well. Parent Sidney Miller, a top literary agent, and his wife Constance invite George and his partner Joley to dinner that evening. There George learns from Constance's step-sister Nina that Joley told her over dinner that he intends to end the relationship. Nina invites George to stay with her since she doesn't want to live with her boyfriend Vince. George and Nina become best mates. When Nina, fed up with Vince, finds out she's pregnant, she asks George to help her raise the child. George accompanies her to her first scan. One day, Nina and George almost have sex when Joley calls, inviting George to go with him to George's old college. There they meet Rodney and his partner Paul; George and Paul are attracted to each other.

After her bag is stolen, Nina meets Louis, the cop who takes her home. Paul (still living with Rodney) and George start dating. George, Nina, Rodney and Paul spend Thanksgiving together. At George's brother's wedding Nina goes into labour. A few years later, Nina's daughter Molly is in a school play directed by George. In the audience are Louis (now Nina's partner); Sidney, Constance and their daughter; and George and Paul, now openly a couple.

Why is it that all the best men are gay? This rather contemporary question is at the heart of this otherwise traditional romantic comedy by Nicholas Hytner (*The Madness of King George, The Crucible*). 'Affection' is a complex feeling, a desire lurking somewhere between fondness and sexual attraction. It's an astute emotion to explore cinematically, allowing *The Object of My Affection* to replicate in some measure the satisfying but unconsummated feeling engendered by the classic Hollywood romances it's indebted to. Censorship did the woman's film a service by dispensing with the problem of sex. Babies, as in Ophuls' *Letter From an Unknown Woman* (1948), arrived from the brief encounter elided by a judicious cross-fade. So, in the 90s when physical contact is assumed to be part of relationships, the next best substitute for the melodrama hero is a gay man. Thus Nina and George take up dancing lessons, share informal pasta meals, and go window-shopping for baby clothes.

Having established this idea of the perfect male/female pairing, *The Object of My Affection* appears surprisingly uncomfortable about dealing with gay sex. Up until the baby-clothes sequence, the narrative (as well as Nina) has conveniently forgotten George's sexuality. In the baby store, George recognises an ex-lover, so when Nina later asks George, "Do you think many married couples are as happy as we are?" before starting to kiss him and unbutton his shirt, you know that the bubble of her fantasy has already burst. Either George renounces his sexuality or he renounces this dreamy half-state. Mercifully he does the latter by starting up with Paul. But the film still seems uneasy about gay sex and maintains a coy, chaste distance from what George actually gets up to.

Because it's striving so hard to be a politically correct romance with a broad appeal, *The Object of My Affection* ends up being equivocal about just about every sort of sex, and presents an equally ambivalent image of heterosexuality. On the one hand it's seen as something one makes do with. Sidney and Constance function as a couple but there's little tenderness there. Likewise, one suspects that Nina's union with Louis is primarily about not wanting to be left alone. Yet on the other hand, coupledom is the happy ending that we and all the characters want for Nina. Ultimately, though, the film doesn't believe its own doctrine, since it gives us the impossible yet ideal trio of Nina, George (both now with other lovers) and Molly skipping off down the street at the end.

As this ending suggests, in its working through of the conundrum it sets itself, *The Object of My Affection* becomes overly schematic. This is most apparent in the paralleling of the two focal couples: George/Nina and Rodney/Paul. Nina's dilemma—that she is in love with a man who only feels a deep affection for her and admits that the person he really *wants* is Paul—is directly mirrored by the position of Rodney (Paul's older partner). The two bond when Rodney warns Nina: "Don't fix your life so you're left alone." The script's schematic tendency also pervades the editing. There are, for example, the juxtaposed sequences of Nina and George working at the beginning which set up the idea that they're so alike they're bound to get on. Later, there are the two scenes showing Constance and George's brother both vowing to set their respective siblings up with appropriate partners. The narrative even opens and closes with parallel school-play sequences.

For such a formulaic genre movie to work, the writing and acting should convey a rather unreal sense of surprise at the events having turned out the way they do. In *The Object of My Affection* the performances are the weak link (apart from Nigel Hawthorne in his first gay role), as the characters fail to respond to or to change because of what happens to them. *The Object of My Affection* is a neat film which sets itself a potentially interesting romantic premise that it nevertheless fails to do very much of interest with.

TIME, 4/20/98, p. 81, Richard Schickel

Opposites attract. If we didn't believe that slightly dubious premise, our culture—not to mention our inner lives—would be infinitely poorer: no *Wuthering Heights*, no *Bringing Up Baby*. On the other hand, to be strictly fair, had we been spared that thought we would also have been spared *Abie's Irish Rose* and *Guess Who's Coming to Dinner*? You win some, you lose some.

Right now in the realm of movie romance, we're on a major losing streak. For we live in a world where all the old dramatically and comedically interesting barriers to love's fulfillment have tumbled. Class, race, religion, all the things that used to keep a man and woman apart until the final reel—and even sometimes through eternity—have lost their potency. Or, to put the point a little more carefully, in a time when the very idea that society actually contains implacable opposites is—smokers and nonsmokers aside—officially discouraged, it's hard to think of anything that might give plausible pause to potential lovers.

You'd think maybe sexual preference might have some potential in this regard. Wendy Wasserstein, the playwright, obviously does. She's been trying to get an adaptation of Stephen McCauley's novel *The Object of My Affection* off the ground for something like a decade. It offers a gay guy named George (Paul Rudd) getting jilted, taking a room with a straight woman named Nina (Jennifer Aniston) and having them fall into, yes, affection. On her part, though, that develops into something a little more intense, especially when she contrasts his sweetness to the abrasiveness of her straight lover, Vince (John Pankow). Those feelings grow when she discovers that she's pregnant and that George is a much more supportive prenatal companion than Vince. Maybe, she thinks, he'd be a better father too. As for sex, well, as someone once said, nobody's perfect. And George does encouragingly tell her that he once had a not entirely disagreeable heterosexual affair.

It's a nice muddle, especially since Wasserstein provides the couple with all kinds of complications. She has rich, interfering relatives (Alan Alda and the divinely bitchy Allison Janney). He soon has a new gay flame (Amo Gulinello) whose worldly-wise longtime companion (wonderfully portrayed by Nigel Hawthorne) gets hurt as hard as Nina does. But it's also too much of a muddle.

There is no logical way to arrange the kind of romantic reconciliation the writer, director (Nicholas Hytner) and we desperately want to enjoy. For neither Wasserstein nor Rudd quite wants to come to grips with the fact that George, despite his sweet smiles, is a careless, selfish man. Eliding the consequences of that problem, Wasserstein turns the whole bunch into an extended family—even adding a sweet-souled black policeman to the mix as Nina's consolation prize. Wasserstein can spritz New York-smart talk with the best of them, but she can't make us believe this mass conversion to sociopolitical correctness, with everybody loving and forgiving everybody despite the fact that the harms they have dealt one another remain essentially unresolved.

One of this movie's implications—and it's a common enough one these days—is that sensitivity is a quality impossible to find in straight guys. *City of Angels* takes that idea to the next logical plane: the celestial one. It suggests the only hope that Maggie Rice (Meg Ryan), a surgeon who is loveless as well as sleepless in Los Angeles, has for sympathetic understanding is not to be found in this world. Luckily for her, she has caught the eye of a sweetie-pie seraph named Seth (Nicolas Cage), an angel so eager for earthly pleasures—the taste of a pear, the touch of a woman—that he's willing, when he happens to spot the right girl, to give up angelic status, but not, of course, his angelic temperament, to sample them.

This premise, sans the feminist spin, was the basis of a very good movie, *Wings of Desire*, which *City of Angels* (as written by Dana Stevens and directed by Brad Silberling) travesties in the course of remaking. In the Wim Wenders—Peter Handke original of a decade ago, the object of their otherworldly hero's affection was not a neurotic overachiever, but a trapeze artist whose simplicity was what attracted him. More important, that movie did not intimate, as the new version does, that perfect love must of necessity be tragically brief. It proposed instead that a life of feeling was bound to be a messy business but that there was more fun to be found in the flux of things, grabbing what happiness you can, enduring what disappointments you must, than in pursuing an impossible ideal .This is not bad advice to the lovelorn of either sex.

VILLAGE VOICE, 4/21/98, p. 72, Dennis Lim

While *City of Angels* evinces staggering lapses of taste and common sense at every turn, *The Object of My Affection*—an adaptation of Stephen McCauley's light-footed 1987 novel—represent's a well-meaning but miscalculated missed opportunity. A model of its kind, McCauley's book is a funny, casually insightful take on youthful romantic anxiety, tracking the relationship between twentysomethings George and Nina, a gay man and a straight woman who, more in denial than in love, fall into a deceptively cozy living arrangement. The film's failings have less to do with lead actors Paul Rudd and Jennifer Aniston or director Nicholas Hytner than screenwriter Wendy Wasserstein, who's abridged, altered, tweaked, and generally taken the luster off McCauley's story.

Wasserstein adds a handful of new characters, and in virtually every instance, there's neither a comedic nor a dramatic payoff. The worst offenders are Nina's social-climbing stepsister (Alison Janney) and her name-dropping hotshot-agent husband (Alan Alda), both pointless and unfunny caricatures. Sufficiently cute and likable, the leads just about carry the film—even if Aniston's Nina isn't much more than Rachel without Rachel-hair. George is the exceedingly rare gay Hollywood character who isn't a bundle of stereotypes, for which Rudd deserves credit as much as Wasserstein and McCauley do. The film's not as witty as it should have been and more coy than it needed to be (and, unlike the book, it refuses to leave a single loose end hanging, flashing forward to an annoyingly pat coda), but it affords glimpses, however fleeting, of two decent people trapped in a believably confusing mess. From an industry that spews out refuse like *City of Angels* without a second thought, I'll take my emotional truths where I can find them.

Also reviewed in:
CHICAGO TRIBUNE, 4/17/98, Friday/p. A, Michael Wilmington
NEW YORK TIMES, 4/17/98, p. E22, Janet Maslin
VARIETY, 4/13-19/98, p. 27, Todd McCarthy
WASHINGTON POST, 4/17/98, p. B4, Rita Kempley
WASHINGTON POST, 4/17/98, Weekend/p. 57, Michael O'Sullivan

OFF THE MENU: THE LAST DAYS OF CHASEN'S

A Northern Arts Entertainment release. *Producer:* Alicia Sams and Julia Strohm. *Director:* Shari Springer Berman and Robert Pulcini. *Director of Photography:* Ken Kobland and Sandra Chandler. *Editor:* Robert Pulcini. *Music:* Mark Suozzo. *Running time:* 90 minutes. *MPAA Rating:* Not Rated.

WITH: Steve Allen; Angela Bassett; Jackie Collins; Matt Dillon; Gerald Ford; Merv Griffin; Bob Hope; Samuel Jackson; Jessica Lange; Sally Kirkland; Jay Leno; Johnny Mathis; Suzanne Pleshette; Don Rickles; Donna Summer; Quentin Tarantino; Yanni; Fay Wray.

LOS ANGELES TIMES, 5/15/98, Calendar/p. 8, Kevin Thomas

While staying at a L.A.-area bed-and-breakfast, New York filmmakers Shari Springer Berman and her husband, Robert Pulcini, learned from the B&B's owner, Raymond Bilbool—also Chasen's banquet captain—that the landmark restaurant would soon be closing. They seized the opportunity to document the restaurant's final two weeks in late March 1995.

The result is "Off the Menu: The Last Days of Chasen's," an irresistible piece of social history assembled with wit and panache. Above all, their affectionate yet tart film is a heartbreaking tribute to the restaurant's key longtime staffers, individuals who were lucky enough to find work they loved and who dedicated themselves to an institution they cherished and surely hoped would outlive them.

In 1936, vaudeville performer Dave Chasen opened a modest restaurant on Beverly Boulevard at Doheny Drive on the edge of West Hollywood. Chasen's specialty was a chili that he had, according to legend, concocted in Frank Capra's kitchen—and which Elizabeth Taylor famously had shipped to Rome while filming "Cleopatra." Good food, a gemutlich atmosphere and Chasen's many show-business friends and acquaintances guaranteed its success. Over the years, Chasen's expanded greatly but always kept its atmosphere of warm red-leather booths and wood paneling.

For nearly 60 years Chasen's hosted not only Hollywood's greatest stars but also heads of state and the famous in every field. According to columnist Army Archerd, Ronald Reagan proposed to Nancy Davis at Chasen's. Indeed, Reagan is one of the four presidents who posed with the restaurant's legendary, affable headwaiter, Tommy Gallagher.

Berman and Pulcini include a montage of the stars arriving at Chasen's over the decades for gala parties and reminiscences from a host of celebrities, ranging from Fay Wray to Sharon Stone and including producers A.C. Lyles, David Brown and Charles Fries.

Chasen's was the most enduring restaurant of Hollywood's Golden Era, but its era was dying out literally. (Alfred Hitchcock, who dined en famille every Thursday at the same booth, and James Stewart were longtime regulars.) It became a bastion of elegance and class, exclusive and expensive, in which were served great food impeccably. In short, it became the refuge of the older crowd, and its rich menu and formal dress code did not attract Hollywood's younger generations, who flocked to a series of trendier, more casual places, most notably Wolfgang Puck's Spago.

Still, its staffers, while reluctant to point fingers, do make it clear that they feel they had been let down by indifferent, unimaginative management once advancing age and illness at last forced Dave Chasen's beautiful and chic widow Maude to retire.

Once the restaurant had posted its closing notice, it not surprisingly became booked solid once again. "It's like when somebody's sick," observes bartender Pepe Ruiz. "Nobody calls, but everybody goes to the funeral." Celebrated for his blazing Flame of Love martini, Ruiz is one of several key Chasen's employees whom the filmmakers gradually move to the fore once the rich and famous have told their stories.

Shrewdly, memorably and rightly, Berman and Pulcini focus on the people who made Chasen's work all those years. They include Ronnie Clint, the restaurant's handsome, silver-haired British-born general manager; Val Schwab, who checked coats for years, receiving $200 regularly from Hitchcock—and $1 from Stewart; the sentimental Gallagher, for whom the restaurant became so much of his life that his son says it was his "other woman"; Onetta Johnson, the ladies' room attendant who inspired Donna Summer's song "She Works Hard for the Money"; and above all, Bilbool, an amusingly mercurial and very sharp perfectionist. (Actor Adam Heller swears he landed his featured Broadway role in "Victor/Victoria" emulating Bilbool's carriage and manner while auditioning for the part of a Parisian nightclub owner.)

At the time "Off the Menu: The Last Days of Chasen's" was completed, things looked bleak for the restaurant's heritage, with talk of a smaller-scale resurrection in a mall to be built once the restaurant was torn down. Three years later, however, Chasen's was able to relocate to Canon Drive in Beverly Hills and still opens the original location for special events.

NEW YORK POST, 6/19/98, p. 50, Larry Worth

Any film that starts with Jimmy Durante singing "I'll Be Seeing You" is off to a great start. As crooned by the master showman, it's a poignant tune that details happy memories, forever gone.

That's why it's a perfect opening for "Off the Menu," a lovely documentary that details the glory years of Chasen's. Along with the Brown Derby, Chasen's was one of Los Angeles' most famous celebrity restaurants. And also like the Brown Derby, Chasen's had to make way for the future.

The film begins with the announcement that the 59-year-old restaurant was to be razed for a strip mall. That sets off a mix of reveries from stars (Sharon Stone, Jack Lemmon and on and on) as well as staffers (the jovial head waiter, coat check woman, martinet-like banquet room manager, etc.)

Thankfully, directors Robert Pulcini and Shari Springer Berman include plenty of vintage clips, starting with Chasen's storied opening in 1936 and giving way to visits from Bogie and Bacall, Ol' Blue Eyes,' Liz Taylor and Elvis, never mind '90s names such as Courtney Love and Quentin Tarantino.

It all makes for fascinating material, whether detailing how Taylor had the restaurant's renowned chili sent to Rome while filming "Cleopatra" or gossipy exchanges about Ronald Reagan proposing to Nancy on the premises. Broken up by title cards like "Rod Steiger and his publicist do lunch," the goodies never stop.

There's even a women's room attendant who inspired Donna Summer's hit song, "She Works Hard for the Money." Indeed, it's those kind of heartfelt reveries that lend the production such soul.

So when the film concludes on April 1, 1995 with a tear-soaked bash to mark the joint's last night, one can't help feeling sad. As "Off the Menu" so lovingly points out, it was truly the end of an era.

VILLAGE VOICE, 6/23/98, p. 135, Michael Atkinson

A simultaneously shameless and shaming dirge for showbiz's ancient regime, *Off the Menu: The Last Days of Chosen's* is no more or less than its title promises: a chronicle of the famous eatery's shutting down after broadening the waistbands of the famous for 60 years. It's strictly old-school night; for every Sharon Stone (caught lamenting the passing of famous landmarks in idiotic interview-speak), there are 20 Fay Wrays and Jane Wymans, waxing nostalgic about the restaurant that, with its gallingly fatty foods and immense cocktails, may have been responsible for many of their costars' untimely last exits. Directors Robert Pulcini and Shari Springer Berman have segmented the movie according to legendary staff members, notably Tommy Gallagher, the loudmouthed, "shanty Irish" waiter who told movie stars what they should eat, and Pepe Ruiz, the Edison-like barkeep seen here scorching brandy with orange peel oil (as narrated by a rapt Ed McMahon).

What the filmmakers didn't understand is that, in terms of Hollywood, sardonic irony cooks off instantly—the real thing is already completely self-mocking and aware of its daffiness. What's left feels more like sincere genuflection before celebrity, and the abject worship of media-sanctified mediocrity can be stultifying. Granted, it's hard not to appreciate the story of Daryl Gate's date trying to steal a lamp, or the glimpse of a letter (dated five days before the Watergate arrests) in which Nixon thanked Chasen's for air-mailing its famous chili, which he shared with Henry Kissinger and Bebe Rebozo. But *Off the Menu* soon grows dull, tells you far more than you ever wanted to know about the ingestive habits of Rod Steiger, and demonstrates again, seemingly in spite of itself, that Hollywood is a hell of empty skull chambers and vapor-thin sentiment.

Also reviewed in:
NEW YORK TIMES, 6/19/98, p. E26, Lawrence Van Gelder
VARIETY, 4/14-20/97, p. 94, Todd McCarthy

OGRE, THE

A Kino International release of a Studio Babelsberg/Renn Productions/Recorded Picture Company co-production in association with WDR and France 2 Cinema. *Executive Producer:* Claude Berri, Jeremy Thomas, and Lew Rywin. *Producer:* Ingrid Windisch. *Director:* Volker Schlondorff. *Screenplay:* Jean-Claude Carriere and Volker Schlondorff. *Story (based on the novel "Ther Erl King" by):* Michael Tournier. *Director of Photography:* Bruno de Keyzer. *Editor:* Nicolas Gaster. *Music:* Michael Nyman. *Sound:* Karl Heinz Laabs. *Casting:* Karin

Beewen. *Production Designer:* Ezio Frigerio. *Art Director:* Didier Naert. *Costumes:* Anna Sheppard. *Running time:* 116 minutes. *MPAA Rating:* Not Rated.

CAST: John Malkovich (Abel); Armin Mueller-Stahl (Count of Kaltenborn); Gottfried John (Chief Forester); Volker Spengler (Hermann Goering); Marianne Sagebrecht (Frau Netta); Heino Ferch (SS-Officer Raufeisen); Dieter Laser (Professor Blattchen); Agnes Soral (Rachel); Sasha Hanau (Martine).

LOS ANGELES TIMES, 1/8/99, Calendar/p. 4, Kevin Thomas

Volker Schlondorff's "The Ogre," adapted from Michel Tournier's celebrated novel "The Erl King," is a superb companion piece to the director's Oscar-winning 1979 film of Gunter Grass' "The Tin Drum." Both deal with the specter of the Third Reich in epic and ironic fashion, with mythological overtones.

"The Ogre" marks a triumphant return to filmmaking for Schlondorff, who devoted five years to establishing Studio Babelsberg, former home of the legendary UFA studios and East Germany's subsequent DEFA organization. (In a sad commentary on art film distribution, "The Ogre," an English-language production three years in the making, was actually completed two years ago. "The Tin Drum" will be the second feature today and Saturday, Fritz Lang's "M" Sunday through Tuesday and G.W. Pabst's "The 3 Penny Opera" Wednesday and Thursday.)

"The Ogre" is a wrenching, richly imaginative tale of innocence, corruption and redemption. It opens in 1925 at a bleak, strict seminary outside Paris, where a miserable, ill-treated orphan boy named Abel wishes that the entire place would burn down. By accident it does, conferring on Abel a sense that he possesses special powers.

When we next catch up with him, it's 1939, and Abel (John Malkovich), near-sighted and still childlike, is a Paris auto mechanic whose identification with youngsters will inevitably be misinterpreted. A series of events catapults Abel from French soldier to prisoner of war in Germany, where he ends up a servant at Hermann Goering's vast country estate. Here Abel, always an outsider in his native country, receives unexpected opportunities.

Until this moment, "The Ogre" unfolds as an odyssey of a naive yet intelligent misfit, but with Abel's entry into Goering's baroque world, the film takes on a darkly satirical tone as it depicts the excesses of the field marshal (Volker Spengler), a man of legendary appetites and deadly iron whims who, when he tenses up, calms himself by thrusting his hands in a giant champagne glass filled with jewels.

Not far from Goering's estate is an elite military school, headquarters in a magnificent ancient castle, which is also the home of Count von Kaltenborn (Armin Mueller-Stahl), who belongs to an ancient line of knights—and is actually a member of the Resistance. When Goering departs, Abel ends up at the academy and, for the first time in his life, feels at home.

Now we're at the heart of the matter. Here is where the scions of Germany's purest Aryan aristocrats are steeped in physical culture and theories of genetic superiority. For all its discipline and demented thinking, the academy, with the warm and kindly Frau Netta (Marianne Sagebrecht) as its housekeeper, has a surprisingly gemutlich atmosphere. That's because everyone is caught up in Hitler-worship and the myth of Teutonic ascendancy.

But as the war wears on, Abel finds himself asked to swoop down on peasant boys to fill out the academy's thinning ranks; no wonder, too, he earns the nickname "The Ogre" across the countryside. Only gradually will Abel come to see the light, which keys the film's stupendous climactic sequence.

"The Ogre," which invites endless connections to German myth and legend, evokes that sense of a longing for an ultimately treacherous artificial paradise that experimentalist Hans Jurgen Syberberg explored so imaginatively in his monumental trilogy, "Karl May," about the German novelist who wrote of an American West he never saw; "Ludwig: Requiem for a Virgin King," about Bavaria's ill-fated builder of fantasy castles and palaces and mentor to Richard Wagner; and "Hitler: A Film From Germany," which envisioned Hitler as a master manipulator of a heady, seductive German Romantic tradition.

"The Ogre" is in all ways a remarkable accomplishment by a master director, working with a perfectly cast Malkovich and the cream of Germany's character actors, and with some of Europe's most distinguished film craftsmen, starting with Schlondorff's co-adapter Jean-Claude Carriere.

Malkovich's plain features and strong physical presence combine with his silky charisma to create an unsettling Abel, at once so vulnerable and so dangerous; his Abel seethes with the outsider's longing and cunning, intermingled with tenderness and complicated by naivete.

In addition to the always formidable Mueller-Stahl, Sagebrecht and Spengler, Malkovich is supported by Gottfried John as Goering's chief forester and the epitome of the intelligent yet obedient soldier, Heino Ferch as the academy's proponent of health and strength, and Dieter Laser as its crazed science professor.

"The Ogre" is a glorious-looking film of both intimacy and scope. Goering's Jagerhof, a cathedral-like structure in a kind of East Prussian folk Deco style, was re-created at Babelsberg, and much of the academy was filmed at Marienburg Castle, one of the most imposing monuments of the Order of German Knights. (There is a parade ground, complete with torches on pillars that looks like pure Albert Speer.) Production designer Ezio Frigerio and cinematographer Bruno de Keyzer give the film an even, burnished glow, and Michael Nyman has composed a magisterial score that is alternately witty and elegiac.

If there is any justice, "The Ogre" will move to another theater once it has completed its New Beverly run. But don't count on it.

NEW YORK POST, 12/11/98, p. 67, Thelma Adams

Before making the disastrous neo-noir "Palmetto," starring Woody Harrelson, German director Volker Schlondorff proved he hadn't entirely lost the beat of "The Tin Drum" with "The Ogre."

The English-language drama, co-written by Schlondorff and Jean-Claude Carriere, is only now being released. Made two years before "Palmetto," it is, like "Drum," another Teutonic fable about WWII as seen through the eyes of the outcast, the innocent, the simple-minded and the delusional.

The so-called ogre, a repellent everyman named Abel (a monotone John Malkovich), began life as an orphan and suffered abuse in a repressive Catholic school. When maltreated, he wished the school would catch fire; it did.

This event convinced Abel that fate, real and cruel, was on his side. Once grown, Abel is unfairly accused of child molestation, inducted into the French army and imprisoned by the Germans.

A chameleon with no loyalty to the French, Abel finds himself in the employ of Reichsmarshall Goering. Ultimately, the co-opted French prisoner ends up riding through the German countryside on horseback, accompanied by snarling Dobermans, rounding up German boys for the Hitler Youth.

Abel is exhilarated by his new job, intoxicated by the fire and flags of the Nazi regime and the beauty of the young boys he pursues. He is unaware that he has become a figure of fear, an ogre. He has ridden out of Grimm, a frightening forest figure, a thief of children, a headless horseman incapable of recognizing his own complicity in the horror of Nazism.

Episodic and engrossing, cruel and darkly funny, "The Ogre" is an adult fairy tale about the battle between innocence and corruption, good and evil, moral responsibility and collusion, played out in the forests that spawned both Grimm and Goering.

NEWSDAY, 12/11/98, Part II/p. B8, Jack Mathews

On first blush, casting John Malkovich in the title role of "The Ogre" sounds like great common sense. Few actors can match his resume for onerous sociopaths, and what could be more onerous than a man who roams the Prussian countryside recruiting children for Hitler Youth?

But Malkovich's Abel Tiffauges, a simple-minded Paris auto mechanic turned POW, is the antipode of an ogre. He's an innocent, ignorant of man's true capacity for evil, and so certain of his security in the hands of fate, and of the security of children placed in his hands, that he swallows whole the promise of a Nazi utopia. He is part Pied Piper, part Forrest Gump, an amiable idiot wandering off the path of good intentions into the heart of darkness.

"The Ogre," adapted from Michael Tournier's 1970s novel "The Erl King," explores the hypnotic appeal of Nazism, with Tiffauges as its symbol of complicity. That he is a prisoner of the Germans is a mere factoid. For Tiffauges, in fact, it's better than being a civilian in France, where he had been taunted all his life, and—just before being drafted into the army—had been wrongly accused of abusing a young girl he had merely tried to help.

From the beginning of his POW existence, Tiffauges is less a prisoner than a trustee, roaming freely away from the camps to commune with nature, always to return, and doing the bidding of his Nazi superiors with an endearing obedience. Like Gump, he humbles from one coincidence to another, coming out ahead each time, until he arrives at the Kaltenborn Castle, which has been taken over by the Nazis for Hitler Youth training.

Schlondorff takes forever—well, close to an hour—to get to the novel's main attraction, but once he does, "The Ogre" is riveting drama.

The director, who famously worked the fable form in his classic "The Tin Drum" (1979), sets out to get beyond the chilling image of blond, blue-eyed German kids sieg-heiling and singing odes to the Fatherland and see them as what they were, children at a severe form of play. Call it Extreme Scouting. The boys, some looking no older than 11 or 12, are on a camping adventure, being both nurtured and driven, entertained and disciplined, given purpose for their lives—to save their country—and the training to kill.

They get to take target practice with real guns, and it's fun, until one of the boys wanders into the backfire of a bazooka and is set ablaze. They learn to march, and it's fun, until they're marched into combat. They are treated as men, and it's fun, until some are pulled out for medical experimentation.

In Tiffauges' fuzzy brain, pride obliterates suspicion, and he continues to vacuum the hills of its able farm boys. And it's fun, until he witnesses the roadside slaughter of some Jewish children, and brings one home alive, and puts himself at risk by hiding him.

Malkovich can play one note longer than any actor alive, but it's perfectly effective in this instance. Tiffauges is ultimately more perceptive than he seems, but he is a slow study. Before we dismiss him as a fool, however, we should remember the millions of people who were just as slow, and wonder, what was their excuse?

VILLAGE VOICE, 12/15/98, p. 141, J. Hoberman

Not quite Norman Bates, the eponymous hero of *The Ogre,* Michael Tournier's celebrated 1970 novel, is a gentle, if gigantic, pederast, captured by the Germans during World War II, who falls in love with the magic kingdom of East Prussia and, as in a fairy tale, comes to serve the Nazis as a sort of spellbound huntsman.

Perhaps Volker Schlondorff imagined Tournier's ambitious allegory would be a companion piece to his 1979 adaptation of *The Tin Drum.* The result, with John Malkovich in the title role, is a high-Euro pudding mix of accents and intentions (literary, prurient, moral). Slack and stilted, the movie's first third is a typically enigmatic, smirky Malkovich show; the second, wherein his character gets a menial job at Hermann Goering's rustic-deco hunting lodge, is eccentric enough to make even the star seem normal, at least as compared to the Nazi leader, played with pop-eyed avidity by Volker Spengler.

When a local count (the inevitable Armin Mueller-Stahl) kills a great stag, Goering sends everyone to the eastern front. The ogre, however, lands at a nearby military school. Dressed like death and accompanied by a pack of hounds, he is given the job of combing the countryside for new recruits to this Riefenstahlian realm of torch-lit singing and near-nude wrestling. Schlondorff, who seems to be ignoring the situation's homoerotic kitsch, would need the medieval conviction of mid-'50s Ingmar Bergman to carry this off. The only evil the movie projects is the purity of its own liberal confusion.

Also reviewed in:
NEW YORK TIMES, 12/11/98, p. E16, Stephen Holden
VARIETY, 9/9-15/96, p. 116, David Stratiton

ONE TOUGH COP

A Stratosphere Entertainment release of a Patriot Pictures presentation of a Bregman production. *Producer:* Michael Bregman and Martin Bregman. *Director:* Bruno Barreto. *Screenplay:* Jeremy Iacone. *Story (based on the novel "One Tough Cop" by):* Bo Dietl. *Director of Photography:* Ron Fortunato. *Running time:* 90 minutes. *MPAA Rating:* R.

CAST: Stephen Baldwin (Bo Dietl); Chris Penn (Duke Finnerty); Mike McGlone (Rickie La Cassa); Gina Gershon (Joey O'Hara); Paul Guilfoyle (Frankie "Hot" Salvano); Amy Irving (FBI Agent Jean Devlin); Victor Slezak (FBI Agent Bruce Payne).

LOS ANGELES TIMES, 9/18/98, Calendar/p. 16, Kevin Thomas

[The following review by Kevin Thomas appeared in a slightly different form in **NEWSDAY, 10/9/98, Part II/p. B.]**

"One Tough Cop" is one dull movie. Yet again we're presented with a fearless NYPD policeman (Stephen Baldwin) who may bend the rules but gets the job done time after time only to be reprimanded by the brass who then takes credit for his heroics. At the end of this predictable picture we're told that except for the former policeman Baldwin plays, Bo Dietl, everyone else is fictional, but this does not come exactly as a surprise.

The problem is that writer Jeremy Iacone, in adapting Dietl's book, keeps on piling on the complications. Dietl has a partner, Duke (Chris Penn), every bit as brave and canny as he is, but plagued with an escalating gambling problem. That Bo's lifelong best friend (Michael McGlone) has grown up to be a leading Mafioso looks to be helpful to Duke's plight, but this fast friendship between cop and crook has fallen under the scrutiny of the FBI, represented by a pair of the nastiest, toughest agents (Amy Irving, Victor Slezak) imaginable.

At just this moment—wouldn't you know?—Bo and Duke are faced with tracking down whoever raped, beat and mutilated a nun in a Harlem convent. Despite official obstacles in investigating this terrible case—based on an actual incident—Bo has time to begin an affair with his Mafioso pal's gorgeous mistress (Gina Gershon).

Now all this and more may have happened to Dietl, but nothing in "One Tough Cop" is convincing because it unfolds in so mechanical and impersonal a manner under Bruno Barreto's by-the-numbers direction. Time after time the well-cast Baldwin and Penn work up a scene impressively, and the film looks to catch fire only to be dampened by rigid adherence to formula filmmaking. The one director who might have made this movie work is Sidney Lumet, who has brought a sense of irony and conflicting loyalties to similar material.

A handsomely designed and photographed film, "One Tough Cop" has the look of a Lumet picture—but without the feeling.

NEW YORK POST, 10/9/98, p. 46, Thelma Adams

TV's "Homicide" has ruined me for run-of-the-mill cop movies like Bruno Barreto's "One Tough Cop." At best, it has a gritty "Serpico" feel (it was produced by Martin Bregman and his son, Michael). At worst, I could sense Huggy Bear hovering on the fringe.

There's no reason for "One Tough Cop" to be so '70s. It's set uptown in 1985, the year of the hideous Harlem nun rape/mutilation that then-Mayor Koch called, "The most heinous crime in the history of New York City." Not that His Kochship doesn't exaggerate, but it was one tough case.

Two beat cops solved the crime and the NYPD apparently robbed them of their righteous glory. Cop-turned-author Bo Dietl made the collar and co-wrote the autobiographical novel that inspired Jeremy Iacone's screenplay.

"One Tough Cop" opens with one of those shameless set-pieces we've come to expect before the titles, the adrenaline surge that marks the boundary between fresh air and popcorn fumes. An enraged father shoots his estranged wife in a crowded market, grabs their daughter and threatens to blow off her pigtails.

Enter Dietl (Stephen Baldwin). He removes his shirt to show the Puerto Rican perp he has nothing up his sleeve but tattoos. He also shows the audience his doughy torso; yes, he's eaten a lot of White Castle sliders for the role.

Cop isn't about dollies in distress. It's not even about a violated nun. It's about men—real men—and loyalty.

"One Tough Cop" focuses on Dietl and his partner Duke Finnerty (Chris Penn): Together, they're two chunky NYPD tough guys. They're sinners in search of salvation by making the streets safe for the ordinary citizens they can never be.

Why can't they be ordinary? Why can't they follow the rules that bind the rest of us? For one thing, Dietl's bosom buddy is mob capo Rickie LaCassa (the weak Mike McGlone as a silly songbird of a hood). And loyalty gets divided when Dietl slips the tongue to LaCassa's slutty mistress (Gina Gershon) and Duke goes deep in debt with LaCassa's crew.

Baldwin—pigeon-toed, squinty-eyed, bearded—carries the movie bareback. The movie finds its fleeting moments of truth in his blue-chip eyes. Penn does his china shop bull routine—but that's the role as written: an alkie, gambler, scofflaw cop.

With Dietl's kneejerk anti-authoritarianism and Duke's drooling drunk, it's no wonder they aren't the most popular boys in the precinct—or among the FBI. When Dietl refuses to rat on LaCassa, a foul-mouthed femme fed tells him: "Say goodbye to your career." Say hello to Hollywood.

Also reviewed in:
CHICAGO TRIBUNE, 10/9/98, Friday/p. H, Michael Wilmington
NEW YORK TIMES, 10/9/98, p. E14, Stephen Holden
VARIETY, 10/5-11/98, p. 69, Dennis Harvey

ONE TRUE THING

A Universal Pictures release of a monarch Pictures/Ufland production. *Executive Producer:* William W. Wilson III and Leslie Morgan. *Producer:* Harry Ufland and Jesse Beaton. *Director:* Carl Franklin. *Screenplay:* Karen Croner. *Story (based on the novel by):* Anna Quindlen. *Director of Photography:* Declan Quinn. *Editor:* Carole Kravetz. *Music:* Cliff Eidelman. *Music Editor:* Alex Gibson. *Choreographer:* Jerry Mitchell. *Sound:* Allan Byer and (music) Bruce Botnick. *Sound Editor:* Randle Akerson. *Casting:* Rick Pagano. *Production Designer:* Paul Peters. *Art Director:* Jefferson Sage. *Set Decorator:* Leslie A. Pope and Elaine O'Donnell. *Set Dresser:* Dennis Zack, Bruce Swanson, Clifford Klatt, Jim Power, Robert Klatt, Robin Koenig, and Dennis Murray. *Costumes:* Donna Zakowska. *Make-up:* Sharon Ilson. *Make-up (Meryl Streep):* J. Roy Helland. *Make-up Special Effects:* Mathew Mungle. *Running time:* 120 minutes. *MPAA Rating:* PG-13.

CAST: Meryl Streep (Kate Gulden); Renee Zellweger (Ellen Gulden); William Hurt (George Gulden); Tom Everett Scott (Brian Gulden); Lauren Graham (Jules); Nicky Katt (Jordan Belzer); James Eckhouse (District Attorney); Patrick Breen (Mr. Tweedy); Gerrit Graham (Oliver Most); David Byron (Senator Sullivan); Stephen Peabody (Harold); Lizabeth MacKay (Dr. Cohen); Mary Catherine Wright (Clarice); Sloane Shelton (Mrs. Best); Michele Shay (June); Bobo Lewis (Muriel); Marylouise Burke (Louisa); Marcia Jean Kurtz (Marcia); Diana Canova (Diana); John Deyle (Santa/Mayor); Hallee Hirsh (8 Year Old Ellen); Jeffrey Scaperrotta (4 Year Old Brian); Todd Cerveris (Casey); Anna Alvim (Nurse Teresa); Julie Janney (Hospital Nurse); Susan Stout (Tweedy's Secretary); Greg Hedtke and Christian James (Magazine Executives); Lauren Toub and Ashley Remy (Halloween Girls); Saul Stacey Williams (Graduate Student); Julianne Nicholson and Ambler Kain (College Students); Yolande Bavan (Nari); Benjamin Andrews and Kathryn Walsh (Party Kids); James E. Graseck (Violinist); Doug Allen (Club Band Leader).

CHRISTIAN SCIENCE MONITOR, 9/18/98, p. B3, David Sterritt

Meryl Streep is today's busiest actress, with a pair of new movies this season: "One True Thing," opening today, and "Dancing at Lughnasa," due in a couple of months. "Dancing" is the more eagerly anticipated of the two, since it's based on Brian Friel's popular play, a favorite with many theatergoers.

"One True Thing" is the better movie, though, using imaginative filming and deeply felt performances to transform a soap-opera story into an affecting screen experience.

Streep plays Kate Gulden, a smart but modest woman who has devoted her life to her ambitious daughter, Ellen, her lackadaisical son Brian, and dominating the household—her egotistical husband, George, who places his needs ahead of every other priority. Each member of the family is challenged when Kate is diagnosed with a serious illness, requiring new degrees of care and concern from all around her.

Ellen passes the test by downgrading her big-city career and returning home to nurse her mother. George professes much solicitude for Kate, but his self-centered habits are too ingrained to be overcome in a hurry.

Already distressed at the waning of her professional life, Ellen finds herself caught in the crossfire between her parents and in a conflict between her own adult personality and long-ago memories awakened by her renewed closeness to a very difficult father.

A seasoned professional to her bones, Streep always seems willing to give up her own spotlight for the sake of a larger ensemble. Her portrayal of Kate is remarkable not only for its lack of movie-star glamour, but also for its untiring sense of balance, allowing Renée Zellweger's moving performance as Ellen to become the story's driving force.

William Hurt rounds out the principal cast with his most stirring work in a long time, making George's complex personality as engaging as it is aggravating—and injecting his scenes with an emotional depth that compensates for some regrettably shallow touches in the screenplay, written by Karen Croner from Anna Quindlen's novel.

Carl Franklin has directed "One True Thing" with a sure and sensitive touch, showing a stronger flair for domestic drama than for the crime-centered action of his previous pictures.

This is not a happy tale, and its ending will have moviegoers reaching for every handkerchief they can find. But its compassion is as clear as the talents of the folks who made it.

LOS ANGELES TIMES, 9/18/98, Calendar/p. 1, Kenneth Turan

What the movie business calls women's pictures get scant respect in Hollywood. The phrase signals dismissal and denigration, a way to casually brush off works that deal with emotions more than explosions, that think the complexity of personal relationships is the most compelling subject around.

But women's pictures, as "One True Thing" proves, are really human stories, accessible to anyone who is willing to feel. Based on Anna Quindlen's novel about a mother and daughter brought closer by the prospect of death, "One True Thing" demonstrates that the power of simple things, the transcendent nature of the ordinary, can make for riveting filmmaking.

It's satisfying somehow that Carl Franklin, working from a dependable script by Karen Croner, should be the director who makes this point so strongly. Though the success of his previous features, "One False Move" and "Devil in a Blue Dress," is grounded in their psychological acuity, they're best remembered for being dark, brooding pieces where physical violence is more of a threat than the emotional kind.

It's also appropriate that Meryl Streep, without question the outstanding American actress of her generation, should be the star here. Her role as Kate Gulden—mother, suburban house frau and faculty wife—is one of the least self-consciously dramatic and surface showy of her career, but Streep adds a level of honesty and reality that makes it one of her most moving.

Equally fitting is that "One True Thing," a film that illustrates the narrowness of gender and genre classification, should be about a daughter who comes to question, through the most painful experiences of her life, everything she believes about a woman whose lifestyle she can't consider without shuddering. "My mother was like dinner," novelist Quindlen has her protagonist say. "I needed her in order to live, but I did not pay much attention to what went into her."

Ellen Gulden (Renee Zellweger) grew up in suburban Langhorne, but she moved to Manhattan after graduating from Harvard. A journalist who writes for New York Magazine, she was proud of being someone, again in Quindlen's phrase, "who ate ambition for breakfast and anyone who got in her way for lunch."

Never close to her mother growing up, Ellen considered herself her father's daughter. George Gulden (William Hurt) is a charismatic professor of American literature and a National Book Award winner, and Ellen, embarrassed when her mother calls her "my brilliant daughter," wants nothing more than her father's faintest word of praise.

These family dynamics are visible at a surprise birthday party Kate throws for her husband, where Ellen, scornful and vaguely contemptuous of the choices her mother has made, first mocks this thoroughgoing homemaker for caring which knife is the right one for cutting bread and then clumsily cuts her finger with it. When someone says, "There's no place like home," Ellen immediately responds, "Thank God."

If it wasn't for her father's insistence, Ellen would never have moved back to Langhorne when Kate is diagnosed with cancer. She's got her off-and-on boyfriend in the city and a big story she's working on for the magazine about a senator with personal problems. But when her father turns censorious and says, "You've got a Harvard education, but where is your heart?," she inevitably gives in.

It's not only Ellen who's wary about the journey back, it's Kate as well. While Ellen mocks the Minnies, her mother's group of civic-minded housewives who do things like decorate the town's Christmas trees, Kate is horrified at the thought of anyone else being caring and nurturing around her house.

Much of the drama here involves a daughter who says, "The one thing I never wanted to do was live my mother's life," gradually and subtly realizing that she never understood this woman who is shrewd enough to nail Jane Austen on being condescending to conventional female characters. Ellen also comes to see that there are aspects to her adored father and her parents' marriage that she had no idea existed.

Summarized like this, "One True Thing" tends to sound schematic, and though the film has those elements to it, Franklin's intuitive restraint and sense of balance keep it honest. His direction brings both dignity and decency to what would have been overly obvious material in other hands; letting emotional situations degenerate into treacle is out of the question with him in charge.

Also benefiting from Franklin's steady, focused hand is Zellweger, whose effectiveness has fluctuated between the two poles of "Jerry Maguire" and "A Price Above Rubies." Zellweger's strength, which she gets to emphasize here, is how accessible and close to the surface her emotions are. As her mother's condition worsens, Ellen increasingly seethes with all kinds of resentments, and she feels free to act out what's troubling her in a way her mother never attempted.

As for Streep, this performance is the equal of her best work because she doesn't condescend to a character who is happy to be ordinary and self-effacing. Only gradually does Ellen's vision clear enough to give her and us a second sight into her mother's strength, spirit and purpose, and once that comes it makes the painful physical collapse Kate goes through that much more wrenching.

If there is an acting weakness in "One True Thing," it is William Hurt's performance as the father. While George Gulden is not supposed to be comfortable with ordinary emotions, the flat, imitating sourness that Hurt projects on screen makes him a more distant character than he should be and telegraphs the inevitability of Ellen's change of heart more than is necessary.

Screenwriter Kroner, most of whose work has been for television, has shrewdly put together a script that makes numerous minor departures from Quindlen's novel, including eliminating one of Ellen's brothers (the remaining one is played by Tom Everett Scott) and adding plot strands to beef up different aspects of Ellen's increasingly strained relationship with her dad.

The film's most interesting choice vis-a-vis its source is to downplay the original's melodrama. While the film delicately frames Ellen's story in discreet questioning by a district attorney investigating the possibility that her mother's death was a mercy killing, in Quindlen's novel the D.A.'s search becomes a major public event, involving jail time, newspaper headlines and large amounts of O.J.-type publicity.

It's fascinating that Franklin, whose films have tended toward storm and fury, was astute enough to see the importance of paring away even the suggestion of sensationalism the book offers. While films like "One True Thing" traditionally smother the viewer, Franklin's measured direction creates the space necessary for audiences to react fully, allowing us the freedom to step forward and embrace the emotion, making it completely our own.

NEW YORK, 9/28/98, p. 88, David Denby

One True Thing, based on a novel by Anna Quindlen, is journalistically conceived in terms of cultural opposites. Ellen (Renée Zellweger), a hard-driving *New York* Magazine reporter who likes to wear black, goes home to visit her parents and is greeted by her mother (Meryl Streep) in ribboned pigtails and blue-and-white dirndls. Mom is a homemaker; she enjoys cooking, dressing up, and trimming Christmas trees, and Ellen has always rejected her and her way of life, admiring instead her father (William Hurt), an allegedly great college teacher and critic-novelist. When the father insists that Ellen bag her career and look after her mother, who is seriously ill with cancer, Ellen comes to realize that she has misjudged them both. I have admired the work of director Carl Franklin in the past, but this movie is like an O'Neill family drama without the juice. Zellweger does fine, but Streep, despite an anguished outburst near the end (the only time the movie comes fully alive), is the wrong actress for this role, and Hurt gives a dim, recessive performance—he's too sheepish to be a convincing villain in this angry-guilty feminist morality play. The movie may, I admit, strongly affect feminist career women who feel uneasy about surpassing their stay-at-home moms, and that kind of emotional response is never to be scorned. But this viewer, an easy crier, shed not a tear: The material is too pat, too obvious, too firmly reined in by intelligent but enfeebling cliché.

NEW YORK POST, 9/18/98, p. 51, Thelma Adams

"One True Thing" might be a first: a post-feminist weepy. Harvard-educated reporter Ellen Gulden (Renee Zellweger) is her father's daughter. She's rational, cerebral and ambitious—and she's climbing the ladder at New York magazine by digging up dirt on a coke-friendly senator.

When Ellen returns home to fictional Langhorne for the birthday of her academic father, George (William Hurt), she learns that her mother, Kate (Meryl Streep), has cancer.

This visit is the beginning of the end for Kate and the start of a new life for Ellen. When George insists that his daughter leave Manhattan to nurse her mother—and sew on his buttons—Ellen begins to realize the pluses and minuses of being Daddy's girl.

Think Rosalind Russell abandoning her Manhattan typewriter and shoulder pads to care for her ailing mother in Podunk. But "One True Thing" doesn't work the territory for comic material; its saving grace is that it doesn't milk it for cheap sentimentality, either.

Based on the Anna Quindlen best-seller, with a tightly woven, shrewd script by Karen Croner and directed with restraint and compassion by Carl Franklin ("One False Move"), this domestic drama positions the lump in the audience's throat early on and doesn't let go until it exacts its weight in tears.

Streep makes an inspired entrance. Mama Kate fetes her husband's birthday by tossing a "come as your favorite literary character" costume party. She's adorably retro dressed in blue gingham, yarn braids and homemade ruby slippers; she's Dorothy from "The Wizard of Oz." It's no coincidence that the lesson of that book, and this film, is that there's no place like home.

Kate has the repulsion-attraction of a Martha Stewart, the manic, maligned contemporary goddess of the hearth. She's the prefeminist model of perfect motherhood, and this gives Ellen, dressed in New York black, the shakes. But once Ellen moves home, she discovers that her heroic, intellectual father isn't half the man her mother is.

As Kate sickens, Ellen slowly comes to see both parents as the dimensional, flawed, disappointed and loving humans that they are. She discovers that, whatever failings exist in her parents' marriage, Kate is the "One True Thing" in George's life.

This is the kind of weepy we expect Streep to steal, but her performance is generous and naked in its honesty. She pulls from Zellweger the performance of the young actress' career, an emotional arc that rings true with Zellweger's sparest performance to date. Hurt does what he does best; since "The Big Chill," he's specialized in the damaged intellectual whose biggest hurdle is his own spiritual weakness.

By the end, Ellen learns to bake a cherry pie, plant daffodils and appreciate her mother's legacy without sacrificing her ambition. With red-rimmed eyes beneath a turban hiding her chemo-matted hair, Kate gives Ellen the lowdown on her marriage: It might not be perfect, but what's the alternative? The one true thing might very well be accepting the lies we create to survive. There's no place like home—and it doesn't have to be Oz.

NEWSDAY, 9/18/98, Part II/p. B2, Jack Mathews

As an ambitious student at Barnard College, the future Pulitzer Prize-winning journalist Anna Quindlen was too self-absorbed to devote much time to trying to understand her relationships with the parents who'd formed her. But when she dropped out of school to help her father care for her dying mother, she was given a crash course in the family's psychology, enduring pain and epiphanies that decades later would inspire an exquisitely moving autobiographical novel "One True Thing."

In Carl Franklin's film version of that book, Quindlen's alter ego, Ellen Gulden, is an aggressive young New York magazine writer who's shamed by the father she worships into returning to their small hometown to take care of a mother whom she can barely abide. "One True Thing" is about how that experience alters Ellen's perceptions of her parents, and by implication, shapes the rest of her life.

A four-hankie weepie in the tradition of "Terms of Endearment" and "Marvin's Room," "One True Thing" is a sharply written (by Karen Croner) and compassionately directed movie featuring two of the most wrenching and emotionally honest performances of the year from Zellweger, as Ellen, and Meryl Streep, as her mother, Kate.

The existing relationship between mother and daughter when disease forces them together is not one of hostility. It's worse; it's a total disconnect. Through Ellen's voice-over narration and effectively employed flashbacks, we learn that from early childhood, Ellen rejected her mother's sunny disposition, mistaking it for superficiality and ignorance, while taking her father's intellect for wisdom on high.

Kate Gulden's Betty Crocker lifestyle, her devotion to homemaking and her ladies-club activities are an anathema to career-minded Ellen, and her disdain hovers over their relationship like a dark cloud. Meanwhile, Ellen covets the attention of her father (William Hurt), a distinguished college English professor and sometime novelist with a National Book Award hanging on his wall.

Neither of Ellen's perceptions about her parents is accurate. Mom is smarter and stronger than Ellen thinks, and Dad, who enlists her as family caregiver to avoid his own responsibilities, is weaker and less talented than she thinks. He is, as she'll come to know, both a philanderer and a bit of a literary phony. Buckle up, as Bette Davis famously said, for a bumpy ride.

The weakest dramatic element of Quindlen's book, the mystery as to whether Kate Gulden's death is a suicide or a mercy killing, is the weakest element of the film, as well. The story is not about euthanasia or the right to a dignified death, though the issues are touched upon. It's about external reckoning, of overriding your perceptions and ego to absorb the truth around you.

Building the story around Ellen's deposition as a murder suspect gives the book and the film a handy structure, but it inevitably leads to an anticlimax. How Kate Gulden died is not important; it's how she lived, and how she facilitated the lives around her. Streep, who inhabits the emotional lives of her characters like no other actress of her generation, is sensational as a buoyant spirit, sinking under the weight of disease.

Nonjudgmental and tolerant to what most of us would regard as a fault, Kate is a woman at peace with herself and her choices. In the film's most powerful scene, she not only justifies her life to her daughter, but with wisdom she can use. Streep's impassioned reading of this scene rip your heart out.

Zellweger is more than an able costar for Streep. Tom Cruise's wife in "Jerry Maguire" was her meatiest role to date—"One True Thing" is, after all, Ellen's story— and she gives an astonishingly seamless performance, as a woman transformed by her emotional journey. The investigative reporter's life becomes her own best subject.

Hurt has a more problematic challenge. The role of George Gulden is expanded here in an attempt to turn the film into a more equitable three-character story, and some of the add-ons ring false. Hurt plays George as an extremely conflicted person, a man who loves his wife but doesn't have the strength to comfort her. The more we see of him, the more unsympathetic he becomes, making his final pass at redemption an empty experience for the audience.

The ending of "One True Thing" is Carl Franklin's only misstep. The director's previous pictures—the violent chase film "One False Move" and the film noir "Devil in a Blue Dress"—hardly qualify as prep work for heavy family drama. However, he shows a masterful touch with his material, and a sure hand in directing two of the year's great performances from Streep and Zellweger.

NEWSWEEK, 9/21/98, p. 99, Yahlin Chang

Ellen Gulden is an ambitious, overcaffeinated Harvard grad embarking on a promising journalism career in New York. She wears all black and a permanent scowl. At 24, she still craves her father's approval—George is an esteemed author and professor—but she has to fight just to get his attention. And she's got only contempt for her mother, Kate, a dotty housewife who spends her days baking and reupholstering the furniture in flowery fabrics. Then Kate's diagnosed with cancer, and George forces Ellen to move home. Stranded in small-town Massachusetts, she feels like she's the one who's dying.

"One True Thing", directed by Carl Franklin and based on a novel by Anna Quindlen, is primarily a coming-of-age story. The heroine grows up by going home, shedding her illusions and seeing her parents for what they really are—a weak and stunted man underneath his literary polish and a brave, wise woman with secrets of her own. Kate (Meryl Streep) turns out to be the real heroine in this movie—the tenaciously cheerful caretaker in a family of grumps, genuinely excited about making her kids cinnamon toast even as she deteriorates.

Streep is brilliant, gradually tempering her rosy-cheeked joy with layer after layer of fatigue and agony. William Hurt, as Ellen's father, registers real torment under his zombie-like professorial detachment. As Ellen, Renee Zellweger just can't compete with the pros. You can see her trying—too hard—to play the neurotic reporter. But she's whiny instead of assertive, pouty instead of depressed. Still, Franklin hits just the right tone for this weeper, exercising such restraint that you won't even feel guilty for tearing up.

TIME, 9/21/98, p. 100, Richard Schickel

Kate Gulden (Meryl Streep) is the kind of woman who gives surprise costume parties for her husband's birthday, is worried about her careerist daughter's lack of culinary skills and spends far too much time with like-minded ladies making sure the town Christmas trees are suitably decorated. She is, in short, the kind of person no one, including her loved ones, takes very seriously—until she begins dying before her time.

One True Thing, a patient, unforced adaptation of Anna Quindlen's novel by screenwriter Karen Croner and director Carl Franklin, contains lots of true things about that process. For it immerses us in the awful, vertiginous panic that attends a death in the family—the fierce-wistful attempts to maintain routines in the face of this most exigent of interruptions; the desire to speak certain truths before it's too late and the fear of what consequences such candor might have; the politesse with which you must cover the outrage you feel as the rest of the world glides on about its business while an important part of yours is painfully, poignantly shutting down.

As she succumbs to illness, Kate must take on the final duty of a dutiful life—mediating some kind of truce between her husband George, walled off from reality by his professorial abstractions and his huge but fragile ego (a perfect role for William Hurt, that most self-regarding of actors), and her daughter Ellen, forced to give up an all consuming career to nurse her mother (Renee Zellweger, in a wonderfully clenched performance). This reconciliation Streep encourages in the subtlest of ways. There's no apology for Kate's lifetime of good cheer and common sense, just an opening up of those modest qualities, so that her family and we are gently, unsentimentally embraced and enlightened by their grace and bravery.

Also reviewed in:
NEW REPUBLIC, 10/19/98, p. 30, Stanley Kauffmann
NEW YORK TIMES, 9/18/98, p. E1, Stephen Holden

NEW YORKER, 9/28/98, p. 104, Daphne Merkin
VARIETY, 9/7-13/98, p. 72, Todd McCarthy
WASHINGTON POST, 9/18/98, p. C1, Rita Kempley
WASHINGTON POST, 9/18/98, Weekend/p. 56, Michael O'Sullivan

OPPOSITE OF SEX, THE

A Sony Pictures Classics release of a David Kirkpatrick/Michael Besman production. *Executive Producer:* Jim Lotfi and Steve Danton. *Producer:* David Kirkpatrick and Michael Besman. *Director:* Don Roos. *Screenplay:* Don Roos. *Director of Photography:* Hubert Taczanowsi. *Editor:* David Codron. *Music:* Mason Daring. *Music Editor:* Brent Brooks. *Sound:* Jon Ailetcher. *Casting:* Amanda Mackey Johnson and Cathy Sandrich. *Production Designer:* Michael Clausen. *Set Designer:* Andrew Reeder. *Set Decorator:* Kristin V. Peterson. *Costumes:* Shawn Barry. *Make-up:* Sergio Lopez-Rivera. *Stunt Coordinator:* Gary Wayton. *Running time:* 100 minutes. *MPAA Rating:* R.

CAST: Christina Ricci (Dedee Truitt);   Martin Donovan (Bill Truitt);   Lisa Kudrow (Lucia Dalury);   Lyle Lovett (Sheriff Carl Tippett);   Johnny Galecki (Jason Bock);   William Lee Scott (Randy);   Ivan Sergei (Matt Matteo);   Megan Blake (Bobette);   Colin Ferguson (Tom Dalury); Dan Bucatinsky (Timothy);   Chauncey Leopardi (Joe);   Rodney Eastman (Ty);   Heather Fairfield (Jennifer); Amy Atkins (TV Reporter);   Leslie Grossman (Girl Student);   Emily Newman (Marcia);   Harrison Young (Medical Examiner); Pancho Demmings (Police Officer); Terry L. Rose (Harley Man);   Richard Moore (Harley Man 2);   Susan Leslie (Judy Zale, Policewoman); Margaux St. Ledger (Reporter); Leslie Bevis (World News Reporter); Nicole Tocantins (Bobette's Lawyer);   Becky Wahlstrom (Cashier);   Peter Spears (Doctor Allen); Kristine Keever (Nurse);   David Phelps-Williams (School Principal);   Todd Eckert (Parole Officer).

LOS ANGELES TIMES, 5/22/98, Calendar/p. 2, Kristine McKenna

It's taken five months, but 1998 has finally produced a funny movie. A brilliantly written black comedy in the tradition of "To Die For" and "Flirting With Disaster," "The Opposite of Sex" was worth the wait.

Written and directed by Don Roos, whose comic sensibility is so fast-paced and unfettered that it verges on screwball comedy, the film stars Christina Ricci and Lisa Kudrow, both of whom are sensational in ways both expected and not.

The plot of this wicked little gem is kicked into motion by DeDee Truitt, a jaded 16-year-old played by the remarkable Ricci. A bad-to-the-bone teen queen who's like a hybrid of Lolita and Patty McCormack's "The Bad Seed," DeDee runs away from her white-trash mom and takes refuge at the home of her gay half-brother Bill (Martin Donovan). Once unpacked, she seduces Bill's live-in boyfriend Matt (Ivan Sergei), a human Irish setter who's lovely to look at but dumb as dirt. A pregnancy and robbery ensue, and the chase is on.

As DeDee, Ricci has the showboat role here. Nobody does sarcasm better than Ricci, who's growing up to be one of America's most consistently interesting actresses. However, it's Kudrow who walks away with the picture. Cast as Bill's long-suffering best friend, Lucia, an emotionally wounded woman who's rushed prematurely into spinsterhood, Kudrow is virtually unrecognizable as the actress who plays the ditsy Phoebe on the television series "Friends."

Trembling with indignation at the way the world works, Kudrow's Lucia is as smart as a whip, but she's a big drag nonetheless. "Do you watch 'Ellen'?" DeDee inquires on meeting Lucia, then adds in the voice-over that runs throughout the film: "She had a life once, but she stopped feeding it and it wandered away." By the end of the film you've realized that although the anarchistic DeDee and the uptight Lucia are coming from opposite ends of the moral spectrum, they're essentially alike; they're both so defended against life that they're barely able to live it.

Much of the humor in "The Opposite of Sex" pivots on cliches about gays, and the barbs—which are liberally sprinkled throughout the film by DeDee—are often so pointed that you may find yourself wondering if the film itself is homophobic. One need only remember that DeDee is equal opportunity all the way when it comes to insulting people. Moreover, it's patronizing to tiptoe around the subject of homosexuality as though it's still the love that dares not speak its name. Nobody tiptoes in this movie.

Because Roos knows how to write dialogue, he doesn't need to tart his film up with loud pop songs, and "The Opposite of Sex" is mercifully free of one of those annoyingly hip soundtracks. Also to be applauded is Roos' supporting cast, which is just about perfect. Donovan handles, with his usual aplomb, the thankless job of being the saintly character who's acted upon; Johnny Galecki is absolutely hilarious as a grunge gay fully equipped with an abundance of piercings and a Jeep; Lyle Lovett turns in a beautifully nuanced performance as a lovelorn cop; and Sergei's portrayal of Matt, the clueless beauty who's the object of everyone's affection, is splendid.

"The Opposite of Sex" would be a bitter pill to swallow were it not for the fact that Roos' characters actually learn scmething from their travails, and evolve over the course of the story. DeDee, of course, tries to play it tough to the end, and in the film's final scene, when she threatens to break down and show some heart, she handles it in a surprising way.

NEW YORK, 6/22/98, p. 58, David Denby

A movie without a big publicity machine behind it is now like a soldier without a weapon. Eager to help, critics can fire off their guns, but to what effect?—they may produce little but noise. So here goes nothing: As our deep-dish media experts rattle their brains trying to elucidate the alleged serious meanings of *The Truman Show* (good luck, fellows), a small American movie has opened that's far more entertaining than Peter Weir's empty fable. Don Roos's *The Opposite of Sex* is a work of comic art offering nothing more ambitious than temperament, humor, and sex. It doesn't require much interpretation; it requires only a decent-size audience to appreciate its very tart and original wit, its considerable gift for spontaneous and generous feeling. Don Roos has worked as a screenwriter on commercial movies like *Boys on the Side* and *Single White Female*, and he wrote *Love Field*, an idealistic project about an interracial romance that was perhaps too cautiously conceived to come off. But Roos has now put caution behind him. *The Opposite of Sex*, an independent film, breathes the air of freedom from its opening moments, in which we are warned by the film's narrator, a 16-year-old bitch named Dedee (Christina Ricci), that "if you think I'm just plucky and scrappy, and all I need is love, you're in over your head."

Dedee may be lounging in baby fat, but she's already a fully functioning femme fatale. Sex and money are the only things that matter to this impatient and ruthless trailer-trash vamp. The comic convention of the movie is that Dedee, taking us into her confidence, is always much worse a person than we expect; she's trying to shock us, like all teens, but at the same time she's truly a bad girl, so bad that she turns every one of our sweet, sympathetic impulses ("Oh, but she's just a kid!") into a pang of regret. Dedee is a great, entertaining caricature, an updated teen version of a forties-noir seductress and murderess—Lana Turner without corsets. Christina Ricci has a malevolent smile and rather too much smooth white flesh; her being more arrogant than beautiful is part of the joke. Ricci possesses a devastating way with a nasty line; she could curdle mother's milk from 30 paces.

Running away from home, Dedee moves in with Bill (Martin Donovan), her gay half-brother, who is considerably older—an exceptionally nice, intelligent man but almost pathologically mild (when he finds dirty jokes written about him on his school's bathroom walls, he corrects the grammar). Dedee now has her patsy; she immediately seduces Bill's live-in lover, the handsome, pleasant, but rather stupid young Matt (Ivan Sergei), and soon the two of them with Bill's money in their pockets, escape from his house in Indiana. They are pursued—not just by Bill but also by a fellow teacher, a woman named Lucia. Roos takes a risk here: It isn't immediately clear what Lucia is doing in the movie. It turns out she loves Bill devotedly but for a rather indirect reason. Bill's previous lover—before Matt the bimbo—was Lucia's brother, who died of AIDS (Dedee refers to him graciously as "the dead guy" and steals his ashes in order to extort money from Bill). When the chase moves to Los Angeles, Lucia tags along, and—as played by Lisa Kudrow, from *Friends*—Lucia turns into a major comic creation.

First Helen Hunt, and now Lisa Kudrow: Television sitcoms, not the movies or the stage, seem to be the breeding ground of great new actresses. Kudrow has a long, Modigliani-esque face and body—everything about her in this movie seems attenuated, as if her spirit had passed through a mangle. Her voice is very dry, like parchment rattling in the wind. Lucia is dismayed by the American sexual wonderland—the tramps, the gays and bisexuals, the straight men (represented here by Lyle Lovett) sleeping with other women while their wives are dying. Old-fashioned and loyal, Lucia complains with bitter wit about everybody's sexual arrangements. She's rapidly becoming a classic spinster—the teacher with the precise observations and the nasty tongue, the one with high standards and a deeply romantic nature that never finds fulfillment in an actual relationship. Kudrow's timing is so good that she can make this pained woman very funny; each of her barbed little remarks is a zinger.

Lucia and Bill are the decent and highminded ones; they represent "the opposite of sex"—the opposite of promiscuous Dedee, who has no standards at all. But of course these poles will not remain apart; they become intertwined with one another and form a knot. The movie is a sex comedy, with little patience for fixed positions. Homosexuality and bisexuality (no fuss is made over either) just add to the comic possibilities. Roos moves with great speed and precision—he assumes that the audience can follow every curve he throws at it. He races from comedy to violent B-movie messiness and then back to comedy again, with frequent pauses for discussion and commentary.

Roos was shrewd enough to see that his bad girl, however funny, has only one dimension, so he leaves us with the real people—Bill, Lucia, and Matt, who turns out not to be so stupid after all, as well as with the gentle, persistent seducer played by Lyle Lovett, who is pursuing Lucia. For long periods, Dedee gets to hang around only as narrator. But she's such a wise guy, she narrates events that she doesn't even witness. She omnisciently comments on what's going on, comments on the means of filmmaking itself—telling us, for instance, not to be taken in by some sappy music, which builds false empathy for good old Bill. She's a one-woman Brechtian alienating device—our adviser, our confidante, our friendly amoralist. Roos plays with everything, and he teases us by making Dedee's cynicism so intimate. After all, she has a certain truth. Some of her outrageous demand on life passes into the virtuous people. They want happiness, too. And happiness doesn't lie in the opposite of sex.

NEW YORK POST, 5/29/98, p. 45, Thelma Adams

"She has 'detention' written all over her," schoolmarm Lucia (Lisa Kudrow) says about Dedee, the 17-year-old hellion played by Christina Ricci in "The Opposite of Sex."

The prickly Lucia tells Dedee that if the teen's a blessing in disguise, it's a very "good disguise." Dedee, in turn, rejects relationships, long-term or otherwise.

The Louisiana Lolita characterizes all emotional attachments as "The Opposite of Sex." And I thought the opposite of sex was chastity!

Don Roos' off-kilter sex comedy opens with Dedee fleeing her Cajun trailer park for the sedate Indiana suburb of her gay half-brother, a popular teacher from "In & Out" territory. Dedee and Bill (Martin Donovan) have no more in common than a dead father and some stray DNA.

Dedee moves in with Bill and seduces his foxy young lover, Matt (Ivan Sergei). The two then head for Hollywood after ransacking Bill's safe-deposit box.

Lucia (a welcome departure from Kudrow's cuddly "Friends" persona) and Bill give chase with Sheriff Carl Tippett (Lyle Lovett) in tow. A gun goes off and the plot goes awry in a way that's never quite as wild as the title leads us to expect.

Dedee, in revealing halters, shortshorts and skimpy bikinis that cry out for suntan oil slathered on hot skin, proceeds to ruin her half-brothers charmed life before putting it back together again.

First-time director Roos, best known for writing "Single White Female," structures the movie on the candid confessions of this sizzling bad girl. She's self-aware enough to admit that she's more than "scrappy and plucky," she's a bitch.

It's hard to imagine siblings as opposite as the zaftig Ricci and the patrician Donovan. The Hal Harley hero has played more sensitive males than Alan Alda. He's the ideal foil for Ricci's trailer trash.

Not since Elizabeth Taylor has a child actress made such a smooth transition to adult stardom. Ricci went from "Mermaids" to "Fear and Loathing in Las Vegas," from "Casper" to the forthcoming "Buffalo '66," from virgin to vixen.

Last year, Ricci was robbed of an Oscar nomination for supporting actress for a performance that rivaled co-stars (and fellow non-nominees) Sigourney Weaver and Joan Allen in "The Ice Storm." Ricci provided that drama's emotional center.

At movie's end, Dedee says, mockingly: "I never was the same after that summer." Audiences may never see Ricci the same way after this season, and that's a ferociously good thing.

SIGHT AND SOUND, 1/99, p. 51, Andy Medhurst

Teenager Dedee Truitt runs away from her Louisiana home, helped by her boyfriend Randy. She goes to Indiana to see her schoolteacher half-brother Bill, who lives with boyfriend Matt but is still grieving over his dead lover Tom. Dedee seduces Matt, confirming the low opinion already held of her by Lucia, Tom's sister. Telling Matt she is pregnant by him, Dedee persuades him to steal $10,000 from Bill and run away with her to LA.

Jason, a jealous ex-lover of Matt's, is so angered by Matt's departure he accuses Bill falsely of sexual harassment. Bill is suspended and becomes the target of local hostility. To try and clear his name, he goes to LA with Lucia in search of Dedee and Matt. They are followed by Carl, a sheriff from Indiana who secretly loves Lucia. Bill finds them, but Dedee tries further extortion, threatening to destroy Tom's ashes (which she had stolen earlier). Though she has married Matt, Randy (the baby's real father) reappears and runs off with Dedee. Carl and Lucia become closer. Randy and Dedee have a violent row and she accidentally shoots and kills him.

Matt and Dedee are reunited and flee to Canada. They enlist Jason for another blackmail attempt on Bill, but Bill refuses to pay and instead sets off after them, followed by Lucia and Carl. At the Canadian hideaway, Bill and Matt are reconciled but agree to part. Dedee almost dies giving birth, but both mother and baby survive. Dedee gives the baby to Bill while she does time in jail. Carl and the now-pregnant Lucia are an item and Bill finds romance with Dedee's parole officer. After her release, Dedee plans to venture off alone, but seems to hesitate ...

A potent cocktail of scandalous comedy and challenging sexual politics, *The Opposite of Sex* is a delight on every conceivable level. It falls short of perfection only by failing to include a few spikey dykes. The story twists and hisses like a rattlesnake, the dialogue is almost arrogantly smart and sharp, the values it espouses deliver a stinging slap in the kisser to every brand of moralising conservatism. And amid a uniformly excellent cast there is a central performance of jaw-dropping virtuosity from Christina Ricci, who with this film establishes herself as beyond question the finest actor of her generation. In her awesomely mature hands (she was only 17 when the film was made), Dedee becomes so much more than the monster she might have been. She's a streetwise vigilante in the sex wars, lashing out not from abstract vindictiveness but because that's how to survive in a world run by dumb men who keep their brains in their pants. Dedee is fully aware that her white-trash background means her intelligence will never be taken seriously, so she determines to succeed by unconventional means.

Writer-director Don Roos is clearly besotted with Dedee, to the extent that the film visibly droops when she's off-screen. He gives her lines so blissfully barbed that they draw blood every time. Many of these, in the film's biggest formal gamble, are in the form of Dedee's teasing, deceiving voice-over which toys with audience expectations much as Dedee toys with men. She lays out the whole story before us, warning early on that, "I don't have a heart of gold and I don't grow one later," tricking us with false sequences that are then corrected by what 'really' happened, and issuing splendidly biased pronouncements on life, love and interior design. At one glorious point she tells women in the audience that if their boyfriends groaned at a gay male kiss, then they're most likely closet cases themselves. No wonder, despite the film's unsparing burnout at the expense of certain homosexual sensitivities, the American gay audience has elevated Ricci to heroine status.

It isn't entirely a one-woman show. Lisa Kudrow dispels the suspicion that nobody from *Friends* can act outside the confines of that sitcom, turning Lucia into an impressively complex character. She memorably labels Dedee "the human tabloid', before her icy, snobbish anxieties are softened by circumstance. Her admission to Bill that she fears giving in to emotions is the film's best Ricci-free scene. Ivan Sergei captures Matt's essence as someone so widely regarded as gorgeous he never needs to turn his brain on, while Johnny Galecki (Darlene's put upon boyfriend in *Roseanne*) whines and snipes as an irresistibly weaselly blackmailer, perfectly pinpointing the snide petulance of a certain type of smalltown queen. The film scores a probable first in having one of its important plot developments hinge on his body piercings.

The film's moral centre, as opposed to the amoral earthquake epicentred in Ricci, is Bill, who could have been one of those sexlessly dull gay men Hollywood deems a 'positive image'. Happily Martin Donovan steers judiciously past that trap, demonstrating by his response to neighbourhood prejudice just how mealy-mouthed *In & Out* really was. When bricks come through his window, he turns them into a rockery. Way to go, girl, as I believe they say on *Ricki Lake*. He even gets to end up in the film's concluding romantic couple, a telling example of just how brazenly this film sets out its political stall. Queers stay happy, marriage is just a label, the only rules that matter are the ones that suit you and your loved ones, and preachy Christians end up shot dead—not a bad message for a mainstream film. Stir into that brew the phenomenal Ricci and you have not only the most fabulous film I've seen since *The Adventures of Priscilla Queen of the Desert* but also the best riposte to Tony Blair's 'focus on the family' imaginable.

TIME, 6/15/98, p. 73, Richard Corliss

This is a declaration of love: *The Opposite of Sex* is the smartest, edgiest, most human and handsomely acted romantic comedy in elephant years. It's got enough plot, in 100 spiky minutes, for an entire season of *Melrose Place* (if that show were totally weird and funny). It has two births, two deaths, five sexual affairs and no special effects. Writer-director Don Roos' film also has a gnarled wisdom about modern romance, straight and gay, that makes it a road-movie *Chasing Amy*, a *Heathers* for the whole postnuclear family.

The film offers seven characters in search of a spanking. The main miscreant is Dedee (Christina Ricci), 16-year-old tornado-park trash from Louisiana. Think of all the black widows and blond minxes from old film noir, give them the mouth of a Quentin Tarantino tough, and you have Dedee—not only in your face but down your throat. In the film's first 15 minutes, she desecrates her stepfather's grave, runs away from home with her one-testicled boyfriend, dumps him to visit her gay half brother, seduces his boyfriend and declares she's pregnant. To top it off, Dedee is the movie's narrator: a man eater who in other films would be gazed at and gossiped about, but here gets to tell us what we need to know. At least she's honest about herself. "I don't have a heart of gold," she says at the start. "And I don't grow one later, O.K.?" More than O.K., because Ricci embodies her with a brazenly unsentimental sass.

Here's a quick rundown. Bill (Martin Donovan), Dedee's half brother, has been nursing himself through mourning for his recently dead lover by romping with dishy, semidim Matt (Ivan Sergei), who may also be seeing the queeny Jason (Johnny Galecki). Dedee too has an old boyfriend (William Scott Lee) who keeps getting in the way. The only one not having sex is Lucia (Lisa Kudrow), Bills neighbor and his dead lover's sister. And the only "normal" guy around is ... Lyle Lovett. As we say, it's complicated.

The richest, strangest creature is Lucia, a twisted spinster who loves gay men (most especially her dead brother) with the desperation and security of caring for someone who can never accept her and thus never reject her. She thinks of herself, of course, as the one normal person. "You have a death wish," she tells Bill. "That's so selfish. I have one too, but I direct it toward others." Lucia could be just comedy's favorite device, the useful fool, but Kudrow makes her funny and sympathetic. Her body language is eloquent—she walks like a constipated stork when her arms and tight lips aren't folded in disapproval of the whole rotten world. Attend to the pain in Lucia's eyes and then to the bloom of sexual radiance when she finds a man who says the magic words, "Look for me in any crowded room. And I'll do likewise."

Formally playful and abubble with naughty wit, *The Opposite of Sex* is that rare grownup movie on the summer landscape. As Lucia says, "This is how we do things on the planet Maturia. We have much to teach you." Today's lesson: pay fond attention to these seven characters, who finally realize they are in search of one another. Somehow they will teach and touch you.

VILLAGE VOICE, 6/2/98, p. 166, Dennis Lim

As Dedee Truitt, the casually evil teen-vamp heroine of *The Opposite of Sex*, Christina Ricci delivers a performance untarnished by cuteness, providing in spades the edginess that the film so nakedly craves. As in the repellent *As Good As It Gets*, the humor in Don Roos's glib farce is of the "politically incorrect" variety—Dedee's acid tongue offends on cue—but the movie only sporadically funny, has an exaggerated sense of its own shock value. The insistent rudeness is also something of a disingenuous pose, a fashionably bitter coating for a blindly sweet center.

Too awkwardly paced to pass for screwball, the story stumbles along fairly predictably. When Dedee moves in with her gay half-brother Bill (Martin Donovan, as stoic as he was in Hal Hartley's films), she immediately sets to seducing his obtuse, mannequin-like new boyfriend, Matt (Ivan Sergei). Announcing that she's pregnant, she then makes off with Matt, a stash of Bill's money, and his late lover's ashes—much to the annoyance of the deceased's sister, embittered schoolmarm Lucia (an impressively dowdy Lisa Kudrow).

Imaginatively cast (Lyle Lovett plays the town sherrif), *The Opposite of Sex* is also distinguished by good performances across the board—surprising since every character is, as written, a borderline cartoon. Lucia is as thankless as female roles get, but Kudrow matches comic spark with unexpected gravity. Ricci's voiceover—a sarcastic running commentary flecked with self-reflexive taunts ("This part where I take the gun" It's like, *duh*, important.")—is a grating gimmick, which Roos runs into the ground. When she's onscreen, though, Ricci proves as fearless and ferociously intelligent as ever. She has the nerve and the smarts to remain unsympathetic, which seems like more than the film could handle.

Also reviewed in:
CHICAGO TRIBUNE, 6/19/98, Friday/p. J, Michael Wilmington
NEW YORK TIMES, 5/29/98, p. E18, Janet Maslin
VARIETY, 2/16-22/98, p. 58, Todd McCarthy
WASHINGTON POST, 6/26/98, p. B1, Stephen Hunter

ORGAZMO

An October Films release of a Rogue Pictures presentation in association with Kuzui Enterprises and MOP Worldwide of an Avenging Conscience production. *Executive Producer:* Mark Damon, Kaz Kuzui, and Noriaki Nakagawa. *Producer:* Fran Rubel Kuzui, Jason McHugh, and Matt Stone. *Director:* Trey Parker. *Screenplay:* Trey Parker. *Director of Photography:* Kenny Gioseffi. *Editor:* Trey Parker and Michael R. Miller. *Music:* Paul Robb. *Music Editor:* Ross Levinson and Johnny Caruso. *Sound:* Jon Ailetcher. *Casting:* Katy Wallin and T. Edwin Klohn. *Production Designer:* Tristan Paris Bourne. *Set Decorator:* Mandana Yamin. *Costumes:* Kristen Anacker. *Make-up:* Gyongyi Wilkins and Karen Sherer. *Stunt Coordinator:* Philip Tan. *Running time:* 95 minutes. *MPAA Rating:* NC-17.

CAST: Trey Parker (Elder Joe Young); Dian Bachar (Ben Chapleski, "Choda-Boy"); Robyn Lynne (Lisa, Joe's fiancée); Michael Dean Jacobs (Maxxx Orbison); Ron Jeremy (Clark, "Jizzmaster Zero"); Andrew W. Kemler (Rodgers); David Dunn (A-Cup, "Neutered Man"); Matt Stone (Dave the Lighting Guy); Toddy Walters (Georgi); Casey Lain (Candi); Juli Ashton (Saffi); Masao "Maki" San (G-Fresh, Sushi Bar Owner); Joseph Arsenault (Jimmy the Fish); Jeff Schubert (Tommy the Shark); Desi Singh (Randy the Guppy); Stan Sawicki (Robert White); Jacobus Rose (Homeowner); Susan Timlake (Housewife); Louise Rapport (Old Lady); Ken Merckx (Suzinski, Original Orgazmo); Kristen Anacker (Costumer); Buff Grey (Bilbo, Security Guard); Cathy Fitzpatrick (Older Porn Actress); Marcus Vaughn (White Stunt Cock); Joseph Moore (Ted, Black Stunt Cock); Anna Kazuki (Nasuko, "Ass-Fuck Twin"); Eve (Haruko, "Ass-Fuck Twin"); Jeffrey Bowman (Porn Actor); Fat Lady Stripper (T-Rex); Shalya Laveaux (Greek Porno Actress); John Marlo (Sancho); Farrell Timlake, Tony Mindel, Jason McHugh, (Porno Film Crew); Jerald A. Greenfield and Ron Hall (2nd Film

Crew);   Jamshid (Ben's Father);   Robert Lansing (Young Ben);   T. Edwin Klohn (Video Clerk);   Stanley L. Kaufman (Doctor);   Jill Kelly (Nurse);   James Pierre Comete (Young Boy); Erin Alain and Liane Adamo (Orgazmo Women);   Liane Adamo (Orgazmo Old Lady);   Horrac Vandegelden (Cop);   Eric Stough (Arrestee);   Miyu Natsuki and Mao Yamada (G-Fresh's Daughters);   Stephen Monas (Karaoke).

LOS ANGELES TIMES, 10/23/98, Calendar/p. 12, Kevin Thomas

Warning: Although an end-title disclaimer to Trey Parker's blissfully outrageous "Orgazmo" assures us that "no actual Mormons were used or abused in the making of this film," some members of the Church of Latter-Day Saints may be offended unless they approach the picture in the spirit of zany nonsense in which it was made. What's more, when a young Mormon (Parker) comes to the critical moment of truth in his life, he regains a sense of traditional values that turns him into a hero.

Parker's clean-cut Joe Young is doing his Mormon missionary tour of duty in Hollywood when he knocks on the door of porn-meister Maxxx Orbison (Michael Dean Jacobs). Maxxx is so impressed by Young's martial arts skills in dispatching a phalanx of security goons that he immediately envisions him as the star of his latest opus, a cheesy porno "Batman," in which Young would play the super-stud Orgazmo.

Young is shocked at the proposition until Maxxx antes his offer up to $ 20,000, which surely would go a long way toward paying for the kind of wedding his fiancee (Robyn Lynne Raab) craves. Young reluctantly—very reluctantly agrees—when Maxxx assures him that he will use a double in the sexual interludes.

When Orbison's porno becomes a phenomenal hit, Young's life is turned upside down. His engagement to marry is endangered, and he is thrown into a series of adventures when it becomes clear that Maxxx is involved in a wide range of unsavory underworld activities. As it happens, Orgazmo has a Robin-like sidekick (Dian Bachar), who's an inventor when he isn't acting in porn. Helpfully, he has just invented Orgazmorator, a fancy stun-gun that disarms its victims by zapping them into intense orgasms. So when Joe becomes disenchanted, to put it mildly, with the crooked Maxxx, he becomes a crime fighter, garbed like Batman and armed with the Orgazmorator.

All this is as silly as it sounds, but it's silly in the best sense—inspired wackiness evoking one laugh after another. Parker's no-budget 1994 debut feature, "Cannibal! The Movie," became a cult video before it was finally released theatrically earlier this month. It showed that Parker knew how to get a laugh though technically it was on the level of a home movie. Parker, who broke through with the cartoon comedy "South Park" when it aired on Comedy Central, here had enough of a budget to show that he is capable of developing and sustaining a brisk tempo amid nonstop off-the-wall antics.

Parker and his co-stars are fun, and his cast includes a number of people, including Bachar, who have worked with him on both sides of the camera right from the start of his career as a University of Colorado film student. "Orgazmo," which could be summed up as a martial arts spoof of porn filmmaking with an affectionate nod to comic book heroes, is a natural for midnight movie slots once it's completed its regular runs.

NEW YORK POST, 10/23/98, p. 44, Bill Hoffmann

There's nothing subtle about "Orgazmo," which features such startling images as a leg-humping German shepherd, a 350-pound porn actress in a bikini and a 90-pound weakling with a rubber penis on his head.

Of course, you don't expect an ounce of subtlety from Trey Parker—co-creator of the wildly popular "South Park" TV series—who wrote, directed and stars in this slapdash, NC-17 sex comedy.

What you do expect from Parker are laughs—lots of big, rude laughs. And while there's plenty of rudeness, with the exception of five or six clever gags, "Orgazmo"—a spoof on the porn industry—is a colossal dud.

Parker plays Joe Young, a wide-eyed young Mormon who, pounding the pavement of Hollywood to spread the word, stumbles onto a porno set where a foul-mouthed, mob-connected director hires him on the spot.

In need of cash for his upcoming wedding, the reluctant religiose agrees to join the film and play Capt. Orgazmo, a masked superhero who combats crazed sex offenders (one of whom is played by roly-poly porn legend Ron Jeremy).

The film is—God knows why—a box-office smash, prompting loads of sequels and growing grief for our hero, who has hidden his cash-cow profession from his prissy fiancee by telling her he's doing "Death of a Salesman."

When Joe bails out of the biz and the sleazy crew kidnaps his girl for leverage, our hero is forced to turn into a real-life Capt. Orgazmo to save the day.

With all of the censorship-skirting that Parker does on TV with "South Park," you'd think that, free of restraint, "Orgazmo" would be an adults-only scream.

But the infantile humor has absolutely no bite. One after another, the jokes fizzle.

The cast of young players is certainly energetic and willing, but the material is just too lame for anybody to shine.

Another surprise is the movie's NC-17 rating. Most of the sexual material here can be seen or heard on any given day on Howard Stern's show.

The rating recently caused October Films, the independent-film arm of Universal Pictures, to drop the picture. We don't handle smut, the brass at Universal said.

Hey, guys: You easily could have saved face with the free-speech crowd by simply saying: We just don't handle films that suck.

NEWSDAY, 10/23/98, Part II/p. B11, Jack Mathews

Irreverence alert: People who find no humor in the mocking of religion, particularly those who might feel personally assaulted by the line "I'm no superhero, I'm a Latter-day Saint," are advised to skip this review and its subject, Trey Parker's "Orgazmo."

Morality Alert: People repulsed by the very idea of porn movies, even if the industry is being playfully spoofed, must avoid going any farther here, or risk being turned into pillars of salt.

Taste Alert: If your ears burn at the use of the F-word as a noun, verb, adjective, pronoun or stage direction, save your ears. And if the thought of seeing a nearly naked 400-pound woman simulating sex disgusts you, save your eyes, too.

For those readers still with me—adults only, please—get ready for a good time. "Orgazmo" is a riot of bad taste and impropriety, and destined for the pantheon of midnight movie classics.

Written and directed by Trey Parker, co-creator of TV's scandalously popular "South Park" show, "Orgazmo" manages to send up Mormonism, pornography and the Batman franchise all at once. It's also a rather sweet love story, a buddy movie and a loving homage to the films of Ed Wood.

Parker stars as Elder Joe Young, a Mormon missionary who, while proselytizing door-to-door in suburban Los Angeles, happens onto the set of a porn movie where some goons commence to punch him out. In defending himself, Joe shows such spectacular skill at martial arts that the smarmy porn director (Michael Dean Jacobs) offers him $20,000 to take over the role of the film's title character, Orgazmo.

This dime-store Batman wears a pink outfit with a massive crotch bulge, and rescues women from thugs by zapping them with his Orgazmorator, a ray gun that disables humans (and watchdogs, as we'll see) by turning them orgasmic. The reward for the good efforts of Orgazmo and his Robinesque sidekick Chodo-Boy (Dian Bachar), a diminutive fellow festooned with phalli hiding a Batcave's worth of rockets and techno-gadgetry, is a roll in the hay with the victims.

Assured that a body double will take over for the close-ups, Joe accepts the role, figuring the quick payday will cover the cost of his wedding to fiancee Lisa (Robyn Lynne Raab), who's waiting for him back in Utah. But things get complicated when Orgazmo becomes an overnight cross-over sensation, and the porn ring kidnaps Lisa to force Joe to star in a series of sequels.

Now, it's up to Joe, as Orgazmo, with an operational Orgazmorator, and Choda-Boy at his side, to rescue a real damsel in distress.

If this sounds deliriously sophomoric, Parker would no doubt accept it as a compliment. It's like a Harvard Lampoon movie, done on a classmate's inheritance. It's well-shot and edited, even though its effects are meant to look cheap, and its actors, the fat lady included, have a perfect grasp of the film's deadpan humor.

The real surprise here, though no practicing Mormon is likely to agree, is that Joe and Lisa remain pure and uphold the church's core values. There are huge laughs at their expense, but at the end of the day, they are "Orgazmo's" true heroes.

SIGHT AND SOUND, 4/99, p. 52, Mark Sinker

Joe Young, a Mormon actor just arrived in Hollywood, stumbles on a porno film shoot. Set upon by director Maxxx Orbison's security goons, he impresses Orbison with his martial-arts skills, inadvertently winning the part of Captain Orgazmo, a superhero armed with the Orgazmerator, a ray gun that causes orgasms, who rescues hapless women from unwanted sex with porno villains. Joe is scrupulously religious but needs the money for his forthcoming marriage—he makes Orbison promise that penetration will always be taken care of by a "stunt cock".

Joe meets science graduate Ben Chapleski, who plays his faithful sidekick Choda Boy on screen and has invented a real-life Orgazmerator. After filming, Joe, Ben and two porno starlets visit a karaoke bar whose owner is being coerced by mobsters to pay protection money. Dressed as Orgazmo and Choda Boy, Joe and Ben assault the mobsters. *Captain Orgazmo* becomes the most successful film of all time and a sequel is required. Joe's fiancée Lisa comes to Hollywood, and discovers the nature of Joe's work.

He promises to give it all up, but the mobsters (headed by Orbison) kidnap Lisa to force him to continue. Joe and Ben become Orgazmo and Choda Boy once again, rescuing Lisa and defeating Orbison.

As a light-hearted spoof on the video-porn industry, martial-arts movies and superhero culture, *Orgazmo* is patchy, clumsy and almost unwatchable. Laughs are few and feebly silly at best; as satire, its bite is as non-existent as the acting. When the movie was awarded an adults-only NC-17 rating in the US, its makers orchestrated a fan-driven shout of internet complaint; they knew it to be bland enough for kids to view, the most explicit content being the rubbery dildos making up Choda Boy's uniform. *Orgazmo* has languished for a year or so, its marketability emerging only in the wake of first-time director Trey Parker's subsequent hit, the cult animated series *South Park*. The only interest to be derived here is archaeological. How could Parker have moved so swiftly from big-screen uselessness to wicked cartoon greatness (in a new Golden Age of small-screen animation, no less)? Are there any clues to future talent to be found here?

Not many. *South Park*'s unmistakable fridge-magnet-alphabet colour scheme has its precursor in Maxxx Orbison's vivid set dressing (but Gregg Araki's *Nowhere* takes a similar stylistic device into genuinely subversive delirium). In keeping with its theme—world-historical mayhem unleashed in Midwestern television-obsessed nowhere —*South Park* makes smart use of guest star voices: Isaac Hayes as Chef, George Clooney barking as Sparky the gay dog, "the chick from *Species*" (Natasha Henstridge) as the substitute teacher bundled into a rocket by terrorists and shot into the centre of the sun. By comparison, Orgazmo's wooden, in joke cameos from the barely known porn stars Ron Jeremy and Chasey Lain merely prove that whatever quasi-stellar body magic these names are supposed to carry dissolves with Parker directing them. And how is merely employing the people bearing these names clever or funny, on its own?

That said, there is one moment of grim daring in *Orgazmo*, which if it doesn't touch the many outrageous coups in *South Park,* at least touches something. It features that minor staple of the fetish-porn industry, an overweight woman engaged in sex. The character is called T-Rex (ho ho); the credits list the actress as "The Fat Lady Stripper", her over-dubbed voice a primitive version of Cartman's whine in *South Park,* the sex, as *Orgazmo* shows it, is jumping up and down on a bed. But it half-deliberately connects with a reality of freak-show exploitation and its semi-taboo presence in the continuum of human desire, and the sadness and cruelty involved in such exploitation, including when it's being mocked, as here. The intended comedy comes in the cutaways, to Joe's pop-eyed look of terror. If most aspects of the movie so far have been extremely shaky, Joe himself is a reasonably effective Mormon hero as likable stupe. In such an excessive, deliberately ugly scene, his one-note hick innocence is now revealed as manipulation—this is a hero played by the film's director, after all—and viewers are briefly flipped into unexpectedly edgy uncontrolled territory, with no guide as to appropriate response. If it's laughter, who exactly would we be laughing at?

The central characters in *South Park*'s otherwise adult shenanigans are innocents also, appalled eight-year-olds in a fallen world. But where in the cartoon this device enables a barrage of breathtaking taboo-busting, *Orgazmo* wastes its moment, and flops smugly back into nudge-and-wink nothingness. Save your money doing nothing or have a night in with Kenny.

VILLAGE VOICE, 11/3/98, p. 135, J. Hoberman

Trey Parker's low-budget *Orgazmo*, is a fish-out-of-water comedy that basically reverses Ross's scenario [the reference is to *Pleasantville*: see Hoberman's review of that film.], make the same point. A pair of innocent Mormons, Joe Young (Parker) and his fiancée (Robyn Lynn Raab), leave their black-and-white Utah for the lurid Technicolor of L.A.'s Unpleasantville.

As mighty as the Hollywood monkey for whom he is named, Young finds himself playing the title role in a superhero porn flick called *Orgazmo*. (Don't ask how he agrees; suffice to say, he preserves his chastity with the use of a "stunt cock.") Gary Ross may be girding his loins to fight the cultural wars, but Parker, co-perpetrator of last season's school-yard sensation *South Park*, has no such agenda. Like a 60's hippie, he's chosen to declare the war over and live as though the day were here.

A ridiculous soft-core kung-fu porn film about a ridiculous hard-core one, *Orgazmo* is the kind of movie that improves according to the lateness of the hour. The narrative structure suggests a sort of low-rent, nonmusical *Rocky Horror Picture Show* with Frank N. Furter played by a tediously sleazy porn producer (Michael Dean Orbison). Targeted at a somewhat older demographic, *Orgazmo* is less relentlessly scatological than *South Park*—which broke new ground in entertainment as the first cartoon series to feature a dancing turd. It's also marginally more concerned with sex, although, as Parker proudly told one interviewer, the hairy butts regularly presented to the camera are the "only nudity you see."

Less funny than it might have been—despite the perpetual sight gag of Orgazmo's sidekick Choda-Boy (Dian Bachar) wandering around in costume with willowy dildo planted on his head—Orgazmo was made at the same time as *Boogie Nights* and, masticating similar material (stunt cock, "happy ending," and all) succeeds as a travesty *avant la lettre*. So was the movie branded with an NC-17, rather than *Boogie Nights's* R, because of the repeated Mormon references to their "Heavenly Father"? It's a question to take up with those good folks in Pleasantville.

Also reviewed in:
CHICAGO TRIBUNE, 10/23/98, Friday/p. G, Monica Eng
NEW YORK TIMES, 10/23/98, p. E26, Stephen Holden
VARIETY, 9/22-28/97, p. 40, Emanuel Levy

OUT OF THE PAST

A Zeitgeist Films/Unapix Films release of a Jeff Dupre production.   *Executive Producer:* Andrew Tobias.   *Producer:* Jeff Dupre *Director:* Jeff Dupre.   *Screenplay:* Michelle Ferrari. *Director of Photogrphy:* Buddy Squires.   *Editor:* George O'Donnell and Toby Shimin.   *Music:* Matthias Gohl.   *Narrator:* Linda Hunt.   *Running time:* 64 minutes.   *MPAA Rating:* Not Rated.

VOICES: Stephen Spinella (Michael Wigglesworth); Gwyneth Paltrow (Sarah Orne Jewett); Cherry Jones (Annie Adams Fields); Edward Norton (Henry Gerber); Leland Gantt (Bayard Rustin).

NEW YORK POST, 7/31/98, p. 44, Larry Worth

Ever since Ellen DeGeneres announced her lesbian leanings, people have questioned why she can't keep private things private. A new and thought-provoking documentary offers a pretty good answer.

Jeff Dupre's "Out of the Past" convincingly argues that gay history is continually hushed up. Accordingly, those willing to be counted always start from square one.

Case in point is Kelli Peterson, a gay Salt Lake City high schooler who met after classes with a dozen gay students. They applied for club status in 1995, and ended up battling Utah's state legislature.

Intercut with Peterson's saga are equally sad tales of Boston's answer to Gertrude Stein and Alice B. Toklas, a World War I vet jailed for starting a gay rights group and a civil rights leader being blackmailed into obscurity due to his homosexuality.

Narrated by Gwyneth Paltrow, Edward Norton and Linda Hunt, the accounts are both eye-opening and moving. And though it concludes too neatly, "Out of the Past" demonstrates why it earned top documentary honors at Sundance this year.

Even more impressive is the 27-minute film accompanying it Todd Haynes' 1993 gem, "Dottie Gets Spanked." Haynes, the director of "Poison" and "Safe," weaves a bittersweet tale about a lonely little boy's obsession with the Lucille Ball-like heroine of a sitcom.

Together, "Past" and "Dottie" dovetail into a double feature that smartly sidesteps polemics. Rather than pleading for gay tolerance, they're eloquent arguments for plain old compassion.

NEWSDAY, 7/31/'98, Part II/p. B12, John Anderson

1683, Harvard College teacher Michael Wigglesworth committed to his diaries the sheet-soaking tensions between his fervent religiosity and his suppressed gay yearnngs. Shortly thereafter, he published the 17th-Century bestseller "The Day of Doom," a cautionary fire-and-brimstone tract about divine judgment and secret desires.

In 1996, the state legislature of Utah—which was, last time anyone checked, still part of these United States—passed a law banning all extra-curricular clubs from its schools, rather than allow the Gay Straight Alliance to meet at Salt Lake City's East High.

You have to admit that, when the talk turns to traditional values, sexual hypocrisy is one of the most hallowed. But Utah isn't special in any way, not according to Jeff Dupre's "Out of the Past," a documentary that begins with lesbian high schooler Kelli Peterson's efforts with the Gay Straight Alliance and traces a line of perverted righteousness straight back to Wigglesworth.

Along the way, with narration provided by actress Linda Hunt (other voices include those of Gwyneth Paltrow, Edward Norton and Cherry Jones), we're acquainted with some of the notable gays of American culture—Walt Whitman, Willa Cather, Cole Porter, Bessie Smith—and some of the more fascinating episodes in American sexual/political life, including the weird spiritual alliance between Adam Clayton Powell Jr.and Strom Thurmond over civil-rights leader Bayard Rustin's gayness.

Cutting back and forth between historical anecdote and Peterson's frustrated campaign, Dupre makes the powerful, simple point that the erasing of gays from American history has made every effort for liberation new; you need a past to establish a present and one of the more insidious side effects of homophobia has been to erase that past. By casting his entertaining, educating film with all these figures from history, he gives people like Peterson a sense of tradition and demolishes the argument that gayness is not part of the fabric of national life.

In a revival of another great American tradition—the double bill—"Out of the Past" is being shown with a mini-masterpiece: "Dottie Gets Spanked," a virtual period piece made several years ago by Todd Haynes for a PBS series called "TV Families." Haynes, director of "Poison," "Safe" and the upcoming "Velvet Goldmine," tells the (perhaps) quasi-autobiographical story of 6-year-old Steven (Evan Bonifant), a lonely little boy obsessed with Lucy-like TV star Dottie Frank (Julie Halston). When he wins a contest to visit the set of the show—and sees Dottie being sitcom-spanked by her TV husband (Adam Arkin)—it crystallizes the mysterious/erotic urges that Dottie's been provoking all along.

Haynes never resorts to cliche. Steven's father (Robert Pall) is worried, but kind, his mother (Harriet Harris) supportive without being smothering. The other kids are predictably cruel ("My sister says that you're a feminino!") but "Dottie's" denouement is one of the more poignant and intelligent moments in recent cinema. And with "Out of the Past," it makes, for a delightful, enlightening double feature, one that perhaps the Utah state legislature should take a look at. Maybe at, one of their closeted—I mean, closed-door—meetings.

VILLAGE VOICE, 8/4/98, p. 102, Dennis Lim

The ostensible subject of Jeff Dupre's somber 65-minute documentary (an Audience Award winner at Sundance) Is 17-year-old Kelli Peterson, who caused a furor in 1996 when she founded a "Gay-Straight Alliance" at her Utah high school. Dupre intercuts Peterson's story with historical segments (narrated by name actors, including Edward Norton and a needlessly haughty Gwyneth Paltrow) that detail the lives of forgotten gay and lesbian figures (17th century cleric Martin Wigglesworth, 19th-century novelist Sarah Orne Jewett). The Idea, an admirable one, is to evoke a hidden history of activism, but, as well-researched as Dupre's documentary is, his execution desperately locks imagination. *Out of the Past* seems even drab alongside the film it's being paired with for theatrical release: *Dottie Gets Spanked*, Todd Haynes's exquisite 1993 short, about the formative obsessions and fantasies of a six-year-old boy.

Also reviewed in:
NEW YORK TIMES, 7/31/98, p. E22, Stephen Holden
VARIETY, 2/9-15/98, p. 72, Emanuel Levy

OUT OF SIGHT

A Universal Pictures release of a Jersey Films production. *Executive Producer:* Barry Sonnenfeld and John Hardy. *Producer:* Danny DeVito, Michael Shamberg, and Stacey Sher. *Director:* Steven Soderbergh. *Screenplay:* Scott Frank. *Based on the novel by:* Elmore Leonard. *Director of Photography:* Elliot Davis. *Editor:* Anne V. Coates. *Music:* David Holmes. *Sound:* Paul Ledfore. *Sound Editor:* Larry Blake. *Casting:* Francine Maisler. *Production Designer:* Gary Frutkoff. *Art Director:* Phil Messina. *Set Designer:* Lauren Cory, Keith P. Cunningham, and Mary Finn. *Set Dresser:* Tristan P. Bourne, Harry Frierson, James E. Hurd, Jr., Alexander Kirst, and Chris Patterson. *Special Effects:* Eric Roberts. *Costumes:* Betsy Heimann. *Make-up:* Kathrine James. *Make-up (Jennifer Lopez):* Margot Boccia. *Make-up (Ving Rhames):* Anita Gibson. *Stunt Coordinator:* G.A. Aguilar. *Running time:* 120 minutes. *MPAA Rating:* R.

CAST: George Clooney (Jack Foley); Jim Robinson (Bank Employee); Elgin Marlow (Bank Customer); Donna Frenzel (Teller/Loretta); Manny Suarez (Cop #1/Bank); Keith Hudson (Cop #2/Bank); Luis Guzman (Chino); Paul Soileau (Lulu); Scott Allen (Pup); Catherine Keener (Adele); Ving Rhames (Buddy Bragg); Susan Hatfield (Parking Lot Woman); Jennifer Lopez (Karen Sisco); Dennis Farina (Marshall Sisco); Steve Zahn (Glenn Michaels); Don Cheadle (Maurice Miller); Brad Martin (White Boxer); Albert Brooks (Richard Ripley); James Black (Himey); Wendell B. Harris, Jr. (Daniel Burdon/FBI); Chuck Castleberry (Library Guard); Chic Daniel (Fourt FBI Man); Connie Sawyer (Old Elevator Lady); Phil Perlman (Old Elevator Gent); Keith Loneker (White Boy Bob); Isaiah Washington (Kenneth); Paul Calderon (Raymond Cruz); Gregory H. Alpert (Officer Grant); Viola Davis (Moselle); Mark Brown (Ripley Personnel); Sandra Ives (Receptionist); Joe Hess (Ripley Guard); Betsy Monroe (Waitress/Celeste); Wayne Pere (Executive Guy/Philip); Joe Chrest (Executive Guy/Andy); Joe Coyle (Executive Guy #3); Nancy Allen (Midge); Stephen M. Horn (Federal Marshal).

CHRISTIAN SCIENCE MONITOR, 6/26/98, p. B3, David Sterritt

"Out of Sight" comes from director Steven Soderbergh, who flew to fame with "sex, lies & videotape" a decade ago. The new movie renews a question that has dogged his career ever since: Will he ever duplicate the impact of his first picture, or will his subsequent films lie forever in its shadows?

Soderbergh has tried just about everything to keep his reputation fresh with films like "Kafka," a surrealistic thriller, and "King of the Hill" a Depression-era drama.

Among his remaining options is the Wisecracking Action Picture, which describes the film reasonably well. The hero (George Clooney) is a bank robber on the lam; the heroine (Jennifer Lopez) is a tough-minded policewoman with a soft spot for him.

Soderbergh's screenplay serves up offbeat dialogue and wry ironies, but his self-created Everest of "sl&v" is still waiting to be conquered.

LOS ANGELES TIMES, 6/26/98, Calendar/p. 1, Kenneth Turan

Hollywood has been doing business with Elmore Leonard for decades, and the novelist has quite a store of amusing stories about the unmitigated fiascoes the studios have turned his novels into. Like the time Richard Widmark came up to him on the set of "The Moonshine War" and said, "What's it like to hear your lines all fouled up?" Only he didn't exactly say "fouled."

Those tales, however, have begun to show their age. Recently, in the kind of Hollywood ending reality rarely provides, the movies in general, and screenwriter Scott Frank in particular, have figured Leonard out. A quartet of diverting movies has been made from his books, including Quentin Tarantino's "Jackie Brown" and Paul Schrader's "Touch." Frank, however, has written the best two: First came "Get Shorty," directed by Barry Sonnenfeld, and now, its engaging and consummately entertaining successor, "Out of Sight."

Like a benevolent character in a fairy tale, Leonard has been good to those who've treated him right. His work is a key inspiration behind Tarantino's accomplishments; he gave Schrader an unlooked-for sense of humor and boosted Travolta's career with "Get Shorty." Similarly, "Out of Sight," a wised-up, insouciant love story between a deputy U.S. marshal and the veteran bank robber she's trying to incarcerate, will be a boon to all concerned.

As Jack Foley, whose 200-plus bank robberies place him at the top of the FBI computer, George Clooney is suave and debonair in a role that should silence doubts about his movie star status. And Jennifer Lopez, an actress who can be convincingly tough and devastatingly erotic, uses the part of a law enforcement agent who only gets emotional about her Sig Sauer .38 to solidify her position as a woman you can confidently build a film around.

Being helped even more will be director Steven Soderbergh, whose erratic career after "sex, lies, and videotape" has included self-indulgent misadventures like the unwatchable "Schizopolis." His work in "Out of Sight," however, turns out to be impeccable. He has brought together the year's most diverse and exciting supporting cast (Ving Rhames, Don Cheadle, Dennis Farina, Albert Brooks, Nancy Allen, Catherine Keener, Isaiah Washington, Steve Zahn, Luis Guzman, newcomer Keith Loneker and Michael Keaton in an unbilled cameo) and well understands that a level of criminal reality in Leonard is the key to setting up the comedy.

For what makes the novelist irresistible, aside from his unmatched gift for playful language, is his pleasure in finding it in unlikely places. Leonard's books are Oscar Wilde behind bars, drawing-room comedies set amid the bemused venality of a harsh criminal world. Serious bad guys and almost competent cons crowd his pages as both heroes and villains, and a pleasing combination of tension and humor is one of his trademarks.

Frank has proven himself expert at presenting and framing Leonard's bemused wackiness on screen. Large chunks of the novelist's dialogue get the call, but Frank has also adroitly juggled the book's characters and plot elements and polished a tone that's more romantic than the book's elegiac, somewhat bittersweet mood.

After a prologue that shows how he got there, we hook up with Foley in Florida's medium-security Glades Correctional Institution. With the help of his ex-wife and magician's assistant Adele (Keener) and pals Buddy and Glenn (Rhames, Zahn) from an earlier incarceration at Lompoc, the shrewd Foley is about to piggyback onto someone else's escape attempt.

Karen Sisco (Lopez) is up at Glades too, delivering some paperwork. She stumbles on the escape and ends up, in a seriously bizarre movie first date, sharing the trunk of a getaway car with an apologetic Foley, comparing thoughts on movies and life with the unwashed desperado as casually as if they were flirting over a pair of cappuccinos.

All first dates have to end, even ones in car trunks, but, cynical as they are, both Foley and Sisco have the odd feeling they'd like to see each other again, something which neither her father (Farina) nor his friend Buddy can quite understand. "Why," Buddy asks, far from unreasonably, "would you want to have cocktails with a woman who wants to shoot you?"

Making this second date more amusingly difficult to pull off is Sisco's determination to rearrest Foley and his eagerness to reach Detroit and get to work on a potentially big score involving the homicidal Maurice "Snoopy" Miller (Cheadle) and a wealthy white-collar criminal (a charming Brooks) everyone knows from Lompoc.

As always with the best of Leonard, it's the journey, not the destination, that counts, and director Soderbergh has let it unfold with dry wit and great skill. Making adroit use of complex flashbacks, freeze frames and other stylistic flourishes, he's managed to put his personal stamp on the film while staying faithful to the irreplaceable spirit of the original. Both he and Frank have learned the main lesson of Elmore Goes to Hollywood: What becomes a legend most is, quite simply, respect.

NEW YORK, 7/13/98, p. 42, David Denby

In the extraordinarily entertaining *Out of Sight* George Clooney works for the first time with a smart script and a good director, and his handsome, mocking face, with its chin-down, saucer-eyed stare, suddenly seems the equipment of a star. Clooney plays Jack Foley, a bank robber with the temperament of a con artist. Jack is cunning and smooth, by instinct nonviolent, but he's still a loser who has spent too many years in prison. Something screws Jack up—a lack of ruthlessness, perhaps, or a too-great enjoyment of what he is doing. Jack's buddy (Ving Rhames) picks him up when he breaks out of the pen. When the two of them are confronted by a beautiful federal marshal, Karen Sisco (Jennifer Lopez), they throw her in the trunk of the car, and Jack, hiding, climbs in with her. The movie comes to a halt, and the most outrageous romantic scene in years plays itself out with leisurely calm. Jack and Karen discuss movies; they discuss life. Something in Jack's soothing manner and touch works for Karen: She falls in love with the man she is supposed to apprehend. And this woman is one tough cookie who annihilates any other man who makes a move on her.

Once again, screenwriter Scott Frank has successfully adapted Elmore Leonard (Frank also did *Get Shorty*). Steven Soderbergh, new to the comedy-thriller genre, directs in a style that might be called gentled Quentin Tarantino. As in *Pulp Fiction*, there's a warming friendship between black and white criminals at the center of the movie, and the story moves backward and forward (we see the same people at different times in their criminal careers and in different prisons). The gentler element is Soderbergh's way of stopping his movie now and then, pausing and just observing, as if he were trying to decide what to do next. The contemplative quality is sexy: Even though there's only one sex scene in *Out of Sight*, the movie is erotically imagined. The characters size one another up; they even dream about one another. These encounters move ahead on sheer personality and verve, and Jack and Karen have a love affair that takes place in glances and fantasies as much as in bed. Soderbergh has done something truly original: He has proved that a comedy-thriller can take place as much in the ideas people have about one another as in what they do. Soderbergh, who started out earnestly, with *Sex, Lies, and Videotape*, has become something of a hipster. The story of Karen and Jack and their friends plays itself out with satisfying twists and turns, and when violence comes, it is far more shocking than in most movies. When these people fire their guns, the bullets really hurt.

NEW YORK POST, 6/26/98, p. 53, Thelma Adams

Somewhere between Steven Soderbergh's 1989 indie cash cow "sex, lies, & videotape" and the navel-gazing of last year's "Schizopolis," the maverick director's career seemed to be heading "Out of Sight."

Now, little Stevie's back! His first glossy studio pic is a giddy romantic caper. "Out of Sight" pairs George Clooney and Jennifer Lopez in the most purely entertaining movie of a lackluster summer.

When was the last time you saw an actor and actress set the screen ablaze? We're talking Chemistry 101; we're talking nuclear biology. And don't make any excuses for Anne Heche and Harrison Ford, the Avis of sexy duos.

Clooney and Lopez's con and cop fall in lust in Scott Frank's foxy Elmore Leonard adaptation. Frank was the screenwriter who made "Get Shorty" such a lark—and "Sight" is less labored than "Shorty."

Like Frank, Soderbergh has a relaxed approach to the material. It's a tack that would have helped "Jackie Brown," Quentin Tarantino's overwrought take on Leonard's "Rum Punch."

Soderbergh does the seemingly impossible: He strips Clooney of his I'm-so-cute-it-hurts-me-more-than-it-hurts-you smirk. In the process, the canny director finally turns Clooney into a big-screen star.

In typical snappy Leonard patter, charming bank robber Foley comforts a female bank teller: "First time you're being robbed? You're doing great. Just smile, Loretta." Is it any wonder she drops her cash drawers?

Foley's no easy match for U.S. Marshal Karen Sisco (Lopez). Perched on the opposite side of the law, Sisco is a woman with a taste for men as dangerous as her trusty shotgun.

Lopez's charismatic Sisco always gets her man. She meets Foley during a prison break—his. Foley's pal Buddy (Ving Rhames) tosses the law gal in a car trunk with the escaped con.

After getting up close and personal with Foley and the spare tire in one of the flirtiest scenes since "It Happened One Night," Sisco follows the gentleman thief to the end of the movie. Is it love or just the law?

What makes Leonard such a kick is that the characters aren't superhuman. They're shleppers like us. Their flaws make them endearing and frustrating—and that includes the well-crafted supporting players.

Rhames, Don Cheadle, Albert Brooks and Dennis Farina form a sharp ensemble. Catherine Keener is pitch-perfect as Foley's ex-wife. On the eve of his jailbreak, she blithely tells him over the phone, "Oh, honey, you try not to get shot," as if he were just stopping for milk at the 7-Eleven on his way home from work.

Novelist Leonard's advice to Soderbergh was just have fun. He listened, "Out of Sight" is outtasite, baby.

NEWSDAY, 6/26/98, Part II/p. B3, Jack Mathews

With his novels and screenplays, crime writer Elmore Leonard has been a major contributor to top-end escapist Hollywood entertainment for more than 30 years. But no one, including Leonard, has done his work as much justice as screenwriter Scott Frank and the directors of the 1995 "Get Shorty" and "Out of Sight."

Frank adapted both novels, and with the same delicate, reverent touch. He burrowed into Leonard's occasionally serpentine prose and found the humor, eccentricities, character and sharp dialogue that give the author his unique touch, reshaping the stories for the second medium without losing the style of the first.

The stories are very different. "Get Shorty," directed by Barry Sonnenfeld, is a spoof of Hollywood's longtime affection for mobsters, where "Out of Sight," directed by Steven Soderbergh, is more a parody of star-crossed lovers. And where "Get Shorty" is told in a fairly straightforward narrative, "Out of Sight" craftily intercuts two time periods.

The foreground story of "Out of Sight" follows career bank robber Jack Foley (George Clooney), his partner-in-crime Buddy Bragg (Ving Rhames), and Karen Sisco (Jennifer Lopez), the federal marshal kidnaped by the pair after they escape from a Florida prison. She, in turn, escapes from them, but not before Foley's enormous charm has softened her enough to wonder if she can bring in a man she's falling in love with.

The background story so carefully revisited takes us back two years to a prison in California where Foley, Buddy and their airhead pal Glenn (Steven Zahn) begin to plot a post-parole burglary of fellow convict Richard Ripley (a bald and barely recognizable Albert Brooks). Ripley is a multimillionaire Wall Street cheat (think: Michael Milken) who claims to have $5 million worth of uncut diamonds in his Michigan home. Wanting in on a taste of Ripley's loot is the homicidal hustler Snoopy Miller (Don Cheadle).

Soderbergh, doing his most assured work since "King of the Hill," moves the action fluidly back and forth between the California and Florida scenes, bringing all of the plot and character nuances together by the time the cast reconnoiters Ripley's manse in Michigan.

"Out of Sight" is laced with memorably off-beat scenes, beginning with a drawn-out sequence in the trunk of a car, where the escaped Foley gets to know his kidnap victim. There's another in a hotel's penthouse bar where Karen Sisco rejects the awkward come-ons of some out-of-town salesmen before being swept up in the aura of Jack Foley. This encounter, which ends up in her hotel room, ranks among the best of playfully erotic love scenes.

Clooney's never had a better showcase for his relaxed, coolly romantic manner; he shows genuine charisma in a role that is otherwise as weightless as air. But Lopez is his equal. If "Out of Sight" finds an audience, this is Lopez' breakout performance.

She was terrific in "Selena," as the innocent Tejano singer, and Oliver Stone's film noir "U-Turn," playing a smoldering femme fatale. Here, she strikes a happy compromise, combining intelligence, confidence and sexuality in a package that should be equally appealing to men and women.

The performances are all highlights. There isn't a character actor around with more presence than Rhames, Cheadle throws a few twists into the formula character of sociopathic hood, and Zahn is hilarious as the zonked and under-appreciated Glenn.

Dennis Farina, John Travolta's comic foil in "Get Shorty," has some funny moments as Karen's overly protective father. And there are sharp, unbilled cameos by Michael Keaton, as Karen's married boyfriend, and Samuel L. Jackson, as Foley's latest conspirator.

Quentin Tarantino may have made over Leonard's "Rum Punch" in his own likeness (as "Jackie Brown"), but with "Get Shorty" and "Out of Sight," he's been done proud. If they keep this up, Leonard may never have to soil his hands in Hollywood again.

NEWSWEEK, 6/29/98, p. 66, David Ansen

Inside the trunk of a car is an odd place to begin a romance. But that's where George Clooney and Jennifer Lopez are thrown together early on in "Out of Sight." He's veteran bank robber Jack Foley, and she's no-nonsense Federal Marshal Karen Sisco. Jack had to kidnap Karen when she almost ruined his clever escape from a Florida prison. With his partner in crime (Ving Rhames) at the wheel of the get-away car, Jack chats up his captive in the trunk, impressed by both her taste in movies and her astonishing calm in the face of danger. Sexy, easy to talk to, this gun-toting woman is someone he'd be seriously interested in—under ordinary circumstances.

Unfortunately for Jack and Karen—but lucky for us—there are no ordinary circumstances in "Out of Sight." It gets quirkier, funnier and sexier as it goes, as the bank robber vows to stay out of jail and the marshal vows to capture him—though she can't say for sure whether she wants him for the state or for herself.

"Out of Sight," a smart, tasty adaptation of the Elmore Leonard novel, is a smashing return to form for director Steven Soderbergh, who's had trouble finding his footing since "sex, lies and videotape." His screenwriter, Scott Frank, demonstrated in "Get Shorty" that he knew how to transfer Leonard's grittily loopy voice to the screen. He succeeds again here, though the tone of Soderbergh's comedy is less broad, the colors less primary, than in Barry Sonnenfeld's 1995 movie.

What Soderbergh and Frank both richly appreciate is Leonard's ability to make every character, big or small come to pungent life. Jack's story takes him from prisons in California and Florida to wintry Detroit, where he's involved in a diamond heist at the home of a billionaire (Albert Brooks). Along the way he picks up an unwanted partner—Steve Zahn, hilarious as a stoned, hapless petty criminal—and such dangerous rivals as ex-con Don Cheadle and his weird, threatening brother Isaiah Washington. "Out of Sight" is packed with juicy, vivid performances. In addition to the above, there's Catherine Keener as Jack's ex-wife, a magician's assistant, and Dennis Farina as Karen's proud dad. The comic timing of this superb ensemble is a joy to behold.

And just as one was beginning to doubt whether Clooney would make the leap from TV star to movie star, he comes up with a performance that mixes charm, edge and rage in beguiling fashion. Looking leaner and hungrier and less pleased with himself Clooney turns Jack Foley into a memorable rogue hero, a smart crook who's never been smart enough to stay out of the joint. And he is beautifully matched by Lopez, who also contributes a personal best by making the tough, sexy Fed—a heroine who could have seemed utterly implausible—both credible and irresistible. The chemistry is palpable. What begins, in that car trunk, as one of the weirder cute-meets in movie history, deepens significantly by the time these two connect on a snowy night in a Detroit hotel room—a brief encounter that's poignant, hot and hard to forget.

SIGHT AND SOUND, 12/98, p. 55, John Wrathall

While escaping from a Florida prison, bank robber Jack Foley kidnaps federal marshal Karen Sisco. Hidden together in the boot of the getaway car (driven by his partner Buddy), Jack and Karen feel an unmistakable sexual attraction. But when they change cars, Karen recognises another of Jack's accomplices, ex-con Glenn Michaels, and persuades him to help her escape. The FBI track Jack to a hotel in Miami but, after a tantalising brush with Karen in the lobby, he escapes. Jack and Buddy go to Detroit to scout out their last big crime: stealing uncut diamonds hidden in the mansion of financier Richard Ripley, whom they met in Lompoc (another jail) while he was doing time for insider dealing. But they discover that Glenn is also planning the same job, in collaboration with another Lompoc alumnus, the psychopathic Maurice "Snoopy" Miller.

After Karen arrives in Detroit, Jack finds her at her hotel and they spend the night together. Against their better judgement, Jack and Buddy team up with Maurice and his gang. Tipped off by Glenn, Karen follows them to Ripley's house. Jack finds the uncut diamonds and escapes with Buddy But, unwilling to leave Ripley and Ripley's girlfriend at the mercy of Maurice, Jack returns to the house. In a shootout, Karen kills Maurice, and wounds Jack when he refuses to surrender. Karen escorts Jack back to jail, arranging for him to travel with a convict who has escaped from prison nine times.

Like *Get Shorty*, *Out of Sight* is adapted from an Elmore Leonard novel by Scott Frank and produced by Danny DeVito's Jersey Films (and also features Dennis Farina in a bit part). But while *Get Shorty*'s director Barry Sonnenfeld played Leonard's material as farce, Steven Soderbergh, in this infinitely more sophisticated follow-up, plays it as romantic comedy.

From Jack and Karen's tantalising first encounter in a car boot, washed in the red of the brake lights, the film is fuelled by the sexual tension between the two leads, as opposed to any great suspense about who is going to end up with Ripley's diamonds. Seizing their chance after too many bad films (the nadirs being *Batman & Robin* for him, *Anaconda* for her), George Clooney and Jennifer Lopez are both much more interesting and real here than they have been allowed to be in the past.

With his slicked-back greying hair and bullish walk, Clooney's Jack is all the cooler for being slightly seedy (in the book, Jack is in his late forties). But he's also quite a poignant figure, aware of his shortcomings (Do you know anyone who's done one last score and gone on to lead the good life?" he wonders), while at the same time unable to resist over-reaching himself. Meanwhile, despite her fabulous Bond-girl accoutrements (tight leather coat, shiny weapons), Lopez succeeds in humanising Karen. Her handgun, for instance, is a gift from her doting father (Farina), and her verve as a law-enforcement officer is offset by her dawning realisation that she'd rather have an affair with Jack than send him to prison. The supporting characters, a feature of any Leonard adaptation, are equally engaging, notably Ving Rhames as Jack's born-again Christian accomplice Buddy, who insists on confessing every job in advance to his sister; Steve Zahn as the feckless dopehead Glenn, in way over his head; and an uncredited Michael Keaton as Ray Nicolette, the same FBI agent he played in *Jackie Brown*.

The real star of *Out of Sight*, however, is director Steven Soderbergh. Previously fêted for the intellectual rather than visual qualities of his films, he rises to the challenge of his most mainstream assignment to date with a dazzling display of hip cinematic style. His battery of freeze frames, jump cuts and zooms might seem irritating in less confident hands, but they flow perfectly in tandem with the wonderful, 70s-style score. The flashback-dependent plot structure might not seem radical in the wake of *Pulp Fiction* or *Jackie Brown*, but, as he did with *The Underneath*, Soderbergh experiments with more short-term flashes back and forwards, to events only minutes in the past or future. Aided by veteran British editor Anne V. Coates, Soderbergh uses this intriguing technique to best effect during the tantalising sequence in a hotel bar where Karen and

Jack finally come face to face. Their flirtation is intercut with what would conventionally be the next scene—making love in the hotel room—in a sly and strangely poignant reversal of the famous sex scene in *Don't Look Now* (1973). Another 30 years from now, Soderbergh's sleight of hand may well seem as dated as *The Thomas Crown Affair* (1968), but for the time being, it looks very good indeed.

VILLAGE VOICE, 6/30/98, p. 138, Amy Taubin

Steven Soderbergh's most seductive film since *sex, lies, and videotape, Out of Sight* is also the best Elmore Leonard adaptation ever-jazzier and more affecting than the overblown *Jackie Brown*, the too cute *Get Shorty*, and the routine *52 Pick-Up*. Soderbergh balances a visual style that's part hyperrealism and part comic-book with a stubbornly romantic humanism that puts character front and center. But what's most distinctive about *Out of Sight* is its fluid narrative structure—the way it sashays in and out of flashback, memory, and fantasy sequences.

This doubling back and zooming forward not only keeps you on your toes, it also gives the film a dream-like edge, making it more like a map of desire than a cops-and-robbers action adventure. I don't want to push this too far. *Out of Sight* isn't as haunting a trip through the unconscious as, say, Tourneur's *Out of the Past* (but then, what is?); Soderbergh's sensibility isn't paranoid enough for noir. Even more than Leonard, whose hard-boiled endings deflate his otherwise excellent beach reads, Soderbergh wants to show you a good time.

Jack Foley (George Clooney), a gentleman bank robber who has spent half his life behind bars, breaks out of a Florida jail only to run smack into the gun-toting arms of federal marshal Karen Sisco (Jennifer Lopez). Foley and his partner Buddy Bragg (Ving Rhames), who's driving the getaway car, overpower Karen and throw her in the trunk. Jack climbs in too. Absurdly close quarters and crossed purposes turn chemical attraction into *l'amour fou*. For the rest of the movie, love vies with professionalism: Karen tries to capture Jack before he can make the biggest heist of his life, while what they both really want to do is get inside each other's pants.

Surprise! Clooney can act and so can Lopez. As he proved with Andie MacDowell and James Spader in his debut feature, Soderbergh is a magician when it comes to getting self-conscious actors to give up their protective tricks and mannerisms. Not once during *Out of Sight* does Clooney fall back on that little-boy head cocking-and-smiling routine. There's no strain in his performance. What we see on the screen is a character who's physically comfortable in his own skin but psychologically driven by obsession.

Soderbergh lets the camera linger on the iconic aspects of his stars's physicality: Clooney's big head and blunt features, the voluptuous curve of Lopez's torso (not even R. Crumb could do her ass justice). The two of them don't, in fact, share very many scenes (anticipation is the name of the game), but when they're together they seem extremely well matched. In profile, they even look alike, and the physical similarity partly accounts for the sense of instant recognition (the love-at-first-sight feeling) that passes between Karen and Jack.

Clooney and Lopez are sensitive to each other's rhythms and to the rhythms of Leonard's prose, large chunks of which have been transposed intact from the page to the screen. The chemistry between them is essential to the film's success, but its not the whole story. Soderbergh has surrounded them with an engaging supporting cast. In addition to Rhames, there's Don Cheadle as a homicidal Detroit drug dealer who specializes in "home invasion" and wants to muzzle in on Jack's big score; Catherine Keener as Jack's ex-wife; Dennis Farina as Karen's doting dad, a private dick who keeps his daughter well supplied with guns and body-skimming designer suits; and Albert Brooks as a Milken-type financier who's put a little too much trust in the guys he met in jail while he was doing time for fraud.

The nervous camera movement—quick, jagged pans and even zooms—makes the film feel looser and more spontaneous than it otherwise might.

(Soderbergh veteran Elliot Davis is the DP.) There's a kind of tremble that overtakes the camera in the long scene when Jack and Karen finally get together in a Detroit hotel lounge (big, silvery snowflakes falling outside the windows) that underscores their go-for-broke emotion. The lush, sunbaked color of the Florida scenes—lots of orange and coral—give,sway to a more steely, monochromatic look when the film moves north for its shoot-em-up climax. (By today's standards, the bloodletting isn't all that severe.) Gary Frutkoff's uncluttered but detailed production design emphasizes the comic-book effect. And David Holmes' score with its spare and repetitive syncopated tiffs is truly memorable.

Out of Sight isn't a great film (its mysteries pale a bit on second viewing), but it's generous and sexy, and lots off fun for the eyes and ears. And when I left the theater, people on the street looked so much more interesting and human than they usually do to my jaded eyes. As a special effect, that one can't be beat.

Also reviewed in:
NATION, 7/27-8/3/98, p. 35, Stuart Klawan
NEW REPUBLIC, 8/3/98, p. 28, Stanley Kauffmann
NEW YORK TIMES, 6/26/98, p. E14, Janet Maslin
VARIETY, 6/22-28/98, p. 50, Emanuel Levy
WASHINGTON POST, 6/26/98, p. B1, Stephen Hunter
WASHINGTON POST, 6/26/98, Weekend/p. 46, Michael O'Sullivan

OUTSIDE OZONA

A Tri-Star Pictures release of a Millenium Films presentation in association with Nu Image of a Sandstorm Films production. *Executive Producer:* Avi Lerner, Danny Dimbort, Trevor Short, Boaz Davidson, and John Thompson.   *Producer:* Carol Kottenbrook and Scott Einbeinder. *Director:* J.S. Cardone.   *Screenplay:* J.S. Cardone.   *Director of Photography:* Irek Hartowicz. *Editor:* Amanda Kirpaul. *Music:* Taj Mahal and Johnny Lee Schell.   *Sound:* George Burton II Goen.   *Casting:* Abra Edelman and Elisa Goodman.   *Production Designer:* Martina Buckley. *Art Director:* Hector Velez.   *Set Decorator:* Ivana Letica. *Running time:* 98 minutes.   *MPAA Rating:* R.

CAST: Robert Forster (Odell Parks);   Kevin Pollak (Wit Roy);   Sherilyn Fenn (Marcy Duggan);   David Paymer (Alan Defaux); Penelope Ann Miller (Earlene Demers);   Swoosie Kurtz (Rosalee);   Taj Mahal (Dix Mayal);   Meat Loaf (Floyd Bibbs);   Kateri Walker (Reva Twosalt);   Lucy Webb (Agent Deene);   Lois Red Elk (Effie Twosalt);   Beth Ann Styne (Bonnie Mimms).

LOS ANGELES TIMES, 12/18/98, Calendar/p. 11, John Anderson

[The following review by John Anderson appeared in a slightly different form in
NEWSDAY, 12/18/98, Part II/p. B6.]

Like Jonathan Demme's "Handle With Care" (a.k.a. "Citizens Band") or even the old cult fave "Vanishing Point," J.S. Cardone's "Outside Ozona" is that customized species of road movie in which the characters are spokes and their hub is the radio. Divergent travelers, united only by a lone voice on the airwaves—and, in this case, the serial killer who's out there with them—it could only be an American movie: There's nothing else to bond these road gypsies besides media and death.

Striving for a cross-section of Populist pie, Cardone isn't short of ideas. His major theme, though, is the wheel of luck and how it spins. Why, for instance, is disc jockey Dix Mayal (blues legend Taj Mahal) still stuck behind the mike of a low-wattage country station in Outback, Okla.? Likewise his yes-man station manager, ex-sports star Floyd Bibbs (Meat Loaf)? Why did trucker Odell Parks (Robert Forster) lose his wife to a drunk driver? Why is out-of-gas Reba Twosalt (Kateri Walker) fortunate enough to have Odell come to her rescue? Why can't circus clown Wit Roy (Kevin Pollak) keep a job? Why's he in love with ex-stripper Earlene (Penelope Ann Miller)? And when is it—as the investigating Agent Deene (Lucy Webb) asks—that the highly successful, madly misogynistic Skokie Ripper will run out of luck?

Having structured his entire film on coincidence, Cardone sets us up not only to accept but expect the kind of cataclysmic convergence of characters toward which "Outside Ozona" ambles awkwardly. While the movie is woefully written (his American Indian characters, just for example, sound like Kevin Costner waxing mystic), the performers are generally good, particularly Forster, who took over the role upon the death of J.T. Walsh (to whom the film is dedicated) and cuts a gently macho figure throughout.

Power-shticking along a highway littered with the corpses of Ripper victims, "Ozona" (which suggests both Oz and the old song "Lost in the Ozone Again") weaves its various stories together in a manner that might be called Altman-esque, if it had that kind of fluidity. We get the woeful Earlene and Wit, trying to rob a liquor store; Odell opening his heart to a brassy-but-good-hearted truck-stop waitress (Swoozie Kurtz); and the earthy Taj Mahal, growling through his on-air exchanges with the Gospel-besotted Ripper, coming off like a combination James Carville-Gore Vidal as he rips through the hypocrisy of fundamentalist-fueled hate.

The movie is anchored by a fairly infectious R & B score put together by Taj Mahal and Bonnie Raitt collaborator Johnny Lee Schell. "Outside Ozona" may not be the most revealing CAT scan of American life or the psychology of its killers, but you can't say it doesn't have a sense of humor.

NEW YORK POST, 12/18/98, p. 64, Jonathan Foreman

"Outside Ozona" is the kind of movie that makes you wonder if there isn't too much money available for independent films. While it starts promisingly and has a few dramatic moments, like an exciting climactic car-wreck, J.S. Cardone's talents as a director are hamstrung by his own sophomoric screenplay.

His script is so poor, so predictable, so filled with clumsy dialogue, that the whole movie feels like something spoofed in "The Simpsons" or concocted by Dawson Leary, the ambitious high school cineaste of TV's "Dawson's Creek."

Essentially, "Outside Ozona" is a compendium of road-movie cliches. Driving down a Southwestern highway on a dark night, there's a Bible-quoting serial killer psychiatrist (David Paymer), a nasty bald clown (Kevin Pollak) whose stripper girlfriend (Penelope Ann Miller) has a heart of gold, and a handsome trucker (Robert Forster) who stands up for a beautiful Navajo girl (Kateri Walker) against a racist gas-station owner.

There are also two sisters, one of them a Chicago lawyer's wife (Sherilyn Fenn) who cares only about money and status, the other a nice woman who runs a bakery in rural Kansas (Beth Ann Stynes). Following the trail of the serial killer is an FBI team led by a supersmart female agent (Lucy Webb).

And just as naturally, everyone's destiny will collide just outside the town of Ozona.

So far, so predictable. But then, in a classic example of half-baked Hollywood prejudice, the serial killers predilection for ripping out women's hearts is explicitly linked to Christian fundamentalism. Even Muslems don't get this kind of thoughtless, bigoted treatment.

Only Swoosie Kurtz as a truck-stop waitress and Robert Forster as the rugged trucker—two real pros—manage to triumph over the material.

The late J.T. Walsh helped find financing for "Outside Ozona" and was to have played the trucker. But it is probably just as well that Walsh, a fine actor, ended his career with "Pleasantville" rather than this callow, shallow embarrassment.

VILLAGE VOICE, 12/29/98, p. 128, Tamara Fishman

It starts with a wolf's-eye view of a corpse and, except for an extended coda, ends with the combustible convergence of its seemingly separate characters. In between, *Outside Ozona* provides a quirky look at just who might be driving the backwoods highways of Texas, listening to late-night radio.

Among those tuned to the sounds of the rebellious DJ (whiskey-voiced Taj Mahal) are a gentle, lonely trucker (Robert Forster), a Navajo woman (Kateri Walker) taking her dying grandmother to the Gulf of Mexico, and a serial killer (David Paymer) stalking women. Suspense builds nicely, although director J.S. Cardone relies on too many talking-head close-ups and "I'm acting now" monologues (one by the should-probably-stick-to-singing Meat Loaf as a desperate station manager is especially obvious). Kevin Pollak and Penelope Ann Miller add wry humor as a violent clown and his sleazy stripper girlfriend, whose essence is expressed by her shellacked-on

Day-Glo makeup. The R&B soundtrack smoothly sustains the mood, and ultimately provides uplift. After a close encounter with death, Pollak's Wit reassures Miller's confused Earlene by stating, "I don't think they got soul music in hell."

Also reviewed in:
CHICAGO TRIBUNE, 12/18/98, Friday/p. D, John Petrakis
NEW YORK TIMES, 12/18/98, p. E20, Stephen Holden
VARIETY, 12/21/98-1/3/99, p. 76, Leonard Klady

OYSTER AND THE WIND, THE

A Ravina Producoes e Communicacoes/Riofilme production.   *Executive Producer:* Marcelo Torres.   *Producer:* Flavio R. Tambellini. *Director:* Walter Lima, Jr..   *Screenplay (Portugese with English subtitles):* Walter Lima Jr. and Flavio R. Tambellini.   *Based on a novel by:* Moacir D. Lopes.   *Director of Photography:* Pedro Farkas.   *Editor:* Sergio Mekler.   *Music:* Wagner Tiso.   *Sound:* Marcio Camara.   *Sound Editor:* Tom Paul.   *Art Director:* Clovis Bueno.   *Set Designer:* Vera Hamburger.   *Costumes:* Rita Murtinho.   *Running time:* 112 minutes.   *MPAA Rating:* Not Rated.

CAST: Leandra Leal (Marcela);   Lima Duarte (Father);   Fernando Torres (Daniel);   Fioriano Peixoto (Roberto);   Castrinho (Pepe);   Debora Bloch (Mother).

NEW YORK POST 1/30/98; p. 44, Larry Worth

More often than not, modern-day cinematic fables have unhappy endings, at least for filmgoers. But "The Oyster and the Wind" is more than the rule's exception; it's a tone poem to the art of imagination.

The script, penned and directed by Brazil's Walter Lima Jr., begins with an intriguing mystery. Specifically, an old salt and his shipmates land on an island populated by housekeeper and his teen-age daughter. But while neither father nor child can be found, there's hot food on the stove and, in the beacon, broken glass that's dripping with blood.

So what happened? Well, viewers won't find out for about two hours, but the enigmatic, jigsaw-like, richly complex route to the answer makes for a deliciously mesmerizing narrative.

Revelations come from various sources (the girl's diary, dad's log, one-time friends and acquaintances), with memories and reminiscences often unfolding in a non-linear fashion bordering on the surreal. Along the way, the titular oyster and wind not only figure prominently, but work as apt metaphors for the enigma at hand.

That's all in addition to drop-dead gorgeous scenery of the craggy South American isle, an entrancing score and some duly intriguing performances.

Particularly luminous is Leandra Leal's poignant turn as the lonely young woman. Her penchant for making the incredible seem startlingly credible (as when taking the wind as her lover in a unique look at sexual awakening) make for one striking moment after another.

Almost as compelling are Fernando Torres as the girl's childhood friend-cum-mentor and Lima Duarte as the hard-hearted father with a few too many secrets, ghosts and demons.

Of course, the film isn't without flaws, exemplified by an excess of subplots, Shakespearean overtones ("The Tempest" meets "King Lear") and a cloud of impending tragedy thick enough to close LaGuardia.

But those are minor quibbles within a consistently eloquent and lyrical production. Indeed, "The Oyster and the Wind" is sheer movie magic.

NEWSDAY, 1/30/98, Part II/p. B6, John Anderson

Although its title suggests a gastronomic cause and effect, "The Oyster and the Wind" is about incipient madness, isolation, sensuality and seafaring. Its story—about a lighthouse keeper, his blossoming daughter and her erotic relationship with the wind—suggests a particularly bad-tempered "Tempest."

However. If director Walter Lima Jr. wanted to borrow from Shakespeare he would have been better off borrowing from "Much Ado About Nothing," because for all the attempts at poetics and parable in this tale of bad parenting, there's not a lot going on. Built on layers of ungraceful flashback, "The Oyster and the Wind" often leaves you marooned on a narrative shoal, or looking for a lifeguard.

As the film commences, a handful of sailors arrive on a beach, hollering for José (Lima Duarte) and his daughter, Marcela (Leandra Leal). The flashback ensues almost immediately. José is a sour sort who dominates his daughter, a sweet, inquisitive child who desperately wants to leave the island and see something besides old salts and seagulls. Despite the entreaties of the other men, like Daniel (Fernando Torres), José, refuses to let her leave, even for a doctor's visit. Her mother, it seems, wanted to leave once, too. The tension mounts.

Well, actually, it ebbs and flows, but Lima makes the fatal structural mistake of flashing back to an unfinished past. He adds elements to the history of José and Marcela—the arrival of the cretinish, Caliban-esque Roberto (Floriano Peixoto), for instance—after already having set us up with a scenario we presumed was complete. It's like starting the movie over in the middle.

And frankly, once you've got to the middle it's the point of no return. An overwrought film with rather foreseeable coda, "The Oyster and the Wind" is, unlike no man, an island.

VILLAGE VOICE, 2/3/98, p. 54, Angela Starita

The Oyster and the Wind probes a well-worn fantasy—life on a desert island—and finds in it both ordinary violence and Shakespearean magic. José (Lima Duarte), a lighthouse keeper spent by jealousy, lives with his teenage daughter, Marcela (Leandra Leal), on an unspecified Brazilian island. Realizing that her father has trapped her there, Marcela, the island's true Prospero, takes the wind as her lover, naming him Saulo. She meets him on the beach at night to writhe in the sand—a pleasure that triggers Papa's ferocious envy: unlike his daughter, he has no allies in nature.

The plot unfolds through flashback sequences that cleverly mimic the unreliability of memory—the characters' recollections are out of sequence and sometimes fantastical. Marcela imagines that the island is a ship she commandeers; while it may seem that clouds are moving, she says, it is the island that glides through the sea.

Such scenes are filmed with undeniable beauty, but Lima abruptly switches focus from Marcela's airy daydreams to the coiled fury behind José's self-imposed solitude. The sudden brutality feels forced: even Saulo's skirt-lifting antics turn nasty, as the film's delicate surrealism teeters into absurdity.

Also reviewed in:
NEW YORK TIMES, 1/30/98, p. E16, Lawrence Van Gelder
VARIETY, 9/22-28/97, p. 50, Deborah Young

PALMETTO

A Castle Rock Entertainment release of a Rialto Film production. *Executive Producer:* Al Corley, Bart Rosenblatt, and Eugene Musso. *Producer:* Matthias Wendlandt. *Director:* Volker Schlondorff. *Screenplay:* E. Max Frye. Based on the novel "Just Another Sucker" by: James Hadley Chase. *Director of Photography:* Thomas Kloss. *Editor:* Peter Przygodda. *Music:* Klaus Doldinger. *Sound:* Mark Weingarten. *Casting:* Dianne Crittenden. *Production Designer:* Claire Jenora Bowin. *Set Decorator:* Jane B. Johnson. *Set Dresser:* Ron Erdberg, Cary Whitaker, and Robert Baker. *Special Effects:* Richard Lee Jones. *Costumes:* Terry Dresbach. *Make-up:* Kimberly Greene. *Make-up (Elisabeth Shue):* Desne Holland. *Stunt Coordinator:* Tim Trella. *Running time:* 114 minutes. *MPAA Rating:* R.

CAST: Woody Harrelson (Harry Barber); Elisabeth Shue (Mrs. Donnelly aka Rhea Malroux); Gina Gershon (Nina); Rolf Hoppe (Felix Malroux); Michael Rapaport (Donnelly); Chloe Sevigny (Odette); Tom Wright (John Renick); Marc Macaulay (Miles Meadows); Joe Hickey (Lawyer); Ralph Wilcox (Judge); Peter Paul Deleo (Bartender); Mal Jones (Ed); Salvador Levy (Driver); Richard Booker (Billy Holden); Mikki McKeever (Alda); Bill Larson (Parking Lot Man); Tim W. Terry (Prison Guard); Jim Janey (Policeman); Brett Rice (Crash Site Cop); Vince Cecere (Tow Truck Driver); Don Bright (Crime Scene Cop); Ernie Garrett (TV Anchor); Karin J. Ivester (Forensic Detective); Marcus Thomas (Courtroom Photographer); Douglas J. Mann II (Courtroom Reporter); Jim Coleman and Victoria Tan (Reporters); Stephen McGruder (Convict); Annabelle Weenick (Ted); Wil Kilmer (Bungalow Cop); Ginger King (The Real Rhea); Corey Blevins (Motel Clerk); Duncan Chamberlain (Gallery Maitre D); Peggy Sheffield (Woman Customer); Karen Fraction (Plainclothes Cop).

LOS ANGELES TIMES, 2/20/98, Calendar/p. 8, Jack Mathews

[The following review by Jack Mathews appeared in a slightly different form in **NEWSDAY, 2/20/98, Part II/p. B3.]**

It must be hard being considered something of a legend as a serious filmmaker and never getting a piece of the commercial pie that is shared so generously with the most hackneyed studio directors. It's enough to drive a Costa-Gavras to make a misguided star vehicle like "Mad City," or Gus Van Sant to direct a slick, mainstream production like "Good Will Hunting," or Volker Schlondorff, maker of the classic German film "The Tin Drum," to attempt a thriller as insubstantial as "Palmetto."

Schlondorff has made a career adapting serious literary works—Gunter Grass' "The Tin Drum," Marcel Proust's "Swann in Love," Margaret Atwood's "A Handmaid's Tale" among them. Now, it's time to have some fun, Schlondorff says in the film's production notes, time to make the kind of movie he actually likes to watch. Apparently he likes to watch bad pulp fiction.

Adapted from the 1930s potboiler "Just Another Sucker," by British writer Rene Raymond (under the pen name James Hadley Chase), "Palmetto" is a parade of film noir clichés and caricatures, plus the occasional—these days, practically obligatory—nod to Quentin Tarantino. There's a killer here who, like a plumber nonchalantly unplugging a drain, gets rid of his victims' bodies by vaporizing them in acid baths.

But he's only a minor Tarantino figure, and not particularly amusing at that. The flawed hero of "Palmetto" is Harry Barber (Woody Harrelson), a contemporary, small-town Florida newspaperman whose enterprising reporting on local corruption got him framed and sent to prison two years before the movie starts.

Now, he is being suspiciously released, and though he'd rather start a new life somewhere else, his devoted artist girlfriend, Nina (Gina Gershon), has other plans for him back in Palmetto, and so does the blond bombshell Rhea (Elisabeth Shue) who comes on to him in a neighborhood tavern and makes him an offer he can't refuse.

Before he's had time to find a legitimate job, or even grow a trendy five-day beard, Harry is up to his ears in sultry women—Nina, Rhea and a precocious teenage kidnap target named Odette (Chloe Sevigny)—and in a scheme that could put him right back in the big house. Somehow, Harry has to pick himself up, sharpen his old journalistic skills and beat the game before it beats him.

The attraction of film noir to foreign auteurs is understandable. It's one of the two original American movie forms, and no one's likely to ask Schlondorff to remake "Shane." Film noir allows a filmmaker to indulge his cinematic tastes for psychological atmosphere, human weakness, violence, sexual bargaining and shadowy, mood-lit photography. And Schlondorff has a grand time indulging himself in all of these things.

But "Palmetto" has no foundation below its pedestrian plot. There is no social theme, no aspect of personal revelation, nothing that would move it from the mystery shelf to general fiction, let alone literature.

The characters aren't even interesting. Though Harrelson is great at playing lost underdogs, Harry Barber is just a loser, an easy conquest for Rhea, an incompetent crook and a lousy police press liaison, a job arranged for him—against all odds and reason—by Nina's brother-in-law cop.

There's not a character in "Palmetto" who rings true. Shue, wearing skirts that fit her like stretched Saran Wrap, does some gamy sexual posing, and fine images they are. But it's impossible not to think that she and Gershon, of "Striptease" infamy, should have switched roles. Gershon knows how to make naughty on screen; Shue is overacting in a charade.

Revelations of betrayals, faked identities and double-crosses come in waves in the last half-hour of "Palmetto," but by then, the film has raised the one question it can't answer: Who cares?

NEW YORK, 3/9/98, p. 49, David Denby

Palmetto is an unconvincing, paint-by-numbers pass at American *noir* by the usually ambitious German director Volker Schlondorff *(The Tin Drum)*. The components of the disaster include Schlondorff's inability to get an adequate star performance out of an unfocused Woody Harrelson; his inducing Elisabeth Shue to caricature herself as a femme fatale who emits steam from every pore of her body; his arranging for characters to act stupidly in order to further the plot; and his attempt to excite the audience with such crudities as a vat of flesh-melting acid into which one character falls by accident.

NEW YORK POST, 2/20/98, p. 37, Thelma Adams

The neo-noir is as dead as the western. Case in point: Volker Schlondorff's "Palmetto." It arrives in theaters as welcome as the big, burnt-orange bug that bears its name.

Palmetto is one of those stock noir towns where the chief export is corruption and there's no such thing as a chance encounter. The postman rings twice, the insurance agent offers double indemnity and there's a killer inside every tough guy with a badge.

Written by E. Max Frye, and based on James Hadley Chase's novel "Just Another Sucker," the movie stars Woody Harrelson as the sucker in question. Harry Barber (hairy barber, get it?) gets sprung from prison after two years. He leaves with a chip on his shoulder and a typewriter at his hip.

Barber is hell-bent on escaping Florida's Palmetto, that steaming sewer by the sea. The recovering alkie gets no further than a few sentences of voiceover narration before ex-girlfriend Nina (Gina Gershon) smooches him back into town. What's going to get Barber to take that first drink? Rhea Malroux. As the young wife of a dying millionaire, Elisabeth Shue ("Leaving Las Vegas")is a throwback's throwback. Her sexpot aims her pointed brassiere like six-shooters in a B western.

Soon after they meet, Mrs. Malroux and Barber rendezvous at a rundown hideaway. She makes him a kidnapping offer he should, but can't refuse. He makes martinis. "Sorry, we're all out of twists," he tells Rhea.

And, for the first hour, Barber seems to be right. Frye's script is so familiar that even Forrest Gump could predict the plot turns. Gershon and Chloe ("Kids") Sevigny, playing a terrific teen tramp, provide distraction, but it's not until the second hour that the surprises hit—and by then it's too late.

The German director of "The Tin Drum" and "Circle of Deceit" adds little more to the production than a clever film schooler could. If there's a bitterness to "Palmetto," it's that even the brilliant Schlondorff can lose his edge and end up being just another sucker at the Hollywood trough.

SIGHT AND SOUND, 8/98, p. 53, Nick Kimberley

Journalist Harry Barber, framed by those involved in the corruption he was investigating, has spent two years in jail. Freed early, he returns to Palmetto with his girlfriend Nina, struggles to find work and meets a beautiful woman who offers him the chance to earn $50,000. Intrigued, Harry discovers that she is Rhea, wife of terminally ill millionaire Felix Malroux. Harry arranges to meet Rhea in a beach bungalow, where, as well as seducing him, she details her scheme to fake the kidnapping of her step-daughter Odette and extort $500,000 from Malroux. Harry takes care of the arrangements.

Malroux pays up, but not before his bodyguard Donnelly alerts district attorney John Renick, who employs Harry as police-press liaison on the kidnapping he himself has arranged. Returning to the bungalow, Harry discovers Odette's body. Panicking, he loads it into Nina's car. Nina persuades him to come clean. Donnelly arrives, reveals his involvement, and helps dispose of the body. Nina tries to extricate Harry from the mess he has made.

Renick summons Harry to the bungalow to view another body, which turns out to be the real Odette. Perplexed, Harry goes to Malroux to tell all, only to learn that the woman who dragged him into the kidnapping is not Malroux's wife. Donnelly captures him and prepares to dispose of Harry and Nina in an acid bath. Rhea enters, admits that she is Mrs Donnelly, and that the couple had planned this for months. Donnelly falls into the acid, the police arrive and arrest both Mrs Donnelly and Harry.

It's difficult to measure how far Schlöndorff had his tongue in his cheek while making *Palmetto*. Certainly the movie is not played for laughs, but nor does it take itself very seriously. Perhaps that's better than taking itself too seriously, but it's also its biggest problem. In the plot's tangled web of disguise, deception and betrayal, there are more loose ends than in Hawks' *The Big Sleep*, but no compensating urgency to render them irrelevant. On the other hand, there is an ingratiating languor. And indeed, why should the movie hurry when we know it will all go wrong in the end?

If at first *Palmetto* seems to be yet another in the long list of neo-*noir* movies, its iconography owes more to 50s cinema posters, or perhaps to pulp paperback covers. There are the same gaudy stereotypes, the same cheerfully overblown lack of realism. Far from being a *femme fatale*, Mrs Donnelly (the very name a denial of all things *fatale*) is a graphic artist's lightning sketch of feminine pulchritude, all stiletto heels and uplift bra. At least that's the way Elisabeth Shue overplays her, and the joke is that Harry thinks she's real.

Much is made of the fact that Harry is a journalists but so atrophied are his investigative instincts that when, after his first encounter with the pneumatic Rhea he sets about finding out who she is, he fails to discover that she isn't the rich man's wife, she is his cook. An ironic comment on the low status of political journalists in the cynical 90s? I don't think the movie has such grand ambitions. All it wants is some sad sap to fall flat on his face, and with his edgy insouciance Woody Harrelson fits the bill perfectly. As Harry he dresses in braces and trilby, as if he's in the right movie but the wrong era.

The screenplay derives, at some distance, from James Hadley Chase's novel *Just Another Sucker*, already dated when it was published in 1996. British born and bred, Chase set most of his 80-odd books in America, without troubling himself too much about what America was actually like: he got the facts he needed from novels and movies. Schlöndorff, likewise a foreigner but one who undoubtedly knows America better than Chase did, takes the same approach to authenticity, which is perhaps his sardonic comment on the way Hollywood makes its thrillers these days. (You want something like Hitchcock? I'll give you back-projection so tacky even Hitchcock would have balked.) Schlöndorff and his cast clearly enjoy the game of manipulating clichés, but it's hard to avoid the feeling that, for all concerned, *Palmetto* merely passes the time until something more substantial comes along.

Also reviewed in:
CHICAGO TRIBUNE, 2/20/98, Friday/p. C, Michael Wilmington
NEW YORK TIMES, 2/20/98, p. E14, Stephen Holden
VARIETY, 2/16-22/98, p. 57, Dennis Harvey
WASHINGTON POST, 2/20/98, p. B6, Stephen Hunter

PARALLEL SONS

A Greycat Releasing release of a Eureka Pictures production. *Producer:* James Spione and Nancy Larsen. *Director:* John G. Young. *Screenplay:* John G. Young. *Editor:* John G. Young and James Spione. *Music:* E.D. Menashe. *Sound:* Harrison Williams. *Production Designer:* Cindy Spinas. *Costumes:* Leonardo Iturregui. *Running time:* 93 minutes. *MPAA Rating:* Not Rated.

WITH: Gabriel Mann (Seth); Laurence Mason (Knowledge Johnson); Julia Weldon (Sally); Graham Alex Johnson Seth's Father); Heather Gottlieb (Kristen); Murphy Guyer (Sheriff Mott); Maureen Shannon (Francine); Josh Hopkins (Marty).

NEW YORK POST, 5/1/98, p. B11, Larry Worth

If the racially mixed heroes of "The Defiant Ones" had been bound by love rather than chains, it might have ended up something like "Parallel Sons." That's not to say writer-director John G. Young's indie drama achieves anywhere near the power of Stanley Kramer's 1958 classic. But its present-day story about prejudice and parental conflicts in upstate New York offers some nice moments before degenerating into melodrama.

The protagonists are an adolescent white boy who's impassioned by African-American culture, and a wounded black convict who's a lot more than his rap sheet. Although their relationship gets off to a shaky start, unexpected intimacy comes about—as well as gunplay that leads to tragedy.

Sadly, the script gets increasingly predictable, leading to an elongated finale that stretches credibility to the max. On the plus side, Gabriel Mann and Laurence Mason prove engaging, as does most of the supporting cast.

That's why one can't help being disappointed by the end product. "Parallel Sons" is good enough to wish it were better.

NEWSDAY, 5/1/98, Part II/p. B11, John Anderson

The likeable, hard-working, intelligent, motherless Seth (Gabriel Mann), his white head full of dreadlocks and rap music, his mouth full of "That's phat!" is just a little bit ridiculous to the people of his upper upstate New York town. Nice, but ridiculous. How else could it be? They've known him all his life. He's no threat. He even wants to go to art school.

And Knowledge Johnson (Laurence Mason), the angry black escapee from the nonviolent offender's program? He's the manifestation of a Pataki-land nightmare, a one-man African-American crime-wave-to-be, rumored to have slaughtered half a dozen people down in New York City. Not that they didn't deserve it.

That these two unhappy people come together, educate each other and perpetrate a tragedy is a lot less surprising than how naturally and convincingly they do it—and in a debut feature besides. John G. Young, the writer director of this combination social autopsy/love story, evades cliche and clearly knows his territory, from the casual racism of the people to the inherent loneliness of close-knit communities.

There are a few dramatically awkward moments—mostly in the initial exchanges that occur after Seth takes Knowledge in and nurses him back to health—but most of it is handled with grace and honesty: The way Seth's father (Graham Alex Johnson) feigns authority; the way his young sister Sally (Julia Weldon) immediately interrogates Knowledge; the way Seth's friend Kristen (Heather Gottlieb) grieves at Seth's reflexive rejection of her sexuality.

And while the story is ostensibly about Seth and Knowledge's mutual secret and how it overshadows race and class, there's a transcendent melancholy about human folly that permeates the film, beginning with the beautiful but brief opening sequence: a Brooklyn apartment, a little boy with a gun he's found in a dresser drawer and a camera that looks away—as if to say it's seen enough carnage in Arkansas and North Carolina and Pennsylvania—and anticipates the inevitable gunshot.

"Parallel Sons" isn't a perfect movie, but, frankly, it's exactly what independent cinema is supposed to be, and so rarely is: personal filmmaking, intelligent storytelling, a director with *something to say.* In a movie year like the one we're having, you'd like to walk up to John G. Young and just say thanks.

VILLAGE VOICE, 5/5/98, p. 119, Amy Taubin

Race, albeit from a different point of view, also figures prominently in John G. Young's *Parallel Sons,* [the reference is to *He Got Game;* see Taubin's review of that film.] which premiered in 1995 at Sundance. An unusually intelligent and haunting depiction of sexual passion and the interplay between desire and identification, it has been an audience favorite at a handful of festivals, but had to wait three years to find a distributor willing and able to take a chance on theatrical release.

Set in a small, redneck, upstate town, it's about a white teenager named Seth (Gabriel Mann) who's enamored of black culture—does his blond hair in dreads, plays hip-hop round the clock, makes the *Autobiography of Malcolm X* his bible—although he's never actually met a black person. His black identification is, in part, a displacement of another kind of difference. He's gay, although he's barely admitted it to himself. But, as luck would have it, Knowledge (Laurence Mason), a black man who was wounded escaping from a nearby prison, takes refuge in the diner where Seth works. Seth rescues Knowledge and hides him in his hunting cabin in the woods. Eventually *Parallel Sons* veers unnecessarily into melodrama but not before Seth and Knowledge have admitted their love in a seduction scene that's both lyrical and very hot.

Made on a shoestring budget, Parallel Sons looks surprisingly attractive, but it's carried by the writing and the acting. Mann and Mason couldn't be better and Heather Gottlieb, as an art student who can't understand why Seth isn't boyfriend material (or at least not for her), is almost as good. *Parallel Sons* is the kind of film the indie infrastructure was created to support. In the immortal words of Jack Smith, "What went wrong" What went wrong?"

Also reviewed in:
NEW YORK TIMES, 5/1/98, p. E28, Lawrence Van Gelder
VARIETY, 1/30-2/5/95, p. 50, Leonard Klady

PARALYZING FEAR, A: THE STORY OF POLIO IN AMERICA

A Film Forum presentation. *Producer:* Paul Wagner and Nina Gilden Seavey. *Director:* Nina Gilden Seavey. *Screenplay:* Nina Gilden Seavey. *Screenplay Narration:* Stephen Chodorov. *Director of Photography:* Allen Moore and Reuben Aaronson. *Editor:* Catherine Shields. *Music:* Paul Christianson. *Running time:* 90 minutes. *MPAA Rating:* Not Rated.

CAST: Olympia Dukakis (Narrator).

NEW YORK POST, 3/4/98, p. 46, Larry Worth

Not so many decades ago, Freddy Krueger wasn't around to strike fear in children's hearts. But The Crippler—a murderer whose villainous ways weren't confined to nightmares—proved a real-life horror.

Now, the true story of The Crippler's reign is revealed in the fascinating documentary "A Paralyzing Fear: The Story of Polio in America."

Granted, a showpiece about the once-unknown disease that maimed or killed legions of children from the summer of 1916 until 1955 (when Jonas Salk and Albert Sabin finally developed vaccines) might sound pretty ho-hum. Not the case.

Writer-director Nina Gilden Seavey has seamlessly fused vintage black-and-white clips of polio's most famous victim—President Franklin Delano Roosevelt, running a treatment center for afflicted children—with reports on how parents' paranoia and growing hysteria brought the country to its knees. Better still, interviews with now-grown polio survivors supply a modern-day relevance.

True, Olympia Dukakis' narration is less than inspired. And, yes, the score makes elevator Muzak seem catchy. But "A Paralyzing Fear" remains a memory-inducing journey for those over 40 and an eye-opening education for those who aren't.

VILLAGE VOICE, 3/10/98, p. 66, Jason Vincz

Almost any unpleasantness can make an engaging documentary—thus films on bugs, pet cemeteries, and salesmen. Nina Seavey, the director of A *Paralyzing Fear,* shies away from polio's historical and scientific contexts, saving her real attention for pop-culture artifacts, which she neatly assembles into a sociology of hysterical pathophobia.

Polio has virtually vanished from the national consciousness, but there was a time when this human-waste-borne virus randomly infected 50,000 American children each year, threatening them with paralysis and even death. Seavey reconstructs this nationwide, decades-long form of psychological torture by intertwining paralyzed survivors' recollections with the stories of children whose terrorized parents forbade them to go to school, or slumber parties, or even the corner store for candy. The history of the March of Dimes and its massive private funding of scientific research fascinates, as do rare clips of semi-closeted victim Franklin Roosevelt and period-piece PSAs from Greer Carson, Lucille Ball, and Rock Hudson,

Seavey is less concerned with the science involved in the discovery of the vaccine—phrases like "monkey after monkey died in the experiments" are checked off and discarded without elaboration—and previous plagues, like smallpox, are almost entirely ignored. Still, a film that can inspire in the layperson a curiosity about acquired immunities and the sanitation paradox is making the most of its unpleasantness.

Also reviewed in:
NEW YORK TIMES, 3/4/98, p. E5, Stephen Holden
VARIETY, 3/9-15/98, p. 42, Godfrey Cheshire

PARENT TRAP, THE

A Walt Disney Pictures release. *Producer:* Charles Shyer. *Director:* Nancy Meyers. *Screenplay:* David Swift, Nancy Meyers, and Charles Shyer. *Director of Photography:* Dean A. Cundey. *Editor:* Stephen A. Rotter. *Music:* Alan Silvestri. *Music Editor:* Andrew Silver. *Choreographer:* Keith Young. *Sound:* Sean Rush and (music) Dennis Sands. *Sound Editor:* Dennis Drummond. *Casting:* Ilene Starger. *Production Designer:* Dean Tavoularis. *Art Director:* Alex Tavoularis. *Set Designer:* Dianne Wager, James Bayliss, and Kelly Hannafin. *Set Decorator:* Gary Fettis. *Set Dresser:* Heidi Hublou and Larry White. *Special Effects:* Cliff Wenger. *Costumes:* Penny Rose and (Wedding Gowns) Vera Wang. *Make-up:* Karen Blynder. *Stunt Coordinator:* Freddie Hice. *Running time:* 128 minutes. *MPAA Rating:* PG.

CAST: Lindsay Lohan (Hallie Parker/Annie James);   Dennis Quaid (Nick Parker);   Natasha Richardson (Elizabeth James);   Elaine Hendrix (Meredith Blake);   Lisa Ann Walter (Chessy); Simon Kunz (Martin);   Polly Holliday (Marva Kulp, Sr.);   Maggie Wheeler (Marva Kulp, Jr.); Ronnie Stevens (Grandfather);   Joanna Barnes (Vicki);   Hallie Meyers-Shyer (Lindsay);   Maggie Emma Thomas (Zoe);   Courney Woods (Nicole);   Katerina Graham (Jackie);   Michael Lohan (Lost Boy at Camp);   Christina Toral, Dana Ponder, and Brianne Mercier (Cell Phone Girls); Danielle Sherman, Natasha Melnick, and Amanda Hampton (Girls at Poker Game);   Lisa Iverson (Bugler);   Lisa Cloud and Heidi Boren (Camp Counselors);   Marissa Leigh and Heather Wayrock (Fencing Girls);   John Atterbury (Gareth, the James' Chauffeur);   Hamish McColl (Photographer);   Vandela K. Thommessen (Bridal Gown Model);   Alexander Cole (Richard, Meredith's Assistant);   J. Patrick McCormack (Les Blake);   William Akey (Bellhop with Flowers);   David Doty (Hotel Bartender);   Roshanna Baron (Lady at Pool);   Annie Meyers-Shyer (Towel Girl);   Brian Fenwick (Desk Clerk);   Jonneine Hellerstein (Ship Photographer);   Troy Christian and Denise Holland (QE 2 Dancers);   Terry Kerr (Living Statue);   Bruce Block (Tourist).

CHRISTIAN SCIENCE MONITOR, 7/31/98, p. B3, David Sterritt

Twins have provided story ideas for Hollywood dramas ("The Dark Mirror," "A Stolen Life") and comedies ("Our Relations," "Wonder Man") and thrillers ("Murder by Television," "Dead Ringers") for as long as anyone can remember. Of the examples that proved popular at the box office, few produced more fond and lasting memories than "The Parent Trap," a Walt Disney release that became a family-film favorite in the early 1960s.

Family entertainments aren't as abundant today as they were in those bygone years, so it's a pleasure to revisit "The Parent Trap" in a 1998 version. It is similar to the original but juiced up with new gags and gimmicks that should compete nicely with the action-oriented fare now reigning in multiplexes. It's also more successful than the current "Madeline" at diverting adults along with their kids.

The heroines are 11-year-old identical twins who were separated soon after birth and know nothing of each other's existence. Meeting by coincidence at a summer camp, they become rivals at first, then realize their relationship and start comparing the lives they've led.

Both have been blessed with comfortable homes—Hallie lives with Dad in the California countryside, Annie with Mom in a London town house—but they've missed the joys of a two-parent household. The logical solution is to bring those antagonistic grown-ups back together.

The method: They'll pull the old twin-trick of trading places, move into each other's homes, and dream up some way of reuniting the family. The problem: Dad has fallen for a young beauty who's after his money, and if the twins don't hurry, he'll remarry before their scheme has time to work.

The biggest difference between the two "Parent Trap" versions is the age of the main characters, played by 15-year-old Hayley Mills in the original and 12-year-old Lindsay Lohan in the remake. This opens the door for more preteen-style humor—and more appeal to very young viewers—without disturbing the basic outline of the adult-romance angle. The maneuver works very well, largely because Lohan is a first-rate young performer, loaded with energy and equipped with all the acting skills for her challenging dual role.

Speaking of which, Hollywood technology has taken a stride or two since the split-screen techniques of the 1961 edition, replacing them with computerized effects that allow Lohan's two characters to interact with remarkable realism. Credit goes partly to the actress and partly to cinematographer Dean Cundey, who contributes the expertise he cultivated in pictures like "Jurassic Park" and "Who Framed Roger Rabbit."

For all the lighthearted merits of "The Parent Trap," it's worth noting that despite its setting in the supposedly real world, the movie isn't much more true to life than the out-and-out fantasies just mentioned. The twins' surroundings are so comfy, carefree, and affluent that you may find yourself wondering how they'd solve their problems if they didn't have oodles of money, unlimited leisure, and cooperative servants at their beck and call. Hollywood has always dealt with this kind of dreaminess, of course, but less-privileged youngsters with real-life family challenges will glean little support from this rose-colored fiction.

Back on the positive side, the rest of the cast is as effective as the young star, from Dennis Quaid and Natasha Richardson as the split-up parents to Lisa Ann Walter and Simon Kunz as household helpers who become the twins' romantic accomplices. Nancy Meyers directed the picture from a screenplay she penned with her husband, Charles Shyer, and Hollywood veteran David Swift, who wrote and directed the first "Parent Trap" almost four decades ago.

LOS ANGELES TIMES, 7/29/98, Calendar/p. 1, Kenneth Turan

[The following review by Kenneth Turan appeared in a slightly different form in
NEWSDAY, 7/29/98, Part II/p. B9.]

The premise couldn't be less plausible, but who has ever cared? Since it came out in 1961, "The Parent Trap" has been an embraceable fantasy, a sugarplum vision of a world where parents are perfect though apart and children are the only ones with the sense and savvy to bring them together again.

Beloved though it is, the original Hayley Mills—starring "The Parent Trap" shows its age more than fond memory admits. The filmmaking team of Nancy Meyers and Charles Shyer took on the task of doing it again, and an irresistible family entertainment it turns out to be.

Hewing so closely to the original structure that 1961 writer David Swift shares a screenplay credit, this new "Parent Trap" is right at home in an age when the line "It's scary the way no one stays together anymore" seems even more to the point than it did nearly four decades ago.

It's not only the offspring of broken homes who will be attracted to this film about children planning to trick their split folks into reuniting. Everyone's on-screen life is so completely perfect, each parent such an amalgam of shining beauty and caring virtue, that it's hard not to wish you were a long-lost family member, too.

Adding contemporary comedy to the tale (based on German writer Erich Kastner's "Das Doppelte Lottchen" or "The Double Lottie") is the Meyers & Shyer team, whose past credits include "Private Benjamin," "Irreconcilable Differences" and the remade "Father of the Bride."

Shyer has been the directing half of the team in the past, but Meyers gets her chance this time, and she makes full use of the opportunity. "The Parent Trap" is a glossy, high-energy entertainment, always smooth and clever. Though the film could use a little shortening, it's been directed with an easy touch and has the considerable virtue of not pushing the sentiment harder than it needs to.

In this, in fact in all things, "The Parent Trap" can't be imagined without its 11-year-old redheaded star, Lindsay Lohan. Her bright spirit and impish smile make for an immensely likable young person we take to our hearts almost at once. Lohan's the soul of this film as much as Hayley Mills was of the original, and, aided by a gift for accent and considerably improved technology, she is more adept than her predecessor at creating two distinct personalities for the unknowing twin sisters who meet at Camp Walden in Moose Lake, Maine.

Hallie Parker is a completely California girl down to her painted nails and her love for horses. She lives on an idyllic vineyard in the Napa Valley with handsome and loving father Nick (Dennis Quaid) and has developed quite an affinity for poker and fencing.

Well-behaved Annie James knows a few things about poker and fencing, too, but otherwise she is Hallie's opposite, more Posh Spice than Brat Pack. Annie lives in London with beautiful and loving mother Elizabeth (Natasha Richardson), a designer of exclusive wedding gowns (Vera Wang's are the ones we see).

When Hallie and Annie discover each other at camp, they can't stand what they see, the shared sentiment being "That girl is without a doubt the lowest, most awful creature that ever walked the planet."

That shared enmity leads to a series of ghastly pranks that land both girls in the dread Isolation Cabin, where they discover: A) that they share a taste for Oreos with peanut butter and B) that they are identical twins separated at birth by photogenic and loving parents who somehow decided this was the sane thing to do.

Barely daunted, the twins come up with "a brilliant beyond brilliant idea." They will switch places, so each can meet the parent they've never known. When the time is right they'll reveal themselves, forcing mother and father to meet again to unswitch them.

Everything goes fine when Hallie arrives in London, but back at Napa, Annie discovers that handsome and loving Nick is being stalked by a calculating blond vamp named Meredith Blake (Elaine Hendrix), nicknamed "Miss I'll Just Have Half a Grapefruit," who is intent on marrying him for his money. A series of panicky transatlantic phone calls follows, and soon enough Nick and Elizabeth are headed for that fateful reunion.

Casting Quaid and Richardson as the parents is one of "The Parent Trap's" shrewder moves. Though they've never played roles this dreamy before (who has?), these two are up to the task and display excellent chemistry. Because this is a '90s movie, they've both got household help, and her butler Martin and his housekeeper-nanny Chessy are strongly played by Simon Kunz and Lisa Ann Walter. (In a nice touch, Joanna Barnes, who played the gold digger in 1961, is cast as Meredith's mother.)

"The Parent Trap" manages to have it both ways. It utilizes lines of dialogue from the original while putting Leonardo DiCaprio's photo where Ricky Nelson's used to be, and it also has its own set of unexpected comic moments, like a camper with the chubbiest cheeks working away at the bugle. And having a star like Lohan, a girl whose happiness you can't help but share in, doesn't hurt a bit.

NEW YORK POST, 7/29/98, Thelma Adams

Twins separated at infancy. Next, on "Oprah."

How kids cope: unruliness, manipulation, identity confusion, eating disorders and aggressive behavior. How parents respond: clueless.

What's the solution? Kids usurp parental roles and restore the nuclear family. That's "The Parent Trap."

In 1961, the original Disney version featured Hayley Mills in the dual role of teen twins who meet at summer camp. On the eve of the sexual revolution, divorce was still taboo—and the premise and star were more delicious.

In the late '80s, as baby boomers started to enshrine their favorite childhood flicks, "The Parent Trap" hit TV with three made-for-tube movies. Mills, in child-star recovery, played adult twins as clueless about love as the movie's original parents, tough-but-tender Brian Keith and fiery Maureen O'Hara.

Director Nancy Meyers ("Father of the Bride"), a boomer herself, swoons at the great honor of remaking "Trap." Her high-gloss, soundtrack-driven revision of the 1961 version (co-written with partner Charles Shyer and original writer David Swift) makes less sense than re-releasing the original—like a poor twin's "Gone With the Wind."

In Meyers' poorly paced comedy, it's even less clear 37 years later how parents Dennis Quaid and Natasha Richardson made the "Sophie's Choice" of splitting twins like an infinitive.

Mom and Dad are rich and perfect with fantasy careers: He has a Napa vineyard, she designs wedding gowns in London. Quaid is all rugged smiles and Richardson, after getting down and dirty in "Cabaret," is doing a perfectly marvelous Julie Andrews. They're so caring and cuddly, yet so clueless!

Oprah, help me here. How could folks this adorable be so heinous? Isn't there some split-twin-abuse statute? Certainly, these girls (perky redhead Lindsay Lohan) have special needs the state should protect.

At least, if one twin were evil—a Damien with an omen complex—we could understand the girls' hellish situation. Then as now, the home wrecker is not parental self-indulgence but a blonde bombshell (Elaine Hendrix) with her talons in Dad.

In a neat bit of casting, Hendrix plays the daughter of Joanna Barnes, the golddigger of 1961. In both comedies, these other women get the wicked stepmother-to-be treatment and deliver the same poison apple to a stubborn twin: "I'm going to marry your father and send you to boarding school in Switzerland."

Children of divorce, divorced parents, evil twins and that rare species, children from functional families, stay tuned for our next therapy session: "Dumb Adults, Smart Kids: The Dionne Quints Crack Wise."

NEWSWEEK, 8/3/98, p. 66, Laura Shapiro & Corie Brown

Fox's "Ever After" and Disney's "Parent Trap" are poised to catch the last waves of this family-friendly summer.

Women and preteen girls still love the 1961 "The Parent Trap," starring Hayley Mills as identical twins. Raised separately by their divorced parents, the twins meet by chance at summer camp and scheme to reunite their mom and dad. This affectionate update, directed by Nancy Meyers, retains the fantasy but gives everything else a stylish makeover.

A winning newcomer, Lindsay Lohan, plays the twins with zest. She makes it clear that the twins' plight has more pathos to it than the original permitted. "I hope she likes me. Please like me," prays Hallie, on her way to meet the mother she's never known. As the parents, Natasha Richardson and Dennis Quaid look gorgeous but leave it at that. This film has everything for the all-important female audience: feisty heroines, lots of slapstick, great clothes. Women, kids—and the men that get dragged along—will likely be the force behind "Ever After," Andy Tennant's dark and rugged retelling of the Cinderella story. The movie opens with a 19th-century French noblewoman (Jeanne Moreau) who wants to set the record straight on her famous ancestor. The rousing history she recounts in flashback tells of a young woman (Drew Barrymore) whose fiery convictions get her into trouble and whose mind and muscle get her out again. She needs love, but she doesn't need rescuing.

Cinderella's real name, Moreau says, was Danielle. When her beloved father dies, he leaves her to the harsh care of her stepmother (Anjelica Huston). When her stepmother sells off a beloved old servant, Danielle dresses up like a court lady and argues with the prince (Dougray Scott) about human rights until he agrees to intervene and release the man. Love doesn't quite blossom: the prince is intrigued, but she's appalled by this restless aristocrat who admires passion and principle yet won't act on them.

This complex tale is told with great buoyancy and wit thanks to the splendid performances. "Cinderella" has had hundreds of variants in dozens of cultures, but "Ever After" is the version we've needed for a long time. And like the most successful of this summer's movie crop, it speaks in ways children can understand and adults can appreciate.

SIGHT AND SOUND, 12/98, p. 56, Andy Richards

Two 11-year-olds, Annie James and Hallie Parker, meet at summer camp in Maine and are immediately taken aback at their physical resemblance to each other. They eventually work out that they are identical twins: when their parents split up ten years ago Hallie stayed with their father Nick and Annie with their mother Elizabeth. The twins decide to swap places secretly in order to spend some time with the parents they never knew. Annie goes to stay with Nick, a prosperous Napa Valley vineyard owner who lives with his housekeeper Chessy.

Hallie stays with Elizabeth, a successful London designer who lives with her butler Martin. Annie is dismayed when she learns Nick plans to marry Meredith Blake, a beautiful but opportunistic publicist. Annie warns Hallie about it, so Hallie reveals her true identity to Elizabeth and persuades her to fly to San Francisco to exchange her with Annie.

Nick and Elizabeth meet, and the twins arrange a romantic date for them. Meanwhile, Chessy and Martin fall in love. Nick and Meredith take a camping trip together during which the twins play pranks on Meredith. Furious, she demands that Nick choose between the children and her. Nick unhesitatingly chooses the children. Elizabeth returns to London with Annie, but Nick and Hallie follow them. Nick and Elizabeth reaffirm their love, much to the twins' delight.

The Parent Trap's feelgood fable of mistaken identity and childhood resourcefulness has served film-makers well over the years. This remake of Disney's 1961 Hayley Mills vehicle of the same name has been preceded recently by Andy Tennant's looser update *It Takes Two,* with Kirstie Alley and Steve Guttenberg. The narrative appeal of the core story is clear, based as it is on the wish-fulfilment fantasy of reforming the broken nuclear family, of bringing one's estranged parents back into the fold through the discovery of a sibling (or *doppelgänger)* that one never knew one had.

While Tennant's film was relentlessly vulgar in both its comedy and its characterisations, *The Parent Trap* in the hands of first-time director Nancy Meyers (the producer-writer of *Private Benjamin)* recognises that charm needs a touch of class to make it shine. In this respect, Dennis Quaid and Natasha Richardson are astutely cast as the idealised couple, ensconced on opposite sides of the world in a Napa vineyard and Kensington townhouse respectively. Their environments are so luxurious, and they themselves are so full of love for their daughters, that from the outset the audience is left in no doubt that they belong together. (Elaine Hendrix's grasping Meredith is too much the brash *arriviste* to contend with Richardson's old-world sophistication.) The loyal retainers Martin and Chessy even embark on a modest romance of their own, a prelude to the renewed grand passion of their employers.

The narrative symmetry may lend a predictability to proceedings, but the formal classicism is part of this film's sense of fun, sustained by Lindsay Lohan's winning and skilful double performance as Annie and Hallie, achieved (as was Mills' turn) through an unobtrusive use of split-screen photography and visual effects. "I should never have believed it possible... that one can make up for lost happiness, like a lesson one has missed at school... We owe every second to our two children," claims the father at the end of Erich Kästner's 1949 source novel *Lottie and Lisa.* Lohan, like Mills before her, has charm enough to make such an unlikely sentiment palatable.

Also reviewed in:
CHICAGO TRIBUNE, 7/29/98, Tempo/p. 1, Michael Wilmington
NEW YORK TIMES, 7/29/98, p. E6, Janet Maslin
VARIETY, 7/27-8/2/98, p. 51, Joe Leydon
WASHINGTON POST, 7/31/98, Weekend/p. 48, Michael O'Sullivan

PASSION IN THE DESERT

A Fine Line Features release of a Roland Films production. *Executive Producer:* Joel McCleary and Stephen Dembitzer. *Producer:* Lavinia Currier. *Director:* Lavinia Currier. *Screenplay:* Lavinia Currier and Martin Edmunds. *Adapted from the novella "A Passion in the Desert" by:* Honoré de Balzac. *Director of Photography:* Alexei Rodionov. *Editor:* Nicolas Gaster. *Music:* José Nieto. *Sound:* Michael Stearns. *Casting:* Daphne Becket. *Production Designer:* Amanda McArthur. *Costumes:* Shuna Harwood. *Running time:* 93 minutes. *MPAA Rating:* PG-13.

CAST: Ben Daniels (Augustin Robert); Michel Piccoli (Venture); Paul Meston (Grognard); Kenneth Collard (Officer); Nadi Odeh (Bedouin Bride); Auda Mohammed Badoul (Shepherd Boy); Mohammed Ali (Medicine Man); Habis Hussein, Tasheen Kwalda, and Ismael Al-Hamd (Bedouins); James Peck, Nicolas Sagalle, and Abdul Latif Salazar (Soldiers).

LOS ANGELES TIMES, 6/12/98, Calendar/p. 12, Kenneth Turan

"Passion in the Desert" is an odd and beautiful little film, a largely effective poetic meditation on the emotional connection between a soldier and a leopard that feels very much like love.

"Passion" is based on an atypical novella by the great 19th century French writer Honore de Balzac. While a good deal of Balzac's fiction is set among Paris' teeming boulevards, "Passion" takes us to Egypt in 1798 and the fortunes of a young French officer in Napoleon's invading force.

Augustin Robert (British actor Ben Daniels) is a handsome, even arrogant young captain with a dashing uniform and hair done up in fashionable braids. The trackless desert, he feels, holds no particular mystery. Between the Nile and Red Sea, he says, "You can't get lost in Egypt."

An artist whom Robert is escorting, Jean-Michel Venture de Paradise (veteran French actor Michel Piccoli), feels differently. Assigned by Napoleon to record the timeless glories of the desert and its monuments, Venture has a passion for the unknown and the unseen. He calls the wind "the breath of the desert" and talks about jinns, mysterious spirits that control the night.

As directed by Lavinia Currier (who also produced and wrote the script with assistance from Martin Edmunds), "Passion" is, even in its early stages, notable more for its look than its dialogue. Words are kept to a minimum, and those that are used tend to be awkward and unsatisfying as often as not.

While the money available for costumes was likely minimal, production designer Amanda McArthur and costume designer Shuna Harwood (Oscar-nominated for the stylish, modern-dress "Richard III" starring Ian McKellen) have combined to create a world that feels believably foreign, period and exotic.

And cinematographer Alexei Rodionov (who shot Sally Potter's great-looking "Orlando") has created visuals so bright and vivid that it's possible to simply ignore the moments when the words aren't up to the standard set by the images.

In the aftermath of an attack by Mameluke fighters and a sandstorm that erases everyone's tracks, Robert and his artist get separated from the French troops they're traveling with and, after getting irredeemably lost, from each other as well.

Stumbling onto mysterious stone ruins (these parts of the film were shot in Petra, Jordan), Robert thinks he's by himself. A pair of bright eyes glowing in the dark tells him otherwise: A wild African leopard considers the ruins home as well.

The heart of "Passion in the Desert," structurally as well as metaphorically, is the almost wordless relationship that develops between the soldier and the leopard. Against all logic, the animal seems to take a liking to Robert. Alone amid the silent stones, the two of them play out an elaborate relationship that blurs the line between man and beast, hunter and hunted.

All this sounds a bit dicey, but the largely silent interaction between these two is convincing to a considerable extent—even though the leopard is, as director Currier put it in an interview, "the most dangerous, idiosyncratic and unmanageable of the great cats."

Currier hired animal trainer Rick Glassey, who raised from birth the leopards used in the film. Even so, it took considerable nerve on the part of actor Daniels to appear in the same frame with an animal that was likely as not thinking of ways to eat him. With Rodionov behind the camera, their scenes together have a kind of tense poetry that is unlikely to be forgotten.

NEW YORK POST, 6/12/98, p. 47, Larry Worth

In a time when one action movie is constantly recycled into another clone, "Passion in the Desert" earns an A for originality.

Based on a controversial short story by Honore de Balzac, the film is bound to generate debate. And, granted, it's not for all tastes.

Balzac's treatise pits man vs. nature, showing humans' tendency to destroy what can't be understood. That's obvious from the outset as Napoleon's troops blast Egyptian monuments during France's late-18th-century campaign to control the Nile.

Following a horrifically bloody fight with tribal warriors, a young army captain is separated from fellow soldiers. That's when things *really* get interesting.

Chased into a cave by knife-wielding Bedouins, the captain comes face to face with an even deadlier foe: a full-grown leopard that's ready to pounce. But that's not the end of the story. Rather, it's the beginning of a jaw-dropping series of events that must be seen to be believed.

This the juncture where detractors will have their heyday. But as a big-screen portrait of madness, it's hard to recall a more powerful depiction.

Director-writer Lavinia Currier fearlessly charts her way into some unfamiliar territory. Effortlessly seguing from war story to nature film, she generates sustained tension while exposing some very primal emotions.

Most importantly, Currier imbues her subject with the seriousness and intelligence it deserves, despite an almost fairy-tale quality. That's in addition to consistently dazzling photography. The desert hasn't been as simultaneously beautiful and frightening since "Lawrence of Arabia."

And then there's Ben Daniels as the confused protagonist. His physical and emotional transformation, right down to adopting feline moves, is nothing short of amazing. So are his interactions with the big cat.

Daniels' courageous performance is nicely complemented by trouper Michel Piccoli, playing an increasingly insane painter. Under Currier's daring direction, they help make "Passion" into spellbinding, utterly unforgettable entertainment.

NEWSDAY, 6/12/98, Part II/p. B11, John Anderson

"You can't get lost in Egypt," declares Captain Augustin Robert (Ben Daniels), Napoleon's officer and Descarte's rational man, as he points at his map. "There's the Nile. And there's the sea."

Easy. Simple. Sane. Of course, as the hot winds blow and the sun beats a tattoo on the wandering Roberts and his charge, the aristocratic artist Venture (Michel Piccoli), and hope evaporates as quickly as stolen water, his sentence might as well come advertised as Famous Last Words. The question is, how lost will he get?

As lost as possible. "Passion in the Desert," a most uncharacteristic story by the 19th-Century French novelist Honoré de Balzac—who has inspired two movies opening today, the other being "Cousin Bette"—has been embellished a bit by filmmaker Lavinia Currier. But at its heart is the nature of the relationship that erupts between a man and a leopard, and more importantly the nature of man. It is a magically strange movie, reckless, overheated and purer in its filmic content than one is ever likely to see these days. It's also highly emotional, if one accepts its conclusion that man is forever caught on the horns of a dual and irreconcilable nature.

Currier, making her first feature, is clearly enamored of the story, which poses questions current in Balzac's 1840s about the nature of man, about Rousseauian philosophy and about the status of man vis-a-vis art and nature. (Which is higher? Where are we?) And those questions remain current. But she is most definitely besotted by what develops into the eroticized desert marriage between Robert—whose belief system has crumbled—and the leopard he calls Simoom. (Robert suggests Josephine, but drops it.) She's an animal who asks nothing but faith in her nature—which is supposed to be totally unpredictable, but pales in that regard when compared with man.

As played by the talented Ben Daniels, who exhibits an enormous amount of courage in his intimate scenes with the notoriously quirky cats (three leopards, a solitary and essentially untrainable species, play Simoom), Robert is blond, lithe and catlike. But it's the nature not of cats but of Robert that is central to the story, and Robert, like Simoom, is an exceptional example of his kind.

Certainly, the lumpen, radically democratic infantry of his troop—who fire their cannon on ancient sphinxes, ostensibly because they were built with slave labor for aristocrats—would follow any creed if it fed them. But Robert is different. No artist, he nonetheless supports Venture in his Bonaparte-backed project of sketching desert sculpture, staying with him as the troops pull out, helping him as their water disappears (Venture, ever the artist, steals extra water to mix his paint, then in desperation drinks it). And when he meets Simoom in the ruined desert temple where he's taken refuge from some vengeful Bedouins, what's left of his "civilized" facade collapses.

The film is gloriously shot, cinematographer Andrei Rodionov ("Orlando") making optimum use both of the Jordanian landscapes and of the cats themselves. Editor Nicolas Gaster also deserves special praise for his fairly seamless work. Between the restrictions on how leopards can be used, and the uncooperative nature of the beasts, making the Robert-Simoom scenes must have been a laborious, dangerous process, the sort perhaps undertaken only by a first-time and impassioned director.

VILLAGE VOICE, 6/16/98, p. 160, Leslie Camhi

Of these two films based on works by Balzac, *Passion in the Dessert* is by far the stranger. [The reference is to *Cousin Bette*; see Camhi's review of that film.] You have to admire first-time director Lavinia Currier's audacity in taking on this nearly unfilmable 10-page story. the movie opens with a bit of *English Patient* envy: a wounded hero lies near death in the desert when he's rescued by passing bedouins. Cut to better times: Augustin (Ben Daniels), a captain in Napoleon's army, is accompanying Venture (Michel Piccoli), an artist sketching monuments in Egypt. Lost in a sandstorm, they wander for days amid blinding heat. Augustin survives to find a lost city and a precious source of water guarded by a female panther.

Being a Frenchman, Augustin overlooks her claws and admires her feline beauty. A sensualist by nature, the panther warms to his attentions. Soon she's sharing the spoils of her hunts and her desert survival tactics. The fascination of watching these two blonds carouse amid splendid scenery begins to wane when a male panther interrupts their folie à deux.

Balzac's tale is told secondhand, by an old soldier recalling his youth. I still think it's best as a literary product, half real, half fantasy; cinema suspends our disbelief too entirely. In the story, the panther is both erotic and otherworldly; on screen she's something of a sex kitten. True to our late-20th-century preoccupation with ecology, Currier has turned a novella about the Romantic sublime into a strained and oddly extended story about one man's endurance test with nature.

Also reviewed in:
CHICAGO TRIBUNE, 7/10/98, Friday/p. D, Michael Wilmington
NEW REPUBLIC, 7/6/98, p. 28, Stanley Kauffmann
NEW YORK TIMES, 6/12/98, p. E20, Lawrence Van Gelder
VARIETY, 9/22-28/97, p. 39, Emanuel Levy
WASHINGTON POST, 7/10/98, p. D5, Rita Kempley

PATCH ADAMS

A Universal Pictures release of a Blue Wolf-Farrell/Minoff-Bungalow 78 production. *Executive Producer:* Marsha Garles Williams and Tom Shadyac. *Producer:* Barry Kemp, Mike Farrell, Marvin Minoff, and Charles Newirth. *Director:* Tom Shadyac. *Screenplay:* Steve Oedekerk. *Based on the book "Gesundheit: Good Health Is a Laughing Matter" by:* Hunter Doherty Adams and Maureen Mylander. *Director of Photography:* Phedon Papamichael. *Editor:* Don Zimmerman. *Music:* Marc Shaiman. *Music Editor:* J.J. George. *Sound:* Nelson Stoll, Steve

Maslow, Gregg Landaker, and (music) Dennis Sands. *Sound Editor:* Michael Hilkene. *Casting:* Debra Zane. *Production Designer:* Linda DeScenna. *Art Director:* Jim Nedza. *Set Designer:* Erin Kemp. *Set Decorator:* Ric McElvin. *Set Dresser:* David G. Ronan, Alan E. Easley, Jim Poynter, and Tony Piller. *Special Effects:* David Blitstein. *Costumes:* Judy Ruskin-Howell. *Make-up:* Hallie D'Amore. *Make-up (Robin Williams):* Cheri Minns. *Running time:* 110 minutes. *MPAA Rating:* PG-13.

CAST: Robin Williams (Patch Adams); Daniel London (Truman); Monica Potter (Carin); Philip Seymour Hoffman (Mitch); Bob Gunton (Dean Walcott); Josef Sommer (Dr. Eaton); Irma P. Hall (Joletta); Frances Lee McCain (Judy); Harve Presnell (Dean Anderson); Daniella Kuhn (Adelane); Jake Bowen (Bryan); Peter Coyote (Bill Davis); James Greene (Bile); Michael Jeter (Rudy); Harold Gould (Arthur Mendelson); Bruce Bohne (Trevor Beene); Harry Groener (Dr. Prack); Barry "Shabaka" Henley (Emmet); Stephen Anthony Jones (Charlie); Richard Kiley (Dr. Titan); Douglas Roberts (Larry); Ellen Albertini Dow (Aggie); Alan Tudyk (Everton); Ryan Hurst (Neil); Peter Siiteri (Chess Man); Tim Wiggins (Scared Customer); Helen Tourtillott (Feeble Woman); On West (Instructor); Domenique Lozano (Paserby); Ralph Peduto (Organizer); Ken Hoffman (Big Texan); Jim Antonio and Roy Conrad (E.R. Doctors); Jay Jacobus (Jack Walton); Dot-Marie Jones (Miss Meat); Geoff Fiorito and Samuel Sheng (3rd Year Students); Kathleen Stefano (Margery); Piers MacKenzie (Dr. Hashman); Alex Gonzalez (Hispanic Boy); Ismael "East" Carlo (Hispanic Father); Wanda McCaddon (Woman in Lobby); Wanda Christine (Nurse Klegg); Lorri Holt (Pediatric Nurse); Stephanie Smith (Laughing Nurse); Mary Delorenzo (Nurse); Vivia (Hysterical Woman); Donna Kimball (Waitress); Norman Alden (Truck Driver); Lydell M. Cheshier (Younger Man); Diane Amos and Sonya Eddy (Older Waitresses); Kelvin Yee (Orderly); Doreen Chou Croft (Asian Woman); Bill Roberson (Fred Jarvis); Randy Oglesby (Pinstriped Man); Vilma Vitanza (Maria); Bonnie Johnson (Walcott's Secretary); Jack Ford (Lecturer); Christine Pineda (Hispanic Girl); Karen Michel (Mrs. Davis); James Allen (Ed); Katherine A. Fitzhugh (Mrs. O'Bannon); Kyle Timothy Smith and Jonathan Holder (Davis Sons); Renee Rogers and Shanón Orrock (Receptionists); Don Rizzo (Minister); Andrew Clement (Puppeteer); George Lee Masters, Daniel P. Hannafin, and Roger W. Durrett (Boardroom Doctors).

LOS ANGELES TIMES, 12/25/98, Calendar/p. 2, Jack Mathews

The moment of truth in Tom Shadyac's "Patch Adams," the moment that will test audience willingness to suspend disbelief, comes at about the midpoint of the movie when a man writhing in agony with pancreatic cancer is made to laugh by a doctor acting like a clown.

It's not that such a thing couldn't happen. Maybe it did. "Patch Adams" is based on the true story of a jokester physician, played in the film by Robin Williams, who sees humor, intimacy and bedside manner as vital components of disease therapy.

In his book, the real Patch Adams told how his experiences as a mental patient led him to the therapeutic benefits of laughter, how his application of humor to treatment got him in trouble with medical authorities, and how he began creating his free clinic, the Gesundheit Institute, where illness is combated with humanism.

All that is retold in the movie, but what Patch Adams couldn't do, even with the funniest man alive portraying him, is tell the filmmakers how to apply his healing touch to a movie script. If Patch Adams made that dying man laugh, surely, it didn't happen this way.

Williams may have enough goodwill to get audiences through these awkward moments, but the reactions of the patients and the beguiled nursing staff to the stodgy antics overreach to a level that is almost insulting. Williams knows when material is working, and he knows the sound of an honestly aroused crowd. This ain't it! There are plenty of laughs in "Patch Adams," but most of them emerge from moments when Williams appears to be vamping, or at least working with his own material. As we've discovered in so many of his movies, Williams' internal muse, under the yoke of a script, cannot sustain a character beyond the moment.

Meanwhile, he's stuck in roles that inevitably combine canned humor with overcooked sentiment. There's a sense of laziness or unworthiness about the writing done for him. It's as if the writers know they can't connect with Williams' unique comedy source, so they simply concoct "funny" scenes they hope he'll personalize and elevate. Sometimes he does, sometimes not.

Williams is nothing if not a good sport, and he certainly gives better than he gets from the disjointed script (by Steve Oedekerk and others), particularly during the first half of the film, when we follow Patch's progress from the mental institution to his eventful early years in medical school.

This section is the film's best, but it's still a mixed bag of comedy and bogus drama. Entire scenes occur as hospital room riffs, with Patch doing clown shtick for patients, then being dressed down by the medical school's inhumanly cold Dean Wolcott (Bob Gunton). "Patch Adams" is built on the assumption that administrators are fed ice water intravenously, and that medical students smile at the risk of lowering their grade-point average.

These humorless scrubs include Patch's insufferably serious roommate Mitch (Philip Seymour Hoffman), a would-be third-generation doctor determined to honor his family, and Carin (Monica Potter), who's fighting a virtual army of perceived sexist demons. It's easy to understand why Mitch hates Patch; the guy goofs off constantly and still gets better grades. And Carin's resistance to Patch's romantic pressure is understandable; he's older than most of her professors.

Patch does find a kindred spirit in Truman (Daniel London), another eccentric outsider with unconventional views on doctoring. Together, and with Carin finally won over, they begin to create Gesundheit Institute as a moonlighting venture that will have tragic consequences and place Patch in the dock of med school justice, with his career riding on the outcome.

Shadyac, whose past comedies ("Ace Ventura," "The Nutty Professor") lacked the melodrama of "Patch Adams," has essentially directed two different movies here, a comedy and a romantic tragedy, and the shift in tone is so abrupt you may need to consult a doctor for whiplash. If you get one like Patch, good luck.

NEW YORK, 1/18/99, p. 61, Peter Rainer

When I saw *Patch Adams* at a press screening last month, I held out the faint hope that it would just go away. But no, it's the top-grossing holiday-season movie, which means we're fated to gaze ad nauseam at those movie ads with Robin Williams looking misty as a child's hand reaches up to his improvised clown nose—a red enema bulb. For Williams, this has been a banner year for blubber—first *What Dreams May Come* and now this, a wilted weepie about a real-life doctor who bucks the medical Establishment and trumpets the medicinal value of laughter. (Patch is the antic, smiling-through-tears counterpart to his huggy-bear therapist in *Good Will Hunting.*) I can hardly wait for his next film. A remake of *Stella Dallas*, perhaps?

The common misconception about Williams is that he's a great nutbrain comic who deliquesces into a pool of drool every time he gets real. That's a disservice to the fine, modulated work he's done in the past, in such films as *The World According to Garp, Moscow on the Hudson, Dead Poets Society, and The Birdcage.* But those days are fast receding, and lately he's not very funny either. He's become a Flubberized, fuzzy-wuzzy family comedian, which, eerily, is exactly what happened to another great comic, Richard Pryor, when he crossed into movieland big-time. Nowadays, if you want a memory jog to Williams's past brain-buzzing glories, you have to catch him cracking up on the talk shows, or acting as a presenter on the Oscars. He's gotten punchy. Williams is playing out an old, sad showbiz story—the dulling-out, at premium prices, of a once firebrand talent. Does he really believe slicing margarine is the best use of his cutting edge?

NEW YORK POST, 12/24/99, p. 34, Rod Dreher

If it's Christmas, it must be time for dreaded holiday perennials such as fruitcake, "Jingle Bells," ACLU anti-creche lawsuits and a treacly Robin Williams movie.

This year's sugar bomb, "Patch Adams," in which the terminally twinkly actor plays a doctor who really does believe that laughter is the best medicine, is desperately awful. Worse, it so epitomizes the talented actor's worst instincts on morbid display that Williams' friends, family and fans should contemplate staging an intervention. The guy apparently can't help himself—he's a schmaltz addict.

Coming on the heels of the glucosal "What Dreams May Come," "Patch Adams," which opens tomorrow, establishes Williams as the maestro of movie mawk. You just watch: If Williams is not dragged out of his deepening rut and forced to play a villain—or any role in which he doesn't beg to be loved—he eventually will remake Jerry Lewis' never-released Auschwitz atrocity, "The Day the Clown Cried." You read it here first.

In one key scene, Patch clips the tip off an enema bulb and plonks it on his honker, all to make a sick child laugh. This is the image, with the tot's widdle hand weaching up toward Patch's weally, weally wed nose, that Universal has been using to market the film in its posters and ads. It's a perfect Rorschach test for the movie.

That is, if that photograph makes you smile, and feel all gooey and toasty-warm inside, "Patch Adams" will, too. If, however, it gives you an unexpected appreciation for the bedside manner of Dr. Jack Kevorkian, you've probably already given up on the gifted but misguided Williams.

The title role in "Patch Adams" is tailor-made for the actor, who has made a bad habit of playing manic man-child characters whose ebullient sense of wonder is meant to convert or condemn the repressed mugwumps of the world—you know, the sorts of people who hate mimes and clowns.

Dr. Patch Adams is nothing if not clownish. The movie begins in the nuthouse, with a morbidly depressed Hunter Adams (Williams) checking himself in to save his own life. But he discovers that the psychiatrists are unfeeling automatons who treat their patients like cattle. Hunter, by contrast, makes his fellow asylum inmates laugh, and heals himself thereby.

If only his physician had put him on a Thorazine drip! But, no, Hunter rechristens himself "Patch" and enters medical school. You can tell how kooky and free-spirited he is by his color-splotched shirts. Alas, nobody appreciates Patch's clowning; in fact, they all want to tell him to grow the hell up.

But we know that they are the ones who really need to grow. Patch fertilizes the fallow field with that enema-bulb stunt in the children's ward at the hospital. Then it's off to the races with Williams, who runs wild with his gibbery tics, his comic voices, his ad libs and unrestrained zaniness, like Rip Taylor with his sack of confetti.

Except Rip Taylor is about slapstick looniness, and nothing but.

"Patch Adams" might have been better as a straight-up comedy—"Ace Ventura, M.D." But Williams has to soak his crackling comic bits in bathetic melodrama to the maximum squish point, and ladle on the sanctimony like gravy.

Why? Because we, too, must be healed, must be set free from the mind-forg'd manacles of conformity.

Hmph. I suspect that most of us, if we were dying in a hospital, would want a doctor we could trust, not some failed stand-up comic with a Messiah complex and an enema bulb on his nose. Need I tell you that the whole thing ends up in a courtroom setting, with Our Lord and Savior Patch Adams surrounding himself with the Sick Children, defending his humorist heresy against the med school Sanhedrin?

It's all so depressing—and so familiar to anyone who has followed Williams' career this decade. Who is Patch Adams but a variation on Jack, the "lovable" man-child he played in the woeful movie of the same name?

Is he not an amped-up version of the hyperempathetic, I-love-you-man shrink Williams played in "Good Will Hunting"—who was a near-reprise of Williams' compassionate doctor in "Awakenings"? And who better as a soulmate for Patch Adams than the huggable humanitarian physician Williams played earlier this year in the unwatchably sentimental "When Dreams May Come"?

Of all Williams' roles, Patch Adams comes closest to John Keating, the rousing teacher at a repressed (natch) boys school in "Dead Poets Society." Keating is a lively performer who makes his students love literature and find joy in and hope for a nonconformist life for themselves. Until, of course, they are all cruelly brought low by the dark forces of reaction.

What's ultimately annoying about these woolly headed dreamers is how smarmy and self-righteous they are about their mission. They're like spoiled children whose inability to deal with reality is somehow passed off as a creative virtue, and whose cases can be made only by positing them against cardboard villains, a.k.a. grown-ups.

To be fair, Williams has been very good in other roles, particularly when working for directors who wouldn't allow him to indulge himself—Mike Nichols in "The Birdcage," for example.

But he takes these Mr. Nice Guy parts so often that you can't help wondering what kind of profound anxieties Williams suffers from. The cliche holds that the source of the best comedians' humor is a deep wound they cannot or will not heal. Is Robin Williams so desperate to be liked that he is willing to typecast himself in these schlocky, superficial roles, even at the risk of his reputation?

He obviously has the versatility to play a wider range of characters. What he may well lack is courage.

He'd be advised to find it soon, because if he keeps this up, Williams may drive us all to misanthropy. I'm already dreading his next film, "Jakob the Liar," which sounds a lot like "Life Is Beautiful." In the movie, Williams plays a World War II Polish Jew who keeps the spirits of his ghetto-dwelling comrades high by passing off made-up stories of Nazi defeats.

Now, the idea of keeping the spirits of the oppressed high by lying to them about reality poses an interesting moral dilemma. But knowing Williams will be the one to raise the spirits of suffering Jews suggests a horrible possibility—the idea that the Holocaust is just another force of repression for our hideously lovable Robin to triumph over.

SIGHT AND SOUND, 3/99, p. 46, Kevin Maher

North Virginia, 1969. After a failed suicide attempt Hunter Adams checks himself into Fairfax psychiatric hospital. Because he has a rapport with other patients and is disgusted with current medical practice, he decides to become a doctor himself. Two years later he attends Virginia Medical University. Unhappy with the lack of patient contact, Adams makes secret visits to the college hospital to entertain terminally ill children. Walcott, the dean of studies, finds out about Adams' trips and warns him to keep away from the hospital. Adams falls for one of his classmates, Carin, and continues visiting and entertaining the patients. He is discovered and given a final warning.

Unperturbed Adams decides to set up a free hospital in the countryside of West Virginia with Carin and another medical student, Truman. The hospital, named the Gesundheit Institute, is an immediate success. One night, while Adams and Truman are stealing basic supplies from the college hospital, Carin is murdered by a Gesundheit patient. Walcott learns of Gesundheit and expels Adams from the college for practising without being qualified. Adams goes to the board of appeal to plead his case. At the hearing, Adams defends Gesundheit and demands that doctors care more for their patients. He is reinstated by the board and later graduates.

"You have a gift, you have a way with people—they like you!" is just one of the many platitudinous commendations repeatedly hurled at Robin Williams 'Patch Adams' in this excessively sentimental movie. Playing a benevolent doctor of laughter, Williams returns once again here to the altruistic man-child persona that first gained him fame in the television series *Mork & Mindy* and was honed in such films as *Dead Poets Society, The Fisher King, Jack and Jumanji*. Yet in crafting *Patch Adams* into an archetypal 'Robin Williams vehicle' comedy director Tom Shadyac *(Liar Liar)* and writer Steve Oedekerk (who co-wrote *The Nutty Professor* with Shadyac and others) have merely highlighted how limited and reductive this same wide-eyed persona has become.

The film-makers have taken the admirably radical life of Hunter Doherty Adams as described in the quasi-autobiographical book *Gesundheit: Good Health is a Laughing Matter*, and processed it through the screenwriting mill. Gone are the years spent touring Europe, the trips to Russia, the pleas for world peace, the work in black ghettos and the conscientious objector status—all elements formally and politically problematic for a mainstream movie. Instead, ten days of positive affirmation in a mental institution and a week of arguments with Dean Walcott are transformed, *pace* Joseph Campbell or John Grisham, into the key structural trials of Adams' life. (Incidentally, Adams earned the moniker 'Patch' from the black anti-Vietnam badge he always wore on his doctor's lapel, and not, as the movie so quaintly suggests, from fixing a leaking cup with sticky-tape.)

Then there's Adams himself. Familiar to many Americans from his numerous television appearances, at a lanky six feet and four inches, with long hair and a conspicuous Salvador Dali moustache, he could hardly be physically farther from Williams' short, neatly cropped and clean-shaven hero. Of course, this hardly matters since Williams is clearly playing Williams here. And though *Patch Adams* flirts with the staples of the college flick, the hospital tearjerker and the courtroom drama, the greater part of its effect depends upon how one feels about Williams' slapstick and manic-delivery shtick. Director Shadyac underscores Williams' comic routines with superfluous and frankly relentless reaction shots of patients and hospital staff alike crumpling with laughter. It's an effect that becomes strangely numbing, and it helps convince us that yet again we're watching a showcase for Williams' familiar talents rather than the natural progression of a fictional character.

Finally, and in what can only be described as an immense lapse in judgement, the film-makers have chosen to have real cancer-stricken children playing themselves in the hospital scenes. This means that after some predictable lip-service is paid to dying with dignity and humanity, the children are wheeled out in the movie's closing courtroom scene as a visual punchline to Adams' syrupy rhetoric. That real pain and suffering could be used so casually and insouciantly is a sad indictment of a movie that purports to deal with the altruism of its central character while assuaging only the egotism of its star.

TIME, 12/28/98-1/4/99, p. 177, Richard Corliss

The latest installment in Robin Williams' campaign for screen sainthood casts him as Hunter ("Patch") Adams, a medical student whose belief that "we have to treat the patient as well as the disease" sends him into patients' rooms with balloon animals, an enema-bulb clown nose and a song in his heart (*Blue Skies*).

There's wisdom in the *Reader's Digest* bromide that laughter is the best medicine; we could name two recent invalids whose hearts were lifted by David Sedaris' impression of Billie Holiday singing the Oscar Mayer jingle on NPR. But waking old folks at midnight and making loud mischief seem like a manic camp counselor's idea of fun: indoctrination by comedy. The supporting characters, from the hospital dean (Harve Presnell) to Patch's girlfriend (Monica Potter), are similarly bludgeoned. They begin as skeptics and end, their wills crushed, as dewy believers.

What's even sadder is the talent wasted. Director Tom Shadyac's other films *(Ace Ventura: Pet Detective, The Nutty Professor, Liar Liar)* are bright, off-kilter farces; scripter Steve Oedekerk wrote *Professor*. It is a crime against humority that they and Williams (who in a chair next to Letterman is still our most brilliant word surrealist) renounce the work they've practiced with such abandon and invention for *Patch's* bullying sentimentality. Comics who want to do *Hamlet* often end up, as here, serving big, sticky slices of ham.

VILLAGE VOICE, 12/29/98, p. 128, Dennis Lim

The medical establishment is roundly censured in *Patch Adams,* a movie irresponsible enough to propose that doctors should behave like Robin Williams. The title character is based on a real person, Hunter "Patch" Adams, M.D., an advocate of "humor therapy" and the author of a woolly-headed, self-promoting book called *Gesundheit: Good Health Is a Laughing Matter.* I have no idea what the real Dr. Adams is like, but his screen incarnation is grotesquely familiar, a compendium of Williams's messiah/manchild roles from *Awakenings, Dead Poets Society, Good Will Hunting,* and, most distressingly, *Jack.*

Patch Adams opens as most Robin Williams movies should end, with its protagonist checking into a mental institution. He doesn't stay long, though, his suicidal thoughts abating as soon as he's alerted to the oddly cheering effects of his attention-hound antics. The logical next step is apparently medical school, where Patch's blindingly ugly shirts single him out as a freethinking renegade. Bemoaning the drill-sergeant mentality of his teachers and the unhealthy emotional distance between doctors and patients, he's soon breaking into hospital wards, spreading cheer to sick children and morose adults with slapstick routines that involve enema bulbs, bedpans, and IV stands.

Both the real Patch Adams and the Robin Williams version yammer on at length about the therapeutic qualities of humor; in the film at least, this theoretically sensible school of thought amounts to nothing more than a buffoonish, scarily maniacal bedside manner, which, far from being salubrious, is more likely to trigger relapses and lawsuits. Worse, the movie is intent on presenting its hero as a social visionary when his numerous epiphanies are notable for a surreal impracticality worthy of particularly out-of-it potheads. (Health care too expensive and bureaucratic? Make it free! On a ranch! In the woods!) Its simpleminded mawkishness aside, Patch *Adams* also represents filmic storytelling at its most corrupt. Crude doesn't begin to describe the characters. "Passion doesn't make doctors. I make doctors!" the demonic dean duly thunders. To no avail, of course. Ever the twinkly-eyed altruist, Patch wins over one careerist colleague after another, most conspicuously an icy female classmate (Monica Potter) who's eventually thawed out by Patch's overwhelming virtuousness, and whose subsequent ill fortune occasions a rigged crisis of faith. Patch regains his composure in time for a climactic tantrum before a medical review board, after which the aforementioned sick children file in for a weepy encore. It's an unforgettable image, stunning in its crassness, and a fitting coda for the year's most repugnant movie.

Also reviewed in:
CHICAGO TRIBUNE, 12/25/98, Friday/p. D, Mark Caro
NEW YORK TIMES, 12/24/98, p. E6, Janet Maslin
NEW YORKER, 1/25/99, p. 96, David Denby
VARIETY, 12/21/98-1/3/99, p. 74, Joe Leydon
WASHINGTON POST, 12/25/98, p. C5, Stephen Hunter
WASHINTON POST, 12/25/98, Weekend/p. 8, Rita Kempley

PAUL MONETTE: THE BRINK OF SUMMER'S END

A First Run Features release of a Brink of Summer's End production. *Producer:* Lesli Klainberg. *Director:* Monte Bramer. *Screenplay:* Monte Bramer. *Music:* John Ehrlich. *Running time:* 90 minutes. *MPAA Rating:* Not Rated.

WITH: Linda Hunt (Narrator); Jonathan Fried (Readings).

LOS ANGELES TIMES, 5/22/98, Calendar/p. 16, David Chute

It is sometimes difficult, and perhaps even wrongheaded, to cling to normal critical standards when judging documentaries. The complex force of something real can be overpowering, even when the best that can be said is that the filmmaker doesn't impose himself between the viewer and the material.

Monte Bramer's "Paul Monette: The Brink of Summer's End" is a case in point. A thoroughly conventional clips-and-interviews documentary—standard TV bio stuff—it is nevertheless a powerful record of a life devoted stubbornly, even heroically, to self-expression. The power derives from the material rather than the movie-making, but that doesn't mean the power isn't real, or significant.

An openly gay poet and novelist ("The Long Shot"), Monette won a National Book Award in 1992 for his memoir "Becoming a Man: Half a Life Story." At that point he had already lost two lovers to AIDS and was terminally ill himself. His determination to keep writing every single day, shuffling to the computer clinging to his IV stand, must have required huge reserves of physical courage.

Monette emerges as a role model not just for writers, and not just for gay writers, but for anyone inclined to take the freedom to speak and to create for granted. Monette in one scene displays an "I Am Salman Rushdie" pin conspicuously on his lapel, a clear indication that he understood, and fully intended, the larger implications.

"Becoming a Man" was designed to be the book Monette had longed to read as a young gay man, but couldn't find, because it didn't yet exist; a plain-spoken account of shared experience that rang true and offered useful advice and reassurance. If the award-winning status of the book means anything (always an open question), it's that the work transcends its immediate purpose, that it describes one form of a common human occurrence and makes its universality clear. As

Monette says here: "We all have a closet we have to come out of if we are ever going to be free."

One of the documentary's strongest "subplots" is an assessment of what it cost the writer to arrive at that mature outlook. At the start, according to his editor, Monette was not so much a man who wanted to write as a charismatic young go-getter "who wanted to be a writer." In retrospect, it seems, the only thing missing was a personal experience harrowing enough to stir him to the core, to burn off the impurities.

Monette seems to have been transfigured, transmuted into an artist, by his experience of AIDS, his lovers' and then his own. His first work of nonfiction, "Borrowed Time: An AIDS Memoir," was an unflinching yet affirmative and even romantic account of his life with his companion of 12 years, attorney Roger Horwitz, and of Horwitz's illness and death; it's a book often cited as the first about the plague to cross over strongly to straight readers.

Will "Borrowed Time" survive as the "Diary of Anne Frank" of the AIDS scourge, as Monette himself incautiously suggests? It's an indication of the personal power of his story that we respond to Monette's most extreme positions (like the equivalence implied here between AIDS and the Holocaust) not with acceptance, perhaps, but certainly with understanding. They emerge as consistent extensions of a personality, essential components of a full portrait.

A movie can honestly earn an emotional response in many ways, and distinguished film technique is only one of them. "I'm not dying of AIDS," Monette insists. "I'm dying of homophobia." In this film, and in the most literal possible sense, we can see where Paul Monette was coming from.

NEW YORK POST, 2/6/98, p. 52, Thelma Adams

If there were a tag line for Monte Bramer's heartbreaking documentary about the late gay activist and author, it would be: "Paul Monette insists on joy."

"Paul Monette: The Brink of Summer's End" opens at the Quad today, the third anniversary of his death from AIDS. What makes it so moving is the author's struggle to reconcile joy and despair, love and rage.

Bramer and producer Lesli Klainberg assemble the usual assortment of talking heads, family photos and home movies, while editing three years of footage shot in the author's company at the end of his life. Linda Hunt narrates. Jonathan Fried recites the author's work.

Born in 1945, Monette—a poet, a novelist, an essayist, a New Englander, an Ivy Leaguer—found his voice writing poetry and gay novels ("Taking Care of Mrs. Carroll"). But the National Book Award-winning author found his subject matter, his reason to write, with the loss of his longtime lover, the lawyer Roger Horwitz, in 1986.

Horwitz's death inspired Monette to write "Borrowed Time: An AIDS Memoir," which he followed with his 1992 autobiography, "Becoming a Man: Half a Life Story."

In a brief 90 minutes, we discover that while the AIDS virus cut Monette's life short (he died at 50), he managed to experience a life and a half by facing down his demons, embracing his "differentness," working and loving with all his heart, and insisting on joy. It's a lesson to us all.

VILLAGE VOICE, 2/10/98, p. 104, Mark Huisman

With AIDS a meek headline in the news, welcome is the film that mercilessly reminds us that, no matter the drug or policy debate du jour, people are still dying. *Paul Monette: The Brink of Summer's End* chronicles the life behind works of poetry, fiction, and two sharply observant memoirs, *Borrowed Time* (about the loss of his first lover) and *Becoming a Man: Half a Life Story*.

Director Monte Bramer and producer Lesli Klainberg followed Monette from Hollywood readings and Washington marches to vacations abroad for the two and a half years preceding his death in 1995. The result is a film of quiet intimacy and intense emotional power. It won a well-deserved Audience Award for best documentary at Sundance in 1997 and is a likely Oscar contender.

Condensing any life into 90 minutes is no easy feat. There are standard biopic interviews with friends like actress Judith Light and Larry Kramer. But every anecdote is matched with perfect images. Monette's brother Robert recounts the team they made—two little boys, one gay, the other with spina bifida—as we see photographs of Robert in leg braces and home movies of snow sledding. Cryptococcal meningitis, revealed in closeups of brain scans, is intercut with shots of Monette, lounging in a hammock, writing pad in hand. Snapshots and home videos featuring Monette's lovers, Roger Horwitz, Stephen Kolzak (both lost to AIDS), and Winston Wilde, celebrate the endurance of love.

Of all voices here, Monette's is clearest. Directly addressing the camera or in clips of TV appearances, he exhibits an artist's passion and an activist's determination. Most affecting are passages from Monette's writing, read as yet another elegiac stream of images unfolds.

While the film lacks the graphic nature of 1993's *Silverlake Life,* it confronts death unflinchingly. Here is the epidemic lately ignored by the press: pill bottles and IV drips, a trembling hand, a shrunken frame collapsed in sleep. While Monette kept writing until the day he died—the need to finish one last story seemed to sustain him—the movie explodes the myth that people "live on" through their work. His thoughts and life experiences linger in writing we can easily revisit, but that voice, the mind that gave it to us, is gone forever.

Also reviewed in:
NEW YORK TIMES, 2/6/98, p. E12, Stephen Holden
VARIETY, 2/3-9/97, p. 49, Godfrey Cheshire

PAULIE

A Dreamworks Pictures release of a Mutual Film Company production. *Executive Producer:* Ginny Nugent. *Producer:* Mark Gordon, Gary Levinsohn, and Allison Lyon Segan. *Director:* John Roberts. *Screenplay:* Laurie Craig. *Director of Photography:* Tony Pierce-Roberts. *Editor:* Bruce Cannon. *Music:* John Debney. *Music Editor:* Tom Carlson. *Sound:* Joseph Geisinger. *Sound Editor:* David Hankins. *Casting:* Risa Bramon Garcia, Randi Hiller, and Sarah Finn. *Production Designer:* Dennis Washington. *Art Director:* Tom Taylor. *Set Designer:* John Berger. *Set Decorator:* Denise Pizzini. *Set Dresser:* David Ronan, Alan Baptiste, and Greg Sanger. *Special Effects:* Dave Kelsey and Tracey Levy. *Costumes:* Mary Zophres. *Make-up:* Tracey Levy. *Make-up (Gena Rowlands):* Christina Smith. *Animal Stunt Coordinator:* Boone Narr. *Animator:* Constance Bracewell and Sean Dever. *Running time:* 92 minutes. *MPAA Rating:* PG.

CAST: Gena Rowlands (Ivy); Tony Shalhoub (Misha); Cheech Marin (Ignacio); Bruce Davison (Dr. Reingold); Jay Mohr (Paulie/Benny); Trini Alvarado (Adult Marie); Buddy Hackett (Artie); Hallie Kate Eisensberg (Marie) Matt Craven (Warren); Bill Cobbs (Virgil); Tia Texada (Ruby/Lupe); Laura Harrington (Lila); Charles Parks (Gerald); Peter Basch and Emily Mura-Smith (Grad Students); Hal Robinson (Grandpa); Seth Mumy (Jeremy); Francesca Federico-O'Murchu (Molly); Jerry Winsett (Mr. Tauper); Dig Wayne and Michael Leydon Campbell (Research Assistants); Nicole Chamberlain (Shirley); Tamara Zook (Speech Therapist); Kristie Transeau (Veterinarian).

LOS ANGELES TIMES, 4/17/98, Calendar/p. 21, Bob Heisler

[*The following review by Bob Heisler appeared in a slightly different form in* NEWSDAY, 4/17/98, Part II/p. B6.]

Make an appointment with your kids or borrow some children from your neighbor and see "Paulie," a perfect family movie with the intelligence, humor and hug-me moments to be a great first-date movie, too. Just remember to bring a hankie.

With a wonderful script by Laurie Craig and starring 14 Blue-Crown Conures with Bette Davis eyes, Charlie Chaplin waddles and E.B. White world views, "Paulie" is a classic quest movie: Bird meets girl, bird loses girl, bird travels across the continent to find girl. Setting the movie as a flashback with Paulie recounting his story—to Russian emigre janitor Misha (Tony Shalhoub) who discovers the bird locked in the dungeon of an animal research institute—provides all the explanation needed to make our hero credible. He has the loyalty of Lassie, the vocabulary of Mr. Ed and the knack for meeting people of Stuart Little.

But don't think of "Paulie" as an animal movie; it's a love story that asks the very human question: When should you speak up and when should you remain silent? Paulie learns to talk (in the voice of the busy Jay Mohr) as his human friend Marie tries to overcome her stutter. Marie couldn't talk, Dad couldn't listen and Mom couldn't cope, Paulie tells Misha. The father (fathers, cats and scientists don't fare well here) gets rid of Paulie anyway because he thinks Marie is getting too attached to him. His love for her is a debt that must be repaid.

Epic quest movies are episodic by nature, and Paulie's adventures include a stint in a pawn shop where he learns to sing "What's New, Pussycat?" and insult customers, and where he meets Ivy (Gena Rowlands), an artist who teaches him manners and how to fly. Ivy takes him home to Marie, but the family has moved west to Los Angeles, so off they go in Ivy's Winnebago.

Rowlands fills the screen with a grace and a humanity that teaches Paulie more than just to say "please." When she can no longer drive, Paulie stays with her. When she dies, Paulie recalls her lessons and—for the first time—flies on toward Los Angeles.

He arrives in East L.A., where he gets a steady gig singing backup in a taco-stand band trained by Ignacio (Cheech Marin). He plays Pip to the Gladys Knight of the fair Lupe, the prettiest parrot in L.A., who wins Paulie's heart by repeating his own declarations of affection. It's a great life until Benny (also Mohr) birdnaps Paulie and forces him into a life of crime in exchange for a promise to help him find Marie. This leads to a life sentence as a prisoner of conscience in the research institute in which Misha finds him.

The birds playing Paulie were selected and trained by Boone Narr, who trained the mice in DreamWorks' most successful movie to date, "Mouse Hunt." But Paulie has none of that film's violence or cynicism.

Yes, you can drop the kids at "Paulie" and see something a little more R, but you'd be encouraging Hollywood to keep dividing movies (and us) into silly for children, stupid for young teens, shocking for older teens and sexually dysfunctional for everyone else. And you'd be missing a chance to see what a family movie is supposed to be.

NEW STATESMAN, 7/31/98, p. 42, Gerald Kaufman

It is a relief to find that *Paulie*, though its eponymous hero is a parrot which not only talks but converses almost incessantly, contains not a single bird dropping. Paulie, because of his garrulousness, is taken away from his loving owner and spends the rest of the movie on a mission to make his way back to little Marie.

Emanating as it does from Steven Spielberg's production company Dream Works, *Paulie* is crammed with references to other movies. Paulie himself is an avian ET. His adventures with a group of human ne'er-do-wells owe more than a little to Disney's *Pinocchio*. The middle-aged fairy godmother (a lovely performance by Gena Rowlands), who takes him into her home for a while, seems to be modelled on the comforting role played by Lillian Gish in *Night of the Hunter*. There is also a sly little episode in which the parrot cheers on the marauding birds while watching a televised extract from Hitchcock's *The Birds*.

Paulie, whose special effects are as skilled as those in *Dr Dolittle* but less ostentatious, stretches its exiguous material almost to breaking point. At only 91 minutes, it has its longueurs. Yet it is suffused with touching charm, containing evocative images of huge Spielbergian night skies, magical silhouettes and an exuberant moment (low-flying helicopter shots) when the timid parrot spreads his wings and soars into flight. *Paulie* may not be a big-budget blockbuster, but it has the far more precious quality of being the rare kind of movie that a little girl could love.

NEW YORK POST, 4/17/98, p. 53, Thelma Adams

Who knew the sensible spirit of TV's Mr. Ed would be reincarnated under the feathers of a talking parrot named Paulie?

Those who saw the comedy's title of the same name and shriveled at the idea that it might star Pauly Shore can relax. There's a lot of squawking in this movie, but none of it's from Shore.

John Roberts' comedy, from Laurie Craig's script, is part of a dying breed—and I'm not referring to talking horses. This smart family movie doesn't condescend to the audience and resists pandering to "Dawson's Creek" tastes.

Paulie (the voice of Jay Mohr) is the childhood friend of a gilded little stutterer named Marie (Hallie Kate Eisenberg). When she goes to speech therapy, it's the bird that benefits. This parrot not only talks—he spells!

In the movie's single false note, Marie's dad (Matt Craven) is crueler than Himmler himself. He believes his daughter's friendship with Paulie is keeping her in a fantasy world. He banishes the parrot and breaks Marie's heart.

But sometimes we need evil daddies to get the plot going (think Grimm). Paulie learns "talking just gets you into a lot of trouble."

Then he embarks on an awesome adventure that brings him into contact with three fabulous fairy godmothers: Gena Rowlands, Cheech Marin and Tony Shalhoub.

Even Buddy Hackett takes a bow. Bruce Davison and Mohr (in the flesh) play villains who try to exploit Paulie's talents, and Trini Alvarado makes a sweet grown-up Marie.

"Paulie" is episodic but brimming with warmth and humor. The bird has a finely tuned b.s. meter—a necessity that's increasingly rare in Hollywood family fare.

In one of the screen's wisest treatments of death for a young audience, Paulie explains one character's demise with: "And then one day the cat got her."

And, Paulie the parrot, thanks to animal stunt coordinator Boone Narr, has more acting talent than Quentin Tarantino. But, then again, so did Mr. Ed.

SIGHT AND SOUND, 9/98, p. 51, Amanda Lipman

Misha, a Russian immigrant to Los Angeles, finds a cleaning job at an animal study institute. There he discovers Paulie, a talking parrot. He wins Paulie's trust and the parrot recounts in flashback how he was separated from his first owner, a little girl in New Jersey called Marie, by her unsympathetic father.

From New Jersey, Paulie sets out to find Marie at her new home in LA. On the way, he befriends elderly painter Ivy and mariachi musician Ignacio and his singing parrots. Paulie is kidnapped by small time hustler Benny. Paulie soon becomes his partner in crime but is captured and taken to the animal institute. Realising that the scientists are hoping to use him to further their careers, he refuses to talk any more and is put in the basement where Misha discovers him. Misha helps him find Marie, now a grown woman, and falls in love with Marie himself.

Made by Spielberg's DreamWorks Pictures, *Paulie* has a host of special-effects credits but, to its own credit perhaps, does not look like an SFX film. *Babe,* a previous talking-animal film, appeared mechanical at times, caught up in the complexity of anthropomorphising its large farmyard cast while trying to retain their animal features. *Paulie,* by contrast, feels all the more fluid for only having a parrot to deal with, allowing us to concentrate on his wry, wisecracking journey to happiness.

Paulie is inexplicably able to interact with the human world, and has been given the character of a small-time hustler from New Jersey who finds a temporary partner in Benny, a human NJ hustler (played by Jay Mohr, who also voices Paulie). But while Benny is less than appealing, the unattractive edges of such a character have been smoothed away in Paulie, who retains a sharp, rather crude sense of humour and an amoral eye for making some dishonest cash. Such a personality works very well when combined with the comedy to be found in humanising the bird's beady-eyed expressions and movements.

The film begins and ends with a sentimental relationship between Marie and Paulie, which finally extends to include Misha. But it is no sentimental education. If the diminutive hero learns anything, it is that he can fly if he tries (the idea that Paulie is too scared to fly somehow seems perfectly plausible in a film in which a bird teaches a little girl not to stutter). Fortunately, Paulie holds back on the full-blown self-help implications of this theme, preferring to symbolise it briskly with the odd sunrise. The tendency to didacticism is further diluted by the structure, a picaresque series of largely engaging encounters between Paulie and various inhabitants of the human world. While all the unattractive characteristics in the film belong to the white males—Marie's father, Benny, Doctor Reingold—this is never schematised so as to become the film's guiding light. Gena Rowlands makes a dignified cameo appearance as Ivy, a kindly but determined widowed artist who resolves to teach Paulie manners. Cheech Marin's Ignacio and his performing parrots add a rumbustious, comical tone (and how many films have brought together the stars of *Cheech and Chong* and *Gloria*?).

The only relationship that jars is that with Misha, not because of its critical implications that the US is not quite the dreamland it promises to be for this literature professor, but because, as the film rather disingenuously points out itself, Misha's own stories are too long. Perhaps parodying Russian literature, they are also too relentlessly melancholy, unbalancing the lighter atmosphere of the rest of the film and temporarily losing the interest of a young audience, not to mention an older one.

Also reviewed in:
CHICAGO TRIBUNE, 4/17/98, Friday/p. D, Michael Wilmington
NEW YORK TIMES, 4/17/98, p. E22, Lawrence Van Gelder
VARIETY, 4/20-26/98, p. 43, Todd McCarthy

PECKER

A Fine Line Features release of a Polar Entertainment production. *Executive Producer:* Mark Ordesky, Joe Revitte, Jonathan Weisgal, and Joe Caracciolo, Jr. *Producer:* John Fiedler and Mark Tarlov. *Director:* John Waters. *Screenplay:* John Waters. *Director of Photography:* Robert Stevens. *Editor:* Janice Hampton. *Music:* Stewart Copeland. *Music Editor:* Michael Dittrick. *Sound:* Rick Angelella. *Casting:* Pat Moran, Billy Hopkins, Suzanne Smith, and Kerry Barden. *Production Designer:* Vincent Peranio. *Art Director:* Scott Pina. *Set Decorator:* Patty Burgee. *Costumes:* Van Smith. *Make-up:* Betty Beebe. *Running time:* 87 minutes. *MPAA Rating:* R.

CAST: Edward Furlong (Pecker); Christina Ricci (Shelley); Bess Armstrong (Dr. Klompus); Mark Joy (Jimmy); Mary Kay Place (Joyce); Martha Plimpton (Tina); Brendan Sexton III (Matt); Mink Stole (Precinct Captain); Lili Taylor (Rorey); Patricia Hearst (Lynn Wentworth); Jean Schertler (Memama); Lauren Hulsey (Little Chrissy); Maureen Fischer (T-Bone); Donald Neal (Mr. Bozak); Carolyn Stayer (Miss Betty); Jack Webster (Outsider Al); Alan J. Wendl (Mr. Nellbox); Judith Knight Young ("Fat and Furious" Lady); Anthony Rogers (Billy Heckman, "Death Row Dave"); Billy Tolzman (Seafood Sam); Brian Thomas (Larry the Lughead); Tim Caggiano (Lester Hallbrook); Betsy Ames (Venetia Keydash); Scott Morgan (Jed Coleman); Valerie Karasek (Redd Larchmont); Cindy Sherman (Herself); Joyce Flick Wendl (Street Lady); Liam Hughes (Wild Man of 22nd Street); Greg Gorman (Himself); Irving Jacobs (Guzzles); Mary Vivian Pearce (Homophobic Lady); Kennen Sisco (Art Fan A); Jennifer Zakroff (Art Fan B); Angela Calo (Pregnant Girl); Susan Duvall (Saleswoman); Ruth Lawson Walsh (Sneaky Customer); Adin Alai (Body Builder); Emmy Collins (Hippie); Brigid Berlin (Super Market Rich Lady); Kimberlee Suerth (Beautiful Girl); John Badila (Irate Manager); R. Scott Williams (Stylist); Susan Lowe (Hairdresser); Maris Zalabak (Make-up Artist); Andreas Kraemer (Junkie); Sharon Neisp (Bouncer); Delaney Williams (Construction Worker); Bobby Brown (Average Joe); Regi Davis (Cop A); Tyler Miller (Randy, Blind Photographer); Channing Wilroy (Wise Guy Neighbor); Rosemary Knower (Friend of Mary A); Kate Kiley (Friend of Mary B); Jack French (Old Fart Customer); Doug Roberts (Mr. Heckman, Death Row Dave's Father); Patsy Grady Abrams (Mrs. Heckman, Death Row Dave's Mother); Holly Twyford (Straight Girl); Joshua Shoemaker (Channel 11 Anchor); Sloane Brown (Channel 45 Anchor); Thomas Korzeniowski (Toupé Man); Susan Greenhill (Voice of Miraculous Virgin Mary); Lola Pashalinski (Voice of Pelt Room Announcer).

LOS ANGELES TIMES, 9/25/98, Calendar/p. 2, Kenneth Turan

[The following review by Kenneth Turan appeared in a slightly different form in
NEWSDAY, 9/25/98, Part II/p. B6.]

"Pecker" is a cautionary tale as only John Waters can caution. Think of writer-director Waters as the Frank Capra of an alternate universe and this film as his genially twisted version of "It's a Wonderful Life," and you'll begin to understand.

Having Capra and Waters in the same paragraph would have been unthinkable 25 years ago, when the Baltimore-based filmmaker scalded sensibilities with his outrageous "Pink Flamingos."

But though Waters' director credit appears over a shot of rats having sex, time has softened him a bit (as well as coarsening a lot else), so this latest combination of good humor and bad taste seems downright innocent, even sentimental at times.

Ostensibly named after a lifelong habit of pecking at his food, 18-year-old Pecker (Edward Furlong) is a happy-go-lucky guy who believes "everyone always looks good" through the lens of his thrift-shop camera.

Unfailingly cheerful and upbeat, Pecker will photograph anything, even the cheeseburgers at the Sub Pit snack shop he works at. Always on the lookout for "Pecker moments," he uses his friends and family as subjects and serves as our guide to Waters' version of blue-collar Baltimore, a wacked-out wonderland where everyone lives in a state of tongue-in-cheek innocence.

Pecker's best pal, Matt (Brendan Sexton III), is the boy king of Baltimore's shoplifters, always ready to help out when more film needs to be stolen. Pecker's girlfriend, Shelley (Christina Ricci), is the zealous manager of the Spin 'n' Grin Laundromat, a woman who can never relax because "people with dirty laundry can be animals."

Pecker's family is more of the same. His mom, Joyce (Mary Kay Place), runs a thrift shop where street people who worry about not having any fall colors in their wardrobe can shop in comfort, while dad Jimmy (Mark Joy) runs a bar called the Claw Machine. His main competition is a new place called the Pelt Room, where surly lesbians take it all off, leading to such tongue-twisting lines of dialogue as "No free peeking in the Pelt Room, Pecker." Really.

Pecker's older sister, Tina (Martha Plimpton), is delighted to be working in a male go-go club called the Fudge Palace, while younger sister Little Chrissy (Lauren Hulsey) has a full-blown sugar addiction. As for grandmother Memama (Jean Schertler), she divides her time between selling pitbeef sandwiches (apparently a Baltimore delicacy) and believing that her statue of the Virgin Mary is a talking miracle that says "full of grace, full of grace" at slight provocation.

Sure, these people are a little eccentric, but, gosh darn it, everyone is happy until the evil specter of the Manhattan art world comes to town in the person of Rorey Wheeler (Lili Taylor), Manhattan gallery owner extraordinaire.

Quicker than a New York minute, Rorey has eyeballed Pecker's work, set up a show and bound him over hand and foot to the celebrity machine. Suddenly he's on the cover of Artforum, being called "a teenage Weegee" by the New York Times and featured in a show at the Whitney called, yes, "A Peek at Pecker."

Just as George Bailey in "It's a Wonderful Life" didn't appreciate his ordinary life until it was all but gone, so Pecker and his gang suddenly find that celebrity, being "just like the Jackson family," can be a pastel nightmare for all concerned. But you already knew that, didn't you.

"Pecker" spices its amusing pokes at the New York art world with appearances by real-life photographers Greg Gorman and Cindy Sherman, and the film's theme that "what they call art in New York looks like just plain misery to me" goes down as easy as anything Waters has ever done.

"Pecker's" tone, as always with this director, is wall-to-wall ironic, and the film does have its raunchier moments, like a giant close-up of one of the pelts that made the Pelt Room famous. Mostly, however, the proceedings are surprisingly sweet and cheerful. The John Waters who told Vanity Fair that his greatest achievement was "making trash 1% more respectable" shows just how it's done here.

NEW YORK POST, 9/25/98, p. 53, Larry Worth

Finding middle ground between the outrageousness of "Pink Flamingos" and mainstream acceptance has proven an uphill battle for down-and-dirty auteur John Waters.

He tried and failed to reach a wider audience with "Cry-Baby" and "Serial Mom." And though his latest, "Pecker," marks a step in the right direction, there's still a ways to go.

For the most part, the script promises far more than it delivers, telling of Pecker, a young photographer (Edward Furlong) whose lens not only immortalizes friends and family in his native Baltimore but makes him a SoHo sensation to rival Basquiat.

The plot's familiar themes of exploitation, social prejudice, the price of fame and the sweetness of revenge are nothing special, but within those well-worn tapestries, Waters weaves some rich subjects.

While Pecker is simply a camera-carrying Candide, those surrounding him are delicious eccentrics. Those include Pecker's stain-obsessed, laundry manager amour (Christina Ricci), a mom (Mary Kay Place) who outfits the homeless, an older sister (Martha Plimpton) who emcees at a gay strip club, a bratty younger sister (Lauren Hulsey) with a sugar fixation, a thieving best friend (Brandon Sexton III), an unscrupulous New York gallery owner (Lili Taylor) and a grandmother (Jean Schertler) who sells "pit beef" on the sidewalk between chats with the Virgin Mary.

The performers, without exception, are dead-on. Furlong deserves special credit for imbuing a bland character with enough quirks and inflections to generate interest. And supporting cast members are delightful. The ever-underrated, nearly unrecognizable Plimpton is a standout as the straight-shooting lover of all things gay. Further, characters' dialogue and tongue-in-cheek settings like the Pelt Room and Fudge Palace (draw your own conclusions) provide hilarious touches. Too bad they never add up.

Equally problematic: Waters' labored efforts to ape his classics, such as watching rats copulate, showcasing a gay turn-on called "teabagging," letting lesbian strippers bare all or simply spotlighting regulars Mink Stole and Patty Hearst. The result is more miss than hit.

As it turns out, the salacious title is a tip-off to the production's tease-then-disappoint nature. Clearly, audiences know what "pecker" means. But the script belabors that Pecker earned his nickname from "pecking" at his food as a child. Yeah, right.

Suffice to say that Waters should count his lucky stars. Furlong, Plimpton et al. not only distract from such silliness but do their darnedest to make "Pecker" Divine.

SIGHT AND SOUND, 2/99, p. 50, Mark Kermode

In Baltimore, amateur photographer Pecker takes pictures of his friends and family, which he exhibits in the fast-food store where he works. Glamorous female art-dealer Rorey Wheeler stumbles upon Pecker's work, and whisks him off to New York City. After an exhibition in a gallery, Pecker is fêted as a naive genius while his subjects are sneered at by the metropolis' art cognoscenti.

Back in Baltimore, Pecker's photographs begin to cause trouble. His best friend Matt becomes too well known to be a thief, his girlfriend Shelley receives obscene phone calls and his younger, sugar-obsessed sister Chrissy is visited by a social worker who prescribes Ritalin to calm her down. Meanwhile, his older sister loses her job at the Fudge Palace nightclub because Pecker has photographed its clientele in compromising positions. Its rival the Pelt Room is picketed for showing pubic hair, and Pecker's grandmother Memama loses the ability to talk to her plaster statue of the Virgin Mary.

When a *Vogue* fashion photographer comes to Baltimore he humiliates Pecker's homeless friends by dressing them in designer clothes. Rejecting Rorey's sexual advances, Pecker turns down an exhibition at the Whitney Museum in New York and instead invites the glitterati to come to Baltimore, where they are confronted with pictures of themselves looking ridiculous which Pecker shot in New York. At the ensuing party, the Virgin Mary statue speaks, and the crowd toast the "end of irony."

The greatest irony of John Waters' career is that he has ended up loving and being loved by Baltimore, the town he initially tried so hard to infuriate. From being the most disgusting film-maker in the world, Waters has become something of a local hero, venerated for bringing an element of glitter into an area not known for its star-spangled potential. Nowadays one of the main reasons for visiting Baltimore is to gawp at the place where the trash-maestro first put a camera up someone's fundament and to see where the cast of *Pink Flamingos* inspired one critic to demand: who are these people? Where do they go when the sun comes up? Isn't there a law or something?"

In his fifteenth film, which the writer/director describes as, "my satire of a Woody Allen movie," Waters balances his affection for Baltimore with an equal contempt for New York. For Waters, the Big Apple is full of fraudsters desperate to be different, while Baltimore is packed with genuinely queer folk, a quality which makes *Pecker*. His crowd is much more likable than their big-city counterparts (making Dave Hardin's soundtrack rendition of 'Baltimore, You're Home to Me' sound oddly free of irony). From Pecker's girlfriend Shelley, Christina Ricci's fiercely independent laundromat mistress, to Pecker's grandmother (played by Jean Schertler) who talks to a statue of the Virgin Mary, and his father who staunchly asserts "pubic hair causes crime", all of Pecker's pals are affectionately drawn, rather than vulgar, caricatures.

Waters loves these people—indeed, their quirks seem drawn from elements of his own personality. While it's easy to read Pecker himself as a thinly veiled portrait of the artist, traces of Waters run deep even in sugar-crazed Little Chrissy, whom Pecker thanks for teaching him "that life is nothing if you're not obsessed." Pecker's sister Tina dishes up a classic string of Watersesque MC patter at the Fudge Palace ("This is Death Row Dave! He's a three-time loser who's been sentenced to the chair but he's still got a boner!"), while Shelley becomes the auteur's mouthpiece when she realises true beauty can be found even in "the brilliant green of a grass stain, the subtle yellow of a urine-soaked sheet, or the aqua blue of cold water as it dilutes a violent red blood stain."

As usual, Waters' coy sweetness is tempered by an almost bloody-minded need to offend somebody. So we get to see two rats having sex, a man masturbating on a washing machine, a psychotic child snorting peas up a $10 bill, a lecherous phone caller (Waters himself making pointed use of the word 'vagina', and even a sub-soft-porno-style insert of 'beaver bush' which will presumably keep the film out of some family-oriented video stores. But when delectations of this kind are served up against the comb-and-paper innocence of such ear-tickling pop gems as Paul Evans' 'Happy Go Lucky Me' and Leroy Pullins' 'I'm A Nut', it's hard to imagine how anyone could take umbrage.

Cameos are liberally scattered throughout the film. These include a by-now-expected appearance from Patty Hearst as well as Waters' stalwart Mink Stole supplementing walk-ons for artist Cindy Sherman and art critic Greg Gorman, who lend credibility to Waters' broad swipes at the art world. Edward Furlong, Martha Plimpton and little Lauren Hulsey handle their roles with racey aplomb, but the show is stolen by Christina Ricci, a cross between Jane Russell and Norman Bates who continues to be the most exciting and entertaining screen actress working in and out of Hollywood today. Few people could bring such weight to the role of Pecker's "stain-Goddess" girlfriend, but when she tells an irritating customer to, "get out and take your tired wardrobe with you" it's hard not to stand up and cheer. Not quite on a par with *Cry-Baby* and even less likely to cause a box-office stir than *Serial Mom*, *Pecker* remains a refreshing reminder of Waters's spunky talents, and offers continued proof that there really is a very thin line between treasure and trash.

Also reviewed in:
CHICAGO TRIBUNE, 9/25/98, Friday/p. M, Michael Wilmington
NATION, 10/5/98, p. 44, Stuart Klawans
NEW YORK TIMES, 9/25/98, p. E15, Janet Maslin
VARIETY, 9/14-20/98, p. 39, Emanuel Levy
WASHINGTON POST, 9/25/98, p. B1, Stephen Hunter
WASHINGTON POST, 9/25/98, Weekend/p. 62, Michael O'Sullivan

PEREIRA DECLARES ("SOSTIENE PEREIRA")

A Mikado Film (Italy) and Fabrica de Imagens (Portugal) release of a Jean Vigo International/KG Productions film. *Producer:* Elda Ferri. *Director:* Roberto Faenza. *Screenplay (based on his novel/Italian with English subtitles):* Antonio Tabucchi, Roberto Faenza, and Sergio Vecchio. *Director of Photography:* Blasco Giurato. *Editor:* Franco Casellato. *Music:* Ennio Morricone.

Sound: Eric Vaucher.   *Art Director:* Giantito Burchiellaro.   *Costumes:* Elisabetta Beraldo. *Running time:* 104 minutes. *MPAA Rating:* Not Rated.

CAST: Marcello Mastroianni (Pereira);   Daniel Auteuil (Doctor Cardoso);   Stefano Dionisi (Monteiro Rossi);   Nicoletta Braschi (Marta);   Marthe Keller (Signora Delgado);   Joaquim de Almeida (Manuel);   and with: Teresa Madruga;   Nicolau Breyner;   Filipe Ferrer;   Mario Viegas;   Joao Grosso.

NEW YORK POST, 4/3/98, p. 50, Larry Worth

Marcello Mastroianni died on Dec. 19, 1996. But one couldn't tell from the number of films that keep coming out, all with the late, great superstar front and center. Now, with Robert Faenza's "Pereira Declares," Mastroianni demonstrates again that he was a master to the very end.

The tale, set in Lisbon of 1938, deals with a sedate newspaper writer whose passion for fighting the good fight is reignited by a young colleague. The two take on fascism's growing threat within Salazar's repressive government.

Though Faenza's direction is often plodding, the actors are topnotch. Even when weighed down with padding to make him look hefty, Mastroianni is utterly convincing. Supporting players Daniel Auteil, Marthe Keller and Joaquim de Almeida also rise to the challenge.

Granted, "Pereira Declares" won't be remembered as one of Mastroianni's very best. But his undeniable presence and talent transform a familiar tale into compelling cinema.

VILLAGE VOICE, 4/7/98, p. 72, Leslie Camhi

Subversives are also the subject of *Pereira Declares*, Roberto Faenza's feature set in 1938 Lisbon [The reference is to *Point of Order*: see Camhi's review of that film.] Portugal, under the dictatorship of Salazar, is allied with Fascists in Spain and Italy. Marcello Mastroianni plays Pereira, a widower and the culture editor of a Lisbon daily. Overweight, highly educated, and perpetually melancholy, he shuffles between a grand, derelict apartment, a shabby office, and a local café. His existential anxiety is left for discussions with his skeptical priest and his philosophically minded cardiologist (Daniel Auteuil).

One day Pereira impulsively decides to hire a charming but ill-qualified young assistant. This basically apolitical youth, Monteiro Rossi (Stefano Dionisi), is in love with a militant anti-Fascist. The articles he writes are all unpublishable for ideological reasons, but slowly he wakes Pereira from his long political sleep.

As Pereira, the inimitable Mastroianni seems a bit lost amid rolls of fake flesh, though the hesitancy is also part of his character. Perhaps it's the bane of European coproductions that none of the actors seem really at home, adrift in a vague sea of Portuguese, Italian, and French. Still, it's inspiring to watch this fine cast mull over the political stakes of European culture from the continent's very edge.

Also reviewed in:
NEW YORK TIMES, 4/3/98, p. E26, Lawrence Van Gelder
VARIETY, 4/10-16/95, p. 46, David Rooney

PERFECT MURDER, A

A Warner Bros. release of a Kopelson Entertainment production. *Executive Producer:* Stephen Brown.   *Producer:* Arnold Kopelson, Anne Kopelson, Christopher Mankiewicz, and Peter MacGregor-Scott. *Director:* Andrew Davis. *Screenplay:* Patrick Smith Kelly. *Based on the play "Dial M for Murder" by:* Frederick Knott. *Director of Photography:* Dariusz Wolski. *Editor:* Dennis Virkler. *Music:* James Newton Howard. *Music Editor:* Jim Weidman. *Sound:* Tom Nelson and (music) Shawn Murphy. *Sound Editor:* Bruce Stambler. *Casting:* Amanda Mackey Johnson and Cathy Sandrich. *Production Designer:* Philip Rosenberg. *Art Director:*

Patricia Woodbridge. Set Decorator: Debra Schutt. *Special Effects:* Jeffrey S. Brink. *Costumes:* Ellen Mirojnick. *Make-up:* Naomi Donne. *Make-up (Michael Douglas):* Tom Lucas. *Stunt Coordinator:* Michael Runyard. *Running time:* 105 minutes. *MPAA Rating:* R.

CAST: Michael Douglas (Steven Taylor); Gwyneth Paltrow (Emily Bradford Taylor); Viggo Mortensen (David Shaw); David Suchet (Mohamed Karaman); Sarita Choudhury (Raquel Martinez); Michael P. Moran (Bobby Fain); Novella Nelson (Ambassador Alice Wills); Constance Towers (Sandra Bradford); Will Lyman (Jason Gates); Maeve McGuire (Ann Gates); Stephen Singer (Effete Man at Met); Laurinda Barrett (Met Woman #1); Aideen O'Kelly (Met Woman #2); Reed Birney (Merchant Prince #1); Robert Vincent Smith (Merchant Prince #2); Bill Ambrozy (Merchant Prince #3); Geroge S. Blumenthal (Merchant Prince #4); Iris Alten, Marion Blumenthal, Andrew Sussman, Robynn N. Sussman, Radney Tucker, Beverly Tucker, Bradford Billet (Guests at Met); Robert Bosco Cokljat (Croatian Delegate); Marat Yusim (Russian Delegate); Lee Wong (Japanese Diplomat); Roberta Orlan (Italian Diplomat); Francis Dumaurier (French Delegate); Deen Badarou (African Delegate); Peter Benson (Hansen); Jeff Williams (Nolan); David Eigenberg (Stein); Jean Debaer (Secretary); Michel Moinot (Maitre d'); Gerrit Vooren (Waiter); Monica Parker (Janice Moran); Michael H. Ingram (Albert); Scott Dillin (Detective Scott); Starla Benford (Police Technician); Bob Bowersox (Police Photographer); Joanna P. Adler (Vyczowski); James Georgiades (Policeman #2); Jose Ramon Rosario (Policeman #1); Gerry Becker (Roger Brill); William Bogert (Harrington); Adrian Martinez (Young Tough); Dexter Brown (Porter).

LOS ANGELES TIMES, 6/5/98, Calendar/p. 8, Kenneth Turan

"Trashy but potent" is how dark prince of Wall Street Steven Taylor (Michael Douglas) describes the canvases of sexy, enigmatic artist David Shaw (Viggo Mortensen). "A Perfect Murder," the film they inhabit, tries hard to live up to that description, but the effort is too much to sustain.

Handsomely mounted and richly melodramatic, "A Perfect Murder" benefits from the gift director Andrew Davis ("The Fugitive") has for adding intelligence to pulp shockers. And being based on the play that became Alfred Hitchcock's "Dial M for Murder" gives the film an impressive pedigree.

But in their zeal to "contemporize" that story, to drag it into the anything-goes '90s, the producers and screenwriter Patrick Smith Kelly have changed the moral balance of the picture in a way that hampers audience satisfaction. "A Perfect Murder" begins better than it ends, and the pleasures it offers turn out to be more of a transitory nature.

One of the treats of "A Perfect Murder" is the good, disreputable fun that's been had in typecasting the film's leads, starting with Douglas as the scheming commodities trader who asks questions like "What's our exposure?" and is never ever happy with the answers.

Steven Taylor is essentially a juicy reprise of "Wall Street's" Gordon Gekko for Douglas. In "Perfect Murder" he looks more powerfully reptilian than ever, with a trace of the undead Count Yorga, Vampire, thrown in for variety. Few actors are as well-suited for making these preposterously amoral captains of industry plausible, or have quite Douglas' way with lines like "I've always thought 'bludgeon' has a spur of the moment sound."

Mortensen, though less well known than Douglas, is similarly and expertly cast to type as a character not likely to be mistaken for Jimmy Stewart. Mortensen's Shaw is a sexually charged artist with a studio in Brooklyn who allows paint to stain his hands but never the sheets of his rarely empty bed.

What these two men have in common is a passion for Emily Bradford Taylor, the wife of one an the mistress of the other. A blond heiress with a hefty trust fund (Grace Kelly played the part in the Hitchcock version), Emily has the kind of job assisting the American ambassador to the United Nations that allows her to take extended amorous lunches at Shaw's quintessentially bohemian studio.

When Gwyneth Paltrow, who plays the role with the appropriate aristocratic sheen, first came to notice with a galvanizing performance as a raw, unpredictable young woman in "Flesh and Bone," it would have been difficult to predict her current incarnation as the studio's favorite icy blond object of desire; the ways of Hollywood are murky indeed.

Once again, as in "Great Expectations," Paltrow in effect plays the virgin imprisoned in the tower, a poor little rich girl desperately in need of rescuing, though the '90s being what they are even virgins are more sexually active than they used to be.

"A Perfect Murder" begins with Emily in bed with David, desperately in love and starting to want to get out of her marriage. The question the film posits is how much does husband Steven know and, given that it's inevitable that he find out, what's he going to do about it.

"A Perfect Murder" looks great as photographed by Darius Wolski, and the spectacular Fifth Avenue apartment created by production designer Philip Rosenberg, art director Patricia Woodbridge and set decorator Debra Schutt on an 11,000-square-foot set in Jersey City will have New Yorkers weeping in envy. But the way the critical plot questions are resolved is acceptable but nowhere near as memorable.

For, paradoxically, once everyone's cards are on the table the film's tensions lessen, not increase. Partly it's because the characters' amorality becomes too predictable, and partly it's because Paltrow's character, the one we end up caring about most, is also the film's least developed.

Emily does speak at least two foreign languages fluently (including Arabic with a somber detective played by David Suchet), and has aristocratic Constance Towers (in a far cry from the roles she played for Sam Fuller) for a mother. But she seems to have interested the filmmakers more as a construct than a character. When she tells a friend that she's thinking of leaving Steven because "he has no real idea who I am," it's easier to sympathize with the in-the-dark husband than it should be.

NEW YORK, 6/15/98, p. 49, David Denby

In the swank new thriller *A Perfect Murder*, Michael Douglas plays a cuckolded husband who loves his wife and plots her death at the same time. The performance is the culmination of Douglas's work as an actor; he is superb—complexly nuanced in a way that he has never been before. For years, Michael Douglas has dominated one movie after another with his baleful stare and saturnine temperament. If anything, Douglas was too incisive an actor: In such movies as *Wall Street* and *Fatal Attraction,* his characters were defined by the single emotion of rage; they lacked depth and variety, the play of humor. In *Basic Instinct* and *Falling Down,* Douglas gave way to passion without humanizing passion, and even though one recognized his precision and skill, one could hardly warm to him. What was he so angry about? His face seemed fixed in a sneer. Yet he became a major box-office draw, and since snarlers have rarely become stars (Edward G. Robinson was an exception; Richard Widmark was a star mainly of B movies), something in Douglas obviously fascinated the public. That something, I think, was intelligence, which audiences instinctively reach out to. Douglas has played a certain type of man that we recognize as emblematic of our time—the success, the capitalist, the man who knows the score and prides himself on his perfect control of everything. Yet anger separates this man from other people. Isolated in a momentous job or a big house, cut off from love, friendship, and ease, Douglas the winner is also a loser, and even as we relished the character's mastery, we also relished his unhappiness, which released us from envy.

In *A Perfect Murder,* we don't at first know what has gone wrong between Steven Taylor (Douglas), a wealthy Wall Street investor, and his elegant young wife, Emily (Gwyneth Paltrow). When the movie opens, Emily, who works at the U.N. as a translator, is in bed with her lover, David Shaw (Viggo Mortensen), a soulful young artist—at least, that is what Emily thinks he is. David is soft-spoken and makes haunted-looking portraits; most of all, he is attentive to Emily. Later that day, the Taylors go to some sort of posh benefit at the Metropolitan Museum of Art, and David is there, and from the way Douglas plays the scene—with icy politeness—it is clear that Steven knows that his wife and the artist are having an affair. It is also clear from Douglas's manner—self-sufficient to the point of haughtiness—why the marriage is over. The debonair dark-blue shirts, just a touch flamboyant; the modishly long, swept-back hair—Douglas exudes egotistical well-being. No woman but a masochist could stay in love with this smug rotter for long. He is suffocating his young wife.

Steven has lost Emily's love, and the loss is killing him. It is also amusing him. Douglas's lips, which have gone softly sinister in recent years, quiver slightly; he even smiles, as if enjoying some private joke at his own expense. When Steven goes to see the artist in his Brooklyn loft—a dark, cavernous lair—he confronts him with self-lacerating humor, as if to say, "You're a bum, and still you have ousted me from the marriage bed. Funny, isn't it?" We admire the lucidity of this hateful man. He takes action the way men like him always do in movies: He hires someone to murder his wife.

If all this sounds vaguely familiar, you may want to know that *A Perfect Murder* is based on the same Frederick Knott play that inspired Alfred Hitchcock's *Dial M for Murder* in 1954. Patrick Smith Kelly, the screenwriter, and Andrew Davis, the director, have productively (and rightly) updated the story, moving it from fifties London to contemporary New York, and from an atmosphere of quiet wealth to one of high-level finance and social power. They have also changed the plot in fascinating ways that I won't reveal. Hitchcock accepted and even reveled in the stage-derived claustrophobia of the action; his direction amounted to virtuoso manipulation of limited means (there were many entrances and exits, an enormous fuss about door keys). In the married couple's small apartment, the three principals (Ray Milland, Grace Kelly, and, as the lover, Robert Cummings) mixed and drank many cocktails while exchanging perfectly phrased remarks. Hitchcock's movie, which reeks of the stage, is a great deal of fun, an enduringly fascinating example of dry-ice elegance.

Andrew Davis, the director of *The Fugitive,* one of the best thrillers of recent years, has added pace and heat and explicit sexuality to the material without whipping up phony excitement. His direction is swift and very effective, and the movie, shot in shades of ebony (the color of black marble), looks exceptionally handsome. *A Perfect Murder* is a very proficient and enjoyable big-budget thriller. Yet there is one bizarre structural error. The filmmakers establish with many significant close-ups the character played by the fine British actor David Suchet—a New York police detective of Arab descent, whom Emily can talk to, conspiratorially, in Arabic. Then they drop him out of the movie—he plays no part in the violent denouement. Feminism has intervened in the 45 years since Hitchcock handled this material: A woman must now fight her own battles. What is most memorable about the new version, however, is the emotional complexity of the husband who loves his wife yet whose pride won't allow her to live. By conveying the bitters of private amusement, Douglas transcends the sexual-revenge clichés of the plot. Douglas's objectivity—the ability to see the character as masterful yet also defeated and to take intellectual pleasure from Steven's desperate gamesmanship—brings us close to him. We admire, almost like, this man. Douglas dominates this movie as he has dominated his past movies, but he's never deserved the limelight more.

NEW YORK POST, 6/5/98, p. 47, Thelma Adams

Kill my wife—please!

And what a wife! In Andrew Davis "A Perfect Murder," Gwyneth Paltrow is Emily Taylor, a multilingual stunner with a closet to die for. This heiress isn't so much a character as a catalog of material desires.

If only this thriller—loosely lifted from Alfred Hitchcock's "Dial M for Murder" by Patrick Smith Kelly—came with a 1-800 number.

I'm dying to know more about the chocolate shearling coat, mocha cigarette skirt and suede boots Mrs. Taylor models from the Upper East Side to Brooklyn's Williamsburg.

A symphony in brown, Emily's the most sophisticated of Tootsie Rolls. But Paltrow is no Grace Kelly, the designated victim in "Dial M." Gwyneth's Manhattan moneybags doesn't have the hats—or the icy reserve.

Emily is torn between two men: hubby Steven Taylor (Michael Douglas, in full "morally bankrupt aging capitalist" mode) and David Shaw (Viggo Mortensen), a craggy artist with angst where his wallet should be.

When Taylor (the Ray Milland role) learns that his Wall Street firm is crashing and his wife is double dipping, he sells his soul short with the plan that strikes fear in every heiress' heart: Pay the lover to kill the wife, bagging the cash and ending the affair in one bloody night.

We all know there's no such thing as a perfect marriage—or a perfect murder. Douglas goes chin dimple to chin dimple with Mortensen (the creep who mock-raped Demi Moore in "G.I. Jane"), recruiting the artist for a crime so convoluted, it would take Agatha Christie sleuth Hercule Poirot to untwist it.

Fortunately, a slimmed-down David Suchet (PBS snoop Poirot) steps in to solve the crime. Despite all the drop-dead threads, the gala evenings at the Met's Temple of Dendur and the $200,000 kitchen (and crime scene), the case is just a standard-issue uxoricide (that's a husband killing his wife).

Davis ("The Fugitive") directs with rich surface style and so-so suspense. Why exhume a Hitchcock classic? Douglas' amoral stockbroker Gordon Gekko had the best answer in "Wall Street": "If something is worth doing, it's worth-doing for the money."

NEWSDAY, 6/5/98, part II/p. B7, Jack Mathews

In 1980, when Universal Pictures reissued Alfred Hitchcock's "Dial M for Murder" in its original 3-D format, critics of that '50s process were compelled to rethink their objections. Hitchcock's 1954 thriller studiously avoided stunt shots in which objects are flung off the screen into the audience, and instead used the dimension of depth to enhance the story's claustrophobic setting.

"Dial M," adapted from a stage play, starred Ray Milland as a man plotting the murder of his wealthy and unfaithful wife (Grace Kelly), and the key scenes took place in the couple's study, where, on cue, the killer was to emerge from behind a drape and strangle the woman while her husband listened on the telephone.

While most directors adapting stage material look for ways to open it into a naturalistic setting, Hitchcock used 3-D to go the other way. By placing furniture in the foreground and keeping his cameras moving, he effectively drew the audience into the room with the killer and his prey, ratcheting the tension to an almost unbearable level.

For "A Perfect Murder," the remake of "Dial M," director Andrew Davis ("The Fugitive") didn't have that option. He had to open the story up, and in doing so, expanded it in ways that, while undeniably entertaining, diminish its emotional power.

With Michael Douglas in the Milland role, Gwyneth Paltrow replacing Kelly, and Viggo Mortensen as the boyfriend played earlier by Robert Cummings, this version of "Dial M" attempts to blend old and new-fashioned suspense, and comes off as a slick, cooly calculated, and generally engaging exercise in homage. What it is not is scary.

Though screenwriter Patrick Smith Kelly takes huge liberties with the source material, "A Perfect Murder" preserves the central issues of "Dial M." Douglas' Steven Taylor is an unscrupulous commodities trader dependent on his wife's fortune, which he intends to claim outright—before she can dump him and marry her lover—by having her snuffed during a faked burglary.

It's a perfectly premeditated murder, with an airtight alibi. Except it doesn't happen. During the struggle, the would-be killer is killed by the would-be victim, leaving the husband to vamp a new strategy.

As a vision of vulnerable beauty, Kelly is hard to replace, even by Paltrow, but overall "A Perfect Murder" boasts a stronger cast than "Dial M" Douglas has been playing this buttoned-down villain for years, and he's never been better or more menacing at it. And Mortensen, whose character has been transformed into someone far less innocent, is a more vital and compelling rival than Cummings.

It should be said that the version of "Dial M" that most people saw in 1954, and have been seeing ever since, isn't very compelling, either. By the time "Dial M" was finished, 3-D had fallen out of favor, and the studio released it in "flat," two-dimensional format. It undermined Hitchcock's design, robbed it of its tension, and unfairly cast it as one of the master's minor works.

"A Perfect Murder" may be a better movie than that version of "Dial M,' but it's no fault of Hitchcock's.

NEWSWEEK, 6/15/98, p. 70, David Ansen

Michael Douglas, Gwyneth Paltrow and Viggo Mortensen are caught in what you would think would be a juicy emotional situation in the suspense thriller "A Perfect Murder". Paltrow, a rich heiress, is having an affair with impoverished artist Mortensen, which husband Douglas, a Gordon Gekko-like commodities trader, discovers. But when he confronts Mortensen, it's with an unexpected offer: he'll give his wife's lover $400,000—to murder her. This is the first of many twists in this loose remake of "Dial M for Murder." (In the Hitchcock film, the hired killer and the lover were two different characters.) But all the surprises strenuously cooked up by screenwriter Patrick Smith Kelly can't overcome the movie's inability to make us care about any of its paper-thin characters. Between them, the three stars don't generate enough heat to warm your pinkies.

We expect a reptilian chill from Douglas—few do it so well. However, his villainous role here, as a man coolly willing to murder for his wife's fortune, is perilously close to self-parody. The audience seemed to be having a hard time taking his wickedness seriously; his shiftiest moments elicited laughs. Mortensen's part as a hunky painter hiding his criminal past (he learned art in prison) is badly underwritten. Though he's revealed to be a con man who's bilked women in the past, the movie suggests—I *think*—that he's truly smitten with Paltrow. Now that offers an interesting dilemma—a guy being blackmailed to kill the woman he loves. Amazingly, neither the writer, the actor nor director Andrew ("The Fugitive") Davis takes advantage of the opportunity. The talented Mortensen ("The Indian Runner," "GI Jane") is left high and dry, looking ill at ease in a callow role no one bothered to think through. If the filmmakers exhibit no curiosity about their characters, why should we?

As for our heroine, if she's smart enough to speak Arabic and Spanish, why does she act with consistent idiocy at key moments in the plot, putting herself in unnecessary jeopardy? (Answer: because the movie would be very short if she didn't.) Paltrow, so effective in "Emma" and "Flesh and Bone," where she had an edge of heartless calculation, makes a much less interesting victim. This sketchy part calls for an actress who can bewitch us out of our commonsense quibbles. Paltrow, putting out a bare minimum on the charisma scale, coasts through on wan noblesse oblige. Movie buffs will get a kick out of seeing Constance Towers, former Sam Fuller leading lady, pop up as Paltrow's patrician mother.

The real energy in this slick, handsomely mounted production seems to have gone into the interior decoration. Director Davis, who films Paltrow's excursions into the subway and the slums as if she had entered Dante's Inferno, dwells dotingly on the elegantly chilly appointments of the couple's Fifth Avenue apartment, which features a Stella over the fireplace and a Botero in the next room. And speaking of art, how is it that our near-penniless bohemian artist/ex-con has managed to find himself a photogenic downtown warehouse roughly the size of Grand Central Terminal? Closer to Architectural Digest than Alfred Hitchcock, "A Perfect Murder" would have been more aptly titled "Lifestyles of the Rich and Murderous."

SIGHT AND SOUND, 10/98, p. 48, Peter Matthews

UN adminstrator Emily Taylor, wife of wealthy bond dealer Steven Taylor, has been having an affair with artist David Shaw. After an apparently chance meeting, Steven approaches David, saying he wants to buy some of his work. In fact he wants to pay him to murder Emily—he's known for sometime about the affair and also that David is an ex-convict who preys on wealthy women. David reluctantly agrees. Steven will hide Emily's own key by the servants' entrance to their apartment so David can gain access. Steven's alibi will be his presence at a poker game. On the night the murder is planned, Emily kills the intruder, who turns out to be another criminal David hired. Steven takes Emily's key off the intruder's corpse and puts it back on her keyring before the police arrive. Detective Mohamed Karaman is suspicious, but the evidence suggests this was the justifiable homicide of a burglar. The only oddity is that the intruder had no keys at all on him.

Steven's dodgy bond deals have gone wrong and he stands to lose all his money; if Emily died he'd inherit her huge fortune, giving him a good reason to kill her. Learning of his trouble, she becomes even more suspicious of her husband when she finds that what she thinks is her house key is actually the intruder's house key. In addition, Steven reveals to her David's shady past. Meanwhile, David blackmails Steven with a tape recording of Steven explaining how to commit the murder. Steven pays David off, but then kills him and retrieves the cash. He goes back to the apartment to kill Emily, but once again she bests her assailant and kills him instead. Once again, she is exonerated by Detective Karaman.

The press notes for *A Perfect Murder* describe it as a "sophisticated thriller"—which seems to mean little more than that the story involves rich people and takes in such swank settings as New

York's Metropolitan Museum of Art. It certainly can't refer to the style of film-making. If one were to make a list of the directors *least* suitable for an escapist bauble about deadly skulduggery among the super-elite, the winner might be Ken Loach or Abbas Kiarostami but Andrew Davis would at least rate an honourable mention. As he demonstrated in such pile-driving action flicks as *The Packaqe, Under Siege, The Fugitive and Chain Reaction,* Davis is a ruthlessly efficient technocrat who delivers no-nonsense thrills with an almost exemplary lack of personal engagement. His cinema attains a kind of inhuman, metallic sheen—and that's exactly wrong for an upscale cat-and-mouse game, which requires a talent for chic little fillips of ghoulish perversity if it's to be even halfway amusing.

Alfred Hitchcock bombed out with the same material (based on Frederick Knott's celebrated melodrama) in his stiff, stagy 1954 suspenser *Dial M for Murder.* At least Hitchcock had an excuse: he was reined in from his customary virtuosity by Jack Warner's insistence that the movie be shot in 3-D. But Davis is plainly in love with the hardware of today at his disposal. Maybe that's why *A Perfect Murder* (even the title is anonymous) feels like it was directed by a computer. Never known as a cinematic trailblazer, Davis keeps his camera in the same old grooves—endlessly tracking, prowling and circling to signify that danger lurks everywhere. And since he appears incapable of building a scene by ordinary dramatic means, he falls back on the purely mechanical expedient of crosscutting between several scenes at once (with musical bridges) to simulate tension and movement. It's conceivable that the producers weren't after stylistic nuance, but hired Davis for his ability to charge a theatrical chestnut with the type of undifferentiated kinetic energy that is supposed to appeal to a wide international market. If so, the tactic may have backfired. At the screening I attended, the movie's by-the-numbers blatancy drew laughter from the audience.

Yet Davis' machine-tooled approach gets the job done, and the film narrowly squeaks by. If the execution were even crummier, the premise—millionaire industrialist Steven Taylor schemes to have his beautiful, unfaithful wife Emily "accidentally" killed is such an irresistible trash archetype that one would probably still be suckered by it. In the Hitchcock version, the wife (Grace Kelly) unexpectedly dispatches her attacker with scissors, and so the husband (Ray Milland) calmly sets about making her act of self defence look like premeditated murder. That attempted frame-up was the best gimmick in the earlier movie the one place where Hitchcock could show off his special aptitude for suave sadism. No doubt hoping to make the woman less of a pathetic victim, first-time screenwriter Patrick Smith Kelly has unwisely recooked the scenario. Now Emily implausibly bonds with kindly detective Mohamed Karaman over her ability to speak fluent Arabic, and the result is that she walks around scot-free in the latter half of the film. While there's a fair amount of gore and general unpleasantness, there isn't a whisper of genuine suspense.

Without quite achieving the glacial hauteur of Grace Kelly, Gwyneth Paltrow looks lovely in her slightly *recherché* evening wear. She lends the movie some class. However, it's Michael Douglas who strikes its single note of eccentricity. Douglas' acting range has grown even smaller, and he has begun to pick up the clenched vocal mannerisms of his father Kirk. Yet his peculiarly arch, deliberate way of speaking seems to cut right through to the campy core of the dialogue (sample: "I feel like I'm knee-deep in bohemian cachet"). Screenwriter Kelly spent six years as a stand-up comedian, and so he may not have approached his task entirely cap in hand. Thankfully, neither does Douglas—his patent delight in his own absurdity gives the movie whatever spark it has.

VILLAGE VOICE, 6/16/98, p. 149, J. Hoberman

Those who prefer to visualize criminal passions among the penthouse set could probably do worse than *A Perfect Murder*—which might be more accurately titled "A Degenerate Entertainment."

This remake of the Hitchcock chestnut *Dial M for Murder* has been set in imperial New York, retooled for Michael Douglas, and directed with two-fisted, gore-soaked glibness by action specialist Andrew Davis. Posh and tawdry, albeit less egregious than Warner's recent remake of the not-dissimilar *Diabolique, A Perfect Murder* is too ponderous to be more than barely passable trash-opera. The camera swoops through Manhattan's canyons from one power location to another—the UN, Wall Street, the Metropolitan Museum. Actually, the Met has nothing on the nearby apartment that commodities broker Douglas shares with his unfaithful wife Gwyneth Paltrow—or the vast Brooklyn loft where Paltrow trysts with artist hunk Viggo Mortensen (who, according to the credits is responsible for his own aggressively garish paintings).

The best that can be said for Patrick Smith Kelly's screenplay (the former stand-up's first) is that it's not totally predictable and that none of his characters are particularly likable. Leaving an oily patch on the screen even in his scenes with smarmy Mortensen, Douglas switches from jealous rage to Satanic scheming to faked grievance—it's *acting*! as Jon Lovitz used to say on *SNL*. Scarcely to be outdone, the slumming Paltrow is professionally slim, confident, and poised—even when Davis is fetishistically exposing her silky derriere. Bored or dutiful, Paltrow signals her superiority to the plot, as well as to hubby, with a delicate drift-away upward glance. What's her problem? This is a role that allows her to twirl pearls, challenge Demi Moore as reigning action babe, and speak Arabic as well.

Also reviewed in:
CHICAGO TRIBUNE, 6/5/98, Friday/p. A, Michael Wilmington
NEW YORK TIMES, 6/5/98, p. E12, Stephen Holden
VARIETY, 6/1-7/98, p. 33, Leonard Klady
WASHINGTON POST, 6/5/98, p. F5, Rita Kempley
WASHINGTON POST, 6/5/98, Weekend/p. 58, Michael O'Sullivan

PERMANENT MIDNIGHT

An Artisan Entertainment release. *Executive Producer:* Yalda Yehranian. *Producer:* Jane Hamsher and Don Murphy. *Director:* David Veloz. *Screenplay:* David Veloz. *Based on the book by:* Jerry Stahl. *Director of Photography:* Robert Yeoman. *Editor:* Steven Weisberg and Cara Silverman. *Music:* Daniel Licht. *Sound:* Eric Enroth. *Casting:* Ronnie Yeskel and Richard Hicks. *Production Designer:* Jerry Fleming. *Costumes:* Louise Mingenbach and Lori Eskowitz. *Running time:* 85 minutes. *MPAA Rating:* R.

CAST: Ben Stiller (Jerry Stahl); Elizabeth Hurley (Sandra); Mario Bello (Kitty); Owen Wilson (Nicky); Lourdes Benedicto (Vola); Peter Greene (Gus); Cheryl Ladd (Pamela Verlaine); Fred Willard (Craig Ziffer); Charles Fleischer (Allen from "Mr. Chompers"); Janeane Garofalo (Jana); Jerry Stahl (Dr. Murphy).

LOS ANGELES TIMES, 9/18/98, Calendar/p. 12, Kenneth Turan

He may have been working on "a habit the size of Utah," but Jerry Stahl was never an ordinary addict. He was a show-biz junkie, someone who wrote for television by day and chased highs at night, a health-conscious kind of guy who made sure to exercise and eat organic while drugs were turning him into a walking cadaver.

Yes, that sounds ridiculous, and Stahl's saving grace was that he always knew it. No matter how wretched his situation, Stahl rarely lost his facility with words or his dark sense of humor. They helped make a success of "Permanent Midnight," the aptly named autobiography he wrote about his experiences, and, as translated to the screen by actor Ben Stiller, they are the film version's biggest assets. Added to the accomplished writing and directing job by David Veloz, these qualities go a ways toward making "Permanent Midnight" an involving film, but they don't go far enough.

For even though the filmmakers like to talk about this being a parable about the human condition, in plainer terms "Permanent Midnight" is yet another movie look at drug addiction, a tedious subject that is apparently as irresistible to young filmmakers as heroin is to a user.

While "Trainspotting" escaped the curse of junkie films by adding a bracing jolt of off-the-cuff energy, other addiction films, from "Rush" through "The Basketball Diaries," eventually degenerate, as this one does, into the usual litany of how-low-can-you-go horrors, with the addict regularly debasing himself for fixes his veins are too far gone to accept.

Filmmaker Veloz, who was one of the writers on Oliver Stone's "Natural Born Killers" and will not be remaking "Mary Poppins" any time soon, has the sense to avoid overdoing things in this, his directing debut. But absent a new way of looking at a tired subject, there's only so much interest that a film like this can create.

What is a bit different, and welcome, is Stahl's drop-dead sarcastic and starkly self-deprecating attitude, visible in lines like "smack is the leisure suit of the '90s" and his explanation for moving to L.A. to avoid a drug problem in Pittsburgh: "I miscalculated."

Stiller spent enough time with Stahl (who has a cameo as a doctor in a methadone clinic) to give an uncanny impersonation of the writer, a man rarely seen without dark clothing and darker sunglasses. Though "Permanent Midnight" can't be classified as fun, Stiller's comic energy and timing are essential in providing the film with the numerous bleak laughs that become its trademark.

"Permanent Midnight" opens in a hellish fast-food restaurant in Phoenix where Stahl, on a kind of work-release program from a rehab spot called Whispering Winds, is taking orders.

Through his drive-through window comes the bright and lively Kitty ("ER's" Maria Bello). Instinctively recognizing each other as ex-addicts (he's been clean for 92 days, she for seven years), they retire to a nearby motel where, between quasi-romantic interludes, he narrates flashbacks about the fast-lane life in L.A. that nearly killed him.

Living with Nicky (Owen Wilson), a friend from back home, Stahl is introduced to Sandra (Elizabeth Hurley), a witty, attractive British woman who is looking to marry someone to acquire a green card. She settles on Stahl, but not before he rips his leather pants down the seam on meeting her and then cracks, "Jewish leather, it's designed for humiliation."

Sandra works on a TV show about a lovable puppet alien called "Mr. Chompers," and soon enough she gets Stahl (who wrote for "Alf" in real life) work on the show, a job he nails when he tells the head man that he views Mr. Chompers as "a modern-day Tom Joad, a defender of the common man." Helped by a completely humorless agent (Janeane Garofalo), his career soon takes off.

"Permanent Midnight's" Hollywood segments are clever and amusing, but the more Stahl's life unravels in his demeaning search for drugs, the more the film inevitably goes down along with it. Watching Stahl searching frantically for an unused vein in his neck with a baby fussing next to him (don't ask) may be unnerving, but it is far from irresistible.

NEW YORK POST, 9/16/98, p. 50, Larry Worth

Mark McGwire and Sammy Sosa may be cleaning up on the baseball field, but Ben Stiller is Hollywood's home-run king.

The applause is still going strong for his comedic coup in "There's Something About Mary." And Stiller's startling, no-nonsense turn in Neil LaBute's "Your Friends and Neighbors" won across-the-board raves.

But those were mere warmups for Stiller's brilliant fusing of funnyman skills and searing dramatics in "Permanent Midnight," the film version of sitcom writer-turned-heroin addict Jerry Stahl's autobiography.

The narrative unfolds from the bed of a Phoenix motel room, where supposedly rehabbed Stahl tells his tale to a dishpan blonde crony. Recalling how he arrived in La-La Land with dreams of penning high-level fiction, Stahl slowly reveals how his career, wife and baby daughter were overshadowed by Bunsen burners and syringes.

Clearly, this is no laughing matter. But writer-director David Veloz injects deliciously subtle comedy into the storyline, whether sending up Tinseltown's superficial ways, moguls' game-playing or the dangers of oh-so-tight leather pants.

But the humor is never far from the horror. Harrowing scenes of strung-out desperation—to the point of stabbing a needle in the neck or repeatedly throwing oneself against a high-rise's floor-to-ceiling windows—prove both devastating and remarkable. They're hard to watch, but even harder to look away from.

Under Veloz's skilled guidance, paranoia and self-loathing are as real as the characters. The result: one of the screen's most honest examinations of the fast lane's temptations and tortures.

Granted, some structural drawbacks surface along the way. But those are easily forgiven in view of first-timer Veloz's varied accomplishments.

There's also outstanding work from Elizabeth Hurley as Stahl's confused wife. It's her best screen role to date, though matched every step of the way by Maria (TVs "ER") Bello as the hero's equally tortured soulmate.

Scene-stealing cameos from Janeane Garofalo, Cheryl Ladd, Lainie Kazan, Liz Torres and Fred Willard round out the superb cast. Even so, all eyes remain on Stiller.

Looking appropriately gaunt, sweaty and perpetually panicked, he perfectly balances on a tight-wire between hilarity and horror. In the process, he invests his flawed character with enough humanity for viewers to care about his fate.

In short, Stiller delivers an unforgettable tour de force—much like "Permanent Midnight" itself.

Also reviewed in:
NEW YORK TIMES, 9/16/98, p. E1, Janet Maslin
NEW YORKER, 9/28/98, p. 105, Daphne Merkin
VARIETY, 9/21-27/98, p. 108, Glenn Lovell
WASHINGTON POST, 9/18/98, p. C7, Rita Kempley
WASHINGTON POST, 9/18/98, Weekend/p. 56, Michael O'Sullivan

PHANTOMS

A Dimension Films release of a Neo Motion Pictures production in association with Raven House, Inc.. *Executive Producer:* Bob Weinstein, Harvey Weinstein, and Dean Koontz. *Producer:* Bob Pringle, Steve Lane, Joel Soisson, and Michael Leahy. *Director:* Joe Chappelle. *Screenplay (Based on his book "Phantoms"):* Dean Koontz. *Director of Photography:* Richard Clabaugh. *Editor:* Randolph K. Bricker. *Music:* David Williams. *Sound:* Larry Scharf. *Sound Editor:* Fred Judkins. *Casting:* Don Phillips. *Production Designer:* Deborah Raymond and Dorian Vernacchio. *Art Director:* Daniel Bradford and Ken Larson. *Set Designer:* Jack Bishop. *Set Decorator:* Barbara Cole Kaye. *Set Dresser:* David Lucas. *Special Effects:* Michael F. Arroyo. *Costumes:* Dana C. Litwack. *Make-up:* Leah Rial and Amanda Carroll. *Stunt Coordinator:* Dan Bradley. *Running time:* 91 minutes. *MPAA Rating:* R.

CAST: Peter O'Toole (Timothy Flyte); Rose McGowan (Lisa Pailey); Joanna Going (Jenny Pailey); Liev Schreiber (Deputy Stu Wargle); Ben Affleck (Sheriff Bryce Hammond); Nicky Katt (Deputy Steve Shanning); Clifton Powell (General Copperfield); Rick Otto (Scientist Lockland); Rachel Shane (Scientist Yamaguci); Adam Nelson (Scientist Burke); John Hammil (Scientist Talbot); John Scott Clough (Scientist Shane); Michael De Lorenzo (Soldier Velazquez); William Hahn (Scientist Borman); Robert Himber (Scientist Walker); Bo Hopkins (Agent Hawthorne); Rob Knepper (Agent Wilson); Paul Schmidt (Church Soldier); Dean Hallo (Sergeant Harker); Clive Rosengren (Commanding Officer); Edmund Wilson (Guthrie); Luke Eberl (Tunnel Boy); Rich Beall (Security Guard); Judith Drake (Hilda); Yvette Nipar (Cowgirl).

LOS ANGELES TIMES, 1/23/98, Calendar/p. 8, Kevin Thomas

[The following review by Kevin Thomas appeared in a slightly different form in
NEWSDAY, 1/23/98, Part II/p. B9.]

There's much that's conventional about "Phantoms," a Dean Koontz tale of supernatural terror, but it does develop lofty intellectual ambitions and boasts a dry, witty performance by Peter O'Toole that lifts the level of the film beyond the routine. It should fill the bill for audiences looking for some thrills and chills once they've seen "Scream 2," but it's less than gripping for those of us who aren't among Koontz's legions of fans.

Adapted by Koontz from his novel and directed crisply by Joe Chappelle, "Phantoms" wastes no time in laying on the horror. A doctor, Jenny Pailey (Joanna Going), living in a lovely Victorian village in the mountains of Colorado, is driving home with her L.A.-based sister Lisa (Rose McGowan), who will be staying for a visit. Once inside her home, she finds her housekeeper dead on her kitchen floor and her phone out of order.

It swiftly becomes clear that the sisters; Bryce Hammond (Ben Affleck), the local sheriff; and a couple of his deputies (Liev Schreiber, Nicky Katt) are the only living people in a town of 400 people.

"Phantoms" pulls out all the tricks in the supernatural horror repertoire—screeching sounds, flashes of light, intermittent power failures, monsters and a slew of gory and dazzling special effects—but doesn't come into focus until O'Toole's Timothy Flyte, an authority on ancient epidemics, enters the picture.

Flyte—the only character with much personality and individuality—theorizes that some form of life has surfaced with the capacity to assume or inhabit any other form and to absorb all knowledge possessed by humans.

This leads to debates over the sources of good and evil, and the role ego plays in this destructive force. Flyte's declarations and analyses get awfully technical for the layman, and the amorphous quality of this force of evil has the effect of making the film seem vague and elusive.

Well-crafted in most aspects, "Phantoms" is finally more ambitious than satisfying. It also could have used more humor. But it can't be accused of insulting the intelligence of its audiences.

NEW YORK POST, 1/23/98, p. 47, Thelma Adams

"It's healthier up here," says one sister to another as they drive toward Snowfield, pop. 400.

"Phantoms" is minutes old and we know from the creepy music, the Rocky Mountains shot to look like the Carpathians, and best-selling chiller author Dean Koontz's name below the title that this trip has nothing to do with health.

Pale-skinned, dark-eyed beauties Jenny (Joanna Going) and Lisa Pailey (Rose McGowan) arrive in that cute little mountain town with corny shops like Get Fleeced lining Main Street, and it's very quiet—too quiet.

Before long, Lisa's whining: "It's only a bundt cake, it's only a bundt cake!" She quickly discovers that the baker's been butchered and something's in the oven that doesn't smell like lovin'. The whole town has disappeared—pets, too—leaving only a few distinctly freaky corpses.

Ben Affleck, Liev Shreiber and Nicky Katt, playing a sheriff and his deputies, join Going and McGowan. Together, these attractive young people make one of those now-familiar spooky parties of five.

Before we can say "Scream III," director Joe Chappelle ("Halloween: The Curse of Michael Myers") assures us that "Phantoms" isn't another self-referential gag-fest. This chiller, with a taut script adapted by Koontz from his novel, isn't about knowing winks and Tori Spelling jokes.

"Phantoms" is a slick, intelligent, scary movie aimed at having its audience cling to the armrests in terror while watching good battle evil for the soul of mankind.

Chappelle has even broken through the voguish ageism of current horror. He casts the legendary Peter O'Toole ("Lawrence of Arabia") as a fallen Oxford don turned tabloid reporter named Timothy Flyte.

"How do you fit in here?" Affleck's cleft-chinned, tragedy-torn lawman asks O'Toole's world-weary reporter. The older man responds: "Reluctantly."

However reluctant O'Toole might have been to take the part, he plays Flyte like a trouper. Just to hear the actor say phrases like "undigested remains" in his impeccable accent is worth the price of admission.

VILLAGE VOICE, 2/3/98, p. 122, Dennis Lim

More opportunistic than *Spice World* [see Lim's review of that film] yet less likely to provoke critical condescension, *Phantoms* represents the latest Miramax/Dimension attempt to ride the *Scream* wave, this time with Joanna Going as Neve Campbell, Ben Affleck as David Arquette, Liev Sclueiber as Skeet Ulrich, and Rose McGowan as Rose McGowan. Director Joe Chapelle is an adept shock tactician who knows disappointingly little about suspense. Working from Dean

Koontz's screenplay, he gets off to an agreeably creepy start (as two sisters arrive in a small mountain town to find it deserted and littered with bodies), but the film unravels as soon as it starts to explain itself. Supernatural expert Peter O'Toole forces the plot into a morass of subscientific theorizing and vague existential musing—nothing that couldn't have been more concisely and elegantly depicted in an episode of *The X-Files*.

Also reviewed in:
CHICAGO TRIBUNE, 1/23/98, Friday/p. H, Michael Wilmington
NEW YORK TIMES, 1/23/98, p. E10, Stephen Holden
VARIETY, 1/26-2/1/98, p. 65, Godfrey Cheshire
WASHINGTON POST, 1/23/98, p. D6, Stephen Hunter
WASHINGTON POST, 1/23/98, Weekend/p. 41, Desson Howe

PHOENIX

A Trimark Pictures release of a Lakeshore Entertainment presentation of a Paradox Films production. *Executive Producer:* Tom Rosenberg, Sigurjon Sighvtsson, and Ted Tannebaum. *Producer:* Victoria Nevinny and Tracie Graham Rice. *Director:* Danny Cannon. *Screenplay:* Eddie Richey. *Director of Photography:* James L. Carter. *Editor:* Zach Staenberg. *Music:* Graeme Breen. *Casting:* Rick Pagano. *Production Designer:* Charles Breen. *Costumes:* Alexandra Walker. *Running time:* 113 minutes. *MPAA Rating:* R.

CAST: Ray Liotta (Harry Collins); Anthony LaPaglia (Mike Henshaw); Anjelica Huston (Leila); Daniel Baldwin (James Nutter); Jeremy Piven (Fred Shuster); Tom Noonan (Chicago); Xander Berkely (Clyde Webber); Giancarlo Esposito (Louie); Brittany Murphy (Veronica); Kari Wuhrer (Katie Shuster).

NEW YORK POST, 9/25/98, p. 45, Larry Worth

A movie about good cops gone bad is nothing new. An arresting movie about good cops gone bad, however, is a whole different story.

Granted, "Phoenix"—the story of four policemen in Arizona's capital city who squeeze their duties in between gambling and illegal debt collection services—could have fallen prey to its minutiae-filled dialogue, metaphors and predictable turns. But a surfeit of telling details and palpable ambience make all the difference.

Another big selling point is Ray Liotta's intense work as the fatally flawed protagonist. Actually, playing a jaded boy in blue is nothing new for the "Copland" and "Unlawful Entry" veteran. But there's no signs of sleepwalking here.

Liotta, who also serves as co-producer, delivers his best work since "GoodFellas," providing myriad reasons to forget his egregious miscasting as Ol' Boy Eyes in "The Rat Pack."

There's fine support from Anthony LaPaglia, Jeremy Piven and Daniel Baldwin as badge-wearing cronies and a lovely, poignant performance from Anjelica Huston as a bar owner who's down but definitely not out.

As for director Danny Cannon, his no-nonsense noir-like storytelling comes as an unexpected pleasure, particularly coming from the same man who lensed Sly Stallone's embarrassingly awful "Judge Dredd."

Much like the legendary creature who rises from its ashes, Cannon and Liotta resurrect themselves in "Phoenix," helping it soar above all flaws in the process.

Also reviewed in:
NEW YORK TIMES, 9/28/98, p. E5, Lawrence Van Gelder
VARIETY, 7/20-26/98, p. 48, Leonard Klady

PI

A Live Entertainment release of a Truth & Soul/Harvest Filmworks/Plantain Films presentation of a Protozoa Films production. *Executive Producer:* Randy Simon. *Producer:* Eric Watson. *Director:* Darren Aronofsky. *Screenplay:* Darren Aronofsky. *Story:* Darren Aronofsky, Sean Gullette, and Eric Watson. *Director of Photography:* Matthew Libatique. *Editor:* Oren Sarch. *Music:* Clint Mansell. *Sound:* Ken Ishii and (music) Dominick Tavella. *Casting:* Denise Fitzgerald. *Production Designer:* Matthew Maraffi. *Art Director:* Eileen Butler. *Special Effects:* Ariyela Wald-Cohain. *Make-up:* Ariyela Wald-Cohain. *Stunt Coordinator:* Marc Vivian. *Running time:* 85 minutes. *MPAA Rating:* Not Rated.

CAST: Sean Gullette (Maximillian Cohen); Mark Margolis (Sol Robeson); Ben Shenkman (Lenny Meyer); Pamela Hart (Marcy Dawson); Stephen Pearlman (Rabbi Cohen); Samia Shoaib (Devi); Ajay Naidu (Farrouhk); Kristin Mae-Anne Lao (Jenna); Esper Lao Nieves (Jenna's Mom); Joanne Gordon (Mrs. Ovadia); Lauren Fox (Jenny Robeson); Stanley Herman (Moustacheless Man); Clint Mansell (Photographer); Totumminello (Ephraim); Peter Cheyenne (Brad); David Tawil (Jake); J.C. Islander (Man Presenting Suitcase); Abraham Aronofsky (Man Delivering Suitcase); Ray Seiden (Transit Cop); Scott Franklin (Voice of Transit Cop); Chris Johnson (Limo Driver); Sal Monte (King Neptune).

LOS ANGELES TIMES, 7/24/98, Calendar/p. 6, Kevin Thomas

That first-time filmmaker Darren Aronofsky calls his picture "Pi," the symbol designating the ratio of the circumference of a circle to its diameter, suggests right away that it's not going to be any ordinary science-fiction thriller. Indeed, it is a brilliant intellectual adventure that fans of bold independent filmmaking will want to experience, even though the ending is something of a letdown.

For the last decade, Aronofsky's young hero, Max (Sean Gullette, an actor of formidable resources and concentration) has been attempting to decode a numerical pattern beneath the workings of the stock market. Holed up in a New York walk-up apartment that has become a computer labyrinth, Max is on the verge of a breakthrough. He's also on the verge of a breakdown, shooting up or swallowing large amounts of medication to allay extreme panic attacks.

Worse yet, he's been somehow tracked by a ruthless speculator (Pamela Hart) who will stop at nothing to tap into Max's brainpower. What's more, Max, a nonreligious Jew, has inadvertently attracted the attention of a young Hasidic Jew (Ben Shenkman), who tells him of the numerical significance of the Hebrew mystical doctrine the cabala, and whose rabbi (Stephen Pearlman) ultimately concludes that Max possesses the true name of God, the key to divine knowledge.

There's no denying that the more mathematical skills you have, the more you will be able to get into this most unusual film better than those of us who are incapable of balancing a checkbook. But even we can grasp that, whether he realizes it or not, Max is ultimately on a spiritual journey, for "Pi" makes it increasingly clear that Aronofsky holds, as do many others, that science, nature and religion are ultimately in unity with one another.

Indeed, Max proceeds on three propositions of his own devising: 1) "mathematics is the language of nature"; 2) "everything around us can be represented and understood through numbers"; and 3) "therefore, there are patterns everywhere in nature."

It's not for nothing Aronofsky won a directing prize for "Pi" at Sundance, for his film is a work of dazzling bravura, shot by Matthew Libatique in a stunningly harsh, high-contrast black-and-white, exuding energy and pace, creating one compelling image after another. Yet for all his abundant talent, imagination and intellect, Aronofsky, who skillfully builds suspense interlaced with dark humor, hasn't been able to overcome the paint-yourself-in-a-corner syndrome that afflicts far more prosaic films.

All along, he's been tantalizing us with the possibility that Max has the ability to unlock the secrets of the universe, and naturally that's a pretty tall order for any director to deliver. Yet

Aronofsky might well have dared, at the moment of truth, to try to evoke a sense of the ineffable—a quality that emerges in the greatest moments of such profoundly spiritual directors as Robert Bresson, Carl Dreyer and Yasujiro Ozu. As it is, "Pi" folds its tent in such a way as to validate the sentimental notion expressed by Max's mentor (Mark Margolis), "Life isn't just mathematics."

NEW YORK POST, 7/10/98, p. 46, Thelma Adams

The mood of "Pi," Darren Aronofsky's black-and-white debut that's being billed as a sci-fi thriller, is "Twilight Zone" meets "Eraserhead."

Using spooky voice-over narration and black-and-white images grainier than whole wheat, the winner of the directing award at the Sundance Film Festival sets out to enlighten audiences on the meaning of life via numbers (hence the movie's title).

Max Cohen (Sean Gullette) is a pasty-faced, bug-eyed math genius with a lineage that qoes back to Dr. Frankenstein. Caught between blinding flashes of brilliance and equally blinding seizures, Max accesses his trusty computer for a formula that would reveal a pattern in the chaos of the stock market.

Max sees the potential for a unifying order in nature, a pattern in everything—from the cream spiraling in his coffee to the leaves rustling in apparent randomness on trees overhead to the infinite possibilities in his weekly board games with his mentor, Sol (Mark Margolis).

Max's research makes him popular among Wall Streeters intent on cracking the market and among Orthodox Jewish cabalists who believe that Max has stumbled upon a 216-digit number that, when translated into alphanumeric Hebrew, is God's first name.

When Hasidic sharpy Lenny Meyer (Ben Shenkman) bumps into Max accidentally on purpose at a Manhattan coffee shop, he tells him: "The Torah's just a long stream of numbers. Some say it's a code sent by God."

Dipping into the cabala, chaos theory and deviant psychology makes for an ambitious and ultimately frustrating formula. "Pi" becomes increasingly chaotic as rabid stockbrokers and Hasids circle around the messianic Max.

It's interesting to consider that life's meaning is as close as the swirls in our morning coffee, but—damn it—what is the meaning of life and how do you get there from a 216-digit number?

NEWSDAY, 7/10/98, Part II/p. B10, John Anderson

In John Updike's "Roger's Version," a contrarian take on "The Scarlet Letter," a graduate student wants a research grant so he can find the face of God through math. Grounded in the author's New England Puritan skepticism, the story asked, among other things, whether a God who could be pinned down against His/Her will was really worth finding.

In the irresistible tradition of God-cracking, we now have Darren Aronofsky's "π"—as in pi, the 16th letter of the Greek alphabet, the mathematical symbol denoting the ratio of the circumference of a circle to its diameter, or the ratio itself, having a value of 3.14159265 and on to infinity. Again, math is the route to God. The map, however, isn't Hawthorne and Christianity, but the Torah and Orthodox Judaism: Max Cohen (Sean Gullette), an underfunded but nonetheless paranoid math genius with chronic headaches and a belief in a numerically patterned universe, begins by looking for a system within the stock market. Intellectually seduced by an evangelical Hasid named Lenny Meyer (Ben Shenkman), he ends up searching for the true name of God in the letter-number sequences of the Torah. And what do the book and movie have in common? That computers are the window to heaven? Or that the window to heaven is invariably a mirror?

Hubris is the subtext of "π," so it's ironic (or just unfortunate) that all the film-school-style trickery tweaks the film toward the smugly facetious (one wonders what Godard would have done with all this). Nevertheless, "π" is an engrossing film, a B-movie-inspired mosaic of and theology. How many indie movies might intelligently refer to Archimedes, Faust, Borges, Lynch, the Icarus myth, Chris Marker and "The Day the Earth Stood Still" without seeming arch? For that matter, how many could sustain this film's brand of tension and visual integrity on what must have been its minuscule budget?

With its oily, grainy texture and reverb-ed dialogue reflecting the disintegration of Max' psyche, this debut by Aronofsky (who won the director's prize at the Sundance Film Festival this year) is set in its own impenetrable universe (Chinatown), in ominous subways and greasy spoons and amid the wire-snarled squalor of Max' quadruple-locked apartment. Here, Max and his Rube Goldberg-inspired computer—named Euclid—attempt to apply his implacable tautologies (basically, that numbers define the universe) to the vagaries of equity trading. A group of high financiers led by the relentless Marcy Dawson (Pamela Hart) wants him to crack Wall Street's code, while Lenny is trying to get Max to apply himself to the 216-letter/number sequence that supposedly lies within the Torah—and will reveal the name of God.

Aronofsky's premise is perfect, really—being, as it is, the most provocative question in the history of mankind. Gleaning terrifying possibilities out of real science along its more remote boundaries, he follows a great sci-fi tradition—embodied in Max, who starts finding the spiral patterns of higher numbers everywhere from a periwinkle on a beach to the swirling cream on the top of his coffee. Is the universe in fact subservient to numbers? Or does higher math define itself by explaining what we can't otherwise fathom? Like "π" itself—which in its thus far infinite parade of unraveling integers suggests an elusive beauty in universal chaos—"π" might leave you feeling humbly exhilarated.

SIGHT AND SOUND, 1/99, p. 52, Mark Sinker

Maximillian Cohen is obsessed with numbers, a human calculator seeking patterns in π and the stock market. Suffering from migraines, he injects painkillers and suffers hallucinations. One day he meets Lenny, a Hasidic Jew, who tries to befriend him, saying that the Kabbalah and the Torah are numerical codes sent from God. Max's former teacher Sol, who spent 40 years seeking similar patterns, tells him to take a break. Euclid, Max's computer, spits out some impossible stock predictions and a 216-digit number, then crashes.

Businesswoman Marcy Dawson wants a meeting, but Max evades her. A newspaper says the stock market has just collapsed; Euclid's predictions were correct after all. Max hunts for the 216-digit number in the trash, but it's gone. Lenny and Sol both mention a 216-digit number, but Sol warns Max off his obsessive search. Dawson offers Max a chip to improve Euclid. He hallucinates finding a brain on the subway steps. He finds a shell and looks at it with a microscope. The rebuilt Euclid crashes, again spitting out the number. Max accepts Dawson's offer of the chip, shaves his head, injects himself and collapses. When he wakes, he has the number. Sol tells him that computers become conscious of themselves just before they crash; this number is a sign of this. Dawson menaces Max for the number. Lenny rescues him, but only so the Hasidim can have the number. Max refuses. Sol dies, and Max realises he too had discovered the number. Max trashes Euclid, and, thinking he has a microchip in his head, drills a hole in his skull, destroying his skill at calculation.

A computer age update of *Der Golem* (1920) by way of Jorge Luis Borges, where technology is rendered lethal by an admixture of quasi-Kabbalistic symbols, π is a Hegelian occult thriller that never sheds its sense of its own cleverness (not entirely merited). For a film that's basically about a man chasing the secret of the universe regardless of the cost to sanity and humanity, and despite its teasing claims to knowledge from the frontiers of the knowable, it's often a bit timid.

Part of the problem is that the filmmakers don't understand the maths they're using to sex up their plot. Certainly π when represented digitally never ends; it is a doorway to the infinite, if you like. But to real mathematicians, proofs of π's infinitude are linked to proofs of its 'transcendentality', professional jargon for a very rigorous algebraic form of patternlessness. For many the allure of the various geometrical diagrams flashed before us in montage during the credits derives from their visually 'abstract' mystery rather than their concrete content. Max has a little mantra setting out his philosophy of cosmic patterning: it shows him to be either a rotten mathematician, ignorant of π's proven properties, or else a lunatic, the kind that blitzes Harvard professors with 'disproofs' of Einstein in angry green ink. This latter option, Max as madman, is so overdetermined (he's forever shooting up and seeing things) it wrecks much chance of drama.

In its favour, π looks great, shot in a high-contrast black-and-white 16mm stock that recalls Maya Deren, *Tetsuo*, David Lynch and Cabaret Voltaire's early videos, with a nod to Buñuel that's a plain old bad pun (ants on a brain for bugs in a computer). Seeing the Hasidim in the role reserved by Hollywood for Native Americans—as repositories of ancient wisdoms that rationalists forget at our peril—is refreshing, if no less patronising.

As Max, Sean Gullette gives a one-note performance which sells short the sublimated passion of genuine intellectual obsession (compare recent television footage on *Horizon* of a choked-up Andrew Wiles recalling his solution of Fermat's 'last theorem'). The amused affection shown by female neighbours toward Max—Devi who feeds him, little Jenna who plays calculator games with him—makes up for the pushy corporate cipher that is Marcy Dawson. Max's mentor Sol has the best joke, about Archimedes and common sense—and perhaps the nicest touch is his apartment which captures well the ambience of a *Scientific American* reader's room circa 1974, right down to the Go board instead of chess. But π would be much more fun if it wasn't trying to kid us that it's about so much more than fun.

VILLAGE VOICE, 7/14/98, p. 146, Amy Taubin

Darren Aronofsky's π is a Neo-Expressionist, sci-fi psychodrama that probably cost less than Bruce Willis' *Armageddon* lunch tab. As ingenious as it is derivative, π may well be the weirdest calling card film that ever won big at Sundance; Aronofsky took home the award for this year's best director. His film also won the IFP's Open Palm Award for best first-feature. I'm not saying he's undeserving, but I also think Vincent Gallo is justified in believing he wuz robbed.

Inspired by the true story of the Chudnovsky brothers, Soviet refugee mathematicians who built a supercomputer in their apartment using spare parts, π is a relentless, inside-out portrait of Maximillian Cohen (Sean Gullette), a lonely math genius. Max lives in a one-room Chinatown walk-up (it looks like the set for a Richard Foreman play) with a jerry-built computer named Euclid. When Max was a little boy, he disobeyed his mother by staring bare-eyed, at the sun; as a result he went temporarily blind. This single act of rebellion determines the course of his life. Though punished with massive migraine headaches, he's obsessed with regaining the ecstatic moment he experienced just before he lost his sight—when the order of all things seemed wondrous clear to him. Max believes that this ephemeral vision is reducible to a mathematical formula and that if he can program Euclid correctly, it will spit the formula out.

Since a guy alone in a room communing with a computer is only minimally more interesting to watch than a guy scribbling in a notebook, Aronofsky grafts a skeletal thriller plot to his cyber-premise. Thus, Max is pursued by the representatives of God (a radical Hasidic sect) and of Mammon (an African American Wall Street broker and her henchmen) who believe that Max's formula will unlock the mysteries of both the cabbalah and the stock market. "This is numerology, not mathematics," warns Max's former professor, who suffered a stroke just when he was on the verge of discovering the pattern hidden in the computation of π.

Still, the effect is less a narrative than a kind of whirligig propelled by Max"s mounting hysteria and paranoia. The crash is inevitable—programmed, as it were, into the film's formula. Abstractly, the structure seems quite elegant, but played out on the screen, it wears thin about two-thirds of the way through. Part of the problem is that Aronofsky is no more willing to grapple with what intellectual activity actually involves than were the director and writers of that other math-genius movie, *Good Will Hunting*. And it's the refusal to delve too deeply into the life of the mind that makes the film seem like a Hollywood audition piece.

For sheer kineticism, however, π is pretty extraordinary. Aronofsky confines the film largely to Max's point of view. Sometimes (most notably in the subway-chase scenes) the camera was strapped to the actor's body so that the frantic, careening movement is a true index of Max's terror and desperation. In the last, extended chase sequence (a direct steal from the climactic scene in Orson Welles's *The Trial,* where Tony Perkins flees through the rickety back corridors of the court) you can just about feel that fetid, metallic subway air hitting the back of your throat. (Welles mounted his camera in a wheelchair; when asked how he got it to move so fast, he replied that he hired a Yugoslavian to push it.)

The Trial hangs heavy throughout π. (The scenes where Max's sexy and solicitous next-door neighbor "invades" his apartment exactly parallel those between Perkins and Jeanne Moreau.) Aronofsky makes no bones about his other influences, either—Cronenberg's *Videodrome*, Lynch's *Eraserhead*, the *Sin City* comic books, and '30s Expressionist photography.

Like *Videodrome,* π locates paranoia in the fascination with and fear of technology. Max's symbiosis with Euclid is so extreme that he loses his sense of boundaries. His fear of being penetrated or of having his interior thoughts, feelings, even his organs stolen away, gives the film an uneasy psychosexual charge. At one particularly nightmarish moment, Max discovers a bare, pulsating brain lying on a subway stair. He gives it a furtive poke and feels the pain stabbing inside his skull.

Gullette, who's a double for the anguished, hollow-cheeked protagonist of Buñuel's *Un chien andalou,* is suitably compelling until near the end of the film, when he's left high and dry with nothing to do but scream and clutch his head in agony. Matthew Libatique's cinematography is brilliant throughout, as is Clint Mansell's techno score. More than any other element, the music drives the film and makes it a unique expression of the cusp-of-the-millennium present rather than just another hip trip through the image bank's future-past.

Also reviewed in:
CHICAGO TRIBUNE, 7/24/98, Friday/p. A, Mark Caro
NEW YORK TIMES, 7/10/98, p. E18, Stephen Holden
VARIETY, 1/26-2/1/98, p. 67, Dennis Harvey
WASHINGTON POST, 7/31/98, p. B5, Rita Kempley
WASHINGTON POST, 7/31/98, Weekend/p. 48, Eve Zibart

PLACE CALLED CHIAPAS, A

A Canada Wild Prods., in associaton with the Canadian Broadcasting Corp., with the participation of Telefilm Canada, the National Film Board of Canada/British Columbia Film/BC Arts Council/Canada Council for the Arts.   *Producer:* Nettie Wild, Betsy Carson, and Kirk Tougas. *Director:* Nettie Wild.   *Screenplay (Spanish with English subtitles):* Nettie Wild and Manfred Becker.   *Director of Photography:* Kirk Tougas and Nettie Wild.   *Editor:* Manfred Becker. *Music:* Joseph Pepe Danza, Salvador Ferreras, Celso Machado, and Laurence Mollerup. *Sound:* Velcrow Ripper and Jesus Sanchez Padilla.   *Running time:* 90 minutes.   MPAA Rating: Not Rated.

VILLAGE VOICE, 11/10/98, p. 120, Andrew Hsiao

Has there ever been a more media-friendly revolution than the Zapatista uprising? Nettie Wild's Chiapas journal contains shots of rebel Web sites—launched soon after the guerrillas' spectacular 1994 New Year's Day revolt—and captures a droll *Marie Claire* photo shoot, in which the gun-toting philosopher-subcomandante Marcos poses against the southern Mexico hills.

Still, the doc's early moments are disappointingly uncinematic. Paramilitary thugs threaten to kill Wild's crew—but off-camera. Marcos refuses an interview with the cryptic words "She knows why."

As it turns out, though, Wild's film coalesces around the unseen. Far from the media crush, she joins a lonely jungle trek of indigenous villagers determined to reclaim their homes from the paramilitary; arriving at their village, the group is attacked—as soon as Wild turns her camera off.

This memorable, frightening episode—blank moments above all—drives home how much remains out of view, even in "the first postmodern revolution." Eventually, the pipe-smoking cult of personality does sit for a session of jungle existentialism, but it's to Wild's great credit that by then the villagers' struggle—the human dimension behind the war of symbols—seems just as absorbing.

Also reviewed in:
NATION, 11/23/98, p. 30, Stuart Klawans
NEW YORK TIMES, 11/4/98, p. E3, Stephen Holden
VARIETY, 3/2-8/98, p. 88, David Stratton

PLAYERS CLUB, THE

A New Line Cinema release of an Ice Cube/Pat Charbonnet production. *Executive Producer:* Ice Cube. *Producer:* Patricia Charbonnet and Carl Craig. *Director:* Ice Cube. *Screenplay:* Ice Cube. *Director of Photography:* Malik Sayeed. *Editor:* Suzanne Hines. *Music:* Frank Fitzpatrick. *Music Editor:* Mark Green and Jeff Charbonneau. *Choreographer:* Fatima. *Sound:* Russell Williams. *Sound Editor:* Marc D. Fishman. *Casting:* Kimberly Hardin. *Production Designer:* Dina Lipton. *Art Director:* Keith Neely. *Set Designer:* Laurie Stevens. *Set Decorator:* Cheryle Grace. *Special Effects:* John Hartigan. *Costumes:* Dahlia Foroutan. *Make-up:* Stacye Branché. *Stunt Coordinator:* William Washington. *Running time:* 103 minutes. *MPAA Rating:* R.

CAST: Bernie Mac (Dollar Bill); Monica Calhoun (Ebony); A.J. Johnson (L'il Man); Ice Cube (Reggie); Alex Thomas (Clyde); Faizon Love (Peters); Charles. O. Murphy (Brooklyn); Adele Givens (Tricks); Chrystale Wilson (Ronnie); Tracy C. Jones (Tina); Terence Howard (K.C.); Larry McCoy (St. Louis); Ronn Riser (Professor Mills); Dick Anthony Williams (Mr. Armstrong); Badja Djola (The Doctor); Tiny Lister (XL); Lisa Raye (Diana "Diamond" Armstrong); Jamie Foxx (Blue); John Amos (Freeman); Judy Ann Elder (Mrs. Armstrong); Jimmy Woodard (Miron); Monte Russell (Lance); Oren Williams (Jamal, 4 Years); Jossie Harris and Lalanya Masters (Strippers); Ursula Y. Houston (Dancer); Annie O'Donnell (Lady); Satari (Girl); Bettina Rae (Vanilla); Big Boy (Joe); Gregg McDonald (Cop); Brett Wagner (Guy/Cop Party); Kenya Williams (Student); Nigel Thatch (Morehouse Guy); Mike Duncan (Bodyguard); Luther Campbell (Luke); Samuel Monroe, Jr. (Junior); Master P (Guy); Keith Burke (Guy at Party).

LOS ANGELES TIMES, 4/8/98, Calendar/p. 5, Gene Seymour

[The following review by Gene Seymour appeared in a slightly different form in **NEWSDAY, 4/8/98, Part II/p. B10.]**

By day, she's Diana Armstrong, single mom and journalism major at a historically African American university in Atlanta. At night, she's Diana Diamond and she takes off her clothes and dances for dollars at a strip joint as raucous as the movie with which it shares its name, "The Players Club."

As conceived by rapper-actor Ice Cube, who wrote, directed and co-produced the film, Diamond conveys some of the Mama-don't-take-no-mess confidence of such "blaxploitation" heroines of the 1970s as "Foxy Brown" and "Coffy." She can duke it out, even shoot it out, if the situation requires.

Implausible as such a superwoman might sound, there's enough charm, conviction and charisma in the performance of newcomer Lisa Raye to make you believe in and root for Diamond in her dubious struggle for dignity in undignified surroundings.

Yet one is moved to ask, once again, where Hollywood comes by this impulse for casting beautiful black women as strippers: Vivica A. Fox in "Independence Day," Lela Rochon in "Gang Related" and now a whole club filled with such dynamos as Diamond and Ronnie, the club's star dancer, played with malevolent gusto by another rookie film actor, Chrystale Wilson. They're such strong presences they make you wonder what they'd be like dueling in a courtroom instead of a dressing room.

As was the case with 1995's "Friday," for which Cube wrote the script, "Players Club" is loosely constructed with anecdotes flowing into each other with the ambling, hit-and-miss rhythm of a comedy routine. Also like "Friday," the movie is heavily populated with an all-star lineup of comics, including Jamie Foxx as the club's caustic disc jockey; Bernie Mac as Dollar Bill, the club's slime-ball owner; A.J. Johnson as Dollar's put-upon sidekick; and Adele Givens as a dancer with so much mileage on her that the club empties as soon as she swaggers onstage.

Such casting may lead you to believe that "Players Club" is a laugh riot. But there's also a lot of grim, unsettling stuff, much of it involving Diamond's seemingly naive cousin Ebony (Monica Calhoun). Cube even casts himself as one of the film's unsavory characters.

Despite the coarse edges of "The Players Club," there's a lot to be said for Cube's care in balancing the sweet and sour elements of his narrative. He's far from being a master. But he's a player for sure.

NEW YORK POST, 4/8/98, p. 50, Bill Hoffmann

Is it a poignant social drama? Is it a flashy blaxploitation flick? "The Players Club"—the first directorial effort from rapper-turned-actor Ice Cube—can't make up its mind.

By trying to walk the line between sensitivity and sensationalism, the picture is unable to harness any real power in either genre.

Part of the "The Players Club" focuses on Diamond (LisaRaye), a good-hearted single mom going for a college degree and making ends meet by clerking in a shoe store.

To pull down some real money, she reluctantly signs on as an exotic dancer at a strip joint with the idea of bumping and grinding until she has enough of a nest egg to begin a brand new life. Will she succeed or be sucked into the abyss of sleaze for good?

This plot might have worked had it stood alone. But Ice Cube—who also scripted—relies on a raucous blaxploitation side plot in which sadistic gangsters gun for the strip-club owner, Dollar Bill (Bernie Mac). This leads to endless violence, sadism and other assorted mayhem.

Plenty of nudity and the ongoing threat of sexual assault—of both straight and lesbian varieties—fills the T&A quota several times over.

In wanting to have his cake and eat it too, Ice Cube pulls his punches too often. The flick doesn't push far enough as pure exploitation, and yet it's too sleazy to be taken seriously as a sensitive drama.

Still, it does boast a fine ensemble cast including Monica Calhoun, A.J. Johnson, Jamie Foxx, John Amos, Tiny Lister and Luther Campbell (of "Me So Horny" fame).

The standout, however, is Bernie Mac, who as the jive-talking strip-club czar, proves he's one of the funniest comic actors working today. A howlingly funny man, Mac makes you giggle with even the slightest of askew glances.

As for Ice Cube's directorial skills, they're solid. In one chilling scene, Diamond's cousin Ebony (Calhoun) is raped and beaten off-camera at a stag party. As help arrives, Cube keeps his camera outside the room where she lies, as if he's afraid to go in. As Ebony's friends scream and moan at their discovery, what we don't see is infinitely more chilling than showing it all.

It proves the intense power that subtlety can generate. Not that there's anything wrong with going over the top. It's just too bad Ice Cube couldn't make up his mind one way or the other.

SIGHT AND SOUND, 10/98, p. 49, Linda Ruth Williams

While working in a shoe shop to support her young son, Diana Armstrong meets Tricks and Ronnie who introduce her to The Players Club, a strip and lap-dancing joint where they work. Dollar Bill, the club's proprietor, renames Diana "Diamond" and starts her working that night. Dollar Bill is pursued by his creditor, St Louis, and St Louis' henchmen.

Diana aims to fund her way through college by studying in the day and stripping at night. Her cousin Ebony moves in with her and joins her at the club, but gradually succumbs to alcohol and sleazier work, supplementing her income with performances at private parties organised by Ronnie. At a stag party, she is brutally attacked and raped by Ronnie's brother. After a shootout, St Louis' men set fire to The Players Club, which is destroyed. Diana prepares to graduate; Ebony works in the shoe shop.

The moment the credits of *The Players Club* announce that this is "An Ice Cube Film" a range of expectations are raised. But few viewers will anticipate the 'woman's picture' that *The Players Club* is clearly trying to be. Written and directed by Cube, and featuring him in a minor role, this is nevertheless no vanity project. Instead, the film suggests politically correct intentions with the opening voiceover by protagonist Diamond, which promises a picaresque fable of an intelligent woman making her way in the sex industry.

Unfortunately, the film never quite has the courage of these laudable convictions, and wants to have its sleaze cake and eat it. While Diana may be the narrative's driving voice, she is still the film's prime sexual spectacle, the hard-body whose strip sequence prompts the camera into its most lascivious moves and angles. However, like *Striptease* before it, the spectacles of *The Players Club* necessarily stay safely soft to avoid repelling the mainstream.

Since it can't be a sex film and so reveal anything new about male or female sexuality, then it must settle for something else, and the woman's story is where it pitches up. It is one of the oddest twists of post-feminism that films about strippers are perfectly fine now as long as their women are 'empowered'—narratively or economically in control. Yet this is not without consequences, for *The Players Club* is perhaps one of the least erotic films ever made about the sex industry, try as it might to titillate while it educates. If Paul Verhoeven's *Showgirls,* another obvious point of comparison, was spectacle without sympathy, then *The Players Club* is spectacle which, in its urgent desire to be sympathetic, falls short of being sexy.

These failures are due more to genre confusion than hybridity or experiment, so the best way to view *The Players Club* is in pieces. While it rarely pauses to analyse the complexities of its heroine's situation (Diana's motto—"Make that money, don't let it make you"—is about as profound as it gets), the film repeatedly makes empathetic nods towards the difficulties of a woman juggling a college-level course, childcare problems and a job lap-dancing. How well a director who makes his camera lurk for so long in the women's changing room can comprehend these pressures is another question. Also troubling is the persistent homophobia which casts painted, sassy dykes Ronnie and Tricks, trying incessantly to trap our heroine into the evils of sapphic sex, as more monstrous than the figures found in violent misogynist texts.

Despite this, *The Players Club* mostly has its heart in the right place. It offers some enjoyable comic turns and some well directed scenes: Ronnie's party trick of making a bare-bottomed submissive white policeman respond, "I'm black and I'm proud!" as she whacks him with a bat and intones, "Say it loud!" is perhaps worth the admission price alone. And if Cube hasn't yet mastered the process of synthesising such a meandering narrative, he is already adept at coaxing fine performances from his players. Former erotic dancer Chrystale Wilson and stand-up comic Adele Givens make a spirited double-act as Ronnie and Tricks, played as glittering wicked stepsisters, while newcomer LisaRaye and seasoned young television actress Monica Calhoun convincingly tackle their roles as wise and foolish virgins respectively, innocents negotiating the dark forest of the sex industry. *The Players Club* is an impressive screen debut for a number of its players, not least for Cube himself.

VILLAGE VOICE, 4/21/98, p. 72, Jeannine Amber

In someone else's film, it might have been a clever twist to create a world of gun-toting thugs, a swindling strip-club owner, and a rapist, and then choose as your most dastardly villain a tall, blond stripper whose worst sin is that she likes to eat pussy. But in rapper Ice Cube's directorial debut, *The Players Club,* it's just another bizarre spin in the chaos.

The Players Club is the story of good-girl-in-a-bad-world Diamond, played by scowling newcomer LisaRaye. All Diamond wants is to finish her journalism degree. But kicked out the house by her pops, she turns to stripping to make ends meet. Add a shoot-out, a wayward cousin, a romance, and a catfight, and there's your movie. It could have been a campy romp. Indeed, Bernie Mac is hilarious as stammering club owner Dollar Bill, skillfully avoiding *Martin*-esque slapstick in a role written for a cartoon. But with half the cast trying for social commentary, it feels like he's the only one in on the joke. There's another problem, The movie's about strippers, so where's all the nekkid 'hos?! In someone else's script, the absence of cooch-flashing dance scenes might have been a coy way of telling us that stripping isn't about sex, it's about power. But in *Players Club,* its simply another reason why this film isn't a lot more fun.

Also reviewed in:
CHICAGO TRIBUNE, 4/8/98, Tempo/p. 2, John Petrakis
NEW YORK TIMES, 4/8/98, p. E3, Janet Maslin
VARIETY, 4/13-19/98, p. 28, Joe Leydon

PLEASANTVILLE

A New Line Cinema release of a Larger Than Life production. *Exeuctive Producer:* Michael De Luca and Mary Parent.   *Producer:* Gary Ross, Jon Kilik, Robert J. Degus, and Steven Soderbergh. *Director:* Gary Ross.   *Screenplay:* Gary Ross.   *Director of Photography:* John Lindley.   *Editor:* William Goldenberg.   *Music:* Randy Newman.   *Music Editor:* Chris Brooks, Bruno Coon, and Jim Flamberg. *Sound:* Robert Anderson, Jr. and (music) Dennis Sands. *Sound Editor:* Bruce Stambler.   *Casting:* Ellen Lewis and Debra Zane.   *Production Designer:* Jeannine Oppewall. *Art Director:* Bill Arnold.   *Set Designer:* Mindi Toback, Mark Poll, Randy Wilkins, Dawn Snyder, and Julia K. Levine.   *Set Decorator:* Jay Hart.   *Set Dresser:* G. Roger Abell, Leslie N. Beattie, Michael Driscoll, H. Chris Grantz, Sean Hood, Troy Peters and John J. Slatsky.   *Special Effects:* Eric Rylander.   *Visual Effects:* Chris Watts.   *Costumes:* Judianna Makovsky.   *Make-up:* Susan A. Cabral.   *Stunt Coordinator:* Ernie Orsatti.   *Running time:* 116 minutes. *MPAA Rating:* PG-13.

CAST: William H. Macy (George);   Joan Allen (Betty);   Natalie Ramsey (Mary Sue);   Kevin Connors (Bud);   Jeff Daniels (Mr. Johnson);   Tobey Maguire (David);   Heather McGill (Girl in School Yard);   Paul Morgan Stetler (College Counselor);   Denise Dowse (Health Teacher); McNally Sagal (Science Teacher);   Jane Kaczmarek (David's Mom);   Giuseppe Andrews (Howard);   Reese Witherspoon (Jennifer);   Marissa Ribisi (Kimmy);   Jenny Lewis (Christin); Justin Nimmo (Mark); Kai Lennox (Mark's Lackey #1); Jason Behr (Mark's Lackey #2); Don Knotts (TV Repairman);   Robin Bissell (Commercial Announcer);   Harry Singleton (Mr. Simpson);   John Ganun and Dan Gillies (Firemen);   Paul Walker (Skip);   Dawn Cody (Betty Jean);   Magie Lawson (Lisa Anne);   Andrea Taylor (Peggy Jane);   Lela Ivey (Miss Peters);   Jim Patric (Tommy);   Marc Blucas (Basketball Hero);   Stanton Rutledge (Coach);   Jason Maves (Paper Boy);   Gerald Emmerick (TV Weatherman);   Charles C. Stevenson, Jr. (Dr. Henderson); Nancy Lenehan (Marge Jenkins);   Weston Blakesley (Gus);   Patrick T. O'Brien (Roy);   Jim Antonio (Ralph);   J.T. Walsh (Bib Bob);   Danny Strong (Juke Box Boy);   Kristin Rudrud (Mary);   Laura Carney (Bridge Club Lady);   Marley Shelton (Margaret);   Erik MacArthur (Will);   Adam Carter (Boy in Soda Shop);   David Tom (Whitey);   Johnny Moran (Pete); Jeanine Jackson (Woman);   J. Patrick Lawlor (Thug);   James Keane (Police Chief Dan).

CHRISTIAN SCIENCE MONITOR, 10/30/98, p. B3, David Sterritt

In an age when good directors are celebrated as "auteurs," often getting more publicity than the stars of their pictures, little attention is paid to the screenwriting profession.

Some writers try to correct this by trumpeting the importance of their contributions every chance they get. Others protest in a more practical way—taking over the director's chair themselves, hoping to protect their visions during the perilous journey from page to screen.

This season two noteworthy scribes are making the switch. "Pleasantville" is written and directed by Gary Ross, who counts the hugely popular "Dave" and "Big" among his past accomplishments. "Living Out Loud" comes from Richard LaGravenese, whose writing credits include "The Fisher King" and "The Bridges of Madison County," as well as "Beloved," currently in release.

Both movies are now traveling to theaters after eagerly attended premieres at the recent Mill Valley, Calif., filmfest.

By a pleasant coincidence, "Pleasantville" makes a perfectly matched set with "The Truman Show," one of last summer's best movies. Again the main action takes place in a town where life follows the formulas of a hackneyed TV show. And again the story prompts us to ask ourselves whether the idealized clichés of a picture-perfect community are a genuine utopia or a fraudulent substitute for the stimulating challenges of real human existence.

The heroes of "Pleasantville" are two 1990s teenagers who find themselves mysteriously transported to the never-never-land of a nostalgia-based television comedy. Their neighbors are all too familiar—the doting mom, the friendly malt-shop proprietor, and so on—but despite the nonstop cheeriness they encounter, the new residents can't feel quite at home. The town's insistence on wholesomeness-by-the-numbers has a phony ring, and when the teens try to open people's minds a little, they touch off a ferocious backlash that reveals real frustration and hatred beneath that smiling 1950s facade.

"Pleasantville" concocts an amusing parody of family-values rhetoric, through Ross's script and through the movie's clever visual maneuvers, using the contrast between color and black-and-white cinematography to chart the slowly changing attitudes of the town's stodgy residents. Also impressive is the picture's excellent cast, from Tobey Maguire and Reese Witherspoon as the teen visitors to Joan Allen and William H. Macy as their Pleasantville parents.

The movie has less biting originality than "The Truman Show," but it proves that director Ross retains screenwriter Ross's flair for exploring real-life issues through divertingly far-fetched plots.

LaGravenese leans toward more bittersweet subjects, and in "Living Out Loud" he explores the psychology of the singles scene through a story that steers a wobbly course between comedy and melodrama.

Holly Hunter plays a divorcée whose comfortable life doesn't mask the emptiness she's felt since her husband ditched her. Her solitude is starting to seem overwhelming when she makes a couple of unexpected friends. One is Danny DeVito as the elevator operator in her apartment building, himself devastated by the recent death of his daughter. The other is Queen Latifah as a feisty nightclub singer who's full of advice for others, but frankly uncertain about her own latest romance. As its title suggests, "Living Out Loud" carries the upbeat message that a life of doubt and insecurity is less meaningful than a life of reaching out, taking risks, and just plain having fun. If that message carries less force than one might wish, it's because LaGravenese the director seems less sure of himself than LaGravenese the writer, resorting to occasional gimmicky touches that dilute the moods and meanings for which he's striving. The plot is promising and the acting is earnest, but in the end the movie doesn't quite work. In the current writer-director sweepstakes, it's Ross with his "Pleasantville" who takes home the honors.

LOS ANGELES TIMES, 10/23/98, Calendar/p. 1, Kenneth Turan

Today's world, teenage David is told in school, is not a user-friendly place. The job market is shrinking, the chance of getting AIDS rising, and global drought and famine are practically here. So is it any wonder that he gets more emotional satisfaction from a 1950s black-and-white TV show than from his own life?

The show, aptly named "Pleasantville," has a "Father Knows Best" simplicity and innocence that modern children of divorce cannot resist. You can set your clock by father George coming home every night, putting his hat on the rack and saying, "Honey, I'm here," as wife Betty hands him a martini and joins him in beaming with pride over children Mary Sue and Bud.

Writer-director Gary Ross starts with our nostalgic infatuation with this kind of fantasy past and takes it one stop beyond. Yes, that TV world is fun to daydream about but would anyone actually want to live there? And if a pair of modern teenagers found themselves suddenly trapped in the place, how would they react?

Ross, as his Oscar nominations for the scripts of both "Big" and "Dave" demonstrate, is a talented writer with a gift for warm and clever humor. "Pleasantville," his first shot at directing, turns out to be both a challenge technically and ambitious thematically. While the technical problems have been beautifully solved, "Pleasantville" takes an unexpected dramatic turn and ends up having more on its mind than it can successfully handle.

The infatuation squeaky-voiced high schooler David (Tobey Maguire) feels for "Pleasantville" is, he hopes, about to pay off. A nostalgia network is broadcasting 24 hours of reruns and offering a sizable cash prize to whoever knows the most show trivia, and no one knows more about George, Betty, Mary Sue and Bud than he does.

David, however, has a socially active sister named Jennifer (Reese Witherspoon) who plans to monopolize the TV watching an MTV event with a local hunk. She and David battle over the set's remote control and when it ends up smashed, a repairman from Reliable TV (a charming Don Knotts) magically appears at their door and offers them a substitute.

"This one has a lot more oomph," the repairman says, handing over a shiny silver remote. "You want something that'll put you right in the show." And, sure enough, a pushed button places Jennifer and David literally inside the black-and-white world of "Pleasantville." "It's not possible, is it possible, it can't be possible," they moan.

Though David knows the show inside out, it's still hard for him to adjust to living in a world where there is no color, nothing bad ever happens and firemen haven't heard of fire, working only to rescue kittens trapped in trees.

Party animal Jennifer has even more trouble with "being trapped in Nerdville," though she's somewhat mollified when she discovers that handsome Skip Martin (Paul Walker), the captain of Pleasantville's undefeated basketball team—they never so much as miss a shot—thinks she's "the keenest girl in the whole school."

Just holding hands Pleasantville style, however, is not Jennifer's modus operandi. A worried David pleads with her that doing anything rash "could screw up their whole universe," but Jennifer, believing that "maybe these people don't want to be geeks all their lives," is determined to introduce carnal knowledge to this completely chaste universe.

It's not sex that changes Pleasantville, but the experience of real emotion, and as local folk start to actually feel things, they slowly, one at a time, turn into full-color characters on the screen.

Visual effects supervisor Chris Watts and color effects designer Michael Southard worked closely with filmmaker Ross and cinematographer John Lindley to get these delicate color transitions right, and the result is a satisfying success. Color and black and white exist magically and seamlessly in the same frames, echoing and surpassing the beautiful effects of Michael Powell's 1946 "A Matter of Life and Death." Following on the visual success of "What Dreams May Come," "Pleasantville" further illustrates how limitless the future is for the inventive use of new technologies.

Ross' work as a writer-director is equally felicitous, at least at first. This TV world has been imagined down to its smallest detail, the cast is perfectly chosen (the easily peeved Witherspoon and the always excellent Joan Allen as mom Betty are especially good) and Ross displays an easy touch and a subtle eye for quiet humor.

There comes a point, however, when "Pleasantville" stops being comic and turns didactic. As David and Jennifer stumble into this unexpected world, so audiences suddenly stumble into that other staple of the 1950s, the message picture. Ross' missive is earnest and well-intentioned, but it's difficult not to feel that his film both runs on too long and overreaches its dramatic resources in its attempt to deliver it. It's true, as David says in reference to "pleasant," that "there are so many other things that are so much better," but a surprise civics lesson may not be one of them.

NEW YORK, 11/2/98, p. 118, Peter Rainer

In *Pleasantville*, two nineties teenagers from a broken suburban home are magically zapped by a Yoda-like television repairman (Don Knotts) into the black-and-white world of a fifties *Father Knows Best*-ish television sitcom, also called *Pleasantville*, which has spawned a cult following on cable TV. David (Tobey Maguire), smart and socially awkward, knows every bit of trivia about the show. He's smitten by the fifties—and not even the actual fifties but a pasty, idealized version of them. His twin sister, Jennifer (Reese Witherspoon), is a frisky crumpet. She's hooked on the here and now; that's where the action is.

It was bad enough when the doomsayers were indicting *The Jerry Springer Show* for hollowing out our souls. Now we've got to worry about Nick at Nite. What David and Jennifer discover in moving about the town of Pleasantville is that the ideal is not so ideal after all. Their brave new world is inhabited by dimensionless dweebs. Their Pleasantville parents, George (William H. Macy) and Betty (Joan Allen), are like Ozzie and Harriet with extra treacle. The high-school basketball star, Skip (Paul Walker), is strictly golly-gee. Chattering lassies and Bryl Creemed boys swarm the screen.

It should all be nightmarish, but it isn't. Gary Ross, the screenwriter of *Dave* and (with Ann Spielberg) *Big*, making his directorial debut, isn't interested in doing a *Village of the Damned* number. The citizens of Pleasantville aren't hollow, exactly; they're more like empty vessels waiting to receive the light. Ross finds them poignant. Corseted by confectionery lives, they fumble toward freedom, and as they do, little smudges of color creep into their world. Some of these effects are quite lovely. Tears track down cheeks, leaving flesh tones in their glistening wake; flowers glow red and yellow in the pearly black-and-whiteness. For Ross, the goal is to get it all in color. That's his idea of a world viewed without blinders.

Which is not to say he's too starched for satire. He takes his share of potshots at these villagers. But his bent is one of messianic civic-mindedness—he's also dabbled in speechwriting for the Clinton administration—and he's on a mission here. He wants to do more than save souls. He wants to *invent* them. The un-people of Pleasantville learn that life is not always pleasant, and the realization humanizes them. Amen.

They learn that firemen exist to put out fires—not just to rescue treed cats. They experience a rain shower for the first time. They experience sex. They experience discrimination, too: The black-and-white townies heckle and pummel the "coloreds"—the people whose awakened emotions have literally turned them into living color—before the toughs, too, are transformed. The mayor (the late J. T. Walsh, in his last role) issues an official code of conduct that tries to turn back the clock. (Perry Como is in; Elvis on the jukebox is out.) Books, previously mere props filled with blank pages, are starting to fill up with words. We watch them heaped by angry demonstrators and torched. (Some of the titles: *Huckleberry Finn, The Catcher in the Rye.*)

Such ugliness, we are made to feel, is the price of freedom. But do we really need all this hoo-ha? Hauling in images of race brawls and book burnings collapses what might otherwise have been a frail, fragrant comedy about how our pop fantasies betray us. Yet even the theme of betrayal is suspect. Nobody—not even studio executives—actually mistakes *Father Knows Best* for the real world. Ross is subverting a pop ideal we never believed in anyway. Worse, he wants to be hailed as a truth-teller for his troubles. *Pleasantville* is a prime piece of showbiz sentimentalism: It says that life isn't like Hollywood, yet its frame of reference is almost entirely Hollywood pap—and white, middle-class pap at that. It flatters itself that the peachy-keen sitcoms we sat through as kids—or that our kids sit through in cable-TV reruns—remain defining moments.

Ross wants us to break free from the deadening blandness of this communal upbringing. But his own imagination is often on the same mundane, fifties-sitcom plane. He doesn't bring anything into the mix that might truly jolt the agenda. We get no bulletins from the outside—no Korea, no HUAC, no nothing. The town's kids lap up Mark Twain all right, but we don't hear a thing about the outlawry of, say, Ginsberg or Kerouac or Mailer or Burroughs. The Elvis that we hear on the jukebox is doing "(Let Me Be Your) Teddy Bear"—Elvis at his coziest. Mr. Johnson (Jeff Daniels), the moonstruck soda jerk who pines to be an artist, has a yen for David's mom, Betty, and renders her nude. This is supposed to be shocking, taboo-busting, but his paint-by-the-numbers expressiveness is as cozy as "Teddy Bear." Even Jennifer, who heats up Skip with her grope-a-thons on Lovers' Lane, is chastened for our benefit. In the old movie tradition of bad-girls-gone-good, or sort of good, she ends up turning away from lust. Instead of coming out to play, she stays in her bedroom, claps on an unflattering pair of specs, and reads D. H. Lawrence. (Sublimation is all.)

There's a grandstanding Capra-esque moment near the end of the movie when David, who has seen the light, exhorts the townspeople to embrace what is happening to them and not be afraid. Recognize the sexy and the dangerous, he sermonizes: "All these things are within yourself." This child of TV has come full circle. No more reruns for him. From now on, it's all first-run.

Is anybody likely to feel liberated watching this film? Ross wants change—just not too much. If he had followed the logic of his own conceit and allowed things to get *really* funky, Pleasantville might have turned into another Twin Peaks. David wants people to embrace within themselves the sexy and the dangerous, but the way Ross sets it up, there's no place for that sex and danger to thrive. The film pays lip service to emotional liberation without really allowing for its consequences. It's just a Norman Rockwell portrait with a somewhat racier palette. The actors, trying their damnedest to give their roles some lyricism, end up frozen on the canvas.

Pleasantville is the latest movie to thwack television for poisoning our marrow. After *The Truman Show,* everyone is probably sick of the whole discussion, but here we go again. What's up with all of this? It wasn't so long ago, after all, that Hollywood started churning out affectionate big-screen versions of old TV shows—everything from *The Addams Family* to *The Flintstones.* (The boomers running the studios are reliving their childhoods by fobbing off their favorite thumb-suckers on the rest of us.) Could *Pleasantville* and *The Truman Show* be Hollywood's make-nice response to the attacks leveled against it by politicos for befouling our minds with gratuitous sex and carnage? Publicly the moguls have groused, but privately there has been much wringing of hands. Don't forget: The flip side of Hollywood's errant crassness is an arrant social consciousness. Bigger even than winning the Nobel Peace Prize is copping the Jean Hersholt Humanitarian Award on Oscar night. *Pleasantville* scores well on this playing field; it's positively *clogged* with social consciousness. It wants to make us better citizens by pulling us out of the fantasy machine.

And it does so by turning itself into a massive mea culpa. The film is an apology for the ways in which show business mesmerizes us with false hope. It's saying that if we are disappointed by life, we should look to the shows we grew up on and pay heed. It takes a real movie-colony mind-set to root the world and its problems in the boiler room of the dream factory. Still, Ross could be onto something: Maybe people soaked in pop culture are increasingly looking for an all-purpose pop-culture explanation for why everything has turned out so lousily. As explanations go, this sort of thing makes a superficial kind of sense, and it's more fun to play around with than Marxism or Freudianism or just about any other ism. Just think: You can watch *Ozzie and Harriet* reruns *and* bemoan the sick soul of America at the same time. Or you can take yourself to see *Pleasantville*.

NEW YORK POST, 10/23/98, p. 37, Rod Dreher

Gary Ross' visually ambitious and disarmingly original fantasy "Pleasantville" is, like its fraternal twin, "The Truman Show," a terrific example of a mainstream movie exploring provocative philosophical issues in a superbly crafted and entertaining piece of pop filmmaking.

Far from the predictable slam on 1950s gray-flannel conformity you might expect, "Pleasantville" proves a clever, complex and surprisingly poignant fable about the problem of pain and the temptation to idolize false utopias. Despite that thematic seriousness, writer-director Ross keeps his comedy fleet-footed, playful and vibrantly alive, almost till the end.

Tobey Maguire plays David, a modern-day teen-ager who hides from the ugly chaos of his daily existence. The news is always bad, his sister Jennifer (Reese Witherspoon) is the school slut and his folks are nastily divorced.

Small wonder, then, that David escapes the madness through reruns of "Pleasantville", a 1950s sitcom in which every day is sunny and nothing troubling intrudes on the slap-happy family life enjoyed by George (William H. Macy), Betty (Joan Allen) and their kids, Bud and Mary Sue.

A magical prank pulled by a gnomish TV repairman (Don Knotts!) zaps David and Jennifer into "Pleasantville"—as Bud and Mary Sue. Both morally and visually, their world is black-and-white. The culture-clash gags are sui generis but still hilarious.

Trampy Witherspoon rebels by doing the one thing she's good at: seducing and deflowering the first Wally Cleaver she can find.

Bringing sex to "Pleasantville" causes the town's tightly woven social fabric to burst into color at the seams. (The swell special effects serve the story but don't dominate it.)

This isn't another simplistic Hollywood paean to sexual liberation, though. What has been introduced is not sex, really, but the experience of deep feeling—which brings dimension, conflict and color—literally—to "Pleasantville"'s monochromatic way of life.

But with the discovery of joy—in carnality, in learning, in art—comes confusion and, well, unpleasantness. A neglected wife turns against a husband; a woozy soda jerk (Jeff Daniels) sets the town on its ear with controversial art; anger erupts into violence as the town mayor, Big Bob (J.T. Walsh, in his final role) tries to reimpose order.

Ross slips in the overlong film's final half hour, stacking on the sort of clunky message-movie moralizing that's more than the narrative can handle. (Yes, Virginia, there is a book-burning.)

"Pleasantville" works much better in its graceful moments of awakening. Joan Allen, the very picture of dignified yearning in another of her quietly stunning performances, leads a magnificently subtle cast that helps turn a gimmicky premise into something close to profound.

At its heart, "Pleasantville" is a critique of our susceptibility to television's notions of perfection. With wit and eloquence, it insists we must know misery if we are to know happiness.

The film tells us that the most profound joy may be found in sharing the sorrow of others—and for a mainstream Hollywood movie as much fun to watch as this one, that's really saying something.

NEWSDAY, 10/23/98, Part II/p. B3, Jack Mathews

The scene is repeated millions of times every day, in homes across this great land and beyond. It's the ultimate power game, a struggle for domination, an expression of free will and desire with the immediate future hanging in the balance. Two teenagers are fighting over the remote control.

In "Pleasantville," Gary Ross' wonderfully inventive and brilliantly executed cultural fairy tale, the combatants are David and Jennifer, siblings whose rivalry galvanizes into explosive fury in front of the television set, at a moment when everything is at stake. David, the withdrawn loner, is about to sit down to a marathon of his favorite 1950s TV show, "Pleasantville," while his outgoing sister is planning to watch a rock concert with the high school stud of her dreams.

Tug, scream, push, tug, scream, pull, tug, tug... Zap!

In one magical moment, facilitated by a strange remote control device left behind by an even stranger TV repairman (Don Knotts), David and Jennifer (superbly played by Tobey Maguire and Reese Witherspoon) have been beamed from their contemporary full-color living room into the black-and-white world of "Pleasantville." They've taken over the roles of their sitcom counterparts, Bud and Mary Sue, and are caught in the loving, uncritical gaze of their perfect TV parents, George (William H. Macy) and Betty (Joan Allen).

Two movie characters haven't faced such a massive physical and cultural dislocation since Dorothy and Toto dropped in on the Munchkins, and their experience will be as filled with adventure. But in their case, they're not looking for Oz, they're bringing it.

Ross has proven himself a natural at writing the modern fable. With utter ease, he makes us believe in a boy who takes over a man's body to become a successful Manhattan toy company executive in "Big," and that a small-town John Doe, recruited as a stand-in for the comatose American president he resembles, leaves a stronger nation behind in "Dave."

For his directing debut, Ross wrote himself a story that takes even greater leaps of fancy, and yet grounds this Looking Glass world so thoroughly in his characters, and in the decency that inevitably drives them, that you surrender immediately, unconditionally, and swallow whole most of what follows.

In "Pleasantville," what follows is the culture clash of the century. Two world-wise kids from the cynical '90s are in the midst of people whose existence is charted by writers propagating the myth of wholesome Eisenhower Era prosperity, where dads are always employed, moms are always in their spic-and-span kitchens, and kids always get their homework done before heading to the malt shop.

David and Jennifer react much differently to their new surroundings. He's always dreamed of living the simple "Ozzie and Harriet" life, while Jennifer is appalled at being in the company of squares, and worse, having a black-and-white wardrobe!

What elevates this far above "Twilight Zone" or sitcom gimmickry is the gradual transformation of "Pleasantville" from cardboard utopia to functional community, with the full rubric of social concerns, and its citizens from script-bound automatons to liberated, colorful, flesh-and-blood people of free will.

The chief and most successful conceit of "Pleasantville" is the optical wizardy that allows color to drain in and fill out this evolving world. You've seen commercials where color is woven into black-and-white scenes, but here, it's done almost constantly, to seamless perfection.

Color, of course, comes to those who embrace reality. It happens on Lovers Lane, where Jennifer's seduction of her aw-shucks boyfriend shows him and others that there's more to romance than holding hands. It happens in the malt shop where gentle Mr. Johnson (Jeff Daniels, who played a similar character in Woody Allen's "The Purple Rose of Cairo") discovers the joy of painting with a full palette of colors. It happens at home, where Jennifer gives her mom a nudge onto the feminist track, leaving a befuddled dad wondering where in the heck his dinner is. And it happens in City Hall, where a conservative mayor (the late J.T. Walsh) and others draw the line against change by banning color.

Ross gets a little carried away with political allegory in the late stages, cramming so many yardsticks of discrimination, oppression and Puritan indignation into it that they threaten to drive you out of the fantasy. But this is a minor quibble about a movie that truly earns the stamp of magic. This is fun!

SIGHT AND SOUND, 3/99, p. 49, Andrew O'Hehir

The USA, the present. Teenage brother and sister David and Jennifer are transported by a mysterious television repairman into the fictional world of David's favourite show, a black-and-white 50s sitcom called *Pleasantville*, where they become Bud and Mary Sue Parker, children of the show's central family. David/Bud suggests they play along with *Pleasantville's* universe—where sex is unknown, the basketball team never loses, and all the library books are blank—until he can make contact with the repairman again. But Jennifer/Mary Sue refuses. Instead she seduces Skip, the captain of the basketball team. *Pleasantville's* universe becomes unstable—the basketball team loses, books fill with words and the like.

As carnal knowledge—along with literature, art and geography—begins to spread, certain objects and people in Pleasantville begin to bloom into colour. Betty, Bud and Mary Sue's mother, becomes "coloured" and leaves home to live with Bill Johnson, the diner owner who has taken up modernist painting, while their father George remains in black and white. Mobs of enraged black-and-white citizens destroy Bill's diner and attack "coloureds" in the street until Big Bob, the town's mayor, decrees a restrictive code of conduct aimed at stopping the spread of colour. But David/Bud and Bill paint a mural on the police station, leading to a court case that ends with David/Bud turning the whole town coloured. Jennifer decides she will stay behind in Pleasantville as Mary Sue to pursue her new-found interest in literature, while David uses the repairman's magic remote control to return to his divorced mother in the present day.

It is rare that one can criticise a big-budget Hollywood movie for having too many ideas, and by that standard alone Gary Ross' *Pleasantville* is a signal event. Ross—whose penchant for outsized fantasy was made clear in his screenplays for *Big* and *Dave*—tries to pack his directorial debut with everything from Milton and Blake to *The Wizard of Oz* (1939) and *To Kill a Mockingbird*, (1962) ending up with a muddled liberal fairytale about freedom and tolerance in the Frank Capra tradition. That's nothing to be ashamed of, especially when *Pleasantville* also emulates the visual lustre and genuine, big-hearted sentimentality of Capra's best work. Unlike *The Truman Show*, with which it will inevitably be compared, *Pleasantville's* ideas are visual and cinematic as well as theoretical, making it gloriously enjoyable entertainment without *Truman's* slight but unmistakable aroma of postmortem pedantry.

Sympathetic portrayals of high-school geek losers are endemic in American movies (the popular-jock caste having produced few film-makers, it seems). Even so, Tobey Maguire's performance as David, suddenly transported to a world he understands better than he does his own life, is an exceptionally nuanced one. Wearing the same wry, wounded, older-than-his-years expression he employed so well in Ang Lee's *The Ice Storm* Maguire gives us a lonely young man who wants nothing more than to succeed in the real world. Mastering the minutiae of the *Pleasantville* series is an enthusiasm and an escape, but David doesn't want to live in the show any more than his randy sister does. In fact, it is the wilfully trampy Jennifer (played with the requisite sauciness by Reese Witherspoon) who is responsible for the greater act of imagination. In refusing to restrain her own desires—in order to collaborate with the Pleasantville ethos—she liberates the town into all the chaos and disorder of sensuality.

From a genial spoof of the Fall, featuring Don Knotts' geriatric television repairman as a misguided Jehovah and the unchanging world of a televisual small town as Paradise, *Pleasantville* careens through a dizzying range of cultural, historical and mythic references. When sitcom mom Betty Parker (whose balance of parody and pathos is affectingly captured by Joan Allen) experiences her sexual awakening, the film seems redolent of *The Scarlet Letter*, or perhaps *A Doll's House*. When Big Bob and his band of angry 'black-and-white' men in bowling shirts ban rock 'n' roll and coloured paint, it briefly becomes *Rebel without a Cause*. When it seeks to evoke both Kristallnacht and the Jim Crow South simultaneously, it overreaches itself.

Like *The Wizard of Oz*, whose structure it parallels closely, *Pleasantville* overcomes its moralising and occasional pomposity with magical photographic effects (the scene in which pink cherry blossoms fall on the black-and-white road to Lovers' Lane will linger in viewers' memories for years); moments of dry burnout, as when television dad George Parker (the hilariously deadpan William H. Macy) admits to David/Bud that he has eaten nothing but cocktail olives since Betty's departure, as he understands neither the freezer nor the stove; and commanding central performances. In place of Judy Garland's irrepressible Depression lass, Ross and Maguire offer a rueful 90s boy-Adam who learns what he already knew: perfect systems always decay, so human beings have no option but to choose uncertainty. It's not quite that there's no place like home—in the end, even in Pleasantville, there's no place *but* home.

TIME, 10/26/98, p. 92, Richard Corliss

Ah, the '50s! A decade of picket fences and placid smiles, of front lawns without weeds and a future without care, when children were wise enough to respect their parents—because Father knew best.

Rotten, wasn't it? People did what they were supposed to do, not what they deeply, truly needed to. It was a time of confinement: those wire bras were a chastity belt for bosoms. Haircuts were part of the hypocrisy—boys couldn't hide their ears, but they could, had to, suppress their liveliest instincts. It was the long night of the living dead.

That's the not-so-hidden agenda of Pleasantville, an epic-size, largely entertaining parable of repression and awakening from writer-director Gary Ross. The movie imagines that two teenagers, David (Tobey Maguire) and his randy sister Jennifer (Reese Witherspoon), are magically transported from the '90s into the small, sleepy town of David's favorite '50s sitcom. The "knows-best" father, George (William H. Macy), and his wife Betty (Joan Allen), all starched sweetness, are convinced that David is Bud, a.k.a. Sport, and that Jennifer, now outfitted in a poodle-skirt-and-sweater set, is Mary Sue—Muffin to her doting dad. Weirdest of all, the whole town is in black-and-white. "We're supposed to be at home, David," Jennifer scolds her brother. "We're supposed to be in color."

In outline, *Pleasantville* sounds like the most derivative movie of all time: a bit of *Back to the Future* (teen time travel), a whit of *The Wizard of Oz* (the color of dreams), a plot from *The Purple Rose of Cairo* (with actor Jeff Daniels linking two stories of real and reel life), a lot from *The Truman Show* (except that here everyone in town believes in the grand fiction of a perfectly ordered society). But Ross, who helped create two other fantasies of displacement, *Big* and *Dave*, has more in mind: Follow your heart, not the rules. And '50s bad, '60s good.

Be it known that whatever its message, the movie bubbles over with felicities. The actors, once they get over their early overplaying, are uniformly splendid. Ross gets plenty of smart fun from the collision of '50s and '90s: a "healthy" breakfast loaded with pork products, a mother-daughter sex talk in which Muffin explains the facts of life to Mom. Carpeting the film is Randy Newman's richest score, tremulous and true to the period; those yearning violins express an ache the Pleasantvillagers don't yet know they have.

This Pleasantville, this Bedford Falls, this Brigadoon, this Springfield, you see, is really Stepford—a place so sanitized there are no toilets or double beds, a people so insular they have never known what it's like to feel unprogrammed joy or lust or rage or bravery or intellectual adventure. When they finally open themselves to these emotions (by gazing at a Picasso or hearing Buddy Holly or spending the evening with a naughty girl from the '90s), the people of Pleasantville literally blush into color. They wear their passion on their shamed, fervent faces, on their clothes, like a scarlet letter. And the town burghers, still cocooned in monochrome propriety, are perplexed, vexed, vengeful.

Ross and his team make brilliant use of color technology; the blossoming of each character really does touch the emotions of an openhearted viewer. But the scheme has heavier undertones. For creamy black-and-white read white: white bread, pasty white skin, whites-only neighborhoods, the last decade of white-male culture and, yes, the white sheets of the Ku Klux Klan. For color read colored, as in "colored people" and other oppressed minorities—artists seeking free expression, women in search of the apocalyptic orgasm.

The movie sees this emotional colorizing as a good thing. Waking from the prolonged childhood of the '50s (when Ike was the omnipotent dad), America attended to the culture bubbling under its consciousness—to rhythm and blues, to Lenny Bruce and Redd Foxx, to *Lolita* and *Lady Chatterley's Lover*—and took a heroic leap into the enthralling unknown; the flourishing of art, the liberation of race and gender. Yet it can also be argued that the opening of those emotional pores brought a more debased culture: drug epidemics, teen pregnancy, splatter movies, penis-size jokes on every sitcom, Marilyn Manson and Monica Lewinsky. Perhaps the four-letterization of

America was not an unalloyed blessing, and the handing of artistic freedom to an infantile culture was not a wise gift.

These views are open to debate—a debate the film doesn't acknowledge. The ultimate irony of *Pleasantville* is that it is less a '60s movie than a '50s one; it has the didacticism and sentimentality of the serious Hollywood product of that earlier time. That one and this. Stretching credulity but never hedging a bet, Ross wants universal acceptance for his film, so he finally makes the town so endearing that one of the '90s kids decides to stay there. (Gee, wait til Mom finds out!) He hopes you will too. That's the difference between today's best Hollywood filmmakers and the top independent auteurs. Todd Solondz and Hal Hartley don't care if you like, or even get, *Happiness* or *Henry Fool*. Ross wants to point a finger while you shake his hand.

VILLAGE VOICE, 11/3/98, p. 135, J. Hoberman

At once generous and authoritarian, outgoing and self-absorbed, eager-to-please and ruthless, American entertainment has a natural desire to be everything to everyone--its human embodiment would be Bill Clinton on the campaign trail. But can such an other-directed force ever truly reflect upon itself?

With the elaborately allegorical *Pleasantville*, the entertainment industry strains to ponder just this ontological question. Gary Ross's first directorial outing—after writing speeches for Michael Dukakis and Bill Clinton, as well as the scripts for *Big* and *Dave*—is the latest example of that special-effects-driven American magic realism rooted in *It's a Wonderful Life* and *The Twilight Zone*. The setting is a media hall of mirrors, as contemporary teen twins David (Tobey Maguire) and Jennifer (an overaged Reese Witherspoon) are transported not back to the 1950s but into its representation—the echt, ersatz '50s TV sitcom *Pleasantville*.

The movie *Pleasantville* is just clever enough to recognize its imaginary namesake as a form of sociological camp, attractive for its corny negation of the modern world. (Ross makes an obvious point in juxtaposing the TV show's black-and-white cheerfulness with 1998 teenagers absorbing all manner of depressing stats on jobs, AIDS, and ecology.) The sitcom is essentially the same artificial world as *The Truman Show*, but Ross gives it a less paranoid, more obviously political inflection by having it promoted on the film's equivalent of Nick at Nite with such post-'50s buzz terms as "family values" and "kinder, gentler."

The *Pleasantville* show is a pleasingly skillful simulation, not least in the hyperreal performances of Joan Allen and William H. Macy as the ideal parents. Because this is TV, the rain never falls, and the temperature is always 72 degrees. Toilets and double beds don't exist. "We're like stuck in nerdville," Jennifer moans as, re-outfitted in a cardigan and poodle skirt, she joins her new peer group as they file into school under the American flag. Lived, as opposed to watched on television, *Pleasantville* has no laugh track, but given the simplicity of its moral universe it scarcely needs one.

With the new power of the Internet, it has apparently become easier for the movies to imagine their old enemy TV as our sole cultural referent. Jesus may be conspicuous by his absence from this particular moral regime, but Ross has no difficulty imagining God's representative as a cosmic TV repairman (Don Knotts). Still, *Pleasantville* is not without its Old Testament metaphors. Having already nibbled the apple back in the World, Jennifer introduces sex into this drab Eden—and, by thus raising the excitement quotient, makes it more entertaining. This transformation is signified in showbiz terms by the gradual introduction of color—a miracle reinforced by such biblical tropes as a burning bush and a comforting rainbow.

Funny for about half an hour, *Pleasantville* thereafter becomes an increasingly lugubrious, ultimately exasperating mix of technological wonder and ideological idiocy. (Stop reading here if you plan to be surprised.) The sexual metaphor is wildly inconsistent. Having seduced the gee-whiz captain of the basketball team, Jennifer is free to put on glasses and start reading books. Soon all the cool kids are out on Lover's Lane participating in a Technicolor orgy of secular humanism as they devour *Huckleberry Finn* and *Catcher in the Rye*. Eventually, these proponents of teen sex, '50s rock and roll, and good books become Pleasantville's persecuted "colored" people with the black-and-white "no-changists" of the Chamber of Commerce conducting themselves like Nazi brownshirts.

Say what? *Father Knows Best* as *Triumph of the Will?* Seemingly haunted by the specter of Pat Robertson's cable network and the early stages of the last presidential campaign, when (at the urging of village scold William Bennett) Bob Dole focused his geriatric fire on Hollywood, Ross feels duty-bound to correct the outmoded entertainment of the 1950s, which has somehow lodged itself in the collective brain of the fundamentalist right as the simulation of a lost American past.

Thus does Hollywood defend itself against itself. The clichés are summoned to the rescue. Ross may believe that he is liberating the uptight Eisenhower era with a zipless '60s sexual and cultural revolution, but, if anything, *Pleasantville* is a colorized imitation of New Dealish Capracorn. (Even its feeble Freudian justification for "silly, sexy, dangerous" art is basically '40s: "You can't stop something that's inside you" is a phrase familiar to the most casual devotee of film noir.)

It's wild to see a big-budget Hollywood movie lifting the cudgels for "modern art" (or at least the modern art of 75 years ago), but *Pleasantville* is just as predicated on denial as the TV show it spoofs. Is it churlishly p.c. to note that, all diversity-babble and color metaphors to the contrary, the new, improved Pleasantville is no less comfortably white and heterosexual (or middle-class and suburban) than the old place? Or that the we-are-the-world epiphany that ends the movie is completely mediated by the (newly color) TV and that the coda is a nauseating replica of a 1984 Ronald Reagan "Morning in America" ad?

Proposing that entertainment will solve the "problems" that entertainment has itself created, this hermetically sealed package gives new meaning to the term *bubble brain*. For that alone, the trope "Pleasantville" deserves to become Op-Ed discourse. This is the year's most richly confused social metaphor, and you can stick that in the ads.

Also reviewed in:
CHICAGO TRIBUNE, 10/23/98, Friday/p. A, Mark Caro
NEW REPUBLIC, 11/23/98, p. 28, Stanley Kauffmann
NEW YORK TIMES, 10/23/98, p. E23, Janet Maslin
VARIETY, 9/21-27/98, p. 104, Joe Leydon
WASHINGTON POST, 10/23/98, p. B1, Rita Kempley
WASHINGTON POST, 10/23/98, Weekend/p. 54, Michael O'Sullivan

POLISH WEDDING

A Fox Searchlight Pictures release in association with Lakeshore Entertainment of an Addis/Wechsler production. *Executive Producer:* Nick Wechsler, Sigurjon Sighvatsson, and Ted Tannebaum. *Producer:* Tom Rosenberg, Julia Chasman, and Geoff Stier. *Director:* Theresa Connelly. *Screenplay:* Theresa Connelly. *Director of Photography:* Guy Dufaux. *Editor:* Curtiss Clayton and Suzanne Fenn. *Music:* Luis Bacalov. *Sound:* Ron Ayers. *Casting:* Owens Hill. *Production Designer:* Kara Lindstrom. *Set Decorator:* Ether Robins Richards. *Costume Designer:* Donna Zakowska. *Running time:* 101 minutes. *MPAA Rating:* PG-13.

CAST: Claire Danes (Hala);   Jon Bradford (Sailor);   Lena Olin (Jadzia);   Ramsey Krull (Kris);   Gabriel Byrne (Bolek);   Daniel LaPaine (Ziggy);   Rebecca Morrin and Rachel Morrin (Ziggy and Sofie's Baby);   Mili Avital (Sofie);   Steven Petrarca (Witek);   Brian Hoyt (Kaz); Christina Romana Lypeckyj (Kaszia);   Peter Carey (Piotrusz);   Robert Daniels (Roman's Business Partner);   Rade Serbedzija (Roman);   Ryan Spahn (Kid);   Adam Trese (Russell); Randy Godwin (Nosy Neighbor);   Jeffrey Nordling (Father Don);   Mitchell Mandeberg (Stanley Mislinski);   Sheldon Alkon (Man in Church);   Laurie V. Logan (Helga);   Joanna Woodcock (Woman in Bakery);   Joseph Haynes (Mr. Schuster);   Judy Dery (Mrs. Schuster);   Sparks of Fire (Band at Festival);   Rick Thompson and Seamus McNally (Hecklers);   Cassidy Cirka (Hala's Baby).

LOS ANGELES TIMES, 7/17/98, Calendar/p. 16, Jack Mathews

[*The following review by Jack Mathews appeared in a slightly different form in* **NEWSDAY, 7/17/98, Part II/p. B7.**]

How many people does it take to have a Polish wedding? Four: a pregnant girl, a reluctant groom, a priest and someone to hold the shotgun.

The script for rookie writer-director Theresa Connelly's "Polish Wedding" doesn't quite pause to summarize its plot in the form of an ethnic joke, but that's the general idea. Every marriage and potential marriage in this heartfelt but often tone-deaf domestic comedy originates in careless passion between people who aren't sure how much they even like each other.

Bolek Pzoniak (Gabriel Byrne), a baker in the Polish Detroit community of Hamtramck, and his still lusty wife Jadzia (Lena Olin) got married to legitimize the birth of the first of their five children, and have stayed together all these years more out of familial ritual than love.

That first child, Ziggi (Daniel LaPaine), married Sofie (Mili Avital) to legitimize the birth of their firstborn, and are getting to know each other under the most stressful circumstances.

Now, Hala (Claire Danes), the youngest of the Pzoniak brood and the designated virgin of the coming Procession of the Virgins, is in a family way, thanks to Russell (Adam Trese), the tomcat cop she's been sneaking away to meet in the middle of the night.

Connelly, who grew up in Hamtramck, intends "Polish Wedding" as an homage to the spirit and rootedness of the immigrant families in her blue-collar neighborhood, and her three central characters have certainly been crafted with loving care.

Jadzia, the controlling matriarch of the Pzoniak clan, is a vibrant, passionate woman who remains sympathetic even while expending her sexual energy in an indiscreet, long-running affair with Roman (Rade Serbedzija), a successful businessman.

Hala is her mother's child, recklessly adventuresome, and despite all the warning signs around her—the tension between Ziggi and Sofie, the strain of her parents' marriage—she's on a fast track to parenthood.

Bolek, meanwhile, is the picture of a beaten man, waiting around like a dog, Hala tells him, while his wife is off with her lover. It breaks his heart, but he won't confront her for fear of losing her.

Somehow, Connelly wants us to believe that the family ties here are strong enough to withstand any test, from being cash-strapped in an overcrowded house, to the rambunctious kids getting themselves into trouble, to the passive father being betrayed. It's a hard sell, and Connelly doesn't quite have the storytelling savvy to pull it off.

Each time the film reaches a critical juncture, Connelly's solution is to distract us with slapstick farce. One minute, poor pathetic Bolek is so down in his cups that you're worrying about a suicide; the next minute, he and Jadzia are teamed up with their sons in the madcap kidnapping—complete with jaunty Polish folk music—of Hala's elusive boyfriend.

If the real point of "Polish Wedding" is that life in Hamtramck is so chaotically fraught that each new trauma buries the last, then a mere movie can't do it justice.

NEW YORK POST, 7/17/98, p. 44, Thelma Adams

How do you tell the bride at a Polish wedding?

In Theresa Connelly's episodic tribute to female fecundity, she's the babe in the dirty white dress carrying all the Virgin Mary symbolism.

Set among Detroit's Polish working class, "Polish Wedding" follows generations of women who know how to lift their skirts but not how to unwrap a condom.

What differentiates a Polish wedding from a shotgun marriage is that the angry family members of the fallen virgin, use hockey sticks, not fire power, to corral the reluctant suitor.

Claire Danes is the so-called bride. Her Hala (pronounced like the bread) is a pouty, fluffy, floppy spoiled , MTV-era teenager with Breck girl curls.

Hala dropped out of high school to flirt with men in uniform. At night, the free spirit sneaks out of the house to be chased by Russell (Adam Trese), a green cop with a coverboy torso. After fierce fondling in a vacant lot near the Catholic Church (symbolism alert), Hala returns home for a forbidden smoke with her little brother.

Hala is a slice off the old pickle. Mama Jadzia (Lena Olin), a lusty cleaning lady in Wonderbras, is having a sudsy affair with her boss (the powerful but miscast Rade Serbedzija).

Meanwhile, Papa Bolek, a baker, struggles to keep his wife as desperately as actor Gabriel Byrne grapples with Bolek's thick accent. We know the patriarch is working class because his cigarette ashes fall onto his white undershirt and he talks with his hands.

Newcomer Connelly leads a strong cast into lazy performances. Both Danes and Byrne are actors who need tough love. Olin, one of the sexiest actresses ever to flee Ingmar Bergman, straddles the role of the ubermom with two well-toned thighs.

But the beautiful Swede can't escape the fact that she's forced to play the second lead in a Polish-American road show of Tennessee Williams. Instead of "Summer and Smoke," we get "Pickles and Polka."

VILLAGE VOICE, 7/21/98, p. 124, Andrew Robertson

Shot on location in her working-class hometown of Hamtramck, Michigan, Theresa Connelly's modestly budgeted *Polish Wedding* is a heartfelt but overly languid ode to her upbringing. Padzia Pzoniak (Lena Olin), the matriarch of a large Polish blue-collar household, is devoted to her family, but also longs to be liberated from them. By night she escapes to a not-so-surreptitious affair with a wealthy businessman, while her husband (Gabriel Byrne), a gentle and complacent baker, laments the loss of his once-sturdy marriage. Their swaggering daughter (Claire Danes) seems destined to emulate mom's sexual audacity.

Olin and Danes are both convincingly restless romantics, and Byrne gives an equally persuasive performance as the man who loves them. But the film relies too heavily on the actors to make up for Connelly's awkward script. Slow-footed from the start, *Polish Wedding* winds up mired in sluggish sentimentality.

Also reviewed in:
CHICAGO TRIBUNE, 8/28/98, Friday/p. J., John Petrakis
NEW YORK TIMES, 7/17/98, p. E18, Stephen Holden
VARIETY, 1/26-2/1/98, p. 70, Emanuel Levy

POST COITUM, ANIMAL TRISTE

A New Yorker Films release of an Ognon Pictures and Pinou Film production in association with Canal Plus, the Gan Foundation, Club Med. *Producer:* Humbert Balsan. *Director:* Brigitte Rouan. *Screenplay (French with English subtitles):* Brigitte Rouan, Santiago Amigorena, Jean-Louis Richard, Guy Zilberstein, and Phillipe Le Guay. *Director of Photography:* Pierre Dupouey. *Editor:* Laurent Rouan. *Sound:* Dominique Viellard. *Production Designer:* Roland Deville. *Costumes:* Florence Emir. *Running time:* 97 minutes. *MPAA Rating:* Not Rated.

CAST: Brigitte Rouan (Diane Clovier); Boris Terral (Emilio); Patrick Chesnais (Philippe Clovier); Nils Tavernier (Francois Narou); Jean-Louis Richard (Weyoman-Lebeau); Francois Arnoul (Mme. Lepluche); Emmanuelle Bach (Caroline); Carmen Chaplin (Copine Narou); Gaelle Le Furr (Isabelle).

LOS ANGELES TIMES, 3/10/98, Calendar/p. 14, Kenneth Turan

Mad love is about madness as much as it is about love. And if irrational passion marks the beginning of an affair, what might be called a Newtonian Law of Relationships posits an equal but opposite reaction at the end. "Post Coitum" provides a hauntingly honest and provocative look at what an all-consuming love can in fact consume.

Called "Post Coitum, Animal Triste" in France, a title taken in turn from the Latin homily meaning all creatures are sad after sex, this film deals with the entire arc of one such relationship, examining the glorious passion of obsessive love as well as the accompanying chaos. In its clear-eyed look at the exhilarating and damaging power of raw emotion, "Post Coitum" manages to be at ease with both carnality and love in a way that links it with the grand tradition of French cinema.

Actress Brigitte Rouan not only stars in "Post Coitum," she co-wrote and directed the film as well, and her three-sided participation is the key to its ability to remain nonjudgmental without sacrificing emotional intensity.

Given that the film opens with a sequence of Rouan's Diane Clovier writhing in misery on her bed and screaming the name "Emilio," we know going in that the romance we're watching will not be without its agonies. Yet it is still intoxicating to watch the actress create empathy for Diane throughout the entire cycle of romance, allowing the audience to feel the joy and the pain right along with the character.

Diane Clovier is in her 40s, a confident and stylish editor at one of Paris' more literary publishing houses. Confident enough in fact to barge in on one of her troublesome writers while he's trying to sleep late and demand to know why he isn't producing more pages. The writer, Francois Narou (Nils Tavernier, director Bertrand's son), doesn't respond well, but his roommate Emilio materializes out of nowhere to offer the editor some unexpected words of consolation.

Emilio likes to call himself a plumber, but he's in fact a hydraulic engineer who works designing sanitation systems in the Third World. As played by Boris Terral, he is also seductiveness personified, a sensitive hunk with masses of luxuriant black curly hair, sensuous lips and the perpetually unshaven look only men who resemble models are allowed to cultivate.

Diane looks at Emilio and can't believe what's happening to her. She's happily (if a trifle complacently) married to a lawyer named Philippe (Patrick Chesnais) with two of the best behaved teenage boys in all France as sons, and she is two decades older than Emilio. She tells him, "I've lived a whole life before you," as if it's supposed to mean something, but it doesn't. These two simply can't keep their hands off each other.

One of the best things about "Post Coitum" is that it doesn't moralistically shortchange the pleasure Diane and Emilio share. The couple's exuberant and passionate scenes together, including so-French-you-could-burst moments like traffic-stopping embraces on the Champs-Elysees, underline the hypnotically sensual nature of the relationship. When she tells him, "You've woken me out of a long sleep," he slyly shrugs and replies, "I'm Prince Charming. It's my job."

Paralleling Diane's swooning relationship is her husband's involvement as the lawyer for a neighbor, Madame Lepluche (veteran actress Francoise Amoul), implicated in a different kind of passionate act. When her philandering husband of 43 years asked for a divorce, Madame Lepluche pierced an artery in his neck with a carving fork and watched him bleed to death.

True to her stated intention to show "how painful passion can be, and how stupid it can make you," Rouan gradually darkens "Post Coitum's" tone. As Diane gets more and more obsessively involved with Emilio, she doesn't seem to care or even notice the ways in which she's recklessly jeopardizing everything about her life, from her work to her family, that's been important to her up to now. The only link to her past that remains unaffected is her commitment to help writer Francois through his new novel.

Traditionally, in films from "The Blue Angel" to "Of Human Bondage," this detailing of the price of mad infatuation has been told with men as the protagonists. One of the great assets that Rouan brings to the flip side of the story is a wisdom that stops her from second-guessing her characters while allowing each their humanity. We may ache for Diane in her vulnerability, but we also see how difficult it would have been for her to act otherwise. "In this day and age," one of the characters says, "being in love means compromise. Absolute passion can be a tragedy." "Post Coitum" shows what that statement truly means.

NEW YORK POST, 3/13/98, p. 44, Thelma Adams

In the sexy French film "Post Coitum," director Brigitte Rouan bares and beats her breast.

She plays Diane, an attractive Parisian editrix with a cuddly lawyer hubby and two musical sons who junks career and family for her great passion: Emilio (Boris Terral), a skanky young engineer who digs latrines in the Third World.

It's *lamour fou*, feminist-French-fantasy edition. We sweat with 40-year-old Diane through the good times and rage in the bad after Emilio ends the affair.

Meanwhile, in a clunky parallel plot line, Diane's husband, Philippe (Patrick Chesnais), defends a neighbor. The frumpy hausfrau killed her philandering spouse with a carving fork over the Sunday roast. In prison, the old wife blossoms, freed of jealousy and betrayal.

For all the tragicomedy's early exuberance, Diane and her director become less interesting and more self-indulgent as the plot thins and hysteria takes over. The movie was well received at last fall's New York Film Festival. And Rouan, best known as a star of Agnieszka Holland's "Olivier Olivier" (1992), cut a coquettish figure at the opening-night festivities.

What's troubling about "Post Coitum" is the self-congratulatory treatment of the material. Rouan takes that tired old chestnut—the French male midlife movie—and turns it on its head. Here, it's the woman who's rich and powerful, but who's powerless over the fact that her breasts are sagging and laugh lines are cracking her Lancome foundation.

Diane grabs at Emilio, and lost youth, as frantically as any male French philanderer in the films of Bertrand Blier. What Rouan delivers is a world turned upside down, but it's the same old world. A not-so-radical departure reaches a reactionary conclusion: Women on the verge of menopause can be just as selfish and self-destructive as men of a certain age.

NEWSDAY, 3/13/98, Part II/p. B7, Jack Mathews

You've heard a lot about post-traumatic stress syndrome in the past couple of decades, but how much thought have you given to post-coital depression? If that last condition strikes you as an oxymoron, count your blessings and plan an early candlelight dinner. If you want to know more, drop in on French actress-director Brigitte Roüan's "Post Coitum."

"Post Coitum" is a fresh, emotionally raw, and captivating study of what the French call *amour fou* —mad love—and its effect on a married, middleage Paris book editor who becomes sexually addicted to a man half her age and twice as free. Her case of post-coital depression, overwhelming sadness following sex, is the sum of her experience rather than an incidental account of it, but whatever it is, you don't want it.

Roüan's Diane Clovier is a model of the modern career mother. She has a good job at which she's very good, she has a decent, good-natured lawyer husband, Philippe, and two adolescent sons who tie the family together in a neat, energetic and loving unit. It looks to be an idyllic middle-class existence, and Diane is so content with the ease and rhythm of the day-to-day that she's barely aware of the diminished passion in her marriage.

But the pilot light never really goes out, and when Diane meets Emilio (Boris Terral), the twentysomething stud muffin of every under-attended middleage woman's dreams, the furnace, to coin a purple phrase, is newly ablaze.

Emilio and Diane are at it at every opportunity, during long lunches, in hours stolen from her family time at breakfast and dinner, in an apartment borrowed from her company, in bathroom stalls, on trains, even at an out-of-town business meeting where Diane abandons her boss and clients to romp with Emilio back in her hotel room. In one particularly reckless moment, she takes a Christmas Day call from Emilio, and drops her voice into a girlish whisper, with Philippe sitting nearby.

"Post Coitum" is a comedy drama, in that order. The first half or so, while Diane becomes more and more intoxicated by her affair, and less and less cautious about it, is sophisticated French sex farce. Though you know there are consequences coming, her exhilaration is contagious. The last section, however, is a combination of anger, melancholy, self-pity and depression.

If affairs involved only sex, and were always as good as Emilio and Diane's, and everybody understood it, there would be no White House scandal right now. But people inevitably get hurt, and by the time Emilio begins losing interest in Diane, she's on the verge of losing everything—her family, her job, her will to live.

Once you're past the deceptive lightness of Diane's affair, it's clear that "Post Coitum" is really a story of helpless addiction, with all the nuances of low self-esteem, experimentation, highs and hangovers, dependency, irrational fantasies and cruel withdrawal. The magic in it is that despite her foolish choices, Roüan never allows Diane to become unsympathetic.

Roüan, who's been acting in French films since 1971 and made her directing debut with the 1991 "Overseas," plays Diane with an emotional and physical abandon that might have been impossible to do for any director other than herself. Diane is both self-conscious about her aging body and thrilled by its responsiveness, and in the frequent, uninhibited love scenes, Roüan has the two feelings in a constant state of tension.

The script, which Roüan co-wrote with three others, is terrific at depicting Diane's ill-fated affair, but it doesn't succeed as well in its two subplots. One involves Diane's stormy relationship with a stereotypically neurotic author (Nils Tavernier), the other is about Philippe's preparation for the defense of an abused wife accused of killing her husband. Philippe is a strong character and sensitively played by Patrick Chesnais, but the murder case is an obvious and awkward mechanism for his own soul-searching.

"Post Coitum" is, nonetheless, a fascinating portrait of an ordinary woman going through an extraordinarily dangerous emotional cycle, and Roüan's performance is astonishing.

VILLAGE VOICE, 3/17/98, p. 64, Leslie Camhi

Have you ever spent long hours consoling a friend for the loss of a lover, indulging in minute analyses of rejection, and wondering at the monumental self-obsession of the spurned? If so, *Post Coitum* will seem familiar. Taking its title from Ovid's icy observation that "after intercourse, all animals are sad," French actress Brigitte Roüan's second feature as a director explores the sometimes disastrous aftereffects of midlife passion. Roüan stars as Diane, a successful book editor in her forties, married and with two teenage sons. *L'amour fou* arrives one day in the form of Emilio (Boris Terral), the swarthy, twentysomething roommate of François (Nils Tavernier), one of her authors, who is suffering from a creative crisis.

Emilio, a hydraulic engineer, has an annoying habit of going about with his mouth half-open, but Diane is soon forsaking Philippe (Patrick Chesnais), her cozy attorney husband, for steamy rendezvous with him in restaurants, parks, and hotel rooms. (Philippe, meanwhile, is stuck defending the local baker's wife, who has murdered her adulterous husband.) The affair ends pretty quickly, but the film continues, as we watch Diane fall to pieces.

Great films have been made about erotic delirium, but this isn't one of them. As a writer, Roüan's at her best using humor; as a director, she gets some fine performances (Tavernier and Chesnais in particular); and her pluck as an actress is considerable. But I'd be more inclined to admire her courage in this punishing portrayal of an older woman's passion if there wasn't such a walloping dose of narcissism mixed in with it. In one scene, an abandoned Diane coldly appraises her naked, middle-aged body in the mirror. The truth is, she looks pretty good, and we're meant to think it.

Also reviewed in:
CHICAGO TRIBUNE, 5/1/98, Friday/p. O, Patrick Z. McGavin
NATION, 3/30/98, p. 34, Stuart Klawans
NEW REPUBLIC, 3/30/98, p. 26, Stanley Kauffmann
NEW YORK TIMES, 3/13/98, p. E12, Janet Maslin
VARIETY, 5/26-6/1/97, p. 66, David Stratton

PRACTICAL MAGIC

A Warner Bros. release in association with Village Roadshow Pictures of a Di Novi pictures production in association with Fortis Films. *Executive Producer:* Mary McLaglen and Bruce Berman. *Producer:* Denise Di Novi. *Director:* Griffin Dunne. *Screenplay:* Robin Swicord, Akiva Goldsman, and Adam Brooks. *Based on the novel by:* Alice Hoffman. *Director of Photography:* Andrew Dunn. *Editor:* Elizabeth Kling. *Music:* Alan Silvestri. *Music Editor:* Kenneth Karman, Nic Ratner, and Bunny Andrews. *Sound:* Richard B. Goodman and (music) Dennis Sands. *Sound Editor:* Robert Hein. *Casting:* Amanda Mackey Johnson and Cathy Sandrich. *Production Designer:* Robin Standefer. *Set Designer:* Aric Lashee. *Set Decorator:* Claire Jenora Bowin. *Special Effects:* Bur Dalton. *Costumes:* Judianna Makovsky. *Make-up:* Pamela Westmore. *Stunt Coordinator:* Jeff Dashnaw and Jim Halty. *Running time:* 105 minutes. *MPAA Rating:* PG-13.

CAST: Sandra Bullock (Sally Owens); Nicole Kidman (Gillian Owens); Dianne Wiest (Aunt Jet); Stockard Channing (Aunt Frances); Aidan Quinn (Gary Hallet); Goran Visnjic (Jimmy Angelov); Evan Rachel Wood (Kylie); Alexandra Artrip (Antonia); Mark Feuerstein (Michael); Caprice Benedetti (Maria Owens); Annabella Price (Lovelorn Lady); Camilla Belle (Sally/aged 11); Lora Anne Criswell (Gillian/age 10); Margo Martindale (Linda Bennett); Chloe Webb (Carla); Martha Gehman (Patty); Lucinda Jenney (Sara as an adult); Cordella Richards (Nan); Mary Gross (Debbie); Jack Kirschke (Old Man Wilkes); Herta Ware (Old Lady Wilkes); Ellen Geer (Pharmacist); Courtney Dettrich (Young Sara); John McLeod (Puritan Minister); Trevor Duncan (Sara's Boy); Colby Cochran (Ice Cream Boy); Caitlyn Holley (Ice Cream Girl); Ken Serratt, Jr. (Lovelorn's Lover); Rich Sickler (Dwight); Jeanne Robinson and Deborah Kancher (PTC Moms); Peter Shaw (Jack); Caralyn Kozlowski (Regina).

LOS ANGELES TIMES, 10/16/98, Calendar/p. 2, Jack Mathews

[The following review by Jack Mathews appeared in a slightly different form in **NEWSDAY, 10/16/98, Part II/p. B7.]**

The trailer and advanced hype on Griffin Dunne's "Practical Magic," the story of two witch sisters' attempts to cover up an accidental killing, suggest something on the order of a big-screen version of "Bewitched." But where "Bewitched" had just one romantic sorceress trying to contain her power while indulging ordinary human passions, this one has two—the ever-wholesome Sandra Bullock, an Elizabeth Montgomery surrogate if there could be one, and the ever seductive Nicole Kidman.

Even at today's inflated ticket prices, a two-for-one witch offer like this should be a bargain. So, why isn't it? Why does "Practical Magic," with its big stars and major studio movie budget, feel like a sitcom with the air let out of it?

Let's start with the film's woeful lack of magic. The sisters, and the aunts (Dianne Wiest, Stockard Channing) who raise them, talk a lot about the scope of their power, and occasionally show off by lighting candles with their breath. Otherwise, they can't wrinkle their noses and accomplish much of anything.

Nobody is made to disappear (though some audience members may be tempted), there are no floating objects (though a stick stirs chocolate on its own) and no men are turned into dogs or frogs (though a frog does throw up a man's ring). There is a restless spirit, and a wind-jamming exorcism. But overall, the movie has no more practical magic than a souffle chef.

Dunne, and his screenwriters Robin Swicord, Akiva Goldsman, and Adam Brooks (adapting a novel by Alice Hoffman), play down the magic intentionally. Rather than perform cheap tricks, which can be really expensive these days, they've concentrated on the emotional trappings of being a witch in the 1990s, when, God knows, there's already enough name-calling.

Sally (Bullock) and Gillian (Kidman) Owens, an introspective brunette and a fiery redhead, have learned to live with the name-calling that has followed their family for three centuries. What's harder to deal with is the curse hanging over the head of any man who'd fall for an Owens girl. The curse was put there by Maria Owens 300 years ago, after being stood up at the gallows by her own lover.

The proof of the curse was in the pudding for Sally and Gillian, whose mother died of a broken heart after their father's death. That tragedy caused Sally to swear off any future romance by casting her own spell for a man who couldn't possibly exist. Meanwhile, Gillian was champing at the bit to get started, whatever the consequences.

Now, they're adults, and in trouble. Sally, who'd ignored her oath and fallen in love, is a grieving widow with two children of her own, trying to rescue Gillian from her abusive Bulgarian lover Jimmy (Goran Visnjic). Somehow, in the ensuing blur of tequila, belladonna and violence, Jimmy ends up dead, and the sisters are awkwardly trying to get a pulse through witchcraft.

Soon, there's an angry spirit, as well as a nosy cop named Gary Hallet (Aidan Quinn) hanging around the Owens place, and the whole community is involved.

Most of what went into "Practical Magic" is serviceable. The script has a jaunty, old-fashioned "The Ghost and Mrs. Muir" quality to it; Bullock and Kidman provide spunky star turns, and Channing and Wiest play the eccentric aunts with apt hamminess. It just doesn't add up to anything—or break down—to anything special. For good or bad, there's hardly a memorable scene in it.

You're promised magic, you expect magic.

NEW YORK POST, 10/16/98, p. 45, Thelma Adams

Magic just isn't, well, magical anymore. In Griffin Dunne's "Practical Magic—a whimsical chick fantasy adapted from Alice Hoffman's novel—being a modern-day witch is one step away from being the misunderstood heroine in a romance novel, two steps distant from Martha Stewart.

Sisters Sally (Sandra Bullock, who has inherited the crinky-nosed, needy, you-love-me, you-really-love-me mantle from Sally Fields) and Gillian Owens (the bewitching Nicole Kidman) have the power to bring humans back from the dead with a bit of abracadabra and Redi-Whip.

Sal and Gil can hop broomsticks and fly to Bermuda, dance naked under a solstice moon and whip up love potions in the Osterizer after midnight margaritas.

But, what really worries the sisters? Men.

The Owens family curse bedevils the girls. For generations, bad things happen to men who love Owens women—usually heralded by their arrival of a squeaky death beetle.

Sally and Gilly's biggest challenge isn't the battle between good and evil, white and black magic, which lies at the heart of most supernatural stories. Oh, sigh, like many modern women who can't conjure and aren't cursed, the gals are just afraid to love.

In response, Sally turns inward. She rejects witchcraft and desperately seeks normalcy (despite the fact that, oh my, her coffee stirs itself).

When Sally opens herself to the love, of an average Joe, she has two girls and a short blissful season, followed by that damn beetle. The aggrieved widow determines to teach her daughters spelling, not spells.

Gilly, on the other hand, taunts love by sleeping around. As she asks Sally and their eccentric aunts (the delightful Stockard Channing and Dianne Wiest, deserving of their own twitchier witch movie): "Since is when is being a slut a crime in this family?

As it turns out, in a script that bears the fingerprints of three writers (Robin Swicord, Akiva Goldsman and Adam Brooks) and no singular vision, Gilly's rambling ways do lead to crime.

Gillian picks up a stray, a scarily sexy cowboy. When Jimmy (Goran Visnjic) punches Gilly, Sally flies to the rescue. Kidnapped and threatened with increasing violence, the siblings overreact, like the mascara-stained mortals of TV movies-of-the-week headed for the battered wife defense.

Now, let's pause: Why would a witch brook an abusive male? Couldn't she curse his cowboy boots and send him on an endless walkabout? Turn him into a frog?

No matter. In Dunne's pretty, pretty world of the supernatural, things that go bump in the night are likely to be honeymooners. It's the ludicrous bad boyfriend subplot that rings in the arrival of lawman Gary Hallet (Aidan Quinn), a dream lover to awaken Sally.

We not only get a pat sisterhood-is-powerful message, but damned if this last good man with one green eye and one blue doesn't encourage Sally to get in touch with her inner witch. Where's Fabio when we need him?

SIGHT AND SOUND, 1/99, p. 53, Kevin Maher

New England, the 1690s. Maria Owens, pregnant and unmarried, is accused of witchcraft by her Puritan neighbours and banished to an offshore island. She puts a death curse on any man who is ever loved by an Owens woman. Nearly 300 years later the curse kills Sally and Gillian Owens' father, The girls are sent to live on the now populated Maria's Island with their aunts Frances and Jet, both locally infamous witches. The girls are taught the powers of magic by their aunts and ostracised by the fearful locals.

As adults, Gillian leaves home while Sally stays to live a normal life. Gillian is attracted to a mysterious stranger called Jimmy Angelov. Under the influence of her aunts' magic, Sally falls for and marries a local man, Michael. When she begins to love Michael truly he's killed by a speeding truck. Jimmy starts to abuse Gillian physically. Sally tries to rescue her and ends up accidentally killing Jimmy with an overdose of magic sleeping powder. Using their powers Sally and Gillian try to resurrect Jimmy but fail. They bury him in the family garden. A special investigator, Gary Hallet, questions the women about Jimmy's disappearance. Gary is suspicious of the sisters, yet he and Sally fall in love. Gillian becomes possessed by Jimmy's undead soul. Sally asks all the local women to come round and form a coven. Together they perform an exorcism. Jimmy's soul is banished and the townsfolk are reunited with the Owens women.

With feel-good sisterly values, *Practical Magic*, like *Hope Floats* and *Moonlight and Valentino* before it, is an attempt at updating the 'women's picture', in this case by injecting the supernatural into the genre. Here director Griffin Dunne *(Addicted to Love)* and screenwriters Robin Swicord (Little Women), Akiva Goldsman *(The Client)* and Adam Brooks *(Beloved)* have taken the melodramatic staple of active females and passive males to a problematic conclusion with the 'Owens Family Curse': most of the movie's male characters are killed off. Yet unlike *Practical Magic*'s classic antecedents—King Vidor's *Stella Dallas* (1937) or even Douglas Sirk's *Imitation Of Life* (1959)—Dunne has no idea of how to play his all-female environment. He consistently ignores the inner tensions of this powerfully matriarchal world in favour of disposable saccharine emotions and glib music-promo aesthetics.

Taking his cue from the glamorous domestic witches of *Bell Book and Candle* (1958), and the more recent films *The Craft* and *The Witches of Eastwick* Dunne renders the supernatural powers of his protagonists subordinate to their function as traditional heroines. Their magic becomes simply an accessory, a showy distraction. Hence Sally's coffee spoon stirs by itself, yet only so she can get busy writing her lovelorn letters. Similarly, though Gillian's magic can raise the dead, she seems strangely unable to use it to sort out her relationship with her abusive boyfriend Jimmy. Consequently, the few moments of crowd pleasing effects that eventually arrive in the climactic exorcism jar uncomfortably with the film's otherwise quotidian tone.

Dunne's reaction to this debilitating 'love without lovers' paradox is to shift the focus to random, isolated events, letting the narrative momentum grind to a halt. His version of the women's picture is an endless series of female-bonding tableaux. And so, under a folk-rock soundtrack from Joni Mitchell and Stevie Nicks, we see Gillian driving across the US, Sally setting up a health store, Sally dancing around the house with Gillian and her aunts and Sally connecting emotionally with the local women.

With most of these scenes bathed in a gelatinous yellow glow, and with protagonists Kidman and Bullock engaged in endless outfit changes and makeovers, the movie is certainly easy to watch. But without any single overriding dramatic motor to guide it, this prettiness soon becomes repetitive and ultimately irksome. Like Sally and Gillian, immaculately attired and roaming around their pristine island home, *Practical Magic* is essentially a movie that's all dressed up with nowhere to go.

VILLAGE VOICE, 10/27/98, p. 135, Dennis Lim

The title is, to say the least, an understatement. Witchcraft has rarely looked more prosaic and less sexy than it does in Griffin Dunne's *Practical Magic*. Virtually anti-camp and laughably toothless compared to more youthful witch fantasies like *The Craft* (or, for that matter, the WB's *Charmed)*, the movie does occasionally make a show of invoking some form of Girl Power—specifically, the mild, Lilith-verging-on-Lifetime version. Still, its halfhearted feminism further muted by an unmistakable whiff of New Age, this adaptation of Alice Hoffman's popular novel is basically a cross-generational female-bonding cliché-fest in supernatural drag, with a discordant emphasis on upbeat romantic resolution.

An age-old spell dictates that any man who dares to love an Owens woman will die young, and the task of lifting the ancestral curse falls to yin-yang sisters (blood pacts, broomsticks, and standing in a circle are involved). While Sally (Sandra Bullock), the saintly one, suppresses her witchy powers in the interests of suburban normalcy, Gillian (Nicole Kidman), the slutty one, escapes to some Gomorrah or other, where she hangs out poolside with lots of men. A few years on, reunited and suddenly faced with the dead-body predicament that leads people in movies to behave in a particularly stupid fashion, the sisters turn to their trusty spell book.

Poised and light-footed, Kidman emerges unscathed, as do Stockard Channing and Dianne Wiest as the flaky aunts. But the most glaring problem here is that the implicitly boring good witch is played by the explicitly boring Sandra Bullock; her inevitable coupling with Aidan Quinn's correspondingly insipid cop ranks as one of the most waterlogged screen romances in memory.

Also reviewed in:
CHICAGO TRIBUNE, 10/16/98, Friday/p. A, Mark Caro
NEW YORK TIMES, 10/16/98, p. E10, Janet Maslin
VARIETY, 10/19-25/98, p. 74, Emanuel Levy
WASHINGTON POST, 10/16/98, p. D5, Rita Kempley
WASHINGTON POST, 10/16/98, Weekend/p. 48, Eve Zibart

PRICE ABOVE RUBIES, A

A Miramax Films release in association with Pandora Cinema and Channel Four Films of a Lawrence Bender production. *Executive Producer:* Bob Weinstein and Harvey Weinstein. *Producer:* Lawrence Bender and John Penotti. *Director:* Boaz Yakin. *Screenplay:* Boaz Yakin. *Director of Photography:* Adam Holender. *Editor:* Arthur Coburn. *Music:* Lesley Barber. *Music Editor:* Dan Diprima. *Sound:* William Sarokin. *Sound Editor:* Robert Fitzgerald. *Casting:* Douglas Aible. *Production Designer:* Dan Leigh. *Art Director:* Eryka Seimon Henderson. *Set Decorator:* Leslie E. Rollins. *Set Dresser:* Mitch Towse, John J. Flugel, Dennis Lee Causey, and Robert Currie. *Special Effects:* John M. Ottesen. *Costumes:* Ellen Lutter. *Make-up:* Lori Hicks. *Running time:* 120 minutes. *MPAA Rating:* R.

CAST: Renée Zellweger (Sonia);   Christopher Eccleston (Sender);   Julianna Margulies (Rachel);   Allen Payne (Ramon);   Glenn Fitzgerald (Mendel);   Kim Hunter (Rebbitzn);   John Randolph (Rebbe);   Kathleen Chalfant (Beggar Woman);   Peter Jacobson (Schmuel);   Edie Falco (Felga);   Tim Jerome (Dr. Bauer);   Phyllis Newman (Mrs. Gelbart);   Joyce Reehling (Shaindy);   Shelton Dane (Yossi);   Jackie Ryan (Young Sonia);   Faran Tahir (Hrundi Kapoor);   Martin Shakar (Mr. Berman);   Teodorina Bello (Mrs. Garcia);   Glenn Flesher (Chief Gabbal);   Adam Dannheisser (Young Gabbal #1);   Stephen Singer (Gabbal #2);   Marvin Einhorn (Gabbal #3);   Mark Zimmerman (Doctor);   Richard "Izzy" Lifshutz (The Moel);   David Deblinger (Baruch);   Sam Jennings (Heshle);   Erin Rakow (Tsipi);   Asher Tabak (Yechlel);   Allen Swift (Mr. Fishbeln);   Daryl Edwards (Nelson);   Peter Slutsker (Mr. Sugarman);   Lauren Klein (Sonia's Mother);   Tonye Patano (Earring Woman);   Don Wallace (Ty);   Asia Minor and Roseanna Plasencia (Homegirls);   Jerry Matz (Mr. Engelberg);   Michael Sthulbarg (Young Hassid);   Karen Contreras (Young Woman);   Wai Ching Ho (Lady Vendor);   Mel Duane Gionson (Paranoid Vendor);   Paul J. Q. Lee (Smooth Vendor);   Leyla Aalam (Israeli Woman).

CHRISTIAN SCIENCE MONITOR, 4/10/98, p. B3, David Sterritt

Too few movies focus seriously on women, and fewer still combine this with an interest in religious life. These factors make "A Price Above Rubies" a newsmaking arrival, although the picture's quality doesn't live up to its subject.

Renée Zellweger, who made such a fine showing in "Jerry Maguire" and "The Whole Wide World," plays an Orthodox Jewish woman who feels increasingly stifled in her male-dominated community.

Her husband loves her, but his highly traditional religious views—and rising status as a local Hasidic leader—turn his attention away from her problems.

Accepting a job in New York's fabled "diamond district," she moves toward new levels of professional independence and personal fulfillment. Her enthusiasm for mingling with outsiders is noted with scorn by many of her neighbors and relatives, however, leading to new crises and hard decisions.

"A Price Above Rubies" would have more impact if filmmaker Boaz Yakin didn't allow its energy level to sag in several scenes, and if he avoided some lapses into Hollywood-style sensationalism, including an unnecessary sexual affair between the heroine and her husband's brother.

Zellweger gives a strong performance, and the story etches an intermittently sharp portrait of a subculture caught between a rich historical legacy and a changing contemporary world.

But the movie as a whole achieves far less dramatic power than Yakin's extraordinary "Fresh" four years ago, suggesting that he has tackled a bit more than he's prepared to handle this time around.

LOS ANGELES TIMES, 3/27/98, Calendar/p. 12, Kevin Thomas

[The following review by Kevin Thomas appeared in a slightly different form in **NEWSDAY, 3/27/98, Part II/p. B13.***]*

"A Price Above Rubles," which showcases Renee Zellweger in a challenging role, is yet another movie that gives Brooklyn's Hasidic community a bad rap. As a child, Zellweger's Sonia, precocious daughter of a jewelry merchant, instantly proclaims as a fake the ruby her 10-year-old older brother gives her, and to redeem himself he goes off for a midnight swim in a lake and drowns.

From then on, Sonia possesses a wandering soul, haunted by her brother's death, and could scarcely be a worse choice for the bride of a profoundly religious scholar, Mendel (Glenn Fitzgerald). So puritanical is Mendel that he believes that lovemaking, which is performed "in the sight of God," shouldn't be an act of pleasure. But now that he has awakened his bride sexually without satisfying her, she has "a fire burning up inside" that her ruthless, hypocritical brother-in-law Sender (Christopher Eccleston), a Manhattan jewelry merchant, swiftly attempts to extinguish with a loveless but vigorous seduction—and more important, the offer of a job.

Writer-director Boaz Yakin reduces his characters' Hasidic community to a patriarchic monolith that oppresses women. "A Price Above Rubies" would be so much richer if it took place in a more deeply evoked world of the Hasidim where today women are enlarging the possibilities open to them within the teachings of the Torah. A world in which, like all others, there are trade-offs: solemnly observed rules that in turn can yield meaning; an enclosed world that nevertheless strives to exist in the midst of modern society with its opportunities—not to mention temptations—forbidden by what most of us would consider archaic doctrine.

As it is, the fluffy 1992 Melanie Griffith vehicle "A Stranger Among Us" treated the Hasidim with more respect than "A Price of Rubles." Sonia's new job, purchasing items wholesale for Sender, lifts her spirit and brings her into contact with a handsome Puerto Rican jewelry designer (Allen Payne), who has no idea of how talented he is. Sonia's entire relationship with him smacks of the contrived and self-conscious, but you just know that one way or another it's going to spell big trouble for her.

There's sufficient complexity to Sonia to allow Zellweger to make an impression as a sensual, highly intelligent and deeply conflicted young woman, but no one else—and that includes a mystery lady who follows her as closely as the memory (or ghost?) of her brother—has much authenticity.

"A Price Above Rubies" leaves you feeling that Yakin was trying to create a parable from Sonia's destiny but lacks the sense of style to pull it off.

NEW YORK POST, 3/25/98 p. 45, Thelma Adams

Some Borough Park Orthodox Jews are protesting "A Price Above Rubies." Most probably have not seen Boaz Yakin's fable of a sexually frustrated Brooklyn mother who seeks satisfaction off Brooklyn's 13th Avenue.

If they did catch "Rubies," what might really burn their Shabbos candles is the impression the "Fresh" director gives that the Hasidim have miserable sex lives.

In Yakin's uneven but entertaining diary of an over-heated housewife, Jewish mama Sonia (Renee Zellweger) cuckolds her scholar hubby Mendel (Glenn Fitzgerald) with his brother Sender (Christopher Eccleston). She also flings with Puerto Rican Ramon (Allen Payne) under a prominent crucifix.

What's more, Sonia eats pork! "It's delicious," she says of an egg roll.

Zellweger's Sonia looks the part of a Borough Park matron and stroller-pusher. She carries herself primly in the comfy shoes, flip wig, velvet headband and long skirts popular in the neighborhood.

There are scenes, including a diamond district business deal, in which the "Jerry Maguire" star catches fire. Still, the role has gaps that Zellweger tries to cover by hiding behind her pouty, bee-stung mouth. But it doesn't work.

Eccleston, so painfully good in "Jude," upstages Zellweger, with his more complex villain. As Sonia's sister-in-law, Julianna Margulies, of NBC's "ER," is richly rooted as a raven-haired, iron-willed wife, who has never had a doubt in her life.

Writer-director Yakin pulls back the *tallit*, the prayer shawl, of Borough Park life. But for all of the movie's authentic locations, Yiddish inflections and dramatic circumcision scene, the Orthodox come off like the Amish of "Witness."

SIGHT AND SOUND, 6/99, p. 51, Nina Caplan

New York City, the present. Orthodox-Jewish Sonia is married to Mendel, a religious scholar. They have a son but she feels alienated from him and their community. Mendel's brother Sender, knowing that her father was a jeweller, offers Sonia the job of buyer for his covert jewellery business. She jumps at the freedom, displeasing Mendel. Sonia and Sender begin a passionless affair, but she thrives in the job. She discovers an exquisite ring with an open setting and sets out to discover its maker. Helped by the apparition of her dead brother Yossi and a homeless woman who may also be imaginary, she tracks down jewellery maker and sculptor Ramon.

Sonia's late return from Ramon's prompts Mendel to insist she leave her job. He suggests marriage counselling but the counsellor is a rabbi and Sonia leaves, furious. She pushes a resentful Ramon to make more jewellery. Sender informs the family Sonia is having an affair with a Puerto Rican. Mendel refuses to see her and her sister-in-law Rachel denies her access to her son. Sender offers her a room, which she rejects. Eventually she goes to Ramon's place and after a heartfelt talk, they make love. Sonia retrieves the ring from Sender's workplace and asks Ramon to look after it. She meets Mendel and they agree they're happier apart. He apologises for having forgotten her birthday, and tells her to visit their son regardless of their community's hostility. He leaves her with a birthday present: a ruby.

According to the Bible, "A woman of fortitude, who can find? For her price is far above rubies." She'll need her fortitude, since however high the price, women are still 'for sale' in some cultures. *A Price above Rubies'* heroine Sonia Horowitz simply cannot place her emotions at the service of her intellect as Orthodox Judaism requires. Renee Zellweger's beautiful performance makes clear that it's not a lack of intelligence but excessive passion that makes her such a bad bargain: like Eve, she craves knowledge—of her worth as opposed to her price.

Tradition is the oxygen of the Jewish religion, which may be why films with Jewish subjects tend to focus on the past, mythical biblical *(The Ten Commandments)* or recent *(Schindler's List, Solomon and Gaenor)*. Like the much-mocked *A Stranger among Us*, in which Melanie Griffith finds happiness among the same New York Orthodox community, *Rubies* is contemporary: Sonia's problems are those of self-definition any modern woman encounters, but with better labelled obstacles. When, absorbed by work, she offers her husband Mendel microwave dinners, he voices the resentment of an old-fashioned husband, a role no longer available to his secular or gentile counterparts. Her anguished question, whether he loves her more than God (as her dead brother Yossi did), is actually asking whether he loves her at all, phrased in a language he understands, a curiously childlike language from a woman trying to grow up to a man determined to remain a child of God.

This is partisan stuff. Writer/director Boaz Yakin's determination that we take Sonia's side makes his Jewish community rather one-dimensional (there were angry protests made during the filming). Mendel's religion is a shield, his sister Rachel's a weapon and at no point are the virtues of a close-knit community pointed out. Sonia's displacement is drummed in with metaphor: she is a jewel seeking a setting, a woman in a man's world both at work and home, an intelligent adult whose closest companions are phantoms—Yossi and an old woman from a fairy tale. Sonia's past is as alive to her as the collective past is to her husband, but he wishes to stand still while she burns to advance.

If Sonia is Eve, her brother-in law Sender is undoubtedly the snake, bartering work and information for cold sex until she is cast out of Eden, although this Eden is a long way from paradise. Sender is that rare creature: a deeply unpleasant Jew on film. He could easily have been reduced to caricature, but Christopher Eccleston's magnificent performance outlaws anything so banal. His voice is soft, his logic compelling and the price he asks is well below rubies. But Sonia eventually rejects the freedom he offers in favour of one she makes herself.

VILLAGE VOICE, 3/31/98, p. 64, J. Hoberman

The tale of a 12-year-old drug runner, Boaz Yakin's *Fresh* was remarkable for its glibness— *New Jack City* reframed as an after-school special. Even after the movie shared the Filmmakers Trophy at Sundance, I thought it unlikely that Yakin's mix of bwana exploitation and wannabe cool would reap the critical indulgence extended Leslie Harris or the Hughes brothers. I was wrong. Perhaps confounded by the filmmaker's name, Anthony Lane welcomed Yakin into the "new black cinema."

Yakin's *A Price Above Rubies*, set among the ultra-orthodox Jews of Borough Park, is a scarcely more convincing slice of Brooklyn life. I doubt even *The New Yorker* will mistake it for evidence of a Hasidic nouvelle vague. *A Price Above Rubies* is, however, an enervated, Americanized example of Hasidic Gothic— a strain of Yiddish literature which drew inspiration from the "exotic" folk culture of East European Jewry. Opening on a suitably bogus note, *A Price Above Rubies* establishes the conditions under which a young Hasidic woman might be possessed by the rebellious spirit of her beloved little brother.

Fresh was a glossy synthesis of *Yojimbo, The 400 Blows* and *Searching for Bobby Fischer; A Price Above Rubies* incorporates elements of *The Dybbuk, The Pawnbroker*, and *Yentle* in a free-floating atmosphere of I.B. Singer supernaturalism. Signs of Jewish uncanniness are as obvious as the film's characterizations. We know Sonia (Renée Zellweger) is striving to be a modern woman when (despite her ultra-orthodox upbringing) she rebels against her son's circumcision. We may also note the movie's postmodernity as the bris is staged like a ritual out of *The Godfather.)*

Sonia is oppressed by a combination of patriarchy and prudishness. Dissatisfied with her lot, she challenges her scholarly husband ("Do you love me more than you love God?") and demands that he leave the light on during sex. Although Zellweger's corseted body-language suggests massive overpreparation for the role, the actress's engaging vulnerability is a physical gift. As in *Jerry Maguire*, her flushed, puffy features give the impression that she's spent the last 20 minutes in tears. (Let it be noted here that, as Sonia's unsympathetic sister-in-law, *E.R.*'s Julianna Margulies looks fabulous in a *shaytl.)*

Sonia thinks her husband Mendel (Glenn Fitzgerald)—so sensitive that he passes out cold at his son's bris—is a saint. She's not. When Mendel's bad brother tempts her with employment on 47th Street, she's willing to add sex on the desktop to the job description. A dybbuk made her do it. The least likely scene has the plucky heroine respond to excommunication by using family memories of the Holocaust to guilt-trip a group of elders. The adventures of a young Hasid who breaks from tradition is a powerful story (and a *Voice* perennial). But *A Price Above Rubies* cannot imagine the disorientation such self-deprogramming entails. For Yakin, the religious worldview is a matter of magic realism. Sonia's familiars include a mysterious beggar (Kathleen Chalfant) who's a sister in Lilith.

At one point, Sonia visits Chinatown and smashes tribal taboo by eating an egg roll. She couldn't find a better form of *treyf?* The same might be said for *A Price Above Rubies*. Al Sharpton never protested *Fresh* but Brooklyn's assemblyman Dov Hikind's been agitating for weeks against Yakin's "message of hate"—a "very dangerous movie." Simpleminded would be more like it. Picket lines around *Rubies* will only microwave a very cold latke.

Also reviewed in:
CHICAGO TRIBUNE, 4/3/98, Friday/p. E, Michael Wilmington
NEW YORK TIMES, 3/25/98, p. E5, Janet Maslin
VARIETY, 2/2-8/98, p. 31, Emanuel Levy

PRIMARY COLORS

A Universal Pictures and Mutual Film Company release of an Icarus production.   Executive Producer: Neil Machlis and Jonathan D. Krane.   *Producer:* Mike Nichols.   *Director:* Mike Nichols.   *Screenplay:* Elaine May.   *Based on the novel by:* Joe Klein.   *Director of Photography:* Michael Ballhaus.   *Editor:* Arthur Schmidt.   *Music:* Ry Cooder.   *Music Editor:* Suzana Peric, Bunny Andrews, and Nic Ratner.   *Sound:* Chris Newman and (music) Allen Sides.   *Sound Editor:* Ron Bochar.   *Casting:* Juliet Taylor, Ellen Lewis, Juel Bestrop.   *Production Designer:* Bo Welch.   *Art Director:* Tom Duffield.   *Set Designer:* Sean Haworth.   *Set Decorator:* Cheryl Carasik.   *Set Dresser:* Craig Zimmerman.   *Special Effects:* Alan Lorimer.   *Costumes:* Ann Roth.   *Make-up:* Lynne Eagan.   *Make-up (John Travolta):* Michelle Buhler.   *Stunt Coordinator:* Mark Riccardi.   *Running time:* 140 minutes.   *MPAA Rating:* R.

CAST: John Travolta (Governor Jack Stanton); Emma Thompson (Susan Stanton); Billy Bob Thornton (Richard Jemmons); Kathy Bates (Libby Holden); Adrian Lester (Henry Burton); Maura Tierney (Daisy); Larry Hagman (Governor Fred Picker); Diane Ladd (Mamma Stanton); Paul Guilfoyle (Howard Ferguson); Rebecca Walker (March); Caroline Aaron (Lucille Kaufman); Tommy Hollis (Fat Willie); Rob Reiner (Izzy Rosenblatt); Ben Jones (Arlen Sporken); J.C. Quinn (Uncle Charlie); Allison Janney (Miss Walsh); Robert Klein (Norman Asher); Mykelti Williamson (Dewayne Smith); Jamie Denton (Mitch); Leontine Guilliard (Ruby); Monique L. Ridge (Tawana Carter); Ned Eisenberg (Brad Lieberman); Brian Markinson (Randy Culligan); Geraldo Rivera, Charlie Rose, Larry King, and Bill Maher (Themselves); O'Neal Compton (Sailorman Shoreson); Kevin Cooney (Lawrence Harris); Bonnie Bartlett (Martha Harris); Cynthia O'Neal (Elegant Woman); Chelcie Ross (Charlie Martin); John Vargas (Lorenzo Delgado); Tony Shalhoub (Eddie Reyes); Bianca Lawson (Loretta); Robert Cicchini (Jimmy Ozio); Stan Davis (Jack Mandela Washington); Harrison Young (Sam); Rolando Molina (Anthony Ramirez); Ross Benjamin (Peter Goldsmith); Stacy Edwards (Jennifer Rogers); Kristoffer Ryan Winters (Terry Hicks); Susan Kussman (Ella Louise); Vickilyn Reynolds (Amalee); Robert Symonds (Bart Nilson); Gia Carides (Cashmere McLeod); Robert Easton (Dr. Beauregard); Scott Burkholder (Danny Scanlon); Lu Elrod (Chubby Woman); R.M. Haley (Shipyard Announcer); Henry Woronicz (Pundit); Darice Richman (Linda Feldstein); Rosalie Peck (Retiree); Susan Forristal (Bugger Bugger Woman); James Earl Jones (CNN Voiceover).

CHRISTIAN SCIENCE MONITOR, 3/27/98, p. B3, David Sterritt

Read before the latest round of White House controversies, the 1996 bestseller "Primary Colors: A Novel of Politics" seemed exaggerated in its portrayal of a presidential candidate besieged by ruthless allegations and the weighty burden of a checkered past. Today its tone seems reasonably close to the actual events of recent headlines.

This doesn't mean the fictional tale—written by an anonymous author subsequently revealed to be Joe Klein, a political columnist—is based point-for-point on experiences of the current White House occupant. Many of the book's incidents have no direct counterparts in real life. But that hasn't stopped its Hollywood adapters from playing up resemblances for all they're worth, right down to the Bill Clinton hairdo sported by John Travolta in the central role.

A mass-market movie based on a noisily promoted novel about Washington's most questionable behaviors could easily have turned into a forgettable exercise in wide-screen exploitation. Fortunately for audiences, a team of first-rate talents signed onto the project, headed by director Mike Nichols and scriptwriter Elaine May, longtime partners who recently renewed their creative partnership with "The Birdcage," another razor-sharp social satire.

"Primary Colors" continues their streak, blending sardonic commentary on the political system with a three-dimensional portrait of a would-be president who's at once an incorrigible scoundrel and an utterly sincere "people person" who truly wants to help the little folks ignored by business-as-usual politicians.

Striking an excellent balance between wry cultural critique and crisp entertainment value, the picture is as smart and funny as any comedy-drama in recent memory.

As for the acting, next year's Academy Award race could be half over even before it starts. Travolta gives the wittiest, savviest performance of his career to date—as a Clinton-like comeback kid, he's a natural for the part to begin with—backed up by a dream supporting cast. Standouts include Emma Thompson as the candidate's wife; Kathy Bates as a larger-than-life aide; newcomer Adrian Lester as the African-American campaigner through whose eyes we see the story; and Billy Bob Thornton as one of their cronies.

Sure to capture a walloping share of the box-office vote, "Primary Colors" is the best Hollywood movie so far in this increasingly impressive year.

LOS ANGELES TIMES, 3/20/98, Calendar/p. 1, Kenneth Turan

If, as it's been said, the mark of a music lover is the ability to hear Rossini's William Tell Overture without thinking of the Lone Ranger, so the mark of a cineaste is being able to watch John Travolta and Emma Thompson in "Primary Colors" unimpeded by thoughts of Bill and Hillary Clinton. It's a test most Americans would fail without thinking twice.

Despite the expected author's note disclaimer about its characters and situations not being real, "Primary Colors" the novel is the most celebrated of modern *romans a clef*, a piece of informed but controversial speculation by political writer Joe Klein working under the pen name Anonymous. Not only Jack Stanton and his wife but almost all its characters are based on well-known operatives, from big state governor Orlando Ozio (read Mario Cuomo) to down-home consultant Richard Jemmons (a.k.a. James Carville).

Director Mike Nichols and screenwriter Elaine May have had the skill and the good sense to take the *frisson* this closeness to reality provides and run with it. Despite all the cautions and disclaimers from a legion of pundits, despite our knowledge that this is not the real thing, only a riff on the 1992 Democratic presidential campaign, "Primary Colors" is for the most part such a smart and savvy piece of work it encourages us to feel we're eavesdropping on history. It's a sensation that can be delicious.

In the decades since he and May were the sharpest of stand-up comedy teams, Nichols has become a director, known for putting a high commercial sheen on material, some of which ("Biloxi Blues," "Regarding Henry," "Wolf") has stopped rewarding the effort. Here, that craft (including the top-drawer help of cinematographer Michael Ballhaus, production designer Bo Welch, editor Arthur Schmidt, composer Ry Cooder and costumer Ann Roth) is joined to the slightly subversive pungency of May's sharp and sarcastic script, which includes many of the book's better speeches and knows how to improve on them. If the film overreaches a bit in its attempt to be meaningful (and it does), it still offers more than enough pleasing wit and pizazz to win us over.

The "Primary Colors" story is told through the eyes of Henry Burton (British actor Adrian Lester), a young African American political operative, the grandson of a legend of the civil rights movement, who joins the presidential campaign of an obscure Southern governor named Jack Stanton (Travolta).

Burton was not eager to get on the team of a man he's heard described as "some cracker who hasn't done much in his own state." But as a would-be idealist who strategist Jemmons (a low-key and effective Billy Bob Thornton) accurately diagnoses as having a case of "galloping true believerism" Burton cannot resist Stanton's color-blindness, what appears to be his genuine feeling for America's have-nots, plus the intellectual moxie of his wife, Susan (Thompson).

If "The War Room," the D.A. Pennebaker-Chris Hegedus documentary on the same topic is any measure, "Primary Colors" is excellent at depicting the barely organized chaos of campaigning, following the candidate and his team from their underdog status in New Hampshire through the trials of campaigns in Florida and New York.

These peregrinations are more twisty than usual because of what a profane, take-no-prisoners Stanton loyalist named Libby Holden calls with typical brio the governor's propensity for having "poked his pecker in some sorry trash bins." After a hairdresser named Cashmere McLeod (read Gennifer Flowers) sells her tell-all story to a national tabloid, Holden is hired by the campaign to be a "dustbuster" and discredit tales of womanizing before they can harm the candidate. For

Tennessee-born Kathy Bates, this gleeful, high-energy part is a lifesaver, her best performance since winning an Oscar in "Misery" and good enough to practically steal the entire picture.

Though "Primary Colors" the movie plays a bit softer than the book, partially because it eliminates a brief sexual encounter between the president's wife and the narrator, it does not avoid the questions the original raised about means and ends. How far can you allow yourself to go in cutthroat slander, deception and manipulation in order to keep a good-guys campaign alive? Is venality the price you pay to lead? Is there truth in Stanton's question, "You don't think Abraham Lincoln was a whore before he was a president?" And does Henry Burton really know what he's getting into when he says early on, "I'll take the liar over the man who doesn't care"?

Making the conundrum of compromise more than a dry, academic query are the characters of Jack and Susan Stanton as revealed through the people who play them. Though it's routinely said that adroit casting is the major part of the filmmaking battle, it's unusual to have two actors whose different approaches to their craft are not only complementary but also help illuminate their characters' relationship to each other.

Travolta, more the instinctive movie star than the highly trained technician, has chosen to closely model Gov. Stanton down to his silvery hair and Southern accent, on President Clinton. It's no more than a turn, an amusing and light-fingered impersonation, but like the politician he plays it's an irresistible one. The movie's Stanton is a flawed and contradictory man, baffling and hypnotic in his seamless combination of genuine caring with casual manipulation. This film's accomplishment is illustrating that contradiction, showing how such a man could captivate an intelligent, caring staff—and the American public—despite his evident shortcomings.

Essential in defining Stanton's character is his relationship with wife Susan. Thompson, the more classically trained performer, chose not to base her character on Hillary Rodham Clinton. That combination makes Susan seem twice removed from the governor, adds spice to the head and heart duality that characterizes their dynamic and makes them eerily seem like two halves of the same person.

"Primary Color's" also features strong performances in its minor characters. Especially worth singling out are Larry Hagman as one of the governor's political opponents, Caroline Aaron as an obstreperous friend of Susan's, and Rob Reiner as an irrepressible Miami talk-show host. Characters we see too little of, presumably because the film ran long, include, Maura Tierney as Daisy, Burton's campaign partner in crime (who simply disappears at a certain point), and Diane Ladd, whose Momma Stanton is reduced to the merest cameo.

Entertaining as it mostly is, "Primary Colors" parallels the book in being least successful near its close when it tries to force more serious moral lessons than its story line can comfortably hold. And as risque as its speculations seemed when Klein was still anonymous, the rush of history, epitomized by the tale of Monica Lewinsky, has overtaken and surpassed what's been put on the screen.

But if parallels to reality is the hook that draws us into "Primary Colors," it's the nature of its characters that holds us there. Gov. Stanton commands our interest, in somewhat the same way the president does; he doesn't seem to add up. If we could fully figure him out and pin down the nature of his appeal, we might be able to do the same for both our political process and ourselves. And that would be not a half-bad day's work.

NEW YORK, 3/23/98, p. 82, David Denby

Primary Colors is a portrait of a slob genius (our president, our obsession, our Bill), a large, groping, hungry animal who just happens to possess the most acute antennae in the history of American politics. Is he a noble beast or an ignoble beast? A fallen angel or an ascending devil? His followers, regarding him with admiration and dismay, puzzle over his nature. This entertaining but rather peculiar movie asks extraordinary questions, and I wish it were better equipped to give the answers. In the end, it gives show-business answers—partial answers—and from an odd angle.

Mike Nichols and his longtime collaborator, Elaine May, adapted Joe Klein's novel, and the movie, like the book, begins with the "meaningful handshake"—the grip firm and confiding, and reinforced by a second hand on the recipient's biceps or shoulder. Was there ever such a handshake? It offers more than a mere greeting; it confirms, reassures, consecrates. In New Hampshire, back there in 1992, Bill Clinton—or Jack Stanton, as Klein calls him—is campaigning for the Democratic nomination, laying his meaty digits into the palms of strangers. As the camera stays close to these epic salutations. a question comes to mind with painful intensity: Does he really care about these people—that is, care more than any other politician seeking votes? Is he simply faking? Or is Stanton's moral nature something fearfully complex, a fathomless mystery in which he acts the role of empathy and concern so superbly that he becomes the thing he wills, much like a cynical grandstanding preacher who whips himself into belief in God? In such a case, sincerity is no longer a matter of honesty; sincerity gets dissolved and reconfigured by will. But a will as strong as that propels us into alarming moral turf, for such a man might act dishonorably with a serene sense of his own innocence. If you then judged him as a liar, you would have to deal with his bafflement. In his eyes, he has been betrayed by *you*.

And that is where we are now. *Primary Colors* was published two years ago, but this film adaptation leaps right into the current moment: The president, who is probably lying, feels righteous and angry, and the rest of us are left in the lurch, hoping to solve (i.e., live with) the conundrum of his character. Bill Clinton drives everyone a little crazy. His heart may be in the right place regarding such key issues as race, education, and jobs, yet his judgment is unspeakably bad in ways that hurt him (and us) again and again. Political columnist Joe Klein, himself an early Clinton fan, lost his faith, and by the time he wrote the book, he was split between outsize admiration and outsize disgust. *Primary Colors* is fueled by a sense of betrayal.

But using that sense of betrayal with dramatic intelligence isn't so easy. Klein's disillusion appears to have been displaced into the character of a rather bland African-American political operative-Henry Burton, the grandson of a civil-rights leader. Burton, who joins Stanton's campaign, is forever worrying about the governor's honor. He narrates both the book and the movie, and he's mostly a blank, a character created in order to be disappointed. Adrian Lester, the young British actor who plays him, has a puzzled, indecisive air—but how could it be any different? He's playing a device, not a man of shrewd or interesting judgment. After all, what intelligent campaign operative—or journalist—could be surprised to discover that politicians lie in order to get elected, that they ruthlessly suppress their past indiscretions? One can be disappointed to find out such things about one's hero—that's only natural—but is there any point in overvaluing one's innocence? What matters in *Macbeth* is not what some minor character thinks of the general. What matters is what *we* think. One of the oddities of *Primary Colors* is that Stanton-Clinton gets lost in his own movie, shunted aside by the agonized scruples of his followers.

The filmmakers, following Klein, portray the president-to-be and his circle as foul-mouthed and sexually active. Sitting there, we cannot help thinking, "This crew will soon take over the country." The thought will shock those who want to be shocked—the Republicans, perhaps, and the umbrageous Maureen Dowd, and also, one imagines, ABC News, which, in an awesome accession of self-importance, has recently been preparing the president, as far as anyone can see, not merely for an impeachment hearing but for an encounter with Jehovah himself. The movie will provide evidence (of an ambiguous nature) for those who want to think the worst of the Clintons.

The candidate and his wife, Susan (Emma Thompson)—the Hillary figure—are not exactly cooing lovebirds, though they hang together in the nest. Their relationship is scandalously funny, at times pathetic, at times noble. She calls him a "faithless bastard" and whacks him on the head with a heavy set of keys, and he responds by smiling, shrugging off her blows and accusations, and easing her back into the thing she's so very good at, managing his career. They can sustain this odd Punching-bag-and-Judy act because they need each other; together, they are winners.

Thompson doesn't imitate Hillary Clinton; she talks in her own style, ironic and precise, sometimes with great warmth, at other times coldly, with severe anger. Physically, she's hard and linear, while Travolta is all rolling ease, his body swiveling, rocking—he seems to carry ball bearings in every joint. Travolta has certainly got the manner down pat: He thrusts out his jaw and jiggles his head slightly as he speaks; he ambles and shuffles, throwing his arms bearishly around the shoulders of anyone in sight. Travolta is good, but he's like a stage actor in a preview performance. He hasn't taken easy command of the role yet;, he hasn't harmonized all the imitative tricks so they seem like the natural manner of a real person. You can always see him acting; the performance is a little clownish and awkward, though it has some wonderful moments—the way he flies into infantile rages when thwarted in some petty way, yet smiles placidly when seriously attacked, refusing to fall into obvious anger. Stanton is a man who understands what American people want: They don't want rancor; they want good humor.

Billy Bob Thornton is entertaining as Richard Jemmons, the James Carville stand-in (though no performer could approach the sheer bravura of Carville himself—the swamp rat with a snake's tongue); Kathy Bates, as the Betsey Wright figure Libby Holden, storms into the movie braying "I'm heeere!" and never stops swinging. Bates is like a pile driver with superb timing; she's mesmerizing. It's Libby's job to cover the governor's tracks (one gets the impression she's kicked a ton of dirt), and she talks tough to him, utterly unafraid, a mama who washes the soiled underclothes and has long lost her tolerance of niceties.

These people are always "on," and they curse a blue streak. Is the portrait accurate? *Primary Colors* offers a show-business view of politics, which is no surprise. Forty years ago, Mike Nichols and Elaine May set up shop as observers and satirists. Brilliant before a live audience, they transformed little behavioral quirks and anxieties into first-rate cabaret theater. When Nichols turned to directing movies, he stayed on the surface, observing and re-creating behavior, devoting himself, often with great skill, to attitude, manners, style. The best scenes in his first film, *The Graduate,* played like sophisticated nightclub skits, and in the recent *The Birdcage,* the comedy was noisy and broad, like something in a superb sitcom.

So Nichols and May turn this group of ambitious pols into a jolly gang of hipsters, and though I enjoyed all the smart talk and profane irreverence, I didn't take the picture all that seriously. That is, I took it not as reality but as an entertaining convention, a movieish fantasy of what political life is like—quarrelsome, colorful as hell, unburdened by drudgery and nagging detail. It is certainly a performer's view of running a campaign; it offers personality as performance.

Since the movie is often funny and loose-limbed—a series of riffs—it seems odd, a bit like dirty pool, when it suddenly turns very serious indeed, and even tragic. The question is posed: Will the Stantons use some vicious material against an opponent in the race, a southern governor with a nasty secret (the governor is played by Larry Hagman with tender dignity)? In its overwrought emotionalism, the violent reaction of Stanton's staff to this decision seems to me extreme and dramatically naive. It goes beyond saying, "Jack Stanton is smart, he cares, he wants to deliver, and it's sickening how amoral and undisciplined he is." No, the movie suddenly seems to hold Stanton responsible for honor itself. If *he* fails in honor, the light goes out of life.

The trouble is, the filmmakers haven't created a rich enough portrait of the president-to-be; they haven't shown enough of his talent to warrant this anguish over its betrayal. We see his empathy, his political adroitness, but we don't see any of the famous intellect, the command of detail and policy that everyone says is so impressive. Nichols may have miscalculated. You can't entertain an audience with the slobbiness of the future leader—a man who's the life of the barbecue—and then complain bitterly that he isn't a figure of probity. *Primary Colors* leaves an uneasy feeling in its wake—not only about the president but about the ability of the movies to handle the moral issues he has so persistently aroused.

NEW YORK POST, 3/20/98, p. 43, Rod Dreher

It's OK, but just. Despite its talented cast and the high-minded comic creativity of director Mike Nichols and screenwriter Elaine May, there's a day-late, dollar-short air to "Primary Colors" that makes it something an effective satire can never be: dated, even on opening day.

Here's a busy film that presents the current president of the United States, in thin disguise, as a lying, no-count, philandering, disloyal, self-serving, piggish good ol' boy. And it's still safe and boring! They don't make reality like they used to.

As everybody knows by now, "Primary Colors," is based on journalist Joe Klein's 1996 *roman a clef* about the first Clinton campaign. What gave that book its sting was the dishy pleasure one took in presuming it was a tell-all account of what really happened behind the "Man from Hope" facade.

It presented the conventional (by then) view of Clinton and his entourage: that he was a deeply flawed but somehow appealing man surrounded by loyal supporters, particularly his hard-charging wife, who stuck by him no matter what.

Even though the movie remains largely faithful to the book, all of this is very old news by now, and "Primary Colors" doesn't bring anything fresh or insightful to the tale.

You know your movie's in trouble when court depositions reprinted in the New York Times prove more shocking, unsettling and altogether entertaining.

John Travolta—armed with a paunch, salt-and-pepper hair, and Southern accent as soft and comforting as buttermilk biscuits—plays Democratic presidential hopeful Gov. Jack Stanton.

Stanton's a big boy with big appetite, which include women not his wife, Krispy Kreme doughnuts, and the misty-eyed adulation of crowds.

Henry Burton (Adrian Lester) is an idealistic young political operative, a black George Stephanopoulos, who signs on with the Stanton campaign. But being a bit of a buppie pill, he's forever fretting over the morality of working for a man whose policies he believes in, but whose personal life is a sleazy joke.

The surprisingly slow-paced "Primary Colors" offers up ever trashier episodes of Stantonian sleaze, including the constant betrayal of his hard-as-shellacked-nails wife, Susan (Emma Thompson).

But the anguish Henry feels doesn't come across on screen. Lester plays him well, but the character is so blandly conceived that we don't, well, feel his pain.

Not so with Libby Holden (the wonderful Kathy Bates), who becomes the film's conscience by default. She's a lunatic lesbian politico who works as the Stantons "dustbuster"—a role played by Betsey Wright in real life—cleaning up the fallout from bimbo eruptions so Jack can remain politically viable.

When, near the picture's end, Libby realizes that her once-idealistic heroes have sold out to corrupt politics, her heart breaks hard.

"Primary Colors" is a confusing film, satisfying neither as comedy nor drama. To get laughs, it gives us a president who is a pluperfect scoundrel (Travolta never, by the way, captures the one thing that informed Clinton's roguish charm: his smarts).

But because it wants to preserve our affection for the guy, May's script pulls its comic punches. And when she wants to make the serious point that Stanton, whatever his sins, is as good as it gets these days, "Primary Colors" descends into smarmy, self-serving moralizing.

Stanton tells Henry that Lincoln was a whore" until he got to the White House, where he did great things. Past doesn't have to be prologue, Stanton argues, which is a way of saying character doesn't count.

Who are you going to believe, though: stolid old "Primary Colors" or the juicy evening news? Like I said, reality bites.

NEWSDAY, 3/20/98, Part II/p. B3, Jack Mathews

Mike Nichols' superb adaptation of Joe Klein's anonymously written political black comedy "Primary Colors" was filmed, edited and scheduled for today's release before Linda Tripp ratted out her friend Monica Lewinsky to Ken Starr But that doesn't mean Tripp, Lewinsky, Starr, Paula Jones, Kathleen Wiley and the rest of Bill Clinton's contemporary accusers aren't in it.

They appear in almost every scene of the movie, not in person, or as characters, but as ghosts from the future. The book and the movie are about Clinton's astonishing 1992 presidential campaign, where every crisis seemed to raise his political stock, and the sex scandal of 1998, which is having pretty much the same result, hangs over it like a bonus sequel.

"Primary Colors'" Jack Stanton, played perfectly in the film by John Travolta, has a lot in common with the guy occupying the White House now. He's an engaging, bright, deceptively folksy policy wonk, true believer in the people, and, if a fraction of what we've heard and are hearing is true, an undisciplined sexual predator. The only things that have changed between '92 and '98 are the names, the places, the stakes and the president's popularity. It's higher.

Rumors preceding the movie, which was written by Nichols' old stand-up partner Elaine May, suggested the filmmaker had pulled his punches, out of deference to his friendship with the president. And, indeed, the movie and the book differ in one major regard. In the book, the George Stephanopoulus character Henry Burton (Adrian Lester), an idealistic young campaign aide, has a brief affair with Susan Stanton (Emma Thompson).

It's implied in the movie, but so obliquely that only readers of the book will notice. You can understand why the Clintons might appreciate the alteration. Much of the book is based on fact, most of it is taken as fact, and so far Hillary has been free of any rumors about her own sexual history. But there's a more troubling explanation for the change. Burton, in the book and the movie, is black, and that's a problem for filmmakers aiming at a national audience.

Klein's Burton also has an ongoing sexual relationship with a white co-worker, which begins as "campaign sex" and grows into something that ultimately puts Henry at odds with Jack Stanton. In the Nichols/May adaptation, that's reduced to a minor, almost offhand subplot, without buildup or passion. Henry and Daisy (Maura Tierney) just suddenly appear in bed together, as if they'd drawn each other's name at a funky campaign party. It's Hollywood liberalism at its worst: Keep the character black, but change him to be sexually nonthreatening.

But that's the only reservation you'll read here about the film version of "Primary Colors." This is one of the best political movies ever made, full of rich characters, beautiful performances, wit and insight. It essentially follows the Stanton campaign, from his beginning as a severe, almost unnoticed underdog to his embarrassed denials of stories about draft dodging, student activism and adultery, to his seduction of the common man and his night at the Inaugural Ball.

Along the way, we meet fictional stand-ins for Clinton rivals Paul Tsongas, Mario Cuomo, Richard Gephardt, Bob Kerry and Jesse Jackson, and we get to know the candidate, his strong-willed and long-suffering wife and their team.

Besides Henry and Daisy, who handles day-to-day political advertising, there's a James Carville character, hilariously played by Billy Bob Thornton, a version of the pragmatic Harold Ickes (Paul Guilfoyle), and, best of all, there's Libby Holden (a scene-stealing Kathy Bates), based on Clinton's flamboyant Little Rock chief of staff Betsey Wright.

The story turns on a pair of Klein inventions designed to measure Stanton/Clinton's moral duality. The first comes in an allegation by the teenage daughter of a black restaurant owner and Stanton loyalist that she's carrying the governor's baby. The other is the personal dirt dug up by Libby and Henry about Stanton's major rival, a populist Florida politician played by Larry Hagman. How Stanton reacts to these two events, how far he's willing to go to A) protect himself and B) to win the party's nomination, merge in the film's powerful last act.

Travolta, without attempting an impression of Clinton, captures what reasonable people may see as the essence of the man. White trash savant or flawed genius Stanton is a genuine charismatic. One of the film's most compelling scenes, reportedly based on an actual campaign moment, shows Stanton winning over a group of disenchanted unemployed factory workers with his jolting straight talk about their future in a world that's quickly moving past them.

"Primary Colors" is not a flattering profile of Clinton, by any means. If you believe he inhaled that joint, evaded the draft, slept with Gennifer Flowers, exploited Monica Lewinsky, assaulted Kathleen Wiley and lied about it all, nothing in the movie will change your opinion. But if you're as stumped as his political rivals and many in the media as to how he's able to survive and hold his head up, bolstered by public opinion, "Primary Colors" is a revelation.

NEWSWEEK, 3/23/98,p. 63, David Ansen

There are moments, watching "Primary Colors," when you squirm with a discomfort movies don't usually produce—an embarrassment that feels almost Oedipal. That's the father of our country hastily buttoning up his pants on screen! That's how close to the bone of our current presidential soap opera Mike Nichols's movie can cut, but the obvious resemblance between the fictional Southern candidate Jack Stanton (John Travolta) and his factual doppelganger in the White House doesn't explain why "Primary Colors" is the funniest, shrewdest and saddest movie about American politics since Gore Vidal's "The Best Man." It could have been merely vulgar and opportunistic. But Nichols and screenwriter Elaine May, faithfully following the lead of Joe (Anonymous) Klein's astute novel, know precisely the difference between exploration and exploitation. We may recoil from the grubby details of the Lewinsky affair—but the stinging revelations of "Primary Colors" feel beneficial.

Like most movies about politics, the subject is idealism betrayed. What's different about this one is that it rejects both cynicism and easy moral righteousness. Our attitude toward Travolta's seductive, piggish, charming, Machiavellian, idealistic and corrupt presidential candidate is as profoundly complex and ambivalent as what many of us feel about Clinton himself. The beauty of "Primary Colors" is that it forces us to grapple with the same questions of political faith that haunt its narrator, Henry Burton (Adrian Lester), the idealistic young man who is lured by Stanton's magic into becoming his deputy campaign manager.

Nichols knows this is a movie about performers performing—much of the comic tension in its first half is about trying to figure out if Stanton's act is genuine or phony, if his empathetic tears are for real. Travolta, his voice thickened with a Clintonian rasp, his voracious appetite always on the lookout for votes, doughnuts or women, gives a terrifically entertaining performance, if one that sometimes seems coarser than its model. In choosing to imitate Clinton, Travolta invites comparison, and we have to say Clinton hides his acting better than the actor.

But Stanton isn't the protagonist; he's the enigma around which the farce and tragedy whirl. What a superb cast Nichols has assembled, from the little-known Lester (an English stage actor) to Billy Bob Thornton, whose Carville-like strategist is a lascivious delight. Emma Thompson plays Stanton's smart, attractive wife, Susan, whose gift for instant intimacy can be as pitch perfect as her husband's. Without a wasted motion, she shows us her character's fierce complexity, how her adoration of her husband is mixed with rage and denial. A terrific Larry Hagman reveals unsuspected depths playing Governor Picker, an anti-politics politician who backs into the race and poses a serious threat to Stanton's juggernaut.

Some of the parallels to real life are glaringly obvious—like the scandal involving Gennifer Flowers's stand-in. Cashmere McCleod. But around the time Picker enters the story, the movie sails into deeper, uncharted waters. It's here that Kathy Bates's trouble-shooter Libby Holden, at first a butch comic cartoon, startles us by turning into the movie's moral conscience. "Primary Colors" can turn on a dime from a bawdy campaign-trail comedy to a trenchant glimpse at a complex marriage to a chilling contemplation of the personal wreckage political ambition leaves in its wake. I expected to laugh; I didn't expect to be moved.

"Primary Colors" doesn't offer up the usual story of good guys and bad guys duking it out for control of the country, because the good guy and the bad guy are the same guy, who's embedded in a hardball political system that seems to demand that you be a bad guy if you want to win and get the chance to act like a good guy.

The political pundits have been asking whether this movie will be good or bad for Clinton. Film-business insiders have been pondering whether the Lewinsky scandal will be good or bad for this movie. The only question I can answer is whether the movie is good or bad for moviegoers. That's a no-brainer: it's the most vital Hollywood movie of the new year.

SIGHT AND SOUND, 10/98, p. 50, Leslie Dick

Henry Burton, grandson of a leading 60s civil-rights leader, observes Jack Stanton's campaign for the 1992 Democratic presidential nomination. The campaign, overseen by Richard Jemmons, is chaotic. The team arrives for the first primary in New Hampshire. Burton sees Stanton win over a group of voters in a public library and decides to join the campaign.

Mayor Ozio of New York announces he is not joining the race. Stanton's votes pick up. Jemmons is troubled by allegations about Stanton's radical 60s past and that his womanising might leak out. Libby, a lesbian friend of the Stantons, comes to help the campaign when a scandal breaks: Cashmere McLeod alleges publicly that she had a long-standing affair with Jack, producing an audio tape as proof. Jack and his wife Susan appear on television, admitting their marriage has had problems. Libby discovers Cashmere's tape is faked.

On the evening of the primary election, Stanton comes second, better than expected. Back home in Mammoth Falls, an old friend of Stanton's accuses him of getting his daughter pregnant. Democrat contender Lawrence Harris dies suddenly and Governor Fred Picker joins the race in his place. Libby and Henry uncover details of Picker's gay sex and cocaine use in the 70s, which the Stantons decide to exploit. Libby, disillusioned, kills herself. Stanton wins the presidency.

The partnership of Mike Nichols and Elaine May has acquired enormous cultural credibility in the United States. They're legit—the real thing—partly because of their work in the theatre, a collaboration that goes back 40 years. And Nichols aspires to make movies which capture a historical moment, movies which present a portrait of America. (In some sense he's never got over *The Graduate,* that great presentation of the 60s Generation Gap.)

In *Primary Colors,* the team take on presidential politics and its secrets within the critically significant context of race relations in the US. The opening shots show the Stars and Stripes and a close-up of black/white handshakes: the presidential candidate Jack Stanton's emotionally expressive handshake as he moves down a line of African Americans. Our protagonist, Henry Burton, is himself black, a campaign organiser whose radical girlfriend busts up with him over his willingness to work for the white man. The candidate is John Travolta (doing Clinton to a 'T'), and Henry's commitment to the cause is largely based on Stanton's unselfconscious ability to communicate across the racial divide.

That's the set-up, as outlined in the best-selling novel by 'Anonymous', notorious for its brutal and telling fictionalisation of Bill Clinton's campaign for the Democratic nomination. It's all there in the book: race, sex, drugs, suicide, misplaced loyalty and moral betrayal. But the film cops out: most of the tough stuff in the book, the "hard ball" they play, is simply left out. Mistakenly, Henry Burton is presented as an innocent, with a sweet smile, and no edge at all. He is naive, something no one in the world of presidential politics can afford to be. This situates the audience (who see it all from Henry's point of view) as equally naive, shocked by things everyone who watches television takes for granted.

Plus, most of the sex is excised. In the book, Henry gets to have sex with Mrs Stanton, and the lesbian nutcase, Libby, who's worked with them for 20 years, has also had sex with her in the past. This won't do for Hollywood! In the book, Henry falls for his white co-worker Daisy, and their sexual relationship is central. In the movie, there's a shot where they are lying in bed together waking up, but you don't see them kiss or touch. The campaign's sexual escapades are reduced to the candidate's lack of self-control: he sleeps with the hairdresser, he sleeps with the woman from the teachers' union, he sleeps with the teenage black babysitter—and denies it to her parents. (We know this because when she gets pregnant, he switches the blood sample provided for a paternity test. Despicable!)

The plot unfolds around Henry and Libby digging the dirt on an apparently virtuous Democratic politician, played by Larry Hagman, who turns out to have been, back in the 70s, both gay and into cocaine. In the film only, the gay sex is minimised ("I slept with Lorenzo once, twice maybe") as if the film's mainstream audience could not stomach a character who'd had a real sexual relationship with someone like Lorenzo, a gay Latino ex-lawyer who's spent 20 years in prison for cocaine, now dying of Aids in a Miami halfway house, here representing the lowest depths of depravity. Secrets like these are indeed political death in the US, but does this apparently well-meaning film have to assume the same values?

The moral crisis of the movie is: will the Clintons/Stantons stoop to exploiting the "gay man with Aids" story, in order to discredit a fellow Democrat, a man they respect? Libby is devastated because they don't even hesitate, their immediate response is: "*New York Times* or *Wall Street Journal*?" They justify this on the grounds that if they don't publicise this information now, before the real presidential race has begun, the Republicans will get hold of the same information and use it more effectively later. Henry and Libby stagger off, deeply disillusioned, having genuinely believed this archetypal political couple was different from all the rest. The political undertow seems to be one of heavy handed acceptance. We may shake our heads in dismayed wonder at the way the media has turned US politics into a tragic circus, a whirlwind of soundbites and scandal, but this is a fact of American life, a bit like Stanton fucking the black babysitter: it's contemptible, indefensible, and unavoidable.

The film has all the tedium of American ensemble theatre acting, with everyone careful not to upstage each other. Characters whose outrageous behaviour jumps right off the page are toned down to measured blandness in the movie—even Billy Bob Thorton (as the James Carville character) is quiet. Kathy Bates as the lesbian loyalist should have been allowed really to let rip; Emma Thompson does her stuff, more than competently, despite a slightly disconcerting accent. And it was nice to see John Travolta dancing badly. Ironically enough, the film opened in the US just when Monica Lewinsky was on the news every night (so its release here is well timed as well). Reality proved more ethically complex, more dynamic and much sexier than *Primary Colors*. This movie should have been directed by a non-American with a deep understanding of moral abasement and no fear of excess: Mike Leigh?

TIME, 3/16/98, p. 64, Richard Corliss

There's a poignant little scene halfway into *Primary Colors*. It's primary night in New Hampshire, and candidate Jack Stanton (John Travolta) stands alone on a rainy street, knocking on car windows and importuning drivers for last-minute votes like a squeegee guy cadging a dollar. To hell with the odds; this man won't give up. He will keep asking, charming, wheedling, until people finally collapse under his will to be loved. As a character says in the Joe Klein novel on which the film is based, "The heart is a lonely hustler." but hustling—hey, that's politics. That's entertainment.

Travolta and Bill Clinton both know about perseverance and the uses of charisma. As the actor spread his seductiveness on a movie screen like jelly on toast, so does Clinton work a room or a country, avidly selling his policies and himself, in love with being loved—and with his need to be loved. No wonder that when Travolta met Klein, he said, "I've been waiting my whole life to play this role."

The $65 million comedy opens next week, almost exactly two months after l'affaire Lewinsky broke. But even without the coincidence of a politicians's sex scandals in the film and in surreal real life, the kinship between Clinton and a movie star like Travolta is clear. Both have It—that mixture of swagger, danger and vulnerability. Folks who meet the President typically refer to his heat, to the musk of his personality, whether he is flashing them a thrilled-with-it-all smile or listening, hands folded prayerfully, concentrating with a ferocity that is a virtual assault of attentiveness. And he uses It like a movie star. The confluence of politics and performance finds its nexus in his indefatigable showmanship. He wants to romance not just the Congress or perhaps a stray intern but America, the world.

Other Presidents had an anchorman aura: authoritative, a bit square. Clinton has the urgency of a talk-show host. Or guest ("I want everyone to want me"—today on Jerry Springer). He is the first boyfriend (rather than father) figure in the White House since Jack Kennedy. Bye-bye, Poppy; hello, Elvis. That was the cue for the Southern beau-hunk to go on strutting his sex appeal, occasionally swiveling his ideology and forever crooning his ballads: "For I can't help/ Falling in love with you."

The film's makers deny, with the fervor of a White House aide in front of the skeptical scorps of the press, that *Primary Colors* is really the story of Clinton in the 1992 presidential campaign. "Of course, nobody is going to note the differences," director Mike Nichols sighs. "There's no fun noting the differences. But the whole story doesn't work if it's literally about the Clintons. It does work if it's about the political process and the people who work in it. Can you remember why you started? Can you do anything but run the race and fight the fight? How do you know when you've forgotten your principles, and whom do you turn to? The movie asks a lot of questions, but it doesn't answer anything."

It answers one thing: Nichols and his once and current partner, screenwriter Elaine May, can make a funny, knowing, ultimately judicious film from the deliciously satyric satire that Klein, a former *Newsweek* columnist who now works for the *New Yorker,* published under the pseudonym Anonymous. If you mix the primary colors red, yellow and blue, the result is black. But this is no black comedy. It is a wistful story, about honor (Nichols says) and (we say) about the joy and pain of an idealist's love. Cagily, it asks big, brutal questions. What will we do for someone we love? What will we do for someone we want to love? When this person is a politician and has a shot at becoming the most powerful man on earth, good people can do pretty cruddy things—for the sake, they keep telling themselves, of a noble goal. Faust knew this. So, at every step of the long primary road, does Henry Burton.

It's his story, not Stanton's, so much so that the film could be called *Regarding Henry* (a 1991 Nichols movie that Klein particularly admires). Henry—a young black man so properly educated, so fully integrated into the political élite that another black pegs him as "the white man's Burton"—is the soul up for grabs in *Primary Colors*. He joins the Stanton campaign because he thinks, "This guy could be the real thing." Delicately played by British stage star Adrian Lester *(As You Like It, Company*), Henry is a can-do Candide, a fixer who keeps hoping Stanton is the best of all possible candidates. Ideals are always in danger of being reduced to fairy tales.

"The characters in my book took on lives of their own," says Klein. "They were who they were." Still, insiders had fun guessing who in the Clinton caravan matched the characters Klein created. Henry's is the most elusive: a sort of mythical grandson of Martin Luther King Jr. crossed with former Clinton adviser George Stephanopoulos. Nearly everyone else is an acute comic exaggeration of a familiar friend or foe of Bill's.

Richard Jemmons, the self-proclaimed redneck spin surgeon (played by *Sling Blade's* Billy Bob Thornton), is transparently James Carville. Daisy Green (Maura Tierney in the film) shares résumés with campaign adviser Mandy Grunwald. Libby Holden (Kathy Bates), the manic "dust buster" who tries to cover up Stanton's peccadillos before they make the tabs' front pages, is similar to Betsey Wright, Governor Clinton's chief of staff and trigger-happy troubleshooter. Lawrence Harris (Kevin Cooney), the New England Senator who runs against Stanton until being felled by a heart attack, could be the physically frail Paul Tsongas. Cashmere McLeod (Gia Carides) stands in for Gennifer Flowers. And Fred Picker (Larry Hagman), the white knight who comes out of retirement to threaten Stanton's front-runner status, is a kinder, less kooky, more kinky H. Ross Perot.

The Stantons, TIME has learned, are based on Bill and Hillary Clinton. Susan Stanton (Emma Thompson), with her iron irony and rigid self-confidence, is Jack's severest critic and staunchest defender. For all her feminist executive briskness, she is in love with Jack, or with what she can help him become. In a more sophisticated way than Jack does, she sells loyalty, cunning and, when cornered, sex appeal.

In the book and the movie, Jack is a guest star. His role is not so much supporting as hovering—like God in the Old Testament. He shows up occasionally to bring fear, awe or happiness to the mortals who are at the center of the story. He asks them to slaughter their first principles, hurls plagues of tabloid headlines their way, gives their lives meaning and hope with his captious majesty. Except, of course, that Jack isn't God. In luring his team toward corruption, twisting their idealism into realpolitik, Stanton is Satan.

And spinning this Mephistophelian tale was Klein, the author who insisted on anonymity until he finally, clumsily, owned up after being outed in the Washington *Post*. Klein was unprepared for the book's success and the attendant rumpus about the author's identity. "I wrote two other books and never got American royalty checks," he says. "I was kind of agog for the first weeks after it happened. Agog, delighted, terrified."

A novelist's expectations may be modest, but while writing he can afford to do what a reader does: cast the movie version. Some of Klein's daydreaming proved prescient. "In my mind Libby Holden *was* Kathy Bates. I was also thinking of Emma Thompson as Susan Stanton—because Emma Thompson can do anything!" On his directors' list were Jonathan Demme (Philadelphia), Michael Apted *(Gorillas in the Mist)* and, at the top, Mike Nichols.

For a while, before publication, it seemed as if Klein's book would be a movie only in his head. The directors on his list, including Nichols, passed. Then the buzz got booming, and a fierce bidding commenced. Each suitor was allotted 30 minutes for a pitch. Nichols smartly said. "The reason I want to film the novel is that it's about honor, and that's the thing very good movies are about." That speech, and $1.5 million, put him over. Universal later reimbursed him for the rights (plus an almost equal amount tied to various bonus incentives) and also spent a reported $5 million to get him to direct and produce the film. Then Nichols got May.

As the royal couple of improv comedy, Nichols and May often took eroticism into new areas; in one duologue they replayed the breathless infidelity of *Brief Encounter* in a dentist's chair. The pair, once estranged, reunited professionally with the direction and script for the 1996 hit *The Birdcage*. "We close a circle," Nichols says. "All the difficulties have long been burned away, and only the good parts are left. I can tell her things in our own code, and it comes out infinitely richer."

Right from his first two films in the mid-'60s (*Who's Afraid of Virginia Woolf?* and *The Graduate),* Nichols has trusted original material, pruning carefully, changing little. Nichols and May's film of *Primary Colors* faithfully distills the 366-page book, excising a few colorful critters (like the caricatures of Mario Cuomo and Jesse Jackson) but bringing the rest to seductive life onscreen. The major elision is the one-night stand Henry has with Susan Stanton.

Klein gave the tryst the logic of satire: Henry discovers that not only his boss but even the boss's wife is desperate for sex. It also humanizes Susan, who, out of hurt and curiosity, for once acts spontaneously. The director of *The Graduate* ("Mrs. Robinson, you're trying to seduce me, aren't you?") liked the scene and, over Universal's protests, shot it. Preview groups hated it—perhaps in prim disapproval or perhaps because when the hero of a film has an affair with the leading lady, audiences expect the affair to take over the story. Here it doesn't; it's just an anecdote about the abuse and frustrations of power. Nichols was right to shoot it and right to cut it.

Casting was a series of sensitive political negotiations. Nichols considered Mel Gibson and Liam Neeson for Stanton, but his first choice was a fellow Clinton sympathizer, Tom Hanks. "He was eager," the director recalls. "Then he said the more he looked at certain things in the script, the less he could see himself doing the film. It was the philandering, I think. He's an at-home, family guy." (Carly Simon, another friend of Bill's, also withdrew as provider of the film's music.) Thornton, an Arkansas homeboy, took the Jemmons role only after receiving Clinton's dispensation via television producer Harry Thomason.

Several distinguished actors were approached for the role of Picker. For a time Nichols wanted Jack Nicholson, who has made four films with the director. But Nicholson had a high price tag for a supporting gig. There was another obstacle: a star of Nicholson's wattage would throw the film off balance; viewers would expect Act III to be all about his character, but it's really Kathy Bates' show (when Libby goes on a mission to save and test the Stantons). As he did with the Henry-Susan tryst, Nichols realized he had to serve the story: "I didn't need Jack the King." Instead he cast Hagman—old J.R.—whose soft smile and dazed eyes bring a lovely sense of politics' walking wounded. He is the film's sweetest emotional wreck.

The two British stars, innocent of the intricacies of U.S. politics (imagine an American actor cast as Prime Minister Tony Blair or Northern Ireland firebrand Ian Paisley), had a few all-night cram sessions.

Lester studied the career of the late Commerce Secretary Ron Brown, an early black supporter of Clinton's, and read *The Power Game: How Washington Works* by Hedrick Smith. Says Thompson: "The areas of my ignorance are vast and arid. I read *Politics for Dummies*, I saw the documentary *The War Room*; and I learned a wee bit about women in American politics. It's impressive what women can do, but it's also depressing that the ultimate glass ceiling is First Lady."

Nichols and his wife, ABC News star Diane Sawyer, are friendly with the Clintons; Nichols and May have been hosts of benefits for the President. But the director insists he neither spoke with Clinton about the film nor softened the case against Stanton. "We're all supposed to be friends of the President, which is nuts to begin with," Nichols says, bristling. "The movie is about a man with a talent for the job and the things that get him into trouble. That's the story. Softening it or hardening it—forgive the expression—doesn't come into it."

In fact Klein was in the thrall of the Clinton charisma; his Jack is a figure that rockets off the page. In the film Stanton is less grand and less sexy, and Travolta plays it subdued, a tad mopish. His smile looks startled, as if he had just sniffed ammonia. He has the hardest job: while everyone else gets to crack wise, he has to make political platitudes sound like poetry and Stanton's skunkish behavior smell almost sweet. His Stanton is a large man unsure whether he's big enough for a job he would kill to get.

There were whispers that after a White House conversation with Travolta, Clinton put pressure on Germany to soften its stance toward the Church of Scientology, of which the actor is an outspoken adherent, and that in return Travolta portrayed Stanton more sympathetically. That rumor gets a sneer from Klein ("I don't think Clinton would change policy toward Germany to get better treatment from John Travolta"), but the actor has warm memories of the chat, in which he says Clinton spoke of an old roommate who had been a Scientologist. Travolta insists his performance wasn't swayed by the President but declares he played the role "with a valentine in my heart."

Old political hands did swarm over the set to make the rallies and conferences look real. Former White House press secretary Dee Dee Meyers, who had been approached to be political adviser on the film, later asked about the production, but that was curiosity, not a threat. And Nichols did ask Stephanopoulos whether Henry would decide to stick with Stanton through the election—a question Klein left hanging, as did the original cut of the movie. "Well, of course he stays," Stephanopoulos replied. "He'd want to know how things turned out."

Universal executives believe the Lewinsky scandal may attract more customers. "Of course, we could have been hurt if Clinton had resigned," says Universal Pictures chairman Casey Silver. "People might have been so despondent and depressed that they wouldn't have wanted to go see the movie." But politics or even prurience may matter little to moviegoers. Studio surveys indicated that only 3% had read the book and that audiences rarely mentioned the Clinton connection even when they'd seen the film. At an early screening in Seattle less than 1% noted similarities to scandals in the White House. Says Nichols: "There was one card that read, 'Hilarious, thought-provoking, touching. Reminds me of the Clintons." Yet when virtually the same cut was screened post-Monica, the audience approval rating shot up 10 points. Even Nichols felt he was watching a different film. "The whole thing shifted and deepened."

The shooting of the last scene took place in late January, just after Monica Lewinsky had become a household name. The film's main ad line ("What went down on the way to the top") now had a Letterman leer, and the central mystery (Can Stanton cover up an affair with a young woman?) seemed less like satire than prophecy. But, of course, the timing was just a fluke of the Zeitgeist. As Maura Tierney says, "The reality is something very serious, and the movie is something we made in Hollywood, based on a book that came out more than two years ago. It doesn't seem the same to me at all."

Yet there is more than coincidence to the charges of sexual recklessness that have dogged Clinton; it could be something like fate. Says Klein: "Personally, I have no information at all about Bill Clinton's sex life. But leadership is a complicated business, and leaders are complicated people. Often they've been overendowed with all kinds of emotional qualities—not only libidinous ones but also violent ones. And historically, having an interesting sex life is a leading indicator of success in the presidency."

Nichols has also raised what might be called the Testosterone Theory of public office. As he told the cast during an early readthrough, "We've often thought about our leaders, 'He's a great man and has a real gift with people—too bad he can't keep his dick in his pants.' But the very gift that makes him a great leader is the same thing that keeps him jumping on a lot of women. We tend to split it up into a 'good' side and a 'bad' side. The fact that it's the same vitality is rarely considered."

It is now. Pundits and real people have for the moment decided that Bill Clinton is a good President with some bad habits. As Klein says, "The American people have shown that they're pretty sophisticated about this." They may even be sophisticated about why they go to movies. They didn't buy $124 million worth of tickets for *The Birdcage* because every one of them supported gay family values; they went because they thought they'd have a good time. And as Nichols notes, *Primary Colors* is, in part, about having a good time—the vertiginous good time Henry has trying to get Stanton elected, as if he and Daisy were Mickey Rooney and Judy Garland putting on the big show in their backyard.

Maybe *Primary Colors* is not about loving the man but about loving the work. Early on, when May asked Nichols what he was hoping to say in the film, he told her, "It's secretly *Seinfeld*. It's about the fun friends have together in what turns out to be the happiest time of their lives." As happy as that canny politician John Travolta, parading his charisma in Hollywood. As happy as that consummate showman Bill Clinton, locking eyes and hands with one more member of the universal audience.

VILLAGE VOICE, 3/24/98, p. 65, J. Hoberman

History, a force frequently invoked in *Primary Colors*, has determined that *Primary Colors* would be the most eagerly anticipated Mike Nichols film since ... *Catch-22*. Is it satire? Celebration? Social realism? What's the difference? No less than Nichols's earlier literary adaptation, this one is founded on paradox: as a scarcely veiled portrait of our current president, *Primary Colors* cannot hope to distinguish itself from the image-making spectacle it attempts to represent.

Sooner separate Ronald Reagan from his cue cards or the actual Gulf War from its CNN miniseries than seek to extract *Primary Colors* from the on-going Clinton media event. (An equally telling infotainment symbiosis is *Time* magazine's delightfully unselfconscious decision to celebrate its 75th anniversary as a showbiz institution by running a cover of President John Travolta in his *Primary Colors* drag.)

Mythologizing the now quaint 1992 primary campaign already "documented" by *The War Room's* spindoctor vérité, Joe Klein's anonymously published novel was sensationally vivid—at least in its characterization of candidate Jack Stanton, a Southern governor with a number of character issues and a high-powered wife named Susan. Here, at last, was a plausible portrait of the political animal Homo Clintonus—his all-encompassing handshakes and "aerobic listening";

the way he "snagged a cold, congealed slice of pepperoni, peppers, and onions on his way to the bedroom"; the way he and Susan disposed of their friends.

Not altogether unflattering, Klein's novel made clear that his quasi-fictional creation Clinto-Stan at least had the conviction of his appetites. Indeed, it ultimately proposed that, given the nature of the American media-cracy, a creature like Clinto-Stan was the best that we could expect. The same is true for the movie. As scripted by Elaine May, the movie is remarkably faithful to the book but, as a story now three times told, it lacks edge.

Travolta has mastered the Clinton voice (at least as parodied on *Saturday Night Live*), and he has no difficulty playing the ultimate touchy-feely blubberer. What he lacks is that presidential charisma—he's the reflection in the mirrored shield. Wasting Emma Thompson's comic potential in the Hillary role, relying on an old Willie Nelson song to keep things brisk, orchestrating a bit of bogus feel-good when the Clinto-Stans survive the equivalent of the Gennifer Flowers tapes, *Primary Colors* could take a rumba lesson from *Wag the Dog*. The pace is stately, even geriatric.

As the nominal hero Henry Burton, a Stephanopoulos-type aide given the additional Kleinian fillip of being grandson to a to a martyred civil rights leader, British actor Adrian Lester plays a timid Jiminy Cricket to Travolta's rambunctious Pinocchio. It's Kathy Bates, cavorting through the movie as the Clinto-Stan loyalist Libby Holden, who is the resident Capra hero. She's the one who conjures up the spirit of the founding fathers and cues the teary flashback to the moment of '60s idealism.

Like Libby's big speech, *Primary Colors* exposes with one hand and fabricates new illusions with the other. Still, there's no question that the movie is best when maintaining a dizzy sense of double déjà vu and multiple romans à clef, echoing Vince Foster while intimating Monica Lewinsky. (Imagine how she'll feel when she hears Libby sneer that Jack has "placed his pecker in some sorry trash bins.") The movie loses interest as it veers from gossipy factoid toward fictional contrivance. Is there any point in sorting out the difference?

As *Primary Colors* is really a political Rorschach test, let's just welcome America to the world's biggest, most expensive political focus group. (One scene has an entire bar watching Jack and Susan on TV, rating their perfs like so many Siskel and Eberts.) Was Kenneth Starr a master of strategy for starting his investigation until this scenario installed itself in a few thousand theaters? Could the president have asked for a more sympathetic portrait? Is casting Rob Reiner, auteur of the 1995 Clinton image job (*The American President*, as an affably stupid radio host meant to be a wink?

Hollywood's *Primary Colors* is even more strident than Klein's in hailing Clinto-Stan as the best of all possible chiefs because he's the one who can play our song. (But then, how could the movie industry have failed to identify with Clinton's tropistic people pleasing?) Clinto-Stan's own ultimate self-justification is to ask Henry if he doesn't believe that even Abraham Lincoln was "a whore before he became president." Well, maybe—although not according to John Ford—but I don't think it occurred to him to sell supporters a night in the Lincoln bedroom.

Published to coincide with Clinton's reelection bid, Klein's novel might still package its candidate for potential greatness. What's wild is that the movie continues to hold out the promise of Clinto-Stan's accomplishments—which, we now know, are cheering the Dow to 8500, ending welfare, and schmoozing with Michael Eisner. *Primary Colors* is likely to be the closest Bill Clinton gets to having his face on Mount Rushmore. But don't cry for him, Argentina; it's also the monument he deserves.

Also reviewed in:
CHICAGO TRIBUNE, 2/12/98, Tempo/p. 1, Gary Dretzka
NATION, 4/27/98, p. 35, Stuart Klawans
NEW REPUBLIC, 4/20/98, p. 24, Stanley Kauffmann
NEW YORK TIMES, 3/20/98, p. E1, Janet Maslin
VARIETY , 3/16-22/98, p. 63, Todd McCarthy
WASHINGTON POST, 3/20/98, Weekend/p. N47, Desson Howe

PRINCE OF EGYPT, THE

A Dreamworks Pictures release. *Executive Producer:* Jeffrey Katzenberg. *Producer:* Penny Finkelman Cox and Sandra Rabins. *Director:* Brenda Chapman, Steven Hickner, Simon Wells. *Screenplay:* Philip Lazebnik. *Editor:* Nick Fletcher. *Music:* Todd Homme. *Music Editor:* Adam Smalley. *Sound:* Lon Bender, Wylie Stateman and (music) Alan Meyerson. *Sound Editor:* Neil Anderson, Chris Assells, Greg Hainer, Phil Hess, Chris Hogan, Craig Jaeger, Randy Kelly, Tony Lamberti, Pete Lehman, David McMoyler, Brian McPherson, and Rick Morris. *Production Designer:* Darek Gogol. *Art Director:* Kathy Altieri and Richard Chavez. *Running time:* 93 minutes. *MPAA Rating:* PG.

VOICES: Moses: Val Kilmer. Ramses: Ralph Fiennes. Tzipporah: Michelle Pfeiffer. Miriam: Sandra Bullock. Aaron: Jeff Goldblum. Jethro: Danny Glover. Seti: Patrick Stewart. The Queen: Helen Mirren. Hotep: Steve Martin. Huy: Martin Short. Rameses Son: Bobby Motown. Young Miriam: Eden Riegel. Yocheved: Ofra Haza.

CHRISTIAN SCIENCE MONITOR, 12/18/98, p. 15, David Sterritt

Even in a year when feature-length animations have flourished, "The Prince of Egypt" stands out as a particularly ambitious project. Its subject is the early life of Moses, from his childhood in the Egyptian court to his leadership of the Hebrews out of bondage. Its theme is the rivalry between forward-looking faith and hidebound tradition, represented by the clash between Moses-inspired authority and Rameses' self-willed insistence on an unjust and outmoded order.

The movie takes itself seriously as both entertainment and education, fleshing out its well-known story with pungent visual motifs and larger-than-life character studies. These were developed in consultation with theologians and biblical scholars as well as historians and Egyptologists, according to the DreamWorks studio.

The cast is solid, adding lively voices to the figures on the screen. Val Kilmer and Ralph Fiennes star as Moses and Rameses, respectively, supported by acting voices from Danny Glover as Jethro and Sandra Bullock as Miriam to Michelle Pfeiffer as Moses' wife and Steve Martin as a court magician.

Add this together and "The Prince of Egypt" could be a box-office hit as well as a useful tool for parents who want to make biblical events vivid for today's youngsters.

This said, however, it's too bad the movie doesn't delve more profoundly into its themes.

Take a statement by DreamWorks chief Jeffrey Katzenberg in the movie's publicity notes. "I'm sure there are those who think we're nuts for choosing a Bible story as our first animated feature," the executive says. "But the fact is, this is a great emotional story about a remarkable man who must come to terms with his past, his heritage, and his faith" as well as "the extraordinary relationship between two brothers" drawn into conflict.

There's a lot there about feelings and psychology and heroism, but not much about spirituality. The same syndrome rings through the picture's ad campaign: "Two men, brothers and princes of the greatest empire on earth. A lie made them brothers, but the truth will destroy a dynasty and forever separate them."

This sounds like the sort of hype used to promote Cecil B. DeMille's version of "The Ten Commandments" more than 40 years ago, not to mention dozens of other biblical epics before and since.

It reminds us of Hollywood's willingness to appropriate any and all material for show-business purposes. But it doesn't indicate much depth in the studio's idea of what it wanted to accomplish.

Katzenberg and his partners, Steven Spielberg and David Geffen, might reply that a studio's main goal must always be entertainment, and if a movie can point out worthwhile ideas along the way, that's just a bonus. But this begs the question of why biblical stories are important in the first place.

The history of Moses hasn't gripped hearts and minds for thousands of years simply because, to quote Katzenberg it has "strong emotional journeys; something wonderful about the human spirit; good triumphing over evil," and the like.

All of that can be found in "A Bug's Life" and DreamWorks's own "Antz," among countless other pictures.

It's because of its spiritual dimension that generations have studied, contemplated, and been guided by the Bible in ways that Hollywood's mass-market approach can hardly comprehend.

None of which means "The Prince of Egypt" is not a lively, colorful cartoon that will please many moviegoers, especially in its most ingenious scenes when an Egyptian frieze springs to chilling life with the story of the escape of Moses from early death, for instance. Or when arrogant wizards sing a sardonic number called "Playing With the Big Boys" in the Pharaoh's palace. Still, "The Prince of Egypt" too rarely rises to the lofty challenge of its subject matter. Children may enjoy it and learn from it, but older folks would spend their time more profitably with the book it is based on.

LOS ANGELES TIMES, 12/18/98, Calendar/p. 1, Kenneth Turan

As the slaves of Egypt worked for years building impressive monuments along the Nile, so the hordes of considerably better paid workers at DreamWorks labored mightily (318,000 hours of rendering time for the seven-minute parting of the Red Sea alone) to create "The Prince of Egypt," the animated retelling of one of the Bible's greatest hits—the saga of Moses and the liberation of the Hebrews from bondage to Pharaoh.

From the point of view of the sheer spectacle of animation, the time was certainly well-spent. Using both computer-generated and traditional methods, the 400-member-strong "Prince of Egypt" team (led by directors Brenda Chapman, Steve Hickner and Simon Wells and ramrodded by executive producer Jeffrey Katzenberg) have created a succession of visual wonders.

Even Cecil B. DeMille, who parted those waters twice in silent and sound versions of "The Ten Commandments," would likely be won over by this animated attempt, and miracles like a pillar of fire are potent enough to turn atheists into believers.

Equally impressive is the sense of scale and space the workers have given ancient Egypt. Apparently helped by a new piece of software that combines 2-D and 3-D animation in the same frame, "Prince of Egypt" creates buildings so immense and breathtaking they're capable of inducing vertigo as the camera tours us through them.

But even in an animated feature, visuals alone, no matter how successful, are not enough. And despite having this sturdy biblical tale to work with, despite being faithful enough to the spirit of the story to please a wide swath of scholars and theologians, the creators of "Prince of Egypt" have been unable to relate it in a completely compelling way. Perhaps inevitably, the film's modernizations have distanced the story from its birthright of biblical power.

Much has been made of "Prince of Egypt's" attempts to do without what's become the expected musical comedy structure for modern animation. While cute animal sidekicks have been banished, having a complete lack of humor was apparently unthinkable, so Steve Martin and Martin Short were brought in to voice a pair of wacky Egyptian high priests, Hotep and Huy.

What "Prince of Egypt" also decided it couldn't do without is musical numbers. The film's seven songs, written by Stephen Schwartz with music by Hans Zimmer, are acceptable, but not even vocal talent like the haunting Israeli singer Ofra Haza can make these interludes as memorable as we'd like them to be.

Also problematical is the way this Old Testament story is structured to fit into what's become standard animation forms. We have Tzipporah (Michelle Pfeiffer), the future bride of Moses, turned into a feisty protofeminist who takes no guff from the male sex. And by changing the woman who discovers the baby Moses from the Pharaoh's daughter to his wife (Helen Mirren), the stage is set for having the plot turn on sibling rivalry plus classic father-son conflicts between the Pharaoh Seti (Patrick Stewart) and both blood son Rameses (Ralph Fiennes) and adopted son Moses (Val Kilmer).

Then there's "Prince of Egypt's" penchant for modern, colloquial dialogue. Amid all this visual pomp and splendor, it's disconcerting to have the royal family of Egypt act and sound like the folks next-door. It's not clear that we really want a Moses who walks around the palace saying, "This place, so many memories," and confronts the troubled new Pharaoh with an empathetic "Rameses, please, talk to me."

(Interestingly enough, "Prince of Egypt" does not have a "screenplay by" credit. Under the "story" category, Philip La Zebnik is listed as "writer" and Nicholas Meyer has an "additional screenplay material" credit, but it seems likely that the writing of this film was a kind of collaborative event.)

The film's most effective song is probably its first one, "Deliver Us," which capably sets up the situation of weary Hebrews slaving under the lash of the Egyptians and Moses' mother responding to a wave of infanticide by setting her baby afloat on the Nile.

We catch up to Moses and Rameses when they've become high-spirited young men, prone to damage-causing chariot races and in general acting very much like two irrepressible, irresponsible fraternity brothers at a large Middle Eastern university.

A chance encounter with the captive Tzipporah eventually leads Moses to secret siblings Miriam (Sandra Bullock), another strong woman, and the ambivalent Aaron (Jeff Goldblum). Moses is not happy to hear he's a Hebrew, but a terrifying dream (a bravura piece of animation the filmmakers call the "Hieroglyphic Nightmare") helps convince him.

Circumstances then force Moses to flee to the desert, where he runs into Tzipporah and her father, the jovial Jethro (Danny Glover), and has that celebrated encounter with a burning bush. That sends him back to Egypt to make the legendary request to stepbrother Rameses, the new Pharaoh in town, to let his people go.

One of the unexpected things this version of the biblical story does is create sympathy for characters you never gave a second thought to before. Pity poor Tzipporah,,who has to leave her family and schlep back to Egypt because her husband received marching orders from a bush. And what of the whipsawed Rameses, who couldn't be happier to see his long-lost stepbrother reappear, only to feel betrayed when it turns out his former boon companion has turned into some kind of religious zealot?

"The Prince of Egypt" does a strong job of putting the resulting 10 plagues on screen and is a serious enough venture to encourage viewers to read the original story in Exodus, a nice twist on the old "You've seen the movie, now read the book" campaigns. But if you've grown up on anything like the King James edition of the Bible, this "The Time Is Now" version of the story (as the advertising material refers to it) may be more up to date than you are prepared for.

NEW YORK, 12/21-28/98, p. 147, Peter Rainer

There's a lot of smiting and plaguing going on in *The Prince of Egypt*, but what really hurts is all the kitsch. This is DreamWorks' second bid to wrest the animation crown from Disney—the first was the computer-generated *Antz*, which recently went up against *A Bug's Life*. What return salvo can we now expect from Disney? An animated version of Freud's *Moses and Monotheism?* DreamWorks is claiming that *The Prince of Egypt* —which follows the lawgiver of lawgivers from the bulrushes to the Ten Commandments (but omits the golden calf)—is the first "adult" animated feature. (Nixing, I suppose, everything from *Fantasia* to the collected works of Ralph Bakshi.) What this means is that its "themes" are edifying. The lesson opens with an onscreen disclaimer: "While artistic and historical license has been taken, we believe that this film is true to the essence, values and integrity of a story that is a cornerstone of faith for millions of people worldwide." Guess we're not going to be seeing *Beavis and Butt-head Do Sinai*, eh? What the movie mostly resembles is one of those DeMille biblical epics minus the hoochie-koochie he worked in to show us what a terrible thing sin is. It should be noted that there *is* some skin on view in *The Prince of Egypt*, and, at least on the Egyptian side, it's remarkably aerobicized. This movie may not send people to the Book of Exodus, but there could be a run on Bally's Total Fitness.

Why should we applaud an animated feature for doing the same emptily monumental things as live-action directors? The visual elements of *The Prince of Egypt*—the way it seamlessly combines 2- and 3-D effects—are technically impressive. At least one sequence, the parting of the Red Sea, is a knockout. But in order to get at such moments, you have to listen to Moses fondly telling his brother Ramses, "I remember when you switched the heads of the temple of Ra," or endure the cheese-ball Stephen Schwartz score, with lyrics on the order of: "Deliver us—There's a land you promised us!" Deliver us, indeed.

NEW YORK POST, 12/18/98, p. 65, Rod Dreher

Rabbi A.J. Heschel had a phrase—"moral grandeur and spiritual audacity"—that gets at the heart of what keeps the mostly excellent "The Prince of Egypt" from reaching the Promised Land.

This gorgeous, brave, admirable film is an astonishing work of animation art—but its stellar artistic achievement is seriously undercut by a humdrum script that's like a contemporary translation of the Bible: all prose, no poetry.

DreamWorks SKG has taken great pains to distinguish "The Prince of Egypt," its maiden animation voyage, from the lucrative Disney standard. This story of Moses giving up his privileged life at Pharaoh's court and leading his enslaved Hebrew people out of exile is told with a reverence and sobriety that liberates animated film from the stifling Disney conventions—no cutesy camels here, thank God, and more darkness and complex characterization—while maintaining Disney's second-to-none animation standards.

Actually, "The Prince of Egypt" looks far better than any Disney animated film since "The Lion King." The screen comes alive with one vivid tableau after another, contrasting the cold splendor of ancient Egypt against the beggarly warmth of life among the Hebrews. Several scenes are worth the price of admission by themselves. These include an ingenious three-dimensional hieroglyphic sequence explaining Moses' origins, the plagues that afflicted the stubborn Egyptians, the Angel of Death passing over the land by night and a spectacular parting of the Red Sea that will make your hair stand on end.

The film begins with Moses' mother hiding him in the bulrushes to avoid Pharaoh's death edict on Hebrew babies. He is found, and raised as a prince of the royal court. The picture gets off to a roaring start with a "Ben-Hur"-like chariot race between young adult Moses (voice of Val Kilmer) and his brother, Pharaoh's heir, Rameses (Ralph Fiennes). The two are spoiled best friends—fun-loving, arrogant dandies—with Pharaoh's kingdom their playboy playground.

But when Moses discovers his Hebrew origins, he wrestles with his loyalty to his brother and his own vanity before leaving his life of luxury and privilege to suffer with his enslaved race. He marries a Midianite, Tzipporah (voice of Michelle Pfeiffer), and is commissioned by God, speaking through the fabled Burning Bush, to lead !he Israelites out of bondage.

Moses later clashes with Rameses, now Pharaoh, over the fate of the Hebrews. The film is commendably straightforward and unapologetic about Moses' role as a prophet of the true God, and demonstrates with visual majesty God's sovereignty over the Egyptian pseudo-deities. And the movie does not hold back darker material in an effort to pander to kids; the plagues are appropriately horrible, and the Angel of Death really does take the life of Egyptian firstborn.

For all its fine qualities, "The Prince of Egypt" is not quite un-Disney enough. Moses is still in the flower of his youth in this version, not the grizzled octogenarian of Exodus. We're smack in the middle of the hoariest Disney trope: how one individual can discover his value and make a difference. And that individual, owing to audience considerations, is usually a young person.

"I remember you when you switched the heads on the Temple of Ra," he tells Rameses in a moment of juvenile, "Cairo 90210" nostalgia. The flat, modern-sounding script, aided and abetted by Stephen Schwartz's lame songs, takes the mickey out of Moses. Absent the terrible majesty we behold in Charlton Heston's lurid but commanding Moses in "The Ten Commandments," the oddly passive prophet seems fairly inconsequential.

But there is that stunning finale on the far banks of the God-cleaved Red Sea, a catapulting moment that infuses you with a transcendent sense of wonder. This feeling, said Rabbi Heschel, is the beginning of authentic religion. It is too bad that there wasn't more of that sort of thing throughout "The Prince of Egypt." But you'll be glad you went all the same.

NEWSDAY, 12/18/98, Part II/p. B7, Jack Mathews

If you're thinking of using "The Prince of Egypt," DreamWorks' animated condensation of the story of Moses, as some sort of supervised Bible study for your uninitiated children, be prepared to answer some tough questions, on the spot!

For instance: "Why is God yelling?" "Why is God causing diseases?" "Why is God drowning men like rats?" And, most urgently, "Why is God killing kids?"

The answer, from the evidence presented here, is that God—on his best behavior, a burning bush—is mad as hell at the Egyptians for enslaving Hebrews and isn't going to take it anymore.

He has chosen Moses (voice of Val Kilmer), the adopted slave who grew up a son of the Pharoah Seti (Patrick Stewart). During his great run at Disney, Katzenberg announced that he wanted to test the appeal of animation for an older audience, and his newly assembled animation team, which includes many Disney veterans, made that a test by fire.

"The Prince of Egypt," with a budget estimated at $70 million, is Bible noir, featuring a melancholy hero who becomes the literal staff-bearer of a slave rebellion that will decimate the Egyptians, both innocents and tyrants alike. In fact, its tone of vengeance, and ultimate jubilation, may lead some armchair analysts to wonder how much of Katzenberg's inspiration came from his testy fallout with former pal and Disney boss Michael Eisner. Moses and Rameses.

The problem with "Prince," at least as an animated film, is inherent in the material. The Old Testament is not exactly a paradigm of political correctness, and despite the happy ending for the liberated Hebrews, the story of Moses is one of its more brutal chapters. It's a story that needs time, and a lot of context.

Cecil B. DeMille, combining patience and context, along with plenty of movie star sex appeal, took 3 hours and 40 minutes to tell the story in his 1956 "The Ten Commandments." "The Prince of Egypt," with the most cursory development of its major characters, skims over the bloody saga in a brisk 90 minutes.

Acknowledging its historical and creative liberties in an opening disclaimer, "Prince" starts, as did "The Ten Commandments," with the mother of Moses placing the baby in a cradle and setting him adrift on the Nile. Better to let him take his chances with hungry crocodiles and hippos than face certain death at the hands of the Egyptians.

The film's most child-friendly scenes follow, with the spirited Moses and his brooding adoptive brother Rameses (adult voice by Ralph Fiennes) roughhousing with each other, and in the film's most exhilarating animation sequence, nearly tearing down the sphinx during a wild chariot race over the monument's scaffolding.

But after Moses learns his true identity, rejoins his people and gets his marching order from God, "Prince" plunges into the vicious cycle of threat, violence and retaliation.

There is little comic relief along the way. No cute animals, except for a lumbering, disinterested camel. No children, save those in imminent peril, like Egypt's condemned first-born sons (among them, Moses' would-be nephew). And there are no clever sidekicks, though a pair of panicky court magicians, voiced by Martin Short and Steve Martin, vaguely serve the tradition.

No question, DreamWorks can compete qualitatively with Disney; the animation and music for "Prince" are first-rate. But this seems an odd, if not downright foolhardy, diversion from classic animated storytelling. The magic, whether it's the parting of the Red Sea or a storm of burning hail, is more frightening than bedazzling, and the big musical numbers—one coming after a plague, another after the drowning of the Egyptian pursuers—are morbidly celebratory.

In the end, "Prince" is a movie aimed at a target that may not exist. It's too deep for young children, and not deep enough for adults, and for those in between, there's "Mortal Kombat."

SIGHT AND SOUND, 1/99, p. 54, Leslie Felperin

Ancient Egypt, biblical times. The Children of Israel, slaves in Egypt, grow restless and sing of a deliverer. To quell their spirits, the Pharaoh Seti orders a cull of their children. An Israelite woman sets her son Moses adrift in the Nile in a rush basket to save his life. He is found and adopted by the Queen and grows up thinking himself a blood-brother of Rameses, the heir to the throne.

Moses meets a slave girl, Miriam, who recognises him as her brother. At first disbelieving, Moses learns she speaks the truth. While intervening on behalf of a slave being whipped, Moses accidentally kills an overseer. He wanders in the desert where he remeets a nomadic shepherd woman, Tzipporah, and her family. Moses and Tzipporah marry. Years later, God, the Deity, tells Moses to go back to Egypt and deliver his people. In Egypt Rameses is now Pharaoh. Moses reveals his birth to Rameses and confronts him about the slaves; to prove the power of God, he turns the Nile to blood. Rameses refuses to free them, and God sends via Moses eight more plagues, but only after the tenth, which kills all the first born of Egypt, does Rameses let the Israelites go.

Moses leads his people out of Egypt. At the Red Sea, God parts it so they can cross. Rameses, having changed his mind, pursues the Israelites with his army, but as soon as all the Israelites are ashore, the sea washes back, wiping out the army. The Israelites wander in the desert until they reach Mount Sinai where Moses brings down to them the Ten Commandments, as writ by God.

Once prominent features on the shoreline of Hollywood and the Italian film industry alike, biblical epics have been all but subsumed under the tide of secular films since the 50s. Back then, they were the ultimate literary adaptations: kudos-winning stories of such impeccable pedigree they justified the expense of producing them, while they could also be guaranteed to make back their money internationally, appealing to America's bible-belt and Australasia's Koran-cape alike. And because of their grand scale, biblical epics were ideal for showcasing new film making techniques, from colour to widescreen ratios.

So it makes sense for DreamWorks to choose to resurrect the genre in animated form, thus furthering the company's international box office ambitions and demonstrating its achievements in animation. Given the very different religious sensibilities of today, it also makes sense that DeMille's *The Ten Commandments* is more of a touchstone for *Prince of Egypt* than the Bible itself. The sequence when Pharaoh talks to a young Moses at the palace with his monuments behind him is an almost exact reconstruction of a scene from the 1956 film. Animation can even go one better by lining up Seti's profile exactly with the statue in his honour, underscoring the egotism of his project. And while this film pulls back from including the orgiastic golden calf sequence (its outcome presumably too much of a downer for today's audience), one team obviously had a ball pulling together the montage of the ten plagues—even cattle murrain!

Certainly technically-minded cartoon connoisseurs will feel many shivers of admiration on seeing this. It's almost impossible to tell the difference between computer-generated effects (used to produce travelling scenery shots in a chariot race, a wonderful St. Elmo's fire like burning bush sequence and the Red Sea parting) and the more traditional techniques that create the characters. Though the svelte figures are generally less cutsified than those in, say, *Mulan*, the overall visual methodology isn't markedly different from Disney's. Executive producer Jeffrey Katzenberg was ultimately responsible for the cohesive look of Disney animation from the early 80s, a form-following-function aesthetic that gave each film a distinctive and apt visual signature. He and his team pursue the same strategy here, going for a monumentality that fits the story well and certainly induces some sense of religious awe. Backgrounds dwarf the figures in imposing landscapes, suggesting the scale of this empire and the onerous task of constructing it, but also seeming to mimic a God's-eye view, watching Moses grow up from afar in the palace he shares with his 'brother' Rameses. Where Katzenberg and Co could have been a bit more ambitious is in the use of music. If they really are trying to take the form upmarket and target an all ages audience, something a little more mature than the usual hokey show tunes would have been welcome. Perhaps they should have taken a tip from Martin Scorsese, one of the few US film makers to pursue religious themes in contemporary cinema *(The Last Temptation of Christ, Kundun)* and commissioned a score by Philip Glass.

VILLAGE VOICE, 12/22/98, p. 127, J. Hoberman

Very nearly as solemn as a big-studio, megamillion-dollar Broadway musical cum animated cartoon about slavery, mass murder, and the word of God could possibly be, Prince of Egypt is constrained by an 11th commandment: Thou shalt not animate a singing camel. The only miracles found in Jeffrey Katzenberg's Moses story are those described in the Bible. As the producer told *Time*, "We've edited God, but we have not rewritten him."

Religious injunctions against graven images aside, *Prince of Egypt* is literal-minded enough for all but the most dogged fundamentalist. As entertainment goes, however, this desert spectacle is no *Aladdin*— despite the impressively strong graphics of the vast urban spaces. (The forced perspective and theme decor of this ancient Egypt reproaches even the most elaborate Las Vegas hotel.) The animation is more than credible, with the movie structured around a number of highly designed set pieces—the opening dance of the mud turtles, the crazy vicissitudes of the basket en route to the reeds, the sibling-rivalry chariot race swiped from *Ben-Hur*. The most original passage animates hieroglyphic wall paintings in the service of a historical flashback in which Moses discovers that his adoptive father, Pharaoh Seti, had slaughtered the Hebrew first-born.

A willowy Egyptian queen and an extravagant rope of dromedary drool aside, though, the character animation is more stilted than the statuary, while the characterizations themselves are scarcely more lively. With an uncharacteristically self-effacing Val Kilmer providing a voice for the angular, brooding moses, Patrick Stewart dubbing Seti, and Ralph Fiennes supplying Rameses's plummier tones, *Prince of Egypt* continues the traditional American-freedom-fighter-versus-British-despot arrangement of Hollywood ancient-world epics. The Burning Bush (uncredited) aside, Moses gets his marching orders from the benign and jolly Jethro (Danny Glover), who cuts a Tevya-esque caper and advises the melancholy ex-prince that he "must learn to join the dance."

This homage to *The Lion King* notwithstanding, *Prince of Egypt's* weakest aspect is Stephen Schwartz's stale, sub-*Godspell* score—filled with simpering ballads and tremulous inspirationals. The movie is bold enough to cap the 10 plagues with a burst of fireworks over the Nile and the two brothers singing a duet. (Moses: "You must let my people..." Rameses: "I will never let your people..." Together: "GO!") But the timid Semitic motifs and belated gospel reprise only underscore the blandness. There is no bread of affliction in the Katzenberg Haggadah and that little Hebrew song the slave children sing as they exit Egypt is no "Had Gadyo."

Even the climactic Red Sea parting only serves to confirm Cecil B. DeMille as the master of Biblical hokum. (Unlike Katzenberg, DeMille had a taste for a juicy villain: Edward G. Robinson's renegade sneering "Where's your God now, nyaaah," or Anne Baxter's temptress sighing "Moses, Moses, Moses, you adorable fool!") There will be no dancing around the golden calf here. Still, *Prince of Egypt* has retained a couple of pagan high priests (Steve Martin and Martin Short) to remind us how much religion owes show business. The only truly comic number has the pair frolicking about mid sound-and-light show, taunting Moses for his no-frills staff-to-snake act: "So you think you've got friends in high places... you're playing with the big boys now!" The sequence suggests that while Katzenberg was trying to figure out how to make his Egyptians theologically and politically correct, his animators were studying the "Pink Elephants on Parade" number from *Dumbo*.

Rather than Jerry Falwell, I'd have had the production vetted by Carl Reiner and Mel Brooks. Indeed, it was only when those big stone tablets materialized in Moses's arms just before the end-credits that I realized I'd been watching the prequel to *Raiders of the Lost Ark*.

Also reviewed in:
CHICAGO TRIBUNE, 12/18/98, Friday/p. A, Michael Wilmington
NEW YORK TIMES, 12/18/98, p. E17, Janet Maslin
NEW YORKER, 12/28/98 & 1/4/99, p. 140, Anthony Lane
VARIETY, 12/14-20/98, p. 130, Glenn Lovell
WASHINGTON POST, 12/18/98, p. D1, Stephen Hunter
WASHINGTON POST, 12/18/98, Weekend/p. 51, Michael O'Sullivan

PROPOSITION, THE

A PolyGram Filmed Entertainment release of an Interscope Communications production. *Executive Producer:* Lata Ryan.   *Producer:* Ted Field, Diane Nabatoff, and Scott Kroopf. *Director:* Lesli Linka Glatter.   *Screenplay:* Rick Ramage.   *Director of Photography:* Peter Sova. *Editor:* Jacqueline Cambas.   *Music:* Stephen Endelman.   *Music Editor:* Lori Eschler Frystak. *Sound:* T. J. O'Mara.   *Sound Editor:* Victoria Rose Sampson.   *Casting:* Johanna Ray and Elaine J. Huzzar.   *Production Designer:* David Brisbin.   *Art Director:* Kenneth A. Hardy.   *Set Designer:* Adam Scher.   *Set Decorator:* Tracey Doyle.   *Special Effects:* Brian Ricci.   *Costumes:* Anna Sheppard.   *Make-up:* Jeff Goodwin.   *Stunt Coordinator:* Paul Marini.   *Running time:* 114 minutes.   *MPAA Rating:* R.

CAST: Kenneth Branagh (Father Michael McKinnon);   Madeleine Stowe (Eleanor Barret); William Hurt (Arthur Barret);   Neil Patrick Harris (Roger Martin);   Robert Loggia (Hannibal Thurman);   Blythe Danner (Syril Danning);   Bronia Wheeler (Sister Mary Frances);   Ken Cheeseman (Wayne Fenton);   Jim Chiros (Timothy);   Dee Nelson (Susan Vicar);   Pamela Hart (Skip Taylor);   Wendy Feign (Maid);   Dossy Peabody (Hannibal's Secretary);   Tom Downey

(Torrey Harrington);   Tom Kemp (Arthur's Chauffeur);   Josef Sommer (Father Dryer);   Frank Toste (Father Frank Timothy);   David Byrd (Dr. Jenkins);   Lawrence Bull (Butler Captain); Michael Bradshaw (Butler);   Willy O'Donnell (Andre);   Frank T. Wells (Coroner).

LOS ANGELES TIMES, 3/27/98, Calendar/p. 10, Kevin Thomas

There ought to be a law: A movie as thunderingly bad, as deliriously preposterous as "The Proposition" should at least be fun instead of a dreary, dragged-out bore.

You have to wonder what a ludicrous and lurid period soap opera is doing up there on the big screen in the first place. You wonder even more how its makers attracted such a large and prestigious cast headed by Kenneth Branagh, Madeleine Stowe and William Hurt and including Blythe Danner, Robert Loggia and Josef Sommer.

You might also have thought that Boston high society tear-jerkers went out with Olive Higgins Prouty—of course, the various films of her "Stella Dallas" and "Now, Voyager" will still resonate long after "The Proposition" is forgotten.

It's 1935 and Hurt and Stowe are among the Boston area's richest and most glamorous couples. (Think a Back Bay Henry and Clare Boothe Luce). He's a financier and she's an emancipated woman who writes novels that get banned in Boston, natch. They are madly in love, live in a brick colonial-style palace, but the one thing that would make their happiness complete eludes them: a child. Hurt is sterile, and Stowe wants to experience pregnancy, so adoption is out.

Their lives start to unravel spectacularly with Hurt's choice of a surrogate father, a bright but incredibly naive Harvard law grad (Neil Patrick Harris) who falls in love with the beautiful woman he's paid 25,000 (in 1935 dollars) to impregnate. (C'mon, artificial insemination was possible in 1935.) Soon to complicate matters massively is the arrival of Branagh, the son of Hurt's bitterly estranged London-based brother. Branagh has just been named an assistant priest in charge of charity programs to the church where Hurt and Stowe worship and which they support generously.

There's no point in outlining writer Rick Ramage's dizzying plot complications, real jaw-droppers every one of them. Now an R.W. Fassbinder or a Pedro Almodovar would have played Ramage's script for camp pathos and pitch-dark comedy, working up compassion for mere mortals caught up in absurd and drastic collisions of passion and fate.

What director Lesli Linka Glatter gives us is a clunky, grafted-on proto-feminist sensibility, an unyielding earnestness and an increasingly slow pace clogged further by Stephen Endelman's sticky, syrupy score. Not even David Brisbin's lush production design has any style or much authentic sense of period—the same goes for costume designer Anna Sheppard.

The one good thing you can say for this clinker is that while everyone else is acting their heads off, Hurt is giving us a beautifully, quietly defined man of strength whose love for his wife is truly profound. It's a wonderful, thoughtful performance wasted in the wrong movie.

NEW YORK POST, 3/27/98, p. 44, Larry Worth

Film fans should stock up on condolence cards for Kenneth Branagh, Madeleine Stowe and William Hurt. The ultra-talented thespians embarrass themselves beyond belief in "The Proposition."

Plain and simple, it's idiocy on parade, what with a soap-opera script that makes the bed-hopping silliness of "Melrose Place" seem plausible.

The tall tale is told in flashback, after an aging priest (Branagh) hears about the death of his longtime nemesis, Boston elitist Arthur Barret (Hurt). The not-so-holy one then thinks back to 1935, when he and Arthur first crossed paths. More importantly, he crossed paths with Arthur's lovely wife, Eleanor (Stowe).

Of course, the Barrets have their own problems. Though wealthy beyond belief, they can't get around Arthur's sterility. Since forward-thinking Eleanor insists on carrying the family's heir, a young Harvard grad (Neil Patrick Harris) is hired for the dirty deed.

All that's well and fine, until the boy-toy falls hard for the mother of his child, threatening to expose their liaison to Beacon Hill bluebloods. That's just the beginning, as a nosy housekeeper with her own secrets (Blythe Danner), a scheming attorney (Robert Loggia) and a backup stud

(Tom Downey) enter the picture—along with murder, betrayal and enough coincidences per minute for a Guinness world record.

That might be OK, if director Lesli Linka Glatter was going for fun trash. But she's under the impression that this is serious filmmaking, even while ripping off everything from "The Thorn Birds" to "Rebecca." Therein lies the biggest joke—except for the cast.

Branagh is utterly miscast as a man of the cloth whose mind isn't on God. He's even worse when putting on his narrator's cap, with a sing-song style better suited to a library's story hour. Stowe also appears out of place, with her delivery and manner far too contemporary for the '30s.

William Hurt, meanwhile, goes the gloom-and-doom route as he merely skulks in dark corners. As for Danner and Loggia, they should thank the Lord they're only in supporting roles.

But how does one explain Neil Patrick Harris? TVs former "Doogie Howser" can't find his place in a world of grownup actors, here coming off like Doogie in dressup pants. It's pretty sad.

Clearly, "The Proposition" doesn't merit a second of thought. Just as clearly, that's all that went into it.

SIGHT AND SOUND, 11/98, p. 60, Andy Richards

Boston, 1935. Impotent lawyer Arthur Barret is desperate for an heir, Roger Martin is recruited by Barret's business partner Thurman to impregnate Barret's wife Eleanor. During their several meetings, Roger falls in love with Eleanor. Father McKinnon, newly appointed to Boston, dines at the Barrets. He reveals he is Barret's nephew. McKinnon is ashamed of his family name, particularly of his father's investment in Nazi Germany. Roger arrives at Barret's house, where he demands to see the now-pregnant Eleanor. Barret threatens to kill him if he returns.

Asked to meet Roger at a paupers' graveyard, Eleanor is shocked when she sees his body in an unmarked coffin. She falls into the grave and miscarries. Believing that her husband has had Roger murdered, Eleanor threatens to leave him. She confesses to McKinnon about Roger; they kiss. Syril, Barret's secretary and confidante, tells McKinnon that another surrogate will be arriving to impregnate Eleanor McKinnon breaks into the Barret house and makes love to Eleanor. She dies giving birth to twin boys. McKinnon immediately claims parentage, but overhears Syril confessing to Barret that she herself murdered Roger with arsenic. McKinnon allows Barret to have his children, in return for having Eleanor buried in the paupers' graveyard. Following Barret's death, McKinnon confesses the entire tale to Thurman.

The Proposition must, at some point, have seemed attractive enough on paper to garner its cast of high calibre talent. On the screen, however, the dubious and intermittent pleasures of the film derive from watching this same cast lurch through a series of ill-conceived, melodramatic set pieces, burdened with almost unendurably mannered dialogue.

In fairness, William Hurt preserves a certain dignified stoicism as the wealthy but impotent Arthur Barret, increasingly isolated through the misjudgements of others. Kenneth Branagh, however, seems entirely miscast as the compromised Father McKinnon, and his courtship scenes with Madeleine Stowe's Eleanor are particularly risible.

"Perhaps secrets aren't logical," McKinnon muses in his opening voiceover, almost as if apologising for the glaring narrative shortcomings to come. Indeed, the film's script has a lot to answer for, with certain pivotal scenes excruciating in their clumsiness—particularly Eleanor's fainting fall into Roger's open grave which causes the loss of her baby, and Syril's belated confession of murder. Contrivances of plot result in gross character inconsistencies: Neil Harris' Roger, following the loss of his virginity to Eleanor, shifts from wide-eyed, grovelling *ingénu* to brazen upstart, while Father McKinnon's cold-blooded denial of Barret's rights over Eleanor's children immediately following her death beggars belief.

In addition, the framing of the film's narrative as a confession by McKinnon to Thurman is nonsensical. (Thurman features directly in parts of the story where McKinnon is absent.) Unlike some more accomplished period dramas—for instance, *The Wings of the Dove* or *Howard's End*—Glatter's film only lazily alludes to a wider sociological context (the rise of Nazi Germany; the empowerment of educated women) to lend a spurious depth to its themes of betrayal and misplaced passion. In the end, the drab flatness of the film's visual style deprives the viewer of even the most basic cosmetic pleasure afforded by the weakest costume drama.

Also reviewed in:
NEW YORK TIMES, 3/27/98, p. E29, Stephen Holden
VARIETY, 3/16-22/98, p. 69, Todd McCarthy

PSYCHO

A Universal Pictures and Imagine Entertainment release.   *Executive Producer:* Dany Wolf.
Producer: Brian Grazer and Gus Van Sant.   *Director:* Gus Van Sant.   *Screenplay:* Joseph
Stefano.   *Based on the novel by:* Robert Bloch.   *Director of Photography:* Christopher Doyle.
Editor: Amy Duddleston.   *Music:* Bernard Herrmann.   *Music Editor:* Kenneth Karman.   *Sound:*
Ron Judkins and (music) Shawn Murphy.   *Sound Editor:* Kelley Baker.   *Casting:* Howard Feuer.
Art Director: Carlos Barbosa.   *Set Designer:* Tim Beach, Kristen Davis, Nicole Koenigsberger,
and G. Victoria Ruskin.   *Set Decorator:* Rosemary Brandenburg.   *Set Dresser:* Rhonda Paynter,
Ed Protiva, Glenn Roberts, Kris Fuller, Steven Ladish, Kelly Berry, and Jay Smith.   *Special
Effects:* Erick Brennan.   *Costumes:* Beatrix Aruna Pasztor.   *Make-up:* Elaine Offers.   *Special
Effects Make-up:* Matthew Mungle.   *Body Make-up:* Nadege Schoenfeld. *Stunt Coordinator:*
Mickey Giacomazzi.   *Running time:* 100 minutes.   *MPAA Rating:* R.

CAST: Vince Vaughn (Norman Bates);   Anne Heche (Marion Crane); Julianne Moore (Lila
Crane); Viggo Mortensen (Sam Loomis);   William H. Macy (Milton Arbogast);   Robert Forster
(Dr. Simon);   Philip Baker Hall (Sheriff Chambers);   Anne Haney (Mrs. Chambers);   Chad
Everett (Tom Cassidy);   Rance Howard (Mr. Lowery);   Rita Wilson (Caroline);   James Remar
(Patrolman);   James Legros (Car Dealer);   Steven Clark Pachosa (Police Guard);   O.B. Babbs
(Mechanic);   Flea (Bob Summerfield);   Marjorie Lovett (Woman Customer);   Ryan Cutrona
(Chief of Police);   Ken Jenkins (District Attorney).

CHRISTIAN SCIENCE MONITOR, 12/11/98, p. 15, David Sterritt

The new version of "Psycho" is the latest example, but the scenario has happened many times
before.

It goes like this. A new Hollywood movie is heading our way, and advertisements have been
trumpeting its praises for weeks. But audiences know that a good promotional campaign doesn't
equal a good movie, so on opening day they pick up a newspaper or tune in a broadcast to find
out what the critics think. And the critics don't think anything at all, for the excellent reason that
they haven't seen the picture, which wasn't previewed by its studio on the theory that no reviews
are preferable to the bad reviews its expected to receive.

This doesn't happen every month, but it seems to be occurring more often than it used to. A
recent instance is "The Avengers," a big-budget romp with major stars and stylish characters
drawn from a popular TV show. It promised to be a sure-fire conversation piece, at the least, yet
Warner Bros. refused to screen it in advance, apparently hoping to keep its failings a secret until
the last moment.

But critics eagerly told their readers, viewers, and listeners all about the no-preview policy, a
sure sign that the movie's own makers considered it a loser. The critics then bore out their own
prophecy, making a beeline for the first public showing and panning the picture with uncommon
enthusiasm.

The story of the new "Psycho" is slightly more complicated, since Universal spread the word
that Alfred Hitchcock refused to preview the original version before its 1960 premiere. Like most
excuses, however, this one is less than convincing. It's true Hitchcock orchestrated the premiere
of "Psycho" with exquisite precision, and it's true he kept the picture's content a secret so he
could spring it on the public with maximum impact But he was releasing a movie that held
extraordinary, unprecedented surprises, including a history-making scene that killed off the main
character with shocking abruptness less than halfway through the story.

The new version doesn't hold any such novelties, precisely because almost every moviegoer has
seen, or partly seen, or at least heard about the original.

If the executives at Universal thought they had a similar success on their hands, they would surely have previewed the daylights out of it, if only to gather blurbs for the "quote ads" that have become a woefully predictable part of marketing movies. The fact that they hid the picture speaks volumes about their confidence in it.

Those executives could be mistaken, of course, turning their backs on a movie that's better or more challenging or daring or innovative than they're capable of recognizing.

But sad to say, that's not the case with the new "Psycho." It's so slavishly similar to its predecessor—right down to the symbolic lettering on Marion's license plates—that there's little to spark fresh discussion except the acting. Here the news is mixed.

Anne Heche and Viggo Mortensen are adequate as Marion and her boyfriend, but Vince Vaughn doesn't have a shred of Anthony Perkins's demented magnetism. The best work comes from William H. Macy as the detective and Julianne Moore as Marion's feisty sister.

In the end, ifs hard to imagine why a smart and savvy filmmaker like Gus Van Sant would want to "re-create" this classic in the first place. There's nothing wrong with remaking a masterpiece if the goal is to put the story in a new context, a different time and place, exploring its relevance to new social and historical circumstances. Regrettably, the new "Psycho" doesn't attempt anything so ambitious.

Its occasional changes or additions, including more sexual explicitness attached to Norman's voyeurism, point less to Van Sant's inventiveness than to the diminished subtlety of Hollywood cinema. On this point, it's worth remembering that Hitchcock once claimed he filmed "Psycho" in black-and-white because a single shot in the picture, showing blood swirling down a drain, would have been too disgusting in color. The remake serves up buckets-full of bright red liquid, suggesting that disgust has become just another tool for imagination-starved studios.

LOS ANGELES TIMES, 12/7/98, Calendar/p. 1, Kenneth Turan

There's a word for Gus Van Sant's colorized version of Alfred Hitchcock's "Psycho," a word that so dominates today's marketing-driven movie culture it probably deserves to be written in capital letters. It's not sacrilege, not travesty, not profanation or desecration. The word is gimmick.

For though the "creative team" (a phrase that doesn't often deserve to be in quotes as much as it does here) behind it would have you believe that critics would be offended simply by the notion of redoing "Psycho," that's not the case. No film is a holy object, and certainly not those by Hitchcock, a director who blithely remade his own works, believed passionately in being commercial and liked nothing better, he once said, than playing the audience "like an organ." It's not a crime against art or nature to do to "Psycho" what Gus Van Sant has done, it's simply boring, a waste of time and money, and doomed to be the failure it is.

If anything is troubling about this project it's the charlatanism involved, the attempt, which did not start off impressively at the box office (the opening weekend was $ 10.5 million), to dupe the public into thinking they're getting something they're not. By the same token, what is interesting about "Psycho" is the combination of forces that got it made, forces that neatly encapsulate what carries weight in today's Hollywood, what levers are most effective in getting things done.

If Gus Van Sant and producer Brian Grazer had simply said they were remaking "Psycho," the torrent of revenue-generating publicity they received would never have materialized. But calling it a shot-by-shot re-creation of what happens to unsuspecting Marion Crane (Janet Leigh in the original, Anne Heche here) when she checks in at the lonely Bates Motel was a superb piece of marketing, a gambit that gains in brilliance because at best it is only partly true.

Yes, I know, everyone in America has heard by now about the next-door-to-fetishistic care Van Sant took with "Psycho's" details. The license plate on Marion Crane's car is the same in both versions, the newspaper she buys is folded the same way, many of the scenes are shot just as Hitchcock did (largely wasting superb cinematographer Chris Doyle), and Van Sant has even hired an actor to impersonate Mr. H in his traditional cameo.

Yet, it hardly needs to be said, Hollywood being Hollywood, that despite the piously professed desire to do everything exactly as Hitchcock did (including no screenings for critics), no one felt constrained to stick to the original $ 800,000 budget (Grazer and Van Sant have given conflicting interviews on how the new film's $ 20-million-plus cost relates to the inflation-adjusted original figure) and no one offered to cut admission prices back to 1960s levels.

Similarly, so many details have been changed, some at whim (why a new house for Norman Bates, why a new neon sign for the motel, why give a murder victim a subliminal flashback?) and some to update things to make the story fit more snugly into the late '90s, that the conclusion is unavoidable that the filmmakers have felt free to call the film a re-creation when it suited them and equally free to ignore that dictum when it didn't.

Most of the updates have to do with giving "Psycho" the last thing it needed: a '90s sexual edge. While John Gavin as Marion's boyfriend Sam Loomis kept his pants on in the original, Viggo Mortensen displays an unclothed rear end here. The soundtrack of his opening meeting with Marion has been altered to add the sound of other couples having sex and, in the biggest departure of all, Vince Vaughn's Norman Bates is shown unmistakably masturbating while watching Heche's Marion Crane through his office peep hole.

Other modernizations create problems of their own. The amount of money Marion walks off with has been quite reasonably upped from $40,000 to $400,000, but in order to make that large sum fit in the same size envelope $40,000 did in 1960, it's shown to be composed of $1,000 bills. Unfortunately, those bills do not freely circulate the way $50s and $100s do, and in fact would never be accepted by the used car lot where Marion spends some of them.

One other change is especially troublesome. In the film's original black-and-white opening credits, the "written by" citation reads "Joseph Stefano based on the novel by Robert Bloch." In this version, which Stefano updated, only his name appears in the front credits, with Bloch relegated to a place in the final crawl. It's never too late, apparently, for Hollywood to disrespect an original author.

Yet, paradoxically, though this "Psycho" is most accurately thought of as a faithful remake, it does stick so close to the 1960 plot that there's no point in anyone who's already seen the original to see Van Sant's version.

"Psycho's" creative team talks grandly of its film being just like watching a classic piece of theater with a different cast, but unlike most plays that are revived, the dialogue is not, to put it mildly, what made "Psycho" a sensation. As a member of the opening-day audience 38 years ago, I well remember that it was the completely surprising nature of the film's unusual twists, not what anyone said, that made the experience memorable.

So what about audiences who've never seen "Psycho" before? Even for those innocents, the obstacles to taking pleasure in the new version are considerable.

For one thing, more than for most genres, the enjoyment of a scary movie is a function of its particular time and place. In 1960, prominent cast members didn't die a third of the way into a film, cross-dressers were not appearing on trash TV every other week, the sound of a flushing toilet could cause a censorship crisis, and the sight of Janet Leigh with her shirt off in the opening scene added an unnerving frisson to the film that not even total nudity could duplicate today. For today's younger audiences raised on gore-fests like "Scream," even the famous shower sequence is like weak tea.

Also, the often-overlooked cast dynamics that helped make "Psycho" successful have proved difficult to re-create. While Janet Leigh had no problem playing Marion straight on, Heche, an otherwise excellent actress, is completely at sea in trying to figure out this typically 1960 woman. And while Anthony Perkins as Norman Bates had a brilliant innocence about him, that's something Vince Vaughn, who can't resist tipping his hand with a menacing little laugh, hasn't come within hailing distance of duplicating.

Given that this masquerade version of "Psycho" really had no chance of satisfying any audience (only Bernard Hermann's exceptional score works the same way now as it did then, and that is not nearly enough), it took a combination of two of the most unstoppable forces in Hollywood to get it made.

Force One: A creative person with clout (Van Sant, just off the success of "Good Will Hunting") wanted to do it. To Van Sant, a graduate of the Rhode Island School of Design, the idea of following in the footsteps of Marcel Duchamp and Andy Warhol and doing a riff on a real object is understandably appealing. To him it was a goof, like using (and crediting) one of John Woo's kitchen knives when the props department could have gotten the same one from a cutlery store. And indulging his art school sensibility probably helped Van Sant to forget the awkward truth that "Good Will," though it captured America's heart, was about as aesthetically adventurous as a plain paper cup.

Force Two: One of Hollywood's smartest producers saw the chance to make something out of nothing. The savvy and market-wise Grazer realized at once that the notion of "Psycho" and its celebrated shower scene was embedded in our cultural consciousness, the same way "Batman" had been before it became a big-screen success story. If the film could be made for a price—which it was—and joined to a hip and clever ad campaign ("Check in. Relax. Take a shower."), a powerful opening weekend seemed like a safe bet.

Naturally, Van Sant's "Psycho" ends with an on-screen nod to Alfred Hitchcock, and it's interesting to speculate what the Master of Suspense would have thought. Turning in his grave would not be an option; if anything, Mr. H's commercial instincts would lead to a tip of the hat in Grazer's direction. If Hitchcock actually had to watch the film, his reaction would probably parallel the viewer who said, puzzlement in his voice as Friday's first show ended, "Why bother?" Why indeed.

NEW YORK, 12/21-28/98, p. 148, Peter Rainer

Just about the only thing I got from watching Gus Van Sant's virtual shot-for-shot and line-for-line re-creation of Hitchcock's *Psycho* was a strong desire to revisit the original. I purposely didn't dip into it before I checked out the new one, but an odd thing happens anyway: You replay Hitchcock in your mind on a parallel track. It's as if you were watching two movies—the one before you and the one you *wish* were before you. As anything but some kind of film-school poststructuralist experiment, Van Sant's version has no reason for being. Vince Vaughn's pallid creepiness makes you appreciate why Anthony Perkins scared the bejeepers out of everyone taking a shower for the next quarter-century. As the celebrated stabee, the highly gifted Anne Heche seems more uncomfortable with her role than with her character's predicament. Is it because she's required to act as a double for Janet Leigh, right down to the quaver in her voice? She's ultimately far more straitjacketed than Norman Bates.

NEW YORK POST, 12/5/98, p. 23, Rod Dreher

Gus Van Sant's retread of Alfred Hitchcock's "Psycho" isn't a bad movie, but it's a pretty pointless one. Van Sant set out to re-create Hitchcock's film shot for shot, line for line—with only slight tweaking. "It's more a replica than a remake," he told Entertainment Weekly magazine. Which begs the question: Why bother?

For the record, this "new" version is matchable, but it's not the least bit scary. If this is the first exposure young people have to "Psycho," they'll wonder what all the fuss was about. Truth to tell, after you learn Norman Bates' dark secret, the original "Psycho" isn't very scary, either.

The film reveals its psychological complexity only upon repeated viewings. Inasmuch as this version is a color imitation, the same applies, but it's hard to get past the feeling that you're being had.

Anne Heche re-creates the role of Marion Crane (Janet Leigh in the original). She's the secretary who steals a chunk of change from her office in hopes of buying her boyfriend out of debt. She fatefully stops at the Bates Motel, where a friendly mama's boy named Norman shows her the shower.

Big, burly Vince Vaughn simply won't do as Norman Bates. He can be a frightening guy, all right, but not in this role. Broad-shouldered Vaughn lacks the effete, clammy-palmed shiftiness that made Tony Perkins so unspeakably creepy; Vaughn also has such an authoritative presence you simply don't believe a guy like this could be a crippled slave of his ripe old mum.

The first mistake Van Sant made was to take on such a landmark of cinema history, a film that many, many people have seen and which utterly changed the course of horror-movie history. Violence had never before felt so intimate.

It's every bit as lunatic as trying to remake "The Godfather" or "Pulp Fiction," which are so ingrained in the public's consciousness as to be quite literally inimitable.

The second mistake was to have aped Hitch shot for shot. If you're going to be hubristic enough to remake "Psycho," you should at least have the courage to put your own spin on it, to draw on the techniques of horror filmmaking developed since 1960 in updating this classic tale. What's called for is not re-creation, but interpretation.

Absent anything fresh or new, you have a half-decent film that owes anything impressive about it to the original. If you see it, you will be entertained—but why should you bother? This ersatz "Psycho" is "Beatlemania" for Hitchcock fans.

NEWSDAY, 12/7/98, Part II/p. B3, Jack Mathews

If the words "shower scene" and "Bates Motel" have no meaning for you, welcome to our world. We're the third rock from the sun, Planet Hollywood, and we have a god we hold dear named Alfred Hitchcock. To become one of us, you must now go to a store marked "Video" and ask for something called "Psycho," then find a place with handrails where you can watch it.

Whatever you do, do not go to a store that says "Now Playing: "Psycho." That would be an impostor, a forgery, a fake, a replica, or worse, a remake! That would be Gus Van Sant's "Psycho," an inexplicably confident, scene-by-scene homage to the master's 1960 horror classic. Van Sant's is a movie that manages to be identical to its source without being any good at all. One wonders, in watching Anne Heche, Vince Vaughn, Viggo Mortensen, Julianne Moore and William H. Macy reprise the roles of Janet Leigh, Anthony Perkins, John Gavin, Vera Miles and Martin Balsam, what was going through their heads. Not while they were acting, but when they were accepting the roles.

There was, their agents might have informed them, no room in this project for interpretation, expansion or psychological development of their characters.

Their dialogue is a near-verbatim lift from Joseph Stefano's original script, and though it occasionally allows a line that was vaguely suggestive in 1960 ("I'll lick your stamps," Leigh said to a fully dressed Gavin) to become a full-blown vulgarity in 1998 ("I'll lick your stamps," says Heche, with a gesturing glance at a naked Mortensen), there's little leeway. The actors are asked to hit the same marks, strike the same poses, use the same inflections. Even the camera movements—the tracking, dolly and crane shots—and the editing are identical.

The film (curiously enough, in color) takes place in December, 1998, and at least one of the characters, Sam Loomis, has been logically revamped. Gavin, a darkly handsome and oakly wooden actor whose best role—as a U.S. ambassador—was still ahead of him, was completely unconvincing as both an ardent lover and a hardware store clerk. The Mortensen version is more of an urban cowboy, and in that opening hotel room scene, he does give Marion more credible motivation for robbing her boss' client and making a run for it.

Otherwise, it's the same film, without the same kicks.

That heralded shower is reproduced cut-by-literal-cut. The death of a private detective at the knife-wielding hand of Ma Bates at the top of the stairs is done with identical effects. Moore's Lila Crane, searching the Bates' dilapidated mansion for her sister, follows the same path as predecessor Miles, from bedrooms to attic to fruit cellar, and to the same discovery.

Of the cast members, Vaughn has the most impossible task, and he doesn't have a fraction of the psychotic dimension Perkins brought to the role. But it's almost irrelevant to compare the casts, since there was no creative room for either, and because no remake of a revered film can recreate the innocence of the original audience.

When "Psycho" was released in 1960, there was an immediate national conspiracy. People who'd seen it refused to reveal its secrets to anyone who hadn't. The jolts from its three shocker scenes were gifts to moviegoers who looked to horror films to not only cure their hiccups, but to blast the plaque out of their arteries.

And a big part of that magic was Hitchcock's casting of Leigh, then a major star, as the doomed heroine. Stars simply did not die midway through movies in those days, certainly not while she and the audience were enjoying her shower. Nor did movies restart halfway through with new characters, as "Psycho" is compelled to do after she's gone.

Speaking of showers, we'd be remiss not to acknowledge the Universal Pictures executives who have been sent to theirs for an 18-month slump that merely culminates with "Psycho." As they consider projects in their uncertain future, they could do worse than follow the logic of the film's detective, Armogast.

"If it doesn't jell, it isn't Jell-O."

SIGHT AND SOUND, 2/99, p. 36, Gavin Smith

Gus Van Sant's remake of Alfred Hitchcock's canonical 1960 film *Psycho*—in which thief-on-the-lam Marion Crane (Janet Leigh in the original, Anne Heche here) is murdered by hotel-owner Norman Bates (Anthony Perkins then, Vince Vaughn now)—isn't the self-defeating, perverse exercise it might seem at first glance. It's more a work of 'metacinematic' research. By remaking *Psycho*, the film-makers have managed to replay formally notions of transgression and difference that manifested themselves in Hitchcock's original as themes and subtexts. So Van Sant's *Psycho* is both more and less than a remake. More in the sense that it literalises the notion of remaking by copying or transcribing Hitchcock's 1960 film, less in that it denies the standard remake strategy which demands that the remake transcend its origins by revision *(Cape Fear, Scarface)*.

On the contrary, Van Sant's *Psycho*, with its ritualistic attention to detail, could be described as a re-enactment or, as he has suggested, as the equivalent of a cover version of a classic song. But critically, given that contemporary cinema has been permeated by the strategies and tactics of the original film, Van Sant can neither reproduce the effect Hitchcock's film had on its contemporary audience—its impact—nor escape the burden of its place in film history. If the theme of Hitchcock's *Psycho* is the terrible power of the past and how it blights the present, then it is doubly so for Van Sant—indeed this becomes the new *Psycho*'s organising principle. The weight of the past on the present and the loss of autonomy afflicting Norman Bates become Van Sant's point of departure for this radical project.

Director and cinematographer (Chris Doyle of *Chungking Express* fame) have imposed on themselves a set of extremely tight expressive constraints to minimise deviation from the original movie. Their film uses the same score, is more or less the same running time and, most crucially, employs the same screenplay. If anything, Van Sant's strategy is subtractive rather than additive. Although several anachronisms are wilfully permitted to survive, Joseph Stefano's original script has been subtly abridged and pared so that, despite several enigmatically superfluous added lines, there is even less dialogue here than in the already sparse original.

On the other hand, given that the original derived much of its power from its no-frills black-and-white shooting style, Van Sant's film is in colour and therefore has a completely different effect. And although many scenes are reproduced exactly, this is by no means a shot-for-shot remake. Many shots only approximate those in the original, and in general the pacing seems faster—dialogue is more clipped, shot duration more varied. In many instances, though, there are significant embellishments: the shower scene (from Marion stepping into the bathtub to Norman descending the house) is now a full minute longer and although many shots are identical, it includes a number of new images (a closeup of Marion's dilating pupil as she is stabbed, a blurred Marion's-eye-view of her killer departing; a fleeting, enigmatic image of billowing storm clouds). Van Sant and Doyle's shots, even those reproduced exactly from the original, seem comparatively casual and indefinite, lacking the starkness, deliberation and measurement of Hitchcock's. And the two films have completely different senses of space, particularly interior space. It is in such distinct yet unquantifiable differences that Van Sant's inquiry or research finds its form. The same is true of the film's determinedly muted, enervated tone and air of inconsequentiality.

Van Sant's *Psycho* is fundamentally an investigation of the expressive and thematic possibilities of nuance. Given the same script and more or less the same visual architecture, casting and direction of actors become key. Sure enough, Van Sant gets considerable mileage from the redeployment and reassignment of character values, enough to achieve a small but significant shift of meaning. Rather than using the modern equivalents, he selects actors who largely counter or contradict the original cast's qualities and associations. (Two exceptions: the perfect substitutions of William H. Macy for Martin Balsam as the private detective Arbogast, and Robert Forster in a bad hairpiece for Simon Oakland as the psychiatrist at the end of the film.)

Anne Heche, whose gay sexuality has become a matter of record, emphatically does not project the same sexuality that Janet Leigh brought to the role. Her Marion lacks Leigh's guilt, melancholy and mounting sense of entrapment. Where Leigh's Marion maintained a careful diplomatic distance from her boss' flirtatious client, Heche's Marion responds with ironic/sarcastic indulgence. Where Leigh is solemn, even grim, Heche is light, untroubled, almost breezy. Van Sant has reconceived her as someone lacking moral ballast and emotional complexity. Once alone in the motel room, she considers different hiding places for the money with the giddy excitement of a naughty child having fun. As a direct consequence of this comprehensive moral diminishment of Marion, Heche recedes as a screen presence in comparison with Leigh.

Conversely, Julianne Moore, as Marion's inquisitive sister Lila who comes looking for her, becomes a more commanding presence, giving the character more stature. More brusque in her dealings with her sister's lover Sam, and now delivering a *coup de grace* kick during the climactic struggle with Norman, she's more aggressively independent than Vera Miles' Lila. It's been suggested she's meant to be a lesbian, a reading perhaps substantiated by her dress style and several rebuffs of Sam's sexist arm around her shoulder. If so, this suggests a rethinking of *Psycho* as a kind of horrific farce of multiple sexual misapprehensions in which Norman's attraction to Marion is as unfortunate as Sam's to Lila.

Just as Marion's sexuality is suppressed in this version, Norman seems more outwardly normal: where Perkins is slim and frail, full of nervous movement, Vince Vaughn is a robust, grounded physical presence, more conventionally masculine, though with his babyface looks he exudes boyishness. In place of Perkins' stutter, he sports a vacant, nervous laugh. A Norman Bates with fewer outward indications of abnormality than originally, he becomes all the more subversive of and threatening to the prevailing heterosexual order, epitomised here by the smug hyper-masculinity of Viggo Mortensen's Sam, who sharply contrasts with the smooth but colourless assurance of John Gavin. Van Sant's Sam fondly pats the Gideon Bible in the motel room, but his right-wing credentials are certified by the gun and ammunition cases prominently displayed in his store.

These weapons are part of a chain of visual associations that extends from the toy soldiers, toy musket and poster of a Blackbird military reconnaissance plane in Norman's bedroom to the pictures of guns and military aircraft in the sheriff's office at the end. Although there is something psychologically unsatisfactory and pat in such an indictment of the fetishisation of violence and weaponry in gun-culture America, through these cult-of-violence symbols Van Sant subversively links the normative heterosexual authority represented by Sam and the sheriff with Norman's spoiled infantile sexual identity, striking a small blow against patriarchal values. Still, however low yield the shift in meaning Van Sant accomplishes proves to be, it's enough to justify the experiment: same film, different meaning. Where Hitchcock's Norman is conclusively Other, Van Sant's is one of us.

TIME, 12/14/98, p. 98, Richard Corliss

Remember the big masturbation in scene in Alfred Hitchcock's *Psycho*? The shot of a George Jones-Tammy Wynette record? The visions of a naked woman and a sheep during one of the murders? The spider crawling out of Mother Bates' mummified mouth? All these are in Gus Van Sant's new version of the 1960 horror classic—which suggests he hasn't been quite so slavish as expected.

But, yes, this is a nearly shot-by-shot recapitulation of the film and an almost verbatim rereading of Joseph Stefano's terrific screenplay. Why do it? One reason: it's never been done. Another: *Psycho*, which spawned a festering genre of slasher films, has been ripped off a zillion times—surely it can be remade just this once. And finally: let's set a test for today's actors, encrusted with decades of Method mannerisms. Can they assimilate the smooth delivery of the 1960 cast?

When *Psycho* first appeared, it was a shock. At first the picture seemed like a familiar Hitchcock melodrama of guilty escape: a woman, on the run with stolen money, stops for the night in a tatty motel, chats with the eccentric owner, takes a shower. And then, 44 minutes in, the movie goes a little mad. Exit leading lady, in a whirlpool of blood. New characters appear, are slaughtered or imperiled. What the hell is going on here? Audiences knew (it was one of Hitchcock's most profitable films), but the critics were annoyed, dismissive. It took a while for them to come around. In 1973 one critic (this one) chose *Psycho* as his all-time favorite film.

This time Anne Heche is the thief, Vince Vaughn is Norman Bates—two lonely people who want something from each other and, fatally, get it. Like some of the other actors here, Heche doesn't know the value of seductive repose; she's fidgety, shallow. But Vaughn (a taller, creepier Billy Crystal) understands Norman, his naive charm, his need to watch women, become them, then mete out punishment for the transgression. And William H. Macy is fine as the prying detective. But does any man still wear a hat these days?

Indeed, the whole film is in a style we'll call contempo-retro. It is beautifully shot by Christopher Doyle, who turns the puky green of motel lighting into a circle of Hell, and it features a busy sound track of rattlesnakes and buzzing flies—moral decay in the desert. Everything else is defiantly same-old. This *Psycho* is radical because it has not only the dialogue but also the tempo of a film almost 40 years old.

Modern viewers, used to up-front gore, may find all that subtle talk way too talky. Could we fast-forward to the bloody part? Or, better yet shall we go rent the original? Perhaps that was Van Sant's aim all along: to lead today's children back to a revolutionary masterpiece.

VILLAGE VOICE, 12/15/98, p. 141, J. Hoberman

Just to liquidate all remaining suspense: For all intents and purposes, Gus Van Sant really does "recreate" Alfred Hitchcock's *Psycho*—from the Saul Bass credits that open the movie to the glib psychological "explanation" that closes it—almost shot by shot with the original music.

Van Sant shoots in color, adds a few jokes, makes the autoerotic quality of Norman Bates's sex life a bit more apparent, suggests that one (or more) of the major characters may be queer, and discreetly jazzes up the celebrated montage sequences. The performances are competent if knowing. Elfin and expressive where Janet Leigh was voluptuously self-contained, Anne Heche imports an aura of transgression from her offscreen love life; Vince Vaughn's gestures are often exact copies of Anthony Perkins's, but, assured and physically imposing, he comes across as snide (and too well-dressed) rather than bashful. As the effect is less hyperreal than perversely fastidious, the response for anyone familiar with the original *Psycho* is likely to be restricted to a narrow range between briefly enjoyable déjà vu and mild disappointment. The movie lacks the chutzpah to even be a travesty.

Based on a novel inspired by the case of the Wisconsin cannibal-necrophiliac Ed Gein, the original Psycho represented a new attitude and a new permissiveness. The print ads showing Leigh in her slip and brassiere were a first for an American star. The opening scene was excitingly tawdry, the attitude daringly now. The monster was not Count Dracula from Transylvania but the sick product of an American family. Rather than a beautiful virgin, the victim was a beautiful, sexually active woman. The crimes were horribly graphic and yet the movie was some sort of comedy. Once seen, *Psycho* was even more unsettling for being an elaborate joke from first to last.

Indeed, arguably the most outrageously manipulative movie ever made, Psycho used P.T. Barnum hype to insist upon its aesthetic integrity. The ads famously promised that "No one... *but no one* ... will be admitted to the theater after the start of each performance." Patrons were enjoined against revealing the plot to the uninitiated. That, of course, is impossible now. If Van Sant's *Psycho* demonstrates anything, it's the degree to which movies are an individual experience largely determined (as used to be said of LSD) by "set and setting." I've seen *Psycho* at least 20 times, but I can still remember the shock of my initial viewing—even though the movie was by then nearly a decade old.

Those who first saw *Psycho* during the last weeks of June 1960 describe a unique atmosphere of excited dread. Nor did the movie disappoint them. *Psycho* featured not only an impressively sordid opening and a boffo shock climax, but a highly graphic (not to mention visceral) sex crime, the early exit of a star, and the first flush toilet in a Hollywood production. The plot was almost unsynopsizable. Not since Fritz Lang's *M* had a movie employed so lurid a "case history." Nothing in American movies had remotely suggested a situation in which a nice young man (Perkins was then a teenage idol) lived in incestuous rapport with the preserved cadaver of his murdered mother. The movie inspired irate walkouts and even faintings. The audience response was an unexpectedly violent mixture of shrieks and laughter, while the repeat viewings by teenagers gave the screenings a ritual flavor.

The essence of *Psycho* is not the overrated shower sequence-except insofar as it was faithful to the lessons of Soviet montage theory in suggesting far more than it showed. (The murder of the detective is actually a more artful piece of editing.) The essence of *Psycho* is the way it systematically undermined movie conventions to disorient the viewer and thwart expectations. In this sense, *Psycho* is a descendant of another montage-based shocker, the venerable Buñuel-Dali joke, *Un Chien andalou*. In other words, while *Psycho* is a movie that can be taught, I'm not sure it can still be lived.

Van Sant's *Psycho* has been spun as a sort of Borges conundrum or an art-school Warhol appropriation. But the project's most Warholian aspect is its appreciation of a commercial gimmick. *Psycho* was not only Hitchcock's greatest hit; by some standards, it was the most profitable black-and-white movie since *The Birth of a Nation*. Universal had no need for press screenings when the title alone was worth a quick $10.5 million. Van Sant, however, would have had to cast *Psycho* grossly against type (Jerry Seinfeld as Norman Bates; Roseanne as Marion Crain) or transpose the action to Pleasantville or use some other sort of conceptual grid (cross-dressing, slow-motion) to illuminate the text in any compelling way.

Everything about the personal relations in the original Psycho suggests a present dominated by the dead hand of the past. So, too, Van Sant's movie. How well-made it seems. How powerful the music, economical the staging, creepy the premise, clever the mise-en-scène, crisp and confident the editing. How unfashionably leisurely the pace. Who needs actors?

The most paradoxical aspect of this recreation is its timid fidelity to a movie that smashed the commercial conventions of its day. Thus, Van Sant's *Psycho* is often surprisingly OK. It is, after all, still Psycho—just a superfluous and inferior version.

Also reviewed in:
NEW YORK TIMES, 12/5/98, p. B7, Janet Maslin
VARIETY , 12/7-13/98, p. 53, Godfrey Cheshire
WASHINGTON POST, 12/5/98, p. C1, Stephen Hunter

QUEST FOR CAMELOT

A Warner Bros. release.   *Producer:* Dalisa Cooper Cohen.   *Director:* Frederick Du Chau. *Screenplay:* Kirk DeMicco, William Schifrin, Jacqueline Feather, and David Seidler.   *Based on the novel "The King's Damosel" by:* Vera Chapman. *Editor:* Stanford C. Allen. *Music:* Patrick Doyle. *Songs:* David Foster and Carole Bayer Sager. *Music Editor:* Caoimhin Ó Criochain. *Choreographer:* Kenny Ortega. *Sound:* Christopher Boyes and Tom Myers and (music) Joseph Magee. *Sound Editor:* Alan Robert Murray and Dave Horton, Sr. *Casting:* Julie Hughes and Barry Moss. *Production Designer:* Steve Pilcher. *Art Director:* Carol Kieffer Police and J. Michael Spooner. *Animator:* Lennie K. Graves and Alyson Hamilton. *Running time:* 100 minutes. *MPAA Rating:* G.

VOICES: Jessalyn Gilsig (Kayley);   Andrea Corr (Kayley, Singing);   Cary Elwes (Garrett); Bryan White (Garrett, Singing);   Gary Oldman (Ruber);   Eric Idle (Devon);   Don Rickles (Cornwall);   Jane Seymour (Juliana);   Celine Dion (Juliana, Singing);   Pierce Brosnan (King Arthur);   Steve Perry (King Arthur, Singing);   Bronson Pinchot (Griffin);   Jaleel White (Bladebeak);   Gabriel Byrne (Lionel);   John Gielgud (Merlin);   Frank Welker (Ayden);   Sarah Rayne (Young Kayley).

LOS ANGELES TIMES, 5/15/98, Calendar/p. 2, David Kronke

Sheer fun in animation, it seems, died with Howard Ashman, the immensely gifted lyricist whose clever wordplay and anything-for-a-laugh rhyming made "The Little Mermaid," "Beauty and the Beast" and parts of "Aladdin" so enjoyable.

Since his death in 1991, animated features have become big business, but their spontaneity and sense of surprise have given way to manufactured awe. Films have been transformed from light Broadway musicals to full-blown heavier fare like "Lion King," "Pocahontas" and "Anastasia," with their new agey lessons and Sturm und Drang plagued characters. Recent attempts at straight-ahead humor such as "Hercules" have been hampered by the fact that they just weren't that funny.

Warner Bros. inaugurates its new feature animation division with "Quest for Camelot," a project that unfortunately seems a nearly perfect reflection of troubling trends in animated features. It's clearly concocted to recall and distill elements of recent animated successes—so much so, alas, that it lacks a distinct personality of its own.

Arthurian legend is kind of shunted to the side of the story here. Instead, the story concerns a standard-issue spunky female heroine named Kayley. Her father, one of the knights of the Round Table, was killed by the menacing Ruber, an imposing guy whose eye twitches whenever he's considering something really evil.

Kayley, aided by a young blind man named Garrett and a two-headed dragon named Devon and Cornwall who provide the requisite comic relief, must battle Ruber's monsters to make Camelot safe again. Garrett's blindness is the one adventurous element to the film, but even it seems calculated; his lack of sight is hardly debilitating, yet still provides kids a lesson in acceptance.

It seems obvious that the film was demographically structured so that the monsters would make really cool action figures for boys, while girls play with Kayley dolls and younger kids cuddle with plush Devons and Cornwalls.

A number of name performers are recruited for vocal contributions here, including Pierce Brosnan, Gary Oldman, Sir John Gielgud, Jane Seymour, Gabriel Byrne, Eric Idle, Don Rickles, Bronson Pinchot and Cary Elwes. Some are used fleetingly, others are unrecognizable and others just aren't that impressive; the point to using such brand-name talent seems a bit mystifying.

The songs here, by veteran tunesmiths David Foster and Carole Bayer Sager, are polished to the point of tedium. There's little sense of playfulness. Example: Ruber, the villain, uncorks a banal paean to evil: "Let's go back to war and violence/I'm so bored with peace and silence."

In another number, Garrett gravely intones, "All by myself I stand alone" (is there another way?). Then, Garrett and Kayley together proclaim, "Love took me by surprise/looking through your eyes." Apparently, Camelot is just one big adult contemporary radio station.

The kids with whom I saw "Quest for Camelot" were entertained but not wowed (too many songs, they complained) and spent much of the ride home playing critics, naming the cinematic precedents for much of what they saw. The 4-year-old said the story was a cross between "Anastasia" and "Hercules," and that Garrett looked like the post-Beast Prince in "Beauty and the Beast." The 8-year-old cited "The Lion King" as the inspiration for "Quest's" exotic musical opening, and referenced Devon and Cornwall practically back to Abbott and Costello. When filmmakers can't even convince children that their wares are fresh, a reassessment of creative goals may be in order.

Still, given Warners' venerable, wildly entertaining history in animation, it would be foolish to discount the new feature division out of hand. Consider "Quest for Camelot" a test run that shakes the bugs out of the system, and hope for the sort of anarchy that Bugs and his brood used to create in the future.

NEW YORK POST, 5/15/98, p. 52, Larry Worth

Disney doesn't have to worry about losing its No. 1 slot in 'Toon Town just yet. Not if "Quest for Camelot" is the best the competition can offer.

Basically, this tale of would-be knights and freaky two-headed dragons has the sophistication of a Saturday morning cartoon, with comparable songs and artistry.

On second thought, the simplistic drawings apply more to the characters' inexpressive faces. Far more detail went into the background visuals of dense forests, castle ramparts and moonlit nights.

Of course, the intended audience—kids—will care more about story than technique. Even then, the plot is pretty much by-the-numbers, mixing a spirited heroine, hunky love interest, dastardly villain and animal sidekicks, this time in an Arthurian setting.

Pretty little Kayley longs to buck the Round Table's ranks by becoming the first female knight. Her feelings intensify when Dad's killed by one of Arthur's rogue operatives, the evil Ruber.

Things come to a head years later when Ruber steals—then loses—Arthur's all-powerful sword. He then steals Kayley's mom, forcing the girl to wander through a haunted forest to find Excalibur.

Faster than she could sing "Over the Rainbow," the girl has paired up with a blind young hermit, a silver-winged falcon and a scaredy-cat dragon that talks out of two heads. It would take a pretty wonderful wizard to turn this into compelling cinema, and director Frederik Du Chau doesn't fill the bill.

Du Chau also fails to spark the vocal talents on board, with Cary Elwes, Gary Oldman, Jane Seymour, Pierce Brosnan, Jaleel White, Gabriel Byrne and Sir John Gielgud paling beside Don Rickles and Eric Idle's Abbott and Costello-like dragon.

More surprising still is that Carole Bayer Sager and David Foster's original songs barely register, despite the presence of Celine Dion, Bryan White, LeAnn Rimes and Steve Perry on the soundtrack. Part of the problem is the tunes' inappropriate placement, as when the arrow-pierced hero breaks into "Looking Through Your Eyes."

As such, a computer-generated ogre and animated sendups of everyone from Dirty Harry and Leatherface to Sonny and Cher are left to carry the day. In fairness, they're legitimate highlights, though their humor will be lost on younger viewers.

That makes "Camelot" a tale that's markedly short on magic, plain and simple. So where's Merlin when you really need him?

NEWSDAY, 5/15/98, Part II/p. B9, Bob Heisler

Be vewy, vewy quiet: We're hunting Excalibur.

There will be hipper animated features, from the new Warner Bros. cartoon-movie group, with more outrageous action and zany cultural references—"Animaniacs, the Movie"?—but things are off to an entertaining start with "Quest for Camelot," a seamless grafting of popular animated conceits and pop-anthem-like songs onto the legend of Camelot.

The most popular plot twist—see "Beauty and the Beast," among others—makes the hero a girl. Not just any girl, of course. Kayley (the pure, but spunky voice of Jessalyn Gilsig) wants to become a Knight of the Round Table, in part to avenge the death of her father at the hands of a renegade knight named Ruber (the sinister Gary Oldman), who never learned to share. This is a bad thing in Camelot, land of fairness and equality.

The quest has the proper heroic heft: Ruber and a band of grotesque mutant Swiss-Army-knife henchlings not only steal Excalibur, the source of King Arthur's confidence and sovereignty, but they have kidnaped Kayley's mom (Jane Seymour) and are forcing her to open the gate to Camelot on their behalf. All that stands between Camelot and the road to destruction is Kayley and one small detail. Ruber's large, but inefficient Griffen (Bronson Pinchot) has dropped the sword into the Forbidden Forest and everyone has to go searching for it.

That's where Kayley meets Garrett (Cary Elwes), a blinded stableboy whose mastery of the forest's dangers make him a cool partner and love interest. They, in turn, meet the two-headed, two-named, flight-challenged dragon Devon (a priggish Eric Idle) and Cornwall (a piggish Don Rickles). The dragon provides the comedy relief and irreverence that keep the littlest of kids and their parents in their seats just as the storyline becomes hardened in a thin candy shell.

Cognoscenti will see direct homage to Robin William's Genii in "Aladdin," of course—the impersonations! the out-of-time-sequence images! Cognoscenti will see Disney executives cringing, since their girl-saves-civilization spectacular "Mulan" doesn't open until June 19. Cognoscenti should get over it.

All three (or four) of our friends learn Important Lessons, sing Revealing Songs (by David Foster and Carole Bayer Sager) and reach Beyond Themselves trying to return Excalibur to a dispirited and shakey King Arthur (Pierce Brosnan).

Animators have given this lively set of characters an oddly pastel, soft-focus world. Castle Camelot is a rural outpost with a killer conference room. The Forbidden Forest comes alive as a wide-screen videogame of walking plants, aggressive vines and shifting landscape. And there's a three-dimensional ogre that's either entrancing or disconcerting, depending on your visual perspective.

SIGHT AND SOUND, 8/98, p. 50, Leslie Felperin

King Arthur rules the kingdom of Camelot by virtue of his possession of Excalibur, a magic sword. Sir Lionel, a knight of the round table, serves Arthur faithfully and lives with his wife Juliana and their tomboy daughter Kayley. However, while trying to effect a coup, evil Sir Ruber kills Sir Lionel as a gryphon steals Excalibur, though the sword is lost in flight over the Magic Forest. Kayley escapes into the Forest, pursued by Ruber and his magic-mechanical minions.

Kayley encounters Garrett, a blind hermit who knew her father. Though antagonistic at first the two become friends and set out to find Excalibur. Along the way they befriend a dragon with two bickering heads named Devon and Cornwall and find the magic sword. Unfortunately, Ruber gets hold of Excalibur and attacks Camelot. Kayley battles him. She is joined by the hitherto aloof Garrett and together they trick Ruber into thrusting the sword back into the magic stone from which only Arthur can withdraw it. Ruber and all his magical effects evaporate; Camelot is saved; Kayley and Garrett are both knighted.

The Magic Sword Quest for Camelot makes one dramatic and vital deviation from the traditional tropes of Camelot stories by having a female character, Kayley, as its protagonist. From Sir Thomas Malory onwards, women have tended to feature mostly as objects of exchange or duplicitous agents (see the stock characters of Guinevere and Morgan Le Fay). And yet, as the popularity of the novels of Marion Zimmer Bradley proves, fantasy medievalist fiction based on the core story is particularly favoured by women readers. So mainstream filmmaking efforts such as this are canny to tap into this vein with a feisty female role model whose action figure will make a welcome alternative to girlie Barbie and her ilk for tomboys.

As a film, Warner Bros' first challenge to Disney's effective monopoly on feature animation (joining in combat with Twentieth Century Fox's *Anastasia* and DreamWorks' forthcoming *The Prince of Egypt*) is accessible but unmemorable. Unsurprisingly, it borrows motifs and devices from well-known animation and children's films at will to stimulate the right unconscious myth synapses. The animistic Magic Forest of *trompe loeil* flora that turn fauna recalls the sinister trees of *Snow White and the Seven Dwarfs* (1937). Voiced by Eric Idle and Don Rickles, the quarrelsome two-headed dragon, spouting anachronisms (when it finally flies, we get a few too many aeroplane jokes to ram the point home), invokes Robin Williams' genie in *Aladdin* and performs much the same comedy-relief function as animal sidekicks in innumerable cartoon features.

Just for the grown-ups dragged along, there's an enchanted chicken with axeblade mohican who quotes lines from *Taxi Driver*, Gary Oldman culminating his renumerative sideline in 'cartoon' baddies for action films with a real cartoon here, and an unintentionally hilarious allusion to the cave-death scene in *The English Patient* with the sexes reversed. But having performed rather sluggishly at the box office in the US, *The Magic Sword* won't disturb Disney's chief Michael Eisner's canoeing trips too much. We'll have to wait for *The Prince of Egypt* to see if the Mouse's fur can be mussed by a rival.

Also reviewed in:
NEW YORK TIMES, 5/15/98, p. E10, Stephen Holden
VARIETY, 5/11-17/98, p. 58, Joe Leydon
WASHINGTON POST, 5/15/98, Weekend/p. 56, Michael O'Sullivan

R.I.P. (REST IN PIECES: A PORTRAIT OF JOE COLEMAN)

An Anthology Film Archives presentation of a Prisma Film production with support of the Austrian Film Institute and ORF. *Producer:* Michael Seeber and Heinz Stussak. *Director:* Robert-Adrian Pejo. *Screenplay:* Walt Michelson. *Director of Photography:* Wolfgang Lehner. *Editor:* Robert-Adrian Pejo. *Music:* Hasil Adkins, Charlie Feathers, Link Wray, and Wanda Jackson. *Sound:* Nils Petersen. *Running time:* 90 minutes. *MPAA Rating:* Not Rated.

WITH: Joe Coleman; Hasil Adkins; Bill Coleman; Katharine Gates; Dian Hanson; Jim Jarmusch; Manuel De Landa; Nancy Pivar; Harold Schechter; Martin Wilner.

NEW YORK POST, 4/10/98, p. 50, Larry Worth

It's hard to identify with a guy who cheers on serial killers. But "R.I.P.—Rest in Pieces," a sometimes squirm-inducing documentary about "shock artist" Joe Coleman, gives considerable insight into what makes an admittedly sick pup tick.

Director Robert-Adrian Pejo portrays Coleman as a man of eclectic interests: painting incredibly detailed, Hieronymus Bosch-like works of art one minute, biting heads off live mice the next; he's as deft at crafting icons with a '90s sensibility as pulling out the innards of an autopsied corpse.

Oddly enough, it never feels exploitational, despite pretty graphic moments. But as Coleman chats with everyone from his equally twisted ex-wife to indie filmmaker Jim Jarmusch (providing some absolutely hilarious repartee), he emerges as a man with a unique perspective on the world's ills, and his own.

Though one wishes that director Pejo tapped further into Coleman's troubled background and Catholic roots, "R.I.P." remains a riveting examination of an artist who refuses to Paint—or, play—on the mainstream canvas.

VILLAGE VOICE, 4/14/98, p. 68, Laurie Stone

Joe Coleman, born in 1955, points Bosch-like visions depicting figures that to him are laden with power: serial killers, Jesus, John Brown, himself as Christ. The paintings are allegories of the artist's anxieties, and their dense borders are meant to contain the terrors to the canvas. The work is richly uncensored, bearing witness to the chaotic emotions inspiring it. But sometimes it is better not to hear an artist explain himself. In Robert-Adrian Pejo's bio doc, Coleman appears literal-minded, his words far less suggestive than his images. To him mankind is a disease and "cities are tumors"; nature "wants to encourage death," hence "deviant sexuality" and plagues. Pejo points a credulous camera at Coleman, and no one comments on his views other than to say they are "Catholic." Also a performer, Coleman, in a moment of adolescent hijinks, bites off the head of a mouse he calls Daddy, but mostly the subject is as stolid as the filmmaking. Pointlessly, Jim Jormusch asks Coleman if, in 100 years, there will be a religion of Charles Hanson. Coleman shrugs. The movie offers confession without wisdom, candor without insight.

Also reviewed in:
NEW YORK TIMES, 4/9/98, p. E5, Lawrence Van Gelder
VARIETY, 2/24-3/2/97, p. 94, David Rooney

RATCHET

A Phaedra Cinema release of a Ratchet Productions, LLC film in association with Altar Rock Films, Inc. *Executive Producer:* Hank Blumenthal. *Producer:* George Belshaw. *Director:* John Johnson. *Screenplay:* John Johnson. *Director of Photography:* Joaquin Baca-Asay. *Editor:* James Lyons and Keith Reamer. *Music:* Paul Schwartz. *Running time:* 114 minutes. *MPAA Rating:* Not Rated.

CAST: Tom Gilroy (Elliott Callahan); Margaret Welsh (Catherine Ripley); Mitchell Lichtenstein (Tim Greenleaf); John MacKay (Chief Groves); Nurit Koppel (Julia Webb); Matthew Dixon (Henry Carver); Neal Jones (Sam O'Leary); Robaert Whaley (Deputy Ed).

NEW YORK POST, 2/6/98, p. 46, Larry Worth

Clearly, writer-director John Johnson never heard the old maxim about people in glass houses. How else to explain "Ratchet," a tale about the ripping off of a thriller script that—irony of ironies—rips off high-profile thriller scripts.

The hero is named Elliott Callahan, but Quentin would be a better fit, at least after hearing of Elliott's overnight fame from penning a blood-drenched film noir. Faster than you can say

"Reservoir Dogs," Elliott's quizzed by a fan about his flick's similarity to a Hong Kong actioner. (Is Ringo Lam's "City on Fire" coming to mind?)

During a Nantucket stay to cure writer's block, Elliott steals an aspiring playwright's screenplay. OK, now we're into Ira Levin territory, with "Death Trap" front and center.

Without much warning, the focus then segues to a duplicitous, bisexual blonde who can wield sharp instruments with the best of them. Sound familiar? Heck, Joe Eszterhas could claim a screen credit.

Oddly enough, "Ratchet"'s derivative quality isn't its worst quality. That's because Johnson is not only devoid of original thought, but utterly lacking in style and technique.

At nearly two hours, the film's pacing is positively glacial. And that's not even mentioning the lighting, or lack thereof. Candles would serve just as well, though viewers may be thankful once the storyline takes a particularly sadistic turn.

The cast, meanwhile, could pass for cigar-store Indians. Indeed, Tom Gilroy's sad-sack lead makes Tarantino's acting talents seem Oscar-worthy. And Sharon Stone needn't fear Margaret Welsh as an up-and-coming femme fatale.

Indeed, it's almost fun to see how bad "Ratchet" can get. That's the one area in which Johnson never disappoints.

NEWSDAY, 2/6/98, Part II/p. B6, John Anderson

From Hitchcock to Buñuel (not that *that's* always such a stretch), filmmakers have taken great glee in peeling the delicate caul of gentility from the face of "normal" life. Likewise, the great film noirists by definition have been intent on exposing the flaws in our expectations. And our character.

According to Webster, a ratchet is a mechanism with inclined teeth for propelling an object in one direction. In the case of John S. Johnson's noiresque "Ratchet," the teeth are sharp, the motion is progressively nasty and the objective is to tinker with the motives and motor of mystery.

Consider, for one thing, the "hero": Elliott Callahan (Tom Gilroy), a not-particularly-likeable, not-very-ethical and none-too-courageous screenwriter, who responds to a plea for "family fare" with "Violence is our national pastime." Elliott's penance, and redemption seem inevitable. Johnson has other plans.

A speargun makes an appearance. A nail gun is mentioned. Dread, like a metaphysical El Niño, turns things gothic in the broad daylight.

Elliott has gone to Nantucket, to his agent's borrowed house, to write the script that's going to save his terminal career. In an obvious lift from the life of Quentin Tarantino, Elliott's first film, the ultra-violent "Criminal Intent," was itself a lift—from a Hong Kong action flick (a la. "Reservoir Dogs" and Ringo Lam's "City of Fire").

Elliott, unlike Quentin, really has no talent, so his island quest runs aground—until a local loser (Matthew Dixon) asks Elliott to read his own script.

That Elliott will steal Henry's material is a given. That Henry was a suspect in a grotesque local rape-murder is, perhaps, less than expected. That the other island dwellers—maybe or maybe not including the obviously dangerous artist Julia Webb (Nurit Koppel) and the seemingly wholesome real estate agent Catherine Ripley (Margaret Welsh)—should have such a boneyard of erotic skeletons in their respective closets *is* a surprise.

The cast is good, and Welsh and Gilroy are particularly good. Gilroy, in fact, is an ideal '90s anti-hero, because he makes Elliott, who's really got very few redeeming qualities, not sympathetic but understandable. Elliott's a symptom of his time, and we are too, so it would be tough not to respond in an even reluctantly positive manner.

The ending of "Ratchet" is a flurry of illogical occurrences. Why do characters flee on a boat only to beach themselves so their pursuer can catch up? (Answer: so the pursuer can catch up). But what we have, as Johnson tampers with our expectations, is the movie taking over and having its own fun. It's akin to Toni Morrison's "Jazz," when the book starts talking back. "Ratchet" is no longer content to be just a passive vehicle for its maker's dementia. It wants to assert itself.

Either that or it's just badly edited, but making murder either exciting or surprising these days is like growing geraniums in concrete. Although he occasionally loses a character or two and careens off his own devices at the end of the picture, Johnson has made an intelligent thriller, one with its own sense of malevolent mischief.

VILLAGE VOICE, 2/10/98, p. 61, Abby McGanney Nolan

Cleverly conjoining the usual serial-killer fright with the terrors of writer's block, John Johnson's *Ratchet* follows onetime-wunderkind filmmaker Elliott Callahan (Tom Gilroy) as he tries to restart his career. That *Ratchet* doesn't ultimately deliver on its promise makes its sometimes funny jibes (at Hollywood, agents, and Quentin Tarantino) seem a little too much like sour grapes. Callahan—whose only credit is meant to resemble *Reservoir Dogs*, with its borrowings from Hong Kong and gleeful treatment of torture—has gone to Nantucket to find enough peace to finish a dangerously overdue script; the studio is threatening a lawsuit. There he immediately stumbles upon betrayal, revenge, and murder, as well as an aspiring filmmaker who begs him to read his screenplay.

Gilroy plays the famous hack Callahan, agonizing over his lack of ideas, with wonderful self-loathing; he delivers Callahan's lines ("So his brilliant script was an autobiography. He wasn't a writer, he was a murderer—what a relief") with admirable understatement. The scenes in which our hero debates plagiarism and then gets a taste of his own infamous torture scene (to the tune of "Whistle While You Work") is also well handled. But the nicely paced and acted story devolves into a familiar and none-too-logical murder mystery, with women who are not what they seem and weapons always at the ready. Derivative as he is, Tarantino still comes out ahead.

Also reviewed in:
NEW YORK TIMES, 2/6/98, p. E20, Anita Gates
VARIETY, 9/30-10/6/96, p. 184, David Stratton

RAT'S TALE, A

A Legacy Films release of a Monty Film Production. *Executive Producer:* Christa-Maria Klein. *Producer:* Hans Peter Clahsen.   *Director:* Michael F. Huse.   *Screenplay (German with English subtitles):* Werner Morgenrath and Peter Scheerbaum.   *Based on the book by:* Tor Seidler. *Director of Photography:* Piotr Lenar.   *Editor:* Timothy McLeish.   *Music:* Frederic Talgorn. *Sound:* Olav Gross and Josef Porzchen. *Production Designer:* Austen Spriggs.   *Set Decorator:* Chantal Giuliani.   *Costumes:* Eun-Young Kim.   *Running time:*   89 minutes. *MPAA Rating:* G.

CAST: Lauren Hutton (Evelyn Jellybelly);   Beverly D'Angelo (Mrs. Dollart);   Jerry Stiller (Professor Plumpingham);   Josef Ostendorf (Lou Dollart);

VOICES: Dee Bradley Baker (Monty Mad-Rat, Jr.);   Lynsey Bartilson (Isabella Noble-Rat);   Ray Guth (Old Monty);   Scott MacDonald (Rudi Rake-Rat);   Donald Arthur (Jean-Paul Canalligator).

LOS ANGELES TIMES, 3/20/98, Calendar/p. 12, David Kronke

Kids today, so spoiled. Conditioned to special-effects-laden movies like "Mouse Hunt" and "The Borrowers," they may have little use for such a shockingly low-tech movie like "A Rat's Tale," a marionette-driven story that will inspire cine-savvy children to demand, "Couldn't they have optically erased those wires from the frame?"

Such an old-fashioned art form is seemingly outmatched on the big screen. Marveling to the wonders of puppetry is an entertainment best enjoyed in a live theatrical setting, with children close enough to the marionettes to touch them; a darkened movie house is a fairly unsatisfactory substitution.

This is particularly true in the case of "A Rat's Tale," in which all the film's minor charms come from the puppets. Since it is a movie, storytelling prowess is required, and, alas, the script and human actors alike are perfunctory and stilted. Even rats can still be let down by the material.

Germany's marionette troupe Augsburger Puppenkiste provides most of the characters. Live actors are mixed in, though there's little interaction between the two.

Our hero is Monty Mad-Rat, a shy sewer rat in love with Isabella Noble-Rat, an "uptown" rat. (Yes, even rats have an unfair socioeconomic system, just another thing to dislike about them.) Except for Isabella's yellow scarf, it's a little hard to tell the two apart, and while they're fuzzy and speak with kewpie voices, they're still not what you would call "cute."

A crass developer wants to eradicate the rats to erect an underground parking structure. The rats decide to raise $100,000 to buy the land back from the humans. "Money money money, we gotta find it fast," they chirp tunelessly. "We'll find the greedy human, we'll pay him off with cash." Monty chips in the lion's share by selling some magical shells to an art gallery owner, Ms. Jellybelly (Lauren Hutton). Beverly D'Angelo plays one of Jellybelly's fatuous patrons. " Oh, my God, there's a rat!" she shrieks. Hutton protests: "That's one of my artists!" D'Angelo regains her composure quickly, asking, "Is he established?"

That's really about the only joke that parents will appreciate in the movie. Otherwise, there are many rat puns—"ratwash" replaces "hogwash," rats are encouraged to show "rattitude," and so on.

Good-intentioned as it all is, it doesn't quite enrapture children; it just aids them in killing some time. Patchy storytelling and too-broad human performances (the rats are more subtle than the established actors) don't help.

And, as all children's films must, "A Rat's Tale" dutifully slips in some lip-service to the power of imagination, to having heart and helping your enemies and, yes, even to helping the environment. Rats, whose main job on this planet seems to be spreading filth and disease, seem unlikely ecological spokesvermin.

NEW YORK POST, 3/21/98 p. 22, Larry Worth

Maybe it's apt for a story about rodents to be cheesy, but that's no excuse for the amateurishness of "A Rat's Tale." Combining live action with puppetry, director Michael F. Huse makes no attempt to hide the dolls' strings or the fact that their mouths don't move. That much is fine.

Unfortunately, the marionettes—courtesy of Germany's Augsberger Puppenkiste—prove far less wooden than the story, never mind human co-stars Beverly D'Angelo, Jerry Stiller and Lauren Hutton.

As a pair of star-crossed Manhattan rats (who look like a genetically defective mix of mouse and chipmunk) fight a plan for their kind to be poisoned throughout the city, one can't help rooting for the exterminators.

Long before the endless silliness reaches its predictably happy conclusion, even Barney starts to look good.

Also reviewed in:
NEW YORK TIMES, 3/20/98, p. E12, Anita Gates
VARIETY, 3/23-29/98, p. 88, Leonard Klady

REACH THE ROCK

A Gramercy Pictures release.   *Executive Producer:* Christopher Cronyn.   *Producer:* John Hughes and Ricardo Mestres.   *Director:* William Ryan.   *Screenplay:* John Hughes.   *Director of Photography:* John Campbell.   *Editor:* Jerry Greenberg.   *Music:* John McEntire.   *Sound:* Richard Lightstone and J.B. Sutton.   *Sound Editor:* Hugh Waddell.   *Casting:* Billy Hopkins, Suzanne Smith, and Kerry Barden.   *Production Designer:* Jeffrey Townsend.   *Art Director:* Caty Maxey.   *Set Decorator:* Joe Bristol.   *Set Designer:* Melissa Rigazio.   *Set Dresser:* Helmer A. Claesson.   *Special Effects:* Kevin Pike.   *Costumes:* Ellen Ryba.   *Make-up:* June Weiss.   *Stunt Coordinator:* Rick LeFevour.   *Running time:* 100 minutes.   *MPAA Rating:* R.

CAST: William Sadler (Quinn); Alessandro Nivola (Robin); Bruce Norris (Ernie); Karen Sillas (Donna); Brooke Langton (Lise); Richard Hamilton (Ed); Norman Reedus (Danny).

LOS ANGELES TIMES, 10/16/98, Calendar/p. 16, Kevin Thomas

An overhead shot of a Norman Rockwell small-town Main Street opens "Reach the Rock." It is a hot summer night, and no one is in sight until a young man (Alessandro Nivola) appears, breaking off a flagpole in front of a hardware store. He uses the pole to smash a display window. When a policeman (Bruce Norris) arrives to arrest him, he's sitting on a lawn chair, an electric fan cooling him.

We don't know immediately why Nivola's 21-year-old Robin has committed this particular act of vandalism, but once he arrives at police headquarters it's crystal-clear that he and the sergeant in charge, Phil Quinn (William Sadler), have a decidedly negative history.

A small film that discloses its meanings gradually has been set in motion. It's one that requires patience in watching a bitter but seemingly mundane battle of wits, relieved by Robin's outrageous shenanigans until an unexpectedly jolting finish takes the film to another, more intense level.

All that has gone before is suddenly thrown into sharp relief, highlighting and connecting the immaturity not only of Robin and Norris' none-too-bright Ernie—whose attempt to rendezvous with Karen Sillas' lush, sultry Donna provides the film's running gag—but also of Quinn, who for years has held an unjustified grudge against the town's troubled bad kid.

Although directed by William Ryan in an encouraging debut, "Reach the Rock" bears the familiar mark of its writer/co-producer John Hughes. Indeed, its central situation, a young man held in detention, echoes one of Hughes' best pictures, "The Breakfast Club."

"Reach the Rock" is less ambitious in that it has fewer characters, and its scale seems better suited to the small screen. However, it has the same respect for young people who have reached a crucial turning point in their lives.

"Reach the Rock" has a nice look to it, and Ryan has a sure way with actors and in dealing with inherently theatrical material. Brooke Langton, as the rich girl Robin fell in love with when he was 17, appears only fleetingly until near the film's end. When she arrives, however, she galvanizes the entire film.

NEW YORK POST, 10/16/98, p. 45, Rod Dreher

If I were a teenager, "Reach the Rock" probably would be my favorite film this fall—if I had the patience to stick with it.

John Hughes, the great interpreter of the American teen-age experience, wrote the screenplay, and despite seeming a bit winded at times, he's as sure-footed as ever on familiar (for him) territory. Few filmmakers have Hughes' ability to understand teen angst and convey it without condescension or exploitation.

The disarmingly intimate "Reach the Rock" is a minor film in the Hughes pantheon, which includes Gen-X greatest hits such as "Ferris Bueller's Day Off," "Pretty in Pink" and "The Breakfast Club." But it's a fine little coming-of-age ensemble piece whose acute perceptiveness and unfussy virtues sneak up on you.

Hughes' story, directed by his young protege William Ryan, begins on a hot summer night in small-town Illinois. Bored and restless, Robin (Alessandro Nivola) breaks a window in a downtown store and waits for the town's only patrolman to arrive. Though 21, Robin has a chronic case of arrested development; stuck in the hurt and frustration of his working-class youth, the sour hothead smells like teen spirit.

He's tossed into a cell by Quinn (William Sadler), a police sergeant all too familiar with this smart kid's long juvenile record. He bears a deep grudge against the boy, whom he unfairly blames for the drowning death of his nephew. The two hurl snide, hurtful remarks at each other for much of the night, but these are mostly glancing blows that serve to soften the duo up for the inevitable Big Talk.

Though the film is rather slow, Hughes averts cabin fever by having clever Robin sneak out of jail to wreak mischievous havoc on the sleeping town. This is pretty funny stuff, particularly in how it puts the kibosh on the desperate attempts of dopey Deputy Ernie (Bruce Norris) to score with his sweetie (Karen Sillas). More importantly, it shows what kind of intelligence and daring Robin is wasting on his childish rage.

When Lise (Brooke Langton), Robin's old girlfriend, makes her appearance near the end of this big night, "Reach the Rock" achieves an uncanny level of sympathy with its initially unlikable male protagonists.

Though not as impressive or as ambitious as Hughes' earlier films, "Reach the Rock" is every bit as graceful and revealing in its sympathetic exploration of ordinary lives.

VILLAGE VOICE, 10/27/98, p. 140, Jessica Winter

Former teen-schlock juggernaut John Hughes returns to his old stomping grounds with this script, which follows one night in the life of college-aged ne'er-do-well Robin (Alessandro Nivola). He gets caught vandalizing a storefront in his sleepy Illinois burg, then repeatedly sneaks out of his holding cell and generally makes the wee hours miserable for the no-nonsense sheriff. Meanwhile, Robin's rich-bitch ex-girlfriend wants a heart-to-heart with her old beau before she makes off for the big city. *Reach the Rock* is as hokey and facile as any of the high school comedies Hughes cranked out in the '80s, but it's likable enough in its own shuffling way, since Hughes's empathetic ear for late-adolescent angst remains acute. Especially endearing, odd as it seems, is the hollowness of Robin's rebellion: he has nothing to revolt against but his own shiftless tendencies. Nivola is droll, puckish despite his (amply displayed) muscles, and immensely appealing, but the real star of the movie is the jazzy prog-rock soundtrack, featuring Chicago indie darlings Tortoise and The Sea and Cake.

Also reviewed in:
CHICAGO TRIBUNE, 10/16/98, Friday/p. J, Michael Wilmington
NEW YORK TIMES, 10/16/98, p. E22, Anita Gates
VARIETY, 10/19-25/98, p. 75, Lael Loewenstein

REAL BLONDE, THE

A Lakeshore Entertainment and Paramount Pictures release of a Marcus Viscidi production. *Executive Producer:* Sigurjon Sighvatsson, Ted Tannenbaum, and Terry Mckay.   *Producer:* Marcus Viscidi and Tom Rosenberg.   *Director:* Tom DiCillo.   *Screenplay:* Tom DiCillo. *Director of Photography:* Frank Prinzi.   *Editor:* Camilla Toniolo and Keiko Deguchi.   *Music:* Jim Farmer.   *Music Editor:* Patrick Mullins.   *Sound:* Tom Mather.   *Sound Editor:* Eliza Paley. *Casting:* Avy Kaufman.   *Production Designer:* Christopher Nowak.   *Art Director:* Paul Austerberry.   *Set Decorator:* Gordon Sim and Marlene Rain.   *Costumes:* Jennifer von Mayrhauser.   *Make-up:* Lori Hicks.   *Stunt Coordinator:* Jamie Jones and George Aguilar. *Running time:* 107 minutes. *MPAA Rating:* R.

CAST: Matthew Modine (Joe);   Catherine Keener (Mary);   Daryl Hannah (Kelly);   Maxwell Caulfield (Bob);   Elizabeth Berkley (Tina);   Marlo Thomas (Blair);   Bridgette Wilson (Sahara); Buck Henry (Doctor Leuter);   Dave Chappelle (Zee);   Jim Fyfe (Roy); Tony Hendra (Soap Director);   Daniel von Bargen (Devon);   Beatrice Winde (Wilma);   David Thornton (Alex); Alexandra Wentworth (Raina);   Christopher Lloyd (Ernst);   Kathleen Turner (Dee Dee Taylor); Denis Leary (Doug);   Schecter Lee (Chang);   John Tormey (Harassing Man);   Wayne Parent (Blair's Assistant);   Peter Rex (Pete, Biker Boy);   Kendall Knights (Ken, Biker Boy);   Daniela Olivieri (Kiki);   Bronson Picket (Rubio);   Arturo Fresolone (Javier);   Ray Trail (Dirty Old Man);   Joe D'Angerio (Porno Clerk);   Kedar Brown (Playful Waiter);   Sheila Hewlett (Waitress in Restaurant);   Timm Zemanek (Couple (see following));   Joan Heney (Couple in Restaurant);   Debra McGrath (Cis);   Sean Orr (Stagehand);   Tom Harvey (Whipped Cream Man);   Nahanni Johnstone (Young Woman);   Alex Appel (Sheila);   Djanet Sears (Chantal); Steve Buscemi (Nick); Landy Cannon (Beach Boy); Katie Griffin (Empty V Interviewee); Brian

Frank (Chet);   Vincent Laresca (Trey);   Missy Yager (Lisa);   Karen Woolridge (Nadia);   Peter Keleghan (Successful Actor);   Colin Mocherie (Renny).

LOS ANGELES TIMES, 2/27/98, Calendar/p. 8, Jack Mathews

[The following review by Jack Mathews appeared in a slightly different form in **NEWSDAY, 2/27/98, Part II/p. B11.]**

Flash! The fashion industry is a skin-deep, sexist, reality-distorting business that perpetuates false expectations among men and objectifies women. This just in, too: Television soap operas are facile melodramas exploiting the Sturm und Drang of everyday human relationships. And, stop the presses! Most gorgeous blonds are made, not born.

When Tom DiCillo ("Living in Oblivion") set up his targets for his episodic satire "The Real Blonde," he made sure he wouldn't miss any of them. Media superficiality and the cult of pretty have been fair game since the dawn of the photo age, maybe since the first cave-wall centerfold. But by interweaving a very contemporary love story into these themes, DiCillo has at least given it all a fresh spin.

The gimmicky title comes from a randy subplot about a narcissistic, womanizing soap opera star (Maxwell Caulfield) who's obsessed with finding a head-to-toe natural blond. The story is related to the rest of the movie by its theme—Caulfield's Bob is the ultimate victim of the myth of perfection—but it plays as pure burlesque, a dirty joke expanded into a series of overdrawn, fitfully funny sketches.

Our main interest in "The Real Blonde" is the relationship between Joe (Matthew Modine), a New York waiter and would-be actor, and his girlfriend Mary (Catherine Keener), a makeup artist for a biker-chic fashion photographer (Marlo Thomas). Joe and Mary share a grungy downtown apartment, and are hitting a dead end in their six-year relationship because Joe's self-esteem has collapsed and Mary's latent hostilities toward all men in general are inching toward the surface.

Something has to happen for each of them if they're to remain a couple, and their separate adventures, along with Bob's recurring pursuit of a true blond, give the film a hit-and-miss anecdotal structure that tends to keep the audience at an emotional distance. The most poignant moment in the film is one when Joe expresses his feelings for Mary, and she's nowhere to be seen. He's ad-libbing a love scene while auditioning for a movie role.

Modine, one of our most under-used if not underrated actors, is brilliant in that pivotal scene, where Joe's talent and emotional depth are simultaneously revealed to him, to us and to the awe-struck film people looking on. But there are too many interruptions, too many diversionary trips to Mary's martial arts class, and to Bob's blond pursuit, for us to develop much of a rooting interest in these characters' lives.

Still, there are good moments throughout. In one, Joe's disdain for a sentimental art-house hit named "Il Piano" (yes, the one with a naked Harvey Keitel) gets an entire restaurant squabbling. In another, he provides the perfect put-down of a young anti-Semite who posits the theory that the Holocaust was a fraud. And you'll love the payoff when Bob finally goes to bed with his real blond.

Caulfield, who's done some stints on daytime TV, has a great time mocking the soap world, and Daryl Hannah is terrific as the yellow-haired co-star who ends his search. The large supporting cast includes Buck Henry, as Mary's lecherous shrink; Denis Leary, as her exploitative self-defense instructor; Elizabeth Berkley, as a young actress with more enthusiasm than talent; and Thomas, as the fashion photographer with an uncanny ability to turn catastrophes into art.

NEW YORK, 3/9/98, p. 49, David Denby

Stupidity is an issue in the independent film *The Real Blonde*, in which everyone seems to have suffered an IQ slippage of some 40 points. The writer-director Tom DiCillo had a great idea for a movie—a sexual roundelay set among young models and actors in New York. *The Real Blonde* undresses quite a few people, but the picture is so dully written and uncertainly directed that the audience is left wondering whether the stentorian clichés coming out of the characters' mouths are meant satirically or simply represent DiCillo's idea of how people talk. If the latter, why make a movie about such a collection of simps? The audience can't possibly enjoy the sight of

Matthew Modine floundering around as a failed actor who doesn't seem to know what he wants to do with himself from one second to the next. In such a case, empathy gives way to irritation. The other victims of DiCillo's miscalculations include Catherine Keener, Daryl Hannah, Maxwell Caulfield, Bridgette Wilson, and, as a hypocritical loudmouth agent, a stridently unfunny Kathleen Turner.

NEW YORK POST, 2/27/98, p. 44, Thelma Adams

Flame-haired actress Julianne Moore attracted attention when she dropped her skivvies in Robert Altman's "Short Cuts." No doubt about it, Moore was a real redhead.

In Tom DiCillo's lackluster comedy "The Real Blonde," the writer-director glibly pursues a truth and beauty that are follicle deep. In a Manhattan peopled by wannabes and has-beens, models and actors, who's the real thing, who's a real blonde?

Certainly not the platinum-tressed Sahara (Bridgette Wilson). She's a mannequin as empty as the desert she's named after. Her idea of a spiritual icon is Disney's Little Mermaid.

"Everybody is so superficial," Sahara whines to her makeup artist, Mary (the adorable Catherine Keener). In DiCillo's narrow Manhattan, a makeup artist has the firmest grasp on reality—even if she gets angry when her transparent blouse attracts unwanted attention.

Mary lives with her boyfriend, Joe (Matthew Modine), a full-time waiter and part-time thespian. He whines about acting, sex and selling out to soap operas.

Joe is jealous of fellow actor Bob (Maxwell Caulfield), who lusts after potential real blondes such as body double Tina (Elizabeth Berkley), soap star Kelly (Daryl Hannah) and—who knows?—casting director Dee Dee Taylor (Kathleen Turner).

If this all sounds very soapy, that doesn't keep DiCillo from lampooning the shallowness of soaps. He also satirizes those notoriously hard targets, the modeling and video industries.

Steve Buscemi sports an earring as a squirt of a music-video director, as if to remind us how hilarious he was as the director in DiCillo's more successful satire, "Living in Oblivion." Maybe DiCillo was better off in oblivion.

SIGHT AND SOUND, 6/98, p. 52, Xan Brooks

Manhattan, the present. Struggling, over-idealistic actor Joe and pragmatic make-up artist Mary have been together for six years, but money worries are now threatening their relationship. Meanwhile, Joe's acting friend Bob goes to bed with teenage model Sahara but dumps her when he discovers that she's not a natural blonde. Bob wins a lead role on a daytime soap, while Joe swallows his pride and agrees to appear in a Madonna video. In an attempt to channel her frustrations, Mary enrols on a self-defence course and becomes dangerously attracted to her instructor, Doug.

On set, Joe is drawn to Madonna's body-double Tina, but is fired from the shoot after arguing with the assistant director. The ratings for Bob's soap shoot up and he is offered a five-year contract with script approval. Bob goes to bed with his co-star—'real blonde' Kelly—but is impotent. He insists that the studio kill off Kelly's character and returns to Sahara. Joe auditions for a major movie role and wins the part. Celebrating in a bar, he resists Tina and returns to Mary. The pair decide to have a baby.

Writer-director Tom DiCillo has built his reputation on an unhealthy fascination with the mechanics of popular culture. His debut *Johnny Suede* cast Brad Pitt as a preening wannabe rock star. His follow-up *Living in Oblivion* spotlighted the behind-the-scenes ineptitude of a team of low-budget filmmakers. Last year's *Box of Moon Light* (about a stuffed-shirt jobsworth on a voyage of self-discovery) took DiCillo on an uncharacteristic rural diversion. But his fourth film finds him back in familiar territory. *The Real Blonde* is a lively, day-glo satire on the toilers in the media beanfield. Strutting soap stars, bimbo models, hysterical fashion photographers, icy casting agents: all are gently held up to ridicule, their superficialities exposed, their insecurities examined.

Anchoring the tale is DiCillo-surrogate Joe. Principled, yet just a shade ludicrous among the more sleek movers and shakers of his profession, Matthew Modine's performance is a marvel of subtle dexterity. When working as a tuxedoed waiter, he desperately attempts to retrieve a glob of cream from a diner's shoulder. Having agreed to be an extra in a Madonna video, he over-acts wildly in billowing plaid boxer-shorts, half-hoping to get away with it, yet ultimately suspecting that he's doomed. By turns honourable hero and luckless stooge, Joe makes for a bracing comic creation.

The trouble is that Joe inhabits a confused and contradictory landscape. *The Real Blonde* is a showbiz satire by a showbiz insider, and as such its vision is skewed, infected by the very values it seeks to critique. In the film's opening moments, Joe and Mary are set up as decent, troubled people pulled apart by the media world's shallow, success-at-all-costs ethos. But the film's finale sees DiCillo subtly endorsing the same value system he's just spent an hour-and-a-half hauling over the coals: Joe wins a part as a serial killer in a crass-looking blockbuster, and this patches up his and Mary's floundering relationship.

Similarly troublesome is Joe's use of a *Death of a Salesman* monologue as his audition piece. Spoken in the play by Willy Loman's son Happy, the monologue offers a maudlin hymn to failed ambitions and thwarted promise. DiCillo has claimed that this monologue "is the key to the whole movie because it's about being forced to do something that's beneath you, about having to perform below your potential." And yet Happy is probably *Death of a Salesman's* most unsympathetic character, a wheedling, money-grabbing phoney with no real potential to speak of. If DiCillo truly intends Happy as a reference point for Joe, it makes his assault on New York's showbiz scene still more muddled.

The Real Blonde is not a film that stands close scrutiny. This is a glossy diversion, eased along by nimble direction, bright comedic flashes and Jim Farmer's fine, *Pink Pantherish* jazz score. Perhaps DiCillo is too in bed with his characters, too immersed in his set-up to muster the required edge or distance. Thus, *The Real Blonde* winds up a cartoonish satire on a cartoonish world—form and content in perfect unison.

VILLAGE VOICE, 3/3/98, p. 61, J. Hoberman

A humorously fractured vision of independent film production, Tom DiCillo's *Living in Oblivion* may be counted among *Rashomon's* distant progeny. DiCillo's latest, *The Real Blonde,* is solipsistic in another way—albeit as self-mockingly fashionable as its vibe and finger-snap credit music would suggest.

DiCillo is one of the few Amerindies who can direct comedy, and—having recovered from *Box of Moonlight's* fumbling New Age sincerity—he orchestrates a bit of fun in the land of midlife crisis. Interrupted wake-up sex is ultimately transformed into long-postponed makeup sex as a Downtown, thirtysomething couple, Matthew Modine and the always welcome DiCillo axiom Catherine Keener, are propelled through a screwball comedy (in which each almost sleeps with someone else) to resolve all issues of career, commitment, and procreation.

As Modine plays a struggling actor and Keener a successful yet frustrated makeup artist, the movie thrives on inside baseball—waiter gigs, fashion shoots, the beach-themed Madonna video for which Modine, alone among extras showing up in boxer trunks, is exiled to the back row and then fired for debating the reality of the Holocaust with the opinionated black assistant director. The model is mid-period Woody Allen. A riff on *The Piano* might have been lifted from *Annie Hall* and, like that prototypical modern romance, the couple stuff has the ring of truth—right down to the self-absorption.

The movie's title refers to Modine colleague Maxwell Caulfield's spurious quest for female authenticity—ironically (but not too ironically) embodied by soap queen Daryl Hannah. Fact is, reality itself is kinda blond here. The coolness of casting Elizabeth Berkley as Madonna's body double notwithstanding, *The Real Blonde* seems so imprisoned in its particular worldview that any character who is not a white heterosexual runs the risk of severe stereotyping.

Also reviewed in:
CHICAGO TRIBUNE, 2/27/98, Friday/p. O, Michael Wilmington
NEW YORK TIMES, 2/27/98, p. E10, Janet Maslin
VARIETY, 9/29-10/5/97, p. 62, Lisa Nesselson
WASHINGTON POST, 3/13/98, Weekend/p. 48, Desson Howe

REGENERATION

An Alliance Communications release of a Rafford Films Limited/Norstar Entertainment Inc./BBC Films/The Scottish Arts Council Lottery Fund production. *Executive Producer:* Saskia Sutton and Mark Shivas.   *Producer:* Allan Scott and Peter Simpson.   *Director:* Gillies MacKinnon. *Screenplay:* Allan Scott.   *Based on the novel by:* Pat Barker.   *Director of Photography:* Glen MacPherson. *Editor:* Pia Di Ciaula. *Music:* Mychael Danna. *Sound:* Louis Kramer. *Casting:* Sarah Trevis.   *Production Designer:* Andy Harris.   *Art Director:* John Frankish.   *Costume Designer:* Kate Carin.   *Make-up:* Irene Napier.   *Stunt Coordinator:* Gareth Milne.   *Running time:* 113 minutes. *MPAA Rating:* Not Rated.

CAST: Jonathan Pryce (Dr. William Rivers);   James Wilby (Siegfried Sassoon);   Jonny Lee Miller (Billy Prior);   Stuart Bunce (Wilfred Owen);   Tanya Allen (Sarah);   David Hayman (Dr. Bryce);   Dougray Scott (Robert Graves);   John Neville (Doctor Yealland);   Paul Young (Doctor Brock);   Alastair Galbraith (Campbell);   Eileen Nicholas (Miss Crowe);   Julian Fellowes (Timmons);   David Robb (Dr. McIntyre);   Kevin McKidd (Callan);   Rupert Proctor (Burns); Angela Bradley (Nurse Alison);   Finlay McLean (Huntley);   Jeremy Child (Balfour Graham); Jenny Ryan (Madge);   Andrew Woodall (Willard);   Russell Barr (Sassoon's Soldier);   Kate Donnelly (Lizzie);   Lee Brown (Logan);   Joel Strachan (Martin);   Bob Docherty (Man in Pub); James McAvoy (Anthony Balfour).

LOS ANGELES TIMES, 8/14/98, Calendar/p. 8, Kevin Thomas

"Regeneration" is as bleak as it is thoughtful, a traditional-style Scottish-British-Canadian production with polished dialogue and superlative performances. It should please fans of the well-made British film, but you could wish that director Gillies Mackinnon and writer Allan Scott, in adapting Pat Barker's trilogy of novels, could have found ways to enliven all that's on their minds—war, class, snobbery, friendship, redemption and, eventually, regeneration—and explored it in less theatrical fashion.

Their handsome film is nothing, however, if not ambitious in scope and depth, and it is blessed with a towering, complex portrayal by Jonathan Pryce, in what surely must be one of the most challenging roles of his varied career. He is cast as Dr. William Rivers, a pioneering psychiatrist, who during World War I ran Craiglockart, a military mental hospital housed in a Victorian castle outside Glasgow.

Rivers, who was charged with curing soldiers of shellshock so that they might return to battle, is a patriotic yet highly empathetic man whose demanding work is beginning to exact its toll. He's already near the limits of his resources when he's handed a hot potato: poet Siegfried Sassoon (James Wilby, as fine as he was in "Maurice"), who has demonstrated incredible bravery and remarkable leadership in battle but who has now spoken out against the war. (That Sassoon is gay is mentioned only obliquely by Rivers; so much for the controversy over gays in the military.) Not a pacifist, Sassoon believes that, after three years, the war, which started out for the British as a necessary defense, is being prolonged at a terrible cost in lives.

Sassoon's friend Robert Graves (Dougray Scott) has managed to persuade his fellow poet to choose Craiglockart over certain court-martial. A forthright man, Rivers tells Sassoon he does,not believe he's mad but reminds him that it's his job to persuade him to return to the battlefield. (What Rivers above all has in mind is to stretch out Sassoon's stay until the war is over.)

Upon his arrival, the brilliant, patrician Sassoon, who has lost a cherished friend in battle, is in a mood for martyrdom, but Rivers commences by bringing his formidable powers of persuasion to bear upon him to try to get the poet to see himself in as large a moral, philosophical and social context as possible.

Indeed, "Regeneration," which has been called a cerebral "Saving Private Ryan," includes terrible scenes of warfare, which haunt not only Sassoon but others at Craiglockart. The film's central, presumably fictional, figure, however, Jonny Lee Miller's young Billy Prior, not only has blanked all memories of battle but has also become mute.

As a humble man who has worked his way up the ranks, Billy is enraged at the naivete and folly of Britain's upper-class leadership in battle, but he is otherwise a generic figure, although certainly played effectively by Miller, best known for his role as Sick Boy in "Trainspotting." What the picture needs more of is Sassoon and his friendship with poet Wilfred Owen (Stuart Bunce), whom Sassoon inspired to write a series of poems considered to be the finest to emerge from World War I.

As the film—and the war itself—progresses—Pryce does a heroic job of expressing with subtlety Rivers' increasing sense of inner pressure and conflict. It comes to a head in a dramatic sequence in which a doctor (John Neville) applies a brutal but effective electrical shock treatment to force mute soldiers to speak again. The impressed but even more appalled Rivers sees the treatment as reducing men to fighting machines.

Certainly, "Regeneration" is an intelligent, well-produced picture, but one that would have gained immeasurably from more dynamic and personal direction.

NEW YORK POST, 8/14/98, p. 46, Larry Worth

In the opening scene of "Regeneration," the camera slowly pans a field of dead and wounded World War I soldiers in various forms of decay. Each is part of a garish jigsaw puzzle, semi-mired in a battlefield of gray sludge.

Granted, the tableau will never be compared to the Atlanta boulevard of bleeding Civil War vets in "Gone With the Wind" or the jarring D-Day beach massacre of "Saving Private Ryan."

But it's effective regardless, even as it sets up the gist of "Regeneration." Set in a forbidding Scottish castle-turned-hospital, the multilayered plot concerns the treatment of soldiers whose decay emanates from troubled mental states.

As a sentient British doctor tries to comfort and heal them, he faces a heart-rending dilemma: taking away enough of the soldiers' madness to return them to the trenches' lunacy.

Adapted from Pat Barker's based-on-truth literary trilogy, the material poses fascinating questions. But Gillies Mackinnon's direction sometimes supplies less compelling answers, partially due to languid pacing, musical miscues and a surfeit of flashbacks.

Of more significance, Mackinnon imbues the production with an ineffable sadness, never mind addressing all kinds of love with gossamer subtlety. And then there's his muted cinematography, ranging from stunning Scottish scenery to eerily lensed shots of the war zone (as of a young man's corpse impaled on barbed wire, then left for days due to constant crossfire.)

The fine cast includes ever-impressive Jonathan Pryce as the shrink who falls prey to his wards' woes, James Wilby's bravura turn as a troop leader who won't renounce anti-war sentiments and Jonny Lee "Afterglow," "Trainspotting") Miller as a twentysomething trouper who's struck mute by the atrocities around him. Stuart Bunce and Dougray Scott (Drew Barrymore's prince in "Ever After") lend fine support.

With that much talent, the production should really be more powerful than it is. Even so, the wealth of highlights—both visual and aural—put "Regeneration" squarely in the victor's corner.

NEWSDAY, 8/14/98, Part II/p. B13, Jack Mathews

Before post-traumatic stress syndrome became a common malady of characters in films about Vietnam veterans, filmmakers generally avoided the psychological casualties of war. There was the occasional shell-shocked soldier, and the disconnected returning GIs of such post-World War II films as William Wyler's "The Best Years of Our Lives," But unflinching looks at truly broken men were rare.

"Wounds that you can see—heroes without legs or arms—are acceptable, because it shows a love of country and patriotism and the right stuff," said the late John Huston, whose "Let There Be Light," a 1946 documentary about the treatment of mentally disabled WWII veterans, was suppressed by the U.S. government for 35 years. "But with men who were emotionally injured, who'd been destroyed in their spirits, that's a different question."

The plight of these men, of course, holds out the most profound kind of actual human drama. They're rescued from the depths, feats that were hardly attempted before the First World War, when the military called on the new science of psychoanalysis to patch emotionally wounded soldiers and return them to battle.

That process is the subject of Scottish director Gillies MacKinnon's frequently compelling "Regeneration," adapted from Pat Barker's novel, which in turn was inspired by the actual experiences of two famous Scottish poets who met as mental patients in a military hospital in 1917, and of the doctor who worked with them.

Jonathan Pryce portrays Dr. William Rivers, a psychoanalyst whose compassion and insecurities about his fledgling profession are pushing him to the brink of his own breakdown. James Wilby is the established poet Siegfried Sassoon, and Stuart Bunce is Wilfred Owen, a budding poet who recruits Sassoon as his mentor. Intercutting combat footage to illuminate the traumas of the hospital's patients, MacKinnon attempts to follow in dramatic terms the same course followed by Huston's "Let There Be Light," essentially following a group of men from their arrival at Craiglockart Castle through their treatment. Besides Sassoon and Owen, we become intimately familiar with Billy Prior ("Trainspotting's" Sick Boy, Jonny Lee Miller), an officer struck mute by a battlefield horror.

The title of the film refers directly to a self-mutilating experiment conducted by one of Rivers' professors, who cut the radial nerve in his wrist to test a drug for regenerating damaged nerve cells. Rivers likens that failed experiment to the radical electric shock therapy being used by his colleagues on combat patients. Rivers insists, on following the more humane psychoanalytic tact of peeling away the symptoms to effect real cure, and in the process, becomes more vulnerable himself.

In adapting Barker's novel, MacKinnon and veteran Scottish screenwriter Allan Scott have perhaps attempted too much. They're telling four interrelated and ultimately competing stories at once, and pausing for far too many talky interludes about the state of psychoanalysis in 1917.

The movie is about a bunch of things; the nature of war and heroism, spiritual healing, camaraderie, loyalty, personal principle, the British class system, military priorities. There's even a love story thrown in, about Billy Prior's relationship with a beautiful local girl (Tanya Allen) who appears in his life as an almost literal angel, to reassure him of his masculinity and worthiness. Who needs therapy?

The film would have been better served if MacKinnon had chosen to focus more insistently on the central relationship between Rivers and Sassoon, a cultural hero turned war hero turned protester. It's an anti-war pamphlet written by Sassoon, condemning the continuation of the war as British aggression, that lands him in Rivers' care.

Is Sassoon mentally disabled, or as a man of free will, has he simply come to his senses, as he claims? Figuring that out is the slippery slope Rivers descends, and the outcome of that journey alone would be enough of a drama.

SIGHT AND SOUND, 12/97, p. 52, Stella Bruzzi

Craiglockhart Hospital, Edinburgh, 1917. Siegfried Sassoon arrives to be a psychiatric patient of Dr William Rivers because he's written a letter condemning the war and been declared unstable. Billy Prior (an officer, now mute from shellshock) only communicates with Rivers using notes. At dinner, another patient named Burns vomits up his food. During their second session, Prior is able to talk to Rivers and begins to reveal the events in France that traumatised him.

While playing golf, Sassoon is approached by another poet, an officer also being treated at Craiglockhart: Wilfred Owen. Owen asks Sassoon to sign copies of Sassoon's book of poems, and Sassoon in turn agrees to read some of Owen's poetry. One evening, Prior goes to a local Edinburgh pub and meets a woman named Sarah. He is grounded for two weeks. Prior apologises to Rivers for transgressing hospital rules and agrees to be hypnotised to bring back his war memories. Rivers tells Sassoon that he is against classifying him as sick. The friendship between Sassoon and Owen develops, and Sassoon reads and compliments Owen's poetry. Prior meets Sarah again. They have sex.

Rivers is given a medical by a colleague and told to take some leave. In London, he observes the brutal psychiatric methods of Dr Yealland. Back at Craiglockhart, Prior tells Rivers he wants to return to France. The medical boards who decide the patients' sanity meet; Sassoon deliberately misses his. Burns maintains he is better, but Rivers disagrees. Sassoon attends a second board at which he says his duty is to return to combat. Rivers decides that Sassoon is ready to resume active duty. Sassoon bids Owen goodbye. Owen soon follows him back to France. Later, Rivers reads a letter from Sassoon telling him of Owen's death.

Gillies MacKinnon's adaptation of Pat Barker's novel is a beautiful, intense evocation of the complex emotions the 1914-1918 war wrung from its soldiers; the pity, grief, wildness and even the erotic feelings. What is slightly lost is the meticulousness of Barker's book. The lengthy sessions between Dr Rivers and his patients are pruned right back, and sometimes the narrative suffers as a consequence. The Siegfried Sassoon and Wilfred Owen relationship—left as a clunky and romanticised portrait of homosocial desire—is crassly intercut with Billy Prior and Sarah's consummated affair. But it is Prior who is the most changed. All evidence of his bisexuality is absent and we do not see him die alongside Owen at the end of the film as he does at the end of Barker's trilogy.

Just as Owen's poetry is much subtler than the lumpen irony of Sassoon's, *Regeneration* is more effective when it uses a more nuanced approach. Narratively, the epicentre and point of identification for the audience is Rivers, the doctor who willingly but painfully listens to and absorbs his shellshocked patients' accounts of the war. Rivers hysterically absorbs the repressed anguish of his patients, beginning to stammer like the injured officers and suffering their nightmares. He is an empty vessel, filled by the personalities of others.

This passivity is crucial in illustrating the impact of the war on mere spectators. Towards the end of the film, Rivers has a nightmare. The camera tracks along a line of soldiers, but a subsequent edit reveals them to be figures standing at the end of the hallucinating Sassoon's bed. It's significant because it implies an identification between Rivers and his patients, and the relation between the images they describe to him and what he sees. This empathy with, and the interweaving of, the soldiers' experiences into a shared memory are the film's most moving innovations.

In terms of style, there is a similarly fluid relationship between individual experiences. The film evokes the war's trauma (and the trauma of its recounting) through a series of bleak, virtually monochrome flashbacks to the trenches. Again, a sense of a collective memory is created as each patient recalls in nightmares and therapy sessions a common wrecked, muddy landscape. More surprising, though, is the technical style the film adopts. Ostensibly this is a straightforwardly realist film, but Glen MacPherson's subtle photography works hard but almost imperceptibly at manipulating our emotional responses. Late in the film, there are two juxtaposed sequences: Rivers' trip to observe Dr Yealland's barbaric, physical means of ensuring a 100 per cent success rate for shellshock cures, and Rivers' own subsequent talking session with the recovering Prior. The first is shot in a cold, functional, detached manner—the camera hardly moves, the editing is functional and the lighting stark. Conversely, the second scene exudes warmth, lit using sensuous oranges while the camera moves continuously around the two characters, reminiscent of the work of Max Ophuls. It's as if the camera likes them and cares for these people.

If some of the narrative flow and the detail of Barker's novel have been lost in translation, *Regeneration* the film still retains many of the imaginative depths of those who experienced the Great War which the book plundered. There's a sequence which starts with Owen, having dutifully gone off to write about the war as instructed by Sassoon, reading 'Dulce et Decorum Est' in his flat, nasal tones. This is spoken over a close-up of Owen's face which dissolves softly into the screaming, anguished face of Burns, which in turn dissolves into a symbolic France composed of sludge, a bridge and skeletal trees. Over this image, that of Owen cradling the traumatised Burns is then superimposed. This sequence, like Owen's poetry, runs the risk of being so beautiful that it aestheticises the war experience into abstraction.

But Owen's verse and the film's images coalesce at the end to make psychological sense of the futile battles. Owen returns to the Western Front (and dies in the last gasps of the war). The France we see is a nightmare drained of colour, while an anxious steadicam shot swoops under the bridge we've seen before, past dead soldiers moulded into the mud and comes to rest on the fresh face of Owen. This sequence directly evokes Owen's parable of hell, 'Strange Meeting'. In his concluding letter telling Rivers of Owen's death, Sassoon pointedly sends him Owen's poem 'The Parable of the Old Man and the Young'. Rivers holds the narrative together while Owen furnishes the imagery.

VILLAGE VOICE, 8/18/98, p. 112, Gary Dauphin

Those who take pedigree as a marker of quality won't be disappointed by *Regeneration*, an adaptation of Pat Barker's Booker Prize-winning novel. An unhesitatingly and self-consciously bookish film, *Regeneration* successfully imagines its cast of real-life literary types grappling with literary type questions raised by World War I—duty, art, pain, and healing, against the backdrop of pointless carnage. *Regeneration* is elegiac at the core but prescient around the edges, filmed in the somber backward glances of most WWI movies, but also forward-looking enough to mourn itself. It seems to know its horrors are eventually going to be trumped, not so much disproved as made irrelevant by World War II, or maybe Steven Spielberg.

Plotwise, *Regeneration* is a fictionalization of the 1917 historical encounter between psychologist William Rivers (Jonathan Pryce) and poets Siegfried Sassoon (James Wilby) and Wilfred Owen (a stunned and dreamy Stuart Bunce). Both men are Rivers's patients in a British shellshock ward—the 17-year-old Owen broke down in France, while Sassoon is a virtual political prisoner, committed for writing an illegal antiwar tract. Most of the action orbits around talking cures. Sassoon gives Owen the confidence to write, while Rivers analyzes Sassoon into integrating his fierce opposition to the war with an obsessive determination to protect the men under his command. (That Sassoon is both a decorated, fearless officer nicknamed "Mad Jack" and a gay poet is seen by the good doctor as more of a logistical issue than a psychic contradiction.)

As adapted by Allan Scott and directed by Gillies Mackinnon *(Trojan Eddie, The Playboys, Small Faces)*, *Regeneration* is mostly faithful to its source material, the main departure being the battle scenes that, in the book, take the form of therapy-session dialogue. Everyone gets to play in the novel's round-robin of psychological breakthrough, but Jonathan Pryce's stammeringly earnest acting gives his Rivers greater depth than the written version, his patient's battle scars leaping off them to adhere to their increasingly twitchy therapist. As for Wilfred Owen, he drifts out of the hospital much as he entered, except that by film's end he's taken on the war as his great (and ultimately only) poetic subject. It's tempting to call *Regeneration* an anti-*Saving Private Ryan*, but deep down both films know every war movie needs a sanctified lamb walking willingly into slaughter. The only difference is that in the gap between countries and eras, one film's lamb can easily become the next film's goat.

Also reviewed in:
CHICAGO TRIBUNE, 8/21/98, Friday/p. F, Mark Caro
NEW REPUBLIC, 9/14 & 21/98, p. 34, Stanley Kauffmann
NEW YORK TIMES, 8/14/98, p. E10, Janet Maslin
VARIETY, 8/25-31/97, p. 76, David Rooney

REPLACEMENT KILLERS, THE

A Columbia Pictures release of a Bernie Brillstein/Brad Grey and WCG Entertainment production. *Executive Producer:* John Woo, Terence Chang, Christopher Godsick, and Matthew Baer. *Producer:* Brad Grey and Bernie Brillstein. *Director:* Antoine Fuqua. *Screenplay:* Ken Sanzel. *Director of Photography:* Peter Lyons Collister. *Editor:* Jay Cassidy. *Music:* Harry Gregson-Williams. *Music Editor:* Richard Whitfield. *Sound:* Douglas B. Arnold and (music) Alan Meyerson. *Sound Editor:* Per Hallberg and Karen M. Baker. *Casting:* Wendy Kurtzman. *Production Designer:* Naomi Shohan. *Art Director:* David Lazan. *Set Designer:* Clare Scarpulla. *Set Decorator:* Evette Knight. *Set Dresser:* Grant Sawyer. *Special Effects:* Joe Ramsey. *Costumes:* Arianne Phillips. *Make-up:* Zoltan Elek. *Stunt Coordinator:* Allan Graf. *Running time:* 82 minutes. *MPAA Rating:* R.

CAST: Chow Yun-Fat (John Lee);   Mira Sorvino (Meg Coburn);   Michael Rooker (Stan "Zeedo" Zedkov);   Kenneth Tsang (Terence Wei);   Jurgen Prochnow (Michael Kogan);   Til Schweiger (Ryker);   Danny Trejo (Collins);   Clifton Gonzalez Gonzalez (Loco);   Carlos Gomez (Hunt);   Frank Medrano (Rawlins);   Leo Lee (Lam);   Patrick Kilpatrick (Pryce);   Randall Duk Kim (Alan Chan);   Andrew J. Marton (Stevie);   Sydney Coberly (Sara);   Yau-Gene Chan (Peter Wei);   Carlos Leon (Romero);   Nicki Micheaux (Technician);   Max Daniels (Smuggler); James Wing Woo (Priest);   Albert Wong (Old Man);   Cle Shaheed Sloan and Paul Higgins (Bangers);   Chris Doyle, Joey Bucaro III, Bob Apisa, and Norm F. Compton (Thugs);   James

Lew (Bodyguard);   Thomas Rosales, Jr., Eddie Perez, Mario Roberts, Jimmy Ortega, and Richard Duran (Gangsters);   David Gene Gibbs and Rodger LaRue (Helicopter Pilots).

LOS ANGELES TIMES, 2/6/98, Calendar/p. 1, Kenneth Turan

Some films create heroes, while others are content to worship them. As starry-eyed as it is stylish, "The Replacement Killers" opts for adoration all the way.

The object of veneration this time around is Hong Kong action star Chow Yun-Fat in his American debut. The veteran of some 70 Asian films, Chow achieved cult status over here with too-cool-for-school performances in features like "A Better Tomorrow," "The Killer" and "Hard-Boiled," all directed by the master of Hong Kong action, John Woo.

Now a Hollywood player after the success of "Face/Off," Woo is one of "Killers' " executive producers, which explains this film's pseudo-Woo qualities. Put together by first-time director Antoine Fuqua, "Killers" smartly echoes the master's stylish visuals, but Woo's trademark emotional delirium proves harder to duplicate.

Described in the press kit as the "noted director of Coolio's 'Gangsta's Paradise' video," Fuqua is the most visually gifted of the group of action directors (including "Con Air's" Simon West and "The Rock's" Michael Bay, and characterized by Premiere Magazine as "They're Bold and Brash and Love to Blow Things Up") who entered the business via music videos made for Propaganda Films.

Though the look of "Killers" is nothing if not slick and commercial, Fuqua, cinematographer Peter Lyons Collister and editor Jay Cassidy are adept at literally using smoke and mirrors as well as off-beat camera angles and rapid cutting to establish a moody visual presence. When in doubt, their motto seems to be, cut to bullets breaking glass.

Part of the plan here is to treat Chow Yun-Fat as an ambulatory part of the decor. With his slow, purposeful walk, impeccable clothes and opaque, impenetrable gaze, Chow's every on-screen minute is mythologized by the filmmakers into the portrait of a laconic king of cool, a soulful murder machine who cares and kills in equal measure.

Chow plays John Lee, a Chinese assassin marooned in America who's fallen under the sway of the all-powerful Mr. Wei (Kenneth Tsang), an aphorism-quoting crime lord who says things like, "We shouldn't be chasing our problems, we should be solving them." You got that right, chief.

Wei's problem of the moment is the death of his drug-dealing son at the hands of tough cop Stan "Zeedo" Zedkov (Michael Rooker). Wei wants our guy to commit a murder that will enable Zedkov to share his pain, or else risk the death of his own mother and sister back home in China. But John Lee, in his somber, Zen master of mayhem way, is not so sure this is a good idea.

If that sounds murky, it'll have to stay that way, because Chow, whose idea of a big speech is, "I will need guns," has more dialogue in subtitled Chinese than English. In truth, he's one of those guys who lets his weapons do the talking for him: In one scene he apparently fired off an impressive 546 rounds with two firearms. "His hands became blistered from the repetitive gunfire," the awe-struck press notes report, "and medics were on standby to bandage them throughout the night." Who knew being an agent of mass destruction was this much work?

Trying her best to fit into this super-macho environment, where no one has smiled since the Mesozoic era, is the plucky Mira Sorvino. She plays Meg Coburn, a fabricator of false passports who has the glib street smarts of a gilded gutter rat. Events conspire to have Meg team up with John Lee, and though there were no reports of medics on standby when Sorvino was working, the actress discharges a hell of a lot more rounds than she did in "Romy and Michele's High School Reunion."

Sparely written by Ken Sanzel and clocking in at a brisk 88 minutes, "Replacement Killers" is an improvement over the excessively jokey scripts that burden many current action films, but even with smooth visuals added into the mix, this film is neither transcendent nor transporting. Rather, like a cold and elaborate art piece made by a computer, it's a stranger to emotional connections. Just as the killers of the title have a hard time replacing John Lee, "The Replacement Killers" is Woo wannabe all the way.

NEW YORK POST, 2/6/98, p. 47, Thelma Adams

It takes 87 of 88 ballistic minutes of "The Replacement Killers" before Hong Kong's Cary Grant, Chow Yun-Fat, is allowed to get a dimple. Until then, he's pretty much Charles Bronson—without Bronson's blithe sense of humor.

Back in Hong Kong, Chow has made more than 70 movies. He was diva director John Woo's alter-ego in the action classics "The Killer" and "Hard-Boiled." Now Chow hopes to be more than a pretty "Face/Off," following Woo to Hollywood with dreams for "A Better Tomorrow."

Like British import Grant, who made his American debut as a supporting player in Frank Tuttle's 1932 romantic comedy, "This Is the Night," Chow's first film Stateside doesn't show all his talents.

He's typecast as an honorable but ruthless Chinese assassin, a hurter with a heart of gold.

Chow's John Lee has no problem liquidating coke fiends. But when L.A. kingpin Mr. Wei (Kenneth Tsang) orders Lee to kill Detective Stan Zedkov (Michael Rooker), the cop's son gets caught in the crosshairs. Lee chokes, and we have a moral dilemma approaching Woo proportions.

Like "Face/Off," cops and killers, fathers and sons, find commonalities that blur the line between black and white. But Woo only produced this bullet-happy actioner. He left the directing to music videographer Antoine Fuqua (Coolio's "Gangsta's Paradise").

"Killers" is too busy trying to be cool to be cutting edge. It's too of-the-moment to sustain plot or character development—not that Ken Sanzel's spiraling script gives Fuqua many options.

Fuqua and cinematographer Peter Collister ("Bad Boys") adore the dwarfcam, a kneecap angle that makes both heroes and villains larger than life—and their nostrils dark tunnels into the unknown. Amid the saturated colors bursting from the dark interiors like Elvis on a black velvet painting, virtually everything but water bursts into flame.

Even femme forger Meg Coburn—the gal Friday that Lee hires to fake him a passport—has inferno hair with hellish highlights. Oscar-winner Mira Sorvino steps into the role and out of her clothes. She's clearly a woman who hasn't learned that underwear as outerwear is way over.

The oft-annoying Sorvino's dishy dish is a fair match for Chow. Bossman Wei's second banana (Jurgen Prochnow, wither your career?) snidely tells the captive duo, "you two make a cute couple." We're surprised, but we have to agree with the evil, pock-marked fiend.

NEWSDAY, 2/6/98, Part II/p. B6, John Anderson

Oh yeah, yeah, yeah it's a *dynamite* combination: Asia's most popular leading man, an actress who consistently confirms the Academy Award as the divining rod of mediocrity, a director of music videos and a budget the size of Trenton. What could possibly go wrong?

What you end up wanting in "The Replacement Killers" is a replacement for "The Replacement Killers." Chow Yun-Fat, John Woo's fetish-actor and a subtly complex sex symbol, is, as always, a compelling presence as the Chinese immigrant and invincible assassin John Lee. Forced to commit hired murder for the powerful Terence Wei (Kenneth Tsang)—who keeps Lee's family in China under threat of death—Lee is the kind of tortured hero that Chow can do in his sleep.

Sorvino, however, seems to actually be asleep. That, or phoning her performance in, from Planet Aphrodite. The chemistry between her and Chow, when it isn't caustic is nonexistent. Add to this her character—a forger of documents named Meg Coburn who, when push comes to shove (and it does) displays the martial/military abilities and charisma of—dare we say it?—Demi Moore in "G.I. Jane."

All Lee wants to do is flee the United States and get back to his family (we don't blame him), but Wei has other plans. A detective named Zedkov (Michael Rooker) has killed Wei's son during a bust—Zedkov gave him a chance, but the son chose to draw and die. Wei cannot accept this relatively honorable death, however, and orders Lee to murder Zedkov's son in his father's arms. This Lee cannot do. So after a shootout at Coburn's offices, Lee and Coburn flee—and shoot, and flee and shoot and flee.

Had there been any dramatic tension or ingenuity to the storyline behind "The Replacement Killers," they likely would have been rendered inert by director Antoine Fuqua, he of the unpronounceable last name and MTV rep (he directed the rap artist Coolio's "Gangsta's Paradise" video). Fuqua's visual sense conforms to the storyline in one sense—move or die. But his antic, illogical and inorganic use of manic camera movements and style-for-style's-sake makes for one annoying movie.

It's unfortunate that Chow's Hollywood debut should be in such a misfire of a film, because this really is his moment: an Asian leading man of legitimate acting talents and screen appeal, who can convincingly assume the post-modernist, existential, fin de siecle mien required of our pre-millennial action hero. Chow's got it all. He simply has to start hanging out with a better crowd.

SIGHT AND SOUND, 6/98, p. 54, David Tse

John Lee is a hitman, under the influence of mob boss Terence Wei, who holds Lee's family captive in China. After dispatching a target in a crowded LA nightclub, Lee's next target is detective Stan Zedkov, who killed Wei's drug-dealing son during a police arrest. Lee is unable to pull the trigger at the last minute, and plans to protect his family by secretly returning to China. His meeting with passport forger Meg Coburn is interrupted by Wei's thugs. Coburn refuses to disclose Lee's identity to Zedkov, but Zedkov and his colleagues figure it out by going through the wreckage of her workshop.

Lee and Coburn become uneasy allies as they shoot their way out of a series of traps. A pair of contract killers, Collins and Ryker, are hired by Wei to replace Lee. Lee reveals his job is actually to kill Zedkov's infant son. He thwarts an attempt on the boy's life in a movie theatre. Lee and Coburn go to wipe out Wei and his killers. They succeed, and depart with Zedkov's acquiescence. Coburn gives Lee forged passports for his family, thus ensuring their freedom.

As prolific as Gérard Depardieu and charismatic as Cary Grant, Chow Yun Fat is without question Hong Kong cinema's foremost leading man. He is perhaps best known for his elegant hitman in John Woo's *The Killer*, a role he now reprises for *The Replacement Killers*, his first US movie.

Chow is given full star treatment here, set among a strong supporting cast including Mira Sorvino, Michael Rooker and Danny Trejo. The movie is slickly directed by newcomer Antoine Fuqua who, as a music-video director turned feature film-maker, is not as bombastic and choppy as, say, Michael Bay (*The Rock*). Fuqua's style is more seamless and gliding. His camera caresses the interiors and gadgets with fetishistic delight, or dashes after the actors as they flee from photogenic bursts of gunfire. Wreckage is observed in beautifying slow motion: this is action movie as abstracted kinetic choreography. Like most music-video actors, Fuqua is visually omnivorous and allusive: Sorvino's shadowy workshop seems to be next door to John Doe's flat in *Se7en* and the neon-lit sleazy chic of the Chinatown sequences nods towards *Fallen Angels*—an ironic touch, since Wong Kar-Wai flippantly quotes John Woo in that film.

You can tell the script has been extensively pared down—there are probably no more than 70 lines of dialogue. The reason appears to be not so much to help its Chinese-speaking star (who utters as few words as Alain Delon in *Le Samorai)*, but that Fuqua recognises the material is formulaic anyway, and consciously reduces the story to a skeletal frame on which to hang the visual razzmatazz. The line between pure action cinema and music-video mannerisms is very thin. With wordless set pieces edited (impressively) to thumping hip-hop beats, the film resembles a flashy gangsta rap video, except that people actually fire their weapons here.

The most semiotically rich sequence of the film is a gunfight in a movie theatre. As the battle takes place, we see old newsreel footage of fighter planes and cartoons flickering on the screen in the background. As a juxtaposition of three different representations of violence (realistic, stylised and slapstick), the sequence shows a self deprecating humour on Fuqua's part. However, it could also be read as the indiscriminate levelling of different registers of violence for punchy visual effect.

Chow is used by Fuqua as an enigmatic icon: his character goes by the non-name of John Lee, and he's not encouraged to act, which is a shame. His star entrance at the beginning doesn't really work because we're not convinced his job is dangerous. He seems protected by a bullet-proof aura of Zen detachment amidst the night clubbers and sweaty crooks. (He has a Buddhist monk as a confidant.) The only element resembling a personal statement from Chow and executive producer Woo is the plot device of the all-important passport. (Both Chow and Woo have immigrated to the US as part of the pre-takeover migration fever.) Otherwise, there is a hollow of impersonality and inaction at the heart of this action movie.

Without a human centre, we gravitate towards Sorvino's counterfeiter. Sorvino, often the hearty, funny girl, clearly relishes being cast against type as a mean, grungy *fatale*, and she attacks her role with skill. She never smiles until the final scene, but has stolen the show long before. She makes the movie.

VILLAGE VOICE, 2/10/98, p. 104, Michael Atkinson

Let's call them billboard movies, movies whose sole function is to position their heretofore unproven players as viable box-office cash crops in the public brainpan. Of course, Chow Yun-Fat, in his first Hollywood piston-thrower *The Replacement Killer* has much more cachet and mileage than either Howie Long or Baby Spice, but to the hinterlands he's just the first Asian male lead in a Hollywood film since Bruce Lee. (Boy, does John Lone not count.) And he doesn't even know the drunken monkey—just how to wear sunglasses and evacuate an automatic magazine faster than pork fat through a goose. Correct me if I'm wrong, but what made Chow memorable in his HK Woo days was the high contrast between his boyishly serene baby face and his just-woke-up nonchalance with slaughter. Taken at face value as it is, Chow's cool reaches a comatic sleepiness in *The Replacement Killers* that may well make the Columbia executives wonder why they bothered.

Chow is pressed into hired-assassin service for an underworld kingpin in exchange for his family's safety, but his final chore involves the vengeance shooting of a cop's (Michael Rooker) young son. Rather than go through with it, Chow decides to break camp and enlists the help of a high-tech forger (Mira "I won an Oscar for this? I went to Harvard for this?" Sorvino) to nail down documents. Of course, other assassins come looking for him before he can escape. Eighteen thousand gun booms, 3000 ricochet *b'dings*, and several hundred household items decimated by stray bullets later, a weary Chow restores honor and proves that he can shoot a gun off-frame as well as Seagal or Schwarzenegger, which is to say, at least as well as my mother—given a few lessons.

Directed by Antoine Fuqua, inexplicably famed for the "Gangsta's Paradise" video (which, I seem to remember, is nothing more than clips from *Dangerous Minds* cut with shots of Coolio and Michelle Pfeiffer glaring at each other on a classroom set), *The Replacement Killers* is Woo manqué down to its dress socks; Woo was, it should be noted, an executive producer. Fuqua tries his best to "woo," to assemble violence as an idealized Acme contraption within which you can see the gears of destiny lock teeth, and within which the laws of physics are bowed like a young tree tied to an angry dog. But there's no grace to the mayhem, and no lunatic Woo passion or bathos. The ritualized expenditure of ammo alone does not transcendence make.

Also reviewed in:
CHICAGO TRIBUNE, 2/6/98, Friday/p. C, John Petrakis
NEW YORK TIMES, 2/6/98, p. E19, Stephen Holden
VARIETY, 2/2-8/98, p. 27, Leonard Klady
WASHINGTON POST, 2/6/98, p. B1, Rita Kempley
WASHINGTON POST, 2/6/98, Weekend/p. 41, Desson Howe

RETURN TO PARADISE

A Polygram Filmed Entertainment release of a Propaganda Films production in association with Tetragram. *Executive Producer:* David Arnold and Ezra Swerdlow. *Producer:* Steve Golin and Alain Bernheim. *Director:* Joseph Ruben. *Screenplay:* Wesley Strick and Bruce Robinson. *Director of Photography:* Reynaldo Villalobos. *Editor:* Andrew Mondshein and Craig McKay. *Music:* Mark Mancina. *Music Editor:* Thomas Drescher. *Sound:* William Sarokin and (music) Christopher Ward. *Sound Editor:* Stan Bochner. *Casting:* Eric R. Zuckerman. *Production Designer:* Bill Groom. *Art Director:* Dennis Bradford. *Set Decorator:* Betsy Klompus. *Set Dresser:* Anthony Dimeo, Joseph L. "Pepe" Bird, Gregg Aharoni, Joseph R. Bird, Christopher Ferraro, Gary Levitsky, and Alan Muzeni. *Special Effects:* Steve Kirshofff. *Costumes:* Juliet

Polcsa. *Make-up:* Katherine Bihr. *Make-up (Anne Heche):* Elaine Offers. *Stunt Coordinator:* Jack Gill and Peter Bucossi. *Running time:* 109 minutes. *MPAA Rating:* R.

CAST: Vince Vaughn (Sheriff); Anne Heche (Beth); Joaquin Phoenix (Lewis); David Conrad (Tony); Vera Farmiga (Kerrie); Nick Sandow (Ravitch); Jada Pinkett Smith (M.J. Major); Ming Lee (Mr. Chandran); Joel De La Fuente (Mr. Doramin); Richard Chang (Prosecutor); James Michael McCauley (Famous Divorce Lawyer); Brettanya Friese (Young Woman in Limo); Deanna Yusoff (Woman in Bar); David Zayas (Construction Foreman); Amy Wong (Ticket Agent); Is Issariya (Malaysian Woman in Hammock); Ed Hodson (Features Editor); Kevin Scullin and Glenn Patrick (Doormen); Yusmal Ghazali, Aril Izani, and Kwak Wai (Scruffy Guys); Curzon Dobell (Client); Vincent Patrick (Tavern Waiter); Elizabeth Rodriguez (Gaby); Teoh Kay Yong (Chief Justice); Rebecca Saifer (Hotel Waitress); Rebecca Boyd (Restaurant Hostess); Woon-Kin Chin (Guard); Regina Wu (Bailiff).

CHRISTIAN SCIENCE MONITOR, 8/14/98, p. B3, David Sterritt

[*Return to Paradise* was reviewed jointly with *How Stella Got Her Groove Back*; See Sterritt's review of that film.]

LOS ANGELES TIMES, 8/14/98, Calendar/p. 14, Kenneth Turan

The plot of "Return to Paradise" sounds like the subject of a late-night college dormitory conversation, the kind where implausible situations are given serious consideration. If you could meet anyone in history, who would it be? If you could ensure world peace by giving up sex, would you do it? That kind of thing.

The question here is a little more specific: If you could save the life of someone you knew by voluntarily spending a few years in prison, would you turn yourself in and invite the police to turn the key? And, if an attorney as attractive and dynamic as Beth Eastern, played by Anne Heche, asked you to do it, how much of a difference would that make?

That dilemma is faced by a pair of New Yorkers who probably would never have met if it wasn't for the random camaraderie of post-college travel. Sheriff (Vince Vaughn) is a self-described scam artist, while Tony (David Conrad) is a well-mannered engineering student from a comfortable background.

For five vacation weeks in Malaysia, these two, plus gentle Lewis (Joaquin Phoenix), a tree-hugger whose idea of fun is reintroducing the orangutan into Borneo, become the closest of pals. We see them in extended flashbacks, using drugs, chasing women, calling one another "bro" and acting alternately oblivious to and contemptuous of the local population.

Cut to two years later, with Sheriff still hustling as a limo driver and Tony rising in his profession and engaged to a chic young woman. Into their lives comes attorney Eastern, who tells them that a combination of bad luck and their own culpability has put her client and their old bro Lewis into a Malaysian prison.

Worse than that, in exactly eight days, Lewis will be executed as a drug dealer unless they return to that erstwhile paradise, admit to drug use and spend time in prison. How much time? Three years if they both come back, six if only one makes the trip. As the days tick away on screen, the men have a heck of a choice to make.

Director Joseph Ruben, a man with a definite gift for the melodramatic, was the appropriate choice for this project. In films like "True Believer," "The Stepfather" and "Sleeping With the Enemy," Ruben has made a career out of involving audiences in far-fetched material and he tries his best here.

Working from a script by Wesley Strick and Bruce Robinson (which in turn was based on a little-seen French film called "Force Majeur"), Ruben has ensured that "Return" was well-cast (Jada Pinkett Smith is noteworthy as a take-no-prisoners journalist, as is Phoenix in his role) and added as much energy to scenes as he can.

But though the Strick-Robinson script is solid from line to line, the film's plot is finally too implausible for anyone to rescue. Starting with the unlikely situation described above, it gets unlikelier and unlikelier as it unfolds, with twists and surprises (some of which are not really surprising) piling up to an unnerving extent.

Vaughn's self-involved Sheriff, "Mr. I Look Out for No. I," is superficially similar to his character in the successful "Swingers." But Vaughn turns out to be not the most convincing guy to be having a crisis of conscience on screen.

Counterbalancing his uncertainty, Heche does the best acting in the picture, giving a sharp and focused performance as a passionate advocate who cares terribly about saving her client. More and more, Heche is becoming one of those rare actresses who can be counted on to bring credibility to every film she's in, and "Return to Paradise" benefits greatly from her intensity.

But even Heche's work is no match for the film's fatal tendency to take itself more seriously than the material merits. A potboiler where Heche's character answers the phone in her underwear because she looks cute in foundation garments should not be confusing itself with a Human Rights Watch manifesto. If its to be experienced at all, "Return to Paradise" is best seen as a lively piece of pulp, not a profound exploration of the vagaries of the human soul.

NEW YORK, 8/31/98, p. 154, David Denby

Anne Heche leans into a scene hungrily, eager for information, for connection and intimacy. Her characters always want something, and Heche, her wired, slender body exposed, her softly curved features directed fiercely at the other actors, throws herself into the moment, holding nothing back. Heche burns so brightly she seems slightly phosphorescent—the blonde intensity can be daunting. Yet we can live with her in movie after movie for a rather simple reason: She has a genius for attentiveness. This may not seem like much of a compliment, but how many other actresses are skilled in just that way? Heche acts with a specific person, feeding off the other actor, and she's almost frighteningly direct, with little time for small talk. A strong will might make another woman rigid or bellicose, but Heche's willfulness flows into a spontaneous emotional aliveness; she drives each scene forward to its dramatic point, adding iron to her voice when she has to be tough. She's a woman in motion, and since she takes risks, she appeals to the women in the audience as a heroine. But she appeals to men too—she plays very well with men. I think one could say, in fact, that she has become the outstanding actress of heterosexual love scenes in movies today. There may be a joke there, but I can't seem to find it. Anne Heche makes a good case for professionalism in acting.

Heche injects some life into the rather square moral melodrama of *Return to Paradise*. In a lushly photographed prelude, three American college grads, Sheriff (Vince Vaughn), Tony (David Conrad), and Lewis (Joaquin Phoenix), vacationing in Malaysia, live on a beautiful beach near Penang and smoke a lot of hash. Two of the young men go home, leaving behind Lewis, an earnest environmentalist and animal lover. The movie then skips ahead to New York, two years later, where Heche shows up as Beth, a lawyer working for Lewis. It seems that he was busted for possession of drugs just after Sheriff and Tony left, and will hang in eight days unless they go back to Penang, admit their responsibility, and agree to serve three years in prison each.

Return to Paradise, which was written by Bruce Robinson and Wesley Strick and directed by Joseph Ruben, appears to be a sober new version of the 1978 shocker *Midnight Express*, in which an American (Brad Davis), held for possession of hash in Turkey, was beaten and sodomized. Ruben avoids the lurid, lustful-Turk stuff, the sadomasochistic hysteria that made *Midnight Express* a trial (and a laugh) to sit through. Joaquin Phoenix, with his ugly-beautiful face, is the post-sixties American innocent, and his suffering in prison—he has the shakes and is nearly incoherent—is shocking enough. The sense of the movie appears to be that the boys, by treating the Third World as a pleasure garden, behaved carelessly, but were then punished far in excess of their crimes by petty Malaysian bureaucrats seeking to humiliate the United States. In New York, Beth puts the screws to Sheriff and Tony: Go back, or your friend dies. The trouble with the story is that it's too obvious morally, and too linear as a piece of dramatic construction. The filmmakers would perhaps have done better if they had started in New York and then cut back to Malaysia, so we could learn, bit by bit, who was guilty of what and we could see how the boys' earlier acts meshed with their current behavior. But Robinson, Strick, and Ruben have instead created a conventionally straightforward melodrama of redemption. The Vince Vaughn character is a self-proclaimed Brooklyn "bum"—a cool guy, maybe, but a time-waster who drives a limo because he won't risk doing anything serious. Sheriff is a tame throwback to the kind of character William Holden played 45 years ago—the wised-up American who says he's only out for himself but who has buried good qualities. The way the character has been set up, Sheriff has only one way to turn; if he doesn't go in that direction, there's no movie.

Tall and handsome, with a high forehead and a nervous laugh, Vaughn (the poseur in *Swingers*) eases into a scene, holding himself in reserve. Vaughn may have buried good qualities himself. We're drawn to his actor's pride—he doesn't try too hard to make himself likable, and that quality alone makes him glamorous. But by the end of the movie, Vaughn is stuck making speeches, and the final scenes are frightfully noble. Joseph Ruben *(The Stepfather, True Believer)* works with superb craftsmanship, but the only thing that saves the movie from boredom is the moment-by-moment sexual tension between Heche and Vaughn. She rouses him from his self-love, and he looks at her as if he's never really taken a woman seriously before. We can hardly blame him.

NEW YORK POST, 8/14/98, p. 46, Thelma Adams

Eight days, seven nights: That's how long Anne Heche has to persuade Vince Vaughn and David Conrad that they should fly to Asia—"Return to Paradise"—and share the rap for the drug bust that landed their buddy Joaquin Phoenix in jail on the Malaysian rice diet.

As the impassioned lawyer sent to bring the two New Yorkers to foreign justice to save Phoenix from hanging, Heche trades her last leading man, middle-aged, irascible burnout Harrison Ford, for young, irascible Brooklynite Vaughn. And she still gets to visit exotic foreign lands, bark into a cell phone and wear cool clothes.

"Paradise," directed by Joseph Rubin ("Sleeping With the Enemy") from a script by Wesley Strick and Bruce Robinson, is a primer on how not to spend the summer after college. It's a poor man's "Midnight Express," without the horror and moral weight.

Harvard architect Tony (Conrad), blue-collar college boy Sheriff (Vaughn) and Greenpeace trust-fund hippie Lewis (Phoenix) spend five carefree weeks together living in a seaside shack.

They're young Americans with an unspoken sense of entitlement. They smoke hashish, screw Malaysian women, disregard local laws—and Phoenix gets caught.

The plot, nominally complicated by ambitious reporter Jada Pinkett, telegraphs every twist. The movie's discovery is Vaughn. He has that combination of heft and looks rippled by the threat of violence that marked the young James Caan. The "Swingers" star is the answer to the perennial question, "Where's the beef(cake)?"

Vaughn's Sheriff is the kind of guy who swills beer from long-necked bottles, handles conflicts with his fists and thinks the hard part of making love to a woman is talking afterward—until he meets Beth. He's a loner straight out of the old West, even though he drives limos in Manhattan instead of cattle in Montana.

Sheriff doesn't wear a dusty white hat, but it's clear before the writers pose the bold-faced question—"Would you accept a handful of years in a foreign prison to spare a buddy's life?"—that he'll do the right thing.

There's hardly enough moral dilemma in "Paradise" to fill the average "Twilight Zone." But if Heche has to spend another week with a man, Vaughn's a keeper.

NEWSDAY, 8/14/98, Part II/p.3, Jack Mathews

[*Return to Paradise* was reviewed jointly with *How Stella Got Her Groove Back;* see Mathews' review of that film.]

SIGHT AND SOUND, 1/99, p. 55, Jamie Graham

College graduates Sheriff, Tony and Lewis are enjoying the final days of their five week holiday in Penang, Malaysia. They crash a hired bike and throw it over a cliff. Later Sheriff and Tony leave their hashish supplies with Lewis, who has decided to stay longer.

Two years later cab driver Sheriff and engineer Tony are working in New York. Their lives are disrupted by Beth, a lawyer who informs them that Lewis has spent the last two years in a Malaysian jail and is going to be executed in eight days' time; the police, investigating the missing bike, found the hashish and charged Lewis with trafficking. His only hope is for Sheriff or Tony to come forward and admit that some of the stash was theirs, although they may be jailed as well as a result. Tony says he will return to Malaysia, but only if the reluctant Sheriff agrees as well. Sheriff eventually gives in to Beth's pressure, not least because they have become lovers.

In Malaysia, Beth lets it slip that she is Lewis' older sister. Tony reacts by flying back to New York, but Sheriff stays. After hearing Sheriff's confession, the prosecutors agree to lessen the charges against Lewis, but news arrives of a vehement anti Malaysian article in an American newspaper. The enraged judge sentences Lewis to death immediately. Beth assures the now imprisoned Sheriff that he will be released in six months and promises to wait for him.

A crisis-of-conscience drama in which two friends must decide whether to sacrifice several years of their own lives to save that of a third, *Return to Paradise* (based on Pierre Jolivet's *Force Majeure)* is, as Hollywood product currently goes, a relatively gritty affair. At its best, it has that raw quality so often associated with 70s films such as *Mean Streets*. Particularly impressive is the opening montage of camcorder footage—which follows the trio through five colourful Malaysian weeks—and the brutal conclusion. But the harsher, more effective sequences are diluted by a steady stream of Hollywood clichés and ersatz sentiment. One suspects many of the cruder elements were jostled into place when director Joseph Ruben *(Money Train, Sleeping with the Enemy)*, himself no stranger to slick but crass output, engaged the services of Wesley Strick, author and script-doctor of *The Saint* and *Final Analysis*. However, whatever or whoever the cause, the final blend of arty touches, commercial melodrama, savagery and syrup is an unhappy one.

This is never more evident than in the central relationship between Vince Vaughn and Anne Heche, both of whom surmount considerable obstacles to give excellent performances. As two indie actors who have only recently dipped their toes into the mainstream, they would surely be aware that their characters' falling in love—shoehorned in to make the tragedy more palatable—isn't very credible. And yet they manage to invest their relationship with both passion and tenderness. Such chemistry bodes well for their casting as Norman Bates and Marion Crane in Gus Van Sant's upcoming shot-by-shot remake of *Psycho*.

Vaughn has the added millstone of having to hold our attention as he slowly evolves from cold-hearted loner to saintly saviour, a man willing to go to jail to salvage a friend's life. It's an all important transmutation that the film makers signpost every step of the way. When his Sheriff informs Heche's Beth that, "I don't have that kind of stuff in me," it is patently obvious that he'll find it soon, for the sake of the drama if nothing else. Hence when Lewis hugs Sheriff and tells him, "I knew you'd come back even if you didn't [know it]," one can't help but nod in jaded agreement.

Even the shock ending abruptly introduced, and reinforced by stark natural light—is softened somewhat by at least two slyly placed omens which fortell it. There is Sheriff's early warning to Tony that, "just because you do something good doesn't mean there'll be a happy ending", and a sub plot involving Jada Pinkett Smith as a journalist who wants to break the story early and shame the Malaysian government into releasing Lewis, a clumsy device present only to manipulate the plot's final, horrifying twist. Such cumbersome tactics are sprinkled throughout *Return to Paradise,* their combined weight preventing the film from becoming the hard-hitting moral drama it clearly wants to be.

VILLAGE VOICE, 8/18/98, p. 107, Michael Atkinson

The Midnight Express paradigm—young, complacent Americans dally in the drug trade of a Third Worldish nation and end up exploring the bowels of a medieval criminal system—is, however exotic in spirit, immensely nerve-wracking and far from exhausted. But *Return to Paradise*, a nonstarter directed unsuspensefully by Joseph Ruben and written ungracefully by Bruce Robinson and Wesley Strick, is a how-to guide on shooting the bottom out of the boat. Vince Vaughn, Joaquin Phoenix, and David Conrad are ugly-American buddies hanging out in Malaysia doing hash; after the other two leave, Phoenix is nabbed for trafficking a brick the boys tossed in the trash, and spends two years behind very rusty bars. Hotshot lawyer Anne Heche then pops up in New York to inform limo driver Vaughn and architect Conrad that unless they return and do three years apiece for the hash, Phoenix will hang in a week.

The problem is, after a convincing opening of whacked-out hedonism in the tropics, the movie spends more than a slow hour with Heche in New York as she nags the boys into getting on that plane. (She and Vaughn meet at least eight times to argue.) There's lots of thinking-with-soundtrack, and the film often feels as indecisive as Vaughn, whose should-I-go, should-I-stay Method acting can drive you to spring-clean your wallet. We never even see Phoenix's arrest and imprisonment, arguably the situation's dramatic heart. What the story did not further need is a love story between Heche and Vaughn, but Ruben and co. seem dedicated to subverting what's provocative about the story, down to the casting of Conrad, who registers like a slow tire leak. Still, however underdressed, Heche proves again she can make gumbo from gruel—without a compelling character to work with, she still brings her scenes to a simmer.

Also reviewed in:
NEW YORK TIMES, 8/14/98, p. E9, Janet Maslin
VARIETY, 8/3-9/98, p. 36, Todd McCarthy
WASHINGTON POST, 8/14/98, p. D1, Stephen Hunter
WASHINGTON POST, 8/14/98, Weekend/p. 39, Michael O'Sullivan

RIDE

A Dimension Films release of a Hudlin Bros. production. *Executive Producer:* Bob Weinstein, Harvey Weinstein, and Cary Granat. *Producer:* Reginald Hudlin and Warrington Hudlin. *Director:* Millicent Shelton. *Screenplay:* Millicent Shelton. *Director of Photography:* Frank Byers. *Editor:* Earl Watson. *Music:* Bill Stephney and Byron Phillips. *Music Editor:* Marvin R. Morris. *Sound:* Al McGuire. *Sound Editor:* Mike Le-Mare. *Casting:* Eileen Mack Knight. *Production Designer:* Bryan Jones. *Art Director:* Vera Mills. *Set Decorator:* Rick Ambroise and Cynthia Wigginton. *Set Dresser:* Bernard Jackson, Wayne Miller, Jane Patterson, and Frank Robert. *Special Effects:* Bob Vasquez. *Costumes:* Richard Owings. *Make-up:* Angela Johnson. *Stunt Coordinator:* Cal Johnson. *Running time:* 95 minutes. *MPAA Rating:* R.

CAST: Malik Yoba (Poppa); Melissa De Sousa (Leta); John Witherspoon (Roscoe); Fredro Starr (Geronimo); Cedric the Entertainer (Bo); Sticky Fingaz (Brotha X); Kellie Williams (Tuesday); Idalis De Leon (Charity); Julia Garrison (Blacké); Guy Torry (Indigo); Rueben Asher (Casper); Lady of Rage (Peaches); Dartanyan Edmonds (Byrd); Downtown Julie Brown (Bleau); Luther "Luke" Campbell (Freddy B); Doctor Dre (Eight); Ed Lover (Six); Snoop Doggy Dogg (Mente); Kirsten Camille Hill (Sexy Woman); Thalia Baudin (#65); Gary Anthony Williams (Tiny); Gene Chen (Store Owner); Glenn Morel (Groom); Fred Williamson (Casper's Dream Dad); Michael Pilver (Reat Room Attendant); Tom Chapman (Farmer); Jonathan Bergholz (Sheriff); George Collier (Mechanic); Michael Balin (James); Amber Pyfrom (Little Girl); Terri Lester (Yes Girl #50); Dave Hollister, Redman, Keith Murray, and Erik Sermon (Themselves); Tonya Oliver (Montage Girl).

LOS ANGELES TIMES, 4/1/98, Calendar/p. 3, John Anderson

Given the El Dorado aspects of the rap music industry—which seems to rival only the NBA as the dream career of underprivileged youth—"Ride," a rap-meets-road movie, sort of blows its chance at making any serious comment about the big business of black culture.

At the same time, it's just about as funny as it is vile—a lot of the humor is either scatological, sophomoric or sexist—and its eclectic cast of characters alone is enough to make "Ride" worth the trip.

They include Leta Evans (Melissa De Sousa), a would-be film director from NYU who's lowered her sights to music videos—and, even further, to V World, where the thoroughly unscrupulous Freddy Brown (Luther Campbell) and his imperious director, Bleau Kelly (Downtown Julie Brown), virtually Shanghai her into the job from hell: taking a busload of the label's young and hungry to a video shoot in Florida—via the MIR spacecraft of luxury tour buses.

With less music than you'd expect (by Onyx, Wu-Tang Clan, Naughty by Nature and others) and more formula than you'd hoped, the busload makes its way through Jersey and points south as romances ebb and flow and interpersonal relationships fray and ravel. Tuesday (Kellie Williams) thinks she's pregnant by Brotha X (Sticky Fingaz); Casper (Rueben Asher), of the black-white act Casper and Indigo (Guy Torry), is hoping to meet his father and hoping that he's black.

Poppa (the magnetic Malik Yoba), who plays spiritual guidance counselor to the group and provides the love interest for Leta, can't keep his brother Geronimo (Fredro Starr) under control. Geronimo, meanwhile, is being pursued by Peaches and Byrd—played by the Lady of Rage and Dartanyan Edmonds as the duo who once robbed the entire Apollo Theater audience for booing them off the stage—because he's made off with the money they stole from a comic Asian store owner. (Do hip-hop comedies always have to have a comic Asian store owner?)

Leta's middle-class values/virtues are employed to a certain degree in writer-director Millicent Shelton's script, but any dramatic excavation of black multiculture is only hinted at. In fact, Shelton (her producers are the Hudlin brothers, Reginald and Warrington) uses a lot of shtick and a lot of dubious material that relies on stereotyping and racist attitudes. But, at the same time, she keeps the whole thing moving along maybe not at top speed but with a rhythm, as well as a destination.

NEW YORK POST, 3/28/98, p. 23, Larry Worth

Every map shows that driving from Harlem to Miami is a long haul. But as portrayed in "Ride," it's downhill all the way.

The paint-by-numbers tale puts a group of inner-city misfits on a bus, then waits 90 minutes for the various combatants to inevitably bond. All-too-familiar squabbles, include a stuck-up beauty queen, a white rapper who thinks he's black, a trouble-making thief, a two-timing lover boy, a fresh-faced ingenue, feuding bro's and on and on.

Naturally, the bus is in worse shape than the Titanic, so it's meant to be a running joke as the vehicle huffs and puffs its way to the Sunshine State. Funny concept, huh?

By all appearances, first-time writer-director Millicent Shelton knows zilch about comedy, demonstrated as she seeks humor in armed robberies, parodies the Million Man March or sinks to endless sex yuks.

The rest is just more cliches, whether introducing the dozen-odd protagonists in slo-mo or showing their fates in "American Graffiti"-like codas. Worse, the dialogue is heavy on jive talk, and even heavier on mumbled non sequiturs.

Basically, the action—or lack thereof—is window dressing for a soundtrack, coming via impromptu rap numbers or dreamy montages. Either way, the musical interludes are welcome distractions.

Few saving graces are found in the acting department, though Malik Yoba, Melissa DeSousa, Snoop Doggy Dogg and Downtown Julie Brown try to expand their walking caricatures. Even then, its all in vain.

The bottom line: "Ride" won't take viewers anywhere they haven't been—or would want to revisit.

Also reviewed in:
NEW YORK TIMES, 3/28/98, p. B12, Lawrence Van Gelder
VARIETY, 3/30-4/5/98, p. 41, Lael Loewenstein

RINGMASTER

An Artisan Entertainment release in association with the Kushner-Locke Company of a Steve Stabler/Gary Goldstein production.   *Executive Producer:* Brent Baum, Don Corsini, Richard Dominick, Erwin More, Brian Medavoy, Donald Kushner, and Peter Locke   *Producer:* Jerry Springer, Gina Rugolo-Judd, Brad Jenkel, Steve Stabler and Gary W. Goldstein.   *Director:* Neil

Abramson.   *Screenplay:* Jon Bernstein.   *Director of Photography:* Russell Lyster.   *Editor:* Suzanne Hines.   *Music:* Kennard Ramsey.   *Sound:* Shawn Holden.   *Casting:* Carmen Tetzlaff.   *Production Designer:* Dorian Vernacchio and Deborah Raymond.   *Set Decorator:* Jodi Ginnever.   *Costumes:* Gail McMullen.   *Running time:* 95 minutes.   *MPAA Rating:* R.

CAST: Jerry Springer (Jerry Farrelly); Jaime Pressly (Angel Zorzak); Molly Hagan (Connie Zorzak); Michael Dudikoff (Rusty); Ashley Holbrook (Willie); Wendy Raquel Robinson (Starletta); Michae Jai White (Demond); Tangie Ambrose (Vonda); Nicki Micheaux (Leshawnette); William McNamara (Troy); Dawn Maxey (Natalie); Maximilliana (Charlie/Claire); John Capodice (Mel Riley).

LOS ANGELES TIMES, 11/25/98, Calendar, p. 7, Kevin Thomas

Watching "The Jerry Springer Show" can be like eating potato chips: It's not very good for you but it's hard to stop once you've started. His show invites a seductive condescension with its endless parade of the overweight, overpainted, undereducated, all in a state of jealous rage or bigotry.

What's more it's easy to justify watching low-class types make fools of themselves by telling ourselves that it's probably good therapy for people too poor or ignorant to seek out counseling to vent all this rage on TV. In any event, Springer is a guilty pleasure, like reading a tabloid while standing in a supermarket check-out line.

A movie inspired by his TV show's phenomenal success was surely an inevitability, but that it would be as shrewd and funny as "Ringmaster" could scarcely have been guaranteed. Director Neil Abramson and writer Jon Bernstein start by imagining two sets of people eager to appear on the program and colliding when they do.

On the one hand, there's Connie Zorzak (Molly Hagan), who's fit to be tied that her sluttish teenage daughter Angel (Jaime Pressly) is fooling around with her stepfather Rusty (Michael Dudikoff), a good-looking but lazy layabout. Fireworks ensue but Connie thinks they'd be perfect candidates for Jerry's show. As an added inducement to Jerry's people she decides it might be a good idea if she can assure them she has seduced her daughter's dim fiance (Ashley Holbrook).

Meanwhile, some fine-looking ladies, Starletta (Wendy Raquel Robinson), Vonda (Tangie Ambrose) and Leshawnette (Nicki Micheaux), think that they belong on the show too, along with Demond (Michael Jai White), a handsome, muscular playboy who's been unfaithful to all of them. There are more fireworks when Angel and Demond take notice of each other backstage at the show.

Performances are uniformly sharp and lively, with Hagan and Robinson suggesting some dimension and genuine anguish in the women they portray.

"Ringmaster" creates some deft insights: that for a person like Connie, a Dade City, Fla., doughnut shop employee who lives in a trailer park, the promise of a free trip, though brief, to Hollywood, with the chance to stay in a nice hotel and to appear on TV—regardless of the outrageous circumstances—is the whole point. It's the promise of a thrill that outweighs her anger at her daughter's and husband's behavior.

Springer, whose movie surname is listed in the production notes as Farrelly, is of course playing himself and appears intermittently throughout. He wisely takes a self-deprecating stance, muses about how he'd hoped to have a career like Walter Cronkite, and finds himself constantly mobbed as much as Madonna. He presents himself as a detached, cool observer of the human comedy, but when one of the people in the audience during one of his shows gets up and says such individuals shouldn't be allowed on TV, Springer lashes back indignantly, asserting that the poor and obscure have just as much a right to air their ills on the tube as the rich and famous, who are always detailing their latest detox or lurid incidents in their lives. The man has a point.

NEWSDAY, 11/25/98, Part II/p. B11, John Anderson

If the distributing Artisan Entertainment had any class at all it would hand out shower curtains and Lysol with every ticket to "Ringmaster," which seems to have been cast out of one of the better bus terminals and seems determined to prove that there is no such thing as objective good taste, nor any depths to which Jerry Springer won't sink in the chemical toilet he calls a career.

All of which is, of course, precisely the thing he'd like to hear, since it appeals to the lobotomized audiences that watch his show and won't even notice that they're being cruelly lampooned. The most depressing thing about "Ringmaster"—in which former Cincinnati mayor and trash-talk stablehand Springer plays a clone named Jerry Farelly—is that there's probably a market for it.

White trash? Sure. Black trash, too. All trash, all the time. But what's really offensive about Springer's movie isn't the acrid haze of vulgarity or the sordid characters or the rampant off-handed oral sex or even someone saying, "This trailer ain't big enough for the both of us." It's the movie's attempt to pass itself off as a defense of the poor and disenfranchised. Rich people get on TV all the time, Springer brays. Where else can poor people get on television and totally humiliate themselves?

Or do it for Springer's benefit, of course. The aspiring "guests" in his mockumentary—which presumes people believe that Springer's guests are real—are Connie (Molly Hagan), her daughter Angel (Jaime Pressly), Connie's husband, Rusty (Michael Dudikoff), who's sleeping with both of them, and Angel's fiance, Willie (Ashley Holbrook), whom Connie sleeps with when she finds out about Rusty and Angel. Traditional family values, as long as your name is Manson.

Their counterparts include Starletta (Wendy Raquel Robinson) and Demond (Michael Jai White), who's sleeping with all of Starletta's friends, who are about as savory as she is.

To paraphrase Mencken, no one ever went broke underestimating the good taste of the American people, something Springer proves daily.

VILLAGE VOICE, 12/1/98, p. 128, Gary Dauphin

Like Howard Stern's *Private Parts*, which dared to imagine the mensch behind the King of All (Sleaze) Media, *Ringmaster*'s fictionalized behind-the-scenes look at *The Jerry Springer Show* is an unexpectedly plaintive cri de coeur. Painting its nominal star as a defender of the poor and their right to be as publicly messy as any drug-addicted rock star, *Ringmaster* is a 90-minute "Jerry's Final Thought" pumped up with silicone implants: bawdy, saccharine, and jiggly. It's not every day you get back-to-back lectures on stepfather-stepdaughter incest and the populist dynamics of daytime television outside graduate departments of cultural studies.

The show being the thing, *Ringmaster* orbits around two panels of Jerry guests, one for a segment about step-sex, the other for a bit about traitor homegirls. The white incest panel occupies most of the screen time and gets what little character development there is. Connie (an oddly credible Molly Hagan) is a hardworking, comely mom saddled with a do-nothing second husband and an overly nubile daughter (Jaime Pressly, looking appropriately trashy and inbred). After catching them in bed for what must be the umpteenth time, Connie calls "the people from Jerry" with her troubles, reacting with pathetically touching glee when she's confirmed as a guest. In comparison, the "traitor girlfriends" bunch, being the black panel, provides *Ringmaster* with most of its verbal comedy but little in the way of texture besides neck rolls, extensions, and lots of shrill yelling about "my man."

Director Neil Abramson throws his audience the necessary naughty bones but also lets quaint buds of sentiment bloom in Jerry's unlikely hothouse, the camera lingering over hugely inflated tits as well as hugs, exchanged looks of betrayal, and schoolgirlish squeals of excitement at the prospect of 15 minutes of fame. If anything rings particularly false, it has to be Springer himself, who ghosts the edges of his own movie with a look of freaked-out surprise. Unwilling to admit that he actually enjoys what he does, Jerry mostly reacts and kvetches, providing the not so new information that deep down he really just wants to be loved and understood. Everyone wants that, but as *Ringmaster* proves (in admittedly the broadest of terms), it's getting those things that's the rub.

Also reviewed in:
CHICAGO TRIBUNE, 11/25/98, Tempo/p. 2, Monica Eng
NEW YORK TIMES, 11/25/98, p. E18, Stephen Holden
VARIETY, 11/23-29/98, p. 48, Dennis Harvey

RIVER RED

A Castle Hill Productions release. *Executive Producer:* David Miller and Gary Kauffman. *Producer:* Eric Drilling, Steven Schlueter, and Avram Ludwig. *Director:* Eric Drilling. *Screenplay:* Eric Drilling. *Director of Photography:* Steven Schlueter. *Editor:* Paul Streicher, Paige Lauman, and Steve LaMorte. *Sound:* Robert Ghiraldini. *Casting:* Gabriela Leff. *Production Designer:* Roshelle Berliner. *Art Director:* Josh Outerbridge. *Special Effects:* Drew Jiritano and Greg Jiritano. *Costumes:* Cindy Evans. *Make-up:* Cassandra Mucha. *Stunt Coordinator:* John McLaughlin and Elliot Santiago. *Running time:* 103 minutes. *MPAA Rating:* R.

CAST: Tom Everett Scott (Dave Holden);   David Moscow (Tom Holden);   Cara Buono (Rachel);   David Lowery (Billy);   Denis O'Hare (Father);   Michael Kelly (Frankie);   Leo Burmester (Judge Perkins);   Tibor Feldman (Dr. Fields);   James Murtaugh (Chief Bascomb);   Michael Angarano (Young Tom);   Peter Tambakis (Young Dave);   Ted Travelstead (Gas Attendant);   Marcia DeBonis (Sara);   Christopher Cantwell (Mr. Taylor);   Andrew VanDusen (Convenience Store Clerk);   Jefferson Taffett (Young Store Clerk);   Mella Fazzoli (Timmy the Mechanic);   Charlie Landry (Mike Sanel);   Christopher Petrosino (Store Clerk's Son);   Jenni Gallagher (Denise);   Chris McGinn (Woman in Store);   Andrew Sikking (Liqour Store Clerk);   Louis Ludwig (Elderly Clerk);   John Lally (Mr. Orton);   Trudy Lally (Mrs. Orton);   Gary Kauffman (Prosecutor);   Pete "Conan" Winebrake (Defense Attorney);   John McLaughlin (Guy in Store);   Daniel Prucell (Boy at Sara's);   Ceíli (Mocha).

NEWSDAY, 11/13/98, Part II/p. B5, John Anderson

Aboard the frequently unsound ship of independent American film, the standard escape hatch for any struggling filmmaker who's gotten him or herself into a script and can't get out is to knock somebody off. Godard said all you need to make a movie is a gun and a girl. In '90s indie world, all you generally need is a gun.

There is a gun, and even a girl, in "River Red," the debut feature by Eric Drilling. But the killing at the heart of the film—one of the more intelligently handled and motivated killings in recent film memory—comes at the beginning of the story, not the end. And it sets the stage for what proves to be an intellectually adept psychological portrait of a murderer—a justified murderer, perhaps, but a murderer nonetheless.

Dave (Tom Everett Scott of "That Thing You Do" and "One True Thing," among other things) and Tom (David Moscow, "Hurricane Streets") are the sons of a brutally abusive, alcoholic father (Denis O'Hare) who takes particular pleasure in beating the younger Tom. So one night, while the old man's in a drunken stupor, Dave plunges a screwdriver through his chest. Tom, who's below legal age, takes the rap—and a term in a juvenile detention center—so Dave won't go to prison.

There was, for me at least, a bit of confusion at the outset of the film, because Moscow isn't shot in a way that makes him look particularly young, and the point of switching his clothes for Dave's bloody ones was lost. But it becomes evident before long, and although "River Red" is occasionally low key to the point of inertia, its feel for the atmosphere of "country" living (in this case, New Hampshire) is frank, honest and no Martha Stewart hallucination. The community in which the boys have grown up knew what a louse their father was, but nobody ever did anything. Some, in fact, step away from them now because of the murder. Others, like Billy the bar owner (David Lowery), are effusively helpful. Nevertheless, Dave can't make ends meet and disaster seems imminent.

What "River Red" is really about is Dave's guilt trip. He agonizies over the murder, he tortures himself over Tom's incarceration. After Tom gets beaten at the center, Dave really starts to lose it, and begins robbing convenience stores—ostensibly to keep the bank off his back, but with increasing frequency and an accelerating level of violence. And although he gets romantically involved with Rachel (the charming Cara Buono of "Next Stop, Wonderland"), he cuts Tom off, refuses any collect calls, ceases his visits and spirals toward certain disaster.

The music behind "River Red," mostly of the sullen alternative rock variety, is annoying, and put to annoying use. But the story is thoughtful and sad and rather unusual. And no escape hatches are necessary.

VILLAGE VOICE, 11/17/98, p. 138, Gary Susman

Yet another look into the savage heart of white-trash masculinity, *River Red* explores just how thick blood really is. In a hovel on the outskirts of a New Hampshire town, Dave Holden (Tom Everett Scott) casually kills his father to prevent him from further abusing Dave's younger brother, Tom (David Moscow). Not yet 21, Tom willingly takes the rap and receives a brief juvenile sentence. But there is no escape from Dad's lethal legacy. Refusing the charity of a superfluous job working for a diner owner (Cracker singer David Lowery), Dave broods at home, turns to crime, and becomes a cruel, alcoholic thug like his father. Inevitably, more blood is shed, and the brothers must figure out what it means to do right by each other. Writer-director Eric Drilling gets the gloomy atmosphere right, thanks to admirably subtle work from his cast and an evocative score by Lowery's band mate, Johnny Hickman. There's little insight, however, other than a judge's remark that "We all punish ourselves in different ways"- words to ponder while sifting through this numbingly grim picture.

Also reviewed in:
NEW YORK TIMES, 11/13/98, p. E18, Lawrence Van Gelder
VARIETY, 2/23-3/1/98, p. 87, Leonard Klady

RONIN

A United Artists release of an FGM Entertainment production. *Executive Producer:* Paul Kelmenson. *Producer:* Frank Mancuso, Jr. *Director:* John Frankenheimer. *Screenplay and Story by:* J.D. Zeik and Richard Weisz. *Director of Photography:* Robert Fraisse. *Editor:* Tony Gibbs. *Music:* Elia Cmiral. *Music Editor:* Mike Flicker. *Choreographer:* Cindy Stuart, Dominic Gugliametti, and Alan Beckworth. *Sound:* Mike Le-Mare and (music) John Whynot. *Sound Editor:* Mike Le-Mare. *Casting:* Amanda Mackey Johnson and Cathy Sandrich. *Production Designer:* Michael Z. Hanan. *Art Director:* Gérard Viard. *Set Decorator:* Robert Le Corre. *Set Dresser:* Bruno Lefebvre and Yves Seigneuret. *Special Effects:* Georges Demétrau. *Costumes:* May Routh. *Make-up:* Paul Le Marinel. *Make-up (Robert De Niro):* Ilona Herman. *Stunt Coordinator:* Joe Dunne. *Running time:* 121 minutes. *MPAA Rating:* R.

CAST: Robert De Niro (Sam); Jean Réno (Vincent); Natascha McElhone (Deirdre); Stellan Skarsgard (Gregor); Sean Bean (Spence); Skipp Sudduth (Larry); Michael Lonsdale (Jean-Pierre); Jan Triska (Dapper Gent); Jonathan Pryce (Seamus); Ron Perkins (Man with the Newspaper); Fèodor Atkine (Mikhi); Katarina Witt (Natacha Kirilova); Bernard Bloch (Sergi); Dominic Gugliametti and Alan Beckworth (Clown Iceskaters); Daniel Breton (Sergi's Accomplice); Amidou Ben Messaoud (Man at Exchange); Tolsty (The Boss); Gérard Moulévrier (Tour Guide); Lionel Vitrant (The "Target"); Vincent Schmitt (Arles Messenger); Léopoldine Serre and Lou Maraval (Arles Little Girls); Frédéric Schmalzbauer (German Tour Guide); Julia Maraval (Girl Hostage); Laurent Spielvogel (Tourist in Nice); Ron Hiatt (Fishmonger); Katia Tchenko (Woman Hostage); Dyna Gauzy (Little Screaming Girl); Lilly-Fleur Pointeaux and Amanda Spencer (Little Girls); Dimitri Rafalsky (Russian Interpreter); Vladimir Tchernine (Russian Mechanic); Gérard Touratier (Ice Rink Security Guard); Cyril Prentout (Mikhi's Bodyguard); Henry Moati (Bartender); Christophe Maratier (Armed Police Officer); Pierre Forest (C.R.S. Captain).

LOS ANGELES TIMES, 9/25/98, Calendar/p. 1, Kenneth Turan

They're tense and intense, been there and been around, world-weary and drop-dead professional. They're five hard men with implacable faces and murky pasts brought together to do a dirty job they don't even pretend to understand. If their story sounds familiar, that turns out to be a very good thing.

"Ronin," directed by John Frankenheimer from a script that David Mamet had a noticeable hand in, is an old-fashioned thriller brought efficiently up to date. It's a welcome throwback to the days when the world didn't have to end or tanker trucks explode to get an action audience's attention, and it calls out for traditional adjectives like crisp and gripping that have almost fallen out of fashion in the face of today's bloated fare.

It couldn't be more fitting that a picture this traditional was directed by the 68-year-old Frankenheimer, whose credits go back to 1954 and live television and include features like "Birdman of Alcatraz," "The Manchurian Candidate" and "Seven Days in May."

Working in a lean, laconic style he acknowledges was influenced by French director Jean-Pierre Melville ("Le Samourai"), Frankenheimer brings his experience to bear on a scenario that has been smartly pared down in order to ratchet up the tension, especially in the film's series of heart-stopping car chases.

It was newcomer J.D. Zeik, one of the film's pair of writers, who came up with the idea of doing a contemporary take on the traditional Japanese notion of ronin, masterless samurai who are forced into the humiliating position of working for hire for anyone with the means to pay them.

In modern Paris, five of these freelance operatives, unknown to each other, congregate in a small Montmartre bistro and a nearby warehouse. They include Slavic electronics whiz Gregor (Stellan Skarsgard), British weapons specialist Spence (Sean Bean), American wheelman Larry (Skipp Sudduth), and French jack-of-all-trades Vincent (Jean Reno).

Though he's self-effacing enough to say his worst crime is "I hurt someone's feelings once," it's the fifth man, an American named Sam who emerges as the group's center. Tautly played by Robert De Niro, an actor who's a natural at being both forceful and impassive, Sam probably doesn't remember his last human emotion and nothing short of a tactical nuclear weapon landing in his lap would make him blink.

The contact person/employer for this group is an Irish woman named Deirdre (Natascha McElhone), who fills the lads in on their assignment. They're to lift a silver metal briefcase, heavily guarded by parties unknown in the scenic South of France. It's coveted by the Russians, among other parties, and worth paying each of these men $5,000 a week plus a $20,000 bonus when the deed is done.

If that sounds kind of sketchy, it's going to have to stay that way, because that box and its mysterious contents are a classic McGuffin, a plot device more important for getting "Ronin's" action juices flowing than for what's actually inside.

Making "Ronin" even harder to figure out is the film's self-consciously clipped and elliptical dialogue, lines like "Whenever there is any doubt there is no doubt." The other writing credit reads Richard Weisz, but figuring out that it's a pseudonym for David Mamet (who apparently no longer believes in using his name on shared writing credits) wouldn't have been difficult even if the situation hadn't become public knowledge.

While Mamet's words are occasionally an irritant in his own, more leisurely works, they make a good fit with this film's fast-paced, more cinematic style. Actually, lots of things about "Ronin," including its implausible coincidences, crosses and double-crosses and unnamed super-secret organizations, would cross the line into silliness except that Frankenheimer's fast-moving ability to tighten scenes to their maximum tolerance (aided by Elia Cmiral's ominous, percussive score) leaves us little time to ponder anything.

"Ronin" is especially satisfying in its several impressive car chases, which blast through the old section of Nice and the winding roads of the Cote d'Azur as well as central Paris. Frankenheimer was determined to film these realistically, without digital compositing, and working with stunt coordinator Joe Dunne and car stunt supervisor Jean-Claude Lagniez, he's come up with startling sequences that remind us how exciting the basics of filmmaking can be when skillful people care enough to do them right.

NEW YORK, 10/5/98, p. 52, David Denby

Some of the lesser *noir* movies of the forties, tired examples of a once-flourishing genre, seemed to have little more on their minds than the angle of Dick Powell's hat or the tilt of a torch singer's shoulders in some disreputable after-hours club—style, perceived through a veil of shadows and cigarette smoke. In the same way, John Frankenheimer's comeback film, *Ronin*, is devoted to the panache of tough-looking men in black who chase one another in fast cars and then retire to cafés, where they sit around grimly smoking. That's really all the movie is about: action flourishes and stoical gestures. There is a plot of sorts: post-Cold War intelligence operatives from different countries join together to steal an aluminum case from other cast-off operatives—but the plot is remarkably obscure. In fact, it is indecipherable, and intentionally so, I am sure. The point is that there's no point to the men's activities, that they do what they do because they are professionals who enjoy one another's habits, and therefore what really matters is a gun held at the right angle and a car rammed through narrow streets, endangering every baguette from Paris to Marseilles, while the driver sits calmly at the wheel, in stem repose. The movie is set in France, and everyone smokes, which may be an anachronism but somehow seems a necessary element in the movie's atmosphere of bitter existential coolness. Any display of normal human emotion in this context is a sign of weakness: The one man among the operatives who gets excited and throws up after escaping an ambush is quickly expelled as unworthy of anyone's company.

Many of us enjoy this sort of thing—the action-film hardness, the stiff, snobbish protocols of professionalism, and *Ronin* is fun for a while. An opening title tells us that the Ronin were unemployed samurai, wandering the land in shame after their master has been killed. As the team is assembled, we're willing to be entertained. We've seen enough of these movies to know that the tough international cast is required by the tough realities of international box-office. From America, there's Robert De Niro, streamlined in crewcut and black leather; from France, Jean Reno, with the great protruding nose and shark's teeth. Stellan Skarsgard, rather mild-looking in glasses and suit, represents the Eastern-bloc countries, and there's a willful Irish girl, Natascha McElhone, of the long, beautiful, and melancholy face. She hires the others, paying them well but not all that well. They have no idea whom they represent or what they are fighting for. Mystification is all.

The action begins: Ambushes and chases, and many shootouts, some of them staged, as in an Italian B-movie from 1964, at point-blank range, with anonymous gunmen falling over in pools of blood. In the chases, the men bash dozens of cars, cause trucks to tumble, and remorselessly knock over tables of fruits and vegetables (ah, the old fruits-and-vegetables scene). The police, of course, never spoil the fun, an omission that is routine in these movies, but I gave up on *Ronin* when Frankenheimer moved the chase into a tunnel in Paris bearing a striking resemblance to the one in which Princess Di's limo crashed. Is this exploitation or simple insensitivity? Frankenheimer has had a peculiar, perhaps incoherent, career. He began, in the fifties, with earnest TV drama, then got into movies and made the scathing, masterly political satire *The Manchurian Candidate* and the exciting *Seven Days in May*, and then, after a European interlude, such thrillers as *French Connection II* and *Black Sunday*. After some years of obscurity, he moved back into television, and recently had a TNT triumph with *George Wallace*. He can be congratulated, I supposed, for not using computer-generated special effects in *Ronin*, but his professionalism has a weary, cynical, and retro feel to it.

Like a French action star from 1954, Robert De Niro gives an all but silent, wryly fatalistic performance. De Niro takes a bullet in the side and then, looking in a mirror, directs Reno in the surgical removal of the bullet before politely passing out. This is a pretty good joke on stoical cool, and there are a few others, but the movie's haughty toughness makes no particular sense. The classic Ronin tales are about honor, and bonds cemented by shame, yet the men in *Ronin* routinely betray one another and work for cash. All we can tell is that Robert De Niro is the star, so he's a good guy, and Jean Reno is loyal to him and him alone, so he must be a good guy, too. The rest is existential absurdity: The men perform violence because they don't know what else to do with themselves. Unfortunately, directors like Frankenheimer go on turning out action films because they, too, don't know what else to do with themselves. *Ronin* is well-made, but it's an act of connoisseurship for people who have given up on movies as an art form.

NEW YORK POST, 9/25/98, p. 45, Thelma Adams

Leave the driving to John Frankenheimer. The "French Connection II" director, whose career has veered wildly from the canonized "The Manchurian Candidate" to the campy "The Island of Dr. Moreau," gases up and goes for broke in "Ronin," a high-octane action thriller that's about little else than thrilling action.

If I were hiring someone to direct the final scene of Princess Di's short, tragic life, I'd tag Frankenheimer. He makes hell-raising use of those same Paris tunnels that swallowed Diana, sending black BMWs careering the wrong way through the cement cocoons until the final flameout.

"Ronin" epitomizes the post-Cold War villain deficit. It posits a Russian-Irish schism, a battle over a silver briefcase and its contents. Intent on getting the briefcase without paying the ransom, one cell of spooks hires a ragtag bunch of out-of-work soldiers of fortune to ambush another cell of spooks and score the briefcase.

The movie, from a script by J.D. Zeik and Richard Weisz (the latter a pseudonym for playwright David Mamet), is as much about that briefcase and the political firestorm it could launch as "The Maltese Falcon" is about a black bird. In the end, the case could contain the Starr report or the secret of nuclear fusion or a brand-new pair of ice skates—it doesn't matter.

What matters is the band of mercenaries willing to kill for it. And, yes, how can we get the briefcase into a car and get back on the streets of Paris or Nice or Arles? (As if driving in France weren't death wish enough!)

Irish contact Deirdre (Natascha McElhone) rounds up the team and carries the cell phone. She has very glossy hair for someone on a covert mission bunking with a handful of untouchables in makeshift digs.

Sam (Robert De Niro, with dry wit and familiar mole) is ex-CIA; Vincent (Jean Reno, in cat-chewing-canary mode) is the wily Frenchman; and Gregor (Stellan Skarsgard) is the Eastern bloc computer geek.

Spence (Sean Bean) is the ballsy Brit who upchucks after the first car ride, and if I expose Seamus (Jonathan Pryce), it will ruin what little mystery remains.

These are the latter-day Ronin. The movie explains in bold-face type (and tiny, hand-painted action figures) that the title refers to samurai warriors adrift after their master's death. Known as Ronin, these soldiers avenged their feudal lord and, loyal to the end, committed suicide.

In 1942, director Kenji Mizoguchi revived the legendary soldiers to stir the Japanese in battle. "The 47 Ronin" was an artful bit of propaganda, a call to arms. In 1998, it's a call to buy BMWs.

NEWSDAY, 9/25/98, Part II/p. B3, Jack Mathews

Do you crave car chases? Big, noisy, pointless motor mayhem, in which cars carrying full loads of gun-wielding passengers career through tight streets and oncoming traffic, side-swiping, broadsiding and rear-ending other vehicles, scattering fruit vendors and pedestrians, and creating a wake of exploding, burning metal, plus a caravan of Johnny-come-lately cops?

Have we got the movie for you! The chase sequences in John Frankenheimer's oddly captivating action-thriller "Ronin" may be the best choreographed and most pointless of any ever assembled for a motion picture. "Ronin" makes "Bullitt" and "The French Connection" look like O.J.'s freeway stroll, and with a more exotic backdrop than any of them.

The chases in "Ronin" run through narrow village streets and two-lane country roads in picturesque France, where the story takes place. There's also a discomforting chase through the streets of Paris, presumably plotted and shot before Henri Paul took Princess Diana for her last ride.

There are at least three of these delirious chase sequences in "Ronin," straining credulity beyond any reasonable suspension of disbelief. If any one of them were to actually occur, it would be bigger news than all the other film's events combined.

About those events "Ronin," written by first-timer J.D. Zeik and script doctor David Mamet (under the name Richard Weisz), is a hybrid of '60s Cold War espionage, contemporary international terrorist hunting, and "Seven Samurai." In fact, the movie opens with a brief tale about how in feudal Japan, samurai who failed to protect their masters were exiled to lives as mercenaries. They were called "ronin."

The movie draws a parallel between ronin and the agents, spies and other provocateurs set adrift by the end of the Cold War, left to sell their services to terrorists and international criminals.

Robert De Niro's Sam, an ex-CIA agent, is one of the five mercenaries assembled in Paris to plot an Irish-paid ambush on a gang carrying a valuable metal case. His temp colleagues include French procurement specialist Vincent (Jean Reno), English weapons expert Spence (Sean Bean), Eastern Bloc alum and electronics whiz Gregor (Stellan Skarsgard), and hot-shoe American Larry (Skipp Sudduth), who'll do most of the chase scene's breakneck driving.

Their employer is the dour Deirdre (Natascha McElhone), who is working for a shifty-eyed character named Seamus (Jonathan Pryce) and a mysterious, unseen man in a wheelchair.

The metal case they're after is a classic Hitchcock McGuffin, a device to move the story along, whether its value or meaning is revealed or not. All the mercenaries—and the audience—know is that the case is coveted not only by Irish terrorists but by the Russian Mafia, who have subcontracted one of the mercenaries to steal the case once it's been hijacked from its original holders, whoever they are.

Perhaps "Ronin" itself was intended as one grand McGuffin, an existential thriller that people will watch because it's there. The characters plot, lurk, fight, double-cross and otherwise behave as if what they were doing made some kind of sense and the storytelling shortcuts weren't so obvious. This is the kind of loopy film where a high-tech genius can be traced by amateurs because he continues to use his own cellphone, and where new characters appear out of thin air to bridge plot gaps.

Still, on a purely esthetic level, "Ronin" has its pleasures. It is so well shot and edited, and slyly performed, you begin to tense up despite yourself. Somehow, we develop a rooting interest in Sam, the old veteran who intuitively takes over as the gang's leader, and the coolly competent Vincent, with whom he teams up.

Frankenheimer, a master of '60s political melodrama, seems to have drawn a second wind after a couple decades of mediocre directing. A veteran of '50s live television drama, he returned to work for the small screen with the recent Emmy-winning mini-series on George Wallace, and though "Ronin" is a far and empty cry from his paranoia classic, "The Manchurian Candidate," it's more entertaining than today's run of superhero thrillers.

But you do have to love car chases.

SIGHT AND SOUND, 12/98, p. 58, Richard Kelly

Six former covert operatives are brought together to steal a mysterious, well-guarded briefcase. The operatives' employer is incognito, their contact an Irish revolutionary, Deirdre. The team includes ex-CIA man Sam; French coordinator Vincent; driver Larry; weapons specialist Spence; and ex-KGB electronics wizard Gregor. Spence blunders an early foray to acquire guns, and is discharged. Sam takes command of tactics, and becomes romantically involved with Deirdre. However, she is secretly in contact with the sinister Seamus, their employer.

The team accomplish their mission, but Gregor betrays them and escapes with the briefcase. Via Sam's old CIA contacts, the team track Gregor to Arles, where he is trying to sell the case to Russian ice-skating promoter Mikhi. But Seamus emerges to snatch Deirdre, Gregor and the case. In the fracas, Larry is killed and Sam wounded. Later, Sam and Vincent pick up Seamus and Gregor's trails, but fail to apprehend them. At a Paris sporting arena where Russian ice-skater Natacha Kirilova is performing, Gregor tries to coerce Mikhi by threatening Kirilova's life. Both she and Gregor are shot, and Mikhi makes off with the case—only to be ambushed and killed by Seamus. In the mêlée, Sam finds Deirdre, reveals he is still a CIA operative, and tells her to flee. Sam and Vincent hunt down and kill Seamus.

News reports announce that a peace deal has been struck in Northern Ireland, thanks to the demise of the hardline head of an IRA splinter group. Vincent asks what was in the case but Sam won't say. Sam and Vincent go their separate ways.

Ronin screenwriter, J. D. Zeik, claims, rather touchingly, to have found his inspiration in the pages of James Clavell's novel *Shogun* where the archetypal Japanese legend 'The Tale of the Forty-Seven Ronin' is recounted. These *ronin* were masterless samurai, set adrift in 1701 when their lord was killed by a fellow nobleman. But the *ronin* plotted their revenge meticulously and succeeded in assassinating the nobleman. Then, honour being satisfied, they committed mass *seppuku.* Zeik seems to respect his band of erstwhile cold warriors just as generations of Japanese have admired those bloody-minded *ronin*; here, he's keen to suggest how honour can survive among spooks.

However, it's worth noting the scholarly view that what really mattered to the 47 *ronin* was not the purity of their motive (after all, their hot-headed master probably deserved his demise), but their purity of purpose—however mindless or savage the job, it had to be executed with maximum zeal. There is indeed room for a Hollywood movie on this theme, one that explores what CIA foot soldiers do in their autumnal years once they've finished undermining democracies across the globe. *Ronin* is not that movie. Its resident sage Jean-Pierre (Buñuel alumnus Michael Lonsdale) describes the *ronin* legend to Robert De Niro's Sam, and suggests that ritual suicide might be his only recourse. But Sam's 'retirement' is a charade: he has other plans, which the film-makers seem to consider entirely honourable.

For a tale so implausible, *Ronin* is regrettably po-faced. There's a brief moment of over-the-top stoicism when De Niro, having taken a bullet in a shootout, supervises its extraction without anaesthetic, and then quietly announces he's going to pass out. This would suit some lurid Japanese yakuza flick, or Frank Miller's sci-fi comic-book *Ronin* (which borrows the same legend). But mainly the film is about interminable gear-crashing car chases and bullet-fests, wherein masonry, paintwork and fruit-and-veg stalls all get a good pasting while the above-the-line actors remain largely unperforated.

It's all rather disappointing coming from director John Frankenheimer, who made such sparky political thrillers as *The Manchurian Candidate* and *Seven Days in May* in the 60s. Though his recent television films about Archbishop Romero and George Wallace have been well received, *Ronin* is no improvement on his last theatrical film, *The Island of Dr Moreau.*

There's some interest in the film's shabby treatment of Sean Bean's Spence, the English weapons specialist who turns out to specialise only in gutless vomiting and ineptitude, and hence is roundly humiliated by Sam. Bean, it seems, may essay English machismo for international television audiences, but in a Hollywood picture he must play sorry second fiddle to quiet Americans like De Niro. One detects here a kind of revenge upon Ian Fleming, who always had CIA man Felix Leiter acting the loyal retainer to Her Majesty's imperturbable 007, thus inverting the real pecking order of western Cold War ascendancy. *Ronin* redresses this imbalance, and then some.

Another, less amusing subtext: following Jim Sheridan's *The Boxer, Ronin* is 1998's second big Hollywood release to find its outsized villain among those irredentist elements within Irish Republicanism. But where *The Boxer* sought to credit an increasing pragmatism within the Provisional IRA, *Ronin* wants to raise a cheer for the ongoing international relevance of the CIA, and the agency's goodly efforts on behalf of world peace. This explains *Ronin*'s stupefying finale, by some measure the most rebarbative ingredient in the pudding.

TIME, 9/21/98, p. 100, Richard Schickel

At some point in recent years, action movies began to resemble pop versions of action painting. Their connections with traditional narrative and their concern for realistic representations of the natural world and the way human beings might plausibly behave in that world virtually vanished. Watching a *Die Hard* or *Lethal Weapon* sequel or anything by the Hong Kong action specialist John Woo, you entered a two-dimensional world in which what you mostly thought about was, as it were, the surface of the canvas—the tension and originality with which the director slapped, slathered or slashed his colors on it. Like their painterly progenitors, many of these filmmakers are craftsmen of a rare order. They know how to arrest your eye and grab your attention, purely through the sophistication and intricacy of the technique by which they orchestrate chases, explosions or mass destruction of one sort or another.

The genius of *Ronin* is that it slyly but quite openly acknowledges the abstract state at which the action film has arrived. The title is the Japanese word for samurai who have lost their master and must hire themselves out as amoral and dispassionate mercenaries. The script, by J.D. Zeik and Richard Weisz (a pseudonym for David Mamet), applies the term to former CIA and KGB agents who are now obliged to work for terrorists and other international thugs, with no ideology to justify their exertions. It sets a bunch of them—including Robert De Niro, Jean Reno, Stellan Skarsgard and Natascha McElhone, all enigmatic and excellent—in expensive, nonstop pursuit of an oddly shaped aluminum suitcase.

We never find out much about any of them except that their bills are being paid by Irish terrorists. We know even less about the guys they are trying to beat out of the box. Indeed—and this is the best part of the joke—neither they nor we ever discover what the box contains. It is a McGuffin raised to the level of Platonic ideal.

Unvexed by boring details, which usually just compound the implausibility of action movies anyway, we are free to appreciate the sheer stylishness of *Ronin*. This derives from the counterpoint between Mamet's verbal manner—weary, knowing, elliptical—and director John Frankenheimer's bold visual manner.

Frankenheimer has always liked to hold a large number of people at different depths in his frames, and that serves well the tense interplay of the actors when they're plotting and scheming. It also provides a nice contrast to the car chases that are another Frankenheimer specialty (Remember *Grand Prix*?). He loves sending his vehicles screeching through narrow European streets, and he apparently loves trying to top himself, because there are three such sequences here. They are done the old-fashioned way, by stunt drivers, which gives these thrill sequences an immediacy, a nervy elan that special-effects techies can't quite generate on a computer screen. They also assert the only message this film wants to convey, which is that in action movies it's not what you say but how smashingly you say it that counts.

VILLAGE VOICE, 9/29/98, p. 124, Dennis Lim

Boasting more crushed steel than *Crash*, John Frankenheimer's *Ronin* is a slick, back-to-basics espionage thriller: Cold War nostalgia as an excuse for some deftly orchestrated fender benders. Instead of grafting an elaborate, transcontinental, us-versus-them premise onto the European political landscape (which *Mission: Impossible,* in its own preposterous way, attempted), the filmmakers simply boil the plot down to stock Bond-movie behavior and comically vague babble: a succession of double- and triple-crossing half-explained away by ominously whispered phrases like "the Russians," "the Irish," "the briefcase" (as silly and lazy as macguffins get), and "the man in the wheelchair." The end result is significantly more enjoyable than all the summer's concussive blockbusters put together.

Written by David Mamet (under the pseudonym Richard Weisz) and J.D. Zeik, *Ronin* is so single-mindedly old-timey that it eschews the modish safeguards of high-tech gadgetry and porno knowingness. The shoot-outs and car chases get wearying over two hours, but even if *Ronin* is basically a procession of set pieces disguised as a movie, at least those set pieces are all snappily staged, however daunting the logistics.

The mission at the center of the film—to retrieve the aforementioned case—is far less consequential or interesting than the cosmopolitan Dirty Half-Dozen who've come together to pull it off. Assembled at the behest of a hard-nosed Irish lass (Natascha McElhone) are a cool Frenchman (Jean Reno), a brainy Eastern Bloc type (Stellan Skarsgard), a devious Brit (Sean Bean), a nondescript American (er, Skipp Sudduth), and a wisecracking American, played by Robert De Niro, and hence ringleader by default. It doesn't matter who they are, what exactly they're supposed to do, who hired them, and why. All that counts is that they're soon racing along scenic, narrow European streets at impossibly high speeds, and crashing into, or shooting at, the Bad Guys, innocent bystanders, and each other.

De Niro, Reno, and Skarsgard don't act in any real sense, but they're poised, alert, and kind of cool to look at. Frankenheimer prioritizes atmospherics over pyrotechnics (the prevailing mood is vacuous Melville), though, giving new meaning to "tunnel vision," the director builds up to a relentless, inevitably Diana-haunted pursuit through a Paris underpass, eventually plunging head-on into several lanes of heavy traffic. (He tops that with a sniper sequence so ridiculous it doesn't echo as much as parody the climax of his *Manchurian Candidate.*) *Ronin* only really disappoints when it flirts with the smug, fake intricacy of, say, Mamet's own *Spanish Prisoner*. This is an essentially meaningless movie, and pretending otherwise only detracts from its most appealing qualities.

Also reviewed in:
CHICAGO TRIBUNE, 9/25/98, Friday/p. A, Michael Wilmington
NEW REPUBLIC, 10/19/98, p. 30, Stanley Kauffmann
NEW YORK TIMES, 9/25/98, p. E15, Janet Maslin
VARIETY, 9/14-20/98, p. 34, Todd McCarthy
WASHINGTON POST, 9/25/98, p. B1, Rita Kempley
WASHINGTON POST, 9/25/98, Weekend/p. 62, Michael O'Sullivan

ROUNDERS

A Miramax Films release of a Spanky Pictures production. *Executive Producer:* Bob Weinstein, Harvey Weinstein, Bobby Cohen, and Kerry Orent. *Producer:* Joel Stillerman and Ted Demme. *Director:* John Dahl. *Screenplay:* David Levien and Brian Koppelman. *Director of Photography:* Jean-Yves Escoffier. *Editor:* Scott Chestnut. *Music:* Christopher Young. *Music Editor:* Tanya Noel Hill. *Sound:* Mark Weingarten. *Sound Editor:* Michael Chandler, Ben Wilkins, and Miguel Rivera. *Casting:* Avy Kaufman. *Production Designer:* Rob Pearson. *Art Director:* Rick Butler. *Set Decorator:* Beth Kushnick. *Special Effects:* Edward Brohan and John Ottesen. *Costumes:* Terry Dresbach. *Make-up:* Carla White. *Stunt Coordinator:* Jery Hewitt. *Running time:* 120 minutes. *MPAA Rating:* R.

CAST: Matt Damon (Mike McDermott);   Edward Norton (Worm);   John Turturro (Joey Knish);   Gretchen Mol (Jo);   Famke Janssen (Petra);   John Malkovich (Teddy KGB);   Martin Landau (Abe Petrovsky);   Michael Rispoli (Grama);   Melina Kanakaredes (Barbara);   Josh Mostel (Zagosh);   Lenny Clarke (Savino);   Tom Aldredge (Judge Marinacci);   Paul Cicero (Russian Thug);   Ray Iannicelli (Kenny);   Merwin Goldsmith (Sy);   Sonny Zito (Tony);   Mal Z. Lawrence (Irving);   Peter Yoshida (Henry Lin);   Jay Boryea (Russian Thug #2);   Lenny Venito (Moogie);   Richard Mawe (Professor Eisen);   Michael Lombard (D.A. Shields);   Beeson Carroll (Judge Kaplan);   Matthew Yavne (Professor Green);   Eric LaRay Harvey (Roy);   Dominic Marcus (Dowling);   Brian Anthony Wilson (Derald);   George Kmeck (Prison Guard);   Joe Parisi (Property Guard);   Kohl Sudduth (Wagner);   Charlie Matthes (Birch);   Hans Jacobs (Steiny);   Chris Higgins (Higgins);   Michael Ryan Segal (Griggs);   Kerry O'Malley (Kelly);   Slava Schoot (Roman);   Goran Visnjic (Maurice);   Michele Zanes (Taj Dealer);   Allan Havey (Guberman);   Joe Vega (Freddy Face);   Neal Hemphill (Claude);   Vernon E. Jordan, Jr. (Judge McKinnon);   Jon C. Chan (Johnny Chan);   Lisa Gorlitsky (Sherry);   John DiBenedetto (LaRossa);   Nicole Brier (Sunshine);   Bill Camp (Eisenberg);   Tony Hoty (Taki);   Marlo Mendoza (Zizzo);   Zoe Zaloom (Cronos);   Sal Richards (Johnny Gold);   Josh Pals (Weitz);   John Gallagher (Bartender);   Adam LeFevre (Sean Frye);   P.J. Brown (Vitter);   David Zayas (Osborne);   Michael Arkin (Bear);   Murphy Guyer (Detweiler);   Alan Davidson (Cabbie);   Peter Bucossi and Norman Douglass (Stunt Troopers).

LOS ANGELES TIMES, 9/11/98, Calendar/p. 12, Kenneth Turan

Likable Matt Damon, that most appealing of young actors, is making a career out of working against expectation and playing characters Americans are least at ease with: geniuses.

In "Good Will Hunting," Damon was a math wizard whose casual grasp of arcane matters made older men (and Minnie Driver) unsteady. In "Rounders," he's a master of a less academically oriented body of knowledge, the game of poker.

Damon's presence is one of several things "Rounders" (the name is poker slang for a smart professional player) has going for it, including having another fine actor, co-star Edward Norton, to work off of. The subculture of high-stakes poker is involving and director John Dahl ("Red Rock West," "The Last Seduction") is a celebrated creator of dark and ominous moods.

But like a poker hand that looks promising but doesn't quite play out, "Rounders" is unable to do justice to its potential. Off and on involving, the film's failure to fully capitalize on its assets does not have a convenient villain. Instead, it's the combination of several factors going more wrong than right that proves too much for it to overcome.

Damon plays narrator Mike McDermott, a Manhattan poker whiz good enough to have paid half his law school tuition with his winnings. This despite having to compete against such players as the veteran Joey Knish (John Turturro) and the sinister Teddy KGB (John Malkovich), an eccentric gambler "connected all the way to the top of the Russian mob" who examines Oreos as if they were tea leaves.

The main action of "Rounders" finds Mike nine months into a vow of staying away from cards, a promise taken at the urging of girlfriend and law school cohort Jo (ingenue of the moment Gretchen Mol). Though Las Vegas' World Series of Poker has always been a dream, Mike now considers his playing days to be behind him.

Enter Worm (Norton). Like a brother to Mike, and just as fanatical about poker, Worm has been in prison for a bit and once he gets out he's determined (encouraged by Michael Rispoli's unpleasant loan shark Grama) to start gambling again and to get Mike to play along with him.

Oscar-nominated for "Primal Fear" and impressive in "The People vs. Larry Flynt," Norton is an actor with the gift of disappearing inside his roles, and the energy and confidence he brings to a toothpick-chewing conniver like Worm makes the character the perfect foil for Mike's straight-arrow diligence.

An insidious instigator and peerless wheedler, Worm is the kind of guy who thinks "it's immoral to let a sucker keep his money" and even has an ace tattooed on the inside of his forearm so he'll always have one up his sleeve.

"Rounders" is written by the beginning screenwriter team of David Levien & Brian Koppelman, and the best thing they bring to the story of Mike and Worm, aided by French cinematographer Jean-Yves Escoffier and a top-notch production team, is a sense of verisimilitude, the ability to make this world as real as the ones we're more familiar with.

But it's one thing to give viewers an air of authenticity, it's another to mystify them completely, and one of the most obvious ways "Rounders" falls down is that anyone who lacks a serious knowledge of poker is not going to be able to figure out what happens in several of the film's key hands. Yes, we know who wins and loses, but that's all. The specifics of a hand, the details that build the drama and the tension, will be totally lost to viewers without an intimate knowledge of no-limit Texas hold 'em, among other things.

Another of the film's gradually emerging weaknesses is a lack of plausibility in the story line. Entire subplots, like one involving Mike's law school dean Professor Petrovsky (Martin Landau), are far from believable, and the relationship between Mike and Worm also takes increasingly unconvincing turns.

Finally, as good as a director as he is, Dahl is better at the flashy, gleefully neo-noirs he made his reputation on than at a film whose emphasis is more on character than high-wire plot pyrotechnics. "Rounders" is not badly directed, but it does not set anything on fire either.

Though Damon is an actor who's flatly impossible not to root for, the longer this film lasts the less patience we have to stay with him. Like Malkovich's out of control Russian accent, "Rounders" ends up reaching a place too hard to understand and even harder to believe in.

NEW YORK, 9/21/98, p. 65, David Denby

Rounders is proudly, blissfully wordy. The new writing team of Brian Koppelman and David Levien immersed themselves in the rituals of a highly specialized milieu—the New York underground gambling world—and emerged from it spouting a torrent of fast, knowing talk. "Listen, here's the thing," says Mike McDermott (Matt Damon) before we even know who he is. "If you can't spot the sucker in your first half-hour at the table, then you're the sucker." Okay, we don't want to be suckers. Tell on, for in this movie the triumphs are in the telling as much as the doing. Mike and Worm (Edward Norton), brilliant working-class boys, have been conning and outbluffing poker players since about eighth grade (they are now maybe 25), and when they describe a big pot or even the possibility of a game in Brooklyn or Jersey, they talk in strings of arialike, ecstatic jargon. The voluble, allusive script is itself something of a gamble, since we can't always follow it. But we don't have to know what a "hanger" is or exactly what is meant by playing "high-low at that goulash joint on 79th Street" to get into the spirit. This movie isn't one of David Mamet's tight little one-upmanship jobs. *Rounders*, directed by the neo-*noir* maestro

John Dahl *(Red Rock West, The Last Seduction),* is about gambling as passion, gambling as destiny. *Rounders* penetrates the fervent and silent dens, the warehouse and basement grottoes with their populations of players and hangers-on—men as fixed in their characters as the fellows at the track, the tabloid office, the Mafia espresso bar. *Rounders* is completely enjoyable, and, at its climactic moments, thrilling: Dahl, Koppelman, and Levien take us deep into the night.

At the beginning of the movie, Mike, a law student without parental support, leaves the bed of his beautiful girlfriend, Jo (Gretchen Mol), gathers his cash, and makes his way to a club run by a nasty Russian Mafia thug and brilliant gambler known as Teddy KGB (John Malkovich). Mike narrates his and KGB's moves while they play, including the devastating loss of his entire stash, $25,000, in a single hand of poker. Forced, then, to work as a night-shift truck driver, Mike takes us into his confidence. He is fully conscious of both his addiction and his gift. Nine months later, he is reunited with his childhood friend Worm, who has spent some time in prison, and despite Mike's promises to Jo that he will stay clean, he and Worm immediately get into a game, cheating some rich boys out of their money. In the next few weeks, they win and lose money in games all over bridge-and-tunnel land, run afoul of a violent loan shark, and get beaten up by some cops whose wallets they've considerably lightened. In other words, they experience pure happiness—playing 64 hours at a stretch without so much as a nap.

Mike was headed for a law career, and when his lowlife friend pulls him back into the night, we are divided between exhilaration and dismay. Jo is a smart, elegant woman, a future lawyer herself. If Mike gives up the law and walks out on her, he loses something more valuable than a pot of gold. The lovely Gretchen Mol—small, perfect features, coiffed blonde hair— makes Jo a very ambitious girl who knows exactly what she wants (a husband and a career). Jo's desires and her disapproval of Mike's gambling make perfect sense, but it's a weakness of the movie that she can't, or won't, enter Mike's world and put up a serious fight for him. She never even gets to confront Worm, her adversary, and tell him off. *Rounders* brushes aside sex and love and turns itself into a follow-your-dream movie (Mike's dream, that is, to make it to the high-stakes tables in Vegas). The movie treats gambling the way *The Hustler* treated pool—partly as sport, partly as macho combat, but mainly as spiritual exercise. There are gods who walk the earth. Mike wants to be one of them.

In this ritualized male world, companionship among men rates higher than a woman's love. At first, the relationship between Matt Damon and Edward Norton bears some resemblance to the fiercely combative and loving tug-of-war between the two young mafiosi played by Harvey Keitel and Robert De Niro in Martin Scorsese's *Mean Streets.* Damon has the Keitel role—he's the careful one, the worrier, a studious gambler with an earnest schoolboy face, who doesn't seem like a hustler at all. Deep down, Mike is a cocky guy, but Damon's manner is engagingly modest. Mike prefers the straight-up game, and he wins by studying the body language of the other players (we receive copious and useful instructions).

Norton's Worm, on the other hand, will use any means necessary; he just wants to pocket the money. "If I see a mark, I take him down," he says. Like De Niro's Johnny Boy in *Mean Streets,* he's completely reckless—he tells off everyone who can help him—and he's constantly in trouble, which drags down Mike, who in turn feels responsible for him. Edward Norton has the narrow, long chin and sparse, unappealing facial hair of a wanted-poster recidivist. He's magnetically crass, with a mean-eyed stare that argues for the lowest, most opportunistic understanding of how the world works. And Norton is the quintessence of intelligent lousiness; he's serious enough as an actor not to try to make Worm's nihilism hip. Physically, he's almost bodiless—he shambles and feints, falling back from confrontation like a ghost. Damon, by contrast, never flinches, particularly not at the poker table. He's a winner because he's a truth-teller; that helps him bluff. The center of the movie is the rapturous dialogues between the two men and Mike's growing disgust with Worm, who turns him back into a rounder—a gambler—but who isn't disciplined enough to be a winner. It takes us a while to realize that one of the things *Rounders* is about is the difference between a gambler and a criminal.

John Dahl is clearly moving away from the genre tropes of *The Last Seduction.* This movie is less melodramatic, more realistic and convincing. The dialogues between the two men have some psychological density as well as an irresistible fast-moving rhythm, and the climactic poker duels play slowly and menacingly, with a beautiful tightening tension. The movie knows its own weight. The New York gambling underground is no more than half dangerous, and Dahl doesn't turn it into Iwo Jima. The high-stakes games are violent enough—and alluring. The great cinematographer Jean-Yves Escoffier turns this subworld into a glowing but heavy-toned bath of gold and satin-red whorehouse colors. The boys move around fast, from a New Jersey union hall to a deli on the Lower East Side to a paneled Westchester golf club, and Dahl and Escoffier establish the character of each place, and the nature of the players, in just a shot or two. So many players, so many losers! The movie's fast-moving inclusiveness is vastly entertaining.

Mike receives his most severe rebuke not from Jo but from a supercautious gambler who plays to feed his children. John Turturro, playing this odd poker-room wraith with almost preternatural quiet, doesn't so much appear as materialize; he gives a brilliantly self-effacing performance. His opposite in every way is John Malkovich, who turns the vile KGB into the thickest, richest slice of glazed ham in recent years. Malkovich has always been a dominating actor. As KGB, however, he does more than dominate; he transforms his lurching, slumping malevolence into high comedy. Everything Malkovich does is surprising, and I predict that the sound of people trying to re-create his Russo-Chicago pronunciation of such lines as "I am very unsatisfied" ("veery un-*sat*-tis-fyi-ed") should enliven New York parties from now until Thanksgiving at least. Even in its casual moments, this movie is in love with words.

NEW YORK POST, 9/11/98 p. 55, Rod Dreher

Given the aces-high talent in front of and behind the camera, you'd expect "Rounders" to be a sure bet.

Director John Dahl and actors Matt Damon, Edward Norton, John Turturro and John Malkovich look like the indie equivalent of a royal flush.

It's mostly a bluff: Though "Rounders" is a pretty good movie, "pretty good" is a disappointment when players this skilled raise the ante so high.

Dahl is a master conjurer of darkling lowlife menace, and "Rounders" is a more straightforward drama than his neo-noir thrillers "Red Rock West" and "The Last Seduction."

The supporting performances by Norton, Turturro and Malkovich—all playing stubbly, gimlet-eyed habitues of the illegal gambling scene, are sublime, and the slangy screenplay provides an insidery zing. But watching "Rounders" is like making a meal on savory appetizers while the bland main course sits untouched. The problem is Matt Damon—or, to be fair to him, the character David Levien and Brian Koppleman have written for Matt Damon.

As a poker-playing hotshot (a rounder), Damon plays a New York law student who risks his life and discovers his destiny at the card table.

Damon's Mike McDermott is the movie's heart and soul, but this smart, handsome card shark is surprisingly dull. While it's kicky and amusing to follow Mike on his victory tour through parlors of iniquity, "Rounders" fails to engage us emotionally in the conflicts between responsibility and reckless ambition that cleave Mike's heart. His passivity takes the edge off the drama.

In the terrific opening sequence, Mike fishes fat rolls of bills out of their hiding places and, leaving his girlfriend, Jo (Gretchen Mol), sleeping like an angel, scurries away into the city's underground, where he joins a high-stakes poker game. The game is run by the malicious, casually perverse mobster nicknamed KGB.

Mike is so good at this, he's paid his way through law school on gambling winnings. But tonight, he foolishly bets the lot on one hand, and loses.

Broke and broken, Mike turns to driving a truck for his professional gambler pal Joey Knish (Turturro), making an honest living and his girlfriend happy.

Then his old pal Worm (Norton) gets out of jail after serving time for fraud, and all but keelhauls Mike back into the gambling underground.

As the terrific Norton plays him, Worm is a thoroughgoing rat, a punk, a shifty-eyed grifter whose bright eyes and sparkly patter belie the rancid rot in his bones.

Yet as the screenplay has it, Worm is such an unvaryingly cretinous loser, you wonder why Mike can't see the BAD NEWS sign flashing on his forehead.

Similarly, it's hard to figure Mike when he sees his love life and his law career mortally endangered by his gambling preoccupation, and reacts with a sort of "easy come, easy go" shrug.

The key to all this is the movie's thesis line, delivered by Martin Landau as a wizened law professor.

"We can't run from who we are: Our destiny chooses us," he says. So it's fate. But Mike doesn't work out his destiny as much as falls easily into it. Where's the struggle, the passion that makes for dramatic payoff?

Despite the flush pleasures provided by the film's colorfully shady characters and sumptuously sinister locales, and the courage of its downbeat ending, "Rounders" is never more—or never less than well-crafted entertainment.

NEWSDAY, 9/11/98, Part II/p. B3, Jack Mathews

Matt Damon fans, and that's certainly a growing club, ought to relish John Dahl's "Rounders," a sort of film noir version of "The Cincinnati Kid," with Damon, a working-class math whiz in last winter's hit "Good Will Hunting," once again in the role of a tormented genius.

Damon's Mike McDermott has pretty much the same talent as Will Hunting, too, though his gift for computation is matched by his ability to read body language, an awesome combination for a poker player. Mike can walk in on a game and, before you can say jacks or better, knows what everybody's holding, and who among them is bluffing.

But those are pocket-money games, the kind held on Friday nights, on a rotating basis, in the dining rooms of friends' homes. Mike has larger fish to fry. A struggling law student by day, he's a first-class rounder by night, a poker pro making a living in Manhattan's underworld card dens, dreaming of the day he'll go legit against Amarillo Slim and the like at the televised World Series of Poker in Las Vegas, where the winner's pot is $1 million.

To get there, however, Mike has to beat a man with a terrible accent known as KGB (John Malkovich), a local don of the Russian mob. KGB is also an ice-veined poker player with a taste for Oreo cookies and an opponent's blood, and no blood is sweeter to him than that of a kid who thinks he's a five-card stud.

"Rounders" is an entertaining, if implausible, fable about the American dream, and Dahl ("Red Rock West," "The Last Seduction") finds in Mike's character echoes of the noir antihero he loves. Throughout the film,, Damon narrates, in a jazz-accompanied, high-Chandler tone, the odds stacked against him in life as well as poker, while intimately filling us in on the nuances of the game.

There are smoky rooms, shady characters, roughhousing cops, straight whiskeys, broken noses, and plenty of tense competition and surprises. There's also an earnest, worried girlfriend (Gretchen Mol) determined to keep Mike away from the table, and a sage counselor, a law professor (Martin Landau, in his best basset hound melancholy) given to the non sequitur when he advises Mike to go for the gold, just as he passed over the rabbinate to become a lawyer.

The real energy and entertainment in "Rounders" are in the performances of Damon, who's every bit as riveting on screen as was Steve McQueen's Cincinnati Kid, and Edward Norton, as Worm, Mike's best friend A perpetual bad luck charm. Just paroled from prison, Worm has a well-honed skill at dealing from the bottom of the deck and a compulsion to get caught doing it, even while invading a weekly game held by state police.

Reading the script literally, it would be hard to accept Mike's loyalty to Worm, whose debts and fights he keeps assuming. But Norton is so much fun as the cheating daredevil, you won't want to see him go any more than Mike does. There are other strong performances by Turturro, as Knish the grinder, a one-time rounder content to play it safe for rent money, and Famke Janssen, as a card club hostess.

Malkovich's performance is severely hobbled by that accent. KGB, as proud as he is mean, is a compelling villain, and Malkovich plays him with physically cool malevolence. But when KGB gets excited, it looks as if he's talking and sucking a lemon at the same time, and his words clang like dropped silverware.

Damon and Norton, two of the most compelling screen presences around, compensate for most of the film's dramatic weaknesses, while Christopher Young's superb score and Jean-Yves Escoffier's cinematography create a perfect atmosphere for Dahl's ominous underworld.

NEWSWEEK, 9/14/98, p. 76, David Ansen

Mike McDermott (Matt Damon) is trying to live a straight life—job, girlfriend, law school. It sounds good on paper, but not even the love of a smart, pretty fellow student (Gretchen Mol) can compare with the rush he gets sitting at a high-stakes poker game of Texas Hold'em, sizing up his opponents and knowing he's too skillful to lose.

We know, watching "Rounders," that it won't be long before Mike loses his way. Temptation arrives in the form of Worm (Edward Norton), his best friend and former poker partner. Just released from the joint and 15 grand in debt, the scuzzy Worm has Big Trouble written all over his twitchy face. We've seen plenty of Worms on screen before. He's one of many descendants of Robert De Niro's wild and crazy Johnny Boy in "Mean Streets": the loose cannon who's always going to blow up our hero's plans. For a while, we're willing to overlook the cliché because Norton gives it a nervously exuberant spin and because Damon is so unabashedly appealing as the choirboy card shark. Director John Dahl ("Red Rock West," "The Last Seduction") deals some decent opening cards—the gritty New York milieu of underground poker clubs and such colorful supporting players as John Malkovich's ruthless Russian player Teddy KGB and John Turturro's Joey Knish, Mike's wise gambling mentor.

But there comes a point when a movie needs to take us beyond the familiar, and "Rounders" has no idea how to get there. As Mike and Worm desperately try to win a bundle before Worm's debt collector gets nasty, the screenplay (by David Levien and Brian Koppelman) runs out of invention and grows repetitious. And as Worm's behavior becomes increasingly destructive, our patience with the character expires: we just want him to go away.

All the best stuff is at the poker tables, where we learn the psychological tricks of the trade and get to watch Malkovich have shameless fun with his flamboyant Russian accent. Most everything else, under the hip indie veneer, is Hollywood formula, from Mol's thankless role as the long-suffering girlfriend to the improbable law professor, played by Martin Landau, who spells out the movie's theme for us: "We can't run from who we are." A terrific cast can't overcome writing like that, and all the moody texture Dahl lays on can't disguise the story's lack of tension. Everything in "Rounders" is right there on the surface. Watching it is about as exciting as playing poker with all the cards face up.

SIGHT AND SOUND, 12/98, p. 59, Edward Yardley

New York, the present. Legal student Mike McDermott is a 'rounder', someone who makes money playing poker by working the odds and reading opponents' give-away gestures (their 'tells'). Having built up $30,000, he takes on Russian-mafia, gambling-club owner Teddy KGB at Texas Hold-em, the poker game played at the world championships in Las Vegas, and loses. Mike takes up driving a grocery-delivery van. His girlfriend Jo insists he give up poker, and is angry when he uses his face-reading skills to impress the judges' poker school run by his law-school mentor Abe Petrovsky.

Mike's buddy Worm is released from prison and inveigles Mike into a game hustling rich kids. When Jo finds out, she moves out of their apartment. Meanwhile Worm runs up debts in Mike's name. When confronted, Worm reveals that Grama, a thug sponsored by Teddy KGB, has bought up all Worm's debts. Worm has to find $30,000 fast.

Mike's word buys Worm a few days and Mike goes on a solo marathon of consecutive poker games to save him. But Worm can't resist joining him in a local cops' game and gets caught cheating. They are both beaten up and robbed. Worm goes on the run. Mike asks Abe Petrovsky for help. Petrovsky gives him $10,000. Mike challenges Teddy KGB to another game, wins back his debt, but is goaded into a further game. He spots the Russian's bluffing 'tell': the splitting of an Oreo cookie. In the final hand, Mike has a lock—he can't lose. He persuades Teddy to go all in, wins $30,000, and leaves for the world championship in Las Vegas.

Some cracker-barrel wit once said that there are only two things in life more intense than sex: winning at poker and losing at poker. Despite Hollywood's reverence for the concepts of bluff and risk-taking, to my knowledge there are no great poker movies to demonstrate this maxim. It seems that no director can take an audience innocent of the game, instil the rules and have them experience a gamblees glee and despair, the psychological freefall. Some argue for the merits of *The Cincinnati Kid,* but that's because Steve McQueen looks so cool at the card table. *Kid* is otherwise as dull and mechanical as poker itself is to the uninitiated. More than any other film *Rounders* wants to solve this conundrum, to make keen addicts of us all while we're watching.

Risible poker abounds in movies. Typically, in such films as *Honeymoon in Vegas* or *Maverick,* a couple of set-piece stud games is as much static action as a script can stand. In at least one of these games, against incredible odds, two players will both complete a once-in-a-lifetime hand—a straight flush—with the last card drawn. This has the virtue of creating suspense but it's bogus poker. *Rounders* is likewise built around two games: stand-offs between Matt Damon's honest genius Mike McDermott and John Malkovich's Russian-mafia hood Teddy KGB. The difference here is there's a lot more card-playing in between.

Director John Dahl needs the viewer to understand these contests if they are to retain any sense of drama. His solution is to put down stacks of poker wisdom in a voice-over while we watch McDermott prepare for his first high-stakes game. "If you can't spot the sucker in the first half hour, it's you," he warns, going on to explain the rules of Texas Hold-em, the "Cadillac of poker". We then see McDermott lose, to his own amazement. He can't get over it, and the film requires the self-destructive urges of his slippery asocial pal Worm (a very manic Edward Norton) to snap McDermott out of his disbelief and back to the table.

Whenever the drama finds McDermott playing cards, voice-over remains a first resort. Matt Damon's intimate tone and delivery suit the all night hush of such gatherings (monotony is deterred by the sheer variety of social circumstances he plays in—from gangster clubs to union halls to upscale mansions), enhancing the nocturnal feel established by the low-key lighting and jazz score. It ought to lull us into a receptive state of mind, but despite the best efforts of screenwriter David Levien, even attentive viewers may remain baffled. The final hand of the final game when McDermott knows he can't lose and only has to persuade Teddy that he's bluffing is particularly confusing.

For most of the film, however, Levien's script builds tension nicely without need of suspense. You get an acute sense of McDermott's dilemma: that he's an honest guy cursed with a talent for something most people regard as sleazy. Matt Damon has a good disbelieving stare, and his lower lip hangs with perfect cocky expectancy. In any case Dahl is expert at the kind of low-key genre movie that must convey a consistent downbeat mood while moving on at a fair clip. He proved this with his road noirs *Kill Me Again* and *Red Rock West*, and achieved genre apotheosis with his ballad of a ball-breaking conwoman *The Last Seduction*. It was in that film that Dahl discovered a talent for revealing male sexual unease, and a fearful cool is maintained between the male players in *Rounders* and the women in their lives. McDermott is not even tempted by fellow rounder Petra, though she's as much the drop-dead fantasy woman as Linda Fiorentino in *The Last Seduction*. Again this flaw makes sense of the poker compulsion—poker would drive Mike's career-minded girlfriend Jo (Gretchen Mol) away not only because she is repelled by the duplicity of the game, but also because it's a successful rival to sex.

What stops *Rounders* in its tracks though, with only ten minutes to go, is Malkovich's wretched, tension-ruining turn as Teddy KGB. As soon as his teeth and tonsils are bared, his hilariously mannered stage-Russian accent defuses the mood intolerably. The final game sees the worst kind of kitsch grandstanding, including a ridiculous moment of pique about 'splashing his chips". When McDermott has won and Teddy's henchman are closing in for retribution, Teddy shouts, "giff the myan hiss munnee." When will someone pay Malkovich to leave promising movies alone?

Also reviewed in:
CHICAGO TRIBUNE, 9/11/98, Friday/p. D, Mark Caro
NEW YORK TIMES, 9/11/98, p. E16, Janet Maslin
VARIETY, 9/7-13/98, p. 71, Todd McCarthy
WASHINGTON POST, 9/11/98, p. D5, Rita Kempley
WASHINGTON POST, 9/11/98, Weekend/p. 52, Stephen Hunter

RUDOLPH THE RED-NOSED REINDEER: THE MOVIE

A Tundra Productions release in association with Good Times Entertainment of a Cayre Brothers production. *Executive Producer:* Eric Ellenbogen, Andrew Greenberg, and Seth Willenson. *Producer:* William Kowalchuk. *Director:* William Kowalchuk. *Screenplay:* Michael Aschner. *Story:* Robert L. May. *Editor:* Tom Hok. *Music:* Michael Lloyd and Al Kasha. *Sound*

Editor: Charlie King.   *Casting:* Mary Jo Slater.   *Character Design:* Phil Mendez.   *Running time:* 90 minutes.   *MPAA Rating:* G.

VOICES: John Goodman (Santa Claus);   Eric Idle (Slyly the Fox);   Bob Newhart (Leonard the Polar Bear);   Debbie Reynolds (Mrs. Santa Claus);   Richard Simmons (Boone);   Whoopi Goldberg (Stormella);   Eric Pospisil (Young Rudolph);   Kathleen Barr (Grown-up Rudolph);   Vanessa Morley/Miriam Sirios (Zoey);   Alec Willows (Doggle).

LOS ANGELES TIMES, 10/16/98, Calendar/p. 12, Charles Solomon

"Rudolph the Red-Nosed Reindeer: The Movie" is a saccharine, simple-minded cartoon that feels like an overly long TV special. The quality of the animation (or the lack of it) suggests that the film was created for the home video market, with a nominal theatrical run added to raise its profile: Releasing a Christmas-themed film two weeks before Halloween seems more than a little incongruous.

Rudolph may be "the most famous reindeer of all," but the old song never gave him much of a personality, so director William R. Kowalchuk and screenwriter Michael Aschner try to invent one. The son of Blitzen and Mitzi Reindeer, Rudolph (voice by Eric Pospisil as a child, Kathleen Barr as an adult) is different: He has a red nose that lights up.

He gets teased by all the other fawns except the spunky Zoey (Vanessa Morley/Miriam Sirios), the "doe of his dreams." Meanwhile, two inept elves, Boone (Richard Simmons) and Doggle (Alec Willows), wreck the garden of Stormella, the evil ice queen (Whoopi Goldberg), with their sled.

She demands that Santa Claus (John Goodman, who should not try to sing) turn them over to her for punishment; he refuses. (The film gains an unplanned topical moment when she shouts, "You dare to obstruct justice?") Stormella declares that she'll imprison the next one who crosses her Ice Bridge and summon up a tempest to end all tempests.

Two years later, after being disqualified from the Junior Reindeer Games and learning that his father is ashamed of him, Rudolph runs away. Zoey goes looking for him and crosses the bridge, so Rudolph has to rescue her from Stormella and guide Santa's sleigh through the stormy Christmas Eve. All ends happily and sappily.

The minimal story line is padded with irrelevant side characters, including a vapid polar bear named Leonard (Bob Newhart) and Slyly the Fox (Eric Idle, doing an improbable Brooklyn accent). The four Sprites of Northern Lights explain transitions, carry messages and generally try to keep the plot moving, no easy task, given the inept storytelling in "Rudolph."

Aschner's threadbare script includes every cliche in the cartoon book: "I hate being different," "Go ahead and laugh, everybody else does," "We're all different on the outside, but what really counts is what's inside our hearts."

The superfluous and wincingly awful songs by Al Kasha and Michael Lloyd impede the story rather than advance it.

The animation is weak, even by the standards of Saturday morning kidvid. The characters' motions are uniformly stiff and jerky; the reindeer's antlers seem to flop around because the artists can't keep them in perspective and the dialogue is so badly synchronized to the mouth movements, the film looks as if it were dubbed from another language.

In a pointless production number, Slyly sings, "So for every step forward/There's a step in reverse/Remember, it could always be worse."

Adults who make the mistake of sitting through "Rudolph" with their kids may wonder how.

Also reviewed in:
CHICAGO TRIBUNE, 10/16/98, Friday/p. J, Monica Eng
NEW YORK TIMES, 10/16/98, p. E12, Lawrence Van Gelder
VARIETY, 10/19-25/98, p. 77, Todd McCarthy

RUGRATS MOVIE, THE

A Paramount Pictures and Nickelodeon Movies release of a Klasky/Csupo production. *Executive Producer:* Albie Hecht and Debby Beece. *Producer:* Arlene Klasky and Gabor Csupo. *Director:* Norton Virgien and Igor Kovalyov. *Screenplay:* David N. Weiss and J. David Stem. *Editor:* John Bryant. *Music:* Mark Mothersbaugh. *Music Editor:* Michael Baber, Jennifer Blank, and Kim Naves. *Sound (music):* Shawn Murphy. *Sound Editor:* Kurt Vanzo. *Casting:* Barbara Wright. *Art Director:* Dima Malanitchev. *Effects Animation Designer:* Dexter Reed. *Rugrats Creation:* Arlene Klasky, Gabor Csupo, Paul Germain. *Running time:* 90 minutes. *MPAA Rating:* G.

VOICES: E.G. Daily (Tommy Pickles); Christine Cavanaugh (Chuckie Finster); Kath Soucie (Philip Deville/Lillian Deville/Betty Deville); Melanie Chartoff (Didi Pickles); Phil Proctor (Howard Deville); Cree Summer (Susie Carmichael); Mary Gross (Woman Guest); Kevin McBride (Male Guest); Andrea Martin (Aunt Miriam); Michael Bell (Chas Finster); Melanie Chartoff (Minka); Michael Bell (Grandpa Boris); Tress MacNeille (Charlotte Pickles); Michael Bell (Drew Pickles); Jack Riley (Stu Pickles); Busta Rhymes (Reptar Wagon); Joe Alaskey (Grandpa Lou Pickles); Cheryl Chase (Angelica Pickles); Tony Jay (Dr. Lipshitz); Edie McClurg (Nurse); Hattie Winston (Dr. Lucy Carmichael); Tara Charendoff (Dylan Pickles); Gregg Berger (Circus TV Announcer); Philip Proctor (Igor); Abe Benrubi (Serge); Charlie Adler (United Express Driver); Roger Clinton (Air Crewman); Margaret Cho (Lieutenant Klavin); Steve Zirnkilton, Robin Groth, and Angel Harper (Reporters); Tim Curry (Rex Pester); Whoopi Goldberg (Ranger Margaret); David Spade (Ranger Frank).

LOS ANGELES TIMES, 11/20/98, Calendar/p. 9, Kevin Thomas

"The Rugrats Movie" arrives just in time for the holidays to delight fans of the wildly popular Nickelodeon TV series featuring the adventures of the world's most precocious babies. They're actually perfectly normal kids; it's just that they speak and move and reason at a breathtakingly early age. As a work of animation this Paramount release is fresh and witty, rich in its colors and jaunty in style.

As ideal and welcome a family entertainment as it is, a word of caution is in order. Paramount is proclaiming that it's "an adventure for anyone who's ever worn diapers." Yet for lots of people their enjoyment of "Rugrats" will be in inverse proportion to how much time has passed since they were in diapers themselves. In other words, by all means take the kiddies, but don't be surprised to find your attention wandering.

Directors Norton Virgien and Igor Kovalyov and writers David N. Weiss and J. David Stem begin and conclude their film with a fantasy homage to "Raiders of the Lost Ark," which aptly suggests that from the perspective of the Rugrat kids their adventures are no less amazing. Its story is set in motion when our hero, stalwart 1-year-old Tommy Pickles (voice of E.G. Daily), now has a baby brother, Dil (voice of Tara Charendoff).

Tommy's 3-year-old know-it-all cousin Angelica (voice of Cheryl Chase) warns Tommy that his parents will be neglecting him in favor of Dil, and when the newborn's presence does begin to cramp Tommy's style, he and his friends, worry-wart Chuckie (voice of Christine Cavanaugh) and the easy-going 15-month-old DeVille twins (both voiced by Kath Soucie) who live next door to Tommy, decide to return Dil to the hospital where he was born.

But when Tommy and his pals board his inventor-father's sleigh-like Reptar Wagon, the kids wind up in a forest where all the traditional thrills and chills and resulting life lessons about the value of family, friendship and bravery ensue. Adding to the fun in the wilderness is the presence of a pack of lost circus monkeys.

What is most likely to impress adults is that the world of the Rugrats is not idealized or homogenized. Its people look real and are ethnically diverse, and they live on a street that also looks not unlike one you can find all over Los Angeles. Tommy learns to love and protect Dil, but "The Rugrats Movie" is warm yet minus the gooey sentimentality of so many animated movies for kids. With its lilting score and pleasant occasional songs, this Arlene Klasky and Gabor Csupo production has success written all over it.

NEW YORK POST, 11/20/98, p. 64, Thelma Adams

Don't expect to see this in dueling Disney and DreamWorks cartoons over the holidays: a production number with dancing newborns spraying a golden fountain in the postnatal unit, climaxing in a urine rainbow.

Welcome to the warped world of "The Rugrats Movie." Parents of hip toddlers already know the drill. We've been indoctrinated into the demented world of Nickelodeon's TV series "The Rugrats," where kids are shrewd, moms are confused between diaper reality and postfeminist dictates, and dads are ineffectual.

Directed by TV vets Norton Virgien and Igor Kovalyov from a script by David N. Weiss and J. David Stem, the much-anticipated (at least among the crib set) movie follows the adventures of baby Tommy, his neurotic pal Chuckie, twins Lil and Phil, and pint-sized dominatrix, Angelica.

The feature takes off from the series with the birth of Tommy's younger brother, Dylan a.k.a. Dyl Pickles, and a series of musical production numbers that are more like meat loaf stretchers than additions to the mayhem.

The gang strays from home into a nearby forest. There they fend off a clan of circus monkeys while sending their preoccupied parents into paroxysms of guilt.

"Rugrats the Movie" simply tries too hard and travels too far afield. The series' funniest moments occur closer to home, in the contrast between grounded kids and neurotic parents. While the movie might be "more fun than picking noses," as one kid says, it's not that much more fun.

NEWSDAY, 11/20/98, Part II/p. B7, John Anderson

"Hold onto your diapies, babies!" cries the intrepid Tommy Pickles, leading his pals through a "Raiders of the Lost Ark" of the mind and cracking his jump rope a la Indiana Jones. If you've ever seen "Rugrats" on Nickelodeon, you know the whole group is going back to reality via the safety of the Pickles living room, having survived another risky trip through the imagination. And that all will be well, if less than unhygienic and grammatically fractured.

But there's real adventure afoot in "The Rugrats Movie," the highly anticipated feature debut of the popular, pan-generational TV cartoon. The kids—Tommy (voice of E.G. Daily), the nebbishy Chucky (Christine Cavanaugh), the lookalikes Phil and Lillian DeVille (Kath Soucie) and the venomous, pint-sized dragon lady Angelica Pickles (Cheryl Chase)—get lost in the woods with Tommy's new brother Dylan (Dil) Pickles, run into some bad monkeys who've escaped from a Russian circus, narrowly escape the jaws of a slavering wolf and scare their parents half to death.

To wit, "The Rugrats Movie" doesn't just movie the Rugrats off the TV and into the theaters, it gets them out of the house.

And, overall, it does so successfully, even if the crisis du jour—the birth of Dil Pickles (Tara Charendoff)—pretty much alters permanently the chemistry of the ensemble. At the same time, the basic charms of the show—the homemade feel, the messy babies, their well-meaning but obtuse parents and their ethnic-specific relatives—especially Grandpa Boris (Michael Bell), a real mensch—are all intact. There are better production values, a couple of musical production numbers (one featuring cameo vocals by the likes of Beck, Jakob Dylan, Iggy Pop, Patti Smith, Lisa Loeb, Lou Rawls and the B-52s), deep-focus animation and a few riffs on eternity.

Whether all this is necessary is questionable, but the kids at a recent screening were laughing their heads off. They weren't alone.

Having deemed the newborn Dil "a bad, naughty, stinky baby," the gang starts off to take him back to the "hopsical" in the Reptar, a dinosaur car constructed by Tommy's inventor dad, Stu (Jack Riley). En route, they get lost (instigating a statewide search), ran into the monkeys and have some wild rides through the wood. What's missing from "The Rugrats Movie," perhaps, is the kind of well-oiled mayhem of a Steven Spielberg-produced Baby Herman cartoon, or even the best of "Tom & Jerry." Nevertheless, what's here is a treat for young and old. And as the kids go off to see the "lizard" to find their way home, exchange frank insults ("Mr. Chocolate Pants!!") and fight off the monkeys, you will, as they might say, get juice bumps before things get back to norman.

SIGHT AND SOUND, 4/99, p. 56, Amanda Lipman

Didi Pickles, heavily pregnant, goes into labour during her baby shower, and Tommy Pickles' brother Dylan is born. As the family struggles with the screaming baby, Stu, Tommy's father, races to finish his new toy invention, a 'Reptar' car. Playing at returning baby Dylan to the hospital, Tommy, Chuckie, twins Phil and Lil plus baby Dylan find themselves racing down the road in the Reptar. They end up in a forest where they must deal with a wolf, some monkeys who have escaped from a circus, river rapids, and their own squabbles. Meanwhile Tommy's cousin Angelica roller skates after them in search of her Cynthia doll, which the toddlers have inadvertently taken. Helped by a park ranger, and using one of Stu's aerial inventions, the anxious parents are finally reunited with their children.

If Michael and Eliot, the benighted admen of the gloopy but mesmerising television series *thirtysomething*, had ever had to come up with a cartoon idea, *The Rugrat Movie* would have been it: a freewheeling take on the lives of an extended family, friends and neighbours, crammed with satire, cute observation, irony and sentiment. The characters, from droopy inventor Stu Pickles to his diaper-clad, heroic son, Tommy, are a little freakish but lovable. If the adults are the butt of the satirical humour—such as the ode to modern birth that takes place in a maternity arts centre, where mothers can deliver in Tibetan yak rooms or rustic field areas they are also the backdrop to the colourful lives of the combo of toddlers.

Trapped in their infant bodies and personalities, Tommy, Chuckie, Angelica and twins Phil and Lil live in the fantastic world of their own imaginations while grappling with the real-life adult world. The film turns an adult lens on an infant's eye view and tunes the peculiar logic of the toddler world up to the highest pitch, motivating the kids' lively jaunts and providing adults with plenty of opportunities for observational humour. (Tommy, for instance, turns his father's words about responsibility towards his brother into an adventure around the theme of what he calls "sponsitility".) Crashing up against the realism is the 100-mile-an hour, hyper-cartoon fantasy, with zooming cameras and scary visuals, in which the toddlers lead charmed lives, roller-coastering up and down trees, rivers, busy roads, without the slightest sense that they might get hurt. An approximation, perhaps, of how they experience their lives?

The other elements in the mix are the unashamed dollops of affection and sentimentality. You cannot but love Tommy Pickles in his struggle to come to terms with the fact that his long awaited baby brother is a greedy, selfish monster. But that monster, Dylan, finally learns to love his older brother. By the same token, Tommy's vituperative cousin Angelica has become the heroine of a host of three-year-old girls, who slavishly identify with her. It's as if they understand that if Tommy represents what we would like them to be, Angelica is what we sometimes feel we've got. But while the characters are defined by particular qualities, they do not always play to type: Angelica can be kind and Tommy can be selfish. The extremes that are thrown up, where a devilish child suddenly becomes a darling little creature, seem to hit the mark of real life. And there's something about the film's roving sympathy that gives it surprising depth, mocking and embracing its characters—adults and kids—in quick succession.

TIME, 11/23/98, p. 98, Richard Corliss

A bucolic scene straight out of classic Disney: birdies flutter, bunnies nuzzle, a Bambi-esque deer gracefully grazes. And then—VROOOM!—the idyll is disrupted as a Reptar wagon rumbles through with some screaming toddlers aboard. Danger: Rugrats at work.

That might be an appropriate warning to all the other movies contending for children's movie money in this kid-glutted holiday season: with a brand loyalty earned every day for years on Nickelodeon, *The Rugrats Movie* has a chance to torpedo the competition. Will Disney-Pixar's entomological epic *A Bug's Life* run for cover under the nearest anthill? Will *Babe: Pig in the City*, the squeal—sorry, sequel—to the 1995 surprise hit, turn out to be so much baloney? In December, will *The Prince of Egypt* prove to be a hit of less than biblical proportions, and *Mighty Joe Young* less than all-righty?

The Rugrats creators pretend to be sanguine about the cluttered calendar. Says Gabor Csupo, the Lugosi-accented Hungarian who with ex-wife Arlene Klasky launched the show in 1991: "The biggest problem is most of the time for children there is nothing of quality their whole family can enjoy. I love competition. It's healthy—it makes everybody work harder and do better work. The strong will survive. If you have a kid, they at least want to go every second weekend to the movies. So there are plenty of weekends from now until the Christmas season for every quality film to do well."

Whatever the quality, the quantity is certainly up this year. Disney virtually created, and for a decade has owned, the kidophilic Thanksgiving period with its animated films (*The Little Mermaid, Aladdin*) and live-action retreads (*101 Dalmatians, Flubber*). But this year turkey time looks like a family free-for-all, and *The Rugrats Movie* could grab the golden drumstick.

If it doesn't, it won't be for want of conniving. *The Rugrats Movie*, in which Tommy Pickles finally gets a little brother (Dylan—"Dil"—Pickles) and goes on an arduous adventure with his pals Chuckie, Lil and Phil, has been focus-grouped and marketed to contain hooks for consumers of all ages; you need only be old enough to shout, "Mommy, I gotta see it!" and young enough to work your walker.

In addition to the usual Burger King tie-in, Lincoln Mercury is running commercials that promote both the film and a new minivan. The movie's sound track includes a spectrum of old and new hipsters: Busta Rhymes and Iggy Pop, Lisa Loeb and Lou Rawls, Beck and DEVO (whose co-begetter, Mark Mothersbaugh, wrote the film's score). There is also *The Rugrats Movie* itself, a knowing festival of pop-cultural citations, evocations and plain old rip-offs. Says Albie Hecht of Nickelodeon, which conducted "parent-focused research" to broaden the project's salability: "We worked hard to make sure the themes appealed to adults as well as children." Adds Klasky: "A lot of adults would fall asleep if there were no 'second level.'" Translation: This ain't just kid stuff.

Well, it's stuff for modern kids: the ones who are primal enough to giggle at a peepee rainbow (created by infants in a nursery) and the "pooped in his pantsie" jokes, yet canny enough to finish the film's sentence "Born under Venus, look for a..." In the catchy newborn nursery anthem This World Is Something New to Me, kids may understand the line "This world is such a gas!" followed by an impolite noise, and the baleful "I can barely hear myself suck!" but not the pouty "I miss my old womb," and maybe not the exchange between a female voice ("Man, they cut my cord!") and a male ("Awww, consider yourself lucky"). Side benefit of taking your kids to the movie: it was probably time to explain the miracle of circumcision to them anyway.

There are adults who, through choice or parental servitude, have learned to love the TV show. It seems to understand the baby imperatives (either suck on a bottle or break out of the playpen and scope out the great wide world) while treating the grownup figures with the same genial ribbing the kids get. Tommy the explorer and Chuckie, his friend with the orange shock top and a chronically fretful nature, are attractive opposites; three-year-old Angelica is a finely drawn priss. The animation is distinctive and supple, suggesting Max Fleischer and the Modernist Zagreb school. Who thought to give the kids' heads the shape and apparent consistency of grapefruit? Who unleashed the hyperkinetic floor-level kidcam? Someone with a smart sense of design and fun.

Each *Rugrats* half hour contains two 10-to-12-min. episodes. How to up the ante to 80 minutes without letting the stretch marks show? By creating an epic event. "The only thing we were very much set on," says Csupo, "was to introduce a new Rugrat, a baby brother or sister." And there you have it—a buddy movie where the, ages of the sibling rivals don't quite add up to two.

Along the way there are intermittent pleasures: a nice updating of David Seville's *Witch Doctor* into a wild Tiki Room monkey jamboree; a sweet scene of Tommy and Dil learning to share a blanket. But the charm of the TV show has been coarsened and franticized. The film's writers (David N. Weiss and J. David Stem) and directors (Norton Virgien and Igor Kovalyov) have taken the Spielberg scenario as their template—children separated from their parents, then found—but this one has the harried air of *The Goonies*. And the film may have overestimated its hold on a few core constituencies. At a screening last week, a child sobbed as the monkeys stole Dil; a mother checked her watch a few times.

So let the holiday scramble begin. And beware. While tweens might go for *A Bug's Life*, and pious adults line up for *The Prince of Egypt*, neither film will have the urgency of a small voice saying, over and over, "Take me to Rugrats!" In the Pickles family, as in nearly every other TV brood, the kids run things. The next few box-office weeks will determine whether the same applies to reel life.

VILLAGE VOICE, 12/8/98, p. 138, Richard Gehr

Say what you will about *The Rugrats Movie* (my five-year-old daughter and I enjoyed it at least as much as the next family unit), but its sentimental view of sibling rivalry plays a distant second to the movie's real *duh* of a raison d'être marketing. According to *Fortune,* the film is the cornerstone of an unprecedented intracorporate branding effort for Viacom and its media subsidiaries. Indeed, the most fascinating thing about the TV series—even more than the show-offy animation, dim-witted yuppie parents, and winking film references—was always its self-reflexive attitude toward the merchandise it spewed forth.

That's why it was no surprise to find the Stu Pickles-designed Reptar Wagon, a baby Bondmobile voiced by Busta Rhymes, the movie's literal prime mover. With its Barney-meets-T. Rex appeal, Reptar is an integral element of the *Rugrats* universe. Neither as pathetic as Krusty the Clown nor as dumb as the Dummi Bears, Reptar parades through the 'rats' collective consciousness as an evolving product line that must constantly one-up itself to survive. So while my daughter is passing on Burger King's cheesy Reptar watch, she'd give up college in a second for a Reptar Wagon.

Also reviewed in:
CHICAGO TRIBUNE, 11/20/98, Friday/p. H, John Petrakis
NEW YORK TIMES, 11/20/98, p. E30, Anita Gates
VARIETY, 11/16-22/98, p. 34, Joe Leydon
WASHINGTON POST, 11/20/98, Weekend/p. 50, Michael O'Sullivan

RUSH HOUR

A New Line Cinema release of an Arthur Sarkissian and Roger Birnbaum production. *Executive Producer:* Jay Stern.   *Producer:* Roger Birnbaum, Arthur Sarkissian, and Jonathan Glickman. *Director:* Brett Ratner.   *Screenplay:* Jim Kouf and Ross Lamanna.   *Story:* Ross Lamanna. *Director of Photography:* Adam Greenberg.   *Editor:* Mark Helfrich.   *Music:* Lalo Schifrin. *Music Editor:* Steve McCroskey.   *Sound:* Kim H. Ornitz and (music) John Richards.   *Sound Editor:* Donald J. Malouf and Tim Chau.   *Casting:* Matthew Barry and Nancy Green-Keyes. *Production Designer:* Robb Wilson King.   *Art Director:* Thomas Fichter.   *Set Designer:* Jeff Ozimek and Patte Strong.   *Set Decorator:* Lance Lombardo.   *Set Dresser:* Ara Darakjian, George C. Atamian, Vartan "V.T." Tashjian, Gary Ledyard, and Frankie Beau Lombardo. *Special Effects:* Vincent Montefusco.   *Costumes:* Sharen Davis.   *Make-up:* Melanie Hughes. *Stunt Coordinator:* Terry Leonard and Jackie Chan.   *Running time:* 94 minutes.   *MPAA Rating:* PG-13.

CAST: Ken Leung (Sang);   Jackie Chan (Lee);   Tom Wilkinson (Griffin/Juntao);   Tzi Ma (Consul Han);   Robert Littman (First Caucasian);   Michael Chow (Dinner Guest);   Julia Hsu (Soo Yung);   Chris Tucker (Carter);   Chris Penn (Clive);   Kai Lennox and Larry Sullivan, Jr. (Cops at Diner);   Yan Lin (Consul Secretary);   Roger Fan (Soo Yung's Bodyguard);   George Cheung (Soo Yung's Driver);   Lucy Lin (Exposition Official);   Rex Linn (Agent Whitney); Mark Rolston (Agent Russ);   Elizabeth Peña (Johnson);   Philip Baker Hall (Captain Diel);   Jason Davis (Kid at Theatre);   John Hawkes (Stucky);   Jean Lebell (Taxi Driver);   Wayne A. King (Cigaweed Man);   Manny Perry (Bartender);   Kevin Jackson (Pool Player);   Ronald D. Brown (Pool Hall Doorman);   Clifton Powell (Luke);   Matt Barry (Market Clerk);   Stanley DeSantis and Dan Martin (FBI Gate Guards);   Kevin Lowe (FBI Agent);   Billy Devlin (FBI Agent at Building);   Tommy Bush (Bomb Practice Sergeant);   Barry Shabaka Henley (Bobby);   Albert Wong (Chin);   Ai Wan (Foo Chow Hostess);   Lydia Look (Foo Chow Waitress);   Sumiko (Osumi) Chan and Man Ching Chan (Japanese Tourists);   Christine Ng Wing Mei, Ada Tai, and Arlene Tai (Flight Attendants);   Frances Fong (Socialite);   Robert Kotecki (Convention Center Agent);   Mike Ashley (Male Flight Attendant).

LOS ANGELES TIMES, 9/18/98, Calendar/p. 6, Kevin Thomas

"Rush Hour" effectively teams Jackie Chan and Chris Tucker in a formulaic but funny action comedy that should please fans of both stars. Writers Jim Kouf and Ross Lamanna and director Brett Ratner nicely contrast Hong Kong's martial arts legend and the young motor-mouth comedian in a thriller with wide audience appeal. This New Line Cinema presentation is also good-looking, well-paced and makes fine use of Los Angeles locales, no small accomplishment given their familiarity.

When the little daughter (Julia Hsu) of China's consul-general (Tzi Ma) for Los Angeles is kidnapped and held for ransom for $50 million, the consul appeals for help from ace Hong Kong policeman Lee (Chan), who was also his daughter's beloved martial arts instructor. The two lead FBI agents (Rex Linn, Mark Rolston) assigned to the case are xenophobic, territorial snobs who think Lee could be of no possible help to their investigation.

They want Lee out of the way so badly that they get the LAPD chief (Philip Baker Hall) to assign a cop to do just that—in effect, becoming Lee's baby sitter. The chief has no trouble making a selection: In picking Carter (Tucker), the loosest of loose cannons, he'll get the wild and crazy guy out of his hair for the duration of the case.

Lee and Carter come from such different cultures—a source of broad humor in the film—that it takes them awhile to get into sync, but when they do you know very well they'll leave the FBI at the gate when it comes to going after the kidnappers.

Ratner keeps the picture barreling ahead while showing off his stars to advantage. Chan humorously underplays to the hyper Tucker, leaving his fabled martial artistry to provide the razzle-dazzle, while Tucker allows us to see that Carter, for all his frenetic antics, is smarter and more focused than he initially appears.

Though "Rush Hour" is emphatically a genre piece, it still gives its stars a chance to break out into a couple of comic riffs; another one or two such interludes would not have been unwelcome. There's a funny moment when Carter and Lee discover that both their fathers were cops and become like little boys, debating their fathers' exploits, culminating with each declaring, "My dad can beat up your dad!" Even more amusing is a charming song-and-dance sequence set in Chinatown in which the stars meld their karate and hip-hop moves to the tune of the vintage Edwin Starr Motown hit "War."

For a movie that otherwise works so well "Rush Hour" has an all-too-elliptical sequence set in Hong Kong on the final day of British rule. There's an elaborate formal dinner in which it would appear that the consul-general and his British counterpart ("The Full Monty's" Tom Wilkinson) are marking not only the changeover but celebrating the retrieval of a stolen fortune in Chinese antiquities; Lee played a key role in its recovery.

The treasure trove figures in the plot later on, as does Wilkinson's character. Also a key in the film is "Lone Star's" Elizabeth Peña as a sharp LAPD policewoman, amusingly deft at deflecting Carter's pursuit of her, plus solid support from Chris Penn and Ken Leung, two of the bad guys.

NEW YORK, 10/5/98, p. 53, David Denby

In *Rush Hour*, two kinds of comic virtuosos link up: The eye-popping African-American clown Chris Tucker, whose specialty is motormouthed, high-pitched insult and indignation, and Hong Kong's own Jackie Chan, the stolidly handsome star of dozens of nonsensical martial-arts movies, a man who achieves with his spinning body what Tucker does with words. The movie is no more than a well-produced confection designed for quick payoff in the big cities, but it's pretty consistently funny. Chan is a cop from Hong Kong, Tucker a popinjay on the LAPD. Each man has his own tricky, stylized movement, and each teaches the other how to move his way. The best bit: Chan fighting off assailants while catching a huge, priceless Ming vase that keeps tipping over.

NEW YORK POST, 9/18/98, p. 59, Thelma Adams

Mel Gibson and Danny Glover are the Bogie and Bacall of the odd-couple cop caper. How many lonely screenwriters scrambling on spec have watched "Lethal Weapon"—or "Beverly Hills

Cop" or "48 Hours"—thinking they could re-create the magic and make more dough than the average kidnapper?

Like the omnipresent sitcom couch, the main location for the odd-couple caper is the front seat of a convertible, preferably in L.A. The boys from opposite sides of the tracks bicker and spar. They pull over to beat the daylights out of each other or buy donuts.

The reluctant partners hurl racial epithets in the first act and critique each other's mothers in the second. By the third act, they're inevitably talking girlfriends and baring souls.

In that context, Jackie Chan and Chris Tucker sharing a ride in "Rush Hour" aren't so far-fetched. They're the Roy Rogers and Gabby Hayes of cop couples.

Hong Kong copper Lee (Chan) is fast with his hands. Carter (Tucker) is the shame of the L.A.P.D., an egotist whose methods lead to unplanned urban redevelopment.

Carter and Lee unite to rescue a Chinese diplomat's daughter kidnapped by Asian thugs in L.A. Scripters Jim Kouf and Ross Lamanna don't stress themselves making this kid-in-peril scenario interesting, while director Brett Ratner ("Money Talks") opts for cruise control.

After the disappointments of "Supercop" and "Mr. Nice Guy," action star Chan may find riding shotgun makes for a more accessible Hollywood vehicle. Rising mouth Tucker balances on the thin edge between humor and bigotry, but steals the show from his restrained co-star.

If screenwriters must churn out these carbon-copy capers, there are some duos I'd like to see. Let's put Joan Rivers and Oprah in a Mustang. How about Cameron Diaz and Janeane Garafolo, or Uma and Jada? Walter Matthau and Jack Lemmon would work, or what about William Shatner and Leonard Nimoy?

NEWSDAY, 9/18/98, Part II/p. B7, Gene Seymour

More than any movie star at work today, Jackie Chan understands the direct connection between old-fashioned screen comedy and newfangled screen adventure. He knows the action movie of today requires its participants to break things and blow them up in increasingly elaborate ways. But he also recognizes—indeed revels in—the absurdity of such imperatives.

It is this sly wisdom, along with a cultivated appreciation of the well-built sight gag, that has given a bracing charge to even the lamest of Chan's action pictures. And at the very least, "Rush Hour," the second action feature directed by Brett Ratner ("Money Talks"), offers those unfamiliar with the worldwide Jackie Chan phenomenon an adequate sense of its appeal.

Ratner must know how fortunate he is to have Chan, cast here as a Hong Kong detective who comes to the USA to track down the ruthless kidnapers of an old friend's pre-teen daughter. Where "Money Talks" was weighed down by gratuitous, empty-headed urban carnage, Chan's leathery grace and well-timed physical stunt work give "Rush Hour" buoyancy and charm that you never see when he's offscreen.

Most of the set pieces would amount to the usual dopey mayhem if it weren't for some of the eye-popping hand-and-leg moves performed by Chan. In particular, there's a funny stretch of hand-to-hand choreography involving Chan, several attackers and some valuable-looking Chinese ceramics that's as clever as anything you can recall from a vintage 1930s slapstick short.

If nothing else, Chan's dry, gently smirking cool serves as a buffer against the relentless, motormouth shtick of Chris Tucker, Ratner's "Money Talks" star, who plays an overaggressive, lone-wolf LAPD detective assigned by the FBI to "babysit" Chan. It's in the odd-couple interaction between Tucker's brash African-American and Chan's stoic Chinese that "Rush Hour" bogs down into dull-witted convention and predictability.

For instance, the much-hyped scene in which Chan turns on Tucker's car radio and finds, to his delight, the Beach Boys. If you've seen the commercials, you know Tucker reacts badly to this and changes the station to new-school hip-hop. Wouldn't it have been more original if Chan was the one who dug rap and Tucker's cop was into surf music? Also: Once—just once!—I'd like to see a movie in which a wiseacre black man goes for Chinese food and *doesn't* complain that there's no "soul food" on the menu.

Such reversals might make Tucker's hyperbolic personality easier to take in sustained doses. Once again, Ratner casts him in a role that is long on attitude and short on sympathy. And, no, we're not convinced that he "changes" for the better toward the end. He starts out as a jerk and ends up that way. If you think all this empty-hearted, overly broad posturing is funny and are willing to settle for the tired old stereotyping in sleek packaging, indulge away. But you can do better and so can Tucker, provided he doesn't burn himself out before then.

SIGHT AND SOUND, 12/98, p. 60, Philip Kemp

Hong Kong, the eve of the British handover. Detective Inspector Lee retrieves a haul of priceless Chinese art treasures stolen by Sang, chief henchman of mysterious master criminal Juntao. At a banquet given in honour of Consul Han by former British administrator Tom Griffin, Lee is congratulated by his friend Han, who's about to take up his new post in Los Angeles. Two months later in LA, Sang kidnaps Han's daughter Soo Yung and holds her to ransom. To the FBI's annoyance, Han demands they send for Lee.

To keep Lee out of the way the FBI co-opts James Carter, a maverick LAPD detective in disgrace for his unorthodox methods. Carter at first treats Lee with contempt, but Lee soon gives him the slip and, defying the FBI, involves himself in the case. Developing mutual respect, Lee and Carter track Sang to a Chinatown restaurant, the headquarters of Juntao. But Sang and his boss escape, taking Soo Yung with them.

With an exhibition of the retrieved art treasures about to open in LA, Sang tells Han to bring the ransom to the opening. Griffin, attending to support his old friend, is unmasked as Juntao and makes off with the money while Sang and the gang shoot it out with the FBI. Carter kills Sang, and Lee pursues Griffin to the roof of the hall where a helicopter is waiting. After a fight Griffin falls to his death. Soo Yung is rescued. Carter scornfully turns down a job offer from the FBI and joins Lee on the flight to Hong Kong.

With *Rush Hour* Jackie Chan, Hong Kong's (and maybe Asia's) top movie star, makes his third assault on the US market. In the early 80's he appeared in some slapdash low-budget US films like *The Big Brawl* and *The Protector*. The flop of that second film sent him back to home territory where he asserted control by directing his own films. More recently American distributor New Line and Entertainment in the UK have picked up his Hong Kong movies and released them: *Rumble in the Bronx* and *Mr. Nice Guy,* choppily dubbed and re-edited, showcase Chan's engaging personality and jaw-dropping fight routines, but let him down with risible dialogue and hit-or-miss plotting. *Rush Hour,* his first big-budget Hollywood movie, at last offers Chan production values worthy of his prodigious talent.

The plot doesn't deviate much from the usual Chan formula. Chan's character, amiable and unassuming, is initially written off as an absurd alien irrelevance, but his intelligence, persistence and infinitely resourceful fighting skills win him respect and success. What's new is a tight, well-thought-through script from Jim Kouf and Ross LaManna—the art treasures retrieved in the opening Hong Kong episode provide not only a key plot motivation, but a handy series of props in the finale—and some sharp, witty dialogue. Chris Tucker, as the black LAPD detective who despises his job, gets some of the best lines: "My own mamma ashamed of me," he tells Lee. "She tell everybody I a drug dealer."

The pairing of Chan with Tucker, star of director Brett Ratner's previous film *Money Talks,* pays dividends. Tucker's Eddie Murphy-ish *schtick,* all jive-ass mockery and shrill falsetto disbelief, plays off divertingly against Chan's self-deprecating humour, and their scenes together convey a genuine sense of mutual enjoyment.

The set-pieces, especially a dazzlingly choreographed pool-hall rumble, are as entertaining as ever. If they never quite attain the bone-cracking heights of Chan's best Hong Kong work, that's probably due more to professional Hollywood safety-consciousness than to any caution on the part of the 45-year-old star. (Chan, as ever, executes all his own stunts.) Veteran composer Lalo Schifrin contributes a pulsating score laced with Chinese percussive elements, and Tom Wilkinson makes a stylish presence as the obligatory urbane Brit villain. (Given the specific linkage to last year's British handover of Hong Kong, it's tempting to read in a political subtext about perfidious Albion, but that would probably be loading too much on to a piece of uncomplicated entertainment.)

Rush Hour is easily Jackie Chan's most accomplished calling-card yet for US and international acceptance, and as such it deserves to succeed. And, needless to say, it's rounded off with the multiple outtakes of cock-ups, pratfalls, flubbed lines and the like without which no Chan film would be complete.

Also reviewed in:
NEW YORK TIMES, 9/18/98, p. E12, Janet Maslin
VARIETY, 9/21-27/98, p. 105, Joe Leydon
WASHINGTON POST, 9/18/98, p. C7, Stephen Hunter
WASHINGTON POST, 9/18/98, Weekend/p. 58, Michael O'Sullivan

RUSHMORE

A Touchstone Pictures release. *Executive Producer:* Wes Anderson and Owen Wilson. *Producer:* Barry Mendel and Paul Schiff. *Director:* Wes Anderson. *Screenplay:* Wes Anderson and Owen Wilson. *Director of Photography:* Robert Yeoman. *Editor:* David Moritz. *Music:* Mark Mothersbaugh. *Music Editor:* Michael Baber. *Sound:* Pawel Wdowczak and (music) Robert Casale. *Sound Editor:* John Nutt. *Casting:* Mary Gail Artz and Barbara Cohen. *Production Designer:* David Wasco. *Art Director:* Andrew Laws. *Set Designer:* Daniel Bradford. *Set Decorator:* Alexandra Reynolds-Wasco. *Set Dresser:* Evelyn Colleen Saro. *Special Effects:* Ron Trost. *Costumes:* Karen Patch. *Make-up:* Robert W. Harper and Sally J. Harper. *Make-up (Bill Murray):* Frances Hannon. *Animator:* David Ridlen. *Stunt Coordinator:* David Sanders. *Running time:* 93 minutes. *MPAA Rating:* Not Rated.

CAST: Bill Murray (Herman Blume); Olivia Williams (Rosemary Cross); Jason Schwartzman (Max Fischer); Seymour Cassel (Bert Fischer); Brian Cox (Doctor Guggenheim); Mason Gamble (Dirk Calloway); Sara Tanaka (Margaret Yang); Stephen McCole (Magnus Buchan); Ronnie McCawley (Donny Blume); Keith McCawley (Donny Blume); Connie Nielsen (Mrs. Calloway); Kim Terry (Mrs. Blume); Luke Wilson (Dr. Peter Flynn); Deepak Pallana (Mr. Adams); Andrew Wilson (Coach Beck); Marietta Marich (Mrs. Guggenheim); Hae Joon Lee (Alex); Adebayo Asabi (Mr. Obiamiwe); Al Fielder (Ernie); Collin Platt (Boy Portraying Frank Serpico); George Farish (O'Reilly); Francis Fernandez (Burnum); McCauley Pendergast (Fields); Eric Weems (Willie); Dalton Tomlin (Wrestler); Wally Wolodarsky (Referee); Ella Pryor (Woman Backstage); Paul Schiff (Waiter); Antoni Scarano (Small Boy Artist); Brian Tenenbaum (Contractor); Thayer McClanahan (School Reporter); Patricia Winkler (Mrs. Whitney); Manning Mott (Mr. Holstead); J.J. Stonebraker (Woody); Donny Caicedo (40 Ounce); Ali Ktiri (Benjamin); Michael Maggart (Concierge); Robbie Lee (Isaac); Morgan Redmond (Bellman); Ed Geldart (Security Guard); David Moritz (Dynamite Salesman); J.J. Killalea (Tommy Stalling); William Lau (Mr. Yang); Lucille Sadikin (Mrs. Yang); Steve Eckelman (Tennis Pro); Eric Anderson (Architect); Danny Fine (Coach Fritz); Kyle Ryan Urquhart (Regis); Kumar Pallana (Mr. Littlejeans); Stephen Dignan (Reuben).

LOS ANGELES TIMES, 12/11/98, Calendar/p. 9, Kenneth Turan

Max Fischer is one strange kid, and "Rushmore," the ode to teenage dementia that is his story, matches him in eccentricity. Like the best filmmakers, director Wes Anderson has an idiosyncratic sensibility, the rare ability to create a world that is completely his own. Unique worlds, however, can be off-putting enough to discourage civilians from spending time there. And that is the case with "Rushmore" as well.

Anderson's first film, co-written (as "Rushmore" is) with actor Owen Wilson, was the charming independent hit "Bottle Rocket." "Rushmore" is considerably more ambitious and impressive, but while it has some of its predecessor's blithe charm, it also has a protagonist it takes an act of will to care about.

That would be Max (newcomer Jason Schwartzman), a fixture at snooty Rushmore Academy since Grade 2 and now a 15-year-old 10th-grader. The film opens with a nerd's fantasy of academic heroism and hearty camaraderie, and it's easy to see why Max takes refuge in dreams. Saddled with braces and a chipmunk manner, peering nearsightedly from behind black-rimmed glasses, Max covers up his understandable insecurities with a whining bravado and a grinding self-mythologizing.

Though his father's a modest barber named Bert (an appealing Seymour Cassel), Max says his dad's a neurosurgeon. Though Max's grades (a 37 in geometry is a typical example) threaten to get him expelled, he insists he's so solid academically that he looks on Harvard as his safety school.

What Max throws his life into instead of classwork are his extracurricular activities. Assisted by alter ego and protege Dirk Calloway (Mason Gamble of "Dennis the Menace"), Max is, among many other things, the driving force behind the stamp and coin, chess and calligraphy clubs, captain of the fencing team, president of the Rushmore Beekeepers, founder of the Dodgeball Society and director of the Max Fischer Players. When he says he'd like to stay at the school for all time, you believe him.

Monomaniacal enough to make people uncomfortable, getting increasingly off-putting the more he tries to please, Max finds an unexpected soulmate in the father of hulking twin classmates Ronny and Donny Bloom. Balding, pot-bellied, with a cigarette taking up permanent residence in the side of his mouth, the senior Mr. Bloom (Bill Murray) is a captain of industry gone to seed, a worn-out titan who admires Max as "a sharp little guy."

Mr. Bloom is not the only adult to penetrate the Stygian depths of Max's obsessive adolescence. Max becomes completely infatuated with Miss Cross (Olivia Williams, recovering nicely from being Kevin Costner's love interest in "The Postman"), a first-grade teacher at Rushmore.

While love brings some people out of themselves, it makes Max more like the worst aspects of himself. He becomes, frankly, an impossible person, self-involved, oblivious, malicious and mendacious. "Rushmore was my life," he says to Miss Cross in a rare moment of honesty. "Now you are."

Anderson brings a lot of appealing gifts to "Rushmore," including the ability to construct a film with an unpredictable dramatic arc. He's gotten the entire cast to function beautifully on his particular wavelength and elicited a fine, bittersweet performance, one of his best ever, from Murray. And then there are the out-there plays Max puts on, from a stage version of "Serpico" to a wild Vietnam drama, all wonders to behold.

But you can't have "Rushmore" without Max, and though Anderson obviously planned it this way, the kid is finally too off-putting to tolerate. The Pest as Hero is an interesting concept, and Max certainly has real-world correlations, but wondering if and when and how he's going to grow up is too precarious a journey to undertake without some serious reservations.

NEW STATESMAN, 8/23/99, p. 32, Jonathan Romney

A measure of the oddness of *Rushmore* is the director Wes Anderson's introduction to the published script, co-written with Owen Wilson. Anderson doesn't discuss the film at all, but instead tells a rambling, somewhat awestruck tale of how he persuaded the veteran critic Pauline Kael to come to a screening he arranged for her. Kael apparently didn't like the film much, munched her way through the cookies provided and advised him that Wes Anderson was a terrible name for a movie director.

You can see how Kael might have been bemused. *Rushmore* feels like neither one thing nor another—too patchy, digressive and wayward for an efficient Hollywood comedy product, yet smarter, punchier and more benign than the average US independent movie. It seems to have been made with no target audience in mind, but purely for the perverse amusement of its makers and any kindred spirits. The film, in fact, is as imaginative and compelling a misfit as its hero, Max Fischer, played with steely but effusive malevolence by Jason Schwartzman.

Max is a nightmare version of American can-doism, like a 1950s over-achiever anti-hero transplanted into the wrong decade. A fish-out-of-water alumnus of the exclusive Rushmore Academy, a private boys' school whose values he cherishes like a religion, Max is president of every society from the Debate Team to the Model United Nations, as well as actor-manager founder of the Max Fischer Players. But he's also an academic disaster and threatened with expulsion.

That situation alone could neatly lend itself to a one-gag comedy of the Farrelly Brothers *(There's Something About Mary)* ilk. But *Rushmore*, having made one point, forever rushes on. Max acquires a guru and surrogate father in the shape of self-made industrialist Blume, whose teachings ("Get them in the crosshairs and take them down") strike a terrible chord. Then both

Max and Blume fall for the high-minded new English teacher, Miss Cross (the English actress Olivia Williams, fully recovered from the extraordinary farrago of Kevin Costner's *The Postman*).

As narrative situations pile up almost uncontrollably, *Rushmore* becomes too diffuse to be categorisable as simply a character study or a satire on the American success ethos. It feels at times like a shapeless concert party at which we're entertained variously with off-beat characterisations and ludicrous production numbers (a routine with angry bees, Max's insane stage production of a blood-and-thunder Vietnam extravaganza). Blume is played by Bill Murray at a staggering new level of world-weariness to top even his weatherman in *Groundhog Day*. He's a man who's had it all, digested it uneasily and now drags life's experience around as weightily as his sagging jowls. As for Max, Schwartzman's oddball demeanour sometimes makes his character look like a fancy-dress routine—prissy bow ties, berets and velvet suits, a horrific joke on fogey geekiness. But, given time, Schwartzman unfolds a memorable monster of insecurity and desire. When Max's father comes along—an unassuming barber played by the always majestic Seymour Cassel—the film really takes off, and a whole new acreage of Max's character opens up.

I'd hesitate to call *Rushmore* a great new American film: it doesn't stop you in your tracks in the same way that, say, *Happiness* does. But it is a great anomaly, a film that makes you look twice and scratch your head in puzzlement over where it's come from and where it's going. Despite the school setting, it has next to nothing in common with this year's highly variable slew of teen and high-school pictures. It barely seems to belong to the 1990s, with its secluded academy setting (it was shot partly at Anderson's own alma mater) and eccentric soundtrack of 1960s British invasion hits (The Creation! Unit 4 + 2! Chad and Jeremy, for God's sake!). And it confounds altogether the usual expectations of how fresh, young American directors are supposed to be original. Even a film of pure dissent such as Todd Solondz's *Happiness* fits some sort of recognisable pigeonhole in its sardonic, unforgiving blackness. At the other end of the spectrum, the prevalent standard for street-smart invention is best exemplified by the speedy, rave-attuned, mall-culture mood of Doug Liman's wild-weekend fantasy *Go*, soon to be released here: exhilarating but empty, it's in every way a fast-food trick, a movie-to-go.

Out on a limb of its own, *Rushmore* feels whimsically pensive, quietly industrious and a touch old-fashioned (it has rightly been compared to Elaine May's comedies of the early 1970s). Anderson may not incline to the deep, dark statement, like Solondz, or to polished pulp, like Liman. On the strength of *Rushmore* (his first film, *Bottle Rocket*, is yet to be seen in Britain), I'd see him more as the high-quality comic novelist whose oblique touch all too easily gets him overlooked. But the idea of someone continuing to make comedies this oblique and intelligent fairly gladdens the heart. And, all respect to Pauline Kael, but Wes Anderson's a rather snappy name for a director, I'd say.

NEW YORK, 12/21-28/98, p. 147, Peter Rainer

Rushmore is best approached without sky-high expectations. Wes Anderson, who also directed and co-wrote *Bottle Rocket*, has a fluky sense of timing—he always seems to be picking up the downbeat of a scene and making it the upbeat—and he has an affinity for deadpan obsessives. But beneath it all is a cackling callowness. What I think appeals to people is that Anderson and his writing partner, Owen Wilson, try to make that callowness soulful.

The deadpan obsessive in *Rushmore* is 15-year-old Max Fischer (Jason Schwartzman), a tenth-grader at Rushmore Academy who is on sudden-death academic probation despite (or because of) being captain of everything from the drama club to the Double-Team Dodgeball Society. With his school blazer and pomaded hair and braces, Max is a preternaturally ambitious geek. There's nothing distinctive about his features— his fixations have dulled everything out. His counterpart is one of the academy's benefactors, Mr. Blume (Bill Murray), a clinically depressed tycoon whose face is a road map of zonked woe. These two end up vying for the same sweetheart (Olivia Williams). The film's comic high point comes when Blume runs over Max's bike in his Bentley. People don't act their age in *Rushmore*, and since that's Murray's specialty, he shines. It's his best performance yet.

NEW YORK POST, 12/11/98, p. 66, Thelma Adams

Nothing about Wes Anderson's previous film, "Bottle Rocket," prepares audiences for his quirky second feature, "Rushmore," the achingly funny, absurd comedy that was the sleeper hit at the fall's New York Film Festival.

Rushmore is the name of a tony boys'school and a code word for obsession. It's there that we find Max Fisher (Jason Schwartzman), a scholarship student whose extracurricular activities range from beekeeping to playwriting.

This industrious son of a barber (Seymour Cassel) goes from eccentric to the brink of psychotic when he falls for pretty Miss Cross (Olivia Williams) and battles married millionaire Mr. Blume (Bill Murray) for the widowed teacher's heart.

Newcomer Schwartzman (Talia Shire's son) combines "Risky Business" era Tom Cruise with Stanley Tucci, while Murray delivers a strong comic performance with an undercurrent of pathos.

"Rushmore" opens today for a week to qualify it for Oscars. It will begin a longer run next year.

NEW YORK POST, 2/5/99, p. 55, Jonathan Foreman

A quirky, sometimes hilarious and often touching comic fable, "Rushmore" is at times reminiscent of both "The Graduate" and "Ferris Bueller's Day Off." It is also, at least until its final moments, one of the most original and unpredictable American movies in years.

What makes this film so different is not the love triangle at the heart of its plot, but the bizarre mental universe of its central character, Max (Jason Schwartzman). Max is a scholarship boy at a private school called Rushmore, and he has the obsessive energy of a (mostly benevolent) psychopath. He runs every possible extracurricular club at Rushmore, and he puts on unintentionally hilarious plays, adapted from movies like "Serpico" and "Platoon."

Emotionally immature, Max has a weird, earnest charm. But he also has a hyperactive fantasy life filled with triumph that bleeds into his real life: He plans to attend Oxford, even though he is the worst student in the school. And when he meets sympathetic widowed first-grade teacher Miss Cross (Olivia Williams), he believes he can win her heart and body, if he only marshals all the influence he has amassed at Rushmore and combines it with his own crazed chutzpah.

Max's plan involves the construction of a massive aquarium at the school with the help of a new friend, a steel tycoon named Mr. Blume (Bill Murray). Mr. Blume is a Rushmore alum, has two horrible sons at the school and is a Vietnam veteran. Not only does the aquarium scheme go awry, causing Max's expulsion to an urban public school, but Mr. Blume falls for Miss Cross. Max then decides to destroy his new friend, and applies all his ruthlessness and formidable imagination to the process.

There is something magical about the way that Max draws people like Mr. Blume and Rushmore's irascible principal (Brian Cox) into his own warped adolescent world.

Schwartzman's face and demeanor fit Max's character perfectly. Bill Murray gives a fine, nuanced, alternately moving and funny performance as Mr. Blume. And the supporting cast, including Mason Gamble as Max's friend Dirk and Stephen McCole as a one-eared, foul-mouthed Scottish bully, are all excellent.

NEWSDAY, 12/11/98, Part II/p. B7, John Anderson

The "vision" of so-called visionary film directors all too frequently refers to the reinvention of a minor train of thought, or image, or implication. Wes Anderson, on the other hand, has the audacity to reinvent Bill Murray. As they say, don't try this at home.

It is, however, a marvelous thing to watch. Murray isn't the star of "Rushmore," exactly—that would be young Jason Schwartzman, as the unformed-bordering-on-malformed adolescent dreamer Max Fischer. But Murray does what he's never done before—react, rather than provoke. The result is his most appealing performance ever.

And "Rushmore" itself? Jane Austen had her 15 minutes about three years ago, but few of the adaptations (with the exception of "Clueless") came as close to the contemporary relevance of her mannered comedy as does Anderson and co-writer Owen Wilson's very original trip into adolescent Oz. Its Dorothy is Max, the quintessential towel-dispensing, hallway-monitoring, lunchroom loner at Rushmore Academy, who is an overachiever in everything but his studies. French club, fencing team, model UN, beekeeping society. Max does it all, and when he's put on academic probation by his one-time mentor, Dr. Guggenheim (Brian Cox), he considers every angle of escape except actually cracking a book.

But this is because Max is a dreamer, a liar, a megalomaniac—and a romantic. His disarming self-absorption also makes him the beneficiary of kindness from unlikely comers—Murray's Mr. Blume, for instance, a wealthy industrialist with a by-the-bootstraps attitude who advises Rushmore's less privileged students to eat the rich ("Get 'em in the crosshairs and take them down"). This inspires Max, the son of a barber (a wonderful Seymour Cassell), and he allies himself with Blume—until they both fall head over heels for the lovely first-grade teacher Miss Cross (Olivia Wiliams), a widow who, like Blume, is flummoxed by Max. What we have for much of "Rushmore" is two alpha males striving for the omega of propriety.

"Find out what you love to do and do it for the rest of your life," Max says. "For me it's going to Rushmore." But Max has to leave Rushmore, and the Anderson-Wilson joke is that Max' attempt to remain an adolescent undermines his very essence. Anderson not only reinvents the teenage comedy, he torpedoes its very foundation: The teen years are not the best time of your life. Things can only get better. The tensions between grown-up yearnings and underage limitations are torture. And the reason someone like Bill Gates is such an incredible yutz is that he had to go through puberty.

Anderson (of the near-legendary "Bottle Rocket") makes better use of pop music (The Who, the Stones, early Cat Stevens) than any director since Scorsese. And this film is so rich in skewed charm and sincere sentiment that you don't want it to end. You can't say that about many movies released in '98. Or ever.

NEWSWEEK, 12/7/98, p. 72, Jeff Giles

You think you know a person. Wes Anderson and Owen Wilson have been friends for nearly 10 years. After graduating from the University of Texas, they wrote a caper flick called "Bottle Rocket." Anderson directed the movie. Wilson turned in a hilarious performance as Dignan, a zealous loser who tries to get his buddies excited about a life of crime, shouting orders into a walkie-talkie and launching every half-baked robbery attempt by barking, Let's get lucky!" "Bottle Rocket" was a winning debut. But, like Dignan, it underperformed. Tonight, in a restaurant in Dallas, Wilson reveals just how disillusioned he was when the movie was released in 1996. As he puts it, "I was exploring a career in the armed services." Across the table, Anderson looks up, confused: "What are you talking about? You're making that up, right? You called the *Army*?" And the Navy, it seems. And the Marines.

Wilson's still a civilian, thank heaven. He and Anderson, 30 and 29, have written a new movie. Anderson has directed it—and it's been lauded at film festivals. "Rushmore" will open in New York and Los Angeles for one week in December—to be eligible for awards—and nationwide early next year. It's a marvelous comedy from deep in left field—immaculately written, unexpectedly touching and pure of heart. Max Fischer (newcomer Jason Schwartzman in a priceless performance) is a geeky, loquacious 15-year-old at New Englandy Rushmore Academy. He arrived at the school as a second-grader, having impressed the headmaster with a play he'd written ("A little one-act about Watergate," says Max). Since then, he's become the captain of every club he could find, plus some he had to invent.

As it turns out, Max is adorably delusional: he's a god-awful student, but plans to apply to Oxford and the Sorbonne. Early in "Rushmore," he gets a titanic crush on a lovely young teacher named Miss Cross (Olivia Williams). Soon, he's decided—why ask why?—that he must build Rushmore an aquarium in Miss Cross's honor. On his quest for capital, he befriends a depressed tycoon named Mr. Blume (Bill Murray). Unfortunately, Mr. Blume falls for Miss Cross, too, and he and Max become mortal enemies. "Rushmore" is about being an outsider, about having more passion than you know what to do with, about how young hearts want to be old and old hearts young. Max tries ruining Mr. Blume's life—and don't expect the tycoon to play nice just because he's 35 years older. He drives over Max's bike with his Bentley.

Anderson and Wilson's writing has an exuberance and an innocence you never see in the often nihilistic work of young filmmakers these days. "I thought 'Rushmore' was very unusual and quirky," says Peter Bogdanovich, who directed "The Last Picture Show" and "Paper Moon."

"The movie's very honest—and yet it isn't dirty. It isn't salacious. It isn't trying to be sexy. I think it's a very encouraging sign." Meeting Anderson and Wilson, you get the feeling they couldn't write a black-hearted movie if they tried. In person, the pair appear entirely different from each other. Wilson looks like a fledgling movie star. Anderson—who's 6 feet 1 inch and maybe 135 pounds, whose shirt is always untucked and whose hair is always sticking up in tufts—looks like someone who's come to help you with your homework. But both are bored by slacker characters, and both admit to being squeamish. "I don't like scatological humor, and I know Wes doesn't," says Wilson. "Wes probably doesn't even like the *word* 'scatological'."

The pair's debut, "Bottle Rocket," began its life as a 15-minute short. Producer Polly Platt and director James L. Brooks were intrigued by it, and flew to Dallas to hear the full-length script. The reading took forever—Anderson had used the wrong font size on the screenplay, and the script was far longer than he'd thought. Says Wilson, "I knew it wasn't going so great when [Brooks] started watching a basketball game on TV." Brooks told the guys to trim the screenplay, and later committed to executive-producing the movie for Columbia Pictures. "My self-confidence was at an all-time high doing 'Bottle Rocket'," says Anderson. "I just felt like, 'Wait until we get this in front of an audience!' So it was a real shocker when it was just brutally rejected by the first test audience in Santa Monica."

After disastrous test screenings—and test screenings *tend* to be disastrous for unformulaic pictures—Columbia's devotion to "Bottle Rocket" cooled. The movie grossed less than a million dollars. Still, it inspired a cult following in Hollywood, and launched the acting careers of both Wilson and his brother, Luke. Owen has done edgily funny little turns in "Anaconda" and "Armageddon," and has been cast in Jan De Bont's "The Haunting of Hill House," with Liam Neeson and Catherine Zeta-Jones. Luke can be seen in "Home Fries," opposite his real-life girlfriend Drew Barrymore.

Director Anderson got a boost from "Bottle Rocket," too. Disney scooped up "Rushmore," and Bill Murray's agent, a "Rocket" fan, urged him to read the new script. Murray agreed to work for scale. On the set, he was a funny, avuncular presence. The first day, Anderson delivered his directions to the star in a whisper, so he wouldn't get embarrassed if Murray shot him down. But the actor made a public show of deferring to his director. He hauled equipment, sang "Happy Birthday" to the sound man and—when Disney was urging Anderson to drop a $75,000 shot of Max and Mr. Blume riding in a helicopter—gave the director a blank check. (Anderson ultimately never shot the scene.)

Murray is restrained and wistful in "Rushmore": every bit of affection you ever had for him comes rushing back. It's the 18-year-old Schwartzman, though, who's the real delight here. Schwartzman is the son of Talia Shire and the nephew of Francis Ford Coppola. "I think Jason's performance in 'Rushmore' is a breath of fresh air—he carries the picture," says Uncle Francis, who notes that his nephew also plays drums for a band called Phantom Planet. "This was his first performance in a film, but the kids have always done one-act plays in the summer. Not only did he write a play, but he also acted in several plays that his cousins Sofia and Roman directed." Casting directors considered 1,800 teenagers before finding Schwartzman. He came to his audition wearing not only a prep-school blazer, but also a Rushmore patch that he'd made himself. Max Fischer would certainly approve. You've got to love a kid with school spirit.

SIGHT AND SOUND, 9/99, p. 54, Richard Kelly

Fifteen-year-old Max Fischer is one of the worst students at Rushmore, a prestigious private school. His extracurricular activities lead headmaster Doctor Guggenheim to threaten him with expulsion. Max befriends unhappy industrialist Herman Blume, the school's principal benefactor, then becomes besotted with widowed first-grade teacher Rosemary Cross.

After the premiere of his new play, Max dines with Blume and Rosemary, drunkenly insults her date, and unsuccessfully declares his love. Funded by Blume, Max attempts to build an aquarium in Rosemary's honour on the school's baseball diamond and is consequently expelled.

He enrols at neighbouring Grover Cleveland High, persuades Rosemary to tutor him privately, and ignores the overtures of fellow student Margaret Yang. Blume and Rosemary fall in love. Max's friend Dirk alerts him, and Max informs Blume's wife, who sues for divorce. Max and Blume engage in tit-for-tat hostilities until Max is arrested. Guggenheim has a stroke and, visiting him, Max learns that Rosemary has dumped Blume. Max initiates a truce and convinces Blume to build the aquarium. Rosemary is unconvinced, so Max arranges for her reunion with Blume at the premiere of his new play *Heaven and Hell*. At the party afterwards, Max and Margaret become an item.

Texan director Wes Anderson and his writing partner Owen Wilson are two of the best things to happen to American film this decade. They first kicked up dust with *Bottle Rocket* (1996), a low-budget gem which still awaits a LTK release. Like *Bottle Rocket Rushmore* has three utterly distinctive strengths: a protagonist possessed of unsettling self-assurance, a lovely way with romance, and an inspired soundtrack of offbeat rock and pop.

Bottle Rocket is propelled by Dignan (played by Owen Wilson), an irrepressible borderline psychopath consumed by the pipedream of organising his shiftless pals into a crew of thieves. *Rushmore*'s mettlesome Max Fischer is cut from some of the same cloth: he's "no cynic, no quitter." In *Bottle Rocket*, love blooms winningly between big, amiable Anthony (played by Wilson's brother Luke) and a lithe Paraguayan motel maid called Inez (Lumi Cavazos). The heart of *Rushmore*, meanwhile, is the beautifully tentative affair between melancholy Blume and luminous Miss Cross; the courtship of Max and daffy Korean ingénue Margaret Yang is an added treat.

Both films create a plausible yet off-kilter universe; evidently a shared dramatic sensibility is at work. The perks and pitfalls of precocity seem to obsess Anderson and Wilson: their recurrent scene is that of an adult in serious discussion with a preternaturally alert child. In *Bottle Rocket*, twentysomething Anthony is lectured by his grave prepubescent sister ("What's going to happen to you, Anthony?"). Here, Blume's infidelity earns him a stiff rebuke ("You're a married man, Blume") from Max's chapel partner Dirk, who looks all of 11.

Of course, Max Fischer is himself a compendium of prodigious tendencies, and gives the film a breakneck energy in its first half. But just as we suspect Anderson and Wilson might be overly enamoured of Max, he comes awfully unstuck, and Miss Cross is forced to rebuff him in smarting fashion ("What do you really think is going to happen between us? Do you think we're going to have *sex?*"). Max's subsequent blue period is the only point where the picture isn't wholly tight, but Bill Murray's Blume is always there for ballast, his wounded mid-life winces seeming to issue from a deep well. "Hey, are you okay?", Max asks him, beginning to sense how real love and real loss might bite. "Oh," Blume murmurs, "I'm a little bit lonely these days." The finale sees *Rushmore*'s slender reality yielding once more to Max's fantasy; but clearly for these young film-makers, that's the point, as underlined in the chorus of the Faces' joyous 'Ooh La-La' which closes the show ("I wish that I knew what I know now/when I was younger").

The cast are all terrific. Jason Schwartzman rises to the challenge of Max with unnerving excellence; Olivia Williams is exquisite as Miss Cross; Murray, for whom Anderson and Wilson wrote the role of Blume, is sublime. Further down the list, Anderson shows every sign of building a repertory company: there are pitch-perfect turns from Deepak Pallana, Kumar Pallana and Andrew Wilson (yes, another brother). Director of photography Robert Yeoman *(Rampage, Drugstore Cowboy)* has also carried on from *Bottle Rocket*, as have editor David Moritz, designer David Wasco and costumer Karen Patch: these too look to be fruitful collaborations.

Rushmore is made to be treasured: it feels like an immediate American classic. As a director of wry, wistful, deceptively simple, sharp-edged comedy, Anderson has quickly ascended to the kind of plateau Elaine May reached after her knockout one-two of *A New Leaf* (1970) and *The Heartbreak Kid* (1972). Of course, May only directed twice more in the subsequent three decades, proving too smart for her own good. Here's hoping Anderson, Wilson and their happy band know where they're headed next.

TIME, 12/14/98, p. 98, Richard Schickel

We tend to forget a couple of things about nerds. One is that despite their inability to dress for success, chat up girls or win the big homecoming game, they are often enviably—maddeningly—smart. The other is that their obsessiveness need not be confined to computer hacking. It can embrace—to take the convenient example of Max Fischer—fencing, beekeeping, astronomy, the dramatic arts and, alas, age-inappropriate lust.

Max, who is played with a sort of eerie solipsism by Jason Schwartzman, is the wearying scourge of Rushmore, a slightly tacky private school, and the ambiguous glory of *Rushmore*, a movie that Wes Anderson directed and co-wrote with Owen Wilson, and that may not be quite as lovable as they think it is. There does come a time when you wish someone would impose a long timeout on the indefatigable Max.

On the other hand, you have to admit that there is something brave about moving this character from the place where he usually lurks in the movies—on the comic-relief fringe of a teenage gang—to the center of the action. You also have to admire the creepy arrogance of Schwartzman's performance. We can see that it covers loneliness, social ineptitude, even a certain amount of duplicity. His father is not the neurosurgeon he claims he is, but a barber. Yet the actor never once sues us for sympathy, and it comes as a nice surprise when we find it flowing toward him anyway.

Beyond that, you have to thank all concerned for giving that great minimalist, Bill Murray, his first good role since 1993's *Groundhog Day*. It's oxymoronically difficult to get laughs out of clinical depression, but as Blume, an industrialist driven to despair by his wealth, his wife and his ghastly children, Murray does it brilliantly. He's also the perfect foil for endlessly up-and-doing Max, who is, perhaps, everything Blume once was, all that he can no longer be. Their eccentricities speak to one another—until they both fall in love with pretty, wistful Miss Cross (Olivia Williams), a young widow who teaches first grade. At this point things fall apart. And to some degree so does the movie.

Expelled from school—you can't expect him to keep his grades up with all those extracurriculars nagging at him—Max goes ballistically obsessive in his passion for the teacher. And his friendship with Blume turns into a nasty, near murderous rivalry. Suddenly Max is no longer quite as adorable as we thought he was. And an often deft, frequently droll little movie turns into an increasingly desperate juggling act, first trying to keep too many dark and weighty emotional objects aloft, then trying to bring them back to hand in a graceful and satisfying way. The goodwill *Rushmore* has accumulated in its early passages is not entirely dissipated by this frenzy, but its concluding klutziness does rather spoil the fun.

VILLAGE VOICE, 2/16/99, p. 143, J. Hoberman

You can keep your cutie-pie *Shakespeare in Love*. The season's wittiest, most original, and best-written portrait of the artist as a young (very young) man is surely Wes Anderson's *Rushmore*—the sleeper of the last New York Film Festival, as well as a distinctively dry, droll, and ludicrous romance with an impressively high "huh?" factor.

Anderson, who with his fellow Texan writing-partner Owen Wilson, scored a mild triumph in their 1996 *Bottle Rocket*—a slacker fantasy about a trio of fanciful slackers—has an evident fondness for skewed genre expectations and obsessive personalities. *Rushmore*, which is an even less classifiable tall tale than its predecessor, celebrates a character whom a good percentage of the audience would probably love to beat up—a ferocious 15-year-old go-getter named Max Fischer (Jason Schwartzman).

"Horrid little Max" (per Janet Maslin) is a scholarship student at the Rushmore Academy. Marching double-time to the different drum of his active fantasy life, Max is neither a successful preppie nor a wacky slacker. Indeed, it is not at all easy to characterize this well-groomed, pasty-faced, bizarrely self-assured four-eyes in the monogrammed blazer and red tam-o'-shanter. The terms *nerd* and *dweeb* are utterly inadequate to describe Max's precocious self-importance. He might be a parody of the character Michael J. Fox played in the Reagan-era sitcom *Family Ties* were his sense of getting ahead not so individualized. If Max is, as the apoplectic Rushmore headmaster explains, "one of the worst students we've got," it is because he is too busy with his extracurricular activities (bee-keeping, serving as an alternate on the wrestling team, saving Latin, producing theatrical pageants, etc.) to pass any of his courses.

Anderson's sophomore project—filmed on location at his own alma mater, where by his own account he too was a "lousy" student with grandiose Ivy League dreams—is the story of Max's sophomore year. It begins, none too promisingly, with the hero placed on "sudden-death" probation. Max soon befriends a depressed millionaire, Herman Blume (Bill Murray), whose jock twin sons have perhaps half a brain between them, and develops a formidable crush on a lovely first-grade teacher, Rosemary Cross (Olivia Williams). It is characteristic of Max's machinations that he would inveigle Blume to create a school aquarium in Rosemary's honor.

Even before this stunt, which involves breaking ground on the Rushmore baseball field, gets Max expelled, the film's mood has come gently unmoored. As the befuddled Mr. Blume, a man in a permanent state of acute psychological discomfort, begins to court Ms. Cross, a woman suffering her own confusion and misery, Max discovers their relationship and freaks out—even though this improbable triangle is an Oedipal fantasy that he himself has masterminded (albeit behind his own back).

What makes Max run? Like the movie, he has the effect of baffling people with his schemes. In some respects, *Rushmore* recalls the baroque high-school shenanigans of *Lord Love a Duck* and *Ferris Bueller's Day Off*—both movies about adolescent "genius." But Max really is some sort of theatrical wizard who, no less than Will Shakespeare, has a taste for popular myth and historical pageantry—his plays are bizarre reworkings of '70s movies like *All the President's Men, Serpico*, and *Apocalypse Now* (directed by Jason Schwartzman's real-life uncle).

Nearly as precocious as Max, Anderson, who grew up writing plays and making Super-8 movies starring himself as Indiana Jones, is a master of soft-shoe comedy. The ensuing series of betrayals and acts of vengeance are played out, largely deadpan, through a series of carefully framed sight gags and judicious wide-screen close-ups that have the effect of children's book pop-ups. If the tinkly incidental music suggests Restoration comedy, the musical set pieces are almost all late—'60s Brit pop (not just Chad and Jeremy but "Oh Yoko"). The sensibility is in no way derivative, although the friendly score and engagingly quirky performances suggest the warm, puppy-dog humanism of a young Jonathan Demme.

Bill Murray has been widely praised for his superb shambling walk-through, but Anderson also gets an unexpectedly sweet performance from the often too-wired Seymour Cassell as Max's father. (Although the senior Fischer is a barber, his son routinely upgrades his profession to brain surgeon.) There are also vivid turns from a trio of young performers—Sara Tanaka as Max's female counterpart, Mason Gamble as his squeaky-voiced "chapel partner," and Stephen McCole as his Scottish nemesis. But *Rushmore* is most dependent on Jason Schwartzman's portrayal of the stubborn, obnoxious, pompous, theatrical, ingenious, horny, and persistent Max.

Cheerfully stylized, *Rushmore* pretends to be a kid's film and perhaps it is—at least insofar as the kid in question grew up to make the movie. The story of Max's education is a charming tale of loss and obsession and, as the title suggests, some sort of monument. The motto it recalls is, "The child is father to the man."

Also reviewed in:
CHICAGO TRIBUNE, 2/5/99, Friday/p. A, Michael Wilmington
NATION, 12/28/98, p. 43, Stuart Klawans
NEW YORK TIMES, 12/11/98, p. E31, Janet Maslin
NEW YORKER, 12/7 & 14/98, p. 214, Anthony Lane
VARIETY, 9/14-20/98, p. 33, Todd McCarthy
WASHINGTON POST, 2/5/99, p. C1, Rita Kempley
WASHINGTON POST, 2/5/99, Weekend/p. 39, Desson Howe

SAFE MEN

An October Films release of an Andell Entertainment production in association with Blue Guitar Films. *Producer:* Andrew Hauptman, Ellen Bronfman, Jeffrey Clifford, and Jonathan Cohen. *Director:* John Hamburg.   *Screenplay:* John Hamburg.   *Director of Photography:* Michael Barrett.   *Editor:* Suzanne Pillsbury.   *Music:* Michelle Kuznetsky and Mary Ramos.   *Music Editor:* Thomas Drescher.   *Sound:* Coll Anderson.   *Sound Editor:* Juan Carlos Martinez. *Casting:* Avy Kaufman. *Production Designer:* Anthony Gasparro. *Art Director:* Ondine Karady. *Set Decorator:* James S. Clauer. *Costumes:* Cat Thomas. *Make-up:* Kyra Panchenko. *Stunt Coordinator:* Manny Siverio. *Running time:* 99 minutes. *MPAA Rating:* R.

CAST: Sam Rockwell (Sam);   Steve Zahn (Eddie);   Paul Giamatti (Veal Chop);   Michael Schmidt (Bernie Jr.);   Michael Lerner (Big Fat Bernie Gayle);   Mark Ruffalo (Frank);   Christina

Kirk (Hannah);   Josh Pais (Mitchell);   Mark Shanahan (Party Coordinator); Harvey Fierstein (Leo);   Raymond Serra (Barber);   Ray Iannicelli (Swoop); Jacob Reynolds (Cousin Ira);   Peter Dinklage (Leflore); Michael Showalter (Larry); Adam Morenoff (Victor);   John Tormey (Older Guy);   Don Picard (Gunter);   Carl Don (Hyman);   Allen Swift (Sol);   John Hamburg (Philip); Ali Marsh (Sherry);   Emily Doubilet ("Sweet" Denise Schneider); Sidney Zubrow (Pappy); Mr. Blue (M.C. Victor);   Ellen M. Hauptman (Joyce Kaufman);   Dee Dee Friedman (Barbara); Seth Herzog and Richard Bolster (Gold Trophies); Brian Mullen (Himself);   Ian Helfer (Janusz)

LOS ANGELES TIMES, 8/7/98, Calendar/p. 10, Jack Mathews

[The following review by Jack Mathews appeared in a slightly different form in
NEWSDAY, 8/7/98, Part II/p. B11.]

The art house isn't the first place you'd think to go for empty-headed farce, a staple of the major studios, but that's where you'll find first-time writer-director John Hamburg's "Safe Men," a comedy of mistaken identity that's about as empty-headed as anything out of Hollywood this year. And, in its own clumsy, eager-to-please manner, more fun than most.

Hamburg hits a low percentage of his jokes and proves that he can overreach with the worst of the studio hacks. But there's an amiably goofy quality to the whole enterprise that earns it a lot of forgiveness. And most of that quality comes through the performances of its three stars, Sam Rockwell, Steve Zahn and Paul Giamatti.

This is Giamatti's year. The actor steals the show from veterans Samuel L. Jackson and Kevin Spacey in "The Negotiator," and, as Veal Chop, the right-hand man of Providence Jewish mob boss Big Fat Bernie Gayle (Michael Lerner), he gives "Safe Men" a jolt of comic energy every time he appears.

Veal Chop is the point man on the mistaken identity. Sent by Big Fat to find and hire a pair of first-rate safecrackers, Veal instead tracks down Sam (Rockwell) and Eddie (Zahn), a would-be singing team with neither talent nor, in Sam's case, a memory for lyrics. But they share the real safecrackers' taste for sloe gin, and that's good enough for Veal.

Pretending to be a resident nurse for a wealthy old man, Veal lures Sam and Eddie into a bogus burglary, where they're taken hostage and given the choice by Big Fat of admitting they're the vaunted safecracking team and agreeing to some Big Fat special assignments, or being killed,.

Soon, the bumbling impostors are trying to learn on the job, putting themselves on a collision course with both Big Fat and the two guys they're impersonating, Mitch (Josh Pais) and Frank (Mark Ruffalo), who, judging by the level of their conversations, are the idiot savants of the safecracking trade.

All that is a setup for the film's parade of off-balance gags and the quirky performances of its cast, notably Rockwell, who's hilarious as a romantic mensch with a serious case of reality-avoidance.

Rockwell handles Sam's courtship of a mobster's daughter (Christina Kirk) with a deadpan incompetence that endears him as much to her as the audience.

Scenes with Lerner's over-the-top Big Fat and his obese son, Bernie Jr. (Michael Schmidt), are wearing, but the characters rebound in the film's climactic set piece, which is one of the funniest bar mitzvah scenes since "The Apprenticeship of Duddy Kravitz."

NEW YORK POST, 8/7/98, p. 47, Larry Worth

When two thieves debate the sexiest member "Charlie's Angels," dissect a metaphor's meaning with killers or try to recall the lyrics of "Walk of Life," it can only mean one thing: another Quentin Tarantino wannabe is on the loose.

Granted, such minutiae-filled dialogue indicates a kinder, gentler Tarantino clone. But aspiring auteur John Hamburg still emerges as a witless, imagination-impaired knockoff—much like his directorial debut, "Safe Men."

The plodding plot focuses on Sam and Eddie, two nerdy twentysomethings who spend their evenings as fifth-rate lounge singers. Through a series of coincidences that could only happen in the movies, they're mistakenly ID'd as the hottest safe-crackers in Providence, R.I.

Under pain of death, the city's leading Jewish gangster has forced the boys into a life of crime. Unfortunately, ticket buyers are the ones who end up doing time.

Making filmgoers' 89-minute sentence seem particularly cruel and unusual are a half-dozen sub-plots that kill any modicum of pacing. Specifically, there's a rival racketeer, his Julia Child-like daughter (who serves as Sam's star-crossed love interest), two bona fide safe crackers (one of whom also woos the culinary cutie) and on and on.

Hamburg seems blissfully unaware that some credibility must surface for viewers to buy into the nonsense. But here, it's just mannered gimmicks with no payoffs.

The good news comes via the cast. Specifically, Sam Rockwell retains his status as one of Hollywood's brightest stars-in-the-making. As the goofy, amour-starved protagonist, his timing, subtle mannerisms and understated humor are flawless.

Unfortunately, as with Rockwell's turns in "Box of Moonlight' and "Lawn Dogs," the role only hints at his talent. Even so, he makes the most of every screen moment, meanwhile bringing out the best in co-star Steve ("That Thing You Do") Zahn.

Harvey Fierstein is another plus, playing it straight as a mafioso who's pitted against rotund, ever-yelling mobster Michael Lerner. Paul Giammatti also fares well as Lerner's loyal assistant. But while their abilities make a bad situation more bearable, there's only so much to be done with warmed-over sight gags and strained yuks. Indeed, Hamburg's labored humor will keep viewers from even trying to crack "Safe Men."

SIGHT AND SOUND, 10/98, p. 53, John Wrathall

In a bar in Rhode Island, low-ranking gangster Veal Chop mistakes hopeless wannabe popstars Sam and Eddie for ace safe-crackers Frank and Mitchell. He recruits them to break into his employer's safe. But his employer turns out to be Jewish gangster Big Fat Bernie Gayle, who has set the alleged safe-crackers up so he can pressure them into doing three jobs for him.

Knowing that Bernie will have them killed if they refuse, Sam and Eddie have to pretend they are the "safe men". While trying to crack the safe of local fence Good Stuff Leo, Sam and Eddie are caught by Leo's daughter Hannah. However, attracted to Sam, she lets them go, and starts dating him.

Sam and Eddie are beaten to the second job by Frank and Mitchell. But after consulting a safe cracking manual bequeathed by his long-lost criminal father, Eddie pulls off the third job, breaking into the synagogue safe during Bernie's son's bar mitzvah.

Still not satisfied, Bernie pressures them into one last job: stealing a sporting trophy, the Stanley Cup, from Leo as a bar mitzvah present for Bernie Jr. When Sam tells Hannah that he is going to rob her father again, she breaks up with him. Sam and Eddie open Leo's safe and get the cup, only to be interrupted by Mitchell and Frank; but the four of them decide to team up. In revenge, Leo hires a hitman to cripple Sam and Eddie. But on the day of Bernie Jr's bar mitzvah party, Mitchell and Frank return the cup to Leo, saying that Sam told them to. This gesture wins over Hannah, who hurries to the party in time to call off the hitman. Sam and Hannah are reunited, while Eddie goes into business with Mitchell and Frank.

Which Charlie's Angel is the most shaggable? Which animal is smarter, the raccoon or the pig? What are the relative merits of various shrimp *hors d'oeuvres?* These are among the issues discussed by the assorted safe-crackers and would-be safe-crackers in writer-director John Hamburg's debut feature.

Complete with a pastiche *Shaft*esque score that's heavy on the wah wah pedal (not to mention a vintage Funkadelic track over the opening credits), *Safe Men* certainly owes a debt to Quentin Tarantino, but with the emphasis on the camp rather than the carnage.

While it's not quite broad enough to qualify as a spoof, *Safe Men* does have a few very funny send-ups of the Tarantino style. Reminiscing on that favourite gangster topic, the last time he killed a man, Harvey Fierstein's gravel-voiced fence Good Stuff Leo comes out with an enjoyably ludicrous anecdote about the woman to whom he once sold a pair of flammable polyester trousers, only to see her go up in flames at a barbecue. In similarly farcical vein, the hitman, whose arrival we await in the climactic party scene, turns out to be a dwarf

In that instance, as elsewhere, Hamburg seems to be trying a bit too hard for the laughs. When, in the opening scene, one safe cracker announces that he is "Hamlisch", he then takes it upon himself to spell out this contrived piece of rhyming slang (Hamlisch equals Marvin which equals starvin'), which pretty much kills any laugh the joke might have prompted. Sam Rockwell's rather redundant voiceover seems to spring from the same anxiety on Hamburg's part that people might not be getting all the jokes.

When he allows himself to relax, however, Hamburg is on much better form. The funniest scenes in the film are not the overt comic turns (including Michael Lerner's ranting performance as Big Fat Bernie Gayle, a reprise of his manic studio head in *Barton Fink)* but the oblique flirtations between Sam and Hannah, the daughter of the man Sam is supposed to be robbing. The two leads, Sam Rockwell (last seen in *Box of Moon Light* and *Lawn Dogs*) and Steve Zahn *(Suburbia,* and a very funny cameo in the forthcoming *Out of Sight),* both give refreshingly gentle performances where the material might have allowed for all out slapstick. Making her debut in the role of Hannah, meanwhile, Christina Kirk has something of the otherworldliness of Uma Thurman; not as beautiful, perhaps, but an awful lot more comfortable with comedy.

VILLAGE VOICE 8/11/98, p. 139, Gary Dauphin

Nimble and slight at the same time, *Safe Men* is an unexpectedly sweet coming-of-age comedy; despite being entirely populated by screwups, it still doles out ample helpings of kindness to all involved. Set in Providence, Rhode Island, *Safe Men* follows three young men on vaguely interlocked paths to manhood. There's Sam (a slack-limbed and -jawed Sam Rockwell), a distracted twentysomething who dreams of being a rock star but can't remember his lyrics; his bandmate Eddie (a nervous Steve Zahn), who's wrestling with his father's criminal legacy; and then there's Big Fat Bernie Jr. (a helplessly rotund Michael Schmidt), son of the track suit-clad Big Fat Bernie Sr., Providence's last Jewish mobster. The three are brought together just before Junior's bar mitzvah, when Big Fat Sr. mistakes Sam and Eddie for safecrackers. The hapless musicians are forced by Big Fat and his "intern" Veal Chop (a desperate Paul Giamatti) to tackle three safes before his son's big day, and the pair make a game effort despite not knowing the first thing about burglary. *Safe Men* leads its boys-to-men down a bumbling, wry road to their inevitable little victories: Eddie learns the family business while the perpetually unfocused Sam ambles off after the girl of his dreams, the daughter of Providence's last Jewish fence (Harvey Fierstein, rasping cheerfully away). Writer-director Hamburg's debut is straightforward in terms of visuals, but full of ear-pleasing, random cross talk. The film starts out poking easy, ironic fun, but by the time Sam evokes the title to describe the strange new feeling he's having, it's clear *Safe Men* has been searching for a way to protect and love its weak and fragile band of borderline pathetic losers. It's not very deep, but it's as good a working definition of being a grown-up as any other.

Also reviewed in:
CHICAGO TRIBUNE, 8/7/98, Friday/p. G, Michael Wilmington
NEW YORK TIMES, 8/7/98, p. E21, Lawrence Van Gelder
VARIETY , 2/23-3/1/98, p. 87, Emanuel Levy
WASHINGTON POST, 8/7/98, Weekend/p. 40, Michael O'Sullivan

SALTMEN OF TIBET, THE

A Zeitgeist Films release of a Catpics Coproductions/Duran Film production. *Executive Producer:* Alfi Sinniger. *Producer:* Christophe Bicker and Knut Winkler. *Director:* Ulrike Koch. *Screenplay (Tibetan with English subtitles):* Ulrike Koch. *Director of Photography:* Pio Corradi. *Editor:* Magdolna Rokob. *Music:* Stefan Wulff and Frank Wulff. *Sound:* Andreas Köppen and Uve Haussig. *Running time:* 110 minutes. *MPAA Rating:* Not Rated.

LOS ANGELES TIMES, 9/11/98, Calendar/p. 18, Kenneth Turan

"The Saltmen of Tibet" wasn't filmed in a galaxy far, far away, but it feels as though it might have been. A gentle, meditative documentary filled with spectacular visuals, it allows audiences the rare pleasure of experiencing a traditional way of life that is close to vanishing.

Even in Tibet, apparently, the lifestyle of nomadic salt gatherers, who spend three months of the year taking yak caravans to Lake Tsentso in the country's far north to collect salt and bring it back to their encampment, is considered exotic. Yet seeing it all through the eyes of director Ulrike Koch is a cleansing, revivifying experience that's as restorative as a mountain vista.

Having worked in different capacities on Bernardo Bertolucci's "The Last Emperor" and "Little Buddha" and other films set in Central Asia, Koch is a filmmaker who specializes in this part of the world.

But even she, the notes tell us, had a difficult time finding the saltmen, who face stiff competition from traders who use trucks for hauling salt. However, aided by "Professor Zhang, manager of the 'Frozen Yak Semen Station' and a national hero," Koch, cinematographer Pio Corradi and their crew finally made contact and began shooting.

What we see on screen is quintessentially unhurried and unobtrusive filmmaking. There is no voice-over, the only words that are spoken are in Tibetan, and whatever problems the crew had are scrupulously kept off the screen.

Neither is there any attempt to romanticize what is clearly a physically difficult existence. The aim is rather to immerse us in a simpler life in which no one moves any faster than the slowest yak and everything, including trading the salt for essential barley, is done just as it has been done for time out of mind.

"Saltmen" focuses on a group of four who make the journey, each of whom is given a traditional designation. The Old Mother is the most experienced; his tasks include preparing several strengths of all-important tea. The Old Father takes care of the many sacrificial offerings; the Lord of the Animals (whose mother is shown worrying that he'll catch a cold) watches the livestock; and the young Novice is there to learn how things are done.

Though these men have added such modern touches as wristwatches and sunglasses to their colorful traditional clothes, they still live a life in which religion and ritual are all-important. They're intensely proud of their work, of the innumerable stories and legends that are associated with it, including one that led to a ban on Tibetan women making the trek.

"The Saltmen of Tibet" immerses us in the dailiness of these men's lives as they head out to the salt marshes. We see them fording streams, coping with bad weather and worrying about a suddenly sick yak, all against the backdrop of some of the most memorable scenery in the world.

We also hear a lot about the rules that circumscribe the saltmen's lives as they near the lake where salt is gathered. They must sit correctly, not curse, not do any bad deeds and, most important, converse in a secret salt language that is unknown to outsiders and not translated into English when used on film.

The salt gathering process is also one that necessitates a good deal of singing. There's a song for scraping the salt and another one for sewing the sacks closed before they're loaded onto the yaks. Also featured in the film is the hypnotic ballad singing of a celebrated woman whose specialty is the tale of King Gesar of Ling, one of Tibet's great folk epics.

Somehow, the filmmakers have managed to seamlessly blend in with the nomads, recording their story without getting in the way. Seeing "The Saltmen of Tibet" doesn't create a desire to be included on their next trip, but we're more than pleased to have been taken along and hopeful that the tradition lasts until the current Novice is old enough to be an Old Mother himself.

NEW YORK POST, 7/22/98, p. 44, Larry Worth

Collecting raw salt from the ultra-remote Himalayan lakes is a painstaking process. But watching "The Saltmen of Tibet" do their thing is almost as laborious.

The documentary's two main components are easy to identify: a long, dry-as-dust narrative and dazzling, jaw-droppingly beautiful cinematography. That's why German writer-director Ulrike Koch deserves both criticism and praise.

Starting with the latter, viewers will be totally entranced when the camera does the talking. Peering at Tibet's majestic vistas—arid plains stretching toward snow-capped, mountains, with the sun and clouds creating patterns to rival Motherwell at his most imaginative—is the stuff of a first-rate travelogue.

And scenes of foot-high piles of salt arranged in circles around the marshy waters—the work of the titular nomadic tribesmen—are downright stunning, making the ancient craftsmen's handiwork look like one of the world's seven wonders.

That's why it's so unfortunate that Koch errs in telling the saltmen's story, although the idea is filled with potential. The characters certainly sound bigger than life, starting with Zopon, Lord of the Animals, Pargon the Elder and Bopsa the Novice. Their faces, lined with crevices to rival the Grand Canyon, tell more about their punishing existence than words ever could.

Sadly, the personalities fail to emerge as Koch gets too wrapped up in intestinal problems of yaks, prayers and chants that clock in at more than five minutes, discussions of commerce (how much barley can one buy for a sackful of salt?) and the prep work for the monthlong trek to the lake.

By the time the film reaches a nearly two-hour running time, it's become a demonstration of editing gone awry. For future reference, Koch should remember that less can definitely be more.

Accordingly, the end product is a proverbial mixed bag. Despite what may be the prettiest visuals since "Lawrence of Arabia," "Tibet" could even make Richard Gere's eyelids droop.

NEWSDAY, 7/22/98, Part II/p. B9, John Anderson

The fat lady hasn't sung yet, but she's in the wings. And when the 20th Century finally collapses in its well-deserved heap, will it be remembered for technological advancement and intimate communications, or for the wholesale slaughter of subordinate cultures? A better existence for a greater number? Or was "quality of life" somehow linked to diversity?

"The Saltmen of Tibet," an unnarrated documentary by German filmmaker Uhrike Koch, is—very simply—a beautifully photographed, elegantly observed study of the nomadic "salt people" of northern Tibet, who make their livelihood collecting salt from near-dry Himalayan lakes. It is a celebratory excursion into a curious, anachronistic culture, a glimpse at something we never knew existed, but isn't it fabulous (and fabulously quaint)?

And on the other hand it's a keening eulogy not just for Tibet and its Chinese problem, but for all that's been taken out of the fabric of humankind since the onset of international currency. It's not campaigning for anything; it harbors no hopes of reversing the global trends that may make the saltmen history before another economic cycle runs its course. It simply says, "They were here," and perhaps makes us grateful that we were, too.

And it says what it says very well. Captured by Koch and her cinematographer, Pio Corradi, on a smuggled digital video camera (after the Autonomous Region of Tibet revoked their permit, apparently in an effort to protect its own film production), the footage has been transferred to 35 mm. film and looks spectacular. There are no obvious plays for the audience's affection and none is necessary: The organic unity of land, man and yak—160 of which were taken on the months-long trek to the lake—is as obvious as the salt-hauling truck we see passing by their slow-moving caravan.

Why not get themselves a truck and make a long story short? Koch must have had to fight the urge to make explanatory intrusions into this largely visual essay, but she allows the saltmen to explain themselves in their own way. The trips for salt are highly ritualized, with certain titles accompanying certain duties: The Margen (which means "old mother," although women are forbidden from collecting salt), and the Pargen (father), whose jobs are basically tea and sympathy; the Lord of the Animals, who tends the yaks, and the Novice, who must devote himself to learning the traditions that have directed the salt people for 2,000 years. All salt people must be prudent, especially during the trip itself, because the lake is the eye of the goddess, and if she, is offended—by bad language, for instance, or casual sex—there will be no salt.

And they drive no truck because they can't conceive of it. They probably will in time, but for the moment their particular strain of Buddhism is as inseparable from their day-to-day lives and work as the salt is from their survival. It's a simple philosophy, perhaps, but one that has been lost to all but the most remote peoples, who are considered simple because belief defines identity—and who represent a timeless kind of existence. And for the rest of us here in the 20th Century, it's not a thing to be recaptured, except perhaps during the 110 minutes of a documentary.

VILLAGE VOICE, 7/28/98, p. 118, J. Hoberman

Liberal Hollywood's well-publicized sense of kinship with faraway Tibet is perhaps an expression of solidarity—the identification of one theocratic fantasy realm with another. Hollywood, too, feels itself living in the aftermath of a lost golden age, even if its corporate bosses haven't been quite as ruthless as the Chinese Communists in liquidating the indigenous religious pageantry.

It doesn't take a Richard Gere to maintain "Ich bin ein Tibetan." German filmmaker Ulrike Kochs documentary *The Saltmen of Tibet* may not win her a star on Hollywood Boulevard, but it goes a long way to demonstrate the source of Tibet's appeal. A 110-minute immersion in an otherworldly worldview, Koch's movie opens on a suitably cosmic note, with a woman—classified by the Chinese as a national treasure—singing a cappella from the Tibet national epic that recounts the adventures of King Gesar.

This heroic recitation provides a context for the movie's adventure: A group of wizened nomads embarks upon its annual trek, driving a herd of yak, 45 days each way, to and from the great salt lakes of northern Tibet. The filmmaker too has undertaken an arduous task, following the caravan for its entire three-month journey and shooting, without official permission, on easy-to-conceal Digital video. The transfer to film is superb: *Saltmen* is filled with stunning vistas of empty space, and Koch allows ample time for this empty landscape to promote full planetary perspective. Maybe not since the Lumieres has the flutter of ribbons against the sky seemed more dramatic.

Although *Saltmen* is so leisurely as to be practically ambient, the annual trip is highly scripted. The saltmen (given the jealousy of the lake goddess, only men are permitted this task) are assigned specific ritual identities—Mother, Father, Keeper of the Animals—and, once they arrive at the salt lake, are required to speak a special language as they harvest the salt into piles to be loaded on their yak. The anachronism of the cheap plastic sunglasses the saltmen wear is eclipsed when, like a bad dream foretold, their rival appears. Suddenly, a monstrous truck pulls up to cart away salt. Koch doesn't dwell on this intrusion.

Tibetans are an endangered species—something like the Native Americans of the global village. An end title cites the saltmen as representing "the last feeling of freedom in Tibet. (Only a churl would suggest preceding *Saltmen* with the 1930 Soviet documentary *Salt for Svetana,* which makes much of the primitive conditions in which an isolated region of the Caucausus is compelled to live without salt.) *Saltmen* has no explanatory voiceover. Nor is there any particular acknowledgment of the filmmakers' presence—was Koch the first woman to visit the salt lake? Did the goddess allow her special dispensation?

Blame it on the altitude or the highly ritualized nature of the enterprise—*Saltmen* feels as much a work of the imagination as a documentary.

Also reviewed in:
CHICAGO TRIBUNE, 12/11/98, Friday/p. H, Michael Wilmington
NEW YORK TIMES, 7/22/98, p. E1, Stephen Holden
VARIETY, 12/15-21/97, p. 62, Lisa Nesselson

SAVING PRIVATE RYAN

A Dreamworks Pictures and Paramount Pictures release of an Amblin Entertainment production in association with Mutual Film Company. *Producer:* Mark Gordon, Gary Levinsohn, Steven Spielberg, and Ian Bryce. *Director:* Steven Spielberg. *Screenplay:* Robert Rodat. *Director of Photography:* Janusz Kaminski. *Editor:* Michael Kahn. *Music:* John Williams. *Music Editor:* Ken Wannberg. *Sound:* Ronald Judkins and (music) Shawn Murphy. *Sound Editor:* Richard Hymns. *Casting:* Denise Chamian. *Production Designer:* Tom Sanders. *Art Director:* Daniel T. Dorrance. *Set Decorator:* Lisa Dean Kavanaugh. *Special Effects:* Neil Corbould. *Costumes:* Joanna Johnston. *Make-up:* Lois Burwell. *Make-up (Tom Hanks):* Daniel C. Striepeke. *Stunt Coordinator:* Simon Crane. *Running time:* 170 minutes. *MPAA Rating:* R.

CAST: Tom Hanks (Captain Miller);   Tom Sizemore (Sergeant Horvath);   Edward Burns
(Private Reiben);   Barry Pepper (Private Jackson);   Adam Goldberg (Private Mellish);   Vin
Diesel (Private Caparzo);   Giovanni Ribisi (T/4 Medic Wade);   Jeremy Davies (Corporal
Upham);   Matt Damon (Private Ryan);   Ted Danson (Captain Hamill);   Paul Giamatti (Sergeant
Hill);   Dennis Farina (Lieutenant Colonel Anderson);   Joerg Stadler (Steamboat Willie);
Maximilian Martini (Corporal Henderson);   Dylan Bruno (Toynbe);   Daniel Cerqueira (Weller);
Demetri Goritsas (Parker);   Ian Porter (Trask);   Gary Sefton (Rice);   Julian Spencer (Garrity);
Steve Griffin (Wilson);   William Marsh (Lyle);   Marc Cass (Fallon);   Markus Napier (Major
Hoess);   Neil Finnighan and Peter Miles (Ramelle Paratroopers);   Paul Garcia (Field HQ
Major);   Seamus McQuade (Field HQ Aide);   Ronald Longridge (Coxswain);   Adam Shaw
(Delancey);   Rold Saxon (Lieutenant Briggs);   Corey Johnson (Radioman);   John Sharian
(Corporal);   Glenn Wrage (Boyle);   Crofton Hardester (Senior Medical Officer);   Martin Hub
(Czech Wermacht Soldier);   Raph Taylor (Goldman);   Nigel Whitmey (Private Boyd);   Sam
Ellis (Private Hastings);   Erich Redman and Tilo Keiner (Germans);   Stephan Cornicard (Jean);
Michele Evans (Jean's Wife);   Martin Beaton (Jean's Son);   Anna Maguire (Jean's Daughter);
Nathan Fillion (Minnesota Ryan);   Leland Orser (Lieutenant DeWindt);   Michael Mantas
(Paratrooper Lieutenant);   David Vegh (Paratrooper Oliver);   Ryan Hurst (Paratrooper
Michaelson);   Nick Brooks (Paratrooper Joe);   Sam Scudder (Paratrooper #1);   John Walters
(Old French man);   Dorothy Grumbar (Old French Woman);   James Innes-Smith (MP
Lieutenant);   Harve Presnell (General Marshall);   Dale Dye and Bryan Cranston (War
Department Colonels);   David Wohl (War Department Captain);   Eric Loren (War Department
Lieutenant);   Valerie Colgan (War Department Clerk);   Amanda Boxer (Mrs. Margaret Ryan);
Harrison Young (Ryan as Old Man);   Kathleen Byron (Old Mrs. Ryan);   Rob Freeman (Ryan's
Son);   Thomas Gizbert (Ryan's Grandson).

CHRISTIAN SCIENCE MONITOR, 7/24/98, p. B3, David Sterritt

Steven Spielberg's new movie, "Saving Private Ryan," begins with a burst of battlefield
violence so long, savage, and relentless that it has become a subject of debate even before the
picture's arrival in theaters.

Spielberg evidently wants to avoid the artificiality of many World War II films and resensitize
audiences to the true horrors of combat. This may not be a selling point for people who feel
they're sensitized enough already. And at the other end of spectrum, viewers jaded by the random
destructiveness of "Armageddon" and its ilk may see the gore of "Saving Private Ryan" as just
another nerve-jolting Hollywood spectacle.

After this obstreperous opening, the picture moves into its long centerpiece, about an officer
(Tom Hanks) commanded to take his squad behind enemy lines and rescue an ordinary private.
The reason is that Private Ryans three brothers have all been killed in action, and a compassionate
general is determined to spare the boy's mother from sacrificing all her children. Disgruntled by
the arbitrariness of their assignment, the squad plods off to find the elusive GI, wondering why
their own mothers aren't worthy of similar consideration.

The first and second portions of "Saving Private Ryan" each raise important moral issues. The
opening sequence implicitly poses the question of whether depicting combat in all its hideous
detail serves useful, and progressive purposes—educating the young, discouraging warlike
thinking—or simply blends into today's general din of violent entertainment.

The events involving Private Ryan and his would-be rescuers probe more intricate ethical
matters, asking whether the saving of one man's life can justify putting many others into serious
jeopardy.

The end of the movie extends this question still further, suggesting that the beneficiary of such
treatment may forever wonder if he was worthy of the sacrifices made for him. It's worth noting
that the question of "Why me?" has troubled many survivors of the Holocaust, which was the
subject of "Schindler's List," still Spielberg's most resonant film. It is clearly an issue he cares
deeply about.

What holds "Saving Private Ryan" short of excellence, despite the vigor of its acting and the
impact of Spielberg's technical skills, is its failure to explore these moral dilemmas with all the
depth and dignity they deserve. In the movie's last half hour, they are finessed by a second large-
scale battle scene, as terrifying as the first but also more predictable, more manipulative, more

calculated in its dramatic and psychological effects. It gives the story a rousing conclusion, but its deft exploitation of war-movie conventions also gives combat the sheen of Hollywood excitement that Spielberg avoided at the start of the picture.

This aside, "Saving Private Ryan" is certain to be one of the year's most popular and talked-about movies. As for the awards race that's starting to pick up midsummer steam, Hanks will surely be on the front Oscar lines for his nuanced portrayal of the sensitive squad leader, and GI sidekicks Edward Burns and Matt Damon may well flank him in the supporting-actor category.

Also expect kudos for cinematographer Janusz Kaminski, composer John Williams, and other Spielberg regulars. Although their work here is not the best of their careers, they help make "Saving Private Ryan" a walloping patriotic tale, if not the rich moral lesson it might have been.

CINEASTE, Vol. XXIV, No.1, 1998, p. 68, Thomas Doherty

Old Glory ripples in the breeze. The weary footsteps of an old soldier trudge to a forest of white crosses, their symmetry broken up by the odd Star of David. As the camera tracks backward, the arms of the crosses slice into the edge of the frame, filling the screen with row upon row of bleached white sentinels. While his family watches from a respectful distance, snapping a disrespectful photograph, the man crumples before a grave. A sound bridge mixes up the rough churning of ocean surf, cuing a flashback dissolve from the veteran at the graveside to a squad of wet and scared soldiers huddled in a landing craft crashing through the waves towards Omaha Beach, June 6, 1944, and the past is present for him and us.

So begins Steven Spielberg's *Saving Private Ryan*, an epic war film so commercially successful, critically esteemed, commemorative in spirit, and grand in ambition that it just begs to be trashed. On Academy Awards night next April, it will rake in all the big Oscars during a four-hour, three-hankie ritual of filial piety: the baby boomer sons kneeling before their WWII fathers in a final, fin-de-siécle act of generational genuflection, kind of like the moment at the end of *Field of Dreams* (1989), when the father and the son reconcile by tossing around a baseball, sports and the military being the only arenas where real men are permitted to get all choked up. In fact, the cynical cineaste who fails to bow before the solemn memorial that is *Saving Private Ryan* may be likened to the baseball fan who refuses to stand up for the National Anthem in Fenway Park—and just as liable to be pummeled senseless by the folks in the bleachers. Perfectly timed and pitched (in both senses), *Saving Private Ryan* radiates grace, gravitas, and good intentions. It flickers less as a motion picture than as a ceremonial flame for Americans, on the cusp of the millennium, to look back at the linchpin event of the twentieth century and to meditate upon the cost paid by the men who won the Good War (without the Studs Turkel scare quotes). If *Schindler's List* (1993) sang Kaddish at the Wailing Wall, *Saving Private Ryan* lays a wreath at Arlington Memorial Cemetery.

What *Saving Private Ryan* is not is a radical departure from the combat genre, the first film to show the true face of war. The blurbs and ballyhoo for *The Big Parade* (1925), *All Quiet on the Western Front* (1930), *A Walk in the Sun* (1945), *The Steel Helmet* (1951), *Patton* (1970), and *Platoon* (1986) all played variations of the same theme: heretofore Hollywood combat was antiseptic, but in this film, finally, the hell of war is shown in all its fury and horror, stripped of romance, nobility, and happy endings. Yeah, right—as if *Saving Private Ryan* is sui generis, proclaiming something about war that no film has dared say before: that it is violent and terrifying, that good guys die, that moral verities wilt under fire.

More than any other entertainment film of recent memory, however, *Saving Private Ryan* comes wrapped in an esthetic of realism that is its red badge of pure motives and high purpose. Prepublicity advertising massaged audience reception and dictated the terms for victory: the imprimatur from historians Stephen Ambrose and Paul Fussell and the testimonials of veterans being more avidly solicited than the thumbs-up sign from film critics. Recruiting from the local VFW and American Legion, TV news shows marched D-Day veterans into multiplex mars and recorded their tearful postscreening edits. One can't help but be touched by the stricken reactions, the traumatic memories welling up under the power of the film, but one also can't help but think that these old soldiers don't get out to the movies much anymore. Every FX blow-up and forensic shock in *Saving Private Ryan* has been detonated on celluloid before. "Tom Savini directs *The Longest Day*," a wiseguy might sneer.

Up on screen, the earnest verisimilitude seemed to justify the endorsements from scholars and vets: not just in the unflinching depiction of violence (always the true measure of 'realism' in American cinema), but in the set design, costuming, and supply lines. Like monks bent over an illuminated manuscript, Spielberg and his crew reclaim the attention to martial detail that invested the best of the classic films—the period authenticity in arms, vehicles, uniforms, unit insignia, every stripe and hash mark in pace, down to the distinctive diamond-shaped design of a Hitler Youth dagger. The wartime vernacular and military lingo in Robert Rodat's sparse script is also spot-on, with no subtitles for listeners who can't keep up—though most will be have figured out the GI acronym FUBAR, a less known variant of SNAFU, long before it dawns on the butt of the joke. Harder to break are the habits of late twentieth-century American hygiene: check out the gleam of the Southern California dental work and the sheen of the footwear.

For his part, the planet's most popular director has been in training for a major WWII landing since his first 8mm one-reelers, shot on location in the deserts of the American Southwest. Robert Shaw's riveting soliloquy in *Jaws* (1975), when the flinty shark hunter Quint conjures his night-sea terror after the sinking of the U.S.S. Indianapolis, may be the single most memorable verbal passage in all of Spielbergia. Tally up the misfired comedy of *1941* (1979); *Always* (1985); the sentimental remake of *A Guy Named Joe* (1943); *Empire of the Sun* (1987), the searing vision of childhood set in a Japanese prison camp; and his AFI-certified masterpiece, *Schindler's List,* and the wartime period shadows the Spielberg filmography at least as much as aliens and anthropologists. In retrospect, it seems inevitable that the most awesome spectacle ever recorded by the moving image should eventually attract the undivided attention of the most cinematically inspired of American artists.

Given that pedigree, the prism of WWII (the movie) not WWII (the war) filters *Saving Private Ryan.* Classic Hollywood combat war films from *Battleground* (1949) to *The Big Red One* (1980) leave visible tracks (cf., the Sergeant Zack lookalike from *The Steel Helmet* who appears briefly in the last battle sequence), but the deeper dreamwork is the most popular television show of its time for a suburban youth of a certain age growing up in Phoenix, Arizona—namely *Combat!* (1962-1967), the gritty black-and-white ABC series, directed from a lean, ground-level perspective, often by Robert Altman. Set in the European Theater of Operations after D-Day, *Combat!* was a weekly reiteration of the tropes of the classical WWII combat film and the shooting script for countless adolescent war games.

The terrific hook that is the whispered "Rosebud" of the narrative derives in part from the true story of the Sullivan brothers, five brothers from the same Iowa family, all lost in the sinking of the U.S.S. Juneau in November 1942. (Talk about the visceral impact of a war film: the Hollywood biopic released the next year, *The Sullivans* [1944], was so melodramatically shattering that in some hard-hit home-front neighborhoods the hysterical reaction from grief-stricken audiences forced the film to be pulled from circulation.) The mission: to save the last surviving sibling of a family hit three times by death, to pluck one man from the fog of war and return him safely to home and hearth.

Since the key to genre is the tension between familiarity and variation, the conventional and the original, *Saving Private Ryan* unfolds as an uncharted mine field of sudden terrors interspersed with secure perimeters and safe bivouacs. The tale is bracketed by the present-day time frame of a graveside visit at the Normandy Memorial Cemetery (quiet, serene, respectful), and by a pair of tour de force combat sequences (loud, chaotic, blasphemous). For every radical disruption (GIs shoot surrendering Germans pointblank and crack bad jokes), a soothing nostrum restores equilibrium. Where else but in a WWII film does a GI warn, "I don't have a good feeling about this one," a Nazi prisoner spared from summary execution return for bad result in the last reel, or a green kid turn into the unlikely hero—or does he?

The baptism of fire, the twenty-seven-minute battle overture depicting the landing at Omaha Beach, is already a lesson for the film textbooks, to be as endlessly rewound, frozen, and analyzed as the shower scene in *Psycho.* A sustained fusillade, it manages to induce not just suspense, shock, and disorientation but a kind of combat fatigue. Protected for a moment in the eggshell of the landing craft, racing through the surf to land on the most hostile of shores, GIs vomit in fear, with good reason. The doors open and whole squads are cut to ribbons on the spot, shot, shelled, drowned, and torn apart. Robert Capa *mise-en-scène* and Army Signal Corp eyelines clash in a barrage of kaleidoscopic flashes: the blurry D-Day images of the famous combat photographer spliced into the handheld combat camerawork of burly noncoms hefting 35mm Mitchells, whose lenses peer out from behind parapets and through the slits of pillboxes. Newsreel memories are evoked by angle of sight, jump-cut action, and subtle shifts in film grain, but the newsreels unspooled nothing like this. The jagged suturing of the combat montage seems a ghastly complement to the surgical violations of the human frame: intestines spilling out, a face blown apart, a dazed GI with a bloody stump gripping his detached forearm, a wounded man who suddenly becomes a shredded torso, and the rending of human flesh leaving an oceanfront awash in blood and body parts.

As the first major WWII combat to be fashioned in the modern age of Computer Graphic Imaging, digital sound, and forensic makeup, *Saving Private Ryan* takes full advantage of the shock of the new, of being able to revision, in full-color carnage, a war largely sanitized on the Hollywood screen. Though well established tricks of the trade in action adventure, horror teenpics, and the Vietnam war film, the high-tech tools of verisimilitude have never before been orchestrated for full visceral impact in WWII territory. Lending a full measure of earwitness depth involvement, the combat symphony howling on the soundtrack underscores the visual bombardment—the mosquito buzz of bullets whizzing through the air, the whistles of the incoming 88s, and the three-dimensional presence of zooming aircraft, crunching tank treads, each weapon, shell, and vehicle given its own aural marker. Digitally sweetened (if that's the right word), sound also renders the hallucinatory haze in the backwash of explosions. Thankfully, too, the musical score by John Williams lacks the bombast of the incoming shells. Quietly martial, all gentle trumpets and mild percussion, it wafts in only when the combat recedes, layered almost beneath conscious registration. The guilty secret here is that far from being horrifying and repulsive, the stunning spectacle of sight and sound is a joy to behold and harken to from a theater seat, pure cinema at its most hypnotic and intense. Godard is right: war on screen is always exhilarating.

Up and off the beach, the carnage and confusion settles into the rational purpose of a military target, to take out a German machine-gun emplacement. With dialogue exchanged and tactics formulated, the terror of the D-Day landing recedes, the heartbeat lowers. Spielberg's celebration of spontaneous GI action, above and beyond the call of duty, conforms to the story of D-Day according to historian Stephen Ambrose, the film's spiritual *auteur*: that discrete acts of heroism and initiative by citizen soldiers assured victory on the beach that day. Mustering the remnants of tattered platoons for a forward assault, Captain Miller (Tom Hanks) bellows a line straight from the manual of Sgt. John Ryker of *Sands of Iwo Jima* (1949) or Sgt. Chip Saunders of *Combat!*: "Let's get in this war!"

Scanning the CGI-generated landscape after battle, a crane shot swoops in on the backpack of a dead GI with the stencilled name, "Ryan, S." From the blood-drenched vista of Omaha Beach, the action shifts to the sepia tones of homefront America and the tap-tap-tapping of War Department secretaries typing out bad news borne by telegram, with utterances of official regret murmured in voice-over. The sight of an Iowa farmhouse with four blue stars in the window and a long shot of an Army staff car driving up a dirt road, spied from the vantage of a mother standing at the kitchen sink, is another kind of telegraphed message—she knows, we know she knows, but we know she knows not the worst of it.

The brief homefront sequence makes another crafty maneuver with a saintly portrait of Army Chief of Staff General George C. Marshall. The architect of victory, the indispensable man in the fight against fascism, Marshall has been almost erased from the popular memory of WWII, never granted the big-screen recognition of Patton or Eisenhower (neither of whom is so much as mentioned here, though British Field Marshall Bernard Montgomery warrants the common Yank evaluation of him as an "overrated" martinet.) Breaking ranks with the usual Hollywood formula for portrayals of the officer corps (the higher up in the command, the lower the IQ and moral character), Spielberg treats Marshall as reverently as Jack Warner treated FDR, a decision designed to endear the film to WWII buffs, most of whom think Marshall's picture should be on U.S. currency. "The boy's alive and we're going to find him and we're going to get him the hell out of there," orders the General. Suitably awed, his men answer, "Yes, sir."

Though *Saving Private Ryan* depicts the American military command structure as decent, competent, and courageous, some of the very few dissenting voices in the chorus of hosannas for the film have come from conservative critics who bewail the absence of the blustery pro-

American, anti-Nazi rhetoric once enforced upon Hollywood by the Office of War Information. More wisely, Spielberg and screenwriter Rodat know that the justness of the Good War and the nobility of the enterprise is too obvious to require a recitation of why we fight, that the moral valance is as much a part of the landscape as khaki and cigarettes. Besides, the man who directed *Schindler's List* knows better than to make an antiwar movie about WWII. He's already made a film about the alternative.

After the battle-scarring introduction and stateside orientation, the film settles into a roulette game of ensemble attrition. A multiethnic sampling of homo americanus, the combat squad sent to extricate Private Ryan fits the Warner Bros. mold: the idealized everyman leader Captain Miller (Hanks); the grizzled Sgt. Horvath (Tom Sizemore); the cynical tough guy Pvt. Reiben (Edward Burns); the emotional Eye-tal-ian Carpazo (Vin Diesel); the edgy Jewish guy Melish (Adam Goldberg); the compassionate medic (Giovanni Ribisi); the Johnny Reb marksman (Barry Pepper); and the Milquetoast clerk pressed into infantryman's boots, Corporal Upham (Jeremy Davis). Bearing the symbolic weight of the moral and statistical stakes, the elusive Ryan (Matt Damon) is an Iowa farm boy issued from the pages of *Guadalcanal Diary*. One half expects William Bendix to pop up with a wisecrack about the Brooklyn Dodgers.

If the cannon fodder on Omaha Beach are a blur of bodies and nameless faces, the combat squad personalizes the cost of war: Caparzo, whose heart overrules his head and whose fate punctuates the cold logic of combat ("And that's why we can't take children!" barks Captain Miller); the up-close death of the medic, a physician who cannot heal himself, who knows the diagnosis is terminal when his liver has been hit, and whose comrades ease him into the next world with morphine; and the excruciating duel between a Nazu *ubermensch* and Melish, penetrated by a blade in a deadly pas de deux that plays like an act of coitus. In good WWII fashion, ethnic and religious colors shade in the character details. Catholics clutch rosaries and cross themselves, priests deliver the last rites to gasping soldiers, and the fundamentalist sniper recites scripture. WWII being the crucible of assimilation for Italian Americans, a vowel in the last name occasions a complementary slur. "All the guineas are buying it," cracks Reiben as the men rummage through a pile of dog tags looking for the Irish surname. Oddly, or maybe not so oddly, Spielberg seems off-balance in limning the Jewish guy Melish, an overdetermined Nazi-hater, who breaks down in tears while clutching a Hitler youth dagger ("Now it's a *Shabbat hallah* cutter") and taunts German POWs by waving a Star of David and hissing, *"Juden, Ja, Juden!"*

In the tension between the esthetic of realism and the satisfactions of genre, Tom Hanks is the man on the tightrope. just as the hierarchy of the studio star system worked against the grain of the values of the classic WWII combat film (ensemble players as combat unit doing an unglamorous job of work), the certainty that Hanks will die not in the first but in the last reel works against the chaos theory of war. *(Of course* he will be killed in action: the way to tell a serious war film from a juvenile war film is that in a serious war film the most likable character dies.) Captain Miller is the Frank Capra version of the American soldier, the antithesis of the *Wehrmacht* automaton, a school teacher who becomes a warrior of necessity, not bloodlust, who wants only to finish the job and get back home to his wife in small-town Pennsylvania. He is also a natural leader who might have sprung from a Walter Mitty daydream. "We'll follow the captain through hell," says a character in the James Thurber short story—and Miller's men do. He is made mortal by a mild case of the nerves, a shaky right hand, a physical tic and visual symbol that will have a wrenching emotional payoff in his last seconds of animation.

Filling the quiet spaces between the combat action are discussions of the bond of brotherhood by that rear-echelon essayist Ralph Waldo Emerson, translations of an Edith Piaf tune wafting on a scratching phonograph in the prebattle calm, droll GI commentary ("The Statue of Liberty is *kaput?*" Miller asks drily, harkening to the news from a Nazi loudspeaker. "That's disconcerting."), and meditations on the connect the dots theme ("This time the mission *is* a man."). The patches of verbal eloquence share space with glimpses of austere beauty: a strangely serene landscape after battle; a quiet night in a demolished cathedral; or a combat squad silhouetted against flashes of artillery light at dawn, the Wehrmacht sharing the affinity of cinematographer Janusz Kaminski for the dappled chiaroscuro of the 'magic hour.' "That's quite a view," says Miller, waxing Spielbergian as he gazes out over Omaha Beach, now secure, cluttered with men, equipment, ships, blimps, and bodies. This is not verisimilitude, nor does it pretend to be.

Spielberg's watchmaker's skill with every unit of cinematic grammar is always breathtaking: seeing the gears turning and the bells chiming on cue never diminishes astonishment at the precision of the instrumentation. The shot/reverse-shot duel to the death between two snipers, one who spies the other through his scope and sees the flash of gunfire a split second too late for his own shot; a forward assault rendered through the passive point of view of Corporal Upham; or Miller, near death and beyond caring, futilely firing his pistol at an oncoming tank, impossibly igniting it, as the camera tilts upward to reveal the true source of the explosion, a plane climbing in an arc out of its attack dive. The squadron of P-51s, we may recall, would not be in the sky had not Miller ordered his reluctant men to take out a German radar installation earlier, a decision that caused the death of the beloved medic.

As the latest esteemed addition to the Spielberg canon, *Saving Private Ryan* confirms the schizophrenia in the director, a split auteurist personality separating Steven the Younger from Steven the Elder. On the one side are Spielberg's juvenile knock-offs, where he seems increasingly disengaged and mechanical (the *Indiana Jones* serials and the *Jurassic Park* stuff). On the other side is his adult work where the artistic investment is more than a matter of percentage points taken off the gross box-office receipts—*Schindler's List, Amistad,* and *Saving Private Ryan.* Gone is the easy mesh of artistry and popularity that invested the early prime of *Jaws/Close Encounters/ET.* Between dinosaurs and didacticism, there seems no happy medium. "I'm a 2.35 kind of guy," Spielberg once remarked, but mainly for his juvenilia, not the serious stuff. *Saving Private Ryan* is shot in standard 1.85:1 aspect ratio, not Panavision, presumably to avoid associations with the glory mongering WWII spectacles of the Fifties and Sixties.

Unlike the reporter seeking the psychic key to Charles Foster Kane, Captain Miller and his squad find their Rosebud. Needless to say, he refuses to abandon his fraternity and remains "with the only brothers I have left." "The world has taken a turn for the surreal," says Captain Miller, anachronistically, incorrectly. Actually, this is as classical and traditional as it gets.

In the landscape after battle, with the armored cavalry riding up and the P-51s soaring above, the combat zone is secure enough for the exit line. "Earn it," whispers the dying Miller to Private Ryan, as the camera tilts down to his hand, now stilled. Neither a benediction nor a curse, it is a reminder aimed not at Private Ryan—he has already earned it—but at his posterity, the callow inheritors of the sacrifice of the wartime generation, Spielberg boomers and Damon Gen-Xers alike. So, too, General Marshall's godlike voice-over, which delivers the eulogy for Captain Miller, Sergeant Horvitz, Private Caparzo, T/4 Medic Wade, et al., quoting again from Lincoln's letter to Mrs. Bixby, offering some words of solace that her sons have died on "the altar of freedom."

The words are not ironic and neither is the last image, echoing of the first, of the American flag flying in the harsh breezes of the memorial cemetery at Normandy. This is not the flag that unfurls in *Born on the Fourth of July, Primary Colors,* of *The People Vs. Larry Flynt,* a stained prop of fake glory and scoundrel patriotism, but the real item, the star-spangled banner yet waving, the symbol of Spielberg's American anthem and an emblem of his own eagle eye for hitting his countrymen right where they live.

FILM QUARTERLY, Fall 1999, p. 39, Karen Jaehne

In September 1998, Steven Spielberg received the Knight Commander's Cross of the Order of Merit of the Federal Republic of Germany from President Roman Herzog, who expressed Germany's appreciation to the American Jewish director. "Germany thanks you for work that has given us more than you may realize," said Herzog. The film that made the Germans realize that there were maybe heroes among them would be *Schindler's List.* Yet at that time, Spielberg's subsequent film was also playing in German cinemas—a film that had as its cornerstone the same verse from the Talmud emblazoned on the screen in *Schindler's List:* "Whoever saves one life, saves the world entire."

In making *Saving Private Ryan,* Spielberg inverted that principle to show an entire group setting out to save a single—and virtually unknown—soldier, someone more remote to them than Schindler's people were to him. *Saving Private Ryan* focuses on Captain John Miller's (Tom

Hanks) leading a special squadron detailed to find and save the last son of Mrs. Ryan, whose other three boys have perished on three different fronts. The carnage they must face is so often blamed on their quest that, by the time we meet Ryan himself, he all too readily accepts the burden of guilt. Spielberg's ability to look at World War II first this way, then that, has guaranteed him an altar in the magazine/TV/newsprint edifice that enshrines pop culture—where our latest products are sheltered, framed, hung, and subjected to an examination of ourselves within the work of art. The critical establishment seldom bothers to wire in a feed from Europe, where reactions to Hollywood product can alert us to surprising things about the movies themselves, as well as the auteurs behind them. In Germany, for example, the reception of *Schindler's List* undoubtedly benefitted from the effect of historian Daniel Goldberg tutoring the people in their proper role as willing villains. Spielberg brought relief by focusing on the hero among them and creating a masterpiece dedicated to their past.

By the time President Herzog came to thank Spielberg, he could tacitly include *Saving Private Ryan* for its relatively benevolent portrait of the German soldier—certainly from the point of view of those who could understand the German dialogue of the film. Why the German dialogue was not shared with English-speaking, or rather, non-German-speaking audiences raises an issue that has not yet been addressed.

In a movie where most of what is said serves to register the shock of battle (often with anachronistic profanity), one scene stands out for the nature of the dialogue, precisely because such a scene requires little dialogue. It is the last big sequence, in which Private Mellish (Adam Goldberg), the Jewish enlisted man who has enjoyed taunting German P.O.W.s with his Star of David, is now waiting in a tower for ammunition. Corporal Upham (Jeremy Davies), who only hours before has impressed his comrades with translations of the melancholy *chansons* of Edith Piaf, is chosen for this mission and thus finds himself in the middle of a raging battle relegated to ammo-delivery boy. Mellish is waiting for him to bring more rounds to keep the Germans at bay, but the onslaught of the German forces has left the young corporal petrified, and he hides from the German soldier who enters the tower and heads up the stairs towards Mellish. Upham creeps halfway up the staircase after him, cringing in fear, incapable of rescuing Mellish.

When the German discovers Mellish, he leaps on him. As the two soldiers struggle, we realize the German is also out of ammunition. Their confrontation comes down to a *mano a mano* death match, which, to be sure, has been the core scene of every great war story since *The Iliad*. Mellish and the German roll over on top of each other, kicking, lunging, strangling, until they're down to their knives. They are evenly matched until Mellish's knife is knocked out of his hand, and the German bears down on him with the knife poised at his heart. Mellish pushes up on the German's arm. Their death grip is like two scorpions in a bottle.

To increase the tension of the scene, the German soldier maintains a steady stream of hissing at Mellish. (In sports, this kind of thing is called talking trash and is used to unnerve the opponents, although it was once considered bad sportsmanship.) Most American viewers seem to think the German's words are another kind of torture for Mellish, threatening him or cursing him, because the harsh guttural sounds of the language strike the ear as dreadful, even evil. This is merely a problem of perception, because what the German is saying to Mellish is actually quite different: "Lass uns es beenden...("Let's just end it all.")

In short, the German wants to show the American an easy death. Why? This is not the sadistic, vicious enemy we know from standard issue Nazis in WWII pictures. Is Spielberg trying to humanize the enemy? In this duel to the death, the German soldier seems to bring mercy to the ghastly business of being a soldier. Unfortunately, once Mellish and the German go at each other, there's no mercy until one of them is dead. I believe the entire point of this scene is lost if we do not understand what the German is saying to his victim. The lack of subtitles encourages us to resort to the idea of the evil, hissing German, a cliché that inflates the Teutonic terror enveloping these innocent Americans. (In 1944, Americans were by definition still innocent.)

Spielberg's point in this scene is perhaps less about the two men fighting than about the witness to their fight, Corporal Upham, who is portrayed from his first scene as a bumbler (expecting to bring his Smith & Corona typewriter with him) or a sucker (as he gets set up by the other men in the detail). Here, Upham is the ineffectual intellectual who failed to get Mellish the bullets to defend himself and now must lurk just out of sight eavesdropping on the death for which he is, in some sense, responsible. Certainly, the camera implicates him because the film continuously cuts back to him cringing in shame. Among the Americans with whom we are meant to identify, Upham alone understands what is said. Upham, however, is no threat, and the German soldier can't even be bothered to kill him as he passes him on the stairs after killing Mellish. Upham offers the profile of a man who, after the war, will not be able to live with himself—far more than Private Ryan, who pleads with Captain Miller to let him fight along with his comrades.

A reasonable interpretation of the scene is impossible without understanding the sequence as a microcosm of the war that Captain Miller and his men have come to fight. Mellish must die, but the German who survives goes misunderstood—except by Upham, who is made most miserable by his own cowardice. Corporal Upham, not Private Ryan, offers the best example of a life lived at the expense of his comrade. Among the reasons for the U.S. to enter WWII, the death of Mellish serves to remind us of the Jews being slaughtered by the Germans, while the search for Private Ryan represents the sacrifices made necessary because America entered the war at such a late stage, when so many fronts demanded so much manpower. It is impossible not to think of all that while watching the prolonged wrestling match between Mellish and his killer.

The sacrifice of Mellish reverberates in our memory as we watch the contemporary scenes that open and conclude Spielberg's film. Some 50 years after the end of WWII, Private Ryan turns to his wife with the query, "Have I lived a life worthy of the great sacrifices made for me?" The same question could be asked of Upham, and of course, we could not answer with the same assurance given Ryan, because Upham's cowardice is appalling and serves as foil against which Ryan's insistence on fighting, even when he has an order from the High Command to avoid the battle, is made to seem even more noble.

How did they get into such a complicated mess? As the film opens, the Germans are entrenched above the beach, with an invisible sharpshooter firing mercilessly. The German enemy is always more powerful for being unseen, which is, I propose, the visual equivalent of language not understood. Whenever German soldiers come into view, they are striking for their failure to frighten us—with the sole exception of the German soldier come to slay Mellish. Upon gaining the plateau above the beach, the Americans have their first face-to-face encounter with German soldiers. A row of them emerges, hands in the air, approaching as P.O.W.s, trying to communicate in German. The Americans can't understand them, so they shoot them.

In another scene, Captain Miller's detail, just embarked on its mission, rests under cover of a bombed-out building, and suddenly the back wall collapses, revealing a unit of German soldiers playing cards. Surprised and defenselessness, they cry out—again, in untranslated German—"Don't shoot!" Their hands go up in alarm as Upham gives them a German command: "Haende hoch—ohne zu scherzen." ("Hands up, no kidding.") But suddenly a shot goes off, and the Germans are mowed down. It is a situation ripe for taking prisoners of war, and its morality is complicated by our not knowing who fired that first shot. But the relief felt by Captain Miller's Americans at still being alive makes them all the more suspect, when it comes to Geneva Conventions. This is compounded when we realize the other soldiers have no respect for the German-speaking Upham. This ethical dilemma is expanded and explored in a sequence where Captain Miller's unit does take a prisoner of war, a man so desperate to stay alive that his begging takes the form of a recitation of every American notion cluttering up his mind: "I like American... Steamboat Willie, Betty Boop, Betty Grable, nice gams.... What a dish!... Donald Duck... O-oh say can you sink?... Fuck Hitler..." It is a stream-of-consciousness list of Yankee cultural exports worthy of James Joyce, but it only inspires Captain Miller's men to take aim and fire.

Spielberg has trouble handling a theme with straightforward consistency. In *Saving Private Ryan*, he indulges his artistic schizophrenia in an early scene that lends a comic irony to the enemy. Hanks' little platoon takes a P.O.W. and details him to dig graves. When the Americans are ready to make him fall into his own grave, Miller protects them from their worst instincts. He sticks to the Geneva Convention, but, unable to be burdened with a P.O.W. in his mission, simply grants the German his life and sends him on his way. In the final scene, that soldier has done what a soldier must do—rejoined his ranks. There he is, among the Germans attacking the bridge Miller is defending. In the final moments, they face each other in the village square. "I know that guy," cries the German in friendly tones—in German (again sans subtitles and sadly not understood), but too late. The German soldiers aim and kill Captain Miller.

In the interstices of this ghastly saga, Spielberg has tried to show the impulse to communicate, to say something meaningful, even humane. Alas, it always goes untranslated. The translator himself, as conceived by the story, is basically a jerk—a man who sits around translating songs for his comrades while they wait for the German tanks to mow them down. He would not be such a bad guy hanging around on the Left Bank 20 years earlier, but he's not cut out for a foxhole.

Ultimately, we watch this film as a generation of Americans who have never risked their lives to defend the free world or gone hungry because there was scarcely enough food for the entire family. In short, to those of us who have never made a personal sacrifice for the greater good, Steven Spielberg brings us the ersatz opportunity of the experience we missed because of the Pax Americana. That same peace puts the Germans in a rather similar situation: What have they suffered lately? *Saving Private Ryan* exploits every possible cinematic trick to recreate the emotional reality of a soldier dumped onto an alien beach and into an onslaught of enemy mortar. Whether American or German, the viewer is faced with death, and as the film goes on, the dubious means of dodging death. If you're American, you thank Spielberg for bringing you close to the last justifiable war. On the other hand, a German can thank Spielberg for not showing him as a villain, but rather continuing with a cause begun in *Schindler's* List to restore dignity and credibility to the Germans as having accepted their destiny and faced battle as worthy foes.

Or, knowing how filmmakers tend to deny all interpretations of their films, Spielberg may have indulged the contradictions in his narrative in order to save himself not from the Germans, but, alas!, from the intellectuals.

LOS ANGELES TIMES, 7/24/98, Calendar/p. 1, Kenneth Turan

More than any of his other films, and that includes "Schindler's List," Steven Spielberg's "Saving Private Ryan" won't leave you alone. To see it is to need to talk about it, to wrestle both with the formidable impact of its unprecedented strengths and the surprising resilience of its niggling weaknesses. A powerful and impressive milestone in the realistic depiction of combat, "Saving Private Ryan" is as much an experience we live through as a film we watch on screen.

No one needs to be told about Spielberg's ability as a popular culture taste-maker: Seven of Hollywood's 20 top-grossing films bear his mark as either director, producer or executive producer. But because his skills as a filmmaker are so great, because he can and often does get away with working at a fraction of his capabilities, "Saving Private Ryan" is a startling reminder of exactly how spectacular a director Spielberg can be when he allows himself to be challenged by a subject (in this case World War II) that pushes against his limits.

The son of a combat veteran, Spielberg says the first movies he made as a child dealt with that war, and many critics feel that the 40 minutes showing 1941 Shanghai under Japanese attack that open "Empire of the Sun" rank among the best footage he's ever shot. Spielberg is most effective when he doesn't flinch, when his respect for the material compels him to be as honest as he can, and that is largely the case here.

It's not that "Private Ryan's" story (written by Robert Rodat) of an eight-man squad detailed to find and rescue a soldier in just-invaded Normandy doesn't provide opportunities for conventional movie heroism. It does, and Tom Hanks as laconic squad leader Capt. John Miller gives an indelible performance as an elevated everyman, our ideal vision of how we all hope we'd act under the duress of combat.

But Capt. Miller is not a casually heroic John Wayne knockoff. He's despairing about his role in leading men to slaughter, troubled at the person the war has turned him into, and the periodic trembling of one of his hands reveals he's dangerously close to coming apart.

In this determination not to trivialize the nature of war and what it does to people, "Private Ryan" is often a darker and more pessimistic look at combat and reality than we are used to from either Hollywood or Spielberg. This is a war where American soldiers mock virtue and shoot surrendering Germans, where decent and altruistic actions tend to be fatal, where death is random, stupid and redeems hardly anything at all. Even the usually vivid American flag is, in Janusz Kaminski's remarkable cinematography, bleached out and desaturated.

More than in its attitudes, more even than in its surprising focus on the nature of cowardice, "Saving Private Ryan" reveals its determination to be accurate in the way it presents combat action. Using a trio of superlative operators (Mitch Dubin, Chris Haarhoff, Seamus Corcoran) and relying on the newsreel look of hand-held cameras, "Private Ryan" gets as close to the unimaginable horror and chaos of battle as fiction film ever has, closer in fact than some audience members may want to experience.

After a brief prelude depicting an old veteran, we're not sure exactly who, returning with his family to the American cemetery at Normandy, we flash immediately back to that beach and a shot of Capt. Miller in his landing craft on D-day, June 6, 1944. During the next 20 or so minutes, we are shown the invasion of France with a violence and an intensity that is almost beyond describing.

The slaughter starts immediately and does not let up. Men are enveloped in flames, ripped to shreds by bullets, dead as soon as they set foot on the beach or, in an agonizing mixture of horror and beauty, dying in slow-motion as they are dragged underwater. One man's leg is blown off, another loses an arm and tries awkwardly to pick it up with the other, a third lies in agony as his intestines graphically spill on the ground. Panic, pitiless fear and bloody pandemonium are everywhere; we see the raw terror on everyone's face, and for once we know exactly why it's there.

A great deal has been made about the violence level in "Saving Private Ryan," and though it is horrific, it's a world apart from the pandering, anything-for-a-rush blood sports that characterize business-as-usual Hollywood. There's no attempt to make the violence fun and games, and special pleading is completely absent. Instead, the visual tone is the dispassionate, pitiless one of an all-seeing but uninvolved deity, inviting us to look on this awful destruction and despair.

One of the last shots of the battle focuses on the name "Ryan" stenciled on the backpack of a corpse. A scene in a military office back home produces the information that in fact three of four Ryan brothers have died in action within days of one another. When Army Chief of Staff Gen. George C. Marshall (Harve Presnell) finds out, he focuses on the survivor, Pvt. James Ryan, on the ground somewhere in Normandy. "We are going to send someone to find him," the general says. "And we are going to get him the hell out of there."

That someone turns out to be Capt. Miller, none too happy at being assigned to what he considers "a public relations gambit" as potentially difficult and pointless as finding "a needle in a stack of needles." What is the sense, both he and his men wonder as they head out, in risking all their lives to save just one? "Ryan better be worth it," the captain says. "He better go home and cure some disease or invent a new, longer-lasting lightbulb."

As the squad warily picks its way through the combat zone, we get to know the men we've only caught a glimpse of during the invasion, starting with Sgt. Horvath (Tom Sizemore), the captain's unflappable right hand, and the newly added Cpl. Upham (Jeremy Davis), a timid, bookish translator who's never seen action.

The rest of the guys, besides the compassionate medic Wade (Giovanni Ribisi), are all privates. The biggest talker is Reiben (Edward Bums), who has "Brooklyn, N.Y." written on his jacket, though Caparzo (Vin Diesel) and his mouth are not far behind. Mellish (Adam Goldberg) is angrily aware of what the Nazis are doing to the Jews, and Jackson (Barry Pepper) is a religious Southern sharpshooter who prays "God grant me strength" before taking aim and firing.

Working with casting director Denise Chamian, Spielberg has adroitly cast these roles, mixing actors known mostly to followers of independent film with camouflaged veterans like Sizemore (who does the best, most controlled work of his career), Dennis Farina and Ted Danson (who appear briefly as officers).

But even as we're admiring these performances, we can't help but be aware that this kind of multiethnic squad is one of the most venerable conventions of war movies, can't help noticing that, for instance, sharpshooter Jackson could have stepped right out of "Sergeant York," the 1941 film about World War I starring Gary Cooper.

What nags at you about "Saving Private Ryan" is the way Rodat's script, though solid and well-structured, has not broken through convention, has not elevated itself to a higher level (or even reached the best of the old level) the way the mind-bending scenes of combat have.

As the squad moves through crises toward the elusive Pvt. Ryan, what impacts us most are invariably scenes of action: sometimes fire fights, sometimes unexpected deaths, but never the dialogue the men trade. Just as the soldiers speculate that Capt. Miller has been artfully reassembled from old body parts, so "Private Ryan's" script has been put together from familiar and shopworn material.

Because the script is only workmanlike, it highlights the hitch in Spielberg's otherwise problem-free direction, which is a tendency to be too insistent at obviously sentimental moments. The enabler here is five-time Oscar-winning composer John Williams, who has been on almost all of the director's films but whose bombastic work is more and more a stranger to subtlety.

Pvt. Ryan (handsome, open-faced Matt Damon) is inevitably located, but finding him occurs simultaneously with a brutal, cataclysmic final shootout in a ruined French village constructed with uncanny, hypnotic verisimilitude by production designer Tom Sanders that is as unforgettable as the invasion. (Given that Spielberg preferred, whenever possible, not to storyboard his action ahead of time, the key player in making this and all of "Private Ryan's" action sequences so compelling is wizardly veteran editor Michael Kahn.)

How much we begrudge "Saving Private Ryan" what flaws it has depends in part on how greedy we are for perfection. When he is on his game, as he is here, Spielberg is a master storyteller whose gift for narrative film is unsurpassed. The overdone sentiment (most noticeable in the film's shaky framing story), the occasional over-reliance on conventional elements, are simply part of the package, part of what he needs for security if he's going to push mainstream filmmaking into directions it has never gone before. As far as trade-offs go, it's a hell of a deal.

NEW STATESMAN, 9/11/98, p. 38, Gerald Kaufman

Steven Spielberg's *Saving Private Ryan* is an exceptional film by a great director—a director who, at his finest, can without hyperbole be placed in the pantheon along with the likes of Eisenstein and Renoir. But because Spielberg is probably the most financially successful movie-maker in the history of cinema and because that success has to a considerable extent been based on popcorn entertainments such as *Jaws, Raiders of the Lost Ark* and *Jurassic Park*; his extraordinary technical, visual and imaginative qualities have tended to be played down or taken for granted. His success also arouses jealousy—which is why the Motion Picture Academy cold-shouldered him until *Schindler's List* forced the Oscars out of their grudging mitts.

The hype has none the less been successful in informing most sentient human beings about *Saving Private Ryan*'s subject: the squad of soldiers sent out to bring back, from the Normandy battlefront in 1944, the last remaining brother whose three siblings have all recently been killed in action. It is widely known, too, that the movie opens with a 25-minute sequence depicting the D-Day invasion on Omaha Beach.

There has been lavish praise for that sequence as the most accurate account of warfare ever seen in a fictional film. What has been less subject to comment is its surpassing technical virtuosity, scarcely noticed because the subject matter is so engrossing and so horrifying.

Certainly, what we see is transfixing. Fearful servicemen vomit in the landing craft as they wait to disembark. On shore, a soldier's leg is blown off, with the bloody stump exposed. Another soldier wanders around searching for his severed arm. Guts spill out of a man's stomach. A soldier's tin hat is hit by a bullet; he takes it off to have a look; the side of his head is blown away. The camera does not pause to dwell on these incidents. The audience has to find the detail itself All is drowned in the intolerable din of bullets and shells and screams.

Everywhere there is blood: drenching a soldier's face; suffusing the sea; in an awesome long-shot of the whole battle scene, turning the tide red; staining the camera lens. For, of course, all of this, while apparently random and even chaotic, has had to be organised meticulously for Janusz (*Schindler's List*) Kaminski's hand-held cameras.

The images captured by those cameras had then to be edited, into almost innumerable short takes, by Michael Kahn (*Schindler's List* again, as well as several other Spielberg pictures). And it had to be envisaged and orchestrated by a director of rare skill. This is one of the most masterly montage sequences in the history of the movies.

More than two hours of the film are still to come. After scenes setting up the decision to bring Ryan back, we move to his family home. Mrs Ryan, at work in the kitchen, sees cars in the distance coming along a country road.

She knows instantly that something abominable is about to be told to her, goes out on to the porch, and collapses so slowly that she seems to liquefy. This whole eloquent and moving scene is shot without a word of dialogue.

Back in Normandy, the squad goes off to rescue Ryan, and it goes reluctantly, even sullenly. These are not idealists, but grumbling sceptics: "Where's the sense of risking the lives of these eight of us to save one guy?" As the film moves along, visual flair—a patrol in silhouette against the sky, blood from a wounded man flowing away in the rain—is accompanied by brutally illusionless action.

There is, indeed, one episode more gruesomely disturbing than anything seen in the Omaha Beach sequence. A member of the rescue squad is shot. His frantic comrades try to succour him as he lies on the ground, but, as they attempt to deal with one wound, the blood flows out of other lacerations in his torso like a viscous mess escaping from a leaky plastic bag. It is one of the most disturbing death scenes in cinema and, without any verbal homily, it says all that is capable of being said about war.

Robert Rodat's screenplay dispenses with cliche. American troops shoot down Germans in cold blood. The squad's coward remains a coward, in his terror fails to rescue a comrade he might have saved, does not redeem himself, and ends up brutalised.

Performances are low-key. Tom Hanks, as the captain in command of the squad, distinguishes himself by refusing to distinguish himself. There is a weariness about Captain Miller, a resigned determination to see this unwanted assignment through. He keeps the squad together when it seems it will break up or turn enragedly on itself. He tries to offer a rationale for the mission: that, maybe, "saving Private Ryan was the one decent thing we were able to pull out of this godawful shitty mess". And, if Matt Damon as Ryan cannot avoid being the handsome, baby-faced lead, he too is awarded a role that eschews heroics; far from grateful for being rescued, he flatly refuses to go.

The movie is book-ended by opening and concluding sequences, set in the present day, which emphasise even further the inconsolable regret that war can leave behind. This film, like any other, contains its imperfections and flaws (such as the final, bang-you're-dead battle sequence). But, make no mistake, *Saving Private Ryan* is a screen landmark.

NEW YORK, 7/27/98, p. 44, David Denby

At the beginning of Steven Spielberg's *Saving Private Ryan*, a group of American soldiers landing on Omaha Beach, on D day, face a hell like none other on this earth. As the front gate of the landing-ship drops, German machine-gunners sitting in a bunker above the beach open fire, and many men fall at the exposed mouth of the craft. Some of the Americans—they are Army Rangers, led by Captain John Miller (Tom Hanks)—jump over the side and get hit under the water (we can actually see the bullets, slowed down by the sea, striking their targets). Many who make it out of the boats die in the first few yards of sand. One man still standing searches for his severed arm, picks it up as if it were a log, and wanders around with it aimlessly. As all this goes on, Spielberg rapidly shifts from one nightmare to another: When we are under the water, or inside the head of a stunned soldier, the sound collapses into an indistinct roar; the next second we are above the water, or back in the head of that soldier, now fully conscious, and the noise of bullets and mortar fire has a cutting metallic shriek that approaches agony. The scene is both utterly realistic and entirely hallucinatory. The camera staggers violently, as in a newsreel. The desaturated cinematography has the grayish shades of a corpse.

Before you have watched more than a few minutes of this—and the sequence goes on for perhaps twenty minutes in all—you know that it is one of the greatest, most appalling things ever done in movies. Not just the violence, but the strangeness of it, is overwhelming. In literature, Homer and Tolstoy have attained a comparable cruel magnificence, but there are things here that literature cannot do—a sense of the simultaneity of many little dramas within the struggle to claim the beach; complex shifts of expectation and emotion that occur in just a second or two; and, in every shot, a blood-pounding rage, senses straining to the utmost, which brings men close to extinction and ecstasy at the same time. In this one scene, and in another battle at the end, Spielberg knocks into oblivion every World War II movie ever made; and not even *Platoon* or *Full Metal Jacket* has brought us so close to the experience of men facing live fire at close range. He has also performed, intentionally or not, a devastating critique of what passes for action-film-making in Hollywood these days. I suspect that such ersatz directors as Joel Schumacher *(Batman Forever)* and Michael Bay *(Armageddon)* have hides thicker than armor; if I am wrong, and they have normal skin, they must know by now that their way of making pictures has just been plugged through the heart.

This is a marvelous movie, with superb things throughout, though it needs to be said that the material between the two battle scenes isn't on their transcendent level. Some of it is merely alert, sensitive, and shrewd; and some of it is dully ceremonial (there's a patriotic framing device that could easily have been dropped). *Saving Private Ryan,* which was conceived and written by Robert Rodat, has its oddities of form and emphasis. It begins as an epic, changes into a peculiar little anecdote, and works toward a kind of moral fable—an attempt to say what the war means. After Omaha Beach has been secured, the captain and some of his men are sent on a special mission. It seems that three brothers from Iowa have been killed; the Army wants the fourth brother, Private Ryan, pulled out of the war and sent home. In part, the rescue is a solemn public-relations exercise, but General George C. Marshall (Harve Presnell) truly considers it the only humane thing to do. In France, Captain Miller's men see it differently; the pursuit of Ryan makes no sense to them (eight of them sent to find one man?); they have two or three testy arguments about it, but they follow orders. Looking for Ryan, they wander through ravaged French fields and villages, fight the Germans here and there, and fall into punishing adventures. When they at last find Ryan (Matt Damon), he doesn't want to be saved.

The search for Ryan borders on absurdity at one point, the captain, exasperated, starts asking distraught French refugees about him—yet this is anything but an absurdist movie. The themes of *Saving Private Ryan* are loyalty, self-sacrifice, and death. The business of saving a single soldier gets folded into a larger question: What is the value of a decent gesture—any decent gesture—in war? And we think to ourselves: What could be the value of a decent gesture after what we've seen on Omaha Beach, where life was both enlarged and reduced to a condition of frenzy? The question is explored in different ways, each intensely moving. In a shattered French village, a terrified couple, standing on the exposed second floor of their house (the wall has been blown away), hand a little girl to the Americans for her protection. The girl cries that she doesn't want to leave her parents, and the captain doesn't want to take her—the Ranger who grabs her, against orders, exposes himself to enemy fire. Spielberg stages the scene without an extra shot and without a false emotion, and the episode has a wrenching painfulness that goes miles beyond the conventional heroics of war movies.

In such films as *Empire of the Sun* and *The Color Purple* Spielberg hyped everything into airily beautiful images that often left us baffled. All those people gamboling about in the broiling southern sun in *The Color Purple*—was he crazy? There seemed to be something deficient and Disneyfied in his sense of reality. And it was hard not to view that deficiency in moral terms: This man had grown up at the movies; he didn't know life. Well the problem has vanished. Like everything Spielberg does, the staging of the small encounters and skirmishes in *Saving Private Ryan* has tremendous physical energy, but his work has become soberly exact—which means, since this is war, close to crazy: A soldier, standing near an opening in a wall, with live fire all around him, picks up one little apple after another, chomping into them, discarding them, trying to find one that tastes good. Soldiers are always hungry, and this one's choosiness makes the scene funny.

Spielberg lets a movie breathe now, and sometimes he prolongs moments to the point of discomforting us. After all the years of meaningless movie violence, he wants us to feel some sort of pain. There is anger here, directed at the triviality of other movies. The old John Wayne and Dana Andrews war pictures made death clean and noble; this one makes it squalid and bloody—and noble. When the medic in the platoon gets shot, the men crowd around, laying on hands, and ask him what they should do to help—he would know that. It's a classic episode: It plays in real time, with a gathering tension of fear and hope, and then the certainty of death.

No doubt there will be a kind of resistance: Someone is sure to say that *Saving Private Ryan* is "only" a platoon movie. It is true that the men are separated, as convention dictates, by temperament and ethnic background. There is a Jew (Adam Goldberg), an Italian (Vin Diesel), a southern Bible-quoting sharpshooter (Barry Pepper), a Brooklyn wiseguy (Ed Burns) who complains a lot. The men know one another intimately, but Spielberg wisely soft-pedals the bitching and jokes. (It helps that the actors aren't familiar; a new face keeps cliché at a distance.) Young Jeremy Davies (from *Spanking the Monkey)* plays a skinny, nervous translator who gets pulled into this tough combat unit, and he's certainly not a cliché. He represents the audience—he's terrified—and when he freezes at the crucial instant, he forces us into a moment of grim self-recognition. Two characters are heroic in ways that most of us can't approach or even understand—a tough sergeant, played by that great, round-faced thug Tom Sizemore, and the captain himself, whom the sergeant hopelessly adores and tries to protect.

Hanks is 42. The goofy grin and springy legs are gone; he's a sadder, more realistic presence now, and certainly the right actor to play an ordinary man raised to greatness by war. He doesn't carry the heroic presence or the mythic associations of an action star. He's mostly very quiet, but he has true authority: When he gives an order, there's just enough pressure in his voice to make you understand why the men follow him. Throughout the movie, the horror and strangeness of war play off his face, which registers tiny shifts of tension and disgust. Only one of his scenes doesn't work for me—the one set in a candlelit church, at night, when he justifies a questionable decision, and the writing and playing become too explicit.

How can so painful a movie also be so exciting and pleasurable? Let me mention one factor: Janusz Kaminski, Spielberg's great cameraman, shoots from the middle of the action with a handheld camera, and much of the footage is rough. Yet Spielberg has so scrupulous a sense of the geography of a scene (the Germans are *here,* the Americans have to get *there)* that the footage, edited by Michael Kahn, hangs together beautifully, and we are desperately involved, not just stimulated. That spatial coherence is what some of us have missed in the nonsensical action movies turned out by Hollywood. Spielberg has taken us back to basics—back to art, back to amazement at the film medium itself.

NEW YORK POST, 7/24/98, p. 35, Rod Dreher

Steven Spielberg's "Saving Private Ryan" is a film of such cyclonic visual and emotional power, of such dazzling virtuosity and shattering humanity, that it is difficult to endure, yet alone describe. Savagely beautiful and savagely true, "Saving Private Ryan" is an excruciating masterpiece.

The film's long overture—a half-hour sequence detailing the D-Day assault on Omaha Beach, led by Army Ranger Capt. John Miller (Tom Hanks)—is one of the most astounding passages ever committed to celluloid.

Terrified young men crawl out of the sea and hurl themselves into a fusillade of German bullets and bombs, into the hot maw of hell.

The gore is unprecedented in mainstream filmmaking: A dazed soldier picks up his severed arm, another lies with his guts spilling out of his belly, screaming for Mama.

Using a hand-held camera (the film was shot by Janusz Kaminski) and wondrous sound design (by Gary Rydstrom), Spielberg mercilessly strafes and bombards us with the raw agony of battle, the chaos, the din, the stark terror of velocity and metal.

To watch it sears the eyes and the heart, but to look away seems an obscenity: We need to see this. A more morally justified use of film violence is unthinkable.

When Capt. Miller, lying in a blood-red tide, puts his helmet on and inadvertently douses himself with crimson water, we feel, as perhaps no war movie has made us feel, that we share his initiation, his baptism by blood and fire.

Once ashore, Capt. Miller receives a peculiar assignment straight from the top. A Pvt. James Ryan, who came ashore elsewhere in the invasion, has lost his three brothers in battle.

Washington doesn't want his mother to lose her last boy, so the Army brass orders Miller to put together a squad to find Ryan, trapped somewhere in Normandy, and deliver him home.

It may be regrettable that Robert Rodat's screenplay brings together the stereotypical motley GI crew.

Under the command of Miller and his sergeant (the great Tom Sizemore), there's a Jew (Adam Goldberg), a Bible-quoting Southerner (Barry Pepper), a Brooklyn wise-ass (Ed Burns), and so forth.

Conventional, yeah, but so what? This film has more important things on its mind.

As the squad makes its wary way through the fields and bombed-out towns of northern France—a perilous journey so closely observed it mires the viewer in a state of constant anxiety—the men confront the meaning of war.

It is taken for granted that this war is just. But in the deadly intensity of the here and now, the abstractions that legitimize the war seem ungraspably far away.

We learn that men carry out feats of unbelievable bravery, but also deeds of revolting barbarism, and endure death and the guilt of having others die for them, for love of their buddies.

Don't we know that? Don't we know war is hell? Spielberg, even more than Oliver Stone did in the remarkable "Platoon," makes us see and feel this, and the complexity of human response to war, to a degree those of us who grew up on graphically violent films in a long era of peace had not thought possible.

The cast is tremendous, with Hanks assured of his third Oscar for his understated, immensely affecting performance.

He is conflicted by his mission—putting eight men at risk to save one—and by the killer the war has made him. Yet his Capt. Miller has made his trembling peace with his fate, and you can see why these men would follow him.

Jeremy Davies ("Spanking the Monkey," "Going All the Way") is even more intriguing as Cpl. Upham.

The skinny, bookish Upham has no combat experience, yet is shanghai'd by Miller to be an interpreter. Upham represents us: He is bewildered and stricken by events, and keeps insisting on maintaining civilized standards of conduct in an arena where that isn't always possible.

Upham is cowardly, paralyzed by fear, but it's hard to judge him harshly because, having been shell-shocked by the violent tableaux, you are unsure you would fare much better under the circumstances.

When the squad finally finds Ryan (Matt Damon), he doesn't want them to save him. Miller and his men join Ryan's ragtag unit in a last-ditch defense of a bridge in a wrecked village.

In the quiet moments before the battle, the men survey the catastrophe the war has brought to this quaint French town, the ghostly sound of an Edith Piaf song on a salvaged Victrola sounding a dirge that invades the heart with a piercing, almost annihilating sense of tragedy and loss.

It's been five years since "Schindler's List." I had forgotten movies could do this.

NEWSDAY, 7/24/98, Part II/p. B3, Jack Mathews

Encouraged perhaps by the respectful acceptance of scenes of brutal realism in "Schindler's List," director Steven Spielberg has raised the ante on explicit human destruction to almost unbearable heights in his World War II epic "Saving Private Ryan," delivering what may be the goriest fiction movie ever made.

From the re-creation of the D-Day slaughter at Normandy to a climactic skirmish amid the ruins of a French village, "Saving Private Ryan" fills the screen with exploding heads, severed limbs, leaking bullet holes, spilled intestines, gushing stumps and burning flesh. Hand-held cameras shove us into the middle of the maelstrom, so close to the devastation we can hear bullets smashing bones, feel the splash of blood and saltwater against our face, and see the sweat and vomit of fear mixing with the smoke and dust of battle.

Spielberg occasionally takes us inside the heads of his characters, allowing us to experience the stunned deafness caused by an exploding shell, or peer through the scope of a rifle, just in time to see our own death flash from the barrel of another gun.

At Omaha Beach, a German bullet fired from the bluff above grazes a GI's helmet, making a harmless clang. But before the soldier's eyes can register his luck, another bullet catches him square in the forehead, tearing out the back of his skull. For more than 20 minutes, to the accompaniment of agonized screams, bullet spray and explosions, we're in the midst of a real Armageddon, a literal apocalypse now.

No question, Spielberg has achieved his goal of authenticating the physical and emotional, second-by-second, existential hell of combat. There's never been war footage like this. But the effect on the shell-shocked viewer is nearly pornographic.

All sensible war movies are antiwar movies, and the human themes here have been handled with indelible power before, in such starkly personal films as Stanley Kubrick's "Paths of Glory," Sam Fuller's "The Big Red One" and Oliver Stone's "Platoon." As brilliantly orchestrated and nobly intended as it may be, the graphic verisimilitude of "Saving Private Ryan" often overwhelms the tight human drama at its core. It's hard to stay focused on evolving relationships, never mind the occasionally banal urges of a screenwriter cribbing from "G.I. Joe," when your instincts are to run like hell.

What ultimately saves the movie from that fate, or which may at least keep some audience members from retreating, is the wrenching performance of Tom Hanks as Capt. John Miller, the determined and tormented leader of a squad sent on a mission to rescue a paratrooper caught behind enemy lines.

That paratrooper is young Private Ryan (Matt Damon), whose three brothers have just been killed elsewhere in combat and whose safety is suddenly a priority of the Allied Command.

Gen. George Marshall (Harve Presnell) doesn't want another tragedy like the deaths of the five Sullivan brothers two years earlier to demoralize the folks at home. Reading a letter written to another luckless mother in another war by Abe Lincoln, Marshall makes the decision that in the midst of a campaign that has already cost thousands of lives, every effort must be made to save this one.

Some of the seven men in Miller's squad aren't enthused about celebrating their survival at Omaha Beach by going on a risky PR mission designed to maintain the morale in the Farm Belt. But then, they're fighting the last good war, whose objective was precisely that protecting the folks at home. Once those dynamics are established, "Saving Private Ryan" more or less follows the formula of the cross-section-of-America platoon movies begun during the war itself.

Miller's squad includes the loyal no-nonsense Sgt. Horvath (Tom Sizemore), the resentful Brooklyn loner Pvt. Reiben (Ed Burns), the nerdy, untested translator Cpl. Upham (Jeremy Davies) and the Bible-quoting southern sharpshooter Pvt. Jackson (Barry Pepper). These guys might not be close anywhere else on the planet, but they're going to become family here.

The script, by Robert Rodat ("Fly Away Home"), creates an episodic journey, with the squad going from one random encounter with German troops to another, from one personal conflict to another, on their frustrated search for Ryan. When they finally do find the young soldier, he refuses to abandon his own unit, which is protecting a bridge from an expected German assault. So, Miller and his men join that mission, too, ready to throw their bodies in front of him to bring him back alive.

It's in this last act that "Saving Private Ryan" completes the merger of Spielberg's contradictory impulses—the desire to be taken seriously and the desire to be entertaining. The result is a kind of twisted melodrama, a contrived battle sequence designed to be both repulsive and exhilarating.

After going out of his way not to demonize the German soldiers, to depict them as young men and boys as frightened and innocent as their counterparts, Spielberg can't resist killing a few of them off in ways that seem aimed to satisfy a thirst for revenge. Nobody deserves this carnage, the serious Spielberg says, but some don't deserve it more than others, the showman Spielberg winks.

Enough cannot be said about the physical portion. Tom Sanders' art direction, Michael Kahn's editing, Janusz Kaminski's cinematography all contribute greatly to Spielberg's nightmare vision, and there are images from this film that will never leave you. At the same time, the grisliness of the action is so persistent, and so realistic, it's hard to appreciate its purpose.

Does anyone doubt that war is hell, or think that World War II was somehow less horrific because it was so clearly righteous?

With "Schindler's List," Spielberg also went for a form of documentary realism but he shot that film in black and white, conforming the images to our visual knowledge of those events, which came to us through black and white newsreel footage and documentaries. Our exposure to actual WWII combat footage came to us the same way.

Most people agreed that the bloodletting in "Schindler's List " would have been impossible for audiences to accept in living/dying color. Yet, "Saving Private Ryan" is awash in a purple-red storm of blood. It's as if the vital fluids draining out of unarmed victims are somehow more vital than those from people thrust into battle with rifles in their hands.

Ultimately, your ability to appreciate "Private Ryan's" subtler cinematic achievements—namely, the performances of Hanks, as an ordinary man summoning up extraordinary courage, and Davies, who gives a devastating portrait of cowardice under fire—comes down to the tensile strength of your gut. From a safe vantage point, you have to make the same choice as Miller's men: "Saving Private Ryan" or saving yourself.

NEWSWEEK, 7/13/98, p. 52, David Ansen

The first days were hell. They were seared, they were so unprepared that they hardly knew how to wear their uniforms or carry their guns—and they were only actors. Before filming began on "Saving Private Ryan," Tom Hanks and fellow cast members went through a 10-day boot camp under former Marine captain Dale Dye. They hauled 40 pounds of equipment on five-mile marches through muddy fields on three hours' sleep. After four days, the younger actors all voted to quit the camp, Edward Burns has said. Hanks voted to stay—and then everybody voted again. "It was absolutely necessary to do it right," Hanks told NEWSWEEK earlier this summer. "It probably would have been more fruitful if it were twice as long."

Boot camp gave the cast at least a taste of war. As Hanks put it, "you're cold and wet for about 72 hours and then realize you still have to stand up for the next 76 hours, and you can't help but think, 'My God, and we're just *faking* it.' You can only imagine what it must have been like to be in training in England preparing for an invasion. When it's all for real, lights are blacked out all over the country, and you don't know if you're going to win or not. It's not hard to stand on Omaha Beach now at dawn and imagine the sight of carnage that it was."

Early in "Private Ryan," Steven Spielberg stages an epic Normandy invasion. He shot on the Irish Coast, using many of the same Irish Army extras from "Braveheart." The director didn't storyboard this harrowing sequence. Instead, he approached it like the newsreel photographers who were present on that day in France, using handheld cameras that plunge us into the carnage. All the movie's combat sequences demanded extraordinary vigilance from the cast. "There's a lot of pressure on the actors in this situation not to drop a line, not to mess up," Matt Damon told NEWSWEEK in April. "You have to be Johnny on the spot. There are explosions, there are a lot of special effects and there are stunt people putting themselves in harm's way. It's a real team effort, and everybody has to be on their game."

Spielberg is not the first filmmaker to hit the beach at Normandy. But his unsparing vision of D-Day wouldn't have been possible before Vietnam, which fundamentally changed Hollywood's approach to the war film. In 1962, Darryl Zanuck released his ambitious "The Longest Day," a three-hour epic that told the D-Day story from the American, British, French and German points of view. Zanuck's epic looked down on the events with eagle-eyed omnipotence, striving for the Big Picture. In 1980, with "The Big Red One," writer-director Sam Fuller took the opposite approach: up close, personal, it depicted the invasion as a matter not of strategy but simple survival. In the almost 20 years between these films came Vietnam. As Spielberg wrote in an essay for NEWSWEEK's recent movie issue, "In the 1940s, realism in war movies didn't really matter. After Vietnam, it was all that mattered."

During World War II, it was Hollywood's patriotic duty to create war films that would aid the Allied effort—scripts were even subject to government approval. The slippery questions that faced artists and propagandists equally was just how much reality should be allowed into these war movies. Too graphic a depiction of the horror could demoralize the home front. Yet if the images were too airbrushed and uplifting it could lead to complacency, a weakened resolve. The stark images John Huston captured in his heralded 1944 documentary "The Battle of San Pietro" had to be toned down before the War Department would approve its release. In the interest of democracy and morale, Hollywood showed racially integrated platoons on screen that didn't exist in fact.

Some of the best war movies were made as the war was drawing to a close, victory was in sight and the filmmakers felt freer to pay homage without the false heroics and sentimentality. William Wellman's "The Story of G.I. Joe" (1945) has a near-documentary verisimilitude. A strange, poetic fatalism invades John Ford's laconic "They Were Expendable" (1945), which salutes the sacrifice of our PT boat soldiers in a losing battle for the Philippines.

After Vietnam, filmmakers had no stomach at all for full-tilt heroism. John Wayne had come to symbolize the never-say-die American fighting man, particularly with 1949's "The Sands of Iwo Jima." Now Wayne had become an object of scorn to some. In 1989, Oliver Stone subverted the rah-rah spirit of "Iwo Jima", with "Born on the Fourth of July," the story of paralyzed Vietnam vet Ron Kovic. The symbolic debate between these two kinds of war movies—the inspirational "Iwo Jima" and the angry "Fourth of July"—has raged for three decades. Since Vietnam, nearly all war movies have called themselves antiwar movies, whether they were traditional ("A Bridge Too Far") or surreal ("Apocalypse Now,"). The spirit of gung-ho heroism had to flee into the future—into boys' adventure fantasies such as"StarWars."

What every filmmaker who makes a combat movie must wrestle with—and it will be fascinating to see how Terrence Malick's "The Thin Red Line" copes with it this fall—is the medium's ambiguous relationship to violence. War, as a dramatic subject, is exciting, and the battles are the most exciting part. How do you depict violence without, in some way, promoting it? How do you take the thrill out of danger? Spielberg's solution seems to be an unblinking contemplation of the horrors of war. Undoubtedly there will be those who will object to the shocking gore. Yet if war's violence is made less sickening, isn't it being made more attractive? And there will be those who are offended by the fact that Spielberg has chosen World War II, the "just war," as the subject of his antiwar epic. Back in 1944, John Huston, who eagerly served in the war, heard a variation of this argument from a general who objected that "The Battle of San Pietro" was pacifist. "Well, Sir," Huston replied, "whenever I make a picture that's *for* war—why, I hope you take me out and shoot me."

Guadalcanal in 1942. The closest parallel to Spielberg's tale is the true story of Fritz Niland, of the 101st Airborne, who lost three brothers in a single week in June 1944: two in Normandy on D-Day and a third in the China-Burma theater. As Ambrose tells it in his 1992 book "Band of Brothers," Niland's mother got all three telegrams from the War Department on the same day, prompting the Army to send a chaplain, Father Francis Sampson, to get Fritz out of the combat zone. "Son," the chaplain said, "you're coming with me." Sampson escorted Niland to Utah Beach, where he was flown to London, and then home.

Spielberg may be dealing in fiction, but he still captures the reality of the grunts' war. Hanks's squad is a classic melting pot—Ed Burns as the wisecracking New Yorker, Tom Sizemore as the veteran sarge, Barry Pepper as the Scripture-quoting Tennessee sharpshooter—but there's little we're-all-in-this together talk. Rather, as they make their way through enemy territory, the eight men carry on an intense, profane debate about why one man's life—young Ryan's—is so important that they should risk all of theirs. "Ryan better be worth it," Hanks says at one point in the action. "He better go home and cure some disease or invent a new longer-lasting lightbulb." In an interview with NEWSWEEK earlier this year, Hanks said, "There's no overt sort of patriotic statement or even curve."

For real GIs, that was certainly true on the ground. In the Civil War soldiers would talk politics, and at first World War I was full of romance—until the bleakness of the trenches trumped dreams of martial glory. By the '40s, the grunts didn't want to hear a lot of speeches. In his book "Wartime," Paul Fussell recalls that John Hersey once asked some Marines on Guadalcanal what they were fighting for. "A piece of blueberry pie," they answered. "Scotch whisky." "Dames." "Books." "Music." "Movies." Hersey, Fussell recounts, translated these replies into the real one: "To get the goddamned thing over with and go home." "What you're thinking when you're out there," says John Barnes, who was a 19-year-old in the 116th on D-Day, "is, 'Well, they didn't get me that time'." Churchill's soaring rhetoric from London sometimes embarrassed the grunts in the field.

The GI's had more immediate concerns. At a distance, the narrative of the war runs in a straight line from Normandy to VE Day, but some of the bloodiest fighting unfolded beginning on D-Day Plus One. After spending the night of June 6 under sporadic fire on Omaha, George Roach foraged for a rifle and a helmet. Two hundred men in his company had come ashore the day before, but just eight survived to make a rendezvous near Vierville. They set out into Normandy, but no one had told Roach or his comrades about the hedgerows, the ancient walls of dirt, rock and timber that enclosed the fields in northern France. The roads around the fields were sunken, and shaded by trees; German gunners set up nests in the maze of vegetation. "No terrain in the world," writes Ambrose, "was better suited for defensive action with the weapons of the fourth decade of the twentieth century than the Norman hedgerows." For men like Roach, the battle was inch by inch, hour by hour. "One day I was sitting with my back to a hedgerow, talking to a buddy, when a voice called out, 'Hey, is there a medic over there?' And they passed a guy over and the fellow had no face; it was just gone. But he wasn't dead—you could see the air bubbles where his mouth used to be." Roach pauses, remembering. "It was all so unreal. We were 19, 20 years old—just kids,you know?"

Not for long. The 502d Regiment's Wallace Strobel, who had turned 22 the day before the invasion, was in a hedgerow tending to a lightly wounded friend. Strobel slipped out for a minute to prepare for a night attack, and when he came back his buddy "had been hit by a shell, and he had no head—it had just been blown away." Slaughter was wounded twice: once a rifle bullet went through his helmet; three pieces of it lodged in his forehead, turning his eyes black. Later, after he recovered, he was wounded again, this time in the back by shrapnel. "You're trying to be brave," he says, "but more than once you find yourself upchucking when you're looking at your buddy with his intestines hanging out." He remembers urinating in his trousers while pinned down by an enemy gunner in a beet field in Germany. "You know you're going to die, and you know you're going to die horribly—you tell yourself you're going to get wounded and bleed to death, and no one's going to ever find you."

The Allies put 170,000 men ashore at D-Day; 2 million followed. In September came the Battle of Hurtgen Forest, the subject of "When Trumpets Fade," a new movie now playing on HBO. Rugged and dark, the forest was, according to one sergeant, "a helluva eerie place to fight." The Germans, Ambrose points out, were already dug in, and when they spotted American patrols they would call down presighted artillery designed to explode on contact with the treetops. The result: a rain of hot metal and splinters. "The days were so terrible that I would pray for darkness," said one private, "and the nights were so bad I would pray for daylight."

Close encounters with the enemy could be complicated. In one riveting sequence in "Saving Private Ryan," Hanks stands between his understandably bloodthirsty men and a German prisoner. The scenes have real-life parallels. "It's funny—one minute you want to kill a guy," says Strobel, "and the next you don't." In "Citizen Soldiers'" Ambrose recounts the bleak Christmas of 1944. Pvt. Joe Tatman was trapped with his squad outside Bastogne—well within the Nazi lines. Captured, the Americans were taken to a warm farmhouse, The Germans invited them to join their holiday dinner. The prisoners sang "Silent Night" in English; their captors in German. Then the Nazi captain toasted his guests and told them that the next morning the Americans "would begin their journey to hell"—a German POW camp.

The only way home, GIs liked to say, was through Berlin. The Battle of the Bulge began in December; the men on the front sometimes ate snow when their canteens were empty. Though the Allies would suffer 80,000 casualties, the Führer's were worse -and by stripping his Eastern Front to fight at the Bulge, he gave the Red Army an opening to reach the German capital. On April 30, in his bunker beneath Berlin, Hitler finished his lunch and shot himself. On May 7 Germany surrendered. A few days before, Dick Winters of the 101st had arrived at Landsberg, a slave-labor camp. Looking at "those starved, dazed men," Winters recalled, "left me saying, only to myself, 'Now I know why I am here'."

It had all begun at the beaches. From D-Day to VE Day, 586,628 American servicemen had fallen; 135,576 were dead. Summer-movie goers may slip into the multiplex looking for an escape into a simpler universe. They won't find one in Spielberg's telling. For Bob Slaughter, the movie evokes not just the battle zone but his occasional visits back to Normandy down the decades. He's walked the beaches and wandered through the American cemetery atop the cliffs, where the war dead rest beneath rows of white marble crosses and Stars of David. "The real heroes," he says, "are the guys who didn't get back." And their true monument is the world they made, but never lived to see.

NEWSWEEK, 7/27/98, p. 57, David Ansen

Steve Spielberg has taken Hollywood's depiction of war to a new level. He does it right at the start of "Saving Private Ryan," in a 25-minute sequence depicting the landing of American forces on Omaha Beach in 1944. This is not the triumphant version of D-Day we're used to seeing, but an inferno of severed arms, spilling intestines, flying corpses and blood red tides. To those of us who have never fought in a war, this re-enactment-newsreel-like in its verisimilitude, hallucinatory in its impact-leaves you convinced that Spielberg has taken you closer to the chaotic, terrifying sights and sounds of combat than any filmmaker before him.

This prelude is so strong, so unnerving, that I feared it would overwhelm the rest of the film. When the narrative proper begins, there's an initial feeling of diminishment: it's just a movie, after all, with the usual banal music cues and actors going through their paces. Fortunately, the feeling passes. "Saving Private Ryan" reasserts its grip on you and, for most of its 2 hour and 40 minute running time, holds you in thrall.

Our heroes are a squad of eight soldiers lucky enough to have survived Omaha Beach. Now they are sent, under the command of Captain Miller (Tom Hanks), to find and safely return from combat a Private Ryan (Matt Damon), whose film brothers have already died in action. Why should they risk their lives to save one man? The question haunts them, and the movie.

The squad is a familiar melting-pot assortment of world War II grunts—the cynical New Yorker (Edward Burns) who doesn't want to risk his neck; the Jew (Adam Goldberg); the Italian (Vin Diesel); the Bible-quoting sniper from Tennessee (Barry Pepper); the medic (Giovanni Ribisi). The most terrified is an inexperienced corporal Jeremy Davies) brought along as a translator. Davies seems to express every possible variety of fear on his eloquently scrawny face. Tom Sizemore is also impressive as Miller's loyal second in command. As written by Robert Rodat, they could be any squad in any war movie. But Spielberg and his actors make us care deeply about their fate. Part of the movie's power comes from Hanks's quietly mysterious performance as their decent, reticent leader (the men have a pool going speculating about what he did in civilian life). There's an unhistrionic fatalism in captain Miller, he just wants to get the job done and get home alive, but his eyes tell you he doesn't like the odds.

The level of work in "Private Ryan"—from the acting to Janusz Kaminski's brilliantly bleached-out color cinematography to the extraordinary sound design by Gary Rydstrom-is state of the art. For most of "Saving Private Ryan," Spielberg is working at the top of his form, with the movie culminating in a spectacularly staged climactic battle in a French village. The good stuff is so shattering that it overwhelms the lapses, but you can't help noticing a few Hollywood moments. Sometimes Spielberg doesn't seem to trust how powerful the material is, and crosses the line into sentimentality. There's a prelude and a coda, set in a military cemetery, that is written and directed with a too-heavy hand. But the truth is, this movie so wiped me out I have little taste for quibbling. When you emerge from Spielberg's cauldron, the world doesn't look quite the same.

SIGHT AND SOUND, 9/98, p. 34, John Wrathall

On D-Day, 1944, Captain Miller loses most of his men during an assault on Omaha beach. Afterwards he is singled out for a special mission at the behest of the US chief of staff: three out of four Ryan brothers have been killed in the same week; the surviving Ryan, who is behind enemy lines, must be saved. Miller chooses six of his men, including Privates Reiben and Mellish, plus an interpreter, Corporal Upham. Reaching a town held by US airborne troops, the squad locates Private Ryan. Miller loses one man to a sniper.

The next day, a wounded soldier tells them that Ryan has been sent to the town of Ramelle to guard a bridge against counterattack. En route, they attack a German machine-gun post, losing another man. The only surviving German soldier surrenders. They are about to kill him when Upham persuades Miller to let the man go. Enraged by the futility of their mission, Reiben threatens to desert. They finally track down Ryan outside Ramell, but he refuses to leave his comrades. Miller decides to stay and help defend the bridge.

German tanks attack. Upham, paralysed by fear fails to save Mellish from being killed by the German soldier they spared earlier. After heavy losses, Miller retreats across the bridge, but US planes arrive just in time. The bridge is held, but Miller dies of his wounds. Upham captures the German soldier who killed Mellish and shoots him. The only other survivors are Ryan and Reiben. In the present, the elderly Ryan looks down at Miller's grave, and hopes that his life has proved worth saving.

Like *Schindler's List*, *Saving Private Ryan* ends in the present day, with a survivor of appalling carnage during World War Two contemplating a memorial to the man who saved him. The saviour this time is Tom Hanks' Captain Miller, who in the aftermath of D-Day is sent behind German lines on a mission to rescue Private Ryan, an American soldier whose three brothers have all been killed in action in the same week. Miller's quixotic mission, to save one symbolic American soldier while thousands die around him, inevitably recalls Schindler's struggle to save a thousand out of the six million. In fact, the same tagline could do for both films: "Whoever saves one life, saves the world entire."

Unlike *Schindler's List,* which was based on fact (by way of Thomas Keneally's novel), *Saving Private Ryan* is the invention of screenwriter Robert Rodat (whose best-known work hitherto was as co-writer of *Fly Away Home).* Unusually for Spielberg, it's not a project he initiated himself. But by choosing it he seems to be grasping the opportunity to revisit *Schindler's List,* only this time liberated from the ideological baggage which any Holocaust film must carry.

Working once again with the Polish born cinematographer Janusz Kaminski, Spielberg abandons his usual emphatically storyboarded style in favour of a more urgent, handheld approach, with desaturated colour emulating the look of World War Two colour newsreels.

From the staggering 25-minute opening sequence on Omaha beach during which Miller's troops are shot to pieces as they struggle to disembark from landing craft, the violence has the terrifying immediacy of the ghetto-clearance scenes in *Schindler's List.* But this time there's no equivalent of the little girl in red, the one sentimental spot of colour in a monochrome world. Apart from John Williams' sparingly used music, the climactic, *deus ex machina* appearance of US bombers roaring overhead, and the moment before the final battle when the rumble of approaching German tanks conjures up a memory of *Jurassic Park Saving Private Ryan* is conspicuously free of overt Spielberg touches.

It's meaningless for critics to write of 'realism' in war movies, as most of us have no idea what war really looks like. But the action sequences in *Saving Private Ryan* are extraordinary: utterly believable, horrifyingly graphic in their depiction of death and injury, but somehow matter of fact, so that the worst atrocities are glimpsed out of the corner of one's eye, and the choreography never shows. For sheer gut-wrenching immediacy, the only war film that's comparable is *Come and See*, Elem Klimov's gruelling 1985 account of Nazi massacres in Belarus, which Spielberg would surely have watched while doing research for *Schindler's List,* if not before. One trick in particular recalls Klimov: at the height of the fighting, first on Omaha beach, then again at the very end in the devastated town of Ramelle, as the US soldiers defend a bridge from ferocious Panzer attack, Spielberg fades out the sound and replaces it with the roar inside the shellshocked Miller's head as all hell breaks loose around him.

The unselfconscious directness of Spielberg's *mise en scéne* is matched by Robert Rodat's solidly constructed, unsensationalist script. Although the futility of Miller's mission—losing several men in order to save one—is pointed out by the squad's resident malcontent, Edward Burns' Private Reiben, this isn't a film about the insanity of war. Spielberg's war may be hell, but it has a point. Holding the bridge at Ramelle in the film's climactic battle will, we are told, help the Allies get to Berlin more quickly. (While contemporaries like Francis Ford Coppola, Brian De Palma and Oliver Stone have made films about Vietnam, Spielberg has preferred the more clear-cut moral universe of World War Two. This is his fourth film about that war, not counting the *Indiana Jones* trilogy with its Nazi villains.)

In between the breathtaking action sequences, Rodat subtly sketches in the character and background of Miller and his seven men, including dependable NCO (Tom Sizemore's Horvath), Brooklyn cynic (Reiben) and sensitive Medic (Giovanni Ribisi's Wade). They may sound like stock characters on paper, but it's to the credit of Rodat's writing and some very astute casting that only one of them ever seems like a scriptwriter's contrivance: Private Jackson (Barry Pepper), a superhumanly gifted sniper from the Deep South who prays out loud as he squints down his telescopic sight.

In *Apollo 13,* Hanks never seemed totally convincing as a man of action. But here he is perfectly cast as an ordinary man doing the best he can in impossible circumstances, and gradually losing his grip. The revelation of Miller's peacetime origins, the subject of much speculation among the other soldiers, is brilliantly timed to provide one of the film's most compelling moments. The film's key character isn't Miller, however, or Matt Damon's Private Ryan, but Corporal Upham. An interpreter seconded to Miller's squad after the landing at Omaha, Upham is the character closest to the audience and to Spielberg himself: he knows about war, and can quote Tennyson's "The Charge of the Light Brigade", but he has never seen action. Played by Jeremy Davies, the incestuous teenager from *Spanking the Monkey,* Upham is bright, but nervous and clumsy. From the start he is set up as the innocent who—in time-honoured war-movie tradition—will surely come into his own under fire. There's a running joke about the squad's favourite expression, "FUBAR", an acronym which he understands only when he has experienced the situation it describes first hand (to reveal it here would spoil the joke).

Upham also represents the squad's conscience. When they storm a machine-gun post behind lines, the other soldiers, enraged by the death of their comrade Wade during the assault, are about to kill the only surviving German soldier. Upham is appalled. After talking to the German, who pleads for his life by reeling off every American Pop-culture reference he can think of, Upham persuades Miller to spare him. As they cannot take the prisoner with them on their mission, they have to let him go. Later, during the final battle in Ramelle, Upham is paralysed by fear. Spielberg keeps playing on our expectations that he will snap out of it and do something heroic. But he never does. In fact, in the film's most agonising scene, Upham fails to come to the rescue of Mellish, one of his comrades, as a German soldier slowly, almost tenderly, stabs him to death, telling him it's easier just to give in and die than to keep on fighting. Mellish isn't just any old GI: he's the squad's only Jew, earlier seen defiantly waving a Star of David in the faces of German prisoners of war. The man who kills him turns out to be the same German Upham saved earlier. Only at the very end of the film does Upham finally take action, recapturing the German and shooting him in cold blood. But it's hardly an act of redemption.

All this, in the light of *Schindler's List,* can hardly be coincidental. But what exactly is Spielberg trying to tell us here? That it's all right to kill prisoners of war? Or that American intellectuals like Upham, through their sympathy with the Germans as civilised human beings, somehow condoned the Holocaust? it's open to interpretation. But that itself is a breakthrough in a Spielberg film. The fact that he refrains from telling us what to think, even after setting us up for manipulation, is the ultimate proof—if any more were needed after this magnificent film—that he has come of age as an artist.

VILLAGE VOICE, 7/28/98, p. 113, Amy Taubin

Let's keep our heads, and our various body parts, together about this. Yes, Steven Spielberg's *Saving Private Ryan* is an Academy picture. Come next March, Spielberg, Tom Hanks, cinematographer Janusz Kaminski, and editor Michael Kahn will be cradling their gold statuettes. But far from being a great film, Spielberg's tribute to the grants of World War II has two magisterial action sequences—the opening carnage on Omaha Beach and the closing battle in a bombed-out French village—and lots of standard issue in between.

A high-minded horror film, *Saving Private Ryan* begins, like *Jaws,* with blood and severed limbs in the water and ends like *Jurassic Park,* with frail humans locked in combat to the death with armored monsters (the monsters being German tanks). The two sequences are all the more impressive for being so dissimilar. The Omaha Beach scene has more gore and a higher body count than any movie ever made. It runs on a castration anxiety inspired by close-ups of all those bloody stumps and mutilated torsos and on Spielberg's astounding ability to drive an action forward through space and time. And it's all the more impressive for being both terrifyingly visceral and impersonal to the point of abstraction. We watch hundreds of men shot to ribbons, dying in screaming agony for 30 minutes of narrative time, before we have a due about the individual fictional identity of any of them. Other films, starting with *Birth of a Nation,* have tackled this war-is-bigger-than-the-fate-of-any-one-soldier theme, but no one has taken it to these lengths.

But in fact, Spielberg isn't being quite as radical as the above description implies. Because after all, he does have Tom Hanks. We may not know who Tom Hanks is supposed to be in this particular film when we see him at the beginning of the D-Day landing, looking down at his shaking hand, then dodging through the dying in the water, pointing the way up the beach to his squad, yelling directions that are barely audible through the gunfire. But in another sense, we always know who Tom Hanks is. He's the American Everyman and we always want him to come out alive (although in *Forrest Gump,* I would have preferred for him to have been run over by a bus). Spielberg trusts our long-standing identification with Hanks to give him just the narrative edge he needs to carry us through a half hour of hellish chaos.

The climactic battle for the French village takes a diametrically opposing approach. By that point, we know who Captain Miller (Hanks) is, we know who the men in his squad are (stereotypical though they may be), we know who Private Ryan (Matt Damon) is. And when we hear the approaching rumble of the German tanks, we hear it through their ears, and it's petrifying.

Between these two bravura action sequences, *Saving Private Ryan* is merely a banal war movie with a forced premise and clichéd characters. Having survived the Omaha Beach landing, Captain Miller is assigned to rescue Private James Ryan of the 101st Airborne, who, if he's still alive, is somewhere behind German lines. Ryan's three brothers have been killed in action within days of one another, and the State Department decides that a fourth loss is more than their mother should be asked to bear. Given the staggering number of American casualties during the D-Day invasion, it's extremely unlikely that even the most shell-shocked brass would risk an excellent officer and seven enlisted men for the sake of a mother's feelings. Thus when Miller's men natter on about why eight men should be put in harms way so that one man can go home, you just want to yell at the screen, "Don't worry about it, it would never happen this way except in the movies."

This desperate gasping for a human-interest hook muddies the potentially powerful philosophical dilemma of the film, as personified in the character of Captain Miller. By the time he makes it up Omaha Beach, Miller has already lost 94 men in the course of a half-dozen big campaigns, and the rationale he's accepted—that for each man lost, 10 or 20 will be saved, and thus the Allied victory over Hitler advanced—has began to fray. Miller doesn't doubt that the war is necessary, but doing his part to win it has tamed him into someone he doesn't want to be. Through Miller's character, we can glimpse the reason that World War II continues to fascinate: it's the most necessary of wars, and yet it raises the question that every other war does about the value of an individual human life.

Because Spielberg doesn't have the intellectual chops to dramatize this issue, the film veers wildly between realism and allegory. A horribly disturbing scene in which a German soldier disembowels a Jewish American soldier while an all-American boy cowers in fear is forced to carry the entire weight of the Holocaust.

Miller, Ryan, and the seven men under Miller's command—yup, there's really one Italian, one Jew, one country boy, one college boy, etc.—each get one purple prose speech that's meant to distill his character. Of the supporting cast, only Tom Sizemore as the seasoned sergeant and Barry Pepper as the wired, Scripture-spouting sharpshooter (who, if he weren't in a war, might be massacring civilians from a Texas bell tower) make much of an impression. Damon lights up the screen for one shot, but he's quickly punished for his irrepressible joie de vivre with the longest, most absurdly written monologue of them all. Hanks, of course, is tremendous. Which means that there's never a moment in which he's less than totally involved in what's happening on the screen. As an actor, Hanks has the kind of transparency that Spielberg (rightly or not) aims for as a director but seldom achieves.

Except in the big battle scenes, Spielberg tries too hard to overwhelm you emotionally. And he underestimates either his own powers or the intelligence of his audience. What other excuse could there be for John Williams's bathetic score? It wasn't the sound of grenades and gunfire that made me cringe in my seat covering my ears. It was the mawkish, programmatic music. *Saving Private Ryan* has the densest, most spatially complicated sound design of any Hollywood movie ever made, and just about the most unbearable score.

The music is most overweening in the brief, contemporary update scenes that bookend the narrative. Thoroughly unnecessary, these scenes involve an elderly man and his family visiting the Normandy graveyards. Stomping across the lawn, the teary-eyed but frozen-faced family looks like a cross between a *Saturday Evening Post* cover and *Dawn of the Dead*. The camera closes in on the man's eyes, which gaze into the distance as if remembering. But what exactly is he remembering? Sorry to be so oblique, but I don't want to give away a slippery bit of business that you need to experience firsthand to appreciate its meretriciousness. Spielberg is being either lazy or incredibly manipulative in these scenes, vis-à-vis storytelling and point of view. It may not be immoral filmmaking, but it certainly creeped me out.

Also reviewed in:
CHICAGO TRIBUNE, 7/24/98, Friday/p. A, Michael Wilmington
NATION, 8/24-31/98, p. 33, Stuart Klawans
NEW REPUBLIC, 8/17 & 24/98, p. 24, Stanley Kauffmann

NEW YORK TIMES, 7/24/98, p. E1, Janet Maslin
NEW YORKER, 8/3/98, p. 77, Anthony Lane
VARIETY, 7/20-26/98, p. 45, Todd McCarthy
WASHINGTON POST, 7/24/98, p. B1, Stephen Hunter
WASHINGTON POST, 7/24/98, Weekend/p. 37, Michael O'Sullivan

SAVIOR

A Lions Gate Films release of an Initial Entertainment Group presentation of an Oliver Stone production. *Executive Producer:* Cindy Cowan. *Producer:* Oliver Stone and Janet Yang. *Director:* Peter Antonijevic. *Screenplay:* Robert Orr. *Director of Photography:* Ian Wilson. *Editor:* Ian Crafford and Gabriella Cristiani. *Music:* David Robbins. *Music Editor:* Lee Scott. *Sound:* Bill Fiege. *Sound Editor:* Scott Wolf. *Casting:* Mary Vernieu. *Production Designer:* Vladislav Lasic. *Set Decorator:* Jovan Radomirovic and Ljubomir Mrsovic. *Special Effects:* Petar Zivkovic. *Costumes:* Boris Caksiran. *Make-up:* Giancarlo Del Brocco and Martina Subic. *Stunt Coordinator:* David McKeown. *Running time:* 116 minutes. *MPAA Rating:* R.

CAST: Dennis Quaid (Joshua Rose, "Guy");   Nastassja Kinski (Maria Rose);   Stellan Skarsgard (Dominic);   Natasa Ninkovic (Vera); Pascal Rollin (Paris Priest);   Catlin Foster (Christian Rose);   John McLaren (Colonel);   Irfan Mensur (Drill Sergeant);   Sergej Trifunovic (Goran);   Kosta Andrejevic (Boy on Bridge);   Ljiljana Krstic (Old Lady);   Sanja Zogovic (Girl on Bridge);   Veljko Otasevic (Orthodox Priest);   Marina Bukvicki (Muslim Girl);   Dusan Perkovic (Uncle Ratko);   Ljiljana Blagojevic (Vera's Mother);   Miodrag Krstovic (Vera's Father); Nebojsa Glagovac (Vera's Brother);   Dusan Janicijevic (Old Man);   Renata Ulmanski (Old Woman); Svetozar Cvetkovic (Croat Officer);   Josif Tatic (Chief Executioner);   Cedo Dragovic (Driver);   Vesna Trivalic (Young Woman).

LOS ANGELES TIMES, 11/20/98, Calendar/p. 12, Kevin Thomas

Dennis Quaid has the title role in "Savior" as a mercenary who finds redemption in the hell of rural Bosnia. He also saves the film in that he makes bearable the otherwise unbearable, with a portrayal that ranks among the year's finest, revealing a resonant new maturity as an actor.

Inspired in part by an actual incident, "Savior" was written by Robert Orr, who spent 1993 through 1995 in Bosnia as a photographer's assistant and relief worker and was directed by Serbian emigre Predag Antonijevic and filmed in the Republic of Montenegro.

The film opens in Paris, 1987. Quaid's Guy is sitting in a cafe with his wife (Nastassja Kinski) and small son, whom he is promising to take to the movies. His wife is expressing concern that he's broken so many promises to the child when Guy's friend and colleague Dominic (Stellan Skarsgaard) appears and says that there's an emergency, and that they must go immediately to see the ambassador.

No sooner do the men step outside and cross the street than the restaurant is bombed, killing both Guy's wife and son. Assuming that it is the work of "fundamentalists," apparently meaning Muslim terrorists, Guy calmly leaves the meeting with the ambassador and heads for a nearby mosque, killing a number of people at prayer. Sensing what Guy might do, Dominic follows and shoots down a wounded survivor about to shoot Guy. The next thing we know both men have signed up for the foreign legion.

"Savior" has therefore at the start announced that it's going to be a blood bath and that at times it's going to be hard to follow, which is often the case with a foreign director working in English for the first time. Production notes tell us helpfully that Guy and Dominic are professional mercenaries, but it is unclear in whose employ they are at the beginning of the film or what nation that ambassador is representing. We assume that the foreign legion they join is the French Foreign Legion, but when the film flash-forwards to 1993, and we find them in the service of the Serbs in Bosnia we're left to assume they are no longer with the foreign legion.

Once past this needlessly vague opening, "Savior" settles into a stunning assertion of humanism in the face of unspeakable mounting horror. Still numb from the killing of his wife and child and the massacre that it triggered in him, Guy is initially fairly indifferent to the Serbs' and Croats' savage treatment of each other. But he is finally snapped out of his almost catatonic state when a Serbian soldier, with whom he is partnered, starts kicking a pregnant woman, Vera (Natasa Ninkovic, a lovely and impressive newcomer), in the stomach, causing her to deliver prematurely a remarkably healthy baby, given the circumstances. Vera is from the soldier's Bosnian village, and is returning home in disgrace, having become pregnant by a Muslim.

When Guy shoots the soldier, "Savior" soon takes on the form of suspense thriller with Guy, Vera and the baby she initially rejects striving to make it to the relative safety of Split, where Guy hopes to get mother and child out of the country. Within this form "Savior" reveals a society that has sunk to the bottom-rung level of people killing each other in the most brutal manner possible, fueled by an all-consuming hatred of those different in ethnicity and religion.

The point "Savior" is making—one that surely will provoke disagreement—is that the situation in the former Yugoslavia has gone beyond any meaningful assigning of blame, and that people have been reduced to the level of wild animals striving to survive.

This starkest of backgrounds—and "Savior" has to be one of the most brutal, serious movies ever made—sets off Guy's regaining his humanity, his instinctive replacement of the wife and son he lost with Vera and her baby. Within himself Guy discovers remarkable reserves of courage, resourcefulness and a renewed capacity for love.

This regeneration, persuasively expressed by Quaid, unfolds amid too much incessant danger to become sentimental until the film's final minutes. Murky at the start, needlessly softened at the finish, "Savior" is nonetheless an important and timely achievement.

NEW YORK POST, 11/25/98, p. 56, Bill Hoffmann

"Savior" grabs you by the throat in the first 10 minutes and doesn't let you breathe easy again until the final credits roll. It's as gut-crunching and intense as war movies get—and in the year of "Saving Private Ryan," that's saying something.

Dennis Quaid plays Guy, a professional soldier trying to trade the thrill of war for the sanctity of family life with his wife (Nastassja Kinski) and young son, when a terrorist explosion in a quiet Parisian cafe changes all that.

Quaid goes berserk, and after committing an astounding act of violence, he's off on the run to Bosnia to work as a mercenary for the Serbs.

But just as the World Wars were clear as to who was good and who was bad, there's no easy answer in Bosnia, as Guy finds out in a brutal search-and-destroy mission in which his Serbian fighting buddy viciously attacks a sick old woman.

But Guy—a man who prides himself on taking no sides and feeling no pain—is forced into a personal mission of mercy when he's confronted with a helpless young woman, pregnant after being raped, who's about to be butchered.

He saves her, delivers the baby and tries to get them into safe hands. That's not so easy as the young mother's family rejects her for bringing them "disgrace and shame." So Guy must press on.

For the next hour, "Savior" turns into a nail-biting, high-tension thriller as Guy and his pitiful pair dodge bombs, bullets and squads of bloodthirsty executioners.

You know somebody's not going to survive the trip through this maze of madness. But when climatic live-or-die moment finally comes, it's a poignant and heartbreaking moment.

Stellan Skarsgaard is excellent as Quaid's mate, who decides to quit his career on the front line just a little too late. And Quaid—who is comfortably and gracefully slipping into chiseled middle-age macho—comes off as an edgier Harrison Ford in what is arguably the best role of his career.

NEWSDAY, 11/25/98, Part II/p. B7, John Anderson

Serbian director Peter Antonijevic attempts some nifty sleight-of-hand, or mind, in "Savior," the story of a professional soldier whose wife and son are killed in a terrorist bombing and who responds by going to Bosnia, where he can shoot Croat children while sparing their goats.

The first trick is making a hired killer the hero of your film and not making an independent American comedy. The second is involving God—Who, if anything, has taken a hands-off approach to the war in the former Yugoslavia and might be hard-pressed to find something redemptive in a man who commits mass murder in a mosque and then regularly fondles his dead wife's crucifix. Or who's so obtuse. "I like to find a war where I could fight for something I believe in," says Guy (Dennis Quaid), somewhere in the middle of a bombed-out village he helped bomb out. Look around, man. Everyone but you is fighting for something he believes in, including the Muslims who blew up your wife and child.

Did they really do it? It's an essential question in "Savior," one that director Antonijevic answers rather bluntly: Just after the mother (Natassja Kinski) and son are blown up, and just before he blows town for the French Foreign Legion, Guy walks into the aforementioned mosque and cold-bloodedly wipes out about a dozen Muslims at prayer. As he stands on the sidewalk with his stunned colleague Dominic (Stellan Skarsgard), a wounded Arab appears at the mosque door, pistol in hand. Dominic efficiently shoots him dead, implicating himself in the massacre and presumably absolving Guy, because why else would a Muslim carry an automatic weapon if he weren't a terrorist?

It's crime and loss that sends Guy off to fight other people's wars, and his story is relentlessly cruel. As is the film. It isn't until about an hour in that the first real act of charity occurs, and that act consists of a Serbian mother, Vera (newcomer Natasa Ninkovic) not killing her own baby—a baby begat by Croatian rape, a baby that's caused her to be driven from her home, who's prompted Guy to shoot the homicidal Serb, Goran (a terrifically evil Sergej Trifunovic), and which has Vera's father and brother after them as they hightail it across the countryside (with unlikely impunity, I might add).

In strictly filmmaking terms, Antonijevic's biggest miscalculation is trying to inject levity into a movie that's otherwise devastating in its portrayal of a county tearing itself apart. Guy chasing a goat to get milk for the baby doesn't raise the slightest smile when you've seen fingers amputated and rings stolen, eviscerated bodies and pure madness. Quaid tries very hard, and occasionally succeeds, in making Guy a human being, but the real question you leave the film with is whether redemption really is an option for any of these people.

SIGHT AND SOUND, 7/98, p. 51, John Wrathall

After Joshua Rose's wife and son are killed by an Islamic terrorist bomb he goes to the nearest mosque and opens fire in revenge. He then joins the Foreign Legion, changing his name to Guy. Six years later, Guy is fighting for the Serbs in Bosnia as a mercenary alongside the psychopathic Goran. Guy and Goran escort a Serbian woman POW named Vera back to her village. Raped by the Muslims during captivity, Vera is pregnant. Goran beats her up to force a miscarriage. Guy kills him, and helps deliver the baby. They reach the village, but Vera's father sends her away, ashamed of her half-Muslim baby. They set off for a refugee camp. But when Goran's body is found, the local Serbian warlord orders Vera's father to avenge the killing. Catching up with the fugitives, he shoots and wounds Guy, but his son persuades him not to kill Vera.

Vera decides to follow her father back home. But by the time they reach the village, it has been destroyed. Guy decides to try and get Vera and the baby out of the country. They set off for Split, but their car runs out of petrol. While the injured Guy hides with the baby, Vera goes into the nearest town to ask about the bus to Split. The Croatian militia kill her. Guy escapes and manages to get to Split, where he abandons the baby. But a woman who saw him brings the baby back to him, asking if he is the father. Guy says he is, and she persuades him to keep the baby.

As Emir Kusturica learned to his cost with *Underground,* any film made in Yugoslavia about the civil war will inevitably be raked over for traces of pro-Serbian bias. *Savior* was filmed in Montenegro, the only republic which remains alongside Serbia in post-war Yugoslavia. The director, Peter Antonijevic (who made *Mala),* is a Serb. While he never shies away from depicting Serbian atrocities, they are all committed by Goran, a man whom even his fellow Serbs acknowledge as a psychopath. Sane Serbs, it's implied, wouldn't do such things. The Muslims, meanwhile, aren't actually shown killing anyone, but are responsible for raping Vera, and are later seen marching her family off, presumably to their deaths. Everyone is to blame in this war, but the Croats are the worst of all, massacring a busload of Serbian and Muslim civilians in a scene of astonishing brutality.

As you might expect from a film produced by Oliver Stone, *Savior* doesn't bother with political correctness. Like *Welcome to Sarajevo,* it approaches the war through the story of a westerner's symbolic attempt to save one child: Vera's half-Serb, half-Muslim baby, presumably representing the only hope for the future of Bosnia. But there the similarity ends. Unlike Henderson in *Welcome to Sarajevo,* Dennis Quaid's Joshua/Guy is an active participant in the war. On the one hand, this necessitates a ludicrously contrived opening sequence to establish how an American came to be fighting for the Serbs in the first place. On the other hand, though, Guy's complicity makes the moral dilemmas he faces all the more painful, and gives his redemption real emotional weight. Despite its shaky beginnings, *Savior* builds up to an an agonising climax in the scene when Guy has to watch, armed but helpless to intervene, as Vera is clubbed to death. It's a devastating moment, at once shockingly violent and strangely poetic, as Vera sings a lullaby to her baby, embracing death in the hope that the child may live.

Walking a tightrope between heavy-handed cliché and raw emotional power, *Savior* has the urgency of the better films Stone once directed himself. Or, at its best, it comes across as the sort of film Sam Fuller might have made about Bosnia, less interested in exploring the rights and wrongs of the war than in rubbing our faces in the emotion, the suffering and the sheer horror of it. (And, occasionally, the black humour too: the scene where the battle-hardened Guy has to feed the baby, improvising a nipple out of a condom, is just the sort of bleak touch you could imagine finding in a Fuller film.)

As Guy, Dennis Quaid is cast boldly against type, displaying a dour, rugged quality only previously glimpsed in *Flesh and Bone.* The other international stars, however, fare less well: Stellan Skarsgard has a very unconvincing role as a US embassy official who runs away with Joshua/Guy to the Foreign Legion only to die moments after the film reaches Bosnia. Even more unfortunate, Nastassja Kinski is very subdued in a momentary appearance as Joshua's doomed wife, Among the intriguingly multilingual credits, British cinematographer Ian Wilson *(Edward II, The Crying Game)* stands out for his glowering photography of Montenegro's forbidding landscape.

VILLAGE VOICE, 11/24/98, p. 128, Gary Dauphin

Savior, the latest handwringer set in the former Yugoslavia, announces its intentions up front, promising redemption in the title and delving into mess after bloody mess in an attempt to keep that promise. Flirting with exploitation, *Savior* is a small film built out of extremes. It puts its lead, Guy (Dennis Quaid, whose most salient characteristic is that he's American), through terrorist attack, death of wife and child, shock-fueled killing spree, and escape into the Foreign Legion in its first few minutes, the hysteria only subsiding when he becomes, of all things, a mercenary fighting for Serbia.

Guy's been numbed by years of murder, but his humanity is thawed out by a Serbian woman and her unborn baby. Stumbling home during a prisoner exchange, Vera (Natasa Ninkovic) isn't exactly welcomed by her family. Her rape, the resultant baby, and her failure to commit suicide are seen as a triple shame to Serb national pride. When she's inevitably attacked by a Serb, Guy kills him, Vera and the child's safety becoming the light at the end of his personal tunnel.

Despite the warmth of fulfilled mutual need at its center, *Savior*'s most powerful moments are scenes of frustration. As Guy and Vera try to make it to the safety of a Red Cross outpost, they helplessly watch Vera's kinsmen taken by the enemy, walk into ambushes, and keep walking after Guy is matter-of-factly shot in the side. Directed with understated competence by Predrag Antonijevic, *Savior* sheds little new light on the war in Bosnia, but it does understand how little acts can amount to a kind of heroism. Distrustful of big-picture historical context, *Savior* simply gives all its players equal opportunities to be good or evil, leaving it to God and the audience to sort it all out.

Also reviewed in:
CHICAGO TRIBUNE, 12/11/98, Friday/p. I, Monica Eng
NEW YORK TIMES, 11/25/98, p. E5, Stephen Holden
VARIETY, 6/29-7/12/98, p. 39, Derek Elley

SEE THE SEA

A Zeitgeist Films release of a Fidelite Productions and Local Films production with the particpation of CNC, Procirep.   *Producer:* Marc Missonnier, Nicolas Breviere and Olivier Delbosc.   *Director:* François Ozon.   *Screenplay (French with English subtitles):* François Ozon.   *Director of Photography:* Yorick Le Saux.   *Editor:* Jeanne Moutard.   *Music:* Eric Neveux.   *Sound:* Daniel Sobrino.   *Art Director:* Cecile Vacheret.   *Running time:* 52 minutes.   *MPAA Rating:* Not Rated.

WITH: Sasha Hails; Marina de Van; Samantha; Paul Raoux.

NEW YORK POST, 8/28/98, p. 60, Thelma Adams

"See the Sea" is no ad for French tourism. Francois Ozon's featurette, which thrilled and horrified audiences at MoMA's New Directors/New Films, does for France's vacation isle of Yeu what "Jaws" did for ocean beach communities.

French Wunderkind Ozon (his latest feature, "Sitcom," divided Cannes viewers) has created a taut, two-person (and a baby) thriller characterized by stunning naturalism, monastic economy and a physical dread that rises with the sexual tension.

Sasha (Sasha Hails) awakens each day to her newborn's crying. Separated from her husband, who works on the mainland, she is languid but not relaxed. She tends the baby, bikes to the beach, cooks a solitary dinner, ripples with unreleased sexual desire.

When the backpacker Tatiana (Marina de Van) requests to pitch her tent near Sasha's house, the mother agrees. Where Sasha is passive, Tatiana is aggressive; where Sasha is privileged and maternal, Tatiana is a menacing outcast.

We see the danger, the stormy sea, long before Sasha does. Tatiana enters the house and cracks Sasha's cozy cocoon, in part because the bored young mother wants it crumbled.

Ozon ratchets the tension by having the backpacker behave in small antisocial ways (you should see what she does with a toothbrush) that are horrifying yet require no special effects or tricky camera work.

The young director has not worked out all his ideas and the characters remain opaque to the end (and, at times, downright unbelievable), but Ozon creates a mood of extraordinary foreboding out of small transgressions in ordinary life.

"See the Sea" is paired with the Ozon short "The Summer Dress." It's the story of a young man of ambiguous sexuality who visits a seaside resort with his male lover and has an affair with a woman on the beach.

NEWSDAY, 8/28/98, Part II/p. B7, John Anderson

A kind of "Black Narcissus on the Beach," Francois Ozon's "See the Sea" occupies an environment that's gorgeous and godless (except for the director), and is occupied with sexual desperation and loathing. The result is a moral limbo full of vapors and snakes.

That something horrible is going to happen is never the question, nor need it be. Each progressively sordid moment is its own satisfying creep show.

That Ozon, a young French filmmaker made "See the Sea" only 52 minutes long shows a discernment almost unknown in '90s cinema. It couldn't have been any longer and shouldn't have been—although one can easily envision a Hollywood studio buying the remake rights, puffing it up to feature length and tacking on a happy ending. Studios, however, despite all evidence to the contrary, are concerned with stories. Ozon is concerned with generating dread in the broad daylight.

The plot, as it were, concerns Sasha (Sasha Hails), a bored young mother alone on a wind-swept holiday island off France, where she occupies her days caring for her infant daughter and waiting for her husband to return from some vague business trip. When a strange young woman (Marina de Van) with a backpack shows up at the door and virtually demands to stay and pitch her tent, Sasha is both intimidated and intrigued.

Tatiana, the younger woman, is a *petit bourgeois* monster—intelligent and repellent. Her skin is foul, her hair is lank, her eyes are dead but shifting, and the manifestations of what seems to be her profound self-loathing are too disgusting to recount.

She almost sneers at Sasha's hospitality, but her presence stirs some dormant eroticism in Sasha, whose ennui is so deeply set that she leaves the baby by the water one afternoon while cruising a beach-side grove for some anonymous sex.

The baby (the actress' child, by the way) is incredibly cute and her implicit peril makes Ozon's job—making our skin crawl—easier. But he does this, too, by making the island's beautiful world as random as the evil within it; there's no logic, no origin, just human impulse, anger and will. What's more unnerving than that?

VILLAGE VOICE, 9/1/98, p. 109, Amy Taubin

A scary little movie, François Ozon's *See the Sea* brings to mind such classics of psychological horror as Henri-Georges Clouzot's *Diabolique* and Philip Noyce's *Dead Calm*. It's a voluptuous, heat-of-summer tale that makes the blood run cold.

Sasha (Sasha Hails) and her 10-month-old daughter are on vacation on a sunbaked, underpopulated island off the coast of France. With nothing to do but lie on the beach and tend to the baby, Sasha is a bit bored, a bit irritated, and helplessly horny. Her husband is out of reach by phone, presumably hard at work.

One evening, a backpacker (Marina de Van) knocks on the door and asks permission to set up her tent in Sasha's yard. There's something menacing in the backpacker's body language, something distorted in her expression. She looks like a thickened version of Sasha herself. "It's my husband's property," Sasha says, by way of an excuse for her reluctance to be hospitable. Disavowing her immediate reaction of fear and antipathy, Sasha agrees to let the backpacker camp on the far end of the lawn. But within a day, she gives the backpacker the run of the house, even leaving the baby in her care while she bicycles down to the ferry landing to do some shopping.

Is this masochism or expedience? Is Sasha the kind of guilty middle-class liberal whose fear of offending someone less privileged than herself overcomes even her protective maternal instinct? Or is her maternal instinct already corrupted by feelings of resentment toward the child who curtails her freedom? It's all of this, and more. Ozon has a talent for conveying an enormous amount of psychological complexity and ambivalence with a few lines of dialogue, the movement of an eye, the almost invisible tensing of a muscle. What's more, he leaves us the time and space to project our own experience, fear, and desire onto the situation.

From the moment that we see the backpacker on a cliff above the beach looking down at the mother and child sprawled sleepy and vulnerable in the midday sun, we know a game of cat and mouse has begun. The backpacker intuits a certain passivity in Sasha that makes her perfect prey. She begins by testing her with tiny acts of aggression. She stares too long, she stands just an inch too close, she waits just a second or two before responding to a simple request like "Would you hand me a towel?," she doesn't flush the toilet. Sasha doesn't know whether to interpret this behavior as adolescent bad manners or as something more predatory. The more confused she becomes, the less able she is to confront the situation.

Ozon constructs the narrative so that we always know more than Sasha does. Perhaps if she had seen, as we did, the backpacker dip her host's toothbrush in the shitty water of the toilet she deliberately leaves unflushed, Sasha would pick up the baby and run for the first ferry off the island. What does it matter if her husband thinks she's a fool for being frightened, or if the house is left open to robbers and vandals? Unlike most horror films, in which the heroine's refusal to remove herself from the vicinity of the maniac who's pursuing her seems like plain stupidity or bad plotting, Ozon makes us aware of the psychological and sociological conditioning that governs action or inaction.

Framed and edited with surgical precision, *See the Sea* announces itself as a horror film before a single character appears on screen. The first time I saw the film, I walked in blind. But from the first three shots—a close-up of surf lapping on coarse, reddish sand, a medium shot of a field of high grass, a long shot of a house within which a baby is crying—I understood that something dreadful was going to happen. Violence is implicit in the cutting and suturing of time and space that is basic to all filmmaking. But Ozon's abrupt, disjunctive editing and deliberately cropped compositions ratchet up the violence, making the film's style the correlative of the backpacker's psychotic disassociation and murderous impulses.

All the more effective for its economy, *See the Sea* is exactly the length it needs to be. But its less-than-feature-length 52 minutes is a distributor's nightmare. Zeitgeist Films is releasing it on a double bill with Ozon's 15 minute short, *A Summer Dress*. Slight but chic, it puts a comic spin on the disruptive, ambiguous sexuality that proves so deadly in *See the Sea*.

Also reviewed in:
NEW YORK TIMES, 3/31/98, p. E1, Janet Maslin
NEW YORK TIMES, 8/28/98, p. E23, Janet Maslin
VARIETY, 12/8-14/97, p. 114, David Rooney

SENSELESS

A Dimension Films release of a Mandeville Films, Gold/Miller production. *Executive Producer:* Bob Weinstein, Harvey Weinstein, Cary Granat, Eric L. Gold, and Don Carmody. *Producer:* David Hoberman. *Director:* Penelope Spheeris. *Screenplay:* Greg Erb and Craig Mazin. *Director of Photography:* Daryn Okada. *Editor:* Ross Albert. *Music:* Stephen E. Smith. *Music Editor:* Steve McCrosky. *Sound:* Susumu Tokunow and (music) Martin Kloiber. *Casting:* Junie Lowry Johnson. *Production Designer:* Peter Jamison. *Art Director:* Ann Harris. *Set Designer:* R. Scott Hebertson. *Set Decorator:* Linda Spheeris. *Set Dresser:* Mark "Travis" Little. *Special Effects:* F. Lee Stone. *Costumes:* Betsy Cox. *Make-up:* Jeanne Van Phue and Jo-Anne Smith. *Stunt Coordinator:* Shane Dixon. *Running time:* 88 minutes. *MPAA Rating:* R.

CAST: Marlon Wayans (Darryl Witherspoon); David Spade (Scott Thorpe); Matthew Lillard (Tim LaFlour); Rip Torn (Randall Tyson); Tamara Taylor (Janice); Brad Dourif (Dr. Wheedon); Richard McGonagle (Robert Bellweather); Esther Scott (Denise Witherspoon); Debra Jo Rupp (Fertility Clinic Attendant); Mark Christopher Lawrence (Wig Shop Owner); John Ingle (Economics Professor); Ernie Lively (Coach Brandau); Jennette Goldstein (Nurse Alvarez); Kenya Moore (Lorraine); Constance Zimmer (Zestfully Clean Woman); Ken Lerner (Dean Barlow); Patrick O'Neill and Ross Rayburn (Waiters); Jeanne Diehl (Banquet Guest); Jennie Vaughn (Pastry Chef); Cee-Cee Harshaw (Tonya); Michael Dean Ester (Chet); Greg Grunberg (Steve); Mike Butters (Hockey Referee); Orlando Brown (Brandon Witherspoon); Angelique Parry (April Witherspoon); Tino Williams (Darius Witherspoon); Brenden Richard Jefferson (Lyndell Witherspoon); Greg Wilson (Monte Card Shark); Jeff Garlin (Arlo Vickers); Patrick Ewing (Himself); Michael Brookhurst, Alexander Enberg, and Manu Intiraymi (DI Students); Michael Weatherred (Kern); Vicellous Shannon (Carter); Kevin Cooney (Mr. Thorpe); Ivar Brogger (Economics Coach); Cyia Batten (Punk Waitress); Jack Shearer (Vice Chair Federal Reserve); Joe Basile (Security Guard); Darrel Heath (Shady Guy); Thom Gossom, Jr. (Clothing Salesman); Sierra Pasteur (Smythe/Bates Receptionist); Len Costenza (Board Member); Jeremy Paul Meldrum, Kevin Downes, and Branden Morgan (Smythe/Bates Finalists).

LOS ANGELES TIMES, 2/20/98, Calendar/p. 6, Kevin Thomas

"Senseless" is a terrific showcase for Marlon Wayans, a master at mugging and physical comedy. But it's lots more than that. It's a laff riot that also contains a torrent of scathing social satire that couldn't be more timely in light of the dismantling of affirmative action.

That its defiantly optimistic and determined African American hero never asks for any special breaks only serves to underline just how tough it can be for an impoverished minority young person to get a college education these days. Even though it's a flat-out comedy, "Senseless" sends a message by not resorting to comic exaggeration; it tells it like it is.

Greg Erb and Craig Mazin, who made their screen debut with "Rocket Man," have written a knowing, razor-sharp script. It's perfect for director Penelope Spheeris ("Wayne's World") who puts it across with her usual punch along with her career-long concern for young people making their way in contemporary American society. Smart, sassy, fast and raunchy, "Senseless" can be enjoyed as merely lively entertainment or taken more seriously.

The great thing about Wayans' irrepressible Darryl Witherspoon is that he never feels sorry for himself. An economics major at a university somewhere in the vicinity of Manhattan—in reality, it's mostly USC—he is determined to make it to Wall Street. He's got four jobs as he's trying to make it through school while helping support his mother (Esther Scott) and four younger siblings. But for all his dogged optimism, he's having an increasingly hard time making ends meet.

So when an intense university neurophysiologist (Brad Dourif) starts recruiting human guinea pigs to test a certain green phosphorescent liquid with potentially off-putting side effects, Darryl is the only applicant not scared away. For the $ 3,000 he's to receive, he tells the professor, he'd allow himself to be infected with the Ebola virus.

The elixir's purpose is to heighten the five senses to a degree that defies comprehension. Until he adjusts to his new state he can be driven nearly crazy by the most everyday sounds, for example. But soon he's a kind of swift-thinking superman, which soon lands him as a front-runner for a $ 60,000-a-year job as a junior analyst at a Wall Street firm whose canny CEO is played amusingly by Rip Torn. Darryl's chief nemesis is a world-class snob and put-down artist (David Spade), whose father is a banker. Spade's hilarious Scott Thorpe really isn't a racist. He's just the most ruthless competitor you could possibly imagine.

You just know, of course, that there are going to be temptations and consequences for Darryl in taking that magic medicine, but the way "Senseless" works its way out is unflaggingly inspired. So much of what Darryl so undauntedly has to go through on such a far-from-level playing field is so humiliating you have to laugh at it, for the alternative would just be too grim. How would you like to go through the most crucial interview of your life forced by incredible circumstance to wear a urine-stained pimp suit? "Senseless" toys very effectively with slapstick near-tragedy.

Along with its satire "Senseless" doesn't stint on gross-out humor, but you do wish a gratuitous slur directed at Koreans hadn't made the release cut. Not only do Erb and Mazin seem to have the workings of Wall Street down pat but also the arcane lore of body piercing (which results in a very funny throwaway line); as it happens, Darryl's roommate is a sweet but loopy hockey player (Matthew Lillard) who's deep into body piercing. Lillard's a hoot, and Tamara Taylor is lovely and poised as the classy young lady Darryl pursues.

Production designer Peter Jamison and his associates contribute strongly with a series of settings that span a wide socioeconomic range in telling yet low-key detail, just as Yello's dynamic score heightens the film's nonstop energy. Cinematographer Daryn Okada melds L.A. and Eastern locales with skill. "Senseless" makes lots of sense.

NEW YORK POST, 2/20/98, p. 43, Michael Medved

It would be easy to dismiss "Senseless" as merely a malodorous melange of wretched rectum jokes, but the movie is actually much more than that. It's a collection of crude closeups through, a fish-eye lens, showing grotesque grimaces that would have embarrassed even Jerry Lewis, all employed to tell a stupid, sadistic story that tries to wring laughs out of temporary blindness and deafness.

In the process, it wastes a talented, attractive young cast while squandering the skills of a versatile director.

At least Penelope Spheeris ("The Decline of Western Civilization," "Wayne's World") keeps the gags moving along at a brisk enough pace that you sometimes forget that they're nearly all falling flat.

Marlon Wayans (youngest member of the talented comedic clan) plays a pure-hearted, hard-working scholarship student at prestigious Stratford University who enters a competition to win a plum job at a top Wall Street firm.

Standing in his way is smug, sneering David Spade, frat boy, banker's son, and apparent favorite of the corporate honcho (Rip Torn) who'll ultimately make the choice.

Wayans' only advantage comes when he volunteers for a medical experiment (conducted by spooky Brad Dourif) that injects him with a mysterious glowing-green drug that suddenly heightens all of his senses to a super-human level.

Unfortunately, he greedily overdoses on the wonder drug and soon begins losing each one of his senses, at unpredictable times. When this results in an orgy of unfunny drooling, spastic staggering, pantswetting, tongue-chewing and seizures, it alienates his glamorous, classy new girlfriend (the glamorous and classy Tamara Taylor).

So many botched laugh lines involve the smells and sounds of defecation, and focus with such laser-like intensity on the hero's itchy anus, that the deeper meaning of this project might be more profitably investigated by academic psychologists than by film students.

Ordinary moviegoers will make little sense of "Senseless" and should feel effectively discouraged by the foul fragrance surrounding the entire project.

VILLAGE VOICE, 3/3/98, p. 108, Gary Dauphin

Churning out *Revenge of the Nerds*-type flicks has a long history in hack Hollywood, putting Marion Wayans, the drooling and rubber-limbed star of *Senseless,* in honorable if not quite quality company. The movie tells the story of Darryl, a black senior at a fictional New York City Ivy, angling for a plum Wall Street gig. Darryl's a decent student but lacks connections and time, his world divided between econ classes and the four jobs he's working to pay his tuition and support his mother and three siblings. When a scientist offers Darryl three grand to take an experimental drug, our boy jumps at the chance, the injections giving him super senses, which in turn aid and hinder him, by allowing him to read stock prices or smell a fart at a hundred paces. Wayans's skills as a physical comedian keep *Senseless* from devolving into goo, while waspy rival David Spade is a recurring-bit annoyance. The only real innovation is the movie's weird racial bait and switch, its narrative laying claim to black-image positively even as its black star scratches the crack of his ass with a toilet scrubber and goes on about being somebody's "outbreak monkey." It's a neat trick and you'd almost detect a whiff of irony about if the rest of this movie didn't stink so much.

Also reviewed in:
CHICAGO TRIBUNE, 2/20/98, Friday/p. A, Allan Johnson
NEW YORK TIMES, 2/20/98, p. E26, Janet Maslin
VARIETY, 2/16-22/98, p. 57, Todd McCarthy
WASHINGTON POST, 2/20/98, Weekend/p. 37, Desson Howe

SEVENTH HEAVEN

A Zeitgeist Films release of a Dacia Films/Cinea/La Sept Cinema production with the participation of Canal Plus and the Centre National de la Cinematographie. *Executive Producer:* Françoise Guglielmi. *Producer:* Georges Benayoun and Philippe Carcassonne. *Director:* Benoît Jacquot.   *Screenplay (French with English subtitles):* Benoît Jacquot and Jérôme Beaujour. *Director of Photography:* Romain Winding. *Editor:* Pascale Chavance. *Sound:* Michel Vionnet. *Sound Editor:* Jean-Pierre Laforce. *Casting:* Frédérique Moidon. *Production Designer:* Patrice Arrat. *Set Designer:* Arnaud De Moleron. *Costumes:* Caroline De Vivaise. *Running time:* 88 minutes. *MPAA Rating:* Not Rated.

CAST: Sandrine Kiberlain (Mathilde); Vincent Lindon (Nico); François Berléand (Doctor); Francine Bergé (Mathilde's Mother); Pierre Cassignard (Etienne); Philippe Magnan (Second Doctor); Florence Loiret (Chloé); Léo Le Bevillon (Arthur); Sylvie Loeillet (Nico's Assistant).

LOS ANGELES TIMES, 8/7/98, Calendar/p. 8, Kenneth Turan

When we first see Mathilde, the protagonist of French director Benoit Jacquot's intriguing "Seventh Heaven," she's literally out of focus, a beauty in a daze.

Her face sad, her body language slack, Mathilde (Sandrine Kiberlain) wanders distractedly through a store, stopping only to casually shoplift a toy she later hides in a bag in her closet.

A lawyer by profession, Mathilde is so sunk in a serious depression that she hasn't worked in more than a month. Her orthopedic surgeon husband Nico (Vincent Lindon, Kiberlain's real-life mate) thinks medication is the answer, but no prescription he's written has had much effect. Then, at an art gallery opening, Mathilde gets a glimpse of a man who turns out to make a difference.

"Seventh Heaven" is the eighth theatrical feature for Jacquot, a director who's been working in France since 1975 but only began to gather attention in the U.S. after the recent success of the real-time drama "A Single Girl." His 1990 "The Disenchanted" just played New York; the Isabelle Huppert-starring "The School of Flesh" was well-received in Cannes.

A bit like a more stringent Claude Sautet, Jacquot focuses on adult romantic conundrums in contemporary Paris. His films (this one co-written with Jerome Beaujour) feature intelligent characters enmeshed in difficult, often unsettling situations that always compel our attention.

The man Mathilde spies across a crowded room (a magnetic Francois Berleand) turns out to be a Svengali-type hypnotist and specialist in alternative medicine. Imperious and completely confident, he seems to know just how to deal with all the crises in her life, even the ones she's not completely aware of.

After she has been in such a deep funk you fear she's forgotten how to smile, Mathilde starts to wake up. Watching actress Kiberlain (last seen here as the abandoned first wife in Jacques Audiard's "A Self-Made Hero") flourish and gain self-confidence under this unusual treatment is one of "Seventh Heaven's" pleasures.

As Mathilde grows in assurance, the focus of "Seventh Heaven" begins to change and the ironic twist attached to the film's title becomes clearer. Though mystics consider that there are seven levels of heaven—the seventh equaling a kind of ultimate happiness—the more Mathilde cheers up and gets closer to that plateau, the less the people around her, especially her husband, can handle it.

Getting increasingly involving as it unfolds, "Seventh Heaven" goes beyond examining the power unconscious forces can have in our lives. It focuses as well on how tricky it is to find and maintain a balance in a marriage, on how attached we get to situations we know are making us unhappy and how deranging and disconcerting the onset of unexpected happiness can be.

"Seventh Heaven" is observant and offbeat, like a perceptive short story, and its fascination with adults trying to make their lives work in troubling circumstances is refreshingly mature and open-ended. We're used to expecting this kind of emotionally adept, sophisticated storytelling as a given from the French, and it's nice to see they haven't lost the touch.

NEW YORK POST, 7/31/98, p. 45, Larry Worth

Emotional maelstroms and personality exchanges. It's the stuff of Ingmar Bergman's "Persona" and Robert Altman's "Three Women." Additions to the genre have a lot to live up to.

Then again, those who saw "A Single Girl" and "The Disenchanted" know that Benoit Jacquot isn't easily daunted. And thankfully so, with "Seventh Heaven" as the director's latest gift to cineastes.

As with his previous films, Jacquot gets inside a woman's psyche and explores her dilemma with rarely seen depth. Here, he focuses on Mathilde, a young woman who's not only having sexual problems with her hubby, but is shoplifting at stores, skipping work and fainting without reason.

What's the problem? That's what a free-thinking therapist wants to know as he hypnotizes Mathilde into introspection and *feng shui,* an Eastern philosophy geared to energy channeling. Predictably, Mathilde's increasingly bewildered spouse, a no-nonsense surgeon, isn't buying in. Soon he's not only confused by the malady but angered by the recovery methods. So, the healthier Mathilde gets, the sicker her better half becomes.

The end result? A deliciously offbeat look at marriage in general (the petty arguments, gnawing jealousies) and mismatched partners in particular. Typical of Jacquot's style, he tells his story in a leisurely, decidedly unorthodox manner, mixing his own brand of whimsy and drama with clear-cut homages to everyone from Godard to Hitchcock.

He's also a master of casting, whether putting the focus on minor players (Francois Berleand as a soothing shrink, Francine Berge as Mathilde's supportive mom) or the majors (Vincent Lindon's exasperated husband).

But the real find here is Sandrine Kiberlain, an unconventional beauty whose sophistication and intelligence remind one of a young, more fragile Meryl Streep. Kiberlain's fully nuanced performance as Mathilde justifiably got her nominated for France's Oscar, the prestigious Cesar. Sure enough, there's not an emotion she doesn't register to perfection.

Make no mistake, Jacquot remains the driving force here. But by keeping Kiberlain front and center, "Seventh Heaven" seems downright ethereal.

NEWSDAY, 7/31/98, Part II/p. B7, John Anderson

While our homegrown and perhaps ingrown filmmakers are providing multiopportunities this summer to watch our world and/or fellow human beings blown to bits, French director Benoit Jacquot arrives with the overdue "Seventh Heaven," a movie in which people are actually put back together.

Delicate, dreamlike and dedicated to the proposition that love is pure mystery, Jacquot's latest film is pure cinema, a work based on gesture and restraint and which proceeds with the easy grace of a petal on the wind. following the release here of "A Single Girl" and the recent belated release of 1990's "The Disenchanted," it should establish Jacquot in the public mind as the fascinatingly enigmatic filmmaker he is.

He's also a "woman's director"—not in a modern sense, empathizing all over the place, but in a classic sense, creating situations and circumstances in which the entire sex can be deliciously inscrutable. And, once again, he has cast a completely successful and captivating actress—Sandrine Kiberlain, seen most recently here in "A Self-Made Hero," but never before in such a central role.

Her Mathilde is painfully pale, barely connected to the ground and—having reached the age her father was when he either died or killed himself—has taken up casual shoplifting. She's also developed the rather quaint habit of fainting under pressure, her sex life with her husband, Nico (Vincent Lindon), is in critical condition and the sexy young housekeeper Chloe (Florence Loiret) has made her domestically obsolete. That she shoplifts children's toys, is passive-aggressive with her mother and has the body language of a 12-year-old is indicating some unresolved issues.

At a party, she exchanges looks with a distinguished older man and faints dead away. A day or so later, having been arrested for shoplifting—and fainting again—she comes to only to find the same older man, a doctor (Francois Berleand), in the room. He takes charge of her, treats her to both lunch and a brusque psychoanalytic exam, plants some post-hypnotic suggestions and introduces her to feng shui—the Chinese practice of harmonious living with one's environment. Her bedroom and her study, he says must be switched for maximum happiness. She goes home, moves some furniture and starts to feel better.

Nico? An orthopedic surgeon, he has a scientific mind balanced with paternalistic patience. He's willing to humor Mathilde, but when she starts experiencing orgasm—something she's not done before—he gets nervous: She's faking, she's cheating, she's sleeping with her hypnotist. In one of the film's funnier sequences, he sees a psychiatrist himself, but can't reconcile his logic with what he sees as mumbo jumbo.

Irreconcilable differences? Not quite. Mathilde and Nico are like planets that have fallen out of each other's orbits, and there are stages of re-orientation: awareness of a problem, a realization that it can't be fixed and a reconciling with the fact that they want each other anyway. It's a very adult movie, this "Seventh Heaven," because it acknowledges that while you can't have everything, if you don't ask too many questions, you can get what you need.

VILLAGE VOICE, 8/4/98, p. 53, J. Hoberman

Benoit Jacquot has been making films for better than two decades but it's only recently that this adroit Frenchman, a narrative filmmaker with a documentarian's taste for the accidental and gestural, has established an international presence with his svelte, slightly sleazy, psychologically charged entertainments.

Jacquot's real-time tour de force *The Single Girl* and his terse, fragmentary *The Disenchanted,* both of which had their local runs at Film Forum, demonstrated his facility as a director of stylish young actresses: projecting inner tumult, they search for self-actualization through the labyrinth of contemporary Paris. *Seventh Heaven,* is a more elaborate variation on the theme—given additional art-movie heft with a dollop of French Freud pseudoscience and *Cahiers du Cinema* connoisseurship, namely the elements lifted from the 1949 Otto Preminger thriller *Whirlpool.*

Seventh Heaven trafficks in kleptomania, hypnosis, and marital jealousy—albeit used to somewhat different ends than in *Whirlpool.* Compulsive shoplifting is only one of the psychosomatic ailments suffered by attractively wan Mathilde (Sandrine Kiberlain), the dissatisfied wife of a nervous and perhaps neglectful young surgeon Nico (Vincent Lindon, Kiberlain's real-life husband). One night at a cocktail party staged as an overheated red haze, Mathilde momentarily locks eyes with a mesmerizing older man and promptly faints away. Like the teenage heroine of *The Disenchanted,* Mathilde has been given a sign—and, no less than the earlier film, *Seventh Heaven*'s narrative is an assemblage of clues and details.

As a director, Jacquot seems to equate the making of a movie with the casting of a spell and the pale, dreamily disdainful Kiberlain—she resembles an elegantly elongated Meg Ryan—is, at least initially, the subject of his trance. Soon her character is wandering through Paris, barely avoiding the traffic in her somnambulist state, until she reencounters the mystery man and, following him into a department store, can stage her compulsive scenario for his benefit. The man is the embodiment of a desire that is not entirely sexual. Mathilde is taken off to lunch at an expensive, empty restaurant and subjected to a brusquely impassive analytic session. "Words are words, feelings are feelings," the mystery man explains. "They don't have much in common."

The doctor, as he turns out to be, seems to have synthesized his own blend of Jacques Lacan (subject of an early Jacquot documentary) and the esoteric Chinese practice of feng shui. Thus Mathilde's treatment not only involves hypnosis but reorienting the geographical placement of the conjugal bed, so that the boudoir is switched with the study. (Ah hah!) Before long, however, husband and wife are switching symptoms and Jacquot's attention shifts from her case history to his—complete with a second, deadpan hypno-shrink.

Its mood as smooth and fragile as a Ming vase, *Seventh Heaven is* suffused with strange flute music and chic metaphysics. Jacquot's movie-movie mysticism may not be to every taste. Is the filmmaker sincere? "One can ask what he brings by way of conviction to the story," as Jacquot's mentor Jacques Rivette wrote of Preminger. "Does he believe it? Does he even try to make us believe it?" The answer, according to Rivette, was the filmmaker's quest "not so much to make an unbelievable story believable, as to find, beyond dramatic or narrative verisimilitude, a truth that is purely cinematic." So it is here.

Flaunting its showy introspection in Preminger-esque widescreen, *Seventh Heaven* is posh, fluid, enjoyable filmmaking. Nor is Otto the only '40s filmmaker *Seventh Heaven* evokes. With its elliptical editing, off-center compositions, and sudden, if cushioned, transitions, this story of a magical cure has echoes of a Maya Deren psychodrama. It's an old-fashioned movie—but no less fashionable for that.

Also reviewed in:
NATION, 8/24-31/98, p. 33, Stuart Klawans
NEW YORK TIMES, 7/31/98, p. E12, Stephen Holden
VARIETY, 10/13-19/97, p. 92, David Stratton

SHADRACH

A Columbia Pictures release of a Millennium Films presentation in association with Nu Image of a Bridget Terry production. *Executive Producer:* Jonathan Demme, Steven Shareshian, Avi Lerner, Danny Dimbort, Trevor Short, and Elie Samaha. *Producer:* John Thompson, Boaz Davidson, and Bridget Terry. *Director:* Susanna Styron. *Screenplay:* Susanna Styron and Bridget Terry. *Based on the short story by:* William Styron. *Director of Photography:* Hiro Narita. *Editor:* Colleen Sharp. *Music:* Van Dyke Parks. *Music Editor:* Sherry Whitfield.

Sound: Larry Long, Carl Rudisill, and (music) Jon Baker. *Sound Editor:* John L. Sisti. *Casting:* Tracy Kilpatrick. *Production Designer:* Burton Rencher. *Set Decorator:* Valerie Fann. *Set Dresser:* Matt Fann. *Costumes:* Dona Granata. *Make-up:* Rudolph Eavey III. *Make-up (Shadrach):* Jeff Goodwin and Thomas Holland. *Stunt Coordinator:* John Copeman. *Running time:* 133 minutes. *MPAA Rating:* PG-13.

CAST: John Franklin Sawyer (Shadrach);   Scott Terra (Paul);   Ginnie Randall (Virginia); Darrell Larson (Father);   Deborah Hedwall (Mother);   Jonathan Parks Jordan (Middle Mole); Erin Underwood (Lucinda);   Alice Rogers (Cloris);   Monica Bugajski (Edmonia);   Daniel Treat (Little Mole);   Andie MacDowell (Trixie);   Michael Ruff (Smut);   Muse Watson (Captain); Doug Chancey (Dock Worker);   Harvey Keitel (Vernon);   Rick Warner (Presbyterian Minister); Edward Bunker (Joe Thornton);   Clarinda Hollmond (Chapel Singer);   Melvin Cauthen (Earvin Williams);   Richard Olsen (Seddon Washington);   Olivia Bost (Sweet Betty);   Bill Nelson (Fauntleroy);   Walter Hand (Preacher);   Martin Sheen (Narrator).

LOS ANGELES TIMES, 9/25/98, Calendar/p. 12, Kevin Thomas

Harvey Keitel, that urban icon, might not be the first actor who comes to mind to play a dirt-poor small-town Southerner. So we can only be grateful that Susanna Styron thought of him for her wise and gentle film based on her father William Styron's short story "Shadrach."

The moment Keitel opens his mouth, we know that he's just right as Vernon Dabney, reduced to supporting his wife and seven children as a moonshiner in the Virginia tidelands in the depths of the Depression. Speaking with an authentic-sounding Southern accent, Keitel proceeds to give one of the finest, most distinctive performances of his career. "Shadrach" represents a stretch in a different direction for Keitel, much as "The Piano" did.

The Dabneys are one of those families who are always found living on the edge of town in a ramshackle house surrounded by derelict cars. Dabney's lovely, slightly disheveled wife, Trixie (Andie MacDowell, no less impressive than Keitel, to whom she bemusedly underplays), is a classic earth mother, calm and caring, the perfect antidote to her frustrated, volatile husband, who sees FDR and his New Deal as a threat rather than a deliverance. Her house is a mess, she's given up on her four sons' personal hygiene, but she has three pretty, immaculate daughters, one of whom, Ebonia (Monica Bugajeski), charms 10-year-old Paul Whitehurst (Scott Terra).

The shabby, profane, unrespectable Dabneys are just the sort of people who would fascinate a boy from a very proper middle-class, God-fearing family, and Paul is thrilled when his parents (Darrell Larson, Deborah Hedwall) reluctantly agree to let him stay with them while they're off to Baltimore for three days. That brief period of time, however, is enough to transform Paul's life. Martin Sheen is heard on the soundtrack as the adult Paul—well-played by Terra—thus providing the perspective and insights of maturity.

That's because a very old, very exhausted black man, Shadrach (John Franklin Sawyer, an amazing 83-year-old retired postal worker), turns up in the Dabneys' yard. Gradually they—and we—realize that Shadrach, who says he's 99 years old, was a slave on Vernon's great-grandfather's tobacco plantation. When Shadrach was a young man, Vernon's ancestor sold him and some other slaves to a planter in Alabama, where Shadrach became a sharecropper after the Civil War. Now that he's outlived three wives and anywhere from 12 to 15 children, he has somehow managed to travel 600 miles to come home to die, to be buried on the Dabney plantation.

Talk about the rock tossed into the still pond. The only evidence that Vernon was descended from plantation aristocracy is a picture of a white-columned mansion, hanging askew on his living room wall. The Yankees burned it, and the land on which it stood is where Vernon maintains his moonshine operations. Through Vernon and his resentment at having to deal with Shadrach, we see not the blind redneck racism that we might have expected but the sheer burden, in its myriad aspects, that the institution of slavery has placed on successive generations of whites and blacks alike.

Keitel expresses what a curse the legacy of slavery has been to men like Vernon in one of the transcendent moments of his career, letting Vernon's weariness and despair shine through the exasperated words of bigotry. But Vernon is in fact a decent man, nudged with a good-natured but subtly resolute firmness by Trixie to do the right thing by Shadrach, only to encounter unexpected obstacles that play out with both poignancies and humor.

This flawless, deeply felt yet buoyant and graceful film marks Styron's feature directorial debut, after a varied career as a documentarian, writer and as an assistant to Ken Russell on "Altered States" and Luis Buñuel on "That Obscure Object of Desire."

That she herself has a Southern heritage, adapting (with Bridget Terry) her own celebrated father's story, surely gives the period-perfect "Shadrach" its special resonance.

NEW YORK POST, 9/23/98, p. 51, Thelma Adams

A pregnant teen-ager waddles across a junky yard. Naked legs waggle out the windows of a rusty Model-T in the lazy throes of summer passion. A dirty urchin scoots under the porch. This ain't the New South, baby.

We're heading down that tobacco road of fallen Southern gentry thanks to Shadrach director and co-writer Susanna Styron. William Styron's daughter has built a dubious monument to her writer father by reviving a short story that had rested in peace behind closed book covers.

In books such as "Sophie's Choice," the chaotic world of eccentric adults caught in a historical back draft is viewed through the naive eyes of an innocent bystander. In that novel, a young writer loses his innocence—and learns to love—through contact with Holocaust survivors.

In "Shadrach," 10-year-old Paul Whitehurst (Scott Terra), the only child of churchgoing, middle-class parents, is drawn into the hectic family life of Virginians Vernon and Trixie Dabney (Harvey Keitel and Andie MacDowell), a moonshiner and a drunk.

It's 1935, and the Dabneys have fallen from their slave-owning glory days. Trixie is often heard saying: "Honeychile, will you bring Mama a beer." Vernon voices obscenity strings, which must have made memorizing lines easy for Keitel.

There are fallen gentry—and then there is the Dabneys' chicken-fried American Gothic schtick. This doesn't even touch on the bizarre casting that put Keitel and MacDowell armpit-to-armpit in a fantasy fit for Stanley Kowalski.

Along comes Shadrach (John Franklin Sawyer). The 99-year-old ex-slave trudges from Alabama to Virginia to die on Dabney land, the terra firma of his birth and enslavement.

Shadrach's arrival unifies the Dabneys. He inspires a dignity not so apparent under all those dirty necks: There is a bond of humanity between ex-slave and ex-master rooted in the Virginia soil.

While Paul, escaping his mother's white gloves and telltale cough, sees Shadrach's homecoming through rose-colored glasses, we're not so sure.

To tell the truth, if I were little Paul's mother, it wouldn't be snobbery or racism that would keep me from letting my only son run wild with the Dabneys. It would be the likelihood that he would find a condom on the floor of the old car (he does), inhale Trixie's boozy kisses or —God forbid—fall in love with a Dabney dust muffin.

VILLAGE VOICE, 10/6/98, p. 128, Gary Susman

Based on a semi-autobiographical story by William Styron, with a screenplay cowritten and directed by his daughter Susanna, Shadrach is a didactic Depression-era tale of an ancient former slave (John Franklin Sawyer) who treks to what's left of the plantation he worked on to die and be buried. But Shadrach's dying wish proves difficult to honor for his former owners' struggling descendants, a Snopes-like brood of unwashed boys and slatternly girls, headed by bootlegger Vernon Dabney (Harvey Keitel) and his magnolia-scented wife (Andie MacDowell).

Why does Shadrach return to the fiery furnace where he was forged? Hard to say, since he speaks in a whisper understood only by the youngest Dabney girl and family friend Paul (Scott Terra). Narrator Paul gets to infer the motivations of Shadrach, whom the movie treats like an old dog, even as it praises the Dabneys for treating him humanely. The only fully human character is Vernon, with Keitel bringing to blustery life a complex man who does the right thing by Shadrach without overcoming the prejudices of his time and place. It's Keitel who delivers the film's moral, "Death ain't much," with the rueful knowledge that life ain't much either.

Also reviewed in:
CHICAGO TRIBUNE, 10/16/98, Friday/p. J, John Petrakis
NEW YORK TIMES, 9/23/98, p. E5, Lawrence Van Gelder
VARIETY, 4/20-26/98, p. 45, Emanuel Levy
WASHINGTON POST, 10/16/98, Weekend/p. 49, Michael O'Sullivan

SHAKESPEARE IN LOVE

A Miramax Films/Universal Pictures/The Bedford Falls Company release. *Executive Producer:* Bob Weinstein and Julie Goldstein. *Producer:* David Parfitt, Donna Gigliotti, Harvey Weinstein, Edward Zwick, and Marc Norman. *Director:* John Madden. *Screenplay:* Marc Norman and Tom Stoppard. *Director of Photography:* Richard Greatrex. *Editor:* David Gamble. *Music:* Stephen Warbeck. *Music Editor:* Roy Prendergast. *Choreographer:* Quinny Sacks. *Sound:* Peter Glossop and (music) Chris Dibble. *Sound Editor:* John Downer. *Casting:* Michelle Guish. *Production Designer:* Martin Childs. *Art Director:* Mark Raggett. *Set Decorator:* Jill Quertier. *Special Effects:* Stuart Brisdon. *Costumes:* Sandy Powell. *Make-up:* Lisa Westcott. *Make-up (Gwyneth Paltrow):* Tina Earnshaw. *Running time:* 113 minutes. *MPAA Rating:* R.

CAST: Joseph Fiennes (Will Shakespeare); Gwyneth Paltrow (Viola De Lesseps); Judi Dench (Queen Elizabeth); Ben Affleck (Ned Alleyn); Colin Firth (Lord Wessex); Simon Callow (Sir Edmund Tilney); Geoffrey Rush (Philip Henslowe); Tom Wilkinson (Hugh Fennyman); Steven O'Donnell (Lambert); Tim McMullen (Frees); Steven Beard (Makepeace, the Preacher); Antony Sher (Dr. Moth); Patrick Barlow (Will Kempe); Martin Clunes (Richard Burbage); Sandra Reinton (Rosaline); Bridget McConnel and Georgie Glen (Ladies in Waiting); Nicholas Boulton (Henry Condell); Imelda Staunton (Nurse); Desmond McNamara (Crier); Barnaby Kay (Nol); Jim Carter (Ralph Bashford); Paul Bigley (Peter, the Stage Manager); Jason Round (Actor in Tavern); Rupert Farley (Barman); Adam Barker (First Auditionee); Joe Roberts (John Webster); Harry Gostelow (Second Auditionee); Alan Cody (Third Auditionee); Mark Williams (Wabash); David Curtiz (John Hemmings); Gregor Truter (James Hemmings); Simon Day (First Boatman); Jill Baker (Lady De Lesseps); Amber Glossop (Scullery Maid); Robin Davies (Master Plum); Hywel Simons (Servant); Nicholas Le Prevost (Sir Robert De Lesseps); Timothy Kightley (Edward Pope); Mark Saban (Augustine Philips); Bob Barrett (George Bryan); Roger Morlidge (James Armitage); Daniel Brocklebank (Sam Gosse); Roger Frost (Second Boatman); Rebecca Charles (Chambermaid); Richard Gold (Lord in Waiting); Rachel Clarke (First Whore); Lucy Speed (Second Whore); Patricia Potter (Third Whore); John Ramm (Makepeace's Neighbour); Martin Neeley (Paris/Lady Montague).

CINEASTE, Vol. XXIV, no. 2-3, 1999, p. 78, Kenneth S. Rothwell

[*Shakespeare In Love* was reviewed jointly with *Elizabeth*; see Rothwell's review of that film.]

LOS ANGELES TIMES, 12/11/98, Calendar/p. 1, Kenneth Turan

"Shakespeare in Love" is a ray of light in a holiday film season that was starting to look as gloomy as the scowl on Ebenezer Scrooge's face. A happy conceit smoothly executed, this is one of those entertaining confections that's so pleasing to the eye and ear you'd have to be a genuine Scrooge to struggle against it.

As the title more than hints, "Shakespeare in Love" is a romance (and one played by the irresistible pairing of Gwyneth Paltrow and Joseph Fiennes), but that is not the limit of its attractions. Part knockabout farce, part witty amusement, "Shakespeare" has the drollness we associate with playwright (and co-writer) Tom Stoppard, but it has the rare ability to wear its cleverness with grace and ease.

The idea is shrewder than merely transporting us back to London in 1593, just in time to see young Will Shakespeare (Fiennes) fall in love with Viola de Lesseps (Paltrow), the woman who is to become his "heroine for all time," though that is certainly pleasant.

The trick is rather that we see Will's relationship with Viola have a transforming effect on the play he's writing, tentatively titled "Romeo and Ethel, the Pirate's Daughter." As this duo live through the real-life passions and tragedies of a wide-screen romance, that play in rehearsal gradually but inevitably becomes (of course) "Romeo and Juliet." (Those hoping for "Titus Andronicus" might want to stay home.)

Co-written by Marc Norman and Stoppard, "Shakespeare" benefited from the hand of both writers. It was Norman (whose credits include "Waterworld" and the woeful "Cutthroat Island") who came up with the deft original idea of having Shakespeare's play and life influence each other. Stoppard (whose work includes the thematically similar "Rosencrantz and Guildenstern Are Dead") came on to do a smashing rewrite, adding his touch with language as well as a smart subplot involving Shakespeare's rival Christopher Marlowe (Rupert Everett).

Everett is not the only well-selected supporting player (Michelle Guish is the film's casting director) "Shakespeare" utilizes. Starting at the top with an unflappable Judi Dench as the one-woman armada Elizabeth I and Geoffrey Rush in an unexpected comic role as a snaggle-toothed theater owner, adept co-stars include Ben Affleck as a self-involved actor, Tom Wilkinson as a stage-struck usurer, and Colin Firth (Darcy in the BBC's recent "Pride and Prejudice") as Wessex, the wellborn but impecunious suitor for Viola's hand.

Finally, though, as always in romance, it's the stars that carry the film. Fiennes, the younger brother of Ralph, has the burning eyes and brooding demeanor appropriate for a lover, and he and Paltrow, flourishing once again under a British accent and doing her best work since "Emma," have a winning chemistry. It's no small thing to be completely believable as a besotted couple who can't keep their hands off each other, and that is what the pair accomplish here.

The ringmaster who deserves the credit for keeping all these performers in sync is John Madden, who directed Dench as yet another queen (Victoria) in last year's "Mrs. Brown." Not one for directorial flourishes, Madden represents the pick of the solidly professional directors who've come through the BBC, adept at getting the best out of the material at hand.

It's not Shakespeare or his eventual muse who is introduced first, but theater owner Philip Henslowe (Rush). He's having his feet literally held to the fire by Elizabethan loan shark Fennyman (Wilkinson), who settles Henslowe's debts for the rights to the next play by hot young scribe Will Shakespeare.

The problem is that master Will seems to have misplaced his muse. As he explains to his apothecary-alchemist-astrologer Dr. Moth (Anthony Sher), the Elizabethan version of a therapist, "It's as if my quill is broken, as if the organ of my imagination is dried up, as if the proud tower of my genius is collapsed." And so on.

One of the most amusing aspects of "Shakespeare" is how many Elizabethan versions of modern things are to be found in 1590s London. These jests include water taxi drivers who like to kibbitz and have written scripts of their own; restaurants where the waiter says, "The special today is a pig's foot marinated in juniper-berry vinegar served on a buckwheat pancake"; and the kind of theatrical bitchiness that causes Shakespeare to say to Marlowe, "I love your early work."

Speaking of Marlowe, "Shakespeare" is also clever in the off-handed way it makes use of real historical situations, such as the question of whether Marlowe had a hand in writing Shakespeare's plays and the cloud over the former's death. And students of English drama will be amused to see a teenage version of future playwright John Webster (Joe Roberts) being every bit as bloodthirsty as his later "The Duchess of Malfi" would have you expect.

Will and Viola finally meet when, disguised as a boy named Thomas Kent (women were forbidden on the Elizabethan stage) she tries out for a part in his new play. Will, ever the insightful writer, figures this ruse out (it's one of the film's unspoken jests that he uses cross-dressing in later plays), and we're soon enmeshed in the heights and depths of a relationship we see echoed in the romance and agony of "Romeo and Juliet."

In addition to everything else, "Shakespeare in Love" also functions as a tribute to the magic of live theater. Whenever problems arise, impresario Henslowe says not to worry, his explanation of how the difficulty will be solved is a wide-eyed, "It's a mystery." Anyone wanting to figure out how all the elements for this charming film fell so nicely into place could do worse than looking to that same phrase for an answer.

NEW STATESMAN, 1/29/99, p. 39, David Jays

Unusually for a film about an artist, "Shakespeare in Love" shows its hero at work. He sharpens his quill and ink-steeped fingers scribble mightily—even if he's only practising his signature. This is a nice Tom Stoppard touch (like his playwright in "The Real Thing" who agonises over a suitably profound playlist for "Desert Island Discs"), and typifies the film's rompish generosity. Stoppard has embellished the original screenplay by Marc Norman, going on the razzle with gleeful backchat and groaning pun. The director, John Madden, and his leading players respond with swelling hearts, animating the conceits and travesties.

Shakespeare (Joseph Fiennes) suffers from writer's block, his projected comic epic (Romeo and Ethel the Pirate's Daughter) strangely stalled. Craving a muse, he meets the radiant Lady Viola De Lesseps (Gwyneth Paltrow) and is inspired by love's light wings. She, meanwhile, longs to strut the stage, and scampers to the theatre in doublet and hose, evading her lowering aristocratic suitor (Colin Firth). Events bob through those of "Romeo and Juliet" itself—a balcony, tragicomic duels, cruel mischance and a beady nurse (Imelda Staunton) to grease the plot.

We know everything and nothing about Shakespeare. Everything about the man of property, nothing of the poet's heart. Even the most familiar (inevitably disputed) likeness, in the National Portrait Gallery, disappears into background obscurity, a slightly louche enigma. "Shakespeare in Love" refreshingly disdains any claim to veracity. We know that Shakespeare spent the plague years of the early 1590s writing his erotic narrative poems "Venus and Adonis" and "The Rape of Lucrece," so his amorous ferment here seems appropriate. Though she's hardly the poet's rampant Venus, Gwyneth Paltrow deserves her Botticelli ringlets. Swannecked, she has a duck-billed beauty and she gives a delicious physical performance. Her goatee'd actor has a slacker slouch, released from the starch-spined demands of courtly dress. She does teach the torches to burn bright, and the camera swoons about her in a golden daze.

Joseph Fiennes, who in "Elizabeth" mastered the art of looking doe-eyed in a blouse, plays Shakespeare as a yearning mooncalf. The playwright becomes a snapper-up of suggestion, swooping on advice like the "upstart crow" and plagiarist of Elizabethan scorn. Although scourges of the theatre accused its boy-players of raising a miasma of misplaced eroticism, there is little here of the presumed bisexual Shakespeare of modern criticism (of the 154 sonnets, 126 are addressed to a man), but the film's lovesickness brims into androgyny. Viola inspires the role of Juliet but plays Romeo, and leaves Will poised to create the tear-streaked bewilderment of "Twelfth Night."

The "Today" programme's man of the millennium, Shakespeare still infuses British culture his face on our currency, his works the currency of our lexicon. We balk at genius nowadays, and "Shakespeare in Love" presents a talented hack, tumbling through the market, catching at demand, enmeshed in the perilous business of theatre. Oddly enough, this concurs with biographic trends, which illuminate his working environment and locate inspiration there rather than in the shadowy Dark Ladies and Only Begetters of the sonnets. Park Honan's recent biography was resolutely scholarly, shying at speculation. "Shakespeare in Love" does no more to flesh out his early marriage to an older woman who remained in Warwickshire. Anne Hathaway, poor cow, is kept off-screen, mistress of "a cold bed" in Stratford.

All adrenaline kitsch, Baz Luhrmann's 1996 film of "Romeo and Juliet" found its vigour in the salty tang of Shakespearean prose, discovering a street-smart pungency. This film, in contrast, swims in verse, is drenched in iambic. Stoppard's deft tapestry of allusion is amplified by Madden's romantic direction. The sheer beauty of Shakespeare's antique immediacy—"the sensual life of verse" that Keats acclaimed, that spurred his own "golden-tongued Romance"—informs the movie, and if it is only half the story, it is nonetheless giddying to sit through. Only Geoffrey Rush's bumbling impresario demands, "We haven't the time—talk prose".

Madden has far more fun with "Shakespeare in Love" than with the slow--thawing affections of Mrs Brown. Judi Dench follows her tiggy winkled Queen Victoria with Elizabeth I, a rot-toothed, tart-tongued queen, eyes glinting through a plastered skull. In a thronging London of stalls and slops, the Rose Theatre, weathered and tatty and agog with groundlings, seems far more convincing than the sanitised heritage pot of the current recreated Globe. Madden presents the theatre as a comfortable, welcoming community, where actors juggle happily in the wings and band together in a crisis. It's like the ramshackle Crummles troupe that embraces Nicholas Nickleby and Smike (and Dickens, too, has them rehearse Romeo, Smike as intent on his apothecary's role as "Shakespeare in Love"'s star-struck moneybags). Glorious artifice and granite pragmatism intertwine, and only a wobbly prop sword asserts the division.

NEW YORK, 12/21-28/98, p. 148, Peter Rainer

Shakespeare in Love is a fanciful romp about the young Will who wrote *Romeo and Juliet* and the romantic liaison that may have led to it. Will is played by that other Fiennes, Joseph, who also turned up recently as the Virgin Queen's suitor in *Elizabeth*. He's blandly dashing. His romantic muse is played by Gwyneth Paltrow, who seems to have become the house actress over at Miramax. She's best when she's playing tough cookies, as in *Hard Eight* and *Flesh and Bone,* but filmmakers keep trying to fashion her into the Grace Kelly of the twentysomething set. The surprise here is Ben Affleck who shows off a tip-top comic style as the actor playing Mercutio. Not only is he funny, but he's funny in tights.

NEW YORK POST, 12/11/98, p. 59, Rod Dreher

What a great and glorious surprise "Shakespeare in Love" is!

There are about a million ways director John Madden's fleet-footed romantic comedy about the Bard finding his muse could have gone embarrassingly wrong. It might have delivered a snootful of artist-bio pretension (viz "Total Eclipse"), or a load of modernized shlock, such as Baz Luhrmann's snazzy but empty "Romeo & Juliet."

As it happens, "Shakespeare in Love" is rich, witty, boisterous, and thoroughly enjoyable. Like many of the Bard's plays, the script, written by Marc Norman and polished by Tom Stoppard, cannily combines style, humor and melodrama, making it accessible and fun for the literary crowd and grubby groundlings alike.

The tale begins in 1593, with actor and dramatist William Shakespeare (Joseph Fiennes), a fierce comer on the London theater scene, flummoxed in his attempt to finish his latest play—a romance with the unpromising working title "Romeo and Ethel, the Pirate's Daughter." Snaggle-toothed Philip Henslowe (Geoffrey Rush), owner of the Rose Theater, desperately needs the scribe to finish the thing, or he's out of business. Agonizing over his dramatic impotence, poor Shakespeare even undergoes a session on an Elizabethan-era psychiatrist's couch.

But Shakespeare has a secret admirer: the rich and lovely Viola De Lesseps (Gwyneth Paltrow), a passionate devotee of his writing and, after their eyes meet across a crowded room, of the man himself. He is equally enchanted, and appears at long last to have found his true love and inspiration.

But there's a problem. Viola's social-climbing father intends for her to marry the pompous Lord Wessex (Colin Firth), an impoverished aristocrat who has obtained a royal blessing on his matrimonial designs. And headstrong Viola, while carrying on an affair with randy Bill, schemes to break into the all-male world of the London theater by disguising herself as a boy and trying out for Shakespeare's play.

The drama plays out amid a ripe smorgasbord of uproarious vanity, romantic roundelays, theatrical rivalries—art vs. commerce, Henslowe vs. competitor Richard Burbage (Martin Clunes), Shakespeare vs. playwright Christopher Marlowe (Rupert Everett)—and ardor-flushed derring-do. The great joke here is that Shakespeare draws on the mad swirl of events around him to finish his play. We hear lines and see plot complications develop that we know will make it not only into "Romeo & Juliet," but into the Bard's later works as well.

The cast is, without exception, terrific. Fiennes is captivating as the tortured romantic, and he's surrounded by a dream cast of supporting players. Rush, Firth, Ben Affleck (as the arrogant actor Ned Alleyn) and Simon Callow (as Tilney, the Master of the Revels)—are splendid, but the show is very nearly stolen by Judi Dench. Her Queen Elizabeth is a tough old broad, as haughty and imperious as befits a monarch, yet worldly wise and possessed of a gimlet eye. Dench is on screen for less than 10 minutes, yet makes a stunning impression that will be remembered come Oscar time.

The best thing, though, is the breathtaking performance of Gwyneth Paltrow. She's ravishing, she's vulnerable, she's irresistible—and she's never been better. Her way with Shakespearean dialogue suggests a future on the stage, should she so choose (and after this movie, Paltrow will have her pick of anything.) Glowing with the incandescence of a true movie star, the magnificent Gwyneth illuminates this entire, many-splendored production.

If she were the only good thing about "Shakespeare in Love," it still would have been worth seeing; that she is the crown jewel in a glittering tiara of a film studded with writing and acting gems testifies to the deep pleasures to be found in this remarkable movie.

NEWSDAY, 12/11/98, Part II/p. B6, Jack Mathews

A theater impresario with debts in arrears is having his feet held to the fire—literally, dunked in glowing coals—when he blurts out a teaser for a new play he might be willing to share with his debtor, who runs 1593 London's Rose Theatre. It's a crowd-tickler, the hot foot says, mistaken identities, shipwreck, pirate king, a bit with a dog and love triumphant.

What's it called?

"Romeo and Ethel, the Pirate's Daughter."

Hmmm. Good title.

Thus begins John Madden's "Shakespeare in Love," one of the strangest, funniest, most enchanting, most romantic and—fittingly—best-written tales ever spun from the vast legend of William Shakespeare. It's the story of the creation of "Romeo and Juliet," a play that a slumping Shakespeare (Joseph Fiennes) is inspired to write by debt, panic, sexual dysfunction and a woman (Gwyneth Paltrow) in male drag who becomes his muse.

Don't ask a scholar to explain.

Co-written by playwright Tom Stoppard, in what must have been a frenzy of whimsy, and heretofore undistinguished Hollywood veteran Marc Norman ("Cutthroat Island"), "Shakespeare in Love" tells the story of how young Will, under pressure from competing theaters and being enormously jealous of his better known rival Christopher Marlowe, caught fire in the burning sheets of his new lover's bed and turned "Romeo and Ethel" into the greatest romantic tragedy ever produced.

"Shakespeare in Love" is a picture of perfection, from every angle. The dialogue is hilarious, even when you're not sure whether you're missing a Shakespearean reference (and there are many). The characters, who seem to have one foot in the late 16th Century and one in the late 20th, are totally convincing, even when their tongues are in their cheeks. And it looks as ripe as an Old Globe production come to life, even though the Old Globe is not to be seen.

Best of all are the performances, which are across-the-cast superb, with special mentions due Geoffrey Rush, as Will's befuddled patron, Ben Affleck, as the traveling thespian who portrays Mercutio ("He dies?"), and Judi Dench, a sensation in her three scenes as the proto-feminist Queen Elizabeth. But the best work is center stage, with Fiennes and Paltrow.

Fiennes, who can also be seen wearing tights in the same historical vicinity in "Elizabeth," plays the lovestruck Bard with a star-making combination of passion, humor, matinee idol posturing, cockiness and humility. Will knows he's a hell of a writer, especially of romance ("For sixpence a line, I could cause a riot in a nunnery," he brags to his hourglass-watching analyst), but he's nothing without a muse, and lately, none of his old girlfriends amuses him.

That changes, in a flash, when he meets Viola, at first disguised as the androgynous actor Thomas Kent, during auditions for the role of Romeo in the unfinished play. Viola is the daughter of a nobleman and the arranged fiancee of a New World-bound Lord Wessex (Colin Firth), but what she wants—other than to be suffocated by the love of a poet—is to break the glass ceiling at the theater, where tradition dictates that all roles be filled by males.

Whether Viola, even with the help of Will and the other cast members, can pull this off is just one of many points of comic tension in the film. Stoppard and Norman have taken the themes of "Romeo and Juliet" and placed them before the horse, as it were. Will and Viola's balcony scene becomes the balcony scene of Romeo and his renamed lover Juliet. The feud between the Rose and Curtain theaters, from opposite sides of the Thames, feed the feud between the Montagues and Capulets.

Madden, who directed last year's potent "Mrs. Brown," manages the rare feat of blending farce and genuine emotion, and of turning out a sophisticated comedy that will work for everyone.

NEWSWEEK, 12/14/98, p.78, David Ansen

It's a playwright's nightmare. You're trying to write a crowd-pleasing comedy. You've got the title—"Romeo and Ethel, the Pirate's Daughter"—but the words won't fall trippingly from your pen. The moneymen are at your throat, the theater owner won't front you any cash, you're not speaking to your estranged wife back in Stratford and your new girlfriend is sleeping around. What's a Bard to do?

If you're William Shakespeare (Joseph Fiennes), a struggling young scribe in 1593, you need to find yourself a muse. In "Shakespeare In Love," she arrives in the comely form of Lady Viola (Gwyneth Paltrow), a rich, romantic young woman who yearns to be an actor in an age when women are forbidden to take the stage. She is also, unfortunately, betrothed to Lord Wessex (Colin Firth), an avaricious aristocrat. In this smart and giddily entertaining comedy, Viola inspires young Will to rethink that "Romeo and Ethel" notion. His heart aflame for a woman he can never marry, Shakespeare is inspired to pour out verse more fitting for a tragic love story than a low farce. Maybe the name Ethel should be changed to... something else.

"It's a completely irreverent attitude to history," acknowledges Tom Stoppard, who wrote the dazzling screenplay from Marc Norman's original script. While admitting that the movie takes place in a "parallel world" of fictional invention, he feels "in one sense, it's a pretty good guess about what it might have been like to be young Will Shakespeare. People don't change that much. Four hundred years isn't enough to change the essentials of what a young writer is."

The beauty of this extremely clever movie, directed with fleet, robust theatricality by John Madden, is how deftly it manages to work on multiple levels. As a satire of show business, it is of course as much about the movie business in the 1990s (Thames boatmen fobbing off their manuscripts on Shakespeare; producers haggling over credits) as it is about Elizabethan mores. Everyone wants to be an actor: the financier Fennyman (Tom Wilkinson) is transformed into a stage-struck ingenue when he's given a bit part. Everyone's ego must be assuaged. To persuade the vain young star Ned Alleyn (a drolly conceited Ben Affleck) to take a flashy but supporting role in his new play, Will assures him he has the title role: "Mercutio."

"Shakespeare in Love" works equally well as an impassioned love story. Fiennes and Paltrow's lusty affair has a can't-take-their-hands-off-each-other urgency. In a brilliant montage that is the emotional centerpiece of the movie, their amorous couplings are intercut with the rehearsals of the play, and we see the gestation of both a love affair and a literary masterpiece, and how one feeds the other. Viola and Will are writing "Romeo and Juliet!' in the flesh. While in bed, Viola is his Juliet. Onstage Viola, disguised as the boy Thomas Kent, is playing Romeo, while Juliet is played, of course, by a boy. But by the time the play is given its premiere, the cast has changed, and it is the real models for the roles who are playing their proper parts. When we watch the actors perform bits of the finished play, "Shakespeare in Love" enables us to hear it with fresh ears. For all its irreverence, the movie is finally a celebration of the spellbinding power of Shakespearean language.

Paltrow, who seemed so listless in "A Perfect Murder," seems rejuvenated here; she's at her most charming and sensuous. If you've seen "Elizabeth" you will recognize the same ardent, wide-eyed intensity in Fiennes. Here he gets to use it for comic, as well as romantic, effect. There's not much variety in his performance, but he and Paltrow set off palpable sparks. Geoffrey Rush makes an inspired dive into comedy as the ratty and rattled owner of Shakespeare's theater. Judi Dench is the imperious Queen Elizabeth; she cuts a trenchant and commanding figure.

Ten years ago, when Marc Norman first fleshed out an idea (given to him by his son) for a movie about the young Shakespeare, this was going to be an American production with American actors. Edward ("The Siege") Zwick was the original director, and Julia Roberts the Lady Viola. it fell apart when no appropriate Shakespeare could be found, and Roberts lost interest. Miramax then resurrected the script, buying it from Universal for the $4 million the studio had already sunk into the project. Norman explains that once Stoppard transformed the words, it had to become an English production. "It was an elevated text. American actors couldn't handle it." Director Madden, entrusted with a $25 minion budget, knew how to approach the material: "You find your way into it by taking the emotions very, very seriously. Go for the heart of it and let the comedy take care of itself." That it has. For all its wit and complexity, its hall-of-mirror interplay between life and art, "Shakespeare in Love" is as light and nimble as a breeze. In the winter of a discontented movie season, this glorious sleeper makes moviegoing fun again.

SIGHT AND SOUND, 2/99, p. 53, Philip Kemp

London, 1593. Will Shakespeare, an ambitious young playwright, has promised his new play, *Romeo and Ethel the Pirate's Daughter,* to Philip Henslowe, owner of the Rose Theatre on the South Bank. But Will is blocked and the play unstarted. Henslowe is desperate: deep in debt to brutal loan shark Fennyman, he fears Will may be lured away by Richard Burbage at the Curtain Theatre across the river, favoured by Sir Edmund Tilney, Master of the Queen's Revels.

Viola De Lesseps, a rich merchant's daughter betrothed to Lord Wessex, is enchanted by Will's verse. She joins Henslowe's company disguised as a man calling herself Thomas Kent. At the same time, as herself, she embarks on a passionate affair with Will. Inspired by his love, and following hints from fellow-playwright Christopher Marlowe, Will transforms Henslowe's commission into a love story, *Romeo and Juliet* The company is boosted by the arrival of star actor Ned Alleyn. 'Kent' is cast as Romeo.

Tilney, tipped off that a woman has joined Henslowe's troupe, exposes Viola and closes the theatre on grounds of immorality, but Burbage magnanimously offers the Curtain to his rival. Will takes over as Romeo, while Viola resignedly goes through with the marriage to Wessex. But after the ceremony she escapes to the theatre for the premiere, and when the lad playing Juliet gets stage fright she takes over the role. The play is rapturously received but Tilney arrives to close it down again. He is forestalled by the Queen herself, who feigns to believe Viola is a man, while making it clear she must renounce Will and sail to Virginia with Wessex. Will starts writing *Twelfth Night.* Viola's ship is wrecked and, sole survivor, she wanders on a strange shore.

Shakespeare in Love is a hodgepodge—or, as the Elizabethans might more pungently put it, a gallimaufry and an olla podrida (rotten pot). The main plotline—well-born young woman named Viola dresses up as a boy, joins Shakespeare's troupe and has an affair with the playwright—is pinched straight from Simon and Brahms' classic comic novel *No Bed for Bacon* as are some of the gags, such as Will practising multiple variants of his signature at moments of stress. ("*Shakespaw,* he scribbled viciously.") The stagestruck heavy is a blatant lift from Woody Allen's *Bullets over Broadway,* and the scene-setting pays homage to the Monty Python school of scatological reconstruction: Henslowe, striding through the London streets, treads in a heap of dung and is narrowly missed by the contents of a pisspot. We get romance, slapstick, bedroom farce, satire, jocular anachronisms ("I 'ad that Christopher Marlowe in my boat once," observes a chatty ferryman), starcrossed tragedy, a shipwreck, a full-on swashbuckled swordfight and enough sly literary allusions to sink a concordance.

Which is perfectly fine since the heterogeneous mixture, a rich but satisfying plum-pudding, works splendidly, absorbing its borrowings and negotiating its switches of mood with little sense of strain.(There's only one serious lapse, a jarring descent into *Carry-On* inanity when Will puts on a squeaky voice and pretends to be Viola's female cousin.) Besides, style and subject are ideally matched, since we're dealing with the greatest magpie genius of all time. Shakespeare was notoriously disinclined to devise his own plots, preferring to, snaffle them from Plutarch, Holinshed or whatever dog-eared chapbook came to hand; he cared nothing for unity of mood, tossing dirty jokes into high tragedy in a way that gave the Augustans the vapours; and several of his plays *(Richard II,* for example) contain great chunks written by someone else. *Shakespeare in Love* may fall short of his exalted standard, but it's a film after his own heart.

Tom Stoppard, co-scripting, can likely be credited with some literary gags that may bypass the groundlings (a bloodthirsty small boy, given to tormenting mice, gives his name as John Webster, who later wrote the bloody play *The White Devil* and some of the codfustian dialogue: "If you be man to ride her, there are rubies in the saddlebag." But the chief delight of *Shakespeare in Love,* along with its gamy exuberance, is the acting. The chemistry between Gwyneth Paltrow (after *Sliding Doors,* delivering yet another faultless Brit accent) and Joseph Fiennes inspires relief that the original casting (Julia Roberts and Daniel Day-Lewis) fell through. Around them cavort star turns from Imelda Staunton (born to play the nurse), Colin Firth sending up his arrogant Darcyesque image, Ben Affleck (a nostril-flaring Ned Alleyn), Judi Dench having a ball as Queen Bess, the increasingly superb Geoffrey Rush as the harassed Henslowe, and others too numerous to list. And the final triumphant premiere of Shakespeare's first true masterpiece, while edging dangerously near luvvie-ish self-regard, conveys something of what Nabokov called *shamanstvo*—the 'enchanter-quality' of great theatre. As Rush's Henslowe remarks, smiling beatifically as the whole shambles comes magically together, "It's a mystery."

TIME, 12/14/98, p. 99, Richard Corliss

In general, writer's block is a blessing: it has saved readers reams of lousy literature that never got written. But when young Will Shakespeare (Joseph Fiennes) becomes pen-tied, the future of English literature is imperiled. For his new play he has a title—*Romeo and Ethel, the Pirate's Daughter*—but not a clue. This is a man in search of a muse, which fate, in the form of screenwriters Marc Norman and Tom Stoppard, brightly provides. Viola De Lesseps (Gwyneth Paltrow) has it all: beauty, poise, a dowry and a titled suitor. But what she really wants is to act. *Shakespeare in Love* fancifully retells the creation and premiere of *Romeo and Juliet*. It peoples the London of 1593 with the usual suspects—Christopher Marlowe (crafty Rupert Everett), Queen Elizabeth (Judi Dench, a sly dominatrix)—and some ageless show-biz types: the poverty-pleading producer (Geoffrey Rush), the backer with a lust for limelight (Tom Wilkinson). Director John Madden works in jokes about profit sharing and credit hogging, and a climax in which the real star steps in—for an indisposed leading lady.

But the true, rare glamour of the piece is its revival of two precious movie tropes: the flourishing of words for their majesty and fun, and—in the love play between Fiennes and his enchantress—the kindling of a playfully adult eroticism. Let the kids toy with their Rugrats and hold their Sandler high. *Shakespeare in Love* is a movie to please the rest of us, parched for a game of dueling, reeling romance.

VILLAGE VOICE, 12/15/98, p. 146, Amy Taubin

Everything's awhirl in *Shakespeare in Love:* the camera; Gwyneth Paltrow's dresses and tresses; Joseph Fiennes's eyes, which, when they're not darting this way and that, seem to gyrate in their sockets, like spinning tops. At first, the breakneck pace is entertaining (all these people knocking themselves out for our pleasure), but it soon becomes evident just how inane a film this is. *Shakespeare in Love* proposes that Shakespeare was a blocked writer until he found his muse, and that having found her, he wrote most of *Romeo and Juliet* in the sack. All writers should be so lucky. We could call this the pillow-talk theory of literature.

The film finds young Will (Fiennes), an actor and wanna-be playwright, in deep shit. He's accepted an advance for a comedy titled *Romeo and Ethel, the Pirate's Daughter,* but he lacks the inspiration to write so much as a line. Then, he espies Viola De Lesseps (Paltrow), the beauteous daughter of a wealthy merchant, and his pen takes flight. (in lieu of any signs of writerly intelligence in this Will, we are given many close-ups of his ink-stained fingers.) Viola is mad about the theater, and, despite the fact that women were not allowed to tread the boards of the Elizabethan stage, she auditions (in drag) for the part of Romeo in the still nonexistent play. Captivated by her talent, Will follows her home and discovers her true identity. (Her perky breasts are most convincing.) Soon they're fucking and the iambic pentameter is flowing back and forth between them.

One of the film's genuinely witty observations has to do with Shakespeare's ability to capitalize on other people's ideas. Thus, Christopher Marlowe, London's reigning playwright, gives Will the premise for *Romeo and Juliet,* and Viola, her tongue loosened by the loss of her virginity, offers up the raw material for the play.

There is, however, no wit in having Will write the play as an idealized reflection of his and Viola's forbidden affair. It's as if Will, having discovered that Viola's father won't let her out of the house, languishes alone in Moomba all night writing the potion scene. Which, I'm sure, is exactly the kind of self-aggrandizing image that director John Madden and his gaggle of Miramax overseers (Harvey Weinstein has claimed that this is his Academy Award picture) want to suggest to their target audience. You too can be Shakespeare (or Shakespeare's muse) if you heedlessly hurl yourself into a love affair that can't possibly last more than three weeks and maintain your cynicism about it at the same time.

Unlike Romeo and Juliet, Will and Viola would never give up their ambitions, let alone their lives, for love. Will caddishly forgets to tell Viola that he has a wife and kids squirreled away in Stratford. And as for Viola she offers remarkably little resistance to being married off to a bore with a title. These are not altogether admirable characters. Which would be pretty interesting if the film didn't work at cross-purposes to try to convince us that they are pure magic.

Thus, Paltrow, who once upon a time (in *Seven* and *Flesh and Bone*) seemed such a promising actor, plays every scene as if she's sprinkling fairy dust on her own head. Paltrow has a nice voice but, with no technique for shaping a line of verse, not to mention a character, she relies mostly on heavy breathing to rev up her own feelings. Still, it's impossible not to feel pity for her. With *Shakespeare in Love* opening just weeks after *Elizabeth,* she's in the unenviable position of arriving late at the party and discovering that she's wearing the same dress and hairdo as the new girl of the year. Cate Blanchett, who's so extraordinary as Elizabeth, has an advantage in that she was given a richer script to work with. But she also has a daring that Paltrow lacks. Blanchett is more intent in revealing a character, however abrasive that character can be, than in charming an audience.

Fiennes is not much better here than Paltrow. He has technique, but not much going on underneath. Maybe it's that he doesn't have the kind of features that the camera takes seriously. With his pouty mouth, cupid nose, and the eyes of a spaniel on speed, Fiennes is more calendar boy than leading man. In *Elizabeth,* his shallowness suited the dynamic of the film. Elizabeth could eat her Lord Dudley for breakfast, and, metaphorically speaking, that's just what she did.

With the exception of Judi Dench, whose no-nonsense Queen Elizabeth is an implicit put-down of the youngsters' hyperactivity, most of the supporting cast is as undistinguished as the two leads. Playing Ned Alleyn, the most celebrated actor of his time, Ben Affleck glows as if his skin has just been put through an aluminum-oxide vacuum treatment at Bliss and his hair looks as if it is manicured daily, strand by strand. Affleck doesn't have much to do except hang around looking fatuous and belligerent, but he's very funny doing just that-as long as he keeps his mouth shut.

The script of *Shakespeare in Love* was written by Marc Norman and Tom Stoppard, and you can bet that Stoppard is responsible for the clever Elizabethan in-jokes that let anyone who took one of those Shakespeare-and-his-world courses feel really smart. Among the best conceits is portraying the Jacobean playwright John Webster (author of such bloodbaths as *The Duchess of Malfi*) as a homeless 13-year-old who hangs around the theater because he loves the violence. Showing his talent for revenge at an early age, Webster gets back at Will for not casting him as Juliet by disclosing the truth about Viola's sex. "I saw her boobies," he yells. So did we all, dear, so did we all.

Also reviewed in:
CHICAGO TRIBUNE, 12/25/98, Friday/p. A, Michael Wilmington
NATION, 2/22/99, p. 34, Stuart Klawans
NEW REPUBLIC, 1/4 & 11/99, p. 26, Stanley Kauffmann
NEW YORK TIMES, 12/11/98, p. E16, Janet Maslin
NEW YORKER, 12/21/98, p. 113, David Denby
VARIETY, 12/7-13/98, p. 53, Lael Loewenstein
WASHINGTON POST, 12/25/98, p. C1, Stephen Hunter
WASHINGTON POST, 12/25/98, Weekend/p. 7, Michael O'Sullivan

SHAMPOO HORNS

An Alta Films release of an Elias Querejeta and Esicma production. *Producer:* Elias Querejeta. *Director:* Manuel Toledano. *Screenplay:* Manuel Toledano. *Director of Photography:* Alfredo Mayo. *Editor:* Nacho Ruiz Capillas. *Music:* Angel Illarramendi. *Sound:* Dave Powers. *Art Director:* Jeffrey Rathaus. *Costumes:* Martha Gretsch. *Running time:* 100 minutes. *MPAA Rating:* Not Rated.

CAST: Jason Reeves (Dennis); Tiffany Shepis (Amy); Jason Anthon (Mark); Cheyenne Besch (Herself); Tim Duperron (Tim Twin); Robert Sorce (Robert Twin); Brie Koyanagi (Herself);

Sophia Lamar (Herself);   James St. James (Himself);   Jonathan Lawrence (Himself);   Andrew Gallupi (Tony);   Michael Alig (Himself);   Richie Rich (Himself).

NEW YORK POST, 3/6/98, p. 66, Bill Hoffmann

It's rare that a movie stars a convicted killer, so "Shampoo Horns" arrives today at the Quad with instant notoriety. It features Michael Alig, now doing 20 years for offing a drug pusher and chopping his body to bits.

Alig and a dozen other losers—real-life "club kids" whose pathetic lives center on mindless partying in Manhattan's nightclubs—star in this semi-fictional movie about themselves.

Since it was filmed at Peter Gatien's now-shut Limelight and produced by Gatien's daughter, Jennifer, you'd think the film would be an obnoxious love letter to this sick little subculture.

But "Shampoo Horns" takes a surprisingly downbeat view of the decadent scene, giving it an unexpected poignancy. Its a cautionary, shaggy-dog tale about the pitfalls of too many drugs and too little ambition. Sadly, the club kids themselves, being so egocentric and clueless, will probably love every minute of it.

VILLAGE VOICE, 3/10/98, p. 66, Dennis Lim

Set during the club-kid heyday and starring real-life club denizens (including Michael Alig as himself), Manuel Toledano's *Shampoo Horns* is a stilted first effort that randomly shuffles three doom-laden stories. A maudlin, terminally ill drag queen retires to a hotel room to expire; two fresh-faced college kids venture into the Limelight ("Whatever you do, don't do K," one warns the other); a semi-comatose druggie fantasizes about a fireman. Bad things happen, for which the survivors are that much stronger, or something. Part clubland valentine complicated by hindsight, part ominous morality fable, the film isn't convincing as either.

Also reviewed in:
NEW YORK TIMES, 3/6/98, p. E32, Stephen Holden
VARIETY, 4/21-27/97, p. 66, Deborah Young

SHATTERED IMAGE

A Lions Gate Films release of a Peter Hoffman presentation of a Seven Arts/Schroeder Hoffman production in association with Fireworks Entertainment. *Executive Producer:* Jack Baran, Jay Firestone, Bastiaan Gleben and James Michael Vernon. *Producer:* Peter Hoffman, Barbet Schroeder, Susan Hoffman, and Lloyd Silverman. *Director:* Raul Ruiz. *Screenplay:* Duane Poole. *Director of Photography:* Robby Muller. *Editor:* Michael Duthie. *Music:* Jorge Arriagada. *Production Designer:* Robert De Vico. *Costumes:* Francine LeCoultre. *Running time:* 103 minutes. *MPAA Rating:* Not Rated.

CAST: Anne Parillaud (Jessie);   Wiliam Baldwin (Brian);   Lisanne Falk (Paula Laura);   Graham Greene (Conrad/Mike);   Billy Wilmott (Lamond);   O'Neil Peart (Simon);   Leonie Forbes (Isabel);   Bulle Ogier (Mrs. Ford).

LOS ANGELES TIMES, 12/4/98, Calendar/p. 8, Kevin Thomas

"Shattered Image" is yet another of Raul Ruiz's endlessly convoluted psychological mysteries, not as richly bravura and daring as his recent "Genealogies of a Crime" but more romantic. It stars a perfectly teamed Anne Parillaud and William Baldwin, and it is a film of shimmering elegance that works smashingly well on an almost surreal visual level. It marks an assured English-language debut for Ruiz, a Chilean emigre, long based in Paris and now a French citizen.

Written adroitly by Duane Poole, "Shattered Image" has one of those stories about which it is all but impossible to say anything with any degree of certainty. It does seem clear that Parillaud's Jessie and Baldwin's Brian are an exceptionally attractive Seattle couple honeymooning at a posh

Jamaican resort and that Jessie is deeply disturbed. She apparently has endured a rape and its trauma has been compounded by the death of her wealthy father. She has vivid dreams in which she sees herself as an ultra-cool hired assassin—and her latest assignment is to knock off none other than Brian or a man who is his twin. As for Brian, is he the solicitous husband he seems to be? Or is it the cold-blooded assassin who is real, and Jessie but a figment of her dreams?

Ruiz piles on such questions to such dizzying heights that his picture begins to boggle the mind, like looking too long at a labyrinthine M.C. Escher drawing. It's best to let the film simply wash over you because trying to sort everything out invites a certain tedium. However, it's worth going along with Ruiz because his payoff is so stunning that you realize that as usual he's carefully building toward it every step of the way. Ruiz verges on pure cinema, relying on the camera rather than dialogue to reveal character, tell the story and express his preoccupation with the duality of human nature.

"Shattered Image" is the kind of stylish guessing game in which actors sometimes don't get the credit they deserve in helping make it work. Parillaud, who can always seem a darkly beautiful enigma, deftly moves between the unstable Jessie and the vision of herself in her dreams, a lethal dame as cold-blooded as the actress' memorable "La Femme Nikita." Baldwin similarly changes personalities with equal effortlessness. Among the supporting players is Bulle Ogier as Jessie's chic, trusting mother.

This Seven Arts production is beautifully designed and scored, and has the glow typical of the work of its master cinematographer Robby Muller. "Shattered Image," despite Baldwin's presence and its suspense genre, is no mainstream movie but an art film that demands of the audience not only to make connections for itself but to do so with what it sees rather than what it hears.

NEW YORK POST, 12/4/98, p. 57, Thelma Adams

"LA Femme Nikita" star Anne Parillaud is the Andie MacDowell of France.

Like MacDowell, the gorgeous French mannequin occasionally rises above her very modest acting talents. But her dual turn as a man-hating assassin and a suicidal honeymooner in Raul Ruiz's "Shattered Image" is not one of those roles.

Parillaud plays two Jessies. One is a spiky Seattle brunette whose response to a brutal rape is the aggressive slaughter of males for money. The other is a fragile Manhattan newlywed torn between fear of a mysterious stalker and love for her husband (the unintentionally funny William Baldwin).

Killer Jessie falls asleep after a hard day of capping strangers and awakens into the life of newlywed Jessie. The honeymooner has rough sex with her new hubby while tropical fish look on, then falls asleep; she dreams of being a sleepless killer in Seattle who straddles an anonymous lover (also Baldwin) in a public aquarium.

Is one woman dreaming the other? Is that naughty Baldwin really a murderous rapist?

Oh, "Twilight Zone," what is reality and what is reflection, what is dream and what is nightmare? Are men scum? Do women come in two flavors: victim or man-eater?

Director Ruiz, known for stylish, labyrinthine art films that occasionally make their way into the New York Film Festival, shoots for a more mainstream thriller but misses the target. Or, as Baldwin's honeymooner tells his wife, "It was all just a bad dream."

NEWSDAY, 12/4/98, Part II/p. B7, John Anderson

Consider it a tribute to Luis Bunuel, a symbol of dada-ist victory, that Raul Ruiz' "Shattered Image" seems so flatly predictable and obvious. The anarchic puncturing of artistic convention has become a virtual commonplace of contemporary cinema, after all. And when bourgeoisie-baiting surrealism is the coin of the realm, how insurgent can the surrealist be?

It's a bit sad and a bit irritating, because Ruiz—the Chilean exile, Paris-based filmmaker whose prolific output includes the recent "Genealogies of a Crime" and "Three Lives and Only One Death"—has been recognized for years as one of the world's smarter directors. Even in "Shattered Image," his first English-language film, he shows how deftly he can sabotage expectations and maneuver down the rutted road to Duchampian nirvana. Problem is, it's the same old rutted road.

Fashioning what is only a near-parody of the doppelganger drama—an elastic subgenre that includes "Vertigo" and "The Double Life of Veronique"—Ruiz employs a carload of arch dialogue, fatalistic rainstorms and a heroine who's half hit-woman, half heiress. French actress Anne Parillaud, in a self-referential reprise of her "La Femme Nikita," plays Jessie, a black-wigged vamp in a Seattle bar who responds to a pickup attempt by shooting the hapless Lothario dead in the men's room. The woman has issues. Cut to the Caribbean, where nice mild Jessie is on her honeymoon with a husband (an appropriately oily William Baldwin) who may or may not be after her money. The scars on her wrist signify—what? And what about Dream Jessie? Or, rather, who is Dream Jessie?

Ruiz cuts back and forth between Jessies, but it's Hit-woman Jessie who discusses Bridal Jessie in rational terms, as a dream, examining her motivations and past—such as the rape that haunts her—and which we get in kaleidoscopic fragments. Ruiz intentionally ties his story line in knots, introducing the same actors as multiple characters, playing with the mystery form as a child plays with a lump of clay. One wants to credit the film's whiplash-inducing camera work (by the estimable Robby Muller) and its raft of red herrings to Ruiz' desire to deflate; to laugh at the jungle birds screaming during the sex scenes and the mysterious, never-unexplained Asian man who lurks in the background; to chuckle at the exchanges that hang like swollen mangoes ("Pave paradise; put up a parking lot," Jessie mutters, when hubby talks of island development). And finally, to find a transcending motive among the pulp. But everything in "Shattered Image" is done to death, from the love triangle involving Paula/Laura (Lisanne Falk), to the ominous islanders, to Parillaud's pouty bride-meets-soulless killer. And what's missing is a payoff. Hollywood parodies itself weekly; the all-too-recent "Sliding Doors" was enough of a spoof of the entire subgenre (sans gunfire). Bunuel's revolution was victorious, but Ruiz keeps waging the same campaign.

VILLAGE VOICE, 12/8/98, p. 129, J. Hoberman

Raul Ruiz is said to have directed a hundred films but *Shattered Image* is only the third one to be made in English. This is hardly the madly prolific, go-for-baroque Chilean exile's greatest movie, but it's one destined for a large (and largely unsuspecting) viewership; part of the movie's pleasure is imagining an entire multiplex audience looking around at each other and wondering, "What the fuck?"

Shattered Image begins as a sort of belated sequel to the French punk actioner *La Femme Nikita*. A glamorous assassin named Jessie (the now somewhat haggard Anne Parillaud) whacks a business dude in the men's room of a fashionable Seattle bistro, then goes home to sleep it off—dreaming that she is a timorous newlywed Jessie en route to Jamaica with her solicitous husband Brian (William Baldwin) and somewhat nervous because it seems that she's been having this serial dream that she's some kind of ruthlessly hard-boiled hit chick living in Seattle.

There you have it: Parallel action; parallel lives, particularly as "Seattle Jessie" soon meets her very own equally attentive Brian. Each Jessie has the other Jessie as her nocturnal alter ego and both dreams are presented in installment cliff-hangers, sometimes literally. Repressed "Jamaica Jessie" dreams of having anonymous sex in public places, while man-hating Seattle Jessie dreams of being thrillingly rescued in a romantic location by her new husband.

Shattered Image is an enjoyably cheap and mildly lurid thriller that might have been scripted in an afternoon by Alain Robbe-Grillet, solicited with cash and the promise of a long weekend in Runaway Bay. (In fact, the movie is the first to be written by Duane Poole, whose copious TV credits include producing *The Love Boat*.) The movie is beautifully shot by Robby Müller but there's an intentionally schlocky aspect to the production that suggests a second-generation *To Catch a Thief* rip-off; it has the spirit, if not the style, of the Mexican potboilers that Luis Buñuel used to subvert in the 1950s.

Given this almost normal facade, *Shattered Image* thrives even more than most Ruiz films on peculiar touches and baffling behavior. The two stars struggle through their dialogue as though dubbed into English (particularly Baldwin) and Ruiz further ups the entertainment quotient with his trademark off-kilter compositions. Suave rac-focus shots allow the schizo heroine to ponder her reflection on a razor blade even as the kitschy mise-en-scène keeps changing the painting in her hotel room.

With the revelation that each Jessie has suffered a traumatic rape, the dreams begin getting mixed up. Seattle Jessie seems to fall in love while Jamaica Jessie shows an unexpected flair for self-protective mayhem. In one dream, some guy's trying to kill her; in the other, she has to kill him. But don't expect a resolution to this Möbius striptease. Rather than build toward the usual Ruiz bloodbath, *Shattered Image* chases its tail to come full circle.

Also reviewed in:
NEW YORK TIMES, 12/4/98, p. E9, Stephen Holden
VARIETY, 9/28-10/4/98, p. 56, Godfrey Cheshire

SHOOTING FISH

A Fox Searchlight Pictures release of a Gruber Brothers production in association with Winchester Multimedia, the Arts Council of England and Tomboy Films. *Executive Producer:* Gary Smith. *Producer:* Richard Holmes and Glynis Murray. *Director:* Stefan Schwartz. *Screenplay:* Stefan Schwartz and Richard Holmes. *Director of Photography:* Henry Braham. *Editor:* Alan Strachan. *Music:* Stanislas Syrewicz. *Sound:* Simon Clark and (music) Rafal Paczkowski. *Sound Editor:* Stefan Henrix. *Casting:* Sarah Beardsall and Dianne Crittenden. *Production Designer:* Max Gottlieb. *Art Director:* Sue Ferguson. *Costumes:* Stewart Meachem. *Make-up:* Susie Adams and Luisa Abel. *Stunt Coordinator:* Clive Curtis and Wayne Michaels. *Running time:* 90 minutes. *MPAA Rating:* PG.

CAST: Dan Futterman (Dylan); Stuart Townsend (Jez); Kate Beckinsale (Georgie); Nickolas Grace (Mr. Stratton-Luce); Claire Cox (Floss); Ralph Ineson (Mr. Ray); Dominic Mafham (Roger); Peter Capaldi (Mr. Gilzean); Annette Crosbie (Mrs. Cummins); Jane Lapotaire (Dylan's Headmistress); Phyllis Logan (Mrs. Ross); Rowena Cooper (Jez's teacher); Scott Charles (Samuel, Aged 8); Antonia Corrigan (Antonia, Aged 8); Myles Anderson (Jez, Aged 8); Harry Ditson (IRS man); Jacob Macoby (Dylan, Aged 8); Tom Chadbon (Mr. Greenaway); Vicki Bensted (Bank Clerk); Peter McNamara (Geoff); Nicola Duffett (Mrs. (Ray); Larry Randall and Neil Peplow (Golfers); Arabella Weir (Mrs. Stratton-Luce); Alan Cooke (Car Park Attendant); Andrée Evans (Mrs. Furnival-Jones); Ralph Watson and Harry Gostelow (Vigilantes); Wolf Christian (Mr. Thor); Louis Schwartz (Bandaged Baby); Alan Sollinger (Gasometer Foreman); Cosmo Scurr (Boy with Tennis Ball); Paul Kynman (Chauffeur); Phillip York (Detective); Nicholas Woodeson (Mr. Collyns); Louis Mahoney (Magistrate); John Clegg (Church Vicar); Darren Renouf (Robin); Emily Braham (Bridesmaid); Phil Evans and Otto Jarman (Prison Guards); Adam Fogerty (Bruiser); David Glover (Prison Governor); Catherine Russell (Crematorium Cleaning Lady); Ronald Markham (Crematorium Vicar); Dickie Graydon (Racehorse Trainer); Tim Stern (Panfield); Paul Williamson (Weighing-in Official); Peter O'Sullevan (Race Commentator); Geoffrey Whitehed (1st Owner); Linda Spurier (The Hon. Mrs. Wescot); Ahmed Khalil (Prince Ahmed); Barry Woolgar (Friend of Lady Georgina).

LOS ANGELES TIMES, 5/1/98, Calendar/p. 18, Kevin Thomas

"Shooting Fish," not as inspired or amusing as it might be, leans heavily on the considerable charm of its three young and attractive principals. Their charisma and the film's larky spirit, English locales and elaborate cons might be just enough to divert easily satisfied date-night audiences.

Even so, "Shooting Fish" is an awful lot like lots of other pictures with an overly complicated and improbable plot that you try to follow at your peril. With "Shooting Fish" it's definitely best to sit back and go with its flow.

Dylan (Dan Futterman), an alumnus of the American Friendly Home for Boys, and Jez (Stuart Townsend), who survived an English institution, the Our Lady of Suffering Orphanage, meet in London, where Dylan has fled the U.S. from one of his backfired get-rich-quick schemes.

Dylan is the fearless, fast-talking kind of guy who wouldn't hesitate to try to sell you the Brooklyn Bridge while the shy Jez is an electronics whiz.

When the two join talents in trying to con business types into investing in their dazzlingly innovative computer prototype they hire as a temp typist the lovely Georgie (Kate Beckinsale), a med student in need of some quick cash.

It doesn't take much for Georgie to realize she's signed on with a pair of con men, as daring as they are reckless.

Yet she's beguiled by these nice-looking guys, especially when Dylan lays on his Robin Hood-of-the-'90s rationale: Why he and Jez are merely stealing from the rich to benefit poor orphans. Naturally, both fellows are smitten with Georgie, with Jez developing deep feelings that he's awkward in expressing.

Even if "Shooting Fish" packs nothing like the belly laughs of the deliciously outrageous "Dirty Rotten Scoundrels" (1988), it does reflect director and co-writer Stefan Schwartz's concern for telling details and his ability to make his three stars shine brightly.

Best known as Robin Williams' son in "The Birdcage" and impressive star of the upcoming "1999," Futterman is certainly adept at playing smart, sarcastic men, and Beckinsale, so funny as the unflappable heroine of John Schlesinger's "Cold Comfort Farm," just glows as an aristocrat facing disaster with considerable aplomb. Townsend's Jez has a sweetness that contrasts well with Dylan's brashness.

"Shooting Fish," which has as its production design set-piece a vast, elaborate pad that Dylan and Jez have created within a huge oil storage tank, is smart enough to move fast and to keep its spirits up but, at almost two hours, it overstays its welcome.

That's something Dylan would never do.

NEW YORK POST, 5/1/98, p. 62, Bill Hoffmann

"Shooting Fish" tries desperately to be funny. But it's plain desperate. This forced British farce has been hyped as the worthy successor to "The Full Monty." But the latter has more laughs in a single minute than "Shooting Fish" musters up in its entire, labored running time.

The ridiculous plot involves two twenty-something con men racing around London, ripping off the rich and powerful in a plodding series of unconvincing schemes. They live in a penthouse atop an oil tank (yeah, right!) and for no apparent reason like singing "Do You know the Way to San Jose?"

The lead character Dylan (American actor Dan Futterman) is so smirky and obnoxious, he sinks what small chance the film has of being likable. Stuart Townsend and Kate Beckinsale, both good actors, are wasted.

"Shooting Fish" is like day-old seafood—it stinks.

NEWSDAY, 5/1/98, Part II/p. B7, John Anderson

Fictitious criminals need something sociological, pathological or simply illogical to justify their actions, otherwise they can only be so clever. After all, if they can outsmart the rest of the world, why do it illegally?

So you ask yourself during "Shooting Fish," an occasionally charming, occasionally overbearing comedy, why two charming-if-overbearing geniuses like Dylan (Dan Futterman) and Jez (Stuart Townsend) ever felt they had to scam their way to success to begin with. Yes, they were both orphans—Dylan grew up in the American Friendly Home for Boys, Jez in Our Lady of Suffering Orphanage. Both showed early promise: Dylan as an embezzler, Jez as a mini-Edison capable of wiring, rewiring and hotwiring just about anything.

And even at that young age, theirs was a shared dream, a transatlantic dream, the American dream: home ownership. And not just any home but the stateliest of stately homes. A home with a sprawl. An epic house.

In other words, 47 rooms of their own.

To call "Shooting Fish" a situation comedy would be unfair, but there are lots of situations: a phony insulation scheme that turns a middle-class community into a lynch mob; innumerable free giveaways and phone scams, and a phony talking computer presentation that bilks many owners of businesses (which they must have inherited) out of many thousands of pounds.

It's at this last masquerade that they meet Georgie (Kate Beckinsale), a strikingly beautiful medical student moonlighting as a secretary (this becomes even more unlikely later) who is sharp enough to pull their chestnuts out of the fire but dim enough to believe that the money they're scamming is for poor orphans (the poor orphans being Dylan and Jez). When she later cries, "You lied to me," there's only one suitable response.

Fast-paced and jammed with small escapades, "Shooting Fish" defies synopsis, crumbles under scrutiny, but is entertaining enough that you won't feel like one of Dylan and Jez' victims. There does seem to be one gaping plot hole involving Georgie, her fiance, a charitable foundation and a house (maybe that's four holes), which only gets cleared up at the end of the movie. Of course, one of the keys to a successful con job is sliding by the details.

SIGHT AND SOUND, 10/97, p. 57, Ben Thompson

In a London suburb, two resourceful young men live together in a converted gasometer. Though very different in character—Dylan is a smooth-talking American. Jez a shy British electronics expert—they are bound together by the common dream of some day owning their own stately home. They pursue this goal by entering competitions, managing their household frugally and conning the rich and greedy.

In the course of an elaborate computer scam they meet Georgie, a medical student who temps in offices for extra money. Although she quickly ascertains what the boys are up to, she helps them out of a difficult situation when they say the money is for charity. Later, a loft insulation fraud and a revenge raid on the home of a hoodlum who stole their car both almost end in disaster. However, Jez and Dylan are arrested while trying to pick up a cheque for a bogus invention from Mr Stratton-Luce, who happened to be a victim of the earlier loft insulation scam.

By the time they are sentenced to a three-month jail sentence, the two adventurers have accumulated the £2 million necessary to buy their stately home and Jez has fallen in love with Georgie. Unfortunately, she is about to marry the charmless but wealthy Roger who has convinced her that if she doesn't, her brother, who has Down's syndrome, will be ejected from the residential home now run in her family's ancestral mansion. Worse still, Dylan and Jez learn that the £40,000 they have in £50 banknotes will cease to be legal tender (because the note is being withdrawn) on the day before they are freed from jail.

Georgie's sister Floss explains that Roger has been lying to Georgie. She rushes to the prison, but Jez admits the money was not intended for the good of others. In reprisal, she cons them out of their hoard, hoping to buy the home with it, but Roger is determined to close it down anyway. Georgie buys his favourite racehorse, only to find it is a hopeless loser. Happily, Jez's ingenuity helps the horse to win an important race, and Roger is forced to buy it back at an inflated price. The home is saved. Jez marries Georgie and Floss marries Dylan in a lavish double wedding.

The parameters of what might make a successful British film have broadened greatly since 1993, when director/producer team Stefan Schwartz and Richard Holmes' heroically inconsequential debut *Soft Top Hard Shoulder* won a brace of Scottish BAFTA awards. As if responding to the new possibilities opened up by *Trainspotting* and *Four Weddings and a Funeral*, Schwartz and Holmes have pitched their belated follow-up into the inviting middle ground between the two: blending the pop-driven vitality of the first with and the second's total absence of social or historical context to create what is clearly intended to be—and sometimes is—a jaunty piece of escapist fluff.

The basic story of Dylan and Jez (two orphaned buddies who yearn for country-house living) and their feisty accomplice Georgie has a timeless quality about it, reminiscent of Enid Blyton. There's no reason for every big-screen story to be tied to the rotting jetty of social and economic verisimilitude, but the consequences of floating free can be perilous. While the carefree tone of *Shooting Fish*'s early stages is enjoyable and even refreshing—the camera angles are rakish while the computing, insulation and invention scams are imaginative and deftly handled—the film's later descent into Children's Film Foundation plotting and bizarrely outdated fantasies of *noblesse oblige* are annoying.

For example, why do the film-makers feel it is necessary for Kate Beckinsale's demonically perky Georgie to be a member of the gentry, a temp and a medical student in order for her to truly engage our affections? With so many contemporary excitements on offer in the film, including a soundtrack of chirpy Britpop by the likes of Space and The Supernaturals, falling back on such old-fashioned snobbery is a bit of a let-down. But this irritation is nothing compared to the handling of Georgie's Down's syndrome brother, which feels like little more than a cynical upping of the disablement ante against the deaf character deployed in *Four Weddings and a Funeral*.

Shooting Fish's closing scenes, wherein the lady of the manor and her sister are united with their blushing swains under the benevolent eye of grateful servants and inmates, are mawkish, and the undoubted virtues of much of what has gone before make this scene doubly painful. Yet the design, especially the gasometer interiors, is natty and not unimaginative; the screenplay has some neat one-liners ("we give but we don't like to talk about it, we're very much like Phil Collins in that respect," Dylan says of his and Jez's charitable plans for the money); and the performances of Dan Futterman, Stuart Townsend and Kate Beckinsale are perfectly personable.

But if the film is still a disappointment, its production background sheds useful light as to why. Initially ham-strung by investors' mysterious unwillingness to put money, in Holmes' words, "into something that didn't have some kind of import", *Shooting Fish*'s finance deficit was finally made good by a grant from the Arts Council's lottery fund. For all its producer's insistence that this project was "agenda-free", its supposed lack of an agenda actually constitutes an Agenda with a capital A. It would be stretching a point to say that this film's wilful refusal to engage with any kind of reality exemplifies its makers' generation's retreat into a premature second childhood, but not by much.

Also reviewed in:
NEW YORK TIMES, 5/1/98, p. E30, Stephen Holden
VARIETY, 9/1-7/97, p. 78, Derek Elley

SHOPPING FOR FANGS

A Margin Films release. *Producer:* Quentin Lee. *Director:* Quentin Lee and Justin Lin. *Screenplay:* Dan Alvarado, Quentin Lee, and Justin Lin. *Director of Photography:* Lisa Wiegand. *Editor:* Quentin Lee, Justin Lin, Sean Yeo. *Music:* Steven Pranato. *Sound:* Jeffrey Liu. *Casting:* Josh Diamond. *Art Director:* Deeya Loram. *Running time:* 90 minutes. *MPAA Rating:* R.

CAST: Radmar Jao (Phil); Jeanne Chin (Katherine); Clint Jung (Jim); Lela Lee (Naomi); John Cho (Clarance); Peggy Ahn (Grace); Scott Eberlein (Matt); Daniel Twyman (Dr. Suleri); Jennifer Hengstenberg (Sammi); Dana Pan (May); Roxanne Coyne (Dr. Hali).

LOS ANGELES TIMES, 5/8/98, Calendar/p. 8, Kevin Thomas

Quentin Lee and Justin Lin's droll "Shopping for Fangs," a jaunty dark comedy with serious undertones, may well be a first: an independently made Asian American Gen-X movie that actually gets booked into selected theaters in Los Angeles and Orange counties. (There are plenty more on hold.)

UCLA film school alums Lee and Lin take us into the bustling, prosperous everyday existence of heavily Asian American San Gabriel Valley to acquaint us with two young people for whom everything is far from all right. Radmar Jao's Phil is a pleasant-looking clerk in an accounting firm whose yearning for love seems to be turning him into a werewolf. Meanwhile, Jeanne Chin's beautiful Katherine would seem to have everything: a spectacular-looking husband (Clint Jung), who is absolutely devoted to her, and a spacious, beautifully decorated home.

Yet Katherine, a hesitant woman who speaks barely above a whisper, seems to be coming apart. That her husband Jim is Phil's boss is coincidental, for these two increasingly desperate people are apparently unacquainted.

Lee and Lin suggest in their well-populated picture that on the surface Gener-Asian-Xers are just as trendy and no different from other young people. This in fact may be true for many, but for some there can be hugely conflicting questions of identity, culture and role-playing. We don't know why poor Phil should feel he's vulnerable to lycanthropy, but he clearly has lots of suppressed rage.

With Katherine things are clearer: In therapy, she is confronted with a horrendously traumatic event that occurred in her childhood, which seems to fuel her inability to integrate the traditional role an Asian wife is supposed to play with her need to be a far more assertive, independent woman.

Meanwhile, there are a number of other people in Katherine and Phil's lives whom we come to know and like. Phil has an endearingly busybody sister (Lela Lee), whose writer boyfriend has written a book about, yes, werewolves. Then there's the good-looking gay photographer (John Cho), who hangs out (a lot) at a coffee shop because he's struck up an acquaintance with a glamorous, hard-edged lesbian waitress who, for all her take-no-nonsense style, nonetheless hides behind dark glasses ("I was born with them," she says) and a blond wig.

Laden—but not overloaded—with hip references to other pictures, "Shopping for Fangs" is very much a first feature, one that could have used more clarity and some more polish around the edges. But its cast is fresh and engaging, it manages quite well the tricky business of being funny and serious at the same time and it succeeds in its makers' stated goal of projecting a postmodern Asian American sensibility that's moved beyond the immigrant experience that is the traditional heart of the Asian American cinema.

NEW YORK POST, 5/15/98, p. 58, Larry Worth

Most men complain about losing their hair. Phil has more than he needs, to the point that he's turning into a werewolf.

That's the gist of "Shopping for Fangs," a new age comedy-thriller that's neither comic nor thrilling. It's main claim to fame is an all Asian-American cast and crew, none of whom distinguish themselves amid the nonstop nonsense.

The convoluted scenario features three separate stories, with characters from each constantly crisscrossing. Accordingly, the tale of a lesbian waitress who's stalking one of her customers ties in with that of a housewife suffering from blackouts, who ties in with the overly hirsute hero.

But they're all played so broadly that none of their fates matters. In addition, one plot point that's meant to be a shocking revelation has been obvious from the get-go.

In fairness, the cast of unknowns tries hard, and even gets off an occasional funny line. But co-directors Quentin Lee and Justin Lin make a less than cohesive whole, while the lycanthropic effects appear to be the stuff of joke-shop mustaches and Elmer's glue.

Werewolf doings aside, that's why "Shopping for Fangs" is truly monstrous.

NEWSDAY, 5/18/98, Part II/p. B7, John Anderson

Directors Quentin Lee and Justin Lin are trying a little too hard with their pidgin-Hong Kong camera work and L.A. attitude, but they've certainly created something in "Shopping for Fangs" that's sui generis: The best Asian-American feminist lesbian werewolf movie you're likely to see this year.

Yeah, they're moonstruck, but there's a method to their madness. In their ultra-hipness and off-kilter comedic sensibility, what they're after is both the making of an Asian-centric movie, and the demolishing of stereotype, both inflicted and self-imposed.

Katherine (Jeanne Chin), is the geisha-delicate housewife who is id-deep in disaffection with marriage and domesticity. Her husband, Jim (Clint Jung), is a muscle man who's probably unfaithful. He's also boss to Phil (Radmar Jao), who gets excited when Grace (Peggy Ahn) shows interest. But she only wants to get him into her Bible-study group. Phil reacts by growing a lot of hair very quickly and getting a little, uh, aggressive. Katherine, meanwhile, has lost her wallet and starts getting strange letters and photos from Trinh, a lesbian waitress in a blond wig and sunglasses.

Their stories eventually interconnect, but the dramatic payoff is a lot weaker than the message about assimilation and control. Phil's lycanthropic manifestations aren't just about sex, they're about his suffocating existence at work; similarly Katherine, who's leading a parallel existence she doesn't even know about. Being good, in other words, has its drawbacks.

The actors are uniformly good, the directors are in over their heads, but "Shopping for Fangs" (fangs, apparently, a symbol of finding one's nature) has noble intentions, knows where it wants to go and occasionally gets there.

VILLAGE VOICE, 5/12/98, p. 123, Amy Taubin

Smart, lively, and agreeably modest, Quentin Lee and Justin Lin's *Shopping for Fangs* is a tenderhearted social satire about Asian and Asian American Gen X-ers in the throes of various identity crises. Phil (Radmar Jao), an accounting clerk, starts sprouting a full beard every hour and develops an inexplicable craving for raw meat. Though his doctor's diagnosis is testosterone buildup, he fears he's becoming a werewolf Similarly, Katherine (Jeanne Chin), who's trapped in a boring marriage with a bourgie muscle-man, starts having 24-hour blackouts. Her cell phone, pager, and wallet are in the possession of a mysterious waitress whose blond wig and sunglasses are an obvious disguise. But for what?

Lee and Lin, who cowrote and codirected, handle the horror film metaphors with a humor that verges on slapstick but never gets out of control. The actors have ease and presence (Jao, in particular, is a find). Shot mostly in the San Gabriel Valley (L.A.'s Asian American 'burb), *Shopping for Fangs* has an edgy sense of place. Forget sushi bars. At the Go-Go Cafe, you can nurse a tapioca milk tea or chow down on spaghetti.

Also reviewed in:
NEW YORK TIMES, 5/15/98, p. E23, Anita Gates
VARIETY, 3/24-30/97, p. 35, Derek Elley

SIEGE, THE

A Twentieth Century Fox release of a Lynda Obst production. *Executive Producer:* Peter Schindler. *Producer:* Lynda Obst and Edward Zwick. *Director:* Edward Zwick. *Screenplay:* Lawrence Wright, Menno Meyjes, and Edward Zwick. *Story:* Lawrence Wright. *Director of Photography:* Roger Deakins. *Editor:* Steven Rosenblum. *Music:* Graeme Revell. *Music Editor:* Josh Winget. *Sound:* Allan Byer and (music) John Kurlander. *Sound Editor:* Neal Anderson, Christopher Assells, Dino DiMuro, Hector C. Gika, Gregory J. Hainer, Danny Hegeman, Craig Jaeger, and Patrick Sellers. *Casting:* Mary Goldberg and Mary Colquhoun. *Production Designer:* Lilly Kilvert. *Art Director:* John O. Warnke. *Set Decorator:* Gretchen Rau. *Special Effects:* Paul Lombardi. *Costumes:* Ann Roth. *Make-up:* Kathryn Bihr. *Running time:* 109 minutes. *MPAA Rating:* R.

CAST: Denzel Washington (Anthony Hubbard); Bruce Willis (General William Deveraux); Annette Bening (Elise Kraft/Sharon Bridger); Tony Shalhoub (Frank Hadad); Sami Bouajila (Samir Nazhde); David Proval (Danny Sussman); Lance Reddick (Floyd Rose); Mark Valley (Mike Johanssen); Liana Pai (Tina Osu); Jack Gwaltney (Fred Darius); Chip Zien (Chief of Staff); Victor Slezak (Colonel Hardwick); Will Lyman (FBI Director); Dakin Matthews (Senator Wright); John Rothman (Congressman Marshall); E. Katherine Kerr (Attorney General); Jimmie Ray Weeks (Army General); Amro Salama (Tariq Husseini); Ahmed Ben Larby (Sheik Ahmed Ben Talal); Mosleh Mohamed (Muezzin); Jeremy Knaster (INS Official); William Hill (INS Uniform); Aasif Mandvi (Khalil Saleh); Frank Dielsi (Officer Williams); Wood Harris (Officer Henderson); Ellen Bethea (Anita); David Costabile (Fingerprint Expert); Glenn Kessler (Fibre Expert); Jeffrey Allan Waid (Video Agent); Tom Mcdermott (Phone Bank Agent); Sherry Ham-Bernard (Hub's Secretary); Joseph Hodge (Landlord); Joey Naber (Rashad); Said Faraj (Yousef); Alex Dodd (Ali); Jacquelian Antaramian (Najiba Haddad); Helmi Kassim (Frank Haddad, Jr.); Ghoulam R. Rasoully (Frank Jr.'s Teacher); Joseph Badalucco, Jr. (EMT); Diana Naftal (Injured Woman); Insben Shenkman (Kaplan); A.A. Barton Tinapp (Mayoral); Neal Jones (NYPD Representative); Donna Hanover (District

Attorney);   Peter Schindler (Johnson, FAA);   Hany Kamal (Arab Spokesman); John Henry Cox (Speaker of the House);   Ray Godshall (CIA Director);   Chris Messina (Corporal);   Gilbert Rosales (Mechanic); Jim Shankman (Tariq Husseini);   Matt Servitto and Jourdan Fremin (Journalists);   Anjua Warfield (Match Organizer);   Susie Essman (Protest Speaker);   Rory J. Aylward (Lieutenant);   Jeff Beatty (FBI Undercover Agent);   Graham J. Larson (FBI Agent); Arianna Hugginton, Robert Scheer, Matt Miller (Capitol Week Pundits).

CHRISTIAN SCIENCE MONITOR, 11/6/98, p. B3, David Sterritt

Politics is usually in the air as November gets under way, and sometimes Hollywood takes note by tackling politically relevant subjects. This season's movies are pushing more than the usual number of ideological buttons, although not always in coherent or constructive ways.

"The Siege" jumped from the entertainment pages to the news columns long before its release today, as some Arab-American groups protested what they feared would be its perpetuation of negative ethnic stereotypes. Such anxieties seemed justified, given the movie's plot about an Arab-sponsored terror campaign that prompts the United States government to put New York City under martial law. But the movie turns out to be more complicated than expected.

Parts of it certainly exploit dangerous notions of an Arab community seething with violent fundamentalists eager to die for their fanatically embraced cause. The screenplay's half-hearted disclaimers reassuring us that "most Arab-Americans are decent citizens" hardly outweigh its implicit embrace of fear and suspicion.

In other respects, however, the movie is reasonably thoughtful. Its subplot about cloak-and-dagger rivalry between the FBI and the CIA points to a healthy recognition that government agencies are no more wise or effective than the people who work for them, and its speeches about civil liberties amount to a refresher course on the perils of law-and-order zealotry.

If it's hard to pin the picture down politically, at least it marks an improvement in director Edward Zwick's storytelling style, previously exemplified by "Legends of the Fall," a legendary bore, and "Glory," which glorified white Hollywood stars more than the black Civil War soldiers it was supposedly about. "The Siege" gives sizzling scenes to Denzel Washington as the FBI agent, Annette Bening as the slippery CIA operative, Tony Shalhoub as a loyal Arab-American betrayed by his adopted country, and Bruce Willis as a military commander.

Two other fall movies deal with a different kind of politics, peering at the thuggish neo-Nazism practiced by skinheads and their ilk. This ideology veers perilously close to the sheer evil found in horror stories, and "Apt Pupil" appropriately takes its plot from a novella by Stephen King, the bestselling terror-spinner of all time. The main character is a high-school student who discovers that his elderly neighbor is a Nazi fugitive with a murderous past and blackmails the old fascist into feeding the student's morbid curiosity about the Third Reich, the Holocaust, and the unthinkable crimes associated with them.

"Apt Pupil" conveys some cautionary messages, especially in its suggestion that youngsters may misunderstand or willfully refuse to grasp the full hideousness of this century's worst historical episodes, unless teachers and parents provide forceful educations in these areas. But as directed by Bryan Singer, who made such a smashing impression with "The Usual Suspects" three years ago, the movie contains enough gratuitous gristliness and over-the-top melodrama to forfeit any credentials as a serious exploration of its topic.

This goes double for the appalling "American History X," about a seemingly clean-cut boy who wants to follow in the footsteps of his older brother, an ardent neo-Nazi fresh from prison for a vicious race-related crime. The films pretzel-like plot may not be the fault of director Tony Kaye, who has complained about studio interference. But the movie is so riddled with simplistic psychology, bombastic effects, and ham-fisted insensitivity that nobody involved should be taking much pride in it.

The wickedness of neofascist hatred and bigotry cries out for hard-hitting Hollywood treatment. Next time, though, the filmmakers should show reasonable respect for the intelligence of their own audience.

LOS ANGELES TIMES, 11/6/98, Calendar/p. 1, Kenneth Turan

"The Siege" is a political thriller with more plausibility—and yes, more thrills—than most. It's a "what-if" movie on a stark subject, terrorist bombings in this country, that tries to serve the two masters of drama and reality and does it for longer than you might predict.

Though "The Siege" loses its way in its final sections, the extent of the film's success is considerable, and largely due to the fine performances of stars Denzel Washington and Annette Bening. It's a pleasure to have actors of this caliber working together on what in many ways is, political relevance aside, strictly cops-and-robbers material.

"The Siege" also benefits from being well-crafted. The work of director Edward Zwick and his team is crisply professional, and the film's script, credited to Lawrence Wright and Menno Meyjes & Zwick, is notable for its careful plotting and dialogue that avoids missteps for a good while.

Helping ratchet the tension up is the unfortunate fact that a scenario involving a wave of terrorist bombings hitting New York City is far from out of the question. To watch "The Siege" is to be aware to the point of discomfort that the film's fatal explosions could appear as soon as tomorrow morning's paper.

The terrorist organization in "The Siege" is an Arabic one, and while Arab American organizations are understandably upset at this, the choice has a basis in fact and was clearly not a knee-jerk decision for a film that's more concerned than most to acknowledge the existence of non-terrorist Arabs and present them in a sympathetic light.

After a prologue introducing the fictitious Sheik Ahmed Ben Talal, thought to be behind the bombings of the U.S. base in Saudi Arabia, "The Siege" switches to Manhattan and the charismatic presence of Anthony "Hub" Hubbard, head of the FBI's anti-terrorism task force in New York.

It's difficult to watch Washington giving his usual commanding performance in this, his third film with Zwick (after "Glory" and "Courage Under Fire"), and not harbor the fond wish that our government agents were as capable as this. So intent on his job he at one point doesn't notice that his nose is badly bleeding, Hubbard is adept at pushing his people to track down every lead.

A fake terrorist attack on a city bus introduces Hubbard to the mysterious Elise Kraft (Bening), a woman who is at the very least his match. A CIA agent who knows a great deal about Arab terrorism but is reluctant to share her information, the tough and world-weary Kraft seems ravaged by her experiences, determined not to trust and troubled by that determination.

These collaborators and combatants have numerous scenes together, and the way Bening and Washington handle the script's sharp repartee—toying with an undercurrent of sexual tension but sticking strictly to business—is a textbook case of how crackling acting and empathetic direction can elevate all kinds of material.

Helping the mix is veteran Tony Shalhoub, an actor of Lebanese heritage best known for playing other nationalities (like the uncompromising Italian chef in "Big Night"). Here he plays Hubbard's right hand, Frank Haddad, an Arab American FBI agent who finds his loyalties torn as the situation worsens.

"The Siege" is at its best when Hubbard's FBI team, with Kraft's uncertain cooperation, works frantically to track down the committed bombers who are working their will on the city. The film's script reveals its credible twists a little at a time, and Zwick, who wisely chooses to indicate carnage rather than actually show it, is expert at making the twists tense and nerve-racking.

The film does run into trouble, however, at its key plot turn regarding the willingness of the president to declare martial law (hence the film's poster art of heavily armed soldiers marching across the Brooklyn Bridge) and place the city under the control of by-the-book Gen. William Devereaux (Bruce Willis).

It's not only that Willis, who's made a career out of playing tongue-in-cheek roles, is miscast and not credible in what ought to be a straight-ahead performance. The rationale for going to martial law feels like a contrivance (other countries with bombing problems haven't done it) and the script not only loses a level of plausibility, it comes on increasingly broad-brush and preachy as it gets closer to its conclusion.

But even at its most unbelievable, "The Siege" has the performances of Washington and Bening to fall back on, and a theme that understands that what's difficult is not choosing right from wrong but "choosing the wrong that's more right." It's the rare thriller that's this immediate and that asks audiences to consider, even fleetingly, the dangers we face as a society.

NEW YORK, 11/16/98, p. 62, Peter Rainer

Denzel Washington plays FBI terrorism task Force chief Anthony Hubbard in *The Siege*, combining a ramrod rectitude with a dancer's grace. Whether he's barking rat-a-tat commands to his staff or swiveling with his cell phone, he has a formidable glide—he turns his authoritativeness into a kind of calisthenics. It makes sense that Hub is always in a state of coiled readiness. How else can he get the jump on terrorists? When the bombs start going off in *The Siege* for no apparent reason—no one takes responsibility and no demands are made—his balance is thrown off. This isn't the way the game is supposed to be played.

At the outset, the director, Edward Zwick (Glory), sustains a high level of tension as a false-alarm bomb threat stops a packed city bus in Brooklyn. Soon after, another seized bus brings Hub into a milling, cordoned-off battle zone where nightly-news choppers dangle like dragonflies in mid-air. It's a war theater, and the split-second urgencies have a sickening tempo. You never know when something's going to detonate, and when a bomb finally does, it has the effect of a bad dream expanding inside your head.

The explosions in *The Siege*—and there's one about every twenty minutes—carry a big enough bang to satisfy the action-movie audience. But that's not the crowd Zwick is trying to ambush; he's going after bigger game. He wants to make a cautionary political thriller about the moral consequences of fighting terrorism: Can you slay the monster without becoming the monster?

Zwick is one of the few directors of his generation able to combine action and politics successfully, but *The Siege* ends up hostage to its own overwrought ambition. It starts out as a straightforward white-knuckler and ends up as a kind of paranoiac screed. The longer the movie plays out, the wackier it gets, but the wackiness seems to have been lost on the filmmakers. It's all done with great gravitas: In order to destroy what the FBI determines is an Arab terrorist threat, the White House invokes martial law, and pretty soon decent, upstanding Arab-Americans are being interned in detention camps, a suspect is tortured to death, and the Brooklyn Bridge is vibrating to the thwomp of Army combat boots. General William Devereaux (Bruce Willis), a straight-faced smarty-pants in camouflage fatigues and fashionably angled beret, heads up the charge. "This is the land of opportunity," he broadcasts to the troublemakers. "The opportunity to turn yourself in."

Even though the Arab terrorists and their sympathizers are depicted mostly one-dimensionally, Zwick is careful not to exploit anti-Arab sentiment. It's as if he had a balance sheet; every anti-Arab conceit is rejoindered in triplicate. Hub gets a Lebanese-American partner, Frank Haddad (Tony Shalhoub), who hates the terrorists as much as any native-born Yankee. Representatives from the Arab-American Society declare their love for America. The Arab Anti-Defamation League throws its support behind the FBI. And so on; it's all very p.c. Meanwhile, mostly off-camera, yahoos rant about towelheads.

We're also treated to an FBI-CIA face-off. Hub's nemesis, Elise Kraft (Annette Bening), is an undercover CIA operative who keeps interfering with his investigation. She has deep ties to the Arab community, though and is fond of saying things like "The Palestinians seduce you with their suffering." She means it literally—her bedmate, Samir (Sami Bouajila), is an Arab agent supposedly doing double duty for the Americans. Equipped with infrared cameras, Hub and Frank, all in the name of security, of course, check out Elise and Samir's coupling from the rooftop across the way. In *The Siege,* the FBI may be smarter, but the CIA is sexier.

Hub and Elise don't link up romantically—that would be too corny but they develop a grudging respect for each other's orneriness. That's pretty corny, too, but since they make such a stunning pair, who cares? Washington is one of the few actors around who can make even a nosebleed seem attractive, and Bening gives her character an acuity to go with her blurry beauty. But the paces these two are put through aren't on a much higher level than a standard TV cop series. The cat-and-mouse maneuvers are pretty much pro forma, and since we're ahead of the game, our interest shifts to the bigger question: Is this the way things would really happen if Manhattan and Brooklyn were placed under martial law? Zwick rumbles in the tanks and the troops; he films the streets newsreel-style for that gritty, you-are-there effect. And yet what we see looks more like a science-fiction scenario. It's hard to suppress the thought that Godzilla is lurking around the next skyscraper.

The Siege is an example of what can go wrong when talented people try to create a political thriller with ideas and still satisfy the box office. Instead of dramatizing the ways in which rage and helplessness in the face of terrorism might push even the most free-minded liberal into xenophobia, the film settles for considerably less. It shifts our anger to a convenient, timeworn target, the U.S. military. General Devereaux is as villainous as any Arab terrorist—even more so, since he's operating in a democracy. He's not struggling with his conscience; he seems to *have* no conscience.

At the same time, Zwick uses the military takeover as a way to score family-of-man points: We get a glimpse of a protest rally involving Christians and Muslims and Jews that clearly is in the movie to demonstrate how ecumenical we Americans are in times of crisis. This sanctification of the citizenry is the flip side of the demonization of Devereaux. Neither rings true. And I can't help thinking that all this we-the-people stuff is a way of avoiding the spiky subject of homegrown terrorism. Remember Pogo's "We have met the enemy and he is us"? It's easy enough to make the military the bad guys. It helps take our minds off Oklahoma City. *The Siege* comes on like gangbusters, but it's rife with wishful thinking.

NEW YORK POST, 11/6/98, p. 71, Rod Dreher

"The Siege" is a terrorist action thriller that even the ACLU could love.

You expect Denzel Washington and Bruce Willis to open a can of whup-ass on deserving mad bombers of the Muslim persuasion, but nooooooo. Instead, we get a squish-headed tutorial on multicultural sensitivity, the fragility of civil liberties and the fascistic tendencies of the U.S. military. Oh, yeah—that's just what action audiences want to see.

Despite a crackerjack opening, the picture slides into muzzy-headed plotting that diffuses the tension built by the first two reels. What's more, it blames America for Islamic terrorism, and depicts the U.S. Army as gnarly Nazoids jonesing to torture Arabs. Guilt-ridden limousine liberal, thy name is Ed Zwick.

Zwick is the talented director ("Glory") who has been hammered by Arab-American groups worried that his film about an Islamic cabal whose New York bombing campaign provokes a martial-law declaration in the city would unfairly stereotype Arabs.

A Brooklyn-based underground network of Islamic fanatics plotting to blow up New York landmarks? Oh, gee, that never happens in real life.

Even so, "The Siege" goes exceedingly out of its way to distinguish between the Good Muslim majority and the handful of Bad Muslims who blow up stuff.

These are the shadowy creeps who FBI agent Anthony "Hub" Hubbard (Washington) and his partner, Frank Haddad (Tony Shalhoub), track down after a couple of bombings set the city on edge. Their paths cross with Elise, a sexy CIA operative of dubious loyalty played by Annette Bening.

The terrorists up the ante with a massive Times Square bombing that demolishes a crowded Broadway theater. A TV report informs us that the explosion wiped out "New York's cultural elite," and you think, hey, those jihad berserkers might not be so bad after all.

Still, the U.S. government goes bananas and, after another deadly big bang, sends in evil, white-male, right-winger Gen. Devereaux (Willis, phoning it in) with tanks and troops to round up all the Arabs in town.

Its maladroit politics aside, "The Siege" is simply mediocre filmmaking. The spectacle of Gotham under martial law is supposed to be the payoff, but it packs little visual punch. You call a few helicopters and troop transports a state of siege? The Barneys warehouse sale is more menacing.

Zwick is much better building anxiety and paranoia in the more intimate scenes composing the film's first half, but the characters aren't interesting enough for us to stick with through the rush-job denouement.

Zwick blows an opportunity to explore the patriotic Haddad's divided loyalties and wounded ambivalence. That could have made a tragic, involving and genuinely humanizing story, but would have required the kind of risk-taking the jittery director apparently wasn't game for. After two good reels, Zwick loses his nerve, and his film.

NEWSDAY, 11/6/98, Part II/p. B3, Jack Mathews

The new millennium hangs over the American film landscape these days like a full moon over the wolf packs of Yellowstone. "Deep Impact," "Armageddon," Godzilla," "Jurassic Park." Forget the Year-2000 computer glitch, let's worry about the end of the world.

In Ed Zwick's "The Siege," the potential calamity is envisioned as an elaborate spread of Arab terrorism into the West, an all-Allah war against the great American demon, beginning with New York City, which was left standing by the failed real-life attempt to knock down the World Trade Center in 1993 and a foiled plot to hit a series of Big Apple landmarks.

This time, the terrorists mean business.

"The Siege" is an uncomfortable mix of paranoia and self-conscious butt-covering. Zwick and his staff of writers are exploiting anti-Arab sentiments aroused by the fear of encroaching Middle East terrorism, while at the same time lecturing us against prejudice.

So eager is the film to deflect race-baiting accusations, it includes an embarrassing scene where a man stands at a press conference, identifies himself as head of an Arab anti-defamation organization and declares his group's love of America. (It wasn't enough to discourage protests from real Arab anti-defamation groups.)

Anyway, the result of the mixed message is an action-thriller that plays like a high-stakes game of Ping-Pong, with good Arabs on one side of the table, bad Arabs on the other and our American security icons—the Army, FBI and CIA—forming that little net in the middle.

Each of those patriotic federal entities is nicely represented by a movie star. Denzel Washington is Anthony Hubbard, the FBI field chief in New York, a man of quick action and limitless courage. Bruce Willis is Army Gen. William Devereaux, a deceptively calm figure with the heart of a crazed martinet. And Annette Bening is CIA agent Sharon Bridger, whose background as a trainer of anti-Saddam Hussein operatives in the Middle East has left her with a curious set of loyalties.

The first half of "The Siege," focusing on the fragile alliance between Hubbard and Bridger as they seek out and take down the terrorists responsible for a bus bombing in Times Square, is solid, intimate political drama. Hubbard has the resources and Bridger has the contact, a nervous young Arab teacher (Sami Bouajila) with whom she's having an affair and who is somehow linked to the terrorist leaders.

Washington and Bening, in a relationship best described as cautious flirtation, have an engaging chemistry. However, no sooner is the bus bombing case solved and they're looking into each other's eyes on a dance floor, than a suicide bomber detonates himself in the midst of a packed Broadway theater. That tragedy is followed almost immediately by a massive bombing (600 dead) of the federal building housing Hubbard's entire field force.

With those events, "The Siege" shifts into full-dress action mode. Martial law is declared in New York, with Devereaux gleefully in charge, and the eerily empty streets are suddenly filled with tanks and armed troops. Arab-Americans are roughly herded out of their Brooklyn enclave into makeshift detention camps. Suspected terrorists are tortured and murdered. And agents Hubbard and Bridger are forced underground, where they become enemies of the state in order to save it.

It is a bleak scenario Zwick presents. We are indeed in trouble if our only defenses against the Osama bin Laden zealots are a lone FBI agent and his Arab-American sidekick (Tony Shalhoub), a CIA agent who doesn't know her own heart and an Army run by a closet sociopath. Since his one admirable film, "Glory," subtlety has been an elusive quality for Zwick, and it's thrown to the wind here.

"The Siege" states the obvious, that Army terrorism is no better than any other kind, that ethnic paranoia undermines reason, that there's no foolproof method of keeping terrorists out of the United States, and that living under martial law is no way to live at all.

Thanks, Ed.

SIGHT AND SOUND, 2/99, p. 54, Ken Hollings

New York City, the present. 'Hub' Hubbard heads the joint FBI/NYPD anti-terrorism task force in the wake of the Oklahoma and World Trade Center bombings. After a fake bomb splatters a busload of passengers with paint, his team receives a demand for the release of Sheik Ahmed Ben

Talal, kidnapped in the Middle East on the orders of US General Devereaux. The bombing of New York will begin in earnest unless Talal is freed.

Hubbard finds his investigations shadowed by CIA operative Elise Kraft. When a second busload of passengers are killed by a bomb, the search focuses on Brooklyn's Arab community. Through Kraft, Hubbard contacts Samir Nazhde, a Palestinian CIA informer. Hubbard discovers Kraft was in Gulf War intelligence with Samir and that they are lovers. The task force locates the terrorist cell and wipes it out. However, new bombs blow up a theatre and FBI headquarters. Martial law is declared and Devereaux takes command.

Devereaux's draconian measures result in a suspect being tortured to death and Hubbard strikes out on his own to find the terrorists. Kraft—real name Sharon Bridger—discloses that she helped train Talal's followers in terror tactics against Saddam Hussein until the CIA abandoned them. She helps Hubbard coerce Samir into arranging a meeting with the bombers during a massive civil-rights rally. Samir seems to comply, but reveals he is the last terrorist on a suicide mission to detonate a bomb in the middle of the protestors. Samir shoots Kraft, but is killed by Hubbard. With Devereaux arrested on a murder charge, martial law is suspended.

The Siege attempts to update the bluffs and counterfeints of the Cold War spy thriller, not to advance any ideological point but to obscure the fact that it doesn't have one. Every major flashpoint in recent US foreign policy is mentioned, from Beirut to Haiti, as if citation alone can take the place of argument. "Ask a question, get an atlas," a Washington politician complains at one point, and it's hard not to sympathise.

Director Zwick tackled the meanings of race and conflict in *Glory* and his Gulf War drama *Courage under Fire,* both featuring Denzel Washington, but the issues here have left him giddy. Daring you not to take the whole thing seriously, *The Siege* opens with President Clinton on television in the wake of the Somalia bombing, warning that "America takes care of its own", intercut with video footage of the devastated Federal Building in Oklahoma. Scarred and grainy the raw actuality of these images only undermines the portentous dialogue and glossy production values to come.

When Hubbard (Washington) and his team first swing into action, the crackle of their procedural repartee seems impressive, until you realise its sole purpose is to establish him as a team player. With his FBI coffee mug and his natty monogrammed shirts, Hub's an Organisation man of heroic proportions: an ex-paratrooper who studied law, a Catholic liberal who believes in the system. Compared with Devereaux (Bruce Willis) and Bridger (Annette Bening), he's a total square. While the other characters tend to drift in and out from moral twilight zones as the plot requires, Hub remains front and centre.

Zwick maintains a smooth pace, as Middle-Eastern terrorists bomb the supine citizens of New York into a panicky State Of Emergency. However, unsettling racial divisions are quickly smoothed over once Martial Law is declared. Herded together into wire cages by heavily armed American soldiers, the Arab population of Brooklyn is allowed to demonstrate good citizenship through its capacity for patient suffering.

Willis and Bening, meanwhile, bring grim determination to their dispiriting roles. Unsure if Devereaux is a dangerous fanatic or an authoritarian berserker, Willis tries both, coming up with a weird mix of Ollie North and Colonel Kurtz—the sight of tanks on the streets and camps heaving with captive Arabs seems to turn him on, but we never find out why Bening bears the heaviest burden as not only the movie's sole major female character but also the only one devious enough to operate under an alias. Even the bombers arriving from the Middle East conveniently use their real names.

As soon as Bening is shown smoking hashish with her Palestinian lover, we know she's doomed. Such behaviour would have been criticised during the Cold War as "going native". In this political melodrama which revels in its own sentimental extremism, it represents, in grossly literal terms, how the expediencies of foreign policy create strange bedfellows. No matter how intelligent, perceptive or experienced Kraft/Bridger may be, she still winds up paying for Hubbard's isolationist purity. With its curious blend of cynicism and naivety, *The Siege* tries to tackle serious issues without actually offending anybody. Unless you happen to be a woman, of course.

TIME, 11/9/98, p. 116, Richard Schickel

Which poses the larger threat to democratic institutions: terrorism or the hysterical response to it? This is not the sort of question you normally expect to be addressed in a big-budget action movie. Nor do you expect it to be answered ultimately with a ringing endorsement of the Bill of Rights, since this is an inherently reactionary form, one that tends to favor a muscular approach to crisis management over more reasoned ones, if only because there is more visceral drama to be found at the end of a pointed pistol than in a pointed argument.

Maybe this concern for what our fears of domestic terrorism might someday, not too far off, do to our way of life is just a sort of intellectual McGuffin, designed to make us soppy liberals take *The Siege* more seriously than we ought to. The movie does, after all, present the bruising, intricately staged spectacle of New York City brought to a quaking halt by a series of ever more serious bombings—first a bus, then a crowded theater, then a federal building—mounted by that lately easiest-to-despise of all groups, Arab fanatics. A panicked government institutes martial law, which includes internment camps and occasional descents into torture when no one can think of any better solution to a crisis. As a result, there's plenty of (literally) raw material to keep the action fans happy.

But let's give director Edward Zwick and his fellow screenwriters, Lawrence Wright and Menno Meyjes, credit for complicating their material, and therefore our responses to it, in ways that go well beyond the demands of the genre. They give us an FBI agent in charge of the case—played by that paragon of sexy stalwartness, Denzel Washington—whose heroism lies largely in his ability to reconsider hasty conclusions. They provide him with an assistant of Arab descent (a quietly smoldering Tony Shalhoub), caught in a conflict between duty and disgust when the soldiery snatches his son because he happens to match a terrorist profile. They also add to the team a sassy CIA operative (Annette Bening) who knows more about these terrorists than she can tell because she's in love with one of them. Even Bruce Willis' Army general, leading the troops who take over the city, is given an interesting spin. He's one tough, exceedingly dutiful nut. But we also know he's overcompensating, because in an earlier scene he has given a speech against martial law. He doesn't think policing their own citizens is proper work for soldiers.

There's a lot packed into *The Siege*, and the strains of its plotting sometimes show. So does the effort to disarm ethnic and religious protests by insisting on the distinction between the peaceful Muslim majority and the terrorist minority. These passages are obvious (and probably useless) in ways that the rest of the movie is not. But Zwick, who directed Glory, remains good with both massed action and more intensely intimate confrontations, and better still at finding ways to sound and sustain a humane and compassionate note, no matter how bloody the spectacle out of which it arises.

VILLAGE VOICE, 11/17/98, p. 135, Gary Dauphin

Imagine an action-hero Colin Powell oozing sex appeal and you get the feel of Denzel Washington in humble-patriot mode, a new style All (African) American boy as likely to sacrifice himself for "our way of life" as he is to make a leading lady's knickers moist. In *The Siege,* Denzel is reunited with his director from *Glory* and *Courage Under Fire,* Edward Zwick, the pair turning their earnest attentions to the thorny problem of Middle Eastern terrorism. The movie opens doc-style with footage of the bombed Marine base in Dhahran, Saudi Arabia, but quickly moves to the fictional American kidnapping of a terrorist leader and retaliatory bombings all over Manhattan. Skyscrapers fall, politicians compromise "basic freedoms," martial law is declared, and innocent Arab Americans are imprisoned and abused. Definitely a job for Super Denzel.

Special agent in charge of the FBI's local antiterrorist desk, Denzel is quickly on the case, but since *The Siege* is an intramural debate masquerading as an action movie, his main obstacles are homegrown. Annette Bening seems to be playing on both sides as an oversexed CIA operative, while a giggle-producing Bruce Willis dresses up in Special Forces gear, clenches his jaw, and proclaims: "I am the law!"

The Siege works surprisingly well as an action movie, but its portrayals of Muslims, Arabs, and Arab Americans are a bit of a mess despite stabs at balance and nuance. Typically, race is the film's Achilles' heel, but in the person of SuperDenzel it's also a perverse strength. A walking racial get-out-of-jail-free card, Denzel allows this "liberal" film to indulge in unvarnished flag worship without shame. I don't think *Siege* is a racist film, but like most American movies, it does create a handy Other in order to define an Us. The only difference is that this time the nigger isn't black.

Also reviewed in:
CHICAGO TRIBUNE, 11/6/98, Friday/p. A, Michael Wilmington
NEW REPUBLIC, 12/7/98, p. 27, Stanley Kauffmann
NEW YORK TIMES, 11/6/98, p. E15, Janet Maslin
NEW YORKER, 11/16/98, p. 114, David Denby
VARIETY, 11/2-8/96, p. 49, Todd McCarthy
WASHINGTON POST, 11/6/98, p. D1, Stephen Hunter
WASHINGTON POST, 11/6/98, Weekend/p. 46, Michael O'Sullivan

SILVER SCREEN, THE: COLOR ME LAVENDER

A Planet Pictures release of a Couch Potato Productions film.   *Director:* Mark Rappaport. *Screenplay:* Mark Rappaport.   *Director of Photography:* Nancy Schreiber.   *Editor:* Mark Rappaport.   *Running time:* 100 minutes. *MPAA Rating:* Not Rated.

CAST: Dan Butler (Narrator).

LOS ANGELES TIMES, 7/17/98, Calendar/p. 10, Kevin Thomas

Mark Rappaport's "The Silver Screen: Color Me Lavender" is more exasperating than provocative in its relentless intent to read male homosexual implications into a wide array of vintage Hollywood—and a couple of European—movies.

The documentary's narrator, "Frasier's" Dan Butler, reiterates how everything is open to interpretation, but clearly Rappaport sees only one reading—subliminal hanky-panky between Bob Hope and Bing Crosby in their "Road" movies, between Jerry Lewis and Dean Martin in their comedies, between perennial old codger Walter Brennan and John Wayne or Gary Cooper or James Stewart. The list is endless.

The problem is that Rappaport—director of the far more impressive "From the Journals of Jean Seberg"—has too narrow a perspective. He seems reluctant to acknowledge that heterosexual American males might be from time to time insecure in their masculinity and that comedy involving drag or homosexual innuendo can be a way of releasing that anxiety. To see clips of Hope, with both Crosby and others, is to be reminded of just how funny he is and what a secure man he must be to poke occasional fun at masculine insecurities.

The amazing thing is how, by and large, inoffensive the humor involving homosexuality and effeminacy is in Rappaport's choices of old clips. This is all the more remarkable when you consider how conclusively and powerfully the late Vito Russo's landmark study "The Celluloid Closet" and its subsequent documentary argue that movies have historically been instrumental in the oppression, ridiculing and stereotyping of gays.

Like Russo before him—and critic-historian Andrew Sarris before that—Rappaport calls attention to the proliferation of clearly, if not openly, gay characters in '30s movies played by such character actors as Franklin Pangborn, Eric Blore and Edward Everett Horton, who enlivened many a movie with their sly wit and humor. (Outside the characters played by these three men, the only man in all the clips that seems to be unmistakably gay is Wendell Corey's heavily repressed pal to John Hodiak in the 1947 "Desert Fury.")

Rappaport surveys the screen images of a number of long-ago male stars, some of whom are widely believed to have been gay, and uses film clips to substantiate that assumption. But he never takes into account that they are being directed in roles that they didn't write. (If you have a wide enough array of clips at your disposal, you can argue just about anything.)

He makes an interesting point about Brennan when he reminds us that as a sidekick, he was perennially trying to steer the star away from the girl in hopes of settling down on some ranch with him. But couldn't it be that these codgers, instead of being repressed gays, are more often than not simply afraid they will be abandoned in their old age?

What Rappaport really accomplishes, although this does not seem his intention, is to remind us that males, regardless of sexual orientation, have a simple, sometimes deep, need to bond and that this bond may just be emotional rather than sexual.

What matters finally is not whether movie characters—past, present or future—are gay but whether their portrayal is harmfully irresponsible and offensive. In the meantime, maybe it would be a good thing for everyone to lighten up.

VILLAGE VOICE, 7/21/98, p. 115, J. Hoberman

More playfully subversive and less conventionally hand-wringing than Robert Epstein and Jeffrey Friedman's 1995 clip-anthology *The Celluloid Closet*, Rappaport's *The Silver Screen—Color Me Lavender* takes the position that Hollywood is naturally gay or barely repressed. Rappaport, who first staked a claim to the territory of VCR-cheology with *Rock Hudson's Home Movies*, concentrates mainly on studio comedies from the mid '30s through the mid '50s, subjecting footage to extensive microanalysis or bringing out latent meanings by fooling with the soundtrack.

The Silver Screen begins by surveying the "unproclaimed homosexuals" who populate the world of Fred Astaire-Ginger Rogers musicals. Although Rappaport doesn't make the point that obvious sissies like Eric Blore or Franklin Pangborne were there to inoculate the less-than-macho Astaire against charges of effeminacy, he argues that these pansies disappeared after 1941 because effete behavior was no laughing matter during wartime (don't ask, don't tell)—especially when women were usurping male prerogatives on the home front.

Providing a taxonomy of Carmen Miranda impersonations (not forgetting Daffy Duck's), *The Silver Screen* goes on to celebrate the queeny aesthete played by Clifton Webb in *Laura* (and done "straight" by George Sanders in *All About Eve*) while touching briefly on the open homoeroticism of European sophisticates like Jean Cocteau and Luchino Visconti. But Rappaport is dearly most amused by parsing the Hollywood dance of insinuation and denial. "Defining and redefining masculinity is a particularly American trait" he asserts, piling on evidence of queer behavior by Jerry Lewis, Red Skelton, and, most hauntingly, Danny Kaye.

Having foisted Lin Shaye on the American public, the Farrelly brothers would no doubt appreciate Rappaport's explication of the "grizzled old prospector," namely Walter Brennan, in the many movies where he plays "boyfriend sidekick" to the Humphrey Bogart or John Wayne action hero. Rappaport's most apt contribution may be his deconstruction of Bob Hope's compulsive camping and impugning of Bing Crosby's masculinity: "What could be funnier than a straight guy pretending he's not as straight as he pretends?"

Also reviewed in:
CHICAGO TRIBUNE, 4/28/00, Friday/p. 8, John Petrakis
NEW YORK TIMES, 7/17/98, p. E22, Lawrence Van Gelder
NEW YORKER, 7/27/98, p. 79, Daphne Merkin
VARIETY, 10/20-26/97, p. 75, Derek Elley

SIMON BIRCH

A Hollywood Pictures release in association with Caravan Pictures. *Executive Producer:* John Baldecchi. *Producer:* Laurence Mark and Roger Birnbaum. *Director:* Mark Steven Johnson. *Screenplay:* Mark Steven Johnson. *Story suggested by the novel "A Prayer for Owen Meany"* *by:* John Irving. *Director of Photography:* Aaron E. Schneider. *Editor:* David Finfer. *Music:* Marc Shaiman. *Music Editor:* Scott Stambler. *Sound:* Glen Gauthier and (music) Dennis Sands. *Sound Editor:* Dane A. Davis. *Casting:* Mary Gail Artz and Barbara Cohen. *Production Designer:* David Chapman. *Art Director:* Dennis Davenport. *Set Decorator:* Carolyn A.

Loucks. *Costumes:* Betsy Heimann and Abram Waterhouse. *Make-up:* Marilyn Terry. *Stunt Coordinator:* Alison Reid. *Running time:* 110 minutes. *MPAA Rating:* PG.

CAST: Ian Michael Smith (Simon Birch); Joseph Mazzello (Joe Wenteworth); Ashley Judd (Rebecca Wenteworth); Oliver Platt (Ben Goodrich); David Strathairn (Reverend Russell); Dana Ivey (Grandmother Wenteworth); Beatrice Winde (Hildie Grove); Jan Hooks (Miss Leavey); Ceciley Carroll (Marjorie); Sumela-Rose Keramidopulos (Ann); Sam Morton (Stuart); Jim Carrey (Adult Joe Wenteworth); John Mazzello (Simon Wenteworth); Holly Dennison (Mrs. Birch); Peter MacNeil (Mr. Birch); Addison Bell (Doctor Wells); Roger McKeen (Coach Higgins); Sean McCann (Chief Al Cork); John Robinson (Mr. Baker); Guy Sanvido (Janitor); Gil Filar (Eddie); Marcello Meleca (Howard Ellis); Tim Hall (Pitcher); Tom Redman (First Baseman); Mark Skrela (Third Baseman); Kevin White (Shortstop); Terry V. Hart and Alan Markfield (Umpires); Christopher Marren (Rival Baseball Coach); Tommy Dorrian and Justin Marangoni (Teammates); Tyler Cairns (Sheep); Gino Giacomini (Wise Man); Barbara Stewart (Delivery Room Nurse); David Rigby (Bus Driver); Sam Aaron and David Chapman (Old Men); Wendy Fleming (Mrs. Russell).

LOS ANGELES TIMES, 9/11/98, Calendar/p. 8, Jack Mathews

[The following review by Jack Mathews appeared in a slightly different form in **NEWSDAY, 9/11/98, Part II/p. B7.]**

The sap is flowing early this year in fictional Gravestown, Maine, the primary setting of John Irving's complex novel "A Prayer for Owen Meany" and for filmmaker Mark Steven Johnson's simple "Simon Birch," a syrupy extract of the book.

Simon Birch, an 11-year-old dwarf with a big faith, would be named Owen Meany if Irving felt Johnson had taken a fair run at the novel instead of using its first chapter as a jumping-off point. As it was, the author insisted on the character name change and a distanced writing credit (the movie is "suggested by" the novel rather than "based upon" it), and wished the filmmakers luck.

They'll need it. While Simon/Owen remains a fascinating character, and is played with the ease of a veteran by sixth-grade discovery Ian Michael Smith, Johnson treats him as something like a live-action toy or a smart, exotic pet. He's a comic figure given an endless string of one-liners that play off his size in the same way dirty jokes play off the ages of the characters in Johnson's scripts for the "Grumpy Old Men" movies.

"Simon Birch" is a reminiscence piece, told by Simon's best friend, Joe Wenteworth, looking back as an adult visiting Simon's grave. This is a somber Jim Carrey, who appears briefly in the opening and closing cemetery scenes and provides the narrator's voice throughout.

"He's the reason I believe in God," Joe says, as the story begins, promising an epiphany that doesn't come until the film's climactic sequence.

"Simon" tells the story of an eventful year in the '60s when its elfin hero got himself into a passel of jams that put him on the outs with just about everyone in Gravestown except Joe (Joseph Mazzello); Joe's angelic mom, Rebecca (Ashley Judd); and her good-natured boyfriend, Ben (Oliver Platt).

Simon's religious challenging of Gravestown's humorless Reverend Russell (David Strathairn) and sourpuss Sunday school teacher Miss Leavy (Jan Hooks) have them declaring him an infidel, while, in fact, he's the most religious person in town. Simon, so tiny at birth that he was delivered with a sneeze rather than a contraction, believes he was put on Earth for a reason, and buffers the cruelty and insensitivity of people around him with the knowledge that "things will be different when God makes me a hero."

In the meantime, he's an outcast, even in his own home, where his farm parents are embittered by the misfortune they consider him to be. Bright, smart-alecky, self-denigrating and eagerly pubescent, Simon is a handful who gets himself into big trouble reaching for a handful during a Christmas church pageant, when a female schoolmate bends over the manger where he lies, playing baby Jesus.

Most of Simon's mischief is done as farce, but when he hits a foul ball during a rare at-bat for his Little League baseball team, and it kills a passerby, the tone shifts, and the scene is set—telegraphed may be a better word for it—for his divine act of heroism and redemption.

Paralleling Simon's religious journey is Joe's quest for the identity of his father. Mom won't reveal his name, so Joe, with Simon's help, is sizing up every age-eligible man in Gravestown as a candidate, running afoul of the law while he's at it.

"Simon Birch" is a dreadfully sticky affair. Johnson, on his maiden voyage as director, treats every scene as if it were a bonbon, almost too precious to consume, and Marc Shaiman's score is a running series of mood cues.

Smith, whose own dwarfism resulted from a rare bone disease, seems a natural before the camera, and not just because of his condition. Johnson gets mostly uninspired performances from the pros in his talented cast—Strathaim plays Reverend Russell like the Grim Reaper in a Monty Python sketch—and Smith's contrasting energy and earnestness give the film its few moments of lift.

NEW YORK POST, 9/11/98, p. 69, Thelma Adams

Cholesterol watchers, beware: "Simon Birch" contains more pure schmaltz than Sammy's Famous Romanian Restaurant on Chrystie Street.

Scrape off Marc Shaiman's shameless score, Aaron E. Schneider's lily-gilding cinematography, and Mark Steven Johnson's sentimental direction, and there's a smart, wrenching, inspirational movie "suggested by" John Irving's "A Prayer for Owen Meany."

Birch (the novel's Meany) is the smallest boy in a tiny New England town. The stunted 12-year-old with the big heart has more faith in God than the spiritually cramped hamlet can handle.

Rejected by his hardscrabble parents, Simon (Ian Michael Smith) creates his own family: best friend Joe (Joseph Mazzello), Joe's single mom (Ashley Judd) and her beau (Oliver Platt).

With Coke-bottle glasses, hearing aid and Billy Barty physique, Simon follows Forrest Gump and the Rain Man in being the most prescient human in the 'hood, despite his handicaps. He considers his "condition" a miracle, rather than a curse. Any day now, God will be showing Simon his heroic mission on Earth.

Events test Simon's faith. The pint-sized slugger knocks a baseball out of the stadium during a pee-wee league playoff with tragic results. First-time director Johnson telegraphs that tragedy and the twists, both horrifying and redemptive, yet to come.

By setting the story in the early '70s in a retro-Cleaverville, Johnson has exchanged the post-Vietnam crisis of faith that dominated Irving's novel for Gumpian Middle American myth-making.

Johnson, best known for writing "Grumpy Old Men" and its sequel, transforms the novel's Meany into Simon, possibly the world's smallest stand-up comic (sorry, Gilbert Gottfried).

We spend our time either laughing at Simon's deflating one-liners, or mouth-breathing away the lumps in our windpipes. If we ever doubt how to interpret the mythic events, Johnson drops anvil-heavy symbols. Jim Carrey, as Joe grown up, delivers the connect-the-dots narration, competing with Robin Williams for deepest funnyman.

And yet, the laughs and lumps are there; the issues of friends, family and faith stirringly presented.

"Simon Birch" is not "Home Alone: The Miracle" largely because newcomer Smith, Mazzello, Platt and, especially Judd, breathe life and humor into characters who veer close to Hollywood stock but salvage the novel's idiosyncratic charm.

SIGHT AND SOUND, 7/99, p. 53, Richard Kelly

Revisiting his hometown in adulthood, Joe Wenteworth remembers his best friend Simon Birch, who was born in 1952 and died in 1964. The smallest infant ever delivered at Gravestown Memorial Hospital, Simon grew to be a diminutive boy, well liked by other kids but neglected by his parents. At Sunday school he drove the Reverend Russell to distraction by insisting that he was an instrument of God. Joe was the illegitimate son of town beauty Rebecca, who wouldn't reveal the name of his father. Rebecca was romanced by drama teacher Ben Goodrich, who gradually earned Joe's approval. At a baseball game, Simon's first hit struck and killed Rebecca.

Simon's friendship with Joe survived the tragedy, but the baseball was stolen. Joe was certain his real father was the thief suspecting swimming coach Mr. Baker, Joe and Simon broke into his office, but were caught and sentenced to community service on a church-run retreat. Cast as baby Jesus in a nativity play, Simon disrupted the performance and Russell barred him from the retreat.

Simon retrieved his confiscated collection of baseball cards from Russell's study, and found the missing baseball. He and Ben raced to the retreat, but Russell had confessed to Joe. On the journey home, a road accident caused the school bus to plunge into a river, but Simon's initiative saved the other children. Simon died in hospital, a hero. Joe was adopted by Ben.

Once asked whether his protagonists' lives were 'predestined', Robert Bresson replied, "Aren't we all?" So steadfast was Bresson's conviction he customarily foretold the outcome of his narratives, as in the perfectly transparent title of *A Man Escaped/Un condamné àmort s'est échappé* (1956). *Simon Birch* also signposts its dramatic cruces quite unabashedly, but its version of the transcendent is pure Hollywood, a cereal box with a crackerjack miracle at the bottom.

"Suggested by" John Irving's *A Prayer for Owen Meany,* the screenplay by director Mark Stephen Johnson (scriptwriter of *Grumpy*—and *Grumpier Old Men)* has been carpentered out of episodes from that novel with Irving's approval. The present-day bookends and earnest voiceover fall to Jim Carrey, attempting the sort of kindly cameo essayed by Richard Dreyfuss in *Stand by Me.* The voiceover foretells crucial plot points, such as Rebecca's freakish demise and the finale of Simon's martyrdom. But this is quite in tune with the conviction of our eponymous hero, a child of miraculously low birth weight who maintains that the Almighty has a plan for him.

Essentially this is a tale of two orphans, and it yields to the fantasies with which orphans may console themselves. For a while at least, fatherless Joe has a knockout mom in the shape of Ashley Judd. Simon's parents, meanwhile, are poor, unattractive and care not a whit for him, so he gladly accepts Rebecca's surrogate attentions. So when fate steals Rebecca away, both boys are robbed and Simon joins in Joe's quest to find an upstanding father.

Figuring out the twist in Joe's paternity won't tax many viewers, least of all those who've seen Paul Schrader's *Light of Day.* But as Reverend Russell, the excellent John Sayles alumnus David Strathaim looks uneasy loaning his naturalistic depth to this school-age fable. Small wonder, then, that Joe is won over by Oliver Platt's hugely amiable Ben, a wry, straight-faced clown who courts Joe's favour by bringing a stuffed armadillo to dinner.

Ian Michael Smith also excels as the wiseacre Simon and Joseph Mazzello is very likable as Joe. Elsewhere, an air of *déjà vu* descends. Joyous 60s pop tunes ('Nowhere to Rue,' 'Up on the Roof' and 'Can I Get a Witness') are poured over scenes like so much period gravy. Marc Shaiman's score could have been sparser; instead it spoonfeeds the audience throughout. Aaron E. Schneider's camera sweeps around like a busy broom, and the visual style is all honey-hued shafts of light, as befits matters religiose.

The obligatory deathbed scene is worth a tear or two, but leaves an unpalatable aftertaste. Ultimately this movie tells us it's more or less OK to be different, but you might just have to die for it. Thus the divinely ordained purpose of Simon's life is to surrender it, in a crisis supremely fit for a pint-sized sacrifice, so that 13 correctly proportioned children can live. The feel-good factor hides a neo-Malthusian mean spirit. Should we be feeding this stuff to our kids?

Also reviewed in:
CHICAGO TRIBUNE, 9/11/98, Friday/p. A, Michael Wilmington
NEW YORK TIMES, 9/11/98, p. E18, Stephen Holden
VARIETY, 8/31-9/6/98, p. 94, Dennis Harvey
WASHINGTON POST, 9/11/98, p. D1, Stephen Hunter
WASHINGTON POST, 9/11/98, Weekend/p. 52, Michael O'Sullivan

SIMPLE PLAN, A

A Paramount Pictures and Mutual Film Company release in association with Savoy Pictures. *Executive Producer:* Gary Levinsohn and Mark Gordon.   *Producer:* James Jacks and Adam Schroeder.   *Director:* Sam Raimi.   *Screenplay (based on his novel):* Scott B. Smith.   *Director of Photography:* Alar Kivilo.   *Editor:* Arthur Coburn and Eric L Beason.   *Music:* Danny Elfman. *Music Editor:* Ellen Segal. *Sound:* Ed Novick and (music): Drew Webster.   *Sound Editor:* Michael Wilhoit.   *Casting:* Ilene Starger.   *Production Designer:* Patrizia von Brandenstein.   *Art Director:* James F. Truesdale.   *Set Designer:* Rando Schmook.   *Set*

Decorator: Hilton Rosemarin. *Special Effects:* John D. Milinac.   *Costumes:* Julie Weiss. *Make-up:* Janeen Schreyer.   *Stunt Coordinator:* Chris Doyle.   *Running time:* 120 minutes. *MPAA Rating:* R.

CAST: Bill Paxton (Hank Mitchell);   Billy Bob Thornton (Jacob Mitchell);   Bridget Fonda (Sarah Mitchell);   Gary Cole (Baxter);   Brent Briscoe (Lou);   Becky Ann Baker (Nancy); Chelcie Ross (Carl);   Jack Walsh (Tom Butler);   Bob Davis (FBI Agent Renkins);   Peter Syvertsen (FBI Agent Freemont);   Tom Carey (Dwight Stephanson);   John Paxton (Mr. Schmitt);   Marie Mathay (News Reporter);   Paul Magers (Anchorman);   Joan Steffand (Anchorwoman);   Jill Sayre (Hospital Nurse);   Wayne A. Evenson (Bartender); Timothy Storms (Drinker);   Terry Hempleman (Dead Pilot);   Jay Gjernes (Bearded Man);   Grant Curtis, Soloman Abrams, and Nina Kaczorowski (Bar Patrons);   Thomas Boedy (Priest);   Mary Woolever (Linda); Rhiannon R. Savers (Girl on Sled);   Christopher Gallus (Boy on Sled);   Eric Cegon (Tommy);   Robert Martin Halverson (Detective);   Katie Kelly (Female Detective).

CHRISTIAN SCIENCE MONITOR, 12/4/98, p. 15, David Sterritt

Few end-of-year movies will draw more attention from Oscar-watchers than "A Simple Plan," which features award-caliber performances by two actors in parts ideally suited to their styles.

Bill Paxton, whose laid-back manner lends itself nicely to regular-guy roles, plays an ordinary man who's allowed his life to veer dangerously out of control.

Billy Bob Thornton, who rocketed to fame as the slow-thinking redneck of "Sling Blade," plays an extremely limited man whose unsophisticated thought processes could prove either a saving grace, or a tragic flaw.

Its an unusual partnership, but Paxton and Thornton turn in one of the year's best ensemble acting jobs, which could prove interesting when the motion-picture academy puts on its nominating hat and ponders which of the actors to choose. It's possible that this high-quality movie year has produced so many top-flight performances that neither will receive a nod. But that seems unlikely, and its conceivable that the actors will end up competing against each other.

Adding spice to this Oscar scenario is that "A Simple Plan" was directed by Sam Raimi, who's rarely thought of as a molder of thoughtful portrayals. Glance at his credits, from "The Evil Dead" and, "The Quick and the Dead" to "Army of Darkness" and "Darkman," and you'll have an idea of the wild-and-woolly fantasies that have kept him busy until now. "A Simple Plan" marks his first step into grownup moviemaking, and an impressive step it turns out to be. He could conceivably figure in the Oscar race himself.

Paxton and Thornton play Hank and Jacob Mitchell, two Midwestern brothers. Hank seems contented with his average middle-class life, but can't help wishing his attractive wife and baby-on-the-way could someday be able to rise above the ordinary. Jacob is considerably lower on the social scale, plugging away as a laborer and wondering whether his days will be brightened by even the simplest pleasures.

Then an unexpected moral crisis drops into their laps. Tramping through the woods outside their village, they stumble on a wrecked airplane containing a dead pilot and a huge amount of money. Hank immediately knows the right thing to do—call the cops and turn it in, but Jacob and his friend Lou have a different idea. Since the cash probably comes from some aborted crime, why not keep it for themselves? This would be legally and ethically wrong, of course, but nobody would be hurt and their lives would be eased forever.

Slowly the three men hatch a simple plan to enrich themselves while avoiding all risk. What they don't count on are the wages of sin, which soon appear in the forms of paranoia, suspicion, and jealousy.

There are moments in "A Simple Plan" when Raimi can't rein in his penchant for over-the-top touches, juicing up the picture with suspense-movie tricks or bursts of violence. But most of the time he keeps the action under control, focusing attention on the story's real points of interest: its study of rich and involving characters and its poignant depiction of the sad results of dishonesty, duplicity, and greed.

Paxton and Thornton receive skilled assistance from Bridget Fonda and Brent Briscoe in the supporting cast, and Raimi's camera style makes the most of Scott B. Smith's articulate screenplay. "A Simple Plan" is neither a happy nor a pretty tale, but it builds uncommon dramatic power as its unpredictable plot unfolds.

LOS ANGELES TIMES, 12/11/98, Calendar/p. 2, Jack Mathews

[The following review by Jack Mathews appeared in a slightly different form in **NEWSDAY, 12/11/98, Part II/p. B3.]**

The title of Scott B. Smith's page-turning novel "A Simple Plan," and the smartly condensed script he adapted for director Sam Raimi, describes the solution that a winter hiker comes up with after he and two others happen onto the carcass of a downed single-engine plane, and decide to keep a duffel bag found inside containing more than $4 million in cash.

The plan's architect is Hank Mitchell (Bill Paxton), a married, underpaid accountant for a small mill in a depressed Midwestern town. The others are his good-hearted, but slow-witted, unemployed brother Jacob (Billy Bob Thornton) and Jacob's boozy redneck pal Lou (Brent Briscoe).

Hank's immediate reaction is to want to call the authorities. Lou's is to take the money and run. And Jacob, who has the swing vote, is gridlocked by his divided loyalties to his brother and his overbearing best friend.

Finally, Hank comes up with a compromise. They'll hide the money until the plane is found by others, and then decide, based on the likelihood of being caught, whether to keep it. It's a simple plan set down on a slippery slope, the beginning of a chain reaction of greed, panic, paranoia, betrayal and murder.

The novel's and the movie's underlying assumptions are that the temptation in these stories of found money are universal, that we'd all at least consider the options before making a decision. And for those who would cross the line, there may be no turning back and a total surrender of their conscience.

Hank is a fundamentally decent person, with a pregnant wife, a mortgage and a future that he neither fantasizes nor fears. It's only when the money is in his possession, when he and his briefly appalled wife, Sarah (Bridget Fonda), allow their imaginations to embrace the possibilities, that the larceny in all men's hearts is activated in his.

Paxton, Central Casting's answer to a call for Everyman, is the perfect choice for the role. He's been playing variations on this theme of the ordinary man in extraordinary circumstances throughout his career, most notably as the small-town sheriff in "One False Move" and astronaut Fred Haise in "Apollo 13." Here, he's playing a man who is transformed from upstanding citizen to ruthless killer, without seeming to change at all.

It's a perfectly transparent performance, at once shocking and believable, and for those who prefer their dramatic arcs on a gentle curve, it's one of the year's more memorable efforts.

But most of the attention will be focused on another mesmerizing portrait of a rural simpleton by Thornton, who won an Oscar nomination and stardom as the paroled killer Karl Childers in "Sling Blade." It is Jacob, not his brother, who carries the film's moral compass, and, working with a prosthetic overbite, a rumpled winter wardrobe and a ratty mop of hair, Thornton makes him the most interesting character, as well.

Where Lou would impetuously blow his share of the loot at the soonest opportunity, and Hank would tuck it away like a pension fund to be parceled out in installments, Jacob wants to use his cut to buy and revive the farm where he and Hank grew up. He wants to reclaim his past, when he was loved and cared for, when life itself was a simple plan.

The role of Jacob is greatly expanded from the book, and the unsatisfying way that Smith and Raimi resolve the brothers' relationship in the movie is the only major change—major compromise—made in transporting the novel to the screen.

Raimi, best known for a series of visually stylish gore-fests ("Dark Man," "The Evil Dead") and one wildly quirky western ("The Quick and the Dead"), restrains his appetite for excess in order to focus on the moral deterioration of Hank. The result is a chilling blend of heartland thriller and Scandinavian gothic.

"A Simple Plan," bearing strong physical similarity to the Coen Brothers' "Fargo," is a black and white world accented in green (money) and red (blood). Virtually everything before Alar

Kivilo's camera is staged against a backdrop of knee-deep snow, under an ominous sky, creating for the audience—as it seems to for the characters—a mood of constant and ever-warranted dread.

NEW YORK, 12/21-28/98, p. 146, Peter Reiner

Wintry rural Minnesota gets the dark treatment in *A Simple Plan*. The snowdrifts seem to be covering up some vast horror. When a raven stands out against the blinding white, the effect is pure malevolence—black has never seemed blacker. Director Sam Raimi, working from a script by Scott B. Smith, is known primarily as a gonzo goremeister with a hyperkinetic visual style. Here, he's pared down his act: There's an elemental contrast between the dazzling drifts in this film and the dark figures scurrying across them. This is a morality play conceived literally in terms of black and white.

It's also steeped in the conventions of pulp *noir,* rural-style. We first hear Hank (Bill Paxton) in one of those measured, mournful *noir* voice-overs telling us how his storybook life went awry. In flashback, we see him trudging through his Currier and Ives snowscape to his twinkly pregnant wife, Sarah (Bridget Fonda). She has a Stepford Wife perfectness. The town sheriff (Chelcie Ross) is peachy-keen. The horsefly in this balm turns out to be Hank's slow-witted-but-quick-to-take-offense brother Jacob (Billy Bob Thornton). Compared with Hank's Dudley Do-Right demeanor, Jacob, with his stringy hair, nerd glasses, and overbite, looks like a frostbitten troll. And yet, when the theft-murder-and-double-crossplot kicks in, Jacob turns out to be the one with the scruples.

His best and only friend, Lou (Brent Briscoe), is riding with the brothers in the beginning when they accidentally discover in the remote countryside a crashed small plane and, along with its pilot's corpse, a $4 million cache. The betrayals and paranoia that follow have an inevitability that sometimes veers dangerously close to predictability. The problem with *noir* fatalism is that we can see it coming a mile away—not just because we've been through it before with other movies and books but also because the pulp worldview is essentially limiting. Greed turns good men into bad—it doth make suckers of us all.

Raimi doesn't work up this dark allegory with lots of winks and irony. It's presented straight; there's no *Fargo*-esque folderol to distance us. It all might seem too self-importantly portentous, except the actors don't play it that way. Paxton is probably the best of his generation at playing ordinary-guy heroes. Here he shows us the hero diminished. When the straight-arrow Hank falls from grace, he can't believe he had it in him to be so *depraved.* If this could happen to him, we are made to feel, it could happen to any of us.

Thornton's Jacob has his own ordinary-guy vibe. His slowness, his scrunched ego, have a poignancy. Hank—the decent, upstanding grain-mill employee—represents the malevolence you can't spot right away. Jacob is the decency you can't spot right away. At first the brothers seem like a massive mismatch, but Paxton and Thornton bring out the little filial feints and tics that make their bond believable. They're more convincing than most of the prefab sibs who turn up in movies or sitcoms. These actors get at the sheer oddity of family connection—the way you can seem both inextricably linked and yet from different galaxies. Raimi is good with the other actors as well: Both Fonda and Briscoe pull character switcheroos that make perfect emotional sense.

The measured deliberateness of this movie suggests that Raimi is seeking deliverance from his schlock-horror roots. He shouldn't be so touchy: For flat-out cinematic invention, nothing in this film matches his *Evil Dead* phase. But what he does here he's never done before. He stands back and lets his people, not his pyrotechnics, carry the day.

NEW YORK POST, 12/11/98, p. 67, Jonathan Foreman

Shot against the silent, snow-covered landscapes of a Midwestern winter, "A Simple Plan" looks like a Breughel painting, with the odd nasty detail from Hieronymus Bosch like a crow plucking out the eyes of a corpse.

You might expect such touches from Sam Raimi, the director of "The Evil Dead" horror-comic movies. But you might not expect a tragedy-thriller of such spare intensity, or one which slows to strolling speed for long stretches in the middle.

Which is too bad, because "A Simple Plan" possesses an excellent script, outstanding performances and an emotional acuity that makes it unique among recent thrillers. Raimi and screenwriter Scott B. Smith have sewn together a combination of "Fargo" and "The Treasure of the Sierra Madre" and infused it with the stark, old-fashioned morality at the heart of horror movies and folk tales.

Sure, the superficial lesson of this film is "Don't take an idiot and a drunk as your partners in a criminal conspiracy." But its message is the classic biblical saw that love of money is the root of all evil.

Chasing a fox into the woods, three small-town guys find $4.4 million in a crashed airplane. Should they report the find or keep it for themselves? Hank (Bill Paxton), who is both college-educated and gainfully employed, argues that "you are supposed to earn the American dream, not steal it."

But his semi-retarded brother, Jacob (Billy Bob Thornton), and his brother's redneck pal soon bring him 'round.

Hank insists on keeping the money at his house, and says that they must not tell anyone about it. But once he and his wife (Bridget Fonda, wearing a rather unrealistic pregnancy prosthesis) get a good look at the bag full of $100 bills, moral corruption sets in. Within days, Hank and Lou, the drunken good old boy, are lying and vying for the allegiance of Jacob, and the first of several innocents is dead.

The prospect of wealth awakens old ambitions and reignites old resentments, cutting all three men off from their moral moorings and corroding the bonds between them. It also turns Paxton's wife—who glimpses a gleaming alternative to a destiny of penny-pinching drudgery—into a kind of small-town Lady Macbeth.

The bloody events that follow are for the most part predictable—you know that the lank-haired moron is going to wreck the whole scheme—but no less powerful.

Thornton, who has cornered the market in rural idiots, is outstanding as a man whose slowness masks a rueful psychological insightfulness. Brent Briscoe is superb as Lou, his drunken buddy. And Paxton gives the kind of quietly brilliant performance, as a decent guy gone astray and pummeled by guilt, that would mean a certain Oscar nomination in a just world.

All three riveting performances are the kind that can only be inspired by a first-rate script. And Smith's screenplay is coherent, believable and thematically satisfying in a way that is all too rare today.

In the era of Quentin Tarantino, when it has become so fashionable for moviemakers to affect an amoral, detached attitude to (non-military) violence, it's refreshing to see a film that unashamedly depicts the existence and effects of guilt.

NEWSWEEK, 12/14/98, p. 79, David Ansen

Billy Bob Thornton gives a fascinating performance in the morality tale/thriller "A Simple Plan." Thornton plays Jacob, a dim, unemployed Midwesterner with greasy hair and bad teeth. He's just the sort of pathetic country boy most actors would condescend to. But not Thornton. One afternoon Jacob; his married middle-class brother, Hank (Bill Paxton), and his good ole boy pal Lou (Brent Briscoe) are out hunting in a silent snowy field when they stumble upon a private plane crashed in the woods. Inside, they discover a dead pilot—and $4.4 million in cash. After some agonizing, the men decide to keep the money—a "simple plan" that, of course, will go fatally awry when the accomplices must resort to even greater crimes to keep their plot a secret. Soon these three men, joined by Hank's wife, Sarah (Bridget Fonda), are caught in a rat's nest of greed, paranoia, betrayal and murder.

Fans of director Sam Raimi are in for a surprise. Best-known for such luridly funny cult horror movies as "The Evil Dead" and the cartoonish action flick "Darkman," Raimi eschews his usual frenetic camera moves for an unusually spare, unobtrusive style. Working from Scott B. Smiths adaptation of his own novel, Raimi turns the screws of the relentless plot with quiet precision, aiming for queasily escalating suspense. He wants us to feel the winter chill, hear the squeak of boots on snow, sense the boredom of a small town where numbing routine can spur grandiose dreams of escape. Even Danny Elfman's score goes for understated spookiness.

Yet as well crafted as "A Simple Plan" is, as effective as many of its individual scenes are, I never quite believed that these particular people would descend so avidly into vicious amorality. Fonda's character begins as the voice of conscience, and in the course of one scene turns into a bloodstained schemer worthy of Lady Macbeth. There's something decidedly mechanical about the movie's bleak view of human nature.

The characters seem like puppets jerked around to illustrate a none-too-original theme—except, that is, for Thornton, whose complex, down-home mixture of sensitivity, self-abasement and fear is anything but generic. You can never be sure what this sad but strangely sly man will do or say next. Thornton is the best thing about the movie, but he's so distinctive he doesn't quite mesh with the other actors. You can't help but wonder how he and Paxton could be from the same gene pool. His unsettling character is like a 3-D figure in a two-dimensional landscape: he points up what's lacking in the rest of this intermittently gripping movie.

SIGHT AND SOUND, 6/99, p. 52, Philip Kemp

Smalltown Minnesota. Hank Mitchell works at the local grain store; his wife Sarah is expecting their first child. Just before New Year's Eve, Hank, his slow-witted older brother Jacob and Jacob's friend Lou find a small plane crashed in the woods. The pilot is dead. A bag in the plane contains $4,400,000. Against his better judgement and later supported by Sarah, Hank agrees they should take the money, but insists he keeps it hidden until the plane is found.

Seeing a farmer, Stephanson, heading towards the plane, Jacob strikes him down. Hank, disposing of the body, finds he isn't dead and finishes the job before making the death look accidental. Sarah discovers the money was the ransom for a kidnappings by two criminal brothers, one of whom was the plane's dead pilot. both Jacob and Lou pressure Hank to let them have some of the loot. Lou threatens blackmail. In a drunken playacting game, Hank and Jacob trick Lou into confessing' on tape to Stephanson's murder, but when he discovers their con he pulls a gun. In the shootout Lou and his wife Nancy are killed. Hank convinces local cop Carl the couple had a drunken row.

FBI agent Baxter comes looking for the plane. Carl asks Hank and Jacob to help them search for it. Sarah realises Baxter is the other kidnapper and begs Hank to stay away. Carl locates the plane and Baxter shoots him; Hank kills Baxter. Jacob forces Hank to kill him too and pass it off as Baxter's work. The real FBI tell Hank that some of the banknote numbers are recorded. Hank burns the money.

Early on in *A Simple Plan*, a man cautiously enters the fuselage of a crashed plane. The pilot is sitting in his seat, his head shaking as if in pain or incredulity. Thinking he's still alive, the newcomer speaks to him and starts forward. His movement causes the fuselage to tip, lurching him forward into the pilot—the crows that have been feeding on the dead man's face erupt in a tumult of angry squawks and stabbing beaks.

It's easy to guess how the Sam Raimi we know and love, splatter happy director of *The Evil Dead, Army of darkness, Darkman* and *The Quick and the Dead,* would have built on that scene. Easy to imagine the in-your-face shocks, the crow-haunted nightmares, the vengeful zombie with a half eaten visage chewing its way up the cast list. The humour would have been gleefully ghoulish, the characters and violence pure cartoon, the genre conventions teased and twanged and mercilessly mocked. But *A Simple Plan* is the work of a very different Sam Raimi, a film-maker who here austerely rejects hyped-up camera tricks and jokey shock effects and creates living, complex characters whose fates we care about. The result is easily his finest film to date.

The subtlety and the pervasive sense of unease are matched from the start by Danny Elfman's insidious score (hailed by Paul Tonks in *Gramophone* magazine as "the most daringly original score from Hollywood in years"). like Raimi, Elfman has come a long way from his cartoonish beginnings (a frequent Tim Burton collaborator, he scored the first two Batman films and *A Nightmare Before Christmas*). Here, he sets up the chill, edgy mood with an off-key duet between detuned piano and banjo, like a distorted reflection of small-town rural values; they're joined by an eerie ensemble of flutes, alto through bass. By the time the three men (Bill Paxton, Billy Bob Thornton and Brent Briscoe) stand beside the wrecked plane, debating what to do with the stash of loot fallen literally from the sky, there's little doubt where we're headed. Things are already going badly wrong, and they're going to get worse.

The corrosive effect of an ill-gotten windfall on ordinary lives is no new theme, of course *(Shallow Grave,* to look no further), and the use of bleak, near-monochrome Minnesota snowscapes—in fact shot in Wisconsin, since the Minnesota winter turned disobligingly mild—inevitably recalls the Coen brothers' *Fargo*. But Raimi's film never feels derivative, thanks not least to the strongly individualised performances he's drawn from his lead actors. Paxton proves once again that he's one of the most underrated (and understated) actors in Hollywood, his Hank a "nice, sweet, normal guy" horrified to find himself sucked down to disaster by one brief capitulation to his own worse instincts. As his brother Jacob, Thornton gives a masterfully gauged portrait of a man whose emotional insights—which are as acute as anybody's—are constantly wrong-footed by his mental limitations. His performance is all the more moving for never lapsing into the sentimentality that tinged his similar role in *Sling Blade*. Only Bridget Fonda, as Hank's wife Sarah, doesn't quite come together as a character—not the actress' fault but the script's since it requires her to switch a little too abruptly from moral revulsion to all-out avidity.

But *A Simple Plan* shares with *Fargo* something more than a use of rural winter backdrops: its stern, absolute morality, as starkly black and white as crows against a snowfield. An alternative title, in fact, might have been that of the film which gave Paxton his previous best role: *One False Move*. Hank's single moment of weakness, allowing himself to be persuaded by the less-grounded and their third accomplice Lou (Briscoe) instead of holding out for integrity, leads with horrifying inexorability into the abyss, making their destruction complete. Utterly different in tone as Raimi's earlier films may have been, they held in common with this latest work a sense of the fearful flimsiness of everyday normality. Just one rent in the fabric of things and darkness is let loose.

But while the plot moves with inevitable momentum to its denouement, it's far from predictable. Central to the film's dramatic impact is the way its moral centre shifts, quite unexpectedly, from Hank to Jacob. To begin with Hank clearly occupies the moral high ground: he's honest Mr Normal, the guy we identify with, while Jacob's eager venality aligns him with the shiftless Lou. When Lou describes the cash as, "the American Dream in a goddam gymbag", Hank retorts (a touch pompously), "You work for the American Dream, you don't t steal it." But as Hank embarks on his slow slide into perdition, it's Jacob, a seemingly formless figure with his protruding teeth and cheap taped-up glasses, who takes on the role of conscience. By the time he asks, "Hank, d'you ever feel evil? I do", he is confronting the questions his brother is desperately trying to evade.

The key point of transition is the scene when Hank, blackmailed by Lou to hand over some of the cash, comes to persuade his brother to help him gain counter leverage by framing Lou. As the scene progresses it emerges that for all his slowness of brain, Jacob's scruples are finer than Hank's. Where Hank sees Lou as a contemptible lowlife against whom any tactics are justified, Jacob sees a friend he is being asked to betray. His distress as Hank piles on the pressure is pitiable, and he gives in only when offered the one bribe he can't resist: that Hank will help him regain their father's farm.

Before Raimi took it on, *A Simple Plan* was to have been directed by John Boorman. A scheduling conflict with *The General* obliged him to withdraw.) It may well have been this transfer of moral stature that attracted Boorman to the project; one can imagine the film as a snowbound counterpart to Boorman's *Deliverance,* another study of everyday guys destroyed by a headlong train of events, and of an individual's self-image (Jon Voight then, Paxton now) fractured and degraded under pressure. But Raimi makes the film his own, carrying over from his previous work the sense of encroaching paranoia as formerly solid ground starts to give way beneath the feet and the avenues of escape are blocked off one by one.

Scott B. Smith, scripting from his own novel, charts his characters' descent into hell with remorseless control and impeccable narrative logic. At each step it's made clear how, at that panic-stricken moment and with no benefit of hindsight, these people could hardly have done other than they did. With each turn of the screw the options narrow down, until Hank, broken and weeping, a gun in his hand, finds himself forced into committing the final, lethal act of destruction. His grief is the more lacerating since by doing so he shatters the only thing to emerge from the grim events, a new-found closeness to his formerly estranged brother.

A Simple Plan is bookended by Hank's voice-over. At the outset he reflects how, despite the dullness of his daily round, a man like him should feel blessed in having "a wife he loves, a decent job, friends and neighbours who respect him." At the end, looking back on the betrayals and deaths, the ambitions raised and crushed, the ruin of that modest measure of contentment, he muses sombrely: "There are days when I manage not to think of anything at all. But those days are few and far between." There's more unbearable anguish in those few spare words than in all the gore and mayhem of Raimi's previous output.

TIME, 2/14/98, p. 98, Richard Schickel

Stopping by woods on a snowy day, three men discover a small, crashed plane that contains a dead pilot and a large sum of cash. They devise *A Simple Plan* to make off with the loot, and we are obliged to watch that plan unravel for what seems to be an eternity.

Despite the rural atmosphere, the bracing cold and the presence of people who seem at first glance to be honest rustics, we are not exactly in Robert Frost country here. Hank (Bill Paxton) is smart enough to guess that money in this amount is going to be pursued by its rightful (or, more likely, wrongful) owners, but he's a weak, inexplicably damaged fellow. His brother Jacob (cunningly played by Billy Bob Thornton) is a halfwit, and Jacob's pal Lou (Brent Briscoe) has a heedless temper. Back home, Hank's wife Sarah (Bridget Fonda) quickly turns into this caper's Lady Macbeth.

The movie, adapted from his own novel by Scott B. Smith and directed by Sam Raimi, whose specialty is cultish horror films, has an addled, feckless sobriety about it. These people think they're saying something serious about greed and how it can cloud people's judgment. They want you to think *Fargo* or *The Treasure of the Sierra Madre*. But there's neither intricacy nor surprise in the narrative, and these dopes are tedious, witless company. Mostly you find yourself thinking, "How long until dinner?"

VILLAGE VOICE, 12/8/98, p. 129, J. Hoberman

White-water time: The holidays are upon us and the studio floodgates are open. You can try panning for gold (or even silver) in the new-release deluge, but keep an eye open for those nuggets that could be washed away in the hype for *Prince of Egypt* or *You've Got Mail*.

Take, for example, the innocuously titled *A Simple Plan*. Compared to the fool's gold of a botched botched-caper flick like *Very Bad Things,* Sam Raimi's *A Simple Plan* is the real stuff—a relatively unselfconscious and attitude-free paragon of all-American B-movie virtue. Set in a small town refrigerated by the Minnesota winter (yet more likely to sprout palm trees than to ever see full employment), *A Simple Plan* will remind some people of *Fargo*. But, as Raimi fans know, this hardcore genre filmmaker is both more elemental in his comedy and gothic in his moral imagination than his erstwhile buddies, the Coens.

As straightforward in narrative as it is gut-wrenching in effect, *A Simple Plan* is a sort of slow-motion skid down an icy blacktop—it's a movie you watch with a mounting sense of dread. The well-behaved, uptight working stiff Hank (Bill Paxton) is trapped into a fateful alliance with his dim-witted big brother Jacob (Billy Bob Thornton) and Jacob's equally feckless, marginally less idiotic friend (Brent Briscoe) when, through a series of weird coincidences, the three guys stumble upon a small plane that has crashed in the woods, leaving a corpse and a suitcase stuffed with cash.

Greed is the word. As the casting reunites the two male principals of Carl Franklin's similarly character-driven and comparably all-business sleeper, *One False Move,* so the situation soon comes to suggest a Three Stooges *Treasure of the Sierra Madre*. The nominal brains of the trio, Hank is saddled with the problem of controlling two blabbermouth, mistrustful trolls and $4 million—not to mention his very pregnant wife (Bridget Fonda), who, if not instantly corrupted by the sight of the money, all but dons the green eyeshade to recalibrate her future.

A Simple Plan proceeds from one blunder to the next, until the increasingly paranoid principals have managed to dig themselves into a hole deeper than Bill Gates's pockets. "Nobody would ever believe you'd be capable of doing what you've done," one character tells another. Everyone is flailing on thin ice and, as with all good tundra noirs, the situation is additionally complicated by the fact that it's darned nearly impossible to cover your tracks in the snow.

Raimi puts over this cautionary tale with a few Hitchcockian flourishes and some others that might have been dreamt up in the Middle Ages. Most of the movie's special effects involve the animal kingdom—the crows that circle around the plane wreck, the fox that causes a truck to skid off the road and later visits the henhouse. *A Simple Plan* goes reliably over the top with one domestic bloodbath—perhaps the only scene more alarming than the ongoing spectacle of Thornton, grinning (or grimacing) like a jack-o'-lantern around a prosthetic overbite and beneath a coiffure that, except for its burnt sienna hue, resembles one of Andy Warhol's old wigs.

A Simple Plan is both an extremely credible thriller and an affecting brother-story. As even an apparently "victimless" crime begins to exact its inevitable toll, conjugal love gives way to furious disappointment, small-town coziness turns horribly claustrophobic, security dissolves into desperation, and family ties knot themselves into a noose. It's a tribute to Raimi's single-minded vision that his movie's choked-up ending is as stark in its moral schemata as anything produced in the heyday of silent-movie German Expressionism.

Also reviewed in:
CHICAGO TRIBUNE, 12/11/98, Friday/p. B, Mark Caro
NATION, 1/11 & 18/99, p. 36, Stuart Klawans
NEW YORK TIMES, 12/11/98, p. E16, Janet Maslin
VARIETY, 9/21-27/98, p. 106, Glenn Lovell
WASHINGTON POST, 1/22/99, p. C1, Stephen Hunter
WASHINGTON POST, 1/22/99, Weekend/p. 38, Michael O'Sullivan

SIX DAYS, SEVEN NIGHTS

A Touchstone Pictures release in association with Caravan Pictures of a Roger Birnbaum/Northern Lights Entertainment production. *Executive Producer:* Joe Medjuck, Daniel Goldberg, and Julie Bergman Sender. *Producer:* Ivan Reitman, Wallis Nicita, and Roger Birnbaum. *Director:* Ivan Reitman. *Screenplay:* Michael Browning. *Director of Photography:* Michael Chapman. *Editor:* Sheldon Kahn and Wendy Greene Bricmont. *Music:* Randy Edelman. *Music Editor:* John LaSalandra. *Choreographer:* Kapu Alquiza. *Sound:* Gene Cantamessa. *Sound Editor:* Howell Gibbens. *Casting:* Michael Chinich and Bonnie Timmerman. *Production Designer:* J. Michael Riva. *Art Director:* David F. Klassen. *Set Designer:* Pamela Klamer and Patricia Klawonn. *Set Decorator:* Lauri Gaffin. *Set Dresser:* Douglas McKay, Marco Lopez, Mike R. Berman, and John Marano. *Special Effects:* Larry Cavanaugh and Bruce Steinheimer. *Costumes:* Gloria Gresham. *Make-up:* Ken Chase. *Make-up (Harrison Ford):* Michael Laudati. *Make-up (Anne Heche):* Elaine Offers. *Stunt Coordinator:* Doug Coleman. *Running time:* 146 minutes. *MPAA Rating:* PG-13.

CAST: Harrison Ford (Quinn Harris); Anne Heche (Robin Monroe); Amy Sedaris (Robin's Secretary); David Schwimmer (Frank Martin); Jacqueline Obradors (Angelica); Temuera Morrison (Jager); Allison Janney (Marjorie); Douglas Weston (Phillippe); Cliff Curtis (Kip); Danny Trejo (Pierce); Ben Bodé (Helicopter Pilot); Derek Basco (Ricky); Michael Chapman (Handsome Mechanic); E. Kalani Flores (Tahitian Priest); Ping Wu (Infirmary Orderly); Greg Gorman (Photographer); Hoyt Richards and Odile Broulard (Models); Cynthia Langbridge (Resort Greeter); Jody Kono (Hotel Clerk); Michael Lushing (Front Desk Clerk); Pua Kaholokula (Waitress); Ron Dinson, Jr. and Don Nahaku (Bellboys); Priscilla Lee Taylor (Bathing Suit Girl); Reri Tava Jobe and Natalie Goss (Flight Attendants); Christian Martson and James Edward Sclafani (French Airport Security); Jason S. Nichols (Runway Traffic); Taj Mahal (Himself).

CHRISTIAN SCIENCE MONITOR, 6/12/98, p. B3, David Sterritt

"Six Days, Seven Nights" is billed as a romantic adventure. But with director Ivan Reitman guiding the tour, you know a boatload of gags can't be far away, even if Harrison Ford—not exactly a comedy specialist—is its main box-office draw.

Sure enough, the movie announces its comic intentions almost as soon as David Schwimmer proposes to Anne Heche that they celebrate their betrothal by escaping wintery Manhattan for a week of faraway sunshine.

The pilot of their island-hopping plane (Ford) turns out to be a goofy guy who cares more about lowdown pleasure than high-flying professionalism. Several plot twists and a thunderstorm later, he and Heche are forced to crash-land on an isolated island. There they pepper each other with wisecracks, flee the clutches of modern-day pirates, and—surprise!—fall battily in love with each other. Meanwhile the abandoned boyfriend mourns his fiancée's disappearance for about two seconds, then falls into the arms of a tropical temptress.

"Six Days, Seven Nights" labors mightily to be a frolicsome entertainment, but the results are—well, labored. The dialogue isn't snappy, the story isn't surprising, there's little chemistry between the stars, and you can't help wondering whether people undergoing an ordeal like this would really think about sex every single minute, even in a Hollywood movie.

Disney's decision to market "Six Days, Seven Nights" by emphasizing thrills over laughter suggests that the film's own studio recognized its clunkiness in the humor department. Reitman has struck comic gold with bygone crowd-pleasers like "Dave" and the "Ghostbusters" pictures, so he'll surely bounce back with a really amusing project before long. For now, this is a vacation moviegoers can afford to miss.

LOS ANGELES TIMES, 6/12/98, Calendar/p. 1, Kenneth Turan

"Six Days, Seven Nights" must have sounded irresistible on paper. In fact, on paper it still does.

"Here's Harrison Ford the way you like to see him, the rugged man's man with the crooked grin and gruff charm. Who's he paired with but the lovely Anne Heche, the ingenue of the moment, fresh from winning plaudits in 'Wag the Dog.' And look who's directing! It's laughmeister Ivan Reitman, the king of can't-miss comedies like 'Kindergarten Cop,' 'Beethoven' and 'Twins.' What could go wrong?"

In fact, looked at that way, not much has. "Six Days, Seven Nights" is an acceptable star vehicle, no better or worse than it should be, a well-worn standard diversion that gets the job done without eliciting either howls of fury or paroxysms of delight.

What "Six Days" lacks is what no one thought was necessary, the spark of originality. It's part sex comedy, part screwball romance, part adventure yarn, part anything that writer Michael Browning felt might conceivably hook an audience.

In both conception and execution, "Six Days" is too predictable and by the book to wow anyone. It chooses instead the safer path of echoing everything from "African Queen" to "Romancing the Stone" to (with its outdoor guy tames snippy, already-spoken-for New York magazine gal plot) "The Horse Whisperer."

It's in Manhattan on a particularly snowy day that things begin. Robin Monroe (Heche) is an assistant editor for Dazzle Magazine, a Cosmopolitan clone run by grand dame Marjorie Howell (Allison Janney in a brisk, amusing cameo). Robin's boyfriend Frank Martin (David Schwimmer) is a workaholic attorney, but that's about to change.

Stung by Robin's complaints that they never do anything or go anywhere, Frank has signed the couple up for six days and seven nights on the secluded South Pacific island paradise of Makatea (Kauai in real life). "I want this to be," Frank says in one of those movie lines that you know he's going to wish he hadn't even thought, "the most unforgettable vacation of our lives."

For the unforgettable part of this particular vacation turns out to be pilot Quinn Harris (Ford), owner-operator of one-plane Harris Freight and introduced (in a scene he shares with director of photography Michael Chapman) with grease on his face and a hearty curse on his lips. Though he modestly denies it, Quinn is, as Robin insists, "one of those guy guys. You send them into the wilderness with a pocket knife and a Q-tip and they build you a shopping mall."

Naturally, Robin and Quinn take a dislike to each other at once; how else can we be sure they're meant to connect? Fate throws them together when Marjorie Howell calls from New York and begs Robin to sacrifice a day of her vacation to fly to nearby Tahiti and baby-sit a photo shoot with, no kidding, Vendela and Evander Holyfield.

Quinn's sturdy DeHavilland Beaver turns out to be the only available plane, but halfway into the trip terrible weather comes up awfully fast. Quicker than you can say, "I told you so," the Beaver is disabled by lightning and deposits its two passengers on an uninhabited island without any way off or the means to let the outside world know they're alive.

Not surprisingly, the crash exacerbates the dislike these two feel for each other. But though they loudly insist they're not each other's type, the film sanctions their romantic link by pushing together people they left behind: her boyfriend, Frank, and his girlfriend, Angelica (Jacqueline Obradors, who enlarges a standard party girl part with a gift for comic delivery).

Robin and Quinn work their way through a laundry list of disasters, including snakes in her pants and a band of marauding pirates, that are strictly standard-issue. The appealing professionalism and chemistry of both stars make what's happening on screen more satisfying than it has a right to be.

Ford is intimately familiar with guy guy parts, and he handles this one like the smooth veteran he is. Though Heche has been an impressive actress as far back as independent vehicles like "Walking and Talking" and "Pie in the Sky," she's never before had the chance to exhibit a wisecracking Barbara Stanwyck side, and she handles the opportunity with skill and fine style.

In addition to the work itself, both Ford and Heche probably had ulterior motives for taking on "Six Days, Seven Nights." A serious pilot, Ford no doubt relished the chance to actually fly a plane on film. And Heche (whose relationship with Ellen DeGeneres has been widely publicized) wanted, like all young actresses, the opportunity to establish herself as an A-list romantic lead, something she does flawlessly. Incentives for the audience, however, are not always as gratifying or well-defined.

NEW YORK, 6/22/98, p. 58, David Denby

Some people in Hollywood must be having sex fantasies about female magazine editors, because here's *Six Days, Seven Nights*, another of those romantic fables about a will-driven, sensually undernourished New York editor who leaves the big city, falls into outdoor adventure, and finds fulfillment in the arms of a real man in the loamy (or in this case sandy) wilds. Without the perturbed elegance of Kristin Scott Thomas, who seemed to be playing Tina Brown or Anna Wintour or both, *The Horse Whisperer* would have been unwatchable-swill, really—and Anne Heche, more volatile than Scott Thomas, a comedian by temperament, is pretty much the only reason to see *Six Days, Seven Nights*. The picture is a clownish retread of familiar material from old movies. Director Ivan Reitman, who has given us all some pleasure (in *Stripes* and the *Ghostbusters* movies), can settle for so little at times. *Six Days, Seven Nights* is not as feeble as *Fathers' Day;* it's just lame and tiresome. What has happened to Reitman's instinct for the offbeat, the eccentric, the extravagantly silly?

Heche is initially matched up with David Schwimmer, a man patently wrong for her. I must say I'm amazed by Schwimmer—he seems utterly hapless to me. What is the point of these people's toning up their bodies if they are going to go so limp onscreen? (At least Schwimmer should get rid of his hangdog expression, so critics don't have to use the word *hangdog* so often.) Anyway, Heche and Schwimmer take a vacation in the South Seas, but Heche gets ordered by her boss to do a photo shoot so she and Harrison Ford, a drunken old pilot, take off in an ancient De Havilland Beaver that couldn't make it from here to New Jersey. You may not be astonished to hear that the plane crash-lands on the beach of a deserted island. Of course, they loathe each other; he thinks she's spoiled, not a real woman, etc., and she thinks he's a second-rater and a wreck. They hustle up and down hills and crags, and frequently fall into sand and water, which is not quite the same thing as actually having adventures. There is, of course, the immortal scene in which he pulls a snake out of her underpants (a lewd version of Bogart pulling the leeches off Hepburn in *The African Queen*). The generic elements stack up quickly: The Strange But Satisfying Meal (peacock), the Night of Safety (under a tree that holds an old Japanese warplane), the Unexpected Attack (from scummy pirates, who seem to have been ordered up, complete with ratty hair and tattoos, over a telephone), and so on.

I'm glad that Anne Heche, who has spirit and intelligence, wants to establish herself as a romantic lead, though I regret that she has to scream lines like "There's nothing wrong with my tits!" in order to do so. She has great allure—brimming eyes, a supernal glow—when she warms up to Ford. But what is she warming up to? Ford is certainly eager to shed any mythic baggage that may have accumulated from his former heroic roles. He's too eager: There's hardly a movie star left in him. Ford mugs and staggers, furrowing his brow, thrusting his jaw. For the first time in his life, he's a commonplace actor and just outright bad.

NEW YORK POST, 6/12/98, p. 39, Rod Dreher

"Six Days, Seven Nights" may well be how long it took rookie screenwriter Michael Browning to dash off this watchable but thoroughly routine romantic comedy—yet another polished, if undistinguished, bit of movie product by blandoid director Ivan Reitman.

Harrison Ford and Anne Heche star as two desert-island castaways who battle the hostile elements, snakes, scorpions and pirates as they wait for rescuers. The more formidable foes are hackneyed repartee and a lack of chemistry between the charismatic Heche and the overly gruff Ford, who are destined to fall in love, but only because the movie's straitjacket formula won't have it any other way.

For the record, lipstick lesbian pin-up gal Heche is entirely convincing as a love interest for hetero hunk Ford. After you get past an early scene, in which a snake crawls unwelcome into Heche's pants (har dee har har), the issue quickly fades. If the two don't exactly charm like Hepburn and Bogart in "The African Queen" (or even like Alan Hale and Bob Denver on "Gilligan's Island"), it has nothing to do with Heche's off-screen preferences.

The movie opens in snowbound Manhattan, where a wet-blanket yupster named Frank Martin (David Schwimmer) surprises his magazine editor sweetie Robin Monroe (Heche) with a pair of tickets to a tropical getaway. Once on the sunny, sultry island, Frank proposes marriage, and the lovebirds took forward to a week of betrothed bliss under the South Pacific sun.

And what a destination! By far the best part of "Six Days" is the spellbinding scenery: the azure seas, the opalescent lagoons, the shimmering shorelines and the lush, emerald forests go far in making, up for the ordinariness of the story. The film was shot on location in Kauai, whose tourist industry should benefit handsomely.

Their rum-soaked reverie is interrupted when Robin's boss calls from New York and orders her briefly to nearby Tahiti to supervise a photo shoot. The officious editrix has to engage the services of Quinn Harris (Ford), the harrumphy old salt who flew them to the isolated island paradise in his dumpy four-seater plane. The plane goes down on a lost island.

Circumstances force urban snoot Robin to appreciate the hunter-gatherer skills of the manly-man Quinn. The plot leads them into enough precarious situations to maintain our interest, if not our enthusiasm, and there are a couple of enjoyably snickery moments. But Ford, so commanding in intelligent action roles, proves just as flat-footed and weighty in this romantic comedy as he did in "Sabrina." The lively Heche can only do so much.

"Six Days" makes a persuasive case that when the going gets rough, even the most liberated woman wants a tough guy with oldfashioned values. Though the lonesome beach offers a seductive bed for Robin and her brush-cut Crusoe, the mighty Quinn is too much of an honorable guy to take advantage of her. The movie's message is that love can be born out of shared adversity, and certainly proves itself under those conditions.

Or doesn't, as the case may be. With his fiancee missing, Robin's boyfriend Frank is stuck back at the resort, fretting and drowning his anxieties in mai tais—and finding comfort in the bosomy embrace of Angelica (Jacqueline Obradors), Quinn's exotic-dancer girlfriend. I suppose Schwimmer, one of those wussy males from "Friends," is right for the role, but he's a squishy, whiny bore. Without Ford, the film could be called "Romancing the Drone."

NEWSDAY, 6/12/98, Part II/p. B3, Jack Mathews

Who says they don't make 'em like they used to? Ivan Reitman's "Six Days, Seven Nights," a romantic comedy-adventure featuring attractive stars in an exotic setting, with downed planes, mean pirates, white beaches, great speeches, short tempers, long kisses and tropical drinks, is exactly what they used to make.

In fact, if first time screenwriter Michael Browning's script for "Six Days", could be time-warped back to Hollywood's Golden Age, MGM's Louis B. Mayer would have the South Pacific re-created on the back lot and have Clark Gable and Jean Harlow matching wits and falling in love there within a week.

It's too expensive to rebuild the world in Hollywood these days, and we're too accustomed to actuality to accept anything less. So, Reitman and his stars, a perfectly matched Harrison Ford and Anne Heche, traveled to the South Pacific—rather, to Kauai, which subs for the South Pacific—where this unlikely couple is marooned after a plane wreck.

The title refers to the length of the vacation planned by uptight Manhattan yuppie Frank Martin (a very funny David Schwimmer), who has chosen this romantic tropical location to pop the question to girlfriend Robin Monroe (Heche), a magazine editor. But no sooner do they arrive and he pops the question (and she says yes) than she's called away to supervise an urgent photo shoot in Tahiti.

It's a short, three-hour plane ride away; she'll be back in a flash. But en route, Robin and her boozy, weathered pilot Quinn (Ford) fly into an electrical storm and end up crash-landed on a beach on a remote, unpopulated island. They don't have the means to communicate with anyone but each other, a situation that evolves from a chore to a necessity to restrained passion.

Meanwhile, back at the resort, where word is received that the search for the lost airplane has been called off, the grief-stricken Frank is having to restrain his own passion. The crisis has brought him together with Quinn's sometime girlfriend Angelica (Jacqueline Obradors), a free-spirited, engagingly addled dancer who believes the best way for two people to handle grief is to handle each other. After all, she asks, doesn't everybody go home after a funeral and have sex?

"Six Days" has its tense moments, and its share of special effects, but it's otherwise that rare modern summer movie that succeeds or fails on the strength and chemistry of its stars; both couples—Ford and Heche, and Schwimmer and Obradors—are terrific together.

Ford shows a self-deprecating humor here that we haven't often seen since the "Star Wars" trilogy, and it's a refreshing change from his sober, rigid-backed heroes. He seems finally comfortable with his stardom, seasoned and relaxed enough to sport with his own image. Although he's an astonishingly fit 55-year-old actor, Ford turns Quinn into something of a lovable softy, a rundown rogue who has checked out of society and into the passive life of a liquored beach bum and part-time pilot.

Quinn's relationship with the effervescent, stubborn, indefatigable Robin will change all that, and Heche's performance ought to move her into the front rank of Hollywood leading ladies. She has a natural beauty that benefits from the added glow of her warmly funny personality, and she seems—for Ford's character and for us—to become sexier as her adventure wears on.

Reitman had shown unerring commercial instincts with mostly broad comic fare like "Ghostbusters," "Twins" and "Kindergarten Cop" before stumbling with last summer's "Fathers' Day." "Six Days, Seven Nights" is a pure confection as well, but it's aimed at the same mature audience that made a hit of Reitman's "Dave." Good show.

SIGHT AND SOUND, 8/98, p. 53, Jonathan Romney

Robin Monroe, an assistant editor on a New York fashion magazine, is invited by her boyfriend Frank Martin for a week's holiday on the Polynesian paradise island of Makatea. On arrival he proposes marriage and she accepts. When Robin is called away for an emergency photo shoot in Tahiti, gruff local pilot Quinn Harris agrees to fly her there in his rickety plane. En route a storm breaks out and they are forced to make an emergency landing on an unknown island, wrecking the plane's wheels in the process. Stranded together, Robin and Quinn initially carp at each other but soon feel a mutual attraction. Meanwhile, on Makatea, Frank shares his concern with Quinn's dancer girlfriend Angelica and ends up sleeping with her.

Exploring the island, Robin and Quinn encounter a shipload of pirates who pursue them. Discovering a wrecked seaplane, they use its floats to rebuild their plane and escape the pirates. Back on Makatea, Frank attempts to confess his infidelity to Robin, but she is already contemplating a life with Quinn. About to fly home with Frank, she leaves the plane to be reunited with Quinn.

A fussy, flustered urban girl and a gruff but cuddly tough adrift in an ocean paradise—we hardly need a map to find our way around this familiar island. For atavism and sexual embarrassment, *Six Days Seven Nights* is hardly in the league of Nicolas Roeg's *Castaway*. The teaming of Harrison Ford and Anne Heche is conceived more along the lines of Bogart and Hepburn in *The African Queen* though Ford and Heche's rapport hardly crackles.

This must be the most desultory castaway yarn ever, its plot designed only to wear out its protagonists until they give up and fall into each other's arms. The excuse to get them stranded is Robin's emergency dash to a photo shoot with Vendela and Evander Holyfield— a superficial errand if ever there was one. The perils she and Quinn face—storms, landslides, pirates—are thrown in and cast aside like obstacles in a computer game, as if the narrative had been cribbed from a Lara Croft video game. The film shows scant interest in any of the things that traditionally drive Crusoe tales: there are no DIY survival tactics, and after one idyllic meal of barbecued peacock and fruit cocktail, the duo seem to give up eating entirely.

Ivan Reitman's film has only one plausible function—as a research exercise to test the star quality of Anne Heche, who had short shrift in her most prominent billing so far, *Volcano*. She gives *Six Days* just enough energy to get by, although there's nothing either novel or especially charismatic in her repertoire of eye-rolling and outraged double takes. She and Ford face off briskly, exchanging testy insults in the time-honoured way, but they're hardly Gable and Lombard, or even Doris Day and Rock Hudson to whose ingenuously risqué pairings *Six Days* harks back. In terms of sexual roleplay, it's a 60s movie through and through. Robin struggles through various slapstick indignities to end up making encouraging goo-goo eyes at her hero: "I need you to be a very confident captain," she pleads. Don't expect this to enhance Heche's status with her lesbian audience.

The situation is only updated by innuendo. Robin yanks a flare gun out of Quinn's shorts, he fishes in hers for a poisonous snake—it's this, apparently, that first sparks her interest. 'I'm not sure I trust your equipment," she taunts. "We may be old but we're sturdy," he retorts. But the film severely tests Ford's viability as a romantic figurehead for the Viagra generation. He was already an improbable romantic lead in the recent remake of *Sabrina*, where at least his stuffiness worked to his advantage. Here, he's ill at ease attempting to fill Cary Grant's *Father Goose* (1964) beachcomber shoes.

The rest is by-the-book trimming: David Schwimmer's whimpering boyfriend is a direct descendent of such early 60s urban jerks as Tony Randall and Dick York; Jacqueline Obradors is a Selma Hayek vamp with a comic squeaky voice; and the dreadlocked pirates—headed by Maori actor Temuera Morrison *(Once Were Warriors)*—are stereotypes even Daniel Defoe would have thought twice about using. As the film crawls to its bathetic reunion, the idea that the lovers will now languish together on their island paradise feels like a horrifying prospect. What's Robin going to do for the rest of her life? Mix cocktails? Mend dinghies? Still, the local band is headed by blues legend Taj Mahal, which is as much entertainment as she can reasonably hope for.

VILLAGE VOICE, 6/23/98, p. 140, Amy Taubin

Call it the Tina Brown syndrome. When you want to show a woman so consumed by her career that she's in danger of losing her humanity, make her an editor. Hard on the heels of *The Horse Whisperer* and *High Art* come *Hav Plenty* and *Six Days, Seven Nights*. What these films have in common is a pair of mismatched lovers, one of whom is dedicated to mass-marketing trivia in glossy packages, while the other turns away from consumer culture for something purer or more natural.

In *Six Days, Seven Nights*, Harrison Ford plays a fiftysomething guy named Quinn whose sole ambition is to keep his life as simple as possible. Quinn's desires seem to have had a profound influence on the film as a whole. *Six Days, Seven Nights* has the most minimal of plots. That's one of its charms, the others being Ford's low-key comic performance, Ivan Reitman's light directorial touch, and some very pretty landscape shots of South Pacific islands.

Quinn is a beach bum who makes a living piloting tourists in his ancient single-engine plane. Thanks to unforeseen heavy weather, he ends up stranded on an uninhabited island with Robin (Anne Heche), a vacationing editor who had hired him to fly her to Tahiti for an emergency photo shoot. In the course of foraging for food and fighting off pirates armed with assault rifles, Quinn and Robin fall in love. Meanwhile their respective girlfriend and boyfriend (played by the bodacious Jacqueline Obradors and the whiny David Schwimmer) believing themselves bereaved, find comfort in each others arms. Whenever Reitman runs out of uncomplicated things for Ford and Heche to do or say, he cuts away to Schwimmer ogling Obradors as she shakes her marimbas or strips out of her bikini.

Six Days, Seven Nights has so little on its mind that it practically demands us to think about extracurricular matters—such as star quality. What is it exactly that makes Ford—a fairly ordinary-looking middle-aged man who occasionally enjoys poking fun at his obvious masculinity—a great star and Heche no more than a minor comic actress who can do a triple take without being embarrassing? That there's no chemistry between Ford and Heche has less to do with the fact that we know her as Ellen's real-life girlfriend (were those unflattering lavender dresses really necessary?) than that, cinematically speaking, they're galaxies apart.

Also reviewed in:
CHICAGO TRIBUNE, 6/12/98, Friday/p. A, Michael Wilmington
NEW YORK TIMES, 6/12/98, p. E1, Janet Maslin
VARIETY, 6/8-14/98, p. 66, Todd McCarthy
WASHINGTON POST, 6/12/98, p. B1, Rita Kempley
WASHINGTON POST, 6/12/98, Weekend/p. 44, Michael O'Sullivan

SKIN AND BONE

A Jour de Fete Films release. *Producer:* Claudia Lewis and Gardner Monks. *Director:* Everett Lewis. *Screenplay:* Everett Lewis. *Director of Photography:* Fernando Aruguelles. *Editor:* Andrew Morreale. *Music:* Fernando Arguelles. *Running time:* 114 minutes. *MPAA Rating:* Not Rated.

CAST: B. Wyatt (Harry);   Alan Boyce (Dean);   Garret Scullin (Billy);   Chad Kula (Bruno);   Nicole Dillenberg (Ghislaine);   Susannah Melvoin (Lovely Girl);   Clark Brolly (Frankie).

WITH: Winston Jones;   Gregory Sporleder;   Buzzhead.

LOS ANGELES TIMES, 12/16/98, Calendar/p. 3, Kevin Thomas

Everett Lewis' "Skin & Bone" tells a story as old as Hollywood but he freshens it up with the same cool, detached manner that made his earlier take on L.A. alienation, "The Natural History of Parking Lots," so memorable. Lewis' view of his three male hustlers is both mordant and tender at the same time.

When we meet B. Wyatt's Harry, he thinks he's on the verge of putting prostitution behind him just as Alan Boyce's Dean is about to start. Both are in the employ of Ghislaine (Nicole Dillenberg), who runs her call-boy service largely out of her convertible as she constantly prowls the streets, ostensibly looking for new employees. Hers is a high-end, anything-goes-as-long-as-you-can-afford-it kind of operation, which she conducts with a cell phone and the longest customer checklist you've ever seen. She wants to know precisely what the client wants and in turn wants to make it crystal clear as to what her rates will be.

Harry, who looks to be in his late 20s, is asked by Ghislaine to look after neophyte Dean, tells the boyish youth that what he'll be doing has nothing to do with himself, that it's just an acting exercise. Of course, Dean's first job is so easy and lucrative that he thinks prostitution will be a breeze. The truth is to the contrary, for Ghislaine caters to the degrading and dangerously kinky.

Lewis has stated that "Skin & Bone" is "about giving your soul away and rationalizing the loss as a bonus," and is a metaphor "for the experiences I suffered attempting to make a film at an evil film company." It is in fact key to seeing the film as a metaphor for self-delusion, because in reality both Harry and Dean could make it as independent hustlers and not have to risk their lives all the time working for someone else.

The third hustler is Billy (Garret Scullin), a tall, thin, long-haired youth who has a fatal penchant for picking up the wrong guy, but Harry, who daydreams about a lovely girl, is decidedly the film's central figure. He's likable and earnest and Wyatt, who co-starred in "Natural History," is very convincing in his portrayal. But Harry is crucially out of touch with himself, so much so that he's actually shocked when confronted with the reality of the casting couch. Later he turns down a part in something called "Satanic Youth 4" even though he's never acted in anything except a student production.

Even though "Skin & Bone" is extreme in its depiction of its characters' seedy world, it is nonetheless compelling, for Lewis is a filmmaker of economical style and impassioned commitment. He's drawn impressive performances from everyone in a substantial cast, except for Dillenberg, who is too callow for Ghislaine.

"Skin & Bone," which benefits from Fernando Arguelles' black-and-white camera work and apt music, is tremendously touching, sometimes funny but finally tragic.

NEW YORK POST, 9/25/98, p. 48, Bill Hoffmann

Pain is the name of the game in "Skin and Bone"—a grim, unpleasant tale of three Hollywood hustlers who run a fantasy role-playing business for men.

For a price, buffed-up sickos Henry, Dean and Billy dress up and strip down to beat, bite, pinch, punch and sexually abuse their equally demented clientele.

No wallop to the groin, no blow to the face, no smash to the kidneys is left unrecorded. Viewers will wince and writhe along with those unfortunate characters on the receiving end.

Particularly gruesome is a snuff-film sequence, in which a customer is hog-tied, sexually tortured with a baton and then murdered as a camera rolls.

Is this entertainment? For sadists, sociopaths and serial killers, maybe.

VILLAGE VOICE, 10/6/98, p. 128, Vince Aletti

Everett Lewis's fitfully comic, pitifully pretentious soap opera about a trio of L.A. male escorts runs out of promise so quickly that only the most tenacious (or desperate) viewers will hang on till the sorry end. The boys work for an agency that seems to be run from behind the wheel of a convertible by a black-wigged madam with the whine of a put-upon salesgirl. The clients, a uniformly creepy bunch, mix their sadomasochism with a dash of theater of the absurd. One dresses up as a general in order to be rousted from his car and beaten by hustlers dressed up as cops; another watches from behind a door while a nude escort mops his kitchen floor.

Antics like these make it easier for the rent boys to pretend that they're just actors doing a job. Late in the film, Harry (B. Wyatt), the seasoned leader of the pack and a movie actor wannabe, gets his chance to turn legit. After bending over for a big agent, he's cast in My Bloody Cop, and unaccountably, they love him. But Harry's redemption is too late (and too unbelievable; we've already seen him act); instead of escaping the racket, he and his buddies, like all good whores, get their ugly comeuppance. "Fantasy has its price," "Skin and Bone's" ad line reads; we can't afford it.

Also reviewed in:
NEW YORK TIMES, 9/25/98, p. E25, Anita Gates
VARIETY, 7/1-14/96, p. 39, Dennis Harvey

SLAM

A Metro Tartan release of an Offline Entertainment Group and Slam Pictures presentation. *Executive Producer:* David Peipers and Henri M. Kessler. *Producer:* Henri M. Kessler, Marc Levin, and Richard Stratton. *Director:* Marc Levin. *Screenplay:* Marc Levin, Bonz Malone, Sonja Sohn, Richard Stratton, and Saul Williams. *Story:* Marc Levin and Richard Stratton. *Director of Photography:* Mark Benjamin. *Editor:* Emir Lewis. *Sound:* David Hocs. *Make-up:* Zeal Harris. *Running time:* 103 minutes. *MPAA Rating:*

CAST: Saul Williams (Ray Joshua); Sonja Sohn (Lauren Bell); Bonz Malone (Hopha); Lawrence Wilson (Big Mike); Beau Sia (Jimmy Huang); Andre Taylor (China); Momolu Stewart (Bay/Jail Rapper); Ron Jones and Reamer Shedrick (Do Wop Cops); Allan E. Lucas (Chief C.O.); Dominic Chianese, Jr. (Officer Dom); Jerome Goldman (Jail Class Poet "Why"); DJ Renegade (Party Poet "Diminuendo In Blue"); Liza Jesse Peterson (Slam Poet "Ice Cream"); Taylor Mali (Slam Poet "Like"); Bob Holman (Slam M.C.); Rhozier Brown

(Public Defender); Richard Stratton (Prosecutor); Marion Barry, Jr. (Judge); Margaret Moore (Director (D.C.)); Patricia Jackson (DC Jail Warden); Weusi Baraka (Weed Buyer (Dodge City)); Daniel M. Favors and Johnny Foye (Jail C.O.'s); Jesse Hicks (Command Center C.O.); Carolyn Morris (Hallway C.O.); Leonard A. Thompson, Jr. and Todd Baker (Bullpen Inmates); Joseph Wilson (Poetry Class); Talib Wilson (Thug Life Crew); Kevin Kennedy and Donnell Robinson (Van Inmates).

LOS ANGELES TIMES, 10/21/98, Calendar/p. 5, Kevin Thomas

Saul Williams, a handsome spoken-word poetry whiz, who was featured in the recent documentary "Slam Nation," now stars in Marc Levin's fictional "Slam." A young man with a charismatic presence and a dazzling talent as a poet in recitation, he also proves to be such an accomplished actor you could envision him in a wide range of roles, rhymed or not.

"Slam" has an undeniable power and energy, but you may find it on the whole a surprisingly modest endeavor to have scored so highly at both the Sundance Film Festival, where it took the Grand Jury Prize, and at Cannes, where it won the Camera d'Or and the audience award.

The film's title refers to "slamming," a dynamic combining of the art of performance and poetry that has spawned many competitions. Williams and Levin collaborated on the script with three other actors, but "Slam" seems all of a piece. Essentially, it's an exceedingly simple story in which Ray (Williams) is getting by in a grim, sprawling southeast Washington, D.C., housing project by selling marijuana. It's his bad luck to be found carrying a quarter pound of grass when the cops arrive to investigate a drive-by shooting he has witnessed.

Surprisingly, Ray doesn't know what's in store for him: 18 months to two years in a D.C. jail or the almost absolute certainty of a 10-year sentence should he plead innocent. Just as the realities of jail are hitting him, he's overheard slamming by Lauren Bell (Sonja Sohn), a beautiful writing teacher at the jail who, lamentably, is about to be laid off because of cutbacks. A gifted slammer herself, Lauren is passionately dedicated to reaching the prisoners, virtually all of them black, to break the perpetual cycle of crime that determines their lives. She zeroes in on Ray, recognizing in him a major talent.

Lauren realizes all too well the hard lives these convicts have had in an unjust world, but she refuses to condone crime, especially drug-dealing, as an alternative. She doesn't pretend to have the socioeconomic answers to the injustices of racism but pleads with the men to try to discover freedom within themselves.

When Ray is unexpectedly bailed out, he finds himself at a crossroads, a brief interlude during which Lauren arranges for him to perform. He does, to electrifying effect, thus bringing him to a point at which he must decide what kind of life he will lead.

Levin brings to "Slam" a raw, impressionistic style that expresses its highly charged emotions effectively and goes a long way to offset that there's not much in the way of traditional-style character development.

There are moments when Williams seems a bit too sophisticated for Ray, but he impresses strongly, as does Sohn. There are brief appearances by champion slammers Beau Sia and Taylor Mali, both featured prominently in "Slam Nation," and D.C. Mayor Marion Barry has a cameo, playing a righteous judge, a sly bit of casting.

NEW YORK POST, 10/9/98, p. 46, Larry Worth

Having already earned Sundance's Grand Jury Prize and the Camera d'Or at Cannes, "Slam"—Marc Levin's feature-film debut—has garnered nonstop acclaim. And this time, the buzz is warranted.

Levin's work is nothing less than entrancing as he focuses—often with hand-held camera—on Raymond, a young would-be poet who can't climb out of the 'hood. And after he gets busted on a minor drug rap, his future prospects diminish further still.

But his life is destined to change. Once he gets past a lawyer who tells him he doesn't have a chance, a fetching prison teacher helps Raymond at least consider matters from a healthier perspective.

What could have turned into a gooey love story or unrealistic rehab tale instead sticks to its tough, hard-edged roots. It beats the odds further still as it injects a subplot about poetry slams that gives the production some of its strongest moments.

For that matter, the portrayal of rap on the screen has never before seemed so much an art form. Levin taps its urgency and power, complementing a streetwise tone that drives home the ghetto's never-ending cycle of violence.

On the down side, Levin's rendering of prison horrors seems all too familiar, while some of the photography—arty shots at sunset, with Raymond staring into a body of water—feels manufactured. They're a weak attempt to balance the grittiness of D.C's scarier neighborhoods.

Of course, none of it would matter if acting newcomers Saul Williams and Sonja Sohn didn't deliver such heartfelt, and heartbreaking, performances. In particular, Williams' dreadlocked hero makes his metamorphosis stunningly authentic. One can't help believing that an inner rhythm drives his every action.

Sohn is equally dead-on, typified by a climactic speech about lost dreams and facing one's demons. It's compelling enough to forgive Marion Berry's ill-advised cameo as a judge who just says no to drugs.

Thankfully, such errors are few and far between. Levin's handiwork—along with the unforgettable Williams and Sohn—ensures that "Slam" packs an emotional wallop.

NEWSDAY, 10/9/98, Part II/p. B6, Jack Mathews

With "Slam," writer-director and former documentarian Marc Levin has taken a hand-held camera to the streets and prison cells and smoky clubs of Washington, to capture the rhythm of language, the sense of despair, and the occasional ray of hope that inform life in the ghetto of the nation's capital.

"Slam" is an extraordinary first feature, rough around the edges but raw emotional power at its core, and it deserved its major awards at both the Sundance and Cannes film festivals earlier this year, as well as its coveted spot in the New York Film Festival.

Starring real-life performance poets Saul Williams and Sonja Sohn, "Slam" follows a brief period in the life of Ray Joshua (Williams), a young street rapper who finds the real power of his voice while awaiting a court date behind bars. It's there that he meets Lauren Bell (Sohn), a reformed crack addict and prostitute who teaches writing and, by extension, self-esteem to inmates.

On her way to class one day, Lauren is overwhelmed by Ray's successful effort to rap his way out of a jailyard gang fight, and invites him to join her group. There, he's overwhelmed in kind by the speech she gives about freedom and the responsibility of the individual to keep it. There's a literal meeting of the minds between them, and after he's bailed out of jail, they make it physical, as well.

Soon, she's inviting him to perform at the weekly poetry slam that's become the center of her life, and the verse is pouring out of him onto the notepads he carries around like an artist's sketch book.

But there are complications. Ray has some old gang loyalties back in the projects, where a friend, blinded in a drive-by shooting, is expecting him to avenge the injury. And there are those drug charges hanging over his head. He minimizes them, seeing himself as a victim of a racist system, while Lauren insists that only by taking responsibility can he avoid entering the vicious cycle.

These are emotionally loaded scenes, and Williams and Sohn, both making their acting debuts, aren't always convincing in them. But whatever they lack in acting technique, they more than compensate with passion for their characters and their situations. And their readings of poetry they've written themselves have astonishing power.

You take hope from messages delivered in movies at your own risk; it would be foolish to predict that "Slam" will change life in America's inner cities. Nonetheless, when Sohn, crying genuine tears by my intuition, finishes her speech to the jail inmates, her words, "Don't give anyone the power to take away your freedom," have resonance far beyond a counselor's cliche.

Wherever and whoever you are, they're words to live by.

SIGHT AND SOUND, 4/99, p. 59, Richard Kelly

Washington DC. Raymond Joshua writes rhymes, and deals grass. His connection Big Mike is shot during a deal and Raymond, trying to flee, is arrested. Bail is set high, and Raymond's public defender warns him he will serve time, depending upon the extent of his "cooperation". In custody, Raymond encounters hostility, but consoles himself with poetry. Hopha, the top dog among the inmates, tells Raymond he is a target for homeboys who suspect he ratted on Big Mike. Raymond averts a fight by 'slamming' a rap-tirade against mindless violence. He meets Lauren, who runs a writing workshop for prisoners. She encourages his writing. Impressed by Raymond, Hopha puts up his bail money.

Raymond is reunited with Big Mike, who was blinded in the shooting. He convinces Big Mike and his crew that retaliation only prolongs the cycle of violence. Raymond meets Lauren at a party and they become lovers. She confesses a past of drug addiction and prostitution, and tells him he must take responsibility for his crime. They argue, but Raymond shows up later at a slam club where Lauren recites her verses. Raymond performs to great applause, is reconciled with Lauren, and prepares to meet his judgement.

"They say slavery has been abolished," rapper Ice-T once opined, "except for the convicted felon." Words failed Ice thereafter and he could only add, "Y'all need to think about that." Clearly, Marc Levin has been thinking about it: his debut feature shows how incarceration looms dispiritingly large across the lives of impoverished US blacks. Bars, chains and shades of the prison house dominate *Slam*'s visual scheme, a grim reminder of the vile manner in which Africans were dragged into the Americas. A stern-visaged prison guard warns our hero Raymond: "We're wiping out our race here in Washington DC." True, *Slam*'s opening credits convey a sense that, if you're poor and black in the nation's capital, life in or out of prison is equally dismal: shooting dice, hitting the weight-pile, waiting for something to go down.

Later, as Raymond and Lauren make romance in the lull before he is sentenced for innocuous grass-peddling, they wander through a DC street market, and Lauren purchases a drawing of a slave ship. Formerly a crack-addicted prostitute, she chides Raymond for his exploitative profession, which reduced her to a slave-overseer relationship with her pimp and supplier. Raymond resists Lauren's condemnation; but as he confesses his fear of returning to prison, his description of the sensation of captivity ("I woke up on a fucking ship") carries an eerie resonance.

Such is the socio-political problem *Slam* describes. Does it suggest any solution? Alas, you have to wonder what Levin (an acclaimed documentarian) was thinking of when he hired the woefully disreputable mayor of DC, Marion Barry Jr, to play the judge at Raymond's arraignment. As Barry bemoans how "drugs are killing our communities" and how congress obstructs the mayor's reforming hand, his hypocrisy is so fulsome you might gag. But Barry, however unpalatably, has lived the American Dream of untrammelled opportunism. Lauren, the conscience of this film (played by poet and script contributor Sonja Sohn), plies her own kind of self-help gibberish. Bidding a tearful farewell to her imprisoned pupils, she urges them to shape their own destinies. "We are capitalists," asserts one brother. And there's a general agreement: if only they had the resources, each could make his own way in the world. Alas, as Marion Barry could inform them, the US system offers a convicted felon not much in the way of a fresh start, not even 40 acres and a pack mule—but crime, if nothing else, pays.

Slamming is seen to provide its own form of release from this cage. When Raymond first overhears a cell-prisoner rhyming, and promptly bursts out with a rap of his own, it's an exciting moment. But Raymond's slams swiftly descend, like so much rap, into doggerel and needless profanity. Their advocacy of non-violence is at least heartening. In a hilariously thoughtful moment, gangster Hopha (Bonz Malone, who also had a hand in the script) compares Raymond's rhymes to his reading of Sun Tzu's *Art of War*. Finally, however, the film's chief moral lesson, imparted by Lauren, is that freedom is prison: Raymond must accept punishment, and be redeemed by it. (Has Levin been reading Dostoevsky, or watching Bresson's *Pickpocket?)* So Raymond readies himself for more porridge, but first he's rewarded with those standard-issue Hollywood sweeteners: an audience's adoring applause, and the unconditional love of a pretty woman.

Slam prevails over its scant budget ($1 million), though certain repetitive stylistic quirks (erratic video inserts, moody montages of close up and slo-mo) seem only to ratchet up the running time. We regularly revisit Raymond's attempted flight from the cops, as if in homage to *Sweet Sweetback's Baad Asssss Song* (1971). But there's some nicely arbitrary shot-making. At one pensive moment, Raymond stands by a river in dying sunlight, the water's surface ripples like molten gold, and his gangling frame becomes semi-translucent. In the final sequence, Raymond stalks up to the foot of the George Washington Monument, a 500-foot Masonic obelisk. The camera tilts alarmingly, until the monument's vertical becomes an illuminated walkway. Where to? Levin only knows, but it's a usefully oblique note on which to close.

TIME, 10/19/98, p. 107, Richard Corliss

A film about a dope-dealing poet from the soul-squashing projects of Washington was a winner on the chic slopes and shores of this year's festivals. The poet-pusher is Ray Joshua, played by a scrawny charismatic named Saul Williams; and the film, *Slam,* arrives in theaters laden with laurels from Sundance and Cannes. Burdened, really, for this is a small movie, as vulnerable as it is volatile, about young black men in trouble. Its underworldly corrosiveness can't tide a heart full of hope.

In director Marc Levin's bifocal vision, Ray is a thug and a saint: he sells weed to the locals and buys ice cream for the neighborhood kids. Of course Ray will be nabbed, for a minor crime, and sent to the rathole of a D.C. jail. Another new guy, a rich Asian American (Beau Sia, scary and very funny), is so sure hell be sprung that he spits wild invective at the screws. But Ray knows not to mouth off. Jail for him is a familiar horror: school with the toughest students and faculty.

In jail a poetry teacher named Lauren (Sonja Sohn, who can soar from a whisper to high-calorie emoting in the flick of a verb) encourages the inmates to examine the cycle of violence and put it into verse; they respond with pensive street scat like "I shot three m----f----s, and I don't know why." Well, it's a start. For Ray, it is the start of big things. He falls in love both with Lauren and with the furious folk art of slamming—a mix of hipster poetry contest and hip-hop riffing. Now *Slam* starts to look like a 'hooded update of *The Corn Is Green* and *A Star Is Born*. But hope is never that simple. Ray realizes that the prospect of a meaningful future can be even more frustrating than the certitude of two to five in a D.C. cell.

Shot in a wandering, often annoying quasi-documentary style that might be called *faux vérité*, the movie sometimes seems its own slamfest of verbal and visual attitudinizing. But Levin is attentive to the rhythms and politics of street and prison life: shootings that disrupt a conversation, animosities expressed in up-ended food trays. Gradually, the film's earnestness pays dividends in accumulated passion; its colliding moods—dank pessimism and loopy sentimentality—finally embrace. And it's always nice to see an independent film made by people who aren't secretly angling to produce the next season of *Caroline in the City*. This is more like "Caroling in the Inner City," especially in a strong scene in which Ray silences rival gangs in the prison yard with his raving eloquence.

Slam has a message of desperate do-gooding. It dares to say that education helps. That poetry can teach killers a saving sweetness. That words matter. Even—especially—four-letter ones, when a gifted loser fashions them into images illuminated by the lightning of his rage and fear.

Also reviewed in:
NEW YORK TIMES, 10/3/98, p. B16, Stephen Holden
VARIETY, 1/26-2/1/98, p. 65, Emanuel Levy
WASHINGTON POST, 10/23/98, p. B1, Stephen Hunter
WASHINGTON POST, 10/23/98, Weekend/p. 55, Michael O'Sullivan

SLAMNATION

A Film Forum presentation. *Producer:* Paul Devlin. *Director:* Paul Devlin. *Director of Photography:* John Anderson. *Editor:* Paul Devlin. *Music:* Chris Parker. *Running time:* 91 minutes. *MPAA Rating:* Not Rated.

WITH: Saul Williams; Jessica Care Moore; Beau Sia; Mums the Schemer; Taylor Mali; Daniel Ferri; Marc Smith.

LOS ANGELES TIMES, 10/8/98, Calendar/p. 14, Kevin Thomas

Marc Smith, a construction worker who founded the National Poetry Slam 12 years ago, describes the annual Portland, Ore., competition as when "the art of performance and the art of poetry come together." Judging from Paul Devlin's dynamic documentary, "SlamNation," the delivery counts more than the message, urgent and eloquent as it may be.

Even so, this intense competition certainly does show how alive and potent poetry can be. To be sure, certain personalities dominate, starting with Taylor Mali, a terrific actor who could easily pass as a Matt Damnon-Ben Affleck buddy. Then there's Saul Williams, a lean, intense African American, whose poetry really does sear; he's so riveting it's scarcely surprising that he'll soon be seen as a rapper/poet in "Slam," winner of the grand jury prize at Sundance. Wittiest is Beau Sia, a Chinese American film student who imagines a collaboration with Quentin Tarantino. It could happen.

NEW YORK POST, 7/17/98, p. 45, Larry Worth

Gone are the days of Robert Frost, lovely sonnets about roads not taken and quiet poetry readings.

In the '90s, poetry slams—an electric mix of performance art and the written word, spoken by the oh-so-hip successors to Longfellow and his ilk—are the way to go. And as demonstrated in Paul Devlin's documentary "SlamNation," poetry can generate the excitement of a contact sport.

That's readily apparent as Devlin focuses on the annual contest in which budding and full-fledged poets from across America converge on one city—this time: Portland, Ore.—to spout their stuff and walk off with the grand prize. Judges give scores from 1 to 10, as the audience boos and cheers accordingly.

As in any good documentary, Devlin is savvy enough to showcase individuals rather than the event. That puts several of the most engaging poets front and center, ranging from a spunky newspaper columnist to a guy who takes bodies to the morgue. Their works—sometimes delivered solo, other times in group—prove equally diverse.

Before long, viewers can't help getting caught up in the event's excitement and being simultaneously absorbed by the performers' craft. Further, their backstage competition and strategies—never mind charges of judges' racism—prove equally interesting.

The down side comes from Devlin's herky-jerky editing style, which later evolves into too many static close-ups. And at a running time of 91 minutes, it ultimately gets a bit redundant.

But for most of its duration, "SlamNation" proves an illuminating look at poetry's evolution. Heck, if Robert Frost were alive, he'd probably be its biggest supporter.

VILLAGE VOICE, 7/21/98, p. 120, Justine Elias

Poetry slams, the evolving hybrid of versifying, rap, theater, and open-mike comedy, have been around since the mid '80s, and these spoken-word contests among the exhibitionists of the literary world are still going strong. One of the hits of this year's Sundance festival was *Slam*, Marc Levin's fiction feature about a poet in and out of prison. But before that independent film finds its way into theaters, there is Paul Devlin's *Slamnation*, a modest documentary about the cut-throat behind-the-scenes drama at the National Poetry Slam, a four-day team competition filled with posing, trash-talking, and, occasionally, some superb readings. Much of the film's tension comes from the conflict between two warring factions, the original slammers, like Chicago's Marc

Smith, who touts the art form's "purity" and "blue-collar roots," and flashier adherents like Bob Holman of the Nuyorican Poets Cafe, who is accused of "cheapening what slam is all about" by playing to the crowd—strange, because the contests are scored by judges picked randomly from the audience.

The purity-versus-popularity friction also shows up in a feud between two top slammers; one needles the other by mimicking his ponderous, incantatory reading style, which might be compared to Beat poetry as delivered by a morning-drive disc jockey. Despite several striking performances—including an appearance by poet and former Boston Globe columnist Patricia Smith—*Slamnation* is verbally fascinating but visually dull; the filmmaker is limited by the fact that most of the individual readings are delivered from the same small nightclub stage. The exceptions to this static mood are the finals, which feature lively group performances, and a brief section in which one contestant, a roofer by day, reads one of his works while he's repairing a suburban house—his words, punctuated by the pounding of his nail gun, find the rhythm in real life.

Also reviewed in:
NEW YORK TIMES, 7/17/98, p. E12, Stephen Holden

SLAPPY AND THE STINKERS

A TriStar Pictures and The Bubble Factory release of a Sheinberg production.   *Producer:* Sid Sheinberg, Bill Sheinberg, and Jon Sheinberg.   *Director:* Barnet Kellman.   *Screenplay:* Bob Wolterstorff and Mike Scott.   *Director of Photography:* Paul Maibaum.   *Editor:* Jeff Wishengrad.   *Music:* Craig Safan.   *Sound:* Darren Pascal.   *Casting:* Shari Rhodes, Joseph Middleton, Ronnie Yeskel, and Mary Vernieu.   *Production Designer:* Ivo Cristante.   *Art Director:* Ken Larson.   *Set Decorator:* Michael Claypool.   *Costumes:* Jami Burrows.   *Running time:* 78 minutes.   *MPAA Rating:* PG.

CAST: B.D. Wong (Morgan Brinway);   Bronson Pinchot (Roy);   Jennifer Coolidge (Harriet);   Joseph Ashton (Sonny);   Gary LeRoi Gray (Domino);   Carl Michael Lindner (Witz);   Scarlett Pomers (Lucy);   Travis Tedford (Loaf);   David Dukes (Spencer Dane Sr.);   Spencer Klein (Spencer Dane Jr.);   Sam McMurray (Boccoli).

LOS ANGELES TIMES, 1/23/98, Calendar/p. 10, Bob Heisler

[The following review by Bob Heisler appeared in a slightly different form in **NEWSDAY, 1/23/98, Part II/p. B11.]**

It's not "Free Willy" with a sea lion, but "Slappy and the Stinkers" is a harmless drop-off movie for the elementary-age boys not standing in line for "Spice World."

"Drop-off" as in drop off the kids at "Slappy," pay an older sibling to watch them, then go see something more suitable for anyone over 15. This is not a family movie; you'll be squandering your quality time searching for a life lesson to share.

From the "Rugrats" school of American social criticism—in which parental units are ciphers, even the most kindly adults are addle-brained, and kids with no supervision whatsoever are free to bike from sea to shining sea—the movie asks for a suspension of disbelief far beyond grown-up capacity.

The Stinkers are five 7-year-olds attending the summer enrichment program of Dartmoor Academy by the grace of scholarships. A mix of bright, articulate, inventive and cuter-than-average kids, they are clearly not the prep-school type. Opera appreciation bores them. So does a trip to the aquarium, until they meet Slappy, a sea lion who exhibits a range of emotion from fear and loathing to elation and love. He also passes gas.

You get the idea.

Now the plan to "free" Slappy and let him cavort among the killer whales in the ocean really has nothing to do with the Stinkers' human enemy, the vain and quite stupid principal Morgan Brinway, a role gamely filled by good sport B.D. Wong.

Brinway spends a good deal of the movie being hit by flying objects and getting in the way of the Slappy plot line, which really doesn't require Dartmoor Academy to establish the Stinkers as the "us" in us-against-the-world. On the other hand, when the Stinkers find what should have been their place in the fall TV schedule of the WB network, he'll be a useful foil to have around.

Oddly, Slappy does not want to cavort among the whales in the ocean, nor would you if you had just spent a day eating raw fish at a party in Mr. Brinway's hot tub (and especially since sea lions are a tasty treat for killer whales!). But the evil Boccoli (Sam McMurray)—and you know he's evil because he smokes cigarettes—steals Slappy before the Stinkers can devise a really impossible-but-clever way to get him back to the aquarium. Slappy faces the prospect of spending his days jumping through hoops at a Bulgarian circus.

The Stinkers—a Nickelodeon-ready group featuring a breakthrough performance by Carl Michael Linder as Witz, the one with the glasses who abuses his inhaler in moments of stress—do nothing really bad. Animals are smuggled from zoos and aquariums every day in the movies. They also do nothing particularly good, either, if you think about it. Just don't think about it.

NEW YORK POST, 1/23/98, p. 46, Michael Medved

To get some idea of the puerile pleasures proffered by "Slappy and the Stinkers," think "Free Willy" meets "The Little Rascals" meets "E.T." meets Home Alone" meets "Dead Poets Society" meets, so help me, "Apocalypse Now."

Sure, these and many other oddly assorted old titles are referenced here, but "Slappy also breaks new ...wind, as the first film in history dramatizing the impact of a seal overdosing on laxatives.

The result is a gross, goofball comedy for kids that should entertain most small fry while even winning a few guilty, grudging chuckles from their parents.

The setting is exclusive Dartmoor Academy, where a quintet of 7-year-old scholarship students so thorough annoys the officious prissy headmaster (B.D. Wong) that he dubs them "the Stinkers."

After causing significant property damage with Rube Goldberg inventions (including an experimental aircraft combining a leaf blower, swivel chair and other elements), they develop special sympathy for a seal named Slappy encountered on an aquarium field trip.

Before attempting to return Slappy to his ocean habitat, the young environmentalists bring him to the campus, where the neo-hippie spacecase who works as the school's gardener (the very funny Bronson Pinchot) believes the seal is actually the giant gopher who's been trashing the grounds.

Together, beast and burnout wreak total destruction on parents' day, and the confusion allows an animal thief to steal the seal for sale to a circus.

It's up to the Stinkers to track the bad guy to his mountain hideout and assault him with their home-made weapons.

"Slappy"'s slapsticks's sloppy (try saying that aloud), but it's still reasonably inventive—with big bright colors and an exhilarating log chute ride as a climax.

The kids are alright (there's another reference) but nothing special, hardly candidates for a new "Our Gang" series as the producers seem to intend.

The adult cast is solid and professional—particularly Wong, who displays so much charisma as a stressed-out, egotistical martinet that it's not too painful to watch the indignities heaped upon him.

Director Barnet Kellman (one of the key forces behind both "Murphy Brown" and "Mad About You" on TV) and the distinguished producers make absurdly inflated claims for "Slappy," suggesting that they have "celebrated the spirit of childhood" or provided "a positive role model when kids see themselves using their talents to overcome obstacles."

You'd have to be slap-happy to connect this silliness to such lofty goals, but you'd also have to be a complete sourpuss to altogether resist its spirit of fun.

Also reviewed in:
CHICAGO TRIBUNE, 2/6/98, Friday/p. I, Elaine Richardson
NEW YORK TIMES, 1/23/98, p. E18, Lawrence Van Gelder
VARIETY, 1/26-2/1/98, p. 67, Lael Loewenstein

SLIDING DOORS

A Miramax Films and Paramount Pictures release in association with Intermedia Films of a Mirage production. *Executive Producer:* Guy East and Nigel Sinclair. *Producer:* Sydney Pollack, Philippa Braithwaite, and William Horberg. *Director:* Peter Howitt. *Screenplay:* Peter Howitt. *Director of Photography:* Remi Adefarasin. *Editor:* John Smith. *Music:* David Hirschfelder. *Music Editor:* John Finklea. *Sound:* John Midgley and (music) Chris Scallan. *Sound Editor:* David B. Cohen and Beth Sterner. *Casting:* Michelle Guish. *Production Designer:* Maria Djurkovie. *Art Director:* Martyn John. *Special Effects:* Bob Hollow. *Costumes:* Jill Taylor. *Make-up:* Tina Earnshaw. *Stunt Coordinator:* Helen Caldwell. *Running time:* 105 minutes. *MPAA Rating:* R.

CAST: Gwyneth Paltrow (Helen); John Hannah (James); John Lynch (Gerry); Jeanne Tripplehorn (Lydia); Zara Turner (Anna); Douglas McFerran (Russel); Paul Brightwell (Clive); Nina Young (Claudia); Virginia McKenna (James' Mother); Kevin McNally (Boss Paul); Terry English (Kind Cabbie); Paul Stacey (Man on Tube); Peter Howitt (Cheeky Bloke); Joanna Roth (Suspicious Girl); Neil Stuke (Defensive Bloke); Theresa Kartell (Rachel); Evelyn Duah (James' Receptionist); Linda Broughton (Senior Theatre Nurse); Charlotte Fryer (Intensive Care Doctor); Pip Miller (Consultant); Christopher Villiers (P.R. Steve); Merryn Jones (Mother); Ella Jones (Child); Julie McDowell (Concerned Diner).

CHRISTIAN SCIENCE MONITOR, 5/15/98, p. B5, David Sterritt

[*Sliding Doors* was reviewed jointly with *The Hanging Garden*; see Sterritt's review of that film.]

LOS ANGELES TIMES, 4/24/98, Calendar/p. 1, Jack Mathews

[*The following review by Jack Mathews appeared in a slightly different form in*
NEWSDAY, 4/24/98, Part II/p. B3.]

No matter now you slice it, Helen is having a bad day. She arrived at work at a London PR agency this morning to learn she's been fired. And now, as she races to catch a subway train, one of two unpleasant experiences is just ahead.

If she makes it aboard the train already in the station, she'll get home in time to catch her boyfriend in bed with his ex-girlfriend. If she doesn't, she'll be knocked down by a purse snatcher, have stitches over one eye, and come home to a boyfriend who's rattled by the close call, but safe. Either way, though, Helen's life is going to change.

Writer-director Peter Howitt's cleverly conceived and superbly executed "Sliding Doors" is a romantic comedy about a girl and two hypotheses. When Helen, played with a tangy British accent by Gwyneth Paltrow, reaches the sliding doors of that train, the movie comes to an abrupt halt, announces its intentions of telling us two parallel stories, then proceeds with a seamless flow of interwoven details from each.

In Story A, Helen reacts to the sight of Gerry (John Lynch) and Lydia (Jeanne Tripplehorn) in a thrashing love tangle on her own bed by packing off to stay with her best friend Anna (Zara Turner). Anna will comfort Helen and give her good advice, like treating herself to a make-over, starting her own PR business and going out with James (John Hannah), the gentle, funny Scotsman she met on that otherwise ill-fated subway ride.

In Story B, Helen's eye and her bruised ego will begin to heal, but Gerry will continue seeing Lydia, and Helen, in blind devotion, will double-up jobs as a waitress and a sandwich delivery girl in order to support him. Eventually, the clues will pile up that Gerry's not getting a lot of writing done at home, and the relationship will reach the crisis point. But it's later rather than sooner.

Howitt, a British actor making his debut as a filmmaker, could have taken his story into the hyperbolic reaches of fantasy and offended no one in Hollywood. Instead, he chose to tell two very human stories as they might actually develop. Helen is the same person in both tales, but the circumstances dictate different actions, and those actions create distinctly different rhythms and moods.

Story A is a lively romance, with Helen being lulled out of her funk by James, an infinitely more charming character than Gerry, who appears moping on the sidelines and hoping for a reconciliation. Story B is a low-keyed version of "Fatal Attraction," where Lydia, a sexual predator with the subtlety of Madame Strap, is trying to get Gerry caught and liberated.

There's a lot going on in both of these stories, and occasionally, events that occur at the same place and at the same time are played out both ways, back and forth. It may be Howitt's greatest achievement that we're able to keep the stories straight.

Paltrow is amiably convincing in her dual roles, and Hannah, who appeared in "Four Weddings and a Funeral," the movie with which "Sliding Doors" begs comparison, manages to rise above the conventional rescuer hero. Howitt's missteps are all in the characters of Gerry and Lydia, and in the dreadful performances he elicited from Lynch and Tripplehorn.

NEW YORK POST, 4/24/98, p. 49, Thelma Adams

Soap operas constantly split characters into two: the good and evil twin, the slut and the nun, the sophisticate and the country cousin. The device saves on salaries and gives popular stars twice the exposure—and the chance to wear goofy hair and false teeth.

In Peter Howitt's fractured romance "Sliding Doors," ingenue Gwyneth Paltrow has a case of the not-so-terrible twos. Her character, Helen, divides into two romantic possibilities, two possible futures, launching two generic plots in one charming movie.

After losing her job at a London ad agency, Helen (Paltrow with an Emma Thompson accent) runs for the tube. Will she make it through the sliding doors and onto the subway? And what would happen if she didn't?

At this point, Helen splits in two: the heroine who makes it onto the train and the one left back at the platform. All roads home lead to the same choice. Will she stay with her live-in, philandering novelist Gerry (John Lynch), or ride off with charming Scot, John (the irresistible if plain John Hannah)?

The difference between Helen-on-the-train and Helen-missed-the-train is largely cosmetic. Whether she sports an auburn career-girl hairdo or a platinum pixie, the "Emma" actress displays two sides: appealing and more appealing.

Helen's choices in men are also clear-cut. John quotes Monty Python and listens, really listens; Gerry listens to Elton John while cheating with lingerie-clad Lydia (Jeanne Tripplehorn).

As maddening as Howitt's plot device is, the gazelle-like Gwyneth leaps over such stumbling blocks as an unsatisfactory ending, multiple pregnancies and a one-dimensional rival, to create a contemporary heroine who could give Ally McBeal a run for her time slot.

SIGHT AND SOUND, 6/98, p. 55, Peter Matthews

Helen is fired from her job at a PR company. Disconsolate, she enters the London Underground, intending to return to the flat she shares with her boyfriend Gerry. Two different, intercut stories unfold, according to whether Helen catches or misses her train.

In the first story, Helen boards the train and meets the handsome James. Returning home, she discovers Gerry having sex with his ex-girlfriend Lydia, so Helen leaves him. She runs into James again and the two soon become lovers. At James' suggestion, Helen opens her own PR agency. Gerry tries to effect a reconciliation but Helen rejects him. Later, Helen discovers that she is pregnant by James, but is shocked when she finds out that he's actually married. James tracks her down and explains that in fact he and his wife are getting a divorce. Delirious with joy, Helen staggers into the path of an oncoming car, loses the baby and later dies in hospital.

In the second story, Helen misses the train. An attempted mugging delays her return home, so she doesn't catch Gerry *flagrante delicto*. The next day, she finds temporary work as a waitress.

Lydia and Gerry's affair continues but, tired of waiting for Gerry to leave Helen, Lydia angrily breaks off the liaison. Gerry stays with Helen, who is now pregnant. Lydia finds out that she is also pregnant and calls Gerry and Helen to her flat to inform them. Shocked, Helen falls down the stairs and is seriously injured. She loses the baby. Waking from a coma to find Gerry by her bedside, Helen orders him out of her life. Leaving the hospital, she encounters James who is visiting his mother in hospital. The strangers exchange their first words.

In one scene of writer-director Peter Howitt's new concept-comedy *Sliding Doors*, a character holds up a tabloid newspaper whose headline, referring to last year's *English Patient* sweep, reads: "A Very English Oscar Triumph". That discreet touch perhaps represents the film-makers' attempt to plant a subliminal seed in the minds of audiences and critics. If this small, quirky production has few pretensions to the class or prestige of that fulsome epic, the evident hope is that it will score a transatlantic bull's-eye as a 'sleeper'. Since English moviegoers seem reluctant to support English movies unless they've been previously certified by the US box office, the recent practice has been to appeal to American anglophiles. So *Four Weddings* sold crotchety Englishness by the yard, while *The Full Monty* shrewdly combined the native speciality of drab realism with a Hollywood-style 'feel-good' storyline. In terms of the international market, *Sliding Doors* (financed, it should be noted, by the US production company Miramax) adopts a more defensive strategy. The assumption seems to be that US viewers, while happy to entertain a generic vision of England, will be put off by too rich a display of cultural otherness. It's probably symptomatic that the ability to quote from *Monty Python*—the one English television show most Americans have heard of—is indicated as a measure of the hero James' extreme zaniness (though, straining for balance, the script makes him a Seinfeld-watcher as well).

There's something similarly calculated about the impeccably bland locations, which succeed in divesting London of street life or geographically specifiable features. The characters inhabit cosy 'apartments' (the script insists on the word) situated nowhere in particular. Their romantic wrangles otherwise occur in a hermetic circle of cafés, bars and restaurants. As the frazzled English-rose heroine Helen, (American-born) Gwyneth Paltrow outstrips the indigenous population for sheer vocal plumminess. And since *Four Weddings* hit pay-dirt peddling the varieties of English embarrassment, Paltrow cutely hems and haws through such dialogue as "I know—this is an ideal—sort of—kissing moment".

Ersatz in every other respect, *Sliding Doors* is perhaps most authentically English in the half-hearted way it carries out its own premise. The basic conceit—that the entire course of Helen's life depends on the tiniest hiccup of fate—has a prominent literary antecedent in those Thomas Hardy novels where characters are doomed because they fail to receive a letter or turn a corner at the wrong moment. More optimistically, *It's a Wonderful Life* bucks up its despondent hero by showing the train of disasters that would have ensued had he never been born. Further afield, there are strong parallels with Kieslowski's early film *Blind Chance*, which shows three possible outcomes of its hero's life depending on whether he catches a train or not. Then there's Alain Resnais' and Alan Ayckbourn's whimsical post-modern jaunt *Smoking/No Smoking*, which spins two interminable movies out of shufflings of the same narrative ingredients. But *Sliding Doors* is more daring than the Resnais-Ayckbourn double header in one regard—it briskly crosscuts between our heroine's divergent destinies rather than treating them serially. Despite such expedients as giving one of the Helens a distinctive cropped hairdo, you can't always tell which version of the story you're in. What with all the complicated parallels and contrasts, the movie makes for demanding, cerebral viewing. Nonetheless, did not the mathematical law assert that twice zero is still zero?

First-time director Howitt (best known for his role in the BBC series *Bread*) would appear to have exhausted his creative energy in pitching the initial concept. The characters barely seem to exist independently of it, as none has a credible personal trait or pursuit (Helen's nebulous PR job in particular feels like the last gambit of the desperate screenwriter). But even where the central gimmick is concerned, Howitt drops the ball early on. The movie might have had fun pushing the bifurcations of the plot to the point of baroque extravagance. Instead, both versions keep to the same doggedly cautious tone—somewhere between middle class soap opera and those staid English sitcoms where even the laugh track never sounds convinced.

It's true that Helen comes to a mournful crunch in one of her incarnations, but that brings us to the worst miscalculation of all. It seems plain commercial suicide to leave the audience hovering limbo-like between alternative endings: one feels cheated of that *sine qua non* of romantic comedies—emotional closure. Howitt provides an escape clause in the form of a last-minute twist intended to mollify the viewer (the tragic version could be read as a dream). However, even this cop out finale gets mangled through some sloppy editing, so that *Sliding Doors* becomes a radically 'open' text in spite of itself. Film studies scholars are duly put on notice.

TIME, 4/27/98, p. 68, Richard Corliss

Damn, I missed the train! Good, its sliding doors have opened again to let me through. Which one has happened to frazzled young Helen (Gwyneth Paltrow)? Both. It is the cunning conceit of the British romantic comedy *Sliding Doors* to create and follow alternative futures—both tines of that fork in life's road we all occasionally face and that leaves us wondering, What if?

Ah, the old What if? trick. It has inspired such evocative works as Alan Ayckbourn's play *Intimate Exchanges* (a woman has, or doesn't have, a cigarette, and her choice leads to 16 variations) and Krzysztof Kieslowski's film *Blind Chance* (a man runs for a train and heads into three different realities). In writer-director Peter Howitt's version, the Helen who makes the train home finds her beau Gerry (John Lynch) in bed with his old girlfriend (Jeanne Tripplehorn); the Helen who misses the train gets mugged. And in both cases she meets a seemingly nice fellow, James (John Hannah), to whose wry persistence she increasingly warms.

The film means to be beguiling, and many will find it so. But in this viewer's alternative reality, *Sliding Doors is* way too strained, in narrative logic and in performance, to work. Paltrow either whines or twinkles; Hannah works overtime at being winsome; Lynch has not even a pinch of larcenous charm; Tripplehorn is reduced to stridency and humiliation. The actors appear to be on trial for unknown offenses, and what could be blithe and affecting instead comes on like—oh, like the Spanish Inquisition.

VILLAGE VOICE, 4/28/98, p. 75, Dennis Lim

Five minutes into *Sliding* Doors, Gwyneth Paltrow splits in two. Had this amoeba-like fission occurred throughout the film at five-minute intervals, it would have spawned 1,048,576 Gwyneths (I did the math; I was bored). Writer-director Peter Howitt's high concept isn't nearly as disturbing—he simply flip-flops between two versions of the same woman in an oafishly whimsical reverie about romantic destiny.

The pivotal replication happens on the London Underground, moments after Helen (Paltrow) has lost her job as a publicist. Helen 1—who catches her train—meets dream man James (John Hannah), arrives home In time to find scummy boyfriend Jerry (John Lynch) in bed with his megabitch ex Lydia (Jeanne Tripplehorn), dumps the bastard, gets a fetching blond do, and sets up her own PR firm. Helen 2—who misses the train and is mugged immediately after—is reduced to delivering sandwiches and waiting tables, takes to wearing her brown hair in pigtails, and (though she doesn't seem to be having sex with Jerry) becomes pregnant.

Paltrow, if nothing else, sports a convincing enough English accent—listen for her pitch-perfect utterances of *twat, shag,* and *bollocks.* Hannah's James is a wisecracking blabbermouth who thinks he's much funnier than he is (come back, Hugh Grant, all is forgiven). Worst off, Tripplehorn is required to play an irredeemably grotesque Other Woman and speak some of the worst lines in film history (one metaphor-choked tantrum has her catching the "Jerry Express" out of "Limbo Central" and "Indecision City"). Unduly smug about its flashy conceit and otherwise utterly empty, the film plays like lobotomized Kieslowski, less *Blind Chance* than dumb luck.

Also reviewed in:
NEW YORK TIMES, 4/24/98, p. E14, Stephen Holden
VARIETY, 1/19-25/98, p. 89, Todd McCarthy
WASHINGTON POST, 4/24/98, p. B1, Rita Kempley
WASHINGTON POST, 4/24/98, p. 56, Michael O'Sullivan

SLUMS OF BEVERLY HILLS

A Fox Searchlight Pictures release of a South Fork Pictures production.   *Executive Producer:* Robert Redford.   *Producer:* Michael Nozik and Stan Wlodkowski.   *Director:* Tamara Jenkins. *Screenplay:* Tamara Jenkins.   *Director of Photography:* Tom Richmond. *Editor:* Pamela Martin. *Music:* Rolfe Kent.   *Music Editor:* Steve McCroskey.   *Sound:* Ken Segal and (music) Ken Segal. *Sound Editor:* Andrew Decristofaro.   *Casting:* Sheila Jaffe and Georgianne Walken.   *Production Designer:* Dena Roth.   *Art Director:* Scott Plauche.   *Set Decorator:* Robert Greenfield. *Costumes:* Kirsten Everberg. *Make-up:* Kathryn Bihr.   *Stunt Coordinator:* Dick Ziker.   *Running time:* 91 minutes.   *MPAA Rating:* R.

CAST: Natasha Lyonne (Vivian); Alan Arkin (Murray); Bryna Weiss (Saleslady); Marisa Tomei (Rita); Charlotte Stewart (Landlady); Eli Marienthal (Rickey); David Krumholtz (Ben); Kevin Corrigan (Eliot); Brendan Burns (Cop in Station); Harris Laskawy (Charlie the Cook); Jessica Walter (Doris); Mena Süväri (Rachel); Marley McClean (Brooke); Mary Portser (Mrs. Hoffman); Jock MacDonald (Man at Brymans); Rich Willis (EMS Guy #1); Rock Reiser (EMS Guy #2); Jack Tracy (Cop); Jay Patterson (Dr. Grossman); Natalie Karp (Nurse Curtrell); Carl Reiner (Mickey); Rita Moreno (Belle); Sally Schaub (Waitress).

CHRISTIAN SCIENCE MONITOR, 8/14/98, p. B3, David Sterritt

Now that 90210 is the world's most famous ZIP Code thanks to the TV show, it's not surprising that another branch of Hollywood has decided to explore not the dark side exactly, but the tacky side of Beverly Hills. It's a view complete with run-down apartments, seedy neighbors, and families that move out in the dead of night,so they won't have to pay the past month's rent.

"Slums of Beverly Hills" is less a hard-edged exposé than a mood-shifting satire, though approaching its subject with a wryly ironic touch.

We view the action through the eyes of Vivian, a mid-1970s adolescent with an unsuccessful dad, an irresponsible brother, and an out-of-control cousin whose parents help out with the bills. Vivian oscillates between worrying about this bunch and coping with her own teenage crises, including sexual adventures that give the picture its well-deserved R rating.

"Slums of Beverly Hills" gets much of its energy from a first-rate cast including Natasha Lyonne as the heroine, Alan Arkin as her father, Marisa Tomei as her cousin, and veteran comic Carl Reiner as her crusty old uncle.

Equally impressive are the unpredictable twists of the screenplay by Tamara Jenkins, who also directed the picture after developing it for executive producer Robert Redford—not usually known for such streetwise fare—at the Sundance Institute. She's a newcomer with a future.

LOS ANGELES TIMES, 8/14/98, Calendar/p. 16, Jack Mathews

[The following review by Jack Mathews appeared in a slightly different form in **NEWSDAY, 8/14/98, Part II/p. B7.]**

First-time writer-director Tamara Jenkins opens her coming-of-age comedy "Slums of Beverly Hills" with a scene reminiscent of the opening of John Hughes' 1984 film "Sixteen Candles," but she makes it a lot more meaningful.

In Hughes' movie, Molly Ringwald's character is met on her 16th birthday with an excited grandparent's observation that "she finally got her boobies!" In "Slums," Natasha Lyonne's Vivian is taken to a lingerie shop by her divorced father, Murray Abramowitz (Alan Arkin), who explains to a clerk—as if apologizing for a mutant family gene—that his daughter has suddenly become "stacked like her mother."

Both scenes are played for laughs, but where it's an obvious, easy laugh for Hughes, who built his early career on the cliches of teenage angst and the stereotyping of adults, it's one loaded with meaningful context by Jenkins.

At the beginning of "Slums," we see the otherwise slight 15-year-old Vivian staring at her image in a mirror, taking in the acreage of her first bra and feeling both transformed and deformed. In voice-over narration, she accuses her breasts of changing her life forever. Her older brother Ben (David Krumholtz) can't take his eyes off them, and her father can barely look at her without being reminded of his wife. It's as if the sheer weight of these additions are pulling her forward into a frightening Neverland.

Vivian, her father, Ben and little brother Rickey (Eli Marienthal) are suburban nomads—the movie is set in the mid-'70s—moving from one run-down apartment building to another on the tattered fringes of 90210, trying to stay ahead of the eviction notices while staying within the Beverly Hills school district.

"Furniture is temporary, but education is forever," Murray assures his confused brood.

Murray is a major failure at love and work, but he's determined to do right by his kids, even if it means taking in his wild niece Rita (Marisa Tomei) in exchange for a monthly living allowance from his wealthy, hypercritical brother Mickey (Carl Reiner). All Murray has to do is keep Rita out of trouble and get her into some sort of school.

Much of what follows is more situation-comedy than feature material. It feels like a vague, upscale knockoff of "The Beverly Hillbillies," and Jenkins' eagerness to please with class-conscious jokiness often comes at the expense of her solid underlying issues.

The biggest mistakes are made with Rita, played with typically studied preciousness by Tomei, who joins the family—pregnant and freshly escaped from a drug rehab clinic—and becomes Vivian's mentor. There's a lot of show with the character, and not much go.

But generally Jenkins shows few rookie jitters, and she got excellent performances from the rest of her cast. Lyonne, who also served as the narrator-daughter in Woody Allen's "Everyone Says I Love You," plays Vivian with an irresistible blend of maturity and innocence.

That the 64-year-old Arkin is a little old to be playing fathers with school-age children prompted Jenkins to include a few "Is that your grandfather?" jokes, but the weight of his sensitive portrayal keeps the story grounded. Kevin Corrigan, a neighbor who's being considered by Vivian as a first lover, is also very good.

NEW YORK POST, 8/14/98, p. 47, Larry Worth

It should be a law: Alan Arkin belongs in at least one big-screen film per month. No matter the quality of the production, the veteran actor enlivens and improves everything he touches. The latest proof: "Slums of Beverly Hills."

Arkin plays Murray, a wold-weary dad who in 1976 makes ends meet—of sorts—by dragging his teen-age daughter Viv (Natasha Lyonne) and two sons (David Krumholtz and Eli Marienthal) from one low-rent Beverly Hills condo to another. His reason? To keep the kids In La-La Land's tony school system.

But there's a price to be paid—literally. In order to climb one rung up the social ladder, Murray must take in Rita (Marisa Tomei), the flaky, pill-popping, ultra-seductive runaway daughter of his wealthy brother (deliciously played by Carl Reiner, Arkin's nemesis from 1966's "The Russians Are Coming! The Russians Are Coming!")

As it turns out, the story revolves around Viv and her anxiety at developing C-cup breasts overnight and discovering the vagaries of love, both familial and hormonal.

That much is fine, but first-time writer-director Tamara Jenkins rarely finds the right tone. That's understandably due to her own inexperience and the largely autobiographical nature of the screenplay. It needed more objectivity and fewer sitcom payoffs.

But what's the excuse for more subplots than a season's worth of "90210"? One minute the focus is on dad's dating habits, the next it's about random violence, pot dealing, menstrual cycles, secret languages (a la "Zoom"), vibrators and you-name-it. Anything she missed seems to be an oversight.

Aside from Arkin's sterling screen presence, Lyonne, who was Woody Allen's daughter in "Everyone Says I Love You," is the chief asset. In what should be a star-making part, her mix of cynicism and naivete always convinces. Whether twirling the pile of cotton-candy hair atop her head or staring from her dad's car at palm trees that look like giant daisies, Lyonne is spot-on.

Tomei, meanwhile, is palatable but one-note as the manic Rita, while Kevin Corrigan recycles his charming-weirdo-next-door routine from "Walking and Talking." Small bits from Rita Moreno and Jessica Walter are relatively mannered, too.

The period setting isn't a redeeming factor, exemplified by a few token tube socks and snippets of "Let's Make a Deal." But at least viewers will relate to Monty Hall's guests: If a mixed bag—a la "Slums"— were behind Door No. 1, who wouldn't seek out a better package?

NEWSWEEK, 8/17/98, p. 61, Jeff Giles

When Tamara Jenkins cast Natasha Lyonne in "The Slums of Beverly Hills" she knew she'd have to give the actress different breasts. Lyonne was to play a teen who watches in horror as her sexual development becomes a subject of family banter. So director Jenkins gave her small-chested star prosthetics to wear in her bra. Says Jenkins, "It worked to our benefit because it was the way Natasha's character gets her breasts: they appear overnight and she doesn't know how to operate them." Lyonne was ambivalent about her new figure, and took the falsies out between scenes. "Natasha was 18, and she was reading a lot of existentialism," says Jenkins, 35. "So on her chair there was always a pack of Camel lights, a copy of 'No Exit' or whatever and her breasts."
Lyonne is in fine form in "Slums," if you'll forgive the pun. She leads a marvelous cast in a funny, poignant movie about the way families dole out tenderness and humiliation. It's the summer of 1976. A divorced car salesman named Murray Abramowitz (Alan Arkin) drags his daughter, Vivian (Lyonne), and her brothers from one dumpy apartment building to the next, often sneaking out in the middle of the night to avoid paying rent. (One landlady chases them as they flee the "Beverly Capri," forcing Vivian to abandon a red bean-bag chair in the parking lot.) Vivian survives her adolescence by bonding with an addled cousin (Marisa Tomei) and an earnest pot dealer (Kevin Corrigan)—and by avoiding her weird brother Ben (David Krumholz), who's given to belting out "Luck Be a Lady" in his jockeys. Jenkins, a first-time writer-director, films the proceedings with such a quirky eye the movie looks like a retro postcard.
Jenkins's own parents met in Philadelphia: Dad owned a strip club, Mom was his hat-check girl. (In an early short film, Jenkins portrays her mother as a Blanche DuBois type, well meaning but scarily untethered, like a runaway parade balloon.) After her parents split, Jenkins's father went to Beverly Hills. He tried to sell big American cars during the energy crisis, and shepherded his kids through a dead-broke decade. By the time Jenkins was 15, the family's dysfunction ran so deep that her oldest brother became her legal guardian. Later, she wrote "Slums" with a Guggenheim grant and a stint at the Sundance Institute. Jenkins's father, already in his 50s when she was born, died during filming. They'd had a complicated relationship. But what one takes away from the movie is Vivian's bedrock love for her dad, even if he does bark, "Put on your brassiere!" "Slums" marks the coming of age of a girl—and a filmmaker.

SIGHT AND SOUND, 12/98, p. 61, Liese Spencer

Los Angeles, 1976. Teenager Vivian Abramowitz and her two brothers Ben and Rickey are suburban nomads, moving between cheap motels in order to qualify for a Beverly Hills education while their gambling single father Murray dodges the rent. At a new motel Viv makes friends with her neighbour, a dope dealer named Eliot. Meanwhile, Viv's older, emotionally unstable cousin Rita has been found wandering around on drugs. Murray collects her from the police and she comes to stay. Rita's father offers Murray financial support in return for his promise to see a reluctant Rita through nursing college.
The family move to an upmarket motel, where Rita teaches Viv about sex. Required to provide a urine sample for her first day at college, Rita finds out she's pregnant. Eliot drops Rita at college and takes Viv to a local car park; they have sex, the first time for Viv. Rita phones her boyfriend and tells him she's pregnant; he hangs up on her. Returning to the flat, Viv and Eliot find Rita comatose on sleeping pills. Murray arrives home with a date. Paramedics arrive and revive Rita. The following day, Rita's father and mother arrive. At a family lunch Rita's father bullies Rita and humiliates Murray. Viv stabs his leg with a fork. Rita tells her parents she is pregnant and returns home with them. The Abramowitz's drive off looking for new accommodation.
"Furniture is just temporary, education is forever," Alan Arkin's cash-strapped single father tells his children as he drags them around 70s LA, little realising the kind of Beverly Hills education they are receiving as they trail from one Formica-clad motel room to the next.

Constantly on the run from landlords, Viv (a wonderfully natural Natasha Lyonne) and her brothers learn skin-of-the-teeth survival: how to dump a cardboard box of ornaments while making a midnight getaway; how to turn up midmorning at a new motel so they don't look too desperate. Debut director Tamara Jenkins' deft handling of such scenes combines robust comedy with darker shades. She shows how this barely functioning family, always on the brink of disaster, just about manages to cleave together. Driving through the palm-lined streets at dawn, Jenkins' economic tourists take turns to spot movie stars' homes before heading for a café to eat steaks for breakfast, reassuring rituals which bind them together.

Indeed, one of the great things about this slight but sharply observed rites-of-passage drama is that it's refreshingly free of 'life lessons'. Rather than the usual journey into self knowledge, *Slums* laid-back picaresque paints Viv's eccentric upbringing as an authentic mess of impressions, experiments, humiliations and accidents. In this world the adults are no wiser than the children, who must learn to look after themselves. Lacking a mother, the closest Viv gets to a female role model is the heroically unsuitable Rita. A fabulous, pre-feminist creation played to perfection by Marisa Tomei, Rita is a sweetly sympathetic airhead who just wants to find herself a man and has neither the brains nor the ambition for even a decorative career as a medical receptionist. Still, Rita introduces Viv to the joys of vibrators and depilatory cream, "the Jewish girl's secret weapon."

It's in such details that Jenkins fleshes out her characters and adds flavour to a familiar tale. Viv suffers her burgeoning sexuality as public spectacle—brother Ben notes how "stacked" she is before Dad makes her buy a bra and wear it with her halter-necked top. A subtly played subplot describes Murray's crisis as an older father, mistaken for the children's grandfather and unhappy about settling for asexual 'companionship' with his upmarket girlfriend. Another strand sees Kevin Corrigan's delightfully harmless Charles Manson fanatic hanging around Viv as if she were a bitch in heat.

Switching easily between farce and melancholy irony, Jenkins' film underlines the fragility and strength of family ties. A relaxed pace and naturalistic performances disguise a tight screenplay, which allows room for individual character development without resorting to any trite resolutions. Though not particularly moving or thought-provoking, it's an enjoyable comedy which ends with the family back on the road, their tenuous life glued together by mutual affection.

VILLAGE VOICE, 8/18/98, p. 112, Amy Taubin

As brash, awkward and immodestly engaging as its heroine, Tamara Jenkins's *Slums of Beverly Hills* is a coming-of-age film set in 1976 in the shag-carpeted wrong side of 90210. Fifteen-year-old Vivian Abramowitz (Natasha Lyonne) lives with her father Murray (Alan Arkin), a failed used-car salesman, and her two brothers. When Murray's niece Rita (Marisa Tomei) escapes from a drug rehab clinic, Murray volunteers to look after her—if her rich father helps pay the rent. Ditsy, dependent, man-crazy, and pregnant, Rita is a weird role model for a teenager as ambivalent about her body as Vivian. But Rita knows stuff about sex that Vivian is desperate to understand.

More visceral than *Fast Times at Ridgemount High*, less horrific than *Carrie*, *Slums of Beverly Hills* views adolescent female sexuality through the eyes of a curious, furious girl. Vivian has an antagonistic relationship with her breasts, which seem to have become mountainous overnight. For her, they're foreign objects; for everyone else, family members included, she *is* her breasts, first and foremost. The only way she can cope is to keep her distance from them, maintain an experimental attitude. She goes to a plastic surgeon to find out about getting them reduced. She lets Elliot (Kevin Corrigan), her sweet, Charles Manson-obsessed, pot-dealer neighbor, play with them while they're doing the laundry. "Do you think they're deformed?" she asks, anxious but defiant. "I think they're beautiful" he answers, trying hard not to let excitement upset his cool. Elliot is bewildered by Vivian, who's interested in sex but not seduction. But he also admires her independence, her stubborn determination to figure things out for herself.

Vivian's a unique character—we haven't seen her like onscreen before—but she's sometimes undermined by a movie that's more eager to please than she is. There's a darker comedy buried beneath *Slums of Beverly Hill*'s pertness, one that's closer to Jane Campion's hilarious but dire early short *A Girls Own Story* or to Jenkins's own short, *Family Remains*. The forced sitcom style robs the movie of its organic pace—often, the actors look frozen and stranded, as if waiting for a laugh track—and the irritatingly bouncy score that sounds as if it's been lifted from a bad Italian farce only emphasizes the problem.

Corrigan must have other music playing in his head; with his off-kilter rhythms, he nearly steals the picture. Tomei is adroit though boringly self involved. Lyonne is bright, tough, and vulnerable, but she's too careful an actor to get inside Vivian's feeling of being out of control. Arkin gives a surprisingly muted performance as the 65-year-old single father who's at the end of his rope but tells himself that he's just starting his climb to the top. Arkin's Murray is crazed, despairing, and mysterious. I'd hate for Jenkins to get distracted from her female characters, but maybe next time, maybe she could give Murray a movie of his own.

CHICAGO TRIBUNE, 8/28/98, Friday/p. M, John Petrakis
NEW YORK TIMES, 8/14/98, p. E9, Janet Maslin
VARIETY, 5/25-31/98, p. 64, Emanuel Levy
WASHINGTON POST, 8/28/98, Weekend/p. 41, Michael O'Sullivan

SMALL SOLDIERS

A Dreamworks Pictures and Universal Pictures release. *Executive Producer:* Walter Parkes. *Producer:* Michael Finnell and Colin Wilson. *Director:* Joe Dante. *Screenplay:* Gavin Scott, Adam Rifkin, Ted Elliott, and Terry Rossio. *Director of Photography:* Jamie Anderson. *Editor:* Marshall Harvey. *Music:* Jerry Goldsmith. *Music Editor:* Darrell Hall. *Sound:* Ken King and (music) Bruce Botnick. *Sound Editor:* Eric Lindemann. *Casting:* Denise Chamian. *Production Designer:* William Sandell. *Art Director:* Mark W. Mansbridge. *Set Designer:* Stan Tropp and William Taliaferro. *Set Dresser:* Edward J. Protiva, Louis Terry, Jennifer LaGura, Stacy Doran, and Kristin Frances Jones. *Special Effects:* Kenneth D. Pepiot. *Costumes:* Carole Brown-James. *Stunt Coordinator:* Jim Arnett. *Running time:* 109 minutes. *MPAA Rating:* PG-13.

CAST: David Cross (Irwin Wayfair); Jay Mohr (Larry Benson); Alexandra Wilson (Ms. Kegel); Denis Leary (Gil Mars); Gregory Smith (Alan Abernathy); Gregory Itzin (Mr. Florens); Dick Miller (Joe); Kirsten Dunst (Christy Fimple); Jacob Smith (Timmy Fimple); Jonathan David Bouck (Brad); Kevin Dunn (Stuart Abernathy); Ann Magnuson (Irene Abernathy); Wendy Schaal (Marion Fimple); Phil Hartman (Phil Fimple); Archie Hahn III (Satellite Dish Installer); Robert Picardo (Clean Room Technician); Julius Tennon (Toy World Supervisor); Belinda Balaski (Neighbor); Rance Howard (Husband); Jackie Joseph (Wife); Marcia Mitzman Gaven (Globotech Announcer).

VOICES: Tommy Lee Jones (Chip Hazard); Frank Langella (Archer); Ernest Borgnine (Kip Killagin); Jim Brown (Butch Meathook); Bruce Dern (Link Static); George Kennedy (Brick Bazooka); Clint Walker (Nick Nitro); Christopher Guest (Slamfist/Scratch-It); Michael McKean (Insaniac/Freakenstein); Harry Shearer (Punch-It); Jim Cummings (Ocula); Sarah Michelle Gellar and Christina Ricci (Gwendy Dolls).

LOS ANGELES TIMES, 7/10/98, Calendar/p. 1, Kenneth Turan

"Small Soldiers" is a little boy's fantasy of toys come to life. And like small boys it is often charming and funny, occasionally malicious, and finally too focused on gizmos and effects for its own good.

What if, wonders Gil Mars (Denis Leary), the rapacious CEO of Globotech Industries, toys were so smart that when you played with them they played back? What if they could do in real life everything they do in commercials? Wouldn't that be great for business?

Mars is wondering all this because Globotech, whose motto is "bringing advanced battlefield technology into consumer products," has just bought a toy company called Heartland Play Systems with an eye toward greatly increasing its profits.

Heartland executives Irwin (David Cross) and Larry (Jay Mohr) are not without ideas of their own. The kindly Irwins dreamed up the Gorgonites, sweet-natured aliens lost on Earth, while the ruthless Larry has come up with Maj. Chip Hazard, the hard-driving head of a dreaded force called the Commando Elite.

Not revolutionary ideas, perhaps, but that's where Globotech's access to military technology pays off when these foot-long action figures get built. Powered by the super-secret X-1000 microchip, the Major and his five cohorts have no trouble more than living up to their "everything else is just a toy" tag line.

These toys are supposed to debut on a Monday, but a kindly delivery driver named Joe (the veteran Dick Miller) lets young Alan Abernathy (Gregory Smith), who's minding the family store in a mythical small town, get some a few days early.

New to town, Alan has a crush on Christy Fimple (Kirsten Dunst), the fetching girl next door, whose doltish father (Phil Hartman, in his last role) is a worshiper of all things technological. But even he is unprepared when the Commandos, programmed to consider the Gorgonites deadly enemies, evacuate their boxes and cause all heck to break out.

With his experience directing "Gremlins" and his affinity for 1950s sci-fi schlock, Joe Dante is the obvious person to be in charge here, and he does bring both sweetness and a sense of satiric comedy to the film's human relationships.

Of course, it's not the people whom audiences will be coming to "Small Soldiers" to see; it's the toys. The idea of playthings springing to life is not new (and veterans of "Toy Story" know all about war toys cooperating), but technology marches on, and these toys, combining the animatronic skills of the Stan Winston Studio and the computer-generated images of Industrial Light & Magic, are definitely state of the art.

"Small Soldiers'" best move was the actors it recruited for vocal talent. Tommy Lee Jones does a magnificent job as the gruff Major, and someone had the clever idea of signing up veterans of "The Dirty Dozen" (Ernest Borgnine, Jim Brown, George Kennedy, Clint Walker) for his commando team.

It's not clear which of the four credited writers (Gavin Scott and Adam Rifkin, Ted Elliott & Terry Rossio) wrote the military patter, but with lines like "Gorgonite scum, we have ways to make you talk" and "It's only a flesh wound, sir" (spoken by a toy that's been cut in half) it amounts to a great spoof of classic war movies.

The Gorgonites are finely vocalized as well, starting with the dulcet tones of Frank Langella as Archer, their leader, and continuing with the gang from "This Is Spinal Tap" (Christopher Guest, Michael McKean, Harry Shearer) as his companions. But one of the problems with "Small Soldiers" is that these creatures are not as intriguing as the Commando crew and play rather too much like leftover critters from the "Gremlins" movies.

In fact, just like those films, "Small Soldiers" finally gets too obsessed with its creatures and too involved with the ways and means they use to attack the humans that get in their way. Though it starts promisingly, the picture ends as a standoff between the affection Dante and company bring to the project and its increasingly frenetic and tiresome emphasis on what special effects can make its little people do. Letting the toys take over may make for great merchandising, but it's hell on motion pictures.

NEW YORK POST, 7/10/98, p. 39, Rod Dreher

"Small Soldiers" is that frustrating sort of picture in which the entire plot dilemma could be solved with a baseball bat in about 10 seconds.

But then the human beings in the film would have to act like they had brains in their heads—and we wouldn't have a movie, which in this case wouldn't be much of a loss.

"Small Soldiers" is about a greed toymaker (Jay Mohr) who secretly installs advanced military microchips in the "Commando Elite" line of G.I. Joe-type action figures. The Commandos and their enemies, the misshapen monstrous Gorgonites, are designed to be a new, improved kind of action toy, dolls with real personalities capable of communicating with kids ("toys that play back!").

Alan Abernathy (Gregory Smith), a misunderstood adolescent who runs his dad's suburban Ohio toy store, finds out just how advanced when he convinces a delivery man to hand over an early shipment of the toys. The Commandos, a brigade of jarhead homunculi under the command of

Chip Hazard (voice of Tommy Lee Jones), break out of their boxes during the night, and attempt,to massacre , the Gorgonites.

The Gorgonites go into hiding, and their chieftain, a half-leopard, half-Schwarzenegger named Archer (voice of Frank Langella), is in the protective custody of Alan's backpack. Speaking in the noble, defeated voice of a liberal elder statesman—imagine John Kenneth Galbraith as an emasculated Klingon—wizened but mopey Archer pleads with Alan to realize how maniacally evil the Commandos are, and to get about the business of annihilating them.

But the Commandos are nothing if not persistent, breaking into Alan's house and MacGyverishly crafting assault weapons out of junk in the garage. An enormous amount of credit must be granted to special-effects artist Stan Winston, who makes the plastic Lilliputian fascists come cleverly alive.

Unfortunately, not nearly as much imagination went into giving them personalities. Unlike the delightful animatronic things in "Toy Story" these little buggers are as charmless as robots. Even the wicked beastlings in "Gremlins" a similarly themed effort from "Small Soldiers" director Joe Dante, were loads more fun to watch wreaking havoc in sleepy suburbia. A few wise-cracky nods to other movies—"Patton," "The Hunchback of Notre Dame" and "Apocalypse Now" among them—have no snap.

You have to accept that foot-tall plastic dolls with a bad attitude can terrorize a neighborhood, and defeat much larger opponents. If the movie were smarter and sharper, the implausibility would be worth accepting. But it's just stupid. In one scene, the Commandos fit the Barbie-like dolls of teen dream Christy (Kirsten Dunst) with their own silicon-chip implants; turning them into vicious mini-fembots, who take down two strapping teenagers. Zit-faced Gullivers? Nobody's that gullible.

The movie's underlying theme is that even misfits can defend themselves. Alan's short-tempered dad (Kevin Dunn) rides him hard, but in the end, only Alan can save the day. The Gorgonites, freakish outsiders, are programmed to lose to the Commandos, and we're supposed to find them pitiable. Message: Nerds Are People Too. Let's move on.

There are worse places to park the rugrats this summer (e.g. "Dr. Dolittle"). I suppose the worst that can be said of "Small Soldiers" is that it's dull and mechanical. Which is true of most summer movies.

The late Phil Hartman has a bit part here as a smarmy technophilic next-door neighbor. What a pity that the gifted comic's final movie role was as a cog in this product's gears.

NEWSDAY, 7/10/98, Part II/p. B2, Jack Mathews

Mean little creatures tearing up a small town while spouting glib pop references. If that sounds familiar, you may be thinking of Joe Dante's 1984 "Gremlins," or you may have seen the trailer for Dante's latest film, "Small Soldiers." Same movie, different gremlins.

Dante and "Gremlins" producer Steven Spielberg have reteamed here for a shameless and far less magical knockoff of their previous work, replacing their alien troublemakers from the first film with a line of self-determinant toy commandos.

There are so many parallels between the two stories, it's easier to point out the differences:

● Instead of being created spontaneously from fur balls and water, the commandos are manmade, battery-operated, plastic characters with micro-processors designed by some techno-freak in the Pentagon.

●Where "Gremlins" was mostly a send-up of B horror movies, "Small Soldiers" satirizes the profit-minded toy industry.

●And where the gremlins got their meanness from post-midnight meals, the Commando Elite is motivated by a warped sense of patriotism and a preprogramed mission to find and destroy the Gorgonites, a line of peace-loving monster toys also equipped to think for themselves.

But these differences route us to the same action, the fury of battle between humans and rabid miniatures on the hallowed ground of suburbia. Only this time, the gremlins aren't nearly as cute. Led by Major Chip Hazard (voice, of Tommy Lee Jones), the muscle-bound, muscle-headed commandos are hard, cold killers, programmed to take no prisoners, human or Gorgonite.

The Commando Elite and the Gorgonites are the result of a toy mogul's edict to a pair of ambitious young executives: Make toys that do in real life what they do in commercials, and get them ready in three months. In the rush to make the deadline, corners are cut, risks are taken and a truckload of the defective toys is on its way to Stuart Abernathy's toy store in bucolic Winslow Corners.

In his father's absence, 15-year-old Alan Abernathy (Gregory Smith) talks the 'truck driver (Dante regular Dick Miller) out of one box each of Commando Elite and the Gorgonites, planning to impress dad by selling them before he returns from a business trip. But before Alan can get the toys on the display racks, mortal enemies Chip Hazard and Archer, emissary of the Gorgonites, are out of their boxes, and squaring off for battle.

Archer (Frank Langella) is the "Small Soldiers" talking version of the friendly mogwai in "Gremlins." With a catlike face and a single nubbed horn, Archer is the pet of every imaginative boy's dream, and he and Alan are immediate pals. And they will be friends on the battlefield.

Archer and his ragtag band of Gorgonites are programmed to find Gorgon, their own Promised Land, but they need help from their human friends—Alan, his friend Christy (Kirsten Dunst), and their parents—to fend off the tenacious Commando Elite.

The late Phil Hartman plays Christy's gadget-loving father, and the film leaves us wondering how much of his last performance was edited out. He's certainly a minor character in the finished product. More central to events is Alan's overbearing father (Kevin Dunn) who is making his son pay for a spiritedness that has had him kicked out of two previous schools.

Alan and Christy are sympathetic, conventional heroes, but the real attraction of "Small Soldiers" is the animatronic. and computer generated creatures, and it all comes off, frankly, as a little too mechanical. Dante's gremlins had the advantage of being other-worldly; we could accept the illusion of the animated dolls without wondering how they were made to move.

In "Small Soldiers," the how-did-they-do-that question arises over every scene, and worse, the question doesn't seem particularly hard to answer.

The commandos are static, foot-high plastic puppets, whose mouths move up and down on hinges without forming the contours of speech. They walk with the graceless gait of robots, and even while they're setting off bombs and shooting nails with their makeshift weapons, they never muster up any real sense of danger, or reality.

It's easier to warm up to the Gorgonites and not just because they're friendly, but because they're the most imaginatively designed. One is a long stalk with a Bette Davis eye on the end. Another rotates his arms with a speed that makes him look like a grounded helicopter. Another is a variant of Frankenstein's monster. It is them, not the humans, that audiences will want to see rescued.

Despite the good voice work of such actors as Jim Brown, Bruce Dern, Christopher Guest, Michael McKean, and Harry Shearer, the lesson of "Small Soldiers" is that it's easier to anthropomorphize animals than miniaturized people.

But the main purpose of the film, to create a market for DreamWorks' first line of toys, depends entirely on the verdict at the box office.

SIGHT AND SOUND, 10/98, p. 55, Jonathan Romney

When toy firm Heartland is taken over by conglomerate Globotech, new boss Gil Mars instructs designers Irwin and Larry to market their new action figures. Irwin has invented a range of aliens, the Gorgonites, while Larry develops the Commando Elite, a team of soldiers whom he equips with a deadly military microprocessor. Minding his father's toy store, young Alan Abernathy persuades Heartland delivery man Joe to give him a sample of the first dolls. Unknown to Alan, the figures come to life, and Gorgonite leader Archer sneaks home with him. Alan returns to the shop to find it wrecked. The Commandos, led by Chip Hazard, have declared war on the Gorgonites, who have vanished.

Alan saves Archer from a Commando attack, but the soldiers rearm with weapons constructed from household tools. Alan meets the other Gorgonites, amiable monsters programmed to hide and lose battles. The Commandos infiltrate the house of Alan's neighbour Christy, and transform her Gwendy dolls into female fighting monsters, who take Christy prisoner. Alan uses a decoy to rescue her and, as chaos escalates, Chip is the only Commando to survive the first skirmish. Chip enlists reinforcements from a new shipment of Commandos. Alan, Christy and their parents, together with Irwin and Larry, are besieged by thousands of dolls, but with the Gorgonites' help, Alan destroys the Commandos with a massive power surge. Mars arrives in town to hand out compensation cheques. The Gorgonites sail off in a toy boat in search of their mythical home of Gorgon.

Watching Disney's *Toy Story*, it was hard not to feel shortchanged by the film's concentration on well-behaved rag-and-plastic heroes. The film's real stars, surely, were the briefly glimpsed toys next door—the hideous mutant playthings modified by a maladjusted pre-teen. Joe Dante has made a career out of being just such an unruly presence. He may not be as gothically warped or self-mythologising as Tim Burton, but he's an unpredictable and mischievous intruder in the well-tended suburb originally mapped out by Steven Spielberg, under whose production aegis he has often worked *(Small Soldiers* is a DreamWorks production). Dante's suburbs, cosy as they initially seem, are invariably hotbeds of rancour, small-mindedness and downright idiocy.

Consequently, since his *Gremlins* hit, Dante has fared badly with producers and audiences alike: his films are too wry and, superficially at least, benevolent for the Burton kids, but too dark and cynical for the mainstream. But despite several years in the wilderness, he has consistently followed his own path, making movies that are sly, knowing variants on each other; Dante is nothing if not a self-made auteur, a knowing hit-and-run merchant out of the Roger Connan academy.

As well as providing a riposte to *Toy Story*, whose green plastic commandos were effectively fairy-tale helper elves, *Small Soldiers* is also an acerbic swipe at the US military ethos, a consistent Dante theme. His last film, the (somewhat lacklustre) HBO political satire *The Second Civil War*, portrayed militarism as a storm in a cable-news teacup. *Small Soldiers* could be happening two streets down from Dante's *The 'Burbs*, in which a posse of witless bourgeois launch a commando assault on their non-conformist neighbours. In *Small Soldiers*, Dante lampoons American warfare and its movie glorification. The Commando Elite are grimacing plug-uglies commanded by a GI Joe-style doll with the clipped bark of Tommy Lee Jones; the rest are voiced by the surviving cast members of *The Dirty Dozen* plus Bruce Dern, the weekend guerrilla in *The 'Burbs*. The gags (from four writers including *Mousehunts* Adam Rifkin) come thick and fast: the Commandos besiege Alan's family (just as the US military besieged General Noriega) with the Spice Girls at full blast, before Chip coasts in by toy helicopter to the sound of Wagner, growling, "I love the smell of polyurethane in the morning." The neatest anti-gung-ho twist comes earlier: in what looks like a sugar-coated Spielbergian touch, Gorgonite leader Archer learns about American history by fast-scanning Alan's CD-ROM. But, in a sharp reversal, Chip later gives his troops a pep-talk: framed in front of a jigsaw-puzzle Stars and Stripes, he barks out a speech that is an incoherent patchwork of death-or-glory clichés.

Small Soldiers' target is the Hollywood merchandising plague. Many recent blockbusters have included some ironic commentary on their own spin-off sales prospects, *Toy Story* most wittily of all. But *Small Soldiers* presents merchandise as terrorism—the town is literally invaded by Commando product, which proliferates as endemically as Dante's Gremlins. Globotech is particularly iniquitous not just because it is a big bad arms company, but because of its hypocritical diversification into the domestic sphere. Its corporate video uses the slogan, "turning swords into ploughshares." But ploughshares are turned right back into swords, as the soldiers convert innocent household objects, rigging up weapons from toasters and salad drainers (and the odd chainsaw). In Dante films the home becomes every bit as deadly as in a slasher pic, everything available for destructive DIY reconfiguring. The film's most brilliant instance of this demonic *bricolage* is the Commandos' *Bride of Frankenstein* modification of Christy's Gwendy dolls into bald, scarred battle vixens, which teem murderously over their owner, spitting out with horrid intent such catchphrases as: "Let's get a facial!"

Small Soldiers is, of course, caught in the same paradox as *Toy Story*, which narratively espoused old-fashioned toys like Cowboy Woody over the high-tech packaged glamour of Buzz Lightyear while itself being entirely generated out of state-of-the-art digital technology. *Small Soldiers* wouldn't be possible without Industrial Light & Magic's effects, but it comes across as a comment about the increasing digitisation of Hollywood. The theme is explored right from the start as the Commando assembly line cranks out little metal skeletons that look exactly like James Cameron's Terminator. But Dante's sympathies are more complex than that. His interest clearly lies with anything that has a potential for comic mayhem, rather than the worthy non-violent toys sold by Alan's dad. And for the most part, he is more interested in the snarling malevolence of the Commandos, bad Gremlins to Archer's noble-but-dull Gizmo. It's only when finally unleashed in all their misshapen farcical energy that the Gorgonites really become charismatic.

But the film is more than a play-off between toys nice and nasty, simple and sophisticated. It's a plea for inventiveness, and its most striking effects are not the deceptively simple-looking ones designed by ILM (Archer required 62 times more data than the T Rex in *Jurassic Park)* but all the improvisations cobbled out of cheese graters and wheelbarrows. Dante's omnivorous smash-and-grab approach can use CGI, but a nailgun always comes in handy too—a defiantly homemade approach that you rather wish would rub off on the James Camerons.

VILLAGE VOICE, 7/21/98, p. 124, Dennis Lim

A feature-length commercial bravely doubling as a critique of capitalism, Joe Dante's *Small Soldiers* isn't exactly self-satirizing; for the most part, it simply glosses over its contradictions in the hope that no one will object. Lazy filmmaking, to be sure, but as a marketing strategy, it'll suffice.

When snarly corporate honcho Denis Leary commissions a new line of toys that are "so smart they play back" his inventor lackeys (Jay Mohr and David Cross) take to installing Department of Defense microprocessors in plastic figurines. Soon enough, the toys are alive, and, this being a Joe Dante movie, it turns out that some of them are vicious little fuckers. A lopsided miniaturist battle eventually breaks out in some suburban nowhere, with the buff gung ho, rabidly militaristic Commando Elite (voiced by Tommy Lee Jones, Bruce Dern, and one third of *The Dirty Dozen)* hunting down their designated enemies, a tribe of soft-spoken, grotesquely malformed freaks known as the Gorgonites (Frank Langella and the Spinal Tap quartet), not to mention any humans who get in the way.

Small Soldiers is clearly positioning itself as an edgier *Toy Story*, but while Dante's movie is reliably unsentimental (and even vaguely anarchic), it's also less fun and less visually exciting. (It more closely recalls *Jumanji*'s methodically boisterous rampage through suburbia.) Initially bogged down by its bland kid protagonist (Gregory Smith), the film also hits a few sluggish patches along the way; the computer-generated effects are impressive enough, but they're also necessarily Lilliputian, and somewhat underwhelming.

Once Dante hits his stride, he does engineer a few enjoyably surreal sequences, like the one in which the Commando Elite co-opt Kristen Dunst's doll collection, spinning off an assembly line of murderous Barbie knockoffs (Christina Ricci and Sarah Michelle Gellar provide the voices—an inspired touch, though, as with many of the other cameos, they're not immediately recognizable). But mostly, the film's "grown-up appeal" consists of the always welcome Ann Magnuson (as the hero's confused mother, she gets to deliver straight-faced lines like "Are you on crank?") and some half-assed nods to *Platoon* and *Apocalypse Now*. Ultimately, *Small Soldiers* might work best as a narrowly defined children's movie—a kind of *Toy Story* for little sadists.

Also reviewed in:
CHICAGO TRIBUNE, 7/10/98, Friday/p. A, Michael Wilmington
NEW YORK TIMES, 7/10/98, p. E18, Janet Maslin
VARIETY, 7/13-19/98, p. 54, Leonard Klady
WASHINGTON POST, 7/10/98, p. D5, Rita Kempley

SMOKE SIGNALS

A Miramax Films release of a Shadow Catcher Entertainment production. *Executive Producer:* David Skinner and Carl Bressler. *Producer:* Scott Rosenfelt and Larry Estes. *Director:* Chris Eyre. *Screenplay (based on stories from his book "The Lone Ranger and Tonto Fistfight in Heaven):* Sherman Alexie. *Director of Photography:* Brian Capener. *Editor:* Brian Berdan. *Music:* BC Smith. *Sound:* Douglas Tourtelot. *Casting:* Coreen Mayrs. *Production Designer:* Charles Armstrong. *Art Director:* Jonathon Saturen. *Set Decorator:* Dawn Ferry. *Costumes:* Ron Leamon. *Running time:* 89 minutes. *MPAA Rating:* PG-13.

CAST: Adam Beach (Victor Joseph);   Evan Adams (Thomas Builds-the-Fire);   Irene Bedard (Suzy Song);   Gary Farmer (Arnold Joseph);   Tantoo Cardinal (Arlene Joseph);   Cody Lightning (Young Victor Joseph);   Simon Baker (Young Thomas Builds-the-Fire); Michelle St. John (Velma);   Robert Miano (Burt);   Molly Cheek (Penny);   Monique Mojica (Grandma Builds-the-Fire); Elaine Miles (Lucy);   Michael Greyeyes (Junior Polatkin);   Leonard George (Lester Fallsapart);   John Trudell (Randy Peone);   Darwin Haine (Boo);   Tom Skerritt (Police Chief);   Cynthia Geary (Cathy the Gymnast);   Perrey Reeves (Holly).

LOS ANGELES TIMES, 6/26/98, Calendar/p. 8, Kevin Thomas

On the eve of July 4, 1976, a couple on Idaho's Coeur d'Alene Indian Reservation celebrate the bicentennial of the white man's independence with a lively party that ends in tragedy when their home catches fire, costing them their lives. Their baby boy, however, gets tossed out an upstairs window. Catching it is burly Arnold Joseph, and the boy, Thomas Builds-the-Fire, grows up with Arnold's son Victor.

This tragic incident sets in motion "Smoke Signals," a bittersweet comedy said to be the first full-length feature film written, directed and co-produced by American Indians. It is unlike most other films about Native Americans in that it is neither earnest nor indignant.

Instead, it is a warm film of friendship and reconciliation, and whenever it refers to historic injustices or contemporary issues in Native American culture, it does so with wry, glancing humor. "Smoke Signals" is indeed poignant, but above all it's pretty funny, far more coherent and stylish than the overrated "Powwow Highway" of nearly a decade ago.

Director Chris Eyre and writer Sherman Alexie, drawing from a collection of Alexie's short stories, are sly, laid-back storytellers as they initially cut back and forth between 1988 and the present. When Victor and Thomas are 12—played at that age by Cody Lightning and Simon Baker, respectively—Victor's alcoholic father (Gary Farmer, who was the best thing about "Powwow") leaves home when his wife, Arlene (Tantoo Cardinal), stands up to him decisively. Now 10 years later, Arlene receives word that Arnold has died of a heart attack in his trailer home in the desert outside Phoenix.

The right thing to do is for Victor (Adam Beach) to go to Arizona to settle his father's affairs and bring back his ashes, but he can't afford to go without the financial aid of Thomas (Evan Adams), who in return insists on going along. They have grown into very different young men. Victor is proud, handsome and cynical, whereas Thomas, raised by his grandmother, is a nerdy, nonstop talker who actually wears a suit.

Thomas, who is nice-looking once Victor gets him to change his look—and to shut up sometimes, too—is also exceedingly witty, bright and resourceful. He's such a skilled teller of outrageous tall tales that he charms some young women into giving Victor and him a lift. One of them reacts to hilarious effect when she dryly remarks, "That's a fine example of the oral tradition."

The journey affords the opportunity for the kind of give-and-take that strengthens the young men's friendship and matures them both in the process. The filmmakers are concerned further with the need for reconciliation between father and son and, beyond that, reconciliation with tradition and nature. For Victor had been bitter about his father, his drinking and ultimate abandonment of his family. When he and Thomas arrive in Phoenix, what they learn about Arnold is wholly unexpected and jolting, and inevitably transforming.

Beach, so impressive in the title role of "Squanto: A Warrior's Tale," has a Matt Damon-Ben Affleck kind of charisma, and Adams is a nervy comedian. They are very skilled actors, and you could scarcely get stronger support than from Cardinal and Farmer, who are among the most renowned North American Indian actors. Irene Bedard stands out as a kindly young woman who looked in on Arnold near the end of his life. Tom Skerritt turns up in a cameo as a canny cop.

There is a most inviting and unpretentious yet sophisticated look and feel to "Smoke Signals," and contributing crucially to its expressing its shifting moods are cameraman Brian Capener's easy flow of images and composer B.C. Smith, who blended traditional Native American drums and flutes with classical, rock, blues and country music.

NEW YORK POST, 6/26/98, p. 52. Thelma Adams

Last March, "Smoke Signals" opened the 27th annual New Directors/New Films series at the Museum of Modern Art. Directed by Chris Eyre and based on Sherman Alexie's comic fiction, "Smoke" is a victim of its own flaming buzz from the Sundance Film Festival.

The uneven road comedy tracks two native Americans who leave Idaho's Coeur d'Alene Indian reservation. Victor Joseph (Adam Beach) and Thomas Builds-the-Fire (Evan Adams) head for Phoenix to claim the ashes of Joseph's dead father.

A burning secret in the young men's past links them together. Along the way, the handsome, angry Victor gives the nerdy, bespectacled Thomas lessons in being a warrior. Thomas shows Victor the way to his heart.

Awkward, stilted, heartfelt and universal in its message about forgiving our fathers, Eyre's debut brushes against being a Native American "Northern Exposure," a prime-time comedy drama. In the opening scenes, the K-REZ disc jockey announces "It's a good day to be indigenous."

The movie's high points are the strong acting of Beach, Adams and Gary Farmer as Victor's troubled dad. Alexie's humor bubbles up in sharp one-liners and set pieces like an ode to John Wayne's teeth. But "Smoke Signals" turns ashen well before the road trip's 6 days, 12 hours and 32 minutes come to an end.

NEWSDAY, 6/26/98, Part II/p. B11, John Anderson

"Sometimes, it's a good day to die," muses a character in "Smoke Signals." "Sometimes, it's a good day to play basketball." Sometimes—not often, maybe—it's a good day to go to the movies.

Today would be one of those days—although last Sunday might have been even better. A Father's Day movie if there ever was one, "Smoke Signals"—written by Sherman Alexie, directed by Chris Eyre—is an American Indian movie only if we insist. Its signatures may be the dry jokes, or the upward-inflected voice of the young, shamanistic storyteller Thomas Builds-a-Fire (Evan Adams) or the handsome stoicism of his childhood friend Victor Joseph (Adam Beach). Its author may be Alexie, the noted Amerind novelist who may be more necessary than he is lyrical. Permeating its soul, however, is a transcendent lesson of forgiveness that blows out the borders.

Yes, yes, it's a movie with a message. Also, a road movie, a not-such-good-buddies movie, a myth-saturated odyssey and a bit of an angry glance at the state of Indian life (set largely on Idaho's Coeur d'Alene reservation, its mise-en-scene is mirthfully, grim). But in addition to all this, "Smoke Signals" celebrates the power of storytelling, and the way that existing within a tradition—even just the tradition of the story form itself—verifies our existence.

This is something that Thomas knows instinctively, something that grows out of the horrific July 4th night he was pitched, swaddled, from out of the upper window of his parents' incinerating house into the great arms of Arnold Joseph (Gary Farmer). And it's something Victor rejects—either because Thomas is such a nerd, or because all the stories lead back to Arnold, who would soon abandon him and his mother (Tantoo Cardinal), leaving a reservation-sized cavity in Victor's life.

Regularly flashing back and forth between the younger Thomas and Victor (Simon Baker and Cody Lightning) and their older selves, Eyre establishes the uneasy bonds between Victor, who loses a father to drink and guilt, and Thomas, for whom his savior Arnold was a surrogate father. When a call comes from Arizona saying Arnold has died, Thomas lends Victor the money he needs to get there, on the condition that he go, too. Victor, as poor as he is unhappy, begrudgingly takes Thomas along.

In Arizona, they meet Arnold's friend Suzy Song (Irene Bedard), a role so underwritten it seems like Bedard might have been cast for the print ads (which she dominates). She's fine. The two leads, however, are very good—Adams, particularly, whose Thomas is a strange but endearing creation; Beach, whose Victor thinks sullenness makes him a warrior, is more understated. Farmer, however, who brought such ironic mysticism to Jim Jarmusch's "Dead Man," virtually steals the picture. Of course, he does play the father. And, in terms of "Smoke Signals," if nowhere else, that is the source and direction whence the spirits flow.

TIME, 6/29/98, p. 69, Richard Schickel

A father long lost to drink and mysterious shame has died. Attention must be paid by his angry, damaged son Victor (Adam Beach). A little odyssey to recover the body—and to achieve some sort of posthumous reconciliation—is arranged. Another youth, Thomas (Evan Adams), whose life the dead man saved and whose memories of him are much fonder, intrudes himself on the journey, which eventually brings the young mourners to a new understanding of their shared past and of one another.

Smoke Signals, which is adapted from some of his own short stories by Sherman Alexie and directed by Chris Eyre, obviously wants to get at primal stuff. And in its little way it does. But the largest pleasure of this very small film, which is being promoted as the first feature largely created by Native Americans, lies in the relationship between its two young travelers. Off the reservation where they were born and raised, they present contrasting faces to the outside world. Victor wants to be silent, stoic, dangerously enigmatic—sort of an old-fashioned movie Indian. Thomas, who seems to be Alexie's surrogate, is, in contrast, a slightly nerdy puppy. And a motormouth, spinning funny, folkish tales, trying to humanize his wary friend and ingratiate himself with strangers.

The result is a shrewd portrait, sly, casual yet palpably authentic, of the principal ways members of any minority try to respond to an uncomprehending world. Each learns something useful from the other, and we, incidentally, learn something believable and warming about modern Native life and manners. *Smoke Signals* could be more complex and compelling, narratively, but there's a sweet freshness in its voice that's worth heeding.

VILLAGE VOICE, 6/30/98, p. 140, Michael Atkinson

Chris Eyre's *Smoke Signals,* a lack-luster Sundance remnant, is already nailed up and lifeless, betrayed by the burden of identity-political sermonizing, precious writerlines, and cliché-mongering. A smug and leaden "res" road movie written by Sherman Alexie, Eyre's film acts as if he's the only Indian film ever made, or at least the first Indian film its intended middle-class white audience will see. Victor (Adam Beach), a cool-looking Coeur d'Alene rebel who loves his mother, must travel off-res to retrieve the ashes of his deadbeat dad (Gary Farmer), bringing along jabbermouth goofball Thomas (Evan Adams) for the ride. Functioning better as a *Schoolhouse Rock* lesson on all things great and indigenous (oral tale-telling, hating the white man, bartering, long hair, etc.) than as convincing narrative, Eyre and Alexie's film coasts on fashionable ethnicity. It's an empty vessel, but it probably looks good on a résumé.

Also Reviewed in:
CHICAGO TRIBUNE, 7/3/98, Friday/p. 8, Mark Caro
NEW YORK TIMES, 6/26/98, p. E14, Janet Maslin
VARIETY, 2/2-8/98, p. 29, Tod McCarthy
WASHINGTON POST, 7/3/98, p. D1, Stephen Hunter
WASHINGTON POST, 7/3/98, Weekend/p. 47, Michael O'Sullivan

SNAKE EYES

A Touchstone Pictures and Paramount Pictures release of a DeBart production. *Executive Producer:* Louis A. Stroller. *Producer:* Brian De Palma. *Director:* Brian De Palma. *Screenplay:* David Koepp. *Story:* Brian De Palma and David Koepp. *Director of Photography:* Stephen H. Burum. *Editor:* Bill Pankow. *Music:* Ryuichi Sakamoto. *Music Editor:* Nick Meyers. *Boxing Choreography:* James Gambina. *Sound:* Patrick Rousseau. *Sound Editor:* Maurice Schell and Richard Cirincione. *Casting:* Mary Colquhoun. *Production Designer:* Anne Pritchard. *Art Director:* James Fox, Isabelle Guay, and Real Proulx. *Set Decorator:* Daniel Carpentier. *Special Effects:* Garry Elmendorf. *Costumes:* Odette Gadoury. *Make-up:* Lucille

Demers. *Stunt Coordinator:* Peter Bucossi, Michael Nomad, Mike Scherer, and Eddie Yansick. *Running time:* 99 minutes. *MPAA Rating:* R.

CAST: Nicolas Cage (Rick Santoro);   Gary Sinise (Kevin Dunne);   John Heard (Gilbert Powell); Carla Gugino (Julia Costello);   Stan Shaw (Lincoln Tyler);   Kevin Dunn (Lou Logan);   Michael Rispoli (Jimmy George);   Joel Fabiani (Charles Kirkland);   Luis Guzman (Cyrus);   David Anthony Higgins (Ned Campbell);   Mike Starr (Walt McGahn);   Tamara Tunie (Anthea);   Chip Zien (Mickey Alter); Michaella Bassey and Eva Tep (Tyler's Party Girls);   Paul Joseph Bernardo and Brian A. Wilson (Casino Security);   Jernard Burks (Tyler's Bodyguard);   Mark Camacho (C.J.);   Desmond Campbell and Deano Clavet (Arena Security);   Jean-Paul Chartrand (Ring Announcer);   Chip Chuipka (Zientz/Drunk);   Tara Ann Culp (Lady at Elevator);   Kelly Deadmon (Blonde Reporter);   Frédérick Degrandpré, Sebastien Delorme, Byron Johnson, and Stephen Spreekmeester (College Boys);   Adam C. Flores (Jose Pacifico Ruiz);   George Fourniotis and Guy Kelada (Blue Shirts);   Christina Fulton (Roundgirl);   Kenneth Glegg (Referee);   Alain Goulem (PPV Director);   Dean Hagopian (Latecomer);   Jayne Heitmeyer (Serena);   Eric Hoziel (Rabat, Assassin).   Sylvain Landry (Remote Producer);   Cary Lawrence (Powell's Aide);   Robert Norman Lemieux, Richard Lemire, and Richard Zeman (FBI Agents); Christopher MacCabe and Jacynthe Rene (Couple);   Sylvain Massé, John Thaddeus, and Lance E. Nichols (Cops);   Patrick F. McDade (Lawyer);   William J. Mckeon III (Anthea's Cameraman);   Peter McRobbie (Pritzker);   Christian Napoli (Michael Santoro);   Jason Nuzzo (Coin Cup Grabber);   Patrick Parent (Detective);   Peter Patrikios (Coin Cup Decoy);   James Whelan (Mayor);   Gerard Max Désilus (Tyler's Party Crash Guy).

CHRISTIAN SCIENCE MONITOR, 8/7/98, p. B3, David Sterritt

Nicolas Cage is one of Hollywood's most energetic actors, and Brian De Palma is one of the few filmmakers who's a match for him. Coming in the sticky doldrums of August, their new "Snake Eyes" is a hard-edged effort to wake-and-shake the lethargic late-summer season. It may be too ornery and slippery to succeed, but it certainly shoots off a lot of sparks trying.

Cage plays Rick Santoro, an Atlantic City cop. Taking a break at a championship boxing match, he stumbles onto a plot to assassinate the secretary of defense, who's also at the match after busy weeks of assessing a new antimissile system. Santoro's first task is to aid his best friend, an army commander guarding the official. But the plot turns out to be thicker than anyone suspected, and soon our hero is simultaneously chasing the villains and figuring out where his loyalties should lie.

As a story, "Snake Eyes" has less suspense and surprise than first-rate De Palma thrillers like "Raising Cain" and "The Fury," which still carry a tingle years later. Its not as tight or emotionally compelling as it might have been if David Koepp's sketchy screenplay matched the wide-eyed conviction of Cage's admirably extroverted acting,

As an exercise in pure style, "Snake Eyes" fares better, again justifying De Palma's longtime claim that he's more interested in creating vivid images than making audiences squirm in their seats. The picture is a small-scale symphony of kinetic camera movements, rapid-fire montage sequences, split-screen effects, and long-lasting shots that allow characters and settings to interact more artfully than happens in less-imaginatively filmed movies.

"Snake Eyes" also has a serious theme to ponder: the out-of-control materialism of contemporary life, represented here by a concatenation of follies ranging from excesses of the gambling and prizefighting industries to machinations of the military-industrial complex. It's no coincidence that the movie's most frequently recurring image is a hundred-dollar bill smeared with a criminal's blood. This symbolizes the crassness and corruption that "Snake Eyes" persuasively attacks when not falling prey to its own brand of media-bred sensationalism.

Cage gets solid if uninspired support from Gary Sinise as the military man with a secret, John Heard as a defense contractor, and Julia Costello as a young whistle-blower caught up in the violent events.

But the real heroes are cinematographer Stephen H. Burum and editor Bill Pankow, who help the picture keep popping even when its plot and dialogue go into a slump.

LOS ANGELES TIMES, 8/7/98, Calendar/p. 1, Kenneth Turan

Brian De Palma is a superb technician in search of a great film. Regrettably, "Snake Eyes" is not it, not even close.

A cartoonish entertainment about corruption, assassination and far-flung conspiracies, "Snake Eyes" exists purely as a vehicle for De Palma to show off the kind of wizardly camera work that is his passion.

Collaborating for the seventh time (including "Mission: Impossible," "The Untouchables" and the underrated "Casualties of War") with expert cinematographer Stephen H. Burum, De Palma, the consummate visual stylist, orchestrates wonderfully complex camera movements for "Snake Eyes," a symphony of visual pivots, swirls, feints and dodges.

Maybe technique is all De Palma cares about anymore as a director. Maybe working with a bombastic, disposable script by David Koepp (responsible for both "Jurassic Park" movies) allows him to focus completely on stylistic flourishes. Whatever the reason, the dramatic side of "Snake Eyes" is coarse and undernourished in a way no amount of legerdemain can make up for.

There is, however, no denying that all that pizazz, courtesy of camera operator Gordon Hayman and steadicam operator Larry McConkey, can be exciting to watch. This is especially so in the film's tour de force opening 20 minutes, shot as one continuous, fiendishly complex steadicam shot.

It's a near-hurricane night in Atlantic City, but inside the city's boxing arena, 14,000 jubilant fans are loudly anticipating the latest title defense by heavyweight champion Lincoln Tyler (Stan Shaw), a local hero known as the Executioner.

No one is more excited than Det. Rick Santoro (Nicolas Cage), a flashy and by no means completely honest local cop who is partial to Hawaiian shirts and a lifestyle that includes keeping both a wife and a mistress happy.

Always for sale and easily bought, Santoro is the kind of policeman who doesn't get out of bed unless there's something in it for him. "This isn't a beach town," he says of Atlantic City, "it's a sewer," and no one knows better than he how to bend rules and cover tracks in this shady environment.

Santoro is especially excited to be at the fight because his great seat is a gift from his closest childhood friend. Kevin Dunne (Gary Sinise) is now a clean-cut Navy commander, assigned to head the security detail for a limelight-loving Secretary of Defense who hates to miss a public event.

Then, in the midst of this screaming Jersey crowd and some furious action in the ring, Dunne gets distracted and shots are heard. The secretary is down, as is a mysterious woman in a blond wig (Carla Gugino) who had suddenly materialized at his side. Eager to help his friend, Santoro pulls rank and takes charge of the burgeoning investigation.

As the detective changes his Hawaiian number for a white shirt and tie, he almost miraculously becomes a more professional operative, attempting with Dunne's help to track down and interview witnesses, especially that elusive mystery woman. Wheels appear within wheels, and what looks simple and obvious turns out to be mistakes waiting to be corrected.

Anyone who doesn't quite catch everything that happens during those critical seconds when bullets are in the air doesn't have to worry. The structure of "Snake Eyes" dictates that we'll see those moments again and again, but each time from another point of view as different witnesses and different arena cameras reveal what they saw. It's the always viable "don't believe your eyes" stratagem reworked by De Palma and Koepp (who share story credit) and it brings a measure of dramatic interest to the proceedings.

Aside from that ploy, "Snake Eyes'" story gets increasingly less involving as more and more of it is revealed and the implausible motivations of characters are exposed. Both Koepp's script and De Palma's directing style encourage the actors to be over-emphatic, and macho posturing is high on the list of the film's weaknesses.

"Snake Eyes" has other bravura visual moments after that 20-minute opening, including using a mirror to change the camera's point of view and a traveling shot that floats over several connected hotel rooms from above the ceiling level. But even his usual inventiveness eventually deserts De Palma, and the climax of "Snake Eyes" finds him, like the audience, marking time till it's permissible to head for the door.

NEW YORK, 8/17/98, p. 57, David Denby

Right at the beginning of Brian De Palma's new thriller, *Snake Eyes*, Rick Santoro (Nicolas Cage), a joyously crooked cop, enters the Atlantic City Arena all jazzed up and ready to roll. It's fight night, the heavyweight title is at stake, and as Rick strides in, his wife and mistress call him on his cell phone, his friends greet him with flattery and bribes, and he's thrilled to be alive and feeling so gloriously dirty. Corruption runs in his veins; he's a rat at home in the sewer. Rick rushes through the arena to his seat, ringside, where he greets an old friend, Commander Kevin Dunne (Gary Sinise), a rather severe-looking Navy officer assigned to protect the Scretary of Defense, who is also attending the fight. The bout begins, Dunne gets up to check someone out, the heavy-weight champ is knocked down, and the secretary, no longer protected, takes a bullet in the throat from the rifle of a hidden shooter on the other side of the arena.

All of this is conveyed in a single, enormously long-lasting shot, which De Palma and his great cameraman, Stephen H. Burum, have brought off with a Steady Cam and a group of actors attuned to continuous work in real time. The camera picks up pieces of conversation, moves to look at something else, returns to where it was, picks up the next piece of conversation, and so on. The shot itself is a kind of representation of the exhilaration and the connectedness that Rick feels. There's nothing languorous or wandering about it: Everyone talks a mile a minute, the crowd is screaming, and De Palma creates, and records, the ambience of a big, violent, semi-coherent event. As we watch, amazed, we know that De Palma is trying to top the famous opening shots of Orson Welles's *Touch of Evil* and Robert Altman's *The Player,* that he's piling on difficulties and complications so as to show off his virtuosity. The sequence runs along on sheer nerve and momentum, and as long as it lasts, it seems to offer everything that the cinema can offer in the way of simultaneity and excitement. But this astonishing opening sets up a peculiar problem. Nothing else that De Palma does in the movie can come anywhere close to it. When the shot runs out, the movie also seems to run out—that is, it devolves into a fairly familiar and depressingly unconvincing thriller about an assassination conspiracy and a corrupt man who has the chance to act, for once in his life, with honor. Without the continuous running shot connecting everything to everything, the clichés become obvious, and then overpowering. We remember past movies featuring assassinations, like *The Parallax View,* which was also centered in an arena, and we notice echoes of earlier De Palma movies *(Blow Out, Body Double,* and *Mission: Impossible)* in which evidence of a crime was revealed by one recording device or another. Here the device is video cameras stationed all over the arena and in an adjoining casino and hotel. A certain weariness settles into our response: The dense layering of imagery, we may suspect, now functions less as a commentary on our media-saturated society than as a convenient way for filmmakers to avoid the hard work of plot construction and character development.

Screenwriter David Koepp, who has worked with De Palma in the past, and also with Spielberg (on the *Jurassic Park* movies), isn't discovering anything; he's just making commercial movies—that is, providing story elements and characters that have no independent life or interest or plausibility but offer a workable frame for a director's manipulations. And what Koepp provides turns out to be too straight for De Palma's fluid technique and narrative circularity. When De Palma worked with sillier or more fantastic material in *Carrie* and *Dressed to Kill,* he was freer to play, and his own emotions and ambivalences burst through the excesses. *Snake Eyes* doesn't display any emotion apart from a passion for the moving camera, and in one scene, De Palma hits rock bottom. Cage is beaten to a pulp and then staggers to his feet and tries to rescue a virtuous young woman. Sinise follows with gun drawn, and the sequence goes on forever, with repeated close-ups of Cage's mashed and bloody face. I can't think of another movie that starts so brilliantly and ends so miserably as this one.

NEW YORK POST, 8/7/98, p. 39, Rod Dreher

Nicolas Cage is an immensely talented but notoriously erratic actor, and each one of his movies is a roll of the dice. He craps out in "Snake Eyes," a dreadful suspense thriller that wastes what's best about Cage and most interesting about the story.

It's obvious why the role of Rick Santoro, a sad-sack Jersey police detective, attracted him. Santoro is a tacky featherbedder, a self-satisfied, likable knucklehead who sustains his comfortably sleazy life by engaging in various sorts of petty corruption. Santoro has a wife, a girlfriend, a gambling habit and a moral slackness that's put to the test when a government bigwig is assassinated under his nose.

Like some of Cage's best screen characters, would-be wheeler-dealer Santoro is a complicated loser, and you might be forgiven for thinking (and hoping) that, with "Snake Eyes," Cage was abandoning his unfortunate action-movie jag of recent years for a richer character role.

Not so. After telling us whodunit early on—and it's a revelation any half-wit could have forecast—director Brian De Palma's limply mannered picture settles into a flat conspiracy-thriller routine that gets less plausible as it goes on. De Palma's direction is snazzy and inspired at some points, and confusing at others. David Koepp's screenplay, when it's not plainly stupid, is wholly banal and unconcerned with character development.

Finally, though, Cage's strenuous overacting puts one off of "Snake Eyes." He yells a lot to show he's emotionally engaged, and wrestles his lines to the ground with choke holds so brutal, the ACLU ought to file a cruelty-to-dialogue complaint. We know how good Cage can be, which is part of the reason why "Snake Eyes" is such a letdown.

The film opens on fight night at an Atlantic City casino. A Trumpish magnate (John Heard) escorts the U.S. secretary of defense into the match. In a dizzying, extended tracking shot, the director follows Santoro, clothed like a Leisure Suit Larry, backstage at the arena as he glad-hands the boxing crowd. Unless you're prepared to find a loud, backslapping schlemiel who's in touch with his inner Ted Baxter sympathetic, cash out while you're ahead.

Santoro settles down ringside with childhood friend Kevin Dunne, a decorated naval officer in charge of SecDefs security. He's played with one-note grimness by Gary Sinise, who looks like he crushes ball bearings with his cast-iron jaw. Spotting a busty woman in the crowd, Dunne rushes to investigate, and in his absence, an unseen gunman whacks the Secretary of Defense.

Dunne shoots a Palestinian terrorist, killing the assassin. But he's hysterical with fear that he'll be court-martialed for leaving the Cabinet official's side. An expert in making wiggle room, Santoro advises his pal on how to create a clever cover story. But he also decides to lock down the arena to search for other suspects. Viewing a tape of the fight, Santoro discovers the champ took a dive; following that trail leads him to a political conspiracy behind the killing.

The plot peters out into sheer nonsense halfway through, about the time you realize you're stuck in the kind of movie where the evil guys explain their nefarious doings by blathering the kind of fraudulent lines only bad-movie villains say.

"Snake Eyes" sidewinds to a dopey denouement involving a helpful hurricane and a naive informant (Carla Gugino) trapped for no good reason.

The final sequence is preposterous, suggesting that De Palma and Koepp had no idea how to end this thing, and the kind of movie the dull, contrived "Snake Eyes" might have been had Koepp expended less time spinning fanciful conspiracies and more any time parsing the mystery of the tragic character at the center of this story.

NEWSDAY, 8/7/98, Part II/p. B3, Jack Mathews

During the opening 20 minutes of Brian De Palma's eventful and furiously fast-paced "Snake Eyes," we are introduced to a good-natured but corrupt Atlantic City detective (Nicolas Cage); his best friend, Kevin (Gary Sinise),who is a Naval commander in charge of the security detail for the Secretary of Defense; a couple of pay-per-view TV reporters; two mysterious, bewigged women; a punk bookie; several mob strongmen; a couple of heavyweight fighters, and a boxing arena packed to the rafters with thousands of screaming fans.

By the end of these 20 minutes, one of the boxers will be counted out, the Secretary of Defense will have been shot, his executioner will be dead, the two women will have disappeared and Cage's Rick Santoro will be lying on the floor, splattered with blood, staring into the alert eyes of the boxer who was supposed to be unconscious.

Here's the kicker: All of this is done in one take!

From the opening images in hurricane weather outside the arena to that last frozen look between Santoro and the fallen champ Lincoln Tyler (Stan Shaw) inside, the action is captured by one, presumably well-conditioned Steadicam operator. It is, next to the Omaha Beach sequence in Steven Spielberg's "Saving Private Ryan," the most remarkable opening of any movie in years.

In fact, it's too good an opening for what proves to be an abysmally weak and mundane thriller, underscoring once again that De Palma is the best filmmaker of his generation operating without intellectual ideas or the instincts of a natural storyteller. His films are not just exercises in style over substance, they're exercises in style nullifying substance, and because "Snake Eyes" is so cleverly choreographed, it's one of his most exasperating efforts.

If the technology existed to allow De Palma to shoot an entire movie without a cut (cameras can carry only 20 minutes of film at a time), and he chose a riveting subject, say following Lee Harvey Oswald from his shooting of JFK to his capture at a movie theater across town, he'd make something indelible. What he's working with here is a script by David Koepp, a two-time Razzie nominee (for De Palma's "Mission: Impossible" and the "Jurassic Park" sequel), and it simply collapses under the weight of De Palma's theatricality.

And the collapse is sudden. That dazzling opening, and the ensuing flashbacks, using all the other cameras De Palma had deployed, buys "Snake Eyes" and its cast a lot of time and goodwill. Cage, who's on camera for almost every second of those first 20 minutes, seems energized by the challenge of acting on the fly, under the skin of a character who is in turn energized by the spectacle of boxing and the risks of being a cop on the take.

By the end of the first act, Santoro is an irrepressible antihero, driven by conflicting currents of ego, loyalty, greed and righteousness. Too bad he and Sinise, whose Naval officer has a dark side right out of a Tom Clancy novel, start screaming about halfway through the movie and never stop. It's at this moment, the moment of collapse, that De Palma abruptly shifts his own direction, abandoning all artistic pretense to wallow in the melodrama.

It's as if he's saying, "I've brought you this far, now you're on your own, and you realize that you're nowhere."

I'm recommending this movie because I think the opening, and much of what immediately follows, is worth the price of admission. De Palma has done clever work before, in his Hitchcock phase, which produced "Carrie" and "Dressed to Kill," and he's had moments of brilliance in such standard Hollywood issue as "The Untouchables" and "Mission: Impossible." But "Snake Eyes" is his highlights film.

Looking back, De Palma may have missed his calling. He would have been a terrific, maybe a great, cinematographer under a Scorsese or a Spielberg or a Coppola. On his own, he's left a body of work that makes the heart pound one moment and break the next. There is rarely anything more to a De Palma film than meets the eye.

NEWSWEEK, 8/17/98, p. 61, Jeff Giles

Nicholas Cage has never met a top he couldn't go over. In the opening moments of Brian De Palma's new thriller, the actor is a sunburst of manic energy, playing Rick Santoro, a corrupt Atlantic City, N.J. detective with a Hawaiian shirt and a gold cell phone. ("It's my sewer, and I love it ... I am the king!") Santoro comes to an arena to watch a prizefight with an old friend, Navy Cmdr. Kevin Dunne (Gary Sinise). The fight ends suspiciously fast—just as an assassin takes out the Secretary of Defense. Geez, can't a cop get a day off? Santoro and Dunne seal off the arena before 14,000 witnesses can flee, then the pair unravel some big military conspiracy. "Snake Eyes" has its slow moments, and De Palma could have used 15 more minutes to flesh out the conclusion. But there's plenty of bravura camera work and two terrific supporting turns from Carla Gugino, as a terrified key witness, and Stan Shaw, as the soul-searching heavy-weight champ. De Palma didn't hit the jackpot here, but he certainly didn't roll snake eyes.

SIGHT AND SOUND, 11/98, p. 38, Philip Strick

In the Atlantic City Arena, the Tyler-Ruiz heavyweight boxing championship fight is about to begin as Tropical Storm Jezebel rages outside. Notoriously corrupt police detective Rick Santoro takes a ringside seat alongside his old friend Kevin Dunne who has been assigned to protect Secretary of Defense Charles Kirkland, attending as a guest of tycoon Gilbert Powell. Dunne is distracted by a mysterious redhead just as another girl, Julia, talks confidentially to Kirland. As Tyler is knocked down in the ring, Kirkland is fatally shot.

Taking charge, Rick studies videotapes of the fight and establishes that Tyler threw the fight on a cue but knows nothing more. As Julia, wounded in the shooting, looks for a hiding place, Dunne shoots two agents in his assassination plot, Zientz and Serena, (the redhead). Spotted by surveillance cameras, Julia takes refuge with a casino gambler until Rick reaches her and learns that she saw Dunne with the assassin Rabat before the shooting. She had come to pass proof to Kirkland that the results of recent millile tests were faked.

Rick hides her away while he studies footage taken from a 'flying eye' camera: it clearly incriminates Dunne. Instructed by Powell (whose missile contract is at stake) to ensure Rick's silence, Dunne promises a $1 million pay-off but Rick refuses to reveal Julia's location. Badly beaten up, he staggers to her hideout unaware that Dunne is following. Dunne prepares to shoot them both, but a police vehicle, dodging storm debris, intervenes; cornered, Dunne shoots himself. First hailed as a hero, Rick soon faces corruption charges and imprisonment. Only Julia has faith in him.

The US Secretary of Defense is shot down during a championship boxing match in an Atlantic City casino. Local police detective Rick Santoro (Nicolas Cage), seemingly assisted by his lifelong friend, naval security chief Kevin Dunne (Gary Sinise), gradually uncovers evidence of an elaborate conspiracy. Nothing is ever simple in Brian De Palma's world, but there is a sense of homecoming about *Snake Eyes*. For one thing, he has known Atlantic City well since his childhood. For another, he previously introduced us to the casino's fevered atmosphere in *Wise Guys* (1986), where Danny DeVito's extravagance was typically revealed to be part of a secret masterplan. Although not a gambling obsessive on the scale of David Mamet or James Toback, De Palma shows a flamboyant wildness of spirit and the garish casino-complex setting provides him with a powerful metaphor.

What chiefly distinguishes De Palma's casino is the certainty that the observer profits more than the participant. The House is there to win, and it protects itself with an army of guards and spies. Snake-eyed or not, its owner is a Master of the Universe, at risk only from the risks of his own making. Plutocrats haunt De Palma's work to such an extent that it only takes one glance at the narrow gaze of Gilbert Powell (John Heard) in *Snake Eyes* to identify the true villain of the piece. Really, he's more of a pragmatist: like the elite of *Bonfire of the Vanities,* he is a creature of currency, a natural product of market forces. And the profit motive, as De Palma commented at the time of *Blow Out*, "attacks the moral fibre: it's too strong and powerful—it just engulfs you."

Long since engulfed, Santoro in *Snake Eyes* is nevertheless still at the other end of the scale from Powell. Determined to be a contender one day, he's one of De Palma's habitual twilight people. His attempts to do the right thing spring more from convenience than from principle. A cross between the soldier who refuses to condone atrocity in *Casualties of War* and the foolhardy lawmen of *The Untouchables* Santoro is a deceiver who stubbornly pursues the truth (a paradox liable to self-destruct at any moment). The split-personality theme, another De Palma constant, also resonates here in the contrast between Santoro and Dunne, a high-flyer with a serviceman's respect for authority, whatever its demands. It is ironic that Dunne's downfall comes when, as far as we can tell (he's that devious), he hesitates to betray the obligations of friendship and tries to buy off Santoro rather than killing him.

An original story compiled by De Palma and David Koepp, *Snake Eyes'* script is strikingly unoriginal, a blatant excuse for some variations on their past joint ventures *Carlito's Way* (1993) and *Mission Impossible* (1996)). If Koepp's individual signature so far lacks definition—his other credits include *Jurassic Park, Death Becomes Her* and *The Shadow*, an intriguing miscellany—De Palma's remains sharp and assertive, even to his use of the *Rashomon*-like structure he first employed for *Murder à la Mode* (1968). His trademark, in fact, is repetition, the recycling of a short sequence of events until its meaning becomes roughly intelligible. It may not, of course, be the 'true' meaning, reality being a subjective matter, but it covers most of the angles.

Hence the compulsive use of surveillance equipment within De Palma's stories, which incorporate reporters giving their versions, newspaper headlines, television screens and innumerable snooping devices. He also has a fondness for split-screen images (which he first used in *Dionysus in '69*), a montage of fragments providing context, distraction and an interesting quantity of information overload. From all of these, as in *Blow Out* (1981), conclusions can be drawn and consequences pursued, based on testimony that gradually acquires coherence.

Reinforcing his reputation—following the bewilderments of *Raising Cain* (1992) and *Mission Impossible*—as a weaver of intricacies beyond control, De Palma flings out so much information at the start of *Snake Eyes* that only repetition makes it comprehensible. The film is actually about people who have lost the plot, fugitives on the hunt for solutions. De Palma introduces us to most of the key players with his opening 13-minute Steadicam shot, a headlong rush to the ringside that embraces the champ, the bookie, the drug dealer, the security chief, the target and the boss in one seething trap. We may not fit them all together until later, but clearly all of them are in trouble. And through their midst plunges the wretched Santoro, his reputation in tatters, his wife and mistress barely in check, his arrogance sustained by little more than a badge and a ready fist.

Later the film becomes a series of attenuated pursuits. The wounded Julia (Carla Gugino) is hunted first through casino crowds and then through endless hotel corridors sparsely peopled by lost souls. By the time Santoro, heavily punished, struggles along the ugly route of storage and service areas, the hunt has become dreamlike, presided over by an almost affectionate killer and accompanied by a gentle Ryuichi Sakamoto score until the howl of the tropical storm forces a showdown. Always in favour of some thunderous downpour, De Palma had a grand finale planned for this bit, with a giant globe unleashed from the exterior decor crushing the baddie. What he settles for is a fumbled compromise.

Whether this matters probably depends on the extent to which one is prepared to tolerate Cage mugging away. At least his ingratiating performance is splendidly supported by Gugino and Sinise. Once decoded, the plot makes little sense, even though the jigsaw pieces do seem to fit. It would be difficult to imagine an assassination plan with more prospect of going wrong. But from that breathtaking opening shot through orchestrated bedlam to such ingenious stagings as the overhead shot that glides above a whole row of hotel rooms, this is film-making for the pure fun of it. A 'real time' marshalling of crowds and gadgetry, *Snake Eyes* is a pleasure to watch for its sheer risk-taking expertise.

VILLAGE VOICE, 8/18/98, p. 107, J. Hoberman

The most sensational kiss-off in movies? Try the finale from Orson Welles's re-released *The Lady from Shanghai* a vehicle for the filmmaker's soon-to-be-ex-wife Rita Hayworth. Welles staged a multiple-image shattering shoot-out in a hall of mirrors. The movies, he had learned, were a funhouse in which it was impossible to separate reality from its reflection. You can't smash the proscenium because there is none.

There's a similar claustrophobic principle at work in the tinny surfaces of Brian De Palma's least prestigious, most playful features—I'm thinking of the tawdry, self-mocking thrillers *Dressed to Kill, Blow Out,* and *Raising Cain. Snake Eyes,* which is De Palma's latest effort along those lines, might almost have been as good—it's a brilliant, smoking car-wreck of a movie, constructed around a provocatively excessive premise and seemingly reedited to conform to some more crudely normal sense of celluloid decorum.

De Palma's voluptuous cheesefest takes off from someone knocking off the Secretary of Defense during the second round of a heavyweight championship fight in an Atlantic City casino. With virtually all of the action confined to a single building (and unfolding, more or less, in real time), *Snake Eyes,* is predicated on a formal conceit, and De Palma wastes no time flaunting his virtuosity.

The film's opening shot is the longest, most serpentine continuous take in recent memory. It begins, under the credits and in the midst of a hurricane, with a TV news crew outside the casino and proceeds indoors, via some digitalized sleight of hand, through a maze of corridors into the gaudy central arena, introducing, all the while, the film's major characters—Nicolas Cages manic, gladhanding crooked cop, Gary Sinise's buttoned-down naval commander, Carla Gugino's dame of mystery, Stan Shaws world-weary fighter—as well as the key elements of the conspiracy.

For nearly 20 minutes, De Palma orchestrates a rhapsodic assortment of visual fanfares and flourishes, percussive tilts and sudden swish-pans; he permits Cage to engage in all manner of aggressive wheeling and dealing while, throughout the abbreviated prize fight, keeping the camera fixed on the horde of reacting spectators. *Snake Eyes's* first real cut comes just before the assassination—the burst of machine-gun fire naturally provokes a corresponding montage pandemonium. The effect is grandiose, chintzy, and ultimately metaphysical in its sense of a recoverable past.

Working the border that separates oddball angst from crazy comedy, the madly hustling Cage is a near-perfect De Palma protagonist—he simultaneously bogarts the investigation and pockets a $5000 bribe to let a pay-for-view announcer be the sole newsman on the premises. (Not completely devoid of tact, Cage cautions his designated feed against showing the gore-splattered crime scene. "All right, I won't shoot the spaghetti then," is the newsman's typically De Palmaesque answer.) What you see is what you get. The filmmaker is revisiting the mood of his 1982 *Blow Out*—the last and greatest example of '70s cine-paranoia—and elaborating on the flashback structure of *Mission: Impossible*. Detection, such as it is, means going to the videotape; the dramatized memories subscribe to the opening time-space continuum (albeit from a different angle), with one freeze-frame dictated by Cages querulous "Hold it!"

Snake Eyes works as a thriller, but what give the movie its distinctive cartoon quality is De Palma's compulsive, attention-grabbing flights of hysterical anti-entertainment—background thunder, cosmetic blood, prurient jiggle shots, inappropriate sight gags, flashy split-screen exegeses, a fight scene shot almost entirely from one participants point of view. A leeringly adolescent, proudly ridiculous display of cinematic muscle-flexing, *Snake Eyes* offers ample opportunity to consider just how much Quentin Tarantino owes to the example of De Palma's exuberant two-dimensional crassness and how much De Palma's own self-conscious pyrotechnics are indebted to the example of Orson Welles's shameless showboating. De Palma's perspective can be brazenly Olympian—his camera blithely penetrating solid walls to sail overhead from one hotel room to the next. You know the case will be "solved" once the director introduces the concept of the Zero-Gravity Flying-Eye Camera.

There's no escape from the hall of mirrors here. Played out amid ubiquitous TV monitors and surveillance cameras—a supremely vulgar vision of a plutocratic pleasure dome where corporate logos are plastered on half the walls and everything and every one is assumed to be for sale—*Snake Eyes* is either De Palma's visual metaphor for *Planet Hollywood* or it's nothing. Political assassination is at once spectator event, business decision, and foundation myth. "That's called the first draft of history," the villain sneers, watching a lying TV newscast rationalizing the event after he's erased the videotape evidence of conspiracy.

And, speaking of erasing the evidence, I wonder how many years will pass before we'll get to see *Snake Eyes. The Directors Cut*. Conspiracy or not, some corporate entity has saddled the movie with an ending so abrupt, maladroit, and haplessly "positive" it would embarrass the guys who reedit movies for airplanes. Or perhaps Cage's would-be insouciant sign-off is De Palma's despairingly rancid show-biz cri de coeur: "Oh, what the hell. At least I got be on TV."

Also reviewed in:
CHICAGO TRIBUNE, 8/7/98, Friday/p. A, Michael Wilmington
NATION, 9/7-14/98, 44, Stuart Klawans
NEW YORK TIMES, 8/7/98, p. E12, Stephen Holden
NEW YORKER, 8/17/98, p. 82, Daphne Merkin
VARIETY, 8/10-16/98, p. 41, Todd McCarthy
WASHINGTON POST, 8/7/98, p. D1, Rita Kempley
WASHINGTON POST, 8/7/98, Weekend/p. 40, Michael O'Sullivan

SOLDIER

A Warner Brothers release in association with Morgan Creek of a Jerry Weintraub production in association with Impact Pictures. *Executive Producer:* R. J. Louis, Susan Ekins, and James G. Robinson. *Producer:* Jerry Weintraub. *Director:* Paul Anderson. *Screenplay:* David Webb Peoples. *Director of Photography:* David Tattersall. *Editor:* Martin Hunter. *Music:* Joel McNeely. *Sound:* Andy Wiskes. *Casting:* Mindy Marin. *Production Designer:* David L Snyder. *Art Director:* Tom Valentine. *Set Designer:* Susan Wexler, Daniel R. Jennings, Mick Cukurs, Richard Berger, Peter Clemens, and Clare Scarpulla. *Set Decorator:* Kate Sullivan. *Visual Effects:* Ed Jones. *Costumes:* Erica Edell Phillips. *Make-up:* Steve LaPorte. *Stunt Doordinator:* Dick Ziker. *Running time:* 99 minutes. *MPAA Rating:* R.

CAST: Kurt Russell (Todd); Jason Scott Lee (Caine 607); Connie Nielsen (Sandra); Sean Pertwee (Mace); Michael Chiklis (Jimmy Pig); Gary Busey (Church); Jason Isaacs (Col.

Mekum); Jared Thorne (Noah); Taylor Thorne (Noah); Brenda Wehle (Hawkins); Mark Bringelson (Rubrick); K.K. Dodds (Sloan).

LOS ANGELES TIMES, 10/23/98, Calendar/p. 18, Kevin Thomas

"Soldier," a potent comic-book-style action-adventure fantasy, envisions a not-too-distant intergalactic future when warriors will be selected at birth by the government and trained to become human fighting machines. Over the years Kurt Russell's Todd has become the best of these warriors, a rugged fighter with a scar on the right side of his face and his name, blood type and a chevron tattooed on his left cheek.

His folksy captain (Gary Busey) respects him and his fellow warriors, but along comes Jason Isaacs' Colonel Mekum, one of those lethal idiots who have mysteriously been rising to positions of power from the beginning of time. The colonel announces that Todd and his ilk have been rendered obsolete by a younger breed of warrior that has been "enhanced" via DNA and who knows what else. Busey's Church proposes a contest between Todd and one of the new "models," Jason Scott Lee's Caine 607, who winds up losing the sight in his right eye.

Undeterred, the colonel orders Todd and the other veterans scooped up in an intergalactic dumpster, deposited on a garbage disposal planet. Only Todd survives being crushed to death amid a load of metal debris.

Near the dumping site is a small colony of people stranded since their plane crashed some years before. Once accepting that they weren't going to be rescued, these individuals set about building a community based on peace and harmony, fashioning a village created from what they could scavenge from the dumps. They've been able to grow enough vegetables to feed themselves, although their shanty-town Garden of Eden is menaced from time to time by rather overly symbolic and highly toxic green snakes.

But can a man trained from birth to be a killing machine fit into human society, especially one as civilized as this one? What's more, you know very well we haven't seen the last of the awful colonel or Caine 607.

In its look, scope and special effects, "Soldier" is suitably imaginative and spectacular if often artificial-looking. Russell has no more than five words to say during the film's first hour and not much after that, but he has the presence, depth of character and expressiveness, along with the physicality, to carry "Soldier."

Directed with vigor and finesse by Paul Anderson, "Soldier" was written by "Blade Runner" and "Unforgiven's" greatly gifted David Webb Peoples. "Soldier" isn't as complex as either of those two landmark films, but it is a decent job of work on the part of Peoples. "Soldier" is the kind of picture described as being aimed at young urban males but may have an unexpected resonance for older viewers, who know only too well that obsolescence is something that nowadays extends to human beings and not just to machines.

It's somehow comforting to be sent home by a sleek, violent, well-oiled action-adventure with the notion that experience can still count for more than mere youth.

NEW YORK POST, 10/23/98, p. 44, Thelma Adams

Picture a really crummy future in which warrior-from-birth Todd (Kurt Russell) comes upon a matriarchal hippie commune atop a distant junkyard planet that resembles "Waterworld" unplugged.

Toss in a mute boy, a dewy blonde, a West Point s.o.b. (Gary Busey), two-dozen green snakes and a genetically engineered grunt named Caine 607 (Jason Scott Lee), and you have the hyper-butch fantasy called "Soldier."

It's recycled "Star Trek" from the director of "Mortal Kombat." David Webb Peoples' bare-bones script pits old soldiers like Russell against new soldiers like Lee, all the while trying to hew to Hollywood's now-traditional anti-military stance.

Muscle-bound Russell, the talented leading man with the erratic career, here does his version of Schwarzenegger: The Early, Humor-Challenged Years.

In the groovy colony, Todd has found shelter among the happy villagers in outer space. Unaccustomed to peace, he cuts his finger while slicing carrots for his alluring hostess and keeps on dicing. She asks: What's it like being a soldier? What do you think about? What do you feel? You must feel something?

Todd grits his teeth beyond the grinding-point and grunts: Fear and discipline.

Feelings, nothing more than feelings...

NEWSDAY, 10/23/98, Part II/p. B13, John Anderson

Count among the ham-handed allegories parading into theaters this week "Soldier," which in its simplest terms is about a worker who has given his entire life to a company—to a way of life, to a handful of maxims—and when he hits 40 gets thrown out with the garbage. Literally. What? A sci-fi thriller by Michael Moore?

No, but "Soldier" is a sci-fi thriller from a filmmaker, Paul Anderson, who once upon a time had a hit at the Sundance Film Festival ("Shopping") and has since devoted himself to formulaic, intergalactic flotsam ("Event Horizon," "Mortal Kombat"). Anderson has, therefore, become something of an allegory himself and if one wanted to hazard a guess, he's using this Kurt Russell-powered space wreck to seek some aesthetic revenge.

Speaking of trash: There's a lot of it in "Soldier," and not just in its "Shane"-meets-"Stargate" storyline or shameless theatricality. Our futuristic hero, the very toned and equally taciturn Todd (Russell), was part of a military project begun way back in 1996 that drafted infants from the cradle—the nursery beds of the chosen are marked "I-A"—and reared them in the tradition of Circus Maximus: Visual aids at mercenary school include Doberman pinschers devouring a boar; motivational techniques consist of shooting the slowest kid in gym class.

Todd, a curiously mild name for such a maniac, becomes a credit to his education: The War of the Six Cities. The Battle of the Argentine Moons. From the halls of Montezuma to the shores of the Sea of Tranquility, if butt needed kicking, Todd was our man.

However, DNA-based technology has allowed a new, even more lethal kind of soldier to be made, and when the ruthless technocrat Colonel Mekum (Jason Isaacs) pits his new strain of soldier against those of the more honor-bound Captain Church (Gary Busey), the shaved-headed Caine 607 (Jason Scott Lee) leaves Todd and two others in a crumpled heap. Presumed dead, Todd, whose name is tattooed on his face so he/we won't forget, is dumped along with the rest of the refuse on a Waste Disposal Planet populated by a gentle but soon-to-be-besieged people.

In his recent novel "Underworld," Don DeLillo uses garbage as a big, rank metaphor about modern life and its lack of values. You wonder whether "Soldier" production designer David L. Snyder read the book, because the film's vast mountains of derelict appliances and iron detritus aren't just backdrops, they're a rebuke. They don't, in fact, even seem to belong in this movie, where the machinery, the action and most of the emotions are wrought out of a laughable kind of cynicism, a winking at the audience about just how far Anderson knows he can push the atrophied sci-fi envelope. Still, the garbage possesses a certain visual weight, even a mute sadness.

And muteness is a constant thematic element in "Soldier," which is a strange one for a dialogue-happy screenwriter like David Webb Peoples ("12 Monkeys," "Blade Runner"), unless you consider the "Shane" parallels. Todd can hardly speak, having been trained not to unless ordered, which makes his longing looks at Sandra (Connie Nielsen)—the beautiful blonde who has nursed him back to health—even funnier than they would be otherwise. Her husband, Mace (Sean Pertwee), and their son, Nathan (twins Jared and Taylor Thorne), has been silent since a bout with snake venom. Considering how irritatingly noisy Brandon de Wilde was in "Shane," this version is an improvement.

The community treats the volatile Todd as a threat, naturally, and rejects him (a single tear slo-mo's down the wounded soldier's cheek, in one of Anderson's cheesiest gestures). This sets the scene for his return/vindication/revenge on Mekum's shock troops, who are busy wiping out said community. "Soldier" ultimately becomes a catalog of genre cliches, from Todd's emerging humanity—the only way he'll become a better killer is through love—to the boring and predictable one-man war on/systematic slaying of those who threaten his new home and people. It's all about community, in the end. And what a beautiful thing it is.

VILLAGE VOICE, 11/3/98, p. 140, Gary Dauphin

Unassumingly preposterous, *Soldier* is the kind of flick that comes into its own on cable, fitting in between abysmal Sci-Fi Channel "originals" [sic] and the good stuff everyone's already seen. Offering a passable SF fix, *Soldier* grafts an Arnold-less remake of *Terminator 2* onto the fast-twitch exoskeleton of action flicks made for video-game addicts. (Director Paul Anderson's first film was *Mortal Kombat*.) The title refers to the fighting men of the future, stiff-jointed cannon fodder raised in an emotional Skinner box to follow orders: show no mercy, kill, kill, kill, etc. Todd (a pumped-up Kurt Russell, who opens his mouth about four times) is the best of the Pavlovian best, but genetic engineering has now rendered him obsolete. After taking a drubbing by one of the newfangled test-tube baby types (Jason Scott Lee), Todd's literally thrown out with the garbage, landing on a windy junkyard planet. The plucky local scavengers will, of course, show Todd the meaning of love, hugging, and family just in time for his replacement to show up, with mayhem and payback to ensue. With a cheerful disregard for characterization and visual texture, Anderson relies on his cgi-jocks and set dressers to flesh out David Webb People's by-the-numbers script. Although *Soldier* technically kind of sucks, it's hard to warn anyone away from it with any enthusiasm. *Star Wars: Episode One* is looming on the horizon, and in the meantime certain itches do need to be scratched.

Also reviewed in:
CHICAGO TRIBUNE, 10/23/98, Tempo/p. 2, Michael Wilmington
NEW YORK TIMES, 10/23/98, p. E27, Stephen Holden
VARIETY, 10/26-11/1/98, p. 41, Glenn Lovell
WASHINGTON POST, 10/23/98, p. B5, Rita Kempley

SOLDIER'S DAUGHTER NEVER CRIES, A

An October Films release of a Merchant Ivory Productions production in association with October Films/Capitol Films/British Screen. *Executive Producer:* Richard Hawley and Nayeem Hafizka. *Producer:* Ismail Merchant. *Director:* James Ivory. *Screenplay:* James Ivory and Ruth Prawer Jhabvala. *Based on a novel by:* Kaylie Jones. *Director of Photography:* Jean-Marc Fabre. *Editor:* Noelle Boisson. *Music:* Richard Robbins. *Sound:* Ludovic Henault. *Sound Editor:* Colin Miller. *Casting:* Annette Trumel, Tricia Tomey, and Celestia Fox. *Production Designer:* Jacque Bufnoir and Pat Garner. *Art Director:* Per-Olof Renard and Linwood Taylor. *Set Designer:* James Ferrell. *Costumes:* Carol Ramsey. *Make-up:* Thomas Nellen. *Stunt Coordinator:* Roland Neunreuther and Dean Mumford. *Running time:* 120 minutes. *MPAA Rating:* R.

CAST: Kris Kristofferson (Bill Willis); Barbara Hershey (Marcella Willis); Leelee Sobieski (Channe Willis); Jane Birkin (Mrs. Fortescue); Dominique Blanc (Candida); Jesse Bradford (Billy Willis); Virginie Ledoyen (Billy's Mother); Anthony Roth Costanzo (Francis Fortescue); Anthony Decadi (Schoolyard Tease); Harley Cross (Keith Carter); Isaac de Bankolé (Mamadou); Macha Méril (Madame Beauvier); Nathalie Richard (Madmoiselle Fournier); Bob Swaim (Bob Smith); Luisa Conlon (Young Channe); Samuel Gruen (Benoît/Young Billy); Frédéric Da (Stéphane); Antoine Chain (Billy's Father); Michelle Fairley (Miss O'Shaunessy); Valerie Toledano (Mademoiselle Fauchon); Daniel Teper (Kevin); Alycia Fashae (Salome); Marcos Pujol (Herod); Catherine Alcover (Herodias); Sarah Haxaire (Mademoiselle Devereux); Marie Henriau (Social Worker); Pierre-Michel Sivadier (Mr. Flowers); Scott Thomas (The Jock); Catriona McColl (Mrs. Smith); Freddy Stracham (Dancer); Véronique Bellegarde (Test Monitor); Miranda Raimondi (Melissa); Anne-Cécile Crapie (Mademoiselle Picot); Eric Naccache (Lawyer); Elizabeth Villeminot (Cassandra Smith); Catherine Villeminot (Mary Ellen Smith); Florence Villeminot (Gillis Smith); Emma Scaife (Bethany).

CHRISTIAN SCIENCE MONITOR, 9/18/98, p. B3, David Sterritt

"A Soldier's Daughter Never Cries," the new film by director James Ivory and producer Ismail Merchant, may surprise moviegoers who think they can predict what a Merchant Ivory picture will be like.

The duo established their reputation with movies about India, like "Shakespeare Wallah" and "Heat and Dust." But their new picture, arriving in theaters direct from the Toronto International Film Festival this week, takes place in Paris and a New Hampshire village. They're also renowned for adaptations of literary classics, from "The Bostonians" to "Howards End," but this time they've tackled a little-known book by an uncelebrated author.

Still and all, "Soldier's Daughter" doesn't mark a completely new departure, since the previous two Merchant Ivory pictures have also been fictionalized portraits of unusual people. Neither "Jefferson in Paris" nor "Surviving Picasso" ranks with their most successful work, but they've mastered it this time around.

Based on the life of novelist James Jones as seen through the eyes of his young daughter, "A Soldier's Daughter Never Cries" is as touching, entertaining, and thoughtful as anything Merchant Ivory has given us in its long and distinguished career. Already a strong candidate for best picture of the year, it will surely be a front-line contender for Top 10 lists and Academy Award honors.

The central characters are Bill Willis, a crusty American author based on the real-life writer of "From Here to Eternity" and "The Thin Red Line," and his daughter Channe, based on Kaylie Jones, whose book inspired the movie.

They live in Paris, where Bill is working on various projects and raising his close-knit family, which grows a bit larger when he and his wife adopt a French boy whose teenage mother isn't ready for parenthood.

The story follows the Willis clan through a series of small adventures, capped by their return to the United States, where unfamiliar surroundings—and Bill's declining health—raise fresh, challenges for Channe and her brother.

This doesn't sound like a very thrilling plot, and that's exactly the point. "Soldier's Daughter" thrives less on Hollywood-style drama than on nuances of personality, details of everyday life, and emotions so commonplace that conventional movies rarely take the time to acknowledge them, much less explore them with loving care.

Ivory has always been gifted with sensitivity to subtleties of ordinary living, and he outdoes himself here, aided by a screenplay, which he penned with Ruth Prawer Jhabvala, the usual Merchant Ivory writing partner, who refuses to wrap experience into neatly tied packages.

One of the film's boldest maneuvers is to involve us with a fascinating character named Francis, who becomes Channe's best junior-high friend, and then drop him decisively when the family severs its French connections for a new American life. This may seem abrupt and unsettling, but it's also as lifelike as can be.

Some aspects of the Willis household will displease audiences whose standards rule out the drinking, four-letter language, and frank sexual discussions that crop up frequently among Bill and his brood; while "A Soldier's Daughter Never Cries" focuses on family life, it can hardly be called a family film.

This aside, the movie's deep domestic feelings are unmistakable—and encouraging, at a time when Hollywood's nods to family issues often seem driven more by trendiness than commitment.

Kris Kristofferson is excellent as Bill, blending amiability and irascibility in just the right proportions, and Leelee Sobieski shows that her run-of-the-mill debut in "Deep Impact" merely hinted at the depth of her talent. Barbara Hershey backs them up superbly as Bill's wife, and newcomer Anthony Roth Costanzo almost steals the movie as Channe's opera-loving friend.

Jean-Marc Fabre did the sensuous cinematography, and Merchant Ivory regular Richard Robbins composed the rhythmic, haunting score. All deserve the highest praise.

LOS ANGELES TIMES, 9/18/98, Calendar/p. 8, Kenneth Turan

The things "A Soldier's Daughter Never Cries" does best are as difficult to describe as to accomplish. Somehow, against considerable obstacles, it has captured something true about families and friendship, creating a texture of believable emotions on screen. To watch this touching story of a young girl's coming of age is to feel that someone felt this, someone cared about it, and someone understood how to translate it into film.

"Soldier's Daughter" is based on an autobiographical novel by Kaylie Jones that deals with her own experiences growing up in Paris and the United States in the '60s as the daughter of celebrated novelist James Jones ("From Here to Eternity," "The Thin Red Line").

Behind the scenes is the veteran team of producer Ismail Merchant, director and co-screenwriter James Ivory and his writing partner Ruth Prawer Jhabvala, whose successes include "A Room With a View," "Howards End" and "The Remains of the Day."

Except for that latter film, the 20th century has not been the most fertile ground for the respected Merchant Ivory group, who have stumbled with modern efforts like "Slaves of New York" and "Surviving Picasso." But this film is for the most part different, a positive exercise whose missteps are not fatal to the general spirit of acceptance and love.

What results is a memory piece with a very loose and fluid form, a series of three sketches from childhood whose main dramatic focus is watching a young girl move uncertainly toward maturity. This has been attempted before, and more than once, but "Soldier's Daughter" manages to get under the skin in unpredictable ways.

The film's final success is especially unexpected because "Soldier's Daughter" is the kind of film that starts awkwardly but picks up assurance as it goes along. In fact, its first section, "Billy," comes off as its rockiest and most confusing.

For one thing, the introduction of writer Bill Willis (Kris Kristofferson), his passionate wife Marcella (a spirited Barbara Hershey) and their expatriate life of jazzy parties and lusty poker games feels initially phony and too broadly drawn.

Also, the plot of this first section, involving the decision by the Willises to adopt a small French boy named Benoit, is filled with so many confusing aspects it's no wonder that the family's natural daughter Channe outright rejects the new addition at first.

But the film shows its integrity in the gradual way Channe comes to accept the boy, who changes his name to Billy and as a young man (Jesse Bradford) becomes especially close to his sister.

The teenage Channe is played by Leelee Sobieski, a remarkably poised young actress last seen in "Deep Impact" and soon to be in Stanley Kubrick's "Eyes Wide Shut." It's not a coincidence that the film gains impact in the final two segments, both named after other pivotal men in Channe's life.

The first of those is called "Francis," after Paul Francis Fortescue (beautifully played by Anthony Roth Costanza), a flamboyant young man whose close teenage friendship with Channe is threatened when she starts to take a romantic interest in other boys. Again, the awkwardness and entanglements of those years is tricky material to handle well, but Ivory, who's said that in creating this character "I sometimes drew on myself," knows how to make it valid.

"Daddy," the namesake of the final section, figures more in Channe's life when the Willises move back to America partly because of her father's concern over the onset of hereditary heart disease.

Though the film's title makes it sound as if World War II veteran Bill Willis were a disciplinarian and a hard case, in fact the opposite is true. Firm but kindly and an invariable source of excellent advice, especially where boyfriends are concerned, the senior Willis comes off as the father we'd all like to have had. His daughter's tribute to him, the rest of her family and herself is fond and clear-eyed, and, by all indications here, well-deserved.

NEW YORK, 10/5/98, p. 53, David Denby

I would pan the new Merchant-Ivory production, "A Soldier's Daughter Never Cries," if only there were something on the screen to pan, but the movie, like Jell-O on a child's spoon, keeps slipping out of view. The daughter in question, Channe (Leelee Sobieski), grows up in Paris in the sixties, the offspring of a James Jones-like expatriate writer (the movie is based on a novel by Jones's daughter, Kaylie). Channe endures no more than the routine trials of a teenager's life and is indeed very well loved by her handsome, sexy, all-wise dad (Kris Kristofferson), her smothering, slightly competitive bohemian mom (Barbara Hershey), her resentful adopted brother (Jesse Bradford), her hothouse-flower gay teen friend (Anthony Roth Costanzo), and even the family maid. They all love Channe, as indeed they should, but where's the movie? This is a wan, shapeless, and amazingly conventional piece of work.

NEW YORK POST, 9/18/98, p. 59, Thelma Adams

From here to maturity: the untold story of novelist James Jones' talented daughter. In Kaylie Jones' autobiographical novel, "A Soldier's Daughter Never Cries," she tried to escape the shadow of her warrior father by writing about him.

This strategy was more literary than cinematic. As brought to the big screen by Merchant-Ivory, the story tells us less than we want to know about the larger-than-life author of "The Thin Red Line" and a bit too much about the menstrual cycles of his only daughter.

K. Jones, like the fictional Channe Willis, grew up in haute expatriate bohemianism in Paris. In her teens, the family returned stateside when her father's health faded.

Producer Ismail Merchant and director James Ivory have dealt with the theme of Americans abroad before, most recently with "Jefferson in Paris." Their biggest stumbling block in treating K. Jones' coming-of-age story is creating structure when the source book is not quite E.M. Forster.

Merchant and Ivory, working from a script Ivory co-wrote with their frequent collaborator Ruth Prawer Jhabvala, parse the novel into three uneven acts defined by three males: adopted brother Billy, best pal Francis and Daddy.

The fictional Willis clan—gravel-voiced patriarch Bill (Kris Kristofferson), fiercely maternal free spirit Marcella (Barbara Hershey) and French-born Billy (Jesse Bradford)—are seen through the sensitive eyes of a latter-day Alice in the unstable wonderland of literary celebrity.

Channe, charmingly portrayed by Luisa Conlon as a youth followed by the adolescent Leelee Sobieski, pads through the big events of her short life: sibling rivalry, first sexual encounter, first love, first death.

Her father—tall, serious, as hard-drinking as he is hard-working—is her spiritual center.

In each of the movie's sections there are electric moments of unusual connection. Preteens play sex games with snails in a secluded treehouse. Young siblings cycle in the Parisian apartment in a brief, moving-day memory. A father strides into the foxhole of his teen-age daughter's troubled life and makes things right.

While the performances are forceful (especially Sobieski's) and the characters intriguing, they're missed opportunities—a pageant, not a drama. There is discussion of Dad's temper, signs of excessive drinking, a miscarriage hastily shunted aside, but none of these formative events figures largely enough.

At one key moment, Marcella confronts Channe: You're so selfish. You can't see anyone but yourself. We nod in agreement.

That's the movie's problem; it's preoccupied with the periphery. I hate to make a soldier's daughter cry, but her life just isn't as compelling as dad's.

NEWSDAY, 9/18/98, Part II/p. B7, Jack Mathews

Taking a rare plunge into the near past, the filmmaking team of producer Ismael Merchant, director James Ivory, and screenwriter Ruth Prawer Jhabvala bring their distinguished, ever tasteful touch to bear on an adaptation of Kaylie Jones' semi-autobiographical novel "'A Soldier's Daughter Never Cries."

Jones, the 38-year-old daughter of the late novelist James Jones ("From Here to Eternity"), has provided a reminiscence of growing up in Paris in the '60s and '70s, and of her formative teenage years, in the United States, after her dying father moved the family there in 1974. It's a story of deep family love, within an eccentrically open family unit, with an adopted French brother, an effervescent mom, and a father trying to rip one last novel from his soul before it departs.

The Merchant-Ivory-Jhabvala team has crafted from that a leisurely, rambling, episodic, nearly impressionistic marvel, a story that wrings power and passion from the everyday ordinariness of life as it evolves into a—get this!—functional family.

"A Soldier's Daughter" follows life with the Joneses—under the name of Willis—from the adoption of 6-year-old Benoit in Paris to the death of Bill Willis (Kris Kristofferson) in the United States. Large sections are devoted to the assimilation of Benoit, to daughter Channe's relationship with an effete schoolmate in France, and to the clumsy, painful adjustments of Benoit and Channe to high school life in America.

Bill and Marcella Willis (Barbara Hershey) are alcoholic parents whose tumblers runneth over with love, and who share an unbridled zest for living. If the inevitable downside of their drinking is glossed over, we'll assume their love made the greater impression.

In fact, the device that connects the beginning and end of the story suggests that it is the abandoned Benoit's destiny to become Billy Willis. With one of the most stunningly simple and beautiful images to grace a Merchant-Ivory production, "A Soldier's Daughter" opens with a slowpan of an empty beach, the camera finally pulling back to reveal that we're looking through the window of a cottage. A young pregnant woman appears, silhouetted against the sea, looking out as if trying to glimpse the future over the horizon.

She sits down, caresses her belly, and begins writing in her diary: "I pray that he will be loved, as is his right."

Boy, will he! But first, there is an infancy spent with a family friend, then enough time in an orphanage to make him wary of the kindness of strangers, and to feel unwanted, despite evidence to the contrary. Rejecting any sense of identity, even in choosing his name, he hides behind that of his adopted father.

Channe, on the other hand, inhales the love, and the trust that comes with it, like pure oxygen. It's always there, freely given, creating in her a sense of self-confidence that others take as a kind of mystery. She's allowed to discover life on her own, propped up only when she stumbles, as she does trying to sleep her way to high school acceptance.

Billy and Channe are played by sets of talented actors, Samuel Gruen and Luisa Conlon in the young years, and Jesse Bradford and Leelee Sobieski as teens. Bradford gives a solid, sympathetic performance as the perennially confused Billy; Sobieski is a revelation.

Sharing features with both Laura Dern and Helen Hunt, Sobieski has precociously mastered the fine art of reaction. There's a quiet, penetrating intelligence behind those searching eyes, and she has the ability to express the deepest feelings with the slightest gestures.

Hershey and Kristofferson match up like old lovers. Hershey always seems to have enough energy to light a set, and Kristofferson has a clear affinity with his leathered and weathered, whisky-voiced character.

As for Merchant, Ivory and Jhabvala, "A Soldier's Daughter" ought to provide a lift after swaying under larger-than-life characters in "Jefferson in Paris" and "Surviving Picasso." James Jones is a big, but mortal subject, and they—like his daughter—do well by him.

SIGHT AND SOUND, 10/98, p. 56, Philip Kemp

The mid-60s. Eight year-old Charlotte Anne (known as Channe) lives in Paris with her parents, American author Bill Willis and his party-loving wife Marcella. Since Marcella can have no more children, the couple adopt six-year-old Benoit. Emotionally withdrawn after years in foster homes, the boy gradually comes to accept his new family and decides to call himself Billy, after his adoptive father. Feeling themselves outsiders, both he and Channe have trouble at school. As Channe approaches puberty, she meets Francis Fortescue, an eccentric boy who lives with his British mother. Francis introduces Channe to opera and high culture but, unsure of his own sexuality, never ventures beyond close friendship. Bill, whose health is deteriorating, decides the family should return to the US. Francis declares his love to Channe and vanishes from her life.

The family move to New England, but the youngsters are no happier at their new school. Billy becomes morose and disaffected, while Channe indulges in loveless sex until she meets a boy, Keith Carter, with whom she can enjoy a more stable relationship. Bill's heart condition worsens, and he dies early in 1973. After the funeral, Marcella gives Billy a diary kept by his natural mother, who bore him at age 15. Billy refuses to look at it, giving it to Channe to read instead.

Europeans in India, English in Italy, Americans in Europe—the theme of the expatriate haunts Merchant Ivory's films. Famously expatriate themselves and still, despite their long-established London base, with something of the rootless air that led John Pym to dub them "The Wandering Company", director James Ivory and producer Ismail Merchant detect a melancholy underlying the expat's seemingly glamorous status. Their characters, never fully assimilated to the adopted culture however long they stay, are also unfitted by the alien experience to slot comfortably back into their native society. The US-born Ivory's view of the US—explored in *Slaves of New York* and *Mr. & Mrs. Bridge*, for example has taken on the detached, quizzical tone of the outsider. To explore quintessential Englishness the team went to a Japanese-born author, Kazuo Ishiguro, for *The Remains of the Day*.

This sense of being suspended between two cultures, attracted by both but at home nowhere, pervades A *Soldier's Daughter Never Cries,* adapted from an autobiographical novel by Kaylie Jones (daughter of James Jones, author of the novel *From Here to Eternity*). Ivory has observed in interviews how closely he identifies with the children in the film. His sympathy is evident, but this emotional closeness may be what led him to overlook the fact that the script, co-written by himself with the partnership's regular third member, Ruth Prawer Jhabvala, lacks a few crucial elements—such as structure, focus and plot.

Little more than a string of mood pieces, the film meanders from episode to evocative episode, capturing period detail but never building up a good head of narrative steam. Ostensibly, it's a rites-of-passage movie, following Channe from the acquisition of an adopted brother through adolescence to the loss of her father, but her point of view isn't developed strongly enough to take control of the story. Only in the middle section, with Channe's friendship with her high camp schoolfellow Francis, does the film gain definition. But then Francis vanishes from the action abruptly, the family moves to the US and everything goes shapeless again. Various potential crises—Marcella's drinking, Billy's slide into delinquency—are intimated but never happen, and crucial epiphanies such as Bill's death are sidestepped or elided. Signposts are set up pointing to areas of pain and loss, but as if in deference to its unprepossessing (and irrelevant) title, the film cautiously detours around them.

Few Ivory films are without their incidental pleasures, though. In this case they lie unexpectedly in moments of near-expressionist satire. A glacially serene French headmistress, entering a disrupted classroom, seems to glide as if mounted on castors. When Francis, egged on by his mother (a daffy little cameo from Jane Birkin), serenades his classmates in a ripe countertenor, Ivory perfectly captures their mesmerised reaction, poised hysterically on the cusp between amazement and derision. Best of all is the brief sample of a stupendously awful production of Strauss' *Salome* to which Francis takes Channe. Bulging with late-60s kitsch, it seats its cast on fat inflatable armchairs in boiled-sweet colours. Salome slurps the Baptist's severed head, Herodias shoots up and Herod masturbates feverishly; Herodias kills one character by plunging a syringe into her neck. Such gleeful lampooning reminds us that, before good taste gelled around them, the Merchant-Ivory team chanced their arm on such films as *Savages* (1972) and *The Wild Party* (1974), not to mention the dance number staged on a giant typewriter in *Bombay Talkie* (1970). A touch more raucous bad taste might yet be the making of them.

Also reviewed in:
CHICAGO TRIBUNE, 9/25/98, Friday/p. A, John Petrakis
NEW YORK TIMES, 9/18/98, p. E12, Janet Maslin
VARIETY, 9/7-13/98, p. 71, Emanuel Levy
WASHINGTON POST, 9/25/98, p. B5, Stephen Hunter
WASHINGTON POST, 9/25/98, Weekend/p. 63, Michael O'Sullivan

SOMEWHERE IN THE CITY

An Artistic License Films release.   *Executive Producer:* Paula Brancato and Das Werk. *Producer:* Ramin Niami and Karen Robson. *Director:* Ramin Niami.   *Screenplay:* Ramin Niami and Patrick Dillon.   *Director of Photography:* Igor Sunara.   *Editor:* Ramin Niami and Elizabeth Gazzara. *Music:* John Cale. *Sound:* Antonio Arroyo. *Casting:* Caroline Sinclair. *Production Designer:* Lisa Albin. *Costumes:* S. Betim Balaman. *Running time:* 90 minutes. *MPAA Rating:* Not Rated.

CAST: Sandra Bernhard (Betty); Ornella Muti (Marta); Robert John Burke (Frankie); Peter Stormare (Graham); Bai Ling (Lu Lu); Paul Anthony Steward (Che); Bulle Ogier (Brigitte); Linda Dano (Casting Agent); Bill Sage (Justin); Steven Schub (Jerry); Kim Walker (Molly);

John Fugelsand (Henry);   M.B. Ghaffari (Teddy);   Robert Shapiro (Larry);   Dupre Kelly (2-Kool);   Jimmy Noonan (Brain);   Victoria Bastel (Johnna);   David Pittu (Agent);   Paolina Weber (Nina);   Mike Danner (Super);   Tom Riis Farrell (Edward);   Edward I. Koch (Himself).

LOS ANGELES TIMES, 10/2/98, Calendar/p. 22, Kevin Thomas

"Somewhere in the City" has such an endearing sensibility, good-humored and surprisingly tender, and such a wonderfully improbable cast, that it's tempting to forgive its strained, synthetic stretches and its tendency to meander. It's one of those lots-of-talk, little-action New York indie ventures best left to those who consider it enough that Sandra Bernhard, Italy's lovely Ornella Muti and French icon Bulle Ogier should somehow pop up in the same film—plus a walk-on by a glamorous Karen Black.

On the plus side, these actresses all shine, as does the entire large cast, and there's a vibrant John Cale score, plus numbers from some hot new bands. Working very—very—loosely from Gorky's "Lower Depths," debuting director and co-writer Ramin Niami introduces us to a clutch of desperate characters who live in an old tenement. Bernhard is a man-hungry, neurotic psychiatrist, and Muti is the miserable wife of the building's crude super.

Her lover (Robert John Burke, a Hal Hartley stalwart) is an inept robber whose gang includes the charmingly flashy Ogier. Other residents are a Chinese beauty (Bai Ling), who's prepared to marry just about anybody to get a green card, and a rich kid (Paul Anthony Stewart) desperately trying to be a revolutionary. The best drawn of the residents is a gifted Shakespearean actor (Peter Stormare), frustrated both as an artist and as a gay man. (He's hoping that a featured part in a film version of "I Dream of Jeannie," starring Madonna, will rescue him from TV commercials.)

A lot that happens is funny and sometimes also touching, but Niami's attempts at screwball comedy, which requires absolute precision combined with the illusion of spontaneity, tend to be less than inspired, and his pacing is unsteady, to say the least. To his credit, he and co-writer Patrick Dillon do come up with satisfying and funny finishes for all their people, including a sequence featuring former New York Mayor Ed Koch, deftly playing himself.

"Somewhere in the City," which has invitingly seedy production design from Lisa Albin, is surely somewhat less than satisfying, but Niami leaves a distinctive enough impression to leave you intrigued by whatever he may do next.

NEW YORK POST, 9/18/98, p. 58, Larry Worth

Maybe the screwball comedy should be retired. Clearly, it's one of the hardest genres to pull off.

Since the heyday of Preston Sturges, Howard Hawks and the Marx Brothers, only two auteurs have successfully stepped up to the plate: Peter Bogdanovich with "What's Up Doc?" and Woody Allen for "Sleeper."

It's safe to say that neophyte writer-director Ramin Niami isn't in that league. Proof positive: "Somewhere in the City."

Niami's big-screen debut focuses on a half-dozen eccentric characters residing in an East Village tenement building. Their all-too-familiar stories overlap for 90-odd, seemingly endless minutes.

That means that Sandra Bernhard's man-hunting shrink, who habitually does all the talking instead of her patients, tries to manage the love life of timid green card-seeking Bai Ling. Clearly, it's the blind leading the blind in allegedly funny setup No. 1.

Nos. 2, 3 and 4 aren't any more humorous or original, whether riffing on the gang that couldn't shoot straight, a gay drama coach's travails or a mother-obsessed revolutionary. It's strictly paint-by-numbers stuff.

In fairness, there's one big plus here: the ever-smart and ultra-hip Bernhard. Her deliciously deadpan delivery, spiked with that trademark sneer, provides a welcome distraction from all the been-there, done-that goings-on.

Bai Ling, who made such a memorable impression opposite Richard Gere in Red Corner, doesn't fare nearly as well. In fact, her antics are pretty embarrassing as she goes from virginal innocent to red-wigged punkster.

Veteran European divas Bulle Ogier and Ornella Muti are utterly wasted, as is the usually reliable Robert John Burke. And by the time a bound-and-threatened Ed Koch takes center stage, it's obvious that the director is just trying to fill space.

The bottom line: "Somewhere" goes nowhere fast.

Also reviewed in:
CHICAGO TRIBUNE, 12/25/98, Friday/p. S, John Petrakis
NEW YORK TIMES, 9/18/98, p. E16, Anita Gates
VARIETY, 8/4-10/97, p. 35, Ken Eisner

SONATINE

A Rolling Thunder Pictures release of a Bandai Visual/Shochiku Dai-ichi/Kogyo co-production in association with Right Vision/Right Vision Entertainment/Office Kitano. *Executive Producer:* Kazuyoshi Okuyama. *Producer:* Masayuki Mori, Hisao Nabeshima, and Takeo Yoshida. *Director:* Takeshi Kitano. *Screenplay (Japanese with English subtitles):* Takeshi Kitano. *Director of Photography:* Katsumi Yanagishima. *Editor:* Takeshi Kitano. *Music:* Jo Hasaishi. *Art Director:* Osamu Saseki. *Costumes:* Hirohide Shibata. *Running time:* 94 minutes. *MPAA Rating:* R.

CAST: Takeshi Kitano (Murakama);   Tetsu Watanabe (Uechi);   Aya Kokumai (Miyuki); Masanobu Katsumura (Ryoji);   Susumu Terashima (Ken);   Ren Ohsugi (Katagiri);   Tonbo Zushi (Katajima);   Kenichi Yajima (Takahashi);   Eiji Minakata (The Hit Man).

LOS ANGELES TIMES, 4/10/98, Calendar/p. 10, Kevin Thomas

How many times have you seen the story about the aging gangster—or gunslinger, for that matter—eager to retire but lassoed into one more job? In his sleek, punchy and altogether captivating "Sonatine," Japan's fabled writer-director-tough guy star Takeshi "Beat" Kitano makes it seem as if we've never seen such a tale on the screen. In doing so, Kitano creates one of the most effectively anti-violence violent movies since "The Wild Bunch."

Another admirable rescue from Quentin Tarantino's Rolling Thunder Pictures via Miramax, "Sonatine" is a 1993 release that anticipates the bravura of Kitano's more recent "Fireworks," although it does not have the newer film's transcendent love story.

As Tokyo yakuza Murakama (Beat Takeshi, Kitano's acting name) has settled into middle age, he's got his operation running so smoothly he's beginning to talk about retirement. But now his boss wants him to round up some guys and go to Okinawa to settle a skirmish of some sort between two rival gangs, the Nakamatsu, an affiliate of their Tokyo outfit, and the Anand.

Murakama is especially reluctant because when he went recently on a similar mission to Hokkaido, three of his men were killed. "Something's fishy about this Okinawa job," muses Murakama's loyal lieutenant Takahashi (Kenichi Yajima).

Sure enough, when Murakama and his gang arrive in Okinawa, the elderly Nakamatsu is surprised to see him, saying the problem is minor. Yet moments later a drive-by shooter shatters the window of the seedy office Murakama has been assigned.

At this point, however, Takano deftly shifts gears, suspending plot developments while Murakama and his minions, some of them young punks, decide to lay low at a handsome traditional-style home on a remote deserted beach, the vacation retreat of Takano's burly host (Tetsu Watanabe), the Nakamatsu second-in-command.

Here the punks engage in some dumb macho games. Murakama, comes to the rescue of an attractive young woman (Aya Kokumai), whom one of them has tried to rape. He later becomes involved with her. In this most beautiful of settings, considerable playfulness, camaraderie and humor develop.

Although the warriors hired by a village to protect them from an impending bandit attack in "Seven Samurai" are of far nobler character, there is in "Sonatine" that same beguiling feeling of the calm before the storm. And when the storm finally comes, irony compounds irony to dazzling effect.

"Sonatine," which has a sensational, pulsating Jo Hisaishi score, has style to burn and a terrific cast headed by Kitano, as much a virile screen icon as Humphrey Bogart. In the kill-or-be-killed world of these yakuza, "Sonatine" evokes both the myth of Capone's Chicago and of the not-so-distant feudal past of Japan itself.

NEW YORK POST, 4/10/98, p. 48, Thelma Adams

"We're bad, ain't we," says the middle-aged gangster at the epicenter of Takeshi Kitano's "Sonatine."

Murakama (writer, director and Japanese phenom Kitano) makes the remark while dangling a rival from a giant crane. While dipping the white-shoed villain in the drink, the black-suited Tokyo mobster chats with his lieutenant.

Distracted by their discussion of yakuza politics, the pair forget to pull the victim out of the water during his second dip. A shake-down becomes a murder. So what?

The violence in the existential gangster poem "Sonatine" is as flat and matter-of-fact as the antihero's face. Kitano, the Japanese Harvey Keitel, is a bullplug of a man whose very presence has gravity.

Kitano is known to New York audiences for "Fireworks"—and for saying the words "Merry Christmas, Mr. Lawrence" in that 1983 David Bowie showcase. Kitano booster Quentin Tarantino is releasing the 1993 anti-thriller under his Rolling Thunder banner at Miramax Films.

The blackly comic gangland melt-down makes a radical departure from the gangsta formula when Murakama—and his band of Tokyo hot shots go to Okinawa to settle a gang dispute. Once there, they get caught in political crossfire and retreat to an Oceanside to lick their wounds.

For a third of the movie, the gangsters live in a state of purgatory, of recess. They toss a Frisbee, flirt with local girls. They wait for the coast to clear, literally and figuratively.

This part of the movie is both the most original and most trying. "Sonatine" bursts into the beautiful imagery that ignited "Fireworks" as the gangsters pass time playing fort in the darkness, shooting at each other with Roman candles. The camera captures streamers of red, yellow and blue sparks against a black sky.

Even at rest, violence is central to the yakuzas' activity. For audiences, the rest stop goes on for too long, but we do learn from Murakama that the yakuza lifestyle is a way of mastering the art of dying. And the point is made with a bang.

NEWSDAY, 4/10/98, Part II/p. B12, John Anderson

Part Charles Bronson, part John Garfield, part samurai philosopher, Takeshi Kitano took the western world by storm with "Fireworks," winning the Venice Film Festival and getting some of the best reviews likely to be seen this year. With "Sonatine," another yakuza (Japanese mobster) ballad, we rewind to an earlier Kitano, but the freshness of his vision is just as invigorating.

Kitano, the No. 1 media celebrity in Japan (he hosts TV shows, writes books, contributes columns to numerous magazines and makes television commercials) has a singular film style, one that appropriates the conventions of the gangster film, but imbues them with a weighty humanity and sets them to his own rhythm. His characters are deadly gentlemen, who move from being genteel to murderous in a flash; the violence is always abrupt and stunning. And whether Kitano's protagonist is a cop or a gangster, what he's seen he doesn't forget. Or certainly forgive.

Made in 1993, before the motorcycle accident that damaged his face, "Sonatine" stars Kitano as the weary, lethal Murakawa, a mob underboss who is getting a little bit tired of the life and wouldn't mind stepping down and out—even while keeping a firm hold on his men and power. But when his boss Katajima (Tonbo Zushi) sends him to Okinawa to quell some disturbances in the branch office, Murakama suspects he's being set up.

Okinawa, however, is a relative paradise, where the men under Murakama become seduced by the breezes, and Murakama finds Miyuki (Aya Kokumai), a yakuza groupie whom he saves from a rape—but only after the assailant ticks him off. The concerns of the mob dissolve into the background of their relatively carefree existence. Reminiscent in some ways of the Italian Oscar-winner "Mediterraneo"—in which a group of soldiers spends World War II on an idyllic island—"Sonatine" lulls its characters and viewers with the idea that life may in fact be sweet, then sits us up straight with a return to violent reality. The presence of Murakama's men spark resentments among local mobsters and murder and vengeance—inescapable, Kitano says, to men of murder and vengeance—resume.

SIGHT AND SOUND, 5/94, p. 55, Geoffrey Macnab

Murakawa is a world-weary gangster, listlessly going through the motions of extorting, racketeering and murdering. When warfare breaks out between two rival *yakuza* gangs, his boss Kitajima instructs him to lead a team of hoodlums to Okinawa to help resolve the dispute. Murakawa is unenthusiastic about the mission, and has grave suspicions about Kitajima's lieutenant, Takahashi. Shortly after Murakawa's arrival in town, a bomb explodes in his offices, killing two of his colleagues. More of his team die when a gunfight breaks out in a bar. The chief of the Anan clan claims that Murakawa's services aren't really needed; the war between Anan and Nakamatsu is a trivial dispute which could easily have been ironed out without Kitajima's help.

Rather than risk further casualty, Murakawa and the surviving gang members decide to hide out in a remote beach-house. Awaiting further instruction, they while away the time, hooting frisbees on the beach, playing cards and mock games of Russian roulette, dancing, drinking and pretending to be sumo wrestlers. One evening, Murakawa witnesses a man attempting to rape his wife on the dunes; the man accuses him of being a voyeur and Murakawa kills him in self-defence. In the following days, Murakawa strikes up a relationship with the woman, Miyuki, and she joins his entourage.

The seaside idyll comes to an abrupt end when an assassin massacres the leaders of the Anan clan as they hold a secret meeting, and then appears on the beach and shoots a member of Murakawa's team. Murakawa learns that he and his followers have been 'expelled' by the boss, and that Takahashi has turned up in Okinawa, ostensibly to broker a truce. Murakawa and his men rush to Takahashi's hotel; a gunfight ensues in which Murakawa, one of his followers, and Takahashi are the sole survivors. Murakawa and his cohort take Takahashi back to the beach-hut and torture him. He confesses that Murakawa's entire mission was really just a smokescreen to distract attention while Kitajima discarded his old Anan partners and made a deal with Nakamatsu; Kitajima is due to meet the leader of the Nakamatsu clan to ratify their agreement.

Murakawa and his follower kill Takahashi, then head back to town. They arrange to fuse the lights in the hotel suite where the meeting is to take place. Murakawa sneaks into the hotel and ambushes the crooks, killing Kitajima and most of the Nakamatsu clan. After the shoot-up, he drives back towards the beach-house, where Miyuki is waiting for him, but stops on the road and blows his brains out.

A sort of elegy for a doomed *yakuza*, Takeshi Kitano's exquisite gangster film starts in familiar key as hard-boiled urban thriller, with all the shoot-and-splatter energy of his debut, *Violent Cop*. But it then veers off in a different direction altogether, turning into a lyrical, rather contemplative beach-movie: the narrative is held in suspension as our off-duty hoodlums hole up in a secret coastal resort. Here, to while away the time, they meditate and play: they don ancient costumes, perform traditional dances, and even have a few mock bouts of sumo wrestling in the sand. Kitano may specialize in making crime films, but he began his career as a comedian, and his deft way with visual gags and slapstick is given full rein: the beach sequences have a freewheeling, improvisatory charm utterly at odds with the stylized, very formal gunfights of the early scenes.

To match the good-spirited antics of the gangsters-at-leisure, the film-making itself becomes more flamboyant, using stop-action, slow motion and an array of high-angle shots. The games seem like harmless fun, but they have at least a tenuous relationship with the more serious business of the plot: they all involve guns or conflict of some sort. As they gambol in the sand, shooting flares at one another, playing Russian roulette, it's as if Kitano's characters are providing their own ironic commentary on their lives as racketeers while he gently mocks and stretches genre conventions, which usually demand that the violence be 'for real.'

The seaside interlude isn't simply a coda, but takes up the greater part of the film. In the space of a few minutes, we move from a tautly scripted mainstream thriller into the realm of the art-house movie. Suddenly, mood and atmosphere appear more important than narrative drive: there are self-consciously poetic shots of waves, long country roads and beautiful nighttime skies.

However, even if it has been kept in abeyance for long periods, the storyline has been scrupulously worked out, and comes complete with all the twists, turns and betrayals demanded of the well-constructed, gangster pic. It only takes the smallest of catalysts to set the whole bloody chain of events back in motion. Throughout the idyllic seaside lull, Kitano never lets the audience forget why his characters have gone into hiding. Nor is the possibility of renewed violence ever far away.

"If you're dead scared, it's like having a death wish," Murakawa (played by Kitano himself) tells his girlfriend Miyuki. There is a large measure of pathos in Murakawa's tale. He has grown tired of his life as a *yakuza*, and wants to move on; but it's a generic convention that he won't be allowed to, that he'll have to stay a gangster right till the bitter end. Kitano has a wonderful clown's face, and, as he showed playing the Sergeant in Oshima's *Merry Christmas, Mr Lawrence*, he's expert at suggesting a gentle, melancholy side in even the least sympathetic types.

Still, as a director, Kitano isn't much interested in characterization. All the figures in the film are one-dimensional stereotypes, defined by their roles. They're simply pawns in some bigger scheme of things, and behave as they must. Kitano even underlines the fact, cutting from the hoodlums playing a game with paper warriors to a pair of them wrestling on the beach, moving in the same rigid, mechanical way as the models. The gunfights are like rituals. Nobody betrays the slightest emotion, or shows anything other than an, impassive expression, when they get caught in a scrap. There are several extremely bloody shoot-outs dotted through the film, most of them mounted with an ingenuity which will probably soon have the great magpie Tarantino scurrying to copy them. (*Sonatine*'s denouement is especially effective, it's a kind of shadow-play, where all the lights have been fused, and we simply see the silhouettes of the killer and his victims illuminated by gunfire.) It is to Kitano's credit that the film never seems a coldly formalist exercise, despite the games he plays with genre: Sonatine is both rooted in a Japanese tradition of storytelling and very aware of the Hollywood gangster cycle, but, whatever its antecedents, the picture's sheer verve and originality are all its own.

Kitano, writer and director and editor of "Sonatine," is something of a fatalist, something of a humorist: If you set an enemy s car on fire, he instructs, you may have to walk home yourself. If you beat a fellow senseless and leave him against the men's room door, no one can enter to help him out. Business can, in fact, be conducted while you're hanging an uncooperative businessman off a crane and under water; if you hold him under too long, well, those things happen. The yin and yang of "Sonatine" are humor and violence, and the way Kitano keeps all his elements in balance keeps us off balance, never knowing what's coming but delighted that it is.

VILLAGE VOICE, 4/14/98, p. 59, J. Hoberman

Released this week on the heels of Takeshi Kitano's critically well-received *Fireworks, Sonatine* is actually the expression of an earlier consciousness—the last feature the Japanese actor-director completed before his near fatal 1994 motorcycle accident.

As its title suggests, *Sonatine* is a formal, almost musical, composition—an exercise in ritualized violence and callous whimsy. Kitano directs himself as a world-weary *yakuza* dispatched on a fool's mission from Tokyo to Okinawa to resolve an obscure underworld dispute. As his presence seemingly exacerbates, rather than calms. the situation, he and his cohorts are forced to hide out—or actually, hang out—on an idyllic, isolated beach. At this point, the movie switches from action thriller to something more experimental and romantic.

I'd be surprised if Kitano was familiar with Godard's *Pierrot Fou*, but *Sonatine* shares its three-part structure, including a lengthy central sequence that shifts from orchestrated urban violence to choreographed, seaside nonsense. Killing time rather than rivals, Kitano and his gang engage in all manner of childish antics—the empty beach serving as a suitably cosmic backdrop for their pranks, stunts, and gags. Many of these involve guns, although even a fatal shooting is treated as a form of comedy. "This is a bad joke," the dying man mutters. It is, of course, only a matter of time before the movie returns to "civilization" and betrayal.

Kitano's specialty as both an actor and director is the startling eruption of noncathartic mayhem. His films are highly formalist—crisp editing, blandly harmonious compositions, black humor understated even in its sadism, throwaway visual gags (for a brief moment, some mug's face is squished against a car window as if it were the screen itself). Such tension between the contemplative and the violent mirrors the director's own self-presentation. The characters Kitano plays rarely speak. His dark, unblinking stare has an animal's affectless curiosity. But, although he's typically most expressive when socking someone, his moon face—at once open and opaque—can unexpectedly break into a surprisingly friendly grin. Similarly, a bloody gunfight is as likely to occur inside a crowded elevator as to be shown, in extreme long shot, with muffled automatic fire illuminating a darkened high-rise office suite like a distant electrical storm, or simply reflected on the car tops in the parking lot outside.

Fireworks is a work of considerable ambition, but for me *Sonatine* remains Kitano's most fully achieved film to date. If *Fireworks* self-reflexive audacity is best appreciated after one has seen *Sonatine, Sonatine's* optimal presentation would have surely been on the bottom half of a 42nd Street double bill. As an abstract, implacable gangster flick, it ranks with Sam Fuller's *Underworld U.S.A.*, Jean-Pierre Melville's *Le Samourai*, John Boormans *Point Blank*, John Woo's *The Killer* and Don Siegel's *The Killers*. I can think of no greater compliment.

Also reviewed in:
CHICAGO TRIBUNE, 4/17/98, Friday/p. N, Michael Wilmington
NEW REPUBLIC, 4/27/98, p. 26, Stanley Kauffmann
NEW YORK TIMES, 4/10/98, p. E14, Stephen Holden
VARIETY, 6/7/93, p. 40, Derek Elley

SOULER OPPOSITE, THE

A Buffalo Jump Productions release. *Producer:* Tani Cohen. *Director:* Bill Kalmenson. *Screenplay:* Bill Kalmenson. *Director of Photography:* Amit Bhattacharya. *Editor:* Timothy Snell. *Music:* Peter Himmelman. *Casting:* Laura Adler and Shan Landsberg. *Production Designer:* Jane Anne Stewart. *Costumes:* Lynn Bernay. *Running time:* 104 minutes. *MPAA Rating:* R.

CAST: Christopher Meloni (Barry); Janel Moloney (Thea); Timothy Busfield (Robert); John Putch (Lester); Allison Mackie (Diane); Rutanya Alda (Thea's Mom); Joshua Keaton (Young Barry); Jed Rhein (Young Robert); Steve Landesberg (Himself).

LOS ANGELES TIMES, 10/2/08, Calendar/p. 8, Kevin Thomas

The "Souler Opposite"—a play on "polar opposite"—fits neatly into the romantic comedy genre yet also transcends it with uncommon wit and sensitivity. The result is a spiky, engaging love story that aims considerably higher than the usual lowest common denominator of so many mainstream movies.

In his feature debut, writer-director Bill Kalmenson signals us early on that we may be in for something special. He opens the film with a scene in which a couple of teenage Valley boys are talking about sex, then fast-forwards 20 years—moving from 1971 to 1991—without breaking their conversation. In this way Kalmenson deftly makes the point that in their 30s, Christopher Meloni's Barry and Timothy Busfield's Robert are still talking about women in the same way they did as teens.

Robert is now a dentist whose marriage is not as solid as he thinks it is, and Barry is a struggling stand-up comic who, as he says in his act, "is looking for a woman to like him for who he pretends to be."

The question Kalmenson, himself a stand-up comic and actor, poses with considerable grace and insight: Can a comic who indulges in humor in his act that is inescapably sexist and a feminist college senior find love and happiness? When Barry and Janel Moloney's Thea meet, they certainly do strike each other as polar opposites, but of course this is not the case.

Kalmenson and his actors develop Barry and Thea's exceedingly wary relationship with impressive skill, as Thea becomes willing to look beyond Barry's compulsive jokester personality to a man capable of extraordinary tenderness and vulnerability. Barry has fallen so hard and so fast for Thea that he opens himself completely to her. He wants the same from her, but it never occurs to him that he may not be prepared to receive the total trust he so craves.

That Kalmenson is drawing from personal experience surely gives his film its resonance. Through Barry and Thea we're able to perceive the whole issue of commitment in the skeptical '90s, and it is refreshing to watch people who are smart and don't hide it.

Both Meloni and Moloney are exciting discoveries for those of us who have not seen them before. Possessed of great intensity, Meloni is a mature performer, well-seasoned on TV. Moloney has a style that recalls Diane Keaton but not so strongly that she doesn't come across as a distinctive personality. As a "thirtysomething" alunmus, Busfield is probably better known than the film's stars and is a delight in his own right, heading a substantial supporting cast that includes John Putch as a political campaign organizer who may be the next man in Thea's life. "The Souler Opposite" looks as if it cost more than it probably did and especially benefits from Peter Himmelman's score, as elegant as it is unobtrusive.

NEW YORK POST, 10/16/98, p. 44, Larry Worth

Supposedly, the course of true love never runs smooth. So when a goofy, struggling stand-up comic falls for a brainy beauty in "The Souler Opposite," it's no big surprise. Nor is anything else in this turgid romance.

Much like the beleaguered funnyman's routines, the film delivers precious little punch—or satisfying punch lines. Maybe that's because writer-director Bill Kalmenson appears inspired by the most hackneyed of sitcoms.

In fairness, the performers try their darndest to be appealing, though newcomers Christopher Meloni and Janel Moloney generate few sparks. As the hero's best friend, Timothy (TV's thirtysomething) Busfield consistently steals their thunder.

That's not to say, however, that lightning ever strikes. Indeed, "Opposite" seems likely to attract little more than dust on video stores' shelves.

Also reviewed in:
NEW YORK TIMES, 10/16/98, p. E12, Janet Maslin
VARIETY, 11/3-9/97, p. 102, Glenn Lovell

SOUR GRAPES

A Castle Rock Entertainment release. *Executive Producer:* Barry Berg. *Producer:* Laurie Lennard. *Director:* Larry David. *Screenplay:* Larry David. *Director of Photography:* Victor Hammer. *Editor:* Priscilla Nedd-Friendly. *Music:* Jonathan Wolff. *Music Editor:* Robert Garrett. *Sound:* Robert Janiger. *Sound Editor:* David A. Whittaker. *Production Designer:* Charles Rosen. *Art Director:* Chas Butcher. *Set Designer:* Stan Tropp. *Set Decorator:* Anne D. McCulley. *Set Dresser:* David P. Newell. *Special Effects:* Mike Thompson. *Costumes:* Debra McGuire. *Make-up:* Brad Wilder. *Stunt Coordinator:* Roydon Clark. *Running time:* 91 minutes. *MPAA Rating:* R.

CAST: Jack Burns (Eulogist);   Viola Harris (Selma);   Scott Erik (Teenage Richie Maxwell); Michael Resnick (Teenage Evan);   Steven Weber (Evan);   Craig Bierko (Richie);   Jennifer Leigh Warren (Millie);   Karen Sillas (Joan);   Robyn Peterman (Roberta); Anthony Parziale (Blackjack Dealer);   Abraham Kessler (Crap Dealer);   Fred Goehner (Floor Manager);   Amy Hohn (Waitress);   Denise Bessette (Cocktail Waitress);   Angelo Tiffe (Chauffeur);   Orlando Jones (Digby);   Bari K. Willerford (Truck Driver);   Alan Wilder (Irwin); Hiram Kasten (Male Co-Worker);   Kari Coleman (Female Co-Worker);   Rosanna Huffman (Mr. Bell's Assistant); Philip Baker Hall (Mr. Bell);   Matt Keeslar (Danny Pepper);   Harry Murphy and Tucker Smallwood (Anesthesiologists);   Deirdre Lovejoy (Nurse Wells);   Iqbal Theba (Dr. Alagappan); Tamara Clatterbuck (Nurse Donato);   Helen Anzalone (Nurse Jamison);   Richard Gant (Detective Crouch);   James Macdonald (Detective Frehill);   Ann Guilbert (Mrs. Drier); Harper Roisman (Mr. Drier);   Edith Varon (Fran);   Jack Kehler (Jack);   John Toles-Bey (Lee);

Michael Krawic (Larry);   Sonya Eddy (Nurse Loder);   Jill Talley (Lois);   Bryan Gordon (Doug);   Rachel Crane (Allie);   Julie Claire (Matisse);   Patrick Fabian (Palmer);   Kevin Shinick (Conner);   Meredith Salenger (Degan);   Kristin Davis (Riggs);   Larry David, Jon Hayman, and Linda Wallem (TV Producers);   Ron West (Dr. Isner);   Bruce Jarchow (Dr. Dean);   Marvin Braverman (Bartender);   Arthur Chobanian (Man in Bar);   Jack O'Connell (Homeless Man);   Mark Chaet (Dr. Michaels);   Rande Leaman (Hospital Worker);   Larry Brandenburg (Landlord);   James Gallery (Mr. Lesser);   Tom Dahlgren (Mr. Havelock).

LOS ANGELES TIMES, 4/17/98, Calendar/p. 6, Jack Mathews

[The following review by Jack Mathews appeared in a slightly different form in **NEWSDAY, 4/17/98, Part II/p. B7.]**

Tennis-shoe-sole designer Richie (Craig Bierko) and his brain surgeon cousin Evan (Steven Weber) are sitting at adjacent slot machines in an Atlantic City casino, doing what losers at the blackjack table often do, punishing themselves by getting rid of their pocket change.

Richie is down to one quarter and asks Evan for the other two he needs to maximize his bet, and Evan obliges.

"Here, go crazy," he says, turning over the two coins.

A moment later, the whole place is going crazy, as Richie hits a jackpot worth more than $436,000. The question, posed at this early moment in writer-director Larry David's raucous, thin and wildly uneven "Sour Grapes," is how do they split the money?

Fifty-fifty? One-third for Richie, two-thirds for Evan? How about nothing for Evan, except maybe his two quarters back?

It's time to choose sides. The hard feelings and chaos that follow Richie's decision are the sole purpose of a story that could have been comfortably told in a half-hour sitcom.

In fact, it could have been done as an episode of "Seinfeld," which David co-created, and for which he has won two Emmys (and hit the jackpot himself).

Evan, whom Weber plays with a mixture of charm and adolescent pique, might have been written for Jerry Seinfeld himself.

And there are echoes of the other series regulars in Richie, and the two girlfriends.

In any event, "Sour Grapes" is a 90-minute sketch, in which the jackpot feud in Atlantic City sets off a chain of increasingly ridiculous events.

Evan is a successful doctor and doesn't need the money, he just wants his share of the loot on principle and is willing to pay the cost that includes the breakup of their friendship, the loss of their girlfriends, an attempted mercy killing and a botched testicle operation that turns a heartthrob soap opera star (Matt Keeslar) into a soprano.

Some of this is very funny, but it would probably be a lot funnier with a live audience, made up of people who are on the verge of hysterics even before the show begins.

There's really just a single idea in play, and it's stretched way beyond its playing time.

David's attempts to flesh it out—with desperate subplots about Richie's home-alone sex life; a chubby, middle-aged patient trying to hit on Evans young receptionist; and a few downtown vagrants who become beneficiaries of the fallout—merely amplify the shallowness of the script.

David's direction is weak, too. He gets a solid performance from Weber, but he allows, or at least encourages, antics from newcomer Bierko that make Richie far more irritating than he's intended to be.

It's like being stuck in a room with Kramer through one of his manic cycles.

Still, "Seinfeld" fans facing withdrawal over the end of the series may find sweetness in "Sour Grapes."

With lines like the one from Richie when his girlfriend dumps him—"I've seen you naked, that was my only goal!"—it's clear that we're seeing the beginning of the "Seinfeld" spawn.

NEW YORK POST, 4/17/98, p. 53, Thelma Adams

The mystery is over! After watching Larry David's "Sour Grapes," it's clear why "Seinfeld" wasn't called "David."

David co-created the wildly popular much-ado-about-zip TV sitcom with Jerry Seinfeld. He gave it all up to make movies. This movie. Oy vey.

At one point in writer-director David's flat-footed comedy, he mimics "Friends." On TV there's a faux show called "Guys'n Gals" that's all hair-flipping and wooden camaraderie.

People in glass houses shouldn't throw videotapes. "Sour Grapes," overall, plays like that same lame clip.

Here are the absurd neuroses: One character can't "be in an enclosed space with fruit."

Here are the debates about who's on top in sex and who should pick up the check. And what about those rude elevator jockeys who refuse to hold the door even when they see you running?

The grapes sour over two quarters. First cousins Richie (Craig Bierko) and Evan (Steven Weber) take their friends (Robyn Peterman and Karen Sillas) to Atlantic City. Once there, Richie wins a half-million-dollar-jackpot with Evan's change.

From that point on, the boys feud and their fortunes tank. The complications include a practical joke about a brain tumor, a botched testicle operation, and a running gag about a double-jointed guy who can pleasure himself.

We've learned from the "Seinfeld" school of scripting that plot isn't everything. Comedy is. Weber's Evan (a neurosurgeon!) is doing a Jerry riff, with only one problem. The handsome "Wings" star doesn't have that stand-up zing.

On TV, you could always depend on the ensemble cast, even in the early days when Seinfeld's acting was so wooden you could knock. Bierko's Richie occasionally stretches toward Kramer's physical comedy, but he's severely misdirected.

With all the echoes of the waning super sitcom, "Sour Grapes" feels like a poorly dubbed knock-off on TeleBulgaria. Even the most slavish "Seinfeld" fans will avoid this movie like yesterday's soup.

NEWSWEEK, 4/27/98, P. 72, David Ansen

"Sour Grapes" requires a little patience. Farce is a little like a windup toy: the longer you crank it up, the faster it'll move when it's unleashed. So sit tight while writer-director Larry David, the co-creator of "Seinfeld," sets up his story. Two cousins, brain surgeon Evan (Steven Weber) and sneaker-sole designer Richie (Craig Bierko), take their girlfriends to Atlantic City to gamble. Down to his last quarter, Richie borrows two more from Evan for a last pull at the slot machine—and hits a $436,000 jackpot.

Evan figures his two quarters entitle him to at least half the winnings. Richie thinks otherwise. Each of their girlfriends takes the other guy's side. But things don't get really ugly—and really funny—until they get back to New York and Evan wickedly tells his cousin he has a fatal disease. The nastiness escalates, dragging into it Richie's smothering mom (Viola Harris), a TV star (Matt Keeslar) who has the misfortune of undergoing surgery on one of Dr. Evan's bad days, a homeless man (Orlando Jones) and, inevitably, the police.

"Sour Grapes" is nothing to look at—it's sitcom drab—but David has the requisite ruthlessness of the true *farceur*, willing to follow the tale's dark logic to its dottiest ends. David isn't afraid of bad taste or his characters' bad dispositions: greed, rage and frustration inspire some of his best jokes. When "Sour Grapes" finally hits its stride, the laughs come loud and fast. You'll leave this comedy of loutishness feeling downright cheerful.

SIGHT AND SOUND, 3/99, p. 52, Andy Richards

Richie Maxwell and his cousin Evan, a brain surgeon, are spending the weekend with their girlfriends in Atlantic City. Having exhausted their gambling funds, Richie drops his last quarter into a fruit machine. Evan gives him two more quarters to have a chance of the big prize. Richie wins a jackpot Of $436,214, but offers Evan only $1,000 to cover his gambling losses. Evan insists he's entitled to half of the jackpot. The cousins part acrimoniously.

Evan informs Richie that Richie has an inoperable brain tumour. Knowing his doting mother Selma will be devastated by his death, Richie plans a mercy killing for her. Richie instructs a friendly bum, Digby, to break into his mother's house. Selma collapses from shock, and is hospitalised. Evan calls the next day to tell Richie that the tumour was a joke. Evan botches an operation performed on television soap star Danny Pepper, accidentally emasculating him, which results in Pepper losing his job.

The cousins are both dumped by their girlfriends. Richie is told that Selma needs a brain operation. Richie begs Evan to do it. He successfully performs the operation—and asks for a fee of $218,000.

Returning home, Evan is confronted by Pepper. During the scuffle, the briefcase of money falls from the balcony; Digby finds it. When she discovers that Digby and his friends have moved into her house, Selma has a fatal heart attack. At her funeral, Selma's landlord gives Richie a hefty bill for damages; Richie gives Evan two quarters for a parking meter; and Digby arrives in an expensive car.

The feature debut of Larry David (co-creator with Jerry Seinfeld of the television sitcom *Seinfeld*), *Sour Grapes* provides dispiriting evidence that material rooted in the conventions of the 22-minute television sitcom is not easily accommodated to the expanses of a feature film. Deprived of the safety net of a laugh track and a regular audience's familiarity with established characters, *Sour Grapes* is painfully ill-conceived. Its premise two cousins feuding over the fruit-machine jackpot both of them contributed money towards—is too flimsy a foundation. Its clumsy ragbag of themes and sub-themes—the venality of television networks, male sexual insecurities and so on only demonstrates the film's lack of focus.

Presumably an ad hoc structure appeals to David because he has been constrained for so long by *Seinfeld's* tight format and the constant rapidity with which that show demanded new ideas. However, as a result, *Sour Grapes* lacks identity: its humour varies in tone erratically from the vulgar (a running gag has Craig Bierko's Richie fellate himself) to the self-consciously arch (there's a diversion about Eskimo court procedure) to the tired Jewish-mother material already familiar from *Seinfeld* itself.

Accidental emasculation aside, the film never attains the blackness of comedy for which David seems to be striving. It even opts unwisely for a brief parody of *Seinfelds* ratings rival *Friends*— Danny Pepper's excruciatingly smug show *Guys and Gals*—but this step out of the fictional world merely reminds viewers of the film's inadequacies.

Lacking stars, *Sour Grapes* satisfies itself with lesser-knowns Craig Bierko and Steven Weber, an uncharismatic duo who cannot sustain our interest in the blandly unsympathetic rival cousins they play. A curiously throwaway cameo from Philip Baker Hall (who was masterful in Paul Thomas Anderson's *Hard Eight*), and a severely underdeveloped role for Hal Hartley collaborator Karen Sillas as Evan's girlfriend Joan are also questionable. This kind of casting, perhaps designed to give the production a spurious US-indie flavour, seems redundant and wasteful in a film that fails to play as anything other than over-extended, low-brow television—an impression compounded by the unimaginative televisual style of static master shots jumping back and forth into close-ups. David will have to work harder at extended play in future to escape his sitcom prison.

VILLAGE VOICE, 4/21/98, p. 76, Laurie Stone

Though *Seinfeld's* dark strains spun off of Larry David, one can see the effervescence that Jerry and crew furnish when viewing David's work without them: *Sour Grapes*, a joyless lump of a first film. It's as if the other Larry David, from a dull, alternative universe, made this movie. Craig Bierko as Richie, the completely unlikable winner of a slot machine jackpot, is a cut-rate Jim Carrey, all Doberman aggression and no inventiveness. Misadventures arise from the baseless demand of his cousin Evan (Steven Weber) that he be given half the winnings for loaning him two quarters. The terrors about strong women and minorities that simmer on Seinfeld are rampant here. A woman meant to be a feminist (she likes fucking on top) chooses a guy because his balls have literally been severed. In another bit intended to be hilarious, a cadre of homeless people camp out in a white woman's house and turn it into a filthy ruin.

Also reviewed in:
CHICAGO TRIBUNE, 4/17/98, Friday/p. L, Monica Eng
NEW YORK TIMES, 4/17/98, p. E18, Janet Maslin
VARIETY, 4/13-19/98, p. 27, Leonard Klady

WASHINGTON POST, 5/1/98, p. D5, Stephen Hunter
WASHINGTON POST, 5/1/98, Weekend/p. 54, Michael O'Sullivan

SPANISH PRISONER, THE

A Sony Pictures Classics release of a Sweetland Films presentation of a Jean Doumanian production. *Executive Producer:* J.E. Beaucaire. *Producer:* Jean Doumanian. *Director:* David Mamet. *Screenplay:* David Mamet. *Director of Photography:* Gabriel Beristain. *Editor:* Barbara Tulliver. *Music:* Carter Burwell. *Music Editor:* Todd Kasow. *Sound:* John Patrick Pritchett. *Sound Editor:* Maurice Schell. *Casting:* Billy Hopkins, Suzanne Smith, and Kerry Barden. *Production Designer:* Tim Galvin. *Art Director:* Kathleen Rosen. *Set Decorator:* Jessica Lanier. *Costumes:* Susan Lyall. *Make-up:* Carla White. *Make-up (Steve Martin):* Frank Griffin. *Stunt Coordinator:* Bill Anagnos. *Running time:* 112 minutes. *MPAA Rating:* PG.

CAST: Campbell Scott (Joe Ross);   Rebecca Pidgeon (Susan Ricci);   Steve Martin (Jimmy Dell);   Ben Gazzara (Joe Klein);   Ricky Jay (George Lang);   Felicity Huffman (Pat McCune); Richard L. Freidman, Jerry Graff, and G. Roy Levin (Businessmen);   Hilary Hinckle (Resort Concierge);   David Pittu (Resort Manager);   Christopher Kaldor (Dell's Bodyguard);   Gary McDonald (Ticket Agent); Michael Robinson (Security Person);   Olivia Tecosky (Flight Attendant);   Charlotte Potok (Bookstore Woman);   Paul Butler (Bookbinder);   J. J. Johnston (Doorman);   Emily Weisberg (Secretary);   Stephanie Ross (Receptionist);   Elliot Cuker (Antique Car Dealer);   Scott Zigler (Car Dealer's Assistant);   Steven Hawley (Restaurant Manager);   Jordan Lage (Maitre'd); Steven Goldstein and Jonathan Katz (Lawyers);   Paul Dunn III (Jailer);   Tony Mamet (FBI Agent Levy);   Jack Wallace (Sanitation Man);   Ed O'Neill (FBI Team Lawyer);   Clark Gregg (FBI Sniper); Lionel Mark Smith (Detective Jones);   Jim Frangione (Detective Luzzio);   Allen Soule (Fingerprint Technician);   Mary McCann (Policewoman);   Gus Johnson (Property Clerk);   Isiah Whitlock, Jr. (Trooper);   Harriet Voyt (Airline Employee); Kristin Reddick (Airport Mother); Andrew Murphy (Airport Child);   Jeremy Geidt (Timid Man); Carolyn "Coco" Kallis (Timid Woman);   Neil Pepe (Airport Security);   Charles Stransky (Deckhand);   Takeo Matsushita and Seiko Yoshida (United States Marshals);   Mimi Jo Katano (Japanese Tour Guide);   Sarah Buff (Girl on Subway).

CHRISTIAN SCIENCE MONITOR, 4/10/98, p. B3, David Sterritt

David Mamet's greatest loves are language, games and the slippery lines people draw between the truths and illusions of their lives. The three come together in his best plays, like "American Buffalo" and "Oleanna," and his finest movies, like "Homicide" and his new picture, "The Spanish Prisoner," a thriller so tricky that figuring it out is half the fun.

Campbell Scott plays Joe Ross, the inventor of a high-tech formula with a great commercial future. The company he works for is already counting the millions expected to roll in, but Joe is worried that his boss is planning to cut him out of the profits.

Determined to protect himself, he seeks advice from a new acquaintance who seems to have an inside track on the financial world. But the more Joe learns, the more concerned and confused he becomes. Are his associates on the level? Or is he caught in a con game that grows more unfathomable—and dangerous—with every move?

Like most Mamet stories, "The Spanish Prisoner" asks us to enter a special world more streamlined and stylized than real life. The dialogue is written in Mametspeak—clipped, rhythmic phrases sounding like a sort of punchy poetry—and the plot has so many twists and turns that inattentive viewers may get lost in its labyrinth.

It pays hefty dividends for those who stay with it, though, unfolding a string of surprises in a series of wittily written scenes. Also invigorating are the performances by Scott as the inventor, Steve Martin as his unpredictable new friend, Ben Gazzara as his possibly shady employer, and Rebecca Pidgeon as his would-be girlfriend.

Puzzle pictures are definitely in style these days—much of this movie is like a modestly budgeted version of "The Game," one of last year's most clever surprises—and Mamet is clearly a master of the genre.

LOS ANGELES TIMES, 4/3/98, Calendar/p. 10, Kenneth Turan

When David Mamet directs, Ricky Jay is never far behind. The magician and sleight-of-hand artist has appeared in four of the playwright's five films, including his latest, "The Spanish Prisoner." More important than his work as an actor, however, is the way Jay's presence serves as a thematic touchstone for a director who enjoys making the same kind of gleefully duplicitous film over and over again.

Starting with the aptly titled "House of Games" in 1987, Mamet as a director has been continually fascinated with elegantly mystifying cinematic puzzles. He uses dazzle and deception to build elaborate houses of cards that coldly toy with audience expectations the way playful cats fool around with mice trapped under their paws.

Mamet brings more than a decade's worth of filmmaking experience to his latest project, and his skill as a director has improved considerably. "The Spanish Prisoner" is the smoothest and most convincing of Mamet's elaborate charades and features intriguing performances by Steve Martin and Campbell Scott. But it shares with the writer-director's earlier work a passion for self-consciously creating distance, for holding the audience at arm's length, that remains a rarefied taste.

Given all that, the plot of "The Spanish Prisoner" (the title comes from the name of "the oldest confidence game on the books") is especially difficult to describe. Set in a world where little turns out the way it first appears—"a small world chock-full of coincidences"—the film prides itself on being ahead of us just when we think we've figured it out. Everyone is suspect, even if we're not exactly sure of what, and given the way masks drop simply to reveal still more masks, even revelations can be misleading.

"The Spanish Prisoner" opens on the mythical Caribbean island of St. Estephe, where Joe Ross (Scott) and his colleague George Lang (Jay) are flown down by their secretive boss, Mr. Klein (Ben Gazzara), to talk to a group of potential investors.

Blessed with youthful good looks, Joe is also a brilliant scientist who has come up with a process (no names, please) that will enable Klein's Manhattan-based firm to control an unspecified global market and earn a spectacular amount of money.

Joe is a Boy Scout of sorts, trusting and naive, but not so much so that he is averse to making friends with the rich and successful Jimmy Dell (Martin), whom he meets on the island. Upon returning to New York, Joe and Jimmy strike up a friendship, and the wealthy older man advises Joe when he becomes fearful that Klein may not be planning to cut him in on the wealth his discovery is sure to create.

Joe makes another acquaintance on the island, Susan Ricci (Rebecca Pigeon), a new and very junior employee at Klein's firm. Susan soon develops a gushing crush on Joe, a romantic development that he is not at all sure how to handle.

In placing these characters in a cold and ruthless world filled with "hush-hush developments," where only fools trust anyone and figuring out who is duping who can literally be worth your life, Mamet makes extensive and idiosyncratic use of his own particular ideas of how dialogue should be recited.

While now-classic plays like "American Buffalo" and "Glengarry Glen Ross" show Mamet to be a master of intense, masculine wordplay, the most memorable movies he's written, from "Wag the Dog (directed by Barry Levinson) to "The Verdict" (directed by Sidney Lumet) to the film version of his own "Glengarry" (directed by James Foley), invariably come when someone else is in charge of the players.

That's because Mamet demands that actors recite his words with distancing rhythms and cadences that make the conversations sound as if they took place on an alternative universe that parallels but does not connect to our own. This alienating verbal style puts peculiar emphasis on phrases like "You're a real gent" and "I'm loyal and true and I'm not hard to look at," emphasizing the artificiality of the situations and making any kind of involvement with the characters hard to imagine.

"The Spanish Prisoner" is more involving than Mamet's previous puzzles at least, partially because protagonists Scott and Martin are good enough at handling the director's dialogue to almost make these elaborate verbal charades a success. Martin especially taps sides of him we don't often see as he oscillates between the sinister and the sincere.

What these men can't always overcome is the film's too-elaborate artifice, as well as specific moments where characters do completely implausible things only because the plot insists they do. The problem with "The Spanish Prisoner" is not so much, as one character asks, "If I told you this story, would you believe it?" as, "Even if you believed it, would you care?"

NEW STATESMAN, 9/4/98, p. 39, Kaufman Gerald

Another wimp called Joe [The reference is to *The Land Girls*; see Kaufman's review of that film] (Campbell Scott) is the focus of the action in David Mamet's *The Spanish Prisoner*. But whereas *The Land Girls* hobbles arthritically, Mamet's new film, though almost exactly the same length, snaps and sizzles along. Joe, who works for a huge corporation, has invented something called "The Process" which is worth billions. This Process, though, is simply what Hitchcock called the McGuffin, the device which triggers the chase.

The corporation's boss, Mr Klein (Ben Gazzara), keeps dodging Joe's requests to be recompensed for his invention. Jimmy Dell, a mysterious millionaire (Steve Martin, in a subtly menacing performance which earns forgiveness for all those awful comedies in which he has recently starred), advises Joe on how to handle Klein. A secretary called Susan (Rebecca Pidgeon, Mamet's wife) tells Joe, "I'm stuck on you," warns him against Dell, and helps him when he goes on the run, suspected of murder.

Early in the film, Joe is told of a convoluted confidence trick called "the Spanish prisoner". Mamet, in turn, has created an intriguingly convoluted plot in which each con, when opened up, reveals another. And if Joe is enmeshed by con inside con, the audience is duped even more.

The action starts when the leading members of the corporation fly off to the Caribbean for a brainstorming session. Ask yourself why. Dell offers to buy Joe's plastic camera for $ 1,000. Why? Pat McCune (Felicity Huffman) reveals herself to Susan as an FBI agent. Why? Jimmy keeps inviting Joe to meet his sister, but the sister never shows up. Why not? What is the package that Dell asks Joe to deliver, and why is he furious with him for delivering it?

Everything that happens in *The Spanish Prisoner* is a trick. Every character, even the hobbling old lady you think is just a dress extra, is present for a purpose. Every remark, however apparently trivial, merits careful examination. Joe is advised, "Anybody could be anybody". But in this captivating entertainment, anybody could not only be anybody but may turn out to be somebody else.

Mr. Nice Guy is also a McGuffin film. Almost as soon as it begins, Jackie Chan, the martial arts acrobat, gets involved in a chase that goes on for the whole of the film's 88 minutes. Various luridly criminal gangs pursue each other—and Chan—around Melbourne in quest of the "videotape that exposes all".

Every one of the wildly inventive stunts is for real. There are positively no mockups or computer simulations. In a marvellous comic sequence the villains pursue Chan, who pursues the villains, who pursue Chan through a succession of interlocking doors. In the grand finale, a 120-ton mining truck crushes an enormous fleet of cars, including sundry Rolls-Royces, before destroying an entire mansion (built to Horace Ma's production design at a cost of $ 1.5 million). A balletic tussle on a carpet of thousands of Pepsi cans provides the ultimate in product placement.

NEW YORK, 4/13/98, p. 48, David Denby

At the beginning of David Mamet's *The Spanish Prisoner*, I laughed out loud. Not at the movie (which is pretty good) but at myself, for I had once written of Mamet's dialogue (at the time of the stage version of *Glengarry Glen Ross)* that it represented a new form of naturalism in the theater—an authentic rendering of everyday American speech. In *Glengarry,* the characters talk in rude fragments, in charged broken phrases that reveal some hostile intent that can never be made entirely explicit. I was excited: Here was an invention equal in freshness to the delirious language of Scorsese's hoods in *Mean Streets!* Well, I still love *Glengarry Glen Ross,* but my initial impression of Mamet's language now seems entirely naïve. Whatever the accuracy of Mamet's ear back in the early eighties, that ear has long been shut against the world. What Mamet writes now, precisely, is Mametese. His dialogue is a severe, even extreme, stylization of speech that serves to express his barbed, paranoid view of reality; and it's also the kind of speech—hooded, treacherous, withholding yet bristling—that gets him from one point to another in his closed-off plots, which have the form of very elaborate, very nasty puzzles. However deeply Mamet goes into filmmaking *(The Spanish Prisoner* is the fifth film he has directed), he remains a man of the theater, a director indifferent to the free-and-easy inclusiveness that is the glory of the movies.

In *The Spanish Prisoner,* Campbell Scott, of the serious brow and the serious cleft, plays a young inventor, Joe Ross, a self-made man uneasy among the rich and powerful, yet secretly eager to join their ranks. What it is that Joe Ross has invented we never find out—"the process," it is called, some sort of technological masterpiece that will earn untold millions for Joe's company. At the beginning of the movie, Joe is asked by his boss (Ben Gazzara) to make a presentation to the company's major investors, who have gathered at a posh Caribbean island resort. But Joe feels he's possibly being used—his invention exploited without proper compensation. Some sort of shadowy international businessman (Steve Martin) shows up at the resort and addresses Joe in a way that immediately tests his integrity; he passes the test and is flattered by the businessman's interest. Steve Martin's antagonistic manner (he always seems to be sizing everyone up) turns out to be perfectly suited to Mamet's notion of how the world works. Martin gives a smooth, cool, perfect performance in Mametese. He plays a tough man, friendly but tricky, who doesn't give a compliment easily. The trap has been set.

Mamet keeps the settings simple, breeding mistrust out of the flat walls and corporate colors. He concentrates on dialogue and character, and this movie is warmer, and much closer to psychological realism, than the weirdly schematic *House of Games.* Campbell Scott is tight, wary, proud; he's not an exciting actor, but he's good for Joe, who places a high value on integrity and longs for respect. Scott gives him just enough hunger around the edges of his pride to suggest why he might be a perfect mark. But Mamet has trouble with woman characters, and he has made his wife, Rebecca Pidgeon, quite extraordinarily dislikable—intrusive, insinuating—as a secretary who claims to be Joe's ally. The secretary should be an ambiguous presence, but instead we are shouting at Joe not to trust her from her first appearance.

Why is David Mamet obsessed with con artists? Is he afraid that someone might be smarter than he is, or more cunning? Mamet wants to stay ahead of the game. The con artist may be the kind of artist he instinctively respects—he creates a completely controlled scenario; he turns cruelty into narrative, conjuring an alternate reality for his mark. But Mamet himself would like to be a real artist in movies, and he's about halfway there. As Joe gets more and more isolated, Mamet takes us deeper into fear than he ever has in the past, and that's an achievement. Hitchcock is the model here—the man who made great films about ordinary people getting in way, way over their heads. But to become Hitchcock's equivalent, Mamet has to learn to trust the camera more than he does; he has to stop trying to control everything with language; he has to let loose a little and just give in to the fluency, the ease, the free-flowing pleasure of making a movie.

NEW YORK POST, 4/3/98, p. 51, Thelma Adams

"Beware of all enterprises that require new clothes," Henry David Thoreau once wrote.

The quote appears in the latest catalog for the J. Peterman Co., the retail outlet that's both the butt and beneficiary of a legion of "Seinfeld" gags.

The Walden Pond scribe's wisdom is right above a trio of ordinary-looking shirts advertised as the faded, Sunday gardening togs that readers of the New Yorker magazine wear, the so-called Nicholas County Squire's Shirt.

Communication is everything, say the Peterman copywriters. It's a quote that's also suitable for David Mamet's latest top-drawer puzzler, "The Spanish Prisoner."

With Mamet's clipped dialogue and bold-faced phrasing, the writer-director has a way of infuriating the audience before he takes them to a hard-bitten world of aphorisms that's totally American and uniquely his (think "Glengarry Glen Ross").

The mystery's title refers to a legendary scam. It's Mamet buddy and cult magician Ricky Jay, the historian of grifters, card sharks and elegant rip-offs, who turns up direct from a sold-out run on the Upper West Side to explain the game without giving away the tricks.

With his rabbinical voice, Jay is Mamet's mouthpiece. Before disappearing into the plot forever, Jay's corporate lawyer drops pungent quotes, including Thoreau's opinion on new clothes. "Beware," as the saying goes.

In "The Spanish Prisoner," no one is who he seems to be, whatever the clothes, the hairstyles, the gentlemen's clubs. At the center of a scam to steal a promising formula is brilliant scientist Joe Ross (Campbell Scott).

Ross has invented "The Process" (a Hitchcockian McGuffin if ever there was one). This regular Joe wants to cash in on his potentially profitable discovery, but boss Ben Gazzara is dragging his feet.

The scientist starts the movie as an innocent, a Gregory Peck, a Henry Fonda with glasses. But Ross has an Achilles' heel. He's too nice, he wants to be liked too much. It's through this weakness that con artists intent on taking the formula prey on our Mr. Ross.

But who's in on the con? Is Jay's gambling lawyer a suspect? What about that button-cute secretary, Susan Ricci (Mamet's young wife, Rebecca Pidgeon).

How about Steve Martin's slick, Bentley-buying Jimmy Dell? And isn't there something fishy about how FBI agent McCune (Felicity Huffman) turns up in the Caribbean? And what about the boss—and wait, is anybody really as naive as Ross?

With "The Spanish Prisoner," Mamet holds the audience hostage to the very end. We unravel the plot with amazement and delight. It's the director's most entertaining suspenser to date. He displays Scott, Martin and Jay with the panache of a royal flush. So what if Mamet cheats a little—we're deliciously conned.

NEWSDAY, 4/3/98, Part II/p. B11, Jack Mathews

Before he sat down to write "Spanish Prisoner," somebody must have slipped the formula for Prozac into the software of David Mamet's word processor. It didn't dull the famously cynical playwright-novelist-poet-screenwriter-movie director's keen intellect, but what an attitude change!

"Spanish Prisoner," Mamet's foray into Hitchcockian mystery, works from a familiar Mamet theme, that ruthlessness and guile trump decency and trust in the game of life. But the message is delivered minus the usual bite, minus the anger and certainly minus the hailstorm of profanity that has become as much a part of Mametese as the staccato dialogue. Who would have thought it conceivable that he'd ever make a film with a PG rating?

The good news is that without the fury typical of his work, we get to focus on and appreciate what a brilliant writer Mamet is. "Spanish Prisoner" has little conventional action and almost no violence. It isn't scary, or even particularly suspenseful. Yet, like his first film, "House of Games," it has a thoughtful, unpredictable logic that proves irresistible.

"Spanish Prisoner" is set up with a classic Hitchcock "McGuffin." Joe Ross (Campbell Scott), a bright young engineer with a Manhattan-based electronics firm, has invented something called only "the process" and has been called to a secret meeting in the Caribbean to present the concept to investors. Whatever it is, Ross' invention is going to dominate the market, whatever that is, and every rival in the industry, whoever they are, wants it. Even the FBI is lurking around.

The question that serves as the story's narrative thread is whether the trusting and naive Ross can protect himself and his formula from his enemies and whether he—or the audience—can even figure out who they are. The candidates include Jimmy Dell (Steve Martin), the amiable jet-setter Ross befriends in the Caribbean; Susan Ricci (Rebecca Pidgeon), a colleague with an aggressive crush on him; his hard-living friend Ricky Jay (George Lang), and perhaps even his boss, Klein (Ben Gazzara), who keeps assuring Ross that he'll be rewarded for his work but won't put it in writing.

There's nothing coy in Mamet's homage to Hitchcock. From the "innocent man" theme to the use of a McGuffin to a constantly prowling camera, Mamet is doing Hitchcock as an artist might try his hand at Picasso. But "Spanish Prisoner" doesn't have the dark core, the true menace that made Hitchcock's films so emotionally powerful. In fact, it's a game, a kind of reversal of "The Sting," where we follow the target of an elaborate ruse and get our kicks discovering who's who and how they did what.

At that, Mamet's script is superbly clever. You can get ahead of it once in a while, but it quickly knocks you off track and leads you somewhere else, culminating with a deus ex machina for which you cannot possibly prepare. But even that cheap trick is done with a satisfying flourish.

The pleasures of "Spanish Prisoner" (the title refers to a confidence game) are all for the head. Mamet's doling out brain candy here, but it's tasty stuff. Even the actors seem to be enjoying what they're getting away with. Scott brings tremendous sympathy to a character who doesn't have the arc of a Hitchcock hero, the ordinary man roused to extraordinary feats. There are lambs and wolves in Mamet's world, and though the lambs may grow wary, they never really change.

The better roles belong to Martin, who has never been more fun in a serious role, and Pidgeon, Mamet's wife, who is totally engaging as a love interest who is both more and less than she seems. Just like the story.

SIGHT AND SOUND, 9/98, p. 53, Philip Kemp

Joe Ross, a scientist who has created a hugely valuable new process for the company he works for, is invited to the Caribbean island of St. Estèphe to meet with his boss Joe Klein and the board of directors. Also on the trip are Joe's friend George Lang, the company lawyer, and a young secretary, Susan Ricci. The board congratulate Joe but are evasive when he asks about his bonus. On the island, Joe meets jetsetter Jimmy Dell, who invites him to dinner back in New York and female FBI agent Pat McCune.

In New York, Joe begins to fear that the company is planning to cheat him. Susan supports his fears. Egged on by Dell, Joe agrees to meet a lawyer Dell recommends. But when asked to bring his formula to the meeting Joe grows suspicious and contacts McCune. She confirms the FBI has Dell under surveillance, and meets Joe before his rendezvous to fit him with a wire. Dell fails to show, and Joe discovers the supposed FBI agents have stolen his formula notes.

Reporting the theft to the real FBI, Joe finds that every trace of Dell has vanished—and all his own recent actions incriminate him. He seeks help from George Lang but finds him dead, stabbed with Joe's own knife. He takes refuge with Susan. Realising that photographs of Dell exist on St Estèphe, they make for the airport but encounter roadblocks and head for Boston instead. But Joe remembers proof of Dell's existence still in New York. He turns back and rejoins Susan, but she leads him straight to Dell who prepares to kill him. Joe desperately appeals to the only other people present, a pair of Japanese tourists—who reveal themselves as US Marshals. Dell and Susan are arrested, and Joe learns that the whole scam was masterminded by Klein.

[Editor's note: this review contains several plot revelations.] In one of G.K. Chesterton's *Father Brown* stories, a murderer enters and leaves a block of flats quite unobserved by several people watching the entrance. The key is that, "Nobody ever notices postmen." David Mamet's *The Spanish Prisoner* turns on an updating of that insight: "Nobody ever looks at a Japanese tourist." Mamet plays fair: his pair of tourists show up, clicking indefatigably away, in scene after scene, and he even nudges us with a line of dialogue about the Japanese getting everywhere. But despite this he counts on his audience, like his lead characters, never giving the supposed oriental visitors a second gland—not until they turn out to be something quite different from what they seem.

This, indeed, is the message of the film (reiterated once or twice too often): "You never know who anybody is." Urbane jetsetter Jimmy Dell gives the opposite angle—"People aren't that complicated; they generally look like what they are"—but then Dell (Steve Martin in his best role for years) is the chief joker in the pack, the very spirit of misdirection. *The Spanish Prisoner* gives us Mamet in playful, sleight-of-hand mode, reworking *House of Games* with a few extra twists. There's no great depth here, but a clever convoluted surface that deftly wrong-foots us time and again. Mamet delights in setting up reassuring stock characters, such as Rebecca Pidgeon in the Jean Arthur role of the plucky, adoring girl turning up trumps for our hero, only to reveal that she is wearing a mask as well. Only the hapless Joe Ross is what he seems to be, very much the average Joe, a boy-scoutish innocent far too transparent for his own good.

Campbell Scott's performance as Joe—geeky, twitchy, borderline unsympathetic—recalls Griffin Dunne in Scorsese's underrated *After Hours*, and Mamet's film shares something of the same comedy-of-nightmare flavour. The plot meshes Mamet's relish for scams and conmen (the title derives from a classic con) with his perennial concerns with loyalty, betrayal and deceit. As the trap closes and the components of the intricate scam lock together around him, Joe finds himself transported to a paranoid world (subtly distorted by Gabriel Beristain's camera) where no appearances can be trusted and everyone looks suspicious (in both senses of the phrase). A janitor fixes Joe with a beady stare, a cop strolls casually towards him; Mamet teases us to guess whether these peripheral figures are in on the plot, or are merely potential witnesses to the hero's guilt.

Graham Greene used to divide his books into "novels" and "entertainments". Mamet seems to make a similar distinction between his plays and his films. With the exception of *Oleanna*, adapted from his own stage work, all his films as director have adopted this look-no-hands style: ingenious, labyrinthine artefacts, pulling back from emotional engagement under cover of accomplished black humour. Mamet the director has yet to give us anything as moving, or as penetrating, as Mamet the playwright. But it would be churlish to disparage any of his films on these grounds, least of all *The Spanish Prisoner*, as satisfyingly convoluted a thriller as any since *The Usual Suspects*.

TIME, 4/6/98, p. 72, Richard Corliss

You are a decent sort—ambitious, a bit rigid and guarded, perhaps not the most likable person around, but smart and honest. The stakes are high in your career; pleasures are morphing into pressures. Then you have what seems like an innocuous conversation, and things change. Someone is playing tricks on you, making your life hell. You are the victim of a long con. Hey, it's only business. The American way.

You are the hero of a David Mamet movie, of *House of Games, Homicide, Oleana* or his newest, finest shell game, *The Spanish Prisoner*. In this diamond-hard, ice-cold thriller, young Joe Ross (Campbell Scott) has developed a secret "process" worth billions to his company, whose chief (Ben Gazzara) is slow to give Joe credit and quick to worry about someone stealing the process. In the company Joe has an ally (Ricky Jay) and a No. 1 fan, a perkily sarcastic secretary (Rebecca Pidgeon). But Joe is tempted to confide in Jimmy Dell (Steve Martin), a mysterious fellow with a wise warning: "Always do business as if the person you're doing business with is trying to screw you. Because most likely they are. And if they're not, you can be pleasantly surprised."

Joe will not be pleasantly surprised. To protect himself and the process, he'll be grilled, chased and pretty much treated like another Joseph, in Kafka's *The Trial* (original German title: *Der Prozess*). But don't let the pedigree fool you. *The Spanish Prisoner* is exemplary entertainment. Come expecting a dour jeremiad on man's corruptibility—or even a slice-of-life drama like Mamet's *American Buffalo* or *Glengarry Glen Ross*—and you'll be pleasantly surprised. The villains in *The Spanish Prisoner* (like the war-games con men in Mamet's *Wag the Dog* script) dress well, speak softly and carry a silver stiletto. They kill for sport.

With something of the same method and intent, Mamet writes about Hollywood. His plays, films and essays contain many scalding observations on mainstream filmmaking. Yet from 1981's *The Postman Always Rings Twice* through *The Verdict, The Untouchables, Hoffa* and *The Edge*, Mamet has written solid, burly movies for top producers and stars while pursuing a parallel career with the modestly budgeted films he writes and directs himself. "I'm really fortunate," he says. "I have some good friends and supporters in Hollywood." And he knows that part of his job as a filmmaker is "shaking money out of those suits on the other side of the table. It's a natural antipathy between the suits and the talent, for want of a better word. That's just the way the world is."

Mamet's fictive world was distinctive from the get-go. His plays, beginning with the 1974 *Sexual Perversity in Chicago,* wrapped Pinteresque menace in comically precise diction, like a gamier Damon Runyon. It was Jewish guys talking like Italian guys about life, death and, always, a poignant memory of the perfect woman, long ago or never. ("Bobby," says the dying cop in Homicide, "you remember that girl that time?") But at 50, Mamet has other concerns. The overtly serious work tends to be about Jewishness (in his play *The Old Neighborhood* and novel *The Old Religion*); the nastily comic, about man's love of the scam (the card-shark show *Ricky Jay & His 52 Assistants*, recently off-Broadway, and this spiffy new film).

At 1 hour 50 minutes, *The Spanish Prisoner* clocks in as one of Mamet's longest works. Yet there are ellipses aplenty, in plot and dialogue, to tantalize and mystify the viewer. "I'm always trying to keep it spare," Mamet says. "Trudy Ship, the editor on my first films, said in editing, 'You start with a scalpel, and you end with a chainsaw.'I think that's true of writing too. For me the real division between a serious writer and an unserious one is whether they're willing to cut."

A Mamet shoot isn't solemn. "There's a great atmosphere on the set," says Martin, whom Mamet wanted to work with ever since seeing him in a 1988 revival of *Waiting for Godot,* and who seamlessly joins such Mamet familiars as Pidgeon (the author's wife) and Jay. "You can make a great movie having fun as easily as you can make a great movie having angst." Mamet loves devising practical jokes, keeping the actors loose, writing gags just for the joy of it. He's written 20 or so plays, five original screenplays he's directed, seven scripts for hire, two novels, four children's books and a load of collected essays. Whatever the word is for the opposite of a writer's block—writerrhea?—Mamet has it.

Ask him why he works so hard, and he cites Noël Coward: "Work is more fun than fun." Or, as con artiste Joe Mantegna says in *House of Games,* "What's more fun than human nature?" Like all those purring predators in The *Spanish Prisoner,* David Mamet devotes much of his working life to nothing more or less complicated than playing artful games. On you.

VILLAGE VOICE, 4/7/98, p. 68, Amy Taubin

David Mamet's *The Spanish Prisoner* plays like a film student's attempt to cross Hitchcock's impeccable *North by Northwest* with Brian Singer's crass but catchy *The Usual Suspects.* Mamet's basic strategy is to underline the clues so heavily that you can't help second-guessing yourself. Does Rebecca Pidgeon, playing a self-deprecating but eager secretary, seem too much like Eve Harrington to actually be a two-faced liar? Does Steve Martin, playing a billionaire entrepreneur, seem too much like a con artist to actually be a con artist? And if the headquarters of this billionaire look like a fly-by-night midtown import-export operation, is that because this is a low-budget film and they couldn't afford posh locations or because... and so forth, ad infinitum.

Pidgeon can't act, Martin can, but in any case they're less important than Campbell Scott, who's a wash as the utterly passive hopelessly dense protagonist, the inventor of a formula for something or other so ahead of its time that everyone wants to steal it. The dollar value of this "great whatsit" is so awesome that it can only be written in the off-screen space. I guess this is Mamet's version of a sight gag; it also satisfies his penchant for withholding information. He makes another ham-fisted joke of the classic Hitchcock strategy whereby the viewer, who's been exactly in sync with what the protagonist knows for most of the film, suddenly gets one step ahead of him. But since this isn't a character with whom you're meant to identify, there's no anxiety generated by the fact that you know he's walking into a trap.

The Spanish Prisoner isn't more labored or smug than Mamet's previous films, but it's no improvement either. The only moment I enjoyed was when Ben Gazzara, playing a sleazy CEO, greets a pair of hookers with an unctuous "Hello, girls." He sounded just like he did in Cassavetes's *The Killing of a Chinese Bookie.* Now that was a movie.

Also reviewed in:
NATION, 4/27/98, p. 35, Stuart Klawans
NEW REPUBLIC, 4/27/98, p. 26, Stanley Kauffmann
NEW YORK TIMES, 4/3/98, p. E16, Janet Maslin
NEW YORKER, 4/13/98, p. 107, Anthony Lane
VARIETY, 9/15-21/97, p. 70, Leonard Klady
WASHINGTON POST, 4/24/98, p. B5, Stephen Hunter
WASHINGTON POST, 4/24/98, Weekend/p. 57, Michael O'Sullivan

SPECIES II

Metro Goldwyn Meyer release of an FGM Entertainment Production of a Peter Medak film. *Executive Producer:* Dennis Feldman. *Producer:* Frank Mancuso, Jr. *Director:* Peter Medak. *Screenplay:* Chris Brancato. *Based on characters created by:* Dennis Feldman. *Editor:* Richard

Nord. *Music:* Edward Shearmur. *Music Editor:* Danny Garde.   *Sound:* Steve Nelson and (music) Robert Fernandez.   *Sound Editor:* Gregory M. Gerlich.   *Casting:* Amanda Mackey Johnson and Cathy Sandrich.   *Production Designer:* Miljen Kreka Kljakovic.   *Art Director:* Mark Zuelzke.   *Set Designer:* James Clator, Gerald Sullivan, Maria Baker, and Colin de Rouin. *Set Decorator:* Suzette Sheets.   *Set Dresser:* Liz Weber, Albert Ford, Jr., Eric Lichtfuss, Steve Shifflette, and Thomas Hicks, Jr.   *Special Effects:* Jeff Jarvis.   *Costumes:* Richard Bruno. *Make-up:* Perri Sorel.   *Creatures and Special Makeup Effects:* Steve Johnson. *Stunt Coordinator:* David M. Barrett.   *Running time:* 95 minutes.   *MPAA Rating:* R.

CAST: Michael Madsen (Press Lennox);   Natasha Henstridge (Eve);   Marg Helgenberger (Dr. Laura Baker);   Mykelti Williamson (Dennis Gamble);   George Dzundza (Colonel Carter Burgess, Jr.);   James Cromwell (Senator Ross);   Justin Lazard (Patrick Ross);   Myriam Cyr (Anne Sampas);   Sarah Wynter (Melissa);   Baxter Harris (Dr. Orinsky);   Scott Morgan (Harry Sampas); Nancy La Scala (Debutante);   Raquel Gardner (Debutante's Sister);   Henderson Forsythe, Robert Hogan, and Ted Sutton (Pentagon Personnel);   Gwen Briley-Strand, Valerie Karasek, and Jane Beard (Biologists);   Nancy Young (Tether Console Guard);   Beau James (Administrator);   Tracy Metro (Prostitute);   Irv Ziff (Seedy Motel Clerk);   Melanie Pearson (Hooker);   Felicia Deel (Stripper);   Norman Aronovic (Medical Examiner);   Kim Adams (Darlene);   Dustin Turner (Kid at Supermarket);   Susan Duvall (Woman Shopper);   Andreas Kraemer (Male Teenager);   Lauren Ziemski (Female Teenager);   Donna Sacco (Woman in Crowd);   Sondra Williamson (Woman with Gamble);   Kevin Grantz (Federal Agent);   Zité Bidanie (Press Assistant);   Nat Benchley (Squad Leader);   Mike Gartland (Cobra Pilot);   John C. Pratt, John T. Scanlon, and Herbert R. Schutt, Jr. (Pilots);   Evelyn Ebo (Gorgeous Nurse);   Bill Boggs (Himself);   Richard Belzer (U.S. President);   Alesia Newman-Breen (News Announcer).

LOS ANGELES TIMES, 4/13/98, Calendar/p. 5, John Anderson

[The following review by John Anderson appeared in a slightly different form in NEWSDAY, 4/13/98, Part II/p. B9.]

So much carnage, so much waste, so many stomach-turning examples of inhumanity to man—and that's just the acting and the careers being turned to French-fried guacamole in "Species II," a horror film that shows how little you can do with an unlimited supply of brown gelatin, lo mein and some space-age weaponry that seems to have been fashioned out of $19 hibachi sets.

But that's not the fault of the actors. No, they're indictable on myriad other charges. Marg Helgenberger, Mykelti Williamson, Michael Madsen, Teutonic love goddess Natasha Henstridge and George Dzundza (all but bursting out of his army uniform)—you can just imagine them jockeying for top billing: "I don't want it! No, please, you take it!" Then there's Peter Boyle, who's shown twice in an insane asylum, raving about how he told them not to go to Mars! Then we never see him again. Maybe he got better.

"Species II" takes no prisoners, and gives no joy, not even the ambiguous amusement of watching a film made by people who know how bad their movie is. If only we'd felt somehow that you knew it was bogus when the Mars mission crew returned and, infected with space slime, began having sex with earthlings and reproducing aliens, and Eve (Henstridge), the reconstituted space Valkyrie, began to get hysterical about mating with a fellow space creature, and the military guy (Dzundza) started fouling things up, and Dr. Laura (Helgenberger) started saying: "This is awful. This is awful." If only there'd been a sign, a gesture that said you were sharing our pain. But no.

Director Peter Medak, in recycling the original's tale of a lethal alien in curvaceous female form, has adopted an interesting tack: Bore the audience to such an extent that when one of those snakey, slimy, blood-burping space atrocities pops out of a character's womb, you're completely caught off guard. It's a cheap tactic, but given the tactical advantage, it's the kind of thing that could catch on.

In some ways, "Species II" is the perfect cheap date movie (and if an ad saying that appears somewhere with my name attached, I'm suing): The creepiness will keep you close, the sex scenes are rampant and the bodies beautiful (until they burst open), and there's no chance anyone's going to want to dine out when it's over. In fact, the best advice to give anyone who wants to see "Species II"—other than "don't go!"—is "don't eat!"

NEW YORK POST, 4/11/98, p. 21, Larry Worth

Forty minutes into "Species II," one character asks, "What do you think this is, the f---ing X-Files?"' In a word, no. That would have required an iota of creativity, acting talent and suspense, all of which is sorely lacking from this special-effects-laden idiocy.

The 1995 original, detailing the creation of a gorgeous half-alien centerfold who sprouts tentacles at will, was no work of art. But it's a masterpiece compared to this utterly predictable, blood and slime-filled fiasco.

The tale kicks off after the monstrous mutant from part one has been recycled in a laboratory from frozen egg embryos. When a U.S. spaceship returns from Mars bearing mutant ooze and a newly infected pilot, the otherworldly Adam and Eve feel the call of the wild, and the need to make Alien Jr.

But the scientists who survived the earlier catastrophe have other ideas. Too bad none of them are even vaguely interesting.

Director Peter Medak, whose career has ranged from the ridiculous ("Pontiac Moon," "Zorro, the Gay Blade") to the sublime ("The Krays," "The Ruling Class,") has returned to the former. Even while paying homage to David Cronenberg's "The Brood," he confuses gore with horror and features way too many eyeball closeups. Heck, it could double as a training film for ophthalmologists.

Accordingly, the chief assets here are hulking skeletal creatures and a series of spaceship miniatures. They're certainly competent, though a bit familiar.

Then there's the less-than-stellar cast, led by anti-hero Justin Lazard. Hunky? Yes, even with scales. Talented? That's another matter. And how,to explain the participation of Oscar nominee James Cromwell as Martian boy's dad, or, Peter Boyle as a modern-day Renfield?

Those back from the first "Species" include Natasha Henstridge, again playing beauty and the beast. But this time around, her chief claims to fame are generally covered by strategically placed straps or matronly frocks. As for Marg Helgenberger and Michael Madsen's overly earnest extraterrestrial busters, they can spray bug juice and scream for backup with total conviction.

Helgenberger may even be winking at the audience. When her endangered character at one point states "This is awful, just awful," she doesn't seem to be referencing the dilemma at hand.

SIGHT AND SOUND, 9/98, p. 53, Philip Strick

Patrick Ross returns from Mars with fellow astronauts Sampas and Gamble unknowingly carrying a deadly alien DNA. At a government research laboratory, the same DNA has been used by Doctor Laura Baker to construct Eve, a part-alien being. (Her first incarnation Sil was destroyed.) Eve is being used for tests ordered by Colonel Burgess, who realises, following a series of killings, that another alien is at large, and reunites Laura with security gunman Press Lennox to track it down. The killings, which produce instant 'children', have been perpetrated by Patrick who, concerned about his blackouts, tries to warn his dismissive father, Senator Ross.

Recognising the astronauts as the source of the violence, Laura and Press intervene just as an alien emerges from Sampas. They destroy it but find that Gamble is uninfected because he carries a blood disease. On Burgess' orders, Laura stimulates Eve's alien components, giving her enough telepathic contact with Patrick to tell them where he is. Captured, Patrick meets Eve but escapes again, murders the Senator and retreats to a remote country hideout where his now numerous children are making cocoons. Eve burst from the laboratory and follows him. As the two creatures embrace, she has just enough humanity left to kill him, but dies in the struggle. Laura and Press destroy the cocoons and poison the alien with Gamble's blood—but as Eve's body is carried away a surviving child is in attendance.

An ungainly hybrid, *Species II* represents the fusion of four main influences. The most vital, not surprisingly, is that of the original *Species*, which melded the supermodel looks of Natasha Henstridge with the erotic armour designs of H.R. Giger to highly profitable effect. The adventures that formed this first outing, while blatantly derivative, have been closely paraphrased here: once again a beautiful half-alien girl is subjected to near-lethal experiments in a laboratory cage, bursts through impenetrable glass, and rushes to a climactic assignation, once again trailing a disparate crew of unlikely experts. The main variation on this theme is the introduction of a male half-alien. Limitless impregnation is now his obsessions instead of hers, and the girl—despite her alien skills—has become an ally instead of a threat.

Its shock potential usefully enhanced in this way, *Species II* is a carnival of the absurdly gruesome from its initial countdown, as a gob of alien slime advances on the astronauts, to the bizarre final battle. Evolving persuasively from their work on *Species*, Steve Johnson's effects team create a gleeful gallery of writhing flesh, intrusive tentacles and exploding stomachs, transcended by the suicide sequence in which a head destroyed by a shotgun blast reconstructs itself as the camera revolves around it in fascination. More intriguing is the extraordinary spectacle of a child being hauled aloft by a glutinous strand which sprouts from its nose and leaps for the ceiling. Bogeys and chrysalises, while nothing new in alien infestation fantasies, are seldom presented with such panache.

Visuals apart, the film's deadening array of clichés has to be blamed on its writer Chris Brancato who, although never short of ideas, seems to have run out of fresh words to express them. Struggling heroically with his script, the cast resorts to mockery (Michael Madsen, even more shambling than usual), exaggeration (James Cromwell, daftly overplaying the role of bullying parent), or inertia (Marg Helgenberger, whose muttered "this is awful" evidently comes from the heart). Replacing the Kingsley character from *Species*, George Dzundza impersonates a foul-mouthed wall-eyed authoritarian with such vigour that no risk remains of the proceedings being taken seriously. Which is a pity, as Brancato—the former script consultant to television's *The Outer Limits* and creator of the next alien invasion series *First Wave*—seems intent on serious exploration of alien influence and genetic engineering and will clearly be with us for some time.

Already well seasoned (although, with the exception of some *Twilight Zones*, in entirely different genres), Peter Medak directs with a relaxed professionalism, content to let the effects team show off. The Mars landing is tackled with pleasing if neutral assurance, and later abominations like the brothel motel or the astronauts' exchanges with the Senator are brisk and pragmatic. What may have drawn Medak to the project is its chilling undertow, in which a generation of emotionally damaged children (echoing Medak's previous films *The Krays* and *Let Him Have It*) heads for self-determination bolstered by the loyalty of confused parents. Almost despite itself, *Species II* is full of family ties, measured in characteristic Medak fashion by constant self-questioning and comparison: scene after scene consists of displays, examinations and witnesses. At least there's plenty to look at, if not, sadly, much to think about.

Also reviewed in:
CHICAGO TRIBUNE, 4/15/98, Tempo, p. 2, John Petrakis
NEW YORK TIMES, 4/11/98, p. B13, Lawrence Van Gelder
VARIETY, 4/10-26/98, p. 44, Joe Leydon

SPHERE

A Warner Bros. release of a Baltimore Pictures/Constant c production in association with Punch Productions, Inc. *Executive Producer:* Peter Giuliano. *Producer:* Barry Levinson, Michael Crichton, and Andrew Wald. *Director:* Barry Levinson. *Screenplay:* Stephen Hauser and Paul Attanasio. *Based on the novel by:* Michael Crichton. *Adaptation by:* Kurt Wimmer. *Director of Photography:* Adam Greenberg. *Editor:* Stu Linder. *Music:* Elliot Goldenthal. *Music Editor:* Curtis Roush. *Sound:* Steve Cantamessa. *Sound Editor:* Tim Holland. *Casting:* Ellen Chenoweth. *Production Designer:* Norman Reynolds. *Art Director:* Mark Mansbridge and Jonathan McKinstry. *Set Designer:* Geoff Hubbard. *Set Decorator:* Anne Kuljian. *Special Effects:* Ken Pepiot. *Visual Effects:* Jeffrey A. Okun. *Costumes:* Gloria Gresham. *Make-up:* Allan Apone. *Stunt Coordinator:* Ronnie Rondell. *Running time:* 120 minutes. *MPAA Rating:* PG-13.

CAST: Dustin Hoffman (Dr. Norman Goodman); Sharon Stone (Dr. Beth Halperin); Samuel L. Jackson (Harry Adams); Peter Coyote (Harold C. Barnes); Queen Latifa (Fletcher); Liev Schreiber (Dr. Ted Fielding); Marga Gomez (Jane Edmunds); Huey Lewis (Helicopter Pilot); Bernard Hocke (Seaman); James Pickens, Jr. (OSSA Instructor); Michael Keys Hall and Ralph Tabakin (OSSA Officials).

LOS ANGELES TIMES, 2/13/98, Calendar/p. 1, Kenneth Turan

Science-fiction thrillers are like children with a secret: They want to hold off revealing what they know for as long as possible. With "Sphere," that reticence has a reason: The more the movie explains itself, the more ordinary it becomes.

As the umpteenth entrant in the We-Are-Not-Alone sweepstakes, "Sphere" feels awfully familiar because it is. The notion of encountering alien civilizations was most recently done in "Contact," using the ocean floor as a staging area is straight out of "The Abyss," and even the film's key plot device is yet another reworking of a scenario that 1956's "Forbidden Planet" pioneered.

Trying to make things fresh, or at least comprehensible, "Sphere" made use of four writers, including Michael Crichton (who wrote the original novel), adapter Kurt Wimmer and screenwriters Stephen Hauser and Paul Attanasio. Yet the final result still comes off as standard 1950s silliness with an expensive pedigree, where high-caliber actors Dustin Hoffman, Sharon Stone and Samuel L. Jackson make the best of lines like "I don't get it," "I don't know what's going on here" and the always popular "Oh my God."

A key element in that pedigree, and part of what attracted the actors, is the presence of director Barry Levinson, currently enjoying deserved success with the more casual "Wag the Dog." Though he's done glossy commercial films before (including the Demi Moore-Michael Douglas version of Crichton's "Disclosure"), Levinson's gift is for the personal and conversational, and having him as the director of this kind of thriller is not always a blessing.

"Sphere" starts with the notion that something big and mysterious is happening in the middle of nowhere, more specifically a miles-from-civilization spot in the Pacific. Once psychologist Norman Goodman (Hoffman) arrives on site, he's greeted by a government operative named Barnes (Peter Coyote) and exposed to a number of surprises.

First, he turns out to know the three other celebrated scientists who have also been helicoptered in, including biochemist (and possible old flame) Beth Halperin (Stone), mathematician Harry Adams (Jackson) and astrophysicist Ted Fielding (Liev Schreiber.)

The other surprise is that everyone is here because Goodman, largely as a lark if the script is to be believed, wrote a government paper years ago recommending the group be assembled as a welcome wagon should an alien encounter become a possibility. That time, Barnes says, has arrived.

Submerged deep under the ocean sits an impressive space vehicle with a fuselage half a mile long. Even more intriguing, the ship is covered with close to 300 years worth of coral. How did it get there, what's it been doing underwater for so long, what if anything remains alive inside: that's what our nonplused quartet has to find out from its base in an undersea habitat.

Given this film's title, it will surprise no one that lurking inside the ship is an enormous round object that all but glows in the dark. What it is and what it does are the central "Sphere" mysteries, and those questions are some of the many that, as noted, this film is more inventive at posing than at answering.

It's not just that the puzzle remains to be solved that makes the early parts of "Sphere" more involving. Because Levinson is a director who understands and cares about language, the film's initial exposition is more literate and better acted than usual, with Hoffman and Jackson performing at their standard expert levels and Stone giving one of her better, most restrained performances.

But the creation of tension and suspense, both genre staples even in a psychological thriller, are not the kinds of things that Levinson does really well, and as tempers fray and strange things start to happen underwater, we don't feel the kind of merciless whipsawing that, for instance, Ridley Scott and James Cameron brought to the first two "Alien" films.

The core problem with "Sphere," however, is that despite (or perhaps because of) employing four writers, the script is muddled and unsatisfying, as ponderous on its feet as its protagonists are in their heavy diving suits. If it's true that, as a scientist says about that large sphere, "Perfection is a powerful message," it's one that this film is not in the business of sending.

NEW STATESMAN, 3/20/98, p. 48, Jonathan Freedland

After Dolly the sheep, who needs science fiction? In a world where people can communicate with anyone on the planet within seconds, what's the point of Isaac Asimov? Now that there's water on the moon, and serious talk of a space-station-cum-staging-post for interplanetary flight, why watch *Star Trek*?

Science fact keeps outstripping science fiction. The New York professor Michio Kaku predicts that within 20 years we will talk to our tie clips, surf the net via our spectacles and manipulate our genes as easily as we change socks—unless, that is, we're hit by an asteroid before then. With all that going on, perhaps there's not an awful lot left for the boys in sci-fi to make up.

At first glance *Sphere* seems to belong to the old rockets-and-aliens school. It's based on a novel by Michael Crichton, the futurologist who has always been more comfy with sci than fi. The strength of *Jurassic Park* was the conceit—cloning a dinosaur from a speck of dino DNA, pecked by an historic mosquito and preserved in amber—rather than the characters. *Disclosure* was sold as a hip drama about sexual harassment but the real stars were the computer gizmos. Crichton and his director Barry Levinson even made backing up a text-file look glamorous.

But if *Disclosure* was sci-fi disguised as psychological drama, *Sphere* is the reverse. Officially it's about a team of scientists plumbing the depths of the Pacific Ocean to inspect a spaceship which has lain undisturbed on the sea bed for nearly 300 years. They root around, discover a massive golden orb—the Sphere—poke it a little and endure a terrible sequence of events as a result: alien intelligence, scary sea creatures, maniacally "possessed" computers and only seconds to go before a huge explosion.

But, like the Sphere, *Sphere* is not all it seems on the surface. Dustin Hoffman is not the usual action hero—he is a psychologist. His inclusion in the team amuses his fellow crew member Samuel L Jackson: "Is that what the little green men say these days, 'Take me to your therapist'?"

Later, when they are cooped up in the sub-aqua "habitat" where most of the movie takes place, Hoffman counsels Jackson: "This is my first underwater session."

Time travel, black holes and the possibility of extraterrestrial life are all there, but they are secondary to what goes on inside the heads of Hoffman, Jackson and the crop-topped Sharon Stone. This mind-not-matter notion is *Sphere*'s central idea, and it gives an extraordinary twist to the film which I won't give away.

Still, this is not a perfect sphere. As in *Disclosure*, the characters are developed no further than the plot requires. The barbed exchanges between Hoffman and Stone—dating back to another kind of couch involvement—give off no crackle of chemistry, let alone marine biology. Many will find Hoffman incredible as an action hero: he looks ridiculous in insulated-suit-and-helmet gear (a reminder of that favourite 1970s toy for boys called Little Big Man).

Not for the first time, the excellent Samuel L Jackson is underused. He gets to crack the odd sceptical one-liner, but few that are actually funny. It's worth remembering that Jackson was nominated as best supporting actor for his performance in *Pulp Fiction,* even though he uttered as many lines as John Travolta, who was placed in the best actor category. It might be that kind of Hollywood racism that prompts moviemakers to cast Jackson as a black clown—just the niche African American actors used to occupy in the pre-enlightenment days. If so, director Barry Levinson has wasted Jackson's talent.

B-movie music on the soundtrack, some clunky dialogue—"It's just another blind alley in the maze of our minds"—and a couple of plot gaps threaten to drag *Sphere* down. Which is a pity. Turning a fine idea and some old pros into a good movie should have been simple enough—after all, this ain't rocket science.

NEW YORK, 3/2/98, p. 50, David Denby

At the end of *Sphere*, the three principals—Dustin Hoffman, Samuel L. Jackson, and Sharon Stone—agree, for the good of humanity, to forget everything that has happened to them in the movie up to that point. This is a pact I can only rush to join, and with exactly the same motive. There are some things that humankind is just better off not knowing about.

NEW YORK POST, 2/13/98, p. 45, Michael Medved

Despite significant shortcomings, sci-fi fans will have a ball with "Sphere." The spiffy thriller from director Barry Levinson deploys an A-team cast and special effects that solidly serve the story without ever threatening to overwhelm it.

Peter Coyote plays the no-nonsense head of a super-secret governmental team assigned to investigate a massive, mysterious spaceship that's been located at ocean bottom in a remote stretch of the Pacific.

Initial reports suggest that the huge machine crashed nearly 300 years ago, yet some form of life within the craft seems to have survived.

To make contact, Coyote recruits an elite team including psychologist Dustin Hoffman (who supposedly wrote a long-forgotten government report on alien encounters), nervous astrophysicist Liev Schreiber, world renowned mathematician Samuel L. Jackson and brilliant biochemist Sharon Stone.

In an unnecessary soap opera twist, Stone shared an affair 10 years before with her married therapist, Hoffman, and still burns with resentment over his selfish behavior.

Stone alone seems uncomfortable in her role, projecting her character's severe psychological problems far more convincingly than her towering intellect and technological competence.

Nevertheless, her presence contributes to an unusually rich and complex treatment of the interaction of the various characters, trapped together in an undersea habitat as they investigate the spacecraft.

No responsible reviewer should ruin the script's many diabolical surprises, but despite a few chilling attacks by killer jellyfish and even a giant squid the main source of terror remains subtle and psychological.

The carefully calibrated pacing and gradually unfolding mysteries provide far more thrills, and provoke much deeper speculation, than last year's stodgy and pseudo-intellectual alien epic "Contact."

Unfortunately, even this smart script (co-written by Paul Attanasio of "Quiz Show" and "Donnie Brasco" fame) ultimately resorts to brain-dead action film cliches ...including heaven help, the climactic unstoppable explosion set to detonate in just a few seconds, 10-9-8-7-6 ... !!!

The circular plot and unsatisfying resolution also fail to answer any number of crucial and intriguing questions posed earlier in the story.

Still and all, the shocks and tension that Levinson expertly provides in the movie's crowded core will pump adrenaline through even the most skeptical moviegoers.

Released just a few weeks aft the Levinson-Hoffman collaboration on "Wag the Dog," this totally different but no less impressive venture demonstrates not only the old friends' thoroughgoing professionalism but their truly dazzling versatility.

NEWSDAY, 2/13/98, Part II/p. B2, Jack Mathews

You have to admire a movie that apologizes for its preposterousness right at the start, and Barry Levinson's "Sphere" has much for which to apologize. Adapted from one of Michael Crichton's more feverishly implausible sci-fi novels, "Sphere" manages to evoke visual comparisons to both "Alien" and "The Abyss" while rivaling Ed Wood's "Plan 9 From Outer Space" for sheer silliness.

The apology for this impending disaster is provided by Dustin Hoffman's Dr. Norman Goodman, a psychologist summoned by the government to a spot near Guam where a gigantic spacecraft has been found resting at the bottom of the Pacific Ocean. From the layers of coral grown over its body, the craft has been there for about three centuries, yet something inside is still alive.

This calls for a team of specialists: a mathematician (Samuel L. Jackson) to figure out how to communicate with whatever's in there (if we don't know anything else about aliens, movies have taught us that they're good at math); a biochemist (Sharon Stone) to tell us what they're made of; an astrophysicist (Liev Schreiber) to tell us where they came from, and a psychologist to overcome any deep-seated hostilities they may have.

None of the specialists has been previously briefed on the scope of the mission, and none has any training in deep-sea diving. Yet, here they are, descending one mile to an underwater space station set up next to the craft, preparing to knock on the door and see if anything's home.

Even the characters see this as an asinine plot, so the psychologist quickly offers an explanation/apology. Seems that years earlier, Norman had been asked to submit a report to the space agency, detailing how to handle an encounter with alien life, and he'd thrown in the others' names because he knew them. He was then having an adulterous affair with Stone's biochemist (she's still upset about it), the astrophysicist was a former student, and the mathematician was a colleague.

Norman didn't think the report would actually be *used*. It was one of those academic fleecing of America deals; he wrote it for the $35,000 fee, which made the down payment on his house! Your tax dollars at work.

This would have been a nice place to turn "Sphere" into a "Spaceballs"-styled spoof. Instead, it assumes Norman's explanation has gone down, and plunges into the realm of sci-fi thriller. Yes, there is something alive in that space ship, a mysterious, levitating sphere, with a quivering gold surface that reflects the images of everything except the visitors' getting dangerously close to it. Whatever secrets the sphere houses—the meaning of life, the source of evil, tips to getting tickets to the "David Letterman Show"—horrible things begin to happen.

The habitat is being attacked by a giant squid right out of H.G. Wells' "20,000 Leagues Under the Sea," a book that is having strange effects on Jackson's mathematician. Crew members are being attacked by swarms of clammy jelly fish, cloudbursts of plasmic eggs, and angry sea snakes. The alien, speaking through a computer, is threatening to kill them all, and the specialists, whose dreams are suddenly manifesting themselves in reality, are beginning to suspect each other. All "Sphere" needs to complete the cliché is a last-act race against time, and it has one.

How this script attracted Hoffman is a bigger mystery than the sphere itself. As he proved with "Outbreak," Hoffman is no-action star, and he has scenes here—notably, one where he's seen flailing and screaming in a puddle of snakes—that you don't expect serious actors to attempt. The others in the cast, which includes Peter Coyote as the expedition leader, do their best, but merely end up demonstrating that with material bad enough, anyone can appear to be an amateur.

Otherwise...well, "Sphere" looks good. Production designer Norman Reynolds, whose credits include the "Star Wars" trilogy, and cinematographer Adam Greenberg ("Terminator 2") are used to creating large-scale illusions, and they have at least given this calamity a convincing environment.

SIGHT AND SOUND, 4/98, p. 53, Philip Strick

Summoned by the US Navy to the middle of the Pacific, psychologist Norman Goodman learns that a mysterious spaceship has been discovered on the ocean floor, where it has rested for some 300 years. Under the command of Captain Barnes, Norman is teamed with mathematician Harry Adams, astrophysicist Ted Fielding, and biochemist Beth Halperin, once Norman's lover. They occupy a deep-water habitat beside the craft, and ascertain that it's an American space probe which, after entering a black hole, was flung back in time. It contains an alien artefact, a huge metallic sphere.

Harry vanishes into the sphere and reappears later with no clear account of his experience. Navy staff member Fletcher is killed by a shoal of jellyfish, and another, Edmunds, is ripped apart by unknown creatures, while patterns of numbers suddenly fill the habitat's monitor screens. Harry deciphers them and the team finds itself in communication with an entity called "Jerry". Seemingly eager to entertain them, Jerry subjects the habitat to an attack from a giant squid: only Norman, Beth and Harry survive. Norman deduces that Jerry is in fact Harry, whose fears and nightmares are being converted into reality by the power of the sphere.

Norman and Beth drug Harry, but when Norman is attacked by sea-snakes he realises that he and Beth have also been inside and affected the sphere. Beth primes explosives to destroy both the habitat and spacecraft, and the trio escape. As they use their collective power to erase all memory of what has occurred, the sphere returns to the black hole.

An illusion of rational order and control is provided by the 'chapter' headings—"The First Exchange", "Battle Stations", "Further Analysis", and so on—that punctuate *Sphere*. Originally from Michael Crichton's novel, they offer breathing space between crises as well as stimulating anticipation. At first an irritating mannerism, they actually provide an ironic ambiguity, lending the whole event the authority of an official report, neatly summarised. In fact, each chapter merely builds to a fresh cliff-hanger (Crichton's habitual structural device). The best part of the joke with *Sphere* is that no report is finally made at all, that instead it has, like a *Mission Impossible* communication, destroyed itself. Floating like discarded markerbuoys above uncharted depths, the intertitles falsely reassure us that we have a clue about what's really going on.

Like the book, *Sphere* launches itself headlong into a familiar curiosity: the discovery of an alien craft promising a hoard of answers to everything from interstellar travel to the meaning of life. Both story and images offer the usual circle (the frozen saucer in *The Thing from Another World*, the geodesic globe in *It Came from Outer Space*, the shadow over Manhattan in *Independence Day*) and because true aliens are by their very nature unimaginable it completes an ideological circuit by reflecting back on its would-be explorers before retreating whence it came. Duplicating the theme of *Contact*, *Sphere* puts itself in the 'mankind is not yet ready' department.

Having already tried out most other genres, Barry Levinson turns at last to science fiction. His contribution, accomplished with the same apparent spontaneity he brings to his *Homicide* television series, is both fresh and oddly uncomfortable. Small armies of stalwart specialists have advanced into the oceanic unknown since Captain Nemo, cherishable in such far-apart ventures as *The Atomic Submarine* (1959) and *The Abyss* (1989). But the leading trio in *Sphere* convert this instantly into a voyage of obsessives, adrift in their own humours. When Norman Goodman admits that the team has been assembled from pure fantasy, based on his eagerness for some ready cash, we are recognisably in the company of Levinson's *Tin Men* or *Bugsy*, where if any dreams come true, they are reliably the wrong ones. Bumbling incredulity actually suits Hoffman so well that by contrast Sharon Stone has a disastrous first half, eyes popping and mouth ajar with comments like, "This is great, you guys! Wow!" The role belatedly acquires a tentacular menace but never quite matches up to the haunted zoologist of Crichton's original.

On film, where despite accumulated bruises everyone still looks much the same from start to finish, shifts of personality are less clearly conveyed. In *Sphere*, the actors seem to lose their way. All the same, Samuel L. Jackson's character prompts the film's best scene when his compulsive study of *20,000 Leagues Under the Sea* results in a sudden influx of copies of the novel, all ending with the giant squid episode.

Sadly, Levinson confines the squid itself to a radar-screen green mass, but then he evidently sees his show (in parallel to his *Wag the Dog)* not as a fable about reality but as a circus of manipulated absurdities, with Hoffman once again as the ringmaster. While not exactly the best thing since *Forbidden Planet* (1956) or *Solaris* (1972), those classics of the released subconscious, the result is witty, frustrating, and packed with possibilities.

TIME, 2/23/98, p. 88, Richard Schickel

What in the world is Barry Levinson, the gritty realist of *Diner* and *Tin Men*, doing down, down, down at the bottom of the sea?

Well, as he was in the delicious *Wag the Dog*, the director is looking for a new venue in which to display the thing he loves best—rough, funny dialogue that reveals the morally equivocal motives of highly dubious dreamers. And for a few minutes at the beginning of *Sphere*, which is about the exploration of a spacecraft that has been discovered resting on the bottom of the Pacific Ocean, you think he may be on to something.

For the scientific team assembled by writers Stephen Hauser and Paul Attanasio, adapting an old Michael Crichton novel, is ragtag and cranky. The chief credential of its psychologist (Dustin Hoffman) is a report on how to handle alien encounters, which he admits cribbing largely from sci-fi tales. The biochemist (Sharon Stone) is a pill popper. The mathematician (Samuel L. Jackson) is a cynic, the astrophysicist (Liev Schreiber) is twittily lusting after a Nobel Prize, and the team leader (Peter Coyote) needs to try a little tenderness. In short, the possibilities for amusing dysfunction are potentially larger than we usually find in movies of this kind.

Then, alas, they all head for a submerged "habitat" on the ocean floor, yank on their wet suits and start poking around the wreck. And the standard scare scenes start occurring on a more or less predictable schedule—leaks, explosions, monsters popping out of the dark depths—with a more or less predictable effect on the health, mental and physical, of the intruders, not to mention the quality of the dialogue, which deteriorates largely to murmured suspicions and warning shouts.

The problem turns out to be the eponymous sphere the space capsule carries. It's hard and shiny and has a mysterious power to ferret out, and then manifest, the worst fears of those who fall under its spell. If you have, say, a special aversion to sea snakes, then by golly, they're going to start hurling themselves at your face mask.

The question of the sphere's origin is left unanswered at the end of the film—along with a lot of other loose ends—but it's really no mystery. It probably came from the Forbidden Planet, a realm first explored in the classic 1956 sci-fi adventure movie. Its inhabitants had mastered the technique of invading people's minds, prying their darkest passions out of them and turning them back on their victims. Obviously Hoffman's character isn't the only figure involved with *Sphere* who has a good memory for the classic tropes of dystopian sci-fi.

But that's all right. We're in the realm of homage here, not plagiarism. What's not so good is the failure to make something arresting out of the way the dark side and the bright side of our minds interact. Movies like *Forbidden Planet,* which had neither the technical sophistication nor the skilled actors available to Levinson, worked their metaphors with a sort of leisurely literateness. Here, all meaning is simply lost in the hubbub, drowned out by the modern imperative to deliver a rush of action, however incomprehensible, every few minutes.

VILLAGE VOICE, 2/24/98, p. 122, Gary Dauphin

Drying out the pop-psychological gurgling of the Michael Crichton novel on which it's based, *Sphere* is at best pointlessly assured and at worst waterlogged, powering through the shallows of recent big-screen science fiction like a grown-up who's decided to teach the tykes in the kiddie pool exactly how this little game of Marco Polo is *played*. *Sphere* expends some intelligence on topics like first contact, time travel, and this thing you humans call "the mind," but always from a self-conscious remove, Barry Levinson and his cast never deigning to break much of a genre sweat.

Sphere starts out promisingly enough, bringing a team of academics to the underwater crash site of a 300-year-old UFO. Running counter to trend, the group is made up of many more geeks than guns, notably psychiatrist Dustin Hoffman, mathematician Samuel L. Jackson, and marine biologist Sharon Stone, The team's randomness is the psychiatrist's fault: He once wrote a bogus government report on aliens, cobbling together bits from science-fiction novels and naming friends and a former lay as potential members of the then wildly hypothetical first contact team. ("Who knew anybody read those things anyway?" Hoffman shame-facedly asks.) The team doesn't find much to contact, except, ultimately, themselves, but they do discover that the ship in question is a 21st-century American craft that's somehow traveled back in time, its crew lying dead while a giant golden ball hums away contentedly in the hold. One by one the eggheads walk up to the sphere, prompting nicely constricted cycles of psychological weirdness (their individual fears are "manifested" à la *Event Horizon/Solaris),* but the tension's inevitably doused by sodden, faux-obsessive dialogue about exactly who went into the sphere when no one except, oh, the entire audience was watching.

As alien artifacts go, the sphere is so incidental to the action you have to wonder exactly why director Levinson and screenwriter pat Paul Attanasio wanted to make a sci-fi film in the first place. *Sphere* is gifted with an appropriately dank look, solid performances by Hoffman and Jackson, and a script chock-full of neat, nattering side business straight out of TVs *Homicide*, but the film seems to be actively working against its own positives, Levinson and Attanasio crafting discrete moments of terror and visual wonder but always pulling back into neurotic cross talk as if afraid to be caught marveling at their own handiwork. Tinkering with the suspension of disbelief that makes all science fiction possible is an admirable goal, but the simple fact is that if filmmakers don't believe in their world, no one else will either.

Also reviewed in:
NEW YORK TIMES, 2/13/98, p. E18, Janet Maslin
VARIETY, 2/16-22/98, p. 56, Todd McCarthy

WASHINGTON POST, 2/13/98, p. D7, Rita Kempley
WASHINGTON POST, 2/13/98, Weekend/p. 7, Desson Howe

SPICE WORLD

A Columbia Pictures release of a Spice Girls/Fragile Films production in assocation with Icon Entertainment International and PolyGram Filmed Entertainment. *Executive Producer:* Simon Fuller. *Producer:* Uri Fruchtmann and Barnaby Thompson. *Director:* Bob Spiers. *Screenplay:* Kim Fuller. *Based on an idea by:* Kim Fuller and The Spice Girls. *Director of Photography:* Clive Tickner. *Editor:* Andrea MacArthur. *Music:* Paul Hardcastle. *Music Editor:* Tom Sayers. *Choreographer:* Priscilla Samuels. *Sound:* Colin Nicolson. *Sound Editors:* Glenn Freemantle and Max Hoskins. *Casting:* Vanessa Pereira and Simone Ireland. *Production Designer:* Grenville Horner. *Art Director:* David Walley and Colin Blaymires. *Set Decorator:* Linda Wilson. *Special Effects:* Stuart Brisdon. *Costumes:* Kate Carin. *Make-up:* Marese Langan. *Make-up (Spice Girls):* Karin Darnell. *Stunt Coordinator:* Peter Brayham. *Running time:* 93 minutes. *MPAA Rating:* PG.

CAST: Victoria Adams (Posh/Victoria); Emma Bunton (Baby/Emma); Melanie Chisholm (Sporty/Mel C); Gerladine Halliwell (Ginger/Geri); Melanie Brown (Scary/Mel B); Richard E. Grant (Clifford); Alan Cumming (Piers Cuthbertson-Smyth); George Wendt (Martin Barnfield/Film Producer); Claire Rushbrook (Deborah); Mark McKinney (Graydon/Screenwriter); Roger Moore (Chief); Kevin Allen (Gainer/TV Director); Devon Anderson (Jack); Michael Barrymore (Mr. Step); Richard Briers (Bishop); Simon Chandler (Hospital Parent); Elvis Costello and The Dream Boys, Bob Geldof, Bob Hoskins, Elton John, and Jonathan Ross (Themselves); David Fahm (Enzo/Cameraman); Jason Flemyng (Brad); Neil Fox (Voice of Radio DJ); Stephen Fry (Judge); Llewela Gideon (Nurse); Jools Holland (Musical Director); Barry Humphries (Kevin McMaxford); Craig Kelly (Nervous Guy); Hugh Laurie (Poirot); Meat Loaf (Dennis/Driver); Marian McLoughlin (Hospital Parent); Kevin McNally (Policeman); Naoko Mori (Nicola); Neil Mullarkey (Barnaby); Richard O'Brien (Damien/Photographer); Steven O'Donnell (Jess/Soundman); Bill Paterson (Brian/Café Owner); Jennifer Saunders (Fashionable Woman); Simon Shepherd (Doctor); Cathy Shipton (Midwife); Peter Sissons (Newsreader); Denise Stephenson (Jack/Evie's Mother); Perdita Weeks (Evie); Dominic West (Photographer).

LOS ANGELES TIMES, 1/23/98, Calendar/p. 18, David Kronke

[The following review by David Kronke appeared in a slightly different form in **NEWSDAY, 1/23/98, Part II/p. B7.]**

Sometimes the *zeitgeist* counts for squat. The inexplicable rise of British pop sensation the Spice Girls says nothing about society except that there exists a vocal batch of preteen-mentality kids who don't realize they're really fans of the Archies, only minus the cartoon boys. Spicemania ostensibly celebrates "Girl Power," a form of female self-empowerment based upon the conceptual architecture of earning gobs of money by dressing up as random, ill-defined bimbo archetypes.

Naturally, those responsible for the phenomenon knew enough to strike while the iron was hot and slapped together a movie. Unfortunately, they forgot to factor in post-production time (not that it helped; on a technical level, the film just barely achieves competency) and missed the chance to cash in while Spice Worship was at full-throttle. The inevitable result "Spice World," a movie about four months too late to endure in the pop-culture annals and about four stars too short to be a four-star movie.

One amusing credit in the film reads "Based on an Idea by the Spice Girls and [screenwriter] Kim Fuller." Apart from maybe, "Hey, let's do a movie," it's difficult to imagine what that "idea" may have been. As it peripatetically follows a few days in the life of *Les Femmes d'Spice,* the film is loosely inspired by the Beatles' "A Hard Day's Night," yet is more closely reminiscent of the lamentable vehicle for flash-in-the-pan Vanilla Ice, "Cool as Ice." (The other amusing credit? "Choreographer.")

So basically, the order of the day is a handful of not-quite-mirth-inducing skits that tend to peter out rather than end—many not even featuring the fab femmes. Even my 7-year-old stepdaughter, who loves the group, saw through the folly of padding the movie with pointless bits featuring a hapless documentarian, some crass filmmakers, a tabloid editor who wants to bring the girls crashing down (as if, after this, they'll need help) and occasional appearances by Roger Moore as an inscrutable "Chief" spouting such insipid aphorisms as, "Without something, there is nothing."

The girls banter (Geri Halliwell, or Ginger Spice, is posited as the smart one—let's just say she's no John Lennon), pillow-fight, poke fun at their mediagenic image and play dress-up. They ride around in a mod double-decker bus cribbed from the wacky flat the Beatles shared in "Help!" As screen presences, the young women are engaging in the way someone trying to perk up what she realizes to be an earnest PBS documentary might be, but they lack the frenzied, in-your-face zaniness that might sweep you up despite the weak material. And it's hard to tell whether Victoria Adams, a.k.a. Posh Spice, looks bored throughout the movie because that's how her character is supposed to act or because she really is (should the latter be true, she immediately has the audience's empathy).

Among the rest of the just-collecting-a-paycheck cast, special pity must be accorded Richard E. Grant, a respected thespian trying really hard—probably too hard—in the thankless role of the group's apoplectic manager. Appearances by Elton John, Elvis Costello, Bob Hoskins, George Wendt, "Absolutely Fabulous'" Jennifer Saunders, Kid in the Hall Mark McKinney, Meat Loaf and Jools Holland won't impress Spice fans—who don't care who these people are—or the parents forced to sit through this. To paraphrase the Spice hit "Wannabe," what you'll want—what you'll really, really want—is your money and your 93 minutes back.

NEW YORK POST, 1/23/981 p. 39, Thelma Adams

"Spice World" is not "A Hard Day's Night"—it's not even a bland afternoon matinee. The Pre-Fab Five stumble into the hallowed footsteps of the Fab Four with chunky shoes. They trip on the questionable assumption that audiences will find them adorable.

Not even multimillion-selling albums can guarantee that!

Rarely has irreverence appeared so taxing. As their band director tells the Girls during a rehearsal for their fictional live concert debut: "Absolutely perfect without being any good."

In moviedom's calculated attempt to extend the group's 15 minutes of fame, the Girls—Baby (Emma Bunton), Ginger (Geri Halliwell), Scary (Melanie Brown), Sporty (Melanie Chisholm) and Posh (Victoria Adams)—learn how to get to London's Albert Hall.

The answer isn't practice, practice, practice.

The mighty minis have a gaggle of goosey males in tow. They include a manager on the verge of a nervous breakdown (Richard E. Grant) and a twitty documentary filmmaker (Alan Cumming) in a fruitless search for the band's soul.

Roger Moore spoofs Bond, and scoops a paycheck, as a kitty-carrying Mr. Big. Meanwhile a Hollywood producer (George Wendt) and his aide (Mark McKinney) pitch the idiotic ideas we keep seeing on the screen. Kim Fuller's script was not so much written as compiled.

Director Bob Spiers battles the script's weaknesses with an aggressive strategy: surround the Spices with comic talent. But an appearance by Jennifer Saunders, the star of "Absolutely Fabulous," England's funniest TV series, can't make the band funnier any more than Elton John's cameo can improve its music.

But, I confess, I'm only a visiting alien in "Spice World." I'm not a girl in the 8-to-13 demographic.

If this young audience views the Spice Girls as a collective role model, and repeatedly returns to the theater, they might just make the pop comedy a hit.

But what life lessons will our daughters learn from their idols? Here are a few:

- Girl power is the freedom to pierce one's navel.
- Single motherhood is cool if you have the right girlfriends.
- The Wonder Bra is the greatest invention of the 20th century.

SIGHT AND SOUND, 2/98, p. 49, Mark Sinker

Five days before their important show at the Albert Hall, the five Spice Girls—Geri (Ginger), Mel C (Sporty), Mel B (Scary), Victoria (Posh), Emma (Baby)—are "set to conquer the globe". Travelling by Spicebus, they endure rehearsals, photoshoots, press conferences and warm-up shows. Their manager Clifford reports back to a mysterious boss. They also try to spend time with Nicola, an ex-Spice and old friend, who is pregnant.

Throughout, a film producer and scriptwriter pitch plots to Clifford for a potential film about the Spice Girls, while a documentary is also being made. A tabloid editor wants his sinister photographer to uncover the juiciest story of all: "Spice Girls Split Up". The Girls undergo various ordeals, ever protesting the relentlessness of their routine (the backlash headlines alarm Clifford but not the group). At the final rehearsal, they argue with him and walk out.

After thoughts of pre-fame past and post-fame future, they reunite and take the neglected Nicola out to a club—but her waters break and they rush to hospital. Countless fans await them at the Albert Hall. Now the story being pitched coincides with what we're watching: the baby is born, the photographer is unmasked, and the Spices race across London in the Spicebus. There's a bombscare, they jump the raised Tower Bridge in their bus and arrive just in time. The show begins. During the credits, the Spices notice the audience watching them—and the bomb goes off.

In 1966, NBC put together a pop-rock group so transparently manufactured that a television series was scheduled before they ever played together. The show's success was unprecedented, and The Monkees racked up ten gold discs. But in 1968, the inevitable movie tie-in *Head* was a huge flop: tired of being manipulated, the group soon split. Yet *Head* (directed and written by Bob Rafelson and Jack Nicholson) had an afterlife as a cult movie, more astutely satirical of media formats (some argue) than many more lauded 'counterculture' artefacts. It took nothing seriously, least of all itself (at one point, the four yell "The money's in/we're made of tin/we're here to give you more"). And it kidded relentlessly with the idea of a group's inauthenticity.

Though not really fierce enough to constitute satire, *Spice World* is far too straightforwardly funny and bouncily colourful to be a flop or a cult. (Director Bob Spiers' track record includes *Fawlty Towers* and *Absolutely Fabulous*, scriptwriter Kim Fuller's includes *Red Dwarf*) With fantasy sequences, parodies and much offstage inter-Spice interplay, it sends up the amiable idiocy of pop packaging—and also the slow witted mass-media response to it. The main running gags second-guess so much of the recent 'bad' publicity (ructions with management, tabloid claims that the bubble's burst) that you catch yourself believing that maybe every element in the backlash was generated by and scripted at Spice Central Control. (Kim Fuller is brother to just-ousted manager Simon.) No wonder the tabloids claim to hate it: not only does the plot cast journalists as clowns, its prescience proves how easy it is to lead the professional cynic by the nose.

Just like The Monkees, the Girls guy themselves winningly throughout, and not just their plastic personas (Geri dreamy-clever, Mel C straight-edge impatient, Mel B weirdly motherly, Victoria allergic to mere fun, Emma able to get away with anything). Whole sequences pretend to a cheerful 'real-life' discontent with these images. Baby pouts that she'll still be Baby when she's—awed pause—30. (Yet she can be bought off by management with a single ice-cream, and when the group's in trouble she cutes up instinctively, happy to manipulate their manipulators.)

Actually Baby's fluffmouth line-delivery and Posh's vocal stiffness are probably the film's biggest flaws. Yes, they're in character, but the cartoon rigour of these two caricatures is occasionally beyond the pair's skills as comediennes. Then again, Posh is probably the wittiest physically, the necessary slapstick straight girl. At an assault course, she minces through the first obstacle in her little camouflage frock and high heels, then simply stalks *past* every other pipe-crawl and ropewalk, the essence of haughty dignity.

Most movie-vehicles seem padded in comparison with the concentrated force of records, sleeves, promo videos: which is why the look here is a triumph. The Spices have always known how to wear clothes for freedom, fun and colour-coded impact: here quickchange becomes a fluid essay in just how static real-life fashion is ("we're here to give you MORE"). Many of the sets take the busy cornucopia of Saturday morning children's television, and go for broke: if the colour scheme is an acid-sharp mid-90s take on late-60s pop cool, the texture is often just a Banana-Splits riot of desirable *stuff*. Who wouldn't want to move into the Tardis-like Spicebus (spaceship spacious, all metal and blue velvet) or Roger Moore's fabulous Bond-villain bachelor pad?

Mums and dads unmoved by the less subtle of their offspring's noisy pleasures (Michael Barrymore's jerky dancing; Spicemusic itself) can pass the time unravelling dozens of affectionate references to 70s pop culture, or revelling in the script's self-awareness. Stephen Fry's cameo as a fantasy judge, passing sentence on the group as they sit wide-eyed in fright before him, is a highlight (complete with excellent Gary Barlow gag—later there's an even better Elvis Costello gag). With a pre-teen audience in mind the sex jokes are kept oblique—and as sweetly socially responsible as a *Sugar* problems page.

I ought to explain how, in film theory terms, the sheer control of multiple *mise en scènes*, combined with a deconstructive montage *dénouement*, raises interesting notions of... but "Yeah yeah yeah," interrupts the eight-year-old girl in the row behind me impatiently (as she did when PolyGram's pompous silver-angel logo unfurled onscreen): "Just get to the Spice Girls!" For the real story will start when all these media-wise tots begin fully to grasp how much they *didn't* get of what Girl Power has been promising them. The whole arc of the Spicestory feels like a great trick to have played on you, as leisure-industry tricks go—thrilling uprush followed by nail-baiting will-they fall suspense—and no pop project flirting this much with possible failure can be accused of gutlessness. Tirelessly generous in its energy (just like its stars) *Spice World* is as uncomplicatedly, lovably kicky underneath all the cleverness as a Mel C backflip—maybe even as real. For today at least, that's more than enough. But pop history holds no fury like that of teenybopper let down by unevolving star: if the Spices do ever tumble off the wire, the accompanying maenad wave of disenchantment will make May '68 look like *Playaway*.

VILLAGE VOICE, 2/3/98, p. 122, Dennis Lim

Let's deal with the snipers first. No, the Spice Girls can't act, but if you were expecting them to, you're probably the sort of person who complains that they can't sing. And no, *Spice World* isn't *A Hard Days Night* (it's not even *Abba the Movie)*, but it's never a good idea to compare noncontemporaneous pop bios, and honestly, who cares?

Spice World is ingratiatingly energetic and amiably unpretentious, and it's also an object lesson in spin. A thickly insulated showcase, the film acknowledges every single brickbat ever hurled at the Girls, and nods in vigorous agreement. You think Scary, Sporty, Ginger, Baby, and Posh are vacuous, talentless, hype-driven, backlash-prone, capitalist-tool caricatures? Well, *so do they*, and what's more, they think it's funny. They win.

That said, it's the "Wannabe" and "Say You'll Be There" videos that will be remembered as quintessential Spice artifacts; *Spice World* is not as effective as either, mainly because it's 30 times longer than an average pop song. As for the Girls, some do worse than others. Posh, the one who *(really)* can't sing, is the designated "actress" and has the most lines, but is now in danger of being known as the one who can't sing *or* act. In Ginger's case, it's more evident than ever why, unlike the others (who each have discernible personality traits), she is defined by hair color.

Set during the nerve-fraying week leading up to the Girls' (fictitious) first live performance, *Spice World* weaves in and out of more subplots than even an on-form Robert Altman could ably handle. Evil tabloid editor Kevin McMaxford (Barry Humphries) unleashes his most determined paparazzo (who, post-Diana, takes the form of the Grim Reaper). An obnoxious documentarian (Alan Cumming doing Nick Broomfield) hounds the Girls. A Hollywood producer (George Wendt) pitches a movie idea—which, in a cartoonishly self-reflexive touch, turns out to be *Spice World*. The Girls contemplate a non-future in the dustbin of pop history. They fall out (as they would go on to do in real life) with their manager (Richard E. Grant, as another one of his trademark gay-acting straight men). Their feline-stroking, martini-swilling Svengali (Roger Moore) spouts baffling aphorisms via telephone ("The drummer who is without sticks has no backbeat"). An expectant friend (Naoko Mori) delivers a baby girl (girl power, etcetera). London landmarks fly by in a logistically impossible, high-speed bus ride.

It's hardly a coherent package, and director Bob Spiers *(Ab Fab)* knows it. He cobbles it all together without much thought, giggling under his breath—which is precisely why it works.

Also reviewed in:
CHICAGO TRIBUNE, 1/2/98, Friday/p. A, Greg Kot
NEW YORK TIMES, 1/23/98, p. E18, Janet Maslin
NEW YORKER, 1/26/98, p. 85, Anthony Lane
VARIETY, 12/22/97-1/4/98, p. 58, Derek Elley
WASHINGTON POST, 1/23/98, p. D1, Richard Harrington
WASHINGTON POST, 1/23/98, Weekend/p. 41, Desson Howe

STAR KID

A Trimark Pictures release of a Jennie Lew Tugend/Trimark Pictures production. *Executive Producer:* Mark Amin. *Producer:* Jennie Lew Tugend. *Director:* Manny Coto. *Screenplay:* Manny Coto. *Director of Photography:* Ronn Schmidt. *Editor:* Bob Ducsay. *Music:* Nicholas Pike. *Music Editor:* Paul Rabjohns and Michael Jay. *Sound:* Turtle Island Sound. *Sound Editor:* Dave McMoyler. *Production Designer:* C.J. Strawn. *Art Director:* Michael D. Welch. *Set Decorator:* Irina Rivera. *Set Dresser:* Noah Winter. *Special Effects:* Lou Carlucci. *Costumes:* Ileane Meltzer. *Make-up:* Tina K. Roesler. *Stunt Coordinator:* Gary Paul. *Running time:* 101 minutes. *MPAA Rating:* PG.

CAST: Joseph Mazzello (Spencer Griffith); Joey Simmrin (Turbo Bruntley); Alex Daniels (Cyborsuit); Arthur Burghardt (Cyborsuit Voice); Brian Simpson (Broodwarrior); Richard Gilliland (Roland Griffith); Corinne Bohrer (Janet Holloway); Ashlee Levitch (Stacey Griffith); Danny Masterson (Kevin); Lauren Eckstrom (Michelle); Christine Weatherup (Nadia); Yumi Adachi (Mika); Jack McGee (Hank Bruntley); Alissa Ann Smego (Burgerworld Girl); Fred Kronenberg (Officer #1); Joshua Fardon (Rookie Cop); Bobby Porter (Trelkin/"Nath"); Larry Nicholas (Trelkin/"Tenris"); Rusty Hanson and Terry Castillo-Faass (Trelkins).

LOS ANGELES TIMES, 1/16/98, Calendar/p. 10, Kevin Thomas

[The following review by John Anderson appeared in a slightly different form in **NEWSDAY, 1/16/98, Part II/p. B11.]**

"Star Kid" comes up with a fresh gimmick for the new boy in middle school, you know, the one who is menaced by the usual schoolyard bully and who is tongue-tied when he tries to speak to the prettiest girl in class. The result is a pleasing diversion for youngsters sparked by a winning portrayal by Joseph Mazzello in the title role.

Just when the morale of Mazzello's 12-year-old Spencer is lowest, he sees from his bedroom window what he thinks is a meteor crashing into a car junkyard not too far from his family"s large old suburban home. But the meteor turns out to be none other than the robotic Cy the Cyborsuit. Cy, who could have been created from a mold of Arnold Schwarzenegger, has glassy, green eyes but develops a kindly expression. Once Spencer dons the suit, he becomes an instant Superman. Cy is such a roomy interior that Spencer is able to keep up a dialogue with Cy, who speaks to Spencer from the back side of his face. (This is not as weird as it sounds.)

In any event Cy proves to be no hollow man, and as Spencer humanizes Cy, the robot in turn gives Spencer friendship and encouragement, along with powers that verge on the Kryptonic. Where writer-director Manny Coto has been inspired is in having Cy need Spencer even more than the boy needs him, for there's an urgent reason why Cy has turned up on Earth.

Corinne Bohrer makes a special impression as the kind of teacher we all wish we'd had when we were in seventh grade. Alex Daniels as Cyborsuit and Arthur Burghardt, who provides Cy's voice, are also top-notch.

As a special-effects film, "Star Kid" is serviceable, with the creation of Cy its key accomplishment. It has an overly cluttered look, but it has a lovely Nicholas Pike score and lots of heart, which is what matters most.

NEW YORK POST, 1/16/98, p. 45, Thelma Adams

"If you run away from the thing you're scared of, it doesn't get any better," a science teacher tells Spencer Griffith (Joseph Mazzello), the 12-year-old hero of "Star Kid."

The problem with this bland sci-fi family film is that if you stay in your seat, it still doesn't get any better.

Mazzello's Spencer is one of those pale, red-haired, big-teethed whiners whom the local bully loves to humiliate. After nearly two hours with the drippy lad, we feel the same. Get us to a tetherball court; we'll wrap him in the cord!

Writer/director Manny Cotto—a name that sounds like manicotti and must have gotten him his licks on the playground—is intent on making one of those safe family films that has no clue how sophisticated kids are in modern America.

The famed writer/director of "Dr. Giggles" (snort!) stacks the deck against poor Spencer: His sister calls him fungus, his father wouldn't even include him on a conference call, and his dream girl dresses like a slut. Almost the only being on Earth who pays Spencer any attention is Turbo (Richard Gilliland), the daddy-abused town bully.

As if this weren't enough trouble in Mayberry R.I.P., our latter-day Opie bumps into the future. A Cyborsuit lands in the local junkyard. An unproven experiment, "Cy" has been created by an elf-like race to be worn by living hosts. Spencer discovers the intelligent robot and climbs in. Between whines, he learns a few lessons about superpowers while teaching the universe the finer points of human urination.

In the end, Spencer vanquishes an evil alien who looks like Godzilla's drooling, spiky little brother. He saves the Earth from annihilation, befriends the bully, makes peace with his family and gets the girl. The special effects are nerdy and cheap, the messages easily transferable to Hallmark Cards and the whole effort is tailor-made for a rainy afternoon of Mystery Science Theater 3000.

Also reviewed in:

CHICAGO TRIBUNE, 1/16/98, Tempo/p. 2, John Petrakis
NEW YORK TIMES, 1/16/98, p. E14, Anita Gates
VARIETY, 1/12-18/98, p. 74, Lael Loewenstein

STAR TREK: INSURRECTION

A Paramount Pictures release of a Rick Berman production. *Executive Producer:* Martin Hornstein. *Producer:* Rick Berman. *Director:* Jonathan Frakes. *Screenplay:* Michael Piller. *Story:* Rick Berman and Michael Piller. *Based on "Star Trek" created by::* Gene Roddenberry. *Director of Photography:* Matthew F. Leonetti. *Editor:* Peter E. Berger. *Music:* Jerry Goldsmith. *Music Editor:* Ken Hall. *Sound:* Thomas Causey and (music) Bruce Botnick. *Sound Editor:* James W. Wolvington and Cameron Frankley. *Casting:* Junie Lowry-Johnson and Ron Surma. *Production Designer:* Herman Zimmerman. *Art Director:* Ron Wilkinson. *Set Designer:* Sharon Davis, Alan Kaye, Nancy Mickelberry, Christopher S. Nushawg. *Set Decorator:* John Dwyer. *Special Effects:* Terry Frazee. *Visual Effects:* Dexter Delara. *Costumes:* Sanja Milkovic Hays. *Make-up:* Michael Westmore. *Stunt Coordinator:* Rick Avery. *Running time:* 105 minutes. *MPAA Rating:* PG.

CAST: Patrick Stewart (Captain Jean-Luc Picard); Jonathan Frakes (Commander William Riker); Brent Spiner (Lt. Commander Data); LeVar Burton (Lt. Commander Geordi LaForge); Michael Dorn (Lt. Commander Worf); Gates McFadden (Dr. Beverly Crusher); Marina Sirtis (Counsellor Deanna Troi); F. Murray Abraham (Ru'afo); Donna Murphy (Anij); Anthony Zerbe (Admiral Dougherty); Gregg Henry (Gallatin); Daniel Hugh-Kelly (Sojef); Michael Welch (Artim); Mark Deakins (Tournel); Stephanie Niznik (Perim); Michael Horton (Lieutenant Daniels); Bruce French (Son'a Officer I); Breon Gorman (Lieutenent Curtis); John Hostetter (Bolian Officer); Rick Worthy (Elloran Officer I); Larry Anderson (Tarlac Officer);

D. Elliot Woods (Starfleet Officer);   Jennifer Tung (Female Ensign);   Raye Birk (Son'a Doctor);
Peggy Miley (Regent Cuzar);   Lee Arnone-Briggs (Librarian); Claudette Nevins (Son'a Officer
2);   Max Grodenchik (Alien Ensign);   Greg Poland (Elloran Officer 2);   Kenneth Lane
Edwards (Male Ensign);   Joseph Ruskin (Son'a Officer 3);   Zachary Williams (Ba'ku Child);
McKenzie Westmore (Ba'ku Woman);   Phillip Glasser (Young Ru'afo).

LOS ANGELES TIMES, 12/11/98, Calendar/p. 1, Kenneth Turan

No disrespect intended to the proud Son'a people but, hey, where are the Borg when you need
them?

It was the terrifying and thoroughly alien Borg who made the last "Star Trek" film, "First
Contact," one of the best in the series' 19-year theatrical history. The latest and ninth installment
in that line, "Star Trek: Insurrection," lacks the adrenalized oomph of its predecessor, but no
adventure of the Starship Enterprise is without its gee-whiz affability.

These intergalactic films are one of the few constants in today's movie universe, a reliable brand
name that guarantees that the proceedings won't sink irredeemably below an acceptable level of
Saturday matinee diversion.

Part of the reason for this is the way the true believers who create the "Star Trek" films have
morphed into a kind of self-perpetuating oligarchy, involved not only with feature films but with
the growing handful of TV series that bear the "Trek" trademark.

"Insurrection" director Jonathan Frakes, for instance, co-stars as Cmdr. William Riker on the
big screen and has worked on the series "Star Trek: The Next Generation," "Star Trek: Deep
Space Nine" and "Star Trek: Voyager." The same goes for screenwriter Michael Piller and
producer and co-story creator Rick Berman. If the Federation isn't in your blood, you don't get
a turn at the bridge.

Every "Star Trek" starts with a puzzling incident, and "Insurrection" has the cheerful android
Data (Brent Spiner), the "Next Generation's" Spock surrogate, surprising everyone by turning
hostile. That's serious enough to cause his mentor and commanding officer, Capt. Jean-Luc
Picard (Patrick Stewart), to change plans and investigate.

Data has been attached to a cultural survey team, a joint venture between the Federation and
those sinister Son'a, to monitor the life of the bucolic Ba'ku people. Two more different races
it wouldn't be possible to imagine.

The Son'a led by the mysterious Ru'afo (F. Murray Abraham), are such an ancient and decrepit
people that you almost expect their arms to fall off when they move them. Determined to look
as young as possible, they indulge in so much face-stretching plastic surgery they resemble Men
From Glad, their visages swathed in miles of plastic wrap.

The Ba'ku colony, on the other hand, is the idyllic dream utopia of every 1960s hippie's
fantasy. It's an outer space commune where comely children play in the fields, handsome men
are kindly and considerate and women wear long skirts and make bread with smiles on their
lovely faces.

When hard-driving Picard arrives here in search of Data (the android, not the information), he
discovers that the Ba'ku are not entirely what they seem. New Agers to the core, they do insist
on living in the moment, but it's not because they can't cut it technologically. After all, as one
of their leaders puts it in typical philosophical "Trek"-ese, "where can warp drive take us but
away from here?"

Helping Picard understand these seeming children of nature is a romantic interlude (we're
talking hand-holding, if you must know) he has with the beautiful, mysterious Anij (Donna
Murphy). "A single moment in time," she tells him, "can be a universe in itself." The captain's
log was never like this.

Why, Picard wonders, would anyone be causing trouble for these sweet-natured innocents? And,
when it comes to that, why are the sinister Son'a hanging around the place in the company of
Federation Adm. Dougherty (Anthony Zerbe)? Is a betrayal of the Federation's sacred Prime
Directive in the offing?

Helping Picard unravel these mysteries is the usual "Star Trek" crew, including Geordi of the
electronic eyes (LeVar Burton), Worf the tame Klingon (Michael Dorn), the medically minded
Dr. Beverly Crusher (Gates McFadden) and the half-Betazoid counselor Deanna Troi (Marina
Sirtis).

Also back are the usual bursts of clunky dialogue and cliched situations that echo the old days of Buck Rogers serials more than may be intended. What would a "Star Trek" be without scientific observations like "The metaphasic radiation is in a state of extreme flux" and questions on the order of "When was the last time we aligned the torque sensors?"? Like the series, itself, it's been awhile, but who's counting?

NEW STATESMAN, 1/1/99, p. 38, David Thompson

Star Trek: Insurrection is the ninth cinematic outing for what is arguably science fiction's most successful formulation. Yet the enormous popularity of *Trek*'s expanding fictional universe cannot, it seems, simply be explained by either its escapism or its spectacular distractions.

In keeping with science fiction's tendency toward peculiar hybrids, the world view offered by all of *Star Trek*'s incarnations centres around a curiously liberal militarism which, contradictions aside, allows for an inexhaustible catalogue of acute moral dilemmas and digitally rendered destruction. Gestated during a period of cold war trepidation and unprecedented technological innovation, *Star Trek* presented a canvas on which to sketch the fears of the age and, perhaps more importantly, the hope of surviving it.

That the series still serves much the same function is testament to the enduring poignancy and appeal of its optimistic premise: that all is not yet lost. Its universe may reflect and extend contemporary fears with cybernetic hives and spatial anomalies, but its dramatic significance ultimately derives from reminding us of expansive frontiers and heroic possibilities.

Inevitably for a franchise spanning four decades of space-faring, *Star Trek* has evolved a uniquely elaborate array of fictional hardware and technical jargon, much of it now part of our own cultural mythology. Spin-off merchandising reached new heights of surrealism in 1991, with the publication of an official, 200-page technical manual detailing the innumerable systems and specifications of the Starship Enterprise. The notion of science fiction as a blueprint or inspirational sketch pad of future possibilities had been noted and clearly underlined.

The freedom to extrapolate, exaggerate and invert the familiar may help to explain science fiction's history of prescience. Edwin Abbott's hypergeometrical satire "Flatland", originally published in 1884, remains one of the most popular mathematical texts to be published. Spanning more than a century of reprints, this unlikely clergyman's morality tale has featured in the thinking of Oscar Wilde, Victorian spiritualists and a filing clerk named Albert Einstein. Flatland also gave the beatniks their unhip and archetypal "-square". It remains recommended reading for students of theoretical physics.

H G Wells'"land iron-clad" featured in his ambitious 1901 essay "Anticipations" and famously predated the British army's deployment of tanks on the western front in 1916. The same essay predicted the strategic importance of aerial warfare (albeit conducted using balloons) along with the development of telescopic sights and automatic weapons. Regarding the cultural impact of the car, Wells prophesies: "There will be conspicuous advertisements by the roadside; there will be traffic jams as motor vehicles replace pedestrians... By the year 2000, London will exted to Wales..." Mercifully, not all of Wells' predictions have yet materialised.

Science fiction has also informed less tangible concerns. During the early years of this century, the rise of the "scientific romance" stirred an unprecedented popular consideration of future political and social possibilities, helping to shape the ambitions of both capitalists and bolsheviks. In 1959, the novelist and philosopher Arthur Koestler voiced his fears for the future, warning of how the social extension of Darwinian ideas would dull the qualitative, visionary and moral senses. He feared the emergence of a purely quantitative world view, driven entirely by commercial imperatives, in which human consciousness would count as no more than a tragicomic curio in a meaningless universe. The stark, survivalist ethos offends justifying means outlined in Koestler's "Sleepwalkers" has largely come to pass.

Now, as corporate biotechnology raises questions hitherto unthinkable, the role of science fiction as an intellectual "rehearsal space" appears more pertinent than ever. The moral preoccupations of Dostoevsky and Dickens may warrant continual attention, but the daunting legal, ethical and philosophical issues being raised by our latest technologies demand solutions without precedent in the literature that previously informed our cultural norms. The prospect of human cloning, as autonomous individuals or surgical spare parts, requires the urgent development of new definitions and legal safeguards if we are to retain fundamental distinctions between "person" and "property".

The flexible perimeters of science fiction seem eminently well-equipped to frame such debates and address the possibilities (and improbabilities) of our own increasingly alien environment. Genetic patents, climatic change and postmortem impregnation may once have been confined to the fictional scenarios of J G Ballard or William Burroughs, but the unthinkable and the impossible are becoming facts of life. With the stakes so high and so much to be done, we may need the motivation of Star Trek's bolder, brighter future.

NEW YORK POST, 12/11/98, p. 58, Jonathan Foreman

The latest installment in the "Star Trek" movie series is nowhere near as good as "The Undiscovered Country" (No. 6) or "The Wrath of Khan" (No. 2)—the two best "Star Trek" flicks—but "Star Trek: Insurrection" is definitely the best "Next Generation" movie so far.

It has the essential space battles, the less-irritating characters from the television series (i.e., no Wesley), the usual underlying moral point. Unfortunately, that underlying moral point happens to be a classic Hollywood example of bubble-headed New Age hokum.

The plot centers on a planet that resembles Yosemite National Park and is inhabited only by a community of 600 beautiful, mostly blond, white people.

Their village looks like a luxurious Santa Fe health spa. And no one seems to do any work except for a few white-clad folk happily hoeing vegetables, like members of some '70s cult. This is the Hollywood boomer idea of a rural Arcadia: Somehow the hard labor of low-tech farming and gardening just gets done—presumably by an army of invisible gardeners.

Special radiation on the planet is keeping people young and healthy: Many of the adults look about 45, even though they are actually over 300 years old.

A Federation admiral joins with the bad guys—a really ugly old-looking humanoid race called the Son'A, led by the fine actor F. Murray Abraham—to reap the benefits of the radiation.

Capt. Jean-Luc Picard discovers that the plan will compel the nice California people to move off the planet. He is appalled by such utilitarian ruthlessness.

Influenced by his growing affection for a busty planet babe who teaches him how to live in the moment, Picard decides to don a gray vinyl blazer and take arms against the process. He is immediately joined in rebellion by his pals from the bridge.

The battle commences and the inevitable follows: There is no way that the wrinkled bad guys—who presumably smoke, eat red meat, etc.—will be allowed to displace the shiny, happy people.

The wonderful Patrick Stewart not only keeps a straight face through all this as Picard, but lends the whole movie dignity and style. As Riker, Jonathan Frakes is getting fat and florid—and seems to be developing some of the grating bonhomie of William Shatner—but he does a sterling turn as the director. Given that the worst of the nine "Star Trek" movies suffered from the Shatner-Nimoy effect, whereby a star considered essential to the franchise was allowed to direct it into the ground, this is no small achievement.

NEWSDAY, 12/11/98, Part II/p. B7, John Anderson

There are now enough "Star Trek" movies that number theories have arisen: The even movies are better than the odd, devout Trekkers say. I, for one, am willing to believe them.

At the same time, "Star Trek: Insurrection," the ninth in the Gene Roddenberry-spawned outer-space adventures—which refs to the original "Star Trek," as well as "Next Generation" and "Deep Space Nine"—has, at its core, a fairly profound question: Is the displacement of the few justifiable for the benefit of the many? Think Robert Moses at warp factor 8.

We always suspected that Jean-Luc Picard (Patrick Stewart) was a fundamentalist at heart, and he proves it in "Insurrection." The Ba'ku people, 300-year-old inhabitants of a planet whose "metaphasic radiation" keeps them from aging, are about to be moved out by the Federation of Planets, that usually benevolent organization of which the starship Enterprise is merely a vessel. As anyone even vaguely familiar with the words that William Shatner knows, the "Prime Directive" of the federation forbids federation personnel from tampering, interfering or otherwise molesting a civilization as regards its natural development. The gentle, bread-baking Ba'ku on the other hand, possess the fountain of youth. And Admiral Dougherty (Anthony Zerbe) thinks they should share.

Picard begs to differ. But then, he would. "Star Trek: Insurrection" is so noble and chaste you'd think Ken Starr was a film critic. There is one bathtub scene featuring Counselor Deanna Troi and Commander William Riker (director Jonathan Frakes, who without his beard looks unsettlingly like Shatner). But the warring battleships look like sophisticated cigarette lighters; the alpine backdrops of the Ba'ku planet look like leftovers from a road company "Sound of Music." Picard and his squeeze dujour, Ba'ku babe Anij (Broadway's Donna Murphy, whose painfully earnest expressions seem directed toward the back row of the Shubert Theater) comport themselves like Father O'Malley and Sister Benedict in "The Bells of St. Mary's." Someone must have been thinking of replay rights on Pax TV.

But this "Star Trek," like all those that have gone before it, is for the aficionado. One has to be aware that when Data the android (Brent Spiner) goes berserk, it's totally out of character—and when he sings an excerpt from "H.M.S. Pinafore," it's completely normal. That when the reverse-aging process of the Ba'ku planet has various characters revisiting puberty, the Klingon Worf (Michael Dorn) will be the most acutely affected ("I have a strange craving for the blood of a kolar beast!"). That the rhetoric ("activating secondary protocol...") is mostly blather.

One wishes that when director Frakes imposes comedy relief, there was something to relieve. Or that someone would explain why, when even blind Geordi (LeVar Burton) benefits from the youth-restoring powers of Ba'ku, that Picard doesn't grow any hair. Or why the evil Son'a people—as personified by the very cranky and apostrophied Ru'afo (F. Murray Abraham)—can't get rid of their rather serious psoriasis problem. Or just what the evolutionary theory is behind "Star Trek," where the philosophy seems straight out of Deepak Chopra and sets are inspired by Ed Wood. "Trek"-ites should demand more from their suppliers. If I cared enough, I'd write a letter.

SIGHT AND SOUND, 2/99, p. 55, Kim Newman

The Ba'ku, an agrarian community who have turned away from the technology of the greater universe, retreat to a planet whose properties give them an extended lifespan. The Federation enters into an alliance with the Son'a race who intend to exploit the Ba'ku world, though it means the forcible removal of the Ba'ku. When android Data, a member of the Federation-Son'a expedition, rebels against the mission, his captain, Jean-Luc Picard, arrives to investigate.

Discovering a plot to evacuate the Ba'ku, Picard protests to Federation Admiral Dougherty and Son'a leader Ru'afo. The admiral orders Picard to keep out of the situation but Picard, now romantically involved with Ba'ku Anij, dispatches crewmen Riker and LaForge to complain to the Federation. Picard remains on the planet with crew members Worf, Dr Crusher, Counsellor Troi and Data to fight a rear-guard action against Ru'afo, who sets up an orbital device which will destroy the planet but preserve its life-extending elements.

Picard learns the Son'a are actually an offshoot of the Ba'ku and that the Federation has become mixed up in a blood feud. The *Enterprise* defeats Son'a ships, but Ru'afo murders Dougherty and continues his plan to despoil the planet. Picard defeats Ru'afo in single combat. The Ba'ku and the remaining Son'a reconcile, and the *Enterprise* departs.

It's hard sometimes not to think of the *Star Trek* films as a two-yearly reminder of the way America feels about the world. Since the 60s, Trek has been almost an instrument of American foreign policy, with the Federation as Uncle Sam and the current race of alien villains standing in for whoever successive administrations have wanted to puff up as global baddies. Traditionally the Federation has stood in for the White House, but now, with America impatient at the inability of compromised international task forces to cope with Rwanda and the former Yugoslavia, the Federation itself has become a bureaucratic mess capable of backing the wrong faction in a 'blood feud', and the locus of right-thinking values has shrunk to the *U.S.S. Enterprise* itself.

Though much has been made of the decision of a *Trek* captain to rebel against the Federation, this aspect is underdeveloped here—Picard sides with the good against the bad and sends off his sidekicks to complain to head office while the other series regulars follow his lead unquestioningly. The problem with the Federation is down to one admiral sticking by an alliance forged through deception rather than any larger flaw. The blithe assumption that once the facts are known 'public opinion' will want to leave the Ba'ku alone rather than exploit the magical properties of their world to extend their own lifespans is tantamount to claiming that the American people would accept a decline in their standard of life if it meant fairer treatment of thirdworld peoples. Dougherty's justification for breaking the 'prime directive' (non-interference in alien cultures) is that the Ba'ku are not indigenous to their paradise, an equivocation which means the story isn't about questioning the assumptions of the Trek universe but splitting hairs over the application of the rules.

One of the pleasanter aspects of this Trek film is that it is the first in the series to concentrate on the sort of story they used to do on television. No major characters die (as Speck did in *Star Trek II: The Wrath of Khan*) and no significant upheaval is made in the *Star Trek* universe like the end of the Federation-Klingon Cold War in *Star Trek 6*. In effect, this is a big-budget television episode, in which the *Enterprise* visits a planet which has a problem and solves it. The self contained story introduces the Ba'ku and the Son'a and takes their struggle to a conclusion very much in the simplistic spirit of series creator Gene Roddenberry. These aliens again represent a fantasy of a third-world conflict, but there's a strangely Californian feel to the schism between tree-hugging, new age commune-dwellers and disease-ridden environmental destroyers who want to rape the planet to avoid getting old.

The Trek movie problem is finding something for all the regulars to do while building up new characters and giving the captain a substantial role. As usual, this means the supporting cast—now looking as waxily preserved as the original crew (and this in a film which uses Clive Barker tactics to condemn cosmetic surgery)—potter around in the background handling sub-plots and comic relief. Patrick Stewart is actor enough to handle romance with a humanoid alien and righteous indignation at injustice in a manner that gives the film an edge over series entries which have to rely on William Shatner or Leonard Nimoy. Stewart even resists the impulse to do a double-take when confronted by Anij with such amorous lines as, "It's 300 years since I've seen a bald man."

The quotient of scientific mumbo-jumbo is extremely high, but director Jonathan Frakes (who also plays Riker) scores with a likable combination of action and special effects, notably a high quality battle in a purple cloud sector of outer space known as the 'Briar Patch', and a nice bit of duplicity involving Trek stand-bys (the holodeck, transporter beams) as actual bits of technology rather than futuristic window-dressing. There are likable embarrassments—Picard does a mean mambo—and overworked bits of business that play only to the fans, but this is the first *Trek* film which might play as well, or even better, to audiences unfamiliar with the franchise.

VILLAGE VOICE, 12/22/98, p. 138, Gary Dauphin

Blame it on the aliens in Hollywood, but odd-numbered *Star Trek* movies tend to suck. The best flicks—from number two, *Wrath of Khan* (probably the best in the series), to number eight, *First Contact*—are all even-numbered entries in the franchise, a tiny detail that, like the height of hemlines, bodes well or ill according to logic beyond mere human ken. The latest *Star Trek* flick, *Insurrection,* is the 9th, and although it doesn't suck as completely as some ignoble odd-numbered low points, it doesn't exactly boldly go where no one has gone before.

Although a printed synopsis of *Insurrection*'s plot might read like Greek to the uninitiated, onscreen it scans legibly as would-be blockbusterese. The film opens with starship *Enterprise* android Data (Brent Spiner) mysteriously flipping out while on a run-of-the-mill anthropological mission to the planet Bak'u. Dashing off to see what has gone wrong with Data, the *Enterprise* crew discovers an idyllic farming community (introduced through a sugary mist of violins and smiles) with a secret. It turns out weird radiation keeps the Bak'u population young and healthy. The *Enterprise*'s captain Picard (Patrick Stewart, playing up the busybody element) also discovers a conspiracy: his war-depleted Federation and a grotesque group of space pirates have secretly colluded to steal the planet from its inhabitants. The scheme is clearly a violation of what Picard sonorously calls "who we are," so before you can say Prime Directive, the *Enterprise* crew disobeys orders and comes to the Bak'u's rescue.

Throughout, the one-liners pop as frequently as phaser blasts, but instead of being jaunty, *Insurrection* is hurried and unfocused. There are some typically *Trek* sparks—the Bak'u love interest with the power to slow time, the regeneration of Chief Engineer LaForge's eyes, Data's ongoing education in the ways of natural-born meat—but overall, *Insurrection* adds little to anyone's understanding of *Trek's* world or its characters. Non-fans might find it hard to believe that, despite the fetishistic interplay of alien races and starships, *Trek* is really about people, but the most resonant pleasures in the series have always been personal: James Tiberius Kirk's love for his First Officer Spock, Picard's endlessly fraught sense of duty, the ongoing tension between the good of the many, the few, and the one. There are real flesh-and-blood people who, despite being targets for easy jokes, have had their lives changed by *Treks* pleasures, but it's hard to imagine anyone being struck by lightning during *Insurrection.* At most it engenders nostalgia and begins the long wait for number 10.

Also reviewed in:
CHICAGO TRIBUNE, 12/11/98, Friday/p. A, Michael Wilmington
NEW YORK TIMES, 12/11/98, p. E14, Stephen Holden
VARIETY, 12/14-20/98, p. 131, Joe Leydon
WASHINGTON POST, 12/11/98, p. D1, Rita Kempley
WASHINGTON POST, 12/11/98, Weekend/p. 50, Michael O'Sullivan

STEAM: THE TURKISH BATH

A Strand Releasing release of a Sorpasso Film/Promete Film/Asbrell Productions coproduction in collaboration with RAI Radio Televisione Italiana. *Executive Producer:* Paolo Buzzi and Ozan Ergun. *Director:* Ferzan Ozpetek. *Screenplay (Italian and Turkish with English subtitles):* Stefano Tummolini and Ferzan Ozpetek. *Story:* Ferzan Ozpetek. *Director of Photography:* Pasquale Mari. *Editor:* Mauro Bonanni. *Music:* Pivio De Scalzi and Aldo De Scalzi. *Sound:* Marco Grillo. *Art Director:* Virginia Vianello and Mustafa Ziya Ulgenciler. *Costumes:* Metella Raboni and Selda Cicek. *Make-up:* Gaja Banchelli. *Running time:* 94 minutes. *MPAA Rating:* Not Rated.

CAST: Alessandro Gassman (Francesco); Francesca d'Aloja (Marta); Carlo Cecchi (Oscar); Halil Ergun (Osman); Serif Sezer (Perran); Mehmet Gunsur (Mehmet); Basak Koklukaya (Fusun); Alberto Molinari (Paolo); Zozo Toledo (Zozo).

LOS ANGELES TIMES, 11/25/98, Calendar/p. 11, Kevin Thomas

Ferzan Ozpetek's "Steam: The Turkish Bath" is as seductive as its title. It takes you into the world of one of Istanbul's ramshackle yet picturesque neighborhoods to introduce you to a gentler, more sensual way of life than most of us are used to in the West. This lovely, contemplative film affirms that happiness is possible in this life—that it is worth seeking out right now, for life is ever fragile and fleeting.

Happiness is what Madame Anita, a self-described "Italian adventuress" found when she arrived in Istanbul, sometime after World War II. She married well, though briefly, and invested her divorce settlement in purchasing an old Turkish bath, transforming it into the most popular spa in the city. But even then, the baths were fading—most modern Turks probably didn't have enough time to enjoy them—and Madame Anita had to start selling off her fine paintings and eventually was forced to close it.

Meanwhile, back in Rome, Madame Anita's nephew Francesco (Alessandro Gassman) is caught up in running a highly successful interior design business with his wife, Marta (Francesca d'Aloja), and their associate, Paolo (Alberto Molinari). They're winding up a big project in Milan when Francesco receives word that his aunt has died and that he is her heir. When Francesco, who did not know his aunt or anything about her, flies off to Istanbul, he envisions a quick stay to dispose of her property, only to have his life transformed.

The usual red tape causes enough delays for Francesco to find himself drawn to the city and especially to the family with whom his aunt shared quarters adjacent to the bath. The Osmans (Halil Ergun, Serif Sezer), who once managed the bath, are a warm, hospitable middle-aged couple with two children still living at home, Memo (Mehmet Gunsur), a TV cameraman, and

Fusun (Basak Koklukaya), a 19-year-old student. When Francesco learns that a ruthless real estate developer has started buying up the neighborhood, which resembles a seedy version of the narrow streets on the slopes of San Francisco's Telegraph Hill, he digs in, not only refusing to sell the bath but also inspiring the Osmans to rally the entire neighborhood to refuse to sell their property. He then launches a restoration of the bath.

The film offers a classic journey of self-discovery on the part of Francesco, who finds himself coming to terms with his true sexual orientation as he discovers an older, more satisfying way of life—only to find it as endangered as such ways of life are almost everywhere around the globe. "Steam: The Turkish Bath" is in all aspects graceful—in its performances, in its sinuous style and lush score, which incorporates Turkish melodies of various eras. It's worth letting it cast its spell.

NEW YORK POST, 11/25/98, p. 57, Jonathan Foreman

If "Midnight Express" made Turkey an unfashionable tourist destination for Americans, the lovely, lilting "Steam" may get people running for the next plane to Istanbul.

This Italian-Turkish-Spanish co-production paints a seductive picture of the old city's charming, rickety back streets and those who inhabit them.

Most recent movies about uptight people going somewhere warm and foreign, thereby learning to relax and indulge their sensual side, have been about English folk on vacation in Italy. In "Steam," it is the Italians who need and receive the benefits of travel therapy.

Yes, even Italians need to be educated about the value of taking time to enjoy food and drink and sex. One of them is Francesco (Alessandro Gassman), a handsome yuppie architect in a perpetual hurry who is called to Istanbul when an aunt he barely knew dies and leaves him property in Istanbul's Old City.

While he waits for matters to be straightened out, Francesco moves in with the delightful Turkish family that looks after the property—which turns out to be a Turkish bath.

Francesco finds himself falling under the wholesome influence of the family and the sensuous spirit of the bath itself. He even begins to flirt with the attractive son and daughter of his hosts. As he learns to slow down, and to stop taking cell-phone calls in the middle of dinner, he makes the fateful decision not to sell the baths but to refurbish them instead.

It's at this point that Francesco's even-more-uptight wife, Marta, arrives in town, intending to tell him that she wants to leave him. She notices that her husband is changing for the better and the city begins to have its own relaxing effect on her.

But she also discovers that her husband has embarked on a homosexual relationship—which is treated in a manner as low-key and tasteful as everything else in "Steam."

Like all good travel stories, "Steam" is an affecting tale of self-discovery. Writer Stefano Tummolini and director Ferzan Opetek happily lack the insecure postmodern discomfort with honest sentiment that so afflicts American filmmakers. And they offer a grown-up, subtle account of the disappearance of a humane, warm, but still far-from-perfect way of life.

VILLAGE VOICE, 12/1/98, p. 128, Dennis Lim

Ferzan Ozpetek's handsome first feature, *Steam: The Turkish Bath*, was an obvious contender for Foreign Film Oscar this year, but the Turkish authorities refused to submit the movie for consideration, reportedly because of its gay content. The irony is that, whatever you make of its distinct yet muted homoeroticism, *Steam* is a tourist board's wet dream, albeit one taken to a swooningly romanticized, mildly creepy extreme. Ozpetek's Istanbul is a sensuous, near-mystical realm that exerts a vicelike grip on unsuspecting visitors: a taste of Turkish hospitality, a frolic in a bathhouse, and, evidently, you're hooked for life.

There's a slightly patronizing old-school flavor to the movie's premise—buttoned-down Westerner visits exotic land, undergoes momentous sexual and spiritual awakening—but *Steam* lulls you into believing it. Francesco (Alessandro Gassman, son of director Vittorio), a stoic, urbane Italian designer, travels to the Turkish capital with the intention of selling the property he has inherited from his late aunt (his mother's estranged sister, who fled to Istanbul in her youth and was so entranced she never returned). At first every bit the stereotypically aloof foreigner (his cell phone keeps ringing at inopportune moments), Francesco rethinks his course of action when he learns he has in fact inherited a bath house—traditionally a sanctuary where men indulge "certain caprices." He also starts to respond to the lavish hospitality of his hosts (employees of his aunt's), not least the family's attractive young son (Mehmet Gunsur). Francesco's experiences are paralleled with his aunt's (her letters to his mother, never sent, serve as voiceover), and his transformation is so conclusive by the time his wife, Marta, shows up (to serve divorce papers), she cannot help but find herself curiously drawn to the new Francesco.

Beautifully photographed (by Pasquale Mari), *Steam* is a languid, melancholic, gently intoxicating experience, though Ozpetek jump-starts the film every now and again with strategic use of a propulsive, percussive score. Gassman smolders effectively throughout, but more than that, he also conveys Francesco's gradual awakening credibly and with admirable economy. There isn't all that much beneath *Steam*'s seductively placid surface, but its potentially trite bottom line—that the pursuit of happiness is no less than an imperative—is so heartfelt and so lucidly rendered that, by the end of the film, it has acquired a wholly unexpected poignancy.

Also reviewed in:
NEW YORK TIMES, 11/25/98, p. E12, Anita Gates
VARIETY, 5/5-11/97, p. 70, David Rooney

STEPHEN KING'S 'THE NIGHT FLIER'

A New Line Cinema and New Amsterdam Entertainment release in association with Stardust International Ltd & Medusa Film SpA of a Richard P. Rubinstein production. *Executive Producer:* David Kappes. *Producer:* Richard P. Rubinstein and Mitchell Galin. *Director:* Mark Pavia. *Screenplay:* Mark Pavia and Jack O'Donnell. *Based on a story by:* Stephen King. *Director of Photography:* David Connell. *Editor:* Elizabeth Schwartz. *Music:* Brian Keane. *Sound:* Jay Meagher. *Sound Editor:* John Bowen. *Casting:* Leonard Finger and Lyn Richmond. *Production Designer:* Burton Rencher. *Set Designer:* Andrew Menzies. *Set Decorator:* Timothy Smithwick Stepeck. *Set Dresser:* Alex L. Ferguson, Doug Kelejian, and Kim Kirk. *Visual Effects:* Oliver Rockwell. *Costumes:* Pauline White. *Make-up:* Jeff Goodwin. *Stunt Coordinator:* John Copeman. *Running time:* 99 minutes. *MPAA Rating:* R.

CAST: Miguel Ferrer (Richard Dees); Julie Entwisle (Katherine Blair); Dan Monahan (Merton Morrison); Michael H. Moss (Dwight Renfield); John Bennes (Ezra Hannon); Beverly Skinner (Selida McCamon); Rob Wilds (Buck Kendall); Richard Olsen (Claire Bowie); Elizabeth McCormick (Ellen Sarch); J.R. Rodriguez and Bob Casey (Terminal Cops); Ashton Stewart (Nate Wilson); William Neely (Ray Sarch); Windy Wenderlich (Henry Gates); General Fermon Judd, Jr. (Policeman); Deann Korbutt (Linda Ross); Rachel Lewis (Libby Grant); Kristen Leigh (Dottie Walsh); Simon Elsworth (Duffery Brtender); Jim Grimshaw (Gas Station Attendant); Matthew Johnson (Caretaker); Terry Neil Edlefsen (Drunk); Kelley Sims (Intern).

LOS ANGELES TIMES, 2/6/98, Calendar/p. 10, Kevin Thomas

[*The following review by Kevin Thomas appeared in a slightly different form in* NEWSDAY, 2/6/98, Part II/p. B7.]

"Stephen King's The Night Flier" is a provocative though murky thriller from the horrormeister that's heavy on gore and laced with more irony than perhaps intended. It's far from first-rate King, but his fans probably will feel it delivers the gory goods.

Best of all, it affords a big star role for Miguel Ferrer, a fine and distinctive actor.

Craggy, deep-voiced and rangy, Ferrer is terrific as Richard Dees, star reporter-photographer for a supermarket tabloid called Inside View. Actually, he's been slipping a bit, but he soon sees a way to get back on Page 1: A serial killer, in a black tricorn hat and flowing cape, flying a black Cessna Skymaster 377—it looks like an elegant giant-sized insect—starts landing at small airports along the Eastern seaboard, leaving in his wake a lot of bloody corpses with outsize gashes on their necks.

The film's point is to confront and overpower Dees, the total cynic, with the human suffering he has exploited so relentlessly in his career.

"The Night Flier," adapted by director Mark Pavia and Jack O'Donnell from King's short story, is King's jeremiad against the tabloid press. King raises a valid, currently much-debated point about where to draw the line in contemporary journalism.

But hasn't King himself exploited human nature's appetite for gore, and hasn't he benefited tremendously from the press, in all its stripes, in becoming a zillionaire writer? This blood bath of a movie, which bears King's name in the title, indulges in the very wretched excesses it attempts to criticize. There's a strong sniff of hypocrisy in all this.

Sardonic and commanding, Ferrer is pretty much the whole show, but Julie Entwistle, in her film debut, makes a firm impression as a rookie reporter whom Dees both insults and underestimates. Dan Monahan is fine as their editor, who loves his job with unashamed relish, and so is Michael Moss in the title role.

The film, which has a number of loose ends, is sleek but so dark you sometimes have a hard time seeing what's going on. In some scenes that's a blessing.

NEW YORK POST, 2/6/98, p. 47, Larry Worth

They don't make vampire stories the way they used to. And that's what—at least initially—brings intrigue to "Stephen King's The Night Flier."

In 1998, Dracula's kin still sport long swirling capes, destroy mirrors on principle and sink their fangs into victims' ravaged necks. But they now take wing via a Cessna plane and dine on whoever's tending the airfield.

That much is well and fine, but King's tale—or at least director Mark Pavia's adaptation of it—is more of an "All About Eve" scenario in a tabloid's newsroom.

Sure enough, there's tough-as-nails veteran reporter Richard Dees (a character who first appeared in King's "The Dead one") and the gal who idolizes him, a sweet-faced ingenue. Gloves come off when both are assigned to track the night flier—all while trying to survive visits from their elusive quarry.

Sadly, the, resulting fireworks are flubbed by director Pavia, who consistently mistakes gore for horror. Worse, a paint-by-numbers approach dominates from the requisite opening murder and continues for most of the film.

That's why the conclusion comes as such a surprise, filled with the black humor, suspense and imagination (a black-and-white "Night of the Living Dead" tribute) that the rest of the film so obviously lacks. It's the classic too-little, too-late.

Also wasted is Miguel Ferrer's deliciously arrogant pitbull-cum-scribe. A virtual ringer for his late dad (the Oscar-winning Jose), the young Ferrer's got a built-in eerie quality, nicely mixing with a carriage and old-fashioned presence that demands attention.

The same can't be said for Julie Entwisle's whiny new kid on the block. She's annoying at best, a quality that also defines Dan Monahan's bit as the tab's gore-hungry editor. Spitting out lines like "The fatties in supermarket lines are going to love this," the "Porky's" stalwart rings as true as an Enquirer headline.

That's unfortunate, because the mix of King and vampires—as demonstrated in "Salem's Lot"—can be truly terrifying. Thanks to Pavia, "Night Flier" only hints at the same.

Also reviewed in:
NEW YORK TIMES, 2/6/98, p. E10, Stephen Holden
VARIETY, 2/9-15/98, p. 71, Lael Loewenstein

STEPMOM

A Columbia Pictures release of a Wendy Finerman and a 1492 production. *Executive Producer:* Patrick McCormick, Ron Bass, Margaret French Isaac, Julia Roberts, Susan Sarandon, and Pliny Porter. *Producer:* Wendy Finerman, Chris Columbus, Mark Radcliffe, and Michael Barnathan.

Director: Chris Columbus.   *Screenplay:* Gigi Levangie, Jessie Nelson, Steven Rogers, Karen Leigh Hopkins, and Ron Bass.   *Story:* Gigi Levangie.   *Director of Photography:* Donald M. McAlpine.   *Editor:* Neil Travis.   *Music:* John Williams.   *Music Editor:* Ken Wannberg.   *Sound:* Tod Maitland and (music) Shawn Murphy.   *Sound Editor:* Robert Shoup.   *Casting:* Ellen Lewis.   *Production Designer:* Stuart Wurtzel.   *Art Director:* Raymond Kluga.   *Set Decorator:* George De Titta, Jr.   *Special Effects:* Todd R. Wolfeil and Robert J. Scupp.   *Costumes:* Joseph G. Aulisi.   *Make-up:* Michal Bigger.   *Make-up (Julia Roberts):* Richard Dean.   *Make-up (Susan Sarandon):* Marilyn Carbone.   *Stunt Coordinator:* Phil Nelson.   *Running time:* 120 minutes.   *MPAA Rating:* PG-13.

CAST: Julia Roberts (Isabel Kelly);   Susan Sarandon (Jackie Harrison);   Ed Harris (Luke Harrison);   Jena Malone (Anna Harrison); Liam Aiken (Ben Harrison);   Lynn Whitfield (Dr. Sweikert);   Darrell Larson (Duncan Samuels); Mary Louise Wilson (School Counselor);   Andre Blake (Cooper);   Russel Harper (Photo Assistant);   Jack Eagle (Craft Service Man);   Mak Gilchrist (Rapunzel); Dylan Michaels (Prince);   David Zayas and Jose Ramon Rosario (Policemen);   Lee Shepherd (Desk Sergeant);   George Masters (Maitre'd);   Robert F. Alvarado (Soccer Coach);   Sebastian Rand (Tucker);   Michelle Hurst (Nurse);   Jason Maves (Brad Kovitsky);   Julie Lancaster (Flight Attendant);   Charlie Christman (Stone Fox);   Anthony Grasso (Waiter);   Andrea Dolloff (Cocktail Waitress);   John Sadowski and Matthew Doudounis (Ben's Friends).

LOS ANGELES TIMES, 12/25/98, Calendar/p. 2, Kenneth Turan

Given that Hollywood thinks a big-screen version of "McHale's Navy" is a sure-fire idea for a feature film, it's not surprising that when a genuinely shrewd notion—like the one for "Stepmom"—appears, no one knows quite what to do with it.

The idea, a choice concept for a three-hankie weepathon, was writer Gigi Levangie's, and it was strong enough to attract stars Susan Sarandon and Julia Roberts. Take two women with the best reason to hate each other (the younger one has usurped the older woman's husband) and introduce a better reason to have to try to get along: The older woman has a fatal disease and needs to know her children will be left in good hands.

Given that a full five writers, enough to field a "Stepmom Scribe" basketball team, are listed on the final credits, and that input also came from the two stars, director Christopher Columbus and, for all anyone knows, the craft service guy as well, it's impossible to tell exactly who is responsible for what finally appears on screen.

What is clear, however, is that believing that anything worth doing is worth overdoing, and fearful that even one person somewhere in the back of the theater might not be sobbing, "Stepmom" has taken this viable idea and laid the emotion on thick as thieves. It may be unfair to ask a film like this not to be shamelessly manipulative, but wouldn't it be nice if audiences could be trusted to feel things more or less on their own without layers of unnecessary hokum entering the picture?

The five scribes (in addition to Levangie they are Jessie Nelson & Steven Rogers & Karen Leigh Hopkins and Ron Bass) and director Columbus have a run of lachrymose credits that prefigures what's going on here, including "Corinna, Corinna," "Hope Floats," "What Dreams May Come" and "Nine Months." So it's not surprising that every teary situation imaginable is put through its paces and that all sensitive moments are trumpeted by John Williams' insistent score.

These kids, to be fair, are a handful. Cute, but a handful. Young son Ben (Liam Aiken) is a magician-in-training and prone to disappearing at any moment. And older sister Anna (Jena Malone, the young Jodie Foster in "Contact") is so angry at Isabel she can hardly stand it.

Jackie (Sarandon), the aggrieved Mother Courage, is not interested in making things easier for her successful rival. Which means a good part of "Stepmom" involves Isabel messing up in one way or another so that Jackie or the kids can say terrible things about her, ranging from the comparatively benign "Slugs have a faster learning curve" to the more definitive "That woman is going to have nothing more to do with our children."

Stuck in the middle is the unfortunate Luke, and "Stepmom" benefits greatly from having Harris in the role. In acting terms as well as for plot purposes, his is a stabilizing presence, and Harris' performance does as much as anything in grounding the film and at least pointing it toward believability.

Sarandon and Roberts seem to have great fun sparring with each other, and Roberts does an especially appealing job as the striving stepparent. Though Sarandon is one of those actresses who never gives a bad performance, her work here is not among her best, suffering in subtlety and credibility especially if compared with what she's done before.

Ham-fisted though it mostly is, "Stepmom's" script does have a tiny handful of honest moments, like one of the children asking Luke, "Can you ever fall out of love with your kids?" More typical are times like the snowy middle of the night in the rural Hudson River Valley, when mom Jackie is able to come up with a baby-sitter in a New York minute so she and her daughter can share an ever so picturesque midnight horseback ride.

If this is "keeping it real," which the publicity insists was this production's watchword, reality, like most other things, is not what it used to be.

NEW YORK POST, 12/23/98, p. 40, Rod Dreher

Julia Roberts and Susan Sarandon have been quoted saying how much they hate the title of their new movie, "Stepmom." They probably think it's too generic and personality-free, and they're right. Unfortunately, so is their movie.

The more writers credited on a screenplay, the worse the film tends to be. It took five scribes to come up with this attractive-looking bourgeois bland-fest, but something this soulless and mechanical surely could have been efficiently spat out by scriptwriting software. This is the kind of tooth-rotter that resolves a deep-seated family crisis by having everybody bond during a Motown sing-along. Why do these feel-good warhorses usually make you feel so bad?

La Dolce Julia is Isabel, the willowy younger girlfriend of Luke (Ed Harris). Luke is formerly the husband of Jackie (Sarandon), and still the father of Anna (Jenna Malone) and Ben (a poor kid named Liam Aiken who, through no fault of his own, has his cloying adorableness shamelessly exploited by director Chris Columbus).

Anna and Ben hate Isabel, who shacks up in a droolworthy loft apartment with Luke, no matter how hard she tries to win their affection—and this pleases Jackie to no end. Spiteful Jackie lives in a gorgeous Hudson Valley house where she raises the kids full time and holds a major grudge against the lithe sexpot who stole her husband.

"Stepmom" is so devoted to its easy-listening brand of storytelling that it refuses to let anybody be too hard-edged. We empathize with Jackie for being stoic Mother Courage, but just when she starts to be too bitter a pill to swallow, she comes down with cancer. So now she's a noble sufferer.

And we want to like Isabel for doing her best to make a bad situation work, and for valuing her boyfriend's kids over her career as a fashion photographer (which is suspiciously undemanding here). But her martyr shtick isn't believable. Luke justifies walking out on his family to his hurting kids by telling them tenderly that "feelings change"—and that's meant to go down like warm honey.

Jackie's terminal illness forces the mildly troubled family to work out their differences, and there's not a thing here you don't see coming a mile away. Columbus stretches like taffy every scene with the remotest emotional content, very nearly stopping the movie in its tracks (it takes longer for Jackie to go down than the Titanic).

"Stepmom" is no "Terms of Endearment," which actually contained genuine sentiment. The manipulative Columbus spares us even the sting of death, and the riskiest, most courageous thing in the picture is Sarandon, 52, appearing onscreen without makeup next to Roberts.

As unsatisfying as the "Stepmom" screenplay is, the production values are tops, and it's still pleasurable to spend time with Sarandon and Roberts, who are so lovely and so professional they make even upholstered smarm like this passable. No matter how appealing these ladies are in mediocre roles, they're never more than tasty frosting on a mighty stale Christmas cookie.

NEWSDAY, 12/24/98, Part II/p. B3, Jack Mathews

It helps us to understand why the world is getting another holiday knockoff of "Terms of Endearment" to note that among "Stepmom's" executive producers are its two stars, Susan Sarandon and Julia Roberts. In stories where character conflicts are resolved through terminal illness, the only real changeable element is the cast, and, let's face it, actresses love this stuff!

In effect, "Stepmom" is a co-production of Roberts and Sarandon, who threw their combined star weight behind it, and made it a go for producer Wendy Finerman ("Forrest Gump") and director Chris Columbus ("Mrs. Doubtfire"). And here they are, just three months after Meryl Streep and Renee Zellweger had a similar go at each other in "One True Thing," ready to further enrich the makers of Kleenex.

"Stepmom" is a "good cry" movie aimed at a sentimentally easy female audience. It is heart-on-its-sleeve humbug, in which the most profound issues between people are resolved—or, at least, suspended—during a race to beat a literal deadline.

The movie, which claims more writers (five!) than main characters, follows the arcs of the relationships between successful New York fashion photographer Isabel (Roberts) and her lover's bitter ex-wife Jackie (Sarandon), and between Isabel and her potential stepchildren.

Though we never get a full explanation for the failure of Luke (Ed Harris) and Jackie's marriage, their shared custody of adorable 7-year-old Ben (Liam Aiken) and bratty 12-year-old Anna (Jena Malone), assure contact between Isabel and Luke's family. And for most of the movie, until a biopsy rearranges everyone's priorities, it's the kind of contact you get when you stick your finger in a light socket.

You might rather do the light-socket thing than put yourself through the overwrought hokum that follows. If the filmmakers had set themselves a goal of total predictability, they over-reached. The story, built on a foundation of tortured dialogue, not only follows a prescribed formula, but virtually announces every coming conflict, argument or turn of events, and leads, with everything but a drum roll and a dirge, to an emotion-drenched ending and a final image of shameless manipulation.

If you like everything you've read so far, you will not be disappointed. Roberts and Sarandon weren't wrong about the roles and their opportunities. Isabel and Jackie are strong, independent women who might be great friends under different circumstances, but are instead natural enemies forced into a kind of Cold War detente.

Through the first half of the film, when they're dealing with these dynamics, as two women from different generations having to reconcile their shared responsibility for the older one's children, "Stepmom" has a kernel of dramatic integrity. But the writers can't find the melodrama in that, so they pull out the ultimate catalyst, incurable cancer, and essentially change the subject by raising the stakes.

NEWSWEEK, 12/21/98, p. 68, David Ansen

A good movie is begging to be made on the subject of stepmoms forced to interract with their husbands' resentful kids, and ex-wives suddenly supplanted by new (often younger) women. It's a common situation strangely absent in Hollywood depictions of family life. "Stepmom" aims to fill the void, and bungles the job badly. Julia Roberts is the glamorous interloper in the lives of Ed Harris's two kids. A fashion photographer with such instinctual talent she seems to complete her shoots in two snaps, Julia has few skills in the parenting department. This fact is hammered home relentlessly by earth mom Susan Sarandon, a character who would try our patience were it not revealed that she has terminal cancer. We know that sooner or later everyone will rise nobly to the tragic occasion.

Roberts, Sarandon and Harris are all vastly better than the material (which took five screenwriters to concoct, all presumably adding their own favorite clichés). The stars manage to sneak some semblance of reality into a soap opera so jerry-built that half its dramatic crises would disappear if either of these well-off women ever thought to hire a babysitter. The director, Chris Columbus, hits every emotion square on the head and seems to repeat all his favorite scenes twice. No room for mixed emotions here: the petulant 12-year-old daughter Jena Malone) goes from hating her stepmom to adoring her in the course of a Motown sing-along. It's indicative of Columbus's touch that he takes a naturally cute 7-year-old actor (Liam Aiken) and milks his cuteness so hard it ceases to be genuine. Not a tear was shed by this hard heart, but in fairness I should report that from the midpoint on, my friend Harvey was in dire need of Kleenex.

SIGHT AND SOUND, 2/99, p. 56, Andy Richards

Divorced lawyer Luke Harrison lives in a Manhattan apartment with his girlfriend, Isabel Kelly. Isabel has a successful career as a fashion photographer, but is inexperienced at looking after Luke's two children, 12-year old Anna and seven-year old Ben, when they come round to stay. Their mother, Jackie Harrison, is scornful of the younger woman's attempts to mother her children, who are resentful of Isabel, and long for their father and mother to reconcile. Isabel takes them to one of her photo shoots in Central Park, but they become bored, and Ben gets lost. He is soon recovered, but Jackie is furious with Isabel, and threatens to get a court order preventing her from seeing Anna and Ben again.

After hospital tests, Jackie is told that she has cancer. She secretly embarks on a course of chemotherapy. Luke tells Jackie that he and Isabel are getting married. The children are upset by this news, but Isabel gradually begins to win their affection. As the side effects of her treatment take hold, Jackie is increasingly forced to rely on isabel's help with the children, and eventually reveals her illness to Isabel and her family.

Isabel is told that her quality of work is slipping because of the distraction of the children. She resigns. Isabel offers Anna advice on her love life, and their friendship develops. Jackie asks Isabel to take some photos of her and the children together. Jackie is told that the chemotherapy has failed. She opts to spend her remaining time at home with her children, making her peace with Isabel for their sake. On Christmas morning, Jackie says a formal goodbye to Anna and Ben. She invites Isabel into the family photo, and clasps her hand.

Chris Columbus has made films that evinced a certain cynicism about the workings of conventional families. Both *Home Alone* (in which Macaulay Culkin's Kevin pointed out that "families suck") and *Mrs. Doubtfire* were energetic, irreverent farces, intrigued by forms of domestic dysfunction. Columbus went on to direct *Nine Months* and to produce the Schwarzenegger vehicle *Jingle All the Way*, both of which offered up disturbingly conservative visions of parenthood, the former preoccupied with a regressive conception of 'naturalness' and the latter with a deadening materialism and a fantasist's view of fatherhood. *Stepmom* may switch the emphasis from fathers to mothers, and downplays Columbus' penchant for slapstick sitcom in favour of a more restrained form of melodrama, but the vision follows this deepening conservative trend.

The fulcrum of the drama here is the gradual replacement of Susan Sarandon's idealised career-mother Jackie with Julia Roberts' apprentice mother (and successful young professional) Isabel. The dynamic between the two actresses is the film's strong suit, the tension of the deposed older woman facing off against her younger rival managing to generate sparks whatever the risible excesses of the script. Consequently, Ed Harris' Luke is almost wholly marginalised (significantly, Isabel is the first person Jackie tells she has cancer, not Luke). Sarandon is characteristically effective, but there is something disconcerting about the conception of Jackie. The script tries to strip her of her sexuality, allowing her to respond to Isabel's patronising observation that she is "mother earth incarnate" with nothing more than a stoical smile (the film would be unable to countenance Jackie having a new lover of her own). Following her cancer diagnosis, Sarandon plays Jackie with something of the hard won grace that served her so well as Sister Helen Prejean in Tim Robbins' *Dead Man Walking*. Here, however, it shades uncomfortably close to smug self-righteousness, a willed saintliness that will entail her children always idolising her above Isabel. The reconciliation of the two women, we are reminded, is forced by circumstance rather than actively desired.

Isabel, for her part, is not permitted to sustain a viable alternative to Jackie's earthiness. She is alarmingly eager to jettison her successful, creative career (as Jackie once did) for the children; within the film's terms, career and motherhood are incompatible roles, with creativity diverted into domestic craftwork (*Stepmom* like *Nine Months,* constructs 'motherhood' with reverential awe). There is no mention of a nanny, let alone any discussion of Luke giving up his career, and no mention of Isabel's desire for any children of her own with Luke. Ultimately, *Stepmom* remains too glossy, contrived and schematic to sustain the interest; its pat, melodramatic pronouncements endeavour simply to reconstitute its divided family without interrogating its essential structures. But if the film leaves us little the wiser about the issues facing real step-parents, it at least manages to resolve the thorny ethics of whether or not to take a 12-year-old girl to a Pearl Jam concert on a school night.

TIME, 12/28/98-1/4/99, p. 173, Richard Schickel

The stepmom in question is Julia Roberts, a career-distracted fashion photographer. The baggage her boyfriend (Ed Harris) totes includes bratty kids and an ex-wife (Susan Sarandon) who resents her rival's youth and glamorous career. The ex-wife is a near saintly mother, though, requiring only a bravely endured onslaught of cancer to complete canonization. Her ailment also brings the warring women together in mutual admiration, shuts the kids up and gets everyone gathered, trembling chins up, around the tree for their first and last Christmas as an inspiringly functional extended family. Under Chris Columbus' direction, they make a pretty but utterly misleading picture in which cheap sentiment is used to supply easy, false resolutions to agonizing issues. It doesn't help to tell lies, even saving ones, about such matters. It may even be immoral.

VILLAGE VOICE, 12/29/98, p. 122, Amy Taubin

Stepmom is a woman's picture; *Thelma and Louise* is a chick flick. The only reason to think of them as a pair is that Susan Sarandon costars in both. Poor Sarandon, still doing penance for Louise's transgressions. It wasn't bad enough that she was forced to drive over the edge of the Grand Canyon. Now, she has to die of cancer.

Where chick flicks are exhilarating (they depict women rebelling against traditional roles), women's pictures are all about making women feel weepy (about the unjustness of it all) and guilty (for wanting more than a life of self-sacrifice). "Have a tissue," said the Columbia publicity person to the critics as they exited the advance screening of *Stepmom*. In the world of the woman's picture, two wet hankies trump two thumbs up.

Glossily directed by Chris Columbus and evasively penned by count 'em, five writers including Ron Bass, *Stepmom* is about the relationship between the two wives (or, more exactly, the ex-wife and the wife-to-be) of a successful New York lawyer. Sarandon plays Jackie, the ex-wife who's also a model mother; Julia Roberts plays Isabel, the wife-to-be, who's terrified of kids, but has a great career as an A-list advertising photographer; and Ed Harris plays Luke, a big moneymaker who is a passive-aggressive shit (although the movie poses him as Mr. Right).

Roberts and Sarandon have the makings of an inspired screwball-comedy couple. Roberts is a hysteric; Sarandon is an obsessive. The differences in their worldviews come from deep within their psyches. But *Stepmom* is about cancer and responsibility and a family becoming one through adversity. So what we get as a climactic scene is the two stars sitting across from each other in a restaurant, both crying into their bourbon. It's a pretty perverse form of competition—which one looks better with tear--stained cheeks?

Women's supposedly inherent competitiveness, and how men use it to their advantage, is really what this movie is about. When Jackie can't pick up her kids from school because she's having chemo, Isabel tremulously seizes the opportunity to prove she's got what it takes to be a mom. So what if she leaves two dozen people stranded at a photo shoot? It never seems to occur to anyone that Luke should take some time off from his law practice. With two rival wives, each trying to prove that she's more worthy of love, all he has to do is sit back and adjudicate the occasional catfight.

Loathsome though *Stepmom* is, the eternally coltish Roberts is always a pleasure to watch and Sarandon's mordant wit occasionally comes to the fore. "It should have been me instead of you" Luke says magnanimously on learning that his ex has cancer. "I'll go along with that," Jackie replies. Still, the actresses must take part of the blame for undervaluing their talents (and their sex). They're two of the film's three coproducers.

Also reviewed in:
CHICAGO TRIBUNE, 12/25/98, Friday/p. A, Michael Wilmington
NEW YORK TIMES, 12/24/98, p. E1, Janet Maslin
NEW YORKER, 12/28/98 & 1/4/99, p. 140, Anthony Lane

VARIETY, 12/14-20/98, p. 131, Todd McCarthy
WASHINGTON POST, 12/25/98, p. C1, Rita Kempley
WASHINGTON POST, 12/25/98, Weekend/p. 7, Stephen Hunter

STILL BREATHING

An October Films release of a Zap Pictures production in association with Seattle Pacific Investments. *Executive Producer:* Joyce Schweickert. *Producer:* Marshall Persinger and James F. Robinson. *Director:* James F. Robinson. *Screenplay:* James F. Robinson. *Director of Photography:* John Thomas. *Editor:* Sean Albertson. *Music:* Paul Mills. *Casting:* Amy Lippens. *Production Designer:* Denise Pizzini. *Costumes:* Susanna Puisto. *Running time:* 109 minutes. *MPAA Rating:* PG-13.

CAST: Brendan Fraser (Fletcher McBracken); Joanna Going (Roz Willoughby); Celeste Holm (Ida McBracken); Ann Magnuson (Elaine); Lou Rawls (Tree Man); Angus MacFadyen (Philip); Toby Huss (Cameron); Paolo Seganti (Tomas De Leon); Michael McKean (Roz's New Mark); Chao-Li Chi (Formosa Bartender); Wendy Benson (Brigitte); Junior Brown (Wrong Texan); Jeff Schweickert (Slamm'n Sammy); Bill Gundry (Man with Painting); Joyce Schweickert (Mary); Kathleen Couser (Frances); Melinda Martinez (Birthday Girl); Jennifer Lauray (Birthday Girl's Mother); Tom Balmos (Beer Delivery Man); Margaret Bush (Dress Shop Sales Woman); Liz Mamana (Coffee House Girl); Katie Hagan (Little Girl in Dream); A.J. Mallett (Little Boy in Dream); Steve Lambert (Man in Alley); Jim Cullum (Jazz Band Leader).

LOS ANGELES TIMES, 5/22/98, Calendar/p. 14, Kevin Thomas

At the beginning of Jim Robinson's delightful debut feature "Still Breathing," an attractive young woman, Roz (Joanna Going), is walking down a dark Hollywood alley where her car is parked when a man pulls a gun on her, only to be hit by a car. A shaken Roz calls 911 at a pay phone outside the landmark Formosa Cafe.

At that very second a young man, Fletcher (Brendan Fraser), in San Antonio has a vision of fragmented images of Roz and the Formosa's neon sign in the dark of night. At that moment you know it's just a matter of time before Fletcher locates Roz, the instant woman of his dreams. When they do meet, at the Formosa, Roz assumes Fletcher is the super-rich Texan that her pal Elaine (Ann Magnuson, aptly tart) has lined up to con into parting with major bucks for a worthless piece of art.

"Still Breathing" is really Roz's story. We all know women like Roz, attractive and intelligent, who have come to L.A. in hopes of launching a career and finding love only to find disappointment in either or both instances. A woman of apparent, if vague, artistic aspirations, Roz has in desperation become a crook hiding behind her job description as a "fine arts consultant."

Roz has in fact had such lousy luck with L.A. men that she gets kicks out of relieving guys of large sums of money. She has reached such depths of cynicism that we understand why she hesitated to dial 911. The best she can say for herself is that she's "still breathing."

Fletcher is going to throw Roz for a loop. He's this sweet, sensitive hunk, an artist of various pursuits whose principal work is playing a trumpet with a group of street musicians (who include Lou Rawls, no less) who perform on Alamo Plaza. Roz is not above resorting to sex to close a deal, but here's a guy who doesn't want to rush things.

Robinson brings a great deal of passion, humor and good dialogue to these familiar trappings of romantic comedy. There's a depth and caring to "Still Breathing" that you don't find in the usual major studio fare. The point is not that Roz is not what she seems but that she's lost touch with the person she once was, the person Fletcher and his equally free-spirited grandmother (Celeste Holm, radiant as ever) perceive her to be. Holm's Ida, speaking from experience, zeros right in on Roz, remarking how easy it is for a woman who is smart and beautiful, a formidable combination, to become disillusioned with men.

But because money is such a major item for Roz you wonder about Fletcher and Ida's sources of income. Ida has taken a small but elegant cottage, a tremendously inviting place signifying clearly some measure of wealth, for Fletcher to live in. We can only conclude that Fletcher and Ida don't worry about money because they have enough not to do so.

We are also left to understand that Fletcher's parents are no longer living rather than living elsewhere; in this film, vagueness about finances and death are unnecessarily distracting. Also, Robinson's opening sequence is staged with such swift, elliptical virtuosity it can leave you needlessly confused if you look away from the screen for so much as a second.

Going has real presence and ability, and you hope that she will break out of the promising leading lady category. Fraser looks to be a big star about to happen. He's physically imposing and has an acting range that encompasses the hilarious shenanigans of "George of the Jungle" to the strong, unapologetically gay son of "The Twilight of the Golds" to Fletcher, an intelligent romantic. Fraser has that knack of seeming to inhabit his characters totally—and he has a sense of humor, a crucial ingredient for a good-looking star.

NEW YORK POST, 5/22/98, p. 56, Thelma Adams

I never thought I'd be nostalgic for Brendan Fraser in a loincloth! But George, George, George of the Jungle, didn't you read "Still Breathing" before you signed on for James F. Robinson's exercise in magical phoniness?

George, George, George of the Jungle, watch out for that plot!

Texan Fletcher McBracken (Fraser) is a gentle giant of a rock sculptor and street performer. He harbors a romantic soul as big as his shoe size. One night, Fletch has a vision of his true love, just like his father, and grandpa before him. One word catches his attention: Formosa.

Is this almond-eyed brunet dream girl a China doll or a regular at L.A.'s Formosa Bar?

Fletcher McBracken, a name that catches in your teeth like rangy steak, hops a flight from San Antone to Taiwan via L.A. No slave to frequent flyer miles, he detours at the Hollywood Formosa.

When Roz Willoughby (Joanna Going) arrives at the bar, ready to part a Texan from his money, this comely con artist mistakes Fletcher for her mark.

Going ("Inventing the Abbotts") is attractive in a sulky, "Star Trek" Bajoran bitch-goddess way. Going reminds me of those stuck-up high school dominatrixes who ended bagging groceries at Ralph's until falling into early marriages.

Personally, I don't like Joanna going or coming; her acting style makes Cindy Crawford ("Fair Game") look methodical. This is a glitch in a romantic fantasy where the audience is supposed to want Fletch and Roz to come together against all odds. Couple therapists could send their children to med school on the problems these folks are going to have.

The movie's saving grace is the sunny presence of Celeste Holm as Fletcher's grandmother. But there should be a law that if Fraser doesn't make better movie choices, the talented actor has to appear in a loincloth at least once in every feature. I can't wait for his "Hamlet."

NEWSDAY, 5/22/98, Part II/p. B7, John Anderson

Would one more movie about perfect love, cosmic matchups, divinely inspired romance and fated amour make you just a little bit cynical? How about a movie where Celeste Holm plays the tuba?

"Still Breathing," by James F. Robinson, is, was and ever shall be a foregone conclusion: Its protagonists *will* get together and forever. The only question is: How long will it take?

Second question: How entertaining will it be to watch them run the high hurdles of love, molt away the tortoise-shell finish of emotional resistance and get down? In this case, pretty entertaining, in a hit-and-miss manner. Yes, the movie is shameless, the dialogue precious, the actions unlikely and the reactions even more so. But the actors are fun to watch, even when mouthing gibberish. And there's a patina of wealth enveloping the entire film, and who doesn't like that feeling of vicarious richness?

Take the early mugging scene. Roz (Joanna Going) is walking to her favorite Hollywood bar, reciting in voiceover her philosophy of love (basically, that she used to believe in it, but doesn't anymore). An alley-crawling street thug starts after her, she runs, he grabs her, she Maces him, he pulls a gun, a nicely refinished yellow '70s Firebird (I think) hits-and-runs the guy. She calmy empties his wallet and leaves him bleeding in the street.

What differentiates this from any similar scenes (if there are any similar scenes) is the high-grade accessorizing.

The gun owned by this presumably homeless degenerate is a very expensive large-bore revolver. His jacket is thigh-length leather, his pants look like crushed velvet (purple), the car is gorgeous, and Roz never breaks a sweat.

There's an aesthetic statement being made in this milieu, one complemented by the one we keep seeing in cross-cut: Fletcher (Brendan Fraser), a wild-haired, seemingly discombobulated artist somewhere in a Francis Bacon-inspired Texas mansion, who has this vision of Roz and by mind power steers the Firebird into the thug. It seems that the men in Fletcher's family have always experienced a vision of the women they would love; as his grandma (Celeste Holm) tells him—as they play a Verdi trumpet-tuba duet in a rowboat on a river—his grandfather picked her out of a crowded streetcar and "knew I had a mole on my back even's I was wearing a coat." Fletcher has just had his vision.

His problem—one of many—is that he has caught this incomplete mental glimpse of Roz going into the bar, called the Formosa, so there's this whole diversionary tactic about him going to China to find her. Roz is having her own visions, or dreams, about a little girl and boy and an episode that will haunt her later. But it doesn't keep her from practicing her craft, which is suckering wealthy, lusty men into paying big money for fraudulent art. She's been wounded in love, you see, and larceny equals therapy.

Also, she lives in L.A., which makes her a marked woman in this ode to bucolic Texas, where the air is sweet, the people sweeter and they never put mentally deficient prison inmates to death. Roz will be seduced by both Fletcher and Texas, although it takes her an awfully long time to figure out that Fletcher isn't the wealthy mogul she thought he was. Which makes her less intelligent than we think she is. It's a good thing that both Going and Fraser—who can be so classically handsome one moment and so goofily funny the next—are so attractive. 'Cause it may be called "Still Breathing," but you might occasionally want to check your pulse.

VILLAGE VOICE, 5/26/98, p. 132, Laurie Stone

Roz Willoughby (Joanna Going) runs cons in LA., hanging out at the Formosa Bar and seducing rich men into buying her expensive abstract art. When they move in for their sex candies, she plants medical paraphernalia and AIDS literature around her bedroom, so they will flee In terror. It's a living, and she's sick of men, and her crony Elaine (Ann Magnuson) sneers if she even suggests the possibility of real romance. While Roz is releasing tension by practicing knife-throwing in her apartment and on an off night escaping a leather-clad stalker, Fletcher McBracken (Brendan Fraser) is frothing himself cappuccinos and blissing out on his idyllic San Antonio homestead. His days are spent presenting puppet shows for children and playing Verdi duets with his tuba-tooting grandmother (Celeste Holm), while their adjacent rowboats drift on a lazy river. It's a tradition among the McBracken men to dream up an Ideal mate and then go off and bag her. Fletcher has imagined his, and she's—yes!—the cynical bad girl who needs saving.

In *Still Breathing*, Producer-writer-director James F. Robinson's bland, tedious first feature, love isn't an opportunity for two people to change, only the woman. Despite Fletcher's New Age, sensitive-guy trappings—he's the one to put brakes on sex—he's still smugly in charge, showing you can take the penis away from the man but not the phallus. He never doubts himself, nor recognizes that his romanticism is the flip side of Roz's cynicism, a fantasy projection. Robinson directs Going not as a femme fatale—lest we see Fletcher's ideal as a slut—but as a deer in headlights. Even her capture lacks tension.

Also reviewed in:
NEW YORK TIMES, 5/22/98, p. E14, Stephen Holden
VARIETY, 4/7-13/97, p. 47, Joe Leydon

STOLEN MOMENTS

A First Run Features release. *Director:* Margaret Wescott. *Screenplay:* Margaret Wescott. *Running time:* 92 minutes. *MPAA Rating:* Not Rated.

CAST: Kate Nelligan (Narrator).

NEW YORK POST, 4/10/98, p. 50, Bill Hoffmann

An intelligent, thoughtful exploration of lesbian culture through the ages. It begins with a recent gathering of dyke bikers in the West Village and—via reenactments, films, photos and drawings—travels back in time to ancient Greece, Paris and Amsterdam in the '20s and Germany under the Nazis.

There are many surprises here for the gay-history novice, including the fact that lesbians endured so much persecution. Even in sexually liberated Europe, gay women were once put on trial for the so-called "silent sin—the sin that can't be named" and punished by banishment, prison—even death.

Chock-full of engrossing testimonials from elderly lesbian pioneers, '60s activists and newly out-of-the-closet women, "Stolen Moments" is poignant and knowledgeable without preachy; explicit without being sensational. It's far and away the best movie about lesbians to date.

VILLAGE VOICE, 4/14/98, p. 64, Elisabeth Vincentelli

It may have taken Ken Burns several hours to tell us about baseball lore, but Margaret Wescott needed only 90 minutes to survey the history of lesbians in the western world. Previous documentaries on gay and lesbian history wisely had a narrower focus (the military, Paris in the 1920s, Stonewall) but, undaunted, the Canadian filmmaker felt we were due for a comprehensive overview. The narrative mode here seems to be free association. Leapfrogging across continents and decades, *Stolen Moments* careens from Amsterdam cafés to the Michigan Womyn's Music Festival, from Sappho to Montreal lesbians frolicking in the snow, from Dykes on Bikes to Gertrude Stein. Since source material was hard to come by (underlining the theme of lesbian invisibility), Wescott makes time with supposedly meaningful shots of rooms ... clothes ... women walking by ... women stroking each other's hair ... And when all else fails, she stages live, dioramo-like recreations of a Weimar cabaret or a 1950s American bar. The overall tone, aggravated by Kate Nelligan's ponderous narration, is relentlessly "inspirational"; after a while it's hard not to root for less Gertrude and more Gia.

Also reviewed in:
NEW YORK TIMES, 4/10/98, p. E14, Stephen Holden
VARIETY, 11/24-30/97, p. 67, Brendan Kelly

STOREFRONT HITCHCOCK

An Orion Pictures release of a Clinica Estetico production. *Executive Producer:* Gary Goetzman and Edward Saxon. *Producer:* Peter Saraf. *Director:* Jonathan Demme. *Director of Photography:* Anthony Jannelli. *Editor:* Andy Keir. *Music:* Robyn Hitchcock. *Music Editor:* Thomas Drescher. *Sound:* Chris Newman and (music) John Hanlon. *Make-up:* Carl Fullerton. *Running time:* 81 minutes. *MPAA Rating:* PG-13.

WITH: Robyn Hitchcock; Deni Bonet; Tim Keegan.

NEW YORK POST, 11/18/98, p. 50, Larry Worth

When Oscar-winning director Jonathan "The Silence of the Lambs" Demme is good, he's very good. But when he's bad...

Welcome to "Storefront Hitchcock," a concert film wherein the eclectic auteur basically sets the camera in front of English folkie Robyn Hitchcock and lets it roll for a seeming eternity.

Granted, this is a very different animal from celebrated Demme dramas like "Melvin and Howard," "Something Wild" and "Philadelphia." It's even a long way down from his current Oprah epic, "Beloved."

But as evidenced in his lensing of David Byrne's gyrations in "Stop Making Sense," Demme can make concert films to rival any of his fictional efforts. Sadly, he wasn't so inclined this time around.

Truth be told, Demme was downright lazy. That means viewers simply watch closeups or distance shots of the eccentric troubadour strumming his guitar, playing his harmonica and delivering his unique song list.

Clearly, the fortysomething, generically handsome Hitchcock must be at his most charismatic to hold viewers' attention. But even hardcore fans will be put to the test with ditties like "The Yip Song," wherein he musically addresses death from cancer, which is dedicated to his father.

For the most part, Hitchcock has a passable voice, best demonstrated on amusing numbers like "Filthy Bird" and the cleverly lyrical "Glass Hotel." His crooning is further enhanced at intervals when violinist Deni Bonet or guitarist Tim Keegan provides backup.

But the only other "action" occurs when Hitchcock's wardrobe shifts from one paisley shirt to another, or day becomes night in the storefront window behind him. The changes serve precious little purpose, only indicating that Demme shot the film at different intervals and then pieced it seamlessly together.

Viewers' acid test that boredom has set in occurs when one starts gazing through the titular pane at adjacent store signs, watching their neon outlines glow in the early evening. (Long before the halfway point, it's obvious that California Fashion's logo is a standout.)

Aside from allowing audience members to gaze at the world, the window also invites passers-by to stare in at Hitchcock. Few do.

No offense to Hitchcock, but it's little wonder.

NEWSDAY, 11/18/98, Part II/p. B9, John Anderson

Performers as musically disparate (and kindredly eccentric) as Glenn Gould and Steely Dan have, over the course of their careers, arrived at the same unfortunate conclusions: Live music is dead. Stage sound is too flawed. The studio provides the only real means of controlling one's music and perfecting one's art.

Control is the co-pilot of Jonathan Demme's "Storefront Hitchcock," and it poses a question: What if the performance is your art? Shouldn't the audience-craving entertainer want the same degree of control as the agoraphobic production wonk?

For the singer/songwriter Robyn Hitchcock, the stage is where the work bears full fruit—his traditionalist minstrel posture, stream-of-consciousness-styled lyrics and anti-standard song forms enjoying a thriving marriage to his tidily rambling introductions or "verbals" (in which he can take five minutes telling you why intros are useless). At the same time, his act is best served by intimacy, a quality habitually absent everywhere from the concert hall to the smallest club.

So Demme filmed cult fave Hitchcock with his back against the front window of an empty shop on Manhattan's East 14th Street, playing, talking and singing for four shows over two days (it would have been a great joke if there'd been no audience, but that apparently was not the case), melding them together into one virtually seamless (the seams show when Demme wants them to) performance. Occupying a folk-rock middle ground between Demme's "Stop Making Sense," the Talking Heads concert film, and the Spalding Gray monologue movie "Swimming to Cambodia," "Storefront Hitchcock" shows what a delicate touch the director has, how subtly he can manipulate lighting and camera angles to make Hitchcock's music even more absorbing than it is already.

Time becomes a bit uncertain—we see daylight through the store window, which rapidly becomes dusk, then night, then suddenly day again, with a parted curtain revealing a new, revitalizing backdrop of colored panes decorating the window. People, as they did before, peer in, check their watches, move on. They never distract from Hitchcock's performance. But they do help punctuate the idea that the man can spin such a seductive web of music and language without any of the accoutrements that have come to seem so necessary for the propagation of what Hitchcock calls the "great civilizing force of the late 20th Century," aka rock and roll.

What Demme has done for him, perhaps unfortunately, is provide Hitchcock with a perfect but unmatchable venue for his art, that intimate space that exists between a movie and its audience. No known stage can provide this level of control, not for a pop musician whose work, to use movie terms, exists without car crashes, shootouts or the occasional gratuitous meteor crashing into the planet.

SIGHT AND SOUND, 1/99, p. 57, Neil McCormick

Cult British singer-songwriter Robyn Hitchcock stands in a shop window chatting and playing songs to an unseen audience inside the shop. He is joined intermittently by violinist Deni Bonet and guitarist Tim Keegan. A constant stream of cars and pedestrians can be seen passing behind Hitchcock's back. Occasionally someone will stop and peer through the window. During what appears to be one continuous performance, the background shifts from day to night and back again.

Robyn Hitchcock is not exactly a household name. His seminal band, The Soft Boys, surfaced in the late 70s playing what he himself has described as 'sedate hippie gibberish' when the music industry was being engulfed by punk rock. Confronted by widespread indifference to such singles as '(I Want to Be an) Anglepoise Lamp' they broke up in 1981 though Hitchcock has continued writing and recording in much the same vein ever since, at first backed by a band called The Egyptians but latterly completely solo. He draws on 60s psychedelic pop as the basis for melodic and emotional compositions, blending bitterness, weirdness and surreal humour in unusual settings. Some critics would argue that Hitchcock's sprawling body of work (he has released over 15 albums) remains one of the great undiscovered treasures of modern pop. But there are probably just as many who think it should remain undiscovered.

Rock superstars REM are among Hitchcock's biggest fans and their endorsement in the 80s helped introduce him to the American college audience who comprise his most loyal fan base.

It was after a typically low-key show in New York that Hitchcock was approached by Jonathan Demme about making a movie. At first glance, the very idea of a feature-length concert film being made about an obscure English eccentric by an Academy award-winning American director seems almost as absurd as one of Hitchcock's off-the-wall monologues. Attempting to explain his appeal, Hitchcock has previously commented: "My stuff is not widescreen. It doesn't look good from a distance. It's more like an etching. You have to get right up close and look at it carefully." So what is he doing on the big screen?

Winning new friends and influencing people, probably. Before the enormous success of *Silence of the Lambs* and *Philadelphia*, Demme enjoyed critical acclaim for his simple, performance-based films about author and raconteur Spalding Grey (1978's *Swimming to Cambodia*) and art rock group Talking Heads (1984's *Stop Making Sense)*. Shot over four days and nights in a storefront in New York, *Storefront Hitchcock* follows the same stylistic pattern as the earlier films: a stripped-down minimalism that forces the viewer to focus intently on the performer. It is, in this sense, closer to the etching Hitchcock imagined than to anything routinely thought of as a widescreen experience.

Apart from a somewhat incongruous four-panelled split-screen during a guitar solo, Demme employs few of the techniques usually associated with rock videos and performance movies. There is almost no camera movement (discounting the occasional subtle zoom or slight pan), no rapid-fire cutting or extravagant staging (one song is performed by candlelight, another beneath a single electric bulb), no audience-reaction shots. The only distraction is provided by the intriguing setting. The out-of-focus, constantly moving backdrop of the city and the subtle yet peculiar shifts from day to night create a dreamlike sense of distorted time. Hitchcock truly seems to be in a world of his own, which some would say has always been the case.

Hitchcock is an acquired taste and if you don't acquire it, the film is likely to prove unbearable. His thin, reedy voice will have some wondering whatever might have convinced him he could sing. And his epic monologues (which sometimes resemble jokes without a punchline) are as likely to baffle as many people as they delight. Yet if you have the patience to settle in, relax and slowly adjust to his peculiar point of view, Hitchcock is a revelation. Although there is much humour in his act, he is not a comedian. His songs address a huge span of ideas and emotions and Demme's closeup style allows all Hitchcock's nuance and subtlety to register.

VILLAGE VOICE, 11/24/98, p. 117, Douglas Wolk

At his best, Robyn Hitchcock is a sweetly peculiar songwriter who wanders into the realm of death and back, and laughs quietly at it all; at his worst, he's a dotty nostalgic with a weakness for the easy joke. Jonathan Demme's second concert movie is a simple but nicely presented document of a middling Hitchcock solo performance. Dressed in his habitual awful Hawaiian shirt, Hitchcock plays in front of an unseen audience in an East Village storefront, against a series of odd props and backdrops that appear and vanish for no reason. Demme's got the eye of a fan who wants to proselytize, and the movie is full of loving portraits of his hero's eccentric gestures, his crowlike posture, his delicate, spidery guitar playing.

But *Stop Making Sense* this is not, mostly because Hitchcock seems to be having an off night. Too conscious of the camera, his notorious free-associative between-song spiels uncharacteristically awkward, he takes half an hour or so to shake off his discomfort and settle into cheerfully mocking vile bodies and organized religion ("I don't know what kind of church you like to imagine. I like to imagine a church filled with carcasses"). Hitchcock is great at establishing rapport with an audience, timing his babble about minotaurs and duct tape to their reactions, but watching it on film means observing that rapport from a distance. And the set list dips generously into his lamest recent material, slow, repetitive tunes that meander through forced non sequiturs. Hitchcock enthusiasts will find things to love here—some expansive, meditative guitar solos, a couple of monologues where he lets his id range freely—but the unconverted may wish they could watch without listening.

Also reviewed in:
NEW YORK TIMES, 11/18/98, p. E5, Stephen Holden
VARIETY, 5/4-10/98, p. 86, Dennis Harvey

SUE

An AMKO Productions release. *Producer:* Amos Kollek. *Director:* Amos Kollek. *Screenplay:* Amos Kolleck. *Director of Photography:* Ed Talavera. *Editor:* Liz Gazzara. *Music:* Chico Freeman. *Sound:* Theresa Radka. *Production Designer:* Charlotte Bourke. *Art Director:* Kirsten Kearse. *Costumes:* Seth Hanson. *Running time:* 91 minutes. *MPAA Rating:* Not Rated.

CAST: Anna Thomson (Sue); Matthew Powers (Ben); Tahnee Welch (Lola); Tracee Ross (Linda); John Ventimiglia (Larry); Edoardo Ballerini (Eddi); Austin Pendleton (Bob).

NEW YORK POST, 11/20/98, p. 69, Larry Worth

The title—"Sue"—isn't very catchy. But like the film it represents, the production is refreshingly unadorned, no-nonsense and straightforward.

Basically, this is an unpretentious character study of a lonely thirtysomething woman who's on a downward spiral. Unable to pay rent on her Lower East Side studio, she's on the verge of being evicted. Unable to keep the most menial of jobs, her prospects for rebounding aren't good.

Worse, the chain-smoking protagonist is her own worst enemy. She pushes away all offers of help, partially due to fear of intimacy. Rather, she engages in meaningless sex and depends on the kindness of strangers.

Coincidence or not, Sue's neediness and desperation evoke the fragility of Blanche Dubois, combined with Holly Golightly's eccentricities and a "Looking for Mr. Goodbar" death wish.

But the real reason Sue comes alive is Anna Thomson's heartbreaking portrait of a lost soul who can't stop herself from self-destructing. It's a brave performance, composed entirely of subtle gestures and soulful glances that never beg for sympathy.

And while newcomer Matthew Powers, Tracee Ross (Diana's daughter) and Tahnee Welch (Raquel's daughter) offer great support, it's all Thomson's show. She has a weird, almost ethereal quality and unconventional beauty that make her tough to dismiss.

One only wishes director writer Amos Kollek was Thomson's equal. Instead, he allows too many coincidences for the story to consistently gel. For instance, over a few days, he lets Sue meet more good-hearted Manhattanites—one willing to make a hefty loan to a virtual barfly—than Mother Teresa could have converted in a month.

Kollek proves far more effective at utilizing drab Manhattan locales as a backdrop for the less-than-uplifting goings on. Indeed, the Big Apple hasn't looked this unappealing since Ratso Rizzo walked its sidewalks.

In all likelihood, Sue will never gain Ratso's legendary screen status. But thanks to the complex way Thomson brings her to life one roots for her—and the film—to soar.

NEWSDAY, 11/20/98, Part II/p. B7, John Anderson

The purpose of the tragic figure, we suppose, is to reflect and illuminate. Hardships and anguish aren't of value in and of themselves, but in what they say about a character, and by extension us or our times. Unless, of course, you're a voyeur.

And what, exactly, is Israeli director Amos Kollek? In "Sue," he continues a pattern that was last exercised in "Bad Girls" (1994), the torrid tale of Hell's Kitchen prostitutes and an exercise in sleazy exploitation. In "High Stakes" (1989), one of his more highly regarded films, he had Sally Kirkland playing a stripper/prostitute, trying to retrieve her daughter from the mob. In "Sue," he fashions a tale of another woman lost in New York, who merely sleeps with every man she meets, does so, ostensibly, because her mother has Alzheimer's and doesn't make a lot of sense except as a solitary, clinical case.

"Sue" is supposed to be a consideration of the brutally cold existence foisted upon a tender soul like Sue (Anna Thomson), and might have been worth something had the character been the least bit believable. As conceived by Kollek, Sue is so horribly needy that the people she approaches for affection (everyone, basically) can smell her desperation. What we smell is a sadistic streak running through Kollek's movie, which starts at cold and unloving, gets progressively less welcoming and offers little more than the twisted portrait of a woman on her unstoppable way down.

What you have to give the writer-director credit for, even as he cast his female characters into his self-made hell, is that he almost gets bailed out by his lead actress—again. Just as Kirkland was the salvation of "High Stakes"—and Faye Dunaway made "Double Edge" watchable, and Julie Haggerty elevated Kollek's "Goodbye, New York"—the gifted Anna Thomson ("Unforgiven," "Angela," "I Shot Andy Warhol") gives a wrenching performance, one that rises above Kollek's fairly tortured portraiture. It would be nice to see more of her, although we'd draw the line at "Sue II."

VILLAGE VOICE, 11/24/98, p. 122, Michael Atkinson

A bald attempt at recapturing '70s loser cinema, à la *Midnight Cowboy, Scarecrow,* and *Wanda,* Amos Kollek's *Sue* suffers from invoking the era's desolate grit, but it's hard to argue with its sincerity. Unceremoniously chronicling the unremarkable fall and fall of an anonymous loser in the Big Apple, *Sue* dawdles, dozes, and mopes, in no great hurry to reach its despairing anti-ending. It's something of a *Mouchette* for unemployed Downtowners, with a litany of tolerated woes as long as the smoking lines on Anna Thomson's face. Thomson, who provided memorable bits in *Talk Radio, Unforgiven, The Crow,* and *Angela* has always seemed ruefully smudged, but here she's almost voluptuous, like a smudged Rene Russo. Still, you don't cast the sad-eyed, droopy Thomson as a master of the universe; Sue's a faceless mass, and the most you can hope for is the blissful absence of a surprise redemption. Kollek doesn't let us down.

Sue is not only jobless (her inability to find even degrading employment, despite her résumé, suggests Kollek's script is a few unedited years old), she's behind in her rent, friendless, loverless, not too bright, regularly confronted by sexual predators (many of whom, like the old man in the park who asks to see her breasts, she simply gives in to), and so lonely she begs long-distance operators to stay on her line and listen. Still, her life seems on one level action-packed: a belligerent slut she meets (Tahnee Welch) moves in for a while and initiates a threesome with a schmekel off the sidewalk, and a chance encounter with a hunky writer (Matthew Powers) blossoms into a romance Sue cannot bring herself to enjoy or trust. Kollek sits still enough for the occasional empty moment to get under the skin, but it's Thomson's unrelenting and completely convincing downtroddenness that matters. *Sue* is hardly a world shaker, and it's badly compromised by clumsy supporting perfs and Kollek's cheap taste for local "color," but it never betrays its sympathies.

Also reviewed in:
NEW YORK TIMES, 11/20/98, p. E34, Lawrence Van Gelder
VARIETY, 3/2-8/98, p. 87, Joe Leydon

SUICIDE KINGS

An Live Entertainment release of a Wayne Rice/Dinamo Entertainment production in association with Artisan Film and Mediaworks. *Executive Producer:* Stephen Drimmer. *Producer:* Wayne Rice and Morrie Eisenman. *Director:* Peter O'Fallon. *Screenplay:* Wayne Rice, Gina Goldman, and Josh McKinney. *Based on the short story "The Hostage" by:* Don Stanford. *Director of Photography:* Christopher Baffa. *Editor:* Chris Peppe. *Music:* Graeme Revell and Tim Simonec. *Sound:* Eric Enroth. *Casting:* Wendy Kurtzman and Roger Mussenden. *Production Designer:* Clark Hunter. *Art Director:* Max Biscoe. *Set Decorator:* Traci Kirshbaum. *Running time:* 106 minutes. *MPAA Rating:* R.

CAST: Christopher Walken (Carlo Bartolucci/Charles Barrett); Denis Leary (Lono Vecchio); Henry Thomas (Avery Chasten); Sean Patrick Flanery (Max Minot); Jay Mohr (Brett Campbell); Jeremy Sisto (T.K.); Johnny Galecki (Ira Reder); Laura San Giacomo (Lydia); Laura Harris (Lisa Chasten); Cliff De Young (Marty).

LOS ANGELES TIMES, 4/17/98, Calendar/p. 10, Kevin Thomas

In the admirably swift opening of the psychological mystery thriller "Suicide Kings," a smart B-picture with lots of A-pluses, a shrewd veteran gangster, wonderfully well-played by Christopher Walken, is kidnapped by a bunch of preppy types and whisked off to a suburban mansion.

It seems that the sister of one of the kidnappers (Henry Thomas) has herself been kidnapped and is being held for a $2-million ransom. What to do but zero in on Walken, who's sure to have access to that kind of money? (Thomas has credible reasons for not turning to his own rich father.)

"You didn't think this thing through too good, did you?" asks Walken, though he was initially impressed that these guys could grab him, dope him and tie him in a chair. But once they've pulled off their daring snatch, they seem to have serious problems figuring just how to play out the rest of their caper. They haven't exactly endeared themselves to Walken, having chopped off one of his fingers, explaining that they've already received one of Thomas' sister's fingers from her kidnappers.

If Thomas and his pals seem unsure of what to do next, that's not the case with debuting director Peter O'Fallon and his producer Wayne Rice who wrote "Suicide Kings"' exceedingly clever script with Josh McKinney and Gina Goldman. What ensues is a classic battle of wits, sustained by strong characterizations and a plot packed with surprises.

Early on, "Suicide Kings" deftly establishes the gangster's superiority over his captors. He's much like Beat Takeshi's gangster in the current "Sonatine." Walken's Charlie Barrett (born Carlo

Bartolucci) is a cold-blooded killer, but he has wit, courage and strength of character way beyond what these preppy jerks could imagine. Barrett is at least a man of his word.

As for his captors, in addition to Thomas' ineffectual Avery, they are a med student, T.K. (Jeremy Sisto), who Charlie immediately realizes is on dope; Max (Sean Patrick Flanery), the kidnapped sister's boyfriend; Brett (Jay Mohr), an obnoxious hothead; and Ira (Johnny Galecki).

"Suicide Kings," which takes its title from a game of poker, belongs primarily to Walken and Galecki, cast as a naive rich nerd, and they run with it. Ira has been conned into letting the guys he'd like to have as his pals use the immaculate, elegant home of his parents (who are away, natch) as the place to hold Charlie prisoner. Poor Ira shrieks at the outrage of what's going on, not to mention how disrespectful the guys are of his parents' expensive furnishings (and their liquor supply).

Galecki's Ira is hilarious, but Charlie knows that of the entire group he's the only one worth anything. For Ira, the incident proves to be an unexpected rite of passage.

While "Suicide Kings" takes place primarily in Ira's family mansion, there is lots going on elsewhere involving an amusing Denis Leary as Charlie's hit man, a guy obsessed with expensive boots. Striking a more serious note are Charlie's loyal supporters, his level-headed lawyer (Cliff DeYoung, impeccable as always) and Laura San Giacomo as a madam operating under Charlie's protection. The film's writers provided good material for the film's many actors, all of whom excel under O'Fallon's taut direction. The film benefits from another of Graeme Revell's mood-enhancing scores.

O'Fallon and ace cinematographer Christopher Baffa, sticking to tightly composed shots, make downtown L.A. pass for Midtown Manhattan in acceptable fashion in the film's opening sequences, and "Suicide Kings" has lots of rhythm and pace for a film so substantially confined to one setting. This Live Entertainment release is satisfying, unpretentious fun.

NEW YORK POST, 4/17/98, p. 52, Bill Hoffmann

Damn Quentin Tarantino! "Pulp Fiction" spawned so many imitators of his outrageous, innovative style that a new film genre was born called Tarantino Lite. A few of these efforts were good. Many, many more were bad.

Now comes "Suicide Kings"—the worst of the lot. It's a movie so unconvincing and messy, it deserves its own sub-genre: Tarantino Limp.

The movie tries to pass as a super-hip mix of crime, comedy and crumbling morals, but it ends up a bland blend of hackneyed Hollywood formulas and characters, including brat packers, mobsters, car chases, grisly bursts of violence and even the obligatory strip-club scene.

The plot sinks 15 minutes in. Aging mobster Carlo Bartolucci (Christopher Walken) is kidnapped by four snot-nosed yuppies who tie him up and chop off one of his fingers.

The reason? A sister of one of the yuppies has been kidnapped and *her* finger cut off. They order Carlo to use his muscle to get sis back. If he can't, they'll chop him up piece by piece.

Carlo calls on his righthand man Lono Vecchio (Denis Leary) to find the girl so he can go free.

But by the end, we're praying Leary will locate these idiot yuppies and chop *them* into little pieces.

These obnoxious rich boys don't look like they could pop a paper bag, let alone pull off an abduction. And their improbable scheme puts the story firmly in fantasy land.

There are dozens of plodding twists and turns in the story, and I bet the filmmakers patted themselves on the back as they thought up each one.

Walken—usually good in anything—sleepwalks through his role. Leary is the best thing here because he just plays his usual chain-smoking, foul-mouthed psycho. But unless you're a Leary freak, rent his great stand-up video instead.

The only thing "Suicide Kings" needs is a visit from Dr. Kevorkian to put it out of its misery.

NEWSDAY, 4/17/98, Part II/p. B7, John Anderson

There are wiseguy movies. There are movies made by wise guys. And then there are wiseguy movies made by wise guys. "Suicide Kings," an all-attitude-all-the-time mob film/situation comedy, would fall into this last category, riddled as it is with slickly recycled ideas and a pretty relentless series of winks, nods and irritating (if figurative) elbows in the ribs.

The chief wiseguy is Charlie Barrett, a k a retired and anglicized mobster Carlo Bartolucci, played by Christopher Walken, a k a the biggest scene-stealer alive. The chief wise guy is director Peter O'Fallon, who's had a lot of practice making pretty good television ("Northern Exposure" "thirtysomething," "Party of Five") but hasn't quite severed all ties with his past.

He's smart enough, though, not to give us too much Walken all at once. He sort of sidles up to him, showing his hands, then his profile, giving him up in increments, showing a sense of restraint that will shortly disappear from the rest of the movie.

Charlie's kidnaping—by Avery (Henry Thomas), Max (Sean Patrick Flanery) and Brett (Jay Mohr)—is a relative nuclear explosion. Careering through the Holland Tunnel, the kidnapers try to chloroform Charlie, tie him up and try to load a syringe full of sedative while avoiding tractor-trailers, which have never been able to move through the Holland Tunnel at quite this rate of speed, certainly not in the midst of the kind of traffic jam-demolition derby the yuppie abductors cause. Charlie, barely legitimized animal that he is, almost fights them off, but they subdue him. And once they do, the tunnel becomes miraculously clear of traffic and they blithely enter New Jersey, which is no way to enter New Jersey, or to conclude this kind of sequence.

But things get worse, and not just for Charlie. Bound and wheelchaired, he finds held hostage by the preppies—who now include T.K. (Jeremy Sisto)—so they can trade him for Avery's kidnaped sister, Lisa (Laura Harris). Never mind that Charlie had nothing to do with it: He knows people who know people. And to prove they're serious, they've cut off Charlie's finger—because, he's told, one of Lisa's has just arrived in a box.

So O'Fallon has set the stage for a good old psychological rumble between the immobilized Charlie—who's a bit too glib for someone who's just had a homemade amputation—and his naive captors, who seem to have set themselves up to be killed over love (the "suicide king," after all, the one with the sword through his head, is the King of Hearts). So what happens? We get the cartoonish Ira ("Rosanne's" Johnny Galecki), the neurotic suburban kid whining about how they're messing up his house and running up his father's phone bill. Plus, what feels like an entirely other movie about Lono (Denis Leary), a Charlie henchman who goes about breaking heads while worrying if he paid too much for his stingray-skin boots.

There's clearly more to this setup than is meant to meet the eye, which is OK: A formulaic mystery with easy plot twists and even sloppily appended comedy routines is as palatable as any other piece of mainstreamed entertainment. Except that O'Fallon and his script writers can't pull it off. There are holes in the story, not as wide as the Holland Tunnel, perhaps, but as big as exit ramps—which the filmmakers use to escape from a movie that was, like Charlie, a bit more than they could handle.

VILLAGE VOICE 4/21/98, p. 76, Laurie Stone

Through most of *Suicide Kings*, a jagged, captivating first feature by director Peter O'Fallon, Christopher Walken sits pinned in a chair. The energy usually buzzing out of his fingertips is channeled into his face, the customary pallor of which suits his character, former mobster Carlo Bartolucci, who is bleeding to death. It isn't giving away too much of this Tarantino-kissed, grisly comedy to say that, early on, Carlo is parted from one of his digits. An alcoholic, he doesn't have enough clotting factor.

Carlo's captors are a preppy rat pack, who have abducted the mafioso in order to locate the sister of one of their crew. The woman has been kidnapped and is being held for $2 million ransom. Her rich daddy won't pay, so the lads nab Carlo, figuring that although he isn't the culprit, he will find out who is and come up with the cash—if sufficiently threatened.

Too much tugging on the threads of this plot will leave it in shreds, though O'Fallon, along with writers Josh McKinney, Gina Goldman, and Wayne Rice, weaves a tricky enough web of deceptions. The game of fingering (as it were) the cruelest manipulator, however, is less fun than watching Walken play Cheshire cat to a roomful of fledgling rodents. The film allows him to tweak his movie image as a psycho. He's warmer, funnier, and friendlier than in many a full moon. Flattered by the regard of his keepers, he sees their attraction to crime as their way of earning dick points; the young actors, especially Jeremy Sisto and Scan Patrick Flanery, portray this impulse with equal parts nerve and naïveté. Long past needing to wave his gun, Carlo uses his head to winnow out the shame in each boy and to play them Against each other. Doing another turn as his patented spitting-wire thug, Denis Leary, as Carlo's henchman, has the funniest line, upon discovering the amputated finger: "Fucking sick fucks, it's from all that rap shit."

Also reviewed in:
CHICAGO TRIBUNE, 4/17/98, Friday/p. J, Michael Wilmington
NEW YORK TIMES, 4/17/98, p. E26, Stephen Holden
VARIETY,9/22-28/97, p. 39, Joe Leydon

SWEPT FROM THE SEA

A TriStar release of a Phoenix Pictures presentation with the participation of The Green Light Fund of a Tapson Steel Films production. *Executive Producer:* Garth Thomas and Tim Willocks. *Producer:* Polly Tapson, Charles Steel, and Beeban Kidron. *Director:* Beeban Kidron. *Screenplay:* Tim Willocks. *Based on the short story "Amy Foster" by:* Joseph Conrad. *Director of Photography:* Dick Pope. *Editor:* Alex Mackie and Andrew Mondshein. *Music:* John Barry. *Music Editor:* Clif Kohlweck. *Choreographer:* Stuart Hopps. *Sound:* George Richards and (music) John Richards. *Sound Editor:* Martin Evans. *Casting:* Gail Stevens and Andy Prior. *Production Designer:* Simon Holland. *Art Director:* Gordon Toms. *Set Decorator:* Neesh Ruben. *Set Dresser:* Shirley Robinson and Brian Winterborn. *Special Effects:* Stuart Brisdon. *Costumes:* Caroline Harris. *Make-up:* Amanda Knight. *Stunt Coordinator:* Tom Lucy and Terry Forrestal. *Running time:* 115 minutes. *MPAA Rating:* PG-13.

CAST: Rachel Weisz (Amy Foster); Vincent Perez (Yanko); Ian McKellen (Dr. James Kennedy); Kathy Bates (Miss Swaffer); Joss Ackland (Mr. Swaffer); Tony Haygarth (Mr. Smith); Fiona Victory (Mrs. Smith); Tom Bell (Isaac Foster); Zoë Wanamaker (Mary Foster); William Scott Masson (Mr. Willcox); Eve Matheson (Mrs. Willcox); Dave Hill (Jack Vincent); J.G.R. Ashton-Griffiths (Canon Van Stone); Matthew Scurfield (Thackery); Margery Withers (Widow Cree); Janine Duvitski (Mrs. Finn); Willie Ross (Preble); Janet Henfry (Mrs. Rigby); Paul Whitby (Stefan); Bob Smith (Nikolas); Angela Morant (Iryna); Gerardo Silano (Brother Bodan); Neil Rutherford (Brother Peter); Sanda Huggett (Brother Bodan's Wife); Frederique Feder (Brother Peter's Wife); Ellis Fernandez (Amy's Son, Stefan).

LOS ANGELES TIMES, 1/23/98, Calendar/p. 12, Kenneth Turan

Looking for a movie that's deep-dish romantic and old-fashioned, where passionate love shares billing with the power of the mighty ocean? No, it's not "Titanic" but "Swept From the Sea," a traditional emotional melodrama that benefits from fine acting by Ian McKellen as well as its literary origins.

Though Joseph Conrad's "Amy Foster," the short story the film is loosely based on, is not one of the writer's celebrated works, seeing "Swept From the Sea" underlines why classic fiction is such a hot commodity in Hollywood these days. Writers like Conrad believed in psychology and plot and were good at it, and even this trifling story from a master has the power and means to involve us.

British director Beeban Kidron has always cared about romance, but her films, at least those that have been seen in this country, have been different enough to give even confirmed auteurists pause. Taken together, the bracingly funny "Antonia and Jane," the eccentric "Used People" and the near-fiasco "To Wong Foo, Thanks for Everything, Julie Newmar" leave you with no idea of how Kidron would do with this kind of costume drama.

Helped by the vivid pictorial sense of cinematographer Dick Pope (responsible for Mike Leigh's most recent films), Kidron has done better than expected. Though it has some blemishes, "Swept From the Sea" is always involving, the kind of narrative-oriented, character-based yarn about the power of love that never goes out of fashion.

Newcomer Rachel Weisz, who debuted in "Stealing Beauty" and is soon to be seen in "Land Girls," brings mystery and an essential calmness and self-possession to the complicated role of

Amy Foster. To the other residents of her seaside village in 19th century Cornwall, Amy is distant and strange, but we see her as a kind of nature girl, a pagan sprite enraptured by the sea as the bringer of gifts most rare and wonderful.

Yanko Gooral (Vincent Perez) turns out to be the most unusual of those gifts. A Ukrainian highlander who left home for America, he is deposited by fate at Amy's door. When they meet, each has reason to consider the other an apparition, and there is a kind of rare and unexpected eroticism in the gentle scene of her washing his wounds and offering him food.

The story, as far as he knows it, is begun by Dr. James Kennedy (McKellen). The doctor is introduced displaying complete coldness toward Amy, prompting one of his patients, the wealthy Miss Swaffer (an expert Kathy Bates), to ask, "Why do you hate her so much?" His tale is told reluctantly and by way of explanation.

As the most educated man in the area and the only one who's traveled outside England, it is Dr. Kennedy who guesses that Yanko is not the guttural idiot the villagers take him for but an intelligent man speaking a foreign language. The two men bond through a mutual love of chess, and though Yanko gradually learns English, he cannot change the suspicion the town feels toward him.

Given that Amy is burdened with a similar outsider status, it is inevitable that their need to connect with another human being will lead her and Yanko to each other. One of the film's dramas involves the terrible stresses the xenophobia and small-mindedness of their nominal friends and neighbors place on these two.

As a woman of surprising clarity and absolute faith in her own instincts, Amy is much the stronger of the pair, and Weisz's fey performance also overshadows that of Perez, whose status as one of People magazine's "50 Most Beautiful People in the World" only partly cancels out an awkward fake-Slavic accent.

Other performers also sound false notes, but the commanding figure of McKellen, one of the giants of British theater, outweighs them all A splendid actor, McKellen does an almost magical job with the doctor, playing him with all manner of nuance and caring, turning the character into a complex figure whose thoughts and actions always fascinate.

With its operatic plot line and its throwback insistence that story and character matter, "Swept From the Sea" is the kind of film You have to choose to give yourself over to. "Fate is both inscrutable and without mercy," one character says, and sentiments like that are hard to resist.

NEW YORK POST, 1/23/98, p. 46, Michael Medved

Many movies fail because their actors exude too little charisma or star power, but "Swept from the Sea" fails because its two leads display too much.

Rachel Weisz and Vincent Perez are both so great-looking, so magnetic, so hugely likable that it makes no dramatic sense at all when the other characters abuse, revile and cast out these two sweet-tempered, starry-eyed lovers—virtually banishing them from an isolated, picturesque village on Britain's rugged Cornwall coast.

Even with the film's heavy-handed emphasis on the bigotry and ignorance that supposedly characterized this desolate place some 100 years ago, the hostility of the locals must seem comprehensible onscreen, and in this slow, soggy melodrama it never does.

Very loosely based on Joseph Conrad's 30-page short story "Amy Foster," the plot centers on a strange, haunted girl (Weisz) viewed as a pathetic simpleton by her neighbors.

When an immigrant ship sinks in a storm, hundreds of bodies wash ashore, with only a single survivor (Perez). He's supposed to be an earthy Ukrainian peasant bound for America, hated by the townspeople for his strange language and foreign ways, but the village outcast takes pity on him, ultimately sharing her mystical inner sanctum of a cave by the sea.

Rejected and hated even by her own mother (Zoe Wanamaker), even at a moment of deadly crisis, the heroine and her tender, sensitive mate receive sympathy only from the town doctor (the always capable Ian McKellen), a lonely bachelor whose love for the handsome young man seem anything but disinterested.

Kathy Bates plays another local loner, who tries to use her resources and standing in the community to help the persecuted love birds.

Director Beeban Kidron (best known for her dubious work on "To Wong Foo" and "Used People") captures stunning scenery, the aura of elemental tragedy, and an other-worldly, mystical quality in the unconventional beauty of Weisz.

Unfortunately, the 30-page story that inspired the project hardly provides enough plot to justify a full-length film, and the result feels padded and puffy.

French sex symbol Perez ("Queen Margot," "Cyrano") learned Ukrainian to emphasize the character's fish-out-of-water status, but his performance, with his stringy, long hair and incomprehensible chatter, contains unfortunate echoes of the all-purpose Eastern European oddity of "Taxi"'s Latka Gravas, or even Robin Williams' "Mork."

John Barry's full-bodied music, on the other hand, speaks a universal language, offering surging, rumbling romanticism that has become his specialty, but it will sound better on a soundtrack CD, separated from the film's disappointments and distractions.

NEWSDAY, 1/23/98, Part II/p. B7, Jack Mathews

Think of Beeban Kidron's "Swept From the Sea" as "Titanic" without the ship.

Now, that's a horrible thought to people less than mesmerized by the love story James Cameron contrived for his epic disaster film. But the love story in "Swept From the Sea," the tale of star-crossed lovers in turn-of-the-century coastal England, doesn't have a hint of contrivance to it. The passion between a strangely insular servant girl and the shipwrecked Ukrainian who washes ashore is as deep and consuming as the North Atlantic where Titanic went down.

The themes of "Swept From the Sea," which is adapted from Joseph Conrad's 1901 short story "Amy Foster," are as old as romantic love itself. Amy (Rachel Weisz) and Yanko (Vincent Perez) are a couple bonded first out of loneliness, compassion and mutual attraction, then caring and love, and finally, by a shared strength against the pressures weighing against them.

"Amy Foster" is thought to have been inspired by Conrad's brief stay in London, when he was an impressionable 21-year-old Polish-Russian seaman, and was taken aback by the hostility he faced as a foreigner who could speak no English. The pain of that experience surfaces in Yanko in "Swept From the Sea," after he encounters the wary, close-minded locals of Cornwall.

Dirty, disheveled, and speaking in a tongue familiar to no one, Yanko is immediately taken for a savage, then an idiot, or a dangerous criminal. Only Amy, whose withdrawn manner has her taken for a simpleton herself, sees the gentle, civilized man behind the frightened eyes, and shows him compassion.

Later, the town doctor (Ian McKellen), who has a more open mind than the fishmongers and farmers of the village, finds a common language with Yanko—they both play chess—and begins teaching him English. But the townspeople still feel threatened, by both Yanko and his relationship with Amy, and when the couple announce they intend to marry, all hell breaks loose, both figuratively and literally.

The dramatic images from the storm that batters the craggy coast of Cornwall in the film's climactic scenes are simultaneously exhilarating and frightening, mimicking the tragedy that brought Yanko and Amy together. Which is the more powerful aggressor, Kidron is asking us, nature or man? Which do they have to fear most?

"Swept From the Sea" was filmed by Mike Leigh's regular cinematographer Mike Pope, meaning he's more experienced at capturing emotional storms than meteorological ones. But here, he's got them both, overlapping, clashing, creating a power of almost unbearable intensity.

The love story and the conflicts are relatively straight-forward, conventional literary melodrama, but it's rarely done with the honesty of Kidron and a terrific cast that, besides the two leads, features compelling performances from McKellen and Kathy Bates, the sympathetic land owner who tries to help Yanko and Amy find peace.

But the movie's success hinges on the gripping power of the lovers' relationship, and the actors are superb. Weisz, a British stage actress just making her way into film (she was Keanu Reeves' co-star in "Chain Reaction"), seems to light Amy from within, giving her qualities that are both mysterious and simple, earthy and ethereal, passionate and considered. Perez, the French actor who made his American film debut as the lead in "The Crow: City of Angels," makes us believe Yanko is a man full of life, hope and idealism, even before he begins speaking English.

To borrow an expression from a century later, Yanko and Amy are the most grounded characters in the story.

SIGHT AND SOUND, 5/98, p. 40, Peter Matthews

Cornwall, England. In a remote coastal village towards the end of the nineteenth century, the ailing Miss Swaffer asks her doctor James Kennedy to relate a love story, which started several years before...

An immigrants' ship is lost at sea during a violent storm and the sole survivor is a young Russian named Yanko Gooral, who staggers to a nearby farm.

The only villager to show him kindness is servant girl Amy Foster, who is herself an object of local suspicion because of the unseemly haste with which her parents married. Amy shows Yanko the secret cave where she stores treasures thrown up by the sea. Local eminence Mr. Swaffer and his daughter Miss Swaffer take an interest in Yanko's case, as does Dr. Kennedy, who teaches him English. However, a report of Amy and Yanko's embracing reaches Amy's father Isaac, who then beats Yanko and dunks him in the sea.

Defiantly, Yanko asks Mr Swaffer's permission to wed Amy. However, Amy's mother Mary reveals that Isaac and his father both forced themselves on Mary before her marriage—so Isaac is actually Amy's brother. Appalled, Amy repairs to her cave, but discovers that the bigoted locals have set her sea memorabilia on fire. Yanko rescues her. The persecuted couple are married and Swaffer bestows on them a country cottage. In due course, Amy gives birth to a son. Soon after, Yanko catches pneumonia. Delirious, he tries to harm the baby. Amy seeks assistance from the Swaffers. She returns just in time for Yanko to die in her arms. Disgusted by what he takes to be Amy's desertion of her husband, Kennedy grows estranged from her. As he finishes recounting the sad tale, he realises his error. He goes to Amy and begs her forgiveness.

It would be slightly unfair to say that Beeban Kidron's *Amy Foster* is Joseph Conrad by way of Catherine Cookson—but only slightly. The movie is almost exemplary of present Hollywood practice in that prodigious amounts of thought, care and technical skill have succeeded in turning Conrad's hard nugget of a yarn into a piece of sumptuous mush. As an instance of goofball revisionism, it can't compare with Roland Joffé's irresistibly rubbishy *The Scarlet Letter* since the only big laugh occurs when passionate sea-nymph Amy and her forbidden lover Yanko couple rhythmically while half-immersed in a magical torch-lit pool. A case might be made for Kidron and screenwriter Tim Willocks having 'feminised' a recalcitrant male author by tapping his heretofore unsuspected potential as a bodice-ripper. Judging from the handsome academic compositions and the abundance of water imagery, the film-makers were probably aiming at a classy metaphorical number along the lines of Jane Campion's *The Piano*. Both movies feature tight-lipped, quasi-pagan heroines in touch with primordial nature (Amy spins ecstatically around in the rain when she isn't gathering baubles from the sea). But for all that was high-toned and sanctimonious in Campion's film, it recognised the power of unbroken silence on the screen. Kidron seems to respect Conrad's own rugged core of silence, a care she demonstrates in one grave, wordless sequence where Amy intently washes Yanko's hands and feet. Yet the director's gestures towards austerity are strangled by John Barry's orchestral score, which whooshes up in almost every scene. Loud, bombastic, wholly anonymous and unable to stir any response beyond the most Pavlovian, the music might stand as an emblem of US cinema's current reluctance to tell even the simplest story without overkill.

This is quite a switch of material from Kidron's last film, the drag spectacular *To Wong Foo, Thanks for Everything!, Julie Newmar*. Yet Kidron's talent for close observation (sharpened in a number of television documentaries) comes through in moments when the camera bears down on the lovers' faces to register the flickering play of their intimacies. There are also a few impressive examples of deep-focus staging, giving certain interior scenes the rigidly posed elegance of a William Wyler production circa 1941.

Kidron has worse luck with the exterior shots, for there she must pass the reins to the Steadicam operator and the aerial photographer, who go barrelling merrily over Cornish sea and cliff to whip up the machine-tooled grandeur. Once again, a US movie conflates epic feeling and technological barbarism—though even on this level, it's surprising how little is done with the initial shipwreck or with Yanko's emergence from the primeval wet (a photo opportunity if there ever was one).

While *Amy Foster*'s romantic aspirations and perfunctory shipwreck aren't likely to drain away *Titanic*'s audience, the visual hyperbole is sufficient to crowd out Conrad's Spartan tale. Like many contemporary filmmakers, Kidron seems to think in individual shots and sequences, without bothering much about the overall pacing and continuity. A superior craftsman like Wyler would have known how to sell the revelation of Amy's birth—it lays a dramatic egg here since no one has thought to bring forward her parents' shadowy role in the narrative. Similarly, the pivotal issue of xenophobia lacks bite because the intolerant rustics are presented as an undifferentiated mass, whose characerisation amounts to quaint expressions like "Get you in that house, girl" and "Well, I never did". Yet against heavy odds, the stars make the movie semi-watchable. As Yanko, vincent Perez seems a questionable Russian at first, but he takes hold of the part and lends it a touching air of courtliness. Constrained to near-muteness for long stretches of the picture, Rachel Weisz beautifully conveys Amy's all-consuming need for her lover by checking her bodily movements and acting with her eyes. The broad grin she flashes when Yanko politely declares his interest is like a glint of living reality scratched on the film's hunk of unremitting hardware.

VILLAGE VOICE, 2/3/98, p. 122, Michael Atkinson

Beeban Kidron's *Swept From the Sea* is relatively graceless, a thuddingly melodramatic flesh-out of Joseph Conrad's short story "Amy Foster," in which shipwrecked Ukrainian Vincent Perez ruts with nutty, local Cornwall girl Rachel Weisz in a candlelit tidal-pool cave (another great seduction idea) and incenses the beetle-browed locals. Coiffed like a lost member of Danzig, Perez stumbles over his English believably, but the rest of the Cornish rabble are BBC castoffs tromping around in ratty wool. Told in alternating flashbacks to each other by doctor Ian McKellen and patient Kathy Bates, as if both weren't witness to the entire story, Kidron's cut-rate Brönte-ism comes off as an attempt to revisit the exquisite mediocrity of *Ryan's Daughter,* which is majestic by comparison.

Also reviewed in:
CHICAGO TRIBUNE, 1/23/98, Friday/p. C, Michael Wilmington
NEW YORK TIMES, 1/23/98, p. E10, Stephen Holden
VARIETY, 9/15-21/97, p. 78, Leonard Klady

SWINDLE, THE

A New Yorker Film release of an MK2 Productions/TFI Films Production/CAB Productions/ Television Suisse Romande/ Teleclub/Rhone-Alpes Cinema co-production with the participation of Canal+ and with the support of La Procirep and the Swiss Federal Cultural Office (DFI). *Producer:* Marin Karmitz. *Director:* Claude Chabrol. *Screenplay (French with English subtitles):* Claude Chabrol. *Director of Photography:* Eduardo Serra. *Editor:* Monique Fardoulis. *Music:* Matthieu Chabrol. *Sound:* Jean-Bernard Thomasson and Claude Villard. *Production Designer:* François Benoit-Fresco. *Costumes:* Corinne Jorry. *Running time:* 105 minutes. *MPAA Rating:* Not Rated.

CAST: Isabelle Huppert (Betty); Michel Serrault (Victor); François Cluzet (Maurice); Jean-François Balmer (Monsieur K); Jackie Berroyer (Chatillon); Jean Benguigui (Guadeloupe Gangster); Mony Dalmes (Signora Trotti); Thomas Chabrol (Swiss Desk Clerk); Greg Germain (Chatty Man); Nathalie Kousnetzoff (Blond Woman); Yves Verhoeven (Pickpocket); Henri Attal (Greek Vendor); Gunther Germain (Chatty Man's Friend); Maurice Debranche (Guadeloupe Taxi Driver); Stefan Witschi (Swiss Maitre d'); Rodolphe Ittig (Belgian Dentist); Dodo Deer (Hungarian Dentist); Barbara-Magdalena Ahren (Wife of Hungarian Dentist); Alexander Seibt (Chair-Lift Worker); James Hauduroy (Barman at Hotel Waldhaus); Elie Axas (Flight Attendant); Emmanuel Guttierez (Barman at the Park Hotel); Gilbert Laumord (Tall Black Man); Yvon Crenn (Mafioso); Marie Dubois (Dédette); Brygida Ochaim (Dancer).

NEW YORK POST, 12/23/98, p. 44, Jonathan Foreman

"The Swindle" is a slow, predictable and ultimately empty film that takes a familiar plot—an oddly-matched pair of grifters; get in over their heads—and squeezes all the life out of it.

Written and directed by Claude Chabrol—perhaps the most overrated of the French New Wave filmmakers—it strains to be witty. But it's the sort of assembled-by-numbers film where everything takes too long to happen: Someone says they are going to Paris and you see them go up to the plane, sit in the plane, get off the plane and get into a taxi.

The woman, a blank-faced Isabelle Huppert (whose acting talents have never matched the wonder of her green eyes), picks up businessmen at conventions, slips them mickeys, and then brings in her older male partner (Michel Serrault) to relieve them of most but never all of their cash. When she meets a businessman (Francois Cluzet) who is himself planning to con his gangsterish employers, she and the old man plan to make a really big killing.

Never has the con game seemed more joyless or joblike. In a shallow bid to wring mystery and Gallic mystique out of the kind of story even the worst American B-movies do much better, you never find out if the charmless older man/younger woman team are father and daughter, husband and wife, or just friends. But in the end it's hard to care.

VILLAGE VOICE, 12/29/98, p. 122, Amy Taubin

Claude Chabrol specializes in bleak social comedies and brutal historic melodramas that take a pickax to the economic and power relationships of the bourgeoisie. *The Swindle,* his 50th film, is a failed attempt at frivolity. Isabelle Huppert and Michel Serrault play a pair of con artists, long-term partners who, despite a 25-year age difference, may have been lovers at some time in the past. In any event, this is a symbiotic relationship. Their most ambitious caper takes them from Paris to the Swiss mountain resort of Sils-Maria (where Nietzsche wrote *Thus Spake Zarathustra)* to the Caribbean. The scenery is fetchingly photographed, as is Huppert, who changes wigs as often as others change their underpants. Even in the most tired situations, Chabrol has a few sophisticated filmmaking tricks up his sleeve. Thus the double-crossing protagonists have a visual correlative in traveling shots where it's impossible to tell if it's the cars or the camera that's changed direction.

Also reviewed in:
NEW YORK TIMES, 12/23/98, p. E5, Janet Maslin
Variety, 9/29-10/5/97, p. 63, David Rooney

T-REX:BACK TO THE CRETACEOUS

An Imax Corporation release. *Executive Producer:* Andrew Gellis. *Producer:* Antoine Compin and Charis Horton. *Director:* Brett Leonard. *Screenplay:* Andrew Gellis and Jeanne Rosenberg. *Story:* Andrew Gelllis and David Young. *Director of Photography:* Andrew Kitzanuk. *Editor:* Jonathan Shaw. *Music:* William Ross. *Running time:* 45 minutes. MPAA Rating: Not Rated.

CAST: Peter Horton (Dr. Donald Hayden); Liz Stauber (Ally Hayden); Kari Coleman (Elizabeth Sample); Laurie Murdoch (Barnum Brown); Tuck Milligan (Charles Knight).

LOS ANGELES TIMES, 10/23/98, Calendar/p. 18, John Anderson

[The following review by John Anderson appeared in a slightly different form in
NEWSDAY, 10/23/98, Part II/p. B11.]

The 3-D headgear may make you feel like Rick Moranis in "Spaceballs," or Michael Dukakis peeking out of a tank, but the experience of Imax technology is a trip. And we mean it.

What else do you call a film in which the heroine sniffs dino-dust and starts having hallucinations inhabited by hadrosaurs, pterodactyls and—ta da!—Tyrannosaurus rex? In "T-Rex: Back to the Cretaceous," a nose full of prehistoric powder sends the not-quite-happy Ally (Liz Stauber) on a mind-bender into lizard land, which may or may not be family entertainment.

The technology of Imax has gotten so good that "T-Rex" is often quite stunning: When a hammer-wielding paleontologist sends stone chips flying at your face, you duck. But the expense of the production, presumably, seems to dictate that the movies be as mainstream as possible and geared toward family audiences that want to be educated as well as entertained, so they can feel they got the most for their dollar (especially for films that are less than feature-length). This is not to say that Imax should be going the sex-and-violence route, but there's a certain amount of dramatic entropy that results when you want to be as palatable as possible to as many viewers as possible.

Of course, if you're properly engrossed in the 3-D imagery, you're not listening to the narration anyway, which involves Ally, a child of divorce whose world-renowned paleontologist father Donald Hayden (Peter Horton) keeps leaving her behind when he embarks on his bone-hunting trips.

Wandering around the museum in which he has his offices, Ally knocks a dinosaur egg off her father's desk (why it's perched there is certainly a question) and the resulting vapors knock Ally for a loop.

Ally walks in and out of the Cretaceous period, rescuing a T. rex egg from a predator, seeing the comet-induced nuclear holocaust that wiped the dinosaurs out and bumping into both Charles Knight (Tuck Milligan), the celebrated dinosaur illustrator of the '20s, and Barnum Brown (Laurie Murdoch), "the most famous bone hunter in history." The scenery is spectacular, and director Brett Leonard creates the right situations—Donald and an assistant rappelling down a cliff face, for instance—to best exploit the 3-D properties of the film.

It's a totalitarian medium, though, sort of like something out of "A Clockwork Orange." The Imax camera makes you look where it wants you to, because the point of focus is small. Enjoying the background when a character is speaking, therefore, can be uncomfortable. The Imax technology may be further improved at some time so that this isn't a factor. Or we'll just have to train ourselves in the proper way to watch an Imax movie, because it seems to be sticking around.

NEW STATESMAN, 12/11/98, p. 37, Jonathan Romney

Cinema, according to one notorious adage, is "truth at 24 frames a second". But what is cinema when it comes at 48 frames a second, projected in three dimensions on a screen seven storeys high?

IMAX is an invention calculated to evoke millennial anguish about the future of cinema. At the end of film's first century, visual technology has become so sophisticated that, for some prophets of the medium, nothing could be more archaic than the act of simply sitting and gazing at two-dimensional images. Director Brett Leonard has already dabbled in fantasies of virtual reality in films such as "The Lawnmower Man", and now operates the gargantuan machinery of IMAX 3D in "T-Rex: Back to the Cretaceous". The format, he claims, "is taking cinema to the next place that it's going... [It] creates the closest thing to truly immersive virtual reality that exists on the planet."

IMAX's weapons in its assault on our consciousness are sheer size and phenomenal technology. You watch the 3D projection on a vast screen, through goggles with liquid crystal lenses that flicker in and out of phase 48 times a second. The frames are ten times bigger than normal 35mm film, and therefore contain ten times the customary amount of visual information.

IMAX, which also comes in 2D, reworks the familiar film-going experience with a view to greater intensity and (supposedly) an enhanced sense of reality. But it uses curiously oppressive means to do it. Attuned to 24 frames a second, we find ourselves outpaced by pictures projected at twice that speed: our eyes and minds aren't fast enough to spot the sleight-of-image. We're conned into thinking we see solid objects; we're effectively robbed of the critical distance our perceptions normally maintain in the cinema.

In this respect, IMAX looks not to the future and a more sophisticated viewing process, but towards a mythical past, a more primitive way of seeing. It aims to stir us to naive awe, like that supposedly felt by the very first film-goers when the Lumiere brothers' cinematograph sent an express train rushing seemingly straight into their midst. As so often happens with futuristic technological utopias, the urge is actually for a state of lost innocence. In fact, that's pretty much the theme of "T-Rex", which wants to turn 1990s viewers into primeval gawpers slack-jawed before the big lizards.

In terms of sheer wonder, "T-Rex" is a poor relation to *Jurassic Park*. At 40 minutes, it sacrifices that film's narrative drive for a loose series of tableaux, a spectacular, vaguely instructive prehistoric pageant. Its teenage heroine Ally is mysteriously zapped back to the Cretaceous era, as well as to more recent times for edifying chats with eminent pioneers of paleontology. But for all the film's educational aspirations, you learn next to nothing about dinosaurs, since the distracting solidity of the images makes it almost impossible to register the dialogue.

It goes without saying that what we register is the effects—and not necessarily the most showy, solid ones, either. The film's strangest features stem from the hallucinatory properties of the screen itself. When the camera points up, we seem to be looking up, and when it points down, we look down—shifts of perspective brilliantly exploited in a mountaineering sequence. There are disconcerting changes of dimension: when the camera shows us a vast perspective, the screen itself seems to stretch to infinity, but in close-ups, the screen appears to shrink, presenting objects as if in actual size. Ironically, IMAX's most challenging possibilities may be as a cinema of intimacy and miniature.

With all its unexpected shifts of consciousness, "T-Rex" feels oddly like an acid movie for family audiences. There's even one sequence in which bones and museum artefacts fly at you in mid-air, as if you'd been thrust flailing into the cover of a Carlos Castaneda paperback. In keeping with this incongruously lysergic quality, "T-Rex" provides beauty and idiocy in equal proportions.

What it doesn't provide is anything resembling reality, even though IMAX is haunted by an obsession with the real. Stunts have to be performed by the actors themselves, since stunt doubles would be easily spotted on such a huge screen; and actors must give muted, natural performances, since overacting would be ludicrously amplified. Yet "T-Rex" mostly deals in pure illusion. The dinosaurs may be certified accurate in every detail, yet they are entirely computer-generated. When a T-Rex quizzically flares its nostrils, the only awe we feel is at the extraordinary craft that has gone into creating these finely veiled and gently throbbing orifices, nostrils worthy of a Cellini.

IMAX may never get round to exploring its true potential for disorientation and abstraction—although the most exciting thing I've seen in the format is a trailer for 3D animation, in which amorphous coloured blobs float in your lap or plummet at you from above. But one thing IMAX can never shake off is its own unwieldy gigantism. The raw, facts about the format tend to the crassly numerical—a camera that weighs 240 pounds, computer imagery that demands 50 megabytes per frame ... You can't help thinking that the future of filmic reality is not in the hands of cinema's corporate heavy artillery, but of the footsoldiers with camcorders.

NEW YORK POST, 10/23/98, p. 44, Larry Worth

Was it a giant meteor? A massive heat wave? A volcanic blast? Truth be told, no one knows why the dinosaurs died out.

But there's no getting around what fells the giant reptiles in "T-Rex: Back to the Cretaceous." It's the prehistoric script.

That's a shame, because this is the most anticipated 3-D IMAX film to date. And as such, it's the biggest disappointment.

Advertisements would have one thinking that the residents of Jurassic Park are jumping off the eight-stories high IMAX screen from start to finish. Sad to say, it's precious few dinos for viewers' dollars.

Instead, the plot is like a "Twilight Zone" episode, minus Rod Serling's imagination, wit and style. It concerns a handsome scientist who's seeking bones at big-dig sites, then wandering the halls of a natural history museum with his studious daughter in tow.

After the adolescent unleashes a puff of smoke from an age-old egg (don't ask), she's transported to the land that time forgot. Suddenly, she's discovering some very big footprints that definitely aren't hers.

Even then, the titular monster takes its time making an appearance. And when finally baring its fangs, T-Rex is about as scary as Barney. For that matter, the fossil-to-be seems more from Ray Harryhausen's era than Steven Spielberg's brand of wizardry.

So, are the 3-D effects good? Unquestionably. But director Brett Leonard puts more emphasis on dizzying moments of rappeling off cliffs than the big lizards of 65 million years past. Go figure.

Meanwhile, scenes of domestic frisson make for pretty dopey dramatics. There's little saving grace in the teaming of Peter (TV's "Thirtysomething") Horton and newcomer Liz Stauber as the paternal paleontologist and his onerous offspring.

The best one can say is that pre-teens should find the production fairly diverting, mostly due to its 40-minute length. For everyone else, however, "T-Rex" is all bore and no bite.

VILLAGE VOICE, 10/21/98, p. 140, Gary Susman

With *T-Rex: Back to the Cretaceous,* the Imax 3-D format continues to evolve toward narrative maturity, without bothering to ask whether viewers want it to. You'd think a cyberschlock director like Brett Leonard *(The Lawnmower Man, Virtuosity)* would privilege in-your-face effects shots over hurried character development and emotional conflict.

Teenage Ally (Liz Stauber) is working on a science project whose theory that Tyrannosaurus rex was a nurturing, bird-like parent awkwardly parallels Ally's own yearning for a closer relationship with her work-obsessed paleontologist father (Peter Horton). Wandering the halls of the natural history museum, she imagines herself traveling back in time, talking shop with a couple of legendary fossil hunters and visiting T-rex in the Cretaceous Period, 65 million years ago. The film boasts the most scientifically accurate dinosaurs yet on screen, and when the money shots of pouncing lizards finally come, you'll be duly impressed and thrilled. The movie even conveys a hint of the awe that dino-diggers feel as they reach across the aeons. But before that, you'll be trying to swallow the treacly story and some undigested dollops of hard science and the history of paleontology while your inner eight-year-old whines, "Where are the dinosaurs?"

Also reviewed in:
CHICAGO TRIBUNE, 11/13/98,Friday/p. G, Michael Wilmington
NEW YORK TIMES, 10/23/98, p. E25, Lawrence Van Gelder
VARIETY, 10/26-11/1/98, p. 42, Todd McCarthy

TALK OF ANGELS

A Miramax Films release of a Polaris Films Ltd. production. *Executive Producer:* Harvey Weinstein, Bob Weinstein, and Donna Gigliotti. *Producer:* Patrick Cassavetti. *Director:* Nick Hamm. *Screenplay:* Ann Guedes and Frank McGuinness. *Based on the novel "Mary Lavelle"* *by:* Kate O'Brien. *Director of Photography:* Alexei Rodionov. *Editor:* Gerry Hambling. *Sound:* Peter Glossop. *Casting:* Mary Selway and Camilla-Valentine Isola. *Production Designer:* Michael Howells. *Art Director:* Eduardo Hidalgo. *Set Decorator:* Totty Whately. *Costumes:* Liz Waller and Lala Huete. *Make-up:* Peter King. *Running time:* 97 minutes. *MPAA Rating:* PG-13.

CAST: Polly Walker (Mary Lavelle); Vincent Perez (Francisco Areavaga); Franco Nero (Dr. Vicente Areavaga); Marisa Paredes (Dona Consuelo); Leire Berrocal (Milagros); Penelope Cruz (Pilar); Frances McDormand (Conlon); Ruth McCabe (O'Toole); Francisco Rabal (Don Jorge); Ariadna Gil (Beatriz); Rossy de Palma (Elena); Britta Smith (Duggan); Anita Reeves (Harty); Veronica Duffy (Keogh); Jorge De Juan (Jaime); Ellea Ratier (Leonor).

LOS ANGELES TIMES, 10/30/98, Calendar/p. 12, John Anderson

[*The following review by John Anderson appeared in a slightly different form in* NEWSDAY, 10/30/98, Part II/p. B6.]

There's a touch of the Finzi-Continis about Nick Hamm's "Talk of Angels," even if the country isn't Italy and the family isn't Jewish. Fascism is coming, gentility is going; there's a sense of imminent loss, of sun-drenched-turning-into-blood-drenched Europe that gives a solemn weight to what is otherwise a fairly frivolous film.

Of course, without beating too much about the bush, the reason "Talk of Angels" seems to exist at all is Polly Walker, easily one of the most beautiful women in film—and who, for that reason alone, may not get a lot of starring roles. Her credits include "Enchanted April" and "For Roseanna"; she's had small parts in "Patriot Games" and "Sliver."

But Walker is a lot like Dudley Moore in "Arthur," when he's told that the "right woman" could stop him from drinking: "She'd have to be a pretty big woman," he says. And it would have to be a pretty big story to distract from Polly Walker.

And that we don't have. Walker's character is Mary Lavelle, a convent-educated Irishwoman transplanted to 1936 Spain to work for the family of the imperious intellectual Dr. Vicente Areavaga (Franco Nero), a disillusioned patriot whose radical instincts are rekindled by Mary. His son, the more flagrantly militant Francisco (Vincent Perez), is unhappily married to the stunning Beatriz (Ariadna Gil), who is far more concerned with how Francisco's politics are threatening the Areavagas' station than in the politics themselves.

Francisco and Mary do the gravitational dance, full of 19th-century stage reluctance and aversion to sin. Only a few leading characters are scarred or maimed, at least within the time frame of the film.

Amid all this, Walker remains the primary distraction, and it doesn't help that director Hamm bisects the actress' face with light at every opportunity, whether they're inside or out; it's gilding the lily, so to speak, but it's interesting to watch just how deliberately the cinematography is orchestrated to show the actress at her most radiant. That and Spain. Oh, yes, let's not forget Spain.

Hamm, who is making his feature debut, has a more-than-prestigious cast at his disposal. Luis Bunuel favorite Francisco Rabal is Don Jorge, the child-molesting priest whom Mary exposes. Two Almodovar regulars, Marisa Paredes ("High Heels," "The Flower of My Secret"), who plays Vicente's wife, and Rossy de Palma (in a literal fleeting glimpse) are here, as is Nero and Irish actress Ruth McCabe ("The Snapper," "The Field," "My Left Foot"), who plays O'Toole, the most extroverted of the gaggle of Irish nannies who populate the town.

And, last but not least, Frances McDormand, who does a memorable turn as Conlon, another of the nannies, whose attraction to Mary is not quite in keeping with the liturgy.

But the sum, as they all too often say, is not quite that of the parts. And "Talk of Angels" unfortunately exists in that romance-novel realm in which political concerns are mere adornments for the treacle-dripping issues of the heart.

NEW YORK POST, 10/30/98, p. 47, Larry Worth

Polly Walker's beauty isn't up for debate. She's one of the most ravishing actresses currently gracing the screen.

For that very reason, director Nick Hamm should be thrilled about her presence in "Talk of Angels". After all, she's a consistently lovely distraction from the idiotic, Harlequin romance-like script.

Set in northern Spain of 1936, it concerns a young Irish governess (Walker) who's hired by a bourgeois couple (Franco Nero and Marisa Paredes) to tutor their three daughters. But teacher's the one who gets an education, thanks to lessons from the rebellious older son (Vincent Perez) about the Spanish Civil War—and the bedroom.

The melodrama piles on from there, most hilariously with a subplot about some of the heroine's fellow expatriate nannies. And wouldn't you know it? The most tart-tongued biddy (Frances McDormand) has a big fat crush on the golden girl.

But any allusions to sapphic love—never mind little issues like dawning fascism, prejudice and class consciousness—take a back seat to the bodice-ripping lunacy of the central coupling. An over-the-top score, dime-novel dialogue and soap-opera developments bring matters to the verge of parody.

Hamm's only good idea involves the production's lighting. He arranges literally every camera angle to showcase Walker's physical glories. To her credit, Walker makes the most of her time in the spotlight, calling on the same style and intelligence that distinguished her in "Enchanted April", "Emma" and "Restoration".

As the hot-blooded insurgent, Vincent "Indochine" Perez also tries hard to wade through the ever-rising sap. Meanwhile, Franco Nero and Marisa Paredes, playing the hero's politically mismatched parents, and Frances McDormand's cynical lesbian merit condolence cards from fans.

That's why it's no surprise when end credits show that "Talk of Angels" has been shelved since 1995. Clearly, studio execs suspected—and justifiably so—that "Angels" would never fly.

VILLAGE VOICE, 11/10/98, p. 126, Elizabeth Weitzman

Set in Spain during the tumultuous '30s, this adaptation of Kate O'Brien's once scandalous novel centers around lovely Mary Lavelle (Polly Walker), an Irish girl who becomes a governess for an aristocratic Spanish clan. Mary just wants a little fun, but soon she's caught between the Republican and Fascist ideals held by the family patriarch (Franco Nero) and his wife (Marisa Paredes). To complicate matters, their married, Franco-hating son (Vincent Perez) turns out to be one of those smoldering types convent-educated Mary's only dreamt of.

Wartime ardor can bolster a compelling film or embarrass a weak one. Director Nick Hamm has enough material for either; there are some fine performances, striking locations, and genuine urgency in its depiction of civil war. Had he chosen to flesh out the political and class-related intrigues, he could have created a memorable picture. But because the real action becomes mere backdrop for a pair of furtive, chemistry-free lovers, our frustrations bloom right along with theirs.

Also reviewed in:
NEW YORK TIMES, 10/30/98, p. E16, Stephen Holden
VARIETY, 10/26-11/1/98, p. 42, Lael Loewenstein

TALK TO ME

A Northern Arts Entertainment release of a Pug Films production. *Producer:* George Esguerra. *Director:* George Esguerra. *Screenplay:* George Esguerrs and Robert Foulkes. *Director of Photography:* Randy Drummond. *Editor:* Tom McArdle. *Music:* David McLary. *Sound:* Boaz Atzmon. *Production Designer:* Jori Adam. *Art Director:* Dixie Thomas and Deborah Lanino. *Costumes:* Debra Edelman. *Running time:* 87 minutes. *MPAA Rating:* Not Rated.

CAST: Cheryl Clifford (Betty Cole); Peter Welch (Arnold Dowling); Elizabeth Landis (Ronnie Goldstein); Gary Navicoff (Michael Dowling); Rick Poli (Jerry); Ralph Romeo (Frederick).

NEW YORK POST, 7/3/98, p. 40, Bill Hoffmann

The hottest sex scene at the movies this summer isn't at your local multiplex.

The steamy sequence can only be found at the Quad, where a romantic little gem called "Talk to Me," opens today. But more on that later.

This New York-lensed independent asks the question: Can two lost souls find love and happiness on a slinky phone-chat line?

This being a breezy comedy, the answer is yes—that is, once you sail around all of the weirdos, wackos and pervs that come with the territory.

Tele-dating is the last thing either Betty (Cheryl Clifford) and Arnold (Peter Welch) want to consider as they navigate through the hills and dales of New York City matchmaking.

But after some disastrous dates, the two lonelyhearts call a $1.50-a-minute love line and, once they get past the lechers and losers, fall into a private chat room with each other.

It's here that the film really kicks into high gear with one, of the steamiest—and bravest—sex scenes you'll see this year.

In a lengthy sequence guaranteed to have you panting along, Betty and Arnold, in their separate apartments, strip naked and get all hot and bothered talking sexy to each other.

Both Clifford and Welch play the scene with extraordinary candor—and full frontal nudity—and soon we know their characters are made for each other.

But there are all sorts of barriers that arise—the biggest of which is a major lie Betty told Arnold, who hates phonies.

Meanwhile, Betty's best girlfriend gives the chat line a go and finds herself in a stretch limo with a Eurotrash creep.

Gorgeously filmed in Greenwich Village, SoHo and the Lower East Side, "Talk to Me" digs into the issue that all single Manhattanites struggle with: Is there someone out there for me amid the endless mass of humanity and will I ever find them?

VILLAGE VOICE, 7/7/98, p. 124, Salma Abdelnour

First-time filmmaker George Esguerra pulls off a neat trick: his characters feel real despite being barely individuated. How he achieves this lies somewhere between his thinly sketched outlines—which, though lazy, teem with possibility—and the actors' raw likability. Two urban singles, Betty (Cheryl Clifford) and Arnold (Peter Welch), spend their days in stultifying jobs and their nights whining to equally hapless friends—just like much of the prime-time population.

But Betty and Arnold stand apart from *Friends* and Co. in that they're mousy and unpoised, with emotional baggage the size of a lipstick case; like most of the phone addicts in *Denise Calls Up*, they're rather boring. This flat psychic landscape suggests a huge hole in the screenplay, which Clifford and Welch fill not so much with deft acting as with a game spirit. Betty and Arnold become perversely endearing, so much so that when desperation drives each of them to call a 1-900 love line, it's hard not to cheer them on. But Esguerra bypasses the tenderness of two quivering voices finding each other on a phone wire and opts for instant full-frontal nudity. Within minutes of dialing in, our friends are sprawled on their couches in a masturbatory sweat.

Early consummation drains the plot's nicely building erotic charge, though a detour into romance and betrayal recaptures some tension. With this belated paean to electro-dating, Esguerra offers nothing new, but he does find the pulse in a mostly wooden script.

Also reviewed in:
CHICAGO TRIBUNE, 10/16/98, Friday/p. J, Michael Wilmington
NEW YORK TIMES, 7/3/98, p. E8, Lawrence Van Gelder
VARIETY, 12/16-22/96, p. 83, Emanuel Levy

TARZAN AND THE LOST CITY

A Warner Bros. release of a Dieter Geissler/Alta Vista production in association with Village Roadshow Pictures-Clipsal Film Partnership. *Executive Producer:* Greg Coote, Peter Ziegler, Kurt Silberschneider, and Lawrence Mortorff. *Producer:* Stanley Canter, Dieter Geissler, and Michael Lake. *Director:* Carl Schenkel. *Screenplay:* Bayard Johnson and J. Anderson Black. *Based on the "Tarzan" stories created by:* Edgar Rice Burroughs. *Director of Photography:* Paul Gilpin. *Editor:* Harry Hitner. *Music:* Christopher Franke. *Sound:* Colin McFarlane. *Casting:* Nicole Arbusto, Celestia Fox, and Moonyeen Lee. *Production Designer:* Herbert Pinter. *Art Director:* Emilia Rouz. *Visual Effects:* Julian Parry. *Costumes:* Jo Katsaras-Barklem. *Running time:* 105 minutes. *MPAA Rating:* PG.

CAST: Casper Van Dien (Tarzan);   Jane March (Jane);   Steven Waddington (Nigel Ravens); Winston Ntshona (Mugambi);   Rapulana Stiphemo (Kaya);   Ian Roberts (Capt. Dooley).

LOS ANGELES TIMES, 4/27/98, Calendar/p. 4, Bob Heisler

The Lost City of Opar, the very cradle of civilization, is found in "Tarzan and the Lost City," but the complex, compelling man called Tarzan is lost in this sequel to the 1984 "Greystoke: The Legend of Tarzan, Lord of the Apes."

You will be entertained. Good triumphs over evil in a movie that offers equal parts of "The Lion King," "Indiana Jones and the Temple of Doom" and the Nickelodeon game show "Legends of the Lost Temple."

Certainly co-producer Stanley Canter and director Carl Schenkel have created a Tarzan for our times. But someone should have reminded them that our times have produced such cultural heroes as George Costanza and Homer Simpson.

Caspar Van Dien, the square-jawed hunk from "Starship Troopers," is a Tarzan for our times, all right—all the right moves, all the right abs, all the right relationships and none of the emotional struggle and native intellect that made Edgar Rice Burroughs' ape man a recurring character in the Hollywood sketchbook.

Our Tarzan is always a barefoot step behind the run-of-the-mill cro-European bad guys—a flat collection of plunderers with last names and facial hair led by Nigel Ravens (Steven Waddington doing an uncanny version of the Jim Carrey gap-lipped stare). The African warriors save Tarzan's loincloth a number of times. He gets killed at least once. Still, the story line had enough magic to work well enough as a clash-of-cultures movie without Tarzan at all.

Give Van Dien credit, though. He swings from vines. He yells. He speaks threateningly through clenched teeth. He never steps on a sharp rock while running through the veldt. He talks to the animals. He's a good listener too—mostly to animals, not to his Jane (Jane March). He just never displays any of the self-doubt or even hesitation of a man caught between two worlds.

It's all Jane's fault, of course. That's because Jane is the one who shows signs of modernity—though she only talks about smoking cigars, and she does tend to scream a lot around snakes. But so did Harrison Ford's Indiana Jones.

When Lord Greystoke leaves her days before their wedding to answer a vision from the chief, she waits a respectable period, then goes off to find him. Whither thou goest...very modern that.

NEW YORK POST, 4/25/98, p. 23, Larry Worth

Shouldn't there be a legal limit to the amount of times Hollywood can make Edgar Rice Burroughs—the man who penned umpteen "Tarzan" novels—spin in his grave?

Although Johnny Weissmuller truly gave the ape-man his due, the same can't be said for successors Buster Crabbe, Lex Barker, Denny Miller and Jock Mahoney. Worse still was Miles O'Keeffe (paired with Bo Derek) in 1981's soft-core knockoff while Christopher Lambert voiced the legendary yell to little effect in a 1984 travesty.

So, just when thinking it can't get any worse, along comes Casper ("Starship Troopers") Van Dien in "Tarzan and the Lost City." Relatively speaking, Disney's Jungle Cruise seems pretty authentic.

The story picks up a ways into the saga, after Lord Greystoke (Van Dien)—a.k.a. Tarzan—has deserted the African jungle, where he was raised by apes, and returned to his native England. But on the eve of wedding the beautiful Jane, he again answers the call of the wild.

Apparently, Tarzan pre-dates the psychic Friends Network: By looking into a fireplace's flames, he hears an angry chieftain's cry for help. Natch, he's on the next boat to Africa, trailed by his feisty intended.

Actually, feisty's an understatement: Jane is now a post-modern feminist. Though she carries a parasol, she shoots guns, smokes cigars, drinks Scotch and swings across ravines on her own vine, thank you. So why does she scream every time a shadow crosses her path?

Her schizophrenia also afflicts director Carl Schenkel, who can't decide between adventure a la "Indiana Jones" and nonsense a la "George of the Jungle." Intentionally or not, it veers to the latter, courtesy of pathetic special effects and a bunch of guys in gorilla suits.

And though square-jawed Van Dien fills his black leather loincloth (a present from the voodoo chief to replace Tarzan's knee-length cutoffs!), his English accent doesn't kick in for the first half-hour. For that matter, Van Dien can't thump his chest with credibility.

Jane March is similarly laughable as the jungle's first lady. On the other hand, she pulls off the impossible: making Bo Derek's Jane look good. And as the token villain, over-the-top Steven Waddington calls natives "savages" and punches out ladies with enough glee to rival Billy ("Titanic") Zane's Snidely Whiplash imitation.

That's all in addition to a cross-dressing monkey now known as Jabba rather than Cheetah. After seeing "Lost City;" it's safe to assume the chimp wanted to disappear. Too bad Tarzan and Jane didn't follow suit.

Also reviewed in:
CHICAGO TRIBUNE, 4/30/98, Tempo/p. 10, John Petrakis
NEW YORK TIMES, 4/25/98, p. B14, Lawrence Van Gelder
VARIETY, 4/27-5/3/98, p. 59, Daniel M. Kimmel

TASTE OF CHERRY

A CIBY 2000 and Zeitgeist Films release of an Abbas Kiarostami Productions film. *Executive Producer:* Abbas Kiarostami. *Director:* Abbas Kiarostami. *Director of Photography:* Homayoun Payvar. *Screenplay (Farsi with English subtitles):* Abbas Kiarostami. *Editor:* Abbas Kiarostami. *Sound:* Jahangir Mirshekari and (music) Mohammad Reza Delpak. *Art Director:* Hassan Yekta Panah. *Special Effects:* Asadollah Majidi. *Running time:* 95 minutes. *MPAA Rating:* Not Rated.

CAST: Homayoun Ershadi (Mr. Badii); Abdolhossain Bagheri (Mr. Bagheri, Taxidermist in Natural History Museum); Afshin Khorsid Bakhtari (Worker); Safar Ali Moradi (Soldier from Kurdistan); Mir Hossain Nouri (Clergyman); Ahmad Ansari (Guard in the Tower); Hamid Masouni (Man in Telephone Box); Elham Emami (Girl Near the Museum); Ahmad Jahangiri (Blacksmith); Nasrolah Amini (Gravel Pit Worker); Sepideh Askari and Davood Forouzanfar (Passengers in VW Car); Iraj Alidoost, Rahman Rezal, and Hojatolah Sarkeshi (Museum Ticket Office Personnel); Ali Noornajafi (Soldier from Ilam); Mehdi Bastami (Soldier from Shahrood); Mohamad Azia Ghasaei (Soldier from Hasht-par); Karim Rostami (Soldier from Khalkhal); Kambiz Baradaran and Valiolah Halzael (Soldiers from Kermanshah); Ali Reza Bayat (Soldier from Toysarkaran); Klanoosh Yooshan-Lou (Soldier from Bandar Anzali); Jamshid Torabi and Gholam Reza Fattahi (Soldiers from Karaj); Ali Akbar Abbasi (Soldier from Qom); Rahim Imanie (Soldier from Ardabil); Ali Mohammad Moravati (Soldier from Takab); Ali Mohammad Rezaei and Mahmood Reza Edalati (Soldiers from Malayer); Seyyed Javad Navabi (Soldier from Arak).

FILM QUARTERLY, Spring 1999, p. 52, Steve Erickson

The kind of films that win the Palme d'Or at Cannes usually wear their ambition on their sleeves, practically jumping in the spectators' face and screaming "Love me! I'm a masterpiece!" Yet *Taste of Cherry,* which split the 1997 Palme d'Or with Shohei Imamura's *The Eel,* is one of Kiarostami's smallest-scale films yet, with a cast of four, an exclusive use of exteriors and a tendency to alternate between extreme close-ups of individuals and extreme long shots of landscapes. As *Taste of Cherry* opens, the 50-ish Mr. Badii (Homayoun Ershadi) is driving a Range Rover slowly through a Teheran morning, Looking closely at men gathering on the street for day labor. Clearly, he wants to pick one of them up, although it will be another 20 minutes before we find out why. Were this not an Iranian film, one might suspect that be's a gay man cruising for a hustler. Even though this is an Iranian film, this suspicion, along with more sinister ones, remains quite evident in the reactions of the men he approaches.

Abandoning the city for its desolate outskirts, he finally manages to pick up a shy, extremely nervous young Kurdish soldier (Ali Moradi). The soldier remains uneasy, becoming even more so when Badii finally explains what kind of "job" he's offering six months pay in exchange for. He's driving toward a roadside hole where he intends to commit suicide later that night by taking an overdose of sleeping pills. He wants the soldier to come back at 6am the following morning and check the status of his body. If he's alive, he wants the soldier to help him out of the hole; if he's dead, he wants the soldier to bury him. In response to this proposition, the soldier suddenly bursts out of the car, racing at full speed into the middle of nowhere.

Approaching a deserted construction site, Badii makes small talk with the guard and manages to convince the guard's friend, an Afghani seminary student (Hossein Noori), to go for a ride. When the student hears Badii's request, he smugly quotes the Koran and warns him against committing the sin of suicide. After the two men argue for a while, Badii drives him back to the site. His next passenger is a Turkish taxidermist (Abdolhossein Bagheri), who, as we later find out, works at a natural history museum. Although adamantly opposed to Badii's decision, Bagheri proves the most responsive of the three passengers. He's the only one willing to talk about his personal life. Indeed, he describes a suicide attempt of his own, which was abandoned only after he ate mulberries and realized that life still had plenty to offer him. He, albeit reluctantly, agrees to help Badii.

During these sequences, Kiarostami shot each actor separately and edited the footage together in shot/reverse-shot form to create the illusion of passengers sitting across from Badii. In truth, Kiarostarni himself sat across from the actor. Additionally, none of the actors except Bagheri and Ershadi met each other. The result of these tactics is a palpable increase in the passengers' level of uncertainty.

Each passenger represents a different age group, as well as a different response to Badii's request. The youngest is the soldier, who appears barely out of his teens; the seminarian appears to be in his 20s, and the taxidermist is an experienced middle-aged man. Together, they represent a sum total of potential responses to a suicidal man's despair: sheer terror and panic, and religious and humanist defenses of life's worth. The force of Kiarostami's conviction seems to lie behind the third one, but all three somehow seem inadequate. Implicitly, the film is also addressed to the spectator, requiring us to fill in or work around the missing information and thus placing us in the passenger's seat.

Several of Kiarostami's screenplays, including *The White Balloon* (directed by Jafar Panahi) and *The Key* (directed by Ebrahim Fourozesh), take place in real time. Although *Taste of Cherry* takes place over the course of about 12 hours, much of it feels like real time because of its relentless focus on Badii's plan. Badii concentrates desperately on his goal of committing suicide, never discussing the reasons behind his despair. The film's sense of character exists entirely in the moment. Does he have a family? He implies that he does, and that they've been hurt by his problems, without actually spelling it out. Where does he work? Is he unemployed? He never mentions these issues. These refusals are brilliant maneuvers on Kiarostami's part, allowing the spectator to read into the enormous, eloquent hollows under Badii's eyes any number of motives that would never make it past the Iranian censors.

Instead of talking about his suicidal feelings, Badii passes over and over through a hellish stretch of industrial debris, abandoned machinery, and brown, dry, or dying vegetation. The land itself looks ready to give up. It's an emblematic use of landscape, worthy of Antonioni or Rossellini (or J.G. Ballard, for that matter)—simultaneously a real landscape and a projection of Badii's mental state. At one point, Bagheri suddenly seems to realize that it may not be particularly effective to evoke the wonders of nature in a desert, and suggests that Badii go out of his way to take a prettier route. He does, and it's the first time we see much greenery.

Described on paper, Bagheri's argument against suicide sounds like a series of simplistic platitudes. Of course, life can get better; of course, the world is full of beauty and possibility. But telling these things to a suicidal man is like telling someone in the middle of a panic attack to just relax and stay calm. However, Bagheri's gesture is moving because of what it represents, not because of the wisdom of his words. Unlike the soldier and seminarian, he's willing to go out on a limb and act out of friendship toward a desperate man. To the extent that Badii's motives are readable, his suicidal urges seem to stem mostly from neediness and loneliness. Kiarostami evokes the force of this loneliness by isolating each actor in a closeup. It's an indication of Bagheri's compassion that he and Badii are allowed to appear in the same shot.

Of the five Kiarostami features I've seen, each is structured around a quest whose goal's importance gradually fades as the experience of the quest itself becomes central. *And Life Goes On* and *Through the Olive Trees* both end with final scenes that offer ambiguities rather than a definitive conclusion to the quest. Unless one has seen these films, the ending of *Taste of Cherry* is likely to seem like a bizarre cop-out.

After Badii lies down in the hole, the film fades to black. Then it cuts to a video, apparently shot in spring. The hills are green, with flowers blooming everywhere. The film crew is visible and audible, having just recorded a sound take of soldiers marching. Ershadi lights a cigarette and then hands it to Kiarostami. The soldiers sit down to relax and start picking flowers, as a jazzy funeral march (Louis Armstrong's "St. James Infirmary") begins on the sound track.

The extreme long shots that close *And Life Goes On* and *Through the Olive Trees* both imply a certain measure of distance from the central quest of the narrative. In *And Life Goes On,* a filmmaker (clearly a stand-in for Kiarostami) travels to the earthquake-ravaged region of Koker, where Kiarostami shot *Where Is the Friend's Home?* to find out if the non-professional child actors who starred in that film are still alive. *Through the Olive Trees* takes place on the set of *And Life Goes On,* in which a young man, Hossein, and a young woman Tahereh, are cast as a married couple. In real life, he desperately wants to marry her, but she won't even speak to him.

These films' abrupt endings open up questions about the real-life events behind the films; they suggest that people are more important than characters and experiences more important than narratives. In a far more extreme fashion, the ending of *Taste of Cherry* opens up a similar set of questions. It's a distancing effect, distracting us from the issue of Badii's suicide by reminding us that we're watching a film, but it wouldn't be particularly remarkable if it stopped there. It's also a new beginning. After involving us in the story of one man's isolation and desperation for 90 minutes, it suddenly shows us some of what was lacking from his life: playfulness, an openness to natural beauty, (possibly) meaningful labor. Additionally, after the rigid formal structure that the film follows for most of its length, the looseness of the hand-held videography comes as a relief and a release. We may never know whether Badii lived or died, but we do realize the richness of the life going on around him (and, implicitly, us). If *Taste of Cherry* itself is a funeral march, this final scene shifts it into a new, slightly more upbeat key and rhythm.

François Truffaut once said that, to him, films were more important than life. Kiarostami, who once boasted that he'd only seen a few dozen films in his life, would be horrified at this statement. All of his work points in the opposite direction: towards an engagement with the richness of the world outside the screen. He may have recently become a "critics' darling," but unlike most of his fans, including Western filmmakers like Jean-Luc Godard, Kiarostami isn't a cinephile himself, therefore his explorations never run the risk of getting trapped in a hall of pop-culture-reference mirrors. To a greater or lesser extent, *And Life Goes On, Through the Olive Tree,* and the documentaries *Close Up* and *Homework* all join a suspicion of the image and an awareness of the tremendous power of filmmakers over ordinary people with a belief in the healing power of cinema. In its own, far more oblique fashion, *Taste of Cherry* continues these concerns. While rarely becoming explicitly political, Karostami's inquiries touch on one of the central challenges of our time: the responsibilities, possibilities, and dangers of image-making. It's a shame that there's no one making films like his in the United States, where the class differences between image-makers and image-consumers dwarf the ones in Iran.

LOS ANGELES TIMES, 3/27/98, Calendar/p. 14, Kevin Thomas

Abbas Kiarostami's soaring parable, "A Taste of Cherry," thrusts us inside a Range Rover being driven by a middle-aged man (Homayoun Ershadi) in congested central Tehran.

Throngs of day laborers try to attract his attention, but he keeps going. Clearly he's looking for something or someone as he gradually makes his way to the mountains that give the city its dramatic backdrop.

By the time he addresses a big, ruggedly handsome man who yells, "Clear out or I'll smash your face in," you start wondering whether Ershadi's Mr. Badii, who has the intense, somber demeanor of Jeremy Irons, is, in fact, cruising, a singularly risky activity in such a homophobic culture. What Badii is after is a man to bury him.

He doesn't want to reveal why he wants to end his life beyond saying that he's "exhausted." He has dug a deep hole by a tree alongside a dirt mountain road. In the evening he plans to take a taxi to the hole, jump in and take his full supply of sleeping pills. All the man Badii hopes to hire has to do is to come by at dawn to make sure he's really dead and then fill up the hole.

That's it, but not surprisingly, soliciting for death duty is lots tougher than soliciting for sex, although they seem in this film eerily similar in their solitude and longing.

Badii's search for the individual to do him final honors becomes, with great ease and simplicity, an odyssey in which Kiarostami invites us to consider life's meaning—or lack of same—and to honor the human dignity of the various men he tries to hire. They are poor men who could use the money, men who face life as it comes uncomplainingly.

Every shot in this most contemplative yet economical of films attests to Kiarostami's mastery of his medium—his sense of when it's important for you to be inside the car to see its passengers reacting to one another and when it's important to see the Ranger Rover snaking its way alongside the mountainside, inviting us to weigh what we hear being said rather than what the individual doing the saying looks like. (Kiarostami, otherwise pretty much a one-man band, has an exceptional resourceful cinematographer, Homayoun Payvar.)

There's a strong elliptical quality to Kiarostami's style, which underlines the filmmaker's ability to maintain focus with considerable emotional force and depth and with great precision.

The long-acclaimed Kiarostami's gift in seeming simultaneously unpretentious and profound, his easy way with actors and his expressive sense of place won "A Taste of Cherry" a Golden Palm at Cannes, a first for an Iranian film.

(It took Cannes' top prize to get the film released in Iran, where suicide is an Islamic taboo. But its domestic play-dates came too late to qualify it for this year's Oscars. Iran did submit the exquisite, folkloric "Gabbeh," passed over in the best foreign film nominations.)

Badii gives a young Kurdish soldier (Ali Moradi) a lift, promising to get him to his barracks by 6 p.m. but heading in a different direction, understandably making the well-mannered youth increasingly wary.

Badii's emphasis on telling the soldier to first think of how, in a mere 10 minutes, he could make as much money as half his annual army salary does suggest a sexual overture in the offing, but the soldier freaks out when he at last learns Badii's request.

Along the way, there also will be encounters with, among others, two Afghani refugees, one a cement factory security guard and the other a seminarian who has come to visit the guard, and, most important, an older man (Abdolhossein Bagheri), hunting quail for a university taxidermy course. All will offer their differing views of suicide.

Once having contemplated suicide himself, the older man has an empathy and a maturity that the others lack. At the darkest moment of his life he was brought back from the brink by the delicious flavor of mulberries; he hopes a taste of cherries will do the same for Badii.

He has learned over the years to draw strength from the beauty of nature. He is the kind of individual in whom you perceive extraordinary strength and perception in a seemingly ordinary man.

Suspense starts building as to whether Badii will really go ahead with his plan and how it will end. Will there be a surprise twist that pays off in irony? Suffice to say that Kiarostami, among the handful of Iran's great filmmakers, invites us to do a lot of thinking for ourselves along the way—and afterward.

NEW YORK, 4/6/98, p. 234, David Denby

The quiet bravura of Abbas Kiarostami's *Taste of Cherry* has received the highest praise, both here and abroad. At Cannes, in 1997, the movie shared the Palme d'Or with *The Ice Storm,* and a number of American critics have hailed it as a masterpiece. A masterpiece! I agree that *Taste of Cherry* is an interesting and unusual movie, but still, I wonder—that is, I struggle like an infidel against evil thoughts. First, an acknowledgment: Kiarostami, the most celebrated director of the Iranian cinema, is a man both delicate in his perceptions and generous in his sentiments; he also wields enormous formal control over his material. Yet I can't help thinking that the comparisons to De Sica and Satyajit Ray and other masters betray a degree of critical desperation. Is this movie rich enough—does it show the many-sided vitality of the great movies of the past—to warrant the extravagant praise? Or are critics, depressed by the obvious aesthetic poverty of the world cinema, arguing themselves into it, placing their bets on Kiarostami because they have no other cards to play? That could be a risky game. When an audience is primed to encounter a royal personage in breastplate and plumes, it can turn vindictive when it discovers instead an emperor wearing no clothes.

In the hills outside Tehran, the handsome, fiftyish Mr. Badii (Homayoun Ershadi) drives about in a Range Rover looking for someone to help him commit suicide. Why does he do this? We search for clues. Ershadi has beautiful dark eyes, a powerful forehead, and a cleft chin. His face is a stunning mix of sensuality and severity—it is the face of a prince, a lawgiver, a great artist.

Surely Mr. Badii is a formidable man, healthy and affluent—not at all the type to kill himself. So it is a puzzle.

Mr. Badii picks up a variety of strangers and demands the same favor of each: He is willing to pay good money if any of them will return the next morning to a prearranged spot—a hole by the side of the road—and either pull him out if he is still alive or shovel dirt on his dead body. Badii, it becomes clear, is going to take sleeping pills and await the results; he will make a wager with death and leave someone else to clean up the mess. He alludes briefly to unhappiness, but he never quite tells us why he wants to kill himself, or why he cannot do the act cleanly, decisively, and in solitude. After a while, this baffling fellow seems less a credible human being than an obvious symbol: Here is a man in negation, a man denying the value of life. Most of his passengers, by contrast, offer plain and solid reasons why he should live. Kiarostami has set up his story as a philosophical debate.

At first, the movie's odd look, its strange repetitions and slow, steady rhythms, fascinate the Western moviegoer. Are we not bored with the straight-ahead style of our commercial movies? Mr. Badii drives and drives, wandering ceaselessly around the yellow-brown hills, which seem partly an industrial waste—we see pipes piled up, an abandoned car—and partly a hilly desert in which dirt is moved, in a parody of purposeful human activity, from one excavation site to another. Nothing seems actually built in this place (it could be a vast prison compound in which the prisoners are merely kept busy); and nature barely exists—a colorless tree or bush appears now and then, and at dusk, a few birds can be heard chirping in the gloom. Physically, the movie is handsome in an intentionally monotonous style. We see the car, we see the hills... is Kiarostami teasing us?

Boredom knocks at the door, at first quietly, then insistently. Inside the Range Rover, Kiarostami cuts back and forth between single shots of Badii and his passengers. These simple exchanges (first one man speaks, then the other) are varied, now and then, by views of the dirt road through the windows of the car, or by shots from above of the Range Rover making its way around a curve or passing through some hollow in the terrain. What have we got here? A road movie going in circles? So it would seem, and we get the point: Life is not a breakout into freedom, not a momentous journey from one state of being to another. Life is a constant revisiting of the familiar. If life can be defended as a value, it must be defended for itself, as mere existence, in all its monotony.

The strangers Badii meets have obviously been selected for their representative quality. There is a rather simple fellow, a worker who extracts plastic bags from the mounds of dirt and sells them—an absurd occupation. There is a very shy young soldier; there is also a man guarding an empty outpost, and his friend, a seminarian who recites (rather tonelessly) the standard Islamic injunctions against suicide. Kiarostami likes to use nonactors, and all these men speak flatly, without emphasis. They are not required to dramatize their beliefs. It is enough, for Kiarostami, that they have a job, a function, a station in life. Like Wordsworth's leech-gatherer in the great poem "Resolution and Independence," they are rooted to their spot, their little piece of the enormous dirt pile.

Taste of Cherry is a parable in realistic form. The repetitions and simplicities feel like something out of a folktale. Wisdom, one fears, is in the air. Mr Badii picks up still another passenger, an older man, a taxidermist, and this fellow, unlike the others, is powerfully articulate. He tells Badii a story, recites the lyrics of a song—his words are touching but also banal, for he offers an affirmation of life that never gets tested or dramatized, an affirmation merely stated, as a conclusion beyond proof. Kiarostami almost lets the old man win the debate, but doesn't quite; Badii's powerful gloom is impressive, too. The argument goes back and forth, but still, by the time we get to the end, we may feel that not much has really happened in *Taste of Cherry,* not much has been *shown*. The extreme severity of Kiarostami's formal game cuts things off. And what's at stake when a director doesn't put much life on the screen? Neither despair nor joy can be tested in a vacuum. The old man speaks of the sensual pleasures of life, but sensual pleasure is precisely what is missing from *Taste of Cherry*. This is a movie of great interest—an original work— but it lacks the courage, the surprise, the ravenous hunger for life, of a serious work of movie art.

NEW YORK POST, 3/20/98, p. 51, Larry Worth

If poets laureate were chosen from the cinema world, Abbas Kiarostami would be wearing the crown, based solely on the hauntingly lyrical "Taste of Cherry."

Never fueled by standard cinematic conventions, the veteran Iranian director manages to address religion, philosophies on human suffering and the very meaning of life, as his camera follows a middle-aged man (Homayoun Ershadi) driving a white Range Rover in Teheran's outskirts.

At first, the protagonist appears to be soliciting as he slows his vehicle and asks man after man to jump in. Sure enough, he has a reason for seeking male companionship, but sex is the last thing on his mind.

Rather, the guy has decided to overdose on sleeping pills that night. So he wants to hire someone to shovel dirt into the remote spot he's selected for a grave. Simple, he thinks.

Yet, finding someone to walk in Dr. Kevorkian's footsteps proves anything but easy. Instead, his passengers register everything from fear to compassion to loathing as they debate the hero's intention—at least until a mysterious taxidermist joins the mix.

And that's just the surface story. As the Range Rover traverses hairpin turns and a maze of twisting trails along Teheran's barren hills , the narrative slowly becomes a stunning metaphor for life's choices, and the proverbial paths not taken.

A lesser filmmaker might get heavy-handed fast, but Kiarostami avoids the pitfalls. He also refuses to sentimentalize the subject matter, even while finding beauty in everyday sights: a cloud of dust unearthed by rocks tumbling into a ravine, monster-like construction cranes at sunset or a lightning storm illuminating the darkest of nights.

The sepia-toned photography alone justifies the price of admission, never mind actor Homayoun Ershadi's note-perfect work as the man with a death wish. Surely both factors helped the production win last year's Palme d'Or at Cannes.

In fact, the only false note is an unnecessary coda. The tacked-on footage is reminiscent of Kiarostami's 1995 film-within-a-film triumph "Through the Olive Trees." But here, it's off-putting and breaks the delicately honed mood.

Still, "Taste of Cherry" ranks as one of the most thought-inducing looks at suicide to date, making American efforts like "'Night, Mother" or "Whose Life Is It Anyway?" seem like warm-ups. Indeed, Kiarostami transforms a traditionally downbeat scenario into a glowing work of art.

NEWSDAY, 3/20/98, Part II/p. B11, John Anderson

The appeal of Iranian cinema over the last decade or so owes something to poverty, and something to the Great Satan (Hollywood). While so much of what we see on screen aspires to a state of swollen excess, movies out of Iran, with so little at their makers' disposal, have often achieved the simplicity of parable—and a corresponding spiritual potency as well. Drunk on big budgets, the besotted viewer finds a healing potation in the chaste elixirs of Tehran.

Would we want a steady diet of such cinema? Only if the films were the work of Abbas Kiarostami, whose latest film, "Taste of Cherry," is more evidence of its director's talent for wielding an oxymoronic magic wand: an exhilarating, even life-affirming film about a man plotting his own extermination.

Kiarostami is loath to dictate a course of perception, as it were: What we see for much of the movie, especially at the outset, is the suicide in question, Mr. Badii (Homayoun Ershadi), driving about the city in a circuitous route to his own death. For some, this will signify the self-absorption of the death-wishful personality. For Kiarostami, more likely, it reflects a deep respect for any man who has reached the point of taking his own life, an unwillingness not to watch a man who soon will cease to exist.

What Badii is doing, in his roundabout way, is looking for someone to check his body in the morning—after he's taken an overdose of barbiturates—and bury him if he's dead. The spot he's picked is on a hillside, the excavation of which has turned the landscape into a disintegrating bowl of blowing dust (from such dust he came, and to which Badii wishes to return, ASAP). That the area's sole tree stands by Badii's grave is an indication of paradise to come. But it is not an inspiring landscape. It is a place one wishes to escape.

The propositions Badii makes to the several people are filtered through the viewer's cultural network, with unsavory feedback. What it seems to be at first is a search for sex—to the

Westerner, at least, who may initially feel badly for his urbanized reaction until Badii is rebuffed, even threatened, by one man who clearly shares our suspicions.

The men he does engage in conversation, and attempts to enlist in his plan, get older as Badii progresses through his day. So do their perspectives on death. A young soldier (Safar Ali Moradi), confronted with Mr. Badii's request (for which he plans to pay handsomely), literally runs for the hills. The second, a seminarian (Hossein Noori) refuses on religious grounds; despite his sympathetic nature, he may be using religion as a refuge from his responsibility (something Kiarostami is suggesting is owed a man who has reached the point of suicide). The third, an elderly taxidermist (Abdolhossein Bagheri), agrees to do what Badii asks, but only because he needs the money for his ailing child.

That the soldier is a Kurd and the seminarian an Afghan reflects the rootless nature of life in the modern Mideast, where warfare and revolutions have sent various nationalities scuttling across the landscape looking for work, food and home. The crowds of day-laborers Badii drives by at the beginning of the film—and whom he rejects, for reasons perhaps of class—are another mute indicator of a land in economic upheaval. It was upheaval of a more literal sort—earthquakes—that had ravaged the land in Kiarostami's "Where Is the Friend's House," "And Life Goes On" and "Through the Olive Trees." And in which the will to live, and live ebulliently, had triumphed over the surrounding devastation. In "Taste of Cherry"—where we never actually learn the nature of Badii's despondency—it is the will to die that provides our inspiration.

When "Taste of Cherry" played the New York Film Festival, having won the Cannes Film Festival, the ending, a video postscript showing the protagonist up and about and the soldier-actors waving flowers, caused more than a little consternation. But having seen it again, I find that same ending provides a perfectly modulated and necessarily cathartic closure—while opening up a raft of possible interpretations. Is it heaven? Maybe it's the result of the director's unwillingness to abet a suicide, even in fiction?

Kiarostami has said that the person who kills himself is validating the life the rest of us lead—that the suicide confirms that life is a choice, and the fact that we have a choice makes life livable. And bearable. In "Taste of Cherry," Kiarostami comes as close to defining the sublime nature of living; and the divine nature of choice, as a filmmaker is ever likely to do.

SIGHT AND SOUND, 6/98, p. 57, Julian Graffy

Mr. Badiei, a middle-aged man in a white Range Rover, cruises the outskirts of Teheran. Unemployed labourers lining the streets offer their services but he drives on. He overhears a young man in a telephone box talking about money and offers him a lift and financial help, but the man refuses, as does another man, collecting plastic bags for sale.

Out in the hills, Badiei gives a lift to a young Kurdish conscript. He explains that he intends to kill himself that night. He shows the soldier the pit he has dug and offers him 200,000 tomans to come and bury him the next morning, but the soldier refuses. Driving on he meets an Afghani guard at a cement works whom he also offers a drive, but the man will not leave his post, so instead the driver takes his friend, a young Afghani seminarian. As they loop through the countryside he again broaches his plan, but the seminarian insists that suicide is wrong, and that he cannot help him.

Badiei drives on, eventually picking up another man, Mr Bagheri, who agrees to do the deed, but then attempts unsuccessfully to dissuade him by talking of the joys of life and nature. Badiei drops Bagheri off at the Natural History Museum where he works. He drives away, but returns to insist that Bagheri makes sure he is really dead before burying him. That night a car arrives for Badiei and drives him out through a storm to his pit in the hills.

The next morning as soldiers exercise at dawn, a crew films them, while the actor playing Badiei waits around. When the shoot is over, the conscripts rest by the roadside and the film crew prepares to return to the city

We never learn why Badiei, the hero of *A Taste Of Cherry*, wants to kill himself. For most of the film he remains an enigmatic, excluded figure, watching the world through screens. The windows of his car are later echoed by those of the cement works watchtower and the museum workshop. This reticence and these ubiquitous barriers make him seem, initially, an ominous figure, preying on his victims for God knows what sinister purpose, or later trying to flatter and cajole them into doing something they resist. We sympathise with the 'simple' men he encounters, because although each of them is uprooted and vulnerable, they all seem to have found their place in the world and Kiarostami allows them to explain the motives for their demurral. This respectful attention to unsophisticated but dignified people is familiar from Kiarostami's earlier films. Like them, we are desperate to know what motivates Badiei, but we (like them) are doomed to frustration, subtly indicated by their repeated inability actually to hear what he says to them.

Gradually, however, as Badiei becomes more expansive, and as the camera lingers over the dark bags under his eyes, we come to sympathise with him as well. For he is also our double, both in his troubled quest and in the way his looking at life through screens mimics the very experience of cinema.

Like *Through the Olive Trees* and *Close-Up*, the two Kiarostami films released in London last year, *A Taste of Cherry* is based around a structural repetition, in this case the parabolic loop of Badiei's car along narrow roads through the parched hills above Teheran. But these repetitions are mesmeric rather than irritating, their cumulative effect being to draw the viewer into ever greater complicity with the events and ideas being rehearsed before him.

The film is constructed in a succession of close-ups punctuated by long shots. Characters and landscapes move in and out of focus. Sometimes events are seen and not heard; at others they are heard and not seen. This play of closeness and distance, which is also a play of knowledge and ignorance, reaches its apogee in the film's open, enigmatic ending. Kiarostami veterans will recognise the appearance of the film crew as an obsessive directorial signature, a didactic, manipulative—and perhaps by now otiose—reminder that we are 'only' watching a film, though it is used later and more sparingly here than in his earlier work.

But the open ending can also be interpreted as a more generous directorial impulse: a symbolic handing over of the interpretive baton to the viewer. For as Kiarostami told *Sight and Sound* last year, "there are as many different versions of the same film as there are members of a given audience". One of our tools for deciding how the film ends will be our own eyes and ears, We will sift the evidence we have accumulated, repeating the actions of Badiei as he selected a suitable gravedigger, and of his interlocutors, when they decided whether they could help him. But our conclusion will also be a measure of our own sensibility. Just as viewers willed Hossein and Tahereh to meet, to have met, in the far, far distance at the end of *Through the Olive Trees*, so we clutch at straws here. Was the "longer and more beautiful road" that Bagheri insisted that Badiei take, a road he "did not know", but that led him past resplendent trees into a noisy, peopled town, the road back to life?

Certainly in the hours after their meeting Badiei is finally seen outside his car, contemplating the setting sun, and then the majestic moon that were causes for hope in Bagheri's narrative. Kiarostami has said that the very process of filming *Through the Olive Trees* led him to replace the socially inevitable conclusion that class would keep the lovers apart with the possibility of a happy ending. Perhaps the director's own emotional reaction to *this* film narrative is indicated in his brilliantly subtle deployment of the cherry motif. Bagheri speaks at length not of cherries but of a mulberry tree, which he had chosen for his own suicide, but the succulent taste of whose berries had reclaimed him for life. As a later aside he asks, "You want to give up the taste of cherries?", a question that elicits no immediate response. Yet this 'chance' remark provides the film's title.

TIME, 4/27/98, p. 68, Richard Corliss

Fellow goes to a doctor and says, "Everythings wrong with me, but I don't know what disease I have. I touch my head, and it hurts. I touch my chest, and it hurts. I touch my leg, and it hurts. What's the problem?" The doctor examines him and says, "Your finger's broken."

This joke, told in Abbas Kiarostami's luminous *Taste of Cherry*, hints at the spirit of Iran's vital new cinema: knowing, poignant as simple and universally significant as an Aesop fable. Kiarostami, who is Iran's leading director *(Through the Olive Trees)* and screenwriter *(The White Balloon)*, tells his tales with the grace and gravity of a wise old man in a village square. *Taste of Cherry*, which won the top prize at Cannes last year, is the finest of his shaggy-man stories.

A man named Badii (Homayoun Ershadi) drives around Tehran looking for someone who will do a little job for a lot of money. The profane and sacred task, we eventually learn, is to bury

Badii if he is successful in a suicide attempt and to rescue him if he is not. The story is starkly allusive—we never learn why Badii wants to kill himself—and most of the "action" takes place in the cab of Badii's Range Rover, but the film isn't cramped or schematic. The talk flows persuasively; the picture pulses with art and humanity.

Here is a suspense thriller cast as a Socratic conversation. By Hollywood's pulse, the film may amble, but this is a token of its respect for each speaker's beliefs, its refusal to sentimentalize matters of life or death. Let the rest of the movie world ride a rocket to excess; Kiarostami will find a quiet place and listen to a man's heart right until it stops beating. And then he will listen some more.

VILLAGE VOICE, 3/24/98, p. 70, Amy Taubin

A man in a dusty, white Range Rover is driving slowly through the outskirts of Tehran. He's middle-aged, he seems both depressed and anxious, he bears a striking resemblance to the German actor Bruno Ganz. As he drives, he looks out the side window, scrutinizing the faces of the men who crowd up to the car, asking for work.

Who is this man? What does he want? The most extraordinary aspect of Abbas Kiarostami's *Taste of Cherry* is that the first question is never answered at all and the second only if you believe that what someone says he wants is a reliable indicator of his innermost desire. I use the male pronoun deliberately. The line on Kiarostami is that he makes great humanist films. In fact, he makes great films about masculinity and its vicissitudes.

If you're up on your art movies, you've probably heard about the premise of *Taste of Cherry*, the first Iranian film to win the Palme d'Or at Cannes, But if you're fortunate enough not to be in the know, I strongly advise you not to read further. The best way to see this movie is to walk in absolutely cold. For everyone else, I'll try not to spill the one thing you may think you don't want spilled.

So this lost-looking man is driving around, and after a few minutes, he works up enough courage to ask one or two diffident types if they'd like to make some good money. They react as if he's sexually propositioning them, and there's something in the guy's guilty demeanor that makes one think that's exactly what's going on. As it turns out, the act he wants to pay for is no less intimate than sex-for-hire.

Eventually a young soldier, a Kurdish refugee, gets in the car. The man drives into the rocky hills high above the city. He tells the soldier how the only happy time in his life was the time he spent in the army, how he enjoyed the companionship, the way the men counted in unison during drills. He tries to get the soldier to count along with him. (I didn't cry at all during the movie, but every time I think about this scene I get choked up.) The soldier, of course, is in a panic, suspecting that the driver is some kind of crazy pervert. The man stops the car on a desolate road and shows the soldier a shallow pit barely concealed by some scrubby bushes. He says that he intends to commit suicide in this pit this very night, and all he wants the soldier to do is to come the next morning and bury him if he's dead and help him out if he's still alive. In any case, hell find his payment waiting for him, the equivalent of six months of military salary. The soldier is horrified, Probably more so than if he had asked for a blow job (which come to think of it, he secretly might have been hoping for) and flees.

After unsuccessfully propositioning an Afghan refugee who's in training for Muslim religious orders and who's against suicide on religious grounds, the man finally finds his accomplice, an elderly Turkish taxidermist who needs the money to pay for medical treatment for his anemic son. The taxidermist does his best to talk our protagonist out of his plan by recounting his own youthful suicide attempt. He tried to hang himself from a mulberry tree, but some berries got in his mouth and when he tasted them, he knew he wanted to live. If our protagonist is too imprisoned in his anxiety to find inspiration in this story, we, the viewers, might not be. Because, soon after that, I noticed that the parched yellow-brown landscape had turned softly golden in the late-afternoon sun.

Kiarostami is as much a master of light as he is of subtext, and his "cinema of poverty" (he works on minuscule budgets with nonactors in situations that are as improvisatory as in documentaries) has resulted in some of the richest and most complicated films of the last 20 years. *Taste of Cherry* is no more a film about suicide than *Taxi Driver*, a film that it oddly resembles, is about homicide. Rather, the subject of both films is loneliness and the desperate need of a man to find another person to bear witness—if not to his life than to his death.

That desire for human contact—and the confusion about intimacy, complicity, and power that comes with it—carries a barely repressed homoerotic charge. It's there in the ambiguous opening, in the scene with the soldier, in the casebook Freudian joke about the broken finger that the taxidermist tells. It's also there in the only euphoric moment in *Taste of Cherry*, when the filmmaking crew and the platoon of soldiers that have been recruited as actors enjoy a little downtime and congratulate one another on a job well done.

It's out of a desire for such camaraderie that the protagonist invents his perverse suicide scenario. Kiarostami tricks us into focusing so much on its outcome that it's not until the movie is over that we understand that, just like the protagonist, we've been wearing blinders throughout the journey. It's not death that matters but how to live as a man among men.

Also reviewed in:
CHICAGO TRIBUNE, 5/29/98, Friday/p. D, Michael Wilmington
NATION, 4/13/98, p. 32, Stuart Klawans
NEW REPUBLIC, 4/13/98, p. 24, Stanley Kauffmann
NEW YORK TIMES, 3/20/98, p. E20, Stephen Holden
VARIETY, 5/19-25/97, p. 57, Deborah Young
WASHINGTON POST, 5/15/98, p. D5, Stephen Hunter
WASHINGTON POST, 5/15/98, Weekend/p. 56, Michael O'Sullivan

TEN BENNY

A Palisades Pictures release in association with Cubb Films and Savan Pictures. *Executive Producer:* Paul D. Wheaton, Lisa Roberts, and Michael Brysh. *Producer:* H. M. Coakley and Eric Bross. *Director:* Eric Bross. *Screenplay:* Tom Cudworth and Eric Bross. *Director of Photography:* Horacio Marquinez. *Editor:* Keith Reamer. *Music:* Chris Hajian. *Sound:* John Bross. *Casting:* Lauren Nadler. *Production Designer:* J.C. Svec. *Costumes:* Jana Lee Fong. *Running time:* 98 minutes. *MPAA Rating:* R.

CAST: Adrien Brody (Ray, Jr.); Michael Gallagher (Mike); Tony Gillan (Butchie); Sybil Temchen (Joanne); Lisa Roberts (Linda); James E. Moriarty (Donny); Frank Vincent (Ray Sr.).

LOS ANGELES TIMES, 11/27/98, Calendar/p. 14, John Anderson

[The following review by John Anderson appeared in a slightly different form in NEWSDAY, 11/13/98, Part II/p. B10.]

Judging by the press releases, Terrence Malick's upcoming "The Thin Red Line" is clearly expected to rank with "Fast Times at Ridgemont High" or "The Big Chill" as an incubator of talent-to-be. Anyone involved in the film has already put it on his resume.

Among the Red Liners is Adrien Brody, a featured soldier in the film, who several years ago starred for first-time feature-maker Eric Bross in "Ten Benny" (formerly called "Nothing to Lose"), a "Mean Streets"/"GoodFellas"—inspired New Jersey-based drama that, like most first films or first novels, seems to be a regurgitation of everything that happened to the author before he sat down to make it.

This isn't bad, nor is the fact that Bross so obviously uses Martin Scorsese as a model, although the Bross film, now in release, is a far more temperate tale of kids growing up to do bad things than Scorsese ever made.

What's intriguing, albeit flawed, about his structuring of "Ten Benny" is that the screen time afforded each of his characters is conversely proportionate to his or her appeal. Ray Jr. (Brody), the son of an ex-con (Scorsese regular Frank Vincent, who's arrested during the introductory flashback), is a shoe salesman with dreams (a ten benny is a size 10B, but don't ask me why it's the title).

A born operator, Ray Jr. wants to buy a local business and, to get it, borrows loan shark money to play a sure thing at the track. Given how early in the film the race takes place, the only sure thing is his horse's destiny as the main course at World o'Burgers.

In debt, in distress, Ray Jr. abuses his girlfriend, Joanne (Sybil Temchen), a waitress and wannabe college student, who's long been lusted after by Ray Jr.'s best friend, Mike (Michael Gallagher), a guy with a nice disposition and the charisma of an artichoke. He walks into a room and people don't notice.

We see a lot of Ray Jr., less of Mike and even less of their other pal, Butchie (Tony Gillan), the conscience of the film and its most upstanding character. (Gillan also gives the most magnetic performance.) What we're left to do, as Ray Jr. makes mistake after mistake in pursuit of money and Mike sleeps with Joanne, is wait for Butchie to come around and tell them what jerks they are. Which he does with some aplomb.

Although surnames are avoided with the subtlety of the sausage and peppers at the San Gennaro Festival, the milieu is middle-class, blue-collar Italian. Scorsese might be critical of middle-class Italian gangsters and their families ("GoodFellas"), but Bross smears with a much broader brush, treating characters with something close to condescension. It seems unworthy of the director, who has obvious talent and, unfortunately, an equally obvious story.

NEW YORK POST, 11/14/98, p. 30, Thelma Adams

Meet Butchie, Ray and Mike. The blue-collar boys from Newark's bad side grew up together, riding bikes, dunking baskets and feeling up girls. Suddenly, the blood brothers find themselves entering adulthood with little in common except their cluelessness.

"Ten Benny," which is as flat as the men's 10B shoe that gives it its name, is a poor man's guided tour through the land of big hair and small opportunities. Eric Boss' feature debut, co-written with Tom Cudworth, wastes film watching the shlemiels enter and exit cars.

The boys smoke cigarettes and look soulfully into the lens as they pile on cliches in their march to a moment of inevitable violence.

Adrien Brody, as the sleazy, spit-curled shoe salesman-cum-gambler Ray, has a bruised, big-eyed, skinny Stallone appeal. But the brooding Brody, soon to be seen in Terrence Malick's "The Thin Red Line," can't create a tragic hero out of a stock supporting character.

VILLAGE VOICE, 11/17/98, p. 138, Amy Taubin

On the other side of the gender divide [the reference is to *Dancing at Lughnasa*] is Eric Bross's *Ten Benny*, a saga of 21-year-olds who, three years after their high-school graduation, are still hanging around their depressed New Jersey working-class 'burb. Bross's film has also lingered on the shelf too long. (It was completed in 1996.) In recent years, we've seen too many of these boys-coming-of-age films to distinguish one from the other. For a low-budget debut feature, *Ten Benny is* neatly put together but not exactly inspired. The reason to see it is Adrien Brody's performance as a young greaseball on the make who's only a trace more rational than *Mean Streets's* Johnny Boy. Bross has the sense to keep his camera on him as much as possible. Watch Brody's skinny face as disbelief gives way to panic and rage when a horse he stupidly bet his life on comes in last.

Also reviewed in:
CHICAGO TRIBUNE, 11/20/98, Friday/p. J, John Petrakis
NEW YORK TIMES, 11/13/98, p. E14, Stephen Holden
VARIETY, 4/17-23/95, p. 37, Emanuel Levy

THEORY OF FLIGHT, THE

A Fine Line Features release of a Distant Horizon and BBC Films presentation of a David M. Thompson and Anant Singh production. *Producer:* David M. Thompson, Ruth Caleb, Anant Singh, and Helena Spring. *Director:* Paul Greengrass. *Screenplay:* Richard Hawkins. *Director of Photography:* Ivan Strasburg. *Editor:* Mark Day. *Music:* Rolfe Kent. *Music Editor:* Richard Ford. *Sound:* John Taylor and (music) Mike Ross-Trevor. *Sound Editor:* Dany Longhurst. *Casting:* John Hubbard and Ros Hubbard. *Production Designer:* Melanie Allen. *Art Director:* Tom Bowyer and Sarah Kane. *Visual Effects:* Val Wardlow. *Costumes:* Dinah Collin. *Make-up:* Marina Monios. *Stunt Coordinator:* Andrea Petrides and Jim Dowdall. *Running time:* 100 minutes. *MPAA Rating:* R.

CAST: Helena Bonham Carter (Jane Hatchard); Kenneth Branagh (Richard); Gemma Jones (Anne); Holly Aird (Julie); Ray Stevenson (Gigolo); Sue Jones Davies (Catherine); Gwenyth Petty (Magistrate); Robert Blythe (Farmer); Aneirin Hughes (Doctor); Natasha Williams (Care Worker); Sian Naiomi (Volunteer); Ruth Jones (Becky); Nia Roberts (ASDA Teller); Dilys Price (Mrs. Williams); Jill James (Mrs. Allen); Sidney Williams (Club Owner); Daryl Beeton (Club Organiser); Deborah Sheridan-Taylor (Shop Assistant); Frances Lima (Julie's Colleague).

LOS ANGELES TIMES, 12/23/98, Calendar/p. 5, Kevin Thomas

"The Theory of Flight" takes off into dicey emotional terrain but stays on course with such steady grace and so blithe a spirit that it's all the more satisfying for the various risks it takes along the way. The result is a beguiling romantic comedy that becomes another personal triumph for its stars Helena Bonham Carter and Kenneth Branagh.

Bonham Carter's Jane and Branagh's Richard have spirits that want to soar but, as Jane remarks, they both have gravity problems. Richard is an erstwhile London painter overcome with an obsession to fly, to the point that with homemade wings he intends to jump off the roof of the bank where his loving but conventional girlfriend Anne (Gemma Jones) works.

This act of folly lands him in court, sentenced to 120 hours of community service. He is somehow permitted to elect to serve in a lovely rural community, which conveniently has a big, empty factory where he can construct a biplane a la the Wright brothers.

As for that mandatory service, he ends up as one of Jane's caretakers. Jane is a beautiful, 25-year-old woman in the advanced stages of Lou Gehrig's disease, which has consigned her to a wheelchair and has commenced robbing her of her voice and, as she knows only too well, will soon claim her life.

Once the two adjust to each other, Jane confesses that she is on one final mission: She wants to lose her virginity. She curses that she missed the one chance she had at 17, not knowing that almost immediately thereafter she would be diagnosed as suffering from amyotrophic lateral sclerosis, which involves the degeneration of certain nerve cells and pathways in the brain and spinal cord, leading to a progressive paralysis of the muscles.

Since both share a rebellious temperament—and Richard is an attractive man—Jane would like him to do the honors. And while he allows that she is "for a cripple quite fancy-able," he indirectly pleads impotence, which sends them off on an adventure in search of a man to do the job.

Their odyssey becomes an affirmation of the rights of the physically challenged to live life as fully as possible. If such individuals can by and large win the battle for public access, why shouldn't they extend it for the right to experience personal pleasure? But writer Richard Hawkins has a larger point to make, which is that Jane is really looking for love, whether she realizes it or not.

Hawkins presents the stars and their director, Paul Greengrass, with a twofold challenge right from the start: If Richard's need to reinvent flight smacks of the overly whimsical and symbolic, Jane's terminal disease is an invitation to maudlin tear-jerking. But Hawkins has thought through his material so thoroughly that Richard's obsession works for rather than against the picture. In turn, the film has an amazingly light tone, thanks to its surprisingly amount of humor that

Greengrass has been able to sustain in the face of Jane's bleak predicament. (The picture also gets away with one of those full-bodied '40s-style scores.)

Only an actress with an aristocratic, resolute lack of self-pity and a formidably dry wit could hope to pull off playing Jane, and there could be no better choice than Bonham Carter, who indeed was to the manor born, a member of one of England's most illustrious families. She in turn simulates the effects of Lou Gehrig's disease with the kind of conviction that comes from dedicated research and observation.

Only an actor of Branagh's charm could likewise get away with Richard's "lunacy," to use Jane's word, which she uses about the same time that she points out, deadpan style, that in regard to the invention of the airplane, he's been beaten to it.

If ever there was a movie that required absolutely the courage of its material, "The Theory of Flight" is it. The people who made this film believe in it so deeply that we end up believing in it, too.

NEW YORK POST, 12/23/98, p. 44, Jonathan Foreman

Although it looks at first glance like another must-miss button-pushing tear-jerker, and a cynical Oscar bid by Helena Bonham Carter—"Hey, let's do a love story about a guy who falls in love with a quadriplegic babe!"—"Theory of Flight" is surprisingly upbeat.

It's also unexpectedly enjoyable. In fact, thanks to a bravura performance by Bonham Carter, and despite an abundance of corny movie-land implausibilities "Theory" is a guilty pleasure.

Kenneth Branagh plays Richard, an immature artist who at the beginning of the film tries to launch a homemade hang glider off the building where his girlfriend works and is then sentenced to community service.

He immediately moves to the country, where he rents a house, barn and Land Rover and starts to build a biplane out of scrap and old canvases. So far, so improbably eccentric.

His community service involves taking a disabled girl out for the day, a couple of times a week. Naturally, when he discovers that the young lady in question is a rebellious 25-year-old beauty, wracked by motor-neuron disease (also known as ALS and Lou Gehrig's disease), a degenerative illness that is shutting down her ability to speak and which will eventually kill her, he's not sure he can handle it.

But Jane (Bonham Carter) has a sardonic sense of humor and a surprising penchant for obscenity; speaking isn't easy so she makes each word count. Sick of being treated like a child, she watches cyberporn alone in her room, shoplifts at the supermarket and is desperate to lose her virginity before she dies.

Once the two of them have become friends, and Richard has shown Jane his homemade airplane, Jane tells him about her obsession and persuades him to help her arrange a sexual initiation. You never know why Richard himself doesn't volunteer: after all Bonham Carter manages to look delicious, even while all twisted up in her wheelchair. But instead the two of them resolve to go to London and somehow get the money to procure Jane a gigolo.

Of course, it's inevitable that Richard will get to deflower Jane and his heavily symbolic plane will get off the ground. But apart from director Greengrass' unforgivably wacky speeded-up scene of the two of them careering around a hotel room, the getting there is light-hearted unsentimental fun.

All the same, Greengrass crosses over the believability borderline in some irritating ways. Computerized voice machines, although they can be programmed to say dirty words, cannot be made to go up in tone at the end of a sentence. The plane is obviously unflyable. And Jane is one of those wheelchair-bound people who conveniently never have to go to the bathroom.

Greengrass' direction is uninspired, but there is powerful chemistry between a workmanlike Branagh and (real-life girlfriend) Bonham Carter. And her original, seductive and always believable turn as the difficult-but-lovable Jane raises the movie above all its flaws.

NEWSDAY, 12/23/98, Part II/p. B5, John Anderson

One can/t quite imagine the Lunts playing Richard and Jane of the virtual two-character drama "The Theory of Flight." He's a grizzled artist/provocateur sentenced to 120 hours of community service to her, a wheelchair-bound victim of Lou Gehrig's disease. Their problems are sex and disease. Their common ground is their dysfunction.

But Kenneth Branagh and Helena Bonham Carter, costars off and on the screen, do it, and it's to their credit. Particularly hers. While screenwriter Richard Hawkins' story never quite clears the runway of director Paul Greengrass' TV sensibilities (it is, additionally, a BBC production and feels like one), you have to give Bonham Carter a round of applause, not just for the performance but for what has become an intensive campaign to kick her image from one fin de siecle era into another. Her nude scene in "Wings of the Dove" was a start. Her earthy Orwellian in "A Merry War" showed a willing ability to shrug off the warm, numbing embrace of E.M. Forster and Henry James. And in "The Theory of Flight" she takes the always risky move of playing a handicapped character, one whose mannerisms might have deteriorated into shtick. She's refashioned herself, the way so many aspire and so few do.

Her Jane is frustrated—not just because of her ALS (amyotrophic lateral sclerosis), but because she was always a good girl and never had sex. Now, at 25, struck by a fatal and degrading disease, she watches surreptitious porn on her PC and has a penchant for shoplifting that any good Freudian would link to unfulfilled lust. It's eating at her. The result is a disposition that could peel wallpaper.

Richard (Branagh), part faux Picasso, part Peter Pan, arrives on his court-ordered mission in a flux and gets flummoxed. Banging her head into the windshield as he helps her into the car, boring her with uplifting field trips, he tries, but he's miserable—not as miserable, however, as when the social services send him to waiting on other, more elderly clients. He returns to Jane, they bond (we don't really witness the mechanics of it, but they bond). The result of all this intimacy is Jane's revelation that what she really wants from Richard is his help in getting "shagged." Which sends poor, impotent Richard into a paroxysm of insecurity.

Greengrass succumbs to a number of Richard Lester-inspired antics that distract from the plight of poor Jane, whom Bonham Carter makes convincingly pained when she isn't being funny.

Branagh is a lot less successful as Richard, but Richard is a less successfully drawn character. His homemade airplane, a da Vinci-esque device he's hiding in a barn, supplies the movie's more fantastic element as well as its main metaphor, but it's as hard to swallow Richard's inner life as it is Greengrass' shorthand approach to the development of the Richard-Jane relationship.

But if you nibble at what he gives you, then Bonham Carter's probably got you hooked. She makes you believe both Jane's strong will and her humiliation—such as when a trip to a handicapped-singles club sends her wheeling into the night. She doesn't want a relationship, though, she wants fantasy. And Richard's search for the suitable hustler—which takes him through some of London's better hotel lobbies—leads to the movie's funnier and more poignant sequences.

The climactic (no, that's the wrong word) sex scene is cross cut with Richard's feeble attempts to rob a bank to get the money to pay the hustler, his shotgun being such an obvious substitute for … oh, you know. Forget the plot. The risky moves in "The Theory of Flight" are all Bonham Carter's, who may not get an Oscar but has certainly entered the 20th Century, albeit just under the wire.

SIGHT AND SOUND, 10/99, p. 56, Mike Higgins

Following an attempt to fly from the roof of a London bank, depressed artist Richard is sentenced to be a companion to the wheelchair-bound Jane, who has a motor neurone disease. After a rocky start, the two hit it off. Richard shuns his ex-girlfriend Julie.

At his farm, Richard shows Jane the bi-plane he's building, whereupon she asks him to find a gigolo who will take her virginity. Richard reluctantly agrees to take Jane to London to fulfil her wish. Richard then shocks Jane by planning to rob a bank to pay for the gigolo. She asks Richard whether he will have sex with her; he refuses. The gigolo arrives for Jane; Richard sets off to rob the bank where, it turns out, Julie works. Neither Jane nor Richard go through with it. Julie confronts Richard who passes Jane off as his girlfriend. Richard and Jane fly his plane and have sex. Months later, just before her death, Jane is best man at Richard and Julie's wedding.

The goodwill extended towards Kenneth Branagh ran out about the same time as this former golden boy of British cinema started casting his spouses opposite him. It ought then to have been with trepidation that he and present partner Helena Bonham Carter took on this whimsical odd-couple comedy. What's more, Bonham Carter appears spectacularly against type as a motor-neurone-disease sufferer, a role all the more conspicuous given the warmly received performances of disabled actors Rosemarie Stevenson in *Orphans* and Heather Rose in *Dance Me to My Song*.

Were it not for the fact that Bonham Carter has striven since *Getting It Right* to broaden the repertoire of Merchant-Ivory roles that established her, her turn might be dismissed an Oscar-chasing aberration. Mastering a halting speech pattern and awkward wheelchair-bound posture, her performance is a feat of actorly technique—impressive if a little flashy. The source of this reductive portrait is not Bonham Carter alone, however.

From *Coming Home* to *Crash*, mainstream film has never quite got grips with disabled sexuality, betraying uneasiness which screenwriter Richard Hawkins perpetuates. Whether it's the internet porn Jane consumes forlornly or the electronic speaking device she uses to voice her innermost desires to Richard, these hardware-bound scenes fail to throw any light on Jane's frustrated libido. The script also labours to strike an attitude of easy-going irreverence towards a sensitive subject: "As cripples go, you're really quite fanciable," jokes Richard.

The taint of expediency marks Jane's characterisation. So as not to complicate Richard's reunion with his old girlfriend Julie, Jane conveniently declares that even if sex with Richard is within her reach, she's resigned to the conclusion that a loving relationship is not. Her encounter with the gigolo—she lies frozen with fear throughout—illustrates succinctly whose story Hawkins is more concerned with. Director Paul Greengrass *(Resurrected)* seems far more interested in the character of Richard. The shots of the construction and flight of his plane essay a gentle lyricism which the film denies Jane in depicting her pursuit of sex. Whereas *The Theory of Flight* apologises for Jane's desire, it gives its blessing to Branagh's rumpled malcontent. The analogy between flying and sex isn't just clichéd, it's in bad faith as their equivalence has no echo in the way the film subordinates Jane's neurosis to Richard's.

The character of Richard himself remains infuriatingly vague. Why, for instance, does flying in particular obsess him? With only an improbably patient girlfriend and an understanding judiciary to compare him with, Richard's plight looks more like listless self-pity than troubled alienation. This said, one shot alone, almost Loachian in its muted humanism, suggests that Greengrass had it within him to introduce a subtler shade to the otherwise schematic central relationship. Their initial trip to a park having ended in mutual dislike, Jane and Richard are seen watching a kite over the brow of a hill. It swoops up and dives down out of sight, intimating a vaulting delicacy in their friendship which the film sadly chooses not to pursue.

VILLAGE VOICE, 12/29/98, p. 128, Dennis Lim

Jane, the spunky, ailing heroine of *The Theory of Flight*, would have no trouble telling Dr. Patch exactly where to stick his red rubber nose. [See Lim's review of *Patch Adams*.] If only there were actually more to this character than her illness and her smart mouth. The faulty logic that underlies Paul Greengrass's unwittingly patronizing film (and many like it) dictates that Jane (Helena Bonham Carter), a horny, self-possessed virgin with a terminal motor-neuron disease, and Richard (Kenneth Branagh), an eccentric, impotent misfit who's obsessed with aviation, are a perfect couple, or at least one whose quirky, doomed, mutually challenging relationship illustrates a variety of platitudes about confronting fears and seizing opportunities.

With carefully slurred speech and perennially cocked head, Bonham Carter's performance is one long Oscar-night clip (or, in parts, a parody thereof). Branagh can only do so much, given that Richard Hawkins's script repeatedly leaves him stranded in some awkward corners. Earnest and misguided in equal measure, *The Theory of Flight is* ostensibly a bold and rare attempt at depicting disabled people as sexual beings, but the notion is couched in such spurious and schematic terms that the film never really stands a chance.

Also reviewed in:
CHICAGO TRIBUNE, 1/22/99, Friday/p. A, Michael Wilmington
NEW YORK TIMES, 12/23/98, p. E5, Stephen Holden
VARIETY, 9/23-10/4/98, p. 42, Derek Elley

THERE'S SOMETHING ABOUT MARY

A Twentieth Century Fox release. *Executive Producer:* Peter Farrelly and Bobby Farrelly. *Producer:* Frank Beddor, Michael Steinberg, Charles B. Wessler, and Bradley Thomas. *Director:* Peter Farrelly and Bobby Farrelly. *Screenplay:* Ed Decter, John J. Strauss, Peter Farrelly, and Bobby Farrelly. *Story:* Ed Decter and John J. Strauss. *Director of Photography:* Mark Irwin. *Editor:* Christopher Greenbury. *Music:* Jonathan Richman. *Music Editor:* Lee Scott. *Sound:* Jonathan Earl Stein and (music) Mike Ross. *Sound Editor:* Michael J. Benavente. *Casting:* Rick Montgomery. *Production Designer:* Scott Malchus. *Art Director:* Arlan Jay Vetter. *Set Designer:* Richard Fojo and Nick Farrantello. *Set Decorator:* Scott Jacobson. *Special Effects:* Kevin Harris. *Costumes:* Mary Zophres. *Make-up:* Cindy Jane Williams. *Special Make-up Effects:* Margaret Prentice. *Stunt Coordinator:* Rick Barker. *Running time:* 105 minutes. *MPAA Rating:* R.

CAST: Cameron Diaz (Mary Jenson); Matt Dillon (Pat Healy); Ben Stiller (Ted Stroehmann); Lee Evans (Tucker); Chris Elliott (Dom); Lin Shaye (Magda); Jeffrey Tambor (Sully); Markie Post (Mary's Mom); Keith David (Mary's Stepfather); W. Earl Brown (Warren); Sarah Silverman (Brenda); Khandi Alexander (Joanie); Marnie Alexenburg (Lisa); Dan Murphy (Boss' Brother); Richard M. Tyson (Detective Krevoy); Rob Moran (Detective Stabler); Jackie Flynn (South Carolina Police); Hillary Matthews (Dom's Wife); Willie Garson (Doctor Zit Face/High School Pal); David Shackelford (Coconut Guy); David Goryl (Petey); Lori Glick (Friend 3); Jeffrey P. Lerner and Cory Pendergast (Car Hood Kids); Brett Favre (Himself); Warren Tashjian (Freddie); Kelly Roarke (Girl); Herbie Flynn (Homeless Man); Caryl West (Medical Assistant 1); Ken Rogerson (Pants at Ankles Guy); Brad Blank (Paramedic); Steve Sweeney (Police Officer); Cindy Oliver (Renise); Steve Tyler (TV News Reporter); Maureen Griffin (Wine Waitress); Bob Farrelly (Hot Dog Stud); Mariann Farrelly (Driving Range Sweetie); Jonathan Richman (Jonathan); Tommy Larkins (Drummer); Lenny Clarke (Fireman); Daniel Greene (Pizza House Woman); Michael Budge (Joey Bishop Look-alike); James Gifford (Jimmy); Sean P. Gildea (Prison Warden); Zen Gesner (Bartender); Tracy Anne George (Dancer); Jesse Farrelly and Anna Farrelly (Dom's Kids); Zack Lee (Mary's Little Friend); Valerie Bruce (Nimrod's Cafe Patron); Kelly O'Brien (Office Assistant); Jack Shields, Fallon Shields, and Bob Grundy (Hot Club Barkeeps); Nancy Farrelly (Boardroom Babe); Billy Beauchene, Kathy Beauchene, and Manny Barrows (Insurance Spitballers); Michael Murphy and Sheils Mone (Office Workers); Barbara O'Connor (Ashtray Babe); Tim Sheehan (Camera Hog); Richie Balsbaugh (Cigar Smoker);   Duana Knight, Kelley Schneider, and Meda Thomas (Architect Babes); Michael Cheney (Cell Block Bitch); Paul Pelletier and Monique Pelletier (Cordosa Gawkers); Johnny Mone (Comic Book Kid); Andrew Greenbury and Nick Greenbury (Fish Hook Kids); Phil Rosenberg (Cell Block Masseuse).

LOS ANGELES TIMES, 7/15/98, Calendar/p. 1, Kenneth Turan

The Farrelly brothers can't help it, they get these ideas, cheerfully crude and way over the line: Nothing delights this writing-directing team more than making audiences laugh hard at what conventional good taste says isn't even worth a smile. With "There's Something About Mary," Peter and Bobby Farrelly have hit their own kind of jackpot.

An outrageous goofball farce, "There's Something About Mary" is a giddy symphony of rude and raucous low humor. Co-directors who shared the writing credit with Ed Decter & John L. Strauss, the Farrellys here show a gift not just for finding humor where others have feared to look but for presenting it in a way that is surprisingly close to irresistible.

The Farrellys first made a splash with the Jim Carrey-starring "Dumb and Dumber" and the bowling-themed "Kingpin." With "Mary's" story of a woman everyone falls in love with, they display a sharpened ability to make comic situations build and build. Several of the picture's more out-there sequences, like a desperate attempt to electroshock a dog back to life and a man's dreadful accident with a pants zipper, benefit from how laughs are structured to build and build on each other.

"There's Something About Mary" also displays the Farrellys' most paradoxical quality, their good-natured innocence amid all the bad taste. This enables them to blithely make light of a whole range of potentially offensive comic subjects, like the gaffes of mentally challenged individuals, the pitfalls of masturbation and the travails of people on crutches, without giving major offense.

The Farrellys have a secret weapon, this time around, in its star, Cameron Diaz. A natural comic talent and a major asset in every film she's been in, from successes like "My Best Friend's Wedding" to misfires like "A Life Less Ordinary," Diaz is irreplaceable here. More than being completely believable as the delight of all eyes, her intrinsic, knockout wholesomeness puts a Good Housekeeping seal on the raunchy proceedings, as well as keeping the film alive during those moments when it raggedly slows down to catch its breath.

Diaz's co-stars are just as well cast and just as funny, though both come to humor from different starting points. Although Ben Stiller has done drama, he's mostly known for his impeccable comedy work in movies like 1996's "Flirting With Disaster" and his own "Reality Bites." Matt Dillon has been thought of mostly for serious roles, but the growing list of comedies he's improved ("The Flamingo Kid," "To Die For," "In & Out") reveal him to be surprisingly gifted at deadpan humor.

Working beautifully together, and backed up by comic sidekicks like Chris Elliott, Lin Shaye, Lee Evans and Jeffrey Tambor, this terrific ensemble throws itself into "There's Something About Mary." No matter how far-fetched and preposterous the film's plot becomes, the cast's ability to treat ridiculous situations with complete seriousness creates a whole lot of laughter.

"Mary" starts with a flashback to a Rhode Island high school in 1985 and an astonishingly geeky Ted Stroehmann (Stiller), a loser with more metal on his teeth than the Man in the Iron Mask.

Stepping in to save the mentally handicapped Warren (W. Earl Brown) from a bully, Ted gains stature in the eyes of Warren's gorgeous sister, Mary Jenson (Diaz), the school's blond princess. In the twinkling of an eye they are planning a senior prom together until an ill-timed errant zipper changes everything.

Cut to 13 years later. Ted is a writer living in Providence (the Farrellys' hometown) and still pining for Mary. His best friend, Dom (Elliott), suggests he hire a private detective to track her down, and even suggests a co-worker, Pat Healy (Dillon), who turns out to be a lowlife ladies' man with a thin mustache and a roving eye.

Pat agrees to search for Mary and, in fact, tracks her down in Miami, where she's nominally an orthopedic surgeon but mostly plays golf and looks in on brother Warren. Completely smitten, Pat lies to Ted about what he's discovered and moves to Florida. Using a technique Woody Allen's character employed in "Everyone Says I Love You," but to much more comic effect, he eavesdrops on Mary, finds out her likes and dislikes, and attempts, against hellacious odds, to turn himself into Mr. Right.

Of course, Ted finds out what's happened and heads to Miami himself. His trip, though, is far from smooth, and, in a fine example of crossed-wires comedy, he ends up in prison facing some serious charges before he can continue his romantic quest.

Though "There's Something About Mary" relishes finding opportunities for humor where more prudent filmmakers see roadblocks of political correctness, the Farrellys don't neglect the chance for quick, throwaway moments of verbal and visual wit. And they make excellent use of singer-songwriter Jonathan Richman, who, along with drummer Tommy Larkins, provide a blank-faced musical Greek chorus that periodically comments with bleak irony on Ted's woeful plight.

Bursting with antic ideas and vulgar energy, "Mary" has enough enthusiasm left over to inspire a crazed sequence that runs alongside the closing credits, where the cast sings the rock standard "Build Me Up, Buttercup" while doing the kinds of manic things only the Farrellys could dream up. It isn't high-toned, but it will certainly make you laugh.

NEW STATESMAN, 9/25/98, p. 65, Gerald Kaufman

There is something to offend most everybody in "There's Something About Mary". Which may be why this comedy, written and directed on a relatively low budget by the Farrelly brothers (who made "Dumb and Dumber"), has become a huge box office hit in the United States.

The plot is simple. Mary (Cameron Diaz) is pleasant and unassuming; but men follow her in adoring droves. When she leaves Rhode Island for Florida, her lovelorn swain, Ted (Ben Stiller), employs a private detective (Matt Dillon) to find her. Several more stalkers turn up to complicate matters still further.

These include Dom (Chris Elliott), the friend who instigates Ted's hiring of the detective, but who has a guilty secret which brings out the most disgusting facial blotches (a triumph in the repulsive for Cindy Jane Williams, the Key Make-up Artist). Also on hand is Tucker (Lee Evans), an architect who staggers around on crutches—I said no holds were barred—and talks in a patently bogus English accent (a triumph in articulation for Evans, who actually is English). All of these, except the absurdly trusting Ted, manoeuvre and conspire against each other, adopting stratagems which are simultaneously audacious and treacherous.

And, as far as any kind of story goes, that's it. But around this narrative core the Farrellys have constructed a series of comic edifices, each of which starts with a vulgar, even disgusting, premise and is then subjected to almost interminable elaborations and variations. The result is one of the funniest films of the year—for those who can tolerate excesses which transcend tastelessness. Some will relish it, while others will find it repellent. I found myself laughing aloud, almost despite myself.

The first comic situation signals what lies ahead. Ted gets his penis inextricably caught in his trouser zip. Mary's father, wanting to know why his guest has been in the toilet for half an hour, enters, sees Ted's predicament, and flinches as if in agony himself. He is joined, successively, by Mary's mother, a policeman and a fireman. Each is appalled. Horror is piled on horror, with Ted eventually carted off in an ambulance. And the film has hardly started.

During its two-hour running time there are verbal and visual jokes about mental and physical disability, homosexuality, fetishism and police brutality. As Mary herself comments, political correctness is out. Ted masturbates, and what happens to his semen is beyond the decent imagining of anyone— except, of course, the Farrelly brothers, who would not even claim to be decent.

A small terrier is fed drugs and, when it fails to snap out of a coma, is given artificial respiration, mouth-to-mouth resuscitation and, after these remedies fail, electric shock treatment which sets it on fire. It eventually ends up almost completely coated in plaster of Paris. But never worry, the caveat "No animals were harmed in the making of this film" is presented in especially prominent capital letters.

Most of the gags are sight-gags which—apart from the subject matter—go right back to silent-cinema techniques, with twist piled on twist until the whole comic structure collapses under its own thistledown weight. For, although the jokes are gross and often filthy, the mood is kind and generous. Strolling balladeers, a sort of Greek chorus, provide a running commentary. The end credits are inventive and joyous. Everybody, whatever his role in the plot, is a fool rather than a knave—except for Mary. The California blonde Cameron Diaz portrays her as so drop-dead gorgeous, the only surprise is that the entire male population are not pursuing her.

Ben Stiller is naively sympathetic as Ted, the character whose infatuation with Mary triggers off the action. But the star turn is provided by Matt Dillon, who, with a wicked moustache, a primeval leer, terrible habits and total unscrupulousness, is a villain any audience is bound to root for. When he traces Mary to Miami and instantly falls for her, he reports back to Ted that she now weighs over 200lbs, has four children by three fathers, is confined to a wheelchair, lives in a no-go housing project and is known as "Rollerpig".

His downright dreadfulness is exceeded only by that of a pair of police detectives who beat up Ted after he has been mistakenly arrested on a murder charge. After one of the cops has knocked Ted senseless, the other turns to him and asks, in genuine solicitude: "Are you OK?"

NEW YORK, 8/3/98, p. 53, David Denby

The new romantic comedy *There's Something About Mary*, a film by the Farrelly brothers *(Dumb and Dumber)*, has been extravagantly praised by some of my colleagues, but I'm having a hard time warming to it, and I feel like making trouble. What do we want out of romantic comedy, anyway? Romantic comedy is a lovely form, and a fairly flexible one, too. A romantic comedy can be satirical *(The Lady Eve, Annie Hall)*, tender *(Moonstruck)*, farcical *(Tootsie)*; it can be erotic and profane, or fairly rough, and maybe a great many other things as well. But a romantic comedy, I think, needs two things: It needs to convey the sense that a man and a woman are heading irrevocably for one another and for no one else, and further, that these lovers, whatever trouble befalls them, are in a state of grace, even dazzled by fairy dust. And the trouble with the Farrelly brothers is that in order to get a laugh, they dump on everybody and everything. Their fairy dust smells like manure.

Manure, I admit, has its value. It is the value of shock, of breaking taboos, of liberating secret fears. But does gross-out humor—the Farrelly brothers' specialty—go with romantic comedy? In a kind of prologue, we meet the hero of the movie, Ted (Ben Stiller), a high-school nerd with braces and a hapless way with girls. By some miracle, Mary (Cameron Diaz)—the beautiful and kindly Mary, a blonde with soul—asks him to the senior prom. But when Ted arrives at Mary's house, dressed in a taupe tux, he suffers, in the bathroom, an unspeakable entanglement of his most delicate parts in the zipper of his fly. The police and fire department show up, the whole neighborhood is called in to see this once-in-a-lifetime event, and we get to see it, too—which, I suppose, is a first in the history of cinema.

After this catastrophe, Ted loses Mary, and thirteen years later, having done very little with his life, he's still thinking about her. The trouble is, Ben Stiller acts as if his privates were still caught in a zipper. He goes too far into bumbling masochism; he makes Ted an unappealing character, a jerk. Audiences will put up with fumbling and pratfalls in a lover, but not with sneakiness and cowardice; they want a lover with something game and determined about him. Otherwise he doesn't deserve the girl.

Ted sends a sleazy insurance investigator, Healy (Matt Dillon), to spy on Mary. And of course Healy falls in love with her too. For a while, Ted is forgotten—it is the best part of the movie. Matt Dillon has had the incredible good sense to realize that the sluggish diction that was sexy in a 16-year-old boy is the comic equipment of a 34-year-old man. Dillon has become very good at playing sleazeballs. His Healy wears a pencil-line mustache, the one adornment absolutely certain to destroy Matt Dillon's looks, but we can see that Healy thinks it's cool. In order to impress Mary, he tries to pass himself off as an architect and free spirit, but everything he does is just a little off, or even way off—he wears the wrong clothes, gets his architectural terms backwards, and displays an improper attitude toward the retarded, and Dillon's attempts to retrieve the errors grow more and more desperate. When Healy visits Mary in her apartment, he falls into a misadventure with a dreadful little dog that is on to him. What Matt Dillon does to that dog is one of the wildest and funniest things in recent movie comedy.

While watching this episode, we may feel we're being tested in some way. Do we have the honesty to admit that the abuse of a pesky little dog is funny? And we're tested again by Mary's brother, who is retarded. He's a big sweet guy, but he flies into rages, and wrestles people to the ground, and we're supposed to be able to laugh at him, too. If you don't laugh at him, or at a man on crutches, or at a psychopathic hitchhiker, or at an old woman's withered breasts (shown twice), then you stand accused of hypocrisy, of a craven obeisance to political correctness. And although I laughed at the poor dog, I didn't laugh at these other things.

Haven't any of the movie's fans noticed that the interiors are lit like a TV show, that the staging is generally clumsy? Haven't they noticed that apart from Matt Dillon, most of the actors are unappealing, and that the wonderful Mary, who gets the benefit of Cameron Diaz's good cheer, never observes anything about anyone? The general insensitivity of the atmosphere gets one down after a while. None of these people go together: Friends don't seem like friends, lovers don't seem like lovers. In brief, it's not enough just to have bad taste. You have to have talent, too. Some of the critics write as if bad taste were an actual cause—as if a blow against p.c. were somehow a victory in itself. But anyone who falls into that trap not only loses his judgment but congratulates himself for far too little.

NEW YORK POST, 7/15/98, p. 49, Thelma Adams

There's something about Mary: She has Farrah Fawcett's golden flip, the pop-up nipples of Pamela Anderson, Mary Richards' comic timing, the compassion of Mother Teresa and Arnold Palmer's golf swing.

Played by Cameron Diaz, who made bad karaoke charming in "My Best Friend's Wedding," Mary is irresistible. She's the most deliberate construction since "The Bride of Frankenstein."

But Peter and Bobby Farrelly's sweet and sour comedy "There's Something About Mary"—the funniest movie since Albert Brooks' "Mother," and a comic leap beyond the Farrellys' crass hit "Dumb and Dumber"—is not Mary's Cinderella story. It's Ted Stroehmanns.

Ted who? In a flashback as painfully funny as getting your lip caught in your braces, Ben Stiller dons fright shag and metal mouth to play Stroehmann. The tender-hearted high school nerd wins Mary's loyalty—and a prom date when he defends her retarded brother, Warren (W. Earl Brown), against a local bully.

The prelude to the prom is the scene people will be retelling at the water cooler on Monday. The bathroom humor is pure "Dumb and Dumber," with Ted getting his "package" stuck in the zipper of his tan-and-taupe tux. The zipper incident puts a damper on Ted and Mary's prom night. After high school, they go their separate ways. Ted becomes a Rhode Island writer. Mary ultimately moves her orthopedic-surgeon practice to Miami.

For Ted, even the examined life isn't worth living without Mary. "Crushes don't last for 13 years, right?" Ted asks his best bud, Dom (Chris Elliott).

Is there something about Mary that makes her worth finding? Or is Ted a loser stuck in the past? With Dom's help, Ted hires private eye Pat Healy (the deliciously sleazy Matt Dillon) to find Mary. Healy does find Mary—he finds her irresistible. The detective becomes Ted's rival.

What sets "Mary" apart from the Farrellys' previous comedies ("Kingpin" included) is that the surrounding love story is so good-natured. With quirky comic turns by Lee Evans, Lin Shaye, Jeffrey Tambor and Keith David, there's something about "There's Something About Mary" that the summer of 1998 had not yet seen: an unapologetic comedy hit that rivals Mary's favorite movie, Hal Ashby's offbeat romance "Harold and Maude."

SIGHT AND SOUND, 10/98, p. 57, Danny Leigh

Rhode Island, 1985. High-school senior Ted Stroehmann rescues Warren, the mentally handicapped brother of fellow-student Mary, from a bully. She asks to be Ted's prom date. On prom night, while using the bathroom at her house, he inadvertently catches sight of Mary changing, Panicked, he garrots his penis in his zip. Ted is rushed to hospital.

Thirteen years later, Ted remains fixated on Mary. On the advice of his friend Dom, he hires private detective Pat Healy to locate her. Healy finds Mary and Warren in Miami, but he falls in love with her as well. Healy tells Ted she is now an obese mother of four, and then attempts to seduce her, posing as a sensitive architect. Mary ignores the misgivings of her suspicious English friend Tucker, and dates Healy. Ted pursues Mary regardless of Healy's counsel and arrives in Miami. He is reunited with Mary. Healy is enraged, as is Tucker, who is also obsessed with Mary and a phoney. She learns Ted hired a detective to find her and, horrified, dumps him. Ted, Healy, Tucker, Mary's former lover Brett, and Dom—who admits he is another of Mary's ex-boyfriends—descend on Mary's house. She chooses Brett. Ted leaves, inconsolable. Moments later, Mary rushes after Ted, explaining that, on reflection, she wants to be with him. They kiss.

Aside from the Farrelly brothers, perhaps only John Waters among comic film-makers would blithely confront his audience with an extreme close-up of a prosthetic yet horribly realistic penis throttled between the teeth of a metal zipper. You suspect, moreover, that even Waters in his then peerlessly tasteless *Pink Flamingos* heyday (1972) might have hesitated before employing a moment of such crudity as a central plot device. Yet *There's Something About Mary*'s nightmarish full-frontal is not its most shocking aspect. What takes the breath away is that it appears not only in a mainstream studio product, but in one that is notable for its intelligence, invention and, unlikely as it may sound, compassion.

The scenario bears comparison with one from the Farrellys' debut *Dumb & Dumber*. Another love-struck loser (this time played by Jeff Daniels) has seduced another seemingly unattainable goddess, before again stumbling into calamity in his date's bathroom, this time suffering from diarrhoea. In both structure and vulgarity, the situation mirrors Ted's mutilation almost exactly. Yet the scene in *Dumb & Dumber* hinges on Daniels' character being the world's biggest moron. Ted, on the other hand, is an Everyman, to be laughed at but also, crucially, empathised with. *Mary* finds less amusement in one individual slipping on a banana skin than the way the world is paved with them.

Such universality also keeps the way the film treats mental disability from crossing the line that differentiates the healthily base from the plain ugly. The character of Warren is demonstrably anything but a helpless patsy, and when Healy describes him as a "goofy bastard", the joke is patently on the venal private investigator himself. Remarkably, coming as it does from men who continue to find breasts intrinsically funny, *Mary*'s humour exhibits a strange kind of maturity. Shit, according to the relentlessly scatological Farrellys, not only happens, it happens to us all.

An equally cheering discovery is that the narrative logic, peripheral to many good comedies and virtually all bad ones, is persuasively coherent. The spine of the story could easily support a conventional romantic weepie and, while the film's momentum is often at the mercy of its comic set-pieces, the script works hard not to rely just on these. Of course, however admirable its grain of humanism and fat-free plotline, *Mary* will not be selling tickets (as it already has, in bulk, across America) on their merits. Such attributes are cogs in the machine. More important in many ways is what they help facilitate: a comedy which is, now and again, funny in the purest sense.

Admittedly, to suggest such heights are reached consistently would be misleading. While the innumerable sight gags and one liners are uniformly well executed, some are designed only to elicit an opportunistic snigger, others to prefigure a running joke. But on the half-dozen or so occasions when the Farrellys allow themselves the freedom to run with a simple premise (such as Ted's misfortune in *Mary*'s bathroom), the resulting comic stream-of-consciousness is seldom less than inspired. Certainly, the strength of the performances must take due credit—Stiller in particular plays straight man/walking punchline with admirable restraint—but in these audacious, free wheeling displays, it becomes clear the real stars of *Mary* are the two grown men behind the camera, giggling triumphantly each time one of their actors says the word "dick".

TIME, 7/20/98, p. 62, Richard Corliss

There's surely something about Cameron Diaz; everyone's crazy about her. Maybe it's the throaty laugh, the sinewy silhouette, the radiant smile that seems to wonder at the edges if you really think she's all that gorgeous. Well, she is—and a fine comic actress too. In *My Best Friend's Wedding*, she outdazzled and outcuted Julia Roberts, no contest. Now she has five men—four pathetic losers and Green Bay Packers quarterback Brett Favre—drooling over her in Peter and Bobby Farrelly's latest assault on the already benumbed taste buds of the American moviegoer.

Spanning 13 years and about 463 gross-out jokes (74 of which are funny), *There's Something About Mary* details the hapless love of can't-catch-a-break Ted (Ben Stiller) for smart, tomboyish, good-hearted Mary (Diaz). He tracks her from Rhode Island to Miami Beach with precious little help from an eczematous friend (Chris Elliott), a sleazy detective (Matt Dillon) and an invalid Brit (Lee Evans).

Viewers of *Dumb and Dumber* and *Kingpin* will think themselves prepared for this new Farrelly farrago. They will be mistaken. Not since John Waters' early X-rated farces has a movie so reveled in low humor: a scrotum in zipperlock a genital-attack dog, an icicle earring made of seminal fluids, plus innumerable chicken-choking and dolphin-flogging references.

Any review is irrelevant to this movie; it is either above criticism or beneath contempt. But for those who park their sense and sensibility at the 'plex door, there's plenty to enjoy in the performances, the rowdy innocence of the whole thing, the closing sing-along of *Build Me Up Buttercup*—and the vision of Cameron Diaz in giggly, gangly bloom.

VILLAGE VOICE, 7/21/98, p. 115, J. Hoberman

There's Something About Mary is less an asteroid sent hurtling toward the audience than a great gobby spitball. Duck if you're squeamish. Proudly lowbrow, hopelessly incorrect, visually strident, and awash in bodily fluids, this third and funniest gross-out yuckfest by Peter and Bobby Farrelly goes a long way in establishing the auteurs of *Dumb and Dumber* and *Kingpin* as the conehead's Coen Brothers.

A romantic comedy, if not exactly the sort that Nora Ephron would concoct, *There's Something About Mary* opens in the filmmakers' native Rhode Island and immediately establishes a typically Farrellian state of mind—Ben Stiller playing a high-school senior afflicted with double braces and tormented by an advanced case of the nerds. Although the Farrellys derive considerable amusement from this prologue—which features the spectacle of thirtysomething actors in outlandish fright wigs reenacting their inarticulate, high-school geekiness—the movie's level of humor is even more regressive, closer to that of a vicious 12-year-old.

Invited to the prom by the senior-class goddess and eponymous object of desire (Cameron Diaz), Stiller proves completely hapless—unwittingly alienating her excitable stepfather, innocently sending her mentally retarded brother into a frenzy, inadvertently peeping on her toilette, and then, in a paroxysm of embarrassment and the first of the movies two never-to-be-forgotten bits of business, catching a bit of scrotum in his zipper. Can any amount of Cameron Diaz cheesecake compensate for what is arguably the most excruciatingly visceral castration metaphor in any Hollywood movie since Ronald Reagan had his legs lopped in *King's Row?* Even a cop shows up to gawk.

Thus arrested in his development, Stiller remains fixated on the lissome, unattainable Diaz for the next 15 years. His simian character is so dorky that even Tostitos corn-chip star Chris Elliot feels entitled to give him coolness tips—and so boring in his romantic obsession that his analyst sneaks out to have lunch as Stiller drones on about the trauma that ruined his date. (Is it a mercy or just another sadistic joke that America's shrinks will be on vacation as *Mary* plays the 'plexes?)

To further explicate Stiller's adolescent angst, Jonathan Richman—the king of greasy kid stuff—is on hand as a troubadour, serenading the principals as he periodically strolls on-camera to articulate his own peculiar brand of deadpan, earnestly dopey romanticism: "True love is not nice and it brings up hurt from when you were five years old/Oh pain, pain, pain is true love's name." Indeed. Although worthy of John Waters's *Pink Flamingos* (or even his gruesome *Desperate Living), Mary's* fly-trap scene is scarcely the film's only venture into theater of cruelty.

Mary's rude assortment of muscular dystrophy, psoriasis, and homophobic jokes might have been scripted by the Garbage Pail Kids for the cast of *South Park.* The material written for Farrelly axiom Lin Shaye—here elaborating her sexualized-hag cameos in their previous films—is approached only by the scene in which Stiller's sleazy rival Matt Dillon is compelled to perform CPR on the Shaye character's terrier. (The gag reflex is a double-edged sword in Farrelly world.) A satire of inept male behavior predicated on the fear of sexual rejection, *There's Something About Mary* expresses an anxiety so funky that you can practically smell it. The jovially disgusting ribaldry suggests a hereto equivalent to the old Playhouse of the Ridiculous.

Could this be the Farrellys' moment? Their man Jim Carrey is being touted for an Oscar, *Kingpin's* bowling set up *The Big Lebowski's*, and the most notorious scene in *Dumb and Dumber* was ripped off by the ecstatically over-praised *Henry Fool. There's Something About Mary* towers above the usual summer idiocy on its formal qualities alone—the slapstick timing, adroit sight-gag placement, choreographed Abbott-and-Costello misunderstandings. Dillon's stupid huckster not only sports a set of oversized choppers but—surprising echoes of Groucho Marx. Not the least of the movies triumphs is Cameron Diaz. At once eternal foil and holy grail, perfectly oblivious, always credulous, generous in her affection, she's a woman so perfect she even likes to talk football.

Good sport or plastic mannequin, Diaz's Mary is untouched by the stalking, stinking, all-round vulgarity that surrounds her even when it smears... never mind. As you are sure to hear around the schoolyard, *There's Something About Mary* has the most startling parody of a money shot—ever. Here, too, the unfailing Diaz radiance brings to mind novelist Fred Chappell's observation in his "Twenty-Six Propositions about Skin Flicks" that "If the whole of history, with its prostitution and unrelenting degradation, has not violated women in their essence, how shall the camera accomplish it?"

There's pathos in the pathology here—but, of course, only if you think about it The worst thing about *There's Something About Mary* is the license it will extend to the next 50 gross-out comedies.

Even if homosexual panic were not an essential ingredient in the goulash of Farrelly humor, *There's Something About Mary* would merit a footnote in Mark Rappaport's new movie for its title alone.

Also reviewed in:
CHICAGO TRIBUNE, 7/15/98, Tempo/p. 1, Mark Caro
NEW REPUBLIC, 8/17-24/98, p. 24, Stanley Kauffmann
NEW YORK TIMES, 7/15/98, p. E1, Janet Maslin

VARIETY, 7/13-19/98, p. 53, Todd McCarthy
WASHINGTON POST, 7/15/98, p. D1, Stephen Hunter
WASHINGTON POST, 7/17/98, Weekend/p. 43, Michael O'Sullivan

THIEF, THE

A Stratosphere Entertainment release of an NTV-Profit/Productions Le Pont/Roissy Films coproduction in association with the State Committee for Cinematography of the Russian Federation/Le Centre National de la Cinématographie/Canal +. *Executive Producer:* Sergei Kozlov. *Producer:* Igor Tolstunov. *Director:* Pavel Chukhrai. *Screenplay: (Russian with English subtitles)* Pavel Chukhrai.   *Director of Photography:* Vladimir Klimov. *Editor:* Marina Dobrianskaia and Natalia Kucherenko. *Music:* Vladimir Dashkevich. *Sound:* Iulia Egorova. *Production Designer:* Victor Petrov. *Costumes:* Natalia Moneva and Natalia Aleksandrova. *Make-up:* Nina Kolodkina. *Running time:* 97 minutes. *MPAA Rating:* R.

CAST: Vladimir Mashkov (Tolyan); Ekaterina Rednikova (Katya); Misha Philipchuk (Katya, Age 6); Dima Chigarev (Sanya, Age 12); Amaliia Mordvinova (Doctor's Wife); Lidlia Savchenko (Granny Tania); Anatolii Koshcheev (Cobbler); Ania Shtukaturova (Lame Girl); Ervant Arzumanian (Bookeeper); Natalia Pozdniakova (Bookkeeper's Wife); Olga Pashkova (Actress); Liudmila Selianskaia (Alcoholic); Galina Petrova (Varvara); Viktor Bunakov (Engineer); Iulia Artamonova (Engineer's Wife); Iurii Beliaev (Sania, Age 48); Evgenii Popov (Homeless Man).

LOS ANGELES TIMES, 7/17/98, Calendar/p. 12, Kevin Thomas

As a young woman, a suitcase in one hand, a cloth sack in the other, trudges along a dirt road, a man's voice recalls his youth in Pavel Chukhrai's Oscar-nominated "The Thief." It's a superb film in the classic style of screen storytelling, at once intimate and epic, possessed of lyrical beauty and suffused with that mixture of warmth, suffering and rueful humor so characteristic of Russian films.

The young woman, our soundtrack narrator informs us, is his mother, and only moments later, clutching at the damp earth, gives birth to him. The year is 1946, and his mother, Katya (Ekaterina Rednikova), had been heading toward shelter with relatives in the next town. His father had come home wounded from the war, and died six months before his birth.

We're fast-forwarded to 1952, with Katya and her now 6-year-old Sanya (Misha Philipchuk, a remarkably expressive actor) encountering a handsome young army officer, Tolyan (Vladimir Mashkov), dashing in his uniform, aboard a crowded train. Katya, who has not remarried, is vulnerable to this highly sensual, utterly confident seducer. Moments later they're having sex.

Stopping at a small city, the couple posing as man and wife, and the boy, find shelter in a seedy but inviting boardinghouse. The couple slide into a passionate affair, with little Sanya initially jealous of Tolyan until the man starts taking a paternal interest in the boy. For a moment they're blossoming into a happy family, but it's not to last—especially in a Russian film set in the grim final flowering of Stalin's regime.

A brawny, virile man of easy sexual swagger, Tolyan is a veritable Stanley Kowalski who has completely captivated mother and son before they get to know that he is a career criminal who likes his nomadic life of moving from one town to another, doing a little breaking and entering in each place before moving on. And if a pretty woman crosses his path he'll have his way with her too.

Tolyan does a fine job of toughening up Sanya and giving him paternal affection. In fact, the boy has replaced the image he has had in his mind of the father he never knew with this dangerous newcomer. For Tolyan does not hesitate to use the boy as an accomplice in burglary. Hopelessly in love with the sexy marauder, jealous of his philandering, outraged at his criminal activities, concerned over his impact on her son, Katya hits the vodka bottle and then gathers the strength to try to leave him.

Tolyan is a remarkably charismatic figure, not quite like any other male character in Russian cinema within memory, and in bringing him to life Mashkov combines animal magnetism and intelligence like a young Brando. His Tolyan makes no apologies for what he is and his character keys Chukhrai's larger point; Tolyan's betrayal of mother and son becomes a metaphor for Stalin's betrayal of the Russian people. (Intriguingly, the gregarious Tolyan is always offering toasts to Comrade Stalin, but we're never quite sure whether it's a cynical public relations gesture or an expression of admiration on the part of one thug for another or some unconscious blend of both.)

With its shimmering floating quality so apt for a memory film, and with its spacious visual splendor, "The Thief" has that emotional richness, that breadth of vision, that graceful cascading toward a grand climax, that characterizes Fellini's "Nights of Cabiria," which resurfaced recently. Films like these remind us how rarely we get to have so heartfelt an experience at the movies nowadays.

NEW YORK POST, 7/17/98, p. 44, Thelma Adams

At the center of Alfred Hitchcock's "To Catch a Thief" and Pavel Chukhrai's Russian nominee for last year's best foreign-language film, "The Thief," is a lovable, handsome dark-haired rascal with sticky fingers.

Retired cat burglar Cary Grant wooed Grace Kelly on the Riviera; soldier Tolyan (Vladimir Mashkov) catches widowed mom Katya (Ekaterina Rednikova) on a Russian train following World War II. It's no coincidence that a woman in the next car interrupts the pair's initial small talk by screaming, "Thief! Thief!."

Under the watchful eyes of Katya's son Sanya (Misha Philipchuk), the young woman falls hard for the dashing captain.

The trio leaves the train together, an instant family, and a convenient cover for the bandit. The charismatic Tolyan befriends their new neighbors, then steals their meager goods.

Katya becomes increasingly disillusioned with Tolyan, but no less in love. Sanya, who never knew his father, develops an equally ambivalent relationship: The 6-year-old yearns for Tolyan's fatherly advice but fears the handsome man's more brutal side. All three actors are impeccable, with Mashkov recalling a darker, more sinister Grant.

What became delicious Grant-Kelly fluff for Hitchcock erupts into a sensual, tragic postwar coming-of-age story in Chukhrai's hands. "The Thief" is also a metaphor for a chaotic, fatherless society desperate for leadership turning to, and betrayed by, the charismatic Josef Stalin, a.k.a. Papa Joe.

NEWSDAY, 7/17/98, Part II/p. B7, John Anderson

Legend has it (also, Time magazine reportage, circa 1941) that Josef Stalin regularly beat his sadsack son, Yakov, blew pipe smoke in his face to strengthen his lungs and then beat him again when the boy started smoking. When Yakov was a prisoner of war, his father refused to trade for him with the Germans, and he died in a concentration camp in 1943, leaving little but leaden metaphor as his legacy; it's nearly impossible, after all, not to trace a trajectory from child abuse to the purging of millions.

Ah, but when your enemies are everywhere, tough love is what a boy and a nation need.

In the little theater of "The Thief," Pavel Chukhrai's suspenseful, elegant, Oscar-nominated romance, we study the moral turpitude of the postwar Soviet Union through the eyes of young Sanya (Misha Philipchuk), who was born out of agony on muddy Russian roadside and is traveling with his mother Katya (Ekaterina Rednikova) on a train in her search for work. Seduced (you might say raped) en route by the persuasive Tolyan (Vladimir Mashkov), a charmer in full military regalia, Katya falls head over heals and topples into a fatal love affair.

This isn't feminist backlash, it's big-acreage allegory: Katya is both mother and motherland, exploited for her natural resources (Rednikova is stunning) as well as her guileless trust. Young Philipchuk—whose arched eyebrows and round mouth seem to be saying "oooh" even when he's silent—embodies the entirety of postwar Russian history: He, too, is seduced by Tolyan, who despite being a thief and a scoundrel is the totalitarian father figure the young boy needs.

Director-writer Chukhrai, in cahoots with the talented cinematographer Vladimir Klimov, creates gauzy, golden memory pages, in which the wonders of Sanya's childhood include the heavy breathing from his mother's bed. Window bars, train rails, ladders and iron grates provide a recurring visual motif of confinement; late in the movie, Sanya improvises an ornamental cemetery fence out of a hospital bed, implying dictatorship beyond the grave. But with all the potency of his mise-en-scene and allusions to politics and Freudian-Oedipal arguments, it's the characters who make the really persuasive arguments—Katya and Sanya being caught up in something they should resist but can't and Tolyan (played deftly by the charismatic Mashkov) mixing charisma and brutality into emotional hypnosis.

The allure of violence is always present, sometimes latent, sometimes overt: When Sanya is beaten by kids outside one of the many rooming houses they inhabit (and which Tolyan then robs), Tolyan tells Sanya he must convince his enemies he's willing to kill and maim and then shows him how it's done. It's a power lesson on a 6-year-old's scale, a feeding into the desire for dominance over a person. Or a people. Sanya keeps seeing crisis-generated visions of the biological father he never knew, as if the presence of the real thing (the real Russian spirit, perhaps) might have made a difference. But this is kid stuff. As Chukhrai knows, the ultimate problem is ego.

SIGHT AND SOUND, 8/98, p. 54, Julian Graffy

In 1946 Katia, the young widow of a Russian soldier, gives birth to a son, Sania. Six years later Katia and Sania meet Tolian, a handsome army captain. Katia is immediately attracted to him, and they quickly become a "family". The three get a room in a crowded communal flat, where Tolian charms all the tenants and pays for a group visit to the circus. During the performance he goes out "for a smoke". Suspicious, Katia follows him back to the flat where he is stealing everyone else's valuables. Realising that he is not an officer but a conman, she pleads unsuccessfully with him to mend his ways.

He repeats the scam, now with Katia and Sania's connivance, in a Black Sea resort, and they move on to a bigger town. Here relations between Katia and Tolian deteriorate. Tolian takes Sania along on his next robbery, but they are disturbed and just manage to escape. Katia tells Tolian that she is leaving him, but as she and Sania prepare to get on a train a police patrol appears. Tolian is captured and sentenced to seven years in a prison camp. Katia and Sania catch a glimpse of him at a transit prison. Soon after, Katia dies following a botched abortion. Sania is sent to a children's home.

Six years later, running wild with the lads near the railway, he hears a familiar voice. But the drunken Tolian doesn't recognise him, and scarcely remembers Katia. At night, as Tolian boards a train, Sania shoots him.

The Thief follows in the footsteps of several recent Russian cinematic recapitulations of the Stalin period. It captures the toughness, but also the humanity of the postwar years in a persuasive evocation of life in drab, cavernous communal flats, with their squabbles, shared meals and meagre hopes relieved by trips to the circus and cinema. The film also contains what has become an almost obligatory sign of the Stalin years in recent films—a visit to a Grigori Aleksandrov musical, this time to *Spring* (1947)—and makes particularly effective use of popular song.

There are many other echoes of earlier films. The visions of his dead real father that trouble the six-year-old Sania recall Marlen Khutsiev's *The Ilich Gate* (*I Am Twenty*), (1963), while his recognition of the Stalin tattoo on the conman Tolian's chest reverses a famous scene in Andrei Konchalovsky's *The Story of Asia Kliachina* (1988). And scenes of the 12-year-old Sania suggest Vitalii Kanevsky's *Don't Move, Die and Rise Again!* (1989).

Above all, though, the film enters into a dialogue with the work of Pavel Chukhrai's director-father Grigorii, particularly his *The Ballad of a Soldier* (1959). Like that film, *The Thief* begins with a widowed mother on a country road, and *Ballad*'s story too is punctuated by scenes on the trains that symbolise Russia's vastness. But the meaning of these scenes is reversed, for if *The Ballad of a Soldier* was imbued with symbols of community and sacrifice, the central figure here is a liar and a thief. The novelty of this film's stance is signalled by the very bluntness of its title. *The Thief* contains neither the move to remorse, reform and redemption that would have been compulsory in earlier Soviet films, nor the concern with overarching political exposé that characterised the perestroika years. Instead it offers a convincing mix of unemphatic social observation and emotional melodrama.

All the relationships in the film involve a struggle between trust and treachery against a background of violence and uncertainty. The central figures form a family, first fatherless and then fake. The intoxicating but dangerous relationship between Katia and Tolian is contrasted with those of the sad, enduring couples in the communal flat. But *The Thief* is even more a story of father and son than of man and woman, and here too images of fakery abound. When Sania finally calls Tolian "Daddy", his real father is betrayed and ceases to appear to him. And Tolian also has a fake parent: he tells the credulous boy that Stalin is his father, and in a sense he is right, since Stalin presides over this society, ubiquitous in portraits on posters an flags and in loyal toasts to his kindness and wisdom.

The version of the film shown at the press screening had been shorn of a final sequence, set in 1994, in which the middle-aged Sania, now a colonel in the Russian army serving in what is probably Chechnya, briefly mistakes a dying old street drunk for Tolian. The released version now includes this final scene, but artistically both extra sequences, with Sania aged 12 and Sania aged 48, diminish the film. The story that ends in the transit camp has a coherence and an engaging vigour that keep the gaps in its sometimes threadbare plot at the back of the viewer's mind, but this energy is dissipated by the perfunctoriness and the incredible coincidences of the later scenes. They also spell out unnecessarily a point that has not in fact been lost on the audience—hat this is a story of the fate of the bereft postwar generation (Chukhrai himself was born in 1946).

The Thief contains a trio of powerful performances. Vladimir Mashkov, one of the biggest stars of contemporary Russian cinema, brings a compelling mix of the attractive and the disturbing to Tolian, and Ekaterina Rednikova is beautiful and doomed in the less developed part of Katia. But at the core of the film is the boy, Sania, and here the acting of Misha Filipchuk is spellbinding. Russia has recently seemed to be able to produce a steady stream of wonderful child actors: Iura Visokoborskis in Dmitrii Astrakhan's *Everything Will Be OK*, Lilia Murlykina in Kira Muratova's *Three Stories*, Nadia Mikhalkova in her father's *Burnt by the Sun* and Andrei Chalimon in Jan Sverák's *Kolya*.

Like the last two of these films, *The Thief* was nominated for the Oscar for Best Foreign Language Film. Unlike them it did not win it, but in April it swept the board at the Nikes, the Russian Oscars, where it was nominated in 10 out of 11 possible categories and won five awards, including Best Film.

While this may seem an exaggeration of *Titanic* proportions in a year which also produced Aleksei Balabanov's *The Brother*, Muratova's *Three Stories* and Aleksandr Sokurov's *Mother and Son* (and was probably a riposte from the Russian Academy to its US equivalent), it shows how directly the film's affecting combination of fragile nostalgia and sober, unillusioned reflection can speak to audiences.

VILLAGE VOICE, 7/28/98, p. 113, Justine Elias

A crowded train rattles across a bleak, wintry Russian landscape, and two destitute travelers, a young war widow and her small son, hear another passenger cry out that he's been robbed. Before they can pay much attention to the crime in their midst, a stranger—a handsome, worldly military officer named Tolyan—sits down next to them, and by the end of their journey, the mother is seduced. Six-year-old Sanya (the wistful, wonderfully expressive Misha Philipchuk) won't be such an easy mark. Haunted by hazy visions of his real father, Sanyo at first fears, then worships, and ultimately rejects the man who seems to be offering salvation. In *The Thief*, a 1997 Oscar nominee for best foreign-language film, this boy's troubled life becomes an elegantly told parable about Stalinism's seductive grip on post-WW II Russia.

At first, the homeless family's life is happily transformed: Tolyan moves them into a boardinghouse in a dreary provincial town, upgrading their existence from wretched to meager. But the interloper is not what he seems: Tolyan is a small-time con artist in a stolen military uniform, and his scam is to lure his neighbors out for an evening's entertainment, steal everything they own, and flee to another city. Sanya's mother is both desperately in love and completely disgusted with Tolyan's true nature; her son is in danger of being corrupted by it. This portrait of criminal dictatorship—of a family and of a country—is all the more effective because its intriguing central figure, Tolyan, is played by Vladimir Mashkov, one of Russia's leading film stars, who acts with a sort of brutish charisma. It's easy to be tricked, as Sanya is, into believing that an evil dad might be better than no dad at all.

Also reveiwed in:
CHICAGO TRIBUNE, 8/14/98, Friday/p. D, Michael Wilmington
NEW REPUBLIC, 8/10/98, p. 24, Stanley Kauffmann
NEW YORK TIMES, 7/17/98, p. E12, Janet Maslin
NEW YORKER, 7/20/98, p. 78, Anthony Lane
VARIETY, 9/22-28/97, p. 57, Deborah Young
WASHINGTON POST, 9/4/98, p. D1, Stephen Hunter
WASHINGTON POST, 9/4/98, Weekend/p. 37, Michael O'Sullivan

THIN RED LINE, THE

A Twentieth Century Fox release of a Fox 2000 Pictures presentation from Phoenix Pictures in association with George Stevens, Jr. of a Geisler/Roberdeau production. *Executive Producer:* George Stevens, Jr. *Producer:* Robert Michael Geisler, John Roberdeau, and Grant Hill. *Director:* Terrence Malick. *Screenplay:* Terrence Malick. *Based on the novel by:* James Jones. *Director of Photography:* John Toll. *Editor:* Billy Weber, Leslie Jones, and Saar Klein. *Music:* Hans Zimmer. *Music Editor:* Lee Scott and Adam Smalley. *Sound:* Paul "Salty" Brincat and (music) Alan Meyerson. *Sound Editor:* J. Paul Huntsman. *Casting:* Dianne Crittenden. *Production Designer:* Jack Fisk. *Art Director:* Ian Gracie. *Set Decorator:* Richard Hobbs and Suza Maybury. *Special Effects:* Brian Cox. *Costumes:* Margot Wilson. *Make-up:* Viv Mepham. *Stunt Coordinator:* Glenn Boswell and Raleigh Wilson. *Running time:* 166 minutes. *MPAA Rating:* R.

CAST: Sean Penn (First Sergeant Edward Welsh); Adrien Brody (Corporal Fife); James Caviezel (Private Witt); Ben Chaplin (Private Bell); George Clooney (Captain Charles Bosche); John Cusack (Captain John Gaff); Woody Harrelson (Sergeant Keck); Elias Koteas (Captain James "Bugger" Staros); Nick Nolte (Lieutenant Colonel Gordon Tall); John C. Reilly (Sergeant Storm); Arie Verveen (Private First Class Dale); Dash Mihok (Private First Class Doll); John Savage (Sergeant McCron); Kirk Acevedo (Private Tella); Penny Allen (Witt's Mother); Benjamin (Melanesian Villager); Simon Billig (Lieutenant Colonel Billig); Mark Boone, Jr. (Private Peale); Norman Patrick Brown (Private Henry); Jarrod Dean (Corporal Thorne); Matt Doran (Private Coombs); Travis Fine (Private Weld); Paul Gleeson (First Lieutenant Band); David Harrod (Corporal Queen); Don Harvey (Sergeant Becker); Kengo Hasuo (Japanese Prisoner); Ben Hines (Assistant Pilot); Danny Hoch (Private Carni); Robert Roy Hofmo (Private Sico); Jack (Melanesian Man Walking); Tom Jane (Private Ash); Jimmy (Melanesian Villager); Polyn Leona (Melanesian Woman with Child); Jared Leto (2nd Lieutenant Whyte); Simon Lyndon (Medic 2); Gordon MacDonald (Private First Class Earl); Kazuki Maehara (Japanese Private 1); Marina Malota (Marina); Michael McGrady (Private Floyd); Ken Mitsuishi (Japanese Officer 1); Ryushi Mizukami (Japanese Private 4); Tim Blake Nelson (Private Tills); Larry Neuhaus (Crewman); Taiju Okayasu (Japanese Private 6); Takamitsu Okubo (Japanese Soldier); Miranda Otto (Mary Bell); Larry Romano (Private Mazzi); Kazuyoshi Sakai (Japanese Prisoner 2); John Dee Smith (Private Train); Stephen Spacek (Corporal Jenks); Nick Stahl (Private First Class Bead); Hiroya Sugisaki (Japanese Private 7); Kouji Suzuki (Japanese Private 3); Tomohiro Tanji (Japanese Private 2); Minoru Toyoshima (Japanese Sergeant); John Travolta (Brigadier General Quintard); Terutake Tsuji (Japanese Private 5); Steven Vidler (2nd Lieutenant Gore); Vincent (Melanesian Guide); Todd Wallace (Pilot); Will Wallace (Private Hoke); Joe Watanabe (Japanese Officer 3); Simon Westaway (First Sount); Don Wyllie (Medic 1); Yasuomi Yoshino (Young Japanese).

CINEASTE, Vol. XXIV, nos. 2-3, 1999, p. 83, Tom Doherty

Released six months after *Saving Private Ryan* and inevitably landing in its shadow, Terrence Malick's version of James Jones's *The Thin Red Line* (1998) underscores the comeback of World War II on screen, a fin-de-siècle film cycle born of a baby-boomer desire for intergenerational fealty. (For a literary example of the same impulse, check out Tom Brokaw's devotional best seller, *The Greatest Generation.*) Bucking the zeitgeist (and the Old Man), writer-director Malick casts WWII as background, not foreground, for a wide-eyed environmentalism that seems above, not inside of, the field of war and remembrance. After a twenty-year hiatus from American cinema, the reclusive *auteur* of two of the most sumptuously lensed films of the 1970s, *Badlands* (1973) and *Days of Heaven* (1978), retains a set of natural affinities that are still with dappled nature. Oceans away from Jones's source novel and the previous motion-picture version filmed in 1964, *The Thin Red Line* overlays the ravishing cinematography of *Days of Heaven* onto the narrative contours of *Guadalcanal Diary.* Not surprisingly, in the struggle for generic dominance, the straightforward plotline of the combat film fades before the visual delights of Malick's exuberant pastoralism. No matter how explosive the battlefield action or horrible the carnage, *The Thin Red Line* is languid, meditative, serene, and artful. Look elsewhere for the verisimilitude of wartime newsreels; Malick splashes his canvas with the colors and sights of a biosphere that is never less than gorgeous.

Set in the Pacific theater of operations, *The Thin Red Line* luxuriates in a sense of lace, not history or politics. Where a military tactician scans the battleground for enemy encampments and defensible positions, Malick looks over no-man's land like a natural scientist bent on discovering new species of plant life. In one sense at least, his outlook reflects the original wartime perspective. To American eyes, the combat landscape of the Pacific appeared as alien territory, primeval and Darwinian, the humid jungles and volcanic ash of obscure atolls possessing none of the reassuring familiarity of the postcard monuments of the tourist capitals of Europe. The inhabitants—Melanesian natives and Japanese invaders alike—were no less strange and otherworldly. Moreover, in the Pacific archipelago, against the Japanese, the ground fighting tended to be more vicious, the enemy less liable to be kept at arm's length. Symbolically and significantly, the favored war trophy for veterans of the Pacific war was the samurai sword; for veterans of the European Theater of Operations, a German Luger.

Of course, the other big difference between the two theaters of war was the race of the enemy—and a medium amenable to sinister caricatures and overripe character acting did more than its bit to imprint the racist dimensions of the war against Japan. By the 1960s, however, as the issue of race pressed itself ever more into the forefront of American reconfigurations of its own history, the Japanese role as a pillar of the Axis triad tended to fade from popular depictions of World War II on screen. A touchstone is the *Rashomon*-like epic *Tora! Tora! Tora!* (1970), a balanced appraisal of the attack on Pearl Harbor from the Japanese and American points of view, a film that was basically a bilateral coproduction with Japanese and American directors. In time, American shame over the internment of Japanese Americans and the exterminationist temper of wartime propaganda encouraged a cultural amnesia that served both sides.

Not least, the relative paucity of recent combat films set in the Pacific reflects a powerful profit motive. Hollywood spectacles about Japanese villainy during World War II make dubious exports into a lucrative Japanese market, where box-office rentals sweeten the dividends from North American theaters. Throughout *The Thin Red Line,* whether as a result of revisionist intentions or commercial calculations, Japanese soldiers appear mainly as shadows in the grass or defeated victims of American war crimes (reversing the national identities in a well-known rumor of the Pacific war, a ghoulish GI collects gold fillings from the bodies of dead Japanese).

The stray line of dialog aside, then, Malick's Guadalcanal diary is more a mediation on nature than an evocation of war: the main characters are neither the American GIs of C-for-Charlie Company nor the barely glimpsed Japanese enemy, but the flora and fauna of the rain-forest location. Shot in the Solomon islands and the Daintree Rain Forest in Queensland, Australia, and photographed in spectacular Panavision by John Toll, *The Thin Red Line* shimmers like a big-budget travelogue. The first image reveals the snout of a crocodile, whose elongated reptilian form slithers into the widescreen frame. "What is this war in the heart of nature?," asks the AWOL Private Witt (James Caviezel). "Why does nature vie with itself?" Presumably, the snake is already in the garden, but the beauty of the lush foliage and the innocence of the noble Melanesian savages belies any intimation of a heart of darkness in the heart of nature. Witt swims in the crystal clear ocean, frolics with the native children, and bakes himself bronze in the sun. It is not crocodiles but Caucasians who violate the purity of the prelapsarian paradise. When a U.S. Navy warship cruises into sight on the blue horizon, *"et in arcadia ego"* (I [Death] am also in Paradise) might be stenciled on the bow.

As voice-overs recite the interior monologues of unusually eloquent and philosophical GIs ("War doesn't ennoble men-it turns them into dogs, poisons the soul") and gauzy flashbacks call up the memory of homefront America, a meandering storyline emerges, slowly. The men-boys, really-of Charlie Company must seize the high ground from a well-dug-in emplacement of Japanese machine guns. So orders the demonic Lieut. Colonel Tall (Nick Nolte), a martinet in the Capt. Queeg mold, driven batty not by war but by the tedium of the peacetime military and the humiliation of being "passed over" for the eagle insignia of the bird colonel. Like the cinematic war lovers played by George C. Scott in *Patton* and Robert Duvall in *Apocalypse Now*, he is invincible and charmed, not even flinching when a mortar explodes nearby. Gravel-voiced and gung-ho, the larger than life Colonel Tall is also by far the most animated character in his combat unit, not to say Malick's ensemble of actors. "Go straight up that goddamn hill!," he bellows, not oblivious to the human toll but heedless of the cost.

Less motivated is Captain Staros (Elias Koteas), who balks at the suicide mission, and Sergeant Welsh (Sean Penn), a loner whose still waters run deep. Wisely, Malick delays the onset of violence, foreshadowing the horror to come with the grisly discovery of two bodies of tortured Marines, creating tension simply by having nothing happen the music of the jungle hums, birds peer from the bush, and a Melanesian elder walks by wordlessly, surreally. When the combat erupts, it hits suddenly and matter of factly, but even amid the hard rain of the technology of war the director never goes too long without getting back to nature. In long shot, two forward point men are taken out by single shots, as if cut down by the rain forest itself, and the elemental fluid bottled up in the supply lines is not gasoline but water. "Nature is cruel, Staros," Colonel Tall says when he relieves the soft-hearted Captain from command, picking up on the recurrent theme.

Weighed against its fated frame of comparison, *The Thin Red Line* offers few of the dramatic or cultural satisfactions of *Saving Private Ryan*. Malick lacks Spielberg's sure sense of narrative drive, of luring an audience into the tabula, even of creating a convincing historical past or compelling genre film. Reaching back further into Hollywood tradition highlights Malick's difficulties with the noncinematographical aspects of film. Compared to the squad members of a vintage Warner Bros. platoon, where distinctive accents and rugged physiognomy brought characters instantly and vividly to life, the GIs of Charlie Company are fuzzy, ill-defined, and, at times, downright hard to tell apart from each other. The star actors are recognizable on sight, but some of the newer faces are cast from the same pretty-boy mold. The chorus of voice-overs does little to flesh out and individualize the personalities. Meant to offer a multiple perspective and running commentary on the combat, the interior monologues are mainly recited in the same hushed, dreary, and soporific monotone (though Nolte's raspy urgency is a conspicuous exception).

Certainly, amid the pantheistic sightseeing, a wartime cliché unfolds here and there: GIs gripe in the accents of the Bronx and Dixie; the devoted husband pining for his wife receives a predictable letter at mail call ("It just got too lonely, Jack."); and Private Witt enjoys a prolonged death scene and sentimental graveside homage. Also, as in latter-day combat epics such as *The Longest Day* (1962) and *A Bridge Too Far* (1977), namebrand American stars march by for a few seconds of screen time—John Travolta as an unctuous Brigadier General, Woody Harrelson as a luckless sergeant clumsy with a hand grenade, and George Clooney as a smug officer. Like the Melanesian islanders, however, the thin red line of men in Charlie Company walk through a mythic state of nature beyond history, not Guadalcanal Island or any other real geographical site or battlefield milestone. In case anyone misses the point, Colonel Tall reminds his subordinates that at West Point he read Homer, in Greek: the original wartime myth.

Not that Malick lacks an agenda. In ideology no less than topography, *The Thin Red Line* evokes the Vietnam combat genre, where the worst enemy of the American soldier is his commanding officer, where combat is always chaos without meaning. The taciturn Sergeant Welsh expresses the generic allegiance when he utters a line that is commonsensical in the

Vietnam jungle but heretical in World War 11 territory: "If you die, it's gonna be for nothing." Yet because this is World War II territory, antiwar sentiments require a convenient bout of amnesia, a refusal to engage the historical reality of the Pacific War. Malick portrays the Americans as the invaders of the Solomon Islands, the violent despoilers who rape a virgin land, while the Imperial Japanese, a conquering army not known for magnanimous behavior towards native populations, seem a natural part of the landscape, as indigenous as the Melanesians.

In the end, however, the true bloodlines of *The Thin Red Line* are neither historical nor cinematic but botanical and zoological. Malick revels in the sights of a fecund environment, oozing with natural energy, churning out life and death in equal measure, with equal enthusiasm. Beams of sunlight break through the jungle canopy for a rosy fingered dawn." Owls watch alertly, vampire bats hang ominously, and carrion birds circle eerily. Festive in blue and red, parrots stand out against the browns and greens of the jungle and the khaki of the GI fatigues. Under withering machine-gun fire, a soldier is threatened by a coiling snake, attacked at once by man and nature. Like the amber waves of grain on the Texas prairie in *Days of Heaven,* a Mountainside of tall grass trembles in a gentle breeze, the wafer-thin reeds giving the illusion of cover from shot and shell. Bathed in the reflection of yellow flames, the faces of young GIs glow in the chiaroscuro of Renaissance portraiture. Even the landscape after battle, where vegetative nature and flesh-and-blood men are burnt to a crisp and dogs feast on cadavers, look fertile and biodegradable. Under such radiant cinematography, amid such environmental splendor, Malick's war is not hell but a wondrous part of the great chain of being.

FILM QUARTERLY, Fall 1999, p. 35, James Morrison

A basic tension between irony and ardency informs Terrence Malick's films of the 1970s—*Badlands* (1974) and *Days of Heaven* (1979). The outlaw-lovers-on-the-run template of *Badlands* splits the difference between the socially conscious romanticism of Nicholas Ray's *They Drive by Night* (1947) and the counter-culture mythmaking of *Bonnie and Clyde* (1967), while *Days of Heaven* weds Whitman's poetic ideal of the democratic vista to the interior landscapes of Henry James, with a plot that evokes *The Wings of the Dove* even as it ends with a quasi-Biblical plague of locusts. The later film's sources may on the whole be classically literary, including Mark Twain and Willa Cather, but the film shares some of the aestheticist detachment of the earlier film, a cool distanciation that inheres in the formalist rigor of its imagery and the inexorable languor of its violence. In *Days of Heaven,* aesthetic distance resides in a complex system of modernist narrative ellipses, but collide with an aesthete's passionate lyricism, much as in *Badlands* the continuing hope of innocence, still visible in quicksilver nature, meets the seeming inevitability of corruption.

In Malick's new film, his first in 20 years, this tension is gone. *The Thin Red Line,* based on James Jones' 1962 novel of World War II, pursues the strains of ardent feeling of the director's earlier work but, without seeming to renounce it, forsakes the irony. The core of the film follows an American battalion's fight against the Japanese for a hill at Guadalcanal, and although this core provides dramatic grounding for the movie, it is flanked at both ends, beginning and end, by stretches of storytelling so fragmentary, so mercurial, they're nearly abstract. In *Badlands* Malick sought the stringency of a tone poem, in *Days of Heaven* the breadth of a ballad; in *The Thin Red Line,* the director aspires to the impersonal grandeur of the epic. In each set of narrative possibilities, Malick finds the same association between pain and ecstasy, but in the earlier films the dialectic bred agitation, while in *The Thin Red Line* it has resolved into a strange tranquility. Narrative here remains tied to archetype, a set of given patterns self-consciously recombined, arranged with the impartial sophistication of a chronicler attuned to the gridwork of collective unconsciousness, but the fervently self-reflexive turns of the story, as complex as ever, are no longer in the service of a compulsive skepticism. *The Thin Red Line is* an anti-war movie, but unlike other anti-war movies it superficially resembles, from the hallucinatory inferno of *Apocalypse Now* (1979) to the gung-ho kitsch of *Saving Private Ryan* (1998), it is almost entirely free of anger or bitterness. Its battle scenes are poetically matter-of-fact, among the most powerful ever filmed, but its critique of the ethos of war appears to derive from a vantage point of ultimate quiescence, and in that regard, *The Thin Red Line is* unique among American war films.

In its picture of combat, *The Thin Red Line* falls somewhere between Renoir's *Grand Illusion* (1937), with battle scenes put in, and Jancso's *The Red and the White* (1969) or *Saving Private Ryan*, with the savagery distilled. The representations of battle in *The Thin Red Line* do not shirk the need to confront ferment or unspeakable bestiality. They expose with the single-mindedness of sober, unyielding conviction the fundamental outcome of war: the deaths of boys. With the dulcified logic of an elegy, grievously resigned to past losses but steadfastly borne up against future ones—like the poems of Wilfred Owen—the battle scenes unflinchingly portray relentless casualty, but they do so in a mode of inconsolable lyricism: sudden cuts to the unbearable beauty of a breathtaking, twilit sky that heralds only doom, or protean inserts of a fissured leaf with blinding light streaming through the holes. Even if, Whitmanesque, they romanticize fated male youth, these lyric interludes do not poeticize the soldiers' deaths—the violence is too immediate—but forthrightly show what it is that these deaths violate. As Renoir does in *Grand Illusion*, Malick refuses the salve of villainy. Even the driven battalion commander, Tall (Nick Nolte), who pushes men to their deaths, is himself—in pensive voiceovers—revealed as vulnerable, and although in the clearest gauge of the film's post-Vietnam dispositions we are confronted with the grisly spectacle of Americans gratuitously torturing entrapped Asians, these scenes appear to propose reversion to barbarity as a refutation of the pseudo-rationality of military science.

The narrative structure of the film divests the battle scenes of the excitement or grandeur typical of the genre. For one thing, the big battle scene is displaced from a climactic position in the story, and after it is over, the film goes on for nearly an hour without heeding any narrative compulsions to build further. Malick risks such anticlimax to strip the battle-scenes of trivializing generic functions that apotheosize a plot's setups or generate frivolous suspense. These scenes absorb the heightened energies of elevated rhetoric, to be sure, and they have a hushed, breathtaking sweep, but it is characterized by a diffused sensibility. The primary formal maneuver of these scenes is a sinuous, decentered tracking shot that glides over multiple planes of action, following one character and then shifting to others with just the smallest turns of its roving but precisely defined perspective. In these shots, the camera's gaze seems to be at once restive, unflinching, and tender, and even as it shows how each of the men is alone in his fear, it constantly reveals unexpected connections between them in space. In such shots, Malick has solved the problem of how to represent battle as collective strife, against demands of individualist narrative points-of-view. In battle, the men are deindividuated and sympathetically particularized in the same moment. The fracturing of the narrative line also works to refuse the standard emotional parabola of the war film. We are frequently shown effects *before* causes, shown badly wounded men, for instance, before the fighting itself.

The uses of voiceover in the film similarly contribute to the construction of character, synthesizing impersonal chronicle with stream-of-consciousness poetics. In Malick's previous films, the voiceover was the clearest gauge of irony, revealing the distance between the limited perspectives of the characters and the mordant self-reflexivity of the narration. In *Badlands*, Holly (Sissy Spacek) delivered a patter of dime-novel clichés over a steely procession of tersely contrapuntal images, while in *Days of Heaven* the little sister, Linda (Linda Manz), mixed the florid and the taciturn in artlessly meditative monologues that surprise in their patchwork assembly as surely in what they show she does not know as in what they show she does. These voiceovers ask to be seen as pastiches—of a penny-dreadful false-consciousness or of a kid's tough, slangy talk—yet despite the irony of their deployment, they also comment on the poignancy of misrecognition and the vulnerability of the ignorant or the impressionable. The sentiments uttered in voiceover in *The Thin Red Line* could also easily be heard as clichés. "What is this war in nature?," is the first sentence we hear, murmured earnestly by the AWOL soldier Witt at the start of the film. "I was a prisoner, you set me free.... I drink you like water," says Private Bell in an interior monologue addressed to his wife. "You are my sons," thinks the officer, Staros, leaving his battalion, "my dear sons. I carry you inside me."

These musings are delivered with real, direct conviction, and they are not counterpointed by action or images, as the voiceovers in *Days of Heaven* or *Badlands* are. They are elliptical, however, fleeting and fragmentary, and they no more function to convey exposition than the voiceovers of Malick's previous films do. Indeed, so dispersed are they across the film's many characters—at one point, as we're looking at the lifeless face of a half-buried Japanese soldier, we hear a rumination in what we can only assume to be the dead man's voice—and so ephemeral are they, so moody and mercurial, they serve something like the *opposite* function of a traditional voiceover. Far from seeming to grant any privileged access to the interior lives of the characters, these voiceovers make those interior lives seem *more* mysterious than they would otherwise. They are the fragments of thoughts, prayers, letters home, yet as these forms bleed into one another, and as the voiceovers blur the boundaries of inner and outer—at times what begins as a line of spoken dialogue ends as a voiceover—their address seems finally constant. All the men, together or alone, even at the height of battle, and even if they think they are addressing God or one another or absent lovers, are really talking only to themselves. Their musings would have to be rejected as cliché only if we, as listeners, insisted upon reverting them to a public form, and they claim a measure of their pathos from their forthright platitude, showing a hopeful perseverance of the private, even in the grip of the ultimate, when selves are lost. They are the shards of lost, fleeting voices that, even if we are somehow privy to them, can have no real hearer in the world.

Among other things, *The Thin Red Line* is a mosaic of faces, and the use of actors is determined by the narrative impulse to collectivism—though the jarring appearance of "stars" sometimes undermines this impulse. The dominant scales of the film's perspectives are long shots and close-ups, and by combining these extremes, Malick synthesizes the epic and the intimate. The close-ups work by principles of Eisensteinian typage, shots sometimes gone too quickly to afford recognition of the actor's face, and sometimes lingering, held to suggest an oblique, obtuse meaning beyond the visible. Because the narrative follows no single character as its focus, the viewer is repeatedly surprised by the reappearance of characters in unexpected contexts, and because exposition is presented so elusively, the faces take on meanings they might otherwise not have assumed. As Witt, James Caviezel brings an expressive tranquility to the film, and it is right there in his open, angular face, at once beatific and amused, generous and skeptical. In Jones' novel, Witt is kin to the character of Prewitt from Jones' previous book, *From Here to Eternity,* famously filmed by Fred Zinneman in 1953, and Caviezel's facial resemblance to Montgomery Clift, who played Prewitt in Zinneman's movie, marks the film's allusive distance from more typical war movies. Caviezel also resembles Ben Chaplin, who plays Bell, and the movie exploits the resemblance by courting confusion between the characters, as if to connote visually the final meditation we hear spoken in the film: "Darkness and light, strife and love—are they the workings of one mind, the features of the same face?"

The movie follows the plot of Jones' novel fairly closely, with crucial exceptions, but its final effects are closer to those of another Jones—David—and another James—Joyce. In its mixture of discursive forms, its atomization of character, its plaintive contemplation of the philosophy of war, it bears direct affinities to David Jones' extraordinary novel/poem/palimpsest of World War I, *In Parenthesis* (1939), while in its marshaling of streams-of-consciousness, it suggests *Ulysses*—and the first memory in the film appears to evoke directly the death of Stephen's mother in that novel. The film is delicately allusive—the lyricism of the opening suggests Flaherty and Murnau's *Tabu,* while the battle scenes cite other famous cinematic battles from *Alexander Nevsky* to *Chimes at Midnight*—but the references do not conjure a postmodern citationality. Rather, they function almost subliminally (like allusion in *Ulysses),* introducing a framework of self-consciousness against which to apprehend the story's emotional content. Malick may be adapting a straightforward war story, but he returns to a distinctively modernist heritage to negotiate the relation between aesthetic distance and emotional engagement.

Malick taught philosophy before he turned to filmmaking, and this meditation on the nature of war, or the war in nature, echoes philosophical treatises on the subject from Heraclitus's fragments to Kant's *Perpetual Peace.* By granting such insights to unschooled characters, Malick keeps them from grandiosity and suggests a dialogic, uncontentious interplay of ideas. On the one hand, especially in its lyric mode, the film seems to adopt a Kantian idea of war as the instrument of nature toward the purpose of unifying through differentiation and ordering through the establishment of covenant, accord, or law. On the other hand, the film expresses abhorrence of war to a degree that is astonishing considering its refusal to stir emotional allegiances or proprietary affiliation—as if to express simple rage, or outrage, at the ravages of war would merely reenact the same impulses that brought them about. There is probably no other film that so compellingly represents the horror of war, yet so thoroughly resists the dialectics of conflict. Its tone is mournful, not angry. Watching it, you may feel it is showing you what is slipping inexorably away as you gaze. Look, the film seems to say in shot after shot, *Look: here is what will be lost.*

LOS ANGELES TIMES, 12/23/98, Calendar/p. 1, Kenneth Turan

For months and even years after World War II officially ended, gaunt, sepulchral figures would periodically emerge from the jungles of some South Pacific island—isolated Japanese soldiers who either hadn't known the fighting was over or who so believed in their cause they didn't really care.

Similarly, "The Thin Red Line," adapted from James Jones' novel about the bloody 1942 battle for the Japanese-held island of Guadalcanal, is a film out of time. Its writer and director, Terrence Malick, has not had anything on screen since "Days of Heaven" in 1978. Time has stood still for him, as it did for those Japanese soldiers, and for better or worse, he has made something that has more in common with his own personal and delicate last film. than anything out there today.

For though it has a reported 60 speaking parts, a 213-page script and a cost estimated at $50 million, "The Thin Red Line" is an art film to the core. If it's an epic (and at two hours and 50 minutes it certainly has the length) it's an intimate, dream-time epic, an elliptical, episodic film, dependent on images and reveries, that treats war as the ultimate nightmare, the one you just cannot awaken from no matter how hard you try.

Working with cinematographer John Toll, Malick has retained his eye for crystalline images, and a facility for camera movement so fluid as to seem almost thought-activated. And, from its unnerving opening look at a crocodile floating half above and half below a surface of green slime, "Thin Red Line" has a tendency toward shots that might be metaphorical but then again might not.

At times an almost hallucinogenic surrealism marks the film's slant on combat, a point of view that bookends nicely with "Saving Private Ryan's" frank and effective straightforwardness. It's the sense of being lost and without bearings that Malick emphasizes, the mind-distorting meaninglessness, the awful loneliness and absolute terror of battle. "War doesn't ennoble men, it turns them into dogs," one character says. "It makes them small, mean, ferocious; it poisons the soul."

But while this kind of moody, personal filmmaking can be impressive from moment to moment, it tends to wear thin over nearly three hours. So, hand in hand with its evocative sequences, "Thin Red Line" (the title comes from Jones' image of the line between sane and mad) can feel precious, self-conscious and even self-indulgent. Poetic almost to excess, it keeps a distance from us, holding its emotions apart, as things best studied at a great and philosophical remove.

This situation results from Malick's lack of sustained interest in conventional narrative. "The Thin Red Line" is a story told in fragments and shards, in glimpses of action. The film's concerns are philosophical rather than dramatic, and its extensive voice-over deals not with story points but with ruminations about how to be a man in a world described as "blowing itself to hell as fast as anyone can arrange it."

"This great evil, where does it come from, how did it steal into the world?" is a typical rumination; "How did we lose the good that was given us?" is another.

Much of this voice-over is spoken by two soldiers, Pvt. Witt (James Caviezel) and Pvt. Bell (Ben Chaplin of "The Truth About Cats & Dogs") and it's indicative of a wider lack of concern with coherence that both men have such similar Southern accents and dark good looks that it's anyone's guess at certain moments which one is speaking.

The film starts with a bucolic interlude; Witt has gone AWOL among the peaceful Melanesians of the Solomon Islands, where the simple pleasures of this unspoiled Eden are contrasted, not for the first time, with the horrors created by nominally more advanced civilizations.

At some point (you won't know exactly when unless you pay close attention) the voice-over is picked up by Bell, who is not worried so much about the morality of conflict but rather whether his wife (Miranda Otto)—glimpsed in a series of wistful flashbacks—can stand the strain of the prolonged physical separation mandated by the war.

Both Witt and Bell are members of an Army rifle unit, C-for-Charlie Company, that is the film's group protagonist. "The Thin Red Line" focuses most as a film when these men have to focus most as a combat force, taking part in a suicidal frontal attack on hill 210, a gentle rise fortified by entrenched Japanese machine gun nests.

The resulting action leads to fine specific moments from a group of familiar faces. These include Sean Penn as a first sergeant who's seen it all, John Cusack as a heroic young captain, Woody Harrelson as a sergeant in extremis, Elias Koteas as a captain who desperately wants to keep his men alive and, in the film's best performance, Nick Nolte as a lieutenant colonel who for the sake of his own career just as desperately wants to capture that hill no matter what the cost.

But while these actors and others have individual scenes that will look great on a lifetime achievement clip roll (the muscles on Nolte's neck vibrate as if they're computer-enhanced when he gets angry), they remain isolated instances. The film is too diffuse to connect up in any meaningful way.

There are also actors whose parts are barely cameo-sized, like George Clooney as a captain who doesn't even show up until the last few minutes, and an unbilled and uncomfortable John Travolta as a general. Unluckiest of all are those men (Adrien Brody, John C. Reilly, Arie Verbveen, Dash Mihok, John Savage, David Harrod, Jared Leto) with roles so underdeveloped or so murkily introduced we have no idea who they are. One-line descriptions in the press kit tells you more about these soldiers than anything they do on screen, and it's indicative of something that actress Otto, whose name isn't even in the press kit, has as much if not more screen time than some of the featured folks.

It's been reported that Malick shot close to a million feet of film, several times the norm for a feature, and it's likely that a longer, more illuminating cut of "Thin Red Line" at one time existed. As it stands now, this truncated-feeling film will make the most sense to those who are privy to that extended version. Though there are moments to cherish throughout, "The Thin Red Line" remains a stubbornly personal film, an artwork that only one person will understand and appreciate completely. No one need ask who that person might be.

NEW STATESMAN, 2/26/99, p. 41, Samuel Hynes

Before I went to the screening of Terrence Malick's "The Thin Red Line," I re-read James Jones's novel. The first time I read it, 35 years ago, I thought it was the best novel by an American to come out of the second world war; my second reading confirms that judgement. What makes it so good, and so permanent, is that Jones wrote only about the war he knew—the month or so he spent on Guadalcanal early in 1943, during the closing stages of the campaign there. He wasn't there when the marines made their first beachhead, nor for the desperate fighting for Henderson Field; when he and his lot came ashore five months later, the glory part was over. The Japanese had been defeated by then, but they fought on, as they always did, and so there were still the final battles of annihilation to be fought, one hill at a time.

Jones was determined that the book he wrote would be a "combat novel" and nothing else. He thought nobody had ever written truthfully about modern combat, that other writers had gone on about courage and cowardice when those terms no longer applied. His novel would be different: it would be objective, "photographic", almost a documentary, without any literary embellishments. It would not contain any Big Picture, but simply tell what it had been like for one company, his company—attacking, taking casualties, winning a hill or two, resting and getting drunk, attacking again. It would be a novel of ordinary war, made honest by what it included and by what it left out.

I thought, when I first read "The Thin Red Line," that it would make a good movie, though I could see some problems. A 500-page narrative of a small-scale mopping-up operation, built out of many small incidents, and with many sharply drawn characters, but no part for John Wayne, would be a challenge for a director. Still, if he could simply keep his head down and follow where Jones led him, he might make an authentic war movie, maybe even a great one.

Hollywood thought so, too; within a year a film version appeared, directed by Andrew Marston and starring Keir Dullea. I didn't see it, but those who did found it awkward and overwritten and crowded with incidents—a comic-strip version of the novel, one critic said.

Terrence Malick's version isn't like that: it is a remarkable war movie, honestly scripted and brilliantly shot. There are strong performances by many fine actors—James Caviezel, Ben Chaplin, Elias Koteas, Nick Nolte, Sean Penn—but no star: the centre of the story is dispersed over Charlie Company and its commanders, as it is in Jones's novel. In its combat sequences it is as faithful to the spirit of Jones's book as the transformation from page to film allows. The camera stays down on the ground with the infantrymen, peering over a ridge or running down a grassy slope or slogging through jungle, showing them as they are close-up: dirty, sweaty, scared, confused, lucky or unlucky. And if unlucky then dead because, as one soldier says, it's largely a matter of luck that decides whether or not you get killed; if you happen to be at a certain spot at a certain time, you get it. That's why there are no heroes.

Combat changes men who experience it: Jones believed that, and the film shows it. Combat is a trial or a test that a man passes or fails; if he passes, he becomes a soldier, numbed for a time by what he has done and seen, but able to do it again. In the novel, after an attack, Corporal Fife thinks: "I can kill, too! I can! Just like everybody! I can kill, too!" There is pride in that thought: Fife is a soldier now. His words aren't in the film, but his feeling is, and it is a part of the film's truth. Combat is a transforming, self-defining experience. You see it in the soldiers' faces after fighting. The film has got a crucial point right, because it has followed James Jones.

But before those truth-telling combat scenes appeared before us in the screening-room, before the film had even begun, something occurred to make me apprehensive. Where was the soundtrack coming from? Who were those children, singing in a strange language? Melanesian kids, it turned out, from the film's opening sequence: an island village, women in grass skirts, palm trees, children swimming in the surf—cliches from all the South Sea paradise films you've ever seen: and two army deserters in among them, discovering Eden. Only after that happy world had been established did the story turn to its other world, the troop ship approaching Guadalcanal that is the novel's first episode.

The village scene is innocently beautiful, and so indeed is the entire island when the camera turns from war to landscape, as it does again and again. And not only is the landscape beautiful: Malick has scattered through the film full-frame images of island flora and fauna—flowers, parrots, lizards, an owl, a crocodile, a tree full of bats—sudden patches of colour, like illustrations in National Geographic, all nature vivid to our eyes.

There are other directorial interpolations: voice-overs begin at once, soldiers of Charlie Company reflecting on God and Death and What Does It All Mean?—banalities that shift the balance of the film inward, and unsettle the characterisation. And there are Japanese soldiers, not seen simply as the distant, faceless others they usually are in war films, but at close range, as combatants firing their machine-guns and making suicide charges, and as the losers, surrendering, begging for their lives, and being shot by their captors. What Malick has done is to load Jones's long but spare combat novel with a cargo of ideology. Think about the environment. Think about nature's creatures. Think about what soldiers think. Think about the defeated. Spread your sympathies. War is a bad business. Since Malick was both the script-writer and the director, all of this is his work.

Some of these expansions of the novel come simply from the climate of ideas we live in, a different sense of what truth about war means. Some may perhaps be a consequence of Malick's peculiar situation, a director who has not made a film in 20 years, and must make his re-entry into the trade not simply with a good picture, but with a big, significant one. Perhaps he knew that his film would arrive in the theatres on the heels of Steven Spielberg's "Saving Private Ryan," and aimed to do for the Pacific war what Spielberg had done for D-Day and the invasion of Europe. Whatever the reasons, Malick made a good film, a moving, physical, convincing film, and then put too much into it. I came away editing it in my head, trimming it down to what would be a perfect, classic war film, with all the ideological superstructure gone.

In a couple of weeks Malick's film will meet Spielberg's in the Academy Awards voting, like two gunslingers in a Western walk-down. Both have been nominated for Best Picture and Best Director. My vote, if I had one, would go to Malick both times. In my view "Private Ryan" is 25 minutes of virtual D-Day followed by a conventional special-unit story, a war movie made out of war movies with only the hi-tech spectacles at the beginning and end to distinguish it. "The Thin Red Line" is a lot better than that, partly because of the superior material (Jones's novel), partly because of the small-scale nature of the engagement that is its story, partly because it isn't top-heavy with technology—but mainly, I think, because Malick was thinking about war when Spielberg was only thinking about movies.

NEW YORK, 1/4/99, p. 52, Peter Rainer

In the twenty years since his last film, *Days of Heaven,* Terrence Malick has achieved the notoriety of a prize recluse—an art-house Howard Hughes. Much of this rep is dubious; he has, after all, apparently been writing, or doctoring (unproduced) scripts all along, as well as directing a bit in the theater. Besides, who can blame him for ducking the media juggernaut that has grown like topsy since his salad days? We should just be thankful that Stanley Kubrick (another guy who doesn't talk to the press) didn't also come out with *his* new film this Christmas as planned. Having to deal—or, more precisely, not deal—with these two mysterioso geniuses in the same week would have ripped a black hole in the P.R. cosmos.

Now that Malick has finally deigned to make a new movie, *The Thin Red Line*—an adaptation of James Jones's 1962 World War II novel about an Army campaign in Guadalcanal—his genius rep is being re-scrutinized. I was never an ardent admirer of Malick's. I've always found *Badlands* to be a lyrical-creepy art thing, though I can still summon up with a shiver some of its more virtuoso sequences, like the house-burning with the Carl Orff music laid over it. But *Days of Heaven* is as emotionally glacial as it is visually ravishing. *The Thin Red Line* is new, but it might have been made by the Malick of twenty years ago—it seems to come out of that same seventies fugue state of his in which all action is aestheticized until nothing is left but pretty pictures and patterning. Malick never saw a leaf he didn't want to film through, or a sunset he didn't want to emblematize.

I shouldn't say *all* action, exactly, since for the first hour or so Malick does manage to stage the Army's advance on Japanese artillery in a way that holds you as powerfully, and conventionally, as anything he's ever done. For all his frills, Malick has a rather routinized imagination. We get many hidebound clichés of the war genre in *The Thin Red Line,* including the growling lieutenant colonel (Nick Nolte), neck veins bursting, who orders his captain (Elias Koteas) to take Hill 210 no matter what the cost in lives; or the private (Ben Chaplin) who keeps flashing back to gauzy, rhapsodic interludes with his wife.

We also get the flossier clichés. Private Witt (James Caviezel) is a Kentucky cracker in the book, but he's been transformed into the film's spiritual guide, and Malick can't get enough of his Christlike countenance. Witt is AWOL at the film's beginning—we see him playing in Rousseau-like innocence with the Melanesian natives—but he gives himself up to the war and, with his soulful steadiness, becomes a great resource to his men. His first sergeant (Sean Penn) is fond of saying to him, "In this world a man himself is nothing, and there ain't nothing but this world." Witt, eyes glazed with goodness, responds, "I've seen another world."

Malick gives virtually all the American combatants their own running interior monologues. At times the voice-over gridlock is confounding—we're unsure whose head we're in. The heads are almost always in the clouds; it's like being in a platoon of philosophy majors. With its plodding but pulverizing descriptiveness, Jones's novel brought you inside the ravages of warfare as Malick almost never does. The book is a triumph of the prosaic; the movie, despite some evocative passages, is a poetic washout. Malick's pretty abstractions and ontologies don't have much to do with the terrors of combat. It's a movie about the importance of preserving your refinement in the trenches.

NEW YORK POST, 12/23/98, p. 40, Rod Dreher

"The Thin Red Line" is to the Second World War as "Beloved" was to slavery. Which is to say, writer-director Terrence Malick is so lost in the film's Big Themes and his own aspirations to art that he neglects to tell a story that makes any but the slightest claim on our attention or emotions. It is a gorgeous movie to look at, but otherwise it's a dull, chaotic, maddening, pretentious mess.

With this adaptation of James Jones' combat novel, the reclusive auteur Malick returns to the director's chair 20 years after making the cult classic "Days of Heaven"—which was only his second movie, after "Badlands."

"The Thin Red Line" is about what you would expect from Malick, who is far more gifted at composing and lighting shots than he is at creating characters or telling a story. "The Thin Red Line" is nearly three hours of stunning nature photography punctuated by spasmodic violence, long stretches of throwaway dialogue and war-related rhetorical musings.

Did Malick devise the story line with a Spirograph? The movie is about a U.S. Army company's fight to capture a hill on Japanese-occupied Guadalcanal. Seems straightforward enough, but the druggy narrative windmills lazily and aimlessly out of control, introducing soldiers, then wandering off for no discernable reason, returning to some of them haphazardly, to others not at all.

Audiences drawn to the film by the stellar cast, which includes Sean Penn, Woody Harrelson and John Cusack, will be bitterly disappointed. Blink and you'll miss John Travolta and George Clooney.

As in his previous movies, Malick uses narration, but here it's hard to keep straight who the narrator is at any given moment. And some of the players—particularly the two leads, Jim Caviezel and Ben Chaplin—bear such a strong resemblance to each other it's easy to lose track of which is which. And who cares about these men, anyway? I looked down at my watch and realized the movie was nearly half over, and I didn't know the name of a single character.

This is a key difference between this film and "Saving Private Ryan." Steven Spielberg grounded his exploration of man at war in specific characters and a coherent moral universe. Malick inverts this, showing far more interest in abstract philosophical concepts than in the suffering of flesh-and-blood men fighting an annihilating but reasonable war.

There is nowhere in this meandering film a sense of purpose to the fighting. Guadalcanal is a blasted heath of insanity, a no-man's land where one is given to ponder questions like the following, heard in voice-over:

"Why does nature war with itself?"

"Is there an avenging power in nature?"

"Why can't we stay on the heights, the heights we're capable of?"

"Do you imagine that suffering will be less because you love?"

To which I say: Life is like a box of chocolates; deal with it.

In truth, these aren't silly questions, but they arise in a movie that's so self-consciously arty and so disconnected from the reasonable expectations of its audience that they sound ludicrous. Malick doesn't even try to answer them. You keep wanting him to get his big fat head out of the clouds and get us from point A to point B with a minimum of digression.

The one great strength of "The Thin Red Line," aside from Hans Zimmer's sepulchral score, is cinematographer John Toll's gloriously lush and lyrical photography. Malick's movie concerns itself with the harsh spectacle of Edenic nature despoiled by violent, sinful men. Image after idyllic image of the luminous, Henri Rosseau—like junglescape mesmerizes (it's like "Koyaanisqatsi" with guns and boring dialogue). But sticking with a three-hour film in which the beautifully billowing grass is the most captivating element is an onerous task.

NEWSDAY, 12/23/98, Part II/p. B3, Jack Mathews

With bitter irony, the late novelist James Jones dedicated his World War II combat novel "The Thin Red Line" to "WAR and WARFARE; may they never cease to give us the pleasure, excitement and adrenal stimulation that we need, or provide us with the heroes, the presidents and leaders, the monuments and museums which we erect to them in the name of PEACE."

At the end of the novel, as surviving members of the Army rifle group Charlie Company are retrieved from the beaches at Guadalcanal in the Solomon Islands, the narrator predicts that one of them will write a book about their experiences there, but that none of the others will believe it because they won't remember it the same way.

Whatever writer-director Terrence Malick does with the material between the dedication and the last sentence of the novel, the reclusive poet-auteur has taken to heart Jones' most personal feelings about a mission he observed first-hand, then relived as a recurring dream.

Malick has adapted that dream as much as he has the novel. The film, even at 2 hours and 50 minutes, must necessarily condense Jones' detailed events and downsize his large cast of central characters. But, of course, Malick, a Rhodes Scholar who made two landmark films of the '70s and then disappeared, does far more than that. He has filmed a haunting, scattered reminiscence piece, where the mind is allowed to drift through its memories, and retrieve impressions of the beautiful and the hideous, the serene and the hysterical, the banal and the profound.

These elements are mixed, separated, overlaid and rearranged as Jones' tale of C company's assault of Japanese positions unfolds, and people looking for a conventional war story will be gravely disappointed—especially if they're anticipating the trumpeted appearances of such stars as John Travolta, George Clooney, Woody Harrelson and John Cusack.

The actors are there, having campaigned to work with the legendary Malick, but their fleeting appearances in cameo roles are more a distraction than an attraction. Sean Penn, as the cynical, strong-willed Sgt. Welsh, based on the same character Burt Lancaster played in "From Here to Eternity," and Nick Nolte, as the ramrod Lt. Col. Toll, have central roles, but like everyone else in the film, they disappear for long stretches of time.

Several of the key roles are filled by relative unknowns, including that of Pvt. Witt (Jim Caviezel), whom Jones saw as a soulmate of the character played by Montgomery Clift in "Eternity," and it's often difficult to keep the new faces straight. Compounding that annoyance is Malick's use of disconnected voices that take us inside his characters' minds. It's hard to keep those minds straight, too.

Obviously, conventional film structure is of little interest to Malick, which may explain why he and Hollywood parted so early in his career. Here, he has composed a psychological portrait of combat. Some of it is as pretentious as it sounds; yet, in many ways, "The Thin Red Line" is a more honest depiction of the effects of war than Steven Spielberg's "Saving Private Ryan."

There's sure to be heated debate over which is the better of the year's two epic war films, and I vote for "The Thin Red Line," but they really should be seen as complementary. Where "Ryan" is a visceral, throat-grabbing re-enactment of the physical horror of war, "The Thin Red Line" takes the subject on at the intellectual and philosophical level. The troops in both stories are deep in harm's way, but their perception of their missions are far different.

Tom Hanks' platoon in "Ryan" is on a patriotic quest, to save a soldier's life, in order to save his mother's grief, in order to save America's faith in the value of the individual. The troops in "The Thin Red Line" are in a primitive jungle, fighting people they can't see, for reasons unknown. There's plenty of brutal action in Malick's film, but at its soul are searching questions about life and death, the nature of war and man, glory and waste.

Surely, Malick didn't intend all his voice-over introspection to be taken literally, as if these were the exact thoughts soldiers feel at the moment of truth. Remember, he's putting himself in the mind of Jones, who had put himself in the minds of the other men on Guadalcanal.

If Jones didn't expect the survivors to believe his version of the story, how can Malick expect us to believe his? The likelihood is that not many people will, but those who do will feel something special.

NEWSWEEK, 12/21/98, p. 66, David Ansen

Terrence Malick's two extraordinary '70s movies, "Badlands" and "Days of Heaven," never looked like anyone else's. They had a quality of meditation, at once closely observed and yet seen from afar, that lodged under your skin. "The Thin Red Line" may come 20 years after he last worked, but it is as singular as its predecessors. Strikingly unconventional in form, this adaptation of James Jones's 1962 novel about the men who fought in Guadalcanal in World War II is faithful to the book's harshly realistic view of combat but stylistically almost its opposite. It juxtaposes beauty and horror to fashion a savage and lyrical cinematic poem. Combat scenes of appalling violence are counterpointed by idyllic visions of the natural world—the Eden that becomes ground zero in the Pacific war. Can such beauty and such ugliness be the "workings of one mind, the features of the same face"? That's the big question the movie's spiritual spokesman—a soft-spoken Kentucky soldier named Witt (Jim Caviezel)—asks us to ponder.

More poet than dramatist, more philosopher than psychologist, Malick and his story-telling methods are going to frustrate viewers looking for characters they can identify with, and plots with a beginning, middle and end. Has there ever been a 2-hour-and-45-minute film with less dialogue? Malick prefers to take us inside the minds of his characters, to eavesdrop on their thoughts. He uses multiple voice-overs, which can be confusing: we're not always sure who we're hearing. There's Witt, the idealistic soldier who has gone AWOL to live among the peaceful natives and now must return to battle. Witt's thematic opposite is the cynical warrior Welsh (Sean Penn), who wants nothing more than to achieve numbness in the face of atrocity. We also dip into the raging, resentful mind of Lieutenant Colonel Tall (Nick Nolte), who commands the troop's attack on hill 210—the movie's bravura centerpiece. The ambitious Tall is determined to succeed no matter what the human cost, which puts him on a collision course with Captain Staros (Elias

Koteas), who wants to protect his men. There are dozens of others in this physically eloquent ensemble, deployed like shards in a violent mosaic.

Like "Saving Private Ryan," "The Thin Red Line" is queasily effective at conveying the sheer physical terror of war, the deafening chaos of combat. Unlike Spielberg, who got us rooting for the enemy to be killed, the more abstract Malick makes us feel an eagle-eye compassion for all the dead. One of the most unsettling sequences shows us the almost obscene intimacy between the terrorized Japanese captives and the victors who are toying with their lives.

This epic, however, never lays claim to our emotions the way Spielberg's film does. "The Thin Red Line" is a film of brilliant pieces and dazzling shots, but it's unable to sustain dramatic tension: it soars and sags, then soars and sags again. (Mood-breaking star cameos from George Clooney and John Travolta don't help.) But whatever its shortcomings, you know you're in the presence of a radical talent. Malick conjures up visions you'll never be able to shake. It's good to have him back.

SIGHT AND SOUND, 3/99, p. 53, Geoffrey Macnab

1942. Guadalcanal. US soldiers land on the island, hoping to take it back from the Japanese. At first, they encounter no resistance. C for Charlie company ventures into the jungle, discovering the corpses of some colleagues who've gone before them. Their progress is halted and they sustain many losses when they attempt to climb a hill heavily fortified by the Japanese. Lt. Colonel Tall is adamant that they must take the hill, but Captain Staros is reluctant to commit his men on a mission he fears will kill many unnecessarily so he disobeys Tall's order.

Eventually, a small group of soldiers outflank the enemy and are able to destroy the Japanese machine gun post. The company marches forward, coming face to face with the enemy, who are terrified and in disarray. Many Japanese are killed and captured. Tall, exultant about the success of the operation, announces the company is to have a week's leave away from the front. The men spend their time off by the sea. Private Bell learns his wife (of whom he is always thinking) is leaving him for another man. First Sergeant Welsh, a pragmatist who takes a very cynical view of the motives behind the war, argues with Private Witt, a young idealist who refuses to conform with army rules. Staros is relieved of his command by Tall. The soldiers return to the front. An operation in the jungle goes wrong. Witt's courage saves the company, but he is killed by the Japanese. Bloodied and dishevelled, the soldiers leave the island.

In his first two films, Terrence Malick evoked rustic America with a detail and lyricism which belied the brutal stories he was telling. *Badlands* (1973) seemed as much a Depression-era travelogue as a film about two murderous delinquents. While seeing the locusts ravage the fields in *Days of Heaven* (1978), you were likely to be so enraptured by the imagery you might forget a farmer's livelihood was being destroyed by them. Malick's characters always seemed detached from the events they were witnessing. His use of voiceovers heightened the sense that they were outsiders looking in at a world to which they didn't really belong.

The Thin Red Line, Malick's first film in 20 years, shares a naive, dream-like quality with its two predecessors. The difference here is that the James Jones novel from which the director took his screenplay is not about a few estranged individuals. It is a sprawling, messy account of the experiences of dozens of soldiers in the face of war. The director is far more of a stylist than the novelist whose work he is (at least slightly) bowdlerising. Where Jones gives us long chunks of ungainly but compelling prose, Malick aims for poetic symbolism.

In the first half of the film, he fails to differentiate between individual characters. Before the fighting begins, we're shown Private Witt enjoying an idyllic interlude on an unspoiled island retreat. Witt, at least as conceived by Malick, has more in common with Montgomery Clift's martyr like Prewitt in *From Here to Eternity* (1953) than with the opportunistic, slightly sleazy figure in Jones' book. Here, he's a visionary at odds with military discipline but always open to his surroundings. When, as constantly happens throughout the film, there are cutaways to insects, animals or birds, it is as if we are seeing them through his eyes.

Although Witt is depicted in detail, many of the other characters from the book are mere thumbnail sketches. Sgt. Welsh's grumblings about how the war is being fought for capitalism are reduced to a few asides about "property, property". We don't see the gay affair between two of the soldiers nor does Malick show arguably the most poignant and grotesque scene in the book, in which one GI, while defecating, is surprised by a Japanese soldier. Whereas Jones was able to offer a multiplicity of perspectives and to suggest how each individual soldier was experiencing the same events in radically different ways, Malick can only hint obliquely at what his characters are feeling, however many voiceovers he uses. Surprisingly, Colonel Tall is made more prominent here, with Nick Nolte playing him much the same way as Sterling Hayden did the mad general in *Dr. Strangelove* (1963). It's an impressive portrayal of a career soldier so steeped in military arrogance he's lost his moral bearings. But by putting such emphasis on him, Malick moves the focus away from the pivotal figure of Captain Staros—named Stein in the book so it's hard to understand why his soldiers are so dismayed when Tall relieves him of his command.

In one key sense, this adaptation is absolutely faithful. Like Jones, Malick shows war as something messy and inchoate. He's often accused of not knowing how to fashion a narrative, but that's to his advantage here. The film benefits from its random shifts in mood—the way it changes voices and lurches between moments of breathtaking beauty, stretches of relative tedium and sudden bloody battle scenes. Whatever its ideological bias or historical oversights, *The Thin Red Line* is hugely effective as a film about the absurdity of war. There is no respite. Apart from the scenes in which Bell remembers the wife he misses so much, we never escape the island. Under Witt's benevolent gaze, it may seem a paradise, but the further the soldiers delve into the jungle, the more hellish it becomes. The most frustrating sequence is the assault on the hill crowned by a Japanese machine-gun post. Each time the soldiers near the top they are sent, like Sisyphus, spiralling back by the gunners.

In many war movies, the battle scenes are an end in themselves. (No review of *Saving Private Ryan* neglected to mention how "realistic" the Omaha-beach landings were.) In *The Thin Red Line* the battle scenes merely provide the backdrop to Malick's rambling, quizzical inquiries into military behaviour and the nature of evil; he's more interested in metaphysics than machismo. It is an extraordinary achievement to have made a big-budget war film which seems so utterly personal. For all the dissonant voices, the star cameos, the awesome cinematography, this is Malick's vision alone. The island setting only reinforces the sense that he is a Prospero pulling all the strings.

TIME, 12/28/98-1/4/99, p. 173, Richard Corliss

It's that war again. At the end of a film year dominated by Steven Spielberg's *Saving Private Ryan* (Europe, 1944: D-day and after) comes Terrence Malick's *The Thin Red Line* (the Pacific, 1942: Guadalcanal). The two films, each with a rightful claim to magnificence, are as different as the terrain of their settings and the strengths of their makers. The New York Film Critics' Circle probably got it right last week by naming *Private Ryan* best film and Malick best director.

In *Private Ryan,* the flinty, competent G.I.s have a clear mission. *The Thin Red Line,* from James Jones' 1962 novel, is about military and moral chaos. Its infantrymen are scared and unprepared for the hilltop assault that consumes most of the film. (The Japanese are scared too.) Who are these guys? There's John Travolta, briefly. And Nick Nolte and a nicely unmannerist Sean Penn. And many young faces we must strain to identify. Malick a poker player or a mystic, does not easily yield information. His story is a meadow with a minefield.

Some films deal in plot truth; this one expresses emotional truth, the heart's search for saving wisdom, in some of the most luscious imagery since Malick's last film, the 1978 *Days of Heaven*. The new movie takes up where *Days*—and his haunting *Badlands* of 1973—left off. Each film is a tragedy of small folks with too grand goals; each is narrated by a hick with a dreamy touch of the poetic; each sets its tiny humans against Nature in ferocious rhapsody. *The Thin Red Line* begins with an island idyll, and to Private Witt (Jim Caviezel) it feels like the ideal hallucination. It is really Nature's tease: here is Eden, the way the world was before the Fall. Now go to war and screw it all up.

Malick's palette holds a precise orgy of colors; his camera moves like the sun's rush down a hill (a thrilling shot) that throws a fatal light on the men's position. Most of the G.I.s are doomed to have a past—iridescent memories of the blue Pacific or the wife back home—but no future. And Malick, like a god who made the world so lovely and life so harsh, ornaments their ordeal splendidly. The film is a gorgeous garland on an unknown soldier's grave.

VILLAGE VOICE, 12/29/98, p. 117, J. Hoberman

The year's most enigmatic studio release, written and directed by one of the most puzzling figures in Hollywood, *The Thin Red Line* projects a sense of wounded diffidence. Terrence Malick's hugely ambitious, austerely hallucinated adaptation of James Jones's 1962 novel—a 500-page account of combat in Guadalcanal—is a metaphysical platoon movie in which battlefield confusion is melded with an Emersonian meditation on the nature of nature.

The first and costliest American victory in World War II's Pacific theater was a six-month assault on Japanese-held Guadalcanal, one of the Solomon Islands east of New Guinea. Malick's movie appears to concern a mop-up operation, late in the struggle, with a battalion of mainly green army recruits landing in relief of the marines who initiated the attack on the stronghold. I say "appears" because although *The Thin Red Line* gives a real—if necessarily idealized—sense of an American army in action, there is a sense in which Malick's movie is not so much about World War II as about a particular existential condition.

Saving Private Ryan opens, in a brutal tour de force that is Steven Spielberg's most visceral filmmaking since *Jaws,* with the GIs landing on Omaha beach. (As a way of conditioning audience response, it's as though Hitchcock began Psycho with the shower sequence.) Malick is considerably more contemplative. *The Thin Red Line* starts with a leisurely immersion in a South Pacific paradise as filtered through the consciousness of the pensive Private Witt (Jim Caviezel). It's not too far from Malick's *Days of Heaven,* although the expulsion from this tropical Eden is an hour-plus attempt to storm a Japanese position.

Jones, who saw action and was wounded at Guadalcanal, devoted fully half of his novel to detailing the capture of Hill 209 and so it seems here. Malick orchestrates what could be the longest battle scene in movie history, and one in which shock and hysteria are pervasive. Charging head-on uphill toward an unseen foe, the men drop at random, often from friendly fire. Everybody, with the exception of an almost frighteningly cool captain (John Cusack) is either terrified or crazed.

In essence, this epic battle scene concerns the stripping away of each soldiers self (or its obliteration) and, in the midst of this operation, a philosophical argument breaks out. Colonel Tall (Nick Nolte) screams orders to launch a suicide attack that his subordinate, Captain Staros (Elias Koteas), stuck on a ridge without shelter, refuses to obey. Nor is the debate restricted to strategy or even words. Abetted by Hans Zimmer's brooding score, the entire sequence has the aspect of an extended reverie. Repeatedly, Malick cuts away from the carnage to the image of a young woman—Private Bell (Ben Chaplin) imagining his wife as a battlefield angel—or, even more outrageously, to the light as it changes on the tall grass in the wind.

Guadalcanal, at least as it was portrayed in the 1944 *Guadalcanal Diary* (the key World War II movie released during the war), was the crucible that, more fiery than any urban melting pot, forged the American fighting spirit. *The Thin Red Line* is no less an ensemble film, although its sense of spirit is more expanded. The archetypes are in place—the sensitive mystic (Caviezel) and the cynical sergeant (Sean Penn in a tremendously concentrated performance), the blowhard warrior Colonel Tall and his tender-hearted adversary (Koteas), the efficient good soldier (Cusack) and the fear-crazed survivor (Adrien Brody), to name only a few. But, if battle-heightened awareness imbues these soldiers with a undeniable, albeit transitory, *uebermensch* quality, *The Thin Red Line* is scarcely waving the flag. And if the Japanese—most extensively seen as the wounded, freaked-out, praying denizens of an overrun camp—are hardly individuated and never grated the slightest subjectivity, it is clear that Malick himself is consciously striving for what might be termed a "Japanese" quality of stillness and emptiness in the midst of hell.

For all its documentary detail, Jones's novel was born old-fashioned. It was published a year after Joseph Heller's *Catch-22* initiated a vast shift in American attitudes; Allied Artists' quickie movie version was distinguished mainly for having been released on a double bill with Sam Fuller's *The Naked Kiss.* Malick's version—which unavoidably references the great, flawed Vietnam visions of *Apocalypse Now* and (especially) *Platoon*—is, however, anachronistic in a different way. Not exactly timeless and not primarily a narrative, it's a head movie about death and dying.

The Thin Red Line meanders from Witt's consciousness into Bell's and even briefly Tall's, as if to suggest that they are all one. Tall may instruct the humanist Staros in the cruelty of nature but even that, Malick insists, is in the mind. (It takes only a single communication from the outside world for a previously idyllic Melanesian village to deliquesce into a miasma of fear, conflict, disease, and death.) When, in one crucial scene, the Japanese appear out of the jungle to surround Witt, they appear as woodland spirits. Their helmets are garnished with tree branches; the scene is shot like a ritual. Witt, who has been living inside his head all movie long, can't believe it; he doesn't even think to drop his weapon.

At two hours and 45 minutes, *The Thin Red Line* gives ample evidence of suffering all manner of cuts, if not having been simply hacked into its final shape. But this violence only adds to the movie's brave, strange, eroded nobility. As mystical as it is gritty, as despairing as it is detached, Malick's study of men in battle materializes in our midst almost exactly a century after Stephen Crane's *The Red Badge of Courage*—an exercise in 19th-century transcendentalism, weirdly serene in the face of horror.

Also reviewed in:
NATION, 1/4/99, p. 34, Stuart Klawans
NEW REPUBLIC, 1/25/99, p. 24, Stanley Kauffmann
NEW YORK TIMES, 12/23/98, p. E1, Janet Maslin
NEW YORKER, 12/28/98 & 1/4/99, p. 138, Anthony Lane
VARIETY, 12/21/98-1/3/99, p. 73, Todd McCarthy
WASHINGTON POST, 1/8/99, p. B1, Stephen Hunter
WASHINGTON POST, 1/8/99, Weekend/p. 38, Michael O'Sullivan

THREE NINJAS: HIGH NOON AT MEGA MOUNTAIN

A TriStar Pictures release of a Sheen production in association with Leeds/Ben-Ami Productions. *Executive Producer:* Simon Sheen and Arthur Leeds. *Producer:* James Kang and Yoram Ben-Ami. *Director:* Sean Patrick McNamara. *Screenplay:* Sean Patrick McNamara and Jeff Phillips. *Director of Photography:* Blake T. Evans. *Editor:* Annamaria Szanto. *Music:* John Coda. *Art Director:* Chase Harlan. *Costumes:* Miye Matsumoto. *Running time:* 94 minutes. *MPAA Rating:* PG.

CAST: Hulk Hogan (Dave Dragon); Loni Anderson (Medusa); Jim Varney (Birdie); Victor Wong (Grandpa Mori); Mathew Botuchis (Rocky); Michael J. O'Laskey II (Colt); J. P. Roeske II (Tum Tum); Chelsey Earlywine (Amanda).

LOS ANGELES TIMES, 4/10/98, Calendar/p. 8, Kevin Thomas

"3 Ninjas: High Noon at Mega Mountain" is just as smart and lively as its three predecessors. Martial arts for kids, with their underlying spiritual principles and emphasis on self-defense, are especially welcome at a time when stories of youngsters with guns flood the media.

Exceptionally well-made family entertainment, this "3 Ninjas" is constantly inventive, action-filled and funny, with a flourish of good special effects. Director Sean Patrick McNamara and his co-writer Jeff Phillips and their first-rate cast and resourceful crew deliver the goods.

Ironically, "3 Ninjas" No. 4 opens on a poignant note. The three likable Douglas brothers, Rocky (Mathew Botuchis), Colt (Michael J. O'Laskey II) and Tum Tum (J.P. Roeske II) are winding up their usual summer vacation with their Grandpa Mori (the wonderful Victor Wong), who has trained them to be black-belt karate fighters at his wilderness retreat. Grandpa sadly overhears his two oldest grandsons expressing their growing boredom with karate and their reluctance to return the following summer. Very shortly, of course, the boys are going to be profoundly grateful for all their grandfather has taught them.

For a birthday treat Tum Tum has picked a day at a theme park, Mega Mountain (in reality Denver's Elitch Gardens), because his martial-arts TV hero Dave Dragon (Hulk Hogan, top-billed but a supporting player) is making a personal appearance. Dragon has just announced his show has been canceled, suggesting wistfully that people don't seem to believe in heroes anymore.

So off to Mega Mountain go the brothers and friends, plus their new neighbor Amanda (Chelsey Earlywine). She's an electronics and computer whiz who's the daughter of a movie special-effects expert who's taught her a few tricks of his trade.

Wouldn't you know that this is the very day that the evil Medusa (Loni Anderson) and her henchmen descend upon Mega Mountain and hold its visitors for $10 million in ransom from the park's owner? Naturally, the baddies are ultimately no match for the three ninjas, plus the smart and clever Amanda and the heroic Dave, but the getting there is ingenious, diverting and amusing.

Encased in dominatrix black leather and spike heels, and sporting a blond hooker wig and makeup, Anderson has fun with the nasty Medusa. Just as she's about to blow up—or so she thinks—the cool Amanda, played with spunk and poise by Earlywine, she tells the girl, "Rest in pieces!"

Cast as Medusa's key henchman is Jim Varney, in a long-overdue departure from his Ernest character, whose lean, weaselly presence fondly recalls old-time serials villains. Don't be surprised if the "3 Ninjas" return for a fifth outing—and let's hope that if there is one, there will be more screen time for the droll Wong.

NEW YORK POST, 4/10/98, p. 49, Larry Worth

Along with "Ay-ah!" the titular heroes of "3 Ninjas: High Noon at Mega Mountain" repeat—over and over and over "this is awesome." But no matter how many times they say it, that doesn't make it so.

As the fourth entry of a painfully uninspired series, this version features new actors portraying the trio of adolescent warriors.

At any rate, Rocky, Colt, and Tum Tum are celebrating a birthday at the ultimate amusement park: Mega Mountain. But, as luck would have it, terrorists on self-propelled waterskies are about to invade the pleasure paradise by the bay—and hold helpless tourists hostage.

Forced to do battle with power-mad Medusa (Loni Anderson) and evil henchman Lothar (Jim Varney), the boys are in for the ride of their lives, aided only by hero Dave Dragon (Hulk Hogan) and their foxy young neighbor (Chesley Earlywine).

The rest is all paint-by-numbers. The scenario of a child beating up an adult—usually starting with a kick to the groin—seemed a cliche long before "Home Alone" made it a kiddie-film staple.

In the meantime, writer-director Sean McNamara comes up with some off-putting scenarios for small-fry viewers, as when depicting tortured roller coaster patrons suspended upside down for 10 minutes or water-rafters threatened with drowning. And that's not even mentioning Loni Anderson, walking around in black leather hot pants, an S & M bustier and thigh-high boots, and cracking a mean whip at her pre-teen captives.

Even Jim "Ernest" Varney and Hulk Hogan, performers who've never been accused of great acting, are embarrassing beyond belief. Only the titular trio—Matthew Botuchis, Michael J. O'Laskey II and J.P. Roeske II—earn credit for some impressive acrobatics.

But that hardly merited a fourth "3 Ninjas" installment. At this rate, it would take Hanson's star power to justify a fifth.

NEWSDAY, 4/10/98, Part II/p. B7, Gene Seymour

Here is your choice. You can order a ham-and-beef hero sandwich, heavy on the oil, lots of extra cheese, or you can see "3 Ninjas: High Noon at Mega Mountain." To those struggling to lose weight, the choice would appear a no-brainer. Then again, so's the movie, which contains roughly the same ingredients. (OK, maybe a *little* more cheese ...)

This time, the brothers Douglas—Rocky (Mathew Paul Botuchis), Colt (Michael J. O'Laskey II) and Tum-Tum (James Paul Roeske II)—find themselves having to use the high performance martial arts training given by their still-implausible grandpa (Victor Wong again!) to battle an army of terrorists who've seized control of Mega Mountain amusement park.

Medusa (Loni Anderson, bringing the ham), the gang's snarling, leather-clad leader, doesn't want political prisoners released or land returned. She wants lots of money from the park's owner—presumably to buy more liederhosen—or she'll set off serial accidents on all the rides.

This elaborate shakedown plan not only has the three suburban warriors standing in its way, but the obligatory junior high-tech whiz (Chelsey Earlywine) who happens to carry such super-neato gadgets as a yo-yo with blades. There's also Dave Dragon (Hulk Hogan, providing the beef), a TV action hero who's about to lose his Saturday morning show because it seems "kids don't believe in heroes anymore."

If so, it's hard to believe such lost faith will be revived by this muddle of cartoonish kickboxing and corny slapstick. A band of dreamy 8-year-olds wandering an amusement park could probably imagine themselves in a story that's more interesting than this. And, by the way, if you think action movies for children haven't the right or the means to be funnier and smarter than this, then the bad guys really have won and heroism is dead.

Also reviewed in:
NEW YORK TIMES, 4/10/98, p. E14, Anita Gates
VARIETY, 4/13-19/98, p. 28, Joe Leydon

TOKYO FIST

A Manga Entertainment release of a Kaijyu Theater Co.production. *Executive Producer:* Shinya Tsukamoto. *Producer:* Kiyo Joo. *Director:* Shinya Tsukamoto. *Screenplay (Japanese with English subtitles):* Shinya Tsukamoto. *Based on a story by:* Hisashi Saito and Shinya Tsukamoto. *Director of Photography:* Shinya Tsukamoto. *Editor:* Shinya Tsukamoto. *Music:* Chu Ishikawa. *Sound:* Ichiro Kawashima and (music) Yukio Sekiya. *Production Designer:* Kiyomi Nakazaki and Tomoko Tsukada. *Art Director:* Shinya Tsukamoto. *Special Effects:* Takashi Oda and Hiroshi Sagae. *Costumes:* Hiroko Iwasaki. *Make-up:* Kaori Sasaki. *Special Effects Make-up:* Akira Fukaya. *Running time:* 90 minutes. *MPAA Rating:* Not Rated.

CAST: Shinya Tsukamoto (Tsuda Yoshiharu); Kahori Fujii (Hizuru); Koji Tsukamoto (Kojima Takuji); Naoto Takenaka (Ohizumi, Trainer); Naomasa Musaka (Hase, Trainer); Koichi Wajima (Shirota, Gym Owner); Tomoroh Taguchi (Tattoo Master); Nobu Kanaoka (Nurse).

NEW YORK POST, 5/22/98, p. 66, Larry Worth

Those who can't get enough of corpse-devouring maggots, body-piercing closeups and faces being pummeled into raw meat will have a field day with "Tokyo Fist." All others should proceed with extreme caution.

It's the latest from Shinya Tsukamoto, the writer-director of Japanese cult films "Tetsuo: Iron Man" and its sequel, "Tetsuo: Body Hammer." Fans of either will recall the auteur's penchant for nonstop violence, striking photography and a hybrid of live-action and animation that's both alluring and appalling.

Here, those elements are woven into a romance between an insurance salesman (nicely played by the director), his unstable fiancee (Kahori Fujii) and a young boxer (Koji Tsukamoto, the director's brother). Suffice to say that the trio's S&M-themed "tough love" sessions will have viewers squirming.

Sadly, that's the film's sole reason for being. As such, "Tokyo Fist," is like a one-two punch: simple and groan-producing.

NEWSDAY, 5/22/98, Part II/p. B11, John Anderson

Having achieved cult status with his "Tetsuo: Iron Man" films, Shinya Tsukamoto, moves several steps further with "Tokyo Fist," fusing the emblematic, graphic angst of ANIME (Japan's gothic comic book art) with pure, horror movie gore and a David Cronenberg-inspired view of flesh-as-cracked-mirror. "Tokyo Fist" is no "Tokyo Story" (Yasujiro Ozu's elegant '50s family drama): In this blood-soaked psycho-allegory, Tsukamoto effectively leaves behind anything that the general public in this country associates with Japanese cinema.

His characters are tortured, and his imagery makes it visceral: The action sequences are furious and dangerous, the more sedate moments bubble with unarticulated rage. Black and white sequences that recall a young schoolgirl's murder, which neither Tsuda (Tsukamoto) nor Kojima (brother Koji Tsukamoto) could stop, and which has haunted their later lives. Tsuda responded, by forgetting the incident entirely, becoming a weary, suffocated wage slave; Kojima went into boxing, to some day seek revenge. And his resentment of Tsuda's forgetfulness sparks his pursuit of Tsuda's girlfriend, Hizuru (Kahori Fujii), who's ready to be considered something other than Tsuda's trophy babe.

Tsuda is outraged and enters the ring, training relentlessly for the inevitable showdown with Kojima, whose own career is faltering and who faces a death match with a seemingly invincible boxer from a rival gym. The plot points are far less interesting however, than the way Tsukamoto reflects the slow death-by-society of his characters, in exhilarating displays of sado-masochistic self-mortification and violence. While riveting in their effrontery and psychology, Tsukamoto's pictures are even more horrifying in their unreality: By only slightly overdoing the effects of the mayhem, he makes it appallingly clear just what the violence really means, what it should look like.

Amid the emotional and physical meltdown of the three main characters, the most fascinating is Hizuru, who in her body-piercing and tattoos becomes a kind of Picture of Dorian Gray, reflecting the pointless and destructive anger and pride of the men in her life, a Japanese feminist St. Sebastian. "Tokyo Fist" may be grossly violent, but unlike so many movies its violence has a point, which reflects the souls involved in the film as much as the bodies. It's certainly a horror film, but one whose resident monster is the human psyche.

SIGHT AND SOUND, 4/97, p. 51, David Tse

Tsuda, an insurance salesman in modern-day Tokyo, chances upon his old school friend Kojima who is now a boxer. Kojima shows up uninvited at Tsuda's apartment twice. The second time he tries to seduce Hizuru, Tsuda's girlfriend. Tsuda confronts Kojima, but Kojima savagely beats him. Hizuru experiments with body-piercing, and goes to see Kojima's matches. Tsuda tries to stop her, but this only drives her away. She moves in with Kojima. Tsuda starts training at Kojima's boxing gym.

Hizuru probes Kojima's psyche and sexuality, and begins to dominate the lives of the two men. Kojima recounts a teenage incident that bonded him with Tsuda: after a female classmate was murdered by hooligans, the two boys vowed to learn boxing and seek revenge. The revenge was never executed—Kojima blamed Tsuda for deserting the plan. The two men's recent reunion has reawakened their destructive instincts.

Kojima has a chance to fight a notoriously murderous opponent. Spurred on by Hizuru, Kojima agrees to the match. Stood up by Hizuru, Tsuda wanders the Tokyo streets. Confronting her, Tsuda and Hizuru have an absurd and barbarous fight. The two men finally spar in the gym. The duel is vicious, and Tsuda is hospitalised. Invigorated by this victory, Kojima wins his dangerous agreed match, but is horrifically wounded. Hizuru seems to arrive at some inner peace, and Tsuda is last seen going to work with a glass eye.

The two cult *Tetsuo* films suggested that their director Shinya Tsukamoto was a *manga* fan who knew how to have wicked fun indulging his subconscious. *Tetsuo: The Iron Man* (1989), which concerned a Japanese *salaryman* whose flesh gradually mutates into metal, was a raw industrial-sexual nightmare *à la Eraserhead* and a surprise art-house hit. Its corporate-sponsored sequel, *Tetsuo II: Body Hammer* (1991), found Tsukamoto in the awkward position of fitting his maverick sensibility to the mould of more conventional sci-fi fantasy. His latest film, *Tokyo Fist,* announces the maturation of Tsukamoto's talent. Made after a four-year hiatus, *Tokyo Fist* is vivid, explosive filmmaking. Its violence is exaggerated and confrontational, one would almost call it cartoonish if it were not so charged with a real sense of danger. The subtexts, hidden behind symbolism and special effects in Tsukamoto's previous films, are here brought forward. The 'monsters' of *Tokyo Fist* are not mutated into being—instead they remain within the three main characters themselves.

The plot bears similarities with Curtis Hanson's *Bad Influence* (1990), in which a virile schemer (Rob Lowe) ingratiates himself into the life of an introvert (James Spader), but significantly *Tokyo Fist*'s situation is developed with a surreal dream logic. Provoked by his old school friend

Kojima, now a psychotic boxer, Tsuda, a mild insurance salesman, works out to try to match his enemy. His girlfriend, teased by Kojima, changes from demure to resisting to finally dominating the boxer, developing a liking for unanaesthetised body-piercing. She leaves Tsuda to move in with Kojima, yet attacks his masculinity. The three are trapped in a love-hate triangle, hammering each other first verbally, then literally with their fists.

Despite the wildness, it would be reductive to say the film is just about blood and hyperactivity. It is infused with black humour, and has a fragmented and suggestive approach to narrative. The visuals are cool and sharp as car commercials. In key sequences, the camerawork springs into Tsukamoto's patented reeling, convulsive style. And thanks to the use of Tokyo's ultra-modern environment, the film's surrealism appears high-tech and clinical, allowing the film to develop a tension between the coldness of its setting and the animal heat of its characters.

This is important, because the film offers Tsukamoto another chance to explore his obsession with the organic-inorganic dichotomy. Metal fetishism and car accidents in the first *Tetsuo* film were precursors of the obsessions and events of David Cronenberg's *Crash*. (In *Tetsuo*, metal mutations occur after the *salaryman* performs furtive sex with his girl while a hit-and-run victim looks on.) Tsukamoto shares with Cronenberg an interest in body-horror, mutations and a vision of a technologically saturated society on the verge of inundation. In *Tokyo Fist*, the action is punctuated with images of gleaming skyscrapers and Lynchian close-ups of pulpy meat; the angry, punching fists seem to be battering something more than just flesh.

The film's anti-establishment undertow is matched with an equally strong homoerotic current. Its excessive violence and rapid-fire editing may have special relevance to a society whose *salaryman* corporate culture is famously rigid and conformist, and whose younger generation is fixated on bombastic beat-'em-up video games. One wonders how close the material cuts to Tsukamoto's bones: the weakling role is played by Tsukamoto himself, and the boxer is played by his brother. The sibling rivalry is possibly quite real, and there is a note of self-examination in Tsukamoto's passive yet impassioned performance.

The film's depiction of the vulnerability of both the body and the psychological make-up of its characters is perhaps its strongest suit. Here, not only are characters' bodies mutilated and invaded by external objects, but personalities also become unstable and open to contagion. Nietzsche's words from *Beyond Good and Evil*: "Battle not with monsters, lest ye become a monster, and if you gaze into the abyss, the abyss gazes also into you," might be film's ideal footnote.

VILLAGE VOICE, 5/26/98 p. 136, Gary Dauphin

Hysterics are said to be unable to see their bodies in mirrors, superimposing imaginary secondary bodies that suffer from phantom injuries (hypochondria) or bloat into ghostly obesity (anorexia). By those markers and others, Shinya Tsukamoto's *Tokyo Fist* is a truly hysterical movie, a celluloid catalogue of deeply psychological transformations of—and affronts to—the flesh, all of them imposed not in the mind's eye but onto the screen via the magic of live-action animation.

Unlike the director's previous *Tetsuo* flicks, *Tokyo Fist* hews close to legible plot-lines and characters, the frenetic camera-work and DIY special effects orbiting around Tsuda (Tsukamoto), a Tokyo insurance salesman, and Hizuru (Kahori Fujii), his coolly indifferent flancée. The pair's orderly lives go haywire when Tsuda reconnects with Takuji (Koji Tsukamoto, the director's real-life brother), a high school classmate who's become a low-level club fighter. Takuji has a rep for cowardice and clumsiness in the ring but he quickly breaks the couple up, in the process setting them on gory but somehow liberating programs of self-mutilation/improvement; Hizuru undertakes an extreme course of body piercing and tattooing. Tsuda retreats to Takuji's gym, the soft salaryman figuring a boxer's hardened body will allow him to retake his woman and best Takuji.

As a director, Tsukamoto's basic innovation and kink (take your pick) has been in recasting the tortured and abused flesh that dominates certain sub-genres of Japanese anime as live-action mayhem. Although *Fist's* outlandishly brutal boxing sequences have had people talking *Raging Bull*, the better reference is probably John Carpenter's *The Thing*, Tsukamoto treating his solid actors as if they were as endlessly malleable as latex putty, skewering them with metal, putting their limbs through changes most commonly associated with meat grinding, and, of course, showering them with all manner of bodily fluids. It's hard to say exactly what it's all supposed to mean, but like any cartoon, the net effect can be horrifying, not to mention hysterically and inexplicably funny.

Also reviewed in:
NEW YORK TIMES, 5/22/98, p. E14, Lawrence Van Gelder
VARIETY, 8/21-27/95, p. 69, David Rooney

TOUCH OF EVIL

An October Films re-release of a 1958 Universal International Film production. *Producer:* Albert Zugsmith. *Director's Cut Producer:* Rick Schmidlin. *Director:* Orson Welles. *Screenplay:* Orson Welles. *Based on the novel "Badge of Evil" by:* Whit Masterson. *Director of Photography:* Russell Metty. *Picture Restoration:* Bob O'Neil. *Editor:* Virgil W. Vogel, Aaron Stell, and Edward Curtiss and (re-edit) Walter Murch. *Music:* Henry Mancini. *Sound:* Leslie I. Carey and Frank Wilkinson. *Sound Editor:* Richard LeGrand, Jr. *Art Director:* Alexander Golitzen and Robert Clatworthy. *Set Decorator:* Russel A. Gausman and John P. Austin. *Costumes:* Bill Thomas. *Make-up:* Bud Westmore. *Running time:* 111 minutes. *MPAA Rating:* Not Rated.

CAST: Charlton Heston (Ramon Miguel "Mike" Vargas); Janet Leigh (Susan Vargas); Orson Welles (Hank Quinlan); Joseph Calleia (Pete Menzies); Akim Tamiroff ("Uncle Joe" Grandi); Joanna Moore (Marcia Linnekar); Marlene Dietrich (Tanya); Ray Collins (Adair); Dennis Weaver (Motel Manager); Victor Milian (Manolo Sanchez); Lalo Rios (Risto); Valentin De Vargas (Pancho);   Mort Mills (Schwartz); Mercedes McCambridge (Leader of the Gang); Wayne Taylor, Ken Miller, and Raymond Rodriguez (Gang Members); Michael Sargent (The Boy); Zsa Zsa Gabor (Nightclub Owner); Joseph Cotten (Police Surgeon); Phil Harvey (Blaine); Joi Lansing (Blond); Harry Shannon (Gould); Rusty Wescoatt (Casey); Arlene McQuade (Ginnie); Domenick Delgarde (Lackey); Joe Basulto (Hoodlum); Jennie Dias (Jackie); Yolanda Bojorquez (Bobbie); Eleanor Dorado (Lia); John Dierkes (Police); Keenan Wynn (Bit Part).

CHRISTIAN SCIENCE MONITOR, 8/28/98, p. B3, David Sterritt

More than a dozen years after his death, Orson Welles is on a roll. The first film he ever directed, "Citizen Kane," took the No. 1 spot in the American Film Institute's recent list of the greatest American movies. Its an ironic tribute to Welles's greatness, since this brilliant bio-pic proved too adventurous for audiences in 1941, becoming the first box-office failure of his troubled career.

Now a picture that some connoisseurs savor even more, the 1958 melodrama "Touch of Evil," is heading for theater screens in a "director's cut"prepared from Welles's own instructions and never seen by moviegoers before.

Although most critics rank Welles with the greatest of all filmmakers, his Hollywood reputation took an early dive when "Citizen Kane" lost money, and plummeted further when "The Magnificent Ambersons" flopped a year later. Most of his movies were either tampered with by dollar-conscious studio executives or made outside the Hollywood industry on painfully low budgets.

Welles was deep in this predicament when actor Charlton Heston accepted a leading role in "Touch of Evil" and then insisted that Welles, already slated to play the movie's villain, be hired to direct it. Heston was too powerful a star for Universal Pictures to ignore, so Welles promptly received another of his rare Hollywood filmmaking jobs. He set to work immediately, rewriting the screenplay and mapping out the off-beat camera work that was his visual trademark.

At once elegant and electrifying, the movie's style mirrored its high-intensity plot about a Mexican cop (Heston) dueling with a corrupt American detective (Welles) when he's supposed to be honeymooning with the beautiful bride (Janet Leigh).

Audiences might have found it an exciting addition to the popular "film noir" genre. But it was too unconventional for Universal, which took advantage of Welles's absence. (He was already shooting "Don Quixote" to alter the movie's editing and add material filmed by another director.) Among other changes, they made the movie "tighter" by superimposing the opening credits over the story's first shot, a moving-camera masterpiece that's now considered one of the most legendary achievements in motion-picture history.

Welles had no control over the "final cut," but after watching Universal's version he wrote a 58-page memo suggesting changes that would move the film closer to his intentions and make it a more enjoyable entertainment for everyday audiences, according to researchers who have studied the document in detail. Universal ignored most of the memo and released the movie with little publicity. It failed to catch fire at the box office, and Welles never directed another Hollywood production.

For its current reissue, a team of experts has reedited "Touch of Evil" with the help of Welles's memo, notes, reports, and original film footage, in the hopes of getting Welles's intentions onto the screen four decades later. There's no way to be certain Welles would have found this edition perfect, since he might have modified (or even recanted) his own suggestions.

But there's no questioning the restored edition's brilliance, as sophisticated cinematic art and rollicking Saturday-night fun. The plot flows more smoothly and makes more psychological sense.

Performances by Marlene Dietrich and Dennis Weaver stand out vividly. And the opening shot dances across the screen in all its glory, with no credits to dilute its superbly choreographed power.

NEW STATESMAN, 6/7/99, p. 40, Jonathan Romney

The sense that no Welles film is ever a closed case is reinforced by the new re-edit of his 1958 thriller "Touch of Evil." The film was yanked out of Welles's hands by Universal and recut to make the story easier to follow. He retorted with a 58-page memo that has now been followed meticulously by Rick Schmidlin and the eminent sound designer Walter Murch to approximate Welles's original vision—a more complex, edgy set of cross-cuts and sound cues than we've hitherto seen. The new version will be controversial—the opening tracking shot gains Welles's cacophonous forest of radio sounds, but then it loses Henry Mancini's hothouse Latino theme. The new "Touch of Evil" is a scholarly provocation; in no way tailored to 1990s tastes, it is still, literally and figuratively, the mono mix we're used to.

We still regard Welles's career with churlish dissatisfaction—we agree he made masterpieces, but somehow not enough masterpieces. But what does it mean that he failed, or refused, constantly to make bigger and better? He simply went on making different. It's significant, also, that among his unrealised projects was a "Moby Dick"—not a raging-winds epic such as John Huston's 1956 film, in which Welles appeared, but a straight-to-camera recitation. For if Welles recalls any writer's vision, it is Herman Melville's. He was his own Ahab and whale; in F for Fake, he made his own version of "The Confidence Man;" and finally, he was like Melville's recalcitrant clerk Bartleby, for he preferred not to.

NEW YORK, 9/21/98, p. 65, David Denby

Orson Welles's great 1958 thriller *Touch of Evil* is playing at Film Forum in a re-edited version, supervised by Walter Murch, that comes closer to fulfilling Welles's original intentions than any previous incarnation of the film. *Touch of Evil,* which stars Welles, Charlton Heston, Janet Leigh, and Joseph Calleia, is one of the most intellectually and emotionally demanding movies ever made in Hollywood, and the general effect of Murch's work is to make the story, the overlapped music, and the complex dialogue track a lot clearer and therefore more expressive and intense. Welles overloads the medium: He shoots large round faces, three or more in a frame, from underneath the chins; he sends degraded, comical figures scurrying across the shadowed De Chirico landscapes of an arcaded Mexican border town; he builds conversations that contain allusions within allusions, each character sniffing like a hound at the scent of meaning. *Touch of*

Evil is tough to sit through; it's a jammed, discordant, discomforting experience—a nightmare, in fact, but a nightmare that leaves in the wake of its many complications a moral significance of disturbing perversity and brilliance. Take a deep breath and enjoy it.

NEW YORK POST, 9/11/98, p. 68, Larry Worth

It's got a scarier motel room scene than "Psycho", contains as many classic lines as "Casablanca", showcases the most mesmerizing photography since Citizen Kane and features a legendary cast to rival "The Misfits".

But writer-director-star Orson Welles' "Touch of Evil" has never been acknowledged as a bona fide masterpiece. One reason: It's been released in three different versions over the last 40 years. Now, in what amounts to a modern-day Hollywood miracle, a cut based on Welles' 58-page memo of editing instructions is finally available.

The result is cause for celebration, with audiences able to drink in the master's design for complicated cross-cuts, a soundtrack of ambient sounds and the jaw-dropping opening scene without obscuring credits. Collectively, the changes make for a tighter, more coherent telling of what may be the ultimate film noir.

Basically, it's the tale of two men—and the strong, courageous women who love them—squaring off in a forgotten little town on the Mexican border. But it's really a tale of corruption, perverted justice, unholy alliances and racial prejudice that fascinates, frightens, moves and mesmerizes.

Starting with the latter, Welles' camerawork is a phenomenon, obviously the work of someone who's in love with the medium of film. Every shadow, mirror reflection, obscure angle and tracking shot contribute to the overall package while never distracting from the hothouse plot.

But Welles' appearance in front of the camera is equally impressive. In what may be his best performance ever, he's Hank Quinlan, the corpulent, cigar-chomping, slit-eyed epitome of corruption. Padded to the hilt and generally shot from below, he oozes decay as a good cop gone bad, the kind who's not above framing an individual to close a case.

Quinlan's up against a morally upright Mexican lawman, played convincingly—and sans accent—by Charlton Heston. Janet Leigh is on hand, too, memorably no-nonsense as Heston's newlywed American bride. And then there's Marlene Dietrich's priceless bit as a bewigged madam from Welles' past. She's also the woman who voices the time-honored line to Welles: "Lay off those candy bars. You a mess, honey."

Though never as well-known, Joseph Calleia also merits mention. He's absolutely heartbreaking as Quinlan's weathered deputy—and the man who recalls Quinlan as a law-abiding mentor. He singlehandedly puts the whole character in perspective.

Adding to the labyrinthe of deception: Akim Tamiroff's oily crimelord, Dennis Weaver's eye-popping motel clerk and unforgettable cameos from Mercedes McCambridge, Joseph Cotten, Keenan Wynn and Zsa Zsa Gabor. It's a virtual dream cast, with each member in amazing form.

Accordingly, "Touch of Evil" isn't just the latest recycling of a blast from the cinematic past. It's the chance to revel in what—at least so far—is the year's premiere movie-going event.

NEWSWEEK, 9/14/98, p. 76, Jack Kroll

When Universal Studio hired Orson Welles to act in *Touch of Evil* in 1957, it thought it was getting the down-on-his-luck director to play a fat crooked cop in a B-movie thriller. But Charlton Heston said he'd appear in the film only if Welles directed, so what Universal got was a film noir classic (rewritten by Welles, too). This of course confused the hell out of the studio, so it started reshooting and re-editing, and released the film as the second half of a double feature. Nevertheless, it won the grand prize at the 1958 World's Fair in Brussels and has gained a standing just below Welles's masterworks "Citizen Kane" and "The Magnificent Ambersons." Now Universal is releasing a new version of the film, working from a 58-page memo that Welles fired off after seeing the studio's cut.

This new version, produced by Rick Schmidlin with Oscar-winning editor Walter Murch, restores much of the Wellesian essence that had been smoothed over 40 years ago. Welles's baroque crosscutting has been restored, and relationships have been clarified, such as that between Mike Vargas (Heston), the Mexican lawman, and his American wife, Susan (Janet Leigh), who find themselves in a seedy, sinister border town involved with murder and drugs. Erased is the studio vandalism, which placed credits over the amazing opening sequence, the most famous tracking shot in film history. Young moviegoers who think the MTV-style directors are virtuosos will see a real genius at work, inspiring actors like Akim Tamiroff as a scary-funny crime boss and Marlene Dietrich as a thinking John's madam. Welles's Hank Quinlan is possibly his greatest performance, a wheezing dissonance of honesty and duplicity that may be a terrifying self-portrait.

Also reviewed in:
CHICAGO TRIBUNE, 10/16/98, Friday/p. Q, Michael Wilmington
NATION, 9/21/98, p. 40, Stuart Klawans
NEW REPUBLIC, 9/28/98, p. 30, Stanley Kauffmann
NEW YORK TIMES, 5/22/58, p. 25, Howard Thompson
NEW YORKER, 9/21/98, p. 146, Anthony Lane
VARIETY, 9/7-13/98, p. 73, Todd McCarthy

TRANCEFORMER: A PORTRAIT OF LARS VON TRIER

A Cowboy Booking International release of an AB Memfis Film production in collaboration with Sveriges Television Dokumentar, Swedish Film Institute/Bengt Forslund, Film i Vast/Danish Film Institute/Jorgen Ljungdalh/Danmarks Radio/TV-Fakta. *Director (Swedish with English subtitles):* Stig Bjorkman. *Director of Photography:* Jan Roed, Anthony Dod Mantle, and Bjorn Blixt. *Editor:* Leon Flamholc. *Sound:* Ragnar Samuelsson, Steen K. Anderson, and Thomas Langballe. *Running time:* 52 minutes. *MPAA Rating:* Not Rated.

WITH: Stig Bjorkman and Fredrik von Krusenstjerna (Interviewers).

NEWSDAY, 8/5/98, Part II/p. B11, John Anderson

Two of the more influential, enigmatic and certainly provocative filmmakers of recent years have been a dour Pole and an anxious Dane, both of whom have created films as slippery as their own public personae.

Did they ever meet? It's doubtful, but they do run into each other this week at Manhattan's Film Forum, where "Krzysztof Kieslowski: I'm So-So" and "Tranceformer: A Portrait of Lars von Trier" open a door to the otherwise inaccessible: Kieslowski, who died in March, 1996, was known as a formidable, reluctant and intimidating interview (he was, be was); von Trier, whose various phobias have generally kept his homebound in Copenhagen, is virtually allergic to the press. So what this double bill offers is a Holy Grail—Judge Crater combo platter that will be manna for fans of the directors and a little exotic for everyone else.

The impetus for "I'm So-So" wasn't Kieslowski's delicate health, but his announcement that—with the completion of the soon-to-be-Oscar-nominated "Red"—he would no longer make films. It seemed a dubious resolution (as evidence, Atom Egoyan is planning to direct a screenplay Kieslowski wrote just before his death), but it was enough to prompt colleagues Krzysztof Wierzbicki, cinematographer Jacek Petrycki and soundman Michal Zarnecki to make a film portrait of their mentor and friend.

"I'm So-So" is on one hand a privileged moment with the great director; on the other, it's too reverent and reticent about what it asks Kieslowski—about his films, his mind, his religious perspective (something essential to understanding him) or his hopes for an art form he was apparently forsaking. Wierzbicki takes one eccentric tack: He presents facts about Kieslowski to a number of professionals and solicits their opinion of the man without telling them who he is. But otherwise, "I'm So-So" is more so-what.

Swedish critic Stig Bjorkman takes the talking-head approach to von Trier, but there are more heads and what they say is a bit more interesting. Von Trier himself speaks extensively about his admitted anxieties, the ultraliberal upbringing on which he blames many of his problems and the roots of his filmmaking; an 8mm film he made as a kid, for instance, includes the use of "incorrect" film stock for intended effect and a primitive tracking shot made from a moving bicycle. Interspersed with shots from von Trier's features—"Elements of Crime," "Epidemic," "Europa" (released here as "Zentropa"), the TV epic "The Kingdom" and "Breaking the Waves"—we hear from his various actors and producers and get a portrait-in-motion of a director who, if the response to his new film "Idiots" at Cannes this spring is any indication, will continue to provoke and disturb for years to come.

Also reviewed in:
NEW YORK TIMES, 8/5/98, p. E5, Stephen Holden
VARIETY, 9/15-21/97, p. 80, David Rooney

TROUBLE ON THE CORNER

A Thalia Theater release. *Producer:* Alan Madison and Diane Kolyer. *Director:* Alan Madison. *Screenplay:* Alan Madison. *Director of Photography:* Phil Abraham. *Editor:* Ray Hubley. *Music:* Robert Een. *Production Designer:* Sherri Adler. *Running time:* 104 minutes. *MPAA Rating:* Not Rated.

CAST: Charles Busch (Ms. Ellen); Giancarlo Esposito (Daryl); Edie Falco (Vivian); Tony Goldwyn (Jeff); Tammy Grimes (Mrs. K.); Bruce MacVittie (Sandy); Mark Margolis (Mr. B); Debi Mazar (Ericca); Joe Morton (Detective Bill); Roger Rees (McMurtry); Anna Thomson (Butcher's Wife); Daniel Von Bargen (Butcher).

NEW YORK POST, 12/18/98, p. 64, V. A. Musetto

Alan Madison, who, when he's not making low-budget movies, is a basketball coach at a New York public school.

The setting is a run-down Harlem tenement, which serves as home and office for Jeff, a low-rent shrink ($35 for 50 minutes!) with an odd assortment of patients and neighbors.

Jeff's troubles begin when a giant piece of ceiling plaster falls into the bathroom while his wife (Edie Falco) is taking her customary after-work bath.

Jeff (Tony Goldwyn) loses no time in using the new hole in his ceiling to spy on the upstairs neighbor, Ericca (Debi Mazar), a hand model who keeps her gloves on while having kinky sex. When Ericca becomes a patient ("I want you to cure my loneliness," she implores the doctor), Jeff's behavior gets even stranger. (Think of the Roman Polanski character in "The Tenant.")

Madison, who also wrote the screenplay, has a sharp sense of the macabre, and the movie's ending is as unexpected as it is strange. But he would have done better concentrating on Jeff, his wife and Ericca. The other characters are supposed to add color to the film, but their eccentricity is forced, straight out of Central Casting.

Still, Madison is a filmmaker with obvious talent. Keep an eye on him.

NEWSDAY, 12/18/98, Part II/p. B6, John Anderson

For those too young to remember the old Abbott & Costello TV show, it was essentially an exercise in dada-ist aburdity: A nebbishy guy living in an apartment building—and a world—in which everyone was clearly crazy but who consistently acted like he was the oddball.

Take the whole setup to a deeper darker level and you'd have "Trouble on the Corner," which would be a comedy if it weren't so twisted. Playfully metaphorical—a psychologist being abused by his patients is some kind of black joke—it's also a Swiftian journey through an urban garden of hybrid disturbances.

Tony Goldwyn is Jeff, a psychologist living in an Upper West Side tenement where the infrastructure is as unstable as the patients. And since they can afford him, they don't respect him. His wife, Vivian—a terrific performance by indie queen Edie Falco, who imposes subtlety on a hysterical premise—is the poster girl for passive aggression. And she keeps Jeff, all of whose clients suffer from sexual aberrations, at an erotic arm's length.

The people around him—from a monosyllabic, dog-walking lawyer (Roger Rees) to a Bible-misquoting neighbor (Tammy Grimes), from a sexually tortured butcher's wife (Anna Thomson) to a fantasy-spouting pedophile (Bruce MacVitte)—keep Jeff surrounded by state-of-the-art weirdness. But it's his own combination of hubris, naivete and self-absorption that eventually begin to take him over. And he reaches a point where the only way out is to assume the worst characteristics of his patients. "Trouble on the Corner" does get mired in its own psychoses at times, but it's a promising film from newcomer Alan Madison and allows its talented cast to stretch.

VILLAGE VOICE,12/29/98, p. 122, Laurie Stone

An A-list of New York actors, including Tony Goldwyn, Charles Busch, Debi Mazar, Roger Rees, Edie Falco, and Tammy Grimes, worked for scale in Alan Madison's first feature, *Trouble on the Corner*, and in return got to camp outrageously. The psycho-comedy is a revenge fantasy for therapy patients who believe their shrinks are nuttier than they are. At the center is psychologist Jeff (Goldwyn), a milquetoast with a scary-mommy wife (Falco). We know we're in fairy-tale land because though Jeff has a practice, he lives in a decrepit tenement in the meat-packing district. Around him flap neighborhood eccentrics—the cross-dressing tarot reader (Busch), the pack-rat widow (Grimes)—who act proud to be clichés. By day Jeff hears tales of sexual obsession, at night he's lucky to get a handjob from his wife. When a chunk of ceiling comes down in the bathroom, enabling him to spy on his glamorous neighbor (Mazar), his life begins to crack open, too. Once his vicious, libidinal side takes the reins, the movie careens enjoyably, as Jeff ups his fees and goads patients to murder their spouses. The film is pure silliness, and Rees is especially enjoyable as a Mamet-talking lawyer who makes nary a move without his three bull mastiffs.

Also reviewed in:
NEW YORK TIMES. 12/18/98, p. 32, Lawrence Van Gelder
VARIETY, 10/27-11/2/97, p. 45, Ken Eisner

TRUCE, THE

A Miramax Films release in association with Capitol Films and Channel Four Films of a 3 Emme production/Stephan Films/UGC Images/DaZu Films/T&C Films AG production in association with RAI Radiotelevisione Italiana/Capitol Films of an Independent Film Producers Consortium/Istituto Luce. *Executive Producer:* Guido De Laurentiis. *Producer:* Leo Pescarolo and Guido De Laurentiis. *Director:* Francesco Rosi. *Screenplay:* Francesco Rosi, Stefano Rulli, and Sandro Petraglia. *Based on the book "The Truce" by:* Primo Levi. *Director of Photography:* Pasqualino De Santis and Marco Pontecorvo. *Editor:* Ruggero Mastroianni and Bruno Sarandrea. *Music:* Luis Bacalov. *Sound:* Alain Curvelier. *Production Designer:* Andrea Crisanti. *Art Director:* Andrea Crisanti. *Costumes:* Alberto Verso. *Make-up:* Francesco Freda. *Running time:* 116 minutes. *MPAA Rating:* R.

CAST: John Turturro (Primo); Massimo Ghini (Cesare); Rade Serbedzija (The Greek); Stefano Dionisi (Daniele); Teco Celio (Col. Rovi); Roberto Citran (Unverdorben); Claudio Bisio (Ferrari); Andy Luotto (D'Agata); Agnieszka Wagner (Galina); Lorenza Indovina (Flora); Marina Gerasymenko (Maria Fiodorovna); Igor Bezgin (Egorov); Alexander Iljin (The Mongol); Viachesslav Olhovsky (Lt. Sergei); Anatoliy Vassiliev (Dr. Gotlieb); Tatiana Meshcherkina (Irina); Franco Trevisi (Marshall); Federico Pacifici (Lieutenant); Ernesto Lama (Carmine); Gerda Maria Jurgens (Brigitte); Kasper Weiss (Kapo); Vitalij Rozstalnyj (Gen. Timoshenko); Joachim Wörmsdorf (German General).

LOS ANGELES TIMES, 4/24/98, Calendar/p. 4, John Anderson

[*The following review by John Anderson appeared in a slightly different form in*
NEWSDAY, 4/24/98, Part II/p. B6.]

Suddenly the war is really over. And as the news percolates through the mess hall at the Red Army's camp for displaced persons, a Russian soldier prances onstage with a saber, Auschwitz survivors dance "Cheek to Cheek," and romance—even among people with death lingering in their nostrils—somehow seems a possibility.

It's a scene that's directly about hope and humanity, indirectly about the absurd cruelty of an insane regime, subversively about the takeover of the world by Hollywood, and, as filmed by Italian director Francesco Rosi in his polyglot epic "The Truce," it seems in sympathy with the nature of author Primo Levi himself.

Although the celebrated writer put a weird punctuation on his life's work by throwing himself down a flight of stairs in 1987, he should nevertheless be remembered as an author of humor as well as pain. And a writer who knew that pain could never be quite so acute as when one was laughing through it.

This is a lesson "The Truce" sometimes forgets. Based upon the Levi novel—written nearly two decades after his liberation from Auschwitz and telling of his post-war journey home to Italy—it is a film that's at its best when the characters in it are going about the business of living. And not when it tries to possess the gravity of the Holocaust itself.

An example of this is the opening scene, in which several Russian soldiers approach the gates of Auschwitz and see... well, what they see. But what a mere movie will reproduce can hardly equal the horror of 1945; all the viewer can think is how well-fed the prisoners look, which doesn't seem quite the point.

On the other hand, Rosi—whose films include the neo-realist masterpiece "Salvatore Giuliano"—handles the dark comedy well. When Levi takes up with, or is taken up by, a rakish character called the Greek (Rade Serbedzija), his life and the film get an injection of adrenaline. The Greek treats Levi like a servant, but re-educates him to life in the world and exposes the naturally timid chemist to the joys of braggadocio.

It's Levi's awakening that's at the core of the film, and it takes place throughout, as he and his motley, multiethnic companions make their grueling way through Europe, viewing sabotaged rail line after dynamited road. In John Turturro—as the former chemist, former partisan and writer-to-be Levi—the film has an invaluable asset. His Levi is earnest and haunted, fragile and intelligent. And as the movie proceeds along Levi's road home we get to watch Turturro inhabit a figure who gradually considers himself lucky his soul is still intact. And what we know that he doesn't—about the end of his life—makes the whole thing profoundly sad.

On the other hand, the movie should have gone one way or the other with its myriad languages—subtitle the whole thing, get Turturro to speak Italian, something to clear up the stiltedness that infects much of the picture. As it is, "The Truce" comes only so close to being a testament to a great writer and a great story.

NEW YORK, 5/4/98, p. 125, David Denby

There is a sublime moment in *The Truce*, Francesco Rosi's awkward but moving epic about the chaotic aftermath of World War II. At the beginning of the movie, Primo Levi (John Turturro), a young Italian chemist, has been left behind in Auschwitz by the Germans. Through sheer luck, Levi has survived. He is later to become a superb writer—the outstanding memoirist of the Holocaust—but in the winter and spring of 1945, he cannot make his way home from Poland. He travels with Italian and Greek fellow survivors—a ragtag group of the larcenous and the merely fortunate—through a European civilization that has simply disappeared. In Poland and Russia, dazed German prisoners wander about or try to work in a desultory way; the black market rules everything; the victorious Red Army provides gentle but chaotic administration. Instead of sending the group south, the Russians put the former camp inmates on trains heading north toward Minsk. After a bit, the rail lines, torn up by the war, give out, and Levi and his friends wander across the countryside and settle beside a beautiful lake. For a while they are content just to sit. Then comes the happy moment: One of their group puts together a ramshackle orchestra, and as he begins to conduct Vivaldi, a gaggle of geese, as if on cue, indignantly walk away from the strange new sound. *The Truce*, which is based on Levi's second book, is about the reawakening of the senses, the resurrection of humanity in men and women consigned to death. The survivors reacquaint themselves with food and sleep (but never a sleep without nightmare—Levi committed suicide 42 years later, in 1987); then they take up sensual pleasures of every kind. When the geese magically bestir themselves in response to music, both art and nature spring to life at once.

Francesco Rosi, now 76, is the last remaining genius of the Italian neorealist movement. Though Rosi has often worked on a large canvas (earlier in his career, he made celebrated movies about the Mafia and political corruption), he is perhaps best known here for the intimate social drama *Three Brothers* and the superb movie version of Bizet's *Carmen*. In *The Truce*, Rosi is working under tremendous constraints. He has to create a peculiar moment of disorder, a moment when civilization exists only through its half-remembered echoes, its scattered fragments. *The Truce* is set in transit camps and in makeshift medical centers, in trains and on the road, and the spectacle is modest rather than moving. Rosi captures the oddity of people rushing to and fro without any clear sense of what to do with themselves. Shyly, tentatively, the shattered camp survivors and the exhausted Russians reach for sex and pleasure. The movie is a series of strange, anomalous moments; it's an epic of gestures and uncompleted acts.

There are other difficulties. How do you shoot a post-Holocaust film? At the beginning, at Auschwitz, four horsemen approach the camp out of the mist and white snow. It is the quartet of young Soviet soldiers who led the Red Army into the undefended camp in January 1945. The white-on-white image is almost abstract, like something out of *Fargo*—the soldiers don't appear to be on a road but seem merely suspended in white. In such shots, the great cinematographer Pasqualino De Santis comes close to aestheticizing the concentration camp. It is a sin, but a forgivable sin, I suppose—the camp scenes themselves are shot in tones of the richest gray, as if De Santis, even in this place, could not resist beauty. Later on, however, the lusciousness doesn't require apology—beauty is one of the things that coaxes the ex-inmates back to life. At the transit camp, a Russian soldier, sword slicing the air, entertains the survivors with a very balletic tap to Irving Berlin's "Cheek to Cheek." When they are wandering about, Levi and his friends encounter some little Fragonard babies playing naked in the sunshine.

It's a film of great images, not a dramatic work. Levi's *The Truce* (known in its American edition as *The Reawakening)* is an account of adventure and vagabondage, and by its very nature the material is anecdotal. Men and women encountered on the road or in a transit camp loom up before the author, powerful in their deviousness and charm, and then abruptly disappear in pursuit of their own destiny. The movie repeats this fragmentary construction. There is only Levi himself to hold it together, and Levi is a quiet and guarded young man—an observer, a writer in the making.

Turturro has a long, lean face, liquid eyes, and a mouth drawn small and tight in fear. He watches and holds himself in. In the early scenes of the movie, he is so clenched, so alarmed by his survival, he appears ready to ward off a blow from a camp guard. He is a child with his face at the candy-shop window, staring and staring, longing to break through to people. Levi is not a physically courageous man, but the pride is there, even a haughty sense of his own worth, and when pushed, he will assert himself and speak with great firmness of principle—it is the future interpreter of the Holocaust's depredations who speaks. Turturro gives a sincere, entirely committed performance as Levi. It is, unfortunately, a rather limited piece of acting. We know why he's doing what he's doing, but we may think he still needs to find some way of giving the character more life and variety. As a writer, Primo Levi has his own kind of gentle vivacity; Turturro hasn't found a way of getting that side of Levi into the performance. One feels he is attempting to hold our attention by sheer force of will, by an exercise of high-mindedness rather than imagination.

Levi is attracted to people bolder than himself—such as the self-sufficient tough guy known as "The Greek," a tremendous scoundrel and operator played by the great Yugoslavian actor Rade Serbedzija (from *Before the Rain* and *The Saint*). Serbedzija, a big, humorous man with a beautiful beard and flashing eyes, speaks in three or four languages at once, and he's dazzling in any language. He looks at Turturro's Levi with contempt. The Greek, we are to understand, has a low-minded and mercenary talent: He has a genius for survival. For a while, as if chosen by God, he takes care of the hapless Levi, who will, in the end, turn out to be survival's true genius.

The Truce is not as exciting as other epics, but it preserves the memory of a man who discovered himself at the moment of Europe's dissolution and in his quiet way triumphed over the worst the century had to offer.

NEW YORK POST, 4/24/98, p. 49, Thelma Adams

"Never forget" is a common theme to Holocaust movies from "Partisans of Vilna" to "Schindler's List." It's the coda that concludes Francesco Rosi's "The Truce."

But the dominant spirit of Rosi's picaresque is not tragedy but redemption.

Based on Primo Levi's autobiographical memoir, it follows Jewish writer and chemist Levi (John Turturro) on the journey home from Auschwitz to Italy, after the liberation of the camps.

Levi—nearly shoeless, emaciated, spiritually deadened, hungry, still wearing his concentration-camp stripes as a badge of courage—crossed Europe with a rag-tag group of thieves, musicians, pimps, Italians and a Greek (the forceful Rade Serbedzija).

"The truce" is an inspiring odyssey from an evil Oz back to the gradual awakening toward God of an assimilated middle-class Italian Jew caught in the backdraft of history.

Rosi, who co-wrote the script with Stefano Rulli and Sandro Petraglia, shuns the cliches of Holocaust movies. He also avoids the danger of literary adaptations: an over-dependence on voiceover narration.

Turturro gives the performance of his life, using his comic gifts sparingly for maximum impact. His Levi is lantern-jawed, nearly silent, sucked dry by camp life; he's practically and sexually inexperienced.

This Holocaust survivor is an unlikely hero, and a bigger man for his failings. Levi's no saintly, asexual Jew in the Ben Kingsley/"Schindler" vein.

Rosi ("Christ Stopped at Eboli") creates a passionate, involving, intimate, if occasionally choppy, drama that challenges its audience without cheap sentimentality.

At one point, Levi says: "God cannot exist if Auschwitz exists." But "The Truce" supports a contrary notion: If a man like Primo Levi exists, surely there must be a God.

VILLAGE VOICE, 4/28/98, p. 80, Leslie Camhi

For a host of reasons, the experience of Auschwitz remains unfilmable. Actors cannot be tortured and starved to resemble the inmates of a death camp. And what fiction could possibly compare with the documentary images that are burned into our memories, of living ghosts in shreds of striped clothing, standing behind barbed wire?

Still, filmmakers keep trying. Italian director Francesco Rosi has adapted *The Truce* from Primo Levi's memoir of his liberation from Auschwitz, with decidedly mixed results. Levi's book (known in English by the more optimistic title *The Reawakening)* recounts the author's nine-month odyssey through transit camps in Poland and Russia, back across central Europe, and finally home to Italy. Set in a chaos of uncertain borders, swarming with wounded, displaced persons, it describes a provisional truce, a pause between the *inferno* of Auschwitz and the struggle with memory in which Levi would finally lose his life.

Rosi's film begins as fleeing Germans abandon Auschwitz, killing or evacuating most prisoners, leaving the sickest (Levi among them) to die. Days later, four horsemen of the Apocalypse appear on the horizon: Russian soldiers, silent with shame at such crimes. This memorable image is immediately undercut by the mobs of strangely robust prisoners who surge forth to cheer their liberators.

Bespectacled and hesitant, Primo (John Turturro) stands apart from them. There's much to admire in Turturro's performance; in his encounters with Russian commandants, Polish peasants, and his own thieving or grieving friends, he melds compassion, irony, strength, and fragility.

But at times this Levi also sinks into an almost Christlike saintliness. (The director even provides him with a Mary Magdalene to defend.) The writer, who strove for accuracy, gentleness, and justice, didn't spare himself; he lied, he tells us, and was greedy. The only sin this Levi commits is that of sanctimoniousness. Perhaps it's a problem in translating a memoirist's interior voice into onscreen dialogue. Levi the writer is never a preacher, always a more humble, and more precious, witness; he would never lecture his companions on the meaning of the Hell they'd all just been through.

Also reviewed in:
NEW REPUBLIC, 5/11/98, p. 28, Stanley Kauffmann
NEW YORK TIMES, 4/24/98, p. E16, Stephen Holden
VARIETY, 2/24-3/2/97, p. 78, David Rooney

TRUMAN SHOW, THE

A Paramount Pictures release of a Scott Rudin production. *Executive Producer:* Lynn Pleshette. *Producer:* Scott Rudin, Andrew Niccol, Edward S. Feldman, and Adam Schroeder. *Director:* Peter Weir. *Screenplay:* Andrew Niccol. *Director of Photography:* Peter Biziou. *Editor:* William Anderson and Lee Smith. *Music:* Burkhard Dallwitz. *Music Editor:* Bunny Andrews. *Sound:* Art Rochester. *Casting:* Howard Feuer. *Production Designer:* Dennis Gassner. *Art Director:* Richard L. Johnson. *Set Designer:* Thomas Minton and Odin R. Oldenburg. *Set Decorator:* Nancy Haigh. *Special Effects:* Larz Anderson. *Costumes:* Marilyn Matthews. Makeup: Ron Berkeley and Brad Wilder. *Stunt Coordinator:* Pat Banta. *Running time:* 104 minutes. *MPAA Rating:* PG.

CAST: Jim Carrey (Truman Burbank); Laura Linney (Meryl); Noah Emmerich (Marlon); Natascha McElhone (Lauren/Sylvian); Holland Taylor (Truman's Mother); Brian Delate (Truman's Father); Blair Slater (Young Truman); Peter Krause (Lawrence); Heidi Schanz (Vivien); Ron Taylor (Ron); Don Taylor (Don); Ted Raymond (Spencer); Judy Clayton (Travel Agent); Fritz Dominique, Angel Schmiedt, and Nastassja Schmiedt (Truman's Neighbors); Muriel Moore (Teacher); Mal Jones (News Vendor); Judson Vaughn (Insurance Co-worker); Earl Hilliard, Jr. (Ferry Worker); David Andrew Nash (Bus Driver/Ferry Captain); Jim Towers (Bus Supervisor); Savannah Swafford (Little Girl in Bus); Antoni Corone and Mario Ernesto Sanchez (Security Guards); John Roselius (Man at Beach); Kade Coates (Truman, 4 Years Old); Marcia DeBonis (Nurse); Sam Kitchin (Surgeon); Sebastian Youngblood (Orderly); Dave Corey (Hospital Security Guard); Mark Alan Gillott (Policeman at Power Plant); Jay Salter and Tony Todd (Policemen at Truman's House); Marco Rubeo (Man in Christmas Box); Daryl Davis and Robert Davis (Couple at Picnic Table); R. J. Murdock (Production Assistant); Matthew McDonough and Larry McDowell (Men at Newstand); Joseph Lucas (Ticket Taker); Logan Kirksey (TV Host); Ed Harris (Christof); Paul Giamatti and Adam Tomei (Control Room Directors); Harry Shearer (Mike Michaelson); Una Damon (Chloe); Philip Baker Hall and John Pleshette (Network Executives); Philip Glass and John Pramik (Keyboard Artists); O-Lan Jones and Krista Lynn Landolfi (Bar Waitresses); Joe Minjares (Bartender); Al Foster, Zoaunne Leroy and Millie Slavin (Bar Patrons); Terry Camilleri (Man in Bathtub); Dona Hardy and Jeanette Miller (Senior Citizens); Joel McKinnon Miller and Tom Simmons (Garage Attendants); Susan Angelo (Mother); Carly Smiga (Daughter); Yuji Okumoto, Kiyoko Yamaguchi and Saemi Nakamura (Japanese Family).

CHRISTIAN SCIENCE MONITOR, 6/5/98, p. B3, David Sterritt

It's only June, but the movie of the year may already have arrived. Jim Carrey's new comedy, "The Truman Show," is the smartest, funniest, most original Hollywood movie in ages.

It's also one of the most offbeat. While Paramount clearly feels it has a giant hit on its hands, the picture might prove too peculiar and too packed with sardonic satire on modern entertainment for audiences craving light warm-weather fare.

So along with its own fascinating qualities, "The Truman Show" could be a barometer for the adventurousness of today's multiplex crowd. If its returns are disappointing, filmmakers will think extra hard before taking such risks again.

The plot is so unusual that too much shouldn't be revealed, but moviegoers already know the basics from ads and coming-attractions trailers. Carrey plays Truman Burbank, an ordinary guy with a comfy home, a commonplace job, and all the trappings of a typical middle-class life.

Each time he makes the slightest move to do something different, some glitch pops up to scoot him back to his usual routine. This pattern is so predictable that Truman starts to wonder if something could be wrong with his all-too-smooth existence.

Eventually the situation starts to come clear. He's the unwitting star of a real-life TV series, and everyone from his best friend to his doting mom is playing a fictional role in the drama. Truman is the only one not pretending, and the artificiality of his world is so complete that it's uncertain whether learning the truth will be enough to set him free.

"The Truman Show" was directed by Peter Weir in a return to the bold moviemaking style of "The Last Wave," one of his early films. Its most striking inspiration is to cast Carrey as the hero, since Carrey's screen image is already so artificial that it makes the story seem almost as uncanny for us as for Truman himself.

Top marks also go to writer Andrew Niccol ("Gattaca"). Some aspects of his screenplay have been hit on by filmmakers such as, Hollis Frampton and Paul Bartel, but they've never been explored so thoroughly before. Add a fine supporting cast led by Laura Linney and Ed Harris, and you have as exciting an experience as Hollywood is likely to provide for a long time to come.

CINEASTE, Vol. 23, no. 4, 1998, p. 48, Richard Porton

Released with a blizzard of hype, *The Truman Show* is being hailed as the movie of the Zeitgeist, or at least the decade, even though Peter Weir's comeback film often resembles an extremely lavish—and surprisingly tame—*Twilight Zone* episode. This leisurely cinematic parable is nevertheless noteworthy for unwittingly coopting a critique of our media-saturated society that was initially launched by the most radical segments of the left during the late Sixties. The film's conformist indictment of conformity faintly echoes Guy Debord's lament that the twentieth century marked the advent of the 'society of the spectacle.' Yet when Debord proclaimed in 1967 that reality was becoming indistinguishable from the attempts of propagandists and advertisers to represent or simulate it, he and his fellow Situationists suggested, however naively, that a revival of council communism's anti-Bolshevik leftism was the appropriate antidote to consumerist alienation. Weir and screenwriter Andrew Niccol view their hero's artificially induced schizophrenia as merely an opportunity for innocuous whimsy.

Since the narrative premise of *The Truman Show* is ludicrously simple, *longueurs* are unavoidable and the pace soon becomes soporific. Truman Burbank (Jim Carrey), a bland but affable insurance salesman who lives an in an idyllic suburban community named Seahaven, gradually realizes that his seemingly happy life is a meticulously constructed sham. For thirty years, Truman has remained blissfully unaware of the fact that he is the star of a long-running television series that millions of fans find inexplicably compelling. Eventually, technical snafus—an ersatz rain shower that drenches Truman but leaves the surrounding ground dry, and radio messages which track the hapless everyman's whereabouts—provide evidence that Seahaven is the world's largest sound stage. Literally victimized by the society of the spectacle, Truman's wife, best friend, actors who orchestrate product placements that make commercial interruptions unnecessary. Jim Carrey has observed that this dystopian fable is "insane with metaphors," but the film's allegorical ruse, lacking true satirical bite, soon becomes vacuous.

Weir's coy exploration of our infatuation with prefabricated notoriety is actually a parodic black hole, since it has been linked to everything from the television coverage of the O.J. Simpson and Louise Woodward trials to Jim Carrey's own celebrity-driven neurosis. Alternately, *The Truman Show*'s heavy-handed efforts to evoke Big Themes have inspired comparisons with Philip K. Dick, Robert Heinlein, Don Siegel, and George Orwell. In the final analysis, however, the inability of critics to interpret this movie without using a skein of allusions as a crutch unveils the fact that there is no there there.

Weir and Niccol's propensity to shoot fish—or insane metaphors—in a barrel is probably best explained by their decision to use Truman Burbank's fate as an excuse for lampooning the vision of suburban paradise venerated during the Eisenhower years and once exemplified by treacly sitcoms like *Father Knows Best* and *Leave It To Beaver*. As a case in point, Truman's perky wife, Meryl (Laura Linney), is an unsavory mixture of homecoming queen and Stepford Wife—she can both attend to her hubby's needs with steely devotion and announce, with preternatural glee, that she has made macaroni. This gentle assault on the nuclear family would have been daring during the Fifties, but seems insipid in 1998. After all, even Republican satirists like P.J. O'Rourke now feel free to make fun of straitlaced suburbanites, and parodies of commercials have been standard fare on *Saturday Night Live* for years. For this reason, the film's explicit mockery of Capra's *It's a Wonderful Life* and its saccharine message falls flat.

Show Me The Way To Go Home, the *It's A Wonderful Life* pastiche that Truman watches as his placid existence unravels, unintentionally reinforces the virtues of the admittedly maudlin Capra original. An off-screen announcer, introducing the broadcast of *Show Me The Way To Go Home,* describes this "much-loved classic" as a "hymn of praise to small-town life where we learn that you don't have to leave home to discover what the world is all about and that no one is poor who has friends." Capra obviously ends his film with a string of platitudes, but the genuinely dark vision of postwar America that precedes *It's A Wonderful Life*'s sermonizing conclusion carries much more emotional weight than Weir and Niccol's flippant parody.

At times, the dissection of a 'Trumanesque' world view seems to go beyond facile putdowns of suburban America to cast a jaundiced eye at the chemically-induced happiness of a nation that increasingly accepts antidepressants like Prozac as a form of social control. Although *The Truman Show* pokes fun at America's 'have a nice day' cheerfulness (Carrey and Linney's pasted-on smiles are among the creepiest touches in the film), it proves itself a canny piece of entertainment by providing heaping amounts of 'backstory' that are simultaneously facetious and designed to foster the audience's identification with one-dimensional characters.

Truman's lack of curiosity about the outside world, for example, is explained with a flashback illustrating how, as a child, he became traumatized when his father was supposedly killed during a boating accident. Weir and Niccol manage to ingeniously target media cynicism, while cynically cementing our own identification with Truman's plight. The filmmakers' focus on Sylvia (Natascha McElhone), a former "extra" who enjoyed a few romantic moments with Truman during his college years, is even more glib. If spectators can be cajoled into believing that a lovable ninny controlled by a corporation can still pine for his college sweetheart, they must also conclude that love inevitably triumphs over adversity. At this point, Weir and Niccol's susceptibility to cheap sentimentality exceeds anything ever dreamed up by Capra.

While critics of mass culture have often been unfairly accused of scorning the desires of 'common people' (as if anyone would willingly concede to being 'common'), *The Truman Show* is in fact distinguished by a sneering Hollywood elitism—an overweening contempt for the supposedly 'average' consumers of television programs. All of the ordinary American viewers who avidly follow Truman's escapades are depicted as complete boobs, and many of them are shot with distorting lenses that make them appear especially grotesque. The capsule biographies of these viewers included by Niccol in the published version of the shooting script reiterate the film's condescension. If Muriel Obermath, for example, names all three of her sons after Truman and later abandons "her biological children when none prove as entertaining as the television child she had 'adopted,'" we can only assume that the gullible public are helpless dupes of film and television moguls. Of course, the film is not clever enough to explain why, in this era of Jerry Springer and Internet chat rooms, boorish parking attendants or elderly airheads would be content to passively follow a slow-as-molasses real-time saga. Unlike the more astute critics of contemporary pop culture, Weir and Niccol fail to realize how the pseudoparticipation promoted by 'interactivity' has replaced the Orwellian one-way spectacle denounced by Debord in the Sixties.

The flip side of *The Truman Show*'s derision of the hoi polloi is its self-congratulatory treatment of the production team responsible for televising Truman's life. Christof (Ed Harris), the producer of *"The Truman Show,"* whose name suggests an odd fusion of Christ and the performance artist and tireless self-promoter, Christo, is the movie's nominal villain. High above Seahaven in his 121st floor-Lunar control room, this peculiarly benign Big Brother imperiously asks his technicians to "cue the Sun." Maintaining that "we've become tired of watching actors give us phony emotions, bored with pyrotechnics and special effects," the self-assured puppetmaster claims that he is simply holding the mirror up to life.

Christof's blend of altruism and smugness also mirrors the schizoid agenda of Weir and Paramount Pictures. The studio has successfully marketed *The Truman Show* as a feel-good movie, this year's incarnation of *Forrest Gump*. Weir, for his part, maintains that this $60-million 'art film' can be construed as a wry response to everything from the "controlled coverage" that made the "Gulf War ... a sanitized video game" to the Disneyfication of America. Like Christof, Weir wants to go beyond "phony emotions ... pyrotechnics, and special effects." On the other hand, the money men at Paramount are content to dream of Oscar nominations for Carrey and their film. They are happy that, like Christof's spectacle itself, this controlled experiment in social criticism is not a downer like their star's previous flop, *The Cable Guy*.

Just as Truman Burbank behaves like the proverbial deer caught in the headlights when he becomes aware of his absurd dilemma, Jim Carrey seems somewhat befuddled by his newfound status as a 'serious' actor. *New York* magazine reported that Carrey's publicist was proud that the rubber-faced comedian suppressed his desire to make goofy faces. Everyone behind *The Truman Show* trumpets the fact that Carrey is no longer a vulgar clown, but an incipient Tom Hanks. Unfortunately, Carrey's heroic restraint only contributes to the film's enervated tone. What this antiseptic protest against our tendency to transform reality into a "sanitized video game" needs is some gratuitous mugging or inspired vulgarity. Charlie Chaplin's decision to make serious films like *Monsieur Verdoux* and *A King in New York* was a true expression of his artistic independence and integrity. Carrey's debut as a mainstream leading man is a career move that proves that the star is as much a victim of his handlers' packaging as Truman himself.

The Truman Show is ultimately less fascinating as a work of art than as a social artifact, painstakingly blurring the distinction between lived experience and media hype that it supposedly condemns. Before releasing this 'comedy-drama,' Paramount staged phony demonstrations using actors who implored passersby to "Free Truman Burbank"; the studio's official web set implores net-surfers to enter "Truman's world." Cinesite Digital Studios issued a press release that expressed pride that their special effects aided Weir's examination of "media voyeurism and perception versus reality in today's world." It would be silly to object moralistically to Hollywood's attempt to lambaste itself. After all, small ironies like these are making Weir's modest allegory the pseudoevent, if not the film, of the decade.

LOS ANGELES TIMES, 6/5/98, Calendar/p. 1, Kenneth Turan

His gifts as a comic actor are well-known, but who would have thought that Jim Carrey might simultaneously break your heart as easily as he makes you laugh? It is only one of the accomplishments of "The Truman Show," the nerviest feature to come out of Hollywood in recent memory, that it gives Carrey the role of his career, the opportunity to make exceptional use of his capacities in a film that is as serious as it is funny.

Adventurous, provocative, even daring, "The Truman Show" has been directed with enviable grace and restraint by Peter Weir, whose deliberate tone is essential to the film's multiple and almost contradictory successes. "The Truman Show" is emotionally involving without losing the ability to raise sharp satiric questions as well as get numerous laughs, the rare film that is disturbing despite working beautifully within standard industry norms.

If there is a key to this picture's accomplishment it is the irresistible nature of its carefully worked-out premise, shrewdly conceived by writer Andrew Niccol. "The Truman Show" is concerned with a very particular television program, one whose disconcerting qualities only gradually become completely clear.

The film starts out with a burst of information, running the delicious risk of disorienting us by providing more data than we can quite absorb. Its first shot is a tight close-up of a man in a beret who looks directly at the camera and goes to the heart of the matter: "We've become bored with watching actors giving us phony emotions. We're tired of pyrotechnics and special effects. While the world he inhabits is to some respects counterfeit, there is nothing faked about Truman. No script, no cue cards. It isn't always Shakespeare, but it's genuine. It's a life."

The speaker is Christof (Ed Harris), later described as the "televisionary" who created "The Truman Show." Next comes a credit reading "Hannah Gill as Meryl" and a young woman (Laura Linney) who says, "My life is my life is 'The Truman Show.'" She's followed by "Louis Coltrane as Marlon," a hearty young man (Noah Emmerich) who insists, "It's all true, it's all real. Nothing you see on this show is fake. It's merely controlled."

After this buildup, after the card reading "Truman Burbank as himself," Carrey's familiar face fills the screen. Like Christof, Truman speaks directly to the camera, but, we slowly realize, he's under the impression he's having a completely private moment, playing out a bizarre fantasy of mountain-climbing heroics in the presumed safety of his bathroom mirror. What he can't see that we can is the small word, "LIVE," in the corner of the screen. Truman is on the air, the center of a television program revolving around his life, and everyone knows about it but him.

While this rough premise soon becomes clear, the film is savvy enough to dole out the ramifications and specifics of Truman's situation in artfully spaced doses. Only in bits and pieces do we find out the true dimensions of what has been done to Truman, how it has all been managed, and revealing more than that would spoil the fun.

In the meantime, simultaneously wised-up and in complicity, we become part of the audience watching TV's "Truman Show," just a few of the multitudes eavesdropping without shame on his so-called life in the always-sunny community of Seahaven Island, motto "It's a Nice Place to Live."

Watching Truman trade pleasantries with Stepford wife Meryl and splitting six-packs with always available buddy Marlon is an experience both amusing and uncomfortable. We may be joining the show on day 10,909 but we've entered Truman's world at a critical juncture. Though his environment is always gee-whiz cheerful and sunny (courtesy of Dennis Gassner's expert production design and Peter Biziou's glistening candy-colored cinematography of the real-life Seaside, Fla.), Truman is not completely happy in it. In fact, in ways neither he nor we completely understand at first, his world is threatening to come apart.

It's hints we see first, hints that don't immediately make sense. Why is Truman furtively calling Tahiti information? Why is he buying fashion magazines, ostensibly for his wife, only to clandestinely rip apart the photographs for purposes unknown. The poignancy of seeing Truman feeling trapped and desperate, hiding behind a painted-on smile but deeply unsatisfied for reasons he can't manage to put his finger on, is a classic example of an actor extending himself as far as he can without overreaching.

Carrey tried to push into new territory before, but "The Truman Show" is worlds apart from an unlamented misfire like "The Cable Guy." It's hard to imagine another actor as effective as this halest of well-met fellows, someone who can look completely haunted with a what-me-worry smile parked on his face. In the context of this film, Carrey's trademark high-energy mania plays like the result of the unknowing artificiality of his life, precisely the way someone might get if everyone he knew was secretly more of a co-star than a friend.

In addition to being consistently moving and funny, "The Truman Show," almost as an aside, makes accurate satiric points about conformity, commercialism, the desire to play god, and what can happen when television, or any other medium, permanently blurs the lines between what's real and what's on screen.

Yet despite these subversive underpinnings, what's perhaps most engaging about "The Truman Show" is the way it still delivers vintage Hollywood satisfactions to an audience. With a beleaguered hero determined to live free or die, "The Truman Show" demonstrates a belief in the indomitability of the human spirit that is as four-square as anything Frank Capra put on screen.

Weir is especially critical to "Truman's" success. Benefiting from 14 months of prep time (because Carrey had commitments to a pair of other films), Weir created and sustained the essential low-key tone for this project. He also paid special care to the casting (including small but pivotal roles like Natascha McElhone as the woman who haunts Truman's dreams and Harry Shearer as an especially unctuous TV interviewer).

Like any current film, this venture has precedents, everything from Rod Serling's "Twilight Zone" series to Paul Bartel's prescient 1965 "Secret Cinema." But "The Truman Show" has been so carefully and thoughtfully worked out, it's so much its own film, that viewers will be justified in feeling that they've never seen anything quite like it. And how often can you say that in this derivative age?

NEW STATESMAN, 10/9/98, p. 36, Gerald Kaufman

A recent New Yorker article pointed out: "This summer, Americans' spent 575 million hours in darkened cinemas and saw, at most, two new things: the harrowing D-Day sequence in 'Saving Private Ryan' and the hair gel joke in 'There's Something About Mary.'" The article was discussing, among other matters, the allegation of 149 similarities between a play called "Frank's Life" and the film "The Truman Show."

Yet anyone with the tiniest experience of cinema who has never even heard of "Frank's Life" will have recognised that "The Truman Show" is simply the latest variant—we saw another not long ago in "The X-Files"—of an extremely well-known formula, most memorably exemplified in the classic "Invasion of the Body Snatchers". What matters is not the familiarity of the formula but the imaginativeness and the ingenuity with which the formula has been reinvented. Andrew Niccol (scriptwriter) and Peter Weir (director) have done a dazzling job with a well-worn stock situation: one man, the centre of the action, is alone in failing to realise that he is the victim of a plot in which all around him are co-conspirators.

Truman Burbank (Jim Carrey, a megastar whose willingness to take the star role at a cut-price rate was instrumental in getting this modestly budgeted film made) lives in Seahaven, an archetype of one of those idyllic towns. familiar from Hollywood B-movies. And that is exactly what Seahaven turns out to be: an invention. Its inhabitants are actors playing roles. The one Seahavenite who does not know is Truman himself.

From the day he was born he has been live, on camera, with millions watching throughout the world. Every aspect of his life is a fake, with the simple, indispensable exception that he is living it. Then Truman, by now aged 30, begins to get an inkling that something odd is going on. He blurts out: "I feel as if the whole world revolves around me somehow. Everyone seems to be in on it." When the scenario no longer suffices to keep him under control, the producer, Christof (Ed Harris, sitting in a huge control room that supervises the 5,000 hidden cameras planted in Seahaven) is compelled to improvise.

Truman tries to drive out of town, but is stopped by officials who claim the roads are blocked due to fire.

"The Truman Show," while a very funny comedy, is a black one. Truman, in an upbeat ending, seems to escape the life scripted for him by Christof But does he? This film warns that, manipulated as we are by media which create our perception of the world in which we live, all of us not only could be but are Truman. The bleakest joke of all is that Peter Weir did not even have to build a studio set to depict Seahaven. He simply went to Florida and shot his movie in what the film's production designer, Dennis Gassner, described as the "highly architecturally designed environment" of the "planned community" of Seaside.

NEW YORK, 6/8/98, p. 100, David Denby

A clever but empty movie that is rapidly turning into the most overpraised picture of the year, *The Truman Show* is about a young man who lives in a small town by the sea with houses as white as ... well, as white as the new teeth that wealthy people seem to grow when they turn 60. The gleaming houses of this theme-park paradise are decorated with cute neo-Victorian trim; and in town, where the young man, Truman Burbank (Jim Carrey), works as an insurance salesman, the public buildings are constructed out of okay materials like glass and brick. The designers of *The Truman Show*—director Peter Weir and his wife, the visual consultant Wendy Stites—are witty enough to realize that the plastic utopias of the future will not, in fact, be made out of plastic. In the town of Seahaven, the light comes up bright and warm every day, but sometimes it comes up in a sudden surge, as if God himself had turned on the juice. In fact, God has. The lord of this realm is named Christof (Ed Harris), and he attempts to redeem the fallen world outside Seahaven by offering for our entertainment a perfect Eden of nothingness. Christof is a television "creator," solemn in beret and dark collarless guru garb, and from his control room he wields absolute power over Seahaven, which, in fact, is a huge set built somewhere on the other side of the Hollywood Hills. From the day of his birth, Truman Burbank has been surrounded by actors, his every move captured by hidden cameras placed all over town. He doesn't know any of this, though he's restless and secretly unhappy, and he's beginning to suspect that something in his uneventful life is a bit weird. His banal, sunshiny routine—rising from bed, greeting neighbors, going to work—provides untold reassurance to the people around the world who watch him in bars, in bedrooms, even in throngs before giant screens in Times Square. Some of them never stop watching him.

I give so much of the premise of *The Truman Show* because the premise is the main thing the picture has going for it. In support of its idea, *The Truman Show* turns out to be intricately and merrily designed, with many sportive touches placed in the corners and backgrounds of shots. Conceptual originality isn't nothing—in fact, it's remarkably rare in a large-scale summer movie, a movie that couldn't have been easy to sell to the Christofs who run the film business. Some of the jokes planted by Weir and screenwriter Andrew Niccol run on a delayed fuse, hitting us with teasing slowness—for instance, the posters warning of the dangers of air travel, which, we realize, have been created by Christof to scare Truman into staying home and remaining in the show. It's fun to watch the TV-set reality fall apart now and then as the actuality below and around it unwillingly slips into view—the studio rain shifted a few feet by technicians so it lands on Truman; the spasmodic, stop-and-go movements of the actors jerking themselves into place so they can photograph Truman, as he passes by, with hidden cameras. For a while, the movie has a fizz of strangeness. We watch one reality encasing and controlling another.

What *The Truman Show* doesn't have is dramatic or emotional power—or much meaning either. Jim Carrey plays Truman as a little boy in a large body—as a friendly, grinning dorky American. Carrey acts with his elbows, his shoulders, his ass; he does his abrupt tormented-duck gestures and his half-conscious-schoolboy frown, misery ascending from cheekbones to high, furrowed brow. It's the filmmakers' point, of course, that Truman has been infantilized, kept in the womb, but Carrey is too much a farceur and clown to suggest what inner life might be awakening in the newly rebellious man. He doesn't move us (as, say, James Stewart or even Bruce Willis would have), because he can't show us the nascent self inside the troubled Truman; he can only turn slapstick up or down in volume. He gives a frenetic but emotionally inert performance.

In any case, the movie is being praised not so much for its craft as for its alleged "subversive" implications—the media-age critique, the metaphysics of illusion and inauthenticity. But *The Truman Show* is too vague in its metaphors to mean much of anything (it's about control, it's about surveillance, it's about paranoia ...), and its various satirical thrusts don't go together—if anything, they cancel one another out.

Consider: Weir and Niccol establish the tyranny of total pleasantness. If the *Saturday Evening Post* of the fifties had fornicated with *The Donna Reed Show*, Seahaven might be the result. Yet the members of the viewing audience are so wrapped up in Seahaven's utterly bland existence on TV that they forget to live their own lives. But what's the point of the satire? It doesn't connect with anything. In the real world, the kind of television spectacle the public gets wrapped up in—soap operas, *Jerry Springer, ER,* or a serial documentary like *An American Family* are all full of incident, emotion, and rage (however ersatz). Even *Seinfeld* has crises, albeit of the spluttering, tempest-in-a-teapot variety. In a recent *Times* column, Frank Rich mentioned the O.J. trial, the death of Princess Di, and the L.A. freeway suicide as examples of the kind of TV mania that *The Truman Show is* getting at, but none of these things is more than distantly relevant to the movie. Violence, scandal, and disorder—that's what mesmerizes the audience and turns it into a collective Peeping Tom. An audience watching a man who does nothing is just a conceit—a Warholian nowhere that is hardly a danger to us, hardly an example of something we fear we might become.

If Truman the TV subject had been a man condemned by Christof to a life of violence, and if he had wanted, on the contrary, to live peacefully but wasn't allowed to do so by his creator or his audience—*that* bit of satire would have hit us where we live. (We don't want the people on *Jerry Springer* to behave like adults; we want them to behave like apes.) And again: If Carrey's unconscious Truman had wanted to break out and feel something—by sticking a nail into his palm or killing someone—then the filmmakers' conception of the character might have packed a wallop. But what's onscreen has no punch, no teeth; it doesn't even scratch.

The movie is about as "subversive" as *Forrest Gump,* another soothing film about an innocent stumbling through his existence. This is a profound movie for people who don't like to think, or perhaps for people who are in the media and *of* the media, and can't imagine any life outside it. Weir's metaphoric realization of their situation startles them. Larry King thinks it's a devastating movie, and so does Frank Rich, who has managed, for some years, to write a national column in which he repeatedly deplores the trivialization of politics by show business while himself avoiding such trivialities as the economy, race, and international affairs. That so resourceful a journalist as Rich has become part of the malaise of our media-saturated society is troublesome. *The Truman Show,* however, will not disturb anyone's sleep. Most people, I suspect, will enjoy it as a kind of witty sci-fi escape fantasy (will Truman get out?)—a more creative and extended version of Rod Serling's *Twilight Zone.*

NEW YORK POST, 6/5/98, p. 39, Rod Dreher

Peter Weir's "The Truman Show" is a spectacularly original, utterly ingenious pop parable, a near-perfect fusion of mainstream filmmaking with art-house aspirations. It's not often that movies so fun to lose yourself in give so much to think about after you leave the theater, and rarely do "idea" films trip so pleasurably across the screen.

What if your whole life were a Mentos commercial? That's the lot of Truman Burbank (Jim Carrey), an insurance adjuster who lives in a world of relentlessly upbeat, minty-fresh perfection. His quaint island town, Seahaven, is as well-scrubbed and flawless as Truman's crisp, cheerful white smile.

If you notice that Truman's wife, Meryl (Laura Linney), his best bud, Marlon (Noah Emmerich) and everybody else in this Disneyfied Eden seems straight out of Central Casting, you'd be right. Everything and everyone in town is fake, a grotesquely elaborate stage set constructed for the sake of "The Truman Show," a television program that has been a worldwide hit for nearly 30 years.

Poor Truman is the only person on the planet not in on the joke. He has been raised since birth in the artificial environment, his every moment broadcast via hidden cameras. Viewers feel as if they know Truman, and it's more than a little creepy that everyone is happy to watch this man's life cruelly exploited to feed the public's endless appetite for infotainment. (Princess Diana, this one's for you.)

Part religious allegory, part media satire, the movie is about the existential crisis sparked when Truman begins to doubt that everything around him is what it appears to be. Walking down his street one fine morning, a studio lighting apparatus falls from the sky in front of him. He's puzzled by it, but we know that it comes from the massive dome built over Seahaven to make the weather controllable.

Gradually, Truman notices that things aren't quite right; the tiny cracks in the pristine canvas of his life serve as messages in bottles signaling him that there's an unseen reality behind what's apparent. Under orders from the godlike director Christof (Ed Harris), wife Meryl tries to distract Truman from his quest for knowledge by offering him the anesthetizing joys of sex and consumer products.

He is not deterred, and as scripter Andrew Niccol's absorbing plot unspools, Truman becomes ever more panicked and paranoid. Goaded by the faint memory of Sylvia (Natascha McElhone), a former "Truman Show" cast member with whom he fell in love, Truman becomes desperate to get off the island and go to Fiji, where he believes she lives. But everything about Seahaven society conspires, rather cleverly, to make him afraid to explore outside the boundaries.

We know that ultimately Truman will have to face down his jealous creator. Weir imagines this with dazzling symbolism as a heroic sea journey, a quest in which Truman must conquer his deepest fear to gain self-knowledge, and claim his free will, and become the captain of his soul.

"The Truman Show" raises issues of free will, obviously. Truman's quest for true love and authenticity is a metaphysical rebellion and a refutation of the idea that the human spirit is programmable. The film's more subtle and subversive theme is how we in the audience passively allow media to define the borders of our thinking, how we deform our own character by yielding to the comforting illusions of televised conformity.

My only quibble with the film is Jim Carrey's adequate performance. It's the riskiest role of the comic actor's career, the first time he's really been called upon to act instead of mug spastically (Carrey's moron-movie audience may not follow him here, but he'll win new fans). Carrey's blank but hopeful Truman really does seem like a child molded by TV's false sincerity. Holding back the herky-jerky comic must have been like damming the Amazon, but Weir accomplished it.

Yet it's clear that Carrey is a work in progress. His natural gift is wildly expressionistic, but here he can't quite convey the pathos of a man struggling to discover an inner life (something Robin Williams, equally facile with physical comedy, has learned to do well). If our emotional connection with Truman is never as deep or as moving as should be, everything else about this wondrous movie hits the bull's-eye. I can't wait to see it again.

NEWSDAY, 6/5/98, Part II/p. B3, Jack Mathews

On the 10,909th day of his perfect life, Truman Burbank (Jim Carrey) awakens to a morning that looks pretty much like the 10,908 that preceded it.

There's a perfect sky hanging over his perfect neighborhood in the perfect island community of Seahaven, where pastel neo-Victorian cottages rest on perfectly manicured lawns on perfectly clean streets that lead either to the storybook town square or to the surrounding miles of pristine white sand beaches and aquamarine surf.

Life is a perpetual child's fantasy of a grown-up's world for the genial insurance salesman, whose perfectly dimpled wife and perfectly friendly neighbors fill a domestic picture that could have been drawn up by one of the creative boards at the Wonderful World of Disney.

The life, of course, is too good to be true, but how would Truman know? In Peter Weir's brilliant, magical "The Truman Show," he is an alien in his own universe. Seahaven isn't a town, it's the Hollywood set for a television show. Its sky is a painting on a domed ceiling, its sea is a climate-controlled tank, and besides Truman, every person in it—his wife (Laura Linney), mom (Holland Taylor), dad (Brian Delate) and best friend (Noah Emmerich) included—is an actor in a live TV show that has been airing 24 hours a day, seven days a week for nearly 30 years.

Since his birth—aired live, of course—Truman Burbank has been its plot.

Like "Forrest Gump," "The Truman Show" is the story of an innocent adrift in a corrupt world, and like "Gump," it may knock the legs out from under the so-called blockbusters and steal the summer of '98. But its star, played with something close to measured perfection by Carrey, is no Forrest Gump. He's a smart, good-natured guy who's simply spent his life in a sunny alternate reality created for the amusement and sedation of the television public.

Truman is living the universal fantasy, in a disease-, disaster-, war- and stress-free environment whose sanguine artifice is beamed on Prozac waves into homes around the world, calming the poor, the elderly, the lonely and the working classes with images of a life running its course in paradise.

"Who Needs Europe?" asks a headline in the local paper, assuring members of the TV audience, if not Truman, that no external unpleasantness—like World War II—will invade Seahaven.

It's a benign existence: The only drama in Truman's life occurs when an actor, like the one playing his father or another playing a girl with whom he has a quick infatuation, misbehaves and has to be chased from the show, and it's hard to imagine such a program finding an audience for more than a weekly summation, let alone a womb-to-tomb cycle. Maybe if Truman were a doctor searching for the one-armed man who killed his wife. . .

In any event, it's compelling film material. Whether you take it as a multi-philosophical tract—perception vs. reality, self-determination vs. fatalism, even science vs. creationism—or as pure "Twilight Zone"-style entertainment "The Truman Show" is as fresh and original an idea as has found its way into a movie theater in years, and it's the most profound glimpse at the power of television to control and influence lives since "Network."

"The Truman Show," written by Andrew Niccol ("Gattaca"), creates three separate realities: the completely fabricated world Truman inhabits; the world on the other side of the set, where the show's megalomaniacal director, Christof (Ed Harris, in a sensational performance), choreographs the action surrounding his star, and the world we inhabit, as voyeurs peering through several sets of lenses.

Part of the time, we see Truman as his TV audience sees him, through miniature cameras installed on clothing (the good old "button cam"), behind mirrors, in his car radio. Other times, we watch as if we were simply there in Seahaven, invisible observers to his reactions to the fissures opening around him. And we see him as Christof sees him, through the eyes of God, or at least as the gentle monster Frankenstein meant to create. There's a genuinely creepy scene of Christof, overwhelmed by pride, admiring the sleeping Truman on a giant, green-tinted screen, where he's curled up as if in an amniotic sac. For Christof, it's about the last pleasant moment he'll have with Truman, whose curiosity, stimulated by the falling of a strange object from the sky (it's a stage light) in the opening sequence, is stumbling toward the truth of his existence and a confrontation with his maker.

Carrey is a revelation here. Gone are the talking butt cheeks, the Silly Putty mannerisms and the facial contortions that have earned him unfair comparisons to Jerry Lewis. There's just enough of Carrey's carefree zest-for-life to give Truman a goofy likability; he's an insurance man you'd buy from. And he handles his increasingly dramatic scenes with convincing self-confidence.

There are flaws to "The Truman Show." The recurring characters watching the show—a pair of elderly women, two parking attendants, a man in a bathtub—are more artificial than anybody in Seahaven. And given the longevity of the fraud perpetrated on him, the clues come in too-convenient bunches for Truman.

But those are quibbles in the face of a great achievement. Weir has made some smartly provocative movies about people caught in situations outside their own reference—"The Year of Living Dangerously," "Witness" and "Gallipoli" most notable among them. "The Truman Show" may be his masterpiece.

NEWSWEEK, 6/1/98, p. 62, Jeff Giles

"The Truman Show" has been broadcast live for more than 10,000 days before the star figures out he's on TV. His name is Truman Burbank (Jim Carrey) and, until recently, he was under the impression that be was just an insurance salesman. Now he's discovered that his family and friends are actors, that the eerily perfect island on which he lives is a giant set and that even the most tender and terrible moments of his life were scripted as part of a 24-hour-a-day hit soap opera. Needless to say, he's pissed. So, one night, Truman does something you wouldn't think possible on an island with 5,000 candid cameras: he escapes. The creator of "The Truman Show," a pompous guy in a beret named Christof (Ed Harris), becomes enraged. He cuts the live transmission for the first time ever and orders his mammoth supporting cast to search the set. Christof turns the moon into a searchlight and, when even that doesn't flush out his star, he barks to an assistant, "Cue the sun!" Suddenly, the sun rises over the ocean, and there's daylight in the middle of the night. Not a bad effect. Most directors only think they're God.

Peter Weir's "The Truman Show" is a miraculous movie. It will rattle both your head and heart, and Carrey's raw, life-size performance will surprise you if you still think of him as the poet laureate of potty humor. The movie is an underdog this summer. Will anybody pay to watch Carrey reinvent himself as a Tom Hanks-ish leading man? His fans are awfully young, and some people past puberty refuse to take him seriously. Still, Weir is famous for guiding stars through transition pictures. He led Robin Williams into pure drama with "Dead Poets Society" and even helped Indiana Jones expand his range with the deeply romantic "Witness." Carrey says that after "Truman" had wrapped, he had something of a panic attack. "I called Peter up and was very concerned about the beginning of the movie, concerned that I hadn't given him enough whatever. He said, 'Harrison Ford called me up and did this exact same thing to me. Just relax'."

As a child, Truman Burbank watched his father drown during a storm at sea. He's been terrified of water ever since, so he's never once stepped off Seahaven. At the outset of the movie, he's finally been hit with wanderlust. But everyone, including his relentlessly perky wife (Laura Linney), seems to be conspiring to keep him on the island, and soon there are strange fissures in what he thought was reality. The biggest jolt comes when he runs into the father he thought was dead, then watches him get suspiciously hustled away. Before long, Truman has realized his wife loathes him and is fantasizing about chasing his true love (Natascha McElhone) to Fiji.

On one level, "The Truman Show" is a movie about a young man spinning his wheels in a suffocating marriage. On another, it's about the way the media and the public have conspired to destroy the very idea of a private life. On yet another, it's about the way movies manipulate us, the way we recognize that fact but beg for more. On yet *another*, it's a nifty rumination on whether or not the proverbial Someone is up there, helping us and occasionally hurling thunderbolts. All this makes for an improbable mix of themes. Frankly, this movie could have been ponderous and awful if it hadn't been so immaculately conceived and directed with such a light, deft touch.

"The Truman Show" was written by Andrew Niccol, a New Zealand-born screenwriter. (He also directed last year's Orwellian sci-fi flick "Gattaca": "So you obviously know that I'm a very paranoid person.") "Truman" was filmed at the hyper-idyllic planned community of Seaside, Fla. It was shot with just the right hints of surrealism, and acted to perfection. Carrey is a team player for the first time, paring down his comic riffs and rendering Truman as an innocent, desperate Everyman. Linney is fabulous as an actress who's trying to stick to the script even when she thinks her "husband" has gone nuts. Harris is a nuanced Christof, part doting father figure, part egomaniacal monster. At one point, his assistant says Truman can't die in front of a live audience, and he demands to know why not: "He was born in front of a live audience."

Reality-based TV has been around for ages. In 1973, with the seminal documentary "An American Family," we saw Pat and Bill Loud's marriage implode, while their son Lance came strutting out of the closet. ("I, to this day, am embarrassed," Pat said 10 years later.) In 1992, with MTV's "The Real World," we saw intense Kevin and sexy Julie, like, *totally* dealing with the whole racial thing. Today, as Weir puts it, "you just switch the channel on and the camera's wobbling about, and you're not sure if it's happening now, whether it's re-created or it's real, whether people are acting or if they're unaware they're being photographed." Not that audiences care. During "The Truman Show," fans are seen riveted to the tube. They hate to see Truman suffer, but they utterly miss the irony at work. Christof would stop torturing the poor guy if everybody stopped watching.

Carrey got the "Truman" script from the producer Scott Rudin. It goes without saying that it was of a different caliber than, say, "Ace Ventura 2." As Carrey puts it, "I didn't have to sit down for five weeks and go through it scene by scene and make sure we made a silk purse out of a sow's ear, which I have to do most of the time." The "Truman" script is also the first one that is anywhere near as complicated as Carrey himself. Asked where Truman's very palpable pain comes from, the actor says without hesitating, "Well, that just comes from my life. I've had a lot of trials and a lot of sadness."

Carrey dropped out of high school to help support his family as a janitor. He had such a monumentally fraught relationship with his parents that he had something of a breakdown in his 20s. He had to watch both his mother and father die—and to admit defeat in two marriages—by his mid-30s. Carrey's comedy is often written off as childlike, but in fact many of his performances have been furnace blasts of hostility. (Hilarious ones, of course.) "Truman" digs into the unhappiness behind the anger. It also reveals a bit of Carrey's touchy-feely side. This, after all, is a guy who never met a self-help book he didn't like, a guy who admits to wondering, "What *is* up there? What's God? I've spent my life wanting the roof to be torn off this thing, you know? For somebody to say, 'Yeah, there's a God. Don't worry about it. You're taken care of'." As for Truman Burbank, he knows that Christof sees all. Now he wants to live a life worth watching.

SIGHT AND SOUND, 10/98, p. 36, Leslie Felperin

Truman Burbank lives in the island community of Seahaven which he never leaves, being afraid of water ever since his father died in a boating accident. Married to Meryl, a nurse, and employed as an insurance salesman, Truman seems content. But he is haunted by the memory of Lauren, a girl he once met who was whisked away by her father to Fiji. What Truman doesn't know is that he was adopted at birth by a television company, run by executive producer Christof, and is the star of an all-day television show, filmed on a huge, enclosed set. Everyone around him is really an actor., Millions of people have watched his whole life on television and even know of his secret longing for Lauren (really named Sylvia, now a campaigner for Truman's freedom).

However, Truman starts to become suspicious of his surroundings. Among other clues, he accidentally glimpses the actor who played his father wandering in a crowd. Christof hastily writes an explanatory reunion for Truman and his father, but Truman's curiosity is not assuaged. He tries to drive away with Meryl, only to be forced back. Truman tricks the cameras by creating a dummy-decoy and sets off in a sailboat. Christof almost drowns him with his computer-controlled weather, but Truman reaches the edge of the set. Christof tries to persuade him to stay, but Truman opens the exit door and leaves for the real world.

Film critics and preview audiences are occasionally privileged to experience something extraordinary: they get to see a film absolutely cold, before it is written about, discussed, excerpted and trailered into ubiquity, before their friends feel unable to keep themselves from re-narrating the best bits. I feel extremely lucky to have walked into a preview of *The Truman Show* several months ago completely ignorant of its story. By now, most inquisitive film-goers will already know the film's central conceit: Truman Burbank (Jim Carrey), to all appearances an ordinary 30-year-old insurance salesman in a superficially happy marriage, is unaware that he's also the star of a television show.

Consequently, most British viewers seeing it after reports of its summer success in the US and several spoiling articles over here—about how the film has rebranded Carrey as a serious actor, about what the whole thing says about the invasiveness of the media, and so on—will be robbed of the aesthetic bliss of seeing, like Truman himself, the trick revealed piece by piece.

Despite the reservations voiced elsewhere about the film's philosophical depth, there's no denying that director Peter Weir shows his hand and conceals it with charming dexterity. The film gives it all away at the start with an opening 'credits sequence' for the series-within-the-film, but it's easy not to understand what's going on. Truman's wife Meryl, played by Laura Linney with sinister, apple-cheeked irony, calls Truman's existence and her own "a truly blessed life". The series' creator Christof (Ed Harris, dressed all in black like a cross between a coke dealer and a kabuki stagehand) explains that, "Nothing you see here is faked. It's merely controlled." (This omniscience recalls the hippie-transcendent notion that "everything happens at exactly the right time" in Weir's first 1975 feature *Picnic at Hanging Rock,* which now seems like an eerie pre-echo of *The Truman Show.)* Gradually, we begin to realise the extent of this control and that the darkened, weirdly angled shots are not affected cinematic mannerisms from Weir and Co, but subjective views of cameras within the diegesis, planted on the figures passing Truman by, or hidden in houseplants. By the time Meryl is extolling, with an unnatural degree of enthusiasm, the virtues of a slicing-peeling-paring kitchen gadget (which will become a comical weapon later on) many viewers tuned into the insincere, television tone-of-voice that cues product placement will already have 'got it'.

Yet even if you know *The Truman Show*'s big joke, there are many lesser ones to savour. As with the kitchen gadget, the film delights in showing the hidden, evil nature of innocuous props and set dressing: the outsize moon (scale is wonderfully skewed here—look out for the gag about Mount Rushmore) is Christof's observation deck; the too-friendly, floppy-eared dog next door turns into a snarling attacker when the town goes looking for the missing Truman. Echoing the dome that encases this world, much play is made out of circles and cycles and repetitions: a golf ball is used to explain that Fiji, where Truman's true love is meant to have flown, is so much on the other side of the world that, "you can't get any further away before you start coming back." Similarly, it's in a revolving door that Truman's rebellion begins.

Of course, a major paradoxical gag is the casting of Carrey in the lead, his character endowed with a first name that's just a bit too much of an allegorical nudge. He is an actor who has built a career on a kind of manic insincerity, which made him perfectly suited if irritating as a lawyer who's jinxed into telling the truth for a day in *Liar Liar.* Here, he's supposed to be the only 'sincere' person in his world, the only one who's not lying (although he later learns deception). And yet, with his gestures large as if he's trying to touch the outsized moon, his smile a row of blank Scrabble tiles, there's a sense even in the earliest scenes that he's performing for the cameras—which would be logical for someone around whom life had been choreographed since he was an infant.

What makes Carrey's self-regarding, class-clown persona so useful to the film is that it buttresses one of *The Truman Show*'s major themes, perhaps its most central: solipsism. Many have read *The Truman Show* as an allegory of how television obsessively watches us, of Bentham-Foucault's panopticon gone digitally out of control. What's more poignant and haunting about this movie is that it's really about how we all secretly *want* to be on television and see ourselves as the stars of our own home-life movies; it is impossible to leave the cinema after seeing *The Truman Show* and not, at some point, wonder if the world is watching, not experience a flicker of identification with Truman (who has already been rehearsing different roles in front of his mirror every morning, before he become aware of the plot around him).

This is nothing new. Solipsism is one the defining tropes of literary modernism, threading through James Joyce's *Ulysses* and most of Vladimir Nabokov's work, Borges' fiction and almost every book by Philip K. Dick (see *Time Out of Joint* and *Flow My Tears, The Policeman Said* for close parallels with *The Truman Show).* But cinema and television have appropriated the theme with problematic results. In a book, be it written in the first or third persons, the reader is always aware that a single authorial presence is playing puppetmaster, writing itself is a solipsistic process. Film's collaborative nature (and the collective way we view it) tugs it into the social realm. What is more, it can seldom comfortably accommodate purely subjective viewpoints. We gradually come to realise that these weird shots of Truman in the beginning are the cameras' views of him, but who is filming Christof in his observatory?   What being watches Sylvia watching Truman inside her flat?

Still, *The Truman Show* is a moving exploration of creation-anxiety, of the fear and hope that in a post Darwinian world the only beings with real power are distant public figures and malevolent unknown forces ringfencing our capacity for free will. Solipsism haunts us because it's both a comfort and a terror to think that someone, something has laid all this on for us, but in fiction like *The Truman Show* characters get to make the last moves. I wont give it away here, but the conclusion of the film is both satisfying and chillingly ambiguous: Truman and the viewers get to decide—to paraphrase the series' tagline blazoned on buttons and T shirts worn by the show's viewers—how it's going to end.

VILLAGE VOICE, 6/9/98, p. 143, J. Hoberman

Celebrity is the coin of the American realm and Peter Weir's *The Truman Show*, which opens Friday on a crescendo of buzz, is a movie about celebritude that pushes the conventional wisdom on the subject to its logical extreme.

The movies protagonist, Truman Burbank (Jim Carrey), is not just well-known for being well-known, he's well-known precisely because he's the most well-known person who ever lived. This star was born... at birth. His 15 minutes of fame have been extended into an entire lifetime; his daily existence is broadcast to millions of faithful viewers as the subject of a live, 24-hour-a-day television show. For 30 years, Truman has played a normal person on TV—but, of course, he's not really a normal person, because he's the only one in the world unaware of his celebrity.

A similar premise served as the basis for an early episode of *The Twilight Zone* in which a businessman suddenly found his office transformed into a movie set. It's also an elaboration on Chuck Jones's classic *Duck Amuck,* in which a capricious, unseen animator treats Daffy Duck as the Looney Tunes equivalent of Job. But *The Truman Show*, which was written by Andrew Niccol—the young author-director of last year's *Gattaca*— is an attempt to represent a total system. Just as the ambitious, if stultifing, *Gattaca* offered a sci-fi critique of genetic programming, so *The Truman Show* suggests that stardom too can be rationally produced. This spoof of what Mark Crispin Miller dubbed our National Entertainment State is a scenario that mixes the 1984 nightmare of absolute surveillance with the notion of an idiot-audience hooked on the vicarious thrills of virtual reality (or what André Bazin called the Myth of Total Cinema).

Truman's antiseptic hometown—seemingly modeled on the Disney planned community, Celebration—is a vast, domed movie studio. The show's somber, self important creator, Christof (Ed Harris), broods in the fake sky overhead while the outside world is represented by occasional cutaways to Truman's cretinous devotees watching their idol on TV. Without doubt, *The Truman Show* has the most intriguing metaphysical premise of any Hollywood comedy since *Groundhog Day,* offers the most resonant showbiz metaphor since *The King of Comedy*, and executes the most ingenious mise-en-scène since *Defendinq Your Life.* But what's it up to?

Surrounded as he is by actors, including his wife (Laura Linney), and eternally observed by an unseen audience (not to mention his producer), there would seem to be two ways to allegorize Truman's condition. Either he's delusional, a paranoid schizophrenic, or else an existential victim, the subject of a brainwashed quasi-religious cult. Is it the movie or the town which is constantly awash in reverential theme music? Or has the soundtrack been implanted in our hero's brain? Truman's TV is only the most obvious part of his environment that is custom-programmed to control him.. In the movie's grisliest joke, actors playing doctors have to stage an amputation for his benefit. Truman's wife is at once shrill and soothing, proudly announcing her latest brandname purchase to the hidden camera. (Product placement substitutes for commercial breaks.)

Jim Carrey's Truman is even more insanely cheerful. Like Steve Martin and Bill Murray before him, Carrey is the master of "sincerity"—so much so that he often seems like a simulation himself. Initially oblivious to the production's various mishaps and miscues (a klieg light crashes down onto his street, a rainstorm follows him around), his Truman is just beginning to suspect something peculiar. As he explains to the actor who is cast as his best friend, he's wondering if, somehow, the whole world revolves around him. *The Truman Show* is less funny than clinically hysterical and, although the pathology isn't meant to be individual so much as social, what the movie suggests is the celebrity's view of celebrity.

The film-makers might have done more with the backstage technology that makes the spectacle work, but then *The Truman Show*—like its TV counterpart—is a star vehicle. Crucial to the premise is the idea of high-paid, lowbrow maniac Jim Carrey taking his first "serious" role. Never mind that Carrey basically plays Truman as an overgrown kid, that *The Cable Guy's* karaoke scene alone was more horrific than the entire *Truman Show*—or that, despite its flaws and lapses, *The Cable Guy* itself was a far more serious and provocative social critique. There, truly working without a net, Carrey played a terrifyingly obnoxious personification of mass culture—not exactly a cover-friendly icon for *Time* magazine. (Good ol' boy Andy Griffith never revisited the demonic persona he exhibited in *A Face in the Crowd;* the same may be true for Carrey.)

The Truman Show is good viewing. As Truman struggles against his fate, Christof resurrects the dead, adds a love interest, conjures up natural disasters to keep him in line. Like *Duck Amuck,* the movie builds to a confrontation between the star and his creator—except that this time, the whole world is watching. The filmmakers have succeeded in marshaling our attention, but neither their protagonist nor his interpreter has the depth or range to play the Jesus Christ Prometheus Joseph K Frankenstein monster that the situation warrants. *The Truman Show* winds up by suggesting that this is just entertainment after all—poor dramaturgy, but the acme of social realism.

Also reviewed in:
CHICAGO TRIBUNE, 6/5/98, Friday/p. A, Michael Wilmington
NATION, 6/29/98, p. 35, Stuart Klawans
NEW REPUBLIC, 6/29/98, p. 22, Stanley Kauffmann
NEW YORK TIMES, 6/5/98, p. E1, Janet Maslin
NEW YORKER, 6/15/98, p. 80, Daphne Merkin
VARIETY, 4/27-5/3/98, p. 57, Todd McCarthy
WASHINGTON POST, 6/5/98, p. F1, Rita Kempley
WASHINGTON POST, 6/5/98, Weekend/p. 58, Michael O'Sullivan

TWILIGHT

A Paramount Pictures release of a Cinehaus production. *Executive Producer:* Michael Hausman. *Producer:* Arlend Donovan and Scott Rudin. *Director:* Robert Benton. *Screenplay:* Robert Benton and Richard Russo. *Director of Photography:* Piotr Sobocinski. *Editor:* Carol Littleton. *Music:* Elmer Bernstein. *Music Editor:* Kathy Durning and Thomas Drescher. *Sound:* David R.B. MacMillan and (music) Dan Wallin. *Sound Editor:* Maurice Schell. *Casting:* Ilene Starger. *Production Designer:* David Gropman. *Art Director:* David Bomba. *Set Decorator:* Beth Rubino. *Special Effects:* Larry Fiorito. *Costumes:* Joseph G. Aulisi. *Make-up:* Bron Roylance. *Stunt Coordinator:* Stan Barrett. *Running time:* 96 minutes. *MPAA Rating:* R.

CAST: Paul Newman (Harry Ross); Susan Sarandon (Catherine Ames); Gene Hackman (Jack Ames); Stockard Channing (Verna); Reese Witherspoon (Mel Ames); Giancarlo Esposito (Reuben); James Garner (Raymond Hope); Liev Schreiber (Jeff Willis); Margo Martindale (Gloria Lamar); John Spencer (Captain Phil Egan); M. Emmet Walsh (Lester Ivar); Peter Gregory (Verna's Partner); Rene Mujica (Mexican Bartender); Jason Clarke and Neil Mather (Young Cops); Patrick Y. Malone (Younger Cop); Lewis Arquette (Water Pistol Man); Michael Brockman (Garvey's Bartender); April Grace (Police Stenographer); Clint Howard (EMS Worker); John J. Cappon (Paramedic); Ronald C. Sanchez (Crime Scene Detective); Jack Wallace (Interrogation Officer); Jeff Joy (Carl); Jonathan Scarfe (Cop).

LOS ANGELES TIMES, 3/6/98, Calendar/p. 1, Kenneth Turan

Given Hollywood's current emphasis on things dark and murderous, it was only a matter of time before elderly parties wanted a piece of the action. "Twilight," starring 73-year-old Paul

Newman, 67-year-old Gene Hackman, 69-year-old James Garner and 51-year-old babe in the woods Susan Sarandon, represents the flowering of that inevitable subgenre: geezer noir.

You know you're watching geezer noir when the protagonists make small talk about their prostates, not platinum blonds. Lines like "Not at my age" and "I'm tired" are also giveaways. And when the studio artificially darkens the star's hair color on the key art, you can be sure you've arrived.

It's a shame that Paramount couldn't live with a naturally gray Paul Newman on "Twilight's" poster because his cool and laconic performance as retired private eye Harry Ross is a fine thing. No one on screen has aged better than Newman; his mustache may be faded and his hair thin, but his eyes remain flinty and hypnotic and his ability to be a hero even in repose remains unimpaired.

Newman's less-is-more acting technique has if anything gotten stronger over the years. The actor's presence creates involvement while he's just standing still, and he brings the perfect been-around quality to the sardonic Ross, supplying a world-weariness that carries lines like, "I'm going to pretend you weren't here tonight, which is almost true."

That verbal archness comes courtesy of director Robert Benton (a geezer noir pioneer with 1977's Art Carney-starring "The Late Show") and his co-writer Richard Russo. These two also collaborated on Newman's last film, "Nobody's Fool," which was based on a Russo novel.

"Twilight" has periodic stretches of unforced dialogue, supporting actors like Hackman and Sarandon who know how to handle those moments, and a generally relaxed attitude that provides shelter for the amusing eccentrics that all L.A.-based private eye movies are legally obligated to provide.

Though audiences will appreciate these extras, extras are all they remain. Despite its pluses, despite trying to do all the right things, "Twilight" comes up lacking in both energy and plot, two areas that no noir, geezer or otherwise, can afford to be caught short in.

Newman himself categorized Harry Ross in a recent interview by referring to one of his earlier roles and calling the retired P.I. "a Harper that has lost a couple of big ones. He has found out his old tricks don't work." Once a cop, once married with a family until alcoholism took everyone away, Ross is a gray ghost who's pretty much given up carrying a gun because he fears he's become a danger to himself.

After a brief prologue that outlines the start of his involvement with married movie stars Jack and Catherine Ames (Hackman and Sarandon), their daughter Mel (Reese Witherspoon) and her boyfriend Jeff (Liev Schreiber), the present finds Harry still living at the Ames' house, doing errands and making himself generally useful.

"Twilight's" plot proper begins with a classic film noir line: Jack, who's dying of cancer, hands Harry a package and says, "Give this to a woman named Gloria Lamarr." That's the kind of nominally simple instruction that is fated to lead to all kinds of unforeseen complications, and it does.

What that task does at first is reinvolve Harry with numerous people from his past, including a fellow private eye (Garner), an old flame (Stockard Channing) and a man who may or may not have been a partner (Giancarlo Esposito).

Then things get more serious. Decades-old secrets spill out, murder and blackmail take center stage, and Harry is forced to watch as "people run out of the little bit of luck they have."

While this sounds involving enough, in fact, involving enough is just what it isn't. "Twilight's" sense of relaxation may be an asset at first, but the film. is finally so relaxed it's almost not there. The story line and certain key characterizations (especially Sarandon's Catherine Ames) are too predictable and unconvincing, and there is a lack of energy, of punch, about the whole project that is fatal. If geezer noir is going to catch on, pacemakers are going to have to become standard issue from now on.

NEW YORK POST, 3/6/98, p. 46, Thelma Adams

Even smog looks beautiful at "Twilight," reflecting the last shards of an L.A. sunset.

In Robert Benton's shambling shamus story, the "Nobody's Fool" director reunites with Paul Newman and co-writer Richard Russo. Together, they celebrate life at the far end of the underpass, the wry consolations of age in the shadow of a youth-worshiping culture.

In "Twilight," Newman glows as Harry Ross. A self-described policeman-turned-private detective-turned-drunk, Ross tumbles over an unsolved "suicide" while cleaning up domestic messes for Hollywood's favorite couple: actors Catherine (Susan Sarandon) and Jack Ames (Gene Hackman).

The "suicide" was Catherine's ex-husband—and the body won't stay buried. Along the way, Newman exchanges barbs with nymphet Mel Ames (Reese Witherspoon), old flame Verna (Stockard Channing), fellow P.I. Raymond Hope (James Garner) and loser lover Jeff Willis (the ubiquitous Liev Schreiber).

"Do you expect anybody to believe this?" Verna's policewoman asks Ross after he tells his version of a messy double murder. Not really. The plot holds water better than a California mudslide—but not much better. The pleasure here is watching great actors in their mellowed primes enjoying the hell out of each others company. Newman is stiff-spined with age and slow on the trigger. His eyelids may droop, but they fall over eyes as clear and sharp as "Hud"'s Newman. The actor is in complete charge as his character falls out of orbit under the spell of Sarandon's serene, vaguely melancholy, siren.

Hackman contributes a portrait of cancerous menace basking in privilege. He's a big man used to getting his way and leaving other people to sweep up. Garner, as always, makes controlled casualness seem easy when it's not. The wonderful Channing has a touch of Liza Minnelli; she's a hard-edged softie who grounds every scene she's in.

Director Benton embraces Los Angeles, from its smoggy panoramas to its shoddy canyon-side shacks. Likewise, he gives each character his due: The haves bury the have-nots and the suckers take the bullets, while the lonely detective has no more to his name than a cheap suitcase, a gun, a linen suit and the respect of the last dame in town.

At "Twilight," in Benton's Hollywood Hills, Raymond Chandler meets "The Rockford Files." Despite Elmer Bernstein's grand score, it's not high art, but it's highly entertaining.

NEWSDAY, 3/6/98, Part II/p. B2, Jack Mathews

As Robert Benton's "Twilight" begins to unfold, my first impression is that the film is outrageously over-cast. Paul Newman, Gene Hackman and Susan Sarandon, veteran stars with a combined 18 Oscar nominations, playing the. principals of a detective story that seems as thin and familiar as an episode of "Barnaby Jones"?

Soon after, I begin thinking it's not just over-cast, but badly miscast, as well. At 73, Newman is still a strikingly handsome man, but he does look his age, and from what we learn about his character Harry Ross' background, he must have been 20 years younger on paper.

Finally, as the subtler layers of Benton and Richard Russo's script are peeled back, to reveal a story that is as much about the past as the present, as much about old passions as new and as much about the characters' places in the world before than now, I realize the casting is as perfect as the title.

On the surface, "Twilight" is conventional detective fiction. Harry Ross, former Los Angeles cop and private eye, is drawn out of retirement by his old friend and onetime Hollywood acting great Jack Ames (Hackman). Harry, a recovered alcoholic who's broke and pretty much broken down, owes Jack a favor. Ever since rescuing Jack's reckless teenage daughter (Reese Witherspoon) from a thug with whom she'd ran off to Mexico, and catching a bullet in his leg for his trouble, Harry has been living rent-free above the garage of the Ames' art-deco house, the old Delores Del Rio place in the Hollywood Hills.

Now, it's time to pay the rent, Jack tells him, by way of delivering money to someone who's been blackmailing him. Added incentive: Jack has just learned he has terminal cancer and doesn't want to leave this baggage behind for his wife, Catherine (Sarandon), to deal with.

Harry reluctantly agrees, and after being nearly shot to death by a dying man he encounters at the drop point, is up to his ears in intrigue and betrayal and a 20-year-old murder that only the killer knew had occurred. And who is that? Jack? Catherine? Their old friend Raymond (James Garner), another retired cop, now living on an adjacent Hollywood hill?

There is nothing original or particularly compelling about this mystery. In fact, it is resolved in the mundane way of most contemporary thrillers. So, don't see it for that reason. Its appeal is in the characters themselves, and in the way these old pros—Benton and his cast—work together to create a dense, and convincing, emotional history.

Benton, of course, has plowed this ground before, with his superb 1977 "The Late Show," in which Art Carney played an aging detective trying to solve the murder of his old partner. Ross may be a version of that character, but he's made totally fresh by Newman's performance. Harry inhabits his twilight with a mixture of melancholy and hope, as if he'd arrived at this point in his life with more questions left than answered.

One of those questions is his relationship with Catherine, whom he's shared a mutual, if unconsummated, attraction ever since the three of them became friends. Now that Jack is sick and Catherine is vulnerable, temptation is a greater threat to their chummy triangle than ever.

The psychological tension among Harry, Jack and Catherine is far better delineated than the actions they take. It's as if Benton and Russo were writing on two levels, one using hack melodrama to counter mass audience resistance to geezer love, the other for those who'd find real drama in people having to re-evaluate themselves and their loyalties late in life.

"Twilight" is far from a great movie, but it has great style and a performance from Newman that shows that while his characters may have lost a step, he hasn't.

NEWSWEEK, 3/16/98, p. 72, Peter Plagens

A film-noir hero always has a few miles on him. He's been a cop, a husband, a drunk; now he's a private eye, a divorcé and a teetotaler. Going through that mill has given him the survivor's cynicism he needs in the viper pit of off-boulevard Los Angeles. But hey—holding a slip of paper at arm's length in order to read the address on it? Welcome to geezer noir.

In Robert Benton's "Twilight," Paul Newman—still flinty-handsome at 73—is world-weary shamus Harry Ross. Two years ago, he took a bullet in the upper thigh while extracting the underage daughter of faded movie star Jack Ames (Gene Hackman) from a Mexican tryst. He's still Jack's gofer, living on Jack's charity in Jack's house, in agonizing proximity to Jack's ripely beautiful wife, Catherine (Susan Sarandon), an actress a bit past her prime. She and Harry have eyes for each other, but because of their loyalty to Jack, they've never wound up together in the sack. Then Jack has Harry deliver a mysterious envelope of money. Harry gets shot at, kicked in the ribs and trundled into a police station as a murder suspect. Now he feels entitled to some affection from his boss's wife.

"Twilight" is all formula. Except for some exposed flesh and rude language, the same movie could have been made 50 years ago. But the formula works here because Benton doesn't pretend his movie is anything but an elegant homage. With James Garner as a studio fixer, you've got a male triumvirate who make up in grizzled stealth what they lack in quick reflexes. You've also got the greatest collection of phlegmy voices ever assembled in one movie: Newman sounds like he's gargling bullets. The women are formidable, too: the smoky Sarandon, Stockard Channing as the police lieutenant who always bails out Harry and Margo Martindale as a blowzy blackmailer self-described as having "mucho hair, mucho tits."

But the real central characters in "Twilight" are the classic modern houses used as locations for a story set in the present. Jack and Catherine's was built around 1930 by Cedric Gibbons (who designed the Oscar statuette) for Dolores Del Rio. Their desert hideaway is an unfinished Frank Lloyd Wright project, abandoned in 1946. And Garner's hillside nest is a John Lautner spaceship from the late '40s. As darkly photographed by Piotr Sobocinski, they're relics of a lost idealism, sad silhouettes against a setting sun. "Twilight" lets us pick their locks and move back in, if only for a couple of deliciously gritty hours.

SIGHT AND SOUND, 12/98, p. 63, Robin Dougherty

Puerto Vallarta, Mexico. Private eye Harry Ross—who narrates the story in flashbacks—has been assigned to locate 17-year-old Mel, who has run off with her boyfriend. He surprises the couple in their hotel room but is shot in the leg when Mel grabs his gun. Two years later, we find him living with Mel's parents, Jack and Catherine Ames, as a handyman in Southern California. Jack tells Harry that he's dying of cancer and asks him to deliver an envelope to a Gloria Lamar. Harry and Catherine make love and that night Jack has a heart attack. Jack survives, but things get stickier for Harry. Instead of finding Gloria Lamar, he walks in on another private eye dying of a gunshot wound in her apartment. Harry discovers the dead man had investigated the suicide of Catherine's first husband.

Meanwhile, he runs into his old friend ex-policeman Raymond Hope. Gloria Lamar arranges a rendezvous in which Harry is beaten up by Mel's former boyfriend. Harry tricks the boy into revealing the links between Gloria, Jack and Catherine. He confronts Jack, who denies killing Catherine's first husband. Harry realises Raymond Hope is the murderer. He kills him, then turns himself in.

Paul Newman has played con artists, outlaws, blowhards, cads and any number of alienated characters, but the one thing he's almost never been is a loser. Although he played an ambulance-chasing lawyer in *The Verdict* you never think that his low-life character is going to do anything but come out on top again.

However, in Robert Benton's *Twilight,* the *film noir* formula calls for someone who was never really on the top and may survive, but not in a heroic way. Perhaps once there was a time when Newman could have been convincingly washed-up and pathetic as Harry Ross, the burned-out private eye, but it's doubtful. As delightful as it is to watch the 73-year-old actor tangle with other Hollywood thoroughbreds such as Susan Sarandon, James Garner and Gene Hackman, all edging into the twilight of their own careers, eternal golden boy Newman feels miscast throughout.

The story is meant to be an essay on diminishing possibilities. Harry Ross describes himself as a man who was once a policeman, a father and a husband, then a private eye and finally a drunk. By the time we meet him he's even given up the bottle. He lives rent free—for reasons that never pan out into believable emotional truths—as a sort of handyman at the home of Jack and Catherine Ames. He's half in love with Catherine and she with him. Jack, an old friend, is now dying of cancer and Harry's agreement to Jack's last wish leads him to discover that his friend is being blackmailed.

Harry is meant to be impotent, in spirit if not in actuality (he and Catherine hit the sack early on). He refuses to carry a gun. A story going around says he took a bullet in the penis while trying to bring back Jack and Catherine's runaway daughter from Mexico. Newman's presence contradicts this notion, of course. Although the film's reversal of the traditional *noir* formula—in which the *femme fatale* destroys her husband for her lover—is intriguing, we're ultimately left wondering why Catherine would go for sickly Gene Hackman when there's such a vital house guest in the wings.

As with Newman, there's nothing diminished about the power of Los Angeles at dusk. Benton (who worked with Newman on *Nobody's Fool* and cinematographer Piotr Sobocinski capture its haunting moods, not to mention the near unbearably beautiful shades of chartreuse green and almost-poison red that infiltrate the evening sky in Southern California. But the effect is more cosy than threatening. That's especially true of the scenes shot in the canyon-top home of Raymond Hope, a classic 40s LA dwelling designed by John Lautner, a disciple of Frank Lloyd Wright's. Contemplating the outcome of Harry's visit to James Garner's whiskey-smooth Raymond, viewers won't want to wait for a shoot out. They'll want to pour themselves a drink and take in the view.

VILLAGE VOICE, 3/17/98, p. 64, Amy Taubin

Sorry, I know I should be on the side of a movie whose primary purpose is to prove that you can be incredibly glamorous and desirable and also maintain a sense of humor when you're over 70 (or at least you can if you're a guy and you've spent those 70-odd years being Paul Newman), but Robert Benton's *Twilight* is such a predictable though preposterous little L.A. murder story that I just can't buy any of it.

Yes, Newman, who finally figured out how to make use of the first rule of acting (that it's basically *re-acting)* sometime around *The Verdict* and has been mesmerizing on screen ever since, is thoroughly charming here as an ex-cop and down-on-his-luck private dick. I would have preferred him, though, to be a little less self-protective. I mean, what's the point of having a senior citizen in a sex scene if you're going to frame him from the collarbone up, thereby keeping the tired flesh out of the picture? As for the two other stars, Susan Sarandon and Gene Hackman, playing aging Hollywood royalty with a nasty secret to hide, they have nothing very much to do and very little screen time to do it in. At one point Sarandon is reduced to hurling crockery to prove that, you know, she has feelings too.

Also reviewed in:
CHICAGO TRIBUNE, 3/6/98, Friday/p. H, Michael Wilmington
NEW REPUBLIC, 3/30/98, p. 26, Stanley Kauffmann
NEW YORK TIMES, 3/6/98, p. E22, Janet Maslin
NEW YORKER, 3/16/98, p. 83, Anthony Lane
VARIETY, 3/2-8/98, p. 83, Todd McCarthy
WASHINGTON POST, 3/6/98, Friday/p. D7, Rita Kempley

TWO GIRLS AND A GUY

A Fox Searchlight Pictures release of an Edward R. Pressman production in association with Muse Productions. *Executive Producer:* Michael Mailer and Daniel Bigel. *Producer:* Edward R. Pressman and Chris Hanley. *Director:* James Toback. *Screenplay:* James Toback. *Director of Photography:* Barry Markowitz. *Editor:* Alan Oxman. *Music:* Barry Cole. *Choreographer:* Patricia Moreno. *Sound:* Bill Markle. *Sound Editor:* Bill Markle. *Casting:* Sheila Jaffe and Georgianne Walken. *Production Designer:* Kevin Thompson. *Set Decorator:* Alisa Grifo. *Costumes:* Renata Chaplynsky. *Make-up:* Meredith Soupios. *Stunt Coordinator:* Danny Aiello, Jr. *Running time:* 92 minutes. *MPAA Rating:* R.

CAST: Robert Downey, Jr. (Blake Allen); Heather Graham (Carla); Natasha Gregson Wagner (Lou); Angel David (Tommy); Frederique Van Der Wal (Carol).

LOS ANGELES TIMES, 4/24/98, Calendar/p. 16, Jack Mathews

[*The following review by Jack Mathews appeared in a slightly different form in* NEWSDAY, 4/24/98, Part II/p. B6.]

Any thorough collection of this decade's most bizarre movie moments will have to feature the scene from James Toback's "Two Girls and a Guy" in which star Robert Downey Jr. mocks and lectures himself with his face nearly pressed against a bathroom mirror.

For the minute or two that the scene lasts, Downey is a spectacle of psychological ruin. There's genuine self-hatred in his bulging, reddened face, a cry of desperation in his improvised dialogue and, when he holds a gun to his head, he seems nearly overcome by the desire to pull the trigger.

It's a weird and, in some ways, darkly funny scene. But what makes it truly bizarre is its context. Downey's character, Blake, is a New York actor vamping for time after being confronted by two girlfriends who've just discovered each other while waiting for him outside his SoHo apartment. Blake is embarrassed and temporarily flummoxed, but his guilt seizure in the bathroom is out of all proportion to that crisis.

We don't get the feeling we're watching Blake attacking Blake, for his deception. In fact, he's been doing a great job of rationalizing his behavior with Carla (Heather Graham) and Lou (Natasha Gregson Wagner). The only thing he seems to be upset about is getting caught. What we're really seeing is Downey attacking Downey, for deceiving himself. It's like a classic drug rant, and given Downey's admitted addictions at the time the film was shot, it has the unsettling air of voyeurism.

Toback, directing his first film in eight years, is not above exploiting an actor or an issue. From his brilliant debut film, "Fingers," about a mob henchman with secret ambitions to be a concert pianist, and his nervy expostulations about the meaning of life in his 1990 documentary "The Big Bang," Toback has been a provocative, in-your-face filmmaker.

With "Two Girls and a Guy," Toback was out to exploit Downey, whom he had directed in the 1987 "The Pick-Up Artist," from the beginning. He has told interviewers he got the idea for the movie when he saw the disheveled actor making a handcuffed court appearance on TV and wrote the script in a four-day creative frenzy. The film was shot in just 11 days, with Downey's intuition given free rein.

The result is a flawed tour de force, in a format that at times resembles experimental theater. It's one act, one setting, three characters and a flock of ideas about fidelity, monogamy, commitment and sexuality in the '90s. It starts with the streetwise, sharp-tongued Lou and the quietly confident Carla meeting outside, then breaking into Blake's apartment, where they compare their nearly identical notes about their relationships with him.

Then Blake returns from his two-week job-hunting trip to Los Angeles and, unaware that he has guests, begins calling the four important people in his life—Carla, Lou, his ailing mother and his agent—all the while entertaining a spirited interpretation of "Cum Sancto Spiritu" from Vivaldi's oratorio "Gloria." The immediate picture we get is of a man extremely pleased with himself.

That picture changes only marginally after the girlfriends reveal themselves, and the story accelerates from the amusingly angry and epithet-riddled confrontations to what plays as serious soul-searching. Toback is exploring several issues at once, but none of them very deeply. We come away from the story with little understanding of Blake, and even less of Carla and Lou. Given their initial outrage, their later confessions about their own infidelities are so off the wall, you might expect it all to be a vengeful put-on. Apparently not.

Toback, whose own Wilt Chamberlain-size sex life has been chronicled in magazines, seems to be revealing more of himself than of his characters. The film's heavily touted sex scene, some reciprocated oral sex between Blake and Carla in the shadows of his bedroom, is a near pornographic detour in the story, used to make Toback's point that despite the betrayal, anger and humiliation—or maybe because of them—lust reigns!

"Two Girls and a Guy" takes a lot of dubious side trips and ends with an event so unexpected it could have come from a different movie. Maybe if Toback had taken 11 days to write the script and four to shoot it, things would have worked out better. As it is, "Two Girls" is a small movie with some big moments and a lot of unfinished business.

NEW YORK, 5/4/98, p. 126, David Denby

D. H. Lawrence, describing his own practice, wrote in a letter to a friend that "the old stable ego" in fictional characters was gone, replaced by an ego that goes through allotropic states"—that is, variations so striking that the reader has some difficulty in recognizing that the character is, in fact, a single individual. I thought of this remark when watching Robert Downey Jr.'s performance in James Toback's *Two Girls and a Guy*, because Downey puts out a furious whirlwind of moods, denials, reversals, reinventions, all in the space of a couple of hours (the movie takes place in real time), and his triumph and his tragedy are that he is many persons inside one person.

At the beginning of *Two Girls and a Guy*, two young women (Heather Graham and Natasha Gregson Wagner) are waiting outside a SoHo loft for what turns out to be the same man. Each thinks she is the exclusive girlfriend of the young actor Blake (Downey), and each has been lied to. The two women break into Blake's loft and wait for him, Toback, who a decade ago made *The Pick-Up Artist*, also with Downey, shot the movie very cheaply and quickly (in eleven days), and some of the sound has the hollow tones of post-dubbing. Trying for revelation, Toback has moved in a little too close to his actresses and forced them to run through their lines under great pressure. For a while, the movie feels rushed and cramped, But when Downey enters, the camera backs off, and Downey fills the loft with his personality. Blake doesn't know the women are there, and as he enters, perfectly happy, he sings "Cum Sancto Spiritu" from Vivaldi's *Gloria*, jumping from the tenor to the bass line, then he telephones each woman and his mother and leaves messages for everyone. He sits down at the piano and sings a torch song.

The women come out of hiding, jump all over him, and he lies and retreats. His defense is that he's telling an actor's truth in sexual relationships—he can be whatever he needs to be; therefore, he means what he says when he tells each woman that he loves her. This is nonsense, of course, but it's very revealing of Downey himself, for this is the same Robert Downey who is both a highly creative actor and a heroin addict passing in and out of rehab and jail. Downey can speak soberly of his guilt in court and jokingly of his impending doom to a friend. His identity isn't stable enough to allow him to claim life for himself. In the movie, he glares at himself in a mirror, pulling his features into a grotesque mask, and runs through Hamlet's confrontation with his mother. It appears to be Toback's idea that Blake is too much his mother's son to love any woman, but the psychologizing and the back-and-forth arguments about monogamy and betrayal are less interesting than Downey's moment-by-moment destruction and re-creation of himself. *Two Girls and a Guy* isn't a satisfying movie, but Downey is alarmingly brilliant in it—a man locked in torment who can't find the way out. Let's pray this isn't one of his last performances.

NEW YORK POST, 4/24/98, p. 49, Thelma Adams

There's a potent moment in "Two Girls and a Guy" when actor Robert Downey Jr. stares himself down in a bathroom mirror.

Is Downey wondering how such a talented guy landed in jail among the switchblade set?

Maybe. Downey, as Manhattan actor Blake, looks into the mirror and says: "Stop deceiving yourself."

The image is striking: The mirror reflects fake blood on Blake's face (makeup for a mock suicide). His 5 o'clock shadow is heading toward 10. He looks like the devil, Lucifer, literally.

Director James Toback ("The Pick-Up Artist") rips away Downey's veneer. What do we find? More veneer. The scene is a flashy actor's piece, but it works.

Meanwhile, outside the bathroom of Blake's inherited down-town loft, the two "girls" (this is post-feminism, baby) pace and bond.

Spunky brunette Lou (Natasha Gregson Wagner) is a swinging '90s Gidget. Carla (Heather Graham) has Botticelli angel looks but very earthly desires—and this is New York, not the City of Angels.

Both women thought they'd surprise boyfriend Blake by meeting him at his loft. On the stoop they met each other. Holy monogamy!

Now, Lou and Carla have to decide whether to stand by their man, grill him, or launch a threesome.

"Two Girls and a Guy" is a randy "No Exit." Within the lavish loft, the trio bicker peel away layers of self and clothing, lie, get drunk, get real.

Wagner, a daughter of Natalie Wood, is as wooden as her mother was. But her tinny voice and awkward, frozen-pelvis attempts at dirty dancing make Lou so vulnerable beneath her spiky bravado.

Graham bared all—on skates—in "Boogie Nights" and got "Lost in Space." Here, she gives Uma and Gwyneth a ride for their money; like Michelle Pfeiffer and Jessica Lange, she's a blonde who can act.

As for Downey, he's no role model, but this jailbird can act. He energizes an economical movie that's contemporary, funny, hot—and packs an emotional punch.

NEWSWEEK, 4/27/98, p. 73, David Ansen

Curled back against the wall, like a trapped bear cub surrounded by lionesses, Blake Allen (Robert Downey Jr.), a struggling New York actor, is desperately trying to stave off a hailstorm of verbal abuse. Everyone is screaming. Rude, angry, obscene accusations fill the air. The attackers are Carla (Heather Graham) and Lou (Natasha Gregson Wagner). An hour earlier, standing on the stoop of Blake's New York loft at the start of "Two Girls and a Guy," these two strangers discovered they were both waiting for the same boyfriend. The duplicitous Blake had been seeing each of them three days a week, using the same lines to profess his undying love. Now, having broken into his loft to await his return, they are giving their stunned lover one hell of a surprise party.

James Toback's scorching, thoroughly unformulaic comedy takes place almost entirely in real time, in one location, among these three people. It is more than enough. "Two Girls and a Guy" works the edgy, abrasive, dangerously erotic territory that "bad boy" writer-director Toback covered in such movies as "Fingers" and "Exposed." But where those movies sometimes confused posturing with profundity, "Two Girls" shows Toback at his best—still a provocateur, but his edginess now balanced by humor and even sweetness. In this hothouse chamber piece, Toback wants us to chew on the messy romantic and sexual dilemmas that plague modem relationships. Monogamy vs. promiscuity. Honesty vs. deception. How to reconcile one's dueling appetites for sexual experimentation and commitment, adventure and permanence? His smart, raunchy movie offers no answers (how could it?), but it poses its questions with painfully hilarious honesty.

Blake seems constitutionally incapable of honesty. As Downey plays him, he's a charming narcissist, a slippery chameleon, his boyish vulnerability an open invitation for women to mother him. Downey is sensational—few actors could make Blake so simultaneously funny, appalling and appealing. Wagner (daughter of Natalie Wood), who plays the spunky, motormouthed Lou, and Graham (so good in "Boogie Nights" as Rollergirl), as the sophisticated, sexy Carla, are every bit his match. It turns out they have their own surprising notions—and secrets—about sex and the varieties of romantic experience. How refreshing to encounter a movie that doesn't fit into Hollywood's cookie-cutter categories. This guy, these girls, this movie, are one of a kind.

SIGHT AND SOUND, 2/99, p. 57, Liese Spencer

Two women, Lou and Carla, stand outside a Manhattan apartment each hoping to surprise her actor boyfriend on his return from a trip to Los Angeles. Lou starts chatting to Carla. As they talk it becomes clear that both women are seeing the same man. Lou breaks into the apartment and lets Carla in. Together they wait for Blake to return and compare notes. Through the window, the women see him arrive by taxi and hide. Blake comes into the apartment and leaves loving phone messages for both women. He plays the piano, phones his mother and his agent. Carla reveals herself and cryptically confronts him over his fidelity. Lou emerges and the women ask him how long he has been two-timing them. He has been seeing both women for three days a week each, claiming to visit his ill mother on the other days. Blake goes into the bathroom and pretends to commit suicide using a fake gun. As the day progresses Blake makes repeated calls to his mother, and phones the doctor to express his anxiety over her health. Lou and Carla drink Tequila together. Carla and Blake have sex. Carla and Lou reveal they have both been Unfaithful to Blake. Lou suggests a *ménage à trois,* is rejected and leaves, giving Carla her phone number. Some time later. Blake and Carla phone an undertaker to make arrangements for his mother's funeral.

In 1987, Robert Downey Jr played a compulsive womaniser in James Toback's sunny romantic comedy *The Pick-Up Artist.* Over a decade later, actor and writer/director return to the same territory in *Two Girls and a Guy,* which sees Downey essaying the role of Blake Allen, a duplicitous cad cornered by the women he's two timing and made to squirm under the spotlight of their dual interrogation. On the face of it, the film profiles a daring love triangle (a moderately raunchy sex scene between Downey and co-star Heather Graham Learly cost the film a N-17 rating in the US.) In fact, it's an old-fashioned romance between a director and his star. After *The Pick-Up Artist,* Toback has said that he was left feeling they could do something "far bolder". According to the director, after seeing Downey in handcuffs on his way to prison, he knew he was "ready", and wrote him this vehicle.

A more sombre and dramatic treatment of infidelity than their former collaboration, *Two Girls and a Guy* plays on the off-screen notoriety of both director and star. Toback is a legendary womaniser, Downey a talent tarnished by drug addiction. As it details Blake's feints and evasions, his vanity, aggression and sophistry, Toback's merciless portrait of male selfishness seems an act of contrition from two ex-hellraisers.

In fact, the film is not so much a critique of male narcissism as a product of it. When he wrote him the role, Toback may have believed he was modelling the feckless Blake on Downey (it's certainly impossible not to view Blake's smug amorality and little-boy charm in a harshly ironic light given Downey's history), but the character is closer to his own. What's more, despite its acute observation, Toback's film is less an apology than a celebration of the romantic, male egotist. Sure Blake is weak and ridiculous while the women are strong and dignified, but the bottom line is that they (and we) are supposed to forgive Blake because he's charming. Whether you do or not depends largely on whether you're prepared to indulge Downey as much as Toback. As Blake, Downey proves he has *chutzpah* to spare, but some may still find it hard to understand why two beautiful and intelligent women would be competing for his wheedling mummy's boy.

In a way, Downey's camp performance fits perfectly with the exaggerated, theatrical tone of this obsessive little melodrama. A three-hander set largely in real time, Toback's densely written chamber piece is described by producer Ed Pressman as a "post-romantic" comedy. For Toback it was clearly conceived as a Serious Entertainment, his staccato script rapping out a self-consciously clever anatomy of modern relationships which veers between cerebral farce, emotional bombast (in one scene Blake recites *Hamlet* to underline his Oedipal relationship with his mother) and giddy implausibility.

Powered by Toback's fizzing dialogue and strong performances from all three stars (Heather Graham's cool Carla and Natasha Wagner's streetwise Lou prove more than a match for Downey's showboating charisma), the film sustains its comedy of ideas surprisingly well, working best in a light, comic register. "I'm talking about Mormonism," Wagner's Lou says earnestly, when hinting at a *ménage a trois*. "I think you mean bigamy," Blake replies.

But somewhere along the line the dramatic tension evaporates. Listening to Toback's solipsistic characters relentlessly chewing over their desires becomes an enervating, confessional experience. In the end, *Two Girls and a Guy* is a bit like watching a cross between a Harvard student review and a highbrow edition of *Oprah* with studio sofas replaced by the Japanese-style screens of a fashionable SoHo loft.

TIME, 4/27/98, p. 68, Richard Schickel

He sings chorales, declaims a scene from *Hamlet* and very persuasively fakes a suicide. He is a dutiful son and a shameless stud, a romantic egotist and sometimes a little boy lost. Few movies offer a performer the opportunity to let his talents cascade forth in the breathless rush that *Two Girls and a Guy* provides Robert Downey Jr.

Except that "movie" doesn't seem quite the right term for it. At best, it's a rather murkily photographed one-act play, confined to a single setting and to real time by writer-director James Toback. Indeed, if he had developed his situation—two girls discover that their guy has been blithely having his way with both of them simultaneously—he might have given us a chic, updated version of one of those old-fashioned farces that once upon a time regaled Broadway.

But Toback is a rather serious and self-conscious fellow. So, after a perky start, his work turns into a meandering wrangle. He flirts with a semidaring resolution—a cozy little ménage à trois—but doesn't quite have the gumption to go there. Instead, he lurches into a darkness that contains the promise of redemption (or at least responsible adulthood) for his wayward protagonist. We don't believe it for a second. We do, however, believe in the talent of his actors. The vengeful women—a coolly elegant Heather Graham and a flat-voiced, sharp-minded Natasha Gregson Wagner—are more than mere accompanists to Downey's tour de force; they're full-scale partners, finding arresting dissonances in this unfinished chamber piece.

VILLAGE VOICE, 5/5/98, p. 128, Gary Dauphin

In Jerry Springer America, the triangle is a common graph of human sexuality, not so new carnal math that leaves a potty-mouthed chatfest like *Two Girls and a Guy* teetering on the thin line between energetically out there and gratingly crappy. Confined to one set and babbling mostly in real time, the film's marquee trio is composed of the pretty nine-to-fiver Carla (semi-I Girl Heather Graham), short-haired Downtown chick Lou (Hollywood princess Natasha Gregson Wagner), and Blake, a messy actor who's been bedding the two women (everyone's favorite fuckup Robert Downey Jr.).

Carla and Lou meet accidentally outside Blake's loft, leading to 90 minutes of accusations, confessions, and momentary curiosities that sink without a trace in the murkiness of writer-director James Tobacks aggressively random script. There are some high points. Downey's character is uncannily indistinguishable from junk-media portrayals of Downey himself, and the flick's incessant chatter is occasionally lifted by sudden gusts of weird cross talk. But Blake has no discernible defense or depth beyond Downey's biography, and the women are at best cutouts designed to linger in the frame until what are essentially last-reel cum shots; Carla partaking in an absurd, inexplicable sex scene and Lou disappearing into pat, grinning intimations of kinkiness. The simple fact is that *The Jerry Springer Show* really does do this better five days a week, and with significantly fewer pretensions.

Also reviewed in:
NEW YORK TIMES, 4/24/98, p. E12, Janet Maslin
NEW YORKER, 4/27 & 5/4/98, p. 166, Anthony Lane

VARIETY, 9/1-7/97, p. 77, Todd McCarthy
WASHINGTON POST, 4/24/98, p. B5, Rita Kempley
WASHINGTON POST, 4/24/98, Weekend/p. 56, Michael O'Sullivan

U.S. MARSHALS

A Warner Bros. release of a Kopelson Entertainment/Keith Barish production. *Executive Producer:* Roy Huggins and Keith Barish. *Producer:* Arnold Kopelson and Anne Kopelson. *Director:* Stuart Baird. *Screenplay:* John Pogue. *Based on characters created by:* Roy Huggins. *Director of Photography:* Andrzej Bartowiak. *Editor:* Terrry Rawlings. *Music:* Jerry Goldsmith. *Music Editor:* Kenny Hall. *Sound:* Scott Smith and (music) Bruce Botnick. *Sound Editor:* John Leveque. *Casting:* Amanda Mackey Johnson and Cathy Sandrich. *Production Designer:* Maher Ahmad. *Art Director:* Bruce Alan Miller and Mark Worthington. *Set Designer:* Kerry Sanders, Richard Fernandez, Randall Richards, and David Tanenbaum. *Set Decorator:* Gene Serdena. *Special Effects:* Michael Meinardus and Richard Helmer. *Costumes:* Louise Frogley. *Make-up:* June Westmore. *Stunt Coordinator:* Gary Davis and Dick Ziker. *Running time:* 105 minutes. *MPAA Rating:* PG-13.

CAST: Tommy Lee Jones (Chief Deputy Marshal Samuel Gerard); Wesley Snipes (Mark Sheridan); Robert Downey, Jr. (John Royce); Joe Pantoliano (Deputy Marshal Cosmo Renfro); Daniel Roebuck (Deputy Marshal Biggs); Tom Wood (Deputy Marshal Newman); LaTanya Richardson (Deputy Marshal Cooper); Irène Jacob (Marie); Kate Nelligan (US Marshal Walsh); Patrick Malahide (Lamb); Rick Snyder (Barrows); Michael Paul Chan (Chen); Johnny Lee Davenport (Deputy Henry); Donald Li (Detective Kim); Marc Vann (Deputy Jackson); Michael Guido (Distracted Driver); Robert Mohler (Young Cop); Richard Lexsee (Fireman); Dado (Female Cop); Karen Vaccaro (Hospital Cashier); David Kersnar (Desk Sergeant); Tony Fitzpatrick (Greg Conroy); Don Gibb (Mike Conroy); Cynthia S. Baker (Mama Conroy); Susan Hart (Greg's Girlfriend); Vaitiare Bandera (Stacia Vela); Don Herion (Detective Caldwell); Len Bajenski (Deputy Hollander); Matt Decaro (Deputy Stern); Thomas Rosales, Jr. (727 Prisoner); James Sie (Ling); Christian Payton (1st 727 Deputy); Steve King (727 Pilot); Tracy Letts (Sheriff Poe); Mark Morettini (1st Cop); Kent Reed (Trooper with Dogs); Ray Toler (Earl); Brenda Pickleman (Martha); Max Maxwell (Roadblock Trooper); Peter Burns (State Trooper Captain); Roy Hytower (Tracker); Ian Barford (Royce's Guide); Robert Kurez (Kidnapped Man); Rose M. Abdoo (Donna); Lorenzo Clemons (Stark); Stephen A. Cinabro (Undercover Deputy); Clifford T. Frazier (Minister); Mindy Bell (Deputy Holt); Richard Thomsen (Doorman); Yasen Peyanikov (Janitor); Meg Thalken (Saks Saleswoman); Lennox Brown (Man in Green Cap); Varen Black (Network Reporter); Ammar Daraiseh (Drugstore Clerk); Romanos Isaac (Ship's First Officer); Richard Pickren (Prosecutor); Lynn Wilde (Caldwell's Wife); Amy E. Jacobson (New York Reporter); Cliff Teinert (Swamp Tracker); Ellen Hearn (4th Reporter); Janet Contursi (Chicago Nurse); George J. Hynek, Jr. and Wendell Thomas (New York Paramedics); E. Glenn Ward, Jr. and Marie Ware (Elderly Residents); Rick Lefevour (10th Deputy); Jim Fierro (6th Deputy); Michael Braun (727 Co-Pilot); Perry D. Sullivan (727 Navigator); Terry G. Rochford (NTSB Agent); Tony Paris (Newman's Guide); Ed Fernandez and Richard Wilkie (Detectives); Rick Edwards (7th 727 Deputy); Dale Chick Bernhardt (Royce's Guide); Tressana Alouane (Mike's Girlfriend); Ralph J. Lucci (Bartender); Louis Young (3rd Reporter); David A. Bales (Man in Taxi); Vince DeMentri (Reporter); Chris Bean (Bar Patron).

LOS ANGELES TIMES, 3/6/98, Calendar/p. 10, John Anderson

[The following review by John Anderson appeared in a slightly different form in NEWSDAY, 3/6/98, Part II/p. B7.]

Warner Bros., which probably knows what it feels like to be persecuted and unloved (especially after a year like last year), has put its waning hopes and diminished expectations behind traditional values—one, at any rate: When in doubt, find an idea that has already worked and beat it to death. Then, blow it up.

The idea is "The Fugitive," itself a remake of a TV show, but one that Andrew Davis' direction, Harrison Ford's stolid dignity and Tommy Lee Jones' gruff charm made into a first-rate entertainment. Jones won an Oscar, and it was a popular choice. So popular that he now has his own movie, "U.S. Marshals," in which every subtle aspect of the original has been taken to its seemingly inevitable extreme.

It starts typically/topically enough, with a truck-car wreck in Chicago caused by a cigar-chomping exec talking on his car phone (that he's not a soccer mom can no doubt be credited to the studio's market-research department). The truck driver with the bad luck is Mark Sheridan (Wesley Snipes), who's wanted on a federal arrest warrant for killing several federal agents back in New York. The U.S. marshal leading the pursuit after Sheridan becomes—gasp!—a fugitive, is Sam Gerard (Jones).

The initial escape is like something out of "Con Air"—and "Turbulence" and "Die Hard 2" and "Air Force One" and maybe even "Airplane!": a jumbo jet full of convicts crash-landing, sliding down a hillside into a lake, flipping over and sinking. All prisoners accounted for, sir, except the ruthless, cruel, heartless assassin Mark Sheridan.

But, of course, he's not ruthless and cruel. He's a really nice guy, says his girlfriend (Irene Jacob, in a truly awful performance), and Gerard himself can't quite figure out why, if Sheridan is so ruthless, he hasn't killed any of the Jerry Springer refugees he's taken hostage on his very successful flight to freedom.

Along with those doubts, Gerard has been given "help" in the person of State Department agent John Royce (Robert Downey Jr., who you'd think had enough problems). Gerard doesn't like him, but Royce does provide a foil ("Get yourself a Glock and get rid of that nickel-plated sissy pistol," Gerard says, demeaning both his artillery and his manhood). And he provides a distraction from the precious interplay of Gerard's regular team of deputies, all "Fugitive" veterans, including Joe Pantoliano, who seems to be morphing into Garry Marshall.

As the chase goes on—and on—the most irritating thing about "U.S. Marshals" is the sense that it's a movie-by-committee, that every line and every aerial shot is calculated to seduce, through a sense of either deja vu or how much money is being lavished on screen. So, ultimately, it's a trade-off. Go see it. But you'll feel cheap in the morning.

NEW YORK POST, 3/6/98, p. 41, Rod Dreher

There's a big Harrison Ford-sized hole in "U.S. Marshals," the tepid, overlong and somewhat confusing follow-up to 1993's terrific "The Fugitive."

Tommy Lee Jones returns in his Oscar-winning role as Sam Gerard, the relentless federal agent who this time out bird-dogs Wesley Snipes halfway across the country. If this catch-as-catch-can rehash of "The Fugitive" proves anything, it's that Jones is a lot more fun to watch driving Ford.

That's not exactly fair to Snipes, who does what he can to bring juice to a poorly conceived, underwritten role. Actually, "Fugitive" screenwriters Jeb Stuart and David Twohy are even more acutely missed than is Ford.

The ingenious plotting and compelling characterizations that helped the first film transcend mere thrillerdom have disappeared with nary a trace in John Pogue's ho-hum effort, which plays like a pallid retread of its predecessor.

So "U.S. Marshals" suffers by comparison—what chase movie wouldn't? The film stands only shakily on its own. It's the kind of lazy potboiler that stretches the action out by having the characters behave illogically at crucial junctures, and act on "How-did-they-know-that?" information. (Jones isn't only brainy, he's apparently clairvoyant.)

You want to yell out advice to the characters, but by the time the story starts to rip irreparably at the seams, you're beyond caring how it ends, just as long as it does.

On the bright side, the likable Jones is back as the driven lawman who always gets his man. In this case, it's Mark Sheridan (Snipes), a Chicago tow-truck driver who is drawn into a conspiracy involving espionage and the murder of two federal agents in New York City.

A hit job against Sheridan goes awry on a prison air transport to the Big Apple, causing the plane to crash spectacularly—"Fugitive" fans will marvel at what a shameless rip-off this sequence is—and Sheridan slips away in the confusion.

Fellow passenger Gerard has to suffer the wreck, the flight of his prisoner, and, along with us, the gratuitous abuse of the "Fly the friendly skies" slogan not once, but twice in Pogue's imagination deprived script.

A piqued Gerard assembles his colorless buddy-movie team and sets out through the swamp after the fugitive Sheridan. Gerard's boss (Kate Nelligan) presses on him the services of John Royce (Robert Downey Jr.), a special agent of dubious skill and trustworthiness.

"You're sure you wanna get cute with me?" Jones hisses at Downey. As a matter of fact, Tommy Lee, we'd like that. The film flirts with the comic possibilities inherent in these actors' clash of styles—Downey's oily, smirking urbanity versus Jones' vinegary, tough-guy cool—but never follows through.

This sort of inattention to the human facets of the story mires "U.S. Marshals" in a formulaic funk.

What made "The Fugitive" so emotionally absorbing was the tragic death-grip relationship between Ford and Jones, who both played strongly delineated, sympathetic characters. Though Jones is in fine flinty form in reprise, he has nothing to strike against; hence, no sparks.

There's little pathos between pursuer and pursued in "U.S. Marshals" because, for all his huffing and puffing, Snipes remains a maddeningly opaque figure throughout the film. Tom and Jerry are a more psychologically intriguing cat-and-mouse duo, and "U.S. Marshals" exhausts itself long before Snipes stops running.

SIGHT AND SOUND, 6/98, p. 58, Liese Spencer

In Chicago, police arrest Mark Roberts and put him on a convicts' plane to New York. also on board is US Marshal Samuel Gerard. When a fellow prisoner attempts to shoot Roberts, he breaks a window, causing the plane to crash in the Ohio river. Roberts escapes. Gerard discovers 'Roberts' is actually Mark Sheridan, an ex-CIA operative. Sheridan is wanted for the murder of two Secret Service men and suspected of passing information to a Chinese spy ring.

Gerard is forced to accept CIA agent John Royce on to his team. Tracking Sheridan to New York Gerard and his team also trace the man who planted the gun on the plane, but he is killed by a Chinese agent named Chen. Gerard realises Sheridan has been framed. Gerard and his team pursue Chen and Sheridan around New York, capturing Chen and cornering Sheridan. Royce tries to kill him, but is interrupted by Marshal Newman whom he kills, blaming Sheridan. Finally capturing Sheridan, Gerard guards his fugitive in hospital alongside Royce. There he realises that Royce murdered Newman, and is trying to kill Sheridan to protect his spy ring. When Royce tries to shoot Gerard, the Marshal kills him.

In this redundant sequel to *The Fugitive*, Tommy Lee Jones returns to the role of Marshal Sam Gerard. This time he's chasing Wesley Snipes' former CIA agent, but if the fugitive has changed, the formula remains the same. Stripped of all but the most functional emotion, the film's complex espionage story seems incidental to its string of action sequences. The most spectacular of these comes early in the film, as the convict plane crashes into the Ohio river. After cutting his teeth on the airborne thriller *Executive Decision*, Stuart Baird wrings maximum suspense from his set piece. Moving stealthily from becalmed security fetishism to panicked cuts between the cabin, the sucking hole in the aircrafts side and a guard's coronary, Baird shows the plane ploughing on to a road where it snaps telegraph poles like twigs before coming to an eerie rest underwater.

After a quick head count of survivors, Jones' Gerard growls the catchphrase, "We have a fugitive", and it's back to business as usual. Pins are put on maps, murders pinned on fall guys. The only difference is, of course, that with Jones promoted to the lead, our sympathies are reversed. While he is certainly charismatic enough to carry the film, the emphasis on his Marshal has a strangely unbalancing effect on the film's narrative, like a sequel to *Thelma & Louise* centred on Harvey Keitel's cop.

With a token black woman joining Gerard's team, time is squandered sketching the characters of the deputies rather than developing Snipes' character. Indeed, so cursory is Snipes' romance, and so professional his survival, that he remains a cipher. Instead of a nightmarish game of cat and mouse between individual and state, the film comes to resemble a training film for the US Marshals, with the emphasis on Gerard's managerial skills as he delegates his deputies, encourages his youngest recruit and motivates everyone with his own commitment.

This is not to say that Jones does not make an attractive star: the film has fun sending up his intense persona, dressing him up in a giant chicken costume and later slipping him into a fetching shellsuit. But these gags merely highlight the way the film prioritises Jones' personality over clearly constructed suspense. If there was a certain thrill in the way *The Fugitive* pared down the action formula to one long chase sequence, that pleasure is missing in a sequel which manages to be both obvious and over-plotted.

As an ex-editor of the *Lethal Weapon* films, Baird initially succeeds in pushing the action on while cutting swiftly between a panoply of locations and characters, but in the crucial closing chase sequences he loses pace. After a dull diversion into a graveyard, he belatedly sets up what should be the most breathtaking stunt in the movie. Sadly, Snipes' rooftop Tarzan swing falls flat after Harrison Ford's dam jump, leaving you waiting for the film to tie up its tedious loose ends and reach its predictable finish. When it does, Tommy and his gang of Marshals pile back into their land cruiser looking for all the world like the A-Team, a worrying indication of where this franchise might be going.

VILLAGE VOICE, 3/17/98, p. 59, Gary Dauphin

Harrison Ford is gone, as is the tireless quest for truth, justice, and the one-armed man, but Tommy Lee Jones is forever. When Warners turned *The Fugitive* into a Jones-anchored franchise, they also reimposed the small-screen frame. *U.S. Marshals,* an inflated cop show with Wesley Snipes as this year's guest star, churns out one tautly effective action-movie absurdity after another, but this is still nothing you wouldn't find in a two-hour special episode of *The Pretender,* or maybe *La Femme Nikita.*

Here the innocent-man-on-the-run gambit goes geopolitical, Snipes playing a mysteriously capable fugitive accused of a double murder in the shadow of the United Nations. As before, the film's arc involves the slow dawning of a clue on Jones's craggy features (his range is confined to the small space between pained and maniacal, two timbres Jones fortunately does well). Gerard seems to know early on that his man isn't guilty but he's on him like a hound-dog anyway, the two connected by an invisible rubber band snapping back together via a lucky fingerprint or stakeout whenever the gap between them gets too big. There's also an added spy-jinks frame here to raise the usual gun-and-run stakes (everyone from Chinese intelligence to the State Department is after Snipes) and give Snipes a chance to play technophilic superman. Director Stuart Baird provides his boys with enough toys and running room to make *Marshals* as easily digestible as it is forgettable, but the film's predictable, money-maker format weighs it down from the start. *Marshals* isn't half over before you start imagining the next entry in the franchise, Jones already chasing Chris Tucker from here to the Blockbuster video shelf.

Also reviewed in:
CHICAGO TRIBUNE, 3/6/98, Friday/p. A, Michael Wilmington
NEW YORK TIMES, 3/6/98, p. E27, Stephen Holden
VARIETY, 3/2-8/98, p. 83, Emanuel Levy
WASHINGTON POST, 3/6/98, Weekend/p. 51, Desson Howe

UGLY, THE

A Trimark Pictures release of an Essential Films production in association with the New Zealand Film Commission. *Producer:* Jonathan Dowling. *Director:* Scott Reynolds. *Screenplay:* Scott Reynolds. *Director of Photography:* Simon Raby. *Editor:* Wayne Cook. *Music:* Victoria Kelly. *Sound:* Dick Reade, Michael Hedges, John Boswell, and (music) Nigel Stone. *Casting:* Gaye Donnellan and Maura Fay. *Production Designer:* Grant Major. *Art Director:* Gary Mackay. *Costumes:* Emily Carter. *Make-up:* Dominie Till. *Stunt Coordinator:* Sam Williams. *Running time:* 92 minutes. *MPAA Rating:* Not Rated.

CAST: Paolo Rotondo (Simon Cartwright); Rebecca Hobbs (Dr. Karen Schumaker); Roy Ward (Dr. Marlowe); Vanessa Byrnes (Julie, Age 25); Sam Wallace (Simon, Age 13); Paul Glover (Phillip); Chris Graham (Robert); Jennifer Ward-Lealand (Evelyn, Simon's Mother); Darien Takle (Marge); Cath McWhirter (Helen Ann Millar); Carolyn Beaver (Helen's Friend); Caelem Pope (Simon, Age 4); Finn Johnsen, Phillip Brown, and Tau Luke (Future Cops); Tim Barlow (Police Photographer); Aaron Buskin (Roland); John Steemson and Oliver Hodges (Bullies); Beth Allen (Julie, Age 13); Chris Bailey (Ed Daley); Gary Mackay (Man in Park); Steve Hall and Shane Bessant (Worker Thugs); Katrina Browne (Woman in the Floral Dress); Yvonne Dudman (Melinda Jackson); Hugh D'Calveley (Victim in Alleyway); Sara Pivac (Deaf Girl); Jon Brazier (Frank, the Vet); Michael Dwyer (Alex); David Baxter (Clive).

LOS ANGELES TIMES, 5/15/98, Calendar/p. 11, John Anderson

[The following review by John Anderson appeared in a slightly different form in NEWSDAY, 5/1/98, Part II/p. B6.]

Besides being an object lesson in what not to name one's film, "The Ugly" also serves to make one appreciate the subtle relationship between—and value of—understated camera work and true film horror. Lacking either, "The Ugly" really makes you miss them.

New Zealander Scott Reynolds' debut feature is also so full of false alarms—killings that take place, ex post facto, only in a character's mind, for instance—and so much machine-gun cutting and disco strobe-light accessorizing that you're never quite sure where you are or why.

Reynolds even has the nerve, after showing us institutionalized serial killer Simon Cartwright (Paolo Rotondo) cutting the throat of psycho-specialist Dr. Karen Schumaker (Rebecca Hobbs), to do the whole counterfeit killing over again immediately. After a while, this kind of bait and switch gets tiresome.

Even more tiresome than the uninspired script and hysterical acting of Rotondo and Hobbs, who for most of the movie face off in an interrogation room and let Simon's reign of terror play out in flashback. Dr. Schumaker, who has been called in to assess Simon's treatment—by a hospital staff that consists entirely of two Neanderthal attendants and the Grand Guignol-esque Dr. Marlowe (Roy Ward)—simply can't fathom Simon's urge to eviscerate, which comes from the voices he hears and the grotesque, shrouded, bleeding figures he sees. He's not the only one.

Simon's childhood was very painful. He was dyslexic, kids picked on him, his mother was a cross between Mrs. Danvers and Nurse Ratched—but to use any of these things as an alibi, or even a reason, for Simon's brand of wholesale slaughter is kind of easy as well as offensive. It probably wouldn't seem so if the film. was at all scary or intelligent, but given there's so little else to recommend "The Ugly," righteous indignation will have to do.

SIGHT AND SOUND, 3/98, p. 56, Kim Newman

Dr Karen Schumaker, a psychiatrist, arrives at an asylum, against the wishes of its director Dr Marlowe, to interview Simon Cartwright, a serial killer. Brutalised by two vicious orderlies, Simon seems a personable young man, but he sees himself as deformed.

Karen manages to draw out from Simon some of his history. As a dyslexic child, Simon suffered at the hands of bullies and his tyrannical single mother, Evelyn. When he was 13, a schoolfriend, Julie, told him a treasured letter from his absent father was not, as his mother claimed, a declaration of hatred but an attempt to gain custody. Evelyn threw Julie out of the house and Simon murdered his mother with a straight razor.

After four years in an institution, Simon was released and began to kill, seemingly at random. Simon claims he is compelled to murder by the spectral presences of his earlier victims, but Marlowe suggests this is a cunning lie designed to deceive the psychiatrist. Simon recounts his involvement with the adult Julie: he murdered her brother under the impression he was disposing of a romantic rival, and then became Julie's lover only to murder her too.

When Karen presses Simon for further explanations, he attacks her; she glimpses the ghosts he claims to see before he is subdued. Later, Simon kills the orderlies and escapes, apparently with the connivance of Marlowe. He breaks into Karen's home and murders her in her bed. Karen wakes up, believing this to have been a dream, but her throat is cut and Simon stands over her.

From the first, *The Ugly* takes care to divorce itself from realism: the asylum is an almost deserted hellhole staffed by a single sinister psychiatrist and a pair of grungy thugs, with—aside from protagonist Simon—only one other visible inmate, a harridan allowed to roam the halls and attack visitors. A horror-movie rainstorm rages outside and the characters all wear primary colour costumes that signify their eccentricities: bad shrink Marlowe sports a white cravat and black *Dr. No*-style collarless jacket; nice Dr Karen Schumaker a tailored red suit.

Throughout, writer-director Scott Reynolds delights in almost theatrical alienation effects. Karen literally steps into Simon's past as, drawn into his flashbacks, she listens to his (misleading?) explanations. It is hinted, *à la The Usual Suspects,* that Simon might have made up on the spot the story of his ghostly tormentors—who are nevertheless glimpsed thereafter and even appear to Karen—by elaborating on the word 'visitors' he had read on the psychiatrist's pass. Flashed-in scenes reveal Karen's fears and fantasies as often as Simon's. A crucial point in the interview when Karen unlocks Simon's cuff is shown three times, with Simon's fantasy of murdering Karen and Karen's fantasy of being murdered by Simon followed by the undramatic (but hardly more reliable) reality of the pair continuing their conversation.

The boldest device of all, prefigured perhaps by Mel Brooks' 1977 spoof *High Anxiety* (which was making a joke about *Psycho)* and Russ Meyer's *Beneath the Valley of the Ultra Vixens* (1979), is that all the bloodshed in the film is an oily black liquid. Though, in theory, this ought to make the many scenes of violence more stylised and easier to take, it effectively conditions you by the end of the movie to flinch at the sight of black ink. Thus, the blood in the final shot (Karen's reality?) is as black as that in the more elaborate dream sequence preceding it. Perhaps even stranger is the almost subliminal omnipresence in many scenes of abandoned supermarket trolley, which can be rationally accepted in the various exterior locations, but even turn up in a high-security corridor of an asylum for the criminally insane.

The Ugly feels a lot like a piece of filmed theatre, with its small cast locked up for most of the film's duration and a story told almost entirely in narrated flashbacks. For this reason, the somewhat shrill performances of the entire cast, except for Paolo Rotondo as Simon, seem apt for the rising crescendo of insanity. There is a slight problem with the current overfamiliarity of the serial-killer theme (covered also in this month's *Fallen* and *Kiss the Girls).* It's hard not to feel that the confrontation of a professional woman investigator and a suave killer with the ability "to get inside her head" is simply a parodic spin on *The Silence of the Lambs.*

If *The Ugly*—the title refers to Simon's name for his dark alternate personality, which comes from a copy of *The Ugly Duckling* ripped in half by bullies—has anything new to add, it isn't in psychological depth. Its ingenuity lies instead in the insidious way it turns from character study to gothic horror, infiltrating ghostly apparitions (shrouded figures with black blood pouring from their mouths) into grimy normality. The finale, however, though unsettling, takes a detour into the incomprehensible that tends to reduce the whole film in retrospect into a malicious shaggy dog story. Nevertheless, there is a lot to admire and be disturbed by here.

VILLAGE VOICE, 5/5/98, p. 124, Gary Susman

Scott Reynolds's *The Ugly* is one of the most ambitious, vexing debuts in recent years. The New Zealand writer-director's story unfolds as a complex web of flashbacks and flashforwards meant to mirror the thoughts of an asylum-confined serial killer (Paolo Rotondo) explaining himself to a psychologist (Rebecca Hobbs). Reynolds underlines the killer's point of view through striking use of saturated colors (wounds bleed dark green) and montages of darting-eye camera movements. It's a pity, then, that such assured technique is devoted to such clichéd, distasteful subject matter. Do we really still want to watch a slasher stalk and attack an endless series of victims, or have him explained to us so we can sympathize with him? Reynolds's deliberate ambiguities fudge all questions of moral responsibility, and the time-shifting plot removes both suspense and consequences from the gory violence. Reynolds has a bright future as a genre director (he already has a deal at Miramax's Dimension Films), but *The Ugly* is better appreciated as a calling card than as a movie you'd actually sit through.

Also reviewed in:
NEW YORK TIMES, 5/1/98, p. E28, Stephen Holden
VARIETY, 9/29-10/5/97, p. 64, David Stratton

UN AIRE DE FAMILLE

A Leisure Time Features and Cinema Village Features release of a Telema/Le Studio Canal Plus/France 2 Cinema/Canal Plus/Cofimage 7 production. *Director:* Cédric Klapisch. *Screenplay (French with English subtitles):* Agnès Jaoui, Jean-Pierre Bacri, and Cédric Klapisch . *Based on the play by:* Agnès Jaoui and Jean-Pierre Bacri. *Director of Photography:* Benoit Delhomme. *Editor:* Francine Sandberg. *Music:* Phillippe Eidel. *Production Director:* Patrick Lancelot. *Set Designer:* François Emmanuelli. *Costumes:* Corinne Jorry. *Running time:* 107 minutes. *MPAA Rating:* Not Rated.

CAST: Jean-Pierre Bacri (Henri);   Agnès Jaoui (Betty);   Jean-Pierre Darroussin (Dennis); Catherine Frot (Yolande);   Claire Maurier (Mother);   Wladimir Yordanoff (Philippe).

LOS ANGELES TIMES, 6/19/98, Calendar/p. 4, Kenneth Turan

"Ah, Monsieur Rabelais," an admirer said to the 16th century French writer in a memorable New Yorker cartoon, "there is simply no word to describe your lusty, bawdy sense of humor."

Similarly, there is no one word (and it probably wouldn't be "Rabelaisian") to describe the kind of uproarious, quintessentially French verbal farce that is "Un Air de Famille." Delicate and deliciously directed by Cedric Klapisch, one of France's best young filmmakers, and acted with great sureness, this droll symphony of comic disenchantment is as perfectly balanced and executed as the timepiece of your dreams.

"Un Air de Famille" is based on a hit French play, and its six-character ensemble is made up of original cast members who played their parts on stage for nine months before filming began. Two of the actors, Agnes Jaoui and Jean-Pierre Bacri, wrote the piece and received a Cesar, the French Oscar, for best screenplay, and two more, Jean-Pierre Darroussin and the marvelous Catherine Frot, won supporting actor Cesars for their roles.

Done in real time largely at a single location, a cafe incongruously named Au Pere Tranquille (Tranquil Dad's), "Un Air de Famille" is simplicity itself in outline. It's Friday night, a time when the Menaud family—mother, two sons and their wives and an unmarried daughter—gathers for a weekly family dinner at the cafe run by son Henri (Bacri), who inherited the place from his father.

The film's title translates as "Family Resemblances," and in truth only families can drive each other as crazy as these people do. Quick to take offense, always willing to needle one another for scores that will forever remain unsettled, these whining, complaining relations have been getting on one another's nerves for time out of mind. On this particular Friday, everything will come to a wildly comic head.

All this contentiousness stems from the pugnacious family matriarch, (Claire Maurier, who played the mother in Truffaut's "Four Hundred Blows"), who's always ready with a critical word for whoever crosses her line of vision.

Usually it's underachieving son Henri who gets most of her grief, and tonight, with his wife, Arlette, absent without official leave, Henri returns the favor. He expresses outraged irritation at anything he can think of, from the willingness of female tennis professionals to wear shorts instead of skirts to the slothfulness of his bartender Denis (Darroussin). "Are you cleaning your kneecap?" he snaps when the poor man rests his rag there for a minute. "It's spotless."

Henri even lashes out at his irritable sister Betty (Jaoui), who has problems of her own. She's worried about being 30 and unmarried, she's just told off her boss and she is involved in a phlegmatic relationship with bartender Denis that no one else in the family knows about.

Smiling, self-satisfied brother Philippe (Wladimir Yordanoff), a top executive at the computer company Betty works for, usually has things his own way, but tonight is not an ordinary night.

Philippe represented his firm on local TV earlier in the day, and he's worried about how he came off, not to mention what Betty's fight with her boss will do to his career. And then there is Yolande, familiarly known as Yoyo (Frot).

Yoyo is Philippe's slightly dim wife whose 35th birthday is to be celebrated on this most uncelebratory night. Simple but sweet and genuine, prone to getting tipsy and putting her hand to her lips when she laughs, Yoyo is a singular comic creation, as sympathetic as she is naive, and Frot's performance makes her irresistible.

All of this highly verbal madness is delivered with great style and in a way that seems, as the entire film does, thoroughly French. Here is a family whose members lavish more care on dogs than they do on people, punctuate their dizzying tirades with vivid gestures and grimaces, are quick to take offense and obstinately passionate about each and every one of their opinions. A collection of riotous national stereotypes, in short, and no less amusing for that.

Though director (and co-screenwriter) Klapisch came into the project after it was a stage hit, "Un Air de Famille" benefits considerably from his touch. As he did with his early "Chacun Cherche Son Chat" (When the Cat's Away), Klapisch excels at bringing reality and empathy to unlikely comic material. We know these people as well as we know ourselves, and maybe that's why we laugh so hard at their foibles.

NEW YORK, 7/13/98, p. 42, David Denby

Cédric Klapisch's expert *Un Air de Famille* is about a family in provincial France who gather for a weekly meal in the restaurant they own and who fight with the intimate violence of people whose habits have been grating on one another for years. The movie is a fluidly directed comedy of habit and surprise—delicate, eloquent, very satisfying...

NEW YORK POST, 6/12/98, p. 46, Larry Worth

Jerry Seinfeld isn't the only one who can make "nothing" entertaining. But rather than focusing on four friends, French writer/director Cedric ("When the Cat's Away") Klapisch puts the emphasis on five family members and one servant, as showcased in "Un Air de Famille."

Based on a stage play, the story concerns an aged mother who meets with her grown daughter, two married sons and their wives each Friday night. And on this particular Friday night, the clan will mark one of the wives' birthdays.

The other wife has actually walked out on her husband, a little fact that hubby is desperately trying to cover up during the celebration. Not to worry. Everyone else is too caught up with their own dilemmas to notice.

But what the comedy-drama truly addresses is the various undercurrents that define every such gathering—borne from past baggage, long-held loyalties, condescending attitudes, petty jealousies and the brand of brutal truth that can be exchanged only with a sibling or parent.

Klapisch pulls it all off via universal experiences (getting a gift one hates or enduring endless group photos) and infinite attention to detail, as when a sister casually refers to her brother's "Friday vest."

What passes for action—lots of close-ups of talking heads—is smartly contrasted against idyllic flashbacks (which prove idyllic only because they took place light years ago). But whether in the past or present, Klapisch takes his time establishing each character, making them entirely credible in the process.

A flawless cast helps, with Agnes Jaoui's ever-reasonable daughter and Claire Maurier's overprotective mom standing out. But Jean-Pierre Bacri, Jean-Pierre Darroussin, Catherine Frot and Wladimir Yordanoff also earn applause.

Collectively, they distract from revelations that come too fast and a finale that ties up too neatly. Indeed, the actors—as spurred on by Klapisch—ensure that a moviegoers will relate to "Famille".

NEWSDAY, 6/12/98, Part II/p. B12, John Anderson

It seems slightly perverse, but the highest accolade ever paid to a film director for a stage adaptation is that he or she has "liberated" the playwright's work from the stodgy confines of the stage, made it breathe, made it new. Which always makes you wonder why the airless old recluse deserved any attention to begin with.

There's never any doubt that Cedric Klapisch's "Un Air de Famille (Family Resemblances)," a smartly wrought and wryly funny family meltdown, had its origins on stage. The action takes place almost exclusively in the bar owned by the dyspepsic Henri (Jean-Pierre Baeri), whose wife has left him on the same evening that his family is arriving for a Friday night birthday dinner. Klapisch, whose light romantic touch made his "When the Cat's Away" such a success, imposes a cinematic discipline on the material, finding the right emotional tone in the bar's soft light and using closeups to great effect. But he never intrudes on the material itself, never obscures what is a really good piece of writing, so you never doubt why he wanted to film it in the first place.

It's a tightly wound and intelligent play, one that evokes Odets and Miller, maybe even O'Neill ("The Errant Wife Cometh"?) and was written by Bacri and Agnes Jaoui, who plays Betty. She's the troubled and troublesome younger sister of Henri and Philippe (Wladmir Yordanoff), who drinks a little too much, hasn't settled down at the age of 30 and has just told off her boss—at the job found for her by Philippe. Pompous, overbearing and the family success, Philippe is a corporate climber whose afternoon appearance on the TV news will dominate the evening, even though the family is supposed to be celebrating the birthday of his wife, Yolande (Catherine Frot).

Rounding out the less-than-happy group are Mom (Claire Maurier), who favors Philippe over Henri to the point of obliviousness, and Denis, Henri's all-around employee, who's in love with Betty and serves as a combination Greek chorus and burr under Mom's saddle.

The story and the dialogue lack the cosmic anxieties of a Miller play, or Odets' sense of social place, but it has a knowing sense of simmering family conflict and of the divine joke whose punchline is of how certain people wind up related to certain other people. You believe Henri's family because you believe their combination of passing concern and overriding self-interest. Also, the unwitting jokes ("It's terrible for the children," Yolande says of Henri's separation. "Fortunately, you don't have any."). Think of "Un Air de Famille" as a kind of "Big Night" with frog legs instead of fusilli, and side order of spleen.

VILLAGE VOICE, 6/16/98, p. 160, Dennis Lim

Cédric Klapisch moves from the breezy, deftly choreographed spontaneity of last year's *"When the Cat's Away* to the potentially airless confines of filmed theater. But *Un Air de famille*, based on a play by Agnès Jaoui and Jean-Pierre Bacri (who also have key roles in the film), is a particularly invigorating instance of single-set moviemaking. The writers approximate the conditions of the Mike Leigh family pressure cooker, bringing long simmering tensions to a claustrophobic yet cathartic boil. Klapisch, for his part, stages and shoots the drama with a fair bit of wit, elegance, and formal intelligence.

Set almost entirely in a drab provincial café, the film unspools over the course of an evening get-together. The attendees arc familiar types: shrewish mother (Claire Maurier), sharp-tongued daughter (Jaoui), and two conveniently chalk-and-cheese sons—the café's gloomy proprietor (Bacri), whose wife has just left him, and the mama's boy, a horrendously self-absorbed suit (Wladimir Yordanoff), who won't shut up about his two-minute appearance on TV earlier that day. The occasion is the birthday of the favored son's prim, slightly vacuous wife (Catherine Frot). There is one outsider present—a watchful bartender (Jean-Pierre Darroussin), who provides perspective while generating an all-important ripple of class conflict.

Jaoui and Bacri have an ear for heat-of-the-moment accusations, but the script's strongest feature is the pungent comedy that often seems to erupt out of nowhere. Although Klapisch makes no effort to mask the inherent staginess, he treats his restrictions more imaginatively than most directors would have. As it turns out, the lighting and the Cinemascope photography are almost as psychologically revealing as the acting itself The ironically idyllic flashbacks to childhood that function as act dividers are heavy handed, but otherwise, Klapisch proves an unassumingly shrewd filmmaker, at once instinctive and meticulous.

Also reviewed in:
CHICAGO TRIBUNE, 10/2/98, Friday/p. M, Michael O'Sullivan
NEW YORK TIMES, 6/12/98, p. E12, Janet Maslin

UNDER THE SKIN

An Arrow Releasing release of a Strange Dog production for the British Film Institute and Channel Four Television in association with Rouge Films and the Merseyside Film Production Fund. *Executive Producer:* Ben Gibson. *Producer:* Kate Ogborn. *Director:* Carine Adler. *Screenplay:* Carine Adler. *Director of Photography:* Barry Ackroyd. *Editor:* Ewa J. Lind. *Music:* Ilona Sekacz. *Sound:* Gary Desmond. *Casting:* Vanessa Pereira and Simone Ireland. *Production Designer:* John-Paul Kelly. *Art Director:* Niall Moroney. *Costumes:* Frances Tempest. *Make-up:* Jenny Sharpe. *Running time:* 82 minutes. *MPAA Rating:* Not Rated.

CAST: Samantha Morton (Iris Kelley); Claire Rushbrook (Rose); Rita Tushingham (Mum); Christine Tremarco (Veronica, 'Vron'); Stuart Townsend (Tom); Matthew Delamere (Gary); Mark Womack (Frank); Clare Francis (Elena); Joe Tucker (Sam); Daniel O'Meara (Max); Crissy Rock (Compere); Lisa Millet (Sylvia); John Whitehall (Man at Station); Marie Jelliman (Manageress); Michelle Byatt (Mrs. Smith, Woman in Lost Property); Stella Scragg (Customer); David Brice (Man in Bed); Jack Marsden (Builder); Sean Cauldwell (Man in Club); Sandie Lavell (Woman at Phone Box); Jill Broadber (Conductor).

LOS ANGELES TIMES, 6/5/98, Calendar/p. 14, Kevin Thomas

Carine Adler's "Under the Skin" takes us into the comfortable suburban Liverpool home of a middle-aged woman (Rita Tushingham) who has just been told she has brain cancer, and has anywhere from three weeks to three months to live.

The terrible news and her subsequent swift demise devastate her 19-year-old daughter Iris (Samantha Morton) and her 24-year-old daughter Rose (Claire Rushbrook). Rose is happily married, also in suburbia, but the shocking loss of her mother sends Iris, who always felt her older sister was clearly her mother's favorite, into a potentially lethal downward spiral.

Indeed, the film's arc follows the falling apart of Iris' life. She jettisons both job and longtime boyfriend to move into a seedy apartment and to have a fling with a handsome—and dangerous—stranger (Stuart Townsend), and soon her life dissolves into a series of degrading one-night stands and hard partying at the clubs.

So hungry for love, so acute is Iris' lack of identity, that she frequently wears her mother's wig and old fur coat, making her look like a hooker. As her life descends into an increasingly rapid tailspin, Iris alienates virtually everyone she knows and is plunging to rock-bottom.

All the while, Rose remains maddeningly obtuse to what's happening to her sister. She too is consumed with grief but has the balancing sustenance and security of a husband and child. Rose is so appallingly self-absorbed, and judgmental in regard to her sister, that she unsympathetically leaves her in the lurch.

In her feature debut, Adler shapes her film gracefully and elicits a scorching no-holds-barred, totally selfless portrayal from Morton. The look, the feel of the film and its evocation of place seem just right, and "Under the Skin's" quality of intimacy, coupled with its succinctness and briskness, owes much to cinematographer Barry Ackroyd, long-standing collaborator of director Ken Loach.

Then, out of nowhere, Adler rushes to an incredibly neatly-tied-up-with-a-shiny-ribbon finish, in the process skipping over a much-needed scene with Rose. It would have been wonderful to watch Rose undergo a change of heart, as played by an actress the caliber of Rushbrook, a Mike Leigh alumna who was featured in "Secrets and Lies." Had we been able to watch Rose undergo such a transformation, "Under the Skin" might well have had a chance at fulfilling the bright promise with which it started.

NEW YORK, 6/8/98, p. 101, David Denby

At the beginning of *Under the Skin*, and unnerving and brilliant little English movie, the 19-year-old Iris (Samantha Morton) lies on her bed naked, daydreaming about her mother while drawing on her own body with a black Magic Marker. This opening shot is a movie in itself—the inscribed and mapped landscape of nakedness (the camera follows the pen raptly), the strange preoccupation and forlornness of the girl, the combination of adolescent dreaminess and womanly splendor. *Under the Skin,* which was written and directed by Carine Adler, is a movie about the female body cast in the form of an urban fairy tale. In Liverpool, a mother (Rita Tushingham) has two daughters named after flowers: There is Rose (Claire Rushbrook), the favorite, who is pregnant and happily married, and Iris (Morton), the younger—single, rebellious, and unloved. When the mother quite suddenly dies, Iris feels nothing—or nothing that she can bring to the surface—and she pitches into a downward spiral of alcoholism and sex. Prowling the streets like a prostitute searching for her own Jack the Ripper, Iris is a little crazy, yet she's also just a self-hating girl hungry for connection. One can't help thinking to oneself, This is *the way it happens—this is the way someone loses herself and goes over the edge.*

Samantha Morton, who is 20, has a long, very mobile body and short hair that makes her features seem large and eager and almost scarily ravenous. As Morton sprawls in bed in an erotic fog (Iris's head is filled with luscious dirty thoughts), she abandons herself to acting in a way that no young American actress would dare. Some of the sex scenes are squalid, but the movie itself couldn't be more delicate in feeling. Using a handheld camera, Adler follows her heroine down streets, in and out of bars and a rumpled apartment; the style is rough but lyrically alive and emotionally potent. *Under the Skin* really is a fairy tale after all: No frog prince appears, but the movie doesn't end in an alley, either. Carine Adler has made a genuinely erotic film without a tinge of exploitation. *Under the Skin* is a triumphant debut.

NEW YORK POST, 5/22/98, p. 56, Thelma Adams

"Under the Skin" must be about the naked truth.

Writer-director Carine Adler's raw drama opens with a naked woman sprawled in the foreground.

Iris, the starkers 19-year-old played by Samantha Morton, reclines in her bedroom, doodling on her belly with a felt-tipped pen, her back arched. her heavy breasts lifted to the ceiling like steeples, her downy stomach hair lit like angel wings.

Perhaps the naked truth would be more truthful if the body were that of Ruth Gordon in her "Harold and Maude" phase. But the eye-catching Morton gets under our skin because she is so tormented by her own epidermis: its ethereal beauty, it's prickly desires and its promise of mortality.

Iris has blossomed physically, but she's emotionally stunted. She responds to the news of her mother's terminal cancer with: "She's dying and she hasn't even noticed me yet."

Iris envies her 24-year-old sister, Rose (Claire Rushbrook), her mother's favorite. Rose is middle-class, pregnant and comfortably married. Their lifelong sibling rivalry climaxes when Mum (Rita Tushingham) dies and they try to fill the vacuum together and separately.

This setup of a difficult intimate relationship between sisters is compelling and painful, but newcomer Adler has an edgier agenda. After the funeral, Iris dons her mother's wig and tatty fur mini.

Iris cruises Liverpool. Her grief leads her into a series of increasingly humiliating sexual encounters. A simple warning: Never believe a man with multiple knife scars who blindfolds you and then says, "Trust me."

Once Iris loses her moral compass, Morton continues a performance that recalls the young Tushingham in "A Taste of Honey" and the black-and-white British morality flicks of the '60s. Must women who struggle to find, or free, themselves through sex end up face down in a gutter before they turn their lives around?

As good as Morton is, supported by a faultless Rushbrook ("Secrets & Lies") and a fragile Tushingham, this message is as dated as the British kitchen-sink dramas of the '60s. The chief difference between them: "Under the Skin" has more flesh—*lots* more flesh.

NEWSDAY, 5/22/98, Part II/p. B7, John Anderson

Just as nuclear weapons and the Holocaust have informed virtually every piece of fiction they've touched since the 1940s, AIDS has haunted movie sex since the '80s, and beyond. The effervescent promiscuity of something like "Irma la Douce" has morphed into the death's-head stare of "Savage Nights." "Midnight Cowboy" has moved to "Philadelphia."

In Carine Adler's "Under the Skin," sex doesn't equal death for Iris, the young woman played with such devastating candor by newcomer Samantha Morton. But death equals sex: When her mother (Rita Tushingham) is diagnosed with cancer and dies within weeks, Iris—already a second-class citizen in the love state of Mom and sister Rose (Claire Rushbrook)—delays her grief in an accelerating game of pelvic chicken, or Sex With Strangers.

AIDS isn't what director-writer Adler is about here, even if she can't avoid it. Sure, everyone who cares about Iris—her sister, her friend Vron (Christine Tremarco)— parrots the standard condom warnings, but Iris is beyond mortality. Wearing her late mother's ratty wig and glasses as she picks up men in movie theaters and grinds against them in sweaty bars, Iris has crossed over. She has Norman Batesified her life: She's degrading the mother who never loved her. Or never moved her enough.

Adler's psychology is complex and intriguing, and so are the performances. Morton is so fresh and open in projecting Iris' conflicted emotions that "Under the Skin" is sure to give her the kind of notices that were lavished on Emily Watson for that other sex-martyrdom epic "Breaking the Waves"—a film with which "Under the Skin" shares more than a few similarities, including nervous camera work (here by Barry Ackroyd) and progressively dangerous sex. But in "Breaking the Waves," sex represented slow crucifixion; here, Adler isn't afraid of reflecting the liberation that Iris experiences, even as she grows more ghoulishly degraded. The director's eye is a voyeur, caressing as it probes—my God, it might have been made by a man! Except that Adler turns one's arousal against one, as one watches Iris hit the skids.

While Morton shines, so does Rushbrook, who played the slatternly daughter in Mike Leigh's "Secrets and Lies" and makes Iris's sister Rose just about despicable. It's not just Rose's proprietary air about Mom, or her lordly manner toward her younger sister. Even her walk—dainty/purposeful, beneath her enormously pregnant self—spells self-absorbed witch. Iris, punky, sexy and unemployed, drives the ambitious Rose up the wall—which is part of her plan—even while she craves sisterly solace. In the end, Adler has packed a lot of baggage into one small movie, one that will undoubtedly grow in stature, along with the reputations of Morton and Rushbrook.

SIGHT AND SOUND, 12/97, p. 56, Pam Cook

When their beloved mother dies from a brain turnout, Iris and her sister Rose, who is pregnant, are devastated. In a cinema, Iris picks up a stranger, Tom, and has sex with him. She quits her job and moves out of her boyfriend Gary's home into a bedsit. Her best friend Vron gets her a job at a lost-property office. At a club, Iris picks up a man whom she takes back to her place for sex. Iris asks her sister to give her their mother's ring, but Rose says that she can't find it. After she picks up the ashes from the crematorium, Iris dreams about her mother. Tom and Iris sleep together again, but he leaves quickly, evading her questions. Vron begins to disapprove of Iris' promiscuity. When Rose visits Iris to ask about the ashes, Iris claims to have lost them and the sisters argue. Iris picks up a man in the street and they have rough sex. Afterwards, Iris is upset and tries to contact Tom, but he fails to ring her back. She goes to see the man from the street, who blindfolds her and then urinates on her.

One night, Iris' bag is snatched. She tries to contact Rose, but is told by her husband Frank that she is about to catch a train to London. At the station, Iris asks her sister for money and becomes violently angry when she sees that Rose is wearing their mother's ring. She goes to see Gary and finds him with Vron. Turning up drunk at Rose's house, she tries to seduce Frank but he refuses. Iris wanders the streets in a daze and collapses in the gutter. The next day, Rose comes to see her and apologises for lying about the ring; Iris confesses that she had the ashes all the time. The sisters are reconciled. Later, Iris begins the singing career she had always wanted.

Carine Adler's feature debut is a powerful, uncompromising depiction of grief and emotional disintegration, dealing with the physical and psychic pain and the loss of self aroused by a loved one's sudden death. It portrays mourning not as a dignified process of letting go, but as a complex matrix of stirred-up emotions from anger and guilt to self-hatred and the urge to destroy. Ostensibly, the story is about the reactions of two sisters, Iris and Rose, to the loss of their mother (a brief and touching appearance by Rita Tushingham). Their alienation from one another, and eventual reconciliation, form the central narrative thread. But the film is dominated by the dazzling performance of Samantha Morton (who played a similarly quixotic and disturbed young woman on the ITV series *Band of Gold)*. As Iris, Morton projects a quality of fierce vulnerability and edgy desperation that is both moving and disturbing.

The shock of grief is presented through Iris' perspective, as she struggles to cope with the terrifying absence created by her mother's death. Her dependency on her mother for her own sense of identity is established in the opening shot, as Iris inscribes a stick figure on her naked body while her voiceover tells us that when she was little, she thought her mother was beautiful and wanted to be like her. The huge close-up of Iris' stomach, pores and all, and the childish drawing suggest a physical bond and a psychological regression, the motivating forces behind her breakdown and regeneration.

But they also evoke need and desire, those profound instincts that drive her to seek comfort in a succession of unsatisfactory sexual encounters with men that lead into a downward spiral of self-humiliation. Iris' anger at being abandoned impels her to act out a fantasy in which, dressed in her mother's clothes and a blonde wig, she recreates her as a 'bad' object, promiscuous and self-obsessed, while simultaneously punishing herself for her feelings of guilt.

Iris' masquerade, and her sexual fantasies, have the quality of a children's dressing-up game in which adult sexuality is tried on but doesn't quite fit. The effect is a parody of heterosexual desire, and Samantha Morton's androgynous appearance and tomboy athleticism suggest that even before her mother's death, Iris had not yet settled into a stable sexual identity. Her grief provokes an exaggerated performance of sexuality that masks a longing for something else. In the context of the story, 'something else' can be taken to mean love, attention, power, self-punishment, revenge and relief from pain, among other things. But there seems to be more to it than that. After her mother dies, Iris escapes into a kind of dream state, halfway between sleeping and waking, in which it is sometimes difficult to distinguish between fantasy and reality.

The impression of inhabiting a sexual uncertainty zone is underlined by hypnotic visual effects that create an intense eroticism around Iris' identity crisis, drawing the audience into a world of free-floating, polymorphous desire. The somewhat perfunctory ending, in which Rose and Iris are reconciled and the sisters come to terms with their mother's death, ties up the threads of the story. But it does not entirely defuse the erotic charge around Iris' sexuality. In the final scene, she performs the Gilbert O'Sullivan song 'Alone Again (Naturally)' in a club, a gesture that signals her new-found independence and confidence, but also suggests that her sexual identity remains undecided, and is not so easily settled. After a roller-coaster ride of mixed emotions, *Under the Skin* leaves us with a sense of regeneration, of possibilities opened up by painful, gut-wrenching experiences, and new life tentatively emerging from dark despair.

VILLAGE VOICE, 5/26/98, p. 132, Amy Taubin

In Carine Adler's *Under the Skin,* a young woman acts out angrily, guiltily, and with a desperate, primal need for physical connection and comfort after her mother dies. The movie isn't as cinematically expressive as certain masculine-fantasy flicks about female masochism, namely *Repulsion* and *Breaking the Waves.* But psychologically, *Under the Skin* is truer than either of them. Adler gets inside her characters without being either terrified or awed by what she finds. The film isn't at all sensational, nor does it feel like a talk-show confessional. And that's a major accomplishment considering that it details compulsive, self-destructive sexual behavior.

Iris (Samantha Morton) and Rose (Claire Rushbrook) are sisters. When their mother (Rita Tushingham, in a too-brief appearance) dies, their sibling rivalry is exacerbated. Rose, who's married, is pregnant, and has a career-track job, resents her, sister's irresponsibility and her flamboyant show of grief. Iris remains hungrily attached to the mother, who, she believes, always preferred her sister. There's a stunning sequence near the beginning of the film when Iris and Rose visit their dying mom. "Dance with me, Mom" says Iris. "I'll be the man' " They cha-cha-cha in slow motion. Iris looks ecstatic. In the next scene, the mother is dead and the sisters are sorting through her possessions.

From this point on, *Under the Skin* follows Iris as she goes looking for love in all the wrong places. Costumed in her mother's wig, dime-store sunglasses, and ratty fur coat (they make her look like an underage hooker rather than a middle-aged woman), she picks up guys in movie theaters and clubs, becomes hysterically attached to her one-night stands regardless of the humiliations they inflict, attacks anyone who might possibly offer support, tries to seduce her sister's husband, and, worst of all, apparently throws her mother's ashes into the trash. If this sounds like a dark comedy, it's not. Iris's pain is too intense and raw to be funny—to her. And Adler wants to keep us inside Iris's experience.

That she succeeds so well has a lot to do with Morton's fierce, febrile, and remarkably unselfconscious performance. Morton's delicate features have an angelic purity; her androgynous body suggests an unfixed sexual identity. She can go from zero to 100 emotionally in a split second. She captures the wounded, narcissistic child under Iris's defiant display of eroticism. Watching her, one is never aware of the actress but only of the character. And considering the extremity of the character's erotic hunger and exhibitionism, that's an extraordinary acting feat.

Under the Skin is Adler's first feature and her inexperience sometimes shows. Despite the subtle and mature intelligence that you can sense behind the film, there are occasional awkward and overly schematic scenes. And the sisters overnight reconciliation is not completely convincing. Nor is Iris's final voiceover, which makes the film seem as if it's suddenly turned into *Ruby in Paradise*. Adler doesn't go so far as to suggest that Iris's pain has been completely resolved—there's an unmistakably manic edge to her optimism. But, in trying to wrest a measure of comfort for both the character and the audience, the director comes dangerously close to betraying the despair that underlies the film. That *Under the Skin* is not undone by this lapse into sentimentality is perversely, a proof of its power.

Also reviewed in:
NEW YORK TIMES, 5/22/98, p. E14, Janet Maslin
VARIETY, 9/22-28/97, p. 44, Derek Elley

UNMADE BEDS

A Chelsea Pictures release of a Chelsea Pictures production. *Producer:* Steve Wax. *Director:* Nicholas Barker. *Screenplay:* Nicholas Barker. *Director of Photography:* William Rexer II. *Editor:* Paul Binns. *Music:* Rupert Lord and Tom Parkinson. *Sound:* Brad Bergbom. *Running time:* 93 minutes. *MPAA Rating:* R.

WITH: Mikey Russo; Aimee Copp; Michael De Stefano; Brenda Monte.

LOS ANGELES TIMES, 10/23/98, Calendar/p. 10, John Anderson

[*The following review by John Anderson appeared in a slightly different form in* NEWSDAY, 8/7/98, Part II/p. B7.]

An anthropologist who started out working for the BBC as a radio producer, Nicholas Barker calls his film "Unmade Beds" a study in untruthfulness. Which is to say, simply, fiction. Which is to say, nothing simply at all.

What Barker has made is a documentary cast with fantasy characters and a fantasy about real people. The extent to which he's pushed the format makes for an often excruciating trip into egos and loneliness, which—sad as it might be—can't help but at times be really funny.

Having searched the Manhattan personal ads for four people to build his film around, Barker arrived at the final quartet of "Unmade Beds": Brenda Monte, voluptuous, proud of it and looking for a man to pay her bills; Michael De Stefano, short and a little angry at never clicking with the women he meets; Aimee Copp, zaftig, lonely and ready to resort to donated sperm and single motherhood; and Mickey Russo, a 54-year-old swinger aging out of the singles scene, who uses a lot of tips to bartenders, the mercifully blind Internet and some highly exaggerated tales of his success as a screenwriter to keep himself in the flow.

"Unmade Beds" is not precisely fact-based, although it does uncover truths. All the characters are playing characters based on themselves, but scripted by Barker. The question, naturally, is what Barker chose to use in his film.

Were the stories more revealing (it's hard to imagine)? Did he soften the biographies, or improvise on the tales of the single life they told him? Most curiously, perhaps, is why people would willingly submit their lives to a film that portrays them in such painful, naked ways. Unless they thought it might help them get some dates.

NEW YORK, 8/24/98, p. 52, David Denby

Cruelty in art is like a glass of cold water flung into one's face—unpleasant, humiliating even, but more than successful in refreshing one's attention. *Unmade Beds* is a maliciously funny satire of the New York singles scene—a joke about self-delusion and unhappiness—and it hurts. As I watched it, I became more and more angry at what the movie was doing, but by the end I had been trapped by my own fascination. The talented British writer-director Nicholas Barker makes us complicit in his crimes, both large and small. One response to this, of course, is simply to walk out—that way we don't play Barker's game, and we avoid becoming cruel ourselves. But if we walk out, we miss one of the more original movies of the year.

Many of us are tired of spectacle and endless genre stories, bored by the same emotional and moral issues plugged into the same visually overwrought movies. Now and then, we require some relief—a new way of making movies, even a new aesthetic. Nicholas Barker has come up with both. Barker has worked in recent years as a producer-director for BBC television, but he was trained as an anthropologist, and for this movie about New York singles, Barker and his staff began by doing fieldwork—searching through personal ads and bars, interviewing, videotaping, etc. In the end, he chose four men and women—heteros all—ranging in age from 28 to 54, and filmed them during the summer, fall, and winter of 1996-97. First, the four subjects told him about their dating experiences in that period; Barker then mixed their actual words with inventions of his own, all of which they fed back to the camera. At home, surrounded by the armature of their lives—their furniture and photographs, the laundry on the floor—or driving to work, or out on the prowl in the city late at night, they deliver long and mesmerizing rants, complaining about the opposite sex and lamenting their own failures and frustrations in the singles scene. They act themselves (and with great skill), but in dramatically heightened versions. The film is a hybrid—a documentary with the formal control of fiction.

The funniest and strongest of the four is Brenda Monte, a former lap dancer who needs money to keep up her mortgage payments. Brenda wants a man who will give her the cash without asking for sex. The trouble is that everyone asks Brenda for sex. Or so she says.

This great fleshy bawd, showing off her golden breasts and belly to us, describes an entire male world inflamed by Brenda. Men keep exposing themselves to her, but she remains sternly unimpressed: The male member is easily available anywhere, but dog food, which she steals regularly from the grocer (she pulls out a can of Alpo from her purse), is something solid and real. Brenda is lewd, tough, quick-witted, hilarious—a more vivid character than any fictional personage in recent American movies. Her opposite number in many ways is Mikey Russo, who affects the tough-guy-loner style of a Mickey Spillane hero—dark clothes, cigarette pinched between thumb and forefinger, a tendency to see the world as divided into beautiful babes and mutts. Mikey, 54, a failed screenwriter, lives in fear of being associated with a mutt; he carries a beeper so that a friend may summon him away from an unfortunate blind date.

Brenda and Mikey maintain a fantasy of themselves as irresistible, an image that all too often crashes against the rocks of unsatisfactory or unappreciative partners. But Barker doesn't actually show us any of their dates: He's interested only in the way these two present themselves to the camera—that is, the way they delude themselves. Seduced by their need to justify their actions, and by their desire to be *seen,* his characters brutally and unwittingly expose themselves to our gaze. We become the critical mirror that they can't find, the friend and enemy who sees the truth.

Brenda and Mikey never meet; each character in this movie—a sort of ballad of the lonely city—is the star of a separate narrative line. *Unmade Beds* begins with warmly lit, exquisitely composed shots of anonymous young men and women viewed from outside their windows. We can't hear them; we can only stare at them. Slowly, dreamily, with absolute confidence, they move through their apartments, talk, undress (there are several classic-looking nudes)—it is the state of sensual fulfillment and ease that is denied to the four principal characters. Right from the beginning of the movie, then, Barker turns us into voyeurs: We first see Brenda and Mikey, too, from outside their windows as they sit in the solitary gloom, taking stock.

Barker and his cinematographer, William Rexer II, have appropriated Edward Hopper's paintings as their warrant for voyeurism. The movie's visual style, the wrenching sense of isolation and frustration, comes straight out of Hopper. Barker even re-creates such Hopper works as *Nighthawks,* positioning solitary strangers at the corners of a coffee shop, behind glass windows. We look in at them; they look out. Staring and suspicion form the connection between them and us.

Aimee Copp, a young Valkyrie at 225 pounds, with flowing blonde hair and a self-deprecating giggle, can't get through to a man. Her personal ads attract older men who want to be dominated by a big woman. The most self-aware of the four, she is desperately eager to get married, and she makes jokes out of her own misadventures. "I was dumped by a submissive," she says. And Michael De Stefano, who is 40 and unmarried, has convinced himself that he's striking out because he's too short—it's Michael's *idée fixe.* De Stefano is caught between resentment of the women who have rejected him and self-contempt. They are all caught in similar ways; it is, Barker implies, the common spiritual condition of hetero single life.

These are real people, and we can't help seeing what each of them is doing wrong. They have the classic troubles of losers: The egotism that holds their morale together is exactly the personality formation that makes them impossible as partners. Barker reveals a tragi-comic situation, but there's a redeeming strength to his approach. He allows these four the dignity of their unhappiness. They are what they are; they will hold on to their anger and resentment even though doing so dooms them to failure, and in the end we build a kind of admiration for them. That emotion, when it comes, releases us from the amorality and nastiness of our situation as voyeurs. We laugh at the characters' follies—and then shiver and think, "There but for the grace of God..."

NEW YORK POST, 8/7/98, p. 46, Thelma Adams

The Greater New York area is Loserville in Nicholas Barker's faux feature documentary, "Unmade Beds."

Four singles who you'd never want to answer your personal ad—a zaftig Jersey City gold digger, a lonely Brooklyn mama's boy, a womanizing security guard and an overweight, 28-year-old Kansan desperate to marry before she hits 30—pursue happiness and fail desperately against the dramatic Manhattan skyline.

British anthropologist Barker created three TV series for the BBC. The production notes, defined in general by being shameless, have this to offer on Mr. Barker: "One critic referred to Barker as 'a fly on the wall turned into a vulture.' Another simply calls him a genius."

Barker had never before made a feature film, and it shows in "Unmade Beds," at the Screening Room. He has a keen eye for a subject—and he delights in watching his quartet skewer themselves on their own folly.

But the writer-director pads his "interviews" (they are, in fact, staged recitations of the losers' real-life stories) interwoven with scenes of moving cabs, Central Park skaters' dramatic cloudscapes and peeks into the windows of strangers. Who knew that so many people in Manhattan opened their shades in the nude?

There's a meaty short in "Unmade Beds"—and wickedly funny moments of grand delusion. If anything, Barker has created a cautionary tale about the perils of the personals.

VILLAGE VOICE, 8/11/98, p. 151, Elizabeth Weitzman

Who hasn't wondered about that 110-lb. SW Vixen Wanting Brad Pitt Twin? For his "real-life feature film," director Nicholas Barker combed our city's classifieds for representatives of this singles-seeking-singles culture. He doesn't call his results a documentary, because he turned his four subjects' experiences into a script, which they relived for the camera. (He claims 90 percent is true and "the rest is a pack of lies.") Barker chose his group very well; despite its small size this is a highly entertaining bunch: Brenda, an outspoken, late-thirties exhibitionist, wants a bill payer who won't demand anything too taxing in return; Aimee, a 28-year-old desperate to get married, is sweet, sensible, and 225 pounds; Mikey, an aging, unemployed lothario, insists, "I've never gone out with a mutt and I'm not going to now"; and 15-year want-ad veteran Michael is convinced he'd be long out of the game if he weren't five foot four.

Barker's camera plays confidant as all four obsess over their unsatisfactory romantic situations. Intriguingly, we never see any of their dates, we simply overhear them or get the frustrated reports shared with friends the next day. We get the picture early on, so the movie drags at times. Barker tries to jazz things up with pretentious shots of anonymous lovers spied through apartment windows, none of which are half as interesting as the confessions unfolding in Brenda's pure-white living room or Mikey's outdated bachelor den. It's a shame about that pack of lies, too; all four are so natural in front of the camera that we feel cheated not knowing what they've really been through and what Barker's fabricated to express "larger dramatic truths." Most have been surprisingly honest in their ads, so why does Barker feel the need to make them into something they're not?

Also reviewed in:
CHICAGO TRIBUNE, 10/30/98, Friday/p. L, John Petrakis
NEW YORK TIMES, 8/7/98, p. E7, Anita Gates
VARIETY, 9/29-10/5/97, p. 64, Emanuel Levy

URBAN LEGEND

A TriStar Pictures release of a Phoenix Pictures presentation of a Neal H. Moritz/Gina Matthews production. *Executive Producer:* Brad Luff. *Producer:* Neal H. Moritz, Gina Matthews, and Michael McDonnell. *Director:* Jamie Blanks. *Screenplay:* Silvio Horta. *Director of Photography:* James Chressanthis. *Editor:* Jay Cassidy. *Music:* Christopher Young. *Music Editor:* Richard Whitfield. *Sound:* Tom Mather and (music) Robert Fernandez. *Sound Editor:* Per Hallberg. *Casting:* John Papsidera. *Production Designer:* Charles Breen. *Art Director:* Benno Tutter. *Set Decorator:* Cal Loucks. *Set Dresser:* Brenda McClennin and Carlos Caneca. *Special Effects:* Martin Malivoire. *Costumes:* Mary Claire Hannan. *Make-up:* Leslie Sebert. *Stunt Coordinator:* Matt Birman. *Running time:* 99 minutes. *MPAA Rating:* R.

CAST: Jared Leto (Paul);   Alicia Witt (Natalie);   Rebecca Gayheart (Brenda);   Michael Rosenbaum (Parker);   Loretta Devine (Reese);   Joshua Jackson (Damon);   Tara Reid (Sasha); John Neville (Dean Adams);   Julian Richings (Janitor);   Robert Englund (Professor Wexler); Danielle Harris (Tosh);   Natasha Gregson Wagner (Michelle Mancini);   Gord Martineau (Newsman);   Kay Hawtrey (Library Attendant);   Angela Vint (Bitchy Girl);   J.C. Kenny (Weather Woman);   Vince Corrazza (David Evans);   Balazs Koos (Nerdy Guy);   Stephanie Mills (Felicia); Danny Comden (Blake);   Nancy McAlear (Jenny);   Shawn Mathieson (Hippie Guy);   Cle Bennett (Dorky Guy);   Danielle Brett (Trendy Girl);   Roberta Angelica (Swimming Woman);   Matt Birman (Killer);   Brad Dourif (Gas Station Attendant).

LOS ANGELES TIMES, 9/25/98, Calendar/p. 8, Bob Heisler

[The following review by Bob Heisler appeared in a slightly different form in
NEWSDAY, 9/25/98, Part II/p. B11.]

It won't take you long to recognize the movie college campus of Pendleton U. One professor, one dean, one security guard, one roommate, one boyfriend, one best friend, one secret and one serial killer. With the dialogue-challenged feel of a television movie of the week, "Urban Legend" gathers all the familiar elements and leaves you counting the bodies and waiting for the showdown between pretty good and incompetent evil in which good escapes and evil improbably lives on, despite all laws of nature and human anatomy.

"Urban Legend" is a low-voltage drive-in movie, made strictly by the book: There's not a surprising moment for fans of the my-profs-got-an-ax, let's-put-on-a-scary-movie genre. The stars have TV-familiar faces. One of those familiar faces is killed during the opening credits (see, most recently, "Scream 2"). The killer is thrown through the front window of a vehicle (see, most recently, "Halloween H20"). People keep bumping into one another (cue the loud music, the only truly frightening thing about the movie).

In this semester's version, someone is killing the people around Natalie (Alicia Witt), and the murders sure sound like the kind of urban legends discussed in the American folklore class taught by odd professor Wexler (Robert Englund in yet another horror-movie cameo for Freddy Krueger).

After the second or third death, Natalie is forced to go where no movie-college student dares to go—the library. There she looks up the urban legends she should have been studying all along. (She is not alone at the library. Otherwise she would have to be killed.) She runs into one other student, Sasha (Tara Reid), the campus radio sex chat hostess who's looking up the Kama Sutra she was supposed to have been studying all along. Witt, who has a little Shelley Duvall in her gaze, seems more angry than scared, especially since she's the last to figure out who wants her dead.

She also enlists the help of the campus hunk/morality-challenged journalist (Jared Leto), tangles herself up in Pendleton's own urban legend—a 1973 dormitory massacre curiously missing from its admissions brochures—and finds herself the object of one of the more icky urban legends, the kidney-harvest.

NEW YORK POST, 9/25/98, p. 44, Larry Worth

Ever hear the one about Pop Rocks and Pepsi making someone's stomach explode? How about an escaped maniac who terrorizes young girls on a country lane? And what of Jamie Blanks, the first-time, no-talent director never heard from again after "Urban Legend"?

OK, the latter's wishful thinking. But the others exemplify the title, popular horror tales with which teens scare each other. In this case, they're also the M.O. for a serial killer who's knocking off students in a bucolic New England college.

From the get-go, one roots for the murderer. In the now requisite first-scene bloodbath, the evil one arises from the back seat of a vehicle driven by ever-irritating Natasha Gregson Wagner and resculpts her head with an ax. Given her resume, that's a mercy kill.

It's also as predictable as what follows. Each of the cookie-cutter protagonists takes a turn as potential victim or suspected assassin (this time outfitted in a less-than-menacing ski parka with fur-lined, face-obscuring hood).

The list of those who'll either dispatch or be dispatched include Alicia Witt, Jared Leto, Rebecca Gayheart, Joshua Jackson, Michael Rosenbaum and Tara Reid. Each is as good-looking as he/she is vacuous. The adult actors fare no better, particularly horror veterans Robert (Freddy Krueger) Englund and Brad ("Child's Play") Dourif.

With cheap jolts replacing bona fide suspense, that leaves "Urban Legend" with precious few assets. But that doesn't mean a sequel won't be forthcoming. Therein lies the stuff of nightmares.

SIGHT AND SOUND, 3/99, p. 56, Kim Newman

Pendleton University, New England. Student Michelle, driving home late, escapes from a stuttering gas-station manager. He is trying to warn her about the axe murderer hiding in the back seat of her car. News of her death spreads across campus, especially affecting her estranged friend Natalie who is taking Professor Wexler's course on urban legends. When Damon, a prank-playing friend, is murdered in front of Natalie in a re-enactment of an urban legend, she confides in fellow students Brenda, Parker, Sasha and Paul. Parker floats the theory that a serial killer is recreating urban legends.

Natalie's roommate Tosh is murdered, leaving the message "aren't you glad you didn't turn on the lights?" in blood, but the Dean writes her death off as suicide. Natalie confides in Brenda that she broke her friendship with Michelle after they played a prank based on an urban legend which resulted in a boy's death in a car accident. During a frat party, the killer murders the Dean, Parker and Sasha. Paul, Brenda and Natalie flee. Brenda and Natalie find Wexler's body in the trunk of Paul's car and run from him, but it is actually Brenda—the girlfriend of the boy Michelle and Natalie killed—who is the murderer. Paul and Natalie fight off Brenda, who falls into a river. Later, on another campus, Brenda listens as someone recounts the story of her murder spree as an urban legend.

Urban Legend calculatedly crossbreeds the youth-appeal of Wes Craven's *Scream* (especially the poster design), the novelty serial killer of *Se7en*, and the persecuted guilty-teens motif of *I Know What You Did Last Summer*. This yields a silly but not unlikable formula horror picture, one exactly like the wave of early 80s movies that were name-checked in *Scream 2 (The Dorm that Dripped Blood, The House on Sorority Row, Graduation Day, Final Exam).* Credibility is not a high priority. The guessable revelation of who the guilty party under the hooded parka is glosses the details. For instance, how does this killer get the first victim to make a late-night visit to an out-of-the-way gas station? How can he be sure the stuttering attendant will be unable to warn anyone? How can he swing an axe with killing force inside a small car? And how come the entire plot is directed at the less culpable Natalie rather than Michelle, initiator of the original incident?

The monomaniacal thesis, elaborated both by Robert Englund's blatant red-herring professor and wiseacre Parker, also stumbles because there aren't enough urban legends to go round. Despite references to the 'dog in the microwave' and the 'snack food and soda intestinal explosion' stories, the string of murders that clutters up the second half of the film are just stereotypical stalk-and-hack killings. Some key legends mentioned in the film ('dead granny on the roofrack', for example) are left out, and only a token stab is made at the 'call her name five times' tale, to avoid invoking memories of *Candyman.* That film was more sophisticated in its deployment of urban legends and was actually urban in setting. (Intriguingly, almost all the stories classed as urban legends take place on lonely roads or woods miles away from cities.)

Nevertheless, *Urban Legend* manages somehow to be rather endearing, from Natasha Gregson Wagner's opening bit (what must now, after *Scream,* be called 'the Drew Barrymore position') to the hokey shaggy-dog punchline. Alicia Witt, whose resemblance to Gillian Anderson is a short-term advantage but long-term handicap, is fine as the 'final girl', shouldering all the sensitivity while her friends carry on with the now-obligatory *Scream*-style callousness. (Best excuse for ignoring screams for help: "She's doing a performance piece to commemorate the massacre.") Lithium-chugging, pierced, goth Tosh breaks up the overwhelming preppiness of even the nastiest frat kids, and there's an amusingly transparent murder set-up scene as Damon drives Natalie out to the woods, pretending to be understanding in order to make out with her.

First-time director Jamie Blanks isn't in Wes Craven's league when it comes to timing a sudden lurch-into-the-frame shock, and writer Silvio Horta doesn't have Kevin Williamson's knack for referentially postmortem yet convincing teen talk, but this is a movie that follows rather than makes trends. It may well be most notable for echoing *Halloween H20* by cementing the newest addition to the repertory of slasher clichés: the comic-relief black security guard—chubby middle-aged Loretta Devine, devoted to early 70s Pam Grier movies—can be killed but only if she turns out to be alive after all a few minutes later.

Also reviewed in:
CHICAGO TRIBUNE, 9/25/98, Friday/p. K, Monica Eng
NEW YORK TIMES, 9/25/98, p. E15, Anita Gates
VARIETY, 9/21-27/98, p. 105, Lael Loewenstein

VELVET GOLDMINE

A Miramax Films release of a Zenith Productions/Killer Films production in association with Single Cell Pictures. *Executive Producer:* Scott Meek and Michael Stipe. *Producer:* Christine Vachon. *Director:* Todd Haynes. *Screenplay:* Todd Haynes. *Story:* Todd Haynes and James Lyons. *Director of Photography:* Maryse Alberti. *Editor:* James Lyons. *Music:* Carter Burwell. *Music Editor:* Annette Kudrak and Todd Kasow. *Choreographer:* Lea Anderson. *Sound:* Peter Lindsay. *Sound Editor:* Eliza Paley and Paul Soucek. *Casting:* Susie Figgis. *Production Designer:* Christopher Hobbs. *Art Director:* Andrew Munro. *Costumes:* Sandy Powell. *Make-up:* Peter King. *Running time:* 120 minutes. *MPAA Rating:* Not Rated.

CAST: Ewan McGregor (Curt Wild); Jonathan Rhys Meyers (Brian Slade); Toni Collette (Mandy Slade); Christian Bale (Arthur Stuart); Eddie Izzard (Jerry Divine); Emily Woof (Shannon); Michael Feast (Cecil); Janet McTeer (Female Narrator); Maíread McKinley (Wilde Housemaid); Luke Morgan Oliver (Oscar Wilde, Age 8); Osheen Jones (Jack Fairy, Age 7); Micko Westmoreland (Jack Fairy); Damian Suchet (BBC Reporter); Danny Nutt (Kissing

Sailor); Wash Westmoreland (Young Man); Don Fellows (Lou); Ganiat Kasumu (Mary); Ray Shell (Murray); Alastair Cumming (Tommy Stone); Zoe Boyce (Girl on Subway); Jim Whelan (Mr. Stuart); Sylvia Grant (Mrs. Stuart); Tim Hans (Manchester Teacher); Ryan Pope (Arthur's Brother); Stuart Callaghan and James Francis (Boys in Record Shop); Callum Hamilton (Brian Slade, Age 7); Lindsay Kemp (Pantomime Dame); Carlos Miranda (Pianist); Emma Handy (Mod Girlfriend); Matthew Glamour (Mimosa); Daniel Adams (Curt Wild, Age 13); Brian Torfeh (Bartender); Joe Beattie (Cooper); Sarah Cawood (Angel); David Hoyle (Freddi); Winston Austin (Micky); Ivan Cartwright and Peter King (Cecil's Friends); Justin Salinger (Rodney); Roger Alborough (Middle Aged Man); Peter Bradley, Jr. (30's Style Singer); Jonathan Cullen and William Key (Reporters); Vincent Marzello, Corey Skaggs, and Nathan Osgood (US Reporters); Nadia Williams (Teenage Girl); Brian Molko (Malcolm); Anthony Langdon (Ray); Xaf (Pearl); Steve Hewitt (Billy); Guy Leverton (Trevor); Vinney Reck (Reg); Keith-Lee Castle (Harley).

FILM QUARTERLY, Fall 1999, p. 42, Felicia Feaster

A ravishing tribute to the Ziggy Stardust decade, Todd Haynes' *Velvet Goldmine* traces a line of British homosexual flamboyance from legendary grand-dandy Oscar Wilde to drag cabaret to the 70s gender-subterfuge phenomenon known as glam rock. *Velvet* adopts Wilde's aesthetic philosophy, voiced in *Lady Windemere's Fan,* "It's absurd to divide people into good and bad. People are either charming or tedious." Self-crafted exotics in the mode of Wilde or Beau Brummell, the glam rockers were gender innovators for taking advantage of the association of performance with female sexual display, wedding the macho rock-star pose with the feminine archetype of a preening, glamorous pin-up queen.

Haynes immediately establishes *Velvet*'s debt to Wilde in his phantasmagorical opening shot of an ELO spaceship dropping Wilde from the sky. Mixing rock's hokey spiritualism with a sentimental belief in the transformative nature of gay identity, the moment references the cosmic, kitschy metaphysicality that characterized rock opera, traces of which Haynes retains in his portrait of the rich fantasy life of glam. But what makes *Velvet Goldmine* truly idiosyncratic is the director's reluctance to suggest his clearly beloved social phenomenon of glam is some historical anomaly.

Instead, Haynes' *Velvet Goldmine* envisions the evolution of glam as a continuum of what sartorial critic Anne Hollander sees as the dandy's creed, in which "A man's heroism consisted only in being thoroughly himself." For Wilde, style was subversion, a way for a meritocracy of self-created, individual achievement to rise above aristocracy and bestowed social wealth and class. A green brooch said to be worn by Oscar Wilde is passed between the characters in *Velvet* as a token of their identification with Wilde's self-appointed—in Haynes' terms extraterrestrial-status as outsider.

Referencing the rise of glitter rock stars like David Bowie, Iggy Pop, Bryan Ferry, and the New York Dolls in a fictional mode, *Velvet Goldmine* centers on the efforts of a reporter, Arthur Stuart (Christian Bale), to return to the vanished, charmed years of his British youth on the fringe of the exploding glam scene. The glam movement demarcated the years when Stuart's sexual identity was articulated and given expression by performers Brian Slade (Jonathan Rhys-Meyers) and Curt Wild (Ewan McGregor), homages to Bowie and Iggy. The inspiration for Slade and Wild is a nightclub phantom, Jack Fairy (Micko Westmoreland), who makes his most memorable appearance in *Velvet* in an homage to Kenneth Anger's color-saturated glamour-fugue *Puce Moment* and whose dandy artifice wafts like a heady perfume through the film, grounding glam in the overlapping worlds of gay subculture and old Hollywood glamour.

Haynes sets the terms of Arthur's melancholy in a grim, robotic present which brutally contrasts with flashbacks to his color-saturated, kaleidoscopic glam youth. The colorless Manhattan of the Reagan 80s, rendered in shades of polluted browns and gunmetal greys and dictated by an Orwellian monotony, makes all the more visceral and bittersweet Arthur's lost world of music and possibility. Referencing *Citizen Kane*'s detective-story framing device, *Velvet* has Arthur investigating the event that sounded the death knell of glam: the mock assassination of its seminal peacock, Brian Slade. Haynes' insight in using this flashback structure is showing the unbearable wistfulness, the sense of one's youth and sexual promise evaporated, that hearing the music of the past can inspire. In *Velvet*, glitter is like dust—the reminder of a once beautiful phenomenon's sad traces.

Haynes' shockingly intelligent and visually dazzling film is not only an examination of an isolated rock fad, but a look at how rock stars—and music—become sexual figureheads for our own desires—poster children of the libido. Nowhere is this phenomenon clearer than in the figure of Curt Wild, a character partly modeled on Iggy Pop (but also evoking another self-destructive punk maverick, Kurt Cobain), whose hypnotic performances are glittering shrines to sexuality, rage, and escape from his grim Wisconsin trailer-park past. Wild, who at one point in *Velvet* tells a reporter, "You can't fake being gay," is the integrity of the movement, and with his flight from its bosom, the music is finally reduced to mere surface glitz. The icon of glam's eventual perversion is the plastic pop idol Tommy Stone, whose blandly sinister face haunts Arthur's contemporary Manhattan. The 70s glam fans who once integrated the musical androgyny into their daily lives give way to the cowed, identity-less Tommy Stone disciples who wear plastic masks bearing their idol's face.

Music as an emotional trigger and a means of self-creation is captured with great pathos and humor in Arthur's first purchase of a "swishy" Brian Slade album, which he fondles and studies back in his teenage bedroom like a fetish object (a scene which also laments the death of the tactile, sensory pleasures the LP provided). Haynes shows how the androgynous heroes of glam operate as conduits to Arthur's own homosexuality. They inspire Arthur to put on his first glitter ensemble and parade the youth-clogged streets of London. In a gesture of utterly poignant, tentative self-expression, Arthur imagines himself shrieking to his father while watching Slade on TV, "That's me, Dad! That's me!" It's one of the truest and saddest moments in the film, for the myriad gaps it points out: between desire and being; between a hoped-for sexual life and an actual one; between a life of the present and an imagined future; between Arthur and his poor, colorless, TV-incubated parents.

What makes *Velvet* abrade with its special form of aching wistfulness is the flashback structure which reminds us that Arthur has become the thing he feared: a robotic, lifeless creature, far from the questing adventurer of his youth. In many ways, *Velvet is* an allegory of youth's end, of the wistfulness of hearing the music of your past as some lingering evidence of a former self. The scene encapsulates what gives *Velvet* its unique combination of lofty gender-bending, pop culture insight, and rare sweetness.

Haynes' depth of feeling for the limitations life imposes on his characters is evident in the entrapped SoCal housewife of *Safe* or the singer trapped within an idea of a doll's body in Haynes' Barbie-doll melodrama *Superstar*. The director often uses the most florid and campy forms and foregrounded style to get at, sideways, the real emotional texture of his subject matter, demonstrating how camp, in its purest form, always exhibits an investment and affection for what it's treating. As much as the glam movement was an act of self-creation beyond working class, beyond gender, beyond a stifling, sexually repressed adulthood, Haynes' film is itself a tribute to the giddy transportive power of filmmaking language; one panning the tawdry gold of 70s rock operas *(Phantom of the Paradise, Tommy, The Rocky Horror Picture Show)* reassembled into a theoretical treatise on gender as a performance and pop culture as transformative. Shot in the tongue-in-cheek, gaudy style of 70s rock operas like *Sgt. Pepper's Lonely Hearts Club Band* and *Lisztomania, Velvet* walks a brilliant line between kitsch and homage with its dizzying overabundance of style. Its confirmed gaudiness, sudden swish zooms, faked painted backdrops, and gleams of light flaring against the camera lens reference 70s filmmaking while capturing glam's candy-coated outrageousness and cathartic, polymorphous perversity. Haynes' emphasis on a frenetic visual style shows his investment in film as a liberating, visual language whose aesthetics are as meaning-laden as its themes.

In moments of gilded emotionalism like Brian Slade's on-stage assassination, Haynes taps into the streak of theatricality and effervescent melodrama in music and in these musical films—the kind of histrionics which speak so persuasively to the heightened drama of being teenage. Haynes mixes high and low in a manner many critics tended to write off as scrambled and disconnected, but which somehow, nevertheless, distilled the essence of youth, when pop culture and identity-formation are deliriously intertwined. *Goldmine* adopts the collapsed, elliptical storytelling of rock opera, in which emotional investment with characters is replaced with the emotional urgency of the music.

For a subculture-aligned director like Haynes, glam was an assertion of a sexually gymnastic, playful identity which was embraced and ingested like candy into mainstream life. Haynes suggests glam made the 70s, for a time, the utopian, decadent sexual paradise which the graceless, sloppy hippie years had only promised. Unlike the current retro movement to exhume the decade (making us as sick of the post-70s pastiche as we were of the original), Haynes' film actually manages to make the decade both sexy and culturally viable again. Resurrecting a supposedly tacky fad, Haynes shows not only glam's debt to gay subculture and its influence on performance, but how even the most apparently throwaway pop culture can hold great, life-altering meaning for its fans.

LOS ANGELES TIMES, 11/6/98, Calendar/p. 8, Kenneth Turan

Dazzling and dizzying, confusing and even annoying, "Velvet Goldmine" is a feverish dream of a film, a riot of color and attitude that is all pop decadence, all night long. Believing like its characters that "style always wins out in the end," it flamboyantly displays the skills and the drawbacks of one of the most gifted of independent filmmakers, writer-director Todd Haynes.

Haynes' "Poison" won the Grand Jury Prize at Sundance in 1991. His Julianne Moore-starring "Safe" was as smart and provocative as independent filmmaking gets, and this work, typically, has a lot on its mind, sometimes more than it can successfully handle.

"Velvet Goldmine" is best at spotlighting Haynes' showy visual sense, his gorgeous flair for simply playing around with film. Working as usual with accomplished cinematographer Maryse Alberti, Haynes creates wave after wave of images that seem to ripple across the screen. Even though this film can be difficult to follow and at times displays the less-than-subtle character sense of, say, "The Young and the Restless," it is never less than compulsively watchable.

Haynes' subject in "Velvet Goldmine" is the glam-rock era of the early 1970s, when, a BBC narrator reports, "the streets of London are ablaze with sparkle makeup and glittering frocks," and not just on the women. Artists like David Bowie, Elton John and T. Rex's Marc Bolan mocked the rules of gender fashion, and sexual identity was considered a less than rigid concept.

"Velvet Goldmine" has not so much re-created the look of those days as artistically re-imagined it with an emphasis on the outrageous. Production designer Christopher Hobbs, makeup and hair designer (don't ask) Peter King and wizardly costume designer Sandy Powell (Oscar nominated for both "Orlando" and "The Wings of the Dove") have combined to operatic effect, creating a world that almost literally makes the head spin.

Also attention-getting is the film's extensive soundtrack, intended, an opening on-screen note informs, "to be played at maximum volume." With its seamless melange of original recordings (like T. Rex's "Cosmic Dancer"), covers of originals by current bands, and music written for the film in the glam manner, the music is energizing and practically wall to wall. It contributes to "Velvet Goldmine's" ability to convey the excitement and the danger of rock, the posing, the nihilism, the eagerness to shock and the subverted rage that make this music a perennial threat to the status quo.

Yet another of "Velvet Goldmine's" concerns is conveying the flaunting of pan-sexual androgyny that characterized the period. Furthering that aim is the adroit casting of the two central rock performers and putative lovers, the David Bowiesque Brian Slade, a.k.a. Maxwell Demon (played with grand icy hauteur by Jonathan Rhys Meyers) and the wild American proto-punk Curt Wild (the protean Ewan McGregor, who gets to scream, howl and indulge in full-frontal nudity).

Not everything about this film, however, is impressive. The film's framing device, involving the character of newspaper reporter Arthur Stuart (Christian Bale), often feels awkward. We see Stuart both undertaking a "Citizen Kane"-type investigation of rocker Slade in 1984, 10 years after the man's heyday, and, in extended flashbacks, having his own life as a teenager seriously affected by the glam movement.

After a typically out-there opening sequence linking Oscar Wilde, a mysterious jewel from outer space and a glam-rock avatar named Jack Fairy (Micko Westmoreland), "Velvet Goldmine" takes us to an infamous 1974 Slade concert that had a profound effect on the man's career and the entire glam movement.

The rest of Slade's story is told through interviews Stuart conducts with people such as Slade's burned-out ex-wife Mandy (Toni Collette) and his first manager, Cecil (Michael Feast). Making extensive use of outrageous videos, flashbacks, supposed concert footage and TV interviews with the likes of star-maker Jerry Divine (Eddie Izzard), plus a scene using dolls (which echoes Haynes' mind-bending "Superstar: The Karen Carpenter Story"), the film goes back and forth between several time periods, often not letting the audience know that a flashback has started until we're well into it. It's a mixture that can be intoxicating.

As the opposites who attracted, Rhys Meyers and McGregor are eye-popping characters on stage, but "Velvet Goldmine's" sporadic attempts to investigate them as real people is less successful. With so much emphasis put on images that delight, provoke and outrage, who can wonder that dramatic insight is not always there for the taking.

NEW STATESMAN, 10/23/98, p. 35, Jonathan Romney

"Although what you are about to see is a work of fiction," teasingly announce the opening titles to "Velvet Goldmine," "it should be played at full volume." Todd Haynes's extraordinary panorama of the glamrock years seems certain to face resistance from British audiences, who usually like to know for sure whether they're dealing with fact or fiction. Besides, its hyper-camp polysexual pitch flies violently in the face of 1990s rock-geezer culture. It won't pull the "Lock, Stock and Two Smoking Barrels" audience, that's for sure.

This is not the real glam story, though. Instead of a David Bowie biopic, it's a fantasy about a Bowie-esque young thing called Brian Slade (Jonathan Rhys Meyers), who enjoys a torrid romance with American star Curt Wild (Ewan McGregor), closely modelled on Iggy Pop. Bowie-ires may well hate the film, not only for its cartoon image of the True Facts, but also because Haynes presents his hero as a confused opportunist, a cultural magpie cribbing indiscriminately from a multitude of role models, before cashing in his chips for the conformist rock dreams of the 1980s.

"Velvet Goldmine" should be read as a fantasy, and like the best fantasies, it's fabulously superficial at first sight, before revealing hidden depths and resonances. It uses the Bowie story much as Slade uses the images of history. This is a fan's dream of pop history, by a director who was too young to be in the thick of it at the time. Although "Velvet Goldmine" has been touted as a British film, because of its stars and Film on Four's production involvement, it's very much an American director's fantasy about Englishness—a rifling, at transatlantic arm's length, of motifs from pop's past and the gay history that informed it. The references run from Oscar Wilde, through music hall drag, through the parlare slang of 1960s gay subculture, to the short-lived revolution of glam's mascara-masquerade.

"Velvet Goldmine" is in every sense a made-up story about made-up people. Like Bowie, Slade invents himself piecemeal, but that hardly invalidates him or makes him less "authentic"—a word which has never been much use in pop history. Ever since emerging in the early 1990s as a front runner in what was briefly hailed as the "New Queer Cinema", Todd Haynes has shown a cultural analyst's eye for the paradoxes of identity and the prerogatives of fantasy. His debut feature, "Poison", was inspired by Jean Genet, the high priest of transgressive self-invention and another Bowie hero. In "Velvet Goldmine," he mischievously alludes to his early short "Superstar", a biopic of Karen Carpenter acted out by Barbie dolls. A young girl plays with two boy dolls customised in the guise of Brian and Curt, who declare their passion before falling into a clinch.

That, Haynes reminds us, is what fan fantasy is for—a way of possessing your idols by turning them into your personal toys. The stars in this story are like puppets—of the media, of their audiences, of each other. And, as such, we can't expect them to have any "depth". At a press conference, Slade dazzles with flashes of lapidary philosophical wit—until you realise that the words are all Oscar Wilde's, and that he's reading them from cue cards.

"Velvet Goldmine" is similarly composed of quotations. It's a gaudy patchwork of different film stock, camera styles, spot-on soundtrack pastiches, and wildly differing styles of performance—Rhys Meyers' fazed-Narcissus blankness, Eddie Izzard's punchy Tin Pan Alley hucksterism, Toni Collette's vampy archness as Slade's wife. And central to a film that is justifiably infatuated with look is Sandy Powell's wardrobe, the whole gamut from catwalk dazzle to Oxfam satin-and-tat.

"Velvet Goldmine" recognises that pop revolutions are invariably short-lived and their seismic effects often denied by the very people that caused them. The polysexual youthquake that Slade heralds has its phoney side, too: the film is good on the way that conformist youth culture latched on to Bowie's bisexuality as a flag of convenience, and the extras casting is rife with what used to be derided as the "mascara'd brickie" look. And, although it's not referred to directly, you can't help remembering how glam's direct descendant, punk, rejected its sexual complexity like a puritanical teenager disowning a scandalous aunt.

This flamboyantly complex film can be taken in different ways: as a giddy fan letter, as a serious essay in gay cultural archaeology, as stretching the language of pop cinema beyond the MTV cliches. But even the fact that it often seems superficial and cartoonish should be applauded—this is pure cinematic dandyism, too rare in these downbeat screen days. You'll learn next to nothing about the real history of glam, but a lot about why 1970s teenagers embraced the risque pleasures of expensive guitars and cheap eyeliner.

NEW YORK, 11/16/98, p. 63, Peter Rainer

I suppose it won't do to say that Todd Haynes's *Velvet Goldmine* isn't my kind of movie and leave it at that. It's about the British glam-rock scene in the early seventies, a period I lived through without ever mistaking it for the flowering of the Enlightenment. The fault may be mine. Still, *Velvet Goldmine* doesn't make me want to step inside the time machine. I mean, there was a *reason* David Bowie killed off Ziggy Stardust.

Haynes's last movie, the vastly overrated *Safe,* was all about the aridity of modern life. *Velvet Goldmine* is also about aridity, but—what with all the platform boots and glitter makeup and feather boas and lacquered hair—it's a much trippier ride. Brian Slade (Jonathan Rhys Meyers) is a glamster who gets his first glimpse of glamdom nirvana when he witnesses a concert by the Iggy Pop-ish American singer Curt Wild (Ewan McGregor) as he prances naked and dives through hoops of fire. Pretty soon Brian is a superstar himself, and Curt is on the junkie skids. Then Brian self-destructs, staging his own mock assassination during a concert and incurring the everlasting wrath of his fans when the hoax is revealed. He drops permanently from sight.

Actually, none of this is as linear as I make it sound. Haynes lifts his structure from *Citizen Kane,* of all things, with a reporter tracking down Brian's cohorts on the tenth anniversary of the scam. The flashbacks and flash-forwards and flash-in-betweens are meant to be deliberately disorienting, but where's the Rosebud in all of this? Since everyone in the movie has the approximate human weight of a hologram, we're not really motivated to fit together the puzzle pieces of their lives. Hollow is as hollow does. Haynes is at least a good sport about all this froufrou. He doesn't push the decadence in glam rock; for him, it's just a great big androgynous glitter pageant. But *Velvet Goldmine* should be more startling than it is.

NEW YORK POST, 11/6/98, p. 70, Thelma Adams

Todd Haynes' impressionistic homage to the glam-rock scene of the 70s pilfers liberally from the lives of David Bowie, Angela Bowie, Iggy Pop and others in the sexually ambiguous mascara-and-glitter pantheon.

At last month's New York Film Festival, "Velvet Goldmine" struck the strongest chord with those who had been there, done that and were carried over the movie's dramatic shortcomings by waves of nostalgia.

High points include the score, which mixes original tunes, covers recorded by contemporary musicians and sound-alike songs written expressly for "Velvet Goldmine."

Haynes, best known for the chilly art-house hit "Safe," starring suburban ice princess Julianne Moore, coaxes fantastically overheated performances here. Scot Ewan McGregor ("Trainspotting") grabs center stage doing a dead-on Detroit accent as bad-boy rocker Curt Wild, a rangy chip off Pop.

Relative newcomer Jonathan Rhys Meyers ("The Governess") glitters as bisexual rock star Brian Slade/David Bowie. Toni Collette ("Muriel's Wedding") finds eyeshadows and light in Mrs. Slade. Weak link Christian Bale drops a stitch as a contemporary newspaper reporter looking back on the era and his own close encounter with eyeliner and crushed velvet.

For all the writer-director's passion and exuberance, and his fine eye for subject matter, Haynes is too arty for his shirt. He references everyone from Oscar Wilde to Rainer Werner Fassbinder to Orson Welles. What the structurally soft "Velvet" most closely approaches is Ken Russell's feverish "Lisztomania," starring Roger Daltrey and Ringo Starr.

NEWSDAY, 11/6/98, Part II/p. B6, John Anderson

Let's call it the Todd Tautology: Judging the work of the genuine visionary demands an elevated set of criteria; the work of Todd Haynes demands an elevated set of criteria; ergo, Todd Haynes is a genuine visionary.

Elemental, simplistic, but true nonetheless. From the late '80s to the late '90s, Haynes has created a body of work made up of understated masterpieces, films whose basic set-ups would be enough to satisfy the itches of most directors, but which Haynes has used as mere vehicles to get at profound societal truths. If this sounds like one of the prime purposes of art, and that perhaps Haynes is merely serving his function as an artist, the answer is yes—but consider how few current filmmakers do it, and how well it's done by Haynes.

His never-released "Superstar: The Karen Carpenter Story"—a "biopic" cast entirely with Barbie dolls (or, to avoid trademark infringement, "Barbie-type dolls")—is one of the fetish items of the bootleg-movie world, a "novelty" that never fails to move audiences with its sense of loss and excoriation of pop stardom. "Poison," the Jean Genet-inspired triptych that won honors at Sundance and a sentence in hell from the American Family Association's Rev. Donald Wildmon, used a poultice of B-movie conventions to draw out the psychic venom of modern life. "Safe," the "environmental-disease" film and Julianne Moore's best to date, was a film of exquisite control about a planet run amok. And "Dottie Gets Spanked," ostensibly about a little boy's innocent fixation on a '60s sitcom, embraced issues of sexual identity, family conflict and the endless vagaries of perception.

So: What has he done for us lately? "Velvet Goldmine," his biggest-budget production to date, is on one hand an exercise in flamboyance and excess, a mystery/biography with major costumes and period music (covers of reverential originals by Grant Lee Buffalo, Pulp and Shudder to Think). At its center is Brian Slade (Jonathan Rhys-Meyers), a David Bowieesque glam rocker of the early '70s, who disappeared at the height of his fame after staging a mock assassination and incurring the wrath of his fans. The story is told through the eyes of Arthur Stuart (self-contained cult movement Christian Bale), a journalist working amid the culturally stultified Reagan year of '84 in New York who is assigned by an editor with no other ideas to find out where Slade went.

Structured in "Citizen Kane" style—Arthur's interview of Slade's wife Mandy (Toni Colette, in *her* best work to date) is pure homage to Welles—"Velvet Goldmine" isn't much of a mystery. And although Slade's orbit contains the Iggy Pop-inspired Curt Wild (Ewan McGregor) and a catalog of veiled '70s cultural references, it isn't anthropology, either.

But what it says about the sexual/cultural options offered up by the androgynous spectacle of glam rock is profound and ultimately ingenious. Through his research on Slade, Arthur flashes back to his own sexual awakening and emancipation—a suffocated middle-class London youth set free and uncloseted by the images and popularity of glam rock. The '70s is a decade regularly abused for its music, but what Haynes gives us, within his pulsing, pounding, liberated history, is a era of possibilities—the opportunity, to paraphrase the Army ads, to be all the people you can be.

"Velvet Goldmine," ultimately, is elegiac—about a pop moment that might easily be lampooned, and about how the self-conscious glitter of the '70s has become the self-conscious cynicism of the '90s. How silly it all was, we say, while Matthew Shepard hangs on a fence.

NEWSWEEK, 11/9/98, p. 70, David Ansen

In the fantastical prologue to Todd Haynes's "Velvet Goldmine," a movie about glam rockers in England in the early '70s, who should pop up but an 8-year-old Oscar Wilde. In Haynes's view, Wilde is the spiritual forefather of the self-invented icons of the Ziggy Stardust era, those androgynous rock stars who, for a brief, gaudily hedonistic moment, turned our notions of sexual identity upside down.

Filled with music, spectacular costumes and orgiastic revelry, "Velvet Goldmine" is a brainy three-ring circus. It's so overloaded you're not sure where to focus your attention. Should it be on Brian Slade (Jonathan Rhys Meyers), the beautiful, David Bowie-like star who mysteriously disappeared from the public eye? Is it the central figure, Curt Wild, the Iggy Pop-like loose cannon played by Ewan McGregor with such incendiary abandon he becomes the film's manic heartbeat? Is it the journalist Arthur Stuart (Christian Bale), the former besotted fan of Slade and Wild who is now, 10 years later, trying to uncover the reality behind the glitter?

Haynes's celebration of the gender-bending exuberance of the period plucks powerful nostalgic chords. But people who didn't live through those times may have a harder time connecting, because Haynes ("Poison," "Safe") is unwilling to get too close to his characters. Slade, in particular, is a blank. "A man's life is his image," the film quotes Oscar Wilde. The movie reveals both the truth and the limitations of that remark. One reason glam rock proved so short-lived may have been its devotion to artifice and image. In the end, platform shoes and feather boas made better accessories than philosophies.

SIGHT AND SOUND, 11/98, p. 63, Xan Brooks

Britain, the early 70s. Thomas, an unremarkable lad from Birmingham, reinvents himself as Brian Slade, the sequinned and feathered icon of the emerging glam-rock scene. In 1974, at the height of his fame, Slade fakes his own death and disappears. Ten years later, journalist Arthur Stuart investigates the mystery. Stuart's search brings him into contact with Slade's ex-wife Mandy and former agent Cecil, while the story cuts back and forth between the 70s and 80s.

Slade's history hinges on his relationship with Curt Wild, a drug-addled American rock star whose career Slade attempts to revitalise. Slade's manager Jerry Divine signs Wild to his label but soon loses faith when Slade is unable to complete an album.

Disillusioned, Slade escapes to Berlin and then returns to London to engineer his own death. Curt Wild and fellow pop star Jack Fairy play a farewell concert to glam rock, at which Slade is seen hiding in the shadows at the back of the auditorium. In New York in 1984, Stuart finds the US in thrall to a showbiz evangelist called Tommy Stone. Stuart meets Curt Wild, who confirms his suspicions that Stone and Slade are in fact the same man; a symbol for the shift of the decadent 70s into the reactionary gloss of the 80s.

Brian Slade, muses one of the secondary characters in *Velvet Goldmine*, "was like nothing I'd ever seen before, and in the end like nothing he appeared," a man "walking arm in arm with a lie." As with the man, so with the film. For Todd Haynes' febrile, flamboyant fancy does not so much steer a course through 70s glam as wallow exuberantly in the movement's chaotic lack of structure, its sense of a style dictating a substance. *Velvet Goldmine* (its title culled from an obscure Bowie B-side) is a film born out of paradox: an intellectual thesis on flyweight fakery and fiction; an American's love-letter to an idiosyncratically British phenomenon. It is far and away the most weighty, sprawling and ambitious project the writer-director of *Poison* and [*Safe*] has yet attempted; it contains multitudes.

There is no centre to *Velvet Goldmine*. Haynes' film is extraneous and diffuse. His story functions as a series of fairy lights, each illuminating one small portion of the whole. Some of these are crucial, others misleading red herrings. Similarly, many of the film's inhabitants ring seemingly deliberate (one is never entirely sure) phoney notes. Slade himself is a clear Bowie clone, yet Jonathan Rhys Meyers' portrayal leaves him looking flat and unknowable, strangely colourless behind the frills and make up, Eddie Izzard's manager delivers his lines in a tortuous mimicry of Michael Caine. Meanwhile, Ewan McGregor's Curt Wild (one part Lou Reed, two parts Iggy Pop, and with a Kurt Cobain hair-do) sports a decidedly wobbly American accent. We can never entirely escape the notion that these people are actors assuming a role. And yet, of course, this was the central feature of glam rock, fed by a life-blood of artifice, androgyny and performance. Again: as with the scene, so with the film.

A leading exponent of US independent film-making's New Queer Cinema (a term he has grown to dislike), Haynes approaches British glam from an implicitly queer vantage point. *Velvet Goldmine* emerges as a homage to gay undercurrents throughout British art. A boyish Oscar Wilde crops up at the start, telling his teacher that, "I want to be a pop idol." The pre-stardom Brian Slade ("a shirt-lifter from Birmingham") looks on transfixed as a Danny La Rue-style entertainer electrifies a working men's club. Later, a camp older audience make catty remarks during one of Slade's first gigs. Glam rock, Haynes implies, marked the zenith of queer art—a blurring of the boundaries, an embrace of the Other—before the pendulum swung back towards a rigid and Orwellian 80s. (The sci fi 80s parallel world depicted here, with a US ruled by a non-existent president, is another exercise in artifice and misdirection.)

Haynes shows us that glam rock did not spring out of nowhere, but rather was a cobbled-together patchwork of US rock, British camp and 30s art deco. Likewise, *Velvet Goldmine* arrives awash with second-hand ingredients. Its soundtrack offers an assortment of Iggy Pop staples ("Gimme Danger", "T.V. Eye") and expert Bowie pastiches. Its narrative echoes both *Citizen Kane* and Don DeLillo's rock star-vanishes novel *Great Jones Street*. At one point, Haynes even 'rips off' himself. A brief scene enacted by plastic Brian and Curt figurines playfully recalls his own banned Barbie doll biopic *Superstar: The Karen Carpenter Story*.

For a brief spell in the early 70s, glam rock energised a discerning section of British youth. Dreary bedrooms were festooned with gaudy posters; gauche teenagers strode grey suburban streets in fantastical new get-ups. The success of Haynes' dense, layered, sometimes frustrating, frequently fabulous picture is in catching this ephemeral butterfly-moment, in turning a mirror on a strange and exotic sight. of course, the face in the mirror lies, but only to the extent that art itself is a lie. In all its poses and glamours, then, Haynes' film brilliantly exposes the ideals of youth culture: its celebration of difference, its clumsy questing for the intangible, the potential it offers for individual expression and renewal. Throughout truth is paired with artifice—you can't have one without the other.

VILLAGE VOICE, 11/10/98, p. 115, J. Hoberman

The epigram "Histories, like ancient ruins, are the fictions of empire" may seem more appropriate to Shekhar Kapur's 16th-century period drama *Elizabeth* than Todd Haynes's 1970s-set *Velvet Goldmine* (wherein it appears), but Haynes's ambitious glam-rock opera is an unusually literate and ironically grandiose contribution to the current cycle of lost-scene movies.

Set on a cusp—between the twilight of the orgiastic '60s and the dawn of the deflated '70s—the 1971-73 Glam Era celebrated self-conscious artifice with melancholy pomp. Haynes, who has his movie define its subject as a post-Flower Power mix of "glamour, nostalgia, and just plain outrageousness," has done his homework. A monument to gilded evanescence, *Velvet Goldmine* struggles mightily to re-mythologize a moment in pop history that was born mythologized.

The movie opens, like the Disney *Peter Pan* or Steven Spielberg's *Close Encounters,* from a cosmic perspective with an extraterrestrial visitation upon the sleeping humanity. The alien turns out to be the infant Oscar Wilde, who, in effect, invents the body electric by growing up to tell his schoolmaster that his ambition is "to be a pop idol." Thus theorizing rock as a romantic expression predicated on the creation of a charismatic persona, Haynes anoints Wilde—the ultimate aesthete and consummate public role-player—s founding father (as someone else might argue for Lord Byron or Walt Whitman).

As can be deduced from this hectic prologue, which then jumps ahead a century to present blue-haired glam star Brian Slade's onstage "assassination," *Velvet Goldmine* has no shortage of ideas—most of which are presented from the viewpoint of an ardent fan. To a large degree and with considerable wit, *Velvet Goldmine* is a film à clef. As glitter-encrusted Slade (Jonathan Rhys Meyers) strongly resembles David Bowie (with a few echoes of Marc Bolan) and his consort Mandy (Toni Collette) suggests Angie Bowie, so his American idol, the bare-chested garage-rock madman Curt Wild (Ewan McGregor), is Iggy Pop (inflected by Lou Reed's bio and Kurt Cobain's look).

Velvet Goldmine's most daring intervention is to take glam's extravagantly queer theatricality at its word. Extrapolating a sexual relationship from Bowie and Iggy's 1977 artistic collaboration, Haynes centers his film on Slade and Wild's mad fling. It's a "Tracy and Hepburn for the '70s" in someone's naughty formulation and Haynes flaunts his subversive fantasy further in quoting his own Super-8 classic *Superstar* by initially dramatizing the Slade-Wild affair with a pair of Ken dolls even before the actors get down to being bad boys together. Rhys Meyers may not be as seductive as the script insists, but his focused petulance projects something of Bowie's lunar coldness; as his wife, Collette has a complementary sullenness, but McGregor pogos off with the movie as the lunatic Wild—and he can sing too.

Haynes's freedom to mess with pop personae is crucial insofar as *Velvet Goldmine* is most strikingly organized in terms of stars and fans. Glam rock is not only presented as a pop religion, complete with a fake crucifixion and holy relics, but as a source of cult identity. In one of the most evocative scenes, the humble devotee Arthur Stuart (Christian Bale) risks public humiliation to purchase an early Brian Slade LP. With a concentrated attention otherwise reserved for the spectacle of McGregor chewing on Rhys Meyers's bee-stung lips, Haynes lavishes mega-close-ups on the record jacket, the paper sleeve, and the label, until the whole clunky process of plopping a vinyl disc on a plastic hi-fi is steeped in erotic anticipation. As Kenneth Anger wrote of the early movie stars, never have so few become masturbation fodder for so many. Later and more pathetically, a languorous glam orgy is interpenetrated with scenes of poor glamateur Arthur caught wanking in his parents' house. (Bale seems to exist in a state of perpetual embarrassment.)

Compounding the artifice, Haynes has Arthur double as a reporter in the investigative flashback structure that *Velvet Goldmine* lifts, none too successfully, from *Citizen Kane*. After a most promising beginning, *Velvet Goldmine*'s progress grows increasingly labored, stumbling around the structural roadblocks Haynes has erected in its path. The emphasis on theatrical, elegiac anthems slows the action, rather than jolting it alive. (This may well be Haynes's intention. The movie's most galvanizing number—Bolan's "20th Century Boy"—is strategically withheld until the so-called Death of Glitter concert.) As free-associative as the movie sometimes seems, it is anything but rhapsodic.

Velvet Goldmine is strong enough to bring together, as glam precursors, a number of hitherto unrelated, early-70s Anglo-American movies—*Performance, A Clockwork Orange, The Boy Friend, Born To Boogie, Cabaret,* and *Jesus Christ Superstar* (as well as *The Rocky Horror Picture Show* and Derek Jarman's *Jubilee,* themselves comments on glam). What it lacks is their showbiz vulgarity. More kabuki pageant than melodrama, less edited than assembled, the movie emphasizes structure over fantasy, concept over performance, and—despite an opening request to be "played at maximum volume"—glam over rock. There's a Brechtian presentation—perhaps even a documentary essay—yearning to emerge from this ostensibly commercial enterprise.

Undeniably intelligent, *Velvet Goldmine* is arguably the most cerebral rock'n'roll movie ever made. The movie begs for footnotes, exegesis, disputation—it's an Apollonian orgy. That's not necessarily an oxymoron, but on the big screen in the real world, it's a Pyrrhic victory at best.

Also reviewed iN:
CHICAGO TRIBUNE, 11/6/98, Friday/p. H, Michael Wilmington
NATION, 11/30/98, p. 32, Stuart Klawans
NEW YORK TIMES, 11/6/98, p. E15, Janet Maslin
NEW YORKER, 11/9/98, p. 108, Anthony Lane
VARIETY, 5/25-31/98, p. 56, Todd McCarthy
WASHINGTON POST, 11/6/98, p. D5, Richard Harrington
WASHINGTON POST, 11/6/98, Weekend/p. 47, Michael O'Sullivan

VERY BAD THINGS

A PolyGram Filmed Entertainment release in association with Initial Entertainment Group of an Interscope Communications production in association with Ballpark Productions. *Executive Producer:* Ted Field, Scott Kroopf, Michael Helfant, and Christian Slater. *Producer:* Michael Schiffer, Diane Nabatoff, and Cindy Cowan. *Director:* Peter Berg. *Screenplay:* Peter Berg. *Director of Photography:* David Hennings. *Editor:* Dan Lebental. *Music:* Stewart Copeland. *Music Editor:* Michael Dittrick. *Sound:* Mark Weingarten and (music) Jeff Seitz. *Sound Editor:* Gregory King and Yann Delpuech. *Casting:* Debi Manwiller. *Production Designer:* Dina Lipton. *Art Director:* Michael Atwell. *Set Designer:* Noelle King. *Set Decorator:* Kathy Lucas. *Set Dresser:* Rodney Petreikis. *Special Effects:* Larry Fioritto. *Costumes:* Terry Dressbach. *Make-up:* Jeanne Van Phue and Nancy Baca. *Stunt Coordinator:* Chris Howell. *Running time:* 101 minutes. *MPAA Rating:* R.

CAST: Jon Faveau (Kyle Fisher); Leland Orser (Charles Moore); Cameron Diaz (Laura Garrety); Christian Slater (Robert Boyd); Rob Brownstein (Man); Jeremy Piven (Michael Berkow); Daniel Stern (Adam Berkow); Jeanne Tripplehorn (Lois Berkow); Joey Zimmerman

(Adam Berkow, Jr.); Tyler Malinger (Timmy Berkow); Carla Scott (Tina); Russell B. McKenzie (Security Guard); Pancho Demings (Cop); Blake Gibbons (Suit); Angelo Di Mascio, Jr. (Clerk); Lawrence Pressman (Mr. Fisher); Steve Fitchpatrick (Cop at Hospital); Brian Grandison, John Cappon and Linda Klein (Doctors); Byrne Piven (Rabbi); Bob Bancroft (Barry Morris); Trey Davis (Receptionist); Marilyn McIntryre (Judge Tower).

LOS ANGELES TIMES, 11/25/98, Calendar/p. 2, Kenneth Turan

"Very Bad Things" is a lamentable film whose woeful qualities are heightened by the smugness and self-satisfaction of its creators. The unhappy writing and directing debut of actor Peter Berg, this sour item will undoubtedly wear its negative reviews as badges of honor, marks of having been too real, too honest, and most important, way too hip and trendy for the uninitiated to appreciate.

The opposite is closer to the truth. Not only isn't this kind of superblack comedy groundbreaking anymore, it's become as familiar and tedious a sight from independent filmmakers as directors in backward baseball caps are at Sundance.

And while its delusional creative team talks grandly in the press notes of having made a film "so disturbing that it rocks your world at a deep level," the truth is that this work is hollow, simple-minded and about as profound an experience as stepping in a pile of road kill.

The hallmark of "Very Bad's" depiction of life falling apart for five friends after a bachelor party in Las Vegas gets way out of hand is the almost sadistic glee it takes in its ability to project the most cynical view of human nature imaginable.

Unfortunately, writer-director Berg and his cast are much too pleased with themselves for having gone oh so far, being oh so daring, for any of them to realize just presenting a situation is not an end in itself.

Not at all funny (though it strenuously pretends to be), not at all insightful (though one of its producers speaks with apparent complete seriousness of revealing "the demons inside all of us"), "Very Bad" is a completely pointless exercise, the fake-provocative scrawl of naughty toddlers who think it's enough to say, "Look how bad we've been," for the world to take approving notice. In today's cinematic climate, they're probably right.

Before you can have a bachelor party, you need a potential bride and groom, and that would be Angelenos Laura Garrety (Cameron Diaz) and Kyle Fisher (Jon Favreau). She's obsessed with every detail of a perfect picture-book wedding while he's got his mind on his upcoming bachelor party in Vegas.

Going with him are bickering brothers Adam and Michael Berkow (Daniel Stem and Jeremy Piven), nonverbal garage mechanic Charles Moore (Leland Orser) and real estate agent Robert Boyd (Christian Slater).

It's Boyd who's the mastermind behind the party, the operator who lines up stripper Tina (Carla Scott) to entertain his drunk and coked-up buddies in their hotel room. But a bout of over-athletic sex in the bathroom takes an unhappy turn: Tina's head gets graphically impaled on a wall hook and she dies exploitatively naked in a pool of blood. Laughing yet? Don't worry, things are just getting started.

While decent Adam wants to call the police, hustler Boyd says not so fast. "There are always options," he claims, even in this kind of "major thin-ice situation," and he makes a passionate case for how easy it would be to just bag Tina and then bury her somewhere in the desert on the drive home.

Making that option a little less easy is the appearance of a hotel security guard (Russell B. McKenzie) who, this being the kind of happy-go-lucky film it is, gets promptly butchered as well. Now both bodies have to be cut into pieces and buried in the desert, not once, but twice, because good-guy Adam insists on digging them up to ensure that all the pieces of each body are buried together.

Naturally, all this creates major hostility between the former pals, which plays itself out in complete hysteria, constant screaming and serious nervous breakdowns once everyone gets back to L.A. One by one the guys unravel and lose control in a kind of chain-reaction psychosis. Before this miserable epic is finally over, everyone involved (including the audience) is either maimed or dead or wishing they were.

Berg, best known for his role on "Chicago Hope," has given an interview about the making of "Very Bad" in a recent issue of Movieline that reads like a parody of an actor who's had his head turned by too much stroking.

"I have very little desire to be a movie star," Berg says. "There's something tremendously unsatisfying about it. You make a lot of money, you have a lot of opportunities, you get to sleep with a lot of very beautiful women, you get free food in restaurants. But you service other people's visions. Your privacy is stripped from you. People perceive you as something you're not."

Before anyone gets too depressed about Berg's plight, be assured he's going to break those golden chains and focus on writing and directing. "If I could make 10 more movies like 'Very Bad Things,'" the actor says, "with that kind of creative control, that's a life, man."

For him, maybe. For moviegoers the prospect is considerably more deadly.

NEW YORK POST, 11/25/98, p. 48, Rod Dreher

"Very Bad Things" is the only bright spot among this years bile-sodden black comedies. Not only is it scaldingly funny (though it falls apart at the end), its satirical critique of contemporary manners and morals resonates beyond modish misanthropy or cheap shock value.

"Chicago Hope" actor Peter Berg, who wrote and directed this, his first feature, doesn't have a light touch, and his way-over-the-top application of graphic gore often obscures his surgical slicing and dicing of the self-centered American soul in a culture that has replaced ethics with squishy self-help nostrums. Still, with its moral rigor and savagely mordant grotesquery, "Very Bad Things" suggests that Berg has been reading Flannery O'Connor.

Before Kyle (Jon Favreau) can marry Laura (Cameron Diaz), his four best buddies are going to take him away for a swingin' bachelor party weekend. The boys—Charles (Leland Orser), Robert (Christian Slater) and squabbling brothers Adam and Michael (Daniel Stern and Jeremy Piven)—treat Kyle to a drugs, booze and sex romp in a Vegas hotel suite.

Things go wrong when a hooker dies in a bout of rough sex, and the men kill a guard to hide their initial crime. Talking like Friedrich Nietzsche by way of Tony Robbins, the amoral Robert pep-talks the others into agreeing that they need not let a little thing like this stand in the way of the success that decent fellas like them deserve.

The men cut up the corpses and bury them in the desert. They tell God they're really, really sorry, and vow never to speak of it again.

But each man has a telltale heart, and their various fears and hatreds eat away at the group's confident collusion. By the time the movie ends, each of them, one way or another, wreaks unintentional vengeance on the others for their crimes.

Everybody is cynical as hell in this acid-washed picture, but frighteningly true to life in their belief in their own virtue, their own entitlement, and in their easy willingness to lie to preserve what a young Bill Clinton once called "my political viability." Berg sends these creeps' vanities up in a bonfire that's very amusing and very timely—but, alas, very grisly.

NEWSDAY, 11/25/98, Part II/p. B7, Jack Mathews

You're in Las Vegas hotel room with your four best friends, having one last drug and alcohol-fueled fling before marrying the girl of your dreams, when one of your pals emerges from the bathroom in a blood-soaked robe and announces that he's accidentally killed the hooker hired for the party.

Are you having fun yet?

Wait, in writer-director Peter Berg's very dark, very smug and only occasionally funny black comedy, "Very Bad Things," the party has just begun.

No sooner have you voted (3-2 yea) to dismember and bury the hooker's body in the desert than a hotel security guard shows up, prompting someone to plunge a corkscrew into his heart, and double the night's graveyard duties.

Now, with your wedding just days off, and paranoia dividing that old gang of yours, you have to wonder if any of you will make it to the church on time.

Welcome, once again, to Quentin Tarantino country, which since "Reservoir Dogs" and "Pulp Fiction" has become the arbiter of incoming talent. Berg, a TV star ("Chicago Hope") making his debut as a filmmaker, shows his mettle as a gross-out gagster, and benefits from a terrific last-act performance from Cameron Diaz as the determined bride.

But "Very Bad Things" is otherwise a pretty routine thing, post-Tarantino, and features five guys (Jon Favreau, Daniel Stem, Christian Slater, Jeremy Piven, Leland Orser) who are no fun to be with even before the bachelor party.

NEWSWEEK, 11/30/98, p. 82, David Ansen

We've been through radical chic, shabby chic and heroin chic. Now the black comedy "Very Bad Things" would like very badly to shock you with nastiness chic. Rarely has a movie tried so hard to rub our noses in the vileness of human nature. Writer-director Peter Berg (best known as an actor in "Chicago Hope") is implicitly challenging the audience: *Are you cool enough to laugh at this?* Don't think so, Pete.

The fun begins in Las Vegas, where five thirtysomething guys have gathered for a raunchy bachelor party on the eve of Kyle Fisher's (Jon Favreau) wedding to Laura Garrety (Cameron Diaz). Booze flows, coke is snorted, tables are smashed, an Asian hooker is summoned and, in the middle of servicing the hopped-up Michael (Jeremy Piven), she is accidentally killed. Instead of calling the cops, the manipulative real-estate agent Robert (Christian Slater) proposes burying the body in the desert and just pretending nothing has happened. When a black security guard happens to check out these noisy guests and discovers her body in a blood-stained bathroom, Robert takes it upon himself to kill the guard. Now they have two bodies to chop up, bag and bury, which Berg shows us in luridly graphic detail. Are we laughing yet?

One very bad thing inevitably leads to many very bad things. Berg's scenario is structured as an immoral Rube Goldberg machine, in which every wrong choice sets off an even worse one, until every character has revealed his—or her, as it turns out—capacity for total depravity. The one voice of morality, Michael's brother Adam (Daniel Stern), is, of course, a hysterical nerd and hopelessly uncool. (He will be murdered by his brother; I guess it's called sibling rivalry.) One of the bigger jokes of the film is that Diaz, the hopeful bride, upon learning that her fiancé and his friends are up to their guilty elbows in blood, is completely unfazed. She's so obsessed with having the perfect wedding that she's not about to let a pile of corpses get in her way. Indeed, she's as eager a killer as they. Still not laughing?

Bad behavior can certainly make good comedy—rent Alec Guinness's "The Ladykillers," if you want just one delightful example. And so can bad taste, as John Waters has proved many times over. But Berg's extra-dark comedy is so mechanical, so strained and so pleased with its own ugliness that it quickly curdles. The escalating outrages have a diminishing impact as the filmmaker dutifully fills in his diagram of depravity. This isn't a "vision" of life, but a kid's game of "can you top this?"

"Very Bad Things" owes an obvious debt to the 1994 Scottish comedy "Shallow Grave," but its antecedents stretch back at least as far as "The Treasure of the Sierra Madre," the classic "scorpion in a bottle" drama in which greed turns everyone into a predator. It's a genre that suddenly seems back in vogue—next month brings, "A Simple Plan," a noncomedic variation of the one-crime-leads-to-another theme. Berg obviously thinks he's being brave and daring, but the very ubiquity of this pop nihilism suggests he's merely being trendy. Filmmakers used to have to fight to get their authentically dark visions onto the screen. In the era of nastiness chic, venality and murder are as common—and as much a cliché—as Mom and apple pie. The only truly shocking thing about "Very Bad Things" is how desperately unfunny it is.

SIGHT AND SOUND, 1/99, p. 59, Xan Brooks

Five friends—Kyle, Robert, Charles and brothers Michael and Adam—go for a stag weekend before Kyle's wedding to Laura. In Las Vegas, Michael accidentally kills Tina, a hooker. While attempting to cover up the crime, Robert kills a hotel security guard who blunders in and sees the body. The friends bury the corpses in the desert and return home.

Guilt and tensions begin to surface. Fraternal friction erupts between Michael and Adam. Michael accidentally kills Adam and becomes a nervous wreck. Meanwhile, Adam's widow Lois grows suspicious. Robert kills both Lois and Michael. Distraught, Kyle confesses all to Laura, but she insists the wedding must go ahead. At the ceremony Robert attacks Kyle but is himself attacked by Laura and then dies falling down some stairs. Laura orders Kyle to dispose of Charles, but both end up crippled in a car crash. Laura finds herself in charge of a warped family setup consisting of Adam and Lois' children and the now disabled Kyle and Charles.

Alongside *8 Heads in a Duffel Bag* and the Farrelly brothers' *There's Something About Mary*, *Very Bad Things* is suggestive of an emerging trend, a new sadism at work within left-of-centre US cinema. Directed at a lick by debut writer-director Peter Berg (an actor from *The Last Seduction* and *CopLand*), this scabrous little comedy comes on like some bastard progeny of the 80s Brat Pack movies. A bunch of sharp-suited young blokes get their kicks at a bachelor party. Then things go abruptly haywire and the movie detours into *Treasure of the Sierra Madre* country as the former buddies start clawing at each other like rats in a sack.

Crucial to the success or failure of *Very Bad Things* is the thin generic line it treads. Is Berg's film a black satire on male friendship and marriage etiquette or a comedy with a dubious subtext? Take those initial murders. The culprits are all white, cocksure and reasonably moneyed; their victims are Asian (the prostitute) and black (the hotel worker). Berg may be taking a subtle potshot at the rapacious white male here, but if so, the swipe is very, very subtle. No explicit racial point is made, yet one suspects we're being asked to laugh at these two unfortunates, who both expire in absurdist, comic fashion. Audience identification is always with the perpetrators. The hooker is "a mess... a 105-pound problem" to be disposed of and the security guard a threatening gate-crasher. This queasy set-up established, Berg's film improves dramatically, its impact heavily reliant on firecracker acting from Daniel Stem and Cameron Diaz. As Adam, the most conscience-pricked member of the group, Stem goes nuts in a most entertaining fashion, freaking out at a service station while his obnoxious kids shriek, "We want Whizzers!" in the minivan outside. When Stern exits the film, it's up to Diaz to perk things up. Taking the stock ballbreaker role she has played before to its logical conclusion, she mutates from petty nagger into the yarn's most ruthless and take-charge protagonist. Certainly Christian Slater's rakish Robert (an actor still perfecting his karaoke Jack Nicholson schtick) pales in comparison.

The trouble is that Berg doesn't seem sure how to draw matters to a close. Hence *Very Bad Things* goes from shrill to shriller to shrillest. As the body count mounts up the dark humour turns from *noir* to pitch. By the last quarter, the film flags until an audacious final coda sends it out with a last-gasp flourish. Such problems often mar first films, yet they are also symptomatic of this rising sub-genre. Black burlesques like *Very Bad Things* thrive on shock tactics, on the gut-punch of the audience gross-out. Continually labouring to top the last gag, they run the risk of expiring on successive does of their own poison.

TIME, 11/30/98, p. 111, Richard Schickel

Week after week, the sanctity of human life, the moral niceties of medical ethics, the nobility of self-sacrifice. After all that tenderness, it's easy to see why bright young Peter Berg, one of the *Chicago Hope* ensemble, would want to try a little purgative transgressiveness.

Hence the very black comedy *Very Bad Things*, which he has written and directed. In it, five thirtysomething guys from a Los Angeles suburb go off to Las Vegas for a bachelor party a week before one of them is to be married. It turns wild: a call girl accidentally gets killed, a security guard gets murdered, the boys—led by Christian Slater, doing a nice, nasty turn spouting pop-psych Nietzscheanisms—get started on a cover-up. Guilt and panic soon lead to lethal wrangles, then to variously colorful comeuppances. Meantime, Cameron Diaz is sublimely screwy as the single-minded bride determined not to let anything—including the deadly mishaps that keep shrinking the wedding party—spoil her nuptials.

Within the chicly amoral terms Berg sets—and brutally enforces—Diaz is curiously believable. So is the way in which stunned calm (we're going to get away with this thing) and hysteria (no, we're not) alternate among the well-played accidental criminals. We do find points of identification with them. And heaven knows, some of us are fed up to the teeth with movies glossily restating humane sentiments. Finally, though, Berg's relentless, youthfully enthusiastic assault on conventional pieties grows tiresome. And we begin to choke on laughter that was from the outset pretty dubious.

VILLAGE VOICE, 12/1/98, p. 117, J. Hoberman

The title *Very Bad Things* not only refers to this week's movie but also brings to mind the past few months' plethora of nasty, over-the-top, programmatically un-p.c. black comedies—*Your Friends and Neighbors, There's Something About Mary, Happiness,* and *Celebration.* Even the least of these is vastly superior to this first feature, schematically written and directed at a very high decibel level by actor Peter Berg (Dr. Kronk of *Chicago Hope*).

A rudderless farce about a bachelor party gone fatally berserk, *Very Bad Things* is predicated on the disjunction between the ultimate socially sanctioned act—the impending nuptials of the characters played by Cameron Diaz and Jon Favreau—and the grossly antisocial behavior exhibited by Favreau and his cronies on a wild weekend in Las Vegas. Given the location, the anxiety, and Favreau's presence, *Very Bad Things* might have been a dark successor to *Swingers.* But suaveness, however bogus, is not a major part of the Berg agenda.

Very Bad Things does not do much table setting. There's no way to discuss Berg's opus without alluding to his Grand Guignol centerpiece. Hyperventilating from the jazzy, snarky get-go, the movie goes totally MTV once the boys arrive in Vegas and start jumping around their hotel room, snorting coke, bonging out, and haplessly wrestling with the unexpected deaths of the Asian lap-dancer they've hired and the black security guard who shows up to investigate the mess. It's the heart of badness to be sure, but despite the picture of Don Rickles prominently displayed in the suite, it's actually not all that comic. The overabundance of anguished whining drowns out even the chain saws. (And if you're intrigued by the spectacle of an out-of-control criminal cover-up, you're much better off waiting a few weeks for Sam Raimi's *A Simple Plan.*)

With Favreau as the deer perpetually trapped in the headlights, Christian Slater gives the movie what passes for a *zetz* by taking charge as the group's Iron John cheerleader. Daniel Stern ups the annoyance factor considerably, giving a shrill, one-note performance as a neurotic paterfamilias, with Jeremy Piven playing his fuck-up kid brother. Leland Orser tags along for the ride as a catatonic fifth wheel. As abstract as they are, there's no particular reason to care about these guys. The actors couldn't be sweating more profusely if they were sitting in a sauna, but it's every man for himself—there's not much ensemble chemistry.

Funny or not, *Very Bad Things* has the makings of an angry-white-male screed—although all five chimps together don't convey the polished malice of even one Michael Douglas. Indeed, lacking the courage of its dubious convictions, the movie eventually starts flogging itself. Berg seems pleased that, with the exception of the luckless hooker, the female characters—Diaz and Jeanne Tripplehorn, who plays Stern's wife—give almost as good as they get in the battle of the sexes. Tripplehorn (or her body double) puts on an impressive kick-boxing display, and Diaz is particularly memorable in the thankless, harridan role of Favreau's fanatically marriage-minded fiancée. (When the movie's villain attempts to disrupt the climactic wedding, she takes matters into her own manicured hands: "This is *my* day!")

As in her sensationally blithe performance in *There's Something About* Mary, Diaz never breaks character. (Michelle Pfeiffer's Catwoman notwithstanding, there hasn't been a Hollywood actress who so combines sex appeal with physical comedy since Shirley MacLaine.) Still, Diaz is only a minor attraction in this show. *Very Bad Things* is a guy film, and, as such, it's a dog. The gross-out humor lacks edge, the guilt never kicks in, and the outrages are predictable. It's one flat brewski.

Also reviewed in:
CHICAGO TRIBUNE, 11/25/98, Tempo/p. 9, Michael Wilmington
NEW YORK TIMES, 11/25/98, p. E10, Janet Maslin
VARIETY, 9/21-27/98, p. 107, Derek Elley
WASHINGTON POST, 11/25/98, p. D13, Stephen Hunter

VILLAGE OF DREAMS

A Milestone Film and Video release of a Siglo production in association with Japan Arts Fund. *Producer:* Tetsujiro Yamagami and Koshiro Sho. *Director:* Yoichi Higashi. *Screenplay (Japanese with English subtitles):* Yoichi Higashi and Takehiro Nakajima. *Based on the memoir "The Village of My Paintings" by:* Seizo Tashima. *Director of Photography:* Yoshio Shimizu. *Editor:* Yoichi Higashi. *Music:* Caterina Ancient Music Esemble. *Sound:* Hiroshi Tsurumaki. *Running time:* 112 minutes. *MPAA Rating:* Not Rated.

CAST: Keigo Matsuyama (Seizo Tashima); Shogo Matsuyama (Yukihiko Tashima); Mieko Harada (Mizue Tashima); Kyozo Nagatsuka (Kenzo Tashima);   Hosei Komatsu (Jimma); Kaneko Iwasaki (Toshie); Koichi Ueda (Principal).

NEW YORK POST, 1/30/98, p. 44, Larry Worth

Hopefully it's just a passing phase. But when it comes to Asian-based movies, American moviegoers now look for Jackie Chan, Michelle Yeoh or perhaps Chow Yun-Fat to be kicking butt from first frame to last.

That's why it's so refreshing to have "'Village of Dreams" hearken back to classic, character-driven tales of everyday life and daily drama made famous by Yasujiro ("Tokyo Story") Ozu or Akira ("Ikiru") Kurosawa.

Director Yoichi Higashi's look at pre-teen twin boys in post-World War II Japan spends much time observing the straw-hatted twosome at their favorite fishing hole, or walking home while carrying a pail of catches between them.

Aside from bits about the boys' overly indulgent mother or a dad often kept away on business, the picaresque scenario also has its share of the offbeat. One minute, it's a fish who talks (via subtitles) in haunted waters; the next, it's a trio of Macbeth-like cronies—clad in kimonos, of course—who constantly monitor the twins' actions.

Sure enough, the boys are as cute as can be, but richly deserving of the villagers' dubbing them "the brats." Whether in the school room or on home turf, the pair nicely illustrate what makes children simultaneously lovable and hateful.

Along the way, Higashi illustrates no shortage of truisms, whether spotlighting kids' penchant for cruelty, the foibles of authority figures or life's utterly inexplicable twists.

Bookending the film with shots of the real-life adult brothers upon whom the twins are based, Higashi lenses the scenario with a painter's delicacy and a fine eye for nature's beauty, Japanese customs and long-forgotten rituals. The performances are equally laudable, with Keigo and Shogo Matsuyama proving irresistible as the mischievous siblings.

Accordingly, "Village of Dreams" comprises a lovely two-hour reverie, the kind from which most moviegoers won't want to be roused by the closing credits.

VILLAGE VOICE, 2/3/98, p. 122, Leslie Camni

Whether an effect of time or recession, postwar Japan seems to be rooting around for the lost remnants of tradition. *Village of Dreams* peels back decades of American influence and high technology to reveal a richly spirited rural culture. Director Yolchi Higashi based his film on the autobiographical writings of artist Seizo Tashima, who palled around a small Japanese village in the year's following World War II with his identical twin brother, Yukihiko. Their parents, displaced intellectuals, moved to the country after being "adopted" by a rich, childless landowner. Their father, a civil servant, is usually absent, leaving them in the care of their indulgent schoolteacher mother, in the company of their bossy older sister, and to their own devices.

The twins, it turns out, are Japanese dissidents in the making. Their friends include Senji, an impoverished orphan with attitude galore; and Hatsumi, the daughter of peasants, who comes to school barefoot. Chopping down the neighbor's taro plants and leaving smelly buckets by the rich man's outhouse, they're as troublesome as a pair of *shibaten*, or wood imps, a gaggle of mysterious old women complain. A troika of ancient spirits, they provide one of several touches of magical realism animating this rustic idyll.

There's much to admire in Higashi's subtle film, which captures the lush texture of postwar village life without avoiding its darker intimations: the effects of fascism, war, and poverty. His treatment of childhood sexuality, in particular, is unusually direct and astute. "Get dressed or the thunder god will steal your penis" the twins' sister warns. Their nocturnal emissions following wet dreams of fish are handled with beautiful simplicity.

But children don't take direction easily, and the cute, skinny twins who've been cast here are no exception. They're fine most of the time, when they seem to have dropped in from another world, as self-contained and oddly content as little aliens. But their dialogue is strangely stylized, and when they're compelled to emote, the direction is painfully apparent.

Fiercely loyal to each other, the boys are also virtually indistinguishable. (The real-life adult brothers, successful children's book illustrators who make cameo appearances, seem to bear out this interpretation.) But can twins have identical personalities? The film's reticence on this point shades into effacement, suggesting there's still another story to be told here.

Also reviewed in:
NEW YORK TIMES, 1/30/98, p. E12, Stephen Holden
VARIETY, 3/4-10/96, p. 75, David Stratton

VOYAGE TO THE BEGINNING OF THE WORLD

A Strand Releasing release of a Madragoa Filmes and Gemini Films production with the participation of Instituto Português da Arte Cinematográfica e Audiovisual/Radio-televiâo Portuguesa/Canal +, and CNC. *Producer:* Paulo Bronco. *Director:* Manoel de Oliveira. *Screenplay (Portuguese and French with English subtitles):* Manoel de Oliveira. *Director of Photography:* Renato Berta. *Editor:* Valérie Loiseleux. *Music:* Emmanuel Nunes. *Sound:* Jean-Paul Mugel and (music) Jean-François Auger. *Production Designer:* Maria José Branco. *Costumes:* Isabel Favila. *Make-up:* Dante Trani and Ana Lorena. *Running time:* 93 minutes. *MPAA Rating:* Not Rated.

CAST: Marcello Mastroianni (Manoel); Jean-Yves Gautier (Afonso); Leonor Silveira (Judite); Diogo Dória (Duarte); Isabel de Castro (Maria Afonso); Cecile Sanz de Alba (Cristina); José Pinto (José Afonso); Adelaide Teixeira (Madame); Isabel Ruth (Olga); Manoel de Oliveira (Conductor).

LOS ANGELES TIMES, 7/31/98, Calendar/p. 8, Kevin Thomas

Marcello Mastroianni, who died in Paris in December 1996 at age 72, could not have had a finer valedictory to a great career than Manoel de Oliveira's "Voyage to the Beginning of the World."

When Federico Fellini's "La Dolce Vita" (1960) established Mastroianni as an international star, he came to embody the archetypal European male—handsome, charming, gallant and not just a little world-weary—in a wide-ranging series of roles, many for Fellini, for whom he became an alter ego. Mastroianni was at once a romantic leading man, a gifted comedian and a superb character actor who gave pleasure to audiences around the world.

In "Voyage," Mastroianni's 171st film, he again becomes an alter ego for a great director, Portugal's De Oliveira, who made his first feature in 1929 and who turns 90 this December. As Manoel, Mastroianni plays a renowned Portuguese film director shooting a Franco-Portuguese co-production. One of the stars of his film is a well-known French actor, Afonso (Jean-Yves Gautier), whose father emigrated from Portugal.

Afonso is eager to visit his late father's hometown, a remote mountain village, meet his father's sister and see his grandparents' graves. Manoel decides he and two of his other actors, Judite (Leonor Silveira) and Duarte (Diogo Doria), should accompany Afonso on his journey and serve as interpreters for him. (The film was based on an actual incident that occurred in 1987 to French actor Yves Afonso.)

The first part of the film belongs to Manoel, for in the course of the journey, he and his colleagues drive through a beautiful, rugged region the director knew in his youth. Though debonair and brave, Manoel is clearly frail, and as memories begin to sweep over him, making him all the more aware that he is an old man, he is confronted with a sense of his own mortality, which Mastroianni, in failing health, surely was experiencing himself.

In his last years, Mastroianni came to believe that if he could keep on working, he could go on living, but he must certainly have realized that "Voyage" could well be his farewell. In any event, there's enormous resonance in Mastroianni's portrayal of Manoel, a man who wryly observes that "nostalgia happens when you start losing your sense of irony."

There's a deceptively casual, random air to "Voyage," but it begins to build powerfully once the travelers arrive at their destination, a small mountain village of ancient stone buildings and narrow streets, a place where farmers and shepherds have been living much the same way for thousands of years.

What gives "Voyage" an unexpected punch is that Afonso's Aunt Maria (Isabel de Castro, an actress of amazing resources), a handsome peasant woman, resists acknowledging her nephew because he doesn't "speak our language" and because she regards her brother, who ran away from home at 14 only to become caught up in the Spanish Civil War, as a deserter who was interested in his family only when he needed money.

As Maria's resistance gradually wears down, all that concerns De Oliveira comes into play—the futility of war, a peasant way of life on the verge of extinction and the contrast between Afonso's and Manoel's relations to the past. Afonso, though he has no memories of his own, has the possibility of making a real connection with the past through Maria, whereas Manoel is rich in memories but has outlived all the friends and relatives of his youth. "Long life is a gift from God," Manoel observes, "but it has a price."

Perhaps inevitably, "Voyage to the Beginning of the World" recalls the 1957 Ingmar Bergman classic "Wild Strawberries," in which an elderly professor, returning to his native region to receive an academic honor, is overcome with memories and faced with his shortcomings. "Voyage" is a less formal, less literary work yet has much the same impact.

It also has a wonderful symbol of the human predicament: an old stone statue of a man stuck throughout eternity with a heavy wooden beam resting on his left shoulder—a statue by the roadside remembered well by Manoel from his youth and surely not to be forgotten by his friends.

Mastroianni was an actor who gave his all to every part he ever played. His Manoel is as wise as he is brave and is as fine a performance as Mastroianni ever gave. As long as there are movies, surely Marcello Mastroianni will not be forgotten either.

NEW YORK POST, 6/26/98, p. 52, Larry Worth

As the final film to be graced by the presence of the late Marcello Mastroianni, "Voyage to the Beginning of the World" is appropriately dedicated to his memory.

Better still, director Manoel de Oliveira uses the great actor to wonderful effect. He's cast as a veteran film director named Manoel (a stand-in for the director, it's safe to assume) who embarks on a sentimental journey into his past with three actors from his latest production.

They're on their way to visit one actor's aged aunt in a remote Portuguese village. Along the way, Manoel reminisces as the quartet explores ruin after ruin, mirroring the somber, haunting tone of their ruminations.

Throughout, veteran director De Oliveira's touch proves as masterful as ever. One reason is that he's never afraid of silence, which—particularly here—speaks volumes. The resulting ambience is alternately intimate and eerie.

That's why it's easy to forgive some obviously symbolic metaphors and an ongoing bit about watching scenery through the car's rear window (thus reinforcing the theme about looking at what's past.)

And while Mastroianni does a superb job as the avuncular auteur who's steeped in memories, his fellow cast members hold their own. As the other passengers, Jean Yves Gautier, the stunning Leonor Silveira and Diogo Doria are naturals, making viewers feel they're eavesdropping on a fascinating conversation. And as the distrustful dowager, Isabel de Castro's wonderfully expressive face is reason enough to buy a ticket.

Of course, Mastroianni's dialogue about the specter of death assumes an extra meaning in light of his passing. But the real pleasure here is observing how much his expressive face and mellifluous voice conveyed to the very end.

SIGHT AND SOUND, 7/98, p. 43, Jonathan Romney

Manoel, a veteran Portuguese film director, takes a car journey through Portugal with three of his cast: Judite, Duarte and Afonso, the last a French actor of Portuguese descent visiting the country for the first time. Both Manoel and Afonso are on pilgrimages—the director to the places of his own past, Afonso to those of his father's.

Manoel shows them the Jesuit school he attended across the River Minho that divides Portugal from Spain. In vineyard country, they find a statue he remembers. Known as Pedro Macau and celebrated in a local rhyme, it is the figure of a moustachioed man supporting a beam on his shoulder. In an old spa town, the group visits the ruins of the Grand Hotel where Manoel stayed as a boy.

En route to the village of Afonso's ancestors, Manoel compares the moderate troubles of his own life with the hardships known by Afonso's father, who set out alone for France at the age of 14 and was imprisoned during the Spanish Civil War. They visit Afonso's aunt Maria: at first she is deeply suspicious of this foreigner who cannot speak Portuguese, thinking he has come to claim an inheritance, but Afonso persuades her that the same blood flows in their veins. Maria and her husband José tell the party that their traditional rural life is coming to an end. Villages like theirs are reverting to "the dawn of time".

Afonso promises Maria he will return with his brother. Back at the film studio, Afonso tries on a false moustache and recognises that he, like Manoel, is also Pedro Macau.

Journey to the Beginning of the World has the feel of a final testament, with all the weight of regret and fondness that implies. This is not Manoel de Oliveira's final film—the tireless 90-year-old director has since made a follow up, *Inquiétude,* shown in Cannes this year. However, it was the last appearance of Marcello Mastroianni, playing a film director called Manoel, to all appearances a representation of Oliveira himself.

The film, a sentimental journey through Portugal undertaken by Manoel and his friends, could hardly have been more intimate if Oliveira had played his own role—in fact, he can be spotted hovering silently in the background as Manoel's driver. But the casting of Mastroianni and the peculiar wry tenderness of his presence give the film a special resonance. Even without the fact of the veteran actor's death, it seems that Oliveira is sharing with him an apprehension of mortality: the film is the director's preparation for his own farewell to the past and to cinema.

Oliveira is arguably the most marginal of Europe's major directors, especially for British audiences—his only previous release here (and then only just) was 1993's *Abraham Valley/Vale Abraão.* However, on the festival circuit Oliveira is revered, as much for his longevity as for his varied and highly eccentric output. He made his first film *Douro, faina fluvial* in 1931, but only got into his professional stride as a director in his 70s, exploring the possibilities of a cinema that was often more literary or theatrical than conventionally filmic: most spectacularly with his version of Claudel's play *The Satin Slipper/Le Soulier de satin* (1985) and *Non, or the Vain Glory of Command/Nao ou a vã gloria de mandar* (1990), with its archly stylised *tableaux vivants.*

In recent years, Oliveira has made a *rapprochement* with the European art-house mainstream, using such bankable names (albeit in wilfully thorny narrative settings) as Catherine Deneuve, John Malkovich (both in *0 covento*) and Michel Piccoli (in *Party*). *Journey to the Beginning of the World* is more immediate than recent films, though just as defiantly 'uncinematic'. But Oliveira has often shunned the traditionally cinematic the asceticism and linguistic emphasis of the theatre or the novel, as a sort of detour leading to his own personal reinvention of screen language. *Journey* aspires to the evocative purity of the radio play. Hearing is as important as seeing here—the film is arranged 'musically' in sections and set to the music of Emmanuel Nunes, from the opening atonal cacophony to a gentler arrangement of piano chords as we head further into exploration of the past.

The film's opening section offers us something dauntingly simple, shot with audacious economy by Renato Berta—a series of close-ups of people talking in the back of a car. It promises a sort of film symposium in the guise of a road movie: after all, on most road trips, there's little to do but talk and watch the scenery. At times, Oliveira simply has his camera gaze out of the car's rear window as the road recedes. Between these shots, we meet the passengers: director Manoel (Mastroianni) and the cast of his latest film. There are two Oliveira regulars—wry, saturnine Diogo Dória and, decked out for the voyage in a sailor suit, Leonor Silveira, an actress who combines sly sexuality with a rather patrician intellectual coolness. As Judite, she starts out prodding Manoel into a discussion of their journey and its meaning for him. He reproaches her for merely tolerating him as an old man. She teases him with a reminder of the traditional sexual tensions between actress and director.

The fourth passenger is Afonso (Jean-Yves Gautier), a French actor who has never learned the language of his Portuguese father, nor visited his country. We learn at the end that the film was inspired by the similar experiences of a real-life actor. The film's basis in experience lifts it out of the realm of mere metaphor. Much of the symbolism is conventional, even shop-soiled—memory as a journey, time as a river. But metaphor here is openly recognised as metaphor. Manoel is delighted to rediscover Pedro Macau, a statue remembered from childhood, depicting a man carrying a beam on his shoulder. He immediately identifies it as a "caricature" of his own father's travails. The old metaphors are still the best, the film tells us, because they are rooted in lived values. Appropriately, Pedro Macau endures as a figure of endurance itself.

This may be the most overtly Proustian film ever made, and its most poignant episode is Manoel's return to the hotel he visited as a child. Now a shell, it still carries for him the echoes of his brother's illness and of the young girls he once knew. In this section of the film, words begin to retreat: Oliveira has the camera drift contemplatively over the crumbling walls, then finally lets the hotel vanish round a bend in the road, as if to acknowledge that neither we nor Manoel nor civilisation for that matter will ever pass by here again.

Portugal itself is also at risk of vanishing into the past. The film is an entirely unsentimental enquiry into endangered national identity, by a director who has made a speciality of being linguistically and culturally polyglot. This Portuguese-French co-production has mainly French dialogue, with most of the Portuguese translated back into French for Afonso's benefit. Oliveira seems to put the pragmatic case that Portuguese cinema—and by extension, Portuguese culture—will only survive through dialogue with the outside world. But Afonso's aunt highlights the fragility of Portugueseness itself: only through translation does her culture have a voice on screen. Throughout the reunion with her nephew, her testy refrain returns: "Why doesn't he speak our language?" Afonso persuades her that identity is a matter not of words but of blood. Yet the film questions this argument in its allusions to Sarajevo, where attempts to locate national identity in blood and language have proved equally problematic.

Rather, *Journey* presents identity as a matter of performance: both in the figure of Cristina, a young French woman who has adopted traditional Portuguese identity to the hilt, and in the casting of an Italian star as a French-speaking Portuguese film-maker. What promises to save a culture is the power of transmitted knowledge: autobiography recounted visually and verbally, and the local rhyme about Pedro Macau that Afonso memorises, thereby learning to recognise himself. This intensely philosophical film, one imagines, could only have been made by a director old enough to know memory not as an abstraction but as a reality laden with a lifetime's existential weight. Oliveira's *Journey*, however, is anything but a sombre pilgrimage. Its stately pace is underwritten by a lightness of touch and the cheek of a veteran director and actor who can both afford to dispense with false dignity; the intense meeting with Maria is leavened by Mastroianni gurning at a stuffed fox's head. In a discussion of that peculiarly Portuguese state of soul known as *saudade*, Manoel describes it as what happens "when you lose your sense of irony". Oliveira maintains his irony to the last, even ending his journey on a bad pun. Returning home, Duarte accuses Manoel of wanting to *"voyager à l'oeil"*—meaning "to get a free ride", but also suggesting "to travel with your eyes". And that's what he invites us to do in this sublimely insightful imaginative essay.

TIME, 7/13/98, p. 78, Richard Corliss

The face is gaunt—ravaged but handsome, like a weathered statue—and the skull is nearly visible through the skin. The body is hunched; it needs a cane for support. Getting a first glimpse of Marcello Mastroianni here, the viewer is not surprised that this was the last film he completed before his death in late 1996. Was he only 72? He looks a decade older, frailer. A closeup could be like an autopsy, were it not for the actor's perennial ease and grace before the camera's eye.

But there is no ghoulish sentiment in the rarefied pleasures afforded by Manoel de Oliveira's luminous film. The Franco-Portuguese *Voyage to the Beginning of the World* is a fable about old age reconciling itself to memory and destiny. Two histories intertwine: a veteran director, also named Manoel (Mastroianni), goes back to the places of his childhood; and an ancient Portuguese woman (Isabel de Castro) meets the French-born son (Jean-Yves Gautier) of her long-lost brother. The old woman is wary of her Francophone nephew—she keeps asking, "Why doesn't he speak our speech?"—until the nephew convinces her, in a heartbreaking scene, that blood is thicker than language.

As for Manoel's recollections, they are engaging, autumnal; he wears the wizened smile of a man who knows he is visiting his youth for the last time. It is easy to see this as Mastroianni's testament but it is also Oliveira's. This amazing auteur, whose spare, poignant films *(Doomed Love, The Cannibals)* are rarely seen in the U.S., has been directing since 1929—and has made a film every year of the '90s. Oliveira will be 90 in December. On the evidence of this vigorous *Voyage*, he is just hitting his stride.

VILLAGE VOICE, 6/30/98, p. 142, Gary Dauphin

Made by Portugal's Manoel de Olivera, the only living director to have been active in the silent era, *Voyage to the Beginning of the World* is a peculiar, overly demanding little movie. There are a few memorable moments held in *Voyage's* wrinkled and parchmentlike hand, but the price in getting to them is steep.

Devoid of traditional plot development, *Voyage's* movement is all spatial and chronological, following three actors and their director on a day trip into the Portuguese mountains. The film is stitched together entirely out of their talk. The aging director (played with a kind of pained equanimity by Marcello Mastroianni in his last role) points out sights and takes questions, while the trio is usually shot immobile behind him, listening while the object under discussion remains unseen. One of the actors is the French child of a Portuguese father, and during *Voyage's* last reel his trip to ancestral lands provides a measure of momentum. But de Olivera is more concerned with duration than action, so even that thin thread is looped and knotted around travelogue, local legends, and strangely dispassionate personal confessions that have been bled dry of pain by the years. *Voyage's* pace isn't the fault of old age, for this is certainly the film de Olivera wanted to make. While it wouldn't have killed de Olivera to have wrapped his remembrances in a more accessible package, at 90 he seems beyond worrying that few will want to take this trip with him.

Also reviewed in:
NATION, 7/13/98, p. 36, Stuart Klawans
NEW YORK TIMES, 6/26/98, p. E24, Stephen Holden
VARIETY, 5/19-25/97, p. 55, Deborah Young

WAKING NED DEVINE

A Fox Searchlight Pictures and Tomboy Films release in association with with The Gruber Brothers/Mainstream S.A./Bonaparte Films Ltd/The Isle of Man Commission and Overseas Filmgroup and with the participation of Canal +. *Executive Producer:* Alexandre Heylen. *Producer:* Glynis Murray and Richard Holmes. *Director:* Kirk Jones. *Screenplay:* Kirk Jones. *Director of Photography:* Henry Braham. *Editor:* Alan Strachan. *Music:* Shaun Davey. *Music Editor:* Bob Hathaway. *Sound:* David Crozier. *Sound Editor:* John Downer. *Casting:* Ros Hubbard and John Hubbard. *Production Designer:* John Ebden. *Art Director:* Mark Tanner. *Special Effects:* Bob Hollow. *Visual Effects:* Karl Mooney. *Costumes:* Rosie Hackett. *Make-up:* Anne Oldham. *Stunt Coordinator:* Andy Bradford. *Running time:* 91 minutes. *MPAA Rating:* PG.

CAST: Ian Bannen (Jackie O'Shea); David Kelly (Michael O'Sullivan); Fionnula Flanagan (Annie O'Shea); Susan Lynch (Maggie); James Nesbitt (Pig Finn); Adrian Robinson (Lotto Observer); Maura O'Malley (Mrs. Kennedy); Robert Hickey (Maurice); Paddy Ward (Brendy O'Toole); James Ryland (Dennis Fitzgerald); Fintan McKeown (Pat Mulligan); Matthew Devitt (Tom Tooney); Eileen Dromey (Lizzy Quinn); Kitty Fitzgerald (Kitty); Dermot Kerrigan (Father Patrick); Jimmy Keogh (Ned Devine); Brendan F. Dempsey (Jim Kelly (Lotto Man)); Larry Randall (Father Mulligan); Eamonn Doyle (Dicey Riley, The Fiddleman); Raymond MacCormac (Baudron Player); Rennie Campbell (Rennie).

CHRISTIAN SCIENCE MONITOR, 12/4/98, p. 15, David Sterritt

[*Waking Ned Devine* was reviewed jointly with *Little Voice*; see Sterritt's review of that film.]

LOS ANGELES TIMES, 11/20/98, Calendar/p. 14, Kenneth Turan

The names Ian Bannen and David Kelly may not be familiar, but their mischievous faces will be. Senior citizens with nearly a century of experience between them, they're a pair of droll old souls with the comic wisdom of the ages in their smiles. Together they turn "Waking Ned Devine" into a roguish and delightful comedy of duplicity that's as entertaining as it is sly.

Though it's the first film for writer-director Kirk Jones, a top commercial director from the United Kingdom, "Waking Ned" is part of the great tradition of daft, cheerful British comedies. Linked in spirit to the understated Ealing studio classics of decades past—"Kind Hearts and Coronets" and "The Lavender Hill Mob" to name two—but with a peppy modern brashness added in, this picture proves that laughter and smiles can be coaxed out of the old moves if they're done with deftness and panache.

"Waking Ned" is set firmly in the mythical movie-Ireland of tiny towns and lilting brogues (though in truth filmed on the Isle of Man), where genial eccentrics trade amusing lines and the only telephone is outside the city limits. What would happen in such a place—Tully More by name, population 52—if a local won a 6.8 million-pound prize in the Irish national lottery? What indeed.

It's Jackie O'Shea (Bannen) who first figures out from a small item in the Irish Times that someone in Tully More has hit the jackpot. Good-natured but with a bit of larceny in his bones, Jackie, admittedly "not a great man for telling things the way they are," has a plan to fit the situation.

As he explains it to his lifelong friend Michael O'Sullivan (Kelly), Jackie wants to apply "the very best of Irish brains" to figure out who the winner is before the prize is claimed. Then he'll so ingratiate himself with the lucky individual that "I'll be their best friend by the time they cash the check."

Sounds simple enough, but, as in all classic comedies, nothing goes quite as planned. For once the winner is discovered (no easy task, as it turns out), so many elaborate feints and dodges prove necessary that Jackie's level-headed wife Annie (Fionnula Flanagan) has reason to worry how it will turn out.

Even the honest Michael, who's never told a lie in his life, gets drawn into this increasingly complex and humorous web to the point where he finds himself riding hellbent for leather on a motorbike wearing nothing but a helmet and some sensible shoes. And that's just the beginning of his pains.

All this playful greed plays out against a background of wall-to-wall characters ranging in age from ancient town witch Lizzie Quinn (Eileen Dromey) to fatherless young Maurice (Robert Hickey), who tells the impoverished local priest he wouldn't want his job because "I don't think I could work for someone I never met and not get paid for it."

Maurice's mother, the wild and beautiful Maggie (Susan Lynch), who earns money writing verse for greeting cards, is the heart of "Waking Ned's" subplot, the battle for her fetching hand. Maggie's in love with the luckless Pig Finn (James Nesbitt), but can't abide the smell his poor animals give off.

"If it wasn't for the pigs," she tells Finn many a time, "we'd be settled by now." Will the basket of "fruity soaps" provided by Jackie help Finn clean up romantically? Stay tuned.

All the actors in "Waking Ned" are smooth and practiced performers who inhabit these roles like they've lived them all their lives. But few can touch stars Bannen (nominated for an Oscar back in 1966 for "Flight of the Phoenix") and Kelly. Playing off each other beautifully, with a lifetime of skills in their every move, they create a charming comedy of winks and nods that is inescapably engaging.

"Waking Ned" is, of course, nothing if not traditional, old-fashioned and small-scaled, its humor depending on such familiar situations as a battle of wits between country lads and an official from the big city. No new ground gets broken, nothing is done that hasn't been done before. But if this film doesn't make you want to smile, you've no one to blame but yourself.

NEW YORK, 12/7/98, p. 77, Peter Rainer

What's the Blarney equivalent of glucose shock? My candidate would be "Waking Ned Devine." Compared to all the I.R.A.-themed movies we've been seeing lately, this swatch of stage-Irishness is a walk in the park. Two lifelong mates from Tully More—population 52—figure out that one of their neighbors has won the lottery. David Kelly and Ian Bannen are the dynamic duo who connive to get close to the money. There's a splendidly surreal comic moment when Kelly, who makes Ichabod Crane seem portly, bicycles buck-naked on a country road. Bannen and he have such an easygoing rapport that you can almost forgive the fact that this film seems to have been produced strictly for the tourist trade. It would make the perfect in-flight movie on Aer Lingus.

NEW YORK POST, 11/20/98, p. 65, Rod Dreher

By now, the world needs a sentimental, Guinness-and-shamrocks Irish comedy about as much as a new memoir from a heretofore obscure member of the McCourt family, God love 'em. Even so, "Waking Ned Devine" is a pretty special slice of Celtic kookery and good cheer, an unabashed crowd-pleaser of the quaint 'n' quirky "Local Hero" kind.

The title character lives in the wee Irish coastal village of Tully More, which is holding its breath after it becomes known that the holder of a winning lottery ticket lives there. But who? Crusty old Jackie O'Shea (Ian Bannen) means to find out and wheedle a portion of the pot out of the winner.

After executing a series of cheekily self-serving schemes to ingratiate himself to his neighbors in hopes that the mum multimillionaire will be generous with his winnings, Jackie and his dim, turkey-necked sidekick, Michael O'Sullivan (David Kelly), happen upon the lucky fellow by accident. It's their neighbor Ned Devine, or what's left of him: He's stiff as a board, having died of shock with the winning ticket in his hand.

Jackie hatches a loony plan to pass Michael off as Ned, hoping to fool the national lottery official when he comes to verify the claim. Eventually the whole village gets in on the misbegotten trickery, with chuckleworthy if unsurprising results.

Bannen and Kelly make fabulous small-town codgers, twinkle-eyed paragons of cootish whimsy whose rollicking, raffish company redeems even the most derivative blarney in writer-director Kirk Jones' screenplay.

The gently amusing "Waking Ned Devine" is never more than thoroughly enjoyable light entertainment—but never less, either. The omnipresent uillean pipes and gorgeous landscape shots oversell the Irish thing, to be sure, but in a season of snarling, cynical, black film comedy, the simple, upbeat pleasures of "Waking Ned Devine" hit a singular grace note.

NEWSDAY, 11/20/98, Part II/p. B11, Jack Mathews

What happens when a lottery winner dies on hearing his numbers called, and no one else can use his ticket because he's signed his name on the back?

In writer-director Kirk Jones' Irish lark, "Waking Ned Devine," the death of the title character inspires the entire town of Tully More (population: 52) to hatch a plan to fool the lottery board. Reedy old bachelor Michael O'Sullivan (David Kelly) will claim to be Ned Devine, and everyone else, for a 1/52th share of the massive pot, will back him up.

From that simple premise, complications grow. Can you really expect everyone in town to agree to commit fraud, even cranky old, penny-pinching Lizzy Quinn (Eileen Dromey), who rides around on her motorized wheelchair like Margaret Hamilton on a broomstick? No, she'd be more likely to negotiate a bigger stake.

Can Michael, who's never told a lie in his long life, pull off the ruse when the lottery man shows up?

Will Tully More, corrupted by opportunity, be lost forevermore?

Fear not, think not. "Waking Ned Devine" is as slight a tale as has flickered on a movie screen this year, and some of the most fun.

Dublin stage veteran David Kelly, a man whose body barely qualifies as a bag of bones, is a riot in his dumb-founded guise of Ned Devine, which requires him, in one hilarious sequence, to mount a motorbike in the nude to keep a date with the lottery man. And Ian Bannen and Fionnulla Flanagan are superb as Jackie O'Shea, the determined ringleader of the Tully More con, and the otherwise sensible wife who agrees to go along.

Jones, a director of British TV commercials making his debut in feature films, has a clear affection for the underdog and the oddball, categories that cover just about everyone in fictional Tully More. The film was actually shot in the picturesque village of Cregneash on the rugged red slopes of the British Isle of Man in the Irish Sea. You may not want to live there, but it would be a great place to own, in case you win the lottery.

NEWSWEEK, 11/23/98, p. 83, Jeff Giles

David Kelly, 69, wasn't concerned about shooting the scene in question. He figured that when the day arrived he wouldn't really be riding the motorcycle himself, or, at the very least, he wouldn't really be buck naked. And then the day arrived. In Kirk Jones's adorable debut film, *Waking Ned Devine*, Kelly plays Michael O'Sullivan, a kindly Irishman embarked on a con with his lifelong buddy Jackie O'Shea (Ian Bannen). It seems a fellow villager, Ned Devine, has won a $4 million lottery—and died from shock, still grasping the ticket. Jackie persuades Michael to impersonate Ned and cash in. One day they're swimming in the sea as a lottery official heads to Ned's house to confirm his identity. Michael leaps onto his motorcycle and races, nude, to beat him there. "I was so scared and so cold that all modesty went out the window," says Kelly. "I'd never been on a motorcycle before and I just thought, 'I am going to die.' It was like Steve McQueen time! And the helmet was unbalancing me. Kirk gave me a lovely direction. He said, 'David, I want you to look worried.' And, by God, I looked worried!"

By the time Michael gets on his motorcycle, we all want to go along for the ride. "Ned Devine" is a surpassingly sweet, funny and picturesque movie. It was shot in a tiny village on the Isle of Man. The movie wasn't officially competing at Cannes this year, but director Jones, 34, drove the only print of the movie down from London himself for a screening. By the time the closing credits rolled, the million-dollar offers had already begun. Fox Searchlight ultimately scooped up "Ned Devine" for $4 million. The studio and the press have positioned "Ned" as this year's version of Searchlight's underdog smash "The Full Monty." The movies have nominal things in common-foreign accents, a good heart, an unlikely scheme—but "Ned" isn't as Hollywoodish as "Monty" and doesn't strain as hard for laughs. "I've always felt that hilarious doesn't really work," says Kelly, a longtime stage, screen and television actor from Dublin. "Funny works. But *hilarious*... If I see that in a review—*a hilarious movie!*—I think, 'No, there won't be a laugh in it.' We avoided hilarious."

The real charm of "Ned Devine" lies in its fond take on friendship and community. This is not, thank heaven, one of those movies about how money destroys people. The entire village of Tully More (population: 52) eventually gets in on the scam, bonding together to try to dupe the lottery man. There's Jackie's reproachful wife, Annie (Fionnula Flanagan). There's a young pig farmer James Nesbitt) and the woman who'd marry him if he didn't smell so bad (Susan Lynch). No matter how sneaky the villagers get, you never question their fundamental goodness. And you never tire of watching Michael and Jackie's rare, twinkling rapport. "It's unusual for two old fogies to be playing the leads," says Kelly. "I'd like to think it'll become a trend. You know: *70 is beautiful.*" It's beautiful here—even naked and riding a motorcycle.

SIGHT AND SOUND, 4/99, p. 61, Kevin Maher

Ireland, the town of Tullymore. Jackie O'Shea learns that the winner of the Irish lottery is one of the town's 52 residents. Together with wife Annie and friend Michael, he scrutinises the villagers for sudden changes in fortune. Jackie throws a party for Tullymore's 18 regular lottery players. Only 17 attend; Jackie deduces missing guest Ned Devine is the winner.

Jackie and Michael visit Ned's house and find him in front of the television, dead from shock, holding on to the winning ticket. After noticing Ned has signed the ticket, Michael decides to pretend to be Ned. They phone the lottery board.

Single-parent Maggie declines pig-farmer Finn's offer of marriage. A lottery agent collects the ticket from Michael and announces that he will return in a couple of days to verify Michael's identity with the locals. Jackie informs the community, and promises to split the jackpot among them if they will help with the ruse. All agree except for aged resident Lizzy Quinn. The agent returns during the funeral of Ned Devine but is duped by the townsfolk. At Ned's wake Maggie agrees to marry Finn, but tells Jackie that Ned was her son Maurice's father. Lizzy Quinn is killed in an accident as she tries to inform the lottery of the deception.

From the opening screech of composer Shaun Davey's romantic uilleann pipes to a closing aerial retreat into magical Celtic mists, *Waking Ned* is firmly at the mercy of market forces. Writer-director Kirk Jones has fashioned the movie shamelessly for a US audience that is both familiar and comfortable with the film's vision of a bucolically idealised Ireland. Although distributors Fox are emphasising *Waking Ned*s 'feel good' factor, linking it to their other regional hit *The Full Monty,* the movie has none of the latter's socio-political complexity, and not enough dramatic weight of its own to counter its over-played Oirishry. The central blarneyism in *Waking Ned* is the rustic idyll of Tullymore itself—the screen Irish village *in extremism.* Here, lost to a derivative cinematic legacy stretching from John MacDonagh's sentimental love story *Willy Reilly and his Colleen Bawn* (1918) through the Bing Crosby comedy *Top o' the Morning* (1949), right up to recent efforts like *Hear My Song,* Jones presents an isolated community of aged characters seemingly free from the compunction to work, and easily tempted into playful alcoholism.

Tullymore's closest movie relative in this respect is the mythical town of Inisfree in John Ford's *The Quiet Man* (1952). Both films are rigorously apolitical, beyond the grasp of twentieth-century ideologies, and both feature villages that view the approach of modernity—mechanised farming in *The Quiet Man,* lottery hoopla in *Waking Ned* as an opportunity to revel in their own sheltered community values. The fact that *Waking Ned* was actually filmed on the Isle of Man merely adds to this awkwardly synthetic sense of place.

So rigid are the parameters of this universe that when problematic emotional relationships are introduced, such as the one between single-parent Maggie and her simple suitor Finn, or the slightly sinister interest Father Patrick takes in Maggie's son Maurice, they are turned into wearisome farce or, in the latter case, dropped completely. Even the movie's pivotal relationship of veterans Jackie and Michael, which very occasionally echoes Beckett's decrepit and mutually dependent Vladimir and Estragon, is generally treated as fodder for punchlines. Though actors Ian Bannen and David Kelly attack their roles with gusto, neither of them gets far away from a poor impression of the stereotypical Irishman that Hollywood character actor Barry Fitzgerald specialised in in the 30s and 40s, especially when gloating twinkle-eyed over such lines as: "Murder is a mighty word to be usin' at this time o'night, so it is."

Formally, Jones displays an understated journeyman's control throughout. He gets maximum value from his aerial shots—the movie teems with swooping passes over verdant fields. And despite a simple shooting style, he executes the demise of Lizzy Quinn—crosscut with the festivities at Ned's wake—with *Godfather*-like flair. Ultimately though, with his heavy recourse to received conventions, Jones sells *Waking Ned*'s brand of Irish whimsy as he once sold Mercedes or Absolut Vodka (he worked for ad company Saatchi & Saatchi). What is genuinely regretful is that with the likes of writers Roddy Doyle and Conor McPherson, and such films as the recent eviscerating *Southpaw* as available reference points, he chose to work from such a creatively bankrupt tradition in the first place.

VILLAGE VOICE, 11/24/98, p. 122, Dennis Lim

I wouldn't be surprised if there was a campaign afoot to get *Waking Ned Devine* banned in Ireland. Set against a painfully quaint backdrop of pig-farming, Guinness-swilling village idiocy, this cynical first feature by writer-director Kirk Jones (who's English) takes provincial whimsy to exasperating, borderline-offensive extremes. The subject of an inexplicably ferocious bidding war at Cannes, *Waking Ned Devine* has been anointed this year's *Full Monty* by marketing types, but that's a grossly misleading reference point. In fact, take away the brogues and the picturesque locales, and what you have is a particularly hoary Lemmon-Matthau vehicle.

About as substantial as a sitcom subplot, the movie hinges on a winning lottery ticket that belongs to one of the 52 inhabitants of remote Tully More. A couple of old codgers (Ian Bannen and David Kelly) take it upon themselves to sniff out the winner, who, it turns out, died of a heart attack upon hearing the good news. A predictably glitch-riddled scheme to keep the 6 million pound jackpot ensues. Jones uses this desperately thin material as launchpad for a merciless onslaught of stereotypical Oirishness, complete with wall-to-wall uileann pipes on the soundtrack and numerous teeth-grinding scenarios that are supposed to be comic simply because the characters involved are either Irish or old or naked or drunk or smelly or slow-witted or various combinations of the above. It's instructive that *Waking Ned Devine* is being so aggressively sold as a feel-good comedy; the "good" feeling in question is called condescension.

Also reviewed in:
CHICAGO TRIBUNE, 12/11/98, Friday/p. D, Michael Wilmington
NEW YORK TIMES, 11/20/98, p. E14, Janet Maslin
VARIETY, 9/21-27/98, p. 106, Derek Elley
WASHINGTON POST, 12/11/98, p. D1, Stephen Hunter
WASHINGTON POST, 12/11/98, Weekend/p. 50, Michael O'Sullivan

WAR ZONE

A Film Fatale Inc./Hank Levine Film GmbH co-production. *Producer:* Hank Levine. *Director:* Maggie Hadleigh-West. *Screenplay:* Maggie Hadleigh-West. *Director of Photography:* Todd Leibler and Eileen Schreiber. *Editor:* Kelly Korzan, Fernando Villena, Tula Goenka, Emily Gumpel, and Sara Thorson. *Music:* Cindy Wall, Jack Wall, David Plakke, and Paul Steinman. *Sound:* Dawn Colello and Peter Levin. *Running time:* 76 minutes. *MPAA Rating:* Not Rated.

WITH: Maggie Hadleigh-West; Sheila Adimoolah; Natasha Ali; Gina T. Charbonnet; Trelles Delandro; Gloria Gonzalez; Lori K. Maher.

LOS ANGELES TIMES, 9/17/98, Calendar/p. 14, Kevin Thomas

You have to admire documentarian Maggie Hadleigh-West for her courage and honesty in the making of her "War Zone," and you have to acknowledge that in taking an extreme position as to what constitutes sexual harassment, she has made a highly provocative film—and not in the sexual sense, one hastens to add.

For much of her 78-minute film, shot mainly in New York with additional sequences in New Orleans and San Francisco, Hadleigh-West, who accurately defines herself as "normal-looking," is seen wearing black leggings, black Lycra tank top (sans bra) and black miniskirt, and carrying a video camera. She is accompanied by an unseen cameraman, Robert Pennington, as she walks through city streets, swift to turn her cameras on any man she has caught looking at her in what she considers to be a sexual way. (Of the 1,050 men she taped, 53 turn up in the finished work.)

To her, the action of any man who in her judgment expresses what she considers sexual attraction to her, even if it is the most innocuous-sounding compliment, constitutes sexual harassment. In those cases, she swiftly retaliates, poking her camera in the man's face, accusing him of ogling her or worse and quizzing him relentlessly on what she considers his offensive behavior. Not surprisingly, a number of men react in ways that are unprintable.

Now Hadleigh-West is trying to make an exceedingly important point: that it is her belief that most women feel unsafe on the streets for the simple fact that it can be difficult, if not impossible, to tell if a man's taking notice of a woman is going to lead to some form of sexual assault.

Many of her interviewees, blue-collar and construction worker types, are genuinely taken aback that what they mean as a compliment could be construed as disrespect. Man after man cites the natural attraction of men for women, yet Hadleigh-West never answers them. She also never answers them when they point out that women who dress provocatively might be hoping for some kind of response. Indeed, she apparently doesn't believe that any woman might appreciate any public recognition of her attractiveness. It leads us to conclude that, in the street at least, no man should ever express any reaction to any woman whatsoever because any such expression is inherently sexual and therefore potentially threatening.

Yet her own unwillingness to differentiate between what many women might consider a harmless appreciation from the opposite sex and that which is patently rude, offensive and intimidating complicates her task in raising men's consciousness about their behavior toward women.

She is on firmer ground in her inclusion of several other women in her film. Not surprisingly, a beautiful, young, light-skinned woman who identifies herself as black, and a beautiful Asian woman report ugly racist remarks in the attention they attract, just as a pretty, somewhat plump San Franciscan reports cruel jibes men make about her weight.

"War Zone" is a street film and its men are mostly blue-collar guys, the majority of whom are black. With a couple of jarring exceptions, they are more open and secure in defending themselves than are the white-collar types, who tend to leer rather than speak and resent being caught in the act. Of course, there are plenty of men of all ages and ethnic backgrounds who are stupefyingly obnoxious; the worst-behaved and most arrogant men in the film are young, white, blue-collar males. The coolest person is an elderly man Hadleigh-West accuses of staring at her breasts. He calmly responds that he was merely noticing a bandage on her arm, hoping it doesn't hurt, explaining that he is on his way to the doctor to get a shot of cortisone to ease the pain in his own arm.

NEW YORK POST, 8/12/98, p. 51, Larry Worth

It sounds like a possible sequel to "Saving Private Ryan." Sure enough, "War Zone" is about fighting the good fight, taking out the oppressor and finding one's courage in the process.

But the setting has changed. Rather than the makeshift trenches of Omaha Beach, this combat takes place in modern-day New York (and Chicago, New Orleans, San Francisco, etc.). There, men are the undisputed enemy and writer-director Maggie Hadleigh-West is the justice-seeking heroine.

Armed with her trusty video cam, Hadleigh-West patrols the streets in her black athletic halter and spandex pants, shoving her microphone in the face of any man who calls out. "Do you think I'm flattered by that?" she justifiably demands.

There's a thought-provoking idea in turning the tables on leering construction workers and all those who mistakenly think it's OK to shout "Lookin' good, baby," wolf whistle or worse.

But while cutting harassers down to size should be applauded, one can't applaud Hadleigh-West. She fails to discriminate between men who catcall and men who simply gaze in her direction.

"I look at a pretty woman just like I'd look at a pretty car," one seemingly normal guy reasons. "Oh, so you equate women with cars?" the interrogator responds in a classic case of twisting someone's words.

Badgering and baiting become Hadleigh-West's specialties, making even those who would be her biggest supporters fail to sympathize.

Hadleigh-West also does her bit for female empowerment, as in literally chasing an innocent male bystander up an escalator. Who's harassing whom here? Didn't Hadleigh-West's parents teach her that two wrongs don't make a right?

Yet, she saves the worst for a mind-numbing conclusion:

That any of these men—even those who simply people-watch—is a potential rapist. The point is made by a 911 tape wherein a terrified woman reports a man breaking into her house. Since when did it become acceptable to use a woman's screams and fear of rape to manipulate an audience?

That's not even mentioning how the film gets redundant, nor how interviews with victimized women are used as filler to reach feature-length running time. Is the cachet of Susan Sarandon—whose name is attached to the project as if "presented by Susan Sarandon"—meant to obscure its lack of focus and squandered opportunities?

Ironically, Sarandon's name will draw attention to the fact that Hadleigh-West is her own worst enemy.

VILLAGE VOICE, 8/18/98, p. 112, Amy Taubin

A film at cross-purposes, Maggie Hadleigh-West's *War Zone* doesn't know whether it wants to be an exercise in power or an investigation of male behavior. Consciously wielding her camera as a weapon with which to retaliate against male street abuse, Hadleigh-West challenges the men who check out, comment on, and occasionally grab women's bodies. "Were you looking at my breasts?" she inquires, thrusting a mike and a lens in the guilty party's face. There are about 50 men in the film, and almost every one of them flies into a rage when Hadleigh-West questions what they seem to take as an absolute right. The film reveals the hostility and aggression beneath what the men claim is just their way of being complimentary. There's an awful truth in these revelations. But there's also something skewed: cameras confer a lot of power. By their mere presence, they change the rules of engagement. Not merely caught in the act, but recorded for posterity, the men respond with perhaps more defensive anger than they might if the camera weren't in the picture.

Also reviewed in:
CHICAGO TRIBUNE, 5/21/99, Friday/p. K, John Petrakis
NEW YORK TIMES, 8/12/98, p. E5, Janet Maslin
VARIETY, 4/13-19/98, p. 32, David Stratton

WATERBOY, THE

A Touchstone Pictures release of a Robert Simonds/Jack Giarraputo production. *Producer:* Robert Simonds and Jack Giarraputo. *Director:* Frank Coraci. *Screenplay:* Tim Herlihy and Adam Sandler. *Director of Photography:* Steven Bernstein. *Editor:* Tom Lewis. *Music:* Alan Pasqua. *Music Editor:* Steve Lotwis. *Sound:* Jay Meagher. *Sound Editor:* Elmo Weber and Gregory M. Gerlich. *Casting:* Roger Mussenden. *Production Designer:* Perry Andelin Blake. *Art Director:* Alan Au. *Set Designer:* Derrick Smith. *Set Decorator:* Barbara Peterson. *Set Dresser:* Dan Wilkerson. *Special Effects:* Ken Gorrell. *Costumes:* Tom Bronson. *Make-up:* Erin B. Koplow and Lee A. Grimes. *Make-up (Adam Sandler):* Ann Pala. *Stunt Coordinator:* Allan Graf. *Running time:* 91 minutes. *MPAA Rating:* PG-13.

CAST: Adam Sandler (Bobby Boucher); Kathy Bates (Mama Boucher); Henry Winkler (Coach Klein); Fairuza Balk (Vicki Vallencourt); Jerry Reed (Red Beaulieu); Larry Gilliard, Jr. (Derek Wallace); Blake Clark (Farmer Fran); Peter Dante (Gee Grenouille); Jonathan Loughran (Lyle Robideaux); Al Whiting (Casey Bugge); Clint Howard (Paco); Allen Covert (Walter); Rob Schneider (Townie); Todd Holland (Greg Meaney); Robert Kokol (Professor); Frank Coraci (Roberto); Jennifer Bini Taylor (Rita); James Bates (West Mississippi Lineman); Kelly Hare (Drunk Cheerleader); Dawn Birch (Red's Watergirl); Steve Raulerson (Sheriff Loughran); Chris Mugglebee (Sheriff Jack); Brett Rice (Laski); John Farley (Tony Dodd); Kevin Farley (Jim Simonds); Paul "The Giant" Wight (Captain Insano); Jamie Williams (Young Bobby); Marc Kittay (Youngest Bobby); Matt Baylis (Student); Jack Carroll (Bible College Coach); Tom Nowicki (Community College Coach); Ric Swezey (Male Cheerleader); Matthew Lussier (Redneck); Haven Gaston (Tina); Michael Hold (Central Kentucky Quarterback); Kevin Reid (West Mississippi Quarterback); Mattie Wolf (Cajun Lady); Phyllis Alia (Assistant); Dave Wagner (Announcer); Tina Barr (Cheerleader); Michael Giarraputo (Bourbon Bowl Statistician);

Marty Eli Schwartz (Moderator); Lee Corso, Bill Cowher, Dan Fouts, Chris Fowler, Jimmy Johnson, Brent Musburger, Dan Patrick, Lynn Swann, and Lawrence Taylor (Themselves).

LOS ANGELES TIMES, 11/6/98, p. 20, John Anderson

[The following review by John Anderson appeared in a slightly different form in **NEWSDAY, 11/6/98, Part II/p. B10.]**

The common wisdom on the school of Jerry Lewis-manque idiot comics is that they serve as whipping boys for the self-esteem-starved audiences of the X, Y or Z generations—that their film personae can make anyone feel good about themselves because they're so purposefully pathetic. But that's too glib.

More likely, the appeal of Pauly Shore, the late Chris Farley, Jim Carrey (on most occasions) and their discipline's sine qua non, Adam Sandler, is rooted in the perverse appreciation of truly bad movie making. Audiences weaned on much of the Hollywood product of the last 20 years, with its presumptive posturing, ludicrous plots, cardboard acting and shamelessly manipulated Big Emotion, have become connoisseurs of trash defined not necessarily as something useless but as something discarded. Filmgoers themselves feel discarded by the industry.

Sandler is the most successful practitioner of this art—this lost-audience stroking—precisely because his performances are the least performed, his characters the least realized. He has removed all artifice from acting; in fact, he can barely keep a straight face himself when he adopts the simpleton's voice of most of his characters. Subsequently, there's an intimacy with his audience that bonds them in contempt—not for each other, but for a system that doesn't just produce this kind of thing, it thrives on it.

Sandler's Bobby Boucher is a 31-year-old victim of the locker-room mentality, a testosterone-fueled pecking order of which he occupies the lowest peck. A devoted employee and advanced hydrologist—his water menu includes "distilled," "spring" and "rain"—he is dismissed abruptly by the sadistic coach Red Beaulieu (Jerry Reed) and his world starts to crumble.

Smothered by his mama (Kathy Bates, who's clearly having fun) and enticed by the felonious Vicki Vallencourt (Fairuza Balk), Bobby will be taken on by Coach Klein (Henry Winkler), an old rival of Red's and one who believes—Freudian that he is—that Bobby needs to vent. When he does, all his pent-up hostility makes him the most ferocious linebacker in the South.

Sandler engages in the comedy of cruelty; Mama's kitchen—where she serves up such bayou delicacies as fried anaconda, fried baby alligator and frog-filled muffins—is a Stephen King-inspired nightmare, as is Bates' performance.

"The Waterboy" follows a leadenly predictable path that will be more than familiar to anyone who's seen a recent sports movie, or any Sandler movie: Miserable underdog rises to the top, falls, is redeemed, shows up late for the big game for no reason other than to make a dramatic entrance, has a minor setback, rises again and scores—in agonizing slow-motion—the winning touchdown/home run/25-foot putt.

There are, no doubt, nuances to be discerned in just how a director manipulates these various bits of cheese to build his own personal vision, but like higher math and the deconstruction of Brahms, the subtleties are the purview of an advanced guard of true believers. Fortunately for Sandler, he has plenty.

NEW YORK POST, 11/6/98, p. 70, Thelma Adams

Root canal. Jury duty. "The Waterboy." Adam Sandler's latest comedy is pure pain. The patron saint of latter-day whiners reunites with director Frank Coraci for a movie that is as charmless and flat as "The Wedding Singer" was funny and appealing.

Sandler plays Bobby Boucher, a bayou water boy for a backwater college football team. The 31-year-old aquatic engineer dips his ladle while better, bigger men butt heads for gridiron glory.

Allegedly, Boucher found his calling because his father, a Peace Corps worker, died of dehydration in the Sahara. This is the movie's notion of dry humor. Meanwhile, Mrs. Boucher (Kathy Bates) cleaves to her only son as if he were the last gator in the swamp.

Oscar-winner Bates makes snake 'n' biscuits and a fool of herself in a comedy too broad for this broad (and, yes, we are laughing at her, not with her). Henry Winkler's neurotic football coach moons the audience. There's a reason they retired the Fonz; it's hard to look cool when your face is more leathery than your jacket.

Co-writer Sandler, crossing a speech impediment with a bayou brogue, can't pull a funny gag out of all this leftover "Deliverance" meets "North Dallas Forty" twaddle—unless you find biting the heads off barbecued lizards funny. This is a script even Pauly Shore would have rejected.

SIGHT AND SOUND, 5/99, p. 57, Andrew O'Hehir

Bobby Boucher, a simple 31-year old, lives with his Cajun mother in the town of Jackson's Bayou, Louisiana. He is fired from his job as waterboy for the University of Louisiana's football team, despite his 18 years of loyalty in the face of constant abuse. His mother is delighted, since she wants Bobby to stay home, but he's despondent. He finds an unpaid job as waterboy for SCLSU, a backwoods college whose team has lost 40 games in a row. Coach Klein, who is recovering from a mental breakdown, soon discovers that when Bobby is reminded of all the humiliation he has suffered, he becomes a fearsome defensive player, able to tackle any opponent.

Bobby's fury drives SCLSU to a winning streak and an invitation to the Bourbon Bowl, where they will face the University of Louisiana and its coach Red Beaulieu, who fired Bobby and drove Coach Klein insane. Beaulieu learns that Bobby never attended high school and so is not eligible to play, and Bobby's mother learns to her horror that Bobby has been playing football and seeing a local bad girl named Vicki, both against her wishes. Bobby passes the high-school equivalency examination and the townspeople convince his mother to relent. On the day of the Bourbon Bowl, Bobby shows up at half-time, leads SCLSU to a last-second victory and then marries Vicki with his mother's blessing.

A witless and utterly predictable comic fantasy about a misfit turned hero—think of it as *Forrest Gump*-Lite, if such a thing were possible—*The Waterboy* stands or falls on the nerd chic appeal of its stammering star Adam Sandler. A major box-office draw in the US after his roles in *Happy Gilmore* and *The Wedding Singer*, Sandler is an agreeably buffoonish sketch comedian, a combination of Jerry Lewis, Andy Kaufman and the Three Stooges, with just a dash of Harpo Marx. Like each of those performers his persona is funniest in small doses, and to me he can grow awfully wearisome across the length of a feature film (although millions of moviegoers evidently disagree). Sandler's enormous popularity isn't easy to explain; he himself has wisecracked that he became a multimillionaire despite being neither handsome nor talented. Perhaps his appeal lies in the imperturbable good cheer he projects—Bobby Boucher's paroxysms of rage are funny precisely because Sandler's performance so rapidly returns to the happy median of a man visibly content with life. Seen in this light, he's the perfect comic for America's blindly optimistic long boom.

Between Sandler's wobbly Cajun accent, the film's laundry list of played-out Southern stereotypes and its setting amid the bewildering autumnal rituals of American college football, it's hard to know what sense British and European audiences will make of *The Waterboy*. Admittedly, it's gratifying to watch the polite and easily flustered Bobby pulverise opposing gridiron goons the first few times it happens. But as the virtually identical football-action sequences mount up, the enterprise feels increasingly shoddy and trivial. This is an entertainment designed to make you forget, albeit temporarily, that weak and vulnerable people all over the world are constantly victimised—and maybe there's nothing wrong with that goal. But *The Waterboy* is too dull and shallow to fulfil it; you can't help thinking that a real-world Bobby would never get the girl or play for the varsity team, but would just keep on smiling while he's tripped and spat on.

Imprisoned by the relentless clichés of Sandler and Tim Herlihy's screenplay, even the estimable Kathy Bates can do nothing with the part of Mama Boucher, who lives with a mule named Steve in a cluttered bayou shack where she's forever cooking alligators, snakes and squirrels. Fairuza Balk and Henry Winkler, however, are the film's bright spots. Balk vigorously attacks her role as Vicki, the trailer trash tramp cum love interest who gets to utter the line: "I find Deputy Dawg very, very sexy." Winkler, a seasoned veteran of the broad, televisual comic style on display here (he was the Fonz in the television series *Happy Days)*, plays the lovably hapless Coach Klein with cheerful restraint, even delicacy. The supporting cast of formulaic Louisiana eccentrics features Larry Gilliard Jr. and Jonathan Loughran as Bobby's friendlier team-mates, along with Jerry Reed as the sadistic Coach Beaulieu.

Frank Coraci, who directed Sandler in *The Wedding Singer*, does nothing here to indicate that time ever passes or the weather ever changes in Jackson's Bayou. Every daytime scene has the bland, bright feeling of a Fourth of July parade. His two oft-repeated tricks are: the use of computer graphics to show how Bobby almost schizophrenically conflates his opponents with his tormentors; and the injection of well known football commentators and coaches in forced, peripheral skits. Sandler is not to blame for the fact that audiences eat up his modest talent for clowning, most of it borrowed from other, better comedians. But surely he has the money and the clout to hire more skilful collaborators.

Also reviewed in:
CHICAGO TRIBUNE, 11/6/98, Friday/p. D, Allan Johnson
NEW YORK TIMES, 11/6/98, p. E18, Janet Maslin
VARIETY, 11/9-15/98, p. 32, Glenn Lovell
WASHINGTON POST, 11/6/98, p. D1, Rita Kempley

WEDDING SINGER, THE

A New Line Cinema release of a Robert Simonds/Brad Grey production. *Executive Producer:* Brad Grey and Sandy Wernick. *Producer:* Robert Simonds and Jack Giarraputo. *Director:* Frank Coraci. *Screenplay:* Tim Herlihy. *Director of Photography:* Tim Suhrstedt. *Editor:* Tom Lewis. *Music:* Teddy Castellucci. *Music Editor:* Steve Lotwis and Scott Grusin. *Sound:* Kim H. Ornitz and (music) Gabriel D. Veltri. *Casting:* Roger Mussenden. *Production Designer:* Perry Andelin Blake. *Art Director:* Alan Au. *Set Designer:* Ann Harris. *Set Decorator:* Lisa Deutsch. *Set Dresser:* Matthew L. Gilbert, Russ Anderson, Chris Carlson, Roger Knight, and Larry White. *Costumes:* Mona May. *Make-up:* Vonda Morris. *Stunt Coordinator:* Michael Runyard. *Running time:* 95 minutes. *MPAA Rating:* PG-13.

CAST: Adam Sandler (Robbie); Drew Barrymore (Julia); Christine Taylor (Holly); Allen Covert (Sammy); Matthew Glave (Glenn); Ellen Albertini Dow (Rosie); Angela Featherstone (Linda); Alexis Arquette (George); Christina Pickles (Angie); Jodi Thelen (Kate); Frank Sivero (Andy); Patrick McTavish (Tyler); Gemini Barnett (Petey); Teddy Castellucci, Randy Razz, and John Vana (Robbie Hart Band); Billy Idol (Billy Idol); Kevin Nealon (Mr. Simms); Marnie Schneider (Joyce, Flight Attendant); Carmen Filpi (Old Man in Bar); Robert Smigel (Andre); Todd Hurst (Drunk Teenager); Peter Dante (David's Friend); Phyllis Alia (Mrs. Harold Veltri); Paul Thiele (Mr. Harold Veltri); Jack Nisbet (Father of Groom); Sally Pierce (Grandma Molly); Earl Carroll (Justice of the Peace); Jenna Byrne (Cindy Castellucci); Jason Cottle (Scott Castellucci); Mark Lonow (Father of the Bride); Bill Elmer (Fat Man); Jackie R. Challet (Sideburns Lady); Jimmy Karz (Studliest Kid at Bar Mitzvah); Al Hopson (Grandpa at Bar Mitzvah); Michael Shuman (Bar Mitzvah Boy); Steven Brill (Glenn's Buddy); Angela Payton (Faye); Timothy P. Herlihy (Rudy the Bartender); Matthew Kimble (Drunk at Bar); Sid Newman (Frank); Mark Beltzman (Vegas Air Ticket Agent); Andrew Shaifer and Shanna Moakler (Flight Attendants); Maree Cheatham (Nice Lady on Plane); Al Burke (Large Billy Idol Fan); Bob Hackl, Gabe Veltri, and Josh Oppenheimer (David's Band); Jon Lovitz (Jimmy Moore); Steve Buscemi (David).

LOS ANGELES TIMES, 2/13/98, Calendar/p. 10, Kevin Thomas

"The Wedding Singer" is a sparkling romantic comedy, the kind of picture that glides by so gracefully and unpretentiously that it's only upon reflection that you realize how much skill, caring and good judgment had to have gone into its making. It's light diversion, totally inconsequential in the greater scheme of things—and those are sometimes the hardest kinds of pictures to pull off.

In the title role, Adam Sandler plays Robbie Hart, who isn't getting rich performing with his band at wedding receptions, but he's good at his job. He sings from his heart, and he respects his audience. When we meet him, he's at work, where he announces that in one week the tables will be turned: He'll be getting married himself.

But there's a hitch. At the moment of truth a week later his fiancee (Angela Featherstone) stands him up. A hard-looking type who dresses like a hooker, she later explains that she'd gotten past and present confused; she had fallen for the aspiring rock star in Spandex and silk shirt open to the waist that Robbie had once been, not "just a wedding singer."

A romantic with integrity, Robbie is absolutely devastated, but he has struck up a friendship with a waitress, Julia (Drew Barrymore). The trouble is that Julia is already engaged to a Wall Street banker (Matthew Glave) she's eager to marry. She seems to be the only person who doesn't know that her banker boyfriend is an incorrigible playboy. Clearly, Robbie and Julia are made for each other...

Director Frank Coraci and writer Tim Herlihy, who set their story in 1985, are deft at dealing with the whole question of marriage and how vulnerable people still are to pressure to marry, even if it's to the wrong person. They also understand the pain of loneliness. In one scene, Robbie's raffish pal Sammy (Allen Covert, a formidable scene-stealer) tries to comfort his friend by extolling the pleasures of being a nonstop playboy but winds up admitting, "All I want is someone to hold me and tell me everything's all right."

Everything is more than all right with "The Wedding Singer." Coraci certainly knows how to get Sandler and Barrymore to turn on the charm full force and with absolute conviction. Robbie represents a drastic change of pace for the usually abrasive Sandler, who emerges as a surprisingly appealing romantic lead.

Sandler and Barrymore are in turn surrounded by some amusing, distinctive types. Alexis Arquette is hilarious and touching as Robbie's band's answer to Boy George, and Steve Buscemi and Jon Lovitz turn up in wonderful unbilled cameos—Buscemi as the drunken, ne'er-do-well brother of a bridegroom and Lovitz as a would-be wedding singer. (Billy Idol, a symbol of the '80s if there ever was one, turns up as himself.) Ellen Albertini Dow plays a zesty old lady who takes singing lessons from Robbie—and they pay off.

Set in either Ridgefield, Conn., or Ridgefield, N.J.—we never know which for sure—"The Wedding Singer" was resourcefully filmed in and around Los Angeles. It's a good-looking, period-sensitive, well-designed picture (though one sequence is marred by a mike boom constantly dipping into the frame) that actually sends you home happy.

NEW YORK, 3/2/98, p. 49, David Denby

The naughty profanities that one used to hear 40 years ago in the routines of a Catskills comic anyone can now hear in the albums and movies of Adam Sandler, who is a kind of suburban-sandlot descendant of the old foul-mouthed entertainers. Sandler is young, and his comedy is directed at kids; there's an occasional touch of knockabout cruelty in it as well as a love of the grotesque. Comedy has gotten wilder—or at least coarser—in the past few decades, and I suppose that some of Sandler's jokes would have made the blue-rinse ladies of 1954 cringe more than laugh. Yet Sandler, it must be said, has a soft spot in his heart for old ladies. In his 1996 movie *Happy Gilmore*, he played a wildly undisciplined failed hockey player, an orphan raised by his grandma. When Grandma's house gets impounded by the IRS, he joins a professional golf tour in order to raise money and reclaim the house. Part of the joke of the movie is that this uncouth young man is just sick with love for his grandmother. In Sandler's new comedy, *The Wedding Singer*, set in 1985, he's a suburban New Jersey entertainer at weddings and "functions," a charmer with damp long hair who makes eyes at aunts and uncles as he sings. On the side, he gives voice lessons to an old lady (Ellen Dow), and at the end of the movie, in celebration of her fiftieth wedding anniversary, she, with perfect rhythm and plenty of gusto, sings the Sugarhill Gang rap song "Rapper's Delight." You go, girl! Surely Mel Brooks was never that nice to old ladies.

Adam Sandler can scream, but he doesn't overwhelm us with noise and screeches like Jim Carrey. Huge and alarming, with wildly thrashing limbs and menacing teeth, Carrey wants to swallow the world. Sandler is big, too-rangy and athletic—but he's not that big; he seems like an overgrown suburban boy much in need of fried chicken, mashed potatoes, and a room under the roof to mope in. He's basically a mild fellow who wants to get along and make his way in the world, though from time to time, weird aggressions burst out of him. In *Happy Gilmore*, he wears a hockey uniform even on a snazzy golf course, where he occasionally breaks into club-throwing rages and hires, as a caddy, a filthy bum who takes baths in the fairway water. He's not a conscious rebel; he just hasn't been socialized yet. At the tee, Sandler steps into his drives like a hockey player gathering momentum for a slap shot. Fore! The ball travels more than 400 yards. An outsider, a pretender, Adam Sandler is a seeming loser who has too much determination to be kept down. He's a loser who's really a winner. Other men hate him—he's the adolescent they have painfully left behind—but girls think he's cute. Like Buster Keaton and other great comics, Sandler has a shy, nuzzling way with the ladies. He spends most of *The Wedding Singer* making eyes at Drew Barrymore, who plays a plump angelic blonde.

Part of this comic is a nice Jewish boy. Even the profanities are nothing more than the outrages perpetrated by an adolescent at the family dinner table. The dirty words add savor to the meal-certainly this kid expects to be forgiven before dessert. Like Allen Sherman 30 years ago, Sandler sings silly satirical songs the whole family can enjoy. On Sandler's album *How Did I Get Here?* there's a Hanukkah song with lines like "O.J. Simpson/Not a Jew/But guess who is?/Hall-of-famer Rod Carew." That's a pandering lyric, actually, that the blue-rinse ladies at the Concord might like. Adam Sandler wants to please. On the same album, there's also an extremely profane ballad, in reggae style, dedicated to a terrible lemon of a car. This song is not a put-down of reggae—its mild shock lies in the dirty words falling into the lulling regularities of the ballad. Middle-class kids love Adam Sandler because his foul mouth is something they know they can get away with.

On the other hand, the nice Jewish boy has a streak of anger; he can't be pushed. In *The Wedding Singer,* Sandler begins one of his songs before a crowd in a quiet, mousy voice and then breaks into a murderous punk whine, passing back and forth throughout the song, schizophrenia as entertainment. In *Happy Gilmore,* the nice boy and the surreal bad boy were held in balance; in *The Wedding Singer,* despite a few outbursts, the nice boy wins out, and not with the best results. It's a pleasant movie—very pleasant, in fact—but soft as a down quilt. The wedding singer is not only the life of the party; he's a part-time shrink, a peacemaker who brings people together. Of course, no one takes him very seriously. Why would anyone wed a man who sings at weddings? Will this schlumpy guy defeat an overconfident Wall Street type and win Drew Barrymore? The movie is a tame affair, shot on calm, manicured streets; the interiors are decorated in pastels. Adam Sandler, a gifted young man, may be comfortable in the suburbs, but if he's going to become a big comedy star in the movies, he's got to either blow the place sky-high or get away and find a more challenging turf. He makes comedy about the underside of blandness. In *The Wedding Singer,* the blandness threatens to take over.

NEW YORK POST, 2/13/98, p. 53, Michael Medved

The amiable idiocy of "The Wedding Singer" offers a sweet, sappy love story for Valentine's Day spiced with just enough raucous humor to allow moviegoers to swallow all the syrup without danger of tooth decay.

Though the romantic story may feel tired and familiar, the movie does break new ground in one respect: as one of the first-ever Hollywood attempts to prematurely exploit heartfelt nostalgia for the 1980s. Intrusive references to "Miami Vice," Boy George, DeLoreans and "Dynasty," along with deliberately dated references ("Your love will last forever—like Donald and Ivana, Woody and Mia, Burt and Loni!"), may keep viewers entertained even as interest in the slender plot begins to fade.

That treacly tale unfolds in a nondescript suburb, where warm-hearted Adam Sandler lives in his married sister's basement while eking out a living as a suburban wedding singer.

His performances are genuinely amusing as he shares the joy of even the tackiest couples, looking forward to his own upcoming nuptials to his high school sweetheart (the sexy, muscular Angela Featherstone).

When she stands him up at the altar, he goes into a tailspin, abated only by friendship with a reception hall waitress who is an adorable newcomer in town (Drew Barrymore, in what may be her most innocent role since "E.T.") Unfortunately, she's engaged to a macho, materialist heel (Matthew Glave) who's obviously meant to be no good since he deals "junk bonds" on Wall Street.

The predictable plot, with heartbroken Sandler helping dewy-eyed Drew prepare for her wedding to the wrong guy, generates surprising romantic chemistry between the two leads and the under- "Graduate" ending works especially well—thanks to an amusing flight to Las Vegas complete with cameo by '80s icon Billy Idol. Jon Lovitz and the marvelous Steve Buscemi also make brief, uncredited, but hilarious appearances.

Unfortunately, a few odd excesses sour some of the good-natured sentimentality. In a bar mitzvah scene, was it really necessary to celebrate aggressive tushy-grabbing by dancing couples of all ages as the ultimate in debonair charm?

And why the obsession with alcohol and drunkenness—with all major characters getting plastered at one point or another, and both romantic leads separately demonstrating their sophistication by reaching the retching point?

In fact, the central couple meets one another while watching a blitzed kid of 11-or-so vomiting into a dumpster outside the reception hall. In comments to the press, actress Barrymore observes, "It just doesn't get more romantic than that." But this may be an aesthetic too bizarre even for the outrageous '80s.

NEWSDAY, 2/13/98, Part II/p. B6, John Anderson

Should Ronald Reagan ever make it to Mount Rushmore, as several idolaters have proposed, it should be for his contribution to comedy: Warm, cuddly and perpetually at sea level, he made it verboten to make fun of people who deserve it. Need evidence? Check out "The Wedding Singer," a disappointingly inert comedy starring Adam Sandler as Robbie, the guy who fixes other people's weddings and gets stood up at his own. Set smack in the middle of the Reagan Era, it is virtually devoid of socio-political references (with the exception of the villain being a junk-bond dealer) and so has to scuttle about wildly looking for objects to deride. Old people. Fat people. Gay people. Fashion victims. All accompanied by the worst of '80s rock and enough leather and rivets to build a convertible couch.

So many worthy victims, so little comedic bloodshed. But this has been the trend in movie comedy ever since "Saturday Night Live" became toothless and allowed its performers to leach out like radon into mainstream motion pictures. Where the objective once was to tip sacred cows and puncture pomposity, somewhere in the '80s comedy became either S or M: In the films of the late Chris Farley, for instance, the joke was always himself; with Adam Sandler, it's everyone in the movie who isn't Adam Sandler—or, in the case of "The Wedding Singer," the radiant Drew Barrymore (radiant but inert) who plays Julia, the woman with whom Robbie is meant to be.

Besides being little more than an excuse for a sound track album, "The Wedding Singer" possesses another odd personality quirk found in other period comedies—the type that uses an avalanche of time-specific music and a few ham-fisted visual references to establish time and place. Robbie and Julia may be surrounded by friends like Sammy (Allen Covert), who actually wears a Michael Jackson jacket and single glove, and Monica (Christine Taylor, Marcia in "The Brady Bunch" movies), who reminds us of the tragedy of acid-washed denim. But neither Sammy nor Julia is ever really part of the world around them. OK, Robbie wears a haircut favored by professional wrestlers and serial killers, but otherwise he's a '90s creature. And Julia, too. God help them.

Sandler, in fact, seems ever-ready to burst into laughter, which gives "The Wedding Singer's" many, many maudlin moments a touch of contempt. Of course, it's tough to keep a straight face when Julia, whose irredeemable intended, Glenn (Matthew Glave), refuses to set a date, utters lines like "I think I'm doomed to wander the Earth alone forever." Or when Robbie, trashed by his feckless fiancée, Linda (Angela Featherstone), tosses the little bride from their cake into the grass. It's enough to make you double over.

Despite the lifeless quality of both Tim Herlihy's script and Frank Coraci's direction, the cameos can be quite entertaining (or maybe it's just relative). Steve Buscemi does an excruciatingly funny bit as a best man whose toast to his brother turns into a bitter emotional meltdown. Alexis Arquette, while making transvestitism one more of the movie's tacky gags, is good as the Boy George impersonator, George. And Billy Idol, a real blast from the past, almost salvages the whole movie with his leering sneer during the last part of the picture. Sandler and

Barrymore, however, get to gaze moonily into each other's eyes yet again, by which time your eyes will be rolling along with the credits.

SIGHT AND SOUND, 7/98, p. 56, John Wrathall

1985. Robbie makes his living singing at wedding receptions, but his own wedding ends in disaster when his bride Linda doesn't turn up. To coax him out of his depression, Julia, a waitress who works at the same reception hall, asks Robbie to help with the arrangements for her own impending wedding to bond dealer Glenn. Hanging out together, Robbie and Julia start to fall for each other. But Robbie can't bring himself to say anything to Julia, even after Glenn brags to him that he cheats on her.

On his stag night, Glenn gets into a fight with Robbie and knocks him down. Robbie comes home drunk to find Linda waiting for him. When Julia comes round to see Robbie the next morning, Linda opens the door and hints that she and Robbie are back together. Upset, Julia asks Glenn to take her to Las Vegas so they can get married immediately.

Robbie races to the airport and gets the only remaining seat on a flight to Las Vegas, in first class. Realising that Julia and Glenn are travelling economy on the same flight, Robbie enlists the help of fellow first-class passenger Billy Idol and serenades Julia over the PA. Robbie and Julia finally declare their love for each other, and get married.

The Wedding Singer is the third collaboration between the *Saturday Night Live* team of comedian Adam Sandler and writer Tim Herlihy, and as you might expect from the men behind *Billy Madison* and *Happy Gilmore*, it's not a particularly clever comedy. There's a lot of vomiting, and jokes at the expense of fat people, ugly people (in particular women with hairy faces) and randy old-age pensioners. The 1985 setting, of no importance to the plot, is the pretext for some cheap retro humour. The ironic references to the fashions and cultural icons of the day—from *Miami Vice* to Rubik's cubes—are all pretty obvious, as is the ever-present soundtrack of nostalgia-inducing (if that phrase can possibly apply to the likes of Kajagoogoo, The Thompson Twins and Musical Youth) 80s music. But somehow, for all its simple mindedness, this turns out to be a very winning romantic comedy.

Whereas Sandler's previous films traded on his knuckle-headed antics, his performance here is unexpectedly self-effacing, endowing the lovelorn Robbie with something of the wounded, goofy charm of David Schwimmer's Ross in *Friends,* only with added *chutzpah*. Another pleasant surprise is Sandler's singing: his wonderfully slick opening version of 'You Spin Me Around (like a Record)', for instance, can't fail to bring a smile to the face of anyone who remembers Dead or Alive's original.

But the most engaging thing about *The Wedding Singer* is that where love-interest roles in his previous vehicles (or those of Jim Carrey, for that matter) were mere tokens, Sandler here allows himself to be upstaged by his female co-star. Hitherto, Drew Barrymore has managed to become a celebrity without ever having a leading role in a decent movie (with the possible exception of the 1992 remake of *Guncrazy,* which went straight to video in the UK). As Julia, however, she does wonders with an unremarkable part managing to make lines like "I vomited in my hair" seem touching.

Sandler's regular film team is augmented here by director Frank Coraci who worked with Sandler on music videos. And Sandler and Herlihy's ability to deliver a conventionally charming romantic comedy hasn't dimmed their talent for the occasional moment of inspired ludicrousness. Perhaps the best here comes courtesy of an uncredited Steve Buscemi who, after a wonderfully bitter cameo as a drunken best man in the opening scene, pops up again at Robbie and Julia's wedding to serenade them with a cover version of Spandau Ballet's "True".

VILLAGE VOICE, 2/17/98, p. 111, Gary Dauphin

Nice guys do have to finish first somewhere, which is why you have movies like *The Wedding Singer.* An orgy of sweetness as charming as it is sickly, *Singer* details the mid-'80s travails of Robbie Hart, a New Jersey crooner-for-hire whose fondest wish is to stand at the altar with a girl he can imagine "getting old with." It's a semi-tough comedic road: Robbie (Adam Sandler, in a role ably written specifically for him, or at least his funny-musician bit) gets jilted by his 'burb-vixen fiancée, and soon discovers he really loves Julia (a limp Drew Barrymore), a waitress whose engaged to the wrong person herself. Will Julia realize Robbie's the one? Will Robbie stand up to Julia's jack-off Wall Street fiancé? Will Robbie's best bud Sammy finally stop wearing that gilded Michael Jackson glove? Yep, you betcha, and maybe.

Robbie isn't a very good singer, but his enthusiasm makes up for talent as he belts out '80s tunes like Dead or Alive's "You Spin Me Round (Like a Record)" and moves the crowd at weddings and Bar Mitzvahs alike. The other secret to Robbie's charm is that he's very good in moral and ethical terms, presiding over receptions like the sultan of sentiment, saving the day from drunk best men, making sure the fat kid gets to dance, and so on. His heart is destined to be broken and mended as easily as the clip on a cheap cummerbund. if *The Wedding Singer* has a flaw, it's the '80s thing, the film running mostly on fumes from random audio-visual references designed to provoke laughs just by being there ("Hey! A Delorean!"). Like Robbie Hart, who can only show his feelings when hiding behind a bad suit and microphone, this movie really just wants to be loved, but the shtick gets in the way.

Also reviewed in:
NEW YORK TIMES, 2/13/98, p. E18, Janet Maslin
VARIETY, 2/16-22/98, p. 56, Leonard Klady

WELCOME TO WOOP WOOP

A Goldwyn Entertainment Company release in association with Scala Productions of a Scala/Unthank production. *Executive Producer:* Nik Powell and Stephen Woolley. *Producer:* Finola Dwyer. *Director:* Stephan Elliott. *Screenplay:* Michael Thomas. *Based on the book "The Dead Heart" by:* Douglas Kennedy. *Director of Photography:* Mike Molloy. *Editor:* Martin Walsh. *Music:* Guy Ross. *Music Editor:* Nick Adams. *Sound:* Tony Johnson. *Sound Editor:* Glenn Freemantle. *Casting:* Gregg Apps. *Production Designer:* Owen Paterson. *Art Director:* Colin Gibson. *Set Decorator:* Suza Maybury. *Set Dresser:* John-Paul (Lon) Lucini. *Special Effects:* John Bowring. *Costumes:* Lizzy Gardiner. *Make-up:* Cassie Hanlon. *Stunt Coordinator:* Rocky McDonald. *Running time:* 102 minutes. *MPAA Rating:* R.

CAST: Johnathon Schaech (Teddy); Rod Taylor (Daddy-O); Susie Porter (Angie); Dee Smart (Krystal); Richard Moir (Reggie); Maggie Kirkpatrick (Ginger); Barry Humphries (Blind Wally); Mark Wilson (Duffy); Paul Mercurio (Midget); Stan Yarramunua (Young Lionel); Bob Oxenbould (Moose); Jan Oxenbould (Big Pat); Daniel Rigney (Small Kenny); David Hoey (Dirty Dean); Sarah Osmo (Laverne); Con Demetriou (Darren); Rachel Griffiths (Sylvia); Tina Louise (Bella); Chelsea Brown (Maud); Adryn White (Herbie); Felix Williamson (Jerome); Kevin Copeland (Plato); Shane Paxton (Sonny); Bindi Paxton (Cher); Alan Finney (Barman); Pat Gibbs (Auntie Di); Bella Cooper (Leigh Ann); Cale Morgan (Damien); Baden Jones (Leon); Breanna Sonsie (Tina); Ding (Projectionist).

LOS ANGELES TIMES, 11/13/98, Calendar/p. 14, Jack Mathews

[*The following review by Jack Mathews appeared in a slightly different form in* **NEWSDAY, 11/13/98, Part II/p. B12.**]

Teddy (Johnathon Schaech) can't believe his luck. The cockatoo smuggler made it out of New York after a stripper girlfriend went crazy and killed a pair of mobsters, and now, in the middle of nowhere, on a dusty, two-lane road cutting across barren kangaroo country in Australia's Outback, he's picked up a beautiful, red-haired hitchhiker who's providing—no, compelling!—the best sex of his life.

I love you!" he shouts, in a moment of exhilaration.

"Do you mean it?" she asks.

The next thing he knows, the heavily drugged Teddy is coming to in a pig slough, covered with mud and cake icing, facing a band of people who look as if they've spilled out of a garbage truck.

Among them is a glowing Angie (Susie Porter), giving him the news that they were married while he was out.

Now, he really can't believe his luck.

Welcome to "Welcome to Woop Woop," a raucous, gross-out comedy set in an uncharted village of lowlifes built from refuse on the slopes of an abandoned asbestos mine. It's Stephan Elliott's first film since his international hit "The Adventures of Priscilla: Queen of the Desert," and you might wish he'd rested on his laurels.

Where "Priscilla" found high comedy in a sensitive portrayal of a trio of drag queens crossing the Outback in a pink bus and a glorious wardrobe, "Woop Woop" seeks low comedy among a tribe of former miners who seem to have reinvented themselves as sewer rats. Lizzy Gardiner's costuming for these characters may be as creative as her Oscar-winning designs for "Priscilla," but no one will call it eye candy.

There are many funny moments in "Woop Woop," and two very good performances. One is from Porter, who plays Angie with an unself-conscious abandon that gives the film comic liftoff whenever she appears, and from a nearly unrecognizable Rod Taylor, a former Hollywood leading man who returns to his native Australia to play Teddy's father-in-law, the cruel, iron-fisted ruler of Woop Woop.

There's also a clever conceit. For entertainment, in the absence of television and radio, the denizens of Woop Woop, who earn their meager livings making dog food from kangaroo road kill, are sonically bathed from loudspeakers with the soundtracks of Rodgers & Hammerstein musicals. At night, they gather to watch film versions of "Sound of Music" and "South Pacific," and mime the performances.

But what Elliott has created is a meandering goof in search of a purpose. Though the film is adapted by Michael Thomas ("Backbeat") from a novel, it plays like an extended, and heavily camped-up episode of "Twilight Zone," as drawn by Mad magazine.

Through most of the movie, we simply follow Teddy around the scruffy hovels and refuse stacks of Woop Woop, as he tries to satiate Angie and calm her father, create his own political base from the community's losers, rebuild his commandeered van, and team up with Angie's wiser sister Krystal (Dee Smart) for an escape run.

Schaech, one of the stars of Tom Hanks' "That Thing You Do!," has an amiable presence, but seems as lost in his role as his role is lost in "Woop Woop." You know you're in trouble when the hero of your story is the least interesting one in it.

Also reviewed in:
NEW YORK TIMES, 11/13/98, p. E10, Stephen Holden
VARIETY, 5/26-6/1/97, p. 66, Todd McCarthy

WEST NEW YORK

A White Whale Films Ltd. release. *Producer:* Donna Miller. *Director:* Phil Gallo. *Screenplay:* Phil Gallo and Steve Bretschneider. *Director of Photography:* Jonathan Rho. *Music:* Michael Boldt, Clem Vicari, Jr., Phil Gallo, and Trade Martin. *Production Designer:* Steve Bretschneider. *Running time:* 86 minutes. *MPAA Rating:* Not Rated.

CAST: Frank Vincent (Tom Coletti); Gian DiDonna (Jimmy Vero); Gloria Darpino (Diane Ryan); Brian McCormack (Frank Ryan); Brian Burke (Zeller); Vincent Pastore (Carmine).

NEW YORK POST, 5/27/98, p. 46, Larry Worth

In the murky finale of "West New York," a villainous cop yells to the doe-eyed heroine, "You just don't have a f---ing clue." If so, that's a trait she shares with director, co-writer Phil Gallo.

Precious little rings true in this low-budget look at corruption and love gone awry in the titular New Jersey town. The chief problem is a script that's hopelessly convoluted, substituting cliches for anything even hinting of originality.

At the alleged plot's center is a dirty ex-cop whose criminal dealings with trigger-happy mobsters and bad bank bonds soon endanger everyone in his sphere. A love triangle involving his daughter, her husband and ex-beau is equally dopey.

A succession of explanatory speeches come in one of two flavors: somewhat confusing or downright asinine. Likewise, the acting ranges from palatable (ever-reliable Frank Vincent) to utterly embarrassing (everyone else).

The bottom line: "West New York" doesn't merit even a 90-minute visit.

Also reviewed in:
NEW YORK TIMES, 5/27/98, p. E5, Lawrence Van Gelder

WESTERN

A New Yorker Films release of a Salome SA and Diaphana production. *Producer:* Maurice Bernart and Michel Saint-Jean. *Director:* Manuel Poirier. *Screenplay (French with English subtitles):* Manuel Poirier and Jean-François Goyet. *Director of Photography:* Nara Keo Kosal *Editor:* Yann Dedet. *Music:* Bernardo Sandoval. *Sound:* Christian Fontaine. *Sound Editor:* Emmanuel Augeard. *Art Director:* Roland Mabille. *Costumes:* Sophie Dwernicki. *Make-up:* Françoise Bosc. *Running time:* 121 minutes. *MPAA Rating:* Not Rated.

CAST: Sergi López (Paco Cazale); Sacha Bourdo (Nino); Elisabeth Vitali (Marinette); Marie Matheron (Nathalie); Daphné Gaudefroy-Demonbyns (Hitch-hiker); Karine Lelièvre (Voice of Mr. Letour's Secretary); Jean-Louis Dupont (Policeman); Olivier Herveet (Hospital Doctor); Alain Luc Guhur (Hospital Attendant); Bernard Mazzinghi (Roland, Marinette's Brother); Alain Denniel (Bearded Man in Hospital Ward); Serge Riaboukine (Van Driver); Michele Vivier (Car Driver); Melanie Léray (Guénaëlle); Catherine Riaux (Guénaëlle's Friend); Carole Ledreau (Friend at Wedding); Basile Siekoua (Baptiste); Hélène Foubert (Baptiste's Girlfriend); Marilyne Canto (Marilyne); Hélène Berrou (Hélène); Monette Cardinaux (Monette); Ghislaine Jégou (Ghislaine); Sophie Kervadel (Sophie); Angelina Pochie (Angelina); Diane Valsonne (Diane); Hélène Moreau (Hélène); Vanina Delannoy (Fougère, Hysterical Woman); Marie Lounici and Véronique Bellegarde (Café Patrons); Fabien Kachev (New Salesman); Guy Abgrall (Farmer); Jean-Jacques Vanier (Dr. Yvon Le Marrec); Brigitte Legal (Pharmacist); Michel Le Cossec (Bar Patron); Johan Le Saux (Johan); Tudy Bernard (Tudy); Lena Bernard (Lena); Rudi Desseaux (Rudi); Maxime Guggenbuhl (Maxime); Olivier Guehenneux (Antoine); Maeva Privat (Antoine's Sister); Arthur Privat and Théo Vigouroux (Antoine's Brothers); Gérard Privat (Antoine's Father); Karine Hascoët (Post Office Clerk).

LOS ANGELES TIMES, 8/7/98, Calendar/p. 8, Kevin Thomas

The title of Manuel Poirier's warm and glowing "Western has nothing to do with the American frontier but refers instead to the ruggedly beautiful west coast of Brittany. What's more, the terrain it covers is not geographic but that of the human heart. Winner of the grand prize at Cannes last year among other key awards, "Western" is a delightfully subtle and perceptive blend of romantic comedy and road movie.

Paco (Sergi Lopez), a shoe salesman born in Catalonia, is driving toward the port town of Le Guilvenec when he stops to give a pretty hitchhiker a lift—only to have her replace herself swiftly with a slight, wistful-looking man, Nino (Sacha Bourdo), who she explains has been trying to thumb a ride for more than two hours without success.

In very short order, Paco has his life turned upside down. Nino gets Paco to make a stop—and drives off with his car, which is loaded with shoes. Paco is sitting by the road in a daze when Marinette (Elisabeth Vitali) stops to fix a loose license plate, and he shamefacedly asks her for a ride into town.

The upshot is that Paco loses his job but commences an affair with the lovely Marinette. But no sooner has an idyll begun for Paco than Marinette insists that they take a three-week breather from their relationship to discover how seriously they feel about each other. Meanwhile, Paco has spotted Nino, and after a couple of plot twists, the two end up friends. Nino, a Russian emigre, persuades Paco to hit the road with him during that three-week break.

So sure is Poirier's sense of humor and pathos that all this elaborate but swiftly unfolding plotting becomes an amusing comment on the workings of fate and human nature. At this point, the film shifts gears as it covers Paco and Nino's aimless rambling over the countryside. Nino, it turns out, has been drifting in this manner for the two years since the Frenchwoman—whom he met in Russia and came to France to marry—stood him up.

Although they instinctively seek contact with as many people as they can, what Paco and Nino are really looking for is love. The need for people, men in this instance, to find someone to love in order to anchor their lives, is what "Western" is all about.

That both men are foreigners inherently heightens their sense of isolation. Yet "Western" doesn't attack the French—or Bretons in particular—for being insular. To the contrary, most everyone the two meet are friendly and helpful. The dark, stocky, boyish-looking Lopez and the diminutive Bourdo are immensely likable guys, and their adventures are matters of both humor and pain.

American audiences, so conditioned to a fast clip, may find the film's leisurely paced 123 minutes a bit taxing. But so consistently fresh is Poirier's take that it's worth it to sit back and go with the flow.

NEW YORK POST, 7/24/98, p. 43, Thelma Adams

There have long been cracks in the American melting pot. The shaggy, anti-establishment buddy films like "Scarecrow" or "Easy Rider" exposed those splits and critiqued the stew while reaffirming the bond between men.

In "Western," Peruvian-born Frenchman Manuel Poirer hitches a ride on the road-buddy movie. The writer-directors comedic take on the new polyglot Western Europe won the 1997 Cannes grand jury prize.

Traveling shoe salesman Paco (Sergi Lopez) picks up hitcher Nino (Sacha Bourdo). The runty Russian immigrant repays Paco by stealing the studly Spaniard's car. This slapstick event ends Paco's stable, if boring, life.

Through a series of equally unlikely twists, the salesman finds, pulverizes and then bonds with Nino. The duo—one a chick magnet, the other a chick repellent—hit the road along France's western coast.

Set to Bernardo Sandoval's danceable score, "Western" has many funny, sexy episodes. Lopez and Bourdo connect in time-worn odd-couple style. But, in the end, "Western" retreats from any frontiers Poirer might be exploring, to give us an "it's a small world" multicultural bear hug that's even less believable than Paco and Nino's pairing.

NEWSDAY, 7/24/98, Part II/p. B11, John Anderson

Manning separate tables at an alfresco cafe, three characters in Manuel Poirier's. "Western" play a game called "Good Morning, France." Bonjouring everyone who passes, they score points for a pleasant response, extra points if they get an answer from a woman, and when a sturdy older Frenchman tells the wheelchair-bound Ivory Coaster named Baptiste to "Go back where you came from," he gets no points at all.

Westerns can be set on the Ponderosa or in a Spielbergian-Lucasian galaxy far far away, but they generally have a frontier. In Poirier's road movie-buddy picture, the frontier is borderless *fin de siecle* Europe, a place where nationalities are more oblique and nationalism more rabid. Unexplored territory ranges from the international to the interpersonal; the possibilities—for exploitation or exploration—seem infinite.

And troubling. Set down in this amorphous terrain is Paco (Sergi Lopez), a traveling shoe salesman from Spain who stops for a beautiful hitchhiker only to have her pull a switcheroo for homeless and decidedly unbeautiful Nino (Sacha Bourdo). Not only is Nino not what he bargained for, the little fellow—Italian by way of Russia—steals Paco's car and leaves him stranded.

But like the New Europe, Paco's life is a continual series of unexpected occurrences. In and around his relationship with Nino—whom he spots on the street, hospitalizes and then befriends—he meets the lovely Marinette (Elisabeth Vitali), falls in lust, maybe in love, but she wants to be sure and proposes a three-week moratorium to test their romantic resolve. On his own again, Paco accepts Nino's proposal to hit the road, and see life from the other side.

Director Poirier's wide-screen romance is only part political allegory and mostly odd-couple picaresque (reminiscent of, though lighter than, the Gene Hackman-Al Pacino oldie "Scarecrow"). Unpredictability is the operating engine. Life can change—and Paco's does—with the loss of a wallet, the heist of a car. So much—appearances, posture, maybe nationality—is determined by superficial things. And sex may be the single unifying concept in a world turned topsy-turvy.

That's certainly a concept on Nino's mind. Paco is a natural ladies' man (although, given Lopez' often impenetrable demeanor, this is asking a lot of us). Nino, conversely, would just like to meet and win one woman, any woman, basically, but since he'd be top-seed at the Ratzo Rizzo Look-alike Contest, his luck runs mostly cold. During a pickup date with two waitresses, in fact, Paco manages to bed both his *and* Nino's date (the scene, featuring an utterly discordant four-way conversation, is brilliant). Nino's attitude isn't getting any better, and at a party, when he rails against one woman for the perceived sins of many, Poirier takes his film in temporarily unnerving directions.

The acting is quite good and the unlikely friendship between Paco and Nino convincing. The crossroads come when they meet Nathalie (Marie Matheron), an unmarried mother of a half-dozen kids, who may represent the common maternity of Europe at large or maybe just a woman with a taste for small Russo-Italians. Either way, and despite his occasionally absurdist grace notes, director Poirier plays a warm tune, not an anthem but a ballad.

SIGHT AND SOUND, 5/98, p. 59, Chris Darke

Brittany, the present. Paco, a travelling salesman, picks up a hitchhiker, Nino, who steals his car and merchandise. After being sacked from his job, Paco is helped out by Marinette, who falls in love with him. Spotting Nino, Paco attacks and hospitalises him but a friendship develops between the men. Marinette is nervous about her feelings for Paco and suggests they take a three-week break to test the strength of their attachment. Nino suggests that he and Paco hit the road for the duration.

They stop at a hotel, where Nino chats up a waitress who's more interested in Paco. They dine with the waitress and her girlfriend and both women end up in bed with Paco, much to Nino's chagrin. To placate his friend, Paco proposes they canvas women for a fake questionnaire on their ideal man, but the scheme is a failure.

They find work on a farm but Nino injures Paco's leg with a chainsaw. Paco, still pining for Marinette, meets Nathalie, a single mother. He introduces her to Nino with whom Nathalie falls in love. Shortly afterwards, Nino asks to stay with her. Nino takes Paco to see Marinette but her feelings have not changed and she doesn't want a relationship with him. The two friends return to Nathalie's house where they join the mother and children in a big family meal.

Manuel Poirier's fifth feature film, and his first to be released in the UK, is an amiable picaresque tale that ambles leisurely for two hours along the Normandy coastline. Paco, a Catalan salesman living in France, inadvertently hitches up with Nino, a scrawny Russian émigré who's been on the road for two years since his planned marriage to a French woman fell through. Initially, their meeting appears ill-fated: Paco picks up Nino, only to have his car and its contents of shoe samples stolen by the hitch-hiker. As a result, Paco loses his job but meets and falls in love with Marinette. When Paco spots Nino in the small Breton coastal town of La Guilvinec, he beats him up and hospitalises him for a week. Out of such inauspicious beginnings is born a firm if errant friendship.

Much of the film's comedy is gently observational and revolves around Paco's ease with women, while Nino seems incapable of attracting any female company. The catch is the fact that Paco has decided to accompany Nino on the road as a way of honouring an agreement he's made with Marinette, to test their nascent feelings for one another by agreeing to separate for three weeks. On the road, pining for Marinette, Paco accompanies Nino from town to town, through various short-term amorous escapades and misadventures. They are both, in their way, fishes out of water: Paco a Catalan, Nino a Russian. They fit in, but not quite, with the people they encounter. Poirier, who's cast Sergi Lopez (Paco) in several of his previous films including *La Petite Amie d'Antonio,* creates an affectionate portrait of the dynamics of male friendship, a gentler version of Betrand Blier's *Les Valseuses* (1974). Each tries to do right by the other, even to the rather wonderfully scatterbrained extent of Paco's persuading Nino that the surefire method of locating his ideal woman is for the pair of them to masquerade as opinion pollsters.

As each scheme comes to nothing, their itinerary becomes increasingly fruitless and slowly Nino starts to get the upper hand. A scrawny, desperately optimistic dead-ringer for the young Bob Dylan, Nino finds himself attracted to Nathalie, the mother of *une famille nombreuse,* all of whom she's borne to men who were just passing through. The film's final image is of the pair of them at the crowded family table in Nathalie's house.

Curiously, it's a scene that recalls the closing image of another recent French comedy about two ill-matched and unhappily footloose male companions, Pierre Salvadori's *Les Apprentis*. Infantilised by their lack of female companionship, these are men shown to be desperate for family and security. But that might be over-reading slightly, for *Western* with its fine widescreen photography (by Nara Keo Kosal) of the stark Breton landscape, is an unusual open-air variation on French *intimiste* film-making. Warm and bittersweet, its comedy is generated from a mixture of social embarrassment, odd-couple dynamics and sympathetic observations of its characters.

VILLAGE VOICE, 7/28/98, p. 113, Amy Taubin

In Manuel Poirier's first feature, *Western*, the coast of France is the scene not of tragedy but of farce. This charmless road movie (which, inexplicably, won the Grand Jury prize at Cannes in 1997) features Sergei Lopez as a depressed, lovesick Spanish shoe salesman who buddies up with a girl-hungry Russian immigrant (Sacha Bourdo), the very guy who ruined his life by stealing his car. Their encounters with women are not to be believed—even as blatant male fantasy.

Also reviewed in:
NEW YORK TIMES, 7/24/98, p. E14, Janet Maslin
VARIETY, 5/26-6/1/97, p. 65, Lisa Nesselson

WHAT DREAMS MAY COME

A PolyGram Filmed Entertainment release of an Interscope Communications production in association with Metafilmics. *Executive Producer:* Erica Huggins, Ron Bass, Ted Field, and Scott Kroopf. *Producer:* Stephen Simon and Barnet Bain. *Director:* Vincent Ward. *Screenplay:* Ron Bass. *Based on the novel by:* Richard Matheson. *Director of Photography:* Eduardo Serra. *Editor:* David Brenner and Maysie Hoy. *Music:* Michael Kamen. *Music Editor:* Bill Abbott, Brent Brooks, and Daryl Kell. *Choreographer* Lisa Giobbi. *Sound:* Nelson Stoll and (music) Steve McLaughlin. *Sound Editor:* David Kneupper and Peter Michael Sullivan. *Casting:* Heidi Levitt. *Production Designer:* Eugenio Zanetti. *Art Director:* Jim Dultz. *Set Designer:* Erin Kemp, Dawn Swiderski, Aric Lasher, Jake Strelow, and Alicia Maccarone. *Set Decorator:* Cindy Carr. *Set Dresser:* Emilio Aramendia, John W. Micheletos, Steve Gardner, and Pete Hudson. *Special Effects:* Roy Arbogast. *Visual Effects:* Joel Hynek and Nicholas Brooks. *Costumes:* Yvonne Blake. *Make-up:* Cindy Williams. *Make-up (Robin Williams):* Cheri Minns. *Make-up (Cuba Gooding, Jr.):* Stacye P. Branche. *Make-up (Annabella Sciorra):* Kate Biscoe. *Prosthetic Make-up Effects:* Todd Masters. *Stunt Coordinator:* Charles Croughwell. *Running time:* 106 minutes. *MPAA Rating:* PG-13.

CAST: Robin Williams (Chris Nielsen); Cuba Gooding, Jr. (Albert); Annabella Sciorra (Annie Nielsen); Max Von Sydow (The Tracker); Jessica Brooks Grant (Marie Nielsen); Rosalind Chao (Leona); Josh Paddock (Ian Nielsen); Lucinda Jenney (Mrs. Jacobs); Wilma Bonet (Angie); Maggie McCarthy (Stacey Jacobs); Matt Salinger (Reverend Hanley); Carin Sprague (Best Friend Cindy); June Lomena (Woman in Car Accident); Werner Herzog (Face); Clara Thomas (Emily); Benjamin Brock (Billy); Paul P. Card IV (Paramedic).

LOS ANGELES TIMES, 10/2/98, Calendar/p. 2, Kenneth Turan

Some movies are so cloying and simplistically sentimental they could rouse the Grinch in a saint. "What Dreams May Come" is a hymn to enduring romance off-putting enough that playing the old rock anthem "Love Stinks" at top volume is the only reliable antidote.

Directed by Vincent Ward, written by Ron Bass from a novel by Richard Matheson and starring Robin Williams in one of his trademark lachrymose performances, "Dreams" has the knack of bringing out the most unfortunate tendencies in its collaborators.

New Zealand director Ward, more of a name on the festival circuit than in Hollywood, has alternated between being visually adventurous ("The Navigator") and full-throttle weepy ("Map of the Human Heart").

Seconding that emotion is prolific screenwriter Bass, whose credits range from "Rain Man" and "The Joy Luck Club" to "When a Man Loves a Woman" and "How Stella Got Her Groove Back" and who seems to have never met a tear he didn't like.

As for Williams, his Oscar for "Good Will Hunting" and his three other nominations and assorted honors notwithstanding, the awkward truth remains that he is a brilliant comedian who is no more than a passable actor and whose determination to indulge a personal sweet tooth for schmaltz represents one of the most visible wastes of genius around.

Putting these three people together was a dangerous act, fated to start a chain reaction of hokum powerful enough to flatten everything in its path. Though "Dreams" has the benefit of the extremely inventive use of computer-generated effects, it pushes its love-conquers-all theme so hard that an alternate title could well have been "Men Who Love Too Much and the Women Who Love Them."

Chris Nielsen (Williams) and Annie (Annabella Sciorra) meet Hollywood-style when their boats gently collide on one of Europe's most picturesque lakes. One look apiece and both know they've found their soul mate, and before the credits have finished they're a blissfully married two-career couple (he's a caring physician, she's a talented artist) with a pair of swell children.

But joyous as they are at the outset, that's how miserable Chris and Annie become when, out of nowhere in more ways than one, repeated tragedies hit them, culminating in the death of Chris when he tries to be a good Samaritan at an accident scene.

This sounds awfully sad, but frankly it plays more bothersome than moving. Despite all their hugs, kisses and protestations of undying love, Chris and Annie's relationship is so minimally sketched in, so simplistic in its rendering, that even the entry-level sense of reality needed for us to feel for them is lacking.

Great guy that he is, Chris goes directly to heaven, where he's met by Albert (Cuba Gooding Jr.), a kind of spirit guide who divides his time between detailing how the place works (the afterlife needs more explaining than the federal tax code) and uttering gee-whiz platitudes like "If you're aware you exist, then you do," "Thought is real, physical is the illusion" and the always popular "When you do, you will."

The basic idea here is that we create our own paradises out of what's in our heads. Ward and his effects team show us several different versions of both heaven and hell, and while some look like bad Fellini, others are truly startling visually.

The best heaven of all is the one Chris imagines out of one of his wife's canvases. The result is a vivid painterly world, where the colors are so supersaturated they literally come off in your hands. Created by POP Film and Digital Domain (with Joel Hynek and Nicholas Brooks credited as effects supervisors), it's by far the neatest trick in this production's repertory.

While Chris is getting the hang of being gone, widow Annie is miserable back on Earth. Then she is gone as well, and, like Orpheus before him, Chris, swearing to all and sundry that no couple has ever been in love like the two of them, must journey to the grungiest parts of the afterlife to attempt a reunion everyone says can't be done. "Stick around, chief," he says to doubters in one of the film's clunkiest exchanges. "You ain't seen nothing yet."

"Dreams" is derivative of more than the Orpheus legend. It steals Max Von Sydow from Ingmar Bergman's films about life and death and has bits and pieces of "Ghost" and numerous other tear-jerkers in it. Though the film wants to be on the side of the angels, so to speak, it's life-affirming in the most deadly, calculating way. Watching it is like being in a room with a couple locked in a torrid embrace. It might be fun for them, but what's in it for everyone else?

NEW STATESMAN, 1/15/99, p. 36, James Hall

A meditation on art and ethics, or Hollywood at its most sentimental?

For as long as there have been picture galleries, people have thought of them in utopian terms. William Hazlitt, after an ecstatic visit to Dulwich Picture Gallery, said that a gallery of pictures is like a palace of thought—"another universe built of air, of shadows, of colours".

Yet a need for pictures is equally an admission that the paradise which they describe is in fact lost, or elsewhere. This was brilliantly demonstrated in Andrew Marvell's wittily wistful poem, "The Gallery" (1650). Here the poet's soul has become a picture gallery filled with images of his mistress. However, the pictures in Marvell's gallery clearly attest to his mistress's elusiveness—and to the poet's impotence—for they depict her in innumerable guises, ranging from a"tender shepherdess" (his favourite) to an "inhuman murderess".

In the 19th century, a love of art was routinely understood to involve a rejection of and by the world; for the decadent Goncourt brothers, art collecting was merely "the index of how women no longer possess the male imagination". They returned from shopping expeditions for rococo objets d'art "as if from a night of sexual debauchery". The corollary to this was that human relationships were considered inimical to the production of great art. Professor Rubek, the sculptor in Ibsen's "When We Dead Awaken" (1899), is convinced that if he even so much as desires his model, his artistic vision will be lost. There seemed to be a straight choice—love art, or love life.

The ethics of art appreciation are central to "What Dreams May Come", a deeply flawed but nonetheless fascinating and visually inventive film directed by the New Zealander Vincent Ward. The central characters are a paediatrician, Chris Nielsen (Robin Williams), and his wife, Annie Collins (Annabella Sciorra), who is both a painter and curator of a modern art gallery. Their marriage, though a success on the surface, leads to disaster, with them and their two children dying violent deaths. The bulk of the film deals with their action-packed afterlives in heaven and hell, but the happy resolution of the film requires transcendence—if not outright rejection—of art and culture.

Their peaches-and-cream kiddies are the first to go, killed in a car crash. Annie usually drives them to school, but on the fateful day she has had to attend a meeting at her gallery. She blames herself and subsequently attempts suicide by slitting her wrists. However, as her pictures were already a yuppie-angst mixture of Caspar David Friedrich and Francis Bacon, we are made to believe that Annie was an accident waiting to happen. Throughout the film she is shown communicating with Chris while looking at paintings, rather than face to face. Thus art (and, of course, careerist women) gets the blame.

Chris, who had tried and failed to get his eldest son to be a mirror image of himself, is equally obsessed by painting and routinely talks of women's breasts as "Rubenesque". He is killed when he goes to help a motorist trapped in a motorway pile-up during atrocious weather. (I don't recall any art-related symptoms here—unless the pile-up was caused by an unhealthy appreciation of Warhol's car crash pictures.)

Despite his failings, Chris goes to heaven, where the special effects get big-budget and the plot becomes byzantine. Heaven, we learn, is "big enough for everyone to have their own private universe". Chris's fantasy is a gooey mixture of Monet and action painting: he slips and slides through a day-glo swamp that's made of brightly coloured oil paint. Just when we're beginning to think that Chris's heaven is more ecological disaster than ectoplasmic kindergarten, a chirpy black man ticks him off. "Fantasy's not what you need right now."

Chris soon discovers that Annie has succeeded in committing suicide and is now in hell. The rest of "What Dreams May Come" deals with his attempts to rescue her. Though the film never dispenses with art-inspired fantasy (landscapes by John Martin and Victorian fairy painting are both pastiched), hell is marked out as the realm of culture rather than nature—or, to be more precise, the realm of European culture. Chris's guide is a former shrink, played by Max von Sydow and the only figure in the film clearly labelled "Olde World": Sydow speaks with a strong accent and does a sort of reprise of his role in Bergman's "The Seventh Seal."

Von Sydow takes Chris through a cavernous neo-classical mausoleum, claustrophobically lagged with antique leather-bound books, to a collapsed gothic pile, where a zombiefied Annie is languishing. Hell seems to be for the self-absorbed, those who think and read too much. When the couple regain heaven, it has become a flower-filled hanging garden, and they gaze longingly at each other. No oil-stained canvas comes between them now. If only soggy, simpering Robin Williams didn't bear such an unnerving resemblance to George Bush...

In the end, it's probably just as well that Williams does look like Bush, because this film comes with a strong conservative agenda. It ends up asserting traditional family values. The type of woman it fears most is someone like the Britpack artist Tracey Emin, who is almost a cartoon version of the destructive creator. Emin had two abortions by her late twenties. Just after her second, when she was still an art student, she took all her paintings into the courtyard of the Royal College and smashed them up with a hammer. It took a whole day and by the time she had finished her hands were bleeding. "I downed brushes," she said. "I downed the whole notion of these ideas of creativity. After termination, I couldn't tolerate the idea of painting any more."

Of course, Emin soon went back to art-making with a vengeance. The childless peintre maudit is alive and kicking.

NEW YORK POST, 10/2/98, p. 45, Rod Dreher

Sitting through "What Dreams May Come" is like dropping acid in a Hallmark shop. It's a psychedelic knockout to look at, but everything else about this life-after-death weeper is so mind-blowingly insipid, you want to jump out a 12-story window.

Sorry, that's unfair to Hallmark, whose average "Hall of Fame" TV movie is Strindberg, Sartre and Bertolt Brecht compared to this treacle. "What Dreams May Come" adds still more credibility to the theory that when Robin Williams plays "serious," he puts us at grave risk of a close encounter with the Touching, the Inspirational, the Terminally Twee.

This time out, Williams plays a sainted dead guy who journeys forth from heaven to rescue his wife from hell. In the time it takes for the opening credits to roll, Chris Nielsen (Williams) has met his true love, Annie (Annabella Sciorra), on an Alpine lake, married her, sired two children and lived through those children's deaths in a car crash.

When he is killed a few years later, the accumulated pain of loss and guilt becomes too much for Annie to bear. She commits suicide and goes to You Know Where.

It's brave for any film to attempt to deal with questions of love, suffering, moral responsibility and the fate of the soul. But having raised these profound questions, "What Dreams May Come" has very little of interest to say about them.

In fact, director Vincent Ward's film cheapens the whole enterprise by slathering these themes with sickly sweet sentimentality. Ron Bass' screenplay uses a marshmallow mallet to pound us with a New Age metaphysic so banal and childish, it makes the Teletubbies look like the Council of Trent.

Leaving aside the mystical mush, it's hard to heap too much praise upon the techno-wizards who created the film's dazzling digital effects. Shortly after Chris dies, spirit guide Albert (Cuba Gooding Jr.) leads him to a transitional place: a 3-D version of an Impressionistic oil painting that was Chris' idea of heaven back on Earth. When he squeezes a vividly colored flower, it melts in his hand.

Yet Chris risks the good life in Monet Acres to rescue his suicidal soulmate when he learns she's going to spend eternity in less cheery environs. Accompanied by Albert and a grizzled old goat called the Tracker (Max von Sydow), Chris sails across a stormy gulf separating heaven and hell.

Conceptually, the road to hell is paved with good intentions brilliantly executed, an inventive cross between "Blade Runner" and Hieronymus Bosch. This ought to be fabulously horrifying, yet in the context of a movie that has spent an hour mercilessly gumming at your brain, it comes off as Dante for dimwits.

What a waste of a special-effects budget! These wondrous images only remind you of what a gripping and powerful meditation on the afterlife "What Dreams May Come" could have been had it not been single-mindedly devoted to soothing and uplifting us into ethereal submission.

NEWSDAY, 10/2/98, Part II/p. B7, Jack Mathews

Love conquers all gets the ultimate treatment in Vincent Ward's "What Dreams May Come," an $80-million romantic fantasy-adventure that follows a dead man's soul from heaven to hell as he searches for the ailing soul of his suicidal widow. Some husbands think they're heroes when they bring home flowers.

But not to make light of it. This movie is earnest, with a capital E-A-R-N-E-S-T. Its press notes begin with the advisory, "For those who believe in eternal love, no explanation is necessary; for those who do not, no explanation is possible," and they mean it. No romantic agnostics allowed.

Whether you're a believer or not, "What Dreams May Come" isn't willing to settle for your faith. It wants your spirit. It wants to be your guide on the other side, where you'll see an artistic soul romp in a Monet landscape, or see the souls of children fly, or meet up with old friends who've reclaimed their youth in the afterlife.

All this is shown, in sometimes gloriously inspiring images. There are also images of a dank hell, resembling the graying bowels of an abandoned ship, drained of color and hope. There are also fields of planted, wailing heads, and seas boiling with lost souls. When the mood is good, the film is gorgeous; when it's bad, it's tax day. The big problem is that the main character, Robin Williams' Chris Nielsen, suffers even through the good times, and two hours is too long for Williams to look anguished.

Chris, one might cautiously put it, is being severely tested. After falling madly in love with the artist Annie (Annabella Sciorra), whom he meets on a flashback vacation in picturesque Switzerland, and having two children with her, his mortal dream is burst. First, his children are killed in an accident, precipitating Annie's mental breakdown; then, while en route to a dinner celebrating her recovery, he's crushed in a multi-car tunnel accident.

When he awakens, he's a spirit, getting an intro to heaven from Albert, an old patient (Cuba Gooding Jr.) whose appearance is at first remarkably like the blurred characters in Annie's paintings. Soon, the picture begins to clear, and Chris finds, himself rewarded for his good life with his own private paradise, an impressionist's alpine haven where the flowers and plants squish under his feet like fresh acrylics, and where he can use his imagination to turn his surroundings into the landscapes of his wife's unfinished paintings.

Before Chris can begin to appreciate it, Albert brings word from the mainland that Annie has killed herself, and because of the act has had her soul consigned to a place in hell where pure souls like his can never go. Like hell, he says, getting himself a guide (Max von Sydow, in a frankly mystifying role) and heading south.

The beauty of the bucolic landscapes in Chris' paradise, miracles of optical manipulation, is transcendent, but ohso brief. With a script adapted by Oscar winner Ron Bass ("Rainman") from Richard Matheson's novel, Ward has condensed a man's life—and then some—into two hours of profound suffering.

Williams gives it his melancholy best, but in the end the clearest message of "What Dreams May Come" isn't about the ability of his love to go the distance, but of the audience's ability to go the distance with him.

NEWSWEEK, 10/5/98, p. 88, Jeff Giles

"What Dreams May Come" is a noble but supernaturally dull movie—a story of endless love with the emphasis on endless. Chris (Robin Williams) is a doctor, his wife, Annie (Annabella Sciorra), a painter. They are wealthy. They are rapturously in love. They have two great kids and—as is often the case in movies—a really, really cool kitchen. Early on in Vincent Ward's movie, Chris and Annie lose their children in a terrible accident. Annie blames herself and goes within inches of crazy. Chris's love redeems her, but then he dies in an accident. The good news is that everyone gets to choose his own heaven and that Chris's is one of Annie's canvases—paint oozes out of flowers and the sky is full of van Gogh swirls. The bad news is that there's an angel (Cuba Gooding Jr.) ushering him around and dishing out metaphysical crapola like, "Thought is real. Physical is the illusion. Ironic, huh?" Yeesh. Hell is worse than this?

Funny you should ask. Before long, Annie kills herself. "Dreams" mixes and matches various religious and New Age sentiments, but suicides still go to hell. The angel tells Chris he'll never see his wife again. Chris refuses to believe it. He hires a tracker (Max von Sydow) and heads south on a rescue mission. Williams gives a simpering, overly sentimental performance here—his own wife is apparently an artist, and you get the sense that this movie is a bit of a love song for him—but Sciorra seems convincingly raw and adrift in the world. Von Sydow, though his role is small, is simply a treat. He's old and surly, and you can't help but relate to him: it's like he hates the script, too.

For his part, Ward ("Map of the Human Heart") is an inventive ambitious director. The scene where Chris gets killed is both harrowing and beautiful, and Ward's vision of the afterlife is majestically rendered. (It's heartening to see that not all special-effects guys have been doting on mayhem and meteors.) But "Dreams" remains an impossibly remote, self-serious movie. The dialogue tends to be mawkish, and Chris and Annie's marriage is recounted in a jumbled and tedious series of flashbacks. And, unlike with other boring movies, you can't wish the characters would go ahead and die because they're already dead. What you can do is enjoy the handful of genuinely emotional moments and gaze at the sometimes scary, sometimes gorgeous living paintings that are constantly streaming by. The climax is Hieronymus Bosch's idea of hell. The rest of the movie may be yours.

SIGHT AND SOUND, 1/99, p. 59, Peter Matthews

Chris and Annie Nielsen first meet in Switzerland. They marry and have two children, Ian and Marie. Chris becomes a doctor, Annie a painter. Years later, Ian and Marie die in a traffic accident. Deeply depressed, Annie attempts suicide. Feeling that Chris has abandoned her to her grief, she proposes a divorce. Eventually, the pair are reconciled. Four years later, Chris is killed in another car crash.

Chris finds himself in a landscape resembling Annie's painting of their Swiss idyll. He encounters Albert, an enigmatic guide who turns out later to be his son Ian in disguise. Albert explains that each soul in the afterlife creates his or her own subjective paradise. After Chris tries fruitlessly to make contact with Annie on earth, he expresses a wish to see his children but this can happen only when he is truly ready. Soon after, it is revealed that Leona—Chris' other substitute guide—is in fact Marie. Chris' jubilation is cut short by news that Annie has killed herself. Albert informs Chris that suicides go to hell; he will never see her again. Chris determines to rescue Annie from hell, enlisting the services of the mysterious Tracker, who eventually reveals himself to be Chris' old medical mentor Albert. In hell, trapped in her vision of inferno, Annie doesn't recognise Chris. But when he chooses to stay rather than abandon her, she awakes from her stupor. The soulmates find themselves transported back to paradise, where they are reunited with Ian and Marie. Chris and Annie decide to be reincarnated so that they can fall in love again.

David Byrne once pointed out, "Heaven is a place where nothing ever happens"—so it seems a bad idea to set a movie there. *What Dreams May Come* does dip down to earth occasionally, but since the main character Chris Nielsen dies within the first ten minutes and the film's chief attraction is a digitally synthesised vision of his posthumous bliss, the chances of working up much terrestrial tension are distinctly slim. In the past, Hollywood tended to exploit the hereafter as a plot gimmick—a literal *deus ex machina* for patching up lovers' quarrels or kick-starting the phlegmatic hero (as in *It's a Wonderful Life*). While a celestial envoy might materialise to sort things, eternity itself was held to be off limits—figured by glimpses of the pearly gates with plenty of dry ice. Everyone agreed that paradise didn't pay off dramatically, being the mythical resolution of all human conflict.

But all bets are off in the new Hollywood, and amorphous plotlessness isn't quite the scandal it once would have been. Indeed, *What Dreams May Come* might testify to the widespread view that American cinema has relinquished its storytelling skills and is regressing to the more primitive function of supplying sheer spectacle since its uninvolving characters and sketchy narrative are the flimsiest pretexts on which to hang the latest in technological barbarism. There really isn't much odds between the millennial uplift of *Dreams* and the destructive orgies in *Independence Day*—both are bread-and-circus films triggering generalised emotions inseparable from detachment. Jaw-droppingly dull though this transcendental pageant is for anyone interested in suspense, it seems destined to strike a nerve at the box office. Awash with assurances of immortality, the movie hooks into the desire of audiences to bask in the glow of a pop metaphysics.

Compounded of notions from Buddhism, Christianity, Greek mythology and New Age philosophy, *What Dreams May Come* is at least an admirably ecumenical enterprise. The jumbled theology may have made better sense in Richard Matheson's original 1977 novel; but screenwriter Ron Bass' screenplay is commercially shrewder in enabling viewers to pick and mix. In the war-torn 40s the afterlife was commonly depicted as a great bureaucracy for the processing of souls. Maybe it isn't surprising that in the splintered 90s, heaven is in the eye of the beholder with Chris setting up perpetual housekeeping in one of his wife Annie's paintings. So you can take it with you after all, and there's no pesky God around to horn in on your personalised nirvana. Should you get bored with the uninterrupted serenity, the movie advances the interesting heresy that souls may choose to be reincarnated—as Chris and Annie do, just in time for one of the ickiest fade-outs in screen history.

In short, *What Dreams May Come* offers all the consoling advantages of religion and none of the contractual disadvantages. Bass incorporates the Catholic edict that suicides are damned but this rule exists only to be broken, as it motivates our hero's Orpheus-like search for his abandoned Eurydice. And in fact the eschatological order proves no match for the gumption of an enterprising American—whose trouncing of hell would appear to confirm the national belief in absolute self-determination. As he demonstrated in *The Navigator* and *Map of the Human Heart* director Vincent Ward has a strong visual imagination but scant story sense, so he seems well suited to the film's loose framework. Ward employs lap dissolves, colour coding and associative editing in a kind of continuous melting effect meant to put across the idea that physical reality is an illusion. Indeed, the densely layered hints and undertones almost suggest Hollywood has made its first Tarkovsky movie—that is, if the net result weren't quite so stupefying. Unfortunately, special effects aren't the best way to conjure an ethereal atmosphere, since they can't help conferring a certain literal-mindedness on the proceedings. As André Bazin once remarked, cinema imposes its own irresistible realism, and the Elysian fields here are a shade too solid-looking for comfort. However, the fundamentalists in the audience should approve—why leave them out of this sweepingly latitudinarian snow job?

VILLAGE VOICE, 10/6/98, p. 122, Dennis Lim

With their beckoning tunnels of light and stairways to heaven, soothing mantras of it's-not-so-bad and it's-never-too-late, New Age afterlife movies are primarily feel-good experiences, born of an understandable, even poignant need to not just demystify but rose-tint the unknown. Still, Vincent Ward's *What Dreams May Come*, a bottomless trough of mystic swill, is too confused to even fulfill the paradigm's most basic requirements. At once light-headed and lugubrious, the film's vision of the afterlife makes death even more of a frightful proposition.

What Dreams May Come opens, nauseatingly, with Chris (Robin Williams) and Annie (Annabella Sciorra) meeting on a lake in the Alps, and quickly flashes forward to tragedy, killing off the couple's two young children in a car crash. Cut to a few years hence, and Chris perishes in similar fashion. In the first sign that the film might have been conceived in the proximity of some king-size spliffs, Cuba Gooding Jr. then appears to the newly deceased Chris as a naked, out-of-focus smudge, turning pirouettes and spelling out the metaphysics of the great beyond in stubbornly unhelpful syllogisms. "If you're aware you exist, then you still do. That's why you're here."

If nothing else, afterlife movies can usually be counted on for a certain reductive clarity, reconfiguring matters of divine judgment and karmic payback in the reassuringly earthly vernacular of point systems and plea bargains. But in *What Dreams May Come*, a curiously laissez-faire philosophy applies: your heaven is what you make it (e.g., heaven is an oil painting, heaven is a purple tree, heaven is your daughter transmogrified into a Singaporean flight attendant—don't ask). This is offset by ripples of old-school damnation (suicides go to hell), though, as it turns out, Annie's version of hell (yes, she kills herself) is a dilapidated mansion containing nothing more traumatizing than cobwebs.

In the complete absence of romantic sparks, the film's love-is-stronger-than-death theme never really stands a chance. Sciorra is bland and particularly susceptible to the fits of hysterical cackling that, under Ward's direction, signify Happy Times (maybe those spliffs were on hand again) and Williams, never more dreadful than when serious, resorts to the crinkly-faced simpering that passes for restraint in his book. Ward and screenwriter Ron Bass's attempts to bridge the plot chasms mainly consist of blinding bursts of white light and flashbacks that involve the once-happy family cavorting in a garden. The over-the-top production design—phantasma-gorical without ever conveying a hint of wonder or enchantment—is as flamboyantly moronic as the film deserves.

Also reviewed in:
CHICAGO TRIBUNE, 10/2/98, Friday/p. A, Michael Wilmington
NEW REPUBLIC, 10/26/98, p. 24, Stanley Kauffmann
NEW YORK TIMES, 10/2/98, p. E10, Stephen Holden
VARIETY, 10/5-11/98, p. 67, Todd McCarthy
WASHINGTON POST, 10/2/98, p. D1, Stephen Hunter

WHATEVER

A Sony Pictures Classics release of a Circle/DuArt Films and Anyway Productions film. *Executive Producer:* Jim Pedas, Ted Pedasa, Irwin Young, Bill Durkin, and George P. Pelecanos. *Producer:* Ellin Baumel, Michelle Yahn, and Kevin Segalla. *Director:* Susan Skoog. *Screenplay:* Susan Skoog. *Director of Photography:* Michael Barrow and Michael Mayers. *Editor:* Sandi Guthrie. *Casting:* Adrienne Stern. *Production Designer:* Dina Goldman. *Running time:* 112 minutes. *MPAA Rating:* R.

CAST: Liza Well (Anna Stockard); Chad Morgan (Brenda Talbot); Kathryn Rossietter (Carol Stockard); Frederick Forrest (Mr. Chaminsky); Gary Wolf (Eddie); Dan Montano (Zak); John G. Connolly (Woods); Marc Riffon (Martin).

LOS ANGELES TIMES, 7/17/98, Calendar/p. 8, Kevin Thomas

Coming of age is too universal an experience for filmmakers ever to stop making movies about. Yet when this rite of passage occurs in a typical American high school you begin to wonder whether there's anything left to say.

The answer is yes, at least when the writer-director is as talented and keenly observant as Susan Skoog, who makes it clear that an important new filmmaker has arrived with her wonderful "Whatever," which is at once wrenching and funny.

Skoog proceeds, as all smart filmmakers do, as if her story has never been told before, and in a sense it hasn't, because her young people are so strongly individual. Indeed, her two stars, Liza Weil and Chad Morgan, make you sit up and take notice just as vividly as Skoog does. Surely, we'll be hearing and seeing a lot of these three, not to mention many others involved on both sides of the camera in the making of this impressively well-realized film.

Weil's Anna Stockard is the film's key figure. She lives in Red Bank, N.J., in a spacious old house with her pretty single mother (Kathryn Rossitter) and younger brother. The time is 1981. Anna, who has a grave beauty, radiates wit and intelligence, but she's also very bored. She feels impatient with lots of childish restrictions yet views the world with a decided wariness. She's too smart not to be scared and uncertain beneath a seemingly detached, quizzical personality.

Morgan's Brenda Talbot is a glamorous blond, her looks and sex appeal more obvious than those of Anna, but her good-time girl demeanor hides an unspeakable home life. Anna is the brighter of the two, but Brenda is more worldly, and the two 17-year-olds complement each other perfectly, making it understandable why they are best friends.

Anna is an uneven student, but she's applied for a scholarship to the Cooper Union. The bright spot in high school life is art class, where she has a splendid teacher (Frederic Forrest, in top form), who goes so far to tell her that she may be the most talented painter ever of all his pupils.

In the course of a fairly short yet crucial span of time in her final year, Anna arrives at a crossroads, requiring her to make choices that will affect the course of her life. She makes these decisions in an era that Skoog evokes with precision, not just through pop music—though there's lots of that—but with attitudes that reflect those of the very early '80s.

A series of events, embedded in everyday life, causes Anna to grow up very quickly, to discover the need for courage and determination and to understand her mother, whom she holds in scorn for considering a financially secure second marriage to an uncomely but otherwise seemingly decent man of 60.

Anna's self-discovery unfolds through a wealth of beautifully detailed incidents, alternately amusing and harrowing. Anna and Brenda take off for Manhattan, head for Bleecker Bob's landmark Greenwich Village record store, tour Cooper Union and look at a spacious loft for rent only to find it goes for $4,500 a month. They then let themselves be picked up by a couple of mid-20s men with less than thrilling results for Anna. Back home Brenda involves herself and Anna with more potentially dangerous encounters, while Anna is drawn to a young artist who has a glib line with women.

Skoog seems a natural screen storyteller, which means she's already skilled at the art that disguises itself. Everything in "Whatever" seems to unfold so effortlessly, free of false notes or anything forced. Everything seems exactly right—the dialogue, the luminous, nuanced portrayals of a large cast, the easy and lovely flow of images. "Whatever" is a pleasure regardless of what year you graduated from high school.

NEW YORK POST, 7/10/98, p. 47, Larry Worth

Coming-of-age stories are a dime a dozen. Been there, done that—ad infinitum.

Sure enough, "Whatever"—the latest take on high school is experimenting with sex, drugs and rock 'n' roll—doesn't exactly break new ground. But its blistering honesty and take-no-prisoners approach makes one sit up and take notice anyway.

To her credit, writer-director Susan Skoog refuses to sugarcoat her material. In fact, it gets downright ugly while watching the 17-year-old protagonists indulging in sex of just about every variety.

More striking still, Skoogs approach never feels exploitive. Rather, she makes her point, then quickly moves on and treats the subsequent scene with equal nonchalance. And whatever the subject matter, there's superb attention to detail.

Maybe that's why the characters sometimes seem too real for comfort. But equal credit belongs to the gifted newcomers playing them: Liza Weil and Chad Morgan.

Weil serves as the film's emotional centerpiece, the ordinary-looking Anna, whose unhappy home life and calloused exterior mask her longing to enter art school after graduation. Morgan is the more worldly and glamorous Brenda, a party girl on the fast track to self-destruction.

Together, Weil and Morgan project an utterly natural camaraderie, whether comparing notes on lovemaking techniques or, homework projects. And as the actresses subtly reveal Anna's and Brenda's vulnerabilities, their characters emerge as modern-day Holden Caulfields, sympathetic and off-putting at the same time.

Trouper Frederic Forrest also stands out as an empathetic teacher, the one ray of light in Anna's claustrophobic world. He helps ensure that the film's adults are portrayed with dignity rather than as comic foils to the young hipsters.

On the down side, Skoog's screenplay isn't always the equal of her direction. But even when veering dangerously close to cliche situations, there's always the sharp editing, intriguing photography or hard-rocking score to distract.

That's why, even with its flaws, "Whatever" proves the sharpest, most disturbing look at adolescence since "Kids."

NEWSDAY, 7/10/98, Part II/p. B7, John Anderson

In making her pilgrimage toward the kind of young, female epiphany that's resonated through films like "Ruby in Paradise" or "Gas Food Lodging," Susan Skoog has placed her debut feature, "Whatever," smack dab in the middle of the Dark Ages (aka the Reagan Wonder Years). If you wanted to make a period piece in which self-obliteration was the order of the day, you couldn't have found a more appropriate era.

But logic is elusive otherwise in this kind of Rebelle With a Cause, even if the heroine does in many ways embody her time and place. Jersey girl Anna Stockard (the intriguing Liza Weil) has tepid aspirations involving New York and a painting scholarship, but she's basically a conformist—not the iconoclastic, die-hard dreamer the impulses of genre are pushing her to be. She wants to be considered cool by the doper-drinkers who populate the marathon party that goes on when school isn't rudely interrupting. She wants to look good for a counterculture Casanova like Martin (Marc Riffon) who because he drove his van cross-country has returned as guru-without-portfolio. She can't see through a lot of the high school hype, although her attitude in both the classroom and home does, in fact, stink.

But she's too smart and self-possessed—at least as played by Weil—to be sucked into the self-destructive maw of instant gratification that has her slutty buddy Brenda (Chad Morgan) in its thrall. The hard drugs, the really bad boys (Dan Montano and John G. Connolly) and the whole drink-til-you-puke philosophy of life should be something Anna glides by like a tourist in a rickshaw. And she nearly does.

Within the Anna milieu, no family escapes dysfunction, no marriage remains intact, no children go unscarred. The domestic failures of the fractured parents in "Whatever" are blamed for the children's heedless nihilism, but it's all far too simplistic—and not funny when it tries to be. Between the recycled-sounding screeds about this one's responsibility and that one's responsibility is an unspoken indictment of diminished expectations and laissez-faire paternalism. If you're going to portray a certain era, why not examine its pathology?

"Whatever" has an eclectic sound track that usually leaves little room for emotional nuance, but Skoog tries hard to establish mood and time, carefully cataloging all the period stuff—posters, records, tchotchkes, clothes—and using the hand-held camera work of Michael Mayers and Michael Barrow to instill a sense of organic unease. But all the establishing shots and introductory dialogue only punctuate the fact there's not a lot being established, or introduced.

The point, although it isn't very pointed, is that Anna can go either way with her life—to Cooper Union, or at least toward art, through the guidance of painter-turned-hip-high-school-teacher Chaminski (Frederic Forrest, who contributes some needed energy), or to vagabond licentiousness a la Brenda, whose body has seen more, traffic than 1-95 on the Wednesday before Thanksgiving.

Which way will she go? Oh, if only there were some question. But Anna's scrapes with serious personal damage are just that; she never gets in too deep, never suffers too much. She's the one on the lost safari with the chocolate bars stashed in her underwear, And the problem is we know it.

VILLAGE VOICE, 7/14/98, p. 146, Amy Taubin

Closer to a daytime soap than a movie, Susan Skoog's *Whatever* ploddingly follows its heroine, Anna Stockard (Liza Weil), as she moves from crisis to crisis during her senior year in a suburban New Jersey high school. The film is set, for no apparent reason other than perhaps to correspond with the filmmakers personal experience, early in the Reagan '80s. It's the time of the Pretenders, Siouxsie, and midcareer Iggy, when no one yet knew that the pill alone was not enough to make sex safe.

Anna is an aspiring artist; her fantasy of going to Cooper Union is her only insulation against the indignities of adolescence. Her best friend is a victim of sexual abuse by her stepfather; she tries to obliterate her pain with alcohol and brutal, casual sex. In an attempt to protect her, Anna tags along from one drunken, stoned-out party to another. She, predictably, loses her virginity to an older guy. Not only is it painful, but when she goes back for more, she discovers he has a glamorous girlfriend waiting in the wings. Things go from bad to worse. She hits bottom in Florida tripping on angel dust. Skoog's depiction of a bad trip (lurching, ultra wide-angle slo-mos) is so lame it would have had even stingy Roger Corman demanding reshoots.

Weil is a skillful, intelligent actor (she gives Anna just the right amount of tough-girl act to shield her vulnerability), but her striking resemblance to Lili Taylor reinforces the sense that there's nothing in the film we haven't seen before.

Also reviewed in:
CHICAGO TRIBUNE, 7/17/98, Friday/p. C, Monica Eng
NEW YORK TIMES, 7/10/98, p. E14, Stephen Holden

VARIETY, 2/16-22/98, p. 60, Emanuel Levy
WASHINGTON POST, 7/31/98, p. B1, Stephen Hunter

WHEN I CLOSE MY EYES

A Fine Line Features release of a Fuji Television Network production. *Executive Producer:* Chiaki Matsushita and Shuji Abe.   *Producer:* Koichi Murakami, Hajime Shigemura, Juichi Horiguchi, Jiro Komaki, Tomoki Ikeda, and Masahiko Nagasawa.   *Director:* Shunji Iwai. *Screenplay (Japanese with English subtitles):* Shunji Iwai.   *Director of Photography:* Noboru Shinoda.   *Editor:* Shunji Iwai.   *Music:* Remedios.   *Production Designer:* Terumi Hosoishi. *Costumes:* Chikae Takahashi.   *Running time:* 116 minutes.   *MPAA Rating:* PG-13.

CAST: Miho Nakayama (Hiroko Watanabe/Itsuki Fujii);   Etsushi Toyokawa (Shigeru Akiba); Bunjaku Han (Itsuki's Mother); Katsuyuki Shinohara (Itsuki's Grandfather);   Mike Sakai (Itsuki Fujii as a Young Girl);   Takashi Kashiwabara (Male Itsuki Fujii);   Ken Mitsuishi (Abekasu); Kumi Nakamura (Ms. Hamaguchi);   Ranran Suzuki (Sanae Oikawa);   Emiko Osada (Librarian); Kaori Oguri (Girl in Akiba's Workshop);   Teppei Wataru (Yoshida);   Keiichi Suzuki (Male Itsuki's Father);   Sansei Shiomi (Kajioyaji);   Mariko Kaga (Male Itsuki's Mother).

LOS ANGELES TIMES, 7/10/98, Calendar/p. 10, Kevin Thomas

In a cemetery on a hill overlooking Kobe, Japan, family and friends have gathered to mark the second anniversary of the death of a young man, regarded by one and all as a paragon. Among the mourners is his former fiancee Hiroko (Miho Nakayama), who has not recovered from his death in a mountain-climbing accident; she still feels compelled to write to him at the address in Otaru, the small town in northern Japan in which he lived through his junior high years.

The impulse of Nakayama's grieving Hiroko is understandable, but the film it sets in motion, Shunji Iwai's "When I Close My Eyes," is relentlessly tedious and contrived. Hiroko is of course astounded to receive a reply. It seems that throughout grade school and junior high, Hiroko's dead lover shared the same name with a classmate, a girl named Itsuki Fujii (also played by Nakayama), who is the recipient of Hiroko's letter. An epistolary friendship results, triggering lengthy flashbacks to the two Itsukis' entirely unexceptional childhood.

All of this is part of Hiroko's healing process, yet we'd really like to see more of her with her new fiance Akiba (Etsushi Toyokawa), an uninhibited yet sensitive glassblower, an artist of quirky personality but a man of infinite sensitivity and patience in regard to Hiroko. As her late fiance's best friend—he was with him when he died on the mountain—Akiba realizes all too well that she needs to come to terms with her past so that she can get on with her life with him.

Coping with loss is a perennially viable and major theme, but here it's treated with unrelenting and manipulative tear-jerking in one of the Japanese cinema's least endearing traditions. The film furthermore is overlaid with an insistent hearts and flowers score that may drive you up the wall if it doesn't drive you up the aisle and out of the theater first. That "When I Close My Eyes" gets a U.S. release when almost no Japanese films, including Akira Kurosawa's most recent picture, reach our screens is all the more depressing.

NEW YORK POST, 6/12/98, p. 46, Larry Worth

Many believe that patience is a virtue. Cinematically speaking, "When I Close My Eyes" confirms that logic.

Japanese writer-director Shunji Iwai's romantic drama—concerning two women's memories of a handsome guy who haunts them both—meanders for a third of its running time. But when the plot gels, it hits an emotional bull's-eye.

That's saying a lot, particularly since the plot is pretty hard to swallow. It begins with the two-year memorial service for a young man who died while mountain climbing. Seeking catharsis, his still-grieving fiancee sends a love letter to his old address, then gets a response.

It turns out that the missive was mistakenly sent to his former classmate, a now-grown woman with the exact same name. The ladies become pen pals, exchanging recollections. One talks about the boy who stole her heart; the other addresses the man he became.

But there's one other hitch: The women could pass for twins. In fact, they're played by the same actress, the amazing Miho Nakayama.

Sound confusing? It is at first, much like the current "Sliding Doors" or Krzysztof Kieslowski's "The Double Life of Veronique." But once the setup is established, it leads from one shining moment to another, alternately funny, touching and charming.

Iwai tells his semi-surreal tale in an aptly lyrical fashion, whether spotlighting solitary figures against a snowy landscape or segueing to dreamy flashbacks of puppy love amongst the library stacks.

Ultimately, intertwined themes about coming to terms with ghosts, letting go of fantasies and digesting hidden revelations coalesce into one of the years most heart-tugging finales. And it's all the more wrenching for its subtlety.

Coming from a land where tradition still reigns, "When I Close My Eyes" is a lovely bow to the past that bodes well for Iwai's future.

VILLAGE VOICE, 6/16/98, p. 160, Dennis Lim

A ravishing Japanese heartbreaker that Fine Line bought two years ago and is finally dumping into one Manhattan theater, *When I Close My Eyes* (formerly known as *Love Letter*) packs the emotional wallop that audiences seem to be searching for now (and, judging by the success of *Titanic* and *City of Angels*, finding in the most bizarre places). Written and directed by young first-timer Shunji Iwai, the film—set in snow-covered northern Japan—is a meditation on grief, love, serendipity, and the therapeutic properties of memory. As knowingly as it evokes Proust and Kieslowski, *When I Close My Eyes* works best as an old-fashioned tearjerker. It makes perfect sense that a Meg Ryan remake is being threatened.

See this version instead. I can't think of a Hollywood director who'd have the mental constitution required to recreate the head rush of this uncynical, lovingly crafted film. On paper, the story is preposterous and beyond corny—a young woman (Miho Nakayama) writes a letter to her fiancé who died two years ago and, on impulse, sends it to an address that she finds in his high-school yearbook, inadvertently sparking a correspondence with one of his female classmates (also played by Nakayama), who happens to have the same name as her dead lover. But Iwai's sophisticated yet swooningly sentimental approach is disarming—it's testament to the movie's ample charm that, at all points, you're more than willing to make the necessary leaps of faith.

Also reviewed in:
NEW YORK TIMES, 6/12/98, p. E27, Stephen Holden
VARIETY, 9/11-17/95, p. 111, David Stratton

WHO THE HELL IS JULIETTE?

A Kino International release of a December Error production. *Producer:* Carlos Marcovich. *Director:* Carlos Marcovich. *Screenplay (Spanish with English subtitles):* Carlos Marcovich. *Story:* Carlos Marcovich. *Director of Photography:* Carlos Marcovich. *Editor:* Carlos Marcovich. *Music:* Alejandro Marcovich. *Sound:* Juan Carlos Prieto and Antonio Diego. *Running time:* 92 minutes. *MPAA Rating:* Not Rated.

WITH: Yuliet Ortega; Fabiola Quiroz; Oneida Ramirez; Jorge Quiroz; Obdulia Fuentes; Yolanda Barajas; Victor Ortega; Marco O. Mark; Jose "Don Pepe" Breuil; Michel Ortega; Guillermo; Billy Joe Landa; Kirenia Rosa; Glenda Rayna; Salma Hayek; Benny; Francesco Clemente; Manolin.

NEW YORK POST, 4/2/98, p. 53, Larry Worth

Within five minutes of its opening credits, the titular question—"Who the Hell Is Juliette?"—is superseded by another. What is "Juliette"? Be prepared: The answer isn't easy.

Director Carlos Marcovich has fashioned an oft-confusing film that mixes documentary footage with fictional storytelling, flashy music videos with long moments of silence, color with black-and-white the likes of Kurosawa's "Rashomon" with Truffaut's "Day for Night," Manhattan's excesses with Third World poverty.

The self-conscious mishmash is undeniably innovative. But innovative doesn't necessarily mean successful.

For the most part, Marcovich focuses on two young women: 16-year-old, Havana-born Juliette and a Mexican model named Fabiola. Their lives cross when Juliette gets cast in one of Fabiola's films.

Along the way, both heroines—complemented by a dozen-odd friends—talk directly to the camera about everything from love affairs to kin to making the movie. "You're just trying to get me to say something silly," says one. But that sums up too many of the comments.

The acting, or at least time spent in front of the lens by principals Yuliet Ortega and Fabiola Quiroz, makes for occasionally arresting moments. Ditto for an extended cameo by Salma ("Desperado") Hayek, playing herself.

But thanks largely to herky-jerky camerawork and MTV-like editing, nothing ever really jells. Gradually, "Who the Hell Is Juliette?" becomes a less urgent question than, "Who cares?"

NEWSDAY, 4/1/98, Part II/p. B13, John Anderson

One might well ask what the hell is "Who the Hell Is Juliette?"

A documentary with an identity crisis, the film bounds across the borders of fact and fiction with diplomatic immunity, wants to be what it isn't while reveling in what it is. It has no sense of propriety about its silly jokes, lapses of maudlin sentiment or seizures of theatrical anguish. If it were a person, it would certainly be an adolescent.

It would, obviously enough, be Juliette herself (or, rather, Yuliet Ortega), the 16-year-old, beautiful, guileful, would-be model and part-time prostitute whose mother is dead, whose father is in New Jersey, whose grandmother has raised her close to the streets of Havana—and who is both the subject and fetish of Argentine director Carlos Marcovich, who has made his first feature film an experiment in nerve as well as form.

As put by one of the various talking heads that bob in and out of Marcovich's frame, "I know Yuliet is very pretty, but you can't tell by looking at her." She's an enigma, and this makes her comfortable. What we learn, as Marcovich lifts his Cuban rhythms out of street life, erratic narrative and the pulse of endemic poverty and oppression, is that Yuliet's father fled when she was a baby; a year later her mother committed suicide. How much fault her father bears for that death is unclear, but Yuliet has made him the demon in her life, the cause of all her woes, and says she never wants to see him while really wishing she could.

Marcovich—who is, quite frankly, a bit more glib than he ought to be as he scampers about the beaches and barrios—met Yuliet while making a music video in Cuba. In the cast was a Mexican model named Fabiola Quiroz; Yuliet was cast as Quiroz' sister and the two bonded, with Fabiola getting Yuliet an introduction to an agency in Mexico. Marcovich, seeing where all this is going—and helping it get there—works the triangle among Fabiola's home (New York), the agency (Mexico City) and Havana.

A cameo sequence featuring the actress Salma Hayek and scenes from one of her Mexican movies, creates a kind of questioning framework for Yuliet's dreams of stardom.

The story—which Marcovich further engineers by arranging a reunion between Yuliet and her father—is fairly routine, overall. What's far more intriguing is how he blithely violates the pseudo-traditions of documentary making—the objective camera, the static point of view—to get what he's after. He shows us his boom operator chasing Yuliet with a microphone. He shows us Yuliet wiping sea water off the camera lens. He shows us the comical Don Pepe, crisscrossing the screen for no apparent reason besides comic relief and he shows us some new ways of looking. Of course, he also shows us Yuliet—or is it Juliette?—and manages to make us share at least some of his obsession with this enigmatic creature.

VILLAGE VOICE, 4/7/98, p. 63, J. Hoberman

Carlos Marcovich the maker of *Who the Hell Is Juliette?*, is more self-effacing than Michael Moore but also creepier. The author of *The Big One* is blatantly advertising his own stardom. The author of *Who the Hell Is Juliette?* is covertly pandering to that same desire on the part of his subjects.

More old-fashioned than *The Big One*, Marcovich's film is predicated on the assumption that anything (rather than anything the star does) is a subject for a movie. Ostensibly a portrait of two beautiful young women—one a Mexican model tagged Fabiola, the other the Havana teenager who gives her name to the movie—*Who the Hell Is Juliette?* has intimations of *The Collector*, in which a strange young man kidnaps a woman to keep in his basement as a trophy. The depressed model and hysterical gamine are the prize exhibits in Marcovich's personal (if nonpetting) zoo. Fabiola enacts tragedy, Juliette lives it. Her father split in the Mariel boat lift, her mother committed suicide, and she keeps herself in blue jeans by shacking up with Italian tourists.

A wiry, mischievous smart-mouth with a prematurely hardened face, Juliette received her first taste of stardom in one of Fabiola's music videos, shot in the local color of Cuban decrepitude. She's more bratty than likable, but she is always almost in motion. While vacant Fabiola has little to say, manic Juliette is never at a loss: "You want to know what hurts? My ovaries hurt," she taunts the filmmaker, playfully pelting the camera with stones.

Who the Hell Is Juliette? has the hyped-up global village feet of an MTV spring break. Marcovich compensates for the film's lack of content by leaping across time and space. Fabiola is interrupted by an Astor Place crazy, Marcovich cuts to Juliette handling some Havana street jive. Reaching the point of diminished returns after an hour, this initially lively mosaic doesn't go anywhere—except deeper into its own underlying tautology. Marcovich uses the movie as a means to orchestrate a family reunion and the family reunion as a way to provide a movie ending.

The filmmaker repeatedly shows his crew but, despite the teasings of both Fabiola and Juliette, never approaches his own fascination with his two stars. The real question is not "Who the Hell is Juliette?" but "Who is Carlos Marcovich to ask?"

Also reviewed in:
NEW YORK TIMES, 4/1/98, p. E7, Stephen Holden
VARIETY, 9/29-10/5/97, p. 63, Emanuel Levy

WHY DO FOOLS FALL IN LOVE

A Warner Bros. release of a Rhino Films production.   *Executive Producer:* Gregory Nava, Mark Allan, and Harold Bronson. *Producer:* Paul Hall and Stephen Nemeth. *Director:* Gregory Nava. *Screenplay:* Tina Andrews. *Director of Photography:* Ed Lachman. *Editor:* Nancy Richardson. *Music:* Stephen James Taylor. *Music Editor:* Dan DiPrima. *Choreographer:* Russell Clark. *Sound:* Veda Campbell and (music): Tim Boyle. *Sound Editor:* Christopher Flick. *Casting:* Reuben Cannon. *Production Designer:* Cary White. *Art Director:* John Chichester. *Set Designer:* Clare Scarpulla and Michael Bernard. *Set Decorator:* Jackie Carr. *Special Effects:* Larry Fioritto. *Costumes:* Elisabetta Beraldo. *Make-up:* Mark Sanchez. *Make-up (Halle Berry):* Mary Burton. *Stunt Coordinator:* William Washington. *Running time:* 112 minutes. *MPAA Rating:* R.

CAST: Halle Berry (Zola Taylor); Vivica A. Fox (Elizabeth Waters); Lela Rochon (Emira Eagle); Larenz Tate (Frankie Lymon); Paul Mazursky (Morris Levy); Little Richard (Himself); Alexis Cruz (Herman Santiago); J. August Richards (Sherman); Jon Huertas (Joe); Norris Young (Jimmy); David Barry Gray (Peter Markowitz); Lane Smith (Ezra Grahme); Clifton Powell (Lawrence Roberts); Pamela Reed (Judge Lambrey); Ben Vereen (Richard Barrett); Miguel A. Nunez, Jr. (Young Little Richard); Aries Spears (Redd Foxx); Paula Jai Parker (Paula King); Craig Kirkwood (Eddie Williams); Lucille M. Oliver (Linda); Alex Thomas, Jr. (Jimmy Mac); Mary-Pat Green, Carlease Burke, and Erik Dahlberg (Guards); Ray

Laska (Bailiff);   Renee Raudman (Waitress);   Marcello Thedford ("Coop");   Frankie Jay Allison (Undercover Cop); Raymond O'Keefe (Desk Sgt.);   Cerita Monet Bickelmann (Laura); Loretta Fox (Pam);   Yorgo Constantine (Announcer);   Shirley Caesar (Herself);   James Gleason (Stage Manager);   Brandon D. Morgan (Young Singer in Church Choir);   Charles Walker (Driver);   Kevin Fry (MP);   Ray Proscia (Security Man);   Keith Amos (Man in Hot Tub); J.W. Smith (Postman);   Shashawnee Hall (Preacher);   Shari Albert (Morris' Secretary);   John West (Singer).

LOS ANGELES TIMES, 8/28/98, Calendar/p. 8, Kenneth Turan

"Why Do Fools Fall in Love" is not quite the question asked by this up-tempo, relentlessly cartoonish biopic focusing on the tangled romantic life of an early rock star. "Why Do Fools Fall in Love With Frankie Lymon" is more like it.

As the lead vocalist for the Teenagers, Lymon (played by Larenz Tate) helped turn "Why Do Fools Fall in Love" into one of the biggest hits of 1956. He followed it with "I'm Not a Juvenile Delinquent," "I Want You to Be My Girl" and other songs characterized by his trademark piercing high voice.

Though this success was short-lived, Lymon on a personal level was apparently quite the boy who couldn't say no. When he died of a drug overdose in 1968, just past his 25th birthday, he left behind a marital history worthy of a man several times his age.

It is in fact three wives who face the camera, one after another, each claiming to be Lymon's true love and legal spouse. Here's the glamorous Zola Taylor (Halle Berry), a member of the Platters, one of early rock's supergroups. Next comes the feisty Elizabeth Waters (Vivica A. Fox), a prison-hardened former shoplifter and prostitute. Last in line is Emira Eagle (Lela Rochon), a demure, well-bred Southern educator.

This trio first meets as a group in 1985 in the offices of Morris Levy (Paul Mazursky), the shrewd operator whose company released Lymon's hits. When trading "Miss Thing"-type insults doesn't clear the air, a lawsuit to determine the identity of the true widow and heir to Lymon's royalties becomes inevitable.

Though other people testify in the trial, notably Little Richard playing himself and saying things like "I am the originator, the emancipator, the motivator," most of "Fools" is told in flashback as each woman takes the stand and relates her portion of Lymon's life.

The Taylor sections are the most fun, largely because Taylor knew Lymon when he was at his performing peak and director Gregory Nava, whose last film was "Selena," does an energetic job of re-creating the exuberant rock stage shows of the period.

By the time Waters connected with Lymon, he had become a junkie, and she ended up ruining herself trying to pay for his drugs. As a been-around woman never at a loss for an insulting put-down ("He dropped you like a whore's panties" is one example), Fox gives "Fools'" most engaging performance. Unfortunately, she's also involved in the film's least convincing area, the jarring sections that deal with the troubles brought on by Lymon's habit.

Last to the altar is Eagle, the sister of one of the singer's Army buddies. The Lymon she knew was more of a homebody than a homeboy—someone so different than the man the other two women married that, as someone sarcastically comments, it "seems like anything in a skirt was Frankie's type."

Paralleling the spectacle of these three women battling over Lymon's heritage is the way different elements of this film, directed by Nava from a script by Tina Andrews, are in conflict with one another.

Yes, the three women are gorgeous and talented, and it is fun to see them having at one another. Also a plus is the entertainment value of the film's infectious classic rock soundtrack, which (besides the Teenagers hits sung by Lymon) includes songs like "The Great Pretender," "Try a Little Tenderness" and "Heat Wave."

Hampering this on the negative side, besides the film's awkwardness with its dark moments, is an inability to provide more than the most superficial look at anything. Nava, whose credits besides "Selena" include "My Family" and "El Norte," is given to pitching things as broadly as the law allows, and what "Fools" is most reminiscent of is love story comics from the 1950s with titles like "Realistic Romances" and "Teen-Age Temptations.'

It's a mark of how shallow "Fools" is that even as gifted an actor as Tate (excellent in "Menace II Society" and "Dead Presidents") can't turn Lymon into anything more than a cipher. Half adroit flatterer, half emotional infant, the film's Lymon offers hardly a clue as to why his real-life counterpart was so irresistible to women.

And while "Fools" ends with an on-screen disclaimer that it is "a dramatization based upon certain historical events and the lives of real people," its inability to incorporate key elements of the real Lymon story hampers it dramatically.

For part of Lymon's appeal to women was how uncommonly young he was; the singer's first hit came before he was 14, younger than most romantic leads can play. Similarly, one of the unexamined factors in his turning to hard drugs was apparently the difficulties caused by his voice beginning to change.

Though Nava's soapy directing style makes "Fools" watchable enough in a campy way, the film's unsophisticated nature undermines its better qualities. Absent the kind of star performance Jennifer Lopez gave in "Selena" (and that film's cleaner, more direct story line), cornball dramaturgy can take audiences only so far and not one note further.

NEW YORK POST, 8/28/98, p. 61, Thelma Adams

Cue the egg, "This is your brain." (Crack! Sizzle.) "This is your brain on drugs." Gregory Nava ("Selena") spins the life of '50s doo-wop giant Frankie Lymon into a "This is your brain on drugs drama" when the director poses the doleful question: "Why Do Fools Fall in Love"?

The famed-musician-on-a-downward-spiral movie is not my fave. It peaked with Sidney J. Furie's "Lady Sings the Blues." Oliver Stone didn't open any new "Doors" when he dropped in on Jim Morrison. Clint Eastwood got jazzy and flipped us the "Bird."

Lymon (Larenz Tate)' made his mark—and then his track marks—in the late '50s and early '60s. The Harlem-born soprano and his backup quartet, the Teenagers, cut the 1955 hit "Fools" and found early success touring with Little Richard (who overplays himself with reckless abandon in the movie) and the Platters.

By 1958, Lymon was a baritone has-been. By 1968, the thrill was long gone. The 26-year-old overdosed on heroin in a Harlem bathroom.

Nava re-creates the early scenes with that buoyant energy that makes every character, every set, every song appear on the verge of popping like an over-full balloon. Of course, that bubble has to burst.

No sooner does Lymon confess that his daddy was a drunk who beat his mama than we see the songbird strung out in a cheap apartment with more tracks on his arm than a child's train set.

Tate, like the movie, is more expressive on the upswing; he can do a mean lip-sync, hip-shake combo. When the movie darkens, the "love jones" star flickers and disappears, unable to hold our interest.

Nava, among Hollywood's most well-intentioned directors, rediscovers most of the agony and little of the ecstasy of the. downward-spiral flick. Tina Andrews' screenwriting debut does not help Nava's unremarkable storytelling skills.

In a labored attempt to put a twist on the cliche, the filmmakers tell Lymon's story from the perspective of three women haggling over his estate in the '80s. Platters girl singer Zola (Halle Berry), streetwise Elizabeth (Vivica A. Fox) and schoolmarm Emira (Lela Rochon) each claims to be Frankie's wife and heir.

The wives club angle offers three charismatic black actresses the dubious opportunity to wear bad wigs and age 20 years—disgracefully. They alternately bitch-fight and dish over a tiny man with a legendary soprano who never thought to get divorced before he remarried.

There were good time. As Berry's Zola tells her rivals: "He could sing me right out of my panties." Now *that's* an epitaph.

NEWSDAY, 8/28/98, Part II/p. B7, Gene Seymour

You'd have to be made of dry ice to resist being galvanized by the 45-rpm single that gives this movie its title. It's been more than 40 years since the recording of "Why Do Fools Fall in Love?" made its way to the pop charts, and the song still leaps into your heart the way a puppy jumps onto your lap. It's only when you think of the kid who sings lead vocal that your exuberance is cut by melancholy.

Frankie Lymon, the 13-year-old dynamo credited with writing the song, recorded it in 1956 with other Harlem kids singing backup, all of whom were billed as "The Teenagers." Lymon ran his hot streak for a couple more years, carrying himself with a terrifying assurance that belied his youth. He seemed endowed with every grown-up attribute except maturity. Lymon's decline through the succeeding decade was steep and swift, ending with his death, at 26, from a drug overdose in February, 1968.

In a rock-and-roll history crowded with burnouts, crash victims and casualties of substance abuse, Lymon's story stands out as one of the saddest. The legal wranglings that ensued several years after his death over the royalties from Lymon's first, great hit resound like a bitter, darkly amusing coda.

Screenwriter Tina Andrews walks a perilous line trying to do justice to both the high tragedy of Lymon's rise and fall and the low comedy that ensued when three women (Halle Berry, Vivica A. Fox, Lela Rochon) appeared before a New York judge, roughly a decade ago, each claiming to be Lymon's widow and rightful heir to those aforementioned royalties.

Nevertheless, both Andrews' tangy script and Gregory Nava's humane direction make "Why Do Fools Fall in Love?" (the movie) an old-fashioned blend of farce and soap opera that looks as if it could have been made in the late 1950s, when rock-and-roll and Technicolor romance were in bright-bursting bloom.

At first, you think you've been invited to watch a cat-fight between three of Hollywood's most beautiful African-American actresses. Berry plays Zola Taylor, the poised and icily elegant member of the Platters, who got involved with Lymon while they were touring the country in mid-'50s rock-and-roll shows. Fox is Elizabeth Waters, a rough-and-tumble Philadelphia homegirl who hooked up with Lymon at the crest of his early '60s decline. Rochon is Emira Eagle, a prim, sweet schoolteacher who met Lymon when he was a soldier stationed in Georgia.

Each of their claims to Lymon's estate—is buttressed by testimony that, while conflicting in detail, nonetheless summon a remarkably similar portrait of Frankie (Larenz Tate) as a charismatic, overconfident manchild who can't control his baser instincts or accept his diminishing luster. Tate brings enough callow swagger and boyish vulnerability to his portrayal to make one understand how he could have made all three of these women believe they each belonged to him.

To some extent, Berry, Fox and Rochon are each being asked to embody a type more than a person. Yet they all manage to amplify their roles with some swagger of their own. Fox and Berry are especially fun to watch as their characters make tentative peace offerings to each other during court proceedings.

Nava, whose previous work showed an easy affinity for period atmosphere ("My Family / Mi Familia") and pop music ("Selena"), seems to be more energized than usual by the momentum of this tale. There is one electrifying stretch of moviemaking early on as the camera spins around Frankie Lymon and the Teenagers in performance before a delirious (and predominantly white) audience. You feel the force of a whole world changing before your eyes.

Not everything in the movie gets you as juiced as this sequence and, for raw thrills and pure transcendence, the original recording of "Why Do Fools..." still cuts the movie. (How could it not?) But if there's any real justice, the film should inspire its audiences to reacquaint themselves with that classic and, maybe, the other records from Lymon's brief heyday. His life may have been a hopeless mess, but his music still enchants with its own giddy energy.

VILLAGE VOICE, 9/8/98, p. 121, J. Hoberman

As medieval Christians had the lives of the saints, so we have the showbiz biopic. What was it the poet wrote? Hold infinit-E! in the palm of your hand, and A&E-ternity in an hour?

There's a lot, actually, that can be said about dead celeb of the week Frankie Lymon (1942-1968), This street-smart Harlem kid was America's first black teen idol—a precocious dynamo who, looking even younger than he was, fronted a group of neighborhood guys called the Teenagers and whose soaring boy-soprano powered one of the biggest r&b hits of 1956, the song that gives its title to the movie *Why Do Fools Fall in Love*, directed by Gregory Nava from Tina Andrews's script.

Over their 18 months of fame, Lymon and the Teenagers had four more hit singles, including the droll "I'm Not a Juvenile Delinquent." The group appeared on TV, toured the world, had their faces immortalized on bubble-gum cards, starred with DJ impresario Alan Freed in a couple of rocksploitation quickies, inspired a satellite ensemble featuring Frankie's younger brother Louie, influenced a whole generation of girl groups, and made money for everyone but themselves. Frankie went solo, managed one more hit, and got strung-out—a junkie has-been well before 20. A 1964 comeback was aborted by a drug conviction; less than four years (and several busts) later, he OD'd in the bathroom of his grandmother's West 165th Street apartment.

But this being America, the story has a capper. When Diana Ross's cover version put "Why Do Fools Fall in Love" back on the charts in 1981, three self-proclaimed Lymon widows—including the former Platters singer Zola Taylor—sued for rights to the late Teenager's nonexistent estate. Success, failure, greed, betrayal, a frantic showbiz milieu crammed with colorful hustlers: the movies haven't been offered celebrity material this rich since *Melvin and Howard.* Indeed, taking the lawsuit as her narrative basis, Andrews had the makings of a Brill Building *Great McGinty,* even a doo-wop *Citizen Kane*—if only there had been an Orson Welles or Preston Sturges to direct it.

Although *Why do Fools Fail in Love* is problematic from the moment the too-old, too-tall, terminally bland Larenz Tate is gumped into Lymon's scenes from *Rock Rock Rock,* neither Andrews nor Nava, whose previous contribution to pop star martyrology was the 1997 *Selena,* are without ideas. The issue of appropriation is scarcely hidden. At one point in the proceedings, all three lawyers gang up on the sleazy record mogul Morris Levy (Paul Mazursky), a conflation of the actual Levy and the somewhat less villainous producer George Goldner, while, in a respite from courtroom catfights, Little Richard, resplendently playing himself in an orange lamé ensemble, is called to testify on the exploitation of naive rock pioneers

There are moments when it seems as though this candy-colored potboiler might deliver a smooth, posh kick. The glamorous Zola (Halle Berry) and her rival—spunky shoplifter Elizabeth Waters (Vivica A. Fox) and prim schoolteacher Emira Eagle (Lela Rochon)—give alternately complementary and contradictory testimony on Frankie's passion. Frankie trashes apartments, pitches woo, collapses onstage, drops a dog out a window. But the courtroom structure creates a repetitive, ultimately dull chronology punctuated by grainy inserts of realness and repeated recesses called by Pamela Reed's bemused judge.

Lacking a coherent tone, *Why Do Fools Fall in Love* bops erratically from broad comedy to romantic bathos. The production design is no less uneven. A clever Harlem street set segues to a ridiculous evocation of '60s L.A. An amusing riff on the TV show *Hullabaloo* —in which, following the Kinks and surrounded by frantic fruggers, the rejuvenated Frankie brings down the house—is followed by a less intentionally recherché interlude of candlelit love. Imitating Diana Ross or rehearsing, perhaps, for her upcoming Dorothy Dandridge biopic, Berry plays young Zola as a glazed construction in crinoline and pearls while Fox has twitchy fun inhabiting a character whose entire personality shifts from scene to scene, with Rochon's Emira as their simpering foil.

"That flat-footed little weirdo played all of us," Fox declares at one point. Would that it were so. The spaniel-eyed Tate has the energy to prance and lip-synch his way through the Lymon songbook. He's light on his feet, but his dramatic scenes are even lighter than that—his Frankie is basically the baby-faced McGuffin for the movie's high-heeled histrionics. (There are times when the spirit of Little Richard infuses everything and *Why Do Fools* becomes a veritable Wigstock.) The softcore sex scenes and fierce female bonding suggest a failed lunge toward Terry McMillan country; given the frantic lindy-hopping, the movie has barely enough swing for a single Gap commercial.

As chintzy as *Why Do Fools Fall in Love* ultimately is, the filmmakers wisely allow survivor Little Richard the last word and then inadvertently reduce the preceding two hours to mere prologue by flashing documentary footage of the actual 14-year-old Lymon at the peak of his career. Saint Frankie's exuberantly telegraphed "innocence," transparently feigned and poignantly real, serves to reproach everything that has come before—the movie, the audience, show business, and 20th-century America.

Also reviewed in:
CHICAGO TRIBUNE, 8/28/98, Friday/p. A, Michael Wilmington
NEW YORK TIMES, 8/28/98, p. E10, Lawrence Van Gelder
VARIETY, 8/10-16/98, p. 42, Todd McCarthy
WASHINGTON POST, 8/28/98, p. B1, Jane Horwitz
WASHINGTON POST, 8/28/98, Weekend/p. 42, Michael O'Sullivan

WIDE AWAKE

A Miramax Films release of a Woods Entertainment production. *Executive Producer:* Bob Weinstein, Harvey Weinstein, Meryl Poster, and Randy Ostrow. *Producer:* Cary Woods and Cathy Konrad. *Director:* M. Night Shyamalan. *Screenplay:* M. Night Shyamalan. *Director of Photography:* Adam Holender. *Editor:* Andrew Mondshein. *Music:* Edmund Choi. *Music Editor:* David Carbonara. *Sound:* Brian Miksis and (music) Michael Farrow. *Sound Editor:* Ira Spiegel. *Casting:* Avy Kaufman. *Production Designer:* Michael Johnston. *Set Decorator:* Andrea Fenton. *Set Dresser:* Richard Devine, Doug Fecht, Bill Hennessey, Peggy Khoury, Jay Klein, Chuck Scott, and Gay Studebaker. *Special Effects:* Edward A. Drohan III and Norm Dodge. *Costumes:* Bridget Kelly. *Make-up:* Joseph Hurt. *Stunt Coordinator:* Bill Anagnos. *Running time:* 90 minutes. *MPAA Rating:* PG.

CAST: Joseph Cross (Joshua Beal); Timothy Reifsnyder (Dave O'Hara); Dana Delany (Mrs. Beal); Denis Leary (Mr. Beal); Robert Loggia (Grandpa Beal); Rosie O'Donnell (Sister Terry); Camryn Manheim (Sister Sophia); Vicki Giunta (Sister Beatrice); Julia Stiles (Neena Beal); Heather Casler (Hope); Dan Lauria (Father Peters); Stefan Niemczyk (Frank Benton); Michael Pacienza (Freddie Waltman); Michael Shulman (Robert Brickman); Jaret Ross Barron (Dan); Jarrett Abello (John); Joseph Melito, Jr. (Billy); Peter A. Urban, Jr. (Newman); Jahmal Curtis (Student); Michael Crag Bigwood (Little Boy); Gil Robbins (Cardinal Geary); Marc H. Glick (Father Sebastian); Robert K. O'Neill (Young Priest); Deborah Stern (Mrs. Waltman); Joey Perillo (Mr. Waltman); Jerry Walsh (Football Coach); Liam Mitchell (Gym Teacher); Charles Techman (Janitor); Antoine McLean (Wilson); Arleen Goman (Mrs. Pitman); Mets Suber (Race Starter).

LOS ANGELES TIMES, 3/20/98, Calendar/p. 10, Kevin Thomas

[The following review by Kevin Thomas appeared in a slightly different form in
NEWSDAY, 3/20/98, Part II/p. B6.]

"Wide Awake" is a wonderful family film that deals sensitively, and even with humor, with a fairly unusual situation for the screen: a 9-year-old's struggles with his faith in God.

It conveys just how devastating the death of a beloved grandparent can be on a child, and it depicts Catholic private school life in an affectionate and ultimately positive manner.

"Wide Awake" is a most encouraging second film from M. Night Shyamalan, who at the age of 21 made "Praying With Anger" (1992), a beautiful, accomplished work about a young man, played by Shyamalan, who reluctantly becomes an exchange student in India, the land of his parents' birth, and ends up discovering himself.

As both parents are hard-working physicians, it's not surprising that the key person in the life of Joshua Beal (Joseph Cross) is his widowed maternal grandfather (Robert Loggia), a rugged retiree who lives with the Beals in an impressive Colonial-style stone manor house in suburban Philadelphia. Joshua's grandpa has plenty of time for him, encouraging him in sports and, as a deeply religious man, setting an example for his grandson.

When stricken with fatal bone cancer, Grandpa places his trust in God. But once Grandpa has died, Joshua, as he commences fifth grade, begins to have serious doubts about God's existence and craves a sign that his grandfather is all right and safely ensconced in heaven.

As a writer and a director, Shyamalan does the admirable job of taking Joshua's plight seriously while showing that life goes on and that in its course there will be moments that are still funny, especially since the opposite sex is just beginning to have its impact upon Joshua.

Joshua's parents (Dana Delany, Denis Leary) are busy and seem to have decided to let Joshua work out his spiritual quest for himself. Joshua's best friend Dave (Timothy Reifsnyder) is a flat-out nonbeliever—or so Dave thinks—but Joshua is not to be so easily diverted.

School provides Joshua with more direction. The school's priest forthrightly tells Joshua that doubt goes hand in hand with faith and that believers can always expect to have their faith tested.

The person who connects the most to Joshua's spiritual quest is his religion teacher, Sister Terry, played by Rosie O'Donnell. Sister Terry, who is given to speaking of Jesus going up to bat and facing down the pitcher Judas, is also a world-class listener and, though amused, doesn't make fun of Joshua's attempts to find answers in other religions. Her quiet concern is certainly crucial in keeping Joshua from becoming overly obsessed.

Cross is a marvel, a terrific young actor who expresses beautifully Joshua's conflicting emotions, his clear intelligence and staunch character. Reifsnyder comes across with similarly strong impact. O'Donnell, like Oprah Winfrey, is able to jettison her talk-show personality and lose herself in a role. Shyamalan, who between his two features wrote a number of scripts for others to direct, was indeed fortunate to get O'Donnell to participate—and least of all for her celebrity.

Loggia, whose scenes all take place in flashback, is the kind of caring grandfather everyone would be lucky to have. Pretty much everyone else is peripheral, including Joshua's parents, even though Delany and Leary are effective.

"Wide Awake" is a good-looking picture and is set entirely in a world of privilege. But there's not a never-never land quality to the film; indeed, we're witness to a painful scene in which a student must leave because his parents can no longer afford such an expensive school. Another key moment occurs when Joshua approaches a cardinal to ask him for reassurance only to back off when he discovers inadvertently how seriously ill the man is.

"Wide Awake" is the kind of picture that's hard to bring to conclusion satisfactorily. It does in fact take a leap of faith at the finish that may strike you as a bit too literal. But it's so well set up in advance that you're likely to go along with it.

NEW YORK POST, 3/20/98, p. 50, Larry Worth

An existential children's film?

It seems like a tall order to pull off, and neophyte writer-director M. Night Shyamalan isn't quite up to the task in "Wide Awake." On the other hand, he certainly deserves credit for trying.

Rather than pursuing the typically simple-minded kids' film route, Shyamalan focuses on what a boy experiences after the death of his beloved grandfather. Specifically, the 10-year-old starts to ask about God and his part in the universe.

As the youngster begins fifth grade in a posh Catholic school, be can't stop wondering about heaven and the possibilities of an afterlife. Pretty soon, he's investigating Buddhism, Judaism and just about everything else.

That much is fine, but the questions are more interesting than the answers. Sometimes, Shyamalan opts for forced humor as an easy out. Other times—as when the boy is disturbed by a TV news account of death—the issue is dropped.

Shyamalan also calls on the usual suspects from any academic setting: the loyal best bud, class bully, annoying fat kid, first love, gym teachers who only yell and on and on. Soon, it's as formulaic as the Pythagorean theorem.

On the other hand, the cast is uniformly good. In particular, screen newcomer Joseph Cross, seen earlier this year as Andy Garcia's sickly son in "Desperate Measures," is an appealing hero, cute without mugging for the camera or being saccharine. Timothy Reifsynder follows suit as the favorite school pal.

In all-too-brief supporting roles Rosie O'Donnell is both funny and natural as a savvy, sports-loving nun while Dana Delany and Denis Leary score as refreshingly intelligent parents. Robert Loggia also soars during flashbacks as the late, lamented grandfather.

Indeed, one never doubts that cast and crew went into "Wide Awake" with anything but the best intentions. Yet, spiritual kiddie flick or not, one knows what the road to hell is paved with.

Also reviewed in:
CHICAGO TRIBUNE, 3/27/98, Friday/p. B, John Petrakis
NEW YORK TIMES, 3/20/98, p. E18, Stephen Holden
VARIETY, 3/16-22/98, p. 64, Emanuel Levy

WILD MAN BLUES

A Fine Line Features release of a Sweetland Films presentation of a Jean Doumanian production. *Executive Producer:* J.E. Beaucaire. *Producer:* Jean Doumanian. *Director:* Barbara Kopple. *Director of Photography:* Tom Hurwitz. *Editor:* Lawrence Silk. *Sound:* Peter Miller and (music) Ted Clark and Harry Higgins. *Sound Editor:* Margaret Crimmins and Paul D. Hsu. *Running time:* 104 minutes. *MPAA Rating:* PG.

CAST: Woody Allen (Himself/Clarinet);   Soon-Yi Previn (Herself);   Letty Aronson (Herself/Woody Allen's Sister);   John Doumanian (Himself/Tour Manager);   Nettie Konigsberg (Herself/Woody Allen's Mother);   Martin Konigsberg (Himself/Woody Allen's Father);   Eddy Davis (Banjo/Director of Band); Dan Barrett (Trombone); Simon Wettenthall (Trumpet);   John Gill (Drums); Cynthia Sayer (Piano);   Greg Cohen (Bass);   Richard Jones (Tour Manager/Sound Engineer).

CHRISTIAN SCIENCE MONITOR, 4/24/98, p. B3, David Sterritt

The title of the latest Woody Allen picture, "Wild Man Blues," has an amusing touch of irony.

Directed by nonfiction filmmaker Barbara Kopple, the movie chronicles Allen's experiences as he travels with his Dixieland band on a European concert tour. Since his public image is closer to a hard-working nerd than a freewheeling wild man, audiences may wonder if a new side of his personality becomes visible when he exchanges his film-world persona for his alter ego as a jazz clarinetist.

Not surprisingly, the answer turns out to be a definite no. The only wildness that surfaces during the documentary is in the New Orleans-style music that cascades from his septet during their too-brief concert scenes.

And that's one of the movie's major problems. Clearly impressed by her opportunity to document the off-screen life of this famously private celebrity—and his wife, Soon-Yi Previn, whom he married after a period of tumultuous public scandal—Kopple focuses less on his musical activities than on hiss hours away from the spotlight. We look on as he and Previn check into hotels, exercise in the pool, discuss the previous evening's performance, and so forth.

Most of this material is the opposite of exciting, and there's little chance anyone would watch it for 104 minutes if a usually elusive movie star weren't involved. Allen may have enough devoted fans to give "Wild Man Blues" a modest degree of success, but it's hard to imagine many moviegoers lining up at the box office for the privilege of watching Allen and Previn chat over breakfast—as if a camera crew weren't two feet away during this "intimate" moment—and consult with the concierge when one of their showers doesn't pump out enough hot water.

All of which raises the question of why Allen and Kopple made the picture. Allen's motivation isn't hard to figure out. His troubled family life has been the subject of highly unflattering press coverage, and his recent fiction films—the comedies "Mighty Aphrodite" and "Deconstructing Harry" in particular—seem calculated to rehabilitate his image by demonstrating his concern with personal and artistic integrity. With its lack of flamboyant content, "Wild Man Blues" does the same: it's certain nobody will leave this movie feeling they've been anywhere near a wild man.

Kopple's reasons for making the movie are harder to imagine. Her honors include richly deserved Academy Awards for "Harlan County USA," about a bitterly fought coal-ming strike, and "American Dream" about rifts in organized labor at a Midwestern meatpacking plant. Her involvement with "Wild Man Blues" may be a temporary vacation from such serious fare, or perhaps she just couldn't resist the chance to spend as much time with a controversial movie star.

In any case, she hasn't succeeded in giving her subject the urgency or intensity that surge through her best pictures. Here's hoping she returns to move involving material now that the vacation is over.

LOS ANGELES TIMES, 4/17/98, Calendar/p. 1, Kenneth Turan

A gentle but inescapable irony is involved in titling a documentary about Woody Allen "Wild Man Blues." An amiable crank who enjoys Paris because "I don't like sun," gives cleaners specific instructions "so they'll know what to violate" and in general worries about everything that's not nailed down, Allen is hardly wild in the Hell's Angels sense of the word.

But the title, taken from a New Orleans jazz composition co-authored by Louis Armstrong, indicates that this Barbara Kopple-directed film is meant to focus on Allen the musician, specifically on the hectic 18-cities-in-24-days European tour that the clarinet-playing star and half a dozen players took in the spring of 1996.

Allen, it turns out, not only practices every day, but he's been obsessed with his clarinet and with New Orleans jazz ("It's like taking a bath in honey") since he was a teenager. But while a good portion of "Wild Man Blues" shows Allen and his group playing these lively and easygoing tunes with acceptable skill, the lure of this picture is not its musical presentations.

The key attractions, not surprisingly, are personal. "Wild Man Blues" gives a more intimate glimpse of Allen than he usually allows, ranging from digs about friends' pets ("Even among dogs, that dog I especially hate") to shots of him padding around a Milan hotel suite in a bathrobe as big as the Ritz.

Though she's mentioned only in passing in the press notes, of special interest to Allen watchers are the glimpses given of the woman who's now his wife and whom Allen at one point introduces, with pointed glee, as "the notorious Soon-Yi."

Resilient, forceful and surprisingly self-possessed, Soon-Yi actually comes off quite well. Hers is the take-charge voice of reason that attempts to connect Allen with the real world, reminding him, for instance, that "a compliment is always nice to hear" and that he should converse off-stage with his entire band, not just leader and old pal Eddy Davis.

In fact, cynics have suggested that, protestations to the contrary, Allen may have in part considered this film as a form of damage control to counter the vitriolic press he's encountered for his romance with the daughter of companion Mia Farrow. In that light, the empathetic persona of documentarian Kopple (twice an Oscar winner for "American Dream" and the landmark "Harlan County USA") may have been a factor in his choice over another candidate for the job, "Crumb's" Terry Zwigoff.

Whatever the reasons, Kopple has the skill to make "Wild Man Blues" into a smart and pleasant entertainment that benefits greatly from its subject's impeccable comic timing and superb, off-handed wit. Who else would glance around an over-elaborate Vienna hotel room and crack, "Franz Joseph used to bring his dates here," or refer to a romantic Venetian gondola ride as "a great way to achieve maximum tension."

Entertaining as it is, the combination of Kopple's skill and Allen's penchant for self-revelation makes "Wild Man Blues" perhaps a trifle more honest about his vulnerability and tentativeness than he might have planned. Tom Hurwitz's sympathetic camera catches Allen looking genuinely ill at ease when a mild wave hits his Venetian water taxi, and comments like "I don't want to be where I am at any given moment" are not conspicuously happy ones.

The most talked-about segment of "Wild Man Blues" is its last 10 minutes, when the weary travelers come home to relate their tales of derring-do to a most unlikely and exasperating audience, Allen's 93-year-old mother and 96-year-old father. Though it wouldn't be fair to spoil the surprise and relate exactly what went on, it's enough to say that when Allen finally blurts out, "This is truly the lunch from hell," he definitely has his reasons.

NEW YORK, 4/27/98, p. 57, David Denby

In *Wild Man Blues*, a documentary about Woody Allen's touring with a jazz band in Europe, Woody worries constantly about his laundry. He sends it out in Milan—will the clothes come back breaded? Will something improper be done to his underwear in Madrid? Woody Allen travels from country to country, playing concerts at night while residing with Soon-Yi Previn in hotels filled with marble and burnished wood, and everything has to be just so, In each hotel, the couple takes a suite so Woody has at his disposal a separate bathroom in which to perform unknown rituals and ablutions. Crowds wait outside his window, as if he were a royal personage. It's the hard easy life. *Wild Man Blues,* directed by Barbara Kopple, who usually takes on sterner material (such as the fate of striking coal miners in *Harlan County, U.S.A.*), is a portrait of a man caught out of his milieu—out of New York, where Woody can work and rest exactly the same way every day. In Europe, on tour, he's not in control of his life.

Or so he would have us believe. My guess is that Woody Allen is partly acting the embattled neurotic in order to give Kopple a comic character to build the film around. In any case, this movie is not presented as a fiction; so we are free to peer around the facades that people present to the camera. And the first thing we notice is that Woody Allen's fear of not being in control is actually a way of exercising control over everything. Heaven forbid that he should have to do anything he doesn't want to do! He has plenty of helpers to prevent this calamity from taking place—his sister, who has been working for him on recent films, is along for the ride, and Jean Doumanian, his producer (who also produced this film), shows up now and then. One wonders: Does any artist really benefit from this kind of coddling? Never mind the European tour; I'm speaking of Woody Allen's life in New York. A comforting routine should not be treated, even in comic terms, as a holy rite—not if it produces routine work. The unpleasant genius Richard Wagner wore nothing but silk against his body, but he made superhuman demands on himself when he sat down to work. Even mad Lear was sane enough to keep the needling, truth-telling Fool close by. Of those present on tour, Soon-Yi Previn is actually the toughest on Woody Allen. She's a strong-willed young woman, but she doesn't have a lot to say—as far as we see, conversation between Woody and Soon-Yi centers on his moods, his reputation, his comforts. This amiable home movie has its depressing side.

In *Wild Man Blues,* Woody Allen doesn't make any great claims for himself or his band, but on tour he plays the clarinet with professional dedication and in some cases with great tenderness, and his fans listen with respect to the pleasant low voltage music. In all, Woody's relation to Europe is one of longing and regret. In France and Italy, he is taken very seriously as an artist, and he feels his roots as a moviemaker are there. As he explains at one point, he still makes films under the influence of the Bergman and Fellini movies that meant so much to him as a young man. Yet when he gets to London and Milan and Bologna, he doesn't attempt (as far as we can see) to talk to artists and intellectuals, or to see new European work; instead, he hides in his hotel from the fans in the street and the voracious rich people who lie in wait for him at receptions. In *Wild Man Blues,* he plays the neurotic to entertain us, but he's also genuinely cut off and self-protecting, and there isn't much sign here that he sees anything the slightest bit wrong with his situation.

NEW YORK POST, 4/17/98, p. 53, Thelma Adams

Here's the poop on Woody Allen from Barbara Kopple's documentary "Wild Man Blues":

1) The Academy Award-winning director wears boxers, not briefs.
2) Soon-Yi Previn's favorite Allen movie is "Manhattan."
3) Soon-Yi thinks his "Interiors" is "long and tedious."
4) Soon-Yi has never seen "Annie Hall,' and Woody thinks she should.
5) Allen's mother wanted him to be a pharmacist.

There's hardly enough dirt here to fill a Movieline magazine interview. Kopple, the crusading documentarian of the Oscar-winning "Harlan County, U.S.A." is figuratively, if not literally, in bed with her subject.

The film captures the 1995 European concert tour taken by Allen and his New Orleans-style jazz band. The no-name band with the famed clarinetist played at Manhattan's Michael's Pub for 25 years, then moved to the Cafe Carlyle.

While Allen clearly loves the free-spirited jazz ("like taking a bath in honey"), he has little rapport with his fellow musicians. For those expecting a warm, fuzzy Allen, forget it! He's so self-involved, he can hardly remember the names of his bandmates.

Woody watchers won't want to miss this latest chapter in Allenmania. But those expecting to glimpse the "real" Allen will be disappointed.

The senior citizen on screen is an intelligent toddler, tended to by his sister and young wife as if he were the next Dalai Lama. Every neurosis is indulged (he can't share bathrooms, abide dogs), and every kvetch exalted.

I don't envy Soon-Yi. At one point, the couple are showing off their palatial Milan hotel suite (with private pool) to a guest. When Previn wanders off, Allen notes the change in his lover's status: "This is a kid who was eating out of garbage pails on the streets of Korea!"

The real shocker is that Kopple, who fearlessly posed tough questions in"Harlan County, U.S.A." a documentary about striking Kentucky miners, could make such a slick corporate film plugging Allen.

In scene after scene, European fans rush Allen as if he were Madonna. "Wild Man Blues" becomes inseparable from p.r. spin: See, Allen postures in mock humility, they love me, they really love me. What's Kopple's excuse?

NEWSDAY, 4/17/98, Part II/p. B6, Jack Mathews

This is not a joke: Soon-Yi Previn, now Mrs. Woody Allen, says that she's never seen "Annie Hall" and that, of her husband's movies she has seen, her favorite is "Manhattan." You know, the one where Woody falls in love with a high school girl.

This is a joke: Doing a run-on commentary in his room in Milan, Italy, Allen frets over his laundry, musing that given their location it might come back "breaded."

These moments come to us by way of Barbara Kopple's "Wild Man Blues," an entertaining, authorized documentary of the seven country, 18-city European tour Allen took with his New-Orleans-style jazz band in 1995. It's only partially about the tour, however. Kopple and her crew had unusual access to the private moments between Allen and Previn, and shadowed them everywhere they went in public.

Those seemingly, unguarded moments, when Allen is whining about the discomforts of travel or being chided by Previn for maintaining too much distance from his band members, are more fascinating than the generous concert footage. Allen is a capable clarinetist, but he's no Benny Goodman, and the tour exists solely because of his celebrity appeal.

Since Allen had final approval of the film ("Crumb" director Jerry Zwigoff was reportedly hired first, then fired for demanding final cut), we can assume it's the Woody Allen—the man, his music, and his woman—that he wants us to see. And what we see, at least of him, is what we are used to getting. He has the same neurotic glibness of his characters, and the ability, to be, simultaneously pathetic and hilarious, weak and controlling, open and disdainful.

At times, as Allen faces the press, the paparazzi and his fawning fans, "Wild Man Blues" looks like a remake of "Stardust Memories." If nothing else, the embarrassing scenes of people drenching him with praise prove that those same scenes in "Stardust Memories," which offended so many of his U.S. fans, weren't pure invention.

The revelation of "Wild Man Blues" is Previn, who, despite her identification with "Manhattan," is anything but a dominated child. She comes off as the guiding force in Allen's life, drawing him out of his egocentric cocoon to acknowledge the sincerity, if not the spectacle, of his fans.

As supportive as she is of him, however, she doesn't play the fan herself. She thinks "Interiors" and "Stardust Memories" are boring and, despite Allen's assurances that she'd enjoy "Annie Hall," she hasn't seen it, and has no desire to.

Kopple's transparent documentary style, where the camera seems to be looking through the eyes of an invisible person, gives the personal scenes in "Wild Man Blues" a home movie quality. Whether we're watching Allen and Previn cut through inch-thick Spanish omelettes in their Madrid hotel room ("It looks like it's been vulcanized," Allen complains) or taking a dip in the swimming pool in their decadently posh suite at Milan's Principe de Savoia, there's a clear sense of intimacy between the couple and the audience.

It's a little harder to warm up to the concert scenes. Allen, not to be too cruel about it, strikes a homely, disconnected image on stage. He compares playing New Orleans jazz to "bathing in honey," and there's no doubt about his sincerity, nor his ability to lose himself in the music. Eyes tightly shut, cheeks puffed up, his whole body quivering spasmodically to the rhythm, he's a man possessed.

What he isn't able to do is to draw the audience into that obsession with him. Except to introduce the band and say goodnight, Allen hardly acknowledges that there's anyone else in the room. He makes fun look like work, and the film doesn't show enough of the rest of the band's musical personality to make up for his aloofness.

After one particularly good night, Allen, nudged on by Previn, tells the band how great they were, saying that the Preservation Hall Jazz Band, the very soul of New Orleans, couldn't have done better. We can pardon the hyperbole but the reference shows how lost Allen was in the illusion. The audiences came to see him, a revered filmmaker, and took the music with him. People go to the Preservation Hall to drown in jazz.

NEWSWEEK, 4/13/98, p. 73, Jack Kroll

"Wild Man Blues" may be the only documentary we're ever going to have about Woody Allen, so it's kind of a historic event. How come the famously private Allen invited someone else's camera into his life? Well, he invited it into one part of his life, the musical part. And the camera belongs to Barbara Kopple, the two-time Oscar-winning maker of documentaries like "Harlan County, U.S.A." (1977) and "American Dream" (1991), both about the sometimes violent struggles of workers in Kentucky and Minnesota. Why would the brilliant director of such powerful, socially militant films want to follow the 23-day, 18-city European tour of clarinetist Allen and his pleasant but hardly world-class New Orleans-style jazz band? Not for the music, she admits. "I wanted to do a film about who Woody really is, and what his relationship with Soon-Yi really is." Aha! Soon-Yi Previn was Allen's fiancée at the time of the tour; their relationship, born in controversy, has settled into marriage and now rumors of impending parenthood.

"I told him I needed total access, and he said no problem," says Kopple. "I had a wireless mike on him at all times, 16 or 18 hours a day. I just wanted life to unfold." The result is the only Woody Allen movie not directed by Allen, who, says Kopple, had no part in the shooting or editing process. The man who has raised the schlemiel to Olympian status falls into his accustomed role immediately, hunched miserably on his private plane with Soon-Yi; his sister, Letty Aronson; producer Jean Doumanian, and her Weimaraner. "I don't like dogs," mumbles Allen. "I'm always afraid a dog will lick me. I'd rather be bitten than licked." It's clear that Allen needs no script to play the role of superschlemiel. But how much of this is the real Woody, and how much is it the role-playing of a man who has turned himself into a virtual Woody Allen? The fun of Kopple's fascinating film is to try to spot the reality in the hilarity. In Vienna, Allen explains that he must have his own private bathroom, so he always takes an extra room or suite, just for the john. In Madrid, he makes sure he has "my multivitamins, my baby aspirin, my antibiotics." In Venice, he subjects Soon-Yi to the only unromantic gondola ride in Venetian history. Huddled morosely like a spirit traversing the river Styx on the way to Hades, he speculates that "the gondolier could cut our throats and no one would know." Soon-Yi endures this neurotic odyssey with charming patience. In fact, the thought occurs that Allen may be ratcheting up his schlemielness to help showcase her caring practicality that he so acutely needs. At one point she lectures him sternly about his habit of addressing only his longtime banjo player Eddy Davis and ignoring the other five band members. "Tell them they're good," she exhorts him. "You're in the room with them and don't speak. You look crazy."

Soon-Yi is the element that we have not seen before, the down-to-earth successor to the up-in-the-air leading ladies like Diane Keaton and Mia Farrow. In Milan their lavish hotel suite contains a good-size swimming pool. Serendipitously, this allows us to see Allen and Soon-Yi in shorts and bikini. At 60, he's in good shape; at 27, she's in better. Surveying the Milanese luxury, Allen muses that Soon-Yi was "this kid eating out of garbage pails on the streets in Korea"—which may inspire the thought that it was Mia Farrow, her adoptive mother, who rescued Soon-Yi from that fate.

Besides Soon-Yi, the other revelation is Allen's tremendous popularity in Europe. Everywhere he's besieged by smiling crowds, by *paparazzi,* by pols who bestow gifts and honors. Every concert is sold out; the crowds listen closely to the music, which ranges from retro retread to outbursts of appealing exuberance. The final sequence takes place back in New York with Allen's parents. His father is 96, his mother 93. Father, who has splendid wavy hair, thinks that Allen might have done "more business as a druggist than as an actor." Mother, boldly lipsticked and red-frizzed, says, "I personally don't think it's right to go out with an Asian girl. That's why the Jews will some day be extinct." Soon-Yi, standing right there, laughs. "This is the lunch from hell," says Allen. Kopple has taken us as close to Allen's gene pool, if not his genius, as we're ever likely to get.

SIGHT AND SOUND, 5/98, p. 60, Kevin Macdonald

A feature documentary about an 18-concert, seven-country European tour made by Woody Allen and his New Orleans-style jazz band. The film is predominantly composed of two elements: footage of the jazz band in performance, and observational footage of Allen in Paris, Madrid, Venice, Bologna, Vienna and London. Allen flies between tour dates in a private jet with his girlfriend Soon-Yi Previn and his sister, Letty Aronson. He is mobbed by fans in Venice and Bologna, travels on a gondola, visits a manufacturer of woodwind instruments, stays in many of Europe's most splendid hotels and is presented to local mayors and other dignitaries. Among the topics Allen discusses either in front of (or for) the camera are his relationship with Soon-Yi Previn and how the press have treated them; his abiding love of New Orleans jazz; and his idiosyncratic attitude towards, among other things, showers, dogs and laundry.

Finally Allen, Aronson and Previn, back in New York, pay a visit to Allen's nonagenarian parents. They discuss Woody's childhood, and the jazz lessons he took in his bedroom. The parents reveal that they wanted him to be a pharmacist and express some disappointment that his girlfriend is Asian, not a "nice Jewish girl".

Back in 1995, it was reported that Woody Allen had agreed to let a documentary be made about himself by Terry Zwigoff. This was astonishing news. *Crumb*, Zwigoff's one previous film, was the most frank and disturbing documentary portrait of recent times. It's subject, the counter-culture cartoonist Robert Crumb, was a physically unprepossessing publicity-shy loner, considered by his detractors to be a dirty-old-man, a lover of traditional jazz and blues, a neurotic whose transparently autobiographical creative outpourings acted as catharsis—sound familiar? Zwigoff's coup—and for a documentary-maker, this can be described as nothing less than a coup—lay in gaining access to Crumb's extraordinarily dysfunctional family (an "Addams family without the aristocratic saving graces", as one review described them), whose behaviour revealed exactly why Crumb turned out the way he did.

One can only wonder why Allen would even consider opening himself up for a messy, humiliating public dissection like *Crumb*. Could it have been a bizarre *cinéma vérité* attempt at psychotherapy through the camera? Or perhaps was it an effort to gain the affection of the US public at a time when it was extraordinarily antagonistic towards him, after he left his then-partner Mia Farrow for her adopted daughter Soon-Yi Previn? The truth will never be known, because soon after those initial trade-press reports Zwigoff was off the project.

In place of that unrealised project we have *Wild Man Blues*, part concert film, part holiday video-diary, directed by Barbara Kopple. Primarily known as a political film-maker—her two epics about the Union movement, *American Dream* and *Harlan County USA*, both won Oscars—Kopple appears to have struggled to find a focus here. Shot in a traditional observational style, it lacks any discernible narrative or point of view and about half way through one begins to think, "so what?'

Not that *Wild Man Blues* doesn't have its pleasures. Fans of New Orleans-style jazz will presumably enjoy the extended concert footage although, as with the original concerts, one suspects that most people will see the film because of Allen not his music. There are also many delightful moments for the unreconstructed Woody-phile to savour: the expression of sheer terror on Allen's face when a small wave rocks his boat on the Venetian lagoon; his line on dogs—"I'd rather be bitten than licked"; and his habit of introducing his girlfriend as "the notorious Soon-Yi Previn".

On the level of gossip, it is fascinating, if not a little queasy, to watch Previn and Allen interact, to see him play the geeky little intellectual boy, reliant on her bossy, mothering practicality. Best of all is the final scene, in which Allen, his sister and Previn return to Manhattan and visit Allen's nonagenarian parents. Apparently unimpressed by his son's success, Allen's father refuses to discuss any topic but the quality of the engraving on the awards Allen was presented with during his trip. Meanwhile, Allen's mother tells us how Woody would never persist with any of his studies when he was a child, and should have become a pharmacist. Suddenly, *Wild Man Blues* feels like a real Woody Allen film.

And that's just the problem. Kopple never manages to find an answer to the question "how do you make a film with Woody Allen in it that isn't a Woody Allen film?" The Woody Allen of *Wild Man Blues* is the same angst-ridden, neurotic, sexually insecure—and very funny—Allen recognisable from *Manhattan, Husbands and Wives* or *Deconstructing Harry.* One begins to wonder how many of the apparently candid moments in the documentary are actually performances, Allen once again donning his celluloid persona. Or is it just that Woody Allen has made himself impervious to the prying lens of other people's cameras because he has revealed so much of himself in his own work? It's a question which Terry Zwigoff might have been able to answer but which Barbara Kopple certainly can't.

VILLAGE VOICE, 4/21/98, p. 67, Amy Taubin

The first film Woody Allen directed was *Take the Money and Run.* Let's hope Barbara Kopple, the director of *Wild Man Blues,* a portrait of Allen touring Europe with his New Orleans jazz band, did exactly that. The best thing that can be said about celebrity documentaries is that they pay the rent and buy time for talented film journalists like Kopple to work on less commercial projects (which, these days, means anything other than celebrity documentaries).

As for anyone interested in Woody Allen's musicianship, you'd be better off going to the Café Carlyle, where Allen's been playing weekly gigs since Michael's Pub closed in 1996. Or if you want the skinny on the relationship between Allen and Soon-Yi Previn (and isn't that why we all want to see the movie?), you learn almost as much from seeing the not-so-odd couple on TV for five seconds sitting courtside at a Knicks game. Or if the Allen persona is your fascination, you'll find as much of it on display in his own films. Once a camera is running (it doesn't matter to whom it belongs), Woody Allen plays Woody Allen. It's more than second nature to him. It's the only thing he can do.

For background about the creation of *Wild Man Blues,* I offer the press kit, where it is writ that Allen's current producers, Jean Doumanian and his sister Letty Aronson, thought it would be nice to have a film of Allen, the jazz clarinetist, playing one night stands in 18 European cities. It is also writ that Kopple's terms for signing on as a director was that she would have total access. Kopple says that she and her crew worked 16 to 18 hours a day, filming Allen at work and in his downtime.

What the press kit fails to report are the conditions governing the editing of this accumulated footage. Who had final say about what would appear on the screen and what would go into the trash? Because however expert Allen and Previn are at keeping their own counsel in public, Kopple must have recorded at least a moment or two of behavior less studied than what passes for revelation in *Wild Man Blues.* True, Allen looks physically worn. True, Previn puts him down the way a teenager does her dad. "I've never read anything he's written," she says with a shrug. She says she hasn't seen *Annie Hall* either. Allen also lets slip one or two of his quirkier personal habits (like always renting the room next to his posh suite so he can have a private bathroom). But that's the kind of neurotic nerd stuff that's always played well for Allen.

See Woody acting seasick in a Venetian gondola and Soon-Yi patting his knee. See Woody looking at Rome from his balcony and musing about Fellini. See Woody and Soon-Yi, wrapped in thick five-star-hotel bathrobes eating breakfast tête-a-tête. This is the scene where Soon-Yi trades omelettes with Woody when she finds hers inedible. Some people might say this proves she's a dominatrix. She well may be (although she seems more like an au pair who's bored with her job), but maybe, after seven years of being with the guy, she knows it doesn't matter because he doesn't eat much in the morning anyway.

See Woody bemused by the throngs that gather outside his hotel and pack the auditoriums to hear him play. Allen's films, even the turgid ones like *Interiors,* are big draws in Europe. "I've waited my whole life to see him" gushes one Italian matron. When a beefy British lad is asked what he likes best about the star-autuer-musician, he replies, "his Jewishness."

Devoted to the clarinet since childhood, Allen plays with discipline, enthusiasm, and concentration. He's not a great musician but he is a good performer. Onstage, he's dedicated to working as one with the six other guys in the band. Offstage is another story. One of the things the film never shows is where the sidemen lay their heads when Allen, Previn, and the producers bed down at the Carleton and other similarly palatial addresses. Rising from his table at some postperformance banquet, Allen peeks through the doorway of a side room, comments to Previn that "the guys seem to be chowing down," and then runs off with her to find some cookies.

Shot with a steady handheld camera by Kopple's regular D.P. Tom Hurwitz, *Wild Man Blues* looks pretty enough. Allen's lack of appreciation for the beauty of his surroundings is the film's running gag. The editing, however, is a snooze. Out of desperation, Kopple pumps up the final scene with zip pans and reaction close-ups. Allen and Previn have just returned home; they're sitting around the table with Allen's parents, both in their nineties. "You had so many talents you could have made something of," says the mother. It's the psychoanalytic moment when we see that in marrying Previn, Allen has married his mother (they're similarly self-involved and uninterested in him as an artist) and also married the forbidden fruit. "Of course, I would have preferred for him to have married a Jewish girl," says the mother. On the word *Jewish*, her throat tightens and her voice squeaks like the high notes of a clarinet.

Kopple has made one truly great film. It's not *Harlan County* or *American Dream,* her documentaries about labor struggles. It's *Fallen Champ: the Story of Mike Tyson,* which she made for NBC (and is available on video.) Despite the obvious differences, Allen and Tyson are both paradigms of American masculinity. Outsiders who grew up poor, they rose to fame and fortune by channeling their aggression into socially approved and applauded occupations, boxing and stand-up comedy. And both fell from grace while becoming more complicated as icons because of their relationships with women. In *Fallen Champ,* Kopple shows the historic conditions and intimate circumstances that produced Tyson. It's an American tragedy that stands in relation to *Wild Man Blues* as *Oedipus Rex* does to a lesser episode of *Seinfeld.*

Also reviewed in:
NEW REPUBLIC, 5/11/98, p. 28, Stanley Kauffmann
NEW YORK TIMES, 4/17/98, p. E18, Janet Maslin
VARIETY, 9/1-7/97, p. 76, David Rooney
WASHINGTON POST, 5/8/98, p. F1, Stephen Hunter
WASHINGTON POST, 5/8/98, Weekend/p. 61, Michael O'Sullivan

WILD THINGS

A Columbia Pictures release of a Mandalay Entertainment presentation. *Executive Producer:* Kevin Bacon. *Producer:* Rodney Liber and Stevan A. Jones. *Director:* John McNaughton. *Screenplay:* Stephen Peters. *Director of Photography:* Jeffrey L. Kimball. *Editor:* Elena Maganini. *Music:* George S. Clinton. *Music Editor:* Mike Flicker and Richard Whitfield. *Sound:* Peter J. Devlin and (music) John Whynot. *Sound Editor:* John Morris. *Casting:* Linda Lowry and John Brace. *Production Designer:* Edward T. McAvoy. *Art Director:* Bill Hiney. *Set Designer:* Carlos A. Menéndez. *Set Decorator:* Bill Cimino. *Set Dresser:* Frank A. Torres, Chris Alicia, Jr., Chris Gordon, Bobby Amor, Gary Dunham, Rod England, and Mark Dane. *Special Effects:* Kevin Harris. *Costumes:* Kimberly A. Tillman. *Make-up:* Jeni Lee Dinkel. *Running time:* 113 minutes. *MPAA Rating:* R.

CAST: Kevin Bacon (Ray Duquette); Matt Dillon (Sam Lombardo); Neve Campbell (Suzie Toller); Theresa Russell (Sandra Van Ryan); Denise Richards (Kelly Van Ryan); Daphne Rubin-Vega (Gloria Perez); Robert Wagner (Tom Baxter); Bill Murray (Ken Bowden); Carrie Snodgress (Ruby); Jeff Perry (Bryce Hunter); Cory Pendergast (Jimmy Leach); Marc Macaulay (Walter); Toi Svane (Nicole); Dennis Neal (Art Maddox); Diane Adams (School Secretary); Eduardo Yañez (Frankie Condo); Jennifer Bini (Barbara Baxter); Victoria Bass

(Judge);   Ted Bartsch (Bailiff);   Leonor Anthony (Ken's Secretary);   Antoni Cornacchione (Police Chief);   Robert Deacon (Prisoner);   Tony Giaimo (Dave);   Manny Suarez (Georgie); Janet Bushor (Barmaid); Gina LaMarca (Hooker);   Nancy Duerr, Margo Peace, and Keith Wilson (Reporters).

LOS ANGELES TIMES, 3/20/98, Calendar/p. 20, Jack Mathews

[The following review by Jack Mathews appeared in a slightly different form in **NEWSDAY, 3/20/98, Part II/p. B6.]**

Two sexually precocious high school seniors are washing a Jeep in a residential driveway in suburban Florida, and indulging in a little water fight while they're at it. The water does what water does, making the girls' skimpy clothing cling to their bodies, and clinging does what clinging does—drives men crazy.

But what men? The Jeep's owner, a teacher that one of the girls has a crush on, is in the house. There's no one there to watch the show they're putting on, so who is it for? It must be... us!

Yes, the victims of John McNaughton's offbeat noir thriller "Wild Things" are the members of the audience.

That's not necessarily bad. "Wild Things" wants you to be in on its tricks, it just doesn't want you to get ahead of them. As if you could. The movie has more twists than Chubby Checker, and as soon as you think Stephen Peters' script has used up every conceivable opportunity to twist again, it twists again.

"Wild Things" begins simply enough. In some small, coastal Florida community, popular high school teacher Sam Lombardo (Matt Dillon) is accused by one of his students, one of those car washers, of rape. It doesn't seem likely to us, after watching her soak up and walk into his house. But when a classmate tells police that she, too, was raped by Sam, the community's in an uproar, led by the first girl's tawdry mother (Theresa Russell), a wealthy widow who was briefly Sam's lover.

At his trial, the second accuser, a tattooed, pierced bit of trailer trash named Suzie Toller (Neve Campbell), is tricked by Sam's ambulance chasing lawyer (a hilarious Bill Murray) into admitting that the whole thing had been dreamed up by the other accuser, Kelly Van Ryan (Denise Richard), and Sam is soon receiving an $8.5-million settlement for a libel suit brought against Kelly's mother.

Kevin Bacon's embarrassed cop Pat Duquette isn't buying any of it. He's convinced that Sam and the girls hatched the whole thing, and as he sets out to prove his theory, fear turns to murder turns to betrayal turns to doublecross and it just keeps turning.

Before "Wild Things" ends, with a series of flashbacks that explain all the motives and events that got us there, there are as many twists as characters.

Like "The Usual Suspects," "Wild Things" is clever for clever's sake. Peters and McNaughton, who's come a long way since the hyper realistic "Henry: Portrait of a Serial Killer," are content to obfuscate and mystify, for the satisfaction of fooling us. On its own terms, it works; that is, each ending is well thought-out and vaguely logical. But it doesn't add up to much.

There's been some hype over the film's R rating, as in, how'd they get away with that? There's a menage a trois scene with Dillon, Campbell and an impressively nude Denise Richards, with some passionate girl-girl kissing, and given Campbell's apple-pie image in "Scream," that may come as a shock.

But the real push against the ratings envelope comes from Bacon, who has what may be the most gratuitous male frontal nude scene in a major studio movie, proving that when you're the executive producer, size does matter.

NEW YORK, 4/6/98, p. 236, David Denby

Wild Things, which is about sex and murder in the Everglades, sounded like great fun. A couple of weeks ago, there was even a screening-room buzz that it might be a trash classic. The movie, I had heard, was so happily florid (writhing alligators, steamy couplings, mean swampy stuff), that it rode right over the top of taste and good sense and landed in the blessed arms of Camp. So I was told. But then I saw it, and... no such luck. It is my dreary duty to report that *Wild*

Things, which was written by Stephen Peters and directed by John McNaughton, lacks fantasy and flamboyance, that it lacks, precisely, wild things, and that most of it is just flat. Matt Dillon plays a guidance counselor at what appears to be a very backward high school at the edge of the swamp. The boys are louts, and literally every girl in the school makes eyes at Mr. Dillon. One of them (Denise Richards, of the big pouty lips) accuses him of rape. Is he a louse who sleeps with students? An honorable guy framed by an imaginative teen? Or is there some larger game at stake? What about that $8 million inheritance that everyone is talking about? And the druggy girl with short dark hair (Neve Campbell), a dropout who sits in a bungalow reading Céline—obviously she's up to no good.

The film is up to no good, either. I noticed the same thing in *Wild Things* that I noticed in *The Real Blonde:* Everyone in the movie, no matter what he or she is reading, appears to be as stupid as hell. Is there some weird new disease going around? It's as if filmmakers were afraid the audience might be outclassed by a few lines of snappy dialogue. Years ago, critics used to put down crudely written movies by saying that they resembled the network sitcoms. Now one has to say that they resemble the afternoon talk shows, the never-never land of twin lesbian rapists and incestuous Dalmatians. Angry moviegoers could throw Florida oranges at the screen, I suppose, but somehow I doubt that anyone will get upset. Audiences can't be insulted anymore, though they can easily be bored. The movie's most prominent feature is a series of sudden plot twists and reversals. The press has been sternly advised not to give any of these developments away, and I shall obey, though I can't help pointing out that the twists are so abrupt and mechanical, and so little related to character, that they may very well have been devised by a dirty-minded 10-year-old diddling an interactive video game before nodding off to sleep.

NEW YORK POST, 3/20/98, p. 51, Thelma Adams

This is the '90s, baby.

The "Wild Things" at South Florida's Blue Bay High don't get lectures in sex ed. They get lectured on sex crimes.

Detective Ray Duquette (a reptilian Kevin Bacon) quizzes a crowded school auditorium: "What is a sex crime?" The senior loudmouth answers: "Not getting any."

If not getting any is a crime in director John McNaughton's Everglades hotbed, then the jails are empty.

In fictional Blue Bay, the high school resembles a country club, but the tensions between rich and poor cut through the halls—and the community at large—like a raw gator bite. Facing off across the divide are the school's Betty and Veronica: pouty princess Kelly Van Ryan (Denise Richards) and sulky "swamp trash" Suzie Toller (Neve Campbell).

The cheerleader and the stoner are no scholars, but they're advanced students in sexual gymnastics. Campbell is a "Scream." She abandons the sweet victim role, exchanging "Party of Five" for a *menage a trois*

And Richards, who squashed bugs without mussing her lip gloss in "Starship Troopers," plays out airbrushed Penthouse fantasies. Kelly makes even the act of a washing a car dirty.

Who really is the bad girl" Only their guidance counselor knows for sure—and Sam Lombardo (dreamboat Matt Dillon) is having too much fun to tell. That is, until Kelly cries rape and Suzie backs her up.

Facing criminal charges, Lombardo taps defense attorney Ken Bowden (the loopy Bill Murray). He appears to ignore the obvious: Never hire a shyster who has an office in a minimall, drives a yellow Gremlin and wears a whiplash brace more often than a necktie.

But in the glossy, over-the-top tropics of McNaughton's thriller, logic takes a holiday and double-cross doesn't even begin to describe the plot. Muddying the waters are Kelly's and Suzie's moms (scene-stealer's Theresa Russell and Carrie Snodgress) and a blue-blood attorney played by Robert Wagner.

Critical fave McNaughton ("Henry: Portrait of a Serial Killer") has no trouble getting down and dirty with Stephen Peters' twisted script. It's a flamingo dive into big-money bad taste, "Dynasty" undressed. In Blue Bay, the humans are so hungry with greed and lust that the gators seem law-abiding in comparison.

To use Blue Bay High's favorite adjective; "Wild Things" is skanky—in a good way.

SIGHT AND SOUND, 7/98, p. 57, Kim Newman

Blue Bay, Florida. Highschool teacher Sam Lombardo is accused of raping his student Kelly, the daughter of the socially prominent Sandra Van Ryan. Detectives Ray Duquette and Gloria Perez investigate the allegation, which Gloria suspects is malicious. When Suzie Toller, another student, comes forward to allege Sam raped her too, the case goes to court and Sam is defended by shyster Ken Bowden.

On the stand, Suzie breaks down and admits she and Kelly cooked up the charges to humiliate Sam. He is acquitted. Bowden negotiates an $8.5 million settlement from Sandra, but Duquette tells Gloria he believes Sam, Suzie and Kelly have pulled off a scheme to swindle Sandra. The conspirators celebrate with a troilist party, but Duquette starts to persecute Kelly and Suzie. Sam has Kelly lure the unstable Suzie out to a beach where he bludgeons her with a wine bottle. Though no corpse is found, Duquette discovers some of Suzie's teeth on the beach and goes after Kelly, who is shot dead during an attempted arrest.

Discharged from the force, Duquette joins Sam in the Caribbean; he was in on the plot all along and tidied up by murdering Kelly. On a yacht, Sam tries to dispose of Duquette but kills him only with the help of Suzie, the real mastermind of the whole plot. Suzie fatally poisons Sam and sails off with the money.

The problem with the sub-genre of thrillers about scams where no one is what they seem (such as *Nightmare*, (1936); *A Big Hand for the Little Lady*, (1966); *Tenebre*, (1982); *No Way Out* (1986) is that the demands of the plot require that performances change to match the audience's understanding of the varying levels of perfidiousness. This means it's impossible to create in-depth characterisations. A rare exception is *The Last Seduction* in which Linda Fiorentino reveals from the outset just how ruthless and rapacious she is, but depends on the male characters and the audience reluctance to believe that she doesn't have a heart somewhere. In *Wild Things*, the ultimate author of the complex swindle—whose identity is divulged in the above synopsis but not in this review—is revealed only in the last scene. Thus the star performer is only allowed to show 'real' character in a series of snippets that fill in missing earlier events, including an especially remarkable instance of DIY dentistry. *Wild Things'* clever variant on the end-credit 'out-takes' montage shows not the film-makers at work but the film's fictional plotters pulling off their trick.

The construction of the puzzle also means that niggles that seem like script holes—why doesn't the rogue cop tell the all-powerful matriarch she has been conned and let her settle the scores?—later turn out to be part of the conspiracy. Though it lacks a mediating, sleuth-busybody like Miss Marple or Hercule Poirot, the world of *Wild Things* is surprisingly close to that of Agatha Christie. People are merely their motivations and criminals are willing to go to any lengths—even shooting themselves *à la Death on the Nile*—to get hold of money that could probably be secured with far less discomfort. As in Christie, there is a dissection of a class-ridden society (much is made of Sandra Van Ryan's ability to get Sam Lombardo barred from the yacht club), tempered by an all-encompassing cynicism. Characters from all walks of life are shown up to be equally venal, grasping and rotten.

Given that, by its very nature, the film is forced to be shallow, the fun has to be in the sparkle and John McNaughton, enjoying himself after a run of grim and gritty psychodramas *(Henry Portrait of a Serial Killer, Normal Life)*, sets out to deliver the most attractive and seductive mystery possible. McNaughton realises the lifestyles of the poor and sleazy (represented here by Neve Campbell's Celine-reading tattooed swamp rat, and storefront shyster Bill Murray) are as picturesque and fascinating as those of the rich and worthless (Theresa Russell in a bikini pawing tanned young men). This is a sun-drenched film, with holiday-advert backdrops, a collection of oiled and glamorous people and a peppy soundtrack that evokes the 80s heyday of *Miami Vice*, though the title also prompts a few shots of lurking alligators to suggest how dangerous the waters are.

With a few more sex scenes, this script could easily have passed muster as a top-shelf video 'erotic thriller'. There is a certain generic glee to the lengthy motelroom clinch between Matt Dillon (an amiable dullard segueing slowly into murderous half-smartness) and high-school cuties Denise Richards *(Starship Troopers)* and Neve Campbell *(Scream)*. Taking every opportunity to get the voluptuous Richards into wet swimwear and indulging in some blatant lesbian titillation as she and Campbell pet in the pool, the film could be accused of sexist leering were it not for the equally gratuitous exposure of its attractive male cast. This culminates with an entirely gratuitous Kevin Bacon shower-scene, guaranteed to appeal to freeze frame penis-spotters. But the sex here is all tease, as it is in a plot which turns out to be more concerned with cash than carnality and which allows only the conspirator with the least emotional involvement and the most manipulative sexuality to survive and sail off into the azure Caribbean.

VILLAGE VOICE, 3/24/98, p. 70, Amy Taubin

Exuberantly trashy, John McNaughton's *Wild Things* is a lot of fun until it goes overboard and drowns in its own plot reversals. McNaughton—who is probably as much of a formalist as Kiarostami, but to mucho different ends—references every '50s camp classic from *Picnic* to *Vertigo* to *Beach Blanket Bingo*. The movie is as filled with in-jokes as it is with t&a. The South Florida locations are the biggest hoot: a mansion whose facade is too wide to fit the Cinemascope screen, the courtroom where Manuel Noriega was tried, an iridescent-green swamp that's home to some serious alligators.

Wild Things starts off as a send-up of lurid and steamy, then for a brief moment seems to take lurid and steamy a little bit seriously, and after that gets its kicks by proving just how easily the audience can be had. Matt Dillon plays a high school guidance counselor to die for who's accused of rape by both the richest girl in school (Denise Richards) and the poorest (Neve Campbell). The rich girl has a very bad lip job; the, poor girl likes to hang out in her shack smoking dope and reading Celine. Among the other twisted participants are Kevin Bacon as an enigmatic sex-crimes detective, Theresa Russell as the rich girl's sexually competitive mom, and Bill Murray as an ambulance-chasing lawyer with a nose for funny money. Aside from Campbell, who manages to be both parodic and emotionally intense (and a lot more interesting than she was in *Scream*), the actors are as wooden or hammy as McNaughton needed them to be.

Also reviewed in:
NATION, 4/27/98, p. 36, Stuart Klawans
NEW YORK TIMES, 3/20/98, p. E9, Janet Maslin
VARIETY, 3/23-29/98, p. 87, Leonard Klady
WASHINGTON POST, 3/20/98, Weekend/p. 47, Desson Howe

WILDE

Sony Pictures Classics release of a Dove International, Inc. presentation of a Samuelson Production in association with Dove International Inc./NDF International Ltd/Pony Canyon Inc./Pandora Film/Capitol Films and BBC Films with the participation of The Greenlight Fund. *Executive Producer:* Michiyo Yoshizaki, Michael Viner, Deborah Raffin, Alan Howden, and Alex Graham.   *Producer:* Marc Samuelson and Peter Samuelson.   *Director:* Brian Gilbert. *Screenplay:* Julian Mitchell.   *Story:* from "Oscar Wilde" by Richard Ellmann.   *Director of Photography:* Martin Fuhrer.   *Editor:* Michael Bradsell.   *Music:* Debbie Wiseman.   *Sound:* Jim Greenhorn and (music) Dick Lewzey.   *Sound Editor:* Colin Miller.   *Casting:* Sarah Bird. *Production Designer:* Maria Djurkovic.   *Art Director:* Martyn John.   *Special Effects:* Bob Hollow.   *Costumes:* Nic Ede.   *Make-up:* Pat Hay.   *Running time:* 116 minutes.   *MPAA Rating:* R.

CAST: Stephen Fry (Oscar Wilde);   Jude Law (Lord Alfred Douglas);   Vanessa Redgrave (Lady Speranza Wilde);   Jennifer Ehle (Constance Wilde);   Gemma Jones (Lady Queensberry); Judy Parfitt (Lady Mount-Temple);   Michael Sheen (Robert Ross);   Zoë Wanamaker (Ada Leverson);   Tom Wilkinson (The Marquess of Queensberry);   John Gruffudd (John Gray); Matthew Mills (Lionel Johnson);   Jason Morell (Ernest Dowson);   Peter Barkworth (Charles Gill);   Robert Lang (C.O. Humphreys);   Philip Locke (Judge); David Westhead (Edward Carson);   Jack Knight (Cyril Wilde);   Jackson Leach (Cyril Wilde, age 4);   Laurence Owen (Vyvyan Wilde);   Benedict Sandiford (Alfred Wood);   Mark Letheren (Charles Parker);   Michael

Fitzgerald (Alfred Taylor);   Orlando Bloom (Rentboy);   Bob Sessions (Mine Owner);   Adam
Garcia (Jones);   Joseph May (First Miner);   Jamie Leene (Second Friend);   James D'Arcy
(First Friend);   Orlando Wells (Undergraduate);   Robin Kermode (George Alexander);   Avril
Elgar (Lady Bracknell);   Jean Ainslie (Miss Prism);   Andrew Havill (Algernon);   Biddy Hodson
(Gwendolen);   Judi Maynard (Mrs. Allonby);   Hugh Munro (Chasuble);   Michael Simkins
(Lord Illingowrth);   James Vaughan (Hotel Manager);   Richard Cubison (Head Waiter);
Christine Moore (Nanny);   John Bleasdale (Warder);   Peter Forbes (Detective);   Peter Harding
(Doorman at Cadogan);   Edward Laurie (Cabman);   Geoffrey Leesley (Policeman);   Colin
MacLachlan and Simon Molloy (Prison Officers);   Hywel Simons (Reporter);   Albert Welling
(Arthur);   Arthur Whybrow (Doorkeeper).

LOS ANGELES TIMES, 5/1/98, Calendar/p. 10, Kevin Thomas

"Wilde" has found a perfect Oscar in the formidably talented Stephen Fry, who brings an
uncanny physical resemblance to the Victorian playwright along with a profound grasp of the
great wit's psyche.

Coupled with Julian Mitchell's superb script, drawn from Richard Ellmann's landmark
biography, and director Brian Gilbert's total commitment to it and to his sterling cast, this deeply
moving "Wilde" is likely to remain the definitive screen treatment of Oscar Wilde for years to
come. At the same time "Wilde" is a lustrous period piece with a high degree of authenticity in
decor and costume.

Fry's Wilde is a big, tall, Irishman with a daunting jaw, large, sensitive eyes and a kindly
manner. There is a certain softness within this great looming presence. This Wilde is clearly a
brilliant intellectual, a master of paradox who in his all-too-short life would turn some of the most
felicitous phrases in the English language. The great thing about this Wilde is that, as beautifully
spoken as he is, he does not drip with bon mots every time he opens his mouth. Surely, Wilde
didn't speak in epigrams all the time, any more than Dorothy Parker did.

In an inspired opening sequence, we meet Wilde on his famous 1882 American speaking tour.
He's just arrived in Leadville, Colo., where he's visiting the Matchless silver mine, (the very one,
it would seem, where another celebrated Victorian-era casualty, the once-rich and beautiful Baby
Doe Tabor, was found frozen to death in 1935). Once down inside the mine, Wilde is as clearly
captivated by the young miners' bare chests as they are about his well-spun tale about the great
Renaissance silversmith Benvenuto Cellini.

But as Wilde has yet to confront his true sexual nature, he marries and sires two sons, as is
expected of him. He loves his wife, Constance (Jennifer Ehle), but his eye keeps roving until at
last he's seduced by a young Canadian, Robbie Ross (Michael Sheen), who will be only a passing
sexual fancy but remain his staunchest friend.

In an inspired opening night of his play "Lady Windemere's Fan" Wilde is reintroduced to the
young Lord Alfred Douglas (Jude Law), whom he had met briefly the year before. He is
transfixed by this gilded but deeply troubled youth of the Gilded Age. Lord Alfred, known as
Bosie, has the misfortune to be the son of a brutal homophobic tyrant, the Marquess of
Queensbury (Tom Wilkinson, the boss of the laid-off workers in "The Full Monty").

"Wilde" is above all a love story, and a classic one at that. Here's a man, not unattractive but
a bit ungainly, who's hit the threshold of dazzling acclaim and who falls hard for a beautiful
young man who's been alternately spoiled and beaten but never loved by his parents. Of course
their physical relationship is fleeting, lasting just long enough for Bosie to become the love of
Oscar's life—even if it is ultimately to cost Wilde his life.

One of the many strengths of this film is that it gives us a full-dimensioned portrait of the
mercurial Bosie, who could be outrageously petulant, cruel and shamelessly exploitative but was
intelligent enough to appreciate Wilde's talent (and thereby envy it).

When Wilde surmises that Bosie loves him as much as he could be capable of loving anyone,
you suspect he's right. There's another love story too, between Oscar and the devoted, ultimately
understanding Constance; in the end Wilde feels great remorse for what he has put his wife and
sons through, to the extent that they must change their names and flee the country.

There is sometimes a certain naivete in genius. Taking an Olympian view of life, this Oscar
seems free from the pettiness and narrow-mindedness of lesser mortals. It's as if Wilde were
trying to tell himself that somehow his own high-mindedness would shield him from what we

would perceive as imminent and inevitable scandal, that having learned to be true to his nature would somehow save the day, even though that day was in an age remarkable for its sexual hypocrisy and moral condemnation of homosexuality.

Although Wilde's libel suit, aimed at the Marquess of Queensbury, who privately had labeled Wilde a "Somdomite sic," has always seemed an act of self-destructive folly, Wilde apparently had convinced himself that a public attack on the dreadful Queensbury would prevent him from destroying his son. As it turned out, Wilde's downfall was dizzyingly swift, and he wound up sentenced to two years of hard labor for acts of "gross indecency." His health undermined, he would be dead at only 46 in 1900.

Gilbert clearly gave Fry and Law the confidence to play roles that would require a baring of souls, and they are triumphant. Ehle's Constance comes across as a woman of noble character, initially in denial, but never a fool. Sheen's Ross has a genuine loyalty of a degree that is enviable, a quality shared by Wilde's other staunch friend, Ada Leverson (Zoe Wanamaker). Vanessa Redgrave is Wilde's feisty, steadfast mother, and along with Wilkinson, there is strong support from Gemma Jones as the unhappy Lady Queensbury and Judy Parfitt as Lady Mount-Temple, whose tart observations on the hypocritical appearance-is-everything mores of high society help define the world of Oscar Wilde.

A work of superior craftsmanship, "Wilde" moves quite briskly, and the idea of approaching an unconventional life with a traditional narrative style pays off. Unfortunately, the film is marred by Debbie Wiseman's trite, overly emotional score, which has the effect of needlessly underlining every point along the way that has otherwise been made so subtly. It is especially undermining in its morose tone in the film's final sequences, when the pace naturally slows down as Wilde's life enters its final phase.

Everyone else involved in the making of "Wilde" has done an exemplary job illuminating a man and his era. Wilde was a man undone by trying to lead a double life, but one who nonetheless found the courage to be true to himself. Wilde worried that his instantly banned plays would be forgotten, but they are constantly revived, their place in world literature secure. Nearly a century after his death, he is remembered even more than they—and as a hero.

NEWSDAY, 5/1/98, Part II/p. B7, John Anderson

With all the Wilde-ing being perpetrated on stage and page, it was inevitable that Oscar Wilde—who besides everything else happened to be a writer of some influence—would inevitably hit the big screen again. In retrospect it seems inevitable, too, that Stephen Fry would play him.: The actor is a virtual doppelganger for the most scandalous man in Anglo-Irish letters, and embodies, if nothing else, the gentleness and generosity portrayed in Richard Ellmann's magisterial biography of 1989.

Based on that book, however casually, Brian Gilbert's "Wilde"—which might have taken an exclamation point, given its preoccupation with sex—is actually a too-proper celebration of impropriety, too "Masterpiece Theater," too elegiac; Fry plays Wilde as if he knew all along that his life would end in tatters, each one sadistically shredded by that pathological pipsqueak Lord Alfred Douglas (Jude Law). Maybe Wilde did know, but among the many attributes Ellmann credited to Wilde, a death wish wasn't among them.

"Wilde" doesn't ignore its subject's work entirely—we see him taking his bows after the triumphs of "Lady Windemere's Fan" and "The Importance of Being Earnest." We see him receiving the spark of inspiration for his one novel "The Picture of Dorian Gray" in an art gallery discussion with one of his Adonysian tarts; we hear, on those infrequent occasions when Wilde is with his long-suffering wife, Constance (Jennifer Ehle) and their two young sons, recitations from Wilde's children's story, "The Selfish Giant"—which echoes throughout the film like a verdict and a judgment.

Mostly, however, "Wilde" is concerned with the writer's seduction by his loyal friend Robbie Ross (Michael Sheen), his dalliances with the London "rent boys" who would prove his undoing, and his longtime love for Douglas, who was lovely but spoiled and leads Wilde by the nose into a libel suit against his hatter-mad father, the Marquess of Queensberry (Tom Wilkinson). When the suit has to be dropped—because those rent boys will attest that the so-called libel is true—the government has no choice but to prosecute Wilde for indecency.

The comedian-writer-actor Fry ("Cold Comfort Farm," "Peter's Friends") enacts Wilde's humiliation in court and his deterioration in prison (where Wilde wrote his celebrated "Ballad of Reading Gaol") with great determination and pathos. But the emotional payoff is lacking. Wilde sued Queensberry out of love for Douglas—his "Bosie"—who wanted to use Wilde to get back at his brutal father. Bosie then abandons Wilde, of course; like the scorpion of the fable, it was his nature. The betrayal, however, lacks the drama found in Ellmann, and not just because it's underplayed in the film.

Ellmann had established a Wilde of enormous character, wit and charity, whose ultimate humiliation and degradation were a shame and a hypocrisy. Fry and Gilbert never quite get us to that point; their Wilde is, occasionally, a gasbag. And although it probably shows a deep-seated respect for the words of the writer, even Wilde's bon mots require some kind of presentation. Fry is so offhanded in his delivery that the comedy gets lost.

"Wilde" starts off promisingly enough, with a flurry of hooves, a cloud of dust and a hearty hi-yo ... Oscar. It's Leadville, Colo. 1882, Wilde is 28 and he's making a stop on his celebrated speaking tour of America, lecturing on art and aesthetics before the simple folk, the common clay of the New West—in a mineshaft, before an audience of muscled, sweaty, ill-educated laborers, the candlelight bouncing off their skin like Wilde's words bouncing off their minds. It's a terrific scene and in Fry's face we see the self-knowledge of a great writer, and everything this movie might have been.

NEW YORK POST, 5/1/98, p. 50, Thelma Adams

I'm not wild about "Wilde." Oscars fine, but I'm sure " The Picture of Dorian Gray" author would have had something awfully witty to say about his martyrdom in Brian Gilbert's ever-so-serious bio-pic.

Fruity, he'd say about Stephen Fry's lumbering performance as "The Importance of Being Earnest" playwright, elephantine, obvious, terribly tortured, asexual.

Fry's fine as Jeeves, P.G. Wodehouse's saintly butler, and he's hilarious in supporting roles, but it's hard labor playing a martyr. Ask Willem Dafoe after "The Last Temptation of Christ."

The big cheat about dramas with Wilde as their subject is that they often steal his best lines and rarely add much. It may be convenient for contemporary dramatists to portray the author as a proud victim of society's narrow-mindedness, but what a bloody bore.

Director Gilbert, who got literary with T.S. Eliot in "Tom and Viv," and screenwriter Julian Mitchell ("Another Country"), open their movie with a bogus prologue set in, of all places, a Colorado mine.

Then, amid the luscious interiors of late Victorian London, Gilbert and Mitchell proceed to sap Wilde's life of all apparent drama.

While the story tortures Wilde's pursuit of "the love that dare not speak it's name," it begins with the author's marriage to Constance, (the dewy-eyed Jennifer Ehle) and comes to a halt at her graveside years later.

In between, Wilde discovers a taste for boys (sacrificing his own two sons in the process). Like any fool in a French farce, Wilde falls for a pretty face. Therein lies his downfall.

The lust of his life, Lord Alfred Douglas (Jude Law), leads Wilde away from his family and into a damaging libel suit. If anyone could lead someone astray, it's Law ("Midnight in the Garden of Good and Evil"), the prettiest young actor since Leonardo DiCaprio.

Wilde's lawsuit backfires. Two years of hard labor for gross indecency follow. Prison sobers up Wilde—but not enough to forget his preening aristocratic popinjay, Lord Alfred.

The fact is, having seen actor Law's bottom from every conceivable angle, it's the most unforgettable aspect of "Wilde."

SIGHT AND SOUND, 10/97, p. 65, Tony Rayans

During his 1882 lecture tour of the US, Oscar Wilde visits a silver mine in Colorado and flirts with the miners. Back in London he marries Constance Lloyd; she is soon pregnant with the first of their two children. But when he is seduced by their Canadian houseguest Robbie Ross, Wilde finally admits to himself that he is primarily attracted to men and starts making excuses to his wife so that he can spend time with Ross. His conscience is assuaged by the financial success of *The Picture of Dorian Gray*.

At the triumphant first night of *Lady Windermere's Fan* Wilde is greatly smitten by Lord Alfred Douglas, known as 'Bosie', a student at Oxford. Learning that Bosie is being blackmailed by a male prostitute, Wilde volunteers his own lawyer to deal with the matter—and gets sexually involved with Bosie. Their affair quickly cools (Bosie is in constant need of new excitements) but they remain close friends and make frequent visits to Alfred Taylor's male brothel in Cleveland Street; Wilde finds himself picking up the bills not only for their meals and excursions together but also for Bosie's gambling debts and other expenses. They have many rows. Constance, meanwhile, tells Wilde's old friend Ada Leverson that she blames herself for driving her husband away by devoting herself to the children.

Bosie tries to pacify his tyrannical and curmudgeonly father the Marquess of Queensberry by introducing him to Wilde in a restaurant; the peer seems charmed, but afterwards threatens to disinherit Bosie if he ever again meets Wilde. The relationship does end after one particularly intense row, but Wilde relents when he discovers that Bosie's brother Francis has died. Queensberry repeatedly tries to catch Bosie and Wilde together, without success. After failing to disrupt the first night of *The Importance of Being Earnest* he leaves a note at Wilde's club, calling him a "posing Somdomite".

Scoffing at the misspelling, Bosie urges Wilde to sue Queensberry for libel. Ross (who has remained close to both Wilde and Constance) foresees disaster if the case comes to court, and is proved right when Queensberry's lawyer produces working-class boys from Taylor's brothel to testify against Wilde. Arrested and sentenced to two years' hard labour, Wilde overnight becomes a 'non-person" in London society. Despite the scandal Constance stands by him, visiting him in Reading Gaol and promising never to divorce him—on condition that he never sees Bosie again.

On his release, Wilde hands the manuscript of *De Profundis* to Ada. Mourning Constance, who has died, he travels to France with Ross. His resolve to cut Bosie out of his life soon cracks, and he goes to Italy to find him. Closing captions explain that Wilde left Bosie for good three months later, and died in 1900. Bosie himself died in 1945. Ross died in 1918, and his ashes were reinterred alongside Wilde's in 1950.

The underlying rationale for this bio-pic—the first since the rival Ken Hughes and Gregory Ratoff versions of 1960—comes straight from the tabloid press: *Now It Can Be Told!* "At last, at the end of the twentieth century," the press notes helpfully explain, "it is possible for a film to present a rounded picture of the Irish-born writer, of his hubris and of the consuming passion which brought him down. No longer is there any need to falsify or ignore the sexual elements which are important parts of this story." The film thus climbs into bed with recent initiatives to reclaim Oscar for Gay Awareness, both radical (Neil Bartlett's book *Who Was That Man?*, Derek Jarman's campaign for a memorial to 'Saint Oscar') and conservative (Maggi Hambling's twee sculpture of Oscar gossiping from the grave).

Wilde may well be the first film to show Oscar in bed with boys, entranced by the Cleveland Street brothel and watching Bosie fuck a 'renter' in a hotel room, but it isn't the first to tell the story of a gay intellectual brought down by a consuming passion for an exploitative slut. Fassbinder staked out this ground in disguised but extremely self-aware autobiographical terms in *The Bitter Tears of Petra von Kant*, and Gus van Sant redefined it in street-level, ethnic terms in *Mala Noche*. More recently, Ira Sachs has finessed the story's 'tragic' elements into something more ambiguous in *The Delta*. *Wilde* is nowhere near this league. It doesn't wonder why men like Oscar fall for boys like Bosie in the first place, let alone why Bosie's increasingly cruel and selfish behaviour keeps Oscar coming back for more; rather than trying to grasp the underlying dynamics of such relationships, it settles for 'heritage' soap opera with a muck-raking spin. This approach, like the visual style, is impossibly dated.

Oscar liked to insist that fictional speculations were more important than mere facts, but the film lacks the courage to ditch its feeble aspirations to historiography. Events with repercussions in Oscar's life—noisy first nights in the theatre, the death of Bosie's brother—hang in the background like a nagging conscience, coming into focus only in the arbitrary precision of dates in the opening and closing captions. As 'rounded' biography, though, the film stumbles at the first hurdle when it shies away from imagining how Oscar functioned as a husband, heterosexual partner and father during the early years of the marriage to Constance. Later, there's little about his endless scrabbling for money (the humiliation of his editorship of *The Woman's World* passes unmentioned) and nothing at all about his engrained superstitiousness or his eventual conversion to Catholicism. The one eccentricity in Julian Mitchell's screenplay is the decision to place voice-over readings from Oscar's fairytales on top of the montages which gloss the phases of the life noone can be bothered to dramatise: interludes with the family, the melodramatic horrors of Reading Gaol. The implication that Oscar lived out a fantasy that had to battle real-life ogres such as Queensberry and the Victorian prison system seems, to say the least, tendentious.

Given the overriding emphasis on bad times with Bosie (the rows are dramatised more or less verbatim from Oscar's own recriminatory accounts in *De Profundis*), it's sad that Stephen Fry and Jude Law—both manifestly capable of going deeper—are limited by the film's overall *Masterpiece Theater* approach. The dismal lack of wit behind the camera coupled with the scrupulous avoidance of anything—frontal nudity, for example—which would earn the film an 'R' rating in the US might win Wilde the wide American release the film-makers clearly crave. If so, it's ironic that the film's most upfront bid to catch the interest of the multiplex programmers is also its one and only flash of genuine inspiration. This is the title sequence, in which discreet lettering decorated with the inevitable Beardsley curlicues suddenly gives way to widescreen images of a Colorado mining camp in the early 1880s. (As in the days of Spaghetti Westerns, a Spanish landscape doubles for the Old West.) Oscar's banter with the 'angelic' silver miners—he tells them that the greatest silversmith ever was Cellini, now sadly dead; they ask who shot him—serves no dramatic purpose beyond establishing that Oscar was aware of homosexual feelings long before he married Constance, and has no follow-through in the rest of the film. But the scene is both unexpected and mildly charming, and that's something to be grateful for in a film as dull and superficial as *Wilde* turns out to be.

VILLAGE VOICE, 5/5/98, p. 124, Dennis Lim

As underplayed by Stephen Fry, Oscar Wilde is gentle and somewhat lugubrious, a relatively unflamboyant wit who likes an audience but isn't compelled to milk every epigram for maximum, preening effect. Averting the self-importance of being Oscar, Fry's interpretation (thoughtful and textured, if sometimes slightly off-key) deserves a better showcase than Brian Gilbert's *Wilde*, a plush biopic with little more than a checklist of turning points to dramatize and one-liners to squeeze in.

The film opens in 1882 with an inventively incongruous scene—mid-lecture tour, Wilde arrives at a Colorado silver mine, is lowered down a shaft, and proceeds to deliver a lecture on Cellini to the young, shirtless workers. Cutting away to London high society, Wilde settles almost immediately into a familiar, period-piece torpor.

The best thing you can say about Julian Mitchell's screenplay—which borrows dialogue, character traits, and the occasional insight from Richard Ellmann's authoritative 1987 biography—is that it's a comprehensive pastiche. Doggedly episodic, *Wilde* feels both rushed and overlong. It devotes screen time to a traditionally sidelined topic—Wilde's family life (he was married, with two children)—but has little to say about it. It strives for sexual frankness, but comes off tastefully explicit at best. Oscar's young lovers are, at least, memorably portrayed—Jude Law, all petulant pout as the dread Bosie Douglas, throws a convincing tantrum, and Michael Sheen vividly embodies an often forgotten figure, Robbie Ross, Wildes first seducer turned lifelong friend.

In his epilogue, Ellmann famously concluded that Wilde "belongs to our time more than to Victoria's." Yet the filmmakers are less interested in his continuing legacy than in a cut-and-dried condemnation of Victorian cant (and we get enough of that from Merchant Ivory, thanks very much). For a late-20th-century portrait, *Wilde* is almost insultingly perfunctory. But the film's biggest problem is even more fundamental—its studious respectability would surely have horrified its subject.

Also reviewed in:
CHICAGO TRIBUNE, 6/12/98, Friday/p. H, Michael Wilmington
NEW REPUBLIC, 5/18/98, p. 24, Stanley Kauffmann
NEW YORK TIMES, 5/1/98, p. E22, Janet Maslin

VARIETY, 8/25-31/97, p. 73, Derek Elley
WASHINGTON POST, 5/29/98, p. B1, Stephen Hunter
WASHINGTON POST, 5/29/98, Weekend/p. 48, Michael O'Sullivan

WITHOUT LIMITS

A Warner Bros. release of a Cruise/Wagner production. *Executive Producer:* Jonathan Sanger and Kenny Moore. *Producer:* Tom Cruise and Paula Wagner. *Director:* Robert Towne. *Screenplay:* Robert Towne and Kenny Moore. *Director of Photography:* Conrad L. Hall. *Editor:* Claire Simpson and Robert K. Lambert. *Music:* Randy Miller. *Music Editor:* Carlton Kaller. *Sound:* Bruce Bisenz. *Sound Editor:* Scott A. Hecker. *Casting:* Rick Pagano. *Production Designer:* William Creber. *Art Director:* William Durrell. *Set Decorator:* Cloudia. *Special Effects:* Bobby Riggs. *Costumes:* Grania Preston. *Make-up:* Gary Liddiard. *Stunt Coordinator:* Billy D. Lucas. *Running time:* 118 minutes. *MPAA Rating:* PG-13.

CAST: William Mapother (Bob Peters);   Adam Setliff (Mac Wilkins); Nicholas Oleson (Russ Francis);   Amy Jo Johnson (Iowa's Finest); Lisa Banes (Elfriede Prefontaine);   Billy Crudup (Steve Prefontaine);   Donald Sutherland (Bill Bowerman);   Monica Potter (Mary Marckx); Jeremy Sisto (Frank Shorter);   Matthew Lillard (Roscoe Devine).   Dean Norris (Bill Dellinger); Gabriel Olds (Don Kardong);   Billy Burke (Kenny Moore);   Judith Ivey (Barbara Bowerman); Frank Shorter (Fred Long);   Charlie Jones (Himself);   William Friedkin (TV Director);   David Coleman (BBC Commentator);   Jamie Schwering (Pre, age 6);   Garth Granholm (George Young);   Karen Elliott (Molly Cox);   Greg Foote (Walt McClure);   Ryan S. Warren (Finnish Official);   Ken Merckx (Eugene Register Reporter);   Katharine Towne, Cassandra A. Coogan, and Amy Erenberger (Coeds);   Edwin L. Coleman II (Turn Judge);   Jay Thorson (Pole Vaulter); John Roemer (German Guard);   Wendy Ray (Hayward Field Announcer);   Wade Bell (Starter); Coleman Dow (Bully);   Kim Nickel (Flight Attendant);   Jeffrey Atkinson (Steve Bence);   James Howarth (Arne Kvalhiem);   Avi Haas (Technical Director);   Dawn Aotani and Jim Sevin (Control Room Assistants);   Pat Porter (Lasse Viren);   Steve Ave (Mohammed Gammoudi); Jonathan Pritchard (Dave Bedford);   Tom Ansberry (Emiel Puttemans);   Sol Alexis Sallos (Harold Norpoth);   Thomas DeBacker (Juha Vaatinen);   Ashley Johnson (Ian Stewart);   Brad Hudson (Javier Alvarez);   Todd D. Lewis (Frank Eisenberg);   Tove Christensen (Per Halle); Chris Caldwell (Nikolay Sviridov);   Paul Vincent (Ian McCafferty);

NEW YORK, 9/28/98, p. 75, David Denby

Without Limits, Robert Towne's film about long-distance runner Steve Prefontaine, is beautifully made and features a marvelous performance by Donald Sutherland as the track coach Bill Bowerman, but the movie is no more than moderately interesting. I greatly enjoy Towne's obsessions when they turn to crime *(Chinatown)*, sex *(Shampoo)*, or the morale of lifetime Navy men *(The Last Detail)*, but Towne's two running movies, *Personal Best* and *Without Limits*, both of which he directed as well as wrote (former Olympic runner Kenny Moore collaborated on *Without Limits)*, are forced to return again and again to the spectacle of people running around a track. My own interest in sports tends to be pragmatic: I like statistics and physical data, and the drama of winning and losing, but not a spiritual lesson, and in the end *Without Limits* embalms long-distance running in the higher religiosity of intellectual sports movies—solemn mystico-athletic abstractions about "will" and "desire" and "heart" and "limits." The movie is somehow very profound yet, at the same time, slightly boring. One has to add, however, that *Without Limits* inspires relief, for it displays certain enlarging notions of the self and of the complexity of human motives that have been abandoned in our bizarre current preoccupations.

Consider: We live in a society in which public discourse is dominated by journalists and lawyers. When the journalists are lied to, as they were by the president, their sense of self-importance becomes aroused, even inflamed, and they turn relentless and prosecutorial. The lawyers, most of them, possess little moral or ethical imagination. Whenever serious human understanding is required, they fall back on legalisms that often distort or narrow down the human or constitutional issues involved. This dreary act of reducing conduct to a formula is called being a good lawyer. If you combine inflamed journalistic righteousness and Dickensian legalism, you wind up with what we've got now, the grindingly literal-minded pursuit (and defense) of an obviously lying adulterer who in other respects is an admirable leader. This pursuit takes place within an "information society," and whatever else the Lewinsky affair represents, and however it ends, the affair signifies the final and disgusting apotheosis of that society's inherent logic. In the Marquis de Sade's utopia, everyone would have absolute dominion over everyone else's body. In the information-age utopia, everyone's privacy belongs to everyone else—and with a sense of entitlement, too. The president's pursuers have turned the reading of near-pornography into a duty of citizenship. In ten years—no, five—all this will look insane.

In contrast, there is an artist like Robert Towne. In *Without Limits*, an actual person, Steve Prefontaine, is invested with a private self as well as a public performing self—he's seen, in other words, with the resources of imagination found in fiction, precisely the resources left out of the mortifying spectacle that is now tearing apart the republic. As Towne tells it, Prefontaine, or Pre, the great American long-distance runner (who died, at age 24, in 1975), was a creature of pure will comparable to a medieval ascetic or saint—a man capable of enduring unimaginable amounts of pain in order to achieve the perfection of his effort. "Talent has nothing to do with it," is Pre's mantra.

As Billy Crudup plays him, Prefontaine is an eagle-crested warrior: His mouth set, his severe high forehead fronting the wind (Pre likes to lead the pack), Crudup is shown running in innumerable slo-mo close-ups. This proud animal in flight is lean and muscular, with strong cheekbones and an odd way of running, with his shoulders thrust back. He runs the way a ballet dancer walks—with an exaggerated commitment to the act that is either (according to taste) an assertion of style or an affectation. In all, it's a little hard to judge the performance: Crudup bucks his head as he talks, like a stallion refusing the bit; his temperament is distant; he shies away—there's no richness to his ego. But what seems amateurish about his performance may be what Towne wanted out of him—the cold, unreachable control of an American champion.

Pre is essentially a mystery. He is perceived through the wondering eyes of Bill Bowerman, a formidable personage who never claims to understand his star athlete. Sutherland, who looks eagle-crested himself, with a strong flat crown of white hair and arched eyebrows, gives a shrewd and candid performance. *His* cheekbones are as pronounced as Crudup's, so the two men together, allowing for the difference in height, might be father and son. In this Oedipal drama, the son overcomes his father by running in his own way, without regard for the coach's instructions. At the heart of the movie is a series of races and furious disputes between Bowerman and Pre—the coach's practical wisdom against the athlete's arrogance, experience against genius, human sympathy against inhuman tolerance of pain. It's not a conflict that means a great deal to me, but the respect for human mystery and intransigence displayed in it remains ennobling even if it isn't emotionally satisfying.

NEW YORK POST, 9/11/98, p. 69, Thelma Adams

The athlete runs toward the camera. His cheeks jiggle. His sweat sparkles. His biceps ripple. His feet pound the track. His mutton chops bristle with excitement. He is a thoroughbred. He is man, the animal, at his prime. He is Steve Prefontaine.

Steve who? The Olympic three-miler almost took the gold at Munich in 1972, and died a tragic James Dean death on a dark Oregon road three years later.

For those who have short sports memories and missed Pre, the first Prefontaine bio-pic to cross the finish line, director Robert Towne has done his personal best to bring the tragic yet triumphant story to the screen in "Without Limits."

Towne is not the cinematic athlete he was when he wrote "Chinatown," and the movie has its limits. The story, from a script by Towne and Kenny Moore, is strictly after-school special in its complexity.

In a flashback, Pacific Northwestern thugs pursue a German-American boy through the Oregon woods. A track star is born. He never looks back. He never slows down.

Billy Crudup ("Sleepers") invests the gutsy track star with a stubborn beauty. Is it the young actor's reserve, or Towne's chilly direction, which creates a performance as hard-edged and impenetrable as the endless close-ups of athletes in flat-out competition?

Donald Sutherland takes a break from villainy to play Bill Bowerman. The Oregon coach (and innovative shoemaker) tries to wean Pre of his bad habits. Instead, Bowerman learns a few life lessons from the Rube who broke all the rules. Monica Potter is the deeply religious, doe-eyed blonde Pre chases and tags.

In the course of running through Prefontaine's short life, Towne presents the murder of Israeli athletes by Arab terrorists at Munich in 1972 like another hurdle in the athlete's career; the birth of Nike's running shoes, invented by Bowerman, is given equal weight as a historical footnote.

For all the drama's canonization of a runner who valued guts over everything else, "Without Limits" takes no risks. It's just not all that it could be.

NEWSDAY, 9/11/98, Part II/p. B6 , Jack Mathews

It's indicative of the creative slump and attending panic at Warner Bros. that Robert Towne's superb biographical drama about the great 1970s distance runner Steve Prefontaine arrives under the forgettable title of "Without Limits." Its original title, "Pre," the single-syllable name by which the late runner is still known throughout the world, was dropped after rival Disney's clunky "Prefontaine" got to the starting line first.

Disney's picture was released in January, 1997, triggering both the name change and a year's delay for Towne's infinitely superior version of the same events. Clearly still nervous, Warner Bros. is releasing "Without Limits" in stages, meaning that if it doesn't do well in selected theaters in major cities, it will probably never have a national release.

One could only wish the studio had the confidence and courage of Prefontaine and, like him, trusted its talent. Towne may be best known as one of Hollywood's premiere screenwriters ("Chinatown"), but he's also a fine director whose work includes the exceptional track film "Personal Best," with which he managed to get solid dramatic performances from athletes cast in key dramatic roles.

Here, Towne is working with talented professionals and gets the best out of his two stars, Billy Crudup, as Prefontaine, and Donald Sutherland, as his famous college coach, Bill Bowerman. There were few better performances in 1997, and fewer yet so far this year.

Towne, and co-screenwriter Kenny Moore, a Sports Illustrated veteran who was once a teammate of Prefontaine's at the University of Oregon, concentrate on the last six years of the runner's life, from his senior year in high school to his death in a 1975 car crash. In that brief period, he converted distance races from track-meet tranquilizers into marquee events, set numerous American records, competed in the 1972 Munich Olympics and drafted a nation of Pre admirers.

Prefontaine's trailing blond hair and distinct, gutsy running style, along with his off-field crusade against track and field's corrupt governing body, made him a symbol of his restless generation, a rebel with a righteous cause. After his death, Prefontaine's image became linked in legend with James Dean, as two charismatic figures taken from the sharp ascension of their fame. They even died similar deaths, in crushed sports cars.

Charisma is hard enough to define, let alone dramatize, and nowhere is it more difficult than with sports figures. Good actors can mime almost any famous person's manner, and replicate or lip-synch their voices. But if he can't swing a bat, catch a football or run like the wind, he'll destroy the credibility of a sports movie. And Crudup, in the numerous race sequences intercut with actual event footage, runs like the wind, cutting the spitting image of Prefontaine while doing it.

Crudup's subtle performance also keeps his character in a realistic focus. We get to know a Prefontaine struggling with his looming legend rather than playing off the legend itself, a choice that has doomed many a sports biography. Prefontaine is a hustler on and off the track; he knows that the brashness that comes naturally with him is marketable in a country in the throes of rebellion, and he learns how to use it to massage the media.

Even more impressive is Sutherland's performance as Oregon's legendary track coach Bowerman, a World War II combat hero whose stubbornness met its match in Prefontaine. The father-son relationship that inevitably evolves between diligent coach and gifted player can sink quickly in sentimental quicksand, and it did between these same characters in Disney's film. But it never happens here.

Bowerman, whose foot fetish (he handmakes his runners' shoes, using his wife's waffle iron) will help launch Nike, recognizes Prefontaine's greatness, but doesn't subjugate himself to it. And the give-and-take between them—"I tried to change him, and he tried not to change, that's our relationship," the coach explains—is genuinely moving. Sutherland's restrained work is the best he's done in years, and his delivery of Bowerman's elegant eulogy at Prefontaine's memorial will leave few eyes undamp.

Less is known, or has been revealed, about Prefontaine's romantic entanglements, but the story, as cinema, cries out for a strong love interest, and gets it in Mary Marckx (Monica Potter), the chaste person who is irresistible counterprograming to Pre's parade of eager groupies. The relationship, which allows us glimpses at Prefontaine's vulnerability, is Towne's only sop to the conventions of the genre (and to studio marketing), but he mostly avoids the sentimental traps and brings in a sports movie that belongs in the company of "Jim Thorpe, All-American" and "Chariots of Fire."

Now, those were titles.

SIGHT AND SOUND, 7/99, p. 57, Edward Laurenson

Long-distance runner Steve Prefontaine accepts a scholarship from the University of Oregon, out of admiration for its running coach Bill Bowerman. Bowerman criticises Prefontaine's habit of setting the pace of each race and advises him to run more tactically. An outstanding performance in his first three-mile race at Oregon makes Prefontaine a popular campus figure. But he's frustrated in his attempts to woo fellow student Mary Marckx who's wary of his womanising reputation.

At the 1970 NCAA competition, Prefontaine takes a personal best, despite a painful cut to his foot. He starts dating Mary, but their relationship remains chaste. A trip to Scandinavia brings Prefontaine into conflict with his ruling body AAU over the rights of amateur athletes; Bowerman warns him that this could jeopardise his place in the 1972 Munich Olympics. He qualifies for the games, but is beaten to fourth place in the 5000-metre final, which is won by Finn Lasse Virén. Disappointed, he returns home and takes a job in a bar. Bowerman persuades him to train for the upcoming Montreal Olympics. At his comeback three-mile race in Oregon, he takes turns setting the pace with runner Frank Shorter and thrills the crowd with a time of under 13 minutes. Driving home from a party after the race, Prefontaine has a fatal car accident.

A biopic of US long-distance runner Steve Prefontaine, Robert Towne's *Without Limits* is a strange kind of sports movie. Overlong, full of visual clichés (Towne seems unable to film any race sequence without using slow motion), and saddled with a strident soundtrack, the film feels at times like an over-earnest made-for-television feature— only *Hoop Dreams'* director Steve James got there first with *Prefontaine*. Worse still, *Without Limits* struggles to justify why Prefontaine should warrant a biopic in the first place. Sure, he was an outstanding athlete—Towne's film features meticulous recreations of some of his record-breaking races. Prefontaine's winning charisma was unusual in the otherwise uniform world of athletics. Engagingly played by Billy Crudup, he emerges from the film as something of a sporting firebrand, the kind of cocky maverick that sports giant Nike likes to associate itself with. (Prefontaine was one of the first athletes to endorse Nike's products.) As an icon of our accelerated age, there was even something sadly fitting about his early death in a car crash aged 24.

But this premature death meant that, despite breaking a clutch of college track records, his Olympic ambitions went unrealised. The film opens with the hype surrounding Prefontaine's chances for the 5000 metres at the Munich Olympics. In the film he finishes fourth in that race, and his failure to make the winning podium severely undermines his confidence. It's also a result which affects the dramatic form of the movie. Just as Prefontaine tended to flag in the final lap of his races, *Without Limits* denies us the triumphalist pay-off any other self-respecting sports movie would reward us with as a matter of course—the big race, the winning moment.

By taking Prefontaine's failure at Munich as its biographical starting point, Towne's film bucks the convention of the genre. The film is as much about losing (and coping with defeat) as winning, about unrealised potential as well as sporting achievement. Despite the slightly

Nietzschean ring to the title and the will-to-win credo of the young Prefontaine (echoing the competitive individualism of sports-gear commercials), this is at heart a rather gentle and affectionate portrait.

Towne's film is at its most thoughtful in exploring the dynamic between Prefontaine and his softly-spoken coach. In a beautifully nuanced performance, Donald Sutherland plays Bowerman like an ageing hippie, a far more genial figure than Scott Glenn's Machiavellian coach in Towne's 1982 athletics movie *Personal Best*. In contrast with Prefontaine's self-motivating exhortations, Bowerman is positively Zen in his trackside encouragement ("Running is a way to find meaning in life"). Such comments are admittedly a little gnomic, a far cry from the crisp elegance of Towne's 70s classic *Chinatown*. But given the increasingly aggressive tenor of sports' advertising campaigns (Nike's and Adidas' goods appear here like sly product placements) and the critique of the pressures facing young athletes by *Hoop Dreams*, Bowerman's belief in sport for sport's sake simply adds to *Without Limits* unassuming charm. After all, it's difficult not to like a movie dedicated to celebrating an all-American track star who is beaten in the biggest race of his career by a Finn.

TIME, 9/7/98, p. 75, Richard Schickel

The hero doesn't win the big race. Instead, he dies young and absurdly in an auto accident, leaving his highest promise unfulfilled. No wonder Warner Bros. has been dithering over the release of *Without Limits* for something like a year and a half. In that story line it's kind of hard to find the thing all sports movies implicitly promise—a triumph of the human spirit.

Kind of hard to find much conventional commercial promise in the movie either. Directed and co-written (with Kenny Moore) by Robert Towne, it stars Billy Crudup and Donald Sutherland, not exactly guys you can count on to open a picture. Worse, it follows by a mere two years another movie about its protagonist, the legendary distance runner Steve Prefontaine, which flopped miserably. *Without Limits,* which is a very good movie, will require a stroke of marketing genius to succeed. Or an unusual effort at understanding—a willingness by the audience to set aside generic expectations and engage the movie on its own terms.

This effort has to begin with the recognition that this is only nominally a sports movie. Yes, there was a time, more than a quarter-century ago, when Prefontaine held the American record in every distance from 2,000 to 10,000 m, when his bold front-running style and his self-dramatizing manner made him running's version of a rock star. And, yes, Towne conveys the exhilaration and exhaustion of high-level competition with unprecedented realism and intimacy.

But if Towne the director has a shrewd and patient eye for the small, telling tics of human behavior, Towne the writer says all his best work—which includes the classic *Chinatoum*—is "about a man's relationship to his profession, the willingness to put everything into doing one single thing well," which he finds "purifying and thrilling."

Clearly, Prefontaine, whom Crudup plays with cool ferocity, is his kind of guy. A knothead and a hothead who insisted that "a race is a work of art," he also liked to say he'd rather lose in a way that was aesthetically pleasing to him than win by more closely calculated means.

This put him in conflict with his coach, the almost equally legendary Bill Bowerman (Sutherland), no mean athletic aesthetician himself. He's presented as a more forgiving and gently eccentric kind of obsessive, disapproving of his pupil's stubborn individuality but also watchfully guarding a passion for excellence that matches his own. Theirs is a marvelously subtle wrangle: Prefontaine ran Bowerman's race in the 5,000 m at the 1972 Munich Olympics, and was beaten; but it was Bowerman who brought him back from self-pity (and maybe self-destruction) and onto the comeback trail before Prefontaine was killed.

Whether he would have won at the next Olympics, we'll never know. What we do know is that Towne, a man of ruefully romantic temperament, has found a soulmate in Steve Prefontaine. In an article he once wrote, Towne made an implicit analogy between writing and running. Both involve a rebellious effort to exceed the limits God places on your talent; both demand, as you settle into the starting blocks, an acceptance of whatever fate he whimsically decrees. One hopes that *Without Limits,* seemingly boxed in at the start, breaks free and scores an upset that is, yes, "purifying and thrilling" for the uncompromising spirit it sweetly celebrates.

Also reviewed in:
CHICAGO TRIBUNE, 10/30/98, Friday/p. F, Michael Wilmington
NEW YORK TIMES, 9/11/98, p. E16, Janet Maslin
NEW YORKER, 9/14/98, p. 100, Daphne Merkin
VARIETY, 3/16-22/98, p. 68, Todd McCarthy

WOO

A New Line Cinema release of a New Deal/Gotham Entertainment production. *Executive Producer:* John Singleton, Howard Hobson, and Bradford W. Smith. *Producer:* Beth Hubbard and Michael Hubbard. *Director:* Daisy V.S. Mayer. *Screenplay:* David C. Johnson. *Director of Photography:* Jean Lépine. *Editor:* Nicholas Eliopoulos and Janice Hampton. *Music:* Michel Colombier. *Music Editor:* Jay Bolton. *Choreographer:* Sergio Trujillo. *Sound:* Owen "Sound" Langevin and (music) Gil Morales. *Sound Editor:* Aaron Weisblatt and Bobbi Banks. *Casting:* Robbi Reed-Humes. *Production Designer:* Ina Mayhew. *Art Director:* Vlasta Svoboda. *Set Decorator:* Mike Harris. *Set Dresser:* Robert Hicks, Malcolm Gibson, and Martyn Jefferson. *Special Effects:* Jordan Craig. *Costumes:* Michael Clancy. *Make-up:* Judy Murdock. *Stunt Coordinator:* Alison Reid. *Running time:* 80 minutes. *MPAA Rating:* R.

CAST: Jada Pinkett Smith (Woo/Off the Wall Babe); Tommy Davidson (Tim); Duane Martin (Frankie); Michael Ralph (Romaine); Darrel M. Heath (Hop); Dave Chappelle (Lenny); Paula Jai Parker (Claudette); LL Cool J (Darryl); Aida Turturro (Tookie); Lance Slaughter (Lamar); Dartanyan Edmonds (Shakim); Foxy Brown (Fiancée); Sam Moses (Cabbie); Tiffany Hall (Denise); Girlina (Celestrial); Denosh Bennett (Sister at Concert); Joanna Bacalso (Stunning Woman); Mia Pitts (Voluptuous Woman); Catherine Burdon (Alluring Woman); Lenny Solomon (Violin Player); Silvio Oliviero (Waiter #1); Nick Corri (Maitre'd); Victor Chan (Delivery Biker); Lisa Scarola (Latina Woman); Philip Akin (Roger Smith); Stu "Large" Riley (Beast); David "Rumble" Morgan (Patron); Fawn Boardley (Shanay); Natalie Venetia Belcon (Hootchie); Buddy Lewis (Bartender); Nicci Gilbert (Crayola); Christian Maelen and Desmond Campbell (Officers); Kelley Grando (Barry, Bouncer); Orlando Jones (Sticky Fingas); Esther Jones (Shorty); Tyree Michael Simpson (Big Brother #1); Roland Rothchild (Big Brother #2); Martin Roach (West Indian Brother); Sergio Trujillo (Ricardo\Salsa Dancer); Shyla Marlin (Niece); Robinne Fanfair (Fine Sister at Restaurant); John Stoneham, Jr. (Fine Sister's Date); Russell Hornsby (Guy); Marc Desourdy (Waiter with Pasta); Billy Linders (Waiter with Flambée); Frank Ferrara (Construction Guy); Silvana Gatica (Rosa); David Roberts and Kirk Pickersgill (Disco Girls); Drake Thorens (Delivery Biker); Kevin Louis (Door Person); A.J. Johnson (Doorman); Pat Dias (Salsa Party Photographer).

LOS ANGELES TIMES, 5/8/98, Calendar/p. 12, John Anderson

[The following review by John Anderson appeared in a slightly different form in
NEWSDAY, 5/8/98, Part II/p. B11.]

"Does it always have to be about sex?" asks Woo (Jada Pinkett Smith), the alternately sultry, vulgar, impish and marginally psychotic club kid/feminist agitator who's shrink-wrapped into a sequined halter top and pants that are stretched thinner than your patience. In a movie in which people have proper names for their private parts, this seems an odd question.
A better question: Why can't Pinkett Smith ("The Nutty Professor," "Scream 2")—as attractive and effervescent a screen presence as is currently being misused by Hollywood—find something better to do than play the title role of "Woo," a painfully graceless comedy that reworks "After Midnight," "Blind Date" and "Booty Call" into something monstrous and untoward? Or, for that matter, Tommy Davidson, who plays Woo's besieged blind date, a guy whose manhood is treated the way a baby treats a diaper?

Did we mention boring? The director is Daisy von Scherler Mayer of the remotely amusing, Parker Posey-powered "Party Girl," who is identified here as Daisy V.S. Mayer, perhaps so she can have some escape route on her resume from this more current exercise in pretentiousness, sexism, vulgarity and pandering. In making the film, she seems to have had some communication with the transmigrated souls of Luis Bunuel and Moe Howard. But not enough.

Woo, an all-purpose celebutante-about-town with oceans of attitude, no visible means of support and a wardrobe one size too small, can figure out most things—except the fact that her cousin Claudette (Paula Jai Parker) and Claudette's boyfriend, Lenny (Dave Chappelle), would like some time alone. Lenny, desperate, calls up his hapless, dateless buddy Tim (Davidson) to take Woo off their hands. Given that Woo is the finest, foxiest... I mean, when you see Woo, you say, "WOOOOO!" In other words, companionship shouldn't be a problem, but there you have it.

Anyway, to make a long story short, Woo's best buddy and transvestite astrologer, Celestrial (Girlina), has prophesied that Woo is going to meet the man of her dreams that very night and that he'll be a Virgo. She meets Tim. He's a Virgo. But it takes her the entire movie to figure out they're meant for each other. In this, "Woo" actually resembles Sophocles: If Oedipus had really believed the oracle, he should have known that whatever woman he met and married would be his mother. Likewise, Woo should have committed herself early. And we all would have been spared a great deal of anguish and agony and the urge to go blind.

NEW YORK POST, 5/8/98, p. 51, Larry Worth

It's fair to say that "Woo" is one for the record books: a '90s sex comedy that makes "Booty Call" seem the height of sophistication and restraint. So why would head-turner Jada Pinkett Smith—an actress whose dramatic and comic potential has electrified a half-dozen supporting turns—choose such a pathetic vehicle for her leading-lady breakthrough? Maybe she was drawn in by the cachet of Daisy V.S. Mayer, the director who put Parker Posey on the map with the deliciously madcap "Party Girl." Suffice to say that lightning didn't strike twice. The juvenile script is a half-hearted retread of 1987's "Blind Date," the lame Blake Edwards romp wherein yuppie Bruce Willis suffers a wild night on the town with gorgeous but out-of-control Kim Basinger. This time around, Tommy Davidson is the hapless bookworm who gets paired up with super-sexy Pinkett Smith, quickly discovering that looks can be deceiving. Of course, it's one calamity after another, with Davidson's three testosterone-charged pals popping up to make bad situations worse. Basically, the central twosome take turns being outraged and offended by each other's reactions to whatever form of hell is breaking out around them. But the real hell is what viewers are asked to endure.

That starts with a script that traffics only in stereotypes, never mind a succession of standard battle scenes—the food fight, the club-scene fight, the catfight—that defeat the production's fleeting merits (a surprise cameo and solid soundtrack).

But along with ceaselessly demeaning dialogue ("Is she a ho, or what?"), Mayer deserves much of the blame. Use of cliched dream sequences, speeded-up montages and exploitative skin scenes are just part of a bigger problem: It's a comedy without a single laugh.

That's an accomplishment when "In Living Color" veteran Davidson is in the spotlight, backed by funnymen Dave Chappelle, Duane Martin, Michael Ralph and Darrel Heath. LL Cool J is also wasted in a walk-on as the consummate lover boy.

And that's not even mentioning the total misuse of Pinkett Smith's considerable abilities. Woe to all those thinking they'll see any trace of them in "Woo."

SIGHT AND SOUND, 10/98, p. 60, Kim Newman

New York. Woo, an attractive single woman, is told by Celestrial, her drag-queen fortune teller, that tonight is propitious for her to meet a soulmate with the birth sign Virgo. However, she decides to join her cousin Claudette.

Claudette's boyfriend Lenny, planning an intimate evening of fantasy sex, fixes Woo up with Tim, a struggling paralegal whose last girlfriend encouraged him to buy a flashy car before dumping him. When Woo learns Tim is a Virgo, she agrees to a blind date. Offended by the make-out kit Tim has in his apartment and the sexist attitudes of his friends Frankie, Romaine and Hop, Woo has a mood swing and causes a disruption in a restaurant.

In a club, the couple encounter Lamar, Woo's possessive and violent ex-boyfriend. Tim's car is stolen and they split up. Tim is mugged while Woo consults Celestrial. Woo gets Frankie, Romaine and Hop admittance to the club where Celestrial is partying, and they slowly realise they are dancing with men. Woo searches the city for Tim and takes him to a party where she reconciles with her brother Shakim and his fiancée. They then steal back the car from Tim's ex. They dance in the street to seal their romantic bond, only for a passing truck to crush the car.

Re-running most of the plot of the Blake Edwards far-from classic *Blind Date*, *Woo* straggles from one embarrassing set-piece to another as if bad previews had encouraged the removal of connective tissue. Edwards, at least, made Kim Basinger a functional alcoholic; here, no reason is given for Woo being as insane as she is scripted, making her the worst kind of device for shaking up the scenes she appears in. The film never manages to make any credible connection between its leads even within the fantastical confines of a genre in which we are expected to believe that a mismatched couple who hate each other on sight (justifiably so) are soulmates. Jada Pinkett—billing herself as Jada Pinkett Smith, as if the name-changing example of Joanne Whalley-Kilmer and Patty Duke Astin hadn't taught actresses everywhere a lesson in career management—has a powerful natural appeal. Unfortunately, this collapses under the weight of obnoxiousness piled on Woo by the script. It slowly dawns that the film expects you to sympathise with this self-obsessed, manipulative, near-psychotic twit rather than see her as a monster who is out to destroy Tim's life. Pinkett was on far better form in her cameo in *Scream 2*, which was abbreviated by the knife-wielding killer one wishes would force his way into this movie and put us all out of our misery.

The bland Tommy Davidson (best known for *Booty Call* suffers through repeated references to his resemblance to Sammy Davis Jr, but his homy, superficial Everyman is only marginally more likable than his boorish friends. Though directed by a woman (who wrote and directed *Party Girl* and equipped with requisite scenes in which Woo upbraids the menfolk for their sexism (she doesn't like being called a "ho" or a "bitch"), it's hard not to feel the film wants to get as many cheap laughs as it can from macho idiocy (LL Cool J lives across the way from Tim with a compliant harem) before condemning it. Hop's fate (a fit of self-disgust after he has snogged a transvestite) flirts with homophobia, Lenny and Claudette's 'chicken delight' fantasy is an energetically humourless sex scene worthy of comparison with any given 70s porno movie, and in the film's ridiculing of any woman with larger hips than Jada Pinkett's there's a streak of body fascism which compounds a cheerless experience into an annoying one.

VILLAGE VOICE, 5/19/98, Film Special/p. 134, Gary Dauphin

The unlikely couple brought together in *Woo* are on a blind date, but that doesn't mean audiences haven't been here before. This Jada Pinkett Smith vehicle written by David C. Johnson is a retread of *Booty Call* and anyone who liked that previous outing will appreciate this new night of horrors. Woo is the unexplained moniker of Pinkett Smith's character, a borderline psychotic who's set up with nerdy paralegal Tim (Tommy Davidson, doing 90 minutes of reaction shots). Intended, I imagine, to scan as a hyperactive handful who needs aggressive male keeping-up-with, Woo is really just annoying, a walking compilation of neck rolls who veers wildly from glossy r&b bitch to black valley girl to club kid-cum-drag queen. Woo takes Tim on the town and watches blithely as he suffers a range of indignities, the couple drifting through stylized black New York subcult spaces until they can appreciate each other's quirks. There are a few decent gags (the lowest yet most intriguing involves something called a "Chicken 'Ho"), but overall *Woo* is the usual bottom-feeding crud aimed at black audiences.

Also reviewed in:
CHICAGO TRIBUNE, 5/8/98, Friday/p. K, Monica Eng
NEW YORK TIMES, 5/8/98, p. E12, Stephen Holden
VARIETY, 5/11-17/98, p. 50, Joe Leydon
WASHINGTON POST, 5/8/98, Weekend/p. 62, Michael O'Sullivan

WRONGFULLY ACCUSED

A Warner Bros. release of a James G. Robinson presentation of a Morgan Creek production in a co-production with Constantin Film. *Executive Producer:* Robert L. Rosen, Gary Barber, and Martin Moszkowicz. *Producer:* James G. Robnson, Bernd Eichinger, and Pat Proft. *Director:* Pat Proft. *Screenplay:* Pat Proft. *Director of Photography:* Glen MacPherson. *Editor:* James R. Symons. *Music:* Bill Conti. *Music Editor:* Chris McGeary. *Choreographer:* Mairead O'Brien-Kent. *Sound:* Rob Young and (music) Dan Wallin. *Sound Editor:* Glenn T. Morgan. *Casting:* Karen Rea. *Production Designer:* Michael Bolton. *Art Director:* Sandy Cochrane. *Set Designer:* Gwendolyn Margetson. *Set Decorator:* Lin MacDonald. *Set Dresser:* Rick Patterson, Michael Jovanovski, Cynthia Burtinshaw, and Lorne Poole. *Special Effects:* Bill Schirmer. *Visual Effects:* Keith Hamakawa. *Costumes:* Jori Woodman. *Make-up:* L. Taylor Roberts. *Make-up (Leslie Nielsen):* Robert Ryan. *Stunt Coordinator:* Guy Bews. *Running time:* 85 minutes. *MPAA Rating:* PG-13.

CAST: Leslie Nielsen (Ryan Harrison); Richard Crenna (Fergus Falls); Kelly Le Brock (Lauren Goodhue); Melinda McGraw (Cass Lake); Michael York (Hibbing Goodhue); Sandra Bernhard (Doctor Fridley); Aaron Pearl (Sean Laughrea); Leslie Jones (Sergeant Tina Bagley); Ben Ratner (Sergeant Orono); Gerard Plunkett (Sir Robert McKintyre); Duncan Fraser (Sergeant McMacDonald); John Walsh (Himself); Maury Hannigan (Commissioner Hannigan); Chick Hearn (Basketball Announcer); Brian Arnold (Dan Clellan the News Reporter); Guy Bews, Alexander Boynton, and Rob Daprocida (Security Guards); Mary Black (Woman with I.V.); Michael Bolton (T.V. Stage Manager); Jacques Bourassa (Teenager with Backpack); Ken Boyd (Usher); Johnathon Bruce (Hospital Janitor); Rick Burgess (Prisoner); Charn (Bus Convict); Brian Cochrane (Cop); Arthur Corber (Percussionist); Rick Cross (Ben Hur Oarsman); Cory Dagg, Michelle Hart, Yoko Sakai, and Ingrid Tesch (Reporters); Alex Daikun (Roman); Thea Nielsen Disney, Maura Nielsen Kaplan, and Kanlayaporn Neelaphamorn (Party Guests); Adrien Dorval (Proctor); Mark Fox (Butcher); Mark Francis (Abe Lincoln); Christopher L. Gibson, Charles Paynes, David Prestley, and Marco Roy (Paramedics); Calvin Guo (Japanese Gardener); Ellie Harvie (Ruth the News Anchor); Noah Heney (Parking Attendant); Ingrid Henningsen (Party Guest Out of Focus); Derek Hurst (Patient with Liquid Ears); Ellen Kennedy (Boy in the Eye Musician); P.J. Lespance (Yo Yo Double); Wallace Leung (Conductor); Bev Martin (Mary Lincoln); Mina E. Mina (Arab Diplomat); Barbaree Earl Nielsen (Fainting Pedestrian); Robin Nielsen (Pary Waiter); Jason Payn (Wanted Poster Boy); Pat Proft (Window Technician); Patty Sachs (Waitress at Crash Site); Veena Sood (Nurse); Bill Tarling (Bus Convict); Stephen Tibbetts (Patient); French Tickner (Doctor in ICU); Kenneth "Brother" Vils (Detective Van Atter); Henry O. Watson (Mayor Stopka).

LOS ANGELES TIMES, 8/22/98, Calendar/p. 8, Kevin Thomas

More than anything else, "Wrongfully Accused" reminds us that it's been nearly 20 years since "Airplane!," and that the zany spoof of big popular pictures is in need of a rest. As a sendup (of sorts) of "The Fugitive"—and scenes from a clutch of other movies—the film reveals how stale the formula has become in a summer season that has brought us "There's Something About Mary."

Writer-producer-director Pat Proft, star Leslie Nielsen and others, most notably Richard Crenna, work up a chuckle here and there and elicit a smile every now and then, but Warner Bros. need not worry that it will be "wrongfully accused" of slighting a comic gem by delaying the film's press preview long enough to avoid opening-day reviews. (Since "Wrongfully Accused" was not trying to be anything more than mindless fun, it's actually less depressing than "Dead Man on Campus," the week's other clunker comedy, which Paramount previewed at the last possible minute for critics to make Friday opening-day deadlines.)

Nielsen, who might consider a change of pace himself, plays a klutzy (what else?) violin virtuoso (who steals from Jimi Hendrix, of all people, for his finish) who is framed by gorgeous vamp Kelly Le Brock for the murder of her husband, Michael York. Nielsen is swiftly on the run, with Crenna, in the Tommy Lee Jones part, on his tail. It seems that York has discovered that

Le Brock is actually a political terrorist, involved in a plot to assassinate the U.N. secretary-general. In any event, a blah mystery woman (Melinda McGraw) is apparently the only person on the face of the Earth who believes in Nielsen's protests of innocence, but who is she anyway and what's her angle?

Proft doesn't make us care about her identity or anything else for that matter, for "Wrongfully Accused" is a movie merely going through the paces in mechanical fashion. It could have used considerably more of the wit and elegance of Le Brock and York, who are on screen too briefly, and only Crenna has a role of sufficient characterization to be able to make a substantial amusing impression, as a solemn lawman with a hick drawl. (Sandra Bernhard turns up for what seems less than an instant.)

Perhaps Minnesotans might be a tad more amused than the rest of us by "Wrongfully Accused" because fellow Minnesotan Proft has named his characters after actual locales in his native state. Indeed, although the film was shot in Canada (Vancouver, mainly), where so many mediocre U.S. productions are shot, it's supposed to be set in a Minneapolis suburb, Columbia Heights, where Proft was born and raised.

NEW YORK POST, 8/21/98, p. 65, Larry Worth

The time has finally come for Leslie Nielsen to hang up the banana peel.

The actor who resurrected his film career as a latter-day Clouseau in the "Naked Gun" trilogy shows signs of terminal deja-vu—much like the well-worn gags of "Wrongfully Accused."

Actually, the film-parody genre has gradually become box-office poison. Just weeks ago, "Mafia" attempted to lampoon "The Godfather," only to have a bored public deliver the kiss of death.

In "Wrongfully Accused," the alleged comic spin is on 1993's "The Fugitive." But the results are no funnier than "Mafia," with Nielsen spoofing Harrison Ford's role of a convicted murderer trying to prove his innocence and nab the real killer.

Nielsen not only pursues the handicapped villain—a one-armed, one-legged, one-eyed man in this version—but goes on to attempt skewed salutes of everything from Michael Flatley's "Lord of the Dance" to "Mission: Impossible," "Titanic," "Braveheart," "Fatal Attraction" and "The Usual Suspects."

Clearly, the subject matter is all over the map, which means Nielsen's anemic performance isn't the only problem. Writer-director Pat Proft, who previously co-penned the "Naked Gun" series and both "Hots Shots," isn't a good fit in the director's chair.

Proft mistakenly thinks that recognizing a subject—as when showing the ever-heaving bosoms of "Baywatch" babe knockoffs—is enough to generate laughs. But familiar equals funny only if there's a twist.

A few jolts of unexpected profanity don't help. Nor does a supporting cast that's either seen better days (Richard Crenna, Kelly LeBrock, Michael York) or has yet to become bankable (Melinda McGraw, Aaron Pearl).

Naturally, a few smiles register within 90 minutes of hit-or-miss jokes. And there's one other plus: a brief appearance by Lambchop, the late Shari Lewis' puppet. Seeing her for what may be the last time delivers an unexpectedly poignant moment—the only memorable one that "Wrongfully Accused" provides.

Also reviewed in:
CHICAGO TRIBUNE, 8/24/98, Tempo/p. 2, John Petrakis
NEW YORK TIMES, 8/22/98, p. B12, Anita Gates
VARIETY, 8/24-30/98, p. 28, Leonard Klady

X-FILES, THE

A Twentieth Century Fox release of a Ten Thirteen production. *Executive Producer:* Lata Ryan. *Producer:* Chris Carter and Daniel Sackheim. *Director:* Rob Bowman. *Screenplay:* Chris Carter. *Story:* Chris Carter and Frank Spotnitz. *Director of Photography:* Ward Russell.

Editor: Stephen Mark. *Music:* Mark Snow. *Music Editor:* Jeff Charbonneau. *Sound:* Geoffrey Patterson and (music) Larold Rebhun. *Sound Editor:* John A. Larsen. *Casting:* Liberman/Hirschfeld. *Production Designer:* Christopher Nowak. *Art Director:* Marc Fisichella. *Set Designer:* Easton Michael Smith, Lauren Cory, Dawn Brown, and Fanie Aaron. *Set Decorator:* Jackie Carr. *Special Effects:* Paul Lombardi. *Costumes:* Marlene Stewart. *Make-up:* Michael Mills. *Special Make-up Effects:* Alec Gillis and Tom Woodruff, Jr. *Stunt Coordinator:* Tim Davison. *Running time:* 115 minutes. *MPAA Rating:* PG-13.

CAST: David Duchovny (Agent Fox Mulder); Gillian Anderson (Agent Dana Scully); John Neville (The Well-Manicured Man); William B. Davis (The Cigarette-Smoking Man); Martin Landau (Dr. Alvin Kurtzweil); Mitch Pileggi (Assistant Director Walter Skinner); Jeffrey De Munn (Dr. Ben Bronschweig); Blythe Danner (Jana Cassidy); Terry O'Quinn (Darius Michaud); Armin Mueller-Stahl (Conrad Strughold); Lucas Black (Stevie); Chris Fennell, Cody Newton, and Blake Stokes (Boys); Dean Haglund (Langly, one of the Lone Gunmen); Bruce Harwood (Byers, one of the Lone Gunmen); Tom Braidwood (Frohike, one of the Lone Gunmen); Don S. Williams (Group Elder); George Murdock (2nd Elder); Michael Shamus Wiles (Black-haired Man); Craig Davis and Carrick O'Quinn (Primitives); Tom Woodruff, Jr. and Gregory B. Ballora (Creature 2); T.W. King (FBI Agent on Roof); Luis Beckford (FBI Agent) Steve Rankin (Field Agent); Gary Crubbs (Fire Captain Cooles); Steven M. Gagnon (Last Agent Out); Lawrence Joshua and Glendon Rich (DC Cops); Gunther Jensen (Security Guard); Scott Smith (Technician); Ian Ruskin (The Well-Manicured Man's Valet); Paul Welterlen (Control Room Operator); Joel Traywick (Young Naval Guard); Milton Johns (British Valet); Paul Tuerpi and Michael A. Krawick (Paramedics); Larry Rippenkroeger (Towncar Driver); Josh McLaglen (Buzz Mihoe); Randy Hall (Windbreakered Agent); T.C. Badalato (Fireman); Amine Zary (Tunisian); Glenne Headly (Barmaid).

CHRISTIAN SCIENCE MONITOR, 6/19/98, p. B4, David Sterritt

From novels by Thomas Pynchon and Umberto Eco to movies like "The Truman Show" and TV programs like "The X-Files," conspiracies have filled the air as the millennium approaches. "The truth is out there," an "X-Files" logo proclaims, and it appears some audiences hope to find this in the fictions they consume.

The widely popular "X-Files" series has captivated untold millions since its 1993 première. While much of its success rests on obvious attributes like attractive stars and eye-catching special effects, it taps into deeper concerns with its suggestions that paranormal forces play a strong but hidden part in contemporary affairs, and that our untrustworthy government(s) are more deeply embroiled in this than they'll admit to us ordinary citizens.

The show occasionally touches on philosophical and even spiritual issues, moreover, opening up fascinating possibilities for its future growth. So far, though, series honcho Chris Carter has chosen to play with those possibilities rather than explore them with the open-minded imagination they deserve. The same goes for the "X-Files" movie he's concocted with director Rob Bowman.

The familiar ingredients are all on display: David Duchovny as Mulder, the FBI agent energized by a childhood alien-abduction scene; Gillian Anderson as Scully, his rational-minded but warmly sympathetic partner; series regulars like good guy Mitch Pileggi and ominous guy William B. Davis; Mark Snow's whistling-by-the-graveyard theme music; and lots of plots, subplots, and subsubplots about everything from viral plagues and alien colonization to deadly cornfields and bug-eyed monsters.

This is more than enough material for two hours of summer-movie fun, and "The X-Files" delivers said fun reasonably well. The action scenes are bigger and bolder than their small-screen counterparts, especially when the story travels to the icebound locations that perennially lure Carter and his colleagues. The screenplay reveals partial answers to a number of unsolved mysteries raised by the show over its five-year history. And there are a few hilarious gags.

And yes, series fans, the almost-romance between Mulder and Scully comes delightfully close to blossoming, although more can't be revealed without spoiling one of the movie's most clever moments.

With all this in its favor, "The X-Files" is poised to become a solid warm-weather hit. Still, it's worth pausing to ask whether it couldn't have been more than just a rousing entertainment. By restricting their movie to the same narrow groove as the series, they forfeit their chance to compete with truly imaginative science-fiction classics like "2001: A Space Odyssey' or "Close Encounters of the Third Kind," which take more chances.

Already a major pop-culture phenomenon, the "X-Files" groundswell will surely grow even larger as moviegoers line up at multiplexes. Once the thrills and spills have ended, though, the movie will fade from most memories as quickly as one of Mulder's elusive UFOs vanishes from the star-filled sky.

LOS ANGELES TIMES, 6/19/98, Calendar/p. 1, Kenneth turan

Who hasn't walked into a movie late and tried desperately to catch up with the plot, to make sense of what's on the screen? For those not washed in the blood, that's what it's like to watch "The X-Files" movie. Except instead of being only momentarily tardy, we're five years behind the curve.

That's how long the popular cult TV show has been on the Fox network. And despite impressive billboards for the movie insisting "Only in Theaters," only those familiar with the small-screen series will get many of the film's characters and references. Despite attempts to make "The X-Files" palatable to nonbelievers, its creators couldn't resist a series of complicit winks to the cognoscenti that can only irritate those not in the know.

"The X-Files" movie is put together by many of the same people responsible for the series, starting with writer-producer Chris Carter, the show's creator. Director Rob Bowman has directed 25 episodes over five years, and editor Stephen Mark and composer Mark Snow are both veterans as well. So it's not surprising that what we've got here is essentially a big-budget version of the small screen, kind of a "Triple-X-Files" to reward the faithful.

With its shrewd mixture of paranoia and the paranormal, the way its elaborate mythology combines enigmatic phenomena with potent cabals intent on running the world, "The X-Files" experience resembles "Twin Peaks" crossed with "The Twilight Zone." It's even replete with recurring characters without real names: Who is the Cigarette-Smoking Man (William B. Davis) after all but the Log Lady with a bad nicotine habit?

At the heart of things are Fox Mulder (David Duchovny) and Dana Scully (Gillian Anderson), a pair of FBI agents usually assigned to investigate the inexplicable. The film awkwardly attempts to fill in five years' worth of back story on this pair, letting us know that Mulder is the true believer who thinks his sister was abducted by aliens, while Scully is the cool, unflappable rationalist, someone not quick to believe sinister forces are out to control the universe.

When the movie opens, Mulder and Scully have been reassigned to an anti-terrorism unit in the Dallas FBI bureau, the X-Files having been officially closed. While they're trying to prevent a major bomb from going off, something seriously weird is going on in a small town in rural Texas.

In an echo of something we saw happen 35,000 years ago, a boy stumbles onto an underground cave and gets more than he bargained for from a skull he encounters. Local paramedics are called and suddenly the area is teaming with helicopters, unmarked tanker trucks and impatient men in white quarantine suits. "That impossible scenario we never planned for," a man says into a phone. "We better come up with a plan."

If this sounds vague, it's because "The X-Files" likes it that way. Writer Carter, director Bowman and cinematographer Ward Russell are expert at doling out information one intriguing dollop at a time. Things get more or less explained by the close, but the fun of "The X-Files" is clearly more in the creation of unease than in the cleaning up of mysteries.

Though the inside baseball stuff, like the appearance of three oddballs known as the Lone Gunmen that no one but constant viewers will understand, let alone appreciate, is a continual frustration, the rest of the movie is a properly spooky, always professional diversion that is happiest when it's throwing continual plot complexities into the mix.

At the center of things is Dr. Alvin Kurtzweil (veteran Martin Landau), a renegade scientist who says he was a friend of Mulder's father. His knowledge of all things sinister leads Mulder and Scully to not only the Cigarette-Smoking Man but also the Well-Manicured Man (John

Neville) and an operative who has the audacity to have a real name, albeit the strange one of Conrad Strughold (Armin Mueller-Stahl).

As much as these creepy doings, it's the too-hip relationship between Mulder and Scully (co-workers who never resort to first names and have a lot of conversations on mobile phones) that is a major "X-Files" attraction. Their supercool attitudes, however, are too distant to work as well on the big screen, and the intense interest devotees have in whether they'll ever kiss is not one that beginning viewers should expect to share in.

While it's not the ideal introduction to the phenomenon, this feature is assured of at least an "X-Files"-sized audience. People are always happy to believe, as Hamlet (who would've been a viewer had the show been available) said to a friend: "There are more things in heaven and earth, Horatio, than are dreamt of in your philosophy."

NEW STATESMAN, 8/21/98, p. 44, Gerald Kaufman

Let us pretend that there is no such thing as the cult TV series "The X-Files." Let us pretend that we have never beard of the FBI agents Mulder and Scully, whose self-imposed assignment, week after week, is to combat the US government's cover-up of plans against our planet by scheming extraterrestrials. Let us approach the new full-length movie, "The X-Files," as though it were just that, a new movie, with no external resonance.

What do we have before us? First, two stalwart patriots, the preoccupied Mulder (David Duchovny)—and who would not be a mite preoccupied if he was convinced he had witnessed his kid sister abducted by aliens?—and his smarter, sassier partner, Scully (Gillian Anderson, wearing a perpetual pout and selections from her extensive wardrobe of power-dress outfits).

Arrayed against them, in chiaroscuro lighting supplied by the director of photography, Ward Russell, is a variety of shadowy governmental functionaries whose primary preoccupation is not to protect the US but to prevent Mulder and Scully from thwarting the schemes of FEMA (the Federal Emergency Management Agency—the secret government) "to conceal the truth about the existence of extraterrestrials".

So we come to "the impossible scenario that we have never planned for". It first manifests itself in an opening sequence set 37,000 years ago, when two cavemen are felled, amid much flashy editing and alarming sound effects, by a fatal essence closely resembling chocolate sauce.

Jump forward to the present day when the sauce claims a small boy, whose friends, on encountering Mulder and Scully, dismiss them with the derisive and not unperceptive put down, "Y'all look like door-to-door salesmen". Even so, Scully recognises something is amiss ("This is weird, Mulder!"), especially when she conducts a post mortem—for, conveniently, she is a doctor—on the corpse, which she has with foresight snatched, of a fireman who was prey to the chocolate sauce.

Now they know what they are up against, and fearsome it is. Despite FEMA's attempts to undermine Scully's loyalty to Mulder ("they wanted me to invalidate your investigations into the paranormal"), the partners are on the track of "a plague to end all plagues, a virus that has mutated into a new extraterrestrial biological entity". As one expert puts it: "We are nothing but digestives for the creation of a new race of alien life form." What Mulder and Scully have blundered into is a rerun, in colour and with state-of-the-art special effects, of the 1956 classic "Invasion of the Body Snatchers."

Obviously, they are not going to stand for that. They know full well what happened to Kevin McCarthy and Dana Wynter, and they are not about to let it happen to them. Going into action, they deploy their mobile phones with a relentless addictiveness which would arouse the envy of passengers on Virgin trains.

They receive the assistance of a broody scientist, Dr Alvin Kurtzweil (Martin Landau), who at first seems to be a baddy, then turns out to be a goody, and is consequently bumped off by FEMA. The trail leads, via some inexplicable trips to "the county of Somerset" and the Royal Albert Hall, to a mock-up Antarctica.

The dauntless agents' pursuit of the truth naturally involves perils, most particularly when Scully is assaulted by a killer bee which carries the virus. Never fear. The Well-Manicured Man (John Neville, a regular on the TV series) is at hand to provide Mulder with a syringe which, of course, is far more potent: "The vaccine you hold is the only defence against the virus." FEMA, though enraged ("Mulder has the vaccine!"), is complacent: "Mulder will never make 'it." But smug cinema-goers, confident that X-Files 2 will shortly be in the pipeline, know different. Hurtling through the snow into a bunker somewhat resembling the Spirit Zone in the Millennium Dome (which arouses the disconcerting question: is Peter Mandelson planning a counterpart of FEMA for Blairite Britain?), Mulder tracks Scully down to a storeroom where she is stacked in a deep-freeze. A fairy prince with the mission of waking the Sleeping Beauty, he plunges the syringe into her and, into the bargain, gives her the kiss of life—the nearest the pair get to sexual contact in the movie's two-hour running time. Antarctica implodes; the aliens scuttle off in disgrace. We move to Tunisia, where a telegram announces: "X-Files reopened" (no news to cynical know-alls in the audience) as the end credits roll.

NEW YORK, 7/13/98, p. 42, David Denby

I think it's useless to complain as many people have, that "The X-Files" never makes any damn sense. This is a movie that is not supposed to make any damn sense. The material's unfathomability—its dedication to dark conspiracies, the powerful "they" controlling the chewing-gum supply for the entire world—is what gives the TV show its mass-cult zing of excitement. For the uninitiated, however, the movie is only moderately entertaining. David Duchovny and Gillian Anderson certainly bring a practiced rhythm to their deadpan gibberish dialogues. Duchovny's morosely preoccupied manner, as if he were trying hard to swallow the end of his nose, matches up nicely with Anderson's suppressed excitement as she grazes his face with her eyelashes. Apart from that, one is constrained by duty to point out that the director, Rob Bowman, employs the same horror-film trope over and over. Either Duchovny or Anderson or both enter a dangerous and enclosed place—an alley, a laboratory, a booby-trapped building, a cave, an enormous warehouse. They are menaced by something strange; they escape. If it weren't for one scene involving bees, who are all terrific, none of these encounters would amount to a thing.

NEW YORK POST, 6/19/98, p. 43, Rod Dreher

"The X-Files: Fight the Future" is a corkscrew flume ride down the rabbit hole of stylized paranoia. Which is to say, it's the same swell old dung from series creator Chris Carter, only more of it, and with the kind of special effects you can buy only on a big-film budget.

In bringing the popular TV show to the silver screen, screenwriter Carter and series helmsman Rob Bowman have almost pulled off a neat trick: They advance the plot of a dramatic series that's been running for five years without leaving "X-Files" newbies behind. Mostly.

To me, an infrequent "X-Files" viewer, the film's relentless conspiracy theorizing feels like piling on, leaving plot holes unplugged while on a mad scramble to cover as much ground as possible. But in the X-world of shadows, fog and paranonish goo, apparently nothing succeeds like excess. And if you yield to the seductive siren song of Carter's plangent, creepy-cool atmospherics—and stars David Duchovny and Gillian Anderson, as well as their supporting cast, make it easy to do—"The X-Files" movie unspools as a smart, satisfying summer rip.

Unless you've been captive on an alien spaceship for the last five years, you know that FBI special agents Fox Mulder (David Duchovny) and Dana Scully (Gillian Anderson) are G-persons who investigate the bizarre and unexplained.

Mulder is a true believer. Scully is rationalist skeptic. The pair's world is a house of mirrors in which certain characters, such as the evil Cigarette-Smoking Man (William B. Davis), recur as part of a sinister cabal.

The movie opens with a child falling into a long-hidden cave in the suburban scrublands just outside—where else?—Dallas. The kid succumbs in an especially gross manner to a mysterious oil that has been there since prehistoric times. Before you can say "Zapruder," the feds swoop down on the site with their bio-suits and white tanker trucks.

Enter Mulder and Scully, stuck doing meat-and-potatoes duty in Big D since the agency's X-Files were closed out at the end of the last TV season. The duo discover a massive bomb in a building housing the Federal Emergency Management Agency, and barely escape when it goes kablooey.

Back in D.C., Mulder, morose and drunk and relieving himself on an "Independence Day" poster in the alley behind a bar, is approached by the pale, gruesome Dr. Kurtzweil (Martin

Landau). He tells Mulder that the bombing was a cover story to hide a terrifying truth. (Hint: That mystery oil turns people into the world's most disgusting dollop of flan—and worse.)

The pursuit of truth leads the intrepid Mulder and Scully, the Moose and Squirrel of modish postmodern paranoia, on a fantastic voyage involving killer bees, homicidal fetal aliens and a credulity-straining finale under the Antarctic permafrost. The truth, it seems, is down there.

If "The X-Files" movie disappoints with its kitchen-sink plotting and overreaching scope, there's plenty to cherish in the picaresque moments and the wry lines Carter tosses off like glow-in-the-dark Mardi Gras doubloons.

The bone-dry Duchovny and the vulnerable Anderson do their usual sexy, controlled burn here. They're just as good together on the big screen as they are on the small, which is not easy to do.

(Ask the "Friends" cast.) The "X-Files" movie plays like an expensive, Very Special Episode of the TV show. And with a show this imaginative, that's no bad thing.

NEWSDAY, 6/19/98, Part II/p. B3, Jack Mathews

The best moment in the $60-million, widescreen, industrial-strength film version of Fox TV's "The X-Files" comes when FBI agent Mulder staggers drunk into an alley and urinates on an "Independence Day" poster. It's the only moment where the filmmakers reveal the slightest hint of irony about their mission to introduce the award-winning series' popular characters to a whole new audience.

In a commercial-free two-hour TV show that strives to be constantly on the verge of cosmic epiphany, the alley scene is as much a relief for the audience as it is for Mulder (David Duchovny). For a few moments, at least, we're not in breathless anxiety over evidence of alien life, mutating extraterrestrial viruses, global conspiracies and impending Armageddon.

For those unfamiliar with the series, "The X-Files" is sort of a combination "Twin Peaks," "JFK" and "Invasion of the Body Snatchers," in which agents Mulder and Scully (Gillian Anderson) are on the trail of a world-wide conspiracy involving governments and savage aliens. Running the conspiracy is a cabal of aging white guys, who are apparently in cahoots with other life forms to create a super race, and who put up with the meddling Mulder because to kill him might turn one man's religion into a crusade.

The advance word on the movie episode was that it would tie up the loose ends that have kept the "X-File" faithful on tenterhooks for five years. It does, and it doesn't. Series creator-producer Chris Carter came up with a story that has a beginning, a middle, and a conventional big-budget thriller ending, then tacks on a coda that seems to take it all back. While one conspiracy is revealed, we're assured it's only a drop in a very big bucket. Tune in next week.

Thanks, no.

"The "X-Files" may be heartstopping cult TV, but it's a big bore on the big screen. Though it has the look, the sound and the pyrotechnic effects of a major studio action film, it is very plainly an episode of a television show whose allure is in its premise and its continuing characters and whose pace is that of a story building toward commercials.

Few people who are not already fans of "The X-Files" are going to find much here to hold their interest. In this episode, co-written by Carter and series regular Frank Spotnitz, Mulder and Scully are clued to a conspiracy by a mysterious science-fiction writer (Martin Landau, as bug-eyed intense as he's ever been), who joins Mulder at the "Independence Day" poster and suggests that a boy and two fire fighters thought killed in the bombing of a federal building had actually died of an anti-virus.

Pursuing the case with a determination that gets them in deep doo-doo with their own agency, Mulder and Scully are soon up to their ears in killers, cornfields, African bee swarms and subterranean Antarctic space stations, culminating in a race against the clock as Mulder rushes a vaccine to save his partner—who's infected with the alien disease—and mankind.

For all the talk about aliens, little is shown of them. We see only shadowy figures, with the occasional glimpse of jaws and claws, as they attack people. Whether Carter didn't want to give too much,away, or his production team, which includes regular series director Rob Bowman, didn't know how to do it, their physical absence is a serious flaw in a science-fiction movie.

And for the uninitiated, the "X-Files" cast is a dull lot. Duchovny is a flat, uninteresting actor playing a humorless, uninteresting character, and Anderson, though she's shown great presence in several recent films, is an intentionally aloof and unattractive Scully. I gather from a couple of scenes of near kisses that the show has toyed with the idea of an unfulfilled romance between the agents, but without that context, their relationship is void of anything other than professional trust.

Other series regulars along for this episode are FBI Assistant Director Skinner (Mitch Pileggi), the Cigarette-Smoking Man (William B. Davis), and the Well-Manicured Man (John Neville). Newcomers include Armin Mueller-Stahl, as one of the conspiracy leaders, and Blythe Danner, as the head of the FBI.

SIGHT AND SOUND, 9/98, p. 55, Kim Newman

North Texas, 35,000 BC. Two proto-humans are killed by an alien. The present. Stevie, a young boy, discovers the cavern where the fatal encounter took place, is invaded by a liquid lifeform and is spirited away by a covert task force. In Dallas, FBI agents Mulder and Scully, recently removed from the 'X Files' (a programme of paranormal investigations) look into a bomb threat to a federal building. Special-Agent-in-Charge Michaud orders the building to be evacuated but stays inside. Michaud lets it explode, killing him and seemingly several other people left behind. In Washington DC, Scully faces a hearing board trying to assign blame for the deaths. Conspiracy crank Kurtzweil tells Mulder that the bodies (including Stevie) found in Dallas were already dead when the building exploded and were infected with an extraterrestrial virus.

In Texas, at the site of Stevie's discovery, scientist Bronschweig (the employee of a cartel of conspirators who have opposed Mulder's crusade) finds the virus has gestated inside a human host and hatched into a killer alien, which is buried along with him. Mulder and Scully follow the trail to an installation where they are attacked by virus infected bees. Scully is stung and spirited away in an ambulance by the Dallas bomber. Kurtzweil is killed, and a conscience-stricken English conspirator tells Mulder that the alliance between the aliens and the cartel is shaky. It seems the colonising aliens intend not to enslave humanity but to use people as incubators. The conspirator gives Mulder an antidote for the virus and directs him to a complex in Antarctica, but is then killed.

Escaping from the complex with a recovering Scully, Mulder realises that it is a vast spaceship, which rises from the ice. In Washington, Mulder persuades Scully to stay with the FBI and him. In Tunisia, arch-conspirator Strughold learns the 'X Files' have been reopened.

Raymond Chandler famously claimed that whenever he reached an impasse in a plot, he would have "a man come through a door with a gun." ' *The X Files* creator-writer producer Chris Carter's preferred resort, perhaps influenced by a (terrible) scene in *Jacob's Ladder* , is to have his hero dragged into an alley by a man with an explanation. Twice in this feature based on the hit television series, Mulder seems stumped by circumstances only to have ambiguous father figures (Martin Landau's Kurtzweil, John Neville's Well-Manicured Man) drag him into an alley and deliver lengthy speeches. This saves him the trouble of doing any detective work. Not only do these men provide information on what's going on, but they also hand over an antidote to the alien virus and a map reference for the base in Antarctica where Scully is stashed. If our hero needs this much help to get anywhere, one wonders why the conspiracy cartel bother to worry about him, though they have also refrained for five seasons from getting rid of him as easily as they dispose of Kurtzweil (framed as a child pornographer) and the Well-Manicured Man (the traditional car bomb).

The series has run for long enough to demonstrate its diversity and its limitations. After five years, there are now four distinct types of *X Files* episode: post modern jokey, clever self-satires; straight crime stories with a parapsychological twist; rampaging mutant/monster/paraphenomenon horror tales; and the developing it's-all-a-government-conspiracy strand.

Unfortunately, most of the series is comprised of the fourth and least effective of the types. So this spin-off has to slot in with a run of clunky stories, many told as two-part episodes, in which mystification is all and revelations are doled out at the rate of two or three a season. For the benefit of those who've been paying attention, the movie picks up on minor themes from the show (the infected bees) and the recurring characters (the Cigarette-Smoking Man, here mostly a stooge). However, aside from confirming hints already dropped that the alliance between the aliens and their human quislings is shaky, nothing new is revealed.

Continuing threads, such as the alleged alien abduction of Mulder's sister and his own uncertain paternity (every older male character is a surrogate or possible actual father to the leads), are mentioned in the film's funniest speech but dropped. What has assured the series' crossover mainstream appeal beyond sci-fi cultists is the relationship between Mulder and Scully. In a witty but cruel touch, their repressed attraction seems about to lead finally to something more when they hug in a corridor, close to an epoch-making smooch. Then an alien-infected killer bee trapped under the collar of Scully's severe suit stings her, ruining the moment and precipitating the rest of the plot. David Duchovny and Gillian Anderson are solid in their regular roles, but the expansion to a big screen and the use of the conspiracy theme perhaps makes them less dominant figures than they might be and curbs their comic potential. (Anderson in particular has to be a spoilsport straight person.)

Taken as a film on its own, *The X Files* is mostly an effective conjuring trick. Television director Rob Bowman effectively manages suspense and spectacle in several sequences: Michaud calmly not defusing the bomb that blows him up; Bronschweig realising that his team-mates are burying him alive with a killer alien; the agents exploring automated hives in sinister white marquees before the bees are loosed on them (a textbook example of creepiness turning into horror). But after an hour or so, the random dumbness becomes wearisome as the map hopping storyline ineptly posits one thing after another, with expository speeches sweeping plot debris under the carpet and apparently important characters killed off-screen. The cavernous underground installation that turns out to be an *Independence Day* style spaceship (a rude joke paying back the dismissal of the series in that movie) and the icequake of its take-off are stunning but meaningless effects, offering are stunning but meaningless effects, offering "is-that-it?" answers to long standing mysteries.

TIME, 6/28/98, p. 70, Richard Corliss

From the beginning, the show was swathed in conspiracy; it begged to be suspected of as much far-fetched chicanery as it imputed to all those Trilateral geezers who look like Clark Clifford. Take our hero, Fox Mulder—his first name is the same as the network that owns the show. Mulder's FBI boss, the skinheaded Skinner, is a dead ringer for former Fox chief Barry Diller. And just what is the name of the show? *The X Files*, as the logo clearly states? Or *The X-Files*, as the publicity indicates?

So you can imagine the anxious speculation when Chris Carter's terrific series, which has turned the paranormal and paranoidal into Sunday-night morality plays, becomes a theatrical movie. Will the canonical secrets (about, say, Mulder's lost sister Samantha, purportedly abducted by aliens when she was nine) be explained? Will the shows dense mythology, replayed in the feature film, confound those ignorant of the backstory? Will the film disappoint the X-philes, the most demanding fans around?

In three words: no, yes, maybe. *The X-Files*, directed by series veteran Rob Bowman, looks damned handsome under the big-screen magnifying glass, with a rapturous clarity of golden and dark hues replacing the enveloping murk of the series. The two stars smartly fill their close-ups: David Duchovny (Mulder) adds a bit of cowboy swagger to his Prince of Dweebs intensity, while Gillian Anderson (as Mulder's skeptical partner Scully) radiates a '40s-style pensiveness that alchemizes glum into glam. The characters' devotion to each other—a caring that stops tantalizingly short of sexuaiity—constitutes one of the great unconsummated marriages in popular fiction. And their wondrous solemnity is a tonic in this age of facetiousness.

The movie has enough plot (by Carter and Frank Spotnitz) to stock a half-season of shows. Let's see ... a virus from aliens has been harvested and is about to be spread, by bees and corn oil, across the world—"a plague to end all plagues," whispers kook-savant Dr. Alvin Kurtzweil (Martin Landau), who spends most of his time hiding in a fetid back alley hoping Mulder will show up. The aliens, you see, were earth's original inhabitants, and they are being tracked by that all-round evilest of government conspiracies, FEMA (the Federal Emergency Management Agency). We feel ourselves sliding deeper into Art Bell territory—into the all-night radioland of sci-fi-cobabble. Believe who will. Follow who can.

If the movie declines to enthrall, it is because its creators forgot what makes the show shine. An hour of dense thoughtfulness and outrageous gamesmanship, it often steps ahead of its canniest viewers, never afraid to mystify or end with a shivery question mark. Skull and Mull—braininess and wondering.

But Carter has turned this complex talk show into an action movie, with lots of running and falling and hauling, from North Texas to the Antarctic. It's as if the cleverest grind in class were told he had to retake P.E. before he could graduate. And that's too bad—enough to turn an X-phile into an ex-phile.

VILLAGE VOICE, 6/30/98, p. 133, J. Hoberman

A quick flashback to 35,000 B.C. notwithstanding, *The X-Files* picks up more or less where the season finale ended—with the FBI's special two-person extraterrestrial-conspiracy unit shut down. It's obvious, though, that there's plenty of material yet for the files when an office building is bombed in Dallas as a government cover-up. Soon agents Fox Mulder (David Duchovny) and Dana Scully (Gillian Anderson) are bouncing back and forth between D.C. and Texas, accumulating icky clues and conducting clandestine autopsies. Meanwhile, the Well-Manicured Man meets in London with the rest of the illuminati to explain that their conspiracy is endangered: "The virus has mutated!"

Underlit, moody, and lugubrious, *The X-Files* has a classier look than most summer fare but, despite the cave-ins, violent (if obscure) alien creatures, and presence of Martin Landau as an OB-GYN UFOlogist, it's slow going—not to mention obvious X-ploitation. The movie is basically a long TV episode affording less new info than the pleasure of watching familiar icons on the big screen. See the light sculpt the lush ridges of the Anderson profile. Enjoy agent Mulder, less inhibited than Billy Brown, take a back alley whiz on a poster of Fox's all-time summer blockbuster *Independence Day*. Ponder his absence of affect and her bug-eyed stare of incredulity. Do agents Mulder and Scully finally kiss? Are there black helicopters in Idaho?

Also reviewed in:
CHICAGO TRIBUNE, 6/19/98, Friday/p. A, Michael Wilmington
NEW YORK TIMES, 6/19/98, p. E1, Janet Maslin
VARIETY, 6/22-28/98, p. 50, Todd McCarthy
WASHINGTON POST, 6/19/98, p. B1, Rita Kempley
WASHINGTON POST, 6/19/98, Weekend/p. 47, Michael O'Sullivan

YOUR FRIENDS & NEIGHBORS

A Gramercy Pictures release of a PolyGram Filmed Entertainment presentation of Propaganda Films/Fleece production.   *Executive Producer:* Alix Madigan-Yorkin and Stephen Pevner. *Producer:* Steve Golin and Jason Patric.   *Director:* Neil LaBute.   *Screenplay:* Neil LaBute. *Director of Photography:* Nancy Schreiber.   *Editor:* Joel Plotch.   *Music:* Frankie Pine.   *Music Editor:* Ron Finn.   *Sound:* Felipe Borrero.   *Sound Editor:* Christopher Sheldon and Dane A. Davis.   *Casting:* Mali Finn.   *Production Designer:* Charles Breen. *Art Director:* Melissa Mollo. *Set Decorator:* Jeffrey Kushon.   *Costumes:* April Napier.   *Make-up:* Desne Holland.   *Running time:* 100 minutes. *MPAA Rating:* R.

CAST: Amy Brenneman (Mary);   Aaron Eckhart (Barry);   Catherine Keener (Terri); Nastassja Kinski (Cheri);   Jason Patric (Cary);   Ben Stiller (Jerry).

CHRISTIAN SCIENCE MONITOR, 8/21/98, p. B3, David Sterritt

From its title, you might think "Your Friends & Neighbors" is a friendly, neighborly kind of movie. But you'll know better if you saw Neil LaBute's previous picture, "In the Company of Men," one of last year's most talked-about independent films.

The clue to his new drama is in the ampersand between "friends" and "neighbors," as if this were an advertising slogan or a listing in the classified ads. Old-fashioned human relations don't interest LaBute much. What he wants to probe are the self-centered interconnections that sprout between people in a commercialized, commodified, endlessly competitive society.

LaBute is an equal-opportunity cynic, so he aims his scathingly satirical vision at Generation X in general, without narrowing his attacks to a particular place or profession. The city where his story takes place is never identified, and even the names of his characters are left unspoken.

This contributes to what LaBute calls a "distancing effect," meant to give the movie a sense of objective truthfulness. Audiences can judge the success of this strategy by deciding whether the story is a convincing expose or a sensationalistic diatribe.

The main characters are a half dozen young urbanites who hook one another into a complicated web of friendship, romance, rivalry, deception, and betrayal. On the surface they're everyday friends and neighbors. Just below the surface, so close you can sense it by peering into their eyes, they're preoccupied with their own lowdown lusts, and with the tactics they can deploy—from locker-room gossiping to lying, cheating, and stealing—to satisfy their latest impulses. Needless to say, barriers like marriage, camaraderie, and commitment count for just about nothing in this environment.

Except that it has twice as many characters, "Your Friends & Neighbors" concocts the same sort of atmosphere LaBute gave to "In the Company of Men," about two businessmen who heap emotional abuse on a deaf secretary as revenge against the women they feel have wronged them over the years. Both movies are flawed by LaBute's sledgehammer approach.

The mood is often more coarse, crude, and nasty than needed to make his cautionary points and also by that "distancing effect," which diminishes whatever feelings of empathy or sympathy the story might otherwise inspire its audience.

"Your Friends & Neighbors" has the indie version of a cream cast—Ben Stiller, Catherine Keener, Aaron Eckhart, Amy Brenneman, Jason Patric, and Nastassja Kinski—and Nancy Schreiber's camera work gives the picture more visual life than "In the Company of Men" contained. The music score consists largely of Metallica songs performed by Apocalyptica, suiting the picture's overall tone to perfection.

LOS ANGELES TIMES, 8/19/98, Calendar/p. 1, Kenneth Turan

The milk of human kindness does not flow through Neil LaBute's films. Taking the baleful futility of personal relationships as a theme, his is rather a cinema of humiliation, embarrassment and misery, the celluloid equivalent of a round-the-clock news station that offers all jerks, all the time.

Writer-director LaBute's remarkably sour and cynical view of human nature couldn't be better suited to gather plaudits in the times we live in. His debut film, the neo-provocative "In the Company of Men," won awards at Sundance and elsewhere for its story of a deaf woman callously seduced by two friends.

His new work, "Your Friends & Neighbors," is more of the same. Set among a group of six young professionals in an unnamed city, it once again confuses a kind of juvenile titillation with insight and treats the ability to make audiences squirm as a pinnacle of film art.

Typically, it's the worst of LaBute's characters we encounter first, devil-in-the-flesh Cary (Jason Patric). A frigid and emotionless misogynist, he's discovered trying out potential sex talk while masturbating and tape-recording his efforts for later study. "If I was a chick," he muses to himself, pleased at the result, "I'd believe this."

Though Cary is unattached, his two closest friends are involved with women, and, given LaBute's thesis that relationships consist of varying degrees of agony, hostility and pretense, it's not surprising that they're not happy with their situations.

Jerry (Ben Stiller), a college professor, likes to talk during sex, something that drives his partner Terri (Catherine Keener) over the edge. "Let's just do it, I don't need the narration," she curtly insists, and that's about the nicest thing you'll hear her say. This couple specializes in verbally flaying each other, trading cutting remarks as if they were baseball cards.

As miserable as everyone else, Barry ("Company of Men's" Aaron Eckhart) and Mary (Amy Brenneman) are more lost than malicious, vacuous people whose attempts at connection are feeble and doomed. Given that they're not quite as pompous, self-involved and insensitive as the other characters, they're ripe to become hapless victims of their more rapacious cohorts.

It's Jerry who gets things going, deciding out of habit to attempt to seduce Mary, the wife of his friend. When Terri gets a hint of this, she starts to look appreciatively at Cheri (Nastassja Kinski), an art gallery employee she happens to run into. Bad as everyone's relationships start out, it's a given with LaBute that things are going to get worse, much worse, and that's what transpires here.

Though LaBute treats characters like an inquiring entomologist, using several distancing techniques and examining his specimens at arm's length whenever possible, he does have a flair for writing very playable dialogue. Naturally, it's the darkest characters, Terri and Cary, who have the most glib lines, and actor Patric (one of the film's co-producers) gives the most compelling performance, complete with a monologue on male rape that almost got the film an NC-17 rating.

Part of the reason LaBute's work causes a stir is that that dialogue, raunchier and racier than the norm, offers minor-league thrills on the order of overhearing something private on an airplane or in a restaurant. But LaBute's delight in showing what's behind the facades people are prone to put up comes off as little more than the tittle-tattle of a naughty boy delighted to have caught the grown-ups in compromising situations.

It's not that the kind of bad behavior, especially male, this film revels in doesn't exist. It's that merely presenting the worst view of life in a concentrated form is not by definition compelling or involving—it has to be made that way. The more things are merely presented, the harder it is to say what aspect of the situation is supposed to interest us.

Despite what the modern sensibility dictates, being completely and unalterably bleak about human motivations and relationships is not any wiser, smarter or more realistic than being totally Pollyannaish. Though they are poles apart in every other respect, "Your Friends & Neighbors," that veneer of hipness notwithstanding, doesn't say anything more profound or insightful about the human condition than "The Sound of Music."

NEW YORK, 8/31/98, p. 155, David Denby

When people described Neil LaBute's first movie, *In the Company of Men,* as a satire of male viciousness and corporate rancor, I thought they were kidding themselves: The movie took too much gloating pleasure in sadism, and left too few outlets for sane or even rational behavior, to be anything other than a covert endorsement of what it allegedly deplored. LaBute's new work, *Your Friends & Neighbors*, draws on the same spirit of nihilism and despair, and I think it's safe to say that LaBute, dramatically speaking, has found the world in which he wants to live. The movie is set in Woody Allen territory—educated Manhattan, art galleries, adultery—and its theme is that no one knows how to love, or even how to *make* love. Essentially, we are all masturbators.

The male characters, three friends, are a schlep (Aaron Eckhart) who jerks off next to his sleeping wife, a worm (Ben Stiller) who lies to everyone, and a would-be stud (Jason Patric) who loathes women and is probably gay. The women are only slightly less depressing. There's a prig (Catherine Keener), a mope (Amy Brenneman), and a sweet lesbian (Nastassja Kinski) doomed to have the same inane conversation with every person who comes into her art gallery. These six people manipulate and betray one another in a series of short, desperate scenes that simply don't play—the characters stammer through sentence fragments, or engage in long, preposterous erotic monologues that, oddly, are never mentioned again. LaBute isn't creating drama, he's showing off. This kind of betray-your-friends nastiness is best expressed in the manner of Waugh, Pinter, or Frederic Raphael, in which venom is released as coldly literate wit, and we can enjoy it as a stylization of bad behavior. *Your Friends & Neighbors* is both vicious and earnest, an excruciating combination. I don't ask for pleasantness, but there has to be some way of making us care about the people in a movie, or else we are wasting our time with stumblers and schmucks. Neil LaBute obliterates his characters, his scenes, and, ultimately, himself.

NEW YORK POST, 8/19/98, p. 47, Thelma Adams

When I was a teen, I loved the twangy Charlie Rich chestnut that went something like: "When we get behind closed doors." It seemed like the pleasures of the adult world existed in bedrooms down the block and next door and in my own house—and all I had to do, someday, was open the door.

When writer-director Neil LaBute opens the door on "Your Friends & Neighbors," it's like a little boy raising a rotted log. The bugs and worms of contemporary adult sexual relationships come scurrying out.

In his dark follow-up to the sleeper "In the Company of Men," LaBute follows these sorry specimens with an intense glee before stepping on them with his sneakers.

Now, we're in the company of three men—and three women. Their rhyming names give the game away—Mary, Barry, Terri, Cheri, Cary and Jerry. These are prototypes: bourgie, middle-class whites with too much time on their hands and their hands down each other's pants.

Cary (Jason Patric) tosses the first ball. We see him making rough love to an unseen object, only to discover he's talking dirty to his pillow and timing himself. He's such a chilly guy, he's practicing sounding human for his next soulless conquest.

Then there's Jerry (Ben Stiller), a shallow drama teacher and philanderer who'd chat up his best friend's wife, Mary (Amy Brenneman)—and does. Mary and hubby Barry (Aaron Ekhart, the "Company" villain) have the perfect yuppie marriage on the surface, but when you get behind closed doors...

And Jerry and his girlfriend Terri (the barbed Catherine Keener) can't make love without bickering. LaBute denies them the privileged airbrushed sex of the typical Hollywood movie where every encounter is a Saturday night special. Instead, he's chattering and she stops him cold with: "Let's just do it, I don't need the narration."

Soon, Terri has strayed into the arms of Cheri (Natassja Kinski)—but she still doesn't want the woman to talk during sex. And Jerry pursues Mary and Barry is clueless and Cary makes a confession that's nearly as horrifying as anything "In the Company of Men."

For audiences who want a character to identify with, forget it. While the shuffling beds are farcical, the acting keen, and the laughs constant, the characters neither get what they deserve nor see the light.

In LaBute's darkly satisfying vision, what you see behind doors is not pleasure, but pain. There's nothing neighborly about these friends, nor friendly about these neighbors. LaBute roughly tears back the sheets on the deceptions deployed by many modern couples. He's made their beds; we have to lie in them.

NEWSWEEK, 8/24/98, p. 58, David Ansen

The most detestable character in Neil LaBute's "Your Friends and Neighbors" is a misogynistic lothario played by Jason Patric. He's first seen tape-recording his own simulated sex act, rehearsing the amorous lines he'll use on his next victim. Later he launches into a vicious tirade against one of his (unseen) conquests, who has fouled his designer sheets with her menstrual blood. (On top of his woman-hating, he's anal retentive.) Worse still, he proudly tells his best friend (Aaron Eckhart) how he punished a woman who dumped him by sending her a note on hospital stationery informing her she was HIV-positive. "The bitch deserved it," he smugly explains.

As anyone who saw LaBute's incendiary first feature, "In the Company of Men," knows, this writer-director has a gift for creating loathsome leading men. Chad, the character Eckhart played in that film, was a white-collar sadist who took delight in humiliating both a deaf woman and a corporate rival. "Your Friends and Neighbors" is clearly the work of the same, misanthropically inclined observer. This time his focus is on the sexual relations between men and women. There are six unnamed characters, three men and three women, all of whom are engaged in either inflicting or enduring misery.

Ben Stiller, who plays a drama teacher, announces to his class while rehearsing a Restoration comedy: "It's all about f---ing." LaBute, who would like us to think he is writing a black neo-Restoration comedy for the '90s, clearly agrees. All the characters are introduced in bed, having a bad time. Stiller's razor-edged girlfriend (Catherine Keener) calls an abrupt halt to their coitus to complain about his incessant talking. The hapless Eckhart prefers masturbation to sex with his sweet, masochistic wife (Amy Brenneman), which makes her perk up when the wormy Stiller, her husband's friend, suggests they have an affair. Keener, meanwhile, takes Nastassja Kinski as a lover: what begins happily soon turns as sour as all the other affairs.

The nastiness of "In the Company of Men" felt new, shocking, revelatory. The nastiness of "Your Friends and Neighbors" feels old, mechanical, jejune. Too many writers have mined this scorched turf before—from Strindberg to savage early Edward Albee dramas to Wallace Shawn raging-id plays like "Marie and Bruce." LaBute isn't uncovering any shocking new truths about the human condition. A half hour into "Your Friends and Neighbors," you know everything you need to know about these characters. Dramatically, they've got nowhere to go—LaBute has closed the case against them from the get-go. Too many scenes—such as Patric's unlikely monologue about "the best lay he ever had"—feel as if they're just there for effect.

LaBute can turn an amusingly nasty phrase, but his deliberately theatrical direction makes this all-indoors movie more static than it needs to be. What keeps you in your seat is the acting. Keener, crisply and coolly playing against type, commands the screen. Brenneman says more with her eyes and her body than her sad, needy character says aloud. Patric is the only performer who seems to be trying too hard. Instead of playing against this guy's callousness, he underlines it. Why, you wonder, would anybody spend five minutes with this jerk? A hefty Eckhart is almost unrecognizable as the pathetic cuckold. Stiller, playing a dishonest weasel, is squirmily funny. But coming on the heels of "There's Something About Mary," the movie makes one think he's a glutton for punishment. Made up and shot to look creepy, Stiller gets as much abuse from LaBute as he did from the Farrelly brothers—though here the humiliations are more moral than physical. A couple more roles like these and he'll qualify for a Purple Heart.

SIGHT AND SOUND, 10/98, p. 61, Peter Matthews

Terri and her husband Jerry argue about his talking too much during intercourse. Barry admits to his best friend Cary that he's only sexually fulfilled through masturbation. Barry tries valiantly to perform for his wife Mary, but fails. Barry and Mary invite Jerry and Terri to dinner. Jerry propositions Mary, and she agrees to meet him secretly. At an art gallery, Terri encounters Cheri; they soon begin an affair. Cary later propositions Cheri unsuccessfully. Mary and Jerry arrange a night at a hotel, but Jerry can't perform either. Barry takes Mary to the same hotel room she has just visited with Jerry; once again, he fails to satisfy her.

Cary confesses to Barry and Jerry that his hottest sexual experience involved the gang rape of a male high-school student who had grassed him and his friends up for cheating; annoyed by Barry's teasing, Jerry reveals that his best sexual experience ever was with Barry's wife. Terri discovers Jerry's infidelity with Mary. Cary propositions Terri in a secondhand book store; when she rebuffs him, he gets abusive. Irate that Jerry recommended the hotel room to Barry, Mary tells him their affair is over. Barry confronts Mary, who admits to her fling with Jerry and moves out. Jerry apologises to Barry. Terri tells Jerry about her liaison with Cheri. Jerry insults Cheri at the gallery. Terri moves in with Cheri. Barry tries phone sex, but discovers he is now impotent even with himself. Terri begins to feel irritated by Cheri's need to talk in bed. Cary's new partner is Mary, who weeps all the time, but whom he has managed to make pregnant.

If ours is the age of the plastic feelgood movie, then writer-director Neil LaBute must earn some kind of distinction for single-handedly attempting to counter the tide. In the short history of cinema, there have been relatively few artists who deserve to be called misanthropes. Peter Greenaway is one; LaBute would appear to be another. His second film, *Your Friends & Neighbors*, is a sour, acrid feelbad fable along the lines of his debut feature, the much-praised *In the Company of Men*. The fairly specialised audiences for that film seemed to enjoy the taste of bile in their mouths; it was delectable precisely because one didn't get to sample it every day. Like its predecessor, *Your Friends & Neighbors* aims to strip away the sentimental guff about male-female relationships and expose the ugly, unvarnished truth. In LaBute's universe, everything comes down to the twin engines of power and lust or as Jerry, one of his typical suburban Machiavellis, pithily explains: "It's always about fucking." LaBute plainly wants you to laugh at the compulsive, dysfunctional characters through gritted teeth: they could be your neighbours, they could be yourself. But perhaps I'm not alone in finding his ultra-cynicism offensive—as phoney, shallow and opportunistic as the pieties it inverts.

Jerry is a drama instructor, and in one scene he and a female student perform an extract from William Wycherley's 1672 play *The Country Wife*. No doubt LaBute imagines this movie to be a contemporary version of a Restoration comedy, with the same symmetrical plotting and the same air of sexual ruthlessness. The highly structured storyline unfolds with the neatness of a blueprint or a mathematical equation: six people (two couples and two singles) advance through various combinations and permutations until they arrive pretty much back where they started. In case you're slow to grasp the idea that human behaviour is unchanging throughout the millennia, LaBute decontextualises the action as far as possible (a trick he also employed in *In the Company of Men*). The cyclical narrative occurs in the bedrooms, bars, galleries and supermarkets of some unspecified yuppie land—and there isn't a single exterior shot to help you get your bearings. LaBute's most irritating stunt in this regard is to avoid having the characters refer to each other by name (even the ones listed for convenience in the credits sound spuriously identikit). He might as well come out and admit he thinks everybody's a clone—or at best represents one of a finite number of options in the vaguely social-Darwinist scheme the movie tries to embody.

It's certainly all of a piece in style and content. By and large, LaBute prefers long takes and static, painterly framing. once in a while, he will begin with a tight close-up and then withdraw to a cooler distance (on the few occasions when the camera moves, you're made very aware of it). The effect is of witnessing some human catastrophe like a car crash from far away, shrugging your shoulders philosophically, and saying, "That's life." Probably LaBute's aesthetic (and moral) detachment is what permits the movie's tone of bilious connoisseurship. However, it would be a mistake to confuse the latter with searing emotional truth. It's clear that LaBute means to stop one's breath by including the lengthy monologue where slime bucket Cary expostulates on the spiritual advantages to be gained from committing homosexual gang rape. But besides being psychologically ludicrous, the sequence is too conscious of its own clever malignancy to count as anything more than cheap titillation. The same goes for this whole callow, nasty-minded movie.

VILLAGE VOICE, 8/25/98, p. 123, J. Hoberman

Your Friends & Neighbors, Neil LaBute's follow-up to last summer's cleverest horror film, In the *Company of Men*, is comparably creeped out and claustrophobic—a fascinatingly mean-spirited erotic comedy set in a realm of self-absorbed fantasy and overdetermined intergender misunderstanding.

Venturing into territory where no modern sitcom is yet prepared to go, although not far from the spot where *In the Company of Men* left off, *Your Friends & Neighbors* begins with a flurry of trompe l'oeil nastiness: A sexual athlete rehearses his pillow talk with the help of a tape recorder, a randy professor demonstrates for his students that Restoration comedy is "always about fucking." So, too, LaBute's movie—except that, as subsequent vignettes make abundantly clear, fucking is always about power, failure, and humiliation.

Jerry the drama prof (Ben Stiller) learns that lesson soon enough when his significant other Terri, (Catherine Keener), puts a damper on his verbose lovemaking by asking him to shut up: "This is not a travelogue" (The acerbic Keener has the bitchiest lines in the movie: "Fucking is fucking, it's not a time for sharing," she'll later tell a group of women friends.) Cut from miserable couple A to their friends, miserable couple B. Barry (Aaron Eckhart) fails to respond to his wife Mary (Amy Brenneman)—or is it Mary not responding to Barry, who later tells some guy at work that "nobody makes me come like I do"

Although predicated largely on such one-liners, *Your Friends & Neighbors* develops a narrative when, with Jerry and Terri enjoying a somewhat strained dinner chez Barry and Mary, Jerry takes advantage of an opportune moment to sexually proposition his hostess. Despite Jerry and Mary's fantasies of self-improvement (I'm very optimistic" he tells her as they check into a hotel), adultery proves just as awkward and unsatisfying as every other human relationship in LaBute's movie—although it does set off a realignment of the stars.

Doubling the triangle at the heart of *Company of Men*, *Friends & Neighbors* is enlivened by its ensemble acting. Ben Stiller—the most fearless comic performer in American movies—adds another portrait to his gallery of off-putting neurotics. Stiller's combination of lewd monkey-man and over-analytical nerd draws sparks from both the always estimable Catherine Keener—herself oscillating between cajoling vixen and vicious cojones breaker—and winsome Amy Brenneman, whose Mary is usually a few beats behind the others. Aaron Eckhart, the diabolical seducer of *In the Company of Men*, is punished for his earlier sins—appearing here as a pitiful *zhlub*—while Jason Patric, who coproduced the picture, handles not only the role of an unsympathetic bully but an ostentatiously daring soliloquy.

A sour *La Ronde* of chance meetings and symmetrical repetitions, *Friends & Neighbors* progresses through a series of one-on-one come-ons, trysts, and scenes in which characters confront their unfaithful partners, typically picking a supermarket aisle as the place for a domestic squabble. "I tried to at least fuck outside our calling circle" is one memorable reproach.) As in his first feature, LaBute eschews exteriors and establishing shots. The filming is precise, the editing minimalized, the setups recurring. Each of the principals has an opportunity to meet the gorgeous gallery assistant Cheri (Nastassja Kinski) in situ. But, if *Friends & Neighbors* feels less formally worked out—as well as less politically astute—than the ruthlessly constructed *Company of Men*, it may be that LaBute took advantage of his first feature's success to dust off an earlier script.

Trapped in LaBute's Skinner box, the characters are condemned to repeat their behavioral patterns while metaphors are piled on innuendos and erotic intrigue corkscrews through the most innocuous interaction. What circle of hell do these lying, manipulating characters inhabit? (Or is hell their relationships with withholding, belittling, depressed partners?) Designed to make the viewer squirm, *Your Friends & Neighbors* is more than a little funny, and a good deal more misanthropic than even *In the Company of Men*. I doubt we'd see a crueler sex comedy until Todd Solondz's *Happiness* opens this fall. Although frequently compared to David Mamet, LaBute's is a distinctive sensibility, at once antisensual and lascivious, as punitive as it is provocative.

Perhaps the movie is not apolitical after all. Although the six characters don't have to go very far in search of their author, LaBute doesn't have the generosity to identify them as "our friends and neighbors let alone the guts to call them his. There's a giddy sense of puritan revenge—as though the filmmaker's dream audience would be watching these antics from the stocks.

Also reviewed in:
NEW REPUBLIC, 8/31/98, p. 28, Stanley Kauffmann
NEW YORK TIMES, 8/19/98, p. E1, Janet Maslin
NEW YORKER, 8/24 & 31/98, p. 159, Anthony Lane
VARIETY, 8/10-16/98, p. 43, Emanuel Levy

YOU'VE GOT MAIL

A Warner Bros. release of a Lauren Shuler Donner production. *Executive Producer:* Delia Ephron, Julie Durk, and G. Mac Brown. *Producer:* Lauren Shuler Donner and Nora Ephron. *Director:* Nora Ephron. *Screenplay:* Nora Ephron and Delia Ephron. *Based on the Screenplay "The Shop Around the Corner" by:* Samson Raphaelson. *From the play "Parfumerie" by:* Miklos Laszlo. *Director of Photography:* John Lindley. *Editor:* Richard Marks. *Music:* George Fenton. *Choreographer:* Susan Stroman. *Sound:* Christopher Newman and (music) John Richards. *Sound Editor:* Ron Bochar. *Casting:* Francine Maisler. *Production Designer:* Dan Davis. *Art Director:* Ray Kluga and Beth Kuhn. *Set Decorator:* Susan Bode and Ellen Christiansen. *Costumes:* Albert Wolsky. *Make-up:* Bernadette Mazur. *Stunt Coordinator:* Jerry Hewitt and Peter Bucossi. *Running time:* 110 minutes. *MPAA Rating:* PG.

CAST: Tom Hanks (Joe Fox);   Meg Ryan (Kathleen Kelly);   Parker Posey (Patricia Eden); Jean Stapleton (Birdie);   Dave Chappelle (Kevin Scanlon);   Steve Zahn (George Pappas); Dabney Coleman (Nelson Fox);   Greg Kinnear (Frank Navasky);   Heather Burns (Christina); John Randolph (Schuyler Fox);   Deborah Rush (Veronica Grant);   Hallee Hirsh (Annabel Fox); Jeffrey Scaperotta (Matt Fox);   Cara Seymour (Gillian, Nelson's Fiancée);   Katie Finneran (Maureen, the Nanny);   Michael Badalucco (Charlie, Elevator Attendant);   Veanne Cox (Miranda Margulies, Children's Author);   Bruce Jay Friedman (Vince Mancini);   Sara Ramirez (Rose, Zabar's Cashier);   Howard Spiegel (Henry, Irate Zabar's Shopper);   Diane Sokolow and Julie Kass (Zabar's Shoppers);   Reiko Aylesworth (Thanksgiving Guest);   Katie Sagona (Young Kathleen Kelly);   Kathryn Meisle (Cecilia Kelly);   Nina Zole Lam (Sidne Anne, TV Reporter); Maggie Murphy (Theater Patron);   Mary Kelly (Fox Books Shopper);   Chris Messina (Fox Salesperson); Ronobir Lahri (Man at Café Lalo); André Sogliuzzo (Waiter at Café Lalo); Peter A. Mian (Capeman at Starbucks);   Richard Cohen and Enzo Angileri (Starbucks Customers); Nick Brown (Juggler);   Ann Fleuchaus (Sarah Mancini);   Neil Bonin and Bill McHugh (Party

Guests);   Santiago Quiñoñes (Decorator);   Lynn Grossman (Yvette Fox);   Dolores Sirianni (Mother of Twins);   Nicole Bernadette (Florist).

LOS ANGELES TIMES, 12/18/98, Calendar/p. 1, Jack Mathews

[The following review by Jack Mathews appeared in a slightly different form in **NEWSDAY, 12/18/98, Part II/p. B3.]**

How things have changed, romance-wise. In the old Bert Kalmar-Harry Ruby song "Three Little Words," the phrase that romantics have always died to hear was "I love you." Now, in Nora Ephron's fitfully amusing remake of "The Shop Around the Corner," it's: "You've Got Mail."

Right. "You've got mail!," the phony-excited greeting delivered by the disembodied voice of the AOL.com man, who informs subscribers, upon logging in, that they have messages. Usually, that means there are stacks of electronic junk mail awaiting deletion, along with the occasional request for Keanu Reeves' birth sign and cousin Gert's boring Christmas letter.

But for some romantic adventurers—that is, for people desperate enough to strike up titillating relationships in shared-interest chat rooms—the phrase "You've got mail" is a daily rush of adrenaline, a promise of things that may safely never come.

It is in this state of electronic excitation that we find Ephron's fated lovers, Joe Fox (Tom Hanks) and Kathleen Kelly (Meg Ryan), a pair of thirtysomething Upper West Siders who pass each other in their daily routines without knowing they are e-mail soulmates. What they do know of each other, they hate.

Kathleen runs a second-generation children's bookstore, and Joe is heir to the discount bookstore chain that is about to run her out of business. Her store is named the Shop Around the Corner, in tribute to the Ernst Lubitsch movie that is the source material for "You've Got Mail." In that 1940 film, which was itself adapted from a play, James Stewart and Margaret Sullavan play feuding co-workers in an accessories shop who comfort themselves with thoughts of meeting their pen pal lovers, not knowing how close they really are.

Ephron, adapting the script with her sister Delia, has given this amiable premise a definite '90s spin. The e-mail device works. You can believe Kathleen when, under her log-on ID Shopgirl, she tells Joe's NY152 that the "you've got mail" greeting makes her heart jump. And you can feel their anxiety, as their anonymous relationship warms up to the point where they think they should meet.

Also, the fact that Joe is living with another woman, a narrowly self-focused book editor (Parker Posey), and Kathleen with another man, a residual Marxist columnist (Greg Kinnear, in a very subdued performance) for the New York Observer, gives their relationship a funky-sneaky complicity that's very funny. They can't wait to be alone so they can go online and cheat with some faceless, nameless hunk-babe in the great beyond.

In obvious ways, of course, "You've Got Mail" attempts to recapture the magic of Ephron's "Sleepless in Seattle," which co-starred Hanks and Ryan as romantics from opposite coasts being matched over a radio talk show by the man's young son. Seasoned with healthy scoops of wry commentary and molasses-thick sentiment, "Sleepless" amounted to a feature-length tease, in which the audience had to wait to the very end for the lovers to meet and then settle for some tentative hand-holding.

"You've Got Mail" plays the same waiting game. In fact, one wonders, as the film bores deep into its second, passionless hour, if two so carefully matched stars have ever gone longer without putting their lips together.

In this case, Hanks' and Ryan's characters at least meet, and interact, though it isn't pretty. As NY152, Joe brings out the best in Kathleen. As the bogeyman of the discount book world, he brings out her worst. And where she, as Shopgirl, brings his e-mail alter ego down to earth, Kathleen's face-to-face confrontations with Joe turn his businessman's heart to stone.

There's no denying the chemistry between Hanks, whose comparisons to Jimmy Stewart are becoming annoyingly accurate, and Ryan, whose schoolgirl cuteness is finally taking on a layer of matured confidence. We can see them together, want them to be together, and know we'll get our wish. It's a matter of getting there (and we might also wish that the writing were a little stronger along the way).

Nora Ephron has never really outgrown her columnist's instincts; she tends to write entire scenes that are riffs on fads and lifestyle trends. She is very good at this—witness, a scene in which she mocks the bogus sophistication of Starbucks' habitues—but they don't always propel the story forward. And with something as slight as "You've Got Mail," the seams and gaps are all the more apparent.

NEW YORK, 1/4/99, p. 52, Peter Rainer

Nora Ephron's *You've Got Mail*, starring Tom Hanks and Meg Ryan, is being touted as an updated Upper West Side remake of *The Shop Around the Corner,* one of the most deeply felt of all romantic comedies. It's more like a gentrified variation on Ephron's last Hanks-Ryan confab, *Sleepless in Seattle,* where Ryan falls for Hanks via a radio call-in show and spends the rest of the movie trying to hook up for real. *You've Got Mail* is the cyber version of this lonely-hearts scenario, and it's just as coy and comfy. Watching this movie is a bit like paging through a West Side shopper—everything on the screen seems to carry a price tag, including the people. Zabar's and Starbucks are invoked as if they were local shrines. No doubt they are. But has even Woody Allen been this cozily self-congratulatory about his own nabe? The real romance in this movie isn't between Hanks and Ryan. It's between Ephron and all the Upper West Side citadels of consumerism on gleaming display.

Joe Fox (Hanks) is introducing his monster book-chain's latest branch into the neighborhood a few blocks away from the venerable children's bookstore the Shop Around the Corner, operated by Kathleen Kelly (Ryan). Kathleen inherited the store from her mother; Joe is the scion of the family business. She's perky and crinkly-nosed and cute-as-a-button, especially when she's fighting the good fight against this interloper with his volume discounts and cappuccino bar. In his run-is with her, Joe is cordial, bemused, unsentimental. The gimmick here is that, without realizing it, these two opposing spirits are also carrying on a serious e-mail flirtation. The whole movie is taken up with how they eventually find out the truth about each other.

The world of cyber-romance might seem ripe for satire, but Ephron—who co-scripted with her sister Delia—plays it for heart-felt winsomeness. Online, Joe and Kathleen are supposed to be their "real" selves; he's vulnerable and supportive and she's, well, she's perky and crinkly-nosed. Neither character is substantial enough to sustain *one* entire self, let alone two. Ephron must realize this, and so, in order to make them seem meatier by comparison, she's saddled Joe and Kathleen with live-in lovers who are even less substantial. Joe's girlfriend Patricia (Parker Posey), a book editor, is a shrill motormouth; Kathleen's paramour Frank (Greg Kinnear), a left-wing newspaper columnist, is sweetly ineffectual. (Frank's last name is Navasky, an in-joke; when Barnes & Noble moved into the Upper West Side a few years back and precipitated the closure of nearby Shakespeare & Co., Victor Navasky, publisher and editorial director of *The Nation,* wrote a celebrated good-riddance piece in the *Times* praising the chain and knocking the specialty bookstore's rude-mannered help.)

Although *You've Got Mail* supposedly sides with the children's bookstore, it shares the chain-store mind-set. Starbucks, which Ephron plugs repeatedly, is hardly a mom-and-pop operation. Like Joe Fox's book emporium, the film tries to attract volume business by appealing to everyone. At times it's overstocked; Ephron delays the inevitable with subplots involving Joe's dad (Dabney Coleman) and Kathleen's co-workers (including Jean Stapleton). There are subplots in *The Shop Around the Corner,* too, but here they just seem like busywork. What keeps the comedy coasting is the rapport between Hanks and Ryan. Their teamwork doesn't touch your soul the way Jimmy Stewart and Margaret Sullavan did in the original. Those two weren't just playing opposite each other; they were in deep communion, Hanks and Ryan finesse a different domain: They know how to play out the superficial charms of their superficial characters. They massage the audience with a full repertoire of feel-good frivolities. In this frivolous movie era, it's a useful gift.

NEW YORK POST, 12/18/98, p. 57, Rod Dreher

"You've Got Mail" delivers exactly what you expect—no more, no less—from the lovey-dovey "Sleepless in Seattle" troika of Tom Hanks, Meg Ryan and co-writer-director Nora Ephron. It's a frothy meringue, a larky yuppie skip-to-my-lou through a dreamy Upper West Side (the theme park called Seinfeldland), a slight New York romantic fairy tale puffed up by bubbly cuteness.

So sue me, it works. 'Tis the season for nibbling on festive, sugary trifles, after all, and crowd-pleasers don't come more crowd-pleasing than this.

"You've Got Mail"—the title comes from the chirpy greeting America Online users get when they sign on—is the 1940 Lubitsch gem about pen pals, "The Shop Around the Corner," updated and outfitted for the Infobahn Age. Ryan plays Kathleen Kelly, a lemony-fresh children's bookshop owner whose livelihood is threatened by the book-and-coffee superstore opening down the street.

Her nemesis is Joe Fox (Hanks), the Barnes-&-Ignoble meanie behind the giant book emporium. A promising meet-cute in Kathleen's store goes sour when Joe and Kathleen reconnect at a cocktail party and learn a little more about each other, their mutual regard hardening like candyapple glaze.

Little do the bookselling rivals know that they're secretly falling in love. They correspond online, cloaking their true identities behind screen names. Their e-friendship is more soulful and satisfying than those they share with their live-in lovers (New York Observer writer Greg Kinnear, and book agent Parker Posey—both amusingly vain, careerist Manhattan stereotypes).

The anonymity of connecting online grants them the blessing of honesty without emotional vulnerability—or so they think.

Joe and Kathleen's friendship sweetens into yearning, and tumbles at last into an epistolary romance. When Joe discovers his e-friend's true identity, he keeps it to himself while teasing and nudging their relationship out of cyberspace and onto the streets of the Upper West Side,

Hanks and Ryan seem a little tuckered together this time out, the sparkling charm they had in "Sleepless in Seattle" going down like half-flat champagne. Though they don't exactly burn up the screen, they are cheerily companionable, and for the first time Ryan's cloying doesn't seem terminal.

"You've Got Mail" wouldn't be half as delightful if not for the blushing love affair between Ephron and the Upper West Side. She makes generous use of its locations and photographs them warmly and beautifully (Hanks and Ryan court on the sunny side of every street). Ephron makes the district between Central Park and the Hudson look so beautiful, quaint and homey the rents will be sky-high.

Some Gothamite grumpuses may cavil at the postcard perfection, but any movie that sends you out the door exhilarated that you live in this glorious city is to be welcomed. Still, who among us won't be pea-green with envy over the fabulous apartment newspaper writer Kinnear and small merchant Ryan live in on their salaries? Hey, kids, you got lucky!

NEWSWEEK, 12/21/98, p. 66, David Ansen

Joe Fox (Tom Hanks) and Kathleen Kelly (Meg Ryan) fall in love on the Internet, without knowing each other's real names, addresses or occupations. In the anonymity of cyberspace, they can open their souls to each other, and disregard the fact that both are involved in less-than-perfect relationships: Joe with a brash Manhattan book editor (Parker Posey) and Kathleen with a vain intellectual (Greg Kinnear). But should they take the big leap and meet in the flesh? The twist in "You've Got Mail"—borrowed from Ernst Lubitsch's 1940 "The Shop Around the Corner"—is that unbeknown to them, they *have* met, and detest each other. As the owner of the megachain Fox Books (think Barnes & Noble), Joe not only represents everything Kathleen hates, he threatens to put her cozy little children's bookstore out of business.

Nora Ephron's latest romantic comedy, co-written with her sister Delia Ephron, has several obstacles to overcome. One is *déjà vu*—it's not just the Lubitsch classic that hovers over the enterprise but her own "Sleepless in Seattle." It must also overcome a tepid first half, filled with mildly satirical Upper West Side jokes and flat scenes involving the none-too-interesting staff of Kathleen's bookstore.

But have patience and "You've Got Mail" will reward you. The love story proves surprisingly touching: this is the most heartfelt of Ephron's movies. It's also the first Hollywood film to tap into the romantic revolution brought about by chat rooms and e-mail. The Internet has restored erotic power to the written word, turning us into a nation of Cyranos and Roxanes, falling in love with the incorporeal. "You've Got Mail" only scratches the surface of this ambiguous development, but it's a resonant scratch.

Kinnear and Posey make fine comic foils, and Ryan is at her best and worst. She can still fall into cloying poses, but as the love story deepens, so does her performance. The movie is unimaginable without Hanks. Physically, he may be the least glamorous of great romantic comedians. But nobody can put an ironic topspin on a line of dialogue with quite his flair; nobody can get so much mileage out of a sly double take, and when he must turn on a dime from the sardonic to the sentimental, your heart is his. Thanks to the chemistry these two pros generate, "You've Got Mail" ultimately achieves that lump in the throat that is the romantic comedy's promised land.

SIGHT AND SOUND, 3/99, p. 57, Charlotte O'Sullivan

New Yorkers Joe and Kathleen enjoy a clandestine e-mail relationship. He is heir to Fox & Sons, a company with a chain of discount bookstores; she owns a tiny bookshop, threatened by his new store. But since they use pen names, neither knows the other's real identity. Joe and Kathleen are introduced at a publishing party. Joe's aggression overwhelms Kathleen. Via e-mail, Kathleen confides in Joe about the ruthless capitalist in her life, while he willingly gives advice. Employing the skills of her journalist boyfriend Frank, Kathleen begins a canny media campaign against Fox.

Increasingly enamoured of each other, the e-mail pair decide to meet. When Joe spies Kathleen at the pre-arranged restaurant he realises the truth. He approaches her anyway, but as Joe Fox. Kathleen insults him and goes home, thinking she's been stood up. Kathleen's shop is forced to close and at the same time she realises she doesn't love Frank. Joe undergoes a similar revelation and leaves his ambitious book-editor fiancée Patricia. Still keeping his e-mail identity secret, as himself he woos Kathleen, who is now writing a book. She grows to enjoy his company but when her e-mail pal asks to see her, she agrees. When Joe arrives, Kathleen realises the truth. The pair declare their love.

You've Got Mail is neither a sequel nor prequel to *Sleepless in Seattle,* yet the two films appear unnaturally close. In both, Meg Ryan and Tom Hanks take the lead roles, the well-articulated sentence proves central to the romance, and sexual difference is expressed through cinema. *(The Godfather* substitutes for *The Dirty Dozen* as the perfect 'male' film this time.) The two films have something even more crucial in common, however: an obsession with perfect, dead women. *Sleepless in Seattle,* it could be argued, is about Virginia Woolf's old enemy, "the angel in the house", embodied by Hanks' ideal first wife Maggie. "She made everything beautiful... When I touched her it was like coming home, though to no home I'd ever known," he says of her. Their son is terrified he's "forgetting Mommy", so Hanks lists her qualities to keep the memory fresh. When her ghost appears, it's in a white dress.

You've Got Mail is slightly more original—this time it's the angel in the workplace with whom we're confronted, in the form of Kathleen's soft-focus old mother. Her ghost also pops up, full of tender and supportive grace. And she too is a feminine ideal, both sexually desirable (Joe's uncle Schuyler keeps saying how "enchanting" she was) and virtuous. She was always kind and fair to her employees, as well as a surrogate mother to her customers and their young children. Like Maggie, Kathleen's mother turns everywhere into a home—the female realm, which the realities of a brutal, competitive world can't reach.

What director and co-writer Nora Ephron makes apparent is how closely such a vision accords with a certain strand of feminism. Kathleen angrily tells "sad multi-millionaire" Joe, "No one will ever remember you, but they'll remember my mother." Kathleen's shop has been passed on to her by her mother and Kathleen intends to honour this tradition, declaring, "I'll leave [the shop] to my daughter," which makes her sound like a radical separatist.

But just as *Sleepless in Seattle* worked to free Hanks of his first wife's ghost and to allow him to love a career girl, *You've Got Mail*'s aim is to drag Kathleen away from her mother and into the "male" marketplace. This is where Joe comes in. Ruthless in business, he can show Kathleen how to be "cruel', how to accept the push and shove of business. That this presents a direct threat to her mother's values is made clear. When Kathleen realises that Joe has won, she wails, "It's like my mother died all over again." For Ephron, it's not enough for saintly people to be dead—their ghosts have to be killed off, too. Only then can sinners flourish: Joe never renounces his daddy's business, while Kathleen's happy ending involves her accepting the services of a successful publisher—one of Patricia's friends, and therefore undoubtedly pushy.

You've Got Mail owes much to other films. A loose reworking of Ernst Lubitsch's *The Shop around the Corner* (1940), it begins like a feminist version of *You Can't Take It with You* (1938), Frank Capra's sprightly take on thoughtless businessmen and their love of monopolies—but where the latter shows eccentric 'little guy' Lionel Barrymore successfully beating off the horrors, *You've Got Mail* says if you can't beat 'em, join 'em: a *Working Girl* for the 90s.

The problem is that Ephron doesn't have the courage of her capitalist convictions. In order to distract us from her project, she does everything in her power to make Kathleen seem unthreatening, such as giving her a 'terrible cold' and making her increasingly witless (her ability not to put two and two together is awesome). But there's a more profound betrayal at work here. The quality of the writing is such that you actually don't believe Kathleen loves Joe. His wooing of her is rushed and his banter doesn't seem particularly charming (Hanks, always better playing good guys, looks uncomfortable here). And Kathleen herself becomes such a blank you begin to wonder if she isn't in a comatose state of denial.

You've Got Mail has much in common with *Sleepless in Seattle* but ultimately pales by comparison. The latter's brand of corn was slick and self-conscious; *You've Got Mail*'s is merely confused. Ephron's second attempt to reject the angelic female sphere proves too much. The title punningly says it all—Ephron gives us male, more male than she can handle.

VILLAGE VOICE, 12/22/98, p. 127, J. Hoberman

Jeffrey Katzenberg retells the Book of Exodus and Gus Van Sant re-creates *Psycho,* so Nora Ephron updates Ernst Lubitsch's 1940 *The Shop Around the Corner*. It's a less sacred text, to be sure, and, in any case, Ephron's *You've Got Mail* (written with her sister Delia Ephron) is more like a rerun of her own *Sleepless in Seattle*. The technological gimmick substitutes e-mail for talk radio but the stars are the same. Bounding from her bed in oversized men's pajamas, Meg Ryan is more a cartoon creature than any to be found in *Prince of Egypt*. Tom Hanks is less adorable, but Ephron has taken care to surround him with appropriate props—big dog, little kids, bitch-on-wheels girlfriend (Parker Posey, suggesting an evil-twin mockery of Ryan's pert bunny act). Unbeknownst to their significant others, Hanks and Ryan are carrying on an anonymous cybercorrespondence. In the real world, she operates a quaint children's bookstore while he's about to rock her world by opening a giant discount book emporium. That both live on the Upper West Side not only allows them to cross paths in Zabar's but facilitates a smug and cloying atmosphere—part faux Woody, part *New York Times* "Metropolitan Diary"—that can reference PEN dinners and poke fun at Victor Navasky.

You've Got Mail is not only about PCs; it appears to have been dictated by one. Too sophisticated to subscribe to her own formula but too cynical to do anything else, Ephron strives mightily to keep her unnatural cuteness on life-support. Although *You've Got Mail* is devoid of genuine feeling, a tin-eared selection of strident pop tunes have been strategically dubbed in as emotional cues. The movie is desperate enough to pump up "Somewhere Over the Rainbow" for the big scene. Call it the Ephron touch.

Also reviewed in:
CHICAGO TRIBUNE, 12/18/98, Friday/p. A, Michael Wilmington
NEW YORK TIMES, 12/18/98, p. E1, Janet Maslin
NEW YORKER, 12/28/98 & 1/4/99, p. 139, Anthony Lane
VARIETY, 12/14-20/98, p. 130, Lael Loewenstein
WASHINGTON POST, 12/18/98, p. D1, Rita Kempley
WASHINGTON POST, 12/18/98, Weekend/p. 51, Michael O'Sullivan

ZERO EFFECT

A Columbia Pictures/Castle Rock Entertainment release of a Manifest Film production. *Executive Producer:* Jim Behnke.   *Producer:* Lisa Henson, Janet Yang, and Jake Kasdan.   *Director:* Jake Kasdan. *Screenplay:* Jake Kasdan.   *Director of Photography:* Bill Pope.   *Editor:* Tara Timpone. *Music:* Happy Walters, Manish Raval, and the Greyboy Allstars.   *Music Editor:* Jonathan Karp. *Sound:* Glenn Berkovitz and (music) Todd Burke.   *Sound Editor:* Robert Grieve and Greg King. *Casting:* Mary Vernieu.   *Production Designer:* Gary Frutkoff.   *Art Director:* Philip J. Messina. *Set Designer:* Kelly Hannafin.   *Set Decorator:* Maggie Martin.   *Set Dresser:* Phil S. Blackburn, Jeff Cach, Joel Elsom, Sean Fong, and Nicholas T. Starin.   *Special Effects:* Bob Riggs. *Costumes:* Kym Barrett.   *Make-up:* John Caglione, Jr.   *Stunt Coordinator:* Diamond Farnsworth. *Running time:* 120 minutes.   *MPAA Rating:* R.

CAST: Bill Pullman (Daryl Zero);   Ben Stiller (Steve Arlo);   Ryan O'Neal (Gregory Stark); Kim Dickens (Gloria Sullivan);   Angela Featherstone (Jess);   Hugh Ross (Bill);   Sara DeVincentis (Daisy);   Matt O'Toole (Kragen Vincent);   Michele Mariana (Maid);   Robert Katims (Gerald Auerbach);   Tyrone Henry and Aleta Barthell (Staffers);   Tapp Watkins (Firefighter);   Wendy Westerwelle (Motel Clerk);   Lauren Hasson (Little Kid);   Daniel Pershing (Rahim);   David Doty (Officer Hagans);   J.W. Crawford (Convention Employee); Fred Parnes (Chuck);   Luisa Sermol (Waitress);   Marvin L. Sanders and Doug Baldwin (Astronomers);   Robert Blanche (Paramedic);   Margot Demeter (Clarissa Devereau).

LOS ANGELES TIMES, 1/30/98, Calendar/p. 12, Jack Mathews

[The following review by Jack Mathews appeared in a slightly different form in NEWSDAY, 1/30/98, Part II/p. B3.]

Daryl Zero, the hero of the offbeat mystery comedy "Zero Effect," has mastered the fine art of detachment, honed to perfection his powers of objectivity and observation and developed a sense of deductive reasoning that can be described only as Sherlockian. All of this may confirm his claim to be the world's greatest detective, but there's a side to him that his clients never see; in fact, they never see him! Daryl Zero is afraid of people.

Meet a Philip Marlowe for the phobic '90s and welcome "Zero Effect's" talented 22-year-old writer, director and producer Jake Kasdan. Yes, he's the son of Lawrence Kasdan, and we can only wonder how much the senior Kasdan had to do with the movie's slick, sure-handed production. Maybe it's all in the genes.

In any event, "Zero Effect" is a confident first film and one of the freshest detective yarns to come along in a while. This is not another genre sendup from someone raised on movies. Kasdan's anthropophobic hero is an original, and he's given the film an odd rhythm that keeps the audience from trying to get a step ahead and outguess it.

The title refers to that inevitable moment when Daryl Zero (Bill Pullman) solves whatever mystery he's working on. Throughout the movie, he carries on a busy off-screen narrative, giving away trade secrets, explaining the process, boasting about how he came to solve some previous, colorfully titled job (The Case of the Mismatched Shoelaces, the Case of the Hired Gun Who Made Too Many Mistakes).

The case at hand, which will end up with a title longer than this review, has Zero venturing out of his fortress-like Los Angeles apartment to fly to Portland, where he's been hired by timber baron Gregory Stark (Ryan O'Neal) to find a key to a safe deposit box containing something that will free him from his persistent blackmailer.

Stark didn't hire Zero directly, of course. He had to deal with Steve Arlo (Ben Stiller), Zero's combination assistant, investigator, secretary, gofer and legal and mental health counselor. Zero can do nothing without Arlo because he can communicate with other people only while playing a self-cast role.

So, while Arlo yo-yos back and forth between Portland and Los Angeles, trying to balance his weird job obligations with his commitment to his increasingly fed-up girlfriend (Angela

Featherstone), the boss goes to work. First step, join Stark's health club and observe his client up close. Next, track a blackmail payment and hope to catch the blackmailer red-handed.

Within 24 hours, Zero has found the lost key and the woman apparently behind the scheme. He could send in his bill and go home. But Zero is far too curious and obsessive to walk away from an unsolved mystery, even off the clock. Why, he has to know, is Stark being blackmailed? What's in the safe deposit box? And why would a woman for whom Zero is feeling—what is that, passion?—be involved in such a crime?

Suddenly, the mystery story has become a romance, and a pretty good one. Zero and Gloria Sullivan (Kim Dickens) are an interesting pair of loners who develop an honest relationship even while lying to each other through their teeth.

Pullman is really marvelous in a role that allows him to make his strongest statements without words. It's hard for Zero to carry on a normal conversation, especially with a woman romantically interested in him, and as he agonizes over what to say, Pullman turns the moments into little arias of tortured silence.

Stiller doesn't get as many comic moments as he might; Arlo is essentially a whiny schlepper. But O'Neal makes a terrific heavy out of Stark, and newcomer Dickens is genuinely appealing as the ultimately tragic Gloria.

"Zero Effect" has its rough spots. The neurotic flourishes that Kasdan uses to introduce Zero manage to be both precious and over the top at the same time. For a while, it looks as though the model for Zero is Sean Penn's Jeff Spicoli from "Fast Times at Ridgemont High." And though the dialogue is generally sharp, there are bad patches.

Nonetheless, this is a smartly hip first film for anyone and, though its box-office performance isn't likely to spawn a sequel, we wouldn't mind seeing Daryl Zero in action again.

NEW STATESMAN, 8/14/98, p. 43, Gerald Kaufman

I don't understand those publications which employ several film critics, each alloted one movie a week to review. Unless the same writer sees everything, criteria cannot be established nor comparative assessments made.

Take Jake Kasdan's "Zero Effect". Viewed on its own, this American private-eye comedy possesses weaknesses. Its narrative, about a business tycoon being blackmailed, seems simultaneously prolix and trivial. Its jokes are too thinly scattered; its denouement is too complex.

Yet compare and contrast "Zero Effect" and "To Have and to Hold". This steamy Australian melodrama seems to have everything going for it. Its cast is led by the Turkish-Greek-French Tcheky Karyo (noted for his role in Luc Besson's thriller "Nikita") and Rachel Griffiths (who attracted plaudits in the highly rated—to my mind, overrated—"Muriel's Wedding").

Its theme—a man so obsessed with his dead wife, Rose, that he seeks to turn his new lover into her replica—blends "Rebecca" with "Vertigo." Its fashionable and politically correct background mingles racialism with lawlessness ("rascalism") in the highly photogenic Papua New Guinea. But it fails to work because its director, John Hillcoat, tries too hard. He augments the vividly atmospheric location photography, by Andrew de Groot, with a stereophonic soundtrack of jungle twitterings and cheepings that would seem overdone in a Tarzan picture.

Hillcoat is a great one for meaningful close-ups, of huge bottles pouring Scotch into vat-size crystalware, and of ominous lizards scampering in the undergrowth. The climax, it goes without saying, takes place in a tropical storm.

Although a third principal character, a Papuan named Luther (played by Robert Kunsa with justifiable glumness, since he has been rendered monocular), is introduced solely for the purpose of tidying up the plot when it shows signs of getting totally out of control, the film revolves around Jack (Karyo) and Kate (Griffiths). The latter, an author who has been picked up by Jack while signing copies of one of her romantic novels in a Melbourne bookshop, accompanies him back to his surprisingly luxurious hacienda on New Guinea's Serpik River. Throughout the movie neither of them ever smiles, and who can blame them?

After all, they have to put up pot only with Hillcoat's ostentatious cinematic style but with being required to recite dialogue, by Gene Conkie, that is frequently heavy-handed and, more than occasionally, downright ludicrous. Kate, described as "the only one who can lift him—Jack—from the shadows of the past and make him real again"; utters the definitive understatement, after a series of increasingly weird experiences: "Jack, I feel strange."

Toiling away on her word processor, Kate is slow to pick up the tell-tale vibes emanating from Jack. He, for reasons never explained, spends most of his time in an outhouse filled with TV sets showing multitudinous videos, one of them depicting Rose's drunken and sluttish last days. What Kate sees in the morose Jack, who stumbles through the movie like a zombie, is never clear, though they do sweat away in sporadic nude sex.

Jack, on the other hand, cannot wait to get Kate to model Rose's favourite dress (which is scarlet, for those looking for symbolism). It is impossible to understand why the apparently level-headed Kate does not leave this clearly eccentric fellow after about five minutes of this. Much of this movie seems to be projected in slow motion, and some of it actually is.

Although "To Have and to Hold" is 25 minutes shorter than "Zero Effect", it seems to last much longer—like forever. After Hillcoat's verbosity, Kasdan's unassumingly light touch is doubly welcome. While Hillcoat's movie is portentous, Kasdan's is flip and effervescent, never takes itself seriously and, ingratiatingly, aims at nothing more consequential than giving its audience a good time. Its interesting, indeed charming, location is the rarely filmed north-western American city of Portland, Oregon.

The cast never emotes but, with the lightest of touches, seeks only to please. Bill Pullman (the American president in "Independence Day") sends himself up nicely as the eccentric private eye, Daryl Zero, with Ben Stiller, an MTV comic, as his fed-up sidekick. Ryan O'Neal, once the handsome hero of "Love Story" and now, disconcertingly, aged 57, is the bloated blackmail victim.

Jake Kasdan, son of Lawrence ("Body Heat") Kasdan, both wrote and directed "Zero Effect," which—despite its undoubted merits—shows that this precocious 22-year-old Wunderkind still has a lot to learn. "To Have and to Hold" demonstrates that 38-year-old John Hillcoat has learned more cinematic cliches than are good for him—or for his audience.

NEW YORK, 3/2/98, p. 50, David Denby

The first movie written and directed by young Jake Kasdan, *Zero Effect*, turns out to be a surprisingly intense comedy about a sort of modern-day, digital Sherlock Holmes. Bill Pullman, of the cringing demeanor, plays the world's greatest private eye, a shambling, neurotic genius, immensely needy, entirely guarded, a man who acts with dauntless savoir faire out in the field only to retire to a vault-like apartment filled with Tab and enormous bags of pretzels. This super-nerd, with his assistant (Ben Stiller), undertakes to protect a rich predator (Ryan O'Neal, who is very good) from blackmail. The movie's comic tone is productively unstable—sneakily funny, discordant, at times romantic, filled with a young man's love of the uncanny and the endless power of cool.

NEW YORK POST, 1/30/98, p. 43, Thelma Adams

From "Zero Effect" to "Desperate Measures" to "Deceiver," almost every movie this week showcases a genius. So why aren't all these Einsteins writing screenplays?

Bill Pullman plays the brains in "Zero Effect," a title that neatly reflects the offbeat mystery's boxoffice future. Written and directed by Jake Kasdan, son of Lawrence ("The Big Chill"), the best that can be said about his debut is that it's competent.

"Zero Effect" also has a strong cast (did someone say connections?). Ryan O'Neal, Ben Stiller and newcomer Kim Dickens add gloss to a calling-card movie that should have ended a glorious career at a spot like Sundance.

As Portland lumber baron Gregory Stark (an expressionless O'Neal) says about the case of the lost keys that leads him to hire gumshoe Zero, "It's all very unoriginal." That doesn't keep Kasdan from straining to make something old appear new.

Pullman's sleuth Daryl Zero is a cyber-Sherlock who types his memoirs into a computer. He lives alone in Los Angeles, trades a guitar for a violin and does amphetamines, not cocaine. He can deduce a stranger (Dickens) is a paramedic just by smelling her—it's her eau d'iodine.

The self-described "greatest observer the world has ever known" is a master of disguise like Holmes. His Doc Watson is a former lawyer in expensive suits (the sly Stiller, a controlled comic actor who can shoot from deadpan to dead mad in two seconds).

Pullman steps into the troubled genius role with the intensity he brought to the troubled musician in David Lynch's "Lost Highway" and the troubled Hollywood mogul in Wim Wenders' 'The End of Violence."

While Pullman can play it straight (he saved the planet as the president in "Independence Day"), the actor has become the middle-age boy next door when next door is a dysfunctional Wonderland.

Pullman's biggest problem is that Kasdan is no Sir Arthur Conan Doyle. Zero, the man of solving mysteries, is tossed into a maze of murder, privilege, rape and paramedics that's far from amazing. The final effect is less than zero.

SIGHT AND SOUND, 9/98, p. 57, Edward Lawrenson

In his Portland office, businessman Gregory Stark tells Steve Arlo—who represents LA-based private investigator Daryl Zero—that he is being blackmailed over the contents of a safe-deposit box whose keys he has lost. Zero flies to Portland. He follows Stark making his regular pay-off to the blackmailer and sees paramedic Gloria Sullivan making the pick-up. Suspicious of Stark, Zero searches his office. He discovers the safe-deposit keys and that the blackmailer is Kragen Vincent. Thinking that Zero is an accountant, Gloria asks him do to her tax returns. The next day, Zero realises that Vincent—who served time for the murder of a woman named Clarissa Devereau—is the ailing man whom Gloria regularly visits. Stark confesses to Arlo that he had Vincent kill Clarissa, a young woman who falsely accused him of rape. Vincent now has evidence linking Stark to the murder and is blackmailing him.

Over dinner, Zero realises that Gloria—whom Vincent rescued as a baby from the motel room where he killed Clarissa—is Stark and Clarissa's offspring, living proof that the rape did indeed take place. Zero and Gloria make love. While making yet another payment, Stark has a heart attack; Gloria uses her medical training to save his life. With Zero's help, she leaves the country, in fear of her life from Stark.

In *Zero Effect* private investigator Daryl Zero tells us what it takes to be a good detective: observation and objectivity. But, as this enjoyably assured debut feature from writer-director Jake Kasdan posits, there is also something a little odd, if not unhealthy, about a person driven by what Zero usefully labels "the two Obs". Zero is a confirmed agoraphobic who ventures outside only when on a case. He stands back, "observing" things, with the scopophilic relish of a true fetishist. Indoors, he's not just disengaged from his immediate environment—an attitude that enables his precious objectivity—but wholly withdrawn from it: a recluse, an amphetamine-popping virgin roaming his grungy flat like a stroppy teenager.

The detective as detached recluse is a familiar figure. Most notably, there are the private investigators who stalk the dark streets of *film noir*, hardened loners whose only access to an otherwise senseless world is through the passionless prism of detective work. But despite Bill Pullman's unhinged portrayal of Zero (a cross between a spoilt rock star and Howard Hughes in his final years), the investigator's neuroses are far less deep-seated than those of the embittered *noir* detective. Following a brief romance with Gloria, chief suspect in his case, Zero is at last able to reach some kind of inner equilibrium; as his harried associate Arlo (Ben Stiller's nicely sardonic Watson to Pullman's troubled Holmes) correctly predicts, all Zero really needed was the love of a good woman.

Of course, in *noir* terms—where romance is always a murky affair—such a conclusion would be heresy. Even confirmed bachelor Sherlock Holmes would disapprove, with some justification, for while there's a lightness of touch to the romance between Zero and Gloria which prevents *Zero Effect* from tipping over into sticky sentimentality, this relationship effectively closes the case on the film's ironic investigation into the myriad perversities underlying detection. In its place, Kasdan opts for a nice line in wistful romanticism—the kind Alan Rudolph has made his own—which provides a touching aptness to the location of Zero's first encounter with Gloria: a gym, the familiar haunt of lonely urbanites everywhere. But one can't help feel, as the film abandons its revisionist take on the detective genre in favour of a more traditional, albeit well-told romance that *Zero Effect* isn't half as clever as it would have us think. (This said, the casting of *Love Story* star Ryan O'Neal as the businessman who murders his college sweetheart is wonderfully mischievous.)

Indeed, as a detective story, there's something defiantly old-fashioned about *Zero Effect*. Unlike the postmortem trickery of *Pulp Fiction* and *The Usual Suspects*, the film's resolutely linear plot unfurls with crisp economy—neatly propelled by the Greyboy Allstars' funk soundtrack and enlivened by some smart dialogue, particularly the weary yet affectionate exchanges between Zero and Arlo. Kasdan turns the relative anonymity of his Portland location to his advantage. With its seedy motel rooms, vaguely sinister corporate offices and carparks, this is less a geographically real place than a generic movie-detective stomping ground. Lovingly rendered, this familiar territory is at least made to appear new by Kasdan's sharp eye for comic detail (he has the shifty-looking Arlo push a little girl on a swing to avoid suspicion while meeting Stark, for instance). Zero himself is a living anachronism, a throwback to detective fiction of a less knowing, more straightforward kind: flitting between airport lounges and in and out of disguises, he's the kind of detective MGM would have dedicated a series to in the 30s. Now that his brief fling with Gloria has cleared his head, Zero can redouble his investigative efforts; and from the endless references he makes to past cases ("The Case of the Hired Gun Who Made Way, Way Too Many Mistakes"), his output seems prodigious enough to justify more entertaining ones like this.

VILLAGE VOICE, 2/3/98, p. 54, Gary Susman

One might expect the filmmaking debut of Lawrence Kasdan's son to be a self-indulgent generational whine. Happily, *Zero Effect* shows 22-year-old Jake Kasdan to have a bright and original voice and a flair for classic storytelling.

Daryl Zero (Bill Pullman) considers himself the world's greatest detective, and he may be right. He has Sherlock Holmes-like powers of observation and deduction. The discreet sleuth uses an intermediary, Steve Arlo (Ben Stiller), to deal with clients and preserve his anonymity. For even though he has a full understanding of human psychology, Zero is a paranoiac who is utterly inept at human contact in his personal fife.

Zero is forced to emerge from his shell when he's hired by blackmailed millionaire Gregory Stark (Ryan O'Neal). Although Stark won't explain what secrets he's afraid of exposing, Zero quickly discovers the blackmailer's identity: she's a kindhearted paramedic named Gloria (Kim Dickens). Zero spends the rest of the film getting close enough to his alluring prey to determine her motive.

Aptly, both Bill Pullmans—the decent everyman *(While You Were Sleeping, Sleepless in Seattle)* and the recessive neurotic *(Lost Highway, The End of Violence)*—are on display here. Zero never hints to the other characters that he's tiptoeing through the minefield of his own emotions, yet Pullman lets viewers see what a shaky disguise Zero's bland public face is. By turns goofy, obsessive, arrogant, and shy, Pullman makes Zero fascinating to watch. Pullman's equal in inscrutability is Kim Dickens, who's one of the freshest new female leads in ages. Neither he nor the audience knows if the seemingly guileless Gloria is on to him. Dickens's unpretentious yet intense presence is disarming and devastating.

Also serving as a fine foil to Zero is Ben Stiller, milking for comic exasperation Steve Arlo's struggle between his desire for a normal, stable life with his girlfriend and his need to be needed by his paranoid puppeteer of a boss. Kasdan puts even Ryan O'Neal's dyspeptic stiffness to good use as the nervous, malevolent, banal tycoon. Kasdan's ability to coax idiosyncratic performances is as much a pleasure to discover as his revitalizing spin on a tired genre.

Also reviewed in:
CHICAGO TRIBUNE, 1/30/98, Friday/p. G, Monica Eng
NEW YORK TIMES, 1/30/98, p. E10, Janet Maslin
VARIETY, 1/25-2/1/98 p. 66, Leonard Klady
WASHINGTON POST, 1/30/98, Weekend/p. 49, Desson Howe

ADDENDUM

The following review arrived too late to be included in this or previous issues of FILM REVIEW ANNUAL. The issue of FILM REVIEW ANNUAL in which the credits and film review appears is given in parenthesis after the name of the film.

DEEP CRIMSON (*Film Review Annual, 1998*)

FILM QUARTERLY, Summer, 1999, p. 33, Marvin D'Lugo

When Nicolás Estrella (Daniel Giménez Cacho), an opportunist who preys on gullible, lonely women, shows up on the doorstep of Coral Fabré (Regina Orozco), the single mother of two small children, in Arturo Ripstein's *Deep Crimson (Profundo carmesí, 1996)*, the stage is set for another of the director's explorations into the shadowy world of Mexicans living on the margins of social as well as moral decay. As he did in the four preceding films co-scripted with Paz Alicia Garcíadiego (beginning with *The Realm of Fortune [El imperio de la fortuna,* 1985]) Ripstein presents a Mexico in which characters feel trapped by the sense of their own mediocrity and come to dream of escape through disguise, pretense, and deceit.

Nico's ruse, impersonating a Spanish exile who bears a striking resemblance to Charles Boyer, is built on his understanding of that desire for escape through pretense as though it were an axiom of Mexican cultural identity. Foreignness and the hint of an exoticism rooted in Hollywood movies are two crucial marks that, for Coral, promise some hope of deliverance from her prosaic and claustrophobic world. It gradually becomes apparent, however, that Nico's impersonation of Boyer is also a way for him to escape his own drab existence. Central to the world Ripstein evokes is the discrepancy between who these two characters really are and the self-images they have constructed as part of their pathetic and ultimately tragic masquerade.

The allure of erotic passion that propels both characters is a measure of the allure of the movies; it also reflects the emotional and physical squalor of their own dreary lives. In the dingy mise-en-scène shaded by grim hues of brown and rust that is so evocatively captured by Guillermo Granillo's photography, the couple evokes the desperation of Hollywood 40s noir characters, here transposed into a Mexican landscape that bears no resemblance to the usual scenic images provided by Mexican cinema of the same period.

By having Coral and Nico come together around a movie illusion of idyllic love, Ripstein is able to layer his relentless probing of lives on the edge with a measure of cinematic self-reference that serves as a metacommentary on Mexican culture itself. The key to Nico's seductive charm with women lies in his toupee, which gives his appearance the Boyer-esque touch of a romantic movie idol. As in some biblical parable, the hair(piece) becomes a fetishized object of sexual power, which, tellingly, Nico seems always on the verge of losing, exposing what he calls the freakishness of his baldness. Coral too has her points of vulnerability: her obesity; her two young children, whom she sees as a burden to the realization of her amorous desires; and, finally, her bad breath (which, she explains, comes from her days working as a nurse in a morgue).

This cinematic dimension is key to both the story and the personality of the two protagonists. These characters are motivated less by spontaneous desires than by the illusion of the roles depicted in movies and popular music that they have absorbed as part of their own identities. This is the story of two self-deceiving characters whose deceptions feed off each other, gradually moving the plot from a grotesque kind of farce toward the unrelenting blackness of tragedy that indirectly reveals Ripstein's nihilistic vision of Mexico.

Having callously abandoned her two children to make herself more acceptable to Nico, Coral shifts from passive and vulnerable female to a much more aggressive role by threatening to expose him to the police if he does not let her follow him. But just as quickly, she is able to shift back to a perversely romanticized notion of self-sacrificing love "just like in the movies" when at one point she cuts off her own hair and weaves a new toupee for him after his hairpiece has fallen into the dirt. Through this kind of gesture, the couple forges a symbiotic love that seems to find its logic only in the melodramatic movie plots that the two embrace as their personal imitations of life.

The reciprocity of mutually authenticated illusions becomes the mechanism through which Ripstein charges his episodic plotting. Having convinced Nico that she is his ideal mate, Coral starts to manage his "business affairs" by setting up the dates and charting the itinerary for the chain of seductions that will comprise the rest of *Deep Crimson*. Most of Ripstein's films up to this point have emphasized closed, claustrophobic narratives in which characters feel themselves trapped in place. In his 1972 *The Castle of Purity [El castillo de la pureza]*, for instance, a father incarcerates his entire family in an old house in order to protect them from the sinfulness and depravity of modem society. In contrast, Nico and Coral's search for victims for their con jobs at first gives the film the appearance of an open-ended road movie, with each new change of locale leading to a new victim, which in turn develops a crescendo of deceit, violence, and finally murder. Despite the suggestion of open-endedness, however, Ripstein's signature motif of desperate characters ensnared in traps of their own invention clearly reemerges when the tale is finally spun out.

The action, set in northern Mexico at some point in the 40s, is a neo-noir concoction that foregrounds the stylistics of nostalgia flics but with a decidedly critical edge. The couple's itinerary brings them to revisit the sites of Mexican Golden Age cinema's principal genres: the *cabaretera* and *ranchera* films. (The *cabaretera* or "fallen woman" genre was so named because the plots often involved heroines forced by circumstance to work in a cabaret; the *ranchera* genre took its name from the setting of these films on a ranch and usually involved a singing cowboy and comic sidekicks.) But this is not the clichéd sunny Mexico of happy campesinos or other folkloric stereotypes. *Deep Crimson*'s evocation of Mexico's movie tradition, far from paying homage to the likes of Dolores Del Río, Maria Félix, and Pedro Infante, uses these hints of nostalgia to suggest the impoverishment, decay, and corruption that such a cinema masked for Mexicans.

Ripstein has long stood in opposition to official visions of Mexican culture both in terms of the politics and, more noticeably, the very look of Mexican films. Rejecting the easy stereotypes of cinematic Mexicanness, he has posed in their place a series of questions about the ways Mexican cinema portrays itself. In this film he exploits the retro ambience of the setting and the nostalgic twist of the narrative to make the crucial connection between those popular but false images of Mexico and the way Mexicans come to image themselves.

Deep Crimson paints a relentlessly bleak portrait of a cultural landscape littered with the debris of failed dreams: a deserted *cabaretera*-esque cantina called Bar Intimo, where Coral serves one of Nico's victims a cocktail laced with rat poison as he dances to the rhapsodic strains of a tango; the Home-Run Motel, where Coral bludgeons another widow to death with a religious statue; finally, the dilapidated *rancho,* converted into a car-repair shop, where Nico and Coral commit their most heinous murders. These are spaces of deception and violence, but also the places where the murderers and their victims seem to feed off the false nostalgia of certain self-deluding myths about who they are that eventually fold back on a political landscape.

Deep Crimson is ostensibly a remake of Leonard Kastle's 1969 film, *The Honeymoon Killers,* a low-budget work that has become a cult classic. Over the years, Ripstein and Garcíadiego have frequently returned to what appears to be the model of the remake. Their first collaboration, *The Realm of Fortune,* was a new version of the original Juan Rulfo script of *The Golden Rooster (El gallo de oro),* first directed by Roberto Gavaldón in 1965. Ripstein's 1991 film, *Woman of the Port (La mujer del puerto),* appears to be a more conventional effort at a remake of the famed Mexican melodrama of brothel life in the port of Veracruz made by the Russian emigré Arcady Boytler in 1933. But in each of these films, as in *Deep Crimson* also, the idea of the remake is less an effort to update and re-do an earlier classic than to develop what amounts to a dialogue between certain representations of a Mexican cinematic and cultural past and the contemporary audience. Part of that dialogue with the past is to be noted in the ways Ripstein's protagonists in *Deep Crimson* seem almost conscious of the derivativeness of their identities.

Coral and Nico are drawn to each other by the very self-conscious sense that they are imitating Hollywood illusions. But they are second-rate, doomed actors in a Mexican scenario that bears only a sham resemblance to the world of movies. The often comic discrepancy between the remembered cinematic illusion and its contemporary evocation serves to underscore their pathetic self-deceptions. A pointed sign of the derivativeness that deforms their way of seeing themselves and others comes at the very end of the film, when, after committing murder and infanticide, they turn themselves in to the local police. Barely acknowledging the heinousness of their actions, the two cling to a romantic notion of their deeds. Nico imagines that he and his lover will be the objects of press interviews and notoriety. He quickly discovers that the corrupt police have no intention of following the pattern of movie plots with trial and execution. Instead, the couple is driven to a deserted landscape where they are told to flee so that they can be shot. Realizing that, in this bizarre twist of events, they have ironically achieved the very erotic paroxysm that each has sought, Coral tells Nico, "This is the happiest day of my life." Running for cover from the police, they are shot down, and the final lingering image of the film reveals the two lifeless bodies dramatically extended over a puddle of mud. Here the myth of unbridled passion confronts its final pathetic destiny in a way that transposes this seemingly unpolitical narrative into the contemporary reality of Mexican official corruption. This is the Mexico of the 40s, but it bears a pointed connection to the harsh realities of state violence and official hypocrisy of the 90s.

At its core, *Deep Crimson* reveals Ripstein's effort to demolish certain cultural myths that Mexican cinema has long purveyed to its audience. The most pivotal of these is that of self-sacrificing maternity. The corpulent Coral has been nurtured on a countermyth: the exotic fictions of harlequin novels, radio dramas, popular love ballads, and the Hollywood star system, emblematically embodied by the framed photograph of Charles Boyer over her dressing-table mirror. In the opening scene of the film, we see her reclining luxuriantly in her bed reading a *fotonovela* in a style reminiscent of certain Diego Rivera nudes. But the glossy images of passion that fill her mind collide with the reality of her own maternity, her two small children whom she prefers to hide when Nico first comes calling. Clearly, the myth of motherhood—one of the sacred icons of popular Mexican culture—clashes head-on with her fantasized self-image as a femme fatale. Abandoning her children at the door of a convent in order to follow Nico, Coral rejects her identity as mother, only to reencounter it ironically in Nico himself who, far from being the Charles Boyer of her dreams, turns out to be her surrogate son.

The figure of incest is flaunted when they masquerade as brother and sister; one of their intended victims is revolted to discover what she believes is the couple's incestuous relationship. She is only partially mistaken, for there is indeed something of the incestuous mother and son in this pairing, as Coral's frequent cradling of Nico in her arms to calm him suggests. At the very end of the film, after coaxing Nico to murder another widow, Coral must dispose of the body of the woman's daughter. She grips the lifeless body to her bosom and sighs, "I'm her mother now."

Ultimately, it is this Oedipal narrative that redeems the grifters' farce as tragedy. The maternity that Coral struggles to avoid but which, through a series of ironic twists of fate, she is forced to accept, seems to transform her from one more of Ripstein's self-deceived loners into a figure of truly tragic dimensions.

Ripstein's career has always sought a difficult accommodation between his natural attraction to a Mexican film tradition and a more international, cosmopolitan cinema that disavows the localism of his Mexican roots. What may account for the critical and commercial success of *Deep Crimson* in Europe and the United States is his apparent flaunting of both national and transnational elements as black comedy. Filmed as a French-Spanish-Mexican coproduction, the film shows a Mexico populated by Mexicans who long to be cosmopolitan and Spaniards who are both imposters and real, along with a chain of other starstruck and downtrodden characters.

In one scene, for instance, with a certain autobiographical resonance, Ripstein has Coral and Nico arrive at the home of a Spanish widow, Irene Gallardo, played by Marisa Paredes, the Spanish actress who, in recent years, has become internationally aligned with the films of Pedro Almodóvar. Irene is entertaining her neighbor, Sara Silberman, an atheist-anarchist who makes clear that she does not for one minute believe Nico's preposterous story of being a religious Spaniard on a charitable crusade in the New World. Coral's defensive response is to pose the xenophobic question to Sara Silberman, "You're not from here, are you?" "No, responds Sara. "I *chose* to live in this screwed-up country." Later, in an attempt to explain Sara's cynical views, Irene tells Nico and Coral that her neighbor is a Jew, then adds, "But you can hardly tell." Through this brief comic sequence, as throughout *Deep Crimson*, Ripstein leads his audience to question the assumption of the very existence of a pure and presumably authentic Mexican culture, suggesting that it is an imposture as blatant and farcical as that of the two protagonists.

Yet ultimately Ripstein understands that this culture of subterfuge and imposture is anything but farcical. The characters of *Deep Crimson* self-consciously define the closed circle of their illusions. On the day of her execution, Coral wears the same crimson dress she wore the day she first met Nico. Like the incestuous circle of her relations with him, the dress, once the mark of her farcical actions and self-delusions, now returns as the leitmotif of tragedy. That final scene describes Ripstein's Mexico as tragic farce, a remake of its movie self in which characters play out the outdated and derivative illusions of their lives as tragedy.

Notes

1. Paulo Antonio Paranaguá has detailed much of that intertextual dialogue in Ripstein's work generally, and in *Deep Crimson* in particular. See Paulo Antonio Paranaguá. *Arturo Ripstein: la espiral de la identidad*. Madrid: Cátedra/Filmoteca Española, 1997, pp. 277-89.

AWARDS

ACADEMY OF MOTION PICTURE ARTS AND SCIENCES
71st Annual Academy Awards — March 21, 1999

BEST PICTURE — *Shakespeare in Love*
Other Nominees: *Elizabeth; Life is Beautiful; Saving Private Ryan; The Thin Red Line*

BEST ACTOR — Roberto Benigni in *Life is Beautiful*
Other Nominees: Tom Hanks in *Saving Private Ryan*; Ian McKellen in *Gods and Monsters*; Nick Nolte in *Affliction*; Edward Norton in *American History X*

BEST ACTRESS — Gwyneth Paltrow in *Shakespeare in Love*
Other Nominees: Cate Blanchett in *Elizabeth;* Fernanda Montenegro in *Central Station*; Meryl Streep in *One True Thing*; Emily Watson in *Hilary and Jackie*

BEST SUPPORTING ACTOR — James Coburn in *Affliction*
Other Nominees: Robert Duvall in *A Civil Action*; Ed Harris in *The Truman Show*; Geoffrey Rush in *Shakespeare in Love*; Billy Bob Thornton in *A Simple Plan*

BEST SUPPORTING ACTRESS — Judi Dench in *Shakespeare in Love*
Other Nominees: Kathy Bates in *Primary Colors*; Brenda Blethyn in *Little Voice*; Rachel Griffiths in *Hilary and Jackie*; Lynn Redgrave in *Gods and Monsters*

BEST DIRECTOR — Steven Spielberg for *Saving Private Ryan*
Other Nominees: Roberto Benigni for *Life is Beautiful*; John Madden for *Shakespeare in Love*; Terrence Malick for *The Thin Red Line*; Peter Weir for *The Truman Show*

BEST FOREIGN-LANGUAGE FILM — *Life is Beautiful* (Italy)
Other Nominees: *Central Station* (Brazil); *Children of Heaven* (Iran); *The Grandfather* (Spain); *Tango* (Argentina)

BEST ORIGINAL SCREENPLAY — Marc Norman and Tom Stoppard for *Shakespeare in Love*

Other Nominees: Warren Beatty and Jeremy Pikser for *Bulworth*; Vincenzo Cerami and Roberto Benigni for *Life is Beautiful*; Robert Rodat for *Saving Private Ryan*; Andrew Niccol for *The Truman Show*

BEST ADAPTED SCREENPLAY — Bill Condon for *Gods and Monsters* Other Nominees: Scott Frank for *Out of Sight*; Elaine May for *Primary Colors*; Scott B. Smith for *A Simple Plan*; Terrence Malick for *The Thin Red Line*

BEST CINEMATOGRAPHY — Janusz Kaminski for *Saving Private Ryan* Other Nominees: Conrad A. Hall for *A Civil Action*; Remi Adefarasin for *Elizabeth*; Richard Greatrex for *Shakespeare in Love*; John Toll for *The Thin Red Line*

BEST FILM EDITING — Michael Kahn for *Saving Private Ryan* Other Nominees: Simona Paggi for *Life is Beautiful*; Anne V. Coates for *Out of Sight*; David Gamble for *Shakespeare in Love*; Billy Weber, Leslie Jones and Saar Klein for *The Thin Red Line*

BEST ART DIRECTION — Martin Childs with set decoration by Jill Quertier for *Shakespeare in Love* Other Nominees: John Myhre with set decoration by Peter Howitt for *Elizabeth*; Jeannine Oppewall with set decoration by Jay Hart for *Pleasantville*; Tom Sanders with set decoration by Lisa Dean Kavanaugh for *Saving Private Ryan*; Eugenio Zanetti with set decoration by Cindy Carr for *What Dreams May Come*

BEST COSTUME DESIGN — Sandy Powell for *Shakespeare in Love* Other Nominees: Coleen Atwood for *Beloved*; Alexandra Byrne for *Elizabeth*; Judianna Makovsky for *Pleasantville*; Sandy Powell for *Velvet Goldmine*

BEST MAKE-UP — Jenny Shircore for *Elizabeth* Other Nominees: Lois Burwell, Conor O'Sullivan and Daniel C. Striepeke for *Saving Private Ryan*; Lisa Wescott and Veronica Brebner for *Shakespeare in Love*

BEST ORIGINAL MUSICAL OR COMEDY SCORE — Stephen Warbeck for *Shakespeare in Love* Other Nominees: Randy Newman for *A Bug's Life*; Matthew Wilder (music), David Zippel (lyric) and Jerry Goldsmith (orchestral score) for *Mulan*; Marc Shaiman for *Patch Adams*; Stephen Schwartz (music and lyric) and Hans Zimmer (orchestral score) for *The Prince of Egypt*

BEST ORIGINAL DRAMATIC SCORE — Nicola Piovani for *Life is Beautiful*
Other Nominees: David Hirschfelder for *Elizabeth*; Randy Newman for *Pleasantville*; John Williams for *Saving Private Ryan*; Hans Zimmer for *The Thin Red Line*

BEST ORIGINAL SONG — "When You Believe" from *The Prince of Egypt*, music and lyric by Stephen Schwartz
Other Nominees: "I Don't Want to Miss a Thing" from *Armageddon*, music and lyric by Diane Warren; "The Prayer" from *Quest for Camelot*, music by Carole Bayer Sager and David Foster, lyric by Carole Bayer Sager, David Foster, Tony Renis and Alberto Testa; "A Soft Place to Fall" from *The Horse Whisperer*, music and lyric by Allison Moorer and Gwil Owen; "That'll Do" from *Babe: Pig in the City*, music and lyric by Randy Newman

BEST SOUND — Gary Rydstrom, Gary Summers, Andy Nelson and Ronald Judkins for *Saving Private Ryan*
Other Nominees: Kevin O'Connell, Greg P. Russell and Keith A. Wester, for *Armageddon*; Kevin O'Connell, Greg P. Russell and Pud Cusack for *The Mask of Zorro*; Robin O'Donoghue, Dominic Lester and Peter Glossop for *Shakespeare in Love*; Andy Nelson, Anna Behlmer and Paul Brincat for *The Thin Red Line*

BEST SOUND EFFECTS EDITING — Gary Rydstrom and Richard Hymns for *Saving Private Ryan*
Other Nominees: George Waters II for *Armageddon*; David McMoyler for *The Mask of Zorro*

BEST VISUAL EFFECTS — Joel Hynek, Nicholas Brooks, Stuart Robertson and Kevin Mack for *What Dreams May Come*
Other Nominees: Richard R. Hoover, Pat McClung and John Frazier for *Armageddon*; Rick Baker, Hoyt Yeatman, Alan Hall and Jim Mitchell for *Mighty Joe Young*

BEST DOCUMENTARY FEATURE — *The Last Days*
Other Nominees: *Dancemaker*; *The Farm: Angola, U.S.A.; Lenny Bruce: Swear to Tell the Truth; Regret to Inform*

BEST DOCUMENTARY SHORT — *The Personals: Improvisations on Romance in the Golden Years*
Other Nominees: *A Place in the Land; Sunrise Over Tiananmen Square*

BEST ANIMATED SHORT — *Bunny*
Other Nominees: *The Canterbury Tales; Jolly Roger; More; When Life Departs*

BEST LIVE-ACTION SHORT — *Election Night (Valgaften)*
Other Nominees: *Culture; Holiday Romance; La Carte Postale (The Postcard)*

THALBERG AWARD — Norman F. Jewison

HONORARY AWARD — Elia Kazan

SCIENTIFIC AND TECHNICAL AWARDS

Academy Award of Merit (Oscar Statuette) to:

Avid Technology for "the concept, system design and engineering of the Avid Film Composer for motion picture editing."

Scientific and Engineering Awards (Plaque) to:

Arnold & Richter Cine Technik and Arri USA, Inc for "the concept and engineering of the Arriflex 435 Camera System."

Mark Roberts, Ronan Carroll, Assaff Rawner, Paul Bartlett and Simon Wakley for "the creation of the Milo Motion-Control Crane."

Michael Sorensen and Richard Alexander of Sorensen Designs International and Donald Trumbull for "advancing the state-of-the-art of real-time motion-control, as exemplified in the Gazelle and Zebra camera dolly systems."

Colin Mossman, George John Rowland and Hans Leisinger of Deluxe Laboratories for "the concept and design of the Deluxe High Speed Spray Film Cleaner."

Ronald E. Uhlig, Thomas F. Powers and Fred M. Fuss of the Eastman Kodak Company for "the design and development of KeyKode latent-image barcode key numbers."

Arnold & Richter Cine Technik and the Carl Zeiss Company for "the concept and optical design of the Carl Zeiss/Arriflex Variable Prime Lenses."

Iain Neil for "the optical design", Takuo Miyagishima for "the mechanical design", Panavision, Incorporated for "the concept and development of the Primo Series of spherical prime lenses for 35mm cinematography."

Stephen J. Kay of K-Tec Corporation for "the design and development of the Shock Block."

Derek C. Lightbody of OpTex for "the design and development of Aurasoft luminaires."

Dr. Thomas G. Stockham and Robert B. Ingebretsen for "their pioneering work in the areas of waveform editing, crossfades and cut-and-paste techniques for digital audio editing."

James A. Moorer for "his pioneering work in the design of digital signal processing and its application to audio editing for film."

Robert Predovich, John Scott, Mohamed Ken T. Husain and Cameron Shearer for "the design and implementation of the Soundmaster Integrated Operations Nucleus operating environment."

Gary Tregaski for "the primary design," Dominique Boisvert, Philippe Panzini and Andre Leblanc for "the development and implementation of the Flame and Inferno software."

Roy B. Ference, Steven R. Schmidt, Richard J. Federico, Rockwell Yarid and Michael E. McCrackan for "the design and development of the Kodak Lightning Laser Recorder."

Technical Achievement Awards (Certificate) to:

Ivan Kruglak for "his commitment to the development of a wireless transmission system for video-assisted images for the motion picture industry."

Takuo Miyagishima and Albert K. Saiki of Panavision, Inc. for "the design and development of the Eyepiece Leveler."

Garrett Brown and Jerry Holway for "the creation of the Skyman flying platform for Steadicam operators."

James Rodnunsky, Bob Webber and James Webber of Cablecam Systems and Trou Bayliss for "the design and engineering of Cablecam."

Mike Bolles, Udo Pampel, Michael Mackenzie and Joseph Fulmer of Industrial Light & Magic for "their pioneering work in motion-controlled, silent camera dollies."

Barry Walton, Bill Schultz, Chris Barker and David Cornelius of Sony Pictures Imageworks for "the creation of an advanced motion-controlled, silent camera dolly."

Bruce Wilton and Carlos Icinkoff of Mechanical Concepts for "their modular system of motion-control rotators and movers for use in motion-control."

Ivan Kruglak for "his pioneering concept and the development of the Coherent Time Code Slate."

Mike Denecke for "refining and further developing electronic time code slates."

Richard C. Sehlin, David F. Kopperl, Dr. A. Tulsi Ram and Dr. Carl F. Holtz of the Eastman Kodak Company for "the research and development of the concept of molecular sieves applied to improve the archival properties of processed photographic film."

Edmund M. Di Giulio and James Bartell of Cinema Products for "the design of the KeyKode Sync Reader."

Ed Zwaneveld and Frederick Gasol of the National Film Board of Canada and Mike Lazaridis and Dale Brubacher-Cressman of Research in Motion for "the design and development of the DigiSync Film KeyKode reader."

Dr. Mitchell J. Bogdanowicz of the Eastman Kodak Company and Jim Meyer and Stan Miller of Rosco Laboratories, Inc. for "the design of the CalColor Calibrated Color Effects Filters."

Remy Smith for "the software and electronic design and development," James K. Branch and Nasir J. Zaidi for "the design and development of the Spectra Professional IV-A digital exposure meter."

Manfred N. Klemme and Donald E. Wetzel for "the design and development of the K-Tek Microphone Boom Pole and accessories for on-set motion picture sound recording.

David DiFrancesco, Bala S. Manian and Thomas L. Noggle for "their pioneering efforts in the development of laster film recording technology."

Dr. Douglas R. Roble for "his contribution to tracking technology and for the design and implementation of the TRACK system for camera position calculation and scene reconstruction."

Nick Foster for "his software development in the field of water simulation systems."

Cary Phillips for "the design and development of the 'Caricature' Animation System at Industrial Light & Magic."

Thaddeus Beier for "the design and implementation of ras_track, a system for 2D tracking, stabilization, and 3D camera and object tracking."

Special Awards (Medal of Commendation) to:

David W. Gray for "outstanding service and dedication in upholding the high standards of the Academy of Motion Picture Arts and Sciences."

NATIONAL SOCIETY OF FILM CRITICS
January 3, 1999

BEST PICTURE — *Out of Sight*

BEST ACTOR — Nick Nolte in *Affliction*

BEST ACTRESS — Ally Sheedy in *High Art*

BEST SUPPORTING ACTOR — Bill Murray in *Rushmore*

BEST SUPPORTING ACTRESS — Judi Dench in *Shakespeare in Love*

BEST DIRECTOR — Steven Soderbergh for *Out of Sight*

BEST SCREENPLAY — Scott Frank for *Out of Sight*

BEST FOREIGN FILM — *Taste of Cherry* (Iran)

BEST DOCUMENTARY — *The Farm: Angola U.S.A.*

BEST CINEMATOGRAPHY — John Toll for *The Thin Red Line*

BEST EXPERIMENTAL FILM — Aleksander Sokurov for *Mother and Son*

SPECIAL CITATION — Walter Munch, Rick Schmidlin, and Bob O'Neil for reassembly of Orson Welles' *Touch of Evil* in a form that fit his original intentions.

NEW YORK FILM CRITICS CIRCLE
January 10, 1999

BEST PICTURE — *Saving Private Ryan*

BEST ACTOR — Nick Nolte in *Affliction*

BEST ACTRESS — Cameron Diaz in *There's Something About Mary*

BEST SUPPORTING ACTOR — Bill Murray in *Rushmore*

BEST SUPPORTING ACTRESS — Lisa Kudrow in *The Opposite of Sex*

BEST DIRECTOR — Terrence Malick for *The Thin Red Line*

BEST SCREENPLAY — Marc Norman and Tom Stoppard for *Shakespeare in Love*

BEST CINEMATOGRAPHER — John Toll for *The Thin Red Line*

BEST FOREIGN-LANGUAGE FILM — *The Celebration* (Denmark)

BEST DOCUMENTARY — *The Farm: Angola U.S.A.*

NEW DIRECTOR — Richard Kwietniowski for *Love and Death on Long Island*

GOLDEN GLOBE
56th Annual Awards—January 24, 1999

BEST PICTURE (drama) — *Saving Private Ryan*

BEST PICTURE (comedy or musical) — *Shakespeare in Love*

BEST ACTOR (drama) — Jim Carrey in *The Truman Show*

BEST ACTOR (comedy or musical) — Michael Caine in *Little Voice*

BEST ACTRESS (drama) — Cate Blanchett in *Elizabeth*

BEST ACTRESS (comedy or musical) — Gwyneth Paltrow in *Shakespeare in Love*

BEST SUPPORTING ACTOR — Ed Harris in *The Truman Show*

BEST SUPPORTING ACTRESS — Lynn Redgrave in *Gods and Monsters*

BEST DIRECTOR — Steven Spielberg for *Saving Private Ryan*

BEST SCREENPLAY — Marc Norman and Tom Stoppard for *Shakespeare in Love*

BEST ORIGINAL SCORE — Burkhard Dallwitz with additional music by Philip Glass for *The Truman Show*

BEST ORIGINAL SONG — "The Prayer" from *Quest for Camelot: The Magic Sword*, music and lyric David Foster and Carole Bayer Sager

BEST FOREIGN-LANGUAGE FILM — *Central Station* (Brazil)

LOS ANGELES FILM CRITICS ASSOCIATION
December 12, 1998

BEST PICTURE — *Saving Private Ryan*

BEST ACTOR — Ian McKellen in *Gods and Monsters*

BEST ACTRESS — (tie) Fernanda Montenegro in *Central Station* and Ally Sheedy in *High Art*

BEST SUPPORTING ACTOR — (tie) Billy Bob Thornton in *A Simple Plan* and Bill Murray in *Rushmore* and *Wild Things*

BEST SUPPORTING ACTRESS — Joan Allen in *Pleasantville*

BEST DIRECTOR — Steven Spielberg for *Saving Private Ryan*

BEST SCREENPLAY — Warren Beatty and Jeremy Pikser for *Bulworth*

BEST CINEMATOGRAPHY — Janusz Kaminski for *Saving Private Ryan*

BEST SCORE — Elliot Goldenthal for *The Butcher Boy*

BEST PRODUCTION DESIGN — Jeannine Oppewall for *Pleasantville*

BEST FOREIGN-LANGUAGE FILM — *The Celebration* (Denmark)

BEST DOCUMENTARY — *The Farm: Angola U.S.A.*

BEST ANIMATED FILM — (tie) *A Boys Life* and *T.R.A.N.S.I.T.*

NATIONAL BOARD OF REVIEW

December 8, 1998

BEST PICTURE — *Gods and Monsters*

BEST ACTOR — Ian McKellen in *Gods and Monsters*

BEST ACTRESS — Fernanda Montenegro in *Central Station*

BEST SUPPORTING ACTOR — Ed Harris in *The Truman Show* and *Stepmom*

BEST SUPPORTING ACTRESS - Christina Ricci in *The Opposite of Sex*, *Buffalo 66*, and *Pecker*

BEST DIRECTOR — Shekhar Kapur for *Elizabeth*

BEST FOREIGN-LANGUAGE FILM — *Central Station* (Brazil)

BEST DOCUMENTARY FILM — *Wild Man Blues*

FREEDOM OF EXPRESSION AWARD — Bernardo Bertolucci

CAREER ACHIEVEMENT AWARD — Michael Caine

ENSEMBLE ACTING AWARD — The cast of *Happiness*

SPECIAL ACHIEVEMENT AWARD — Roberto Benigni for producing, writing, directing and starring in *Life Is Beautiful*

BILLY WILDER AWARD — Martin Scorsese

CANNES FILM FESTIVAL

51st Annual Awards — May 24, 1998

BEST PICTURE (Golden Palm Award) — *Eternity and a Day* (Greece)

BEST DIRECTOR — John Boorman for *The General*

BEST ACTOR — Peter Mullan in *My Name Is Joe*

BEST ACTRESS — (tie) Elodie Bouchez and Natacha Regnier in *The Dreamlife of Angels*

GRAND JURY PRIZE — *Life is Beautiful* (Italy)

SCREENPLAY PRIZE — Hal Hartley for *Henry Fool*

JURY PRIZE — (tie) *The Class Trip* (France) and *The Celebration* (Denmark)

CAMERA D'OR (Best First Film) — *Slam* (Australia)

TECHNICAL PRIZE — Vittorio Storaro for his contribution to *Tango*

PALME D'OR (Short Film) — *The Interview* (France)

JURY PRIZE (Short Film) — (tie) *Horseshoe* (United Kingdom) and *Gasman* (United Kingdom)

INTERNATIONAL CRITICS PRIZE (FIPRESCI) — *The Hole* (China)

YOUTH PRIZE — *Last Night* (Canada

INDEX

CAST

Aalam, Leyla, 996

Aamodt, Thor Michael, 607

Aaron, Caroline, 1000

Aaron, Sam, 1164

Abareu, Claudia, 403

Abatantuono, Diego, 87

Abbasi, Ali Akbar, 1293

Abdoo, Rose M., 1371

Abdul-Jabbar, Kareem, 72

Abelle, Janvier, 764

Abello, Jarrett, 1447

Abgrall, Guy, 1426

Aboulela, Amir, 441

Abraham, F. Murray, 1254

Abraham, Richard, 755

Abrahams, Doug, 313

Abrahams, Jon, 364

Abrams, Patsy Grady, 349, 954

Abrams, Soloman, 1167

Acevedo, Kirk, 1319

Ackland, Joss, 390, 1280

Acosta, José Alberto, 789

Adachi, Leanne, 292

Adachi, Yumi, 1253

Adair-Rios, Mark, 317

Adamo, Liane, 915

Adams, Daniel, 1390

Adams, Diane, 1456

Adams, Eboni, 114

Adams, Evan, 1203

Adams, J.B., 583

Adams, Jane, 277, 480

Adams, Kim, 155, 1240

Adams, Polly, 187

Adams, Steve, 1

Adams, Victoria, 1249

Adamson, Christopher, 674

Addison, Bernard, 187, 376

Addy, Mark, 610

Addy, William, 187

Ade, Herbie, 832

Adimoolah, Sheila, 1414

Adkins, Hasil, 1034

Adkins, Seth, 755

Adler, Charlie, 1077

Adler, Joanna P., 959

Adly-Guirgis, Stephen, 781

Adwoa, Kai, 671

Affleck, Ben, 40, 967, 1137

Afrika Bambaataa, 830

Agie, Awaovieyi, 593

Agius, Keith, 820

Aguilar, George, 19

Ahmed, Ali, 618

Ahn, Peggy, 1152

Ahray, Sonsee, 659

Ahren, Barbara-Magdalena, 1284

Aida, Toshiharu, 334

Aikawa, Sho, 334

Aiken, Liam, 512, 888, 1264

Ainslie, Jean, 740, 1461

Aird, Holly, 1304

Ai Wan, 1081

Akerman, Jeremy, 740

Akey, William, 936

Akhurst, Lucy, 652

Akin, Philip, 322, 1471

Alai, Adin, 954

Alain, Erin, 915

Alan, Sayda, 232

Alaskey, Joe, 1077

Alban, Allisa, 550

Alban, Carlo, 519, 572

Albe, Paul, 512

Albert, Shari, 882, 1443

Alborough, Roger, 1390

Albuquerque, Andra, 195

Alcázar, Damián, 789

Alcover, Catherine, 1216

Alda, Alan, 888

Alda, Rutanya, 1227

Alden, Norman, 944

Alderson, Jude, 697

Aldredge, Tom, 664, 1069

Alexander, Barbara, 798

Alexander, Dorothea, 801

Alexander, Erika, 385

Alexander, Harri, 801

Alexander, John, 811

Alexander, Khandi, 1308

Alexander, Terry, 572

Alexandra, Luz, 866

Alexenburg, Marnie, 1308

Alexis, Kim, 540

Alfonsi, Claudio, 686

Alfonsi, Lydia, 686

Al-Hamd, Ismael, 941

Ali, Mohammed, 941

Ali, Natasha, 1414

Alia, Phyllis, 1416, 1419

Aliansk, Hrant, 310

Alidoost, Iraj, 1293

Alig, Michael, 1146

Alkon, Sheldon, 987

Allar, Daniel, 511

Allen, Alfie, 339

Allen, Beth, 1375

Allen, Doug, 903

Allen, Elizabeth, 61

Allen, James, 944

Allen, Joan, 978

Allen, Joe, 40

Allen, Kevin, 1249

Allen, Lily, 339

Allen, Lisa-Erin, 888

Allen, Molly, 232

Allen, Nancy, 920

Allen, Penny, 1319

Allen, Ray, 500

Allen, Robert, 379

Allen, Sage, 40

Allen, Scott, 920

Allen, Steve, 896

Allen, Tanya, 1044

Allen, Woody, 27, 597, 1449

Allendorfer, John, 349

Allison, Cynthia, 811

Allison, Frankie Jay, 1443

Allison, Ralph, 1

Almgren, Susie, 1

Alouane, Tressana, 1371

Alpert, Arnie, 349

Alpert, Gregory H., 434, 920

Altamirano, Pedro, 773

Alteras, Adriana, 623

Alten, Iris, 959

Altman, Bruce, 888

Alvarado, Robert F., 1264

Alvarado, Trini, 951

Alvim, Anna, 903

Ambrose, Lauren, 173

Ambrose, Tangie, 578, 1059

Ambrozy, Bill, 959

Amendola, Tony, 773

Ames, Betsy, 954

Ami, Shoshana, 512

Amini, Nasrolah, 1293

Amiransvili, Amiran, 135

Amis, Suzy, 394

Amos, Diane, 944

Amos, Emma, 390

Amos, John, 975

Amos, Keith, 1443

Amsing, Sean, 313

Anacker, Kristen, 914

Ananishnov, Aleksei, 837

Anderson, Carol, 322

Anderson, Clark, 715

Anderson, Devon, 1249

Anderson, Eric, 874, 1085

Anderson, Gillian, 216, 806, 1476

Anderson, Haskell Vaughn, III, 232

Anderson, Isabelle, 461

Anderson, Jason, 10

Anderson, Julie, 512

Anderson, Kevin, 390

Anderson, Larry, 1254

Anderson, Loni, 871, 1334

Anderson, Mark, 109

Anderson, Myles, 1149

Anderson, Nathan, 448

Anderson, Stanley, 40

Anderson, Steve, 238

Anderson, Todd, 616

Andolini, Mike, 349

Andrade, Roberto, 195

Andrejevic, Kosta, 1123

Andrews, Benjamin, 903

Andrews, Giuseppe, 21, 978

Andrews, Jason, 385

Andrews, Matt, 339

Andrews, Naveen, 811

Angerano, Michael, 1061

Angel, Vanessa, 631

Angelica, Roberta, 1387

Angelo, Susan, 1348

Angileri, Enzo, 1489

Angulo, Alejandro, 709

Aniston, Jennifer, 326, 888

Anker, Jack, 291

Anne-Simone, 292

Ansari, Ahmad, 1293

Ansberry, Tom, 1466

Anscombe, Mike, 310

Antaramian, Jacqueline, 1154

Anthony, Jason, 1146

Anthony, Leonor, 1457

Antonio, Jim, 944, 978

Antunes, Sidney, 195

Anzalone, Helen, 1228

Anzilotti, Perry, 10

Aotani, Dawn, 1466

Apisa, Bob, 1048

Appel, Alex, 1040

Applegate, Christina, 93, 755

Applegate, Royce D., 317

Apsion, Annabelle, 722

Araiza, Gus, 364

Arango, Iván, 789

Arbatt, Alexandre, 751

Archie, John, 540

Arcoraci, Ven, 349

Ardant, Fanny, 339

Ardolino, Maureen, 72

Argiro, Vinny, 155

Argo, Victor, 865

Argueta, Luis, 130

Ariola, Julie, 580

Arkin, Adam, 472

Arkin, Alan, 403, 1193

Arkin, Michael, 1069

Arlyn, Nikki, 237

Armand, Gisken, 607

Armendariz, Pedro, 773

Armour, Annabel, 798

Armstrong, Bess, 954

Armstrong, Neil, 624

Arnette, Jeannetta, 400

Arnold, Brian, 1474

Arnone-Briggs, Lee, 1255

Arnoul, Françoise, 989

Aron, Michael, 369

Aronofsky, Abraham, 970

Aronovic, Norman, 1240

Aronson, Letty, 1449

Arquette, Alexis, 133, 587, 1419

Arquette, Lewis, 19, 1361

Arquette, Patricia, 522, 874

Arquette, Rosanna, 139, 282

Arrington, Brad, 860

Arroyo, Danny, 679

Arsenault, Joseph, 914

Artamonova, Iulia, 1315

Arthur, Donal, 1037

Arthur, Wren, 434

Artrip, Alexandra, 993

Artura, Michael, 33

Arvizu, Camerina, 601

Arzumanian, Ervant, 1315

Asabi, Adebayo, 1085

Ascaride, Ariane, 768

Ashe, Christine, 298

Asher, Rueben, 1057

Ashford, Matthew, 109

Ashikawa, Makoto, 396

Ashley, Elizabeth, 480

Ashley, Mike, 1081

Ashman, Frances, 876

Ashton, Al Hunter, 357

Ashton, John, 780

Ashton, Joseph, 1187

Ashton, Juli, 914

Ashton-Griffiths, J.G.R., 1280

Askari, Sepideh, 1293

Aske, Per Egil, 619

Askew, Luke, 860

Asner, Edward, 493

Assemany, Rita, 195

Assemany, Ruta, 195

Astileanu, Dan, 420

Astin, Mackenzie, 326, 659

Astin, Sean, 155

Ateah, Scott, 10

Athey, Ron, 470

Atholl, Steven, 531

Atkin, Harvey, 740

Atkine, Fodor, 1062

Atkins, Amy, 909

Atkins, Eileen, 52

Atkins, Juan, 831

Atkinson, Jeffrey, 1466

Attal, Henri, 1284

Attenborough, Richard, 339

Atterbury, John, 936

Atterton, Edward, 759

Attfield, Howard, 357

Auber, Brigitte, 759

Aubert, Christian, 225, 369, 448

Aubrey, Juliet, 440

Aubry, Darius, 851

Auclert, Cecile, 759

Audran, Stéphane, 751

Auger, Romain, 411

Augusto, Otávio, 195

Aurelius, Marcus, 114

Aurvag, Trond Fausa, 619

Austell, Jan, 659

Austin, Mark, 477

Austin, Winston, 1390

Auteuil, Daniel, 649, 958

Ave, Steve, 1466

Aviss, Mark, 313

Avital, Mili, 631, 987

Awanzino, Erick, 357

Axas, Elie, 1284

Ayer, Debbon, 659

Ayers, Jeff, 69

Aykroyd, Dan, 27, 119

Aylesworth, Reiko, 1489

Aylward, John, 40

Aylward, Rory J., 1155

Ayres, Rosalind, 441

Aza, Sebastian, 755

Azarie, Hank, 187, 448, 461, 548

Azizi, Rahi, 286

Babbs, O.B., 1023

Babcock, Todd, 441

Babich, Michaline, 684

Babin, Hugh Joseph, 400

Baburkova, Miroslava, 847

Bacalso, Joanna, 1471

Bach, Emmanuelle, 989

Bachar, Dian, 72, 171, 914

Backers, Sonia, 759

Bacon, Kevin, 306, 1456

Bacri, Jean-Pierre, 1377

Badalato, T.C., 1476

Badalucco, Joesph, Jr., 448, 1154

Badalucco, Michael, 749, 1489

Badarou, Deen, 959

Badel, Sarah, 822

Bader, Sheila, 369

Bader, Terry, 271

Badila, John, 954

Badland, Annette, 703

Badoul, Auda Mohammed, 941

Badu, Erykah, 119

Bagheri, Abdolhossain, 1293

Bagley, Lorri, 187, 385

Baier, Robert, 298

Bailey, Chris, 1375

Bailey, D'Army, 563

Bailleul, Sbastien, 694

Bain, Trevor, 310

Baisho, Mitsuko, 334

Bai Yefu, 410

Bai Yu, 410

Bajenski, Len, 1371

Baker, Becky Ann, 187, 1167

Baker, Carly, 589

Baker, Cynthia S., 1371

Baker, Damani, 77

Baker, Dee Bradley, 1037

Baker, Dylan, 187, 480

Baker, Gale, 379

Baker, Jill, 1137

Baker, Ray, 493

Baker, Rupert, 822

Baker, Simon, 1203

Baker, Todd, 1182

Bakhtari, Afshin Khorsid, 1293

Bakula, Scott, 757

Balaban, Bob, 240

Balaban, Neil, 580

Balahoutis, Alexandra, 348

Balan, Ovidiu, 420

Balaski, Belinda, 1197

Baldecchi, Marti, 292

Baldwin, Alec, 798

Baldwin, Daniel, 615, 969

Baldwin, Doug, 1495

Baldwin, Stephen, 468, 902

Baldwin, William, 1146

Bale, Christian, 1389

Baler, Robert, 851

Bales, David A., 1371

Balfour, Eric, 173

Balin, Michael, 1057

Balin, Richard, 578

Balk, Fairuza, 21, 1416

Ball, Angeline, 427

Ball, Seamus, 130

Ballantine, Carl, 847

Ballard, Alimi, 286

Ballerini, Edoardo, 659

Ballora, Gregory B., 1476

Balmaceda, Madeline N., 781

Balmer, Jean-François, 1284

Balmos, Tom, 1269

Balsbaugh, Richie, 1308

Baltz, Kirk, 155

Baluev, Alexander, 286

Bamman, Gerry, 461

Bancroft, Anne, 27, 461, 772

Bancroft, Bob, 1399

Bande, Pal, 531

Bandera, Vaitiare, 1371

Banderas, Antonio, 773

Banderet, Pierre, 768

Bandey, Paul, 247

Banes, Lisa, 1466

Bank-Mikkelsen, Nils, 626

Banks, Boyd, 310

Banks, Ernie, 155

Banks, Lenore, 722

Banks, Linden, 291

Bannen, Ian, 1409

Bannerman, Celia, 652

Bannon, Chad, 872

Bantzer, Christoph, 416

Baracz, Jan, 304

Baradaran, Kambiz, 1293

Barajas, Yolanda, 1440

Baraka, Amiri, 155

Baraka, Weusi, 1182

Baranski, Christine, 155, 857

Barber, Gillian, 313

Barber, Glynis, 294

Barbuscia, Lisa, 19

Bardadi, Meziane, 411

Bardem, Javier, 709

Bardem, Pilar, 709

Barford, Ian, 1371

Barish, Natalie, 593

Barkan, Anna, 531

Barker, Adam, 1137

Barker, Howard, 400

Barkin, Ellen, 379

Barkley, Charles, 500

Barkworth, Peter, 1460

Barlett, Charles, 61

Barlow, Patrick, 1137

Barlow, Tim, 247, 674, 1375

Barnes, Joanna, 936

Barnett, Gemini, 1419

Baron, Chuck, 497

Baron, Roshanna, 936

Baron, Sandy, 522

Baroni, Gil, 686

Barquin, Pedro, 462

Barr, Kathleen, 1076

Barr, Russell, 652, 1044

Barr, Tina, 1416

Barrera, David, 19

Barrett, Bob, 1137

Barrett, Dan, 1449

Barrett, David, 232

Barrett, Laurinda, 959

Barron, Barbara Hubbard, 539

Barron, Jaret Ross, 1447

Barrow, Andrew, 740

Barrows, Manny, 1308

Barry, Alan, 427

Barry, Jason, 832

Barry, Marion, Jr., 1182

Barry, Matt, 1081

Barry, Thom, 757

Barrymore, Drew, 356, 546, 1419

Barrymore, Jaid, 659

Barrymore, Michael, 1249

Bartel, Paul, 109

Barthell, Aleta, 1495

Bartilson, Lynsey, 1037

Bartlett, Bonnie, 1000

Bartlett, Robin, 225

Barton, Mischa, 664

Bartsch, Ted, 1457

Basch, Peter, 951

Basco, Derek, 1174

Basile, Joe, 1129

Basoli, Anna, 572

Bass, Ben, 133

Bass, George, 130

Bass, Victoria, 1456

Bassett, Angela, 563, 896

Bassey, Michaella, 1206

Bassler, Bethany, 811

Bastami, Mehdi, 1293

Bastel, Victoria, 1222

Bastos, Othon, 195

Basulto, David, 21

Basulto, Joe, 1339

Bates, James, 1416

Bates, Kathy, 1000, 1280, 1416

Bateson, Timothy, 674

Batten, Cyia, 1129

Battista, Rich, 448

Batyr, Christopher, 497

Bauche, Vanessa, 773

Baudin, Thalia, 1057

Baun, Jack, 757

Bavan, Yolande, 903

Baxter, Charles Thomas, 576

Baxter, David, 1375

Baxter, Tommie, 187

Bay, Frances, 636

Bayat, Ali Reza, 1293

Baylis, Matt, 1416

Be, Yoshio, 871

Beach, Adam, 1203

Beall, Rich, 967

Beals, Jennifer, 659

Bean, Chris, 1371

Bean, Sean, 1062

Beard, Jane, 1240

Beard, Steven, 1137

Beasley, Alyson E., 434

Beasley, Angela, 434

Beastie Boys, 406

Beaton, Martin, 1100

Beattie, Joe, 1390

Beattie, Ron, 631

Beatty, Bruce, 851

Beatty, Jeff, 1155

Beatty, Ned, 500

Beatty, Warren, 155

Beauchene, Billy, 1308

Beauchene, Kathy, 1308

Beaudene, Raquel, 461

Beauville, Raphaël, 751

Beaver, Carolyn, 1375
Bechir, Pierre, 48
Beckel, Graham, 112, 155
Becker, Gerry, 187, 481, 959
Becker, Merte, 623
Beckett, Diane, 866
Beckford, Luis, 1476
Beckinsale, Kate, 659, 1149
Beckworth, Alan, 1062
Bedard, Irene, 1203
Bedelia, Bonnie, 67
Bednarz, Mark, 434
Beegle, Brian, 757
Beehner, Scott, 659
Beener, Yada, 77
Beeton, Daryl, 1304
Behr, Dani, 697
Behr, Jason, 978
Beint, Michael, 339
Beiser, Brenda, 593
Belack, Doris, 636, 857
Belance, Alerte, 77
Belcon, Natalie Venetia, 1471
Belcourt, Dominique, 390
Beliaev, Iurii, 1315
Bell, Addison, 1164
Bell, Ann, 652
Bell, Daniel, 37
Bell, E.E., 847
Bell, Michael, 1077
Bell, Mindy, 1371
Bell, Nicholas, 271
Bell, Steve, 697
Bell, Tom, 1280
Bell, Wade, 1466
Belle, Camilla, 993
Bellegarde, Véronique, 1216, 1426
Bello, Mario, 965
Bello, Teodorina, 996
Belly, Karine, 759
Belton, Tony, 847
Beltzman, Mark, 1419
Belzer, Richard, 1240
Bemis, Cliff, 857
Bench, Park, 133
Benchley, Nat, 1240
Bendov , Veronika, 674
Benedetti, Caprice, 993
Benedicto, Lourdes, 965
Benfield, John, 247
Benford, Starla, 959
Benigni, Roberto, 686
Bening, Annette, 1154
Benitez, Mike, 540
Benjamin, 126, 1319
Benjamin, Jon, 865
Benjamin, Ross, 1000
Benjamin-Cooper, Michelle, 434
Bennes, John, 1262
Bennett, Alan, 652

Bennett, Andrew, 427
Bennett, Cle, 1387
Bennett, Denosh, 1471
Bennett, Jesse, 237
Bennett, Norman, 550
Bennett, Sophie, 806
Benny, 1440
Benrubi, Abe, 1077
Benson, Chris, 322
Benson, Peter, 959
Benson, Rex, 153
Benson, Ryan C., 679
Benson, Wendy, 1269
Bensted, Vicki, 1149
Bentley, Justine, 631
Bentley, Wes, 77
Benureau, Didier, 201
Ben-Victor, Paul, 232
Berben, Iris, 623
Berbist, Jos, 211
Berdick, Leonard, 587
Berenger, Tom, 434
Berger, Gregg, 1077
Bergeron, Philippe, 448
Bergholz, Jonathan, 1057
Bergin, John, 589
Bergschneider, Conrad, 310
Berg, Francine, 1131
Berkely, Xander, 969
Berkley, Elizabeth, 1040
Berland, François, 1131
Berlin, Brigid, 954
Berman, Elizabeth, 349
Bern, Mina, 187
Bernadette, Nicole, 1490
Bernal, Juan Manuel, 805
Bernard, Lena, 1426
Bernard, Taylor, 232
Bernard, Tudy, 1426
Bernardo, Paul Joseph, 1206
Bernhard, Sandra, 1221, 1474
Bernhardt, Dale Chick, 1371
Berns, Judy Jean, 578
Bernsen, Corbin, 757
Bernstein, Jack, 755
Berrocal, Leire, 1288
Berrou, Hélène, 1426
Berroyer, Jackie, 1284
Berry, Halle, 155, 1442
Berry, Sydney, 550
Bershevitz, Vladimir, 294
Bertelot, Suzanne, 694
Berwick, Arthur, 187
Besch, Cheyenne, 1145
Beshlian, Harout, 232
Bessant, Shane, 1375

Bessette, Denise, 1228
Best, Travis, 500
Besten, Blair, 72
Bethea, Ellen, 1154
Bettany, Paul, 652
Better, Eddie, 850
Better, Sonnie, 850
Betts, Jack, 441
Bevan, Daisy, 339
Bevan, Tim, 339
Bevis, Leslie, 909
Bews, Guy, 1474
Beyer, Troy, 434, 684
Bezace, Didier, 201
Bezgin, Igor, 1344
Bianchi, Massimo, 686
Bianco, Tony Lo, 755
Biase, Mike, 232
Bibic, Vladimir, 187
Bichir, Bruno, 805
Bickelmann, Cerita Monet, 1443
Bickhofer, Anna, 89
Bidanie, Zit, 1240
Biehl, Bonnie, 109
Biel, Jessica, 593
Bieling, Susann, 89
Bierko, Craig, 379, 1228
Big Boy, 975
Bigley, Paul, 1137
Bigwood, Michael Crag, 1447
Bilderback, Nicole, 173
Billet, Bradford, 959
Billig, Simon, 1319
Billingslea, Beau, 472
Binchy, Kate, 822
Bini, Jennifer, 1456
Binkley, James, 310, 385
Binnie, Alex, 470
Binnings, Earl S., 400
Birch, Dawn, 1416
Bird, Emma, 457
Birk, Raye, 1255
Birkett, Jeremiah, 671
Birkin, David, 674
Birkin, Jane, 1216
Birkova, Lena, 847
Birman, Matt, 1387
Birney, Frank, 755
Birney, Reed, 959
Bishop, Rummy, 310, 468
Bisio, Claudio, 1344
Bissell, Robin, 978
Bisset, Douglas, 806
Bisset, Jacqueline, 269
Bjork, 406
Bjorkman, Stig, 1342
Bjorn-Andersen, Michelle, 626
Black, Jack, 348
Black, James, 448, 920
Black, Jay, 75, 847
Black, Louis, 364
Black, Lucas, 1476

Black, Mary, 1474
Black, Varen, 1371
Blackburn, Richard, 322
Blacker, David, 385
Blackman, Joan, 801
Blackman, Sean San Jose, 326
Blades, Ruben, 219
Blaevoet, Hine, 694
Blagojevic, Ljiljana, 1123
Blair, Selma, 173
Blaisdell, Brad, 851
Blake, Andre, 1264
Blake, Craig, 563
Blake, Geoffrey, 811
Blake, Megan, 909
Blakely, Rachel, 819
Blakesley, Weston, 978
Blalock, Steve, 616
Blanc, Dominique, 1216
Blancard, Jarred, 313
Blancehtt, Cate, 339
Blanchard, David, 472
Blanchard, Tara, 21
Blanche, Robert, 1495
Blank, Brad, 1308
Bleasdale, John, 1461
Bleeth, Yasmine, 72
Blethyn, Brenda, 703
Blevins, Corey, 931
Blicker, Jason, 468
Bloch, Bernard, 1062
Bloch, Debora, 929
Block, Bruce, 936
Bloom, Orlando, 1461
Blount, Will, 379
Blucas, Marc, 978
Bluestein, David, 468
Blumberg, Ted, 597
Blumenthal, Geroge S., 959
Blumenthal, Marion, 959
Blundell, John, 876
Bluthal, John, 271
Blythe, Robert, 1304
Boakye, Adusah, 462
Boardley, Fawn, 1471
Boardman, Chad, 109
Boas, Erna, 184
Boas, John, 184
Bobby, Anne, 481
Boccaccio, Gil, 379
Bode, Georg-Martin, 623
Bodle, Jane, 888
Bodnar, Michael, 119
Bodrov, Sergei, Jr., 137
Body, Leslie, 572
Bod, Ben, 1174
Boedy, Thomas, 1167
Boeheim, Jim, 500
Boen, Earl, 857
Bogdanovich, Peter, 816

Bogert, William, 959
Boggs, Bill, 1240
Bohn, Jürgen, 686
Bohne, Bruce, 944
Bohrer, Corinne, 1253
Bohringer, Romane, 201
Boidin, Samuel, 694
Boisen, Ole, 626
Bojorquez, Yolanda, 1339
Boles, Gene, 832
Bollard, Natalie, 272
Bolster, Richard, 1094
Bolton, Michael, 1474
Bolz, Alexandra, 89
Bon Jovi, Jon, 548, 667, 882
Bon, Ross, 631
Bonanni, Maud, 269
Bondam, Klaus, 184
Bondy, Ken, 414
Bonet, Deni, 1272
Bonet, Lisa, 348
Bonet, Wilma, 1429
Boni, Gabrielle, 738
Bonifant, J. Evan, 119
Bonin, Neil, 1489
Bonini, Nathaniel, 587
Bonnal, Frédérique, 768
Bonnevie, Maria, 607
Boocock, Paul, 512
Booker, Jessica, 310
Booker, Richard, 931
Booker, Tom, 554
Boone, Lesley, 593
Boone, Mark, Jr., 40, 584, 615, 1319
Boorem, Mika, 610, 811
Boren, Heidi, 936
Borgnine, Ernest, 72, 1197
Borriello, Bobby, 348
Borsay, Les, 109
Boryea, Jay, 1069
Bosa, John, 540
Bosco, Mario, 385
Bosco, Philip, 834
Bose-Smith, Jason, 21
Bost, Olivia, 1135
Boston, Michael, 699
Boston, Philip, 601
Boswell, Anthony, 578
Boswell, Donnie, Sr., 722
Boswell, Glenn, 272
Bosworth, Catherine, 554
Bosworth, Martin, 349
Botuchis, Mathew, 1334
Bouajila, Sami, 48, 1154
Bouali, Louisa, 764
Boucher, Brigitte, 759
Bouchez, Elodie, 411

Bouck, Jonathan David, 1197
Boudet, Jacques, 768
Bougere, Teagle F., 597
Boulton, Nicholas, 1137
Bourassa, Jacques, 1474
Bourdo, Sacha, 1426
Bourgeois, John, 806
Boutte, Jean-Luc, 646
Bovingloh, Don, 755
Bowen, Jake, 944
Bower, John T., 811
Bowersox, Bob, 959
Bowles, Hamish, 746
Bowlin, Brandon N., 155
Bowman, Al, 640
Bowman, Jeffrey, 914
Bowman, Ronald "Buzz", 757
Boxer, Amanda, 1100
Boyce, Alan, 1180
Boyce, Zoe, 1390
Boyd, Ken, 1474
Boyd, Lynda, 313
Boyd, Rebecca, 1053
Boyle, Alan, 164
Boyle, Lara Flynn, 480
Boyle, Peter, 317
Boynton, Alexander, 1474
Braccia, Marion, 441
Bracco, Elizabeth, 597
Bradfield, Dawn, 265
Bradford, Doug, 126
Bradford, Jesse, 1216
Bradford, Jon, 987
Bradford, Susan, 888
Bradford, Toby, 129
Bradley, Angela, 1044
Bradley, Christopher, 109, 669
Bradley, Peter, Jr., 1390
Bradshaw, Michael, 1021
Bradshaw, Richard, 822
Brady, Don, 722
Brady, Rachel, 589
Braeden, Eric, 780
Braham, Emily, 1149
Braid, Hilda, 822
Braidwood, Kate, 313
Braidwood, Tom, 1476
Branagh, Kenneth, 187, 434, 1020, 1304
Brancato, Lillo, 348
Brandenburg, Larry, 379, 757, 811, 1229
Brandenburg, Otto, 626
Brandon, Mark, 10

Brandon, Michael, 294
Brandt, Max, 583
Brandy, 584
Branklyn, Charles A., 317
Brantley, Betsy, 285, 349, 798
Brantley, Whitt, 112
Brás, Patricia, 195
Braschi, Nicoletta, 686, 958
Brask, Cecilie, 626
Braugher, André, 225
Braun, Craig, 461
Braun, Michael, 1371
Braunstein, Terry, 140
Braverman, Marvin, 1229
Bray, Charles "Chip", 860
Bray, Wilfrid, 310
Braz, Joao, 195
Brazeau, Jay, 10, 313
Brazier, Jon, 1375
Breathnach, Páraic, 165
Breed, Helen Lloyd, 544
Breen, Patrick, 903
Breland, Mark, 500
Brenna, Wayne, 237
Brennan, Brid, 264
Brennan, Kevin, 468
Brennan, Neal, 468
Brennan, Stephen, 427
Brenneman, Amy, 1483
Breslau, Susan, 72
Breton, Daniel, 1062
Brett, Danielle, 1387
Brettingham, Steve, 634
Breuer, Jim, 468
Breuil, Jose "Don Pepe", 1440
Brewster, Jordana, 364
Brewster, Paget, 684
Breyner, Nicolau, 958
Brezner, China, 636
Brice, David, 1380
Bridges, Jeff, 97
Bridges, Lloyd, 755
Bridges-Nicasio, Betty, 871
Bridgewater, Stephen, 379
Brier, Nicole, 1069
Briers, Richard, 1249
Briggs, Jack, 640
Bright, Don, 931
Brightwell, Paul, 1189
Briley-Strand, Gwen, 1240
Brill, Steven, 1419
Bring, Gabriella, 587
Bringelson, Mark, 1214
Brisbin, David, 379
Briscoe, Brent, 1167

Brissart, Jean-Pol, 759
Britton, Connie, 882
Broadbent, Jim, 52, 123, 703
Broadber, Jill, 1380
Brock, Benjamin, 610, 1429
Brock, Kelly Le, 1474
Brocklebank, Daniel, 1137
Brockman, Michael, 1361
Broderick, Charlie, 866
Broderick, Erin, 112
Broderick, Matthew, 448
Brodie, Colin, 349
Brody, Adrien, 1302, 1319
Brody, Raymond, 457
Brogger, Ivar, 1129
Brogren, Paul, 468
Brolin, Josh, 874
Brolly, Clark, 40, 1180
Bromfield, Gerry, 876
Bromley, Joe, 457
Brook, Faith, 822
Brookhurst, Michael, 1129
Brookhurst, Michelle, 173
Brooks, Albert, 317, 920
Brooks, Annabel, 746
Brooks, Avery, 21, 93
Brooks, Diana, 457
Brooks, Jeff, 69
Brooks, Lonnie, 119
Brooks, Nick, 1100
Broomfield, Nick, 640
Brosnan, Pierce, 1031
Broughton, Linda, 1189
Broughton, Paul, 697
Broulard, Odile, 40, 1174
Brown, Benjamin, 584
Brown, Bobby, 954
Brown, Bundy, 831
Brown, Chelsea, 1424
Brown, Dexter, 959
Brown, Donna Marie, 33
Brown, Foxy, 1471
Brown, James, 119, 539
Brown, Jim, 500, 1197
Brown, John, 376
Brown, Junior, 1269
Brown, Kedar, 1040
Brown, Lee, 1044
Brown, Lennox, 114, 349, 1371
Brown, Mark, 540, 920
Brown, Melanie, 1249
Brown, Nick, 1489

Brown, Norman Patrick, 1319
Brown, Orlando, 1129
Brown, P.J., 1069
Brown, Pat Crawford, 611
Brown, Phillip, 1375
Brown, Rhozier, 1181
Brown, Ronald D., 1081
Brown, Sharon, 468
Brown, Sloane, 954
Brown, W. Earl, 1308
Brown, Wedell, 798
Browne, Bernard, 322
Browne, Katrina, 1375
Browne, Roscoe Lee, 61
Brownlee, Mongo, 155
Brownstein, Rob, 1398
Bruce, Honey, 672
Bruce, Johnathon, 1474
Bruce, Kitty, 672
Bruce, Reginald, 497
Bruce, Susan, 276
Bruce, Valerie, 1308
Bruglio, Julia, 581
Brunet, Marc, 764
Bruno, Dylan, 1100
Bruno, Gary, 379
Bruskotter, Eric, 757
Bruynbroek, Frank, 448
Bry, Ellen, 286
Bryant, Lee, 540
Bryce, Mackenzie, 493
Brygmann, Lars, 184
Brynolfsson, Reine, 674
Bubriski, Peter, 18
Bucaro, Joey III, 1048
Bucatinsky, Dan, 909
Buchholtz, Horst, 686
Buck, Cory, 811
Buckford, Kenneth, 563
Buckley, A.J., 313
Buckley, Ellen, 715
Buckley, John, 851
Bucossi, Peter, 1069
Budge, Michael, 1308
Bufalo, Nicholas, 820
Buff, Sarah, 187, 1232
Bugajski, Monica, 1135
Buggy, Niall, 164
Bugin, Mary, 97
Buhr, Gavin, 394
Bukvicki, Marina, 1123
Bull, Lawrence, 1021
Bullmore, Amelia, 822
Bullock, Sandra, 550, 993
Bully, Bryon, 806
Bunakov, Victor, 1315
Bunce, Stuart, 1044
Bunker, Edward, 1135
Bunton, Emma, 1249

Buono, Cara, 865, 1061
Buratti, Verena, 686
Burdon, Catherine, 1471
Burgess, Rick, 1474
Burghardt, Arthur, 1253
Burgio, Danielle, 616
Burke, Adam, 699
Burke, Al, 1419
Burke, Billy, 755, 1466
Burke, Brian, 1425
Burke, Carlease, 1442
Burke, Jenni, 468
Burke, Kathy, 265, 338, 876
Burke, Keith, 975
Burke, Marylouise, 781, 903
Burke, Robert John, 400, 1221
Burke, Stephen, 697
Burkholder, Scott, 874, 1000
Burks, Jernard, 1206
Burmester, Leo, 1061
Burnett, Carol, 834
Burnette, Elizabeth, 232
Burney, Stuart, 308
Burns, Brendan, 1193
Burns, Edward, 882, 1100
Burns, Heather, 1489
Burns, Jack, 1228
Burns, Jere, 847
Burns, Peter, 1371
Burroughs, Hayley, 339
Burrowes, Marcus, 468
Burrows, Darren, 521
Burstyn, Ellen, 282
Burton, Kate, 187
Burton, LeVar, 1254
Burton, Terrance, 97
Busby, Linda, 740
Buscemi, Steve, 40, 97, 597, 1040, 1419
Busch, Charles, 1343
Busch, Ian, 636
Busch, Inga, 623
Busey, Gary, 379, 1213
Busey, Jake, 348, 546
Busfield, Timothy, 1227
Bush, Robert L., 616
Bush, Margaret, 1269
Bush, Tommy, 1081
Bushor, Janet, 1457
Buskin, Aaron, 1375
Bustric, Sergio, 686
Butel, Mitchell, 271
Butler, Chelsea, 282
Butler, Dan, 348, 1162
Butler, Dollie, 578
Butler, Genevieve, 282
Butler, Paul, 1232

Butler, William, 669
Buttafuoco, Joey, 187
Buttafuoco, Mary Jo,
  187
Butterfield, Neil, 659
Butters, Mike, 1129
Butusov, Slava, 137
Buzzhead, 1180
Byatt, Michelle, 1380
Bye, John Ivar, 619
Byers, Lyndon, 832
Byrd, David, 1021
Byrd, Donald, 864
Byrd, Thomas Jeff-
  erson, 155, 500
Byrd, William "Buddy",
  554
Byrne, Antoine, 589
Byrne, Gabriel, 348,
  759, 987, 1031
Byrne, Jason, 427,
  589
Byrne, Jenna, 1419
Byrne, Michael, 33,
  232
Byrne, Patsy, 674
Byrnes, C.J., 554
Byrnes, Vanessa, 1375
Byron, David, 903
Byron, Kathleen, 674,
  1100

Caan, Scott, 348
Caballero, Katia, 751
Caban, Angel, 187
Cabezas, Oyanka, 176
Cabral, Tony, 773
Cabrinha, Pete, 601
Cacho, Daniel Gimenez,
  805
Cadell, Selina, 822
Caesar, Shirley, 1443
Caffrey, Peter, 589
Cage, Nicolas, 225,
  1206
Caggiano, Tim, 954
Cahill, Lynn, 427
Caicedo, Donny, 1085
Cain, Burl, 376
Cain, Robbie, 109
Caine, Charlie, 697
Caine, Michael, 703
Cairns, Tyler, 1164
Caise, Yule, 317
Calderon, Paul, 920
Caldwell, Chris, 1466
Caldwell, Sandra, 322
Calfa, Don, 317
Calhoun, Monica, 975
Call, Allyson, 755
Callaghan, Stuart,
  1390
Callahan, Greg, 448
Callan, Carmel, 589
Callan, Margaret, 589
Callan, Peter, 61, 272
Calleia, Joseph, 1339

Callen, Christopher,
  379
Callender, L. Peter,
  317
Callow, Simon, 1137
Calnan, Richard, 232
Calo, Angela, 954
Caloz, Michael, 1, 738
Calvert, Phyllis, 822
Calypso, Anthony S.,
  77
Camacho, Mark, 1,
  1206
Camargo, Chrisanto,
  195
Camero, Robert, 686
Cameron, Dean, 519
Cameron, Earl, 294
Camilleri, Terry, 1348
Camp, Andrew, 581
Camp, Bill, 1069
Camp, Hamilton, 19,
  318
Campanella, Sauveur,
  764
Campbell, Desmond,
  1206, 1471
Campbell, J. Kenneth,
  155
Campbell, Ken, 40
Campbell, Kim, 109
Campbell, Larkin, 679
Campbell, Luther, 975,
  1057
Campbell, Michael
  Leydon, 951
Campbell, Neil, 461
Campbell, Neve, 385,
  1456
Campbell, Rennie,
  1409
Campbell, Saskia, 61
Campbell, Scott
  Michael, 155
Campbell, Sean, 394
Candela, Michael, 580
Candelario, Wanda,
  497
Canfield, Gene, 781
Cannata, T.J., 755
Cannon, Landy, 1040
Cano, Daniel, 349
Canonica, Sibylle, 89
Canova, Diana, 903
Cantarelli, Dario, 87
Cantarini, Giorgio, 686
Canto, Marilyne, 1426
Canton, Abigail, 733
Cantona, Eric, 339
Cantwell, Christopher,
  1061
Cantwell, John, 126
Capaldi, Peter, 1149
Capizzi, Bill, 61
Caplan, Twink, 871
Capodice, John, 348,
  1059
Cappon, John, 1361,
  1399

Carapezza, Mark, 278
Caravetta, Julio, 10
Carby, Fanny, 822
Card, Paul P. IV, 1429
Cardellini, Linda, 278,
  284
Carden, Paul, 434
Cardinal, Tantoo, 1203
Cardinaux, Monette,
  1426
Cardona, Rene, Jr.,
  304
Cardoso, Pedro, 403
Cardwell, Lena, 888
Carey, David, 427
Carey, Geoffrey, 247
Carey, Peter, 987
Carey, Richenda, 822
Carey, Tom, 1167
Carides, Gia, 1000
Carl, Jann, 155
Carlo, Ismael "East",
  944
Carlo, Johann, 481
Carlson, Beecey, 857
Carlson, Dylan, 640
Carlson, Erika, 773
Carlton, Darryl, 470
Carlyle, Robert, 176,
  440
Carneiro, Marcelo, 195
Carnes, Tara, 369
Carney, Laura, 978
Carney, Zane, 847
Carpentieri, Renato,
  48
Carpio, Maria
  Alejandra, 540
Carpio, Swan, 764
Carr, Howie, 232
Carr, Katie, 822
Carr, Melanie, 292
Carrey, Jim, 1164,
  1348
Carrier, Don, 385
Carrigan, Caroline, 232
Carrière, Normand, 69
Carroll, Beeson, 1069
Carroll, Ceciley, 1164
Carroll, Earl, 1419
Carroll, Jack, 1416
Carroll, James, 310
Carroll, Jolene, 575
Carroll, Kevin, 888
Carroll, Marjorie, 860
Carrot Top, 199
Carruthers, Chris-
  topher, 448
Carson, L.M. Kit, 572
Carter, Adam, 978
Carter, Craig, 522
Carter, Helena Bonham,
  801, 1304
Carter, Jim, 801,
  1137
Carter, Joelle, 554
Carter, John, 187
Carter, Myra, 130
Carter, Richard, 61

Carter, Vercy, 578
Cartlidge, Katrin, 519
Cartmell, Charles, 339
Cartwright, Angela,
  733
Cartwright, Ivan, 1390
Cartwright, Nancy, 448
Carubia, Saverio, 755
Carvell, Marium, 322
Casanova, Delia, 805
Casar, Amira, 764
Cascio, Will, 522
Cascone, Nicholas,
  874
Casey, Bob, 1262
Casey, Donna, 364
Casey, John P., 462
Casino, John, 616
Casler, Heather, 1447
Casnoff, Phillip, 563
Cass, Crystal, 312
Cass, Marc, 1100
Cassadie, Alberto, 201
Cassar, Raymond, 512
Cassel, Seymour, 326,
  1085
Cassel, Vincent, 339
Casseus, Gabriel, 112,
  369
Cassidy, Joanna, 269
Cassignard, Pierre,
  1131
Cassini, John, 472
Cassola, Carla, 269
Castaldo, Craig A., 448
Castellaneta, Dan, 847
Castellarin, Stephanie,
  544
Castellotti, Pete, 187
Castellucci, Teddy,
  1419
Castelotti, Pete, 201
Castillo, Enrique, 521
Castillo, Gilma Tuyub,
  789
Castillo-Faass, Terry,
  1253
Castle, Keith-Lee, 1390
Castle, Ramona, 77
Castle, Robert, 77
Casteberry, Chuck,
  920
Castrinho, 929
Catalano, Laura, 385
Catanese, Kerry, 155
Catano, Adriana, 540
Cates, Georgina, 237
Catillon, Brigitte, 48
Cattell, Todd, 636
Cauldwell, Sean, 1380
Caulfield, Maxwell,
  1040
Cauthen, Melvin, 1135
Cavanagh, Megan, 780
Cavanaugh, Christine,
  1077
Cave, Des, 427
Caviezel, James, 1319
Cawood, Sarah, 1390

Cayouette, Laura, 348,
  636
Cecchi, Carlo, 1260
Cecere, Fulvio, 313
Cecere, Vince, 931
Cedar, Larry, 379,
  874
Cedric the Entertainer,
  1057
Cegon, Eric, 1167
Celio, Teco, 1344
Cellier, Peter, 822
Cenatiempo, John,
  349
Cephers, Troy
  Anthony, 349
Cerqueira, Daniel,
  1100
Cerruti, Nino, 539
Cerveris, Todd, 903
Cervi, Valentina, 48
Cervo, Pascal, 411
Cesario, Jeff, 611
Ceili, 1061
Chaatouf, Kader, 694
Chaatouf, M., 694
Chaatouf, Mme., 694
Chabert, Lacey, 733
Chabrol, Thomas,
  1284
Chadbon, Tom, 1149
Chae, Sunny, 554
Chaet, Mark, 1229
Chaialton, Andrea, 531
Chaifetz, Dena, 308
Chain, Antoine, 1216
Chalfant, Kathleen,
  275, 659, 996
Chalfoun, Carine, 699
Chalk, Garry, 312
Challet, Jackie R.,
  1419
Chalupa, Václav, 674
Chamberlain, Duncan,
  931
Chamberlain, Nicole,
  951
Chambers, Jacob, 348
Chambers, Tom, 477
Chan, Dennis, 634
Chan, Henry, 310
Chan, Jackie, 819,
  1081
Chan, Jon C., 1069
Chan, Kim, 679
Chan, Michael Paul,
  1371
Chan, Moses, 634
Chan, Sumiko (Osumi),
  1081
Chan, Victor, 832,
  1471
Chancey, Doug, 1135
Chandler, Simon, 1249
Chaney, Eoin, 165
Chaney, John, 500
Cheng, Ray, 679
Chang, Richard, 1053

Channing, Stockard, 93, 1361
Chao, Rosalind, 1429
Chaplin, Ben, 1319
Chaplin, Carmen, 989
Chaplin, Geraldine, 247
Chapman, David, 1164
Chapman, Justin, 72
Chapman, Kevin, 832
Chapman, Lonny, 874
Chapman, Michael, 1174
Chapman, Tom, 1057
Chappelle, Dave, 468, 1040, 1471, 1489
Charbonnet, Gina T., 1414
Charendoff, Tara, 1077
Charles, Emile, 697
Charles, Rebecca, 1137
Charles, Scott, 1149
Charn, 1474
Chartoff, Melanie, 1077
Chartrand, Jean-Paul, 1206
Chase, Angie, 860
Chase, Cheryl, 1077
Chase, Chevy, 310
Chase, Johnie, 310, 322
Chase, Maraya, 512
Chatto, Grace, 531
Chau, Emil, 819
Chau-Li Chi, 1269
Chaykin, Maury, 740, 773
Cheadle, Don, 155, 920
Cheatham, Maree, 871, 1419
Cheeseman, Ken, 866, 1020
Chelsea, 640
Chen, Gene, 1057
Chen, Lauren, 888
Chen, Lisa Marie, 806
Cheney, Michael, 1308
Chepovetsky, Dimitry, 593
Chernov, Jacqueline, 540
Cherot, Christopher Scott, 497
Cheshier, Lydell M., 944
Chesnais, Patrick, 989
Chester, Craig, 276
Chester, Rodney, 109
Cheung, George, 679, 1081
Cheung, Joseph, 243
Cheung, Leslie, 634
Cheung, Maggie, 219, 243
Chevrier, Arno, 201
Cheyenne, Peter, 970

Chianese, Dominic, Jr., 1181
Chibas, Marissa, 512
Chieffo, Michael, 798
Chigarev, Dima, 1315
Chiklis, Michael, 1213
Child, Jeremy, 1044
Chin, Glen, 634
Chin, Jeanne, 679, 1152
Chiros, Jim, 1020
Chisholm, Anthony, 77
Chisholm, Melanie, 1249
Chiu, Ann, 806
Cho, John, 1152
Cho, Margaret, 1077
Chong, Phil, 679
Chong, Tommy, 468
Choudhury, Sarita, 959
Chovanian, Arthur, 1229
Chow, China, 93
Chow, Michael, 679, 1081
Chow, William, 634
Chow Yun-Fat, 1048
Choy, Cordelia, 634
Chrest, Joe, 920
Christensen, Laura, 626
Christensen, Margaret, 61
Christensen, Sean, 332
Christensen, Tove, 1466
Christian, Troy, 936
Christine, Wanda, 944
Christman, Charlie, 1264
Christopher, Dyllan, 40
Christopher, June, 317
Christopher, Mike, 540
Chuipka, Chip, 1206
Chunn, Tommy, 578
Chuvalo, George, 310
Ciampi, Daniele, 269
Ciarrocchi, Pat, 369
Cibrian, Eddie, 715
Cicchetti, Mike, 369
Cicchini, Robert, 232, 1000
Ciccolella, Jude, 77
Cicero, Paul, 1069
Cilberg, Frank, 448
Cinabro, Stephen A., 1371
Cinis, Alan, 271
Cirka, Cassidy, 987
Citran, Roberto, 1344
Cividanes, Robert, 187
Claire, Julie, 1229
Carol Ann Susi, 755
Clapczynski, Stefan, 416
Clark, Bill, 369
Clark, Blake, 1416

Clark, Dave Allen, 155
Clark, Jonathan, 703
Clark, Matt, 548
Clark, Mystro, 199
Clarke, Basil, 61
Clarke, Eugene, 322
Clarke, George, 746
Clarke, Jason, 1361
Clarke, Lenny, 832, 1069, 1308
Clarke, Rachel, 1137
Clarke, Richard, 781
Clarke, Victoria, 640
Clarkson, Patricia, 527
Clatterbuck, Tamara, 1228
Clavet, Deano, 1206
Claxton, Jack, 140
Clay, Ray, 500
Clayton, Judy, 1348
Clegg, John, 801, 1149
Cleghorne, Ellen, 40
Clemenson, Christian, 19, 40, 97, 811
Clement, Andrew, 944
Clemente, Francesco, 1440
Clemons, Lorenzo, 1371
Clifford, Cheryl, 1290
Clinton, Roger, 1077
Clooney, George, 414, 920, 1319
Cloud, Lisa, 936
Clough, John Scott, 967
Clover, Andrew, 764
Clunes, Martin, 1137
Cluzet, François, 1284
Clydesdale, Gareth, 61
Coassin, Cinzia, 271
Coates, Dorothy Love, 77
Coates, Kade, 1348
Coats, Steve, 781
Cobbs, Bill, 550, 584, 951
Coberly, Sydney, 1048
Coburn, James, 1
Cochran, Colby, 993
Cochrane, Brian, 1474
Cockburn, Arlene, 457
Cockrum, Dennis, 298
Cody, Alan, 1137
Cody, Dawn, 978
Coen, Alexis Rose, 21
Cohen, Amy, 414
Cohen, Greg, 1449
Cohen, Lynn, 572
Cohen, Marc, 468
Cohen, Ray, 187
Cohen, Richard, 1489
Cokljat, Robert Bosco, 959
Cold, Ulrik, 626
Cole, Alexander, 936
Cole, Gary, 593, 1167
Coleman, Bill, 1034

Coleman, Brady, 546
Coleman, Clarke, 615
Coleman, Dabney, 1489
Coleman, David, 1466
Coleman, Edwin L. II, 1466
Coleman, Gary, 310
Coleman, Jim, 931
Coleman, Joe, 1034
Coleman, Kalena, 126
Coleman, Kari, 1228, 1285
Colgan, Valerie, 1100
Colicchio, Victor, 187
Colina, Luis, 97
Collard, Kenneth, 941
Collette, Toni, 240, 1389
Collier, Marian, 679
Collins, Emmy, 954
Collins, Greg, 40, 349, 448
Collins, Jackie, 896
Collins, Mark, 798
Collins, Ray, 1339
Colomby, Scott, 298
Colton, Michael, 468, 806
Colwell, Joshua, 286
Combs, Jeffrey, 182, 584
Comden, Danny, 1387
Comete, James Pierre, 915
Como, Franie, 755
Compton, Norm F., 1048
Compton, O'Neal, 285, 1000
Conard, Steven Brian, 554
Condon, Dominic, 61
Condron, Patrick, 427
Conley, Jack, 538, 798
Conley, Mark, 109
Conlon, Luisa, 1216
Connelly, Jennifer, 271
Connery, Sean, 52
Connick, Harry, Jr., 550
Connolly, Billy, 597
Connolly, John G., 1436
Connors, Kevin, 978
Conrad, David, 1053
Conrad, Roy, 944
Conroy, Brendan, 165, 427
Conroy, Neile, 427
Consalvi, Ennio, 686
Constantine, Yorgo, 1443
Conti, Ugo, 87
Contreras, Karen, 996
Contursi, Janet, 1371
Conway, Denis, 589
Conway, Kevin, 798

Conway, Lyle, 114
Conway, Tim, 10
Coogan, Cassandra A., 1466
Cook, Ben, 738
Cook, Rachael Leigh, 715
Cooke, Alan, 1149
Cooke, Chris, 583
Cooley, David, 33
Cooley, Terry, 155
Coolidge, Jennifer, 871, 1187
Cooney, Kevin, 155, 240, 1000, 1129
Cooney, Tim, 679
Cooper, Bella, 1424
Cooper, Chris, 461, 554
Cooper, James, 468
Cooper, Rowena, 1149
Copeland, Joan, 888
Copeland, Kevin, 1424
Copp, Aimee, 1384
Coraci, Frank, 1416
Corazza, Vincent, 133, 740
Corber, Arthur, 1474
Corbiletto, Roberto, 269
Corcoran, Jay, 18
Cordova, Amanda, 522
Cordova, Laura, 616
Corduner, Allan, 597
Corey, Dave, 540, 1348
Corman, Maddie, 587
Cornacchione, Antoni, 540, 1457
Cornicard, Stephan, 1100
Corone, Antoni, 1348
Corr, Andrea, 1031
Corrazza, Vince, 1387
Corrente, Damian, 572
Corri, Nick, 1471
Corrigan, Antonia, 1149
Corrigan, Kevin, 140, 512, 595, 1193
Corso, Lee, 1417
Cortese, Joe, 21
Cosentino, Giancarlo, 686
Cosgrove, Daniel, 888
Cosme, Gabriel, 789
Cosmo, James, 61
Costa, James, 755
Costabile, David, 1154
Costanzo, Anthony Roth, 1216
Costanzo, Robert, 10
Costas, Bob, 72
Costello, Elvis, 1249
Costelloe, John, 187
Costenza, Len, 1129
Costesu, Petre, 420
Costigan, Ken, 597
Costini, Angela, 434

Cotten, Joseph, 1339
Cotterill, Chrissie, 876
Cottle, Jason, 1419
Cotton, Antony, 746
Cotton, Jerry, 699
Cottreel, Genevive, 694
Cottreel, Marjorie, 694
Cottrell, Mickey, 33
Coulson, Bernie, 492
Council, Richard, 130
Countess Koulinskyi, 457
Courier, David, 275
Couser, Kathleen, 1269
Cover, Franklin, 19
Covert, Allen, 1416, 1419
Cowen, Shuulie, 216
Cowher, Bill, 1417
Cox, Alan, 822
Cox, Brian, 298, 1085
Cox, Claire, 1149
Cox, Jennifer Elise, 379
Cox, John Henry, 1155
Cox, Veanne, 512, 1489
Coyle, Brendan, 427
Coyle, Joe, 920
Coyote, Peter, 944, 1243
Crabb, Bill, 434
Crable, Bradley, 758
Craig, Aaron, 686
Craig, Daniel, 339, 746
Cramer, Kendal, 457
Crane, Chilton, 394
Crane, Rachel, 1229
Cranitch, Lorcan, 265
Cranshaw, Patrick, 19
Cranston, Bryan, 1100
Crapie, Anne-Ccile, 1216
Craven, Matt, 951
Crawford, Eve, 806
Crawford, George, 376
Crawford, J.W., 1495
Crawford, Shontonette, 497
Creech, Don, 512
Creed-Miles, Charlie, 876
Cregg, Ian, 674
Cremer, Ute, 89
Cremins, Robert "Bobby", 500
Crenna, Richard, 1474
Crenna, Yvon, 1284
Criswell, Lora Anne, 993
Crivello, Anthony, 755
Croft, Doreen Chou, 944
Crompton, Ben, 674
Cromwell, James, 60, 285, 1240
Cronauer, Gail, 860

Cronaur, Gail, 699
Cronin, Jeanette, 271
Cronin, John, 427
Cropper, Steve, 119
Crosbie, Annette, 1149
Crosby, Denise, 286
Cross, David, 1197
Cross, Harley, 1216
Cross, Joseph, 298, 610, 1447
Cross, Rick, 1474
Crowder, Daniel, 52
Crowe, Ian, 390
Crowley, Amelia, 589
Crowley, Donnacha, 427
Crubbs, Gary, 1476
Crudup, Billy, 521, 832, 1466
Crum, Denny, 500
Cruttenden, Hal, 822
Cruz, Alexis, 1442
Cruz, Anthony "Az", 75
Cruz, Anthony Jesse, 755
Cruz, Ernesto Gomez, 805
Cruz, Gary, 448
Cruz, Gregory Norman, 19
Cruz, Maria Fernandez, 773
Cruz, Monica Fernandez, 773
Cruz, Penelope, 522, 709, 1288
Cruz, Ricardo, 357
Cruz, Tania, 789
Cruzat, Liza, 631
Cryer, Jon, 539
Crystal, Billy, 847
Crystal, Lindsay, 847
Csitos, Michelle, 874
Csokas, Marton, 126
Cubison, Richard, 1461
Cuccioli, Robert, 187
Cudlitz, Michael, 851
Cuervo, Alma, 187
Cuevas, Jose-Luis, 304
Cuker, Elliot, 1232
Culbertson, Rod, 339
Culkin, Kieran, 806
Culkin, Michael, 269, 722
Cullen, Jonathan, 1390
Cullum, Jim, 1269
Culp, Tara Ann, 1206
Cumming, Alan, 1249
Cumming, Alastair, 1390
Cummings, Jim, 61, 1197
Cunha, Telma, 195
Cunningham, Bill, 434
Cunningham, Jocelyn, 477
Curry, Christopher, 155

Curry, Mark, 40
Curry, Tim, 1077
Curtin, Jane, 27
Curtis, Charlie, 349
Curtis, Cliff, 291, 1174
Curtis, Clint, 114, 291
Curtis, Grant, 1167
Curtis, Jahmal, 1447
Curtis, Jamie Lee, 472, 548
Curtiz, David, 1137
Cusack, John, 216, 1319
Cutell, Lou, 857
Cuthbert, Jon, 394
Cutler, Wendy, 369
Cutrona, Ryan, 1023
Cuttell, Ricki, 357
Cvetkovic, Svetozar, 1123
Cyr, Myriam, 1240
Czajkowski, Peter, 531
Czerny, Henry, 887
Czypionka, Hansa, 89

D J Spooky, 831
Da, Frédéric, 1216
Dado, 1371
Dafoe, Willem, 1
Dagg, Cory, 1474
Daggett, Jensen, 757
Dahlberg, Erik, 1442
Dahlgren, Tom, 1229
Daike, Yuko, 396
Daikun, Alex, 1474
Daily, E. G., 61, 1077
Dakinah, Gbatokai, 184
Dalmes, Mony, 1284
Deloise, Sean, 187
d'Aloja, Francesca, 1260
Dalton, Kristin, 871
Daltrey, Roger, 697
Daly, Peter Hugo, 427
Daly, Shane, 310
Daly, Tim, 888
Damon, Mark, 282
Damon, Matt, 1069, 1100
Damon, Una, 286, 291, 1348
Dempf, Sarah, 225
Danare, Malcolm, 448
Dance, Charles, 531
Dane, Lawrence, 133
Dane, Shelton, 996
Danes, Claire, 674, 987
D'Angelo, Beverly, 21, 1037
D'Angerio, Joe, 1040
Daniel, Chic, 920
Daniels, Alex, 1253
Daniels, Ben, 75'i, 941
Daniels, Jeff, 978

Daniels, Max, 1048
Daniels, Robert, 987
Danner, Blythe, 882, 1020, 1476
Danner, Mike, 1222
Dannheisser, Adam, 996
Dano, Linda, 1221
Danson, Ted, 548, 1100
Dantas, Nelson, 403
Dante, Peter, 1416, 1419
Denton, Steve, 563
Danyliu, Andre, 313
Danza, Ton, 595
Daprocida, Rob, 1474
Darabont, Frank, 616
Daraiseh, Ammar, 1371
D'Arbanville, Patti, 187
D'Arcy, James, 1461
Darga, Christopher, 286
Darnell, Chad, 434
Darpino, Gloria, 1425
Darr, Lisa, 442
Darroussin, Jean-Pierre, 768, 1377
Darrow, Danny, 888
Darrow, Tony, 187
Darst, Danny, 434
da Silva, Estelina Moreira, 195
da Silva, José Pereira, 195
Davenport, Eric, 109
Davenport, Johnny Lee, 1371
David, Angel, 1366
David, Ingolf, 626
David, Keith, 40, 1308
David, Larry, 1229
David, Zdenek, 674
Davidovich, Lolita, 441
Davidson, Alan, 1069
Davidson, Tommy, 1471
Davidtz, Embeth, 369, 434
Davies, Eleanor, 310
Davies, Glynis, 313
Davies, Jeremy, 1100
Davies, Oliver Ford, 822
Davies, Robin, 1137
Davies, Sue Jones, 1304
Davis, Bob, 1167
Davis, Bridge D., 497
Davis, Craig, 1476
Davis, Deryl, 1348
Davis, Eddy, 1449
Davis, Felix, 652
Davis, Frank, 369

Davis, Hope, 597, 865
Davis, Jason, 755, 1081
Davis, Jeff, 874
Davis, Judy, 187
Davis, Julie, 580
Davis, Kristin, 1229
Davis, Michael, 69
Davis, Ossie, 317
Davis, Paula, 722
Davis, Regi, 954
Davis, Robert, 1348
Davis, Stan, 1000
Davis, Tom, 119, 500
Davis, Trey, 1399
Davis, Vaginal, 470
Davis, Vicki, 811
Davis, Viola, 920
Davis, William B., 1476
Davison, Bruce, 33, 951
Davy, Susan, 119
Dawkins, Harold, 563
Dawson, Rosario, 500
Day, Simon, 1137
Daydodge, Billy, 19
Daykin, Ariana, 531
D'Calveley, Hugh, 1375
de Alba, Cecile Sanz, 1405
de Almeida, Joaquim, 958
De Backer, Thomas, 1466
de Bankol, Isaac, 1216
De Caro, Vincenzo, 201
de Castro, Felicia, 1915
de Castro, Isabel, 1405
de Costa Filho, José Pedro, 195
Deacon, Robert, 1457
Deadmon, Kelly, 1206
Deakins, Mark, 1254
Deal, Jenilee, 811
Deal, Mark, 811
Dean, Erin J., 722
Dean, James F., 318
Dean, Jarrod, 1319
Dean, Loren, 348
Deavers, Dorothy, 722
Deayton, Angus, 339
Debaer, Jean, 959
Debatin, Jackie, 580
Deblinger, David, 996
deBoer, Nicole, 256
Debonis, Marcia, 882, 1061, 1348
Debranche, Maurice, 1284
Decadi, Anthony, 1216
Decaro, Matt, 1371
Deckert, Blue, 546
Decleir, Jan, 210
De Crispino, Sam, 349
Decter, Duke, 601
Deda, Herildo, 195

Deegan, Karl, 428
Deel, Felicia, 1240
Deer, Dodo, 1284
DeGeneres, Ellen, 318
de Gooyer, Rijk, 327
Degrandpré, Frédérick, 1206
De Jesus, Manuel, 773
De Juan, Jorge, 1288
DeKay, Tim, 19
de la Cruz, Mariano López, 789
De La Cruz, Mark, 593
De La Fuente, Joel, 1053
de la Huerta, Paz, 888
Delamere, Matthew, 1380
De Landa, Manuel, 1034
Delandro, Trelles, 1414
Delannoy, Vanina, 1426
Delany, Dana, 1447
de la Osa, Kristian, 751
de la Paix, Yvonne, 847
De La Soul, 406
Delate, Brian, 544, 1348
Delbaere, Sébastien, 694
DeLeo, Peter Paul, 540, 931
De Leon, Idalis, 1057
Delgado, Damián, 789
Delgarde, Domenick, 1339
Delia, Matty, 882
Dell, Michael, 581
Dellums, Erik Todd, 317
Delorenzo, Mary, 944
De Lorenzo, Michael, 967
Delorme, Sebastien, 1206
Del Sherman, Barry, 19
Del Toro, Benicio, 379
de Lima, Marcos, 195
de Linha, Preto, 195
de Lint, Derek, 286
De luca, Aaron, 48
Demas, Rick, 468
DeMentri, Vince, 1371
Demeter, Margot, 1495
Demetriou, Con, 1424
Demings, Pancho, 909, 1399
de Montalembert, Thibault, 646
Dempsey, Brendan F., 1409
De Munn, Jeffrey, 1476
Dench, Judi, 1137
Deneuve, Catherine, 425

Dengler, Dieter, 701
Denicourt, Marianne, 646
De Niro, Drena, 461
De Niro, Robert, 461, 672, 1062
Dennehy, Ned, 427
Denniel, Alain, 1426
Dennis, Alfred, 857
Dennis, Rachel, 751
Dennison, Holly, 1164
Dente, Joey, 755
Denton, Samuel, 468
de Oliveira, Manoel, 1405
de Oliveira, Vinícius, 195
de Palma, Rossy, 1288
Depardieu, Gérard, 759
Depp, Johnny, 379
De Quevedo, Rafael, 789
Derangre, Grégory, 764
De Ravenel, Ariel, 746
Dern, Bruce, 1197
De Roxtra, Ron, 860
Derringer, Robb, 636
Dery, Judy, 987
DeSalvo, Anne, 519
De Santis, Silvia, 48
De Santis, Stanley, 155, 240, 1081
De Santo, Daniel, 468
Descano, John, 369
Deschamps, Jérôme, 649
Deseure, Mélinda, 694
Désilius, Gerard Max, 1206
De Silva, Pietro, 686
Deslandes, Christophe, 764
Desmond, Dan, 225
Desmond, Paul, 232
Desormeaux, Danielle, 1
Desourdy, Marc, 1471
De Sousa, Melissa, 1057
De Souza, Ralf, 531
Desplechin, Fabrice, 646
Despont, Thierry W., 245
Desseaux, Alexis, 751
Desseaux, Rudi, 1426
De Stefano, Michael, 1384
Destry, John, 313
Desure, Francis, 694
de Tavira, Jose Maria, 773
Dettrich, Courtney, 993
De Vargas, Valentin, 1339
De Vincentis, D.V., 114

Devincentis, Sarah, 1495
Devine, Loretta, 322, 1387
DeVito, Danny, 715
Devitt, Matthew, 1409
Devlin, Billy, 40, 1081
Devos, Emmanuelle, 40, 646
De Wees, Rusty, 112
Dexter, Annabelle Raine, 477
Dexter, Sally, 390
Deyle, John, 903
De Young, Cliff, 1277
de Zern, Tim, 580
Diamond, Keith, 298
Dias, Jennie, 1339
Dias, Pat, 1471
Diaz, Cameron, 379, 1308, 1398
Diaz, Guillermo, 468, 587
Diaz, Joey "Coco", 72
Dib, Mohammed, 411
Dibben, Damien, 746
DiBenedetto, John, 1069
DiCaprio, Leonardo, 187, 759
Dickens, Kim, 461, 798, 1495
DiConcetto, Karen, 512
DiDonna, Gian, 1425
Diehl, Jeanne, 1129
Diehl, John, 522, 832
Dielsi, Frank, 1154
Dienst, Jonathan, 448
Dierkes, John, 1339
Diesel, Vin, 1100
Dietrich, Marlene, 1339
DiFilippo, Ted, 757
DiFilippo, Tim, 757
DiFilippo, Tom, 757
DiGennaro, Julius, 140
Diggs, Taye, 563
Dignan, Stephen, 1085
Dillane, Stephen, 294, 390
Dillen, Lori, 616
Dillenberg, Nicole, 1180
Diller, Phyllis, 146
Dilley, Leslie, 286
Dillin, Scott, 959
Dillon, Hugh, 492
Dillon, Matt, 896, 1308, 1456
Dillon, Paul, 216
Di Mascio, Angelo, Jr., 1399
Ding, 1424
Dinklage, Peter, 1094
Dinson, Ron, Jr., 1174
Dion, Celine, 1031
Dionisi, Stefano, 958, 1344
Dionisios, 789
Dionisotti, Paola, 674

Di Re, Flo, 811
Director, Kim, 500
Dirty Baby, 126
Dish, Madame, 669
Disney, Thea Nielsen, 1474
Ditson, Harry, 1149
Dixon, Jerry, 578
Dixon, Phil, 624
Dixon, Richard, 801
Dixon, Terrell, 61
Djola, Badja, 975
Dobell, Curzon, 1053
D'Obici, Valeria, 87
Dobrin, Marilyn, 888
Dobtcheff, Vernon, 294, 531
Docherty, Bob, 1044
Doctor Dre, 1057
Dodd, Alex, 448, 1154
Dodds, K.K., 1214
Dodds, Megan, 356
Doerner, Derrick, 601
Dohring, Jason, 286
Dolan, Julie, 72
Dolan, Michael, 722
Dollison, Ed, 860
Dolloeris, Helle, 184
Dolloff, Andrea, 1264
Dolven, Rolf, 619
Doman, John, 699, 798
Dominique, Fritz, 1348
Don, Carl, 1094
Donald, Juli, 232
Donatto, Jean, 546
Donella, Chad E., 312
Donnelly, Jamie, 174
Donnelly, Kate, 1044
Donnelly, Tony Michael, 369
D'Onofrio, Vincent, 860
Donohue, John F., 715
Donovan, Elisa, 871
Donovan, James, 427
Donovan, Martin, 715, 909
Dooley, Paul, 240
Dooley, Sean, 715
Dorado, Eleanor, 1339
Doran, Matt, 1319
Dorff, Stephen, 114
Dria, Diogo, 1405
Dorian, Patrick Shane, 601
Dormer, Richard, 130
Dorn, Michael, 1254
Dorr, Sabi, 851
Dorrian, Tommy, 1164
Dorsey, Ayoka, 77
Dótria, Diogo, 1405
Dorval, Adrien, 394, 1474
Dor, Edna, 674, 876
dos Santos, Antonio, 195
Dotson, Rhonda, 225, 851

Doty, David, 936, 1495
Doubilet, Emily, 1094
Doucette, Jeff, 318
Douche, David, 694
Doudounis, Matthew, 1264
Doughty, Kenny, 339
Douglas, Shirley, 69
Douglas, Suzzanne, 563
Douglass, Norman, 1069
Dougthy, Richard Bruce, 757
Doumanian, John, 187, 1449
Dourif, Brad, 133, 874, 1129, 1387
Douthitt, Buff, 522
Dow, Coleman, 1466
Dow, Ellen Albertini, 385, 944, 1419
Dowd, Ann, 33
Dowling, John, 764
Down, Gerald, 652
Downes, Kevin, 1129
Downey, Jim, 310
Downey, Robert, Jr., 434, 1366, 1371
Downey, Tom, 1020
Downtown Julie Brown, 1057
Dowse, Denise, 232, 978
Doyle, Ann, 427
Doyle, Chris, 243, 1048
Doyle, Eamonn, 1409
Doyle, Kathleen, 187, 882
Doyle, Tony, 357, 589
Doyle-Murray, Brian, 318
Drago, Joe, 298
Dragovic, Cedo, 1123
Drake, David, 276
Drake, Dolores, 593
Drake, Judith, 40, 967
Drayton, Stanley, 75
Dream Boys, The, 1249
Dreger, Reg, 468
Dreville, Valerie, 646
Drew, Amanda, 822
Drewy, Chris, 550
Dreyfuss, Richard, 636
Driscoll, Robyn, 394
Driver, John, 308
Driver, Minnie, 457, 493
Dromey, Eileen, 1409
Droog, Bernhard, 210
Duah, Evelyn, 1189
Duarte, Lima, 929
Dubois, Marie, 1284
Dubsky, Miroslav, 847
Duce, El, 640
Ducey, John, 286

Duchovny, David, 1476
Duclos, Philippe, 646
Dudikoff, Michael, 1059
Dudman, Yvonne, 1375
Duering, Carl, 294
Duerr, Nancy, 540, 1457
Duffett, Nicola, 1149
Duffy, Donna M., 298
Duffy, Karen, 187
Duffy, Veronica, 1288
Duggan, Judy, 722
Duhaney, Kevin, 322, 468
Dukakis, Olympia, 755, 935
Dukes, David, 441, 1187
Dulli, Greg, 832
Dumas, Charles, 286
DuMaurier, Francis, 462, 959
Dunbar, Adrian, 427
Duncan, Michael "Big Mike", 155, 871
Duncan, Michael Clarke, 40, 975
Duncan, Trevor, 993
Dunford, Andrew, 123
Dungey, Merrin, 286
Dunn, David, 914
Dunn, Donald, 119
Dunn, Kevin, 19, 448, 1197, 1206
Dunn, Morissey, 740
Dunn, Nora, 10, 155
Dunn, Paul III, 1232
Dunne, Mark, 428
Dunne, Murphy, 119
Dunne, Robin, 93
Dunn-Hill, John, 69
Dunphy, Jerry, 155
Dunst, Kirsten, 1197
Dunsworth, Christine, 477
Duong, Anh, 527
Duperron, Tim, 1145
Dupont, Jean-Louis, 1426
Dupree, Whitney, 539
Duque, Chris, 636
Duran, James, 130
Duran, Richard, 1049
Durand, Chris, 472
Durano, Giustino, 686
Duris, Romain, 420
Durning, Charles, 519
Durrett, Roger W., 944
Dutton, Anthony, 390
Dutton, Charles, 112
Dutton, Simon, 269
Duvall, Clea, 173, 364
Duvall, Robert, 232, 285, 434
Duvall, Shelley, 546

Duvall, Susan, 954, 1240
Duvall, Wayne, 493
Duvitski, Janine, 1280
Dwyer, Michael, 1375
Dye, Dale, 1100
Dye, Richie, 434, 758
Dyktynski, Matthew, 820
Dyrholm, Trine, 184
Dysart, Richard, 493
Dzakeli, Aleksi, 135
Dzundza, George, 1240

Eagle, Jack, 1264
Earl, Elizabeth, 357
Earle, Mari, 640
Earlywine, Chelsey, 1334
Earnhardt, Dale, 72
Eastman, Rodney, 909
Easton, Robert, 1000
Eaton, Robert Vernon, 93
Eaves, Dashiell, 77
Ebbe, Annevig Shelde, 626
Eberl, Luke, 967
Eberlein, Scott, 1152
Ebo, Evelyn, 1240
Eccleston, Christopher, 338, 996
Echevarria, Nicholas, 304
Eckelman, Steve, 1085
Eckert, Todd, 909
Eckhart, Aaron, 1483
Eckhouse, James, 903
Eckstrom, Lauren, 1253
Edalati, Mahmood Reza, 1293
Eddy, Sonya, 944, 1228
Edelson, Kenneth, 187
Edlefsen, Terry Neil, 1262
Edmonds, Dartanyan, 155, 1057, 1471
Edmonds, Kenneth "Babyface", 497
Edmonds, Tracey E., 497
Edwards, Daryl, 996
Edwards, David, 468
Edwards, Don, 554
Edwards, Eric, 114
Edwards, Kenneth Lane, 1255
Edwards, Neville, 322
Edwards, Rick, 1371
Edwards, Stacy, 1000
Edward-Stevens, Michael, 61
Egan, Aeryk, 278
Egan, Robert M., 757
Ehle, Jennifer, 1460

Ehrlich, Joy, 349
Eichenberger, Rebecca, 888
Eigeman, Chris, 659, 816
Eigenberg, David, 959
Eilber, Janet, 811
Einbinder, Chad, 318
Einhorn, Marvin, 996
Einhorn, Trevor, 72
Eisenberg, Halie Kate, 951
Eisenberg, Ned, 232, 1000
Eizenia, Laura, 349
Ejogo, Carmen, 52
Ekstrand, Laura, 527
Elam, Kiant, 21
Elbaz, Aaron, 540
el-Cherif, Nour, 302
Eldard, Ron, 285
Elder, Judy Ann, 975
el-Emary, Safia, 302
Elfaro, Efrine, 789
Elfman, Bodhi, 348, 448, 798
Elfman, Jenna, 174, 318, 636
Elgar, Avril, 1461
Elise, Kimberly, 77
Elizondeo, Humberto, 773
Elk, Lois Red, 927
Ellerinel, 584
Ellin, Doug, 631
Elliott, Chris, 1308
Elliott, David James, 240
Elliott, Karen, 1466
Elliott, Sam, 97, 522
Elliott, Shawn, 572
Ellis, Chris, 40, 448, 546
Ellis, Leland, 578
Ellis, Sam, 1100
Elman, Bodhi, 40
Elmer, Bill, 1419
el-Nabaoui, Khaled, 302
Eloui, Laila, 302
Elrod, Lu, 97, 1000
Elroy, James,
Elspas, Jacob, 576
Elspas, Rebecca, 576
Elspas, Sarah, 576
Elsworth, Simon, 1262
Elvin, Justin, 480
Elwes, Cary, 1031
Emami, Elham, 1293
Embry, Ethan, 173, 312
Emelie, Michelyn, 322
Emerick, Gerald, 755
Emerson, Michael, 597
Emmerich, Noah, 832, 1348
Emmerick, Gerald, 978
Emoto, Akira, 334

Enberg, Alexander, 1129
Eng, Melinda, 187
Engle, Marie, 554
English, Terry, 1189
Englund, Robert, 284, 780, 1387
Ennis, John, 611
Enos, John III, 114
Entwisle, Julie, 1262
Eonnet, Eloise, 751
Epperson, Van, 61
Erenberger, Amy, 1466
Ergener, Sibel, 657
Ergun, Halil, 1260
Erickson, Christian, 759
Erik, Scott, 1228
Erl, 114
Erpichini, Mario, 87
Ershadi, Homayoun, 1293
Erskine, Howard, 187
Erwin, Bill, 200
Esary, Doreen, 10
Eshun, Kodwo, 831
Esperanza, Katia, 470
Espinosa, Sergio, 773
Espinoza, Salvador, 176
Esposito, Giancarlo, 969, 1343, 1361
Esposito, Jennifer, 500, 584, 882
Essman, Susie, 1155
Ester, Michael Dean, 1129
Estevez, Joe, 578
Estis, Erika, 850
Etherson, Edward J., 155
Ettinger, Cynthia, 286
Eusébe, Marie-Noëlle, 751
Evangelista, Daniella, 313
Evans, Auriol, 531
Evans, Elia Mae, 578
Evans, Lee, 1308
Evans, Michele, 1100
Evans, Phil, 1149
Evans, Roy, 801
Evans, Troy, 379
Eve, 914
Evenson, Wayne A., 1167
Everett, Chad, 1023
Everett, Lee, 126
Evetts, H.P., 522
Ewing, Patrick, 1129
Eyraud, Matthew R., 581
Eyre, Peter, 269

Fabian, Patrick, 1229
Fabiani, Joel, 1206
Fabrizio, David, 442
Facinelli, Peter, 173

Fahey, Dennis S., 349
Fahm, David, 1249
Fair, William, 286
Fairbrass, Craig, 624
Fairchild, Morgan, 539
Fairfax, Sisoe, 822
Fairfield, Heather, 909
Fairley, Michelle, 1216
Faison, Donald, 173
Falco, Edie, 572, 996, 1343
Falk, Lisanne, 1146
Fallick, Mary, 322
Fallon, Siobhan, 636, 851
Falomi, Alfiero, 686
Faltisco, Robert, 448
Falty'n, Martin, 847
Fan, Roger, 1081
Fanfair, Robinne, 1471
Farabaugh, Brian, 448
Faraday, Jim, 477
Faragallah, Ramsey, 187
Faraj, Said, 1154
Fardon, Joshua, 1253
Farina, Carolyn, 659
Farina, Dennis, 920, 1100
Farish, George, 1085
Farley, Chris, 19
Farley, John, 19, 1416
Farley, Kevin, 310, 1416
Farley, Rupert, 1137
Farmer, Gary, 1203
Farmer, Ken, 860
Farmiga, Vera, 1053
Farrell, Rom Riis, 1222
Farrelly, Anna, 1308
Farrelly, Bob, 1308
Farrelly, Jesse, 1308
Farrelly, Mariann, 1308
Farrelly, Nancy, 1308
Farçat, Morgane, 751
Fashae, Alycia, 1216
Fate, Jayson, 631
Fat Lady Stripper, 914
Fattahi, Gholam Reza, 1293
Faurschou, Jannie, 626
Faveau, Jon, 1398
Favors, Daniel M., 1182
Favre, Brett, 1308
Favreau, Jon, 285, 887
Fawcett, Alan, 69
Faye, Denise, 864
Fazzoli, Mella, 1061
Feast, Fred, 703
Feast, Michael, 1389
Featherstone, Angela, 595, 1419, 1495
Feder, Frederique, 1280
Federico-O'Murchú, Francesca, 951

Federman, Wayne, 611
Fedtke, Daniela, 686
Fee, Kathleen, 738
Feeney, Caroleen, 67
Fehr, Brendan, 312
Feign, Wendy, 1020
Fein, Amanda, 286
Fein, Caitlin, 286
Feldman, Tibor, 1061
Feldshuh, Tovah, 215
Felice, Lina, 385
Fellowes, Julian, 1044
Fellows, Don, 1390
Felton, Tom, 123
Fenn, Sherilyn, 927
Fennell, Chris, 1476
Fenwick, Brian, 936
Feore, Colm, 225
Ferch, Heino, 899
Fergerson, Pearline, 232
Ferguson, Chamblee, 860
Ferguson, Colin, 909
Ferguson, J. Don, 757
Ferguson, Myles, 10
Fernandes, Maria, 195
Fernandez, Ed, 1371
Fernandez, Ellis, 1280
Fernandez, Esteban, 130
Fernandez, Francis, 1085
Ferrara, Frank, 1471
Ferrara, Juan, 304
Ferre, Cameron, 610
Ferrell, Patrick, 872
Ferrell, Will, 871
Ferrer, Filipe, 958
Ferrer, Miguel, 1262
Ferrero, Martin, 442
Ferri, Daniel, 1186
Feuer, Cindra, 527
Feuerstein, Mark, 993
Fichtner, William, 40
Fickert, Mark, 860
Field, Arabella, 448
Field, Susan, 357
Fielder, Al, 1085
Fiennes, Joseph, 339, 1137
Fiennes, Ralph, 52
Fierro, Jim, 1371
Fierstein, Harvey, 1094
Figenschow, Kristian, 607
Figueroa, Efrain, 298
Filar, Gil, 1164
Filabeen, Bernard, 694
Filho, Bertho, 195
Filho, Diogo Lopes, 195
Filion, Jean, 69
Fillion, Nathan, 1100
Fillmore, Bruce, 740
Filpi, Carmen, 1419
Fine, Danny, 1085
Fine, Travis, 1319
Fink, John, 72

Finley, Cameron, 550
Finley, Felicia, 500
Finnegan, John, 165
Finneran, Katie, 1489
Finney, Alan, 1424
Finnighan, Neil, 1100
Fiore, Antimo, 631
Fiorito, Geoff, 944
Fiorucci, Elio, 385
Firmin, Tyne, 126
Firth, Colin, 1137
Firth, Peter, 811
Fischer, Maureen, 954
Fischer, Thomas, 390
Fischnaller, Eddie, 603
Fitchpatrick, Steve, 1399
Fite, Mark, 448
Fitzgerald, Ciaran, 427
Fitzgerald, Dan, 540
Fitzgerald, Donegal, 187
Fitzgerald, Glenn, 996
Fitzgerald, Gregg, 165
Fitzgerald, Helen, 240
Fitzgerald, Kitty, 1409
Fitzgerald, Leah, 876
Fitzgerald, Melissa, 832
Fitzgerald, Michael, 1461
Fitzgerald, Patrick, 1277
Fitzgerald, Rob Roy, 174
Fitzgerald, Wilbur T., 434
Fitzhugh, Katherine A., 944
Fitzpatrick, Cathy, 914
Fitzpatrick, Gabrielle, 819
Fitzpatrick, James, 40
Fitzpatrick, Tony, 1371
Flaherty, Lanny, 546
Flanagan, Fionnula, 1409
Flanagan, Jesse, 97
Flanagan, John, 390
Flanders, Keeley, 531
Flanery, Sean Patrick, 332, 1277
Flea, 97, 379, 1023
Fleischer, Charles, 965
Fleming, Cliff, 298, 554
Fleming, Shara P., 497
Fleming, Wendy, 1164
Flemyng, Jason, 291, 1249
Flesher, Glenn, 996
Fleuchaus, Ann, 1489
Flick, David, 298
Flig, Henrik, 626
Flippo, Mike, 282
Floberg, Bjorn, 607
Flood, Kevin, 427
Florek, Dann, 493
Flores, Adam C., 1206

Flores, E. Kalani, 1174
Flores, Jose, 304
Florian, Luc, 751
Floyd, Eddie, 119
Floyd, Kari Leigh, 636
Flygare, Claus, 626
Flynn, Herbie, 1308
Flynn, Jackie, 1308
Flynn, Tony, 428
Flynt, Larry, 640
Flythe, Mark, 33
Foch, Nina, 575
Fogarty, Mary, 857
Fogerty, Adam, 1149
Foley, Dave, 146
Foley, Liam, 339
Fommel, Antonio, 686
Fonda, Bridget, 816, 1167
Fong, Frances, 1081
Fong, Tig, 93
Fontana, Peter, 798
Fontani, Amerigo, 686
Foo Fighters, 406
Foote, Greg, 1466
Forbert, Steve, 67
Forbes, Leonie, 1146
Forbes, Peter, 1461
Ford, Gerald, 896
Ford, Harrison, 1174
Ford, Jack, 944
Ford, Steven, 40
Foreman, Jamie, 338
Forest, Pierre, 1062
Forge, Scarlet, 40
Forgerty, Adam, 703
Forlani, Claire, 781
Forman, Jamie, 876
Formicola, Fil, 715
Forouzanfar, Davood, 1293
Forrest, Frederick, 1436
Forristal, Susan, 1000
Forster, Kurt, 245
Forster, Robert, 927, 1023
Forsythe, Henderson, 1240
Forsythe, William, 394
Forte, Marlene, 671
Forte, Smith, 886
Foster, Al, 1348
Foster, Catlin, 1123
Foster, Steffen, 69
Foster, V. J., 155
Foubert, Hélène, 1426
Fourniotis, George, 1206
Fouts, Dan, 1417
Fowells, Julie, 470
Fowler, Chris, 1417
Fowler, Jonathan, Jr., 21
Fowler, Monique, 187
Fox, Alejandro Acosta, 540
Fox, Anthony, 427
Fox, Edward, 733

Fox, Kerry, 477
Fox, Lauren, 970
Fox, Loretta, 1443
Fox, Mark, 1474
Fox, Neil, 1249
Fox, Paul, 339
Fox, Rick, 500
Fox, Ronny, 876
Fox, Vivica A., 1442
Foxhall, Scott, 758
Foxx, Jamie, 975
Foy, Darren D., 601
Foye, Janet, 61
Foye, Johnny, 1182
Foyt, Victoria, 294
Fraction, Karen, 931
Frain, Ben, 339
Frain, James, 338, 531
Frakes, Jonathan, 1254
Francese, Paulette, 871
Francis, Clare, 1380
Francis, James, 1390
Francis, Lynne, 634
Francis, Mark, 1474
Frangione, Jim, 1232
Frangipani, Stefano, 686
Frank, Brian, 1041
Frank, Dan, 886
Frank, David Roland, 572
Franklin, Aretha, 119
Franklin, Candide, 119
Franklin, Cherie, 317
Franklin, Paula Bellamy, 578
Franklin, Scott, 970
Franklyn-Robbins, John, 822
Franko B., 470
Franks, Bo, 860
Franz, Dennis, 225
Fresca, Jason, 286
Fraser, Brendan, 441, 1269
Fraser, Duncan, 1474
Fraser, Laura, 247, 759
Fraser, Tiffany, 798
Fratkin, Stuart, 448
Frazier, Clifford T., 1371
Frazier, John, 40
Fredericks, David, 394
Freeman, Al, Jr., 322
Freeman, Brent, 798
Freeman, Kathleen, 119, 593
Freeman, Morgan, 93, 285, 385, 493
Freeman, Rob, 1100
Freidman, Richard L., 1232
Freitas, Stela, 195
Fremin, Jourdan, 1155
French, Bruce, 1254
French, Jack, 954

French, Michael Bryan, 584
Frenzel, Donna, 920
Fresolone, Arturo, 1040
Fribo, Louise, 626
Fried, Jonathan, 949
Fried, Manny, 140
Friedkin, William, 1466
Friedman, Bruce Jay, 1489
Friedman, Dee Dee, 1094
Friedman, Glenn, 679
Friel, Anna, 652
Friels, Colin, 271
Frierson, Eddie, 318
Frierson, Leon Curtis, 155
Friese, Brettanya, 1053
Frisch, Arno, 416
Frogner, Lars, 619
Frost, Roger, 801, 1137
Frot, Catherine, 1377
Fruitman, Jason, 385
Fry, Cory, 10
Fry, Ed, 715
Fry, Kevin, 232, 1443
Fry, Stephen, 232, 1249, 1460
Frye, Steve, 554
Fryer, Charlotte, 1189
Fuchel, Kurt, 850
Fuchs, Jason, 755
Fuentes, Obdulia, 1440
Fugees, 406
Fugelsand, John, 1222
Fuhrman, Lisa, 493
Fujii, Kahori, 1336
Fujitani, Miki, 396
Fukuzaki, Rob, 448
Fulco, Fernando, 195
Fullerton, Andrew, 165
Fulton, Christina, 1206
Fultz, Mona Lee, 546, 550
Fuqua, Joseph, 275
Furlong, Edward, 21, 954
Furlong, John, 615
Furth, George, 155
Futterman, Dan, 1149
Future Sound of London, 831
Fyfe, Jim, 1040

Gabor, Zsa Zsa, 1339
Gabriel, Michelle, 243
Gabteni, Choukri, 751
Gage, Kevin, 284
Gagnon, Steven M., 1476
Gainey, M. C., 780
Gaizidorskala, Marina, 481

Galbraith, Alastair, 1044
Gale, Alison, 874
Gale, Valerie, 339
Galecki, Johnny, 909, 1277
Galiena, Anna, 667
Galindo, Xiomara Cuevas, 155
Gallacher, Frank, 271
Gallagher, Jenni, 1061
Gallagher, Joe, 589
Gallagher, John, 1069
Gallagher, Maureen, 798
Gallagher, Michael, 1302
Gallanders, James, 133
Gallante, Jayme, 72
Gallery, James, 1229
Gallin, Scotty, 540
Gallin, Tim, 722
Gallo, Vincent, 139
Gallop, Tom, 798
Galloway, Jack, 822
Gallupi, Andrew, 1146
Gallus, Christopher, 1167
Gamble, Brittany, 679
Gamble, Mason, 1085
Gambon, Michael, 265
Gammell, Robin, 155
Gammon, James, 522
Gandolfini, James, 232, 369, 806
Ganoung, Richard, 109
Gant, David, 269, 294
Gant, Mtume, 572
Gant, Richard, 97, 448, 1228
Gantt, Leland, 918
Ganun, John, 978
Ganus, Paul, 773
Garay, Soo, 119
Garber, Dennis E., 616
Garbus, Martin, 672
Garcia, Adam, 1461
Garcia, Andy, 298
Garcia, Daniel, 578
Garcia, David, 578
Garcia, Kaylissa Keli, 773
Garcia, Kelsie Kimberli, 773
Garcia, Paul, 1100
Garcia, Virginia, 357
Garcin, Henri, 327
Gardner, Raquel, 871, 1240
Garello, Stefania Orsola, 201
Garito, Ken, 215
Garland, Life, 155
Garlin, Jeff, 1129
Garner, James, 1361
Garofalo, Janeane, 237, 965
Garrard, Pilar, 751
Garrel, Maurice, 48

Garrett, Brad, 146
Garrett, Ernie, 931
Garrison, Julia, 1057
Garson, Willie, 715, 1308
Gartland, Mike, 1240
Garvey, Michael, 72
Garza, Eduardo Cavazos, 860
Gascoine, Jill, 72
Gassman, Alessandro, 1260
Gasteyer, Ana, 780
Gaston, Haven, 1416
Gates, Katharine, 1034
Gates, Ransom, 379
Gatica, Silvana, 1471
Gatien, Jennifer "Nen", 75
Gatiss, Dean, 740
Gaudefroy D, Daphné, 1426
Gault, Willie, 540
Gaultier, Jean-Yves, 1405
Gaunt, Fred, 703
Gauthier, Alain, 69
Gauzy, Dyna, 1062
Gaven, Marcia Mitzman, 1197
Gavin, Don, 832
Gavin, James W., 679
Gay, Benjamin T., 434
Gayheart, Rebecca, 1387
Gayle, Jackie, 155
Gazzara, Ben, 97, 139, 480, 1232
Geary, Cynthia, 1203
Gebehr, Vera, 626
Geer, Ellen, 857, 993
Geffner, Deborah, 715
Gehman, Martha, 993
Geidt, Jeremy, 866, 1232
Geldart, Ed, 1085
Geldof, Bob, 1249
Gelfant, Alan, 865
Gellar, Sarah Michelle, 1197
Gelman, Kimiko, 109
Gelose, Norma, 140
Genaro, Tony, 773, 811
Gendreau, Alain, 69
George, Jason Winston, 369
George, Kent, 442
George, Leonard, 1203
George, Matt, 601
George, Melissa, 271
George, Tracy Anne, 1308
Georges, Liz, 811
Georgeson, Tom, 652
Georgiades, James, 959
Geraghty, Clive, 427

Gerardino, Ana Susana, 461
Gerasymenko, Marina, 1344
Gerber, Bill, 187
Gerber, Mark, 61
Germain, Greg, 1284
Germain, Gunther, 1284
Gershon, Gina, 902, 931
Geschwind, Marc C., 540
Gesner, Zen, 1308
Getz, Ileen, 187
Getzoff, Daniel, 679
Geyer, Gudrun, 837
Ge You, 346
Ghaffari, M.B., 1222
Ghasaei, Mohamad Azia, 1293
Ghazali, Yusmal, 1053
Gherebenec, Gheorghe, 420
Ghilmoinou, Nadir, 694
Ghini, Massimo, 1344
Ghostley, Alice, 857
Giacomini, Gino, 1164
Giaimo, Tony, 1457
Giamatti, Paul, 130, 851, 1093, 1100, 1348
Giangiulio, Nicholas J., 448
Giannelli, Steve, 448, 611
Giannotti, Claudia, 48
Giantonelli, Thomas Giuseppe, 448
Giarraputo, Michael, 1416
Gibb, Don, 1371
Gibbons, Blake, 1399
Gibbs, David Gene, 1049
Gibbs, Elika, 339
Gibbs, Keith, 72
Gibbs, Matyelok, 356
Gibbs, Nigel, 225
Gibbs, Pat, 1424
Gibbs, Reedy, 252
Gibson, Christopher L., 1474
Gibson, Mel, 679
Gibson, Scott, 310
Gibson, Terel, 77
Gideon, Llewela, 1249
Gidley, Pamela, 755
Gielgud, John, 339, 1031
Giering, Frank, 416
Gifford, James, 1308
Gigeroff, Lex, 740
Gijn, Aitana Sánchez, 201
Gil, Ariadna, 1288
Gil, Arturo, 310

Gilbert, Nicci, 1471
Gilborn, Steven, 317
Gilchrist, Mak, 1264
Gildea, Sean P., 1308
Giles, Annabel, 390
Giles, Liz, 339
Gill, Jack, 298
Gill, John, 652, 1449
Gill, Will, Jr., 578
Gillan, Tony, 1302
Gilleron, Ren, 694
Gillett, Aden, 123
Gillett, Chris, 310
Gillette, Anita, 126, 215
Gilliard, Larry, Jr., 865, 1416
Gillies, Dan, 978
Gilliland, Richard, 1253
Gillis, Mary, 379
Gilloran, Dave, 866
Gillott, Mark Alan, 1348
Gilmore, Jimmie Dale, 97
Gilmour, Alexa, 93
Gilroy, Tom, 1035
Gilsfort, Peter, 626
Gilshenan, Darren, 272
Gilsig, Jessalyn, 554, 1031
Gingerich, Peter, 126
Ginter, L. L., 798
Giocante, Vahina, 764
Gioiello, Bruno, 187
Gionson, Mel Duane, 996
Giovinazzo, Carmine D., 109
Girlana, 1471
Giroday, François, 448
Giunta, Vicki, 1447
Giuntoli, Neil, 511
Givens, Adele, 975
Gizbert, Thomas, 1100
Gjernes, Jay, 1167
Glagovac, Nebojsa, 1123
Glahn, Therese, 184
Glamour, Matthew, 1390
Glantzman-Leib, Lila, 481
Glasser, Phillip, 1255
Glassman, Andrew, 40
Glave, Matthew, 1419
Glazer, Nathan, 37
Gleason, James, 1443
Gleeson, Brendan, 129, 164, 427, 589
Gleeson, Paul, 1319
Glegg, Kenneth, 1206
Glen, Georgie, 1137
Glenn, Charles, 77
Glenn, DeFoy, 322
Glenn, Scott, 176, 394
Gless, Sharon, 57
Glick, Lori, 1308

Glick, Marc H., 1447
Glossop, Amber, 1137
Glover, Denny, 27, 77, 679
Glover, David, 1149
Glover, Joan, 722
Glover, Paul, 1375
Glück, Wolfgang, 416
Glymph, Avery, 500
Goass, Philip, 1348
Gobbi, Giorgio, 201
Goddard, Mark, 733
Goddard, Trevor, 291
Godenzi, Mina, 819
Godfrey, Julie, 61
Godfrey, Patrick, 356
Godley, Michael, 52
Godreche, Judith, 759
Godshall, Ray, 1155
Godwin, Christopher, 52
Godwin, Randy, 987
Goede, Jay, 385
Goehner, Fred, 1228
Goessens, Fred, 210
Goggins, Walton, 757
Gogibedasvili, Dato, 135
Gogin, Michael Lee, 379
Going, Joanna, 332, 967, 1269
Gold, Richard, 1137
Goldberg, Adam, 61, 1100
Goldberg, Whoopi, 563, 1076, 1077
Goldberger, Kurt, 850
Goldblatt, Max, 847
Goldblum, Jeff, 539
Golder, Sid, 876
Goldman, Jerome, 1181
Goldman, Lorry, 448
Goldsmith, Merwin, 1069
Goldstein, Jenette, 379, 715
Goldstein, Jennette, 1129
Goldstein, Mark, 755
Goldstein, Steven, 1232
Goldwyn, Tony, 1343
Golonka, Arlene, 669
Goman, Arleen, 1447
Gomes, Manoel, 195
Gomez, Carlos, 349, 851, 1048
Gomez, Marga, 1243
Gomez, Mateo, 587
Gomez, Michael, 97
Goncalves, Mauricio, 403
Gong Li, 219
Gonzalez, Alex, 944
Gonzalez, Clifton
Gonzalez, 1048
Gonzalez, Gloria, 1414

Gonzalez, Oscar Zerafin, 773
González, Dan Rivera, 789
Goodall, Louise, 176
Gooding, Cuba, Jr., 1429
Goodman, Brian, 832
Goodman, John, 97, 119, 123, 369, 1076
Goodson, Mark, 72
Goodwin, Kia Joy, 888
Goodwin, Michael, 722
Goody, Bob, 123
Goorjian, Michael, 493
Gorby, Maebh, 427
Gordon, Bryan, 1228
Gordon, Danso, 21
Gordon, Eve, 593
Gordon, Joanne, 970
Gordon, Joel, 322
Gordon, Liz, 119
Goritsas, Demetri, 1100
Gorlitsky, Lisa, 1069
Gorman, Breon, 1254
Gorman, Greg, 954, 1174
Goryl, David, 1308
Goshmir, Simon, 294
Goss, Natalie, 1174
Gosselaar, Mark-Paul, 278
Gossom, Thom, Jr., 1129
Gostelow, Harry, 1137, 1149
Gottfried, Gilbert, 318
Gottlieb, Heather, 934
Gottlieb, Jasper, 210
Gottlieb, Marius, 210
Gough, John, 531
Gould, Elliott, 21, 93
Gould, Graydon, 294
Gould, Harold, 847, 944
Goulem, Alain, 1206
Gowdy, Curt, 72
Gowen, Peter, 164, 265
Grace, April, 216, 1361
Grace, Howard, 703
Grace, Nickolas, 1149
Grady, Ed, 722
Graff, Jerry, 1232
Graham, Chris, 1375
Graham, Gerrit, 903
Graham, Heather, 733, 1366
Graham, Katerina, 936
Graham, Lauren, 874, 903
Graham, Robert, 546
Graham, Stuart, 164
Grainger, Gawn, 740
Grandison, Brian, 1399
Grando, Kelley, 1471

Granholm, Garth, 1466
Granli, Elizabeth, 563
Grant, Beth, 317, 664
Grant, Edward II, 271
Grant, Jessica Brooks, 1429
Grant, Kate Jennings, 888
Grant, Lisa Ann, 286
Grant, Matt, 634
Grant, Oliver, 75
Grant, Richard E., 801, 1249
Grant, Sylvia, 1390
Grant, Tom, 640
Grantz, Kevin, 1240
Graseck, James E., 903
Grassi, Alessandra, 686
Grasso, Anthony, 1264
Gratson, Katie, 860
Graves, Rupert, 822
Gray, David Barry, 664, 1442
Gray, Gary LeRoi, 1187
Gray, Jack Mclaughlin, 851
Gray, Leah, 882
Gray, Rick, 575
Gray, Sam, 187
Gray, Shari, 789
Graydon, Dickie, 1149
Grayson, Jerry, 130
Greaves, Kristoffer, 61
Greco, Paul, 512
Green, Clinton, 322
Green, Fanni, 888
Green, Judy, 819
Green, Mary-Pat, 1442
Green, Seth, 173, 349
Greenberg, Mitch, 715
Greenbury, Andrew, 1308
Greenbury, Nick, 1308
Greene, Daniel, 1308
Greene, Graham, 1146
Greene, James, 944
Greene, Peter, 965
Greenfield, Jerald A., 914
Greenhill, Susan, 954
Greenwood, Bruce, 313
Greer, Judy, 631
Greer, Stuart, 112, 434
Gregg, Bradley, 874
Gregg, Clark, 1232
Gregg, David, 764
Gregory, André, 187
Gregory, Karen, 703
Gregory, Peter, 1361
Gremmels, Becket, 860
Grenham, Sheila A., 126
Grenier, Adrian, 187, 572

Gresham, James, 75
Gress, Googy, 611
Grey, Buff, 914
Grey, Martin, 857
Grey, Sally, 339
Greyeyes, Michael, 394, 1203
Grieco, Richard, 871
Griego, Penny, 349
Griffin, Eddie, 40
Griffin, Gerry, 286
Griffin, Katie, 1040
Griffin, Laura-Shay, 758
Griffin, Mary, 385
Griffin, Maureen, 1308
Griffin, Merv, 896
Griffin, Steve, 1100
Griffith, Melanie, 187, 722
Griffith, Thomas Ian, 615
Griffiths, Rachel, 531, 1424
Griffiths-Malin, Emma, 722
Grimes, Tammy, 527, 1343
Grimm, Tim, 798
Grimshaw, Jim, 369, 434, 722, 1262
Grodenchik, Max, 1255
Grody, Kathryn, 789
Groener, Harry, 944
Groll, Father, 89
Gros, Jean-Benoît, 694
Gross, Mary, 993, 1077
Grossman, Leslie, 173, 909
Grossman, Lynn, 1490
Grosso, Joao, 958
Grosvenor, Vertamae, 78
Grote, Andy, 385
Groth, Robin, 1077
Groves, Marianne, 201, 751
Gruen, Samuel, 1216
Gruffudd, John, 1460
Grumbar, Dorothy, 1100
Grunberg, Greg, 72, 1129
Grundy, Bob, 1308
Gschnitzer, Julia, 603
Guadagni, Nicky, 256
Gudgell, Wallace, 679
Guehenneux, Olivier, 1426
Guerra, Emiliano, 773
Guest, Christopher, 1197
Guggenbuhl, Maxime, 1426
Gugino, Carla, 1206
Gugliametti, Dominic, 1062

Guhur, Alain Luc, 1426
Guidall, George, 597
Guidera, Anthony, 40
Guido, Michael, 1371
Guilbert, Ann, 1228
Guilfoyle, Paul, 902, 1000
Guillermo, 1440
Guilliard, Leontine, 1000
Guimaraes, Luiz Fernand, 403
Guinee, Tim, 114, 615
Gulinello, Amo, 888
Gulka, Jeff, 10
Gullette, Sean, 970
Gumbert, Noah, 271
Gumbert, Satya, 271
Gundry, Bill, 1269
Gunn, Anna, 348
Gunn, Peter, 357
Gunning, Charles, 860
Gunsur, Mehmet, 1260
Gunton, Bob, 944
Guo, Calvin, 1474
Gurrola, Juan-Jose, 304
Gurwitch, Annabelle, 109
Gusenbauer, Christoph, 603
Gustafson, Neil, 866
Guth, Ray, 1037
Guttierez, Emmanuel, 759, 1284
Guybet, Christophe, 751
Guyer, Murphy, 934, 1069
Guzmán, Diego Méndez, 789
Guzmán, Ermenehildo Sáenz, 789
Guzman, Luis, 920, 1206
Guzmán, Patricio, 218
Guzzo, Francesco, 686
Gwaltney, Jack, 1154

Ha, Benita, 740
Haas, Avi, 1466
Habich, Matthias, 89
Hacker, Trevor St. John, 390
Hackett, Buddy, 951
Hackl, Bob, 1419
Heckman, Gene, 27, 348, 1361
Haddon, Dayle, 187
Hadleigh-West, Maggie, 1414
Hae Joon Lee, 1085
Hagen, Katie, 286, 1269
Hagen, Marianne, 587
Hagen, Molly, 1059
Haglund, Dean, 1476

Hagman, Larry, 1000
Hagopian, Dean, 1206
Hahn, Archie, 318, 1197
Hahn, William, 967
Hahn-Petersen, John, 626
Haine, Darwin, 1203
Hakuryu, 396
Hald, Mette, 626
Haleva, Jerry, 97, 755
Haley, R.M., 1000
Hall, Albert, 77
Hall, Brian, 173
Hall, Irma P., 77, 944
Hall, Michael Keys, 1243
Hall, Philip Baker, 349, 538, 1023, 1081, 1228
Hall, Randy, 1476
Hall, Robert David, 851
Hall, Ron, 914
Hall, Shashawnee, 636, 1443
Hall, Steve, 1375
Hall, Suzanne, 697
Hall, Tiffany, 1471
Hall, Tim, 1164
Hall, Walter C., 522
Hall, Willie, 119
Halligan, Tim, 636
Helliwell, Gerladine, 1249
Hallo, Dean, 967
Halston, Julie, 187, 275
Helverson, Robert Martin, 1167
Halzael, Valiolah, 1293
Hamacher, Al, 758
Ham-Bernard, Sherry, 1154
Hamburg, John, 1094
Hamer, Lillie Shaw, 349
Hamilton, Callum, 1390
Hamilton, Derek, 312, 394
Hamilton, Lisa Gay, 77, 472
Hamilton, Quancetia, 322
Hamilton, Richard, 1039
Hamilton, Trip, 722
Hammil, John, 967
Hammond, Blake, 755
Hammond, Darrell, 119
Hammond, Louis, 674
Hammonds, Margaret, 722
Hampton, Amanda, 936
Han, Bunjaku, 1439
Han, David, 349
Han, Si, 330
Hancock, Sheila, 740

Hand, Gary, 679, 798
Hand, Walter, 1135
Handfield, Don, 286
Handley, Taylor, 610
Handy, Emma, 1390
Handy, Jacob, 636
Handy, Zachary, 636
Haney, Anne, 1023
Hanfstingl, Franz-
  Hermann, 89
Hanks, Tom, 1100,
  1489
Hanna, Gillian, 674
Hanna, Lisa, 563
Hannafin, Daniel P.,
  944
Hannah, Bobby, 93
Hannah, Daryl, 434,
  519, 1040
Hannah, John, 1189
Hann-Byrd, Adam, 472
Hanndy, Preston B.,
  572
Hannigan, Alyson, 278
Hannigan, Maury,
  1474
Hanover, Donna, 187,
  1154
Hans, Tim, 1390
Hansen, Holger Juul,
  626
Hansen, Kevin, 593
Hansen, Monika, 623
Hansen, Nyree, 634
Hanson, Dian, 1034
Hanson, Rusty, 1253
Harada, Ann, 481
Harada, Mieko, 1404
Harden, Marcia Gay,
  298, 781
Harder, Teresa, 795
Hardester, Crofton,
  1100
Hardfloor, 831
Hardig, Stephen, 758
Harding, Jan Leslie,
  512
Harding, Peter, 624,
  1461
Härdle, Carmen, 89
Hardt, Katreen, 512
Hardwicke, Edward,
  338
Hardy, Dona, 1348
Hardy, Nita, 434
Hardy, Robert, 822
Hare, Kelly, 1416
Hargett, Hester, 112
Hargreaves, Chris-
  topher, 697
Hargreaves, Janie, 247
Harimoto, Dale, 448
Harker, Amanda, 659
Harland, Franz, 304
Harley, Kieran, 427
Harmon, Angie, 664
Harmon, Cynde, 313
Harmon, Mark, 379
Harper, Angel, 1077

Harper, Hill, 78, 497,
  500
Harper, James, 40
Harper, Ron, 857
Harper, Russel, 1264
Harper, Tess, 308
Harrell, James N., 550
Harrelson, Brett, 284
Harrelson, Woody,
  521, 931, 1319
Harrington, John, 584
Harrington, Laura, 951
Harris, Baxter, 1240
Harris, Danielle, 1387
Harris, Ed, 1264, 1348
Harris, Estelle, 200,
  847, 857
Harris, George, 751
Harris, Hank, 798
Harris, Henry, 755
Harris, Jamie, 764
Harris, Jared, 480,
  733
Harris, Jill, 33
Harris, Jonathan, 146
Harris, Jossie, 975
Harris, Julie, 67
Harris, Kemp, 866
Harris, Kim, 497
Harris, Laura, 364,
  1277
Harris, Michael, 580,
  578
Harris, Moira, 216
Harris, Neil Patrick,
  1020
Harris, Quinn, 500
Harris, Reggie, 512
Harris, Ricky, 493
Harris, Viola, 1228
Harris, Wendell B., Jr.,
  920
Harris, Wood, 187,
  1154
Harris, Zelda, 500
Harrison, Cathryn, 294
Harrison, Gregory, 10
Harrison, Hank, 640
Harrison, Jasmine, 286
Harrison, Noel, 294
Harrison, Stanley Earl,
  308
Harrod, David, 1319
Harrold, Jamie, 587
Harryhausen, Ray, 811
Harryson, Annelie, 269
Harshaw, Cee-Cee,
  1129
Hart, Anita, 616
Hart, Bob Eric, 780
Hart, Ian, 164, 348,
  832
Hart, Jillian, 119
Hart, Michelle, 1474
Hart, Pamela, 866,
  970, 1020
Hart, Susan, 1371
Hart, Terry V., 1164
Hartley, Steven, 616

Hartley, Theodore R.,
  811
Hartman, Phil, 1197
Hartmann, Peter, 626
Hartner, Rona, 420
Hartnett, Josh, 364,
  472
Hartridge, Walter, 434
Hartsock, Charlie, 286
Harvey, Don, 1319
Harvey, Eric LaRay,
  1069
Harvey, Pat, 755
Harvey, Phil, 1339
Harvey, Tom, 1040
Harvie, Ellie, 1474
Harwood, Bruce, 1476
Hascoüt, Karine, 1426
Haskins, Clem, 500
Hassen, Kulani, 322
Hasson, Lauren, 1495
Hasuo, Kengo, 1319
Hatfield, Mert, 722
Hatfield, Susan, 920
Hathaway, Amy, 601
Hatosy, Shawn, 364
Hauduroy, James,
  1284
Haughton, Mark, 634
Haugk, Charlie, 540
Hauguth, Axel, 89
Hauptman, Ellen M.,
  1094
Hauser, Cole, 521
Havens, John C., 659
Havens, Richie, 406
Haverson, Nick, 531
Havey, Allan, 1069
Havill, Andrew, 1461
Hawes, Keeley, 52
Hawk, Jeremy, 339
Hawke, Ethan, 461,
  860
Hawken, Pamela, 61
Hawkes, John, 546,
  584, 1081
Hawkins, Anika, 369
Hawkins, Brittany, 77
Hawkins, Dana, 540
Hawley, Steven, 1232
Hawthorne, Nigel, 751,
  888
Hawtrey, Kay, 310,
  1387
Haxaire, Sarah, 1216
Hay, Jaida, 10
Haybeard, Roy, 130
Hayden, Cynthia, 369
Hayek, Salma, 364,
  385, 805, 1440
Hayes, Clyde, 434
Hayes, Deryl, 394
Hayes, Isaac, 595
Hayes, Laura, 578
Hayes, Sean P., 109
Haygarth, Tony, 1280
Hayman, David, 1044
Hayman, Jon, 1229
Haynes, Joseph, 987

Haynie, Jim, 155
Haysbert, Dennis, 757
Hayward, J.C., 40
Hazen, Kelley, 798
Headey, Lena, 822
Headly, Glenne, 61,
  1476
Heald, Anthony, 291
Healy, Darren, 427
Healy, Dermot, 165
Heard, John, 1206
Hearn, Chick, 1474
Hearn, Ellen, 1371
Hearn, George, 69
Hearst, Patricia, 954
Heath, Darrel, 1129,
  1471
Hébert, Françoise, 69
Heche, Anne, 1023,
  1053, 1174
Hecker, Gary, 364
Hedaya, Dan, 232,
  871
Hedges, Ami, 428
Hedges, Mark, 272
Hedley, Jack, 211
Hedtke, Greg, 903
Hedwall, Deborah,
  1135
Hefferman, Kevin, 882
Hegel, Jon, 171
Heigl, Katherine, 133
Heimbinder, Susan,
  657
Heinrich, Denise, 540
Heitmeyer, Jayne,
  1206
Helen, Jimmy, 601
Helfer, Ian, 1094
Helgenberger, Marg,
  1240
Heller, Randee, 155
Hellerstein, Jonneine,
  936
Helman, Hannes, 686
Helmond, Katherine,
  379
Helms, Jesse, 280
Helsel, Dee Ann, 584
Hely, Kevin, 589
Hemeida, Mahmoud,
  302
Hemingway, Mariel,
  738
Hemon, Oliver, 759
Hemphill, Neal, 1069
Hempleman, Terry,
  1167
Henderson, Andrew,
  357
Henderson, Bill, 679
Henderson, Florence,
  539
Henderson, Michael,
  385
Hendley, Elleanor Jean,
  369
Hendra, Tony, 1040
Hendrie, Chris, 379

Hendrix, Elaine, 936
Hendrix, Natalie, 434,
  758
Heney, Joan, 1040
Heney, Noah, 1474
Henfrey, Janet, 357,
  674, 822, 1280
Hengstenberg,
  Jennifer, 1152
Henley, Barry
  "Shabaka", 155,
  369, 563, 944,
  1081
Hennigan, Dee, 550
Henning, Golden, 611
Henningsen, Ingrid,
  1474
Henriau, Marie, 1216
Henriksen, Bjarne, 184
Henriques, Mark, 468
Henritze, Bette, 888
Henry, Buck, 1040
Henry, Gregg, 1254
Henry, Tyrone, 1495
Henson, Elden, 806
Henstridge, Natasha,
  1240
Hentoff, Nat, 672
Heras, Mario, 601
Herek, Lori Viveros,
  539
Herion, Don, 1371
Herlihy, Timothy P.,
  1419
Herman, Andrew, 72
Herman, Paul, 349
Herman, Stanley, 970
Hermstad, John
Henning Gobring, 795
Hernandez, Coati
  Mundi, 385
Hernández, Pedro, 789
Herndon, Kimberly,
  758
Herod, Geoffrey, 740
Hershey, Barbara,
  1216
Herveet, Olivier, 1426
Hervey, Shane, 674
Herzog, Seth, 1094
Herzog, Werner, 701,
  1429
Heslov, Grant, 349
Hess, Jayne, 576
Hess, Joe, 920
Hess, Zdenek, 674
Heston, Charlton, 40,
  1339
Hetherington, Kate,
  531
Heung Hoi, 634
Heuring, Lori, 860
Hevner, Suzanne, 781
Hewitt, Jennifer Love,
  173, 584
Hewitt, Paul, 232
Hewitt, Steve, 1390
Hewlett, David, 256
Hewlett, Sheila, 1040

Heyerdahl, Chris, 1
Hibbs, Tisa, 550
Hickey, Joe, 931
Hickey, Paul, 427
Hickey, Robert, 1409
Hickey, Tom, 164
Hickman, Dwayne, 871
Hicks, Barbara, 294
Hicks, Dwight, 40
Hicks, Jesse, 1182
Hicks, Tehitia, 601
Hicks, Taral, 75
Higgins, Chris, 1069
Higgins, David
  Anthony, 1206
Higgins, Michael, 597
Higgins, Paul, 1048
Higgs, Scot Brien, 722
High, Wally, 119
Highfield, Bill, 271
Highmore, Edward,
  339
Highsmith, Steve, 369
Hill, Christian, 715
Hill, Dave, 1280
Hill, James, 155
Hill, Kirsten Camille,
  1057
Hill, Lauryn, 497
Hill, William, 597,
  1154
Hilliard, Earl, Jr., 1348
Hillinger, Wolfgang,
  686
Hillman, Ty, 554
Himber, Robert, 967
Himes, John, 385
Hinckle, Hilary, 1232
Hinderstein, Deborah,
  310
Hinds, Catriona, 129
Hines, Ben, 1319
Hines, Damon, 679
Hinkley, Brent, 19
Hinson, Tyler, 77
Hinton, Raymond, 468
Hirsberg, David, 434
Hirsch, Hallee, 722
Hirschfield, Jeffrey,
  740
Hirsh, Hallee, 903,
  1489
Hirt, Chritianne, 394
Hitchcock, Robyn,
  1272
Hoag, Bill, 448
Hoag, Judith, 40
Hoath, Florence, 457
Hobbs, Rebecca, 1375
Hoch, Danny, 1319
Hochevar, Slavko, 119
Ho Chow, 468
Hocke, Bernard, 851,
  1243
Hodge, Joseph, 1154
Hodge, Patricia, 667
Hodges, Oliver, 1375
Hodges, Tom, 581

Hodgkinson, John, 390
Hodson, Biddy, 1461
Hodson, Ed, 1053
Hoey, David, 1424
Hoffman, Dustin, 1243
Hoffman, Ken, 944
Hoffman, Phil, 97,
  480, 840, 944
Hoffman, Rick, 679
Hofland, Michael, 759
Hofmo, Robert Roy,
  1319
Hogan, Gabriel, 740
Hogan, Hulk, 1334
Hogan, Robert, 1240
Hogan, Susan, 312
Hogerty, John, 554
Hogg, B. J., 130
Hohn, Amy, 597,
  1228
Hoijtink, Elisabeth,
  1327
Holbrook, Ashley,
  1059
Holbrook, Hal, 575
Hold, Michael, 1416
Holden, Jill, 369
Holden, Marjean, 616
Holder, Jonathan, 944
Hole, Henrik, 619
Holger, Ernst Frowein,
  686
Holland, Buck, 379
Holland, Denise, 936
Holland, Jools, 1249
Holland, Matt, 69
Holland, Todd, 1416
Holley, Caitlyn, 993
Holliday, Kene, 155
Holliday, Polly, 936
Hollis, Tommy, 1000
Hollister, Dave, 1057
Hollmond, Clarinda,
  1135
Holly, Lauren, 882
Holm, Bentine, 619
Holm, Celeste, 1269
Holman, Bob, 1181
Holman, Bruce, 232
Holmes, Katie, 313
Holmes, Stephen, 313
Holmes, Tom, 575
Holt, Chris, 349
Holt, Lorri, 944
Holt, Nick, 385
Hooker, John Lee, 406
Hooks, Brian, 77
Hooks, Jan, 1164
Hoosier, James G., 97
Hoover, Howard, 119
Hope, Bob, 896
Hope, Nicholas, 512
Hopewell, Nancy, 679
Hopkins, Anthony,
  773, 781
Hopkins, Barbara
  Barnes, 322
Hopkins, Bo, 860, 967
Hopkins, Josh, 934

Hopkins, Kaitlin, 699
Hopkins, Karen Leigh,
  755
Hopkins, Paul, 21
Hopkins, T. Dan, 19
Hoppe, Rolf, 931
Hopper, Dennis, 780
Hopson, Al, 1419
Horan, Gerard, 674
Horler, Sacha, 61
Horn, Stephen M., 920
Horne, Viviane, 339
Hornsby, Russell, 1471
Horovitz, Avrohom,
  539
Horrocks, Jane, 703
Horton, Michael, 1254
Horton, Peter, 1285
Horwitz, Alan, 866
Hosking, Craig, 298,
  679
Hoskins, Bob, 247,
  1249
Hostetter, John, 1254
Hoty, Tony, 1069
Houghton, Peter, 819
Hounsou, Djimon, 291
Houston, Candy
  Brown, 874
Houston, Thelma, 385
Houston, Ursula Y.,
  975
Hove, Anders, 626
Howard, Chit, 1361
Howard, Clint, 1416
Howard, David S.,
  781
Howard, Rance, 1023,
  1197
Howard, Terence, 975
Howard, Tom, 715
Howard, Traylor, 310
Howarth, James, 1466
Howe, Irvin, 37
Howell, Mark Eric, 126
Howell, Norm, 298
Howitt, Peter, 1189
Hoyland, William, 746
Hoyle, David, 1390
Hoyt, Brian, 987
Hoziel, Eric, 1206
Hsu, Julia, 1081
Hub, Martin, 1100
Hubbard, Valorie, 512
Hudak, Thomas, 634
Hudaverdi, Kenan, 876
Huddleston, David, 97
Huddleston, Michael,
  616
Hudson, Brad, 1466
Hudson, Gwenne, 468
Hudson, Keith, 497,
  920
Huertas, Jon, 1442
Huertas, Luisa, 773
Huffman, Felicity,
  1232
Huffman, Rosanna,
  1228

Huggett, Richard, 61
Huggett, Sanda, 1280
Hugginton, Arianna,
  1155
Hughes, Aneirin, 1304
Hughes, Barnard, 857
Huges, Jordan, 806
Hughes, Liam, 954
Hughes, Miko, 798
Hughes, Sean, 164
Hughes, Tresa, 308
Hugh-Kelly, Daniel,
  1254
Hugho, Kimo, 601
Hui, Michael, 219
Huie, Kimberly, 286
Hulsey, Lauren, 954
Hume, Gary, 746
Humphries, Barry, 667,
  1249, 1424
Humphries, Harry, 40
Hundley, Dylan, 659
Hung, Samo, 819
Hungerford, Bob, 282
Hunt, Barbar Leigh,
  801
Hunt, Bonnie, 146,
  631
Hunt, Denise, 563
Hunt, Eamonn, 589
Hunt, Linda, 949
Hunter, Heather, 500
Hunter, Holly, 715
Hunter, Jack, 140
Hunter, Kelly, 674
Hunter, Kim, 996
Hunter, Shedric, Jr.,
  182
Huppert, Isabelle, 649,
  1284
Hurley, Elizabeth, 965
Hurst, Derek, 1474
Hurst, Michelle, 1264
Hurst, Ryan, 944,
  1100
Hurst, Todd, 1419
Hurst, Tommy, 740
Hurt, John, 740
Hurt, Mary Beth, 1
Hurt, William, 271,
  733, 903, 1020
Huss, Toby, 1269
Hussein, Habis, 941
Huston, Anjelica, 140,
  356 969
Hutton, Lauren, 385,
  1037
Huxtable, Ada Louise,
  245
Hyche, Heath, 857
Hyland, Edward James,
  888
Hyland, Sarah, 888
Hynek, George J., Jr.,
  1371
Hynes, Tyler, 738
Hytower, Roy, 1371
Hütel, Paul, 626
Hébert, François, 69

Iannaccone, Robert,
  860
Iannicelli, Ray, 1069,
  1094
Ice Cube, 578, 975
Ichihara, Etsuko, 334
Idle, Eric, 1031, 1076
Idol, Billy, 1419
Ifans, Rhys, 265
Iijima, Miyuki, 618
Iljin, Alexander, 1344
Imada, Jeff, 679
Imanie, Rahim, 1293
Imrie, Celia, 123, 531
Indovina, Lorenza,
  1344
Ineson, Ralph, 1149
Infeld, Geoffrey, 581
Ingerman, Randi, 684
Ingle, John, 1129
Ingleby, Lee, 356
Ingram, Chris, 385
Ingram, Michael H.,
  959
Innes, Laura, 285
Innes-Smith, James,
  1100
Inoue, Tetsu, 831
Inscoe, Joe, 575
Intiraymi, Manu, 1129
Irizarry, Alaina, 497
Irons, Jeremy, 219,
  722, 759
Ironside, Michael, 216
Irrera, Dom, 97
Irving, Amy, 902
Irving, Martha, 477
Irwin, Jennifer, 119
Irwin, Robert, 245
Isaac, Romanos, 1371
Isaacs, Jason, 40,
  1213
Isabelle, Katharine, 312
Isherwood, Simon, 10
Ishibashi, Takeaki, 757
Ishide, Jim, 40
Islander, J.C., 970
Issariya, Is, 1053
Itsumi, Taro, 396
Ittig, Rodolphe, 1284
Itzin, Gregory, 379,
  1197
Ivanek, Zeljko, 232
Iverson, Lisa, 936
Ives, Sandra, 920
Ivester, Karin J., 931
Ivey, Dana, 597, 1164
Ivey, Judith, 1466
Ivey, Lela, 978
Iwasaki, Kaneko, 1404
Izani, Aril, 1053
Izzard, Eddie, 52, 1389

J., Myra, 155
Jacinto, Jinny, 69
Jack, 1319
Jackman, Kenneth,
  679

Jackson, Dee Jay, 313
Jackson, Ernie, 593
Jackson, Jeanine, 978
Jackson, Joshua, 33, 1387
Jackson, Kevin, 1081
Jackson, Mario, 155
Jackson, Patricia, 1182
Jackson, Philip, 247, 703
Jackson, Reggie, 72
Jackson, Reuben, 187
Jackson, Samuel L., 851, 896, 1243
Jacob, Irne, 1371
Jacobi, Derek, 126, 746
Jacobs, Hans, 1069
Jacobs, Irving, 954
Jacobs, Michael Dean, 914
Jacobson, Amy E., 1371
Jacobson, Peter, 232, 461, 996
Jacobus, Jay, 944
Jacoby, Bobby, 173
Jacott, Carlos, 659, 816
Jaglom, Sabrina, 294
Jaglom, Simon Orson, 294
Jahangiri, Ahmad, 1293
Jain, Aditi, 462
Jain, Shobha, 462
James, Beau, 1240
James, Brion, 601
James, Brooklyn, 77
James, Christian, 903
James, Grant, 860
James, Jess, 434, 442
James, Jill, 1304
James, Lennie, 674, 733
James, Reginald, 497
James, Shane, 434
James-Gannon, Hayley, 531
James-Gannon, Melissa, 531
Jamieson, Greg, 820
Jamshid, 915
Jane, Tom, 1319
Janey, Jim, 931
Janger, Lane, 587
Janicijevic, Dusan, 1123
Janis, Ryan, 232
Jann, Jessica, 679
Jannasch, Charles, 740
Janney, Allison, 187, 597, 888, 1000, 1174
Janney, Julie, 903

Janssen, Famke, 187, 291, 364, 434, 832, 1069
Janssen, Pete, 364
Jansson, Kim, 626
Jao, Radmar, 1152
Jaoui, Agns, 1377
Jarchow, Bruce, 636, 1229
Jaregard, Ernst-Hugo, 626
Jarman, Chris, 722
Jarman, Otto, 1149
Jarmusch, Jim, 1034
Jarrett, Gregg, 434
Jarrett, Phil, 322
Jay, Kenneth, 247
Jay, Ricky, 1232
Jay, Tony, 1077
Jean-Baptiste, Marianne, 816
Jeannin, Marcel, 1
Jean-Thomas, David, 857
Jeffers, Christine, 740
Jefferson, Brenden Richard, 1129
Jeffrey, Myles, 61, 857
Jeffreys, William C. III, 369
Jégou, Ghislaine, 1426
Jelliman, Marie, 1380
Jen Wei Chang, 679
Jenco, Sal, 715
Jenkins, Ken, 1023
Jenkins, Noam, 385
Jenkins, Richard, 597
Jenkins, Roy, 871
Jenney, Lucinda, 993, 1429
Jennings, Brent, 699
Jennings, Byron, 232
Jennings, Sam, 996
Jensen, Birger, 626
Jensen, David, 860
Jensen, Gunther, 1476
Jensen, Henning, 626
Jensen, Soren Elung, 626
Jensen, Vita, 626
Jenson, Niles, 109
Jeremy, Ron, 385, 914
Jerome, Howard, 310
Jerome, Tim, 996
Jessula, Emilie, 751
Jeter, Michael, 379, 944
Jewesbury, Edward, 822
Jia Hongshen, 410
Jiang Wen, 346
Jillette, Penn, 379
Jimmy, 1319
Joachim, Suzy, 313
Jobe, Reri Tava, 1174

Jocelyn, Matthew, 759
Johannessen, Runar, 619
Johansson, Scarlett, 554
John, Chris, 587
John, Elton, 1249
John, Gottfried, 899
Johns, Milton, 1476
Johnsen, Finn, 1375
Johnson, Geir, 619
Johnson, A. J., 578, 975, 1471
Johnson, Alexander, 40
Johnson, Amy Jo, 1466
Johnson, Andray, 114
Johnson, Anne Marie, 322
Johnson, Ariyen, 155
Johnson, Ashley, 1466
Johnson, Bonnie, 944
Johnson, Bryon, 1206
Johnson, Calen, 77
Johnson, Chris, 970
Johnson, Corey, 1100
Johnson, Crystal N., 75
Johnson, Graham Alex, 934
Johnson, Guri, 607
Johnson, Gus, 500, 1232
Johnson, Hassan, 75
Johnson, Jack, 733
Johnson, Jimmy, 1417
Johnson, John H., 40
Johnson, Julie, 69
Johnson, Karl, 746
Johnson, Ken, 61, 114, 757
Johnson, Kristina Eliot, 798
Johnson, Lauri, 225, 851
Johnson, Marcus, 271
Johnson, Matthew, 1262
Johnson, Michael, 133
Johnson, Richard, 72
Johnson, Shann, 119
Johnson, Theodore Tour, Jr., 679
Johnston, Darrell, 265
Johnston, J.J., 1232
Johnston, Jay, 611
Johnston, Jim, 364
Johnston, Michelle, 857
Johnstone, Nahanni, 1040
Jolani, Wael, 294
Jones, Baden, 1424
Jones, Ben, 1000
Jones, Charlie, 1466
Jones, Cherry, 554, 918

Jones, Dot-Marie, 944
Jones, Elia, 1189
Jones, Esther, 1471
Jones, Gemma, 1304, 1460
Jones, Harry, 390
Jones, Hatty, 751
Jones, James Earl, 1000
Jones, Jason Edward, 448
Jones, Jedda, 155
Jones, Jeff, 322
Jones, L. Q., 773
Jones, Leslie, 1474
Jones, Lewis, 339
Jones, Mal, 539, 931, 1348
Jones, Merryn, 1189
Jones, Michael Steve, 636
Jones, Nasir, 75
Jones, Neal, 277, 1154
Jones, Nicola, 93
Jones, O-Lan, 1348
Jones, Orlando, 1228, 1471
Jones, Osheen, 1389
Jones, Richard, 860, 1449
Jones, Roby, 357
Jones, Ron, 500, 1181
Jones, Rupert Penry, 531
Jones, Ruth, 1304
Jones, Stephen Anthony, 944
Jones, Tamela, 173
Jones, Tammi Katherine, 497
Jones, Tiffany, 500
Jones, Timothy, 271
Jones, Toby, 247, 674
Jones, Tommy Lee, 1197, 1371
Jones, Tracy C., 975
Jones, Ursula, 357
Jones, Walker, 597
Jones, William James, 252
Jones, William Todd, 733
Jones, Winston, 1180
Jordan, Alan, 540
Jordan, Jonathan Parks, 1135
Jordan, Michael, 500
Jordan, Vernon E., Jr., 434, 1069
Joseph, François, 832
Joseph, Jackie, 1197
Joshua, Lawrence, 1476
Joss, Jonathan, 19
Jostyn, Jennifer, 286
Jover, Arly, 114
Jovovich, Milla, 500
Joy, Jeff, 1361

Joy, Mark, 954
Joy, Robert, 369
Joyce, Anne, 554
Joyner, David, 69
Juan, Jean-Marie, 201
Judd, Ashley, 1164
Judd, General Fermon, Jr., 1262
Judge, 601
Jun, Hu, 330
Jung, Calvin, 679
Jung, Clint, 1152
Jungmann, Eric, 364
Junker, Ruth, 626
Junqueria, Caio, 195, 403
Jurado, Katy, 522
Jurgens, Gerda Maria, 1344
Jutras, Roch, 69

Kachev, Fabien, 1426
Kackley, R. J., 758
Kaczmarek, Jane, 978
Kaczorowski, Nina, 1167
Kaelin, Kato, 72
Kaga, Mariko, 1439
Kagan, Diane, 781
Kagan, Elaine, 847
Kahan, Steve, 679
Kahler, Wolf, 390
Kahn, Madeline, 146
Kaholokula, Pua, 1174
Kain, Ambler, 903
Keina, James K., 601
Kajanus, Georg, 304
Kajanus, Johanne, 304
Kaldor, Christopher, 1232
Kalember, Patricia, 544
Kaler, Berwick, 440
Kellis, Carolyn "Coco", 1232
Kamaar, Al, 539
Kamal, Hany, 1155
Kamin, Daniel T., 860
Kampwirth, Stephan, 89
Kanakaredes, Melina, 269, 1069
Kanaoka, Nobu, 1336
Kancher, Deborah, 993
Kane, Billy, 298
Kane, Dyan, 462
Kaneshiro, Takeshi, 373
Kang, Stan, 369
Kanter, Marlene, 225
Kantor, Calman, 420
Kapanadze, Keti, 135
Kaplan, Maura Nielsen, 1474
Kaplan, Michael, 40
Karam, Jena, 860
Karasek, Valerie, 954, 1240
Karen, James, 33

Karfo, Robin, 636
Karkowsky, Adam, 349
Karl, George, 500
Karp, Izetta, 578
Karp, Natalie, 1193
Karras, Alex, 140
Kartell, Theresa, 1189
Kartsivadze, Niko, 135
Karz, Jimmy, 1419
Karn, Michelle, 109
Kashiwabara, Takashi, 1439
Kass, Julie, 1489
Kassim, Helmi, 1154
Kasten, Hiram, 1228
Kasumu, Ganiat, 1390
Katano, Mimi Jo, 1232
Katims, Robert, 1495
Kato, Masaya, 448
Katsulas, Andreas, 755
Katsumura, Masanobu, 1223
Katt, Nicky, 903, 967
Kattan, Chris, 871
Katz, Jonathan, 1232
Katz, Phyllis, 318
Kauffman, Gary, 1061
Kaufman, Michael, 155
Kaufman, Stanley L., 915
Kava, Caroline, 403
Kavanagh, John, 164, 265
Kavanagh, Stuart, 634
Kavner, Julie, 318
Kawara, Sabu, 334
Kay, Barnaby, 1137
Kazan, Lainie, 93
Kazuki, Anna, 914
Keach, Stacy, 21
Keane, James, 978
Keaneally, Laura, 272
Keaney, Dermot, 247
Kearny, Geré, 428
Keaton, Joshua, 1227
Keaton, Michael, 298, 610
Keats, Richard, 578
Keaulana, Brian L., 601
Keaulana, Buffalo, 601
Kechiouche, Salim, 411
Keegan, Donna, 298
Keegan, Tim, 1272
Keelan, John, 10
Keenan, Kathy Baldwin, 554
Keener, Catherine, 920, 1040, 1483
Keeslar, Matt, 659, 1228
Keever, Kristine, 909
Kehler, Jack, 97, 679, 1228
Keiner, Tilo, 1100
Keitel, Harvey, 414, 1135

Keith, Warren David, 97
Kelada, Guy, 1206
Kelamis, Peter, 593
Keleghan, Peter, 1041
Kell, Michael, 187
Kelleher, Tim, 298, 851
Keller, Joel S., 477
Keller, Marthe, 958
Keller, Mary Page, 851
Kellner, Catherine, 277
Kellner, Deborah, 811
Kellogg, Mary Anne, 871
Kellor, Garrison, 105
Kelly, Craig, 1249
Kelly, Daragh, 427
Kelly, David, 1409
Kelly, Dupre, 1222
Kelly, Eamon A., 589
Kelly, Jill, 500, 915
Kelly, Joe, 349, 757
Kelly, Joseph Patrick, 40
Kelly, Katie, 1167
Kelly, Mary, 1489
Kelly, Michael, 1061
Kelly-Miller, Lois, 781
Kelly, Moira, 269, 519, 749
Kelly, Terry, 394
Kelsey, Herb, 434
Kelsey, Tamsin, 313
Kelty, Gavin, 165, 427
Kemble, Josh, 298
Kemler, Andrew W., 914
Kemp, Lindsay, 1390
Kemp, Sacha, 578
Kemp, Tom, 1021
Kempson, Rachel, 294
Kenia, Sheyla, 195
Kennaway, George, 531
Kennedy, David, 746
Kennedy, Ellen, 1474
Kennedy, George, 1197
Kennedy, Jamie, 240, 348
Kennedy, Kevin, 1182
Kennedy, Maria Doyle, 129, 427
Kenny, J.C., 1387
Kenny, Jack, 593
Kenny, Jon, 674
Kent, Anne, 427, 589
Kent, Jennifer, 61
Keogh, Jimmy, 1409
Keramidopulos, Sumela-Rose, 1164
Kermode, Robin, 1461
Kern, Richard, 153
Kerr, E. Katherine, 597, 866, 1154
Kerr, Eddie, 746
Kerr, Terry, 936

Kerrigan, Dermot, 1409
Kersnar, David, 1371
Kervadec, Sophie, 1426
Kerwin, Brian, 816
Kess, Georgina, 385
Kjessler, Abraham, 1228
Kessler, Glenn, 1154
Kesting, Hans, 210
Ketscher, Annette, 626
Keung, Eric, 349
Key, Steve, 798
Key, William, 1390
Keyes, Tony, 679
Khaderni, Shahri, 10
Khaled, Alaa, 173
Khalil, Ahmed, 1149
Khosla, Surinder, 187
Kibbe, David, 126
Kiberlain, Sandrine, 1131
Kidder, Janet, 133
Kidman, Nicole, 667, 993
Kiely, Mark, 441
Kier, Udo, 40, 114, 626
Kierann, Anthony, 272
Kierney, Tyde, 379
Kightley, Timothy, 1137
Kihistedt, Rya, 286
Kikai, Hiromi, 396
Kikkenborg, Natalie B., 888
Kiley, Kate, 954
Kiley, Richard, 944
Killalea, J.J., 1085
Killen, Paula, 153
Killian, Robyn, 349
Kilmer, Wil, 931
Kilner, David, 764
Kilpatrick, Laurie, 811
Kilpatrick, Patrick, 1048
Kim, Jin S., 572
Kim, Randall Duk, 1048
Kimball, Donna, 944
Kimble, Matthew, 1419
Kimura, Kazuya, 455
Kind, Richard, 146
Kinery, Micheline, 304
Kinevane, Pat, 427
King, B.B., 119
King, Erik, 298
King, Ginger, 931
King, Jama, 140
King, Janel, 140
King, Kip, 871
King, Larry, 155, 349, 1000
King, Peter, 1390
King, Regina, 348, 563, 811
King, Steve, 1371
King, Suzy, 697

King, T.W., 1476
King, Wayne A., 1081
Kingi, Henry, 615
Kingston, Graeme, 593
Kinimaka, Alekai, 601
Kinimaka, Titus, 601
Kinnear, Greg, 1489
Kino, Lloyd, 448
Kinsey, Lance, 636
Kinski, Nastassja, 699, 1123, 1483
Kirk, Christina, 1094
Kirkland, Ajgie, 97
Kirkland, Sally, 896
Kirkman, Tim, 280
Kirkpatrick, Maggie, 1424
Kirksey, Logan, 1348
Kirkwood, Craig, 1442
Kirschke, Jack, 993
Kirton, Mike, 540
Kishimoto, Kayoko, 395
Kishina, Ai, 396
Kissner, Jeremy James, 461
Kitano, Takeshi, 455, 1223
Kitazawa, Kiyoko, 396
Kitchen, Michael, 822
Kitchin, Sam, 539, 1348
Kittay, Marc, 1416
Klein, Dan, 755
Klein, Lauren, 996
Klein, Robert, 866, 1000
Klein, Spencer, 1187
Kleinhans, Martha-Marie, 1
Kleyla, Brandon, 441
Klieman, Rikki, 232
Klohn, T. Edwin, 915
Klyn, Vince, 601
Kmeck, George, 1069
Knaster, Jeremy, 1154
Knatchbull, Melissa, 390
Knepper, Rob, 967
Knight, Duane, 1308
Knight, Jack, 1460
Knight, Phil, 105
Knight, Shirley, 699
Knight, William, 578
Knights, Kendall, 1040
Knode, Helen, 613
Knott, Robert, 522
Knotts, Don, 978
Knower, Rosemary, 954
Knowles, Harry, 364
Knowlton, Sarah, 888
Knutson, Ashley, 798
Ko, Andrew, 572
Ko, Eddy, 679
Koaho, Mpho, 322
Kobayashi, Banbino, 396

Kobayashi, Ken, 334
Kobayashi, Victor, 871
Koblizkova, Sylvie, 674
Koch, Daniel, 67
Koch, Edward I., 1222
Koci, Pavel, 674
Koechner, David, 310
Kohn, Richard, 575
Koklukaya, Basak, 1260
Kokol, Robert, 1416
Kokumai, Aya, 1223
Kolaas, Harald, 619
Komatsu, Hosei, 1404
Komenich, Rich, 511
Konigsberg, Martin, 1449
Konigsberg, Nettie, 1449
Konishi, Hiroyuki, 334
Konishi, Muneyuki, 396
Kono, Jody, 1174
Koole, Ricky, 327
Koos, Balazs, 1387
Kopit, Neal, 811
Koppel, Nurit, 1035
Korbutt, Deann, 1262
Kordelle, Kessia, 77
Korikova, Elena, 408
Koromzay, Alix, 874
Korsmo, Charlie, 173
Korte, Donald, 851
Korzeniowski, Thomas, 954
Koshcheev, Anatolii, 1315
Kostychin, Constantin, 408
Kosugi, Shaw, 396
Koteas, Elias, 33, 369, 538, 715, 1319
Kotecki, Robert, 1081
Kotva, Vaclav, 847
Kousnetzoff, Nathalie, 1284
Kovac, Mario, 470
Koyanagi, Brie, 1145
Kozlowski, Caralyn, 993
Krabbé, Jeroen, 269, 356
Kraemer, Andreas, 954, 1240
Kraemer, Mattias, 348
Kraft, Scot, 611
Krag, James, 798
Krah, Kim, 140
Krape, Evelyn, 61
Krassner, Paul, 672
Krause, Peter, 1348
Krauss, Margareta Lucia, 686
Krawick, Michael, 1228, 1476
Kreiner, Michael "Pogo", 603
Kremer, Hans, 795

Kress, Nathan, 61
Krich, Gretchen, 512
Krieger, Deborah, 871
Kriss, Mandy, 349
Kristen, Marta, 733
Kristofferson, Kris, 114, 1216
Kristol, Irving, 37
Krivitska, Tatiana, 408
Krog, Evald, 626
Kronenberg, Fred, 1253
Kronenfeld, Ivan, 715
Krstic, Ljiljana, 1123
Krstovic, Miodrag, 1123
Kruk, Richard, 119
Krull, Ramsey, 987
Krumholtz, David, 1193
Krystle, Erin, 669
Krystyan, Vieslav, 385
Ktiri, Ali, 1085
Kudrow, Lisa, 240, 909
Kuhn, Daniella, 944
Kuhon, Monica, 601
Kula, Chad, 1180
Kulich, Vladimir, 394
Kulish, Kyle, 187
Kunis, Mila, 636
Künnecke, Evelyn, 623
Kunstmann, Doris, 416
Kunz, Simon, 936
Kuoch, Koing, 886
Kurez, Robert, 1371
Kurth, Wally, 580
Kurtz, Marcia Jean, 903
Kurtz, Swoosie, 927
Kurup, Shishir, 225
Kusatsu, Clyde, 448
Kushner, Celia, 593
Kussman, Susan, 1000
Kuzelka, Jan, 674
Kuznetsov, Yuri, 137
Kwalda, Tasheen, 941
Kwan, Brian, 317
Kynman, Paul, 1149

Labao, Cece Neber, 679
Laborit, Emmanuelle, 89
Lacey, Deborah, 155
Lacopo, Jay, 19
Lacroix, Peter, 313
Ladd, Cheryl, 965
Ladd, Diane, 1000
Lady of Rage, 1057
LaFayette, John, 232, 317
Laffen, Pat, 427
LaFont, Bernadette, 425
Lage, Jordan, 1232
Lahri, Ronobir, 1489
Lai, Leon, 243, 373

Lain, Chasey, 914
Lake, Don, 19
Lake, Michael, 271
Lally, John, 1061
Lally, Trudy, 1061
La Londe, Mike, 554
Lam, Nina Zole, 1489
Lam, Steven, 679
Lama, Ernesto, 1344
Lamar, Sophia, 1146
LaMarca, Gina, 1457
Lamb, Jennifer, 97
Lambert, Steve, 1269
Lambton, Anne, 21, 746
Lampley, Jim, 72
Lancaster, Julie, 1264
Lancelot, Patrick, 48
Landa, Billy Joe, 1440
Landau, Martin, 1069, 1476
Lander, John-Michael, 18
Lander, Patrick, 40
Landes, Michael, 326
Landesberg, Steve, 1227
Landesman, Rocco, 834
Landey, Clayton, 232
Landi, Marielle, 601
Landis, Elizabeth, 1290
Landis, Max, 119
Landolfi, Krist Lynn, 1348
Landry, Charlie, 1061
Landry, Sylvain, 1206
Landré, Lou, 210
Lang, Johnny, 119
Lang, Robert, 1460
Lang, Stephen, 313, 870
Langbridge, Cynthia, 1174
Langdon, Anthony, 1390
Lange, Artie, 310
Lange, Jessica, 247, 575, 896
Langella, Frank, 722, 1197
Langer, A. J., 780
Langford, Lisa Louise, 481
Lano, Jenya, 114
Lansbury, Kate, 356
Lansing, Joi, 1339
Lansing, Robert, 915
Lansink, Leonard, 623
Lantton, Brooke, 1039
Lao, Kristin Mae-Anne, 970
LaPaglia, Anthony, 969
La Paine, Daniel, 269, 385, 987
Lapotaire, Jane, 1149
Larby, Ahmed Ben, 1154

Laresca, Vincent, 1041
Larkin, Robert, 866
Larkin, Sheena, 1, 69
Larkins, Tommy, 1308
La Rosa, Kevin, 286
Larouche, David, 69
Larouche, Edouard, 69
Larrivey, Wayne A., 349
Larsen, Nils, 173
Larsen, Thomas Bo, 184, 626
Larson, Bill, 931
Larson, Darrell, 1135, 1264
Larson, Graham J., 1155
Larson, Mark S., 886
Larson, Tom, 583
LaRue, Rodger, 1049
Lasardo, Robert, 874
La Scala, Nancy, 1240
Laser, Dieter, 899
Laska, Rey, 1442
Laskawy, Harris, 1193
Lasser, Louise, 480
Latham, David, 512
Lathna, Sanaa, 114
Lau, William, 1085
Laudenbach, Phillippe, 646
Lauer, Andrew, 593
Laumord, Gilbert, 1284
Lauray, Jennifer, 1269
Laurie, Dan, 1447
Laurie, Edward, 1461
Laurie, Hugh, 123, 247, 759, 1249
Laurie, Piper, 364
Laursen, Linda, 184
Lavaud, Alice, 751
Laveaux, Shalya, 914
La Vecchia, Antoinette, 308
Lavell, Sandie, 1380
Laverty, Frank, 427
Lavia, Lorenzo, 48
LaVorgna, Adam, 593
Law, Jude, 1460
Lawlor, J. Patrick, 978
Lawrence, Andy, 610
Lawrence, Cary, 1206
Lawrence, Christopher B., 349
Lawrence, Jeremy D., 126
Lawrence, Jonathan, 1146
Lawrence, Mal Z., 1069
Lawrence, Mark Christopher, 1129
Lawrence, Steve, 119
Lawson, Bianca, 1000
Lawson, Maggie, 978
Lawson, Richard, 563
Layfield, Crispin, 652
Lazar, Paul, 77, 512
Lazard, Justin, 1240

Lazarev, Alexandre, 408
Lazzarini, Patrizia, 686
Lea, Ursula, 697
Leach, Jackson, 1460
Leach, Nigel, 624
Leadbitter, Bill, 740
Leahan, Cathrine, 232
Leake, Damien, 811
Leal, Leandra, 929
Leaman, Rande, 1229
Leary, Denis, 146, 749, 832, 1040, 1197, 1277, 1447
Leavins, Chris, 477
Leavy, Pat, 165, 427
LeBaron, Brian, 379
Lebboroni, Raffaella, 686
Lebel, David, 69
Lebell, Jean, 1081
Le Bevillon, Lo, 1131
LeBlanc, Matt, 733
LeBrecht, James, 69
Le Cossec, Michel, 1426
Leder, Bryan, 659
Ledoyen, Virginie, 1216
Ledreau, Carole, 1426
Lee, Carmen, 634
Lee, Cherish, 21
Lee, Dan, 679
Lee, Fay Ann, 512
Lee, Grace, 636
Lee, Jason, 348, 631, 1213
Lee, Kaiulani, 232, 575
Lee, Lela, 1152
Lee, Leo, 1048
Lee, Miki, 819
Lee, Oliver, 531
Lee, Paul J. Q., 996
Lee, Robbie, 1085
Lee, Robert E., 72
Lee, Robinne, 497
Lee, Schecter, 1040
Lee, Shannon, 114
Lee, Sheryl, 615, 887
Lee, Stephen, 448, 851
Lee, Zack, 1308
Leeds, Phil, 636
Leene, Jamie, 1461
Leesley, Geoffrey, 1461
Lefevour, Rick, 1371
LeFevre, Adam, 1069
Leffers, Morten Rotne, 626
Le Furr, Gaelle, 989
Lefèbvre, Jean-Claude, 694
Lefèbvre, Laetitia, 764
Legal, Brigitte, 1426
Leggett, Jay, 538
Le Gros, James, 348, 1023

Le Guerrier, Renée Madeleine, 69
Leguizamo, John, 317
Lehmann, Karin, 89
Lehr, John, 816
Leigh, Janet, 472, 1339
Leigh, Katie, 61
Leigh, Kristen, 1262
Leigh, Marissa, 936
Leigh, Taylor, 715
Leitch, Megan, 492
Leite, Gildásio, 195
Leite, Sonia, 195
Leland, Grace, 652
Leland, Jacob, 652
Lelièvre, Karine, 1426
Lelio, Anna, 48
Le Mat, Paul, 21
Lemieux, Robert Norman, 1206
Lemire, Richard, 1206
Lemmon, Jack, 857
Lenancker, Alain, 694
Lenehan, Nancy, 978
Lennix, Harry, 216
Lennox, Kai, 978, 1081
Lennstrom, Stephen, 332
Leno, Jay, 896
Leomiti, K.C., 40
Leon, Carlos, 97, 1048
Leona, Polyn, 1319
Leonard, Robert Sean, 659
Leoni, Te, 285
Leopardi, Chauncey, 909
Le Prevost, Nicholas, 652, 1137
Léray, Melanie, 1426
Lerel, Laurence, 649
Lerici, Barbara, 201
Lerner, Jeffrey P., 1308
Lerner, Ken, 1129
Lerner, Michael, 187, 448, 1093
Leroy, Zoeunne, 1348
Le Saux, Johan, 1426
Leslie, Susan, 909
Lespance, P.J., 1474
Lesser, Robert, 448
Lester, Adrian, 1000
Lester, Terri, 1057
Letheren, Mark, 1460
Letizia, Maria, 686
Leto, Jared, 1319, 1387
Letscher, Matt, 773
Letts, Dennis, 699
Letts, Tracy, 1371
Leung, Ken, 1081
Leung, Wallace, 1474
Levani, 114
Leverone, Gene, 781
Levert, Matt, 798

Leverton, Guy, 1390
Levin, Charles, 232
Levin, G. Roy, 1232
Levine, Walter, 119
Levinson, Carrie, 511
Levitch, Ashlee, 1253
Levitch, Peter, 819
Levitch, Timothy, 253
Levitt, Joseph Gordon, 472
Levy, Adam, 457
Levy, Eugene, 19
Levy, Katharine, 390
Levy, Salvador, 931
Lew, James, 679, 1049
Lewetz, Stephan, 89
Lewicki, Jennifer, 339
Lewis, Andrea, 322
Lewis, Bobo, 903
Lewis, Bret, 72
Lewis, Buddy, 1471
Lewis, Carol Jean, 77
Lewis, Cornelius, 286
Lewis, David, 10
Lewis, Gary, 176
Lewis, Huey, 1243
Lewis, Jason, 866
Lewis, Jennifer, 806
Lewis, Jenny, 699, 978
Lewis, Juliette, 414
Lewis, Mark, 357
Lewis, Rachel, 1262
Lewis, Robert, 313
Lewis, Todd D., 1466
Lewis, Tyrone, 75
Lewis, Vicki, 448
Lexsee, Richard, 1371
L'Heureux, Grard, 97
Li, Donald, 1371
Li, Jet, 679
Librizzi, Rosa, 634
Lichtenstein, Mitchell, 1035
Lieber, Mimi, 155
Lien, Jennifer, 21
Lierop, Toy Van, 540
Lifshutz, Richard "Izzy", 996
Lifton, Robert Jay, 509
Li Geng, 410
Lightning, Cody, 1203
Lill, Denis, 822
Lillard, Matthew, 1129, 1466
Lillesee, Britta, 626
Lilly, Kabriel, 385
Lima, Danny, 93
Lima, Edivaldo, 195
Lima, Frances, 1304
Limas, Jim Adhi, 201
Lin, Lucy, 1081
Lin, Yan, 1081
Lindberg, Chad, 798
Lindbjerg, Lalainia, 312
Linde, Betty, 593
Linden, Andy, 746
Linders, Billy, 1471
Lindgren, Axel, 19

Lindner, Carl Michael, 636, 1187
Lindon, Vincent, 1131
Lindsay, Delia, 531
Lindsay, Elizabeth, 866
Lindsay, Peter, 819
Lindsay, Elizabeth, 155
Lindsay, Joseph, 182
Lineback, Richard, 575, 780
Lineham, Hardee T., 93
Lineham, Niamh, 427
Linehan, Rosaleen, 165, 522
Ling, Bai, 1221
Linn, Rex, 857, 1081
Linnestad, Eli Anne, 619
Linney, Laura, 1348
Liotta, Ray, 969
Lipinski, Eugene, 1
Lipman, David, 597
Lipnicki, Jonathan, 318
Lippin, Renee, 187
Lipton, Sam, 126
Lira, Nanego, 195
Lira, Soia, 195
Lisi, Joe, 481
Lister, Tommy "Tiny", Jr., 578, 975
Lithgow, John, 232, 548
Little, Brock, 601
Little Richard, 1442
Littmen, Robert, 1081
Litz, Nadia, 806
Liu, Matty, 601
Liufau, Sidney, 114
Liu Jie, 410
Lively, Andrea, 540
Lively, Ernie, 1129
Livingston, Bill, 755
Livingston, Paul, 61, 271
LL Cool J, 182, 472, 1471
Lloyd, Christopher, 1040
Lloyd, Eric, 847
Lo, Ming, 317
Locke, Kourtney, 578
Locke, Philip, 1460
Lockhart, June, 733
Lockwood, Vera, 755
Loder, Kurk, 75
Loeillet, Sylvie, 1131
Loevy, Karen, 294
Loewi, Fiona, 740
Loftin, Lennie, 874
Logan, Laurie V., 987
Logan, Phyllis, 1149
Loggia, Robert, 539, 1020, 1447
Logue, Donal, 114, 400
Logue, Karina, 282
Lohan, Lindsay, 936
Lohan, Michael, 936
Lohman, Lenore, 269

Lohmeyer, Peter, 623
Loiret, Florence, 1131
Lojodice, Giuliana, 686
Lombard, Michael, '1069
Lombardo, Concetta, 686
Lombardozzi, Domenick, 385
Lomena, June, 1429
London, Daniel, 944
Loneker, Keith, 920
Long, Howie, 394
Long, Hudson Lee, 722
Long, Jess H., 442
Long, Jodi, 187
Long, Martha, 550
Long, Nia, 497
Longley, Janine, 385
Longridge, Ronald, 1100
Lonow, Mark, 1419
Lonsdale, Michael, 1062
Look, Lydia, 1081
López, Antonio de la Torré, 789
López, Iguandili, 789
López, Irene Olga, 97, 857
Lopez, Jennifer, 27, 920
Lopez, Sergi, 1426
Lorbeer, Julia, 89
Lord, Justin, 322
Lordon, John, 851
Lords, Traci, 114
Loren, Eric, 1100
Lother, Susanne, 416
Loughran, Jonathan, 1416
Louis, Kevin, 1471
Louis-Dreyfus, Julia, 146
Louise, Tina, 1424
Lounici, Marie, 1426
Loustau, Kate, 339
Love, Courtney, 640
Love, Darlene, 679
Love, Faizon, 975
Love, Mary, 860
Lovejoy, Deirdre, 1228
Lover, Ed, 1057
Lovett, Lyle, 379, 909
Lovett, Marjorie, 33, 1023
Lovitz, Jon, 480, 1419
Löw, Victor, 210
Lowe, David, 759
Lowe, Kevin, 1081
Lowe, Susan, 954
Lowery, David, 1061
Loza, Richard, 176
Lozano, Domenique, 944
Lucai, Victoria, 414
Lucas, Allan E., 1181
Lucas, Joseph, 1348
Lucci, Ralph J., 1371

Lucy, 477
Ludwig, Ken, 834
Ludwig, Louis, 1061
Ludwig, Salem, 888
Luft, Lorna, 847
Luke, Tau, 1375
Lumbly, Carl, 563
Lumsden, Richard, 52
Lund, Julie, 781
Lund, Rold Arly, 619
Lunderskov, Lasse, 184
Lunoe, Lars, 626
Luotto, Andy, 1344
Luppi, Federico, 789
Lusby, Scott, 448
Lushing, Michael, 1174
Lussier, Matthew, 1416
Lutz, Mike, 364
Luzia, Dona, 195
Lyles, Leslie, 659
Lyman, Will, 959, 1154
Lynch, Aubrey, 864
Lynch, John, 798, 1189
Lynch, Kelly, 548
Lynch, Michael A., 757
Lynch, Susan, 1409
Lyndon, Simon, 1319
Lynn, Amanda, 540
Lynn, Meredith Scott, 109, 580, 871
Lynne, Robyn, 914
Lynskey, Melanie, 356
Lyonne, Natasha, 636, 1193
Lyons, Antonio David, 21
Lyons, Jennifer, 173
Lyons, John, 119
Lyons, Paula, 866
Lypeckyj, Christina Romana, 987
Lysenko, Stefan, 755

Ma, Ramond, 679
Ma, Tzi, 1081
Ma Xiaoqing, 410
Mabe, Ricky, 738
Mabius, Eric, 664
Mac, Bernie, 975
McAdam, Margaret, 176
McAlear, Nancy, 1387
MacArthur, Erik, 978
Macaulay, Marc, 461, 539, 931, 1456
McAuliffe, Casey, 860
McAvoy, James, 1044
McBeath, Tom, 394
McBride, Chi, 798
McBride, Kevin, 1077
McBurney, Simon, 247
MacCabe, Christopher, 1206
McCabe, Pat, 165

McCabe, Ruth, 1288
McCabe, Vinnie, 165
McCaddon, Wanda, 944
McCafferty, Frankie, 130
McCain, Frances Lee, 944
McCain, Micah, 72
McCambridge, Mercedes, 1339
McCann, Mary, 1232
McCann, Sean, 1, 1164
McCerlie, Colin, 292
McCarthy, Francis X., 72, 286
McCarthy, Jenny, 72
McCarthy, Maggie, 390, 531, 801, 1429
McCarthy, Patrick, 187
McCarthy, Thomas J., 369
McCarthy, Tyson, 271
McCarty, Walter, 500
McCarver, Tim, 72
McCauley, James Michael, 1053
McCawley, Keith, 1085
McCawley, Ronnie, 1085
Maccione, Aldo, 201
McClanahan, Thayer, 1085
McClean, Marley, 1193
McClurg, Edie, 146, 539, 1077
McCole, Stephen, 1085
McColl, Catriona, 1216
McColl, Hamish, 936
McComb, Heather, 33
McConaughey, Matthew, 860
McConaughey, Rooster, 860
McConnachie, Brian, 187
McConnel, Bridget, 1137
McCord, Sarah, 597
MacCormac, Raymond, 1409
McCormack, Brian, 187, 1425
McCormack, Catherine, 265, 269, 652
McCormack, Eric, 539
McCormack, J. Patrick, 40, 936
McCormack, Mary, 285
McCormick, Elizabeth, 1262
McCormick, Shannon, 674

McCouch, Grayson, 40
McCoy, Larry, 975
McCullough, Lonnie, 857
McDade, Patrick F., 1206
McDaniel, Drucie, 369
Mcdermott, Tom, 1154
McDonald, Audra, 888
MacDonald, Barry, 10
McDonald, Bill, 832
McDonald, Chris, 310, 364, 644
McDonald, Gary, 1232
MacDonald, George, 832
MacDonald, Gordon, 1319
McDonald, Gregg, 975
MacDonald, James, 798, 1228
MacDonald, Jock, 1193
McDonald, John, 851
Macdonald, Kelly, 247, 339
Macdonald, Norm, 310, 317
McDonald, Peter, 589
McDonald, Robin, 715
MacDonald, Scott, 1037
McDonnell, Blue, 860
McDonough, Brenna, 349
McDonough, Matthew, 1348
McDormand, Frances, 751, 1288
McDowell, Larry, 1348
MacDowell, Andie, 1135
McDowell, Julie, 1189
McDowell, Roddy, 146
McElduff, Ellen, 715, 882
McElhatton, Michael, 589
McElhenney, Rob, 232
McElhone, Natascha, 822, 1062, 1348
Macellari, Maria Rita, 686
McElvaney, Siobhan, 165
Macero, Teo, 830
McEwan, Russell, 470
McFadden, Gates, 1254
MacFadyen, Angus, 1269
McFerran, Douglas, 1189
McFerrin, Julia, 616
McGee, Carl A., 601
McGee, Gwen, 798

McGee, Jack, 200, 580, 1253
McGee, Mark, 857
McGill, Bruce, 664
McGill, Heather, 978
McGinley, Sean, 129, 165, 427
McGinley, Ted, 757
McGinn, Chris, 1061
McGinnis, Sue, 832
McGlone, Mike, 902
McGlynn, John, 674
McGonagle, Richard, 811, 1129
McGough, Philip, 674
McGovern, Barry, 427
McGovern, Chris, 882
McGowan, Rose, 967
McGrady, Michael, 1319
McGrath, Brian, 427
McGrath, Debra, 1040
McGrath, Doug, 187, 480
McGrath, Matt, 597
McGrath, Pat, 165
McGraw, Melinda, 1474
McGraw, Sarge, 522
McGregor, Ewan, 703, 874, 1389
McGregor-Stewart, Kate, 715
McGruder, Stephen, 931
McGuire, Elly, 563
McGuire, Maeve, 959
Macht, Gabriel, 888
McHugh, Bill, 1489
McHugh, Jason, 171, 914
Maciejewski, Michael, 140
McIlvaine, Mary, 888
McIntosh, Yanna, 322
MacIntyre, Gandhi, 61
McIntyre, Gerry, 864
McIntyre, Marilyn, 1399
McIntyre, Roger, 448
Macisaac, Ashley, 477
McIvor, Emma, 427
McKane, Matthew, 715
McKay, David, 674
Mackay, Gary, 1375
McKay, John, 870, 1035
MacKay, Lizabeth, 903
Mackay, Mathew, 738
MacKay, Michael Reid, 33
McKean, Michael, 1197, 1269
McKee, Lonette, 500
McKeen, Roger, 133, 1164
McKeever, Mikki, 931

McKellen, Ian, 33, 441, 1280
McKenna, Seans, 477
McKenna, Virginia, 1189
Mackenzie, J.C., 500
McKenzie, Matt, 441, 857
MacKenzie, Peter, 757
Mackenzie, Piers, 944
McKenzie, Russell B., 1399
Mckeon, William J. III, 1206
McKeown, Fintan, 1409
McKewley, Robert, 740
Mackichan, Doon, 123
McKidd, Kevin, 1044
Mackie, Allison, 1227
McKinley, Mairead, 1389
McKinney, Mark, 659, 871, 1249
Mackintosh, Martha, 652
Mackintosh, Steven, 652
McKnight, Esau, Jr., 114
MacKriel, Peter, 674
MacLachlan, Colin, 1461
McLaglen, Josh, 1476
MacLaren, Alyson, 10
McLaren, John, 1123
McLaughlin, Cliff, 317
McLaughlin, Ian, 624
McLaughlin, John, 1061
MacLean, Ali, 173
McLean, Antoine, 572, 1447
McLean, Finlay, 1044
McLellan, B.J., 738
McLeod, John, 993
McLeod, Shannon, 581
McLiam, Eanna, 427
McLoughlin, Marian, 1249
McLymont, Karen, 819
McMillan, Babs, 61
McMullan, Tim, 269, 1137
McMurray, Sam, 1187
McNally, Kevin, 1189, 1249
McNally, Seamus, 987
McNamara, Desmond, 1137
McNamara, Peter, 1149
McNamara, William, 1059
Macnee, Patrick, 52
McNeil, Eric Keith, 75
McNeil, Marguerite, 740

MacNeil, Peter, 477, 1164
MacNeille, Tress, 1077
Macoby, Jacob, 1149
McPherson, Conor, 589
McPherson, Selma, 563
McQuade, Arlene, 1339
McQuade, Seamus, 1100
McQueen, Armelia, 155
McQueen, B.J., 310
McRobbie, Peter, 1206
McShane, Michael, 146
McSorley, Gerard, 165
McSwain, Monica, 173
McTavish, Patrick, 1419
McTeer, Janet, 1389
MacVittie, Bruce, 385, 519, 1343
McWhirter, Cath, 1375
Macy, William H., 232, 538, 978, 1023
Maddox, Rose, 522
Madrid, Carmen, 789
Madrid, Salvador, 201
Madruga, Teresa, 958
Madsen, Michael, 1240
Maehara, Kazuki, 1319
Maelen, Christian, 587
Maffia, Robert, 153
Mafham, Dominic, 1149
Magdalena, Deborah, 540
Magers, Paul, 1167
Maggart, Michael, 1085
Magnan, Philippe, 1131
Magnuson, Ann, 1197, 1269
Magnusson, Magnus, 740
Maguire, Anna, 357, 1100
Maguire, Tobey, 379, 978
Mahan, Kerrigan, 318
Maher, Bill, 1000
Maher, Lori K., 1414
Mahmoud, Abdallah, 302
Mahmud-Bey, Sheik, 130
Mahon, John, 40
Mahoney, John, 27
Mahoney, Louis, 1149
Mainz, Steven, 851
Maisonett, Robert, 277
Makin, Nigel, 740
Malahide, Patrick, 1371
Malau, Lillemor, 623

Malcolm, Graeme, 130
Maldonado, Miguel, 888
Maleki, Chris, 448
Malgras, Frederic, 764
Mali, Taylor, 1181, 1186
Malicki-Sanchez, Keram, 21
Malina, Joshua, 155
Malinger, Tyler, 1399
Malkovich, John, 759, 899, 1069
Mallett, A.J., 1269
Malloy, Matt, 481, 597
Malone, Bonz, 1181
Malone, Jena, 1264
Malone, Katherine, 33
Malone, Patrick Y., 1361
Malone, Tom, 119
Maloney, Janet, 298
Maloney, Peter, 888
Malota, Marina, 1319
Maltby, Lauren, 593
Malthe, Natassia, 312
Mamana, Liz, 1269
Mamet, Tony, 1232
Manahan, Kent, 369
Man Ching Chan, 1081
Mancini, Al, 61
Mancuso, Penny, 1
Mandeberg, Mitchell, 987
Mandvi, Aasif, 1154
Mandylor, Louis, 755
Manesh, Marshall, 97
Mangani, Christina, 751
Mangione, Carlotta, 686
Manheim, Camryn, 275, 480, 798, 1447
Maniaci, Jim, 40
Mann, Aimee, 97
Mann, Alex Craig, 379
Mann, Denn, 61
Mann, Douglas J. II, 931
Mann, Gabriel, 527, 934
Manni, Vic, 40, 348
Manning, Michael, 75
Manojlovic, Miki, 48
Manolin, 1440
Manon, Christian, 61
Mansell, Clint, 970
Manson, Ted, 757
Mantas, Michael, 652, 1100
Mantegna, Joe, 187
Manza, Ralph, 448
Maples, Marla, 480
Mapother, William, 1466
Mara, Mary, 232
Marander, Tracy, 640

Marangoni, Justin, 1164
Maratier, Christophe, 1062
Maraval, Julie, 1062
Maraval, Lou, 1062
Marc, Christian, 357
Marceau, Sophie, 390
March, Jane, 1291
Marchett, Jeffrey, 888
Marchi, Carl, 140
Marclay, Christian, 831
Marcos, Antonio, 195
Marcus, Dominic, 1069
Marcus, Eric, 481
Marcus, Michael, 308
Marder, Jordan, 21
Margolis, Mark, 970, 1343
Margolyes, Miriam, 61
Margulies, David, 187
Margulies, Julianna, 860, 996
Mari, Gina, 871
Maria, Nick Santa, 540
Mariana, Michele, 1495
Marich, Marietta, 1085
Marienthal, Eli, 400, 610, 1193
Marin, Cheech, 951
Marini, Lou, 119
Marino, Dan, 539
Marino, Vincent, 468
Maris, Stella, 531
Mariye, Lily, 811
Mark, Emmanuel, 385
Mark, Larry, 155
Mark, Marco O., 1440
Markfield, Alan, 1164
Markham, Ronald, 1149
Markie, Biz, 406
Markinson, Brian, 225, 349, 1000
Marko, Monica, 10
Markova, Nadine, 304
Marks, Aviva, 294
Marks, Leo, 781
Marlene, Lydia, 434
Marlene, Maria, 195
Marlin, Shyla, 1471
Marlo, John, 914
Marlow, Elgin, 920
Marlow, Janet, 187
Marlow, Zuzana, 313
Marlowe, Nora, 77
Marni, Heather, 187
Marotte, Carl, 806
Marquez, William, 773
Marr, Sally, 672
Marren, Christopher, 1164
Marsac, Laure, 538
Marsden, Jack, 1380
Marsden, James, 312
Marsh, Ali, 1094
Marsh, William, 1100
Marshall, Chris, 119
Marshall, Nancy, 740

Martell, Gillian, 247
Martin, Alexander, 173
Martin, Andrea, 1077
Martin, Bev, 1474
Martin, Brad, 920
Martin, Christian, 746
Martin, Dan, 1081
Martin, Dick, 10
Martin, Duane, 364, 1471
Martin, Helen, 155, 578
Martin, Lily, 294
Martin, Richard, 10
Martin, Rudolf, 527
Martin, Sandy, 636
Martin, Steve, 1232
Martindale, Margo, 993, 1361
Martineau, Gord, 310, 1387
Martinez, Adrian, 959
Martinez, Joaquin, 857
Martinez, Lizzie Curry, 789
Martinez, Melinda, 1269
Martinez, Olivier, 201
Martinez, Raul, 773
Martini, Maximilian, 1100
Marton, Andrew J., 1048
Martson, Christian, 1174
Mary Alice, 322
Marz, Pablo, 578
Marzello, Vincent, 1390
Mascoli, Cinia, 87
Mashimo, Fritz, 40
Mashkov, Vladimir, 1315
Maskell, Neil, 876
Mason, Anthony, 187
Mason, Jessica, 751
Mason, Laurence, 934
Mason, Luba, 308
Mason, Margery, 674
Mason, Raymond Matthew, 317
Masouni, Hamid, 1293
Massar, Mark, 540
Massey, Anna, 294
Masson, William Scott, 1280
Mass, Sylvain, 1206
Master P, 578, 975
Masters, George, 944, 1264
Masters, Lalanya, 975
Masterson, Chris, 21
Masterson, Danny, 364, 1253
Masterson, Mary Stuart, 306
Masterson, Owen, 442
Mastroianni, Marcello, 958, 1405

Matarazzo, Heather, 385, 572
Matarazzo, Neal, 298
Mathay, Marie, 1167
Mather, Cotton, 93
Mather, Neil, 1361
Matheron, Marie, 1426
Matheson, Eve, 1280
Matheson, Hans, 674
Mathiesen, Maria, 607
Mathieson, Shawn, 1387
Mathis, Johnny, 896
Mathis, Lynn, 860
Mathison, Cameron, 385
Matsuda, Seiko, 40
Matsuda, Shoko, 396
Matsumi, Satowa, 396
Matsushita, Takeo, 1232
Matsuyama, Keigo, 1404
Matsuyama, Shogo, 1404
Matthau, Walter, 857
Matthes, Charlie, 1069
Matthews, Dajon, 77
Matthews, Dakin, 1154
Matthews, Eddie, 860
Matthews, Hillary, 1308
Matthews, Kathleen, 40
Matthews, Regina Mae, 860
Matthow, Michelle, 857
Matthys, Michael, 72, 364
Matz, Jerry, 996
Mauceri, Patricia, 587
Maurel, Julien, 751
Mauri, Paco, 789
Maurier, Claire, 1377
Maves, Jason, 978, 1264
Mawe, Richard, 1069
Maxey, Dawn, 1059
Maxie, Judith, 313
Maximilliana, , 1059
Maxwell, Chenoa, 497
Maxwell, Max, 1371
Maxwell, Rupam, 357
May, Jim, 292
May, Joseph, 1461
Maybury, Paul, 61
Mayböck, Gertraud, 603
Maynard, Judi, 1461
Mayne, Kenny, 72
Mayor, Greg, 126
Mayoral, Beatriz, 349
Mayus, Jefferson, 247
Mazar, Debi, 575, 1343
Mazieres, Jean-Pierre, 357

Mazursky, Paul, 27, 1442
Mazzello, John, 1164
Mazzello, Joseph, 1164, 1253
Mazzinghi, Bernard, 1426
Mazzola, Jeff, 187
M'bo, Emile Abossolo, 751
Meadows, Tim, 406
Meaney, Colm, 832
Meardon, Marily Murphy, 832
Meat Loaf, 112, 806, 927, 1249
Mechoso, Julio Oscar, 636
Medel, Fernando, 789
Medlock, Ken, 758
Medonca, Carla, 531
Medrano, Frank, 349, 369, 631, 1048
Meehan, Howard, 298
Meehan, Miles, 664
Meer, Alicia, 187
Mehler, Tobias, 312
Mehrens, Timm, 626
Mehta, Ajay, 659
Mei, Christine Ng Wing, 1081
Meier, John, 298
Meier, Richard, 245
Meingast, Martin, 795
Meisle, Kathryn, 1489
Mekhnéche, Léa, 89
Meldrum, Jeremy Paul, 1129
Meleca, Marcello, 1164
Melendez, Ray, 364
Melia, Frank, 427
Melinand, Monique, 425
Melito, Joseph, Jr., 1447
Mello, Selton, 403
Mellor, Steve, 187
Melnick, Natasha, 936
Meloni, Chris, 379, 1227
Melvoin, Susannah, 1180
Mendes, Helen, 527
Mendes, Mário, 195
Mendez, Eva, 871
Mendicino, Gerry, 310
Mendillo, Tag, 631
Mendocino, Gerry, 93
Mendoza, Marlo, 130, 1069
Meneghel, Susanne, 416
Menezes, Maria, 195
Mensur, Irfan, 1123
Mercado, Hector, 669
Mercier, Brianne, 936
Merckx, Ken, 914, 1466

Mercurio, Paul, 1424
Mergenthaler, Carl, 348
Méril, Macha, 1216
Merlin, Joanna, 225
Merlin, Serge, 764
Merrill, Dina, 811
Merritt, Theresa, 546
Mesa, Cristbal Guzmán, 789
Mescolini, Franco, 686
Meshcherkina, Tatiana, 1344
Meskin, Amnon, 294
Mesquida, Roxane, 764
Messaoud, Amidou Ben, 1062
Messina, Chris, 1155, 1489
Messinese, Francesca, 686
Messing, Debra, 187
Meston, Paul, 941
Metcalf, Laurie, 155, 216
Metrano, Art, 563
Metro, Tracy, 1240
Mettia, Rudy, 40
Meyer, Breckin, 385
Meyer, Daryl, 540
Meyers, Jonathan Rhys, 457, 1389
Meyers-Shyer, Annie, 936
Meyers-Shyer, Hallie, 936
Meylan, Gérard, 768
Meyler, Tony, 310
Mia, 618
Mia X, 578
Mian, Peter A., 1489
Miano, Robert, 1203
Miceli, Justine, 269
Michael, Devon, 699
Michael, Rebecca, 740
Michael Moon Band, 187
Michaels, Al, 72
Michaels, Bret, 601
Michaels, Dylan, 1264
Michaels, Jimmy, 611
Michaels, Monica, 75
Michaely, Joel, 173
Micheaux, Nicki, 1048, 1059
Micheaux, Nikki, 847
Michel, Karen, 944
Michelsen, Charis, 583
Michelson, Charis, 527
Mick, Gabriel, 461
Middleton, Inger Lise, 686
Middleton, James, 282
Miehe-Renard, Tine, 626
Miguel, Bruno, 385
Miguel, Nigel, 21
Mihok, Dash, 1319
Mikala, Monica, 755

Milavich, Ivana, 349
Miles, Ben, 801
Miles, Elaine, 1203
Miles, Peter, 1100
Miles, Robin, 659
Miley, Darren, 427
Miley, Peggy, 857, 1255
Milford, Penelope, 511
Milhoan, Michael, 155
Milian, Victor, 1339
Millbern, David, 441
Miller, Andrew, 256
Miller, Corey, 578
Miller, Dick, 1197
Miller, Jeanette, 1348
Miller, Jeff, 18
Miller, Joe McKinnon, 1348
Miller, Jonny Lee, 1044
Miller, Ken, 1339
Miller, Larisa, 472
Miller, Larry, 199
Miller, Matt, 1155
Miller, Michael, 634, 715
Miller, Penelope Ann, 927
Miller, Pip, 1189
Miller, Reggie, 500
Miller, Sam, 876
Miller, Stephen E., 313
Miller, Tenny, 563
Miller, Tracy, 232
Miller, Tyler, 954
Millet, Lisa, 1380
Millgate, Gabby, 61
Milligan, Tuck, 1285
Millman, Gabriel, 187
Mills, A.G. Zeke, 860
Mills, Jessica, 631
Mills, Judson, 442, 757, 811
Mills, Matthew, 1460
Mills, Mort, 1339
Mills, Stephanie, 1387
Mills, Zeke, 546
Milos, Sofia, 755
Mimica, Marin, 272
Minakata, Eiji, 1223
Minda, Mina E., 1474
Mindel Tony, 914
Miner, Rachel, 512
Mingalone, Dick, 187
Ming Lee, 1053
Minifie, Valerie, 390
Mininni, Lisa, 806
Minjares, Joe, 1348
Mink Stole, 669, 954
Minor, Asia, 996
Minor, Bob, 434
Miragliotta, Frederick, 271, 820
Miranda, Carlos, 1390
Miranda, Leontina Santos, 601
Miranda, Telmo, 806
Miriam, Jennifer, 860

Mirsky, Eytan, 481
Mirylees, Kika, 531
Misura, Nick, 593
Mita, Elena, 269
Mita, Federico, 269
Mitchell, Alexandra, 593
Mitchell, Alexandria, 394
Mitchell, Daryl, 546
Mitchell, John Cameron, 276
Mitchell, Liam, 1447
Mitchell, Radha, 527
Mitsuishi, Ken, 1319, 1439
Mixmaster Morris, 831
Mixon, Jamal, 155
Mixon, Jerod, 155
Mixon, L. Christian, 400
Mizrahi, Isaac, 187
Mizukami, Ryushi, 1319
Moakler, Shanna, 1419
Moan, Bjorn, 607
Moati, Henry, 1062
Mocherie, Colin, 1041
Modine, Matthew, 1040
Moench, Monica, 237
Moffett, Joel, 126
Moglia, Ronald, 304
Mohamed, Mosleh, 1154
Mohammed-Khani, Mina, 815
Mohler, Robert, 1371
Mohr, Jay, 755, 951, 1197, 1277
Moinot, Michel, 959
Moir, Richard, 1424
Moist Towelette, 669
Mojdehi, R., 815
Mojica, Monique, 1203
Mok, Karen, 373
Mokae, Zakes, 636
Mokone, Tsepo, 481
Mol, Gretchen, 187, 1069
Moldovan, Florin, 420
Molina, Alfred, 129, 597
Molina, Angela, 709
Molina, Rolando, 1000
Molinari, Alberto, 1260
Molko, Brian, 1390
Mollo, Nick, 652
Molloy, Simon, 1461
Moloney, Janel, 1227
Moloney, Robert, 312
Moltena, Luis, 269
Momma, 669
Monahan, Dan, 1262
Monas, Stephen, 915
Mone, Johnny, 1308
Mone, Sheila, 1308
Mongo, 874
Monjo, Justin, 271

Monk, Damian, 61
Monk, Debra, 155
Monk, Gregg Joseph, 232
Monks, Michael, 493
Monkton, Patrick, 123
Monroe, Betsy, 920
Monroe, Samuel, Jr., 975
Monroe, Steve, 173
Montagu, Francois, 759
Montano, Dan, 1436
Monte, Brenda, 1384
Monte, Sal, 970
Montenegro, Fernanda, 195
Montgomery, Chuck, 512, 857
Montgomery, Poppy, 278
Montiel, Cecilia, 414
Montiel, Nazario, 789
Montue, Ted, 851
Moody, Gary, 860
Moody, Geoffrey, 669
Moody, Jim, 187
Moog, Robert, 831
Moon, Philip, 97
Moore, Abra, 860
Moore, Anthony, 33
Moore, Christine, 1461
Moore, Deborah, 155
Moore, Elizabeth Jaye, 112
Moore, Jack, 448
Moore, Jessica Care, 1186
Moore, Joanna, 1339
Moore, Joseph, 914
Moore, Julianne, 97, 216, 1023
Moore, Kenya, 1129
Moore, Margaret, 1182
Moore, Michael, 105, 601
Moore, Muriel, 1348
Moore, Richard, 909
Moore, Roger, 1249
Moore, Sam, 119
Moore, Shemar, 497
Moore, Terry, 811
Moore, Tom, 834
Moore, Zachary, 546
Moorer, Allison, 554
Moradet, Aurelle, 764
Moradi, Safar Ali, 1293
Morales, Vasquez, 773
Moran, Dan, 187, 481
Moran, Janet, 165
Moran, Johnny, 978
Moran, Michael P., 959
Moran, Rob, 1308
Morant, Angela, 1280
Morato, Nina, 649
Moravati, Ali Mohammed, 1293
Morayta, Paco, 773

Mordvinova, Amaliia, 1315
Moreau, Hélène, 1426
Moreau, Jeanne, 357
Moreau, Marguerite, 811
Morel, Glenn, 1057
Morel, Paul, 411
Morell, Jason, 1460
Moreno, Ayesha, 601
Moreno, Esther, 618
Moreno, Rita, 1193
Morenoff, Adam, 1094
Morettini, Mark, 1371
Moreu, Kristin, 864
Morfogen, George, 215
Morgan, Branden, 1129
Morgan, Brandon D., 1443
Morgan, Cale, 1424
Morgan, Chad, 1436
Morgan, David "Rumble", 1471
Morgan, Denise, 512
Morgan, Michele, 155
Morgan, Patrick, 155
Morgan, Scott, 954, 1240
Morgan, Tracy, 468
Morgan, Trevor, 69
Morgan, Wesley, 746
Mori, Naoko, 1249
Moriarity, Aoife, 427
Moriarty, Cathy, 306
Moriarty, Edmund, 652
Moriarty, James E., 1302
Moritz, David, 1085
Moritzen, Henning, 184
Morley, Jill, 512
Morley, Vanessa, 1076
Morlidge, Roger, 801, 1137
Mormino, Carmen, 857
Moroder, Giorgio, 831
Morrin, Rachel, 987
Morrin, Rebecca, 987
Morris, A. Lee, 187
Morris, Carolyn, 1182
Morris, Jeff, 119
Morris, Mack, 578
Morris, Michael, 759
Morris, Phil, 237
Morrison, Jon, 876
Morrison, Shaun, 75
Morrison, Temuera, 1174
Morrissey, David, 531
Morrissey, Erin, 540
Morrone, Dina, 40
Morrow, Donald, 379
Morrow, Mari, 278
Morse, David, 851
Morse, Laila, 876
Morshower, Glenn, 448
Morstad, Geir, 619

Mortensen, Viggo, 959, 1023
Mortimer, Emily, 339
Morton, Joe, 33, 119, 1343
Morton, Sam, 1164, 1380
Mortz, Juli, 155
Moscow, David, 572, 1061
Moseley, Bill, 613
Mosenson, Scott, 155
Moses, Mark, 286
Moses, Sam, 1471
Moskovis, Eduardo, 403
Moss, Larry, 61
Moss, Michael H., 1262
Moss, Paige, 173
Mostel, Josh, 461, 1069
Motley, Paul, 155
Motoki, Masahiro, 455
Mott, Manning, 1085
Motta, Bess, 310
Motta, Esperança, 195
Mottola, Greg, 187
Moulvrier, Gérard, 1062
Mounir, Mohamed, 302
Mouritsen, Ryan, 238
Mowat, Rick, 187
Moxley, Gina, 165
Moxley, Paul, 61
Moyer, Mike G., 715
Moynihan, Daniel, 339
Mr. Blue, 1094
Mr. Dan, 109
Mr. Oh, 755
Mucci, David, 468
Mueller-Stahl, Armin, 899, 1476
Mugglebee, Chris, 468, 1416
Muhammed, Benjamin F., 75
Mühe, Ulrich, 416
Muhoumatsu, 396
Mujica, Rene, 1361
Muldoon, Margaret, 540
Mulheren, Michael, 308
Mulkey, Chris, 155
Mullarkey, Neil, 1249
Mullen, Brian, 1094
Mullen, Marie, 165, 265
Muller, Turk, 153
Mulligan, Brian, 40
Mulligan, Terry David, 312
Mulot, Christian, 751
Mulrooney, Kelsey, 851
Mulzer, Hubert, 89
Mums the Schemer, 1186
Mumy, Seth, 951

Munafo, Mark, 448
Mundi, Coati, 130, 500
Mungo, Howard, 578
Munro, Debbie, 580
Munro, Hugh, 1461
Munro, Lochlyn, 278, 871
Munro, Ronn, 369
Mura-Smith, Emily, 951
Murdoch, Laurie, 1285
Murdock, George, 1476
Murdock, R. J., 1348
Muresan, Gheorghe, 847
Murfi, Mikel, 165
Murnik, Peter, 493
Murphy, Andrew, 1232
Murphy, Brian, 470
Murphy, Brittany, 969
Murphy, Charles. O., 975
Murphy, Dan, 1308
Murphy, Donna, 1254
Murphy, Eddie, 317, 539
Murphy, Elizabeth, 740
Murphy, Gary, 758
Murphy, Harry, 1228
Murphy, Johnny, 589
Murphy, Lynn, 820
Murphy, Maggie, 1489
Murphy, Matt, 119
Murphy, Michael, 1308
Murphy, Tom, 427
Murphy, Vinnie, 427
Murray, Bill, 1085
Murray, Keith, 1057
Murray, Matthew, 72
Murtaugh, James, 659, 1061
Musaka, Naomasa, 1336
Musburger, Brent, 1417
Muser, Wolfgang, 40
Musser, Larry, 313
Musy, Gianny, 269
Muti, Ornella, 1221
Mydcarz, Anthony, 140
Myers, Bruce, 457
Myers, Leroy, 758
Myers, Lou, 155, 563
Myers, Mike, 385
Mygind, Peter, 626
Myrin, Arden, 587, 597

Naber, Joey, 1154
Naccache, Eric, 1216
Nacer, Miloud, 768
Nachtergaele, Matheus, 195, 403
Naderer, Johann, 603
Naelen, Christian, 1471

Naftal, Diana, 1154
Nagai, Yoichi, 396
Nagashima, Toshiyuki, 455
Nagatsuka, Kyozo, 1404
Nagler, Shawna, 155
Nahaku, Don, 1174
Naidu, Ajay, 847, 970
Naidu, Vayu, 751
Naiomi, Sian, 1304
Najimy, Kathy, 133, 550
Nakahara-Wallett, Kellye, 317
Nakamura, Kumi, 1439
Nakamura, Mari, 396
Nakamura, Midori, 888
Nakamura, Suzy, 286
Nakayama, Miho, 1439
Nance, Richard, 550
Nani, 751
Nanjera, Maricruz, 789
Nannerello, George, 282
Napier, Markus, 1100
Napoleon, Titius, 72
Napoli, Christian, 1206
Nardi, Andrea, 686
Naruse, Keigo, 618
Nascarella, Arthur, 349, 385, 481, 500
Nash, David Andrew, 1348
Natale, Alan, 18
Nation, Steve, 634
Natsuki, Miyu, 915
Navabi, Seyyed Javad, 1293
Navarro, Lol, 789
Navicoff, Gary, 1290
Naya, Shindai, 396
Nazary, Ali, 860
Neal, Dennis, 1456
Neal, Donald, 954
Neal, Jonathan Roger, 155
Nealon, Kevin, 1419
Needham, Peter, 390
Neelaphamorn, Kanlayaporn, 1474
Neeley, Martin, 1137
Neely, William, 1262
Neeson, Liam, 362, 674
Neff, Kathy, 40
Negin, Louis, 385
Negron, Rick, 864
Nehls, Roger, 715
Neill, Sam, 554
Neisp, Sharon, 954
Nelligan, Kate, 1272, 1371
Nelson, Adam, 967
Nelson, Dee, 1020
Nelson, Everton, 876
Nelson, Fill, 1135
Nelson, Novella, 959
Nelson, Peter, 634

Nelson, Rebecca, 512
Nelson, Tim Blake, 1319
Nelson, Willie, 468
Nemeth, Vincent, 759
Neri, Francesca, 709
Nero, Franco, 1288
Nesbitt, James, 440, 1409
Neuhaus, Larry, 1319
Neumann, Birthe, 184, 626
Neuwirth, Bebe, 187, 364
Neuwirth, Chantal, 751
Neves, Manula-Manuel José, 195
Neville, John, 1044, 1387, 1476
Nevins, Claudette, 1255
Nevinson, Nancy, 822
Nevolina, Anglika, 408
Newbery, Shirley, 652
Newbigin, Flora, 123
Newbold, Richard, 746
Newcott, Rosemary, 434
Newhart, Bob, 1076
Newman, Emily, 909
Newman, Mimi, 674
Newman, Paul, 1361
Newman, Phyllis, 996
Newman, Sid, 1319
Newman-Breen, Alesia, 1240
Newton, Cody, 1476
Newton, Thandie, 77, 667
Nezu, Jimpachi, 455
Ngo, Rosy, 126
Ngor, Haing S., 538
Nguyen, Tina, 684
Nicholas, Eileen, 1044
Nicholas, Larry, 1253
Nicholas, PJ, 697
Nicholas, Raymond Leslie, 634
Nichols, Dave, 468
Nichols, Jason S., 1174
Nichols, Lance E., 1206
Nichols, Marisol, 173, 755
Nichols, Taylor, 659, 864
Nicholson, Julianne, 903
Nicholson, Shawan, 109
Nickalls, Grant, 310
Nickeln, Kim, 1466
Nicksay, Lily, 851
Nicolae, Petre, 420
Nielsen, Barbaree Earl, 1474
Nielsen, Bjarre G., 626

Nielsen, Connie, 1085, 1213
Nielsen, Leslie, 1474
Nielsen, Robin, 1474
Nielson, Rick, 105
Niemczyk, Stefan, 1447
Nieminen, Henric, 601
Nieves, Espher Lao, 970
Nigrini, Ron, 806
Nigsch, Dietmar, 603
Nikaido, Miho, 512
Nimmo, Justin, 978
Ninkovic, Natasa, 1123
Nipar, Yvette, 967
Nisbet, Jack, 1419
Nishimura, Deborah, 40
Nishizawa, Hitoshi, 396
Nissen, Claus, 626
Nissman, Michael, 126
Nivola, Alessandro, 1039
Nixon, Marni, 587
Niznik, Stephanie, 1254
No, David, 819
Nobre, Socorro, 195
Nolan, Jeanette, 554
Noland, Charles, 298
Nolot, Jacques, 48
Nolte, Brawley, 1
Nolte, Nick, 1, 874, 1319
Noonan, Jimmy, 1222
Noonan, Tom, 969
Noornajafi, Ali, 1293
Norby, Ghita, 626
Nordling, Jeffrey, 987
Noronha, Antoinieta, 195
Noronha, Antonieta, 195
Norris, Bruce, 232, 1039
Norris, Dean, 851, 1466
Northup, Harry, 77
Norton, Alex, 674, 703
Norton, Edward, 21, 918, 1069
Norton, Jim, 21
Norton, Ken, 310
Norton, Richard, 819
Norvind, Eva, 304
Nossek, Ralph, 674
Notarfrancesco, Sonny, 820
Nottle, Dean, 61
Nouri, Mir Hossain, 1293
Nowicki, Tom, 1416
Noyce, Richard, 21
Noyes, Joanna, 1
Ntshona, Winston, 1291
Nucci, Danny, 749
Nunes, Paulino, 468

Nunez, Miguel A., Jr., 1442
Nunn, Bill, 500
Nutt, Danny, 1389
Nuzzo, Jason, 1206

O'Blenis, Edward, Jr., 332
Obradors, Jacqueline, 1174
Obregon, Claudio, 805
O'Brien, Kelly, 1308
O'Brien, Maureen, 652
O'Brien, Mick, 428
O'Brien, Patrick T., 978
O'Brien, Richard, 271, 357, 1249
O'Bryan, Sean, 593
O'Callaghan, Richard, 269
Ocampo, Yvette, 114
Ochaim, Brygida, 1284
Ochoa, Maricela, 798
Ochoa, Steven, 888
O'Connell, Deirdre, 225
O'Connell, Jack, 597, 1229
O'Connell, Jerry, 174
O'Connor, Barbara, 1308
O'Connor, Derrick, 291
O'Connor, Gladys, 468
O'Connor, Joseph, 339
O'Connor, Kevin J., 291, 441, 538
O'Connor, Raymond, 847
O'Connor, Shane, 165
O'Connor, Sinéad, 165
Oddy, Christine, 310
Odeh, Nadi, 941
Odett, Keith, 21
O'Donnell, Annie, 975
O'Donnell, Rosie, 1447
O'Donnell, Steven, 1137, 1249
O'Donnell, Willy, 1021
Odzonikidze, Nino, 135
O'Fatharta, Macdara, 165
Ogier, Bulle, 1146, 1221
Oglesby, Randy, 944
Oguri, Kaori, 1439
O'Hagan, Michael, 441
O'Hampton, Jack, 652
O'Hanlon, Ardal, 165
O'Hara, Catherine, 546
O'Hara, Denis, 1061
O'Hea, Brendan, 339
O'Herlihy, Cornelia Hayes, 441
Ohsugi, Ren, 1223
Ok, Anne, 462
Okamura, Yoichi, 618
O'Kane, Deirdre, 129

Okayasu, Taiju, 1319
O'Keefe, Jodi Lyn, 472
O'Keefe, Raymond, 1443
O'Kelly, Aideen, 959
O'Kelly, Donal, 589
Okking, Jens, 626
Okonedo, Sophie, 440
Oksen, Lene Laub, 184
Okubo, Takamitsu, 1319
Okumoto, Yuji, 1348
O'Lague, Ruben, 40
O'Laskey, Michael J. II, 1334
Oldman, Gary, 733, 1031
Olds, Gabriel, 1466
O'Leary, Jer, 165
Oleson, Nicholas, 21, 1466
Olga, 457
Olhovsky, Viachesslav, 1344
Olin, Lena, 987
Oliveira, Jorsebá Sebastiao, 195
Oliver, Cindy, 1308
Oliver, Cory, 72
Oliver, James, 679
Oliver, Lucille M., 1442
Oliver, Luke Morgan, 1389
Oliver, Nicole, 593
Oliver, Roland, 801
Oliver, Tonya, 540
Olivero, Silvio, 310
Olivey, Alan, 540
Olivier, George, 703
Olivieri, Daniela, 1040
Oliviero, Silvio, 1471
Olley, Ray, 746
Ollivier, Alain, 48
Olmstead, Dan, 77
Olney, Warren, 349
Olohan, John, 165
Olsen, Craig, 669
Olsen, Richard, 1135, 1262
Olson, Eric, 349
Olson, Jeff, 237
Olson, Lute, 500
O'Malley, Des, 427
O'Malley, Kerry, 1069
O'Malley, Maura, 1409
O'Malley, Mike, 286
O'Meara, Daniel, 1380
Omiyanomatsu, , 396
Omoumi, N., 815
Oms, Alba, 130
O'Neal, Cynthia, 1000
O'Neal, Gerard, 304
O'Neill, Owen, 427
O'Neal, Ryan, 1495
O'Neal, Shaquille, 500
O'Neil, Ed, 1232
O'Neill, Anne, 165
O'Neill, Colleen, 126, 427

O'Neill, Margaret, 882
O'Neill, Patrick, 1129
O'Neill, Robert, 1447
O'Neill, Tommy, 427
Onimaru, 618
Ono, Yoko, 406
Oparei, Debbie, 271
Opie, Cathy, 470
Oppenheimer, Josh, 1419
O'Quinn, Carrick, 1476
O'Quinn, Terry, 1476
Orbital, 831
Orchid, Bruce, 679
Orchid, Christina, 679
Orefice, Carmen Dell, 187
O'Reilly, Ciaran, 130
O'Reilly, Cyril, 112
Orenstein, Joan, 477
Orizaga, Yolandeo, 773
Orlan, Roberta, 959
O'Rourke, Robert, 349
Orr, Sean, 1040
Orrock, Shann, 944
Orser, Leland, 1100, 1398
Ortega, Armando, 857
Ortega, Jimmy, 615, 1049
Ortega, Michel, 1440
Ortega, Oscar Garcia, 789
Ortega, Victor, 1440
Ortega, Yuliet, 1440
Orth, Elisabeth, 603
Oruche, Phina, 563
Osada, Emiko, 1439
Osborne, Holmes, 1
Osborne, Kent, 634
Osgood, Nathan, 1390
O'Shaughnessy, Maureen, 271
O'Shea, Milo, 165
Osmo, Sarah, 1424
Osokow, David Alan, 72
Ossman, David, 146
Ostendorf, Josef, 1037
Ostrow, Ron, 155
Osugi, Ren, 395
O'Sullivan, Aisling, 165
O'Sullivan, Frank, 589, 674
O'Sullivan, James, 379
O'Sullivan, Máire, 427
O'Sullivan, Paul, 310
O'Sullivan, Peter, 1149
Ota, Kohsuke, 396
Otasevic, Veljko, 1123
O'Toole, Jeffrey, 427
O'Toole, John, 427
O'Toole, Kate, 265
O'Toole, Matt, 1495
O'Toole, Peter, 967
Ottman, Mary, 33
Otto, Barry, 819
Otto, Miranda, 1319

Otto, Rick, 967
Oubramová, Zoja, 674, 847
Ousdal, Sverre Anker, 607
Outlaw, Paul, 18
Overby, Rhona, 349
Overton, Rick, 847
Owe, Beard, 626
Owen, Laurence, 1460
Owen, Sarah, 339
Owens, Eamon, 164, 427
Owens, Chris, 173, 312
Owens, Ciarán, 165
Oxenbould, Bob, 1424
Oxenbould, Jan, 1424
Oz, Frank, 119
Ozawa, Shoichi, 334

Paalgaard, Suzanne, 619
Pachin, Eugen, 408
Pachosa, Steven Clark, 1023
Pacienza, Michael, 1447
Pacifici, Federico, 1344
Packer, David, 19
Pacula, Joanna, 847
Paddock, Josh, 1429
Paetkau, David, 313
Pagan, Michael J., 369, 563
Page, Corey, 278
Pagh, Klaus, 626
Paglia, Camile, 512
Pai, Liana, 1154
Paige, Jordan, 385
Paige, Tony, 500
Pais, Josh, 232, 1094
Palagonia, Al, 500
Pall, Subash Singh, 176
Palladino, Aleksa, 187
Palladino, Erik, 173
Palladino, Michael, 245
Pallana, Deepak, 1085
Pallana, Kumar, 1085
Palma, Enrike, 773
Palmer, Andrew, 563
Palmer, Gretchen, 578
Palmier, Marina, 886
Palminteri, Chazz, 569
Palomino, Cris Thomas, 616
Pals, Josh, 1069
Paltrow, Gwyneth, 461, 575, 918, 959, 1137, 1189
Pamintuan, Angelica, 349
Pan, Dena, 1152
Pandey, Ramesh, 580
Panettiere, Hayden, 146, 888
Pankow, John, 888

Pantaeva, Irina, 187
Pantoliano, Joe, 1371
Paolini, Joseph, 126
Paolone, Catherine, 636, 857
Papajohn, Michael, 847
Paquin, Anna, 569
Par, Michael, 550
Paredes, Marisa, 686, 1288
Parent, Wayne, 1040
Parfitt, Judy, 356, 1460
Parhm, A. J. Alexander O., 540
Parillaud, Anne, 759, 1146
Paris, Tony, 1371
Parisi, Joe, 1069
Park, Steve, 298
Park, Uni, 310
Parker, Monica, 959
Parker, Norman, 155
Parker, Paula Jai, 1442, 1471
Parker, Trey, 72, 171, 914
Parker, Zane, 237
Parker-Jones, Jill, 546
Parkinson, Matthew, 61
Parks, Charles, 951
Parks, Michael, 282, 414, 870
Parnes, Fred, 1495
Parrilla, Domencio "Macio", 468
Parris, James, 75
Parrish, Amy, 857
Parry, Angelique, 1129
Parsons, Grant, 801
Parsons, Ian, 477
Parziale, Anthony, 1228
Paseka, Lawton, 448
Pashalinski, Lola, 448, 954
Pashkova, Olga, 1315
Paskel, Eric, 448
Pasteur, Sierra, 1129
Pastor, Rosana, 129
Pastore, Vincent, 755, 1425
Patano, Tonye, 996
Pate, Curt, 554
Pate, Tammy, 554
Patellis, Anthony, 587
Paterson, Bill, 530, 1249
Patinkin, Mandy, 789
Patocka, Jiri, 674
Paton, Angela, 722
Paton, Eliot, 272
Patric, Jason, 1483
Patric, Jim, 978
Patrick, Dan, 72, 1417
Patrick, Glenn, 1053
Patrick, Robert, 364
Patrick, Vincent, 1053

Patrikios, Patric, 1206
Patron, Emmanuel, 759
Patterson, Jay, 225, 232, 493, 1193
Patterson, Patrick, 119
Patton, Stephanie, 286
Patton, Will, 40
Patzwald, Julie, 313
Paulin, Vivica, 871
Paulos, Nick, 173
Paulson, Jay, 173
Paun, Jean, 420
Paun, Luninita, 420
Pavement, 406
Paxton, Bill, 811, 1167
Paxton, Bindi, 1424
Paxton, John, 1167
Paxton, Shane, 1424
Payan, Diana, 390
Paymer, David, 811, 927
Payn, Jason, 1474
Payne, Allen, 996
Paynes, Charles, 1474
Payton, Angela, 1419
Payton, Christian, 1371
Paz, Jennifer, 173
Peabody, Dossy, 1020
Peabody, Stephen, 903
Peace, Joshua, 93
Peace, Margo, 462, 1457
Pearce, Daniel, 448
Pearce, Darren, 298
Pearce, Mary Vivian, 954
Pearl, Aaron, 1474
Pearlman, Stephen, 554, 970
Pearlstein, Randy, 278
Pearson, Melanie, 1240
Pearsonstorm, Jay S., 434
Peart, O'Neil, 1146
Peck, James, 941
Peck, Rosalie, 1000
Pecora, Robert, 886
Pedtrchenko, Victor, 119
Peduto, Ralph, 944
Peels, Derek, 93
Peeples, Nia, 119
Peil, Mary Beth, 857
Peirez, Susan, 671
Peixoto, Fioriano, 929
Pellegrino, Frank, 187
Pellegrino, Mark, 97
Pellerin, Michael, 740
Pelletier, Monique, 1308
Pelletier, Paul, 1308
Pelmear, Donald, 339
Peluso, Stephen R., 114
Pendergast, Cory, 1308, 1456

Pendergast, McCauley, 1085
Pendleton, Austin, 215, 1275
Penkava, Petr, 674
Penn, Chris, 282, 902, 1081
Penn, Kim Maree, 634
Penn, Richard, 317
Penn, Robin Wright, 569
Penn, Sean, 569, 1319
Penney, Rene, 477
Pepe, Neil, 1232
Peplow, Neil, 1149
Pepper, Barry, 348, 394, 1100
Pepper, Warren, 758
Pére, Marilia, 195
Perce, Julie R., 434
Perchtold, Norbert, 603
Pere, Wayne, 920
Pereira, Zezao, 195
Perella, Marco, 546
Perez, Eddie, 1049
Perez, Gary, 671
Perez, Jose, 773
Perez, Vincent, 1280, 1288
Perfort, Holger, 626
Perillo, Joey, 851, 1447
Perino, Joe, 806
Perkins, Brian, 531
Perkins, Merle, 18
Perkins, Pat P., 722
Perkins, Ron, 1062
Perkovic, Dusan, 1123
Perlman, Phil, 920
Peroni, Donna, 126
Perry, Jeff, 1456
Perry, Manny, 1081
Perry, Matthew, 19
Perry, Steve, 1031
Pershing, Daniel, 1495
Pertier, Michell, 864
Pertwee, Sean, 1213
Pesci, Joe, 679
Pesenti, Laetitia, 768
Peterman, Robyn, 1228
Peterson, Kari, 238
Peterson, Liza Jesse, 1181
Peterson, Seth, 173
Petrarca, Steven, 987
Petrie, Alistair, 822
Petrocelli, Richard, 572
Petrof, Alita, 703
Petrosino, Christopher, 1061
Petrova, Galina, 1315
Petrusonis, Anthony T., 851
Petty, Dini, 310
Petty, Gwenyth, 1304
Peyanikov, Yasen, 1371

Peña, Elizabeth, 284, 1081
Pfanzelter, Günther, 686
Phelan, Anthony, 61
Phelan, Michael, 888
Phelps-Williams, David, 909
Phifer, Mekhi, 497, 584
Philipchuk, Misha, 1315
Philips, Gina, 715
Phillippe, Ryan, 385, 548, 699
Phillips, Joseph C., 684
Phillips, Lara, 153
Phillips, Lou Diamond, 93
Phillips, Neville, 822
Phoenix, Joaquin, 237, 1053
Phoenix, Summer, 364
Picard, Don, 1094
Picardo, Robert, 1197
Piccirillo, Mario, 715
Piccoli, Michel, 425, 941
Pickard, Raymond, 123
Pickelsimer, David Alan II, 282
Pickens, James, Jr., 155, 563, 1243
Pickersgill, Kirk, 1471
Picket, Bronson, 1040
Pickett, Wiley, 811
Pickett, Wilson, 119
Pickleman, Brenda, 1371
Pickles, Christina, 1419
Pickren, Richard, 1371
Pickup, Ronald, 722
Pidgeon, Rebecca, 1232
Pierce, Bradley, 123
Pierce, David Hyde, 146
Pierce, Linda, 659
Pierce, Sally, 1419
Pierce, Wendell, 155
Pierrot, Frédéric, 48
Pierson, Ronda, 540
Pike, Tamsin, 531
Pileggi, Mitch, 1476
Pilkington, Joe, 165
Pilmark, Soren, 626
Pilver, Michael, 1057
Pinchot, Bronson, 1031, 1187
Pine, Larry, 187
Pineda, Christine, 944
Pinkett, Jada, 1053, 1471
Pinnock, Emil, 77
Pino, Mariangela, 715
Pinto, José, 1405
Pippen, Scottie, 500

Pirver, Nancy, 1034
Pismichenko, Svetlana, 137
Pitillo, Maria, 448
Pitino, Rick, 500
Pitt, Brad, 781
Pittarello, Massimo, 48
Pitts, Mia, 1471
Pittu, David, 1222, 1232
Pivac, Sara, 1375
Piven, Byrne, 1399
Piven, Jeremy, 969, 1398
Place, Mary Kay, 954
Planer, Nigel, 652
Plasencia, Roseanna, 996
Platt, Collin, 1085
Platt, Oliver, 155, 269, 317, 597, 1164
Plein, Linda, 1399
Pleshette, Suzanne, 896
Plimpton, Martha, 954
Plotnick, Jack, 199, 441
Plum, Mette Munk, 626
Plum, Paul, 866
Plunkett, Gerard, 1474
Pniewski, Mike, 434
Pochie, Angelina, 1426
Pointeaux, Lilly-Fleur, 1062
Polanco, Iraida, 888
Poland, Greg, 1255
Pole, Edward Tudo, 674
Poletto, Vince, 819
Poli, Rick, 1290
Polito, Jon, 97
Polk, Patrik Ian, 497
Pollack, Sydney, 232
Pollak, Kevin, 140, 927
Polley, Sarah, 477
Pomerance, Hope, 481
Pomeroy, Christopher, 597
Pomers, Scarlett, 1187
Poncelet, Thomas, 294
Ponchon, Alix, 751
Ponder, Dana, 936
Ponterotto, Donna, 851
Pontes, Everaldo, 195
Pool, Austin John, 310
Pooley, Alex, 357
Pooley, Robin, 67
Poon, Alice, 468
Pope, Caelem, 1375
Pope, Carly, 313
Pope, Don, 522
Pope, Ralph, 187
Pope, Ryan, 1390
Popov, Evgenii, 1315
Porchiella, Cristiana, 686

Portal, Robert, 822
Porter, Bobby, 1253
Porter, Charlaine, 806
Porter, Ian, 1100
Porter, Maria, 512
Porter, Nyree Dawn, 531
Porter, Pat, 1466
Porter, Steven M., 19
Porter, Susie, 1424
Portno, Richard, 847
Portnow, Richard, 379
Portser, Mary, 1193
Posey, Parker, 240, 1489
Pospisil, Eric, 593, 1076
Post, F.W., 860
Post, Markie, 1308
Post, Tim, 1
Poston, Tom, 636
Potok, Charlotte, 1232
Potter, Monica, 944, 1466
Potter, Patricia, 1137
Potts, Faith, 575
Pouncie, Ocie, 282
Poupaud, Melvil, 425
Powell, Charles, 1
Powell, Clifton, 182, 291, 967, 1081, 1442
Powell, Tim, 539
Powers, Matthew, 1275
Pozdniakova, Natalia, 1315
Pozsik, Gary P., 758
Pramik, John, 1348
Pratt, John C., 1240
Pratt, Kyla, 69, 317
Pratt, Lauren Varija, 888
Pratt, Susan, 882
Prentout, Cyril, 1062
Presnell, Harve, 944, 1100
Press, Jacob, 575
Pressly, Jaime, 1059
Pressly, Jamie, 173
Pressman, David, 448
Pressman, Lawrence, 811, 847, 1399
Prester, Nino, 686
Preston, Carrie, 798
Preston, Kelly, 539, 610
Preston, Stewart, 176
Pretlow, Wayne, 866
Previn, Soon-Yi, 1449
Price, Annabella, 993
Price, Dilys, 1304
Price, Tara, 550
Priest, Dan, 584
Priestley, Jason, 740
Prince, Daisy, 187
Prinsloo, P. J., 312
Prinslow, P. J., 593
Prinz, Werner, 603

Prinze, Freddie, Jr., 584
Pritchard, Jonathan, 1466
Pritchett, Polly, 822
Privat, Arthur, 1426
Privat, Gérard, 1426
Privat, Maeva, 1426
Prochnow, Jurgen, 1048
Proctor, Phil, 318, 1077, 1077
Proctor, Rupert, 1044
Prodigy, 831
Proft, Pat, 1474
Proscia, Ray, 1443
Proval, David, 1154
Prucell, Daniel, 1061
Pruyn, Serena, 806
Pryce, Jonathan, 1044, 1062
Pryor, Ella, 1085
Prückner, Tilo, 603
Pudwell, Laura, 310
Pujol, Marcos, 1216
Pullman, Bill, 1495
Pultar, Maylin, 601
Purdy, Richard, 522
Purl, Linda, 811
Purvery, Edward, 339
Putch, John, 225, 1227
Pyfrom, Amber, 1057
Pyper-Ferguson, John, 492

Qian, Zu-Wu, 679
Quaid, Dennis, 936, 1123
Quaid, Randy, 493
Quarles, Norma, 659
Queen Latifah, 715, 1243
Quentin, John, 247
Quie, Diana, 667
Quigley, Mark, 427
Quijada, Franciso, 187
Quinlan, Kathleen, 232, 664, 847
Quinn, Aidan, 993
Quinn, Colin, 871
Quinn, Elizabeth, 740
Quinn, Ian, 40
Quinn, J.C., 282, 538, 1000
Quinn, Thomas M., 349
Quinoñes, Santiago, 1490
Quiroz, Fabiola, 1440
Quiroz, Jorge, 1440
Qu Lixin, 410

Raaberg, Birgitte, 626
Rabal, Francisco, 1288
Rabal, Liberto, 709
Rabelo, José, 481
Radecki, Barbara, 385

Rademaker, Sean, 888
Radley, Ken, 61
Rae, Bettina, 975
Rafalsky, Dimitri, 1062
Rage Against the Mac, 406
Ragno, Joe, 277
Rahm, Kevin, 237
Rahman, Seif Abdel, 302
Raider-Wexler, Victor, 580
Railsback, Steve, 312
Raimondi, Miranda, 1216
Rakow, Erin, 996
Ralph, Michael, 1471
Ramcu, Mandra, 420
Ramcu, Radu, 420
Ramirez, Oneida, 1440
Ramirez, Sara, 1489
Ramiriz, Luis, 789
Ramish, Trish, 871
Ramm, John, 1137
Ramos, Armando, 540
Ramos, José, 195
Ramsay, Bruce, 538
Ramsey, Natalie, 978
Ramiriz, Nandi Luna, 789
Rand, Sebastian, 1264
Randall, Chad, 601
Randall, Ginnie, 1135
Randall, Larry, 1149, 1409
Randazzo, Steven, 187
Randle, Charlotte, 269
Randle, Kenneth, 155
Randle, Rush, 601
Randle, Tony Romas, 155
Randolph, John, 996, 1489
Rands, Noel, 634
Ranft, Joe, 146
Rankin, Heather, 477
Rankin, Louie, 75
Rankin, Steve, 798, 1476
Rapaport, Michael, 595, 931
Raphael, Marilyn, 187
Raposo, Matthew, 468
Rapp, Anthony, 275
Rapport, Louise, 914
Rasmussen, Frode, 607
Rasouly, Ghoulam R., 1154
Ratier, Ellea, 1288
Ratner, Ben, 394, 1474
Ratzenberger, John, 146
Raudman, Renee, 1443
Raulerson, Steve, 1416
Raven-Symon, 317
Rawls, Lou, 1269
Ray, Connie, 550
Ray, Danny, 119

Ray, George E., 77
Ray, Ruth, 583
Ray, Wendy, 1466
Rayburn, Ross, 1129
Raymond, Dominique, 48
Raymond, Jennie, 740
Raymond, Ted, 1348
Raymond, Usher, 364
Rayna, Glenda, 1440
Rayne, Sarah, 1031
Raynor, Lavita, 75
Razack, Noorie, 634
Razz, Randy, 1419
Ricca, Marco, 403
R.D. Grandos and the Ventures, 126
Rea, Stephen, 129, 164
Read, Rufus, 480
Rebouças, Iami, 195
Reck, Vinney, 1390
Rector, Jerry, 857
Reddick, Kristin, 1232
Reddick, Lance, 461, 1154
Reddin, Keith, 722
Redgrave, Lynn, 441
Redgrave, Vanessa, 285, 294, 822, 1460
Red Hot Chili Pepper, 406
Redman, 1057, 1100
Redman, Tom, 1164
Redmond, Morgan, 1085
Redmond, Sarah-Jane, 313
Redner, Gwyne, 601
Rednikova, Ekaterina, 1315
Reed, Darryl Alan, 798
Reed, Jerry, 1416
Reed, Kent, 1371
Reed, Pamela, 1442
Reedus, Norman, 1039
Reehling, Joyce, 996
Reel Big Fish, 72
Rees, Roger, 866, 1343
Reese, P. G., 497
Reeves, Anita, 165, 1288
Reeves, Jason, 1145
Reeves, Perrey, 1203
Regan, Judith, 715
Regan, Liam, 589
Reggie, Arthur III, 155
Reid, Ann, 740
Reid, Bradley, 310
Reid, Ferguson, 434
Reid, Jim, 428
Reid, Kevin, 1416
Reid, R. D., 468
Reid, Roger, 540
Reid, Tara, 97, 1387
Reid, Valerie, 636

Reifsnyder, Timothy, 1447
Reilly, Corinne, 174
Reilly, John C., 216, 1319
Reiner, Carl, 1193
Reiner, Rob, 1000
Reinhardt, Shanti, 109
Reinhold, Judge, 548
Reinton, Sandra, 1137
Reis, Michele, 373
Reiser, Rock, 1193
Reisman, Arnie, 866
Reiter, Donovan, 1
Reitman, Joseph D., 237
Reitz, Tymme, 886
Remar, James, 1023
Remy, Ashley, 903
Renaday, Peter, 857
Renaud, Ritch, 10
Rene, Jacynthe, 1206
Renegade, DJ, 1181
Renfro, Brad, 33
Rennie, Callum, 492
Réno, Jean, 448
Reno, Susan, 715
Renouf, Darren, 1149
Renzi, Maggie, 789
Resnick, Michael, 1228
Reubens, Paul, 318
Rex, Peter, 1040
Rey, Antonia, 888
Reyes, Judy, 671
Reynolds, Clarence, 539
Reynolds, Debbie, 379, 1076
Reynolds, Jacob, 1094
Reynolds, Molly, 153
Reynolds, Simon, 831
Reynolds, Vickilyn, 1000
Rezabek, Rozz, 640
Rezaei, Ali Mohammad, 1293
Rezai, Rahman, 1293
Rhames, Ving, 920
Rhee, Simon, 679
Rhein, Jed, 1227
Rhind-Tutt, Julian, 674
Rhoads, Terry, 715
Rhymes, Busta, 1077
Riaboukine, Serge, 1426
Riach, Ralph, 269, 457
Riaux, Catherine, 1426
Ribisi, Giovanni, 400, 1100
Ribisi, Marissa, 978
Ricci, Christina, 139, 379, 909, 954, 1197
Rice, Brett, 540, 931, 1416
Rice, Diana, 69
Rice, Gigi, 871
Rice, Nicholas, 119
Rice, Robyn, 126

Rich, Duffy, 578
Rich, Glendon, 1476
Rich, Richie, 1146
Richard, Adrian, 155
Richard, Jean-Louis, 646, 989
Richard, Nathalie, 1216
Richards, Beah, 77
Richards, Cordella, 993
Richards, Denise, 1456
Richards, Hoyt, 1174
Richards, J. August, 1442
Richards, Lou, 715
Richards, Sal, 1069
Richards, T.R., 348
Richardson, Ian, 271
Richardson, Kevin Michael, 72
Richardson, LaTanya, 1371
Richardson, Natasha, 936
Richardson, Nolen, 500
Richardson, Shaun D., 740
Richings, Julian, 256, 492, 1387
Richman, Darice, 1000
Richman, Jonathan, 1308
Richter, Marc, 623
Richwood, Patrick, 40
Rickles, Don, 310, 896, 1031
Rideau, Stephane, 411
Rideau, Wilbert, 376
Ridge, Monique L, 1000
Ridgeway, Esther, 119
Ridgeway, Gloria, 119
Ridgeway, Gracie, 119
Riding, Anthony, 746
Riebel, Aladin, 764
Riegert, Peter, 519
Riehle, Richard, 298, 379, 679, 798, 811, 857
Riehs, Milan, 674
Rietman, Mark, 211
Rietti, Robert, 531
Riffon, Marc, 1436
Rifkin, Ron, 851
Rigby, David, 1164
Rigby, Terence, 338
Rigney, Daniel, 1424
Riley, Jack, 1077
Riley, Sharon, 119
Riley, Stu "Large", 1471
Rimmer, Maureen, 294
Rios, Lalo, 1339
Riovega, Elodie, 539
Rippenkroeger, Larry, 1476
Riser, Ronn, 975
Rispoli, Michael, 1069, 1206
Ristic, Suzanne, 10

Ritter, John, 133
Rivas, Geoffrey, 887
Rivera, Ava, 155
Rivera, Geraldo, 1000
Rivers, Victor, 773
Rizzo, Don, 944
Rizzo, Ray, 272
Roach, Martin, 1471
Roarke, Kelly, 1308
Robards, Jason, 77, 349
Robb, David, 1044
Robbins, Gil, 1447
Robbins, Stephen, 457
Roberson, Bill, 944
Roberts, Conrad, 773
Roberts, Doris, 847
Roberts, Doug, 349, 944, 954
Roberts, Francesca P., 857
Roberts, Ian, 1291
Roberts, Joe, 1137
Roberts, Julia, 1264
Roberts, Kim, 322
Roberts, Kitty, 703
Roberts, Layla, 40
Roberts, Leonard, 500
Roberts, Lisa, 1302
Roberts, Mario, 1049
Roberts, Ndehru, 130
Roberts, Nia, 1304
Roberts, Pascale, 768
Roberts, Robin, 500
Robertson, Woody, Jr., 575
Robillard, Kim, 546, 798
Robinson, Adrian, 1409
Robinson, Aemilia, 385
Robinson, Aliya, 77
Robinson, Donnell, 1182
Robinson, Hal, 951
Robinson, Jeanne, 993
Robinson, Jim, 920
Robinson, John, 1164
Robinson, Michael, 1232
Robinson, Paul Michael, 72
Robinson, Todd, 866
Robinson, Troy, 298, 616
Robinson, Wendy Raquel, 1059
Robison, Ian, 593
Robison, Mark Steven, 112
Robson, Wayne, 1, 256
Rocco, Alex, 146
Rocco, Rinaldo, 48
Rocha, Kali, 888
Roche, Eammon, 887
Roche, Jim, 78
Rochford, Terry G., 1371

Rochon, Lela, 93, 634, 1442
Rock, Chris, 317, 679
Rock, Crissy, 1380
Rockwell, Sam, 187, 664, 1093
Rodriguez, Carlos, 587
Rodriguez, Christina, 364
Rodriguez, Elizabeth, 587, 1053
Rodriguez, Freddy, 173
Rodriguez, J.R., 1262
Rodriguez, Raymond, 1339
Rodriques, Joao, 195
Rodriquez, Marta, 89
Roe, Channon, 173
Roebuck, Daniel, 1371
Roemer, John, 1466
Roemer, Michael, 850
Roeske, J.P. II, 1334
Rogell, Gregg, 468
Rogers, Alice, 1135
Rogers, Anthony, 954
Rogers, Ashley, 282
Rogers, Danny, 298
Rogers, Ingrid, 187
Rogers, Mimi, 733
Rogers, Renee, 944
Rogerson, Ken, 1308
Rogerson, Ryan, 740
Rohr, Tony, 165
Rois, Sophie, 603
Roisman, Harper, 1228
Rojas, Luz Maria, 304
Rojo, Maria, 805
Rokicki, Joe, 610
Roland, John, 888
Roland, Scott, 860
Rolf, Frederick, 187
Rolffes, Kirsten, 626
Rolle, Esther, 322
Rollin, Pascal, 1123
Rollins, Henry, 610
Rois, Dominic, 357
Rolston, Mark, 493, 1081
Rom, Lori, 500
Roman, Emilio, 310
Roman, Frank, 857
Romano, Christy, 512
Romano, Frank, 379
Romano, Larry, 1319
Romanyuk, Sergiy, 408
Romeo, Ralph, 1290
Romero, Humberto, 789
Romero, Kaylan, 811
Romijn, Rebecca, 310
Ronan, Paul, 130
Roncalli, Guido, 48
Rooker, Michael, 282, 1048
Rooney, Mickey, 60
Root, Stephen, 636
Rosa, Gideon, 195
Rosa, Kirenia, 1440

Rosa, Skip, 187
Rosales, Gilbert, 615, 1155
Rosales, Thomas, Jr., 1049, 1371
Rosales, Tommy, 615
Rosario, Jose Ramon, 959, 1264
Rosas, Antonio, 886
Rose, Charlie, 1000
Rose, Ian, 697
Rose, Jacobus, 914
Rose, Margot, 232
Rose, Mitchell, 581
Rose, Terry L., 857, 909
Roselius, John, 1348
Rosen, Julieta, 773
Rosenbaum, Michael, 1387
Rosenberg, Alan, 37
Rosenberg, Ira, 126
Rosenberg, Phil, 1308
Rosenfield, Nancy, 679
Rosengren, Clive, 967
Rosethall, Joann, 316
Rosier, Bill, 636
Ross, Chelcie, 1000, 1167
Ross, Chris, 697
Ross, Hugh, 1495
Ross, Jonathan, 1249
Ross, Katharine, 543
Ross, Matt, 548, 659
Ross, Sandi, 119, 322
Ross, Stanley Ralph, 61
Ross, Stephanie, 1232
Ross, Tracee, 1275
Ross, Willie, 1280
Rossatti, Alberto, 269
Rossellini, Isabella, 597
Rossetter, Kathryn, 1436
Rossi, Toni, 583
Rostami, Karim, 1293
Roth, Joanna, 1189
Roth, Jordan, 587
Roth, Tim, 282
Rothchild, Roland, 1471
Rothhaar, Will, 610
Rothman, John, 1154
Rottger, John, 298
Rotundo, Paolo, 1375
Rouan, Brigitte, 764, 989
Roughly, Lill, 801
Round, Jason, 1137
Rountree, Stephen, 245
Rourke, Mickey, 139
Rovere, Gina, 686
Rovre, Liliane, 48
Rowat, Ruby, 69
Rowden, David, 615
Rowe, Brad, 109
Rowe, James, 339

Rowlands, Gena, 550, 806, 951
Rowley, Terry, 876
Rox, Robbie, 310
Roy, Marco, 1474
Roy, Mathieu, 69
Rozelaar-Green, Frank, 390
Rozstalnyj, Vitalij, 1344
Rubeo, Marco, 1348
Rubin, Alan, 119
Rubin, David, 294
Rubinek, Saul, 67
Rubin-Vega, Daphne, 1456
Ruby, Dave, 278
Ruckebusch, Sophie, 694
Rudd, Paul, 888
Rudeberg, Laura, 686
Rudin, Stuart, 882
Rudolph, Lars, 603
Rudrud, Kristin, 978
Rue, Sara, 173
Ruff, Michael, 1135
Ruffalo, Mark, 385, 1093
Ruffini, Gene, 512
Ruffo, A. Frank, 310
Rufo, Joseph Jumbo, 755
Ruggier, Carole, 715
Ruggiero, Allelon, 369
Ruivivar, Anthony, 527
Ruiz, Edoardo, 48
Ruiz, Hernan, 811
Rummel, John, 140
Rumney, Jon, 531
Rumnock, Bob, 369
Runte, Kurt Max, 593
Runyan, Tygh, 312
Rupert, Michael, 275
Rupp, Debra Jo, 240, 1129
Ruppe, Diana, 512
Rush, Deborah, 1489
Rush, Ed, 831
Rush, Geoffrey, 339, 674, 1137
Rushbrook, Claire, 1249, 1380
Rushton, Kevin, 468
Ruskin, Ian, 1476
Ruskin, Joseph, 1255
Russ, William, 21
Russell, Anthony, 715
Russell, Catherine, 1149
Russell, Grant, 269
Russell, John Raphael, 369
Russell, Kurt, 1213
Russell, Monte, 448, 975
Russell, Theresa, 1456
Russo, John, 583
Russo, Laura, 857
Russo, Mikey, 1384

Russo, Rene, 679
Russom, Leon, 97
Ruth, Isabel, 1405
Rutherford, Bill, 272
Rutherford, Neil, 1280
Rutledge, Stanton, 978
Ruttan, Susan, 636
Ruud, Michael, 780
Ryan, Amanda, 338
Ryan, Andy, 40
Ryan, Jackie, 996
Ryan, Jenny, 1044
Ryan, Jessie, 601
Ryan, Meg, 225, 569, 1489
Ryan, Thomas Jay, 512
Ryder, Shaun, 52
Ryder, Winona, 187
Ryland, James, 1409

Saad, Karim, 764
Saban, Mark, 1137
Sabato, Antonio, Jr., 93
Sacco, Donna, 1240
Sachs, Patty, 1474
Sachtleben, Horst, 89
Sack, George, Jr., 554
Sadikin, Lucille, 1085
Sadler, Nicholas, 874
Sadler, William, 313, 1039
Sadowski, John, 1264
Saether, Andrine, 619
Sagal, McNally, 978
Sagalle, Nicolas, 941
Sage, Bill, 527, 1221
Sagebrecht, Marianne, 899
Sagona, Katie, 1489
Saifer, Rebecca, 1053
St. James, James, 1146
St. James, Mark, 581
St. Jean, André, 69
St. John, Jahnni, 781
St. John, Michelle, 1203
St. Juste, Margie, 497
St. Ledger, Margaux, 909
Saito, James, 512
Sakai, Kazuyoshi, 1319
Sakai, Mike, 1439
Sakai, Yoko, 1474
Salama, Amro, 1154
Salama, Hani, 302
Salamanca, Richard, 587
Salazar, Abdul Latif, 941
Saleem, Damon, 182
Salem, Pamela, 441
Salenger, Meredith, 1229
Salerno, Nini, 87
Salgado, Marcus, 114

Sali, Richard, 310
Salimbeni, Enrico, 48
Salinger, Emmanuel, 646
Salinger, Justin, 1390
Salinger, Matt, 1429
Sallos, Sol Alexis, 1466
Salsedo, Frank Sotonoma, 19
Salter, Jay, 1348
Salvail, Eve, 187
Salvato, Laura, 715
Salvianti, Massimo, 686
Samadpour, T., 815
Samaha, John, 61
Samel, Udo, 623
Sammel, Richard, 686
Sampson, Tiffany, 512
San, Maseo "Maki", 914
Sánchez, Celeste Cornelio, 789
Sánchez, Domingo Pérez, 789
Sanchez, Joanna, 857
Sanchez, Mario Ernesto, 1348
Sánchez, Raúl, 789
Sanchez, Ronald C., 1361
Sanchez-Gijon, Aitana, 749
Sancho, José, 709
Sandberg, Paul Michael, 442
Sandburg, Laura Kellogg, 216
Sander, Otto, 623
Sanders, Ajai, 611
Sanders, Jay O., 857
Sanders, Marvin L., 1495
Sandiford, Benedict, 1460
Sandler, Adam, 1416, 1419
Sandler, Henry, 349
Sandoval, Diego, 773
Sandow, Nick, 715, 882, 1053
Sanford, Garwin, 394
Sanford, Glenn D., 882
San Giacomo, Laura, 1277
Sansone, John, 140
Santagata, Toni, 87
Santana, Inaldo, 195
Santiago, Saundra, 519
Santiago, Socorro, 481, 572
Santoni, Reni, 174, 317
Santos, Cicero, 195
Sanvido, Guy, 1164
Sanz, Jorge, 129
Sanz, Margarita, 805

Saperstein, Richard, 733

Sapienza, Al, 448

Sarafian, Richard, 155

Sarandon, Chris, 738

Sarandon, Susan, 1264, 1361

Sargent, Michael, 1339

Sarkeshi, Hojatolah, 1293

Sarruf, Valerie, 390

Sarsgaard, Peter, 759

Saso, Theresa, 470

Sasser, Danny, 364

Sastre, Ines, 87

Satari, 975

Sato, Koichi, 455

Sato, Makoto, 334

Saudek, Molly, 69

Saunders, Cliff, 310

Saunders, George P., 580

Saunders, Jennifer, 1249

Saunders, Kendall, 313

Saunders, Paul, 468

Savage, John, 699, 1319

Savant, Doug, 448

Savchenko, Lidlia, 1315

Savers, Rhiannon R., 1167

Sawalha, Nadim, 52

Sawicki, Stan, 72, 914

Sawyer, Connie, 920

Sawyer, John Franklin, 1135

Saxon, James, 674

Saxon, Rold, 1100

Sayer, Cynthia, 1449

Sayre, Jill, 1167

Scaife, Emma, 1216

Scales, Alonzo, 500

Scales, Melodie, 703

Scanda, Tiare, 805

Scanlon, John, 798, 1240

Scaperotta, Jeffrey, 903, 1489

Scarano, Antoni, 1085

Scarborough, Adrian, 746

Scarfe, Jonathan, 1361

Scarola, Lisa, 1471

Schaad, Jutta, 89

Schaal, Wendy, 1197

Schade, Birge, 89

Schade, Doris, 89

Schaech, Johnathon, 575, 1424

Schaffel, Marla, 580

Schanz, Heidi, 1348

Schatz, Mike, 757

Schaub, Sally, 1193

Schecter, Harold, 1034

Scheer, Robert, 155, 1155

Schell, Maximillian, 285, 615

Schertler, Jean, 954

Schiavelli, Vincent, 640

Schiff, Paul, 1085

Schiff, Richard, 285, 317, 715

Schindler, Peter, 847, 1155

Schirripa, Steve, 379

Schluter, Ariane, 327

Schlüter, Henning, 623

Schmalzbauer, Fréd-éric, 1062

Schmidt, Dwight, 48

Schmidt, Michael, 1093

Schmidt, Paul, 967

Schmidtberger, Mary, 187, 715

Schmidtke, Ned, 798

Schmiedt, Angel, 539, 1348

Schmiedt, Nastassja, 1348

Schmitt, Vincent, 1062

Schneider, Kelley, 1308

Schneider, Marnie, 1308

Schneider, Rob, 634, 1416

Scholl, Kiff, 109

Schoot, Slava, 1069

Schram, Bitty, 631

Schreiber, Liev, 967, 1243, 1361

Schroder, Lise, 626

Schub, Steven, 298, 1221

Schubert, Jeff, 914

Schull, Rebecca, 857

Schulte, Mark, 882

Schulze, Matt, 114

Schulze, Paul, 595

Schutt, Herbert R., Jr., 1240

Schuurman, Betty, 210

Schwab, Kirstin, 603

Schwan, J.P., 860

Schwartz, Louis, 1149

Schwartz, Marty Eli, 1417

Schwartzberg, Antonette, 187

Schwartzman, Jason, 1085

Schwarz, Austin, 554

Schwarz, Dustin, 554

Schwarz, Simon, 603

Schweickert, Jeff, 1269

Schweickert, Joyce, 1269

Schweiger, Til, 1048

Schwering, Jamie, 1466

Schwimmer, David, 33, 631, 1174

Scialla, Fred, 715

Sciorra, Annabella, 816, 1429

Sclafani, James Edward, 1174

Scott, Bryon, 369

Scott, Campbell, 519, 597, 1232

Scott, Carla, 1399

Scott, Donna, 349

Scott, Dougray, 285, 356, 1044

Scott, Eric Brice, 173

Scott, Esther, 1129

Scott, Fiona, 312

Scott, Jason-Shane, 109

Scott, Judson, 114

Scott, Stuart, 500

Scott, Tom Everett, 278, 903, 1061

Scott, Willard, 539

Scott, William Lee, 909

Scotto, Rosanna, 888

Scragg, Stella, 1380

Scriba, Mik, 851

Scroope, Doug, 271

Scruggs, Sharon, 659

Scudder, Sam, 1100

Scullin, Garret, 1180

Scullin, Kevin, 1053

Scurfield, Matthew, 1280

Scurr, Cosmo, 1149

Seabrook, Christine, 434

Seagal, Steven, 847

Seago, Howie, 89

Seagren, Steve, 631

Sealy-Smith, Alison, 322

Sears, Djanet, 1040

Sears, Ross, 860

Sebastian, Lobo, 757

Sedaris, Amy, 1174

Seder, Sam, 866

Sefton, Gary, 1100

Segal, Jason, 173

Segal, Lore, 850

Segal, Michael Ryan, 11069

Seganti, Paolo, 1269

Segar, Leslie "Big Lez", 1497

Segel, Jason, 278

Segovia, Alexis, 89

Seibt, Alexander, 1284

Seiden, Ray, 970

Seiler, Sonny, 434

Seivwright-Adams, Troy, 322

Seki, Tokio, 396

Sekkelsten, Adne Olav, 619

Seldes, Marian, 1, 187, 306

Selianskaia, Liudmila, 1315

Sellers, Stan, 317

Sellon-Wright, Keith, 19

Serban, Angela, 420

Serban, Aurica, 420

Serban, Ioan, 420

Serban, Isidor, 420

Serban, Vasile, 420

Serbedzija, Rade, 987, 1344

Sergei, Ivan, 909

Sermol, Luisa, 1495

Sermon, Erik, 1057

Serra, Raymond, 1094

Serraf, Patrick, 764

Serrano, Nestor, 851

Serratt, Ken, Jr., 993

Serrault, Michel, 48, 1284

Serre, Lopoldine, 1062

Servidio, Kristy Ann, 554

Servitto, Matt, 1155

Sessions, Bob, 1461

Sessions, John, 247

Setliff, Adam, 1466

Setrakian, Ed, 277

Settle, Matthew, 584

Severin, Laurel, 89

Severina, Dona, 195

Sevigny, Chloe, 659, 931

Sevin, Jim, 1466

Sewell, Rufus, 269, 271

Seweryn, Andrzej, 425

Sexton, Brendan III, 572, 954

Seymour, Brandi, 659

Seymour, Cara, 1489

Seymour, Caroline, 130

Seymour, Dorin, 461

Seymour, Jane, 1031

Seymour, Shaughan, 740

Sezer, Serif, 1260

Shack, Andrew, 578

Shackelford, David, 1308

Shadix, Glenn, 200

Shaff, Edmund, 857

Shaffer, Paul, 119

Shaffner, Catherine, 575

Shaifer, Andrew, 1419

Shainberg, Steven, 538

Shakar, Martin, 996

Shalhoub, Tony, 232, 597, 951, 1000, 1154

Shamburger, Douglas, 318

Shamshak, Sam, 155

Shanahan, Mark, 1094

Shandling, Garry, 318, 569

Shane, Rachel, 967

Shankman, Jim, 1155

Shannon, Harry, 1339

Shannon, Maureen, 934

Shannon, Michael, 216

Shannon, Molly, 481, 871

Shannon, Polly, 310

Shannon, Vicellous, 173, 1129

Shapiro, Robert, 1222

Shaps, Cyril, 457

Sharian, John, 733, 1100

Sharif, Bina, 481

Shaud, Grant, 27

Shaw, Adam, 1100

Shaw, Emme, 866

Shaw, Fiona, 52, 164

Shaw, Morgana, 546

Shaw, Peter, 993

Shaw, Stan, 1206

Shawn-Williams, Nigel, 322

Shawzin, Gregg, 232

Shay, Michele, 500, 903

Shaye, Lin, 715, 1308

Shear, Claudia, 715

Shearer, Harry, 19, 448, 1197, 1348

Shearer, Jack, 851, 1129

Shebby, Brianna, 126

Shebby, Danielle, 126

Shedrick, Reamer, 1181

Sheedy, Ally, 527

Sheehan, Nora, 806

Sheehan, Tim, 1308

Sheen, Martin, 832, 1135

Sheen, Michael, 1460

Sheffield, Peggy, 931

Shell, Ray, 1390

Shelton, Marley, 978

Shelton, Sloane, 903

Shendi, 477

Sheng, Samuel, 944

Shenkel, Leslie, 187

Shenkman, Ben, 970

Shenkman, Insben, 1154

Shepherd, Lee, 1264

Shepherd, Simon, 1249

Shepherd, Suzanne, 715, 722

Shepis, Tiffany, 1145

Sheppard, Ellen, 369

Sher, Antony, 1137

Sher, Sy, 715

Sherbedgia, Rade, 811

Sheridan, Joe, 759

Sheridan-Taylor, Deborah, 1304

Sherman, Cindy, 954

Sherman, Danielle, 936

Sherry, James, 593

Shestack, MarciaRose, 313

Shields, Fallon, 1308

Shields, Jack, 1308

Shiels, Ciara A., 500

Shiina, Kippei, 455

Shimono, Sab, 93

Shimwell, David, 530

Shindler, James, 686

Shinick, Kevin, 1229

Shinohara, Katsuyuki, 1439

Shinra, Banshou, 396

Shinsui, Sansho, 334

Shiomi, Sensei, 1439

Shipman, Robert, 310

Shippley, Sandra, 832

Shipton, Cathy, 1249

Shirzad, M., 815

Shosib, Samia, 888, 970

Shodeinde, Fash, 626

Shoemaker, Joshua, 954

Short, Paul, 21

Short, Sylvia, 584

Shorter, Frank, 1466

Showalter, Michael, 1094

Shroyer, Sonny, 434

Shtempel, Alexander, 294

Shtukaturova, Ania, 1315

Shue, Elisabeth, 247, 931

Shulman, Michael, 1447

Shuman, Michael, 1419

Sia, Beau, 1181, 1186

Sicari, Joseph R., 755

Sicilia, Joseph, 310

Sicily, 563

Sickler, Rich, 993

Sie, Allison, 349

Sie, James, 1371

Siegler, Ben, 369

Sieh, Jeanette, 550

Sieker, Richard M., 679

Siekoua, Basile, 1426

Sieras, Diego, 773

Sierra, Gregory, 615, 755

Sietz, Adam, 187

Sikes, Lori Beth, 434

Sikking, Andrew, 1061

Silano, Gerardo, 1280

Silberg, Tusse, 740

Silles, Karen, 1039, 1228

Silva, Eliane, 195

Silva, Rebecca, 348

Silveira, Leonor, 1405

Silverberg, Evan, 481

Silverio, Susanne, 603

Silverman, Jonathan, 857

Silverman, Laura, 468

Silverman, Sarah, 155, 1308

Silverstein, Salik, 820

Silverstone, Ben, 722

Silvstedt, Victoria, 72

Simionescu, Adrian, 420

Simkins, Michael, 1461

Simmons, Earl, 75

Simmons, J.K., 187, 252

Simmons, Richard, 1076

Simmons, Tom, 1348

Simmons, Vincent, 376

Simmons, Xavier, 75

Simmrin, Joey, 1253

Simms, Tasha, 593

Simola, Liisa, 304

Simon, Cheung, 634

Simon, Georgia, 755

Simonds, Dave, 512

Simonds, Lincoln, 847

Simons, Hywel, 1137, 1461

Simpson, Brian, 1253

Simpson, Michael Philip, 626

Simpson, Sean, 697

Simpson, Tyree Michael, 1471

Sims, Adam, 733

Sims, Bronwyn, 866

Sims, Kelley, 1262

Sinclair, Malcolm, 801

Sinden, Grace, 33

Singer, Mildred, 33

Singer, Norbert D., 33

Singer, Ritchie, 271

Singer, Stephen, 959, 996

Singh, Desi, 914

Singleton, Harry, 978

Sinise, Gary, 1206

Siragusa, Peter, 97

Sirianni, Dolores, 1490

Sirico, Tony, 187

Sirios, Miriam, 1076

Sirtis, Marina, 1254

Sisco, Kennen, 954

Sissons, Peter, 1249

Sisto, Jeremy, 1277, 1466

Sisto, Meadow, 173, 252

Sitschi, Stefan, 1284

Sitteri, Peter, 944

Sivadier, Pierre-Michel, 1216

Sivero, Frank, 1419

Sivertsen, Mark, 615

Siviero, Marco, 631

Sizemore, Tom, 349, 1100

Skaggs, Corey, 1390

Skalnik, Michelle, 312

Skarsgard, Stellan, 607, 1062, 1123

Skerritt, Tom, 1203

Skinner, Beverly, 1262

Skjaerstad, Robert, 619

Skold, Tim, 601

Skortstad, Ben, 874

Skrela, Mark, 1164

Skulski, Brooke, 155

Skye, Ione, 326

Slade, Gloria, 119

Slater, Blair, 593, 1348

Slater, Callison, 349

Slater, Christian, 493, 1398

Slaughter, Lance, 1471

Slavin, Millie, 1348

Sleep, Wayne, 339

Slezak, Victor, 902, 1154

Sloan, Cle Shaheed, 1048

Sloan, Matt, 72

Sloan, Tina, 187

Slutsker, Peter, 996

Smaghe, Steve, 694

Small, Robert, 539

Smallman, Nick, 339

Smallwood, Tucker, 1229

Smart, Amy, 284

Smart, Dee, 1424

Smart, Jean, 857

Smashing Pumpkins, 406

Smee, Anthony, 531

Smee, Derek, 801, 822

Smego, Alissa Ann, 1253

Smiga, Carly, 1348

Smigel, Robert, 1419

Smiley, Leigh, 77

Smit, Cate, 659

Smith, Adam C., 40

Smith, Andrew, 740

Smith, Bee-Be, 155

Smith, Bob, 1280

Smith, Britta, 1288

Smith, Charles Martin, 286

Smith, Clifford, 75

Smith, Danny, 93

Smith, Dari Gerard, 317

Smith, Dean, 500

Smith, Eboni, 679

Smith, Edward, 578

Smith, Errol, 540

Smith, Gregory, 636, 1197

Smith, Ian Michael, 1164

Smith, J.W., 1443

Smith, Jacob, 1197

Smith, John Dee, 1319

Smith, Kurtwood, 286

Smith, Kyle Timothy, 944

Smith, L. H., 434

Smith, Lane, 522, 1442

Smith, Lionel Mark, 1232

Smith, Lillian, 77

Smith, Liz, 801

Smith, Marc, 1186

Smith, Paul, 282

Smith, Philip R., 631

Smith, Robert Vincent, 959

Smith, Roger Guenveur, 500

Smith, Ron Clinton, 758

Smith, Scott, 1476

Smith, Sean, 313

Smith, Shawnee, 40

Smith, Stephanie, 944

Smith, Tucker, 519

Smith, Will, 348

Snider, Barry, 130

Snider, Dee, 284

Snipes, Wesley, 114, 322, 1371

Snow, Rachel Lena, 550

Snodgress, Carrie, 1456

Snoop Doggy Dogg, 182, 468, 1057

Snowball, Yolanda, 715

Snyder, Kim, 461

Snyder, Rick, 1371

Soares, Malcolm, 195

Sobeck, Tara, 554

Soberanes, Esteban, 789

Sobieski, Leelee, 285, 1216

Sogliuzzo, Andr, 1489

Sohn, Sonja, 1181

Soileau, Paul, 920

Sokolow, Diane, 1489

Sol, Alex, 21

Solari, Matthew, 126

Solarino, Ken, 130

Solberg, Shayn, 10

Solda, Maurizio, 201

Sollinger, Alan, 1149

Solomon, Lenny, 1471

Somera, Leon C., Jr., 634

Somerville, Phyllis, 597

Sommer, Josef, 944, 1020

Sommerfield, Peter, 271

Sommers, Jana, 292

Sonic Youth, 406

Sonnenberg, Maurice, 187

Sonsie, Breanna, 1424

Sood, Veena, 1474

Soral, Agnes, 899

Sorce, Robert, 1145

Sorel, Nancy, 580

Sorensen, Cindy L., 578

Sorensen, Thomas Jungling, 795

Soronen, Tim "Stuffy", 414

Sorvino, Mira, 1048

Sorvino, Paul, 155, 634

Sosa, Roberto, 789

Sosa, Sammy, 631

Soto, Roberto, 155

Soucie, Kath, 1077

Soucy, Jin Hi, 434

Soule, Allen, 1232

Soupy Sales, 539

Southerland, Boots, 860

Sozzani, Anna, 269

Spacek, Sissy, 1

Spacek, Stephen, 1319

Spacey, Kevin, 146, 569, 851

Spade, David, 1077, 1129

Spahn, Ryan, 987

Sparks of Fire, 987

Sparrow, Walter, 357

Spears, Aries, 1442

Spears, Peter, 909

Speed, Lucy, 801, 1137

Spence, Bruce, 271

Spence, Sebastian, 394

Spencer, Amanda, 1062

Spencer, Dorian, 872

Spencer, Jaime, 109

Spencer, John, 851, 1361

Spencer, Julian, 1100

Spengler, Volker, 899

Sperdakos, George, 119, 310

Spiegel, Howard, 1489

Spielvogel, Laurent, 1062

Spijkers, Jaap, 211

Spinella, Stephen, 276, 461, 918

Spiner, Brent, 1254

Spinuzza, Doug, 851

Spirtas, Kevin, 33

Spoke, Suanne, 636

Spore, Richard, 583

Sporleder, Gregory, 237, 1180

Spottag, Jens Jorn, 626

Sprague, Carin, 1429

Spreekmeester, Stephen, 1206

Spreer, Stefan, 89

Springall, Alejandro, 789

Springer, Jerry, 631, 1059

Spurrier, Linda, 531, 1149

Squibb, June, 781

Squire, Mike, 631
Stabile, Nick, 133
Stacey, Paul, 1189
Stack, Robert, 72
Stadlen, Lewis J., 597
Stadler, Joerg, 357, 1100
Stahelski, Chad, 616
Stahl, Jerry, 965
Stahl, Nick, 312, 1319
Stahlbrand, Sandi, 133
Staines, Christopher, 822
Stallone, Sylvester, 27
Stamp, Terrence, 749
Standing, John, 822
Stanisavijevic, Selestina, 89
Stanley, Florence, 155, 857
Stanton, Harry Dean, 379, 806
Stanton, Robert, 798, 866
Stapleton, Jean, 1489
Starr, Fredro, 1057
Starr, Mike, 1206
Stauber, Liz, 173, 1285
Staunton, Imelda, 1137
Staunton, Kim, 539
Stavola, Charlie, 232
Stayer, Carolyn, 954
Stedman, Anne, 860
Steedman, Tony, 822
Steemson, John, 1375
Steen, Jessica, 40
Steen, Paprika, 184
Steers, Burr, 659
Stefano, Kathleen, 944
Steffand, Joan, 1167
Steger, Lawrence, 470
Stein, Mary, 60
Stein, Saul, 500, 595
Steinberg, David, 847
Steinberg, Matthew, 310
Steiner, Tommy Shane, 546
Steinline, Lenny, 575
Stender, Thomas, 626
Stender-Petersen, Dorrit, 626
Stepanova, Olga, 481
Mary Ellen Trainor, 679
Stephens, Duane, 238
Stephens, Nancy, 472
Stephens, Toby, 247
Stephenson, Denise, 1249
Stepic, Irene A., 114
Sterk, Michael, 326
Sterling, Philip, 847
Sterling, Raymond, 758
Stern, Daniel, 1398
Stern, Deborah, 1447
Stern, Tim, 1149

Stern, Tom, 601
Sternard, Mitchell, 126
Stetler, Paul Morgan, 978
Stevens, Fisher, 403
Stevens, Joe, 860
Stevens, Leslie, 326
Stevens, Miceal, 75
Stevens, Ronnie, 936
Stevenson, Charles C., Jr., 978
Stevenson, Christopher, 232
Stevenson, Cynthia, 10, 480
Stevenson, Elvira, 357
Stevenson, Ray, 1304
Steward, Paul Anthony, 1221
Stewart, Ashton, 1262
Stewart, Barbara, 1164
Stewart, Charles, 40
Stewart, Charlotte, 1193
Stewart, Jon, 364, 468
Stewart, Mike, 601
Stewart, Momolu, 1181
Stewart, Patrick, 1254
Stewart, Paul, 1
Sthulbarg, Michael, 996
Stickney, Phyllis Yvonne, 563
Sticky Fingaz, 1057
Stiers, David Ogden, 636
Stiles, Julia, 1447
Stiller, Ben, 965, 1308, 1483, 1495
Stiller, Jerry, 1037
Stiphemo, Rapulana, 1291
Stirling, Richard, 822
Stockbridge, Peter, 339, 801
Stockhausen, Karlheinz, 831
Stojanovich, Christina, 550
Stoker, John, 93
Stokes, Blake, 1476
Stoller, Fred, 200
Stoltz, Eric, 519, 816
Stone, James, 470
Stone, Laura, 310
Stone, Matt, 72, 171, 914
Stone, Sharon, 27, 806, 1243
Stonebraker, J.J., 1085
Stoneham, John Sr., 93
Stoneham, John, Jr., 1471
Stoner, Jeremy, 294
Storm, Mark, 758

Stormare, Peter, 40, 97, 798, 1221
Storms, Timothy, 1167
Story, Kim, 61
Story, Tom, 575
Stough, Eric, 915
Stout, Mary, 539
Stout, Susan, 903
Stowe, Madeleine, 1020
Stracham, Freddy, 1216
Strachan, Joel, 1044
Stralka, Benjamin, 286
Stransky, Charles, 1232
Strathairn, David, 67, 1164
Stratt, Jonathan, 740
Stratton, Cherie, 887
Stratton, Richard, 1182
Strauss, Kim, 126
Straw, Brien, 758
Streep, Meryl, 265, 903
Street, Simon, 563
Stribling, Rick, 414
Strickland, Amzie, 593, 636
Stringfield, Sherry, 385
Stripling, Randy, 860
Stritch, Elaine, 636
Strnad, Petr, 674
Ströhman, Bianca, 751
Strong, Brenda, 112
Strong, Danny, 978
Strong, Jeff, 153
Strong, Rider, 847
Strother, Frederick, 77
Studi, Wes, 291
Stuke, Neil, 1189
Sturiano, Terry, 572
Styles, Luke, 272
Scott, R. Williams, 954
Styne, Beth Ann, 927
Suarez, Manny, 920, 1457
Suber, Mets, 1447
Subkoff, Tara, 659
Sucharetza, Marla, 461
Suchet, Damian, 1389
Suchet, David, 959
Sudduth, Kohl, 385, 1069
Sudduth, Skipp, 385, 1062
Suerth, Kimberlee, 954
Suggs, Harold, 860
Sugisaki, Hiroya, 1319
Suhorukov, Viktor, 137
Sullivan, Jackie, 832
Sullivan, Larry, Jr., 1081
Sullivan, Perry D., 1371
Sullivan, Quinn, 155
Sullivan, Sarah, 679
Sullivan, Sean, 385

Summer, Cree, 1077
Summer, Donna, 896
Summerour, Lisa, 798
Sumpton, Christopher R., 313
Sun, Jade, 601
Sundby, Karl, 619
Sundown, Monica, 522
Sundquist, Bjorn, 619, 795
Sung, Elizabeth, 679
Suplee, Ethan, 21
Suriano, Phil, 755
Surman, John, 674
Sussman, Andrew, 959
Sussman, Robynn N., 959
Sutcliffe, David, 468
Sutherland, Donald, 369, 1466
Sutherland, Kiefer, 271
Sutherland, Victor, 385
Sutton, Pete, 349
Sutton, Ted, 1240
Suvri, Men, 1193
Suzrez, Moises, 773
Suzuki, Keiichi, 1439
Suzuki, Kimmy, 462
Suzuki, Kouji, 1319
Suzuki, Ranran, 1439
Svane, Toi, 1456
Svarre, Steen, 626
Sveen, Helge, 619
Sviland, Maria, 601
Swafford, Savannah, 1348
Swaim, Bob, 1216
Swain, Dominique, 722
Swann, Lynn, 1417
Swanson, Hannah, 811
Swayze, Patrick, 112
Sweeney, Birdy, 165
Sweeney, Kelley, 554
Sweeney, Matthew, 187
Sweeney, Steve, 876, 1308
Sweet, Jack, 866
Swezey, Ric, 1416
Swift, Allen, 996, 1094
Swingler, Dwayne, 448
Swinton, Tilda, 746
Symonds, Robert, 1000
Syversen, Marit, 619
Syvertsen, Peter, 1167
Syverud, Henning, 619
Syyouk, Igor, 119
Szubanski, Magda, 60

Tabak, Asher, 996
Tabakin, Ralph, 1243
Táborsky, Miroslav, 195
Taffett, Jefferson, 1061

Tagawa, Cary-Hiroyuki, 615
Taguchi, Tomoro, 334, 1336
Tahash, Brian, 755
Tahir, Faran, 996
Tai, Ada, 1081
Tai, Arlene, 1081
Taj Mahal, 927, 1174
Takenaka, Naoto, 455, 1336
Takeshi, Beat, 395
Takeuchi, Warren T., 291
Takle, Darien, 1375
Taliferro, Michael "Bear", 40
Talley, Jill, 1228
Tallman, Bob, 522
Talukdar, 746
Talwar, Sanjay, 310
Tamabukuro, Sujitaro, 396
Tambakis, Peter, 1061
Tambor, Jeffrey, 317, 781, 1308
Tamez, Art Michael, 550
Tamiroff, Akim, 1339
Tamura, Motoharu, 396
Tan, Philip, 679
Tan, Victoria, 931
Tanaka, Fumiya, 830
Tanaka, Sara, 1085
Tanchon, Daniel, 694
Tanji, Tomohiro, 1319
Tannehill, Eugene "Bishop", 376
Tanner, Jeff, 369
Tannous, Glenn, 679
Taplin, Terry, 674
Tarantino, Quentin, 414, 896
Taras, Barry, 69
Tardieu, Andre, 758
Tarling, Bill, 1474
Tartack, Kerry, 860
Tarver, Milt, 379
Tashjian, Warren, 1308
Tataryn, Sean, 669
Tate, Larenz, 1442
Tatic, Josif, 1123
Tavernier, Nils, 989
Tawil, David, 970
Taylor, Andre, 978, 1181
Taylor, Christine, 1419
Taylor, Don, 1348
Taylor, Holland, 866, 1348
Taylor, Jennifer Bini, 539, 1416
Taylor, Joseph Lyle, 500
Taylor, Joshua, 448
Taylor, Ken, 811
Taylor, Koko, 798

Taylor, Lawrence, 1417
Taylor, Lili, 595, 597, 954
Taylor, Michael L., 578
Taylor, Patrick, 385
Taylor, Priscilla Lee, 1174
Taylor, Raph, 1100
Taylor, Regina, 851
Taylor, Robert, 129
Taylor, Rod, 1424
Taylor, Ron, 1348
Taylor, Russi, 61
Taylor, Ryan, 313
Taylor, Tamara, 1129
Taylor, Wayne, 1339
Taylor, Zachary, 659
Tchenko, Katia, 751, 1062
Tchernine, Vladimir, 1062
Teague, Marshall, 40
Techman, Charles, 1447
Tecosky, Olivia, 1232
Tedford, Travis, 1187
Tedlie, Dan, 481
Teinert, Cliff, 1371
Teixeira, Adelaide, 1405
Telesco, Dominic, 140
Telljohn, Sumiko, 155
Temchen, Sybil, 1302
Temple, Lew, 860
Tenenbaum, Brian, 1085
Tenney, Jon, 548
Tennon, Julius, 1197
Tensun, Justin, 385
Teodosiu, Valentin, 420
Tep, Eva, 1206
Tepfer, Daniel, 1216
Terada, Chiho, 334
Terajima, Susumu, 395
Terashima, Susumu, 1223
Terkel, Studs, 105
Termo, Leonard, 448
Terra, Scott, 1135
Terral, Boris, 989
Terry, Kim, 1085
Terry, Tim W., 931
Tesch, Ingrid, 1474
Testud, Sylvie, 89
Texada, Tia, 126, 951
Thaddeus, John, 1206
Thalken, Meg, 1371
Thatch, Nigel, 975
Theba, Iqbal, 72, 1228
Thedford, Marcello, 1443
Theirse, Darryl, 580
Thelen, Jodi, 1419
Theriault, Janine, 1
Theriot, Logan "Bones", 376

Theron, Charlize, 187, 811
Thewlis, David, 97
Thiele, Paul, 1419
Thirkeld, Stephen D., 624
Thomas, Alex, 975, 1442
Thomas, Brian, 954
Thomas, Carmen, 114
Thomas, Clara, 1429
Thomas, Clare, 751
Thomas, Heather, 847
Thomas, Henry, 870, 1277
Thomas, Jay, 308
Thomas, JoAnn D., 155
Thomas, Jonathan Taylor, 593
Thomas, Kristin Scott, 554
Thomas, Leonard, 851
Thomas, Maggie Emma, 936
Thomas, Marcus, 931
Thomas, Marlo, 1040
Thomas, Meda, 1308
Thomas, Robin, 155
Thomas, Scott, 1216
Thomas, Sean Patrick, 173
Thomas, Wendell, 1371
Thomerson, Tim, 379
Thommessen, Vandela K., 936
Thompson, Barry, 857
Thompson, Dee, 758
Thompson, Emma, 472, 1000
Thompson, Ernest, 866
Thompson, Heather, 888
Thompson, John, 500
Thompson, Leonard A., Jr., 1182
Thompson, Randy, 298
Thompson, Rick, 987
Thompson, Sophie, 265
Thompson, Tyler, 10
Thomsen, Richard, 1371
Thomsen, Ulrich, 184
Thomson, Anna, 1275, 1343
Thomson, Scott, 611
Thorens, Drake, 385, 1471
Thorne, Callie, 866
Thorne, Jared, 1214
Thorne, Taylor, 1214
Thorne-Smith, Courtney, 199
Thornton, Billy Bob, 40, 548, 1000, 1167

Thornton, David, 232, 527, 575, 659, 1040
Thorp, William L. IV, 434
Thorson, Jay, 1466
Thurman, Dechen, 587
Thurman, Uma, 52, 674
Tibbetts, Blake Anthony, 33
Tibbetts, Stephen, 1474
Tickner, French, 1474
Tidona, Andrea, 686
Tiefenbach, Dov, 806
Tierney, Brigid, 1
Tierney, Lawrence, 40
Tierney, Maura, 1000
Tiffe, Angelo, 1228
Tighe, Darren, 440
Tignini, Eric, 298
Tilden, Peter, 636
Tilly, Jennifer, 133
Timlake, Farrell, 914
Timlake, Susan, 914
Tinapp, A.A. Barton, 1154
Tingle, Jimmy, 866
Tittor, Robert, 19
Tobolowsky, Stephen, 112
Tocantins, Nicole, 909
Toda, Toshi, 448
Todd, Tony, 182, 1348
Todeschini, Bruno, 646
Togunde, Victor, 173
Toji, Takao, 396
Tokoyama, Megumi, 455
Toledano, Valerie, 1216
Toledo, Zozo, 1260
Toler, Ray, 1371
Toles-Bey, John, 1228
Tolson, Dicon, 697
Tolsty, 1062
Tolzman, Billy, 954
Tom, David, 978
Tomei, Adam, 1348
Tomei, Concetta, 286
Tomei, Marisa, 1193
Tomita, Tamlyn, 715
Tomlin, Dalton, 1085
Tomlin, Lily, 636
Tompkins, Paul F., 610
Tomson, Shaun, 601
Tootle, Chip, 434
Tootle, Grace, 434
Torabi, Jamshid, 1293
Toral, Christina, 936
Torfeh, Brian, 1390
Torgan, Kendra, 624
Tormey, John, 1094
Torn, Rip, 1129
Torney, John, 1040
Torres, Angelina Calderon, 615

Torres, Fernanda, 403, 929
Torres, Liz, 857
Torres, Robert, 187
Torry, Guy, 21, 1057
Toste, Frank, 1021
Toth, Richard, 674
Totumminello, 970
Toub, Lauren, 903
Tougas, Erin, 313
Touratier, Grard, 1062
Tourtillott, Helen, 944
Toussaint, Lorraine, 112
Toutebon, Joe, 77
Tovar, Luis Felipe, 789, 805
Tove, Birthe, 626
Towers, Constance, 959
Towers, Jim, 1348
Towles, Tom, 318
Towne, Katharine, 1466
Townsend, Stuart, 1149, 1380
Townsend, Tommy, 860
Toyokawa, Etsushi, 1439
Toyoshima, Minoru, 1319
Tracy, Jack, 1193
Tracy, Virgil, 703
Trail, Ray, 1040
Trang Thanh Le, 400
Transeau, Kristie, 951
Travelstead, Ted, 1061
Travis, Nigel, 746
Travis, Randy, 112
Travolta, John, 232, 1000, 1319
Travolta, Margaret, 798
Travolta, Sam, 232
Traynor, Rosemary, 271
Traywick, Joel, 1476
Treat, Daniel, 1135
Tregouet, Yann, 48
Trejo, Danny, 1048, 1174
Tremarco, Christine, 1380
Tremblay, Luc, 69
Trese, Adam, 595, 987
Trevisi, Franco, 1344
Trieb, Tatjana, 89
Trifunovic, Sergej, 1123
Trigueiro, Ingrid, 195
Tripplehorn, Jeanne, 832, 1189, 1398
Triska, Jan, 33, 1062
Trivalic, Vesna, 1123
Troughton, Scott, 434
Troy, Thomas, 349
Troya, Verne J., 379
Trudell, John, 1203

True, Jim, 1
True, Rachel, 468
Trujillo, Horacio, 789
Trujillo, Sergio, 1471
Trump, Donald, 187
Truter, Gregor, 1137
Tsang, Eric, 243
Tsang, Kenneth, 1048
Tse, Elaine, 527
Tsu, Irene, 243
Tsuda, Kanji, 396
Tsuji, Terutake, 1319
Tsukamoto, Koji, 1336
Tsukamoto, Shinya, 1336
Tsunami, Edamame, 396
Tsurmi, Shingo, 455
Tubbe, Bruce, 806
Tucci, Stanley, 597
Tuck, Michael, 40
Tucker, Beverly, 959
Tucker, Chris, 1081
Tucker, Joe, 1380
Tucker, Radney, 959
Tudyk, Alan, 944
Tuerpi, Paul, 679, 1476
Tuesday, Ruby, 669
Tugend, Jennie Lew, 679
Tuiasosopo, Peter Navy, 72
Tullio, Paolo, 165
Tung, Jennifer, 1255
Tunie, Tamara, 1206
Tunney, Robin, 870
Turk, Brian, 232
Turman, Glynn, 563
Turner, Arnold F., 317
Turner, Dustin, 1240
Turner, Frank C., 10
Turner, Frantz, 578
Turner, Graham, 703
Turner, Kathleen, 1040
Turner, Marcus, 10
Turner, Michele, 497
Turner, Pamela, 176
Turner, Tyrin, 75, 699
Turner, Zara, 1189
Turturro, Aida, 369, 1471
Turturro, Aida, 187
Turturro, John, 97, 500, 1069, 1344
Tushingham, Rita, 1380
Twyford, Holly, 954
Twyman, Daniel, 1152
Tyler, Diane, 481
Tyler, Liv, 40
Tyler, Steve, 1308
Tyson, Richard M., 1308
Tyzack, Margaret, 822
Tzintzadze, Guio, 135

Ubach, Alanna, 240

Uecker, Bob, 757
Ueda, Koichi, 334, 1404
Uhrig, Steve, 349
Ulmanski, Renata, 1123
Ulmschneider, Craig, 187
Ulrich, Skeet, 860
Ulrichsen, Marianne O., 607
Umbers, Mark, 746
Underwood, Blair, 285
Underwood, Erin, 308, 1135
Underwood, Sheryl, 155, 578
Unger, Jan, 674
Upjohn, William, 272
Upton, John, 61
Urban, Peter A., Jr., 1447
Urbaniak, James, 512
Uria, Joseph, 286
Urquhart, Kyle Ryan, 1085
Usher, David, 93
Utt, Angie, 77

Vaccaro, Karen, 1371
Vacco, Angelo, 173
Vachon, Paul, 69
Vahle, Dirk, 298, 554
Vajakas, Lena, 385
Valdes-Kennedy, Armando, 109
Váldez, Francisco, 789
Valenti, Duke, 40
Valentine, Owen, 575
Valentino, Charles, 851
Valeska, Etta, 583
Valley, Mark, 1154
Valsonne, Diane, 1426
Van, Alex, 757
Vana, John, 1419
Van Allen, Willam, 806
Van Damme, Jean-Claude, 634
Vandegelden, Horrac, 915
Van Den Berg, Dirk Kersten, 686
van den Dop, Tamar, 210
van der Donk, Eric, 327
van der Grijn, Wim, 211
Vanderloo, Mark, 187
Van der Veen, Ben, 379
Van Der Velden, Naomi, 272
Van Der Wal, Frederique, 187, 1366
Van Dien, Casper, 1291

VanDusen, Andrew, 1061
van Eyle, Marisa, 210
Van Hekken, Joey, 601
Van Horn, Sara, 580
van Huet, Fadja, 210
van Overbeke, Marie-Josée, 694
Vanier, Jean-Jacques, 1426
Van Keeken, Frank, 40
Van Lear, Philip, 216
Vann, Marc, 1371
Van Swearingen, Guy, 851
van Warmerdam, Alex, 327
Van Winkle, Dick, 703
Van Wormer, Steve, 780
Varela, Leonor, 759
Vareze, Anne, 40
Vargas, Jacob, 521
Vargas, John, 1000
Varney, Jim, 1334
Varon, Edith, 1228
Varrez, Ash, 751
Vassiliev, Anatoly, 1344
Vastine, Lisa, 442
Vaughan, Peter, 674
Vaughan, James, 1461
Vaughn, Betty, 497
Vaughn, Jennie, 1129
Vaughn, Judson, 1348
Vaughn, Marcus, 914
Vaughn, Robert, 72
Vaughn, Vince, 237, 1023, 1053
Vaus, Lyn, 866
Vega, Isidra, 1069
Vega, Joe, 1069
Vega, Vladimir, 339
Vegh, David, 1100
Veinotte, Troy, 477
Velásquez, Armando Martínez, 789
Velasquez, Hector, 225
Velez, Daisy, 857
Vlez, Lauren, 587
Velter, François, 357
Veltri, Gabe, 1419
Venable, Janine, 580
Venci, Zdenek, 674
Venegas, Arturo, 751
Venito, Lenny, 1069
Ventimiglia, John, 882, 1275
Vera, Veronica, 304
Vereen, Ben, 1442
Verhoeven, Yves, 201, 1284
Vernoff, Kaili, 882
Vernstad, Alice, 304
Vernstad, Paul, 304
Veronis, Nick, 277
Verveen, Arie, 1319
Vesey, Melanie, 512

Viard, Karin, 649
Vickerage, Lesley, 801
Victory, Fiona, 1280
Vidal, Eric, 578
Vidler, Steven, 1319
Viegas, Mario, 958
Vieluf, Vince, 237
Vigouroux, Tho, 1426
Villa, Giovanna, 686
Villalpando, David, 773, 789
Villari, Libby, 364
Villeminot, Catherine, 1216
Villeminot, Florence, 1216
Villeneuve, Bernard, 411
Villiers, Christopher, 1189
Vils, Kenneth "Brother", 1474
Vince, Pruitt Taylor, 129
Vincent, 112, 130, 1319
Vincent, David, 18
Vincent, Frank, 75, 1302, 1425
Vincent, Jan-Michael, 139
Vincent, Louis, 649
Vincent, Paul, 1466
Vinson, Victor, 40
Vint, Angela, 1387
Vinyard, Doris, 21
Virkner, Helle, 626
Visnjic, Goran, 993, 1069
Vitale, Dick, 500
Vitali, Elisabeth, 1426
Vitanza, Vilma, 944
Viterelli, Joe, 755
Viteychuk, Chris, 364
Vitrant, Lionel, 1062
Vivia, 944
Vlahos, Sam, 21
Vogel, Tony, 674
Voges, Torsten, 97
Voight, Jon, 348, 427
Vokoun, Pavel, 674
Vollans, Michael, 310
Voltaire, Jacqueline Walters, 789
Von Bargen, Daniel, 232, 364, 1040, 1343
von Sydow, Max, 1429
Vooren, Gerrit, 959
Vorstman, Frans, 210
Voyt, Harriet, 1232
von Krusenstjerne, Fredrik, 1342
von Moers, Stefan, 89
von Sinnen, Helle, 623

Wachsman, Melanie, 581
Wada, Jey, 679
Waddell, Karen, 468
Waddington, Steven, 1291
Wadham, Julian, 801
Wagner, Agnieszka, 1344
Wagner, Brett, 975
Wagner, Dave, 1416
Wagner, Henrik, 247
Wagner, Natasha Gregson, 400, 1366, 1387
Wagner, Paul, 866
Wagner, Robert, 1456
Wahl, Bob, 140
Wahlberg, Mark, 93
Wahlstrom, Becky, 909
Wai, Kwak, 1053
Wai Ching Ho, 481, 996
Waid, Jeffrey Allen, 1154
Wajima, Kochi, 1336
Walken, Christopher, 27, 1277
Walker, Amanda, 357
Walker, Charles, 1443
Walker, Clint, 1197
Walker, Fuchsia, 864
Walker, Jake, 616
Walker, Jiggs, 78
Walker, John Haynes, 349
Walker, Kateri, 927
Walker, Kelvin, 126
Walker, Kim, 1221
Walker, Michael J., 349
Walker, Paul, 780, 978
Walker, Polly, 1288
Walker, Rebecca, 1000
Walker, Robert, 539
Wallace, Andrew, 759
Wallace, Basil, 182
Wallace, Don, 996
Wallace, Jack, 1232, 1361
Wallace, John, 500
Wallace, Laurie, 540
Wallace, Sam, 1375
Wallace, Todd, 1319
Wallace, Will, 1319
Wallem, Linda, 1229
Walling, Jessica, 597
Wallis, Bill, 801
Walls, Kevin Patrick, 114
Wallyn, Grard, 694
Walsh, Dylan, 332
Walsh, Gwynyth, 252
Walsh, J.T., 851, 978
Walsh, Jack, 1167
Walsh, Jerry, 369, 1447

Walsh, John, 245, 1474
Walsh, Kate, 511
Walsh, Kathryn, 903
Walsh, M. Emmet, 200, 1361
Walsh, Ruth Lawson, 954
Walter, Harriet, 457, 801
Walter, Jessica, 1193
Walter, Lisa Ann, 936
Walter, Tracey, 77, 298, 811
Walters, Hugh, 390
Walters, John, 357, 1100
Walters, Keith, 522
Walters, Mark, 364, 546
Walters, Toddy, 171, 914
Walton, Bill, 500
Walton, Gary H., 155
Walton, John, 61
Waltz, Lisa, 857
Wameling, Gerd, 623
Wanamaker, Zoë, 1280, 1460
Wanlass, Lynn, 369
Wan-Lei, Chen, 373
Ward, Dick, 123
Ward, E. Glenn, Jr., 1371
Ward, Fern, 563
Ward, Fred, 269
Ward, Jackilynn, 349
Ward, Joshua, 349
Ward, Paddy, 1409
Ward, Roy, 1375
Ward, Sela, 385
Warden, Jack, 155, 199, 310
Warden, Rick, 624
Ward-Lealand, Jennifer, 1375
Ware, Herta, 993
Ware, Marie, 1371
Ware, Paul, 448
Ware, Tim, 757
Warfield, Anjua, 1155
Warmoth, Greg, 40
Warne, Andrew, 155
Warner, David, 667
Warner, Gary, 448
Warner, Martin Charles, 755
Werner, Rick, 369, 1135
Warren, Jennifer Leigh, 1228
Warren, Ryan S., 1466
Warwick, Michael, 379
Washington, Denzel, 369, 500, 1154
Washington, Isaiah, 155, 920
Washington, Jascha, 348

Watanabe, Joe, 1319
Watanabe, Tetsu, 395, 1223
Wataru, Teppei, 1439
Watkins, Doug, 885
Watkins, Tapp, 1495
Watkins, Tionne "T-Boz", 75
Watkins, Tuc, 587
Watson, Ashleigh, 77
Watson, Emily, 531
Watson, Greg, 866
Watson, Henry O., 1474
Watson, Muse, 584, 1135
Watson, Ralph, 1149
Watt, Reichle, 349
Wattley, Danny, 394
Watts, Naomi, 269
Waugh, Scott, 298
Wax, Ruby, 123
Wayans, Marlon, 1129
Wayne, Dig, 951
Wayrock, Heather, 936
Weatherly, Michael, 659
Weatherred, Michael, 1129
Weathers, Doug, 434
Weatherup, Christine, 1253
Weaver, Dennis, 1339
Weaver, Doug, 679
Weaver, Lee, 155, 448, 563
Weaving, Hugh, 61
Webb, Chloe, 860, 993
Webb, Danny, 740
Webb, Lucy, 927
Webb, Rudy, 806
Webb, Veronica, 540
Webber, David, 52
Weber, Jake, 269, 781
Weber, Paolina, 1222
Weber, Steven, 1228
Webster, Derek, 448
Webster, Jack, 954
Wedersoe, Erik, 626
Weedon, Emily, 133
Weeks, Heather, 531
Weeks, Jimmie Ray, 1154
Weeks, Perdita, 1249
Weems, Eric, 1085
Weenick, Annabelle, 931
Wegener, Klaus, 626
Wehle, Brenda, 1214
Weintraub, Scott, 232
Weir, Arabella, 1149
Weir, Michael, 477
Weireter, Peter, 298
Weisberg, Emily, 1232
Weisinger, Tina, 872
Weiss, Bryna, 1193
Weiss, Kasper, 1344

Weisz, Rachel, 652, 1280
Weitz, Bruce, 285
Wei Ye, 410
Welbers, Nicolas, 764
Welch, Jason, 349
Welch, Michael, 1254
Welch, Peter, 1290
Welch, Raquel, 199
Welch, Tahnee, 1275
Weldon, Julia, 933
Welker, Frank, 1031
Well, Liza, 1436
Welles, Orson, 1339
Welling, Albert, 1461
Wells, Elizabeth Diane, 758
Wells, Frank T., 1021
Wells, Junior, 119
Wells, Orlando, 1461
Wells, Timothy, 636
Welsh, James, 703
Welsh, Margaret, 1035
Welterlen, Paul, 1476
Wenderlich, Windy, 1262
Wendl, Alan J., 954
Wendl, Joyce Flick, 349, 954
Wendt, George, 1249
Wenham, David, 271
Wenn, Joslyn, 310
Went, Johanna, 470
Wentworth, Alexandra, 1040
Wenz, Tyler Daniel, 755
Werking, Noel, 349
Werntz, Gary, 285
Werntz, Hannah, 286
Wert, Douglas, 888
Wescoatt, Rusty, 1339
Weseluck, Cathy, 593
Wesley, John, 578
West, Bob, 69
West, Caryl, 1308
West, Dominic, 1249
West, John, 1443
West, On, 944
West, Pamela, 539
West, Red, 584
West, Ron, 1229
West, Tegan, 519
West, Timothy, 356
Westaway, Simon, 61, 1319
Westbam, 831
Westerman, Frederic, 764
Westerwelle, Wendy, 1495
Westhead, David, 1460
Westmore, McKenzie, 1255
Westmoreland, Micko, 1389
Westmoreland, Stoney, 448

Westmoreland, Wash, 1390
Weston, Celia, 187
Weston, Douglas, 1174
Wettenthall, Simon, 1449
Wetzel, Jeffrey, 540
Wheeler, Alice, 640
Wheeler, Bronia, 1020
Wheeler, Ed, 448
Wheeler, Jane, 69
Wheeler, Maggie, 936
Whelan, James, 1206
Whelan, Jim, 1390
Whitaker, Kenn, 155
Whitaker, Lucinda, 758
Whitby, Paul, 1280
White, Adryn, 1424
White, Bernard, 225
White, Betty, 493, 539
White, Bradley, 888
White, Bryan, 1031
White, Freeman III, 114
White, Giovahann, 93
White, Harrison, 578
White, Jaleel, 1031
White, Jane, 77
White, Joe, 339
White, John Patrick, 173
White, Karen, 832
White, Kevin, 1164
White, Lloyd, 310
White, Michael Jai, 1059
White, Michelle Christine, 21
White, Myrna, 434
White, Peter, 40
White, Welker, 882
Whited, Renita, 866
Whitehall, John, 1380
Whitehead, Geoffrey, 1149
Whiteman, Frank, 286
Whitfield, Lynn, 1264
Whitfield, Mitchell, 580
Whiting, Al, 1416
Whitlock, Isiah, Jr., 1232
Whitman, Mae, 434, 550
Whitmey, Nigel, 1100
Whittenshaw, Jane, 822
Whybrow, Arthur, 1461
Wicherley, Don, 427
Widdoes, Kathleen, 519
Wiehl, Chris, 173
Wiest, Dianne, 554, 993
Wieth, Julie, 626
Wiggins, Norris, Jr., 77
Wiggins, Tim, 944
Wiggins, Wiley, 364

Wight, Paul "The Giant", 1416
Wiig, Esther Marie, 304
Wilby, James, 1044
Wilcox, Cristina, 539
Wilcox, Ralph, 931
Wilde, Aaron, 109
Wilde, Bob, 313
Wilde, Lynn, 1371
Wilder, Alan, 232, 1228
Wildgruber, Ulrich, 603
Wilds, Rob, 1262
Wiles, Michael Shamus, 298, 369, 851, 1476
Wiley, Meason, 546, 550
Wilhelm, Jody, 282
Wilkie, Richard, 1371
Wilkinson, Tom, 457, 1081, 1137, 1460
Willard, Fred, 965
Willerfore, Bari K., 1228
Willes, Chris, 593
Willett, Blake, 512
Williams, Barbara, 636
Williams, Branden, 173, 472
Williams, Clarence III, 468
Williams, Colleen, 322
Williams, Cress, 369
Williams, Cynda, 182
Williams, Delaney, 954
Williams, Dick Anthony, 975
Williams, Don S., 1476
Williams, Elizabeth, 834
Williams, Gary Anthony, 1057
Williams, Gigi, 187
Williams, Glynn, 860
Williams, Harland, 468
Williams, Harold M., 245
Williams, Heathcote, 247
Williams, Jamie, 1416
Williams, Jeff, 959
Williams, Jermaine, 155
Williams, Keith Leon, 114
Williams, Kellie, 1057
Williams, Kenya, 975
Williams, Lawrence, 578
Williams, Lia, 390
Williams, Mark, 123, 1137
Williams, Michelle, 472
Williams, Nadia, 1390
Williams, Natasha, 1304
Williams, Olivia, 1085
Williams, Oren, 975

Williams, Rhys, 10
Williams, Robin, 944, 1429
Williams, Ron, 623
Williams, Roxanne, 427
Williams, Roy, 500
Williams, Saul, 903, 1181, 1186
Williams, Sidney, 1304
Williams, Tino, 1129
Williams, Treat, 291
Williams, Zachary, 1255
Williamson, Felix, 1424
Williamson, Fred, 1057
Williamson, Kate, 522
Williamson, Kendall, 462
Williamson, Mykelti, 1000, 1240
Williamson, Paul, 1149
Williamson, Scott, 19
Williamson, Sondra, 1240
Willis, Bruce, 40, 798, 1154
Willis, Katherine, 364
Willis, Rich, 1193
Willis, Susan, 364
Willows, Alec, 1076
Wilmot, David, 427, 589
Wilmot, Ronan, 165, 427
Wilmott, Billy, 1146
Wilner, Martin, 1034
Wilroy, Channing, 954
Wilson, Alexandra, 1197
Wilson, Andrew, 1085
Wilson, Brian A., 1206
Wilson, Brian Anthony, 1069
Wilson, Bridgette, 1040
Wilson, Chrystale, 975
Wilson, Dolan, 758
Wilson, Edmund, 967
Wilson, Greg, 1129
Wilson, Jody, 539
Wilson, Joseph, 1182
Wilson, Keith, 1456
Wilson, Kristen, 317
Wilson, Lambert, 667
Wilson, Lawrence, 1181
Wilson, Luke, 546, 1085
Wilson, Mark, 1424
Wilson, Mary Louise, 1264
Wilson, Owen, 40, 965
Wilson, Reno, 369, 811
Wilson, Rita, 1023
Wilson, Scott, 237
Wilson, Stuart, 348, 773
Wilson, Talib, 1182

Wilson, Warren,   33
Winde, Beatrice, 1040,
     1164
Windle, David, 746
Winebrake, Pete
     "Conan", 1061
Winfree, Rachel, 636
Winfrey, Oprah,   77
Wing Woo, James,
     1048
Winkler, Henry, 1416
Winkler, Patricia,
     1085
Winsett, Jerry, 951
Winston, Don, 282
Winston, Hattie, 715,
     780, 1077
Winston, Matt, 472
Winstone, Ray, 876
Wint, Maurice Dean,
     256
Winters, Kristoffer
     Ryan, 1000
Winters, Michael, 286
Wirtz, Patty, 69
Wisdom, Robert, 811
Wise, Jim, 872
Withers, Margery,
     1280
Witherspoon, Ashanti,
     376
Witherspoon, John,
     155, 578, 1057
Witherspoon, Reese,
     978,1361
Witt, Alicia, 1387
Witt, Katarina, 1062
Wohl, David, 1100
Wolande, Gene, 232,
     851
Wolf, Fred, 310
Wolf, Gary, 1436
Wolf, Mattie, 1416
Wolfe, Jeff Joseph,
     634
Wolfe, Traci, 679
Wolfert, Nicholas, 461
Wolfgang, Penny, 140
Wolford, Steve,   21
Woller, Kirk B.R., 798
Wollheim, Norbert, 850
Wolodarsky, Wally,
     1085
Wolter, Ralf, 623
Womack, Mark, 1380
Wong, Albert, 349,
     1048, 1081
Wong, Amy, 1053

Wong, B.D., 1187
Wong, Delbert,   40
Wong, Donna, 114
Wong, Lee, 959
Wong, Michael
     Fitzgerald, 634
Wong, Victor, 1334
Wong, Wyman, 634
Wood, Evan Rachel,
     306, 993
Wood, Jody 472,
Wood, John, 52
Wood, Julie Tolentino,
     470
Wood, Tom, 1371
Woodall, Andrew,
     1044
Woodard, Alfre, 322
Woodard, Jimmy, 975
Woodbine, Bokeem,
     19, 93, 182
Woodbury, Judith, 679
Woodcock, Joanna,
     987
Woodeson, Nicholas,
     52, 1149
Woodhouse, Michael,
     75
Woodlawn, Holly, 109
Woodruff, Tom, Jr.,
     1476
Woods, Courtney, 936

Woods, D. Elliot, 1255
Woods, Dana, 578
Woods, Denise, 798
Woods, James, 615
Woodward, Joanne,
     850
Woof, Emily, 1389
Woolever, Mary,
     1167
Woolgar, Barry, 1149
Woolrich, Abel, 773
Woolridge, Karen,
     1041
Woolvett, Gordon
     Michael, 133
Woon-Kin Chin, 1053
Workman, Fred, 540
Wörmsdorf, Joachim,
     1344
Woronicz, Henry, 715,
     1000
Worrall, Chaylee, 512
Worret, Christopher,
     40
Worth, Nicholas, 669

Worthington, Wendy,
     636
Worthy, Rick, 1254
Wrage, Glenn, 1100
Wray, Fay, 896
Wren, Joshua, 674
Wright, Arlaine, 310
Wright, Bruce, 851
Wright, Cecil, 740
Wright, Jeff, 72, 187
Wright, Karl T., 317
Wright, Mary Cath-
     erine, 187, 903
Wright, N'Bushe, 114
Wright, Steven, 61
Wright, Tom, 931
Wu, Ping, 1174
Wu, Regina, 1053
Wuhrer, Kari, 631,
     969
Wyatt, B., 1180
Wyatt, Dale, 847
Wycherley, Don, 589
Wyllie, Don, 1319
Wynands, Dan, 679
Wynkoop, Christopher,
     500
Wynn, Keenan, 1339
Wynne, Avril, 272
Wynter, Sarah, 1240

Xaf, 1390
Xifo, Ray, 72, 308,
     369
Xocua, Guadalupe, 789
Xocua, Miguel, 789
Xu Qing, 346

Yada, Yuzo, 396
Yager, Missy, 1041
Yajina, Kenichi, 396,
     1223
Yakushiji, Yasuei, 396
Yakusho, Koji, 334
Yamada, Mao, 915
Yamaguchi, Akifumi,
     618
Yamaguchi, Kiyoko,
     1348
Yamamoto, Kay, 317
Yamamoto, Keiko, 396
Yamamoto, Shizuko,
     618
Yanagi, Yurel, 396
Yang, Jamison, 448
Yanne, Matthew, 1069
Yanni, 896
Yannuzzi, Carmen, Jr.,
     75

Yarmoush, Michael,
     738
Yarramunua, Stan,
     1424
Yasbeck, Amy, 857
Yates, Cecilia, 61
Yau-Gene Chan, 1048
Yaez, Eduardo, 1456
Yeager, Ben, 379
Yeager, Steve, 757
Yearwood, Richard,
     322
Yee, Kelvin, 944
Yee, Nancy, 349
Yenque, Teresa, 130
Yeung, Kristy, 243
Yiasoumi, George,
     123, 339
Yoakam, Dwight, 860
Yoba, Malik, 1057
Yong, Teoh Kay, 1053
Yooshan-Lou,
     Klanoosh, 1293
Yordanoff, Wladimir,
     1377
York, Michael, 385,
     1474
York, Philip, 1149
Yorker, Jade, 500
Yoshida, Peter, 1069
Yoshida, Seiko, 1232
Yoshino, Yasuomi,
     1319
Yoshiyuki, 618
Youell, Michelle, 781
Young, Aden, 247
Young, Charlie, 373
Young, Damian, 888
Young, Harrison, 909,
     1000, 1100
Young, Jonathon, 394
Young, Judith Knight,
     954
Young, Louis, 1371
Young, Nancy, 1240
Young, Nina, 1189
Young, Norris, 1442
Young, Paul, 1044
Young, Ricardo Miguel,
     575
Young, Rozwill, 369
Youngblood, Sebastian,
     1348
Yow, David, 153
Yu, Ting, 243
Yuan, Roger, 679
Yusim, Marat, 959
Yusoff, Deanna, 1053

Zaborowski, Jan, 619
Zabriskie, Grace,   40
Zacapa, Daniel, 857
Zago, Catherine,   48
Zahn, Steve, 888, 920,
     1093, 1489
Zakroff, Jennifer, 954
Zalabak, Maris, 954
Zellinger, Monika, 416
Zaloom, Zoe, 1069
Zander, Johnny, 173
Zandn, Philip, 626
Zanes, Michele, 1069
Zappa, Ahmet, 610
Zappa, Dweezil, 611
Zary, Amine, 1476
Zayas, David, 671,
     1053, 1069, 1264
Zegers, Kevin, 10
Zeller, Torben, 626
Zellweger, Renee, 282,
     903, 996
Zeman, Richard, 1206
Zemanek, Timm, 1040
Zerbe, Anthony, 1254
Zeta-Jones, Catherine,
     773
Zhang Yongning, 410
Zhukova, Mariya, 137
Zidek, Libor, 674
Ziemski, Lauren, 1240
Zien, Chip, 1154,
     1206
Ziff, Irv, 1240
Zigler, Scott, 1232
Zimmer, Constance,
     1129
Zimmerman, Joey,
     1398
Zimmerman, Mark, 996
Zingaretti, Luca,   48
Zirnkilton, Steve, 1077
Zitin, Brandon, 369
Zito, Sonny, 1069
Zogovic, Sanja, 1123
Zook, Tamara, 951
Zoppi, Gaia, 269
Zubrow, Sidney,
     1094
Zucker, Charlotte, 72
Zucker, Danielle, 72
Zuiderhoek, Olga, 327
Zukovic, Dan, 312,
     657
Zuniga, Jose, 572,
     866
Zushi, Tonbo, 1223

PRODUCERS

Abe, Shuji, 1439
Abell, Keith, 512
Abrahamsen, Svend, 625
Abrams, Peter, 755
Ainsworth, Susan, 684
Akkad, Moustapha, 471
Alexander, Beth, 597
Ali, Malik B., 511
Ali, Waleed B., 511
Allan, Mark, 1442
Allard, Patricia, 48
Almodóvar, Agustin, 709
Amin, Mark, 199, 1253
Anderson, Darla K., 145
Anderson, Wes, 1085
Arad, Avi, 114
Arnold, David, 1052
Aufiero, Dorothy, 544
Aukin, David, 129
Avati, Antonio, 87
Avellan, Elizabeth, 364
Aviram, Nitzan, 509
Aykroyd, Dan, 119
Azoff, Irving, 610

Backström, Tomas, 607
Bacon, Kevin, 1456
Badalato, Bill, 755
Baden-Powell, Sue, 317
Baer, Matthew, 610, 1048
Bain, Barnet, 1429
Baker, Bruce, 669
Baker, Todd, 433
Baldecchi, John, 291, 1163
Ball, Chris J., 822
Balsan, Humbert, 302, 989
Baran, Jack, 1146
Barber, Gary, 757, 1474
Barclay, Jane, 264
Barish, Keith, 1371
Barker, Clive, 441
Barnathan, Michael, 1263
Barreto, Lucy, 403
Barry, Jeff, 610
Bass, Ron, 563, 1263, 1429
Battista, Franco, 738
Baum, Brent, 1058
Baumel, Ellin, 1436
Bay, Michael, 40
Bayly, Stephen, 822

Beasley, William S., 584
Beaton, Jesse, 903
Beatty, Warren, 155
Beaucaire, J.E., 187, 1232, 1449
Beckman, Chris, 886
Beddor, Frank, 1308
Beece, Debby, 1077
Beer, Steven C., 519
Behnke, Jim, 1495
Beigel, Herbert, 400
Belshaw, George, 1035
Belzberg, Leslie, 119
Ben-Ami, Yoram, 1334
Benayoun, Georges, 1131
Bender, Lawrence, 996
Benegui, Laurent, 411
Benzinger, Suzy, 201
Berg, Barry, 1228
Berg, Russel, 201
Berman, Bruce, 992
Berman, Rick, 1254
Bernardi, Barry, 291
Bernart, Maurice, 1426
Bernheim, Alain, 1052
Bernstein, Armyan, 312
Berri, Claude, 649, 898
Berry, Tom, 738
Besman, Michael, 909
Besson, Luc, 875
Bevan, Tim, 96, 123, 338, 521
Bicker, Christophe, 1096
Bierman, Robert, 801
Bigel, Daniel, 1366
Bigwood, James, 75
Birnbaum, Lillian, 195
Birnbaum, Roger, 539, 1081, 1163, 1174
Bjorkman, Stig, 1342
Blumentahl, Hank, 864
Boe, Peter, 619
Boorman, John, 427
Borgli, Petter, 607
Bouchareb, Rachid, 693
Bozman, Ron, 77
Bradshaw, Joan, 285
Braithwaite, Philippa, 1189
Brancato, Paula, 1221
Branco, Paulo, 425
Braschi, Gianluigi, 685
Bregman, Martin, 902
Bregman, Michael, 902
Bressler, Carl, 1202
Brest, Martin, 781
Breviere, Nicolas, 1127
Brezner, Larry, 636
Briggs, David, 126

Brillstein, Bernie, 1048
Bronco, Paulo, 1405
Bronfman, Ellen, 1093
Bronson, Harold, 379, 1442
Brooks, Paul, 624
Broomfield, Nick, 640
Bross, Eric, 1302
Brown, David, 285
Brown, G. Mac, 1489
Brown, Stephen, 958
Bruckheimer, Jerry, 40, 348
Brugge, Pieter Jan, 155
Brundig, Reinhard, 219
Brunton, Colin, 255
Bryce, Ian, 493, 1099
Brysh, Michael, 1302
Brhat, Jean, 693
Bullock, Sandra, 550
Burg, Mark, 433
Burns, Edward, 882
Bush, Thomas J., 511
Bushell, David, 284, 595
Bushell, David L., 869
Buzzi, Paolo, 1260

Calamari, Joseph, 114
Caleb, Ruth, 1304
Cannold, Mitchell, 772
Canter, Ross, 636
Canter, Stanley, 1291
Canton, Mark, 610
Caplan, Sarah, 269
Caracciolo, Joe, Jr., 954
Carcassonne, Philippe, 1131
Carmody, Don, 385, 1129
Carraro, Bill, 21
Carson, Betsy, 974
Carson, L.M. Kit, 572
Carter, Chris, 1475
Cartsonis, Susan, 390
Casamayou, Jean François, 674
Cassavetti, Patrick, 379, 1288
Castleberg, Joel, 816
Cavallo, Robert, 225, 369
Chaffin, Stokely, 584
Chaiken, Jennifer, 580
Chan, Peter, 243
Chang, Terence, 93, 1048
Chan Ye-Cheng, 373
Charbonnet, Patricia, 975
Chasman, Julia, 987
Chernov, Jeffrey, 298, 539

Cherot, Christopher Scot, 497
Cherot, S.J., 497
Chosed, Scott, 580
Chow, Raymond, 243
Christiansen, Bob, 322
Chua Lam, 819
Clahsen, Hans Peter, 1037
Clark, Jason, 548
Clark-Hall, Steve, 739
Claussen, Jacob, 89
Claybourne, Doug, 773
Clifford, Jeffrey, 1093
Coakley, H. M., 1302
Coats, Pam, 841
Coen, Ethan, 96
Cohen, Bobby, 385, 1069
Cohen, Dalisa Cooper, 1031
Cohen, David, 253
Cohen, Jonathan, 1093
Cohen, Tani, 1227
Cohn, Arthur, 195
Colichman, Paul, 441
Collins, David, 544, 589
Columbus, Chris, 1263
Compin, Antoine, 1285
Cooper, Saul, 751
Coplaert, Carl, 569
Corley, Al, 930
Corrigan, Kieran, 427
Corsini, Don, 1058
Cort, Robert W., 857
Cotone, Mario, 685
Cotte, Greg, 1291
Cowan, Cindy, 1123, 1398
Cox, Penney Finkelman, 27, 1014
Craig, Carl, 975
Crean, Linda, 215
Creste, Didier, 656
Crichton, Michael, 1242
Cronyn, Christopher, 1038
Cruise, Tom, 1466
Crystal, Billy, 847
Csupo, Gabor, 1077
Curling, Chris, 129
Currier, Lavinia, 941
Curtis, Sarah, 457
Curtis, Simon, 822
Cusack, John, 216

Damon, Mark, 282, 914
Daniels, Ron, 664
Danton, Steve, 909
David, Pierre, 738

Davidson, Boaz, 927, 1134
Davis, Andrew Z., 348
Davis, Bridget D., 497
Davis, John, 67, 306, 317
Davis, Julie, 580
De Faria, Walt, 123
DeFina, Barbara, 521
Degus, Robert J., 978
Dekrone, Jane, 127
De Laurentiis, Aurelio, 87
De Laurentiis, Guido, 1344
De Laurentiis, Raffaella, 112
Delbosc, Olivier, 1127
De Luca, Michael, 733, 978
Dembitzer, Stephen, 941
Demme, Jonathan, 77, 1134
Demme, Ted, 831, 1069
Dennis, Brian, 492
De Palma, Brian, 1205
Dershowitz, Elon, 369
DeShazer, Dennis, 69
Desplechin, Arnaud, 646
Deutchman, Ira, 385
DeVito, Danny, 715, 920
Devlin, Dean, 447
Devlin, Paul, 1186
De Walt, Suzanne, 216
Dietrich, Ralph S., 622
Dillon, Paul, 216
Dimbort, Danny, 927, 1134
DiMilia, Robert E., 308
Di Novi, Denise, 19, 992
Divincentis, D.V., 216
Dollard, Alicia, 886
Dominick, Richard, 1058
Donner, Lauren Shuler, 155, 1489
Donner, Richard, 679
Donovan, Arlene, 1361
Dorman, Joseph, 36
Doumanian, Jean, 187, 1232, 1449
Dowling, Jonathan, 1374
Drazan, Anthony, 569
Drilling, Eric, 1061
Drimmer, Stephen, 1277
Duncan, Chip, 332
Dunning, John, 139

du Plantier, Daniel Toscan, 201
Dupre, Jeff, 918
Durk, Julie, 1489
Durkin, Bill, 1436
Dwyer, Finola, 1424

East, Guy, 237, 531, 1189
Eastman, Brian, 390
Eaton, Andrew, 440
Eckert, John M., 93
Edmonds, Kenneth "Babyface", 497
Edmonds, Tracey E., 497
Eichinger, Bernd, 1474
Einbeinder, Scott, 927
Eisenman, Morrie, 1277
Ekins, Susan, 52, 1213
Ellenbogen, Eric, 1075
Emmerich, Roland, 447
Emmerich, Ute, 447
Engelman, Robert, 114
Ephron, Delia, 1489
Ephron, Nora, 1489
Ergun, Ozan, 1260
Erickson, C.O., 312
Esguerra, George, 1290
Estes, Larry, 1202
Ettinger, Wendy, 834

Faires, Jay, 406
Fantl, Michele, 126
Farrell, Mike, 943
Farrelly, Bobby, 1308
Farrelly, Peter, 1308
Fast, Adam, 885
Fay, William, 447
Feig, Erik, 584
Feldman, Dennis, 1239
Feldman, Edward S., 1348
Fellner, Eric, 96, 123, 338, 521
Ferri, Elda, 685, 957
Fiedler, John, 954
Field, Ted, 1020, 1398, 1429
Fields, Simon, 806
Fienberg, Gregg, 441
Filley, Jonathan, 597
Finerman, Wendy, 1263
Finestra, Carmen, 390
Finnell, Michael, 1197
Firestone, Jay, 1146
Fischer, Markus, 613
Fitzgerald, Thom, 476
Fleck, John, 240
Foley, Maureen, 544
Form, Andrew, 631
Forrest, David, 441
Forte, Kate, 77
Foster, David, 773

Foster, Gary, 298
Frankfurt, Peter, 114
Fraser, Nick, 640
Freeman, Morgan J., 572
Freeman, Paul, 471
Freixa, Ricardo, 749
French, Robin, 593
Friendly, David, 306, 317
Frilseth, Anne, 607
Fritsch, Manfred, 603
Froemke, Susan, 245
Fruchtmann, Uri, 1249
Fry, Carla, 733
Fuller, Simon, 1249

Gale, David, 278
Galin, Mitchell, 1262
Gallagher, Helen M., 201
Garbus, Liz, 376
Gardiner, Tracey, 697
Garfield, Louise, 476
Garner, Chip, 671
Garvin, Thomas, 195
Geels, Laurens, 210
Geisler, Robert Michael, 1319
Geissler, Dieter, 1291
Gelbart, Arnie, 476
Gellis, Andrew, 1285
Gelsberg, Ulrich, 129
Gerrans, Jon, 587
Giarraputo, Jack, 1416, 1419
Gibbs, Barbara, 60
Gibson, Ben, 746, 1380
Gibson, Jeremy, 105
Gigliotti, Donna, 1137, 1288
Gill, Mark, 865
Gilman, Gayle, 376
Gilroy, Grace, 133
Giritlian, Virginia, 699
Giuliano, Peter, 1242
Gladstein, Richard N., 385, 569
Glatzer, Peter, 282
Gleben, Bastiaan, 1146
Gleicher, Marvin, 432
Glickman, Jonathan, 539, 1081
Glickman, Rana Joh, 414
Glynn, Kathleen, 105
Godsick, Christopher, 1048
Goetzman, Gary, 77, 1272
Gold, Eric L., 1129
Goldberg, Daniel, 1174
Goldberg, Jerry, 669
Goldfine, Phillip B., 312
Goldsman, Akiva, 733
Goldsmith, Richard, 610

Goldstein, Gary W., 1058
Goldstein, Julie, 806, 1137
Goldstone, John, 294
Golin, Steve, 1052, 1483
Golutva, Aleksandr, 837
Gonda, Lou, 788
Goodman, Gregory, 538
Goos, Richard, 379
Gordon, Mark, 112, 493, 951, 1099, 1166
Gorman, James, 674
Graham, Alex, 1460
Granat, Cary, 874, 1057, 1129
Grazer, Brian, 797, 1023
Green, Whitney, 636
Greenberg, Andrew, 1075
Greene, Robyn M., 497
Grey, Brad, 309, 1048, 1419
Grosso, Daniel K., 201
Gruber, Frank, 886
Grunstein, Pierre, 649
Guglielmi, Françoise, 1131
Gund, George, 831

Hacker, Melissa, 850
Hackett, John, 325
Haddad, Patrice, 48
Haebler, Christine, 492
Hafizka, Nayeem, 1216
Hagemann, Martin, 837
Hald, Birgitte, 184
Hall, Dolly, 385, 527
Hall, Paul, 1442
Hamburger, David S., 569
Hammel, Thomas M., 394
Hamsher, Jane, 33, 965
Hanley, Chris, 139, 1366
Hannah, David, 252
Herbert, Tim, 33
Hardin, Ian, 171
Hardy, John, 920
Harel, Sharon, 264
Hargrave, Cynthia, 572
Harris, J. Todd, 67, 306
Harris, Lynn, 114
Harris, Mark R., 441
Hartley, Hal, 512
Hartley, Ted, 810
Harvey, Rupert, 199

Hauptman, Andrew, 1093
Hausman, Michael, 1361
Hawley, Richard, 1216
Hecht, Albie, 1077
Heckerling, Amy, 871
Heiduschka, Veit, 416
Helfant, Michael, 1398
Helgeland, Alex, 795
Heller, Peter, 182
Hensleigh, Jonathan, 40
Henson, Lisa, 1495
Herek, Stephen, 539
Herskovitz, Marshall, 269
Herzog, Werner, 701
Heuer, Jonathan, 578
Heuser, H. Michael, 569
Heylen, Alexandre, 1409
Heyward, Andy, 779
Hibbin, Sally, 176, 457
Hill, Grant, 1319
Hird, Christopher, 697
Hjort, Karen, 639
Ho, Koshiro, 1404
Ho, Leonard, 819
Hoberman, David, 593, 851, 1129
Hobson, Howard, 1471
Hoffman, Peter, 1146
Hoffman, Susan, 298, 1146
Holland, Gill, 280, 572
Holmes, Richard, 1149, 1409
Hope, Ted, 480, 882
Hopkins, Stephen, 733
Horberg, William, 1189
Horiguchi, Juichi, 1439
Hornstein, Martin, 1254
Horton, Charis, 1285
Howden, Alan, 1460
Howsam, Gary, 216
Hsu, Melinda, 126
Hu, Marcus, 587
Hubbard, Beth, 1471
Hubbard, Michael, 1471
Hudlin, Reginald, 1057
Hudlin, Warrington, 1057
Huggins, Erica, 1429
Huggins, Roy, 1371
Hughes, John, 1038
Hurd, Gale Ann, 40, 278

Ice Cube, 975
Iino, Hisa, 333
Ikeda, Tomoki, 1439
Inaba, Akinori, 219

Isaac, Margaret French, 1263
Isomi, Toshihiro, 618

Jacks, James, 1166
Jackson, Ruth, 531, 652
Jacobson, Tom, 810
Jacquot, Benoît, 1131
Jaffe, Stanley R., 751
Jaglom, Henry, 294
Janger, Lane, 587
Jarchow, Stephen P., 441
Jeannedeau, Yves, 218
Jenkel, Brad, 1058
Jensen, Peter Aalbaek, 625
Johns, Richard, 624
Johnson, Mark, 546
Jones, Steven A., 1456
Joo, Kiyo, 1336
Jordan, Neil, 164
Judelewicz, Pascal, 764
Judson, Stephen, 362
Jung, Christophe, 330

Kabillio, Eli, 885
Kahn, Harvey, 332
Kang, James, 1334
Kaplan, Alan, 67
Kappes, David, 1262
Karlsen, Elizabeth, 703
Karmitz, Marin, 1284
Kasdan, Jake, 1495
Kasdan, Lawrence, 546
Kassar, Mario, 722
Katz, Gail, 810
Katzenberg, Jeffrey, 1014
Kauffman, Gary, 1061
Kazan, Nicholas, 369
Kehela, Karen, 797
Kellek, Amos, 1275
Kelly, Alexandra, 171
Kelmenson, Paul, 1062
Kemler, Andrew, 171
Kemp, Barry, 943
Kent, Nicholas, 531
Kenworthy, Duncan, 664
Kessler, Henri M., 1181
Khoury, Gabriel, 302
Kiarostami, Abbas, 1293
Kidney, Ric, 797
Kidron, Beeban, 1280
Kilik, Jon, 500, 978
King, Sandy, 615
King, Zalman, 601
Kirkpatrick, David, 909
Kirschner, David, 133
Klainberg, Lesli, 949
Klasky, Arlene, 1077

Klein, Christa-Maria, 1037
Koch, Mark W., 112, 733
Kohner, Pancho, 751
Kolyer, Diane, 1343
Komaki, Jiro, 1439
Konrad, Cathy, 1447
Koontz, Dean, 967
Kopelson, Anne, 958, 1371
Kopelson, Arnold, 958, 1371
Kottenbrook, Carol, 927
Kowalchuk, William, 1075
Kozlov, Sergei, 1315
Krane, Jonathan D., 1000
Krausz, Danny, 603
Kroopf, Scott, 1020, 1398, 1429
Kufus, Thomas, 837
Kunming, Chen, 346
Kurdyla, Ted, 369
Kushner, Donald, 1058
Kuzui, Fran Rubel, 914
Kuzui, Kaz, 914

Labadie, Jean, 219
Ladd, Alan, Jr., 759
Lahti, James, 772
Lake, Michael, 1291
Landaas, Robert William, 332
Landis, John, 119
Landsberg, Cleve, 72
Lane, Steve, 967
Larsen, Nancy, 933
Lashbrook, Rick, 631
Lassally, Romi, 546
Laubacher, Robert, 544
Leach, Sheryl, 69
Leahy, Michael, 967
Lee, Deborah, 461
Lee, Quentin, 1152
Lee, Spike, 500
Lee, Stan, 114
Leed, Rick, 390
Leeds, Arthur, 1334
Lenkov, Peter M., 199
Lennard, Laurie, 1228
Lerner, Avi, 927, 1134
Levin, Marc, 1181
Levine, Hank, 1414
Levinsohn, Gary, 112, 493, 951, 1099, 1166
Levinson, Barry, 546, 1242
Levinson, Stephen, 631
Levy, Robert L., 755
Levy-Hinte, Jeff, 400, 527
Lewis, Brad, 27

Lewis, Claudia, 1180
Liber, Rodney, 1456
Linde, David, 480
Link, Andr, 139
Linson, Art, 461
Lloyd, Christopher, 325
LoCash, Robert, 72
Locke, Peter, 1058
Loeb, Joseph III, 394
Longinotto, Kim, 316
Lorimore, Alec, 362
Lotfi, Jim, 909
Louis, R.J., 1213
Low, Stephen, 772
Ludwig, Avram, 1061
Luff, Brad, 1387

Ma, Maria, 406
Macaulay, Scott, 400
McCleary, Joel, 941
McCormick, Patrick, 1263
MacDonald, Laurie, 773
McDonnell, Michael, 1387
McFadzean, David, 390
McGauley, Victor, 322
MacGillivray, Greg, 362
MacGregor-Scott, Peter, 958
McGuinn, Patrick, 126
Machenko, Mykola, 407
Machlis, Neil, 1000
McHugh, Jason, 171, 914
Mckay, Terry, 1040
McLaglen, Mary, 550, 992
McMahon, Patricia, 327
McMillan, Terry, 563
Madden, David, 857
Madigan-Yorkin, Alix, 1483
Madison, Alan, 1343
Mailer, Michael, 1366
Mancini, Don, 133
Mancuso, Frank, Jr., 1062, 1239
Mankiewicz, Christopher, 958
Mann, Mary Beth, 280
Marcovich, Carlos, 1440
Marignac, Martine, 135
Marignane, Guy, 420
Mark, Laurence, 291, 887, 1163
Markey, Patrick, 554
Master P, 578
Mathis, Catherine, 656
Matsushita, Chiaki, 1439
Matthews, Gina, 1387
Medavoy, Brian, 1058
Medjuck, Joe, 1174
Meek, Scott, 1389

Meh, Mehra, 255
Meistrich, Larry, 75, 512, 595, 869
Menage, Chiara, 746
Menager, Christophe, 330
Mendel, Barry, 1085
Mendillo, Tag, 631
Merchant, Ismail, 1216
Mestres, Ricardo, 1038
Meyerson, Aaron, 780
Michaels, Joel B., 722
Michaels, Lorne, 871
Michel, Eric, 218
Milchan, Arnon, 225, 269, 851
Miller, Bennet, 253
Miller, Bill, 60
Miller, David, 1061
Miller, Donna, 1425
Miller, George, 60
Miller, J.B., 253
Miller, R. Paul, 788
Miller, Robert, 587
Miller, Theodore, 253
Minoff, Marvin, 943
Missonnier, Marc, 1127
Mitchell, Doug, 60
Mitran, Doru, 420
Miura, Kanji, 455
Monks, Gardner, 1180
Moore, Kenny, 1466
Mora, Jorge Estrada, 749
Moravec, Petr, 674
More, Erwin, 1058
Morgan, Kathy, 216
Morgan, Leslie, 903
Mori, Masayuki, 395, 1223
Moritz, Neal H., 584, 1387
Morris, Redmond, 164
Morrissey, John, 21
Mortimer, David, 105
Mortorff, Lawrence, 1291
Moseley, David, 109
Moszkowica, Martin, 1474
Motokki, Katsuhide, 455
Mruvka, Alan, 306
Murakami, Koichi, 1439
Murphy, Don, 33, 965
Murray, Glynis, 1149, 1409
Muska, Susan, 127
Musso, Eugene, 930
Myron, Ben, 69

Nabatoff, Diane, 1020, 1398
Nabeshima, Hisao, 1223
Nabulsi, Laila, 379

Nagasawa, Masahiko, 1439
Nakagawa, Noriaki, 914
Nansun Chi, 634
Nathanson, Michael, 269
Nava, Gregory, 1442
Nemeth, Stephen, 67, 306, 379, 1442
Netter, Gil, 72
Neufeld, Mace, 112, 733
Nevinny, Victoria, 969
Nevins, Sheila, 672
Newirth, Charles, 225, 546, 943
Niami, Ramin, 1221
Niccol, Andrew, 1348
Nichols, Mike, 1000
Nicita, Wallis, 1174
Nicksay, David, 851
Niederhoffer, Galt, 572
Niitsu, Taketo, 455
Nikkah-Azad, V., 815
Nolte, Nick, 1
Nordahl, Dag, 619
Norman, Marc, 1137
Nozik, Michael, 882, 1193
Nugent, Ginny, 951

Obel, Michael, 874
Obst, Lynda, 550, 1154
Ogborn, Kate, 1380
Ogden, Jennifer, 563
O'Hara, Robin, 400
Ohlsson, Bertil, 667
Okuyama, Kazuyoshi, 333, 455, 1223
Olafsdottir, Greta, 127
Oldman, Gary, 875
Oman, Chad, 40, 348
Ordesky, Mark, 954
Orent, Kerry, 1069
Orr, Betty, 255
Ostrow, Randy, 1447
Ouaknine, Jacky, 407
Owen, Alison, 338

Paleologos, Nicholas, 569
Palmer, Isaac, 772
Panahi, Jafar, 815
Pang Ming, 410
Parent, Mary, 978
Parfitt, David, 1137
Parker, Trey, 171
Parkes, Walter, 285, 773, 1197
Par, Lisa Katselas, 822
Paseornek, Michael, 139, 519
Paterson, Andy, 531
Patric, Jason, 1483
Patton, Jody, 788

Paxton, Michael, 57
Peak, Kearie, 21
Pearson, Noel, 264
Pedas, Jim, 1436
Pedas, Ted, 1436
Peipers, David, 1181
Pelecanos, George P., 1436
Pennebaker, Frazer, 834
Penotti, John, 996
Perlovich, Vladimir, 657
Perry, Steve, 679
Persinger, Marshall, 1269
Pescarolo, Leo, 1344
Pevner, Stephen, 1483
Pfeffer, Rachel, 232, 554
Piel, Jean-Louis, 219
Pilcher, Lydia Dean, 219
Pink, Steve, 216
Pleshette, Lynn, 1348
Plympton, Bill, 582
Pojhan, Aladdin, 601
Pollack, Sydney, 1189
Pollock, Dale, 779
Porter, Pliny, 1263
Poster, Meryl, 1447
Potter, Barr, 471, 615
Powell, Nik, 703, 1424
Pressman, Edward R., 1366
Pringle, Bob, 967
Proft, Patr, 1474
Putz, Uli, 89

Querejeta, Elias, 1145

Rabins, Sandra, 27, 1014
Rachmil, Michael, 757
Radcliffe, Mark, 1263
Radclyffe, Sarah, 246, 674
Raffin, Deborah, 1460
Randall, Stephen, 269
Ranvaud, Don, 195
Raphael, Paul, 667
Redford, Robert, 232, 554, 882, 1193
Reed, Aaron, 864
Reher, Kevin, 145
Rehme, Robert, 112, 733
Reichebner, Harald, 622
Reisman, Linda, 471
Reitman, Ivan, 1174
Relph, Simon, 652
Remlov, Tom, 607
Renzi, Maggie, 788
Reo, Ray, 309
Resnick, Gina, 240
Revitte, Joe, 954

Rice, Tracie Graham, 969
Rice, Wayne, 1277
Rich, Lee, 298
Ridpath, Deborah, 684
Ripp, Artie, 779
Ripstein, Alfredo, Jr., 805
Rival, Pierre, 407
Robbins, Mitchell B., 865
Roben, Charles, 225
Roberdeau, John, 1319
Roberts, Julia, 1263
Roberts, Lisa, 1302
Robinson, James F., 1269
Robinson, James G., 757, 1213, 1474
Robson, Karen, 1221
Rogers, Beau, 441
Rokisky, Rita J., 325
Rosen, Robert L., 1474
Rosenberg, Rick, 322
Rosenberg, Tom, 969, 987, 1040
Rosenblatt, Bart, 930
Rosendahl, Carl, 27
Rosenfelt, Scott, 1202
Rosenow, James, 252
Rosner, Louise, 394
Ross, Gary, 978
Roth, Daryl, 587
Rotholz, Ron, 75
Rousselet, Philippe, 764
Roven, Charles, 369
Rubenstein, Anthony, 657
Rubinstein, Richard P., 1262
Rudin, Scott, 232, 1348, 1361
Rugolo-Judd, Gina, 1058
Ryan, Lata, 1020, 1475
Rywin, Lew, 898

Saalfield, Catherine Gund, 469
Sackheim, Daniel, 1475
Sackman, Jeff, 139, 519
Saint-Jean, Michel, 1426
Salerno, Robert, 75
Saly, Lilian, 48
Samaha, Elie, 1134
Sams, Alicia, 896
Samuelson, Marc, 1460
Samuelson, Peter, 1460
Sandoz, Giles, 768
Sanger, Jonathan, 1466

Saperstein, Richard, 733
Saphier, Peter, 112
Saraf, Peter, 1272
Sarandon, Susan, 1263
Sarkissian, Arthur, 1081
Saunders, David, 601
Saxon, Edward, 77, 1272
Schamus, James, 480
Scheidlinger, Rob, 246
Schiff, Paul, 1085
Schiffer, Michael, 1398
Schindler, Deborah, 563
Schindler, Peter, 847, 1154
Schippers, Ton, 327
Schlösser, Katrin, 837
Schlueter, Steven, 1061
Schmidlin, Rick, 1339
Scholz, John P., 275
Schroeder, Adam, 1166, 1348
Schroeder, Barbet, 298, 1146
Schwary, Ronald L., 781
Schweickert, Joyce, 1269
Schwimmer, David, 631
Scorsese, Martin, 521
Scott, Allan, 1044
Scott, Ridley, 237
Scott, Tony, 237
Seavey, Nina Gilden, 935
Seeber, Michael, 1034
Segalla, Kevin, 1436
Segan, Allison Lyon, 493, 951
Selianov, Sergei, 137
Sender, Julie Bergman, 1174
Serpico, Jim, 831
Shadyac, Tom, 943
Shainberg, Steven, 538
Shamberg, Michael, 715, 920
Shareshian, Steven, 1134
Shaw, Peter, 801
Sheen, Simon, 1334
Sheinberg, Bill, 1187
Sheinberg, Jon, 1187
Sheinberg, Sid, 1187
Shepherd, Bill, 822
Sher, Stacey, 715, 920
Sherwin, Robert, 308
Shestack, Jon, 312
Shigemura, Hajime, 1439
Shivas, Mark, 589, 1044

Short, Trevor, 927, 1134
Shu Kei, 410
Shwarztein, Meyer, 738
Shyer, Charles, 936
Siefert, Lynn, 246
Sienega, Corey, 133
Sighvatsson, Sigurjon, 969, 987, 1040
Sikora, Jim, 153
Silberschneider, Kurt, 1291
Silver, Joel, 679
Silverman, Lloyd, 1146
Simmons, Rudd, 521
Simon, Neil, 857
Simon, Randy, 970
Simon, Stephen, 1429
Simonds, Robert, 309, 468, 1416, 1419
Simpson, Peter, 1044
Sinclair, Nigel, 237, 531, 1189
Singer, Bryan, 33
Singer, Joseph M., 317, 797
Singh, Anant, 1304
Singleton, John, 1471
Sinniger, Alfi, 1096
Skinner, David, 1202
Skotchdopole, James W., 348
Slater, Christian, 1398
Sloss, John, 658, 788, 860
Smith, Bradford W., 1471
Smith, Gary, 1149
Smith, Leslie L., 275
Smith, Russell, 759
Snider, Dee, 284
Snipes, Wesley, 93, 114, 322
Soderbergh, Steven, 978
Soisson, Joel, 967
Sollo, Frederick, 569
Solomon, Frances-Anne, 746
Sonnenfeld, Barry, 920
Soria, Mireille, 356
Spellman-Silverman, Erica, 519
Spielberg, Steven, 285, 773, 1099
Spione, James, 933
Spring, Helena, 1304
Springer, Jerry, 1058
Stabler, Steve, 1058
Stack, Jonathan, 376
Startz, Jane, 806
Steel, Charles, 1280
Steel, Dawn, 225, 369
Steinberg, Michael, 1308
Stern, Jay, 1081
Stern, Jonathan, 772

Stern, Tom, 601
Stevens, George, Jr., 1319
Stewart, Allyn, 751
Stier, Geoff, 987
Stillerman, Joel, 831, 1069
Stillman, Whit, 658
Stipe, Michael, 1389
Stocker, Kurt, 603
Stoltz, Eric, 816
Stone, Matt, 171, 914
Stone, Oliver, 1123
Stone, Robert, 851
Stone, Webster, 851
Stoneman, Rod, 129, 589
Stover, Susan A., 527
Strange, Michael, 10
Stratton, Richard, 1181
Stricker, Michael, 622
Stroh, Etchie, 306
Strohm, Julia, 896
Stroller, Louis A., 1205
Stussak, Heinz, 1034
Sutton, Saskia, 1044
Swerdlow, Ezra, 1052

Tadross, Michael, 610
Talalay, Rachel, 123
Tambellini, Flavio R., 929
Tan, Jimmy, 346
Tannenbaum, Jeremy, 433
Tannenbaum, Ted, 969, 987, 1040
Tapson, Polly, 1280
Tarantino, Quentin, 414
Tarlov, Mark, 954
Tarr, Susan, 246
Tec, Roland, 18
Temple, Amanda, 400
Terry, Bridget, 1134
Thomas, Betty, 173
Thomas, Bradley, 1308
Thomas, Garth, 1280
Thomas, Jeremy, 898
Thompson, Barnaby, 1249
Thompson, David M., 1304
Thompson, John, 927, 1134
Tisch, Steve, 21
Tobias, Andrew, 918
Tobias, Glen A., 433
Todman, Bill, Jr., 757
Toffler, Van, 278
Tolomelli, Elisa, 195
Tolstunov, Igor, 1315
Tonnerre, Martine de Clermont, 195
Topei, David, 136
Topping, Jenno, 173, 317

Torres, Marcelo, 929
Touges, Kirk, 974
Trench, Tracey, 356, 593
Tsang, Eric, 243
Tsao, Willy, 330
Tsuge, Yasushi, 395
Tsukamoto, Shinya, 1336
Tucci, Stanley, 597
Tugend, Jennie Lew, 1253
Turman, Lawrence, 21
Tyrer, William, 822

Ufland, Harry, 903
Urbanski, Douglas, 875
Ursini, Amedeo, 699

Vachon, Christine, 480, 1389
Van Sant, Gus, 1023
van Warmerdam, Alex, 327
van Warmerdam, Marc, 327
Van Wyck, Jim, 40, 679
Vance, Marilyn, 306
Vernon, James Michael, 1146
Veronis, Nick, 277
Victor, Daniel J., 512
Vince, Anne, 10
Vince, Robert, 10
Vince, William, 10
Viner, Michael, 1460
Viscidi, Marcus, 1040
Visser, Matthias, 126
von Alberti, Irene, 304

Wachsberger, Patrick, 379
Wagner, Paul, 935, 1466
Wald, Andrew, 1242
Waldleitner, Luggi, 89
Walker-McBay, Anne, 860
Walkow, Gary Alan, 886
Wallace, Randall, 759
Walpole, Robert, 589
Wang, Wayne, 219
Warner, Aron, 27
Watson, Eric, 970
Wax, Steve, 1384
Weber, Charles, 216
Wechsler, Nick, 987
Weide, Robert B., 672
Weinstein, Bob, 364, 385, 806, 874, 967, 996, 1057, 1069, 1129, 1137, 1288, 1447

Weinstein, Harvey, 364, 385, 806, 874, 967, 996, 1057, 1069, 1129, 1137, 1288, 1447
Weintraub, Jerry, 52, 1213
Weisgal, Jonathan, 954
Weisman, Matthew, 394
Weiss, Robert K., 871
Wendlandt, Matthias, 930
Werk, Das, 1221
Wernick, Sandy, 1419

Wessler, Charles B., 1308
Wheaton, Paul D., 1302
Wick, Douglas, 575
Wild, Nettie, 974
Willenson, Seth, 1075
Williams, Hype, 75
Williams, Marsha Garles, 943
Williams, Matt, 390
Williams, Michael, 543
Willocks, Tim, 1280
Wilson, Colin, 1197
Wilson, Owen, 1085
Wilson, William W. III, 903
Windelov, Vibeke, 625

Windisch, Ingrid, 898
Winfrey, Oprah, 77
Winkler, Knut, 1096
Wisnievitz, David, 232
Wlodkowski, Stan, 1193
Wöbke, Thomas, 89
Wolf, Deny, 1023
Wolstenholme, John, 801
Wong Kar-Wai, 373
Woo, John, 93, 1048
Woods, Cary, 1447
Wooley, Stephen, 703
Woolley, Stepehn, 164
Woolley, Stephen, 1424

Wooton, Patty, 27
Wuhrmann, Daniel, 48

Xu Wei, 410

Yahn, Michelle, 1436
Yamagami, Tetsujiro, 1404
Yamner, David, 253
Yang, Janet, 1123, 1495
Yauch, Adam, 406
Yehranian, Yalda, 965
Yoshida, Takio, 395, 1223
Yoshizaki, Michiyo, 129, 219, 1460

Young, Irwin, 1436
Yuan, Zhang, 330

Zaillian, Steven, 232
Zanuck, Richard D., 285
Zarpas, Chris, 237
Zide, Warren, 93
Ziegler, Peter, 1291
Zimmer, Christopher, 739
Zucker, David, 72
Zugsmith, Albert, 1339
Zurlo, Rosemarie, 201
Zwick, Edward, 269, 1137, 1154

DIRECTORS

Abrahams, Jim, 755
Abramson, Neil, 1058
Adler, Carine, 1380
Alcorn, Keith, 432
Allen, Woody, 187
Almodóvar, Pedro, 709
Altman, Robert, 433
Anderson, Brad, 865
Anderson, Paul, 1213
Anderson, Wes, 1085
Angelou, Maya, 322
Antonijevic, Peter, 123
Arcadias, Laurence, 432
Arnfred, Morten, 625
Aronofsky, Darren, 970
August, Bille, 674
Avati, Pupi, 87
Aviram, Nitzan, 509

Bailey, John, 715
Baird, Stuart, 1371
Balabanov, Aleksei, 137
Bancroft, Tony, 841
Barker, Nicholas, 1384
Barreto, Bruno, 403, 902
Baumbach, Noah, 816
Bay, Michael, 40
Beatty, Warren, 155
Becker, Harold, 797
Benigni, Roberto, 685
Benton, Robert, 1361
Berg, Peter, 1398
Berman, Shari Springer, 896
Beyer, Troy, 684
Bierman, Robert, 801
Blanks, Jamie, 1387
Bolofo, Koto, 656

Boorman, John, 427
Booth, Mike, 432
Bornedal, Ole, 874
Bowman, Rob, 1475
Boyum, Steve, 780
Bramer, Monte, 949
Breashears, David, 362
Breathnach, Paddy, 589
Brest, Martin, 781
Briggs, David, 126
Brinkerhoff, Joel, 432
Broomfield, Nick, 640
Bross, Eric, 1302
Burns, Edward, 882

Campanella, Juan J., 749
Campbell, Martin, 773
Cannon, Danny, 584, 969
Cardone, J.S., 927
Carpenter, John, 615
Chabrol, Claude, 1284
Chahine, Youssef, 302
Chan, Peter, 243
Chapman, Brenda, 1014
Chappelle, Joe, 967
Chechik, Jeremiah, 52
Chelsom, Peter, 806
Cholodenko, Lisa, 527
Christopher, Mark, 385
Chukhrai, Pavel, 1315
Coen, Joel, 96
Cohn, Alan, 278
Collins, Vince, 432
Columbus, Chris, 1264
Condon, Bill, 441
Connelly, Theresa, 987
Cook, Barry, 841

Coraci, Frank, 1416, 1419
Coto, Manny, 1253
Cox, Jan, 432
Cuarón, Alfonso, 461
Currier, Lavinia, 941
Cybulski, Mary, 216

Dahl, John, 1069
Dante, Joe, 1197
Darby, Jonathan, 575
Darnell, Eric, 27
David, Larry, 1228
Davis, Andrew, 958
Davis, Julie, 580
Davis, Tamra, 468
DeBartolo, Tiffanie, 325
DeCoteau, David, 669
Demme, Jonathan, 77, 1272
Demme, Ted, 831
de Oliveria, Manoel, 1405
De Palma, Brian, 1205
Desplechin, Arnaud, 646
Deutch, Howard, 857
Devlin, Paul, 1186
DiCillo, Tom, 1040
Dobkin, David, 237
Donar, David, 432
Donner, Richard, 679
Dorman, Joseph, 36
Dornhelm, Robert, 129
Downing, Tod, 126
Drazen, Anthony, 569
Drilling, Eric, 1061, 1061
Du Chau, Frederick, 1031
Duigan, John, 664, 667

Dumont, Bruno, 693
Dunne, Griffin, 992
Dupre, Jeff, 918

Eisenhardt, Bob, 245
Elfont, Harry, 173
Eling, Stefan, 432
Ellin, Doug, 631
Elliott, Stephan, 1424
Emmerich, Roland, 447
Enright, Amanda, 432
Ephron, Nora, 1489
Eriksen, Gordon, 671
Esguerra, George, 1290
Eyre, Chris, 1202

Faber, Christian, 864
Faenza, Roberto, 957
Farrelly, Bobby, 1308
Farrelly, Peter, 1308
Fitzgerald, Thom, 476
Fogel, Eric, 432
Foley, Maureen, 544
Fons, Jorge, 805
Fortenberry, John, 871
Frakes, Jonathan, 1254
Frankenheimer, John, 1062
Franklin, Carl, 903
Frears, Stephen, 521
Freeman, Morgan J., 572
Froemke, Susan, 245
Fuqua, Antoine, 1048

Gallo, Phil, 1425
Gallo, Vincent, 139
Garbus, Liz, 376
Gatlif, Tony, 420

Gibbons, Rodney, 738
Gilbert, Brian, 1460
Gilliam, Terry, 379
Glatter, Lesli Linka, 1020
Goldbacher, Sandra, 557
Goldberg, Howard, 332
Gomer, Steve, 69
Gomez, Nick, 595
Gorris, Marleen, 822
Gosse, Bob, 869
Gray, F. Gary, 851
Greengrass, Paul, 1304
Guest, Christopher, 19
Guzmán, Patricio, 75, 218
Gudiguian, Robert, 768
Gyllenhaal, Stephen, 548

Hacker, Melissa, 850
Hadleigh-West, Maggie, 1414
Hamburg, John, 1093
Hamm, Nick, 1288
Haneke, Michael, 416
Hartley, Hal, 512
Haynes, Todd, 1389
Hedden, Roger, 519
Hegedus, Chris, 834
Herek, Stephen, 539
Herman, Mark, 703
Herskovitz, Marshall, 269
Herzog, Werner, 701
Hewitt, Peter, 123
Hickner, Steven, 1014
Higashi, Yoichi, 1404
Hoblit, Gregory, 369
Holland, Todd, 636
Hooks, Kevin, 112

Hopkins, Stephen, 733
Howitt, Peter, 1189
Hung, Samo, 819
Huse, Michael F., 1037
Hutton, Timothy, 306
Hytner, Nicholas, 887

Ice Cube, 975
Imamura, Shohei, 333
Iosseliani, Otar, 135
Ishii, Takashi, 455
Ivory, James, 1216
Iwai, Shunji, 1439

Jenkins, Tamara, 1193
Johnson, John, 1035
Johnson, Mark Steven, 1163
Johnson, Tim, 27
Johnston, Heather, 671
Jones, Kirk, 1409
Jordan, Neil, 164

Kalmenson, Bill, 1227
Kaplan, Deborah, 173
Kapur, Shekhar, 338
Kasdan, Jake, 1495
Kaufer, Jonathan, 67
Kaye, Tony, 21
Kellman, Barnet, 1187
Kelly, Sarah, 414
Kiarostami, Abbas, 1293
Kidron, Beeban, 1280
King, Zalman, 601
Kirkman, Tim, 280
Kitano, Takeshi, 395, 1223
Klapisch, Cdric, 1377
Koch, Ulrike, 1096
Kollek, Amos, 1275
Kopple, Barbara, 1449
Kovalyov, Igor, 1077
Kowalchuk, William, 1075
Krishtofovich, Vyachleslav, 407
Kwietniowski, Richard, 739

LaBute, Neil, 1483
LaGravenese, Richard, 715
Landis, John, 119
Lasseter, John, 145
Lea, Frances,
Leder, Mimi, 285
Lee, Iara, 831
Lee, Quentin, 1152
Lee, Spike, 500
Lehmann, Michael, 847
Leland, David, 652

Leonard, Brett, 1285
Levin, Marc, 1181
Levinson, Barry, 1242
Lewis, Everett, 1180
Lima, Walter, Jr., 929
Link, Caroline, 89
Linklater, Richard, 860
Loach, Ken, 176
Longinotto, Kim, 316
Low, Stephen, 772
Luna, Bigas, 201
Lyne, Adrian, 722

McAnuff, Des, 246
McDonald, Bruce, 492
MacGillivray, Greg, 362
McGuinn, Patrick, 126
McKinney, Brandon, 432
MacKinnon, Gillies, 1044
McNamara, Sean Patrick, 1334
McNaughton, John, 1456
Madden, John, 1137
Madison, Alan, 1343
Main, Stewart, 126
Malick, Terrence, 1319
Mamet, David, 1232
Marcovich, Carlos, 1440
Martin, Michael, 578
Martin, Richard, 10
Matthews, John, 126
Maybury, John, 746
Mayer, Daisy V.S., 1471
Maysles, Albert, 245
Mazziotti, Thomas F., 215
Medak, Peter, 1239
Merlet, Agnes, 48
Meyers, Nancy, 936
Mignatti, Victor, 136
Miller, Bennet, 253
Miller, George, 60
Miller, Troy, 610
Miner, Steve, 471
Mir-Hosseini, Ziba, 316
Moffett, Joel, 126
Montgomery, Tyron, 432
Moore, Michael, 105
Morel, Gael, 411
Muska, Susan, 127

Nalluri, Bharat, 624
Natali, Vincenzo, 255
Nava, Gregory, 1442
Niami, Ramin, 1221
Nichols, Mike, 1000
Nicholson, William, 390

Nittoli, Tony, 432
Normand, Michael, 308
Norrington, Stephen, 114
Nutter, David, 312

O'Connor, Pat, 264
O'Fallon, Peter, 1277
O'Haver, Tommy, 109
Olafsdottir, Greta, 127
Oldman, Gary, 875
Oremland, Paul, 697
Ozon, François, 1127
Ozpetek, Ferzan, 1260

Panahi, Jafar, 815
Parello, Chuck, 511
Parisot, Dean, 546
Parker, Trey, 171, 914
Pate, Jonas, 282
Pate, Joshua, 282
Pavia, Mark, 1262
Paxton, Michael, 57
Pejo, Robert-Adrian, 1034
Pennebaker, D.A., 834
Peretz, Jesse, 400
Pieplow, John, 284
Pirozek, Sarah, 406
Plympton, Bill, 432, 582
Poirer, Manuel, 1426
Pradal, Manuel, 764
Proft, Pat, 1474
Proyas, Alex, 271
Pulcini, Robert, 896
Purves, Barry, 126

Raimi, Sam, 1166
Rappaport, Mark, 1162
Ratner, Brett, 1081
Redford, Robert, 554
Reinhard, Jud, 613
Reitman, Ivan, 1174
Reynolds, Scott, 1374
Rideau, Wilbert, 376
Roberts, John, 951
Robinson, James F., 1269
Rodriquez, Robert, 364
Roos, Don, 909
Rosenow, James, 252
Rosi, Francesco, 1344
Rosler, Alexander, 795
Ross, Gary, 978
Rouen, Brigitte, 989
Rozowitzky, Stefan, 603
Ruben, Joseph, 1052
Ruiz, Raoul, 425, 1146
Ryan, William, 1038

Saalfield, Catherine Gund, 469
Saget, Bob, 309
Salles, Walter, 195
Salomon, Mikael, 493
Sanford, Arlene, 593
Santucci, Walter, 432
Sayles, John, 788
Schenkel, Carl, 1291
Schlondorff, Volker, 898, 930
Schrader, Paul, 1
Schroeder, Barbet, 298
Schwarta, Stefan, 1149
Scott, Darin, 182
Scott, Tony, 348
Seavey, Nina Gilden, 935
Semler, Dean, 394
Shadyac, Tom, 943
Shelton, Millicent, 1057
Sherwin, Robert, 308
Shyamalan, M. Night, 1447
Sikora, Jim, 153
Silberling, Brad, 225
Singer, Bryan, 33
Skinner, Emily, 432
Skjoldbjaerg, Erik, 607
Skoog, Susan, 1436
Sletaune, Pal, 619
Sloan, Brian, 587
Smith, Leslie L., 275
Soderbergh, Steven, 920
Sokurov, Aleksandr, 837
Solondz, Todd, 480
Sommers, Stephen, 291
Soth, Chris, 394
Spheeris, Penelope, 1129
Spielberg, Steven, 1099
Spiers, Bob, 1249
Sprecher, Jill, 240
Stack, Jonathan, 376
Stave, Karl, 432
Stillman, Whit, 658
Sturgis, Jeff, 432
Styron, Susanna, 1134
Sullivan, Kevin Rodner, 563

Tac, Roland, 18
Tennant, Andy, 356
Thomas, Betty, 317
Tibaldi, Antonio, 699
Tintori, John, 216
Toback, James, 1366
Toledano, Manuel, 1145

Towne, Robert, 1466
Travers, Kathryn, 432
Treut, Monika, 304
Tsui Hark, 634
Tsukamoto, Shinya, 1336
Tucci, Stanley, 597
Tucker, Anand, 531

Underwood, Ron, 810

Van Diem, Mike, 210
Van Sant, Gus, 1023
van Warmerdam, Alex, 327
Veloz, David, 965
Veronis, Nick, 277
Vincent, Christian, 649
Vinterberg, Thomas, 184
Virgien, Norton, 1077
von Sherler Mayer, Daisy, 751
von Trier, Lars, 625

Walkow, Cary, 887
Wallace, Randall, 759
Walz, Martin, 622
Wang, Wayne, 219
Ward, Vincent, 1429
Warren, John, 757
Waters, John, 954
Weide, Robert B., 672
Weir, Peter, 1348
Welles, Orson, 1339
Wells, Simon, 1014
Wescott, Margaret, 1272
Whitaker, Forest, 550
Wierzbicki, Krzysztof, 639
Wild, Nettie, 974
Williams, Hype, 75
Winterbottom, Michael, 440
Wong, Che-Kirk, 93
Wong Kar-Wai, 373
Wu Ming, 410

Yakin, Boaz, 996
Yamamoto, Masashi, 618
Young, John G., 933
Yu, Ronny, 133
Yuan, Zhang, 330

Zaillian, Steven, 232
Zamm, Alex, 199
Zhou Xiaowen, 346
Zucker, David, 72
Zukovic, Dan, 657
Zwick, Edward, 1154

SCREENWRITERS

Abrahams, Jim, 755
Abrams, Anthony, 278
Abrams, J.J., 40
Adair, Gilbert, 739
Adams, Hunter
Doherty, 943
Adler, Carine, 1380
Alcott, Louisa May, 738
Alcott, Todd, 27
Alexie, Sherman, 1202
Allen, Woody, 187
Allin, Michael, 593
Almodóvar, Pedro, 709
Alvarado, Dan, 1152
Amigorena, Santiago, 989
Anderson, Brad, 865
Anderson, Wes, 1085
Andrews, Tina, 1442
Arabov, Iruii, 837
Armstrong, Mike, 831
Aronofsky, Darren, 970
Aschner, Michael, 1075
Atkins, Eileen, 822
Attanasio, Paul, 1242
Avati, Pupi, 87
Aviram, Nitzan, 509
Aykroyd, Dan, 119

Bacri, Jean-Pierre, 1377
Bagnall, Alison, 139
Baker, Noel S., 492
Balabanov, Aleksei, 137
Balzac, Honore de, 246, 941
Banks, Russell, 1
Barker, Nicholas, 1384
Barker, Pat, 1044
Bass, Ron, 563, 1264, 1429
Baumbach, Noah, 816
Beatty, Warren, 155
Beaujour, Jrme, 1131
Becker, Manfred, 974
Bemelmans, Ludwig, 751
Benguigui, Jean, 1284
Benigni, Roberto, 685
Bennett, Ronan, 129
Benoit, Jean-Louis, 201
Benton, Robert, 1361
Berg, Peter, 1398
Berman, Rick, 1254
Bernstein, Jon, 1059
Bernstein, Marcos, 195
Berry, Caspar, 624
Beyer, Troy, 684
Bijelic, Andre, 255

Black, J. Anderson, 1291
Bloch, Robert, 1023
Bloom, Steve, 610
Bodden, Anthony, 75
Bolofo, Claudia Mapula, 656
Bonitzer, Pascal, 425
Boorman, John, 427
Bornedal, Ole, 874
Boston, Michael, 699
Bostwick-Singer, Eugenia, 841
Boyce, Brandon, 33
Boyce, Frank Cottrell, 531
Bram, Christopher, 441
Bramer, Monte, 949
Brancato, Chris, 1239
Brennan, Neal, 468
Briggs, David, 126
Broder, Adam Larson, 278
Brooks, Adam, 77, 992
Bross, Eric, 1302
Browning, Michael, 1174
Burns, Edward, 882
Burroughs, Edgar Rice, 1291
Busia, Akosua, 77

Cahill, Tim, 362
Callaway, Trey, 584
Campanella, Juan, 749
Canals, Cuca, 201
Cardone, J.S., 927
Carducci, Joe, 153
Carneiro, Joao Emanuel, 195
Carriere, Jean-Claude, 219, 898
Carter, Chris, 1475, Cartwright, Jim, 703
Cerami, Vincenzo, 685
Cesario, Jeff, 610
Chabrol, Claude, 1284
Chahine, Youssef, 302
Chapman, Vera, 1031
Chappelle, Dave, 468
Chase, James Hadley, 930
Chevarria, Jorge Guerricae, 709
Chodorov, Stephen, 935
Cholodenko, Lisa, 527
Christopher, Mark, 385
Coen, Ethan, 96
Coen, Joel, 96
Colan, Gene, 114
Condon, Bill, 441
Connelly, Theresa, 987

Conrad, Joseph, 1280
Cooper, Merian C., 810
Costello, Fleur, 624
Coto, Manny, 1253
Cox, Alex, 379
Craig, Laurie, 951
Cray, Robert, 697
Crichton, Michael, 1242
Croner, Karen, 903
Crystal, Billy, 847
Csupo, Gabor, 1077
Cudworth, Tom, 1302
Currier, Lavinia, 941

Darby, Jonathan, 575
David, Larry, 1228
Davies, Tod, 379
Davis, Julie, 580
DeBartolo, Tiffanie, 325
Decoin, Didier, 201
Decter, Ed, 1308
DeMicco, Kirk, 1031
DeMonaco, James, 851
de Oliveira, Manoel, 1405
De Palma, Brian, 1205
DeShazer, Dennis, 69
de Souza, Steven E., 634
Desplechin, Arnaud, 646
Devlin, Dean, 447
Dewhurst, Keith, 652
DiCillo, Tom, 1040
Dicicco, Kevin, 10
Dickens, Charles, 461
Dietl, Bo, 902
Dillon, Patrick, 1221
Dobbs, Lem, 271
Dominy, Jeannine, 269
Dorman, Joseph, 36
Dostoevsky, Fyodor, 886, 887
Douglas, Leroy, 578
Downing, Todd, 126
Drummond, Randy, 1290
Duigan, Virginia, 667
Dumas, Alexandre, 759
Dumont, Bruno, 693
Duncan, Lois, 584
du Pré, Hilary, 531
du Pré, Piers, 531

Edmunds, Martin, 941
Eisenhardt, Bob, 245
Elfont, Harry, 173
Ellin, Doug, 631

Elliott, Ted, 447, 773, 1197
Ellmann, Richard, 1460
Emmerich, Roland, 447
Ephron, Delia, 1489
Ephron, Nora, 1489
Erb, Greg, 1129
Eriksen, Gordon, 671
Esguerrs, George, 1290
Eskow, John, 773
Evans, Max, 521
Evans, Nicholas, 554

Faenza, Roberto, 957
Farrelly, Bobby, 1308
Farrelly, Peter, 1308
Feather, Jacqueline, 1031
Feinmann, Jose Pablo, 749
Feldman, Dennis, 1239
Ferrari, Michelle, 918
Ferrell, Will, 871
Fitzgerald, Thom, 476
Flackett, Jennifer, 751
Foley, Maureen, 544
Fordewijk, F., 210
Fox, Kevin, 851
Foyt, Victoria, 294
Franck, Dan, 649
Frank, Scott, 920
Freeman, Morgan J., 572
Frey, James, 631
Friedman, Lewis, 72
Friel, Brian, 264
Frobenius, Nikolaj, 607
Froemke, Susan, 245
Frye, E. Max, 930
Fuller, Kim, 1249

Gabeira, Fernado, 403
Gallo, Phil, 1425
Gallo, Vincent, 139
Gatlif, Tony, 420
Geels, Lauren, 210
Geller, Lynn, 749
Gellis, Andrew, 1285
Gellis, Andrew, 1285
George, Matt, 601
Germain, Paul, 1077
Gibson, Channing, 679
Gillham, Dan, 887
Gilliam, Terry, 379
Gilligan, Vince, 546
Gilman, David, 67
Gilroy, Tony, 40
Glazer, Mitch, 461
Goble, Myron, 322
Goldbacher, Sandra, 457

Goldberg, Harris, 593
Goldberg, Howard, 332
Goldman, Bo, 781
Goldman, Gina, 1277
Goldsman, Akiva, 733, 992
Golin, Larry, 749
Gomez, Nick, 595
Gough, Alfred, 679
Goyer, David S., 114, 271
Goyet, Jean-François, 1426
Grant, Susannah, 356
Green, Walon, 521
Greenberg, Matt, 471
Grisham, John, 433
Grisoni, Tony, 379
Gross, Larry, 219
Guedes, Ann, 1288
Gullette, Sean, 970
Gudiguian, Robert, 768
Gyllenhaal, Stephen, 548

Hadleigh-West, Maggie, 1414
Halberg, Jonny, 619
Hale, Boyd, 19
Hamburg, John, 1093
Handke, Peter, 225
Haneke, Michael, 416
Harr, Jonathan, 232
Hartley, Hal, 512
Hauser, Stephen, 1242
Hawkins, Richard, 1304
Hayes, Al, 433
Haynes, Todd, 1389
Healy, Matt, 237
Hedden, Roger, 519
Hensleigh, Jonathan, 40
Herlihy, Tim, 1416, 1419
Herman, Mark, 703
Herzfeld, Jim, 780
Herzog, Werner, 701
Higashi, Yoichi, 1404
Hirst, Michael, 338
Ho, Ivy, 243
Hoffman, Alice, 992
Holmes, Richard, 1149
Hopkins, Karen Leigh, 1264
Horta, Silvio, 1387
Howitt, Peter, 1189
Hsiao, Rita, 841
Huggins, Roy, 1371
Hughes, John, 1038
Hugo, Victor, 674
Huth, Angela, 652

Iacone, Jeremy, 902
Ice Cube, 975
Imamura, Shohei, 333
Iosseliani, Otar, 135
Irving, John, 1163
Ishii, Takashi, 455
Ivory, James, 1216
Iwai, Shunji, 1439

Jacquot, Benoît, 1131
Jaglom, Henry, 294
Jahnson, Randall, 773
Jakoby, Don, 615
Janszen, Karen, 306
Jaoui, Agnès, 1377
Jenkins, Tamara, 1193
Jhabvala, Ruth Prawer, 1216
Johnson, Bayard, 1291
Johnson, David C., 1471
Johnson, Denis, 538
Johnson, John, 1035
Johnson, Mark Steven, 610, 1163
Johnston, Heather, 671
Jones, James, 1319
Jones, Kaylie, 1216
Jones, Kirk, 1409
Jones, Nasir, 75
Jordan, Neil, 164
Jud, Reinhard, 613
Judson, Stephen, 362

Kalmenson, Bill, 1227
Kamps, John, 123
Kaplan, Deborah, 173
Kasdan, Jake, 1495
Kattan, Chris, 871
Kazan, Nicholas, 369, 548
Kelly, Patrick Smith, 958
Kennedy, Douglas, 1424
Kern, Will, 216
Kiarostami, Abbas, 1293
Kimmel, Bruce, 364
King, Stephen, 33, 1262
King, Zalman, 601
King-Smith, Dick, 60
Kirkman, Tim, 280
Kitano, Takeshi, 395, 1223
Klapisch, Cédric, 1377
Klasky, Arlene, 1077
Klass, David, 298
Klein, Joe, 1000
Kloss, Thomas, 930
Knott, Frederick, 958
Koch, Ulrike, 1096
Koenig, Ralf, 622
Koepp, David, 1205

Kolleck, Amos, 1275
Konner, Lawrence, 797, 810
Koontz, Dean, 967
Koppelman, Brian, 1069
Koren, Steve, 871
Kouf, Jim, 1081
Kourkov, Andrei, 407
Kramp, Mario, 622
Kwietniowski, Richard, 739

LaBute, Neil, 1483
LaGravenese, Richard, 77, 554, 715
Lamanna, Ross, 1081
Lamprell, Mark, 60
Landis, John, 119
Lasseter, John, 145
Laszlo, Miklos, 1489
Laverty, Paul, 176
Lazebnik, Philip, 841, 1014
Le Guay, Phillipe, 989
Leach, Sheryl, 69
Leavitt, Charles, 806
Lee, Quentin, 1152
Lee, Spike, 500
Lehner, Wolfgang, 613
Leland, David, 652
Lemkin, Jonathan, 679
Lenero, Vicente, 805
Leonard, Elmore, 920
Levangie, Gigi, 1264
Levi, Primo, 1344
Levien, David, 1069
Levin, Larry, 317
Levin, Marc, 1181
Levin, Mark, 751
Lewis, Everett, 1180
Lifton, Robert Jay, 509
Lima, Walter, Jr., 929
Lin, Justin, 1152
Link, Caroline, 89
Linklater, Richard, 860
LoCash, Robert, 72
Lofting, Hugh, 317
Lopes, Moacir D., 929
Loriga, Ray, 709
Low, Alex, 772
Low, Stephen, 772
Luna, Bigas, 201
Lyons, James, 1389

Ma, Fibe, 819
McArdle, Tom, 1290
McCabe, Patrick, 164
McCauley, Stephen, 887
McCulley, Johnston, 773
Macdonald, Norm, 309
McEnery, Donald, 145
McEwan, Ian, 400
McGovern, Jimmy, 440

McGuinn, Patrick, 126
McGuinness, Frank, 264, 1288
McKenna, David, 21
McKinney, Josh, 1277
McManus, Michael, 755
McMillan, Terry, 563
McNamara, Sean Patrick, 1334
McPherson, Conor, 589
Macpherson, Don, 52
Madison, Alan, 1343
Mahfouz, Naguib, 805
Main, Stewart, 126
Malick, Terrence, 1319
Malone, Bonz, 1181
Mamet, David, 1232
Mancini, Don, 133
Manson, Graeme, 255
Marconi, David, 348
Marcovich, Carlos, 1440
Marmo, Malia Scotch, 751
Marshall, Neil, 624
Master P, 578
Masterson, Whit, 1339
Matheson, Richard, 1429
Matthews, John, 126
Mauldin, Nat, 317
May, Elaine, 1000
May, Robert L., 1075
Maybury, John, 746
Maysles, Albert, 245
Mazin, Craig, 1129
Mazziotti, Thomas F., 215
Mendelsohn, Aaron, 10
Merlet, Agnes, 48
Meyer, Turi, 199
Meyers, Nancy, 936
Meyjes, Menno, 1154
Michelson, Walt, 1034
Mickelberry, William, 112
Mieczkowski, Rondo, 669
Milesi, Jean-Louis, 768
Millar, Miles, 679
Miller, George, 60
Mitchell, Julian, 1460
Moore, Kenny, 1466
Moore, Michael, 105
Morel, Gael, 411
Morgenrath, Werner, 1037
Morris, Judy, 60
Morrison, Toni, 77
Mungo, Carrie, 578
Muska, Susan, 127
Mylander, Maureen, 943

Nabokov, Vladimir, 722

Nakajima, Takehiro, 1404
Natali, Vincenzo, 255
Nelson, Jessie, 1264
Niami, Ramin, 1221
Niccol, Andrew, 1348
Nicholson, William, 390
Norberg, Greg, 755
Norman, Marc, 1137
Normand, Michael, 308
Norton, Mary, 123
Nursall, Tom, 593
Nutter, Mark, 19

O'Brien, Kate, 1288
O'Donnell, Jack, 1262
Oedekerk, Steve, 943
O'Haver, Tommy, 109
Olafsdottir, Greta, 127
Oldman, Gary, 875
Oremland, Paul, 697
Orr, Robert, 1123
Orwell, George, 801
Osborn, Ron, 781
Ozon, François, 1127
Ozpetek, Ferzan, 1260

Panahi, Jafar, 815
Pang Ming, 410
Parello, Chuck, 511
Parker, Trey, 171, 914
Parkin, Frank, 636
Parks, Rick, 356
Pate, Jonas, 282
Pate, Joshua, 282
Pavia, Mark, 1262
Paxton, Michael, 57
Peardson, Ryne Douglas, 797
Penn, Zak, 27
Peoples, David Webb, 1213
Peretz, Jesse, 400
Peters, Charlie, 636
Peters, Stephen, 1456
Petraglia, Sandro, 1344
Philbrick, Rodman, 806
Phillips, Jeff, 1334
Pikser, Jeremy, 155
Piller, Michael, 1254
Plater, Alan, 801
Pogue, John, 1371
Poirier, Manuel, 1426
Pool, Robert Roy, 40
Poole, Duane, 1146
Powell, Paul Henry, 440
Pradal, Manuel, 764
Proft, Pat, 1474
Proyas, Alex, 271

Quindlen, Anna, 903

Raba, David, 569
Ramage, Rick, 1020
Ramsey, Ben, 93

Ranft, Joe, 145
Raphaelson, Samson, 1489
Rappaport, Mark, 1162
Raskin, John, 548
Rea, Stephen, 129
Reed, Aaron, 864
Reinhard, Jud, 613
Reitinger, Richard, 225
Rendell, Ruth, 709
Reno, Jeff, 781
Reynolds, Scott, 1374
Rice, Wayn, 1277
Richard, Jean-Louis, 989
Richey, Eddie, 969
Rifkin, Adam, 1197
Roberts, Jonathan, 610
Robinson, Bruce, 1052
Rodat, Robert, 1099
Roddenberry, Gene, 1254
Rogers, Steven, 550, 1264
Roos, Don, 909
Rose, Ruth, 810
Rosenberg, Jeanne, 1285
Rosenberg, Scott, 312
Rosenow, James, 252
Rosenthal, Margaret, 269
Rosenthal, Mark, 797, 810
Rosi, Francesco, 1344
Rosler, Alexander, 795
Ross, Gary, 978
Rossio, Terry, 447, 773, 1197
Roth, Eric, 554
Rouan, Brigitte, 989
Rubin, Bruce Joel, 285
Ruiz, Raoul, 425
Rukov, Mogens, 184
Rulli, Stefano, 1344
Rusconi, Jane, 575
Russo, Richard, 1361
Ruzowitzky, Stefan, 603
Ryan, David, 400

Saalfield, Catherine Gund, 469
Saito, Hisashi, 1336
Salerno, Shane, 40
Salles, Walter, 195
Sampson, Kevin, 697
Sanders, Christopher, 841
Sandler, Adam, 1416
San Souci, Robert D., 841
Sanzel, Ken, 1048
Sayles, John, 789
Scheerbaum, Peter, 1037
Schiff, Stephen, 722
Schifrin, William, 1031

Schlöndorff, Volker, 898
Schrader, Paul, 1
Schulman, Tom, 539
Schwartz, Mark Evan, 738
Schwartz, Stefan, 1149
Scott, Allan, 1044
Scott, Derin, 182
Scott, Gavin, 123, 1197
Scott, Mike, 1187
Seavey, Nina Gilden, 935
Sebastiano, Frank, 309
Seidler, David, 1031
Seidler, Tor, 1037
Seltzer, David, 847
Septien, Al, 199
Serlin, Beth, 89
Serran, Leopoldo, 403
Shapiro, Peter, 831
Shaw, Bob, 145
Shelton, Millicent, 1057
Shyamalan, M. Night, 1447
Shyer, Charles, 936
Siefert, Lynn, 246
Sikora, Jim, 153
Simon, Neil, 857
Singer, Raymond, 841
Skoog, Susan, 1436
Sletaune, Pal, 619
Sloan, Brian, 587
Smith, Leslie L., 275
Smith, Scott B., 1166
Snider, Dee, 284

Soderbergh, Steven, 874
Sohn, Sonja, 1181
Solondz, Todd, 480
Sommers, Stephen, 291
Spice Girls, 1249
Spotnitz, Frank, 1475
Sprecher, Jill, 240
Sprecher, Karen, 240
Stahl, Jerry, 965
Stanford, Don, 1277
Stanton, Andrew, 145
Stanush, Claude, 860
Steakley, John, 615
Stefano, Joseph, 1023
Stem, J. David, 1077
Stevens, Dana, 225
Stillman, Whit, 658
Stoppard, Tom, 1137
Stratton, Richard, 1181
Strauss, John J., 1308
Strick, Wesley, 1052
Styron, Susanna, 1134
Styron, William, 1134
Swicord, Robin, 992
Swift, David, 936

Tabucchi, Antonio, 957
Tamasy, Paul, 10
Tambellini, Flavio R., 929
Tang, Edward, 819
Tarantino, Quentin, 414
Tarr, Susan, 246
Tashima, Sizo, 1404

Tec, Roland, 18
Tengan, Daisuke, 333
Tennant, Andy, 356
Terry, Bridget, 1134
Theroux, Paul, 219
Thomas, Michael, 1424
Thompson, Hunter S., 379
Thompson, Jim, 538
Toback, James, 1366
Toledano, Manuel, 1145
Tolkin, Michael, 285
Tomikawa, Motofumi, 333
Tournier, Michael, 898
Towne, Robert, 1466
Traeger, Michael, 278
Treut, Monika, 304
Tsukamoto, Shinya, 1336
Tucci, Stanley, 597
Tummolini, Stefano, 1260
Turner, Michael, 492

Van Diem, Mike, 210
van Mega, Ruud, 210
van Warmerdam, Alex, 337
Vaus, Lyn, 865
Vecchio, Sergio, 957
Veloz, David, 965
Veronis, Nick, 277
Vincent, Christian, 649
Vining, Dan, 112
Vinterberg, Thomas, 184

Volodo, Koto, 656
von Trier, Lars, 625
Vorsel, Niels, 625

Wade, Kevin, 781
Walker, Clark Lee, 860
Walkow, Gary Alan, 886, 887
Wallace, Naomi, 664
Wallace, Randall, 759
Walz, Martin, 622
Wang, Wayne, 219
Wasserstein, Wendy, 887
Waters, John, 954
Watkins, Doug, 885
Watson, Eric, 970
Wechter, David, 364
Weide, Robert B., 672
Weiss, David N., 1077
Weiss, Matthew, 869
Weisz, Richard, 1062
Weitz, Chris, 27
Weitz, Paul, 27
Welles, Orson, 1339
Wenders, Wim, 225
Wescott, Margaret, 1272
White, Mike, 278
White, Stephen, 69
Wierzbicki, Krzysztof, 639
Wild, Nettie, 974
Williams, Hype, 75
Williams, Paul, 427
Williams, Saul, 1181
Williamson, Kevin, 364, 584
Willocks, Tim, 1280

Wilson, Owen, 1085
Wimmer, Kurt, 1242
Wolf, Fred, 309
Wolfe, Tom, 19
Wolfman, Marv, 114
Wolterstorff, Bob, 1187
Wong Kar-Wai, 373
Woolf, Virginia, 822
Wright, Jeff, 72
Wright, Lawrence, 1154
Wu Ming, 410

Xiabo, Wang, 330

Yakin, Boaz, 996
Yamamoto, Masashi, 618
Yglesias, Rafael, 674
Yoshimura, Akira, 334
Yost, Graham, 493
Young, David, 1285
Young, John G., 933
Youssef, Khaled, 302
Yuan, Zhang, 330

Zaillian, Steven, 232
Zamm, Alex, 199
Zappia, Robert, 471
Zeik, J.D., 1062
Zhou Xiaowen, 346
Zilberstein, Guy, 989
Zucker, David, 72
Zukovic, Dan, 657
Zwick, Edward, 1154

CINEMATOGRAPHERS

Aaronson, Reuben, 935
Abraham, Phil, 1343
Ackroyd, Barry, 176, 1380
Acord, Lance, 139
Adair, Sandra, 860
Adefarasin, Remi, 338, 1189
Ahern, Lloyd, 173
Aim, Pierre, 751
Albert, Arthur, 309
Alberti, Maryse, 480, 1389
Anderson, Jamie, 857, 1197
Anderson, John, 1186
Anderson, Lea, 1389
Archambault, Georges, 738
Aronson, John, 601

Aruguelles, Fernando, 1180
Astakhov, Sergei, 137
Atherton, Howard, 291, 722

Baca-Asay, Joaquin, 1035
Baffa, Christopher, 1277
Ballhaus, Michael, 1000
Barnard, Evan, 406
Barrett, Michael, 1093
Barrow, Michael, 1436
Bartkowiak, Andrzej, 679, 1371
Bartley, John S., 312
Basulto, Armando, 671
Bazelli, Bojan, 269
Beato, Affonso, 709

Benjamin, Mark, 1181
Beristain, Gabriel, 1232
Bernstein, Steven, 468, 816, 1416
Berta, Renato, 1405
Bhattacharya, Amit, 1227
Biddle, Adrian, 164, 539
Biziou, Peter, 1348
Blixt, Bjorn, 1342
Blossier, Patrick, 201
Bonet, Barrin, 37
Boyd, Russell, 317
Braham, Henry, 652, 1149, 1409
Breashears, David, 362
Briessewitz, Uta, 865
Brooker, Trevor, 123
Brownscombe, Peter, 37
Burnett, Marcus, 831

Burum, Stephen H., 1205
Butler, Bill, 282
Byers, Frank, 1057

Calahan, Sharon, 145
Callaway, Tom, 182
Calvache, Antonio, 578
Cameron, Alistair, 697
Campbell, John, 1038
Capener, Brian, 1202
Carpenter, Russell, 851
Carter, James L., 969
Carvalho, Walter, 195
Cavali, Bernard, 768
Champetier, Caroline, 646
Chandler, Sandra, 896
Changwei Gu, 439, 569

Chapman, Michael, 1174
Chediak, Enrique, 364, 1387
Cheek, Norwood, 280
Chressanthis, James, 1387
Churchill, Joan, 640
Clabaugh, Richard, 967
Cody, Alan, 780
Colli, Tonino Delli, 685
Collins, Andy, 703
Collister, Peter Lyons, 1048
Connell, David, 1262
Coppola, Roman, 406
Corradi, Pio, 1096
Coulter, Michael, 847
Cundey, Dean, 636, 936
Curtis, Oliver, 739

Danitz, Brian, 105
Davis, Elliot, 664, 920
Deakins, Roger, 96, 1154
Deasy, Seamus, 427
de Borman, John, 806
De Buitéler, Ci, 589
Deguchi, Keiko, 1040
de Keyzer, Bruno, 896
de la Roche, Wayne, 37
Delhomme, Benoit, 48, 1377
Del Ruth, Thomas, 631
Denault, Jim, 240, 595
De Santis, Pasqualino, 1344
Deschanel, Caleb, 550
Desmond, James, 834
Devonish, Kerwin, 497
Donnelly, John, 582
Doob, Nick, 834
Downing, Todd, 126
Doyle, Christopher, 373, 1023
Dufaux, Guy, 987
Dunn, Andrew, 356, 575, 992
Dupouey, Pierre, 989

Edwards, Eric, 237
Escoffier, Jean-Yves, 1069
Estus, Boyd, 37
Evans, Blake T., 1334
Evans, Kelly, 684

Fabre, Jean-Marc, 1216
Farkas, Pedro, 929
Fedorov, Aleksei, 837
Feitshans, Buzz IV, 112
Felperlaan, Marc, 327
Fenner, John, 123
Filac, Vilko, 219
Fortunato, Ron, 875, 902
Foster, John, 850
Foulkes, Robert, 1290
Fraisse, Robert, 1062
Freeman, David, 123
Fuhrer, Martin, 1460
Fujimoto, Tak, 77

Gallo, Christopher, 414
Gardiner, Greg, 548
Georgevich, Dejan, 252
Gibson, Sue, 822
Gillham, Dan, 886
Gilpin, Paul, 1291
Gioseffi, Kenny, 914
Gissen, Amy, 126
Giurato, Blasco, 957
Gordon, Mark J., 538
Graves, Chris, 171

Greatrex, Richard, 1137
Greenberg, Adam, 1081, 1242
Gruszynski, Alexander, 385
Guichard, Eric, 420

Hagen, Ron, 699
Hall, Conrad L., 232, 1466
Hambling, Gerry, 1288
Hammer, Victor, 1228
Hartowicz, Irek, 927
Heller, Brian, 544
Hennings, David, 780, 1398
Henriques, Samuel, 376
Herrington, David, 119
Hobson, Def, 440
Holender, Adam, 996, 1447
Honisch, Alexander, 622
Hurwitz, Tom, 1449

Idziak, Slawomir, 789
Irwin, Mark, 1308
Ito, Hiroshi, 618
Ivanov, Stefan, 425

James, Peter, 860
Jannelli, Anthony, 1272
Jian, Zhang, 330
Jobin, Daniel, 476
Jodat, F., 815
Johnson, David, 531
Johnson, Jill, 850
Jonze, Spike, 406
Jordan, Lawrence, 369
Jörgen, Jeffrey, 563

Kaluta, Vilen, 408
Kam, Milton, 587
Kaminski, Janusz, 1099
Katz, Robin, 67
Katz, Stephen M., 441
Kaye, Tony, 21
Keating, Kevin, 850
Kelsch, Ken, 597
Kenaston, Nils, 277
Kenny, Francis, 871
Kibbe, Gary B., 615
Kimball, Jeffrey L., 1456
Kimmel, Adam, 19, 831
Kitzanuk, Andrew, 772, 1285
Kivilo, Alar, 1166
Klimov, Vladimir, 1315
Kling, Elizabeth, 992
Kobland, Ken, 896

Kohnhurst, Michael, 511
Komatsubara, Shigeru, 334
Kosal, Nara Keo, 1426
Kovacs, Laszlo, 610
Kravetz, Carole, 903
Kress, Erik, 625

Lachman, Ed, 1442
Lam, Raymond, 819
Landerer, Christopher, 304
Lapoirie, Jeanne, 411
Laustsen, Dan, 874
Layton, Vernon, 584
Lehner, Wolfgang, 613, 1034
Leibler, Todd, 1414
Lener, Piotr, 1037
Lenoir, Denis, 649
Leonetti, Matthew F., 1254
Lpine, Jean, 1471
Le Saux, Yorick, 1127
Lesnie, Andrew, 60
Letarte, Pierre, 755
Levy, Peter, 733
Lewis, David, 199
Lewis, Tom, 1416
Libatique, Matthew, 970
Lindley, John, 978, 1489
Lohmann, Dietrich, 285
Lubezki, Emmanuel, 461, 781
Lubtchansky, William, 135
Lu Gengxin, 346
Lyster, Russell, 1059

Ma, Jingle, 243
McAlpine, Donald M., 1264
McCurdy, Sam, 624
McKinney, Ashley, 280
MacMillan, Kenneth, 19, 264
MacPerson, Glen, 1044, 1474
Maibaum, Paul, 1187
Maloney, Denis, 67
Mantle, Anthony Dod, 184, 1342
Marcovich, Carlos, 805, 1440
Mari, Pasquale, 1260
Markowitz, Barry, 1366
Marquinez, Horacio, 1302
Mason, Steve, 72
Mathieson, John, 746
Mayers, Michael, 136, 1436
Mayo, Alfredo, 1145
Meheux, Phil, 773

Menzies, Peter, Jr., 493
Mervis, Mark, 109
Metty, Russell, 1339
Miller, Bennett, 253
Millo, Yoram, 509
Mindel, Dan, 348
Molloy, Mike, 1424
Monti, Felix, 403
Moore, Allen, 935
Morris, Nic, 390
Mullen, M. David, 657
Müller, Jorge, 75, 218
Müller, Robby, 1146
Muratore, Robert, 171
Muska, Susan, 127

Narita, Hiro, 593, 1134
Nasr, Mohsen, 302
Navarro, Guillermo, 325
Newby, John, 308
Nowak, Danny, 93, 492
Nuttgens, Giles, 801
Nykvist, Sven, 187

Okada, Daryn, 471, 1129
Olafsdottir, Greta, 127
O'Neil, Bob,

Papamichael, Phedon, 943
Pau, Peter, 133
Pavicevic, Goran, 284
Payvar, Homayoun, 1293
Pecorini, Nicola, 379
Pennebaker, D.A., 834
Perrin, Bob, 376
Persson, Jorgen, 306
674
Peterman, Don, 810
Petersson, Mark, 544
Petrycki, Jacek, 639
Phelan, Kate, 126
Pierce-Roberts, Tony, 951
Pollack, Ekkehardt, 304
Pollock, Christophe, 764
Pontecorvo, Marco, 1344
Pope, Bill, 1495
Pope, Dick, 1280
Pratt, Roger, 52
Prinzi, Frank, 882, 1040
Putnam, Mark, 580

Quinn, Declan, 903

Raby, Simon, 1374
Rachini, Pasquale, 87

Reiker, Tami, 527
Rexer, William II, 1384
Rho, Jonathan, 1425
Richardson, Robert, 554
Richmond, Tom, 400, 1193
Robin, Jean-Francois, 667
Rodionov, Alexei, 941, 1288
Roed, Jan, 1342
Rogers, Derek, 255
Roll, Gernot, 89
Rowe, Ashley, 457
Russell, Ward, 1475

Saalfield, Catherine Gund, 469
Saiedzadeh, Zahra, 316
Sakharov, Alik, 57
Sarossy, Paul, 1
Sasakibara, Yasushi, 455
Sayeed, Malik, 75, 500, 975
Schlueter, Steven, 1061
Schmidt, Eric, 850
Schmidt, Ronn, 1253
Schneider, Aaron E., 1163
Scholz, John P., 275
Schreiber, Eileen, 1414
Schreiber, Nancy, 1162, 1483
Schwartzman, John, 40
Seale, John, 225
Sekula, Andrzej, 129, 246
Semb, Helge, 795
Seresin, Michael, 797
Serra, Eduardo, 1284, 1429
Shimizu, Yoshio, 1404
Shinoda, Noboru, 1439
Shulman, Daniel, 749
Sigel, Newton Thomas, 33, 369
Silk, Lawrence, 1449
Sissel, Sandi, 69
Slovis, Mike, 215
Smith, Chris, 105
Sobocinski, Piotr, 1361
Southon, Mike, 10
Sova, Peter, 1020
Spiller, Michael, 512, 869
Squires, Buddy, 918
Stapleton, Oliver, 521, 887
Steiger, Ueli, 447
Stevens, Robert, 954
Stoffers, Rogier, 210
Storaro, Vittorio, 155
Strasburg, Ivan, 1304

Suhrstedt, Tim, 757, 1419
Sunara, Igor, 1221
Suschitzky, Peter, 759

Taczanowski, Hubert, 216, 332, 909
Talavera, Ed, 1275
Tattersall, David, 1213
Terendy, John, 153
Thomas, Andrew, 126
Thomas, John, 278, 519, 658, 1269

Thurmann-Andersen, Erling, 607
Tickner, Clive, 1249
Toll, John, 1319
Toniolo, Camilla, 1040
Tougas, Kirk, 974
Tovoli, Luciano, 298
Tsukamoto, Shinya, 1336

Van de Sande, Theo, 114

Van Leeuw, Philippe, 693
Vassdal, Kjell, 619
Vendler, Alex, 640
Villalobos, Reynaldo, 1052
von Haller, Peter, 603

Wages, William, 322
Waite, Trevor, 440
Wexler, Howard, 669
Widmer, Gretchen, 18

Wiegand, Lisa, 1152
Wild, Nettie, 974
Wilson, Ian, 1123
Winding, Romain, 1131
Windon, Stephen F., 394
Winestine, Zack, 864
Wolski, Dariusz, 271, 958
Wong, Arthur, 634
Wood, Oliver, 810
Wright, Bill, 801

Yamamoto, Hideo, 395
Yanagishima, Katsumi, 1223
Yang Shu, 410
Yates, Paul, 830
Yeoman, Robert, 965, 1085

Zeitlinger, Peter, 701
Zielinski, Jerzy, 546

EDITORS

Albert, Ross, 1129
Albertson, Sean, 1269
Allen, Stanford C., 1031
Altschuler, Jon, 18
Amundson, Peter, 447
Anderson, Brad, 865
Anderson, William, 1348
Anwar, Tariq, 246, 887
Arcidi, Anthony, 582
Aron, Donn, 538
Atkins, Mark, 640
Audsley, Mick, 52

Bacalov, Luis, 1344
Bertz, Geof, 672
Beason, Eric L, 1166
Becker, Manfred, 974
Bedford, James Gavin, 601
Beldin, Dale, 119
Beltrami, Marco, 364
Berdan, Brian, 1202
Berger, Peter E., 1254
Betancourt, Jeff, 109
Bilcock, Jill, 338
Billeskov-Jansen, Janus, 674
Bini, Joe, 701
Binns, Paul, 1384
Binns, T. David, 578
Blye, Toni, 275
Boisson, Noelle, 1216
Bonanni, Mauro, 1260
Bondelli, Roger, 356
Bornstein, Charles, 182
Bowers, George, 563
Bradsell, Michael, 1460
Brandt-Burgoyne, Anita, 593
Brenner, David, 722, 1429
Bricker, Randolph K., 133, 967

Bricmont, Wendy Greene, 1174
Briggs, David, 126
Brown, Barry Alexander, 246, 500
Brown, Nicholas, 757
Bryant, John, 1077
Butusov, Slava, 137

Cambas, Jacqueline, 1020
Cannon, Bruce, 951
Capillas, Nacho Ruiz, 1145
Carroll, Bryan H., 757
Casellato, Franco, 957
Cassidy, Jay, 1048, 1387
Catalena, Mark, 126
Ceppi, François, 649
Chang, William, 373
Chan Ki-hop, 243
Chaskel, Pedro, 75, 218
Chavance, Pascale, 1131
Cherot, Christopher Scott, 497
Chestnut, Scott, 1069
Cheung, Peter, 819
Chew, Richard, 550
Chiate, Debra, 278
Choukroun, Pierre, 694
Christensen, Pernille Bech, 625
Clayton, Curtiss, 139, 987
Coates, Anne V., 920
Coburn, Arthur, 269, 996, 1166
Codron, David, 864, 909
Congdon, Dana, 306
Cook, Wayne, 1374
Cooke, Tricia, 96
Corrao, Angelo, 252
Corriveau, Andre, 738
Corwin, Hank, 554

Crafford, Ian, 1123
Cristiani, Gabriella, 1123
Curtiss, Edward, 1339

Dartonne, Monique, 420
Davies, Freeman, 554
Davis, Julie, 580
Davis, Mona, 376
Davis, Ron, 427
Day, Mark, 1304
Dedet, Yann, 1426
de Koning, Jessica, 210
Deschamps, Yves, 694
Desseine, Valerie, 764
Devlin, Paul, 1186
Di Ciaula, Pia, 1044
Dixon, Humphrey, 264, 664, 667
Dobrianskaia, Marina, 1315
Downing, Todd, 126
Driscoll, Deb, 865
Ducsay, Bob, 291, 1253
Duddleston, Amy, 1023, 527
Duthie, Michael, 1146

Earl, Christopher, 57
Eisenhardt, Bob, 245
Eliopoulos, Nicholas, 1471
Ellis, Mike, 703
Ellis, Peter B., 887
Elmiger, Suzy, 597
Escudier, Harley, 640

Fardoulis, Monique, 1284
Fenn, Suzanne, 987
Fiedler, Milenia, 639
Finfer, David, 631, 1163
Flamholc, Leon, 1342

Fleum, Seth, 857
Fletcher, Nick, 1014
Folsey, George, Jr., 309
Friedkin, Jay, 60
Fries, Tom, 325
Fuller, Brad, 875

Gamble, David, 1137
Gaster, Nicolas, 898, 941
Gazzara, Elizabeth, 1221, 1275
Gedigier, François, 646
Gengenbach, Pal, 619
Gibbs, Tony, 1062
Gibson, J.Kathleen, 816
Goenka, Tula, 1414
Goldblatt, Mark, 40
Goldenberg, William, 978
Graef, Sue, 882
Granger, Tracy, 595
Greenberg, Jerry, 21, 1038
Greenbury, Christopher, 1308
Gregory, Jon, 715
Gumpel, Emily, 1414
Guthrie, Sandi, 1436

Hacker, Melissa, 850
Hafitz, Andrew, 658
Halsey, Richard, 69
Hamilton, Steve, 512
Hampton, Janice, 954, 1471
Hardin, Ian, 171
Harkema, Reginald, 492
Harris, Daniel, 640
Harvey, Marshall, 1197
Hegedus, Chris, 834
Heim, Alan, 21
Helfrich, Mark, 1081
Henry, Bill, 684

Heredia, Paula, 406, 831
Higashi, Yoichi, 1404
Hill, Jim, 199
Hines, Suzanne, 975, 1059
Hirakubo, Masahiro, 129, 521
Hirsch, Paul, 493, 810
Hitner, Harry, 1291
Hoenig, Dov, 271
Hoffman, Sabine, 572
Hofstra, Jack, 394
Hok, Tom, 1075
Honess, Peter, 797
Hoy, Maysie, 1429
Hoy, William, 759
Hubley, Ray, 1343
Hunter, Martin, 1213
Hutshing, Joe, 781

Iglesias, Alberto, 201
Ikebe, Shinichiro, 334
Iosseliani, Otar, 135
Iwai, Shunji, 1439

Jablow, Michael, 173, 548
Jaglom, Henry, 294
Jakubowics, Alain, 306
Jaynes, Roderick, 96
Jones, Leslie, 1319
Jones, Robert C., 155
Jordan, Lawrence, 610
Judson, Stephen, 362
Juergens, Mark, 277

Kahn, Michael, 1099
Kahn, Sheldon, 1174
Kakesu, Syuichi, 618
Kamen, Jay, 871
Katz, Virginia, 441
Kawashima, Akimasa, 455
Keefe, Tom, 511
Keir, Andy, 77, 1272
Kelly, Michael, 841

Keraudren, François, 587
Kiarostami, Abbas, 1293
Kirpaul, Amanda, 927
Kitano, Takeshi, 395, 1223
Klein, Saar, 1319
Klier, Simone, 623
Klingman, Lynzee, 225, 575, 715
Kloomok, Darren, 749
Klotz, Joe, 280
Korzanl, Kelly, 1414
Kucherenko, Natalia, 1315
Kushner, Jeff, 284
Kwong Chi-leung, 243

Lacerda, Felipe, 195
Lahti, James, 772
Lambert, Robert K., 1466
LaMorte, Steve, 1061
Lange, Bruce, 10
Langford, Jan, 697
Lauman, Paige, 1061
Lawson, Tony, 164
Lebental, Dan, 282, 1398
Lebenzon, Chris, 40, 348
Lecorne, Guy, 48, 693
Lee, Quentine, 1152
Leighton, Robert, 575
Leonard, David, 75
Levine, Michael, 253
Levy, Vincent, 330
Lewis, Emir, 1181
Lewis, Tom, 1419
Lin, Justin, 1152
Lind, Ewa J., 1380
Linder, Stu, 1242
Lipartija, Marina, 137
Littleton, Carol, 77, 1361
Lofstrom, Markus, 657
Loiseleux, Valrie, 1405
Lorente, Isabel, 457
Lovejoy, Ray, 733
Lunger, Jeff, 304
Lusser, Patrick, 471
Lyons, James, 400, 1035, 1389

McArdle, Tom, 519
MacArthur, Andrea, 1249
Maganini, Elena, 1456
McGuinn, Patrick, 126
Mak Chi Sin, 634
McKay, Craig, 1052

Mackie, Alex, 1280
McLeish, Timothy, 1037
Manhardt, Mary, 376
Marciano, Eric, 304
Marcovich, Carlos, 1440
Mark, Stephen, 1476
Marks, Richard, 1489
Marshall, Neil, 624
Martin, Pamela, 1193
Maslansky, Judd, 864
Mastroianni, Ruggero, 1344
Mekler, Sergio, 929
Menke, Sally, 874
Mignatti, Victor, 136
Mirrione, Stephen, 240
Mitrecey, Karina, 656
Mondshein, Andrew, 1052, 1280, 1447
Monroe, Julie, 722
Moore, Nick, 652
Morgan, Randy Jon, 312
Moritz, David, 1085
Morreale, Andrew, 308, 1180
Morris, Jonathan, 176
Morse, Susan E., 187
Moutard, Jeanne, 1127
Murch, Walter, 1339
Muska, Susan, 127

Nahler, Britta, 603
Nedd-Friendly, Priscilla, 1228
Neil-Fisher, Debra, 112
Nevius, Steve, 332
Niami, Ramin, 1221
Noble, Thom, 773
Nord, Richard, 1239

O'Donnell, George, 918
Okayasu, Hajime, 334
Olafsdottir, Gerta, 127
Oppenheim, Jonathan, 37
Orland, John, 885
Oskarsdottir, Valdis, 184
Ota, Yoshinori, 395
Ottman, John, 33
Overas, Hakon, 607
Oxman, Alan, 480, 1366

Paggi, Simona, 685
Panahi, Jafar, 815
Pankow, Bill, 1205

Parker, Trey, 914
Pejo, Robert-Adrian, 1034
Peltier, Kenout, 201
Pennebaker, D.A., 834
Peppe, Chris, 1277
Percy, Lee, 298, 385
Peroni, Geraldine, 433
Pillsbury, Suzanne, 1093
Pires, Jay, 658
Plisco-Morris, Sabrina, 112
Plotch, Joel, 1483
Poll, Jon, 636
Press-Aviram, Naomi, 509
Prior, Peck, 584
Prochaska, Andreas, 416
Przygodda, Peter, 930
Puett, Dallas, 679
Pulcini, Robert, 896

Qing Qing, 410

Rabinowitz, Jay, 1
Rae, Dan, 575
Rappaport, Mark, 1162
Rask, Kirsten Bonnen, 795
Rathéry, Isabelle, 195, 403
Rawlings, Terrry, 1371
Reamer, Keith, 1035, 1302
Reichwein, Michiel, 822
Reiner, Jeffrey, 72
Ressler, Karina,
Reticker, Meg, 105
Reynolds, Emer, 589
Richardson, Nancy, 322, 1442
Rodriguez, Robert, 364
Rokob, Magdolna, 1096
Rolf, Tom, 554
Rommel, Patricia, 89
Rondinella, Thomas R., 215
Roose, Ronald, 19
Rosenbloom, David, 285
Rosenblum, Steven, 269, 1154
Ross, William, 1285
Rotter, Stephen A., 936
Rouan, Laurent, 989
Rubell, Paul, 114
Russell, Robin, 93

Rutenbeck, James, 544

Salem, Rachida Abdel, 302
Salcedo, José, 709
Salfa, Amadeo, 87
Salfas, Stan, 237
Sandberg, Francine, 1377
Sanders, John, 255
Sarandrea, Bruno, 1344
Sarch, Oren, 970
Sarmiento, Valeria, 425
Sasia, Bernard, 768
Savage, Carlos, 805
Sayles, John, 789
Scalia, Pietro, 93
Scantlebury, Glen, 40, 701
Schaffer, Lauren, 57
Schmidt, Arthur, 1000
Schwartz, Catherine, 411
Schwartz, Elizabeth, 1262
Schwarz, Jeffrey, 669
Seabrook, Melinda, 10
Semel, Stephen, 847
Semenova, Leda, 837
Shanks, Susan, 476
Sharp, Colleen, 1134
Shaw, Jonathan, 1285
Shields, Catherine, 935
Shimin, Toby, 918
Ship, Trudy, 539
Shipton, Susan, 739
Shugart, Joe, 601
Siegel, David J., 447
Silkensen, Steve, 671
Silverman, Cara, 965
Simpson, Claire, 1466
Sixel, Margaret, 60
Smith, John, 1189
Smith, Lee, 1348
Smith, Nicholas C., 546
Snell, Timothy, 1227
Spione, James, 933
Staenberg, Zach, 969
Standke, Rainer, 701
Stell, Aaron, 1339
Stensgaard, Molly Malene, 625
Stokes, Terry, 755
Strachan, Alan, 1149, 1409
Streicher, Paul, 1061
Sumovska, Eleonora, 408

Symons, James R., 1474
Szanto, Annamaria, 1334

Taylor, Chris, 153
Taylor, Tobin, 699
Teschner, Peter, 317
Thompson, Sara, 1414
Tibaldi, Antonio, 699
Tichenor, Dylan, 569
Timpone, Tara, 1495
Travis, Neil, 1264
Tronick, Michael, 781
Tsukamoto, Shinya, 1336
Tulliver, Barbara, 1232
Tunsil, Aljernon, 469

Unkrich, Lee, 145
Urioste, Frank J., 679

Villena, Fernando, 1414
Vince, Barrie, 316
Virkler, Dennis, 958
Vogel, Virgil W., 1339

Wagner, Christian, 851
Wahrman, Wayne, 232
Walker, Lesley, 379
Walsh, Martin, 531, 806, 1424
Warden, Rachel, 869
Warschilka, Edward A., 615
Watson, Earl, 1057
Webb, Stan, 27
Weber, Billy, 155, 1319
Weide, Robert B., 672
Weisberg, Steven, 461, 965
Wiegmans, Rene, 327
Wimble, Chris, 390
Wishengrad, Jeff, 1187
Wolf, Jeffrey, 751, 831
Wong Ming Lam, 373
Wright, John, 291
Wu, David, 133

Yeo, Sean, 1152
Young, John G., 933

Zimmerman, Don, 468, 943
Zuckerman, Lauren, 414

MUSIC

Abbott, Bill, 364, 722, 1429
Adams, Nick, 1424
Adkins, Hasil, 1034
Altman, John, 703
Alvarez, Lucia, 805
Anderson, Deva, 77
Andrews, Bunny, 992, 1000, 1348
Arguelles, Fernando, 1180
Arnold, David, 447
Arriagada, Jorge, 425, 1146
Aserud, Bent, 795
Auinger, Sam, 613

Baber, Michael, 1077, 1085
Bacalov, Luis, 987
Badami, Bob, 155, 348
Bad Livers, 860
Baerwald, David, 569
Ball, Lionel, 578
Barber, Lesley, 996
Barry, John, 797, 1280
Bartek, Steve, 780
Batt, Mike, 801
Begley, Philip, 264
Beller, Marty, 253
Berger, Cary, 414
Bernstein, Bill, 554, 781
Bernstein, Elmer, 1361
Bernstein, Richard, 875
Betanzos, Rick, 476
Beville, Matt, 414
Bird, Jeff, 869
Blackstone, Wendy, 749
Blank, Jennifer, 1077
Bohren, Geir, 795
Boldt, Michael, 1425
Bolton, Jay, 1471
Bonilla, Marc, 182
Borne, Steve, 597
Boswell, Simon, 246
Braden, Don, 671
Bretschneider, Steve, 1425
Briting, Jeff, 57
Brook, Michael, 1
Brooks, Brent, 909, 1429
Brooks, Chris, 978
Broughton, Bruce, 636, 733
Brown Brothers, The, 127
Bryant, Katherine Jane, 816
Buckley, Martina, 657
Buckley, Richie, 427

Burwell, Carter, 96, 441, 521, 1232, 1389

Cale, John, 1221
Cannom, Greg, 114
Carbonara, David, 751, 1447
Carlin, Patricia, 733
Carlin, Patty, 636
Carlson, Tom, 114, 593, 951
Carpenter, John, 615
Carpenter, Michael, 684
Caruso, Johnny, 914
Castellucci, Teddy, 1419
Caterina Ancient Music, 1404
Chabrol, Matthieu, 1284
Chan, Frankie, 373
Charbonneau, Jeff, 312, 975, 1476
Chiu Tseng-hei, 243
Choi, Edmund, 1447
Christianson, Bob, 885
Christianson, Paul, 935
Churchill, Sharal, 580
Clapton, Eric, 679, 875
Clarke, Stanley, 322
Clausen, Alf, 468
Clinton, George S., 112, 1456
Cmiral, Elia, 1062
Coda, John, 1334
Cole, Barry, 1366
Coleman, Lisa, 497
Colombier, Michel, 563, 1471
Connell, Michael, 52, 164
Conti, Bill, 1474
Cooder, Ry, 1000
Coon, Bruno, 978
Coonce, Cole, 657
Cooper, Ray, 379
Copeland, Aaron, 500
Copeland, Stewart, 403, 699, 954, 1398
Cowen, Jeanine, 544
Criocháin, Caoimhin O, 1031
Crivelli, Carlo, 764
Crooke, John, 280
Cullo, Stephen, 75
Curtis, Christo, 60
Cuvillier, Richard, 694

Dallwitz, Burkhard, 1348
Danna, Mychael, 1044

Danza, Joseph Pepe, 974
Daring, Mason, 789, 909
Dashkevich, Vladimir, 1315
Davey, Shaun, 129, 1409
Debney, John, 593, 951
Delia, Joe, 882
DeMichele, Gary, 597
Denesles, Olivier, 694
Denison-Kimball Trio, 153
Diener, Joanie, 112
Diprima, Dan, 996
DiPrima, Dan, 1442
Dittrick, Michael, 954, 1398
Dol, Roeland, 410
Doldinger, Klaus, 930
Doyle, Patrick, 461, 1031
Drescher, Thomas, 264, 1052, 1093, 1272, 1361
Dudley, Anne, 21
Dun, Tan, 369
Durning, Kathy, 1361

Eaton, Dina, 123, 447
Edelman, Randy, 1174
Een, Robert, 816, 1343
Ehrlich, John, 949
Eidel, Phillippe, 1377
Eidelman, Cliff, 903
el-Mougy, Yohia, 302
el-Tawil, Kamal, 302
Elfman, Danny, 232, 1166
Ellis, Peter B., 886
Endelman, Stephen, 1020

Farmer, Jim, 1040
Feathers, Charlie, 1034
Fenton, George, 176, 269, 356, 715, 887, 1489
Ferreras, Salvador, 974
Fiedel, Brad, 332
Finkles, John, 385, 1189
Finn, Ron, 1483
Fitzpatrick, Frank, 975
Flamberg, Jim, 978
Flicker, Mike, 112, 1062, 1456
Folk, Robert, 757
Ford, Jane, 580
Ford, Richard, 21, 1304

Foster, David, 1031
Fox, Celestia, 1216
Franke, Christopher, 1291
Freeman, Chico, 1275
Frizzell, John, 584
Frizzelli, Gianni, 755
Frystak, Lori Eschler, 145, 1020

Gallo, Phil, 1425
Gallo, Vincent, 139
Garcia, Roel A., 373
Garde, Danny, 1239
Garrett, Robert, 1228
Gatlif, Tony, 420
Gavin, Alastair, 440
George, J.J., 468, 757, 943
Gershman, Gerry, 587
Gibbs, Richard, 309, 317
Gibson, Alex, 860, 903
Glen, Andy, 703
Glennie-Smith, Nick, 759
Goddard, Daniel, 746
Goetz, Stuart, 269
Gohl, Matthias, 918
Goldenthal, Elliot, 164, 1242
Goldsmith, Jerry, 291, 1197, 1254, 1371
Goodman, Joel, 245, 850
Goodpaster, Amanda, 33, 237, 471
Governor, Mark, 887
Grassby-Lewis, Richard, 739
Green, Mark, 975
Gregson-Williams, Harry, 27, 123, 282, 348, 1048
Greyboy Allstars, 1495
Gron, Zig, 679
Gronski, Vladimir, 408
Grusin, Dave, 550
Grusin, Scott, 1419
Grusin, Stuart, 173
Guettel, Adam, 37
Gunning, Christopher, 390

Hajian, Chris, 199, 1302
Hall, Darrell, 1197
Hall, Ken, 291, 841, 1254, 1371
Hamilton, Page, 216
Handel, Georg Friedrich, 416

Handsome Family, 153
Hardcastle, Paul, 1249
Harrison, George, 362
Harrison, Jim, 806
Hartley, Hal, 512
Hassaishi, Jo, 1223
Hathaway, Bob, 531, 1409
Henrikson, Jim, 285, 773, 810
Hernandez, Coati Mundi, 385
Herrmann, Bernard, 1023
Higham, Michael, 338
Hill, Tanya Noel, 1069
Himmelman, Peter, 1227
Hirschfelder, David, 338, 1189
Hisaishi, Joe, 395
Hitchcock, Robyn, 1272
Hoffman, Jeffrey, 126
Holbek, Joachim, 619, 625, 874
Holmes, David, 920
Homme, Todd, 1014
Horner, James, 285, 773, 810
Howard, James Newton, 958
Hunt, Linda, 918

Iglesias, Alberto, 709
Illarramendi, Angel, 1145
Imbert, Matthieu, 694
Insects, The, 739
Isham, Mark, 114, 433
Ishikawa, Chu, 1336
Ivanovich, Mikhail, 837

Jackson, Wanda, 1034
Jacobs, Susan, 385
Jay, Michael, 1253
Jensen, Geir, 607
Johanson, Shari, 1, 385
Johnson, Laurie, 52
Jones, Trevor, 271, 298, 806
Jordan, Jeremy, 669
Judson, Tom, 304

Kajanus, Georg, 304
Keller, Carl, 225, 114, 173, 1466
Kamen, Michael, 679, 1429
Kaplan, Will, 317, 546, 610

Karman, Kennet, 539,
857, 992, 1023
Karp, Jonathan, 1495
Kasha, Al, 1075
Kasow, Todd, 96,
1232, 1389
Keane, Brian, 595,
1262
Kell, Daryl, 679, 1429
Kelly, Dominic, 414
Kelly, Victoria, 1374
Kennedy, Christopher,
19
Kent, Rolfe, 1193,
1304
Kitay, David, 173, 871
Kloser, Harald, 129
Kohlweck, Clif, 797,
1280
Kondor, Robbie, 480
Kramer, Tom, 369,
563, 610, 874
Krush, DJ, 618
Kudrak, Annette, 1389
Kuznetsky, Michelle,
1093
Kymlicka, Milan, 738

Lane, Kevin, 247, 379
Laraio, John, 325
Larson, Nathan, 400
LaSalandra, John,
1174
Lawrence, David, 519
Lazer, Alan Ari, 109
Lee, Helena, 433
Leadley, Simon, 271
Legg, James, 308
Legrand, Michel, 751
Lepage, Robert M., 75,
218
Levinson, Ross, 914
Levy, Krishna, 48
Levy, Stuart, 75
Licht, Daniel, 965
Lindsey, Steve, 569
Lisanti, Joe, 658
Lloyd, Michael, 1075
Lock, Brian, 652
Lockett, Tommy, 269
Loose, William, 126
Lopez, Peter C., 215
Lord, Rupert, 1384
Lotwis, Steve, 309,
1416, 1419
Luna, 816
Lundy, Curtis, 376
Lurie, John, 237

McCroskey, Steve,
1081, 1129, 1193
McElheron, Maureen,
582
McEntire, John, 1038
McGeary, Chris, 69,
385, 563, 1474
McGlashan, Don, 697
Machado, Celso, 974

Machida, Ko, 618
McKnight, Tracy, 527
McLary, David, 1290
McNamee, Steve, 256
McNaughton, Robert
F., 511
McNeely, Joel, 52,
1213
Mader, 240
Mael, Ron, 634
Mael, Russell, 634
Magee, Joseph, 1031
Mancina, Mark, 1052
Mancini, Henry, 1339
Mannion, Willie, 264
Mansell, Clint, 970
Marcovich, Alejandro,
1440
Marianelli, Dario, 589
Marino, Dean Richard,
322
Martin, George, 119,
471
Martin, Trade, 1425
Mascagni, Pietro, 416
May, Daniel, 362
Melvoin, Wendy, 497
Menashe, E.D., 933
Meyers, Nick, 715,
887, 1205
Milano, Thomas, 493,
575
Millar, Cynthia, 306
Miller, Randy, 1466
Mills, Paul, 1269
Min, Xiang, 330
Mollerup, Laurence,
974
Morales, Mio, 864
Morelenbaum, Jaques,
195
Morgan, Lorri, 127
Morricone, Ennio, 155,
722, 957
Morris, Marvin R.,
1057
Mothersbaugh, Mark,
278, 1077, 1085
Mozart, W.A., 416
Mullins, Patrick, 789,
882, 1040

Naves, Kim, 1077
Neidhart, Deedee, 613
Neveux, Eric, 1127
Newborn, Ira, 67, 72
Newman, Randy, 145,
978
Newman, Thomas,
554, 781
Nieto, Jos, 941
Nunes, Emmanuel,
1405
Nussio, Glinka, 837
Nussio, Otmar, 837
Nyman, Michael, 898

Ortolani, Riz, 87

Ottman, John, 471
Otto, Brian, 864
Otttman, John, 33

Parker, Chris, 1186
Parker, Trey, 171
Parkinson, Tom, 1384
Parks, Van Dyke, 1134
Pasqua, Alan, 1416
Peric, Suzana, 77, 298
1000
Perlman, Laura, 759
Pheloung, Barrington,
531
Phillips, Byron, 1057
Pike, Nicholas, 1253
Pine, Frankie, 1483
Pinto, Antnio, 195
Piovani, Nicola, 685
Plakke, David, 1414
Poledouris, Basil, 674
Portman, Rachel, 77,
546
Pranato, Steven, 1152
Preisner, Zbigniew,
639
Prendergast, Roy, 461,
1137

Quittner, Katherine,
225

Rabin, Trevor, 40,
348, 548, 610
Rabjohns, Paul, 114,
1253
Ragazzi, Claudio,
865
Ramos, Mary, 1093
Ramsey, Kennard,
1059
Randles, Robert, 225
Raoul, Nathalie, 694
Ratner, Nic, 461, 992,
1000
Raval, Manish, 1495
Reiser, Niki, 89
Remedios, 1439
Revell, Ashley, 133
Revell, Graeme, 93,
133, 851, 969,
1154, 1277
Rhees, Jan, 69
Ribicoff, Jacob, 406
Richards, Brian, 27,
123, 441
Richardson, Jay, 364,
546
Richardson, Lis, 394,
819
Richman, Jonathan,
1308
Rittersbusch, Esther,
837
Robb, Paul, 914
Robbins, David, 1123

Robbins, Richard, 1216
Robinson, J. Peter,
394, 819
Robinson, Peter
Manning, 538
Roby, John, 476
Rophé, Eric, 694
Rosen, Allan K., 631
Ross, Guy, 1424
Roush, Curtis, 674,
1242
Rubin, Angie, 780,
781
Ryan, Michael T., 539

Safan, Craig, 1187
Sager, Carole Bayer,
1031
Sakamoto, Ryuichi,
746, 1205
Sanborn, David, 679
Sanchez, Isabelle, 694
Sanders, Rich, 171
Sandoval, Bernardo,
1426
Sanko, Anton, 284
Sano, Dena, 114
Saracene, Tony, 277
Satie, Erik, 603
Sayers, Tom, 1249
Scheer-Demme,
Amanda, 601, 831
Schell, Johnny Lee,
927
Schifrin, Lalo, 1081
Schoen, Gaili, 294
Schwartz, Paul, 1035
Scott, Lee, 1123,
1308, 1319
Segal, Ellen, 232,
1166
Sekacz, Ilona, 822,
1380
Shack, Andrew, 578
Shaffer, Paul, 119
Shaiman, Marc, 847,
943, 1163
Shapiro, Theodore, 572
Shearmur, Edward,
457, 667, 1239
Silver, Andrew, 857,
936
Silvestri, Alan, 539,
857, 936, 992
Simonec, Tim, 1277
Skies, Roni, 864
Slaski, Christopher,
624
Slusser, David, 471
Smalley, Adam, 282,
441, 521, 1014,
1319
Smith, BC, 1202
Smith, Stephen E.,
1129
Snow, Mark, 312,
1476
Sobel, Curt, 550

Sokolov, Elliot, 136
Sommer, Marc, 646
Stambler, Scott, 1163
Steiner, Armin, 10
Steinman, Paul, 1414
Stephney, Bill, 1057
Stevens, April, 127
Stewart, Bob, 10
Suozzo, Mark, 658,
896
Sutton, Graham, 123,
356
Sweet, Matthew, 173
Syrewicz, Stanislas,
1149

Taj Mahal, 927
Talgorn, Frederic, 1037
Taylor, Stephen James,
1442
Tec, Roland, 18
Tellefsen, Christopher,
219
Thompson, Walter,
252
Timmins, Michael, 869
Tiso, Wagner, 929
Tomey, Tricia, 1216
Tozer, Schaun, 492
Treloggen, Abby, 584,
755
Trevis, David, 634
Trumel, Annette, 1216

Vanston, Jeffrey CJ,
19
Vicari, Clem, Jr., 1425
Viklicky, Emil, 622
Vitarelli, Joseph, 631
Vollack, Lia, 33

Wall, Cindy, 1414
Wall, Jack, 1414
Walters, Happy, 1495
Wannberg, Ken, 1099,
1264
Warbeck, Stephen,
1137
Washington, Dinah,
127
Wedron, Craig, 400
Weidman, Jim, 958
Weissman, Maisie, 500
Wenger, Brahm, 10
Westlake, Nigel, 60
Whelan, Bill, 264
Whitfield, Richard,
1048, 1387, 1456
Whitfield, Sherry, 1134
Wilder, Matthew, 841
Williams, Alan, 772
Williams, David, 967
Williams, John, 1099,
1264
Wilson, Terry, 72, 871
Winget, Josh, 93, 851,
1154

Wiseman, Debbie, 1460
Wolff, Jonathan, 1228
Wood, Steve, 362
World Famous Blue, 105

Wray, Link, 1034
Wulff, Frank, 1096
Wulff, Stefan, 1096

Yared, Gabriel, 225
Yasukawa, Goro, 455

Young, Christopher, 493, 575, 1069, 1387

Zaafour, Frouz, 694
Zehavi, Oded, 509

Zelinskaia, Vera, 837
Zhao Jiping, 346
Zimmer, Hans, 1319
Zippel, David, 841
Zorn, John, 416
Zourabichvili, Nicolas, 135

PRODUCTION CREW

Aaron, Fanee, 1476
Abades, Reyes, 176
Abel, Luisa, 1149
Abell, G. Roger, 978
Abraham, Yasmine, 400
Abroms, Rachel, 114
Acheson, James, 759
Adair, Catherine, 72
Adam, Jori, 1290
Adamovich, Roman, 408
Adams, Charmian, 531
Adams, Susie, 1149
Adams, Victoria, 348
Adler, Laura, 1227
Adler, Sherri, 1343
Aguilar, G.A., 887, 920
Aguilar, George, 597
Aharoni, Gregg, 1052
Ahern, Ken, 414
Ahmad, Maher, 1371
Ahuna, Archie K., 636
Aible, Douglas, 996
Aida, Toshiharu, 334
Aiello, Danny III, 722
Aiello, Danny Jr., 1366
Ailetcher, Jon, 909, 914
Akerson, Randle, 903
Alan-Dittmar, David, 57
Alberts, John, 105
Albin, Lisa, 1221
Alder, Daril, 847
Aleksandrova, Natalia, 1315
Alicia, Chris, 539
Alicia, Chris, Jr., 1456
Allday, David, 356
Allder, Nick, 733
Allen, Linda, 19
Allen, Melanie, 1304
Alonso, Mat, 768
Alquiza, Kapu, 1174
Altieri, Kathy, 1014
Altman, Matthew, 447
Altman, Stephen, 433
Alvanos, Peter "Beetle", 282
Alvarez, Ignacio, 580
Alvarez, Miguel Angel, 789
Amann, Walter, 416

Amarante, Cássio, 195
Ambroise, Rick, 1057
Ambrose, June, 75
Amies, Caroline, 652
Ammon, Ruth, 831
Amor, Bobby, 1456
Amy, Christopher, 755
Anacker, Kristen, 914
Anagnos, Bill, 1232, 1447
Andersen, Lars Kolding, 625
Andersen, Mark, 715
Anderson, Coll, 1093
Anderson, George, 636
Anderson, Hawley, 715
Anderson, Larz, 1348
Anderson, Neal, 1154
Anderson, Neil, 1014
Anderson, Richard L., 27
Anderson, Robert, Jr., 978
Anderson, Russ, 1419
Anderson, Steen K., 1342
Anderson, Susan, 544
Andreatta, Jolie Anne, 601
Andres, Jo, 597
Andrews, Slamm, 282
Angelella, Rick, 954
Aouni, Walid, 302
Apone, Allan, 1242
Apps, Gregg, 1424
Aquila, Deborah, 278
Aquino, Ruben A., 841
Aramendia, Emilio, 1429
Arbogast, Roy, 1429
Arbuckle, Jamie, 282
Arbusto, Nicole, 1291
Archer, Tim, 738
Arenal, Julie, 461
Armstrong, Charles, 1202
Armstrong, Matt, 527
Armstrong, Vic, 112
Arnett, Jim, 1197
Arnett, M. James, 285
Arnold, Bill, 978

Arnold, Douglas B., 1048
Arnold, Joseph B., 237
Arrat, Patrice, 1131
Arroyo, Antonio, 1221
Arroyo, Michael F., 967
Artmont, Steve, 857
Artz, Mary Gail, 19, 806, 1085, 1163
Ash, Rick, 403
Ashman, Louis, 18
Askew, Campbell, 356
Asp, Anna, 674
Asselin, Chris, 1014, 1154
Astle, Martin, 652
Atamian, George C., 1081
Ateah, Scott, 10
Atria, Benni, 685
Atwell, Michael, 773, 1398
Atwood, Colleen, 77, 369
Atzmon, Boaz, 1290
Au, Alan, 1416, 1419
Augeard, Emmanuel, 1426
Auger, Jean-François, 1405
Auguste, Mark, 338
Augustine, Paige, 379
Auinger, Sam, Aulisi, Joseph G., 1264, 1361
Austerberry, Paul, 468, 1040
Austin, John P., 1339
Avery, John, 697
Avery, Rick, 119, 1254
Ayers, Ron, 987

Baca, Nancy, 1398
Bach, David, 441, 578
Bacharach, Jean, 176
Becher, Hans, 841
Baer, Hanania, 294
Bailey, Annelise, 626
Baker, Jon, 1135
Baker, Karen M., 1048
Baker, Kelley, 1023
Baker, Maria, 1240
Baker, Maxyne, 322

Baker, Rick, 811
Baker, Robert, 930
Baker, Vivian, 461, 575, 757
Baksht, David, 805
Balaman, S. Betim, 1221
Baldwin, Alice, 664
Ballance, Colleen, 757
Ballance, Jack, 433
Bamberger, Bernhard, 416
Banchelli, Geja, 1260
Bancroft, Tom, 841
Banister, Patrick, 312
Banks, Bobbi, 1471
Banta, Pat, 1348
Baptiste, Alan, 951
Barber, Lynn, 112
Barbosa, Carlos, 1023
Barchi, Petra, 277, 572
Barden, Kenny, 385
Barden, Kerry, 527, 659, 954, 1038, 1232
Barden, Stephen, 133, 256
Barker, Michelle, 67
Barker, Rick, 1308
Barosky, Michael, 664, 887
Barre, Perine, 759
Barrett, Alison, 60
Barrett, David M., 1240
Barrett, Kym, 1495
Barrett, Nicki, 60
Barrett, Stan, 1361
Barringer, Daniel W., 155, 225
Barrow, Carlotta, 822
Barry, Matthew, 1081
Barry, Shawn, 909
Bartholomew, Julia, 109
Bartlett, Kip, 112
Bartz, Axel, 271
Bashford, Anthony, 886
Bates, Jonathan, 264, 664, 674
Bates, Kenny, 40
Bauer, Joe, 634
Baum, Jenny, 33

Baumung, Ekkehart, 701
Baylis, Michele, 697
Bayliss, James, 936
Bayonas, Katrina, 709
Baytos, Eddie, 860
Beach, Lisa, 312
Beach, Tim, 1023
Beardsall, Sarah, 1149
Beattie, Leslie N., 978
Beauchamp, Eric, 578
Beauchamp, Kevin, 578
Beauchamp, Wayne, 578
Beaudet, Michel, 1
Beavan, Jenny, 356
Beck, Philip, Jr., 33
Beck, Tony, 312
Becket, Daphne, 941
Beckett, Ray, 176
Beckworth, Alan, 1062
Bedford, Louise, 697
Bedig, Jason, 317
Beebe, Betty, 954
Beewen, Karin, 898
Behrens, Kim, 587
Belardinelli, Charles "O.G.", 19
Belgrave, Michael A., 755
Bell, John, 27
Bell, Robert, 733
Bellens, Danny, 416
Bellfort, Tom, 385
Bellissimo, Thomas "Brooklyn", 19, 21
Benavente, Michael J., 317, 1308
Bendall, Haydn, 801
Bender, Lon E., 759, 841, 1014
Benitanai, Kenichi, 334
Benoit-Fresco, François, 1284
Benson, John, 593
Benson, Mark, 886
Benson, Phil, 364
Bensson, Mark, 887
Bentley, Peter, 282
Bentley-Griffin, Shay, 757
Benzinger, Suzy, 187
Beraldo, Elisabetta, 958, 1442

Bergbom, Brad, 1384
Berger, Howard, 615
Berger, John, 951
Berger, Richard, 1213
Bergin, Joan, 264
Bergstrom, Jan, 173, 278
Berke, Mayne, 610
Berkeley, Ron, 1348
Berkovitz, Glenn, 1495
Berliner, Roshelle, 1061
Berman, Danielle, 199
Berman, Mike R., 1174
Berman, Sandy, 575, 857
Bernard, Michael, 1442
Bernay, Lynn, 1227
Berry, Kelly, 1023
Bertrand, Claude, 649
Beschastnaia, Ekaterina, 837
Bestrop, Juel, 1000
Betanzos, Rick, 476
Beveridge, Chrissie, 773
Beville, Dean, 112
Bews, Guy, 1474
Bickerton, Angus, 733
Biel, Timothy, 684
Bieling, Susann, 89
Bigger, Michael, 882, 1264
Bihr, Kathryn, 1053, 1154, 1193
Bing, An, 330
Bird, Joseph L. "Pepe", 1052
Bird, Joseph R., 1052
Bird, Sarah, 1460
Birman, Matt, 1387
Biscoe, Kate, 1429
Biscoe, Max, 237, 869, 1277
Bisenz, Bruce, 1466
Bishop, Dan, 857
Bishop, Jack, 967
Bivins, Ray, 282, 780
Black, James Kyler, 21
Black, Jean, 97, 781
Blackburn, Phil S., 1495
Blaise, Aaron, 841
Blake, Larry, 920
Blake, Perry Andelin, 468, 1416, 1419
Blake, Yvonne, 1429
Blau, Fred, 40
Blaymires, Colin, 1249
Bleckman, Robert, 847
Blitstein, David, 225, 546, 944
Bloch, David, 447
Bloom, Leslie, 781
Blundell, Christine, 176
Blynder, Karen, 936
Blyth, Graham, 582
Blythe, Bernhard, 527
Bo, Eli, 607

Boccia, Margot, 920
Bochar, Ron, 298, 1000, 1489
Bochner, Stan, 715, 1052
Bode, Susan, 461, 887, 1489
Boland, Andrew, 589
Bolger, David, 264
Bolles, Harry, 497
Bolles, Susan, 595
Bolton, Michael, 1474
Bomba, David, 232, 1361
Bonetto, Aline, 751
Bonnie, Louisa, 584
Born, Dominique, 48
Borne, Steve, 75
Borrero, Felipe, 550, 1483
Bosc, Françoise, 1426
Boss, Clay, 173
Boston, P. J., 601
Boswell, Glenn, 271, 1319
Boswell, John, 1374
Boswell, Merideth, 810
Botnick, Bruce, 291, 841, 903, 1197, 1254, 1371
Bourke, Charlotte, 277, 1275
Bourne, Tristan, 914, 920
Bowen, Deidre, 256
Bowen, John, 1262
Bowern, Sarah, 697
Bowin, Claire Jenora, 930, 992
Bowring, John, 1424
Bowyer, Tom, 1304
Boyd, Michael T., 364
Boyes, Chris, 1031
Boylan, Debbie, 589
Boyle, Marc, 52
Boyle, Tim, 33, 674, 1442
Brace, John, 1456
Bracewell, Constance, 951
Bradford, Andy, 1409
Bradford, Daniel, 967, 1085
Bradford, Dennis, 285, 1052
Bradley, Dan, 967
Bradley, Stewart, 291
Braive, Charles, 772
Bramon-Garcia, Risa, 493
Branagan, John, 847
Branche, Stacye P., 975, 1429
Branco, Maria José, 975, 1405

Brandau, Thomas, 610
Brandenburg, Rosemary, 1023
Brander, Peter, 619
Brassart, Brigitte, 420
Braswell, Mariko, 96
Brattvik, Carina, 619
Braumberger, Heidi, 764
Brayham, Peter, 1249
Brazier, Kevin, 739
Brebner, Veronica, 457
Breen, Charles, 631, 969, 1387, 1483
Breindel, Scott, 658
Brennan, Erick, 1023
Brewer, Charlie, 857
Bridges, Mark, 173
Brincat, Paul "Salty", 1319
Brink, Connie, 781
Brink, Jeffrey S., 959
Brisbin, David, 1020
Brisdon, Stuart, 1137, 1249, 1280
Brisson, Jean-Claude, 195
Bristol, Joe, 1038
Broad, Suzan, 390
Brocher, Sylvie, 751
Brockmann, Les, 67
Brodie, Bill, 119
Brohan, Edward, 1069
Bromell, John T., 112
Bronson, Tom, 1416
Bronson-Howard, Aude, 781
Brooks, Nicholas, 1429
Brookshire, Jim, 550
Bross, John, 1302
Brot, Murielle, 764
Brous, Nancy, 572
Brown, Bart, 860
Brown, Bobby, 364
Brown, Brenton, 468
Brown, Dawn, 1476
Brown, Deborah, 519
Brown, Debra, 69
Brown, Kerrie, 60
Brown, Ross, 471
Brown-James, Carole, 1197
Brubaker, Tony, 77
Bruce, John, 40, 610, 882
Bruchon, Catherine, 411
Bruno, Richard, 1240
Bryant, Katherine Jane, 67
Buckley, Emma, 746
Buckley, Martine, 927
Bucossi, Peter, 659, 664, 1053, 1206, 1489
Budd, Tracy, 119
Bueno, Clovis, 929
Bufnoir, Jacques, 1216

Bühler, Michelle, 232, 1000
Bullock, Sandra, 1014
Burch, Jackie, 584, 636, 755
Burchiellaro, Giantito, 958
Burgee, Patty, 954
Burke, Todd, 1495
Burnett, Michael, 284
Burnham, Vin, 733
Burrough, Tony, 461
Burrows, Jami, 1187
Burtinshaw, Cynthia, 1474
Burton, Mary, 155, 1442
Burton, Willie, 77, 278
Burwell, Lois, 531, 1099
Bush, John, 703
Bush, Robin Michel, 615
Butcher, Charles, 584, 1228
Butler, Eileen, 970
Butler, Rick, 1069
Buttgereit, Jorg, 622
Byer, Allan, 96, 500, 903, 1154
Byrd, Donald, 864
Byrne, Alexandra, 338

Caben, Wilfred, 500
Cabral, Kelly, 810
Cabral, Susan A., 978
Cach, Jeff, 1495
Cady, Jill, 615
Caff, Carla, 195
Caglione, John, Jr., 1495
Caksiran, Boris, 1123
Calder, Frances, 738
Caldwell, Helen, 1189
Callahan, James, 500
Cellen, Nik, 822
Calvert, Frank, 847
Camara, Marcio, 929
Camargo, Denise, 773
Cameron, John, 37
Campana, Enrico, 93
Campayno, Joe, 539
Campbell, Janet, 738
Campbell, Veda, 1442
Camron, Robert, 317
Caneca, Carlos, 1387
Canelos, Damian, 497
Cannon, Reuben, 322, 615, 1442
Canonero, Milena, 155
Cantamessa, Gene, 1174
Cantamessa, Steve, 1242
Cao Jiuping, 346
Caprara, Walter, 201
Carasik, Cheryl, 1000

Carbone, Franco-Giacomo, 109
Carbone, Marilyn, 1264
Carden, Paul Timothy, 155
Cardenas, Charisse, 493
Cardwell, Shane, 385
Carey, Leslie I., 1339
Carin, Kate, 1044, 1249
Carlhian, Sophie, 544
Carlos, Juan, 1440
Carlson, Chris, 1419
Carlucci, Lou, 114, 173, 1253
Carpentier, Daniel, 1205
Carr, Cathy, 57
Carr, Cindy, 1429
Carr, Jackie, 1442, 1476
Carrafa, John, 658
Carrett, G. John, 544
Carroll, Amanda, 967
Carroll, Shawn, 749
Carruth, Scott, 886
Carseldine, Jenny, 271
Carter, Emily, 1374
Carter, Juliet, 865
Carter, Ruth E., 563
Carter-Narcisse, Marietta, 851
Cartwright, Caroly, 500
Carwardine, Bruce, 309, 806
Casale, Robert, 1085
Casillas, Raul, 10
Cassara, Carl, 847
Cassel, Ferne, 631
Cast, Frank Saint, 764
Castaeda, Rigoberto, 789
Castle, Danny, 550
Cate, Russell, 256
Causey, Dennis Lee, 781, 996
Causey, Thomas, 155, 1254
Cavanaugh, Larry, 1174
Ceniceros, John, 40
Cesari, Bruno, 201
Chalmers, Kirstin, 294
Chelon, Luc, 425
Chamberland, Francesca, 69
Chambliss, Scott, 636
Chamian, Denise, 1099, 1197
Chan, Jackie, 819, 1081
Chan, Julius, 60
Chan, Shirley, 219
Chandler, Michael, 1069
Chang, William, 373

Chaplynsky, Renatta, 1366
Chapman, David, 1163
Charette, Cynthia, 593
Chase, Ken, 1174
Chau, Tim, 539, 1081
Chau Sai-Hung, 819
Chavez, Richard, 1014
Chen, Christopher, 10
Chenoweth, Ellen, 1, 554, 722, 1242
Chesley, Martha, 476
Chesney, Peter, 97
Chester, Gary, 75, 369
Chiang, Peter, 123
Chichester, John, 1442
Childs, Martin, 1137
Chilvers, John, 133
Chinelli, Rick, 715
Chinich, Michael, 1174
Chinlund, James, 139
Chojecki, Mechelle, 527
Chopin, Kathleen, 1
Choukroun, Pierre, 48
Cho Wing, 819
Christiansen, Ellen, 1489
Christl, Lisy, 416
Christopher, Lynn, 379
Christopher, Tom, 860
Church, Karen, 580, 593
Chusid, Barry, 114
Cicek, Selda, 1260
Cimino, Bill, 1456
Cirincione, Richard, 1205
Cisterna, Fred, 886, 887
Claesson, Helmer A., 1038
Clancy, Michael, 751, 1471
Clark, John, 356
Clark, Nick, 37
Clark, Roydon, 1228
Clark, Russell, 369, 563, 1442
Clark, Simon, 1149
Clark, Ted, 1449
Clator, James, 1240
Cletworthy, Robert, 1339
Clauer, James S., 1093
Clausen, Michael, 909
Clay, Paul, 806, 819
Claypool, Michael, 1187
Clayton, Guy, 232
Clayton, R. Gilbert, 40
Claytor, James F., 317
Clegg, Fergus, 176
Clemens, Peter, 1213
Clement, Michel, 738
Clifford, Jeff, 652
Cloudia, 1466

Clydesdale, Ross, 119, 133
Coates, Nelson, 312, 715
Cochrane, Alexander, 593
Cochrane, Sandy, 291, 1474
Cohen, Barbara, 19, 806, 1085, 1163
Cohen, David B., 1189
Cohen, Harry, 362
Colbert, Joanna, 119, 133, 468
Cole, David, 19
Colello, Dawn, 1414
Coleman, Doug, 225, 1174
Coley, Aisha, 500
Collin, Dinah, 1304
Collins, Jake, 511
Colmenero, Jack, 546, 550
Colquhoun, Mary, 1154, 1205
Combris, Anne-Laure, 746
Combs, Gary, 291, 554
Comerford, Jon, 739
Condren, Patrick, 164
Cone, William, 146
Conna, Edward, 237
Cook, Leslie, 521
Cooney, Tim, 679
Cooper, Clifton T., 112
Cooper, Sandy, 593
Copeman, John, 664, 1135, 1262
Coppard, Yvonne, 733
Corbett, Ann Marie, 291
Corbin, Lisa S., 97
Corbould, Chris, 394
Corbould, Neil, 1099
Cordero, Humberto, 865
Cordice, Sharyn, 75
Corenblith, Michael, 810
Cormier, Phil, 865
Corsalini, Stephanie, 587
Cory, Lauren, 920, 1476
Cossu, Walter, 686
Costa, Damian J., 461
Cotter, Jemima, 746
Cottignoli, Alberto, 87
Coufal, Don, 847
Court, Gretchen Rennell, 554
Cowitt, Allison, 733
Cox, Betsy, 1129
Cox, Brian, 1319
Cox, Monty, 72
Craig, Jordan, 1471
Craig, Louis, 1
Craig, Stuart, 52

Crane, Simon, 1099
Cranham, Gina B., 317
Creber, William, 1466
Crespo, Jos Luis, 709
Cresson, Françoise, 390
Crimmins, Margaret, 469, 572, 1449
Crisanti, Andrea, 1344
Cristante, Ivo, 1187
Crittenden, Dianne, 930, 1149, 1319
Cronkhite, Kendel, 27
Crosby, Douglas, 882
Cross, Kevin, 860
Croughwell, Charles, 285, 1429
Crowther, Graeme, 356
Crozier, David, 531, 1409
Cruse, William, 369
Cukurs, Mick, 447, 1213
Cummings, Peg, 285
Cunliffe, Shay, 225, 232
Cunningham, Keith P., 920
Currie, Mark, 93
Currie, Robert, 781, 996
Curry, Martha, 739
Curtis, Christo, 60
Curtis, Clive, 1149
Curvelier, Alain, 1344
Cusack, Pud, 773

D'Amore, Hallie, 225, 232, 847, 944
Dabe, Marc, 563
Dagort, Phil, 546
Dahl, Nancy, 578
Dalton, Bur, 317, 992
D'Ambrogio, Cori, 135
Damiani, John, 173
Dane, Mark, 1456
Danger, Amy, 538
Danziger, Neil, 480
Darakjian, Ara, 1081
Dare, Daphne, 176
Darnell, Karin, 1249
Darrow, Harry, 780
Dashnaw, Jeff, 992
Da Silva, Rosalina, 291
Davenport, Dennis, 806, 1163
Davis, Bill, 112
Davis, Catherine, 597
Davis, Dan, 1163, 1483, 1489
Davis, Gary, 1371
Davis, Jason, 521
Davis, Jennifer A., 348
Davis, Kristen, 1023
Davis, Leonora, 674
Davis, Nick, 52

Davis, Sharen, 317, 1081
Davis, Sharon, 1254
Davison, Steve, 715
Davison, Tim, 1476
Daweachu, Agi Ariumsaichan, 622
Day, Gary, 153
Day, Kate, 739
Day, Terra, 441
de Bruijn, Gert, 822
de Bruijn, Robert, 210
de Cossio, José Maria, 709
De Chauvigny, Emmanuel, 135
De Cosmo, Matteo, 587
de Hoogd, Marcel, 210
de Laubier, Marie, 420
De Luca, Raffael, 87
De Moleron, Arnaud, 1131
de Paco, Felipe, 709
de Rossi, Giannetto, 759
de Rouin, Colin, 755, 1240
De Scalzi, Aldo, 1260
De Scalzi, Pivio, 1260
De Titta, George, Jr., 1264
de Van, Marina, 1127
De Vico, Robert, 306, 1146
De Vivaise, Caroline, 1131
Dean, Richard, 722, 781, 1264
Deasy, Brendan, 164, 427
Decristofaro, Andrew, 1193
DeGovia, Jackson, 847
DeHaven, Bonita, 584
Del Brocco, Giancarlo, 1123
Del Paso, Felipe Fernández, 789
Del Rosario, Linda, 394
DeLara, Dexter, 1254
Delpak, Mohammad Reza, 1293
Delpuech, Yann, 1398
Demers, Lucille, 1205
Demetrau, Georges, 1062
Denson, Debra, 874
Deprez, Therese, 480, 882
Derrien, Yannick, 759
DeSanto, Susie, 550
DeScenna, Linda, 944
Desmond, Gary, 1380
Detoro, Kathleen, 278, 493
Detweiller, Chad, 865
Deutsch, Lisa, 1419

Deveau, Marie Sylvie, 806
Develle, Jeanne, 139
Dever, Sean, 951
Deverell, Tamara, 385
Deville, Debbie, 284, 587
Deville, Roland, 989
Devine, Alicia, 176
Devine, Michael W., 757
Devine, Richard, 1447
Devlin, Peter J., 539, 1456
Devries, Devora, 105
Dexter, John, 96
Diamant, Ilana, 634
Diamond, Gary, 610
Diamond, Josh, 1152
Diaz, Ken, 773
Dibble, Chris, 390, 1137
Dicicco, Mary, 865
Dick, Jaro, 310
Diego, Antonio, 1440
Dillett, Pat, 237
Dilley, Leslie, 285
Dimeo, Anthony, 1052
DiMuro, Dino, 1154
Dinkel, Jeni Lee, 1456
Dittrick, Michael, 403
Dixon, Shane, 1129
Djurkovic, Maria, 1189, 1460
Dodd, Patrick, 291, 780
Dodge, Norm, 1447
Donaldson, Kevin, 587
Donati, Danilo, 685, 686
Donne, Naomi, 887, 959
Donnellan, Gaye, 1374
Donnelly, Maggie, 129
Dopaso, Andrea, 860
Doran, Stacy, 1197
Dorrance, Daniel T., 1099
Dougherty, Marion, 679
Douglas, Michael, 959
Dowdall, Jim, 123, 1304
Downer, John, 1137, 1409
Downer, Wayne, 322
Doyle, Chris, 1167
Doyle, Tracey, 232, 1020
Dresbach, Terry, 930, 1069, 1398
Driscoll, Michael, 978
Drohan, Edward A. III, 1447
Drummond, Dennis, 936
Drysdale, Dorothy, 580
Duffield, Tom, 1000
Dultz, Jim, 1429

Duncan, Emilia, 403
Dunham, Gary, 1456
Dunlop, Eddie, 615
Dunn, John, 615, 664, 887
Dunne, Joe, 797, 1062
Dunsford, Ann A., 757
Dunsworth, John, 476
Duo Guoxiang, 346
Dupuis, Stephan, 291
Durante, Stephen, 539
Durrell, William, 1466
Dutertre, Annette, 302
Duvall, Sonya, 282
Dwernicki, Sophie, 1426
Dwyer, John, 1254

Eagan, Lynne, 40, 1000
Earnshaw, Tina, 356, 1137, 1189
Easley, Alan E., 944
Eastside, Lori, 385, 539
Eavey, Rudolph III, 1135
Ebden, John, 1409
Eber, Robert, 237
Ebner, Heinz, 603
Eckert, David, 33
Eddo, Scott, 112
Ede, Nic, 1460
Edelman, Abra, 10, 927
Edelman, Debra, 1290
Eden, Jill, 819
Eder, Hannes, 416
Edwards, Sarah, 610, 659
Edwards, Tricia, 531
Efinger, Tom, 480, 527
Egorova, Iulia, 1315
Eidenbenz, Florian, 135
Elliott, William, 755
Einarson, Sturla, 619
Eisenmann, David, 146
Elam, Greg W., 546
Elam, Kiante, 550
Elek, Katalin, 448
Elek, Zoltan, 1048
Elias, Gloria, 578
Elliott, John M., Jr., 285
Elliott, William, 317, 755
Ellis, Mary, 112
Elmendorf, Garry, 1205
Elsom, Joel, 1495
Emerson, Beth, 97
Emir, Florence, 989
Emmanuelli, François, 1377
Engel, Jann, 447
Engel, Volker, 447
England, Rod, 1456

Engleman, Leonard, 797
English, Jane, 114
Ennis, Victor Ray, 757
Enroth, Eric, 965, 1277
Erdberg, Ron, 930
Eriksen, Jennifer L., 671
Eskowitz, Lori, 965
Estabrook, Dan, 400
Ettinger, Wendy, 176
Eulner, Frank, 461, 471, 554
Evans, Cindy, 1061
Evans, Martin, 1280
Everberg, Kirsten, 1193
Everton, Deborah, 471

Fabris, Bill, 126
Fann, Matt, 1135
Fann, Valerie, 1135
Farhat, Jon, 317
Farnsworth, Diamond, 1495
Farr, Judy, 356
Farrantello, Nick, 1308
Farrell, Victoria, 527, 587
Farrow, Michael, 97, 441, 493, 521, 1447
Fatima, 975
Fauquet-Lemaitre, Dominique, 394
Faur, Brigitte, 411
Favila, Isabel, 1405
Fay, Dale, 593
Fay, Maura, 819, 1374
Fecht, Doug, 1447
Fechtman, Robert, 447
Felce, Christine, 316
Feldman, Leslee, 27
Fenton, Andrea, 1447
Fenton, Mike, 733
Ferbrache, Richard, 133
Ferguson, Alex L., 1262
Ferguson, Sue, 1149
Fernandez, Benjamin, 348
Fernandez, Richard, 1371
Fernandez, Robert, 19, 317, 394, 679, 780, 1240, 1387
Ferraro, Christopher, 1052
Ferreira, Nelson, 634
Ferrell, James, 664, 1216
Ferretti, Dante, 781
Ferry, April, 699
Ferry, Dawn, 1202
Fettis, Gary, 936

Feuer, Howard, 77, 298, 1023, 1348
Fichter, Thomas, 1081
Fiege, Bill, 1123
Fiennes, Ralph, 1014
Figgis, Susie, 52, 164, 1389
Finger, Leonard, 1262
Finlayson, Bruce, 394, 441
Finn, Mali, 1483
Finn, Mary, 857, 920
Finn, Sarah, 951
Fioramonti, Glory, 575
Fioritto, Larry, 1361, 1398, 1442
Fischnaller, Nicole, 603
Fishman, Marc, 237, 975
Fisichella, Marc, 1476
Fisk, Jack, 1319
Fitzgerald, Denise, 970
Fitzgerald, Robert, 996
Flack, Stephanie, 546
Flaksman, Marcos, 403
Fleming, Frank, 819
Fleming, Jerry, 965
Fleming, Rachael, 440, 667
Flick, Christopher, 1442
Flick, Stephen Hunter, 874
Flugel, John J., 781, 996
Fojo, Richard, 539, 1308
Foley, Maurice, 589
Fong, Jana Lee, 1302
Fong, Sean, 1495
Fonne, Runa, 607
Fontaine, Christian, 201, 1426
Ford, Albert, Jr., 1240
Ford, Roger, 60
Foroutan, Dahlia, 975
Forrestal, Terry, 338, 1280
Forsayth, Rick, 806
Fortune, Bruce, 369
Foster, Geoff, 247
Foster, Terrence, 182
Fotinos, Eleny, 887
Fowler, Jo Ann, 10
Fox, Celestia, 822, 1291
Fox, James, 1205
Fox, K.C., 317
Foy, Nancy, 317
France, Marie, 123
Francesco, Jake Notar, 819
Frankish, John, 1044
Frankley, Cameron, 871, 1254
Fraser, Eric, 312
Fraser, Jennifer, 578
Fraser, Tim, 294
Frazee, Terry, 1254

Frazier, John, 40, 493
Freda, Francesco, 1344
Fredburg, Jim, 369
Freeborn, Dennis, 461
Freeman, Laurie, 634
Freemantle, Glenn, 1249, 1424
French, Callie, 572
Frey, Chad S., 114
Frick, John, 699, 860
Friedman, Alan "Doc", 871
Friel, Greg, 176
Frierson, Harry, 920
Frigato, Emita, 48
Frigerio, Ezio, 899
Frithiof, Berndt, 619
Frogley, Louise, 1371
Frutkoff, Gary, 920, 1495
Fuhrer, Chelsea, 512
Fukaya, Akira, 1336
Fuller, Ian, 390, 652
Fuller, Kris, 1023
Fullerton, Carl, 77
Fulton, Larry, 550
Fung, William, 634

Gaborieu, Dominique, 420
Gadoury, Odette, 1205
Gaeta, Frank, 394
Gaffin, Lauri, 679, 1174
Gaily, Paul, 781
Gainceva, Ludmila, 135
Galer, Andrea, 390, 739
Galich, Steve, 379, 610
Gallagher, Helen M., 187
Galline, Frank, 757
Galvin, Tim, 77, 1232
Gambina, James, 1205
Gammelsrod, Tom, 607
Gang, Wu, 330
Gannon, Ted, 587
Ganton, Douglas, 93
Garcia, Francois, 738
Garcia, Jose Antonio, 447
Garcia, Risa Bramon, 237, 951
Garcia, Esther, 709
Gardiner, Lizzy, 1424
Gardner, Hal, 112
Gardner, Steve, 1429
Gardner, Suzanne, 511
Garfield, Hank, 72, 615
Garlington, Marshal, 362
Garner, Pat, 1216
Garrison, Miranda, 72

Garrity, Joseph T., 19
Garwood, Norman, 269, 733
Gasparro, Anthony, 1093
Gassner, Dennis, 1348
Gastel, Angelo, 403
Gatson, Frank, Jr., 715
Gausman, Russel A., 1339
Gauthier, Diane, 738
Gauthier, Glen, 119, 1163
Gautrelet, Sylvie, 649
Gehr, Rocky, 773
Geisinger, Joseph, 951
Geleng, Antonello, 48
Georgiades, Ben, 225
Geraghty, Mark, 264
Gerard-Hirne, Claire, 764
Gerlich, Gary S., 468
Gerlich, Gregory M., 1240, 1416
Germain, Perry M., 114
Getzler, Sandy, 298
Ghiraldini, Robert, 1061
Giacomazzi, Mickey, 1023
Gibbens, Howell, 1174
Gibbs, George, 338, 759
Gibson, Anita, 500, 920
Gibson, Colin, 60, 1424
Gibson, Jane, 247, 390
Gibson, Malcolm, 1471
Giger, H.R., 622
Giguere, Edi, 240
Gika, Hector C., 1154
Gilbert, Lance, 780
Gilbert, Matthew L., 1419
Gill, Jack, 1053
Gillis, Alec, 1476
Gilman, John H., 109
Ginnever, Jodi, 1059
Giobbi, Lisa, 1429
Giovanni, Judi, 563
Girard, Stephanie, 539
Giulani, Chantal, 1037
Glass, Terry, 674
Glossop, Peter, 822, 1137, 1288
Glover, Denny, 1014
Gobruegge, Les, 847
Goddard, Richard, 851
Goen, George Burton II, 927
Gogol, Derek, 1014
Gold, Nina, 123
Goldberg, Harvey, 119
Goldberg, Mary, 291, 1154
Goldblum, Jeff, 1014

Goldman, Dina, 136, 215, 1436
Goldsmith, John, 225
Goldsmith, Laura, 237
Goldstein, Libby, 72
Golitzen, Alexander,
Golub, Michael, 789
Gómez, Antxon, 709
Good, Tim, 322
Goodman, Elisa, 10, 927
Goodman, Richard Bryce, 810, 992
Goodwin, Jeff, 1020, 1135, 1262
Gorak, Chris, 379
Gordon, Antoinette Judith, 278
Gordon, Chris, 1456
Gorrell, Ken, 1416
Gottlieb, Max, 1149
Goudier, Jean, 764
Goulder, Ann, 480
Gow, Ronald, 624
Grace, Cheryle, 975
Grace, Martin, 264
Gracie, Ian, 1319
Graef, Vicki, 468
Graf, Allan, 1048, 1416
Grafmuller, Joe, 715
Graham, W. Steven, 554, 722
Granata, Dona, 1135
Grande, Greg, 114
Grant, Jacques, 411
Grant, Peter, 674
Grantz, H. Chris, 978
Graves, Lennie K., 1031
Graysmark, Jo, 703
Greco, Carolyn, 216
Green, Patricia, 119, 133, 385
Greenberg, Dana Allyson, 282
Greenberg, Jeff, 871
Greenberg, Jill, 461
Greene, Kimberly, 356, 546, 930
Greenfield, Robert, 1193
Greenhorn, Jim, 875, 1460
Green-Hughes, Evan, 530
Green-Keyes, Nancy, 1081
Greenwood, Sarah, 457, 801
Greiner, Wendy, 580
Gresham, Gloria, 1174, 1242
Gretsch, Martha, 1145
Greville-Masson, Marc, 601
Grieve, Robert, 610, 847, 1495
Griffin, Frank, 1232

Griffin, Wayne, 93
Griffiths, Chris, 21
Griffiths, Frank, 291
Griffiths, Stephen, 739
Grifo, Alisa, 1366
Grignon, Rex, 27
Grigorian, Greta, 240
Grillo, Marco, 1260
Grimes, Lee A., 1416
Groff, Lee Ann, 284
Groom, Bill, 1052
Gropman, David, 232, 1361
Gross, Holger, 291, 851
Gross, Olav, 1037
Groult, François, 195, 411, 764
Grubbs, Stephen, 309
Guaglione, Eric, 841
Guaita, Vittoria, 87
Guay, Isabelle, 1205
Guegan, Philippe, 411, 759
Guenther, Kimberly, 679
Guerra, Robert, 781
Gugliametti, Dominic, 1062
Guidasci, Magali, 40
Guillermin, Michelle, 699
Guimaraes, Oliva, 403
Guish, Michelle, 457, 801, 1137, 1189
Guzauski, Mick, 563

Habberstad, Jeff, 493
Hackett, Rosie, 1409
Haigh, Nancy, 379, 1348
Hails, Sasha, 1127
Hainer, Greg, 1014, 1154
Halbert, Stephen, 874
Halili, Caroline, 580
Hall, Bob, 468
Hall, Doug, 21
Hallberg, Per, 269, 447, 1048, 1387
Haller, Michael, 569
Halty, Jim, 992
Hamakawa, Keith, 1474
Hambrook, Danny, 457
Hamburger, Vera, 929
Hamilton, Alyson, 1031
Hammond, Diane, 77
Hammond, Fae, 876
Hamzaoui, Aziz, 764
Hamzaoui, Karim, 768
Hamzaoui, Malek, 768
Hanan, Michael Z., 1062
Hanania, Caroline, 667, 806

Hancock, Mike, 493
Hankins, David, 951
Hanlon, Cassie, 1424
Hannafin, Kelly, 298, 936, 1495
Hannan, Georges, 477
Hannan, Mary Claire, 569, 1387
Hannon, Frances, 1085
Hansell, Jeff, 37
Hansen, Peter Christian, 625
Hanson, Luana, 876
Hanson, Seth, 1275
Haraguchi, Tomoo, 395
Hardin, Kimberly, 975
Harding, Kathleen, 252
Hardwicke, Catherine, 860
Hardy, Ken, 112, 1020
Hargreaves, Patricia, 10
Harkins, Isabel, 521
Harlan, Chase, 1334
Harman, Lee C., 554
Harper, Charlotte, 477
Harper, James, 715
Harper, Robert W., 1085
Harper, Sally J., 1085
Harrell, Michael D., 575
Harris, Andy, 1044
Harris, Ann, 584, 755, 1129, 1419
Harris, Barbara, 60
Harris, Caroline, 457, 1280
Harris, Daniel, 640
Harris, Kevin, 539, 1308, 1456
Harris, Mike, 133, 1471
Harris, Rob, 390
Harris, Zeal, 1181
Hart, Christine, 806
Hart, Jay, 978
Hart, Patricia L., 511
Hart, Philippe, 746
Hartigan, John, 471, 563, 975
Hartl, Petr, 674
Harvey, Judith, 271
Harwood, Shuna, 652, 941
Haussig, Uwe, 1096
Hawkins, Bill, 810
Haworth, Sean, 1000
Hay, Pat, 1460
Hays, Sanja Milkovic, 114, 1254
Haze, Ofra, 1014
Hebden, Gilly, 733
Hebertson, R. Scott, 1129
Hecker, Scott A., 119, 781, 1466
Hedegaard, Rie, 184

Hedge, Dave, 171
Hedges, Michael, 1374
Heflin, Karoline T., 603
Hegarty, Jennifer, 264
Hegeman, Danny, 1154
Heimann, Betsy, 797, 920, 1164
Hein, Robert, 187, 597, 992
Heinrichs, Rick, 96
Helland, J. Roy, 903
Helmer, Richard, 1371
Hemdane, Hamed, 302
Hemming, Lindy, 703
Henault, Ludovic, 411, 1216
Henderson, Eryka Seimon, 996
Henderson-Martin, Cathy, 601
Henighan, Craig, 256
Henn, Mark, 841
Hennessey, Bill, 1447
Hennessy, William, 77
Henriques, Edouard, 97
Henrix, Stefan, 521, 1149
Hergersberg, Jochen, 622
Herman, Ilona, 461, 1062
Hermer-Bell, Lindsey, 322
Hernandez, Sandra, 500
Herrera, Boris, 218
Hertzog, Careen, 123
Hervieux, Mario, 738
Herwitt, Jennifer, 33
Hess, Phil, 1014
Hetland, Carla, 394
Hewitt, Dominic, 427
Hewitt, Jery, 1069, 1489
Heyman, Lawrence, 550
Hibbs, Edward, 669
Hice, Freddie, 584, 936
Hicks, Lori, 996, 1040
Hicks, Michael, 112
Hicks, Richard, 965
Hicks, Robert, 1471
Hicks, Thomas, Jr., 1240
Hidalgo, Eduardo, 1288
Hidderley, Tom, 322
Higgins, Harry, 1449
Hilkene, Michael, 755, 944
Hill, Bruce, 715
Hill, Owens, 987
Hiller, Randi, 237, 493, 951
Hills, Graham, 751
Hills, Joan, 123, 822
Hinds-Johnson, Marcia, 173

Hiney, Bill, 72, 1456
Hirschberg, Lora, 127
Hix, Kim, 615
Hliddal, Petur, 715
Hobbs, Al, 493, 810
Hobbs, Christopher, 1389
Hobbs, Richard, 271, 1319
Hobbs, William, 269
Hobel, Mara, 136
Hocs, David, 1181
Hodges, Joseph, 715
Hofstedt, T. Daniel, 841
Hogan, Chris, 1014
Holden, Shawn, 441, 1059
Holland, A. Todd, 114
Holland, Desne, 930, 1483
Holland, Simon, 1280
Holland, Thomas, 1135
Holland, Tim, 146, 1242
Hollow, Bob, 703, 1189, 1409, 1460
Holm, Morten, 184
Holt, Paul, 601
Holtshousen, Bryce, 886
Holtzman, Robert, 77
Homan, Gina, 780
Hood, Sean, 978
Hooker, Buddy Joe, 610, 781
Hoover, Richard, 33, 874
Hopkins, Billy, 385, 527, 575, 658, 954, 1038, 1232
Hopps, Stuart, 1280
Horgan, Kieran, 164, 264
Horiuchi, Senji, 395
Horner, Grenville, 1249
Horton, Dave Sr., 1031
Horton, John, 822
Hoskins, Max, 1249
Hosoishi, Terumi, 1439
Hospes, Dave, 312
Hotoda, Goh, 746
Houston, Ken, 369, 379
Hovey, Dean, 322
Howard, Angela, 511
Howard, Frederick, 21
Howell, Chris, 1398
Howell, Lee, 580
Howell, Shawn, 521
Howells, Michael, 356, 1288
Howitt, Peter, 338
Hoyos, Luis G., 291, 447, 851
Hsu, Paul, 469, 572, 1449
Hubbard, Geoff, 40, 1242

Hubbard, John, 390, 1304, 1409
Hubbard, Ros, 390, 1304, 1409
Huber, Sabina, 886
Hublou, Heidi, 936
Hudson, Pete, 1429
Huete, Lala, 1288
Hughes, Julie, 1031
Hughes, Melanie, 1081
Hui, Raman, 27
Hulme, Paul, 21, 225, 461
Hummelvoll, Gudny, 619
Hunter, Clark, 237, 869, 1277
Huntsman, J. Paul, 285, 1319
Hurd, James E., Jr., 920
Hurpeau, Frederique, 411
Hurt, Joseph, 1447
Husby, David, 394
Huss, Deborah, 601
Hutcherson, Marty, 403
Hutman, Jon, 554, 722
Huzzer, Elaine J., 1020
Hverven, Pal Morten, 607, 619
Hymes, Gary, 112, 155
Hymns, Richard, 554, 1099
Hynek, Joel, 1429

Iacoponi, Enrico, 686
Ibsen, Nora, 795
Igawa, Shigeko, 334
Ilson, Sharon, 493, 610, 903
Imada, Jeff, 615
Inagaki, Hisao, 334
Ireland, Simone, 338, 531, 1249, 1380
Isaacs, Jhane, 578
Isaksen, Eva, 619
Ishii, Ken, 970
Ishioka, Kevin, 40, 291, 851
Isoda, Norihiro, 395
Isola, Cam-illa-Valentine, 1288
Iturregui, Leonard, 933
Ivanov, Kalina, 129
Iwasaki, Hiroko, 1336

Jackness, Andrew, 597
Jackson, Bernard, 1057
Jackson, Bill, 1
Jackson, Gemma, 123
Jackson, John E., 21

Jackson, Pat, 860
Jackson, Regan, 75
Jacobson, Scott, 1308
Jacoby, Ellen, 684
Jaeger, Craig, 1014, 1154
Jaffe, Sheila, 67, 403, 869, 1193, 1366
James, Katherine, 715, 920
James, Whitney L., 232
Jamison, Peter, 1129
Jamison-Tanchuck, Francine, 851
Janiger, Robert, 1228
Jannasch, Emmanuel, 739
Jansen, Joann Fregeletto, 379
Jarvis, Jeff, 1240
Jay, Jina, 427
Jeans, Sarah, 640
Jefferds, Vincent, 69
Jefferies, John D., 72, 584
Jefferson, Martyn, 1471
Jelier & Schaaf, 210
Jennings, Daniel, 40, 1213
Jensen, Gary, 33
Jensen, Lisa, 857
Jensen, Nils C., 550
Jeung, Kathy, 40
Jianquin, Shen, 330
Jiritano, Drew, 480, 1061
Jiritano, Greg, 1061
Joachim, Joe, 603
John, David, 674
John, Martyn, 1189, 1460
John, Priscilla, 356, 703
Johnson, Amanda Mackey, 539, 759, 909, 958, 992, 1062, 1240, 1371
Johnson, Angela, 1057
Johnson, Bill, 119
Johnson, Bo, 173, 298
Johnson, Broose, 841
Johnson, Cal, 282, 757, 1057
Johnson, Glen W., 60
Johnson, Jane B., 930
Johnson, Junie Lowry, 1129
Johnson, Martin, 176
Johnson, Richard L., 1348
Johnson, Steve, 1240
Johnson, Tony, 1424
Johnston, Joanna, 1099

Johnston, Martha, 225
Johnston, Michael, 575, 1447
Johnston, Michelle, 857
Jolly, Trevor, 282
Joly, Peter, 52, 123
Jones, Allison, 285
Jones, Bryan, 1057
Jones, Ed, 1213
Jones, Gary, 298
Jones, Jamie, 1040
Jones, Kristin Frances, 1197
Jones, Mike, 477
Jones, Richard Lee, 930
Jones, Roxanne, 173
Jones, Sue, 875
Jordan, Michael, 275
Jordan, Steven, 72, 871
Jorry, Corinne, 1284, 1377
Joseph, Adam, 601
Joseph, Eddy, 164, 733
Joson, Jocelyn, 512
Jovanovski, Michael, 1474
Joyce, Andy, 322
Judkins, Fred, 312, 967
Judkins, Ronald, 1023, 1099
Julienne, Rémy, 751
Juliusson, Karl, 619
Junxia, Guo, 410
Justice, Matthew, 114

Kaahanui, Michael Jr., 601
Kaczenski, Chester, 563
Kane, Sarah, 1304
Kanter, Christoph, 416
Kaplan, Bill, 348
Kaplan, Michael, 40
Karady, Ondine, 1093
Kardos, Derrick, 882
Karl, Peter, 37
Karp, Judy, 789
Kartashov, Vladimir, 137
Kasarda, John, 461
Kasch, Brian, 433, 874
Katsaras-Barklem, Jo, 1291
Kaufman, Avy, 232, 1040, 1069, 1093, 1447
Kaufmann, Susan, 187, 434, 631
Kavanagh, Michael, 385, 806
Kavanaugh, Lisa Dean, 1099

Kawashiima, Ichiro, 1336
Kaye, Alan, 1254
Kaye, Barbara Cole, 967
Kaye, Elizabeth, 332
Kaye, Simon, 356, 733
Kearns, Patrick, 312
Kearse, Kirsten, 1275
Keast, James, 801
Keating, Trish, 312
Keegan, Donna, 472
Keen, Gregory, 310
Keffer, Lelan, 521
Keil, Jeanet, 625
Kelejian, Doug, 1262
Kellogg, Mary Anne, 871
Kelly, Bridget, 1447
Kelly, John-Paul, 1380
Kelly, Peter J., 348
Kelly, Randy, 1014
Kelsey, Dave, 72, 575, 951
Kelson, David M., 780
Kelter, Jerie, 755
Kemp, Erin, 944, 1429
Kemp, Larry, 232
Kempster, Steve, 40, 348, 610
Keogh, Liz, 271
Kern, David, 550
Kes, Risa, 89
Keyer, Philip J., 332
Keywan, Alicia, 133
Khan, Ralis, 572
Kharat, Michel, 751
Khoury, Peggy, 1447
Kidd, Barbara, 876
Kilmer, Val, 1014
Kilpatrick, Tracy, 1135
Kilpe, Kristina, 77
Kilvert, Lilly, 225, 1154
Kim, Eun-Young, 1037
King, Charlie, 1076
King, Greg, 610, 847, 1398, 1495
King, Ken, 1197
King, Noelle, 773, 1398
King, Peter, 52, 703, 1288, 1389
King, Richard, 601
King, Robb Wilson, 1081
Kingi, Henry, Jr., 114
Kingsbury, Neil, 739
Kin-kwun, Poon, 373
Kirk, Kim, 1262
Kirkland, Geoffrey, 298
Kirschner, David, 173, 317
Kirshbaum, Traci, 237, 869, 1277
Kirshoff, Steve, 461, 1052
Kirst, Alexander, 810, 920

Kirzinger, Ken, 394
Kittle, Tom, 433
Kitzmeyer, Bruce, 882
Klamer, Pamela, 1174
Klassen, David, 493, 679, 1174
Klatt, Clifford, 903
Klatt, Robert, 903
Klatt, Rose, 477
Klaudi, Inge, 468
Klawonn, Patricia, 40, 1174
Klein, Helga, 603
Klein, Jay, 1447
Kleven, Max, 19
Kljakovic, Miljen Kreka, 1240
Klohn, T. Edwin, 914
Kloiber, Martin, 1129
Klompus, Betsy, 1052
Klopp, Kathe, 847
Klopper, Nancy, 390, 797
Kluge, Ray, 1264, 1489
Kneupper, David, 1429
Knight, Amanda, 1280
Knight, Eileen Mack, 1057
Knight, Evette, 1048
Knight, Roger, 1419
Knipp, Jeff, 857
Kobielski, Kaz, 93
Koenig, Robin, 903
Koenigsberger, Nicole, 1023
Kohler, Allison Gordon, 394
Kolodkina, Nina, 1315
Kolpin, Vill, 500
Komarov, Shelley, 860
Koplow, Erin B., 1416
Köppen, Andreas, 1096
Koretz, Elliott L., 27
Korven, Mark, 255
Kosko, Gary, 285
Kosse, Grit, 837
Kramer, Deina, 578
Kramer, Den, 587
Kramer, Joel, 851
Kramer, Katherine, 554
Kramer, Louis, 1044
Kraner, Douglas, 584
Kratter, Tia W., 146
Krause, Stephen, 114, 433
Kreiner, Jillian Ann, 284
Kress, Ronna, 69, 664
Kretschmer, John, 282
Kris, Andy, 105
Kuehn, Brad, 19
Kuhn, Beth, 1489
Kühne, Kathy, 210
Kuljian, Anne, 1242
Kunin, Drew, 219, 247, 521
Kunz, Peter, 664

Kupershmidt, Alex, 841
Kurland, Jeffrey, 715
Kurlander, John, 133, 364, 851, 1154
Kurtzman, Robert, 615
Kurtzman, Wendy, 269, 306, 1048, 1277
Kushner, Jeff, 595
Kushnick, Beth, 1069
Kushon, Jeffrey, 1483
Kwan, Mable, 634
Kwan Lee Na, 634

Laabs, Karl Heinz, 898
Ladish, Steven, 1023
Lafferty, Craig, 21
Laforce, Jean-Pierre, 48, 768, 1131
Lafran, Laurent, 768
LaGura, Jennifer, 1197
Lahoda, Ladislav, 674
Lakoff, Dean, 232
Lamb, Irene, 294
Lambert, Ruth, 145
Lamberti, Tony, 1014
La Monica, Matthew "Boomer", 480
Lamont, Neil, 52
Lamothe, Diane, 69
Lancaster, Jonathan, 394
Lancelot, Patrick, 1377
Landaker, Gregg, 27, 944
Lande, Ellen, 795
Landrum, Bill, 96
Landrum, Jacqui, 96
Landsberg, Shan, 1227
Lane, Mark, 468
Lane, Michael, 282
Langan, Marese, 1249
Langballe, Thomas, 1342
Langevin, Owen, 133, 468, 1471
Lanier, Jessica, 1232
Lanino, Deborah, 1290
Lantieri, Michael, 285
LaPlante, François, 1
La Plante, Greg, 57
Laporte, Steve, 1213
Larman, Patricia, 739
Larrea, Robert Taz, 572, 587
Larsen, Chris, 126
Larsen, Deborah, 434, 811
Larsen, John A., 317, 1476
Larsen, Thomas B., 184
Larson, Ken, 967, 1187
Lasher, Aric, 992, 1429
Lasik, Vladislav, 1123

Lather, Barry, 119
Lathrop, Craig, 93
Lau Chi-Ho, 93
Laudati, Michael, 1174
Lavoie, Carol, 133
Laws, Andrew, 1085
Lazan, David, 1048
Lazarowitz, Les, 187
Leach, John Paul, 176
Leamon, Ron, 1202
LeBrecht, James, 69
Lebredt, Gordon, 310
Le Corre, Robert, 247, 1062
LeCoultre, Francine, 1146
Lederman, Diane, 882
Ledermann, Nicki, 480
Ledfore, Paul, 920
Ledyard, Gary, 1081
Lee, David, 385
Lee, George R., 40
Lee, Ken, 746
Lee, Kevin, 497, 500
Lee, Moonyeen, 1291
Lee, Tony, 182
Lefebvre, Bruno, 1062
Lefebvre, Stéphane, 69
LeFevour, Rick, 1038
Leff, Gabriela, 1061
LeFlora, Julius, 75, 578
Lefton, Sue, 338, 822
LeGrand, Richard, Jr., 72, 468
Lehman, Pete, 1014
Lehmann, Jette, 625
Leigh, Dan, 996
Le-Mare, Mike, 1057, 1062
Le Marinel, Paul, 1062
Lenander, Lars, 291
Leonard, Terry, 811, 1081
Lerner, Fred, 860
Less, Megan, 322
Lester, Dan, 584
Letica, Ivana, 927
Leung, James, 634
Leveque, John, 1371
Levin, Peter, 1414
Levine, Julia K., 857, 978
Levitsky, Gary, 781, 1052
Levitt, Heidi, 575, 1429
Levon, Jacquetta, 746
Levy, Bruno, 48
Levy, Stuart, 715, 751
Levy, Tracey, 951
Lewis, Ellen, 597, 781, 978, 1000, 1264
Lewis, Garrett, 348
Lewzey, Dick, 1460
Liberman/Hirschfeld, 1476
Librizzi, Rosa, 634

Lichtfuss, Eric, 1240
Liddiard, Gary, 554, 679, 1466
Liddle, George, 271
Lievsay, Skip, 77, 96
Light, Sarah, 271
Lightstone, Richard, 1038
Lindela, Toy, 312
Lindauer, Jack, 669
Lindauer, John, 199
Lindemann, Eric, 1197
Lindholm, Lars Christian, 625
Lindsay, Peter, 703, 1389
Lindsay-Stewart, Karen, 751
Lindsey, Otto, 757
Lindstrom, Kara, 987
Linn, Marc, 578
Lippens, Amy, 780, 1269
Lipton, Dina, 975, 1398
Liroff, Marci, 610
Little, Mark "Travis", 1129
Littlejohn, Victor, 77
Litwack, Dana C., 967
Liu, Jeffrey, 1152
Lockett, Stevie "Black", 578
Lohman, Melissa P., 512
Loiseleux, Valerie, 1405
Lojodice, Leda, 685
Lombardi, Paul, 298, 1154, 1476
Lombardo, Frankie Beau, 1081
Lombardo, Lance, 1081
Lomma, Jeannie, 669
Lomofsky, Sharon, 67, 519
Long, Larry, 1135
Longhurst, Dany, 1304
Longhurst, Graham, 751
Lopez, Marco, 1174
López, Rosa Amelia, 76
Lopez-Rivera, Sergio, 909
Loquasto, Santo, 187
Loram, Deeya, 1152
Lorena, Ana, 1405
Lorimer, Alan, 1000
Loublier, Jean-Paul, 649
Loucks, Carolyn, 806, 1163, 1387
Love, Lisa, 312, 394
Lowe, Georgina, 294
Lowry, Linda, 1456
Lowry-Johnson, Junie, 72, 1254
Lucas, Billy D., 1466

Lucas, David, 967
Lucas, Kathy, 1398
Lucas, Michael Shawn, 136
Lucas, Tom, 959
Lucini, John-Paul (Lon), 1424
Lucky, Joseph, 173, 584
Lucy, Tom, 1280
Luczyc-Wyhowski, Hugo, 247, 751, 875
Ludvigsen, Hans-Peter, 625
Lui, Bill, 634
Lui Fung-Shan, 819
Luk, Ben, 634
Luker, Malcolm, 759
Luling, Eric, 112
Lulla, Claus, 512
Lundy, Nicholas, 75
Lusby, Joshua P., 285
Lutter, Ellen, 996
Lyall, Susan, 1232
Lyngsoe, Birthe, 625
Lyons, John, 96
Lyons, Loren, 232

Ma, Horace, 819
Maayan, Yehuda, 886, 887
Mabille, Roland, 1426
McAlpine, Andrew, 539
McArthur, Amanda, 941
McAteer, James, 133
MacAvin, Josie, 164
McAvoy, Edward T., 1456
McCaffrey, Valerie, 21, 271
Maccarone, Alicia, 1429
McCarthy, Anne, 173, 364
McCarthy, Jeanne, 155, 240
McClaren, Merdyce, 636
McClennin, Brenda, 1387
McComas, Tania, 471, 851
McCorkle, Pat, 751
McCormack, Lynda, 322
McCormick, John, 37
McCormick, Keith, 847
McCullagh, Tom, 129, 589
McCulley, Anne D., 72, 1228
McCulloch, Jeff, 477
MacDonald, Alan, 746

MacDonald, Lin, 593, 1474
MacDonald, Marilyn, 801
McDonald, Rocky, 1424
McDowell, Alex, 379
McElvin, Ric, 944
McFarlane, Colin, 1291
McGahey, Michelle, 271
McGee, Robert, 109
McGuire, Al, 1057
McGuire, Debra, 1228
McGuire, Joseph R., Jr., 664
McHenry, David, 739
McIntosh, Daniel, 512
McIntyre, Dianne, 77
McKay, Douglas, 1174
Mackay, Gary, 1374
MacKay, Lynne, 133
McKee, Joseph, 109
McKenney, Haven, 37
McKeown, David, 1, 1123
McKernin, Kathleen, 33, 874
McKinstry, Jonathan, 1242
Mackintosh, Louise, 256
Mackintosh, Ray, 256
MacLane, Rich, 578
McLaughlin, John, 1061
McLaughlin, Stephen, 164, 457, 1429
Maclean, Mary Ellen, 476
McLeod, John, 364, 860
Macleod, Zo, 589
MacMillan, David, 225, 232, 1361
McMillan, Stephanie, 52
McMoyler, David, 773, 1014, 1253
McMullen, Gail, 1059
McNabb, Mark Hopkins, 285
Macneal, Kelly, 67
McPherson, Brian, 1014
McQueen, Glenn, 146
MacRae, Sandy, 390
McSherry, Rose Marie, 291
McTaggart, Dennis, 703
Magee, Joseph, 72
Maginnis, Molly, 810
Magnus, Diana, 256
Mahon, Kevin, 882
Maisler, Francine, 33, 563, 920, 1489
Maitland, Tod, 75, 554, 1264

Majidi, Asadollah, 1293
Major, Grant, 1374
Makaro, J.J., 312
Maki, Russell, 601
Makovsky, Judianna, 461, 722, 978, 992
Malanitchev, Dima, 1077
Malchus, Scott, 1308
Malherbe, Annet, 327
Malin, Mary, 755
Malivoire, Martin, 119, 310, 468, 1387
Malouf, Donald, 550, 539, 1081
Mamet, Allen, 77
Manchester, Lawrence, 75
Mangini, Mark, 225, 679
Mani, Maya, 593
Manning, Lee, 679
Mansbridge, Mark, 1197, 1242
Manthey, Karen, 636
Manwiller, Debi, 1398
Manzo, Lenny, 865
Maraffi, Matthew, 970
Marano, John, 1174
Marcotte, Pamela, 240
Marcus, Caryn, 527
Margetson, Gwendolyn, 1474
Margiotta, Karen, 247
Margiotta, Mary, 247
Marin, Mindy, 269, 1213
Marini, Paul, 1020
Markle, Bill, 1366
Marks, Glen, 746
Marsh, Laurie, 312
Marsh, Terence, 369
Martin, Maggie, 1495
Martin, Steve, 1014
Martin, Walt, 278
Martinez, Juan Carlos, 1093
Martinez, Lizzie Curry, 789
Martinez, Tony, 1
Martz, Neal, 77
Maskovich, John D., 447
Maslansky, Stephanie, 129
Maslow, Steve, 27, 943
Massalas, Valorie, 441
Masson, Jacqueline R., 601
Masters, Todd, 1429
Masterson, Brian, 427
Masuda, Masako, 291
Mather, Tom, 1040, 1387
Mathews, James Grey, 757
Matsuda, Kazuo, 334

Matsumoto, Miye, 1334
Matthews, Marilyn, 1348
Maxey, Caty, 1038
Maxwell, John H., 72, 755
May, Mona, 871, 1419
Maybury, Suza, 1319, 1424
Mayhew, Ina, 1471
Mayrs, Coreen, 1202
Mays, Richard F., 285
Mazahn, Richard, 468
Mazon, Graciela, 773
Mazur, Bernadette, 1489
Mazur, Johanna, 10
Meachem, Stewart, 1149
Meagher, Jay, 369, 379, 575, 1262, 1416
Meehan, James, 379
Meinardus, Mike, 348, 1371
Meiselmann, Peter V., 199
Mellery, Véronique, 764
Meltzer, Ileane, 1253
Mendez, Phil, 1076
Menéndez, Carlos, 1456
Meneses, José, 176
Menz, Bernardo, 709
Menzies, Andrew, 546, 1319
Mepham, Viv, 1319
Mercer, Randy Houston, 781
Mercurio, Joseph, 722
Messina, Kristen Toscano, 857
Messina, Phil, 920, 1495
Meyers, Drew, 112
Meyerson, Alan, 27, 40, 123, 1014, 1048, 1319
Michael, Chuck, 33
Michael, Danny, 781
Michaels, Wayne, 1149
Micheletos, John W., 1429
Mickelberry, Nancy, 1254
Mickelson, Pam Dixon, 773, 810, 847
Middleton, Joseph, 1187
Midgley, John, 1189
Miksis, Brian, 139, 400, 1447
Milinac, John D., 584, 1167
Miller, Bruce Alan, 1371

Miller, Christina G., 497
Miller, Colin, 1216, 1460
Miller, Jonathan, 114
Miller, Peter, 1449
Miller, Wayne, 1057
Mills, Michael, 1476
Mills, Rick, 37
Mills, Robert, 298
Mills, Vera, 1057
Milne, Gareth, 674, 1044
Milner, Digby, 123
Mingenbach, Louise, 33, 874, 965
Minns, Cheri, 944, 1429
Minton, Thomas, 1348
Miquel, Lloren, 176
Mirojnick, Ellen, 959
Mirren, Helen, 1014
Mirshekari, Jahangir, 1293
Mitchell, Ed, 199
Mitchell, Jerry, 903
Miyauchi, Michiyo, 395
Mocanu, Leana, 420
Mohr, Margaret, 93
Moidon, Frederique, 649
Moidon, Frdrique, 1131
Molina, 709
Mollo, Melissa, 1483
Monaci, Gina, 237
Moneva, Natalie, 1315
Monios, Marina, 1304
Montagna, Peter, 847
Montefusco, Vincent, 1081
Montgomery, Rick, 1308
Montiel, Cecilia, 773
Montoya, Charlie, 521
Mooney, Karl, 1409
Moore, Christina, 746
Moore, Michael M., 57
Moore, Randy E., 550
Moore, Wendy May, 256
Moraes, Silvia, 685
Morahan, Jim, 123
Morales, Gil, 1471
Morales, Leslie, 521
Moran, Pat, 954
Morelli, Tony, 593
Moreno, Patricia, 1366
Morgan, Glenn T., 1474
Morganti, Tullio, 685
Moriceau, Norma, 60
Moroney, Niall, 1380
Morris, Jeffray, 669
Morris, John, 584, 1456
Morris, Rick, 1014
Morris, Todd, 860
Morris, Vonda, 434, 1419

Mose, Caleb, 37
Moser, Heidi, 89
Mosko, Gil, 72
Moss, Barry, 1031
Mossum, Lena, 176
Motavalli, M., 815
Motown, Bobby, 1014
Motyer, John F., 1474
Mourus, Paul, 410
Mowat, Donald J., 93
Mowat, Douglas A., 550
Mrkic, Branka, 882
Mrsovic, Ljubomir, 1123
Mucha, Cassandra, 1061
Mugel, Jean-Paul, 201, 1405
Mumford, Dean, 1216
Mungle, Mathew, 21, 317, 903, 1023
Munro, Andrew, 667, 1389
Munro, Christa, 550
Murakami, James J., 348
Murdock, Judy, 563, 1471
Murphy, Jennifer, 546
Murphy, Paul, 139
Murphy, Shawn, 52, 232, 447, 958, 1023, 1077, 1099, 1264
Murray, Alan Robert, 1031
Murray, Dennis, 903
Murray, Douglas, 291
Murtinho, Rita, 929
Muscal, Michael, 133
Musky, Jane, 887
Mussenden, Isis, 519, 636
Mussenden, Roger, 93, 310, 593, 1277, 1416, 1419
Muzeni, Alan, 1052
Myers, Gary, 312
Myers, Ruth, 285
Myers, Tom, 1031
Myhre, John, 338, 664
Mylanus, Roland, 210

Nadler, Lauren, 1302
Nadoolman, Deborah, 119
Naegelen, Nicolas, 420
Naert, Didier, 247, 899
Nakase, Hirofumi, 334
Nakazaki, Kiyomi, 1336
Napier, April, 1483
Napier, Irene, 1044
Narr, Boone, 951
Nasrallah, Nahed, 302
Nassau, Robert, 671
Nay, A. J., 155

Nay, Maria, 216, 797
Nedza, Jim, 944
Neely, Keith, 975
Neighbour, Trevor, 112
Neilson, Phil, 369, 1264
Nellen, Thomas, 1216
Nelson, Steve, 21, 298, 364, 1239
Nelson, Tom, 461, 958
Neskoromny, Andrew, 285
Nestor, Greg, 155
Neuner, Willy, 416
Neunreuther, Roland, 1216
New, Gary, 325
Newell, David P., 1228
Newkirk, Dale, 874
Newman, Chris, 1000, 1272, 1489
Newman, Walter, 285
Newman, William J., II, 291
Ng, Dora, 243
Nichols, Robert Tate, 550
Nicholson, Charles, 348
Nicolson, Colin, 1249
Nicotero, Gregory, 615
Niehaus, Anja, 622
Nielsen, Lene, 625
Niemmi, Collin, 69
Nixon, Kathryn, 480
Nolens, Marc, 822
Nomad, Michael, 1206
Noonan, Donna, 738
Norlin, Eric, 10
Norman, Michel, 751
Normington, Alice, 531
Norris, Guy, 60
Norris, Patricia, 521
Novack, David, 253
Novick, Ed, 1166
Nowak, Christopher, 1040, 1476
Numme, Karen, 580
Nushawg, Christopher S., 563, 847, 1254
Nutt, John, 1085
Nye, Ben, Jr., 636
Nytro, Kari, 607

Oates, Joan, Jr., 781
Obermeyer, David, 631
O'Brien, William F., 155
O'Brien-Kent, Mairead, 1474
Oda, Takashi, 1336
O'Donnell, Elaine, 903
O'Farrell, Michael, 93, 722
Offers, Elaine, 1023, 1053, 1174
Ogu, Susan, 67
Ohanneson, Jill, 546

O'Hara, Karen, 77
O'Kane, Deirdre, 589
Okun, Jeffrey A., 722, 1242
Oldenburg, Odin R., 1348
Oldham, Anne, 1409
Olexiewicz, Dan, 21
Oliney, Alan, 539
Olsson, Kim, 625
Olsson, Lis, 625
O'Mara, T. J., 1020
Oppewall, Jeannine, 978
Orbom, Eric, 563
O'Reilly, Valli, 155, 715
Orloff, Lee, 114, 493, 857
Ornitz, Kim, 797, 1081, 1419
Orr, William H., 593
Orsatti, Ernie, 21, 317, 369, 978
Orsatti, Noon, 21, 379
Ortega, Kenny, 1031
Osborne, Aaron, 199
Osmo, Ben, 60, 271
Ospina, Ermahn, 364
O'Sullivan, Máire, 379, 427
Ottesen, John, 77, 996, 1069
Outerbridge, Josh, 1061
Overd, Greg, 886
Owings, Richard, 1057
Oxford, Kelly, 759, 841
Ozeki, Tatsuo, 395
Ozimek, Jeff, 1081

Paczkowski, Rafal, 1149
Padilla, Jesus Sanchez, 974
Pagano, Rick, 903, 969, 1466
Pain, Keith, 269, 733
Pais, Greg, 582
Pala, Ann, 317, 1416
Paley, Eliza, 875, 1040, 1389
Palmisano, Conrad E., 679
Paneh, Hassan Yekta, 1293
Panaro, Hugh, 136
Panchenko, Kyra, 1093
Panova, Alina, 887
Papadopoulis, Ioannis, 1009
Papalia, Greg, 317, 755
Papsidera, John, 1387
Parenti, Steve, 722
Paris, Richard, 394
Parise, Tina, 275

Park, Kevin "Noogie", 291
Park, Tim, 97
Parke, Dave, 10
Parker, Connie, 593
Parker, Daniel, 52
Parker, John, 550
Parker, Rick, 1040
Parr, Steve, 739
Parra, Salvador, 789
Parrillo, Anthony D., 225
Parry, Julian, 1291
Parsidera, John, 216
Pascal, Darren, 1187
Pascuzzo, Christopher, 232
Pashley, Wayne, 60
Pasternak, Beth, 310
Pasztor, Beatrix Aruna, 1023
Patch, Karen, 1085
Paterson, Maeve, 427
Paterson, Owen, 1424
Patnode, Darren, 860
Patrick, Ben, 67, 182
Patrick, Brian, 468
Patrick, Shane, 860
Patterson, Chris, 920
Patterson, Geoffrey, 33, 1476
Patterson, Jane, 1057
Patterson, Rick, 1474
Pattison, Paul, 819
Paul, Gary, 1253
Paul, Rick, 511
Paul, Tom, 929
Paul, Victoria, 112
Paulsen, Fred, 847
Pauley, Bob, 146
Paull, Francie, 109
Paulsen, Kjersti, 619
Paynter, Rhonda, 1023
Pearce, Frazer, 440
Pearce, Hayden, 440
Pearce, Michael, 578
Pearse, Grant, 10
Pearson, Rob, 1069
Pellicoro, Paul, 887
Penley, Paul, 715
Pennell, Peter, 379
Pepiot, Ken, 1197, 1242
Pepperdine, Judy, 822
Peranio, Vincent, 954
Pereira, Vanessa, 271, 338, 531, 1249, 1380
Perez, José, 819
Perry, Kelly, 126
Persoff, Joshua, 348
Persov, Vladimir, 837
Pescucci, Gabriella, 247, 269, 674
Peters, Paul, 903
Peters, Troy, 978
Petersen, Beau, 471
Petersen, Nils, 1034

Peterson, Barbara, 1416
Peterson, Kristin V., 909
Petreikis, Rodney, 1398
Petrides, Andrea, 822, 1304
Petrov, Victor, 1315
Petruccelli, Kirk M., 114
Peyton, Robin, 780
Pfeiffer, Michelle, 1014
Pfeiffer, Sarah, 18
Pharr, Melinda, 546
Phillips, Arianne, 1048
Phillips, Don, 860, 967
Phillips, Erica Edell, 1213
Phillips, Helene, 755
Phillips, Janna B., 615
Philpotts, John, 871
Picerni, Charles, Jr., 348
Pickering, Lisa, 390
Pierce, Denney, 21
Pierret, Brian, 819
Pietila, Bonita, 886, 887
Pietsch-Lindenberg, Andreas, 304
Pike, Kevin, 1038
Pilcher, Steve, 1031
Piller, Tony, 944
Pina, Scott, 954
Pinnock, Anna, 733
Pinter, Herbert, 1291
Pisani, Michael, 112
Pizzini, Denise, 951, 1269
Platteau, Antoine, 646
Plauche, Scott, 1193
Plympton, Bill, 582
Po, Javier, 764
Poirier, Laurent, 646
Pokromski, Waldemar, 416
Polek, Leonie, 327
Polcsa, Juliet, 597, 1052
Police, Carol Kieffer, 1031
Poll, Mark, 978
Ponte, Gideon, 139
Poole, Lorne, 1474
Poon Men-Wah, 819
Pope, Leslie A., 903
Popienko, Dena, 865
Porath, Jonathan, 1272
Porro, Joseph, 291, 448
Porter, Alan L., 232
Porzchen, Josef, 1037
Posnansky, Tessa, 21
Pospisil, John, 27
Potter, Chuck, 282
Powell, Anthony, 52

Powell, Greg, 733
Powell, John, 27
Powell, Joni Meers, 33
Powell, Nick, 457, 652
Powell, Sandy, 164, 530, 1137, 1389
Power, Jim, 903
Powers, Dave, 1145
Poynter, Jim, 944
Pratt, Anthony, 164, 759
Prentice, Margaret, 1308
Preston, Grania, 1466
Price, James E., 348
Price, Matthew, 500, 882
Price, Sarah, 105
Price, Wynona, 322
Prichett, Darrell D., 615
Pride, Tad, 60, 271
Prior, Andy, 1280
Pritchard, Anne, 1, 1205
Pritchard, Terry, 264
Pritchett, Darrell D., 291
Pritchett, John, 433, 860, 1232
Protat, Marie-Angle, 69
Protiva, Ed, 1023, 1197
Proulx, Real, 1205
Puisto, Susanna, 1269
Pullman, Jeff, 37, 869
Purdy, Jill, 256
Purdy, Lynda, 738
Purves, Barry, 126

Quade, Rich, 146
Quaglio, Laurent, 201
Quertier, Jill, 1137
Quirk, Patrick, 801
Quist, Jerry, 797

Raboni, Metella, 1260
Rackard, Anna, 129, 164
Racki, Branko, 310, 739
Radka, Theresa, 1275
Radomirovic, Jovan, 1123
Rae, Kori, 146
Raes, Tony, 60
Raggett, Mark, 1137
Raglan, Rex, 10
Rain, Marlene, 1040
Rajau, Albert, 759
Ramirez, Eric, 317
Ramirez, Oscar, 773
Ramsey, Carol, 1216
Ramsey, Janine, 749
Ramsey, Joe, 1048
Randall, Chad, 601, 610

Randall, Glenn, 773
Rankin, John, 133
Raoux, Paul, 1127
Rathaus, Jeffrey, 1145
Ratliff, Richard, 847
Rau, Gretchen, 225, 554, 1154
Ray, Johanna, 1020
Ray, Robyn, 199
Raymond, Deborah, 967, 1059
Rea, Bill, 636
Rea, Karen, 1474
Reade, Dick, 1374
Rebhun, Larold, 312, 1476
Redbourn, Michael, 589
Ree, Veslemoy Fosse, 607
Reece-Thorne, Cyndi, 114
Reed, Dexter, 1077
Reeder, Andrew, 909
Reed-Humes, Robbi, 1471
Reeves, Brian, 634
Regan, Patricia, 664
Reich, Liora, 247
Reid, Alison, 1164, 1471
Reiss, Ron, 493, 610
Renard, Per-Olof, 1216
Rencher, Burton, 1135, 1262
Renna, Bob, 575
Reta, Thomas, 114, 471, 847
Reynolds, Chris, 457
Reynolds, Craig, 593
Reynolds, Norman, 1242
Reynolds, Richard, 447
Reynolds-Wasco, Alexandra, 1085
Rhodes, Shari, 1187
Rhodes, Simon, 285, 298, 664, 773, 806, 810
Rial, Leah, 967
Riccardi, Mark, 232, 1000
Ricci, Brian, 831, 1020
Ricco, Rick, 468
Rich, S. Mark, 521
Richards, Esther Robins, 987
Richards, George, 1280
Richards, Gregory, 865
Richards, John, 269, 356, 593, 887, 1081, 1280, 1489
Richards, Paul, 865
Richards, Randall, 112, 1371

Richardson, Geoff, 10
Richardson, Lucy, 338
Richens, David, 822
Richmond, Lyn, 1262
Ridlen, David, 1085
Riegel, Eden, 1014
Rigazio, Melissa, 1038
Riggs, Bob, 1466, 1495
Rillie, Jim, 739
Rio, Sérgio Machado, 195
Ripper, Velcrow, 974
Ritenour, Scott, 584
Riva, J. Michael, 493, 679, 1174
Rivera, Irina, 1253
Rivera, Miguel, 1069
Rivers, Glenn, 433
Rizzo, Michael, 886, 887
Robert, Frank, 1057
Roberts, Eric, 920
Roberts, Glenn, 317, 847, 1023
Roberts, L. Taylor, 1474
Robertson, Brandi, 580
Robinson, David, 749, 781
Robinson, Philip, 457, 801
Robinson, Robert Lee, 755
Robinson, Shirley, 1280
Robison, Barry, 546
Robitaille, Ginette, 1
Rocchetti, Manlio, 461
Rochester, Art, 1348
Rockburn, David "Rocky", 322
Rockwell, Oliver, 1262
Rodgers, Aggie Guerard, 539
Rodgers, Mic, 679
Rodman, Terry, 797
Roesler, Tina K., 1253
Rolfshoj, Annette, 625
Rollins, Leslie E., 996
Roman, Lisa, 21
Romanillos, Pres Antonio, 841
Romano, Pat, 871
Ronan, David, 951, 944
Rondell, R.A., 448, 1242
Roneli, Chandler, 684
Ronne, David, 584, 755
Roper, Louise, 312
Rose, Penny, 936
Rosemarin, Hilton, 554, 1167
Rosen, Charles, 1228
Rosen, Kathleen, 543, 1232
Rosenberg, Alex, 857

Rosenberg, Philip, 958
Rosenthal, Laura, 187, 882
Rosenzweig, Steve, 512
Ross, Mike, 546, 1308
Ross, Morag, 164, 674
Ross-Trevor, Mike, 530, 1304
Roth, Ann, 575, 1000, 1154
Roth, Dena, 1193
Rouda, Saul, 37
Rousseau, Patrick, 1, 1205
Rousseaux, Jean-Yves, 768
Routh, May, 1062
Rouz, Emilia, 1291
Rovin, David, 582
Roy, Mark, 37
Roylance, Bron, 1361
Rozenberg, Corinne, 411
Rozett, Mark, 640
Ruben, Neesh, 1280
Rubeo, Mayes C., 789
Rubin, David, 225, 369, 851
Rubin, Sheila, 685
Rubino, Beth, 1361
Rudisill, Carl, 757, 1135
Rudolph, Elisabeth, 112
Rundell, Steve, 77
Runyard, Michael, 959, 1419
Rupp, Jacob, 593
Rush, Sean, 936
Ruskin, G. Victoria, 1023
Ruskin, Judy L., 554
Ruskin-Howell, Judy, 944
Russell, Rhona, 294
Rutter, Ellen, 385
Ryack, Rita, 847
Ryan, Robert, 1474
Ryba, Ellen, 1038
Rydstrom, Gary, 146
Rygh, Eva, 619
Rylander, Eric, 978

Saccio, Michael A., 781
Sacks, Quinny, 1137
Sagae, Hiroshi, 1336
Sage, Jefferson, 903
Saito, Masami, 395
Sakas, Iliana, 572
Saklad, Steve, 797
Samantha, 1127
Sampson, Victoria Rose, 1020
Samson, James, 441
Samuels, Priscilla, 1249

Samuelson, Ragge, 619
Samuelsson, Ragnar, 1342
Sánchez, Carlos, 789
Sanchez, Mark, 1442
Sandell, William, 1197
Sanders, David, 1085
Sanders, Kerry, 1371
Sanders, Rosy, 457
Sanders, Tom, 1099
Sandrich, Cathy, 539, 759, 909, 958, 992, 1062, 1240, 1371
Sands, Dennis, 539, 554, 781, 857, 936, 944, 978, 992, 1163
Sands, Jill Greenberg, 546
Sands, Kevin, 10
Sandvik, Liv, 619
Sanford, Julia S., 112
Sanger, Greg, 951
Santiago, Elliot, 1061
Santiago, Hugo, 493
Santo, Evaldo Souza, 411
Saro, Evelyn Colleen, 546, 550, 1085
Sarokin, William, 597, 996, 1052
Sasaki, Kaori, 1336
Saseki, Osamu, 1223
Saturen, Jonathon, 1202
Sauls, Larry, 112
Sawhill, Steve, 546, 550
Sawyer, Grant, 554, 1048
Sawyer, Tricia, 806
Saylor, Steven M., 40
Scali, Maria, 865
Scallan, Chris, 1189
Scarpulla, Clare, 554, 1048, 1213, 1442
Scharf, Larry, 967
Schell, Maurice, 1205, 1232, 1361
Scher, Adam, 874, 1020
Scherer, Mike, 1206
Schillinger, Georgie, 603
Schirle, Scott, 109
Schirmer, Bill, 1474
Schleinig, Robert, 865
Schlesinger, David, 615
Schmook, Randy, 298, 1166
Schnee, Bill, 755
Schneider, Tricia, 631
Schoenfeld, Nadege, 1023
Schöpping, Michel, 210

Schreyer, Janeen, 1167
Schutt, Debra, 722, 959
Schwalm, Jim, 493
Schwan, Jeff P., 860
Sciabelli, Anne, 362
Scott, Alexis, 139
Scott, Chuck, 1447
Scott, Helen, 294
Scott, Jeanette, 364, 860
Scribner, Robert, 679
Scruggs, Tom, 77
Scupp, Robert J., 1264
Sebert, Leslie, 310, 1387
Segal, Ken, 1193
Seidman, Sara, 282
Seigneuret, Yves, 1062
Seirton, Michael, 369, 575
Seitz, Jeff, 1398
Sekiya, Yukio, 1336
Selemon, Mark, 500
Sellers, Patrick, 1154
Selway, Mary, 264, 269, 733, 746, 1288
Sen, Jupiter, 457
Senior, Alan, 356
Serdena, Gene, 1371
Serdinova, Lyudmila, 408
Serveira, Gita, 764
Severino, Randy, 715
Sevleyan, Maya, 768
Sforza, Fabrizio, 269
Shankman, Adam, 19, 27
Shannon, Laura Jean, 869
Shannon-Smith, Jane, 278, 857
Sharp, Rick, 298
Sharpe, Jenny, 1380
Shaw, Michael, 749
Shaw, Polar Bear, 112
Shea, Mike, 291
Sheaks, Christine, 471
Sheen, Edna M., 369
Sheets, Suzette, 546, 1240
Sheldon, Christopher, 1483
Sheppard, Anna, 899, 1020
Sher, Robert, 322
Sherer, Karen, 914
Sherman, Richard, 441, 548
Sheward, Lee, 703
Shewchuk, Steve, 119
Shibata, Hirohide, 1223
Shields, Darlene, 477
Shifflette, Steve, 1240
Shircore, Jenny, 247, 338, 652

Shock, Amy, 33
Shohan, Naomi, 1048
Sholl, Oliver, 447
Shopmaker, Susan, 572
Short, Jonathan, 112
Short, Martin, 1014
Short, Paul, 21
Shorter, Kate, 19
Shoup, Robert, 385, 1264
Shriver, Chris, 597
Sides, Allen, 1000
Silverman, Carol, 75
Silvestri, Domenic, 40
Silvi, Maurizio, 48
Sim, Gordon, 1040
Simard, Diane, 1
Simkin, Margery, 379, 715
Simmons, Brian, 822
Simon, Mark, 500
Simonet, Jean-Michael, 135
Simons, Jef, 847
Simpson, George, 679
Simpson, Rick, 40, 155
Sinclair, Caroline, 1221
Sinclair, Winsome, 75
Sirrs, Janek, 97
Sisti, John L., 1135
Siverio, Manny, 500, 1093
Skinner, William Ladd, 447
Slater, Mary Jo, 433, 684, 1076
Slatsky, John J., 978
Slider, Dan, 885
Slotnick, Sara, 595, 882
Sluiter, Ric, 841
Smalley, Adam, 27
Smarz, Nena, 72
Smith, Caroline, 390
Smith, Charles Ewing, 414
Smith, Christina, 21, 550, 951
Smith, Derrick, 1416
Smith, Easton Michael, 317, 575, 1476
Smith, J.D., 155
Smith, Jay, 1023
Smith, Jimmy, 664
Smith, Jo-Anne, 1129
Smith, Julie K., 874
Smith, Laurel, 282
Smith, Russell J., 521
Smith, Scott, 1371
Smith, Suzanne, 385, 527, 658, 954, 1038, 1232
Smith, Van, 954
Smithwick, 1262
Smoke, Bob, 746
Snik, Jeanette, 210
Snyder, David L., 1213

Snyder, Dawn, 471, 978
Snyder, Doug, 18
So, Jorge, 403
Sobrino, Daniel, 1127
Solomon, Gary, 882
Soodor, Taavo, 93, 476
Sorel, Perri, 1240
Soucek, Paul, 658, 1389
Soupios, Meredith, 1366
Sparapani, Flavia, 269
Sparrman, Goran, 126
Spears, Michelle, 109
Speckman, Gary R., 40
Spellman, Chris, 97, 539
Spencer, Katie, 457
Spencer, Ted, 658
Spheeris, Linda, 1129
Spiegel, Ira, 1447
Spints, Cindy, 933
Spooner, J. Michael, 1031
Spriggs, Austen, 1037
Squarciapino, France, 201
Stambler, Bruce, 958, 978
Stamper, Peggy, 112
Standefer, Robin, 992
Starger, Ilene, 936, 1166, 1361
Starin, Nicholas T., 1495
Stateman, Wylie, 810, 1014
Stearn, Andrew, 93
Stearns, Michael, 941
Stears, John, 773
Steele, Jon Gary, 21
Stefanovic, Jasna, 256
Stein, David, 500
Stein, Jonathan Earl, 1308
Steiner, Armin, 636
Steinheimer, Bruce, 1174
Steinmeier, Mac, 416
Stensel, Carl, 871
Stepeck, Timothy
Stephenson, David, 123, 269, 338, 759
Sterling, Hamilton, 19
Stern, Adrienne, 1436
Sterner, Beth, 1189
Stevens, Gail, 1280
Stevens, Laurie, 975
Stewart, Dean, 468
Stewart, Jane Anne, 1227
Stewart, Marlene, 348, 1476
Stewart, Patrick, 1014
Steyer, Martin, 837

Stockton, Philip, 789, 887
Stoeckinger, Mark, 155, 851
Stoll, Nelson, 943, 1429
Stone, Casey, 471
Stone, F. Lee, 1129
Stone, Nigel, 1375
Stoneham, John, Jr., 93, 133, 256
Storer, Stephen, 780
Storvick, Tim, 291
Stoughton, Diana L., 112
Strachan, Kathy, 589
Strait, Walter, 699
Stratford, Peter, 593
Stratton, Rick, 40
Strawn, C.J., 1253
Strebel, Thomas, 89
Strelow, Jake, 1429
Stremovski, Georgui, 408
Striepeke, Daniel C., 1099
Strober, Carol, 580
Stroman, Susan, 1489
Stromberg, Robert, 269
Strong, Patte, 810, 1081
Stuart, Cindy, 1062
Studebaker, Gay, 1447
Sturm, Dieter, 521
Subic, Martina, 1123
Sudick, Dan, 851
Sullivan, Gerald, 1240
Sullivan, Jerry, 715
Sullivan, Kate, 1213
Sullivan, Peter Michael, 1429
Sundahl, Eric, 173
Surma, Ron, 1254
Susik, Tamara, 10
Sutton, J.B., 1038
Sutton, Linda Lee, 715
Svec, J.C., 1302
Svoboda, Vlasta, 1471
Swanson, Bruce, 903
Swayze, Patsy, 550
Swee, Daniel, 887
Sweeney, Matt, 679
Swiderski, Dawn, 471, 1429
Sykes, Steve, 757
Sykes, Tim, 697
Syson, Lucinda, 356

Tagliaferro, Pat, 19
Takahashi, Chikae, 1439
Takaka, Shinichi, 395
Taliaferro, William, 40, 1197
Tan, Philip, 914
Tanenbaum, David, 1371

Tanenbaum, Jim, 471, 871
Tanner, Mark, 1409
Tarrire, Bruno, 195
Tashjian, Vartan "V.T.", 1081
Tatopoulos, Patrick, 448
Tavella, Dominick, 970
Tavernier, Elisabeth, 425
Tavoularis, Alex, 936
Tavoularis, Dean, 155, 936
Taylor, Bec, 271
Taylor, Christopher M., 199, 240
Taylor, Don, 703
Taylor, Jill, 1189
Taylor, John, 1304
Taylor, Juliet, 187, 781, 1000
Taylor, Linwood, 1216
Taylor, Tom, 951
Teaney, Ken, 362
Temime, Jany, 210
Tempest, Frances, 1380
Temple, Barry, 841
Ternes, Edward, 269
Terry, Louis, 1197
Terry, Marilyn, 1164
Tetzlaff, Carmen, 1059
Thillye, Peter, 772
Thoen, Mia, 527
Thomas, Bill,
Thomas, Cat, 1093
Thomas, Dixie, 1290
Thomas, Victoria, 155, 521
Thomas, Wynn, 500
Thomasson, Clive, 119
Thomasson, Jean-Bernard, 1284
Thompson, Kevin, 385, 1366
Thompson, Laini, 348
Thompson, Mike, 1228
Thornburn, Gretchen, 819
Thune, Vida, 619
Thurbetr, Geof, 865
Tidgwell, David, 841
Till, Dominie, 1254
Tillman, Kimberly A., 1456
Timan, Noah, 527, 671
Timmerman, Bonnie, 40, 1174
Timoney, Ann Marie, 176
Timperley, John, 733
Tissier, Nathalie, 751
Toback, Mindi, 40, 510, 978
Tocci, James, 539
Tokunow, Susumu, 1129

Tokunow, Sysyny, 563
Toms, Gordon, 1280
Tonelli, Steno, 87
Toniolli, Bruno, 703
Torres, Frank A., 1456
Torres, Suzan, 285
Touges, Ginger, 659
Tourtelot, Douglas, 1202
Townsend, Jeffrey, 1038
Townsley, Andy, 176
Towse, Mitch, 781, 996
Traechai, Prisana, 634
Trani, Dante, 1405
Tranier, Valrie, 764
Trella, Tim, 521, 930
Trevis, Sarah, 1044
Trifunovich, Neil, 554
Trigg, Derek, 247
Tropp, Stan, 610, 1197, 1228
Trost, Ron, 1085
Trowbridge, Patrick, 77
Truesdale, James, 575, 797, 1166
Trujillo, Bernardo, 773
Trujillo, Sergio, 1471
Tsukada, Tomoko, 1336
Tsukamoto, Shinya, 1336
Tsurumaki, Hiroshi, 1404
Turlure, Philippe, 759
Turner, Rebecca, 67
Turtle Island Sound, 1253
Tussman, Glenn, 476
Tutter, Benno, 1387
Twetaki, Joel, 530

Ularu, Mihaela, 420
Ulgenciler, Mustafa Ziya, 1260

Vacheret, Cecile, 1127
Valentine, Thomas, 285, 1213
Vallerin, Christian, 649
Vance, Cindy, 886, 887
Vanderhope, Gareth, 60
Vanderwalt, Lesley, 60
Van Domburg, Jack, 795
Van Lierop, Toy Russell, 317, 539
Van Phue, Jeanne, 1129, 1398
Vanzo, Kurt, 1077
Van Zeebroeck, Bruno, 755

Varab, Jeffrey J., 841
Vasquez, Bob, 1057
Vaucher, Eric, 958
Vaughn, Jeff, 310
Vazquez, Alejandro, 709
Vázquez, Alex, 789
Vega, Ed, 364
Veilleux, Jacques A., 93
Veira, Ellen, 400
Velez, Hector, 927
Veltri, Gabriel D., 1419
Venturi, Fabio, 155, 685
Verardi, Cecelia M., 461
Vérité, Daniel, 751
Vernacchio, Dorian, 967, 1059
Vernieu, Mary, 173, 364, 1123, 1187, 1495
Verso, Alberto, 1344
Vertigan, Jeanne, 822
Vetter, Arlan Jay, 1308
Vianello, Virginia, 1260
Viard, Gérard, 1062
Vicari, Tommy, 757
Vidosa, Antonio, 69
Viellard, Dominique, 989
Villand, Claude, 1284
Villarreal, Gabriella, 699
Vincelette, Sophie, 146
Vionnet, Michel, 1131
Virwani, Brian, 669
Vitarelli, Nicholas, 631
Vivian, Marc, 970
Vögel, Barbara, 603
Vogt, Bob, 461
Vogt, Chris, 461
Vojvoda, Michael J., 317
Von Bartheld, Peter, 500
von Brandenstein, Patrizia, 797
von Martius, Katherine, 89
von Mayrhauser, Jennifer, 1040

Waddell, Hugh, 1038
Wager, Dianne, 155, 936
Waggoner, Peter, 105
Wagner, Karyn, 780
Waine, David, 441
Wald-Cohain, Ariyela, 970
Waledisch, Françoise, 48
Walken, Georgianne, 67, 403, 869, 1193, 1366

Walken & Jaffe, 865
Walker, Alexandra, 969
Walker, Greg, 434
Wallace, Christine
  Cullen, 759
Wallace, Derek, 427
Waller, Liz, 1288
Walley, David, 1249
Wallin, Dan, 631, 851,
  1361, 1474
Wallin, Katy, 914
Walpert, Jeff, 119
Walsh, Frank, 652
Walsh, Thomas A.,
  575, 615
Waltenberg, Andrzej
  Rafal, 210
Wams, Henk, 210
Wang, Vera, 936
Ward, Christopher,
  1052
Ward, Jeff, 114, 500
Ward, Tom, 77
Wardlow, Val, 1304
Warnke, John O., 225,
  1154
Warren, Gene, 332
Warren, Tom, 187
Warson, Joe, 684
Wasco, David, 1085
Washington, Dennis,
  951
Washington, William,
  975, 1442
Watanabe, Noriko, 554
Waterhouse, Abram,
  1164
Watters, George II,
  348
Watts, Chris, 978
Wayne, David, 237
Wayton, Gary, 909
Wdowczak, Pawel,
  1085
Weathered, Paul, 595
Webb, James E., 636
Webb, Le'Von, 21
Webb, Maggie, 822
Weber, Elmo, 1416
Weber, Karen, 865
Weber, Liz, 1240
Webster, April, 447
Webster, Dan, 810

Webster, Drew, 1166
Wedde, Wolfgang, 619
Weil, Jason, 755
Weingarten, Mark, 19,
  930, 1069, 1398
Weinger, Don, 27
Weisblatt, Aaron, 1471
Weiss, Julie, 379,
  1167
Weiss, June, 1038
Weitz, Jory, 114
Welch, Bo, 1000
Welch, Michael D.,
  1253
Welker, Alexandra, 780
Wells, Cynthia, 57
Wenger, Cliff, 936
Wenham, Peter, 390
West, Mary, 471
West, Tom, 77
Westcott, Lisa, 1137
Wester, Keith A., 40
Westman, Gucci, 139
Westmore, Bud,
Westmore, June,
  1371
Westmore, Michael,
  1254
Westmore, Pamela,
  550, 992
Weston, Paul, 847
Wexler, Jeff, 847
Wexler, Susan, 1213
Whately, Totty, 1288
Wheeler, Lynn, 271
Whist, Joel, 312
Whitaker, Cary, 930
White, Carla, 597,
  1069, 1232
White, Cary, 364,
  1442
White, Gord, 119,
  133
White, Larry, 936,
  1419
White, Michael, 40
White, Pauline, 1262
White, Tracey, 182
Whitlock, Fleur, 739
Whitman, Dale, 37
Whittaker, David A.,
  1228
Whittaker, Ian, 269

Whynot, John, 112,
  1062, 1456
Wiesel, Karin, 385
Wigginton, Cynthia,
  1057
Wilborn, Charles, 722
Wilder, Brad, 1228,
  1348
Wilder, Glenn, 394
Wilhoit, Michael,
  1166
Wilkerson, Dan, 1416
Wilkins, Ben, 1069
Wilkins, Gary, 634
Wilkins, Gyongyi, 914
Wilkins, Randy, 978
Wilkinson, Frank,
Wilkinson, Gary, 697
Wilkinson, Ron, 1254
Willett, John, 471
Willett, Susan, 544
Williams, Aaron, 136
Williams, Cindy, 1308,
  1429
Williams, Craig, 597
Williams, Derek, 146
Williams, Harrison, 933
Williams, Jennifer, 298
Williams, Joss, 52
Williams, Keith, 757
Williams, Russell, 851,
  975
Williams, Sam, 1374
Williams, Steven D.,
  563
Willis, Artemis, 659
Willis, Simon J., 589
Wilson, David, 492
Wilson, Linda, 1249
Wilson, Margot, 1319
Wilson, Raleigh, 1319
Wilson, Stuart, 652
Wimmer, Isi, 603
Wingrove, Ian, 652
Winslow, Ellie, 77
Winston, Charles E.,
  325
Winter, Clive, 52
Winter, Noah, 1253
Winterborn, Brian,
  1280
Winther-Larsen, Bente,
  619

Wiskes, Andy, 1213
Wolcott, Dean, 285
Wolf, Frank, 146, 841
Wolf, Leslie, 57
Wolf, Scott, 1123
Wolfeil, Todd R., 1264
Wolifson, Shauna,
  271
Wolsky, Albert, 1489
Wolvington, James W.,
  1254
Wong, Chris, 219
Wong, Ellen, 348
Wood, Carol Winstead,
  278
Wood, Durinda, 19
Woodbridge, Patricia,
  887, 959
Woodman, Jori, 1474
Woodruff, Donald B.,
  173, 348
Woodruff, Rod, 746,
  876
Woodruff, Tom, 1476
Worthen, James A.,
  477
Worthington, Mark,
  1371
Wratten, Alison, 822
Wright, Barbara, 1077
Wright, Terri L., 860
Wright, Tory, 739
Wu Jiang, 410
Wulfenstein, Wayne,
  780
Wurtzel, Stuart, 1264
Wynbrandt, Denise,
  631

Wiki, Andreas, 89

Xavier, Waldir, 195

Yagher, Kevin, 133
Yamada, Yoshio, 334
Yamamoto, Akir, 395
Yamazaki, Teru, 455
Yamin, Mandana, 914
Yansick, Eddie, 1206
Yanxiu, Li, 410
Yarhi, Dan, 119
Yarid, Joe, 216
Yates, Ron, 369

Yawn, Richard E., 631
Yeatman, Hoyt, 810
Yee Chung-man, 243
Yeskel, Ronnie, 550,
  965, 1187
Yetman, Steven J.,
  282
Yoho, Robert, 572
Yoon, Seok H., 199
York, Patty, 379, 860
Yoshikawa, Takefumi,
  395
Young, Keith, 936
Young, Rob, 291, 312,
  593, 1474
Yuen Bing, 634
Yurtchuk, Vera, 755

Zack, Dennis, 903
Zakowska, Donna,
  903, 987
Zamperla, Neno, 269
Zane, Debra, 546,
  944, 978
Zanetti, Eugenio, 1429
Zarnecki, Michael, 639
Zea, Kristi, 77
Zed, 48
Zeitoun, Solange, 425
Zhai Lixin, 410
Zhang Deqian, 346
Ziegler, John, 715
Zijlstra, Ben, 327
Ziker, Dick, 1193,
  1213, 1371
Zimmerman, Craig,
  1000
Zimmerman, Herman,
  1254
Zimmerman, Jeremy,
  652
Zivkovic, Petar, 1123
Zolfo, Victor, 447
Zoller, Debbie, 521
Zone, Philippe, 589
Zophres, Mary, 97,
  306, 951, 1308
Zuckerman, Dori, 601
Zuckerman, Eric R.,
  1052
Zuelzke, Mark, 1240
Zukova, Lena, 135
Zurlo, Rosemarie, 187